FestWrld: Peru-1998
Jermyn, Leslie. *Festivals of the World: Peru.* Gareth Stevens Pub., 1998.

FestWrld: Phil-1999
Mendoza, Lunita. *Festivals of the World: Philippines.* Gareth Stevens Pub., 1999.

FestWrld: Russia-1997
Whyte, Harlinah. *Festivals of the World: Russia.* Gareth Stevens Pub., 1997

FestWrld: Saudi-1999
O'Shea, Maria. *Festivals of the World: Saudi Arabia.* Gareth Stevens Pub., 1999.

FestWrld: SouthKorea-1998
Ho Siow Yen. *Festivals of the World: South Korea.* Gareth Stevens Pub., 1998

FestWrld: Thailand-1998
Whyte, Harlinah. *Festivals of the World: Thailand.* Gareth Stevens Pub., 1998.

FestWrld: Turkey-1999
O'Shea, Maria. *Festivals of the World: Turkey.* Gareth Stevens Pub., 1999.

FestWrld: Ukraine-1998
Bassis, Vladimir. *Festivals of the World: Ukraine.* Gareth Stevens Pub., 1998.

FestWrld: Viet-1997
McKay, Susan. *Festivals of the World: Vietnam.* Gareth Stevens Pub., 1997.

FiestaTime-1965
Milne, Jean. *Fiesta Time in Latin America.* Ward Ritchie Press, 1965.

FolkAmerHol-1999
Cohen, Hennig, and Tristram Potter Coffin, eds. *The Folklore of American Holidays.* 3rd ed. Gale Research, 1999.

FolkCal-1930
Long, George. *The Folklore Calendar.* 1930. Reprint. Omnigraphics, 1990.

FolkWrldHol-1999
Griffin, Robert H., and Ann H. Shurgin, eds. *The Folklore of World Holidays.* 2nd ed. Gale Research, 1999.

FoodFestDanube-1969
Perl, Lila. *Foods and Festivals of the Danube Lands.* World Pub. Co., 1969.

FunAlsoRises-1998
Davis, Alan. *The Fun Also Rises.* Greenline Pub., 1998.

GdAnctWrld-1986
Grant, Michael. *A Guide to the Ancient World.* H. W. Wilson Co., 1986.

GdUSFest-1984
Shemanski, Frances. *A Guide to Fairs and Festivals in the United States.* Greenwood, 1984.

GdWrldFest-1985
Shemanski, Frances. *A Guide to World Fairs and Festivals.* Greenwood, 1985.

GodsSymbAncMex-1993
Miller, Mary, and Karl Taube. *An Illustrated Dictionary of the Gods and Symbols of Ancient Mexico and the Maya.* Thames and Hudson, 1993.

HarvFestWrld-1995
Corwin, Judith Hoffman. *Harvest Festivals around the World.* Silver Burdett Press, 1995.

HinduRelCustManners-1960
Thomas, Paul. *Hindu Religion, Customs and Manners.* D.B. Taraporevala Sons & Co., 1960.

HinduRelYr-1921
Underhill, M. M. *The Hindu Religious Year.* Oxford University Press, 1921.

HolSymbols-2009
Henderson, Helene, ed. *Holiday Symbols and Customs.* 4th ed. Omnigraphics, 2009.

IllFestJapan-1993
Illustrated Festivals of Japan. Japan Travel Bureau, 1993.

IndianAmer-1989
Eagle/Walking Turtle. *Indian America.* John Muir Pub., 1989.

IntlThFolk-1979
Merin, Jennifer. *International Directory of Theatre, Dance, and Folklore Festivals.* Greenwood Press, 1979.

JapanFest-1965
Bauer, Helen, and Sherwin Carlquist. *Japanese Festivals.* Doubleday & Co., 1965.

LatinoLife-1995
Goring, Ruth. *Latino Life.* Rourke Pub., 1995.

Matsuri-1993
Ashkenazi, Michael. *Matsuri.* University of Hawaii Press, 1993.

MuhFest-1988
Von Grunebaum, Gustave E. *Muhammadan Festivals.* Olive Branch Press, 1988.

MusFest-1987
Ahsan, M.M. *Muslim Festivals.* Rourke Enterprises, 1987.

MusFestAmer-1990
Rabin, Carol Price. *The Complete Guide to Music Festivals in America.* 4th ed. Berkshire Traveller Press, 1990.

MusFestEurBrit-1980
Rabin, Carol Price. *Music Festivals in Europe and Britain.* Berkshire Traveller Press, 1980.

MusFestWrld-1963
Stoll, Dennis Gray. *Music Festivals of the World.* Pergamon Press, 1963.

NatlHolWrld-1968
Dobler, Lavinia. *National Holidays around the World.* Fleet Press Corp., 1968.

NewCentClassHandbk-1962
Avery, Catherine B., ed. *The New Century Classical Handbook.* Appleton Century-Crofts, 1962.

OxClassDict-1970
Hammond, N.G.L., and H.H. Scullard. *The Oxford Classical Dictionary.* 2nd ed. Clarendon Press, 1970.

OxDictSaints-1987
Farmer, David Hugh. *The Oxford Dictionary of Saints.* 2nd ed. Oxford University Press, 1987.

OxDictWRel-1997
Bowker, John, ed. *The Oxford Dictionary of World Religions.* Oxford University Press, 1997.

OxYear-1999
Blackburn, Bonnie, and Leofranc Holford Stevens. *The Oxford Companion to the Year.* Oxford University Press, 1999.

PatHols-2006
Henderson, Helene, ed. *Patriotic Holidays of the United States.* Omnigraphics, 2006.

RelFestSriLank-1982
Welbon, Guy R., and Glenn E. Yocum, eds. *Religious Festivals in South India and Sri Lanka.* Manohar, 1982.

RelHolCal-2004
Bellenir, Karen. *Religious Holidays and Calendars.* 3rd ed. Omnigraphics, 2004.

RomFest-1925
Fowler, W. Warde. *The Roman Festivals of the Period of the Republic.* Macmillan and Co., 1899. Reprinted in 1925.

RoundYr-1950
Pike, Royston. *Round the Year with the World's Religions.* 1950. Reprint. Omnigraphics, 1993.

SaintFestCh-1904
Brewster, H. Pomeroy. *Saints and Festivals of the Christian Church.* 1904. Reprint. Omnigraphics, 1990.

SeasFeast-1961
James, E.O. *Seasonal Feasts and Festivals.* 1961. Reprint. Omnigraphics, 1993.

SikhFest-1989
Kapoor, Sukhbir Singh. *Sikh Festivals.* Rourke Enterprises, 1989.

SpanFiestas-1968
Epton, Nina. *Spanish Fiestas.* A.S. Barnes and Co., 1968.

StoryWrldHol-1924
Humphrey, Grace. *Stories of the World's Holidays.* 1924. Reprint. Omnigraphics, 1990.

UndIslam-2004
Gulevich, Tanya. *Understanding Islam and Muslim Traditions.* Omnigraphics, 2004.

WildPlanet-1995
Clynes, Tom. *Wild Planet.* Gale Research, 1995.

WrldBuddhism-1984
Bechert, Heinz, and Richard Gombrich, eds. *The World of Buddhism.* Thames and Hudson, 1984.

YrbookEngFest-1954
Spicer, Dorothy Gladys. *Yearbook of English Festivals.* 1954. Reprint. Omnigraphics, 1993.

YrFest-1972
Palmer, Geoffrey, and Noel Lloyd. *A Year of Festivals.* Frederick Warne, 1972.

YrJapanFest-1974
Epstein, Sam, and Beryl Epstein. *A Year of Japanese Festivals.* Garrard Pub. Co., 1974.

For additional information on the sources used in this book, see the Bibliography in Appendix 13.

W9-ARC-998
WITHDRAWN FROM OUR COLLECTION
HUDSON

REF 394.26 HOL

Holidays, festivals, and celebrations
of the world dictionary : detailing
more than 3,000 observances from
all 50 states and more than 100 na-

For Reference

Not to be taken from this room

Holidays, Festivals, and Celebrations of the World Dictionary

*Detailing More Than 3,000 Observances from
All 50 States and More Than 100 Nations*

4th Edition

HUDSON PUBLIC LIBRARY
WOOD SQUARE
HUDSON, MA 01749

Holidays, Festivals, and Celebrations of the World Dictionary

Detailing More Than 3,000 Observances from All 50 States and More Than 100 Nations

4th Edition

A Compendious Reference Guide to Popular, Ethnic, Religious, National, and Ancient Holidays, Festivals, Celebrations, Commemorations, Holy Days, Feasts, and Fasts, Including Contact Information and Web Sites. Supplemented by Special Sections on Words Relating to Time, Calendar Systems, Phases of the Moon, the World's Major Living Religions, Facts about the U.S. States and Territories, Legal Holidays by State, Facts about the U.S. Presidents, Facts about Countries around the World, Legal Holidays by Country, Tourism Information Sources; and by an Annotated Bibliography and Chronological, Historic, Ancient, Folkloric, Calendar, Promotional, Sports, and Subject Indexes

Edited by
Cherie D. Abbey

P.O. Box 31-1640
Detroit, MI 48231-1640

HUDSON PUBLIC LIBRARY
WOOD SQUARE
HUDSON, MA 01749

Omnigraphics, Inc.

Cherie D. Abbey, *Editor*

Tanya Gulevich, Helene Henderson, Amy Keyzer,
and Sue Ellen Thompson, *Contributing Editors*

Brian Baughan, Laurie DiMauro, Sheila Fitzgerald, Joan Goldsworthy, Justin Karr,
Leslie Karr, Eve Nagler, Rhoda Wilburn, and Tom Wiloch, *Writers*

Allison A. Beckett and Mary Butler, *Research Staff*

* * *

Peter E. Ruffner, *Publisher*
Matthew P. Barbour, *Senior Vice President*

* * *

Elizabeth Collins, *Research and Permissions Coordinator*
Kevin M. Hayes, *Operations Manager*
Cherry Stockdale, *Permissions Assistant*
Shirley Amore, Martha Johns, and Kirk Kauffmann, *Administrative Staff*

Copyright © 2010 Omnigraphics, Inc.
ISBN 978-0-7808-0994-9

Special thanks to Frederick G. Ruffner for his role in creating this book.

Library of Congress Cataloging-in-Publication Data

Holidays, festivals, and celebrations of the world dictionary : detailing more than 3,000 observances from all 50 states and more than 100 nations : a compendious reference guide to popular, ethnic, religious, national, and ancient holidays. / edited by Cherie D. Abbey. -- 4th ed.

    p. cm.

    Includes bibliographical references and indexes.

    Summary: "A comprehensive dictionary that describes more than 3,000 holidays and festivals celebrated around the world. Features both secular and religious events from many different cultures, countries, and ethnic groups. Includes contact information for events; multiple appendices with background information on world holidays; extensive bibliography; multiple indexes"--Provided by publisher.

    ISBN 978-0-7808-0994-9 (hardcover : alk. paper) 1. Holidays--Dictionaries. 2. Festivals--Dictionaries. I. Abbey, Cherie D.

    GT3925.H64 2010

    394.26--dc22   2009041138

The information in this publication was compiled from sources cited and from sources considered reliable. While every possible effort has been made to ensure reliability, the publisher will not assume liability for damages caused by inaccuracies in the data, and makes no warranty, express or implied, on the accuracy of the information contained herein.

This book is printed on acid-free paper meeting the ANSI Z39.48 Standard. The infinity symbol that appears above indicates that the paper in this book meets that standard.

Printed in the United States of America.

Table of Contents

Dedicated to the Memory of
Leslie Alan Shepard,
June 21, 1917 – August 20, 2004

Les Shepard's contributions have informed and enlivened the catalogs of Omnigraphics and Gale Research since the 1960s. In addition to penning the graceful forewords to the first three editions of this publication, he edited the now classic *Encyclopedia of Occultism and Parapsychology* for Gale. Les brought a vast store of knowledge and diverse interests to everything he did. The book world will miss his warmth, wit, peaceful spirit, and dedication to the advancement of knowledge throughout the world.

Peter E. Ruffner
Publisher

Foreword to the Fourth Edition

Holidays, festivals, and celebrations of the world ... what could be more important? Although many people are inclined to view holidays and celebrations as fun, at best, and occasions for unproductive behavior, at worst, this question may seem unusual. However, that is the secret of holidays—they are much more than they seem.

Holidays, Festivals, and Celebrations of the World Dictionary, 4th edition, includes special occasions of all kinds, not just official holidays. In fact, many of our most joyful activities are not legal holidays at all. Halloween, for instance, is widely celebrated throughout the United States and Canada, as well as in Ireland, and it is growing in popularity throughout Europe. But is not an official holiday; we do not receive a day's rest from employment on October 31. Instead it is a "popular" holiday in the truest sense: people are motivated to celebrate it regardless of the often hostile views toward it held by both church and state. With its ever-increasing popularity Halloween has, in the U.S., become the second-largest revenue-producing occasion on the calendar, second only to the mighty Christmas season. Looking further at Halloween, we can see just how complex such occasions actually are.

Halloween is generally thought by scholars to be derived from an ancient Celtic festival of the dead and the new year, called "Samhain" (pronounced "sawen"). The American Halloween grew in popularity in the 19th century with the great influx of Irish immigrants. By the mid-20th century Halloween was known primarily as a children's festival, but since the 1970s it is celebrated increasingly by people of all ages, often with large, urban costume processions. Halloween provides an occasion for parody and satire—the foibles and feet of clay of politicians and celebrities are frequently mocked in costumed display. Moreover, Halloween has become a primary festival of autumn, with its pumpkins, apples, nuts, squash, and other harvest-seasonal fruits and vegetables. In turn, these are linked to images of death (skeletons, fake graves, and ghosts), perhaps suggesting that the lives and deaths of people are intimately related to the natural cycle of growth, harvest, and new life. Further, Halloween is the Eve of All Saints Day and is in this way connected to Christian ritual. Neo-pagans prefer to relate to it as Samhain, while many devout Christians condemn the imagery of devils, seeing Halloween as a satanic occasion. So there is no one "right" interpretation of Halloween, no one "right" way to celebrate it.

Internationally, traditional celebrations of All Saints Day (November 1) and All Souls Day (November 2), both religious and secular, are quite common. The American-style Halloween is making inroads, however, due to the influence of television programs imported from the U.S. and the efforts of such commercial interests as candy manufacturers. While they have had some success, there is also frequent resistance to the idea of abandoning the national and traditional customs of, for instance, France. The government of Mexico, which observes this period as the Days of the Dead, has actively attempted to stop the American Halloween from crossing the border. In these cases, Halloween has become a symbol, not of harvest or death, but of cultural imperialism.

Halloween, then, a night of the year that most people view as inconsequential fun, is in fact an extension of peoples' religious, regional, or ethnic identities, and has become another area of globalized industrial and cultural contestation.

The holidays and celebrations included in this encyclopedia all have their hidden dimensions: those of identity, for instance, whether regional, as in community festivals; religious, such as saints' days; occupational, such as blessings of the fleet, or blessings of tools; or gender and sexuality, such as Gay Pride Day. Holidays are also important markers of season and transition through the year. Our celebrations are opportunities for people to come together, to share—and to create—their sense of groupness, of belonging. Holidays and celebrations anchor people in time and place.

Nor are they all fun and games. Unfortunately, they can exclude people from backgrounds other than that being celebrated. In Northern Ireland, for instance, with its history of political and sectarian violence related to religion and national heritage, not everyone is Irish on Saint Patrick's Day (March 17). Nor are they all British on Orangemen's Day (July 12). Catholic parades and celebrations of March 17 have been restricted to local neighborhoods, while the large July 12 parades dominate the main streets and highways of the cities and towns. As a result, riots have occurred over parade routes and other public displays. Not all celebrations are greeted with enthusiasm, and they are often—as in the case of the Pride Day celebrations—the objects of derision and intense resistance.

Many of our holidays and holy days are derived from the biographies of great leaders. In this way, the rites of passage of the life cycle becomes institutionalized (e.g. Christmas, or the birthday of Buddha or Martin Luther King, Jr.). Rituals mark such transitions as birth, marriage, and death, as well as seasonal, solar, and lunar transitions. The latter are our seasonal holidays and festivals. In all cases, however, people, families and friends, celebrate with traditions both old and new. The memories created are among peoples' most treasured. The holiday materials saved in boxes from schoolchildren, the family recipes, the photographs—these are what people will run back into the burning building to save. Holidays and celebrations may be ephemeral, may be fun, may allow for otherwise disreputable behavior (such as heavy drinking). But fun, and periods of license, are not unimportant. Setting aside time to acknowledge our collective past, to celebrate our values, and to have the opportunity to suspend the rules for a while—this is something that only human beings seem to do. Holidays and celebrations mark moments of life and history that we consider MOST important, not least. But they disguise their profound purpose with fun.

Holidays, festivals, and celebrations of the world … what could be more important?

Jack Santino
Department of Popular Culture
Bowling Green State University

Foreword to the Third Edition

This is the third edition of an indispensable guide to one of the important and enduring subject areas of everyday life.

The celebration of special days and seasons, both religious and secular, is universal. From primitive times onwards, special rites and festivals have marked the religious mysteries of existence—the enigma of birth, life, death, and rebirth in the environment and in individual human experience. Such celebrations fulfilled a deep-seated urge in the human psyche, evoking profound emotions associated with the changing pattern of the year, the promise of spring, the joys of summer, the harvest, the decline of the year through fall to the rigors of winter, and the promise of a new spring. The divine source of this mystery was to be acknowledged and propitiated so that human prosperity and fertility flourished in the struggle for existence throughout the passing of time.

In individual experience, the day of birth and also of death of oneself and members of the family and tribe had special meaning. The achievements of gifted men and women of special talents and deeds who guided and safeguarded tribes and nations were also celebrated in orally transmitted texts, ballads, and stories, marked by special rites and festivals.

Inevitably such celebrations involved a measurement of time, so that seasonal festivals could take place at appropriate dates in the cycle of the year. But for thousands of years, primitive and pantheistic concepts of the universe inhibited the exact timing of festivals. In the natural division of time, the solar day is the daily revolution of the earth and the alternation of light and darkness, the solar year is the circle of seasons of the earth's revolution around the sun. Months are the divisions resulting from the lunar phases of the moon. But the division of time into hours, days, or months is more arbitrary, and it was not until early Roman times that the calendar month as such was formalized for civil convenience; the word "calendar" itself derives from the Latin *Kalendae*. By 46 B.C., the time of Julius Caesar, the Roman civil calendar had become three months out of phase with the true astronomical year. That year was called *ultimus annus confusionis*, "the last year of the muddled reckoning." The Julian calendar reform in the first century B.C., which became the standard of Western countries, corrected the discrepancy and regularized a calendar based on the solar cycle. Though far more accurate, the Julian calendar still resulted in a discrepancy, since the "average" year of 365.25 days—requiring the insertion of an extra leap year day once every four years—became progressively out of step with the real solar year of 365.242199 days.

In a papal bull of February 24, 1582, Pope Gregory XIII inaugurated the Gregorian calendar, which required the deletion of ten days from the calendar (to bring it back into phase with the astronomical year) in October 1582, and the occasional adjustment whereby three out of every four "century" years are not leap years (1700, 1800 and 1900 were not leap years; the year 2000 was). October 4, 1582, was followed by October 15 in the calendar, much to the confusion of the populace. But the Gregorian calendar was eventually adopted, at least for civil purposes, throughout the West and remains a worldwide standard to this day. Meanwhile, of course, other ancient calendars, such as the Jewish and Islamic, have continued to exist side by side with the Gregorian calendar. *Holidays, Festivals, and Celebrations of the World Dictionary* includes a discussion on the history of ancient and modern calendars and clarifies such complexities.

ix

Different religions have continued to find common ground in the concept of special days to mark the supreme mysteries of life. Three of the great world religions—Judaism, Christianity, and Islam—have all recognized a holy day of rest from the week of toil for special worship. The Sabbath of Judaism was moved by Christians from Saturday to Sunday, while for Muslims, "the day of assembly" in a mosque is Friday.

Many different religions meet in their interpretation of festival times of the year. With the rise of Christianity in Europe, some of the old pagan festivals were retained by the new Church, although given different religious associations. Yet behind the feasting and merrymaking of Christmas, one might still hear dim echoes of ancient winter solstice festivals of light, the Roman Saturnalia, the Druidic rites with mistletoe, and the strange gods of Saxon mythology.

In addition to religious festivals, the ancient Romans made a distinction between religious and secular events, and the institution of secular holidays has since proliferated in the countries of the world. Even so, secular holidays still have their roots in the concept of some special significance of certain days necessitating a break in the daily toil of normal life. The very word "holiday" is derived from "holy day."

Secular holidays excite deep emotions. We love to celebrate the birthdays of family members and friends with greetings and gifts. So, too, we feel a strong sense of belonging to a social group or nation observing holidays that unite us in common ties of special interest, ethnicity, or national pride.

In the past, the great festivals and holidays were kept alive by folk memory, or by the many almanacs sold by peddlers giving the dates of fairs and other events and anniversaries, together with lunar information, tides, eclipses, and even prophecies, spiced with quaint aphorisms and proverbs. In 1732, Benjamin Franklin became author-editor-publisher of the *Poor Richard* series of almanacs that popularized such pithy folk wisdom as "God helps them that help themselves" and "Necessity never made a good bargain." The British counterpart of *Poor Richard* was the *Vox Stellarm* of Dr. Francis Moore, first published in 1700, descendants of which are still published annually under the title *Old Moore's Almanack*.

In nineteenth-century Britain, antiquaries published various volumes of discursive lore, listing the significance of days of the calendar, festivals, and holidays, and their history. The best of these was the delightful work *The Book of Days: A Miscellany of Popular Antiquities in Connection with the Calendar, Including Anecdote, Biography & History, Curiosities of Literature, and Oddities of Human Life and Character*, by Robert Chambers (two volumes, 1862-64, reissued by Omnigraphics in 1990). Such books are fascinating to browse through for their out-of-the-way information and bygone lore, but although many of the festivals and holidays discussed are still celebrated, there have been scores of newer holidays in the U.S. and worldwide in the twentieth century.

The range of festivals and secular holidays in the various countries of the world is now vast. In modern times the proliferation of national and local events has also resulted in scores of special group days, and even whimsical and bizarre observances, ranging from Buzzard Day in Hinckley, Ohio, to the Rat's Wedding Day in China.

Publication of the first edition of *Holidays, Festivals, and Celebrations of the World Dictionary* in 1994 provided a truly comprehensive annotated reference work giving information on national and international festivals and holidays, with descriptive entries covering religious, cultural, ethnic, historical, popular, and sports celebrations from all over the world, with special sections on calendar systems, and tables of state and national public holidays. In addition to a General Index of people, places, institutions, and other keywords, easy reference was facilitated by special indexes of Chronological, Religious, and Special Subjects (including Ancient/Pagan, Calendar, Folkloric, Historical, Pro¬motional, and Sporting entries).

The second edition in 1997 was greatly enlarged and updated by hundreds of new entries covering state, national and legal holidays, and independence, republic, and national days for countries of the world. There were also special sections of biographical information, annotated bibliographies, and other valuable additions.

Now the present third edition is even further enlarged and updated. There are more than 400 new entries, an expanded section on calendar systems, and a perpetual calendar, together with a combining of the Ethnic and Geographic, Religious Groups, Subject, and General (Alphabetical and Keyword) indexes, while retaining the existing index access. There is also the newer technical information on web sites, e-mail addresses, and other contacts.

This is a key reference work for general and professional use, for schools and public libraries, but it is also a multi-purpose dictionary. Ministers of different denominations will find it valuable for its broad coverage of the festivals of Christianity and those of other world religions. Business people planning promotional journeys will find its information of special value when visiting foreign countries and different states in the U.S. Politicians and other dignitaries will find it useful in marking the local and national importance of given days. Schoolchildren can learn about the meaning of individual holidays and the observances of different religions and ethnic groups as well as the popular fun festivals of various states and countries.

All kinds of travelers will value the listings of public holidays in the U.S. and other countries, and it will also add special interest to the planning of personal vacations at home and abroad. In addition to the often spectacular festivals of the world, there are now scores of lighthearted or tongue-in-cheek popular holiday events, such as the Great American Duck Race in Deming, New Mexico, or the Garlic Festival in Gilroy, California. From state to state and country to country there are humorous, quaint, and diverting events which have become great tourist attractions. Journalists will find this an invaluable desk book for news stories on the significance of days.

The wide range of international coverage reflects the history and cultural identity of many countries. This has special significance for the U.S., which has always been a melting pot of nationalities, each with their own traditions and customs. Side by side with the memory of such ethnic and cultural identity goes the assimilation of specifically American history and culture. In turn, this helps to bring harmony and understanding in the host community and towards other countries and peoples of the world, enhancing pride and pleasure in honouring the great events of world history and culture, the men and women who brought them about, and sharing the excitement and happiness of festival days.

Leslie Shepard
Dublin, Ireland

Preface

This revised and expanded fourth edition of *Holidays, Festivals, and Celebrations of the World Dictionary (HFCWD)* contains up-to-date information about more than 3,000 holidays, festivals, celebrations, commemorations, holy days, feasts and fasts, and other observances from all parts of the world, including more than 500 entries that are new to this edition. Entries include events for which people come together for a day or periods of up to a few days or (rarely) weeks for special activities, celebrations, commemorations, or rituals. These events have a story to tell, in that each is significant, unusual, or somehow remarkable. Holidays and festivals for more than 100 countries, as well as events specifically observed in every state of the United States, are included.

The entries cover holidays and festivals that are popular, secular, religious, or a combination thereof. The majority of entries covers events still celebrated or observed, but a few ancient and discontinued events are included because allusions to them still appear in literature or art, or occur in discourse.

Birth or death anniversaries of famous individuals generally are not included, nor are simple anniversaries of historical events. But those few such events that are regularly observed with significant celebrations or special activities, or that have particular cultural significance, such as COLUMBUS DAY, MARTIN LUTHER KING, JR.'S BIRTHDAY, MAWLID AL-NABI, or PEARL HARBOR DAY, are included.

Most entries in *HFCWD* have national or wide regional significance, but some local events that are offbeat, colorful, distinctive, or bizarre have also been included, such as the DETROIT ELECTRONIC MUSIC FESTIVAL, the GREAT FALLS SKI CLUB MANNEQUIN JUMP, the MOBILE-PHONE THROWING WORLD CHAMPIONSHIP, and the WORLD ROCK PAPER SCISSORS CHAMPIONSHIP. Entries for well-known days of religious significance, such as CHRISTMAS, ROSH HASHANAH, and RAMADAN, contain information seldom found in other current reference sources.

Audience

HFCWD is intended for elementary, middle, and high schools, academic and public libraries, as well as churches, synagogues, mosques, community affairs groups, and others interested in learning about festive events.

Organization

Main Entries and Alternate Forms

The book is arranged alphabetically by name of holiday. Main entries appear in boldface. All main entries are numbered, and these numbers are used in the indexes. Well-known alternate names of the main entry appear in parentheses immediately after the main entry, e.g., Hanukkah (Chanukah). Common alternate forms appear in boldface within the text of the entry, and cross-references to other entries in the book appear in SMALL CAPITAL letters.

Order of Main Entries

Since people looking for information on a given subject may not know its official title, main entries have been written with the key words first. Thus, words such as *birthday, death of, feast, festa, festival, fête, fiesta, national,* and *international* have been transposed to the end of the main entry, as in BAB, BIRTH OF THE; BASTILLE, FESTIVAL DE LA; and OLD-TIME FIDDLERS' CONTEST, NATIONAL.

The rationale for organizing events derived from people's names can be particularly difficult. Some event names use only the person's last name, while other events use the first and last. To simplify the search process for readers, events where a person's name forms the first part of the event name are alphabetized under the person's last name, as in FAWKES (GUY) DAY and PARKER (CHARLIE) JAZZ FESTIVAL.

Spelling and Forms Used for Main Entries

HFCWD deals with events that relate to many cultures, the original names of which involve a number of alphabets and non-Roman writing systems. As much as possible, spellings and forms for main entries were standardized for ease of access. The following were used as guides on spelling standardization:

- For Hindu and Islamic calendars and events: *The Encyclopedia of Religion*, Mircea Eliade, ed., Macmillan, 1987.

- For Jewish calendar and events: *The Jewish Holidays: A Guide and Commentary*, Michael Strassfeld, Harper & Row, 1985, as well as *The Encyclopedia of Religion* by Eliade.

- For Asian and African holidays and events no single standard was used. The form used is that appearing most often in the sources consulted. For many Hindu, Islamic, and Asian terms, diacriticals unfamiliar to the non-specialist were omitted.

- General sources consulted were *Encyclopedia Britannica* (15th edition, 1995), *Columbia Encyclopedia* (fifth edition, 1993), *Merriam-Webster's Biographical Dictionary* (1995), and *Merriam-Webster's Geographical Dictionary* (third edition, 1997).

Dates

On the line below the main entry, the date of celebration or observance is given in italics. For those entries whose date is based on a lunar calendar, we have shown the approximate date in the Gregorian calendar followed by the lunar date. The exception is for events based on the strictly lunar Islamic calendar, where only the Islamic month and day are given. See appendix 2, *Calendars throughout History: An Overview of Calendar Systems around the World*, for a detailed explanation of the Islamic calendar.

Religious Holidays

For the most part, entries for religious holidays are spelled and described in terms of the major religion that observes them. If only some followers of a major religion observe a holiday, or if different branches or sects commemorate something different (or nothing at all) on a given holiday, the entry specifies the practice of the particular group. ST. JOHN THE BAPTIST'S DAY, for instance, is recognized by most Christians, and so is described (and indexed) as "Christian," despite the fact that some Christians do not venerate saints. The holy day of ASHURA is observed quite differently by Sunni and Shi'ite Muslims, and so both practices are described.

Christian Denominations

For Christianity, references to the West or Western Church generally include the Roman Catholic Church, the branches of the Anglican Communion, and major Protestant denominations. References to the East or Eastern Church include Orthodox Christians, such as Greek and Russian Orthodox; "separated" churches, such as the Nestorian Church, the Syrian churches, the Coptic Orthodox Church in Egypt, the Armenian Orthodox Church, and the Ethiopian Orthodox Church; and the Uniate churches, or Eastern Catholics, including the Malabar Church in India and the Melchite and Maronite churches.

Sources

Abbreviated reference source titles are provided for entries as applicable, followed by the relevant page number(s) where one can find information in that source. A key to the abbreviations appears on the inside front and back covers of the book. For a complete bibliographic listing of all sources used, see the Bibliography in the Appendices.

Contact Information

Names, addresses, phone and fax numbers, and web sites (when available) are included for entries on contemporary public festivals and other events. In some cases, the organization(s) listed are actual sponsors. In others, an embassy or tourist office is given; such agencies are not necessarily responsible for the event, but they are provided as likely sources of information about the event. In a few cases, entries discuss events in several locations, but we have maintained a limit of no more than three contacts per entry. Generally excluded are such religious or contemplative holidays as EASTER, HANUKKAH, KARWACHOTH, and LAYLAT AL-MIRAJ—for which the obvious contact would be a local church, synagogue, temple, or mosque, although in some cases, web sites of churches and religious organizations do provide additional information—as well as holidays that tend to be private or domestic observances, such as MOTHER'S DAY and APRIL FOOLS' DAY. More general contact information is provided in Appendix 8, *Tourism Information Sources for the U.S. States and North America*, and Appendix 12, *Tourism Information Sources for Countries around the World*.

New Entries

More than 500 new entries have been added to this edition. They include independence days, national days, republic days, and liberation days around the world. More religious holidays appear in this edition, and more celebrations of Native North Americans. There are dozens of new entries on holidays and festivals in many countries, such as Azerbaijan, Czechoslovakia, Croatia, Eritrea, Liberia, Malawi, Moldova, Myanmar, North and South Korea, Palau, Rwanda, Timor-Leste, and more. Coverage of festivals in the United States has been expanded as well, ranging from those celebrating American heritage (such as the KUNTA KINTE HERITAGE FESTIVAL in Maryland) to the offbeat (NATIONAL MANLY MAN FESTIVAL AND SPAM COOK-OFF in Washington), the disgusting (TARANTULA FEST AND BARBECUE in California), the nostalgic (WOODWARD DREAM CRUISE in Michigan), and the solemn (PATRIOT DAY/SEPTEMBER 11 DAY in New York).

Special Features New to This Edition

As well as adding more than 500 new entries to this new edition, we have also updated 10 appendices and three indexes. In addition, three new appendices have been added that further expand understanding of world holidays: Appendix 4, *Phases of the Moon from 2009 to 2020*; Appendix 5, *Overview of the World's Major Religions*; and Appendix 10, *Facts about Countries around the World*. A full list of the book's appendices is included below.

Appendices

1. *Glossary of Words Relating to Time*
   This section includes a descriptive listing of words relating to periods of time.

2. *Calendars throughout History: An Overview of Calendar Systems around the World*
   This section includes an overview of the evolution of calendar systems throughout history and throughout the world.

3. *Comparative Table of Calendar Systems*
   This section shows the relationship among various calendar systems, including Gregorian, Jewish, Hindu, Jain, Buddhist, Sikh, and Burmese calendars.

4. *Phases of the Moon from 2009 to 2020 Given in Eastern Standard Time* (NEW!)
   This section explains the importance of the moon to the world's religions and includes charts that show the phases of the moon.

5. *Overview of the World's Major Religions* (NEW!)
   This section provides basic information about the world's major religions, including when and where originated, founder(s), theological orientation, major sacred texts, denominations and sects, estimated number of adherents around the world, and a listing of the main holidays in chronological order by the religion's calendar.

6. *Facts about the U.S. States and Territories*
   This section includes a range of information for each of the 50 states, the District of Columbia, Puerto Rico, and the U.S. territories.

7. *Legal Holidays by State*
   This section lists legal public holidays in each of the states, the District of Columbia, Puerto Rico, and the U.S. territories.

8. *Tourism Information Sources for the U.S. States and North America*
   This section includes tourism information sources for the United States, Canada, and Mexico.

9. *Facts about the U.S. Presidents*
   This section lists all U.S. presidents in the order in which they held office, includes basic biographical information, and lists notable landmarks commemorating them, along with contact information and web sites.

10. *Facts about Countries around the World* (NEW!)
    This section provides basic information about the independent nations of the world: official name (in English); capital city; internet country code; flag description; national anthem, motto, and symbols (when available); geographical description of location; total area; brief climate description; proper terms for nationality; population numbers; languages spoken; and information on ethnic groups and religions.

11. *Legal Holidays by Country*
    This section lists legal public holidays around the world in alphabetical order by country.

12. *Tourism Information Sources for Countries around the World*
    This section includes tourism information sources for countries around the world, except the United States, Canada, and Mexico (see Appendix 8). The listings are in alphabetical order by name of the country.

13. *Bibliography*
    This section includes an annotated listing of sources cited or consulted in *HFCWD*, as well as other sources for further reading.

Indexes

Several indexes provide reference to entries (as appropriate) for each of the following categories. In all indexes in this edition, references to entries are given by entry numbers, not page numbers.

1. *Chronological Index—Fixed Days and Events*
   Indexes events that are celebrated at a specific time.

2. *Chronological Index—Movable Days*

   Indexes events whose date of celebration is not fixed, particularly those that are observed according to non-Gregorian calendars and those that depend on the date of Easter.

3. *Special Subject Index*

   Divides events into six categories:

   Ancient/Pagan—Indexes events rooted in ancient times.

   Calendar—Indexes events that deal specifically with the calendar.

   Folkloric—Indexes events rooted in folklore and tradition.

   Historic—Indexes commemorations of specific events in history.

   Promotional—Indexes festivals that promote something, such as a location or activity.

   Sporting—Indexes events that are based on or revolve around sports, games, etc.

   Some events may be categorized in more than one of the above special subjects. For instance, ST. PATRICK'S DAY is listed under the Historic Index, because it commemorates a historical person, and the Folkloric Index, for all the folk legends and traditions associated with St. Patrick and his feast day.

4. *General Index*

   Lists names of festivals and holidays by keyword, religious groups, ethnic groups, geographic locations, names of individuals, institutions, and other items of significance appearing within the text of the entries. For example, foods, animals, music, customs, and activities closely associated with an event are indexed—both those that are the subject of an observance and those that play significant roles in observances. Also indexed are celebratory elements common to various cultures.

Acknowledgments

Holidays, Festivals, and Celebrations of the World Dictionary would not have been possible without the assistance, inspiration, and diligence of many people. Special thanks go to Frank R. Abate and Jacquelyn S. Goodwin for developing the first edition of the *Dictionary*. We also thank Barbara Carlson, Donna Rhein, Kathleen Mallory, and Marian J. Darling for editorial and research work on the first edition.

We also wish to recognize the assistance provided by a number of clergy members, especially Rabbi Carl Astor of Congregation Beth-El, the Rev. Ralph W. Merrill of St. James Episcopal Church, and the Rev. Constantine J. Simones of St. Sophia Hellenic Orthodox Church, all in New London, Connecticut; and the Rev. Paul E. Lutz of St. Paul Lutheran Church, Old Saybrook, Connecticut. Their prompt responses to our many questions and their willingness to look up arcane information were indispensable.

For their contributions to the third edition, we are deeply grateful to Tanya Gulevich, David Henderson, Amy Keyzer, Carol H. Munson, Lori Packwood and Writers Research Group, Mary Ann Stavros-Lanning, Jenifer Swanson, and Sue Ellen Thompson.

For their work on the fourth edition, we would like to thank Brian Baughan, Laurie DiMauro, Sheila Fitzgerald, Joan Goldsworthy, Justin Karr, Leslie Karr, Eve Nagler, Rhoda Wilburn, and Tom Wiloch. Special thanks go to Helene Henderson, whose editorial expertise and knowledge of the material contributed greatly to this edition as well.

Finally, we must extend many thanks and best wishes to the countless festival sponsors, embassy and consulate personnel, and tourism professionals who helped put the formidable job of accurate coverage within the realm of possibility.

Even with all the essential contributions of the individuals mentioned above and others, we must add that the responsibility for any errors or omissions in *HFCWD* rests solely with the editor.

Comments and Suggestions

We welcome your comments on *HFCWD* and suggestions for events that warrant coverage in future editions. Please address correspondence to:

Editor, *Holidays, Festivals, and Celebrations of the World Dictionary*
Omnigraphics, Inc.
PO Box 31-1640
Detroit, MI 48231-1640
Email: editorial@omnigraphics.com

Holidays, Festivals, and Celebrations of the World Dictionary

A

◆ 0001 ◆ **Aban Parab**
February, March, October; 10th day of Aban, the eighth Zoroastrian month

In the Zoroastrian calendar, each of the 30 days of the month bears the name of the *yazata*, or spiritual being, who is believed to preside over that day. Similarly, each of the 12 months bears the name of the yazata who rules over that month. When the day and the month both share the same name, as they do on the 10th of Aban, it is considered a name-day feast. The yazata of the month of Aban is the female waters. On name-feast days Zoroastrians attend services in a fire temple, a meeting hall, or a private home.

Because of discrepancies in the calendars used by widely separated Zoroastrian communities around the world, there are now three different calendars in use, and the 10th of Aban can fall either in October, March, or February according to the Gregorian calendar.

Followers of the Zoroastrian religion, which was founded by the prophet Zoroaster (or Zarathushtra, who is believed to have lived around 1200 B.C.E.), today live primarily in Iran and northwestern India, although smaller communities exist in Pakistan, Sri Lanka, Canada, the U.S., England, and Australia.

SOURCES:
RelHolCal-2004, p. 68

◆ 0002 ◆ **Abbey Road on the River**
Memorial Day Weekend

Even decades after the final Beatles recording, the music of the Fab Four from Liverpool, England, is still compelling enough to draw thousands of rock fans together for a single Beatles event. Abbey Road on the River, which takes place along the banks of the Ohio River in Louisville, Ky., is the largest celebration of the band's music in North America. As many as 25,000 town residents attend—along with Beatles fans from all over the world—to see dozens of tribute bands perform on six stages.

The first Abbey Road on the River, in 2002, took place along the banks of the Cuyahoga River in Cleveland, Ohio. The festivities were moved to their present location in 2006. Once a three-day affair, the festival has expanded to five days, with performances by more than 40 bands at the four outdoor venues of the Riverfront Plaza Belvedere as well as in two indoor theaters in town.

Festival highlights include shows of complete albums, including a 30-member performance of the *White Album*. In addition to the live music, the event also offers a film festival, lectures, and vendors selling a variety of merchandise, collectibles, and artwork.

CONTACTS:
Abbey Road on the River
2673 Green Rd.
Shaker Heights, OH 44122
216-378-1980
www.abbeyroadontheriver.com

◆ 0003 ◆ **Abbotsford International Air Show**
August

Widely recognized as Canada's national air show, this three-day event is an opportunity for the aviation industry to display the latest developments in civilian aircraft. Since the first show was held in 1962, it has included aerobatic performances by the Canadian Armed Forces, the Royal Air Force, the Snowbirds Jet Team, and the U.S. Air Force's Thunderbirds. Aviation-related equipment is on display, and there is a large banquet featuring well-known personalities in the aviation and aerospace fields. The show is held at the airport in Abbotsford, British Columbia, and is regularly attended by upwards of 200,000 people.

CONTACTS:
Abbotsford International Airshow Society
1276 Tower St., Unit 4
Abbotsford, BC V2T 6H5 Canada
604-852-8511; fax: 604-852-6093
www.abbotsfordairshow.com

SOURCES:
GdWorldFest-1985, p. 31

◆ 0004 ◆ **Abdu'l-Baha, Ascension of**
November 28

The Ascension of Abdul'l-Baha is a holy day in the Baha'i religion that commemorates the death of Abbas Effendi, known as Abdu'l-Baha, in 1921 in Haifa, Palestine (now Israel). The eldest son of Mirza Husayn Ali, known as Baha'u'llah, the prophet-founder of the Baha'i faith, he was named the leader of the Baha'i community in his father's will, which also appointed him to interpret Baha'i writings. In turn, Abdu'l-Baha appointed his eldest grandson, Shoghi Effendi (1896-1957) as his successor and Guardian of the Cause. Today the affairs of the worldwide Baha'i community are administered by the Universal House of Justice, a body that meets in Haifa and is elected every five years.

CONTACTS:
Bahai National Center
1233 Central St.
Evanston, IL 60201
800-228-6483 or 847-733-3400; fax: 847-733-3578
www.us.bahai.org

Bahai International Community
866 United Nations Pl., Ste. 120
New York, NY 10017
212-803-2500; fax: 212-803-2566
www.bahai.org

SOURCES:
AnnivHol-2000, p. 197
ConEncyBahai-2000, p. 14
RelHolCal-2004, p. 157

♦ 0005 ♦ Abdullah's (King) Birthday in Jordan
January 30

Since 1999, the year Abdullah II bin al-Hussein succeeded his father, King Hussein, as national monarch, Jordan has celebrated the king's birthday. It is typical on this date for the Royal Hashemite Court of Jordan to publish various well-wishes that arrive from Arab leaders, Western leaders, and other international dignitaries.

Before 2007, the country also observed the day as an official national holiday by closing all its banks and stores. However, that year King Abdullah announced that in order to help "boost productivity and dedication," banks and businesses would remain open on his birthday. He also asked citizens to do the same on the birthday of his late father, another public holiday.

CONTACTS:
Jordan Embassy
3504 International Dr. N.W.
Washington, D.C. 20008
202-265-1606; fax: 202-667-0777
HKJEmbassyDC@jordanembassyus.org

♦ 0006 ♦ Abha Festival
Six weeks in July-August

Situated in the mountains and blessed with mild weather in an otherwise harsh climate, the city of Adha, Saudi Arabia, is also a popular tourist attraction that boasts amusement parks, a shopping district, and a hotel industry. The Abha

Festival, which lasts about six weeks, was established in 1998 to help sustain the city's appeal among tourists. In past years, over 1.5 million visitors have traveled to the city and attended the festival's sports competitions, religious activities, and concerts featuring Arab pop stars. The concert series, which has the distinction of being Saudi Arabia's first public music event, first took place during the inaugural Adha Festival.

The summer festival's main event has consistently been the music program. Its performers cater to younger Saudis, who have been the target audience over the years. Other youth-oriented activities include sailing competitions, horse racing, and soccer.

Addressing general anxieties about the negative impact of popular culture on young festival-goers, organizers ensure the program maintains moral standards by coordinating with officials of the Commission for the Promotion of Virtue and Prevention of Vice.

CONTACTS:
Saudi Arabia Embassy
601 New Hampshire Ave. N.W.
Washington, D.C. 20037
202-337-4076; fax: 202-944-5983
www.saudiembassy.net

♦ 0007 ♦ Aboakyer Festival
April or May

The Effutu people of Winneba, Ghana, celebrate the **Deer-Hunting Festival** by making an offering to the god Penkye Otu. Two groups known as the Asafo companies, each consisting of about 150 people ranging in age from young boys to grandfathers, compete in a deer hunt that begins at dawn with the pounding of drums and the ringing of bells. When the first deer is caught, the victorious company brings it back alive and presents it proudly to their chief. Then the animal is taken back to the village, where dancing and drumming continue in an effort to placate Penkye Otu so that he will bring them a bountiful year.

CONTACTS:
Ghana Tourist Board
P.O. Box 4386
Accra, Ghana
233-21-666314; fax: 233-21-244611
www.touringghana.com

SOURCES:
FestGhana-1970, p. 33
FolkWrldHol-1999, p. 272

♦ 0008 ♦ Aboriginal Day, National
June 21

To foster respect and appreciation for the traditions and cultures of Canada's indigenous peoples, the government in 1996 designated the summer solstice as National Aboriginal Day. Long before the national holiday was established, this day of the year had been observed by Canada's Inuit, Métis, and First Nations peoples as a summer celebration commemorating Aboriginal heritage. Coordinating with National Aboriginal organizations, the Canadian government made June 21 an official holiday with the objective of including all citizens in the observance.

Celebrations take place throughout Canada's provinces and territories and are organized by the regional offices of Indian and Northern Affairs Canada and Canadian Heritage. Some festivities are modest celebrations like summer barbecues and picnics, while others exhibit a stronger focus on culture and tradition by holding canoe races, powwows, and awareness events.

Since becoming an official holiday, National Aboriginal Day has been designated the opening day of Celebrate Canada! This 11-day celebration also includes St-Jean Baptiste Day, Canadian Multiculturalism Day, and CANADA DAY.

CONTACTS:
Indian and Northern Affairs Canada
Ottawa, ON K1A 0H4 Canada
www.ainc-inac.gc.ca/index-eng.asp

♦ 0009 ♦ **Abu Simbel Festival**
February 22 and October 22

This festival celebrates the two days of the year on which the light of the rising sun can reach the 180-foot deep innermost chambers of Abu Simbel, the great temple of Ramses II, in Egypt. The temple was designed so that only on these two days in February and October does the sun shine on the four gods in the sanctuary: Ptah, Amen-Re, Ramses, and Re-Horakhty. This temple, the most colossal in Egypt, was built by Ramses II between 1300 and 1233 B.C.E., and is famous for its four 65-foot statues of the seated Ramses. It is actually two temples—one for Ramses and one for queen Nefertiti—and is extraordinary for its grandeur, beauty, and history. It was unknown to the European world until Swiss explorer Johann Burckhardt found it in 1812. The Italian Giovanni Belzoni excavated the entrance and explored the temple in 1816. In 1964, when the new Aswan Dam was to be built, creating a lake that would have drowned the temple, it was cut into 2,000 pieces and reassembled at a site about 180 feet higher. It is not as perfect as it was at the foot of the cliff—but it was saved.

It is thought that there must have been ritual celebrations in ancient times on the days when the sun penetrated the sanctuary. Today, television covers the event, and people gather to see the sunrise and to meditate. The sun now shines on the sanctuary a day earlier than it did before the temple was moved.

CONTACTS:
State Information Service, Egypt Ministry of Information
3 Al Estad Al Bahary St.
Nasr City, Cairo Egypt
20-2261-7304; fax: 20-2261-7308
www.sis.gov.eg

♦ 0010 ♦ **Academy Awards Ceremony**
Late February or March

The glamour and glitz of Hollywood is on full display at the annual movie awards known as the **Oscars** or the Academy Awards. Presented every year since 1929 by the Academy of Motion Picture Arts and Sciences, these awards are presented for outstanding achievements in filmmaking during the preceding year.

Some of the best star-gazing occurs before the actual awards ceremony. That's when some of the film industry's best-known actors and actresses arrive in limousines, wearing everything from tuxedos and designer evening gowns to far less conventional outfits. After the awards—which include Oscars for Best Actor, Best Actress, Best Director, and Best Picture—are handed out, numerous after-show parties are held at various Los Angeles homes and restaurants.

CONTACTS:
Academy of Motion Picture Arts and Sciences
8949 Wilshire Blvd.
Beverly Hills, CA 90211
310-247-3000; fax: 310-859-9619
www.oscars.org

SOURCES:
FunAlsoRises-1998, p. 87

♦ 0011 ♦ **Acadian Day**
Two weeks in August

The original Acadians were 17th-century French colonists who settled in the area known as Acadia, which covered what is now Nova Scotia as well as Prince Edward Island, and parts of northern Maine and Quebec. Their French-speaking descendants in the Maritime Provinces continue to honor their heritage by holding many local Acadian Day celebrations, usually during the summer months.

Fifty thousand people attend the **Acadian Festival** in Caraquet, New Brunswick, the largest of these celebrations. The festival takes place for 14 days in August each year and includes Acadian dance performances, cabaret, and concerts as well as sporting contests and a blessing of the fleet. The highlight of the festival is "L'Acadie en Fête," a huge celebration involving Acadian musicians, singers, artists, and actors.

CONTACTS:
Festival acadien de Caraquet
220 Boul St-Pierre Ouest, Bureau 312
Caraquet, NB E1W 1A5 Canada
506-727-2787; fax: 506-727-1995
www.festivalacadien.ca/contenu.cfm?id=108

Tourism New Brunswick
P.O. Box 6000
Fredericton, NB E3B 5H1 Canada
www.tourismnbcanada.com

SOURCES:
DictDays-1988, p. 1
GdWrldFest-1985, p. 37

♦ 0012 ♦ **Acadian Festival**
Length varies, usually three-four days at the end of June

The Madawaska Territory, which at one time ran along the Canadian border between Maine and New Brunswick, was settled by a small group of farmers who were chased out of Acadia by the English in the late 18th century. As the settlements grew, they were separated into Canadian and American communities, with Edmundston on the Canadian side and Madawaska and St. David on the American side of the St. John River.

In 1978 the local historical society in Madawaska proclaimed June 28 as Acadian Day in the state of Maine, and since that time it has been the site of an Acadian (or French-Canadian) festival lasting anywhere from one day to a week. Regular events include French music and dancing, an Acadian Supper featuring *pot en pot* and *fougère,* a parade with bands and marching units from both Maine and Canada, and an Acadian mass followed by a procession to the white marble cross that marks the site of the original Acadian settlement. The festival usually coincides with a reunion of the original 13 families who settled here.

CONTACTS:
The Acadian Festival Committee
328 St. Thomas St.
Madawaska, ME 04756
207-728-6055; fax: 207-728-3611
www.acadianfestival.com

♦ 0013 ♦ **Acadiens, Festivals**
Third weekend in September

A combination of several festivals (food, music, crafts, and more) to celebrate Cajun culture in Lafayette, La., known as the capital of French Louisiana. When they were expelled from Nova Scotia by the British in the 1770s, the French Acadian farmers settled in the area around Lafayette in a region of 22 parishes that came to be known as Acadiana. The word "Cajun" comes from Acadian.

One part of the celebration is the Bayou Food Festival, which offers a range of Cajun cooking from crawfish gumbo to alligator sausage to corn maque-chou. The Louisiana Crafts Festival features handmade Cajun crafts and demonstrations by blacksmiths, decoy carvers, alligator skinners, and storytellers. The Festival de Musique Acadienne features centuries-old music sung in French. Modern crafts are also on exhibit, and lectures and workshops on the Acadian language and history are part of the weekend.

CONTACTS:
Lafayette Convention & Visitors Commission
1400 N.W. Evangeline Trwy.
Lafayette, LA 70501
800-346-1958 or 337-232-3737; fax: 337-232-0161
www.festivalsacadiens.com

♦ 0014 ♦ **Accession of H.H. Sheikh Zayed as Ruler of Abu Dhabi**
August 6

On August 6, 1966, His Highness Sheikh Zayed bin Sultan Al Nahyan overthrew his brother, Sheikh Shakhbut Bin-Sultan

Al Nahyan, in a bloodless palace coup in the Persian Gulf country of the United Arab Emirates (UAE). Sheikh Zayed became the ruler of Abu Dhabi, the country's principal city. In 1971, Sheikh Zayad was appointed president of the country and held that post until his death in 2004. Sheikh Zayed's family had been rulers in the UAE for many years: his grandfather ruled the UAE from 1855 to 1909, and his father ruled from 1922 to 1926.

Sheikh Zayed's reign was marked by reform and the development of a modern, liberalized state. He used his nation's oil wealth to better the lives of his people. Education was his top priority, and many schools and colleges were built under his direction. He promoted sports among young people, both men and women, and built stadiums, training facilities, and a number of youth hostels and centers. Sheikh Zayed also built a modern army with state-of-the-art equipment and training. The troops have participated in UN peacekeeping activities, including the construction of an airport in Kosovo. Unusual in a Muslim nation, the media were allowed a large measure of freedom, although they could not directly criticize Sheikh Zayed or his family. Speaking of his policies, Sheikh Zayed was quoted as saying, "What is the benefit of wealth if it is not utilized to raise the standard of the people of the country?"

The day of Sheikh Zayed's accession to power is celebrated with a parade featuring floats carrying posters with Sheikh Zayed's portrait and pictures showing the development that the UAE has enjoyed due to his reign. A caravan of camels and other animals follows the floats. Other activities have included an opera concerning the ruler's life.

CONTACTS:
Embassy of the United Arab Emirates
3522 International Ct. N.W., Ste. 400
Washington, D.C. 20008
800-823-6911; fax: 202-243-2432

♦ 0015 ♦ **Adae-Kese**
January

This is the highlight of the ceremonial year among the Ashanti people in Ghana. Adae-Kese commemorates the day on which priest Okomfo Anokye called down from heaven the Ashantis' Golden Stool. Elaborate stools are important fixtures in Ashanti culture. When someone passes away, that person's stool is treasured by his or her survivors and honored periodically. The Golden Stool is that of King Osei Tutu, the founder of the Ashanti kingdom.

During the Adae-Kese festival, people clean their ancestral stools and offer food to the gods and ancestors. The current king and the Golden Stool sit in state, while people from the community and, often, the president of Ghana pay homage to him. All of this takes place in Kumasi, where the king's palace is located. The museum there houses a second, copycat golden stool used to deceive the British, who demanded that the stool be turned over to them after hearing that it was the source of the Ashanti king's powers.

The Adae festival is held every 40 days throughout the year, but the January celebration is the largest and most important.

CONTACTS:
Ghana Tourist Board
P.O. Box 4386
Accra, Ghana
233-21-666314; fax: 233-21-244611
www.touringghana.com

SOURCES:
FestGhana-1970, p. 7
WildPlanet-1995, p. 183

♦ 0016 ♦ Adam's Peak, Pilgrimage to
December-April

A footprint preserved in stone is a sacred site at the top of a mountain in Dalhousie, Sri Lanka. Depending on one's religious tradition, the footprint belongs to Adam (Muslim), the Buddha, St. Thomas (Christian), or Lord Shiva (Hindu). Pilgrims have made the climb for over 1,000 years.

There are two routes to the summit of Adam's Peak, one of which takes about three hours while the other takes seven hours. Though the terrain is rugged, many pilgrims make the ascent by the light of lanterns so they can arrive at the break of dawn and catch a spectacular view of the western coastline. According to local tradition, a woman who reaches the top will be reincarnated as a man.

CONTACTS:
Living Heritage Trust of Sri Lanka
1 Horton Terrace
Colombo, 7 Sri Lanka
94-11-269-1685; fax: 94-11-722-88177
www.sripada.org

SOURCES:
Wild Planet-1995, p. 290

♦ 0017 ♦ Adar Parab
March, April, November; ninth day of Adar, the ninth Zoroastrian month

Adar Parab is one of the "sacred name days" in the Zororastrian calendar, where the name of the day and the name of the month coincide. Adar, the spiritual being or *yazata* for whom both the day and the month are named, presides over fire and is associated with light and warmth. Parsis—as the Zoroastrians living in India are called—traditionally give their household fires a rest on this day by not cooking and by offering special prayers. It is also customary to recite the portion of the *Avesta* (Zoroastrian sacred writings) known as the *Atash Niyayesh*, "Fire Litany."

Fire is the most important symbol for the followers of Zoroaster (also known as Zarathushtra), a Persian religious leader believed to have lived around 1200 B.C.E. They have fire temples where fires burn constantly, as well as fires that are kindled in prayer halls and private homes for special services performed outside the temple.

The Zoroastrian calendar has 12 months of 30 days each, plus five extra days at the end of the year. Because of discrepancies in the calendars used by widely separated Zoroastrian communities around the world, there are now three different calendars in use, and the 9th of Adar can fall either in March, April, or November.

SOURCES:
DictWrldRel-1989, p. 829
RelHolCal-2004, p. 68

♦ 0018 ♦ Adelaide Festival
Two weeks in February-March in even-numbered years

Adelaide, South Australia, metamorphosed from an isolated, culturally deprived city to a major center of art and culture worldwide, thanks to a group of visionary businessmen who originated this biennial festival of the arts in 1960. In 2004 the Adelaide Festival program included more than 50 performances, exhibitions, and workshops in dance, music, film, theater, opera, and the visual arts, featuring artists from all over the world. A writers' week is also featured. Events in the festival take place in the Festival Theatre, parks, churches, the Adelaide Town Hall, and other locations.

See also ADELAIDE FRINGE FESTIVAL

CONTACTS:
Adelaide Festival
Level 9, 33 King William St.
P.O. Box 8221 Sta Arcade
Adelaide, SA 5000 Australia
61-8-8216-4444; fax: 61-8-8216-4455
www.adelaidefestival.org.au

SOURCES:
GdWrldFest-1985, p. 8
IntlThFolk-1979, pp. 19, 21

♦ 0019 ♦ Adelaide Fringe Festival
Three weeks in February-March during even-numbered years

Originating in the 1970s as an innovative, cutting-edge alternative to the established ADELAIDE FESTIVAL, the Adelaide Fringe Festival today enjoys a synergistic relationship with its sister event, contributing to the vibrant atmosphere of this Australian city during the autumn months. Held biennially for a three-week period, the Fringe features the latest in the underground and experimental arts created by independent artists from Australia, Europe, and the United States. The program includes comedy, dance, film, music, physical theater, dramatic theater, and visual arts. Audience attendance in 2002 was nearly 200,000, making the Adelaide Fringe one of the largest and most popular arts festivals in the world.

CONTACTS:
Adelaide Fringe Inc.
105 Hindley St.
P.O. Box 3242
Adelaide, SA 5000 Australia
61-8-8100-2000; fax: 61-8-8100-2020
www.adelaidefringe.com.au

♦ 0020 ♦ **Administrative Professionals Week**
Last full week of April

Professional Secretaries Week was started in 1952 by Professional Secretaries International—now called the International Association of Administrative Professionals (IAAP)—an organization devoted to the education and professional development of secretaries, executive assistants, information specialists, and office managers. It takes place during the last full week in April, with Administrative Professionals Day observed on Wednesday. Many IAAP chapters sponsor special events throughout the week—such as educational seminars or luncheons with guest speakers for secretaries and their bosses—but Wednesday is the day when managers and executives are supposed to give their office support staff a special token of their appreciation.

How do secretaries want to be recognized on this day? According to the 2001 IAAP survey, most of them want company-wide special events or training and educational sessions. What do they get? Lunch is the most common form of recognition, followed by flowers or other gifts.

CONTACTS:
International Association of Administrative Professionals
10502 N.W. Ambassador Dr.
P.O. Box 20404
Kansas City, MO 64195
816-891-6600; fax: 816-891-9118
www.iaap-hq.org

SOURCES:
AnnivHol-2000, p. 72
DictDays-1988, p. 109

♦ 0021 ♦ **Admission Day**
Varies from state to state

Many American states celebrate the anniversary of their admission to the Union by observing a public holiday on or near the actual day. Sometimes the day is referred to by the name of the state—as in Colorado Day, Indiana Day, Nevada Day, or WEST VIRGINIA DAY—and is marked by special celebrations. Other states let the anniversary of their admission pass unnoticed. In Vermont, Admission Day coincides with TOWN MEETING DAY.

For a listing of all states, *see* Appendix.

♦ 0022 ♦ **Advent**
From the Sunday closest to November 30 to December 24 in the West; from November 15 to December 24 in the East

The Advent season marks the beginning of the Christian year in Western Christianity. Its length varies from 22 to 28 days, beginning on the Sunday nearest St. Andrew's Day and encompassing the next three Sundays, ending on CHRISTMAS EVE.

In the Roman Catholic Church and those of the Anglican Communion the third Sunday is called Gaudete Sunday, from the first word of the introit, "Rejoice." Rose-colored vestments may replace the purple, and flowers may be on the altar. Originally a period of reflection and penitence in preparation for CHRISTMAS—in much the same way that LENT is in preparation for EASTER—Advent has sometimes been referred to as the **Winter Lent**. But over time the restrictions of Advent have become greatly relaxed. Today it is usually associated with the Advent calendars that parents give their children to help them count the days until Christmas.

In Orthodox (Eastern) Christianity, the church year begins on September 1, and Advent begins on November 15. The Advent fast is called the **Little Lent**, because it's shorter than the Great Lent preceding Easter.

SOURCES:
AmerBkDays-2000, p. 802
BkFestHolWrld-1970, p. 127
DaysCustFaith-1957, p. 302
DictWrldRel-1989, pp. 5, 154, 175
EncyChristmas-2003, pp. 3, 7, 8, 10
EncyRel-1987, v. 3, p. 441
FolkWrldHol-1999, p. 680
HolSymbols-2009, p. 7
OxYear-1999, p. 598
RelHolCal-2004, pp. 83, 115
SaintFestCh-1904, p. xiii

♦ 0023 ♦ **Advent (Germany)**
Sunday nearest November 30 through December 24

Many German households observe Advent with an Advent wreath. Traditionally fashioned from a fir branch entwined with gold and silver ribbons or bits of red thread, the wreaths also contain holders for four candles. German families display the wreath on a tabletop or suspend it from the ceiling. One candle is lit on each of the Sundays in Advent. An old Roman Catholic tradition called for lighting the candles on Saturday instead. Many German households light a "Star of Seven," a seven-branched candelabrum, on CHRISTMAS EVE, and at midnight carry the lit "star" though the dark to the village church for the Christmas Eve service.

SOURCES:
BkFestHolWrld-1970, p. 128
EncyChristmas-2003, pp. 3, 6, 7, 10, 276
FestWestEur-1958, p. 79
FolkWrldHol-1999, p. 680
OxYear-1999, p. 598

♦ 0024 ♦ **AFC Asian Cup**
Every four years

Since 1956, the Asian Football Confederation has held the AFC Asian Cup tournament every four years to determine the best soccer team in Asia. The winner of the contest goes on to compete for the FIFA Confederations' World Cup, the soccer world's highest honor. To avoid conflict over audience with the Olympic Games, which are also held every four years, the Asian Football Confederation held their most recent competition in 2007 and will hold future tournaments every four years from that date forward.

In 2007, 25 national teams vied for the AFC Asian Cup, with that number whittled down to 16 in the preliminary rounds. Over the years, several national teams have dominated the competition. Japan, Saudi Arabia, and Iran have won the AFC Asian Cup three times. South Korea has won twice. Iran's team boasts the best overall numbers for tournament play.

The 2007 winner was Iraq, which defeated Saudi Arabia by a score of 1-0. It was the first time that Iraq had won the coveted sports prize. Many Iraqis saw the soccer win in larger terms, pointing out that the team was composed of Kurd, Sunni, and Shiite players who were able to work together to win a victory. They hoped it foreshadowed a spirit of cooperation in national politics as well.

CONTACTS:
Asian Football Confederation
AFC House, Jalan 1/155B, Bukit Jalil
Kuala Lumpur 57000 Malaysia
www.the-afc.com/eng/index.jsp.html

♦ 0025 ♦ **Africa Industrialization Day**
November 20

In 1989 the UNITED NATIONS designated November 20 as Africa Industrialization Day. Observances center around mustering international support for the industrialization of Africa.

CONTACTS:
United Nations
Dept. of Public Information, Ste. S-1070L
New York, NY 10017
212-963-6842; fax: 212-963-6914
www.un.org

♦ 0026 ♦ **Africa Malaria Day**
April 25

Africa Malaria Day is sponsored by an international organization called Roll Back Malaria, whose members include representatives from the World Health Organization, UNICEF, the UNITED NATIONS, the World Bank, and various member countries, organizations, and agencies. The goal of this organization is to reduce the worldwide number of malaria cases by one-half by the year 2010.

Malaria kills about 3,000 people a day, which adds up to about 1,000,000 people per year. Most of these people are children, and nine out of ten of them live in sub-Saharan Africa.

Africa Malaria Day is a day dedicated to raising public awareness about malaria prevention and treatment, as well as the economic and social toll the disease takes on poor countries. Activities include special media campaigns, demonstrations of the proper use of treated mosquito netting, lectures about the disease, and other educational events. Roll Back Malaria chose April 25 as the date of their newly created holiday in order to commemorate the April 25, 2000, Summit on Malaria, held in Abuja, Nigeria. The first Africa Malaria Day was held the following year in 2001. The United Nations has declared 2001-2010 as the Decade to Roll Back Malaria.

CONTACTS:
World Health Organization
Ave. Appia 20
Geneva, 1211 Switzerland
41-22-791-2111; fax: 41-22-791-4824
www.rbm.who.int

♦ 0027 ♦ **African American Day Parade**
Last Sunday in September

The African American Day parade is the largest black parade in the United States and attracts a crowd of approximately 900,000 annually. Held on the last Sunday of September in the Harlem neighborhood of New York City, the parade progresses up Adam Clayton Powell Boulevard from 111th Street to 142nd Street. The African American Day parade has been held annually since 1969 to promote unity, justice, and economic empowerment. It features many African-American business, social, and political leaders, as well as performers, marchers, and floats representing more than 300 organizations, including a wide range of colleges and bands from throughout the region. Among the participants are step dancers, drum and bugle corps, service organizations, professional associations, philanthropic organizations, cultural heritage groups, and social clubs. The parade celebrates African heritage and black achievement in all areas, and past grand marshals include such luminaries as congressional representative Shirley Chisholm, New York mayor David Dinkins, filmmaker Spike Lee, Reverend Al Sharpton, and actor Denzel Washington.

CONTACTS:
African American Day Parade, Inc.
P.O. Box 501
College Station
New York, NY 10030
212-348-3080
www.africanamericandayparade.org

SOURCES:
AAH-2007, p. 3

♦ 0028 ♦ **African American Women in Cinema International Film Festival**
Late October or early November

The African American Women in Cinema International Film Festival is a three-day event held in New York City since 1998. The festival celebrates the accomplishments of black and other minority women in the film industry and seeks to expand their professional opportunities. Sponsored by African American Women in Cinema, Inc., a nonprofit organization that works to support minority women filmmakers, the festival takes place in late October or early November and includes film screenings (short and long films), social events, acting workshops, and panel discussions on a variety of subjects in cinema and entertainment. Workshop and discussion forums include such topics as audition techniques, the film editing process, understanding film financing, empowering women through movies, and selecting film music. Events take place at several venues throughout the city. The festival concludes with a brunch and award ceremony on Sunday.

CONTACTS:
African-American Women in Cinema Organization, Inc.
545 Eighth Ave., Ste. 401
New York, NY 10018
212-769-7949; fax: 212-871-2074
aawic.org

SOURCES:
AAH-2007, p. 21

◆ 0029 ◆ **African/Caribbean International Festival of Life**
Independence Day weekend

Introduced in 1993, the African/Caribbean International Festival of Life (IFOL) is a music and culture celebration held in Washington Park in Chicago during the first week of July. The family-oriented festival draws more than 150,000 attendees over a four-day period extending from Thursday through Sunday of Independence Day weekend. IFOL showcases reggae, calypso, world beat, R&B, hip-hop, jazz, blues, and Latin music. In addition, it features dance performances, food, clothing, arts, crafts, and a variety of activities and games designed for family entertainment. IFOL organizers sponsor the event to promote peace, love, and unity among nations, stressing the dual themes of "Bringing nations together" and "Living together as one." Festivalgoers can purchase a one-day pass or a festival pass good for all four days. A portion of the proceeds from the festival is donated to charity to support programs for children in crisis.

CONTACTS:
African/Caribbean International Festival of Life
Martin's International Culture, Inc.
1325 S. Wabash Ave., Ste. 307
Chicago, IL 60605-2536
312-427-0266 or 877-973-4423; fax: 312-427-0268
www.festivaloflife.com

SOURCES:
AAH-2007, p. 24

◆ 0030 ◆ **African Liberation Day**
May 25

While other holidays seek to commemorate the events and achievements of the past, African Liberation Day focuses attention on a goal that has not yet been fully realized: the liberation of all African people. The observance of this day can be traced back to April 15, 1958, when the Conference of Independent African States was held in Accra, Ghana. Attendees declared April 15 African Freedom Day, and between 1958 and 1963 this observance was supported by leaders worldwide, including President John F. Kennedy, MALCOLM X, and Senator Hubert Humphrey in the United States.

As British and European colonies in Africa continued to win their independence during the 1950s and 60s, and as the civil rights movement in the United States began to achieve some success, 31 independent African countries met on May 25, 1963, to form the Organization of African Unity. They changed the name and the date of what now became African

Liberation Day. In 1999 the group reorganized into the African Union.

Today, observances worldwide include marches, parades, rallies, and conferences. These events focus on celebrating freedom from colonialism, educating people about the progress of the African liberation movement, and speaking out against oppression. There are also sporting contests and tribal dances, particularly in Chad, Zambia, and other African states where it is a public holiday.

CONTACTS:
African Union
P.O. Box 3243
Addis Ababa, Ethiopia
251-1-151-7700; fax: 251-1-151-7844
www.africa-union.org/root/au/index/index.ht

SOURCES:
AfrAmerHol-1991, p. 43

◆ 0031 ◆ **African Methodist Quarterly Meeting Day**
Last Saturday in August

The **Big August Quarterly** of the African Union Methodist Protestant Church takes place annually in Wilmington, Delaware. It honors the establishment of the A.U.M.P. Church in 1813 as the "Mother Church" for African Americans. The first independent black congregation in Wilmington was started by an influential black religious leader named Peter Spencer, who, along with 41 like-minded African Americans, left the town's Asbury Methodist Church in 1805 because its white members refused to let them participate fully in the services. In the years before the Civil War the Big August Quarterly drew slaves from all around, who obtained special passes permitting them to attend the weekend of gospel music, impassioned preaching, and family get-togethers.

Its founders modeled the Big August Quarterly on the quarterly meetings held by Quakers. Many thousands of people from Delaware and its neighboring states came to these stirring religious festivals. Although it no longer draws the crowds it used to, the Big August Quarterly has undergone a resurgence in recent years. It features soul food, musical entertainment, and an opportunity for people to reminisce about the Big August Quarterlies of the past.

SOURCES:
AAH-2007, p. 29
FolkAmerHol-1999, p. 350
RelHolCal-2004, p. 100

◆ 0032 ◆ **African World Festival**
Third weekend in August

The African World Festival is a cultural festival held annually on the third weekend of August in Detroit, Mich. With more than one million visitors each year, it is one of the largest ethnic festivals in the United States. Sponsored by the Charles H. Wright Museum of African-American History, the festival has been in existence since 1983.

The African World Festival is held at Hart Plaza overlooking the Detroit River and includes entertainment, arts, education, and cultural exhibits. Festival events take place over a three-day weekend, operating from Friday through Sunday. Traditional African dancers and drummers perform, and musicians entertain audiences in the plaza's amphitheater with various styles of African-influenced music, including such genres as reggae, blues, gospel, and jazz. An annual Greek step show features sorority and fraternity dance teams. African and world goods are available from more than 150 vendors in the marketplace, and the Taste of the Diaspora food court offers cuisine ranging from African specialties to all-American favorites. The African Family Village offers arts, crafts, games, spoken word performances, and music for families with children.

CONTACTS:
Charles H. Wright Museum of African American History
315 East Warren
Detroit, MI 48201
313-494-5800; fax: 313-494-5855
www.maah-detroit.org

SOURCES:
AAH-2007, p. 36

♦ 0033 ♦ **Agonalia**
January 9

In Roman mythology, Janus is the god of beginnings and of doorways. The worship of Janus is believed to have been started by Romulus, one of the legendary founders of Rome. Usually depicted with two faces, one looking forward to the future and the other looking back to the past, his image appeared on an early Roman coin with a ship's prow on the reverse side. Roman boys used to toss these coins, calling out "heads or ships" just as youngsters today play "heads or tails." During the festival in honor of Janus known as the Agonalia, the *rex sacrorum* or officiating priest sacrificed a ram. Offerings of barley, incense, wine, and cakes called *Januae* were also common.

Numa Pompilius, the legendary second king of Rome, honored Janus by dedicating the famous *Ianus geminus*, the arcade at the northeast end of the Roman Forum, to him. It was believed that passing through this arcade brought luck to soldiers on their way to war.

SOURCES:
AmerBkDays-2000, p. 1
DictFolkMyth-1984, p. 539
DictRomRel-1996, p. 4
FestRom-1981, p. 60
OxYear-1999, p. 29

♦ 0034 ♦ **Agriculture Fair at Santarém, National**
10 days beginning first Friday in June

The most important agricultural fair in Portugal is held for 10 days in June each year at Santarém, capital of the rich agricultural province of Ribatejo. Although the focus of the **Ribatejo Fair** is on farming and livestock breeding, there is also a colorful program of bullfighting, folk singing, and dancing, as well as a procession of *campinos*, or bull-herders. Many other European countries exhibit farm animals and machinery at the **Feira Nacional de Agricultura**. Santarém is also the site of an annual gastronomy festival in October, which focuses on traditional cooking from all over the country.

CONTACTS:
Ribatejo Tourist Office
Campo Emilio Infante da Camara
Casa do Campino
Santarem, 2000-014 Portugal
043-33-33-18
www.ribatejo.com/ecos/linguas/english.html

SOURCES:
IntlThFolk-1979, p. 312

♦ 0035 ♦ **Agua, La Fiesta de**
First Sunday in October

A festival held in San Pedro de Casta, Lima Department, Peru, the **Water Festival** accompanies the annual cleaning and maintaining of the river canals. The town mayor goes to the cave where Pariapunko, a deity of water, is believed to reside and implores him to flood the community with fresh water. Then La Toma, the gate that holds back the Carhuayumac River, is opened and the water is allowed to course through the newly repaired canals. A procession of horsemen follows the path of the water as it makes its way to the gorge of Carhuayumac.

SOURCES:
FolkWrldHol-1999, p. 589

♦ 0036 ♦ **Agwunsi Festival**
August-September

Agwunsi, or Agwu, is the god of healing and divination among the Igbo people of Nigeria. He is also the patron of doctors, because he gives herbs and other medicines their power to cure. On Agwunsi feast day, patients who have been healed send animals as a token of gratitude to the doctors who cured them.

SOURCES:
FolkWrldHol-1999, p. 550

♦ 0037 ♦ **Air Races and Air Show, National Championship**
September, four days ending on second weekend after Labor Day

The National Championship Air Races and Air Show is a four-day nostalgia trip for air buffs, held since 1964 in Reno, Nev. About 95 to 100 aircraft are generally registered for the races, providing some 180,000 spectators with the sight and sound of piston-engine planes flying around closed-pylon race courses. The planes entered include such World War II planes as the powerful P-51 Mustang and the bent-wing Chance-Vought F2G Corsair; the eerie sound the Corsair made was called "whistling death" by the Japanese of World War II. The race is the only one in the world that covers all four classes: Unlimited (vintage and modified warbirds and homebuilt racers), AT-6 (World War II pilot trainers), Formula One (super-midget planes), and Biplane (double-winged barn stormers). Air shows of military demonstrations, parachuting exhibits, and military fly-bys are also some of the events.

CONTACTS:
Reno Air Racing Association
14501 Mt. Anderson St.
Reno, NV 89505
775-972-6663; fax: 775-972-6429
www.airrace.org

SOURCES:
GdUSFest-1984, p. 115

♦ 0038 ♦ Airing the Classics
Sixth day of sixth lunar month

In China the **Double Sixth** is the day when Buddhist monasteries examine the books in their library collections to make sure that they haven't been damaged. It commemorates the time when the boat carrying the Buddhist scriptures from India was upset at a river crossing, and all the books had to be spread out to dry. Also known as **Tiankuang Jie,** or **Heaven's Gift Day,** it is traditional in some regions to set linens and books, as well as bath water, out in the sun. Setting aside a special day for "Airing the Classics" is especially important in hot, wet climates, where books are more vulnerable to mold and insects.

SOURCES:
EncyRel-1987, v. 3, p. 326
FolkWrldHol-1999, p. 415
OxYear-1999, p. 702

♦ 0039 ♦ AirVenture
Late July–early August

Begun in 1953 as a part of the Milwaukee Air Pageant, the AirVenture has grown to become one of the largest conventions of any kind in the world. Sponsored by the Experimental Aircraft Association, the annual event draws together enthusiasts of homemade flying craft, designers of more serious craft, and a host of individuals, companies, and government agencies involved in the aviation and aeronautics industries.

Some 10,000 aircraft of all kinds are on display at the convention. Included in this number are homebuilt airplanes, antique planes, classics, military craft, ultralight flying vehicles, and rotorcraft. In addition, over 500 forums are conducted by aviation leaders, NASA researchers, Federal Aviation Agency personnel, and aircraft designers. Some 800 exhibitors set up booths covering some one million square feet to display their aviation products and services. Workshops explain the details of constructing your own working aircraft. In the afternoon, there is a three-hour air show. In the evening, live entertainment performances feature NASA astronauts, test pilots, and leading aviation personalities. An estimated 750,000 people attend the convention every year.

CONTACTS:
Experimental Aircraft Association
EAA Aviation Center
3000 Poberezny Rd.
Oshkosh, WI 54902
920-426-4800
www.airventure.org

♦ 0040 ♦ Aizu Byakko Matsuri
September 22-24

Aizu was at one time the sturdiest castle in northeast Japan, but it was destroyed in the battle between the Emperor's forces and the Shogun's forces known as *Boshin-no-eki* in 1868. The *Byakkotai,* or White Tiger Band, a band of young men who vowed to lay down their lives in defense of the castle, saw what they thought was fire rising from the walls. Thinking it had fallen into enemy hands, they kept their vow and killed themselves. To commemorate their courage, there is a procession of 500 warriors, led by the highly selective Byakkotai corps, and a lantern procession through the streets of Aizu Wakamatsu, where the original members of the White Tiger Band are buried.

CONTACTS:
International Relations Section of City
City of Aizu Wakamatsu Hall
3-46 Higashi Sakae-machi
Aizu Wakamatsu-shi, Fukushima-ken 965-8601 Japan
81-2-4239-1201; fax: 81-2-4239-1400
www.city.aizuwakamatsu.fukushima.jp

SOURCES:
IllFestJapan-1993, p. 111
JapanFest-1965, p. 191

♦ 0041 ♦ Ak-Sar-Ben Livestock Exposition and Rodeo
September

Billed as the "World's Largest 4-H Livestock Show," the Ak-Sar-Ben ("Nebraska" spelled backwards) Livestock Exposition and Rodeo in Omaha dates back to 1928, when its purpose was to get the state's young people interested in livestock breeding. It started out as a nationwide breed show, but thoroughbred racing became an important part of the event when, during the 1930s, parimutuel racing became legal—as long as it was administered by nonprofit organizations.

The exposition lasts five days and features a World Championship Rodeo, a Catch-a-Calf contest, and entertainment by well-known country and western stars. But the show's main purpose historically has been to showcase 4-H activities.

CONTACTS:
Knights of Ak-Sar-Ben Foundation
302 S. 36th St., Ste. 800
Omaha, NE 68131
402-554-9600; fax: 402-554-9609
www.aksarben.org

SOURCES:
GdUSFest-1984, p. 111

◆ 0042 ◆ **Akshya Tritiya**
April-May; third day of the waxing half of the
Hindu month of Vaisakha

The Hindu observance of Akshya Tritiya in India combines fasting and festivities. *Akshya* means "exempt from decay," and the devotions performed on this day are believed to last forever. Hindus fast and worship Vishnu, along with his consort Lakshmi, with holy Ganges water, *tulsi* or basil leaves, incense, flowers, lamps, and new clothes. Bathing in the Ganges River is a popular way to demonstrate one's devotion. This is also the day on which the mountain passes of Sri Badrinarain in the Himalayas open again after the long, snowy winter.

Svetambaras Jains also fast on the third day of the waxing half of Vaisakha. They call this day **Aksaya Tritiya**, and it commemorates the fast observed by the first Tirthankara, whose name was Risabha and who was given some sugar cane juice to break his fast. The Svetambaras or "white-clad" Jains are the dominant group in northern India, and they are called this because they believe that monks should be clothed. The other major Jain sect, the Digambaras or "sky-clad" sect, believe that total nudity is required of monks, although Indian law requires that Digambara monks wear a loincloth in public.

SOURCES:
RelHolCal-2004, pp. 168, 195

◆ 0043 ◆ **Akwambo (Path-Clearing Festival)**
Date varies

How and when the Akwambo Festival is observed by the Fante people, particularly in the Agona and Gomoa regions of Ghana, varies from place to place. It was first observed by the migrant ancestors of these people, whose primary task when they arrived in a new place was clearing paths to the rivers and other watering places. A day was set aside for this purpose, and for clearing the paths leading to farms and other communal places as well. Everyone who used these routes was expected to attend and help in the work or contribute financially.

In some places, path clearing is no longer necessary because there are paved roads. But the festival is still observed, especially at Agona Nkum, where it is part of a week-long celebration. A traditional part of the festivities is the parade of the Asafo groups. Each town has a number of Asafo companies which, during colonial times, functioned as militias. The literal translation of *asafo* is "people of war." Today they are community associations which together include representatives from nearly every family in town, but the military influence is still seen in the flags and weapons carried by members.

On path-clearing day in Agona Nkum the Asafo companies lead a procession beyond the town's borders where they pay homage to Oburata Kofi, the god of the well. Then, amid firing guns, dancing, and drumming, the procession returns to town, where community members meet with the town chief and other leaders to discuss town laws and other communal matters.

CONTACTS:
Ghana Embassy
3512 International Dr. N.W.
Washington, D.C. 20008
202-686-4520; fax: 202-686-4527
www.ghanaembassy.org

SOURCES:
FestGhana-1970, p. 40

◆ 0044 ◆ **Al Bustan International Festival of**
Music and the Arts
February and March

The Al Bustan International Festival of Beirut, Lebanon, annually presents a program of music dance, marionettes, and theater, usually centered on a specific theme. Past events have been devoted to the culture of a particular country or city, or to a special subject.

The festival was founded in 1994 to help revive Lebanon's cultural life after 17 years of war. While chamber music dominates the program, the festival also includes works of opera, orchestral music, and choral music. Each year, the festival offers more than 30 performances over the five-week festival period in February and March. During the festival, participating artists offer master classes and workshops at the National Conservatoire in Beirut and other institutions throughout Lebanon. A visual arts exhibition accompanies every festival, and it has commissioned musical works by such contemporary composers as John Taverner.

CONTACTS:
Al Bustan Festival
Mail Box 343
56 Gloucester Rd.
London SW7 4UB UK
www.albustanfestival.com

Lebanon Embassy
Washington, DC 20008
202-939-6300; fax: 202-939-6324
lebanonembassyus.org

◆ 0045 ◆ **Alabama Blueberry Festival**
Third Saturday in June

The Alabama Blueberry Festival is a one-day celebration of the blueberry in Brewton, which is in the only area of Alabama still shipping blueberries commercially. The celebration, dedicated to Dr. W. T. Brightwell, whose improved varieties of the Rabbiteye blueberry were introduced here in 1961, features tours of the local blueberry farms. Events include live entertainment, children's rides, arts and crafts, an antique car show, a food contest, and food booths selling all kinds of locally prepared blueberry dishes, among them cobbler, waffles, ice cream and cakes. Attendance is about 28,000.

CONTACTS:
Greater Brewton Area Chamber of Commerce
1010-B Douglas Ave.
Brewton, AL 36426
251-867-3224; fax: 251-809-1793
www.brewtonchamber.com

♦ 0046 ♦ **Alahamady Be**
First new moon in March

Alahamady Be is NEW YEAR'S DAY in Madagascar, the fourth largest island in the world, located off the southeastern coast of Africa. The Malagasy new year traditionally begins in March. Alahamady Be is celebrated with the appearance of the year's first new moon. Festivities last for two days. People put on their best clothes, feast, give presents, and sing religious songs. The celebration is particularly festive in the capital city of Antananarivo, which means "town of a thousand warriors." The townspeople make their way to the sacred royal hill known as Ambohimanga, meeting at what was once the site of the queen's palace to offer prayers to the departed. When these devotions are completed it's time to eat.

A favorite food is *romazava*, which is made from meat and herbs and eaten with rice. Sausages, vegetables, and wine made from rice or cane sugar often round out the meal. The feasting is an opportunity for families and friends to get together and wish each other luck in the coming year. Because it is not unusual in Madagascar for Christian beliefs to be combined with traditional customs and practices, Christian hymns are often sung on New Year's Day.

CONTACTS:
Madagascar Embassy
2374 Massachusetts Ave. N.W.
Washington, D.C. 20008
202-265-5525; fax: 202-483-7603
www.madagascar-consulate.org

SOURCES:
FestWrld: Madag-1999, p. 8

♦ 0047 ♦ **Alamo Day**
March 6

The cry "Remember the Alamo!" has particular significance for the natives of Texas, which was once part of Mexico. In 1836 a garrison of Texans took a stand against the Mexican army at a Franciscan mission in San Antonio named after the grove of cottonwood trees (*alamo* in Spanish) that surrounded it. Led by Lieutenant William Barret Travis, the band of 187 volunteers, including border heroes Davy Crockett and James Bowie, was besieged for 13 days by 3,000-5,000 Mexicans under the leadership of General Antonio López de Santa Anna. Travis refused to surrender and the Alamo was overrun by the opposing army on the morning of March 6. Only women and children among the defenders survived.

The heroic action at the Alamo gave the Texans time to organize the forces necessary to save their independence movement. Six weeks after the Alamo's fall, General Sam Houston defeated and captured Santa Anna at the battle of San Jacinto (*see* SAN JACINTO DAY), forcing him to sign a treaty recognizing Texas' independence. Since 1897, this day has been celebrated as **Texas Heroes' Day**.

The Daughters of the Republic of Texas (DRT) have managed the Alamo since 1905. DRT is an organization founded by daughters of Texas veterans in 1891 to promote the study and celebration of Texas history.

CONTACTS:
Daughters of the Republic of Texas
P.O. Box 2599
San Antonio, TX 78299
210-225-1391; fax: 210-229-1343
www.thealamo.org

San Antonio Living History Association
5310 San Pedro Ave.
San Antonio, TX 78212
210-273-1730
www.sanantoniolivinghistory.org

Library of Congress
101 Independence Ave. S.E.
Washington, DC 20540
202-707-5000; fax: 202-707-8366
www.loc.gov

SOURCES:
AmerBkDays-2000, p. 187
AnnivHol-2000, p. 40
DaysCustFaith-1957, p. 97
DictDays-1988, p. 2

♦ 0048 ♦ **Alasitas Fair**
January 24

Each year on January 24 a large marketplace in La Paz, Bolivia, is full of merchants who traditionally call out, "*Alasitas*," an Aymara word meaning "buy from me," to potential buyers of their miniature wares. Shoppers can find tiny replicas of just about every kind of object—cars, houses, foods, furniture, clothes, tools, household goods, and, especially, money—and seek those which represent items they would like to have in the coming year. After purchasing the miniature object of one's desire, the next step is to take it to church to have it blessed.

Presiding over all this downsized commerce is Ekeko, an Aymara god of material wealth, fertility, and good luck. Ekeko is represented as a portly little man who wears a backpack full of goods and whose arms are stretched out, as if in an attitude of acquisition. Many people keep ceramic figures of Ekeko in their homes for good luck.

CONTACTS:
Bolivian Embassy
3014 Massachusetts Ave. N.W.
Washington, D.C. 20008
202-483-4410; fax: 202-328-3712
www.bolivia-usa.org

SOURCES:
AnnivHol-2000, p. 14
BkFestHolWrld-1970, p. 17
BkHolWrld-1986, p. Jan 24
DictFolkMyth-1984, pp. 33, 342
FolkWrldHol-1999, p. 46

♦ 0049 ♦ **Alaska Day**
October 18

An official holiday in America's 49th and largest state, Alaska Day commemorates the formal transfer of Alaska from Russia to the United States on October 18, 1867. The event, which took place at Sitka, was a sad one for the Russian colonists who had already made Alaska their home, and it must have seemed that Mother Nature was conspiring against them. A strong wind caught the Russian flag during the transfer ceremony, tangling it in the halyards. The seaman who was finally hoisted up to free it dropped the flag by mistake, and another gust swept it into a group of Russian bayonets. The tattered remains were presented to the weeping wife of Prince Dmitri Maksoutsoff, the last Russian governor.

Today the lowering of the Russian flag and the raising of the Stars and Stripes is reenacted every year as part of this five-day festival in Sitka. Other events include a parade and a period costume ball.

After the transfer, Alaska was eventually organized as a territory and maintained this status until it became a state on January 3, 1959 (*see also* Appendix).

CONTACTS:
Anchorage Convention & Visitors Bureau
524 W. 4th Ave.
Anchorage, AZ 99501
800-478-1255 or 907-276-4118
www.travelalaska.com

Sitka Convention and Visitors Bureau
P.O. Box 1226
Sitka, AK 99835
907-747-5940; fax: 907-747-3739
www.sitka.org

SOURCES:
AmerBkDays-2000, p. 717
AnnivHol-2000, pp. 3, 174
DictDays-1988, p. 3

♦ 0050 ♦ Albania Independence Day
November 28

The Albanian people proclaimed their independence from the Turks on this day in 1912. The Turks had first invaded this part of Europe around 1400, but under the leadership of a brave chief named Skanderbeg, the Albanians held them off for more than 20 years. After his death, however, the Turks conquered Albania, and they continued to rule the country for more than 400 years. It wasn't until the end of the Balkan War that Turkish rule was abolished and a proclamation of independence was issued on November 28, 1912.

Independence Day is a public holiday observed throughout Albania and is marked by a festive parade in Tirana, the capital. It is closely followed by Liberation Day on November 29, the day on which the invasions of German and Italian troops during World War II were terminated in 1944.

CONTACTS:
Albanian Embassy
2100 S. St. N.W.
Washington, D.C. 20008
202-223-4942; fax: 202-628-7342
www.embassyofalbania.org

SOURCES:
AnnivHol-2000, p. 196
NatlHolWrld-1968, p. 210

♦ 0051 ♦ Albania Republic Day
January 11

Republic Day was a national holiday in Albania, also known as **Anniversary Day**, which commemorated the founding of the Communist government on January 11, 1946, until April 15, 1991, when the first Parliament since the fall of the Soviet Union convened.

CONTACTS:
Albanian Embassy
2100 S St. N.W.
Washington, D.C. 20008
202-223-4942; fax: 202-628-7342
www.embassyofalbania.org

♦ 0052 ♦ Alberta Heritage Day
First Monday in August

The province of Alberta, Canada, celebrates its cultural heritage on the first Monday of August. The Legislative Assembly of Alberta made this day an official provincial holiday by passing the Heritage Act of 1974, which also decreed that the observance can occur on the preceding Saturday or Sunday.

The holiday's date differs from that of other Canadian heritage celebrations, which are usually held on the third Monday of February. Despite continuous attempts by the Heritage Canada Foundation to make Heritage Day a national holiday, Alberta has maintained its own calendar date.

A notable annual event scheduled just before Alberta Heritage Day is the Crowsnest Pass Doors Open and Heritage Festival. Held since 2006, this tourist-friendly event takes place in the Canadian Rockies and includes heritage hikes, storytelling, and tours of historical sites and local architecture.

CONTACTS:
Heritage Community Foundation
Ste. 54
9912-106 St.
Edmonton, AB T5K 1C5 Canada
www.heritagecanada.org

♦ 0053 ♦ Albuquerque International Balloon Fiesta
First full week in October

The Albuquerque International Balloon Fiesta is one of the world's largest gatherings of hot-air balloonists. More than 1,000 balloons, some more than six-stories high, present dizzying colors and designs in the skies of New Mexico for a nine-day fiesta that attracts nearly a million spectators. Besides the daytime ascensions, illuminated balloons light up the night skies. The fiesta also boasts fireworks and food of all sorts.

See also HOT AIR BALLOON CLASSIC

CONTACTS:
Albuquerque International Balloon Fiesta Inc.
4401 Alameda N.E.
Albuquerque, NM 87113
888-422-7277 or 505-821-1000; fax: 505-828-2887
www.balloonfiesta.com

♦ 0054 ♦ **Aldeburgh Festival of Music and the Arts**
June

The English fishing village of Aldeburgh, located on the North Sea about 100 miles from London, may seem an unlikely place for an international music festival. But it was here that English composer Benjamin Britten, singer Peter Pears, and writer-producer Eric Crozier—who together led a touring opera company, the English Opera Group—founded the Aldeburgh Festival in 1948. Then as now, the festival embraced the community as both audience member and participant, and sought to bring together established and new artists. Britten and other composers often premiered their works at the festival, many of which were inspired by the people and landscape of Aldeburgh. When the festival grew out of its performance spaces, a new venue, the Snapes Maltings Concert Hall, was built in 1967 on the site of a former malt brewery barn.

Today, in addition to the 17-day festival, activities continue year-round through Aldeburgh Productions and include classical, folk and jazz concerts; opera; contemporary dance; the Britten-Pears School for Advanced Musical Studies; the Snape Proms; and the Easter Festival.

CONTACTS:
Aldeburgh Productions
Snape Maltings Concert Hall
Snape, Suffolk IP17 1SP United Kingdom
44-17-2868-7110; fax: 44-17-2868-7120
www.aldeburgh.co.uk

SOURCES:
GdWrldFest-1985, p. 89
IntlThFolk-1979, p. 155
MusFestEurBrit-1980, p. 42
MusFestWrld-1963, p. 21

♦ 0055 ♦ **Aldersgate Experience**
Sunday nearest May 24

On the evening of May 24, 1738, John Wesley (1703-1791), co-founder of the Methodist Church, visited a house on Aldersgate Street, London, to join a group reading of Martin Luther's preface to the *Epistle to the Romans*. At about quarter to nine, just as they were reading Luther's description of the change that God works in man's heart, Wesley underwent a conversion experience. "I felt my heart strangely warmed," he says in his account of the evening. From that time until his death in 1791, Wesley considered it his mission in life to tell people about his experience and to invite them to share his beliefs. The anniversary of this event is commemorated by the Methodist Church on the Sunday nearest May 24.

SOURCES:
DaysCustFaith-1957, p. 127
EncyRel-1987, v. 15, p. 370
RelHolCal-2004, p. 96

♦ 0056 ♦ **Alexandra Rose Day**
June; Saturday

Sometimes called **Alexandra Day** or simply **Rose Day**, this day commemorates the arrival of Queen Alexandra (1844-1925), wife of the English king, Edward VII, in England on June 26, 1862. In 1902 the much-loved queen founded the Imperial Military Nursing Service, and in 1912 she started Alexandra Rose Day. The Danish-born queen died 13 years later, but the day is still celebrated by selling rose emblems to raise money for hospitals.

See also HOSPITAL WEEK, NATIONAL

SOURCES:
DictDays-1988, p. 3

♦ 0057 ♦ **Algeria Independence Day**
July 5

On this day in 1962, more than 100 years of French rule in Algeria came to an end as France officially recognized a referendum for independence that was passed by a vote of the Algerian people on July 1. Algerians had struggled for independence, or at least equality with the French occupants of their land, with organized movements for revolution since the end of World War I. Independence Day is a legal holiday in Algeria.

Another important celebration takes place on ALGERIA NATIONAL DAY, which commemorates the day the successful revolution against the French began.

CONTACTS:
Algerian Embassy
2118 Kalorama Rd. N.W.
Washington, D.C. 20008
202-265-2800; fax: 202-667-2174
www.algeria-us.org

SOURCES:
AnnivHol-2000, p. 112

♦ 0058 ♦ **Algeria National Day**
November 1

This national holiday, also known as **Revolution Day,** commemorates the day in 1954 Algerians began their revolution against the French, who had ruled since 1830. Huge crowds of people celebrate in the capital city of Algiers on the Mediterranean coast.

CONTACTS:
Algerian Embassy
2118 Kalorama Rd. N.W.
Washington, D.C. 20008
202-265-2800; fax: 202-667-2174
www.algeria-us.org

SOURCES:
AnnivHol-2000, p. 183
NatlHolWrld-1968, p. 198

♦ 0059 ♦ All-American Soap Box Derby
First Saturday in August

The Soap Box Derby is a youth racing program that has been run nationally since 1934. The idea came from an Ohio journalist named Myron Scott, who was assigned to cover a race of gravity-propelled cars built by young boys in his hometown of Dayton and was so impressed by the event that he began to develop a similar program on a nationwide scale. In 1935 the race was moved to Akron because of its hilly terrain, and the following year a permanent track was constructed through the efforts of the Works Progress Administration (WPA).

The World Championship finals held at Derby Downs in Akron consist of three racing divisions: the Stock Division for girls and boys ages 9-16 competing in simplified cars built from kits; the Kit Car Division for youngsters competing in more advanced models, although still using standardized kits and shells; and the Masters Division for girls and boys ages 11-16 who want to test their creativity and design skills. They can build a car from scratch or purchase and assemble a Masters Kit and shell.

Competitors arrive on the Monday before the race and spend the week working on their cars, participating in trial runs, and relaxing before the big race on Saturday. The home-built cars used in the derby today bear little resemblance to derby cars in the 1930s, many of which were actually built out of soap boxes.

CONTACTS:
All-American Soap Box Derby
1000 George Washington Blvd.
P.O. Box 7225
Akron, OH 44312
330-733-8723; fax: 330-733-1370
www.aasbd.com

SOURCES:
AnnivHol-2000, p. 147
GdUSFest-1984, p. 137

♦ 0060 ♦ All Saints' Day
November 1 in the West; first Sunday after
Pentecost in the East

In Roman Catholic, Anglican, and many Protestant churches, the first day of November is a celebration of all the Christian saints—particularly those who have no special feast days of their own. Also known as **All-Hallomas** or **All Hallows' Day**, the idea for this holy day goes back to the fourth century, when the Greek Christians kept a festival on the first Sunday after PENTECOST (in late May or early June) in honor of all martyrs and saints. When the Pantheon at Rome was converted into a Christian place of worship in the seventh century, Pope Boniface IV dedicated it to the Virgin and all the martyrs, and the anniversary of this event was celebrated on May 1.

CONTACTS:
Greek Orthodox Archdiocese of Australia
221 Dorcas St.
South Melbourne, VIC 3205 Australia
61-3-9696-2488; fax: 61-3-9696-3583
www.greekorthodox.org.au

SOURCES:
AmerBkDays-2000, p. 745
BkDays-1864, vol. II, p. 520
DictFolkMyth-1984, pp. 36, 181, 573, 1056
FestSaintDays-1915, p. 197
FestWestEur-1958, pp. 17, 47
FolkAmerHol-1999, p. 427
FolkWrldHol-1999, p. 632
OxYear-1999, pp. 440, 441
RelHolCal-2004, pp. 105, 123
SaintFestCh-1904, p. 470

♦ 0061 ♦ All Saints' Day (France)
November 1

Both All Saints' Day, **La Toussaint**, and ALL SOULS' DAY, *Le Jour des Morts*, are widely observed in France. All Saints' Day is, in fact, a legal holiday in France. Church services in memory of all the saints are held on November 1, but by evening the focus turns toward the dead. Cemeteries everywhere are crowded with people who come to clean and decorate the family graves. All Souls' Day, November 2, is dedicated to prayers for the dead who are not yet glorified. Church services are often followed by visits to the churchyard, and families get together to pay homage to the deceased.

In Brittany, pancakes and cider are set out for the dead on the eve of All Souls' Day, and children play practical jokes in the cemeteries—such as placing lit candles inside skulls, or rattling bones in empty pails—to frighten visitors.

SOURCES:
DictFolkMyth-1984, p. 842
FestWestEur-1958, p. 47

♦ 0062 ♦ All Saints' Day (Louisiana)
November 1

ALL SAINTS' DAY is celebrated in many areas of the United States where there are large Roman Catholic populations. In New Orleans, for example, it is a legal holiday on which Catholics gather in local cemeteries and decorate the graves with flowers. The descendants of the French Canadian (also known as Acadian or Cajun) settlers around St. Martinsville, Louisiana, observe this day in the traditional French manner by laying wreaths and bouquets on even the most obscure graves and, as darkness falls, by lighting candles throughout the cemeteries in anticipation of ALL SOULS' DAY on November 2.

SOURCES:
AmerBkDays-2000, p. 746
DictDays-1988, p. 3

♦ 0063 ♦ All Saints' Day and All Souls' Day (Guatemala)
October 31-November 2

Throughout Latin America, ALL SAINTS' DAY, November 1, and ALL SOULS' DAY, November 2, are treated like a single holiday. In Guatemala, the Indian villagers of Todos Santos (which means "All Saints") stretch these celebrations honoring the dead into a three-day-long affair by adding October 31. Families pay homage to the dead on All Souls' Day by decorating the graves of their loved ones and offering flowers, corn, squash, and orange slices at church. They position them on the floor of the church, pour some coffee into the flower blossoms, and then shake droplets of brandy over the whole display.

These solemn offerings are in stark contrast to the highlight of the festival, wild horse races, in which many of the riders have been drinking since the previous night. In the town of Santiago Sacatepequez people fly huge kites in the graveyard and many attach prayers and notes to their deceased loved ones to the kites' tails.

CONTACTS:
Guatemalan Tourist Board
7A Avenida
Zona 4, Centro Civico 1-17 Guatemala
502-2421-2810; fax: 502-2421-2891
www.visitguatemala.com/nuevo/mainE.asp

SOURCES:
FiestaTime-1965, p. 163

♦ 0064 ♦ **All Saints' Day and All Souls' Day (Peru)**
November 1-2

In parts of Peru, the normally solemn celebration of ALL SAINTS' DAY and ALL SOULS' DAY gives way to some lively courtship rituals. In Arequipa and Cuzco, for example, many of the young men deliver cakes in the form of a baby, decorated with colored candies to their sweetheart's home. There they hold a mock baptismal ceremony in which they play the role of godfather. This entering into the ritual relationship of *compadrazgo*, or godfathership, often paves the way for marriage later on. On November 2 the young men of Tomaiquiche village visit their girlfriends' homes at dawn to sing to them. The girls reward their suitors by opening a window or door and dousing them with drops of urine. Although this may not seem like a traditional token of love, urine is kept in a closed container in some homes because it is believed to have curative powers.

CONTACTS:
Commission on the Promotion of Peru
Calle Uno Oeste No. 50, piso 13th
Urb. Corpac
Lima, 27 Peru
51-1-4224-3131; fax: 51-1-224-7134
www.promperu.gob.pe

SOURCES:
FiestaTime-1965, p. 163

♦ 0065 ♦ **All Souls' Day**
November 2 in the West; second Saturday prior to Lent and the day before Pentecost in the East

People held festivals for the dead long before Christianity. It was St. Odilo, the abbot of Cluny in France, who in the 10th century proposed that the day after ALL SAINTS' DAY be set aside in honor of the departed—particularly those whose

souls were still in purgatory. Today, the souls of all the faithful departed are commemorated. Although All Souls' Day is observed informally by some Protestants, it is primarily a Roman Catholic, Anglican, and Orthodox holy day.

In many Catholic countries, people attend churches, which are appropriately draped in black, and visit family graves on this day to honor their ancestors. In Shropshire and Cheshire, England, children still go out "souling" from house to house, although they are no longer given the traditional "soul cakes" that were supposed to rescue souls from purgatory. The evening of November 1 is often called **All Souls' Eve** and is a time to decorate graveyards and light candles in memory of the dead.

Orthodox Christians commemorate the dead on the second Saturday before Lent begins and on the day before Pentecost.

In Mexico, it is a national holiday called the DÍA DE LOS MUERTOS (or **Day of the Dead**). In the United States, Día de los Muertos is celebrated in areas where there is a large Mexican-American population.

In Portugal, November 2 is known as **Día dos Finados** (All Souls' Day), and the day is observed with special masses and processions to cemeteries. Similar celebrations are held for All Souls' Day in Ecuador, El Salvador, the French West Indies, Macao, and Uruguay.

In Italy **Il Giorno dei Morti** begins at dawn with a solemn Requiem for the dead. Church bells toll and people decorate the graves of their family members with flowers and candles. But Il Giorno dei Morti is not entirely a somber occasion. In Sicily the children who have prayed for the *morti*, souls of the departed, leave their shoes outside doors and windows, where they are filled with gifts. In Rome, it is customary for young people to announce their engagements on All Souls' Day. The man sends the engagement ring to his fiancée in a small white box, which in turn is packed in an oval container filled with *fave dei morti*, "beans of the dead"—little bean-shaped cakes made of ground almonds and sugar combined with eggs, butter, and flour.

SOURCES:
DaysCustFaith-1957, p. 282
DictFolkMyth-1984, p. 38, 184, 842, 1051, 1052
FestSaintDays-1915, p. 200
FestWestEur-1958, pp. 17, 47, 100
FolkAmerHol-1999, p. 427
FolkWrldHol-1999, p. 635
HolSymbols-2009, p. 19
OxYear-1999, p. 441
RelHolCal-2004, p. 105
SaintFestCh-1904, p. 472

♦ 0066 ♦ **All Souls' Day (Cochiti Pueblo)**
November 2

The Cochiti Pueblo Indians, who occupy the northernmost of the Keresan-speaking pueblos along the Rio Grande west of Santa Fe, refer to this day as **"Their Grandfathers Arrive from the West Feast"** (or **"Their Grandfathers Arrive from the Dead Feast"**). Converted to Catholicism by Spanish missionaries in the late 17th century, the Cochiti Indians regard ALL SOULS' DAY as an opportunity to persuade the visiting spirits of the departed that they have not been forgotten and that their kin are prospering. Each family fasts, setting out bowls of food in the corner of the house and leaving the door open for the returning spirits. The family's material goods—in the form of blankets, shawls, and jewelry—are displayed on the walls, and candles are lit so that the dead can find their way to their former homes. The men congregate in the *kiva*, or ceremonial chamber, where they spend the night singing and cutting up small pieces of food as offerings for the dead.

Similar ceremonies are held at other Indian pueblos in New Mexico. At Taos Pueblo, for example, the church bell rings all night while candles burn and food is brought to the graves in the churchyard. At the Zuni Pueblo around this same time, **Grandmothers' Day** is celebrated by making offerings of food to the dead. The men and boys spend the day going from house to house singing and receiving food.

CONTACTS:
Pueblo Cultural Center
2401 12th St. N.W.
Albuquerque, NM 87104
866-855-7902 or 505-843-7270; fax: 505-842-6959
www.indianpueblo.org

♦ 0067 ♦ Allen (Richard), Birthday of
February 14

The son of two slaves, Richard Allen (1760-1831) was born in Philadelphia on this day. By the time he was 26 years old, he had saved enough money to buy his way out of slavery, and soon after that he established an African-American congregation that met on Sunday afternoons in St. George's Methodist Church. Because he didn't want his church to exist solely as an arm of a European-American church, Allen bought some land and set up America's first African-American church in an old blacksmith shop. His followers were known as Allenites.

A new church building, completed in 1794, was dedicated by Francis Asbury, America's first Methodist bishop. Allen's work among African Americans expanded at such a rapid rate that in 1816 he had to expand the organization of his church nationwide. Members of the African Methodist Episcopal (AME) Church commemorate the birth of their founder and first bishop on this day.

CONTACTS:
First Episcopal District of the African Methodist Episcopal
  Church
3801 Market St., Ste. 300
First District Plaza
Philadelphia, PA 19104
215-662-0506; fax: 215-662-0199
www.1stdistrict-ame.org

African Methodist Episcopal Church
500 8th Ave. S
Nashville, TN 37203
615-254-0911; fax: 615-254-0912
www.ame-church.com

SOURCES:
EncyRel-1987, v. 1, pp. 97, 211

♦ 0068 ♦ Alma Highland Festival and Games
May, Memorial Day weekend

Like other American cities and towns founded or settled primarily by Scots, Alma, Michigan, celebrates its Scottish heritage by holding a traditional Highland Festival for three days in late May each year. The festival was originated by a local resident who attended the Scottish games in Boston in 1962 and decided that a similar event should be held in Alma, a city founded by Scots and with a Scottish name.

Activities include Scottish athletic events, border collie demonstrations, fiddling contests, an arts and crafts show, piping, drumming, and highland dancing. Participants come from all over the United States and Canada, and some even come from Scotland. The food served at the festival includes meat pies, haggis (a traditional Scottish dish made from the heart, liver, etc. of a sheep or calf, minced with suet and oatmeal, seasoned, and boiled in the stomach of the animal), bridies (hot sausage or meat rolls), and shortbread.

See also GRANDFATHER MOUNTAIN HIGHLAND GAMES AND GATHERING OF SCOTTISH CLANS; HIGHLAND GAMES; and VIRGINIA SCOTTISH GAMES

CONTACTS:
Alma Highland Festival
110 W. Superior St.
Alma, MI 48801
989-463-8979; fax: 989-463-6588
www.almahighlandfestival.com

SOURCES:
GdUSFest-1984, p. 91

♦ 0069 ♦ Almabtrieb
September

The **Return from the Mountain Pasture** is an autumn festival that takes place around Salzburg, Austria, and other areas in the German Alps on the day that the cattle are driven down from the mountain pastures to their winter shelter. The cattle are decorated with flowers and the *Sennerinnen*, or herding girls, who lead them wear traditional costumes that vary from place to place. Sometimes the cattle are brought to their final destination on flower-decked boats that ferry them across the mountain lakes. Once the cattle are safely in for the winter, the farmers hold welcome-home feasts which are followed by music, dancing, and singing.

See also ALPAUFZUG and COW FIGHTS

CONTACTS:
National Park Administration Salzburg
Neukirchen am Grv. 306
Salzburg, A-5741 Austria
43-656-2408-4933
www.salzburg.gv.at/en/en-index

SOURCES:
FestWestEur-1958, p. 70

♦ 0070 ♦ Aloha Festivals
September-October

Aloha Festivals is a celebration of Hawaiian culture. Once a week-long event called Aloha Week, it's now a two-month affair with 300 events that starts in Honolulu in early September and runs through the end of October, with a week of festivities on every island of Hawaii. The celebrations include canoe races between the islands of Molokai and Oahu, coronations of royal courts as commemorations of the former Hawaiian monarchy, street parties, cultural events, parades, and pageantry.

CONTACTS:
Aloha Festivals
P.O. Box 15945
Honolulu, HI 96830
800-852-7690 or 808-589-1771; fax: 808-589-1770
www.alohafestivals.com

SOURCES:
GdUSFest-1984, p. 41

♦ 0071 ♦ Alpaufzug
May or June

Also known as **Alpine Cattle Drive**, an old custom in Switzerland is this springtime "ascent to the mountains," when goats and cows are driven to higher pasture. In the cantons of Appenzell in eastern Switzerland and also in the Alpine canton of Valais, there are picturesque festivals, with herders and their families dressing in traditional costume (the Appenzell men wear red vests and yellow knicker-type pants) and everyone enjoying the cattle show and Cow Fights that establish the leader of the herd. In August and September, bringing the herds back down to the valleys, known as *Alpabfahrten*, also prompts festivals, and the cow that has been the greatest milk producer is feted and decked with flowers.

See also Almabtrieb

CONTACTS:
Appenzellerland Tourismus AI
Hauptgasse 4
Appenzell, 9050 Switzerland
41-71-788-9641; fax: 41-71-788-9650
www.appenzell.ch/en

SOURCES:
BkHolWrld-1986, Apr 17
FestWestEur-1958, p. 229

♦ 0072 ♦ Alpenfest
Third week in July

At an altitude of 1,348 feet, Gaylord is one of the highest incorporated communities in Michigan. Five rivers rise nearby and flow in different directions. Gaylord receives nearly 150 inches of snow each year and the town's main streets are lined with Swiss-style architecture. The annual Alpenfest is basically a celebration of summer.

A highlight of the festival is the "Burning of the Boog." People write their troubles on slips of paper and place them in the Boog—a 300-pound, 10-foot-high monster—which is then burned, giving spectators a chance to watch their troubles literally go up in smoke. The festival also boasts a number of outdoor cafes which host "the World's Largest Coffee Break."

CONTACTS:
Gaylord/Otsego Chamber of Commerce Information Center
101 W. Main St.
P.O. Box 513
Gaylord, MI 49734
800-345-8621 or 989-732-6333; fax: 989-732-7990
www.gaylordchamber.com

♦ 0073 ♦ Amalaka Ekadashi
February-March; 11th day of waxing half of Hindu month of Phalguna

Among Hindus, who respect all animate and inanimate things because they are manifestations of the Universal Spirit, this is a day for worshipping the Alma tree (Amalaka), where Vishnu is believed to live. An Amalaka tree is ceremonially bathed and watered, a fast is observed, and Brahmans are given gifts.

Amalaka Ekadashi also marks the beginning of the Holi or spring festival in India, where people splash each other with colored water and red powder (an aphrodisiac), indulge in eating and drinking, and generally behave in an uninhibited manner.

SOURCES:
RelHolCal-2004, p. 183

♦ 0074 ♦ Amalgamated Order of Real Bearded Santas International Conference
Third Sunday in January

The Amalgamated Order of Real Bearded Santas (AORBS) is an international organization "dedicated to training Santas and enhancing their portrayal of Santa Claus for the benefit of your family and community." To be a member of AORBS, one must be a gentleman who has a real beard and has portrayed Santa Claus at least once, in any venue—from playing the role of Santa for his own kids on Christmas Day to playing Santa throughout the year.

The AORBS formed in August 1994 when 10 men were selected to play the role of Santa in a commercial for a German mail-order company named OTTO. Over the course of the approximately 14 hours of filming, the men quickly became friends. They decided to meet for lunch at a future date. They chose to meet in January because all of them would be very busy through December.

The Santas met for their first lunch on January 15, 1995. At the end of the meeting, they decided they would meet every year on the third Sunday of January. It was during this meeting that they also decided on the name for their group.

Over the years, membership in this group grew to the point that they decided to hold a convention. In July 2006, AORBS held the first Discover Santa Convention. Nearly 300 Santas and 200 Mrs. Clauses from countries around the world (Scandinavia, Germany, Russia, the United States, and Japan) attended the three-day convention in Branson, Mo. The convention received lots of media attention, which led to an increase in AORBS membership. By 2007, the organization had over 1,300 member Santas.

AORBS organizes events in various locations throughout the year, but they continue to meet every January. Because there are now so many AORBS members, many of the annual lunches have grown to more than just a simple lunch gathering.

CONTACTS:
Amalgamated Order of Real Bearded Santas, Inc. (AORBS)
c/o Nicholas Trolli
1100 Newportville Rd.
Apt. 803
Croydon, PA 19021
www.aorbsinc.com

♦ 0075 ♦ **Amarnath Yatra**
July-August; full moon of Hindu month of Sravana

Amarnath Yatra is a pilgrimage to the Amarnath cave, high in the Kashmir Himalayas, near Pahalgam in northern India. This cave holds a natural ice lingam, the Hindu phallic symbol of Lord Shiva. The trek to the cave, at an altitude of about 12,700 feet, is along narrow, winding mountain trails. The thousands of pilgrims who make this trip include everyone from *sadhus* (holy men) walking barefoot over the stones and snow to wealthy people being carried by coolies. People can make the yatra, or pilgrimage, for a few months during the year when the paths are accessible, but the full moon day of Sravana has special significance to the devout, since tradition holds that Shiva first made himself manifest in the lingam on this day.

CONTACTS:
Directorate of Information, Jammu and Kashmir Government
Opposite Pratap Park, Abhi Guzar Lal Chowk
Srinagar, Jammu & Kashmir 190 001 India
91-194-2452294; fax: 91-194-2452227
www.jammukashmir.nic.in

♦ 0076 ♦ **Amazon & Galapagos Day**
February 12

Two significant events happened in Ecuadoran history on the same date: the discovery of the Amazon River headwaters by Spanish explorer Francisco de Orellana in 1542 and the incorporation of the Galapagos Islands in 1832. The country established the Amazon & Galapagos Day holiday during the presidency of Jaime Roldós Aguilera (1979–1981). Festivities typically focus more attention on the Amazon story and the biodiversity of that region than on Ecuador's inclusion of the Galapagos.

According to legend, Orellana and his exploration party of Spaniards and native peoples successfully arrived from the city of Quito to the grand river's headwaters only after defeating a group of warrior women known as "the Amazons." Following their discovery of the river, they sailed its course to where it emptied into the Atlantic Ocean. The alter-

native name for the holiday, **Dia del Oriente** (Orient Day), is a reference to the eastward destination of the explorers.

In observance of the anniversary, Ecuadoran presidents have visited the Amazon and paid homage to the historic expedition of 1542. Other activities include traditional dances, the presentation of folklore, and other cultural festivities.

CONTACTS:
Ecuador Embassy
2535 15th St. N.W.
Washington, D.C. 20009
202-234-7200; fax: 202-667-3482

SOURCES:
AnnivHol-2000, p. 26

♦ 0077 ♦ **American Birkebeiner**
Last weekend in February

The Birkie started in 1973 as a 55-kilometer cross-country ski race from Hayward, Wis., to Telemark Resort in the neighboring town of Cable, with only 35 skiers competing. Now it is the largest and most prestigious cross-country ski race in North America, an event that attracts top cross-country skiers from all over the world. In addition to the 55-kilometer Birkie, there is also the Kortelopet or "short race" of 23 kilometers, which is open to competitors ages 13 and up. Other races held during the three-day festival include the Barnebirkie (for children) and the 10K Family Fun Ski.

The American Birkebeiner is part of the Worldloppet, an international series of 12 marathon races held in Japan, Switzerland, Sweden, Norway, France, Germany, Austria, Finland, Italy, Canada, Australia, and the United States.

The American race was patterned after the Birkebeiner Rennet in Lillehammer, Norway. During the 13th century, a foreign invader was about to capture Norway's infant prince and heir to the throne. He was saved by two Viking warriors—called "Birkebeiners" for the birch-bark leggings they wore. These men took the child and skied 55 kilometers to safety. The baby eventually became the great Norwegian king, Haakon Haakonsson.

See also VASALOPPET

CONTACTS:
American Birkebeiner Ski Foundation
10527 Main St.
P.O. Box 911
Hayward, WI 54843
800-872-2753 or 715-634-5025; fax: 715-634-5663
www.birkie.com

SOURCES:
GdUSFest-1984, p. 210

♦ 0078 ♦ **American Folklife, Festival of**
Last weekend in June to first weekend in July

Since 1967 the Festival of American Folklife has been held on the National Mall in Washington, D.C., to celebrate the richness and diversity of American and world cultures. Since that time the Festival has presented more than 15,000 musicians, craftspeople, storytellers, cooks, workers, performers, and other cultural specialists from every region of the United States and from more than 45 other nations. Recent festival programs have included musicians from the former Soviet Union, demonstrations of African-American coil basketry and Italian-American stone-carving, the performance of a Japanese rice-planting ritual, and exhibits illustrating the occupational cultures of working people—taxicab drivers, firefighters, waiters, and railway workers.

The Festival is designed to expose visitors to people and cultures who would not ordinarily be heard in a national setting. It emphasizes folk, tribal, ethnic, and regional traditions in communities throughout the U.S. and abroad. Each year the festival features a particular state (or region) and country. One year, for example, the featured region was "Family Farming in the Heartland." More than 100 farmers from 12 Midwestern states came to the nation's capital to talk to visitors about changes in farming methods and farm life, and to demonstrate both modern and traditional farming skills. The featured country was Indonesia, and there were demonstrations of Buginese boat-building and traditional mask carving, in addition to an all-night Indonesian shadow-puppet show.

CONTACTS:
Center for Folklife and Cultural Heritage Capital Gallery
600 Maryland Ave. S.W., Ste. 2001 MRC 520
Washington, D.C. 20024
202-633-6440; fax: 202-633-6474
www.folklife.si.edu

SOURCES:
MusFestAmer-1990, p. 219

◆ 0079 ◆ **American Indian Heritage Month**
November

In 1914 Red Fox James of the Blackfeet tribe rode a pony 4,000 miles to present his request—endorsed by the governors of 24 states—that a day be set aside in honor of American Indians, or Native Americans, a name many prefer. The first general American Indian Day was observed on the second Saturday in May 1916, but throughout the 20th century, the observance and its date were left to the individual states, and they have varied widely. Since 1995 the month of November has been observed as American Indian Heritage Month.

Few would argue that the plight of American Indians today is not a grim one, with unemployment, illiteracy, and high school drop-out rates among the highest in the country. Although the largest Indian populations can be found in Oklahoma, Arizona, California, New Mexico, and North Carolina, many other states have come up with ways to draw attention to their unique contribution to American culture and to the need for improving their condition. Most celebrations focus on educational and promotional events, displays of Native American art and dance, and agricultural fairs.

CONTACTS:
Indian Health Service Heritage Committee
801 Thompson Ave., Ste. 400

Rockville, MD 20852
301-443-7261; fax: 301-480-3192
www.ihs.gov

SOURCES:
AnnivHol-2000, pp. 164, 181
BkFest-1937, p. 204

◆ 0080 ◆ **American Royal Livestock, Horse Show and Rodeo**
October-November

Also known as the **American Royal**, or simply the **Royal**, this is the oldest and one of the largest livestock shows and rodeos in the United States. It dates back to the period just after the Civil War, when Texans returning from the battlefield discovered that their cattle herds had multiplied unchecked. They were forced to conduct massive roundups that reached as far west as Kansas City, Missouri, which soon became a center for the consignment of cattle. Meat packers started building plants there to accommodate the supply, and breeders began to show their stock. The National Hereford Show, held in the Kansas City Stockyards in 1899, is now considered the first American Royal. Over the years the Hereford breeders were joined by breeders of other cattle as well as sheep, swine, and poultry. Draft and carriage horses were first shown at the Royal in 1903.

Although the Royal has suffered some setbacks over the years—including a fire that nearly destroyed the American Royal Building in 1922 and a serious flood in 1951—it has continued to expand and now draws more than 300,000 visitors. Beginning in June, there are special tours and instruction for school children, 20,000 of whom come to the show to learn more about agribusiness. The main events occur in October and November. The **American Royal Rodeo** is the final rodeo of the season on the professional circuit, featuring over 700 professional riders and offering more than $100,000 in prize money. There are also livestock auctions, horse and livestock shows, country music concerts, barbecue competitions, and a parade through downtown Kansas City that has been called America's largest hometown parade.

CONTACTS:
American Royal
1701 American Royal Ct.
Kansas City, MO 64102
816-221-9800; fax: 816-221-8189
www.americanroyal.com

◆ 0081 ◆ **American West, Festival of the**
July-August

This eight-day festival was started in 1972 by Glen L. Taggart, president of Utah State University in Logan, and takes place from late July to early August. Designed to educate people about America's pioneer and Indian cultures at the close of the 19th century, the festival includes a multimedia historical pageant; a cowboy poetry gathering; an exhibit of Western art, photographs, and engravings; a display of vintage steam tractors; an Old West parade of antique horse-drawn wagons; and demonstrations of pioneer cooking. Various celebrities—

including actors Robert Redford, Peter Strauss, and James Drury—have participated in past festivals, and Jimmy Stewart did the taped narration that still accompanies festival events.

Proceeds from the yearly festival have been used to establish a center for the Outlaw-Lawman History Association at Utah State University, a Western Writers' Conference, and two Western magazines. The events are held on the USU campus and in surrounding areas.

CONTACTS:
American West Heritage Center
4025 S. Hwy. 89-91
Wellsville, UT 84339
800-225-3378 or 435-245-6050; fax: 435-245-6052

SOURCES:
GdUSFest-1984, p. 189

♦ 0082 ♦ **America's Cup**
Held whenever the Cup is challenged, usually every 3-4 years

The America's Cup races are the world's longest-running international sporting event. The event is named for the trophy, originally called the Hundred Guinea Cup by the Royal Yacht Squadron of Great Britain, that was won by the 100-foot schooner *America* in a race around the Isle of Wight in 1851. The Cup was given by the schooner's owner, J. C. Stevens, to the New York Yacht Club, which successfully defended it against international challenges for 130 years. In 1984, the challenger *Australia II* defeated the American defender *Courageous* in races off Newport, Rhode Island, marking the end of the longest winning streak in international sports. In 1987, the American challenger *Stars & Stripes*, sailing for the San Diego Yacht Club, regained the Cup in races off Perth, Australia. *Stars & Stripes* successfully defended the cup in 1988 against New Zealand, and in 1992 *America*³ retained the Cup for the United States by defeating the Italian boat four races to one.

The race is usually held every three to four years, with challengers coming from England, Canada, France, Sweden, Italy, New Zealand, Australia, Japan, and other countries. The rules require that the defenders and challengers sail in closely matched boats built to the same general specifications, but designs have varied over the years as sailing technology has grown more sophisticated. A new class of boats, the America's Cup class, was introduced in 1991.

The New Zealand team won the Cup in 1995 and again in 2000. The Swiss team took the Cup in 2003 and 2007. The 2007 event was held in Spain, the first time since 1951 that it was held in Europe.

CONTACTS:
America's Cup
P.O. Box 2500
Olympic Valley, CA 96146
530-386-2190
www.americascup.com

SOURCES:
AmerBkDays-2000, p. 601
HolSymbols-2009, p. 23

♦ 0083 ♦ **Amherstburg Heritage Homecoming**
September

During the period of slavery in America, a secret network of people was established to help slaves escape to freedom. This network became known as the Underground Railroad. The Underground Railroad used several routes, with one route ending in Amherstburg, Ontario.

In 1793, Upper Canada passed the Anti-slave Law, which ended the importation of slaves into Upper Canada. It also granted freedom to all born after that date when they reached the age of 25. This made Upper Canada a safe place for slaves hoping to escape the tyranny of American slave owners. Amherstburg could easily be reached by crossing the Detroit River, which runs between Detroit and Windsor, Ontario, so this became the destination of many escaped slaves.

Amherstburg became a main center in the history and development of the community of black Canadians. Blacks participated in all aspects of business and community life. They were innkeepers, grocers, tobacconists, millers, and shoemakers. The core of the black community was the church. Nazery African Methodist Episcopal Church (now the site of The North American Black Museum) was established in 1848, and the First Baptist Church was established in 1849.

The Amherstburg Heritage Homecoming is an annual multi-family reunion for the families and friends of those whose ancestors found freedom in Amherstburg, and the descendants of those who aided, supported, and welcomed them as citizens and neighbors.

The idea of having a multi-family reunion came up during various family reunions around town. In September 2002, several families got together at the First Baptist Church in Amherstburg to discuss the multi-family reunion idea. During this meeting, the group decided that, if possible, the event should occur on the historic EMANCIPATION DAY date.

Within a few months of this first meeting, an Executive Committee was formed, and many more families became involved. Over the next year, many people worked to make the reunion a reality. This was to be an event where the children could share with pride their heritage and a day where they could remember the sacrifices made by their ancestors to implement an important and positive change.

During the Amherstburg Heritage Homecoming weekend, activities include a re-enactment of the slave crossing, a parade, music, religious services, picnics, arts and crafts, and other fair-type festivities.

CONTACTS:
Amherstburg Heritage Homecoming
519-736-2340
www.uwindsor.ca/users/e/ernest/main.nsf

♦ 0084 ♦ **Amurdad, Feast of**
July, November, December; seventh day of Amurdad, the fifth Zoroastrian month

The Feast of Amurdad is one of the "sacred name days" in the Zoroastrian religion, where both the day and the month share the name of the same *yazata* or spiritual being—in this case Amurdad, who presides over plants and is represented by fruits and flowers. Amurdad also stands for immortality.

The Zoroastrian calendar has 12 months of 30 days each, plus five extra days at the end of the year. Because of discrepancies in the calendars used by widely separated Zoroastrian communities around the world, there are now three different calendars in use, and the 7th of Amurdad can fall either in July, November, or December.

Followers of the Zoroastrian religion, which was founded by the prophet Zoroaster (also known as Zarathushtra, who is believed to have lived around 1200 B.C.E.), today live primarily in Iran and northwestern India, although smaller communities exist in Pakistan, Sri Lanka, Canada, the U.S., England, and Australia.

SOURCES:
RelHolCal-2004, p. 67

♦ 0085 ♦ **An tOireachtas**
Early November

The original *Oireachtas*, or "Assembly," dates back to the ancient kingdoms of seventh-century Ireland. In 1897 Conradh na Gaeilge revived the tradition of assembly and discussion that had begun centuries earlier by founding what is now Ireland's oldest annual cultural festival. An tOireachtas is a 10-day celebration of Irish culture and language, and it includes lectures, debates, literary and stage competitions, concerts, art exhibitions, storytelling, and performances of traditional Irish song, music, and dance. A highlight of the festival is the *sean-nós*, or traditional singing in the Irish language. The sean-nós singing competitions culminate in the *Corn Uí Riada*, the final competition for the coveted Ó Riada Trophy.

Sponsored by the Gaelic League, the festival is held in a different venue each year. It is similar to the EISTEDDFOD in Wales and the GAELIC MOD in Scotland.

CONTACTS:
Tourism Ireland
345 Park Ave., 17th Fl.
New York, NY 10154
800-223-6470 or 212-418-0800; fax: 212-371-9052
www.antoireachtas.ie

SOURCES:
IntlThFolk-1979, p. 237

♦ 0086 ♦ **Anant Chaturdashi**
August-September; 14th day of waxing half of Hindu month of Bhadrapada

Among Hindus, this is a day for worshipping and meditating on the god Vishnu. A day-long fast is observed, with offerings of fruits, sweets, and flowers to Vishnu. A thread colored in turmeric paste and having 14 knots is tied on the upper right arm while meditating in the belief that it will protect the worshipper from evil and bring prosperity and happiness. The

Pandava princes in exile observed this fast on the advice of Sri Krishna and as a result, they defeated the Kauravas and regained their lost kingdom (*see* BHISHMA ASHTAMI).

SOURCES:
BkFest-1937, p. 160
RelHolCal-2004, p. 174

♦ 0087 ♦ **Anastenaria**
May 21-23

Anastenaria is a firewalking ceremony in Greece, in the communes of Agia Eleni near Serres and of Langada near Thessalonike. Men and women, some holding red kerchiefs and some carrying icons of St. Constantine and St. Helen—in whose honor the ceremonies are held—dance barefooted on red-hot coals while folk musicians play. The custom is supposed to have originated in an ancient form of worship that was brought by travelers from Kosti in Eastern Thrace and adapted to Christian beliefs.

Firewalking has been practiced in many parts of the world and has been thought at times to ensure a good harvest and at other times to purify the participants.

CONTACTS:
Greek National Tourist Organization
645 Fifth Ave., 9th Fl.
New York, NY 10022
212-421-5777; fax: 212-826-6940
www.visitgreece.gr

SOURCES:
OxYear-1999, p. 215

♦ 0088 ♦ **Anchorage Festival of Music**
June

A major cultural event in Alaska, the Anchorage Festival of Music was established in 1956 by Mary Hale, an arts patron who lived in the city, and Robert Shaw, the world-famous maestro of choral music. Since its inception, this classical music festival has brought local, national, and international orchestral and choral musicians together to perform in chamber recitals and concerts during the month of June. The festival also has an educational component in its Summer Music Conservatory, cosponsored by the Anchorage Festival of Music and the University of Alaska at Anchorage, a program for musicians ages 11-18 with prior instrumental and/or vocal experience. In addition to featuring such works as those of Ludwig van Beethoven (1770-1827), Wolfgang Amadeus MOZART (1756-1791), and Gioacchino Rossini (1792-1868), the festival presents some contemporary classics—hit songs from popular Broadway shows.

CONTACTS:
Anchorage Festival of Music
550 W. 7th Ave.
P.O. Box 103251
Anchorage, AK 99510
907-276-2465; fax: 907-276-2540
www.anchoragefestivalmusic.com

SOURCES:
MusFestAmer-1990, p. 21
MusFestWrld-1963, p. 285

♦ 0089 ♦ Anchorage Fur Rendezvous
Begins on the second Friday in February

The Anchorage Fur Rendezvous, also called the **Rondy** and sometimes the **Mardi Gras of the North**, is a 10-day city-wide celebration held in Anchorage, Alaska. The Rondy has its origins in the days when fur trappers, joined by miners, capped off a season of trapping by carousing in Anchorage; this annual rendezvous was formalized as a winter carnival in 1936.

Highlighting the celebration is the World Championship Sled Dog Race, a 75-mile race run in three 25-mile legs on three successive days, starting and ending in Anchorage. Contestants come from throughout the United States. Among the scores of other events and exhibits are parades, the Miners and Trappers Ball, Eskimo blanket tossing, Eskimo dances, a snowshoe baseball game, wristwrestling matches, and performances of an old-time melodrama. Special Alaskan foods sold include sourdough pancakes.

See also IDITAROD TRAIL SLED DOG RACE

CONTACTS:
Greater Anchorage, Inc.
400 D St., Ste. 200
Anchorage, AK 99501
907-274-1177; fax: 907-277-2199
www.furrondy.net

SOURCES:
AmerBkDays-2000, p. 138

♦ 0090 ♦ Andersen (Hans Christian) Festival
Mid-June through July

Since 1965, the city of Odense, where Danish author Hans Christian Andersen (1805-1875) lived as a child, has honored its native son with festival activities during the summer. Each year, the Hans Christian Andersen Festival presents a choreographed musical production of one of Andersen's fairy tales at the Funen Village outdoor amphitheater. The play is performed once a day, with a cast of about 85 children and young adults. Past performances have included "The Tinder Box," "The Ugly Duckling," "Little Claus and Big Claus," and "Simple Simon." From mid-June through July, the fairy tale castle in the garden behind the Hans Christian Andersen Museum is the site of the Hans Christian Andersen Parade, with 30-minute shows three times a day. Playing the roles of 35 favorite Andersen characters, the troupe performs scenes from the writer's most popular fairy tales.

See also CHILDREN'S BOOK DAY, INTERNATIONAL

CONTACTS:
Odense Tourist Bureau
Radhuset
Odense C, DK-5000 Denmark
45-66-12-75-20; fax: 45-66-12-75-86
museum.odense.dk/?lang=en

H. C. Andersen Festspillenes Sekretariatet
Sct. Knuds Kirkestraede 9, 2
Odense C, DK-5000 Denmark
45-70-27-40-77; fax: 45-70-27-40-78

SOURCES:
GdWrldFest-1985, p. 73

♦ 0091 ♦ Andorra National Day
September 8

The Principality of Andorra, located in the Pyrénées Mountains between France and Spain, was founded by the Emperor Charlemagne, who recovered the region from the Muslims in 803. (*See also* ST. CHARLEMAGNE'S DAY.) His son later granted part of his empire to the Spanish bishop of Urgell, and by the late 13th century the citizens of Andorra were ruled by two princes, one in Spain and one in France. Until recently, the principality had been governed jointly by the bishop of Urgell and the king, and, later, the president of France.

On September 8, 1278, Andorra's first constitutional document, known as the "Pareatges," was signed. Among other things, it stated that each of the co-rulers would receive a token tribute each year known as the Questia. Originally, the French king received $2 biennially; the bishop $8, plus six hams, six cheeses, and 12 hens in alternate years. On March 14, 1993, the people of Andorra voted to abandon this mode of government and institute a parliamentary system.

The people of Andorra celebrate their National Day by honoring Jungfrau von Meritxell, their patron saint. Pilgrims climb to her hilltop sanctuary near the villages of Encamp and Canillo, where her statue was found by a shepherd under an almond tree (some say a rose bush) blooming out of season. The pilgrims stop to refresh themselves with drinks that have been cooled in the nearby springs, and after the sermon they celebrate by dancing and eating lamb grilled on slabs of slate.

CONTACTS:
Ministry of Tourism
C/ Prat de la Creu, 62-64
Andorra la Vella, AD500 Andorra
376-875-700; fax: 376-860-184
www.andorra.ad/en-US/Pages/default.aspx

SOURCES:
AnnivHol-2000, p. 151

♦ 0092 ♦ Angam Day
October 26

Nauru is an island in the Pacific, about 2,200 miles northeast of Sydney, Australia, and 2,400 miles southwest of Honolulu. Over the past 100 years, the existence of Nauruans has been threatened a number of times—by tribal disputes in the 1870s, which reduced the population to fewer than 1,000, and by an influenza epidemic in 1919. During World War II, two-thirds of the population was deported by the Japanese to the Caroline Islands to build airstrips.

Although the population has increased substantially since then, it is still a cause for concern. Angam Day (angam means "hope") on October 26 commemorates the various occasions when the Nauruan population has reached 1,500, which is considered the minimum number necessary for survival.

CONTACTS:
Nauru Mission to the UN
800 Second Ave., Ste. 400D
New York, NY 10017
212-937-0074
www.un.int

♦ 0093 ♦ **Angelitos, Los**
October 30

For the Mayan Indians living near Cancún in southeastern Mexico, October 30 was a day devoted to children who had died, the *angelitos*, or "little angels." It was customary for families to put flowers on their doors and to cook up treats for the angelitos who would visit them that night. Los Angelitos marked the beginning of the period during which all the dead were commemorated. Mexicans celebrate the Day of the Dead, or DÍA DE LOS MUERTOS, on ALL SOULS' DAY, November 2.

SOURCES:
BkHolWrld-1986, Oct 30

♦ 0094 ♦ **Angkor Photography Festival**
Late November

The first annual photography event in Southeast Asia, the Angkor Photography Festival takes place in Siem Reap, a town in northwestern Cambodia near the ancient ruins of Angkor. The photographic selections of this exhibition typically focus on the regions of South Asia, Southeast Asia, and the Far East, although the festival welcomes submissions from all over the world.

The festival caters to two genres in the field—humanistic (or concerned) documentary photography and fine art photography. Festivalgoers view works in print exhibitions and outdoor projections set up in different Siem Reap locations.

The festival was co-founded by journalist Gary Knight, photographer Christophe Loviny, and gallerist Jean-Yves Navel in 2005. Their mission—beyond displaying excellent photographs—was to pool the resources of compassionate artists to serve Cambodia's marginalized groups. Each festival, which lasts roughly 10 days, offers youths free workshops led by established photographers. One such workshop offered in 2007 festival used photography to empower women with HIV to document their situation.

CONTACTS:
Ankor Photography Festival Center
Carnets d'Asie
333 Sivatha St.
Siem Reap, Kambodscha Cambodia
www.angkorphotofestival.com

♦ 0095 ♦ **Angola Independence Day**
November 11

This national holiday commemorates Angola's formal independence from Portugal on this day in 1975, after battling for autonomy since the beginning of the 20th century.

CONTACTS:
Angola Embassy
2100-2108 16th St. N.W.
Washington, D.C. 20009
202-785-1156; fax: 202-822-9049
www.angola.org

SOURCES:
AnnivHol-2000, p. 189

♦ 0096 ♦ **Angola National Heroes Day**
September 17

National Heroes Day in Angola is celebrated on the birthday of the man considered to be the nation's founder, Antonio Agostinho Neto. Born in 1922 in the Bengo province and educated as a doctor, Neto was a powerful force in Angolan history, as well as one of the country's foremost poets. He led the Popular Movement for the Liberation of Angola (PMLA) in the fight for Angola's independence from Portugal. Neto continued to lead that group through years of civil war that raged in Angola after Portugal withdrew and various nationalist groups struggled for power. He also served as Angola's first president, holding office from 1975 until his death in 1979.

National Heroes Day honors Neto, his ideals for his country, and his accomplishments, as well as those who lost their lives in the struggle for Angolan independence. In addition to ceremonies and speeches, special sports events are often held on this day, including competitions in basketball, cycling, football, chess, swimming, volleyball, and other athletics.

CONTACTS:
Angolan Embassy
2100-2108 16th St. N.W.
Washington, D.C. 20009
202-785-1156; fax: 202-822-9049
www.angola.org

♦ 0097 ♦ **Anjou Festival**
July

Every summer the Festival d'Anjou, a celebration of the performing and visual arts held in Angers, France, gives young artists an opportunity to work with and learn from professionals in their fields through the educational workshops offered during the festival. Some of the world's best-known dance and theatrical groups have come to perform at the festival since its founding in 1975. Most of these performances are held either outdoors or inside abbeys, castles, and churches.

CONTACTS:
French Government Tourist Office
444 Madison Ave., 16th Fl.
New York, NY 10022
800-391-4909 or 212-838-7800; fax: 212-838-7855
martinique.org

Association du Festival d'Anjou
1, rue des Arenes

Angers, 49100 France
33-2-4124-8877; fax: 33-2-4124-8878
festivaldanjou.com

SOURCES:
IntlThFolk-1979, p. 98

♦ 0098 ♦ **Anna Parenna Festival**
March 15

Anna Parenna was a Roman goddess who represented the circle or ring of the year—Anna being the feminine form of *annus* (meaning "year") and March, the month her festival was observed, being the first month of the Roman calendar. Anna was usually depicted as the old woman of the year that had just passed, while Mars was the god of the first month of the new year. According to legend, in 494 B.C.E. the ancient Roman *plebs*, or common citizens, fled the city to put political pressure on the patricians (aristocracy), who needed the plebs for the army. They took refuge on the Mons Sacer, a mountain near Rome. They began to run out of food and suffer starvation. Anna, an old woman from Bovillae, brought them cakes every day. When peace was reestablished, the people made her one of their deities and added *Parenna* (meaning "enduring" or "lasting throughout the year") to her name.

On the day of her festival, the plebs of Rome went to the Campus Martius, a large field outside the walls of the city, and lay about on the grass, often pitching tents or constructing simple huts out of stakes and branches with togas stretched across the top. They spent the day drinking, dancing, and singing, returning to the city at night in a state of deep intoxication. As they drank, they often prayed to Anna to let them live as many years as the number of cups of wine they had swallowed.

SOURCES:
ClassDict-1984, p. 48
DictRomRel-1996, p. 9
FestRom-1981, p. 90

♦ 0099 ♦ **Annakut Festival**
October-November; first day of waxing half of Hindu month of Kartika

This Hindu festival is observed on the day following DEWALI in northern India. It celebrates an event in Krishna's life in which he lifted the Govardhan Mountain on his little finger for seven days, to protect the cows and people of Vrindavana (now in the state of Uttar Pradesh) against the deluge of rain sent by Indra, god of the heavens and rains. People come to the nearby town of Vrindavan from all over India to visit and worship at Mount Govardhan on this day. Those who cannot make the trip worship at home and give gifts to Brahmans. Hindus all over the world celebrate this day by preparing hundreds of different food dishes and taking them to temples to offer to the gods.

CONTACTS:
India Tourist Office
1270 Avenue of the Americas, Ste. 1808
New York, NY 10020

800-953-9399 or 212-751-6840; fax: 212-582-3274
www.tourisminindia.com

SOURCES:
RelHolCal-2004, p. 177

♦ 0100 ♦ **Annapolis Valley Apple Blossom Festival**
Five or six days beginning last week in May

Nova Scotia's Annapolis Valley is widely known for its apple orchards, which begin to flower in late May or early June. The area's first Apple Blossom Festival was held in 1933 in the town of Kentville, but since that time it has grown into a nearly week-long celebration whose events are held throughout the 60 towns and villages of the Annapolis Valley. In addition to a children's parade, sporting events, tours to view the apple blossoms, apple pie baking and eating contests, and a cooking competition, the festival includes the crowning of "Queen Annapolisa," who is chosen from among 18 local princesses.

The festival is also designed to draw attention to the area's historic background as "The Land of Evangeline," the heroine of Henry Wadsworth Longfellow's long narrative poem about the expulsion of a group of Acadians and their subsequent settlement in Louisiana.

CONTACTS:
Apple Blossom Festival Committee
217 Belcher St.
Kentville, NS B4N 1E2 Canada
902-678-8322; fax: 902-678-3710
www.appleblossom.com

SOURCES:
GdWrldFest-1985, p. 44

♦ 0101 ♦ **Annual Lantern Ceremony**
Eve of Patriots' Day (the third Monday in April)

The Annual Lantern Ceremony takes place every year on the eve of Patriots' Day, a public holiday observed in Massachusetts and Maine on the third Monday in April. Patriots' Day commemorates the American Revolutionary War battles of Lexington and Concord on April 19, 1775. The ceremony is held at the Old North Church in Boston (formal name: Christ Church in the City of Boston), which was built in 1723 and is the oldest standing church building in the city. It permanently entered the American history books on the evening of April 18, 1775. That night, the church sexton, Robert Newman, displayed two lanterns from the church steeple, signaling Paul Revere's fateful message that the British would come to Lexington and Concord "by sea" (i.e., across the Charles River), not by land.

The Annual Lantern Ceremony commemorates the lighting of the two lamps that launched a remarkable episode in U.S. history. The centerpiece of the ceremony each year is a keynote address by a notable leader of the Boston area or beyond. Notable past speakers have included President Gerald Ford, Chief Justice Margaret Marshall, and journalist Nina Totenberg.

CONTACTS:
Old North Church
193 Salem St.
Boston, MA 02113
617-523-6676; fax: 617-725-0559

◆ 0102 ◆ Annual Session of the National Baptist Convention, USA
First Week in September

The Annual Session of the National Baptist Convention, USA, which convenes during the first week of each September in a designated U.S. city, is the major business meeting of the group's boards, auxiliaries, and member churches. It lasts for five days and can attract up to 40,000 delegates. Each annual session typically has a theme, such as "Christian Music for the 21st Century," "The Call to Faithfulness in the Gospel Ministry," or "The Heavenly Vision and the Morals of the Church." During the annual session, delegates deal with business issues. However, they also share Christian fellowship and, through a series of forums, explore such issues as health and wellness, social justice, and empowerment, often with emphasis on their impact on the African-American community. Delegates also hear a keynote speech by the convention's national president and by such guest speakers as Barack Obama.

The National Baptist Convention, USA, founded in 1886, is the country's largest and oldest African-American religious convention, with about 7.5 million members. The group marked its 127th annual session in 2007.

CONTACTS:
National Baptist Convention, USA, Inc.
1700 Baptist World Center Dr.
Nashville, TN 37207
866-531-3054 or 215-895-4094; fax: 215-895-4094
www.nationalbaptist.com

◆ 0103 ◆ Annunciation of the Blessed Virgin Mary, Feast of the (Belgium)
March 25

The Feast of the Annunciation or LADY DAY is known in Belgium as **Notre Dame de la Prospérité**, due to a folk belief that seeds planted on this feast day will certainly sprout. This day is also associated with weather lore: traditional Belgian belief has it that a clear, starry sky before sunrise is a good omen for the next harvest.

According to legend, the Lord asked the animals and birds to pass the Feast of the Annunciation in silent contemplation. When the cuckoo ignored this command and continued its brazen, loud calling, God punished the bird by forbidding it to build its own nest, thus dooming it to wander forever.

SOURCES:
FestSaintDays-1915, p. 59
FestWestEur-1958, p. 6

◆ 0104 ◆ Annunciation of the Lord
March 25

Formerly called the **Annunciation of the Blessed Virgin Mary** by the Roman Catholic Church, this day celebrates the appearance of the Archangel Gabriel to the Virgin Mary announcing that she was to become the mother of Jesus. The date for this feast couldn't have been fixed until the date of CHRISTMAS was established, and obviously the two dates had to be nine months apart. In England, the Feast of the Annunciation is commonly called LADY DAY. Greek Orthodox Christians refer to this day as the Annunciation of the Theotokos.

Annunciation usually falls during LENT, and is kept as a feast day in the midst of the Lenten fast. If it should happen to fall on MAUNDY THURSDAY or GOOD FRIDAY, it is transferred to a date following EASTER. According to medieval superstition, it was a bad omen when Easter and the Annunciation fell on the same day.

In Sweden it was called *Varfrudagen*, "Our Lady's Day." Common pronunciation turned it into *Vaffeldagen*, or "Waffle Day." This is the source of heart-shaped waffle irons: the waffles commemorate the heart of the Virgin Mary.

CONTACTS:
Marian Library/International Marian Research Institute
University of Dayton
Dayton, OH 45469
937-229-4214; fax: 937-229-4258
www.udayton.edu

Greek Orthodox Archdiocese of Australia
242 Cleveland St.
Redfern, NSW 2016 Australia
61-2-9698-5066; fax: 61-2-9698-536
www.greekorthodox.org.au

SOURCES:
AmerBkDays-2000, pp. 3, 232
BkDays-1864, vol. I, p. 417
BkHolWrld-1986, Mar 25
DaysCustFaith-1957, p. 86
EncyChristmas-2003, p. 33
EncyEaster-2002, p. 3
EncyRel-1987, v. 3, p. 441
FestSaintDays-1915, p. 56
FestWestEur-1958, pp. 6, 213
FolkWrldHol-1999, p. 223
OxYear-1999, p. 133, 503
RelHolCal-2004, p. 92
SaintFestCh-1904, p. 146

◆ 0105 ◆ Anthesteria
February-March

Anthesteria was a spring festival held for three days annually in ancient Athens during the Attic month of Anthesterion (February-March). Its purpose was to celebrate the beginning of spring, the god Dionysus, and the maturing of the wine stored during the previous year. The first day was celebrated by tasting the new wine from the previous vintage. This was known as the Pithoigia, or "opening of the casks." The second day, the Choes, or "pitcher feast," was a merry celebration of the marriage of the chief archon's (magistrate's) wife to Dionysus. A festival of the dead was held on the third day. This was called the Chutroi, or "feast of pots." This was a time of mourning to honor the dead, and to placate or expel ghosts. The three days of the Anthesteria incorporated the theme of birth-growth-death.

SOURCES:
DictFolkMyth-1984, p. 64
EncyRel-1987, v. 1, p. 306
OxClassDict-1970, p. 67

◆ 0106 ◆ Anthony (Susan B.) Day
February 15; August 26

Susan Brownell Anthony (1820-1906) devoted her life to the temperance, anti-slavery, and women's suffrage movements. After the Civil War ended in 1865, she focused all of her energies on getting women the right to vote. That goal was achieved in 1920 with the passage of the 19th Amendment to the Constitution of the United States, sometimes called "the Anthony Amendment." She was elected to the Hall of Fame for Great Americans in 1950, and was honored in 1979 when she became the first American woman to have her likeness on a coin: the Susan B. Anthony dollar.

Tributes to Anthony take place on her birthday, February 15, in various parts of the country. Sometimes a memorial service is held in the crypt of the Capitol in Washington, D.C., where there is a statue of the pioneers in the women's suffrage movement: Anthony, Elizabeth Cady STANTON, and Lucretia Mott. Ceremonies honoring Anthony are often held at her grave in Rochester, New York, near the home where for more than 40 years she lived and frequently met with other influential reformers. Women's organizations, such as the National Organization for Women (NOW), usually play a major role in sponsoring memorial observances.

Some states observe Susan B. Anthony Day on August 26, the day on which the 19th Amendment was ratified.

CONTACTS:
Susan B. Anthony House
17 Madison St.
Rochester, NY 14608
585-235-6124; fax: 585-235-6124
www.susanbanthonyhouse.org

SOURCES:
AmerBkDays-2000, pp. 456, 609
DictDays-1988, p. 115
OxYear-1999, p. 79

◆ 0107 ◆ Antigua and Barbuda Independence Day
November 1

Antigua and its dependency, Barbuda, became officially independent from England in 1981. Antigua had been settled by English people as early as 1632. It did not gain self-rule until 1967.

This small state also observes the first Monday and Tuesday in August as a legal holiday known as ANTIGUA CARNIVAL, during which a festival celebrates the islanders' cultural heritage.

CONTACTS:
Antigua and Barbuda Embassy
3216 New Mexico Ave. N.W.
Washington, D.C. 20016
202-362-5122; fax: 202-362-5225
www.antigua-barbuda.org

SOURCES:
AnnivHol-2000, p. 183

◆ 0108 ◆ Antigua Carnival
July-August

Antigua and Barbuda was the first nation in the British Caribbean to abolish slavery, in 1834. This distinction moves Antiguans to celebrate for 11 days in the summer.

The initial Carnival celebrations, which date back to 1957, took place earlier in the year, between May and July. However, the festival was later moved to its current position on the calendar to coincide with the already established celebration of the slaves' emancipation. Today, Antiguans begin celebrating the Carnival in late July and continue until the first Tuesday in August.

Music, competitions, and pageantry dominate the proceedings, most of which take place in the capital city of St. John's. Calypso music can be heard throughout the celebration, and the annual calypso competition produces a Calypso Monarch. Other contests include a steel band competition and two beauty pageants, which crown Caribbean Queen and Miss Antigua. Every Carnival also features street parades that are famous for their elaborate glittering costumes.

All the proceedings essentially lead up to J'Ouvert, the party on the first Monday in August. At 4:00 A.M. thousands of people fill the streets of St. John's for street dancing, which is accompanied by the sounds of steel drums and brass instruments.

CONTACTS:
Antigua and Barbuda Department of Tourism and Trade
25 S.E. 2nd Ave., Ste. 300
Miami, FL 33131
305-381-6762; fax: 305-381-7908
www.antiguacarnival.com

SOURCES:
FolkWrldHol-1999. p. 475

◆ 0109 ◆ Antigua National Heroes Day
December 9

Antigua has four citizens who have been designated as National Heroes, and December 9 is a public holiday to honor and celebrate all of them. The date is the birthday of one of the four, Sir Vere Cornwall Bird, the first prime minister of Antigua, who is considered the father of the nation. The others are King Court, who led a slave revolt in 1736; Dame Ellen Georgian Nellie Robinson, a pioneer in education; and Sir Vivian Richards, one of the world's greatest cricket players, who was captain of the West Indies team from 1985 to 1991.

Speeches and ceremonies honor the accomplishments of the National Heroes on this day. In 2007, in the capital city of St. John's, a ceremony took place at Heroes Park, involving Prime Minister Baldwin Spencer and children from various schools in the area. Spencer also laid a wreath at the monument honoring King Court. Also in 2007, postage stamps were issued memorializing the four National Heroes.

CONTACTS:
Consulate of Antigua and Barbuda
610 Fifth Ave., Ste. 311
New York, NY 10020
212-541-4117 or 212-541-4589; fax: 212-757-1607

Embassy of Antigua and Barbuda
32 New Mexico Ave. N.W.
Washington, DC 20016
202-362-5122; fax: 202-362-5225

♦ 0110 ♦ **Antique and Classic Boat Rendezvous**
Last weekend in July

Every July since 1975, classic wooden yachts of pre-1952 vintage have gathered for the annual Antique and Classic Boat Rendezvous at Mystic Seaport Museum in Mystic, Connecticut. Although some boats built as early as 1890 have participated, most date from the 1920s to the 1940s. Many are one-of-a-kind and have been kept in mint condition by their owners. More than 50 boats from throughout the Northeast participate each year, making it one of the largest gatherings of its kind.

The boats can be viewed at dockside on Friday evening and early on Saturday. Sunday afternoon the vessels begin their colorful parade down the Mystic River to Noank, led by the museum's 84-year-old steamboat, *Sabino*, with a Dixieland jazz band on board. The boats are "dressed" with brightly colored signal flags, and many carry crews in period costumes as they compete for awards in various categories.

CONTACTS:
Mystic Seaport Museum
75 Greenmanville Ave.
P.O. Box 6000
Mystic, CT 06355
888-973-2767 or 860-572-5315; fax: 860-572-5393
www.mysticseaport.org

♦ 0111 ♦ **Anzac Day**
April 25

A national holiday in Australia and New Zealand, Anzac Day takes its name from the initial letters of "Australia and New Zealand Army Corps." It commemorates the landing of the Anzac troops on the Gallipoli Peninsula in European Turkey on April 25, 1915, during World War I. Like MEMORIAL DAY in the U.S., this day is celebrated with veterans' parades and church services. Observed as a holiday since 1920, Anzac Day now honors those who have died in both world wars as well as in Korea and Vietnam.

CONTACTS:
Anzac Day Commemoration Committee of Queensland
P.O. Box 391

Aspley, QLD 4034 Australia
61-7-3263-7118; fax: 61-7-3263-7118
www.anzacday.org.au

History and Heritage Units, Ministry for Culture and Heritage
P.O. Box 5364
Wellington, New Zealand
64-4-471-4027; fax: 64-4-499-4490
www.nzhistory.net.nz

SOURCES:
AnnivHol-2000, p. 68
BkHolWrld-1986, Apr 25
DictDays-1988, p. 4
OxYear-1999, p. 174

♦ 0112 ♦ **Aoi Matsuri**
May 15

One of the three major festivals of Kyoto, Japan, the **Hollyhock Festival** is believed to date from the sixth century. The festival's name derives from the hollyhock leaves adorning the headdresses of the participants; legend says hollyhocks help prevent storms and earthquakes. The festival owes its present form to the time in the Heian period (792-1099) when imperial messengers were sent to the Kyoto shrines of Shimogamo and Kamigamo after a plague (or a flood) that came about because the shrines were neglected. Today the festival, which was revived in 1884, consists of a re-creation of the original imperial procession. Some 500 people in ancient costume parade with horses and large lacquered oxcarts carrying the "imperial messengers" from the Kyoto Imperial Palace to the shrines.

See also GION MATSURI and JIDAI MATSURI

CONTACTS:
Japan Information Network, Japan Center for Intercultural
   Communications
2-7-7 Hirakawacho
Chiyodaku
Tokyo, 102-0093 Japan
81-3-3263-5041; fax: 81-3-3230-4107
home.jcic.or.jp

Kyoto City Tourism & Culture Information
233-5 Daimon-ji-cho, Atarashimachi-dori
Oike-sagaru, Nakagyo-ku
Kyoto, 604-8315 Japan
81-7-5811-6388; fax: 81-7-5813-3250
www.kyotoguide.com

SOURCES:
GdWrldFest-1985, p. 122
HolSymbols-2009, p. 29
JapanFest-1965, p. 30

♦ 0113 ♦ **Apache Maidens' Puberty Rites**
July 4

The Apache Maidens' Puberty Rites are a celebration of the coming-of-age of girls of the Mescalero Apache Tribe, held for four days and four nights around the FOURTH OF JULY in Mescalero, N.M. Besides the puberty rites, there are other events: a rodeo, a powwow with cash prizes for dancers, a parade on July 4, and the nighttime Dance of the Mountain Gods.

The rites are related to the belief that soon after the creation of the world, White Painted Woman appeared in the east as a beautiful young woman, moved to the west, and disappeared when she was old. On the first and last days of the ceremonial, the girls must run around a basket four times, symbolically going through the four stages of life (infancy, childhood, adulthood, and old age). On the last day, their faces are painted with white clay and they enact the role of White Painted Woman, taking on her qualities and preparing for a rewarding adult life. On each of the four nights, the girls dance in the Holy Lodge, which was set up on the first day, while singers sing of the creation and beat time with deer-hoof rattles. The celebrations also involve feasting and elaborate ceremonial dresses.

In the 1800s, the U.S. government forbade the Apaches to congregate, but in 1911 decreed that they could congregate on July 4 to celebrate the nation's birthday. The Apaches then chose that date for their most important cultural ritual as an insult to their conquerors.

CONTACTS:
Mescalero Apache Tribe
P.O. Box 227
Mescalero, NM 88340
505-464-4494; fax: 505-464-9191

SOURCES:
DictWrldRel-1989, p. 531
EncyNatAmerRel-2001, p. 102
HolSymbols-2009, p. 32
IndianAmer-1989, p. 301

◆ 0114 ◆ Apollonian Games
July 6-13

Apollo was an ancient Greek god, but his fame had spread to Rome where he was adopted as a healing god during a plague in the fifth century B.C.E. A couple of hundred years later, after a setback in the Second Punic War against Hannibal's forces, religious officials decided to appeal to Apollo by holding games in his honor. The Romans first held the **Ludi Apollinares**, or Apollonian Games, in 212 B.C.E. Originally the Games took place on July 13; they turned into an eight-day event due to the event's success.

From the very start, the Apollonian Games showed a Greek influence. There were chariot races and "scenic shows" or theatrical productions—a Greek custom. An ox with gilded horns was sacrificed to Apollo, and everyone feasted. Of the eight days, two were devoted to games and races in the Circus Maximus, a huge outdoor arena, and the other six were devoted to plays in the theaters and market fairs.

See also LUDI; PLEBEIAN GAMES; ROMAN GAMES

SOURCES:
BkFairs-1939, p. 60
DictRomRel-1996, p. 134
FestRom-1981, p. 159
RomFest-1925, p. 179

◆ 0115 ◆ Apparition of the Infant Jesus
September 18

The ancient Villa de Eten in Peru is inhabited by many descendants of the Mochicas—a pre-Inca culture that flourished in northern Peru from the 3rd century B.C.E. to the 7th century C.E. Town residents still speak the ancient Mochica language, preserved in no other place in Peru. Two of their most important fiestas celebrate the apparitions of the infant Jesus, which took place on June 2 and September 18, 1649. After the second apparition, a tidal wave destroyed the village. The chapel of the apparitions, however, remained standing. Hence the villagers named it *La Capilla de los Milagros* (Chapel of the Miracles).

Townsfolk host a three-day festival commemorating this event, beginning on September 18. Preparations for the fiesta, which include candle making and other festive pursuits, begin several weeks beforehand. A special mass is held on the eve of the fiesta, and it is followed by fireworks and lighted balloons. Festivities continue the following day with a procession to the chapel with the images of Mary Magdalene, St. Peter holding the keys to heaven, and Senor del Mar (Lord of the Sea). Dance groups accompany the procession, each performing to its own tunes and wearing its own distinctive costumes. When the procession returns from the chapel, it stops at altars that have been set up along the way. A huge wheel of fireworks is set off when the procession reaches the church.

CONTACTS:
Commission for the Promotion of Peru
Calle Uno Oeste No. 50, piso 13th
Urb. Corpac
Lima, 27 Peru
51-1-4224-3131; fax: 51-1-224-7134
www.promperu.gob.pe

SOURCES:
FiestaTime-1965, p. 148

◆ 0116 ◆ Apple and Candle Night
October 31

Another name for HALLOWEEN among children in the Swansea area of Wales. The traditional game of "Apple and Candle" is played by suspending a stick from the ceiling with an apple fastened to one end and a lit candle to the other. The object is to eat the apple without using hands and without getting burned by the swinging candle. To make the game more challenging, players are sometimes blindfolded and the stick is twirled around before the game begins.

See also MISCHIEF NIGHT

SOURCES:
DictDays-1988, p. 4
DictFolkMyth-1984, p. 869
FestSaintDays-1915, p. 192
FolkWrldHol-1999, p. 604

◆ 0117 ◆ Appleseed (Johnny), Birthday of
September 26

John Chapman—better known as Johnny Appleseed for his lifelong dedication to planting apple seedlings all over the

American Midwest—was born on this day in 1774. While some frontier settlers thought he was a saint, or at the very least a religious fanatic, with his tin pot hat and coffee-sack tunic, the Indians regarded him as a great medicine man since he planted herbs as well as apples.

Since 1962 Johnny Appleseed's birthday has been observed in his hometown of Leominster, Massachusetts, on the first Saturday in June as **Johnny Appleseed Civic Day**. There is usually a ceremony at the monument that marks the site of Chapman's birthplace. In 1966 the day was celebrated with a ceremony marking the issue of a commemorative stamp bearing an image of the pioneer horticulturalist. His birthday is also honored in Ashland, Ohio, where he lived for more than 25 years, and at harvest festivals in apple-growing regions throughout the United States. In fact, the last week in September has been observed as Johnny Appleseed Week in Ohio since 1941.

See also JOHNNY APPLESEED FESTIVAL

CONTACTS:
Johnny Appleseed Heritage Center, Inc.
2179 State Rt. 603
Ashland, OH 44805
800-642-0388; fax: 419-368-8369
www.jahci.org

Leominster City Hall
25 West St.
Leominster, MA 01453
978-534-7500
www.leominster-ma.gov

SOURCES:
AmerBkDays-2000, p. 673
BkHolWrld-1986, Sep 26
DictFolkMyth-1984, p. 555

♦ 0118 ♦ **Appleseed (Johnny) Festival**
Third full weekend in September

A legend in his own time, John Chapman—better known as "Johnny Appleseed"—was born in Leominster, Massachusetts, on September 26, 1774. Although facts about his early life are hard to come by, there is a story that he fell in love with a woman named Dorothy Durand and that the families of the two lovers were bitter enemies. When Dorothy's family moved West, Johnny followed. But she died of a broken heart before he found her, the legend says, and many years later he returned to place apple blossoms on her grave.

Chapman knew that there was money to be made in the apple nursery business. By the 1790s he was planting apple trees in western Pennsylvania, and by the turn of the century, he'd moved on to Ohio. He had an uncanny knack for selecting the most advantageous spot near a new settlement, begging or leasing a plot of land to plant his trees, and then selling the saplings to frontier farmers.

Ironically, his trees and apples were never of the best quality, because he refused to improve his stock by grafting superior branches onto his seedlings. One settler in Fort Wayne, Indiana, where Chapman arrived in 1834, complained that his

apples were "so sour they would make a pig squeal." It was supposedly in Fort Wayne that he died in 1845, although no one is certain exactly where he is buried.

Chapman has been commemorated in Fort Wayne since 1974 with a two-day fall festival held at Johnny Appleseed Park. The festival includes traditional music and entertainment, demonstrations of pioneer arts and crafts, visits to the alleged gravesite, and discussions with "The Living Lincoln," who talks with visitors about the social issues of the period in history he shared with Johnny Appleseed.

CONTACTS:
Johnny Appleseed Festival Inc.
1502 Harry Beals Dr.
Fort Wayne, IN 46805
260-427-6003; fax: 260-427-6020
www.johnnyappleseedfest.com

♦ 0119 ♦ **Appomattox Day**
April 9

The Civil War ended on April 9, 1865, in the village of Appomattox Court House, Virginia, when Lieutenant General Ulysses S. Grant of the Union army accepted the surrender of General Robert E. LEE of the Confederacy. The Confederate soldiers were allowed to keep their horses and return to their homes; the officers were allowed to retain their side arms and swords as well. Thus ended the bloody four-year conflict that had cost more than half a million lives.

The most widespread celebration of Appomattox Day took place in 1965 during the Civil War centennial year. Thousands of people attended the ceremonies at the Appomattox Court House National Historical Park. Participants included the Union leader's grandson, Ulysses S. Grant III, as well as Robert E. Lee IV, great-grandson of the Confederate leader. The day was noted across the country—but particularly in the South—with costumed pageants, books and articles reflecting on the war, and concerts of martial music. Although the anniversary is not observed on a yearly basis, reenactments of the historic surrender are held periodically.

CONTACTS:
Appomattox Court House National Historical Park
Hwy. 24
P.O. Box 218
Appomattox, VA 24522
434-352-8987; fax: 434-352-8330
www.nps.gov

Appomattox County Visitor Information Center
P.O. Box 704
5 Main St.
Appomattox, VA 24522
804-352-2621; fax: 804-352-2621
www.appomattox.com

SOURCES:
AmerBkDays-2000, p. 266

♦ 0120 ♦ **April Fools' Day**
April 1

There are many names for this day—including **All Fools' Day**, **April Noddy Day**, **Gowkie Day**, **Huntigowk Day**, and **St. All-Fools' Morn**—just as there are many practical jokes to play on the unsuspecting. One theory about its origin points to Noah as the first "April Fool." It is said that on that day he mistakenly sent the dove out to find dry land after the flood. Another points to the adoption of the Gregorian calendar in 1582, when NEW YEAR'S DAY was officially moved from March 25 to January 1. People who forgot about the change were often mocked by their friends, as they continued to make New Year visits just after the old March date.

The simplest pranks usually involve children who, for example, tell each other that their shoelaces are undone and then cry "April Fool!" when the victims glance at their feet. Sometimes the media get into the act, broadcasting fictitious news items designed to amuse or alarm the public. British television, for example, once showed Italian farmers "harvesting" spaghetti from trees. The French call it **Fooling the April Fish Day** (the fool being the *poisson d'avril*) and try to pin a paper fish on someone's back without getting caught.

In Mexico children play April Fools'-type pranks on December 28, HOLY INNOCENTS' DAY.

SOURCES:
AmerBkDays-2000, p. 247
BkDays-1864, vol. I, p. 460
BkFest-1937, p. 17
DaysCustFaith-1957, p. 92
EncyEaster-2002, p. 9
EncyRel-1987, v. 1, p. 213
FestSaintDays-1915, p. 58
FestWestEur-1958, p. 34
FolkAmerHol-1999, p. 191
FolkWrldHol-1999, p. 268
OxYear-1999, p. 142

♦ 0121 ♦ **Arab International Festival**
Mid-June

The Arab International Festival takes place annually over a three-day weekend in mid-June in Dearborn, Mich. Dearborn's eastern section is noted for its large Arab-American population as well as Arab restaurants, bakeries, and businesses.

The festival was founded in 1996 to showcase and celebrate the heritage and culture of the area's Arab-American residents, as well as the diverse backgrounds of the people of metropolitan Detroit. Ethnic music, performances, food, and merchandise are all featured at the festival, along with amusement rides and such pastimes as coffee-cup reading and henna treatments. As many as 300,000 people have attended the non-alcoholic, family-oriented festival during its opening hours from Friday evening to Sunday night. The festival's sponsors are the local American Arab Chamber of Commerce, the Arab Community Center for Education and Social Services (ACCESS), and the city of Dearborn.

CONTACTS:
American Arab Chamber of Commerce
12740 W. Warren Ave., Ste. 101

Dearborn, MI 48126
313-945-1700; fax: 313-945-6697
www.americanarab.com

♦ 0122 ♦ **Arabic Music Festival**
November

The Arabic Music Festival is an annual event that celebrates classic, traditional Arabic music. The main venue for the event is the Cairo Opera House, which was opened in 1988 after the original building was destroyed by fire in 1971. Located on Gezira Island in the Nile River, the Opera House is part of a cultural district that includes the Museum of Egyptian Modern Arts and the El Hangar Theatre. The Arabic Music Festival was first held there in 1992.

Since then, the festival has been an occasion when the top Arabic instrumentalists, singers, and ensembles from around the world gather to perform. Homage is paid to established performers, and upcoming new talent is frequently introduced here. A cash prize is given to the musical act judged to be the best in the festival. Awards are also given to those who have made significant contributions to the field of Arabic music in the previous year. A conference to discuss topics related to Arabic music is another part of the event. In 2007, the festival lasted 10 days, during which 41 concerts were staged at five different theaters, some in Alexandria as well as in Cairo. Participants included musicians from 20 countries. Some of the best-known performers included Mohamed Tharwat, Mohamed Al-Tokhi, Sherien Abdul Wahab, Carole Samaham Molhim Zein, and Maded Al-Mohandes.

CONTACTS:
Cairo Opera House
P.O. Box 11567
El Borg Gezira
Cairo Egypt

Egypt State Information Service
3 Al Estad Al Bahary St.
Nasr City, Cairo
www.sis.gov.eg

♦ 0123 ♦ **Arapaho Sun Dance**
Mid-summer

The Sun Dance is a major religious event for many Native Americans, including the Cheyenne, Shoshone, and other Plains Indian tribes. The Arapaho people on the Wind River Reservation, outside Fort Washakie, Wyoming, hold the Sun Dance in mid-summer. To prepare for this sacred ceremony, they create a space for the dance to take place and particular objects are placed within this space, including a buffalo head, symbolizing strength, comfort, and abundance, and fresh sage, which represents the breath of life.

The dancers focus their gaze on the buffalo head as they move toward and away from it. The dance can have many purposes—to cure a loved one who is ill, to bring rain, to avoid death and other calamities, to ensure the tribe's prosperity, or to give thanks. It can last for up to three days.

See also SIOUX SUN DANCE; SOUTHERN UTE TRIBAL SUN DANCE

CONTACTS:
Wind River Visitors Council
P.O. Box 925
Lander, WY 82520
800-645-6233 or 307-856-7566
www.wind-river.org

SOURCES:
CustHolWrld-1962, p. 102
EncyNatAmerRel-2001, p. 289

♦ 0124 ♦ Arbaeen
20th day of Islamic month of Safar

In the year 680 C.E., Imam al-Hussein died during the Battle of Taf in Karbala, Iraq. He was the grandson of the Prophet Mohammad The martyrdom of Hussein was such a pivotal event in Islamic history that it has inspired two Shi'ite Muslim holidays of mourning: ASHURA and Arbaeen. ASHURA, the holy day that commemorates the day Hussein fell to his Sunni enemies, is more widely observed, but Arbaeen still retains significance and elicits fervent expressions from the faithful.

The holy day falls on the 40th day after the anniversary of Hussein's death and marks the date when the martyr's decapitated head, which had been carried off as a trophy to Damascus, was finally reunited with his body.

The most popular way that Iranian Shi'ites observe this holiday is by carrying out *ziarats*—pilgrimages to a holy shrine. The holiest of shrines to Hussein lies in Karbala, the Iraqi city where the fateful seventh-century battle took place. Karbala receives most of its pilgrims from Iraq and Iran. Celebrations have seen Shi'ite-Sunni violence during periods of elevated tension between these two groups.

CONTACTS:
Iran's Ministry of Foreign Affairs
Imam Khomeini Sq.
Tehran Iran

♦ 0125 ♦ Arbaeen Pilgrimage
February 28

In the year 680 C.E., Imam al-Hussein died during the Battle of Taf in Karbala, Iraq. He was the grandson of the Prophet Mohammad and, for Shiite Muslims, one of the three holiest figures in their religion. To commemorate his passing, Shiites from around the world hold the week-long Arbaeen Pilgrimage to his gravesite 40 days after his death. This period of 40 days is the traditional Muslim mourning period following a death. Imam al-Hussein's tomb is in the town of Karbala, about 50 miles south of Baghdad.

Karbala is one of the holiest cities for Shiite Muslims. It has more than 100 mosques and 23 religious schools in its old quarter. For Shiite Muslims, the city is also believed to be a gate to paradise. Many elderly believers come to the city to die, hoping to enter paradise more easily.

During the regime of Iraqi dictator Saddam Hussein, the Arbaeen Pilgrimage was banned. Clashes between pilgrims and the Iraqi military resulted in the arrest of thousands of people and the deaths of hundreds more. Since his overthrow in 2003, the number of people celebrating the Shiite holiday has grown every year. While there have been deaths from attacks made by Sunni suicide bombers, the Arbaeen Pilgrimage has been a largely peaceful affair in which some seven million people participate.

CONTACTS:
Embassy of the Republic of Iraq
3421 Massachusetts Ave. N.W.
Washington, D.C. 20007
202-742-1600
www.iraqiembassy.us

♦ 0126 ♦ Arbor Day
Last Friday in April

Julius Sterling Morton (1832-1902), one of the earliest American conservationists, settled on the treeless plains of Nebraska in 1855, where he edited the Nebraska City *News* and developed a lifelong interest in new agricultural methods. Believing that the prairie needed more trees to serve as windbreaks, to hold moisture in the soil, and to provide lumber for housing, Morton began planting trees and urged his neighbors to do the same. On April 10, 1872, when he first proposed that a specific day be set aside for the planting of trees, the response was overwhelming: a million trees were planted in Nebraska on that day alone.

All 50 states now observe Arbor Day—usually on the last Friday in April—and the idea has spread to other countries as well. Most observances take place in the public schools, where the value of trees is discussed and trees and shrubs are planted. At the White House, the president, first lady, or a presidential designate plants a special tree on the grounds each year on Arbor Day. But it is in Nebraska City, Nebraska, that Morton is best remembered as the originator of Arbor Day, with celebrations taking place on or near his birthday, April 22. A special ceremony is held at Arbor Lodge, Morton's homestead and one of the earliest known attempts at conservation and beautification in America.

Some states call this day **Bird and Arbor Day**, emphasizing the planting of trees that are attractive to birds.

CONTACTS:
The National Arbor Day Foundation
100 Arbor Ave.
Nebraska City, NE 68410
888-448-7337 or 402-474-5655; fax: 402-474-0820
www.arborday.org

SOURCES:
AmerBkDays-2000, p. 303
AnnivHol-2000, p. 66, 72
BkFestHolWrld-1970, p. 86
BkHolWrld-1986, Apr 24
DictDays-1988, p. 5
GdUSFest-1984, p. 109

♦ 0127 ♦ Arctic Circle Race
Mid-April

The first Arctic Circle cross-country ski race was held in Sisimiut, Greenland, in 1996. Organizers bill the event as the "world's toughest ski race" not only because of its length but also because of the uncertain weather conditions and terrain. Athletes must spend two nights camped in a tent in order to complete the race. The event lasts three days and covers 160 kilometers. Dog sleds follow the skiers as a safety precaution. In recent years the event has attracted participants from over 20 countries.

CONTACTS:
Arctic Circle Race Secretariat
P.O. Box 258
Sisimiut, 3911 Greenland
299-86-68-30; fax: 299-86-68-51
www.greenland-guide.gl

♦ 0128 ♦ **Ardwahist, Feast of**
*April, August, September; third day of
Ardwahist, the second Zoroastrian month*

The Feast of Ardwahist is considered a "sacred name day" in the Zoroastrian religion because both the day and the month share the name of the same *yazata* or spiritual being—in this case Ardwahist, who stands for truth and righteousness and presides over fire and energy. Ardwahist is represented by the ceremonial fire that plays such a central role in Zoroastrian worship, and that burns continually in most Zoroastrian temples.

The Zoroastrian calendar has 12 months of 30 days each, plus five extra days at the end of the year. Because of discrepancies in the calendars used by widely separated Zoroastrian communities around the world, there are now three different calendars in use, and the 3rd of Ardwahist can fall either in April, August, or September.

Followers of the Zoroastrian religion, which was founded by the prophet Zoroaster (also known as Zarathushtra, who is believed to have lived around 1200 B.C.E.), today live primarily in Iran and northwestern India, although smaller communities exist in Pakistan, Sri Lanka, Canada, the U.S., England, and Australia.

SOURCES:
RelHolCal-2004, p. 66

♦ 0129 ♦ **Argentina Flag Day**
*June 20 in Rosario; celebrated as a national
holiday on the third Monday in June*

The Argentine flag was designed and first raised on February 27, 1812, by Lt.-General Manuel Belgrano, during a battle with the forces of the Spanish crown. Stories about the origin of the design vary, but one popular version states that Belgrano, noting that both Spanish and Independence forces wore the yellow and red of Spain, was inspired to create the new flag of two light blue stripes and one white. The colors are variously said to have been in honor of the Virgin Mary, inspired by the sky, or drawn from a coat of arms of the Spanish monarchy. In any case, Belgrano's flag was first

raised at the village of Rosario, in two artillery batteries—one on the banks of the Parana River, and another at a site on an island directly opposite Rosario. On June 20, 1816, the Argentine Congress officially approved Belgrano's flag as the symbol of the independent Argentine nation. In later years, a sun was added to the white stripe of the original design. While this is now required on official ceremonial flags, flags without the sun symbol are also used and are known as "ornamental flags."

Belgrano died on June 20, 1820, and this date was declared Flag Day in 1938. It is now celebrated as a national holiday on the third Monday in June, but in Rosario, June 20 is also marked as a civic and school holiday. Across the country, the day may be marked with flag ceremonies and various other celebrations, but in Rosario, the festivities are most extensive. Many of the activities there take place near the National Flag Memorial, a large complex featuring a 70-meter tower commemorating the revolution and containing Belgrano's crypt.

The 50th anniversary of the Flag Memorial was celebrated in 2007. In addition to the usual parades, flag ceremonies, and speeches by government officials, celebrations in Rosario that year featured the inauguration of a new blue-and-white lighting system for the monument. There were also concerts, sporting events, a national artisans fair, and a reenactment of Belgrano's 1812 entry into Rosario.

CONTACTS:
Embassy of Argentina
1600 New Hampshire Ave. N.W.
Washington, D.C. 20009-2512
202-238-6400; fax: 202-332-3171
www.embassyofargentina.us

♦ 0130 ♦ **Argentina Independence Day**
July 9

Independence Day in Argentina is a national holiday commemorating the day in 1816 when delegates from various provinces of the country met at the home of the prominent Bazán family, in Tucumán, to proclaim their independence from Spanish rule. The Bazán home has been preserved and is now a museum known as the Casa Histórica de la Independencia.

The ideal of Argentine independence had been growing for many years before 1816, fostered by the American and French Revolutions. Argentine confidence that a war for independence could be won was bolstered when British forces invaded Buenos Aires in 1806 and 1807, and were driven back by Argentine forces. After much discussion among the various Argentine factions and military campaigns at various places around South America, independence was declared and the United Provinces of South America was formed. Civil war and various forms of government followed, but the date of the original Independence Day celebration has been continuously honored. It is now marked across the country by speeches and patriotic displays, as well as parties, family reunions, and live music. In 2007, Independence Day was the occasion of a freak snowstorm in the capital city, Buenos Aires. Prior to that day, it had not snowed in Buenos Aires since 1918.

CONTACTS:
Embassy of Argentina
1600 New Hampshire Ave. N.W.
Washington, D.C. 20009-2512
202-238-6400; fax: 202-332-3171
www.embassyofargentina.us

♦ 0131 ♦ **Argentina National Day of Memory for Truth and Justice**
March 24

Argentina's National Day of Memory for Truth and Justice is a public holiday that commemorates all those who lost their lives or otherwise suffered under the National Reorganization Process, a military dictatorship that seized power in Argentina on March 24, 1976. The junta held power for eight years, and in that time, at least 30,000 citizens were kidnapped, tortured, and executed for their political views. Many of those detained by the secret police were never heard from again, nor were their bodies ever found. Even after democracy was restored, amnesty laws and pardons ruled out trials of those behind the atrocities for several years. The Day of Memory for Truth and Justice is meant not only as a day to remember the dead, but also as a day to continue to seek justice for the human rights violations that were committed during the years of military rule.

In 2006, the 30th anniversary of the coup, there were vigils to remember the dead and missing, as well as demonstrations calling for prosecution of the perpetrators. In Buenos Aires, President Nestor Kirchner unveiled a plaque bearing the words "Never Again." Photographs of some 3,500 of the victims were displayed, and plaques bearing the names of the dead and the missing were unveiled around the city. In Buenos Aires and around the country, art exhibitions, poetry readings, prayer services, and other cultural events are dedicated to remembering the events of March 24 and its aftermath. Argentines living in other countries may also gather on this day for cultural events honoring the victims of the coup and the years of atrocities that followed it.

CONTACTS:
Embassy of Argentina
1600 New Hampshire Ave. N.W.
Washington, D.C. 20009-2512
202-238-6400; fax: 202-332-3171
www.embassyofargentina.us

♦ 0132 ♦ **Argentine National Day**
May 25

Argentina was one of a number of Spanish colonies controlled by the Spanish viceroy in Lima, Peru. When the colonies became too large to be controlled from one site, a separate viceroyalty was formed in 1776, with its headquarters in Buenos Aires.

On May 25, 1810, Buenos Aires declared its independence from the viceroyalty but continued to pledge loyalty to the Spanish crown. May 25 is observed throughout the country as the anniversary of the revolution. Independence from Spain wasn't declared until July 9, 1816—an event that provoked a long series of civil wars in which rival political leaders fought for national control. Both days are national holidays and are observed with religious services at the cathedral and special performances at the Colón Theatre in Buenos Aires. The city's *Plaza de Mayo* (May Square) was named for the month in which independence was declared.

The Argentine flag is honored with a legal holiday on June 20, **Argentine Flag Day**.

CONTACTS:
Embassy of Argentina
1600 New Hampshire Ave. N.W.
Washington, D.C. 20009
202-238-6400; fax: 202-332-3171
www.embassyofargentina.us

SOURCES:
AnnivHol-2000, pp. 87, 114

♦ 0133 ♦ **Argungu Fishing Festival**
February-March

The Argungu Fishing Festival is held along a sacred mile of the Sokoto River, a tributary of the Niger River, near Argungu, Kebbi State, in northwestern Nigeria. About 5,000 men from throughout Nigeria take part in the approximately 45 minutes of frenzied fishing. Using nets with calabashes (gourds) as floats, they can catch perch of up to 140 pounds. The largest perch are presented to the emirs, or rulers, who hold the festival.

CONTACTS:
Embassy of the Federal Republic of Nigeria
3519 International Ct. N.W.
Washington, D.C. 20008
202-986-8400; fax: 202-362-6541
www.nigeriaembassyusa.org

SOURCES:
BkHolWrld-1986, Feb 10

♦ 0134 ♦ **Århus Festival**
Nine days beginning first Saturday in September

Since 1965 the Danish city of Århus has been the site of a nine-day festival whose cultural and sporting events run the gamut from opera to fishing competitions. Queen MARGRETHE II traditionally gives the opening speech, followed by a performance by the Danish National Radio Symphony Orchestra. Festival events include jazz, classical, and rock concerts, a cross-country race, public debates, children's programs, poetry readings, and theatrical productions. The New York City Ballet and the Alvin Ailey American Dance Theatre have performed there, as have the Israel Philharmonic Orchestra, the Orchestre de Paris, and such world-renowned soloists as Isaac Stern, Vladimir Ashkenazy, Boris Christoff, and Claudio Arrau.

The program varies from year to year, but the events are always held in a variety of indoor and outdoor sites throughout the city, including the Århus Theater, an art nouveau building from the turn of the 20th century; the new Århus Concert Hall, built in 1981; and the area's many parks, churches, and coffee shops. Århus is also the site of Marselisborg Castle, the Danish royal family's summer residence.

CONTACTS:
Aarhus Festuge
Officersbygningen
Vester Alle 3
Arhus C, DK-8000 Denmark
45-87-30-83-00; fax: 45-87-30-83-19
www.aarhusfestuge.dk

SOURCES:
GdWrldFest-1985, p. 71
MusFestEurBrit-1980, p. 37

♦ 0135 ♦ Armed Forces Day (Egypt)
October 6

Armed Forces Day in Egypt is an important national holiday marking the surprise attack on Israel that began the October War of 1973 (also known as the YOM KIPPUR War). Egypt's ally in the war was Syria. The war ended with a cease-fire secured by the United States, and was declared a victory by Egyptian President Anwar Sadat. It strengthened his position and enabled him to seek an honorable peace with Israel. In 1974 and 1975, agreements were signed that paved the way for the return of the SINAI Peninsula to Egypt in April 1982; Israel had occupied the peninsula since the Six-Day War of 1967, in which Egypt had been crushed. In 1977 Sadat made his dramatic trip to Jerusalem to address the Israeli Knesset (Parliament); a year later, Sadat, Israeli Prime Minister Menachem Begin and United States President Jimmy Carter held talks at Camp David, Md., that led to the Israeli-Egyptian peace treaty of 1979.

The holiday is celebrated with grand parades, speeches by government officials, and fireworks. It was while reviewing a military parade on this day in 1981 that Anwar Sadat was assassinated by opponents of peace with Israel.

CONTACTS:
State Information Service, Egypt Ministry of Information
3 Al Estad Al Bahary St.
Nasr City, Cairo Egypt
20-2261-7304; fax: 20-2261-7308
www.sis.gov.eg

♦ 0136 ♦ Armed Forces Day (United States)
Third Saturday in May

Before President Harry S. Truman proclaimed the third Saturday in May as Armed Forces Day in 1949, the three major branches of the United States armed forces—the Army, the Navy, and the Air Force—held elaborate celebrations on three different days during the year. Although the service units continue to celebrate their own days on April 6 (Army), October 27 (Navy), the second Saturday in September (Air Force), and November 10 (Marine Corps), the purpose of Armed Forces

Day is to promote the unification of the branches under the Department of Defense (which took place in 1947) and to pay tribute to those serving in all the armed forces.

While commemorations of the individual service units are usually confined to military bases, the celebration of Armed Forces Day entails much broader participation. In addition to the huge parade held on this day each year in New York City, the armed forces often hold "open house" to acquaint the public with their facilities and to demonstrate some of the latest technological advances.

CONTACTS:
Office of the Assistant Secretary of Defense, U.S. Department of Defense
1400 Defense Pentagon
Washington, D.C. 20301
703-428-0711
www.defenselink.mil

SOURCES:
AmerBkDays-2000, p. 368
AnnivHol-2000, p. 91
DaysCustFaith-1957, p. 137
DictDays-1988, p. 5
PatHols-2006, p. 47

♦ 0137 ♦ Armenia Constitution Day
July 5

On July 5, 1995, four years after Armenia gained independence from the Soviet Union, the national government adopted a new constitution. Constitution Day, a public holiday, commemorates the creation of a new governmental framework and the beginning of another era for this small country, which for over seven decades had been a Soviet satellite.

The government rewards the public sector with a day off on Constitution Day. Victory Park, located in the capital city of Yerevan, usually stages performances that feature traditional music and dance.

Some Armenian communities settled abroad also conduct their own Constitution Day ceremonies. In 2006, the American University of Armenia Department of Law commemorated the day by hosting a panel discussion on Mkhitar Gosh, a 12th-century Armenian scholar and author of a set of laws that profoundly influenced the country's present-day legal code.

CONTACTS:
Armenian Embassy
2225 R St. N.W.
Washington, D.C. 20008
202-319-1976; fax: 202-319-2982
www.armeniaemb.org

♦ 0138 ♦ Armenia Earthquake Memorial Day
December 7

On December 7, 1988, a severe earthquake struck in Armenia, causing catastrophic damage to the entire country's infrastructure and virtually destroying the cities of Spitak, Leninakan (now Gyumri), Kirovakan (now Vanadzor), and

Stepanavan. Hundreds of small villages were completely obliterated by the quake and its aftershocks. At its epicenter, the earthquake was estimated to have the destructive force of 10 atomic bombs the size of those dropped on Hiroshima during World War II. More than 25,000 people were killed in the disaster, with another 140,000 injured and more than one million left homeless, in a disaster zone that measured about 30,000 square kilometers.

That day is now remembered each year as a national holiday, marked across the country with prayer, memorial services, and a moment of silence. In 2006, Armenian president Robert Kocharian and other government officials laid a wreath of flowers at the memorial to the earthquake victims in front of St. Savior Church in Gyumri and attended an open-air religious service.

CONTACTS:
Armenian Embassy
2225 R St. N.W.
Washington, D.C. 20008
202-319-1976 or 202-319-2982
www.armeniaemb.org

Armenian Tourism Development Agency
374-154-2303 or 374-154-2306
www.armenianinfo.am

♦ 0139 ♦ Armenia First Republic Day
May 28

The people of Armenia lived for hundreds of years under foreign domination. Then, in 1917, the Russian Revolution and the collapse of the Russian empire allowed Armenia the opportunity to create a modern republic. The Democratic Republic of Armenia (DRA) was formed in 1918. Also known as the First Republic of Armenia, the DRA was short-lived but important, as it represented the beginning of the modern quest for democracy and independence in Armenia.

The new republic faced serious problems from within and without its borders. In 1920, it was invaded by the Bolshevik Army of Russia and made part of the Transcaucasian Socialist Federative Soviet Republic, and eventually part of the Soviet Union, for more than 70 years. Yet the establishment and brief life of the First Republic is still seen as a proud victory for Armenia. On the holiday, titles and medals are awarded to Armenians of outstanding achievement, and there are speeches by government officials, fireworks displays, concerts, and dancing.

CONTACTS:
Armenian Embassy
2225 R St. N.W.
Washington, D.C. 20008
202-319-1976 or 202-319-2982
www.armeniaemb.org

Armenian Tourism Development Agency
374-154-2303 or 374-154-2306
www.armenianinfo.am

♦ 0140 ♦ Armenia Independence Day
September 21

On September 21, 1991, the Armenian people voted in favor of independence from the U.S.S.R.; they were granted independence on December 26 of that year, by which time the former Soviet Union had collapsed. Armenia had been part of the Soviet Union since the 1920s.

CONTACTS:
Armenian Embassy
2225 R St. N.W.
Washington, D.C. 20008
202-319-1976; fax: 202-319-2982
www.armeniaemb.org

Armenian Tourism Development Agency
374-154-2303 or 374-154-2306
www.armenianinfo.am

SOURCES:
AnnivHol-2000, p. 158

♦ 0141 ♦ Armenia Motherhood and Beauty Day
April 7

Motherhood and Beauty Day is a national holiday in Armenia, celebrated each year on April 7. It comes not long after another national holiday, Women's Day, which is celebrated on March 8. Women's Day is meant to honor all women, but Motherhood and Beauty Day is dedicated especially to those who have become mothers.

On this occasion, the unique qualities and beauty of each woman are to be appreciated. Children and adults alike show their affection for their mothers with special visits, cards, and gifts. Sending flowers to one's mother is an especially popular way to mark this holiday. Another tradition associated with Motherhood and Beauty Day is the gift of a twig that has fresh sprouts on it. The symbolism of the budding twig, and the holiday's placement in the springtime, are indicators that the celebration may trace its roots back to ancient fertility cults, such as the cult of Anahit. The month-long period between Women's Day and Motherhood and Beauty Day is unofficially regarded as an ongoing opportunity to celebrate all women.

CONTACTS:
Armenian Embassy
2225 R St. N.W.
Washington, D.C. 20008
202-319-1976; fax: 202-319-2982
www.armeniaemb.org

Armenian Tourism Development Agency
374-154-2303 or 374-154-2306
www.armenianinfo.am

♦ 0142 ♦ Armenian Martyrs' Day
April 24

Armenian Martyrs' Day is a day of remembrance for the one million Armenians who died in the Turkish massacre of 1915-16. On April 24, 1915, Turks arrested Armenian political and intellectual leaders in Istanbul, killing 250 of them. That was the start of deportations, forced marches in the desert, rapes, and imprisonments that killed half the Armenian population in Turkey.

Armenian communities throughout the world observe this day. In the United States, many state governors issue proclamations of remembrance, and special programs, with speeches and prayers, are held in state capitals. There are also special services in Armenian churches.

CONTACTS:
Armenian Embassy
2225 R St. N.W.
Washington, D.C. 20008
202-319-1976; fax: 202-319-2982
www.armeniaemb.org

Armenian Tourism Development Agency
374-154-2303 or 374-154-2306
www.armenianinfo.am

SOURCES:
AnnivHol-2000, p. 67

♦ 0143 ♦ **Artcar Fest**
Last weekend in September

Artcar Fest, an annual parade in the San Francisco Bay area since 1997, is dedicated to promoting and celebrating those people who enjoy decorating their cars in artistic ways. The cars are not specially decorated for the event—these cars have been permanently altered in an artistic fashion, are legally registered, and are normally used to go to work, school, and shopping by their owners.

Founded by Philo Northrup and Harrod Blank, two artcar enthusiasts who had been decorating cars since the 1980s, the Artcar Fest parade of cars stretches for more than a mile and takes a full hour to roll by. Many of the owners see themselves as creating mobile sculptural works of art. Some of the designs are whimsical and fun. The Sashimi Tabernacle Choir, for example, is a car decorated with 250 computer-controlled singing fish and lobster sculptures. Together, the fish can perform a repertoire of songs while the car is being driven. The Radio Flyer is a car shaped like a giant red wagon, complete with handle, and named after the famous brand of children's toy wagon.

CONTACTS:
Artcar Fest
415-385-7229
artcarfest.com

♦ 0144 ♦ **Arts and Crafts Fair, International**
October-November, every two years

Burkina Faso, a small sub-Saharan African country with limited natural resources, is continually seeking ways to boost its economy. The International Arts and Crafts Fair, which takes place in the capital city, Ouagadougou, is part of a national development plan that heavily promotes the African handicraft sector. Along with showcasing the works of Burkinabé craftspeople, the 10-day exposition also displays crafts from over 30 other African countries as well as European and Asian nations. Organizers have reported annual attendance totals at over 350,000, making it one of the world's largest handicraft fairs.

The International Arts and Crafts Fair was founded in 1988 by the Salon International de l'Artisanat de Ouagadougou (SIAO), a government organization, and over the years the group has helped expand the Fair's capacity. Exporters from all over the world have traveled to the fair to peruse the many statues, textiles, leatherwork, jewelry, pottery, and ceramics on display. Ever year the SIAO has ensured that an international forum remains a fixture at the exposition. This forum creates opportunities for craftspeople and other industry figures to discuss and seek solutions to ongoing issues in the international handicraft market.

CONTACTS:
Ouagadougou International Arts and Crafts Fair
Directorate-General
01 BP 3414
Ouagadougou Burkina Faso
www.siao.bf/english/index.htm

♦ 0145 ♦ **Arts and Pageant of the Masters, Festival of**
July-September

This festival features a display of art works in arty Laguna Beach, Calif., along with breathtaking *tableaux vivants*—living pictures that recreate master art works. Since the 1940s, artists have created the tableaux to reproduce paintings by such varied masters as Leonardo da Vinci, Henri Matisse, and Winslow Homer. They don't stop there; they also transform delicate pieces of jewelry, sculptures, antique artifacts, and even scenes from postage stamps into life-sized works of art. The tableaux, presented for 90 minutes each evening, are created by some 300 models who have used 1,000 yards of fabric and 100 gallons of makeup. Example of a tableau: three gilded men and two gilded styrofoam horses appear in a setting that reproduces a five-inch Scythian gold comb.

CONTACTS:
Festival of the Arts / Pageant of the Masters
650 Laguna Canyon Rd.
Laguna Beach, CA 92651
800-487-3378 or 949-494-1145; fax: 949-376-1143
www.foapom.com

SOURCES:
GdUSFest-1984, p. 18

♦ 0146 ♦ **Asanha Bucha Day (Asanha Puja Day)**
First full moon of eighth lunar month

Celebrated in Thailand on the first full moon of the eighth lunar month, Asanha Bucha Day marks the first public sermon given by Buddha, which took place at Deer Park in Benares, India. In this initial sermon, Buddha presented the Four Noble Truths to five ascetics. While the ascetics believed in self-mortification, he taught that the cessation of desire was the key to enlightenment. Upon hearing this message, the five men reached enlightenment and became the first Buddhist priests or Sangha. The day also marks the beginning of Vassa, the Buddhist lent period also known as the Rains Retreat.

Ceremonies are held in Buddhist temples throughout the country. Elaborate wax candles are lit and kept burning throughout lent. In the city of Ubon, a Candle Festival is held in which a parade of candles is followed by a contest for best candle design and a beauty contest. In Saraburi, monks from the local temple will walk through the town with their alms bowls. On this day, townspeople will put flowers into their bowls instead of food, and the monks offer these flowers at the temple in honor of the Buddha. Asanha Bucha Day has become a popular day for young Thai men to enter the monkhood.

CONTACTS:
Royal Thai Embassy
1024 Wisconsin Ave. N.W.
Washington, D.C. 20007
202-338-9700
www.thaiembdc.org

◆ 0147 ◆ Asarah be-Tevet (Fast of the Tenth of Tevet)
Between December 13 and January 10; Tevet 10

Asarah be-Tevet is a Jewish fast day commemorating the beginning of the siege of Jerusalem by the Babylonians under King Nebuchadnezzar in 586 B.C.E. that was a prelude to the destruction of the First Temple. The fast begins at first morning light on the 10th day of the Jewish month of Tevet.

In Israel it is also a day to remember the victims of the Holocaust. However, Jews outside Israel observe Yom ha-Shoah as HOLOCAUST MEMORIAL DAY.

CONTACTS:
Union of Orthodox Jewish Congregations of America
11 Broadway
New York, NY 10004
212-563-4000; fax: 212-564-9058
www.ou.org

◆ 0148 ◆ Ascension Day
Between April 30 and June 3; 40 days after Easter

Ascension Day is one of the earliest Christian festivals, dating back to the year 68. According to the New Testament, Jesus met several times with his disciples during the 40 days after his Resurrection to instruct them in how to carry out his teachings. Then on the 40th day he took them to the Mount of Olives, where they watched as he ascended to heaven.

Reflecting both Christian and pagan customs, Ascension Day celebrations include processions symbolizing Christ's entry into heaven and, in some countries, chasing a "devil" through the streets and dunking him in a pond or burning him in effigy—symbolic of the Messiah's triumph over the devil when he opened the kingdom of heaven to all believers.

Other customs attached to this day include "beating the bounds"—switching young boys with willow branches as they are driven along parish boundaries, not only to purify them of evil but to teach them the limits of their parish. This gave rise to the name **Bounds Thursday** in England, where it

is also sometimes called **Holy Thursday**, though in the rest of the world that term applies to MAUNDY THURSDAY.

In Germany it is sometimes called Father's Day because Protestant men have *herrenpartien*, "outings," on this day. In Sweden many people go out to the woods at three or four o'clock to hear the birds at sunrise. It is good luck if a cuckoo is heard from the east or west. These jaunts are called *gök-otta*, or "early cuckoo morning."

See also BANNTAG; HOLY THURSDAY

CONTACTS:
Holy Apostolic Catholic Assyrian Church of the East
P.O. Box 1977
Fort Macleod, AL T0L 0Z0 Canada
403-553-2731; fax: 403-553-3141
www.cired.org

Greek Orthodox Archdiocese of Australia
242 Cleveland St.
Redfern, NSW 2016 Australia
61-2-9698-5066; fax: 61-2-9698-536
www.greekorthodox.org.au

SOURCES:
AmerBkDays-2000, p. 346
BkFest-1937, p. 135
DictFolkMyth-1984, pp. 49, 1156
DictWrldRel-1989, p. 65
EncyEaster-2002, p. 13
EncyRel-1987, v. 3, p. 440
FestSaintDays-1915, p. 113
FestWestEur-1958, pp. 64, 165, 215
FolkAmerHol-1999, p. 241
FolkWrldHol-1999, p. 337
OxYear-1999, p. 629
RelHolCal-2004, pp. 95, 121

◆ 0149 ◆ Ascension Day (Portugal)
Between April 30 and June 3; 40 days after Easter

Also known as *Quinta Feira da Espiga*, or Ear of Wheat Thursday, ASCENSION DAY in Portugal is associated with wishes for peace and prosperity. Traditionally, in rural communities, people gather olive branches, wheat sheaves, poppies, and daisies and fashion them into bouquets. The olive and wheat are symbolic of an abundant harvest; the poppy represents tranquility, and the daisy stands for money. Many Portuguese preserve a sprig of wheat in their homes as a symbol of prosperity. Another Ascension Day custom is to cull healing plants and herbs to be used later in concocting homemade medicines or magic potions.

SOURCES:
BkFest-1937, p. 268
FestWestEur-1958, p. 165

◆ 0150 ◆ Ash Wednesday
Between February 4 and March 10

The first day of LENT in the West. For 14 centuries the season of Lent has been a time for self-examination and penitence in preparation for EASTER. The name comes from the Saxon *lengten-tide*, referring to the lengthening of the days and the coming of spring. This 40-day period of abstinence recalls the fasts of Moses, Elijah, and Jesus, all of which—according to scripture—lasted 40 days. It was originally begun in the Western Church on a Sunday. But since Sundays were feast days, in the latter part of the sixth century Pope Gregory I moved the beginning of Lent ahead four days.

Gregory is also credited with having introduced the ceremony that gives this day its name. When public penitents came to the church for forgiveness, the priest would take some ash (made by burning the palms used on PALM SUNDAY of the previous year) and mark their foreheads with the sign of the cross as a reminder that they were but ashes and dust. Eventually the practice was extended to include all who wished to receive ashes.

In the East, ashes are not used, and Lent begins on the Monday before Ash Wednesday.

On Ash Wednesday in Iceland, children try to hook small bags of ashes or stones to the back of people's clothing.

See also SHROVE TUESDAY

CONTACTS:
CRI/Voice Institute
4801 N.W. 62nd St.
Oklahoma City, OK 73122
801-497-0946
www.crivoice.org

SOURCES:
AmerBkDays-2000, p. 131
BkDays-1864, vol. I, p. 240
BkFest-1937, p. 299
DaysCustFaith-1957, p. 64
DictFolkMyth-1984, pp. 82, 535
EncyEaster-2002, p. 19
FestWestEur-1958, p. 194
FolkAmerHol-1999, p. 106
FolkWrldHol-1999, p. 151
HolSymbols-2009, p. 50
RelHolCal-2004, p. 91
SaintFestCh-1904, p. 115

♦ 0151 ♦ **Asheville Mountain Dance and Folk Festival**
First Thursday, Friday, and Saturday in August

The Asheville Mountain Dance and Folk Festival is the oldest festival of its kind in the country, held since 1928 in Asheville, N.C. Dedicated to traditional southern Appalachian music, it draws more than 400 performers: dulcimer sweepers, tune bow and mouth harp players, mountain fiddlers, and dancers who compete in smooth- and clog-dancing. Bluegrass and old-time bands also are on hand. ("Bluegrass" is not named for the Kentucky grass, but for the Blue Grass Boys, a band formed in 1938 by Bill Monroe, whose style of country popular music is still widely imitated; *see also* BLUE-GRASS FAN FEST).

Other events of the weekend include a quilt show and the Gee Haw Whimmy Diddle World Competition at the Folk Art Center, which usually draws about 50 contestants. The whimmy diddle, an Appalachian whittled folk toy, is a notched wooden gadget with a propeller on one end; when a stick is rubbed across the notches, the propeller spins. The idea of the contest is to control the spin, to make the propeller gee (turn to the right) and haw (turn to the left). The winners of cash prizes are those who get their whimmy diddle to change the direction of rotation the most times. There is also a cash prize for the Most Unusual and World's Largest Whimmy Diddle.

CONTACTS:
Asheville Convention and Visitors Bureau
P.O. Box 1010
Asheville, NC 28802
828-258-6101
www.folkheritage.org

SOURCES:
MusFestAmer-1990, p. 226

♦ 0152 ♦ **Ashokashtami**
March-April; eighth day of the waxing half of the Hindu month of Caitra

Lord Lingaraj, a name for the Hindu deity Shiva, receives praise and adoration from Hindus on Ashokashtami, a day in the lunar month of Caitra (March-April in the Gregorian calendar). The festival takes place in Bhubaneswar, a small city in eastern India and the capital of Orissa. Two venerated sites host the festival: the Lingaraja Temple, believed to be the city's oldest temple, and the Rameshwar Temple, located just over a mile away. Thousands of people living in Bhubaneswar and throughout Orissa attend the festival to watch a traditional procession that features a giant wooden chariot carrying a Lingaraj idol and other deities.

The festival is inspired by the world-famous CAR FESTIVAL OF JAGANNATHA, which takes place in Puri, another city in Orissa. For the Ashokashtami procession, the wooden chariot begins at the Lingaraja Temple and, with the assistance of hundreds of attendees, the processional with the heavy cart proceeds to the Rameshwar Temple. Lingaraj and the other deities remain at the temple for four days before they are returned.

CONTACTS:
Orissa Department of Tourism
Paryatan Bhawan
Museum Campus
Bhubaneswar, Orissa 751014 India
www.orissatourism.gov.in

SOURCES:
RelHolCal-2004, p. 185

♦ 0153 ♦ **Ashura**
First 10 days of Islamic month of Muharram

On the 10th of Muharram in the year 680, Muhammad's grandson Hussein (also spelled Husain) was killed in a skirmish between Sunnis and the small group of Shi'ite supporters with whom he was travelling to Iraq. They had been cut off from water and had suffered for 10 days before the men were killed and the women and children taken to Damascus, Syria, along with the heads of the men. His battlefield grave in Kerbela, about 60 miles southwest of Baghdad, became a pilgrimage site almost immediately, and to this day it remains a devotional center for Shi'ite Muslims around the world. Many aging Shi'ites settle in Kerbela or ask in their will to have their bodies carried to the holy city. So many dead have been sent to Kerbela that the town has been transformed into one vast burial ground.

This Islamic holy day, celebrated in the first month of the Islamic year, was derived by Muhammad from the Jewish fast of YOM KIPPUR; he later changed it to an optional fast day and it is so observed by modern-day Sunni Muslims. But for Shi'ites throughout Asia, the festival is dedicated to Hussein and begins on the first day of Muharram, when people put on their mourning clothes and refrain from shaving or bathing. The story of Hussein's martyrdom is recited in Muslim halls, with as much elaboration as possible. The celebration culminates on the 10th day of Muharram, in a large procession designed as a reenactment of Hussein's funeral, with many men whipping themselves bloody with whips and knives to take on the pain of Hussein. Since the early 19th century, the **Hussein Day** celebration has culminated in the performance of a *ta'ziyah,* or passion play, in which Hussein's life, death, and burial are recreated in a loose sequence of 40 to 50 scenes.

The Fatimid dynasty (969-1171) transferred Hussein's head to Cairo and built the Mosque of the Hasanain ('the two Hasans': Hasan and his brother, Hussein) over the relic. It is an especially holy place and is venerated also by Sunnis.

In India non-Shi'ites frequently take part in the processions, whereas in Iraq they would not be tolerated. Small replicas of Hussein's tomb, called *Ta ziyehs* (from the Arabic *aza,* meaning "mourning"), are carried and buried in the local "Kerbela" grounds: India is so far from Kerbela, Iraq, that Indian Shi'ites consecrate local lands so they, too, may be buried in "Kerbela" grounds.

In Jamaica and Trinidad the festival is called HOSAY and is celebrated by Muslims and Hindus as a symbol of East Indian unity. In Guyana, it is called **Tadja** and is now celebrated by Afro- and Indo-Guyanese, after having been outlawed in the 1930s because of clashes between Muslims and Hindus when it coincided with DURGA PUJA.

In West Africa the holy day is combined with African beliefs, and ensuring prosperity is of uppermost importance: everyone eats as much as possible, inviting poor people to join them, because a full belly ensures prosperity. The Hausa give a fowl or goat's head to each member of the household, which they eat with their backs to each other. In Senegal, Guinea, and Sierra Leone, the dried head and feet of the ram killed at 'ID AL-ADHA are cooked and eaten. Symbolic bathing in rivers and purification by leaping over small fires are followed by torchlight parades and contests.

In Turkey, the 10th of Muharram is called **Yevmi Ashurer,** (day of sweet soup or porridge) and commemorates Noah's departure from the Ark onto Mount Ararat. They must share Allah's gifts with others, so everyone makes *ashurer,* which is a sweet soup or porridge made of boiled wheat, dried cur-

rants, grain, and nuts, similar to that supposedly made by Noah and stored in the bins of the Ark. Each person is assigned a day to invite his neighbors to come and share it.

CONTACTS:
Embassy of Iraq
3421 Massachusetts Ave. N.W.
Washington, D.C. 20007
202-742-1600; fax: 202-462-5066
www.iraqiembassy.us

SOURCES:
AnnivHol-2000, p. 233
BkFest-1937, p. 237
ConEncyIslam-1991, p. 52
EncyRel-1987, v. 1, p. 462
FolkWrldHol-1999, p. 433
HolSymbols-2009, p. 53
MuhFest-1988, pp. 51, 85
OxYear-1999, pp. 732, 734
RelHolCal-2004, p. 144
UndIslam-2004, p. 261

♦ 0154 ♦ **Asian Games**
Every four years; November

The Olympic Council of Asia has been organizing the Asian Games since 1951. Every four years, the best athletes from throughout Asia are chosen to compete in the games, which are supervised by the International Olympics Committee.

Not all Asian countries participate in the games. Israel is kept out of the competition due to objections by several Arab nations. Taiwan was kept out for several years due to a conflict with communist mainland China. Australia was disqualified from participation when it was judged to be an Oceanic country. In 1994, the Olympic Council of Asia drew protest for admitting five former Soviet republics into the games.

The Asian Games draw 10,500 athletes from some 45 countries who compete in 39 sporting events. Among the contests are handball, karate, rowing, chess, bowling, and swimming. As in the Olympics, each competition awards a gold, silver, and bronze medal to the three best athletes. A torch is also carried from the site of the last games to the site of the next games, a process that involves some 3,000 persons.

The 15th Asian Games were held in the Persian Gulf country of Qatar in 2006. China won the most medals, followed by South Korea and Japan. The 16th Asian Games will be held in China in 2010.

CONTACTS:
Olympic Council of Asia
P.O. Box 6706
Hawalli 32042 Kuwait
www.ocasia.org

♦ 0155 ♦ **Aspen Music Festival**
Late June to late August

One of the finest and most important musical events in the United States, this event was founded in 1949 in Aspen in the Colorado Rocky Mountains. Symphonic orchestra and chamber-music concerts are staged in the white-tented amphitheater designed by Finnish-born architect Eero Saarinen, and smaller presentations in a renovated opera house and a church. Programs range from baroque to modern. Each season new compositions are introduced by "composers in residence"; Virgil Thomson and Aaron Copland have been among them. A school of music operates along with the festival and has an enrollment of more than 900 students.

Aspen was a wealthy silver-mining town in the 1880s, but lost its glitter when silver prices collapsed in the 1890s. Its rebirth began in the late 1930s, largely because of the enterprise of Chicago industrialist Walter Paepcke, who thought Aspen would be suitable for a Platonic community. It is now a popular though pricey skiing resort.

CONTACTS:
Aspen Music Festival and School
2 Music School Rd.
Aspen, CO 81611
970-935-3254; fax: 970-925-8077
www.aspenmusicfestival.com

SOURCES:
GdUSFest-1984, p. 23
MusFestAmer-1990, p. 42
MusFestWrld-1963, p. 277

♦ 0156 ♦ **Ass, Feast of the**
Around Christmas, December 25

This festival recalling the flight of the Holy Family (Jesus, Mary, and Joseph) into Egypt to escape King Herod reached its peak during the Middle Ages in France. It was customary to have a girl carrying a baby and riding an elaborately decorated ass led through the streets to the church, where a mass was said. But the celebration gradually took on comic overtones, with the priest and congregation imitating the braying of an ass at appropriate times during the service and the ass itself being led into the church and given food and drink. By the 15th century the feast had obviously become nothing more than an occasion for laughter, and it was suppressed thereafter by the Church, although it didn't completely die out until years afterward.

See also FEAST OF FOOLS

SOURCES:
BkDays-1864, vol. I, p. 112
DictFolkMyth-1984, p. 84
EncyChristmas-2003, p. 247
EncyRel-1987, vol. 3, p. 99
FestSaintDays-1915, p. 254

♦ 0157 ♦ **Assumption of Our Lady (Santa Marija)**
August 15

The Republic of Malta is a small country in the central Mediterranean that consists of seven islands. In 1814, Malta became a crown colony of the British empire. Under British rule, the Maltese Islands helped the Allies during World War I. Hundreds of Maltese served as soldiers in the British regiments, and Malta allowed the British to use its dockyard and

hospitals. Thousands of sick and wounded soldiers were brought to Malta for treatment, thereby earning the country the title of the "Nurse of the Mediterranean."

Malta also played an important role during World War II. The bravery its people showed during the war led to the country being awarded the George Cross, which is now displayed on its flag

During World War II, Malta served as a military base for Great Britain's ships, submarines, and military airplanes. For two years, the Axis powers (Italy, Germany, and Japan) attacked Malta, trying to take over the country in an attempt to control the Mediterranean. As supply convoys approached, the Axis military would attack and destroy them. By the summer of 1942, supplies were so low that many Maltese were close to starvation, and the country would soon be forced to surrender.

Operation Pedestal was planned and executed by the British Royal Navy. Fourteen merchant ships carried badly needed supplies to Malta for both the military and civilian population. Those merchant ships were guarded and escorted by 64 warships. The Italian and German air forces were prepared for the convoy and attacked the ships as they approached. The *SS Ohio*, an American oil tanker, soon became a main target. The ship withstood two days of bombings and was severely crippled. However, the Allied warships were able to prop her up and escort her safely to Malta's Valletta Grand Harbour. Only five of the 14 merchant ships reached Malta. These ships and their crews were met with cheers of joy and appreciation. It gave the people hope that they were saved. Within months after Operation Pedestal, the Axis powers gave up on their attempts to take over Malta.

Today in Malta, the country celebrates the feast of the Assumption of Our Lady, a national holiday that commemorates the success of Operation Pedestal. Many believe that it was through the intervention of Our Lady that Operation Pedestal was able to succeed. On this day, church services across the country start with a prayer of thanksgiving, and the names of the five surviving merchant ships are read.

Feast days, including the feast of Santa Marija, are a big part of life on the Islands. In Malta, this holiday and many of the other holidays are celebrated *festa*-style—with fireworks, decorated streets, and carts throughout the villages selling many different foods, including traditional sweets and delicacies such as Maltese nougat.

CONTACTS:
Malta Tourism Authority
Auberge D'Italie
Merchants St.
Valetta VLT 1170 Malta
www.visitmalta.com

♦ 0158 ♦ **Assumption of the Blessed Virgin Mary, Feast of the**
August 15

Assumption Day, called the **Dormition of the Most Holy Mother of God** in the East, commemorates the belief that when Mary, the mother of Jesus, died, her body was not subjected to the usual process of physical decay but was "assumed" into heaven and reunited there with her soul. Like the IMMACULATE CONCEPTION, the Assumption wasn't always an official dogma of the Roman Catholic Church—not until Pope Pius XII ruled it so in 1950. It was, however, a pious belief held by most Orthodox Christians and some Anglicans. It is regarded as the principal feast day of the Virgin Mother.

This festival may be a Christianization of an earlier Artemis harvest feast, and in some parts of Europe it is still called the **Feast of Our Lady of the Harvest**. The people of Queven, France, actually reenact the Assumption by lowering a wooden angel from the tower of the church and then making her rise again toward "heaven." In Elche, Spain, a two-day enactment of the apocryphal Gospels is performed each year (*see* MYSTERY PLAY OF ELCHE). It is the national holiday of the Acadians in the Maritime Provinces of Canada, and is called *tinta marre* (meaning "a racket"). At 6 P.M. on the 15th, pots and pans are banged, whistles blown, and drums beaten. On the nearest Sunday, boats are decorated and sail past the dock where the priest blesses the fleet. Messina, Sicily, celebrates with a two-week festival including a human tableau of the Assumption and giant figures believed to symbolize the mythical founders of the city, Zancleo and his wife. The girl who portrays the Madonna is allowed to pardon one criminal.

In São Paulo and other parts of southern Brazil, the feast is called **Nosa Senhora dos Navegantes**, "Our Lady of the Navigators." Pageants are held on decorated canoes, each carrying a captain, a purser, three musicians, and two rowers. They travel to small villages to entertain and feast. Towns may have a church procession with musicians whose costumes and demeanors depict the Three Wise Men.

See also BLESSING OF THE GRAPES; MARYMASS FESTIVAL

CONTACTS:
Marian Library/International Marian Research Institute
University of Dayton
Dayton, OH 45469
937-229-4214; fax: 937-229-4258
www.udayton.edu

Greek Orthodox Archdiocese of Australia
242 Cleveland St.
Redfern, NSW 2016 Australia
61-2-9698-5066; fax: 61-2-9698-536
www.greekorthodox.org.au

SOURCES:
BkFest-1937, p. 172
DaysCustFaith-1957, p. 206
DictFolkMyth-1984, pp. 886, 1065
FestSaintDays-1915, p. 169
FestWestEur-1958, pp. 15, 47, 184, 203
FolkAmerHol-1999, p. 341
FolkWrldHol-1999, p. 494
OxYear-1999, p. 334
RelHolCal-2004, pp. 99, 124

♦ 0159 ♦ **Assumption of the Virgin Mary, Feast of the (Guatemala)**
August 15

Roman Catholics believe that the body of Mary, rather than undergoing death and decay, entered heaven along with her soul, an event that is commemorated in the Feast of the Assumption (*see* ASSUMPTION OF THE BLESSED VIRGIN MARY, FEAST OF THE). In the Guatemalan town of Santa Cruz del Quiché, the Feast of the Assumption is combined with the Fiestas Elenas (August 16-20) and celebrated for nearly a week.

The fiesta's highlight is the famous Snake Dance. Also known as the Dance of the Jesters, this was a Native American dance that the Spanish priests tried to stamp out. They were not successful because the secret societies that executed the dances did so in caves and other secret locations unknown to the Spanish.

The dance involves the use of live snakes, some of them poisonous, which are captured in the mountains and brought back to town in jars. In order to prevent the snakes from poisoning anyone, the venom is removed in advance or else someone sews the snakes' mouths shut. As the energy of the dance reaches its peak the snakes are released and permitted to writhe about on the dance floor. Each of the dancers scoops up a snake and lets it wrap itself around his limbs while continuing to dance. Occasionally the snake goes down a dancer's blouse or jacket, and the audience roars with laughter if the snake manages to escape through a trouser leg.

One of the dancers wears a fur-trimmed suit and carries a stuffed fox. As he lunges at the audience in a threatening way, kids approach him from behind and yank on the fox's tail. According to legend, the stuffed fox represents the earth's fertility, while the serpent symbolizes the rain that bestows life on the earth. It is probably related to the feathered serpent, a predominant Mesoamerican symbol.

CONTACTS:
Guatemala Tourist Commission
299 Alhambra Cir., Ste. 510
Coral Gables, FL 33134
888-464-8281 or 305-442-0651; fax: 305-442-1013
www.guatemala.travel.com.gt

SOURCES:
DictSymb-1971, p. 289
FiestaTime-1965, p. 129

♦ 0160 ♦ **Assumption of the Virgin Mary, Feast of the (Hasselt, Belgium)**
Third and fourth Sundays in August every seven years

In Hasselt, the capital of the Belgian province of Limburg, the festival known as *Virge Jesse* (Virgin of the Line of Jesse) takes place on the third and fourth Sundays in August every seven years. Local lore states that in medieval times an image of the Virgin was propped up against a great tree which stood at the crossroads near the present-day site of Hasselt. Those whose journeys took them past the image often stopped there to pray for safe travels and to make an offering to the Virgin. By the 14th century, tales concerning the Virgin's blessings began to attract pilgrims from far and near the image at the crossroads.

Today's ceremonies feature a procession with a dark, ancient image of the Virgin, said by townsfolk to be the same one that once stood against the tree at the crossroads. Bearers carry the image, draped in a black velvet mantle, through town and under a progression of arches that represent important episodes in the city's past.

Assumption Day is an official holiday in Belgium.

CONTACTS:
Belgian National Tourist Office
220 E. 42nd St., Ste. 3402
New York, NY 10017
212-758-8130; fax: 212-355-7576
www.visitbelgium.com

SOURCES:
BkFest-1937, p. 46
FestWestEur-1958, p. 15

♦ 0161 ♦ Assumption of the Virgin Mary, Feast of the (Italy)
August 15

Colorful processions through the streets and displays of fireworks mark the celebration of the Feast of the Assumption in Italy, as they do in Italian-American communities throughout the United States. In Sicily and rural areas outside of Rome, a **Bowing Procession** is the day's main event. A statue of the Virgin Mary is carried through the town to a ceremonial arch of flowers, where a group of people holding a statue of Christ awaits her arrival. Both statues are inclined toward each other three times, and then the Christ figure precedes that of Mary back to the parish church for a special benediction. The journey to the arch symbolizes Mary's sojourn on earth, the arch itself represents the gate of heaven, and the trip back to the church represents her entrance into heaven.

CONTACTS:
Italian Government Tourist Board
630 Fifth Ave., Ste. 1565
New York, NY 10111
212-245-5618; fax: 212-586-9249
www.italiantourism.com

SOURCES:
DaysCustFaith-1957, p. 207

♦ 0162 ♦ Aston Magna Festival
Five weekend evenings from early July to early August

The Aston Magna Festival has been held since the 1970s, continuing its tradition of bringing music of the baroque period and beyond to today's audiences using historically accurate instruments and performance practices. The oldest festival of its kind, this annual event in the Berkshires of Massachusetts is an outgrowth of the Aston Magna Foundation for Music and the Humanities, which was founded in 1972 by Lee Elman and harpsichordist Albert Fuller to study all aspects of music composed in the 17th and 18th centuries. Today the mission of the foundation is "to enrich the appreciation of music of the past

and the understanding of the cultural, political, and social contexts in which it was composed and experienced."

For five consecutive weekends in July and August, a 21st-century audience can enjoy a musical experience closely resembling that of an earlier era as the works of MOZART, Monteverdi, the Bach family, Schubert, Beethoven, Corelli, Purcell, Haydn, and other composers are performed on period instruments. Concerts are held on Fridays at Bard College, with the same program presented on Saturdays at St. James Church in Great Barrington, Massachusetts. Programs have featured vocal and instrumental works ranging from Elizabethan and Italian madrigals and cantatas to piano sonatas, concertos, and symphonies.

CONTACTS:
Aston Magna Foundation for Music and the Humanities
323 Main St.
P.O. Box 28
Great Barrington, MA 01230
800-875-7156 or 416-528-3595
www.astonmagna.org

SOURCES:
MusFestAmer-1990, p. 73

♦ 0163 ♦ Atatürk Remembrance (Youth and Sports Day)
May 19

On May 19, 1919, Mustafa Kemal Atatürk landed with his forces at the Black Sea town of Samsun, Turkey, to begin his fight against the Allies who had occupied the Ottoman Empire at the end of World War I. Four years later, Atatürk had successfully overcome the last of the Allied forces and Turkey was declared a free republic. He ushered in an era of reform, development, and an increasingly Western approach to government and society. Because Turkish youth have always engaged in sporting events to celebrate the day, it has also become known as **Youth and Sports Day** as well.

In the capital city of Ankara, the celebration of the day begins with a 21-gun salute at 7:00 in the morning, the time when Atatürk arrived in Samsun. Then the president and other government officials visit the Atatürk Mausoleum before moving on to the 19 Mayis (May 19th) Stadium. Members of the Turkish Air Forces Youth Team have performed parachuting exhibitions in several cities across Turkey.

CONTACTS:
Embassy of the Republic of Turkey
2525 Massachusetts Ave. N.W.
Washington, D.C. 20008
202-612-6700; fax: 202-612-6744
www.turkishembassy.org

♦ 0164 ♦ Athens Festival
End of June through September

The feeling of ancient Greece comes alive among the ruins every summer in Athens, where the Acropolis and Parthenon help set the stage for the Athens Festival. Harkening back to the city's heritage, music, dance, and theater performances are presented in the Herod Atticus Odeon, a Roman-style, open-air hillside theater originally built in C.E. 161 that seats thousands. Since 1955 orchestral and chamber music, classical and popular theater, opera, ballet, and modern dance have been performed there by both Greek and international artists, among them the Paris Symphony Orchestra, the Kirov Opera, the Peking Opera, the Alvin Ailey American Dance Theater, the English Bach Festival, the National Theatre of Greece, the Old Vic Company, and the Bolshoi Ballet.

CONTACTS:
Athens Festival
23 Hadjichristou St.
Athens, GR-117 42 Greece
30-210-928-2900; fax: 30-210-928-2941
www.greekfestival.gr/?lang=en

SOURCES:
GdWrldFest-1985, p. 101
IntlThFolk-1979, p. 192
MusFestEurBrit-1980, p. 107
MusFestWrld-1963, p. 231

♦ 0165 ♦ Ati-Atihan Festival
Third week in January

One of the most colorful festivals in the Philippines, held in Kalibo, the capital city of the province of Aklan. Originally falling on the Feast Day of Santo Niño (the infant Jesus), the celebration combines Christian and non-Christian elements.

Its origins are in the 13th century, when 10 families fled Borneo and landed on the Philippine island of Panay. There the resident Ati people gave them land. The Ati (also called Negritos or Pygmies) were small dark people, and after receiving the land, the story goes, the Malayan people blackened their faces to look like the Ati. Years later, the Spanish Christians, having converted much of the country, persuaded the inhabitants to darken their skin, wear warlike clothing, and pretend they were Ati to frighten away the Muslims. They were victorious over the Muslims and attributed their victory to Santo Niño. At that time, religion came into the festival.

Ati-Atihan means "to make like Atis." During the present-day festival, revelers cover their skin with soot and wear Ati costumes that are patchworks of coconut shells, feathers, and fronds. They converge on the main streets and around the town plaza and, to the beat of drums, shout "Hala Bira" ('Go on and fight!'), pound their spears, and repeatedly dance a two-step dance. From a distance, the celebrants look like a solid mass of people lurching and swinging in a frenzied rhythm.

See also DINAGYANG and SINULOG

CONTACTS:
Philippine Tourism Center
556 Fifth Ave.
New York, NY 10036
212-575-7915; fax: 212-302-6759
www.wowphilippines.com.ph

SOURCES:
GdWrldFest-1985, p. 152
IntlThFolk-1979, p. 288

♦ 0166 ♦ Audubon Day
April 26

John James Audubon (1785-1851) was America's foremost ornithological illustrator. After studying drawing in Paris under the French painter Jacques Louis David, Audubon struggled for many years to make a living from his art, shuttling back and forth between Europe and the United States and supplementing his income by giving drawing lessons, turning out portraits, playing the flute or violin at local dances, and at one time running a general store.

In 1820 he began a flatboat excursion down the Mississippi River to seek out new varieties of birds to paint. Eventually he had enough bird portraits to publish in book form. *Birds of America,* produced with the help of engraver Robert Havell, Jr., contains 435 hand-colored plates and was published in "elephant folio" format to accommodate the life-sized portrayals of birds on which Audubon insisted.

After his death in 1851, Audubon's wife Lucy returned to teaching to support herself. One of her students, George Bird Grinnell, became the editor of *Forest and Stream* magazine and in 1886 organized the Audubon Society for the study and protection of birds. Today there are many branches of this organization, known as the National Audubon Society, and it remains dedicated to the conservation of wildlife and natural resources. Its members honor Audubon on his birthday, April 26. In some states, Audubon Day and ARBOR DAY are celebrated together by planting trees in bird sanctuaries.

CONTACTS:
National Audubon Society
225 Varick St., Fl. 7
New York, NY 10014
212-979-3000; fax: 212-979-3188
www.audubon.org

SOURCES:
AmerBkDays-2000, p. 314
AnnivHol-2000, p. 69
BkHolWrld-1986, Apr 13

♦ 0167 ♦ Auntie Litter's Annual Earth Day Parade and Celebration
April 22

Auntie Litter's Annual Earth Day Parade and Celebration are held each Earth Day, April 22, in Birmingham, Ala. The character "Auntie Litter," dressed in distinctive stars and green-and-white stripes, is the mascot for an environmental education and awareness program that promotes its green campaign through the Earth Day event.

The message of Auntie Litter is to conserve natural resources, eliminate litter, and to embrace the three Rs: reduce, reuse, and recycle. During Auntie Litter's parade, hundreds of schoolchildren and supporters march for a cleaner Earth. The accompanying celebration features educational exhibits, live entertainment, science demonstrations, and costume competitions. Auntie Litter, Inc., a non-profit organization, was founded in 1990. The Earth Day parade and celebration have been held each year since 1992.

CONTACTS:
Auntie Litter, Inc.
1776 Independence Ct., Ste. 304
Birmingham, AL 35216
205-879-3009; fax: 205-879-3049
www.auntielitter.org/index/html

♦ 0168 ♦ Austen (Jane) Festival
Last week of September

Along with being famous for its ancient Roman ruins, the town of Bath, England, is also known as the home of renowned English novelist Jane Austen (1775–1817). The writer's residence in the town, located 100 miles west of London, was short—a mere five years at the turn of the 19th century. However, the author's foray in the city was significant enough to inspire the creation of an annual festival in September.

Since 2001, Austen aficionados have converged on Bath for over a week to celebrate with music, walking tours, films, and the famous Regency Promenade, in which a large group in period costume parade the Georgian terraces of Bath. The festival boasts that it is the largest European promenade featuring the fashion of Britain's Regency era, the period during which Austen wrote. Other well-attended events are workshops, lectures, and readings, which often reference *Northanger Abbey* and *Persuasion*, two Austen novels mainly set in Bath.

Many festival goers delve deeper into Austen's personal history and the influence Bath had on her by visiting the Jane Austen Centre, a permanent exhibit situated in one of the city's Georgian town houses.

CONTACTS:
Jane Austen Festival
40 Gay St.
Queen Sq.
Bath BA1 2NT UK
www.janeausten.co.uk/festival/index.html

♦ 0169 ♦ Australia Day
January 26

The anniversary of the first British settlement in Australia on January 26, 1788, was formerly known as **Foundation Day** or **Anniversary Day**. Captain Arthur Phillip and his company of British convicts arrived first at Botany Bay, and when that proved to be an unsuitable location they moved on to Port Jackson, where the city of Sydney was eventually established. They built a penal colony there to help relieve overcrowding in the British prisons.

First officially celebrated in Sydney in 1818, Australia Day has been a public holiday since 1838. It used to be observed on either January 26 or the nearest Monday, but since 1994 it has been observed on January 26 with celebrations all over the country.

CONTACTS:
National Australia Day Council
Old Parliament House
King George Terr.
Parkes, ACT 2600 Australia
61-2-6120-0600; fax: 61-2-6273-6277
www.australiaday.gov.au

SOURCES:
AnnivHol-2000, p. 14
DictDays-1988, p. 7
IntlThFolk-1979, p. 11
NatlHolWrld-1968, p. 16

♦ 0170 ♦ Australian Open Tennis
January

The Australian Open is the year's first event in the Grand Slam of tennis, followed by the FRENCH OPEN, the UNITED STATES OPEN, and WIMBLEDON. It is played on synthetic hard courts at Sydney, Australia, and Melbourne, Australia, and known officially as the **Australian Championships.** Tennis took root in Australia in 1880 at the Melbourne Cricket Club. The championship for men began in 1905, and the women's championship in 1922. The matches became an "open" (to both amateurs and professionals) in 1969.

Margaret Smith Court, an Australian known for her powerful serve and volley, is the all-time champion in the women's division of the open; she won the title 11 times between 1960 and 1973. In 1970, she was the second woman to win the Grand Slam; Maureen Connolly had swept the four tournaments in 1953, and Steffi Graf won all four in 1988.

Top multiple winners in the men's division of the Australian Open have been Roy Emerson, who took six titles (1961 and 1962-67); Jack Crawford, Ken Rosewall, and Pat Wood, who each won four; and Rod Laver, Adrian Quist, and Mats Wilander, who each won three.

In 1990, for the first time in Open Grand Slam history, the eight singles titles for men and women were won by eight different players.

CONTACTS:
Tennis Australia
P.O. Box 6060
Richmond South, VIC 3121 Australia
61-3-9286-1177; fax: 61-3-9650-2743
www.australianopen.com

♦ 0171 ♦ Austria National Day
October 26

National Day commemorates the day in 1955 when Soviet occupation forces left Austria, after taking control in 1945. The Austrian State Treaty of May 15, 1955, ensured that Austrians would regain sovereignty over their country on July 27. By October 26, it was once again a free, independent country.

Though a national holiday in Austria, people do not get the day off from school or work, mainly because of the idea that one's country is best served by working. Schools hold special presentations, and the president delivers a speech.

SOURCES:
AnnivHol-2000, p. 178

♦ 0172 ♦ **Author's Day, National**
November 1

The idea of setting aside a day to celebrate American authors came from Nellie Verne Burt McPherson, president of the Bement (Illinois) Women's Club in 1928. McPherson was a teacher and an avid reader throughout her life. During World War I, when she was recuperating in a hospital, she wrote a fan letter to fiction writer Irving Bacheller, telling him how much she had enjoyed his story, "Eben Holden's Last Day A'Fishin." Bacheller sent her an autographed copy of another story, and McPherson realized that she could never adequately thank him for his gift. Instead, she showed her appreciation by submitting an idea for a National Author's Day to the General Federation of Women's Clubs, which passed a resolution setting aside November 1 as a day to honor American writers. In 1949 the day was recognized by the U.S. Department of Commerce.

Sue Cole, McPherson's granddaughter, was largely responsible for promoting the observation of National Author's Day after her grandmother's death in 1968. She has urged people to write a note to their favorite author on this day to "brighten up the sometimes lonely business of being a writer." Flying the American flag on November 1, according to Mrs. Cole, is another way of showing appreciation for the men and women who have created American literature.

SOURCES:
AnnivHol-2000, p. 184

♦ 0173 ♦ **Autumnal Equinox**
September 22-23

The sun crosses the plane of the earth's equator twice a year: on or about March 21 (*see* VERNAL EQUINOX) and again six months later, on or about September 22 or 23. On these two occasions, night and day are of equal length all over the world. In the Northern Hemisphere, September 22 or 23 is the first day of autumn.

Autumnal Equinox Day is a national holiday in Japan, observed on either September 23 or 24 to celebrate the arrival of autumn and to honor family ancestors.

See also HIGAN; SHUNBUN-NO-HI

CONTACTS:
Lab for Particles and Fields
Code 672, Goddard Space Flight Center
Greenbelt, MD 20771
301-286-0447
www-istp.gsfc.nasa.gov

The Royal Observatory Greenwich
The National Maritime Museum Greenwich
London, SE10 9NF United Kingdom
44-20-8312-6565; fax: 44-20-8312-6632
www.rog.nmm.ac.uk

SOURCES:
AmerBkDays-2000, p. 665
BkDays-1864, vol. II, p. 364
DictDays-1988, p. 37
FolkWrldHol-1999, p. 565

♦ 0174 ♦ **Avani Mulam**
August-September; during the Hindu month of Bhadrapada

According to Hindu mythology, the god Indra showed his displeasure with the king of Madurai by sending a drought, during which the river completely dried up. When a sudden, heavy rainfall threatened to flood the river's banks, the king ordered everyone in Madurai to help build a dam to conserve the precious water. The portion of the dam assigned to one old woman was never completed, because she was too busy cooking for the other hungry laborers. One of the workmen who came to her for food was actually the god Sundara, who saved the dam from leaking by throwing a small handful of earth in the gap left by the old woman.

Although Avani Mulam is observed throughout India, the grandest celebration is in Madurai, Tamil Nadu, where an image of Sundara, with a golden basket and a golden spade, is carried in a procession from the river to the temple.

CONTACTS:
India Tourist Office
1270 Avenue of the Americas, Ste. 1808
New York, NY 10020
800-953-9399 or 212-751-6840; fax: 212-582-3274
www.tourisminindia.com

SOURCES:
BkFestHolWrld-1970, p. 107

♦ 0175 ♦ **Aviation Day**
August 19

National Aviation Day honors the birthday of the American inventor and early manufacturer of airplanes, Orville WRIGHT (1871-1948), as well as the progress that has been made in manned flight since the Wright Brothers made their historic 120-foot flight at Kitty Hawk, North Carolina, in 1903. President Franklin D. ROOSEVELT proclaimed August 19 as Aviation Day in 1939, and since that time celebrations have been sponsored in a number of states by organizations involved in aviation. Parachute jumping, glider demonstrations, films, airplane rides, and displays of new and antique aircraft are popular events on this day, and open house celebrations are often held at local airports. One of the more impressive observations of Aviation Day occurs when military aircraft fly in formation, often at lower-than-usual altitudes, over airports or other locations where celebrations are being held.

SOURCES:
AmerBkDays-2000, p. 598
AnnivHol-2000, p. 139

♦ 0176 ♦ **Avignon Festival**
July

The month-long **Festival d'Avignon** was founded in 1947 by Jean Vilar, a well-known French actor and director. Invited to direct the first annual drama festival at Avignon, Vilar selected bold and innovative productions to be performed at the Court of Honor at the Popes' Palace (*Palais des Papes*), a large outdoor stage. This new kind of theater attracted an eager audience. In the 1960s Vilar expanded the festival's offerings to include dance, cinema, and musical theater.

The International Centre for Creative Research, a residence for artists, was established in the 1970s at the site of a 14th-century monastery, with exhibitions and concerts held during the festival. About the same time, fringe theater sprouted in conjunction with the festival. In the 1980s the festival once again reinvented itself by introducing audiovisual media, presenting more international theater productions, and inviting contemporary poets to do readings.

Throughout its evolution, the Avignon Festival has not strayed from the fresh experimentation which was Vilar's hallmark, thus continuing to attract new audiences after more than 50 years of existence. The festival presents a different program each year, with about 40 performances given in 20 venues including the Popes' Palace, cloisters, and churches, and approximately 120,000 people in attendance.

CONTACTS:
Avignon Festival et Compagnies
5, rue Ninon Vallin
Avignon, 84000 France
33-4-9085-1308
www.festival-avignon.com/index.php?lg=en

SOURCES:
IntlThFolk-1979, p. 99
MusFestEurBrit-1980, p. 74

◆ 0177 ◆ **Awoojoh**
Various

A thanksgiving feast in the West African nation of Sierra Leone, the Awoojoh honors the spirits of the dead, who are believed to have influence over the fortunes of the living. It may be held at any time of year, and the guests include not only friends and relatives but, in a small community, the entire village. The day begins with a family visit to the cemetery, where a libation is poured over the relatives' graves and the dead are invited to join in the thanksgiving celebration. Two kola nuts, one red and one white, are split in half and thrown upon the grave, and the pattern in which they fall is believed to carry a message from the ancestors. It is essential for all family quarrels to be settled before the feast begins.

Many popular African dishes—such as fried bean cakes, fried plantains, rice bread, and "Awoojoh beans"—are served, but the highlight of the meal is an elaborate stew, a portion of which is set out for the dead ancestors or thrown to the vultures, who are believed to embody the souls of the departed. Although the practice of holding a thanksgiving feast originated with the Yoruba, who came to Sierra Leone from Nigeria, Christians and Muslims give them as well.

SOURCES:
FolkWrldHol-1999, p. 545
HolSymbols-2009, p. 68

◆ 0178 ◆ **Awuru Odo Festival**
Biannually in April

Among the Igbo people of Nigeria, the Odo are the spirits of the dead, who return to the earth to visit their families every two years. They arrive sometime between September and November (*see* ODO FESTIVAL) and depart in April. Before they leave, there is a big theatrical performance known as the Awuru Odo in which masked players, representing the Odo spirits, reenact the story of their visit to the living and the agony of their departure. The performance takes place on a ritual stage in the market square.

Because the Odo festival occurs only once every two years, elaborate preparations are made to welcome the returning spirits. The masks used in the performance are refurbished or new ones are made. Fences are put up around the shrines where the Odo will worship. Many of these preparations are carried out in secrecy by the men, while the women, who are totally excluded from and can have no knowledge of the activities, are responsible for providing enough food for the celebration.

SOURCES:
FolkWrldHol-1999, p. 262

◆ 0179 ◆ **Ayathrem (Ayathrima; Bringing Home the Herds)**
February, March, October; 26th-30th day of Mihr, the seventh Zoroastrian month

This is the fourth of the six great seasonal feasts known as *gahambars* in the Zoroastrian religion. The gahambars traditionally provided the Zoroastrians, who were at one time a primarily agricultural people, with periodic respites from their labor and an opportunity to give thanks for their earthly blessings. Each of the six gahambars correlated with a phase of agricultural production—midsummer, bringing in the harvest, etc.—and honored one of the six things created by God: sky, water, earth, plants, animals, and humankind. The importance of the gahambars has diminished somewhat, now that so many Zoroastrians live in urban areas, but they are still observed in rural communities where farming rules the patterns of daily life.

The meaning of the word *Ayathrem* is not entirely clear. It is thought to refer to the time of prosperity and nourishment (*thrime* comes from *thrâ*, meaning "to thrive"), which may also be why it is identified with the breeding season for cattle.

The gahambars were typically joyous festivals that included such activities as intricate rituals, specific prayers, and the sharing of food.

The Zoroastrian calendar has 12 months of 30 days each, plus five extra days at the end of the year. Because of discrepancies in the calendars used by widely separated Zoroastrian communities around the world, there are now three different calendars in use, and Ayathrem can fall either in October, March, or February.

SOURCES:
RelHolCal-2004, p. 68

◆ 0180 ◆ **Ayerye Festival**
Between September and December

Fante communities in southern Ghana have organized themselves into local military companies called *asafo* groups for at least the last few hundred years. The Ayerye Festival celebrates and maintains this tradition of local self-defense. When young men come of age, their fathers traditionally give them guns; the Ayerye Festival is a kind of communal initiation occasion, in which the older men share their experience and skills with the new young initiates in order to help prepare them to take their places some day. There are mock battles and competitions designed to help the young men develop their skills.

CONTACTS:
Ghana Embassy
3512 International Dr. N.W.
Washington, D.C. 20008
202-686-4520; fax: 202-686-4527
www.ghanaembassy.org

SOURCES:
FestGhana-1970, p. 44

♦ 0181 ♦ **Aymuray (Song of the Harvest)**
May 3

The South American Indians known as the Incas had an empire that flourished during the 15th and early 16th centuries and extended along the Pacific coast and Andean highlands from the northern border of what is now Ecuador to central Chile. They celebrated a harvest festival in May, which month they called *Aymuray*, which means "the song of the harvest."

Today, many Quechua Indians, who are descended from the Incas, still live in this region—most of them in Peru, and many continue to celebrate this ancient festival. They choose a tree to be the focus of the action and hang fruit and other objects on its boughs. Then they perform a traditional dance called the *Ayriwa*, "dance of the young corn," around the tree. Singing of the harvest song, the Aymuray, follows, and people shake the tree loose of its gifts and share them amongst each other.

Elsewhere in Peru, Aymuray has been largely combined with the Christian Feast of the EXALTATION OF THE CROSS. There are bonfires and music everywhere, as well as altars with crosses, which people take in processions to church.

SOURCES:
CelebNature-1969, p. 126
DictFolkMyth-1984, p. 99
FiestaTime-1965, p. 88

♦ 0182 ♦ **Ayyam-i-Ha**
February 25-March 1

Also known as **Days of Ha**, the Ayyam-i-Ha are intercalary days (extra days inserted in a calendar) in the Baha'i calendar. The calendar is made up of 19 months of 19 days each (361 days), plus the period of four days (five in leap years) of Ayyam-i-Ha added between the 18th and 19th months, which allows for the year to be adjusted to the solar cycle.

The days are set aside for rejoicing, hospitality, gift-giving, special acts of charity, and spiritually preparing for the Baha'i fast, from March 2-20. March 21 is New Year's Day, NAWRUZ, and the first day of the Baha'i calendar.

The new calendar was inaugurated by Mirza Ali Mohammad, known as the BAB, founder of the Babi religion from which the Baha'i faith emerged. Baha'is believe that the new age of unity they foresee should have a new calendar free of the associations of the older calendars.

The Baha'i observe nine days on which work connected with trade, commerce, industry, and agriculture should be suspended. These days are the first, ninth, and 12th days of the Feast of RIDVAN, Nawruz, the anniversaries of the Bab's birth, declaration, and martyrdom, and the birth and ascension of BAHA'U'LAH.

CONTACTS:
Bahai National Center
1233 Central St.
Evanston, IL 60201
800-228-6483 or 847-869-9039
www.bahai.us

SOURCES:
AnnivHol-2000, p. 33, 37
ConEncyBahai-2000, p. 53
OxYear-1999, p. 695
RelHolCal-2004, p. 157

♦ 0183 ♦ **Azerbaijan Day of the Martyrs**
January 20

On January 20, 1990, Soviet troops entered the Azerbaijan capital city of Baku to quell protests by Azerbaijani nationals, who were agitating for freedom from Soviet rule. Shooting down people in the streets, Soviet soldiers were responsible for the deaths of 131 people; 744 others were wounded, and 841 were illegally arrested. The events have come to be known as "Black January." Although the day was very grim, it is considered to be the birth of independent Azerbaijan and a crucial event leading to the collapse of the Soviet Union, due to the public outcry that followed it. The Soviet Union lasted only about one more year after the events in Azerbaijan.

The national holiday on January 20 honors those who died at the hands of the Soviet troops. Flags are flown at half-mast across the country, and a minute of silence is observed at noon. The tragedy is commemorated at Martyrs' Lane, a cemetery and park in Baku where photographs of the victims decorate the tombstones. Here, the president of the nation lays a wreath at the Eternal Fire that honors the dead of Black January.

CONTACTS:
Azerbaijan Embassy
2741 34th St. N.W.
Washington, D.C. 20008
202-337-3500; fax: 202-465-6438
www.azembassy.com

♦ 0184 ♦ **Azerbaijan Independence Days**
May 28; October 18

Azerbaijan observes two independence days. The May 28, 1918, establishment of the Democratic Republic of Azerbaijan provides the occasion for the older independence celebration. Two years later, Azerbaijan came under Soviet rule. By 1991, the growing perestroika (social and economic reform) movement in the former U.S.S.R. created the opportunity for Soviet republics to break free, which, one by one, they proceeded to do. Azerbaijan declared its intention to once again become an independent nation on August 30, 1991. Azerbaijan's new independence day commemorates the declaration of independence made by the Supreme Soviet of Azerbaijan on October 18, 1991. After the U.S.S.R. ceased to exist as a geopolitical entity in December 1991 (which became official on January 1, 1992), Azerbaijan became an official independent state on December 26, 1991.

CONTACTS:
Embassy of the Republic of Azerbaijan
2741 34th St. N.W.
Washington, D.C. 20008
202-337-3500; fax: 202-337-5911
www.azembassy.us

SOURCES:
AnnivHol-2000, p. 174

♦ 0185 ♦ **Aztec Rain Festival**
Varies

For about 100 years the Aztecs ruled much of Mexico until the invasion of the Spanish explorer Hernando Cortes and his troops in 1521. They observed a number of festivals associated with rain and the god of rain and lightning, Tlaloc. One was held in February, when a priest performed various rituals to encourage rainfall at the beginning of the agricultural year.

Another festival was held in March, when flowers had begun to bloom. Because these were the first arrivals of new life from the earth, they were offered to Tlaloc and other rain gods. A third festival to encourage rainfall was held in the autumn. Tlaloc was believed to live in a mountain and at this festival, people fashioned small mountains and images of the gods.

A bit of modern folklore attaches to the Aztec rain god. In 1968 a group of students clambered up a statue of Tlaloc in Mexico City and sat on his head. Some speculated that the god did not take kindly to this and made it pour rain during the OLYMPIC GAMES held in the city that year.

SOURCES:
CelebNature-1969, p. 138
EncyRel-1987, vol. 14, p. 542
GodsSymbAncMex-1993, p. 166

B

♦ 0186 ♦ **Baalbeck Festival**
July and August

The Baalbeck Festival takes place in July and August in the town of Baalbeck, Lebanon. This festival features music, dance, and drama performances by world-famous artists and ensembles. Performances take place Friday and Saturday evenings, in addition to some Thursday and Sunday evenings. They are staged in the town's remarkable Roman ruins, which it bills as the most intact Roman temples in the world. The festival officially began in 1956, though various groups had used the setting in previous years for special performances. Lebanon's long civil war (1975-1996) put a stop to the festival, but the performances resumed again in 1997. The Baalbeck Festival honors Lebanon's historical position as the crossroads of the West and the Middle East by featuring both European art forms, such as opera and ballet, and Middle Eastern music, dance, and poetry. In addition, it commissions new works from writers and composers.

CONTACTS:
Baalbeck International Festival
Karakone El Druze, Osman Ben Affan St., Doursoumian Bldg.
P.O. Box 11-4215 Riad El Solh
Beirut, 1107 2160 Lebanon
961-1-373150; fax: 961-1-373153
www.baalbeck.org.lb

♦ 0187 ♦ **Bab, Birth of the**
October 20

Birth of the Bab is a holy day in the Baha'i religion to celebrate the birthday in 1819 of Mirza Ali Mohammad in Shiraz, Persia (now Iran). In 1844, Mirza Ali declared himself the Bab (meaning "gate") and foretold the coming of one greater than he. The day, on which work is suspended, is a happy social occasion for Baha'is.

See also BAB, DECLARATION OF THE and BAB, MARTYRDOM OF THE

CONTACTS:
Bahai National Center
1233 Central St.
Evanston, IL 60201
800-228-6483 or 847-869-9039; fax: 847-733-3578
www.us.bahai.org

Bahai International Community
866 United Nations Pl., Ste. 120
New York, NY 10017
212-803-2500; fax: 212-803-2566
www.bahai.org

SOURCES:
AnnivHol-2000, p. 175
ConEncyBahai-2000, p. 55
DictWrldRel-1989, p. 86, 87
RelHolCal-2004, p. 156

♦ 0188 ♦ **Bab, Declaration of the**
May 22-23

Declaration of the Bab is a joyous Baha'i festival to celebrate the Bab's announcement in 1844 in Shiraz, Persia (now Iran), that he was the "gate" (which is the meaning of Bab) to the coming of the promised one of all religions. This proclamation is considered the beginning of the Baha'i faith, although the religion was founded after the Bab's death.

The Bab, who was born Mirza Ali Mohammad, founded an independent religion known as the Babi faith which grew out of Shi'ite Islam. At the time of this proclamation, the Bab also announced that it was his mission to herald a prophet who would be greater than he (paralleling St. John the Baptist as the forerunner of Jesus; *see* ST. JOHN'S DAY). After his proclamation, the Bab assembled 18 disciples.

This day is holy to Baha'is and a day on which work is suspended. Its observation begins at about two hours after sunset on May 22.

See also BAB, BIRTH OF THE and BAB, MARTYRDOM OF THE

CONTACTS:
Bahai National Center
1233 Central St.
Evanston, IL 60201
800-228-6483 or 847-869-9039; fax: 847-733-3578
www.us.bahai.org

Bahai International Community
866 United Nations Pl., Ste. 120
New York, NY 10017
212-803-2500; fax: 212-803-2566
www.bahai.org

SOURCES:
AnnivHol-2000, p. 86
ConEncyBahai-2000, p. 56
DictWrldRel-1989, pp. 86, 87
OxYear-1999, p. 694
RelHolCal-2004, p. 155

♦ 0189 ♦ **Bab, Martyrdom of the**
July 9

Martyrdom of the Bab is a solemn commemoration of the day in 1850 when the Bab, the first prophet of the Baha'i faith, was executed in Tabriz, Persia (now Iran). Prayers and readings mark the Baha'i holy day, and work is suspended.

After founding the Babi, a new religion growing out of Shi'ite Islam in 1844, the Bab was repeatedly exiled and imprisoned by Muslim rulers and priests who opposed the idea that the Bab would provide another avenue to the truth. They saw the Babis as revolutionaries and heterodox despoilers. A committee of priests demanded the Bab's execution, and he was led to the town square and tied to a post in front of 750 riflemen. The Baha'i's say that shots were fired, but they only severed the ropes binding him. When the smoke cleared, the Bab was found in his cell completing the work he had been doing before the volley of shots—dictating holy words to a scribe. He was taken before a second regiment of riflemen, and this time he was killed. His body was disposed of in a ditch, but was retrieved by his followers and eventually placed in a mausoleum on Mount Carmel in Haifa, Israel, where the Baha'i headquarters is today.

See also BAB, BIRTH OF THE and BAB, DECLARATION OF THE

CONTACTS:
Bahai National Center
1233 Central St.
Evanston, IL 60201
800-228-6483 or 847-869-9039; fax: 847-733-3578
www.us.bahai.org

Bahai International Community
866 United Nations Pl., Ste. 120
New York, NY 10017
212-803-2500; fax: 212-803-2566
www.bahai.org

SOURCES:
AnnivHol-2000, p. 114
ConEncyBahai-2000, p. 57
DictWrldRel-1989, pp. 86, 87
RelHolCal-2004, p. 155

♦ 0190 ♦ **Babin Den**
January 20

In Bulgaria the old women who helped deliver babies—much like the modern midwife—were called *baba*, or grandmother. It was widely believed that the baby received some of the baba's wisdom, and it was customary for the baby's parents to bring the baba flowers on a particular day each year, called **Grandmother's Day** or **Day of the Midwives**. Eventually the children grew up, but they would continue to visit their baba each year.

Most babies in Bulgaria today are born in hospitals, so the children bring flowers to the doctors and nurses who assisted at their birth. Another traditional activity on this day involves boys dunking girls in the icy waters of rivers and lakes, supposedly to bring them good health in the coming year.

See also GRANDPARENTS' DAY

SOURCES:
BkFest-1937, p. 66
BkHolWrld-1986, Jan 20

♦ 0191 ♦ **Baby Parade**
Second Thursday in August

Started in 1901 by Leo Bamberger, founder of New Jersey's Bamberger's Department Store chain, the Baby Parade that takes place along the boardwalk at the seaside resort of Ocean City on the second Thursday in August each year allows children up to the age of 10 to participate and compete for prizes. There are four different divisions: Division A is for children in decorated strollers, go-carts, wagons, etc., and is further divided into three sections according to the age of the child; Division B features children in comically decorated vehicles, as well as walkers; Division C is for floats; and Division D is for larger commercial and noncommercial floats. The children are reviewed by the judges as they walk or wheel along the boardwalk from Sixth Street to Twelfth Street, and every child who enters receives a sterling silver identification bracelet. Cash prizes are given to the best entry in each division. More than 50,000 spectators are drawn to the **Ocean City Baby Parade** each year.

CONTACTS:
Ocean City Chamber of Commerce
854 Asbury Ave.
P.O. Box 157
Ocean City, NJ 08226
609-399-1412; fax: 609-398-3932
www.oceancityvacation.com

SOURCES:
GdUSFest-1984, p. 118

♦ 0192 ♦ **Bach Festival**
Late July for 10 days during odd-numbered years

Although the Bavarian city of Ansbach, Germany, has no particular connection to Johann Sebastian Bach, it has been the site of a biennial Bach Festival, the **Bachwoche Ansbach**, since 1947. Only music by Bach (or one of his family members) is played, and only on authentic instruments from Bach's time, such as the 1776 fortepiano. Even the concerts are held in buildings that were standing during Bach's lifetime, such as the 15th-century St. Gumbertus Church with its baroque organ.

Well-known vocalists, instrumentalists, and ensembles from all over the world are invited to the 10-day festival to perform Bach's motets, cantatas, organ, and orchestral works. The audience can experience not only the music but the fine acoustics and period architecture of the historic sites where the festival is held. The Palace of Carl Wilhelm Friedrich, for example, allows 500 festival-goers to listen to Bach in its rococo-style ballroom.

CONTACTS:
Bach Festival
Karlsplatz 7
Ansbach, 91522 Germany
49-981-150-37; fax: 49-981-155-01
www.bachwoche.de

SOURCES:
MusFestEurBrit-1980, p. 95

♦ 0193 ♦ **Bachok Cultural Festival**
May or June

This two-week cultural festival held in Bachok, Kelantan, Malaysia, features traditional Menora and Ma'yong dance-drama troupes, who often perform at Irama Beach. In addition to giant top-spinning and kiteflying competitions, the festival includes *wayang kulit*, or shadow plays, which are not normally seen in public but are performed privately at weddings, anniversaries, and other important celebrations. A puppeteer called *To'Dalang* (Father of the Mysteries) manipulates the puppets from inside an enclosed bamboo stage, and then their shadows are cast upon a screen in front of the audience. Most of the shadow plays are based upon either the *Ramayana* or *Mahabharata* epics from India. The plays are accompanied by a small band of five or six players with drums, a gong, a flageolet (a small, end-blown flute), and sometimes a Malay violin.

CONTACTS:
Malaysian Tourism Promotion Board
818 W. 7th St., Ste. 970
Los Angeles, CA 90017
800-336-6842 or 213-689-9702; fax: 213-689-1530
www.tourismmalaysiausa.com

SOURCES:
GdWrldFest-1985, p. 131
IntlThFolk-1979, p. 266

♦ 0194 ♦ **Bad Durkheim Wurstmarkt (Sausage Fair)**
September

Although called Bad Durkheim Wurstmarkt, or **Sausage Fair**, this is actually Germany's biggest wine festival. The name is said to have originated about 150 years ago because of the immense amounts of sausage consumed. Today there are dozens of wheelbarrow stands selling sausage and also chicken and shish-kebab. The religious origins of the feast are traced to 1417, when the villagers sold sausages, wine, and bread from wheelbarrows to pilgrims going to Michelsberg (St. Michael's hill) on MICHAELMAS (ST. MICHAEL'S DAY).

The opening day of the festival features a concert and a procession of bands, vineyard proprietors, and tapsters of the tavern stalls with decorated wine floats. The official opening is conducted by the mayor of Bad Durkheim and the German

Wine Queen, and is followed by the tapping of the first cask. The following days are a medley of fireworks, band playing, dancing, and singing through the night. At the three dozen or so tavern stalls, wine is served in glasses called *Schoppen* that hold about a pint. Before the festival is over, some half a million people will have drunk more than 400,000 Schoppen.

From July through late October, there are numerous other wine festivals, mainly in the villages of the Rhine and Moselle valleys. Among them are Bockenheim, Deidesheim, and Schweigen-Rechterbach.

CONTACTS:
German National Tourist Office
122 E. 42nd St.
New York, NY 10168
800-651-7010 or 212-661-7200; fax: 212-661-7174
www.cometogermany.com

♦ 0195 ♦ **Baekjung**
15th day of the seventh lunar month

In Korea the 15th, or full moon day, of the seventh lunar month is observed with Buddhist and folk agricultural traditions. *Baekjung* means "one hundred kinds," referring to the great number of fruits, vegetables, and grains that flourish at this time of year. There are Buddhist ceremonies at which samples of one hundred of these foods are offered to Buddha.

In farming areas, people celebrate this day as a "weeding party" often called *Homi Ssisi* or *Homi ssiggi*—"hoe cleaning," since, by this time in the season, most of the hard work of farming is completed. The farm worker judged to be the hardest worker is feted with a parade around the village. Then his employer provides food and drink for a village-wide party.

CONTACTS:
Korea Foundation
10-11F, Diplomatic Center Bldg., 2558 Nambusunhwanno,
 Seocho-gu
Seoul, 137-863 Korea
82-2-3463-5684; fax: 82-2-3463-6086
www.koreana.or.kr

SOURCES:
AnnCustKorea-1983, p. 129

♦ 0196 ♦ **Baha'i Day of the Covenant**
November 26

The Baha'i Day of the Covenant is a Baha'i holy day. It commemorates the covenant BAHA'U'LLAH, founder of the faith, made with humanity and his followers, appointing ABDU'L-BAHA as the head of the Baha'i religion who would interpret Baha'i teachings. Abdu'l-Baha chose the date when followers requested an occasion to remember his importance.

CONTACTS:
Baha'i National Center
1233 Central St.
Evanston, IL 60201
800-228-6483 or 847-733-3559; fax: 847-733-3578
www.us.bahai.org

SOURCES:
AnnivHol-2000, p. 196
RelHolCal-2004, p. 157

♦ 0197 ♦ Bahamas Emancipation Day
First Monday in August

The English settled in the Bahamas during the mid-17th century and brought African slaves with them to work in the cotton fields. Slavery was formally abolished in the British Empire by the Abolition Act of 1833, but it wasn't until 1838 that the slaves in the Bahamas were freed.

Emancipation Day in the Bahamas is observed on the first Monday in August. Businesses are closed, and a regatta is held at Black Point, near Staniel Cay, in the Exuma island group.

See also Fox Hill Festival

CONTACTS:
Bahamas Tourism Office
60 E. 42nd St., Ste. 1850
New York, NY 10165
212-758-2777; fax: 212-753-6531
www.bahamas.com

SOURCES:
AnnivHol-2000, p. 145

♦ 0198 ♦ Bahamas Independence Day
July 10

The Bahama Islands gained independence from Great Britain at 12:01 A.M. on this day in 1973. The islands had been a British colony for nearly 250 years, but are now a commonwealth, with their own prime minister and parliament.

Businesses are closed on the tenth, a legal holiday, but festivities go on for a week with parades and celebrations. A fireworks display at Clifford Park on July 10 tops off the week.

CONTACTS:
Bahamas Embassy
2220 Massachusetts Ave. N.W.
Washington, D.C. 20008
202-319-2660; fax: 202-319-2668
www.bahamas.gov.bs

SOURCES:
AnnivHol-2000, p. 115

♦ 0199 ♦ Bahamas Labor Day
June 7; national holiday is celebrated on first Friday in June

Labor Day is a national holiday in the Bahamas, celebrated on the first Friday in June in order to create a long weekend for workers. The traditional date of Labor Day in the Bahamas, however, is June 7, in commemoration of a significant workers' strike that began on that day in 1942.

Labor Day is meant to honor and celebrate workers and the importance of their contributions to the nation and society. In the capital city, Nassau, thousands of people come to watch a parade through the streets, which begins at midmorning. Bands in colorful uniforms, traditional African *junkanoo* performers, and members of various labor unions and political parties are all part of the procession, which ends up at the Southern Recreation Grounds, where government officials make speeches for the occasion. For many residents and visitors to the Bahamas, the afternoon of Labor Day is a time to relax at home or perhaps visit the beach.

CONTACTS:
Embassy of the Bahamas in the United States
2220 Massachusetts Ave. N.W.
202-319-2660 or 202-319-2667; fax: 202-319-2668

♦ 0200 ♦ Baha'u'llah, Ascension of
May 29

This marks the anniversary of the death in 1892 of Mirza Husayn Ali, known as Baha'u'llah, founder of the Baha'i religion. "Ascension" is not meant literally, but is considered the ascension of the spirit. The day is one of nine Baha'i holy days on which work is suspended. It is observed by gathering together at 3:00 A.M., the time of Baha'u'llah's death in Acre, Palestine (now Israel), for prayers and sometimes readings from Baha'i historical works.

CONTACTS:
Bahai National Center
1233 Central St.
Evanston, IL 60201
800-228-6483 or 847-869-9039; fax: 847-733-3578
www.us.bahai.org

Bahai International Community
866 United Nations Pl., Ste. 120
New York, NY 10017
212-803-2500; fax: 212-803-2566
www.bahai.org

SOURCES:
AnnivHol-2000, p. 89
ConEncyBahai-2000, p. 77
RelHolCal-2004, p. 155

♦ 0201 ♦ Baha'u'llah, Birth of
November 12

The anniversary of the birth in 1817 of Baha'u'llah, the founder of the Baha'i religion, is a holy day on which work is suspended. Mirza Husayn Ali, later known as Baha'u'llah ("Glory of God"), was born in Tehran, Persia (now Iran). He was an adherent of Islam, and later a follower of the Bab, who founded the Babi faith, an independent messianic religion. Thirteen years after the Bab's execution in 1850, Husayn Ali declared himself the messenger of God, foretold by the Bab.

See also Ridvan, Feast of

CONTACTS:
Bahai National Center
1233 Central St.
Evanston, IL 60201

800-228-6483 or 847-869-9039; fax: 847-733-3578
www.us.bahai.org

Bahai International Community
866 United Nations Pl., Ste. 120
New York, NY 10017
212-803-2500; fax: 212-803-2566
www.bahai.org

SOURCES:
AnnivHol-2000, p. 190
ConEncyBahai-2000, p. 73
DictWrldRel-1989, pp. 87, 89
RelHolCal-2004, p. 156

♦ 0202 ♦ **Bahia Independence Day**
July 2

The consolidation of Brazilian independence in the state of Bahia is remembered each year with a procession following the path that the Brazilians took when they defeated Portuguese troops there in 1823. Folkloric characters like the *caboclo*, who symbolizes the superiority of native strength over the colonizers, have worked their way into this primarily civic celebration.

CONTACTS:
Bahia Tourism Authority
Av. Simon Bolivar S/N
Centro de Convences da Bahia-1dg Pisa
Salvador, Bahia 41750-230 Brazil
55-71-3117-3000; fax: 55-71-3371-0110
www.bahiatursa.ba.gov.br

♦ 0203 ♦ **Bahrain National Day**
December 16

Bahrain is a small (260 square miles in area) country of islands in the Persian Gulf. After being a British protectorate for more than 100 years, Bahrain became independent in 1971. National Day is a legal holiday observed on December 16 with fireworks, laser shows, and acrobatic and magic performances.

CONTACTS:
Ministry of Information
P.O. Box 253
Manama, Kingdom of Bahrain
973-17871111; fax: 973-17682777
www.info.gov.bh/en

♦ 0204 ♦ **Baile de las Turas (Dance of the Flutes)**
Varies, June-October

Indigenous peoples, including the Ayamas, living in Venezuela's Falcón and Lara states celebrate the Baile de las Turas at various times during the harvest season in thanksgiving for the corn crop. In Maparari, Lara state, Las Turas is held on September 23-24. Roman Catholic-influenced religious processions and services honoring the Virgen Mary blend with traditional religious dance and music over two days. "Tura" refers to the end of the corn harvest as well as to the two different kinds of flutes used in the ceremonies: a

smaller, shorter flute which creates a sharp sound and a larger flute with a deeper tone.

CONTACTS:
Venezuelan Embassy
1099 30th St. N.W.
Washington, D.C. 20007
202-342-2214; fax: 202-342-6820
www.embavenez-us.org

SOURCES:
FiestaTime-1965, p. 135

♦ 0205 ♦ **Bal du Rat Mort (Dead Rat's Ball)**
First Saturday in March

A huge carnival and ball, Bal du Rat Mort is concentrated in the casino of Ostende, Belgium, but also spread out all over the town. The carnival began at the end of the 19th century, launched by members of the Oostende Art and Philanthropic Circle (Circle Coecilia) who named the affair for a café on Montmartre (a hilly part of northern Paris, home to many artists) where they had whiled away pleasant hours. People are masked at the ball, and there's a competition for the best costume.

CONTACTS:
Bal Rat Mort Site
St. Sebastiaanstraat 26 bus 9
Koninklijke Coeciliakring
Oostende, B 8400 Belgium
32-59-50-05-12; fax: 32-59-50-05-12
www.ratmort.be/bal/engels/index_frame.htm

Oostende Tourist Office
Monacoplein 2
Oostende, B 8400 Belgium
32-59-70-11-99; fax: 32-59-70-34-77
www.ratmort.be/bal/engels/index_frame.htm

♦ 0206 ♦ **Balfour Declaration Day**
November 2

Jews, particularly those in Israel, observe Balfour Declaration Day in memory of a turning point in modern Jewish history. On November 2, 1917, Arthur J. Balfour, British Secretary of State for Foreign Affairs, sent a letter to Lord Rothschild indicating that the British government was in favor of establishing a national home for the Jewish people in Palestine. Although this may not seem to be as significant an event as ISRAEL INDEPENDENCE DAY, the Jewish people felt that the British government's commitment to their cause was very important. The day on which it was made has been kept as a semi-holiday ever since.

CONTACTS:
Israel Ministry of Foreign Affairs
9 Yitzhak Rabin Blvd.
Kiryat Ben-Gurion
Jerusalem, 91035 Israel
972-2-530-3111; fax: 972-2-530-3367
www.mfa.gov.il

SOURCES:
AmerBkDays-2000, p. 665

AnnivHol-2000, p. 185
DaysCustFaith-1957, p. 282
DictWrldRel-1989, p. 89

♦ 0207 ♦ Ball-Catching Festival (Tamaseseri)
January 3

Each year on January 3, two teams of Japanese men wearing only loincloths compete for a ball that weighs about 18 pounds and measures about 12 inches in diameter. It is believed that whoever can raise the ball above his or her head will have good fortune. Because they also believe that merely touching the ball brings good luck, spectators also enter the fray of the competition. Throughout the struggle, the competitors are continuously splashed with cold water, which also soaks the crowd watching the spectacle in cold winter air.

The two ball-catching teams consist of the Land Team, made up of farmers who work the fields, and the Sea team, composed of fisherman. They believe that the size of the harvest or of the catch during the New Year is determined by which team wins the ball and gives it to a waiting Shinto priest—with the winning team bound for the greater yield. A 500-year-old tradition, the ball-catching festival is said to have its roots in the legend of the dragon god (ryujin) offering two balls to the Empress Jingu (170-269). It takes place at Hakozaki Shrine City, Higashi-ku,Fukuoka City, Japan. It is one of the three main festivals of Kyushu, the southernmost of the four main islands that make up Japan.

CONTACTS:
Japan National Tourist Organization
515 S. Figueroa St., Ste. 1470
Los Angeles, CA 90071
213-623-1952; fax: 213-623-6301
www.jnto.go.jp/eng/index.html

♦ 0208 ♦ Balserías
On or around February 12

The Guaymía people of Chiriqui Province in Panama meet near February 12 to catch up on tribal affairs. This is also an occasion for the single men to hold an unusual competition amongst each other for available young women. The men line up in rows so that they face each other and hold small logs of balsa, a light wood. The men then try to eliminate each other from the contest by throwing the logs at each other's ankles with such force that they injure each other. The only allowable way for the men to avoid broken bones and other injuries is to constantly leap and dance out of the way of the logs. Those who manage to survive this frenzy intact and without being harmed are allowed to choose from among the young women.

CONTACTS:
Panama Embassy
2862 McGill Terr. N.W.
Washington, D.C. 20008
202-483-1407; fax: 202-483-8413
www.embassyofpanama.org

SOURCES:
FiestaTime-1965, p. 30

♦ 0209 ♦ Baltic-Nordic Harmonica Festival
July

The Baltic-Nordic Harmonica Festival is an international music festival that celebrates and showcases all types of harmonica playing. It has been held in the historic seaside resort town of Parnu, Estonia, each year since 2002. Most of the events are held at the Kuursaal, a summer theater that holds several small areas for performances and gatherings. Participants have come from far beyond the Baltic, from countries including Italy, France, Holland, Germany, and the United States. In 2007, more than 2,000 people attended the festival. Participants and visitors attend harmonica workshops and take part in, or listen to, competitions in a number of categories. They may even have a chance to hear something as unusual as a harmonica chorus. The overall winner of the competitions is awarded a prize of 1,000 Euros.

CONTACTS:
Elmar Trink, festival director
Piccolo Harmonica Club
80018 Parnu, Estonia
www.piccolo.ee

♦ 0210 ♦ Baltic Song Festivals
Summer

Massive festivals of song and dance, emphasizing folk music and national culture, in the Baltic countries of Estonia, Latvia, and Lithuania. These festivals came to symbolize nationhood, especially after the countries came under Soviet domination.

The first all-Estonian song festival, called the *Laulupidu,* was held in Tartu in 1869 with 845 performers singing to 15,000 people. Nationalist leaders, led by J. V. Jannsen, publisher of the first Estonian-language newspaper, had organized the festival to demonstrate that their culture had survived its conquerors.

In 1975 the festival drew 30,000 on stage and 200,000 spectators, and when it ended, the people rose and sang their unofficial anthem, "My Fatherland Is My Love," as tears streamed down their cheeks. The anthem was written during World War II by Lydia Koidula, daughter of Song Festival originator Jannsen, and put to music by Gustav Ernesaks. In 1988, as political activities heightened, there were spontaneous song fests throughout Estonia. Recently, the festival has been held at the Song Festival Amphitheater outside Tallinn.

In Latvia, the first Song Festival was held in 1873 at the Keizardarzs (the Czar's Garden), a park created in 1721 and named for Czar Peter I. Janis Cimze began collecting the melodies of folk songs in 1869, and these songs, some more than 1,000 years old, were performed by thousands of singers in huge choirs at the first and later festivals.

In Lithuania, each region has its own distinct musical style. Northeastern Aukstaitija, for example, is known for a kind of polyphonic round not found in any other region or in neighboring countries. The rhythms are syncopated, and the rounds sound very dissonant.

The old town of Vilnius is the site each May of "Skamba kankliai," performances by vocalists, instrumentalists, and dancers. Vilnius also hosts the song festival, Dainu Svente, with huge choirs and dancers, every four years (1998, 2002, 2006, etc.).

CONTACTS:
Culture Events Department, Riga City Council Culture
  Department
Riga Congress House
5 Krisjana Voldemara St.
Riga, 1010 Latvia
371-2-732-0941; fax: 371-2-732-6035
www.culture.lv/en

Vilnius Tourist Information Centre
Vilniaus g. 22
Vilnius, LT-01119 Lithuania
370-5-2629660; fax: 370-5-2628169
www.turizmas.vilnius.lt

Estonian Song and Dance Celebration Foundation
Suur-Karja 23
Tallinn, 10148 Estonia
372-6-273-120; fax: 372-6-273-125
www.laulupidu.ee/eng.php

♦ 0211 ♦ **Banff Festival of the Arts**
May-August

The Banff Arts Festival grew out of the Banff Centre School of Fine Arts, which was founded in 1933 in this mountain town nestled in the Canadian Rockies. Every summer since 1971, students and faculty of the school, along with internationally renowned artists, have presented a vast array of programs in jazz, vocal jazz, orchestral and chamber music, opera, drama, dance, literature, journalism, visual arts, Aboriginal arts, and film.

CONTACTS:
Banff Centre for the Arts
107 Tunnel Mountain Dr.
P.O. Box 1020
Banff, AL T1L 1H5 Canada
403-762-6180; fax: 403-762-6345
www.banffcentre.ca

SOURCES:
GdWrldFest-1985, p. 28
IntlThFolk-1979, p. 59
MusFestAmer-1990, p. 158

♦ 0212 ♦ **Bangladesh Independence Day**
March 26

This public holiday celebrates the declaration of the existence of the state of Bangladesh on March 26, 1971. When India gained independence from Britain in 1947, the region that is now Bangladesh was part of Bengal, India. It became East Pakistan and was governed together with West Pakistan as one country. The movement for autonomy in East Pakistan began in 1949. By early 1971, differences between East and West Pakistan had led to war. India entered the war in November in support of East Pakistan, and independence was assured within a month (*see* BANGLADESH VICTORY DAY).

Bangladeshis observe their national holiday of independence in the capital city of Dhaka with memorial ceremonies, a boat race on the Buriganga river, and other festivities.

CONTACTS:
Bangladesh Embassy
3510 International Dr. N.W.
Washington, D.C. 20008
202-244-0183; fax: 202-244-2771
www.bangladoot.org

SOURCES:
AnnivHol-2000, p. 51

♦ 0213 ♦ **Bangladesh Victory Day**
December 16

This public holiday in Bangladesh commemorates the end of the war with Pakistan in 1971 and the official creation of the state of Bangladesh, after months of fighting and years of struggle to gain autonomy.

See also BANGLADESH INDEPENDENCE DAY

CONTACTS:
Bangladesh Liberation War Museum
5 Segun Bagicha
Dhaka, 1000 Bangladesh
880-2-955-9091; fax: 880-2-955-9092
www.liberationmuseum.org

SOURCES:
AnnivHol-2000, p. 208

♦ 0214 ♦ **Bank Holiday**
Various

In England there are typically six "bank holidays"—weekdays when the banks are closed for business: NEW YEAR'S DAY, GOOD FRIDAY, EASTER MONDAY, Early May Bank Holidays, Spring Bank Holiday (in late May), August (or Summer) Bank Holiday, CHRISTMAS, and BOXING DAY. These official public holidays were established by law in 1871 and are traditionally spent at local fairgrounds.

In the United States, the Great Depression of 1929 had caused many people to withdraw their savings, and the banks had trouble meeting the demand. In February 1933 the Detroit banks failed and this caused a country-wide panic. President Franklin D. Roosevelt proclaimed his first full day in office (March 6, 1933) a national "Bank Holiday" to help save the country's banking system. The "holiday" actually lasted 10 days, during which "scrip" (paper currency in denominations of less than a dollar) temporarily replaced real money in many American households.

SOURCES:
AnnivHol-2000, pp. 91, 146
DictDays-1988, pp. 6, 8

♦ 0215 ♦ **Banntag**
Between April 30 and June 3; Ascension Day

In the canton of Basel in Switzerland, this is a day when village citizens walk the village boundaries. *Banntag* means community- or town-boundary day.

Until the Reformation, Ascension Day was a time for the blessing of the fields and checking of boundary markers. The religious aspect of the day declined, and now Ascension Day, which is a public holiday in Basel, is seen as a community festival. Citizens of Basel canton, accompanied by a local official, flag bearers, and musicians, walk along the boundaries to a certain spot where the president of the town council greets them and discusses town topics. In some communities, the walk is followed by a church service and community meal.

CONTACTS:
Switzerland Tourism
608 Fifth Ave.
New York, NY 10020
877-794-8037 or 212-757-5944; fax: 212-262-6116
www.myswitzerland.com

♦ 0216 ♦ **Baptism of the Lord, Feast of the**
January, Sunday following Epiphany

Jesus' baptism by John the Baptist in the River Jordan has always been considered a significant manifestation of Jesus' divinity, and has been celebrated on Epiphany by the Orthodox Church since the end of the second century. However, in 1961 the Roman Catholic Church began to celebrate it as a separate feast in its own right. The original date for the feast was January 13, but when the Church calendar was reorganized in 1969, the Feast of the Baptism of the Lord was moved to the Sunday following the Epiphany. The Church omits the observance in years when it coincides with the Epiphany, especially in places like the United States, where celebration of the Epiphany has been shifted from the traditional January 6 observance to the Sunday between January 2 and 8.

See also Timqat

CONTACTS:
Greek Orthodox Archdiocese of Australia
242 Cleveland St.
Redfern, NSW 2016 Australia
61-2-9698-5066; fax: 61-2-9698-536
www.greekorthodox.org.au

SOURCES:
AnnivHol-2000, p. 5
EncyChristmas-2003, p. 217
RelHolCal-2004, p. 89

♦ 0217 ♦ **Barbados Independence Day**
November 30

After having been a British colony since the 17th century, Barbados became independent on this day in 1966. A ceremony took place near the capital city of Bridgetown, during which the British flag was lowered and replaced by the Barbados flag, and the national anthem was sung.

Today, festivities extend through the month of November with the National Independence Festival of the Creative Arts.

This is a talent show of all ages in singing, dancing, writing, and acting. On Independence Day, festivities culminate with a parade and the final appearance of performers, and exhibits of art work and photography are on display.

See also Barrow Day, Errol

CONTACTS:
Barbados Tourism Authority
800 Second Ave., 2nd Fl.
New York, NY 10017
800-221-9831 or 212-986-6516; fax: 212-573-9850
www.visitbarbados.org

SOURCES:
AnnivHol-2000, p. 198
NatlHolWrld-1968, p. 215

♦ 0218 ♦ **Barbados Jazz Festival**
January

Established in 1994 to bring world-renowned jazz performers to the West Indies, the Barbados Jazz Festival has featured such musicians as Luther Vandross, Kenny G, Roberta Flack, and Ray Charles. Indoor performances are held at the Sir Garfield Sobers's Gymnasium and Sunbury Plantation House. There are also open-air concerts at Farley Hill National Park and Heritage Park.

CONTACTS:
S&R Rentals & Production
A1 Stepney
St. George, Barbados
246-437-4537; fax: 246-437-4538
www.barbadosjazzfestival.com

♦ 0219 ♦ **Bar-B-Q Festival, International**
Second weekend in May

A two-day mouth-watering event in Owensboro, Ky., which calls itself the Bar-B-Q Capital of the World. In the course of the weekend, 10 tons of mutton, 5,000 chickens, and 1,500 gallons of burgoo are cooked and served. Kentucky burgoo is a thick soup made of chicken, mutton, beef, tomatoes, cabbage, potatoes, onions, and corn.

The festival had its beginnings at the turn of the century when the many Roman Catholic churches in the area had summertime picnics in their parishes. Each church had a cooking team to vie with the others in cooking the best barbecue. Eventually, the idea struck someone that there could be a city-wide barbecue if all the church barbecues were combined. Out of that grew the present festival, which now attracts more than 40,000 people.

The barbecue-pit fires are lit on Friday afternoon on the banks of the Ohio River, and the chicken and meat—always mutton, not beef—is barbecued when the coals are red. The Roman Catholic parish chefs still compete, but the cooking contest has expanded to be open to anyone. Events besides cooking and eating include arts and crafts exhibits, bluegrass and country music, street dancing, and contests of pie eating, keg throwing and horseshoe throwing. There are also likely to be political speeches.

CONTACTS:
International Bar-B-Q Festival
P.O. Box 434
Owensboro, KY 42301
800-489-1131 or 270-926-6938
www.bbqfest.com

♦ 0220 ♦ **Bard of Armagh Festival of Humorous Verse**
Late November

The town of Armagh, Northern Ireland, located southwest of Belfast, is featured in a famous ballad called "The Bard of Armagh." That poem's title inspired the name of the Bard of Armagh Festival of Humorous Verse, an annual three-day event that has taken place since 1993. Poets appear before audiences to recite their works and compete for best poem.

The festival debuted as part of the November Keady Fair before becoming an event in its own right. To determine the official entries, a selection process was established that ensures each poem does not exceed a length of 200 words and features humorous verse suitable for a family audience.

The first two days are devoted to competition heats, which are held at several venues. The third day is devoted to finals, which usually take place at the Armagh City Hotel.

CONTACTS:
J. Makem
34 Fergort Rd.
Derrynoose, County Armagh Northern Ireland
www.bardofarmagh.com

♦ 0221 ♦ **Barnum Festival**
Late May-early July

Bridgeport, Connecticut, was the home of Phineas Taylor Barnum (1810-1891) and the birthplace of Charles Sherwood Stratton (1838-1883), known by his circus name of "General" Tom Thumb, a 28" tall man who was the main attraction of Barnum's 19th-century circus, the Greatest Show on Earth. Barnum was also Bridgeport's mayor in 1875, and his contributions to the city included bringing in new industrial jobs and building a number of parks. Since 1949 he has been honored with a festival beginning in late May and extending through the FOURTH OF JULY. Occasionally it continues through July 5, which is Barnum's birthday, or beyond. The idea behind the festival, which is sponsored by the P.T. Barnum Foundation, Inc., is to get away from Bridgeport's industrial image and to promote the city's circus heritage.

One of the highlights of the festival is the event known as "Champions on Parade," the largest senior drum corps competition in the Northeast. It takes place on the Saturday evening before July 4. On Sunday there is a Barnum Memorial Ceremony at the cemetery where he is buried. Many of the events focus on Barnum's circus background, including entertainment by clowns and a visit to the Barnum Museum,

where there is a miniature replica of his circus. The festival is preceded by the selection of an honorary Tom Thumb and Lavinia Warren, Thumb's wife, from among the area's schoolchildren. There is also an honorary Jenny Lind (the Swedish-born soprano who toured the United States under Barnum's sponsorship). Other figures associated with Barnum and his circus are recognized in this way as well.

CONTACTS:
P. T. Barnum Foundation
1070 Main St.
Bridgeport, CT 06604
866-867-8495 or 203-367-8495; fax: 203-367-0212
www.barnumfestival.com

SOURCES:
AmerBkDays-2000, p. 506
GdUSFest-1985, p. 28

♦ 0222 ♦ **Baron Bliss Day**
March 9

Baron Bliss Day is a public holiday in Belize honoring Englishman Henry Edward Ernest Victor Bliss (1869-1926). When he died on March 9, Bliss bequeathed his entire estate to Belize City.

On this day each year a morning mass and wreath laying is held at his tomb in the Fort Point area. Then there is a regatta in the harbor, a cycle race, and a kite contest.

SOURCES:
AnnivHol-2000, p. 41

♦ 0223 ♦ **Barrow (Errol) Day**
January 21

A national public holiday that honors Barbados' first prime minister. Errol Barrow was born in 1920, earned a law degree in England, then returned to Barbados. He became finance minister in 1959 and prime minister in 1961. He was reelected in 1966 and, soon after, Barbados became independent of Great Britain (*see* BARBADOS INDEPENDENCE DAY). Barrow was voted out in 1976, but regained office in 1986; he died the next year.

CONTACTS:
Barbados Tourism Authority
800 Second Ave., 2nd Fl.
New York, NY 10017
800-221-9831 or 212-986-6516; fax: 212-573-9850
www.visitbarbados.org

♦ 0224 ♦ **Bartholomew Fair**
August 24

Although ST. BARTHOLOMEW'S DAY isn't really celebrated anymore, for more than 700 years (1133-1855) it was the day on which the Bartholomew Fair was held at Smithfield on the outskirts of London. What began as an opportunity for buying and selling cloth eventually turned into a major event. Almost every type of commodity could be purchased there, and a number of sideshows and other crude sources of entertainment were available as well—earning the Fair its present-day reputation as "the Coney Island of medieval England."

Eventually the entertainment aspects of the Fair outweighed its commercial purposes, and although it was very much a part of English life there was a movement to close it down. In 1822, thousands of people rioted in protest against the threat of closing the Fair. But finally, in 1855, it was permanently abolished.

St. Bartholomew's Day is also known for the massacre of the Huguenots (Protestants) in France, which began at the instigation of Catherine de Medici in Paris on the night of August 23-24, 1572, and spread throughout the country for two more days until between 5,000 and 10,000 had been killed.

SOURCES:
BkDays-1864, vol. II, p. 264
DaysCustFaith-1957, p. 217
DictDays-1988, p. 9
FestSaintDays-1915, p. 176
OxYear-1999, pp. 343, 344

♦ 0225 ♦ Bascarsija Nights
July

One of Bosnia and Herzegovina's biggest events, Bascarsija Nights is a month-long celebration of culture. Artistic expressions ranging from street theater to classical symphony make up this festival held in the country's capital, Sarajevo. Over the course of July, about 150,000 people attend between 40 to 50 free events, held in open-air stages throughout Sarajevo and on the city's central stage opposite the Town Hall. Both local and guest artists from other European countries are invited.

Film director Sejfudin Tanovic and other arts enthusiasts began setting up the festival in 1988. Initially, the festival program was extensive but was limited to a single night. Over the years more dates were added until the entire month was booked. The festival gathered more momentum particularly after peace was reached following the Bosnian War (1992–1995).

One well-established tradition of the festival is the opening night performance by the Sarajevo Symphony Orchestra. This prestigious event typically draws a large audience including local and foreign officials. The remaining days are marked by more events offering sophisticated entertainment—theatre, book readings, opera, ballet, art exhibits—as well as popular fare like rock concerts, movie screenings, and folklore presentations.

CONTACTS:
Sarajevo Arts Agency
Dalmatinska St. 2/1
Sarajevo 71000 Bosnia and Herzegovina
www.sarajevoarts.ba/index_eng.html

♦ 0226 ♦ Basket Dance
Late September or October

The most important of the three harvest ceremonies performed by the Hopi Indians, the Basket Dance includes vari-ous ritual activities that serve to remind people that life is temporary and that they must comply with the Creator's plans. It is observed primarily by women who are members of the Lakon and Owaqöl societies. First they spend several days in a kiva (a sacred ceremonial room) to fast, pray, and chant. Other preparations include creating a sand painting, fashioning prayer plumes from feathers, building an altar, and getting costumes ready.

When the women emerge from the kiva, they chant while presenting baskets to the four directions of the compass, lifting them, then lowering them. Their movements are designed to bring cold, wet weather so that the crops will grow the following spring. Afterward, the women traditionally toss the baskets to the onlookers.

CONTACTS:
Hopi Cultural Center
P.O. Box 67
Second Mesa, AZ 86043
520-734-2401; fax: 520-734-6651
www.hopiculturalcenter.com

Frank H. McClung Museum
1327 Circle Park Dr.
Knoxville, TN 37996
865-974-2144; fax: 865-974-3827
mcclungmuseum.utk.edu

SOURCES:
DancingGods-1931, p. 168
EncyNatAmerRel-2001, pp. 154, 208
EncyRel-1987, vol. 10, p. 520
RelHolCal-2004, p. 259

♦ 0227 ♦ Basque Festival, National
First weekend in July

A sports-music-dance-barbecue celebration of Basque heritage, held annually since 1962 in Elko, Nev. Basque people settled in the West, largely in Nevada and Idaho, in the late 1800s, many becoming shepherds and sheep ranchers.

Participants in the festival wear the traditional red, white, and green of the Basque provinces of Spain. The men also wear the traditional Basque beret.

The festival begins on Friday with social and exhibition dancing. On Saturday there's a parade of more than 50 floats, and major contests of weightlifting, sheep hooking (sheep are hooked with a crook, dragged to a designated spot, and tied by one leg), sheepdog-working, yelling, and dancing the native *jota*. Each year, there is also a three-event contest of log chopping, weightlifting, and a strength-and-endurance event in which contestants race to pluck each of 30 beer cans (they were ears of corn in the old country) from a line and deposit them in a trash can.

Some years, when contestants from Spain are present, there are pentathlons—five-event contests that largely involve lifting, dragging, and walking with enormous weights (for example, a 1,200-pound granite slab is dragged).

On Sunday, the events wind up with a big barbecue of steak, marinated lamb, and spicy sausages called *chorizo*. Music and dancing are important parts of the festival, and *bertsolaris,* troubadours, entertain with song improvisations in the Basque language.

Another Nevada Basque festival is in Reno in July. The Gooding, Idaho, Basque club holds its annual Basque Association Picnic in July.

CONTACTS:
Elko Basque Club
P.O. Box 1321
Elko, NV 89803
775-738-9957; fax: 775-738-5525
www.elkobasque.com

SOURCES:
GdUSFest-1984, p. 112

♦ 0228 ♦ **Basset Hound Games**
Third Sunday in July

The Basset Hound games are held annually at Legion Park in Woodburn, Ore., as a way to bring together Basset Hound owners and their dogs in a day of light-hearted activities. The dogs compete in such custom-tailored Basset Hound events as longest ears, marathon napping, and the best howl. The public is welcome to view the games. The event is run by and raises money for Oregon Basset Hound Rescue, a non-profit group that fosters abandoned Basset Hounds and places them in permanent homes.

The Basset Hound Olympics were launched in 1990 by the Emerald Empire Basset Hound Fanciers as an event where their dogs could compete equally, whether they were show dogs or family pets. From the start, it benefited Basset Hound rescue efforts. It was turned over to the Oregon Basset Hound Rescue in 2007.

CONTACTS:
Oregon Basset Hound Rescue, Inc.
Box 5071
Salem, OR 97304
503-351-0649 or 360-607-9274
www.oregonbassethoundrescue.com/index.html

♦ 0229 ♦ **Bastille Day**
July 14

The Bastille was a 14th-century fortress that became a notorious state prison in Paris. An angry mob assaulted the Bastille—which had come to symbolize the French monarchy's oppression of the people—on July 14, 1789, freeing the political prisoners held there and launching the French Revolution.

Although the building itself was razed a year after the attack, the Bastille became a symbol of French independence. July 14 has been celebrated since that time in France as **Fête Nationale**, as well as in French territories in the Pacific, with parades, fireworks, and dancing in the streets. This period in French history is familiar to many through Charles Dickens's portrayal of it in *A Tale of Two Cities.*

In Tahiti and the rest of French Polynesia it is called **Tiurai** or **Heiva**, and is celebrated for most of the month. The festival includes European-type celebrations plus Polynesian competitions that include both men and women, and a play about the enthronement of a Tahitian high chief. The highlight is the nightly folklore spectacle—a competition of music and dance among groups from throughout French Polynesia who have practiced all year for the event.

See also NIGHT WATCH

CONTACTS:
The French Government Tourist Office
825 Third Ave., Fl. 29
New York, NY 10022
514-288-1904; fax: 212-838-7855
www.franceguide.com

SOURCES:
AnnivHol-2000, p. 117
BkDays-1864, vol. II, p. 59
BkHolWrld-1986, Jul 14
FolkWrldHol-1999, p. 440
HolSymbols-2009, p. 75
NatlHolWrld-1968, p. 113
OxYear-1999, p. 293

♦ 0230 ♦ **Bastille Day (Kaplan, Louisiana)**
July 14

The French-speaking town of Kaplan, Louisiana, where most of the inhabitants are descended from French Canadians (Acadians), claims to hold the only community-wide celebration of BASTILLE DAY in the United States. The celebration there on July 14 includes fireworks, amateur athletic competitions, and a "fais do-do" or Acadian street dance.

The custom of observing Bastille Day was started by Eugene Eleazer, a French immigrant who became mayor of Kaplan in 1920. With the exception of a brief interruption during World War II, the town has held its fête every year since 1906. Smaller Bastille Day celebrations are held elsewhere in Louisiana, including New Orleans and Baton Rouge, where French traditions still run strong.

CONTACTS:
Vermilion Parish Tourist Commission
1907 Veterans Memorial Dr.
P.O. Box 1106
Abbeville, LA 70511
337-898-6600
www.vermilion.org

♦ 0231 ♦ **Bastille, Festival de la**
Weekend closest to July 14

Because the storming of the BASTILLE on July 14, 1789, marked an important turning point in the history of France, members of the Club Calumet in Augusta, Maine, chose this day (or the nearest Friday, Saturday, and Sunday) to celebrate the state's French-Canadian (or Acadian) heritage. Events include entertainment by Cajun bands, French folk dancers and Maine cloggers, a huge fireworks display, and a parade through downtown Augusta.

In 1991 the festival honored 85 visitors from Paris—all members of the Sarthois Club who were in this country as part of an exchange with its sister club, Le Club Calumet. But the festival is not limited to the French or descendants of the original Acadian settlers. More than 13,000 visitors come to Augusta each year to participate in the festival. About one-fourth of Maine's current population is of Acadian descent.

See also ACADIAN FESTIVAL

CONTACTS:
Calumet Club
334 Northern Ave.
P.O. Box 110
Augusta, ME 04338
207-623-8211; fax: 207-623-3360
www.calumetclub.com

♦ 0232 ♦ **Bat Flight Breakfast**
Second Thursday in August

Carlsbad Caverns in southern New Mexico was proclaimed a national monument in 1923 not only for its geologic formations but for its teeming bat population. Carlsbad's summer colony of Mexican free-tailed bats, whose numbers vary from one hundred thousand to a million, migrates to the cave each spring. They eat, sleep, digest, communicate, mate, and raise their young while hanging upside-down. The accumulation of guano—a valuable source of fertilizer—can reach depths of up to 40 feet.

Although many visitors to the park witness the bats' spectacular outbound flight at sunset, when they leave the cave in a dense black cloud for their night's feeding in the Pecos River Valley, far fewer are there to witness their return—except those who attend the annual Bat Flight Breakfast. Started in the late 1950s by a group of park employees who wanted to encourage people to witness this natural phenomenon, the breakfast soon became an annual tradition. About 400 people arrive at the cave before sunrise on the second Thursday in August and eat sausages and scrambled eggs in their official yellow "bat breakfast hats" while they wait for the bats to return to their roosts. It is said that the bats generate an eerie sound as they rocket downward with folded wings.

When a television crew was there to film the event in 1989, the bats failed to return as expected. No one is sure how or when they got back into the cave, but 13 hours later, at sunset, they left in droves as usual.

CONTACTS:
Carlsbad Caverns National Park
3225 National Parks Hwy.
Carlsbad, NM 88220
505-785-2232; fax: 505-785-2133
www.nps.gov

♦ 0233 ♦ **Bataan Day**
April 9

A national legal holiday in the Philippines in commemoration of the disastrous World War II Battle of Bataan in 1942, in which the Philippines fell to the Japanese. It is also known as **Araw ng Kagitingan** or **Heroes Day** in the Philippines. Also remembered on this date are the 37,000 U.S. and Filipino soldiers who were captured and the thousands who died during the infamous 70-mile "death march" from Mariveles to a Japanese concentration camp inland at San Fernando. Ceremonies are held at Mt. Samat Shrine, the site of side-by-side fighting by Filipino and American troops.

CONTACTS:
Philippine Tourism Center
556 Fifth Ave.
New York, NY 10036
212-575-7915; fax: 212-302-6759
www.wowphilippines.com.ph

SOURCES:
AnnivHol-2000, p. 59

♦ 0234 ♦ **Bath International Music Festival**
Late May to early June

Located about 100 miles west of London, the city of Bath was already known for its mineral hot springs and 18th-century architecture when the idea for a music festival germinated and in 1948, a children's festival was held. Lack of funds and public interest nearly extinguished the festival over the next decade, but it gained a new spark with the appointment of violinist Yehudi MENUHIN as artistic director in 1959. During his tenure in the 1960s, the festival became an event of international scope and featured dance, theater, and not-to-be-missed parties in addition to opera and orchestral music. In subsequent years, film presentations, art exhibitions, and children's events were also part of the program.

Today, the 17-day festival presents all types of music—classical, jazz, contemporary, early, world—performed by local and international musicians and features some 150 events, including concerts, lectures, gatherings, workshops, open rehearsals, and educational programs. Festival events take place not only in many of Bath's well-preserved historic buildings, but also in the city streets and on the riverfront.

CONTACTS:
Bath Festivals
2 Church St.
Abbey Green
Bath, BA1 1NL United Kingdom
44-12-2546-2231; fax: 44-12-2544-5551
www.bathmusicfest.org.uk

SOURCES:
GdWrldFest-1985, p. 89
MusFestEurBrit-1980, p. 43
MusFestWrld-1963, p. 24

♦ 0235 ♦ **Baths of Caracalla**
First week in July to second week in August

Originally designed as a social gathering place for men in third-century Rome, the Baths of Caracalla became the unusual setting for open-air opera in 1937. Held every summer, the Bath Operas feature grand Italian operas such as Giuseppe Verdi's *Aida*, which are produced by the Rome Opera Company in lavish style. Ballet performances produced by local and international dance companies are also on the program. The events take place in the evening on one of the world's largest stages—100 feet long and 162 feet wide. While the acoustics are far from ideal, more than 10,000 spectators generally fill the bleachers to enjoy this one-of-a-kind musical extravaganza.

CONTACTS:
Italian Government Tourist Board
630 Fifth Ave., Ste. 1565
New York, NY 10111
212-245-5618; fax: 212-586-9249
www.italiantourism.com

SOURCES:
MusFestEurBrit-1980, p. 113

♦ 0236 ♦ Battle of Britain Day
September 15

In England, September 15, 1940, is remembered as the day of the biggest daylight bombing raid of Britain by the German Luftwaffe. The German air attacks had begun in June 1940, and beginning September 7 bombs rained on London for 57 consecutive nights. The Royal Air Force (RAF), while greatly outnumbered, had a secret advantage—radar—and the early-warning chain gave RAF pilots a half-hour's notice of German planes taking off from France. The Luftwaffe was finally defeated in April 1941, ending the first extended battle ever fought for control of the air. Winston Churchill, in a speech in August 1940, was referring to the RAF pilots when he said, "Never in the field of human conflict was so much owed by so many to so few."

Today the RAF, as well as civilian aviation organizations, commemorate the anniversary with air displays of various kinds.

CONTACTS:
Royal Air Force Museum
Grahame Park Way
London, NW9 5LL United Kingdom
44-20-8205-2266
www.rafmuseum.org.uk

SOURCES:
AnnivHol-2000, p. 155
OxYear-1999, p. 374

♦ 0237 ♦ Battle of Flowers (Jersey, Channel Islands)
Second Thursday in August

First held in 1902 as part of the celebration honoring the coronation of Edward VII and Queen ALEXANDRA, the **Jersey Battle of Flowers** takes place on Jersey in the British Channel Islands every August. It begins with a parade of floats covered in flowers, many of which are quite elaborate and take

months to prepare. In past years, floats have included a working windmill and large birds made completely out of flowers. Another popular theme is significant events in the island's history, including the 1871 Battle of Jersey. Award-winning floats in 2000 included Shangri-La, Alien Invasion, and Lord of the Rings. In addition, each year there is a special float for Miss Battle, the queen of the event.

Spectators no longer engage in a flower-throwing melee after the parade. These days the first event is the town parade two days before the battle, which exposes the year's exhibits to the public for the first time. Then the "battle" consists of a competition for the finest floats. Finally, a moonlight parade Friday night displays the floats with their illuminations and concludes with a fireworks finale.

CONTACTS:
The Jersey Battle of Flowers (Events) Ltd.
Meadow Bank
St Lawrence, Jersey JE3 1EE United Kingdom
44-15-3473-0178; fax: 44-15-3476-8985
www.battleofflowers.com

SOURCES:
AnnivHol-2000, p. 147
GdWrldFest-1985, p. 98

♦ 0238 ♦ Battle of Flowers (Vienna, Austria)
Summer

The Battle of Flowers is the culmination of a huge flower festival in the capital city of Vienna, Austria. Hundreds of floats are elaborately decorated with flowers, often to symbolize a particular aspect of Austrian history or culture. Sometimes they re-create entire scenes from Austrian operettas or ballets. The people of Vienna dress up in their best clothes and hats—similar to what Americans do on EASTER—to watch the parade, which is reviewed by government officials and the leaders of various cultural organizations.

Similar "Battles of Flowers" are held in other Austrian cities, such as Linz, Salzburg, and Innsbruck. A particularly famous one is held on a lake in south Upper Austria known as the Traun See, where barges and boats, rather than floats, are decorated with flowers.

CONTACTS:
Hans Christian Andersen Festival
Store Klaus 16
Odense N, DK-5270 Denmark
45-36-59-44-464
www.hcandersenfestspil.dk

♦ 0239 ♦ Battle of Germantown, Reenactment of
First Saturday in October

In October of 1777, George WASHINGTON's battle strategy to recapture Philadelphia from the British called for an assault on the little community of Germantown to the northwest of the city. The British soldiers took refuge in a new stone house, Cliveden, that had just been built by Benjamin Chew. Although the house was pounded by cannon balls, the stone walls withstood the assault and Washington's men were eventually forced to retreat. The thick fog proved to be a decisive factor, hindering the movements of Washington's soldiers at a point where they appeared to be on the verge of winning. Although the Americans were defeated, the Battle of Germantown was considered a moral victory, especially when it was followed two weeks later by the victory of General Horatio Gates at Saratoga.

Since the early 1970s, there has been a reenactment of Washington's defeat by the British in Germantown, now a suburb of Philadelphia, on the first Saturday in October. British and American troops stage a mock battle from house to house. At Cliveden, which now belongs to the National Trust for Historic Preservation, visitors can still see the scars left by American bullets.

CONTACTS:
Cliveden of the National Trust
6401 Germantown Ave.
Philadelphia, PA 19144
215-848-1777
www.cliveden.org

SOURCES:
Battle of Lexington and Concord *See* **Patriots' Day**

◆ 0240 ◆ **Battle of New Orleans Day**
January 8

When 5,400 British soldiers attacked near the Chalmette plantation outside New Orleans on January 8, 1815, they were met by a ragtag army of militiamen, sailors, and pirates fighting from behind barricades. The defending U.S. troops were led by General Andrew JACKSON, whose stunning victory—the British suffered some 2,000 casualties, while the Americans lost only eight men—made him a national hero.

This day is no longer as widely celebrated as it was before the Civil War, but it remains a legal holiday in Louisiana, where it is also known as **Jackson Day** or, in honor of Jackson's nickname, as **Old Hickory's Day**. The battlefield is located in Jean Lafitte National Historic Park, which sponsors commemorations and hosts living history encampments during the second weekend in January each year.

CONTACTS:
National Park Service, Chalmette Battlefield
419 Decatur St.
New Orleans, LA 70130
504-589-3882; fax: 504-589-3851
www.nps.gov

SOURCES:
AmerBkDays-2000, p. 36
AnnivHol-2000, p. 6
DictDays-1988, pp. 9, 61, 84
FolkAmerHol-1999, p. 41
OxYear-1999, pp. 29, 36

◆ 0241 ◆ **Battle of Olustee Reenactment**
Weekend in mid-February

The Battle of Olustee Reenactment commemorates the largest battle in Florida during the Civil War. A Confederate victory, the Battle of Olustee (also known as the Battle of Ocean Pond) was fought on February 20, 1864, and a reenactment has taken place on a February weekend each year since 1977.

Knowing that Union soldiers were on the way to secure strategic positions in northeast Florida, Confederate troops fortified a highly defensible position about 10 miles west of Lake City. They occupied a narrow, forested area of dry land with an impassable swamp on one side and a lake on the other. When Union soldiers attacked, the Confederates were able to repel them, though both armies suffered staggering casualties. Each side had about 5,000 men in the battle, but Union losses were heaviest, with 203 killed, 1,152 wounded, and 506 missing. Confederate casualties totaled 93 killed, 847 wounded, and 6 missing.

The Battle of Olustee is also known for the participation of the 54th Massachusetts Regiment, one of the most famous African-American fighting units in the war and the one represented in the film *Glory*. However, other black regiments also took part in the Battle of Olustee, including the 8th United States Colored Troops of Pennsylvania and the 35th United States Colored Troops of North Carolina. Noting the participation of black fighting units in the original battle and its reenactment, Blue/Grey Army, Inc., which sponsors the event, emphasizes that the reenactment and festival are not intended to glorify war or the Confederacy. Rather, through these events the organizers hope to honor the memory of the soldiers who participated on both sides during the Civil War, to encourage the study of local history, and to make known the horror of war. The sponsors state that war "is not something we celebrate, but it is something we should remember."

The reenactment has expanded over the years to include a weekend street festival in Lake City. Associated events include a beauty pageant, history displays and lectures, a music festival, an arts and crafts fair, Blue-Grey 5-K and 1 Mile Fun Runs, and a Blue/Grey Square Dance. Saturday morning features the Olustee Civil War Parade, with hundreds of participants in period costumes representing all facets of life during the Civil War. Descendants of the battle also participate. The Battle Reenactment, with about 2,000 reenactors, is the largest annual Civil War reenactment in the Southeast. It takes place at Olustee Battlefield State Park on Sunday afternoon before an audience of as many as 50,000 spectators.

CONTACTS:
Blue-Grey Army, Inc.
P.O. Box 2224
Lake City, FL 32056-2224
386-755-1097
www.olusteefestival.com

Olustee Battlefield Historic State Park
P.O. Box 40
Olustee, FL 32072
386-758-0400
www.floridastateparks.org/olustee

Olustee Battlefield Citizens Support Organization
P. O. Box 382
Glen St. Mary, FL 32040
battleofolustee.org

SOURCES:
AAH-2007, p. 45

♦ 0242 ♦ **Bawming the Thorn Day**
Saturday nearest Midsummer Day, June 24

This is the day on which people in Appleton, Cheshire, England, celebrate the centuries-old tradition of bawming the thorn, or decorating the hawthorn tree that stands in the center of their town. Children dance around the tree after draping its branches with flowers, flags, and ribbons. According to local legend, the original hawthorn tree was planted there in 1125 by a returning crusader. It was thought to have been a cutting from the hawthorn allegedly planted in Glastonbury, England, by Joseph of Arimathea, who buried Jesus after his crucifixion.

CONTACTS:
Cheshire County Council
Duke St.
Chester, Cheshire CH1 1RL United Kingdom
44-12-4460-2574; fax: 44-12-4460-3812
www.cheshire.gov.uk

SOURCES:
BkHolWrld-1986, Jun 29

♦ 0243 ♦ **Bayfest**
Weekend in late September

In Corpus Christi, Texas, Bayfest began in 1976 as a multicultural celebration that provided entertainment for families while also raising money for local charities, which is still its focus today. Festival entertainment includes tejano, mariachi, and other Latin music; rock and roll and country music; a carnival; dancing; and games. Bayfest is held on a beach bordering the Gulf of Mexico and also features ethnic and carnival foods, arts and crafts, fireworks, and the Bayfest Run.

CONTACTS:
Bayfest Inc.
P.O. Box 1858
Corpus Christi, TX 78403
361-887-0868; fax: 361-887-9773
www.bayfesttexas.com

SOURCES:
LatinoLife-1995, p. 39

♦ 0244 ♦ **Bayou Classic**
Thanksgiving weekend

The State Farm Bayou Classic is a sporting event held annually in New Orleans, La., that combines the intensity of a great college football rivalry with the pageantry and celebratory atmosphere of a cultural festival. The Bayou Classic centers on the annual football game between two historically black universities: Grambling State University of Grambling, Louisiana, and Southern University of Baton Rouge. Held each year since 1974, the Classic attracts more than 70,000 football fans to the Louisiana Superdome on Thanksgiving weekend to see the nationally televised game between the Grambling Tigers and the Southern Jaguars.

In addition to such football traditions as tailgate parties and a coaches' luncheon, the Bayou Classic includes numerous fraternity and sorority parties, a battle of the marching bands, a Greek step show, a quiz bowl competition, a gospel music brunch, an employment fair, college fair, fan festival, golf tournament, and community service activity, including building a children's playground in New Orleans one recent year. Altogether more than 200,000 people participate in the Bayou Classic football game and related educational and social events.

CONTACTS:
State Farm Bayou Classic
www.statefarmbayouclassic.com

Grambling State University
403 Main St.
Grambling, LA 71245
800-569-4714 or 318-247-3811
www.gram.edu

SOURCES:
AAH-2007, p. 159
HolSymbols-2009, p. 77

♦ 0245 ♦ **Bayreuth Festival**
Late July through end of August

An internationally famous month-long festival in Bayreuth (pronounced buy-ROIT), Bavaria, Germany, celebrating the music of Richard Wagner. It features six to eight Wagner operas and is usually sold out a year in advance. Performances are in the Festspielhaus (Festival Theater) designed by Wagner himself specifically for the presentation of his works. The festival was launched with the first complete performance of the four-opera *Der Ring des Nibelungen* (The Ring of the Nibelung), triumphantly presented in the new Festspielhaus on Aug. 13, 14, 16, and 17, 1876. Except for wartime interruptions, the festival has been staged every year since then. Wagner had moved to Bayreuth in 1874, and lived in the house he called *Wahnfried* (Peace from Delusion) until his death in 1883. During those years, he composed his last work, the sacred festival drama *Parsifal*, and it was produced at Bayreuth in 1882. The festival was directed after Wagner's death by his wife Cosima; their son Seigfried took over as director in 1930, and grandsons Wieland and Wolfgang Wagner revived it after World War II, in 1951.

CONTACTS:
Bayreuther Festspiele GmbH
Festival Hill 1-2
Bayreuth, 95445 Germany
49-921-787-80
www.bayreuther-festspiele.de

SOURCES:
GdWrldFest-1985, p. 83
MusFestEurBrit-1980, p. 97
MusFestWrld-1963, p. 47

♦ 0246 ♦ **Be Kind to Animals Week**
First full week in May

The oldest week of its kind in the United States, Be Kind to Animals Week was first observed in 1915. Established by Dr. William O. Stillman, the leader of the American Humane Association at the time, this week was dedicated to helping animals and to publicizing the achievements of the nation's humane societies.

Today, Be Kind to Animals Week is observed by thousands of animal shelters across the country. They host special media events, promote education on the humane treatment of animals, and try to remind people of the debt that humankind owes to both wild and domestic animals.

CONTACTS:
American Humane Association
63 Inverness Dr. E
Englewood, CO 80112
303-792-9900; fax: 303-792-5333
www.americanhumane.org

♦ 0247 ♦ **Beaches, Day of the (Día de las Playas)**
December 8

In Uruguay, December 8 is known as the Day of the Beaches because it marks the official opening of the beach season on the coast known as the "Uruguayan Riviera." There are ceremonies in which a priest blesses the waters, sailing regattas, horseback riding competitions, and an international shooting contest at Carrasco. Sometimes this day is referred to as **Family Day** or **Blessing of the Waters Day**.

CONTACTS:
Uruguay Tourist Bureau
1077 Ponce de Leon Blvd.
Coral Gables, FL 33134
877-878-4829 or 305-443-9764; fax: 305-443-7802
www.turismo.gub.uy

SOURCES:
FiestaTime-1965, p. 178

♦ 0248 ♦ **Bear Society Dance**
Varies

This ritual dance is performed by the Bear Society, an Iroquois Indian group known for its ability to cure the victims of "bear sickness," a type of mental illness of which the victim is aware, but which he or she cannot control. The illness is caused by the bear spirit, and ceremonial foods that would please the spirit are an important part of the ritual. The dance is held in the patient's home or in the longhouse. As part of the ritual, members of the society blow berry juice on the patient.

There are actually two dances: one is a curing rite, and the other can be performed at any time, even without a patient present. The first consists of slow chants, a round dance with a stomp step, and finally the pairing of dancers. Patients cured by the ritual become members of the society.

SOURCES:
DictFolkMyth-1984, p. 724
EncyNatAmerRel-2001, p. 15

♦ 0249 ♦ **Beargrease (John) Sled Dog Marathon**
First week in February

This annual dog-sledding festival commemorates John Beargrease (1861-1911), the son of a Chippewa chief who was known for delivering mail by sled dog along the North Shore of Minnesota from 1887 to 1900. Beargrease was often the only connection to the outside world for people living in this remote area in the latter part of the 19th century. For his skill in negotiating the shifting ice on Lake Superior, he was known as the "renowned pilot of Lake Superior."

The festivities begin with a mushers banquet the evening before preparations begin for the big race. The next day veterinarians make sure each dog is marathon-ready, then a cutest puppy contest rounds out the afternoon. On Race Day, opening ceremonies pay respects to John Beargrease before the mushers take off. The Marathon itself is divided into two divisions: Mid-Distance racers follow a 150-mile course, while Marathon mushers cover about 420 miles.

CONTACTS:
John Beargrease Sled Dog Marathon
P.O. Box 500
Duluth, MN 55801
218-722-7631; fax: 218-625-5302
www.beargrease.com

♦ 0250 ♦ **Befana Festival**
January 5

Sometimes referred to simply as **La Befana**, this is the TWELFTH NIGHT festival in Italy where the *Befana*, a kindly witch, plays much the same role that Santa Claus plays in the United States on CHRISTMAS EVE—giving toys and candy to the children who have been good and a lump of coal or a pebble to those who haven't. According to legend, the Befana was sweeping her house when the Magi, or Three Wise Men, stopped by on their way to Bethlehem. But when they asked her to accompany them, she said she was too busy. She later changed her mind and set out to find the Christ Child, but she got lost. Every year la Befana passes through Italy in her continuing search for the *Gésu Bambino*, leaving gifts for children.

The festival begins on EPIPHANY EVE, when the Befana is supposed to come down the chimney on her broom to leave gifts in children's stockings. In Rome, the Piazza Navona is thronged with children and their parents, who shop for toys and exchange greetings. Bands of young people march around, blowing on cardboard trumpets, and the noise level in the square can be deafening. In the countryside, bonfires are often lit on Epiphany Eve, and people try to predict the weather by watching the direction in which the smoke blows.

See also DÍA DE LOS TRES REYES

SOURCES:
BkFest-1937, p. 178
DictFolkMyth-1984, p. 131
EncyChristmas-2003, p. 50
FestSaintDays-1915, p. 16
FestWestEur-1958, p. 87
FolkWrldHol-1999, p. 17
OxYear-1999, p. 22

♦ 0251 ♦ **Beiderbecke (Bix) Memorial Jazz Festival**
Third weekend in July

Leon "Bix" Beiderbecke (1903-1931) was an American jazz cornetist, pianist, and composer whose unique style on the horn and tragically short life made him a Jazz Age legend at the age of 28. But it wasn't until 1971, on the 40th anniversary of Bix's death, that the seeds of an annual festival commemorating him were planted. That year, Bill Donahoe's Bix Beiderbecke Memorial Jazz Band arrived in Bix's hometown of Davenport, Iowa, to pay tribute to him by playing at his gravesite and elsewhere in the city. An enthusiatic response and desire to preserve Bix's memory and music led to the formation of the Bix Beiderbecke Memorial Society, which established the first official festival in 1972. This annual, four-day jazz festival, popularly known as the "Bix Bash," features concerts by some of the world's best jazz bands as well as the Bix Jazz Society Youth Band, tours of Bix's boyhood home, a Bix Jazz Brunch on Sunday, a jazz liturgy at the First Presbyterian Church, and a concert at Bix's grave in Oakdale Memorial Gardens. Many of the concerts are held at LeClaire Park on the banks of the Mississippi River, where musicians perform in a bandshell, as well as indoor venues.

CONTACTS:
Bix Beiderbecke Memorial Society
P.O. Box 3688
Davenport, IA 52808
888-249-5487 or 563-324-7170; fax: 563-326-1732
www.bixsociety.org

SOURCES:
MusFestAmer-1990, p. 192

♦ 0252 ♦ **Beijing Opera Festival**
Early December, held triennially

The traditional form of theatre known as Beijing Opera, or Peking Opera, is a national treasure in China. The Beijing Opera Festival is the country's most recognized event featuring this dramatic genre, which distinguishes itself from other opera styles with its elaborate costumes and martial arts displays. Scheduled every three years and always in a different city, the two-week festival is co-organized by the Ministry of Culture, local government, and the Beijing Opera Art Foundation.

About 20 shows are typically featured on each program, and festival organizers bestow awards in various categories to the best productions. The festival also offers workshops in addition to staging performances.

In 1995, the inaugural festival was held in Tianjin, located in northeast China. After the 1998 festival in Beijing, the Ministry of Culture decided to move the next two festivals to southern cities in the hope of fostering greater interest in the region, which has been less engaged historically with Beijing Opera than the northern Chinese.

CONTACTS:
Ministry of Culture
Jia 83

Donganmen Bei Jie
Dongcheng Qu
Beijing 100722 China

♦ 0253 ♦ **Beiteddine Festival**
July and August

The Beiteddine Festival, held in a magnificent 200-year-old palace in this town in the Chouf region of Lebanon, has presented world-class offerings in the arts since 1985. Organizers defied the struggles of Lebanon's civil war by staging this celebration of human culture. Many performers are Lebanese, but artists from around the world also are invited. The 2001 festival, for example, included a concert by Elton John, a production of Victor Hugo's *Notre Dame de Paris*, and Turkish folk musician Kudsi Erguner, as well as a performance by the popular Lebanese singer Fairouz.

CONTACTS:
Beiteddine Festival
Starco Ctr., Bloc C, Fl.4
Beirut, Lebanon
961-1-373430; fax: 961-1-373440
www.beiteddine.org

♦ 0254 ♦ **Belarus Independence Day**
July 3

After nearly 70 years under Soviet rule, Belarus declared its sovereignty on July 27, 1990, and issued its declaration of independence on August 25, 1991. Belarus officially became autonomous on December 26, 1991, as did other former Soviet republics. On April 2, 1997, however, a treaty was signed to unite Belarus with the Russian Federation. Thus, Belarus reverted to its earlier Independence Day, July 3, which commemorated the liberation of the capital, Minsk, from German occupation in 1944. April 2 is another public, though working, holiday in Belarus, Unification Day of the Peoples of Belarus and Russia.

CONTACTS:
Belarus Embassy
1619 New Hampshire Ave. N.W.
Washington, D.C. 20009
202-986-1604; fax: 202-986-1805
www.belarusembassy.org

♦ 0255 ♦ **Belfast Festival**
Late October through early November

A two-week-long arts event held annually since 1962, the Belfast Festival is organized primarily by Queen's University in Belfast. The festival offers a broad selection of artistic genres, including classical music, jazz, comedy, literature, and popular music. The festival program features local and international artists. Luminaries who have appeared throughout the festival's long history include comedian Rowan Atkinson, musicians Jimi Hendrix and Dizzy Gillespie, and actors Laurence Olivier and Billy Connolly.

Founded by Michael Emmerson, a Queen's University student, the festival started as a humble affair but continued to expand over the decades, eventually becoming Northern Ireland's premier arts festival.

By 2006, the program featured 36 venues and audience totals of more than 100,000 people. Around that time, government funding for the festival began to decline. The Save the Belfast Festival Campaign, launched by the *Belfast Telegraph,* successfully recruited a new major funding source and ensured the festival would remain in operation for at least the next few years.

CONTACTS:
Queen's University Belfast
University Rd.
Belfast, Northern Ireland BT7 1NN UK
www.belfastfestival.com

♦ 0256 ♦ **Belgian-American Days**
August

Ghent, Minnesota, named after the famous city in Belgium, is the state's only predominantly Belgian community. The annual Belgian-American Days celebration gives the descendants of Ghent's original Belgian settlers an opportunity to compete in the traditional Belgian sport of *rolle bolle,* which is similar to lawn bowling or Italian bocci. The game is played on bare ground or grass, with stakes set 30 feet apart. The eight-pound disc called a *bolle* is rolled from one stake to the other. The bolle that lands closest to the stake scores. Teams usually consist of three players, and the first team to score eight points wins the game. As many as 300 bollers participate in the championship round held during the event.

Although rolle bolle is the biggest attraction, the festival also features a softball tournament, parades, a firemen's dinner, and a street dance.

CONTACTS:
Marshall Area Chamber of Commerce
317 W Main St.
Marshall, MN 56258
507-532-4484; fax: 507-532-4485
www.marshall-mn.org

♦ 0257 ♦ **Belgium Independence Day**
July 21

This public holiday, also known as the Belgium **National Day**, commemorates Belgium's independence from the Netherlands on July 21, 1831. Belgians had struggled against their rulers for 15 years. A revolt began in 1830, and the next year, the state of Belgium was formed and King Leopold I (1790-1865) was made its first king.

Belgians sing "La Brabançonne," the national anthem, and observe their independence with festivities, especially in the capital city of Brussels.

CONTACTS:
Belgian Federal Government Online
3330 Garfield St. N.W.
Washington, D.C. 20008

202-333-6900; fax: 202-338-4960
www.belgium.be

SOURCES:
AnnivHol-2000, p. 121
NatlHolWrld-1968, p. 119

♦ 0258 ♦ **Belize Independence Day**
September 21

On September 21, 1981, Belize gained independence from Britain. Belize was formerly known as British Honduras and had been internally self-governing since 1965.

Independence Day is a national public holiday in Belize. Celebrations begin more than a week before the 21st with dances, pageants, sporting events, and concerts, and culminate with parades and patriotic ceremonies.

CONTACTS:
Belize Tourist Board
64 Regent St.
P.O. Box 325
Belize City, Belize
501-227-2420; fax: 501-227-2423
www.travelbelize.org

SOURCES:
AnnivHol-2000, p. 158

♦ 0259 ♦ **Belize National Day**
September 10

A public holiday in Belize commemorating the Battle of St. George's Caye, fought in 1798 between the Spanish and the English over possession of the area. English loggers had settled in what is now Belize in the early 17th century. British pirates used to hide in the cays there waiting for opportunities to plunder passing Spanish ships. It is also known as **St. George's Caye Day**. Numerous festivities take place on the days leading up to the holiday, including a grand carnival parade.

CONTACTS:
Belize Tourist Board
64 Regent St.
P.O. Box 325
Belize City, Belize
011-501-227-2420; fax: 011-501-227-2423
www.travelbelize.org

SOURCES:
AnnivHol-2000, p. 152

♦ 0260 ♦ **Bella Coola Midwinter Rites**
November-February

The *kusiut* is a traditional masked dancing society of the Bella Coola, Kimsquit, and other Indian tribes of coastal British Columbia. The society performed dramatic curing dances during the midwinter ceremonial season, which began with the opening rite in November and ended in February. Most involved feats of juggling as well as masked mime. Some were used by initiates to prove that they had received a supernatural "call" to join the society.

Among the more frightening was the series of five *kusiotem* dances: the stomach-cutting dance, the beheading dance, the drowning dance, the burning dance, and the fungus dance. All involved elaborate masks and deception. The beheading dance, for example, was simulated with a false head, and the drowning dance used a dummy and a trap door.

Nowadays membership in the kusiut is open to all men, though the number of spectators is decreasing. As a result, the society's status is deteriorating.

SOURCES:
DictFolkMyth-1984, pp. 596, 946, 963, 1186
EncyNatAmerRel-2001, p. 333

♦ 0261 ♦ **Belmont Stakes**
June; fifth Saturday after Kentucky Derby

The final race of the Triple Crown of horseracing, the Belmont Stakes is traditionally run on the fifth Saturday after the KENTUCKY DERBY (the third Saturday after the PREAKNESS STAKES). Founded in 1867, it takes place at the Belmont Park Race Track in western Nassau County on Long Island, named for August Belmont, a well-to-do German who played an important role in establishing horseracing in New York.

The horse that sweeps the Triple Crown receives a $1 million bonus in addition to the winner's share of the purses, but in years when no horse wins the Triple Crown, the bonus goes to the horse competing in all three races and scoring the highest on a 5-3-1 point system for finishing first, second, or third. The chances of a single horse winning all three races are relatively slim: in 114 years only 11 horses have managed to do it.

Many breeders pay more attention to the Belmont than they do to the other races when it comes to selecting stud prospects because they believe that in the long run, Belmont winners make better sires.

CONTACTS:
New York Racing Association
Aqueduct Racetrack, 110-00 Rockaway Blvd.
Jamaica, NY 11420
800-437-1611 or 718-641-4700; fax: 718-738-8890
www.nyra.com

♦ 0262 ♦ **Beltane**
May 1

Beltane (also spelled **Beltine** or **Beltein**) is the Celtic name for the first day of May (*see* MAY DAY), which divided the ancient Celtic year in half. It was believed that each day began with the setting of the sun the night before, so Beltane was celebrated by lighting bonfires to honor the sun god. Cattle were driven through the "Beltane fire"—or between two fires—to protect them from disease before putting them out to pasture for the new season. Sometimes people followed the same rit-

ual to forestall bad luck and to cure barrenness. Contact with the fire was symbolic of contact with the life-giving sun.

Along with LAMMAS (August 1), Hallowmas (ALL SAINTS' DAY, November 1), and CANDLEMAS (February 2), Beltane was one of the British QUARTER DAYS, or term days, when rents were due and debts were settled. The day is still observed in parts of Ireland, the Scottish Highlands, Wales, Brittany, and the Isle of Man, with most of the celebrations revolving around fire and reflecting ancient fertility rites.

See also MIDSUMMER DAY

SOURCES:
AmerBkDays-2000, p. 334
BkDays-1864, vol. I, p. 571
DictFolkMyth-1984, pp. 135, 181, 203, 304, 789
FestSaintDays-1915, p. 104
OxYear-1999, pp. 190, 205
RelHolCal-2004, p. 272

♦ 0263 ♦ **Benin Independence Day**
August 1

On August 1, 1960, Benin declared its independence from France, ending 70 years as a French colony. Independence Day is a national holiday observed throughout the country, especially in the capital city of Porto Novo.

CONTACTS:
Embassy of the Republic of Benin
2124 Kalorama Rd. N.W.
Washington, D.C. 20008
202-232-6656; fax: 202-265-1996
www.beninembassy.us

SOURCES:
AnnivHol-2000, p. 128
NatlHolWrld-1968, p. 130

♦ 0264 ♦ **Benin National Vodoun Day (Traditional Religions Day)**
January 10

Vodoun is an ancient, African, pantheistic religion. When it was brought to the Americas by African slaves, it was blended with elements of Christianity into what is known as "voodoo." The present African country of Benin, situated on the former kingdom of Dahomey, is known as a center of Vodoun culture, and the city of Ouidah is the home of Vodoun's Supreme Chief, Daagbo Hounon.

Vodoun was scorned and suppressed by European colonists in Dahomey. It continued to be practiced, often in secret, even by those indigenous people who outwardly accepted conversion to Christianity. Benin gained independence in 1960, but Vodoun continued to be banned during the 18 years Mathieu Kerekou was at the head of the government. He found the Vodoun practices and rites unacceptable to the socialist philosophy of his regime.

Kerekou lost power in 1991, and Benin's new democratic government soon showed its respect for Vodoun, which is still practiced by an estimated 65% of the country's population. January 10 was proclaimed National Vodoun Day/Traditional Religions Day, and Vodoun and other traditional religions were given officially recognized status, along with Christianity and Islam. The government, in conjunction with UNESCO, sponsored an event called "Ouidah 92: The First International Festival of Vodoun Arts and Cultures." Works of art were commissioned to honor the ancient kingdom of Dahomey and other aspects of Benin's history and traditions. Because the port of Ouidah was a major point of departure for slave ships, many of the works concerned the slave trade. They are permanently installed throughout the city and are focal points for the celebration of National Vodoun Day/Traditional Religions Day in Ouidah.

The day is celebrated throughout Benin, but most elaborately in Ouidah. There are various processions, Vodoun rituals, dances, and even an international film festival held in conjunction with the holiday. The celebration's central activity, however, is the re-enactment of the journey from the slave auction block in the center of town to the ships in the harbor. Led by the Supreme Chief of Vodoun, followers travel the three-kilometer "Route of the Slaves," pausing to pray and make offerings to the gods and ancestors at the memorials that have been erected along the way. The final stop is a sculpture at the water's edge, called "Gate of No Return." After reaching the end of the route, participants can enjoy music, food vendors, and artists in town and on the beach. Many people of African descent from North and South America visit Benin to make this pilgrimage along the Route of the Slaves.

CONTACTS:
Embassy of Benin
2124 Kalorama Rd. N.W.
Washington, D.C. 20008
202-232-6656; fax: 202-232-1196
www.beninembassy.us

♦ 0265 ♦ **Bennington Battle Day**
August 16

During the Revolutionary War, Colonel Seth Warner and 350 of his Green Mountain Boys, a group of soldiers from Vermont, played a vital role in defeating the British forces who had come to capture the American supply depot at Bennington, a town in southern Vermont near the New York border. The anniversary of the fighting that took place along the Walloomsac River on August 16, 1777, is a legal holiday in Vermont, and a 306-foot tower has been erected in the town of Old Bennington, two miles west of Bennington proper. A statue of Seth Warner stands nearby. Across the state border in New York's Rensselaer County, the Bennington Battlefield State Park includes the site where the heaviest fighting took place.

The Bennington Battle Monument State Historic Site hosts historic reenactments and displays on the weekend nearest August 16.

CONTACTS:
Vermont State Historic Sites
Vermont Division for Historic Preservation

National Life Bldg.
P.O. Box 20
Montpelier, VT 05620
800-837-6668 or 802-828-3211; fax: 802-828-3206
www.historicvermont.org

SOURCES:
AmerBkDays-2000, p. 589
AnnivHol-2000, p. 137
DictDays-1988, p. 11

♦ 0266 ♦ **Bera Festival**
August-September; last Thursday of the Hindu month of Bhadrapada

Wherever there is a large body of water in Bengal, a region encompassing eastern India and Bangladesh, agricultural communities are likely to celebrate the Bera Festival. Holy men known as fakirs supervise the preparation of ornately decorated floats (*bera* means "raft" or "float" in Hindi), which are constructed in honor of Khaja Khizir, the patron saint of the waters. The festival is essentially a Muslim tradition, although it draws from Hindu regional customs. It takes place during the Bangla month of Bhadra, which falls sometime between August and September.

The ancient raft custom existed before the 13th century, but it was only with the arrival of Turkish rulers during that time that the celebration shifted its focus on Khaja Khizir. At that point *nawabs*, or viceroys, of regional cities like Murshidabad and Dhaka became followers of the saint and decreed that the raft festival honor him.

The centerpiece of the festival, the raft, is made out of local banana trunks that are lashed together to make a square platform. On top of the platform are placed 20-foot boats. The float is then decorated with flags, flowers, and other trappings, and finally is pushed into the water to be received by Khaja Khizir.

CONTACTS:
Bangladesh Parjatan Corporation, National Tourism Organization
233 Airport Rd.
Tejgaon
Dhaka 1215 Bangladesh
www.bangladeshtourism.gov.bd

♦ 0267 ♦ **Berchtold's Day**
January 2

In Switzerland, the day after NEW YEAR'S DAY is known as **Berchtoldstag** and is celebrated primarily by children. Groups of playmates organize parties that feature nut eating and nut games followed by singing and folk dancing. A popular game is the building of "hocks" composed of four nuts placed close together with a fifth balanced on top. The children begin gathering and stockpiling nuts for Berchtold's Day festivities early in the fall.

SOURCES:
AnnivHol-2000, p. 3
BkFest-1937, p. 316

♦ 0268 ♦ Bergen International Festival
12 days from late May to early June

The Bergen International Festival is the major cultural event in Norway, and features more than 100 events in music, drama, folklore, opera, ballet, and the visual arts. Most of the musical events are held in Bergen's Viking Castle, Haakon's Hall (built in 1250), at the Grieg Concert Hall, at Edvard Grieg's home (known as "Troldhaugen"), and at Lysoen, the island home of composer and violinist Ole Bull. It was, in fact, Edvard Grieg—the composer and founder of the Norwegian nationalist school of music—who originated the idea for a musical festival and who first sponsored such a festival back in 1898. But the Bergen International Festival as it exists today didn't really get started until 1952. Although the primary attraction is music—ranging from classical to jazz, new music from around the world, organ concerts, military band performances, and folklore opera—children's programs, literary events, and art exhibits are featured as well.

CONTACTS:
Bergen International Festival Foundation
Sentrum
P.O. Box 183
Bergen, N-5804 Norway
47-5521-0630; fax: 47-5521-0640
www.fib.no/index_e.asp?ID=3&segment=2

SOURCES:
GdWrldFest-1985, p. 144
IntlThFolk-1979, p. 286
MusFestEurBrit-1980, p. 126
MusFestWrld-1963, p. 186

♦ 0269 ♦ Bering Sea Ice Golf Classic
Third Saturday in March

This golfing challenge, played on a six-hole course with bright orange golf balls, takes place on the frozen Bering Sea off Nome, Alaska, at a time when the winds can be gale-strength. Par is 41, but winners have claimed scores as low as 23. Entry fees benefit the Lions Club. The tournament, not a wholly serious affair, coincides with the final days of the IDITAROD TRAIL SLED DOG RACE that starts about the first of March and ends in Nome about two weeks later.

CONTACTS:
Nome Convention and Visitors Bureau
P.O. Box 240 H-P
Nome, AK 99762
907-443-6624; fax: 907-443-5832
www.nomealaska.org

♦ 0270 ♦ Bermuda College Weeks
March-April

College Weeks began as **Rugby Weeks** in the 1950s, when Ivy League rugby teams came to the island of Bermuda to spend their spring holidays and compete against Bermudian and British teams. But parties and socializing soon took precedence over the rugby competition, and College Weeks became a time for young people from colleges and universities all over the United States to meet in Bermuda and get an early start on the summer season.

The Bermuda government organizes and pays for all of the activities that are scheduled during this period, issuing courtesy cards that entitle college students free admission to everything from a "Get Acquainted" dance at one of the major hotels to beach parties, boat cruises, and steel band concerts. Scores of moped-riding college students take advantage of the island's hospitality, making Bermuda one of the most popular SPRING BREAK destinations.

CONTACTS:
Bermuda Department of Tourism
675 3rd Ave., 20th Fl.
New York, NY 10017
800-223-6106 or 212-818-9800; fax: 212-983-5289
www.bermudatourism.com

SOURCES:
GdWrldFest-1985, p. 22

♦ 0271 ♦ Bermuda Day
May 24

Bermuda Day, formerly COMMONWEALTH DAY, is a public holiday and the highlight of Bermuda Heritage Month. Since 1979, there are a variety of cultural activities during May, including historical exhibits, musical concerts, and thanksgiving services in area churches. Festivities on May 24 include a parade that ends up in the middle of a festival at Bernard Park in Hamilton. It is also a popular day for Bermudians to hit the beaches. Runners participate in a marathon race, and there are also races for cyclists and skaters. May 24 is the beginning of dinghy-racing season—about every other Sunday boaters race in St. George's Harbor.

CONTACTS:
Bermuda Department of Tourism
675 3rd Ave., 20th Fl.
New York, NY 10017
800-223-6106 or 212-818-9800; fax: 212-983-5289
www.bermudatourism.com

♦ 0272 ♦ Bermuda Festival
January-February

The winter season on the island of Bermuda brings on a schedule of performing arts events known as the Bermuda Festival, which began in 1976. Yehudi MENUHIN was instrumental in organizing the first festival and performed on its 20th anniversary in 1996. Offerings include theater, dance, opera, classical, and modern music performances from around the world. The 2002 Festival brought the dazzling Shanghai Circus to the island.

CONTACTS:
Bermuda Festival Ltd.
Jardine House, 33-35 Reid St.
P.O. Box HM 297
Hamilton, HM 12 Bermuda
441-295-1291; fax: 441-295-7403
www.bermudafestival.org

SOURCES:
GdWrldFest-1985, p. 22
IntlThFolk-1979, p. 50
MusFestAmer-1990, p. 157

♦ 0273 ♦ Bettara-Ichi
October 19

The annual **Pickle Market** or **Sticky-Sticky Fair** is held near the Ebisu Shrine in Tokyo, Japan, to supply people with what they will need to observe the EBISU FESTIVAL on the following day, October 20. One of the seven Shinto deities of good luck and the patron deity of tradesmen, Ebisu has a limited following in Tokyo. But the fair that is held the day before is very popular. People buy wooden images of Ebisu, good-luck tokens, and most important of all, the large, white, pickled radish known as *bettara* that is so closely identified with the fair.

The Sticky-Sticky Fair was named after the way the pickled radishes were sold. Stall keepers used to dangle them from a rope so the buyer wouldn't get his hands sticky from the malted rice in which the radishes had been pickled. People would carry them home by swinging them from their ropes, calling out "Bettara! Bettara!" so that others would make way for them. But mischievous young boys would often deliberately swing the sticky pickles around in a crowd to tease the women and girls, who were all dressed up in their holiday clothes.

CONTACTS:
Tokyo Convention & Visitors Bureau
Kasuga Business Center Bldg. 10F, 1-15-15 Nishikata
Bunkyo-ku
Tokyo, 113-0024 Japan
81-3-5840-8892; fax: 81-3-5840-8895
www.tcvb.or.jp/en/index_en.htm

SOURCES:
BkFestHolWrld-1970, p. 114
BkHolWrld-1986, Oct 19
DictFolkMyth-1984, p. 336
JapanFest-1965, p. 200

♦ 0274 ♦ Bhairava Ashtami
November-December; eighth day of the waning half of the Hindu month of Margasirsa

Among Hindus, *Bhairava* means "frightful" or "terrible." He is a manifestation of Shiva, a terrifying character who is worshipped to obtain success, prosperity, the removal of obstacles, and recovery from illness. He is often referred to as *Danda-pani* because he punishes sinners with a *danda* (staff or rod). Another of Bhairava's names is *Swaswa*, which means "he whose horse is a dog." He is often depicted accompanied by a dog or riding on one.

On Bhairava Ashtami Hindus worship Bhairava with sweets and flowers. Dogs everywhere are treated to milk, sweets, and other delicacies. At night, worshippers keep a vigil and spend the time telling stories about Bhairava. They also offer libations to their dead ancestors.

SOURCES:
Dict.Hindu-1977, p. 41
RelHolCal-2004, p. 180

♦ 0275 ♦ Bhishma Ashtami
January-February, eighth day of waxing half of Hindu month of Magha or during Hindu month of Kartika (October-November)

In Hindu mythology Bhishma was the son of King Shantanu. When his father decided he wanted to marry a beautiful young maiden named Satyavati, her parents would not permit it because it was Bhishma who was heir to the throne, and if she had sons they could not inherit the kingdom. To allow the marriage to go forward, Bhishma vowed never to marry and have children of his own, nor to accept the crown. Shantanu then married Satyavati, and she bore him two sons.

The two sons died without producing any offspring, but Satyavati had two grandchildren by a son who had been born before she married the king. Bhishma ended up raising these two and taking charge of the training of their children, who were known as the Kauravas and the Pandavas (*see also* ANANT CHATURDASHI). In the battle that was eventually fought between the two groups of offspring, Bhishma sided with the Kauravas and was so badly wounded it was said that there was barely a space of two fingers' width on his body that had not been pierced by an arrow. Since he had been allowed to choose the time of his death, he waited on his death-bed of arrows for 58 days, during which he delivered many religious discourses. He later became the model for modern ascetics who lie on nail-studded beds, and to this day is considered a great example of self-denial, loyalty, and devotion.

During the festival held in his honor, libations are offered to Bhishma with barley, sesame, flowers, and water from the sacred Ganges River.

CONTACTS:
India Tourist Office
1270 Ave. of the Americas, Ste. 1808, 18th Fl.
New York, NY 10020
800-953-9399 or 212-586-4901; fax: 212-582-3274
www.indiatouristoffice.org

SOURCES:
DictFolkMyth-1984, p. 139
RelHolCal-2004, p. 182

♦ 0276 ♦ Bianou
April

A celebration of the end of the winter season in the market town of Agadés (or Agadéz), Niger. The festivities are held for three days, and start with the sound of distant drumming and chanting of the *muezzin* calling Muslims to prayer. As people assemble, the drummers appear. Behind them come the Tuareg nomads, wearing long blue robes and spinning around in their special dance, the *guedra*. The Tuareg turbans are folded in a way that suggests a cock's comb, since the cock is the symbol of the new season. Agadés is in northern

Niger in the Sahara Desert. It was the seat of a Tuareg sultanate in the 15th century, and has been a crossroads for Fulani cattle herders, Tuareg traders, and Hausa merchants. The nomadic peoples also hold an annual gathering in Ingal town in August to take a census, at which time medical care is given by the national government.

See also CAMEL MARKET

CONTACTS:
Embassy of the Republic of Niger
2204 R St. N.W.
Washington, D.C. 20008
202-483-4224; fax: 202-483-3169
www.nigerembassyusa.org

♦ 0277 ♦ **Bible Week, National**
November, begins the Sunday before
Thanksgiving

A week devoted to encouraging people to read the Bible, in the belief that it will arouse a positive spiritual force in a world plagued with problems. National Bible Week is promoted by the National Bible Association (originally the Laymen's National Committee), a non-denominational group of businessmen founded in 1940 and devoted to the application of the Golden Rule in daily life. A huge audience listened to the NBC radio program that was broadcast to kick off the first National Bible Week scheduled for December 8-14, 1941; PEARL HARBOR had been bombed just hours before.

CONTACTS:
National Bible Association
1865 Broadway
New York, NY 10023
212-408-1390; fax: 212-408-1448
www.nationalbible.org

SOURCES:
DaysCustFaith-1957, p. 275

♦ 0278 ♦ **Big Iron Farm Show and Exhibition**
Three days in mid-September

The Upper Midwest's largest agricultural exposition, the **Big Iron** is held at the Red River Valley Fairgrounds in West Fargo, North Dakota. Established in 1981 so that farmers would have a place where they could come to view the latest innovations in farming and agricultural equipment, the Big Iron prides itself on being a business event rather than a carnival. In the words of one organizer, "We don't distract people with music, pots and pans, and dog and pony acts." However, for those who would like a little entertainment mixed in, a skid steer rodeo is held each day.

The three-day show regularly attracts more than 70,000 visitors, who come to see not only the farm equipment that is on exhibit but field demonstrations of tillage, crop-spraying, irrigation, and other equipment.

A special program for women takes place on "Ladies' Day." Seminars on such subjects as "Heirloom Art" and "The Changing Role of the Rural Woman" are offered, as well as other activities designed to inform and entertain women who participate in the running of a family farm.

CONTACTS:
Red River Valley Fair
P.O. Box 797
West Fargo, ND 58078
800-456-6408 or 701-282-2200; fax: 701-282-6909
www.bigironfarmshow.com

♦ 0279 ♦ **Big Singing**
Last Sunday in May

Big Singing in Benton, Kentucky, takes place on the last Sunday in May. The event brings together more than 100 singers trained in the tradition of shape-note singing. Together they enjoy a communal picnic lunch and spend the day singing hymns written in an almost-extinct style of musical notation called shape notes.

A book titled *The Southern Harmony and Musical Companion* increased the popularity of this kind of singing in 19th-century America, and so it is sometimes called Southern Harmony singing. The notation assigns each note a particular shape, thus aiding those who don't read music to figure out the tune. The distinctive harmonies of shape-note singing result from the fact that each part is composed of only four different notes, again making it easier for the singers to learn their part.

The Big Singing in Benton dates back to 1884. Historical records reveal that in the 1920s and 1930s over 10,000 people attended this event annually. As more people became familiar with the melodies and harmonies of American pop music, however, the popularity of shape-note singing faded away. The Benton Big Singing is currently sponsored by the Society for the Preservation of Southern Harmony Singing.

CONTACTS:
Marshall County Chamber of Commerce
17 U.S. Hwy. 68 W
Benton, KY 42025
270-527-7665
www.marshallcounty.net

♦ 0280 ♦ **Bilby Day, National**
Second Sunday of September

Bilbies are nocturnal marsupials in Australia. The animal is not well known compared to the other iconic animals of Australia, the koala and the kangaroo, a fact that conservationists hope to rectify by raising awareness on National Bilby Day. The event takes place in Charleville, a town located west of Brisbane in northeastern Australia, where the bilbies are part of a captive breeding program run by the Queensland Parks and Wildlife Service.

Founded by two local wildlife preservations, National Bilby Day was officially launched in 2005 and arrives at the tail end of Australia's Threatened Species Week. The day's activities are organized by the Save the Bilby Fund, which collects money from year-round fund-raising operations. For past observances, the fund has received a large donation from the manufacturer of a popular chocolate bilby.

A warm-up night, called the "Nocturnal" party, brings people together before the main event the next day. On Bilby Day many of the stalls that are set up cater toward youth. Booths sell bilby stuffed animals and offer face-painting and bilby ears to dress children up like the beloved critters. Choirs perform songs that shed light on the endangered animals, and wildlife experts are on hand to give talks on the current status of bilbies and other endangered species.

CONTACTS:
Save the Bilby Fund
P.O. Box 155
Charleville, Queensland 4470 Australia
www.savethebilbyfund.com

♦ 0281 ♦ **Bill of Rights Day**
December 15

The first 10 amendments to the U.S. Constitution of 1787—referred to collectively as the Bill of Rights—were ratified on December 15, 1791 (*see* CITIZENSHIP DAY). This landmark document protected American citizens from specific abuses by their government and guaranteed such basic rights as the freedom of religion, freedom of speech, and freedom of the press. In 1941 President Franklin D. ROOSEVELT designated December 15 as Bill of Rights Day and called upon Americans to observe it with appropriate patriotic ceremonies.

On December 10, 1948, the UNITED NATIONS General Assembly unanimously adopted the Universal Declaration of Human Rights, and member countries of the U.N. began to observe December 10 as Human Rights Day. In the United States, the observance extends from December 10 to December 17 and is referred to as Human Rights Week. Since it encompasses December 15, the two events are now observed together and are typically celebrated with essay contests on the importance of freedom and democracy, special radio and television shows, and speeches on the themes of personal freedom and human rights.

In Massachusetts, the week of December 8-15 has been celebrated as Civil Rights Week since 1952. It honors not only the ratification of the Bill of Rights but the adoption of the state's first code of laws, the Body of Liberties, on December 10, 1641.

CONTACTS:
U.S. Government Printing Office
732 N. Capitol St. N.W.
Washington, D.C. 20401
866-512-1800 or 202-512-1530; fax: 202-512-2104
www.gpo.gov

SOURCES:
AmerBkDays-2000, p. 831
DaysCustFaith-1957, p. 314

♦ 0282 ♦ **Billboard Latin Music Awards**
April

Since 1989, Billboard magazine has sponsored the week-long Billboard Latin Music Conference in which some 1,000 music executives, musicians, managers, composers, agents, media, and other industry insiders gather for programs, showcases, parties, and networking events.

At the end of the week, the conference presents the Billboard Latin Music Awards in over 50 categories. The awards are chosen based on record sales, radio airplay data, and position on the weekly Billboard music charts. In addition to those awards for musical performance, the conference also bestows the Spirit of Hope Award, for an artist's humanitarian work during the year, and the Lifetime Achievement Award. Since 1999, the awards ceremony has been broadcast on the Telemundo television network.

CONTACTS:
Billboard.com
www.billboard.com/bbcom/index.jsp

♦ 0283 ♦ **Billiken (Bud) Day**
Second Saturday in August

Bud Billiken is the "patron saint" of Chicago's African-American children. Created in 1923 by Robert S. Abbott, the founder of the *Chicago Daily Defender* newspaper, Bud Billiken is a symbol of things as they should be—not necessarily as they are—and his day is primarily a children's event. There is a parade held on the second Saturday in August each year that goes on for several hours, complete with marching bands, baton twirlers, floats holding celebrities and politicians, and units from the Navy, Air Force, and National Guard. The formalities end when the parade reaches Washington Park in the Grand Boulevard area of Chicago, where families have picnics and cookouts.

CONTACTS:
Chicago Convention and Tourism Bureau
2301 S. Lake Shore Dr.
Chicago, IL 60616
877-244-2246 or 312-567-8500; fax: 312-567-8533
www.choosechicago.com

♦ 0284 ♦ **Billy the Kid Pageant**
First weekend in August

It was in Lincoln, New Mexico, that the legendary American outlaw Billy the Kid (William Bonney, 1859?-1881) was brought to be hanged in 1881 after a frontier feud known as the Lincoln County War. He made his escape from a building that was once referred to as the Big Store—a combination general store, post office, billiard room, and private hotel that was later used as a courthouse. Today, the building has been restored as a state museum and courthouse.

The reenactment that takes place on the first Saturday and Sunday in August every year features Lincoln residents—many of them descendants of the individuals who originally played a part in the court proceedings and Billy's subsequent escape. First presented in 1940, the pageant involves almost everyone in town and is designed to be as historically accurate as possible. Festival activities surround Billy the Kid's "last escape" throughout the weekend to give the town a late 19th-century feeling, such as weaving and horseshoeing demonstrations, encampments, and an appearance by the Fourth Texas Cavalry.

CONTACTS:
Ruidoso Valley Chamber of Commerce
720 Sudderth Dr.
P.O. Box 698
Ruidoso, NM 88345
877-784-3676 or 505-257-7395; fax: 505-257-4693
www.ruidosonow.com

SOURCES:
AmerFestGuide-1956, p. 131

◆ 0285 ◆ Biological Diversity, International Day for
May 22

In 1994 the UNITED NATIONS declared December 29 International Day for Biological Diversity. In the year 2000 they changed the date to May 22 in order to draw more attention to the observance. They also wished to honor the May 22, 2000, signing of the Convention on Biological Diversity.

CONTACTS:
United Nations, Department of Public Information
Rm. S-1070L J, K, L
New York, NY 10017
212-963-6842; fax: 212-963-6914
www.un.org

◆ 0286 ◆ Birmingham International Festival
April

Formerly known as the Birmingham Festival of the Arts, this display of performing and visual arts honors a different nation each year, and has been held since 1951 in Birmingham, Ala. A two-week long affair, the festival celebrates the chosen country's theater, literature, history, music, customs, and food with films, lectures, exhibits, and book-and-author luncheons. Traditional dance and folk music ensembles from the honored country perform at the street festival on the third weekend in April amid food and craft booths, storytellers, artists, and musicians.

But the rest of the festival—a renowned educational program—begins in early March when teachers from around the state gather for a workshop to learn about the featured country. Then during the second and third weeks in April they hold events in schools throughout the state highlighting the country's folklore, art, history, and traditions.

CONTACTS:
Birmingham International Center
1910 3rd Ave. N, Ste. 100
Birmingham, AL 35203
205-252-7652; fax: 205-252-7656
www.birminghaminternationalcenter.org

SOURCES:
GdUSFest-1984, p. 3
MusFestAmer-1990, p. 20

◆ 0287 ◆ Bishwa Ijtema
Weekend in December–February

Bishwa Ijtema (sometimes spelled Vishwa Ijtema) brings together Muslim believers to Tongi, a northern suburb of the capital of Bangladesh, Dhaka. The three-day event is organized by the Tablighi Jamaat, a missionary organization. English speakers refer to the festival as the World Muslim Congregation (*ijtema* is Arabic for "public gathering"). After the PILGRIMAGE TO MECCA (HAJJ), it is considered one of the largest Muslim gatherings in the world.

Since 1966, Muslims from Bangladesh and other countries have congregated at Tongi's 190-acre venue along the banks of the Turag River, where they pray, discuss the Quran, and receive instruction from religious scholars. The number of people attending has increased over the decades, expanding to an estimated three million in 2008. Devotees pour into crowded boats and climb rooftops to watch the proceedings. In order to meet the language needs of various believers, translations are provided in English, Arabic, Urdu, and Bangla.

Unlike other Muslim gatherings that may have a political perspective, Bishwa Ijtema forbids political speeches and encourages prayers for harmony and world peace.

CONTACTS:
Bangladesh Parjatan Corporation, National Tourism Organization
233 Airport Rd.
Tejgaon
Dhaka 1215 Bangladesh
www.bangladeshtourism.gov.bd

◆ 0288 ◆ Bisket Jatra
April 13 or 14

The festival of the new year in Nepal, **Nava Varsa** or **Navabarsha**, is celebrated with exchanges of greetings and in some areas with ritual bathing. The most important celebration is Bisket Jatra, which means the "festival after the death of the serpent." In Bhaktapur, the new year is celebrated by parading images of gods in chariots. The main attraction of the festival is the erection of a ceremonial pole—a lingam or phallic symbol. This is a peeled tree trunk as much as 80 feet in length that is erected using bamboo and heavy ropes while crowds watch. On New Year's Day, the pole is torn down.

There is a legend behind this ceremonial pole. The daughter of the king of Bhaktapur was insatiable and demanded a new lover every night, but she left her lovers dead by morning. Then a brave prince appeared to try his luck. He managed to stay awake through the night, and saw two thread-like wisps emerging from the princess's nostrils. These wisps turned into poisonous snakes, so the prince drew his sword and killed them. Of course the prince and princess lived happily ever after. This story is recalled with the raising of the pole of Bisket Jatra.

Most holidays in Nepal are set by the lunisolar calendar, but New Year's Day is an exception and always falls in the middle of April.

CONTACTS:
Kantipur Online
Subidhanagar, Tinkune
Kathmandu, BA 8559 Nepal
977-1-4480100; fax: 977-1-4470178
www.kantipuronline.com

♦ 0289 ♦ **Black and White Ball**
Early June in odd-numbered years

This biennial ball, which began in the 1950s, has been the biggest one-night fundraising event for the arts held in the United States, drawing some 16,000 black-tie partygoers to San Francisco's Civic Center area for music, dancing, food, cocktails, and socializing—all for the benefit of the San Francisco Symphony's education and outreach programs. From 9:00 P.M. until 2:00 A.M., attendees can walk throughout the several-block area to catch an eclectic mix of live music—classical, jazz, rock and roll, blues, swing, funk, reggae, salsa, country—performed by more than 30 groups in 13 indoor and outdoor venues. They can also feast on hors d'oeuvres prepared by nearly 90 of the city's fine dining establishments. In addition to the black and white attire of the revelers, black and white decorations adorn the venues. The high-energy Bash Before the Ball, presented by the San Francisco Symphony's young professional's group, Symphonix, provides a pre-ball warm-up.

CONTACTS:
San Francisco Symphony, Davies Symphony Hall
201 Van Ness Ave.
San Francisco, CA 94102
415-552-8000; fax: 415-431-6857
www.sfsymphony.org

SOURCES:
FunAlsoRises-1998, p. 121

♦ 0290 ♦ **Black Christ, Festival of the**
October 21

There are two legends associated with the observance of the **Black Christ Festival** in Portobelo, Panama. One says that during a cholera epidemic on the Isthmus, the people found a crate floating on the water near the beach. When they brought it ashore and opened it, they discovered a statue of a black Christ. They brought it into the church and, within a few days, the cholera had completely disappeared from Portobelo, even though it continued to rage elsewhere.

The other legend concerns a ship carrying the black Christ statue from Spain to Cartagena, Colombia. The ship stopped for supplies in Portobelo, but when it attempted to leave, it was turned back five times by sudden storms. The crew finally threw the crate containing the statue overboard, but local residents rescued it and put it in a place of honor in their church. The image of the black Christ, which is made of dark brown coco-bolo wood, has been credited with everything from miraculous cures to helping the city win the national lottery.

The people of Portobelo honor their patron saint, El Jesús Nazarene, by carrying the statue in procession on a decorated platform through the city streets. Pilgrims come from all

over Panama, as they have for more than 300 years, to celebrate with folk dancing, music, and songs.

See also BLACK NAZARENE FIESTA

CONTACTS:
Embassy of Panama
2862 McGill Terr. N.W.
Washington, D.C. 20008
202-483-1407; fax: 202-483-8413
www.embassyofpanama.org

SOURCES:
GdWrldFest-1985, p. 148

♦ 0291 ♦ **Black Christ of Esquipulas, Day of the**
January 15

For many people in Central and South America, the pilgrimage to the Black Christ of Esquipulas begins well in advance of the January 15 festival. Quite a number of Indians make the journey to Esquipulas—located in southeastern Guatemala along the borders with El Salvador and Honduras—entirely on foot, and look down upon those pilgrims who travel by horseback or in cars. Many don wide-brimmed straw hats, to which they attach gray Spanish moss and *chiches* (breasts), a yellow fruit that resembles a gourd. Indians making the journey from Quezaltenango blacken their hands with the juice from a special fruit. Folk belief teaches that this act aids Christ in enduring his pain.

Prior to the Spanish Conquest, Indians came to site of modern-day Esquipulas for religious rituals and trade. Once the Spaniards arrived the chief of the local tribes, whose name was Esquipulas, comprehended that it would be useless to resist the Europeans and decided instead to cooperate with them. The Spaniards honored him by founding a town which bore his name. They also built a Roman Catholic church and hired a well-known artist to sculpt a statue of Jesus. Since the local Indians thought that all Europeans were wicked, the priests requested that the artist carve the statue from balsam wood, a wood whose color was close to that of the natives' skin. Over the 400 years that have elapsed since then, the statue has darkened to black due to constant exposure to candle smoke and incense. Many legends involving answered prayers and miraculous cures have enhanced the Black Christ's reputation.

Ceremonial sites resembling altars, built from rocks brought by pilgrims, are scattered through the hills surrounding Esquipulas. The pilgrims stop to pray at these sites in their journeys to and from Esquipulas.

Only Quiché Indians from western Guatemala—believed to be the only Indians in the country who have not intermarried with whites—can perform some of the sacred rituals associated with this pilgrimage, such as dressing the image of the Black Christ. The pilgrimage is a good example of a Christian ritual that is closely tied to the practices of an indigenous population.

CONTACTS:
Guatemala Tourist Commission
7th Ave. 1-17 Zone 4, Civic Ctr.

Guatemala City, Guatemala
502-331-3333; fax: 502-331-8893
www.guatemala.travel.com.gt

SOURCES:
FiestaTime-1965, p. 10

◆ 0292 ◆ **Black Cowboys Parade**
Saturday in October

A salute to the black cowboys who helped settle the West, held since 1975 in Oakland, Calif. Hundreds of mounted cowboys and marching bands participate in the parade, the only one of its kind in the nation. There are also arts and crafts exhibits and food booths.

CONTACTS:
Oakland Convention & Visitors Bureau
463 11th St.
Oakland, CA 94607
510-839-9000; fax: 510-839-5924
www.oaklandcvb.com

Library of Congress
101 Independence Ave. S.E.
Washington, DC 20540
202-707-5000; fax: 202-707-2076
www.loc.gov

◆ 0293 ◆ **Black Diaspora Film Festival**
February

The St. Joseph's Historic Foundation, Inc. (SJHF), was founded in 1975 to advance "cultural understanding through diverse programs that examine the experiences of Americans of African descent—locally, nationally, and globally." It is an African- American cultural and educational institution deeply rooted in the historic Hayti community of Durham, N.C.

African Americans started to settle on the southwest edge of Durham shortly after the Civil War. During the slavery era, the term "Hayti" was used by white people when referring to black settlements. This area originally provided a labor pool for Durham's tobacco warehouses, but it soon began to prosper. When Booker T. Washington visited Hayti in 1911, he described it as "a city of Negro enterprises" whose citizens were "shining examples of what a colored man may become."

The Hayti Heritage Center, which is the former St. Joseph's African Methodist Episcopal Church, sponsors the annual Black Diaspora Film Festival. The festival celebrates African-American cinema by highlighting established and emerging filmmakers and films while showcasing the contributions and uniqueness of the black artistic tradition in film. The films that are selected embody the richness of black culture and recognize universal themes that exist among all cultures.

CONTACTS:
Hayti Heritage Center
804 Old Fayetteville St.
Durham, NC 27707
919-683-1709; fax: 919-682-5869
www.hayti.org/14th-annual-black-diaspora-film-festival/#more-102

◆ 0294 ◆ **Black Friday**
Various

Black Friday usually refers either to the infamous Wall Street Panic of September 24, 1869, when Jay Gould and James Fisk tried to "corner" the gold market, or to September 19, 1873, when stock failures caused the Panic of 1873. In England, it is often used by workers to describe May 12, 1926, the day on which the General Strike was ended. It is occasionally used to refer to GOOD FRIDAY.

Shoppers and retailers in the United States sometimes refer to the day after THANKSGIVING as Black Friday because it marks the beginning of the CHRISTMAS commercial season and is traditionally a frenetic day of shopping.

SOURCES:
DictDays-1988, p. 12

◆ 0295 ◆ **Black Hills Passion Play**
June-August

One of Europe's oldest productions, the Passion Play—which recreates events during the last seven days of the life of Christ—was first presented on the American stage in 1932. It was brought to the United States from Germany by Josef Meier, who, until his retirement in 1991, continued to produce and direct the drama three nights a week from early June through the end of August in an outdoor amphitheater in Spearfish, South Dakota.

Known as the Black Hills Passion Play since 1939, when the company settled in Spearfish, the huge outdoor production features Roman soldiers on horseback, a camel caravan, and pigeons escaping from cages as merchants and moneylenders are driven from the Temple.

The amphitheater, which seats 6,000, was built specifically for the Passion Play and claims to have the world's largest stage. A series of permanent sets are used to portray Bethany, the home of Mary and Martha; the palace of Pontius Pilate, the Roman governor; the Temple; the Garden of Gethsemane; the Tomb; and Mount Calvary.

CONTACTS:
Black Hills Passion Play
100 Saint Joe St.
P.O. Box 489
Spearfish, SD 57783
800-457-0160 or 605-642-2646; fax: 605-642-7993
www.theblackhillspassionplay.com

◆ 0296 ◆ **Black History Month**
February

Black History Month grew out of **Negro History Week**, which was established in February 1926 by African-American historian Carter G. Woodson, who founded the Association for the Study of African-American Life and History. Expanded in 1976 to a month-long observance, this celebration of the contributions and achievements of African Americans was initially designed to encompass the birthday of the abolitionist orator and journalist Frederick Douglass (1817-1895) on February 14 as well as Abraham LINCOLN'S BIRTHDAY. The event is widely observed by schools, churches, libraries, clubs, and organizations wishing to draw attention to the contributions of African Americans.

Douglass was a fugitive slave who assumed this name when, by posing as a sailor, he escaped to New Bedford, Massachusetts. His former master's wife had secretly taught him to read and write, and after his escape Douglass became a skilled orator who lectured widely in favor of abolition. He settled for a while in Rochester, New York, where he founded an anti-slavery newspaper, and eventually ended up in Washington, D.C., where he held a number of government positions. One of his former residences there now houses the Museum of African Art and the Frederick Douglass Institute.

CONTACTS:
The Association for the Study of African-American Life and
 History
CB Powell Bldg.
525 Bryant St., Ste. C142
Washington, D.C. 20059
202-865-0053; fax: 202-265-7920
www.asalh.org

SOURCES:
AAH-2007, p. 9

♦ 0297 ♦ Black Madonna of Jasna Gora, Feast of the
August 15

The most famous icon in Eastern Europe can be found at the monastery on Jasna Gora, in the city of Czestochowa, Poland. The *Czarna Madonna*, or Black Madonna, is so called because of the dark complexion in the portrait of the Virgin Mary that, according to legend, was painted by St. Luke on a linden wood tabletop built by the apprentice carpenter, Jesus of Nazareth. Each year on August 15, the feast of the ASSUMPTION, hundreds of thousands of pilgrims attend the **Feast of Our Lady of Czestochowa** to seek forgiveness for their sins, recovery from injury or illness, or to offer gratitude for a favor granted. With their rosaries in hand, the pilgrims—some on their knees—climb Jasna Gora, which means the "Hill of Light," to attend mass at the monastery, celebrated above them, on the high monastery walls, by priests in golden chasubles.

More than 80 miracles have been documented at the shrine, which is only one of many dedicated to the Virgin Mary throughout the country. King John II Casimir proclaimed the Virgin Mary to be the Queen of Poland in 1656 after an unlikely victory over the Swedes at Jasna Gora prevented the latter from overrunning the monastery and looting its treasures. Mary is the patron saint of Poland, and Assumption Day is a national holiday.

CONTACTS:
Polish National Tourist Office
5 Marine View Pl.
Hoboken, NJ 07030
201-420-9910; fax: 201-584-9153
www.polandtour.org

♦ 0298 ♦ Black Music Month
June

Black Music Month is observed in June each year in the United States. Created by music industry executives Kenny Gable and Ed Wright as a way to celebrate and promote black music, the special designation has been proclaimed each year since 1979 by the incumbent U.S. president.

Black Music Month concerts and activities are typically planned and sponsored on a local level by such organizations as arts councils, chambers of commerce, music associations, museums, charitable foundations, radio stations, and theme parks. At the White House in Washington, D.C., a concert and reception is held each year that features various genres of African-American music, including R&B, jazz, blues, and hip hop. In addition television networks present programming showcasing black performers in concert as well as documentary and feature films about the development and influence of African-American musical forms.

Throughout the country during Black Music Month public and private organizations host numerous educational programs and cultural festivals recognizing the achievements of black musicians. In Detroit, Mich., the Charles H. Wright Museum of African American History focuses on a different musical genre each week in a month-long series of concerts, workshops, films, and lectures. Similarly, in the Harlem neighborhood of New York City, an area that was a center of black music and the arts during the Harlem Renaissance of the 1920s, a series of concerts, forums, and ceremonies commemorate the development of jazz, hip hop, and R&B.

CONTACTS:
Charles H. Wright Museum of African American History
315 East Warren
Detroit, MI 48201
313-494-5800; fax: 313-494-5855
www.maah-detroit.org

Greater Harlem chamber of commerce
200A W. 136th St.
New York, NY 10030-7200
212-862-7200; fax: 212-862-8745
harlemdiscover.com

International Association African American Music
P.O. Box 382
Gladwyne, PA 19035
610-664-8292; fax: 610-664-5940
www.iaaam.com/home.html

SOURCES:
AAH-2007, p. 68

♦ 0299 ♦ Black Nazarene Fiesta
January 1-9

The **Fiesta of Quiapo District** is the largest festival in Manila, Philippines. It is held each year in honor of the Quiapo District's patron saint—the Black Nazarene, a life-sized statue of Jesus carved from blackwood, whose shrine is located in Quiapo's baroque church. The traditional nine-day fiesta features nightly cultural events, band concerts, and fireworks. On the last day of the festival there is a procession of barefoot men pulling a carriage that holds the 200-year-old statue of Christ on the way to Calvary. Those members of the procession who are not pulling the carriage carry candles and circle throughout the district.

See also BLACK CHRIST, FESTIVAL OF THE

CONTACTS:
Philippine Tourism Center
556 Fifth Ave.
New York, NY 10036
212-575-7915; fax: 212-302-6759
www.wowphilippines.com.ph

SOURCES:
AnnivHol-2000, p. 7
GdWrldFest-1985, p. 153

♦ 0300 ♦ **Black Poetry Day**
October 17

Jupiter Hammon, the first African-American poet to publish his own verse, was born on this day in 1711 and lived most of his life in the Lloyd Neck area of Huntington, Long Island. Hammon was a slave—first to the merchant Henry Lloyd, lord of the Manor of Queen's Village (now Lloyd Neck), and later to Joseph Lloyd, an American patriot who moved to Hartford, Connecticut, during the Revolution. Hammon eventually returned to Lloyd Neck as slave to Joseph's grandson, John Lloyd. Hammon learned how to read and was allowed to use his master's library. On Christmas Day, 1760, he published his first poem, "An Evening Thought," at the age of 49. He went on to publish other poems and a number of prose pieces as well.

Black Poetry Day was first proposed in 1970 by Stanley A. Ransom of Huntington, who was concerned that there were no celebrations to honor the contributions African Americans have made to American life and culture. When Ransom relocated to Plattsburgh, New York, he brought Black Poetry Day with him. Although it is celebrated all over the state, it has yet to be formally proclaimed a state holiday. Oregon has already proclaimed October 17 as Black Poetry Day, and schools elsewhere have taken advantage of the opportunity to encourage African-American students to express their thoughts and feelings through poetry. Other celebrations include inviting guest poets to do readings and meet with students at SUNY-Plattsburgh. In 1985, the African-American poet Gwendolyn Brooks spoke at SUNY-Plattsburgh in honor of Jupiter Hammon's contribution to American culture. Other poets who have visited in the past for Black Poetry Day include Nikki Giovanni, Lucille Clifton, Ntozake Shange, Derek Walcott, Michael Harper, and Yusef Komunyakaa. In 1993 Rita Dove, an African American, was named poet laureate of the United States.

CONTACTS:
Educational Opportunity Program
Plattsburgh State University
103 Algonquin Hall
Plattsburgh, NY 12901
518-564-2263; fax: 518-564-2295
www.plattsburgh.edu

♦ 0301 ♦ **Black Ships Festival**
Third weekend in May in Shimoda, Japan; last full weekend in July in Rhode Island

Kurofune is what the Japanese called the black ships that Commodore Matthew C. Perry anchored off Shimoda, Japan, on July 8, 1853. He forcefully negotiated the Treaty of Kanagawa—the first treaty between the United States and Japan—in 1854. The treaty opened trade between the two countries and ended two centuries of self-imposed isolation for Japan.

In 1934, Shimoda began commemorating the arrival of Commodore Perry and his black ships. It is the site of the first American consulate in Japan, placed there by the Japanese to keep the "barbarians" (Americans) away from the capital, then called Edo. The first consul-general, Townsend Harris, arrived in August 1856. Twenty years later, Shimoda became the sister city to Newport, Rhode Island, where Perry was born.

In 1984, Newport began celebrating a reciprocal Black Ships Festival emphasizing Japanese art, culture, and education. Events include Japanese tea ceremonies, ikebana (flower arranging), origami (paper folding), kendo (martial arts), Sumo wrestling, Japanese kite flying, and traditional Japanese performing arts. In 1986 the Black Ships Festival was expanded to form the Japan-America Society of Rhode Island, which now sponsors the festival and works to develop cooperation and understanding between the citizens of Rhode Island and Japan.

CONTACTS:
Marketing & Events Inc.
28 Pelham St.
Newport, RI 02840
401-847-7666; fax: 401-846-5600
www.newportevents.com

Shizuoka Prefecture Tourist Association
Mizunomori Bldg. 2F
14-1 Minami-machi
Chubu, Shizuoka Prefecture 422-8067 Japan
81-5-4202-5595
www.shizuoka-guide.com

SOURCES:
JapanFest-1965, p. 152

♦ 0302 ♦ **Black St. Benito, Fiesta of the**
December 29

This fiesta is celebrated by a number of locales in the state of Zulia, Venezuela, and is especially popular in Bobures. The streets are decorated and people adorn the windows of their homes with white flags two days before the fiesta begins, and the events of December 29 are supervised by the *chimbángueles* or vassals of the saint. After early morning mass, the chimbángueles put St. Benito's statue on a litter and surround it with flowers. They then carry it through the streets while performing an unusual bouncing kind of dance in which they continually move forward and backward to the accompaniment of seven drums, each of which sounds a different tone. They are followed by groups of women who shake green branches in the saint's face. Throughout the long procession, St. Benito's image is sprinkled with perfumes and presented with drinks of homemade whiskey.

When Africans first arrived in Venezuela, they formed brotherhoods to help them preserve their ancient religious practices. Today's chimbángueles are direct descendants of these brotherhoods, and their members are divided according to a rigid hierarchy into chiefs, captains, major-domos, and slaves.

CONTACTS:
Consulate General of the Bolivarian Republic of Venezuela
7 E. 51st St.
New York, NY 10022
212-826-1660; fax: 212-644-7471
www.consulado-ny.gov.ve

SOURCES:
FiestaTime-1965, p. 189

♦ 0303 ♦ **Black Storytelling Festival and Conference, National**
November

The National Association of Black Storytellers meets annually in November for its National Black Storytelling Festival and Conference. The event, open to both performers and listeners, features workshops and performances by a diverse range of storytellers, including those who dance, play instruments, or recite poetry. All are united by an interest in the African and African-American oral tradition. At the conference, daytime workshops are offered in various aspects of storytelling, while evenings are devoted to concert performances and special story-telling circles. A "master liar's contest" is considered a festival favorite. Also on offer is an African-American market place with cultural instruments, clothing, jewelry for sale, as well as demonstrations, games, and casual storytelling.

The National Association of Black Storytellers was founded by storytellers Mary Carter Smith and Linda Goss in 1982. The first festival of black storytelling was held in 1983 in Baltimore, Md. Its festival and conference now draws thousands of participants and listeners.

CONTACTS:
National Association of Black Storytellers
P.O. Box 67722
Baltimore, MD 21215
410-947-1117 or 410-489-6747; fax: 410-489-2428
www.nabsinc.org

♦ 0304 ♦ **Blackbeard Pirate Festival**
Saturday and Sunday in early June

The Blackbeard Pirate Festival takes place in Hampton, Va., on a two-day weekend in early June. The festival acknowledges Hampton's history as a key colonial port from which tobacco was exported to England and various manufactured commodities were imported into the new world. The area's wealth attracted the notorious 18th-century Caribbean pirate Blackbeard. The dress, music, and customs of swashbucklers like Blackbeard provide the inspiration for this historical

event, which aims to recreate waterfront life in Hampton as it was in 1718. The festival launched in 2000.

The event features tours of replicas of three "tall ships" similar to the ones Blackbeard and his mates may have plundered. A street fair offers live music with historical and maritime themes, as well as refreshments and children's events. Several historical re-enactments can include such incidents as an invasion of Hampton Harbor by pirates seeking revenge for Blackbeard's death and a duel between pirates fighting with pistol and cutlass. Visitors can watch demonstrations of 18th-century crafts, navigation, cooking, and medicine at living history exhibits. The event also features a Grand Pirates Ball for adults, and a Saturday night fireworks display.

CONTACTS:
Virginia Air and Space Center
600 Settlers' Landing Rd.
Hampton, VA 23669
757-727-0900
www.blackbeardpiratefestival.com

♦ 0305 ♦ **Blajini, Feast of the (Sarbatoarea Blajinilor)**
April-May; second Monday after Easter

Among rural people in Romania there is a widespread belief in the existence of the *Blajini*, the "Meek" or "Kindly Ones"— a lost race who don't understand the ways of human beings, keep to themselves, and live in a fairy-land "by the Sunday-water." They are beloved by God because of their purity and innocence. On the Monday after EASTER MONDAY, Romanian women and children throw red Easter egg shells on running streams, since they believe that all the world streams eventually flow into a single river, alongside of which live the Blajini. Their hope is that the Blajini will find the shells and know it is time to celebrate the EASTER feast.

SOURCES:
BkFest-1937, p. 277
FolkWrldHol-1999, p. 249

♦ 0306 ♦ **Blavatsky (Helena Petrovna), Death of**
May 8

The anniversary of the death of Helena Petrovna Blavatsky (1831-1891) is commemorated by members of the Theosophical Society, which was founded in New York in 1875 by Blavatsky and Henry Olcott. Theosophy, a pantheistic philosophical-religious system that seeks to learn about reality through mystical experience and by finding esoteric meanings in sacred writings, is regarded as the precursor of American Hinduism. Olcott and Blavatsky moved to India in 1878, and the international headquarters for the Theosophical movement remains in Adyar (near Madras) today.

Blavatsky believed that she possessed extraordinary psychic powers, although in 1884 the Indian press accused her of concocting spiritualist phenomena. When the London Society of Psychical Research declared her a fraud the following year, Blavatsky left India and never returned. She did, however, complete her most important work, *The Secret Doctrine* (1888), an overview of Theosophical teachings, along with numerous other books, before her death in 1891.

CONTACTS:
Theosophical Society in America
1926 N. Main St.
P.O. Box 270
Wheaton, IL 60189
630-668-1571; fax: 630-668-4976
www.theosophical.org

SOURCES:
DictWrldRel-1989, pp. 320, 757
EncyRel-1987, vol. 2, p. 245

♦ 0307 ♦ **Blessed Sacrament, Feast of the**
First weekend in August

The **Festival of the Blessed Sacrament** held annually in New Bedford, Massachusetts, coincides with a similar festival on the Portuguese island of Madeira. The American festival, which was first held in 1914, celebrates the safe arrival of the Portuguese immigrants who came to New Bedford in the early 19th century after braving rough seas and stormy weather en route.

The descendants of these immigrants, many of whom served aboard American whaleships, give thanks each year by holding what they would like to think of as the largest Portuguese feast in the world on the first weekend in August. Preparations for the festivities go on throughout the year, and the events include a parade, Portuguese folkloric dancers and singers, Portuguese specialties such as *cabra* (goat) and *bacalhau* (codfish), and a colorful procession to the Immaculate Conception Church. The festival is held at Madeira Field, although the events extend throughout the city. New Bedford, once a thriving New England whaling port, remains home to a large Portuguese-American community.

CONTACTS:
Club Madeirense S.S. Sacramento Inc.
50 Madeira Ave.
New Bedford, MA 02746
508-992-6911
www.portuguesefeast.com

SOURCES:
GdUSFest-1984, p. 87

♦ 0308 ♦ **Blessing of the Bikes**
Between April and June

In 1996, Father Robert McElwee of the Frontenac Sacred Heart Church in Frontenac, Kans., began a Blessing of the Bikes for local motorcycle enthusiasts. Motorcycles are popular in his part of Kansas, and Father McElwee believed that the blessing ceremony would bring some people into church who might not otherwise attend. He held the event in the spring, just as motorcycle riding season begins. The first blessing involved sprinkling holy water on six motorcycles. But over the years the event began to attract thousands of motorcycle enthusiasts from across the country. The Blessing was so popular in

2005 that Father McElwee needed the assistance of two other priests from nearby parishes. The blessing that year took the three men 45 minutes to complete. For 2006, Father McElwee shared the Blessing of the Bikes with churches in the nearby towns of Joplin, Mo., Fort Scott, Kans., and Pittsburg, Kans. Besides motorcycles, people also bring such wheeled vehicles as children's bicycles and wheelchairs to be blessed.

The celebration includes a number of other events throughout the county, including jumps by the Green Beret Parachute Team, races at the Mo-Kan Dragway, a street concert in Pittsburg, and a concert at Foxtown.

While there is no charge to have a bike blessed, sales of related items such as T-shirts, food, and raffles are used to support scholarships at the nearby Harley-Davidson Technical School and local charities.

CONTACTS:
Sacred Heart Church
100 S. Cherokee
Frontenac, KS 66763
620-231-7747; fax: 620-232-7006
www.sacredheartsek.com

♦ 0309 ♦ **Blessing of the Grapes (Haghoghy Ortnootyoon)**
Sunday nearest August 15

In ancient times people in Armenia dedicated their grape harvest to Astrik, the goddess of the hearth, in a New Year celebration called *Navasard*. Nowadays the festival is associated with the Feast of the Assumption, and is celebrated on the Sunday nearest August 15, which is the feast day. No one is supposed to eat grapes until this day, when a tray filled with them is blessed in the church. Each member of the congregation is given a bunch of grapes as he or she leaves, and parties are held after the church ceremony in homes and in the vineyards. It is also traditional for women named Mary to entertain their friends on this, their name day.

SOURCES:
BkFest-1937, p. 27
BkFestHolWrld-1970, p. 109
BkHolWrld-1986, Aug 25
DaysCustFaith-1957, p. 207
FestSaintDays-1915, p. 172

♦ 0310 ♦ **Blessing of the Shrimp Fleet**
First weekend in May

In the coastal town of Bayou La Batre, the "Seafood Capital of Alabama," the shrimp blessing has been celebrated since 1950. It is usually held on the first Sunday in May. The "main street" of the town, founded in 1786, is actually the bayou, where trawlers are often tied up three or four deep. Shrimp is the mainstay of commercial fishing here, and more than 350 shrimp boats work out of the town, while several hundred other vessels operate in the waters off the port harvesting oysters, crab, and finfish. Seafood products landed in the port have a dockside value of $33 million annually, but the total seafood industry, including processors, is thought to produce $300 million for the local economy. Boat building and repair are also major industries.

The fleet blessing began simply: a priest went up and down the bayou blessing the boats tied to the docks. From the start, a wreath has been lowered into the bayou to honor fishermen lost at sea. Now some 25,000 people come for the highlight and final event of the weekend: the blessing ceremony by the priest of St. Margaret Roman Catholic Church and a parade of between 50 and 100 boats decorated with pennants, bunting, and papier mâché figures. Other events include contests in oyster shucking, shrimp heading, and crab picking; seafood and gumbo dinners; a land parade; a fiddler-crab race for children; and the crowning of the Fleet Queen. The affair is sponsored by St. Margaret Church.

In the port city of Biloxi, Mississippi, **Blessing of the Fleet** is a celebration of the start of the fishing season, where seafood is the major industry. It is also held over the first weekend in May. The blessing began in 1924 when sailing craft made up most of the fleet.

Today up to 80 boats parade past the Blessing Boat, where the pastor of St. Michael's Roman Catholic Church (known as the Church of the Fisherman) stands and bestows the blessings. The boats are decorated with flags and elaborate three-dimensional plywood constructions of such figures as mermaids, shrimp, paddlewheels, and fishnets. There are also schooner races, net-throwing and oyster-shucking contests, the crowning of a king and queen, and street dances known as *fais-do-do*. Supposedly "fais-do-do" was the song sung to children to tell them to go to sleep, and the dance got its name because adults danced when the children slept. The weekend also offers lots of local food—mullet, boiled shrimp, and Biloxi bacon.

CONTACTS:
St. Margaret Catholic Church
13790 S. Wintzell
P.O. Box 365
Bayou La Batre, AL 36509
334-824-2415; fax: 334-824-2415
www.fleetblessing.org

St. Michael Catholic Church
177 First St.
P.O. Box 523
Biloxi, MS 39530
228-435-5578
www.stmichaelchurchbiloxi.com

Library of Congress
101 Independence Ave. S.E.
Washington, DC 20540
202-707-5000; fax: 202-707-2076
www.loc.gov

SOURCES:
GdUSFest-1984, p. 100

♦ 0311 ♦ **Blessing the Sun (Birchat Hahamah)**
March-April; every 28 years on the first Wednesday in Jewish month of Nisan

According to Jewish tradition, God made the sun, the moon, and the stars on the fourth day of Creation—a Wednesday, according to ancient reckoning—and once every 28 years the sun returns to the same astronomical position that it held on that day. The Talmud says that the turning point of this 28-year sun cycle occurs at the VERNAL EQUINOX on a Tuesday evening (the first in the month of Nisan) at 6:00 P.M. in Jerusalem. But since the sun is not visible at that time in all parts of the world, the blessing isn't recited until the following morning at sunrise. The blessing is said while standing, and the sun must be visible.

The last blessing of the sun occurred on April 8, 1981, with about 50,000 Jews gathered at the Wailing Wall in Jerusalem, Judaism's holiest shrine. Similar celebrations took place on top of Israel's highest building in Tel Aviv and at the Empire State Building in New York City. The next **Blessing of the Sun** will take place in 2009.

SOURCES:
FolkAmerHol-1999, p. 199

♦ 0312 ♦ **Bloomsday**
June 16

James Joyce's novel *Ulysses* describes the events of a single day in Dublin: June 16, 1904. First published in Paris in 1922 because it had been banned elsewhere, *Ulysses* caused an uproar when it finally did appear in Ireland, and for a time, Joyce was reviled by the people of Dublin. But since 1954 Bloomsday—named after the novel's main character, Leopold Bloom—has been a Joycean feast day, observed with a number of events throughout Dublin that commemorate its illustrious author and the lives of his characters. There is a ritual pilgrimage along the "Ulysses Trail" (the path followed by Leopold Bloom), public readings from the novel, costume parties, and parades. Joyce fans can visit the Martello Tower, where the author lived, the James Joyce Centre, and Davy Byrne's Pub, where Leopold Bloom stops on his day-long odyssey. Restaurants specialize in serving the dishes that Bloom ate: kidneys for breakfast, gorgonzola cheese and burgundy for lunch.

CONTACTS:
James Joyce Centre
35 N Great Georges St.
Dublin, 1 Ireland
353-1-8788547; fax: 353-1-8788488
www.jamesjoyce.ie

Dublin Tourism
Tourism Centre
Suffolk St.
Dublin, 2 Ireland
353-1-6057700; fax: 353-1-6057757
www.visitdublin.com

SOURCES:
AnnivHol-2000, p. 101
DictDays-1988, p. 13
OxYear-1999, p. 252

♦ 0313 ♦ **Blowing the Midwinter Horn**
December-January; beginning of Advent through Sunday after Epiphany

The custom of **Midwinterhoorn Blazen** in the province of Overijssel, Netherlands, is believed to have originated more than 2,000 years ago. The local farmers make their winter horns out of pieces of curved birch wood. The horns are about 45 inches long and when soaked in water, they produce a piercing wail that carries for miles over the frozen countryside. Although in pagan times the blowing of the horns was thought to rid the earth of evil spirits, today the horns announce the coming of Christ.

In Oldenzaal, a special melody composed by the area's champion hornblower is played from the four corners of the local church tower, beginning at dawn on Advent Eve and continuing until Three Kings' Day (Epiphany).

SOURCES:
BkHolWrld-1986, Dec 15
FestWestEur-1958, p. 143

♦ 0314 ♦ **Bluegrass Fan Fest**
Third weekend in October

This festival for bluegrass music fans follows a week-long trade show of the International Bluegrass Music Association (IBMA), held the third week in September in Owensboro, Ky. Owensboro was the choice for the event's location because Bill Monroe (1912-1996)—the founder of the seminal bluegrass group, The Blue Grass Boys, and father of bluegrass music—was born in Ohio County, 30 miles from the city. More than 40 bluegrass groups perform, and proceeds from admission sales go to a trust fund for IBMA members.

CONTACTS:
International Bluegrass Music Association
2 Music Circle S, Ste. 100
Nashville, TN 37203
888-438-4262 or 615-256-3222; fax: 615-256-0450
www.ibma.org

♦ 0315 ♦ **Boat Race Day (Okinawa, Japan)**
May; 14th day of fifth lunar month

On Okinawa, the largest of the Ryukyu Islands southwest of Japan, the 14th day of the fifth month is both a religious festival and a sporting event. In Minatogawa, for example, this is the **Festival of the Gods of the Sea**. The villagers first go to the religious sites to make offerings and pray, and then they attend the boat races held in the estuary of the river. In Taira, it is the day on which fishing canoes from Taira race against competitors from the neighboring village of Kawata.

CONTACTS:
Okinawa Convention and Visitors Bureau
1831-1 Oroku
Naha, Okinawa 901-0152 Japan
81-9-8898-3000; fax: 81-9-8898-2202
www.ocvb.or.jp/index.php

SOURCES:
FolkWrldHol-1999, p. 376

♦ 0316 ♦ **Boat Race Day (Thames River)**
Late March or early April

This is the annual rowing race between the Oxford and Cambridge University "eights" (as the crews of the eight-oared rowing shells are called) that takes place on the Thames River in England. The race is scheduled to be held on a day when there's an incoming spring tide, which usually occurs in late March or early April. Beginning in Putney and ending four-and-a-half miles downriver at Mortlake, the race attracts large crowds of spectators—many of whom are hoping for the drama of an unexpected capsizing.

CONTACTS:
Oxford University, Information Office
Wellington Sq.
Oxford, OX1 2JD United Kingdom
44-18-6527-0000; fax: 44-18-6527-0708
www.ox.ac.uk

SOURCES:
DictDays-1988, p. 14

♦ 0317 ♦ **Bog Snorkelling Championship, World**
Last Monday in August

Peat bogs are areas of wetlands that are plentiful around the United Kingdom, so in the 1980s folks in the small town of Llanwrtyd Wells, Wales, decided to make annual, if wacky, use of one. They clear a 60-yard path through the black, smelly waters of the Waen Rhydd peat bog outside town. Competitors must traverse the trench twice using any but standard swim strokes. Snorkels and flippers are required wear. A newer event takes place in the same bog in July—the World Mountain Bike Bog Snorkelling Championship; participants in this race can skip the flippers, but still must wear snorkels, as they try to cycle two lengths in the fastest time.

CONTACTS:
Tourist Information Centre
Ty Barcud
Llanwrtyd Wells, Wales LD5 4RB United Kingdom
44-15-9161-0828; fax: 44-15-9161-0666
www.llanwrtyd.com

♦ 0318 ♦ **Boganda Day**
March 29

In the Central African Republic, Boganda Day marks the anniversary of the death of Barthélémy Boganda, the nation's first prime minister. Boganda was killed in a plane crash on March 29, 1959. He had been a driving force in the creation of the Central African Republic, which became a self-governing republic in 1958. Boganda was also a leader in the movement to unite black African nations. He designed his new country's green, yellow and red flag to represent the ideal of African unity. Boganda was flying between cities in the Central African Republic when his plane went down. At the time of the accident, there was of speculation that sabotage caused the crash.

Boganda Day is a national holiday in the Central African Republic. All banks, official government offices, businesses, and schools are closed.

CONTACTS:
Central African Republic Embassy
1618 22nd St.
Washington, D.C. 20008
202-483-7800; fax: 202-332-9893

♦ 0319 ♦ **Boggy Bayou Mullet Festival**
Third full weekend in October

A festival of seafood, folk culture, sports, and pageants, the Boggy Bayou Mullet Festival has been held since 1976 in Niceville, Fla. It celebrates the unappreciated mullet, the underdog of seafood, and serves up 10 tons of fried and smoked mullet, plus vast quantities of "mullet dogs," mullet filets on buns. Attendance can reach upwards of 200,000.

Niceville is a small town about 50 miles east of Pensacola in the Florida panhandle. But people kept calling Niceville "Nashville," so, to publicize the town and to promote mullet the Boggy Bayou Festival was begun. Mullet, abundant in the local Gulf waters, is a cheap source of high-quality protein but has had a bad reputation among seafood fanciers because of its feeding habits. Mullet are bottom-feeding vegetarians, and they taste like what they eat. The people of Niceville know that only mullet caught from waters with clean bottoms—like those on Florida's Gulf Coast—are worth eating.

This sleepy bayou town's festival has exploded into a fully rounded affair. It has beauty pageants to name not only the Queen of the Mullet Festival but also Miss Teen Mullet Festival, Junior Miss Mullet Festival, and Little Miss Mullet Festival. Entertainment is on stage all weekend and arts and crafts are on display. Then there is the food. Beyond the mullet, these are samplings from the food booths: Cajun specialties like crawfish pie, gumbo, and gator sausage; American Indian staples of fried bread and *pasole*, which is like pizza; barbecued rabbit, stingray and barracuda on a stick, fried oysters, boiled shrimp, apple dumplings, strawberry pie, and Mexican fried ice cream.

CONTACTS:
City of Niceville
208 N. Partin Dr.
Niceville, FL 32578
850-729-4008
www.niceville.org

♦ 0320 ♦ **Bok Kai Festival**
Usually February or March; second day of second month of Chinese lunar year

The Bok Kai Festival is a two-day event in Marysville, Calif., that began as a Chinese religious event to honor Bok Eye (or Bok I), the god who has the power to control flooding and the waters of irrigation and the rains. The festival, held since the 1880s, is now more of a cultural tribute to the Bok Kai legend.

Chinese immigrants came to northern California in the 1850s to find work in the gold fields or on the railroads being built through the Sierra Nevada mountains. When the railroads were completed, they settled in Marysville, which became the third largest Chinese community in the country, after San Francisco and Sacramento.

Between 1825 and 1862, three floods caused hundreds of fatalities in the Marysville area. In 1865, the Chinese first built a temple on the Yuba River, naming it Bok Kai Mui, meaning temple (Mui) on the north (Bok) side of the stream (Kai). (The temple was destroyed by fire and rebuilt in 1880.) Several gods were placed in the temple, but Bok Eye, meaning Northern or Dark North God, was the central deity. By building the temple in his honor, the Chinese people hoped to protect the city from future flooding.

The celebration of **Bomb Day**—Bok Eye's birthday—began in the 1880s. Today the celebration of Bomb Day with the Bok Kai Festival is a community-wide affair, drawing thousands of visitors from as far as Hong Kong. The day is named for the bombs, huge firecrackers that are fired off during the festival. A parade is another highlight of the festival, and a 150-foot dragon is the highlight of the parade. It winds its way along the parade route on the legs of 100 volunteers, accompanied by floats and marching bands, Clydesdale horses and a Wells Fargo stagecoach—more than 100 entries in all. The current dragon is the second one to be used in the parade. The first, brought to the United States before 1900, was retired in 1937 and now rests in the temple.

Besides the parade, there are vendors' markets for foods and crafts, demonstrations of martial arts, lion dancing, art displays, and performances by celebrated Chinese artists; these have included a master of Chinese brush painting, a pianist from China, and a composer and poet.

The Bok Kai Temple in Marysville is the only religious shrine to Bok Eye outside of Asia and is a designated historical landmark.

CONTACTS:
The City of Marysville Bok
P.O. Box 1844
Marysville, CA 95901
www.bokkaitemple.org

♦ 0321 ♦ **Bolivia Independence Day**
August 6

Bolivians proclaimed their independence from Spain in 1809, but it took 16 years of struggle to actually gain it in 1825. Spain had ruled the area since the 16th century. The country was named for its revolutionary hero, Simon Bolívar, who, with José SAN MARTÍN, led the Battle of Ayacucho in 1824 that resulted in the end of Spanish rule of Bolivia and Peru.

Independence Day is a public holiday, celebrated over two days including August 6, with parades and dancing in the streets of La Paz and Sucre.

CONTACTS:
Embassy of Bolivia
3014 Massachusetts Ave. N.W.
Washington, D.C. 20008
202-483-4410; fax: 202-328-3712
www.bolivia-usa.org

SOURCES:
AnnivHol-2000, p. 132
NatlHolWrld-1968, p. 134

◆ 0322 ◆ Bologna Festival
Last full weekend in July

In 1906 a bologna maker named T. J. Minnie set up his shop in Yale, Michigan. Over the next several decades, a number of other bologna makers settled in Yale, but today only one remains: C. Roy Inc., which produces Yale Bologna. The annual Bologna Festival, established in 1989, is designed to attract true bologna lovers with its booths serving bologna rings, bologna hot dogs, bologna and sauerkraut, and fried bologna sandwiches. A King and Queen Bologna are crowned, and they ride through town on the C. Roy float in the Big Bologna Parade wearing crowns made out of bologna rings.

CONTACTS:
St. Clair County
200 Grand River Ave., Ste. 203
Port Huron, MI 48060
810-989-6900; fax: 810-985-3463
www.stclaircounty.org

◆ 0323 ◆ Bolshevik Revolution Day
November 7

Bolshevik Revolution Day commemorates the October Revolution of 1917, when the Bolsheviks overthrew the Russian government by seizing power in Petrograd (formerly St. Petersburg, later named Leningrad, and in 1991, after the collapse of the Communist Party, renamed St. Petersburg). The coup took place on November 7 (October 25 on the Julian calendar) and through the years was celebrated as a national holiday marking the start of the Soviet regime. Celebrations were particularly lavish in Moscow, with grand military parades and fly-overs and the Soviet leadership reviewing the parade from atop the Lenin Mausoleum. In Leningrad, the Soviet Baltic fleet sailed up the Neva to drop anchor across from the Winter Palace.

All this ended in 1991. With the Soviet Union disintegrating, the state holiday was still in place, but marches and demonstrations were banned in Moscow. In the newly renamed St. Petersburg, Mayor Anatoly A. Sobchak attended Russian Orthodox services (formerly forbidden) with the Grand Duke Vladimir Kirillovich Romanov, son of a cousin of the last czar.

SOURCES:
AnnivHol-2000, p. 187
BkFest-1937, p. 286
NatlHolWrld-1968, p. 202

◆ 0324 ◆ Bom Jesus dos Navegantes
January 1

In Salvador, Brazil, the festival known as Bom Jesus dos Navegantes is celebrated on NEW YEAR'S DAY. A procession of small boats decorated with flags and streamers carries a statue of the **Lord Jesus of Seafarers** from the main harbor to the outlying beach of Boa Viagem. Thousands of spectators line Salvador's beaches to catch a glimpse of the spectacle. According to legend, sailors participating in the event will never die by drowning.

A similar procession takes place on the same day in Angra dos Reis, 90 miles south of Rio de Janeiro.

CONTACTS:
Bahia Tourism Authority
Av. Simon Bolivar S/N
Centro de Convences da Bahia-1dg Pisa
Salvador, Bahia 41750-230 Brazil
55-71-3117-3000; fax: 55-71-3371-0110
www.bahiatursa.ba.gov.br

SOURCES:
Bon Festival *See* **Obon Festival**

◆ 0325 ◆ Bombing of Darwin, Anniversary of the
February 19

On February 19, 1942, Japanese bomber and fighter planes conducted a devastating air raid on the town of Darwin, the capital city of Australia's Northern Territory. A total of 243 people—service personnel and civilians—died in the attack, which was the first of a long series of bomb raids that the Japanese launched on Darwin and nearby locations during World War II. The bombing on Darwin was the first attack during the war on Australian soil, and it is sometimes called the "Pearl Harbor of Australia," a reference to the Japanese attack on Hawaii in December 1941.

As a tribute to honor the dead and to remember those who defended Darwin, an annual commemoration is held in Bicentennial Park by the Cenotaph, a marble monument to those slain in World War I. The service begins at 9:30 A.M., and at 9:58, the exact time the attack began in 1942, a World War II air raid siren sounds. During some observances, Australian regiments will re-enact the historic attack. Ground units will shoot their guns, and fighter planes will perform fly-bys over the memorial site.

CONTACTS:
Tourism NT
G.P.O. Box 1155
Darwin, Northern Territory 0801 Australia
www.travelnt.com

Darwin City Council
Harry Chan Ave.
Northern Territory 0801
www.darwin.nt.gov.au

◆ 0326 ◆ Bona Dea Festival
May 1

The ancient Roman festival known as the Bona Dea, or **Maia Maiesta Festival**, was celebrated only by women; no men were allowed to observe or participate in the festivities. Variously described as the sister, daughter, or wife of Faunus, the rustic Roman fertility god, Bona Dea was a deified woman, a chaste matron who was killed by a suspicious husband. Because she revealed her prophesies only to women, Bona Dea's temple was cared for by women, and all of her rites were restricted to women.

The festival of Bona Dea was observed on May 1, the day on which her temple had been dedicated on the Aventine Hill in Rome. The ceremonies were performed by vestal virgins and a group of very respectable matrons, although the rituals associated with the festival apparently included remnants of phallic worship and the telling of indecencies which were not to be repeated to the uninitiated. The observance of the Bona Dea festival undoubtedly contributed to the Roman belief that May was an unlucky month for marriage.

See also MEGALESIA and OPALIA

SOURCES:
AmerBkDays-2000, p. 333
DictFolkMyth-1984, p. 867
DictRomRel-1996, p. 31
FestRom-1981, p. 116
FestSaintDays-1915, p. 110
OxYear-1999, p. 183

♦ 0327 ♦ **Bonden Festival (Bonden Matsuri)**
February 16-17

At the Bonden (or Bonten) Festival at Yokote in the Akita Prefecture of Japan, each district of the city has a team of 20-30 young men to carry its *bonden* in a race to the Asahiokayama-jinja shrine. The bonden is a ten-foot bamboo pole, draped with heavy cloth and topped by a circular platform holding a figure of the Animal of the Year, a custom inspired by the traditional east Asian calendar in which each year is named after a particular animal (the rat, ox, tiger, rabbit, dragon, snake, horse, monkey, cock, dog, or boar). As the groups make their way through the city, several from each team carry the bonden, passing it to teammates when they tire. Those carrying the bonden shake and spin it as they go, gradually increasing their pace until, at the end, they are running. The steep incline that leads to the Shinto shrine constitutes the last leg of the race. Here the racers begin to jostle one another, often pushing members of competing teams to the ground in a frenzy to be the first to the top. The team that arrives first wins the privilege of offering its bonden to the *kami,* or god.

There are bonden festivals elsewhere in Japan. At the Kawawatari Bonden Festival, for example, the bonden must be ferried across the river to a shrine on the far bank.

CONTACTS:
Japan National Tourist Organization
1 Rockefeller Pl., Ste. 1250
New York, NY 10020
212-757-5640; fax: 212-307-6754
www.jnto.go.jp

Daily Yomiuri Online (Japanese online newspaper)
Japan
81-6-6366-1896; fax: 81-6-6366-1897
www.yomiuri.co.jp/dy

SOURCES:
IllFestJapan-1993, p. 23
JapanFest-1965, p. 128
YrJapanFest-1974, p. 29

♦ 0328 ♦ **Bonfim Festival (Festa do Bonfim)**
January; one week to 10 days ending the second Sunday after Epiphany, January 6

There is a church in Salvador, Bahia, Brazil, known as Our Lord of the Happy Ending (*bonfim*). It was built by the captain of a ship that was wrecked off the coast of Bahia in 1875. The captain promised God that if his men survived, he would build a church in gratitude. Today during the Bonfim Festival, hundreds of Brazilian women dress in the traditional white dresses of colonial Bahia and form a procession to the church. The *bahianas* balance jars of water, scented with blossoms, on their heads. The washing of the steps at Bonfim Basilica on the second Thursday after Epiphany is the highlight of the festival.

Though Brazil is nominally a Roman Catholic country, many Brazilians adhere to various Afro-Brazilian cults. Candomblé is one such belief system popular in Bahia, and the Lord of the Happy Ending is Oxalá, a Candomblé deity.

CONTACTS:
Bahia Tourism Authority
Av. Simon Bolivar S/N
Centro de Convences da Bahia-1dg Pisa
Salvador, Bahia 41750-230 Brazil
55-71-3117-3000; fax: 55-71-3371-0110
www.bahiatursa.ba.gov.br

SOURCES:
BkHolWrld-1986, Jan 23
FolkWrldHol-1999, p. 32

♦ 0329 ♦ **Bonfire Night**
Various

There are a number of holidays that are referred to by this name. GUY FAWKES DAY (November 5) in England is sometimes called Bonfire Night, and in Scotland the name is applied to the Monday nearest May 24th, the former Empire Day (*see* COMMONWEALTH DAY). The original bonfires were actually "bone-fires" in which human or animal bones were burned to appease the gods. But nowadays bonfires are lit primarily for amusement. Other traditional bonfire nights include June 23, the eve of MIDSUMMER DAY, when fires were lit to cure disease and ward off evil spirits, and the WINTER SOLSTICE, when bonfires heralded the return of the sun.

SOURCES:
DictDays-1988, p. 14

♦ 0330 ♦ **Bonneville Speed Week**
Four days in late September

Bonneville Speed Week is a competition to set speed records on the Bonneville Salt Flats near Wendover, Utah (now called the **World of Speed**). The salt flats were once under Lake

Bonneville, which was formed about two million years ago and covered 19,000 square miles in what are now Utah, Nevada, and Idaho. The Great Salt Lake to the east of the flats is all that remains of that prehistoric lake. Bonneville is so flat that it is the only place in the United States where the curvature of the earth can be seen. Its salt surface is as hard as concrete by summer's end, and the many miles of unobstructed space create an anomaly of nature found nowhere else in the world. These conditions are ideal for land speed racing.

Speed Week has been held since 1949. About 300 cars and motorcycles come here from all over the world to try to break land speed records. The one-mile automobile speed record was set in 1983 by Britain's Richard Noble who zipped over the flats in the Thrust 2 at 633.468 mph. The first person to set a speed record on the Bonneville Salt Flats was Teddy Tetzlaff who drove a Blitzen Benz 141 mph in 1914.

CONTACTS:
Utah Salt Flats Racing Association
P.O. Box 27365
Salt Lake City, UT 84127
801-485-2662; fax: 801-583-3765
www.saltflats.com

♦ 0331 ♦ **Boone (Daniel) Festival**
First full week in October

Held annually since 1948 in Barbourville, Kentucky, this week-long festival honors the frontiersman Daniel Boone (1734-1820), who in 1775 was the first to carve a trail through the Appalachian Mountains from eastern Tennessee all the way to the Ohio River. For 50 years Boone's "Wilderness Road" was the major route for settlers heading west.

An important part of the festival is the signing of the Cherokee Cane Treaty. Descendants of the original Cherokees who hid in the Smoky Mountains to avoid being forced to move to Oklahoma in 1838-39 sign a treaty each year that provides them with cane, which still grows along the Cumberland River, that they can use to make baskets. Other festival events include an old-fashioned barbecue featuring pioneer and American Indian foods, traditional Indian dances, a long-rifle shoot, and competitions in such activities as hog-calling, wood-chopping, and fiddling.

CONTACTS:
Knox County Chamber of Commerce
196 Daniel Boone Dr., Ste. 205
Barbourville, KY 40906
606-546-4300; fax: 606-546-4300
www.knoxcochamber.com

SOURCES:
AmerBkDays-2000, p. 427

♦ 0332 ♦ **Borglum (Gutzon) Day**
August 10

On this day in 1927, sculptor John Gutzon de la Mothe Borglum began carving the faces of four American presidents out of Mount Rushmore in the Black Hills of South Dakota.

He chose this site because of its smooth-grained granite and the way it dominated the surrounding terrain. It took 14 years to bring the mountain sculpture to its present appearance, but because of delays caused by lack of funds and bad weather, only six and a half years were actually spent in carving. Gutzon Borglum died before the national memorial could be completed, but his son, Lincoln, continued to work on the project until funds ran out in 1941. Since that time no additional carving has been done, nor is any further work planned other than maintenance of the memorial.

The four presidents whose faces emerge from the granite cliffs were chosen as symbols of the birth and growth of the United States during its first 150 years. George WASHINGTON signifies the struggle for independence and the birth of the republic, Thomas JEFFERSON the idea of representative government, Abraham LINCOLN the permanent union of the States and equality for all citizens, and Theodore Roosevelt the 20th-century role of the U.S. in world affairs.

August 10 is observed at Mount Rushmore each year with patriotic music and speeches. The 50th anniversary celebration in 1991 included a formal dedication of the monument and a summer-long extravaganza featuring appearances by former presidents, television personalities, and famous South Dakotans.

CONTACTS:
Library of Congress
101 Independence Ave. S.E.
Washington, D.C. 20540
202-707-5000; fax: 202-707-2076
www.loc.gov

Mount Rushmore National Memorial
13000 Hwy. 244, Bldg. 31, Ste. 1
Keystone, SD 57751
605-574-2523; fax: 605-574-2307
www.nps.gov

Keystone Chamber of Commerce
110 Swanzey St.
P.O. Box 653
Keystone, SD 57751
800-456-3345 or 605-666-4896
www.keystonechamber.com

♦ 0333 ♦ **Borrowed Days**
March 29, 30, 31

According to an old Scottish rhyme, the last three days in March were "borrowed" from April, in return for which March promised to destroy three young sheep. But the weather proved to be an obstacle, and the promise was never fulfilled. Other references to the **Borrowing Days** go back even farther. Both an ancient calendar of the Church of Rome and a 1548 book known as the *Complaynt of Scotland* allude to the days at the end of March as being more like winter than spring. Whatever their origin, it seems likely that the wet, windy weather that so often comes at the end of March gave rise to the notion that this month had to "borrow" some additional time.

In the Scottish Highlands, there is an ancient belief that February 12, 13, and 14 were "borrowed" from January, and that it was a good omen for the rest of the year if the weather was as stormy as possible on these days. But if they were fair, no further good weather could be expected through the spring.

SOURCES:
BkDays-1864, vol. I, p. 448
DictDays-1988, p. 14
OxYear-1999, p. 144

♦ 0334 ♦ Bosnia and Herzegovina Statehood Day
November 25

Bosnia and Herzegovina are two adjoining regions in the Balkans that were ruled by Croatian kings in medieval times. They were united into a province under the Turkish Ottoman Empire. From Turkish control, the area passed into Austria-Hungary's realm until Bosnia became part of Yugoslavia in 1918. It was in the capital city of Sarajevo that Austrian Archduke Ferdinand was assassinated, sparking the first World War.

Statehood Day commemorates the November 25, 1943, assembly of the first joint Bosnian and Herzegovinan parliament. In 1946 Bosnia and Herzegovina became part of the newly formed Yugoslav federation.

Bosnia and Herzegovina declared independence from Yugoslavia on March 1, 1992. Bloody conflict between Serbs, Muslims, and Croats escalated into a Serbian ethnic cleansing program to oust the Muslim and Croatian populations, which NATO peacekeeping troops, deployed in 1995-96, stemmed. In March 1994 the Croat and Muslim factions signed an agreement to be united into the Federation of Bosnia and Herzegovina. The Dayton Agreement of December 14, 1995, established a democratic government and constitution.

CONTACTS:
Embassy of Bosnia and Herzegovina
2109 E. St. N.W.
Washington, D.C. 20037
202-337-1500; fax: 202-337-1502
www.bhembassy.org

♦ 0335 ♦ Bosra Festival
September 1-10

The city of Bosra, Syria, holds an arts festival during the first 10 days of September. Begun in 1985, the festival features singers, poets, and other performing artists from the Middle East and beyond. Visitors also enjoy displays of visual arts and handicrafts.

CONTACTS:
Syrian Arab Republic
Daraa Governorate
Daraa, Syrian Arab Republic
963-15-235000; fax: 963-15-243119
www.bosrafestival.com

♦ 0336 ♦ Boston Marathon
Third Monday in April

The oldest footrace in the United States was first held on Patriots' Day, April 19, 1897. Organized by members of the Boston Athletic Association (BAA), the race involved only 15 runners. Nowadays the Boston Marathon draws anywhere from 7,000 to more than 9,000 official starters, who must meet established qualifying times. Several thousand additional runners participate on an unofficial basis. In 1972, it became the first marathon to officially admit women runners, and in 1975 a wheelchair division was created.

The 26.2-mile course begins exactly at noon in Hopkinton, Massachusetts, includes the infamous "Heartbreak Hill" (a section of Commonwealth Avenue in Newton Centre, Massachusetts, that marks the race's 21st mile), and ends near Copley Square in the Back Bay Area.

Well-known American winners of the Boston Marathon include the "old" John Kelley, who won twice and last completed the race in 1992 when he was 84; the "young" John J. Kelley (no relation), who was the first American victor in the post-World War II era; and "Tarzan" Brown, who in 1938 took a break at the nine-mile mark for a quick swim in Lake Cochichuate.

Among the women, Rosa Mota of Portugal was the first to win three official Boston Marathon titles. And few people will forget the infamous Rosie Ruiz in 1980, who many believed tried to defraud the BAA by showing up at the end of the race to capture the women's laurel wreath, the traditional symbol of victory, without having actually run the full distance; this was substantiated by television coverage of certain checkpoints. Jackie Gareau of Canada was later declared the women's winner, although Ruiz continued to insist that she'd run the race fairly.

By 1988 the Boston Marathon became the Olympic Marathon trial for nine African countries, leading to what organizers call "the African running revolution." In 1988, a Kenyan runner, Ibrahim Hussein, won the Marathon, becoming the first African to do so. Since then, from 1988 to 2008, all but one winner in the men's division hailed from Africa. That impressive run included two Ethiopians, with all the rest of the winners coming from Kenya.

CONTACTS:
Boston Athletic Association
40 Trinity Pl., 4th Fl.
Boston, MA 02116
617-236-1652; fax: 617-236-4505
www.bostonmarathon.org

SOURCES:
AnnivHol-2000, p. 73
HolSymbols-2009, p. 92

♦ 0337 ♦ Boston Massacre Day
March 5

Once observed in New Jersey as **Crispus Attucks Day**, March 5 marks the anniversary of the 1770 street fight between a group of colonial American protesters and a squad of British troops quartered in Boston—an event that reflected the unpopularity of the British regime in colonial America and set the stage for the American Revolution. A British sentry was pelted with stones and snowballs by a mob of about 50 people. He called for help, and Captain Thomas Preston sent several soldiers. The soldiers fired and five of the protesters were killed. One of them was Crispus Attucks, a runaway slave who'd spent 20 years as a whaleman. It was Attucks who led the crowd from Dock Square to King Street (now State Street), where the confrontation occurred, and who later became known as the first martyr of the American Revolution.

The name "Boston Massacre" was invented by the colonists and used as propaganda to force the removal of the British troops.

In Massachusetts, the anniversary of the Boston Massacre is observed annually with patriotic songs and speeches recalling Attucks's sacrifice. On the 200th anniversary of the massacre in 1970, and again five years later on the 200th anniversary of the outbreak of the Revolutionary War, the Charlestown Militia Company staged a reenactment of the event.

CONTACTS:
Boston National Historical Park
Charlestown Navy Yard
Boston, MA 02129
617-242-5642; fax: 617-242-6006
www.nps.gov

Library of Congress
101 Independence Ave. S.E.
Washington, DC 20540
202-707-5000; fax: 202-707-2076
www.loc.gov

SOURCES:
AmerBkDays-2000, p. 185
AnnivHol-2000, p. 39
OxYear-1999, p. 108

♦ 0338 ♦ **Boston Pops**
First week in May through middle of July

Henry Lee Higginson, who established the Boston Symphony Orchestra in 1881 to provide culture-hungry Bostonians with classical music, nonetheless believed that in the summer, "concerts of a lighter kind of music" should be presented. On July 11, 1885, his idea became a reality when the audience enjoyed refreshments along with light classics at the first Promenade Concert, held at the Boston Music Hall. It wasn't long before people began to refer fondly to these summer music concerts as "the Pops," a name which became official in 1900. That same year, the Pops moved into the newly built Symphony Hall, which has been its home ever since.

World-class acoustics and the accommodation of cabaret-style seating have made Symphony Hall the perfect indoor venue for the Boston Pops for over one hundred years. Arthur Fiedler led the orchestra into a new era when he was appointed conductor in 1930. Under Fiedler's direction, the Pops gained a wider audience and national recognition via radio broadcasts (instituted in 1952) and public television

presentations (beginning in 1970). In the mid-1970s, two new Pops traditions were established: "Boston's FOURTH OF JULY" on the Charles River ESPLANADE, and Christmas Pops concerts. Composer John Williams, best known for his film scores, was named conductor of the Pops in 1980 after Fiedler's death. He was succeeded in 1995 by Keith Lockhart, former associate conductor of the Cincinnati Pops Orchestra.

Throughout its history the Boston Pops has tailored its programs around American music and musicians, medleys of popular songs, and familiar movements of favorite classical works, and it has featured such artists as Leontyne Price, Itzhak Perlman, Mandy Patinkin, Joel Grey, Doc Severinsen, and Cleo Laine.

Outside of its official concert season at Symphony Hall, where it performs Tuesday through Sunday evenings in spring and summer, the Pops also tours the United States and makes studio recordings, further cementing its reputation as "America's Orchestra."

CONTACTS:
Boston Symphony Orchestra
Symphony Hall
301 Massachusetts Ave.
Boston, MA 02115
617-266-1492
www.bso.org

SOURCES:
MusFestAmer-1990, p. 209

♦ 0339 ♦ **Botswana Independence Day**
September 30-October 1

Botswana became independent from Great Britain on September 30, 1966. Since 1885, the region had been a British colony called the Bechuanaland Protectorate. The biggest Independence Day festivities are held in the capital city of Gaberones, and includes the singing of the national anthem, "Fatshe La Rona" (Blessed Country).

President's Day is another national holiday, observed on two days in mid-July.

CONTACTS:
Embassy of the Republic of Botswana
1531-1533 New Hampshire Ave. N.W.
Washington, D.C. 20036
202-244-4990; fax: 202-244-4164
www.botswanaembassy.org

SOURCES:
AnnivHol-2000, p. 163
NatlHolWrld-1968, p. 179

♦ 0340 ♦ **Botswana Sir Seretse Khama Day**
July 1

July 1 is the birthday of Sir Seretse Khama, the man who led the nation of Botswana out of colonialism and laid the foundation for a modern democracy in his country. Khama was born in 1921, when Botswana was still known as Bechuanaland, a British protectorate. He was the eldest son of Khama III, the *kgosi* or king of the Bamangwato people. Upon his father's death, Seretse Khama became *kgosi* at the age of four, with his uncle, Tshekedi Khama, acting as his guardian and regent. Khama was educated at boarding schools in South Africa and began college there, but finished his education in England. It was there he met and married Ruth Williams, a white Englishwoman. Shortly thereafter, he returned to his home country with his wife.

The interracial marriage caused an outcry both among tribal leaders and the pro-apartheid leadership of Bechuanaland's powerful neighbor, South Africa. Khama was able to win his own people over, but South African authorities were profoundly threatened by the marriage of a black tribal leader to a white woman. They stirred up a dispute with England regarding the legitimacy of Khama's claims to chieftancy. Due to this pressure from South Africa, Khama and his wife were exiled to England in 1951, and the following year, this exile was declared permanent. By 1956, however, public outcry about the way they had been treated resulted in the couple's return to Bechuanaland.

Khama formed the Bechuanaland Democratic Party and became the last colonial prime minister of Bechuanaland, serving in that post from 1965-66. He was also honored with knighthood in 1966. On September 30, 1966, Bechuanaland became the independent country of Botswana, with Khama as its president. He held this post until his death in 1980. When Botswana became independent, it was widely assumed the country would have to be dependent on one of its wealthier neighbors, for Botswana was so poor that its tax base seemed too small to support the country. Yet through Khama's initiatives, Botswana was able to develop an independent, export-based economy.

Sir Seretse Khama Day is a national holiday, honored across Botswana as a day to remember Khama's contributions to his homeland. In celebrations in Serowe, which is Botswana's capital as well as Khama's birthplace, people proceed from various points to the main town center, where musical and religious groups have gathered. Traditional dances, such as the *tsutsube,* are performed. Speeches and ceremonies are made at the city's statue honoring Khama, and a wreath is laid at his grave in the royal cemetery.

CONTACTS:
Botswana Embassy
1531-3 New Hampshire Ave.
Washington, D.C. 20036
202-244-4990; fax: 202-244-4164
www.botswanaembassy.com

◆ 0341 ◆ **Bottle Kicking and Hare Pie Scramble, Annual**
Between March 23 and April 26; Easter Monday

This 700-year-old event is the highpoint of the local calendar in the small village of Hallaton in Leicestershire, England. Opposing teams from Hallaton and the neighboring town of Medbourne scramble to maneuver two out of three small

wooden beer kegs across a goal line in a game that has been described as being "unsurpassed for sheer animal ferocity." The chaos on the field may have something to do with the fact that players drop out of the game from time to time and have "a pint."

The event begins when the local rector blesses the Hare Pie—originally made of hare but now of beef. After handing out slices to some of the villagers, he scatters the remainder on the rectory lawn, where people scramble for it. Then comes the contest for the beer-filled kegs.

Where did these activities originate? According to legend, a village woman was crossing a field when she was attacked by a bull. A running hare diverted the bull's attention and she escaped. She bequeathed a field to the town in gratitude. The connection between the legend and the modern festivities is vague.

CONTACTS:
Hallaton Village Museum
Hog Ln.
Hallaton, Leicestershire LE16 8UE United Kingdom
44-18-5855-5305
www.hallaton.org

Harborough District Council, Council Offices
Adam & Eve St.
Market Harborough, Leicestershire LE16 7AG United Kingdom
44-18-5882-8282
www.harborough.gov.uk

◆ 0342 ◆ **Boun Phan Vet**
October-November; 12th lunar month

In the Laotian capital of Vientiane, rituals honoring events in the country's history as well as the origins of the Laotian people are held on this day in That Luang, the temple where the Buddha's relics have been traditionally housed. Outside the capital Laotians from various communities observe Boun Phan Vet at different times of the year, using the occasion to pay homage to Prince Vessantara, who is believed to be an incarnation of the Buddha. These observances include feasts, dramatic performances, love song contests, rooster fights, and parties at which the villagers entertain neighbors from other villages. This is also a time for young men to be ordained into the *sangha,* or community of Buddhist monks.

CONTACTS:
Lao Embassy
2222 S St. N.W.
Washington, D.C. 20008
202-332-6416; fax: 202-332-4923
www.laoembassy.com

SOURCES:
FolkWrldHol-1999, p. 665

◆ 0343 ◆ **Boundary Walk (Grenzumgang)**
Various

Boundary Walk festivals are held in many German towns. The custom dates back to the Middle Ages, when landowners and church officials, accompanied by armed men, periodically reviewed the boundaries to see that marking stones were in place and that hunting or fishing rights were observed. Eventually town and village boundaries were surveyed in the same way, with a huge feast ending the ceremony.

CONTACTS:
German National Tourist Office
122 E. 42nd St.
New York, NY 10168
800-651-7010 or 212-661-7200; fax: 212-661-7174
www.cometogermany.com

SOURCES:
FestWestEur-1958, p. 73

♦ 0344 ♦ **Bouphonia (Buphonia)**
End of June

The ancient Greek ceremony Bouphonia was held in Athens each year as part of the festival known as **Dipolia** or **Diipolia**. Wheat and barley, or cakes made from them, were placed at the altar of Zeus on the Acropolis. Oxen were driven around the altar, and as soon as one of them nibbled on the grasses or ate the cakes, he was killed with an ax, which was then thrown into the sea. The flesh of the ox was eaten, but his hide was stuffed with straw and sewn together. Then the stuffed animal was set up and yoked to a plow.

According to legend, a man called Sopatrus killed an ox in anger after the animal had eaten some of the cereal he was offering as a sacrifice. He felt so much remorse that he buried the ox and fled to Crete. When a famine ensued, the festival known as Bouphonia was instituted. It was customary for the killing of the ox to be followed by a ceremonial trial for those who had participated in its murder, after which the knife used to slit its throat and the ax used to fell it were thrown into the sea.

SOURCES:
DictFolkMyth-1984, p. 158
EncyRel-1987, vol. 3, p. 126
NewCentClassHandbk-1962, pp. 222, 410

♦ 0345 ♦ **Bowlegs (Billy) Festival**
First full week in June

The oldest and one of the biggest festivals in northwest Florida is held in Fort Walton Beach to commemorate the pirate William Augustus Bowles, also known as Capt. Billy Bowlegs. Bowles arrived in what's now known as the Florida panhandle in 1778 when the Spanish, English, and Americans were maneuvering for control of the Gulf shores. He put together a force of Indians and "White Banditti," created his own throne, and formed the State of Muskogee. To support it, he ran raids on the Gulf of Mexico and on the mainland. He was finally seized and imprisoned in Morro Castle in Cuba, where he starved himself to death in 1803.

This is not a particularly joyous saga, but the light-hearted affair of the Billy Bowlegs Festival goes on for a week. The festival began in 1954 and today attracts about 40,000 spectators. Activities begin with fireworks on Friday night. The following day, the pirate captain and his red-kerchiefed "krewe" members storm the city from the pirate ship *Blackhawk*. As events move on there are musical concerts, a treasure hunt, arts and crafts, numerous food vendors, and sports events that include a midnight run. More than 100 floats take part in a torchlight parade, and parade participants rain gold doubloons and assorted trinkets on the clamoring crowds.

CONTACTS:
Greater Fort Walton Beach Chamber of Commerce
34 S.E. Miracle Strip Pkwy.
P.O. Box 640
Fort Walton Beach, FL 32549
850-244-8191; fax: 850-244-1935
www.fwbchamber.org

♦ 0346 ♦ **Boxing Day**
December 26

The term "Boxing Day" comes from the little earthenware boxes that servants, tradespeople, and others who rendered services to the public used to carry around on the day after CHRISTMAS to collect tips and year-end bonuses. Although the custom of distributing gifts (usually money) to public servants and employees has continued, it often takes place before Christmas rather than after, and boxes have nothing to do with it. But the name has remained, and Boxing Day is still observed in England, Canada, Australia, and many other nations. In South Africa, it is known as the **Day of Good Will**. If December 26 falls on a Saturday or Sunday, the following Monday or Tuesday is usually observed as a public or BANK HOLIDAY.

SOURCES:
BkDays-1864, vol. II, p. 764
BkHolWrld-1986, Dec 26
DaysCustFaith-1957, p. 322
EncyChristmas-2003, p. 79
FolkWrldHol-1999, p. 765
NatlHolWrld-1968, p. 79
OxYear-1999, p. 534

♦ 0347 ♦ **Boy Scouts' Day**
February 8

The Boy Scout movement was started by a British cavalry officer, Robert S. S. Baden-Powell, who was well known not only for his heroic defense of Mafeking in southern Africa during the Boer War, but also for his publication of a military pamphlet, "Aids to Scouting," which emphasized the need for a strong character and outdoor survival skills among British soldiers. King George V ordered Baden-Powell to retire from the military so that he could help British boys learn about camping, hiking, signaling, plant identification, swimming, and other such activities. Baden-Powell's 1908 book, *Scouting for Boys*, was an immediate success, and he devoted the rest of his life to the task of promoting the scouting movement.

The Boy Scouts of America, the nation's largest youth organization, was founded on February 8, 1910. A Chicago publisher, William D. Boyce, who had experienced the courtesy and helpfulness of a young scout firsthand while staying in London, decided that young American boys needed the same kind of training. Two existing organizations—Dan C. Beard's Sons of Daniel Boone and Ernest Thompson Seton's "Woodcraft Indians"—had already introduced boys to the same idea, and the Sons of Daniel Boone eventually merged with the Boy Scouts of America. Cub Scout "Blue and Gold" dinners, flag ceremonies, parents' nights, shopping center demonstrations, and the presentation of advancement awards are popular ways of celebrating this day, which is part of **Boy Scout Month**, an annual anniversary celebration extending throughout February.

CONTACTS:
Boy Scouts of America
P.O. Box 152079
Irving, TX 75015
972-580-2000; fax: 972-580-2502
www.scouting.org

SOURCES:
AmerBkDays-2000, p. 126
AnnivHol-2000, p. 24

◆ 0348 ◆ Boys' Dodo Masquerade
Full moon of Islamic month of Ramadan

A children's entertainment introduced by Muslim Hausa traders during the mid-19th century, the **Dodo Masquerade** performed in Burkina Faso (formerly Upper Volta), has changed considerably over the years, and now reflects the local largely non-Muslim Mossi culture. As the RAMADAN season approaches, boys between the ages of 12 and 16 form groups consisting of a principal singer, a chorus, five or more dancers, a drummer, a few costumed wild animals based on local folklore, and a leader who dresses in military style. The boys decide on their roles and dance steps, which are usually variations on a dozen well-known patterns. Each dancer wears knee bells made from tin can tops and carries two sticks decorated by painting or peeling the bark away in special patterns.

On the night of the full moon during the Islamic month of Ramadan, the boys in their masks and costumes perform their dance for each household or compound while the chorus sings. Younger boys (seven to 12 years of age) started forming their own "Petit Dodo" groups and by the mid-1950s, little boys were dancing Dodo in many Mossi villages.

CONTACTS:
Embassy of Burkina Faso
2340 Massachusetts Ave. N.W.
Washington, D.C. 20008
202-332-5577; fax: 202-667-1882
www.burkinaembassy-usa.org

SOURCES:
FolkWrldHol-1999, p. 669

◆ 0349 ◆ Brady (Captain Samuel) Day
Second week in July

The body of water that is the focal point of the village of Brady Lake, Ohio, has more than aesthetic value to the residents. Captain Samuel Brady, an American frontiersman who fought in the Revolutionary War, was a scout in what was then called the Northwest Territory. He escaped a group of Wyandotte Indians by hiding under the surface of the lake and breathing through a hollow reed. The importance of this event is reflected in the fact that both the community and the lake were named after Captain Brady, and every summer (on a date that has not yet been firmly fixed), the escape is reenacted on the shores of the lake.

When the level of Brady Lake began to drop suddenly in the late 1970s, the residents pulled together to deal with the problems triggered by the water shortage rather than trying to sell their homes in anticipation of falling real estate values. The Captain Brady Day celebration has become an important unifying event for the people of Brady Lake, who view the lake as a symbol of their solidarity and peaceful way of life.

CONTACTS:
Village of Brady Lake
6500 Lakeview Dr.
Brady Lake, OH 44211
330-673-5998
www.villageofbradylake.com

SOURCES:
FolkAmerHol-1999, p. 324

◆ 0350 ◆ Braemar Highland Gathering
First Saturday in September

In the 11th century, King Malcolm held a gathering of the Scottish clans in Braemar to test their strength and to choose the hardiest soldiers. Competitors were asked to toss the caber—a pole 16' to 20' long and weighing 120 pounds—in such a way that it landed on its other end, much the way loggers used to toss logs across a river. The Braemar Gathering is still an annual event in the village of Braemar in Scotland, and the participants are still required to wear kilts and toss the caber. But the event has been expanded to include traditional Highland dancing, bagpipe music, games, and other athletic competitions as well.

See also HIGHLAND GAMES

CONTACTS:
Braemar Royal Highland Society
Coilacriech
Ballater, Aberdeenshire AB35 5UH United Kingdom
44-13-3975-5377; fax: 44-13-3975-5377
www.braemargathering.org

SOURCES:
AnnivHol-2000, p. 147
BkHolWrld-1986, Sep 6

◆ 0351 ◆ Bratislava Music Festival
Late September to early October

With its royal classical musical heritage—Joseph Haydn (1732-1809), Wolfgang Amadeus MOZART (1756-1791), Ludwig van Beethoven (1770-1827), Franz Liszt (1811-1886), and Anton Rubinstein (1829-1894) all performed there—Bratislava was already primed to host an international music festival, founded in 1965 with support from the Ministry of Culture of the Slovak Republic. The two-week festival presents choral, orchestral, and chamber music; opera; musical theater; and ballet. Through a project of the International Music Council and UNESCO, young artists have had the opportunity to perform alongside world-famous musicians at the festival since 1969, launching many professional careers.

CONTACTS:
Music Centre
Michalska 10
Bratislava, 815 36 Slovak Republic
421-2- 5920-4811; fax: 421-2-5443-0379
www.hc.sk/src/index.php?lg=en

SOURCES:
GdWrldFest-1985, p. 67
IntlThFolk-1979, p. 87

♦ 0352 ♦ **Brauteln**
Between February 3 and March 9; Shrove Tuesday

The **Wooing a Bride Ceremony** in Sigmaringen, Germany, is part of a CARNIVAL custom that dates back to 1648. After the Thirty Years' War was over, hunger and disease were widespread in Sigmaringen. This discouraged young men from marrying and starting families. The population dropped so quickly that the mayor offered to reward the first young man brave enough to become engaged with the *Brauteln*, or bride-wooing ceremony, during which the lucky bachelor was carried at the head of a colorful procession around the town square.

Today the custom continues. On SHROVE TUESDAY any man who has married in the last year, who has just moved into town with his wife, or who has arrived at the 25th or 50th anniversary of his marriage is invited to be *brautelt*. Heralds dressed in traditional costumes carry the men around the town pump to the accompaniment of drummers and pipers.

CONTACTS:
Sigmaringen Fremdenverkerhrsamt (Tourist Office)
Schwabstrasse 1
Sigmaringen, 72488 Germany
49-75-711-06-223
www.northlincs.gov.uk

SOURCES:
FestWestEur-1958, p. 57

♦ 0353 ♦ **Brazil Independence Day**
September 7

A declaration of independence was made by Pedro di Alcântara (1798-1834) on this day in 1822. Brazil had been a colony of Portugal since the 16th century. Alcântara, better known as Pedro I, became the first emperor of Brazil in 1823 and ruled until 1831.

Independence Day is a public holiday in Brazil, and there are celebrations in Brasilia, the capital, with parades of military personnel and floats decorated with flowers.

See also INCONFIDÊNCIA WEEK

CONTACTS:
Brazilian Embassy
3006 Massachusetts Ave. N.W.
Washington, D.C. 20008
202-238-2700; fax: 202-238-2827
www.brasilemb.org

SOURCES:
AnnivHol-2000, p. 151
NatlHolWrld-1968, p. 158

♦ 0354 ♦ **Brazil Proclamation of the Republic Day**
November 15

November 15 is a public holiday commemorating the proclamation of the Republic of Brazil during the rule of Pedro II (1825-1891), who reigned from 1831 to 1889.

CONTACTS:
Brazilian Embassy
3006 Massachusetts Ave. N.W.
Washington, D.C. 20008
202-238-2700; fax: 202-238-2827
www.brasilemb.org

SOURCES:
AnnivHol-2000, p. 191
NatlHolWrld-1968, p. 158

♦ 0355 ♦ **Bread and Roses Festival**
First Monday in September; coincides with Labor Day in the United States

The Bread and Roses Festival is a one-day, free event held in Lawrence, Mass., each year on LABOR DAY, the first Monday in September. The Festival, which has been held on the town common annually since 1985, commemorates the Bread and Roses Labor Strike that occurred in Lawrence in 1912, when most of the town's 30,000 textile workers walked off the job in protest of low wages and harsh working conditions. Many of the strikers were women and children, including a large proportion of recent immigrants. The strike gained its name from a sign reportedly carried by female protesters, proclaiming, "We want bread and roses, too," indicating that they sought both fair compensation for their work and respect from their employers.

The Festival combines multicultural arts, poetry, dance, and music with themes of labor activism and social protest. Trolley and walking tours visit sites connected with the history of the strike and include exhibits of period artifacts and a demonstration of wool carding and spinning. In addition, information booths, ethnic food, and commemorative merchandise vendors are on site, as well as a petting zoo, pony rides, and a domino tournament.

CONTACTS:
Bread and Roses Heritage Committee, Inc.
P.O. Box 1137
Lawrence, MA 01842-1137
978-794-1655
www.breadandroses.net

SOURCES:
PatHols, pp. 180-81, 183

♦ 0356 ♦ **Bregenz Festival**
July-August

Lake Constance in Bregenz, Austria, provides the setting for the Bregenz Festival, which features opera, symphonic and chamber music, theater, and ballet in a variety of indoor and outdoor venues, including the Festival House on the banks of the lake and a floating stage on the lake itself. The summer festival was established in 1946 to culturally refresh a war-weary public.

CONTACTS:
Bregenzer Festspiele
Platz der Wiener Symphoniker 1
P.O. Box 311
Bregenz, A-6900 Austria
43-5574-407-0; fax: 43-5574-407-400
www.bregenzerfestspiele.com/en

SOURCES:
GdWrldFest-1985, p. 11
IntlThFolk-1979, p. 31
MusFestEurBrit-1980, p. 17

♦ 0357 ♦ **Bridge Crossing Jubilee**
First weekend in March

This annual event in Selma, Alabama, commemorates "Bloody Sunday," which occurred on March 7, 1965, when a group of about 525 African-American demonstrators gathered at Browns Chapel to demand the right to vote. They walked six blocks to Broad Street, then across the Edmund Pettus Bridge, where they were met by more than 50 state troopers and a few dozen possemen on horseback. When the demonstrators refused to turn back, they were brutally beaten. At least 17 were hospitalized, and 40 others received treatment for injuries and the effects of tear gas.

The attack, which was broadcast on national television, caught the attention of millions of Americans and became a symbol of the brutal racism of the South. Two weeks later, the Reverend Martin Luther KING, Jr. and 3,200 civil rights protesters marched the 49 miles from Selma to the state capital, Montgomery—an event that prompted Congress to pass the Voting Rights Act.

Every year on the first weekend in March, the Bridge Crossing Jubilee commemorates both the bloody confrontation at the Pettus Bridge and the march from Selma to Montgomery that followed. Events include a parade, a Miss Jubilee Pageant, a mock trial, and a commemorative march to the bridge. Every five years, celebrants continue all the way to Montgomery.

CONTACTS:
National Voting Rights & Museum
1012 Water Ave.
P.O. Box 1366
Selma, AL 36702
334-418-0800; fax: 334-418-0278
www.selmavotingrightsmuseum.org

Selma-Dallas County Chamber of Commerce
912 Selma Ave.
Selma, AL 36701
800-457-3562 or 334-875-7241
www.selmaalabama.com

SOURCES:
AAH-2007, p. 78

♦ 0358 ♦ **Bridge Day**
Third Saturday in October

Bridge Day is both a celebration of the New River Gorge Bridge in Fayetteville, West Virginia, and a day of bliss for daredevils. The bridge, completed in 1977, is the world's longest steel-arch span and is the second highest bridge in the nation (after the Royal Gorge Bridge over the Arkansas River in Colorado). Its arch span is 1,700 feet, with a rise of 360 feet, putting it 876 feet above the New River Gorge National River. On Bridge Day, celebrated since 1980, parachutists jump from the bridge onto the river's banks below. The less bold walk over the bridge. About 200 vendors offer food, crafts, and souvenirs for sale. Attendance is about 150,000.

CONTACTS:
Fayette County Chamber of Commerce
New River Convention and Visitors Bureau
310 Oyler Ave.
Oak Hill, WV 25901
800-927-0263 or 304-465-5618
www.nps.gov/neri/bridgeday.htm

♦ 0359 ♦ **Bridge Walking (Dari Balgi)**
15th day of the first lunar month

According to Korean folklore, anyone who wants to avoid foot problems for the year should cross a bridge on the night of the 15th, or full moon, day of the first lunar month. Walking over 12 bridges is said to keep away bad luck altogether. Not surprisingly, Koreans of all ages are outdoors on this night looking for bridges to walk across.

The custom of bridge walking goes back centuries. It was particularly popular during the Middle Ages. So many people crowded the bridges that officials decided that men could cross bridges on the full moon night, but women had to wait until the next night. No one knows exactly how or why this custom originated, but the words for "bridge" and "foot" sound alike in Korean.

See also TAEBORUM

SOURCES:
AnnCustKorea-1983, p. 65
FestWrld: SouthKorea-1998, p. 10

♦ 0360 ♦ **British Columbia Day**
First Monday in August

British Columbia, Canada's westernmost province, joins several other communities in holding a civil holiday on the first Monday in August. For local residents, this day honors the pioneers who established the colony of British Columbia in the 19th century. Although the Legislative Assembly of British Columbia introduced the holiday in 1974, its official status was not ratified until 1996.

There are a number of events that take place in the province's capital, Victoria, but the most popular is the "Symphony Splash," an annual performance of modern and classical music by the Victoria Symphony Orchestra. Held on a barge on the city's Inner Harbor, the concert draws thousands of tourists and locals.

CONTACTS:
British Columbia Protocol and Events Branch
P.O. Box 9422
Stn. Prov. Govt.
Victoria, BC V8W 9V1 Canada
www.protocol.gov.bc.ca

SOURCES:
AnnivHol-2000, p. 145

♦ 0361 ♦ **British Open**
Summer (usually July)

The Britiash Open is the oldest and one of the most prestigious international golf championship tournaments in the world. It is officially the **Open Championship of the British Isles,** but in Great Britain it is known simply as the **Open.** It began in 1860 at the then 12-hole Prestwick course in Scotland and is now rotated among select golf courses in England and Scotland. Scot Willie Park won the first tournament, which is memorable for the tourney's highest single-hole stroke total—21.

Other notable years in the Open:

In 1901, Scot James Braid, who became one of Scotland's greatest golf heroes, won the first of five Open championships.

In 1907, Arnaud Massy of France was the first player from outside Great Britain to win.

In 1910, the Open's 50th anniversary was celebrated at St. Andrews (considered by many to be the premier golf course of the world) in a tempest of a rainstorm that put some of the greens under water.

In 1914, at Prestwick, the great triumvirate of golf, Braid and Englishmen John Henry Taylor and Harry Vardon, entered the match with each having five Open titles behind them. Vardon won with a final total round of 78.

In 1921, Bobby Jones (Robert Tyre Jones Jr.), the legendary golfer and lawyer from Atlanta, Ga., lost his temper at the par-three 11th hole at St. Andrews and shredded his score-card while the gallery gaped.

In 1926, that same Bobby Jones won the cup; it was the first time in 29 years that an amateur had won.

In 1930, Jones won and went on to sweep the UNITED STATES OPEN and the British Amateur and U.S. Amateur for golfing's Grand Slam, after which he retired. The feat hasn't been equaled. (Later, in 1958, Jones became the first American since Benjamin FRANKLIN to receive the Freedom of the Burgh of St. Andrews.)

In 1973, Gene Sarazen, celebrating his 50th anniversary of play, shot a first-round hole-in-one on the par-three, 126-yard eighth hole (known as the Postage Stamp) at Royal Troon. In the second round, he deuced the hole.

In 1975, American Tom Watson won the first of five championships.

In 1977, Watson and fellow American Jack Nicklaus left the field behind them and dueled to a dramatic final round; Watson won by a stroke with a 72-hole total score of 268.

The Open has a special cachet for golfers since Scotland is considered, if not the birthplace of golf, the place where it developed into its present form played with ball, club, and hole. (At one time, pub doors were the target). The game may actually have originated in Holland, where they called it *kolven,* but golf in Scotland goes back before 1457. That year, Scottish King James II banned "fute-ball and golfe" because they interfered with his subjects' archery practice. The ban didn't take. Golf was confined pretty much to Scotland until 1603 when King James VI of Scotland also assumed the throne of England and brought golf there, even though many English sportsmen sniffily derided it as "Scottish croquet."

CONTACTS:
Royal and Ancient Golf Club
St. Andrews
Fife, Scotland KY16 9JD United Kingdom
44-13-3446-0000; fax: 44-13-3446-0001
www.randa.org

♦ 0362 ♦ **Broadstairs Dickens Festival**
June

This nine-day festival commemorating the 19th-century novelist Charles Dickens and his association with the English town of Broadstairs features a play adapted from a different Dickens novel each year. The actors are members of the Broadstairs Dickens Players' Society, and they spend about eight months preparing for their June performance. During the festival, the entire town is transformed: people wander through the streets in Dickensian costumes, play croquet and other games popular during the 19th century, and attend bathing parties and social events with a Victorian theme. There are also concerts of Victorian music, exhibits, and lectures on Dickens.

Charles Dickens lived for many years in Bleak House, overlooking the harbor of Broadstairs. The festival was started by a later inhabitant of Bleak House, Gladys Waterer, in 1936. Although all of Dickens's works have been adapted and performed at the festival at least once, the town's nostalgia for its most famous citizen shows no signs of flagging.

CONTACTS:
Broadstairs Dickens Festival
10 Lanthorne Rd., Broadstairs
Kent, CT10 3NH United Kingdom
44-18-4386-1827
www.broadstairsdickensfestival.co.uk

SOURCES:
GdWrldFest-1985, p. 90
IntlThFolk-1979, p. 157

♦ 0363 ♦ **Brotherhood/Sisterhood Week**
Third week in February

Every year since 1934, Brotherhood Week has been proclaimed by the president of the United States, sponsored by the National Conference for Community and Justice (formerly, the National Conference of Christians and Jews), and observed by the country as a whole. The original idea was to set aside a week each year when people of all faiths would get together, discuss their differences, and reaffirm the human brotherhood that underlies the variations in their religious beliefs.

Now known as Brotherhood/Sisterhood Week, schools, churches, synagogues, civic groups, and other organizations across America celebrate by bringing together people of different faiths and backgrounds.

The decision to celebrate Brotherhood/Sisterhood Week near WASHINGTON'S BIRTHDAY called attention to George Washington as a symbol of America's commitment to freedom from racial and religious prejudice. When Washington was president he wrote a letter to the Hebrew congregation in Newport, Rhode Island, in which he assured them that in this country there would be "to bigotry no sanction, to persecution no assistance." This quotation has become practically a slogan for the National Conference for Community and Justice which, in addition to organizing this observance, is engaged in a continuing effort to promote interfaith relations.

CONTACTS:
National Conference for Community and Justice
475 Park Ave. S., 19th Fl.
New York, NY 10016
212-545-1300; fax: 212-545-8053
www.nccj.org

SOURCES:
AnnivHol-2000, p. 34
DaysCustFaith-1957, p. 60
DictDays-1988, p. 15

♦ 0364 ♦ **Bruckner Festival, International**
Three weeks in September

Linz, Austria, is the setting for a festival devoted to the works of composer Anton Bruckner (1824-1896), best known for his nine symphonies and three Masses. Although a number of famous composers have lived and worked in Austria—

among them Beethoven, Mahler, and Brahms—Bruckner's roots there go back to the fifth century. On the 150th anniversary of his birth in 1974, therefore, it seemed appropriate to institute a festival in his honor.

The Orchestra of Linz and other well-known orchestras perform Bruckner's symphonies, piano and organ compositions, sacred choral and orchestral works, and Masses in the Brucknerhaus, a concert hall built in 1974, as well as in other locations throughout the city. Choral concerts are usually performed in the Augustinian monastery in St. Florian (near Linz) where Bruckner was organist from 1848-55 and where he is buried.

CONTACTS:
Oberosterreich Tourismus Information
Freistadter Strabe 119
Linz, A-4041 Austria
43-732-2210-22; fax: 43-732-7277-701
www.oberoesterreich.at/english

Brucknerfest Linz
Untere Donaulaende 7
P.O. Box 57
Linz, A-4010 Austria
43-732-7752-30; fax: 43-732-7612-2170
www.brucknerhaus.at/www1/en

SOURCES:
MusFestEurBrit-1980, p. 21

♦ 0365 ♦ **Brunei National Day**
February 23

Brunei is an independent sultanate on the island of Borneo in the Malay Archipelago. The country is officially named Brunei Darussalam. It had been a British protectorate since 1888. The sultanate gained independence in 1984 and observes its National Day each year on February 23. Many people prepare months in advance to participate in colorful crowd formations, a favorite National Day event, and prayer services take place at mosques around the officially Muslim country.

CONTACTS:
Government of Brunei Information Department
Berakas Old Airport
Bandar Seri Begawan
Darussalam, BB 3510 Brunei
673-2-380527; fax: 673-2-381004
www.brunei.gov.bn

SOURCES:
AnnivHol-2000, p. 31

♦ 0366 ♦ **Buccaneer Days**
Early April through first weekend in May

During Buccanner Days, the city of Corpus Christi, Tex., by proclamation of the mayor, is under pirate rule, similar to the GASPARILLA PIRATE FESTIVAL in Tampa, Fla. Buccaneer Days, now also known as **Buc Days**, began in 1938 to honor the discovery of Corpus Christi Bay by Spanish explorer Alonzo Alvarez Pineda in 1519. It has become a month-long carnival, calling to mind the days of the early 19th century when the settlement was a hideaway for pirates, who did a brisk trade in contraband. Pirates sail into town, capture the mayor, and demand revelry throughout the city. Events include a professional rodeo, sailboat regattas, parades, sporting events, concerts, a coronation and ball, and fireworks on the bayfront.

CONTACTS:
Buccaneer Commission
P.O. Box 30404
Corpus Christi, TX 78463
512-882-3242; fax: 512-882-5735
www.bucdays.com

♦ 0367 ♦ **Budapest Music Weeks**
September-October

Music by the Hungarian composers Bela Bartók (1881-1945) and Franz Liszt (1811-1886) is a standby at the music festival held in Budapest from the last week in September through late October each year. But the festival was founded in 1959 to commemorate the 150th anniversary of the death of Franz Josef Haydn (1732-1809), the Austrian composer who spent 30 years at the Esterházy Palace as court composer to Prince Nicolaus Esterházy.

The festival always includes works by Hungarians—Zoltan Kodály (1882-1967), Gyula Illyés, and Zsigmond Móricz as well as Bartók and Liszt—but there are works by composers from other countries as well. Performances of symphonic, chamber, and organ music are held daily, usually in the Budapest Opera House, the Erkel Theatre, the Academy of Music, and in nearby churches and castles. For one week in October, there is a "festival within a festival": the Contemporary Music Series, in which the latest works by Hungarian and foreign composers are premiered.

The Budapest Autumn Festival is held over the last two weeks in October and presents plays, art exhibits, films, and musical and dance performances.

CONTACTS:
Filharmonia Budapest
Kazinczy u. 24-26
Budapest, H-1075 Hungary
36-1-302-4961; fax: 36-1-302-4962
www.filharmoniabp.hu/page.asp

SOURCES:
IntlThFolk-1979, p. 199
MusFestEurBrit-1980, p. 109
MusFestWrld-1963, p. 145

♦ 0368 ♦ **Budget Day**
April 9

As a general term, Budget Day refers to the day on which a government official presents the budget for the following year. In England, however, there is a tradition of having the Chancellor of the Exchequer carry the dispatch box containing papers relating to the government's revenues and expenditures for the coming year from the Prime Minister's resi-

dence at 10 Downing Street in London to the House of Commons on April 9.

The word "budget" originally referred to a leather wallet or bag, and the Chancellor of the Exchequer carried the government's financial papers in such a bag. The expression "to open one's budget" meant "to speak one's mind." Eventually the word came to stand for the contents of the bag, and the Chancellor of the Exchequer was said to be "opening the budget" when he presented his annual statement to the House of Commons. The modern meaning of the word dates from the mid-18th century.

CONTACTS:
Parliament of the United Kingdom Information Service
House of Lords
London, SW1A 0PW United Kingdom
44-20-7219-3000; fax: 44-20-7219-0620
www.parliament.uk

SOURCES:
AnnivHol-2000, p. 60
DictDays-1988, p. 16

♦ 0369 ♦ **Buena Vista Logging Days**
February

In the 1800s, the logging of Minnesota's pine forests near Bemidji was in full swing. During the winter timber harvest, lumberjacks guided teams of Percheron horses, who hauled logs along ice-covered roads. Although the timber industry still works the woods around Bemidji, the golden days of the Minnesota logging boom only lasted 50 years. But the area continues to remember, recreate, and celebrate the skills of the old-time lumberjack by holding a festival at Buena Vista village and logging camp located north of Bemidji. Each year participants dressed in red plaid wool shirts demonstrate log scaling and compete in axe chopping and crosscut-sawing contests. They also guide teams of Percheron, Belgian, and Clydesdale draft horses in log loading and hauling demonstrations.

Visitors are transported to the logging camp aboard horse-powered sleighs and are served lumberjack camp meals all day long. Buena Vista village is also the home of the Lumberjack Hall of Fame, where up to 100 of the old lumberjacks are honored and inducted during the festival. Many of those fabled laborers of the north woods, some of whom are nearly 100 years old, attend the festival each year.

CONTACTS:
Buena Vista Ski Area
19276 Lake Julia Dr. N.W.
Bemidji, MN 56601
800-777-7958 or 218-243-2231
www.bvskiarea.com

♦ 0370 ♦ **Buergsonndeg**
February-March; first Sunday in Lent

On this day, young people go to hills in the countryside throughout Luxembourg to build bonfires to celebrate the sun and to mark winter's end. Though this custom can be traced to pre-Christian times, in modern times it is associated with LENT.

CONTACTS:
Institute Grand-Ducal
Section de Linguistique, d'Ethnologie et d'Onomastique
2a, rue Kalchesbruck
Luxembourg, L-1852 Luxembourg
352-247-88640; fax: 352-260-94788
www.institutgrandducal.lu

♦ 0371 ♦ Buffalo Days Powwow
Third weekend in July

UNESCO designated the Head-Smashed-In Buffalo Jump site near Fort Mcleod, Alberta, Canada, as a World Heritage Site in 1981. For more than 5,500 years this natural land formation was used by northern Plains Indians to hunt and slaughter buffalo. Hunters on horseback would herd a large group of buffalo to the edge of the cliff and trigger a stampede so that some would run over the edge to their death. The interpretive center located at the jump provides tours and information and features exhibits on the area's Plains Indian culture.

The Buffalo Days Powwow is held at the site every July. Attendees enjoy dance competitions, foods, crafts, and a teepee village.

CONTACTS:
Head-Smashed-In Buffalo Jump Interpretive Centre
P.O. Box 1977
Fort Macleod, AL T0L 0Z0 Canada
403-553-2731; fax: 403-553-3141
www.head-smashed-in.com

SOURCES:
EndurHarv-1995, p. 280

♦ 0372 ♦ Buffalo Soldiers Commemorations
July 28 and other dates

In 1992 the U.S. Congress passed a law designating July 28 as Buffalo Soldiers Day in the United States. This day commemorates the formation on that date in 1866 of the first regular Army regiments comprising African-American soldiers.

African-American soldiers fought for the Union during the Civil War. But it was not until after the war that permanent all-black regiments were established, maintaining the U.S. armed forces policy of segregation. The African-American regiments were deployed in the southwest and in the plains states to serve U.S. interests against Native American tribes, to protect important shipments, and to construct roads and trails. A long-standing debate ranges around the origin of the term "Buffalo Soldier," with some maintaining that the nickname reflected the toughness of the soldiers and others claiming that it was a disparaging racial term used by Native Americans to describe the dark-skinned soldiers they met in battle. The segregated regiments served in the Spanish-American War, World War II, and other conflicts, before being disbanded during the 1940s and 1950s as the U.S. armed forces embraced integration.

Since 1992, Buffalo Soldier Commemorations have been held throughout the country and typically include reenactments, museum displays, educational forums, prayer services, and dedication or groundbreaking ceremonies for sculptural or other permanent memorials. A monument to the Buffalo Soldiers was dedicated at Fort Leavenworth, Kans., on the first Buffalo Soldiers Day in 1992 by General Colin Powell, who had originated the idea of a memorial to the black soldiers when he was stationed at the fort. Ceremonies and reenactments honoring the Buffalo Soldiers are not limited to July 28, however. Communities throughout the United States present special programs designed to educate audiences about the history of the Buffalo Soldiers throughout the year, particularly during Black History Month in February and on such patriotic holidays as Memorial Day and Veterans Day, with displays of memorabilia and speeches recounting the accomplishments of the troops.

CONTACTS:
Buffalo Soldier Educational and Historical Committee
P.O. Box 3372
Fort Leavenworth, KS 33207
garrison.leavenworth.army.mil/sites/about/Buffalo.asp

Buffalo Soldiers National Museum
1834 Southmore
Houston, TX 77004
713-942-8920; fax: 713-942-8912
www.buffalosoldiermuseum.com

SOURCES:
AAH-2007, p. 89

♦ 0373 ♦ Buffalo's Big Board Surfing Classic
February

This event features two days of surfing contests at Makaha Beach, Oahu, Hawaii, where the surf is sometimes 20 feet high. The classic is a tribute to "Buffalo" Keaulana, one of the state's premiere watermen. Old-timers ride the waves on the huge wooden surfboards that were used in Hawaii's early days; other events include canoe surfing, team bodyboarding, and tandem surfing. There are also food booths and Hawaiian entertainment.

CONTACTS:
Hawaii Visitors Bureau
2270 Kalakaua Ave., 8th Fl.
Honolulu, HI 96815
800-464-2924 or 808-923-1811; fax: 808-924-0290
www.hvcb.org

♦ 0374 ♦ Bulgaria Day of Liberation from Ottoman Domination
March 3

Bulgaria Day of Liberation from Ottoman Domination, celebrated each year on March 3, commemorates the day in 1878 when the Peace Treaty of San Stefano was struck between Russia and Turkey. The signing of this treaty put the nation of Bulgaria back on the map after an absence of about five centuries.

The Ottoman or Turkish Empire had consumed Bulgaria at the end of the 14th century. During the 18th century, a group of Bulgarians began working to revive the national identity of Bulgaria and to encourage Bulgarians to fight for their freedom (*see also* LEADERS OF THE BULGARIAN NATIONAL REVIVAL DAY). In 1876, Georgi Benkowski led a rebellion against the Turks, but it was forcefully put down by the Ottoman forces, and some 30,000 people were killed. In 1877, Czar Alexander II of Russia declared war on the Ottoman Empire, motivated by concern for the Orthodox Christians living in Bulgaria. A joint force of Russian and Bulgarian forces defeated the Ottoman troops at Shipka Pass, which led to the Treaty of San Stefano. Independence did not come instantly; Bulgaria was under Russian administration from 1877 to 1879.

In 1880, March 3 was celebrated in Bulgaria as the anniversary of the enthronement of Alexander II as the Russian Emperor. As Alexander's support had been critical to Bulgarian independence, he was and is seen as a liberator and a hero in Bulgaria. In 1888, March 3 was first observed as Bulgaria's Day of Liberation. It was pronounced a national holiday in 1978 and has been included in the official list of holidays since 1990. The Day of Liberation from Ottoman Domination is considered the most important holiday related to Bulgarian independence. Throughout Bulgaria, citizens pause on this day to pay tribute to those who helped Bulgaria to become a modern, independent country. Festivities marking the day often include parades, concerts, religious services, cultural exhibitions, and fireworks. Those who died fighting for Bulgaria's freedom are honored by the placement of ceremonial wreaths upon their graves.

CONTACTS:
Embassy of the Republic of Bulgaria
1621 22nd St. N.W.
Washington, D.C. 20008
202-387-0174 or 202-299-0273; fax: 202-234-7973
www.bulgaria-embassy.org

SOURCES:
AnnivHol-2000, p. 38

♦ 0375 ♦ **Bulgaria Independence Day**
September 22

On September 22, 1908, Prince Ferdinand (1861-1948) of Bulgaria declared the country's independence from the Turkish Ottoman Empire, which had ruled since the 14th century. In 1944 the former Soviet Union invaded Bulgaria and imposed its communist system for nearly 50 years. Like many other eastern European countries, Bulgaria became an independent republic with a new constitution in 1991. In 1998 the Bulgarian Parliament reinstituted September 22 as Bulgarian Independence Day. It also declared September 6 Unification Day to mark the unification of Bulgaria with Eastern Rumelia, previously under Ottoman control, in 1885.

CONTACTS:
Embassy of the Republic of Bulgaria
1621 22nd St. N.W.
Washington, D.C. 20008
202-387-0174; fax: 202-234-7973
www.bulgaria-embassy.org

♦ 0376 ♦ **Bulgarian Culture Day**
May 24

This Bulgarian national holiday—formerly known as **Holy Day of Letters**—promotes Bulgarian culture and honors two brothers, St. Cyril (c. 827-869) and St. Methodius (c. 815-844), missionaries to Moravia. They are believed to have invented the Slavonic alphabet, also known as the Cyrillic alphabet. What is certain is that through their evangelization efforts, they helped spread the use of the new alphabet, and they are both widely regarded as the country's patrons of education and culture. In 1980, Pope John Paul II declared them patrons of Europe. The brothers started out preaching Christianity in what are now the Czech and Slovak Republics, but their followers fled to Bulgaria when they were persecuted, and Cyrillic became the official alphabet there. It is still used in the former Soviet Union, Serbia, and other Slavic countries as well.

Special religious services, concerts, festivals, and student parades are held throughout Bulgaria on this day, which is also known as **Saints Cyril and Methodius's Day** and **Day of the Founders of the Slavonic Alphabet**. An impressive liturgy, celebrated at the cathedral in Sofia, is one of the highlights.

CONTACTS:
Embassy of the Republic of Bulgaria
1621 22nd St. N.W.
Washington, D.C. 20008
202-387-0174; fax: 202-234-7973
www.bulgaria-embassy.org

SOURCES:
BkFest-1937, p. 71
BkHolWrld-1986, May 24
EncyRel-1987, vol. 4, p. 191
OxYear-1999, p. 203

♦ 0377 ♦ **Bull Durham Blues Festival**
September

The Carolina blues style of music (also known as Piedmont blues) is different from traditional blues. Rather than expressing stories of bad luck, hard times, and lost love, Carolina blues balance sorrow with celebration. These songs are often light and upbeat, encouraging listeners to dance.

Since 1988, the St. Joseph's Historic Foundation, Inc. (SJHF) has held a blues festival at the Durham Athletic Park in North Carolina, where the Durham Blues baseball team used to play.

The SJHF, an African-American cultural and educational institution, was founded in 1975 to "advance cultural understanding through diverse programs that examine the experiences of Americans of African descent—locally, nationally, and globally." SJHF is deeply rooted in the historic Hayti community of Durham. Funds raised from the Bull Durham Blues Festival support the programs and operations of the Foundation and Hayti Heritage Center, which is the former St. Joseph's African Methodist Episcopal Church, a National

Historic landmark. The Hayti District is an area on the southwest edge of Durham, where African Americans settled shortly after the Civil War.

According to the SJHF, the festival serves many purposes. These are as follows: "To increase awareness and appreciation for Durham's rich musical heritage in the Blues, particularly as a showplace for the Piedmont blues style made popular in this part of the Southeast; to increase awareness and appreciation for the Blues as a unique American art form that is reflective of the African American experience; to develop the local audience, particularly within the African American communities in the region, for the Blues which is often more popular overseas than in the United States; to become a national showcase for the finest in contemporary and traditional blues artists in North Carolina and the rest of the United States."

During the three-day festival, many of the best and best-known contemporary blues artists perform for audiences from over 175 North Carolina cities, 25 states, and five countries. As with many music festivals around the country, good food is plentiful in the various restaurants and other venues around Durham.

CONTACTS:
Hayti Heritage Center
804 Old Fayetteville St.
Durham, NC 27707
919-683-1709; fax: 919-682-5869
www.bulldurhamblues.org

♦ 0378 ♦ Bulu Festival
June

To the Dogon people who live in southeastern Mali in West Africa, *bulu* means "rejuvenate." It celebrates the beginning of the planting season. The festival continues for six days during which people ritually renew the life of the community with visits, feasts, and tying up any loose ends amongst each other, as well as their connection with the spiritual realm by offering sacrifices and creating new paintings for sanctuaries. The main communal ritual takes place at the house of the *hogan*, the most powerful priest in the community. Using millet grain saved from the previous year's crop, he enacts a ceremonial planting of grain for the current season in order to encourage a good crop.

CONTACTS:
Mali Embassy
2130 R St. N.W.
Washington, D.C. 20008
202-332-2249; fax: 202-332-6603
www.maliembassy.us

SOURCES:
EncyRel-1987, vol. 4, p. 394

♦ 0379 ♦ Bumba-Meu-Boi Folk Drama
June, including June 24, St. John's Day

The Bumba-Meu-Boi is a Brazilian folk drama that is popular in Brazil and especially noteworthy in cities and small towns in the state of Maranhão. The play tells the story of a bull (or, in some versions, an ox) that is slain and then brought back to life. The characters include a sea captain riding a wicker hobby-horse, the bull or ox, the cowboys Chico and Birico, Catirina (the pregnant wife of Chico), the Doctor, and the Chorus. A colorful procession announces the arrival of the players, who sometimes stage playful attacks on the spectators lining the streets. Performances usually take place in a room of the house belonging to the most important family in town, or else in front of a church or in the town's main square.

CONTACTS:
Government of Maranhao, State Department of Tourism
Rua da Palma
Centro, Brazil
55-98-3212-6215
www.turismo.ma.gov.br/en/index.html

SOURCES:
FolkWrldHol-1999, p. 389

♦ 0380 ♦ Bumbershoot
September, four days over Labor Day weekend

Bumbershoot is the premier festival of Seattle, Wash., held since 1971 and now a wide-ranging round-up of many arts. It started as Festival '71, but became Bumbershoot in 1973. Bumbershoot is British slang for umbrella, and the festival is supposed to be an umbrella for the arts; the word also calls to mind Seattle's rainy climate.

In recent years, Bumbershoot attractions have included Japanese Kabuki theater, Russian rock, robot art, flamenco dancing, and readings by contemporary writers. In 1991, performers included: Foday Musa Suso, a hereditary musician and oral historian of the Mandingo people of West Africa; Roger Ferguson, the former National Flat-Pick Guitar Champion, presenting bluegrass music; and the Mazeltones, singing Jewish music in Yiddish, Hebrew, and English. The food offerings yield Cajun-style salmon, Pennsylvania Dutch funnel cake, Italian calzone, Lebanese falafels, Thai beef sticks, strawberry shortcake, etc. In other words, Bumbershoot is a gallimaufry of music, dance, theater, visual and literary arts, children's activities, food, and crafts. It's held at the Seattle Center, the site of the 1962 World's Fair, and attracts about 250,000 people.

CONTACTS:
One Reel
P.O. Box 9750
Seattle, WA 98109
206-281-7788; fax: 206-281-7799
www.bumbershoot.org

♦ 0381 ♦ Bun Bang Fai (Boun Bang Fay; Rocket Festival)
April-May; full moon day of Hindu month of Vaisakha; second weekend in May

Bun Bang Fai is a rain ceremony celebrated in Laos and northeastern Thailand during Buddhist VESAK or Vesakha Puja, observed on the full moon day of the sixth Hindu month

(Vaisakha). The Bun Bang Fai (*bun* or *boun* means "festival" in Lao) pre-dates Buddhism and is intended to insure good crops.

In Laos, this is one of the country's wildest celebrations, with music and irreverent dances, processions, and merrymaking. The celebration ends with the firing of bamboo rockets into the sky, supposedly prompting the heavens to commence the rainy season and bring water to the rice fields. Prizes go to the fastest, highest, and brightest rockets.

In Thailand, the celebration is usually on the second weekend in May and is especially festive in Yasothon, with villagers shooting off huge rockets. Before the shooting, there are beauty parades, folk dances, and ribald entertainment.

CONTACTS:
Lao Embassy
2222 S St. N.W.
Washington, D.C. 20008
202-667-0076; fax: 202-332-4923
www.laoembassy.com

Tourism Authority of Thailand
611 N. Larchmont Blvd., 1st Fl.
Los Angeles, CA 90004
800-842-4526 or 323-461-9814; fax: 323-461-9834
www.tourismthailand.org

SOURCES:
BkHolWrld-1986, May 26
FolkWrldHol-1999, p. 381

♦ 0382 ♦ **Bunch (Madam Lou) Day**
Third Saturday in June

Bunch day is an annual reminder of the rowdy gold-mining days of Central City, Colo., held to honor the town's last madam. The event features bed races, a Madams and Miners Ball, and the selection of a Madam of the Year. In addition, there are tours of old mining rigs and trains that take visitors into the heart of the mountains to see colorful veins of ore.

Central City was settled in the Gold Rush of 1859 and became known as the Richest Square Mile on Earth—some $75 million in gold was mined there. One of the miners was a man named John Gregory, who dug up a fortune. New York newspaper editor Horace Greeley heard about Gregory Gulch and went west to take a look, after which he supposedly wrote, "Go west, young man." The phrase isn't found in his writings, because this advice was first given by John Babsone Soulé in an article for Indiana's *Terre Haute Express.* Greeley reprinted the article in his *New York Tribune* under Soulé's byline; nevertheless Greeley has been remembered for the inspiring phrase and both Gregory and Soulé have faded into history.

CONTACTS:
Central City
141 Nevada
Central City, CO 80427
303-582-5251
www.centralcitycolorado.us

♦ 0383 ♦ **Bunka-no-Hi (Culture Day)**
November 3

Bunka-no-Hi is a Japanese national holiday on which medals are awarded by the government to those who have made special contributions in the fields of arts and sciences. Winners are not always Japanese; the American Apollo 11 astronauts—Neil Armstrong, Edwin "Buzz" Aldrin, and Michael Collins—are among past honorees. This is also the anniversary of Japan's current constitution in 1946.

The day was formerly celebrated as the birthday of Emperor Meiji, who ruled from 1868 until his death in 1912 and was the great-grandfather of Emperor Akihito (b. 1933). The years of his reign were a time of turning away from feudalism and toward Western rationalism and science, and were known as the age of *bummei-kaika*—"civilization and enlightenment."

Today, this holiday serves to promote the love of freedom, peace, and cultural development.

CONTACTS:
Japan Information Network, Japan Center for Intercultural
   Communications
2-7-7 Hirakawacho
Chiyodaku
Tokyo, 102-0093 Japan
81-3-3263-5041; fax: 81-3-3230-4107
home.jcic.or.jp

SOURCES:
AnnivHol-2000, p. 185
JapanFest-1965, p. 205

♦ 0384 ♦ **Bunker Hill Day**
June 17

Observed primarily in Boston, Mass., Bunker Hill Day commemorates the Revolutionary War battle of June 1775 between 2,200 British troops under the leadership of General William Howe and half that number of Americans under Colonel William Prescott. In fact, Breed's Hill was fortified, not nearby Bunker Hill, and that is where the British attacked the rebels three times, eventually driving them out of their hastily constructed barricade, but only after losing more than 1,000 men. The American revolutionaries, who had exhausted their small store of ammunition, ended up fighting the British bayonets with the butts of their muskets.

Although the Americans were driven from their fortification and lost some 450 men, the battle boosted their confidence and has always been looked upon as one of the great heroic battles of the American Revolution. A 221-foot granite obelisk in Charlestown, just north of Boston, marks the site of the battle on Breed's Hill, which itself is only 87 feet high. This day is sometimes referred to as **Boston's Fourth of July**.

CONTACTS:
Boston National Historic Park
Charlestown Navy Yard
Downtown Visitor Ctr.
Boston, MA 02129
617-242-5642; fax: 617-242-6006
www.nps.gov

The Freedom Trail Foundation
99 Chauncy St., Ste. 401

Boston, MA 02111
617-357-8300; fax: 617-357-8303
www.thefreedomtrail.org

SOURCES:
AmerBkDays-2000, p. 454
AnnivHol-2000, p. 101
BkDays-1864, vol. I, p. 790
DictDays-1988, p. 16

♦ 0385 ♦ **Burbank Day**
March 7

The birthday of naturalist and plant breeder Luther Burbank (1849-1926) is observed in California in much the same way ARBOR DAY is observed in other states—that is, with activities promoting the value of natural resources and the protection of trees and birds. Burbank moved from his native Massachusetts to Santa Rosa, Calif., in 1875 and spent the rest of his life there experimenting with new varieties of fruits, flowers, and vegetables. Among his other achievements, he is credited with introducing the Shasta daisy. All in all, he developed more than 800 new strains and varieties of fruits, flowers, and forage plants, drawing worldwide attention to the science of plant breeding and helping farmers learn how to use their land more productively.

Burbank was fortunate enough to be honored by the citizens of Santa Rosa during his lifetime. The Rose Carnival was held intermittently between 1894 and his death in 1926. Then, in 1950, the three-day Luther Burbank Rose Festival was instituted. This celebration, which takes place annually in mid-May, includes flower shows, music and sporting events, and a Rose Festival parade. On March 7 a birthday and Arbor Day celebration is held at the Luther Burbank Home and Gardens.

CONTACTS:
Santa Rosa Convention and Visitors Bureau
9 Fourth St.
Santa Rosa, CA 95401
800-404-7673 or 707-577-8674; fax: 707-571-5949
www.visitsantarosa.com

SOURCES:
AmerBkDays-2000, p. 189
AnnivHol-2000, p. 40

♦ 0386 ♦ **Burgoyne's (John) Surrender Day**
October 17

British General John Burgoyne (1722-1792) is best remembered for his defeat by the colonial American forces in the Saratoga campaign of 1777, during the Revolutionary War. The plan was to have British troops from the north, south, and west unite at Albany, New York, thus isolating New England from the other rebellious colonies. Burgoyne led his troops south from Canada by way of Lake Champlain, capturing Fort Ticonderoga, New York, on July 6, 1777. But they were stopped at the Hudson River by the American forces commanded by General Philip Schuyler and, later, General Horatio Gates, with the assistance of General Benedict

Arnold. Burgoyne was eventually forced to surrender to Gates near Saratoga Springs, New York, on October 17, 1777.

Historians regard the surrender at Saratoga Springs as the turning point in the Revolutionary War. The Americans' victory gave them a psychological advantage and persuaded France to ally itself with the colonists against England, its traditional rival.

The anniversary of Burgoyne's surrender is observed in New York State, particularly in the communities surrounding the Saratoga National Historical Park near Stillwater, New York. A well-known painting of Burgoyne's surrender by John Trumbull hangs in the U.S. Capitol Rotunda in Washington, D.C.

CONTACTS:
Saratoga National Historic Park
National Park Service
648 Route 32
Stillwater, NY 12170
518-664-9821; fax: 518-664-9830
www.nps.gov/sara/f-sara.htm

SOURCES:
AmerBkDays-2000, p. 713
AnnivHol-2000, p. 174
BkDaysAmerHist-1987, Oct 17

♦ 0387 ♦ **Burial of the Sardine**
Between February 4 and March 10; Ash Wednesday, the first day of Lent

The custom of burying a thin slice of meat, nicknamed "the sardine," on ASH WEDNESDAY is common throughout Spain and is thought to have originated in an old fertility custom symbolizing the burial of winter in early spring. The **Entierro de la Sardina** also symbolizes the burial of worldly pleasures and serves as a reminder that people must abstain from eating meat on Fridays throughout the 40 days of LENT. After the burial is over, people attend Ash Wednesday church services.

Another Spanish custom is to make a figure of an ugly old woman out of stucco or cardboard or figures representing the King and Queen of CARNIVAL and to burn or drown these personifications of Carnival on Ash Wednesday or SHROVE TUESDAY.

See also CARNIVAL IN PANAMA

SOURCES:
BkFest-1937, p. 299
DictFolkMyth-1984, p. 82
EncyEaster-2002, p. 52
FestSaintDays-1915, p. 49
FestWestEur-1958, p. 194

♦ 0388 ♦ **Burkina Faso Independence Day**
August 5

Formerly called Upper Volta, Burkina Faso gained independence from France on August 5, 1960, an event commemorated as a national holiday each year. The area had been a French protectorate since the 1890s.

CONTACTS:
Embassy of Burkina Faso
2340 Massachusetts Ave. N.W.
Washington, D.C. 20008
202-332-5577; fax: 202-667-1882
www.burkinaembassy-usa.org

SOURCES:
AnnivHol-2000, p. 131

♦ 0389 ♦ **Burkina Faso Republic Day**
December 11

On this day in 1958 Upper Volta (now Burkina Faso) voted to become an independent republic within the French community. It was then internally self-governing until it achieved independence in 1960 (*see* BURKINA FASO INDEPENDENCE DAY). This is considered the most important national holiday in Burkina Faso, with many events held in the capital city of Ouagadougou.

CONTACTS:
Embassy of Burkina Faso
2340 Massachusetts Ave. N.W.
Washington, D.C. 20008
202-332-5577; fax: 202-667-1882
www.burkinaembassy-usa.org

SOURCES:
AnnivHol-2000, p. 206
NatlHolWrld-1968, p. 224

♦ 0390 ♦ **Burning Man Festival**
September, Labor Day weekend

The Burning Man is a counterculture festival held in Nevada's Black Rock Desert near Gerlach over LABOR DAY weekend. Conceived by Larry Harvey in 1986 to honor the SUMMER SOLSTICE, an eight-foot, wooden human figure was burned on Baker Beach in San Francisco in front of a small crowd of about 20. This act of "radical self-expression," as Harvey later called it, would evolve into an annual event drawing thousands of people from all over the world. In 1990 when the police intervened and banned the actual burning of the Man, the event was moved to the desert.

Fueled by the Internet, other media, and word of mouth, Burning Man has become a populist phenomenon, where participants set up a temporary "city," creating their own community, for a few days. "No spectators" is the motto, and people are expected to interact with one another, produce and display artwork and fashion, play music, dance, do spontaneous performances—as long as they actively participate. The 50-foot-high, neon-lit Man towers over Black Rock City until the climax of the festival on Saturday night. While more than 15,000 desert dwellers watch, the figure is ignited and the Man becomes a fiery blaze, with previously loaded fireworks shooting out of him into the night sky. The next day, participants dismantle their city and leave the desert as

they found it, with no trace of the Burning Man festivities—until the next year.

CONTACTS:
Burning Man Project
P.O. Box 884688
San Francisco, CA 94188
415-863-5263
www.burningman.com

SOURCES:
FunAlsoRises-1998, p. 183
WildPlanet-1995, p. 611

♦ 0391 ♦ **Burning of Judas**
Between March 22 and April 25; Easter

La Quema de Judas takes place throughout Venezuela on the evening of EASTER Sunday. Unlike the many solemn rituals organized by the Roman Catholic Church during HOLY WEEK, Judas burning is a local affair, organized by villages and neighborhoods. The preparations go on all week, beginning with the selection of an appropriate Judas—usually a public figure in the community, but sometimes an individual well known throughout the state or nation—against whom the group has decided to stage a protest. The women construct a life-sized effigy of this person, making sure to include elements of dress or appearance that leave no mistake about its identity. The men build a wooden stand in a central location where the Judas figure will be placed.

On Easter afternoon, the people proceed to the house where the effigy has been stored for safekeeping and demand that Judas Iscariot, the disciple who betrayed Jesus, be turned over for punishment. The Judas effigy is placed on the stand, where everyone gets a chance to hit or kick it. At dusk the leader of the group recites the complaints that the people have against this individual—a document known as "The Testament of Judas," which is often written in verse and quite humorous. Then the event leaders pour gasoline on the Judas and set flame to it. The drinking, dancing, and fireworks continue late into the evening.

Although no one seems to know exactly how the custom originated, accounts of it have been traced back as far as 13th-century Spain.

See also HOLY SATURDAY IN MEXICO

SOURCES:
EncyEaster-2002, p. 328
FolkWrldHol-1999, p. 245

♦ 0392 ♦ **Burning of the Ribbons (Queima das Fitas)**
May

The Burning of the Ribbons is an eight-day festival that transforms the Portuguese city of Coimbra into a lively festival with music and merriment abounding. The event is centered around a tradition, dating from the 19th century, that is perpetuated by students at the University of Coimbra (the oldest in Portugal). At the end of the second semester (typically in May), the students ceremoniously burn the ribbons (one per day) that represent each of the eight faculties at the institution: Letters, Law, Medicine, Sciences & Technology, Pharmacy, Economics, Psychology & Education Sciences, and Sports Sciences & Physical Education.

Over the course of the eight days, numerous concerts and performances take place. Other highlights include sporting events, a gala ball, and a traditional nighttime serenade at the steps of the Old Cathedral of Coimbra. Thousands of students, townspeople, and tourists gather for the spirited performance. Another high point is the *cortejo*, an elaborate parade featuring floats bearing the respective colors of each faculty. They are accompanied by placards displaying criticisms of particular teachers, of politicians, and of the education system.

CONTACTS:
Portuguese National Tourist Office
590 5th Ave.
4th Fl.
New York, NY 10036
800-767-8842 or 646-723-0200; fax: 212-764-6137
www.visitportugal.com

♦ 0393 ♦ **Burning of the Socks**
March 21, spring equinox

This pungent event takes place in Eastport, Maryland, on the day of the VERNAL EQUINOX. Once a mere suburb of Annapolis, Eastport seceded when the bridge that connected them with the rest of the city was closed for repairs. Local residents reorganized themselves as the "Maritime Republic of Eastport," a little town with an independent spirit, a sense of humor, and a love of local tradition. The town's motto: "We like it this way."

The burning of the socks began in the mid-1970s when a man named Bob Turner, upon leaving his job at the boatyard on the first day of spring, decided to burn his socks in tribute to the coming warmer weather. When he later became the owner of the Annapolis Harbor Boatyard, he invited his employees to stay after work on the first day of spring, burn their socks, and drink a beer in honor of the occasion. Turner's personal custom caught on with others and became a local tradition. The Eastport Yacht Club now organizes the yearly event at which people drink beer, eat oysters, and burn socks, all in the name of driving away winter and welcoming spring.

CONTACTS:
Eastport Yacht Club
317 First St.
P.O. Box 3205
Annapolis, MD 21403
410-263-0415; fax: 410-216-9263
www.eastportyc.org

The Maritime Republic of Eastport
P.O. Box 3455
Eastport, MD 21403
410-990-9025; fax: 410-263-3434
www.themre.org

♦ 0394 ♦ **Burning the Clavie**
January 11

The Burning of the Clavie takes place in Burghead, a fishing village in the region of Moray, Scotland, on January 11, or Old New Year's Eve (*see* OLD CHRISTMAS DAY). Local residents make the clavie themselves by sawing a tar barrel into a larger and smaller half, breaking the larger half into pieces and stuffing it inside the smaller half along with tinder and tar. Once this is done they nail the clavie to a stout post. According to tradition, the clavie must be made without the use of store-bought tools. Therefore a local blacksmith makes the nail, which is hammered to the post with a stone.

At dusk the Clavie King sets the clavie on fire and leads a procession in which the burning barrel is dragged around the harbor and town. The procession stops at the homes of prominent townspeople, and paraders toss a chunk of the clavie through their doors, a custom said to bring good luck to the inhabitants. The parade proceeds to a high headland along the coast, where the flames from the clavie ignite a huge bonfire. At the end of the festivities, the clavie tumbles down the hill. Town inhabitants gather pieces of the clavie to take home with them, using them to light a New Year fire believed to keep witches and evil spirits away for a year.

Because the headland where the bonfire takes place is also the site of a ruined Roman temple, some people believe that the celebration is a survival of an ancient Roman custom. Others trace the festival back to Scandinavia, while another group suspects that it comes from the Druids, members of a pre-Christian religious order that developed among the ancient Celts.

CONTACTS:
Aberdeen and Grampian Tourist Board
Exchange House
26/28 Exchange St.
Aberdeen, AB11 6PH United Kingdom
44-12-2428-8811; fax: 44-12-2428-8838
www.agtb.org

SOURCES:
OxYear-1999, p. 31
YrFest-1972, p. 120

♦ 0395 ♦ **Burning the Devil**
December 7

La Quema del Diablo takes place in Guatemala. Men dressed as devils chase children through the streets from the start of ADVENT until December 7, the eve of the IMMACULATE CONCEPTION. On this day, trash fires are lit in the streets of Guatemala City and other towns, and the devils' reign of terror comes to an end.

CONTACTS:
Guatemalan Embassy
2220 R St. N.W.
Washington, D.C. 20008
202-745-4952; fax: 202-745-1908

SOURCES:
EncyChristmas-2003, p. 320
FolkWrldHol-1999, p. 691

♦ 0396 ♦ Burning the Moon House
February; 15th day of the first lunar month

The festival known as **Dal-jip-tae-u-gee** in the Kyongsang provinces of Korea pays tribute to the moon by watching it rise through a moon house or moon gate—a carefully constructed pile of pine branches which are set on fire. The moon gate is usually built on the top of a hill or at the seashore, where it is easier to see the moon rise through the flames. Jumping over the flames is believed to ward off evil, and the direction in which the moon gate collapses is an indication of whether the coming year will bring good luck or bad.

In other parts of Korea, a similar moon festival known as **Dal-ma-ji** is celebrated on the eve of the first full moon of the lunar year. People climb hills and build bonfires (without the "gate") to welcome the moon. Various folkloric beliefs concerning the harvest and the weather are associated with the color and brightness of the moon on this night.

See also TAEBORUM

SOURCES:
AnnCustKorea-1983, p. 61
FolkWrldHol-1999, p. 90

♦ 0397 ♦ Burns (Robert) Night
January 25

Burns Night is the anniversary of the birthday of Scottish poet Robert Burns, who was born in 1759 in a clay cottage that blew down a week later and died in 1796. The day is celebrated not only in Scotland but also in Newfoundland, where there is a sizeable settlement of Scots, and wherever there are devotees of this lusty poet.

The celebrations generally take the form of recitations of Burns's poetry ("Tam O'Shanter" is a standard), the imbibing of quantities of single-malt Scotch whiskey, and the serving of haggis, a Scottish dish made of a sheep's or calf's innards (liver, heart, etc.) cut up with suet and oatmeal, seasoned, and boiled in the stomach of the animal. At the point of the carving of the haggis, it is traditional to recite "To a Haggis," with its line, "Great chieftain o' the pudding race!"

In the course of things, the Selkirk grace is also read: *"Some hae meat, and canna eat/ And some wad eat that want it/ But we hae meat and we can eat/ And sae the Lord be thanket."* And other favorite lines will be heard—for example, "O, my luve's like a red, red rose," and "O wad some Pow'r the giftie gie us/ To see oursels as others see us!" The evening always ends, of course, with "Auld Lang Syne."

CONTACTS:
Edinburgh Convention Bureau
29 Drumsheugh Gardens
Edinburgh, Scotland EH3 7RN United Kingdom
44-13-1473-3666; fax: 44-13-1473-3877
www.edinburgh.org

SOURCES:
AmerBkDays-2000, p. 86
BkHolWrld-1986, Jan 25

DictDays-1988, p. 16
FolkWrldHol-1999, p. 47
OxYear-1999, p. 49

♦ 0398 ♦ Burry Man Day
Second Friday in August

The "Burry Man" has appeared on the streets of South Queensbury, West Lothian, Scotland, annually for over 600 years. He wears a headdress made of flowers that completely hides his face, and his body is costumed with a thick mat of teazle burrs and thistles. With a staff in each hand, he walks from house to house without uttering a word. Nevertheless, people address him politely and often offer him money, in return for which he bestows good fortune on their home.

Some say that the ceremonies of Burry Man Day commemorate King Malcolm III's escape from the British, which he accomplished with the aid of a thick covering of burs and flowers. Another theory contends that the Burry Man is a remnant of an old custom connected with the gathering of fair tolls. This theory draws strength from the fact that he appears on the day before Ferry Fair.

CONTACTS:
Royal Botanic Garden Edinburgh
20A Inverleith Row
Edinburgh, Scotland EH3 5LR United Kingdom
44-13-1552-7171; fax: 44-13-1248-2901
www.rbge.org.uk

Edinburgh and Lothians Tourist Board, Edinburgh and Scotland
   Information Centre
3 Princes St.
Edinburgh, Scotland EH2 2QP United Kingdom
44-84-5225-5121
www.edinburgh.org

SOURCES:
YrFest-1972, p. 53

♦ 0399 ♦ Burundi Independence Day
July 1

This national holiday commemorates Burundi's independence from Belgium, which had control over the country since the end of World War II, on this day in 1962. Before the war, Germany had counted Burundi among its African territories. Since independence, the country has suffered from devastating ethnic violence between the Hutus, who constitute the majority of the population, and the Tutsis, who are in the minority.

CONTACTS:
Burundi Embassy
2233 Wisconsin Ave. N.W., Ste. 212
Washington, D.C. 20007
202-342-2574; fax: 202-342-2578

SOURCES:
AnnivHol-2000, p. 110
NatlHolWrld-1968, p. 97

♦ 0400 ♦ Busan Sea Festival
August

Every August, beginning in 1999, the municipal government of the seaside town of Busan (Pusan) in South Korea has sponsored a nine-day Sea Festival on its main beaches. The festival kicks off with an opening ceremony featuring performances by popular singers and other entertainers and culminates that night in a spectacular fireworks display. Over the course of the festival, a variety of water sports are offered, as well as the Hanbada Festival for the Disabled and championship competitions in windsurfing and beach volleyball.

CONTACTS:
Korea National Tourism Organization
737 N. Michigan Ave., Ste. 910
Chicago, IL 60611
800-868-7567 or 312-981-1717; fax: 312-981-1721
english.visitkorea.or.kr

◆ 0401 ◆ Buskers' Festival
Late August

"Buskers" are vagabond musicians. They were common in the streets of 14th-century Ferrara, Italy, when it was ruled by the Dukes of Este. They still roam the streets of the world's cities, although they may be difficult to find because they usually have no fixed address and no manager or agent to contact. But Stefano Bottoni, artistic director of Ferrara's Buskers' Festival, manages to track them down and persuade them to come for a seven-day celebration of music that ranges from salsa to Celtic laments, and from MOZART to New Orleans jazz. They are not paid anything, nor are they given a stage to perform on, but since 1988 hundreds of them have wandered the city's narrow streets for a week in August, improvising their own kind of music and jamming with other itinerant musicians. Nearly 700 buskers come from all over the world to perform in Ferrara's squares and alleyways, with its spectacular medieval and Renaissance architecture as their backdrop. The week ends with a jam session in front of the walls of the castle in the center of the town.

CONTACTS:
Ferrara Buskers Festival Association
Via De'Romei 3
Ferrara, Emilia-Romagna 44100 Italy
39-532-2493-37; fax: 39-532-2070-48
www.ferrarabuskers.com

◆ 0402 ◆ Butter and Egg Days
First weekend after last Wednesday in April

This is a promotional event in Petaluma, Calif., that recalls the historic days when Petaluma was the "World's Egg Basket," producing millions of eggs that were shipped all over the world. The first Butter and Egg Days was a modest affair in 1983; it now draws about 25,000 for a parade with floats, bands, bagpipers, and children dressed as such things as butter pats and fried eggs. There are also street fairs, an antiques show, an egg toss, a butter-churning contest, and the presentation of the Good Egg award to a Petaluma booster.

The seed of this event was laid in 1918 when the first Egg Day parade was held. With the food shortages of World War I, people were being urged to eat less meat, and Petalumans decided to promote the idea of eating more eggs. Petaluma had the eggs; there were more hatcheries here than anywhere else. In 1878, the incubator developer L. C. Byce had established the Petaluma Incubator Co., which allowed great numbers of baby chicks to be artificially hatched. The town became a thriving poultry center, and boasted the world's only chicken pharmacy. The Egg Days, which ran from 1918 to 1926, brought the town national attention. These were huge celebrations, with nighttime illuminations, balls, chicken rodeos, and parades with gigantic Humpty Dumptys and white leghorn chickens. The chicken-and-egg industry waned in the 1950s, and the dairy industry moved in, which is now honored along with eggs.

CONTACTS:
Petaluma Visitors Program
210 Lakeville St.
Petaluma, CA 94952
877-273-8258 or 707-769-0429
www.visitpetaluma.com

◆ 0403 ◆ Butter Sculpture Festival
15th day of first lunar month

The celebration of the Buddhist New Year (LOSAR) in Tibet is followed by MONLAM, a two-week prayer festival. On the 15th day, everyone goes to a monastery to view the butter sculptures. The most famous are at Jokhang Monastery in Lhasa, Tibet's capital. Completed over a period of months, the huge sculptures are made out of yak butter pigmented with dyes. They are fastened to 30-foot-high frames for display purposes and illuminated by special butter lamps. Each monastery maintains a workshop where its own artists shape the cold-hardened butter into depictions of legends, or other themes, different each year.

SOURCES:
BkHolWrld-1986, Mar 9
FolkWrldHol-1999, p. 86

◆ 0404 ◆ Butter Week (Russia)
February-March, the week preceding Ash Wednesday

CARNIVAL is known as Butter Week or **Maslyanitsa** (also rendered Maslenitsa) in Russia because Russians consume so many rich foods throughout this week, the last before the seven-week Lenten fast. *Bliny,* Russian-style pancakes served with sour cream or butter, are eaten all week long and have come to symbolize the feast. People enjoy one rich meal after another as the week proceeds. LENT begins on the Monday following the last Sunday in Butter Week. On this day observant Russian Orthodox Christians remove meat and dairy products from their diets.

Around the turn of the 20th century, the Carnival celebration in St. Petersburg ended with a ceremony in which a folk figure called Prince Carnival rode through town in a cart pulled by 10 horses and bade farewell to the people. He was represented as a tipsy man, sitting before a table covered with food.

When the Prince departed, the people celebrated the end of Carnival with a display of fireworks. In many areas people enjoy winter sports such as skiing, sledding, ice skating, and snowball fights during Butter Week. In some places people mark the end of Carnival by making huge hand-sewn dolls that represent winter and tossing them onto burning bonfires.

CONTACTS:
Department of Tourism
47 Myasnitskaya St.
Moscow, 107084 Russia
7-495-207-7176; fax: 7-495-207-3745
www.russiatourism.ru

SOURCES:
BkFest-1937, p. 289
EncyEaster-2002, p. 382
FolkWrldHol-1999, p. 165
OxYear-1999, p. 641

♦ 0405 ♦ Buzzard Day
Sunday following March 15

About 75 turkey vultures, also known as turkey buzzards, return to Hinckley, Ohio, each March 15 to spend the summer. While these carrion-eating birds may lack the charm of the Swallows of San Juan Capistrano, thousands of people celebrate them at the Hinckley Buzzard Day Festival, held since 1958 on the first Sunday after March 15. It features tours, hikes, and talks by naturalists at Metro Park, where the buzzards roost.

The vultures' return was first documented by a park patrolman who logged their arrival date for 23 years. Why the birds return, however, isn't known. One theory recalls the Great Hinckley Varmint Hunt on Dec. 24, 1818, when 475 men and boys lined up along Hinckley's borders and moved inward, slaughtering predators that were killing farm animals. The tons of carrion, of course, provided fine repasts for vulturine tastes.

CONTACTS:
Hinckley Township
1410 Ridge Rd.
P.O. Box 344
Hinckley, OH 44233
330-278-4181; fax: 330-278-2023
www.hinckleytwp.org

SOURCES:
AnnivHol-2000, p. 44
FolkAmerHol-1999, p. 129

♦ 0406 ♦ Byblos Festival
May-September

The ancient city of Byblos in Lebanon has hosted an international music festival since the late 1960s. Performances of orchestral, chamber music, and jazz concerts are held throughout the summer. There are also plays, operettas, ballet, and modern dance recitals. Most of the events are held in the 12th-century castle built by the Crusaders out of the stones and granite columns of ancient Roman temples and public buildings.

Byblos, also known as Jubayl or Jebeil, is one of the oldest continuously inhabited towns in the world. The precursor of the modern alphabet was developed in Byblos, and the ancient Phoenicians exported their papyrus to the Aegean through the city. The English word "Bible" is derived from *byblos*, the early Greek name for papyrus.

CONTACTS:
Lebanon Ministry of Tourism
550 Central Bank St.
P.O. Box 11-5344
Hamra, Beirut Lebanon
961-134-0940; fax: 961-134-0940
www.byblosfestival.org
www.destinationlebanon.gov.lb

SOURCES:
IntlThFolk-1979, p. 264

C

♦ 0407 ♦ Cabrillo Day and Festival
Week including September 28

Juan Rodríguez Cabrillo was the Portuguese explorer who discovered California on September 28, 1542, when he sailed into the bay that would eventually be called San Diego. He went on to explore the upper California coast, naming both Catalina and San Clemente islands after his ships, but he failed to discover San Francisco Bay before being driven south again by a severe storm.

In the San Diego area, Cabrillo Day celebrations were relatively modest until the early 1960s, when the week-long Cabrillo Festival became a yearly event. Activities include Portuguese-American music and dancing, the placing of a wreath at the base of Cabrillo's statue on Point Loma, and a costumed reenactment of the discovery of San Diego Bay.

CONTACTS:
Cabrillo National Monument
National Park Service
1800 Cabrillo Memorial Dr.
San Diego, CA 92106
619-557-5450; fax: 619-226-6311
www.nps.gov

SOURCES:
AmerBkDays-2000, p. 676

♦ 0408 ♦ Caitra Parb
March-April; eight days before the full moon of Hindu month of Caitra

A Hindu festival held in Orissa, India, Caitra Parb begins eight days before the purnima (full moon). Throughout the celebration people fast, dance, and hunt. Heads of the families pay homage to their forefathers in the presence of the village priest, or *Jani,* and family members put on festive new costumes. Animal sacrifice plays a prominent part in the celebration, which also signals the beginning of the mango season.

CONTACTS:
Department of Tourism, Government of Orissa
Paryatan Bhawan, Museum Campus
Bhubaneswar, Orissa 751 014 India
91-674-432177; fax: 91-674-430887
www.orissatourism.gov.in

SOURCES:
RelHolCal-2004, p. 185

♦ 0409 ♦ Caitra Purnima
March-April; 10 days in Hindu month of Caitra

In southern India, Caitra Purnima is a time for Hindus to worship Chitra Gupta, also known as "the scribe of the gods." Tradition holds that while Brahma was meditating, Chitra Gupta was brought into being. He serves as the scribe to Yama, the ruler and judge of the dead. Some Hindus believe that it is Chitra Gupta who maintains the accounts of their good and bad deeds in the *Agrasamdhani* (main records).

At Kanchipuram, near Madras in Tamil Nadu State, the image of Chitra Gupta is taken out in a procession. Devotees bathe in the holy waters of the River Chitra, which flows from the nearby hills.

CONTACTS:
Tamil Nadu Tourism
Tourism Complex, No. 2 Wallajah Rd.
Chennai, Tamil Nadu 600 002 India
91-44-25383333; fax: 91-44-25381567
www.tamilnadutourism.org

SOURCES:
DictHindu-1977, p. 63
RelHolCal-2004, p. 185

♦ 0410 ♦ Calaveras County Fair and Frog Jumping Jubilee
Third weekend in May

This event is a four-day county fair, established in 1928, at the Frogtown Fairgrounds near Angels Camp, Calif. It includes the official, original frog-jumping contest based on Mark Twain's story, "The Celebrated Jumping Frog of Calaveras County," as well as a children's parade, livestock competitions, a professional rodeo, a demolition derby, fireworks, and art exhibits. About 3,500 frogs are jumped in daily contests leading up to the Grand Finals on Sunday, in which there are 75 to 100 frog contestants. Jumps are measured from starting point to the landing point of the third hop. The world's record is 21' 5¾", set in 1986 by Rosie the Ribiter.

There are cash prizes for winners in various divisions, and anyone breaking Rosie's world record will win $5,000.

Mark Twain wrote the story of the jumping frog in 1865 and claimed it was told to him as the true story of an episode in Angels Camp in 1849. In his story, the original frog, named Dan'l Webster, was owned by one Jim Smiley, who educated it to be a fine jumper. When a stranger came along, Smiley bet him $40 Dan'l Webster could out-jump any frog in Calaveras County. The time arrived for the contest, but the stranger had secretly filled Dan'l Webster with quail shot, and the frog couldn't move. The stranger took the money and left, saying (according to Twain), "Well, *I* don't see no p'ints about that frog that's any better'n any other frog."

CONTACTS:
39th District Agricultural Association
P.O. Box 489
Angels Camp, CA 95222
209-736-2561; fax: 209-736-2476
www.frogtown.org

SOURCES:
BkHolWrld-1986, May 22

♦ 0411 ♦ Calendimaggio
Three days beginning the first Thursday after May 1

According to legend, ST. FRANCIS OF ASSISI used to walk through the streets of Assisi at night, singing. During one of these nocturnal outings, he had a vision of the *Madonna Poverta,* or Lady Poverty, after which he renounced his inheritance and even his clothes and began a new life tending those who suffered from leprosy.

In Assisi, Italy, in early May each year, long processions of *messeri* (gentlemen) and *madonne* (ladies), escorted by knights and esquires, compete with each other in singing and music at the Piazza del Comune. In addition to commemorating the town's patron saint, these singing contests serve as an official welcome to May, which is known as the month of love.

CONTACTS:
Umbria Touristic Promotion Board
Via Mazzini, 21
Perugia, Umbria 06100 Italy
39-75-5759-51; fax: 39-75-5736-828

SOURCES:
FestEur-1961, p. 115
OxDictSaints-1987, p. 167

♦ 0412 ♦ Calgary Exhibition and Stampede
July

The 10-day Calgary Exhibition and Stampede, originally called the **Calgary Stampede**, is Canada's largest rodeo event, similar to CHEYENNE FRONTIER DAYS in the United States. The stampede offers a world-class rodeo competition in saddle bronc and bareback riding, steer wrestling, calf roping, and bull riding, as well as a chuck wagon race that carries a $175,000 prize. Most of the rodeo events are held in the

130-acre Stampede Park in downtown Calgary, but there's also a Wild West town called Weadickville (named for Guy Weadick from Cheyenne, Wyoming, who founded the event in 1912), an Indian Village populated by representatives of five Indian tribes from the nearby Plains, a Frontier Casino with blackjack tables and roulette wheels, and agricultural and livestock exhibits.

CONTACTS:
Calgary Stampede Ticket Office
P.O. Box 1060, Sta. M
Calgary, AL T2P 2K8 Canada
403-261-0101; fax: 403-265-7187
www.cs.calgarystampede.com

SOURCES:
GdWrldFest-1985, p. 28

♦ 0413 ♦ Calgary International Children's Festival
Late May, during the week following Victoria Day

Children, parents, and teachers are entertained and educated every year at the Calgary International Children's Festival. This five-day event takes place in downtown Calgary, located in the Canadian province of Alberta. The festival features storytelling, dance, music, puppetry, and physical comedy, all catering to a young audience. The performances take place in and around the EPCOR CENTRE, located in the Olympic Plaza Cultural District.

The program of the festival, which was launched in 1989, reflects the organizers' emphasis on creativity and cultural sensitivity. Teacher guides are provided to instructors looking to ensure an educational experience for students. A large corps of volunteers helps run the event, and through the financial contributions of donors and sponsors, an outreach program has been established to provide free admission to economically disadvantaged children.

CONTACTS:
Calgary International Children's Festival Office
205 8 Ave. S.E.
Calgary, AB T2G 0K9 Canada
www.calgarychildfest.org

♦ 0414 ♦ Cali Fair (Sugar Cane Fair, Salsa Fair)
Last week in December

Santiago de Cali, the third-largest city in Colombia, is the capital of one of the country's most prosperous regions, the Valle del Cauca. The rich cultural identity of this city (often called simply "Cali") and the surrounding area have been celebrated each year since 1957 at the Cali Fair. Although it is billed as a "town fair," suggesting a small country festival, the Cali Fair is a major event that draws thousands of local residents and tourists from around the world. Cali is the center of Colombia's sugar industry and is also known as the home of the best salsa dancing in Colombia. The celebration of sugar and salsa is a prominent part of the festival, which is also known as the **Sugar Cane Fair** and the **Salsa Fair**.

The Fair opens with the *cabalgata,* an elaborate cavalcade of riders mounted on fine horses, which moves through the streets of the city. Other parades take place throughout the duration of the Fair. There are numerous artisans selling their crafts, street performers, and other forms of entertainment. There are beauty contests, cultural exhibitions, concerts, and sporting events, including a marathon along the Cali River. A Bullfighting Festival is also part of the celebration. Held at La Plaza de Toros de Cañaveralejo, the Bullfighting Festival showcases the top bulls and matadors from the Americas and Europe.

Many parties and dances take place around the city during the Cali Fair. A salsa marathon is one of many dance events held each year. There are also contests for tango and just about every other kind of Latin American dance. It is said that during Fair time, Cali is the home of the best salsa dancing in the world.

CONTACTS:
Offices of the City of Santiago de Cali
Santiago de Cali, Valle del Cauca Colombia
www.cali.gov.co

Tourism Promotion Fund of Colombia
Calle 69
No. 11-66
Bogota, Colombia
www.turismocolombia.com

♦ 0415 ♦ **Calico Pitchin', Cookin', and Spittin' Hullabaloo**
March-April; Palm Sunday weekend

This event is a celebration highlighting a tobacco-spitting contest and recalling the 19th-century heyday of Calico, a silver-mining ghost town in southern California about 10 miles north of Barstow. The contest for World Tobacco Spitting Champion began in 1977 and has led to two mentions in the *Guinness Book of World Records* for distance in juice-spitting: Randy Ober of Arkansas spat a record 44' 6" in 1980 and then topped that record the next year with 47' 10". Other contest categories are accuracy in juice-spitting and distance in wadspitting (wads are required to be at least half an inch in diameter). Contestants have come not only from the United States but also from Great Britain, Germany, and Japan.

The hullabaloo also features a stew cook-off and flapjack racing, plus more standard fare such as a horseshoe-pitching contest, egg-tossing, greased-pole climbing, and bluegrass music.

The date of the event recalls the time of year in 1881 when the miners arrived and named the town Calico because they thought the reds, greens, and yellows of the rock formations looked like a calico skirt. It was the location of one of the largest silver strikes in California, producing about $86 million in silver during the 20 years it flourished. When silver prices sank, so did Calico. In San Bernardino County, Calico is visited by tourists year-round.

CONTACTS:
San Bernardino Convention & Visitors Bureau
1955 Hunts Lane, Ste. 102

San Bernardino, CA 92408
909-891-1151; fax: 909-888-5998
www.san-bernardino.org

♦ 0416 ♦ **California Avocado Festival**
October

The California Avocado Festival is held every October in Carpinteria, Calif. The three-day, free event features music, arts and crafts, activities (including a golf tournament), and a kids' block party with games, face-painting, and crafts. It also celebrates the avocado. At the Avocado Expo tent, competitors vie to win the awards for best guacamole and biggest avocado. There are cooking demonstrations and a display of the largest vat of guacamole in the world. About 100,000 visitors enjoy each year's avocado celebration.

The festival began in 1986, when a group of community leaders in Carpinteria met to organize an ongoing weekend event to help raise money for local non-profit organizations. Carpinteria is an avocado-growing area located in Santa Barbara County, the third-largest producer of avocados in North America. It seemed natural to put the rough-skinned green fruit at the center of the event. Now the festival benefits more than 40 non-profit groups, whose volunteers work at the festival. And the festival itself is a volunteer-run event, with just one part-time paid staff person. A non-profit group itself, the festival generates its own annual operating revenue.

CONTACTS:
California Avocado Festival
P.O. Box 146
Carpinteria, CA 93014-0146
805-684-0038
www.avofest.com

♦ 0417 ♦ **California Gold Rush Day**
Weekend nearest January 24

The anniversary of James W. Marshall's discovery of gold in 1848 while overseeing the construction of a sawmill near Coloma, Calif., is commemorated with an annual celebration at the Marshall Gold Discovery State Historic Park on the weekend nearest January 24. An employee of John A. Sutter, a wealthy landowner and entrepreneur, Marshall noticed flakes of gold in the streambed as he was inspecting work on the mill. Although Sutter and Marshall tried to keep the discovery secret, over the next year approximately 60,000 to 100,000 gold prospectors flocked to California. The surface deposits of gold eventually dwindled, but both Sutter and Marshall had already been ruined by the gold rush they tried to forestall. Sutter died bankrupt in 1888, and Marshall died five years later, living alone in a crude cabin just a short distance from where he'd first noticed the gleam of metal.

Marshall's cabin is now part of the Marshall Gold Discovery State Historic Park, and Sutter's adobe home is part of a museum and park in Sacramento.

CONTACTS:
Marshall Gold Discovery State Historic Park
310 Back St.

P.O. Box 265
Coloma, CA 95613
530-622-3470
www.parks.ca.gov

SOURCES:
AmerBkDays-2000, p. 83
AnnivHol-2000, p. 14

◆ 0418 ◆ **Calinda Dance**
June 23

The Calinda Dance was a 19th-century Voodoo ritual observed on the eve of ST. JOHN'S DAY in New Orleans. Performed by Sanité Dédé, a Voodoo priestess who confined herself to a very small space and imitated the undulations of a snake, the Calinda was so sensual that in the frenzied group dance that followed it, the dancers tore off their clothing and engaged in an orgy.

Although most Voodoo ceremonies were held in secret, the New Orleans authorities allowed slaves to dance in Congo Square on Sunday afternoons where the authorities could keep an eye on them. This marked the end of the orgy climax and resulted in a combination of the original snake dance with an African war dance. But the Calinda remained so threatening to whites that it was banned as obscene in 1843, shortly before Voodoo enjoyed its greatest popularity under the leadership of Marie Laveau. Laveau presided over the gatherings in Congo Square and turned the St. John's Eve celebration into a public show to which whites and even some newspaper reporters were invited.

SOURCES:
FolkAmerHol-1999, p. 264

◆ 0419 ◆ **Cambodia Constitution Day**
September 24

After a long and troubled history, Cambodia became a constitutional monarchy in 1993. Constitution Day marks the anniversary of the formal adoption of the Constitution of Cambodia on September 24, 1993. Under the constitution, the king is head of state, but the elected National Assembly has legislative power. The prime minister is appointed by the king from representatives of the political party with the largest number of seats in the Assembly.

Constitution Day is also the anniversary of the recoronation of King Norodom Sihanouk, who was overthrown by General Lon Nol in 1970. September 24 is a national holiday in Cambodia. All banks, state offices, and most businesses are closed.

CONTACTS:
Royal Embassy of Cambodia
4530 16th St. N.W.
Washington, D.C. 20011
202-726-7742 or 202-726-8268; fax: 202-726-8381
www.embassyofcambodia.org

◆ 0420 ◆ **Cambodia Independence Day**
November 9

Cambodia was a French protectorate for 90 years before it gained independence from France on November 9, 1953. Independence Day, which marks that event, is a national holiday. The principal celebrations are held in the capital city of Phnom Penh, beginning with a morning ceremony at Independence Monument on the crossroads of Norodom and Sihanouk Boulevards, usually with the King of Cambodia in attendance. Later in the day, there is a gala parade held in front of the Royal Palace in Phnom Penh, with colorful floats and marching bands. Shops are adorned with national flags. After dark, the Royal Palace and other important buildings and monuments are lit up. A large fireworks display is held near the riverbanks of the Royal Palace.

CONTACTS:
Royal Embassy of Cambodia
4530 16th St. N.W.
Washington, D.C. 20011
202-726-7742 or 202-726-8268; fax: 202-726-8381
www.embassyofcambodia.org

Tourism of Cambodia
262 Monivong Blvd.
Khan Daun Penh
Phnom Penh, Cambodia
www.tourismcambodia.com

◆ 0421 ◆ **Cambodia National Culture Day**
April 3

This event was created in 1999 by the Cambodian government as a way to promote the country's arts and culture. The yearly event is composed of displays, exhibits, live theatrical performances, and conferences held throughout the country. The festival honors the living elder masters in different artistic and cultural fields.

The Ministry of Culture and Fine Arts coordinates many of the events and uses the occasion to take stock of Cambodia's cultural infrastructure, including its historic temples, pagodas, and other landmarks important to the country's heritage and tourism.

CONTACTS:
Ministry of Culture and Fine Arts
227 Norodom Blvd.
Phnom Penh, Cambodia
mcfa.gov.kh

Royal Embassy of Cambodia
4530 16th St. N.W.
Washington, DC 20011
202-726-7742 or 202-726-8268; fax: 202-726-8381
www.embassyofcambodia.org

◆ 0422 ◆ **Cambodia Queen Sihanouk's Birthday**
June 18

Her Majesty Norodom Monineath Sihanouk is the mother of King Norodom Sihamoni of Cambodia. The birthday of the Queen Mother is a national holiday in Cambodia, with government offices, schools, and many businesses closed. The holiday is a relatively quiet one, with no lavish festivities normally planned. This is in contrast to the three-day celebration of King Sihanouk's Birthday, the former king and the husband of Queen Sihanouk.

CONTACTS:
Royal Embassy of Cambodia
4530 16th St. N.W.
Washington, D.C. 20011
202-726-7742 or 202-726-8268; fax: 202-726-8381
www.embassyofcambodia.org

Tourism of Cambodia
262 Monivong Blvd.
Khan Daun Penh
Phnom Penh, Cambodia
www.tourismcambodia.com

♦ 0423 ♦ **Cambodia Victory Day (Victory over Genocide Day, Nation Day)**
January 7

This national holiday is also called **Victory over Genocide Day** and **Nation Day**. It marks the day in 1979 that Vietnamese troops entered Cambodia and began an assault that ended the bloody regime of the Khmer Rouge. It is estimated that as many as two million Cambodians were killed during the nearly four years that Pol Pot of the Khmer Rouge ruled the country. The celebration is viewed with mixed emotions by many Cambodians, since the holiday also marks the beginning of Cambodian dependence on Vietnam.

Victory Day is celebrated with patriotic speeches by government officials, remembrance services for the victims, as well as cultural displays of the era.

CONTACTS:
Royal Embassy of Cambodia
4530 16th St. N.W.
Washington, D.C. 20011
202-726-7742 or 202-726-8268; fax: 202-726-8381
www.embassyofcambodia.org

Tourism of Cambodia
262 Monivong Blvd.
Khan Daun Penh
Phnom Penh, Cambodia
www.tourismcambodia.com

♦ 0424 ♦ **Cambodian New Year (Khmer New Year)**
Three days in mid-April (varies according to lunar calendar)

This three-day New Year holiday, also known as **Khmer Year**, is a major celebration in Cambodia. The first day is called *Moha Sangkran*, which means "New Angel." The tradition on this day is for families to welcome the angel who looks after the world in the coming year. To do so, people clean their houses and themselves and prepare a feast of such traditional foods as peanut curries, noodles, and tree mushrooms. Families bring food to offer Buddhist monks and gather for blessing and prayer. Another activity is the building of a small sand "mountain." Each bit of sand that is added is believed to increase the chance for health and happiness in the coming year.

The second day is known as *Wanabot* or *Vana Bat*. It is a day of gift giving to parents and other elders or persons worthy of respect. Many people also give gifts of charity on this day and perform acts of community service. More sand is added to the mountain.

The final day is called *Loeung Sack*. On this day the monks bless the sand mountains. This is also the day for people to wash their Buddha statues, which is thought to be a kind deed that will bring good luck and long life. The bathing also symbolizes hope for sufficient rainfall for the rice harvest. Many people also spray water on each other in a spirit of fun.

Throughout the new year celebration, children and adults gather to dance and play traditional games. Many streets in Cambodia are crowded with celebrants. The holiday often ends with a fireworks display.

CONTACTS:
Royal Embassy of Cambodia
4530 16th St. N.W.
Washington, D.C. 20011
202-726-7742 or 202-726-8268; fax: 202-726-8381
www.embassyofcambodia.org

Tourism of Cambodia
262 Monivong Blvd.
Khan Daun Penh
Phnom Penh, Cambodia
www.tourismcambodia.com

♦ 0425 ♦ **Camel Cup Carnival**
Early July

What began in 1971 as a friendly camel race between two Alice Springs Lions Club members has grown into a major Australian event that generates more than $250,000 annually for charity. Camels thrive in Alice Springs, which has one of the driest and harshest climates in Australia, and therefore it is not surprising that camel races play the same role there that horse races do in other, less arid parts of the country (*see* HOBART CUP DAY; MELBOURNE CUP DAY).

Today the Camel Cup takes place at Blatherskite Park in Alice Springs and is only one of several camel-oriented events, which are accompanied by the eating and beer-drinking that are a hallmark of so many Australian festivals. Other events include polo on camels, helicopter rides, rickshaw races, the Miss Camel Cup competition, and fireworks.

CONTACTS:
Camel Cup Committee Inc.
P.O. Box 3233
Alice Springs, NT 0871 Australia
61-8-8952-6796
www.camelcup.com.au

Alice Springs Town Council
93 Todd St.
P.O. Box 1071
Alice Springs, NT 0871 Australia
61-8-8950-0500; fax: 61-8-8953-0558
www.alicesprings.nt.gov.au

SOURCES:
WildPlanet-1995, p. 421

♦ 0426 ♦ **Camel Market**
Usually July

An important annual camel-trading fair in Guelmime (also spelled Goulimime or Goulimine), Morocco, a walled town that historically was a caravan center. Located on the northwest edge of the Sahara, the market is attended by the wanderers of the desert—the Shluh (a Berber people from southern Morocco), as well as the blue-veiled Tuareg men known as the Blue Men. The Tuaregs wear a blue *litham*, a double strip of blue cloth worn over the head and covering all but the eyes, sometimes giving their faces a blue tint. They also wear blue robes over their white *djellabahs*. The story is that an English cloth merchant visited the port and trading city of Agadir in the 1500s with calico dyed indigo blue. The Tuaregs liked the blue cloth and have had a predilection for it ever since.

The camel market brings together thousands of these nomads and their camels. They come to sell and trade baby camels as well as animal skins and wool. Hundreds of tents are pitched, and there is constant activity and noise: camel races, shouted bartering, and, at night, performances of the erotic *guedra* dance.

See also BIANOU and CURE SALÉE

CONTACTS:
Moroccan National Tourist Office
20 E. 46th St., Ste. 1201
New York, NY 10017
212-557-2520; fax: 212-949-8148
www.visitmorocco.org

♦ 0427 ♦ **Camel Races, International**
September, weekend after Labor Day

The International Camel Races are possibly the only camel races in the United States, and are a reminder of a peculiar 19th-century experiment. The races have been held since 1954 in Virginia City, Nev., the one-time mining town that was considered the richest place on earth in the 1860s. In 1991, a team from Alice Springs, Australia, won the races.

The town is the site of the celebrated Comstock Lode, which yielded nearly $300 million in gold and silver in the two decades after its discovery in 1859. The wealth also gave the territory strategic importance: President Abraham LINCOLN wanted Nevada as a state on the side of the North to support anti-slavery amendments, and he also needed the mineral riches to finance the Civil War. Nevada became a state in 1864, and gold and silver were dug from the mines—with the help, briefly, of camels.

It was thought that camels could work like mules in the mines, and camels in the Federal Camel Corps were shipped to Nevada from Texas (where they were used in the army cavalry). The army had originally brought about 120 camels to the U.S. from Africa and Asia in the mid-1850s to carry cargo from Texas to California. But they didn't last long; their hoofs didn't adapt to the rocky terrain, so they were allowed to roam wild, and apparently died out.

There are some camels kept in town today, though, and others are imported for the races. The three-day race weekend now includes a Camel Hump Ball (a dance and barbecue); a parade with about 70 units, including belly dancers and bagpipe players; and a race of ostriches pulling chariots.

When the camel race was being held in 1961, the movie *The Misfits* was being filmed nearby. Director John Huston came to the races, borrowed a camel, and won.

CONTACTS:
Virginia City Convention and Tourism Authority
86 S. C St.
P.O. Box 920
Virginia City, NV 89440
800-718-7587 or 775-847-7500; fax: 775-847-0935
www.visitvirginiacitynv.com

♦ 0428 ♦ **Cameroon National Day**
May 20

A public holiday commemorating the people's vote to establish a united Republic of Cameroon on May 20, 1972, this day is also known as **Constitution Day**.

CONTACTS:
Cameroon Embassy
2349 Massachusetts Ave. N.W.
Washington, D.C. 20008
202-265-8790; fax: 202-387-3826
www.ambacam-usa.org

SOURCES:
AnnivHol-2000, p. 84

♦ 0429 ♦ **Cameroon Youth Day**
February 11

This national holiday in the west African nation of Cameroon celebrates the country's young people. School children and youth groups participate in parades, often accompanied by university students in marching bands. Government officials watch the processions, along with many other onlookers. Businesses sell food and merchandise along the parade routes. Many schools and youth groups also organize art exhibits and sports activities.

The theme of Youth Day is to encourage Cameroon's young people to renounce violence and other unsavory behaviors and to embrace education, sports, and artistic activities. The country's president traditionally makes a nationally broadcast speech on Youth Day, commenting on the achievements of the country's young people and outlining the government's plans to improve education and youth employment opportunities.

CONTACTS:
Embassy of Cameroon
2349 Massachusetts Ave. N.W.
Washington, D.C. 20008
202-265-8790; fax: 202-387-3826
www.ambacam-usa.org

♦ 0430 ♦ **Camp Fire Founders' Day**
March 17

The organization originally known as the Camp Fire Girls was founded on March 17, 1910, around the same time that the Boy Scout movement was getting its start in Great Britain (*see* BOY SCOUTS' DAY). Now it is coeducational and is known as Camp Fire USA. The organization stresses self-reliance, and membership is divided into five different age levels, ranging from Sparks (pre-school) to Horizon (grades 9-12). Skilled adults work with these young people in small groups, helping them to become acquainted with nature's secrets and to learn a variety of crafts. Interaction with adults is also emphasized as a way of learning about career choices, hobbies, and other interests.

Camp Fire's founding is observed by the group's members as part of **Camp Fire Boys and Girls Birthday Week**. The Sunday nearest March 17 is **Camp Fire Boys and Girls Birthday Sunday** and is a day when Camp Fire Boys and Girls worship together and participate in their church or temple services.

CONTACTS:
Camp Fire USA
1100 Walnut St., Ste. 1800
Kansas City, MO 64106-2197
816-285-2010; fax: 816-285-9444
www.campfireusa.org

SOURCES:
AnnivHol-2000, p. 46

♦ 0431 ♦ **Canada Day**
July 1

The British North America Act went into effect on July 1, 1867, uniting Upper Canada (now called Ontario), Lower Canada (now Quebec), New Brunswick, and Nova Scotia into a British dominion. Canadians celebrate this day—which was formerly known as **Dominion Day**—with parades and picnics, somewhat similar to FOURTH OF JULY festivities in the United States.

In Detroit, Michigan, and Windsor, Ontario, which are on opposite sides of the Detroit River and are connected by a vehicular tunnel and the Ambassador Bridge, this is also one of the days on which the International FREEDOM FESTIVAL is held.

CONTACTS:
Canadian Heritage
15 Eddy St.
Gatineau, QC K1A OM5 Canada
819-997-0055
www.pch.gc.ca/index_e.cfm

SOURCES:
AnnivHol-2000, p. 110
BkHolWrld-1986, Jul 1
DictDays-1988, pp. 18, 32
GdWrldFest-1985, p. 55
NatlHolWrld-1968, p. 98

♦ 0432 ♦ **Canadian International Military Tattoo**
Second weekend in June

An annual event preserving an ancient military tradition, the Canadian International Military Tattoo takes place in Hamilton, a town in the province of Ontario. The evening of entertainment features military bands, drum corps regiments, and pipe bands from Canada and other countries, all performing for residents of Hamilton and the surrounding area. The event often celebrates anniversaries related to Canada's national and/or military heritage and features civilian as well as military musical acts.

The first tattoo took place in 1992 and marked Canada's 125th birthday. In 1999, the Hamilton International Tattoo—as it was then called—faced the threat of being discontinued, but a group of volunteers rallied to preserve it. Around that time the Canadian International Tattoo Association was formed with the sole mission of coordinating the event and ensuring its continuation.

In 2008, the Tattoo celebrated the 400th anniversary of the founding of Quebec City and declared as its theme *Je me souviens* (a popular Quebec slogan that means "I remember").

CONTACTS:
Canadian International Tattoo Association
101 York Blvd.
Hamilton, ON L8R 3L4 Canada
www.canadianmilitarytattoo.ca

♦ 0433 ♦ **Canadian National Exhibition**
August-September

The first Canadian National Exhibition was held in 1879 in Toronto. The fair moved briefly to Ottawa, but it returned to Toronto and was called the **Toronto Industrial Exhibition** until 1921, when the name was changed to reflect its nationwide appeal. Located on the shores of Lake Ontario, about 10 minutes from downtown Toronto, the fairgrounds occupy 350 acres of lawns, gardens, pavilions, and Victorian-style buildings. Events include an air show, a horse show, celebrity appearances, and much more. The Exhibition claims to be the oldest and largest of its kind in the world.

CONTACTS:
Canadian National Exhibition
Exhibition Place
210 Princes Blvd.
Toronto, ON M6K 3C3 Canada
416-263-3800; fax: 416-263-3838
www.theex.com

SOURCES:
GdWrldFest-1985, p. 53

♦ 0434 ♦ **Canberra Day**
Third Monday in March

Canberra, the capital city of Australia, was founded on March 12, 1913. Unusual in that it is one of the few world capitals planned from the ground up, the city and its giant ornamental pond, Lake Burley Griffin, were built out of a depression in a dusty plain about 200 miles southwest of Sydney.

The city's founding is celebrated on the third Monday in March each year, which marks the end of the two-week Canberra National Multicultural Festival. The festival is an outdoor community event that encompasses everything from hot-air balloon rides and a car show to fireworks and musical performances.

CONTACTS:
Canberra National Multicultural Festival
P.O. Box 2154
1 Constitution Ave.
Canberra, ACT 2601 Australia
61-2-6207-0162; fax: 61-2-6207-5862
www.multiculturalfestival.com.au

SOURCES:
AnnivHol-2000, p. 54
IntlThFolk-1979, p. 8

♦ 0435 ♦ **Candelaria (Bolivia)**
February 2

Candelaria or CANDLEMAS is a major holiday in Bolivia, where the Virgen de Candelaria is the country's patroness. The festivities focus on her shrine in the normally placid town of Copacabana on Lake Titicaca, where visitors begin to arrive in the week that precedes the festival. Aymará, Quechua, and Chiriwano Indians can be recognized by their colorful native costumes and musical instruments, and most begin dancing as soon as they arrive and continue till the end of the festival. The image of the Virgin Mary that stands on a revolving platform in the church is not the same one that is carried in the procession on February 2; a duplicate dressed in elaborate robes and precious jewels is used instead, because many years ago it was discovered that every time the statue was moved, big storms or other natural disasters were likely to follow.

CONTACTS:
Bolivian Embassy
3014 Massachusetts Ave. N.W.
Washington, D.C. 20008
800-777-5777 or 202-483-4410; fax: 202-328-3712
www.bolivia-usa.org

SOURCES:
FiestaTime-1965, p. 21
WildPlanet-1995, p. 461

♦ 0436 ♦ **Candelaria (Peru)**
February

A lively celebration of CANDLEMAS is held in Puno, Peru, for about two weeks, including February 2. On that day priests and laypeople form a huge procession that carries the statue of the Virgin Mary through streets carpeted with yellow flowers. Preparations begin more than a week before, however, with church decorating, feasts, and fireworks. By the second week, hundreds of dancers and musicians have arrived to join the main procession, accompanying it with indigenous dances and colorful costumes.

CONTACTS:
Commission for the Promotion of Peru
Calle Uno Oeste No. 50, piso 13th

Urb. Corpac
Lima, 27 Peru
51-1-4224-3131; fax: 51-1-224-7134
www.promperu.gob.pe

SOURCES:
FiestaTime-1965, p. 25
WildPlanet-1995, p. 487

♦ 0437 ♦ **Candle Auction**
Saturday following April 6

The old custom of "selling by candle" is still observed in scattered locations throughout England, among them the village of Tatworth in Somerset. Every year on the Saturday following April 6, which was LADY DAY according to the old Julian calendar, six acres of valuable watercress-growing land are leased to the highest bidder. The bidders gather behind locked doors in a room illuminated only by a candle stuck to a board. A pin is inserted into the candle an inch below the flame, and the bidding begins as the candle is lit. As the candle burns, the melting wax eventually releases the pin. When the pin falls out, the bidding is closed. The person who got the last bid in before the pin dropped will be able to use the land in the year to come. The idea here is that each bidder will have sufficient time to think before making an offer higher than the one previously presented.

Similar candle auctions are held on different dates at Congresbury, also in Somerset; at Old Bolingbroke, Lincolnshire; at Grimston and Diseworth in Leicestershire; and at Aldermaston in Berkshire, where an acre of church land is let every third year.

CONTACTS:
British Tourist Authority
551 Fifth Ave., Ste. 701
New York, NY 10176
800-462-2748
www.visitbritain.us

SOURCES:
YrbookEngFest-1954, p. 46
YrFest-1972, p. 88

♦ 0438 ♦ **Candlemas**
February 2

After observing the traditional 40-day period of purification following the birth of Jesus, Mary presented him to God at the Temple in Jerusalem. According to a New Testament gospel, an aged and devout Jew named Simeon held the baby in his arms and said that he would be "a light to lighten the Gentiles" (Luke 2:32). It is for this reason that February 2 has come to be called Candlemas (or **Candelaria** in Spanish-speaking countries) and has been celebrated by the blessing of candles since the 11th century. In both the Eastern and Western churches, it is now known as the **Feast of the Presentation of Christ in the Temple**; in the Roman Catholic Church, it was formerly called the **Feast of the Purification of the Blessed Virgin Mary**. In the United States, February 2 is also GROUNDHOG DAY; in Great Britain it is said that the badger comes out to test the weather. The old rhyme is as follows:

If Candlemas Day be dry and fair,
The half of winter's to come and mair.
If Candlemas Day be wet and foul,
The half of winter's gone at Yule.

See also CANDELARIA; MIHR, FESTIVAL OF

CONTACTS:
Orthodox Church in America
P.O. Box 675
Syosset, NY 11791
516-922-0550; fax: 516-922-0954
www.oca.org

SOURCES:
AmerBkDays-2000, p. 111
BkDays-1864, vol. I, p. 212
BkFest-1937, p. 226
DaysCustFaith-1957, p. 45
DictFolkMyth-1984, pp. 181, 186, 787
EncyChristmas-2003, p. 95
FestSaintDays-1915, p. 27
FestWestEur-1958, p. 105
FolkAmerHol-1999, p. 69
FolkWrldHol-1999, p. 113
OxYear-1999, pp. 61, 63
RelHolCal-2004, pp. 90, 117
SaintFestCh-1904, p. 90

♦ 0439 ♦ **Candlewalk**
December 31

The American custom of seeing the old year out and the new year in with some type of WATCH NIGHT service can be traced back to England. John Wesley, the founder of the Methodist Church, advocated these kinds of services, believing NEW YEAR'S EVE an appropriate time for religious observance. The first watch night services in the United States were held in St. George's Methodist Church in Philadelphia in the year 1770. Nowadays this type of service may be referred to as a "candlelight" service.

In some areas the African Methodist Episcopal Zion Church holds distinctive Watch Night services. In rural Bladen County, North Carolina, an observance known as the Candlewalk combines pagan fertility rites with the Christian worship of the Virgin Mary. On CHRISTMAS EVE the women and the girls of the church walk deep into the swamp or forest, while the men and boys are threatened with a death curse if they follow. According to local legend, this period of withdrawal is for the purpose of sexual instruction. When the women return, they do so in a single file procession, bearing lighted torches or candles and singing ancient hymns in pidgin English, which some have misidentified as an African language. The women blow out their candles as they come into the church.

The New Year's Eve Watch Night ritual usually takes place close to midnight. It involves prayers, hymns, and sermons. Participants often dress in white and carry lit candles.

SOURCES:
FolkAmerHol-1999, p. 544

♦ 0440 ♦ **Candy Dance Arts and Crafts Faire**
Last full weekend in September

In 1919, the Candy Dance began in the town of Genoa, in northern Nevada, as a way to raise funds to install street lights. Lillian Virgin Finnegan, daughter of a local judge, proposed a dance where candy would be distributed to dancing couples, followed by a midnight supper at the local hotel. The townswomen made a variety of candies for the occasion, and the event raised enough money to install the needed lights. The following year, however, the town was having trouble paying the electric bill for those lights, and so the Candy Dance returned.

This annual event raising funds to pay for the street lights soon became a popular event, attracting dancers from Reno and Carson City to join the fun. More than two tons of candy is now consumed during the dance weekend. In the 1970s, an arts and crafts fair featuring 300 booths of merchandise was added to the two-day event. Locals dressed as Wyatt Earp and his cohorts roam the town, engaging in gunfights. Activities for children include candle-making, face-painting, and tattoos. The Candy Dance Arts and Crafts Faire, as it is now officially known, provides a substantial part of Genoa's annual operating budget.

CONTACTS:
Town of Genoa
P.O. Box 14
Genoa, NV 89411-0014
775-782-8696; fax: 775-782-2779
www.genoanevada.org

♦ 0441 ♦ **Cannes Film Festival**
May

The **International Film Festival** held in the resort city of Cannes on the French Riviera is probably the best known of the hundreds of film festivals held all over the world each year. Sponsored by governments, industry, service organizations, experimental film groups, or individual promoters, these festivals provide filmmakers, critics, distributors, and cinema enthusiasts an opportunity to attend showings of new films and to discuss current trends in the industry. The festival at Cannes is held at the Palais des Festivals, and its founding in 1947 marked a resurgence for the film industry, which had been shattered by World War II. The festival has also been responsible for the growing popularity of foreign films in the United States.

Other important film festivals are held in Berlin, London, San Francisco, New York, Chicago, Venice, and Karlovy Vary in the Czech Republic. Some cater to the films of just one country, some to specific subjects, and some are special festivals for student filmmakers.

CONTACTS:
Cannes Film Festival
3 rue Amelie
Paris, 75007 France
33-1-4561-6100; fax: 33-1-5359-6110
www.festival-cannes.fr/en.html

♦ 0442 ♦ **Cantaderas, Las**
Late September or early October

The Fiesta of Las Cantaderas is held in the town of León, Spain. It dates back to a time when four parishes—San Marcelo, Mercado, San Martín, and Santa Ana—were required to contribute four to six young girls, 8-12 years old, as an annual tribute to the Moors. No family could escape this requirement, and any family without a daughter needed to provide a girl and costume her. When the king of León finally freed the population of this burden, the girls sang and danced in the streets to celebrate.

These days the *cantaderas* form a parade, starting at the town hall. They dance and sing their way down the street, directed by a woman called the *sotadera*, who is costumed in a veil and sequined, silk turban. The girls bear fruit baskets or other offerings, which they later give to the bishop. Although civil authorities regard these gifts as a voluntary offering, church authorities still see them as a necessary ceremony going back to feudal times.

CONTACTS:
Tourist Office of Spain
666 Fifth Ave., 35th Fl.
New York, NY 10103
212-265-8822; fax: 212-265-8864
www.okspain.org

SOURCES:
SpanFiestas-1968, p. 173

♦ 0443 ♦ **Capac Raymi**
December

The Capac Raymi was an Inca festival observed around the time of the December solstice (which is the SUMMER SOLSTICE in the Southern Hemisphere and the WINTER SOLSTICE in the Northern Hemisphere). The Inca Empire flourished in the Andean regions of South America, including Peru, Ecuador, and the northern parts of Chile and Argentina during the 15th and 16th centuries, until the Spanish arrived in 1531. The Capac Raymi served as an initiation ceremony for the young men of the ruling class. When the solstice arrived, the boys' ears were pierced in order to insert the large ear spools worn by Inca royalty.

See also INTI RAYMI

SOURCES:
DictFolkMyth-1984, p. 190

♦ 0444 ♦ **Cape Minstrels' Carnival**
January

The **Annual Minstrels' Carnival** in Cape Town, South Africa, was inspired by the animated singing and dancing of African-American musicians and singers of the United States. Bands are organized during the year, money is raised to purchase the materials needed for their costumes, and on NEW YEAR'S DAY, Second New Year (January 2), and the week

or so that follows, the bands take over the city, displaying their costumes and performing their music in the streets.

This roisterous carnival is offset by string bands, the members of which are decorously dressed and parade with great dignity while playing sacred and other songs during the CHRISTMAS and New Year season.

CONTACTS:
Cape Town Routes Unlimited
P.O. Box X9108
Cape Town, 8000 South Africa
27-21-426-5639; fax: 27-21-426-5640
www.tourismcapetown.co.za

SOURCES:
FolkWrldHol-1999, p. 14

♦ 0445 ♦ **Cape Verde Independence Day**
July 5

This public holiday commemorates Cape Verde's independence from Portugal on this day in 1975.

CONTACTS:
Cape Verde Embassy
3415 Massachusetts Ave. N.W.
Washington, D.C. 20007
202-965-6820; fax: 202-965-1207

SOURCES:
AnnivHol-2000, p. 113

♦ 0446 ♦ **Cape Vincent French Festival**
Saturday before July 14

Cape Vincent, New York, is in the Thousand Islands, where Lake Ontario meets the St. Lawrence River, an area with a strong French heritage. At one time, there was so much feeling for NAPOLEON among the local residents that they built a cup-and-saucer style house (a local architectural style in which the ground floor is wider than the second floor) where they hoped he might decide to spend his exile. However, it was one of Napoleon's followers, Le Roy de Chaumont, who first settled here in the 1800s.

Launched in 1968, the festival immediately drew an astounding number of visitors, many of them French Canadians. It takes place, appropriately enough, on the Saturday before BASTILLE DAY and features a wide variety of French foods as well as a pageant and a parade of decorated carts. A French mass is held at St. Vincent de Paul's Church, and the evening ends with a waterfront display of fireworks.

CONTACTS:
Cape Vincent Chamber of Commerce
P.O. Box 482
Cape Vincent, NY 13618
315-654-2481
www.capevincent.org

SOURCES:
GdUSFest-1984, p. 123

◆ 0447 ◆ **Carabao Festival**
May 14

A feast in honor of San Isidro Labrador (St. Isidore the Farmer), the patron saint of Filipino farmers, held in Pulilan, Bulacan province, the Philippines. The feast also honors the *carabao*, or water buffalo, the universal beast of burden of the Philippines. Farmers scrub their carabao, then decorate them with flowers to parade with the image of San Isidro. A carabao race is held, and at the finish line, the animals kneel while the parish priest blesses them. The festival is also marked by exploding firecrackers and the performance of the Bamboo Dance, where dancers represent the tinikling bird, a menace to the rice crop. Among the games played is *palo sebo*—climbing a greased pole to get the prize at the top.

See also ST. ISIDORE, FESTIVAL OF; SAN ISIDRO IN PERU, FIESTA OF; SAN ISIDRO THE FARMER, FEAST OF

CONTACTS:
Philippine Tourism Center
556 Fifth Ave.
New York, NY 10036
212-575-7915; fax: 212-302-6759
www.wowphilippines.com

SOURCES:
FolkWrldHol-1999, p. 357
GdWrldFest-1985, p. 153

◆ 0448 ◆ **Caramoor International Music Festival**
Mid-June to mid-August

In the 1930s, Walter and Lucie Rosen gave private concerts for their friends in the music room of their Mediterranean-style country estate in Katonah, New York, known as Caramoor. Their devotion to music led to the establishment of the Caramoor Festival in 1946. Small opera productions, chamber music, and children's programs are held in the estate's open-air Spanish courtyard, while the Venetian Theater, which incorporates Greek and Roman marble columns from a 15th-century Italian villa, has a stage large enough to accommodate a symphony orchestra and full-scale opera. Such world-class singers as Beverly Sills, Jessye Norman, and Charles Bressler have performed there, as have well-known instrumentalists Alicia De Larrocha, Misha Dichter, Garrick Ohlsson, and Philippe Entremont. Concerts are held Thursdays through Sundays for nine weeks during the summer. The festival is the summer home of the Orchestra of St. Luke's and St. Luke's Chamber Ensemble.

CONTACTS:
Caramoor
149 Girdle Ridge Rd.
Katonah, NY 10536
914-232-5035; fax: 914-232-5521
www.caramoor.com

SOURCES:
MusFestAmer-1990, p. 99

◆ 0449 ◆ **Carberry Day**
Friday the 13th

The students and faculty at Brown University in Providence, Rhode Island, celebrate the fictitious academic exploits of Professor Josiah Stinkney Carberry every Friday the 13th. It all began in 1929, when a young faculty member at Brown posted a notice saying that J. S. Carberry would give a lecture on "Archaic Greek Architectural Revetments in Connection with Ionian Philosophy" at eight o'clock, on a certain evening. Ben C. Clough, a retired Latin professor spotted the hoax and decided to join in the fun by inserting the word "not" between "will" and "give." After that, the joke took on a life of its own, and the ubiquitous Professor Carberry began to send postcards and telegrams with news of his latest exotic research trips. Articles under his name began appearing in scholarly journals and, in 1966, Brown gave Carberry a bona fide M.A. degree—awarded, of course, *in absentia*.

On Carberry Day, small brown jugs appear around the campus, and students and teachers fill them with change. The money goes to a book fund that Professor Carberry has set up "in memory of my future late wife, Laura."

CONTACTS:
Brown University
45 Prospect St.
Providence, RI 02912
401-863-1000; fax: 401-863-3700
www.brown.edu

SOURCES:
FolkAmerHol-1999, p. 42

◆ 0450 ◆ **Caribbean Festival (Feast of Fire)**
July

The annual Caribbean Festival in Santiago de Cuba, also known as the **Feast of Fire**, is dedicated to preserving and promoting the cultural traditions of the Caribbean. Casa del Caribe, a cultural center in Santiago de Cuba, organizes the event, along with several other Cuban groups. In addition to numerous performances of music and dancing, there are exhibitions of culinary arts, painting, crafts, drama, religious rituals, and poetry. Each year the festival gives special focus to one of the Caribbean countries. There are academic conferences that explore ways to promote and develop cultural understanding among the Caribbean nations and workshops on storytelling, music, and other traditional arts. Awards are presented to those who have made notable contributions to the culture of the region. Thousands of people from many nations attend the event, enjoying the street festivities and performances at the four main stages and many smaller venues. The "Serpent Parade" is a high point of the Festival, with throngs of dancing people winding their way through the streets of Santiago de Cuba.

CONTACTS:
Casa del Caribe
Calle 13 no. 154
Vista Alegre
Santiago, Cuba

◆ 0451 ◆ **Caribou Carnival and Canadian Championship Dog Derby**
Last weekend in March

The Caribou Carnival is a Canadian festival of winter sports and entertainment that includes competitions in snow and ice sculpting and beard growing. But the highlight of the carnival is the Championship Dog Derby. Offering more prize money than any other dog sled competition in the Northwest Territories, the grueling three-day race takes mushers 150 miles across Great Slave Lake.

In addition to sports, the carnival features a Mushers' Ball, a talent show, fireworks, and an ugly truck and dog contest. It is held in Yellowknife, the capital of the Northwest Territories, a vast region that stretches from the northern boundaries of the Canadian provinces to within 500 miles of the North Pole.

CONTACTS:
Yellowknife City Hall
4807-52 St.
P.O. Box 580
Yellowknife, NT X1A 2N4 Canada
867-920-5600; fax: 867-920-5649
www.yellowknife.ca

SOURCES:
WildPlanet-1995, p. 555

♦ 0452 ♦ **Caricom Day**
On or near July 4

CARICOM stands for the "Caribbean Community," an organization established on July 4, 1973, for the purpose of supporting a common market, coordinating foreign policy, and promoting cooperation among the 15 member states of the Caribbean: Antigua and Barbuda, Bahamas, Barbados, Belize, Dominica, Grenada, Guyana, Haiti, Jamaica, Montserrat, St. Kitts-Nevis, St. Lucia, St. Vincent and the Grenadines, Suriname, and Trinidad and Tobago. Caricom Day is celebrated on or around July 4 in Barbados, Guyana, and St. Vincent. In Antigua and Barbuda, it is celebrated on the first Saturday in June.

CONTACTS:
Caribbean Community
P.O. Box 10827
Georgetown, Guyana
592-222 0001-75; fax: 592-222 0171
www.caricom.org

SOURCES:
AnnivHol-2000, p. 112

♦ 0453 ♦ **Carifest**
June

The northern climate of Calgary, Alberta, may make the city an unlikely venue for celebrating Caribbean culture. But every summer Carifest helps transform the cold locale into a sunny and vibrant scene with Caribbean music, dancing, and food. After the Toronto Caribana, it is the largest Caribbean festival in Canada.

This five-day affair is organized by the Caribbean Community Council (CCC), which consists of various island associa-

tion representatives. The CCC established Carifest in 1981 with a mission to offer local Caribbean residents a celebration reminiscent of their homeland. The organization also saw the need to expose all Calgarians to Caribbean culture and to celebrate the city's multicultural character.

The calypso, soca, and reggae music of the Caribbean enlivens the mood at the parade that kicks off the festival week. The procession always includes a special appearance by Miss Carifest, who is selected at a beauty pageant preceding the festival. More music is featured at the main event, the Sunshine Festival, which takes place at Prince's Island Park in downtown Calgary. In addition to its performances, the Sunshine Festival also draws large crowds with crafts and spicy Caribbean food.

CONTACTS:
Caribbean Community Council
101, 3208 – 8th Ave. N.E.
Calgary, AL T2A 7V8 Canada
www.carifestcalgary.ca

♦ 0454 ♦ **Carillon Festival, International**
First full week in June

The only event of its kind in the world, the International Carillon Festival in Springfield, Illinois, attracts carillonneurs from France, Belgium, Germany, Brazil, New Zealand, and the Netherlands as well as from the United States. The centerpiece of the festival is the Rees Memorial Carillon, housed in a tower given to the community by Thomas Rees, publisher of the *Illinois State Register* from 1881 to 1933. Rees first became interested in the art and skill of playing bell music while visiting Holland and Belgium. The tower holds 66 bronze bells cast by a 300-year-old Dutch foundry and covering a range of five-and-a-half chromatic octaves. The bells are played manually by means of a keyboard.

The festival, instituted in 1962, features the music of Johann Sebastian BACH (1685-1750), Franz Schubert (1797-1828, *see also* SCHUBERTIADE), Wolfgang Amadeus MOZART (1756-1791), Edvard Grieg (1843-1907), and other compositions arranged for the carillon and played by internationally acclaimed masters of the instrument. The performances take place in Springfield's Washington Park, where listeners can sit the recommended 300 or more feet away.

CONTACTS:
Thomas Rees Memorial Carillon
Washington Pk.
Springfield, IL 62703
217-753-6219; fax: 217-546-3139
www.carillon-rees.org

SOURCES:
MusFestAmer-1990, p. 55

♦ 0455 ♦ **Carinthian Summer Music Festival**
July-August

Austria, birthplace of Wolfgang Amadeus MOZART, is also home to this summertime classical music festival. For six weeks spanning July and August, the world's most renowned conductors and orchestras perform in various locations in the country's southernmost province, Carinthia.

The performance sites for the festival's symphonic pieces are as impressive as the roster of performing artists, which has included composer Leonard Bernstein and flautist James Galway. Ossiach Abbey, an 11th-century monastery, has remained a main venue site since it hosted the first Carinthian festival, in 1969. Ensembles play at the abbey's church and its baroque hall, Villach's Congress Centre, Glanegg Castle, as well as other scenic settings throughout the mountainous province. The Festival has built its musical reputation on the rare genre known as the "church opera."

Organizers encourage families to take part in the proceedings by offering age-appropriate events for children. For individuals looking for an academic approach, there are instructional courses and opportunities to engage in dialogue with composers and musicians.

CONTACTS:
Carinthian Summer Festival
Stift Ossiach
1 Ossiach (Stift)
Ossiach 9570 Austria
www.carinthischersommer.at

♦ 0456 ♦ **Carling Sunday**
Between March 8 and April 11 in the West;
between March 21 and April 24 in the East

Carling Sunday is the fifth Sunday in LENT, and is also known as **Passion Sunday**. Its name possibly derives from "care." It is traditional in Great Britain to eat a dish of parched peas cooked in butter, called a *carling*, said to be in memory of grain Jesus' disciples picked on the Sabbath.

SOURCES:
BkDays-1864, vol. I, p. 336
BkFest-1937, p. 56
DictDays-1988, p. 19
EncyEaster-2002, p. 463
FestSaintDays-1915, p. 53
FolkWrldHol-1999, p. 169
OxYear-1999, p. 615

♦ 0457 ♦ **Carmentalia**
January 11 and 15

It was unusual in ancient Rome for a single deity to have two separate festival days only a few days apart, and a number of explanations—none of them conclusive—have been offered for why the second festival in honor of the goddess Carmenta was instituted. The only thing that is certain is that the goddess's most prominent characteristic was her gift of prophecy, and that it was primarily women who frequented her temple near the Porta Carmentalis, a gate at the foot of the southern end of the capitol. Carmenta was also a birth-goddess, and although it might seem unusual to celebrate birth in the middle of winter, January happens to be exactly nine months after April, then the most popular time for marriages.

Carmenta had her own priest, or *flamen,* whose duties on her festival days were confined to the preparation of offerings of grain or cereal. There was a taboo against animal skins in Carmenta's cult, perhaps because the slaughter of animals was antithetical to a goddess of birth. The women known as *Carmentes* were similar to midwives—wise old women whose skills and spells assisted women in childbirth, and who had the power to tell their fortunes.

SOURCES:
ClassDict-1984, p. 127
FestRom-1981, p. 62
OxYear-1999, p. 31
RomFest-1925, p. 290

♦ 0458 ♦ **Carnaval Miami**
First two full weeks in March

Carnaval is the biggest event in Miami, Fla., honoring Hispanic culture. Held since 1938, it is estimated that one million people attend each year. The highlight and grand finale of the festival is the famous Calle Ocho Open House. This is non-stop, wall-to-wall entertainment along 23 blocks of Southwest Eighth Street (*Calle Ocho*): 40 stages with more than 200 troupes offering live music, dancing, and folkloric performances. There are more than 600 vendors of ethnic food. Other events are the Miss Carnaval Miami beauty contest; a grand *paseo* or parade with floats; limbo dancers, samba groups, and steel bands from the Caribbean; a footrace; a laser display; fireworks; and concerts of international stars.

CONTACTS:
Carnaval Miami
Kiwanis of Little Havana
701 S.W. 27 Ave., Ste. 900
Miami, FL 33135
305-644-8888; fax: 305-644-8693
www.carnavalmiami.com

♦ 0459 ♦ **Carnea**
August-September

The Carnea, also spelled **Karneia**, **Karnea**, or **Carneia**, was one of ancient Sparta's three principal religious festivals—the other two being the Hyacinthia and the Gymnopaidiai—which were observed in many parts of the Peloponnesus as well as in Cyrene, Magna Graecia, and elsewhere. It was the ultimate expression of the cult of Apollo Karneios, the ram god of flocks and herds and of fertility in general. It was held during the month of Carneus (August-September) and dates back to 676 B.C.E. The Carnea was both a vintage festival and a military one, Apollo being expected to help his people both by promoting the harvest and by supporting them in battle. Young men called *staphylodromoi,* or "grape-cluster-runners," chased after a man wearing garlands. It was considered a good omen for the city if they caught him and a bad one if they didn't.

No military operations could be held during this festival, and it is said that the Spartans might not have been defeated by the Persians at Thermopylae if the Carnea hadn't prevented the movement of their main army.

SOURCES:
DictFolkMyth-1984, pp. 67, 192
OxClassDict-1970, p. 206
RelHolCal-2004, p. 273

♦ 0460 ♦ **Carnival**
Various dates, from Epiphany to Ash Wednesday Eve

The period known as Carnival—probably from the Latin *caro* or *carne levara*, meaning "to take away meat" and "a farewell to flesh"—begins anytime after EPIPHANY and usually comes to a climax during the last three days before ASH WEDNESDAY, especially during MARDI GRAS. It is a time of feasting and revelry in anticipation of the prohibitions of LENT.

Carnival is still observed in most of Europe and the Americas. It features masked balls, lavish costume parades, torch processions, dancing, fireworks, noisemaking, and of course feasting on all the foods that will have to be given up for Lent. Ordinarily Carnival includes only the Sunday, Monday, and Tuesday before Ash Wednesday (*see* FASCHING), but sometimes it begins on the preceding Friday or even earlier. In Brazil, Carnival is the major holiday of the year.

See also KARNEVAL IN COLOGNE and SHROVE TUESDAY

SOURCES:
BkDays-1864, vol. I, pp. 65, 236
BkFest-1937, pp. 4, 29, 38, 54, 67, 95, 102, 111, 120, 132, 146, 166, 179, 219, 241, 249, 259, 267, 289, 298, 316, 328
DictFolkMyth-1984, pp. 105, 178, 181, 192, 193, 197, 220, 370, 397, 543, 568, 629, 747, 749, 757, 759, 787, 807, 842, 844, 947, 977, 980, 1082
EncyEaster-2002, p. 51
EncyRel-1987, vol. 3, p. 98
FestWestEur-1958, pp. 6, 23, 34, 55, 56, 89, 124, 151, 163, 191, 211, 230
FolkAmerHol-1999, p. 88
FolkWrldHol-1999, p. 132
GdUSFest-1984, pp. 5, 68, 133
GdWrldFest-1985, pp. 4, 24, 64, 96, 133, 147, 175
HolSymbols-2009, p. 106
IntlThFolk-1979, pp. 44, 82, 278
OxYear-1999, p. 603
RelHolCal-2004, p. 91

♦ 0461 ♦ **Carnival (Argentina)**
February-March

The celebration of CARNIVAL in Argentina has decreased in the larger cities, but it remains the most popular celebration of the year in the more sparsely inhabited northern zone. In the province of Jujuy, men and women wearing colorful blankets perform *carnivalito*, a traditional round dance where couples continually vary a few simple figures while their leader waves a handkerchief or ribboned stick and calls out for changes in a high voice. Although this dance at one time was associated with an ancient harvest festival, its significance in this context has been long forgotten. In some places people dance for a few hours a day. These festivities may continue for as long as a month.

The *tincunaco* ceremony is an important part of the Carnival celebration in other areas of Argentina. The ceremony symbolizes the sacred ties that unite a mother and her child's godmother. It takes place under an arch made from a branch taken from a willow tree and decorated with fruit, sweets, cheese, blossoms, and lanterns. The mothers line up on one side of the arch, the godmothers on the other. They move toward one another until they meet under the arch. There they touch foreheads and pass a child made from candy from one to the other. The celebration usually draws to a close with the mock funeral of Pukllay, the spirit of Carnival. One woman, chosen to act as Pukllay's wife, cries about her husband's death. The others tap drums and sing Carnival tunes. Pukllay—usually a rag doll dressed in native costume—is laid to rest in a freshly dug grave showered with blossoms and sweets.

CONTACTS:
National Secretariat of Tourism, Tourist Information Centers
Av. Santa Fe 883
Buenos Aires, C1059ABC Argentina
54-11-4312-2232; fax: 54-11-4302-7816
www.turismo.gov.ar/eng/menu.htm

SOURCES:
FiestaTime-1965, p. 53

♦ 0462 ♦ **Carnival (Aruba)**
February-March; three days before Ash Wednesday

Preparations for the CARNIVAL celebration on the island of Aruba begin months before the actual event. There is a calypso competition at the end of January, followed by a steel band competition to see who gets to perform in the Carnival parade in Oranjestad. Then there's a tumba contest, "tumba" being the native music of the Netherlands Antilles. The actual celebration begins three days before ASH WEDNESDAY and ends at midnight on MARDI GRAS.

The highlight is the Carnival Main Parade, which takes eight hours to wind its way through the streets of Oranjestad. It includes elaborate floats and people in colorful costumes dancing the jump-up, a dance performed to a half-march rhythm. The three-day festival comes to an end with the Old Mask Parade, followed by the traditional burning of "King Momo."

CONTACTS:
Aruba Tourism Authority
One Financial Pl., Ste. 2508
Ft. Lauderdale, FL 33394
954-767-6477; fax: 954-767-0432
www.aruba.com

SOURCES:
GdWrldFest-1985, p. 4

♦ 0463 ♦ **Carnival (Bolivia)**
February-March

While Carnival celebrations were formerly held throughout Bolivia, the tendency in recent years has been for people to gather in the larger cities, such as La Paz, Sucre, Cochambamba, and Oruro, where the dancing and drinking can go on for a week (*see also* CARNIVAL OF ORURO). *Pepinos*, masked clowns that wear striped clothing and carry cardboard rods, are found only in La Paz. They wander through the crowds talking in high-pitched voices so that no one will know who they are. Thus disguised they strike at random passersby—who often hit back—with their cardboard batons. Those who wish to dress as pepinos must apply to the police for a special license and wear it throughout the festival so that all can see it. In this way, festivalgoers can identify pepinos that cause injury to people or property.

CONTACTS:
Bolivian Embassy
3014 Massachusetts Ave. N.W.
Washington, D.C. 20008
202-483-4410; fax: 202-328-3712
www.bolivia-usa.org

SOURCES:
FiestaTime-1965, p. 46

♦ 0464 ♦ **Carnival (Brazil)**
*Between January 30 and March 5; four days
preceding Ash Wednesday*

CARNIVAL is the largest popular festival in Brazil, the last chance for partying before LENT. The most extravagant celebration takes place along the eight miles of Copacabana Beach in Rio de Janeiro, where, since the 1930s, the parades, pageants, and costume balls go on for four days, all accompanied by the distinctive rhythm of the samba. The whole city is decorated with colored lights and streamers, and impromptu bands play on every street corner. Banks, stores, and government offices are closed until noon on ASH WEDNESDAY.

The high point of the Carioca (as the natives of Rio are known) Carnival is the parade of the samba schools (*Escola de Samba*), which begins on Carnival Sunday and ends about midday on Monday. The samba schools are neighborhood groups, many of whom come from the humblest sections of Rio, who develop their own choreography, costumes, and theme songs. The competition among them is as fierce as the rivalry of top sports teams. A single samba school can have as many as two to three thousand participants, so the scale of the parade can only be described as massive. People spend months learning special dances for the parade, and must often raise huge sums of money to pay for their costumes, which range from a few strategically placed strings of beads to elaborate spangled and feathered headdresses. Each samba school dances the length of the Sambadrome, a one-of-a-kind samba stadium designed by Oscar Niemeyer and built in 1984 to allow 85,000 spectators to watch the samba schools dance by. Viewing the parade from the Sambadrome is usually an all-night affair.

In recent years, more and more of Carnival has moved into clubs, the Club Monte Libano being one of the most famous. The Marilyn Monroe look-alike contest held by transvestites on Sugarloaf Mountain is among the most unusual events.

CONTACTS:
Rio de Janeiro Tourism Authority
Praca Pio X, 119 - 9? andar - Centro
Rio de Janeiro-RJ-, Cep 20040-020 Brasil
55-21-2271-7000; fax: 55-21-531-1872

SOURCES:
BkHolWrld-1986, Feb 25
DictFolkMyth-1984, p. 193
EncyEaster-2002, p. 38
EncyRel-1987, vol. 3, p. 102
FolkWrldHol-1999, p. 136
GdWrldFest-1985, p. 24

♦ 0465 ♦ **Carnival (Colombia)**
*February-March; Friday through Tuesday before
Ash Wednesday*

From the Friday preceding ASH WEDNESDAY until SHROVE TUESDAY, the Colombian city of Barranquilla celebrates CARNIVAL. There are costume balls, folklore shows, water festivals, and, on the night before Ash Wednesday, the ceremonial burial of "José Carnaval," the spirit who rules over the festivities. Each *barrio*, or neighborhood, chooses its own beauty queen and holds informal parties, while the city's wealthier inhabitants hold pageants and formal balls, competing to see who can come up with the most ornate costume. *Ron blanco*, the local white rum, is the favored drink, and residents dance in the streets to African and Indian rhythms. The Battle of Flowers on the opening day of the festival involves many elaborate floats decorated with the country's exotic flora.

CONTACTS:
Colombian Embassy
2118 Leroy Pl. N.W.
Washington, D.C. 20008
202-387-8338; fax: 202-232-8643
www.colombiaemb.org

SOURCES:
GdWrldFest-1985, p. 64

♦ 0466 ♦ **Carnival (Cuba)**
Late July to early August

The celebration of CARNIVAL in Havana, Cuba, dates back to the earliest years of the republic, when it featured *comparsas*, or groups of Afro-Cuban dancers, and parades of local officials and other distinguished people in carriages or on horseback. The first floats, many of them imported from New Orleans, appeared in 1908, but from then on, the people of Havana began to design and construct floats of their own and to establish what soon became one of the best-known Carnival celebrations in all of the Americas.

The comparsas remain the highlight of Carnival. About 18 of these dance groups, which come from all parts of the island, entertain Carnival goers with well-orchestrated spectacles of song, dance, and gorgeous costume. Some of the comparsas—composed of ordinary people from all walks of life—have been in existence for nearly 100 years. Each brings its own band and pauses at several points along the parade route to present its choreographic spectacle. This usually includes a conga line, whose characteristic step may represent an attempt to mimic the foot-dragging gait of slaves in chains.

Under the dictatorship of Fidel Castro, Carnival has become somewhat more restrained. Floats and dramatic spectacles are often utilitized for propaganda purposes and to ridicule the country's political enemies. In recent years Carnival has been held over two or more weeks in late July and early August and associated with National Day on July 26 (*see* CUBA LIBERATION DAY).

SOURCES:
FiestaTime-1965, p. 38

◆ 0467 ◆ Carnival (Goa, India)
February-March; Saturday through Tuesday before Ash Wednesday

In Goa, a region on the southwest coast of India, CARNIVAL is known as **Intruz** because it leads into the period of LENT. Social conventions are relaxed, and people wearing masks toss *cocotes* and *cartuchos* (small paper packets containing flour and sawdust) at one another, or squirt each other with syringes of perfumed colored water—much like what goes on during the Hindu festival of HOLI. In Panaji, the capital of Goa, there is a huge parade in honor of King Momo, the Lord of the Revels, on SHROVE TUESDAY. There are floats with dancers and bands playing swing music, stilt-walkers dressed up as Walt Disney characters, tableaux, and grotesque figures in African masks. The entire procession can take as long as four hours to pass, ending at the Church of Our Lady of the Immaculate Conception. Afterward, there is dancing in the town squares, public halls, and on the beaches, with older people doing the tango and waltz while the young people dance to popular music. The festivities end at dawn on ASH WEDNESDAY, when most attendees head for church services.

CONTACTS:
Goa Tourism Development Corporation Ltd.
Trionara Apts, Dr. Alvares Costa Rd.
Panaji, Goa 403 001 India
91-832-2424001; fax: 91-832-2423926
www.goa-tourism.com

SOURCES:
FolkWrldHol-1999, p. 140

◆ 0468 ◆ Carnival (Haiti)
February-March; three days preceding Ash Wednesday

Although the official CARNIVAL holiday in Haiti takes place during the last three days before ASH WEDNESDAY, the celebration actually begins on the first Sunday after EPIPHANY, when *bandes* or groups of costumed dancers begin to appear in the streets of the cities and suburbs. They often carry a sort of maypole, plant it in someone's yard, and then braid a simple pattern with the colored streamers as they dance to the rhythm of drums. The dancers often travel with *marchandes* who sell rum, candy, and rolls from the trays they carry on their heads. After the neighbors have gifted the dancers with a few coins, the whole entourage packs up and moves on to the next location.

The last three days before Ash Wednesday are particularly boisterous and exciting in Port-au-Prince, the capital. Almost everyone appears in costume, blowing noisemakers or playing musical instruments. Floats are pulled through the streets, decorated with bird feathers, palm fronds, flowers, and seashells as well as more mundane materials such as bottle caps, ribbons, and fabric. Because the merrymakers wear masks, they feel free to make fun of political leaders and local institutions. Although the Port-au-Prince celebration is the largest in Haiti, even wilder ones are held in Jacmel, Cap Haitien, Cayes, and Jérémie.

See also CARNIVAL LAMAYOTE; RARA

CONTACTS:
Haitian Embassy
2311 Massachusetts Ave. N.W.
Washington, D.C. 20008
202-332-4090; fax: 202-745-7215
www.haiti.org

SOURCES:
BkHolWrld-1986, Feb 9
FestWrld: Haiti-1999, p. 8
FiestaTime-1965, p. 40

◆ 0469 ◆ Carnival (Hungary) (Farsang)
January 6 to Ash Wednesday (February-March)

This is the time of year when most weddings are celebrated in Hungary, and when dances, parties, and festivities are held. In some parts of the country, villagers perform the symbolic burying of King Marrow Bone, who represents life's indulgences. Prince Cibere, whose name recalls the sour bran soup served throughout LENT, begins his 40-day reign on ASH WEDNESDAY.

In southern Hungary, masks known as *busó* that are passed down from one generation to the next are worn during MARDI GRAS. They are made out of carved wood painted with ox blood, with animal skins covering the top and ram's horns emerging from either side. Although at one time only adult married men could wear these masks, young unmarried men now wear them, shaking huge wooden rattles, shooting off cannons, and teasing women with long sticks topped by sheepskin gourds. In Slovenia, these masks have dangling red tongues, and the men wearing them run around in groups carrying clubs covered at one end with the skins of hedgehogs. The Busó parade in Mohács is said to be the biggest carnival event in Hungary.

CONTACTS:
Hungarian National Tourist Office
350 Fifth Ave., Ste. 7107
New York, NY 10118
212-695-1221; fax: 212-695-0809
www.gotohungary.com

SOURCES:
BkFest-1937, p. 166
FolkWrldHol-1999, p. 140

♦ 0470 ♦ **Carnival (Malta)**
February-March; before Ash Wednesday

Carnival in Malta includes five days of pre-Lenten festivities, a custom since the 1500s. There are some festivities in the villages, but the main activities are in the capital city of Valletta. Here the traditional events include a parade with floats, brass bands, and participants wearing grotesque masks, as well as open-air folk-dancing competitions. A King Carnival reigns over the festival.

CONTACTS:
Malta National Tourist Office
65 Broadway, Ste. 823
New York, NY 10006
212-430-3799; fax: 425-795-3425
www.visitmalta.com

SOURCES:
FolkWrldHol-1999, p. 142

♦ 0471 ♦ **Carnival (Martinique and Guadeloupe)**
January-March, until Ash Wednesday night

CARNIVAL celebrations on the French Caribbean island of Martinique and its sister island of Guadeloupe begin the Sunday after NEW YEAR'S DAY with weekend parties and dances in the larger cities and towns. But they reach a climax during the last few days before LENT. On the Sunday before Lent, there are parades with marchers in exotic costumes dancing to the beat of the *beguine*, a Congolese ritual dance. Stores and offices are closed on Monday, an official holiday that is spent singing and dancing, with masked balls that go on far into the night. SHROVE TUESDAY is a day for children to dress up in red-devil costumes and carry homemade tridents as they parade through the streets.

The celebration continues right through ASH WEDNESDAY, when thousands of masked, costumed she-devils (many of whom are men in drag) have a parade of their own. Everyone wears black and white, and dark-skinned faces are smeared with ash. Effigies of King Vaval and his alter ego, Bois-Bois, tower over the procession. That night the effigies are burned, and Vaval's coffin is lowered into the ground.

CONTACTS:
Martinique Promotion Bureau
444 Madison Ave., 16th Fl.
New York, NY 10022
800-391-4909 or 212-838-7800; fax: 212-838-7855
www.martinique.org

SOURCES:
GdWrldFest-1985, p. 133

♦ 0472 ♦ **Carnival (Mexico)**
February-March

CARNIVAL celebrations in Mexico vary from one town or region to the next, but almost all involve folk and ritual dances. In Tepeyanco and Papalotla, Tlaxcala State, *paragueros* ("umbrella men") perform exaggerated polkas and mazurkas during Carnival, wearing headdresses shaped like an umbrella. In Santa Ana Chiautempan and Contla, also in Tlaxcala State, *los catrines*—men dressed as women, or "dandies"—carry umbrellas as they mock high-society dances. Other dances performed during Carnival include the *moros, diablos,* and *muertos* taken over from the Spanish, as well as the *arcos* and *pastoras,* which are danced with flowered arches. In Morelos, the Carnival dancers are known as *chinelos.* Although they were formerly disguised as black Africans, nowadays they wear long embroidered satin gowns, hats topped with ostrich plumes, and masks with horn-shaped black beards.

Carnival in Mexico is known for drama as well as dance. In Zaachila, Oaxaca State, there is a mock battle between priests and devils. In Huejotzingo, Puebla State, an elaborate drama staged over a period of three or four days dramatizes the exploits of the bandit Agustin Lorenzo and the woman with whom he elopes. Carnival is celebrated in Mexico City with fireworks, parades, street dancers, and costume balls.

See also ST. MARTIN'S CARNIVAL

CONTACTS:
Mexico Tourism Board
21 E. 63rd St., Fl. 3
New York, NY 10021
800-446-3942 or 212-821-0314; fax: 212-821-0367
www.visitmexico.com

SOURCES:
DictFolkMyth-1984, pp. 193, 197, 220, 759
IntlThFolk-1979, p. 278

♦ 0473 ♦ **Carnival (Panama)**
February-March; four days preceding Ash Wednesday

The celebration of CARNIVAL in Panama begins on the Saturday before ASH WEDNESDAY, when the Carnival Queen and her courtiers enter Panama City. They are greeted by King Momus, the god of gaiety. The Queen leads a parade through the streets, to the accompaniment of *murgas,* or walking bands. Sunday is Pollera Day, when the women bring out the brilliantly colored, hand-embroidered, multilayered *pollera* dresses that are often handed down from one generation to the next. Monday is the day when the *comparasas*—precision dance troupes dressed in elaborate costumes—compete for prizes. On Tuesday, the last day of the celebration, there is a Grand Parade of floats, walking bands, dancers, and all the groups that have performed or paraded on previous days. The festivities continue throughout the night, ending at dawn with the "burial of the fish" ceremony. A mock funeral is held for a dead fish, which is then dumped into the ocean or a swimming pool.

See also BURIAL OF THE SARDINE

CONTACTS:
Embassy of Panama
2862 McGill Terr. N.W.
Washington, D.C. 20008
202-483-1407; fax: 202-483-8413
www.embassyofpanama.org

SOURCES:
FolkWrldHol-1999, p. 144
GdWrldFest-1985, p. 147

♦ 0474 ♦ **Carnival (Peru)**
February-March

In Peru, it is customary during CARNIVAL for people to throw water and flour at each other. Sometimes the flour and water are thrown from a balcony on whoever happens to be walking beneath. Groups of young people often stage battles in which the boys throw the girls into fountains or bathtubs and vice versa. At Carnival dances, even well-bred young men and women squirt water at each other from special syringes sold for this purpose. Water-throwing battles are common between sailboats on lakes and in private homes. A particularly colorful celebration is held in Cajamarca.

Although Carnival is celebrated throughout Peru, the events are not as elaborate as those in neighboring Brazil.

CONTACTS:
Commission for the Promotion of Peru
Calle Uno Oeste No. 50, piso 13th
Urb. Corpac
Lima, 27 Peru
51-1-4224-3131; fax: 51-1-224-7134
www.promperu.gob.pe

SOURCES:
BkFestHolWrld-1970, p. 37

♦ 0475 ♦ **Carnival (Portugal)**
February-March; three days preceding Ash Wednesday

The pre-Lenten festivities in Portugal reach a peak on the last three days before ASH WEDNESDAY. There was a time when the CARNIVAL celebration in Lisbon was characterized by sexual banter and horseplay, with battles involving eggs, oranges, flour, and water. But the present-day public festivities are more restrained. People decorate their cars with masses of flowers, and as the cars parade through town, they pelt their friends and neighbors with blossoms while the bystanders try to retaliate.

There are balls, parties, and dances in the cities, but in rural areas many of the more uninhibited Carnival traditions persist. The *folía* (literally, "madness"), a fertility dance associated with the Portuguese Carnival celebration, is named after the quick and crazy movements of the participants. Mummers and musicians, the burial in effigy of King Carnival, and traditional folk plays are also part of these rural Carnival observances.

CONTACTS:
Portuguese National Tourist Office
590 Fifth Ave., 4th Fl.
New York, NY 10036
800-767-8842 or 212-354-4403; fax: 212-764-6137
www.visitportugal.com

SOURCES:
BkFest-1937, p. 267
BkFestHolWrld-1970, p. 34
DictFolkMyth-1984, p. 397
EncyRel-1987, vol. 3, p. 101

♦ 0476 ♦ **Carnival (Spain)**
February-March; three days preceding Ash Wednesday

CARNIVAL in Spain is an occasion for feasting and partying. Bullfights, masquerade parties, weddings, and dances are held in almost every town and village. The Prado Museum in Madrid resembles a huge street fair, with masqueraders, battles of flowers, showers of confetti, and throngs of vendors. In Catalonia, the northeastern section of Spain, Carnival is observed with the *baile de cintas* or *baile del cordon*, the Spanish ribbon or maypole dance. Another traditional Spanish dance associated with Carnival is *los seises* ("the six"), similar to the English Morris dance. When los seises were on the verge of being suppressed in 1685, they were preserved by papal edict for as long as the costumes lasted. With good care and numerous repairs, they have lasted to this day.

Throwing flowers and confetti at bystanders from blossom-decked cars is another Carnival tradition in Spain. Some towns even stage a battle of flowers. A particularly colorful celebration is held in Valencia, where the orange trees are in bloom at this time of year.

The city of Santa Cruz de Tenerife hosts what many consider the most Brazilesque Carnival celebration in Spain. Parades and musical and dance contests fill the days leading up to ASH WEDNESDAY, when there are fireworks and the traditional BURIAL OF THE SARDINE.

SOURCES:
BkFest-1937, p. 298
BkFestHolWrld-1970, p. 34
DictFolkMyth-1984, pp. 105, 178, 980
EncyRel-1987, vol. 3, p. 101
FestWestEur-1958, p. 191

♦ 0477 ♦ **Carnival (Switzerland)**
February-March; usually the three days preceding Ash Wednesday

The Swiss actually observe CARNIVAL, or **Fasnacht**, at two different times: in the Roman Catholic cantons, it is observed according to the Gregorian calendar; the Protestant cantons follow the Julian calendar and celebrate it 13 days later.

In Basel, the lights of the city go out at 4:00 A.M., when fife and drum bands perform in the market square. Then members of the Carnival guilds, wearing wild masks and costumes, parade through the streets with lanterns on long poles or perched on their heads, to the accompaniment of pipers and drummers. Frightening masks are also worn during the Carnival celebration at Flums, where they represent such notions as war, death, or disease. At Einsiedeln, "Carnival Runners" dash through the city's thoroughfares from Sunday to ASH WEDNESDAY morning, displaying frightening masks and huge jangling bells strapped to their backs. The masks and bells found in many Swiss Carnival traditions are believed to have survived from ancient times, when people "drove out winter" with loud sounds and frightening masks.

In some parts of Switzerland it is the children who parade through the streets at Carnival, singing and carrying the national flag. The boys dress in costumes that offer clues to their fathers' professions and the girls masquerade as fairies.

CONTACTS:
Switzerland Tourism
Swiss Center
608 Fifth Ave.
New York, NY 10020
877-794-8037 or 212-757-5944; fax: 212-262-6116
usa.myswitzerland.com

Basel Fasnacht Online
Glockengasse 7
Basel, 4051 Switzerland
www.fasnacht.ch/?pm_1=21&mid=21

SOURCES:
BkFest-1937, p. 316
BkHolWrld-1986, Mar 4
EncyEaster-2002, p. 593
FestWestEur-1958, p. 230
FolkWrldHol-1999, p. 147

♦ 0478 ♦ Carnival (U.S. Virgin Islands)
Last two weeks in April

Unlike CARNIVAL in New Orleans, Brazil, and elsewhere in the world, where it is a pre-Lenten celebration, the Virgin Islands Carnival is held after EASTER, toward the end of April. It dates back to the days when Danish plantation owners gave their slaves time off to celebrate the end of the sugar cane harvest. Although the first Carnival in 1912 was a great success, it wasn't held again for four decades. Since 1952, it has been an annual event in the capital city of Charlotte Amalie on the island of St. Thomas, and nowadays the Carnival observance in St. Thomas ranks second only to the TRINIDAD AND TOBAGO CARNIVAL.

Preliminary events begin a week or more beforehand, and the official Carnival period runs from Sunday until midnight the following Saturday. It begins with the opening of Calypso Tent, a week-long calypso song competition for the coveted title of "Calypso King." The celebrations include the crowning of a Carnival Queen, children's parades, a J'Ouvert morning tramp, steel bands, and dancing in the streets. The climax comes on Saturday with the grand carnival parade, featuring limbo dancers, masked figures, and mock stick-fights between Carib Indians and "Zulus." The celebration winds up with one of the most elaborate all-day parades in the Caribbean, featuring the Mocko Jumbi Dancers. These are colorful dancers on 17-foot stilts whose dances and customs derived from ancient cult traditions brought to the islands by African slaves.

CONTACTS:
US Virgin Islands Department of Tourism
P.O. Box 6400

St. Thomas, VI 00804
800-372-8784 or 340-774-8784; fax: 340-774-4390
www.usvitourism.vi

SOURCES:
AnnivHol-2000, p. 73
BkFestHolWrld-1970, p. 36
GdUSFest-1984, p. 221

♦ 0479 ♦ Carnival (Venice)
Begins between February 3 and March 9; ending on Shrove Tuesday night

The CARNIVAL celebration in Venice, Italy, is more sophisticated and steeped in tradition than the flashy celebrations that take place in Rio de Janeiro and New Orleans (*see* CARNIVAL IN BRAZIL; MARDI GRAS). Costumes for the event are often drawn from the stock characters of Italian popular theater from the 16th through 18th centuries—including Harlequin, a masked clown in diamond-patterned tights; Punchinello, the hunchback; and Pierrot, the sad white-faced clown adapted by the French from the commedia dell'arte. There are also traditional costumed characters such as *La Bautta* (the domino), *Il Dottore* (the professor or doctor of law), and the Renaissance count or countess.

Italian university students, usually in more innovative costumes, pour into Venice as ASH WEDNESDAY draws near. The rhythm of the celebration quickens, evidenced by a number of spectacular costume balls. The costume ball given at Teatro La Fenice—a benefit for charity—is known for attracting film stars, members of European nobility, and other rich and famous people.

CONTACTS:
Comune di Venezia
San Marco, Venice 04136 Italy
39-41-2748-111
www.comune.venezia.it

SOURCES:
EncyEaster-2002, p. 305
FolkWrldHol-1999, p. 141

♦ 0480 ♦ Carnival Lamayote
February-March; before Ash Wednesday

CARNIVAL, the biggest holiday of the year in Haiti, is distinguished from other Carnival celebrations by the preparation of wooden boxes, decorated with tissue paper and paint, known as *lamayotes*. Haitian boys put a "monster"—usually a mouse, lizard, bug, or other small animal—inside these boxes. During Carnival they dress up in masks and costumes and try to persuade people to pay them a penny for a peek inside their box.

See also RARA

SOURCES:
BkHolWrld-1986, Feb 9
RelHolCal-2004, p. 91

◆ 0481 ◆ Carnival Memphis
May-June

CARNIVAL celebrations in Memphis, Tennessee, take the form of parties sponsored by the city's "krewes" (private social clubs) throughout the spring. Each Krewe's "king," "queen," and other royal officers are selected each year and preside over some of these functions, the most important of which take place in May and June. Once composed of two separate events—the "Cotton Carnival" attended primarily by whites and the "Cotton Maker's Jubilee" attended primarily by blacks—the event has become slightly more integrated in recent decades. In the one major event open to the public, the Carnival parade, royalty from both black and white clubs ride through the streets together.

Cotton has been an important crop to the people of Memphis since before the Civil War, when the city served as the largest inland port and cotton market in the American South. The Cotton Festival began in 1931—a faint echo of the city's long abandoned MARDI GRAS celebrations—as a means of cheering up the populace during the Depression. The Cotton Maker's Jubilee got its start in 1935. Cotton remains an important aspect of the city's economy, as Memphis continues to serve as one of the world's largest cotton markets.

CONTACTS:
Carnival Memphis
1060 Early Maxwell Blvd.
Memphis, TN 38104
901-278-0243; fax: 901-278-0271
www.carnivalmemphis.org

◆ 0482 ◆ Carnival of Binche
February-March; seven weeks preceding Shrove Tuesday

Carnival of Binche is the most famous pre-Lenten carnival in Belgium and one of the most unusual in Europe. Festivities in Binche, a town of 10,000 population, begin seven weeks before LENT starts and culminate on MARDI GRAS with day-long rites of elaborately costumed, orange-throwing clowns called *Gilles*, which means, roughly, "fools" or "jesters." Some 200,000 visitors come for the Mardi Gras weekend.

The Gilles—about 800 men and boys—wear suits stuffed with hay and decorated with appliqued rearing lions, crowns, and stars in the Belgian colors of red, yellow, and black. Heavy bells hang at their waists, and their headdresses—four feet tall and weighing up to seven pounds—are topped by ostrich plumes. In the early morning, the Gilles wear masks with green spectacles and orange eyebrows and moustaches, but these are doffed later in the day when the ostrich headdresses go on. The rites start at daybreak when the Gilles gather in the main square of Binche. To the beating of drums, they march and dance through the streets, stomping their wooden shoes and pelting spectators with oranges. Fireworks at midnight officially end the carnival, but dancing often goes on until dawn of ASH WEDNESDAY.

The most accepted legend explaining the carnival traces its origins to a fete in 1549. Spain had just conquered Peru, and

Mary of Hungary, regent of the Netherlands, gave a sumptuous reception at her Binche palace for her nephew, Philip II of Spain. Supposedly, the costumes of the Gilles are patterned on the wardrobe of the Incas, and the thrown oranges represent the Incan gold. A document from 1795 is the earliest to describe the mask of the Gilles.

Some people have suggested that the English word "binge" comes from Binche.

CONTACTS:
Belgian Tourist Office
220 E. 42nd St., Ste. 3402
New York, NY 10017
212-758-8130; fax: 212-355-7675
www.visitbelgium.com

SOURCES:
BkFest-1937, p. 38
BkFestHolWrld-1970, p. 34
FestWestEur-1958, p. 6
FolkWrldHol-1999, p. 133
IntlThFolk-1979, p. 44

◆ 0483 ◆ Carnival of Blacks and Whites
January 4-6

The Carnival of Blacks and Whites, held each year in Pasto, Colombia, is one of the oldest Carnival celebrations in South America. In 2002, it was officially declared part of the nation's cultural heritage. This Carnival has four distinct sections, drawn from different aspects of its traditions and history, but the main event commemorated is an annual day of freedom that was granted to slaves during the 1600s. According to tradition, in 1607 there was a slave uprising in Remedios that badly frightened the Spanish masters. The slave population in Popayán played on this fear and demanded at least one day of freedom to offset a similar revolt. They were given January 5 as their own, and on that day they took over the streets, danced to African rhythms, and blackened the city's white walls with coal. This celebration was brought to Pasto by the Ayerbe family in the mid-1800s. By the late 1880s, it had become quite elaborate and had taken on the traditional Carnival use of masks and costumes.

Pre-Carnival festivities begin on December 28, HOLY INNOCENTS' DAY. This day honors the infants slain by King Herod as he sought to destroy the Christ child. In Colombia, it is a day to play pranks on friends and neighbors, usually involving hiding and trying to squirt them other with water. On January 3, pre-Carnival festivities continue with "el Carnavalito," featuring a special children's parade.

The Carnival officially opens on January 4, with a parade that commemorates the arrival in Pasto of the Castañeda family. Some say that the Castañedas are a caricature of the Ayerbe family, while others believe the Castañedas were a large country family that passed through or settled in Pasto in the early 20th century. Whatever the historical truth, in the parade and Carnival the Castañedas are presented as a zany group that includes a pregnant teenaged bride and many misbehaving children. They are overburdened with luggage, mattresses, and cooking equipment.

The following day, January 5, is the Day of the Blacks, on which the slave revolt is remembered. Revelers celebrate in the streets, and, using special paints and cosmetics designed for the occasion, they paint themselves, their friends, and the town's walls and buildings black. Festivities continue on January 6 with the Day of the Whites. White paints and cosmetics are used as they were the day before, and white powder is also thrown. The Carnival reaches its peak on this day with a final parade consisting of costumed groups, musical and dance ensembles, and elaborate floats that may have been a year in the making.

CONTACTS:
Corporación Carnaval de Negros y Blancos de Pasto
Calle 19, Carrera 25
Casa Don Lorenzo
Plazoleta Galán
Pasto, Nariño Colombia
www.colombia.travel/en

Tourism Promotion Fund of Colombia
Calle 69
No. 11-66
Bogota, Colombia

♦ 0484 ♦ Carnival of Flowers
Late September-early October

The **Toowoomba Carnival of Flowers** held in Queensland, Australia, is responsible for the city of Toowoomba being known as "Australia's Garden City." Since 1950 the eight-day event has included tours of home and city gardens, floral exhibits in all the city shops, a competition for home gardeners, and a special display of exotic and native orchids by the Toowoomba Orchid Society. The highlight of the festival is the Floral Parade, which features thousands of flower-decorated floats and girls in floral costumes. The festival's performing and visual arts section includes theater, music, children's plays, jazz, films, and arts and crafts exhibits.

CONTACTS:
Visitor Information Centre
Cnr. Kitchener & James St.
Toowoomba, QLD 4350 Australia
61-7-4688-6439; fax: 61-7-4688-6910
www.tcof.com.au

SOURCES:
GdWrldFest-1985, p. 7
IntlThFolk-1979, p. 18

♦ 0485 ♦ Carnival of Ivrea Orange-Throwing Battle
Week before Lent

The highlight of the annual pre-Lent carnival—held every year for generations in Ivrea, Italy—is the massive orange-throwing battle that involves thousands of combatants in the town's streets and squares. The battle evokes, rather than re-enacts, past events in the town's long history—in this case,

key insurrections that the townspeople launched against undesirable leaders. One of the most notorious of these was the medieval Count Raineri di Biandrate, a tyrant who tried to seize maidens' virginity before their weddings. Much of the carnival's activities are inspired by a legendary revolt by the townspeople in 1194 against the Count. They killed him and destroyed his castle, and liberty triumphed.

On the Sunday before LENT, the battle of the oranges is pitted between throwers on foot—who represent the townspeople—and others on decorated horse-drawn wagons, who represent the tyrant's officers. Anyone is welcome to take part. The fight rages all over town, often continuing through MARDI GRAS, or the Tuesday before Lent. The streets become thick with orange peels and the air acrid with their scent. On ASH WEDNESDAY, religious solemnity takes over, and peace is restored for another year.

CONTACTS:
Consortium for the Organisation of the Historic Carnival of Ivrea
Antico Palazzo della Credenza
Ivrea 10015 Italy
www.carnevalediivrea.it

♦ 0486 ♦ Carnival of Oruro, Bolivia
Between February and March; week preceding Ash Wednesday

The CARNIVAL celebrations in Oruro, Bolivia, continue for an entire week and include music, dancing, eating and drinking, and offerings to *Pachamama*, or Mother Earth. But the highlight is the parade that begins with a series of vehicles carrying items made from gold and silver, jewels, exquisitely embroidered cloth, and antique coins and bills. Next are the Diablos, costumed with horns made from plaster, colored lightbulbs in place of eyes, teeth made from shards of mirrors, and hair fashioned out of tail hairs taken from horses or oxen. They are led by Lucifer and two Satans and accompanied by five cavorting female devils. Then come the Incas, who portray famous people from the time of the Spanish conquest, and the Tobas, who perform war dances. The llama drivers, or *llameros*, are next, followed by the *Callahuallas*, or witch doctors, and a number of other companies, each with its own distinctive costumes and role in the procession. The parade ends with the entry of all the masked groups into the church for a mass in honor of the Virgen del Socavón.

CONTACTS:
Bolivian Embassy
3014 Massachusetts Ave. N.W.
Washington, D.C. 20008
202-483-4410; fax: 202-328-3712
www.bolivia-usa.org

SOURCES:
EncyRel-1987, vol. 1, p. 476
FolkWrldHol-1999, p. 134

♦ 0487 ♦ Carnival of the Devil
January 2-8 in alternate years

The Carnival of the Devil, held every other year in Riosucio, Caldas, Colombia, is considered so important to Colombia's identity that it has been given official status as part of the nation's cultural heritage. At this unusual festival, a "good" devil is worshipped and celebrated with song and dance. Rather than a representation of absolute evil, he is a playful, happy figure, one who embodies human weaknesses and unsatisfied longings. During the festival, tributes are offered to this devil by artists, poets, writers, and other revelers.

The roots of this festival are very old. It was first officially held in 1847, when the towns of Quiebralomo and Montaña were combined. One of the most striking aspects of the festival is its blending of traditions from different cultures. The people of Quiebralomo had been celebrating the Christian festival of EPIPHANY, or the visit of the Three Wise Men to the infant Jesus, since the 16th century. Even in that celebration, European and African customs had been mixed. Elements from the ancient, native Indian cultures of Colombia were added when the two towns joined their celebrations. These include worship of the earth, the sun, and the jaguar. The slanted eyes and other features of the big cat (a sacred animal that represents the astral king) have been incorporated into many devil masks. *Guarapo*, a beverage made of fermented maize, is drunk from *calabazos*, or drinking vessels made from gourds.

The festivities begin when the devil takes his throne. Parades, fireworks, bullfights, crafts shows, and other amusements are ongoing, along with contemporary art and music performances by groups known as *cuadrilas*. Spectators and participants alike may dress in colorful devil costumes and masks, which are often painstakingly handcrafted. The costumed revelers represent the main demon's court of lesser devils. At the close of the Carnival, the devil makes a speech promising to return in two years, bringing his little demons back with him.

CONTACTS:
Tourism Promotion Fund of Colombia
Calle 69
No. 11-66
Bogota, Colombia
www.colombia.travel/en

♦ 0488 ♦ Carnival of the Laetare
Weekend of Laetare Sunday (fourth Sunday of Lent)

Throughout the history of the Catholic Church, various communities designated the fourth Sunday of Lent, known as Laetare Sunday, as a day for carousing—a rare moment of joy in an otherwise somber season. Some believers view the party as a great motivator to persevere through the remainder of their Lent sacrifice. Stavelot, a municipality in the Walloon region of Belgium, developed its own peculiar tradition for this holiday: Carnival of the Laetare, or **Carnival of the Blanc-Moussis (White Brethren)**.

According to legend, the monks of the region joined the carnival celebration in the late 15th century. The local abbot-

prince did not approve of the monks' participation, and in mocking rebellion, the people subsequently honored the monks by putting on habits themselves. To add fuel to the fire, they even added a laughing mask with a long red nose to the costume.

The many Blanc-Moussis who populate the festival still remain the central focus today. During the parade, which is held on Sunday, the costumed men stand on floats and shower the crowds with confetti and inflated pig bladders. Throughout the weekend, there are also live music performances and fireworks displays.

CONTACTS:
Belgian Tourist Office (Headquarters for United States and Canada)
220 E. 42nd St., , Ste. 3402
34th Fl.
New York, NY 10017
212-758-8130; fax: 212-355-7675
www.visitbelgium.com

♦ 0489 ♦ Carnival Thursday
Between January 29 and March 4; Thursday before Shrove Tuesday

This is the day on which pre-Lenten celebrations, such as CARNIVAL, traditionally begin, ending several days later on SHROVE TUESDAY night. These celebrations often take the form of wild revelry, which is perhaps why it also has been referred to as **Mad Thursday**.

SOURCES:
DictDays-1988, pp. 19, 72

♦ 0490 ♦ Carriacou Parang Festival
Weekend before Christmas, December 25

The Carriacou Parang Festival has been held annually since 1977 to sustain the musical tradition of house-to-house serenading by acoustic string bands at Christmas time. Located in the Caribbean Sea, Carriacou is the largest of the sister islands of Grenada, of which it is a dependency. Carriacou is just 13 square miles in size, with a population of mixed Scottish and African ancestry.

The Parang Festival is held in the form of a musical competition. Organized parang groups from villages throughout Carriacou, its neighboring island Petit Martinique, and Grenada compete for cash prizes and a challenge trophy. Groups comprise not more than eight members, all dressed in colorful outfits to reflect the festive season. Some of the instruments used include the bass drum, iron, guitar, quarto, violin, marack (shack-shack), mandolin, saxophone, tambourine, and others. Groups make two appearances, first to perform a "test-piece" Christmas carol selected by the festival committee. In their second appearance, groups perform a song of their choice. Groups are judged on appearance as well as performance.

In 1987, the festival was extended from one day to two, so that international entertainers could perform for the people of Carriacou and Petit Martinique. As a result, the Saturday night of the festival is known as "foreign entertainers' night." The festival was founded and is run by the Mt. Royal Progressive Youth Movement, a non-profit youth organization dedicated to developing its community and serving the less fortunate in society.

CONTACTS:
Mt. Royal Progressive Youth Movement
www.grenadines.net/carriacou/parang.html#aboutparang

Granada Board of Tourism
P.O. Box 293
St. George's, Grenada
www.grenadagrenadines.com/index2.html

♦ 0491 ♦ Carthage, International Festival of
Early July to late August

The International Festival of Carthage features classical music, jazz, folk music, theater, films, and ballet. It was founded in 1963 by the Tunisian Ministry of Cultural Affairs to bring foreign productions to Tunisia and to introduce the Tunisian public to the cultures of the West. Both Tunisian and foreign artists and ensembles—many of them from Romania, Spain, France, Germany, the Czech Republic, and the former U.S.S.R.—appear at the festival, which is held in a Roman amphitheater. Well-known American stars who have appeared there include James Brown, Joan Baez, Ray Charles, and Cab Calloway. The two-month Carthage Festival is held concurrently with the Festival of Hammamet, which also includes performances of music, dance, folklore, and theater in an open-air setting.

CONTACTS:
Tunisian Tourism Office, Tunisian Embassy
1515 Massachusetts Ave. N.W.
Washington, D.C. 20005
202-862-1850; fax: 202-862-1858
www.tunisiaguide.com

SOURCES:
GdWrldFest-1985, p. 178
IntlThFolk-1979, pp. 358, 361

♦ 0492 ♦ Carthaginians and Romans Fiesta
10 days in late September

Cartegena, located on the Mediterranean Sea in southeastern Spain, is an ancient city steeped in the history of the Carthaginian and Roman Empires. Founded as the central Carthaginian hub in 227 B.C.E., the city was conquered two decades later by the Romans. Today, for 10 days in late September, thousands of local people celebrate the Carthaginians and Romans Fiesta by dressing in period costume and reenacting this pivotal era in history. The festival has been an annual event since 1989.

The festivities open with a ceremonial lighting of a sacred fire, which is followed by the official presentation of the Carthaginian troops and the Roman Legions. During the festival the soldiers stay in Carthaginian and Roman camps, each constructed in a historically accurate style.

Over the next several days, festival attendees witness a series of reenactments, including a Roman circus; the wedding of Carthaginian commander Hannibal and his wife Himilce; the sea battle that preceded the Roman conquest of the city; and the victorious march by the Roman Legions through the streets of Cartegena. On the festival's final day, both sides make one more procession through the city.

CONTACTS:
Tourist Office of Spain
666 Fifth Ave.
35th Fl.
New York, NY 10103

Spanish Tourism Institute (Turespaña)
6 Jose Lázaro Galdiano
Madrid, Spain
www.tourspain.es

♦ 0493 ♦ Caruaru Roundup
September

Roundups started out as nothing more than the yearly task of bringing the cattle together in the winter for branding. But in parts of Brazil they have developed into folkloric celebrations involving the participation of hundreds of cowboys who compete in "downing the steers." The roundup in the city of Caruaru in Pernambuco state is one of the largest. In addition to steer-roping contests, viola players and *repentistas* (verse improvisers) entertain the people with their music and rhyming descriptions of the day's activities. Local food specialties are served during the three-day event.

CONTACTS:
Brazilian Embassy
3006 Massachusetts Ave. N.W.
Washington, D.C. 20008
202-238-2700; fax: 202-238-2827
www.brasilemb.org

♦ 0494 ♦ Casals Festival
Early June

This event is a two-week music festival held in San Juan, Puerto Rico, to celebrate the memory of Pablo Casals (1876-1973), the world-renowned Spanish-born cellist and conductor. An outspoken opponent of Fascism and the regime of Francisco Franco, he was forced to leave Spain and moved to France in 1936. Twenty years later he moved to Puerto Rico, the birthplace of his mother. There he initiated this music festival.

Through the years internationally known artists, among them Rudolf Serkin, Andrés Segovia, Arthur Rubenstein, Isaac Stern, and Yehudi Menuhin (*see also* MENUHIN FESTIVAL), have appeared at the festival. Programs offer a variety of composers, from BACH to Bartók.

CONTACTS:
Puerto Rico Tourism Company
666 Fifth Ave., 15th Fl.
New York, NY 10103
800-866-7827
gotopuertorico.com

SOURCES:
GdUSFest-1984, p. 220
MusFestAmer-1990, p. 156

♦ 0495 ♦ Cassinga Day
May 4

On May 4, 1978, South African forces attacked a SWAPO (South West Africa People's Organization) base located in the old Angolan mining town of Cassinga. Hundreds of Namibians died during the attack. Although Namibia eventually won its political independence in 1990 and is currently ruled by the SWAPO party government, a national holiday is declared every year on the anniversary of the attack to commemorate those who died in their country's struggle for independence.

CONTACTS:
Namibian Embassy
1605 New Hampshire Ave. N.W.
Washington, D.C. 20009
202-986-0540; fax: 202-986-0443

♦ 0496 ♦ Castor and Pollux, Festival of
July 15

In Greco-Roman mythology, Castor and Pollux were twin gods who helped shipwrecked sailors and received sacrifices for favorable winds. Worshipped as the Dioscuri (from the Greek *Dioskouroi*, or "sons of Zeus"), their cult was a popular one in 484 B.C.E., when, according to legend, the twins fought on the side of the Romans in the Battle of Lake Regillus and brought word of their victory to Rome. A temple was built for them in the Forum, and it was here that the annual festival in their honor was celebrated on July 15.

Castor and Pollux were renowned for their athletic ability and are usually depicted as horsemen. They shared the same mother, Leda, but Castor was the son of Tyndareus and was therefore mortal, while Pollux was the son of Zeus and immortal. When they got into an argument with Idas and Lynceus, another set of twins, Castor was slain. Pollux was heartbroken because, as an immortal, he could not join his brother in death. Zeus finally allowed them to stay together, dividing their time between the heavens and the underworld. Eventually they were transformed into the constellation known as Gemini (The Twins), which, before the invention of the compass, was an important aid to navigation.

SOURCES:
NewCentClassHandbk-1962, p. 408
OxClassDict-1970, p. 213

♦ 0497 ♦ Castroville Artichoke Festival
Third weekend in September

The Castroville Artichoke Festival is one of the oldest agricultural festivals in California, held in Castroville, which calls itself the "Artichoke Center of the World." The two-day festival began in 1959 with a barbecue and parade; there is still a parade, and the lead float traditionally carries the Artichoke Queen and a huge green artichoke replica. Other events include a classic car show, a fun run, and displays of "AGROart"—sculptures composed of fruits and vegetables. Food booths offer artichoke cookies and french-fried artichokes. Attendance may reach 14,000.

Castroville, founded in 1863 by Juan Bautista Castro, was an agricultural community from the start. In 1888 sugar beets became an important crop on the land west of Castro's settlement. When beet prices declined in 1921, Andrew J. Molera, the owner of the land, decided to grow artichokes, which were new to the U.S. market. He provided the plants for the first crop and leased the acreage to farmers. By 1925, more than 4,000 acres of artichokes were being cultivated, and by 1929 artichokes were the third largest cash crop of the Salinas Valley.

CONTACTS:
Castroville Festivals
P.O. Box 1041
Castroville, CA 95012
831-633-2465
www.artichoke-festival.org

♦ 0498 ♦ Caturmas
June through September

The Jains follow an ancient Indian religion popularized by MAHAVIRA. The name of the religion derives from *jinas*, meaning "spiritual victors." There have been 24 jinas so far in this age of the world, according to Jainism. Nonviolence, or *ashima*, is one of Jainism's primary tenets, and devout Jains go to considerable lengths to avoid harming other living beings, including adhering to a vegetarian diet.

Jains observe a retreat known as Caturmas during the rainy season in India, during which travel is curtailed and fasting is frequent. Some speculate that this tradition is based in the Jains' concern for the many small insects that come out during the rainy season, whom they do not wish to kill unnecessarily by traveling about.

SOURCES:
EncyRel-1987, vol. 7, p. 507
OxDictWrldRel-1997, p. 487
RelHolCal-2004, p. 195

♦ 0499 ♦ Cavalcata Sarda
Second to last Sunday of May

This famous procession—or *cavalcata*—was originally held in Sassari, Sardinia, Italy, more than 900 years ago to celebrate a victory over Saracen invaders. Today the procession consists of costumed groups from over 100 Sardinian villages. Wearing the traditional dress of their region, participants in the Cavalcata Sarda often ride through the streets in ox-drawn carts. After the procession is over, the celebration continues with singing and dancing.

CONTACTS:
Italian Government Tourist Board
630 Fifth Ave., Ste. 1565
New York, NY 10111
212-245-5618; fax: 212-586-9249
www.italiantourism.com

SOURCES:
BkHolWrld-1986, May 23
GdWrldFest-1985, p. 118

♦ 0500 ♦ Cavalhadas
50 days after Easter

During the Pentecost season, Brazilian Catholics celebrate Festival of the DIVINE HOLY SPIRIT (Festa do Divino). This festival, believed to have been established by Portugal's Queen Isabel in the 13th century, observes the ascension of Christ into heaven, which is commemorated by Christians worldwide. One distinctly Brazilian tradition during the three-day festival is the Cavalhadas, a ceremony that reenacts the Christian knights' defeat of the Moors on the Iberian Peninsula during the Middle Ages.

Cavalhadas has been an annual observance since 1819. It is held throughout Brazil, although the most popular celebration takes place in the historic city of Pirenópolis in the country's central region. A smaller festival takes place in Amarantina, located farther to the south.

Among the feast's expressly religious activities are masses, processions, and the recitation of novenas. The festival's most-attended event is the staging of the knight tournament itself, which in Pirenópolis occurs in the city's bull ring. All the actors ride on horseback, with the Christian knights, dressed in blue, squaring off against the Moors, in red.

CONTACTS:
Brazilian Embassy
3006 Massachusetts Ave. N.W.
Washington, D.C. 20008-3634
202-238-2700; fax: 202-238-2827
www.brasilemb.org

SOURCES:
FolkWrldHol-1999, p. 339

♦ 0501 ♦ Central African Republic Independence Day
August 13; December 1

On December 1, 1958, the region now known as Central African Republic became a republic within the French Community. The republic achieved independence from France on August 13, 1960. Both days are celebrated as national holidays.

CONTACTS:
Central African Republic Embassy
1618 22nd St. N.W.
Washington, D.C. 20008
202-483-7800; fax: 202-332-9893

SOURCES:
AnnivHol-2000, p. 135
NatlHolWrld-1968, p. 218

♦ 0502 ♦ Central City Opera Festival
Late June to mid-August

Central City Opera Festival is a festival of opera, operetta, and cabaret in the one-time mining town of Central City, Colo. Performances are staged in the Old Opera House, built in 1878 and since restored to its original Victorian elegance. On opening night, "flower girls" present the audience with fresh flowers, which are thrown on stage to the cast at the end of the performance.

Inaugurated in 1932, the **Opera Festival** was not only the first summer opera festival in the country but also the first to espouse singing opera in English, a tradition that continues. *The Ballad of Baby Doe*, an opera that depicts the love story of the real-life silver king, Horace Tabor, who left his wife for the beautiful and much younger Baby Doe, was commissioned by Central City.

Cabaret opera is presented in the historic Teller House next to the Opera House. Built in 1872, this was once the grandest hotel in the west, host to President Ulysses S. Grant and other notables.

One of the presentations is *Face on the Barroom Floor*, which was commissioned on the 100th anniversary of the opera house. The saloon of the Teller House is the site of the "face" made famous in the poem by H. Antoine D'Arcy. The poem tells the story of the drunken vagabond who comes into the bar, asks for whiskey, and explains that he was once a painter who fell in love with beautiful Madeline—and that she was stolen away by his friend. "That's why I took to drink, boys," the vagabond says, and then offers to draw Madeline's portrait on the barroom floor:

Another drink, and with chalk in hand the vagabond began
To sketch a face that well might buy the soul of any man.
Then, as he placed another lock upon the shapely head,
With a fearful shriek, he leaped and fell across the picture—dead.

CONTACTS:
Central City Opera House Association
400 S. Colorado Blvd., Ste. 530
Denver, CO 80246
800-851-8175 or 303-292-6500; fax: 303-292-2221
www.centralcityopera.org

SOURCES:
GdUSFest-1984, p. 25
MusFestAmer-1990, p. 167

♦ 0503 ♦ Central Maine Egg Festival
Fourth Saturday in July

This one-day event in Pittsfield, Maine, was started in 1972 by two journalists who were tired of hearing about their state's potato crop and wanted to focus attention on central Maine's egg and chicken industry. Today its primary attraction is the world's largest skillet—a 300-pound teflon-coated frying pan, five feet in diameter, that is used to cook more than 4,000 eggs for those attending the festival breakfast. The giant skillet, designed and donated by the Alcoa Corporation, is stored in an airplane hangar.

A festival highlight in years past was the World's Largest Egg Contest, in which only chicken eggs could be entered. Since entries came from all over the world, special tests often were conducted to reveal imposters. The winning egg was plated with gold. Other events include an "Egglympics," a chicken barbecue, a street dance, and fireworks.

CONTACTS:
Central Maine Egg Festival Committee
P.O. Box 82
Pittsfield, ME 04969
207-257-4209
eggfestcraftah.com

SOURCES:
GdUSFest-1984, p. 77

◆ 0504 ◆ **Cerealia (Cerialia)**
April 19

Ceres was the ancient Roman goddess of grain and of harvests, often identified with the Greek goddess Demeter. People held festivals in her honor in various locations, but the Cerealia originated in Rome, where she was worshipped at her temple on the Aventine Hill along with two other deities, Liber (a fertility god) and Libera, his female counterpart. The temple became a center of activity for the plebeians, or common people, who usually suffered when there was a grain shortage.

The festival known as Cerealia was observed at various locations only by Roman matrons, who, for several days preceding the festival, abstained from wine and other carnal pleasures. People who were in mourning were not allowed to appear at the celebration. For this reason, the Cerealia was not observed after the Battle of Cannae, when 50,000 Roman troops were killed by Hannibal.

There is a theory that APRIL FOOLS' DAY is a relic of the ancient Roman Cerealia, also held in April. According to legend, when Ceres's daughter Proserpine was carried off to the underworld by Pluto, Ceres heard the echo of her screams and tried to follow her voice. But it was a fool's errand, for it was impossible to locate the echo's source.

The THESMOPHORIA was a similar festival observed in ancient Greece.

SOURCES:
AmerBkDays-2000, p. 247
ClassDict-1984, p. 140
DictRomRel-1996, p. 45
FestRom-1981, p. 102
OxClassDict-1970, p. 223
OxYear-1999, p. 160

◆ 0505 ◆ **Cervantes Festival, International**
October

Spanish novelist, poet, and playwright Miguel de Cervantes (1547-1616) is best known for his creation of *Don Quixote* (1605), a novel that describes the adventures of an elderly knight and his pragmatic squire, Sancho Panza. Cervantes is honored in a three-week festival held in Guanajuato, Mexico, featuring orchestral music, opera, theater, dance, film, and

folklore. At the festival's opening ceremony, statues of Don Quixote and Sancho Panza are lit up by fireworks.

Although most festival events are held in the Teatro Juarez and the Teatro Principal, amateur Mexican actors often give street performances of Cervantes's famous one-act plays in the Plaza de San Roque. Various musical performances are a popular attraction, as are art exhibits, children's theater, and folkloric dance ensembles.

CONTACTS:
Mexico Tourism Board
21 E. 63rd St., Fl. 3
New York, NY 10021
800-446-3942 or 212-821-0314; fax: 212-821-0367
www.visitmexico.com

SOURCES:
GdWrldFest-1985, p. 134
IntlThFolk-1979, p. 269

◆ 0506 ◆ **Chad Independence Day**
August 11

On August 11, 1960, Chad became an independent country after struggling against the French since they first claimed Chad as a French territory in the 1890s.

Celebrations of this national holiday—including parades, dancing, and singing—are often moved to January 11 because of the heavy rains in August.

CONTACTS:
Chad Embassy
2002 R St. N.W.
Washington, D.C. 20009
202-462-4009; fax: 202-265-1937

SOURCES:
AnnivHol-2000, p. 135
NatlHolWrld-1968, p. 15

◆ 0507 ◆ **Chad Republic Day**
November 28

This national holiday commemorates the establishment of the republic on this day in 1958, which afforded Chad some autonomy, though it was a French territory until it attained full independence (*see* CHAD INDEPENDENCE DAY).

CONTACTS:
Chad Embassy
2002 R St. N.W.
Washington, D.C. 20009
202-462-4009; fax: 202-265-1937

SOURCES:
AnnivHol-2000, p. 197

◆ 0508 ◆ **Chagu-Chagu Umakko**
June 15

People in Morioka, a horse-breeding district of Iwate Prefecture in Japan, hold the Chagu-Chagu Umakko Festival to honor the god of horses. The parade begins at the Komaga-ta-jinja shrine and ends at the Morioka Hachimangu shrine, a distance of just under 10 miles. Using white ropes, people lead richly decorated horses. When they reach the shrine, the riders make an offering of a picture of a horse, and prayers are said for the horses' well-being and the owners' financial success.

Chagu-chagu refers to the sound of the bells that are hung on the horses' heads. *Umakko* comes from *uma*, the word for "horse" in the local dialect. The horses and their riders, mostly young women and children, make a very picturesque sight as they ride along the paths between the rice paddies in summer.

CONTACTS:
Japan National Tourist Organization
1 Rockefeller Pl., Ste. 1250
New York, NY 10020
212-757-5640; fax: 212-307-6754
www.japantravelinfo.com

SOURCES:
IllFestJapan-1993, p. 74
JapanFest-1965, p. 159
WildPlanet-1995, p. 319

♦ 0509 ♦ **Chakri Day**
April 6

A national holiday in Thailand to commemorate the enthronement of Rama I, who founded the Chakri Dynasty in 1782. He was born Chao Phraya Chakri in 1737 and had become Thailand's leading general when a palace coup took place in Thon Buri. Officials invited the general to assume the throne; he did, and one of his first acts was to move the capital across the river to Bangkok. The dynasty he established has headed the country to this day, although the end of absolute monarchy came in 1932. The king was given the title Rama after his death. Ceremonies on April 6 honor his deeds and the founding of Bangkok as the capital.

CONTACTS:
Tourism Authority of Thailand
611 N. Larchmont Blvd., 1st Fl.
Los Angeles, CA 90004
800-842-4526 or 323-461-9814; fax: 323-461-9834
www.tourismthailand.org

SOURCES:
AnnivHol-2000, p. 58

♦ 0510 ♦ **Chalanda Marz (First of March)**
March 1

In Engadine, located in the Inn River valley of eastern Switzerland, the arrival of spring is celebrated with the ringing of bells. Young people put on herdsmen's costumes with wide leather belts from which they hang as many cow bells as they can collect. Smaller bells hang from their necks or are strapped across their chests. These "herdsmen" are followed by other young boys with bells around their necks who represent the cows. They go from house to house, clanging their bells as loudly as possible to scare off winter and serenading people with traditional spring songs. Sometimes they are given money, but more often they are rewarded with cakes, apples, or eggs. An evening feast is made out of the food, and afterward there are games and dancing. The money goes to the village schoolmaster, who saves it for a class picnic or excursion.

SOURCES:
AnnivHol-2000, p. 37
FestWestEur-1958, p. 226

♦ 0511 ♦ **Chalk Sunday**
Between February 8 and March 14; first Sunday of Lent

In rural Ireland it was at one time customary to brush chalk on single men and women as they entered the church on the first Sunday of LENT. Because Roman Catholics were not permitted to hold weddings during Lent, those who were still unmarried at the beginning of the Lenten season had to remain so until EASTER—if not longer. Back when it was less common for young people to stay single well into their 20s and 30s, marking them with chalk was a way of chiding them for their unmarried status.

SOURCES:
FolkWrldHol-1999, p. 167

♦ 0512 ♦ **Chamizal Festival**
Early October

The Chamizal Festival, formerly known as the **Border Folk Festival**, has been held at the Chamizal National Memorial in El Paso, Texas, since 1973. It is celebrated in early October and features Latino food, music, and dance as well as traditional crafts and children's activities and entertainment.

The location of the festival is significant, for it was here that Mexican claims to El Chamizal, a wedge of land on the Texas side, were first filed in 1895. The dispute, which involved relocating the Rio Grande's channel, was finally resolved in 1963, an event that is commemorated by the Chamizal National Memorial.

CONTACTS:
Chamizal National Memorial
National Park Service
800 S. San Marcial
El Paso, TX 79905
915-532-7273; fax: 915-532-7240
www.nps.gov/cham

SOURCES:
LatinoLife-1995, p. 39

♦ 0513 ♦ **Chandan Yatra**
April-May; beginning on the third day of the waxing half of the Hindu month of Vaisakha and lasting 42 days

Indian Hindus celebrate several festivals during the new year, which in their holiday cycle arrives in Vaisakha, a month falling sometime between April and May. Within Vaisakha there are festivals whose observance takes place during a particular moon phase. One such festival, Chandan Yatra, is held during the waxing half of Vaisakha. During the festival, believers honor various Hindu deities, but most of their devotions are reserved for Lord Jagannatha, an expression of Krishna.

Depending on the festival site, Chandan Yatra lasts between three and six weeks and is celebrated throughout Orissa, a state located on India's eastern coast. Festival locations within Orissa include Puri, Baribapada, Balanga, and one of Hinduism's four holy places, Bhubaneshwar. Traditionally, the most elaborate celebration has always taken place at Puri, which is the final destination of a 42-day-long procession carrying icons of Lord Rama, Lord Krishna, and other deities. The various icons are gathered from temples along the way of the procession. At the final site, a large water tank in Puri called the Narenda, the idols are placed in decorated boats and undergo sacred baths to the accompaniment of music.

Festivals in other towns are typically only three weeks long. They are observed in a similar fashion to the Puri ceremony, with a daily procession from the temple to the water tank.

CONTACTS:
Orissa Department of Tourism
Paryatan Bhawan
Museum Campus
Bhubaneswar, Orissa 751014 India
www.orissatourism.gov.in

Bharatonline—Savion Travel Services Pvt. Ltd.
A-88, First Fl., Sector 4
Noida, Uttar Pradesh 201301 India
www.bharatonline.com

◆ 0514 ◆ Chaomos
At least seven days, including December 21, the winter solstice

Chaomos is the winter festival of the Kalasha (also known as Kalash Kafir) people, who live in valleys in the northwestern corner of Pakistan, about 20 miles north of Chitral. The festival honors Balomain, a demigod who once lived among the Kalasha and did heroic deeds. Every year, his spirit comes to the valleys to count the people, collect their prayers, and take them back to Tsiam, the mythical land where the Kalasha originated, and to Dezao, the omnipotent creator god.

The celebration begins with the purification of women and girls: they take ritual baths, and then have water poured over their heads as they hold loaves of bread cooked by the men. A man waves burning juniper over the head of each woman, murmuring, *"Sooch"* ("Be pure"). On the following day, the men and boys are purified. They, too, take ritual baths and are then forbidden to sit on chairs or beds until evening when the blood of a sacrificed goat is sprinkled on their faces. The celebration continues with singing and chanting, a torchlight procession, dancing, bonfires, and festive eating of special bread and goat tripe.

Kalash means "black," and the people (thought to have descended from Alexander the Great) are called that because

of the women's black robes. The Kalasha are among the people who live in Afghanistan in the area called Nuristan ("land of light"). This entire region was once known to the Muslims as Kafiristan ("land of infidels"), but in 1896 the Afghan Kafirs were forcibly converted to Islam. The Kalasha still maintain their old religion, a mixture of ancestor and fire worship. Their pantheon of gods, besides Dezao, includes Sajigor, the "great" god, Mahandeu, the "wise" god, and Surisan, who protects cattle.

Chaomos is one of the four annual festivals of the Kalasha; others are the spring festival in mid-May, the harvest festival in mid-August, and the autumn festival that marks the walnut and grape harvest.

CONTACTS:
Sarhad Tourism Corporation
13-A Khyber Rd.
Peshawar, Northwest Frontier Province, Pakistan
92-91-921-1091; fax: 92-91-921-0871

◆ 0515 ◆ Charleston Sternwheel Regatta
Labor Day weekend

The Sternwheel Regatta was a celebration of its river-town history by Charleston, W.Va. The highlights were the sternwheel and power-boat races on the Kanawha River. There were also many other events, including concerts, parades, a car show, a distance run, and the "Anything That Floats Race." The regatta began in 1971 and attracted about a million spectators before it was retired in 2008.

CONTACTS:
Charleston Regatta Commission
P.O. Box 20185
Charleston, WV 25362
304-545-0244
www.sternwheelregatta.com

◆ 0516 ◆ Charlottetown Festival
June-October

The Charlottetown Festival is devoted entirely to musicals by Canadians. Held from mid-June through mid-October on Prince Edward Island, the festival presents three full-scale musicals every year. One of these is always *Anne of Green Gables*, a story about rural life on the island at the turn of the century, written by island-born novelist Lucy Maud Montgomery. In fact, *Anne of Green Gables* was the first musical presented at the festival when it was founded in 1965.

The festival also offers plays for children, Sunday evening pop concerts, and a series of short plays and musical events. The full-scale musicals and most of the festival's events are held at the Confederation Centre of the Arts in Charlottetown, the capital of Prince Edward Island.

CONTACTS:
Confederation Centre
145 Richmond St.
Charlottetown, PE C1A 1J1 Canada
902-628-1864; fax: 902-566-4648
www.confederationcentre.com

SOURCES:
GdWrldFest-1985, p. 55
IntlThFolk-1979, p. 75

◆ 0517 ◆ Charro Days Fiesta
Between January 31 and March 4; four days beginning the Thursday of the weekend before Ash Wednesday

The pre-Lenten festival known as Charro Days has been held each year since 1938 in the border towns of Brownsville, Texas, and Matamoros, Mexico, on opposite sides of the Rio Grande. A major border-crossing point, the two towns have a rich Spanish-Mexican heritage which is reflected in the fiesta. Male residents of the two cities wear the *charro* costume— a cross between the costume worn by the Spanish dons who once ruled Mexico and the Mexican horseman's outfit. Women wear the *china poblana*—a regional costume once worn by a little Chinese girl who was befriended by the Mexicans and has since become a kind of fairy princess to them.

Fiesta events take place in both Brownsville and Matamoros, and include a huge children's parade, costume dances in the street, and other events with Mexican and Latin themes. The festival has been known to attract as many as 400,000 visitors, many of whom wear costumes and participate in the events.

CONTACTS:
Charro Days Committees
P.O. Box 3247
Brownsville, TX 78523
956-542-4245; fax: 956-542-6771
www.charrodaysfiesta.com

SOURCES:
AmerBkDays-2000, p. 118
AnnivHol-2000, p. 35

◆ 0518 ◆ Cheese Rolling
May-June, Monday after Pentecost

In Gloucestershire, England, cheese rolling is believed to have been a popular annual sport for at least 500 years. It is held on WHIT-MONDAY in Birdlip. Cooper's Hill, which is located in Birdlip near Brockworth and is a thousand feet high, is famous for its fine pasture lands. Rolling the cheese down this hill traditionally reminded villagers of their rights to graze their sheep there.

Early in the evening, the event leader, sporting a white smock and top hat, rolls the "cheese" (nowadays, three or four large wooden discs) down the hill. People chase after them, and the first to capture one of the discs receives a small prize. The game is quite tricky, because the descent down Cooper's Hill is very steep, and people often end up tumbling down the side more quickly than the discs.

Cheese rolling is a MAY DAY custom in Stilton, where men and women in teams of four compete to roll the wooden cheese.

CONTACTS:
Stilton Community Association
8 Caldecote Rd.

Stilton, Peterborough PE7 3RH United Kingdom
44-17-3324-1206
www.stilton.org

SOURCES:
YrbookEngFest-1954, p. 238
YrFest-1972, p. 40

◆ 0519 ◆ Cheese Sunday
Between February 8 and 28; Sunday before Lent

The week before Orthodox Christian LENT is known as Cheese or Dairy Week—especially in regions of Greece and Macedonia—because it is the last opportunity for people to eat dairy products. It is usually characterized by dancing, masquerading, and generally uninhibited behavior. At sunset on the final Sunday, people attend an evening church service during which the priest and congregation exchange mutual forgiveness for their sins. The last dish eaten on Cheese Sunday, or **Cheesefare Sunday**, is usually eggs.

Following custom, the last egg left over from the meal may be hung from a string in the middle of the ceiling. People sitting around the table hit it with their foreheads to get it swinging and then try to catch it in their mouths. Another variation of this game is to have someone hold a stick with an egg swinging from a string or thread on the end. People sit in a circle with their mouths open, trying to catch it. The popular saying, "With an egg I close my mouth, with an egg I shall open it again," refers to the hard-boiled Easter eggs that will mark the end of the Lenten fast.

In the Orthodox Church, the second Sunday before the beginning of Great Lent is called Meat Fare Sunday because it is traditionally the last day on which meat may be eaten until EASTER.

SOURCES:
BkFestHolWrld-1970, p. 35
EncyEaster-2002, p. 58
FolkWrldHol-1999, p. 126
OxYear-1999, p. 641

◆ 0520 ◆ Cheese Week (Sima Sedmitza)
Between February 8 and 28; week preceding Lent

Bulgarians call the week preceding the start of Orthodox Christian LENT Cheese Week. During this time Bulgarians try to eat up all their cheese, lard, milk, and fish, since these foods will be forbidden in the coming Lenten fast. People visit their parents, godchildren their godparents, and young people call on the elderly during this week, customarily offering a lemon (to men) or an orange (to women).

Young people play a traditional game that involves dangling a piece of Turkish taffy, a bit of cheese, or a hard-boiled egg from the ceiling with a bit of string. One person sets the object in motion while contestants try to catch it with their teeth. In some zones people burn bonfires. The boys jump through the fire while the girls dance around them—possibly a remnant from an ancient custom ensuring fertility.

SOURCES:
BkFest-1937, p. 67

♦ 0521 ♦ **Chelsea Flower Show**
Late May

For more than eight decades, England's Royal Horticultural Society (RHS) has held a flower show in London on the grounds of the Royal Hospital in Chelsea. The highlight of this five-day event is the full-sized show gardens that are planted and landscaped in the space of only three weeks by some of Britain's top garden designers. There are also scientific displays of the latest advances in gardening; booths for flower arranging and garden design; and trade stands showing everything from antique garden statuary to the very latest in garden tools and machinery. Experts are also on hand to give people advice on courtyard gardens, window boxes, hanging baskets, and other less elaborate forms of gardening.

The Chelsea Flower Show is followed by other RHS-sponsored shows that span the entire calendar, among them the Hampton Court Palace Flower Show in July, the Westminster Shows held every month in the Royal Horticultural Halls, and the Malvern Spring and Autumn Shows.

CONTACTS:
Royal Horticultural Society
80 Vincent Sq.
London, SW1P 2PE United Kingdom
44-84-5260-5000; fax: 44-20-7233-9502
www.rhs.org.uk

SOURCES:
GdWrldFest-1985, p. 95

♦ 0522 ♦ **Cheltenham International Festival of Music**
Early July

Established in 1945 to give first performances of works by British composers, the two-week Cheltenham International Festival of Music has since expanded its scope considerably. Its musical repertoire now includes both British and foreign composers offering operas as well as symphonic, chamber, and choral music. The festival commissions a handful of new works each year and often highlights British works that have been neglected. Composers whose works have premiered there include Malcolm Arnold, Thea Musgrave, Alan Rawsthorne, and Sir Michael Tippett. Special master classes are also offered each year on such subjects as string quartets, piano trios, and brass instruments, while children and adults can participate in other educational programs.

Recitals and chamber music concerts are held in the Pittville Pump Room, Cheltenham Spa's most important Regency structure. Operas are presented in the Everyman Theatre, and symphony concerts take place in the Town Hall. Other locations include local churches, abbeys, and castles. Cheltenham Spa is well known for its mineral springs, its Regency architecture, and its proximity to other attractions in the Cotswold Hills area of England.

CONTACTS:
Cheltenham Arts Festivals Ltd.
109-111 Bath Rd.
Cheltenham, Gloucestershire GL53 7LS United Kingdom
44-12-4277-4400; fax: 44-12-4257-3902
www.cheltenhamfestivals.co.uk

SOURCES:
MusFestEurBrit-1980, p. 50
MusFestWrld-1963, p. 245

♦ 0523 ♦ **Cherokee National Holiday**
September, Labor Day weekend

The Cherokee National Holiday has been held since 1953 in Tahlequah, Oklahoma. To commemorate the signing of the 1839 Cherokee Constitution and the establishment of the Cherokee Nation, thousands of Cherokee Indians get together for a four-day celebration in early September. There is an all-Indian rodeo, a native dance competition, a powwow, and a parade with colorful floats and Cherokees in ceremonial dress. Native American arts and crafts—including baskets, flutes, dolls, and jewelry—are on display, and visitors can sample Native American foods. Games and sports offered at the festival include a golf tournament, a horseshoe tournament, a cornstalk shoot, a blowgun shoot, and a traditional Indian marble game.

CONTACTS:
Cherokee Nation
P.O. Box 948
Tahlequah, OK 74465
800-256-0671 or 918-456-0671
www.cherokee.org

♦ 0524 ♦ **Cherokee Strip Day**
September 16

September 16, 1893, was the date of the last and largest of the "land runs" that opened western Indian territories to white settlement. The Cherokee Strip encompassed more than six million acres of mostly grassy plains where white homesteaders wanted to graze their animals. Anyone who wanted to claim and settle the 160-acre parcels had to line up on the morning of September 16 and race to plant his flag at a chosen spot. The lure of free land attracted an estimated 100,000 prospective settlers, mostly young men who could withstand the harsh climate.

Cherokee Strip Day is a festival day in Oklahoma—particularly in the communities of Ponca City, Enid, and Perry—towns that sprang up as a result of the 1893 run. The celebrations last several days and include parades, picnics, dances, and rodeos.

See also OKLAHOMA DAY

CONTACTS:
Oklahoma Tourism and Recreation Department
15 Robinson St., Ste. 801
Oklahoma City, OK 73105
800-652-6552 or 405-521-2409; fax: 405-521-3992
www.oklatourism.gov

SOURCES:
AmerBkDays-2000, p. 649
AnnivHol-2000, p. 156

♦ 0525 ♦ Cherry Blossom Festival (Hawaii)
February-March

The Cherry Blossom Festival in Hawaii is an annual Japanese cultural celebration held in Honolulu, usually from mid-February until the first week in April. The beauty of cherry blossoms is almost sacred in Japan, but the cherry blossoms of this festival are purely symbolic; cherry trees don't grow in Hawaii. The festival offers a variety of events: presentations of Kabuki drama, traditional Japanese dances, martial arts, and Japanese films, as well as demonstrations of such arts as weaving and paper-doll making. The celebration was created in 1953 by the Honolulu Japanese community to "bridge the cultural gap by sharing with others the essence of the Japanese heritage."

See also HANAMI

CONTACTS:
Honolulu Japanese Junior Chamber of Commerce
2454 S. Beretania St., Ste. 205
Honolulu, HI 96826
808-949-2255; fax: 808-627-8841
www.cbfhawaii.com

SOURCES:
GdUSFest-1984, p. 43

♦ 0526 ♦ Cherry Blossom Festival (Northern California)
April

More than 2,000 Japanese Americans and performers from Japan participate in this festival in San Francisco's Japantown that takes place over two consecutive weekends in April. Based on HANAMI, a traditional festival in Japan, this celebration of Japanese culture and customs includes exhibitions of Japanese art and dancing, kimono and obi (the sash worn with a kimono) demonstrations, tea ceremonies, and bonsai exhibits. The climax of the festival is a three-hour parade from City Hall to the Japan Center at Post and Fillmore Streets. The parade includes singers and dancers, floats, Akita dogs, Taiko drummers, the Cherry Blossom Queen, and the traditional Taru Mikoshi, a portable shrine piled so high with casks of sake—an alcoholic beverage made from rice—that it takes 100 men to carry it. The festival lasts for seven days, covering two weekends in April. It was first held in 1968 to mark the official opening of San Francisco's Japan Center.

CONTACTS:
San Francisco Convention and Visitors Bureau
900 Market St., Ste. 900
San Francisco, CA 94103
415-391-2000; fax: 415-974-1992
nccbf.org

SOURCES:
GdUSFest-1984, p. 22

♦ 0527 ♦ Cherry Blossom Festival, National
Between late March and early April

The National Cherry Blossom Festival in Washington, D.C., is held whenever the cherry trees planted around the Potomac River Tidal Basin bloom—usually between March 20 and April 15. The 3,000 trees were a gift to the city of Washington from the city of Tokyo, Japan, in 1912, and today they are the focal point of a two-week festival celebrating the friendship between the two countries. Most of the original trees died because the water in the Basin flooded their roots. Their replacements were more carefully planted and now thrive. Dates for the festival are set a year in advance to avoid coinciding with EASTER and HOLY WEEK observances.

The festival has been in existence since 1948, although earlier celebrations included re-enacting the original planting and crowning a Cherry Blossom Festival Queen. Today the festivities include formal receptions for the 52 festival princesses (representing the 50 states, the District of Columbia, and the territory of Guam) and a Cherry Blossom parade through downtown Washington.

See also MACON CHERRY BLOSSOM FESTIVAL

CONTACTS:
Official Website of the National Cherry Blossom Festival
1250 H St. N.W., Ste. 1000
Washington, D.C. 20005
202-661-7584; fax: 202-661-7599
www.nationalcherryblossomfestival.org

National Mall & Memorial Parks
900 Ohio Dr. S.W.
Washington, DC 20024
202-426-6841
www.nps.gov

SOURCES:
AmerBkDays-2000, p. 262
AnnivHol-2000, p. 72
GdUSFest-1984, pp. 43, 203

♦ 0528 ♦ Cherry Festival, National
Second week in July

An annual event since 1926, Michigan's National Cherry Festival takes place in Traverse City, "The Cherry Capital of the World," where 70 percent of the world's red cherries are grown. Traditionally held for a full week in July, the time of the cherry harvest, the festival features both traditional and offbeat events involving cherries: cherry pie-eating and cooking contests, a cherry wine competition, displays of cherries and cherry products, free tours of the cherry orchards, a cherry smorgasbord luncheon, and the weighing-in of the world's largest cherry.

The festival began in 1924 with a ceremony to bless the cherry blossoms and ensure a good crop. Now it draws upwards of half a million visitors and includes three major parades, national high school band competitions, canoe races, and a water ski tournament among the more than 100 different events. Former President Gerald R. Ford, a Michigan native, officiated at the festival in 1975.

CONTACTS:
National Cherry Festival
109 Sixth St.
Traverse City, MI 49684
231-947-4230; fax: 231-947-7435
www.cherryfestival.org

SOURCES:
GdUSFest-1984, p. 94

♦ 0529 ♦ **Chestertown Tea Party Festival**
Late May

When the British passed the Boston Port Act closing the Port of Boston until complete restitution had been made for the tea destroyed during the Boston Tea Party, it unleashed a wave of anger throughout the American colonies. Shortly after the news reached Chestertown, Maryland, the brigantine *Geddes* dropped anchor in Chestertown harbor on May 13, 1774. Word went out that the *Geddes* was carrying a small shipment of tea, and 10 days later a group of local residents boarded the ship and dumped the tea in the Chester River.

Every year during the Chestertown Tea Party Festival the rebellion is reenacted. The local merchants gather at the town park, where they voice their opposition to the British tax on tea. The crowd winds its way down High Street to the river, where the "colonists" board a ship—usually a reproduction of an historic vessel—and throw its cargo of tea (and some of its crew) into the river. Other festival events include a colonial parade with fife and drum corps, exhibits and demonstrations of 18th-century American crafts, walking tours of Chestertown, clog dancing and fiddling, horse-and-carriage rides, and tall ship cruises. Typical Eastern Shore foods are served, such as Maryland fried chicken, barbequed ribs, "chitlins," crab cakes, she-crab soup, and fried clams.

CONTACTS:
Kent County
Tourism Dev. Office
400 High St.
Chestertown, MD 21620
410-778-0416; fax: 410-778-2746
www.chestertownteaparty.com

Library of Congress
101 Independence Ave. S.E.
Washington, DC 20540
202-707-5000; fax: 202-707-2076
www.loc.gov

♦ 0530 ♦ **Cheung Chau Bun Festival**
April-May; date decided by divination; usually about eight days between the end of third lunar month and 10th day of fourth lunar month

This festival is one of the most spectacular events in Hong Kong, celebrated only on Cheung Chau (which means "Long Island" in Chinese), one of the outlying islands of Hong Kong. It is believed that restless ghosts roam the island during the eight-day festival. Some believe they are the spirits of islanders massacred by 19th-century pirates. Others claim they are people who diied of a plague in the early 20th centu-

ry or that they are spirits of people whose remains were disturbed by people building new houses.

Three bamboo-and-paper towers, up to about 60 feet high and covered with sweet pink and white buns, are dedicated to the spirits and intended to placate them. People burn paper replicas of houses, cars, and money. The buns placed highest in the towers traditionally are held to be the luckiest, and people used to climb up the towers in a race to get them. But after a serious accident in 1978, the buns now are passed down the towers.

At the island's Pak Tai Temple, rites are held to honor Pak Tai, known as a Taoist king of the Dark Heaven or the Underworld. He is worshipped as a god of the sea who defeated a demon king and the king's allies, a tortoise and a serpent. The temple holds many small wooden statues of Pak Tai, all with a tortoise under one foot and a serpent under the other.

To pay homage to the animals and fish who serve as residents' food, only vegetarian dishes are served during the festival, and some people also make offerings to the animals' spirits.

In the highlight of the festival, the images of the temple gods are carried in a procession of lion and dragon dancers and children aged about five to eight, who are costumed as legendary Chinese figures. These children seem to float above the procession, but in reality they are held up by poles to which they are attached as adults carry them through the streets.

CONTACTS:
Hong Kong Tourism Board
115 E. 54th St., 2nd Fl.
New York, NY 10022
212-421-3382; fax: 212-421-8428
www.discoverhongkong.com

Cheung Chau Bun Festival
CHEUNGCHAU.ORG
China
www.cheungchau.org

SOURCES:
BkHolWrld-1986, May 25
GdWrldFest-1985, p. 105
IntlThFolk-1979, p. 197
WildPlanet-1995, p. 309

♦ 0531 ♦ **Cheyenne Frontier Days**
Last full week of July

What began in 1897 as an attempt to keep alive the sports and customs of the Old West has grown into a week-long festival that regularly attracts over 300,000 visitors. Cheyenne, Wyoming, was one of the wealthiest cattle-raising cities in the world in the 1880s, and now it celebrates its colorful history by staging one of the world's largest outdoor rodeos. The festival also includes parades of covered wagons, stagecoaches, and other old-time vehicles; ceremonial Indian dances; the crowning of a "Miss Frontier" queen; and pageants recreating events from Cheyenne's past. Cheyenne residents make pancakes for all with batter mixed in a concrete mixer.

CONTACTS:
Cheyenne Frontier Days
P.O. Box 2477

Cheyenne, WY 82003
800-227-6336 or 307-778-7200; fax: 307-778-7213
www.cfdrodeo.com

SOURCES:
AnnivHol-2000, p. 127
BkHolWrld-1986, Jul 28
DictDays-1988, p. 45
GdUSFest-1984, p. 215

♦ 0532 ♦ Chhau Mask-Dance Festival
Mid-April

Chhau is a form of dance rooted in the religious beliefs of Indian folk culture. Different regions of India practice their own unique style of Chhau, incorporating various folk, classical, and traditional elements. The masked dancers are often silent and use stylized movements to illustrate the conflict between good and evil to the accompaniment of drums, pipes, and cymbals. The dramatic situations that give shape to the dances are often drawn from episodes in the *Ramayana* and the *Mahabharata*, two famous epic poems of India.

The Seraikella Chhau dance held every April in the Singhbhum District of Bihar State reflects variations that are unique to the region. The influence of the martial arts can be seen in the dance, but the predominant mood is lyrical. Seraikella is also the home of the Government Chhau Dance School, which sponsors the two-day festival.

In the Mayurbhanj Chhau Dance, also held in the middle of April, the dancers do not wear masks but hold their facial expressions as still as possible, as if to imitate a mask. Unlike other forms of Indian dance, the Chhau dancers use all of the space available to them, and there are many long entrances and sweeping gestures.

CONTACTS:
Ministry of Tourism, Government of India
Rm. No 123, Transport Bhawan, No. 1, Parliament St.
New Delhi, Delhi 110 001 India
91-11-23715084; fax: 91-11-23715084
www.tourisminindia.com

Government of Orissa
Dept. of Tourism, Museum Campus
Paryatan Bhawan
Bhubaneswar, Orissa 751 014 India
91-674-432177; fax: 91-674-430887
www.orissagov.nic.in

SOURCES:
IntlThFolk-1979, p. 203

♦ 0533 ♦ Chiao Festival (Rite of Cosmic Renewal)
Every 60 years

Also spelled **Jiao**, this ancient festival is traditionally held about every 60 years all over Taiwan. The specific date is determined by a committee of the local priest and town leaders. The Rite of Cosmic Renewal serves to "rededicate" the local temple as well as renew the whole community. The festival can also be held more frequently in order to raise funds for repairing the temple.

People prepare for this important occasion by performing acts of penance and purification, cleansing, repairing and adorning the temple, and inviting the gods and family ancestors to attend the festival, which may last about three days.

Several priests may be enlisted to perform the various rituals of the Chiao Festival, some of which are carried out in private. Public rituals include a presentation of offerings, readings from sacred works, lighting a new fire outside and inside the temple, and dances. People go to enormous effort to prepare a huge banquet for the last day of the festival, to which all the deceased are formally invited by the "floating of the lanterns" the day before. Elaborate floats accompany representatives of each family in the community in a procession to a nearby body of water into which everyone releases a paper lantern on a small raft. The following day the entire community looks like a smorgasbord, with dishes set out in front of homes and more food filling the temple. The festive atmosphere is enhanced by puppet shows, operas, and other attractions.

CONTACTS:
Taipei Economic & Cultural Office
Information Division
90 Park Ave., 31st Fl.
New York, NY 10016
212-557-5122; fax: 212-557-3043

♦ 0534 ♦ Chicago Gospel Music Festival
First weekend in June

Since 1985 the city of Chicago, Ill., has celebrated its heritage as the birthplace of gospel music by hosting a three-day festival showcasing local, national, and international performers. The African-American composer Thomas A. Dorsey of Chicago's Pilgrim Baptist Church published the first gospel music in Chicago in 1926. A transplant from Georgia, Dorsey developed a vibrant, upbeat musical style that combined traditional spirituals and hymns with blues and jazz rhythms. In the following decades the genre spread from its roots in the black church to become a significant influence on American music and culture.

Each year the festival hosts about 275,000 fans, who enjoy 50 free performances on three stages in a lakefront setting at Millennium Park. It is the largest free music festival in the world devoted exclusively to gospel music. In addition to the entertainment offerings, the festival hosts a fine art fair, including works in such media as fiber, glass, painting, photography, and wood.

CONTACTS:
Chicago Gospel Music Festival
Mayor's Office of Special Events
121 N. LaSalle St., Rm. 703
Chicago, IL 60602
312-744-3315; fax: 312-744-8523
www.chicagogospelmusicfestival.us

SOURCES:
AAH-2007, p. 97

♦ 0535 ♦ Chicago Jazz Festival
August-September, four days preceding Labor Day

In the 1920s a four-block area along Chicago's State Street, known to the black community as "the Stroll," was the mecca of the jazz world. It was here that jazz took root in the city, establishing Chicago as a center for this uniquely American music. Shortly after the great composer-bandleader Duke Ellington died in 1974, a group of Chicago musicians got together to hold a concert in his honor; after that, the Ellington Concert became an annual event. A similar memorial concert was held for saxophonist John Coltrane in 1978, and the following year these two events merged with the jazz festival already being planned by the Jazz Institute of Chicago. Now it is the most extensive free jazz festival in the world, drawing an estimated audience of 400,000 and featuring such well-known artists as Sarah Vaughan, Ray Charles, Dave Brubeck, Herbie Hancock, George Benson, and Wynton Marsalis.

A number of major jazz events have occurred at the festival, such as the world premiere of Randy Weston's *African Sunrise* by Dizzy Gillespie and the Machito All-Star Orchestra in 1984, or the rendition of "Happy Birthday" sung in honor of Charlie Parker, the great jazz improviser, who was born on August 29, 1920, and died March 12, 1955.

CONTACTS:
Jazz Institute of Chicago
410 S. Michigan Ave., Ste. 943
Chicago, IL 60605
312-427-1676; fax: 312-427-1684
www.chicagojazzfestival.org

SOURCES:
MusFestAmer-1990, p. 191

♦ 0536 ♦ **Chickaban**
During Mayan month of Xul

The ancient Mayan feast known as Chickaban, observed at Mani in the Yucatán state of Mexico, was held in honor of the feathered serpent and storm god Kukulcán. Before the feast, the tribal chiefs spent five days fasting, dancing, and worshipping their idols. At the feast itself, offerings were made to Kukulcán, who came down from the sky to join them.

According to the myth, Kukulcán came to the Mayas from the west with 19 attendants, all bareheaded and wearing long robes and sandals. He built Chichén Itzá, the ancient Mayan city, and ruled over the four points of the compass and the four elements of air, earth, fire, and water. Kukulcán is usually depicted with a serpent's body, a jaguar's teeth, and the long plumes of the quetzal bird. He is holding a human head in his jaws and is seated on the cross-shaped symbol of the compass.

SOURCES:
DictFolkMyth-1984, p. 594

♦ 0537 ♦ **Chief Joseph Days**
Last full weekend in July

Chief Joseph (1840-1904) was the chief of the Nez Perce Indians. When the U.S. government tried to force the Nez Perce Indians to relocate to a reservation in 1877, the chief decided instead to lead about 800 of his followers on a long journey to Canada. After many battles with the white soldiers who were pursuing him and who outnumbered his warriors by ten to one, Chief Joseph and his people were captured within 40 miles of the Canadian border and sent to reservations in Oklahoma, where many of them became ill and died.

Chief Joseph, who spent the rest of his life in exile and who pleaded with President Theodore Roosevelt to let his people return to their ancestral home, is honored with a four-day festival every July in Joseph, Oregon. Established in 1945, the festival features one of the largest rodeos in the Northwest, a traditional Indian dance contest, a Nez Perce encampment and powwow, parades, dances, a golf tournament, and a cowboy church service.

CONTACTS:
Chief Joseph Days and Rodeo Encampment
P.O. Box 13
Joseph, OR 97846
541-432-1015
www.chiefjosephdays.com

♦ 0538 ♦ **Chief Seattle Days**
Third weekend in August

A three-day inter-tribal festival to honor Chief Seattle (1786-1866), for whom Seattle, Washington, is named. He was head of the Suquamish and Duwamish Indian tribes in the Puget Sound area of Washington. His name in the Lushootseed language was *See-ahth.* The festival is held at the Port Madison Indian Reservation in Suquamish, 40 miles south of Seattle. Besides featuring traditional Indian dances and drumming and dancing contests, it has a distinctive northwestern flavor, with salmon and clam bakes and canoe races. Other highlights are a horseshoe tournament, storytelling, and the election of a Chief Seattle Days Queen. The festival closes with the blessing of Chief Seattle's grave.

Chief Seattle and his father were both friendly to white settlers and helped them. He was the first to sign the Port Elliott Treaty in 1855, which set aside reservations for the Suquamish and other Washington tribes.

In a moving speech made in 1854 to a large group of Indians gathered to greet Isaac Stevens, the new United States Indian superintendent, Chief Seattle spoke of the passing away of the Indian tribes, fleeing at the approach of the white man. "Let him be just and deal kindly with my people," he said, "for the dead are not powerless. There is no death, only a change of worlds."

It is uncertain whether Chief Seattle actually uttered these words. The only known translation of Seattle's speech was made from the recollection of Dr. Harvy Smith 33 years later. The waters were made even muddier when, in 1971, Ted Perry, a screenwriter who now teaches at Middlebury College in Vermont, wrote a speech for the Chief that was included in a film on ecology. Mr. Perry knew the script was fiction, but others did not. Perry's apocryphal speech has been attributed to Chief Seattle ever since.

In 1992 a children's book based on an embellished version of Perry's script, *Brother Eagle, Sister Sky* by Susan Jeffers, made the *New York Times* Best Seller list and the great Chief Seattle slipped further into the mists of legend.

CONTACTS:
Suquamish Tribal Council
Port Madison Indian Reservation
P.O. Box 498
Suquamish, WA 98392
360-598-3311; fax: 360-598-3135
www.suquamish.nsn.us/csd.html

SOURCES:
IndianAmer-1989, p. 215

♦ 0539 ♦ Children's Book Day, International
April 2

This day, which is observed by countries all over the world, was first suggested by the International Board on Books for Young People (IBBY). They chose Hans Christian Andersen's birthday, April 2, because the Danish author's stories—which include "The Little Match Girl," "The Steadfast Tin Soldier," "The Ugly Duckling," and "Thumbelina"—have been favorites among children of all nationalities. The celebrations include contests in which children illustrate their favorite books, as well as the adoption of foreign pen pals. Every two years the IBBY sponsors the Hans Christian Andersen medals, which are awarded to a children's book author and a children's book illustrator for their contributions to children's literature.

See also ANDERSEN (HANS CHRISTIAN) FESTIVAL

CONTACTS:
International Reading Association
(U.S. section of IBBY)
800 Barksdale Rd.
Newark, DE 19714
302-731-1600; fax: 302-731-1057
www.usbby.org

International Board on Books for Young People
Nonnenweg 12
Postfach
Basel, 4003 Switzerland
41-61-272-2917; fax: 41-61-272-2757
www.ibby.org

SOURCES:
AnnivHol-2000, p. 56
BkHolWrld-1986, Apr 2

♦ 0540 ♦ Children's Day
Various

Many countries have set aside a day on which children are allowed to participate in church services, in government, and in various cultural and recreational activities. In the United States, Children's Day was first celebrated in June 1856 at the Universalist Church in Chelsea, Massachusetts. By 1868 its date had been set on a nationwide basis as the second Sunday in June.

Children's Day is also celebrated in the Democratic Republic of Congo (Dec. 25), Iceland (April 24), Indonesia (June 17), Japan (*see* KODOMO-NO-HI), Nigeria (May 27), and Turkey. The Turkish Children's Day on April 23 gives 400 students the educational opportunity to take seats in the national government in Ankara. The same thing takes place on a smaller scale in cities and towns all over the country.

See also TURKEY NATIONAL SOVEREIGNTY AND CHILDREN'S DAY and URINI NAL

SOURCES:
AnnivHol-2000, pp. 66, 68, 109, 190, 194
BkFestHolWrld-1970, p. 80
DaysCustFaith-1957, p. 157
RelHolCal-2004, p. 97

♦ 0541 ♦ Children's Day (former Yugoslavia)
December; three Sundays before Christmas

On the third Sunday before Christmas, known as **Dechiyi Dan** or Children's Day, parents in the former Yugoslavia tie up their children and refuse to release them until they have promised to be good.

And, although many people think that MOTHER'S DAY originated in the United States, Slavs traditionally set aside a Sunday in December to visit their mothers and bring them small gifts. Young children, on the other hand, honor their mothers by tying them up and refusing to release them until they have paid a "ransom" of sweets and goodies. Sometimes the mother hides small gifts under her mattress so that if the children tie her up before she gets out of bed in the morning, she'll have something to offer them. Considering that mothers tied up their children on the previous Sunday, this custom isn't as outrageous as it seems.

The Sunday following Materitse is *Ochichi* or *Ocevi* (Father's Day). Boys and girls tie their fathers to his chair or bed. The ransom in this case is even higher, as the father must promise to buy them coats, shoes, dresses, or other expensive items before they let him go. These promises are usually fulfilled a short time later as CHRISTMAS gifts.

SOURCES:
BkFest-1937, p. 344
FolkWrldHol-2000, p.

♦ 0542 ♦ Chile Battle of Iquique Day (Día de las Glorias Navales)
May 21

This national holiday in Chile is often called **Dia de las Glorias Navales** in Spanish ("The Day of the Glorious Navy"). From 1879 to 1881, the Chilean navy fought an alliance of Peru and Bolivia in the War of the Pacific (also known as the Chile-Peruvian War). The war grew out of a dispute over export tariffs that Bolivia levied on Chile for nitrate deposits mined in Bolivia's Atacama Province. Peru joined the Bolivian side, and the Chilean navy blockaded the Peruvian port of Iquique. The Chilean victory in the Battle of Iquique on

May 21, 1879, was a turning point in a war that Chile eventually won decisively.

The holiday is celebrated throughout Chile with festivals, military parades, and speeches. Sporting events, including boat and bicycle races, are held in honor of the holiday. Many people dress in traditional costumes as a symbol of national pride.

CONTACTS:
Embassy of Chile
1732 Massachusetts Ave. N.W.
Washington, D.C. 20036
202-785-1746; fax: 202-659-9624
chile-usa.org

◆ 0543 ◆ **Chile National Unity Day**
First Monday in September

In 1973, Chilean General Augusto Pinochet led a military coup that toppled the government of President Salvador Allende. Allende had been democratically elected, and his administration was replaced by a military dictatorship led by Pinochet. The government created a national holiday, celebrated on September 11, to mark the anniversary of the 1973 military coup. In 1998 the Chilean legislature voted to abolish the September 11 holiday. In its place, the legislature created National Unity Day, which has been celebrated since 1999.

Many Chileans have bitter memories of the years of military rule, when many citizens were arrested and never seen again. The purpose of National Unity Day is to promote reconciliation and justice in Chile. The holiday is celebrated annually on the first Monday in September.

CONTACTS:
Embassy of Chile
1732 Massachusetts Ave. N.W.
Washington, D.C. 20036
202-785-1746; fax: 202-887-5579
www.chile-usa.org

◆ 0544 ◆ **Chilembwe (John) Day**
January 15

John Chilembwe Day is a national holiday celebrated annually on January 15 (some sources state January 17) in the southeast-African country of Malawi. Reverend John Chilembwe was born in the 1860s in the African nation of Nyasaland, now known as Malawi. A Baptist minister, he spent considerable time abroad in America, where he was exposed to the radical abolitionist thought of John Brown and Booker T. Washington. Returning to Africa, Chilembwe opened a series of schools. Dismayed by the treatment of local peoples at the hands of plantation owners, whom he charged with racism and exploitation, he and a group of 200 followers staged an uprising. They attacked plantations and killed three white staff members along with several African workers. When the revolt failed to gain popular support, Chilembwe tried to flee to neighboring Mozambique. He and a group of his followers were caught and killed on February 3, 1915.

John Chilembwe is now memorialized as a hero for African independence and resistance to colonialism and is celebrated in modern Malawi, which attained its independence in 1964. His image on a Malawi banknote attests to his enduring popularity as a national figure and a symbol of Malawi freedom and patriotism.

CONTACTS:
Malawi Embassy
2408 Massachusetts Ave. N.W.
Washington, D.C. 20008
202-797-1007

◆ 0545 ◆ **Chilseog (Seventh Evening)**
Seventh day of the seventh lunar month

Chilseog is the Korean version of the SEVEN SISTERS FESTIVAL, based on an old Chinese legend about two stars known as the Herdsman and the Spinning Maiden. The Herdsman star, located in the Aquila constellation, and the Spinning Maiden star, Vega in the Lyra constellation, are in love but can only meet once a year—on the seventh day of the seventh lunar month, when it is believed that crows and magpies fly up into the heavens to form a bridge across the heavenly river, as the Milky Way is called.

On this night it is customary for young Korean women to pray for celestial assistance in sewing and to honor the stars by penning verse about them.

SOURCES:
AnnCustKorea-1983, p. 127
FolkWrldHol-1999, p. 456

◆ 0546 ◆ **Chilympiad (Republic of Texas Chili Cookoff)**
Third weekend in September

A chili cookoff in San Marcos, Tex., is called the "largest bowl o' red" competition in the world, which it probably is. Hundreds of chili chefs compete for the state championship, being judged on showmanship as much as recipes. Participation in the Chilympiad is a preliminary to entering the TERLINGUA CHILI COOKOFF in November. Besides the Chilympiad's gastronomic attractions, there are also concerts, arts and crafts, a parade, and carnival.

CONTACTS:
Chilympiad Office
P.O. Box 188
San Marcos, TX 78667
512-396-2233
www.sanmarcos.net/chilympiad

◆ 0547 ◆ **China National Days**
October 1-2

This public holiday commemorates the founding of the People's Republic of China in the capital of Beijing in 1949. Observances take place on October 1-2.

CONTACTS:
China National Tourist Office
370 Lexington Ave., Ste. 912
New York, NY 10118
888-760-8218 or 212-760-8218; fax: 212-760-8809
www.cnto.org

SOURCES:
AnnivHol-2000, p. 165
NatlHolWrld-1968, p. 182

♦ 0548 ♦ Chincoteague Pony Swim and Auction
Wednesday before the last Thursday in July

The Chincoteague Pony Swim and Auction is an annual salt-water roundup of the famous wild ponies of Assateague Island off the Delmarva Peninsula. The volunteer firemen of Chincoteague Island, the largest inhabited island on the Eastern Shore of Virginia, become cowboys for a day. They ride to Assateague, round up as many as 250 or 300 foals, mares, and sires, and then guide them into the water to swim across the channel to Chincoteague. There the ponies are penned in corrals, and the next day some foals are sold at auction and the rest of the herd swims back to Assateague.

Legend says the ponies, which are considered stunted horses rather than true ponies, are the descendants of mustangs that survived a shipwreck of a 16th-century Spanish galleon. Another story holds that the ponies were left behind by pirates who used the island as a hideout and had to leave in a hurry. Still a third (and most probable) version is that English colonists, having brought the ponies to the New World, turned them loose on Assateague and Chincoteague when they began to damage mainland crops.

The annual penning probably started with the colonists, who rounded up foals and yearlings to invigorate their workhorse supply. It took its present form in 1925 when the newly formed Chincoteague Volunteer Fire Company decided to add a fund-raising carnival to the regular pony penning.

Now a week of festivities surrounds the roundup, with midway rides, country music, and oysters and clams to eat. Tens of thousands come to watch the excitement from land and small boats.

A book featuring the event, *Misty of Chincoteague* by Marguerite Henry, was published in 1947 and became a children's classic. A movie based on the book appeared in 1960.

CONTACTS:
Chincoteague Chamber of Commerce
P.O. Box 258
Chincoteague, VA 23336
757-336-6161
www.chincoteaguechamber.com

SOURCES:
AmerBkDays-2000, p. 550
GdUSFest-1984, p. 199

♦ 0549 ♦ Chinhae Cherry Blossom Festival
Early April

The Cherry Blossom Festival is held in Chinhae, South Kyongsang, Korea, the headquarters of the Korean Navy. The purpose of the festival is to enjoy the thousands of blossoming cherry trees and also to honor Korea's illustrious Admiral Yi Sun-shin. Admiral Yi defeated the Japanese in several sea battles during the latter's invasions of the late 16th century. He is famous for developing "turtle boats," the first ironclad naval vessels, with 26 cannons on each side; though outnumbered, they proved superior to the Japanese boats. While the cherries bloom, there are daily events—a memorial service, parades, sports contests, music and dance performances, and folk games.

CONTACTS:
Korea National Tourism Organization
1 Executive Dr., Ste. 100
Fort Lee, NJ 07024
800-868-7567 or 201-585-0909; fax: 201-585-9041
www.kntoamerica.com

♦ 0550 ♦ Chinkashiki (Fire Control Ceremony)
September 17

Chinkashiki is a ceremony performed by Shinto priests at shrines around Tokyo and elsewhere in Japan. The priests walk in somber procession around a bed of burning coals until they work themselves into a kind of trance. Next, the priests gather up some salt, throw some of it into the fire and smear the remainder on their feet before walking over the burning coals in as dignified a manner as possible. The purpose of the ceremony is to demonstrate to the assembled crowds that Shinto religious beliefs and practices can tame fire and destroy its power to hurt human beings.

Shinto is the indigenous Japanese religious tradition. It has no founder, no official sacred scriptures, and no fixed system of doctrine or ethics, but it relies heavily on traditional rites and festivals.

CONTACTS:
Japan National Tourist Organization
1 Rockefeller Pl., Ste. 1250
New York, NY 10020
212-757-5640; fax: 212-307-6754
www.japantravelinfo.com

SOURCES:
JapanFest-1965, p. 190
OxDictWrldRel-1997, p. 892

♦ 0551 ♦ Chitlin' Strut
November, Friday and Saturday after Thanksgiving

The Chitlin' Strut is a feast of chitlins or chitterlings (hog intestines), held in the small town of Salley, S.C. The affair features a "hawg-calling" contest, country music, arts and crafts, a parade, lots of chitlins (about 8,000 pounds are devoured each year), and chicken for those not enamored of chitlins. (Former President George Bush has said he is a chitlin fan.) Chitlins are prepared by cleaning them well, boiling them until they are tender, and then, after coating them in egg and crumbs, frying them in deep fat until they're crackling crisp.

Salley was named for Col. Dempsey Hammond Salley, who donated the site in the 19th century.

The Chitlin' Strut began in 1966 to raise money for the town's Christmas decorations. The Strut now draws as many as 50,000 people, and Salley, with a population of 700, has used the revenues from it to pay for such necessities as trash cans, signs, and even a fire truck.

CONTACTS:
Chitlin' Strut
161 Railroad Ave. N.
P.O. Box 484
Salley, SC 29137
803-258-3485; fax: 803-258-3484
www.chitlinstrut.com

Library of Congress
101 Independence Ave. S.E.
Washington, DC 20540
202-707-5000; fax: 202-707-2076
www.loc.gov

SOURCES:
GdUSFest-1984, p. 171

♦ 0552 ♦ **Chochin Matsuri (Lantern Festival)**
Various

Chochin are cylindrical lanterns made out of paper stretched over a split bamboo frame. These colorful, festive lanterns appear at many Japanese festivals, but they play a special role in Nihonmatsu's Chochin Matsuri on October 4-6 and Akita's Kanto Festival in August. *Kanto* are huge decorations made from 46 chochin hung from a 30-foot pole with nine cross-poles. Each kanto can weigh more than 100 pounds, and there are 160 kanto displayed at the festival in Akita. Not surprisingly, this event is also known as the **Balancing Festival**, since young men perform stunts in which they try to balance the kanto on their chins and foreheads for the entertainment of the crowd.

One of the best-known Chochin festivals is held on August 26-27 in Ishiiki town at Hazu in Aichi Prefecture. The primary attractions are 12 huge chochin, each about 30 feet high and 18 feet across, that are hoisted by means of pulleys up three huge pillars at the Suwa Shrine. According to a local legend, the lanterns commemorate the bonfire that destroyed a dragon who once threatened the shoreline community. As night nears, priests begin to illuminate the lanterns—a process that may take several hours. At the end of the festival the lanterns are lowered after religious dances and songs have been offered.

CONTACTS:
Akita City Hall
1-1-1 Sanno
Akita, Akita Prefecture 010-0951 Japan
81-1-8866-2033; fax: 81-1-8866-2278
www.city.akita.akita.jp/en/default.htm

City of Nihonmatsu, Nihonmatsu Film Commission
403-1 Kanairo

Nihonmatsu, Fukushima Prefecture 964-8601 Japan
81-2-4323-1111; fax: 81-2-4322-5411
www.city.nihonmatsu.lg.jp

SOURCES:
IllFestJapan-1993, p. 96
JapanFest-1965, pp. 176, 185, 193

♦ 0553 ♦ **Choctaw Indian Fair**
Begins first Wednesday after Fourth of July

This is a four-day annual gathering of the Mississippi band of Choctaw Indians. Held since 1949 in Philadelphia, Mississippi, it features—besides dances, crafts exhibits, and pageantry—the Choctaw Stickball World Series. Choctaw stickball, the forerunner of lacrosse, is played with long-handled sticks with pouches at the ends for carrying and pitching a leather ball. It is called the "granddaddy of games" and is thought to be the oldest field sport in America. More than 20,000 visitors usually attend the fair.

CONTACTS:
Mississippi Band of Choctaw Indians
101 Industrial Rd.
Philadelphia, MS 39350
601-656-5251
www.choctaw.org

SOURCES:
GdUSFest-1984, p. 102
IndianAmer-1989, p. 242

♦ 0554 ♦ **Choctaw Trail of Tears Walk**
May or June

As European settlers migrated west, the Choctaw Indians were forced from their Mississippi and Louisiana settlements. In the 1830s thousands of Choctaw people suffered from starvation, disease, and cold, wet weather for which they were ill-equipped, having had to leave all their possessions behind, and thousands died during the movement to reservations in what is now Oklahoma.

Each year many Choctaw families and friends gather in Skullyville, Oklahoma, where the dead were buried. There is an annual historic reenactment of the walk, known as the "Trail of Tears" walk, and other events. Traditional Choctaw foods are served, and Choctaw baskets, renowned for their intricate patterns, are on display.

CONTACTS:
Choctaw Nation
P.O. Drawer 1210
Durant, OK 74702
800-522-6170 or 580-924-8280; fax: 580-924-4148
www.choctawnation.com

Skullyville Cemetery of the Choctaw Nation of Oklahoma
Hwy. 9 E
Spiro, OK 74959
www.skullyville.com

SOURCES:
EndurHarv-1995, p. 242

♦ 0555 ♦ **Chongmyo Taeje (Royal Shrine Rite)**
First Sunday in May

Chongmyo Taeje is a Confucian memorial ceremony held at Chongmyo (or Jongmyo) Shrine in Seoul, Korea, to honor the kings and queens of the Yi, or Joseon, Dynasty (1392-1910). The shrine, in a secluded garden in the center of Seoul, houses the ancestral tablets of the monarchs. Each year elaborate rites are performed to pay homage to them, and a number of royal descendants, robed in the traditional garments of their ancestors, take part. The rites are accompanied by court music and dance. The ceremony is a grand expression of the widespread Confucian practice of honoring ancestors, either at home or at their graves.

CONTACTS:
Cultural Properties Administration
139, Seonsa-ro (920, Dunsan-dong)
Seo-gu
Daejeon, 302-701 Korea
82-42-481-4650; fax: 82-42-481-4759

♦ 0556 ♦ **Christ the King, Feast of**
November, Sunday before Advent begins

In 1925, Pope Pius XI established the last Sunday in October as the Feast of Christ the King. He did so in order to remind people of Christ's everlasting authority over the people of the earth, thereby signaling the church's resistance to the rising tide of secular values and ideas in politics as well as in social matters. This Roman Catholic feast day was adopted by the Episcopal Church as well as other churches of the Anglican Communion. In 1970 the Roman Catholic Church moved the feast to the last Sunday before ADVENT begins, as did the Episcopal Church and some other churches in the Anglican Communion.

SOURCES:
ChristYr-1991, p. 86
DaysCustFaith-1957, p. 276
OxYear-1999, p. 636

♦ 0557 ♦ **Christkindlesmarkt**
Early December through Christmas Eve

Christkindlesmarkt is the biggest and best known of the CHRISTMAS markets of Germany. The market in Nuremberg, Bavaria, Germany, has been held since 1697 in the city's *Hauptmarkt* ("main market"), the site of the famed 60-foot-high *Schöner Brunnen* ("beautiful fountain") and the 600-year-old redstone Church of Our Lady. More than 100 booths are set up to offer only goods directly related to Christmas—dolls, wooden soldiers, tinsel angels, picture books, and painted boxes. Food booths sell Nuremberg's specialties—*Lebkuchen*, or gingerbread, and *Zwetschgenmännlein*, which are little people-shaped confections made of prunes, figs, and raisins, with heads of painted walnuts. A post office branch is set up to cancel letters with a special stamp, and rides are offered in an old horse-drawn mail coach.

The three-week festival is inaugurated with choral singing, the pealing of church bells, and illumination of a crèche. A

week or two before Christmas, some 10,000 people parade with lanterns to the Imperial Castle overlooking the city to sing carols. Other major Christmas markets are held in a number of German cities. Munich has the oldest Christmas market; it has been held annually for about 600 years and features daily musical programs. In Rothenburg-on-the Tauber, the market is a month-long "Winter's Tale" of 150 events that include stagecoach rides, plays, and concerts. In Berlin, a miniature village for children is featured.

CONTACTS:
Nuremberg Christkindlesmarkt
Congress- und Tourismis-Zentrale
Postfach 42 48
Nuremberg, 90022 Germany
49-91-123-36-166; fax: 49-91-123-36-166
www.christkindlesmarkt.de/english

SOURCES:
AnnivHol-2000, p. 217
BkFestHolWrld-1970, p. 129
BkHolWrld-1986, Dec 4
EncyChristmas-2003, p. 154
FestWestEur-1958, p. 80

♦ 0558 ♦ **Christmas**
December 25

The most popular of the Christian festivals, also known as the **Feast of the Nativity of Our Lord**, Christmas (from "Christ's Mass") celebrates the birth of Jesus of Nazareth. The exact date of Jesus' birth is not known, and for more than three centuries it was a movable feast, often celebrated on EPIPHANY, January 6. The Western Church chose to observe it at the end of December, perhaps as a way of countering the various pre-Christian festivals celebrated around that time of year. Some believe that Pope Julius I fixed the date of Christmas at December 25 in the fourth century. The earliest reference to it is in the Philocalian Calendar of Rome in 336. Although the majority of Eastern Orthodox churches have celebrated the Nativity on December 25 since the middle of the fifth century, those that still adhere to the old Julian calendar—called Old Calendarists—mark the occasion 13 days later, on January 7. The Armenian Churches continue to celebrate OLD CHRISTMAS DAY on January 6.

The Christmas season in the church begins on Christmas Eve and ends on Epiphany, unlike the commercial season that may begin any time after HALLOWEEN.

December 25th is a holy day of obligation for Roman Catholics, who must attend one of the three masses priests are permitted to say in honor of the occasion. These services are celebrated at midnight on CHRISTMAS EVE and at dawn and, usually, mid-morning on Christmas.

As a holiday, Christmas represents a strange intermingling of both Christian and the pagan traditions it replaced. Many of the secular customs now associated with Christmas—such as decorating with mistletoe, holly, and ivy; indulging in excessive eating and drinking; stringing lights in trees; and exchanging gifts—can be traced back to early pagan festivals like the SATURNALIA and ancient WINTER SOLSTICE rites.

Another example is burning the YULE log, which was part of a pre-Christian winter solstice festival celebrating the return of the sun in the middle of winter. Even the Christmas tree, a German custom introduced in Britain by Queen Victoria's husband, Albert, may trace its history back to ancient times

One of the most universal Christmas traditions is the crèche, a model of the birth scene of Christ, with Jesus in the manger, surrounded by the Holy Family and worshipping angels, shepherds, and animals. Many families have their own crèche, with the three Wise Men set apart and moved closer each day after Christmas until they arrive at the manger on Epiphany. In Austria, the crèche is not put away until CANDLEMAS Day.

In Belgium, the manger also appears in shop windows, constructed of the material sold by the shop: bread at the bakery; silks and laces at dressmakers; a variety of materials from the hardware store; butter and cheese from dairies; and cravats and neckties at the haberdashers.

In Chile the crèche is called a *pesebre*. Some homes leave their doors open so people passing by can come in and say a brief prayer to the *Niño Lindo* (beautiful baby).

In Italy it is a *presépio* and is placed on the lowest shelf of a *ceppo*, which is a pyramid of shelves, lit with candles, used to display secular Christmas decorations and ornaments.

In Poland, where the crèche is called a *yaselko*, it is believed to be the origin of the Christmas folk play called the King Herod play, based on Herod's order to kill all male babies in Bethlehem (*see* HOLY INNOCENTS' DAY). Thirteenth-century Franciscan monks brought the crèche to Poland. Eventually the wax, clay, and wooden figures were transformed into *szopka*, puppets that performed Christmas mystery plays, which told of the mysteries of Christ's life. Later, the monks acted the parts played by the puppets and were called "living szopka." In time, the plays were blended with characters and events from Polish history. The performers are called "Herods" and go from house to house in their villages where they are invited in to sing carols, act, and later to eat and drink with the family.

In Burkina Faso (until 1984 called Upper Volta), in western Africa, the population is mostly in Ouagadougou, the capital, and there the children make nativities (manger scenes) around the entrance to their compound. They are ready on Christmas Day so friends and neighbors can come by and, if they like them, leave a few coins in the dish provided. Some are made of paper and set on a pedestal, others of mud bricks with a thatch roof, while others are in the form of the local round house and have the bricks covered with a coat of concrete and a masonry dome instead of thatch. All of this is ornately decorated with strings of plastic packing peanuts, bits of shiny metal, tinsel, plastic, and flashlight bulbs. Some are modeled after pictures of European churches, but the child who can build a multi-storied nativity is thought very clever. On the wall of the compound behind the nativity is painted a white panel on which are affixed pictures of the Holy Family, crosses, hearts, arrows, stars, and anything else that comes to the mind of the young creator.

In Japan, since the end of World War II, Christmas has become a very popular holiday, even for non-Christians. Christmas dinner is replaced with a commercial Christmas cake, called "decoration cake," (*dekoreshon keki*), covered with ridges and waves of frosting. Grandfather Santa Claus brings the gifts, but stockings are hung on the pipe for the bathtub stove, which is the nearest equivalent to a fireplace in Japanese homes. NEW YEAR'S postcards are much more important than Christmas cards, and the most elaborate use of evergreen trees is also saved for New Year's. Christmas parties are a kind of blending with *bonenkai*, "closing of the year parties," which may only be attended by men and professional women: geishas, waitresses, entertainers. All women can attend Christmas parties, which is one of the reasons why the Japanese consider Christmas to be democratic.

Secular Christmas customs have continued to evolve. The Christmas card didn't become popular until the 19th century in England; Santa Claus's reindeer were an American invention at about the same time. Modern Christmas celebrations tend to focus on the worldly—with such traditions as the office Christmas party, sending out greeting cards, and Christmas specials on television taking the place of church services and other religious observances for many. The movement to "put Christ back into Christmas" has not lessened the enjoyment of this holiday as much for its social and commercial events as for its spiritual significance. The way Christmas is celebrated today is actually no worse—and in many ways much less excessive—than the hedonistic medieval celebration, where the feasting and revelry often extended all the way from Christmas to Candlemas (February 2).

See also GANNA; KOLEDOUVANE; LIGHTING OF THE NATIONAL CHRISTMAS TREE; MISA DE GALLO; and POSADAS

CONTACTS:
Christian Resource Institute
4712 N. Hammond
Warr Acres, OK 73122
www.crivoice.org

Greek Orthodox Archdiocese of Australia
242 Cleveland St.
Redfern, NSW 2016 Australia
61-2-9698-5066; fax: 61-2-9698-536
www.greekorthodox.org.au

SOURCES:
AmerBkDays-2000, pp. 3, 851
BkDays-1864, vol. II, pp. 733, 744
BkFest-1937, pp. 10, 11, 20, 35, 49, 62, 73, 93, 99, 108, 117, 130, 140, 150, 155, 175, 192, 216, 223, 234, 247, 254, 256, 272, 281, 287, 296, 305, 314, 323, 333, 345
DaysCustFaith-1957, pp. 319, 351
DictFolkMyth-1984, pp. 182, 193, 229, 501, 554, 571, 591, 628, 689, 761, 779, 854, 1063, 1065, 1133
EncyChristmas-2003
EncyRel-1987, vol. 3, p. 460
FestSaintDays-1915, p. 231
FestWestEur-1958, pp. 20, 30, 53, 83, 104, 148, 158, 186, 208, 222, 241
FolkAmerHol-1999, p. 497
FolkWrldHol-1999, p. 716
HolSymbols-2009, p. 125
OxYear-1999, pp. 514, 601
RelHolCal-2004, pp. 86, 116
SaintFestCh-1904, p. 37

♦ 0559 ♦ Christmas (Greece)
December 25

According to Greek folklore, supernatural beings with unusual powers are present upon earth during the 12 days between CHRISTMAS EVE and EPIPHANY. The name for these spirits is *kallikantzari,* and they wander about during the Christmas season causing mischief. They are ugly and unkempt, and their favorite way of getting into the house is through the chimney, much like the traditional Santa Claus. Christmas masqueraders often dress in animal skins to represent these demons of the WINTER SOLSTICE, and their jangling bells are supposed to drive the spirits away. Children born on CHRISTMAS must be baptized immediately to rid them of the evil influence of the kallikantzari.

CONTACTS:
Greek Embassy
Press and Information Office
2211 Massachusetts Ave. N.W.
Washington, D.C. 20008
202-332-2727; fax: 202-265-4931
www.greekembassy.org

SOURCES:
BkFest-1937, p. 154
EncyChristmas-2003, pp. 312, 401
FestSaintDays-1915, p. 230

♦ 0560 ♦ Christmas (Malta)
December 25

The Republic of Malta is a small country in the central Mediterranean that consists of seven islands. The Maltese Islands have a strong Catholic population that celebrates many religious holidays throughout the year. Because of the strong Catholic influence, several of the holy days are national holidays in Malta.

Religious holidays, such as CHRISTMAS and EASTER, are widely celebrated in Malta. Maltese families tend to be very close-knit, and the holidays are a time to strengthen the sense of community and reinforce family bonds.

On CHRISTMAS EVE, it is traditional to attend Midnight mass and then eat a large Christmas breakfast. In most churches, at 11 P.M. on Christmas Eve there is the "Priedka tat-Tifel," which consists of a young boy (or girl, in some parishes) reciting by heart the events leading up to the Nativity.

On Christmas Day, families prepare large Christmas lunches and give thanks with their relatives for all that they have. Also, the streets are lined with carts selling a wide assortment of foods, including the more traditional sweets and delicacies. As in many other countries around the world, Maltese families exchange presents at Christmas time.

CONTACTS:
Malta Tourism Authority
Auberge D'Italie
Merchants St.
Valetta VLT 1170 Malta
www.visitmalta.com

♦ 0561 ♦ Christmas (Marshall Islands)
December 25

The United Church of Christ in the Marshall Islands of Micronesia has an unusual approach to the traditional lighting of the CHRISTMAS tree. Members of the church's Stewardship Council conceal a decorated tree inside a large wooden cross. While they are singing Christmas carols and hymns, the cross opens slowly and the tree rises from it. The singers set off firecrackers as the tree rises, and then lower their voices and sing more softly as the tree descends back into the cross. When their singing is over, the two sides of the cross come apart and the tree remains standing, symbolic of the birth, death, and resurrection of Christ.

See also KURIJMOJ

SOURCES:
BkFestHolWrld-1970, p. 154
EncyChristmas-2003, p. 462
FolkWrldHol-1999, p. 743

♦ 0562 ♦ Christmas (Norway)
December 25-26

CHRISTMAS, known as **Juledag** in Norway, is generally a quiet day. After attending morning church services, most Norwegians return home to be with their family and friends. December 26, however, is another matter. Referred to as Second Christmas Day, or *Anden Juledag,* it is spent eating, drinking, and going to parties, festivities that continue until January 13. Holiday breakfasts are popular, often accompanied by *aquavit* and other strong drinks. Traditional foods served at these Christmas get-togethers include *lutefisk* (dried cod), *lefse* (a thin potato roll served with butter or cinnamon and sugar), and *fladbröd* (a flat, hard Norwegian bread).

During the German occupation of Norway, when King Haakon was living in England, a Norwegian boat stationed there would be sent to Norway to bring back a Norway spruce each year as a gift for the king at Christmas. The custom of bringing a Norwegian tree to England was continued after the war, and every Christmas a huge Norwegian spruce stands in London's Trafalgar Square.

CONTACTS:
Norwegian Embassy
2720 34th St. N.W.
Washington, D.C. 20008
202-333-6000; fax: 202-337-0870
www.norway.org

SOURCES:
BkFest-1937, p. 254
BkFestHolWrld-1970, p. 140
EncyChristmas-2003, p. 567
FestWestEur-1958, p. 158
FolkWrldHol-1999, p. 745

♦ 0563 ♦ Christmas (Puerto Rico)
December 25

CHRISTMAS celebrations in Puerto Rico combine island traditions with more contemporary customs, such as Santa Claus and imported Christmas trees. Singers, often dressed as the Three Kings (or Magi), go from door to door singing ancient carols known as *aguinaldos* to the accompaniment of guitars. It is customary to offer gifts to the singer, and over the years the term "aguinaldos" has also come to stand for the gift itself. Sometimes the strolling carolers are asked inside to sample special Christmas dishes, such as roast pig and rice pudding. Christmas pageants and parties, which begin in early December, often extend right up until the Feast of the Three Kings on EPIPHANY (January 6).

In the Dominican Republic, on the island of Hispaniola just west of Puerto Rico, a major Christmas attraction is the animated *nacimiento* (Nativity scene) at the Church of San José. This mechanized toy village features miniature trains and figures of people going about their jobs.

SOURCES:
FolkAmerHol-1999, p. 509
FolkWrldHol-1999, p. 751

♦ 0564 ♦ **Christmas (Romania) (Craciun)**
December 25

From CHRISTMAS EVE until NEW YEAR'S EVE, boys in Romania go from house to house singing carols, reciting poetry and legends, and carrying the *steaua*, which is a large wooden star covered with gilt paper, decorated with ribbons and bells, and illuminated from within by a burning candle. Dramatic performances of the story of Jesus' birth can be seen in many Romanian towns and villages, with a cast of traditional characters that includes King Herod, the Magi, a clown, and a comical old man. Puppet shows are also popular.

Turte, a special kind of cake consisting of many layers of thin dough with melted sugar or honey and crushed walnuts in between, is the food most often associated with Christmas in Romania. The many-layered dough is representative of the swaddling clothes of the infant Jesus. As the housewife prepares the turte on the day before Christmas Eve, she walks into the yard followed by her husband wielding an ax. They go around to each tree in the yard, and the husband threatens to cut it down because it no longer bears any fruit. The wife intervenes, persuading the husband that the tree will be full of fruit the following summer. The custom may derive from a pagan ceremony.

CONTACTS:
Embassy Of Romania
1607 23rd St. N.W.
Washington, D.C. 20008
202-332-4846; fax: 202-232-4748
www.roembus.org

SOURCES:
BkFest-1937, p. 281
BkFestHolWrld-1970, p. 142
DaysCustFaith-1957, p. 351
FolkWrldHol-1999, p. 751

♦ 0565 ♦ **Christmas (Russian Orthodox)**
January 7

This celebration of the birth of Jesus is observed by the Russian Orthodox Church under the Julian calendar. The calendar trails behind the Gregorian calendar by 13 days.

Before the 1917 Revolution, Orthodox CHRISTMAS was widely observed in Russia, Ukraine, Belarus, and Georgia. After the Revolution, churches were closed and people practicing religion were persecuted. In 1991, after the Soviet Union had been officially dissolved, Christmas was observed openly and as a state holiday in Russia for the first time in 70 years.

In Moscow, banners were strung up and Nativity scenes were displayed in Red Square. On radio and television, there were nonstop programs telling the Christmas story and showing villagers wearing embroidered folk costumes and carrying tambourines as they made the rounds to offer Christmas bread at every house. On CHRISTMAS EVE, tens of thousands jammed Red Square for performances by choirs and bellringers and gala fireworks over the multi-colored onion domes of St. Basil's Cathedral. Midnight services were celebrated in churches. At the Kremlin, a Christmas charity ball was held to raise money for orphan children.

Before the Revolution, Christmas in Russia was a great feast celebrated with decorated trees, strolling carolers, and gifts. There was a legend of "Father Frost" or "Grandfather Frost," who wore a red robe and black boots and had a long white beard. Tchaikovsky's "Nutcracker Suite" was, of course, associated with the holiday. When Joseph Stalin was in power, some aspects of the old Christmas, such as the tree and the gifts from Grandfather Frost, were added to the New Year's celebrations. Then January 7 became a holiday observed only by those who dared to go to church.

See also OLD CHRISTMAS DAY; RUSSIAN WINTER FESTIVAL

SOURCES:
AmerBkDays-2000, p. 35
BkFest-1937, p. 296
BkFestHolWrld-1970, p. 142
DictFolkMyth-1984, p. 230
EncyChristmas-2003, p. 651
FolkWrldHol-1999, p. 752

♦ 0566 ♦ **Christmas (South Africa)**
December 25

Because South Africa is in the Southern Hemisphere, CHRISTMAS is a summer holiday. The tinsel and evergreen boughs that decorate homes, churches, parks, and shopping malls offer a stark contrast to the weather, which encourages people to spend the day at the beach or in the shaded mountains. But Christmas traditions persist: English-speaking children hang up their stockings in anticipation of the arrival of Father Christmas, carolers sing by candlelight on CHRISTMAS EVE, and Christmas pageants are performed. One of the most popular activities for children is to produce pantomimes based on such classic tales as "Babes in the Woods." BOXING DAY, December 26, is also observed as a holiday, a time for giving boxes of food and clothing to the poor.

For black South Africans Christmas is a day for feasting and exchanging gifts. It marks the culmination of a CARNIVAL-like week of singing, dancing, and eating.

SOURCES:
BkFestHolWrld-1970, p. 152
EncyChristmas-2003, p. 728
FolkWrldHol-1999, p. 753

♦ 0567 ♦ **Christmas (Spain) (Pascua de Navidad)**
December 25

The **Feast of the Birth** is observed in Spain by attending church services, feasting, and listening to Christmas music. It is a Spanish custom for public servants—such as the mail carrier and the garbage collector—to leave cards with holiday messages for their customers, a reminder of the services they have rendered in the past or hope to render in the coming year. In return, they are given *aguinaldos*, or gifts of money. In Madrid and other large cities, it is not uncommon to see a police officer directing traffic on CHRISTMAS Day, surrounded by parcels of all sizes and shapes. Christmas is also a time for processions of the *gigantes*, or giant figures, which dance to the music of fife and drum.

Spanish children receive their gifts at EPIPHANY, which commemorates the coming of the Magi to Bethlehem, bearing gifts for the Christ child. Children leave their shoes on the window sill or balcony and fill them with straw and carrots or barley for the Magi's horses to eat. In Cadiz, children still observe the traditional rite of "Christmas swinging" on swings that are set up in the courtyards. At one time the custom may have been intended to help the sun in its climb to the highest point in the sky.

SOURCES:
BkFest-1937, p. 305
BkFestHolWrld-1970, p. 145
EncyChristmas-2003, p. 731
FestWestEur-1958, p. 208

♦ 0568 ♦ **Christmas (Sweden) (Juledagen)**
December 25

Swedes rise early on CHRISTMAS to attend *Julotta*, six o'clock church services. The church is lit with hundreds of candles and the congregation sings nativity hymns. In rural areas, lit candles are placed in farmhouse windows and people travel to church by sleigh. Each sleigh carries a torch, and when people arrive at the church they all throw their torches into a bonfire.

Unlike the American Santa Claus, the Swedish Father Christmas, or *jultomte*, is small and thin, more like a leprechaun than a jolly, white-bearded man. The *tomte*, "little man," is a mythical character similar to an elf who can be either troublesome or benevolent, depending on how well he is treated. Because midwinter was considered a dangerous season in pre-Christian times, full of evil spirits, it was important to treat the tomte well by putting out food and drink for him. Over the generations, the jultomte has become a more gener-

ous spirit, who distributes gifts rather than receives them. Even when he appears in a red costume with a white beard, however, he is always depicted as being very thin.

See also ST. KNUT'S DAY; ST. LUCY'S DAY

CONTACTS:
Scandinavian Tourism Inc.
P.O. Box 4649, Grand Central Sta.
New York, NY 10163
212-885-9700; fax: 212-885-9710
www.visit-sweden.com

SOURCES:
BkFest-1937, p. 314
EncyChristmas-2003, pp. 392, 393
FestWestEur-1958, p. 222
FolkWrldHol-1999, p. 755

♦ 0569 ♦ **Christmas (Syria)**
December 25; January 1

The Syrian Santa Claus is the camel, who brings gifts to children on NEW YEAR'S DAY. According to legend, the youngest of the three camels that carried the Magi to Bethlehem fell down, exhausted by the journey. The Christ child blessed the animal and granted it immortality. Syrian children set out water and wheat for the camel before they go to bed, and when they awake in the morning, they find gifts, or, if they've been naughty, a black mark on their wrists. Another custom associated with the Magi is carried out on CHRISTMAS EVE, when vine stems are burned in the middle of the church to warm the Magi after their long journey.

CHRISTMAS itself is a family festival in Syria. A special dinner is prepared, and afterward friends and relatives pay social calls on one another. Among Syrian Americans, it is customary to serve guests Oriental coffee and holiday cakes such as *baklawa, burma,* and *mulabas,* as well as nuts, oranges, candies, and Syrian wines.

SOURCES:
BkFest-1937, p. 333
BkFestHolWrld-1970, p. 150
EncyChristmas-2003, p. 751

♦ 0570 ♦ **Christmas Bird Count**
December 14-January 6

The CHRISTMAS Bird Count, also known as CBC, is an international event sponsored annually by the National Audubon Society. Under a system that the society calls "citizen science," volunteers join a count that takes place on one day during the designated CBC period, December 14–January 5. Each group of volunteers, known as a Christmas Bird Count Circle, is assigned a specific geographic area and asked to record the number and species of birds they see. Each circle has a compiler, who organizes the volunteers and records the data that they gather according to a specific methodology. Counts take place in all 50 states, every Canadian province, parts of Central and South America, Bermuda, the West Indies, and Pacific Islands. The data gathered every year helps the Audubon

Society and scientists worldwide to understand the status and distribution of bird populations in early winter.

The Christmas Bird Count began at the turn of the last century. At that time, people often competed during the holiday season to see who could shoot the most birds and game. Ornithologist Frank Chapman, an officer in the just-developing Audubon Society, proposed a new holiday tradition—a "Christmas Bird Census" that would encourage people to count birds rather than kill them. At the first count, birders in 25 North American locations spotted about 18,500 individual birds. During the 2006 count, nearly 58,000 volunteers tallied almost 70 million birds. Over the decades, generations of volunteers have supplied vital information for the longest-running database in ornithology.

CONTACTS:
National Audubon Society
700 Broadway
New York, NY 10003
212-979-3000; fax: 212-979-3188
www.audubon.org

♦ 0571 ♦ **Christmas Eve**
December 24

Christmas Eve or the **Vigil of Christmas** represents the culmination of the ADVENT season. Like CHRISTMAS itself, Christmas Eve celebrations combine both religious and secular events. Perhaps the most widely anticipated by children is the arrival of Santa Claus—known as *Sinterklass* by the Dutch settlers of New York, who were the first to introduce the idea of St. Nicholas's annual appearance on this day; the original Santa Claus was the tall, saintly looking bishop, Nicholas of Metz. It wasn't until the 19th century that he became the jolly, overweight, pipe-smoking figure in a red fur-trimmed suit that children in the United States recognize today. The modern Santa Claus was largely the invention of two men: Clement Moore, who in 1822 wrote his now-famous poem, "A Visit from St. Nicholas," and Thomas Nast, a cartoonist who did numerous illustrations of Santa Claus based on Moore's description. In any case, it is on Christmas Eve that Santa Claus climbs down the chimney and fills the children's stockings that have been hung by the fireplace mantel. Before going to bed children around the world leave milk and food out for the one who brings the presents, be it Santa Claus, the baby Jesus, the Christmas elf of Denmark, the Christmas goat of Finland (called *Joulupukki*), or the Swedish *tomte*, or little man, who resembles Puck or a leprechaun.

The midnight church service celebrating the birth of Jesus Christ is the main Christmas Eve tradition for many Christians of all denominations and even of non-believers, especially if there is a good organist, soloist, or choir. In most European countries, a large but meatless meal is eaten before church, for it is a fast day. Some families, especially those with grown children, exchange gifts on Christmas Eve rather than on Christmas Day. Caroling—going from house to house singing Christmas carols—began in Europe in the Middle Ages. The English brought the custom to America, where it is still very popular.

In Venezuela, after midnight on Christmas Eve, crowds of teenagers roller skate on the Avenida de los Caiboas. After an hour or so, they attend a special early mass called *Misa de Aguinaldos*, "Mass of the Carols," where they're greeted at the door with folk songs. Then they skate home for Christmas breakfast.

In Newfoundland and Nova Scotia, Canada, mummers, or *belsnickers*, go from house to house. Once inside they jog, tell licentious stories, play instruments and sing, and generally act up until the householder identifies the person under the mask. Then the mummer takes off his or her costume and acts like a normal visitor.

In the 19th century, in what is now New Mexico, bundles of branches were set ablaze along the roads and pathways. Called *farolitos* and *luminarias*, these small fires are meant to guide the Travelers to the people's homes on Christmas Eve. Residents are ready to give hospitality to anyone on that night, especially Joseph and Mary with the Christ Child. They wait in faith for the Travelers' three knocks on their door. But modern fire codes overtook the ancient faith, and firefighters began to extinguish the small piles of burning pine branches for fear a spark would start an inferno. Small brown paper bags partially filled with sand and holding a candle eventually replaced the open fires. Inevitably merchants began to sell wires of electric lights to replace the candles, and plastic, multi-colored sleeves to imitate lunch bags, and the modern luminarias began to appear at holidays like HALLOWEEN and the FOURTH OF JULY.

Last-minute shopping is another Christmas Eve tradition, and stores often stay open late to accommodate those who wait until the last minute to purchase their Christmas gifts.

In Buddhist Japan, Christmas Eve is for lovers, a concept introduced by a Japanese pop star and expanded by trendy magazines. It is a Western rite celebrated with a Japanese twist. The day should be spent doing something extra special (expensive), and should end in a fine Tokyo hotel room, most of which have been booked since the previous January; even the cheapest rooms go for exorbitant prices. Being alone on this night is comparable to being dateless on prom night in the United States.

Uncle Chimney is the Japanese version of Santa Claus. Youngsters may be treated to a $29 (or more) barrel of Kentucky Fried Chicken (10 pieces of chicken, five containers of ice cream, and salad) if their parents don't mind lining up for two hours. The reason for the chicken is that many Japanese think Colonel Sanders resembles Santa Claus. Another culinary tradition is strawberry shortcake with a plastic fir tree on top. This was introduced 70 years ago by a Japanese confectioner as a variant of plum pudding. While the origins of this form of Christmas are unclear, many people say it dates from the 1930s, well before the United States occupation in 1945 after World War II.

See also BEFANA FESTIVAL; DÍA DE LOS TRES REYES; GIANT LANTERN FESTIVAL; POSADAS; ST. NICHOLAS'S DAY; "SILENT NIGHT, HOLY NIGHT" CELEBRATION; TOLLING THE DEVIL'S KNELL; WIGILIA

SOURCES:
AmerBkDays-2000, p. 850
BkDays-1864, vol. II, p. 733
BkFest-1937, pp. 9, 20, 22, 35, 48, 62, 73, 92, 98, 107, 116, 129, 139, 154,
    175, 191, 215, 222, 234, 252, 272, 280, 287, 296, 304, 313, 322, 333, 344
BkHolWrld-1986, Dec 24
DaysCustFaith-1957, p. 350
DictFolkMyth-1984, pp. 549, 591, 1063
EncyChristmas-2003
FestSaintDays-1915, pp. 8, 228
FestWestEur-1958, pp. 27, 28, 50, 82, 83, 102, 120, 156, 206, 219, 239
HolSymbols-2009, p. 137
OxYear-1999, p. 510
RelHolCal-2004, p. 85

♦ 0572 ♦ Christmas Eve (Armenia)
January 5 by the Julian calendar; January 18 by the Gregorian calendar

On CHRISTMAS EVE in Armenia it is traditional to eat fried fish, lettuce, and boiled spinach. The spinach is eaten to pay tribute to the Virgin Mary, who, according to legend, ate spinach on the evening before Jesus' birth. After a morning church service on CHRISTMAS DAY, the men exchange brief social calls and are served coffee and sweets. On the third day after Christmas, it's the women's turn to make and receive calls.

SOURCES:
BkFest-1937, p. 22
DaysCustFaith-1957, p. 351
EncyChristmas-2003, p. 36

♦ 0573 ♦ Christmas Eve (Baltics)
December 24

Many people in Estonia attend church on CHRISTMAS EVE. The holiday dinner, which follows the church service, typically includes roasted pig's head or blood sausages, turnips, and potatoes. For dessert there is cranberry soup, and of course plenty of Estonian vodka, which is made from the potatoes for which the country is famous. Many of the Christmas tree ornaments are edible, and real candles—often made by dipping a lamb's wool thread into hot sheep fat—are used to light the tree.

In Latvia, the tree is the only Christmas decoration, and it is laden with gilded walnuts, artificial snow, tinsel, small red apples, and colored candies. After the traditional Christmas Eve dinner, which consists of roast pork, goose and boar's head, and little meat-filled pastries known as *piradzini,* the candles on the tree are lighted and the gifts piled beneath it are distributed and opened.

In Lithuania family members break and consume delicate wafers, or *plotkeles,* on Christmas Eve as a token of peace. The family puts a little hay under the tablecloth as a reminder that Jesus was born in a stable. The *kucios,* or Christmas Eve supper, consists of fish soup followed by cabbage, fried and boiled fish, sauerkraut, and a huge pike served with a hearty, dark gravy. Dessert is *kisielius,* a pudding-like dish that is composed of cream of oats, sugar, and cream.

CONTACTS:
Estonian Ministry of Foreign Affairs, Press and Information
    Department
Islandi valjak 1
Tallinn, 15049 Estonia
372-6-317-000; fax: 372-6-317-099
www.vm.ee/eng

SOURCES:
BkFest-1937, pp. 107, 215, 222
EncyChristmas-2003, pp. 225, 421, 427

♦ 0574 ♦ Christmas Eve (Bethlehem)
December 24

Located only a few miles from Jerusalem in an area that is part of the biblical land of Palestine, Bethlehem is known as the birthplace of Jesus and has long been regarded as a holy place by Christians. A church was eventually built on the site, and the crypt beneath it, known as the Grotto of the Nativity, is reputed to be the site of the original manger. Because there have been so many arguments over the years about which Christian church should control the sanctuary, it is jointly owned by the Armenian, Orthodox, and Roman Catholic churches. A Roman Catholic mass is held there at midnight on CHRISTMAS EVE, and because pilgrims from all over the world attend, most of them end up watching the service on a large closed-circuit television screen in nearby Manger Square. The highlight of the service occurs when a carved wooden figure of the Christ Child is laid in a manger in the Grotto of the Nativity.

Protestants hold an outdoor service in Shepherds' Field where, according to tradition, the shepherds kept watch over the flocks on the first Christmas Eve.

CONTACTS:
Palestine Ministry of Tourism and Antiquities
Manger St.
P.O. Box 534
Bethlehem, Palestine
970-2-274-1581; fax: 970-2-274-3753
www.visit-palestine.com

SOURCES:
EncyChristmas-2003, p. 62

♦ 0575 ♦ Christmas Eve (Denmark) (Juleaften)
December 24

The celebration of CHRISTMAS in Denmark actually begins on Little Christmas Eve (December 23) and continues well into the NEW YEAR. It is customary to make enough apple fritters on Little Christmas Eve to last three days. In rural areas, farmers tie a sheaf of grain to a pole in the garden so that the birds can feed from it. Even city dwellers tie bunches of grain to their balconies.

The traditional CHRISTMAS EVE dinner starts with *risengrød* (rice porridge). Like Christmas puddings elsewhere, there is an almond hidden inside the porridge. Whoever finds it receives a prize. The risengrød is followed by roast goose stuffed with prunes and apples and decorated with small

Danish flags. After dinner, family members often dance around the Christmas tree, sing carols, and exchange gifts.

The *Julenisse,* or Christmas gnome, is a small bearded man dressed in gray with a pointed red cap who, according to Danish legend, lives in attics or barns and is responsible for bringing a family good or bad luck. On Christmas Eve the Julenisse is given a generous portion of risengrød with an extra helping of butter.

CONTACTS:
Royal Danish Embassy
3200 Whitehaven St. N.W.
Washington, D.C. 20008
202-234-4300; fax: 202-328-1470
www.denmarkemb.org

SOURCES:
BkFest-1937, p. 98
EncyChristmas-2003, p. 192
FestWestEur-1958, p. 27

♦ 0576 ♦ Christmas Eve (Finland) (Jouluaatto)
December 24

Before sitting down to the traditional CHRISTMAS EVE dinner, many Finns go to church and place flowers and lighted candles on the graves of departed family members. Then the family gathers around the table and listens to the head of the household read a Christmas prayer. The meal itself includes *lipeäkala* (the Christmas fish) and ham, various breads, a kind of plum cake known as *torttuja,* and the traditional rice pudding in which an almond has been hidden. According to superstition, the boy or girl who finds it will be married before the next Christmas. The tree is decorated with homemade paper or wooden toys, gingerbread cookies, gilded walnuts, and other treats.

CONTACTS:
Ministry of Foreign Affairs of Finland
Department for Communication and Culture
P.O. Box 176
Helsinki, 00161 Finland
358-9-1600-5; fax: 358-9-1605-5901
www.formin.finland.fi

SOURCES:
BkFest-1937, p. 116
EncyChristmas-2003, p. 602

♦ 0577 ♦ Christmas Eve (France) (Veille de Noël)
December 24

CHRISTMAS EVE church services in Paris can be quite elaborate, while those in rural areas of France are usually very simple. No matter where it takes place, the Christmas Mass involves burning candles, Christmas carols, bells, and a crèche or miniature Nativity scene. Most homes also have a crèche. In Provence, the crèche includes not only the Holy Family, but small clay figures called *santons* representing traditional village characters—the butcher, baker, basket maker, flute players, etc.—who come to adore the infant Jesus. In Marseilles, there is a SANTON FAIR in the weeks preceding

Christmas that is attended by people from all over Provence who want to purchase the traditional santons, made from molds that have been used for generations.

After the midnight service is over, families return to their homes for the *réveillon,* or traditional Christmas Eve meal, which includes *pâté de foie gras,* oysters, blood sausage, pancakes, and plenty of French wine. It is customary for the newspapers to calculate how many kilograms of blood sausage have been consumed at réveillon. Many families serve goose because, according to a Provençal legend, the goose clucked a greeting to the Wise Men when they drew near the baby Jesus.

In France children leave a pair of shoes out for *Père Noël,* the French gift bringer, to fill with treats.

In some parts of France, people celebrate Christmas Eve with the *Fête des Bergers,* the Shepherds' Mass or Shepherds' Festival. The event revolves around a procession led by shepherds and shepherdesses dressed in traditional, local costumes. A simple farm cart, led by a ram, is decorated with bells, flowers, and candles. The shepherds and shepherdesses put a lamb in the cart and lead it in a procession around the church. Then a shepherd picks up the lamb and gives it to the priest, a gesture that is said to represent the offering of a newborn lamb to the infant Jesus.

CONTACTS:
French Embassy
4101 Reservoir Rd. N.W.
Washington, D.C. 20007
202-944-6000; fax: 202-944-6166
www.info-france-usa.org

Department of Canadian Heritage and France's Ministry of
   Culture
150 John St., Ste. 400
Toronto, ON M5V 3T6 Canada
416-973-5400; fax: 416-954-2909
www.canadianheritage.gc.ca

SOURCES:
BkFest-1937, p. 129
BkHolWrld-1986, Dec 24
EncyChristmas-2003, pp. 262, 644
FestWestEur-1958, p. 50

♦ 0578 ♦ Christmas Eve (Italy) (La Vigilia)
December 24

The *presépio,* or Nativity manger, with its miniature figures of the Holy Family, angels, shepherds, and Three Kings plays a major role in the Italian observance of CHRISTMAS and is thought to have originated with ST. FRANCIS OF ASSISI more than 700 years ago. The presépio is set up on the first day of the Novena (the nine days preceding Christmas); on each subsequent morning, the family gathers before the presépio to light candles and offer prayers. Although manger figures are on sale in every market and village fair, in many families the manger is an heirloom that has been handed down for generations. The setting for the manger is usually built at home from cardboard, moss, and bits of twig, and it can be quite elaborate.

Christmas Eve is a family affair. After lighting candles before the presépio, a meatless meal known as the *cenone*, or *festa* supper, is served. It usually consists of some type of fish (eel is popular among the well-to-do), fowl, artichokes cooked with eggs, fancy breads, and Italian sweets such as *cannoli* (cheese-filled pastry), nougat, and other delicacies.

The YULE log plays a more important role than the Christmas tree. The children may tap it with sticks, requesting certain gifts. Few presents are given on Christmas Eve, since EPIPHANY is the time for gift-giving. The evening concludes with a church service at midnight.

In parts of Calabria and the Abruzzi, itinerant bagpipers, or *zampognari*, come down from the mountains and go from house to house playing pastoral hymns before the home-made mangers. They are given gifts of food or money.

See also BEFANA FESTIVAL

SOURCES:
BkFest-1937, p. 191
EncyChristmas-2003, p. 365
FestSaintDays-1915, p. 229
FestWestEur-1958, p. 102

♦ 0579 ♦ **Christmas Eve (Moravian Church)**
December 24

Members of the Moravian Church—named after Moravia, a region in the former Czechoslovakia (now part of the Czech Republic)—fled to America to escape persecution in the mid-18th century. They established a number of communities in Pennsylvania, one of which is called Bethlehem and known as "America's Christmas City." As Christmas approaches, the Moravians carry on the Old World tradition of building a Christmas "putz" (from the German word *putzen*, meaning "to decorate") or Nativity scene, which can range from a simple mantle decoration to an elaborate miniature landscape.

On the afternoon of CHRISTMAS EVE, they hold a children's "love feast" consisting of music, meditation, and a simple meal—usually sweet buns and mugs of sweetened coffee—served in the church. Then, after dinner, they assemble again in the church for the Christmas Eve Vigil, a service devoted almost entirely to music. The church lights are dimmed and handmade beeswax candles are distributed to the entire congregation while the children's choir sings a favorite Moravian hymn. A similar observance is held in Winston-Salem, North Carolina, now a historical restoration at which the Moravian way of life is preserved.

CONTACTS:
Moravian Church in North America
P.O. Box 1245
Bethlehem, PA 18016
610-867-0593; fax: 610-866-9223
www.moravian.org

Moravian Music Foundation
Southern Music Archives, Research Library and Main Office
457 S. Church St.
Winston-Salem, NC 27101
336-725-0651; fax: 336-725-4514
www.moravianmusic.org

Old Salem Online
P.O. Box F Salem Station
Winston-Salem, NC 27108
888-653-7253 or 336-721-7300; fax: 336-721-7335
www.oldsalem.org

SOURCES:
DictWrldRel-1981, p. 493
EncyChristmas-2003, pp. 64, 438, 632
OxDictWrldRel-1997, p. 655
RelHolCal-2004, p. 86

♦ 0580 ♦ **Christmas Eve (Switzerland)**
(HeiligerAbend)
December 24

There are a number of superstitions and folk beliefs surrounding CHRISTMAS EVE in Switzerland. One is the belief that animals gain the power of speech at midnight on Christmas Eve because they were present at Jesus' birth. Farmers give their horses, cows, goats, and other animals extra food on this night, but it's considered bad luck to overhear what the animals say. Old people claim that they can predict the weather for the next 12 months by peeling off 12 layers of onionskin and filling them with salt. Young lovers who want to find out who they will marry are told to drink from nine different fountains while the midnight church bells are ringing on Christmas Eve. If they rush to the church, their future mate will be standing on the steps.

Christkindli, or the Christ Child, who travels in a sleigh pulled by six reindeer, brings Swiss children their gifts. In the area surrounding Hallwil in the canton of Lucerne, a girl dressed in white robes, glittering crown, and a veil portrays the Christ Child. Other children, wearing white garments and carrying baskets of gifts and lanterns, accompany her on her rounds. Some families wait until the Christkindli enters the house to light the candles on the Christmas tree. In many homes the tree is kept hidden until after Christmas Eve supper, when the parlor doors are opened and the tree is displayed in all its glory.

In Zurich cakes known as *Tirggel*, whose main ingredients are flour and honey, are served at Christmas time. The cakes are believed to have originated as a pagan offering. They are made by pushing dough into intricate molds, shaped like characters from folktales, cartoons and other popular subjects. The finished cakes are tough and glossy, so it is not uncommon for them to be kept for months, or even years, and to be used as decorations around the house.

CONTACTS:
Swiss Embassy
2900 Cathedral Ave. N.W.
Washington, D.C. 20008
202-745-7900; fax: 202-387-2564
www.swissemb.org

SOURCES:
BkFest-1937, p. 322
EncyChristmas-2003, p. 114
FestWestEur-1958, p. 239

◆ 0581 ◆ **Christmas Eve Bonfires**
December 22, 23, and 24

The state of Louisiana contains four parishes (the equivalent of counties) called the river parishes, named for their position along the Mississippi River. This cluster of communities, located between Baton Rouge and New Orleans, forms part of the state's Cajun Country, a region that has preserved distinctive ethnic traditions. One such community, St. James Parish, has a popular Cajun tradition that takes place during the three days before CHRISTMAS in the towns of Gramercy, Lutcher, and Paulina.

According to the festival organizers, the tradition of the CHRISTMAS EVE bonfires most likely came from such European countries as France and Germany, the home countries of many early settlers of the St. James area. In those and other European nations, fires commonly marked the Christmas season, as well as St. John the Baptist's Feast Day Eve on June 23. The tradition of fires on these occasions in turn most likely sprang from pagan rituals marking, respectively, the winter and summer solstices.

The Christmas bonfire tradition in Louisiana dates back to the 1880s. There are several theories about how the current practice originated, but the most common explanation is that the bonfires lit the way for the arrival of Papa Noel, the Cajun version of Santa Claus. After World War II, the bonfire structures expanded into more elaborate creations, taking different forms and reaching 25 feet high.

Once restricted to small fires built by family groups, the tradition now calls for dozens of huge blazes lining the levee for miles along the local River Road. Some residents begin building the bonfires the day after Thanksgiving. In the weeks leading up to Christmas, local residents work together to collect materials and to construct the bonfires. A bonfire is lit on each of the two days before Christmas Eve. Then, on Christmas Eve, nearly 100 bonfires are ignited before a large crowd. Fire chiefs give a signal at 7:00 P.M. Christmas Eve (weather permitting) and the fire-tenders simultaneously ignite the fires. The event draws thousands of revelers to the area for the bonfires as well as a series of pageants, music performances, and cook-offs accompanying the main event.

The local community of Lutcher provides a preview of the Christmas Eve bonfires with an annual Festival of the Bonfires that takes place in a public park on a weekend early in December. The three-day event features live music, food, crafts, and carnival rides, as well as the lighting of a single bonfire on each night of the festival. This preview festival celebrated its 18th anniversary in 2007.

CONTACTS:
St. James Parish
P.O. Box 106
Convent, LA 70723
800-367-7852 or 225-562-2266

◆ 0582 ◆ **Christmas Pastorellas (Mexico)**
December 25-January 6

CHRISTMAS Day in Mexico is traditionally a quiet family day, especially following the POSADAS season and the midnight mass known as the *Misa de Gallo*, or "Mass of the Cock," that many attend on CHRISTMAS EVE. But Christmas in Mexico, which extends until DÍA DE LOS TRES REYES (EPIPHANY) on January 6, is also celebrated with *pastorellas*, or pageants, showing how the Wise Men and shepherds overcame obstacles to visit Jesus in the manger in Bethlehem.

These celebrations, which date from colonial days when Spanish missionaries used pageants as a way of teaching Mexicans the story of the Nativity, are performed throughout Mexico in public squares, churches, and theaters. Most of the pageants represent a humorous mix of tradition, politics, and social affairs.

CONTACTS:
Mexico Tourism Board
21 E. 63rd St., Fl. 3
New York, NY 10021
800-446-3942 or 212-821-0314; fax: 212-821-0367
www.visitmexico.com

SOURCES:
EncyChristmas-2003, p. 598

◆ 0583 ◆ **Christmas Shooting**
Christmas Eve and New Year's Eve

Christmas Shooting is a very noisy custom in Berchtesgaden, Bavaria, Germany. About 200 marksmen gather at midnight above the Berchtesgaden valley and shoot rifles and mortars for an hour. The salvos echoing off the mountains can be heard for many miles. It is believed that the custom of making a loud racket began as a pagan rite to drive away evil spirits.

CONTACTS:
Visitors' Center Berchtesgadener Land
Bahnhofplatz 4
Berchtesgaden, 83471 Germany
49-18-058-65-200; fax: 49-86-529-67-402
en.berchtesgadener-land.com

SOURCES:
EncyChristmas-2003, p. 717

◆ 0584 ◆ **Chrysanthemum Festival**
September-October, including the ninth day of ninth lunar month

The Chrysanthemum Festival was the last of the five sacred festivals of ancient Japan. It lasted over the ninth month and sometimes into the tenth month of the Buddhist lunar calendar, although the ninth day of the ninth month was known as **Chrysanthemum Day**, primarily an occasion for paying visits to one's superiors. Also known as **Choyo**, the festival was a unique tribute to the gardening and artistic skills of the Japanese, who developed a method for growing chrysanthemums within a wire or bamboo frame in the shape of a human figure. The boughs were guided around the frame such that the flowers bloomed only on the outside, clothing the figure in flower blossoms. The heads, hands, and feet of these more-than-life-sized figures would be made of wax or paste, but their costumes were made entirely of chrysanthemums, with blossoms of different sizes and colors used to achieve as realistic an effect as possible.

Formerly, *kiku ningyo* exhibitions were numerous, and could still be seen in the parks of big cities in the early part of the 20th century. But the cost of growing the flowers and erecting the figures became prohibitive, and the exhibits eventually died out. In Japan, Korea, and Okinawa today, Chrysanthemum Day is a fairly unimportant holiday, observed in scattered locations by eating chrysanthemum cakes (a dumpling made from yellow chrysanthemum petals mixed with rice flour) and drinking chrysanthemum wine.

SOURCES:
DictFolkMyth-1984, p. 540
FolkWrldHol-1999, p. 576
JapanFest-1965, p. 186
OxYear-1999, p. 703

♦ 0585 ♦ **Chuckwagon Races, National Championship**
September, weekend of Labor Day

The National Championship Chuckwagon Races take place at Dan Eoff's "Bar Of" Ranch in Clinton, Ark., each Labor Day weekend from Friday through Sunday. About 150 teams consisting of a wagon and four horses compete in five divisions for the National Champion title. Division winners are awarded silver belt buckles. They also take home a share of $20,000 worth of prizes, including jackets, saddles, and "Chuckwagon Bucks"—prize money that can be spent at the western-themed Trade Show held at the event. The races are for amateurs and open to all. The weekend can attract more than 20,000 spectators, many of whom camp out on the 700-acre ranch.

In addition to chuckwagon racing, events include bronc fanning, so called because riders attempt to calm ornery mounts by fanning them with their cowboy hats. The annual Snowy River Race is a tribute to the film *The Man from Snowy River,* which featured a downhill chase on horseback into a river. The 16 entrants in the race ride their horses up and then furiously down a steep hill, straight into the mouth of a stream, where the race finishes. Live music and dances add to the weekend's festivities.

Eoff and his family launched the races in 1986 as a Labor Day party for friends after attending a chuckwagon race in Cheyenne, Wyoming, in 1985. Eight wagons competed in the first race. More than 20 years later, that party has grown to be the largest chuckwagon race in the United States.

CONTACTS:
Bar Of Ranch
2848 Shake Rag Rd.
Clinton, AR 72031
501-745-5250 or 501-745-8407
chuckwagonraces.com

♦ 0586 ♦ **Chugiak-Eagle River Bear Paw Festival**
Mid-July

The Bear Paw Festival is a five-day community festival in the towns of Chugiak and Eagle River, near Anchorage, Alaska. Relatively new, it has established itself and achieved popularity with its Ugly Truck and Dog Contest, in which contestants compete for a combined score that rates the lack of beauty of both their vehicles and canine companions. Other events are a parade, a rodeo, arts and crafts displays, a beauty pageant, and carnival rides.

CONTACTS:
Chugiak-Eagle River Chamber of Commerce
P.O. Box 770353
Eagle River, AK 99577
907-694-4702; fax: 907-694-1205
www.cer.org

♦ 0587 ♦ **Chulalongkorn Day**
October 23

Chulalongkorn Day is a national holiday in Thailand commemorating King Chulalongkorn (Rama V), the king who abolished slavery and introduced numerous reforms when the country was still called Siam. He succeeded to the throne in 1868 when he was 15 years old, was crowned in 1873, and ruled until his death in 1910. He had been a pupil of Anna Leonowens, who taught the young prince about Abraham LINCOLN. The story of her stay in the royal court, and her teaching of the royal children and concubines, was told in Margaret Landon's book, *Anna and the King of Siam.* The book was the basis for the popular Broadway musical, *The King and I.*

CONTACTS:
Thailand Government
Public Relations Dept.
Rama VI Rd.
Bangkok, 10400 Thailand
66-2-618-2323; fax: 66-2-618-2358
thailand.prd.go.th

SOURCES:
AnnivHol-2000, p. 176

♦ 0588 ♦ **Chung Yeung**
September-October; ninth day of ninth lunar month

A Chinese holiday, Chung Yeung is the second family-remembrance day of the year. It's customary, as on the festival of QING MING, for families to visit the graves of ancestors, tend their gravestones, and make offerings of food, which are eaten after the ceremonies are completed.

It's also traditional on this day for people to go to the hills for picnics and kite-flying. This is done because, according to an ancient legend, a scholar was warned by a soothsayer that disaster would fall on the ninth day of the ninth lunar month. He took his family up into the mountains. When the family returned to their village, they found every living thing dead. They gave thanks that they had been spared. The custom of flying kites stems from traditional lore, which holds that kites can convey bad luck up into the sky.

The day is also known as **Ch'ung Yang**, **Double Nine Day**, and the **Festival of High Places**. It is a public holiday in some places, including Hong Kong and Macau.

CONTACTS:
Hong Kong Tourism Board
115 E. 54th St., 2nd Fl.
New York, NY 10022
212-421-3382; fax: 212-421-8428
www.discoverhongkong.com

SOURCES:
AnnivHol-2000, p. 240
BkFest-1937, p. 81
BkHolFestWrld-1970, p. 117
BkHolWrld-1986, Oct 15
DictFolkMyth-1984, pp. 225, 1106
EncyRel-1987, vol. 3, p. 327
FolkAmerHol-1999, p. 380
FolkWrldHol-1999, p. 574
HolSymbols-2009, p. 147

♦ 0589 ♦ **Ch'un-hyang Festival**
May

This celebration in Namwon, Jeollabuk-do, Korea, honors Ch'un-hyang, a symbol of female virtue. She is the heroine of the ancient Korean story, *Ch'un-hyangjon,* which tells of the love between a commoner and a nobleman. During the festival, her story is reenacted, and other events include a *p'ansori,* or "narrative song" contest, a swinging competition, traditionally enjoyed by young women, and a Miss Ch'un-hyang beauty pageant.

Ch'un-hyang was the daughter of a *kisaeng,* or female entertainer, and she and a nobleman's son, Yi Mongnyong, fell in love and were secretly married. Soon after, he was transferred from Namwon to Seoul. The new governor of Namwon was corrupt and licentious, and he wanted Ch'un-hyang. But even though she was beaten, she didn't give in to his advances. Finally Yi Mongnyong returned to Namwon as provincial inspector. He punished the governor and took Ch'un-hyang as his official bride. To Koreans, this is a favorite tale of love and fidelity and also a symbol of the resistance by common people to privileged classes.

CONTACTS:
City of Namwon
Cultural Information Center
Namwon
Jeollabuk-do, Korea
82-63-620-6544; fax: 82-63-620-6535
www.namwon.go.kr/en

SOURCES:
GdWrldFest-1985, p. 128

♦ 0590 ♦ **Chuseok (Gawi or Hangawi)**
15th day of the eighth lunar month

The MID-AUTUMN FESTIVAL, which is observed in China, Japan, Vietnam, and other Asian countries, is celebrated in Korea as well, where it is called *Chuseok* or **Hangawi**. This fall harvest festival is marked on the 15th day of the eighth lunar

month and is a major national holiday in Korea. Like THANKSGIVING in the United States, Chuseok finds many people on the move in Korea as they travel to spend the holiday with their families.

Koreans traditionally begin the day with a religious service at home to remember their ancestors. Then they visit the graves of their departed family members and clear away the weeds and grasses around the tombs; this is not only a symbolic act of honoring their ancestors, but also a practical matter, because of the increased chance for grass fires during the typically dry autumn season. Then people go home and enjoy foods traditional to the season. Various rice-based dishes incorporating fresh fruits and vegetables are popular. Other customary games and activities include wrestling for men, a women's circle song and dance called *Gang-gang-sullae* in the south, and in rural areas, a cow or ox game, in which two men or boys in a cow or ox costume visit each house in the neighborhood and beg for something to eat; if the householder feeds them, they perform a dance. Taking walks in the evening and admiring the moon is also a favorite activity on Chuseok, since the holiday falls on the full moon day of the eighth month.

CONTACTS:
Korea National Tourism Organization
1 Executive Dr., Ste. 100
Fort Lee, NJ 07024
800-868-7567 or 201-585-0909; fax: 201-585-9041
www.kntoamerica.com

SOURCES:
AnnCustKorea-1983, p. 135
FestWrld: SouthKorea-1998, p. 20
FolkWrldHol-1999, p. 508
HolSymbols-2009, p. 150

♦ 0591 ♦ **Cinco de Mayo**
May 5

Cinco de Mayo or the **Fifth of May** is a national holiday in Mexico commemorating the Battle of Puebla on May 5, 1862, in which Mexican troops under General Ignacio Zaragoza defeated the invading French forces of Napoleon III. Although the battle itself represented only a temporary setback for the French, the Mexicans' victory against overwhelming odds gave them the confidence they needed to persevere until finally triumphing on April 2, 1867.

The anniversary of this event is celebrated not only in Mexico but in many American communities with large Mexican-American populations—especially in the southwestern states of Texas, Arizona, and southern California. The events include parades, patriotic speeches, bullfights, barbecues, and beauty contests. Olvera Street in Los Angeles is particularly known for its Cinco de Mayo celebration.

CONTACTS:
Mexico Tourism Board
21 E. 63rd St., Fl. 3
New York, NY 10021
800-446-3942 or 212-821-0314; fax: 212-821-0367
www.visitmexico.com

University of California
405 Hilgard Ave.
Los Angeles, CA 90095
310-825-4321
www.ucla.edu

SOURCES:
AmerBkDays-2000, p. 343
AnnivHol-2000, p. 77
DictFolkMyth-1984, p. 1065
FolkWrldHol-1999, p. 329
HolSymbols-2009, p. 152
OxYear-1999, p. 198

♦ 0592 ♦ Circumcision, Feast of the
January 1

The Feast of the Circumcision, which commemorates the circumcision of the infant Jesus on the eighth day after his birth, was first observed by the Eastern Orthodox and Roman Catholic churches in the sixth century or earlier and was adopted by the Anglican Church in 1549. It is known by a number of different names: Roman Catholics, who used to call it the **Octave of the Birth of Our Lord** or the **Circumcision of Jesus,** now mark the day as the **Solemnity of Mary, the Mother of God.** Episcopalians call it the **Feast of the Holy Name of Our Lord Jesus Christ**—a reference to the fact that Jesus was officially given his name on this day. Lutherans refer to it as the **Feast of the Circumcision and the Name of Jesus.** And Eastern Orthodox churches call it the **Feast of the Circumcision of Our Lord.** Old Calendar Orthodox churches observe it 13 days later in accordance with the Julian, or Old Style, calendar.

SOURCES:
AmerBkDays-2000, p. 3
BkFest-1937, p. 326
DaysCustFaith-1957, p. 17
EncyChristmas-2003, p. 248
FolkWrldHol-1999, p. 11
OxYear-1999, p. 6
RelHolCal-2004, p. 88
SaintFestCh-1904, p. 50

♦ 0593 ♦ Círio de Nazaré
Second Sunday in October

The Brazilian festival known as the Círio de Nazaré is a great "Candle Procession," which attracts pilgrims from all over the country. The Círio de Nazaré has been celebrated since the late 18th century. It traditionally takes place on the second Sunday in October and winds through the city of Belém in the state of Pará on its way to the Nazaré Basilica. There the statue of Our Lady of Nazaré is venerated for 15 days during the festival. The statue is carried on a wooden framework pulled by thousands of people as payment for prayers that have been answered by the saint. The origins of the festival lie in a miracle that is said to have occurred in the early 1700s, when a wooden image of the saint disappeared from someone's home and then reappeared a couple of days later in the same place. To people in Pará, this festival is on a par with CHRISTMAS, with much feasting and exchanging of gifts.

CONTACTS:
Brazil Tourism Office
3006 Massachusetts Ave. N.W.
Washington, D.C. 20008
800-727-2945 or 202-238-2802; fax: 202-238-2827
www.embratur.gov.br

SOURCES:
FiestaTime-1965, p. 156

♦ 0594 ♦ Citizenship Day
September 17

Citizenship Day is an outgrowth of two earlier patriotic celebrations. As the anniversary of the signing of the Constitution of the United States in 1787, September 17 was first observed in Philadelphia shortly after the outbreak of the Civil War as **Constitution Day.** Then in 1940 Congress set aside the third Sunday in May as **"I Am an American" Day,** which honored those who had become U.S. citizens during the preceding year. The two holidays were combined in 1952 and called Citizenship Day.

A number of states and cities hold special exercises on September 17 to focus attention on the rights and obligations of citizenship. Schools make a special effort to acquaint their students with the history and importance of the Constitution. Naturalization ceremonies, re-creations of the signing of the Constitution, and parades are other popular ways of celebrating Citizenship Day. Several states observe the entire week in which this day occurs as Constitution Week.

CONTACTS:
Ben's Guide to Government
U.S. Government Printing Office
732 N. Capitol St. N.W.
Washington, D.C. 20401
888-293-6498 or 202-512-1530; fax: 202-512-1262
bensguide.gpo.gov

National Constitution Center
525 Arch St.
Independence Mall
Philadelphia, PA 19106
866-917-1787 or 215-409-6600
www.constitutioncenter.org

SOURCES:
AmerBkDays-2000, p. 653
AnnivHol-2000, p. 156
DictDays-1988, p. 21
PatHols-2006, p. 63

♦ 0595 ♦ Clearwater County Fair and Lumberjack Days
Third weekend in September

This international lumberjack event attracts loggers from throughout the world to little Orofino, Idaho (population 3,000). Goldminers came to Orofino to establish the state's first settlements in the 1860s, and more settlers came at the turn of the century to stake out timber claims. Lumbering is now a major part of Orofino's economy. Lumberjack Days began in the early 1940s as a local contest and kept growing.

The events begin on Thursday, a children's parade is held on Friday, and the lumberjack events come on the weekend. The logging competitions include log birling, ax throwing, chopping, chain-saw events, a speed pole climb (130 feet), jack-and-jill sawing, and a skidding, or weight-pulling, contest. The cash prizes total more than $30,000 and attendance is about 6,000.

CONTACTS:
Orofino Chamber of Commerce
P.O. Box 2346
Orofino, ID 83544
208-476-4335
www.orofino.com

◆ 0596 ◆ Clipping the Church Day
First Sunday in July

The old English custom of "clipping the church" entails embracing the church by joining hands around it and performing a simple dance step, advancing and retreating three times. In Guiseley, Yorkshire, the custom traditionally was observed on St. Oswald's Day, August 5, but now takes place in July, during the Festival of Guiseley. There is a special service followed by a procession outside the church where all sing "St. Oswald's Ballad."

In other areas of England, it is observed on whatever day is appropriate to the church calendar. Sometimes a "puppy-dog pie"—a round cake with almond paste on top and a small china dog inside—is baked on the day of the church-clipping ceremony.

Some observers believe that this custom dates back to the ancient pagan festival known as the LUPERCALIA, which included a sacred dance around the altar and the sacrifice of goats and young dogs—hence the puppy-dog pie. At one time it was customary for children to run through the streets after the clipping ceremony crying, "Highgates!"

CONTACTS:
St. Oswald's Parish Church
Church St.
Guiseley, Yorkshire LS20 9BE United Kingdom
44-19-1383-0830
www.oswalds.org.uk

SOURCES:
EngCustUse-1941, p. 5

◆ 0597 ◆ Closing the Gates Ceremony
December 18

The celebration that takes place on this day in Londonderry, Northern Ireland, commemorates the siege of 1688, when James II, at the head of a 20,000-man army, stormed the Protestant city's walls. Londonderry's governor, Colonel Lundy, wanted to surrender and was eventually let down over the walls and permitted to join the king's forces. The governor's scheme to deliver the city to the British was foiled by 13 boy apprentices who managed to shut the Ferryquay Gate just as the British were about to enter the city. The siege lasted for 105 days, during which thousands of Londonderry citizens died of starvation or disease. A ship named the *Mountjoy* finally broke the blockade that had been set up on the River Foyle and brought food to the city's starving inhabitants.

The celebrations held annually on December 18 are set up by the Association of the Apprentice Boys of Derry. The festivities include an historical pageant, the climax of which is the burning of Colonel Lundy's effigy.

SOURCES:
YrFest-1972, p. 88

◆ 0598 ◆ Clown Festival, International
August

Begun in 1995, the International Clown Festival has been held annually at the Bakken amusement park near Copenhagen, Denmark. The festival was founded by the Danish clown Benny Schumann, the grandson of famed European clown Charlie Rivel. The event attracts performing talent from Italy, Belgium, Denmark, Spain, and Russia. While giving the public the chance to see a range of clown performances from around the world, the festival also allows the performers the opportunity to meet and learn from each other as well.

The festival has highlighted both those clowns who perform in the time-honored manner familiar to the general public and those who experiment with different costumes, characters, and approaches. Among the latter are Lars Lottrup, who climbs inside of a large balloon (optional) and disappears; Galina and Yuri Emeliyanovs, the duo known as Pilula, who perform on the high wire with a giant baby carriage; and the Jashgawronsky Brothers, who make music using common garden tools. Two awards are given out (optional) each year: the World Artist and Clown Award and the Golden Nose.

CONTACTS:
International Clown Festival
Lundingsvej 6
Rungsted Kyst. DK-2960 Denmark
www.schumann.dk/real/festival/?lang=en

◆ 0599 ◆ Coca-Cola 600
May, Memorial Day weekend

The Coca-Cola 600 is the longest race of the four big races of the NASCAR (National Association for Stock Car Auto Racing) Sprint Cup circuit (formerly the Winston Cup). The race is held at Lowe's Motor Speedway in Charlotte, N.C. The track, which opened in 1960, installed special lights in 1992 to be the first super speedway ever to have nighttime racing. The track is a mile-and-a-half long, and the 600-mile race covers 400 laps. Lowe's Motor Speedway is also the home track for NASCAR, and many racing teams are based near the speedway.

The 2009 event was the 50th running of the Coca-Cola 600, which has become a MEMORIAL DAY tradition. In the week preceding the 600, the Charlotte 600 Festival offers a variety of downtown events, including a parade.

See also DAYTONA 500; WINSTON 500; and SOUTHERN 500

CONTACTS:
National Association for Stock Car Auto Racing
1801 W. International Speedway Blvd.
Daytona Beach, FL 32115
386-253-0611; fax: 386-681-4041
www.nascar.com

600 Festival Association
6324 Performance Dr.
Concord, NC 28027
704-455-6814; fax: 704-455-1900
www.600festival.com

♦ 0600 ♦ **Cock Festival**
February 2

Popular throughout Castilla and northern Spain, the **Fiesta del Gallo**, or Cock Festival, usually takes place on CANDLE-MAS, and it symbolizes the renewal of life or of the harvest. It involves two groups of young people, 12 men and 12 women, who together comprise a kingdom, or *reinado*, with a king and queen who officiate at this and other festivals throughout the year. Young ladies, clothed in white garments and led by the queen, exit the church immediately after the mass and proceed to the town square carrying a live cock. There they meet the mayor of the village whose permission they must ask to kill the cock.

Just how the killing takes place varies from town to town. Sometimes the cock is tied by the legs to a pole, and the queen attacks it with a wooden sword. Sometimes it's buried in the ground with just its head showing. Any young man who wishes to try may be blindfolded, turned around several times, and allowed to attack the cock if he can find it. In some villages of northern Spain, blindfolded men on horseback strike at the cock with wooden swords as it swings from a rope that has been stretched across the street. After the cock is killed, there is a feast.

CONTACTS:
Tourist Office of Spain
666 Fifth Ave., 35th Fl.
New York, NY 10103
212-265-8822; fax: 212-265-8864
www.okspain.org

SOURCES:
DictFolkMyth-1984, p. 1062

♦ 0601 ♦ **Collop Monday**
Between February 2 and March 8; Monday before Shrove Tuesday

In England, the day before SHROVE TUESDAY was called Collop Monday, a "collop" being a slice of meat or bacon. It was traditionally a day for getting rid of all the meat in the house in preparation for LENT.

SOURCES:
DictDays-1988, p. 22
EncyEaster-2002, p. 510
OxYear-1999, p. 606

♦ 0602 ♦ **Colombia Battle of Boyacá Day**
August 7

Colombia, known as New Granada in the early part of the 19th century, was then ruled by Spain. Simón Bolívar, the leader of the independence movement in South America, began a military campaign to liberate Colombia in 1817. He achieved a major victory at the Battle of Boyacá on August 7, 1819, when he surprised the Spanish forces crossing a bridge and routed them.

Colombians celebrate this national holiday with parades and festivals throughout the country. Ceremonies take place at the cemeteries where the fallen soldiers of the battle are buried.

CONTACTS:
Embassy of Colombia
2118 Leroy Pl. N.W.
Washington, D.C. 20008
202-387-8338; fax: 202-232-8643
www.colombiaemb.org

♦ 0603 ♦ **Colombia Independence Day**
July 20

On the day that they celebrate their independence from Spain, Colombians in the capital city of Bogotá often visit an historic place known as *La Casa del Florero* (The House of the Flowerpot). It was here, in the 19th century, that a Colombian storekeeper was asked to lend a large flowerpot to the Spaniards for an important occasion. Rather than let them use it, he broke the flowerpot. A riot ensued—the beginning of the revolt against Spain.

There are Independence Day parades throughout the country on July 20, some with uniformed cavalry performing acrobatic feats on horseback. Schoolchildren march in their uniforms, and dancers perform in the costumes of their region. In the afternoon, people watch athletic games and listen to singing groups perform their favorite folk songs. Because July is a winter month in Colombia, almost everyone wears *ruanas*, which are square shawls of brightly colored wool with a slit in the center for the head, and *alpargates*, or rope-soled canvas sandals.

When Colombia first became a republic in 1819, it included Venezuela, Ecuador, and Panama as well. Venezuela and Ecuador became separate states in 1830, and Panama withdrew in 1903.

CONTACTS:
Colombian Embassy
2118 Leroy Pl. N.W.
Washington, D.C. 20008
202-387-8338; fax: 202-232-8643
www.colombiaemb.org

SOURCES:
AnnivHol-2000, p. 120
NatlHolWrld-1968, p. 117

♦ 0604 ♦ **Columbus Day**
Second Monday in October

When the Italian explorer Christopher Columbus (1451-1506) persuaded King Ferdinand and Queen Isabella of Spain to provide financial backing for his plan to find a new route to the Orient by sailing west, he was confident that only about 2,400 miles of ocean separated the two continents—a gross underestimation, as it turned out. And when he first landed in the Bahamas on October 12, 1492, he believed that he'd reached the East Indies. Despite these errors in judgment, Columbus is credited with opening the New World to European colonization, and the anniversary of his landing on the Bahamian island of San Salvador is commemorated not only in the United States but in Italy and most of the Spanish-speaking nations of the world.

Also known as **Landing Day**, **Discoverers' Day** (in Hawaii), DISCOVERY DAY, **Hispanity Day** in Spain, and in many Latin American countries as **Día de la Raza** or **Day of the Race**, the second Monday in October is celebrated in this country with parades, patriotic ceremonies, and pageants reenacting the historic landing. A mammoth parade up Fifth Avenue in New York City is a Columbus Day tradition.

In 1991, the spirit of political correctness affected Berkeley, California, as Columbus Day was cancelled in favor of Indigenous Peoples Day. Likewise, the Student Senate at the University of Cincinnati declared that myths about Columbus may not be studied or discussed—the University is "a Columbus-myth-free-campus."

CONTACTS:
Library of Congress
101 Independence Ave. S.E.
Washington, DC 20540
202-707-5000; fax: 202-707-2076
www.loc.gov

SOURCES:
AmerBkDays-2000, p. 703
BkDays-1864, vol. II, p. 437
BkFest-1937, p. 18
BkHolWrld-1986, Oct 12
DaysCustFaith-1957, p. 255
DictDays-1988, pp. 22, 31
FolkAmerHol-1999, p. 419
OxYear-1999, p. 412
PatHols-2006, p. 73

♦ 0605 ♦ **Common Ridings Day**
Various dates in June and July

Many Scottish border towns hold a ceremony known as Common Ridings or **Riding the Marches** in June or July. The marches are border districts between England and Scotland and England and Wales. The custom dates back to the Middle Ages, when it was often necessary to reconfirm boundaries destroyed by fire in order to retain royal charters. Originally this was done only as the need arose, but eventually it became a yearly event.

The two main observations of Common Ridings occur in Selkirk and Haywick in June. In Selkirk, the event is combined with a commemoration of the 1513 Battle of Flodden, in which King James IV of Scotland and 10,000 others were

killed. The Royal Burgh Standard Bearer leads a cavalcade of 200 riders around the borders of the town common.

CONTACTS:
Selkirk Community Council
Newtown St.
Boswells, Scotland TD6 0SA United Kingdom
44-18-3582-6626; fax: 44-18-3582-5059
www.selkirk.bordernet.co.uk

♦ 0606 ♦ **Commonwealth Day**
Second Monday in March

From 1903 until 1957, this holiday in honor of the British Empire was known as **Empire Day** and was celebrated on May 24, Queen Victoria's birthday. Between 1958 and 1966, it was called **British Commonwealth Day**. Then it was switched to Queen ELIZABETH II's official birthday in June, and the name was shortened to Commonwealth Day. It is observed annually on the second Monday in March.

In Canada it is still celebrated on May 24 (or the Monday before) and referred to as **Victoria Day**.

CONTACTS:
Commonwealth Secretariat
Marlborough House
Pall Mall
London, SW1Y 5HX United Kingdom
44-20-7747-6500; fax: 44-20-7930-0827
www.thecommonwealth.org

Royal Commonwealth Society
25 Northumberland Ave.
London, WC2N 5AP United Kingdom
44-20-7930-6733; fax: 44-20-7930-9705
www.rcsint.org

SOURCES:
AnnivHol-2000, p. 87
DictDays-1988, pp. 23, 36, 125

♦ 0607 ♦ **Comoros Independence Day**
July 6

Comoros proclaimed its declaration of independence from France on this day in 1975, after more than 100 years under French rule. It is commemorated with a national holiday.

CONTACTS:
Comoros Mission in the U.S.
450 E. 50th St.
New York, NY 10022
212-972-8010; fax: 212-983-4712

SOURCES:
AnnivHol-2000, p. 113

♦ 0608 ♦ **Compitalia**
Early January

The Compitalia were festivals celebrated in ancient Rome in early January (between the 3rd and the 5th, according to some accounts) in honor of the *lares*, or deities of the household farm and family. *Compita* were places where roads or farm paths crossed each other and were considered sacred. Small tower-like shrines were often built there, and people would hold sacrifices at the shrines at the end of the agricultural year. The shrines were left open in four directions so that the lares had access to them. Sometimes farmers would also hang a broken plough there to indicate that a job was done.

The institution of the Compitalia is attributed to either Tarquin the Proud (also known as Tarquinius Superbus because of his proud and insolent nature) or Servius Tullius. There is some indication that the original sacrifices were human, but that Brutus, the first consul of Rome, eventually substituted dolls and the heads of poppies for human figures. Slaves enjoyed a brief period of freedom during the Compitalia, and the spirit of the ancient festival survived in PLOUGH MONDAY, an occasion for servants to celebrate the completion of their ploughing.

SOURCES:
ClassDict-1984, pp. 162, 608
DictFolkMyth-1984, p. 604
DictRomRel-1996, p. 51
FestRom-1981, p. 58
FestSaintDays-1915, p. 19

◆ 0609 ◆ **Conch Republic Independence Celebration**
Week including April 23

In 1982 the United States Border Patrol set up a roadblock on U.S. Highway 1, just north of the Florida Keys. The new checkpoint created massive traffic jams, threatened the region's tourist industry, and angered residents of the Keys, who resented having to prove their American citizenship each time they attempted to drive to the Florida mainland.

On April 23, 1982, after trying in vain to get the courts to stop the blockade, the residents of the Florida Keys, under the leadership of Key West Mayor Dennis Wardlow, seceded from the United States of America. Wardlow announced that the Florida Keys would henceforth become an independent nation known as the Conch Republic. The besieged Republic maintained the secession for one minute, after which time Wardlow surrendered to the United States Navy and called for $1 billion in foreign aid and war relief to restore the damage done to the Keys by the federal government. Though the Republic didn't last, the stunt succeeded in pressuring the U.S. government to lift the roadblocks. Indeed, the motto of the tiny nation later became "we seceded where others failed."

Each year lighthearted residents of the Keys celebrate the short-lived independence of the Conch Republic, which they affirm still exists as a "state of mind." The festival takes place for an entire week surrounding April 23. It features conch-blowing contests, real drag races—in which drag queens race each other down the street—a reenactment of the secession, mock naval battles, bed races, food and crafts booths, a pancake-eating contest, numerous public parties held in bars and clubs, and more.

CONTACTS:
The Conch Republic Office of the Secretary General
509 Whitehead St., Ste. 1
Key West, FL 33040
305-296-0213; fax: 305-296-8803
www.conchrepublic.com

◆ 0610 ◆ **Concordia Day**
November 11

A public holiday on the island of St. Maarten in the West Indies, Concordia Day commemorates the 1648 agreement to divide the island between the Dutch and the French. To this day, St. Maarten is the smallest territory shared by two sovereign states, with only a stone monument and two hand-lettered signs marking the boundary.

Concordia Day celebrates the long-standing peaceful coexistence of the two countries by holding parades and a joint ceremony with French and Dutch officials at the obelisk border monument. November 11 is also the anniversary of the island's discovery in 1493 by Christopher COLUMBUS, who named it after ST. MARTIN, on whose feast day it was discovered.

CONTACTS:
St. Maarten Tourist Office
675 Third Ave., Ste. 1806
New York, NY 10017
800-786-2278 or 212-953-2084; fax: 212-953-2145
www.st-maarten.com

SOURCES:
AnnivHol-2000, p. 189

◆ 0611 ◆ **Confederados Reunion**
April

The "Confederados" are the descendants of a small band of Southerners who fled the United States at the end of the Civil War to establish a new life in Brazil. Led by Colonel William Hutchinson Norris, an Alabama state senator who arrived in December 1865 and purchased a large farm about 80 miles northwest of São Paulo, the newcomers found the area's reddish soil reminiscent of Mississippi clay and the climate perfect for growing cotton and watermelons. As the word spread, thousands of Southerners followed—an estimated 2,900 a year landed in Rio de Janeiro between 1867 and 1871, and many more arrived at other Brazilian ports. They settled in a number of places, but the most successful colony was the one started by Norris. Americana, as it is known today, is a center for the textile industry in Brazil.

Many of the Americans missed their homeland and eventually returned there; the number of Confederados living in and around Americana leveled off at about 500 by the turn of the century. They hold four gatherings a year, the largest and most important of which—known as the **Festa Confederada**—takes place in April. In celebration of their heritage, they eat hot dogs and candied apples, drink cold beer, dance in hoop skirts and Civil War uniforms, and display the flag of the Confederate States of America. The April reunion takes place in a small local cemetery between Americana and Santa Barbara, where more than 400 of their ancestors are buried.

CONTACTS:
Prefeitura Municipal de Americana
Av. Brasil, 85
Vila Medon, 13465-901 Brazil
55-19-3475-9000
www.americana.sp.gov.br

♦ 0612 ♦ **Confederate Memorial Day**
Varies from state to state

Observed in memory of the Confederate soldiers who died in the Civil War, Confederate Memorial Day is widely observed in the southern United States. It grew out of a number of smaller, more localized responses to the bloodshed of the War between the States. In Vicksburg, Mississippi, for example, a group of women got together in 1865 to decorate the graves of more than 18,000 men who had been killed during the siege of Vicksburg. A similar event took place the following year in Columbus, Mississippi, where the women laid magnolia blossoms on the graves of the enemy soldiers as well. Today, the last Monday in April is a legal holiday in Mississippi.

The dates on which Confederate Memorial Day is observed vary from state to state and are often linked to some local historical event. In Texas it is called **Confederate Heroes Day**, and is observed on January 19, Robert E. LEE's birthday. Alabama (April 23), Florida (April 23), Georgia (Monday nearest April 26), and South Carolina (May 10) also observe Confederate Memorial Day as a legal holiday. In Tennessee (June 3), the day is a special observance.

SOURCES:
AmerBkDays-2000, pp. 316, 425
AnnivHol-2000, pp. 72, 91
DictDays-1988, p. 23

♦ 0613 ♦ **Confucius's Birthday (Teacher's Day)**
September 28

A time to commemorate the birth of the teacher Confucius, perhaps the most influential man in China's history. In Qufu, Shandong Province, China, the birthplace of Confucius, there is a two-week-long **Confucian Culture Festival**. In Hong Kong, observances are held by the Confucian Society at the Confucius Temple at Causeway Bay near this date.

Confucius, the Latinized version of the name K'ung-fu-tzu, was born in 551 B.C.E. during the Warring States Period and developed a system of ethics and politics that stressed five virtues: charity, justice, propriety, wisdom, and loyalty. His teachings were recorded by his followers in the *Analects* and formed the code of ethics called Confucianism that is still the cornerstone of Chinese thought. It taught filial obedience, respect, and selflessness; the Confucian "golden rule" is "Do not do unto others what you would not want others to do unto you." Confucius died at the age of 73 in 479 B.C.E.

During the Cultural Revolution, Confucianism lost favor, and in the late 1960s Red Guards defaced many of the build-

ings in Qufu. They have since been restored, and the festival held there from late September into October attracts scholars from China and abroad. The festival opens with a ceremony accompanied by ancient music and dance and includes exhibitions and lectures on the life and teachings of Confucius and on Chinese customs.

Commemorations in Taiwan take the form of dawn services at the Confucian temples. The Confucius Temple in Tainan was built in 1665 by Gen. Chen Yunghua of the Ming Dynasty and is the oldest Confucian temple in Taiwan.

CONTACTS:
Taiwan Government Information Office
4201 Wisconsin Ave. N.W.
Washington, D.C. 20016
202-895-1850; fax: 202-362-6144
www.gio.gov.tw

Hong Kong Tourism Board
115 E. 54th St. 2/F
New York, NY 10022
212-421-3382; fax: 212-421-8428
www.discoverhongkong.com

Information Office of Jinan Municipal People's Government
182, Jing™er Road
Jinan, Shandong China
86-531-8207-5603
www.china-sd.com

SOURCES:
AnnivHol-2000, p. 161
BkFest-1937, p. 76
DictWrldRel-1989, p. 191
EncyRel-1987, vol. 4, p. 38

♦ 0614 ♦ **Congo Independence Day Celebration**
August 13-15

The **Three Glorious Days**, or **Trois Glorieuses**, constitute a national holiday in the Republic of Congo, commemorating the independence gained from France on August 15, 1960.

CONTACTS:
Republic of Congo Embassy
4891 Colorado Ave. N.W.
Washington, D.C. 20011
202-726-5500; fax: 202-726-1860

SOURCES:
AnnivHol-2000, p. 136
NatlHolWrld-1968, p. 142

♦ 0615 ♦ **Congo National Days**
March 18; June 5

The Republic of Congo has two historical holidays in addition to its independence day: the assassination of President Marien Ngouabi on March 18, 1977, and the beginning of the civil war on June 5, 1997, which restored President Denis Sassou-Nguesso to power.

CONTACTS:
Republic of Congo Embassy
4891 Colorado Ave. N.W.

Washington, D.C. 20011
202-726-5500; fax: 202-726-1860

♦ 0616 ♦ Connecticut Early Music Festival
Two weeks in June

The term "early music" refers to music from the medieval, renaissance, baroque, and classical periods, up to and including Beethoven and Schubert, performed on period instruments.

Since 1983, when harpsichordist Igor Kipnis and flutist John Solum co-founded the Connecticut Early Music Festival, the residents of southeastern Connecticut have been able to hear the music of such composers as Henry Purcell (c.1659-1695), Wolfgang Mozart (1756-1791), Luigi Boccherini (1743-1805), Georg Telemann (1681-1767), Johann Sebastian Bach (1685-1750), François Couperin (1668-1733), Antonio Salieri (1750-1825), Christoph Gluck (1714-1787), Arcangelo Corelli (1653-1713), Antonio Vivaldi (1678-1741), Claudio Monteverdi (1567-1643), Georg Frideric Handel (1685-1759), Joseph Haydn (1732-1809), Franz Schubert (1797-1828; *see also* Schubertiade), and Ludwig van Beethoven (1770-1827) performed on such unusual instruments as the cornet, slide trumpet, sackbut, viola da gamba, and the clavichord. The concerts are held in small rooms or churches so that the subtleties of the instruments can be heard—particularly the Noank Baptist Church in Noank and the Harkness Chapel at Connecticut College in New London.

CONTACTS:
Connecticut Early Music Festival
P.O. Box 329
New London, CT 06320
860-444-2419; fax: 860-439-2695
www.ctearlymusic.org

SOURCES:
MusFestAmer-1990, p. 46

♦ 0617 ♦ Constitution Week
Week beginning September 17

Since 2004, the National Constitution Center in Philadelphia, Pa., has hosted Constitution Week, beginning on September 17th, Constitution Day. The event celebrates September 17, 1787, the day the U.S. Constitution was signed. On August 2, 1956, the Congress set aside Constitution Week and asked that the president establish it each year by proclamation. Some presidents, including Ronald Reagan, were faithful in doing so, but the event has lapsed over the years.

Constitution Week begins with a public reading of the Constitution by a rotating group of 100 readers, including politicians, firefighters, nurses, and many others. During Constitution Week, the center provides classrooms across the country with suggested reading lists, class projects, constitution-related games and activities, and other materials to raise the awareness of the nation's children about the U.S. Constitution. Beginning in 2006, the week also includes the two-day Peter Jennings Institute for Journalists and the Constitution,

which brings journalists together to discuss a range of constitutional issues. In addition, a two-day Constitutional Convention composed of adult and youth delegations from all 50 states discuss and debate constitutional issues. The convention releases a "Report Card on the Constitution" in which the health of constitutional practices is evaluated. The convention is videotaped and made available to schools.

The National Constitution Center was established by the U.S. Government in 1988 to promote a greater understanding of the nation's constitution and its relevance in the daily lives of citizens today. The center has over 100 interactive exhibits and displays of film, documents, text, artifacts, and sculpture. It also houses the Annenberg Center for Education and Outreach, which coordinates national educational efforts about the constitution.

CONTACTS:
National Constitution Center
535 Arch St.
Philadelphia, PA 19106
215-409-6600
www.constitutioncenter.org

♦ 0618 ♦ Constitution Week (Mesa, Arizona)
Week of September 17

Mesa, Ariz., has consistently celebrated the Congressionally established Constitution Week for over 30 years.

Held at the Mesa Amphitheater, the celebration includes a school band concert, the chance for children to meet the Founding Fathers and ask them questions, a Constitution Quiz (the two winning students receive airline tickets to Washington. D.C.), a Boy Scouts parade of flags, the high school color guard ROTC, and live music. Educational activities include information about the lives and activities of America's Founding Fathers, an in-depth examination of the U.S. Constitution and the Bill of Rights, and a class on how to qualify for the Boy Scouts' "Citizenship in the Nation" Merit Badge.

Mesa students at all grade levels learn about the U.S. Constitution during the week. Local politicians visit classrooms to give talks about the legislative process. Mesa students also participate in the National Anthem Project, meant to encourage citizens to sing the country's national anthem.

CONTACTS:
Mesa Public Schools
63 East Main St., #101
Mesa, AZ 85201-7422
480-472-0000
www.mpsaz.org/main2

♦ 0619 ♦ Consualia
August 21 and December 15

The infamous rape of the Sabine women occurred at the first Consualia in ancient Rome. Consus, originally an agricultural deity but also regarded as the god of good counsel and the guardian of secrets, is said to have advised Romulus, the founder of Rome, to abduct the Sabine women as wives for his supporters.

The sanctuary dedicated to Consus in 272 B.C.E. was located on the Aventine Hill in Rome. Sacrifices were held there during his festival, and there were also horse and chariot races in the Circus Maximus, the large arena that lay between the Palatine and Aventine hills. There were actually two festivals in honor of Consus, one on August 21 and the other on December 15.

SOURCES:
AmerBkDays-2000, p. 555
DictFolkMyth-1984, p. 248
DictRomRel-1996, p. 52
FestRom-1981, p. 177

♦ 0620 ♦ **Coolidge (Calvin) Birthday Celebration**
July 4

The village of Plymouth Notch, Vermont, contains what many consider to be the best preserved and most authentic of all presidential homesites. It was here that Calvin Coolidge (1872-1933), 30th president of the United States, spent his boyhood and was sworn in as president by his father following the death of Warren Harding in 1923. The Coolidge Homestead was donated to the state of Vermont by John Coolidge, the President's son, in 1956. The state eventually acquired his birthplace, the general store and post office owned by his father, the homes of his mother and stepmother, his paternal grandparents' farmhouse, the family church, and the cemetery where the President and six generations of Coolidges are buried.

On the FOURTH OF JULY each year, the anniversary of Coolidge's birth, there is a noontime march from the green near the Plymouth Post Office to the Notch Cemetery, led by a Vermont National Guard colorguard with a bugler and a chaplain. The White House sends a wreath, which is laid at the President's tomb. Townspeople, tourists, and descendants of the Coolidge family listen to a brief graveside prayer service followed by the playing of taps. Next to the President's grave are those of his father, his wife, and his son, Calvin Coolidge, Jr., who died at the age of 16 during his father's White House years.

CONTACTS:
Calvin Coolidge Memorial Foundation
P.O. Box 97
Plymouth, VT 05056
802-672-3389; fax: 802-672-3369
www.calvin-coolidge.org

SOURCES:
AmerBkDays-2000, p. 502

♦ 0621 ♦ **Cooperatives, International Day of**
First Saturday in July

In 1992 the UNITED NATIONS established International Day of Cooperatives on the first Saturday in July. They chose this date to honor the founding of the International Cooperative

Alliance one hundred years earlier. Today the organization represents 760 million people who belong to various cooperatives in 100 countries. In 1994 the United Nations affirmed their commitment to International Day of Cooperatives in recognition of the crucial role that cooperatives play in economic and social development.

CONTACTS:
United Nations, Department of Public Information
Rm. S-1070L J, K, L
New York, NY 10017
212-963-6842; fax: 212-963-6914
www.un.org

♦ 0622 ♦ **Coopers' Dance**
January-February every seven years (2012, 2019, 2026...)

The famous Coopers' Dance, a 500-year-old custom, is performed in Munich, Germany, every seven years throughout the CARNIVAL season. The coopers, who make the barrels in which beer is stored, are highly respected in this city known for its breweries.

According to tradition, the first Coopers' Dance of the Carnival season is performed on EPIPHANY in front of the Minister-President's office building, where thousands of spectators gather in the streets to watch. The dance is performed by 25 colorfully dressed coopers, who swing hoops of fir branches and keep time with the music by beating on barrels with their tools. Individuals, clubs, and other organizations may order a Coopers' Dance to be performed, but so many of these orders come in during Carnival that they cannot all be filled.

CONTACTS:
Munich Tourist Office
Sendlinger St. 1
Munich, D-80331 Germany
49-89-233-96-500; fax: 49-89-233-30-233
www.muenchen.de/home/60093/Homepage.html

SOURCES:
FestEur-1961, p. 48

♦ 0623 ♦ **Coptic New Year (Feast of El-Nayrouz)**
September 11

Members of the Coptic Orthodox Church, the native Christian church in Egypt, celebrate the New Year on September 11 because it is the day on which the Dog Star, Sirius, rises in the Egyptian sky, announcing the flooding of the Nile and the new planting season.

To commemorate the martyrs of the church, red vestments and altar clothes are used on this day. A food of special significance on this day is the red date: red recalls the martyrs' blood, the light-colored flesh of the date symbolizes their purity, and the stony pit symbolizes their steadfast faith. The Coptic New Year is also celebrated by Canadians of Egyptian descent and by Egyptian communities elsewhere.

SOURCES:
FolkWrldHol-1999, p. 555

♦ 0624 ♦ **Corn Palace Festival**
Last week in August

The world's only Corn Palace was built in Mitchell, South Dakota, in 1892. It was home to the Corn Belt Exposition, designed to encourage farmers to settle in the area by displaying its corn and wheat crops on the building's exterior. A second and larger Corn Palace was built in 1905 to accommodate the growing crowds, and in 1937 a third Corn Palace was completed, this time with the addition of Moorish-looking minarets, turrets, and kiosks. The outside of the Palace is covered entirely with decorations consisting of dock, wild oats, bromegrass, blue grass, rye straw, and wheat tied in bunches. Corn of different colors, sawed in half lengthwise and nailed to the outside walls, is also used to complete the design, which changes every year. The decorating process usually begins in mid-summer and is completed in time for the festival.

Entertainment at the festival has reflected changing public tastes over the years. Stage revues in the 1920s gave way to the "big bands" of the '30s and '40s. Standup comedians and television entertainers in the '50s and '60s have yielded to country and western stars today.

CONTACTS:
Mitchell Corn Palace Festival
P.O. Box 250
Mitchell, SD 57301
866-273-2676 or 605-995-8427
www.cornpalacefestival.com

SOURCES:
GdUSFest-1984, p. 173

♦ 0625 ♦ **Corn-Planting Ceremony**
February-April

Corn is more than a staple for the Quiché Mayan Indians of Guatemala. In addition to eating it themselves and feeding it to their animals, they use the husks to thatch their huts. The Quiché Mayans also believe that their ancestors were made of ground corn paste.

The corn-planting season begins in February and lasts until April and requires considerable preparation. The fields must be burned and made ready for sowing, and the men who plant the corn perform numerous purification rituals. Churches hold special masses at the beginning of the planting season, and people bring seeds to church for blessings. On the eve of the first day of planting, people light candles, burn incense, and pray for the well-being of their crop. Afterwards, a huge feast and festivities, including fireworks, fortify the farmers before their work begins.

SOURCES:
FiestaTime-1965, p. 59

♦ 0626 ♦ **Cornouaille Festival**
One full week in late July

The Celtic heritage of the Breton people comes alive every year in Quimper, a town in the district of Cornouaille. Located in Brittany, a region in northwestern France, Quimper has hosted this festival of traditional dance, music, storytelling, food, and games for more than 70 years. People dress in Breton costumes, which include elaborate lace bonnets for the women and shallow, brimmed hats for the men. Many of Brittany's inhabitants still speak the ancient Celtic language brought to the region by its first settlers some 2,500 years ago.

CONTACTS:
Cornouaille Festival
P.O. Box 1315
Quimper, Cedex 29103 France
33-2-9855-5353; fax: 33-2-9855-3560
www.festival-cornouaille.com

Quimper Office of Tourism
Place de la Resistance
Quimper, 29000 France
33-2-9853-0405; fax: 33-2-9853-3133
www.quimper-tourisme.com/en

SOURCES:
FestWrld: France-1998, p. 8

♦ 0627 ♦ **Corpus Christi**
Between May 21 and June 24; Thursday after Trinity Sunday

Also known as the **Feast of the Most Holy Body of Christ**, the **Day of Wreaths**, and in France as the **Fête-Dieu**, Corpus Christi is a Roman Catholic festival that has been celebrated in honor of the Eucharist since 1246. In commemoration of the Last Supper on the day before Jesus' crucifixion, worshippers receive Communion and, in some countries, the consecrated bread (or Host) is paraded through the streets, held by the priests in a monstrance. In Spain and Provence, these processions can be quite elaborate, with saints and characters from the Bible following a path decorated with wreaths and strewn with flowers.

In Portugal the feast is known as **Día de Corpo de Deus** and has been one of the major religious observances—both on the mainland and in the Azores—since medieval times. In the city of Ponta Delgada, on San Miguel in the Azores, the people make a flower-petal carpet almost three-quarters of a mile in length. Over this carpet passes a colorful procession of high-ranking clergy and red-robed priests, who are followed by a group of first communicants (those who are to receive communion for the first time)—the young boys wearing dark suits and scarlet capes and the girls wearing white dresses and veils. The climax of the ceremony comes when the bishop raises the silver monstrance and exposes the Blessed Sacrament, the Body of Christ.

CONTACTS:
Portuguese National Tourist Office
590 Fifth Ave., 4th Fl.
New York, NY 10036
800-767-8842 or 212-354-4403; fax: 212-764-6137
www.visitportugal.com

SOURCES:
BkDays-1864, vol. I, p. 686
BkFest-1937, pp. 124, 186, 303

DaysCustFaith-1957, p. 156
DictFolkMyth-1984, pp. 253, 747, 749, 754, 787, 980, 1065
FestSaintDays-1915, p. 131
FestWestEur-1958, pp. 67, 98, 165, 198, 234
FolkAmerHol-1999, p. 249
FolkWrldHol-1999, p. 346
IntlThFolk-1979, pp. 275, 276
OxYear-1999, p. 633
RelHolCal-2004, p. 96
SaintFestCh-1904, p. 263

◆ 0628 ◆ Corpus Christi (England)
Between May 21 and June 24; Thursday after Trinity Sunday

In England, before the Reformation, there was a famous procession in London on CORPUS CHRISTI Day. Beginning at Cheapside, a group of clergymen would move down the street chanting the paternoster, or Lord's Prayer. Over the years they perfected their timing so that just as they reached a certain corner, they sang, "Amen." To this day, there is a street corner in London known as the "Amen Corner," and the street leading to it is known as "Paternoster Row." The procession then turned the corner and proceeded down another street, still known as "Ave Maria Lane."

Although the feast of Corpus Christi is no longer observed in England, there was a time when the city guilds were involved in processions on this day and often performed what were known as Corpus Christi plays. These were pageants based on a scriptural subject or religious mystery, named after the *pagiante*, the large, partitioned cart in which they were presented.

SOURCES:
BkFestHolWrld-1970, p. 69
FestSaintDays-1915, p. 133

◆ 0629 ◆ Corpus Christi (Germany) (Fronleichnamsfest)
Between May 21 and June 24; Thursday after Trinity Sunday

CORPUS CHRISTI Day in Germany is celebrated with colorful processions where the Sacrament and other holy symbols are carried through villages. Small-town streets are decorated with flowers and greenery, and children dressed in white and wearing wreaths of flowers accompany women in regional costume and local clergy. Sometimes people display pictures of Christ and spread carpets in front of their houses in honor of the day.

The most picturesque of these processions take place in Bavaria, where Corpus Christi is a legal holiday. Some are held on lakes rather than in the streets, with flower-decked boats carrying members of the procession and worshippers across crystal clear waters. The processions at Lake Staffelsee and Lake Chiemsee in Upper Bavaria are among the most dramatic.

CONTACTS:
German National Tourist Office
122 E. 42nd St.

New York, NY 10168
800-651-7010 or 212-661-7200; fax: 212-661-7174
www.cometogermany.com

SOURCES:
FestSaintDays-1915, p. 137
FestWestEur-1958, p. 67
FolkWrldHol-1999, p. 346

◆ 0630 ◆ Corpus Christi (Mexico)
Between May 21 and June 24; Thursday after Trinity Sunday

A Roman Catholic holiday commemorating the Eucharist, CORPUS CHRISTI is often observed in Mexico with symbolic battles between the Moors (Muslims) and the Christians, particularly in the states of Puebla and Veracruz. Although costumes vary from one area to the next, the Moors can usually be distinguished by their turbans and crescents, while the Christians often wear either elaborate plumed helmets with visors or derby hats with pink masks. The battle between them may last four or five hours, at the end of which the Moors are defeated and their leader is symbolically buried.

Another spectacle that takes place on Corpus Christi is the *Danza de los Voladores*, or Flying Pole Dance, performed by the Totonac Indians in Papantla in Veracruz State. Four dancers dressed as birds stand on a small platform atop a 70-foot tree that has been stripped of its branches. By carefully winding ropes around the tree and around themselves, they are able to hurl themselves into space and circle the tree 13 times before landing on the ground feet first. The four dancers multiplied by the 13 circles equals 52, the number of years in the ancient Aztec calendar cycle. Other versions of the Flying Pole Dance are performed in Pahuatlan and Cuetzalan, Puebla State.

Religious processions are common in Mexico on Corpus Christi, as is the *reposiar*, a small shrine or altar set up along the procession's path, covered with a lace-trimmed altar cloth and decorated with candles, flowers, and garlands. As the priest makes his rounds of the village, he stops at each of these shrines and gives his benediction. Local tradespeople set up a "mock" market along the path of the procession at which they display miniature objects of their trade. A builder, for example, makes doll houses, while restaurant owners serve small portions of food in miniature dishes and weavers make tiny blankets. The inch-long breads made by the bakers are used by the children as money to buy other miniature wares.

See also MOORS AND CHRISTIANS FIESTA

CONTACTS:
Mexico Tourism Board
21 E. 63rd St., Fl. 3
New York, NY 10021
800-446-3942 or 212-821-0314; fax: 212-821-0367
www.visitmexico.com

SOURCES:
BkFestHolWrld-1970, p. 70
DictFolkMyth-1984, pp. 253, 749
IntlThFolk-1979, p. 275

♦ 0631 ♦ Corpus Christi (Switzerland)
(Fronleichnamsfest)
Between May 21 and June 24; Thursday after
Trinity Sunday

Many of the ceremonies observed on CORPUS CHRISTI in Switzerland have come down from the Middle Ages. Although customs may vary from one canton to the next, this festival is almost always observed with elaborate processions of clergy in their best robes, people in picturesque regional costumes, and soldiers in historic uniforms. The priest who leads the procession often walks on a carpet of flowers.

In Fribourg, people decorate their houses with Gobelins (tapestries) as the bishop of Fribourg carries the Holy Sacrament through the streets. In the cantons of Appenzell, the processions include women in native costume, Capuchin monks in their robes, and young girls with white dresses and wreaths of flowers in their hair.

It is customary to throw the church doors open on Corpus Christi and to decorate the altar and aisles with garlands and greens. Outdoor village altars with flowers and candles are often erected in secluded places.

CONTACTS:
Switzerland Tourism
608 Fifth Ave.
New York, NY 10020
877-794-8037 or 212-757-5944; fax: 212-262-6116
www.myswitzerland.com

SOURCES:
FestWestEur-1958, p. 234

♦ 0632 ♦ Corpus Christi (Venezuela)
Between May 21 and June 24; Thursday after
Trinity Sunday

The Christian feast of CORPUS CHRISTI was established in Spanish America by royal decree in the latter part of the 16th century. The celebration was supposed to resemble that held in Spain, with performances and parades of people dressed up as dragons, devils, and giants. Although the dragons and giants have disappeared over the years, the Corpus Christi devils remain an important part of the festival, particularly in San Francisco de Yare in Venezuela.

The devil dancers are welcomed with a blast of fireworks at nine o'clock on the morning of the feast. Spectators gather in the Plaza Bolívar, waiting as the drumbeats become increasingly louder. Then more than 1,000 devils appear, disguised in red garments and horrible-looking masks from which protrude both the horn and the snout of an animal, usually an ox or a pig. Each dancer holds one or more maracas in his right hand and a thin rod from which dangles a small sack in his left. Cowbells and rattles are tied to each dancer's waist, and the noise they make as they leap around and shake the maracas can be deafening.

The appearance of the Sacred Host in the doorway of the church is a sign that the procession around the plaza is about to begin. The devils dance about in a frenzy, while the man at the head of the procession acts as if he is beating them with the whip he carries. When the Sacred Host is taken back to its sanctuary, the devils start crying and attempt to enter the church, but they are shut out. They become increasingly frantic, until finally they fall on their knees and toss their horned masks on the ground as a gesture admitting their defeat.

After the dance is over, the devils go to their leader's house, where everyone dances the *bamba*, a traditional dance of Spanish origin.

CONTACTS:
Venezuelan Tourism Department
7 E. 51st St.
New York, NY 10022
212-826-1660; fax: 212-644-7471
www.embavenez-us.org

SOURCES:
FiestaTime-1965, p. 105

♦ 0633 ♦ Cosby Ramp Festival
First Sunday in May

A festival started in 1951 to honor an obnoxious plant—the ramp. Held on Kineuvista Hill near Cosby, Tenn. (which is near Knoxville), the festival is touted as the first and largest of the ramp celebrations.

The ramp, related to the onion, is scientifically designated *Allium triccorcum lilaceae*. The name "ramp" supposedly was a shortening of *rampson*, the name of a similar plant. Devotees of the ramp say it has a mouth-watering, sweet flavor with a hint of garlic; they also concede that it has an astoundingly strong smell—like that of a wild onion multiplied a thousand times. It was once used in medicinal tonics, the theory being that the odor was enough to ward off germs and certainly germy people. It is rich in vitamin C and was the first spring vegetable for mountain people. Ramp harvest festivals of an informal sort are an old Appalachian custom handed down from the Indians, who taught the European settlers how to cook ramps.

Several days before the festival, a group of ramp pluckers goes into the mountains to pick and clean the ramps. The festival lunch, of course, features fried ramp with eggs cooked with streaked meat, a kind of bacon. The festival music is bluegrass, gospel, and country, and the events include the crowning of the Maid of Ramps. About 5,000 to 6,000 attend.

The Polk County Ramp Festival, a similar but smaller affair, is held in late April in Benton, Tenn. It has bluegrass music all day, and awards are given to the oldest and youngest ramp eaters, the largest family, and the person who has come the farthest distance (winners of this last have even come from outside of the U.S.).

CONTACTS:
Cosby Ramp Festival
Kineuvista Hill
Cosby, TN 37821
423-623-1009
www.cosbyrampfestival.org

Library of Congress
101 Independence Ave. S.E.
Washington, DC 20540
202-707-5000; fax: 202-707-2076
www.loc.gov

♦ 0634 ♦ **Cosmonauts Day**
April 12

On April 12, 1961, Russian cosmonaut Yuri Gagarin became the first man to travel in outer space. His one-hour-and-48-minute flight aboard the Vostok 1 caught the world's imagination and filled the Soviet people with pride. April 12th was declared Cosmonauts Day in Gagarin's honor.

Official ceremonies on this day begin in the Moscow suburb of Korolyov, well-known as the center of Russian rocket production, where officials and former cosmonauts lay flowers at a statue of Gagarin. Participants then walk to Red Square and Gagarin's grave at the Kremlin Wall Necropolis. They then proceed to Gagarin's statue in Cosmonauts Alley, a nearby walkway that leads to the Monument to the Conquerors of Space, and end at Gagarin's grave in the Novodevichy Cemetery.

The general public celebrates the day in a less formal manner. Some place flowers at statues of Gagarin in various cities, while others attend space-themed art and film exhibitions or fashion shows featuring designs based on cosmonaut spacesuits and helmets. Moscow's Institute of Medico-Biological Problems, which produces the food and beverages that cosmonauts use in space, has opened its doors for the general public to taste samples of space food, including vacuum-packed vodka. In 2007, Russian and American astronauts aboard the international space station celebrated the day with a six-course meal provided by Martha Stewart.

CONTACTS:
Embassy of the Russian Federation
2650 Wisconsin Ave. N.W.
Washington, D.C. 20007
202-298-5700; fax: 202-298-5735
www.russianembassy.org

♦ 0635 ♦ **Costa Rica Annexation of Guanacaste Day (Guanacaste Day, Día de Guanacaste)**
July 25; Monday nearest July 25

Annexation of Guanacaste Day is a Costa Rican national holiday also known as **Guanacaste Day,** or **Día de Guanacaste** in Spanish. It marks the annexation of Guanacaste, the northern part of the Nicoya peninsula, from Nicaragua. The inhabitants of Guanacaste voted to join the state of Costa Rica on July 25, 1824.

The holiday is celebrated with street fiestas, folk dancing, horse parades, and cattle shows. There are organized activities in major parks. Bullfights are a traditional part of the celebration in the Nicoya peninsula, where the holiday festivities typically last for several days.

CONTACTS:
Embassy of Costa Rica
2114 S St. N.W.
Washington, D.C. 20008
202-234-2945 or 202-234-2946; fax: 202-265-4795
www.costarica-embassy.org

♦ 0636 ♦ **Costa Rica Independence Day**
September 15

On this day in 1821, Costa Rica achieved independence, after having been ruled by Spain since the early 1500s. EL SALVADOR, GUATEMALA, HONDURAS, and NICARAGUA also declared independence from Spain on September 15, 1821.

On the evening of September 14, the president traditionally lights a torch representing liberty in the old capital city of Cartago and, on Independence Day, gives a speech to schoolchildren. There are more speeches and dancing in San José, the modern capital.

CONTACTS:
Costa Rican Embassy
2114 S. St. N.W.
Washington, D.C. 20008
202-234-2945; fax: 202-265-4795
www.costarica-embassy.org

SOURCES:
AnnivHol-2000, p. 155
NatlHolWrld-1968, p. 163

♦ 0637 ♦ **Costa Rica National Arts Festival**
March or April

One of Central America's most famous celebrations of creative expression, the National Arts Festival in Costa Rica draws international artists from over 30 countries and also serves as a promotional engine for its domestic art scene. The annual weeklong event features theater, dance, music, painting, and the fine arts.

The first festival took place in the national capital of San José in 1989. It was then called the International Theatre Festival and featured the theme "San José for Peace," an allusion to a harmonious political climate that for decades has fostered Costa Rica's rich cultural life. Beginning in 1992, the event became a permanent fixture on the country's calendar and thereafter was known as the National Arts Festival.

Shows and exhibitions take place throughout the month of March. Both the site of the festival and its program alternate each year: in even-numbered years, San José hosts the festival and invites international submissions; in odd-numbered years, a city outside the capital coordinates a plan of events that exclusively features Costa Rican artists.

CONTACTS:
Festival de las Artes
Tercer Piso
Teatro Popular Melico Salazar
San José 8569-1000 Costa Rica
www.festivaldelasartescostarica.com

◆ 0638 ◆ Côte d'Ivoire Independence Day
August 7

Côte d'Ivoire (Ivory Coast) was granted independence from France on August 7, 1960. It had been a French colony since 1893.

Independence Day is a national holiday in Ivory Coast, celebrated with parades, dancing, and fireworks.

CONTACTS:
Cote d'Ivoire Embassy
3421 Massachusetts Ave. N.W.
Washington, D.C. 20007
202-797-0300

SOURCES:
AnnivHol-2000, p. 203
NatlHolWrld-1968, p. 139

◆ 0639 ◆ Cotton Bowl Game
January 1

This great college football game was inaugurated in 1937 and pits the Southwest Conference champion against another nationally ranked team. The game is preceded by a music festival, an art contest, and a NEW YEAR'S EVE parade of marching bands.

CONTACTS:
AT&T Cotton Bowl Classic
P.O. Box 569420
Dallas, TX 75356
888-792-2695; fax: 214-634-7764
www.attcottonbowl.com

SOURCES:
AmerBkDays-2000, p. 12

◆ 0640 ◆ Country Christmas Lighted Farm Implement Parade
First Saturday of December

Yakima Valley, Wash., has taken a conventional tradition—the Christmas parade—and added an interesting twist. The Country Christmas Lighted Farm Implement Parade, which takes place in the town of Sunnyside, showcases as many as 70 farm vehicles decorated with hundreds—sometimes thousands—of lights. Some people consider the parade the premier lighted parade of the U.S. northwest.

An annual event since 1989, the parade has drawn as many as 25,000 spectators and has been covered by the national media. Entries in the ceremony include tractors, combines, grape pickers, semi-trucks with flatbeds, and even horse-drawn floats.

The parade route starts in downtown Sunnyside and goes 1.5 miles through the downtown area across Yakima Valley Highway. Other activities that accompany the celebration are a breakfast with Santa and Christmas caroling.

Participants and spectators value the event because it preserves the tradition of a rural Christmas celebration and promotes the agricultural heritage of the Yakima Valley.

CONTACTS:
Sunnyside Chamber of Commerce
230 E. Edison
P.O. Box 360
Sunnyside, WA 98944
509-837-5939; fax: 509-837-8015
www.sunnysidechamber.com

◆ 0641 ◆ Country Dionysia
December

Like the HALOA, the Country DIONYSIA was an ancient Greek celebration that was originally a fertility festival with a strong phallic emphasis. Both were observed during the latter part of the month of Poseideon (December), at the time of year when the days were at their shortest. The Country Dionysia, in fact, was not tied to a single date but was celebrated all over Attica on dates that were determined by local custom. Like CHRISTMAS festivities, it was something that everyone—even slaves—participated in. It was also a time for traditional games, particularly *askoliasmos* ("standing on one leg"), which involved trying to stand on top of a goatskin that had been blown up like a beachball and then covered in grease. There were other contests that also entailed standing on one leg and jumping the longest possible distance, or trying to touch the other players with the leg that was held off the ground.

In its earlier days, the Country Dionysia included a simple procession in which someone carried a jar of wine and a vine, someone dragged a he-goat, someone held a wicker basket of raisins, and someone held a phallus. But over time, it became an elaborate event with gold vessels, expensive costumes, and teams of horses.

SOURCES:
FestAth-1977, p. 100
OxClassDict-1970, p. 350

◆ 0642 ◆ Country Music Fan Fair, International
Mid-June

The International Country Music Fan Fair is a country feast of music held over a long weekend in downtown Nashville, Tenn., also known as "Music City, U.S.A." and the home of the Grand Ole Opry. The 20th anniversary of the Fan Fair was celebrated in 1991 with a "grand ole party" attended by country music's brightest stars. Yearly attractions include stage shows and concerts, autograph-and-picture-taking sessions with big-name stars, some 300 booths and exhibits, fan-club banquet dinners, and a celebrity auction that gives bidders a chance to buy such items as Junior Sample's overalls from TV's "Hee Haw" or Dolly Parton's boots.

The Grand Ole Opry was founded by George Dewey Hay, who was called "the Solemn Ole Judge," and began weekly radio broadcasts from Nashville in 1925. The music developed from ballads of rural laborers in the 1920s through the string bands and cowboy music of the 1930s into honky-tonk and rockabilly music after World War II. In 1941, the Opry was staged live at the Ryman Auditorium in Nashville, and in

1974 it moved to Opryland U.S.A. This all led to the Fan Fair, which is billed as "The Closest Thing to Hillbilly Heaven."

CONTACTS:
CMA Music Festival, Dept. T
P.O. Box 24480
Nashville, TN 37202
800-262-3378
www.fanfair.com

SOURCES:
GdUSFest-1984, p. 178
MusFestAmer-1990, p. 251

♦ 0643 ♦ Cow, Festival of the
January 25

The **Fiesta de la Vaca** takes place in the village of San Pablo de los Montes, in the Spanish province of Toledo, on St. Paul's Day. While the religious procession and mass that are a traditional part of the observance of the feast of San Pablo are going on, a group of young men form a counter-procession in the opposite direction. One of them plays the role of the cow, *La Vaca*, while another is dressed as Mother Sow, *Madre Cochina*. A third is dressed as a shepherd, and there are others ringing cow bells. Every time the group passes the image of the saint, they call out, "Here goes the cow!"

After the mass is over, the mayor and the town councilmen follow the priest to the town hall for the *correr de la Vaca*, or Race of the Cow. La Vaca and the rest of the young men in the group run from the church to the town hall, La Vaca menacing the spectators with his horns. After the Cow arrives at the town hall, the young men are greeted by the mayor, and a celebration with wine follows. Everyone goes home when the church bells ring at noon.

It is believed that the Festival of the Cow is the remnant of a pagan festival and that it survived in opposition to the Christian festivities. Today, however, the two exist quite peacefully side by side.

CONTACTS:
Tourist Office of Spain
666 Fifth Ave., 35th Fl.
New York, NY 10103
212-265-8822; fax: 212-265-8864
www.okspain.org

SOURCES:
DictFolkMyth-1984, p. 1063

♦ 0644 ♦ Cow Fights
March or April and September or October

Each spring the winner of the cow battles, or **Kuhkämpfe**, held in the canton of Valais, Switzerland, is crowned Queen Cow of the village herds. A championship tournament is held in September or October in Martigny's amphitheater after the cows are herded down the mountains for the winter (*see* ALMABTRIEB). The cow fights began in the 1920s in Martigny, and today crowds fill the streets for the event. Refreshments of choice include wine and sausages, but no beef. The Queen

Cow is adorned with a flower garland between her horns and a large bell hanging from a decorated collar. The calf of a Queen Cow can fetch up to 10 times the price of a regular calf.

The term "cow fights" is a bit misleading, however; as a rule, cows don't often exhibit much aggressive behavior, though their owners do. Much of the event consists of cows standing around, grazing, drooling, or even attempting to step out of the fighting arena. Sometimes, though, some cows can be provoked into pushing another cow, letting loose with some barbarous mooing, or—on momentous occasions—butting heads. A group of animal rights activists from Austria descended on the 1993 Fights, but dropped their protest when they witnessed what actually goes on.

See also ALPAUFZUG

CONTACTS:
Valais Tourisme
Rue Pre-Fleuri 6
Sion, 1951 Switzerland
41-27-327-3570; fax: 41-27-327-3571
www.valais.ch/en/welcome.cfm

SOURCES:
FestWestEur-1958, p. 228

♦ 0645 ♦ Cow Parade
Varies

The Cow Parade is the world's largest public art exhibition. Since its inception in 1999, the Cow Parade has made appearances in cities all over the world, including Sydney, Auckland, Tokyo, Moscow, Istanbul, Warsaw, Copenhagen, Barcelona, Paris, Buenos Aires, Rio de Janeiro, and Mexico City, as well as over a dozen locations in the U.S.

In each location, the event revolves around fiberglass statues of cows. The undecorated figures are turned over to local artists who then adorn the cows in creative ways. Their designs are frequently based on themes and events with special significance to their locality. After the artists have completed the work on the cows, the statues are displayed in various public locations around the host city. The exhibition continues for several weeks, after which the statues are auctioned off, with proceeds benefiting charities designated by local organizers of the Cow Parade. Besides being a means to raise money for charitable causes, the Cow Parade is meant to bring art to the masses. The cow statues may not represent high art, but they are highly accessible and demonstrate that art can be playful as well as serious.

Although there are some variations, the cows used are usually those created by Pascal Knapp, a Swiss sculptor. The cow was chosen as a subject because of its status as an animal that is known and valued around the world. Knapp designed three cows to be used in the competitions: a standing cow, a grazing cow, and a cow lying at rest.

Since its first staging in 1999, the Cow Parade has grown dramatically. New artists are challenged and inspired by the work of previous entrants. More than 3,000 cows have been decorated, and they have been viewed by more than 100 million people. Through the Cow Parade, millions of dollars have been raised for charities; in Chicago's auction in 1999, approximately $3 million was raised for local charities, with the average price of a cow being about $25,000. Miniature replicas of the cows have also become valued collector's items.

CONTACTS:
Cow Parade
860-561-0000
www.cowparade.com

♦ 0646 ♦ **Cowboy Poetry Gathering, National**
Last week in January

The National Cowboy Poetry Gathering is a celebration of the old tradition of cowboy poetry—and of other cowboy art—in the buckaroo town of Elko, Nev.

Poetry by cowboys has a long history; cowboys traditionally recited poetry as they rode on cattle drives, but it was a private, little-known custom. A poem by Allen McCanless published in 1885 has these lines:

My ceiling the sky, my carpet the grass,
My music the lowing of herds as they pass
My books are the brooks, my sermons the stones,
My parson's a wolf on a pulpit of bones…

The gathering, which began in 1985 with about 50 working cowboys, has become a six-day affair that now includes folk-music concerts, western dances, exhibits of cowboy gear, and workshops not only on writing but also on such topics as horse-hair braiding and photography. In 1992, the Hispanic *vaquero* (cowboy) was honored with performances and exhibits. Poetry remains the heart of the festival, and the poets—all working ranch people—include men, women, and children as young as six or eight. The poetry includes doggerel and limericks, but is mostly in ballad form with narratives like those of Rudyard Kipling's.

Close to 300 cowboys, cowgirls, and ranchers participate, and between 6,000 and 8,000 people from all over the world attend the various events. Tickets go on sale in October and are instant sell-outs. The gathering has spawned other cowboy-poetry festivals throughout the West (*see also* DAKOTA COWBOY POETRY GATHERING).

Hal Cannon, director of the Western Folklore Center in Salt Lake City, was the force behind the first gathering, and the Center still sponsors it. The goals of the gathering are to represent the voices of working ranch people through their poetry, music, and folklife; to promote a dialogue between urban and rural people of the American West; and to nurture understanding between pastoral peoples throughout the world. The Center provides a live webcast of events from the Elko Convention Center Auditorium.

CONTACTS:
Western Folklife Center
501 Railroad St.

Elko, NV 89801
775-738-7508; fax: 775-738-2900
www.westernfolklife.org

♦ 0647 ♦ **Craftsmen's Fair**
One week in early August

Although craft fairs can be found all over New England during the summer months, the Craftsmen's Fair at Mt. Sunapee Resort in Newbury, N.H., is considered to be the oldest continuously held craft fair, dating back to 1934. The fair features more than 200 craftspeople who sell their work and display their skills through demonstrations in such diverse areas as decoy carving, printmaking, weaving and spinning, basket making, embroidering, pipe making, and blacksmithing. Visitors to the **League of New Hampshire Craftsmen's Fair** can buy clothing, pottery, leaded glass, lampshades, character dolls, marionettes, jewelry, blown glass, leather goods, and just about any other craft they can imagine. There is also a juried craft exhibit, which is open only to members of the League.

CONTACTS:
League of New Hampshire Craftsmen
205 N. Main St.
Concord, NH 03301
603-224-3375; fax: 603-225-8452
www.nhcrafts.org

SOURCES:
GdUSFest-1984, p. 117

♦ 0648 ♦ **Cranberry Day Festival**
Second Tuesday in October

Wampanoag Indians on Martha's Vineyard and Cape Cod, Massachusetts, celebrate Cranberry Day, their most significant annual holiday, on the second Tuesday in October. The tribe cultivates 200 acres of wild cranberries. In earlier times, this festival lasted several days as people harvested the cranberries and used them in festive dishes. These days, children get the day off from school to join the day's activities, which include picking cranberries, a lunch-time bonfire during which stories of previous Cranberry Days and other community legends are told, and a celebration in the evening with dancing, singing, and a huge potluck meal.

CONTACTS:
Wampanoag Tribe of Gay Head
20 Black Brook Rd.
Aquinnah, MA 02535
508-645-9265; fax: 508-645-3790
www.wampanoagtribe.net

SOURCES:
EndurHarv-1995, p. 48

♦ 0649 ♦ **Cranberry Harvest Festival**
October, Columbus Day weekend

Also known as the **Massachusetts Cranberry Festival**, this annual event has celebrated the harvesting of cranberries in

South Carver, Massachusetts, since 1949. The idea for the festival came from Ellis D. Atwood, founder of the Edaville Railroad, and Robert Rich of Ocean Spray Cranberries. Rides through the cranberry bogs on the old Edaville steam train are still a popular festival attraction, as are the cranberry-baking and pie-eating contests, the crowning of the Cranberry Queen, and musical and other performances. The highlight of the festival, of course, is the harvesting of the cranberries themselves, which are a traditional part of the American and Canadian THANKSGIVING feasts.

CONTACTS:
Cape Cod Cranberry Growers' Association
3203 Cranberry Hwy., Ste. B
East Wareham, MA 02538
508-759-1041
www.cranberries.org

♦ 0650 ♦ **Crandall (Prudence) Day**
September, Saturday of Labor Day weekend

The official celebration of Prudence Crandall Day in Canterbury, Connecticut, only dates back to 1987, but Crandall herself has been recognized for some time as a pioneer in the education of young African-American girls. Born in 1803 in Hopkinton, Rhode Island, and educated at the Friends' School in Providence, she established a private academy for girls in Canterbury in 1831. Although her school was widely recognized as one of the state's best, she lost many of her white patrons when she admitted a young African-American girl. Rather than bow to social pressure, she opened another school for "young ladies and little misses of colour"—an act for which she was socially ostracized.

Eventually the Connecticut legislature passed a Black Law (repealed in 1838), which prohibited setting up schools for nonresident African Americans in any Connecticut city or town without the local authorities' approval. Crandall ignored the new law and was arrested, tried, and convicted. Although the verdict was reversed by the court of appeals in July 1834, this only served to strengthen the opposition of the people of Canterbury. Crandall moved to Illinois later that year with her husband, a Baptist clergyman. In a belated attempt to make amends, Connecticut provided Crandall with an annuity. She died in Kansas in 1890. In 1995 the state legislature proclaimed her the official state heroine.

Prudence Crandall Day events include craft demonstrations from the 1830s, period children's games, and at least one activity directly relating to Crandall herself. One year, for example, an actor portraying Crandall gave an interpretation of her character. Most of the festival events are held at the Prudence Crandall Museum, located in the house where Crandall lived and taught.

CONTACTS:
Prudence Crandall Museum
Routes 14 & 169
P.O. Box 58
Canterbury, CT 06331
860-546-9916
www.chc.state.ct.us

CT Commission on Culture & Tourism, State of Connecticut
One Constitution Plaza, 2nd Fl.
Hartford, CT 06103
860-256-2800; fax: 860-256-2811
www.cultureandtourism.org

♦ 0651 ♦ **Crane Watch**
March-April

There are actually two events in Nebraska that celebrate the world's largest concentration of sandhill cranes: the Crane Watch in Wood River and **Wings Over the Platte** in Grand Island. Both take place during a six-week period in March and April when 70 percent of the world's sandhill cranes—over a half million birds—crowd a 150-mile stretch of the Platte River between Grand Island and Sutherland. Arriving from west Texas, New Mexico, southern California, and central Mexico, the cranes rest and feed in the area before continuing their migration to Canada and Alaska.

The Crane Meadows Nature Center serves as an information center for the many visitors who come to see the cranes, and there are guided tours to the most advantageous viewing areas. Other events associated with the Crane Watch include wildlife displays, outdoor photo seminars, and nature workshops.

CONTACTS:
Grand Island/Hall County Convention and Visitors Bureau
309 W. 2nd St.
P.O. Box 1486
Grand Island, NE 68802
800-658-3178 or 308-382-4400
www.visitgrandisland.com

Crane Meadows Nature Center
9325 S. Alda Rd.
Wood River, NE 68883
308-382-1820
www.nebraskabeautiful.com

Northern Prairie Wildlife Research Center
Operation Crane Watch
8711 37th St. S.E.
Jamestown, ND 58401
701-253-5500; fax: 701-253-5553
www.npwrc.usgs.gov

♦ 0652 ♦ **Crawfish Festival (Breaux Bridge, Louisiana)**
First weekend in May

The Crawfish Festival is a time to celebrate and eat the small crustaceans (also called crayfish and crawdads) in Breaux Bridge, La., a small Cajun village. Since 1959, by act of the state legislature, the village has been officially called the "Crawfish Capital of the World."

Crawfish is related to the lobster, and local folk say the crawfish is really the Acadian lobster that followed them to the bayou lands of southern Louisiana. The Cajuns are descendants of the French Canadians whom the British drove from the colony of Acadia (now Nova Scotia) in the 18th century. They still speak their own patois, a combination of French forms with words borrowed from American Indian, African,

Spanish, English, and other languages; they often still live in small, self-contained communities.

The festival is a three-day event, featuring crawfish races (on a special circular table, with betting allowed), a parade, Cajun music night and day, a crawfish cookoff, crawfish races, and a World Championship Crawfish-Eating Contest. In the latter, contestants start out with a dishpan of five pounds of crawfish and eat for two hours. The prize is a trophy and crawfish to take home. As many as 100,000 visitors come to this village of 7,600 for the festival.

CONTACTS:
Breaux Bridge Crawfish Festival Association
P.O. Box 25
Breaux Bridge, LA 70517
337-332-6655; fax: 337-332-5917
www.bbcrawfest.com

Louisiana Travel Promotion Association
1165 S. Foster Dr.
Baton Rouge, LA 70806
225-346-1857; fax: 225-336-4154
www.louisianatravel.com

SOURCES:
GdUSFest-1984, p. 66

♦ 0653 ♦ **Crazy Horse Ride and Veterans' Powwow**
Early June

The Crazy Horse Ride and Veterans' Powwow are annual events held in early June by members of the Oglala Lakota Sioux tribe of the Pine Ridge Indian Reservation in Pine Ridge, S.D. In 2007, the Veterans' Powwow celebrated its 22nd year of honoring all armed-service veterans with drumming, dancing, and singing. A three- or four-day day event, it also features a Saturday parade and daily specials and tributes to veterans and soldiers in active duty.

In 1998, Charles Brewer founded the Crazy Horse Ride, to take place just before the Veterans' Powwow, to honor the great Oglala Lakota Sioux warrior chief, Crazy Horse. Brewer also wanted to express gratitude for warrior culture and to pay tribute to all war veterans. The four-day horse ride begins in Fort Robinson, Nebraska, where Crazy Horse was killed in 1877, and it terminates in Pine Ridge at the grounds of the Veterans' Powwow. About 200 people typically take part in the ride, many of them children and young people from the Pine Ridge Indian reservation. The powwow and ride are open to all.

CONTACTS:
Pine Ridge Indian Reservation
P.O. Box 150
Pine Ridge, SD 57770
605-867-5762

♦ 0654 ♦ **Cree Walking-Out Ceremony**
Early spring

Among Cree Indians in Canada, it is customary for small children to be carried when they go outdoors until they are initiated through the Walking-Out Ceremony. The springtime ceremony provides an occasion for the first time a child walks on his or her own (or with a little adult help) outside, signifying movement toward adulthood and greater responsibility. The toddlers' families and friends assemble in a special tent. The children are dressed in traditional costumes and, in some places, are given toy tools and utensils, representing the real tools and utensils they eventually will use. For the walking out, each child walks through the doorway and proceeds about 20 feet to a tree, circles the tree, then returns to the tent, where a huge fuss is made over each child's new accomplishment. After all the toddlers have completed the walk, everyone enjoys a feast.

CONTACTS:
Tourist Office, Ouje Bougoumou Cree Nation
203 Opemiska Meskino
P.O. Box 131
Ouje-Bougoumou, QC G0W 3C0 Canada
418-745-3905; fax: 418-745-3544
www.ouje.ca

SOURCES:
EndurHarv-1995, p. 200

♦ 0655 ♦ **Creek Green Corn Ceremony**
Late summer

This ceremony is a religious harvest festival, not open to the public, held in late summer by the Muskogee-Creek Indians on the ceremonial grounds in Okmulgee, Oklahoma. Each tribal group conducts its own Green Corn Ceremony on one of 12 such Creek ceremonial grounds in the state.

The dances for the ceremony are performed not to the beat of drums, but to the rhythm of turtle and gourd rattles. Women are designated "shell-shakers," and they dance in groups of four with shells (or sometimes today with juice cans filled with pebbles) around their ankles. Children are included in ceremonies from the earliest age: women dancers with babies carry them into the ceremonial circle. One dance, known as the ribbon dance, honors women and is performed only by women and girls.

Other elements of the festival are stickball games and cleansing ceremonies, but the affair is essentially religious. To worship the Great Spirit, Creeks perform rituals relating to wind, fire, water, and earth.

Seminoles and Yuchis in Oklahoma also celebrate the Green Corn. In some ceremonies participants purge themselves with emetics and submit to ceremonial scratching on their legs and arms.

SOURCES:
EncyNatAmerRel-2001, p. 108
EncyRel-1987, vol. 4, p. 467

♦ 0656 ♦ **Cricket World Cup**
Varies

Held every four years, the Cricket World Cup is the premier contest in the sport of cricket, a bat-and-ball sport that originated in England. A series of qualification tournaments are played before the World Cup finals, during which teams from 16 nations square off to determine the world champion. The host country or region for each finals tournament is determined by the sport's governing body, the International Cricket Council (ICC).

Although the sport is centuries old, the tournament itself has only existed since 1975. Around the time of the World Cup's inception, the cricket community was facing pressure to expand its membership, which had previously consisted of a handful of present and former countries of the British Commonwealth. The ICC responded by creating a different kind of membership status for new competitors. By 2007, the ICC had designated six slots in the World Cup Finals for these new teams—the other 10 were reserved for the teams of the old guard, known to cricket fans as Test-playing countries.

Over the course of the first nine tournaments, played between 1975 and 2007, Australia dominated the competition, garnering a World Cup trophy in 1987 and later three straight consecutive titles between 1999 and 2007.

CONTACTS:
International Cricket Council
P.O. Box 500070
Dubai, United Arab Emirates
icc-cricket.yahoo.net

♦ 0657 ♦ **Croatia Anti-Fascist Resistance Day (Anti-Fascism Day)**
June 22

This holiday in Croatia, also called **Anti-Fascism Day**, dates back to the Second World War. After Nazi Germany invaded and conquered Yugoslavia in 1941, Croatia became a German puppet state under a government of Croatian fascists, called the Usta e. One of the resistance groups that sprang up to oppose the fascist government was called the Partisans. It was headed by a half-Croatian Communist leader called Tito (his real name was Josip Broz), who later appointed himself president for life of Yugoslavia.

Anti-Fascist Resistance Day is a national holiday in Croatia. Like most warm weather holidays in the country, it is celebrated with outdoor barbeques and fireworks.

CONTACTS:
Embassy of Croatia
2343 Massachusetts Ave. N.W.
Washington, D.C. 20008
202-588-8497; fax: 202-234-2363
croatiaemb.org

♦ 0658 ♦ **Croatia Independence Day**
October 8

This holiday is celebrated in Croatia to mark the day in 1991 that the Croatian Parliament voted to cut constitutional ties with Yugoslavia. The Croatians had declared their independence three months earlier, on June 25 (CROATIA STATEHOOD DAY), but a three-month moratorium was placed on imple-

mentation of the decision to give European negotiators a chance to broker an agreement. Those talks failed, and Croatia proceeded with its plan for independence.

Offices, businesses, and schools in Croatia are closed on Independence Day.

CONTACTS:
Embassy of Croatia
2343 Massachusetts Ave. N.W.
Washington, D.C. 20008
202-588-8497; fax: 202-234-2363
croatiaemb.org

Croatian National Tourist Board
Iblerov trg 10/IV
10000 Zagreb
Croatia
www.croatia.hr/English/Home/Naslovna.aspx

♦ 0659 ♦ **Croatia Statehood Day**
June 25

Croatians mark this national holiday to commemorate the country's declaration of independence from Yugoslavia on June 25, 1991. This holiday is distinct from the country's Independence Day on October 8, when the implementation of the declaration went into effect.

Offices, businesses, and schools are closed in Croatia on Statehood Day. Wreaths are laid and candles lit at sites of fallen soldiers, including the graves of national heroes. Past celebrations have included a ceremonial line-up of military troops in the central square of the country's capital, Zagreb, and speeches by the country's leaders, including the president.

CONTACTS:
Embassy of Croatia
2343 Massachusetts Ave. N.W.
Washington, D.C. 20008
202-588-8497; fax: 202-234-2363
croatiaemb.org

Croatian National Tourist Board
Iblerov trg 10/IV
10000 Zagreb
Croatia
www.croatia.hr/English/Home/Naslovna.aspx

♦ 0660 ♦ **Croatia Victory and Homeland Thanksgiving Day**
August 5

On this date in 1995 the Croatian Army defeated Serbian forces at the city of Knin in a decisive battle called Operation Storm. The victory enabled Croatia to regain control of the Serbian-declared breakaway Republic of Serbian Krajina.

The main celebration of this national holiday takes place in Knin, where thousands gather to watch a parade and to listen to speeches by the country's leaders. Church bells toll, and wreaths are laid in honor of those who died in the war. The national flag is hoisted on top of the medieval fortress overlooking southern Knin as part of the celebration.

CONTACTS:
Embassy of Croatia
2343 Massachusetts Ave. N.W.
Washington, D.C. 20008
202-588-8497; fax: 202-234-2363
croatiaemb.org

Croatian National Tourist Board
Iblerov trg 10/IV
10000 Zagreb
Croatia
www.croatia.hr/English/Home/Naslovna.aspx

♦ 0661 ♦ **Crom Dubh Sunday**
Last Sunday in July

Crom Dubh was an ancient Celtic god believed to live near the town of Cloghane in County Kerry. During the festival of LUGHNASADH, August 1, people would go up to nearby Mount Brandon to pick berries, then join the festivities in Cloghane at the foot of the mountain. The mountain was named for ST. BRENDAN, who is said to have converted Crom Dubh to Christianity. Thereafter the trek up Mount Brandon became a Christian pilgrimage site.

Today Cloghane hosts a revived Lughnasadh festival over the last weekend in July. In addition to the pilgrimage up Mount Brandon, there are traditional musical and dance performances, poetry readings, sheep-shearing events, boat races, and many other events.

See also REEK SUNDAY

CONTACTS:
Dingle Peninsula Tourism
Comharchumann Turasoireachta Chorca Dhuibhne
Dingle, County Kerry Ireland
353-66-9151188; fax: 353-66-9151270
www.dingle-peninsula.ie

♦ 0662 ♦ **Cromwell's Day**
September 3

As a British general, Puritan statesman, and Lord Protector of England from 1653-58, Oliver Cromwell is remembered today more for his actions as a general and a statesman than for his efforts within the narrow field of Puritanism. Each year the Cromwell Association in England holds a special service near Cromwell's statue outside the Houses of Parliament on September 3. The date is particularly appropriate. It was on this day in 1650 that Cromwell won the battle of Dunbar, inflicting 3,000 casualties and taking 10,000 prisoners at a cost of only 20 British lives. It was on the same day a year later that he won a decisive victory at the battle of Worcester against the Scots. And it was also the day on which he died.

CONTACTS:
Cromwell Association
190 Cemetery Rd.
Scunthorpe, North Lincolnshire DN16 1NU United Kingdom
www.olivercromwell.org

SOURCES:
BkDays-1864, vol. II, p. 308

DictDays-1988, p. 24
OxYear-1999, p. 360

♦ 0663 ♦ **Cronia (Kronia)**
Midsummer

In Greek mythology, Cronus (or Kronos) was lord of the universe before the Olympian gods took power. He was the son of Uranus, whom he eventually castrated with a sickle given to him by his mother, Gaea. Once he succeeded his father as ruler of the universe, his reign was so peaceful it was known as the Golden Age. Because he had been warned that one of his children would eventually overthrow him, Cronus swallowed his sons as they were born. But the youngest son, Zeus, managed to escape this fate and was the victor in a 10-year war against his father and the other Titan gods.

The only important festival held in honor of Cronus in classical times was the Cronia, held at Athens, Rhodes, and Thebes in midsummer and resembling the Roman SATURNALIA in terms of the unrestrained behavior that accompanied it. Some say that when Cronus was defeated by Zeus, he fled to the west and established another Golden Age in Rome, where he was known as Saturn.

Cronus is usually depicted holding a curved object, perhaps the sickle he used to castrate Uranus. After the defeat of Cronus, the universe was divided among his three sons: Zeus ruled the sky, Hades the underworld, and Poseidon the sea.

SOURCES:
DictFolkMyth-1984, p. 263
NewCentClassHandbk-1962, p. 340

♦ 0664 ♦ **Crop Over**
Last three weeks in July to first Monday in August

This harvest festival in Barbados was originally celebrated in the 1800s by slaves at the end of the sugar-cane harvest. A procession of carts and animals decorated with flowers would bring the last load of cane to the plantation owner, who would then provide a feast for the laborers. One of the carts carried an effigy known as Mr. Harding, made from sugar-cane refuse and dressed in a black coat, top hat, and mask. The effigy represented the cruel gangdrivers and symbolized the hard times that lay ahead for the laborers until the next crop.

Today, Crop Over is a civic celebration, which was revived in 1974. It takes place during the last three weeks of July and usually ends on the first Monday in August. There are historical displays, craft shows, fairs, cane-cutting contests, open-air concerts, calypso music and dancing, and "stick licking"—a self-defense sport similar to fencing. By the last weekend of the festival, the celebration moves to the island's capital, Bridgetown, which is transformed into a huge open-air bazaar where people can shop and listen to live bands.

Monday is the finale, known as the **Kadooment**—a public holiday—which includes the judging of costumed bands at the National Stadium and a grand calypso procession.

CONTACTS:
Barbados Tourism Authority
800 Second Ave., 2nd Fl.
New York, NY 10017
800-221-9831 or 212-986-6516; fax: 212-573-9850
www.barbados.org

SOURCES:
FolkWrldHol-1999, p. 521
GdWrldFest-1985, p. 17

◆ 0665 ◆ Crosses, Festival of the (Fiesta de las Cruces)
Late April

The Mayas of Quintana Roo, Mexico, celebrate the Fiesta of the Patron Crosses in late April. Although its origins are not fully understood, the festival's main feature is an unusual dance or pantomime known as *okoztah-pol*. Festival participants slaughter, cook, and consume a pig. The pig's head is reserved, decorated, and set upon the altar. The following day nine girls, bearing bowls of *pinole* (a powder of toasted corn) and spoons made from agave leaves, circle round a table in the atrium of the church. Two men come into the atrium, one carrying a rattle made from a gourd, the other carrying the decorated head of the pig, which he announces is for sale.

The men barter for the pig's head, while the girls circle nine times in one direction and nine times in the other, keeping track of their circuits by laying cigarettes on the table. The man with the pig's head impersonates the pig, which attempts to escape its captors. The pig impersonater is caught and given to the festival organizer for the price of a hundred cigarettes. Everyone else eats the pinole.

CONTACTS:
Mexico Tourism Board
21 E. 63rd St., Fl. 3
New York, NY 10021
800-446-3942 or 212-821-0314; fax: 212-821-0367
www.visitmexico.com

SOURCES:
FiestaTime-1965, p. 63

◆ 0666 ◆ Crossing of the Delaware
December 25

What is now known as Washington Crossing State Park is the site of the historic event that took place on CHRISTMAS night in 1776, when General George WASHINGTON and the Continental Army crossed the Delaware River just before the Battle of Trenton. **Washington's Crossing of the Delaware** is reenacted on December 25 each year, beginning at Washington Crossing, Pennsylvania (formerly McKonkey's Ferry), and ending on the opposite bank at Washington Crossing, New Jersey.

St. John Terrell, an actor and producer, inaugurated this observance in 1953; he played the part of George Washington himself for a number of years. The costumed actors who cross the river in a specially made Durham boat, similar to those originally used by Washington and his men, try to reproduce the scene exactly as it is depicted in the well-known painting by

Emanual Leutze: Vermont's Green Mountain Boys sit in the bow, Gloucester fishermen from Massachusetts man the oars, and General Washington stands with one foot on the gunwale. The actor who portrays Lieutenant James Monroe carries the 13-star flag seen in the painting—an anachronism, since the flag had not been adopted in 1776.

CONTACTS:
Washington Crossing State Park
355 Washington Crossing-Pennington Rd.
Titusville, NJ 08560
609-737-0623
www.state.nj.us

SOURCES:
AmerBkDays-2000, p. 856

◆ 0667 ◆ Cross-Quarter Days
February 1, May 1, August 1, November 1

The cross-quarter days are the four traditional Celtic festivals celebrated by Neopagans. Along with the QUARTER DAYS, they make up the "Wheel of the Year." These holidays "cross" the quarter days (the solstices and the equinoxes) by falling about halfway in between, thus dividing the year into four parts of approximately three months each. They are also known as IMBOLC (February 1), BELTANE (May 1), LAMMAS (August 1), and SAMHAIN (November 1). These Gregorian calendar dates are less than exact, however; February 6, May 6, August 6, and November 6 actually fall closer to the halfway point between the equinoxes and solstices. (*See also* VERNAL EQUINOX, AUTUMNAL EQUINOX, SUMMER SOLSTICE, WINTER SOLSTICE)

SOURCES:
CelebSols-1993, p. 11
RelHolCal-2004, p. 269

◆ 0668 ◆ Crow Fair
Third weekend in August

The Crow Fair is one of the biggest powwows in the U.S., held since 1918 at Crow Agency, Mont., about 65 miles southeast of Billings. The fair, held Thursday through Sunday, is hosted by the Crow tribe but attracts thousands of other Indians (Peruvian Incas and Alaskan Eskimos were among those attending in 1991), who set up more than 1,000 tepees on the camp grounds.

Dancing at the fair includes not only traditional Plains Indian dances but also the Crow Hop, which is similar to a war dance and is unique to the Crows. It was originally a men's dance, but now women also take part, and all wear clothes of buckskin, feathers, quills, and bells to add a counterpoint to the drum beats.

There are rodeos with cash prizes, horse races, a relay of bareback riding, art exhibits, and demonstrations of such crafts as pipe carving and jewelry designing with turquoise and silver.

CONTACTS:
Crow Tribal Council
P.O. Box 159

Crow Agency, MT 59022
406-638-3700; fax: 406-638-3881
www.crowtribe.com
www.crow-fair.com

SOURCES:
EndurHarv-1995, p. 299
GdUSFest-1984, p. 107
IndianAmer-1989, p. 33

◆ 0669 ◆ Cruft's Dog Show
Three days in February

Charles Cruft was an English salesman who went to France to collect orders for "dog cakes" and so impressed the French dog breeders that they invited him to organize the canine section of the Paris Exhibition of 1878. Eight years later Cruft organized his first dog show in London, which won the patronage of Queen Victoria, an ardent dog lover. Now more than 10,000 dogs representing 150 breeds compete for the Best in Show title, and Cruft's Dog Show is considered to be the largest and most widely attended dog show in Britain.

CONTACTS:
Crufts, The Kennel Club
1-5 Clarges St.
Piccadilly, London W1J 8AB United Kingdom
44-87-0606-6750; fax: 44-20-7518-1058
www.the-kennel-club.org.uk

SOURCES:
EndlessCaval-1964, p. 32
GdWrldFest-1985, p. 94

◆ 0670 ◆ Cuba Liberation Day
January 1; July 26

This national public holiday commemorates the overthrow of the military government of Fulgencio Batista (1901-1973) led by Fidel Castro (b. 1926) that succeeded on January 1, 1959. July 26 is National Day, another public holiday marking the beginning of the revolution Castro led in 1953.

CONTACTS:
Cuban Mission to the U.N.
315 Lexington Ave.
New York, NY 10016
212-689-7215; fax: 212-689-9073
embacuba.cubaminrex.cu

SOURCES:
AnnivHol-2000, pp. 1, 123

◆ 0671 ◆ Cuban Anniversary of the Beginning of the Wars of Independence
October 10

This official holiday in Cuba marks the day in 1868 when Cuba declared its autonomy from Spain. The declaration, called the Grito de Yara, began the Ten Years' War (1868-1878), which was the first of three wars that Cuba fought against Spain for its freedom.

Schools and offices in Cuba are closed on this day.

CONTACTS:
Ministry of Tourism
Calle 19
No. 710
Vedado
Havana, Cuba
www.cubatravel.cu

◆ 0672 ◆ Cuisinières, Fête des la
Early August

With the possible exception of the celebration at CARNIVAL, this is the most colorful event of the year in the French West Indian island of Guadeloupe. The **Women Cooks' Festival** begins with a morning service at the cathedral and a parade of women in Creole dress. The highlight of the festival is the five-hour feast prepared by the dozen or so members of the Association of Women Chefs. The Creole dishes they prepare include *blaffs* (a fish or shellfish dish in a sauce; the name comes from the sound made by the fish as it is plunged into boiling water), *boudins* (sausage), and *crabes farcis* (stuffed crabs). It has been said that "one fistful of the tiny hot peppers that are vital to Creole cooking is generally considered enough to blow up an average European city."

CONTACTS:
French Government Tourist Office
444 Madison Ave., 16th Fl.
New York, NY 10022
800-391-4909 or 212-838-7800; fax: 212-838-7855
www.us.franceguide.com

SOURCES:
GdWrldFest-1985, p. 104

◆ 0673 ◆ Cultural Olympiad
Varies

As the name implies, the Cultural Olympiad is the cultural arm of the OLYMPIC GAMES. When it was first held in 1948, the **Olympic Arts Festival** took place during the games; but since the Barcelona Games in 1992, it has started immediately after the preceding summer or winter Olympic Games end and continued right up until the next Olympics. The 1992 Cultural Olympiad, for example, began immediately after the Seoul Games in 1988. Similarly, the 1996 Cultural Olympiad began in 1993 with a program called "Winterland," a tribute to the 1994 Winter Games host country, Norway. It ended on April 25, 1995, with a gathering of eight NOBEL literature laureates for two days of free-wheeling discussions that covered many topics.

CONTACTS:
Cultural Olympiad
Hellenic Cultural Heritage S.A.
Bouboulinas 42
Athens, 106 82 Greece
30-210-889-4800; fax: 30-210-889-4805
www.london2012.com/get-involved

Commission for Culture and Olympic Education
Chateau de Vidy

Lausanne, 1007 Switzerland
41-21-621-6111; fax: 41-21-621-6216
www.olympic.org

♦ 0674 ♦ Cure Salée
September-October

The Tuareg, a largely nomadic ethnic group found primarily in Algeria, Niger, Mali, and Libya, converge with their camels and cattle on a place known as Ingal just after the first rains of the season arrive. An oasis in the Sahara region of northern Niger, Ingal has palm groves and date plantations and is a favorite grazing ground. The **Salt Festival** takes its name from the salt contained in the new grass, which is essential to the animals' diet. Each Tuareg group participating in the Cure Salée follows a very specific transhumance or seasonal migration route, some traveling hundreds of miles.

In Tamacheq, the language of the Tuareg, the event is known as **Tanekert** or **Tenekert**. The return of the rains is also celebrated with dancing, singing, and camel races.

CONTACTS:
Niger Embassy
2204 R St. N.W.
Washington, D.C. 20008
202-483-4224; fax: 202-483-3169

SOURCES:
BkHolWrld-1986, Sep 11

♦ 0675 ♦ Curium Festival (Kourion Festival)
July

The ancient city of Curium, or Kourion, on the southwest coast of Cyprus, about 12 miles west of Limassol, was buried by volcanic lava in 365. Extensive excavation in recent decades has uncovered a stadium, a basilica and sanctuary of Apollo, and a Roman amphitheater that dates from 50 to 175 C.E. Curium has been the setting for an annual drama festival since 1961. Also known as the **Ancient Greek Drama Festival**, performances are held in the restored amphitheater, which seats 2,400. Both international and Cypriot drama companies participate in the festival, which focuses on the classical Greek dramatists and Shakespeare. There are also moonlight concerts overlooking Episkopi Bay.

CONTACTS:
Cyprus Tourism Organization
13 E. 40th St.
New York, NY 10016
212-683-5280; fax: 212-683-5282
www.cyprusembassy.net

SOURCES:
GdWrldFest-1985, p. 66
IntlThFolk-1979, p. 81

♦ 0676 ♦ Custer Buffalo Roundup and Arts Festival
Weekend nearest last Monday in September or first Monday in October

In South Dakota, buffalo still roam at the Custer State Park in the Black Hills. And every fall, the Old West comes further alive as cowboys, cowgirls, and park staff round up the thundering herd of 1,500 bison and channel the animals into corrals. This annual event helps the park manage and maintain a healthy bison population. Calves are branded and vaccinated, and a number of the animals are sold at auction, which keeps the herd thinned and is an important source of revenue for the park. In addition to the roundup, artists from around the state display their work, and the Custer Chamber of Commerce hosts a chili cook-off.

CONTACTS:
Custer State Park
13329 US. Hwy. 16A
Custer, SD 57730
605-255-4515; fax: 605-225-4460
www.custerstatepark.info

SOURCES:
WildPlanet-1995, p. 596

♦ 0677 ♦ Cynonfardd Eisteddfod
Last Saturday in April

When the Welsh began to emigrate to the United States during the latter part of the 19th century and the early years of the 20th, many were drawn to the coal-mining areas of northeastern Pennsylvania. Among them was a minister, Dr. Thomas C. Edwards, who emigrated in 1870 and established a church society designed to teach English to Welsh children by having them read and memorize music, hymns, songs, poetry, and other literary selections in the tradition of the Welsh EISTEDDFOD. This group became known as the Cynonfardd Literary Society—the Cynon being a stream in South Wales where Edwards had lived as a child. Edwards patterned the society's activities after the Welsh National Eisteddfod, and by 1889 the Cynonfardd Eisteddfod was well established.

Believed to be the oldest continuous Eisteddfod outside of Wales and the only one of its kind in the United States today, the Cynonfardd Eisteddfod was originally held on March 17, ST. PATRICK'S DAY, probably because the coal mines were closed on that day so the Irish miners could celebrate.

Now it is held at the end of April, and the competition is limited to recitations and vocal and instrumental selections. Competitors range in age from under five years old to adults, and the prizes are generally modest—two dollars, for example, for the child under five years who sings the best "Twinkle, Twinkle Little Star," or $50 for the prize-winning senior citizen who sings a Welsh hymn. Literary recitations include selections from the Bible, Henry Wadsworth Longfellow, and other well-known American authors. All performers in both the poetry and music competitions must memorize their selections.

CONTACTS:
Dr. Edwards Memorial Congregational Church
668 Main St.
Edwardsville, PA 18704
570-287-4581

♦ 0678 ♦ **Cyprus Independence Day**
October 1

Cyprus gained independence from Great Britain on August 16, 1960. On that day, British governor Hugh Foot departed amid much ceremony, and Greek Cypriot freedom fighters landed on a plane from Athens with a heroes' welcome. The new Cypriot president, Archbishop Makarios III (1913-1977), gave a speech inspiring Cypriots to improve their new nation.

Independence Day is observed as a public holiday on October 1 each year.

CONTACTS:
Embassy of the Republic of Cyprus
2211 R St. N.W.
Washington, D.C. 20008
202-462-5772; fax: 202-483-6710
www.cyprusembassy.net

SOURCES:
AnnivHol-2000, p. 165
NatlHolWrld-1968, p. 145

♦ 0679 ♦ **Czech Festival, National**
First full weekend in August

The town of Wilber, Nebraska, site of the annual Czech Festival, has been designated by the U.S. Congress as the "Czech Capital of America." Patterned after the well-known Pennsylvania Dutch Festival in Kutztown (*see* KUTZTOWN FESTIVAL), the purpose of the festival is to recognize contributions of Czech immigrants and to foster Czech culture.

Folk dance groups come from all over the state, and local residents wear Czech costumes and dance the *beseda*, or polka, in the streets. Foods prepared by the town's residents and served at the festival include a number of Czech specialties, such as roast duck, sauerkraut, dumplings, and *kolaches* (sweet buns). There is even a kolache-eating contest.

On the second day of the festival, awards are presented for special achievements in promoting both Nebraska and Czech culture.

CONTACTS:
City of Wilber
101 W. 3rd
Wilber, NE 68465
800-494-5237 or 402-821-3233
www.ci.wilber.ne.us

Library of Congress
101 Independence Ave. S.E.
Washington, DC 20540
202-707-5000; fax: 202-707-2076
www.loc.gov

SOURCES:
GdUSFest-1984, p. 112

♦ 0680 ♦ **Czech Statehood Day (St. Wenceslas Day)**
September 28

Czech Statehood Day marks the assassination of Duke Vaclav Wenceslas of Bohemia (western Czech Republic). During his seven-year reign in the 10th century, Wenceslas was known for spreading Christianity among his subjects and helping Prague become the center of trade in central Europe. Wenceslas was murdered by his brother Boleslav on September 28; historians disagree on the precise year, which is thought to be between 929 and 935. Wenceslas was canonized as a saint due to his martyr's death as well as several purported miracles that occurred in the wake of his murder. He is traditionally considered the patron saint of the Czech people. Legends and fictional accounts have sprung up over the centuries about "Good King Wenceslas."

Czech Statehood Day is a public holiday celebrated throughout the Czech Republic. Every year the Czech president awards St. Wenceslas medals to people who contributed to Czech statehood. This ceremony takes place at Prague Castle, where a memorial wreath is placed on the statue of St. Wenceslas. In addition, a pilgrimage takes place at Stara Boleslav, the site of St. Wenceslas' murder.

CONTACTS:
Office of the President of the Czech Republic
Prague Castle
119 08 Prague 1
Prague Czech Republic
www.czech.cz/en

♦ 0681 ♦ **Czechoslovak Independence Day**
October 28

The Republic of Czechoslovakia was founded on October 28, 1918, when the National Committee in Prague proclaimed independence from the Austrian Hapsburg emperors and took over the administration of an independent Czechoslovak state. They were supported in this move by President Woodrow Wilson, who sent a note to the Austro-Hungarian foreign minister urging that the various nationalities of the empire be allowed to determine their own political future.

Independence Day was widely celebrated in Czechoslovakia until the Communists seized power there in 1948 and turned it into a Soviet satellite. But it continued to be recognized in the United States with special banquets, addresses, religious services, cultural programs, and the laying of a wreath at the tomb of President Wilson at the Cathedral of St. Peter and St. Paul (also known as the National Cathedral, or Washington Cathedral) in Washington, D.C.

Communities with large Czech or Slovak populations such as New York City, Los Angeles, Wilber, Nebraska, and Newark, New Jersey, may also mark the occasion.

This day should not be confused with Czechoslovak Liberation Day, a national holiday observed on May 9 to commemorate the country's liberation by the Soviet army and U.S. forces at the end of World War II.

CONTACTS:
Embassy of the Czech Republic
3900 Spring of Freedom St. N.W.

Washington, D.C. 20008
202-274-9103; fax: 202-363-6308
www.mzv.cz/washington

SOURCES:
AnnivHol-2000, p. 179

D

◆ 0682 ◆ D-Day
June 6

The day is also known as **Allied Landing Observances Day**. It marks the start of the Allied invasion of occupied France in 1944, which led to the final defeat of Hitler's Germany the following May. The assault, led by U.S. Gen. Dwight D. Eisenhower, was carried out by airborne forces and the greatest armada the world had ever known. About 3,000 ships transported 130,000 British, Canadian, and American troops across the English Channel to land on the beaches of Normandy, which are known historically by their invasion code names: Utah Beach, Omaha Beach, Gold Beach, Juno Beach, Sword Beach.

Airborne troops began parachuting into Normandy at 15 minutes past midnight on June 6, and Landing Craft Transports plowed through the surf to spill troops onto the beaches starting at 6:30 A.M. About 10,000 troops were killed or wounded that day. Each year, simple ceremonies at the Normandy cemeteries commemorate the men who fell.

CONTACTS:
Normandy Tourist Board
14, rue Charles Corbeau
Evreux, 27000 France
33-2-3233-7900; fax: 33-2-3231-1904
www.normandie-tourisme.fr/normandy-tourism-109-2.html

National World War II Museum
945 Magazine St.
New Orleans, LA 70130
504-527-6012; fax: 504-527-6088
www.ddaymuseum.org

SOURCES:
AmerBkDays-2000, p. 422
AnnivHol-2000, p. 97
DictDays-1988, p. 29

◆ 0683 ◆ Dae, Feasts of
December-January, April-May, May-June; 1st, 8th, 15th, and 23rd of Dae, the 10th Zoroastrian month

The Feasts of Dae occur during the month of Dae on the four days that are ruled by Dae, which is the name for the creator aspect of Ahura Mazda, the Wise Lord and primary deity of the Zoroastrian religion. Because there are four days in each month named after and dedicated to the Creator—the 1st, 8th, 15th, and 23rd—there are four name-day feasts in the month of Dae where the same *yazata*, or spiritual being, presides over both the day and the month.

It was on the first of Dae that the king of Persia used to descend from his throne, dressed entirely in white, and suspend the duties of his attendants and make himself available to anyone who wanted to speak to him. He would hold meetings with small landowners and farmers, sharing a meal and reminding them that the continued existence of their culture depended upon each one of them.

The Zoroastrian calendar has 12 months of 30 days each, plus five extra days at the end of the year. Because of discrepancies in the calendars used by widely separated Zoroastrian communities around the world, there are now three different calendars in use, and the Feasts of Dae can fall either in December-January, April-May, or May-June.

Followers of the Zoroastrian religion, which was founded by the prophet Zoroaster (also known as Zarathushtra, believed to have lived around 1200 B.C.E.), today live primarily in Iran and northwestern India, although smaller communities exist in Pakistan, Sri Lanka, Canada, the U.S., England, and Australia.

SOURCES:
RelHolCal-2004, p. 69

◆ 0684 ◆ Daedala
Spring

This is the name given to two festivals held in ancient Boeotia, which was a part of Greece, in honor of the reconciliation of Hera and Zeus. According to the myth, Hera and Zeus quarreled and Hera went away to Euboea and refused to return to his bed. To trick her into coming back and on the advice of Cithaeron, Zeus dressed up a carved oak-trunk to resemble a bride and let it be known that he planned to marry Plataea, the daughter of Asopus. Hera was so angry she tore the clothes from the statue, discovered the deception, and was so pleased that the two were reconciled.

The **Little Daedala**, held every six years, involved going to an ancient oak grove and cutting down trees for images. Every 59 or 60 years the **Great Daedala** was held, and all Boeotia joined in the celebration. All the images that had been collected over the years during the Little Daedala were carried to the top of Mt. Cithaeron, where they were burned on an altar along with sacrifices to Zeus and Hera.

SOURCES:
DictFolkMyth-1984, p. 273
NewCentClassHandbk-1962, p. 356

♦ 0685 ♦ Dahlonega Gold Rush Days
October

Gold Rush Days are a celebratory reminder in Dahlonega, Ga., of the town's heyday as a gold-rush town. The nation's first major gold rush was here in 1828, and the area around Dahlonega boomed; a federal mint built in 1838 operated for 23 years and coined more than $6 million. Mining continued into the beginning of the 20th century, and today visitors can pan for gold at several locations. The name of the town is pronounced dah-LON-a-gah; it is derived from the Cherokee name *Talonega*, meaning "golden." The festival includes arts and crafts exhibits, country cooking, and beard-growing and hog-calling contests.

CONTACTS:
Dahlonega Jaycees
E. Morrison Moore Pkwy.
P.O. Box 774
Dahlonega, GA 30533
706-864-7247
www.dahlonega.org

♦ 0686 ♦ Daimonji Okuribi (Great Bonfire Event)
August 16

In Japan, the belief that the souls of the dead return to earth during the OBON FESTIVAL gave rise to the custom of lighting great bonfires to guide the souls back to heaven after their yearly visit. This custom is known as Daimonji Okuribi, the Great Bonfire Event. In the city of Kyoto, an enormous flammable structure, built in the shape of the Chinese character *dai*, meaning "big," is set on fire on the hill in back of the Zenrinji Temple. The character is 530 feet tall and 510 feet wide, providing a spectacular display for city residents. The festival begins at 8:00 P.M., when the fires are lit. After this, more fires are lit on other mountains nearby. Hotels charge a fee to those who wish to watch the festival from their roofs, thereby insuring a view of all five okuribi. The banks of the Kamogawa River provide another popular viewing area.

According to legend, an apparition of a burning temple once appeared at the foot of the mountain, and this event inspired the yearly bonfires. Similar bonfires are held at Yokote and Hakone on the same night.

CONTACTS:
Kyoto City Tourism & Culture Information
233-5 Daimon-ji-cho, Atarashimachi-dori
Oike-sagaru, Nakagyo-ku

Kyoto, 604-8315 Japan
81-7-5811-6388; fax: 81-7-5813-3250
www.kyotoguide.com

SOURCES:
IllFestJapan-1993, p. 98
JapanFest-1965, p. 180

♦ 0687 ♦ Daimyo Gyoretsu
Third weekend in August

The Daimyo Gyoretsu is the largest parade of the year in Yuzawa, Japan. It commemorates the annual journey of the *daimyo*, or feudal lord, to Edo (present-day Tokyo) during the Tokugawa period (1600-1868). In order to suppress the possibility of unrest, the Edo shogun, or supreme military ruler, would compel the daimyo from all over Japan to make periodic visits to the capital city. Because the daimyo had to be accompanied by a large entourage, these visits were hugely expensive, leaving them with little money left over for plotting a revolution.

The contemporary Daimyo Gyoretsu consists of a lord's parade and a *mikoshi* parade—mikoshi being the elaborately decorated portable shrines to which the gods were believed to descend during the festivals held in their honor. In addition to the 200 costumed figures who march in these two sections of the parade, there are also floats holding dioramas based on Japanese history and mythology. The tail end of the parade consists of a series of trucks decorated with lanterns that carry dancers, kids, and floats with papier-mâché statues. It is far less formal than what precedes it, and the participants usually wear shorts and brightly colored *happi* coats (traditional Japanese short jackets).

The parade starts at 8:00 in the morning and lasts about five hours, although there is a two-hour break at midday. The route varies slightly from year to year, depending on which of Yuzawa's neighborhoods is in charge of running the parade. Other Japanese cities hold similar Daimyo Gyoretsu festivals, including Hakone on November 3 and Sanjo on May 15-16.

CONTACTS:
Japan National Tourist Organization
1 Rockefeller Pl., Ste. 1250
New York, NY 10020
212-757-5640; fax: 212-307-6754
www.japantravelinfo.com

SOURCES:
JapanFest-1965, pp. 152-204
Matsuri-1993, p. 54

♦ 0688 ♦ Dairy Festival
July

The dairy capital of Michigan is appropriately named Elsie in honor of the cow in Borden's ads, and although it has fewer than 1,000 residents, there are 20 working dairy farms in the area. One of them is Green Meadow Farms, which boasts the largest herd of registered Holsteins in the United States.

For three days in July each year since 1986, the town of Elsie serves gallons of ice cream at bargain prices. Green Meadow Farms is open to visitors, and there are competitions in cow milking, ice cream eating, and even milk drinking, with competitors using a baby bottle. The 14-foot-tall fiberglass Holstein in the center of town is a popular place for the festival's 20,000 visitors to have their photographs taken.

CONTACTS:
Village of Elsie
125 W. Main St.
Elsie, MI 48831
989-862-4273; fax: 989-862-5287
www.elsie.org

♦ 0689 ♦ Dakota Cowboy Poetry Gathering
May, Memorial Day weekend

The Dakota Cowboy Poetry Gathering was founded by Bill Lowman, a cowboy poet who had attended a similar event in Nevada in 1985 (*see* COWBOY POETRY GATHERING) and decided that the Badlands of North Dakota should host its own cowboy poetry festival. Two years later the first "Real Cowboy Review" was held in Medora, with 40 poets and musicians participating. The crowds drawn to the event have continued to grow, and the performers often travel long distances to share their poetry, songs, and stories inspired by life on the ranch.

The Medora gathering prides itself on featuring only "the Real Ones"—those cowboys who "have spent a lifetime looking down the top of a cow." It tries to discourage "novelty cowboys, movie cowboys, or rodeo cowboys" who don't really live the life portrayed in their poems. This burgeoning interest in cowboy poetry is largely the result of research done by folklorists who wanted to draw attention to the cowboys' passion for rhyme and tale-spinning and to keep the tradition alive.

CONTACTS:
City of Medora
P.O. Box 418-A
Medora, ND 58645
701-623-4828
www.medorand.com

Library of Congress
101 Independence Ave. S.E.
Washington, DC 20540
202-707-5000; fax: 202-707-2076
www.loc.gov

♦ 0690 ♦ Dalai Lama, Birthday of the
July 6

This celebration is held on July 6 for the birthday of the current Dalai Lama, the spiritual and political head of Tibet. The name Dalai means "ocean" and was given to the ruling lama in the 16th century by the Mongol leader Altan Khan. The title suggests depth of wisdom.

The present Dalai Lama, Tenzin Gyatso (b. 1935), who was enthroned in 1940 at the age of five, is the latest in the line that began in the 14th century. Each Dalai Lama is believed to be the reincarnation of the preceding one, and when a Dalai Lama dies, Tibetan lamas search throughout the country for a child who is his reincarnation.

Tibet had been a sovereign country until 1949, when China invaded eastern Tibet and sporadic warfare followed. In 1959, a popular uprising exploded at Lhasa but was suppressed, and the Dalai Lama and most of his ministers and about 80,000 Tibetans escaped across the Himalayas. The Dalai Lama has lived since then in exile in Dharmsala, India. Today there are some 80,000 Tibetans in India, 30,000 in Nepal, and 3,000 in Bhutan.

The birthday is observed today by exiles in India with incense-burning ceremonies to appease the local spirits, family picnics, and traditional dances and singing. The incense burning is a rite pre-dating Buddhism.

See also UNIVERSAL PRAYER DAY

CONTACTS:
Office of Tibet
Tibet House, 1 Culworth St.
London, NW8 7AF United Kingdom
44-20-7722-5378; fax: 44-20-7722-0362
www.tibet.com

SOURCES:
EncyRel-1987, vol. 4, p. 200
OxDictWrldRel-1997, p. 254

♦ 0691 ♦ Dally in the Alley
Saturday in early September

Dally in the Alley is a one-day visual and performing arts fair that takes place on the Saturday after Labor Day in the North Cass neighborhood of Detroit, Mich. Located in an area with a reputation as a center of creativity and also as a somewhat seedy neighborhood, the Dally began as a community block party and art fair in 1977. The art show expanded into a performing arts festival and moved to its current location in 1982, when it became known as the "Dally in the Alley," the name of an English pub song.

The original festival site was a service alley that dates back to the era when homeowners in the area maintained horses and carriages. Over the years, however, the Dally has expanded beyond the alley proper, taking over neighboring streets with vendor stalls, art displays, and four stages presenting a variety of original music acts throughout the day and night, including rock, techno, hip-hop, folk, country, and jazz artists, among others.

The Dally is sponsored by and benefits the North Cass Community Union, a nonprofit neighborhood organization that supports community preservation issues. Each year more than 30,000 visitors attend the festival, which includes music, a curated art show, poetry and writing workshops, children's activities, food, and refreshments—particularly beer, a beverage closely associated with the founding of the event.

CONTACTS:
Dally in the Alley
4632 Second Ave.

Detroit, MI 48201
dallyinthealley.com

♦ 0692 ♦ **Damba**
August

Observed in August by many people in the Northern and Upper Regions of Ghana, Damba may have been originally an Islamic festival, though its real origins are uncertain. There are two parts to the Damba festival: the Somba Damba, which marks MAWLID AL-NABI, the Prophet Muhammad's birthday, and the Naa Damba, which celebrates the naming of Muhammad. The celebration continues for 10 days, with drumming and crowds of dancers in front of the chief's house every night.

The Damba festival includes everyone in the community. Muslims hold evening prayers every night leading up to the Somba Damba, while others join in singing and dancing. But it is the Naa Damba, or chief's celebration, that is the main event. People recite from the Qur'an as they dance near a cow or bull that will be slaughtered for the following feast.

Afterward everyone congregates in front of the chief's house, dressed up in his or her finest garb. As drummers play, the chief and his entourage emerge from the house. Everyone gathers into two semicircles, leaving a large space in the middle for the dancers, the last of whom will be the chief himself.

A highlight of the festival occurs the next day, when horse-owners decorate their animals and parade them around town, stopping at the homes of friends. Later in the day a final grand procession marks the official end of the Damba festival.

CONTACTS:
Embassy of Ghana
3512 International Dr. N.W.
Washington, D.C. 20008
202-686-4520; fax: 202-686-4527
www.ghanaembassy.org

SOURCES:
FestGhana-1970, p. 57

♦ 0693 ♦ **DanceAfrica**
Late May and early June

DanceAfrica is a festival of dance that takes place annually in New York City during the Memorial Day weekend in late May; it then restages on a somewhat smaller scale during the first weekend in June in Washington, D.C. Founded by choreographer Chuck Davis and headquartered at the Brooklyn Academy of Music, the festival began in 1977 as a means of counteracting the negative stereotypes of African dance presented in film and other media. Davis conceived of the festival as a way to provide a "cultural bridge" showing the range and beauty of traditional African dance and its influence on contemporary American dance forms.

Each DanceAfrica festival features an international cast of dancers and musicians and showcases such forms as African folk dance, Afro-Caribbean fusion, and African-American dance theatre. In addition, the weekend includes African music and film presentations, master classes, and an outdoor marketplace featuring African-themed arts, food, clothing, and crafts.

CONTACTS:
DanceAfrica in New York
Brooklyn Academy of Music
Peter Jay Sharp Bldg.
30 Lafayette Ave.
Brooklyn, NY 11217
718-636-4100
www.bam.org

DanceAfrica in Washington, D.C.
Dance Place
3225 8th St. N.E.
Washington, DC 20017
202-269-1600; fax: 202-269-4103
www.danceplace.org

SOURCES:
AAH-2007, p. 115

♦ 0694 ♦ **Dancing Procession**
Between May 12 and June 15; Whit Tuesday

The **Sprangprocession** in Luxembourg has been held on Whit Tuesday, which falls 52 days after EASTER, since the eighth century. It honors St. Willibrord (St. Wilfred), the patron saint of Luxembourg, whose feast day is celebrated November 7. The dance that is performed by thousands of participants in the procession through the narrow streets of Echternach has remained basically unchanged. It traditionally involved taking three steps forward and two back to the accompaniment of local bands playing the same melody that was played more than 500 years ago. These days so many people participate, the backward steps are eliminated and instead people step to the left, then to the right. The procession ends up in the basilica, where the remains of St. Willibrord (658-739) are buried.

There are a number of legends that attempt to explain the origin of the Dancing Procession. According to one of them, St. Willibrord came to Luxembourg from northern England to convert the people to Christianity. He saved them from a plague by promising that if they subjected themselves to physical punishment, the plague would end. The people danced to the same tune that is played today, hopping up and down until they were completely exhausted and, as promised, the plague disappeared.

Another story is that a crusader returned from the Holy Land to discover that his dead wife's greedy relatives had taken over his property and branded him a murderer. As he was about to be hanged, he asked permission to play one last tune on his violin. The haunting melody mesmerized the onlookers, who started dancing and were unable to stop. The condemned man walked away from the scaffold, and the procession that is held each year is penance for his unjust condemnation.

A more prosaic explanation is that, in the late eighth century, people afflicted with tremors and various kinds of paralysis reported being healed at St. Willibrord's grave. From that time on, people have performed the dance near his grave for protection from illness. In 1999 University of Kiel neurologist Paul Krack, a native of Echternach, published an article examining the tradition's relationship to outbreaks of hysteric chorea (a disorder that causes involuntary movements) and other movement disorders.

CONTACTS:
Luxembourg National Tourist Office, The Luxembourg House
17 Beekman Pl.
New York, NY 10022
212-935-8888; fax: 212-935-5896

SOURCES:
BkHolWrld-1986, Jun 3
FestWestEur-1958, p. 112
GdWrldFest-1985, p. 128

◆ 0695 ◆ Dartmouth Winter Carnival
Weekend in February

The students of Dartmouth College in Hanover, New Hampshire, have been celebrating Winter Carnival since 1910, when they decided to hold their own mini-OLYMPICS to shake off the winter blues. Soon other colleges were invited to join in the athletic events, which included ski jumping and snowshoe races. By the 1920s, there were so many parties and balls associated with the weekend that it was called "The Mardi Gras of the North."

The event became even more popular after it was featured in the 1939 movie *Winter Carnival*. Students from other colleges, some as far away as Florida, came to Hanover to join in the fun, and eventually drunkenness and vandalism became a problem.

Carnival events nowadays are limited to Dartmouth students and their guests. Teams from a dozen or so northeastern colleges and universities compete in Nordic and Alpine skiing, ski jumping, hockey, basketball, gymnastics, and other sports. But the highlight for many is the snow sculpture competition on the Dartmouth green. Because snow has been so scarce in some recent winters, the sculptors sometimes have had to rely on snow trucked in from nearby ski areas, scraped off parking lots, and recycled from skating rinks.

CONTACTS:
Dartmouth College, Student Activities Office
303 Collis Ctr.
Hanover, NH 03755
603-646-3399; fax: 603-646-1386
www.dartmouth.edu

◆ 0696 ◆ Daruma Ichi (Daruma Doll Fair)
Various

Daruma are papier-mâché tumbling dolls that are sold at doll markets held at various times throughout the year. They are symbolic of sturdy character and hard-headedness as well as joy. Custom encourages people to buy dolls that have no eyes painted in. Then the doll owner makes a wish and gives the doll one eye. The other eye is painted in when the wish has been fulfilled.

During the Daruma Ichi held in Takasaki (January 6-7), Tokyo (March 3-4), and other Japanese cities, these dolls are sold in stalls erected on the grounds of shrines or temples. They are similar in shape to the famous Russian "nesting" dolls, and they are often made by farmers as a hobby in their off-hours and sold during the winter months.

CONTACTS:
Japan Information Network, Japan Center for Intercultural
  Communications
2-7-7 Hirakawacho
Chiyodaku
Tokyo, 102-0093 Japan
81-3-3263-5041; fax: 81-3-3230-4107
home.jcic.or.jp/en

SOURCES:
IllFestJapan-1993, p. 138
JapanFest-1965, p. 117

◆ 0697 ◆ Dasa Laksana Parvan (Time of the Ten Characteristics)
August-September; fifth to 13th day of the waxing half of Hindu month of Bhadrapada

Dasa Laksana Parvan is a Jain festival observed by the Digambara, or "sky-clad," sect, which is the dominant sect in southern India. Its members are called "sky-clad" because they believe that total nudity is required of monks; even images of the Jinas or spiritual teachers should not be clothed.

This festival usually falls during the latter part of the rainy season, and it may last 10 days instead of eight. Scripture readings focus on different portions of the holy text describing the 10 characteristics to which Jains aspire: forbearance, gentleness, uprightness, purity, truth, restraint, austerity, renunciation, lack of possession, and chastity. The Svetambara, or "white-clad," Jains—the dominant sect in northern India, which believes that monks and images of the Jinas should be clothed—observe a similar festival, known as PARYUSHANA, just before Dasa Laksana Paryan begins.

SOURCES:
OxDictWrldRel-1997, p. 487
RelHolCal-2004, p. 196

◆ 0698 ◆ Data Ganj Baksh Death Festival
Islamic month of Safar, days 18-19

This festival is an occasion for massive pilgrimages to the Mausoleum of Data Ganj Baksh in Lahore, Pakistan. Data Ganj Baksh, which means "He Who Gives Generously," was the name given to Syed Ali Abdul Hasan Bin Usman Hujwiri (also rendered Ali Hajweri or al-Hujwiri), a scholar and author who lived most of his life in Lahore and died in 1072. He wrote *Kashful Mahjub* (or *Kashf al-mahjub*), the oldest Persian treatise on Sufism. It is a text on the fundamentals of Sufism and it reviews Islamic mysticism, linking each famous master to a particular doctrine. Ali Hujwiri is one of the most popular saints in Pakistan, and every day hundreds of pilgrims pray at his shrine and ask for blessings and favors. On his *urs* (death festival), thousands throng to the shrine for celebratory activities and prayers.

SOURCES:
DictWrldRel-1989, pp. 719, 720
UndIslam-2004, p. 390

♦ 0699 ♦ **Dattatreya Jayanti**
November-December; full moon day of Hindu month of Margasirsa

Dattatreya's birthday is celebrated all over India. One legend has him as the son of Anusuya, an exceptionally devoted and virtuous wife. The wives of Brahma, Vishnu, and Shiva decided to test her virtue by sending their husbands, disguised as beggars, to ask her to give them alms while in the nude. Anusuya avoided the trap by transforming them into babies and suckling them. When her husband, Atri, returned from his morning bath and discovered what had occurred, he turned them into one child with three heads and six hands. The wives begged for their husbands' return, and when Anusuya restored them to their original forms, they blessed Anusuya, Atri, and their son Dattatreya.

On Dattatreya's birthday, Hindus rise early and bathe in sacred streams, fast, and spend the day in worship and prayer. They also meditate on sacred works that include the *Avadhuta Gita* and *Jivanmukta Gita*. Recently, Dattatreya is identified with the triad of Brahma, Vishnu, and Shiva, for it is believed that portions of these deities were incarnated in him. He is usually depicted with three heads and six hands.

SOURCES:
RelHolCal-2004, p. 180

♦ 0700 ♦ **Davis Cup**
November-December

The Davis Cup is the oldest international men's tennis competition, inaugurated in 1900 and credited with drawing world attention to the game. Tennis was then a young sport; the first U.S. national championship games were played in 1881. The competition was fathered by Dwight F. Davis, who was U.S. doubles champion with Harvard teammate Holcombe Ward in 1899-1901. Davis believed international competition would boost the game's popularity and had a 13-inch-high silver bowl crafted by a Boston silversmith; it was to be called the International Lawn Tennis Challenge Trophy but became known as the Davis Cup.

From the first, the championship was open to all nations. The first games, held at the Longwood Cricket Club in Chestnut Hill, Massachusetts, had only two contestants: a British Isles team and the American team (captained by Davis). The Americans won, 3-0. The Brits did better—but still lost—in 1902. In 1903, they won, and it was not until 1913 that the U.S. regained the cup.

There was growing interest in the cup. Four nations competed in 1919, and that number grew to 14 in 1922 and 24 in 1926. From the start, teams have consisted of two singles players and a doubles team. There are five matches—four singles and one doubles. Each match is awarded one point, and the first team to win three points wins the cup. In women's tennis, the Federation Cup, inaugurated in 1963 and played each year in the spring, is considered the equivalent of the Davis Cup.

The United States dominated the Davis Cup in the 1920s, spurred by William T. ("Big Bill") Tilden II, who was a member of the Davis Cup team for 11 years. France won in 1927 and went on to win the next five years up through 1932. Great Britain was a power in the 1930s, and Australia and the United States dominated in the 1940s, 1950s, and 1960s; in the late 1970s and the 1980s the winners had a multi-national flavor. In 1980, Czechoslovakia became the first Communist country to win the Davis Cup. The United States won in 1990, but in 1991, playing in Lyons, France, the French team knocked out the champion U.S. team 3-1 and owned the cup for the first time in 59 years. The French team (led by Guy Forget, Henri Leconte, and coach Yannick Noah) kissed, hugged, leapt over the net, lay down on the court, and danced a conga line. Sweden dominated the 1990s, winning in 1994, 1997, and 1998.

CONTACTS:
International Tennis Federation
Bank Lane
Roehampton
London, SW15 5XZ United Kingdom
44-20-8878-6464; fax: 44-20-8392-4744
www.itftennis.com

The International Tennis Federation
Bank Lane
Roehampton
London, SW15 5XZ United Kingdom
44-20-8878-6464; fax: 44-20-8392-4744
www.daviscup.org

♦ 0701 ♦ **Davis's (Jefferson) Birthday**
First Monday in June

The only president of the Confederate States of America, Jefferson Davis, was captured and imprisoned after the Civil War but never brought to trial. Since he refused to ask the federal government for a pardon, he went to his grave deprived of the rights of citizenship, including all of his former privileges and properties. It wasn't until October 17, 1978, that his citizenship was restored, posthumously, by President Jimmy Carter when he signed an Amnesty Bill designed to "finally set at rest the divisions that threatened to destroy our nation."

Davis's memory is honored by many white southerners in the United States, and his birthday (June 3) is a legal holiday in Alabama and Florida. In Mississippi the observance is combined with MEMORIAL DAY. In Texas it is observed as CONFEDERATE MEMORIAL DAY, a time when the graves of Confederate soldiers are decorated and memorial ceremonies are held.

At Arlington National Cemetery in Virginia, the Confederate Memorial Services are held each year on the Sunday nearest

June 3, and a speaker usually pays tribute to those who died while serving the Confederacy. Another important ceremony is the Massing of the Flags, which is held at the Jefferson Davis Monument in Richmond, Virginia. The flags of the various Southern states are presented in the order in which they seceded from the nation.

SOURCES:
AmerBkDays-2000, pp. 150, 418
AnnivHol-2000, p. 95
DictDays-1988, p. 61

♦ 0702 ♦ **Days of '76**
Last week in July

This celebration held each year in Deadwood, South Dakota, is an attempt to revive the spirit of the gold rush days. It is timed to coincide as closely as possible with the anniversaries of the deaths of "Calamity Jane" Canary (August 1, 1903) and "Wild Bill" Hickok (August 2, 1876), two of Deadwood's most famous residents.

The festivities begin with a Professional Rodeo Cowboys Association rodeo. Then there is a three-mile-long historical parade that includes floats portraying the various stages of, and characters in, Deadwood's history—from the earliest settlers to the coming of industry and tourism. A kids' carnival and a rodeo are in town during the festival, and street dances featuring country music take place Thursday through Saturday night.

A highlight is the reenactment of the capture and trial of Jack McCall, who shot the much-admired U.S. Marshal James Butler "Wild Bill" Hickok in the back, and who was eventually hanged. The shooting, capture, and trial are reenacted every afternoon from Memorial Day to Labor Day.

Visitors can also tour long-abandoned gold mines and Mount Moriah cemetery where Calamity Jane, the famous frontierswoman, Wild Bill Hickok, and the brilliant young minister Henry Weston "Preacher" Smith are buried.

CONTACTS:
Deadwood Chamber of Commerce & Visitors Bureau
767 Main St.
Deadwood, SD 57732
800-999-1876 or 605-578-1876; fax: 605-578-2429
www.deadwood.org

SOURCES:
GdUSFest-1984, p. 172

♦ 0703 ♦ **Daytona 500**
February

The Daytona 500 is the richest of the four biggest NASCAR (National Association for Stock Car Auto Racing) Sprint Cup races (formerly the Winston Cup). It's the final event of Speedweeks at Daytona International Speedway in Daytona Beach, Fla., which lasts more than two weeks. The speedway is a 2.5-mile oval, and racers must complete 200 laps. The all-time champion of the Daytona 500 is Richard Petty, who won seven times (1964, 1966, 1971, 1973, 1974, 1979, and 1981).

The Daytona Speedway, which has a seating capacity of 102,900, has been operating since 1959, but stock-car racing at Daytona dates back to 1936, and car racing has been going on here since the early days of cars. Between 1902 and 1935, 13 automobile speed records were set on the beach by racing greats Barney Oldfield, Sir Henry Segrave, and Sir Malcolm Campbell, who broke existing records five times.

The speedway was the creation of William H. G. (Bill) France, a mechanic and racer who moved to Daytona Beach in 1934 in the heyday of beach racing. He gave up driving to organize and promote races and in 1947 founded NASCAR. He had the idea of building the Daytona track in 1953, but financial and political problems delayed its opening until 1959. When he died in 1992, he was known as the father of stock-car racing.

Today the Speedway presents eight weeks of racing events. Speedweeks starts with a 24-hour endurance race; this race and the 24 Hours of LE MANS (France) are the only two 24-hour races for prototype sports cars in the world.

The stock-car racing world lost one of its legends on February 18, 2001, when seven-time Winston Cup champion Dale Earnhardt, Sr., 49, died from head injuries sustained in a crash during the final lap of the Daytona. His son, Dale, Jr., was in one of two cars ahead of him when he slammed into the wall at about 180 miles per hour in an attempt to overtake Sterling Martin, who was in third place at the time. Michael Waltrip won this particularly dramatic race, which had seen the lead change 49 times and in which an 18-car crash that caused one injury also occurred. Earnhardt characteristically took dangerous risks on the track, earning him such nicknames as "Ironhead" and "Intimidator." Earnhardt's death raised yet more questions about NASCAR race safety; during the 2000 season three drivers died in car wrecks from similar injuries: Adam Petty, grandson of racing star Richard Petty, Kenny Irwin, and Tony Roper.

The "crown jewels" of the NASCAR circuit are the Daytona 500, the WINSTON 500, the COCA-COLA 600, and the SOUTHERN 500.

CONTACTS:
Daytona International Speedway
1801 W. International Speedway Blvd.
Daytona Beach, FL 32114
386-254-2700
www.daytonaintlspeedway.com

National Association for Stock Car Auto Racing
1801 W. International Speedway Blvd.
Daytona Beach, FL 32115
386-253-0611; fax: 386-681-4041
www.nascar.com

♦ 0704 ♦ **DC Black Pride Festival**
Last weekend in May

The D.C. Black Pride Festival is a social, educational, and fundraising festival originating in the African-American lesbian, gay, bisexual, and transgender community of Washington, D.C. The central mission of the festival is to raise awareness of and pride in black lesbians, gays, bisexuals, and transgenders and to support organizations fighting HIV/AIDS and other health issues. The event serves as the model for numerous black pride festivals held throughout the United States.

Held each year since 1991 on the long Memorial Day weekend, the D.C. Black Pride Festival draws about 25,000 to the Washington Convention Center, where displays include a health and wellness fair, as well as specialty merchandise and food vendors. In addition to activities centered in the exhibition hall, entertainment and social events extend throughout the preceding week. Included are a town hall meeting on the state of black gay men's health, workshops on various lifestyle topics, a basketball tournament, and worship services. A fashion show, film festival, comedy showcase, and poetry slam are among the entertainment offerings, and a pageant is held to select Mr. and Ms. D.C. Black Pride. Throughout the festival, various social events offer music, dancing, and refreshments.

CONTACTS:
DC Black Pride
P.O. Box 77071
Washington, D.C. 20013
202-737-5767
www.dcblackpride.org

SOURCES:
AAH-2007, p. 75

♦ 0705 ♦ **DC Caribbean Carnival**
Last full weekend in June

Held annually in Washington, D.C., during the last weekend in June, the D.C. Caribbean Carnival is a colorful pageant celebrating the rich cultural life of the Caribbean region. The festival is organized by the nonprofit D.C. Caribbean Carnival, Inc., which conceived the event as a way to foster appreciation of Caribbean culture and to promote cross-cultural understanding.

Since beginning with nine bands in 1993, the carnival has nearly tripled in size, with groups representing every country in the Caribbean. The festival highlight is the opening-day parade that features more than two dozen calypso and steel drum bands accompanied by thousands of costumed masqueraders representing such themes as "Quest for Gold," "Party Time," and "Angels and Jumbies." The parade originates at the intersection of Georgia Avenue and Missouri Avenue N.W. and ends at Banneker Field, where the site has been transformed into "De Savannah," an international marketplace. Entertainment continues throughout the weekend, and craft and food vendors offer regional arts and cuisine. More than 300,000 people attend each year.

CONTACTS:
DC Caribbean Carnival, Inc.
4809A Georgia Ave. N.W., Ste. 112
Washington, D.C. 20011
202-726-2204; fax: 202-726-8221
www.dccaribbeancarnival.org

Washington, D.C., Convention and Tourism Corporation
901 7th St. N.W., 4th Fl.
Washington, DC 20001-3719
202-789-7000; fax: 202-789-7037
www.washington.org

SOURCES:
AAH-2007, p. 119

♦ 0706 ♦ **Dead, Feast for the**
Annually or semiannually

An Iroquois Indian ceremony, the Feast for the Dead—the **'Ohgiwe**—is an attempt to placate the spirits of the dead. Sometimes the 'ohgiwe was used as a healing ceremony, for it was believed that an offended spirit could cause sickness or loss of sleep. Often it was held in the longhouse in the spring or fall as a communal ceremony.

The ceremony itself consists of two long dances, a ritual during which pieces of cloth are waved back and forth and distributed to all the singers and dancers, and the ceremonial carrying out of the kettle or drum. There are social dances after the feast is over, and a mock-struggle over special cakes that have been prepared for the dead.

SOURCES:
DictFolkMyth-1984, p. 816
EncyNatAmerRel-2001, p. 85
EncyRel-1987, vol. 7, p. 286
HolSymbols-2009, p. 257

♦ 0707 ♦ **Dean (James) Festival**
September

James Dean (1931–1955), the legendary film actor and star of *Rebel Without a Cause*, remains the subject of adulation even decades after his early death in an automobile accident. The star's hometown of Fairmount, Ind., contributes to the ongoing tribute by dedicating an annual four-day festival to the icon.

The festival's origins date back to 1975, the same year the Fairmount Historical Museum was founded. Several notables from the town have their own displays, but the main exhibit pays homage to James Dean. During the event, which is officially called **Museum Days/Remembering James Dean**, thousands of fans survey Dean memorabilia and his personal items.

Additional events take place at locations throughout the town. There are free showings of the star's most celebrated films, a James Dean look-alike contest, fashion shows, and a trivia contest. Another tradition, the James Dean Car Show, has existed since 1980.

CONTACTS:
Fairmount Historical Museum
203 E. Washington St.
Fairmount, IN 469258
765-948-4555
www.jamesdean.com/community/festival/index.htm

♦ 0708 ♦ Decorated Horse, Procession of the
Between May 21 and June 24; Corpus Christi

According to legend, during the Crusades the ship in which the French King Louis IX was traveling and bearing the Eucharist was wrecked on the beach at Brindisi, Puglia province, Italy. The local archbishop salvaged the sacred Host and carried it with him as he rode through the town on a white horse. To commemorate this event, the current archbishop of Brindisi carries the Most Holy Sacrament in a procession that takes place on CORPUS CHRISTI each year. He rides at the head of the procession on a white horse caparisoned in gold, passing through galleries of silk draperies and a constant rain of flowers thrown by spectators. This event is sometimes referred to as the **Procession of the Caparisoned Horse**.

Corpus Christi is celebrated with flowers and colorful processions in other Italian towns and villages as well—those occurring at Genzano and Perugia, Umbria province, being among the more spectacular.

CONTACTS:
Italian Government Tourist Board
630 Fifth Ave., Ste. 1565
New York, NY 10111
212-245-5618; fax: 212-586-9249
www.italiantourism.com

SOURCES:
BkFest-1937, p. 186
FestWestEur-1958, p. 98

♦ 0709 ♦ Deep Sea Fishing Rodeo
Weekend of July 4

This event is the "World's Largest Fishing Rodeo," according to its promoters, and a four-day event staged from Gulfport, Miss. The Mississippi Gulf Coast area is reputed to be one of the world's best natural fish hatcheries, with an abundance of species of fresh-water, salt-water, and deep-sea game fish. The rodeo's fishing waters are the Mississippi Sound of the Gulf of Mexico and the bayous and creeks within a range of 200 miles north of the Mississippi shoreline.

The rodeo began in 1949 and today attracts from 15,000 to 20,000 people and entrants from 48 states. Prizes are awarded for the top weight in 28 categories of fish. Besides fishing, there are also all the peripherals of a festival: arts and crafts exhibits, dances, a midway, fireworks, bands, and the coronation of a Rodeo Queen.

CONTACTS:
Mississippi Deep Sea Fishing Rodeo Inc.
P.O. Box 3957
Gulfport, MS 39505
228-863-2713
www.mississippideepseafishingrodeo.com

♦ 0710 ♦ Defenders' Day
September 12

Defenders' Day, a legal holiday in Maryland, celebrates the anniversary of the battle of North Point. The battle took place near Baltimore on September 12, 1814; two days later, the unsuccessful British attack on Baltimore's Fort McHenry inspired Francis Scott Key to jot down the words of "The Star-Spangled Banner." For this reason the two events are celebrated more or less in conjunction on September 12, a day that is sometimes referred to as **National Anthem Day**.

A 56-foot monument at Calvert and Fayette Streets in Baltimore commemorates the 1814 battle, and the star-shaped Fort McHenry is a national monument and an historic shrine. Defenders' Day is celebrated with a number of patriotic events, including an annual mock bombardment of the fort on the weekend nearest September 12.

CONTACTS:
Fort McHenry National Monument and Historic Shrine
National Park Service
End of E. Fort Ave.
Baltimore, MD 21230
410-962-4290; fax: 410-962-2500
www.nps.gov

Maryland Secretary of State
State House
Annapolis, MD 21401
888-874-0013 or 410-974-5521; fax: 410-974-5190
www.sos.state.md.us

SOURCES:
AmerBkDays-2000, p. 640
AnnivHol-2000, p. 153
DictDays-1988, p. 30

♦ 0711 ♦ Delaware Big House Ceremony
Late October

The Lenape Indians—formerly referred to as Delaware Indians by early European settlers—once lived in what is now New Jersey, southeastern New York, eastern Pennsylvania, Delaware, and parts of western Connecticut, but like many other native peoples, most eventually moved to the western territories. Their faith was known as the Big House Religion, and each autumn the Lenape observed the Big House Ceremony, a 12-day long affair in which members of the tribe would camp around the lodge and celebrate their homecoming. The ceremony included purification rites, a deer hunt, drumming and dancing, and a sacred feast. The Big House was a large log building with doorways positioned facing the east and the west, and was the gathering place for sacred communal observances. The last known Big House Ceremony was held in 1924.

SOURCES:
EncyNatAmerRel-2001, p. 19
EndurHarv-1995, p. 56

♦ 0712 ♦ Democratic People's Republic of Korea Founding Day
September 9

The founding of North Korea (official name: Democratic People's Republic of Korea) on September 9, 1948, is observed throughout the country as a national holiday. The whole of the Korean peninsula (i.e., present-day North and South Korea) was under the control of Japan from 1910 until the end of World War II. When Japan surrendered in August 1945, the U.S.S.R took control of the northern half of the peninsula, while the southern half came under control of the United States. Despite attempts to unify the two regions, by 1948 it was clear that their sharp political differences made reunification impossible. On August 15, 1949, the Republic of Korea was established in the south. Less than a month later, the Democratic People's Republic of Korea, under the leadership of then-Premier Kim Il-Sung, was founded in the North.

Much of the observance of North Korea's founding day centers on adulating Kim Il-Sung, the founding leader. This is true of many of the political holidays in North Korea, reflecting the "cult of personality" that was a facet of Kim's distinctive political philosophy. The main public celebrations take place in the capital city, Pyongyang, and can include such events as government banquets in the late Kim's honor, political meetings, concerts, and displays of song and dance. Officials and citizens also lay flowers before the monuments to Kim in the capital. Similar displays and flower-laying also take place in towns and cities throughout North Korea.

CONTACTS:
Permanent Representative of the Democratic People's Republic of
   Korea to the United Nations
820 Second Ave.
New York, NY 10017
212-972-3105; fax: 212-972-3154
www.korea-dpr.com

♦ 0713 ♦ **Democratic Republic of Congo**
Independence Day
June 30

The Democratic Republic of Congo (formerly Zaire) gained independence from Belgium on this day in 1960. It had been a Belgian colony since 1907, and powerful movements had struggled for self-rule since the 1950s. The people celebrated the first independence day with fireworks and bonfires in the capital city of Léopoldville (now Kinshasa).

CONTACTS:
Embassy of the Democratic Republic of Congo
1800 New Hampshire Ave. N.W.
Washington, D.C. 20009
202-234-7690; fax: 202-234-2609
kinshasa.usembassy.gov

SOURCES:
NatlHolWrld-1968, p. 92

♦ 0714 ♦ **Denmark Constitution Day**
June 5

This public holiday commemorates the constitution signed on June 5, 1849, that made Denmark a constitutional monarchy, and the one signed on June 5, 1953, that created parliamentary reforms.

A parade takes place in Copenhagen, and other festivities are held in villages throughout Denmark.

CONTACTS:
Royal Danish Embassy
3200 Whitehaven St. N.W.
Washington, D.C. 20008
202-234-4300; fax: 202-328-1470
www.denmarkemb.org

Royal Danish Ministry of Foreign Affairs
Asiatisk Plads 2
Copenhagen, DK-1448 Denmark
45-33-92-00-00; fax: 45-32-54-05-33
www.um.dk/en

SOURCES:
AnnivHol-2000, p. 96
NatlHolWrld-1968, p. 33

♦ 0715 ♦ **Denver Black Arts Festival**
Weekend in mid-July

The Denver Black Arts festival, inaugurated in 1987, is an annual cultural exhibition and celebration held each July in Denver City Park West. With more than 100,000 visitors annually, it is one of the largest African-American cultural events in the western United States.

The festival features events from a wide array of art forms. From the performing arts, music shows are featured on four different stages and include African, blues, gospel, hip hop, jazz, reggae, soul, and world beat acts. In addition, dancers perform in a variety of genres, including African, modern, and tap, sharing their talents through dance workshops. A theater emphasizes the strong oral traditions in African and African-American society through presentations of drama, storytelling, and poetry. A musical competition, the "Mile High Challenge," features drum and drill teams from throughout the region. Friday's special events include a program of youth activities designed for those under age 18. On Saturday the "Carnivale du Promenade," also known as the "Boogaloo Celebration Parade," starts at the intersection of Colorado Boulevard and 22nd Avenue and travels through the park to 17th Avenue and Esplanade.

An art fair features visual arts such as carving, drawing, glass works, painting, photography, and textiles as well as a sculpture garden. A number of exhibits allow participants to try techniques and crafts for themselves, including making herd sticks and Kente cloth and adding their work to a mural that is painted throughout the festival. Children may participate in a historical scavenger hunt that invites them to visit various locales within the park to gather information and win prizes.

African goods, including carvings, clothing, and jewelry, are available from vendors in an area known as "Watu Sokoni" ("People's Marketplace"). In addition, a community outreach fair features exhibit booths by clubs, agencies, and other organizations providing health and housing services, as well as employment and education assistance. In a food court area, vendors offer African, Caribbean, and Southern cuisine.

CONTACTS:
Denver Black Arts Festival
2721 Welton St.
P.O. Box 300577

Denver, CO 80203
720-309-2302; fax: 303-377-4631
denbaf.org

SOURCES:
AAH-2007, p. 122

♦ 0716 ♦ **Departure of the Continental Army**
Saturday nearest June 19

On December 19, 1777, George WASHINGTON and between 11,000 and 12,000 of his Continental Army soldiers marched into Valley Forge, about 18 miles north of Philadelphia, to set up camp for the winter. The men were exhausted, hungry, and poorly equipped. Severe winter weather didn't make their stay at Valley Forge any easier, and they received only irregular supplies of meat and bread. Between 2,000 and 3,000 of the men died from typhus, typhoid, dysentery, and pneumonia before the winter was over.

It was largely through Washington's leadership and the efforts of Baron Friedrich Von STEUBEN that the dispirited army was turned into a well-trained, dependable fighting force by the following summer.

The anniversary of the day the Continental army marched out of Valley Forge in pursuit of the British, who were moving toward New York, is still celebrated with an historic reenactment that takes place on or near June 19 at the Valley Forge National Historical Park each year. In addition, the Army's return to Valley Forge is commemorated on December 19, and there is a muster roll in February.

CONTACTS:
Valley Forge National Historical Park
1400 N. Outer Line Dr.
King of Prussia, PA 19406
610-783-1077; fax: 610-783-1060

SOURCES:
AmerBkDays-2000, p. 839

♦ 0717 ♦ **Derby Day**
Early June

Derby Day is the most prestigious horse race in the world. The idea for the race arose at a dinner party in 1779 and was eventually named for the Earl of Derby, one of the guests who was present that evening. Derby Day is held annually at the Epsom Racecourse in Surrey, England, on the second day of the summer meeting, usually in early June. Many companies in England give their employees the day off so they can join in the picnicking that takes place near the course.

Like its American counterpart, the KENTUCKY DERBY, the festivities surrounding the Derby last far longer than the race itself, which covers a mile and a half and is over in just a few minutes. Only three-year-old colts and fillies can enter, which means that the race can never be won by the same horse twice.

CONTACTS:
Epsom Downs Racecourse
Epsom Downs

Surrey, KT18 5LQ United Kingdom
44-13-7272-6311; fax: 44-13-7274-8253
www.epsomderby.co.uk

SOURCES:
DictDays-1988, p. 30
OxYear-1999, pp. 218, 232

♦ 0718 ♦ **Detroit Electronic Music Festival**
Memorial Day Weekend

The Detroit Electronic Music Festival (DEMF) is a four-day celebration of electronic dance music held annually on Memorial Day weekend in Detroit, Mich. Developing out of the techno (or "house") music scene that originated in the city's dance clubs during the late 1980s and '90s, the festival presents an entertainment lineup that features DJs and music acts from the local area as well as from around the globe.

Since its inception in 2000, it has become one of the largest electronic music festivals in the United States. Events take place Friday through Monday on multiple stages at Hart Plaza, a park along the Detroit River, which borders Detroit and Windsor, Ontario, Canada. More than one million attendees participated in the first three festivals, which were free to the public, but that number declined after paid admission was required beginning in 2003. The festival attracted approximately 75,000 people in 2008. In addition to live music, the festival hosts a market area with food and beverage vendors as well as merchandise stalls and social action organizations. Detroit Electronic Music Festival is produced by Paxahar Promotions Group and financially supported by the City of Detroit and a number of commercial sponsors.

CONTACTS:
Detroit Electronic Music Festival
c/o Paxahau Promotions Group, LLC
326 Hilton
Ferndale, MI 48220
248-584-1646; fax: 248-584-1647
www.myspace.com/detroitmusicfest

♦ 0719 ♦ **Detroit International Jazz Festival**
Labor Day weekend

The Detroit International Jazz Festival (DJF) is a celebration of the jazz music genre held annually in Detroit, Mich., on Labor Day weekend. Billed as the world's largest free jazz festival, the DJF takes place over a period of four days, beginning on Friday evening and concluding on the Monday holiday. It presents more than 100 musical acts on six stages and attracts approximately 750,000 spectators.

Founded in 1980 by philanthropist Robert McCabe and a group of community supporters, the festival was initiated as a means of celebrating the rich musical legacy of the Detroit area, bringing world-class entertainment to the streets of Detroit and revitalizing tourism to the city. The first festivals were located in Hart Plaza, a waterfront park overlooking the Detroit River and Windsor, Ontario, Canada. Associated with the Montreux International Jazz Festival in Switzerland during its first decade, the festival partnered with the Detroit Music Hall from 1991 to 2005.

In 2006 it came under the management of record company executive and philanthropist Gretchen Carhartt Valade. Through Valade's efforts, a nonprofit foundation was established to fund and oversee festival operations, guaranteeing the continuation of DJF and fueling its expansion. The festival area now extends from Hart Plaza three blocks north on Woodward Avenue to Campus Martius Park. Each year the performance lineup includes local and national jazz acts and covers the spectrum of the jazz genre, including funk, fusion, salsa, Afro-rhythms, R&B, and gospel. While such high-profile artists as Herbie Hancock, Dave Brubeck, and Regina Carter headline the show, student ensembles and emerging artists are also featured throughout the weekend, and special programming for young fans is provided at the KidBop area. Refreshments are available at restaurants located within the festival area as well as from food and beverage vendors in Hart Plaza and on the street.

CONTACTS:
Detroit International Jazz Festival
660 Woodward Ave., Ste. 13
Detroit, MI 48226
313-447-1144; fax: 313-447-1145
www.detroitjazzfest.com

♦ 0720 ♦ **Devathani Ekadashi**
October-November; 11th day of waxing half of Hindu month of Kartika

Devathani EKADASHI is a Hindu festival, observed in rural areas, that celebrates the waking of Vishnu. Hindus believe that Vishnu's battle with the great demon Shankhasura was so exhausting that he went to sleep for a period of four months afterward. Each year, Vishnu slumbers from the 11th day of the waxing half of Asadha (June-July) until the 10th day of the waxing half of Kartika (October-November). On the 11th day, he awakens. During his long sleep, Hindu marriages and other ceremonies are not observed.

Hindu women celebrate the festival by fasting, worshipping Vishnu, and singing hymns in praise of various gods and goddesses. Newly ripened crops, such as sugarcane and waternuts, may be eaten on this day for the first time, and it also marks the end of the period during which marriages and other ceremonies cannot be held.

SOURCES:
RelHolCal-2004, p. 178

♦ 0721 ♦ **Devi Dhura**
July-August; the day before and the full moon day of the Hindu month of Sravana

Held at the same time as RAKSHA BANDHAN, the Hindu festival observed by brothers and sisters in honor of their relationship, a two-day festival is observed in the small Himalayan town of Devi Dhura in Uttar Pradesh, India. Hindus gather at the shrine of Varahi Devi or Bhagwati, an incar-

nation of Durga. She is the patron goddess of the approximately 200 villages in the area. Animal sacrifices—originally male buffaloes, but often bulls or goats today—are made at the shrine on the day before Raksha Bandhan. Processions from the other villages stream in to Devi Dhura. Generally these are led by dancers, followed by the animals, the priest, and members of the community. As hundreds of goats and bulls are killed, people use the blood to mark their foreheads.

On the second day, the *bagwals* assemble at Kholi Khan, a flat yard next to the shrine. These are groups of men, wearing turbans and carrying sturdy cane shields, who have been selected from six of the villages to participate in an unusual stone-throwing ritual. Each man is given six to eight stones to throw, and the battle that ensues is not a symbolic act but a true fight in which injuries are common and often severe. The stoning can last as little as 20 minutes or as long as two-and-a-half hours, and spectators watch from a safe distance.

Although there are many legends that account for this tradition, none really offers a satisfactory explanation. It is apparently a well-established custom by which Hindus show their faith not only by shedding the blood of animals but also their own. It is believed that the blood lost by the stone-throwing participants amounts to that which would be shed in the sacrifice of one human being.

CONTACTS:
Uttar Pradesh Tourism Department, Directorate of Tourism
Rajarshi Purshottam Das Tandon Paryatan Bhavan
Vipin Khand, Gomti Nagar
Lucknow, Uttar Pradesh C-13 India
91-522-2308916; fax: 91-522-2308937
www.up-tourism.com

SOURCES:
FestIndia-1987, p. 62

♦ 0722 ♦ **Dew Treading**
Between April 30 and June 3; Ascension Day

Both city and country dwellers in the Netherlands continue to observe the old folk custom known as **Dauwtrappen** ("dew treading") on ASCENSION DAY, which is also a public holiday. People take their children to the fields—or, in the case of city dwellers, to the suburbs—to walk through the morning dew and gather spring flowers. According to an old superstition, the Ascension Day dew possesses supernatural growing and healing powers. In the country, it is customary for friends and neighbors to meet each other at an inn for a big breakfast afterward.

SOURCES:
FestWestEur-1958, p. 133

♦ 0723 ♦ **Dewali (Divali, Deepavali, Festival of Lights)**
October-November; 15th day of waning half of Hindu month of Kartika

The word *dewali* means 'a row or cluster of lights', and the week-long festivities are illuminated by lamps, fireworks, and bonfires. The holiday means different things in different parts of Asia. In northern India it marks the beginning of the Hindu New Year. In Gujarat and Malaysia, families clean and whitewash their homes and draw elaborate designs (called *alpanas*) on their floors with colored powder to welcome Lakshmi, the Hindu goddess of wealth and prosperity. Then they set up rows of little clay lamps, decorating their courtyards, windows, and roofs with light in the belief that Lakshmi won't bless a home that isn't lit up to greet her.

In the Punjab and Mauritius, Dewali celebrates the coronation of Rama (an incarnation of Vishnu) after his conquest of Ravana, the ruler of Sri Lanka, who had stolen his wife. In West Bengal it is a Kali festival. In Maharashtra the lights fend off King Bali, the ruler of the underworld. The Jains commemorate the death of their great hero, MAHAVIRA, on this day, called Deva Dewali, in the city of Pava in Bihar. In Nepal it is TIHAR, a multi-holiday that celebrates the New Year and Lakshmi, sisters honor brothers, and mandalas are prepared for each member of the family.

Dewali is as important to Hindus as CHRISTMAS is to Christians. It is celebrated by the world's 500 million Hindus with gift exchanges, fireworks, and festive (typically vegetarian) meals.

CONTACTS:
Ministry of Tourism, Government of India
Rm. No 123, Transport Bhawan, No. 1, Parliament St.
New Delhi, Delhi 110 001 India
91-11-23715084; fax: 91-11-23715084
www.tourisminindia.com

SOURCES:
BkFest-1937, p. 161
BkHolWrld-1986, Nov 1
EncyRel-1987, vol. 4, p. 374
FolkAmerHol-1999, p. 425
FolkWrldHol-1999, p. 620
GdWrldFest-1985, p. 110
RelHolCal-2004, pp. 179, 195

♦ 0724 ♦ **Dhan Teras**
October-November; 13th day of waning half of Hindu month of Kartika

Dhan Teras or **Dhanvantri Trayodashi** is observed two days prior to DEWALI, the Hindu Festival of Lights. It is held in honor of Dhanvantri, the physician of the gods and the father of Indian medicine, whom doctors in particular worship on this day. According to Hindu mythology, the gods and the demons tried to produce the elixir known as *amrita* by churning up the ocean. Dhanvantri rose up out of the water bearing a cup filled with it. He is also credited with inventing the traditional system of Indian medicine known as Ayurveda.

On this day Hindus rise at dawn and bathe, put on new robes, and fast. In the evening, they light an earthen lamp before the door of the house and break their fast. It is considered an auspicious day to purchase new utensils.

SOURCES:
RelHolCal-2004, p. 179

♦ 0725 ♦ **Dhungri Fair**
May

This is a festival celebrated by Hindu women from the hills near Manali, at the north end of the Kullu Valley in the Himachal Pradesh State of India. A small wooden temple known as the Hidimba (or Dhungri) Temple stands among a woods of cedar trees near Manali. The women gather here to honor the goddess Hidimba, who fell in love with Bhima and became his wife in the famous Hindu epic *Mahabharata*, with a traditional dance.

The temple is known for its intricately chiseled door. Hindu legend has it that the craftsman who carved it had his right hand chopped off by order of the king who hired him. The king wanted his temple to stand alone as a great and unique work. However, when the same carver went on to construct a yet more elaborate temple at Chamba, this time using his left hand, the unfortunate worker got his head chopped off.

CONTACTS:
India Tourist Office
1270 Ave. of the Americas, Ste. 1808, 18th Fl.
New York, NY 10020
800-953-9399 or 212-586-4901; fax: 212-582-3274
www.indiatouristoffice.org

SOURCES:
WildPlanet-1995, p. 246

♦ 0726 ♦ **Día de la Santa Cruz (Day of the Holy Cross)**
May 3

The Day of the Holy Cross, known elsewhere as the EXALTATION OF THE CROSS, is an important one throughout Latin America. Crosses that are normally found in the churches are repaired and repainted, or decorated and carried in procession through the streets.

In Mexico the Day of the Holy Cross is primarily observed by miners, masons, and construction workers. They make elaborately decorated crosses and place them on buildings where they are working. Anyone who is constructing a new building is obligated to throw a party for the workers on this day. Fireworks are set off, and the occasion is treated as a fiesta.

In Peru, Indians hold an all-night vigil on May 2, watching over the wooden crosses they have collected from the churches, roadsides, and mountaintops. The next morning, the crosses are taken to church for the priest's blessing.

In the Andes, the Day of the Cross celebrations have taken the place of the ancient Inca ceremonies known as AYMURAY. In Guatemala, too, the Day of the Cross has replaced an annual pilgrimage to Lake Amatitlán for the purpose of fulfilling certain fertility rites. After the Spanish Conquest, the Spanish priests took advantage of this huge gathering to establish their own Christian celebration. The contemporary festival held in the village of Amatitlán on May 2 and 3 revolves around Indian dancing, music, and water sports as well as prayers and church services.

In Venezuela, the celebration is known as **Velorio de Cruz**. People set up special altars in their homes that include crosses, lighted candles, and images of the saints. Roving musicians and poets from all over the country come to perform in front of these altars. While playing their instruments, they improvise rhymed couplets and other poetic forms.

CONTACTS:
Commission for the Promotion of Peru
Calle Uno Oeste No. 50, piso 13th
Urb. Corpac
Lima, 27 Peru
51-1-4224-3131; fax: 51-1-224-7134
www.promperu.gob.pe

SOURCES:
AnnivHol-2000, p. 76
BkFest-1937, p. 228
BkFestHolWrld-1970, p. 93
BkHolWrld-1986, May 3
FiestaTime-1965, p. 87

◆ 0727 ◆ Día de los Charros
September 14

In Mexico the *charros*, whose name means "loud" or "flashy," are skilled horsemen who were originally *rancheros* (ranchers) of mixed Spanish and Indian blood who took pride in their horses and amused themselves by holding riding competitions with each other. They decorated the harnesses with silver and wore elaborately embroidered costumes.

Today's Mexican charros are more sportsmen than cowboys or ranchers. Most belong to one of the many charro associations, each of which has its own ranch and arena for rodeos. It is on September 14, the day before the MEXICO FESTIVAL OF INDEPENDENCE, that many of the charro associations organize parades and rodeos. The *jaripeo*, or rodeo, generally consists of 10 or more events involving special horse-handling skills and exhibitions of various tricks. Bringing a running horse to a full stop by lassoing its front feet is known as a *mangana*, and the *cola* involves riding very close to a running steer and grabbing its tail, which the charro then twists around his own right leg, forcing the steer to fall on its back and do a complete roll. Perhaps the most difficult trick is the *paso de la muerte* (death's pass), where the charro pursues a wild horse, switching from his own horse's saddle to the back of the wild horse at full gallop.

The typical charro's costume features a pair of snug pants together with a long-sleeved top called a *guayabera*, a waist-length jacket, a bow tie, and a sombrero (wide-brimmed hat). These Mexican horsemen generally carry guns, symbolic of the role the charros have played in Mexico's wars.

See also CHARRO DAYS FIESTA

CONTACTS:
Mexico Tourism Board
21 E. 63rd St., Fl. 3
New York, NY 10021
800-446-3942 or 212-821-0314; fax: 212-821-0367
www.visitmexico.com

SOURCES:
FiestaTime-1965, p. 141

◆ 0728 ◆ Día de los Muertos
November 2

Día de los Muertos, or **Day of the Dead**, is a national holiday in Mexico and is observed in Hispanic communities throughout the U.S. Many Mexicans believe that the spirits of the dead return to enjoy a visit with their friends and relatives on this day. Long before sunrise, people stream into the cemeteries laden with candles, flowers, and food that is often shaped and decorated to resemble the symbols of death. Children eat tiny chocolate hearses, sugar funeral wreaths, and candy skulls and coffins. But the atmosphere is festive.

In many homes people set up *ofrendas*, or altars, to the departed. These are decked with lighted candles, special foods, and whatever the dead enjoyed when they were alive.

See also ALL SOULS' DAY; ANGELITOS, LOS

CONTACTS:
Mexico Tourism Board
21 E. 63rd St., Fl. 3
New York, NY 10021
800-446-3942 or 212-821-0314; fax: 212-821-0367
www.visitmexico.com

SOURCES:
FolkWrldHol-1999, p. 636
HolSymbols-2009, p. 184

◆ 0729 ◆ Día de los Tres Reyes
January 6

Throughout most of Latin America and Spain, EPIPHANY is called el Día de los Tres Reyes (**Three Kings Day** or **Day of the Wise Men**). It marks the end of the CHRISTMAS season that began on December 16 with POSADAS. In Mexico, on the night of January 5 children stuff their shoes with hay and leave them out for the Wise Men to fill with sweets and gifts—much as children elsewhere leave their Christmas stockings out for Santa Claus to fill on CHRISTMAS EVE. And just as letters to Santa Claus are a popular custom in the United States, Mexican children often write letters to the Magi (the Three Wise Men), listing their good deeds and suggesting what gifts they would like to receive.

In Venezuela, children leave straw by their beds so that the Magi's camels will have something to eat. On the morning of January 6 they awake to find the straw gone and gifts delivered in its place.

See also BEFANA FESTIVAL and TWELFTH NIGHT

SOURCES:
BkFest-1937, p. 225
DictFolkMyth-1984, p. 346
EncyChristmas-2003, pp. 451, 489, 733
FolkWrldHol-1999, p. 20

◆ 0730 ◆ Día de Negritos and Fiesta de los Blanquitos
January 5-6

In Popayán, in Colombia's Cauca Department, the CHRISTMAS season ends with the festivities that take place on January 5 and 6. But rather than honoring the Three Wise Men (*see* DÍA DE LOS TRES REYES), who are said to have reached Bethlehem on January 6, the wild celebration that takes place here comes closer to MARDI GRAS.

During the morning hours of January 5, known as the Día de Negritos or **Day of the Black Ones**, boys equipped with black shoe polish chase the girls and try to smear them with their blackened hands. By evening, older boys have joined in the fun, and no one who dares to leave the house is safe. There are parades in the afternoon with people in costume, decorated cars, and the music of *chirimíasi* (roving groups of musicians who play Colombian music on traditional instruments). At least one member of each group is dressed as a devil carrying a spike or horsewhip, which he uses to tease and frighten spectators. Afterward, the poor crowd into the main square, where beef and other foods donated by the town's wealthier inhabitants are distributed.

The following day, January 6, is known as the Fiesta de los Blanquitos (Festival of the White Ones). Instead of chasing the girls with shoe polish, the boys use talcum powder and wheat flour, which turns into a gluey substance when people dump water from their balconies on the victims. The rowdiness of the two-day celebration is not enjoyed by everyone, however. Older Colombians remember the days when well-dressed gentlemen sauntered beneath the windows of beautiful young women, who favored them by coming to the door and permitting a beauty mark to be dabbed on their faces.

CONTACTS:
Embassy of Colombia
2118 Leroy Pl. N.W.
Washington, D.C. 20008
202-387-8338; fax: 202-232-8643
www.colombiaemb.org

SOURCES:
FiestaTime-1965, p. 5

♦ 0731 ♦ **Día del Puno**
November 5

Each year a festival takes place in Puno, Peru, during the first week in November to mark the legendary birth of the first Inca ruler, Manco Capac, and his wife Mama Ocllo. It is said that they were the children of the Sun, intended to be the first rulers of the Inca people, and were born on an island in Lake Titicaca. On November 5, the date associated with their birth, a parade of reed boats, called *balsas*, accompanies an elaborately decorated boat that takes a couple playing the roles of Manco Capac and Mama Ocllo to an island in the lake. There the birth is dramatically reenacted.

Festivities include performances of traditional dance and musical groups, sporting events, exhibits, and a crafts fair.

CONTACTS:
Commission for the Promotion of Peru
Calle Uno Oeste No. 50, piso 13th
Urb. Corpac

Lima, 27 Peru
51-1-4224-3131; fax: 51-1-224-7134
www.promperu.gob.pe

SOURCES:
FestWrld: Peru-1998, p. 20

♦ 0732 ♦ **Diamond Head Crater Celebration**
April or May

In 2006, for the first time in 30 years, music was played inside the Diamond Head Crater on the Hawaiian island of Oahu. The Diamond Head Crater Celebration, created to present Hawaiian culture and music alongside national acts, was organized by Ron Gibson and Mark Mellick of GM Entertainment. The Diamond Head Crater is an extinct volcano outside of the city of Honolulu. It is both a Hawaii state monument and a United States National Natural Landmark.

Crater concerts held during the 1960s and 1970s drew about 40,000 people, but the congestion, parked cars, and trash eventually led to the shows being discontinued. A number of changes were made when the shows were reinstated in 2006. Seating is limited to 7,500 people. Concert-goers are bussed into the site to minimize their impact on the crater environment. Blankets and low-backed beach chairs are permitted in the open-grass seating area.

The six-hour concert has included a number of nationally known musical acts, including the Steve Miller Band, Linda Ronstadt, and Earth, Wind, and Fire. The Honolulu Symphony also performs. The Polynesian Cultural Center presents a program of Pacific island music and dance. A Crater Cabaret presents local musical favorites and dancing. Hawaiian restaurants and breweries provide the food and beverages.

CONTACTS:
Diamond Head Crater
Honolulu, HI 96815
808-735-7000
www.cratercelebration.com

GM Entertainment
1103 9th Ave.
Honolulu, HI 96816

♦ 0733 ♦ **Dicing for the Maid's Money Day**
Last Thursday in January

In the 17th century, dicing (throwing dice) for money was a favorite English pastime in which large sums of money could be won or lost. However, the annual dicing competition that still takes place in Guildford, England, is for the relatively modest sum of 11 pounds, 19 shillings.

In 1674 a local resident named John How established a fund of 400 pounds, which in his will he said he wanted invested and the proceeds distributed each year to a local "maid" or house servant who had served faithfully in the same position for at least two years. The will also stipulated that two servants should throw dice for the gift, and that the one who threw the highest number should receive the entire amount. In 1702, however, another, larger fund was begun by John

Parsons. Today, whoever throws the higher number receives the How prize, which is smaller than the Parson prize, which goes to the woman who throws the lower number.

In the presence of the mayor, trustees, and assembled townspeople, the two women chosen to participate in this event each year take turns shaking the dice in a special hide-covered, silver-banded dice box which has been used for this purpose over the past century. According to the official Maid's Money receipt book, the recipients of the prizes in recent years have been older women who have served faithfully in the same family for many years. But the gift was originally designed for young, unmarried women who might need the money for a dowry.

CONTACTS:
Tourist Information Centre
14, Tunsgate
Guildford, Surrey GU1 3QT United Kingdom
44-14-8344-4333; fax: 44-14-8330-2046
www.guildford.gov.uk

SOURCES:
AnnivHol-2000, p. 18

♦ 0734 ♦ **Dinagyang**
Last weekend in January

The Dinagyang is a dancing-in-the-streets carnival on the island of Panay in Iloilo City, Philippines, held a week after the ATI-ATIHAN in Kalibo and the SINULOG in Cebu. Like these festivals, Dinagyang venerates the Santo Niño, or Holy Infant. In Iloilo (pronounced EE-lo-EE-lo) the participation of tribal groups adds to the festival's color, but, unlike the exuberant Kalibo crowds, the spectators in Iloilo are quiet.

CONTACTS:
Philippine Tourism Center
556 Fifth Ave.
New York, NY 10036
212-575-7915; fax: 212-302-6759
www.wowphilippines.com.ph

♦ 0735 ♦ **Dinosaur Days**
July

Dinosaur Days is a new celebration of very old bones: the dinosaur fossils that rest in Dinosaur, Colo., near Grand Junction, in the Dinosaur National Monument. About 140 million years ago, when the area of Grand Junction was semi-tropical, dinosaurs roamed here. In 1900, the remains of a brachiosaurus, one of the biggest of the dinosaurs, was found four miles west of downtown. Hence, the Dinosaur Days, which started in 1986 and consist of festivities with a reptilian theme.

A foot race, called the Pterandon Ptrot, starts things off and is followed by a parade of dinosaurs and cave men (anachronisms are allowed) and a street dance (with a rock band, of course) named the Stegosaurus Stomp. There are also lectures and tours at the quarry.

CONTACTS:
Dinosaur National Monument
4545 E. Hwy. 40
Dinosaur, CO 81610
970-374-3000; fax: 970-374-3003

♦ 0736 ♦ **Dionysia (Bacchanalia)**
Various dates

The Dionysia was a festival in ancient Greece in honor of Dionysus (also called Bacchus), the son of Zeus and god of wine, fertility, and drama. There were a series of Dionysian festivals: the Oschophoria, the rural or COUNTRY DIONYSIA, the Lenaea, the ANTHESTERIA, the urban Dionysia, and the most famous—the City or Great Dionysia.

The Great Dionysias were held in the spring (March or April) in Athens for five or six days, and their centerpieces were the performances of new tragedies, comedies, and satyric dramas. These took place in the Theater of Dionysus on the side of the Acropolis and were attended by people from throughout the country. The earliest tragedy that survives is *Persai* by Aeschylus, from the year 472 B.C.E. The dramatists, actors, and singers were considered to be performing an act of worship of the god, and Dionysus was thought to be present at the productions.

The City Dionysias were a time of general springtime rejoicing (even prisoners were released to share in the festivities) and great pomp. The statue of Dionysus was carried in a procession that also included representations of the phallus, symbolizing the god.

Dionysus was both a merry god who inspired great poetry and a cruel god; the Greeks realistically saw wine as something that made people happy and also made them drunk and cruel. Thus, like the god, his festivals seem to have combined contrasting elements of poetry and revelry.

The small rustic Dionysias were festive and bawdy affairs held in December or January at the first tasting of new wine. Besides dramatic presentations, there were processions of slaves carrying the phallus, the singing of obscene lays, youths balancing on a full goat-skin, and the like.

The Leneae, held in Athens in January or February, included a procession of jesting citizens through the city and dramatic presentations. The Oschophoria ("carrying of the grape cluster"), held in the fall when the grapes were ripe, was marked by a footrace for youths.

SOURCES:
DictFolkMyth-1984, pp. 830, 867
EncyRel-1987, vol. 4, p. 358
NewCentClassHandbk-1962, p. 399
OxClassDict-1970, p. 350

♦ 0737 ♦ **Dipri Festival**
March-April

The Dipri Festival is a celebration held by the Abidji tribe in Gomon, Côte d'Ivoire (Ivory Coast). The Abidjis are one of about 60 ethnic groups in the country, which became a French colony in 1893 and attained independence in 1960 (*see* CÔTE D'IVOIRE INDEPENDENCE DAY). First, relatives or neighbors meet on the evening before the celebration to reconcile their differences. Then, during the festival, people go into frenzied trances as they are possessed by *sékés*—beneficient spirits—and stumble, dazed, in the street. Some people, supposedly led by the spirits, plunge knives into their bodies and then, with the guidance of the sékés, are healed with poultices of raw eggs and herbs. This festival serves several purposes: it resolves conflicts between generations and in the community, it drives away evil spirits, and it purifies the celebrants.

CONTACTS:
Embassy of the Republic of Cote d'Ivoire
2424 Massachusetts Ave. N.W.
Washington, D.C. 20008
202-797-0300; fax: 202-483-8482

♦ 0738 ♦ Disabled Persons, International Day of
December 3

The years 1983-92 marked the United Nations Decade of Disabled Persons, a period during which great strides were made in raising awareness and enacting laws to improve the situation of individuals with disabilities. At the conclusion of this 10-year observance, December 3 was proclaimed the International Day of Disabled Persons. The U.N. General Assembly appealed to its members to observe this day with activities and events designed to promote the advantages of integrating disabled persons into every area of social, economic, and political life.

CONTACTS:
United Nations, Department of Public Information
Rm. S-1070L J, K, L
New York, NY 10017
212-963-6842; fax: 212-963-6914
www.un.org

♦ 0739 ♦ Disarmament Week
October 24-30

The United Nations' Disarmament Week, observed between October 24 and October 30, was established in 1978. It begins on October 24, the anniversary of the founding of the United Nations, now observed as UNITED NATIONS DAY. Observance revolves around raising public awareness of the dangers of the arms race and the need for international disarmament.

CONTACTS:
United Nations, Department of Public Information
Rm. S-1070L
New York, NY 10017
212-963-6842; fax: 212-963-6914
www.un.org

♦ 0740 ♦ Discovery Day
November 19; December 5

There are a number of different days referred to by this name, all of which relate to the voyages of Christopher COLUMBUS.

In Trinidad and Tobago, August 1 was Discovery Day, in honor of Columbus's discovery of the two islands on his third voyage to the Western Hemisphere. Since 1985, however, August 1 has been observed as TRINIDAD AND TOBAGO EMANCIPATION DAY. In Haiti, Discovery Day is a legal holiday celebrated on December 5, commemorating its discovery by Columbus in 1492. And in Puerto Rico, which Columbus found on his second voyage in 1493, Discovery Day is celebrated on November 19.

See also MAGELLAN DAY

SOURCES:
AnnivHol-2000, pp. 193, 203
BkHolWrld-1986, p. 176

♦ 0741 ♦ Distaff Day
January 7

After the 12-day CHRISTMAS celebration ended on TWELFTH NIGHT or EPIPHANY, **St. Distaff's Day** was traditionally the day on which women resumed their chores, symbolized by the distaff, a tool used in spinning flax or wool. It was also called **Rock Day**, from the German word *rocken*—"rock" being another name for the distaff. The "spear side" and the "distaff side" were legal terms used to distinguish the inheritance of male from that of female children, and the distaff eventually became a synonym for the female sex as a whole. Distaff Day was not really a church festival, but it was widely observed at one time in England.

Although the women had to return to work after Twelfth Night was over, the men apparently had plenty of time to amuse themselves by setting the flax on fire, in return for which they would get buckets of water dumped on their heads.

SOURCES:
AnnivHol-2000, p. 6
BkDays-1864, vol. I, p. 68
DaysCustFaith-1957, p. 22
DictDays-1988, pp. 32, 96
EncyChristmas-2003, p. 663
FolkWrldHol-1999, p. 25
OxYear-1999, p. 28
SaintFestCh-1904, p. 57

♦ 0742 ♦ Divine Holy Spirit, Festival of the (Festa do Divino)
May-June; around Pentecost (50 days after Easter)

Portuguese colonists brought their PENTECOST celebration, the **Festa do Divino**, to Brazil in the 17th century. This religious festival is still celebrated today in many Brazilian cities. One of the most traditional celebrations takes place in Diamantina, Minas Gerais State. The week-long festivities include masses and fireworks, culminating in the "parade of the Emperor."

Festa do Divino celebrations can also be found in two of Brazil's most beautiful colonial-era towns: Alcântara, Maranhão State, and Paraty, Rio de Janeiro State. The townspeople dress up in colonial costumes, with many playing the roles of prominent figures from Brazilian history. The climax is a visit from the "Emperor," who arrives with his servants for a procession and mass at the church square. He frees prisoners from the town jail in a symbolic gesture of royal generosity, and strolling musicians known as *Folias do Divino* serenade the townspeople day and night.

The Feast of the Holy Ghost is celebrated by the fishermen living in and around Tietê, São Paulo State, Brazil, and represents a tradition that began several centuries ago in Portugal to commemorate the Descent of the Holy Ghost upon the Apostles. On Pentecost all the fishermen dress in white with sashes and long stocking caps. Each carries an oar in one hand, and during the procession to the river, they form a double line facing each other. As they make an arch by crossing their oars, a dove, symbolic of the Holy Spirit, is carried beneath it on a ribbon-decorated crown.

The townspeople follow the fishermen and the musicians to the river's edge, where all the fishing canoes have been decorated with bunting for the occasion. The white-clad fishermen climb into their canoes, standing while holding their oars upright, and the current carries the floating regatta downstream. The event comes to a close in the parish church, where the men bring their oars to be blessed so they will have a plentiful catch in the coming year.

See also HOLY GHOST, FEAST OF THE

CONTACTS:
Brazilian Embassy
3006 Massachusetts Ave. N.W.
Washington, D.C. 20008
202-238-2700; fax: 202-238-2827
www.brasilemb.org

SOURCES:
FiestaTime-1965, p. 95

◆ 0743 ◆ **Djibouti Independence Day**
June 27

On this day in 1977, Djibouti gained autonomy from France, after more than 100 years under French rule. It is observed as a national holiday.

CONTACTS:
Embassy of Republic of Djibouti
1156 15th St. N.W., Ste. 515
Washington, D.C. 20005
202-331-0270; fax: 202-331-0302

SOURCES:
AnnivHol-2000, p. 107

◆ 0744 ◆ **Doan Ngu (Summer Solstice Day)**
May-June; fifth day of fifth lunar month

Doan Ngu is a celebration of the SUMMER SOLSTICE in Vietnam. Offerings are made to spirits and ghosts and to the god of

death to fend off epidemics. In addition, human effigies are burned, providing souls to staff the army of the god of death.

CONTACTS:
Embassy of Vietnam
1233 20th St. N.W., Ste. 400
Washington, D.C. 20036
202-861-0737; fax: 202-861-0917
www.vietnamembassy-usa.org

◆ 0745 ◆ **Doctors' Day**
March 30

Since 1933 this day has been set aside to honor America's physicians. It is the anniversary of the day in 1842 on which Dr. Crawford W. Long removed a tumor from the neck of a man while the patient was anesthetized by ether. Dr. Long was the first acclaimed American physician to use ether as an anesthetic agent in a surgical procedure.

Although Doctors' Day highlights the achievement of Dr. Long, the issue of who really discovered general anesthesia is far from clear. In addition to Dr. Long, Gardner Colton, Horace Wells, and Charles Jackson have also claimed credit for the discovery, although some used nitrous oxide gas while others used ether. It was William Thomas Morton who first demonstrated the use of ether as a general anesthetic in front of a gathering of physicians on October 16, 1846, at Massachusetts General Hospital.

The red carnation is the official flower associated with Doctors' Day. The American Medical Association promotes various activities to mark this day, including walk-a-thons and blood drives.

CONTACTS:
American Medical Association
515 N. State St.
Chicago, IL 60610
800-621-8335
www.ama-assn.org

SOURCES:
AnnivHol-2000, pp. 53, 173

◆ 0746 ◆ **Dodge City Days**
Late July through early August

Dodge City's name alone is enough to conjure up memories of the Old West for the residents of Kansas and the surrounding states who come here to celebrate Dodge City Days every summer. Held annually in late July and early August, the main purpose of the festival is to keep the area's history alive. There are staged shootouts between "Marshal Dillon" and the bad guys, a Professional Rodeo Cowboys Association rodeo, a horse show, and parades featuring costumed characters from the Old West on horseback.

First held in 1960, Dodge City Days now attracts crowds of up to 50,000—most of whom are tourists. In recent years the festival has featured entertainment by top country-and-western music stars, and the events have expanded to include a golf tournament, auto racing, and other decidedly non-traditional activities that have little to do with Dodge City's Old West heritage.

CONTACTS:
Dodge City Area Chamber of Commerce
311 W. Spruce
P.O. Box 939
Dodge City, KS 67801
316-227-3119; fax: 316-227-2957
www.dodgecitychamber.com

SOURCES:
GdUSFest-1984, p. 60

♦ 0747 ♦ **Dodge National Circuit Finals Rodeo**
Third week in March

The Dodge National Rodeo event is the finals competition for cowboys competing in the regional circuit system of rodeos, held since 1987 in Pocatello, Idaho. About 200 top cowboys and cowgirls compete each year for their share of a purse worth thousands of dollars and gold championship buckles. Competitions for cowboys are in saddle bronc, bull riding, calf roping, bareback riding, team roping, and steer wrestling; the women compete in barrel racing. For youngsters, there's mutton bustin'—riding sheep. Opening ceremonies spotlight the Pocatello Rodeo Queen and her court. Post-rodeo parties are held each night. Attendance at the finals runs about 40,000.

The circuit system was introduced to allow weekend cowboys who can't compete full-time in rodeos to compete in one of 12 regions in the United States.

See also NATIONAL FINALS RODEO

CONTACTS:
Dodge National Circuit Finals Rodeo
324 S. Main
P.O. Box 4541
Pocatello, ID 83205
208-233-1546; fax: 208-233-1553
www.dncfr.org

♦ 0748 ♦ **Dodge (Geraldine R.) Poetry Festival**
September in even-numbered years

Since the first Dodge Poetry Festival was held in 1986, the biennial gathering has grown into a four-day event that draws upwards of 5,000 people—including television crews—for what has been described as "a grueling but exhilarating marathon of poetry activity." Readings, panel discussions, and talks by some of America's most famous poets have made the restored village of Waterloo in rural southern New Jersey synonymous with the word "poetry" for the students, writers, and interested spectators who flock to the festival, which is sponsored by the Geraldine R. Dodge Foundation. Mrs. Dodge was a local philanthropist.

Many of the events take place outdoors and include music, food, and strolling performers, giving the whole affair the flavor of a bona fide festival rather than the typical writers'

conference. Coverage of the Dodge Festival by the award-winning PBS series "The Power of the Word," hosted by Bill Moyers, is thought to have contributed to the festival's broad public appeal. The 2008 festival brought such luminaries as Lucille Clifton, Billy Collins, Maxine Kumin, Naomi Shihab Nye, and Charles Simic.

CONTACTS:
Geraldine R. Dodge Foundation
163 Madison Ave.
P.O. Box 1239
Morristown, NJ 07962
973-540-8442; fax: 973-540-1211
www.dodgepoetry.org

♦ 0749 ♦ **Dog Days**
July 3-August 11

The Dog Days are known as the hottest days of the year in the Northern Hemisphere and usually occur in July and early August. In ancient times, the sultry weather in Rome during these months often made people sick, and they blamed their illnesses on the fact that this was the time of year when Sirius, the Dog Star, rose at about the same time as the sun. Because Sirius was the brightest star, it was thought to add its heat to the sun, producing hot, unhealthy weather. The ancients used to sacrifice a brown dog at the beginning of the Dog Days to appease the rage of Sirius.

Although there are many different ways of calculating which days in any given year are the dog days, and how long they last, it is impossible to be precise. Nowadays it is generally assumed that they fall between July 3 and August 11—slightly later than they occurred in ancient times.

Because of their association with the Dog Star, various beliefs have sprung up involving the behavior of dogs during this period. In the 16th century it was believed that dogs went mad during the Dog Star season. Another name for this time of year, the **canicular days**, comes from the Latin word *canis* meaning "dog."

SOURCES:
BkDays-1864, vol. II, p. 5
DictDays-1988, p. 32
DictFolkMyth-1984, p. 918
OxYear-1999, p. 595

♦ 0750 ♦ **Doggett's Coat and Badge Race**
August 1

Established in 1716 by Thomas Doggett, an actor and one of the owners of the Drury Lane Theatre in London, the **Waterman's Derby** is an annual rowing race held on the Thames River between Old Swan Pier and Cadogan Pier. Six young boatmen who have just completed their apprenticeships must row against the tide for a distance of four and a half miles. The winner receives a new pair of breeches, an orange coat, and—because the original race was to commemorate the crowning of King George I—a badge with the Hanoverian white horse on it. There are cash prizes as well: originally, 10 pounds for the winner, and six, five, four, three, or two pounds for the other rowers, according to the order in which they complete the race. When Doggett died in 1721, he left a legacy that would ensure the continuation of both the race and its prizes.

Nowadays, the prizes are significantly higher, beginning at 250 pounds for first place. The race is administered by the Fishmongers' Company, of which Doggett was a member.

CONTACTS:
Company of Watermen and Lightermen
16 St-Mary-at-Hill
London, EC3R 8EF United Kingdom
44-20-7283-2373; fax: 44-20-7283-0477
www.watermenshall.org

Fishmongers Company
Fishmongers Hall
London Bridge
London, EC4R 9EL United Kingdom
44-20-7626-3531; fax: 44-20-7929-1389
www.fishhall.co.uk

SOURCES:
AnnivHol-2000, p. 129
OxYear-1999, p. 318

♦ 0751 ♦ **Dogwood Festival**
April

The Dogwood Festival is a night-and-day celebration of the pink and white dogwoods (and azaleas) blooming everywhere in Atlanta, Ga. The founders of the first festival in 1936 thought the event could make Atlanta "internationally known for its beauty during the blooming of the dogwood trees and be the beginning of an annual pilgrimage to the Gate City of the South." The festival comes close to doing that, even though it lapsed during World War II, and didn't really get going again until 1968.

Now this gala event each year attracts about 100,000 people who come not only to see the trees but also for numerous concerts, a hot-air balloon exhibit, an artists market, canine frisbee, and rock climbing. Children's activities include puppet making, games, and a kite-making workshop.

CONTACTS:
Atlanta Dogwood Festival
887 W. Marietta St. Studio S-105
Atlanta, GA 30318
404-817-6642; fax: 404-817-9508
www.dogwood.org

♦ 0752 ♦ **Dol Purnima**
February-March; full moon day of Hindu month of Phalguna

The Dol Purnima festival is celebrated throughout India by followers of Krishna. It occurs on the same day as the birthday of Chaitanya Mahaprabhu (1486-1534), also known as Gauranga, the 16th-century Vishnavite saint and poet of Bengal regarded as an incarnation of Krishna. It is therefore a significant festival for Hindus, who carry an image of Lord Krishna, covered with colored powder and placed in a swinging cradle, through the streets as they sing songs composed especially for the occasion.

CONTACTS:
India Tourist Office
1270 Ave. of the Americas, Ste. 1808, 18th Fl.
New York, NY 10020
800-953-9399 or 212-586-4901; fax: 212-582-3274
www.indiatouristoffice.org

SOURCES:
BkFest-1937, p. 163
FolkWrldHol-1999, p. 185
RelHolCal-2004, p. 184

♦ 0753 ♦ **Doleing Day**
December 21

It was customary at one time in England on ST. THOMAS'S DAY for the poorer inhabitants of the parish to call on their wealthier neighbors and receive a gift or "dole" of food or money. In return, they would give their benefactors a sprig of holly or mistletoe.

The custom of "going a-gooding," as it was called, gave rise to the name **Gooding Day** in parts of Sussex; in other areas it was referred to as **Mumping (Begging) Day**, since those who had to beg were said to be "on the mump." Children would often spend St. Thomas's Day begging for apples.

SOURCES:
BkDays-1864, vol. II, p. 724
DictDays-1988, pp. 32, 49, 78
EncyChristmas-2003, p. 693
OxYear-1999, p. 506

♦ 0754 ♦ **Dom Fair**
November-December

The **Hamburger Dom**, or Dom Fair, is one of the most famous CHRISTMAS fairs in the world. It was named after its original location, which was in the open square in front of the Dom, or cathedral, in Hamburg, Germany. Today the fair is held in the Heiligengeistfeld, or Holy Ghost Field, in the middle of the city. It features booths filled with toys, gingerbread, crafts, and other temptations for holiday shoppers. The Fair begins in November and doesn't close until just before Christmas, giving shoppers from Hamburg and the surrounding area plenty of time to buy their gifts.

CONTACTS:
Hamburg Tourist Office
Steinstrasse 7
Hamburg, 20095 Germany
49-40-300-51-300; fax: 49-40-300-51-333
www.hamburg-tourism.de/en

SOURCES:
FestWestEur-1958, p. 79

♦ 0755 ♦ **Dominica Independence Day**
November 3

On this day in 1978, Dominica gained independence from Britain as it became a member of the Commonwealth. It is celebrated as a national holiday for three days, including November 3.

CONTACTS:
Dominica Festivals Commission
23 Great Marlborough St.
Roseau, Dominica
767-448-4833; fax: 767-448-0229
www.wcmfstore.com

SOURCES:
AnnivHol-2000, p. 185

♦ 0756 ♦ **Dominican Republic Independence Day**
February 27

In the 1830s Juan Pablo Duarte (1813-1876)—known as "the father of Dominican independence"—organized a secret society known as *La Trinitaria* to fight the Haitians. After a long struggle, independence was finally declared on February 27, 1844. Although disorder, dictatorships, and intermittent peace characterized the Dominican Republic's history until the U.S. Marines occupied it from 1916 to 1924 to keep peace between rival political groups, February 27 is still observed as the country's Independence Day and is celebrated with parades and political meetings.

The site of the proclamation, Independence Park, contains a shrine known as the *Altar de la Patria*, "the nation's altar," honoring the three founders of the Republic—Duarte, Ramón Mella, and Juan Sánchez Ramírez. Duarte's birthday, January 26, is also a public holiday, celebrated as Duarte Day.

Dominican Republicans usually celebrate CARNIVAL along with Independence Day. Thousands gather in the capital, Santo Domingo, for the traditional day-long parade and street party.

CONTACTS:
Dominican Republic Tourism Office
136 E. 57th St., Ste. 803
New York, NY 10022
888-374-6361 or 212-588-1012; fax: 212-588-1015
www.godominicanrepublic.com

SOURCES:
AnnivHol-2000, p. 15, 33
NatlHolWrld-1968, p. 27

♦ 0757 ♦ **Dominican Republic Independence Restoration Day**
August 16

During the 19th century, the Dominican Republic won its autonomy from Haiti, only to quickly lose it again over a decade later to Spain. The country reclaimed its freedom after winning a two-year-long war with Spain in 1865. Only 14 men were present for the historic raid that marked the beginning of that war, on August 16, 1863. The freedom fighter Santiago Rodriguez led his small contingent up Capotillo Hill in the capital city, Santo Domingo, where they raised the Dominican flag.

Thus, to pay tribute to its complicated history, Dominicans celebrate independence twice a year: on DOMINICAN REPUBLIC INDEPENDENCE DAY and on Dominican Republic Independence Restoration Day, which commemorates the official beginning of the War of the Restoration in 1863. Celebrations take place throughout the island, but the most prominent celebrations are in Santo Domingo and the other main city, Santiago.

Customary festivities include parades, street fairs, and performances of the national anthem and other compositions. Troops will also present a military review before government officials.

CONTACTS:
Embassy of the Dominican Republic
1715 22nd St. N.W.
Washington, D.C. 20008
202-332-6280; fax: 202-265-8057

Dominican Republic Tourism Office
136 E. 57th St., Ste. 803
New York, NY 10022
888-374-6361 or 215-588-1012; fax: 212-588-1015

♦ 0758 ♦ **Dominican Republic Our Lady of Altagracia (Feast of the Virgin of Altagracia, Feast of Our Lady of Altagracia)**
January 21

The Virgin Mary is considered by many Catholics to be the patron saint of the Dominican Republic. A cloth painting of Mary that is 13 inches (33 cm) wide by 18 inches (45 cm) high is the focus of a yearly celebration in the island nation. Many religious legends have sprung up over the centuries about the portrait. It was painted by a Spanish artist and brought to the Dominican Republic by two Spanish brothers in the early 1500s. The portrait, which was crowned by a gold and silver tiara by Pope John Paul II in 1978, is located in a basilica in the city of Higuey, in the province of Altagracia.

Every year on January 21, thousands of pilgrims visit the Higuey cathedral to worship. The feast day is a national holiday in the Dominican Republic. It is marked by all-night church services, singing, dancing, and festivals in many Dominican towns.

CONTACTS:
Embassy of the Dominican Republic
1715 22nd St. N.W.
Washington, D.C. 20008
202-265-8057 or 202-939-0971; fax: 202-265-8057
www.domrep.org

♦ 0759 ♦ **Dominican Republic Our Lady of Mercedes Day**
September 24

A national holiday that illustrates the strong influence of Spanish colonialism and the Catholic Church on Dominican culture, this feast day honors Mary the mother of Jesus, often referred to by Dominicans by her patron saint title—Nuestra Señora de Mercedes (Our Lady of Mercedes). Observance of this celebration dates back to 1615, the year the Mercedians, a Spanish order, established the feast day.

According to legend, before returning to Spain Christopher Columbus placed a cross atop a hill overlooking El Cibao, a region on the northern end of the island. In 1495, during a battle between the Spanish and the native Taino Indians, the Lady of Mercedes appeared, scattering the frightened Indians and thereby securing the Europeans' victory. There were subsequent visitations reported at the site, and eventually settlers marked the spot by erecting a church and pilgrimage site they named Iglesia Las Mercedes.

Every year Iglesia Las Mercedes receives thousands of worshippers, many of whom arrive on the saint's day to pay homage. Another church in Santo Domingo, the Church of Las Mercedes, also attracts many followers on September 24. Typical ceremonies at the church in the capital city include masses throughout the day, the Blessing of the Waters, and a procession from the church through Santo Domingo's Colonial Zone.

CONTACTS:
Embassy of the Dominican Republic
1715 22nd St. N.W.
Washington, D.C. 20008
202-332-6280; fax: 202-265-8057

♦ 0760 ♦ Dongji (Winter Solstice)
11th lunar month; around December 21

In Korea the WINTER SOLSTICE falls during the 11th lunar month. Perhaps because the winter solstice month was regarded as the first month of the year under the old calendar system in Korea, many people consider the day of the solstice to be the day on which they become one year older—a kind of communal birthday.

Red bean stew with glutinous rice flour balls is a favorite seasonal dish, particularly on Dongji (also rendered *Tongji*). This food is not only eaten as a means of warding off disease, but is also offered to the family ancestors, spread around the front door or gate of the house, and, throughout the year, prepared and taken to people who are in mourning. The color red is traditionally thought to repel evil spirits and all misfortune.

One legend behind this belief holds that a disobedient son, who happened to dislike red bean porridge, died on Dongji day and became a smallpox spirit. Thus, putting red porridge stew around the house will keep him away.

CONTACTS:
The Korea Foundation
10F Diplomatic Center Bldg., 2558 Nambusunhwanno
Seocho-gu, Seoul 137-863 South Korea
82-2-3463-5684; fax: 82-2-3463-6086
www.koreana.or.kr

SOURCES:
AnnCustKorea-1983, p. 153

♦ 0761 ♦ Doo Dah Parade
January

Since 1977, the city of Pasadena, Calif., has been the scene of the Doo Dah Parade, a parody of the nationally known Rose Parade. The Rose Parade is held in conjunction with the Rose Bowl football championship, which is held in the same city.

The Doo Dah Parade encourages outrageous, surreal, and imaginative floats, costumes, and themes from all those who participate. The parade takes place in Old Pasadena. Among the groups who have participated are the Fabulous Sons of Ed Wood, Howdy Krishna, Stupidiotic Evolution, Tequila Mockingbird, Horses on Astroturf, and the Doo Dah House Band. Every year an official queen of the Doo Dah Parade is chosen, and she and her court lead the procession.

Sponsored by the nonprofit Light Bringer Project, the parade raises money for the group's art projects, including the Metro Gallery and the Pasadena Chalk Festival.

CONTACTS:
Light Bringer Project
P.O. Box 968
Pasadena, CA 91102
626-205-4029
www.pasadenadoodahparade.info

♦ 0762 ♦ Dosmoche
February; first lunar month

Early in the new Tibetan Year the Dosmoche festival is held in Leh in the Ladakh region of Jammu and Kashmir State, India. A large *dosmo*, or pole, decorated with streamers and religious symbols is erected. The lamas make a food and drink offering to the Buddha and the gods after the dosmo is in place as a ritual to drive away evil spirits for the new year. Later the dosmo is torn down and burned, symbolizing that the spirits have been driven away.

SOURCES:
FolkWrldHol-1999, p. 789

♦ 0763 ♦ Double Tenth Day
October 10

Double Tenth Day is a national holiday in Taiwan to commemorate the Chinese Revolution of October 10, 1911. The revolt marked the end of the Ching, or Qing, Dynasty that had been established in 1644 by the Manchus, and it led to the founding of the Republic of China on January 1, 1912.

It took the Ching rulers several decades to complete their military conquest of China and by 1683, when Taiwan became part of the empire, they governed all of China. The Ching Court's period of glory was in the time of the first three emperors, but after 1795 the court began a slow decline. By the end of the 19th century, Japan and the Western powers had reduced China to what SUN YAT-SEN called a "subcolony," the court was weak and corrupt, and a group of national capitalists was fomenting uprisings. Sun Yat-sen was one of the leaders of this nationalistic group; he was a

Jeffersonian figure who wanted a Western-style government with a parliament and separation of powers.

In October 1911, when a revolt in Wuchang (in the province of Hubei) succeeded, supportive uprisings broke out in other cities. The fall of the Manchus followed. Sun Yat-sen, who was in Denver, Colo., at the time of the October revolt, returned to Shanghai and was elected provisional president of the new republic. He is thought of today as the father of modern China, and his birthday on Nov. 12 is also a national holiday in Taiwan.

For several weeks before Double Tenth Day, the plaza in front of the Presidential Office Building in Taipei, Taiwan, is illuminated. Here there are massive parades and rallies on the holiday, displays of martial arts, folk dancing, and other cultural activities. dazzling display of fireworks is presented over an island in the middle of the Tanshui River.

CONTACTS:
Taiwan Government Information Office
4201 Wisconsin Ave. N.W.
Washington, D.C. 20016
202-895-1850; fax: 202-362-6144
www.gio.gov.tw

SOURCES:
AnnivHol-2000, p. 171
NatlHolWrld-1968, p. 189

♦ 0764 ♦ **Douglass (Frederick) Day**
February 14

Frederick Douglass Day in the United States is celebrated on February 14, the date traditionally believed to have been Douglass's birthday. Born into slavery in 1818 in Maryland, he escaped to freedom in 1838 and eventually made his home in New Bedford, Mass., where he became active in the international abolitionist movement. After the Civil War he served in the U.S. government as a marshal in the District of Columbia and as a minister to the Republic of Haiti and the Dominican Republic.

Each year Douglass's birthday is commemorated with a ceremony at his former home, Cedar Hill, which is now the Frederick Douglass National Historic Site in Washington, D.C. The event, which attracts about 300 people, features speakers on human rights, recitations of excerpts from Douglass's speeches, tours of the home, music performances, and a wreath-laying ceremony. In addition, activities including lectures, readings from his works, and film presentations about his life are also planned in New Bedford, in Rochester, N.Y., where Douglass's grave is located, and in many other locations throughout the country.

CONTACTS:
Frederick Douglass National Historic Site
1411 W St. S.E.
Washington, D.C. 20020
202-426-5961
www.nps.gov/frdo/index.htm

New Bedford Friends Meeting House
83 Spring St.

New Bedford, MA 02740-5934
508-979-8828

SOURCES:
AAH-2007, p. 170

♦ 0765 ♦ **Down Home Family Reunion**
Third weekend in August

Introduced in 1992, the Down Home Family Reunion is an annual celebration of west African folk life held in Abner Clay Park in Richmond, Va., during the third weekend in August. The reunion draws approximately 25,000 attendees during two days of events and offers music and dance performances, storytelling presentations, traditional foods, a heritage marketplace, and children's activities.

The festival is organized by the Elegba Folklore Society, Inc., a nonprofit group that sponsors the activities in an effort to demonstrate the close connection between west African folk life and the cultural traditions of African Americans. With many hands-on and interactive exhibits, the festival showcases the strong influence of west African culture on life in the American South. Many performers and participants are African. Saturday's activities are free and emphasize family participation in craft demonstrations and a variety of cultural exhibits. Sunday's lineup concludes with a concert at dusk that features music and spoken word performances by national and local acts.

CONTACTS:
Elegba Folklore Society
101 E. Broad St.
Richmond, VA 23219
804-644-3900
elegbafolkloresociety.org

Richmond Metropolitan Convention & Visitors Bureau
401 N. 3rd St.
Richmond, VA 23219
800-370-9004 or 888-742-4663
www.visit.richmond.com

SOURCES:
AAH-2007, p. 126

♦ 0766 ♦ **Downtown Hoedown**
Second weekend in May

The Downtown Hoedown is a three-day celebration of country music held annually on the second weekend of May in Detroit, Mich. Since it began as a one-day, outdoor concert in 1983, the Hoedown has become one of the largest events of its kind in the United States and as of 2008 was known as the "World's Largest Free Country Music Concert."

The Hoedown is hosted and sponsored by radio station 99.5 FM WYCD and is considered a premier showcase for new country artists. Among those who have risen to fame after playing at the Hoedown are Garth Brooks, Reba McEntire, Rascal Flatts, and Josh Turner. Musical acts perform on multiple stages Friday through Sunday in a riverfront setting at

Hart Plaza, a park along the Detroit River, which borders Detroit and Windsor, Ontario, Canada. Local artists start the show at noon and such Nashville stars as Trace Adkins, Josh Gracin, and Trisha Yearwood headline the show in the evening. In addition to music and dancing, the festival offers food and beverage vendors, mechanical bull rides, and a shopping area. Estimated attendance for the three-day weekend is between 800,000 and one million.

CONTACTS:
Downtown Hoedown
c/o 99.5 WYCD
26555 Evergreen Rd., Ste. 675
Southfield, MI 48076
248-799-0600; fax: 248-358-9216
www.wycd.com

♦ 0767 ♦ **Dozynki Festival**
August 15

For many Christians around the world, August 15 is the Feast of the ASSUMPTION. But in Poland, it is also a time for celebrating the harvest. During the wheat harvest festival known as **Dozynki Pod Debami**, or **Festival under the Oaks**, the reapers make wreaths out of grain, flowers, nuts, and corn. When they present their wreaths to the master and mistress of the estate on which the wheat is grown, they are invited in for a feast, which is followed by dancing.

For Americans of Polish descent living in Orange County, New York—one of the richest onion-growing areas in the United States—the Dozynki Festival underwent a revival in 1939 under the name of the **Feast of Our Lady of the Flowers**. In the village of Florida, the streets were banked high with piles of onions, and there was a huge parade with floats depicting the arrival of the Polish immigrants in America and various aspects of the onion production industry. There was a costumed pageant in which the onion farmers presented the Lord and Lady of the Manor with a huge wreath of onions and flowers, followed by the Onion Dance, which had been created especially for the festival.

CONTACTS:
Library of Congress
101 Independence Ave. S.E.
Washington, D.C. 20540
202-707-5510; fax: 202-707-2076
www.loc.gov

SOURCES:
FolkAmerHol-1999, p. 341
FolkWrldHol-1999, p. 495

♦ 0768 ♦ **Drachenstich (Spearing the Dragon)**
Mid-August

This annual event centers around the performance of an open-air play, *Drachenstich*, in Fürth, Germany, in the Bavarian Forest. The climax of the play is a battle between a knight on horseback and a huge (about 50 feet long and 10 feet tall), fire-spewing dragon. The knight, of course, wins—by thrusting his spear into the dragon's throat, thereby piercing a pig's

bladder filled with ox blood. Besides the dragon-sticking, the celebrations include various merrymaking events and a street procession. The play has been performed for about 500 years and is thought to be the oldest folk play in Germany.

CONTACTS:
Tourist Information
Drachenstich-Festspiele
Schlossplatz 1
Furth im Wald, D-93437 Germany
49-99-735-09-70; fax: 49-99-735-09-85
www.drachenstich.de

♦ 0769 ♦ **Dragon Boat Festival**
May-June; fifth day of fifth lunar month

Chu'ü Yüan (343-289 B.C.E.) was a Chinese poet and statesman of the Ch'u kingdom who drowned himself in the Mi Lo River to protest political corruption and injustice. The colorful dragon boat races that take place on lakes and rivers throughout China, Hong Kong, and Taiwan on this day are a reenactment of the search for his body, which was never found. Although the shape of the boats has changed over time, most are narrow shells about 30-feet long with a dragon's head at the prow.

It is said that rice dumplings were cast on the water to lure fish away from the martyr's body. Chinese people in the United States and other countries celebrate the Dragon Boat Festival, which occurs on TUAN WU, or Double Fifth Day, by eating special dumplings made of steamed rice wrapped in bamboo leaves called *tsung tzu* or *zong ze*. This is also a traditional time for performing customs intended to drive away evil spirits and illness.

CONTACTS:
Hong Kong Tourism Board
115 E. 54th St. 2/F
New York, NY 10022
212-421-3382; fax: 212-421-8428
www.discoverhongkong.com

Taiwan Government Information Office
4201 Wisconsin Ave. N.W.
Washington, DC 20016
202-895-1850; fax: 202-362-6144
www.gio.gov.tw

SOURCES:
BkFest-1937, p. 79
BkHolWrld-1986, Jun 18
DictFolkMyth-1984, p. 1130
EncyRel-1987, vol. 3, p. 326
FolkAmerHol-1999, p. 221
FolkWrldHol-1999, p. 369
GdWrldFest-1985, p. 106
IntlThFolk-1979, p. 197

♦ 0770 ♦ **Druids' Summer Solstice Ceremony**
June 23

Stonehenge, the ancient stone circle located on Salisbury Plain in Wiltshire, England, is believed to have been built between about 3050 and 1600 B.C.E. The alignment of the monument's stones have led some to theorize that its builders were sun worshippers: at the SUMMER SOLSTICE, when viewed from the center of the monument, the sun rises through the entrance and just between two of the large stones.

In popular lore, Stonehenge has been associated with the ancient Celtic priests known as Druids. However, Stonehenge was built more than 2,000 years before Druids existed. Nonetheless, today modern Druids and other Neopagans gather at Stonehenge for ceremonies, although the date has been pushed forward a couple of days to avoid the crowds of tourists who flock to Stonehenge on the solstice. Wearing white robes and scarlet hoods, the Druids keep a vigil throughout the night, and when the first rays of the rising sun shine on the Altar Stone, they walk in procession around the circle, gathering at the Altar Stone to recite prayers and salute the rising sun.

Neopagans holding ceremonies in the 1980s had several run-ins with the police, so English Heritage—the British government agency that administers the national monument—closed the monument to solstice celebrations. Since 1998, however, English Heritage has gradually been allowing more and more visitors access to the monument. More than 14,000 Druids and other Neopagans peacefully saw in the summer solstice at Stonehenge in 2001.

CONTACTS:
English Heritage
P.O. Box 569
Swindon, Wiltshire SN22YP United Kingdom
44-87-0333-1181; fax: 44-17-9341-4926
www.english-heritage.org.uk

SOURCES:
EngCustUse-1941, p. 79
FolkCal-1930, p. 137
YrFest-1972, p. 48

◆ 0771 ◆ Drymiais
March 1-3

In Macedonia, the first three days of March are known as Drymiais and are associated with a number of superstitious beliefs. No trees are pruned or planted during this period because it is believed that they will wither. The same fate awaits trees that are pruned or planted during the last three days of March or on any Wednesday or Friday during the month.

The first day of March is traditionally considered to mark the beginning of spring. One custom is for Macedonian mothers to tie pieces of red and white yarn, twisted together, around their children's wrists on this day (*see also* MARTENITZA). When they see a swallow, the children throw the skein of yarn to the bird as an offering or place it under a stone. If they lift the stone a few days later and find a swarm of ants beneath it, they can expect a healthy and prosperous year.

SOURCES:
FolkWrldHol-1999, p. 198

◆ 0772 ◆ Duarte Day
January 26

The birthday of national hero Juan Pablo Duarte (1813-76) is an official day of remembrance in the Dominican Republic. Dominicans recognize other founding fathers—Ramón Mella and Juan Sanchez Ramírez—but these figures do not figure nearly as prominently in history as Duarte does. Known as the father of national independence, Duarte organized *La Trinitaria* in 1838, a secret resistance group whose efforts against the Haitian occupiers culminated in the Dominican Republic's declaration of independence on February 27, 1844.

Dominicans honor Duarte Day with public fiestas in major towns throughout the country. The stateliest ceremony takes place in Independence Park, located in the capital city, Santa Domingo. The park, which also hosts ceremonies for DOMINICAN REPUBLIC INDEPENDENCE DAY, features *Altar de la Patria* (the nation's altar), a mausoleum to the nation's heroes. On Duarte Day, dignitaries and citizens pay their respects at the gravesites of Duarte, Mella, and Sanchez by adorning the altar with flowers.

CONTACTS:
Embassy of the Dominican Republic
1715 22nd St. N.W.
Washington, D.C. 20008
202-332-6280; fax: 202-265-8057

Dominican Republic Tourism Office
136 E. 57th St., Ste. 803
New York, NY 10022
888-374-6361 or 215-588-1012; fax: 212-588-1015

◆ 0773 ◆ Dublin Irish Festival
First weekend in August

During the 19th century, a large Irish immigrant population settled in communities throughout the United States. One particular enclave established north of Columbus, Ohio, took the name of the capital of Ireland. In 1987, the first Dublin Irish Festival was held to commemorate the city's rich ethnic heritage.

The first festival was a humble affair, consisting of a small gathering of Irish dancers. The magnitude of the 20th anniversary, with over 93,000 people arriving from all over the world, showed how much the festival had grown in popularity over two decades. That same year, 10,036 festival attendees danced the Irish Jig at one time, setting a Guinness World Record for the largest Irish dance.

One of the festival's main events is the Columbus Feis, in which competitors square off in performances of a Gaelic dance known as the ceilidh (KAY-lee). The Feis, as well as shows taking place on six different stages, comprise the festival's music and dance component. Other activities include listening to storytelling and folklore at three cultural stages, eating traditional Irish food, shopping for imported Irish goods, and watching sheepherding demonstrations.

CONTACTS:
Dublin, Ohio Convention & Visitors Bureau
9 S. High St.
Dublin, Ohio 43017
800-245-8387 or 614-792-7666; fax: 614-760-1818
www.dublinirishfestival.org

♦ 0774 ♦ **Dubrovnik Summer Festival**
Mid-July to mid-August

Centuries of artistic legacy come to life each year in Croatia at the Dubrovnik Summer Festival, an international festival of music, dance, and theater. Approximately 80 performances, including opera, ballet, drama, art exhibitions, and poetry readings are offered during the course of the festival. They are staged at a variety of open-air and indoor venues, bringing to life the beautiful Renaissance and Baroque architecture of Dubrovnik.

As early as the 1920s, attempts had been made to organize an arts festival in Dubrovnik that would take advantage of the region's rich cultural heritage and its many fine stages. Many performances took place, but planning for a full-fledged festival was not realized at that time. In the aftermath of World War II, there was an upsurge of interest in the arts, as people sought healing and a new identity following the horrors of the war years. As a result, many arts festivals were established at that time, including the Dubrovnik Summer Festival.

The first full festival season in Dubrovnik took place in 1950, and it included orchestra and choral performances, five plays, and an evening of poetry. In 1956, Dubrovnik's annual Games were accepted as a member of the European Festivals Association. In the early years of the festival, the material was almost exclusively Croatian, but as the years passed, the festival expanded to include classics from the wider European tradition, including Shakespeare, Molière, Goethe, and the Greek tragedians. In 2007, performers at the festival included artists from approximately 20 countries, including the United States, Brazil, India, and China.

CONTACTS:
Dubrovnik Summer Festival
Od Sigurate 1
20 000 Dubrovnik, Croatia
www.dubrovnik-festival.hr

Croatian National Tourist Board
Iblerov trg 10/IV
10000 Zagreb, Croatia
www.croatia.hr

♦ 0775 ♦ **Dukang Festival**
December 15

The Dukang Festival is a trade fair and festival held in Yichuan in the Henan Province of China. This was the homeland of Dukang, who is supposed to have discovered alcoholic beverages 4,000 years ago (as Dionysus, in Greek mythology, invented wine). A Chinese folk tale tells of Dukang's beverage intoxicating the eight deities, and a poem contains the line, "Who other than Dukang can relieve me of my grief?" Dukang has become a synonym for liquor, and is also the name of a distillery in Yichuan.

The trade fair highlights not only wines and spirits but also cooking oil and food products, electrical appliances, dyes, and other manufactured goods. The festival features performances by opera troupes and dance ensembles.

CONTACTS:
China National Tourist Office
370 Lexington Ave., Ste. 912
New York, NY 10118
888-760-8218 or 212-760-8218; fax: 212-760-8809
www.cnto.org

♦ 0776 ♦ **Dulcimer and Harp Convention**
Second weekend in June

Founded in 1962 by Jean and Lee Schilling, this annual festival takes place at the Folk Life Center of the Smokies in Cosby, Tenn., which is dedicated to the study and preservation of southern Appalachian folk traditions. There is a modern amphitheater on the Center's 19-acre grounds in the foothills of the Great Smoky Mountains where most of the musical demonstrations and concerts are held. There are also workshops for those who play the musical saw, jew's harp, mountain dulcimer, hammered dulcimer, autoharp, bowed psaltery, and banjo. Both renowned instrumentalists and amateurs from all over the United States attend the two-day festival, which includes jam sessions, craft displays, and special activities for children.

CONTACTS:
Folk Life Center of the Smokies
P.O. Box 8
Cosby, TN 37722
423-487-5543

SOURCES:
MusFestAmer-1990, p. 228

♦ 0777 ♦ **Dulcimer Days**
Third weekend in May

The hammered dulcimer is a stringed musical instrument in which the strings are beaten with small hammers rather than plucked with the fingers. It is a favorite with American folk musicians, many of whom gather in Coshocton, Ohio, each year for the **Mid-Eastern Regional Dulcimer Championships**. The competition takes place near Roscoe Village, a restored 1830s canal town. In addition to the musical competition there are exhibits, workshops dealing with the hammered and mountain dulcimers—the latter being a narrow folk-zither with three to five metal strings—and jam sessions. The winners of the Dulcimer Days competition are given a chance to compete in the national competition held each year in Winfield, Kansas.

CONTACTS:
Roscoe Village Foundation
600 N. Whitewoman St.
Coshocton, OH 43812
800-877-1830 or 740-622-9310; fax: 740-623-6555
www.roscoevillage.com

♦ 0778 ♦ **Dundee International Guitar Festival**
July

The seaside town of Dundee, Scotland, is hardly a European epicenter; nonetheless, it has become the site of one of

Europe's most prominent classical guitar festivals. Virtuosos come from the world's most prestigious conservatories to perform and lead master classes over the course of one weekend. The first festival in 1991 was a local affair, but over the years it has expanded to become an internationally recognized event.

The festival's concerts and educational programs cater particularly to young guitar students. Along with featuring international greats like Paul Galbraith and John Williams, the program also features a Young Artists Platform that puts aspiring guitarists in the spotlight. Many of the instructional subjects are designed in response to students' suggestions; and reduced rates are available for the younger players who cannot afford the full admission.

CONTACTS:
Dundee Guitar Festival
Dundee Contemporary Arts
152 Nethergate
Dundee DD1 4DY Scotland
dundeeguitarfestival.com

♦ 0779 ♦ **Dunmow Flitch Trial**
Every four years in July (2012, 2016, 2020…)

The custom of awarding a flitch of bacon ("flitch" refers to the side of a hog) to any married pair who have neither regretted their union nor quarrelled for a year and a day since their wedding dates back to the 13th century in England. The trial formerly took place on WHIT-MONDAY, but these days it is held every four years in July. Robert Fitzwater instituted the practice during the reign of King Henry III (1216-72), although in the beginning the flitch of bacon was only given to men, since a "happy marriage" at the time was defined as one that was satisfactory to the husband. The wife's views on the success of her marriage were not considered until the beginning of the 18th century.

While kneeling on two sharp stones in the churchyard, the applicant had to take an oath before the prior and villagers of Dunmow that he had never repented of his marriage, waking or sleeping, for a year and a day. If they believed him, he would be carried through the streets in an ancient wooden chair. Given the fact that there were only three prizewinners between 1445 and 1510, it must be assumed that the standard to which the applicants were held was very high.

Today, claimants for the Dunmow Flitch are required to answer questions about their marriage at a mock trial, presided over by a judge. A jury consisting of six spinsters and six bachelors gives the verdict, and the proceedings are usually lighthearted, although there are always some genuine candidates for the flitch as well as those who only take part for amusement.

CONTACTS:
Official Dunmow Flitch Trials Committee
Dunmow Flitch Judge
28 High St.
Great Dunmow, Essex CM6 1AH United Kingdom
44-13-7187-2816; fax: 44-13-7187-2324
www.dunmowflitchtrials.co.uk

Dunmow Town Strategy Group
Foakes House
47 Stortford Rd.
Great Dunmow, Essex CM6 1DG United Kingdom
44-13-7187-2406; fax: 44-13-7187-8378
www.great-dunmow.co.uk

SOURCES:
EngCustUse-1941, p. 64
FolkCal-1930, p. 115
YrFest-1972, p. 41

♦ 0780 ♦ **Durga Puja**
September-October; waxing half of Hindu month of Asvina

There are various Hindu festivals on the Indian subcontinent that celebrate the victory of good over evil.

The festival in Calcutta, India, in the state of West Bengal, honors Durga, who rides a lion and destroys demons. She is one aspect of the Mother Goddess and the personification of energy, and is famous for slaying the buffalo demon, Mahisasura. During the 10 days of Durga Puja, the city becomes one great festival, with deafening music and fireworks. Before the *puja* (a Sanskrit word meaning "worship" or "homage"), artisans have constructed clay figures over straw-and-bamboo frames, some of them 10 feet high. Stages are set up for these figures in neighborhoods throughout the city, and for four days throngs of people admire the clay tableaux, often showing Durga on a lion slaying demons. (Artist Aloke Sen's images have become famous because his demons have the faces of ordinary men and women and represent such evils as lust, anger, vanity, and greed.) On the fourth night, the images, which are genuine works of art and have cost as much as $20,000, are taken down from the stages, placed on bamboo stretchers, and carried—to the music of hundreds of bagpipers and other musicians—to the banks of the Hooghly River and tossed in. As they float toward the mouth of the Ganges, they dissolve back into clay, straw, and bamboo.

Navaratri. In the states of southern India this festival is known as Navaratri (nine nights), and also involves the worship of the goddesses Lakshmi and Sarasvati. Lakshmi is linked with wealth and good luck, and Sarasvati is associated with a river of that name, as well as with fertility, wisdom, and education. The festival is a time for visiting friends and relatives, and houses are decorated with displays of toys and dolls and images of gods. In the state of Gujarat there are nine days of music and dancing devoted to the nine forms of the goddess Ambaji, as well as competitions of *garba* dancing.

Dussehra (or **Dashara**). In other parts of India the festival also celebrates the victory of Lord Rama over Ravana, and is known as Dussehra (or Dashara).

During the 10 days of Dussehra, scenes from the epic poem *Ramayana* are enacted. The epic tells the story of Lord Rama who wins the lovely Sita for his wife, only to have her carried off by evil 10-headed Ravana, demon king of Lanka. Ultimately, Rama slays Ravana, and the forces of good triumph over evil. The dramatizations with music, held throughout northern India, are considered at their best in Delhi. On the 10th day, immense effigies of Ravana, his brother, and his son (all of them stuffed with firecrackers) explode in dramatic bursts of flame and noise (*see also* RAMA LEELA FESTIVAL).

In the northern mountains of Himachal Pradesh, the festival begins with a procession of deities to the town of Kulu from the little hill temples of neighboring villages. Accompanying the deities are villagers blowing large horns, ringing bells, and beating drums. When a deity arrives in Kulu, it is placed before Raghunathji, the presiding god of Kulu Valley, who is in an honored position in a tent. Outside, there is folk dancing and music. On the final day of the festival, a bull is sacrificed as a gift to the gods.

Mysore, in the state of Karnataka, celebrates the victory of goddess Chamundi over demon Mahisasura with regal pomp. The palace of the maharajah is illuminated, there are torchlight and daylight parades, and deities on decorated barges in a floodlit lake. On the final day, there is a grand procession of magnificently caparisoned elephants, the camel corps, the cavalry, and the infantry.

Dasain. In Nepal, the festival is called Dasain, or Bada Dasain. It comes at the end of the long monsoon period when days are clear and the rice is ready for harvesting, and lasts for 10 days.

In Nepal, Buddhists also celebrate this festival and special events are held at Buddhist shrines in Patan and Bhaktapur. The Nepalese also modify the *Ramayana* story to include the goddess Durga's victory over the forces of evil represented by the demon Mahisasura. Since Durga is bloodthirsty, there are thousands of animal sacrifices.

Before the festival begins, Nepalese clean their houses and set up ferris wheels and swings in their villages. On the first day of the festival, a water jug called a *kalash* is filled with holy water, and barley seeds are planted in cow dung on the outside of the jug. During the festival, the seeds are sprinkled with the water, and ceremonies are performed around it.

The first big day of the festival is the seventh day, Fulpati, meaning "day of flowers." A royal kalash holding flowers is carried by Brahmin priests from the ancestral palace in Gurkha to Katmandu. Cannons boom, the king and queen review troops, and then revere the flowers at the Hanuman Dhoka Palace, the old residence of kings.

The eighth night is known as Kalratri, or "black night." At midnight, at Hanuman Dhoka, eight buffaloes and 108 goats are beheaded. During the next day, thousands of buffaloes, goats, and chickens are sacrificed in temples, military posts, and homes as people ask Durga for protection. Blood is sprinkled on the wheels of vehicles, and at the airport, a goat is sacrificed for each Royal Nepal Airlines aircraft.

The 10th day, Vijaya Dashami, commemorates the day that Durga (or Rama) appeared riding a lion to slay the Mahisasura (or Ravana). On this day, people wear the fresh shoots of the barley in their hair and visit older relatives to receive the red *tika* blessing on their foreheads. In towns of the Katman-

du Valley, there are masked dances and processions of priests carrying wooden swords, symbolic of the sword used to kill the buffalo demon.

Caitra Dasain, observed in the month of Caitra (March-April), is similar to Bada Dasain, but observed with less pomp. On this earlier occasion, the goddess is worshipped and animal sacrifices are made to her.

CONTACTS:
Ministry of Tourism, Government of India
Rm. No 123, Transport Bhawan, No. 1, Parliament St.
New Delhi, Delhi 110 001 India
91-11-23715084; fax: 91-11-23715084
www.tourisminindia.com

SOURCES:
BkFest-1937, p. 161
BkHolWrld-1986, Oct 13
DictWrldRel-1989, p. 280
FolkWrldHol-1999, p. 581
GdWrldFest-1985, p. 110
OxYear-1999, p. 720
RelHolCal-2004, p. 176

♦ 0781 ♦ **Durham Miners' Gala**
Second Saturday of July

With the emergence of coal mining in the 17th century, England began enjoying the fruits of a lucrative industry. But the miners did not always receive fair compensation. Soon after founding the first union in 1869, a group of mine workers in northern England initiated a campaign to lobby their pit bosses, who met regularly to set mining wages at the Royal County Hotel in the city of Durham.

Soon an annual tradition developed in which mine workers arrived at the hotel in grand style, bringing with them brass bands and colorful silk banners that identified their unions. What began as a formal protest became a grand party, and by 1871, the first official Durham Miners' Gala was held.

Today, the gala is less political in nature. It has become more of a heritage celebration of coal mining, an industry that has steadily decreased over the years. The event usually features about 30 community brass bands, which march through the streets of Durham with banners representing member organizations of the National Union of Mineworkers. The procession ends at the Racecourse of Durham University, where attendees gather to hear speeches from trade union leaders and politicians.

CONTACTS:
Durham Mining Museum
c/o Thornley Community Centre
Hartlepool St.
Thornley DH6 3AB UK

♦ 0782 ♦ **Dutch Liberation Day**
May 4-5

Liberation Day, or **National Day**, in the Netherlands celebrates May 5, 1945, the day on which the Nazi forces were driven out of Holland by the Allies. Although the Dutch had succeeded in remaining neutral during World War I, the country was invaded by the Nazis in May 1940 and rapidly overrun. Despite the occupation, however, the Dutch managed to make a significant contribution to the Allied cause by building up an effective resistance. The liberation of Holland in 1945, in which the resistance played a leading part, was an important step toward the subsequent defeat of the Nazis.

Many Dutch cities hold special concerts on this day. Special commemorations are held in Amsterdam and around the country on May 5 each year, as well as on May 4, Remembrance Day.

CONTACTS:
National 4 and 5 May Committee
Nieuwe Prinsengracht 89
Amsterdam, 1018 VR Netherlands
31-20-718-3500; fax: 31-20-718-3501
www.4en5mei.nl

SOURCES:
AnnivHol-2000, p. 77

E

♦ 0783 ♦ **Eagle Dance**
Early spring

Many North American Indians associate the eagle with supernatural powers, particularly the power to control thunder and rain. In the Jemez and Tesuque pueblos in New Mexico, the eagle dance takes place in the early spring. Two dancers, representing male and female, wear feathered caps with yellow beaks and hold wings made out of eagle feathers. They circle each other with hopping and swaying motions.

The Comanches hold an eagle dance where a single dancer imitates the eagle, who according to legend is the young son of a chieftain who was turned into an eagle when he died. Dancers in the Iowa tribe's eagle dance carry an eagle feather fan in their left hands, while the Iroquois eagle dance features feathered rattles and wands.

Among some tribes, eagle feathers are believed to exert special powers. The Sioux wear them in their war bonnets for victory, while the Pawnee, Yuchi, Delaware, and Iroquois Indians use them in ceremonial fans or brushes or as ornaments.

SOURCES:
DictFolkMyth-1984, p. 333
EncyNatAmerRel-2001, p. 74
EncyRel-1987, vol. 4, p. 466

♦ 0784 ♦ **Earhart (Amelia) Festival**
Weekend closest to July 24

To celebrate the birthday of noted aviator and Atchison native Amelia Earhart, the town of Atchison, Kans., holds the Amelia Earhart Festival on the weekend closest to her July 24th birthday. Earhart was born in Atchison in 1897 and lived there with her grandparents until 1908. The winner of many world records in the history of aviation, Earhart was the first woman to fly across the Atlantic Ocean on her own. In 1937, while attempting to fly around the world, Earhart went missing over the Pacific Ocean and is presumed to have crashed.

The festival began in 1997 to mark the 100th anniversary of the hometown heroine's birth. Among the weekend events are aerobatic performances over the Missouri River, including an exhibition of wing-walking, a birthday party for Earhart, including free cake, an outdoor country music concert, a one-hour trolley tour of Earhart-related sites in town, a children's stage featuring puppet shows and live animals, a toy airplane contest, talks and documentary films about Earhart's life, and a riverside fireworks display set to music. The Amelia Earhart Pioneering Achievement Award is also presented to a woman who has contributed to the field of aviation.

CONTACTS:
Atchison Chamber of Commerce
200 S. 10th St.
Atchison, KS 66002
800-234-1854
www.atchisonkansas.net

♦ 0785 ♦ **Earth Day**
April 22

The first Earth Day was observed on April 22, 1970, for the purpose of drawing public attention to the need for cleaning up the earth's air and water and for conserving our natural resources. Since that time the idea has spread, and Earth Day is now observed regularly throughout the United States and in many other countries (though there were some years of slack observance until the late 1980s).

Typical ways of celebrating Earth Day include planting trees, picking up roadside trash, and conducting various programs for recycling and conservation. Schoolchildren may be asked to use only recyclable containers for their snacks and lunches, and environmentally concerned families often try to give up wasteful habits, such as using paper towels or plastic garbage bags.

"Earth" days have been observed by other groups as well. The day of the VERNAL EQUINOX is also observed by some as Earth Day.

CONTACTS:
Earth Day Network
1616 P St. N.W., Ste. 340
Seattle, WA 98104
202-518-0044; fax: 202-518-8794
www.earthday.net

SOURCES:
AmerBkDays-2000, p. 223
AnnivHol-2000, p. 66

♦ 0786 ♦ East Timor Independence Day
May 20

On May 20, 2002, about half of a small island in the Lesser Sundra group became the Democratic Republic of East Timor after being an unwilling and brutalized province of Indonesia for the previous two decades and under Portuguese colonial rule for hundreds of years before that. Among the approximately 200,000 attendees at the independence ceremony in the capital city of Dili were Bishop Carlos Belo and Jose Ramos Horta, who won the NOBEL Peace Prize in 1996 for their efforts toward building the peaceful independence of this Roman Catholic region within Indonesia, the largest Muslim country in the world.

CONTACTS:
East Timor Government, Department of Tourism
Apartado 194
Dili, Timor-Leste
670-331-0371; fax: 670-333-9179
www.turismotimorleste.com/en

Prime Minister's Office, Government Palace
President Nicolau Lobato Ave.
Dili, Timor-Leste
www.timor-leste.gov.tl

♦ 0787 ♦ Easter
Between March 22 and April 25 in the West and between April 4 and May 8 in the East; first Sunday after the first full moon on or following the vernal equinox

Easter is the principal feast of the Christian year, despite the popularity and commercialization that surrounds CHRISTMAS. According to the Gospel of John, Mary Magdalene came to the cave where Jesus had been buried and found the tomb empty. An angel of the Lord told her that Jesus had risen. The anniversary of his resurrection from the dead is joyfully celebrated by Christians every year with special services, music, candlelight, flowers, and the ringing of church bells that had remained silent during LENT.

For Greek Orthodox Christians, the sorrow of GOOD FRIDAY lifts with the service of the Holy Resurrection on Saturday night in a dimly lit church. At midnight, all lights are extinguished, the door to the altar opens and the priest, holding a lighted candle, appears and proclaims that Christ is risen. The congregants light their candles from the priest's, bells ring, people turn to each other and say, *Christos Anesti,* "Christ is risen," and receive the reply, *Alithos Anesti,* "He is risen indeed."

Easter is a movable holiday whose day of observation has for centuries been painstakingly calculated. This is because its day of observance is determined initially by the lunar calendar, like PASSOVER, but then must be put into terms of the solar calendar. The Council of Nicea in 325 C.E. set the formula for calculating the date of Easter still in use today. After many centuries of controversy among Christians, Western Christendom settled on the use of the Gregorian calendar (Eastern Christians use the Julian calendar to determine Easter), decreeing that Easter shall be celebrated on the Sunday after the full moon on or following the VERNAL EQUINOX. If the full moon is on a Sunday, Easter is held the next Sunday. In the East, Easter can occur between April 4 and May 8, but it must come after Passover has ended.

The name for Easter may have come from *Eostre,* the Teutonic goddess of spring and fertility, whose feast was celebrated around this same time. There is also a Germanic goddess named Ostara who was always accompanied by a hare—possibly the ancestor of our modern Easter Bunny. The association of both the rabbit and eggs with Easter is probably the vestige of an ancient springtime fertility rite.

Although Easter has retained a greater religious significance than Christmas, many children in the United States think of it as a time to get new spring clothes, to decorate eggs, and to indulge in the chocolate and jelly beans that the Easter Bunny has left in their Easter baskets.

In Belgium, throughout Walloonia, the priest gives a number of unconsecrated priest's wafers to young children to sell to householders. The proceeds are given to the needy parish families, and the wafers are nailed over the front doors to protect the families from evil.

In Ethiopia, Easter is called **Fasika** and is welcomed in the capital city of Addis Ababa at dawn with a 21-gun salute.

CONTACTS:
Christian Resource Institute
4712 N. Hammond
Warr Acres, OK 73122
www.cresourcei.org

Greek Orthodox Archdiocese of Australia
242 Cleveland St.
Redfern, NSW 2016 Australia
61-2-9698-5066; fax: 61-2-9698-536
www.greekorthodox.org.au

Orthodox Church in America
P.O. Box 675
Syosset, NY 11791
516-922-0550; fax: 516-922-0954
www.oca.org

SOURCES:
AmerBkDays-2000, p. 238
BkDays-1864, vol. I, p. 423
BkFest-1937, pp. 6, 16, 24, 30, 42, 57, 70, 87, 96, 113, 121, 133, 148, 168, 185, 211, 219, 228, 241, 249, 260, 268, 276, 287, 292, 301, 309, 317, 330, 339
DaysCustFaith-1957, pp. 108, 353
DictFolkMyth-1984, pp. 129, 181, 212, 334, 561, 628, 687, 789, 854, 947
EncyEaster-2002
EncyRel-1987, vol. 3, p. 439
FestSaintDays-1915, p. 73
FestWestEur-1958, pp. 9, 24, 35, 61, 95, 108, 126, 130, 152, 164, 213, 231
FolkAmerHol-1999, p. 167
FolkWrldHol-1999, p. 224
GdUSFest-1984, p. 144
HolSymbols-2009, p. 215

OxYear-1999, pp. 621, 643, 791
RelHolCal-2004, pp. 78, 94, 111, 121
SaintFestCh-1904, p. 162

♦ 0788 ♦ Easter (Bulgaria)
Between April 4 and May 8

Although midnight church services are widespread throughout Bulgaria on **Velikden** (The Great Day), or **Vuzkresenie** (Resurrection Day), the EASTER service held in the cathedral in Sofia, the capital, is by far the most impressive. Just before midnight on Easter morning, the traditional hour of Christ's resurrection, a procession of church dignitaries in elaborate vestments follows the archbishop from the cathedral to Alexander Nevsky Square, which is already filled with thousands of worshippers carrying unlighted candles. As the midnight chimes peal, the archbishop blesses the people and the thousands of candles are lit. A service in the cathedral follows.

Easter celebrations in Bulgaria last a full week, known as *Svetla Nedelya,* or the Week of Light, because folklore has it that the sun did not set in Jerusalem for eight days after the resurrection of Christ. One tradition during this week is the national dance known as the *Choro,* which is performed by a circle composed of equal numbers of male and female dancers who begin with a very slow movement that gradually quickens in pace.

CONTACTS:
Embassy of the Republic of Bulgaria
1621 22nd St. N.W.
Washington, D.C. 20008
202-387-0174; fax: 202-234-7973
www.bulgaria-embassy.org

SOURCES:
BkFest-1937, p. 70
FestSaintDays-1915, p. 82

♦ 0789 ♦ Easter (Chile)
Between March 22 and April 25

HOLY WEEK or Semana Santa, the week that precedes EASTER, is a very solemn period in Chile, most of whose inhabitants are Roman Catholic. It is a time to remember the death and resurrection of Christ, and the primary activity for adults is going to church to pray. Children, on the other hand, drag large dolls, who represent Judas, through the streets of their neighborhood in carts or wagons, stopping at houses to request coins. These coins represent the 30 pieces of silver given to Judas for turning Jesus over to the authorities. When the day is over, children set fire to the dolls, under their parents' supervision. On Easter Sunday itself, there are Easter egg hunts and baskets filled with chocolates.

Cuasimodo is the first Sunday following Easter. In the villages and little towns of rural central and southern Chile, religious processions take place, led by priests, who bring Holy Communion to those who are too sick or elderly to make it to church. This is a tradition that extends back more than 100 years, when many Chileans lived too far out in the country to travel to church on Cuasimodo. Because bandits were common and likely to attack the priest, he would usually be accompanied by cowboys known as *huasos*. Although there are no longer any bandits, huasos still like to display their horsemanship on Cuasimodo, when horse-riding contests are frequently held. Today cyclists also escort the priest.

CONTACTS:
Embassy of Chile
1732 Massachusetts Ave. N.W.
Washington, D.C. 20036
202-785-1746; fax: 202-887-5579
www.chile-usa.org

SOURCES:
FestWrld: Chile-1998, p. 20

♦ 0790 ♦ Easter (Cyprus)
Between April 4 and May 8

On EASTER Sunday in Cyprus, fireworks are set off, ships in ports blow their whistles, and bonfires are built to burn Judas. People go home for a late dinner starting with red-dyed hard-boiled eggs and then a special soup and often cheese pie (*tiropita*). It's customary to tap the eggs against each other; whoever cracks the other's egg will have good luck in the coming year. Often there is feasting on lamb roasted on spits over open fires; other traditional foods are *kokoretsi*, a sausage made of lamb innards and herbs, and *lambropsomo*, an Easter bread with a whole red-dyed egg in the center. In the countryside, the feasting is accompanied by fairs and dancing in regional costume. Passersby are offered lamb, red eggs, and wine and are toasted with "Christos Anesti."

SOURCES:
FolkWrldHol-1999, p. 227

♦ 0791 ♦ Easter (Czech Republic)
Between March 22 and April 25

In the Czech Republic, EASTER (**Velikonoce**) is celebrated as both a religious holy day and a seasonal festival that marks the end of winter.

For breakfast on Easter Sunday (*Nedele velikonocní*), Czechs eat *mazanec*, a traditional raisin-filled sweet bun spiced with nutmeg, topped with almonds, and marked with a cross before baking. Roast lamb or goat is the customary Easter dinner fare. The day itself is filled with preparations for traditional activities that take place the following day on EASTER MONDAY, known as Whipping Monday.

On that day young boys and adolescents visit the homes of girls they admire to sing carols and whip the girls symbolically with pomlázka—pussy willow branches that have been braided into wands and decorated with colored ribbons. In return, the girls give boys such treats as *kraslice* (decorated eggs) or chocolate. The pussy willow branches symbolize youth and fertility. Though the custom is dying out in larger cities, the ritual, which is documented in writings extending back as far as the 14th century, continues in villages.

CONTACTS:
Embassy of the Czech Republic
3900 Spring of Freedom St. N.W.
Washington, D.C. 20008
202-274-9100; fax: 202-966-8540
www.mzv.cz/wwwo/?zu=washington

SOURCES:
EncyEaster-2002, p. 76

♦ 0792 ♦ Easter (Egypt)
Between April 4 and May 8

EASTER in Egypt is celebrated by the nation's population of Christians, about seven percent of the total population (or 12 million people). The majority of Christians in Egypt belongs to the Coptic Orthodox branch of the church, which is based in Alexandria and Cairo. The Coptic Orthodox Church dates back to the first century and was founded by the apostle Mark, one of the four gospel authors. Significant numbers of Egyptians also belong to various Eastern and Roman Catholic rites, including the Greek Orthodox Church, the Coptic Catholic Church, the Melkite Greek Catholic Church, or to Protestant denominations such as the Coptic Evangelical Church.

In preparation for Easter, the high feast commemorating the resurrection of Jesus, Coptic Orthodox adherents observe a period of LENT comprising 55 days of fasting. During this time all foods derived from animals are prohibited, including meat, fish, eggs, and milk. A diet limited to vegetables and beans is followed during HOLY WEEK, the week leading up to Easter Sunday, and during this period people attend church services every day. On Saturday night, they attend a long Easter Vigil service, which continues through much of the night, ending in the early hours of Easter Sunday morning. Families then return home to break the long period of fasting and celebrate with a feast of roasted turkey or lamb with grape leaves. Children receive small gifts of money or clothing. In Cairo the pope of the Coptic Orthodox Church presides over a national Easter service in the Great Cathedral of St. Mark that is attended by thousands of the congregation as well as numerous government and religious dignitaries. A public holiday celebrating the beginning of spring is held on the day after Easter, and this is a popular day for picnics and visiting family and friends.

CONTACTS:
Coptic Orthodox Church in Egypt
His Holiness Pope Shenouda III
www.copticpope.org/index.php

Coptic Orthodox Church Network
P.O. Box 6909
East Brunswick, NJ 08816
www.copticchurch.net

SOURCES:
EncyEaster-2002, p. 171

♦ 0793 ♦ Easter (Germany) (Ostern)
Between March 22 and April 25

The first recorded evidence of a rabbit being associated with EASTER dates from the 16th century in Germany, although the custom may be even older. The Easter hare still brings eggs to German children and hides them in out-of-the-way places, although in the past, the stork, the fox, and the cuckoo have played the same role. In many parts of Germany, little "rabbit gardens" are built for the Easter Bunny, using moss or grass as a nest for the eggs. Egg-gathering and egg-rolling are both popular activities at Easter, as are contests to see who can devour the greatest number of eggs.

Perhaps a remnant of ancient sacrificial rites, bonfires are built on high points of land in northern Germany. Although usually built out of huge piles of tar-soaked barrels and old tree roots and limbs, in the North Rhine-Westphalian village of Luegde, bonfires are made by tying twigs and straw to seven-foot wheels, lighting them, and rolling them down the hill. The flaming wheels, symbolic of the sun, weigh about 800 pounds each. Every time one of them reaches the bottom of the hill, the spectators shout for joy, for it is believed that this will bring a special blessing to the land and a bountiful harvest.

Water is also associated with Easter celebrations in Germany. One old custom entails girls in the Harz Mountains, Thuringia, and other regions rising at dawn to draw "Easter water" from the rivers. If they do so in complete silence and then bathe in the water, they will be blessed with beauty throughout the year. Easter morning dew is used for the same purpose.

"Easter smacks," or *Schmeckostern*, are traditional beatings that the men and women give to each other in various parts of Germany to bring them luck, to protect them from disease, and to keep them young and healthy. The men beat the women on EASTER MONDAY, and the women beat the men on Easter Tuesday. The new life contained by a green branch is supposed to be bestowed on the one who is beaten with it.

CONTACTS:
German Embassy in Ottawa, Canada
1 Waverley St.
Ottawa, ON K2P OT8 Canada
613-232-1101; fax: 613-594-9330
www.germanembassy.co.uk

SOURCES:
BkFest-1937, p. 133
BkFestHolWrld-1970, p. 60
DictFolkMyth-1984, p. 335
EncyEaster-2002, p. 227
FestWestEur-1958, p. 61

♦ 0794 ♦ Easter (Hollywood, California)
Between March 22 and April 25

The early Christians believed that on EASTER morning, the sun danced in honor of the resurrection of Christ. This led to the custom of rising before dawn to witness the phenomenon and may be the reason why sunrise services on Easter morning are common throughout the United States.

At the Hollywood Bowl, a huge outdoor amphitheater in the Hollywood Hills, California, the Easter sunrise service is a spectacle on a scale that only Hollywood could produce. First held in 1921, the service is attended by about 30,000 people who spend the night in the stadium. About 50,000 calla lilies decorate the stage, where a huge choir and a symphony orchestra perform the *Hallelujah* chorus from Handel's *Messiah* and traditional Easter hymns. Some 250 teenagers form a "living cross" just after dawn.

CONTACTS:
Hollywood Bowl
2301 N. Highland Ave.
Hollywood, CA 90078
323-850-2000
www.hollywoodbowl.com

SOURCES:
BkFestHolWrld-1970, p. 59

♦ 0795 ♦ **Easter (Italy) (La Pasqua)**
Between March 22 and April 25

In many Italian towns and villages sacred dramas commemorating episodes in the EASTER story or from the Bible are held in the *piazzas* on Easter day. Pastries called *corona di nove* are baked in the form of a crown; in America, these pastries are often made in the shape of rabbits instead. Other traditional foods of the season include *capretto* (lamb) and *agnello* (kid).

In Florence, the Ceremony of the Car, or *Scoppio del Carro,* is held on HOLY SATURDAY. Inaugurated by the ancient Florentine family of de'Pazzi, the custom involves a decorated wooden car filled with explosives, which is drawn into the piazza by white oxen and placed before the cathedral doors. A wire runs from the high altar inside the cathedral to the car in the piazza. As the mass ends, a dove-shaped rocket is ignited at the altar and sent shooting out along the wire. When it reaches the car, it sets fire to the explosives. Tuscan farmers believe that if the rocket does its job well, their harvests will prosper in the coming year. If it fails to ignite the *carro* or if something else goes wrong, their crops in the coming season will be poor.

CONTACTS:
Italian Government Tourist Board
630 Fifth Ave., Ste. 1565
New York, NY 10111
212-245-5618; fax: 212-586-9249
www.italiantourism.com

SOURCES:
BkFest-1937, p. 185
EncyEaster-2002, p. 313
FestSaintDays-1915, p. 75
FestWestEur-1958, p. 95

♦ 0796 ♦ **Easter (Netherlands) (Paschen, Paasch Zondag)**
Between March 22 and April 25

The lighting of bonfires is a common occurrence on EASTER or Easter Eve in the Netherlands. The fuel is collected weeks in advance, and neighboring towns often compete with each other to see which can build the biggest fire. As the flames get higher, the villagers join hands and dance around the fire. In ancient times, bits of charred wood carried home from the

bonfire were believed to protect people's houses from fire and other disasters during the year.

In the village of Denekamp, in the province of Overijssel, two young men who represent the comic characters known as Judas and Iscariot—Judas being "the clever man" and Iscariot being "the stupid man"—prepare the Easter bonfire and help set up the "Easter pole," which is a tall fir tree that has been stripped of its branches, cut down, and carried to the hill where the bonfire will be lit. Judas sets a ladder against the tree, climbs up, and starts auctioning it to the highest bidder. The crowd hoots and jeers at him and at Iscariot, who replaces him. At eight o'clock in the evening the fire is lit, and the townspeople dance and sing a very old hymn whose dialect words and meanings are understood only by local people.

In the eastern Netherlands village of Ootmarsum, the VLÖGGELEN, or "winging ceremony," is held on Easter Sunday and Monday.

See also EASTER MONDAY IN THE NETHERLANDS

CONTACTS:
Netherlands Board of Tourism & Conventions
355 Lexington Ave., 19th Fl.
New York, NY 10017
888-464-6552 or 212-370-7360; fax: 212-370-9507
www.us.holland.com

SOURCES:
BkFest-1937, p. 241
EncyEaster-2002, p. 120
FestWestEur-1958, pp. 126, 130

♦ 0797 ♦ **Easter (Norway) (Paske)**
Between March 22 and April 25

EASTER in Norway is a popular time to go to mountain resorts and enjoy winter sports. From MAUNDY THURSDAY through EASTER MONDAY, the towns and cities are deserted, but every mountain inn and hotel is packed to overflowing with those who come to ski, skate, toboggan, and enjoy watching others pursue such activities. Ice carnivals, sports competitions, dances, and concerts are also popular, and many mountain resorts hold special out-of-doors Easter services for skiers.

Norwegians who observe the holiday at home dye and decorate Easter eggs after boring small holes in the ends and blowing out the yolk and white, or by carefully cutting the shells in half and then pasting them together again with strips of paper. The decorated eggs are hidden all over the house, and on Easter morning, everyone hunts for the eggs that have been concealed for them by other family members.

SOURCES:
BkFest-1937, p. 249
FestWestEur-1958, p. 152

♦ 0798 ♦ **Easter (Poland) (Wielkanoc)**
Between March 22 and April 25

After attending the EASTER church service, Polish families gather to share a cold meal, for the day is considered too sacred to light a fire. The head of the family cuts up a colored egg and gives a piece of it to everyone present. Each person then offers an Easter greeting to the others. The meal itself usually consists of ham, sausages, salads, *babka* (the Polish national cake), and *mazurki,* or sweet cakes filled with nuts, fruit, and honey.

On EASTER MONDAY, people don old clothes and engage in a water-throwing game known as *smigus.* Children often throw decorated eggshells into a stream, in hopes that their Easter wishes will reach those who live beneath the earth.

CONTACTS:
Polish American Journal
P.O. Box 328
Boston, NY 14025
800-422-1275 or 716-312-8088
www.polamjournal.com

SOURCES:
BkFest-1937, p. 260
EncyEaster-2002, p. 500
FolkWrldHol-1999, p. 238

♦ 0799 ♦ Easter (Russia) (Paskha)
Between April 4 and May 8

EASTER is one of the most important holidays of the Russian year. A great deal of attention is devoted to the preparation of *koulich,* a very tall Easter cake made according to a traditional recipe and a major part of the Easter meal that breaks the Lenten fast. Pillows are often placed around the pan while the dough is rising, because any jarring might cause the cake to fall. Husbands often complain that they've been kicked out of the house because their heavy footsteps are disturbing the koulich. The finished cake is usually marked with the initials X and B, which stand for the Russian words meaning "Christ is risen."

On Easter Sunday and Monday the men visit each other, but Easter Tuesday is reserved for the women to call on their friends. In rural areas it is customary for children to swing, dance, and play games and musical instruments on this day. Church bells ring throughout the Easter holiday.

CONTACTS:
Moscow City Tourist Information Center
Gostiny Dvor, 4, Ilyinka
Moscow, 103012 Russia
7-395-232-5657
eng.menu.ru

SOURCES:
BkFest-1937, p. 292
EncyEaster-2002, p. 539

♦ 0800 ♦ Easter (Spain)
Between March 22 and April 25

After attending EASTER morning mass, many Spanish people throng the cafes and restaurants to break their Lenten fast. In the afternoon, residents of Madrid, Seville, and other cities usually attend bullfights. In villages in southern Valencia,

such as Jumilla and Alcañiz, the coming of Easter is marked by a *tamborada*—three days of non-stop drumming. Residents of Hellin are treated to the pounding of 8,000 to 10,000 drums between Holy Wednesday and Easter Sunday.

The shop windows of confectioners and pastry cooks are filled with elaborate displays of cakes around Easter. Sometimes a farmyard is made out of pastry, with hens, cocks, and monkeys. A special pastry known as a *mona* (female monkey) contains a hard-boiled egg, and elaborate and ingenious monas are often given as Easter presents.

In the region of Spain known as Catalonia, HOLY WEEK *pasos* (tableaux) are formed by men standing on each other's shoulders to form a kind of circular pyramid, with a small child standing on the top. Easter pasos often illustrate a biblical scene, such as the Descent from the Cross.

CONTACTS:
Tourist Office of Spain
666 Fifth Ave., 35th Fl.
New York, NY 10103
212-265-8822; fax: 212-265-8864
www.okspain.org

SOURCES:
BkFest-1937, p. 301
EncyEaster-2002, p. 565
FestSaintDays-1915, p. 84
FolkWrldHol-1999, p. 239

♦ 0801 ♦ Easter (Sweden) (Påskdagen)
Between March 22 and April 25

EASTER in Sweden is a time for winter sports. Thousands of people from Stockholm and other southern cities board special excursion trains and spend the Easter holidays in the northern provinces, where winter sports are at their peak.

On either MAUNDY THURSDAY or Easter Eve, children often dress up as witches and call on their neighbors, much as children in the United States do on HALLOWEEN. Sometimes they slip a secret "Easter letter" under the door or in the mailbox. Bonfires are popular in the western provinces of Sweden, with competitions to see which village can build the biggest fire. The witches and bonfires are reminiscent of pagan ceremonies to ward off evil, and in rural areas people still hang crossed scythes in their stables or paint crosses over their doors to protect themselves against the evil spread by Easter hags flying around on their broomsticks.

SOURCES:
BkFest-1937, p. 309
EncyEaster-2002, p. 590
FestWestEur-1958, p. 213
FolkWrldHol-1999, p. 240

♦ 0802 ♦ Easter (Ukraine)
Between April 4 and May 8

Decorating eggs is the EASTER custom for which Ukrainians are known all over the world. The *pysanky* eggs are not cooked because the raw egg shell absorbs the color better.

The initial design is drawn on the shell with a *pysar,* or small, metal-tipped writing tool, dipped in beeswax. When the egg is dipped in the first dye (usually yellow, the lightest color), the wax prevents any dye from being absorbed. When the next layer of the design is drawn on the shell, it will remain yellow while the rest of the egg is dyed a darker color (usually orange or red). This layering process continues until the desired artistic effect is achieved. Then the egg is held over a candle flame to melt off the wax and is coated with shellac or varnish. A woman who is particularly adept at decorating Easter eggs is called a *pysarka.*

The eggs are presented as gifts to friends and relatives on Easter morning. One of the decorated eggs that has been hard-boiled is shelled, sliced up, and served at the beginning of the Easter dinner to symbolize the end of the Lenten fast. Sometimes the eggs are used in a game where children try to strike each other's eggs with their own. But due to the eggs' religious significance and the work that goes into decorating them, the shells are never dropped on the ground or discarded. If broken, they are usually thrown into fire or water.

CONTACTS:
Ukrainian Museum
222 E. 6th St.
New York, NY 10003
212-228-0110; fax: 212-228-1947
www.ukrainianmuseum.org

SOURCES:
EncyEaster-2002, p. 617
FolkAmerHol-1999, p. 179
FolkWrldHol-1999, p. 241

♦ 0803 ♦ **Easter (Yaqui Indians)**
Between March 22 and April 25

Although they were originally Mexican, the Yaqui Indians resettled in Arizona, and most of them now live near Tucson or Phoenix. During HOLY WEEK they perform a series of dances and pageants that combine Christian, Native American, and Spanish customs. They act out their own version of the biblical events associated with EASTER, using spectacular masks and costumes and incorporating the complicated symbolism of their native culture as well as such recognizable Christian figures as Jesus, the Virgin Mary, Judas, and Pilate.

When the Yaqui lived in Mexico, a group of ritual clowns known as the Chapayekas played the role of police during the Easter week celebrations. They wore masks made out of goat or wild pig skin with long ears and snouts (*chapayekas* means "long slender noses") and huge horns. They maintained a ritual silence and communicated only by sign language. Today they still play a part in Yaqui Easter observances, performing dances during Easter processions and church services.

CONTACTS:
Pascua Yaqui Tribe
7474 S. Camino de Oeste
Tucson, AZ 85746
520-883-5000; fax: 520-883-5014
www.pascuayaqui-nsn.gov

SOURCES:
DictFolkMyth-1984, p. 212
EncyRel-1987, vol. 4, p. 437
IndianAmer-1989, p. 274

♦ 0804 ♦ **Easter Egg Roll**
Between March 23 and April 26; Monday following Easter

Starting in the middle of the 19th century, it was customary for young children to roll EASTER eggs on the lawn of the Capitol Building in Washington, D.C. But Congress objected to the damage they inflicted on the grass and in 1878 stationed guards there to halt the practice. President Rutherford B. Hayes, who enjoyed children, said they could use the White House lawn. President Franklin D. ROOSEVELT stopped the custom during World War II, but then it was restored again in 1953 by President Dwight D. Eisenhower.

Today the Egg Roll takes place on the Ellipse behind the White House, and children up to age eight are invited to participate. In addition to rolling their own hard-boiled eggs, the children hunt for about 1,000 wooden eggs—many of them signed by past presidents or celebrities—that have been hidden in the grass. A crowd of up to 10,000 adults and children gathers for the annual event, and sometimes the president greets the crowd from the balcony of the White House.

CONTACTS:
President's Park
White House Liaison
1100 Ohio Dr. S.W.
Washington, D.C. 20242
202-208-1631; fax: 202-208-1643
www.nps.gov

National Archives and Records Administration (NARA)
Prologue: Quarterly Journal of the NARA
700 Pennsylvania Ave. N.W.
Washington, DC 20408
866-272-6272 or 301-713-6800
www.archives.gov

SOURCES:
AmerBkDays-2000, p. 243
BkFest-1937, p. 16
EncyEaster-2002, p. 161

♦ 0805 ♦ **Easter Festival (Osterfestspiele)**
Begins between March 15 and April 18 and ends between March 22 and April 26; Palm Sunday through Easter Monday

Salzburg's Easter Festival was founded by the famous conductor Herbert von Karajan (1908-1989) in 1967 to honor the works of Richard Wagner (1813-1883), and it remains one of Europe's most elite and elegant music festivals. Those who attend pay top prices, but in return they get to hear some of the world's greatest performers. The Berlin Philharmonic Orchestra is the festival's resident ensemble, and the chorus of the Vienna State Opera or the Choir of the Society of Friends of Music in Vienna perform the choral works. Von Karajan himself conducted all of the concerts, which include the works of Johann Sebastian BACH (1685-1750), Ludwig van Beethoven (1770-1827), Johannes Brahms (1833-1897), Gustav Mahler (1860-1911), Wolfgang Amadeus MOZART (1756-1791) and Giuseppe Verdi (1813-1901), until his death in 1989. Now various conductors are invited. A full-scale opera is performed twice during each nine-day festival in the *Grosses Festspielhaus* (large festival hall), which is known for its unique acoustics and seats more than 2,000.

CONTACTS:
Salzburg Easter Festival
Herbert von Karajan Platz 9
Salzburg, A-5020 Austria
43-662-8045-361; fax: 43-662-8045-790
www.osterfestspiele-salzburg.at/en

SOURCES:
MusFestEurBrit-1980, p. 20

♦ 0806 ♦ **Easter Fires**
March-April; Easter eve

The tradition of hillside fires on EASTER eve in Fredericksburg, Tex., is thought to have begun many years ago, soon after the town's settlement by German farmers in 1846. A pioneer mother, to calm her children, told them the fires burning on the town's hillside had been lit by the Easter Bunny to boil their Easter eggs. In reality, the fires were those of Indians who were watching the settlement. Since the 1940s the fires have blazed at the Gillespie County Fairgrounds in Fredericksburg in an Easter pageant with a cast of more than 600 that portrays the local legend.

CONTACTS:
Gillespie County Fair & Festivals Association
P.O. Box 526
Fredericksburg, TX 78624
830-997-2359; fax: 830-997-4923
www.gillespiefair.com

♦ 0807 ♦ **Easter Monday**
Between March 23 and April 26; Monday after Easter

Although EASTER Sunday is the culmination of HOLY WEEK and the end of LENT, the following Monday (also known as **Pasch Monday**) is observed as a public holiday in many nations, perhaps to round off the long weekend that begins on GOOD FRIDAY. In London there is a big Easter parade in Hyde Park on this day.

A curious English tradition associated at one time with Easter Monday involved "lifting" or "heaving." Forming what children call a "chair" by crossing hands and grasping another person's wrists, the men would lift the women on Easter Monday—sometimes carrying them for a short distance down the street or to the village green—and on Easter Tuesday the women would lift the men. A similar retaliatory game involved taking off each other's shoes. This is thought to have a connection with the resurrection of Christ. Polish children play *smigus,* a water-throwing game.

SOURCES:
AmerBkDays-2000, p. 242
BkFest-1937, pp. 16, 57, 261
DictDays-1988, pp. 8, 11, 35, 55, 56, 122
EncyEaster-2002, p. 122
FestSaintDays-1915, p. 91
OxYear-1999, p. 625

♦ 0808 ♦ **Easter Monday (Netherlands)**
Between March 23 and April 26; Monday after Easter

EASTER MONDAY, or **Paasch Maandag**, is celebrated in the Netherlands with games played with Easter eggs. *Eierrapen,* or hunting for eggs, is a favorite pastime among younger children. *Eiertikken,* or hitting hard-boiled eggs together, is a sport for children of all ages. In rural areas, the eggs are still dyed with coffee grounds, beet juice, onion skins, and other vegetable substances. Then they're packed in baskets and carried to an open field for the eiertikken contest. At a given signal, the children line up and try to break the shell of an opposing team member's egg (the two eggs must be the same color) by knocking them together. The winner keeps the opponent's egg, and the boy or girl who collects the most eggs wins.

Another Easter game, which was popular in the 16th and 17th centuries and was still played in the 20th, is called the *eiergaren.* Played by both children and adults who assemble in the main streets of villages on Easter Monday, the game involves a tub of water with a huge apple floating in it. The tub is placed in the middle of the road and 25 eggs are placed at intervals of about 12 feet along the same road. One person must eat the apple with his hands tied behind his back while a second contestant has to run and gather up all the eggs in a basket before the apple is eaten. Whoever finishes his or her task first is the victor.

SOURCES:
BkFest-1937, p. 242
EncyEaster-2002, p. 123
FestWestEur-1958, p. 131

♦ 0809 ♦ **Eastern States Exposition**
September, starts the second Friday after Labor Day

Also known as the **Big E**, the Eastern States Exposition is an agricultural and industrial fair in West Springfield, Mass. It's sponsored by all six New England states and runs to the end of September. The first exposition in 1917 attracted 138,000 visitors; these days, attendance tops one million.

The exposition is known for its Avenue of the States, where each New England state has erected a permanent replica of its original State House. (The New Hampshire State House uses New Hampshire granite for its columns.) In the buildings are displays of state products, for example, Maine potatoes, New Hampshire maple syrup, Vermont cheese, Massachusetts cranberries, Rhode Island clam cakes, and Connecticut apples.

The livestock show is the largest in the East, and the Eastern States Horse Show is one of the oldest and most prestigious equestrian events in the country. Besides hunters, jumpers, harness, and saddle horses, there are draft horses in dress harness.

Today the exposition also features a parade, a circus, and international exhibits.

CONTACTS:
Eastern States Exposition
1305 Memorial Ave., Rte. 147
West Springfield, MA 01089
413-787-0271; fax: 413-787-0127
www.thebige.com

♦ 0810 ♦ **Ebisu Festival**
October 20

This Japanese festival is named after Ebisu, one among seven Japanese gods of luck, who is the protector of businessmen and fishermen. According to legend, all the other gods leave their shrines during October, which is known as "the godless month," and gather at the temple of Izumo to discuss issues of great importance. Because he is deaf, Ebisu cannot hear the summons and does not accompany them. The Ebisu Festival, observed on October 20, is a time for members of trade associations and political and literary societies to get together and socialize. Because Ebisu presides over trade and business, the festival is also a time to pray for prosperity. The main celebration takes place in Nara, where the streets leading to the Ebisu shrine are lined with booths selling figures of Ebisu and other objects that stand for wealth and good fortune. In the western part of the country, some shrines celebrate the Ebisu Festival in January.

Ebisu is a folk deity who probably originated in a cult of luck in fishing. To this day, Japanese fishermen bring up stones from the bottom of the sea at the beginning of the fishing season and make them into a shrine to Ebisu. As they cast their nets, they have also been known to call out "Ebisu!" to invoke the god's power. In urban areas, however, the Ebisu Festival is mostly celebrated by merchants, although even here the god is often depicted as carrying a fish.

See also BETTARA-ICHI

CONTACTS:
Japan National Tourist Organization
1 Rockefeller Pl., Ste. 1250
New York, NY 10020
212-757-5640; fax: 212-307-6754
www.japantravelinfo.com

SOURCES:
IllFestJapan-1993, p. 22
JapanFest-1965, pp. 116, 200
OxDictWrldRel-1997, p. 302

♦ 0811 ♦ **Ecuador Independence Day**
August 10

Independence Day, or **National Day**, in Ecuador celebrates its independence movement of 1809. Freedom from Spanish rule was finally achieved on May 24, 1822. That event is com-

memorated each year on May 24 with another holiday called Battle of Pichincha Day.

Patriotic festivities are held throughout the country, but particularly in the colorful capital city of Quito.

CONTACTS:
Embassy of Ecuador
2535 15th St. N.W.
Washington, D.C. 20009
202-234-7166; fax: 202-667-3482
www.ecuador.org

SOURCES:
AnnivHol-2000, pp. 86, 134
NatlHolWrld-1968, p. 140

♦ 0812 ♦ **Ecuadoran Civicism & National Unity Day**
February 27

Public displays of patriotism are commonplace for Ecuadorans on this national holiday, observed on the anniversary of the Battle of Tarqui in 1822. Leading that military campaign against the Spanish loyalists was Antonio José de Sucre, who is considered the liberator of Ecuador and Peru. In 1948, Ecuadoran president Carlos Julio Arosemena Tola established Civicism and National Unity Day by executive decree.

The flag of Ecuador is prominently featured during the day's celebrations. Along with receiving a public display at government and private buildings, the flag also appears in the traditional ceremonies at schools throughout the country. Students with exemplary academic records will have the honor of being flag bearers in official parades, and all students are expected to deliver an oath and kiss the flag as a symbol of their allegiance.

CONTACTS:
Ecuador Embassy
2535 15th St. N.W.
Washington, D.C. 20009
202-234-7200; fax: 202-667-3482

SOURCES:
AnnivHol-2000, p. 33

♦ 0813 ♦ **Eddy (Mary Baker), Birthday of**
July 16

This is the day on which Mary Baker Eddy (1821-1910), founder of the Church of Christ, Scientist, was born. After spending much of her early life as a semi-invalid due to a spinal malady, Eddy suffered a serious fall in 1866 and underwent a healing experience that led her to the discovery of Christian Science. Based on the largely forgotten healing aspects of Christianity, the First Church of Christ, Scientist was established in Boston in 1879, and two years later, Eddy founded the Massachusetts Metaphysical College, where she taught until 1889. She dedicated her entire life to spreading the word about Christianity's power to heal. Her most important written work was *Science and Health with Key to the Scriptures,* published in 1875.

The basic premise of Christian Science is that only mind and spirit are real; matter is an illusion, and therefore subject to decay and dissolution. Sickness and death are only real in that they seem real to humans; through prayer and spiritual development, this error can be overcome. Mary Baker Eddy's birthday is observed by Christian Science churches around the world.

CONTACTS:
First Church of Christ, Scientist
210 Massachusetts Ave.
Boston, MA 02115
800-775-2775 or 617-450-2000; fax: 617-450-7575
www.tfccs.com

SOURCES:
AmerBkDays-2000, p. 528
DictWrldRel-1989, p. 168
RelHolCal-2004, p. 125

♦ 0814 ♦ **Edinburgh International Festival**
August

The capital city of Edinburgh (pronounced ED-in-bo-ro), Scotland, is transformed during the last two weeks of August and, in some years, into the first week of September, when it hosts what is probably the most prestigious arts festival in the world. Theater and dance companies, orchestras, chamber groups, and soloists from all over the world perform at the city's major venues, and there are art exhibitions and poetry readings as well. Many important new works have been commissioned specifically for the festival—one of the most famous being T.S. Eliot's *The Cocktail Party*. A highlight of the festival, which has been held since 1947, is the traditional Military Tattoo performed nightly at Edinburgh Castle, which is perched high above the city on a rocky promontory. Marching bands from all over the world perform along with Scottish pipe bands at the tattoo, which ends with a farewell song from a lone piper standing on the floodlit battlements.

There is also a "Fringe Festival" that goes on at the same time—an arena for new talent and amateur entertainers. Although student drama and street theater predominate, the quality of the productions in recent years has sometimes made it difficult to distinguish Fringe events from the "official" ones. The number of Fringe performances has increased dramatically as well—from only a few in 1947 to more than 9,000 in 1989. But the three defining features of the earliest Fringe events still hold true today: none of the performers are officially invited to take part; they must use small and unconventional theater spaces; and they all assume their own financial risks, surviving or sinking according to public demand.

CONTACTS:
Edinburgh International Festival
The Hub
Castlehill
Edinburgh, Scotland EH1 2NE United Kingdom
44-13-1473-2000; fax: 44-13-1473-2002
www.eif.co.uk

Edinburgh Fringe Festival
180 High St.

Edinburgh, Scotland EH1 1QS United Kingdom
44-13-1226-0026; fax: 44-13-1226-0016
www.edfringe.com

Edinburgh Military Tattoo
The Tattoo Office
32 Market St.
Edinburgh, Scotland EH1 1QB United Kingdom
44-13-1225-4783; fax: 44-13-1225-8627
www.edintattoo.co.uk

SOURCES:
GdWrldFest-1985, p. 99
IntlThFolk-1979, pp. 184, 185
MusFestEurBrit-1980, p. 132
MusFestWrld-1963, p. 8

♦ 0815 ♦ **Edison (Thomas) Festival of Light**
Mid-January through mid-February

Most people associate Thomas Alva Edison (1847-1931) with his famous laboratory in Menlo Park, New Jersey. But when he was 38 years old, a widower and seriously ill, his doctors sent him to Florida for a long vacation. There he discovered giant bamboo growing along the Caloosahatchee River. He established his winter home in Fort Myers and planned to use the bamboo fiber to make filaments for his new incandescent electric lamp bulbs.

The Edison Festival of Light, held annually in Fort Myers for more than three weeks, encompassing his birthday (*see* EDISON'S BIRTHDAY), began as a three-day event in 1938. Highlights of the festival include concerts, the coronation of the King and Queen of Edisonia, a children's parade, fireworks, exhibits of Edison's various inventions, and exhibits of regional inventors. The Grand Parade of Light—a nighttime procession of more than 100 bands, floats, and marching units—is the festival's grand finale. Edison's winter home and his Florida laboratory are open to the public year-round.

CONTACTS:
Edison Festival of Light
1300 Hendry St.
Fort Myers, FL 33901
239-334-2999; fax: 239-334-7418
www.edisonfestival.org

SOURCES:
GdUSFest-1984, p. 35

♦ 0816 ♦ **Edison's (Thomas) Birthday**
February 11

Although Thomas Alva Edison (1847-1931) is best known as the inventor of the incandescent electric light, his real achievement was to produce the first incandescent lamp of any practical value—one that could be produced inexpensively and distributed widely. In 1882 Edison lost a patent infringement case to Joseph Wilson Swan, who was developing an incandescent light at the same time in England. As a compromise, the two men combined their resources and formed the Edison and Swan Electric Lamp Company.

Edison's genius is credited with a number of other important inventions, among them the carbon transmitter (which brought Alexander Graham Bell's newly invented telephone into general use and led to the development of the microphone), the dictating machine, a method for transmitting telegraphic signals from ship to ship (or ship to shore), the Kinetoscope (which made the motion picture a reality), and the phonograph.

See also EDISON FESTIVAL OF LIGHT

CONTACTS:
Thomas Edison Birthplace Museum
9 Edison Dr.
Milan, OH 44846
419-499-2135
www.tomedison.org

Henry Ford Museum at Greenfield Village
20900 Oakman Blvd.
Dearborn, MI 48124
800-835-5237 or 313-271-2455
www.thehenryford.org

SOURCES:
AmerBkDays-2000, p. 131

♦ 0817 ♦ **Edmund Fitzgerald Anniversary**
On the Sunday closest to November 10

On November 10, 1975, the 26,000-ton ore carrier *SS Edmund Fitzgerald*, the largest ship on the Great Lakes in its time and known as "The Queen of the Great Lakes," sank during a deadly storm in Lake Superior. In commemoration of that tragedy, a number of events are held.

The primary event is held at the Mariners' Church in downtown Detroit, Mich. As the names of the 29 lost crewmen are read out, a family member or friend of the deceased rings a ship's bell. Beginning in 2006, the church has expanded its service to a 30th ring to remember all those sailors who have been lost on the Great Lakes, some 30,000 lives lost in 6,000 shipwrecks over the years. Additional events were held for the 30th anniversary of the sinking in 2005. At the Great Lakes Shipwreck Historical Society and Museum in Whitefish Point, Mich., near where the sinking occurred, a ship's bell recovered from the wreck was rung in a special ceremony. At the Dossin Great Lakes Museum on Belle Isle in the Detroit River, 29 lanterns were placed around an anchor that came from the *Fitzgerald*.

CONTACTS:
S.S. Edmund Fitzgerald Online
www.ssefo.com

Mariners' Church of Detroit
170 E. Jefferson
Detroit, MI 48226-4391
313-259-2206
marinerschurchofdetroit.org

Dossin Great Lakes Museum
100 Strand Dr.
Belle Isle
Detroit, MI 48207
313-821-2661
www.detroithistorical.org/exhibits/index.asp

♦ 0818 ♦ **Egungun Festival**
June

The Egungun is a secret society among the Yoruba people of Ede, Oyo State, Nigeria. The major Egungun festival takes place in June, when members of the society come to the market place and perform masked dances. The masks they wear represent ancestral spirits and may cover the whole body or just the face. It is considered dangerous to see any part of the man who is wearing the mask—an offense that was at one time punishable by death.

The masqueraders all dance simultaneously, although each has his own drum accompaniment and entourage of chanting women and girls. The festival climaxes with the appearance of Andu, the most powerful mask. It is believed that the spirits of the deceased possess the masqueraders while they are dancing, and although it promotes a feeling of oneness between the living and the dead, the festival also inspires a certain amount of fear.

CONTACTS:
Embassy of the Federal Republic of Nigeria
3519 International Ct. N.W.
Washington, D.C. 20008
202-986-8400; fax: 202-362-6981
www.nigeriaembassyusa.org

SOURCES:
DictFolkMyth-1984, p. 341
FolkWrldHol-1999, p. 384

♦ 0819 ♦ **Egypt Revolution Day**
July 23

This national holiday is the anniversary of the military overthrow of the monarchy on July 23, 1952. The new government formally instituted the Republic of Egypt on June 18, 1953. In Cairo on July 23, parades and other festivities take place to commemorate the republic.

CONTACTS:
State Information Service, Egypt Ministry of Information
3 Al Estad Al Bahary St.
Nasr City, Cairo Egypt
20-2261-7304; fax: 20-2261-7308
www.sis.gov.eg/En

SOURCES:
AnnivHol-2000, p. 122
NatlHolWrld-1968, p. 122

♦ 0820 ♦ **Egyptian Days**
Various

Up until the 17th century in England, these were commonly thought to be unlucky days throughout the year. Popular almanacs would list them as days on which to avoid such important activities as weddings, blood letting (a standard way of treating various illnesses), and traveling. No one knew why certain days were considered unlucky. In fact, which days were Egyptian Days seems to have depended upon which almanac was consulted; apparently, there was never any standard list that was widely circulated.

Although it is not known for sure why they were referred to as the Egyptian Days, it's possible that they were first computed by Egyptian astrologers or were somehow related to the Egyptian plagues. They were also known as the **Dismal Days**, from Latin *dies mali* (meaning "evil days").

SOURCES:
BkDays-1864, vol. I, p. 41
DictDays-1988, pp. 31, 36
OxYear-1999, pp. 195, 360, 590

◆ 0821 ◆ **Eight-Hour Day**
Various

Each of Australia's states celebrates the improvements that have been made in working conditions with its own LABOR DAY. The Eight-Hour Day holiday is marked with parades and celebrations to commemorate trade union efforts to limit working hours. In many places, people still chant the unions' slogan: "Eight hours' labor, eight hours' recreation, and eight hours' rest!," which, by happenstance, is the basis of St. Benedict's Rule of Life for religious orders.

In Queensland Labour Day is celebrated on the first Monday in May; in New South Wales, the Australian Capital Territory, and South Australia it's the first Monday in October; in Western Australia it's the first Monday in March; and in Tasmania and Victoria it's the second Monday in March. In New Zealand, Labour Day is observed on the first Monday in October.

CONTACTS:
Ministry for Culture and Heritage
P.O. Box 5364
Wellington, New Zealand
64-4-471-4027; fax: 61-4-499-4490
www.nzhistory.net.nz

SOURCES:
AnnivHol-2000, pp. 54, 91, 180
BkHolWrld-1986, Mar 5
DictDays-1988, pp. 36, 65

◆ 0822 ◆ **Eisteddfod**
Early August

The **Royal National Eisteddfod of Wales** dates back to the 12th century. Its purpose is to encourage the preservation of Welsh music and literature, and only those who sing or write in Welsh may enter the competitions. The annual event opens with the blowing of trumpets, followed by all kinds of musical and literary contests—harp playing, solo and choral singing, dramatic presentations, and poetic composition. Prizes and degrees are awarded to the winners.

The National Eisteddfod is held in northern Wales one year and southern Wales the next. Other Eisteddfodau are held in Welsh communities elsewhere from May to November.

See also CYNONFARDD EISTEDDFOD

CONTACTS:
Eisteddfod Genedlaethol Cymru
40 Parc Ty Glas, Llanisien
Cardiff, Wales CF4 5WU United Kingdom
44-29-2076-3777; fax: 44-29-2076-3737
www.eisteddfod.org.uk

SOURCES:
AnnivHol-2000, p. 147
BkFest-1937, p. 60
BkHolWrld-1986, Aug 3
DictFolkMyth-1984, p. 342
GdWrldFest-1985, p. 100
IntlThFolk-1979, p. 191
MusFestEurBrit-1980, p. 150

◆ 0823 ◆ **Eka Dasa Rudra**
Once every 100 years

Eka Dasa Rudra is a series of processions, ceremonies, and sacrifices held every 100 years at Pura Besakih, the "mother temple" of Bali, Indonesia. The temple, which comprises about 30 separate temples honoring a great variety of Balinese and Hindu gods, was probably built about 1,000 years ago and is on the slopes of the volcanic mountain, Gunung ("Mount") Agung.

On March 17, 1963, the Eka Dasa Rudra was under way when Agung catastrophically erupted and killed more than 1,500 people. Since the sacrifices were interrupted, the Eka Dasa Rudra was started again 16 years later and completed in the period from late February to early May of 1979. Images of gods were carried 19 miles down the mountain to be washed in the sea: entire villages gathered along the route. In all, it is estimated that more than 100,000 people participated in the ritual. The climax came during the Taur rites when 23 priests offered prayers and sacrificed animals—ranging from an eagle to an anteater—to appease forms of Rudra, a Hindu demonic manifestation. Thousands of pilgrims traveled by truck and foot to Besakih.

The complex Balinese religion is largely a blend with Hinduism; the majority of Balinese hold to the Bali Hindu faith, also known as Agama Tirtha.

CONTACTS:
The Embassy of The Republic of Indonesia
2020 Massachusetts Ave. N.W.
Washington, D.C. 20036
202-775-5200; fax: 202-775-5365
www.embassyofindonesia.org

SOURCES:
EncyRel-1987, vol. 2, p. 48

◆ 0824 ◆ **Ekadashi**
11th day of each waxing and waning moon

Ekadashi is the Hindi word for "eleventh." Hindus observe 24 11th-day fasts during the course of the Hindu year, although some are more important than others. Each Ekadashi is held in honor of a different Hindu legend and has specific religious duties associated with it. Eating rice, however, is prohibited on all Ekadashi. According to legend, a demon was born of the sweat that fell from Brahma's head on this day, and Brahma instructed it to inhabit the rice grains eaten by people on Ekadashi and to turn into worms in their stomachs.

See also AMALAKA EKADASHI; DEVATHANI EKADASHI; NIRJALA EKADASHI; PUTRADA EKADASHI

SOURCES:
RelHolCal-2004, p. 167

◆ 0825 ◆ El Pochó Dance-Drama
January 20

ST. SEBASTIAN'S DAY is celebrated throughout Latin America, but the event that takes place in Tenosique in Tabasco State, Mexico, on this day is unique. The dance-drama known as *El Pochó* involves most of the townspeople and anywhere from 15 to more than 60 dancers. Dancers each play one of three main characters. The *cojóes* are played by men who will engage in a struggle with the *tigres*, also played by men. The *pochoveras* are played by women.

On the morning of January 20 everyone gathers at the pre-arranged location, a house or a plaza. The pochoveras enter in their long skirts and embroidered blouses and perform the initial dance. Then the cojóes enter, wearing masks with exaggerated features, representing the best and worst in humans. Soon the tigres (jaguars) invade the dance space, and the cojóes and tigres play at hunting each other until, finally, they join forces to chase the audience.

SOURCES:
FiestaTime-1965, p. 15

◆ 0826 ◆ El Salvador del Mundo, Festival of
First week in August

The patron saint and namesake of El Salvador—El Salvador del Mundo (the Savior of the World)—is honored with a national festival. Festival proceedings commence the week before the saint's day, on August 6, which is also the same day as the FEAST OF THE TRANSFIGURATION. Some Salvadorans refer to the festival as **Fiestas Agostinos** (August Feasts).

The observance of the festival dates back to 1525, the year that the city of San Salvador, the present-day capital, was founded. The grandest of the celebrations take place in that city, but there are also observances throughout the rest of the country and in Salvadoran communities settled abroad.

The main events of the festival are a religious procession, a large fair, various sporting events, a beauty contest, and a riotous party featuring street floats and dancers. The religious ceremony takes place in front of the national cathedral and entails a spectacle known as *la bajada* (the descent). This ritual features an old wooden image of Christ that is paraded through the streets and then lowered inside a wooden shell. There the sculpture's purple garments are removed, and it emerges from the shell appareled in gleaming white robes, a symbolic representation of Christ's transfiguration.

CONTACTS:
El Salvador Embassy
2308 California St. N.W.
Washington, D.C. 20008
202-265-9671; fax: 202-234-3834

◆ 0827 ◆ El Salvador Independence Day
September 15

El Salvador joined with other Central American countries in revolt against Spanish rule in 1821, and revolutionary leader Father José Matías Delgado declared El Salvador to be independent. On this same day, COSTA RICA, GUATEMALA, HONDURAS, and NICARAGUA also declared their independence.

Independence Day is a national holiday in El Salvador.

CONTACTS:
Embassy of El Salvador
1400 16th St. N.W., Ste. 100
Washington, D.C. 20008
202-265-9671; fax: 202-232-3763
www.elsalvador.org

SOURCES:
AnnivHol-2000, p. 155
NatlHolWrld-1968, p. 165

◆ 0828 ◆ Eldon Turkey Festival
Second Saturday in October

While people in most parts of the United States think about turkeys only as THANKSGIVING day approaches, it is a year-round concern for the turkey farmers of Eldon, Missouri, and the surrounding area, where over two million turkeys are raised annually. There is also a large wild turkey population, which makes turkey hunting a popular local sport.

Since 1986, Eldon has held the Turkey Festival designed to educate the public about domestic turkey production, turkey-farming operations, and the health benefits of turkey-food products. The festival is also an opportunity for numerous conservation and turkey-hunting organizations to provide information on safe hunting practices, wild turkey-calling techniques, and efforts to increase the wild turkey population.

Events at the October festival include turkey races (with the turkeys on leashes), a turkey egg toss, sales of turkey foods, and exhibits on the production of domestic turkeys.

CONTACTS:
Eldon Chamber of Commerce
203 E. First St.
Eldon, MO 65026
573-392-3752; fax: 573-392-0634
www.eldonchamber.com

◆ 0829 ◆ Election Day
Tuesday following the first Monday in November

Election Day, the day on which Americans vote for their elected officials, is held on the Tuesday after the first Monday in November. Americans vote for their president and vice president every four years on that Tuesday. They vote for their U.S. representatives every two years during even-numbered years, and they vote for their U.S. senators every six years—one-third of the U.S. senators are up for reelection every two years. Americans also vote for their state senators, state representatives, and many local officials on this day.

This date was set by Congress in 1845 to correct abuses caused by having allowed each state to appoint its electors any time before the date in December set for their convening. At that time, the nation was primarily rural, so Election Day was set for late fall, after the harvest would be brought in. At that time, many people would have to travel on foot to their courthouse or county seat to cast their vote, which could take a full day. So Election Day was set on a Tuesday to avoid conflict with Sunday church services.

To encourage people to vote, ten states now consider Election Day a legal holiday, and five additional states require employers to give their employees several hours off to allow them to vote. In other states, some employers give their employees the day off. Even so, millions of Americans do not take advantage of what may be their most valuable privilege.

CONTACTS:
Federal Election Commission
999 E. St. N.W.
Washington, D.C. 20463
800-424-9530 or 202-694-1100; fax: 202-219-8504
www.fec.gov

SOURCES:
AmerBkDays-2000, p. 752
AnnivHol-2000, p. 199
DictDays-1988, p. 36
PatHols-2006, p. 83

♦ 0830 ♦ **Election of the Lord Mayor of London**
September 29

Since 1546 MICHAELMAS has been the day on which the Lord Mayor of London is elected each year. The election occurs in the Guildhall, in front of which a high wooden fence has been erected. There are a number of doors in the fence, and a beadle of one of the city's Livery Companies, dressed in uniform and a three-cornered hat, waits in back of each door. It is the beadle's job to guard the Guildhall and see that persons without authorization are not allowed into the election ceremony.

Two candidates for the job are chosen from among the city aldermen who have already served a term of office as sheriff. The ceremony begins when the current Lord Mayor, two sheriffs, and 26 aldermen in their scarlet gowns walk from the Mansion House to Guildhall, where they sit on a platform that has been strewn with herbs, a medieval protection against both plague and witchcraft. The candidates proceed to the Aldermen's Court, a body consisting of 13 aldermen whose job it is to interview the candidates and select the one who will serve as mayor.

Once the voting is over, both the new and the old Lord Mayors appear together on the porch of the Guildhall, and then

an ornate horse-drawn coach carries them to the Mansion House, which has been the Lord Mayor of London's official residence since 1753.

See also LORD MAYOR'S SHOW

SOURCES:
YrFest-1972, p. 153

♦ 0831 ♦ **Election of the Mayor of Ock Street**
Saturday nearest June 19

The town of Abingdon, England, has long been famous for its Morris dancers, who rank among the best in England. During the 18th century, it was customary for the people of Abingdon to kill and roast a black ox on St. Edmund of Abingdon's Feast Day, or another day nearby. The feast day is June 19, the day before St. Edmund's Fair. The meat would be distributed among the town's needy folk.

In 1700 an argument arose during the ox roast over who would get the horns. It was decided that the only fair way to settle the argument was to have a real fight, so the town was divided into two opposing teams by drawing an imaginary line along Ock Street. Using torches, sticks, stones, and bare fists, the western part of Abingdon, led by a man by the name of Hemmings—one of the town's Morris dancers—took possession of the horns. The crowd hailed him as the "Mayor of Ock Street."

Today, only people who live on Ock Street may vote for the mayor, which they do by placing paper ballots into a soapbox. The winner is usually a member of the Hemmings family, and he toasts his election by drinking from a special applewood chalice, or bowl, with a silver rim, which is believed to be more than 200 years old. He is carried through the streets in a flower-decorated chair by the Abingdon Morris dancers, who follow behind the "hornbearer," a man holding a pole on which is mounted a black-horned ox head. They stop at each of Ock Street's many pubs, where all the dancers have a drink and join in the celebration.

CONTACTS:
Abingdon Traditional Morris Dancers
19 Spring Gardens
Abingdon, Berkshire OX14 1AZ United Kingdom
44-12-3552-7064
www.abingdonmorris.org.uk

SOURCES:
YrbookEngFest-1954, p. 83
YrFest-1972, p. 47

♦ 0832 ♦ **Elephant Festival**
Mid-February

The Elephant Festival is held annually in February in the Paklay district of the Sayaboury province in northwestern Laos as a celebration of the Asian elephant. Co-sponsored by the nonprofit ElefantAsia conservation organization, the festival also exists to raise awareness of the increasing threat of extinction that faces the 50,000 elephants throughout Asia. Activities at the event include a majestic parade of more than 70 elephants;

offerings of fruit and flowers; an elephant race, show, and museum; a traditional elephant Baci ceremony; as well as the chance to see elephants at their bath. In addition, there are such activities as a tug-of-war contest, a drawing competition, film, music performances, food stalls, and a night market.

CONTACTS:
ElefantAsia
c/o OTIEC
22 rue de l'arcade
Paris 75008 France
www.elefantasia.org

Lao National Tourism Administration
Tourism Marketing and Promotion Dept.
P.O. Box 3556
Lane Xang Ave.
Hatsady Village, Chanthabouly District, Ventiane Capital Lao PDR
www.tourismlaos.gov.la

♦ 0833 ♦ **Elephant Round-Up**
Third weekend in November

The Elephant Round-Up is an internationally famous show of 200 or more trained elephants held annually in the provincial capital of Surin, Thailand. The Suay people of the area have traditionally captured and trained wild elephants to work in the northern Thailand teak forests. The Round-Up gives the trainers the opportunity to demonstrate their elephants' intelligence, strength, and obedience. A tug-of-war is staged where elephants are pitted against Thai soldiers. There are also log-pulling contests, a soccer game with two teams of elephants kicking a giant soccer ball, elephant basketball and other sports. A highlight is the spectacular array of elephants rigged out to reenact a medieval war parade. Besides the elephant demonstrations, there are cultural performances and folk dancing.

CONTACTS:
Tourism Authority of Thailand
611 N. Larchmont Blvd., 1st Fl.
Los Angeles, CA 90004
800-842-4526 or 323-461-9814; fax: 323-461-9834
www.tourismthailand.org

SOURCES:
BkHolWrld-1986, Nov 16
GdWrldFest-1985, p. 175

♦ 0834 ♦ **Eleusinian Mysteries**
Lesser Eleusinia in February-March; Greater Eleusinia in September-October

In ancient Athens, the Eleusinia was the most celebrated of all religious ceremonies. Often referred to as the **Mysteries** because anyone who violated the secrecy surrounding the festival rites would be punished by death, the Eleusinia consisted of two celebrations: The Greater Eleusinia was observed for a week or more in September or October; the Lesser Eleusinia was observed in early spring. Those who had been initiated at the lesser mysteries were allowed to participate in the greater mysteries the following year, when the secrets of the festival would be revealed to them.

The Eleusinia was based on the legend of Demeter, a goddess associated with the harvest, and her daughter Persephone, who was carried off by Pluto to live in his underground kingdom. Although the secrecy that accompanied the Eleusinian mysteries has made it difficult to reconstruct exactly what went on there, it is believed that they were intended to encourage a bountiful growing season. The men and women who were initiated during these ceremonies were believed to live happier and more secure lives, and when they died, they were granted a place in the Elysian Fields, the mythical place where the souls of the virtuous went after death.

CONTACTS:
Tufts University, Department of the Classics
321 Eaton Hall
Medford, MA 02155
617-627-3213; fax: 617-627-2896
www.ase.tufts.edu

SOURCES:
AtticFest-1981, pp. 139, 192
ClassDict-1984, p. 220
DictFolkMyth-1984, p. 512
EncyRel-1987, vol. 5, p. 83
OxClassDict-1970, p. 716

♦ 0835 ♦ **Elfreth's Alley Fete Day**
First weekend in June

Elfreth's Alley is a well-preserved street of privately owned 18th-century homes in Philadelphia. It is the only street in the city that has survived architecturally since the alley first opened in 1702. The 30 houses on the street, dating from 1713 to 1811, have all remained private residences, with the exception of the Mantua Maker's House, which is now a museum open to the public.

The idea of holding an "at home" day dates back to 1934, when a group of residents formed the Elfreth's Alley Association. Now called **Fete Day**, it is a day on which many of the houses are open to visitors, with members of the Association acting as hostesses in Colonial dress. On Fete Day in 1963, the Alley's distinctive character and historical value were officially recognized by its designation as a Registered National Historic Landmark. Over the years the Elfreth's Alley Association has played an active role in renovating the street's cartway and brick sidewalks, as well as saving some of the houses from destruction.

CONTACTS:
Elfreth's Alley Association
126 Elfreth's Alley
Philadelphia, PA 19106
215-574-0560
www.elfrethsalley.org

SOURCES:
GdUSFest-1984, p. 160

♦ 0836 ♦ **Elfstedentocht**
December, January, or February

The day of this famous ice skating race in the Netherlands depends on the weather and the thickness of the ice. In the 18th century, young men in the northern part of the country, known as Friesland, would try to skate all the canals that connected the province's 11 towns. Today the **Eleven Cities Race** covers the same 124-mile course, but increasingly mild winters have made its timing less dependable. As many as 16,000 men and women have competed in the race at one time, which takes several hours to complete.

CONTACTS:
De Friesche Elf Steden Association
P.O. Box 569
Leeuwarden, 8901 BJ Netherlands
31-58-215-5020; fax: 31-58-213-8520
www.elfstedentocht.nl

SOURCES:
BkHolWrld-1986, Jan 22

♦ 0837 ♦ Elijah Day
July 20

Considered to be among the greatest of prophets, Elijah is commemorated on this day in both the Roman Catholic and Orthodox churches. An Old Testament Jew who is revered by Jews and Muslims as well, Elijah's story appears in chapters 17 and 18 of the first book of Kings, with the final episode appearing in Second Kings, chapter two. It tells of Elijah's sojourn in the desert, where he was fed every morning and evening by ravens. It also tells about the miracles he performed, replenishing the meal and oil supplies of a widow who fed him despite a severe famine and bringing her son back to life when he died.

The highpoint of Elijah's ministry occurred when he called the priests who worshipped Baal, the pagan fertility god, to the top of Mount Carmel and challenged them to a contest that would prove who was the true God. When the pagan priests failed in their efforts to ask Baal to set fire to their sacrifice, Elijah called on his God, who immediately consumed with fire not only the sacrifice but the altar itself and the dust and water surrounding it. When Elijah died, it is said that he was taken up to heaven in a fiery chariot by a whirlwind.

SOURCES:
DayRel-1990, p. 139
DaysCustFaith-1957, p. 187

♦ 0838 ♦ Elimination of Racial Discrimination, International Day for the
March 21

International Day for the Elimination of Racial Discrimination is observed annually on March 21, the anniversary of the day in 1960 when, at a peaceful demonstration against the apartheid "pass laws" in Sharpeville, South Africa, police opened fire and killed 69 black South Africans. The observation of this day was initiated by the UNITED NATIONS General Assembly in 1966, when it called on the international community to redouble its efforts to eliminate all forms of racial

discrimination and to remember "the victims of Sharpeville and those countless others in different parts of the world who have fallen victim to racial injustice."

CONTACTS:
United Nations, Department of Public Information
Rm. S-1070L J, K, L
New York, NY 10017
212-963-6842; fax: 212-963-6914
www.un.org

♦ 0839 ♦ Elisabeth (Queen) International Music Competition
May

One of the world's most prestigious music competitions and the largest musical event in Brussels takes place throughout the month of May each year. Open to young competitors from around the world, the competition focuses on violinists one year, composers the next, pianists the third year, and singers the fourth year. It is timed to coincide with the birthday of Queen Elisabeth of Belgium, who supported and encouraged violinist-composer Eugène Ysaÿe when he started the event in 1937.

Although billed as a competition, the public is invited to attend every stage of the contest, from the initial tests at the Royal Conservatory of Music to the winner's performance with full orchestra at the Beaux Arts Palace. Members of the jury, many of whom are past winners of the competition, also perform for the public one evening during the month-long competition, and a distinguished musician is invited to give the opening concert.

CONTACTS:
Secretariat of the Queen Elisabeth Competition
20 Rue aux Laines
Brussels, B 1000 Belgium
32-2-213-40-50; fax: 32-2-514-3297
www.cmireb.be/en

SOURCES:
MusFestEurBrit-1980, p. 33

♦ 0840 ♦ Elizabeth II (Queen) Birthday
June

Queen Elizabeth II was born on April 21, 1926, but her birthday is officially observed on a Saturday in June by proclamation each year (it may be changed if the weather is really foul). A good explanation for the discrepancy in dates is that April weather is notoriously bad in London.

The celebration includes Trooping the Colour. The "colour" referred to here is the regimental flag. When British soldiers went to battle, it was important that they be able to recognize their flag so they could rally around it. "Trooping the Colour" was a marching display put on for new recruits so they would know what their regiment's flag looked like.

In 1805 the ceremony became an annual event to celebrate the king or queen's official birthday. Today, a different regiment is chosen each year to parade its flag before Queen Elizabeth II, who sits on horseback and inspects the troops in their brightly colored uniforms as they pass before her in London's Horseguards Parade, a large open space in Whitehall. Then she rides in a carriage back to Buckingham Palace. Although the event attracts thousands of tourists, many Londoners turn out for the traditional ceremony as well.

Queen's Birthday is a national holiday in Australia, where it is celebrated on the second Monday in June. It was first observed there in 1788, not long after the country was settled. June 4, the birthday of King George III, was set aside at that time as a holiday for convicts and settlers. After George V died in 1936, the date of his birth, June 3, was set aside to honor the reigning king or queen. Bermuda holds an annual military parade on Hamilton's Front Street in honor of the Queen.

CONTACTS:
The British Monarchy Official Web Site
Buckingham Palace
London, SW1A 1AA United Kingdom
44-20-7930-4832
www.royal.gov.uk

SOURCES:
AnnivHol-2000, pp. 65, 109
BkHolWrld-1986, Jun 13
DictDays-1988, p. 112
NatlHolWrld-1968, p. 78

♦ 0841 ♦ **Ellensburg Rodeo**
September, Labor Day weekend

The Ellensburg Rodeo is the richest rodeo in the state of Washington and also one of the top 25 rodeos of the Professional Rodeo Cowboys Association. Prize money in recent years has been more than $200,000, and an estimated 20,000 people visit Ellensburg on this weekend. Events include a parade and displays of hand crafts, especially weaving and bead work, by the people of the Yakima Indian nation. Yakimas, many in feathered headdress, open each performance of the rodeo with a solemn horseback ride down a steep hill that overlooks the arena.

CONTACTS:
Ellensburg Rodeo
609 N. Main St.
Ellensburg, WA 98926
800-637-2444 or 509-962-7831; fax: 509-962-7830
www.ellensburgrodeo.com

♦ 0842 ♦ **Elvis International Tribute Week**
Week including August 16

This week-long event pays tribute to rock and roll singer Elvis Presley—"The King of Rock and Roll." The tribute takes place in Memphis, Tenn., largely at Graceland, the 15,000-square-foot mansion that Elvis called home and that is now his gravesite, museum, and a rock and roll shrine.

Born in 1935 in a two-room house in Tupelo, Miss., Elvis moved to Memphis when he was 12, and came to fame in the 1950s with hits like "Hound Dog," "Don't Be Cruel," and "All

Shook Up." As a white man singing a black sound, he swept the music world and helped create the Memphis Sound. He was charismatic and sexy and gyrated his hips while performing in a fashion that sent the females in his audiences into a screeching frenzy. This won him the nickname, "Elvis the Pelvis." When he first appeared on television on the "Ed Sullivan Show," the hip shaking was considered too risque, and he was photographed only from the waist up. He appeared in 33 motion pictures and made 45 recordings that sold over a million copies each. He died at Graceland of an overdose of prescription drugs on Aug. 16, 1977.

A candlelight vigil is held on the evening of Aug. 15 at Graceland. Thousands of Elvis's fans, each carrying a candle, pour through the gates and walk to the gravesite. Other events of the week include a Nostalgia Concert by singers and musicians who worked with Presley; a Sock Hop Ball for "flat-top cats and dungaree dolls," in which Elvis songs and other classics of the 1950s and 1960s are played; and an art exhibit and contest, with art depicting Elvis or his home. The Elvis Presley Memorial Karate Tournament draws about 500 competitors from all over the world and reflects Presley's interest in karate—he studied the martial arts for years and was the first movie star to use karate in films.

For those who cannot attend in person, the official Elvis web site provides a live webcast of the vigil.

CONTACTS:
Graceland/Elvis Presley Enterprises Inc.
3734 Elvis Presley Blvd.
P.O. Box 16508
Memphis, TN 38186
800-238-2000 or 901-332-3322; fax: 901-332-1636
www.elvis.com

SOURCES:
AnnivHol-2000, p. 137

♦ 0843 ♦ **Emancipation Day (Canada)**
August 1 or the nearest Saturday

Emancipation Day commemorates August 1, 1834, the date that England's Abolition of Slavery Bill took effect, ending slavery throughout the British Empire. As a result of the law, more than one million slaves were freed in the British colonies, including Canada. While August 1 is not a public holiday in Canada, it is marked by many communities, particularly in Ontario, where many sites of importance to African-Canadian history are located. Public ceremonies typically take place in Toronto, Windsor, Amherstburg, and other cities and towns. But two sites of particular historical interest, the city of Owen Sound and Uncle Tom's Cabin in Dresden, organize Ontario's most prominent Emancipation Day observances. They take place on the Saturday nearest August 1.

Owen Sound was the northern-most terminus for the Underground Railroad, the network of people that helped slaves escape from the American South to the North and to Canada. Many escaped slaves settled in Owen Sound to become integral members of the community. Since 1862, the town has held a picnic to commemorate both Emancipation Day and the U.S. abolition of slavery, which took effect on January 1, 1863. The picnic, attended by local groups and many visitors, has come to incorporate music, crafts, and black-history exhibits as well as food and games.

The Uncle Tom's Cabin site in Dresden comprises the former home of Reverend Josiah Henson and other period buildings, as well as a major exhibit and interpretive centre on black history in North America. Henson, an escaped slave, settled in Ontario in 1830. He established the Dawn Settlement, a community that nurtured former slaves' self-sufficiency and success. Harriet Beecher Stowe used him as the model for the title character in *Uncle Tom's Cabin,* her renowned anti-slavery novel. The Uncle Tom's Cabin site marks Emancipation Day with a day-long program of educational and cultural events, including storytelling, dance, drama, and speeches.

CONTACTS:
Emancipation Picnic Committee
1303 Knights Bridge Ct.
Burlington, ON ON L7P 3K8 Canada
www.emancipation.ca

Uncle Tom's Cabin Historic Site
29251 Uncle Tom's Rd.
Dresden, ON N0P 1M0 Canada
www.uncletomscabin.org/index.htm

♦ 0844 ♦ **Emancipation Day (Hutchinson, Kansas)**
First weekend in August

Emancipation Day typically commemorates the day African-American slaves were freed in the United States. That event is celebrated annually in Hutchinson, Kansas, on the first weekend in August.

During the post-Civil War era, former slaves in the region celebrated Emancipation Day as "Lincoln Day" in Atchinson, Kansas, on September 22. That was the anniversary of the date in 1862 when President Abraham Lincoln issued the Emancipation Proclamation that would take effect the following year. By the late 1890s, the celebration had been moved to Hutchinson in order to take advantage of its more central location. In 1931 the local government proclaimed August 4 Emancipation Day and made it a legal holiday within the African-American community.

Since that time, a program of activities has been conducted each year. While the activities vary somewhat from year to year, the weekend typically kicks off with a social event on Friday night and features a parade on Saturday morning that begins at the intersection of 12th and Main. Following the parade and opening ceremonies, participants gather for a picnic in the park with food and drink vendors. The holiday program also includes sports, such as a basketball, boxing, or golf, as well as a teen night at a local swimming pool. Entertainment includes concerts featuring jazz, blues, or Gospel performers, and the weekend concludes with an ice cream social on Sunday afternoon.

CONTACTS:
Hutchinson Reno Arts & Humanities Council
23 East 1st Ave.

Hutchinson, KS 67501
620-662-1280

Hutchinson/Reno County Chamber of Commerce
P.O. Box 519
117 N. Walnut
Hutchinson, KS 67504-0519
620-662-3391
www.hutchchamber.com

SOURCES:
AAH-2007, p. 146

♦ 0845 ♦ **Emancipation Day (Tallahassee, Florida)**
May 20

Emancipation Day in Tallahassee, Florida, is celebrated each year on May 20. That date marks the anniversary of the day in 1865 when Union General Edward M. McCook announced from the steps of his headquarters in central Tallahassee that President Abraham Lincoln had ended slavery in Florida under the terms of the Emancipation Proclamation.

Since 1997 the site of McCook's headquarters, now known as Knott House and open to the public as a state historical museum, has hosted an annual reenactment of the proclamation. A local actor dressed in period costume for the occasion delivers McCook's address from the steps of the white-columned antebellum mansion. A free public celebration follows, with additional speeches, period entertainment, and a picnic across the street in Lewis Park. In addition, trolley tours are conducted to local African-American heritage sites, including a cemetery where African-American Union soldiers were laid to rest.

Long-celebrated by the local African-American community at various sites throughout the area, the observance of Emancipation Day includes a wreath-laying ceremony at Old City Cemetery and a number of educational and cultural functions during the preceding week.

CONTACTS:
Knott House Museum
301 E. Park Ave.
Tallahassee, FL 32301
850-922-2459
www.flheritage.com/museum/sites/knotthouse

John G. Riley Center/Museum of African-American History & Culture
419 E. Jefferson St.
Tallahassee, FL 32301
850-681-7881; fax: 850-681-7000
www.rileymuseum.org

SOURCES:
AAH-2007, p. 142

♦ 0846 ♦ **Emancipation Day (United States)**
January 1

President Abraham Lincoln issued his famous Emancipation Proclamation freeing the slaves on January 1, 1863. Although some states have their own emancipation, or freedom, celebrations on the anniversary of the day on which they adopted the 13th Amendment, the most widespread observance takes place on January 1 because it is both a traditional and a legal holiday in all the states. In Texas, and other parts of the South and Southwest, the emancipation of the slaves is celebrated on June 19 or JUNETEENTH, the anniversary of the day in 1865 when General Gordon Granger arrived in Texas to enforce Lincoln's proclamation.

Celebrations are more common in the southern United States, where they frequently center around public readings of the original Emancipation Proclamation.

CONTACTS:
U.S. Government Printing Office
732 N Capitol St. N.W.
Washington, D.C. 20401
888-293-6498 or 202-512-1530; fax: 202-512-2104
www.gpoaccess.gov

SOURCES:
AAH-2007, p. 131
AmerBkDays-2000, p. 6
AnnivHol-2000, p. 2
EncyChristmas-2003, p. 210
FolkAmerHol-1999, p. 24
PatHols-2006, p. 97

◆ 0847 ◆ Emancipation Day (Washington, D.C.)
April 16

In Washington, D.C., April 16th is celebrated as EMANCIPATION DAY, commemorating the day in 1862 when President Abraham Lincoln signed into law the District of Columbia Emancipation Act. This law was enacted nine months prior to the Emancipation Proclamation that freed slaves throughout the United States on January 1, 1863. At the time of their emancipation, slaves from the District of Columbia were offered $100 to relocate to colonies outside the United States. In addition, former masters who had remained loyal to the Union during the Civil War were compensated $300 for each freed slave. More than 3,000 slaves were freed under this agreement.

Commemoration of the event was celebrated with parades and festivities annually from 1866 through 1901. The holiday was revived in 2002, and since 2005 the date has been a legal holiday in the District. Events are scheduled throughout the preceding week, including lectures, speeches, reenactments, and a wreath-laying ceremony at the Emancipation Memorial in Lincoln Park near Capitol Hill. The observance culminates in a day of festivities and entertainment that begins with a parade down Pennsylvania Avenue in the morning and ends with evening fireworks on April 16th.

CONTACTS:
District of Columbia Emancipation Day Foundation
4101 S. Dakota Ave. N.E.
Washington, D.C. 20017
202-529-4833
www.dcemancipation.org

District of Columbia Mayor's Office
Emancipation Day
John A. Wilson Bldg.

1350 Pennsylvania Ave. N.W.
Washington, DC 20004
202-727-1000
www.dc.gov/emancipationday

SOURCES:
AAH-2007, p. 149
PatHols-2006, p. 108

◆ 0848 ◆ Emancipation Day Festival
August; varies

On August 1, 1834, the government of Upper Canada formally enacted the Emancipation Proclamation, which freed slaves in Canada. Word of this proclamation spread south to the United States, and thousands of American slaves sought to follow the North Star to find freedom in Canada.

Amherstburg, Ontario, was one of the first communities to hold celebrations in honor of this historic decree. Soon the celebrations spread to other cities, including Windsor. The Emancipation Day celebrations drew tens of thousands of Canadians and Americans. Over the years, Emancipation Day celebrations have included an Emancipation Day parade featuring floats, marching bands, precision drill teams, and dignitaries. The various festivities at Emancipation Day celebrations also included booths selling food and handicrafts.

During the 1930s women of color were often barred from entering mainstream beauty pageants. In 1931 Walter Perry organized the first annual Miss Sepia Pageant in Windsor, which helped bring beautiful and talented young black women into the spotlight. Contestants competed in the evening gown, swimwear, and talent categories. During the Emancipation Day parade, floats featuring the Miss Sepia contestants were always very popular.

CONTACTS:
Emancipation Picnic Committee, Emancipation Celebration
  Festival
1303 Knights Bridge Ct.
Burlington, ON L7P 3K8 Canada
www.emancipation.ca

◆ 0849 ◆ Ember Days
Four times a year

The Ember Days occur four times a year, at the beginning of each of the natural seasons. Traditionally they are marked by three days of fasting and abstinence—the Wednesday, Friday, and Saturday following, respectively, ASH WEDNESDAY, PENTECOST (Whitsunday), EXALTATION OF THE CROSS, and ST. LUCY'S DAY. In 1966, the Roman Catholic Church replaced them with days of prayer for various needs and withdrew the obligation to fast. The Anglican Communion still observes them. The four weeks in which these days occur are called Ember Weeks, and the Friday in each of these weeks is known as **Golden Friday**. The word "ember" itself derives from an Old English word referring to the revolution of time.

Some scholars believe that the Ember Days originated with the old pagan purification rites that took place at the seasons of planting, harvest, and vintage. The idea of fasting on these days was instituted by Pope Calixtus I in the third century. By the ninth century it was observed throughout Europe, but it wasn't until 1095 that the dates were fixed. In the Roman Catholic Church and the Church of England, since the sixth century, priests have been ordained on an Ember Saturday.

SOURCES:
BkDays-1864, vol. II, p. 687
DaysCustFaith-1957, p. 163
DictDays-1988, p. 48
DictWrldRel-1989, p. 237
OxYear-1999, p. 600
RelHolCal-2004, p. 83
SaintFestCh-1904, p. 253

♦ 0850 ♦ **Encaenia Day**
June

In general terms, *encaenia* (pronounced en-SEEN-ya) refers to the festivities celebrating the founding of a city or the dedication of a church. But in Oxford, England, Encaenia Day— sometimes referred to as **Commemoration Day**—is the day at the end of the summer term when the founders and benefactors of Oxford University are commemorated and honorary degrees are awarded to distinguished men and women. The ceremonies take place in the Sheldonian Theatre, designed by Christopher Wren when he was a professor of astronomy at the university, built between 1664-68. Based on a classical amphitheater, the Sheldonian offers an exceptional and often-photographed view from its cupola of Oxford's spires and gargoyles.

CONTACTS:
Oxford University, Information Office
Wellington Sq.
Oxford, OX1 2JD United Kingdom
44-18-6527-0000; fax: 44-18-6527-0708
www.ox.ac.uk

SOURCES:
DictDays-1988, pp. 23, 36

♦ 0851 ♦ **Enescu (George) Festival**
August and September (in odd-numbered years)

The George Enescu Festival is held in Bucharest, Romania, over three to four weeks in August and September in odd-numbered years. More than 3,000 musicians, many of them distinguished artists, take part in Romania's celebration of its only famous classical-music composer, George Enescu (1881-1955). In addition to an extensive program of concerts and recitals, prestigious competitions are held at the same time for composers, pianists, and violinists. The rest of the country joins in with related concerts in other parts of Romania.

In 1958, the then-communist regime in Romania launched the festival to honor an artist who had been driven out by their policies: Enescu had died in Paris just three years earlier. Concert venues are centered around Bucharest's Enescu Square and include the Sala Mare a Palatului (Palace Hall) and the Ateneul Roman (Romanian Atheneum), a neoclassi-

cal rotunda. Music lovers flock to the festival, whose ticket prices are far lower than many of its counterpart classical-music festivals in Europe.

CONTACTS:
Artexim
Calea Victoriei nr.155
corp D1, sc.8, et.2
sector 1
Bucharest 010073 Romania
www.festivalenescu.ro

Romanian National Tourist Office
14 E. 38th St., 12th Fl.
New York, NY 10016
212-545-8484; fax: 212-251-0429
www.romaniatourism.com

♦ 0852 ♦ **Enkutatash**
September 11

The **Ethiopian New Year** falls on the first day of the Ethiopian month of Maskarem, which is September 11 on the Gregorian calendar. It comes at the end of the rainy season, so the wildflowers that the children gather and the tall grass that rural people use to cover their floors on this day are plentiful. Small groups of children go from house to house, singing songs, leaving small bouquets of flowers, and hoping for a handful of *dabo*, or roasted grain, in return. In some parts of Ethiopia it is customary to slaughter an animal on this day. For traditional reasons this is either a white-headed lamb or a red chicken.

CONTACTS:
Ethiopian Embassy
3506 International Dr. N.W.
Washington, D.C. 20008
202-364-1200; fax: 202-587-0195
www.ethiopianembassy.org

Ethiopian Tourism Commission
P.O. Box 2183
Addis Ababa, Ethiopia
251-1-517-470; fax: 251-1-517-533
www.tourismethiopia.org

SOURCES:
AnnivHol-2000, p. 153
FolkWrldHol-1999, p. 556

♦ 0853 ♦ **Enlighteners, Day of the (Den na Buditelite)**
November 1

A holiday in Bulgaria, this day commemorates the patriots, writers, and revolutionaries who helped to ignite the spirit of Bulgarian nationalism. Thanksgiving services are held in churches, and elsewhere patriotic speeches, parades, and folk music mark this yearly event. Also known as the **Day of the Awakeners**, it is largely observed by schools and municipalities.

CONTACTS:
Embassy of the Republic of Bulgaria
1621 22nd St. N.W.
Washington, D.C. 20008

202-387-0174; fax: 202-234-7973
www.bulgaria-embassy.org

SOURCES:
BkFest-1937, p. 72

♦ 0854 ♦ Eo e Emalani i Alaka i Festival
Second Saturday in October

The Eo e Emalani i Alaka i Festival is an annual outdoor celebration that takes place, rain or shine, on the second Saturday in October in Koke'e State Park, Kaua'i, Hawaii. It is a joyous commemoration of the journey of Hawaiian Queen Emma Naea Rooke in 1871 from her beach house in Lawa'i to the upper reaches of Kilohana Viewpoint, where she wanted to see for herself the legendary, sweeping views reaching to Wainiha. The Queen, with nearly 100 companions, was led by a legendary guide, Kaluahi, recommended by Eric Knudsen of Waimea.

At the festival, the nature-loving Queen Emma is represented by a woman from the halau (a school where hula-dancing is taught). She and an entourage re-enact Queen Emma's entrance to the mountain meadow, where they are greeted by numerous Hawaiian hula dancers who offer ancient chants and special dances to the royal party. Guests at the free festival are asked to observe royal protocol, such as standing when the Queen enters or leaves the royal tent set up for the occasion. In addition to the historical re-enactment, the day's activities include a photographic exhibit and demonstrations of local crafts, including lauhala (fan and matt) weaving and Ni'ihau shell lei-making. Approximately 2,500 local guests and visitors attend each year's festival, sponsored by the Koke'e Natural History Museum in Kekeha, Kaua'i.

CONTACTS:
Koke'e Natural History Museum
P.O. Box 100
Kekaha, HI 96752
808-335-9975; fax: 808-335-6131
www.kokee.org/emalani.html

♦ 0855 ♦ Epidaurus Festival
Weekends from July to September

The Epidaurus Festival is marked by theatrical productions of ancient Greek tragedy and comedy at the theater built in the third century B.C.E. in Epidaurus, Greece, about 90 miles southwest of Athens. This open-air theater, the best preserved in Greece, can seat 14,000, and the acoustics are so fine that those seated in the top row can hear a whisper on stage. The performances, also known as the **Festival of Ancient Drama**, are presented by various theaters in the area. Summaries of the Greek-language plays are available to the audience in English.

CONTACTS:
Epidaurus Festival
23 Hadjichristou & Makriyanni St..
Athens, GR-117 42 Greece
30-210-9282900; fax: 30-210-92-82-941
www.greekfestival.gr/?lang=en

SOURCES:
GdWrldFest-1985, p. 102
IntlThFolk-1979, p. 193
MusFestEurBrit-1980, p. 108

♦ 0856 ♦ Epiphany, Christian Orthodox
January 6 (Gregorian calendar) or January 19 (Julian calendar)

EPIPHANY is a celebration by the Eastern Orthodox Christian churches of the baptism of Jesus in the River Jordan and the manifestation of his divinity when a dove descended on him. For Orthodox Christians around the world it is called **Blessing of the Waters Day**. In honor of the baptism of Christ, the church's baptismal water is blessed, and small bottles of the holy water are given to parishioners to take home. In many American cities, the priest leads the congregation to a local river which he blesses. Many places throughout the world mark the day with a blessing of the waters and immersion of a cross in seas, lakes, and rivers. At the port of Piraeus, Greece, the local priest throws a cross into the sea, and the diver who retrieves it is thought to be blessed with good luck in the coming year.

In pre-revolutionary Russia, priests and church officials led a procession to the banks of streams or rivers, breaking the ice and lowering a crucifix into the water. Those brave enough to jump into the icy waters to recover the crucifix were thought to be especially blessed. In the north, diving for the cross is frequently done on September 14 (*see* EXALTATION OF THE CROSS), when the water is warmer.

The holy day of the Epiphany is celebrated in colorful fashion in Tarpon Springs, Fla., at one time a sea sponge center with the largest sponge market in the world. The community has a strong Greek influence, going back to the beginning of the 20th century when sponge divers from Greece came here to take part in the growing sponge industry. On Epiphany, up to 100 young men from Greek Orthodox churches compete in diving for a gold cross. The cross has been tossed into the bayou by the chief celebrant from the town's St. Nicholas Greek Orthodox Church, and the person who retrieves it will be specially blessed.

Events of this holiday begin the day before with a blessing of the sponge fleet. The next morning, after the church service and a blessing of the waters, there is a parade of school and civic groups led by ecclesiastical dignitaries in their vestments. Many of the paraders wear Greek costume. After the parade, when the cross has been retrieved, the day becomes festive, with bouzouki music, dancing, and feasting, especially on roast lamb. Epiphany has been observed in this manner at Tarpon Springs since 1904, and now attracts about 30,000 people.

In Greece, Epiphany is one of the country's most important church days, especially in the port towns where diving for the cross takes place. After services, on the eve of Epiphany in Cyprus, priests visit houses to cleanse them from demons known as *Kallikantzari*. According to Cypriot tradition, these evil spirits appear on earth at CHRISTMAS, and for the next 12 days play evil tricks on people. On the eve of their departure, people appease them by throwing pancakes and sausages onto their roofs, which is where the demons dwell.

See also EPIPHANY, FEAST OF THE

CONTACTS:
St. Nicholas Greek Orthodox Cathedral
18 Hibiscus St.
Tarpon Springs, FL 34689
727-937-3540
www.epiphanycity.org

Orthodox Church in America
P.O. Box 675
Syosset, NY 11791
516-922-0550; fax: 516-922-0954
www.oca.org

Library of Congress
101 Independence Ave. S.E.
Washington, DC 20540
202-707-5000; fax: 202-707-2076
www.loc.gov

SOURCES:
BkFest-1937, pp. 3, 144, 289, 335
DictWrldRel-1989, p. 237
EncyChristmas-2003, p. 217
FestSaintDays-1915, p. 17
FolkAmerHol-1999, p. 35
FolkWrldHol-1999, p. 15
OxYear-1999, p. 21
RelHolCal-2004, p. 117

♦ 0857 ♦ **Epiphany, Feast of the**
January 6

One of the oldest Christian feasts (celebrated since the end of the second century, before the establishment of the CHRISTMAS holiday), Epiphany (which means "manifestation" or "showing forth") is sometimes called **Twelfth Day**, THREE KINGS' DAY, DÍA DE LOS TRES REYES (in Latin America), the **Feast of Jordan** (by Ukrainian Orthodox), or OLD CHRISTMAS DAY.

It commemorates the first two occasions on which the divinity of Jesus was manifested: when the Three Kings (or Magi) came to worship the infant Jesus in Bethlehem, and when he was baptized by John the Baptist in the River Jordan and the Holy Spirit descended in the form of a dove and proclaimed him the Son of God. The Roman Catholic and Protestant churches emphasize the visit of the Magi when they celebrate the Epiphany; the Eastern Orthodox churches focus on the baptism of Jesus. The blessing of lakes, rivers, and seas plays a central role in their celebrations.

In France **Le Jour des Rois** (the **Day of the Kings**), sometimes called the **Fête des Rois**, is celebrated with parties for children and adults alike. The highlight of these celebrations is the *galette des rois*, or "cake of the Kings"—a round, flat cake which is cut in the pantry, covered with a white napkin, and carried into the dining room on a small table. An extra piece is always cut, which is traditionally called *le part à Dieu* ("God's share") and is reserved for the first poor person who comes to the door.

The youngest person in the room oversees the distribution of the pieces of cake, one of which contains a bean or tiny china doll. The person who finds this token becomes king or queen for the evening. He or she chooses a consort, and for the remainder of the evening, every move the royal couple makes is imitated and commented upon by the other guests, who take great delight in exclaiming, for example, "The King drinks!" or "The Queen coughs!"

In many parts of France, the celebration begins on the evening of January 5 and involves collecting and distributing food and gifts for the poor (*see* EPIPHANY EVE IN FRANCE).

Now observed by a growing number of Protestants as well as Roman Catholics and Orthodox Christians, Epiphany refers not only to the day itself but to the church season that follows it—a season whose length varies because it ends when LENT begins, and that depends on the date of EASTER.

See also BEFANA FESTIVAL; FOUR AN' TWENTY DAY; EPIPHANY, CHRISTIAN ORTHODOX; TIMQAT; and TWELFTH NIGHT

SOURCES:
AmerBkDays-2000, p. 28
BkDays-1864, vol. I, p. 62
BkFest-1937, pp. 3, 119, 144, 289, 335
BkFestHolWrld-1970, pp. 19, 20, 22
DaysCustFaith-1957, p. 20
EncyChristmas-2003, p. 217
EncyRel-1987, vol. 3, p. 441
FestSaintDays-1915, pp. 15, 17
FestWestEur-1958, p. 33
FolkAmerHol-1999, p. 27
FolkWrldHol-1999, pp. 15, 20
OxYear-1999, pp. 21, 28
RelHolCal-2004, p. 89

♦ 0858 ♦ **Epiphany (Germany) (Dreikönigsfest)**
January 6

Boys dressed up as the Three Kings go from house to house caroling on EPIPHANY in Germany. Because they take with them a long pole from which dangles a star, they are known as Starsingers, or *Sternsinger* (*see also* EPIPHANY IN SWEDEN and NEW YEAR'S DAY IN GERMANY). In western and southern Germany, salt and chalk are consecrated in church on this day. The salt is given to animals to lick, while the chalk is used to write the initials of the Three Kings—*C.M.B.* for Caspar, Melchior, and Balthasar—over the house and stable doors to protect the household from danger and to keep out the evil spirits.

According to folk belief, a mysterious witch known as *Frau Perchta* (also Berchta or Bertha) wanders about the earth causing trouble between CHRISTMAS and Epiphany. In Upper Bavaria, according to tradition, peasants wearing wooden masks go around cracking whips and symbolically driving out Perchta, who is actually an ancient German fertility goddess and custodian of the dead. It is for this reason that Epiphany is also known as **Perchtennacht**. The Perchta masks, which can be terrifying in their ugliness, are often handed down from one generation to the next.

See also PERCHTENLAUF

SOURCES:
BkFest-1937, p. 131

EncyChristmas-2003, pp. 56, 221, 282
FestSaintDays-1915, p. 9
FestWestEur-1958, p. 54
FolkWrldHol-1999, p. 17

◆ 0859 ◆ Epiphany (Labrador)
January 6

The *naluyuks* that visit children on EPIPHANY in Labrador, Canada, are a combination of Santa Claus and the bogeyman. They go from house to house on January 6, their bodies covered in bearskin or an oversized coat with a mask over their faces and a stick in their hands along with a bag of gifts that has been donated ahead of time by parents. Children regard the coming of the naluyuks with great trepidation; Eskimo parents tell tales of a bogeyman figure, the naluyuk, to frighten them into good behavior.

When the naluyuks enter the house, the children perform a Christmas carol or hymn for them, and the naluyuks show their approval by pounding their sticks on the floor. After the singing, the children are asked various questions regarding their behavior over the past year. If the naluyuks are pleased with the answers, they hand each child a gift from their bag.

SOURCES:
FolkWrldHol-1999, p. 16

◆ 0860 ◆ Epiphany (Portugal) (Día de Reis)
January 6

EPIPHANY plays and pageants are common in Portugal, particularly in rural areas of the country. Bands of carolers go from house to house singing and begging for gifts. Sometimes family groups visit one another, standing at the door and asking to come in so they can sing to the Christ Child. After they sing their carols, the guests are entertained with wines and sweets.

It is common for parents to give parties for their children on Epiphany Day. The Epiphany cake, or *bolo-rei*, is a favorite tradition at these parties. Baked in the shape of a crown or ring, the cake contains many small trinkets and a single dried bean. Whoever finds the bean is crowned king of the party and must promise to make the cake the following year. At adult parties, the person who finds the bean is expected to pay for the following year's cake.

Epiphany is also a time when the traditional Portuguese dances known as *mouriscadas* and *paulitos* are performed. The latter is an elaborate stick dance in which the dancers, who are usually male but may be dressed as women, manipulate sticks or staves (substitutes for swords) in two opposing lines.

CONTACTS:
Portuguese National Tourist Office
590 Fifth Ave., 4th Fl.
New York, NY 10036
800-767-8842 or 212-354-4403; fax: 212-764-6137
www.visitportugal.com

SOURCES:
BkFest-1937, p. 266

DictFolkMyth-1984, pp. 346, 1082
FestWestEur-1958, p. 160

◆ 0861 ◆ Epiphany (Russia)
January 19

On January 19th, members of the Russian Orthodox Church ritually bathe in a river or lake. The day marks the baptism of Jesus Christ in the River Jordan, an event called the Epiphany. Bathing outside on that day, Orthodox Catholics believe, washes away sin. As believers cut holes in the ice with chainsaws and plunge into the frigid water, priests chant prayers to bless the water. Altars and crosses made of ice and snow are sometimes constructed near the bathing site.

Authorities advise against the practice, especially in the freezing temperatures of a Russian winter. Still, in 2006, some 2,000 persons were said to have participated in the ritual in the Moscow area alone.

CONTACTS:
Cathedral of the Epiphany in Elokhovo
Spartakovskaya ul. 15
Moscow 107066 Russia

◆ 0862 ◆ Epiphany (Spain) (Día de los Reyes Magos)
January 6

EPIPHANY is the day when Spanish children receive their gifts, and it is the Three Kings, rather than Santa Claus, who bring them. On Epiphany Eve the children fill their shoes with straw or grain for the Three Kings' horses to eat and place them on balconies or by the front door. The next morning, they find cookies, sweets, and gifts in their place.

In many cities throughout Spain, the Three Kings make a spectacular entry on Epiphany Eve, to the accompaniment of military bands and drummers in medieval dress. The Kings themselves usually ride horses, although in the Canary Islands they arrive by camel. One custom was for groups of people to walk out toward the city boundary to meet the Kings, some carrying ladders and some making a huge racket with horns, bells, and drums. Occasionally, those with ladders would pause in the procession while someone climbed a ladder to look for the Kings.

CONTACTS:
Tourist Office of Spain
666 Fifth Ave., 35th Fl.
New York, NY 10103
212-265-8822; fax: 212-265-8864
www.okspain.org

SOURCES:
BkFest-1937, p. 297
DictFolkMyth-1984, p. 1063
EncyChristmas-2003, p. 733
FestWestEur-1958, p. 188

◆ 0863 ◆ Epiphany (Sweden) (Trettondag Jul)
January 6

The **Night of the Three Holy Kings** was celebrated in Sweden during the Middle Ages with ecclesiastical folk plays commemorating the Magi's finding of Jesus in the manger. It is still customary for *Stjärngossar*, or Star Boys (*see also* EPIPHANY IN GERMANY), to present pageants dramatizing the journey of the Three Kings to Bethlehem. They wear white robes and cone-shaped hats with pompons and astronomical symbols on them. They carry paper star lanterns on long poles, illuminated from within by candles.

In rural areas, the Star Boys go from house to house, accompanied by other children dressed in costumes to resemble biblical characters, singing folk songs and hymns. The group almost always includes someone dressed up as Judas, wearing a huge false nose and carrying a purse or money bag jingling with the 30 pieces of silver he received for betraying Jesus.

SOURCES:
BkFest-1937, p. 307
EncyChristmas-2003, p. 735
FestWestEur-1958, p. 210
FolkWrldHol-1999, p. 18

♦ 0864 ♦ **Epiphany Eve (Austria)**
January 5

At one time the 12 nights between CHRISTMAS and EPIPHANY were known as "Smoke Nights" in Austria because people went through their houses and barns burning incense. Now the ceremony takes place on only one night, January 5. Also known as the **Vigil of Epiphany**, there is traditionally a special feast on this night during which an Epiphany cake is served. Three beans are concealed in the cake—two white, one black—and whoever finds a bean in his or her portion gets to dress up as one of the Three Wise Men or Holy Kings. The one with the black bean dresses up as the African king, Balthasar, by rubbing his face with soot or shoe polish. On Epiphany Day the three kings are the guests of honor at the table.

After the Epiphany Eve meal is served, to follow an old custom, the father or head of the household takes a shovelful of coal and burns incense on it. He walks through the house and outbuildings spreading smoke from the incense, followed by the oldest son, who sprinkles holy water in his path. The rest of the family follow, with the youngest child carrying a piece of chalk on a plate that has been blessed in morning mass. After each room and outbuilding has been blessed, the father takes the chalk and writes the initials of the Three Kings—C for Caspar, M for Melchior, and B for Balthasar—over every door leading to the outside. The ritual is believed to protect the household from evil in the coming year.

See also PERCHTENLAUF

CONTACTS:
Embassy of Austria
3524 International Ct. N.W.
Washington, D.C. 20008
202-895-6700; fax: 202-895-6750
www.austria.org

SOURCES:
BkFestHolWrld-1970, p. 21

EncyChristmas-2003, pp. 221, 771
FolkWrldHol-1999, p. 15

♦ 0865 ♦ **Epiphany Eve (France)**
January 5

On the eve of *Le Jour des Rois* ("the Day of the Kings") it is customary in France to give food, clothing, money, and gifts to the parish poor. In Alsace, children go from door to door dressed as the Three Kings, asking for donations of eggs, bacon, and cakes. In Normandy, children make their neighborhood rounds carrying Chinese lanterns and empty baskets, in which they hope to collect food, clothing, and money. In Brittany, someone dressed as a beggar leads a horse, decorated with ribbons and mistletoe, through the streets. There are empty baskets hanging from the saddle in which donations are carried. In Provence and some other parts of southern France, children go out on Epiphany Eve to meet the Three Kings, carrying cakes and figs for the hungry Magi and hay for their camels. Even though they may not meet the Three Kings on the road, they can see their statues standing near the altar of the church, where an Epiphany mass is celebrated at night.

SOURCES:
BkFest-1937, p. 119
DictFolkMyth-1984, pp. 182, 581
EncyChristmas-2003, p. 404
FestWestEur-1958, p. 33
FolkWrldHol-1999, p. 16

♦ 0866 ♦ **Equal Opportunity Day**
November 19

At the dedication of the Gettysburg National Cemetery in southern Pennsylvania on November 19, 1863, President Abraham LINCOLN delivered the GETTYSBURG Address. This 270-word speech is considered one of the greatest in American history, though it didn't receive much attention at the time. Equal Opportunity Day is observed at Gettysburg National Cemetery each year, where ceremonies commemorating Lincoln's address are held under the sponsorship of the Sons of Union Veterans and the Lincoln Fellowship of Pennsylvania. Sometimes this day is referred to as **Gettysburg Address Day**.

CONTACTS:
Library of Congress
101 Independence Ave. S.E.
Washington, D.C. 20540
202-707-5000; fax: 202-707-2076
www.loc.gov

Ben's Guide to Government
U.S. Government Printing Office
732 N. Capitol St. N.W.
Washington, DC 20401
888-293-6498 or 202-512-1530; fax: 202-512-1262
bensguide.gpo.gov

Gettysburg National Cemetery
97 Taneytown Rd.
Gettysburg, PA 17325
717-334-1124; fax: 717-334-1891
www.nps.gov

SOURCES:
AnnivHol-2000, p. 194

♦ 0867 ♦ Equatorial Guinea Independence Day
October 12

On this day in 1968, Equatorial Guinea became independent from Spain after being one of its colonies for nearly 300 years. On October 12—the same day on which COLUMBUS DAY is celebrated elsewhere in the world—Equatorial Guinea celebrates its autonomy with a national holiday.

CONTACTS:
Embassy of Equatorial Guinea
2020 16th St. N.W.
Washington, D.C. 20009
202-518-5700; fax: 202-518-5252

SOURCES:
AnnivHol-2000, p. 171

♦ 0868 ♦ Equirria
February 27 and March 14

Tradition holds that Romulus, one of the mythical founders of Rome, began the Equirria. This festival was held on both February 27 and March 14. The Equirria mainly involved racing horses and was dedicated to Mars, the Roman god of war. Scholars don't know why there were two annual Equirrias little more than two weeks apart from each other, but one theory is that these were occasions to publicly begin training horses and men for the military excursions Roman soldiers undertook in the spring. There is also a question of whether the later Equirria was related to the MAMURALIA, also observed on March 14.

SOURCES:
DictRomRel-1996, p. 69
FestRom-1981, p. 82
RomFest-1925, p. 44

♦ 0869 ♦ Eradication of Poverty, International Day for the
October 17

The UNITED NATIONS named October 17 the International Day for the Eradication of Poverty in 1992. In doing so, the U.N. followed the lead of some non-governmental organizations that had already dedicated the day to promoting awareness of the plight of the extremely poor. The U.N. observance focuses especially on the needs of the destitute in developing countries.

CONTACTS:
United Nations, Department of Public Information
Rm. S-1070L J, K, L
New York, NY 10017
212-963-6842; fax: 212-963-6914
www.un.org

♦ 0870 ♦ Erau Festival
September

This Indonesian festival takes place in Tenggarong, in the province of East Kalimantan on the island of Borneo. Some of the most isolated people in the world live in the surrounding area, where the dense jungle has made contact among neighboring villages difficult and where, until recently, raiding parties were common.

Today the Erau Festival is celebrated for as long as a week around September 24, the anniversary of the city's founding, though many of the ceremonies performed during the festival go back much further. The festival opens with special blessing and purification ceremonies, followed by musical and dance performances, art exhibits, and more traditional Dayak ceremonies.

CONTACTS:
Data and Information Centre, Indonesian Culture & Tourism
  Board
Sapta Pesona Bldg., 21st Fl.
Jalan Medan Merdeka Barat 17
Jakarta, 10110 Indonesia
62-21-3838717; fax: 62-21-3452006
www.indonesiatourism.go.id

SOURCES:
WildPlanet-1995, p. 359

♦ 0871 ♦ Eritrea Independence Day
May 24

Eritrea is a small country on the Red Sea, northeast of Ethiopia, of which it was a part until 1993. Eritreans struggled for 30 years for independence from Ethiopia. Internationally observed elections in 1993 decided the outcome as all but 0.2 percent of Eritreans voted to become independent, which became official on May 24, 1993. A border dispute with Ethiopia caused war from 1998 until 2000, when the UNITED NATIONS resolved the issue.

CONTACTS:
Embassy of Eritrea
1708 New Hampshire Ave. N.W.
Washington, D.C. 20009
202-319-1991; fax: 202-319-1304
www.embassyeritrea.org

♦ 0872 ♦ Eritrean Martyrs' Day
June 20

Following its defeat of Ethiopian government forces in 1991 to establish national independence, Eritrea instituted an official holiday to pay tribute to those who died for the country's liberation. The struggle, which lasted from 1961 to 1991, claimed the lives of an estimated 65,000 freedom fighters and tens of thousands of civilians.

Many Eritreans observe Martyrs' Day by filing into mass mourning processions that conclude at the "Martyrs' Graveyards" located throughout the country. On the eve of Martyrs' Day in 1997, the government expanded the national tribute by opening the National Martyrs' Park, situated in a forest and wildlife preserve outside the capital city, Asmara.

Individuals arrive to pay their respects to the dead by finding names engraved on the National Martyrs' Monument and walking through museums that depict the 30-year struggle for independence.

CONTACTS:
Eritrean Embassy
1708 New Hampshire Ave. N.W.
Washington, D.C. 20009
202-319-1991; fax: 202-319-1304
www.embassyeritrea.org

Ethiopian Tourism Commission
P.O. Box 2183
Addis Ababa, Ethiopia
www.tourismethiopia.org (click on "Cultural Attractions")

♦ 0873 ♦ **Eritrean Start of the Armed Struggle Day**
September 1

Between 1961 and 1991 the small country of Eritrea in eastern Africa waged a war of independence against Ethiopia. An important holiday that recognizes Eritrean sacrifices during this prolonged campaign is the Start of the Armed Struggle Day, also known as **Bahti Meskerem**. The day's festivities take place in the country and in Eritrean communities throughout the world.

The anniversary commemorates the first shot fired in 1961 at Mount Adal, in the country's western region. Leading the attack was Idris Hamid Awate, founder of the Eritrean Liberation Army and a celebrated martyr.

In the years since Eritrea's independence was approved by popular referendum in 1993, this anniversary has been less of a war cry against Ethiopia and more an occasion to simply remember the contributions of freedom fighters. Typically, observances include a moment of silence in honor of the martyrs, the singing of the Eritrean national anthem, and public statements by dignitaries.

CONTACTS:
Eritrean Embassy
1708 New Hampshire Ave. N.W.
Washington, D.C. 20009
202-319-1991; fax: 202-319-1304
www.embassyeritrea.org

Ministry of Information of the State of Eritrea
P.O. Box 872
Asmara, Eritrea
www.shabait.com

♦ 0874 ♦ **Esala Perahera (Arrival of the Tooth Relic)**
July-August; Sinhalese month of Esala

Esala Perahera is a celebration in Kandy, Sri Lanka (formerly Ceylon), that lasts 10 nights and pays homage to the sacred relic believed to be a tooth of the Buddha. Kandy, originally the capital of the independent kingdom of Kandy in the Sri Lankan highlands, is the site of the Dalada Maligava, or Temple of the Tooth, where the relic is kept. The celebration originated in the fourth century when the king of Kandy declared that the tooth be paraded annually so people could honor it.

Processions are held each night for 10 nights, and the tooth is paraded in an elaborate *howdah* (platform) on the back of an ornately decorated elephant. Dozens of richly caparisoned elephants follow, and there are also drummers beating big bass drums and small tom-toms, horn blowers, the famous Kandyan dancers, acrobats, and torch bearers holding aloft baskets of blazing *copra* (coconut meat). Representatives of the major Hindu temples also are part of the processions.

CONTACTS:
Kandy Municipal Council
D.S. Senanayake Veediya, Town Hall
Kandy, Sri Lanka
94-81-222-2275; fax: 94-81-222-2274
www.kandycity.org

Temple of the Sacred Tooth Relic
Dalada Veediya
Kandy, Sri Lanka
www.sridaladamaligawa.lk

SOURCES:
BkHolWrld-1986, Aug 20
DictWrldRel-1989, p. 135
EncyRel-1987, vol. 2, p. 549
FolkWrldHol-1999, p. 468
GdWrldFest-1985, p. 165
IntlThFolk-1979, p. 344

♦ 0875 ♦ **Esbat**
Full moon of each month; sometimes at the new moon and sometimes at both the full and new moons

"Wicca" is the term used by many believers in modern Neopagan witchcraft to describe themselves because it doesn't carry the negative connotations of the words "witch" and "pagan." Many Wiccan covens (assemblies of witches) hold regular meetings, known as Esbats, on the most convenient evening nearest the full and/or new moon. Esbat rituals typically use color, nature symbolism, candles, and symbolic acts to enhance the attributes of a particular moon—the Oak Moon, the Wolf Moon, the Storm Moon, etc. There are 13 moons in one solar year.

The rituals associated with the Esbats, which are usually known by heart, serve as a form of worship, a means of teaching, an aide to meditation, and a form of communication between the worshipper and the gods. Esbat meetings are usually open only to initiates, because they are specifically intended to develop members who are in training for the Wiccan priesthood.

SOURCES:
RelHolCal-2004, p. 267

♦ 0876 ♦ **Escalade (Scaling the Walls)**
Weekend in mid-December

Escalade is a celebration in Geneva, Switzerland, of the victory of the people of Geneva over the attacking French Savoyards. On the nights of Dec. 11 and 12 in 1602, the French soldiers tried to scale the city ramparts, but were ferociously turned back. Among the remembered defenders is Mère Royaume, who poured a pot of scalding soup on the head of a Savoyard soldier.

To mark the victory, people carrying torches and wearing period costumes and armor proceed through the old city on both banks of the Rhone River. Historic figures, like Mère Royaume, are always represented. Shops sell chocolates that look like miniature soup pots. These commemorate Royaume's courageous act. At several points on the route, the procession stops while a herald on horseback reads the proclamation of victory. The procession winds up at St. Peter's Cathedral, where the citizens sing patriotic songs and a huge bonfire concludes the celebration. From there revelers can feast on Mère Royaume's soup and tour the Passage de Monetier. Open to the public only at this time of year, this secret passageway under the Cathedral runs along the old city walls.

On the first Saturday in December a local sports club organizes various races to celebrate, ranging from two to nine kilometers, around the St. Pierre Cathedral. In the evening everyone can participate in the most popular event: the soup pot, or *La Marmite*, race. Runners cover 3.4 kilometers while dressed in costume which can range from witches and skeletons to the more modern and innovative.

CONTACTS:
Geneva Tourism
Rue de Mont-Blanc 18
C.P. 1602
Geneva, 1211 Switzerland
41-22-909-7070; fax: 41-22-909-7011
www.geneva-tourism.ch

Course de l'Escalade
P.O. Box 3687
Geneva, 1211 Switzerland
41-22-318-5320
www.escalade.ch

♦ 0877 ♦ Esplanade Concerts
July 4

Arthur Fiedler (1894-1979), a violinist for the Boston Symphony Orchestra, started this outdoor concert series on July 4, 1929. The first concerts were held under a temporary wooden shell along the banks of the Charles River in Boston, which has since been replaced by the Hatch Memorial Shell, a gift presented to the city in 1940. The concerts are free, and it is not uncommon for hundreds of thousands to gather on the grassy riverbank or listen to the concerts from boats moored in the Charles River lagoon for the FOURTH OF JULY holiday. A musically synchronized fireworks display follows the concert.

During the Bicentennial celebration in 1976, the Boston Pops Esplanade Orchestra performed a spectacular rendition of Tchaikovsky's *1812 Overture*. The music was accompanied by the firing of live cannons, the ringing of nearby church bells, and fireworks.

See also BOSTON POPS

CONTACTS:
Boston's Fourth of July
222 Berkeley St. 14th Fl.
Boston, MA 02116
888-484-7677 or 617-267-2400; fax: 617-267-3303
www.july4th.org

SOURCES:
MusFestAmer-1990, p. 211

♦ 0878 ♦ Essence Festival
Early July

The Essence Music Festival bills itself as the "the nation's largest annual African-American event and gathering of musical talent." The three-day event was launched in 1995. From 1995 through 2005, a combined total of two million fans have taken part in the event. Featured performers have included such renowned African-American musicians as Alicia Keys, Aretha Franklin, Destiny's Child, Earth, Wind & Fire, Gladys Knight, Prince, and Kanye West.

The festival began in New Orleans in 1995 as a one-time event to celebrate the 25th anniversary of *Essence*, the African-American lifestyle magazine, but its success inspired *Essence* to make it an annual event. After the devastation of Hurricane Katrina, the festival temporarily relocated from New Orleans to Houston in 2005. The following year, it returned to New Orleans. According to *Essence* magazine, the festival is a multigenerational event where far-flung African-American families and friends reunite.

CONTACTS:
Essence Magazine
135 W. 50th St.
New York, NY 10020
212-484-8000
www.essence.com/essence

♦ 0879 ♦ Estonia Independence Day
February 24

On this day in 1918, Estonia issued a declaration of independence from the new Soviet Russia, which was followed by war with the Soviets to maintain Estonian liberty. On February 2, 1920, the war ended with the Tartu Peace Treaty which guaranteed Estonia's independence for all time. The Soviets went on to break this pact, however, and Estonia was under Soviet control for 75 years.

Following a strong independence movement during the late 1980s, Estonia officially declared its independence from the former U.S.S.R. on August 20, 1991, a day which is also commemorated with a public holiday. LATVIA and LITHUANIA had also declared independence from the disintegrating Soviet empire. On September 6, independence was formally recognized by the former Soviet Union.

Estonians celebrate their Independence Day with a parade, church services, speeches, and concerts in the capital city, Tallinn.

CONTACTS:
Estonian Ministry of Foreign Affairs, Press and Information
  Department
Islandi valjak 1
Tallinn, 15049 Estonia
372-6-317-000; fax: 372-6-317-099
www.vm.ee/eng

SOURCES:
AnnivHol-2000, p. 31

♦ 0880 ♦ **Estonia Restoration of Independence Day**
August 20

In the 20th century, Estonia was a sovereign state from 1919 to 1940. At that time, it was forced to become a socialist republic of the Soviet Union. Then, in 1991, the Soviet Union collapsed, and the three Baltic countries of Estonia, Latvia, and Lithuania regained their independence. On August 20 of that year, Estonia formally re-established its independence following a national referendum.

Throughout 2008, the country celebrated its 90th anniversary as a republic. The government encouraged citizens to devote the entire month of August to appreciating the blessings of independence and to remembering the Estonian patriots who suffered through exile and resistance during the Soviet era.

Estonia Restoration of Independence Day is one of three days on which the national flag must be hoisted on state buildings. (The other two days are ESTONIA VICTORY DAY and ESTONIA INDEPENDENCE DAY.)

CONTACTS:
Estonia Embassy in Washington
2131 Massachusetts Ave. N.W.
Washington, D.C. 20008
202-588-0101; fax: 202-588-0108
www.estemb.org/embassy

Estonian Ministry of Foreign Affairs
Press and Information Dept.
Islandi Väljak
Tallinn 15049 Estonia

♦ 0881 ♦ **Estonia Victory Day**
June 23

In light of the multiple times Estonia has lost its sovereignty, the independence celebration known as Victory Day bears special significance for citizens. This date commemorates the Battle of Võnnu in 1919, in which a joint force of Estonians and Latvians claimed a decisive victory against their Baltic German adversaries. The celebration falls a day before the same date as two time-honored celebrations, MIDSUMMER DAY and the ST. JOHN'S DAY (Jaanipäev in Estonian). As a result of the synchronicity of the festivals, various traditions and observances have melded together.

The military triumph in 1919 marked the end of 700 years of German control. The present-day government has framed the holiday as a celebration of Estonian freedom and sovereignty. The president and other dignitaries attend the offi-

cial Victory Day ceremonies in the capital city, Tallinn. Festivities include a parade, a speech by the president, and a military review.

The holiday transitions from the political to the traditional when the president orders citizens to take torches from the official bonfire held in honor of Victory Day to light the hundreds of bonfires in the country that initiate Midsummer and St. John's Eve celebrations.

CONTACTS:
Estonia Embassy in Washington
2131 Massachusetts Ave. N.W.
Washington, DC 20008
202-588-0101; fax: 202-588-0108
www.estemb.org/embassy

Estonian Ministry of Foreign Affairs
Press and Information Dept.
Islandi Väljak
Tallinn 15049 Estonia

♦ 0882 ♦ **Ethiopia National Day**
May 28

A military junta called the Derg brought an end to the Ethiopian Empire and HAILE SELASSIE'S rule September 12, 1974. Haile Selassie (born Tafari Makonnen, 1892-1975) was crowned in 1930, inheriting the throne from a long line of regents. According to tradition, he was the 111th ruler descended from King Solomon and the Queen of Sheba.

The Derg socialist military regime was overthrown by the Ethiopian People's Revolutionary Democratic Front (EPRDF) in 1991, commemorated by the May 28 holiday. A constitution was adopted in 1994 and Ethiopia's first multiparty elections were held in 1995.

CONTACTS:
Ethiopian Embassy
3506 International Dr. N.W.
Washington, D.C. 20008
202-364-1200; fax: 202-587-0195
www.ethiopianembassy.org

Ethiopian Tourism Commission
P.O. Box 2183
Addis Ababa, Ethiopia
www.tourismethiopia.org (click on "Cultural Attractions")

♦ 0883 ♦ **Ethiopia Patriots' Victory Day**
May 5

Emperor Haile Selassie of Ethiopia made a grand entrance into the capital city, Addis Ababa, on May 5, 1941, to mark the end of the Italian occupation. Selassie had deliberately chosen that date because exactly five years earlier, the Italians had entered the city and initiated a period of occupation that halted Ethiopia's long legacy of sovereignty. However, the intervention of British forces and other Allies, as well as the heroics of Ethiopian patriots, helped preserve Ethiopia's independence. Ever since, Ethiopians have annually commemorated Selassie's famous arrival into the capital.

In Addis Ababa, government leaders, diplomats, patriot associations, and city residents turn out to honor veterans who fought in the resistance movement between 1935 and 1941. A dignitary often lays a wreath before one of the city's monuments commemorating Ethiopia's various military victories. Army brass bands also perform to mark the occasion.

CONTACTS:
Ethiopian Embassy
3506 International Dr. N.W.
Washington, D.C. 20008
202-364-1200; fax: 202-587-0195

Ethiopian Tourism Commission
P.O. Box 2183
Addis Ababa, Ethiopia
www.tourismethiopia.org (click on "Cultural Attractions")

SOURCES:
AnnivHol-2000, p. 77

♦ 0884 ♦ **Ethiopia Victory of Adwa Commemoration Day**
March 2

Ethiopia enjoys rare distinction as an African country that successfully shook off European domination for centuries. One pivotal moment of resistance was the Ethiopian army's historic victory over invading Italian troops in the Battle of Adwa. The two-day battle, fought in northern Ethiopia in 1896 and led by Emperor Menelik II, ended on March 2. The great military feat stands as a turning point in the history of modern Africa. The anniversary is thus a significant patriotic holiday for Ethiopians.

Festivities take place throughout the country, with official ceremonies in the capital, Addis Ababa, and Adwa, the historical market town located near the battle site. Past celebrations in the capital have featured addresses by national leaders, with messages focusing on Ethiopia's forefathers and their achievements. People will also leave wreaths at the foot of the Menelik Monument, which commemorates the victory led by the Ethiopian emperor.

The celebration in 2005 was a milestone because it occurred the day before the Italian government returned to Ethiopia the Axum obelisk, a 4th-century relic that the Fascist forces looted during a brief period of conquest and occupation in the 1930s.

CONTACTS:
Ethiopian Embassy
3506 International Dr. N.W.
Washington, D.C. 20008
202-364-1200; fax: 202-587-0195

Ethiopian Tourism Commission
P.O. Box 2183
Addis Ababa, Ethiopia
www.tourismethiopia.org (click on "Cultural Attractions")

♦ 0885 ♦ **Eton Wall Game**
November 30

Every year on St. Andrew's Day, England's prestigious Eton College holds the famous Eton Wall Game, a variety of rugby that has its own highly technical rules and is different from all other forms of the game. The game is played between two teams: the Collegers, who are boys receiving scholarships and living in the old College, and the Oppidans (which means "townspeople"), who live in boarding-houses in town.

The rules are so complex and mysterious that even the spectators are often confused, although the players seem to understand how to play the game. The object of the game is to win goals by maneuvering the ball into the opposing team's "calx," designated by a chalk line on a garden wall at one end of the field and by a mark on a tree at the other. The game is made up of many scrimmages along the brick wall that marks off the college athletic field for which the game is named, and goals are almost never scored.

CONTACTS:
Eton College
Windsor, Berkshire SL4 6DW United Kingdom
44-17-5367-1000; fax: 44-17-5367-1159
www.etoncollege.com

SOURCES:
EngCustUse-1941, p. 169
YrFest-1972, p. 86

♦ 0886 ♦ **Europalia**
October-December

Since its founding in 1969, the European arts festival known around the world as Europalia has presented a comprehensive survey of the diverse cultural and artistic aspects of a specific country. The first several festivals were devoted to European cultures: Italy, the Netherlands, Great Britain, France, Germany, Belgium, Greece, Spain, and Austria. But in 1989 the decision was made to devote the festival to a major culture from outside Europe: Japan. In 1993 the festival's founders moved its focus to the American continent, devoting the three-month festival to a display of cultural events representing Mexico.

While most of the festival events take place in Brussels, other cities in the Netherlands, France, Luxembourg, and Germany also host events, which include art, photography, and craft exhibitions; theater, dance, and orchestral performances; literary and scientific colloquia; and film retrospectives. Europalia '93 Mexico, for example, offered 14 exhibitions, 76 concerts, eight ballet performances, 22 theatrical productions, 17 literary events, 187 films, and nine traditional folk events. Discussions with the well-known writers Octavio Paz and Carlos Fuentes were a highlight of the festival.

CONTACTS:
Europalia
Koningsstraat 10
Brussels, B 1000 Belgium
32-2-507-85-95; fax: 32-02-513-5488
www.europalia.be/home.php?lng=en

SOURCES:
IntlThFolk-1979, p. 45

◆ 0887 ◆ Evacuation Day
March 17; September 1; November 25

"Evacuation Day" has been used to describe a number of dates in history on which military forces have withdrawn from a city or country. The best-known evacuation in the United States took place on March 17, 1776, during the early part of the American Revolution. British troops were forced out of Boston when the British commander, General Sir William Howe, conceded defeat to American General George WASHINGTON in a move that he hoped would save the British fleet. Bostonians have been celebrating the day ever since. Because of the large Irish-American community in Boston, the popularity of this holiday is often attributed to its being coincident with ST. PATRICK'S DAY.

Another well-known evacuation took place a few years later on November 25, 1783, when the British were forced out of New York City.

In England, "Evacuation Day" has also been used to refer to September 1, 1939, and the two days following, when over a million children and adults were evacuated from London and other cities considered to be likely targets for bombing during World War II.

SOURCES:
AmerBkDays-2000, pp. 211, 794
DictDays-1988, p. 37
OxYear-1999, p. 474

◆ 0888 ◆ Evamelunga
September 8

Evamelunga, which means **"The Taking Away of the Burden of Sin"** is a day of thanksgiving for Christians in Cameroon. Families put on their best clothes and flock to the thatched-roof churches, which are decorated with flowers and palm leaves for the occasion. Church choirs and school choruses sing songs expressing gratitude for the arrival of the first missionary who brought them the story of Jesus in the late 19th century. After the church services are over, the feasting and singing continue late into the evening.

SOURCES:
FolkWrldHol-1999, p. 523

◆ 0889 ◆ Exaltation of the Cross, Feast of the
September 14; formerly May 3 by Roman Catholics

The holiday known as the Exaltation of the Cross by the Eastern Church, where it is one of the 12 great feasts, is also known as the **Elevation, Recovery,** or **Adoration of the Cross**. In the West, it is known as **Holy Cross Day** (by the Anglican Communion), the **Triumph of the Cross** (by Roman Catholics), and also the **Invention of the Cross** (from Latin *invenire*, meaning "to find"). It commemorates three events: the finding of the cross on which Jesus was crucified, the dedication in 335 of the basilica built by Emperor Constantine enclosing the supposed site of Jesus' crucifixion on Golgotha, and the recovery in 629 by Emperor Heraclius of the relic of the cross that had been stolen by the Persians.

According to tradition, St. Helena, mother of Emperor Constantine, found the cross on a visit to Jerusalem, being enabled to identify it by a miracle. Many relics from the cross were distributed among churches throughout the world. (In the late 19th century, Rohault de Fleury catalogued all the known relics in the world; he estimated that they constituted less than one-third of the size of the cross that was believed to have been used.)

In addition, St. Helena discovered the four nails used in the Crucifixion, and the small plaque hung above Jesus that bore the sarcastic inscription "INRI" (*Iesus Nazarenus Rex Iudaeorum*, Latin for "Jesus of Nazareth, King of the Jews"). Two of the nails were placed in Constantine's crown, one was later brought to France by Charlemagne, and the fourth was supposedly cast into the Adriatic Sea when Helena's ship was threatened by a storm on her return journey.

On September 13, 335, bishops met in Jerusalem for the dedication of the basilica of the Holy Sepulchre built by order of Constantine. Many believe this date marks the discovery of the remains of the cross during excavations on the site of the Temple of Venus. On the 14th, a relic enshrined in a silver-gilt receptacle was elevated for veneration.

The relic was taken to Persia in 614 after the Persian army of King Choesroes occupied Jerusalem. When Heraclius of Constantinople defeated the Persians on the banks of the Danube in 629, he brought the sacred relic to Constantinople (now Istanbul). On September 14, 633, it was carried in a solemn procession to the Church of the Holy Wisdom (Hagia Sophia in Greek; Saint Sophia in English) where it was elevated for all to adore, recalling Jesus' words, "And I, if I be lifted up from the earth, will draw all men unto me" (John 12:32).

Former names for this day are **Crouchmas** (**Cross Mass**), **Holy Rood Day**, and **Roodmas**, *rood* referring to the wood of which the cross was made.

In the Philippines, there is a nationwide celebration commemorating the discovery of the Holy Cross of Calvary by St. Helena. It is known as **Santacruzan**. Nine-day pageants are held in May with local men and women playing the parts of biblical characters. There are processions with floats of each town's patron saint, and costumed young women and their escorts parade under flower-decked arches. In Lucban, Quezon Province, multicolored rice wafers, called *kiping*, are shaped into the form of fruits and vegetables and displayed as window ornaments.

See also DÍA DE LA SANTA CRUZ; EPIPHANY, ORTHODOX; MASKAL

CONTACTS:
Greek Orthodox Archdiocese of Australia
242 Cleveland St.
Redfern, NSW 2016 Australia
61-2-9698-5066; fax: 61-2-9698-536
www.greekorthodox.org.au

Orthodox Church in America
P.O. Box 675

Syosset, NY 11791
516-922-0550; fax: 516-922-0954
www.oca.org

Philippine Tourism Center
556 Fifth Ave.
New York, NY 10036
212-575-7915; fax: 212-302-6759
www.philippinetourism.us

SOURCES:
BkDays-1864, vol. I, p. 586; vol. II, p. 340
BkFest-1937, pp. 152, 295
BkHolWrld-1986, May 3
DaysCustFaith-1957, pp. 118, 234
FestSaintDays-1915, pp. 110, 177
FolkAmerHol-1999, pp. 213, 381
FolkWrldHol-1999, p. 324
OxYear-1999, pp. 194, 371
RelHolCal-2004, pp. 101, 114
SaintFestCh-1904, pp. 224, 404

♦ 0890 ♦ **Excited Insects, Feast of**
On or around March 5

Known as **Kyongchip** or *Gyeongchip* in Korea and as **Ching Che** in China, the Feast of Excited Insects marks the transition from winter to spring. It is the day when the insects are said to come back to life after hibernating all winter. In China, it is the day when "the dragon raises his head," summoning the insects back to life, and people perform various rituals designed to prepare for the onslaught and begin the task of restoring fertility to the earth. In Korea, this is one of 24 days in the lunar calendar that marks the beginning of a new season. Farmers prepare their fields and begin planting their barley, cabbage, and other vegetables.

SOURCES:
FolkWrldHol-1999, p. 204

F

◆ 0891 ◆ Faces Etnofestival
Weekend in late July or early August

Faces is a multicultural arts festival held annually in Billnäs, Finland, a town in the southern part of the country about 40 miles from Helsinki. Each summer more than 12,000 visitors gather for three days celebrating world cultures with performances in music, dance, theater, and poetry. Ten different stages showcase a range of acts from musical theater and improvisational comedy to reggae, punk, and country. Musicians, actors, clowns, writers, and other participants come from many countries around the world, including Argentina, Sweden, South Africa, Australia, and Russia; Finnish folk and popular music is also highlighted. In addition, workshops, exhibits, and vendors promote fine art, music, crafts, and world cuisine. Yoga, graffiti art, fire dancing, Scandinavian myths, and herbal remedies, are among the many unusual areas of interest included in the program. Activities in the Small Faces area are designed especially for children, including tribal drumming workshops and felting lessons.

The festival, which is sponsored by the humanitarian aid group Etnokult, has been held each year since 1998 as a means of promoting global diversity, equality, and understanding. A symposium held on the festival Saturday challenges those in attendance to reflect on developments in multiculturalism and globalization. The festival's name derives from the idea that coming together in a celebration of diversity helps to give a "face" to otherwise unfamiliar ethnicities and cultures. On the final day of the festival a benefit Peace Concert is held, with proceeds contributing to an international aid project such as hospital construction in a developing nation. The festival operates two campgrounds near the event site for those who wish to stay overnight, with one offering parking for recreational vehicles.

CONTACTS:
Faces Etnofestival
Bruksvägen 8
Billnäs Finland
www.faces.fi

◆ 0892 ◆ Fairbanks Winter Carnival
Second week in March

The Winter Carnival is a week of festivities in Fairbanks, Alaska, highlighted by sled dog races. The carnival opens with the two-day Limited North American Sled Dog Race, and concludes, on the last two days, with the Open North American Sled Dog Race. Other events include dances, a parka parade, a campstove chili contest, a native potlatch, snow- and ice-sculpting contests, snowshoe races and softball, musical and dramatic presentations, and a trade fair.

CONTACTS:
Fairbanks Convention and Visitors Bureau
550 First Ave.
Fairbanks, AK 99701
800-327-5774 or 907-456-5774; fax: 907-452-2867
www.explorefairbanks.com

◆ 0893 ◆ Fairhope Jubilee
Summer, usually August

The Jubilee marks a natural phenomenon greeted by the citizens of Fairhope, Alabama, with a rush to the shores of Mobile Bay. Fairhope, on a bluff over the bay, has two miles of beach. At a certain time, when the bay is calm and there is an east wind and a certain feel to the air, bottom-dwelling fish and crustaceans are trapped between a low-oxygen water mass and the shore. They become sluggish because of the shortage of oxygen and can't swim, so townsfolk rush out with buckets, cooking pots, crab nets, long poles, and wash basins to harvest them. The harvest may include flounder, shrimp, blue crab, stingrays, eels, and smaller fish such as shiners, anchovies, and hogchokers.

It's impossible to predict when the phenomenon will occur except that it's always in the summer and usually in August. Sometimes there is more than one occurrence; sometimes it will happen five days in a row. This event depends on a number of very specific circumstances: an overcast day, a gentle wind from the east, a rising tide.

Here's what happens: a deep-water pocket of very salty water stagnates and collects plant matter. This food supply and the warm temperatures cause a population explosion of microorganisms that consume great quantities of oxygen. A gentle east wind comes along and moves the upper-layer water offshore. Then the rising tide pushes the oxygen-poor bottom water toward the shore, and the bottom sea creatures are pushed in front of it. They act as though they're in a stupor because they're trying to get oxygen; they move slowly and don't try to swim. Eels will leave the water and burrow tail-first into the moist sand, leaving their heads in the air with mouths open.

Supposedly the event got its name because the first person seeing the marine migration called out, "Jubilee!"

CONTACTS:
City of Fairhope
P.O. Drawer 429
Fairhope, AL 36533
251-928-2136; fax: 251-928-6776
www.cofairhope.com

◆ 0894 ◆ Famadihana
Between June and September

The Malagasy people of Madagascar, an island off the southeast coast of Africa, believe that their deceased ancestors have become intermediaries between the living and God. Because they will spend eternity in their new existence, tombs are built to be much sturdier and more elaborately decorated than houses. The Famadihana is a celebration in which people exhume the remains of their ancestors, treat them to a grand feast and party, replace their burial clothes, and then reintern them. The specific date of a family's Famidihana is determined by a spiritual leader, but, for hygenic reasons, it always takes place sometime during the winter months, when the weather is dry.

SOURCES:
FestWrld: Madag-1999, p. 14

◆ 0895 ◆ Family Month, National
Second Sunday in May through the third Sunday in June

National Family Month is observed during the five-week period between MOTHER'S DAY in May and FATHER'S DAY in June. It is timed to coincide with the end of the school year, when families start spending more time together, and also to focus attention on mothers and fathers as the most powerful support system for their children.

National Family Month was started by KidsPeace, a private, not-for-profit organization that has dedicated itself to helping children attain the confidence and develop the courage to face and overcome crises since 1882. KidsPeace has also established National Kids Day, observed on the third Saturday of September. The organization believes that such observances provide opportunities for parents, grandparents, and caregivers to be more involved in the lives of the children for whom they are responsible. Families are urged to spend time doing things together during this five-week period, whether it is taking a family vacation or simply doing chores around the house.

CONTACTS:
KidsPeace
5300 KidsPeace Dr.

Orefield, PA 18069
800-257-3223 or 610-799-1930; fax: 610-776-1694
www.kidspeace.org

◆ 0896 ◆ Family Week
Begins on the first Sunday in May

In America, Protestant churches, Roman Catholic churches, and Jewish congregations observe **National Family Week**. While each has its own way of celebrating this event, the emphasis is on the strength that a family can find in religion. Members of the congregation are encouraged to examine their own lives from the perspective of how they have contributed to the religious life of their families, and groups often meet to discuss how to deal with social conditions that are having an adverse effect on family life. National Family Week begins on the first Sunday in May and leads up to MOTHER'S DAY and, among Christians, to the **Festival of the Christian Home**.

Many other countries observe a **Family Day**, as well, particularly in Africa. In Angola, Family Day is observed on December 25; in Namibia, December 26. Family Day is also the name by which EASTER MONDAY is known in South Africa.

SOURCES:
DaysCustFaith-1957, p. 133
RelHolCal-2004, p. 95

◆ 0897 ◆ Farvardegan Days
March, July, August; 26th-30th days of Spendarmad, the 12th Zoroastrian month, plus five intercalary days

Also known as **Farvadin** or **Farvardin**, this is a Zoroastrian festival celebrated by the followers of Zoroaster in Iran and India. The 10-day **Remembrance of the Departed** commemorates the spirits of the dead (*fravashis*), who have returned to God, or Ahura Mazda, to help in the fight against evil. People perform ceremonies for the departed at home shrines or fire temples.

Farvardegan is celebrated in March by the Fasli sect, July by the Kadmi sect, and August by the Shahenshai sect. Zoroaster (or Zarathushtra) was a Persian prophet and reformer, now believed to have lived around 1200 B.C.E., whose teachings influenced Judaism, Christianity, and Islam. The largest Zoroastrian groups remaining today are in India, where they are known as Parsis, and in Iran.

SOURCES:
AnnivHol-2000, p. 42
RelHolCal-2004, p. 69

◆ 0898 ◆ Fasching
Between February 2 and March 8; the two days before Ash Wednesday

Known in southwest Germany as **Fastnacht**, in Bavaria and Austria as **Fasching**, and as **Karneval** in the Rhineland, this is a Shrovetide festival that takes place on the two days immediately preceding Ash Wednesday, otherwise known as Rose Monday and Shrove Tuesday. It features processions of masked figures, and is the equivalent of Mardi Gras and the last day of Carnival.

Fastnacht means "eve of the fast," and the wild celebrations that typically take place during this festival are a way of making the most of the last hours before the deprivations of Lent.

In the Black Forest area of southern Germany, these pre-Lenten festivities are called **Fastnet**. The celebrations date back to the Middle Ages and were developed by craftsmen's guilds. Today's carnival clubs (*Narrenzünfte*) still use the same wooden masks and traditional costumes in their parades as their ancestors did. The rites of Fasnet are distinctive: in Elzach, wooden-masked Schuddig Fools, wearing red costumes and large hats decorated with snail shells, run through the town beating people with blown-up hogs' bladders; in Wolfach, fools stroll around in nightgowns and nightcaps; in Überlinger on the Bodensee and Villingen, they crack long whips, toss fruit and nuts to the children, and wear foxes' tails and smiling wooden masks. Carnival ends with *Kehraus*, a "sweeping out."

See also Karneval in Cologne

CONTACTS:
German National Tourist Office
122 E. 42nd St., 20th Fl., Ste. 2000
New York, NY 10168
800-651-7010 or 212-661-7200; fax: 212-661-7174
www.cometogermany.com

Austrian National Tourist Office
120 W. 45th St., 9th Fl.
P.O. Box 1142
New York, NY 10036
212-944-6885; fax: 212-730-4568
www.austria.info

SOURCES:
BkFest-1937, pp. 29, 132
BkHolWrld-1986, Feb 25
DictFolkMyth-1984, pp. 192, 370, 977, 1082
EncyEaster-2002, p. 219
FestWestEur-1958, pp. 55, 56
FolkWrldHol-1999, p. 139
RelHolCal-2004, p. 91

◆ 0899 ◆ **Fasinada**
July 22

Fasinada is a commemoration of a miraculous event on the tiny island of Gospa od Skrpjela (Our Lady of the Chisels) off Montenegro (formerly in Yugoslavia). The island, according to the story, was once nothing more than a rock. One stormy night, a shipwrecked sailor clung to the rock and vowed that if he survived he would build a church to the Virgin Mary. He did survive, and sailors dumped stones there until an island was formed; in the 17th century a church was built on the pile of rocks. The festival includes a procession to the island of boats decorated with garlands of flowers and loaded with rocks. The rocks are piled up to reinforce the shores of the island, and then the participants enjoy folk dancing and country sports and games.

CONTACTS:
Embassy of Serbia and Montenegro
2134 Kalorama Rd. N.W.
Washington, D.C. 20008
202-332-0333; fax: 202-332-3933
www.serbiaembusa.org

◆ 0900 ◆ **Fast Day**
Fourth Monday in April

At one time it was customary for the governors of the New England states to proclaim days of public fasting and prayer, usually around the middle of April. But after the Revolutionary War, enthusiasm for the custom began to wane. Because the day's spiritual significance had faded by the 19th century, Massachusetts abolished its Fast Day in 1895 and began to observe Patriots' Day in its place. Maine followed suit a few years later.

New Hampshire is now the only state that continues to observe Fast Day as a legal holiday, maintaining a tradition that can be traced back to 1679. No longer an occasion for abstinence, it is usually regarded as an opportunity for outdoor recreation and spring chores. Although the date is set by law, the governor of New Hampshire issues a yearly proclamation designating the day on which it will be observed.

CONTACTS:
New Hampshire Almanac, New Hampshire State Library
20 Park St.
Concord, NH 03301
603-271-2143; fax: 603-271-2205
www.nh.gov

SOURCES:
AmerBkDays-2000, p. 322
DictDays-1988, p. 39

◆ 0901 ◆ **Fastelavn**
Between February 2 and March 8; Monday before Ash Wednesday

The Monday before Lent begins is a school holiday for children in Denmark. Early in the morning they enter their parents' bedrooms swinging "Lenten birches"—twigs covered with silk, crepe paper, or ribbon. As they poke or smack their parents they cry out, "Give buns! Give buns!"—referring to the traditional *Fastelavnsboller,* or Shrovetide buns, which their parents give them to put a stop to the beating. This custom probably has its roots in ancient purification rites, where people used to beat one another with switches to drive out evil.

Various games are played with the buns, such as suspending one by string from a chandelier and trying to take a bite of it. Later in the day, the children dress up in costume and go from door to door, where they are given coins, candy, and more buns.

CONTACTS:
Embassy of Denmark
3200 Whitehaven St. N.W.

Washington, D.C. 20008
202-234-4300; fax: 202-328-1470
www.ambwashington.um.dk

SOURCES:
BkFest-1937, p. 95
BkHolWrld-1986, Feb 24
FestWestEur-1958, p. 23

◆ 0902 ◆ **Fastens-een**
Between February 3 and March 9; the day before Ash Wednesday

The eve or day before ASH WEDNESDAY has been given a number of names in Scotland and northern England, including Fastens-een, **Fastens-eve**, **Fastens-Even,** and **Fastens Tuesday**. All refer to the Lenten season that is about to begin, "Fasten Day" being the Old English form of "Fast Day." **Fastingong** was an early English expression for SHROVE TUESDAY, which was also called **Fastingong Tuesday**. In certain English dialects the word "fastgong" means "fast-going" or "approaching a time of fast."

No matter what the day is called, the day before LENT begins in the West is traditionally a time for carnival-like celebrations.

See also CARNIVAL; COLLOP MONDAY; FASCHING

SOURCES:
BkDays-1864, vol. I, p. 236
BkFest-1937, p. 54
DictDays-1988, pp. 9, 15, 39, 42

◆ 0903 ◆ **Father's Day**
Third Sunday in June

Sonora Louise Smart Dodd from Spokane, Washington, suggested to her minister in 1910 that a day be set aside for honoring fathers. Her own father was a Civil War veteran who raised his six children on the family farm after his wife died in childbirth. The Ministerial Association and the Spokane YMCA picked up on the idea, and in 1924 Father's Day received the support of President Calvin Coolidge. But it wasn't until 1966 that a presidential proclamation established Father's Day as the third Sunday in June. Although it began as a religious celebration, today it is primarily an occasion for showing appreciation through gift-giving.

See also CHILDREN'S DAY, MOTHER'S DAY

CONTACTS:
National Center for Fathering
P.O. Box 413888
Kansas City, MO 64141
800-593-3237 or 913-384-4661; fax: 913-384-4665
www.fathers.com

SOURCES:
AmerBkDays-2000, p. 467
AnnivHol-2000, p. 109
BkHolWrld-1986, Jun 21
DaysCustFaith-1957, p. 158
DictDays-1988, p. 39
HolSymbols-2009, p. 251

◆ 0904 ◆ **Faunalia**
December 5 and February 13

In Roman mythology Faunus was a god of the forest who was also associated with fertility. It was believed that eerie noises in the woods came from Faunus. The Faunalia was mostly celebrated by farmers and other rural workers on December 5 with feasting and games. For a time, city-dwellers adopted the festival and observed it on February 13.

Faunus was known as the brother, father, or husband of BONA DEA. Lupercus, the fertility god associated with the LUPERCALIA, was also identified with Faunus, as was Inuus, the fertilizer of cattle. The Fauni, or fauns, were spirits of the forest who resembled the satyrs of Greek legend.

SOURCES:
DictFolkMyth-1984, p. 372
DictRomRel-1996, p. 73
FestRom-1981, pp. 72, 201
NewCentClassHandbk-1962, p. 479
OxClassDict-1970, p. 432
RomFest-1925, p. 256

◆ 0905 ◆ **Fawkes (Guy) Day**
November 5

On the night of November 4, 1605, 36 barrels of gunpowder were discovered in a cellar beneath the Houses of Parliament in London. The conspirators of the so-called Gunpowder Plot, who planned to blow up King James I and his government to avenge their laws against Roman Catholics, were discovered and arrested, and on January 31 eight of them were beheaded. While Guy Fawkes didn't originate the plan, he was caught red-handed after someone tipped off the king's ministers. And he was among those whose heads were displayed on pikes at London Bridge.

The following year, Parliament established November 5 as a national day of thanksgiving. Children still make effigies of Guy Fawkes and ask passersby for money ("Penny for the Guy") which they spend on fireworks. The effigies are burned in bonfires that night, and fireworks traditionally fill the skies over Britain in remembrance of the failure of the Gunpowder Plot.

CONTACTS:
House of Commons Information Office
House of Commons
London, SW1A 2TT United Kingdom
44-20-7219-3000; fax: 44-20-7219-5839
www.parliament.uk

Gunpowder Plot Society
160 S.W. 12 Ave., Ste. 108
Deerfield Beach, FL 33442
954-427-3542
www.gunpowder-plot.org

SOURCES:
BkDays-1864, vol. II, p. 546
BkFest-1937, p. 61
BkHolWrld-1986, Nov 5
DaysCustFaith-1957, p. 284
DictDays-1988, pp. 51, 90, 96

FestSaintDays-1915, p. 199
FolkAmerHol-1999, p. 439
FolkWrldHol-1999, p. 644
OxYear-1999, p. 448

♦ 0906 ♦ FeatherFest
Late March-Early April

Begun in 2002, the Galveston Island FeatherFest is intended to celebrate the "birds and natural heritage of the Upper Texas Coastal area." Some 300 species of birds are found on Galveston Island in the springtime as they stop at the island during their migration north.

The four-day FeatherFest allows bird enthusiasts the chance to go on field trips to photograph and watch the birds. Prominent environmental writers, naturalists, and artists are the leaders of these field trips. Visitors may also enjoy kayak and boat trips into the wilderness. Seminars, workshops, and lectures on the wildlife in the community are also available. In addition, a FeatherFest Photo Contest is held. Other highlights have included an exhibition of nature photographs at the Galveston County Historical Museum. In the evenings, visitors attend informal gatherings. In 2007, the Houston String Quartet performed an original piece by Houston composer Ken Booker.

CONTACTS:
Galveston Island Nature Tourism Council
Galveston Featherfest
P.O. Box 1468
Gaveston, TX 77553-1468
888-425-4753 or 409-392-0841; fax 409-737-2264
www.galvestonfeatherfest.com

♦ 0907 ♦ Feralia
February 21

This ancient Roman festival marked the culmination of a week-long celebration in honor of the *manes*, spirits of the dead. It began on February 13 with the PARENTALIA, a private celebration in honor of deceased family members, and ended on February 21 with a public celebration known as the Feralia. This was the day on which offerings and gifts were placed on the graves of the deceased and the anniversary of the funeral feast was celebrated. The Feralia was similar to the later Christian holiday, ALL SOULS' DAY.

SOURCES:
DictFolkMyth-1984, p. 673
FestRom-1981, p. 74
FestSaintDays-1915, p. 191
OxClassDict-1970, p. 434
OxYear-1999, p. 85

♦ 0908 ♦ Fes Festival of World Sacred Music
May - June

The prevailing spirituality of the holy city of Fez in Morocco was the inspiration for the annual Fes Festival of World Sacred Music, which was launched in 1995. Artists from all over the world perform the sacred music of the world's reli-gions in all its various styles during the week-long festival. The main evening concerts take place at Bab Makina, the reception court of a 14th-century royal palace. The Moorish Palace of Dar Bat'ha is the site of many of the afternoon concerts. Another striking performance site is the Roman ruin of Volubilis, with the ancient Arc of Triumph as a backdrop. The festival, now considered among the world's premier music festivals, draws distinguished artists from the world over, as well as hundreds of enthusiastic visitors each year.

In 2000, festival organizers launched the Festival in the City to run alongside the Sacred Music festival. Free of charge and open to all, it features concerts, Sufi nights, workshops, and art exhibitions, and lends a festive air to the city streets. Another feature of the festival is Fes Encounter, an annual gathering of academics, social activists, and politicians, who debate a pressing current issue, which can range from conflict resolution to social justice.

CONTACTS:
Festival des Fes des Sacred Music de Monde
Sidi Wl Khayat
BP 629
Fes-Medina 30200 Morocco
www.fesfestival.com

Morocco National Tourist Office
20 E. 46th St., Ste. 1201
New York, NY 10017
212-557-2520; fax: 212-949-8148
www.visitmorocco.org

♦ 0909 ♦ Festa da Luz (Festival of Light)
Two weeks beginning the second Sunday in October

The two-week Festival of Light held every year in Belém, Pará State, Brazil, honors Our Lady of Nazareth. Her image is carried through the streets to the cathedral on Saturday night in a *berlinda* or glass enclosure set upon wheels. But it is the Sunday morning procession that is the most important. Church and civic leaders accompany the image as it again rolls through the streets in the berlinda. Behind comes the "Miracle Car"—a heavy platform inscribed with images of the miracles performed by the Virgin—carried on the shoulders of strong men who perform this service as a form of penance. Adults and children of all ages and circumstances follow, many dressed in hair shirts, walking in bare feet, or carrying a heavy load as a form of penance.

The festival takes its name from the lights that decorate the square in front of the church and that outline the building itself. There are booths selling a wide variety of goods and instrumental groups supply continuous music. The pilgrimage that accompanies the Festival of Light dates back to the year 1700 and often draws as many as 100,000 participants.

CONTACTS:
Brazilian Embassy
3006 Massachusetts Ave. N.W.
Washington, D.C. 20008
202-238-2700; fax: 202-238-2827
www.brasilemb.org

SOURCES:
FiestaTime-1965, p. 156

♦ 0910 ♦ Festa del Grillo
Between April 30 and June 3; 40 days after Easter

In most European countries, ASCENSION DAY is a holiday when families go to the country to have picnics or just to spend the day outdoors. On Ascension Day in Florence, Italy, crowds gather in the Cascine—a public park along the banks of the Arno River—to celebrate the Festa del Grillo, or **Cricket Festival**, the chirping cricket being a traditional symbol of spring. Food stalls are set up in the park, and there are balloons and other souvenirs for sale.

Although people used to catch their own crickets, today they can buy them in brightly painted wood, wicker, or wire cages, where they are kept with a large lettuce leaf to sustain them. The children carry their crickets through the park and later hang the cages outside their windows. If the *grillo* sings to them, it means they'll have good luck.

SOURCES:
BkFestHolWrld-1970, p. 105
BkHolWrld-1986, May 21
FestSaintDays-1915, p. 116
FestWestEur-1958, p. 97

♦ 0911 ♦ Festival-Institute at Round Top, International
Early June to mid-July

This teaching institute and music festival was founded by world-renowned pianist James Dick in 1971. Dick wanted to establish a center where talented student musicians could make a smooth transition to a professional career. He started out with a 10-day workshop, but now the institute offers advanced lessons, coaching, and various seminars. The emphasis is still on pianists, but there is also instruction in strings, woodwinds, brass, chamber music, and orchestra. The faculty is composed of internationally known musicians who not only teach at the Institute but perform as soloists at the concerts given there.

Round Top is the smallest incorporated city in Texas, with a population of less than 100. It was named for a building with a rounded roof that was at one time a landmark for arriving stage coaches. Just north of the town square is the scenic 200-acre Festival Hill grounds. Concerts are held in the acoustically excellent 1,200-seat festival concert hall and the Edythe Bates Old Chapel, built in 1883. The campus is open all year to visitors and hosts various events, including an Early Music Festival during MEMORIAL DAY weekend, "August-to-April Concert Series," herb workshops, retreats and conferences, and guided tours.

CONTACTS:
International Festival-Institute at Round Top
248 Jaster Rd.
P.O. Box 89
Round Top, TX 78954
979-249-3129; fax: 979-249-5078
www.festivalhill.org

SOURCES:
GdUSFest-1984, p. 185
MusFestAmer-1990, p. 139

♦ 0912 ♦ Festivities for the Day of National Rebellion
July 25-27

This three-day national holiday is celebrated throughout Cuba. It commemorates an attack that took place on July 26, 1953, when rebel forces led by Fidel Castro struck the Moncada army barracks in Santiago de Cuba. Although the attack was unsuccessful, it is remembered as the beginning of the rebellion that eventually ousted the dictatorship of Fulgencio Batista in 1959.

The holiday is an occasion for displays of national pride and mass rallies organized by the state. Crowds of 100,000 are common in Havana, where a carnival, live music, singing, dancing, and flag waving mark the occasion. Santiago de Cuba also has a large carnival, and other cities in the country host celebrations as well.

CONTACTS:
Ministry of Tourism
Calle 19
No. 710
Vedado
Havana, Cuba
www.cubatravel.cu

♦ 0913 ♦ Festivus
December 23

The holiday of Festivus first originated on the "Seinfeld" television program in the 1990s. Regular series character Frank Costanza, father of Jerry Seinfeld's friend George Costanza, invented the holiday when he found that the usual year-end holidays did not fulfill him. Festivus, he explains, is "for the rest of us." To mark Festivus, which he insists his family celebrate, a plain aluminum pole is placed in a bucket of cement. One by one, those present grab the pole and air their grievances about how other people disappointed them in the past year. Frank begins this segment with the phrase: "I gotta lot of problems with some of you people!" After this gripe session comes a contest called the "feats of strength," in which all those present try to subdue the head of the household, and which usually devolves into a wrestling match.

The residents of Erie, Penn., have taken the imaginary holiday of Festivus to heart. Many people in the city and nearby communities throw Festivus parties featuring the aluminum pole and the feats of strength, all in the spirit of good fun.

♦ 0914 ♦ Fiesta Day
Late February

Held for more than 50 years, Fiesta Day celebrates the multicultural heritage of those who settled Ybor (Ee-bore) City, which is part of Tampa, Florida. Cuban, African-Cuban, Italian, and Jewish immigrants made Ybor City their home in the 1880s, and their influence is still felt in Tampa's Historic District, where this festival takes place. Celebrants can enjoy the diverse food, drink, music, and arts and crafts that reflect the character of Ybor City.

CONTACTS:
Ybor City Visitor Information Center, CC Event Productions Inc.
1710 Republica de Cuba
P.O. Box 76189
Tampa, FL 33605
877-934-3782 or 813-248-0721; fax: 813-248-0431
www.cc-events.org

♦ 0915 ♦ Fiesta sa EDSA (People Power Anniversary)
February 25

The Fiesta sa EDSA is a commemoration of the bloodless People Power Revolution in the Philippines on Feb. 22-25, 1986, in which the dictatorial regime of President Ferdinand Marcos was toppled. The revolution began because Marcos and Corazon C. Aquino both claimed victory in a presidential election filled with fraud and violence.

Two key government officers, Minister Juan Ponce Enrile and Armed Forces Vice Chief of Staff Fidel Ramos, rebelled in protest of Marcos's oppression and demanded his resignation. They holed up at military camps at the Epifanio de los Santos Highway (EDSA), which borders Manila on the east. Pro-Marcos forces threatened to annihilate them, but two million unarmed people surged toward the camps. With offerings of flowers, food, and prayers, they provided a human shield and overcame the military's firepower. Fourteen years of Marcos's rule ended, and Corazon C. Aquino became the first woman president of the Philippines (1986-92). Ramos was elected president in 1992 and served until 1998.

The day is marked with ceremonies at the site of the revolution in Quezon City, a part of metropolitan Manila.

CONTACTS:
Embassy of Philippine
1600 Massachusetts Ave. N.W.
Washington, D.C. 20036
202-467-9300; fax: 202-467-9417
www.philippineembassy-usa.org

♦ 0916 ♦ Fiestas Patrias
September 18-19

Fiestas Patrias is the great national two-day holiday in Chile celebrating Independence Day, September 18, and Army Day, September 19. Independence Day commemorates the anniversary of Chile's first movement toward independence from Spain on September 18, 1810, when a group of Chilean leaders took over the government. Spain had colonized much of South America since the 16th century. By 1814 Chileans were involved in a war with the Spanish, who were opposed to the new local government. The citizens of Chile finally declared their independence on February 12, 1818.

Army Day is observed with a military parade in Santiago, in which the army, navy, air force, and national police display their weapons, equipment, and uniforms. In the days preceding the holiday, *fondas* (fairs) pop up throughout Chile, with carnival rides and food stalls.

Fiestas Patrias is a popular time for Chilean rodeos. *Huasos* or cowboys compete against one another by attempting to pin a calf against the wall of the *medialuna* or arena with their horse—unlike the calf-roping that takes place at American rodeos—and are awarded points based on which part of the horse is touching the calf.

Because September marks the beginning of spring in Chile, Fiestas Patrias is also a popular occasion for kite flying. A favorite sport is kite fighting, in which people cover the kite strings with small sharp pieces of glass in order to try to cut others' kite strings.

CONTACTS:
Embassy of Chile
1732 Massachusetts Ave. N.W.
Washington, D.C. 20036
202-785-1746; fax: 202-887-5579
www.chile-usa.org

SOURCES:
AnnivHol-2000, p. 157
FestWrld: Chile-1998, p. 16
NatlHolWrld-1968, p. 174

♦ 0917 ♦ Fifteenth of Av (Tu be-Av; Hamishah Asar b'Av)
Between July 23 and August 21; Av 15

During the time of the Second Temple in Jerusalem (dedicated between 521 and 517 B.C.E. and destroyed in 70 C.E.), this was a Jewish folk festival in which young women would dress in white and dance in the vineyards, where young bachelors would come to choose their brides.

There are a number of explanations for why the festival was celebrated this way. According to the Talmud, the 15th day of Av was the day when members of different tribes were allowed to intermarry. It was also the day when the cutting of trees to burn on the altar ceased, because the heat of the sun was diminishing and there was some concern that the trees wouldn't dry properly. It's also possible that the holiday was adapted from an ancient SUMMER SOLSTICE festival.

Although in modern times there have been attempts by the new settlements in Israel to turn this day into one of music and folk dancing, the idea doesn't seem to have caught on. The Fifteenth of Av is marked only by a ban on eulogies or fasting.

CONTACTS:
Union of Orthodox Jewish Congregations of America
11 Broadway
New York, NY 10004
212-563-4000; fax: 212-564-9058
www.ou.org

♦ 0918 ♦ Fig Sunday
Between March 14 and April 18; Palm Sunday

The custom of eating figs on PALM SUNDAY gave rise to the name Fig Sunday, or **Fig Pudding Day**, in England, when children would buy figs and either eat them or bring them home to their mothers to make fig pudding. The name may have come from Jesus' cursing of the barren fig tree on the day after his entry into Jerusalem, as told in the 11th chapter of the Gospel of Mark.

SOURCES:
DictDays-1988, p. 41
EncyEaster-2002, p. 439

♦ 0919 ♦ **Fiji Day**
October 10

It took 96 years for Great Britain to transfer its claim on Fiji to the island nation's indigenous leadership. However, Fijians still celebrate the date of the signing of the 1874 Deed of Cession, the document that initiated the protracted process that culminated in Fiji's independence in 1970.

The anniversary is celebrated nationwide. The main events take place at the Site of Cession in the town of Levuka, located on the island of Ovalau, and in the present-day capital city, Suva.

In Levuka, festivities focus on the historical aspects of Fiji Day. Fijians will dress up in traditional garb to re-enact of the Deed of Cession. In Suva, leaders, dignitaries, and citizens gather in historic Albert Park for addresses by the president and the prime minister. There is also a parade by military forces, the singing of the national anthem, and a ceremonial firing of cannons. In other communities throughout the islands, Fijians hold oratory contests and stage cultural performances.

CONTACTS:
Ministry of Fijian Affairs, Culture & Heritage
P.O. Box 2100
Government Buildings
Suva, Fiji
www.culture.gov.fj

Embassy of the Republic of the Fiji Islands
2000 M St. N.W., Ste. 710
Washington, DC 20036
202-466-8320; fax: 202-466-8325
www.fijiembassydc.com

SOURCES:
AnnivHol-2000, p. 181

♦ 0920 ♦ **Fiji National Youth Day**
Date varies

The island nation of Fiji puts a strong emphasis on national initiatives that serve its young citizens. One of the goals of Fiji's Ministry of Youth and Sports is to increase youth participation in civic life, and in particular, to coordinate programs that help raise the employment rate among the country's youth. National Youth Day highlights this agenda through a series of activities that are coordinated by regional agencies and take place at various locations. The ceremonies are held on a different date each year.

Customarily, the minister who supervises youth initiatives will give a commencement address that officially opens the celebrations, outlines the plan concerning youth, and describes the theme of the year's celebrations. Past celebration themes have included "Tackling Poverty Together" and "Breaking Barriers."

The regional festivities include mural painting, team building activities, youth marches, and competitions in oration and traditional storytelling.

CONTACTS:
Fiji Ministry of Youth
P.O. Box 2448
Suva, Fiji

Ministry of Fijian Affairs, Culture & Heritage
P.O. Box 2100
Government Buildings
Suva, Fiji
www.culture.gov.fj

Embassy of the Republic of the Fiji Islands
2000 M St. N.W., Ste. 710
Washington, DC 20036
202-466-8320; fax: 202-466-8325
www.fijiembassydc.com

♦ 0921 ♦ **Fiji Ratu Sir Lala Sukuna Day**
Last Monday of May

The people of Fiji honor one of the nation's most prominent leaders, Ratu Sir Lala Sukuna, on the Monday nearest his death anniversary (May 30). Sukuna (1888–1958) was a decorated hero in World War I before he became a politician. Over the course of holding various government posts, he helped prepare Fiji for independence from Great Britain. The island nation gained independence in 1970, 12 years after his death.

For many Fijians, memories of the 2000 anniversary are marred by cataclysmic events that took place around the time of the observance. George Speight led a military takeover that briefly removed President Ratu Sir Kamisese Mara and stirred up animosity between native Fijians and Indian residents.

In 2005, the prime minister led an effort to reclaim the holiday's positive connotations by highlighting Sukuna's harmonious economic plan, which protected the land rights of native Fijians but still left room for foreign investment. Adopting a theme of "Unity in Diversity," the celebration included a church service commemorating Ratu Sukuna's life and an exhibition at Fiji Museum devoted to the statesman. Festivities extended for a week and culminated with a final ceremony on the May 30th anniversary.

CONTACTS:
Ministry of Fijian Affairs, Culture & Heritage
P.O. Box 2100
Government Buildings
Suva, Fiji
www.culture.gov.fj

Embassy of the Republic of the Fiji Islands
2000 M St. N.W., Ste. 710
Washington, DC 20036
202-466-8320; fax: 202-466-8325
www.fijiembassydc.com

SOURCES:
AnnivHol-2000, p. 91

♦ 0922 ♦ **Fillmore Jazz Festival**
Weekend closest to Independence Day

Sponsored by the Fillmore Merchants Association in San Francisco, Calif., the Fillmore Jazz Festival is the largest free jazz festival in the western United States. The festival comprises two full days and nights of musical entertainment on three stages and occupies Fillmore Street from Jackson to Eddy Streets. An annual event held on the weekend closest to Independence Day, each year it attracts approximately 90,000 visitors from the Bay Area, the state, and throughout North America.

The first Fillmore Jazz Festival was held in 1985 to celebrate the musical heritage of the ethnically diverse Fillmore neighborhood, where such jazz luminaries as Ella Fitzgerald, Duke Ellington, Count Basie, and Billie Holliday performed during the 1940s. In addition to offering performances of standards from the 20th-century golden age of jazz, the lineup features local and national acts offering funk, fusion, salsa, Afro-rhythms, and R&B. The festival showcases the ethnic diversity of the neighborhood through a variety of gourmet food vendors and artists in addition to the entertainment schedule.

CONTACTS:
Fillmore Jazz Festival
Fillmore Merchants Association
2130 Fillmore St. #155
San Francisco, CA 94115
415-441-4093
www.fillmorejazzfestival.com

Steven Restivo Event Services, LLC
Fillmore Jazz Festival
P.O. Box 151017
San Rafael, CA 94915
800-310-6563; fax: 415-456-6436
www.sresproductions.com/events.html

SOURCES:
AAH-2007, p. 156
PatHols-2006, p. 166

♦ 0923 ♦ **Finland Independence Day**
December 6

Sweden and Russia contended for Finland for almost 700 years. The Finnish people lived under Russian control beginning in 1809. The Finnish nationalist movement grew in the 1800s, and when the BOLSHEVIKS took over Russia on November 7, 1917, the Finns saw a time to declare their independence. They did so on December 6 of that same year. This day is a national holiday celebrated with military parades in Helsinki and performances at the National Theater. It is traditionally a solemn occasion that begins with a parade of students carrying torches and one flag for each year of independence.

CONTACTS:
Ministry of Foreign Affairs of Finland
Department for Communication and Culture
P.O. Box 176
Helsinki, 00161 Finland
358-9-160-05; fax: 358-9-1605-5901
www.formin.finland.fi

SOURCES:
AnnivHol-2000, p. 203
NatlHolWrld-1968, p. 221

♦ 0924 ♦ **Finnish Sliding Festival**
First weekend in February

Patterned after the traditional event in Finland that celebrates Fat Tuesday or SHROVE TUESDAY before the beginning of LENT, the Finnish Sliding Festival, or **Laskiainen**, has been held in White, Minnesota, every winter for more than 50 years. It features two large ice slides which are constructed at the edge of Loon Lake. People bring their sleds or toboggans for an exciting ride down the slide onto the frozen expanse of the lake. For those who want more thrills, there is a *vipukelka* which resembles a kind of merry-go-round on ice.

Other activities at the weekend event include log-sawing contests, Finnish music and dance performances, and traditional Finnish foods such as oven pancakes and pea soup.

CONTACTS:
Iron Trail Convention and Visitors Bureau
403 N. First St.
Virginia, MN 55792
800-777-8497 or 218-749-8161; fax: 218-749-8055
www.irontrail.org

♦ 0925 ♦ **Fire Festivals**
February 1, May 1, August 1, November 1

The bonfire has deep symbolic significance in Celtic culture and Neopagan practice. The Greater Sabbats, the four traditional festivals that mark the CROSS-QUARTER DAYS—IMBOLC, BELTANE, LAMMAS, and SAMHAIN—are often referred to as Fire Festivals. In conjunction with the Quarter Days these four days comprise the Celtic/Neopagan cycle known as the "Wheel of the Year." A bonfire ceremony is customary on the four sabbats among observing Neopagans in the United Kingdom, the United States, and other countries where such traditions are observed.

For three of the Cross-Quarter Days, the symbolic meaning of fire has significance within a sabbat's particular context. For example, for Imbolc (February 1) the emphasis is on the daylight that believers anticipate in the coming spring season. Lighting bonfires during Beltane (May 1) is a way of honoring the sun god. During Samhain (November 1), both the heat and light of fire have great significance since both elements are lacking during the approaching winter.

Historical accounts of bonfires during Lammas are unavailable because the sabbat has only been included in modern-day fire festivals.

CONTACTS:
Pagan Federation
BM Box 7097
London WC1N 3XX United Kingdom
www.paganfed.demon.co.uk

SOURCES:
AmerBkDays-2000, p. 334
RelHolCal-2004, pp. 270, 272

◆ 0926 ◆ Fire Prevention Week, National
Week including October 9

National Fire Prevention Day is October 9, the anniversary of the Great Chicago Fire of 1871, which killed more than 250 people, left 100,000 homeless, and destroyed more than 17,000 structures. The people of Chicago celebrated their restoration of the city by holding festivities on the anniversary of the fire, but it was the Fire Marshals' Association of North America that decided in 1911 to observe the day in a way that would raise the public's consciousness about fire prevention. President Woodrow Wilson issued the first National Fire Prevention Day proclamation in 1920, and every year since 1925 the week in which October 9 falls has been observed nationwide as National Fire Prevention Week.

Each year the National Fire Protection Association (NFPA) announces a theme for National Fire Prevention Week and sets up programs to educate the public about a particular aspect of fire prevention. In 1994, for example, the theme was the importance of keeping smoke detectors in good working order, and the theme for 1995 was avoiding the major causes of home fires—lighted cigarettes, unattended cooking equipment, and auxiliary heat sources. Planning and practicing fire drill escape plans was the theme for 1998, 1999, and 2000. The NFPA provides a Community Awareness Kit each year to help communities plan their own fire prevention activities.

CONTACTS:
National Fire Protection Association
1 Batterymarch Pk.
Quincy, MA 02169
800-344-3555 or 617-770-3000; fax: 617-770-0700
www.nfpa.org

◆ 0927 ◆ Firecracker Festival
January-February

Firecrackers are a traditional element of TET, the Vietnamese New Year celebration, and one town really takes its firecrackers seriously. Each year 16 families are selected to compete in producing the most spectacular display for the town of Dong Ky in Vietnam's Ha Bac Province. These are no ordinary firecrackers, but huge, elaborately decorated affairs that may require two dozen men to carry and up to $500—more than an average family's annual earnings—to create. Each firecracker is paraded through town and set up on a special tripod for firing. After all the firecrackers have been set off, a panel of judges determines the winning family.

CONTACTS:
Vietnam National Administration of Tourism

80 Quan Su Rd.
Hanoi, Vietnam
84-4-942-1061; fax: 84-4-826-3956
www.vietnamtourism.com/e_pages/news/index.a

SOURCES:
FestWrld: Viet-1997, p. 12

◆ 0928 ◆ First Day of Summer (Iceland)
Thursday between April 19-25

In Iceland the First Day of Summer is second in importance only to CHRISTMAS and NEW YEAR'S DAY. It is a legal holiday observed on the Thursday that falls between April 19 and April 25, a time of year that marks the end of the long northern winter. The custom of giving gifts on this day was widespread by the middle of the 19th century, although they were usually homemade articles or, in some areas, a share of the fisherman's catch.

Special foods associated with the First Day of Summer include summer-day cakes—flat rye breads up to a foot in diameter—on top of which the day's share of food for each person would be piled. Since the turn of the century it has also been a popular day for young people to give speeches, poetry readings and dramatic performances, or to engage in singing, dancing, and sports.

SOURCES:
BkHolWrld-1986, Apr 22
FolkWrldHol-1999, p. 297

◆ 0929 ◆ First Foot Day
January 1

The custom of firstfooting, or being the first to cross the threshold of a home in the early hours of NEW YEAR'S DAY, was so popular in England and Scotland during the 19th century that the streets were often more crowded between midnight and one o'clock in the morning than they would normally be at midday. If the "First Foot," traditionally a man, was to bring the family luck, he had to arrive with his arms full of cakes, bread, and cheese for everyone to share. He should be dark-haired, not fair, and must not have flat feet.

Today the custom may still be observed in Britain and in scattered areas of the United States.

SOURCES:
BkDays-1864, vol. I, p. 27
BkFest-1937, p. 51
BkFestHolWrld-1970, p. 3
EncyChristmas-2003, p. 252
FolkAmerHol-1999, p. 13
FolkWrldHol-1999, p. 8
OxYear-1999, p. 10

◆ 0930 ◆ First Fruits of the Alps Sunday
Fourth Sunday in August

The Alpine dairymen of Vissoie, Valais Canton, Switzerland, show their appreciation to the parish priest by presenting him with cheeses known as *les prémices des Alpes,* or the "first fruits of the Alps," on the fourth Sunday in August every year. Because they live in huts and graze their herds in the mountains all summer, the dairymen rely on the priest's visits so they can attend mass and receive the Holy Sacraments. In return, they give him all the milk their herds yield on the third day after their arrival in the mountains by making it into cheeses.

At the end of August, the justice of the peace of Val D'Anniviers counts, inspects, and weighs the cheeses brought back to Vissoie with the returning herds. After High Mass, the dairymen of the district march in procession to the altar, each carrying his own cheese, and stand before the town's red-and-black-robed magistrates. After giving the first fruits of the Alps to the priest, the dairymen once more form a procession and march to the parsonage, where a feast is held in the courtyard.

SOURCES:
BkFestHolWrld-1970, p. 105
FestWestEur-1958, p. 236

♦ 0931 ♦ **First Monday Trade Days**
Thursday through Sunday before first Monday of each month

The First Monday Trade Days are a colossal trading bazaar that each month brings 100,000 to 300,000 people to the small town of Canton, Tex. (population 2,800). This legendary affair in northern Texas has its origins in the 1850s when the circuit court judge came to Canton on the first Monday of the month to conduct court proceedings. Farmers from the area would gather to sell or trade horses, hunting hounds, and other dogs, conduct other business in town, and watch the occasional hanging. The judge no longer holds court in Canton, but the trading event continues.

Now the flea market starts on a Thursday, runs through the weekend, and offers merchandise and food at more than 3,000 exhibition stalls.

Scottsboro, Ala., also has well-known First Monday Trade Days attended by thousands, and this custom is observed in most southern states. Commonly, the markets are held on the streets surrounding the county courthouse. Fiddling and storytelling are often part of the day's activities. The name for the event differs; in some places, it's **Court Day**. In Abingdon, Va., it's **Jockey Day** because of the horse races held along with the trading.

CONTACTS:
First Monday Trade Days
P.O. Box 245
Canton, TX 75103
903-567-6556; fax: 903-567-2923
www.firstmondaycanton.com

♦ 0932 ♦ **First Night (Boston, Massachusetts)**
December 31

First Night originated in Boston as an annual NEW YEAR'S EVE celebration of the arts. This citywide festival was first held in 1976 to change the drinking and partying that have traditionally marked New Year's Eve celebrations in most American cities into a night of family entertainment. It has proved so successful that 65 other cities in the United States and Canada have followed Boston's lead.

To bring both inner city and suburban communities together, 1,000 artists in Boston offer a wide variety of artistic events and performances at 70 indoor and outdoor sites in Boston's Back Bay, Beacon Hill, South End, downtown, and waterfront areas. In recent years more than one million residents and visitors have been drawn to places in the city where they would not normally walk after dark.

CONTACTS:
First Night Boston
36 Bromfield St., Ste. 204
Boston, MA 02108
617-542-1399; fax: 617-426-9531
www.firstnight.org

SOURCES:
EncyChristmas-2003, p. 254

♦ 0933 ♦ **Firstborn, Fast of the**
Between March 26 and April 23; Nisan 14

The Fast of the Firstborn is the only fast in the Jewish calendar which is neither an atonement for sin nor a fast of petition. Observed only symbolically by firstborn male Jews on the day before PASSOVER, its main purpose appears to be to remind Jews of the Angel of Death's slaying of the Egyptians' firstborn sons and the miraculous escape of their own sons. The obligation to fast can be avoided by participating in a *siyyum*—the study of a particular passage of the Talmud.

SOURCES:
DaysCustFaith-1957, p. 111
OxYear-1999, p. 727
RelHolCal-2004, p. 50

♦ 0934 ♦ **Fisher Poets Gathering**
Three-day weekend in late February

The Fisher Poets Gathering annually brings together poets, musicians, and story-tellers with an interest in fishing, particularly the lives of commercial fishers. Performances and meetings take place in various venues in the historic coastal town of Astoria, Ore., which boasts a still-working waterfront and a rich maritime history.

The centerpieces of the Fisher Poets Gathering are poetry and prose readings, story telling, and open microphone sessions in the evenings. Daytime workshops are available in such areas as creative writing, video-making, painting, and photography. Attendees can also enjoy live music, panels and lectures on fishing-industry issues, and art exhibits. Participants' literary contributions range from poignant personal memoirs to bawdy songs. The gathering was founded in 1998 by local writer Jon Broderick.

CONTACTS:
Astoria-Warrenton Area Chamber of Commerce
111 W. Marine Dr.
P.O. Box 176
Astoria, OR 97103-6807
503-325-6311 or 800-875-6807; fax: 503-325-9767
www.clatsopcollege.com/fisherpoets/contact_fpg.html

♦ 0935 ♦ **Five-Petalled Rose Festival**
Third week in June

The Festival of the Five-Petalled Rose takes place in Cesky Krumlov in the Czech Republic. The town prospered during the Renaissance, and today's festival permits residents and visitors to relive some of the town's past glories. Cesky Krumlov's magnificent castle adds to the festival's atmosphere, and some of the events take place there. Festival highlights include swordplay demonstrations, plays and street dramas, processions of people in Renaissance costume, a medieval feast, a historical market, demonstrations of Renaissance crafts, contemporary and Renaissance musical entertainment, and medieval games, military exercises, and dances. The festival takes its name from the five-petalled rose found on the coat of arms of the Rosenbergs, the noble family that lived in the castle during the late medieval and Renaissance periods.

CONTACTS:
Cesky Krumlov Municipal Offices
Namesti Svornosti No. 1
381 01 Cesky Krumlov
Cesky Krumlov, 381 01 Czech Republic
420-380-766-314
www.ckrumlov.info/docs/en/kaktualita.xml

♦ 0936 ♦ **Flag Day**
June 14

On June 14, 1777, the Continental Congress replaced the British symbols of George WASHINGTON'S Grand Union flag with a new design featuring 13 white stars in a circle on a field of blue and 13 red and white stripes—one for each state. Although it is not certain, this flag may have been made by the Philadelphia seamstress Betsy Ross who was an official flagmaker for the Pennsylvania Navy. The number of stars increased as the new states entered the Union, but the number of stripes stopped at 15 and was later returned to 13.

President Woodrow Wilson issued a proclamation that established June 14 as Flag Day in 1916, but it didn't become official until 1949. This occurred as a result of a campaign by Bernard J. Cigrand and the American Flag Day Association.

It is observed across the country by displaying the American flag on homes and public buildings. Other popular ways of observing this day include flag-raising ceremonies, the singing of the national anthem, and the study of flag etiquette and the flag's origin and meaning. Each year more than 3,000 schoolchildren form a living American flag at Fort McHenry National Monument in Baltimore, Md., near where Francis Scott Key wrote "The Star-Spangled Banner" (*see also* DEFENDERS' DAY).

CONTACTS:
National Flag Day Foundation
418 S. Broadway
P.O. Box 435
Baltimore, MD 21231
410-563-3524
www.flagday.org

Fort McHenry National Monument and Historic Shrine
National Park Service
End of S. Fort Ave.
Baltimore, MD 21230
410-962-4290; fax: 410-962-2500
www.nps.gov/fomc

SOURCES:
AmerBkDays-2000, p. 444
AnnivHol-2000, p. 100
BkHolWrld-1986, Jun 14
DictDays-1988, p. 42
HolSymbols-2009, p. 264
PatHols-2006, p. 117

♦ 0937 ♦ **Flagstaff Festival of the Arts**
July

This major performing and visual arts festival of Arizona is held in Flagstaff on the campus of Northern Arizona University. The affair began in the early 1960s as a music camp and became a full-fledged festival in 1966. It ran one week that year, and today is a four-week festival with more than 48 events: symphonic and chamber music concerts, ballet, theater, film showings, and art exhibits. From 1966 to 1977, Izler Solomon directed and conducted the festival orchestra, which is composed of musicians from major U.S. orchestras.

CONTACTS:
Flagstaff Convention and Visitors Bureau
211 W. Aspen
Flagstaff, AZ 86001
800-379-0065 or 928-774-9541; fax: 928-556-1308
www.flagstaffarizona.org

SOURCES:
MusFestAmer-1990, p. 23

♦ 0938 ♦ **Flanders Festival**
May-November

The Flanders Festival, or **Festival van Vlaanderen**, is one of the longest and most diverse music festivals in Europe. The season extends from spring to late autumn, with events taking place in eight cities spread over the five Flemish provinces of Belgium. In the medieval city of Bruges, for instance, the festival takes place in August and features baroque and early classical music. In Ghent it includes opera as well as symphonic music. Other cities participating in the festival include Antwerp, Brussels-Leuven, Courtrai, Limburg, Mechelen, and Vlaas-Brabant.

Established in 1958, the Flanders Festival grew out of the Brussels World Fair. The world's most famous performers, opera companies, and ensembles perform—often in more than one city—in settings that range from concert halls to abbeys and stadiums.

CONTACTS:
Flanders Festival
Kasteel Borluut
Kleine Gentstraat 46
Gent, B 9051 Belgium
32-9-243-94-94; fax: 32-9-243-9490
www.festival-van-vlaanderen.be/index.php?id

SOURCES:
GdWrldFest-1985, p. 18
IntlThFolk-1979, p. 43
MusFestEurBrit-1980, p. 30

◆ 0939 ◆ Fleadh Cheoil
Late August

The Fleadh Cheoil (Festival of Music) is a national festival that has been promoting Irish traditional music and dance through competition for more than 50 years. It takes place in late August, although the location changes from year to year. The festival also features less formal music sessions and street performances, as well as Irish art, parades, and pageants.

CONTACTS:
Comhaltas Ceoltoiri Eireann
32 Belgrave Sq.
Monkstown, County Dublin, Ireland
353-1-28-00295; fax: 353-1-2803759
www.comhaltas.ie

SOURCES:
WildPlanet-1995, p. 58

◆ 0940 ◆ Fleet Week (Hampton Roads, Virginia)
October

The Hampton Roads area of southeastern Virginia and northeastern North Carolina features one of the world's largest natural harbors. The cities of Norfolk, Virginia Beach, and Newport News are located here. The U.S. Navy, Marines, Air Force, and Army have facilities in the area, as does NASA.

The Hampton Roads community sponsors an annual Fleet Week to honor the military personnel who are stationed in the area for the work they perform on behalf of the nation. The event is also a celebration of the U.S. Navy's official birthday in October.

Among the Fleet Week activities are a 5K run, a golf tournament, free outdoor music concerts, a chili cook-off, a family day at Norfolk's Town Point Park, and a half marathon run. Military personnel attend the music concerts for free. The Virginia Zoo offers special programming at this time, also free to military personnel and their families.

Local motorcycle enthusiasts sponsor the "Rumble through the Tunnels," a fundraiser in which hundreds of motorcycles ride through several of Hampton Roads tunnels.

Fleet Week ends with a parade of ships and planes along the downtown Norfolk waterfront. Navy tugs spray water into the air, helicopters fly overhead, and frigates, submarines, and landing craft sail by.

CONTACTS:
Department of the Navy
1200 Navy Pentagon
Room 4B463
Washington, D.C. 20350-1200
www.navy.mil/swf/index.asp

◆ 0941 ◆ Fleet Week (New York City)
May

To give citizens of New York City the chance to meet Navy, Coast Guard, and Marine personnel firsthand, the Navy has sponsored an annual Fleet Week since 1987.

During the week-long event the public is allowed to tour Navy and Coast Guard vessels, including amphibious assault vessels, destroyers, and cruisers. They can also view fighter jets, helicopters, aerial refueler tankers, anti-submarine trackers, bombers, and cargo planes.

As part of the event, personnel from the Marines, Coast Guard, and Navy learn from each other and from New York's police and firefighters. In 2007, Marines toured the Fire Academy at Randall's Island and learned about the training courses for New York City firefighters. Navy sailors toured the New York Police Department's Aviation unit at Floyd Bennett Field in Brooklyn. The police aviation unit handles air-sea rescues and provides aerial back-up for the city's police. Sailors, along with members of the New York Jets football team, also visited Project Hope, a nonprofit organization that provides inner-city families with food, resources, and counseling.

CONTACTS:
Fleet Week New York City
www.fleetweek.navy.mil

Official New York City Web site
www.nyc.gov/portal/site/nycgov/?front_door=true

◆ 0942 ◆ Fleet Week (San Diego, California)
September

In 1997, community and business organizations in San Diego, Calif., organized the first Fleet Week to honor the sailors and marines who are stationed in that city. Service personnel are thanked for "Serving America Twice," as military personnel and as volunteer workers in the San Diego community. A large number of the sailors and marines use their free time to work as volunteer firefighters, scout leaders, coaches for youth teams, or in other community service positions. By 2001, the annual event was taken over by the newly formed San Diego Fleet Week Foundation. While called a "week," the San Diego Fleet Week lasts for more than a month, with various activities around the city.

San Diego Fleet Week begins with the Port of San Diego Sea and Air Parade featuring Navy aircraft carriers, destroyers, cruisers, submarines, amphibious craft, and frigates, as well as Coast Guard cutters. Military jets and helicopters fly overhead.

Some 100,000 people turn out to watch the parade. Later, naval ships docked at Broadway Pier are open to visitors.

The Marine Corps sponsors a one-day boot camp for civilians interested in experiencing the obstacle course and drill fields used by real recruits. The Marine Corps Air Station Miramar Air Show features vintage airplanes as well as the latest in military aviation. Some 200 booths offer hands-on displays. An evening fireworks display ends the air show.

San Diego State University holds the Fleet Week Football Classic in which their football team plays the U.S. Air Force Academy team.

CONTACTS:
Fleet Week San Diego
5330 Napa St.
San Diego, CA 92110
800-353-3893
www.fleetweeksandiego.org

♦ 0943 ♦ Fleet Week (San Francisco, California)
October

To celebrate the men and women who serve in America's armed forces, San Francisco has held an annual Fleet Week since 1981.

The week-long event features members of the U.S. Navy, Coast Guard, and Marines. After a parade of ships, the public is allowed to visit a number of Navy and Coast Guard vessels docked in San Francisco Bay. In 2007, the Coast Guard demonstrated their search and rescue capabilities. In 2008, aerial shows will feature the Navy's Blue Angels precision flight team, the Canadian Air Force's Snowbirds flight team, and Team Oracle. Other Air Force and Navy aircraft have also participated in Fleet Week, including fighter aircraft and historic planes. There have also been fireworks displays over San Francisco Bay.

CONTACTS:
San Francisco Fleet Week
650-599-5057
www.military.com/fleetweek

♦ 0944 ♦ Flemington Fair
Late August through Labor Day, first Monday in September

The **New Jersey State Agricultural Fair** is held in Flemington from the end of August and continuing right through LABOR DAY. The event is a traditional agricultural fair that was started by a group of local farmers in 1856, making it one of the oldest state fairs in the country. It features a statewide 4-H lamb show and sale, a tractor pull, a horse and pony pull, and all types of car racing (mini-stocks, modified stocks, midgets, and super sprints). The fair also offers programs and exhibits of flowers, the 4-H organization, nurserymen, and various commercial enterprises.

CONTACTS:
Flemington Agricultural Fair, Flemington Fairgrounds
Rte. 31

Flemington, NJ 08822
908-782-2413; fax: 908-806-8432

SOURCES:
GdUSFest-1984, p. 117

♦ 0945 ♦ Flemish Community, Feast Day of the
July 11

Each of the autonomous regions of Belgium observes its own feast day. The Feast Day of the Flemish Community is one of several celebrations observed by the citizens of Belgium's autonomous regions, which include three linguistic communities—the Flemish, French, and German. Feast days in other regions of Belgium include FEAST DAY OF THE FRENCH COMMUNITY, FEAST DAY OF THE GERMAN-SPEAKING COMMUNITY, IRIS FEST, and WALLOON REGIONAL DAY.

The Flemish Community, whose political territory encompasses the historic region of Flanders in northern Belgium, celebrates its heritage on the anniversary of The Battle of the Golden Spurs in 1302. The battle, which ended in the Flemish defeat of France, marked the beginning of regional autonomy for this ethnic group.

Many inhabitants believe that if that untrained force of Flemish tradesmen had not overcome their professional French opponents in 1302, the region might still be under French control. The "golden spurs" refer to the 600 spurs that fell from the vanquished French knights on the battlefield, which were retrieved and later preserved as tokens of the Flemish victory.

On the feast day all Flemish governmental offices close for the holiday. Various cities, municipalities, and private groups hold cultural events; local Flemings and those resettled throughout the world pause to give a toast to Flanders; and many individuals gather to hear the minister-president of the Flemish Community deliver a speech marking the anniversary.

CONTACTS:
Belgium Embassy
3330 Garfield St. N.W.
Washington, D.C. 20008
202-333-6900; fax: 202-333-3079
www.diplobel.us

♦ 0946 ♦ Flight into Egypt
December 26

Many congregations within the Eastern Orthodox Church commemorate the Holy Family's flight into Egypt on December 26. According to the Gospel of St. Matthew, King Herod wanted to seek out and kill the infant Jesus. But an angel warned Joseph, the husband of Jesus' mother, Mary, of the danger and instructed him to take the family to Egypt for safety and to remain there until Herod's death. Two days later, according to the Gospel, all of the male children under two years of age in Bethlehem were massacred, an event that is commemorated on HOLY INNOCENTS' DAY.

SOURCES:
EncyChristmas-2003, p. 255
RelHolCal-2004, p. 116

♦ 0947 ♦ **Float Festival**
January-February; night of full moon in Tamil month of Thai (Hindu month of Magha)

The Float Festival is held at the temple city of Madurai in the state of Tamil Nadu, India, to commemorate the birth of Tirumala Nayak, a 17th-century king of Madurai. The center of the festival is the Mariamman Teppakulam pond surrounding a temple on an island. Images of the goddess Meenakshi and her consort are floated on a flower-bedecked raft to the illuminated temple, and a spectacular array of lit floats moves in procession around the pond, accompanied by music and chanted hymns. Thousands of pilgrims from all over India attend this enormously popular festival.

CONTACTS:
Tamil Nadu Tourism
Tourism Complex, No. 2 Wallajah Rd.
Chennai, Tamil Nadu 600 002 India
91-44-25383333; fax: 91-44-25381567
www.tamilnadutourism.org

SOURCES:
RelHolCal-2004, p. 183

♦ 0948 ♦ **Floating Lantern Ceremony (Toro Nagashi)**
August

This Buddhist ceremony is held in Honolulu, Hawaii, around the anniversaries of the end of World War II and the atomic bombing of HIROSHIMA. The festival is part of the annual Buddhist Bon season of July and August in which the spirits of departed ancestors are welcomed back to earth with prayers, dances, offerings, and by setting afloat more than 1,000 colorful paper lanterns bearing the names of the dead.

See also OBON FESTIVAL

CONTACTS:
Hawaii Visitors Bureau
2270 Kalakaua Ave., 8th Fl.
Honolulu, HI 96815
800-464-2924 or 808-924-0259; fax: 808-924-0291
www.hvcb.org

SOURCES:
RelHolCal-2004, p. 221

♦ 0949 ♦ **Floralia**
April 27-May 3

An ancient Roman festival held in honor of Flora, the goddess of flowers and gardens, the Floralia was instituted in 238 B.C.E. It was originally a movable feast whose date depended on the condition of the crops and flowers in any particular year at the end of April and beginning of May.

In 173 B.C.E., after severe storms had proved disastrous for the cornfields and vineyards, the Roman Senate made it an annual festival extending for six days—from April 27, the anniversary of the founding of Flora's temple, through May 3. Traditionally, the first person to lay a wreath or garland on the temple's statue of Flora was destined to have good fortune in the months that followed.

From the beginning, the Floralia was characterized by wild and licentious behavior on the part of the celebrants. The games, dances, and dramatic productions involved in the celebration were usually lewd, and courtesans are said to have performed mimes in the nude. The obscene nature of the festivities was undoubtedly due to their origins in earlier pagan fertility rites designed to promote the earth's fruitfulness. But when the festival was introduced into Rome, it became a good excuse for excessive drinking and carrying on.

The Floralia, which originally featured small statues of Flora that children would decorate with flowers, is believed to have been the precedent for Christian-oriented MAY DAY celebrations, which often included dolls or images of the Virgin Mary.

SOURCES:
AmerBkDays-2000, pp. 247, 333, 334
ClassDict-1984, p. 244
DictRomRel-1996, p. 81
FestRom-1981, p. 110
OxYear-1999, p. 176
SeasFeast-1961, p. 169

♦ 0950 ♦ **Floralies**
April-May, every four to six years

The famous flower festivals of the cities of Ghent and Liège in Belgium combined to hold one joint festival every four to six years at the Hall des Foires de Liège. The first combined festival was held in 2003. Hundreds of horticulturists from around the world show their best products to be judged for cash prizes. The showing attracts about 700,000 visitors.

Ghent was one of the centers of a thriving horticultural industry, and the Floralies there began in 1809 at the Frascati Inn where 50 plants were arranged around a bust of Napoleon. In 1814, it is believed that John Quincy Adams and other U.S. delegates visited the flower show; they were staying in Ghent during negotiations preceding the signing of the Treaty of Ghent, which ended the War of 1812. The Floralies in Liège have been held since 1830.

CONTACTS:
La Foire Internationale de Liege
Ave. Maurice-Denis 4
Liege, B 4000 Belgium
32-4-227-19-34; fax: 32-4-227-18-95
www.fil.be/fil/main.php?lan=4

♦ 0951 ♦ **Florence Musical May (Maggio Musicale Fiorentino)**
May-June

The **Florence May Festival** was first held in 1933, and it wasn't long before it had established itself as one of the most important international festivals in Italy. It offers chamber and symphonic music, ballet, and dance, and is recognized as a pioneer in its efforts to revive rare foreign and Italian operas. Most of the larger events are held in the Teatro della Pergola or the more modern Teatro Comunale, home of the festival's resident opera company.

In the past, when operas were staged outdoors, the city fathers had to ban the Vespa motor scooters that young Florentines use to get around, for fear that the noise would ruin the listening experience for festivalgoers.

Many of the world's greatest singers have performed at the festival, among them Maria Callas, Renata Tebaldi, Mario del Monaco, and Boris Christoff. The festival regularly commissions new opera and dance productions, using funds received from the Ministry of Culture.

CONTACTS:
Teatro del Maggio Musicale Fiorentino Foundation
Corso Italia 16
Firenze, Tuscany 50123 Italy
39-55-2779-1; fax: 39-55-2872-22
www.maggiofiorentino.com

SOURCES:
GdWrldFest-1985, p. 117
IntlThFolk-1979, p. 242
MusFestEurBrit-1980, p. 114
MusFestWrld-1963, p. 100

♦ 0952 ♦ **Flores de Mayo (El Salvador)**
May

In the late 18th century the Roman Catholic Church set aside the month of May to honor the Blessed Virgin Mary. The religious ceremonies held in honor of the Virgin in El Salvador during this month are called Flores de Mayo (Flowers of May), probably because there are so many wildflowers in bloom at this time of year.

The town of San Vincente celebrates the fiesta in a distinctive way. Each day, between four and five in the afternoon, there is a procession through the streets of town. It starts at the house of the *capitana*, the woman who directs the festival on that day. The women who have worked on the festival and their friends march through town scattering candy, anise seeds, and sweetmeats. Men throw flowers, corn, and grain from the sidelines. At six o'clock the image of the Virgin Mary is carried from the capitana's house to the church in procession, and a second and even more elaborate procession takes place later that night. These processions take place throughout the month-long observance. Each day a different capitana takes charge of the day's activities.

Although "la Flor," as the procession is known, is the highlight of each day's activities, there is also music every morning as men and women playing guitars and marimbas stroll through the streets. Sometimes a jester wearing a mask rides through the town on horseback, handing out announcements of coming events. Another procession takes place at midday, consisting of a parade of cars that have been specially decorated for the fiesta. People wearing masks follow on foot.

CONTACTS:
Embassy of El Salvador
1400 16th St. N.W., Ste. 100
Washington, D.C. 20008
202-265-9671; fax: 202-232-3763
www.elsalvador.org

SOURCES:
FiestaTime-1965, p. 85

♦ 0953 ♦ **Flores de Mayo (Philippines)**
May 31

Flores de Mayo ("May flowers") festivals take place throughout the Philippines during the month of May. Children create offerings of flowers and bring them to their churches in the afternoon. Parades make their way through towns and villages, with girls wearing traditional costumes followed by their relatives and friends singing Hail Marys.

The festival ends on May 31 with fiestas everywhere. In big cities like Manila, Flores de Mayo is one of the largest festivals of the year, featuring May Queens and fancy dress balls. In the smaller towns and villages, the last day of the month is a day to celebrate the birthday of their patron saint.

CONTACTS:
Philippine Tourism Center
556 Fifth Ave.
New York, NY 10036
212-575-7915; fax: 212-302-6759
www.wowphilippines.com.ph

SOURCES:
FolkWrldHol-1999, p. 365

♦ 0954 ♦ **Floriade**
April-October, every 10 years (2002, 2012, 2022,...)

Once every 10 years, the Netherlands organizes a World Horticultural Exhibition called the Floriade. The grounds for the 1992 exhibition were the Zoeteneer, outside Amsterdam. They cover 230 acres with lakes, gardens, theme pavilions, restaurants, and environmental displays—including a miniature Netherlands with dykes and canals that visitors can flood and drain at will.

What has been billed as the greatest flower show on earth runs from early April through early October and attracts about three million visitors. Magnificent displays of bulbs and flowers, plants and trees, and fruits and vegetables are divided into seven thematic areas: transport, production, consumer, environment, future, world, and recreation. In addition to the many open-air activities, there are extensive indoor attractions in the numerous halls, greenhouses, and pavilions.

The 2002 Floriade was held in the park in the city of Haarlemmermeer. A unique feature of this event was the milling about of 25 CyberCabs—new, automatically propelled vehicles resembling golf carts—which drove visitors to the top of a hill in the park to enjoy spectacular views of the festival.

CONTACTS:
Dutch Horticultural Council
P.O. Box 2002
Hoofddorp, 2130 GE Netherlands
31-23-562-2002; fax: 31-23-562-0002

♦ 0955 ♦ Florida Heritage Festival
March-April

The celebration, formerly known as the **De Soto Celebration**, in Florida is in honor of the young Spanish explorer Hernando de Soto (c. 1500-1542), who arrived on the west coast of Florida, probably near Tampa Bay and the present-day town of Bradenton, in 1539. With his band of several hundred conquistadores (conquerors), de Soto set out on a 4,000-mile trek through the wilderness north to the Blue Ridge Mountains, across them, south along the Alabama River to present-day Mobile, across the Mississippi River into what is now Arkansas, and explored further to the south and west. It was the first time a European had explored the North American interior.

The De Soto Celebration held each year from late March through most of April in Bradenton goes back to 1939. In past years, a group of costumed conquistadores would reenact de Soto's landing, coming ashore in longboats and skirmishing with the "Indians" in full view of a grandstand full of spectators then pressing onward until they reached Bradenton, where they would raid the county courthouse. Today they capture the De Soto Square Mall.

Other festival events include a children's parade, a grand parade, a bottle boat regatta, and a seafood fest with live entertainment, arts and crafts, and boat cruises with the conquistadores.

CONTACTS:
Hernando De Soto Historical Society
910 Third Ave. W.
Bradenton, FL 34205
941-747-1998; fax: 941-747-7953
www.desotohq.com

SOURCES:
GdUSFest-1984, p. 33

♦ 0956 ♦ Flower Festivals of St. Rose and St. Margaret Mary Alacoque
August 30 (St. Rose) and October 17 (St. Margaret Mary Alacoque)

On the Caribbean island of St. Lucia, two floral societies known as the Roses and the Marguerites have preserved the royal pageant traditions of their former European colonizers. Each of these groups boasts a royal family as well as a large number of general supporters. They regularly pay tribute to their namesake flowers as well as their patron saints: Rose of Lima (1586–1617) and Margaret Mary Alacoque (1647–1690). The societies no longer enjoy a dominant role in the Caribbean island's social structure but still enjoy a reputation for hosting the *grand fêtes* that mark the respective feast days.

In an intensive process of preparing for the two *fêtes*, the Roses and the Marguerites each hold a series of dress rehearsals known as *séances*. During these events, a main performer, the *shantwel*, leads society members in call-and-response singing accompanied by various folk instruments.

The feast day opens with a church service, which is followed by a street procession presenting the host society's royal entourage. The evening program includes a banquet, the much-awaited performance by the shantwel, and folk dances such as the Quadrille, the *Mappa*, and the *Belair*.

CONTACTS:
St. Lucia Tourist Board
800 Second Ave., 9th Fl.
New York, NY 10017
800-456-3984 or 212-867-2950; fax: 212-867-2795
www.stlucia.org

Permanent Mission of St. Lucia to the United Nations
800 Second Ave.
9th Fl.
New York, NY 10017
212-697-9360; fax: 212-697-4993

♦ 0957 ♦ Folk Festival, National
Summer or fall, depending on location

Unlike other music festivals, the National Folk Festival (NFF) does not have a home base. Rather than assuming a permanent residence, this traveling festival works in partnership with a host community for periods of three years. The three-day NFF is a celebration of traditional music, dance, and crafts with an emphasis on the ethnic music styles that have shaped American culture through various eras.

The festival is organized by the National Council for the Traditional Arts (NCTA), which has been producing celebrations of the traditional arts since 1934. The NCTA's aim is to produce a show in the same city for three years, thereby laying the groundwork for a locally produced festival to continue after the National Folk Festival moves on to another city. Since the event is presented free of charge, planning and operations depends largely on the efforts of volunteers.

The traveling framework of the festival has had success in a handful of cities, including Bangor, Maine (host city of NFF in 2002-2004), and Richmond, Va. (2005-2007), which are now sites of regional folk festivals that continue to attract large audiences. Butte, Mont., was chosen to host the festival in the years 2008-2010.

CONTACTS:
National Council for the Traditional Arts
1320 Fenwick Lane, Ste. 200
Silver Spring, MD 20910
301-565-0654; fax: 301-565-0472
www.ncta.net

♦ 0958 ♦ Folklore, National Festival of
Every four years in autumn

Albania celebrates its cultural heritage with the National Festival of Folklore, which takes place in the southern city of Gjirokastra. Since 1968, the festival has drawn local artists and performers; Albanian troupes from neighboring countries like Kosovo, Montenegro, and Macedonia; and performers from more distant countries like Italy, Turkey, and the United States. It is an occasion to present traditional music, folk art, clothing, and locally made jewelry. The event, which takes place every four years, draws tourists as well as local Albanians.

Gjirokastra, which historians believe was founded as early as the fourth century, has a rich history that is appropriate to the festival's traditional feel. The open square of Gjirokastra Castle, which dates back to the sixth century C.E., is the main performance site. There, dance troupes face off in competitions and singers often perform ballads to the accompaniment of the çifteli, a two-string long-necked mandolin. Crafts people also entice shoppers with their copper jewelry and other wares.

CONTACTS:
Albanian Institute of Tourism and Environmental Developments
Rr., Sulejman Delvina
Zayed Center
Tirania, Albania
www.tourismalbania.com

♦ 0959 ♦ **Folkmoot**
Two weeks in mid- to late July

This two-week festival is held in the mountains at the entrance to the Great Smoky Mountains National Park in western North Carolina. It features more than 350 folk musicians and dancers from countries as diverse as Ecuador, Italy, Malaysia, Turkey, Peru, Israel, Slovenia, China, and the Philippines.

Events include a Parade of Nations, a bazaar with local and regional artisans and food vendors, a special children's program, and performances by the folk dancers and musicians. Many of the events take place in the nearby towns of Waynesville and Asheville.

CONTACTS:
Folkmoot USA
112 Virginia Ave.
P.O. Box 658
Waynesville, NC 28786
877-365-5872 or 828-452-2997; fax: 828-452-5762
www.folkmootusa.org

♦ 0960 ♦ **Fools, Feast of**
On or around January 1

A mock-religious festival popular during the Middle Ages in Europe, particularly France, the Feast of Fools had much in common with the Roman SATURNALIA. During the holiday period around CHRISTMAS and NEW YEAR'S DAY, various classes of the clergy took turns reversing the normal procedures in the church. On January 1, the Feast of the CIRCUMCISION, for example, the priests were in charge; on HOLY INNOCENTS' DAY, December 28, the choirboys held sway. The group to whom the day belonged would nominate a bishop and archbishop of fools, ordaining them in a mock ceremony and then pre-

senting them to the people. Masked and dressed in women's clothing, they would dance and sing obscene songs, play dice or eat at the altar, burn old shoes in the censers, and engage in other activities that would normally be unthinkable. The revelry died out around the time of the Reformation.

The Feast of Fools was similar, but not identical, to the FEAST OF THE ASS that was observed in France around Christmas time.

SOURCES:
DictFolkMyth-1984, p. 374
EncyChristmas-2003, p. 244
EncyRel-1987, vol. 3, p. 99; vol. 6, p. 526
FestSaintDays-1915, p. 253
OxYear-1999, p. 34
SeasFeast-1961, p. 278

♦ 0961 ♦ **Footwashing Day**
Early summer; Sunday

According to the Gospel of John, before the Last Supper Jesus washed the feet of his disciples and instructed them to follow his example of humility and love. Although it was originally performed on MAUNDY THURSDAY, in most American Protestant sects it takes place at other times and occasionally at more frequent intervals.

For some mountain people of Kentucky, this observance takes place only once a year, but the preparations go on for weeks beforehand. On Footwashing Day, the women take turns washing each other's feet, and on the opposite side of the church the men do the same thing. Refreshment stands have been set up so children can eat while their parents are participating in the ritual. After the service, the people who live near the church invite the rest of the participants to eat with them.

SOURCES:
FolkAmerHol-1999, p. 273
RelHolCal-2004, p. 97

♦ 0962 ♦ **Forefathers' Day**
December 21 or 22

Observed primarily in Plymouth, Massachusetts, and by various New England societies throughout the country, Forefathers' Day commemorates the landing of the Pilgrims, who arrived in 1620 on the *Mayflower* and established the second English colony in North America. (The first colony successfully established was in JAMESTOWN, Virginia, in 1607.)

The Old Colony Club of Plymouth was the first group to observe the anniversary in 1769, but since this was only 15 years after the New Style Calendar went into effect, there was some confusion about how many days should be added to the original December 11 date of the landing. All dates before 1700 were supposed to have 10 days added, and all dates after 1700 were supposed to have 11 days added. Somehow a mistake was made, and Old Colony Club members still celebrate Forefathers' Day on December 22. Wearing top hats and led by a drummer, they march down the main street of Plymouth. After firing a small cannon, they return to their Club for breakfast and toasts to the Pilgrims.

Transplanted New Englanders who have formed New England societies in other parts of the country, however, observe the occasion on December 21, as does the General Society of Mayflower Descendants, which sometimes refers to it as **Compact Day**. The Pilgrim Society, which was founded in 1820 by a group of people interested in the history of Plymouth, holds its annual meeting on December 21 and serves a traditional dinner of succotash, stew, corn, turnips, and beans.

CONTACTS:
Plimoth Plantation
137 Warren Ave.
P.O. Box 1620
Plymouth, MA 02362
508-746-1622; fax: 508-746-4978
www.plimoth.org

SOURCES:
AmerBkDays-2000, p. 843
AnnivHol-2000, p. 211
DictDays-1988, p. 43

♦ 0963 ♦ **Forgiveness, Feast of**
August 1-2

The **Festa del Perdono**, or Feast of Forgiveness, is observed annually in Assisi, Italy, where St. Francis built his humble hermitage, known as the *Porciúncula* ("little portion"), in the 13th century. It was here on a small plot of land containing a ruined chapel that St. Francis experienced his religious conversion and began to preach and gather disciples. He restored the chapel and claimed it as his "portion" or "little inheritance." In 1209 he received papal permission to establish the Franciscan monastic order, the Friars Minor, urging his followers to maintain the chapel as a sacred place.

Porciúncula also refers to the plenary indulgence that used to be given to those who visited this sanctuary on August 2, the date set by Pope Honorius III in 1221. Although in the beginning the indulgence could only be gained in the Porciúncula, the privilege was eventually extended to all churches having a connection with the Franciscan order, and the time for visiting the sanctuary was extended to the period between the afternoon of August 1 and sunset on August 2.

St. Francis instituted the two-day Feast of Forgiveness because it upset him that by going off to fight in the Crusades a sinful man could escape punishment in purgatory. Believing that there should be a more peaceful means to gain salvation, St. Francis received the Pope's permission for Roman Catholics to make an annual pilgrimage to Assisi to renew their relationship with the church.

The August 2 feast was brought to New Mexico by the early Spanish settlers, and it is still observed in the small town of Arroyo Hondo, about 80 miles north of Santa Fe. Although at one time it involved two processions—one beginning at the village church's main entrance and another, a quarter of a mile away, involving only members of the flagellant brother-

hood—today the celebration in Arroyo Hondo that once drew large crowds has nearly died out.

See also St. Francis of Assisi, Feast of

CONTACTS:
Italian Government Tourist Board
630 Fifth Ave., Ste. 1565
New York, NY 10111
212-245-5618; fax: 212-586-9249
www.italiantourism.com

Order of Friars Minor
Via S. Maria Mediatrices 25
Rome, 00165 Italy
39-6-6849-19; fax: 39-6-6380-292
www.ofm.org

SOURCES:
FolkAmerHol-1999, p. 335

♦ 0964 ♦ **Fornacalia**
Around February 17

The Fornacalia, or **Feast of Ovens**, was observed no later than February 17, which was also the day of the Quirinalia festival honoring the ancient Roman god Quirinus. The Fornacalia was designed to benefit the ovens (*fornices*) that parched grain and was held to placate the goddess Fornix, who presided over them. It lasted a week, during which each household made an offering of *far*, flour of the oldest kind of Italian wheat, roasted in the oven and then crushed in an ancient mill and served in the form of cakes. The rituals involved in the Fornacalia were observed primarily by the *curiae*, or tribal divisions of Rome, and it was celebrated in February on different days—one day for the state and one for each of the curiae. According to Ovid, those who were uncertain which curia they belonged to ended up observing this festival on February 17 instead of on the proper day. At this time a general offering of cakes was made by the whole community.

SOURCES:
FestRom-1981, p. 73
FestSaintDays-1915, p. 43
NewCentClassHandbk-1962, p. 641
OxClassDict-1970, p. 444
OxYear-1999, p. 82

♦ 0965 ♦ **Forty Martyrs' Day**
March 9

The "Forty Martyrs of Sebaste" were Roman soldiers quartered in Armenia in 320. Agricola, the governor of the province, told them that under orders of the Emperor Licinius, they would have to make a sacrifice to the Roman gods. As Christians, they refused to do so. Agricola told them to strip themselves naked and stand on the ice of a nearby pond. All died from exposure during the night. They are greatly revered in the Eastern Christian Church. This day is observed in the Orthodox church in Syria as **Id al-Arba'in Shahid**. In Greece, special foods are prepared: cake with 40 layers of pastry, stew with 40 herbs, 40 pancakes, etc. In

Romania, little cakes called *sfintisori* ("little mints") are baked and given to and received from every passerby. *Coliva*, a cake of cooked corn and honey, is also traditional. Farm tools are readied for work, and hearth ashes are spread around the cottage to keep the serpent from entering (each home is said to have a serpent protecting it).

CONTACTS:
Orthodox America, Nikodemus Orthodox Publication Society
P.O. Box 383
Richfield Springs, NY 13439

SOURCES:
BkFest-1937, p. 328
FolkWrldHol-1999, p. 206
OxYear-1999, p. 111

♦ 0966 ♦ **Fossey (Dian) Day**
December 27

Over the course of her career, American conservationist Dian Fossey (1932–1985) conducted groundbreaking research on Rwanda's mountain gorillas, a species long victimized by wide-scale poaching. Her advocacy on behalf of the gorillas also helped ensure their preservation. At the age of 53, Fossey was murdered in her cabin at a research center in the Virunga Mountains on December 27, 1985. For Rwandans and conservationists, the anniversary of her death honors a legacy that draws attention to the plight of a rare animal species and helps promote eco-tourism.

Ceremonies take place in Volcanoes National Park, which is the site of Fossey's murder and contains a permanent memorial to the zoologist. Individuals typically perform traditional dances, while government officials deliver speeches and lay wreaths on her grave site.

CONTACTS:
Dian Fossey Gorilla Fund International
800 Cherokee Ave. S.E.
Atlanta, GA 30315-1440
800-851-0203 or 404-624-5881; fax: 404-624-5999

♦ 0967 ♦ **Foster (Stephen) Memorial Day**
January 13

Stephen Collins Foster (1826-1864) was a composer whose popular minstrel songs and sentimental ballads have found a lasting place in American music. When he died at the age of 37, suffering from poverty and alcoholism, he left behind more than 200 compositions—among them "Camptown Races," "Beautiful Dreamer," "My Old Kentucky Home," "Oh! Susanna," "Swanee River," and "Jeanie with the Light Brown Hair."

January 13, the anniversary of Foster's death, was proclaimed as Stephen Foster Memorial Day in 1951. In Florida, this day is part of Stephen Foster Memorial Week, established by the state legislature in 1935.

One of the most widely known observances takes place at the Stephen Foster Center in White Springs, Florida, on the Sun-day nearest January 13. The events commemorating Foster's contributions to American music include performances by musical groups from schools and universities throughout the state and daily concerts from the 97-bell carillon tower. During the preceding October, the so-called "Jeanie auditions" (named for Foster's wife, the subject of "Jeanie with the Light Brown Hair") are held to determine the winner of a music scholarship for 18- to 21-year-old Florida women. The winner often appears at the Memorial Week festivities and performs some of Foster's songs.

CONTACTS:
Stephen Foster Folk Culture Center State Park
P.O. Box G
White Springs, FL 32096
386-397-2733

SOURCES:
AmerBkDays-2000, p. 58
AnnivHol-2000, p. 9

♦ 0968 ♦ **Founder's Day**
May 29

Many organizations and institutions celebrate a Founder's Day. In London, the old soldiers at the Royal Hospital in Chelsea hold a Founder's Day parade on May 29, the birthday of Charles II (1630-1685), the hospital's founder and one of England's most popular monarchs. May 29 is also Royal Oak Day (*see* SHICK-SHACK DAY).

CONTACTS:
Royal Hospital Chelsea
Royal Hospital Rd., Chelsea
London, SW3 4SR United Kingdom
44-20-7881-5200; fax: 44-20-7881-5463
www.chelsea-pensioners.org.uk

♦ 0969 ♦ **Four an' Twenty Day**
January 18

When England and Scotland switched from the Julian to the Gregorian calendar in 1752, 11 days were dropped to make up for the additional time that had accumulated during the use of the Julian calendar. Four an' Twenty Day (or **Old Twelfth Day**) is a Scottish expression referring to the day on which TWELFTH NIGHT used to be celebrated before the switch.

SOURCES:
DictDays-1988, p. 43

♦ 0970 ♦ **Fourth of July**
July 4

In Philadelphia, Pennsylvania, on July 4, 1776, the Continental Congress approved the final draft of the Declaration of Independence. John Hancock, the president of the Congress, was the first to sign the document, using a clear and distinctive hand, thus giving rise to the expression "John Hancock" for one's signature.

As the most important national holiday in the U.S., **Independence Day**, often called the Fourth of July, is traditionally celebrated with fireworks displays, family picnics, parades, band concerts, and patriotic speeches. It is observed throughout the United States and U.S. territories.

CONTACTS:
U.S. Government Printing Office
732 N. Capitol St. N.W.
Washington, D.C. 20401
866-512-1800 or 202-512-1530; fax: 202-512-2104
www.gpo.gov

Fourth of July Celebrations Database
James R. Heintze, librarian
American University Library
Washington, DC 20016
202-885-3205; fax: 202-885-3226
www.american.edu

SOURCES:
AmerBkDays-2000, p. 500
BkFest-1937, p. 18
BkHolWrld-1986, Jul 4
DaysCustFaith-1957, p. 169
FolkAmerHol-1999, p. 276
GdUSFest-1984, pp. 165, 201, 220
IntlThFolk-1979, p. 90
OxYear-1999, p. 281
PatHols-2006, p. 127

♦ 0971 ♦ **Fourth of July (Denmark)**
July 4

The Fourth of July celebration held in Aalborg, Denmark, each year since 1912 was started by an American of Danish descent, Dr. Max Henius of Chicago. He bought 200 acres of land in Rebild and deeded the land to King Christian X, with the stipulation that his fellow Danish Americans be allowed to celebrate the Fourth of July there every year.

The area is now a national park to which about 35,000 people come to observe America's Independence Day. A replica of the Liberty Bell is rung, the national anthems of both countries are sung by stars from the Royal Danish Opera, military bands perform, and there are bilingual readings of the Declaration of Independence and the Gettysburg Address. As a permanent shrine for Americans of Danish ancestry, there is a replica of the log cabin in which Abraham LINCOLN lived as a young boy.

CONTACTS:
Aalborg Tourist and Convention Bureau
Ossteragade 8
P.O. Box 1862
Aalborg, DK-9000 Denmark
45-99-31-75-00; fax: 45-99-31-75-19
www.visitaalborg.com/international/en-gb/menu/tour

SOURCES:
GdWrldFest-1985, p. 70

♦ 0972 ♦ **Fox (George), Death of**
January 13

George Fox (1624-1691) was the founder of the Society of Friends, or Quakers, which he organized in 1650 to protest the overly formal religion of his time. An English preacher and missionary, Fox believed that creeds and scriptures were unimportant in religion; all that really counted was the divine light of Christ as it manifested itself in all people. Church was merely a gathering of friends who were guided by the Inner Light and who were thus able to provide guidance for each other. There was no need for an ordained ministry.

In the early days, the "Friends" set themselves apart from the rest of the world by dressing in black and speaking in biblical style. They were known for their efforts in the abolition of slavery, prison reform, temperance, and education. In the United States, William Penn received a land grant that subsequently became the Quaker colony of Pennsylvania (*see* PENNSYLVANIA DAY). Quakers all over the world observe the anniversary of their founder's death in their meetinghouses.

CONTACTS:
Friends General Conference
1216 Arch St., Ste. 2B
Philadelphia, PA 19107
215-561-1700; fax: 215-561-0759
www.fgcquaker.org

SOURCES:
DayRel-1990, p. 11
DaysCustFaith-1957, p. 71
OxYear-1999, p. 34
RelHolCal-2004, p. 89

♦ 0973 ♦ **Fox Hill Festival**
Second week in August

For more than 100 years this day has been celebrated at Fox Hill Village in Nassau, a seaside resort on the island of New Providence in the Bahamas, to commemorate the abolition of slavery. Bahamian foods, singing, and dancing contribute to a carnival atmosphere, although there are services in local churches in the morning that feature gospel and Bahamian religious songs.

See also BAHAMAS EMANCIPATION DAY

CONTACTS:
Bahamas Tourism Office
60 E. 42nd St., Ste. 1850
New York, NY 10165
212-758-2777; fax: 212-753-6531
www.bahamas.com

SOURCES:
GdWrldFest-1985, p. 16

♦ 0974 ♦ **Frankenmuth Bavarian Festival**
Second weekend in June

Religious leaders in Bavaria sent a group of 15 Franconians to Michigan's Saginaw Valley in 1845 to set up a mission for the Indians. Although the mission eventually moved elsewhere, the settlement known as Frankenmuth, meaning "courage of the Franconians," retained its Bavarian roots and soon attracted other German immigrants. In fact, for many years after the beginning of the 20th century, German remained the community's principal language.

The Frankenmuth Bavarian Festival, held in June each year to celebrate the town's German heritage, takes advantage of the town's Old World atmosphere and Bavarian architecture, which includes a glockenspiel tower that plays traditional German melodies, while carved wooden figures depict the legend of the PIED PIPER of Hamelin. There is also a replica of the 19th-century Holz Brücke, Frankenmuth's covered wooden bridge that spans the Cass River. The festival features a dance tent resembling a German *biergarten* with German dance bands and beverages, as well as farm tours, arts and crafts displays, a parade featuring the festival's Bavarian Princess, and well-known entertainers of German origin.

CONTACTS:
RAM Productions
P.O. Box 204
Frankenmuth, MI 48734
800-386-3378 or 989-652-3378; fax: 989-652-4633
www.frankenmuthfestivals.com

♦ 0975 ♦ **Frankfurt Book Fair (Buchmesse)**
Second week in October

The world's largest annual trade show for the book publishing industry is held annually for five days in Frankfurt, Germany. It attracts exhibitors from about 110 countries and is attended by more than 250,000 people, of whom about 7,000 are publishers, editors, and exhibitors.

Trade fairs have been a tradition in Frankfurt for at least 800 years, and, in even earlier times, its location on the Main River in the heart of the continent made the community a crossroads of trade. Book fairs were held in Frankfurt in the 16th century, when the city had become the center of German publishing. In 1579, the book fairs came under the supervision of the imperial censorship commission, and gradually the center of publishing shifted to Leipzig.

The world wars severely restricted publishing in Europe, but the industry reemerged afterwards. Because Leipzig was in Soviet-controlled East Germany, the publishing trade center moved back to Frankfurt for the first time since about 1650. The book fair had been chiefly an event for German publishers before 1939, but it grew in a few years to be the world's preeminent book fair. In its present international form, the fair is officially dated to 1949.

CONTACTS:
Ausstellungs-und Messe GmbH
Frankfurter Buchmesse
Reineckstr. 3
Frankfurt, Hesse 60313 Germany
49-69-210-20; fax: 49-69-210-22-27
www.frankfurt-book-fair.com

♦ 0976 ♦ **Franklin's (Benjamin) Birthday**
January 17

This holiday is a commemoration of the birth of Benjamin Franklin—printer, scientist, inventor, statesman, diplomat, writer, editor, wit, and aphorist. Born in Boston on this day in 1706, Franklin helped edit, and was a signer of, the Declaration of Independence. He also helped to frame the Constitution. The commonsense moralities of his *Poor Richard's Almanac* became catch-phrases in his time and are still quoted today—for example, "Make haste slowly"; "Fish and visitors smell in three days"; "He that goes a-borrowing, goes a-sorrowing."

Franklin invented bifocals, proposed Daylight Saving Time in 1786, and unsuccessfully recommended the wild turkey rather than the bald eagle as the national bird. When he died in 1790 in Philadelphia, he was given the most impressive funeral that city had ever seen: 20,000 people attended.

Since 1991, the Bower Award and Prize in Science—a cash prize of more than $300,000—has been presented on Jan. 17 by the Franklin Institute in Philadelphia to a person who has made a scientific contribution of a practical nature in the manner of Franklin. Also in Philadelphia, the Franklin Institute Science Museum holds a two-day "birthday bash" that often involves people dressing as Franklin. The celebration takes place on the weekend preceding Martin Luther KING, Jr. Day, which is the Monday after Jan. 15.

CONTACTS:
Franklin Institute Science Museum
222 N. 20th St.
Philadelphia, PA 19103
215-448-1200
sln.fi.edu

Library of Congress
101 Independence Ave. S.E.
Washington, DC 20540
202-707-5000; fax: 202-707-8366
www.loc.gov

SOURCES:
AmerBkDays-2000, p. 65
AnnivHol-2000, p. 10
DictDays-1988, p. 44

♦ 0977 ♦ **Frawardignan, Feast of**
April, September, August; 19th day of Frawardin, the first Zoroastrian month

This is a "sacred name day" feast on which the month and day names coincide in the Zoroastrian calendar. But unlike most other name-day feasts, which refer to *yazatas* or spiritual beings, the 19th day of Frawardin honors the spirit of those who are living, dead, and not yet born. On this day a special ceremony is performed in memory of people from the community who have died. This thanksgiving service can be held in a fire temple, a meeting-hall, or a private home.

The Zoroastrian calendar has 12 months of 30 days each, plus five extra days at the end of the year. Because of discrepancies in the calendars used by widely separated Zoroastrian communities around the world, there are now three different calendars in use, and the Feast of Frawardignan can fall either in April, August, or September.

Followers of the Zoroastrian religion, which was founded by the prophet Zoroaster (also known as Zarathushtra, believed to have lived around 1200 B.C.E.), today live primarily in Iran and northwestern India, although smaller communities exist in Pakistan, Sri Lanka, Canada, the U.S., England, and Australia.

SOURCES:
RelHolCal-2004, p. 66

♦ 0978 ♦ Freedom Day, National
February 1

National Freedom Day commemorates the abolition of slavery in the United States. On that date in 1865, President Abraham Lincoln signed the 13th Amendment to the U.S. Constitution, making slavery illegal. The purpose of the day is to celebrate the freedom from slavery for all people and to acknowledge the importance of freedom and harmony in American society. Freedom Day is not a federal holiday. Government offices and banks are open for business.

Freedom Day was conceived by U.S. Army Major Richard Robert Wright Sr., a former slave who was a distinguished officer, educator, civil rights activist, and banking entrepreneur. He worked hard to have Freedom Day recognized as a holiday. In 1948, President Harry Truman signed a bill declaring February 1 as National Freedom Day. However, over the years, there have been few formal observances. In fact, a strong drive is underway to adopt June 19, or JUNETEENTH, as it is known, as the American holiday to celebrate the end of slavery. This was the date in 1865 when news reached slaves in Texas—two and a half years after the fact—that Lincoln had signed the Emancipation Proclamation. The traditional Texan celebration of the day was revived in recent years and has spread nationwide. Many would like to see it replace February 1 as the national holiday to mark slavery's demise.

CONTACTS:
U.S. Library of Congress
101 Independence Ave. S.E.
Washington, D.C. 20540
202-707-5000
www.loc.gov/help

Juneteenth World-Wide Celebration
www.juneteenth.com

♦ 0979 ♦ Freedom Festival, International
Late June to early July

The International Freedom Festival takes place each summer in the neighboring cities of Windsor, Canada, and Detroit, Michigan. The festival began in 1958 as a means of promoting tourism and providing local residents with summertime activities. It celebrates the historically friendly relationship between Canada and the United States. The festival starts in late June and ends in early July to celebrate CANADA DAY on July 1 and the U.S. FOURTH OF JULY. Events have included a rope-pulling contest across the Detroit River, a tug-boat race,

a chili-cooking contest, a variety of concerts, carnival rides, a Canada Day parade and party, fireworks displays, and special events for children, the elderly, and the disabled.

CONTACTS:
The Parade Company
9500 Mt. Elliott, Studio A
Detroit, MI 48211
313-923-7400; fax: 313-923-2920
www.theparade.org

♦ 0980 ♦ Freedom of Entry Ceremony
April 28

Inaugurated in 2007, this ceremony honors the Royal Malaysian Navy with a series of traditional rituals that date back to medieval times. It takes place in the Malaysian seaport town of Kota Kinabalu on the island of Borneo. Along with the public symbolic gestures that confer the navy's right to protect the city, the ceremony also features several entertaining exhibitions and shows intended to attract tourists.

In the entry ceremony, which borrows from British and Australian military tradition, the navy marches through the city streets with "swords drawn, drums beating, band playing, colors flying, and bayonets fixed." As a public confirmation of the navy's right to march, Kota Kinabalu's Lord Mayor will present a special scroll before the assembled crowd. Another of the ceremony's symbolic elements is the assortment of parade colors, which are meant to help soldiers reassemble in the event of their separation during battle.

Additional events include a boat demonstration, helicopter aerial displays, tours of navy ships, and performances by the navy band and silent drill teams. The inaugural event drew 2,000 people, and government officials announced that they intended to make the ceremony an annual tradition.

CONTACTS:
Sabah Tourism Board
51 Gaya St.
88000 Kota Kinabalu
Sabah, Malaysia
www.sabahtourism.com

Malaysia Embassy
3516 International Ct. N.W.
Washington, DC 20008
202-572-9700; fax: 202-572-9882
myperwakilan.mfa.gov.my/am/washington

♦ 0981 ♦ Freeing the Insects
Late August-early September

There is a festival in Japan on May 28 during which vendors sell insects in tiny bamboo cages. Those who purchase the diminutive pets keep them in or near the house during the summer months so that they can hear their songs in the evening. Then, on a day in late August or early September, they gather in public parks and at temples or shrines to set the insects free. When the creatures realize they have been released, the former captors listen to them burst into their individual sounds.

The custom of freeing the insects, also known as the **Insect-Hearing Festival**, is more common in the countryside. Although no one seems to know its exact origin, it is reminiscent of Italy's FESTA DEL GRILLO, where crickets are purchased in cages and kept as good luck tokens or harbingers of spring.

SOURCES:
FolkWrldHol-1999, p. 551
JapanFest-1965, p. 185

♦ 0982 ♦ **French Community, Feast Day of the (La fête de la Communauté française de Belgique)**
September 27

Each of the autonomous regions of Belgium observes its own feast day. Feast Day of the French Community (La fête de la Communauté française de Belgique) is a celebration of linguistic heritage and national independence. Feast days in other regions of Belgium include FEAST DAY OF THE FLEMISH COMMUNITY, FEAST DAY OF THE GERMAN-SPEAKING COMMUNITY, IRIS FEST, and WALLOON REGIONAL DAY.

Three linguistic communities make up Belgium's population—the French, Flemish, and German. There are four million French speakers in Belgium, and most of them live in the federal region of Wallonia, located in the south. Feast Day of the French Community, which largely takes place in the Walloon cities of Namur, Liege, Huy, and Charleroi, is a public assertion of the linguistic and ethnic rights of French speakers. It also marks the historic date in 1830 when the Dutch army withdrew from Brussels to end the union with Holland and its king, William I. This event allowed Belgium to declare its sovereignty.

For the greater part of the 20th century, the holiday took place on the final Sunday of September. The Walloon Assembly, a group leading the burgeoning Walloon Movement, decided in 1975 to switch to the late September date to mark the days in 1830 when Belgians successfully resisted foreign domination. By focusing on this page in history, the leaders hoped to inspire a similar movement of preserving autonomy from Belgium's dominant group, the Flemish speakers of Flanders.

All schools and administrative buildings are closed for the feast day. Past celebrations have extended three days and have offered a program of plays, sports competitions, and free music concerts.

CONTACTS:
Belgium Embassy
3330 Garfield St. N.W.
Washington, D.C. 20008
202-333-6900; fax: 202-333-3079
www.diplobel.us

♦ 0983 ♦ **French Open Tennis**
May-June

Officially known as the **French Championships**, the French Open is one of the four major tournaments that make up the Grand Slam of tennis. (The others are the AUSTRALIAN OPEN,

the UNITED STATES OPEN, and WIMBLEDON.) The French National Championship, played at the Stade Roland Garros in Auteil, France, on red-clay courts, was instituted in 1891 but wasn't opened to players from other nations until 1925. It became an open (to both amateurs and professionals) in 1968.

In 1974, Bjorn Borg of Sweden, 18 years old, became the youngest French Open winner. He went on to become a six-time winner—1974, 1975, 1978-81—putting him ahead of the former champion, Henri Cochet, the winner in 1926, 1928, 1930, and 1932. In the women's division, the players who have won the most titles since 1925 have been American Chris Evert Lloyd (seven wins: 1974, 1975, 1979, 1980, 1983, 1985, and 1986) and Australian Margaret Smith Court (five wins: 1962, 1964, 1969, 1970, and 1973). In 1990, 16-year-old Monica Seles of Yugoslavia took the youngest-champion honors from Borg when she beat German Steffi Graf. But Graf went on to win five times (1987, 1988, 1993, 1995, and 1996).

CONTACTS:
Federation Francaise de Tennis
Stade Roland Garros, 2 Ave., Gordon Bennett
Paris, 75016 France
33-1-4743-4800; fax: 33-1-4743-0494
www.fft.fr

♦ 0984 ♦ **French Quarter Festival**
Mid-April

The French Quarter Festival celebrates Louisiana's distinctive musical and culinary traditions. Held in New Orleans, the festival features performances by local and other Louisiana musicians as well as those foreign musicians influenced by Louisiana's musical traditions. Scores of bands perform at various sites throughout the French Quarter (also called the Vieux Carré). Sixty local restaurants operate food booths on the festival grounds, offering spectators the best in Louisiana cooking. The festival began in 1983. In recent years close to 300,000 people have attended this three-day event.

CONTACTS:
French Quarter Festivals, Inc.
400 N. Peters St., Ste. 205
New Orleans, LA 70130
800-673-5725 or 504-522-5730; fax: 504-522-5711
www.fqfi.org

♦ 0985 ♦ **Fritter Thursday**
Between February 5 and March 11; day after Ash Wednesday

At one time in England, each day of the week during which LENT began had a special name: COLLOP MONDAY, SHROVE TUESDAY, ASH WEDNESDAY, Fritter Thursday, and Kissing Friday. Fritter Thursday took its name from the custom of eating apple fritters—fruit-filled cakes deep-fried in fat—on this day.

SOURCES:
DictDays-1988, p. 45

♦ 0986 ♦ **Frost Saints' Days**
May 11, 12, 13

These three consecutive days in May mark the feasts of St. Mammertus, St. Pancras, and St. Servatus. In the wine-growing districts of France, a severe cold spell occasionally strikes at this time of year, inflicting serious damage on the grapevines. Although scientists claim that the unseasonable frost is caused by air currents blowing off a late breakup of polar ice in the north, some in rural France have believed that it is the result of their having offended one of the three saints, who for this reason are called the "frost saints."

In Germany, too, feelings toward these three saints are mixed, especially among those whose livelihood depends on agriculture. They call them "the three severe lords," and farmers believe that their crops are not safe from frost until May 13 has passed. French farmers have been known to show their displeasure over a cold snap at this time of year by flogging the statues and defacing the pictures of Mammertus, Pancras, and Servatus.

SOURCES:
DaysCustFaith-1957, p. 122
FolkWrldHol-1999, p. 354
OxYear-1999, pp. 204, 205

♦ 0987 ♦ **Fur Trade Days**
Second weekend in July

Chadron, Nebraska, was at one time a frontier town with a reputation for lawlessness. Shootouts in the local saloons were a regular occurrence. But in 1893 a local newspaper came up with a way of putting the town's high spiritedness to better use. They organized the 1,000 Mile Horse Race from Chadron to Chicago—a publicity stunt that made Chadron a household name. Nine men, including one former outlaw, competed in the race. John Berry, the winner, reached Chicago in 13 days, 16 hours.

Today Fur Trade Days is an attempt to recreate the excitement of the town's active frontier trading days in the mid-1800s. Activities include a buffalo cookout, horseshoe pitching and buffalo chip-throwing contests, and a primitive rendezvous with a black powder shoot.

CONTACTS:
Chadron/Dawes County Area Chamber of Commerce
706 W. Third St.
P.O. Box 646
Chadron, NE 69337
800-603-2937 or 308-432-4401; fax: 308-432-4757
www.chadron.com

♦ 0988 ♦ **Furrinalia**
July 25

Furrina (or Furina) was an ancient Roman deity whose reason for existence has been largely forgotten. She might have been associated with a spring or springs, and some experts regard her as a spirit of the darkness. Others say she was the goddess of robbers. All that is known for certain is that she possessed a grove (on the slopes of the Janiculum, a ridge near the Tiber River), a festival (the Furrinalia, on July 25), and her own *flamen*, or priest, named Furrinalis. Although Furrina belongs to the earliest of Roman religions, the Furrinalia continued to be observed in later Roman times. It was in Furrina's grove that the Roman tribune Gaius Sempronius Gracchus ordered his slave to kill him in 121 B.C.E.

SOURCES:
ClassDict-1984, p. 246
DictFolkMyth-1984, p. 428
DictRomRel-1996, p. 90
FestRom-1981, p. 168
OxClassDict-1970, p. 451
OxYear-1999, p. 306

♦ 0989 ♦ **Fyr-Bål Fest**
Weekend nearest June 21

The Fyr-Bål Fest held every year in Ephraim, Wisconsin, reflects the town's Swedish and Norwegian heritage by incorporating customs traditionally associated with Scandinavian MIDSUMMER celebrations. The two-day festival is presided over by a "Viking chieftain," chosen on the basis of his contributions to the community. On the first evening the chieftain, whose identity has been kept secret, arrives by boat at Ephraim on the shores of Lake Michigan, where he is greeted by children dressed as elves. After a coronation ceremony, he proclaims the official opening of summer and lights a bonfire in which an effigy of the Winter Witch is burned. Other groups along the shores of adjacent Eagle Harbor then light their own bonfires.

In addition to the bonfire, traditional Scandinavian events at the festival include folk dancing and welcome mats in doorways made out of evergreen boughs woven together. There is also a trophy race at the Ephraim Yacht Club.

CONTACTS:
Ephraim Historical Foundation
P.O. Box 165
Ephraim, WI 54211
920-854-9688; fax: 920-854-7232
www.ephraim.org

G

♦ 0990 ♦ Gable (Clark) Birthday Celebration
Saturday nearest February 1

The American film actor William Clark Gable was born in Cadiz, Ohio, on February 1, 1901. For almost a quarter of a century he was Hollywood's leading male star, playing such romantic heroes as Rhett Butler in *Gone With the Wind* (1939).

The Clark Gable Foundation, Inc., was formed in the actor's hometown of Cadiz in 1985 for the purpose of preserving and promoting Gable's memory. Since 1987 it has hosted an annual celebration of Gable's birthday on or near February 1, an event that has been attended by John Clark, Gable's son; Joan Spreckles, his step-daughter; and a number of the original cast members of *Gone With the Wind*. There are booths for Gable memorabilia and showings of his films. The celebration is attended by several hundred collectors and fans.

CONTACTS:
Clark Gable Foundation Inc.
138 Charleston St.
P.O. Box 65
Cadiz, OH 43907
740-942-4989
www.clarkgablefoundation.com

♦ 0991 ♦ Gabon Independence Day
August 16-18

Gabon gained official independence from France on August 17, 1960, after more than a century of domination.

August 17 is a public holiday, but celebrations often extend to the days before and after Independence Day, with parades and dancing.

CONTACTS:
Embassy of the Republic of Gabon
2034 20th St. N.W., Ste. 200
Washington, D.C. 20009
202-797-1000; fax: 202-332-0668
www.gabonembassy.org.za

SOURCES:
AnnivHol-2000, p. 138
NatlHolWrld-1968, p. 146

♦ 0992 ♦ Gaelic Mod
August

Held in August at the Gaelic College of Celtic Arts and Crafts in St. Ann's, Nova Scotia, the Gaelic Mod is patterned after a similar event observed in Scotland every October. A mod is a competition that involves Gaelic singing, highland dancing, bagpipe playing, and athletic skills—not unlike the Welsh EISTEDDFOD, although the latter is primarily a music and literary event. The Canadian Gaelic Mod includes visits by Scottish clan chiefs and performances by bagpipe bands and highland dance groups. The first mod was held in 1939 when the Gaelic College was founded. Its students and teachers perform all over the world.

CONTACTS:
Gaelic College
P.O. Box 80
Englishtown, NS B0C 1H0 Canada
902-295-3411; fax: 902-295-2912
www.gaeliccollege.edu

SOURCES:
GdWrldFest-1985, p. 46
IntlThFolk-1979, p. 67

♦ 0993 ♦ Gai Jatra
One week beginning the day after the full moon in August

Gai Jatra is an eight-day carnival-type festival in Nepal, also known as the **Cow Festival**. The largest observances take place in Kathmandu, though people observe Gai Jatra throughout the country. It is sponsored by families who had deaths during the year and is intended to help the dead complete a smooth journey to heaven. Cows are believed to ease the journey and open the gates of heaven with their horns; therefore, during the festival, cows decorated with flowers and teenagers dressed as cows process through the streets. Dancing, singing, and performances satirizing the government and society are also part of the celebrations. These diversions stem from a legend that, after the death of a queen's child, the king sent clowns to console the queen.

CONTACTS:
Nepal Tourism Board, Tourist Service Center

Bhrikuti Mandap
P.O. Box 11018
Kathmandu, Nepal
977-1-4256909; fax: 977-1-4256910
www.welcomenepal.com

SOURCES:
BkHolWrld-1986, Oct 8
FolkWrldHol-1999, p. 463

♦ 0994 ♦ **Gallup Inter-Tribal Indian Ceremonial**
*Second week in August, Wednesday through
Sunday*

This event is a major inter-tribal celebration held at Red Rock State Park near Gallup, New Mexico. The ceremonial originated in 1922, and now more than 50 tribes from the United States, Canada, and Mexico participate. Average attendance is 30,000.

The ceremonial activities include competitive dancing, a barbecue, and all-Indian professional rodeos, in which cowboys compete for silver belt-buckle prizes in such events as calf roping and bronco riding. There are also three evenings of Indian ceremonial dancing, with the Hoop, Deer, Buffalo, and other dances performed by different tribes.

The markets here present some of the country's finest displays of Indian fine arts—Navajo rugs, katchinas, jewelry, pottery, basketry, beadwork, leatherwork, sculptures, and painting. There are also silversmiths, weavers, and potters at work on their crafts.

On Saturday morning, downtown Gallup is the scene of the Ceremonial Parade, with tribal bands playing traditional and contemporary music. It is called the country's only all-Indian non-mechanized parade—all participants are walking, on horseback, or in wagons. On Saturday night, a Ceremonial Queen is crowned.

CONTACTS:
Gallup Inter-Tribal Ceremonial Association
202 W. Coal Ave.
Gallup, NM 87301
505-863-3896; fax: 505-863-9168
www.newmexico.org

♦ 0995 ♦ **Galungan**
Every 210 days

Galungan is a major 10-day religious festival commemorating the Balinese New Year that is celebrated throughout the Indonesian island-province of Bali every 210 days. (The Balinese calendar followed for holidays is a 210-day cycle.) This is a Bali Hindu festival (Balinese religion is a mix of traditional Balinese and Hindu practices and beliefs), during which the gods are thought to come to earth. Balinese festivals include rituals in the temples, where small thrones are symbolic seats for the gods to occupy; cockfights, a combination of sport and gambling; offerings of foods, fruit, and flowers to the temple by the women; and card games, music, and dancing.

Numerous temple festivals are held during the year in individual Balinese villages, but Galungan is island-wide.

CONTACTS:
The Embassy of the Republic of Indonesia
2020 Massachusetts Ave. N.W.
Washington, D.C. 20036
202-775-5200; fax: 202-775-5365
www.embassyofindonesia.org

SOURCES:
GdWrldFest-1985, p. 112
IntlThFolk-1979, p. 218

♦ 0996 ♦ **Galway Oyster Festival**
Last weekend in September

In Galway, Ireland, the opening of the oyster season is celebrated with parties, music, and an oyster-opening competition. A young woman chosen to preside over the activities as the Pearl presents the first oyster to the mayor, who traditionally stands on Clarenbridge Pier in his scarlet robes waiting to open and taste it. Banquets are held in the evening and local pubs serve oysters by the bucketful, washed down by beer.

CONTACTS:
Galway Oyster Festival
Aras Failte
Galway, Ireland
353-91-522066; fax: 353-91-527282
www.galwayoysterfest.com

SOURCES:
GdWrldFest-1985, p. 114

♦ 0997 ♦ **Gambia Independence Day**
February 18

Gambia gained independence from Britain on February 18, 1965, and became a constitutional monarchy. On that day, people gathered in Bathurst for music, dancing, and the replacement of the Union Jack with the Gambian flag. A public vote in 1970 made the Republic of the Gambia a British Commonwealth.

Independence Day is a national holiday in Gambia.

Embassy of the Gambia
1424 K St. N.W., Ste. 600
Washington, D.C. 20005
202-785-1399; fax: 202-785-1430
www.gambiaembassy.us

SOURCES:
AnnivHol-2000, p. 29
NatlHolWrld-1968, p. 25

♦ 0998 ♦ **Gambia Revolution Day**
July 22

The tiny country of Gambia, a former British colony in West Africa, celebrates the anniversary of a coup in 1994 that ousted the country's president, Sir Dawda Jawara, and ushered in a military government. Following the bloodless coup, which was staged by a group of soldiers led by Lieutenant Yahya

Jammeh, the government made the transition to civilian leadership and the people elected Jammeh president.

The commemoration is essentially a vehicle to show the Gambian people's approval of their president. Since the 1994 coup, there have been a number of public changes to foster support for the celebration: the name of a major park in the capital city, Banjul, was changed from MacCarthy Square to July 22 Square, and the president commissioned the construction of the Arch 22, a tall gateway also in Banjul.

Past celebrations have included the unveiling of new development initiatives as well as cultural festivities. Dissident leaders in Gambia have voiced their disapproval of the anniversary, which they feel does not honor the country's legacy because it commemorates an unconstitutional overthrow of the government.

CONTACTS:
Embassy of the Gambia
1424 K St. N.W., Ste. 600
Washington, D.C. 20005
202-785-1399; fax: 202-785-1430
www.gambiaembassy.us

♦ 0999 ♦ Gandhi Jayanti (Mahatma Gandhi'sBirthday)
October 2

A national holiday in India to commemorate the birth of Mohandas Karamchand Gandhi, who came to be known as Mahatma ("great soul") Gandhi. At this time pilgrimages are made from throughout the country to the Raj Ghat on the banks of the Yamuna River in Delhi where Gandhi was cremated. Many communities also hold spinning and weaving sessions in his honor.

Gandhi, often pictured in a simple white cotton robe at a spinning wheel, was the leader of the movement for Indian nationalism, the 20th century's great prophet of nonviolence, and a religious innovator who encouraged a reformed, liberal Hinduism.

He was born in 1869 in Porbandar, India, and educated both in India and England. He went to South Africa as a young lawyer, was shocked by the racial discrimination, and led the African Indians in a nonviolent struggle against repression. Returning to India, he became a dominant political figure, and, in the struggle for independence, was jailed several times. His protests often took the form of fasts.

In the 1930s, he worked for rural people trying to eradicate discrimination against the untouchable caste and promoting hand spinning and weaving as occupations for the poor and as a way to overcome the British monopoly on cloth. The ashram (a religious retreat center) he established near Ahmedabad became the center of his freedom movement. In the 1940s, he helped heal the scars of religious conflict in Bengal and Bihar; in 1947 his fasting put an end to the rioting in Calcutta. On January 30, 1948, on his way to an evening prayer meeting in Delhi, he was shot and killed by a Hindu fanatic. Albert Einstein was among his great admirers.

CONTACTS:
Ministry of Tourism, Government of India
Rm. No 123, Transport Bhawan, No. 1, Parliament St.
New Delhi, Delhi 110 001 India
91-11-23715084; fax: 91-11-23715084
www.tourisminindia.com

Official Mahatma Gandhi eArchive
Mahatma Gandhi Foundation, N.T. Malusare Ln., Irla off S.V. Rd.,
   Vile Parle (West)
Rishiket Apt., Ground Fl.
Mumbai, Mumbai 400 056 India
91-22-26704605; fax: 91-22-26704603
web.mahatma.org.in

M. K. Gandhi Institute for Nonviolence
Christian Brothers University
650 E. Parkway, S.
Memphis, TN 38104
901-452-2824; fax: 901-452-2775
www.gandhiinstitute.org

SOURCES:
AnnivHol-2000, p. 166
BkHolWrld-1986, Oct 2
DictWrldRel-1989, p. 271

♦ 1000 ♦ Ganesh Chathurthi
August-September; waxing half of Hindu month of Bhadrapada

Ganesh Chathurthi is a lively seven- to ten-day long festival to worship the elephant-headed Ganesh, the Hindu god of wisdom and success. He is also the remover of obstacles, so he is also called Vighnesa, or Vighneswara. The festival is especially colorful in the Indian states of Tamil Nadu, Maharashtra, Andhra Pradesh, and Karnataka, and is the best-known event in Bombay.

Everyone pays homage to huge clay images of Ganesh made by highly respected artists, and he is also propitiated with street performances, competitions, processions, and yoga demonstrations. In Bombay, at the end of the week of celebration, as sacred songs are chanted, an image is taken to the sea and immersed to ensure prosperity for both land and water.

It is said that Ganesh, the son of the gods Shiva and Parvati, so annoyed his father one day that Shiva cut off his head. But Shiva then repented, and replaced his head with that of an elephant. Today people ask for Ganesh's help in undertaking new projects.

The story behind the festival in Nepal is that the day, called **Ganesh Chata**, celebrates a bitter dispute between Ganesh and the moon goddess. Therefore, the Nepalese try to stay inside on this night and close out the moonlight.

CONTACTS:
Ministry of Tourism, Government of India
Rm. No 123, Transport Bhawan, No. 1, Parliament St.
New Delhi, Delhi 110 001 India
91-11-23715084; fax: 91-11-23715084
www.tourisminindia.com

Maharashtra Tourism Development Corporation
Express Towers, 9th Fl.
Nariman Point, Mumbai 400 021 India

91-22-22024482; fax: 91-22-22024521
www.maharashtratourism.gov.in

SOURCES:
BkFest-1937, p. 162
BkHolWrld-1986, Sep 5
DictFolkMyth-1984, p. 440
DictWrldRel-1989, p. 273
EncyRel-1987, vol. 4, p. 60
FolkWrldHol-1999, p. 511
RelHolCal-2004, p. 174

♦ 1001 ♦ **Ganga Dussehra**
May-June; Hindu month of Jyestha

According to Hindu mythology, the Ganges River in India originally flowed only in heaven. In the form of a goddess, Ganga, the river was brought down to earth by King Bhagiratha in order to purify the ashes of his ancestors, 60,000 of whom had been burned under a curse from the great sage Kapila. The river came down reluctantly, breaking her fall on the head of Shiva so that she wouldn't shatter the Earth. By the time she reached the Bay of Bengal, she had touched the ashes of the 60,000 princes and fertilized the entire region.

On Ganga Dussehra, the 10th day of the waxing half of the month of Jyestha, Hindus who are able to reach the Ganges take a dip in the river to purify their sins and remedy their physical ills. The largest crowds assemble at the Uttar Pradesh towns of Hardwar, Mukteshwar, Varanasi, and other locations on the banks of the Ganges that have legendary significance. Those who live far away from the Ganges immerse themselves in whatever river, pond, or sea they can get to on this day.

Part of the Hindu faith includes the hope of bathing in the Ganges at some point during one's life. Upon death, a Hindu's body is generally cremated and the ashes are immersed in its holy water to assure peace for the soul.

See also KUMBH MELA

CONTACTS:
Uttar Pradesh Tourism Department, Directorate of Tourism
Rajarshi Purshottam Das Tandon
Vipin Khand, Gomti Nagar
Lucknow, Uttar Pradesh C-13 India
91-522-2308916; fax: 91-522-2308937
www.up-tourism.com

SOURCES:
DictFolkMyth-1984, p. 671
FolkWrldHol-1999, p. 378
RelHolCal-2004, p. 169

♦ 1002 ♦ **Gangaur**
*March-April; first through 18th days of the
Hindu month of Caitra*

Gangaur is one of the highlights of the festival year in the state of Rajasthan, India. It is observed in celebration of Gauri, another name for Parvati, Shiva's wife. This is largely a girls' and women's festival, but boys and men get to enjoy

the elaborate processions that take place in cities around the state, such as Jaipur, Bikaner, Jodhpur, and Udaipur, where there is also a boat procession on Pichola Lake.

The festival begins the day after HOLI and continues for 18 days, during which women fast, dress in their best clothes, adorn themselves with intricate henna designs, and pray—married women, for the well-being of their husbands and marriages, and single women, to find good husbands. The festival culminates with feasting and processions of the goddess' image celebrate the union of Gauri and Shiva, representing happy married life.

CONTACTS:
Ministry of Tourism, Government of India
Rm. No 123, Transport Bhawan, No. 1, Parliament St.
New Delhi, Delhi 110 001 India
91-11-23715084; fax: 91-11-23715084
www.tourisminindia.com

SOURCES:
FestIndia-1978, p. 76
RelHolCal-2004, p. 184

♦ 1003 ♦ **Ganna (Genna)**
January 7

The CHRISTMAS celebration in Ethiopia, which is officially called **Leddat**, takes place on January 7 (*see* OLD CHRISTMAS), observing the Coptic Orthodox calendar. But it is more popularly known as Ganna, after the game that is traditionally played by boys, young men, and occasionally elders, on this day. According to legend, the shepherds were so happy when they heard about the birth of Jesus that they used their hooked staffs to play ganna—a game similar to field hockey. Pilgrims gather in the spectacular medieval churches in Lalibela for services, music, and food.

SOURCES:
AnnivHol-2000, p. 6
BkFestHolWrld-1970, p. 151
BkHolWrld-1986, Jan 7
EncyChristmas-2003, p. 228
FolkWrldHol-1999, p. 28
GdWrldFest-1985, p. 74

♦ 1004 ♦ **Gansabhauet**
November 11

Gansabhauet is an old and peculiar festival involving a dead goose, held only in the country town of Sursee, Lucerne Canton, Switzerland, on St. Martin's Day (*see* MARTINMAS). A dead goose is hung by its neck in front of the town hall, and young men draw lots to take turns trying to knock it down with a blunt saber. (*Gansabhauet* means "knocking down goose.")

The young men, blindfolded and wearing red robes and big round masks representing the sun, get only one try at the bird. While the men whack at the goose, children's games take place: they scale a stripped tree, race in sacks, and compete in seeing who can make the ugliest face.

Gansabhauet was first mentioned in 1821. Its real origin is uncertain, although it is thought that it may have something to do with the old practice of handing over payment in kind to the landlord.

CONTACTS:
Switzerland Tourism, Swiss Center
608 Fifth Ave.
New York, NY 10020
877-794-8037 or 212-757-5944; fax: 212-262-6116
www.myswitzerland.com

◆ 1005 ◆ Garifuna Settlement Day
November 19

Garifuna Settlement Day honors the heritage of the Garifuna people, a unique ethnic group in the Caribbean and Central America. Their ancestors were Nigerian captives, who were sent in 1635 from West Africa to the New World to work on plantations and in mines. They were shipwrecked off St. Vincent island, an accident that offered freedom to those who survived. Those who reached the island were taken in by the Carib Indians, who were of South American origin but had lived there for some time. Intermarriage gave rise to the Garifuna, a people that combined the spiritual and artistic traditions of Africa, the Caribbean, and South America.

The Garifuna got along well with the French settlers who arrived later in the 17th century, but when the British came, there was friction. War broke out, and the Garifuna and their French allies eventually surrendered to the superior British forces in 1796. The Garifuna people were then exiled and imprisoned on another island, Baliceaux. More than half of them died there. Those who survived were moved again the following year. Packed onto ships under appalling conditions, they were sent to Roatán Island, near the coast of Honduras. Legends say that the captives hid cassava, one of their staple foods, under their clothing, where it was watered and kept alive by their sweat. Released at Roatán, they quickly settled in Honduras, establishing fishing villages and taking up their former lifestyle.

In 1832, a civil war caused many Garifuna, under the leadership of Alejo Beni, to leave Honduras and settle in Dangriga, Belize. They arrived there on November 19. In 1941, that date was declared Garifina Settlement Day in Dangriga by Thomas Vincent Ramos, one of the community's leaders. In 1943, Garafina Settlement Day was declared a bank and public holiday in the southern districts of Belize, and it is now celebrated throughout the country. The activities often include a reenactment of the landing of the Garifuna in boats. There may be Thanksgiving Masses held in the Catholic churches, followed by long sessions of traditional drumming and dancing. Garifuna crafts and food are sold and displayed. Events to raise awareness and appreciation of Garifuna culture are common, including special days to dress in traditional clothing, a Miss Garifuna Belize beauty pageant, parades, and rallies.

CONTACTS:
Embassy of Belize in the United States
2535 Massachusetts Ave. N.W.
Washington, D.C. 20008
202-332-9636; fax: 202-332-6888
www.embassyofbelize.org

◆ 1006 ◆ Garland Day
May 12; May 29

On May 12, or **Old May Day**, the children of the Dorset fishing village of Abbotsbury still "bring in the May." They do this by carrying garlands from door to door and receiving small gifts in return. The May garlands are woven by a local woman and her helpers, who are regarded as the town's official garland-makers. Each garland is constructed over a frame and supported by a stout broomstick, which is carried by two young people as they go about the village. Later, the garlands are laid at the base of the local war memorial.

At one time this was an important festival marking the beginning of the fishing season. Garland Day used to center around the blessing of the wreaths, which were then carried down to the water and fastened to the bows of the fishing boats. The fishermen then rowed out to sea after dark and tossed the garlands to the waves with prayers for a safe and plentiful fishing season. This ceremony may be a carry-over from pagan times, when sacrificial offerings were made to the gods of the sea.

Another Garland Day celebration is held in Castleton, Derbyshire, on May 29 or SHICK-SHACK DAY. The Garland King (or May King) rides on horseback at the head of a procession of musicians and young girls, who perform a dance similar to the HELSTON FLORA DAY furry dance. The "garland" is an immense beehive-shaped structure that fits over his head and shoulders, covered with greenery and flowers and crowned with a special bouquet called the "queen." This is laid at the war memorial in Castleton's marketplace.

CONTACTS:
Visit Britain
551 Fifth Ave., Ste. 701, 17th Fl.
New York, NY 10176
800-462-2748 or 212-986-2266; fax: 212-986-1188
www.visitbritain.us

SOURCES:
AnnivHol-2000, p. 81
DictDays-1988, p. 46

◆ 1007 ◆ Garma Festival
August

Although the Garma Festival is a relatively new event, it celebrates one of the oldest living cultures on earth, the Yolngu of Australia's Northern Territory. The cultural life of this Aboriginal people, whose history stretches back over 40,000 years, is the focus of this festival, which takes place over four days in August. In the spirit of *garma*, a Yolngu word that describes a "two-way learning process," indigenous Australians gather with non-indigenous Australians and international visitors for cultural exchange.

The festival was introduced in 1998 by the Yothu Yindi Foundation, an organization committed to preserving Yolngu culture. Each year people from all over the globe come to Arnhem Land, located in the Northern Territory, for a hands-on experience with the Yolngu.

The centerpiece event of the festival is the daily *bunggul* ceremony, an afternoon gathering that features dances and music performed in traditional dress. Educational activities include classes on how to play the *yidaki* (didgeridoo); fields trips into the bush to collect native plants and foods; and an overview of spear-making. Every year the festival includes an academic forum that investigates issues facing the Yolngu and other indigenous peoples.

CONTACTS:
Garma Festival
G.P.O. Box 2727
Darwin, Northern Territory 0801 Australia
www.garma.telstra.com

♦ 1008 ♦ Gasparilla Pirate Festival
Early February

A 164-foot reproduction pirate ship sails up Florida's Tampa Bay and into the Hillsborough River with its cannons booming. About 500 costumed pirates lower themselves over the side and "capture" the city of Tampa and its mayor, raising the pirate flag over city hall. Thus begins the **Gasparilla Pirate Invasion**, one of the nation's largest and best-attended celebrations. The mock invasion is followed by a three-hour victory parade featuring members of a men's club known as Ye Mystic Krewe, which started the pirate festival in 1904.

The festival is named for José Gaspar, an 18th-century Spanish pirate who terrorized the Florida coast from around 1783 until his death in 1821, when he wrapped a length of anchor chain around his waist and leapt into the sea brandishing his sword rather than be captured by a U.S. Navy warship.

CONTACTS:
Eventmakers Corporation
3701 W. Azeele St.
Tampa, FL 33609
813-353-8070; fax: 813-353-8075
www.eventmakers-fl.com

SOURCES:
AmerBkDays-2000, p. 127
AnnivHol-2000, pp. 34, 35
BkHolWrld-1986, Feb 7
FolkAmerHol-1999, p. 74
GdUSFest-1984, p. 37

♦ 1009 ♦ Gaspee Days
May-June

The British revenue schooner *Gaspee* was sent to the American colonies to reinforce various British revenue laws, including the Townshend Acts of 1767. Because of these laws, colonists had to pay taxes to the British on imported goods they bought from England. As a result, smuggling was common. The colonists at Rhode Island burned the ship on June 10, 1772, in what many regard as the first act of rebellion leading up to the Revolutionary War.

Since 1966 the event has been commemorated in a festival that includes a symbolic reenactment of the burning, a fife and drum muster, and a colonial parade. There are also numerous athletic events and a gala ball. The events, which take place in both Cranston and Warwick, Rhode Island, were proclaimed part of the "Year of the Gaspee" in 1972, the bicentennial of this early stage in the struggle for independence.

See also RHODE ISLAND INDEPENDENCE DAY

CONTACTS:
Gaspee Days Committee
P.O. Box 1772
Warwick, RI 02888
401-781-1772
www.gaspee.com

SOURCES:
AmerBkDays-2000, p. 341
GdUSFest-1984, p. 166

♦ 1010 ♦ Gawai Dayak
Late May to early June

Gawai Dayak is a rice harvest festival of the Dayak people of Sarawak, Malaysia, on the northern coast of Borneo. Some aspects of the celebrations have remained essentially the same for centuries. They take place in longhouses, the bamboo-and-palm-leaf structures built on stilts that are shared by 20 or 30 families. At midnight on the eve of Gawai Dayak, a house elder conducts the chief ritual: while sacrificing a white cock, he recites a poem to ask for guidance, blessings, and a long life. Other events include the selection of the most beautiful man and woman to be king and queen of the harvest, dancing, a feast of rice, eggs, and vegetables, and the serving of traditional *tuak*, rice wine.

CONTACTS:
Sarawak Tourism Board
6th & 7th Fl., Bangunan Yayasan Sarawak
Jalan Masjid Kuching
Yayasan Sarawak, 93400 Malaysia
6082-423-600; fax: 6082-416-700
www.sarawaktourism.com

SOURCES:
BkHolWrld-1986, Jun 2
GdWrldFest-1985, p. 132

♦ 1011 ♦ Gedaliah, Fast of (Tsom Gedalyah, Tzom Gedaliahu)
Between September 8 and October 6; Tishri 3
(first day following Rosh Hashanah)

Nebuchadnezzar, the Babylonian king, destroyed Jerusalem and the First Temple and carried away most of the Jews into slavery in 586 B.C.E. But he left behind a few farmers and families under the supervision of a Jewish governor named Gedaliah ben Ahikam to clean up after the army and to administer affairs in the devastated land. Eventually some Jews who had managed to hide out in the hills came back to the area and joined the thousand or so who had been left behind.

Things progressed well until a few hot-headed traitors, who accused Gedaliah of collaborating with the enemy, murdered him and the small garrison of soldiers Nebuchadnezzar had stationed there. Many of the farmers took their families and fled in terror to Egypt; the rest were either killed or taken to Babylon, bringing about Judah's final collapse. The Fast of Gedaliah commemorates the man who was assassinated at a time when he was needed most.

SOURCES:
DaysCustFaith-1957, p. 245
OxYear-1999, p. 726
RelHolCal-2004, p. 53

♦ 1012 ♦ Geerewol Celebrations
Rainy season, late June to mid-September

Geerewol Celebrations are elaborate week-long festivities held by the Wodaabe people of Niger as a kind of male beauty contest. The festivities also serve the important purpose of allowing young men and women to meet prospective mates outside their circle of cousins.

There are two main dances to the celebrations, the *yaake* and the *geerewol*.

The yaake is the dance for demonstrating charm. The men paint their faces with pale yellow or red powder and borders of black kohl around their eyes; they also shave their hairline to heighten the forehead. They dance in a line, leaning forward on tiptoe to accentuate their height, and contorting their faces with rolling eyes, pursed lips, and inflated cheeks. Their charm and personality is judged based on these expressions.

The geerewol is held to select the most beautiful men. In this dance the men line up wearing beads on their bare chests and turbans adorned with ostrich feathers on their heads. For a couple of hours they chant and jump and stomp while selected young unmarried women kneel and scrutinize them. These women are the judges; eventually they walk toward the dancers and indicate their favorites by swinging their arms.

The Geerewol celebration ends at sunrise after an entire night of dancing when the host group presents the departing guests with roasted meat.

CONTACTS:
Niger Embassy
2204 R St. N.W.
Washington, D.C. 20008
202-483-4224; fax: 202-483-3169
www.nigerembassyusa.org

African Ceremonies Inc.
230 W. 41st St.
New York, NY 10036
fax: 207-794-7330
www.africanceremonies.com

♦ 1013 ♦ General Clinton Canoe Regatta
May, Memorial Day weekend

Originally a re-creation of the historic trip down the Susquehanna River by General James Clinton during the Revolutionary War, this well-known canoe regatta now has three divisions, one for professionals and two for amateurs, based on the type of canoe used. The professional race, which has gained national recognition as the **World Championship Flat Water Endurance Race**, is the longest one-day race of its kind and covers a 70-mile stretch of the river between Cooperstown and Bainbridge, New York. When it was first held in 1962, it was a one-day affair, but now the regatta and the events associated with it extend for three and a half days over the MEMORIAL DAY weekend. There are cash prizes, and the event attracts canoeists from Canada, Michigan, Minnesota, and Wisconsin.

In addition to the races, a carnival and many other activities for spectators are held at General Clinton Park. It was, in fact, money raised by the races that enabled the Bainbridge Chamber of Commerce to purchase the riverfront land on which the park now stands.

CONTACTS:
Bainbridge Chamber of Commerce
P.O. Box 2
Bainbridge, NY 13733
607-967-8700; fax: 607-967-3207
www.canoeregatta.org

SOURCES:
GdUSFest-1984, p. 122

♦ 1014 ♦ George Tupou V (King), Birthday of
August 1

Located in the Pacific Ocean some 1,250 miles north of New Zealand, the island nation of Tonga consists of about 150 islands, 36 of which are inhabited. With a population of about 120,000, Tonga is ruled by a royal family that goes back to 1831. August 1st marks one event in the recent history of the royal family.

With the death of King George Tupou IV at the age of 88 in September 2006, his son became King George Tupou V. His coronation took place on August 1, 2007. The new king's birthday is in May, but he decreed in 2007 that his birthday would be changed to August 1st and officially celebrated on that day. The first birthday celebration included such foreign dignitaries as Samoa's Head of State, the Korean Ambassador to Tonga, and the British High Commissioner to Tonga.

CONTACTS:
General Consulate of Tonga in San Francisco
360 Post St. , Ste. 604
San Francisco, CA 94108
415-781-0365

♦ 1015 ♦ Georgia Day
February 12

Also known as **Oglethorpe Day**, February 12 commemorates the day in 1733 when James Edward Oglethorpe and 120 other Englishmen landed in Savannah, Georgia, to establish a new colony. The earliest European settlers observed the day by firing salutes and offering toasts in Oglethorpe's honor. For almost 200 years thereafter, the celebrations were confined to major anniversaries of the event, and it wasn't until 1933 that February 12 became a "special day of observance" in the Georgia schools. In 1965 the anniversary of the state's founding was officially proclaimed Georgia Day.

On February 12 there is a procession through the historic town of Savannah and a luncheon. Since 1966 there has been a reenactment of Oglethorpe's landing, with costumed residents playing the roles of Georgia's first European settlers and of the American Indians who greeted them upon their arrival.

CONTACTS:
Savannah Convention and Visitors Bureau
101 E. Bay St.
Savannah, GA 31401
877-728-2662 or 912-644-6400; fax: 912-644-6499
www.savcvb.com

Georgia Secretary of State
Capitol Tours and Information Desk
214 State Capitol
Atlanta, GA 30334
404-656-2844; fax: 404-656-0513
www.sos.state.ga.us

SOURCES:
AmerBkDays-2000, p. 137
AnnivHol-2000, p. 26
GdUSFest-1984, p. 39

♦ 1016 ♦ **Georgia Harmony Jubilee**
Late April

Established in 2004, the week-long Georgia Harmony Jubilee celebrates the 1896 founding of Fitzgerald, Ga., by a group of some 2,000 Northern Civil War veterans and local Southerners. The idea came from Indianapolis newspaper publisher P.H. Fitzgerald, who was impressed when the state of Georgia donated huge quantities of food to help out drought-stricken towns in the North and Midwest. He saw that the wounds of the Civil War had finally healed. Fitzgerald proposed a town where elderly Northern veterans could retire to live with their former enemies. He organized the American Tribune Soldiers' Colony Company, which purchased 60,000 acres of virgin forest in southern Georgia for the project. The city's core is formed by seven streets named after Confederate Civil War generals, seven streets named after Union Civil War generals, and four named after Civil War ships. Sidewalks in the town are painted blue and gray in remembrance of the colors worn by the two armies.

The spirit of harmony—the ability of two former enemies to come together to form a new community 30 years after the end of the American Civil War—is the focus of the annual celebration. Highlights include a staging of *Our Friends, the Enemy,* a play about the town's founding, musical concerts, historical seminars, a tour of historic homes, arts and crafts, and a parade featuring flag bearers from all 50 states.

CONTACTS:
Fitzgerald Area Convention and Visitors Bureau
115 S. Main St.

Fitzgerald, GA 31750
800-386-4642 or 229-426-5033; fax: 229-426-5037

♦ 1017 ♦ **Georgia Independence Day**
May 26

Georgia Independence Day celebrates the republic's brief period of independence from Tsarist Russia from May 26, 1918, until its forced incorporation into the Soviet Union in 1922. Georgia declared its independence from the former Soviet Union on April 9, 1991, but the national holiday commemorates the country's original independence earlier in the century.

CONTACTS:
Republic of Georgia Embassy
2209 Massachusetts Ave. N.W.
Washington, D.C. 20008
202-387-2390; fax: 202-387-0864
www.usa.mfa.gov.ge

♦ 1018 ♦ **Georgia Peanut Festival**
October

A harvest festival paying tribute to Georgia's top crop is held in Sylvester, the Peanut Capital of the World. More peanuts are produced in the region around Sylvester than anywhere else in the state, and Georgia accounts for nearly half the U.S.'s peanut production and supplies five percent of the world's total production. Furthermore, Georgia's peanuts are a $2.5 billion industry. In other countries, the end products of peanuts are usually oil and meal; Georgia's harvest is largely used for salted and roasted peanuts and peanut butter.

This festival, which comes at the end of the peanut harvest time, began in 1964. Highlights through the years have included an appearance by George Bush, Sr. in 1979 to kick off his unsuccessful drive for the Republican presidential nomination, and the making of the World's Largest Peanut Butter and Jelly Sandwich in 1987. The sandwich measured 12½ feet by 12½ feet.

Events of the festival include a beauty pageant to choose a Little Miss Peanut, Junior Miss Peanut, and Georgia Peanut Queen; a peanut-syrup-and-pancakes eating contest; a peanut-recipe contest for school children; concerts; clogging exhibitions; a kiddy parade and a grand parade (the state's largest commodity parade) with 150 to 200 entries, including floats, horses, antique cars, and people dressed as peanuts.

CONTACTS:
Sylvester-Worth County Chamber of Commerce
301 E. Franklin St.
P.O. Box 768
Sylvester, GA 31791
229-776-7718; fax: 229-776-7719

♦ 1019 ♦ **Georgiritt (St. George's Parade)**
March-April, Monday after Easter

St. George is honored each year at Traunstein in Bavaria, Germany, and in other Bavarian villages on EASTER MONDAY to mark April 23, the day on which he is said to have been martyred in 303. The Georgiritt, or St. George's Parade, commemorates the legend of George's victory over the dragon that was threatening the pagan city of Sylene by demanding that humans be sacrificed to feed it. St. George killed the dragon, saved the king's daughter (who was next in line to be sacrificed), and converted Sylene's 15,000 citizens to Christianity.

Because St. George is usually depicted on horseback, the farmers of Traunstein decorate their own horses with garlands and ribbons and ride them across the fields and three times around the parish church. After the local priest blesses the horses and other farm animals, the procession turns toward the village. The festival ends with ritualistic sword dances that have been handed down from medieval times.

See also ST. GEORGE'S DAY

SOURCES:
FestWestEur-1958, p. 64

♦ 1020 ♦ **Geranium Day**
April and May

Since the 1920s this has been a day in England to collect money for the blind. It represents a joint effort by a number of charities dedicated to helping the blind and is organized by the Greater London Fund for the Blind. Although at one time real geraniums were given to those who made donations, these days contributors receive a sticker with a red geranium on it. And there are now two collection days—one in the City of London in April and one in the greater London area in May.

The choice of the geranium—a flower without a strong scent—seems unusual as a symbol for the blind, but it may have been chosen simply because the poppy (*see* MEMORIAL DAY) and the rose (*see* ALEXANDRA ROSE DAY) were already being used for fund-raising purposes. It may also have been chosen for its symbolic meaning: consolation.

CONTACTS:
Greater London Fund for the Blind
12 Whitehorse Mews, 37 Westminster Bridge Rd.
London, SE1 7QD United Kingdom
44-20-7620-2066; fax: 44-20-7620-2016
www.glfb.org.uk

SOURCES:
DictDays-1988, p. 47

♦ 1021 ♦ **German-American Day**
October 6

Descendants of the earliest German settlers have observed October 6 as **German Pioneer Day** or **German Settlement Day** since 1908, commemorating the day on which the first permanent German settlement in America was established at Germantown, Pennsylvania, in 1683. But it wasn't until 1987 that October 6 was formally designated German-American Day by President Ronald Reagan.

According to the 2000 census, German Americans are the largest ancestry group in the United States—almost 43 million people reported they were of German ancestry—and their traditions and institutions have had a wide-ranging impact on the American way of life.

This day is often observed by attending programs and events that promote an understanding of the contributions of German immigrants—for example, lectures on German history, art, music, and literature; exhibits featuring German artifacts; performances of German music and hymns; and church services that acknowledge German-American members of the congregation. Ohio observes German-American Heritage Month throughout October, and smaller celebrations are held in more than 2,000 communities across the country. In recent years, October 6 has also become a time to celebrate GERMAN UNIFICATION DAY (October 3).

CONTACTS:
German American National Congress
4740 N. Western Ave.
Chicago, IL 60625
773-275-1100; fax: 773-275-4010
www.dank.org

United German-American Societies of Greater Chicago
6540 N. Milwaukee Ave.
Chicago, IL 60631
630-653-3018; fax: 630-668-5243
www.germanday.com

SOURCES:
DictDays-1988, p. 47

♦ 1022 ♦ **German-American Volksfest**
July-August

The German-American Volksfest is a cultural fair and carnival held each summer in Berlin, Germany, that celebrates American life and the close relationship of the German and American peoples.

The Volksfest was first celebrated in 1961, closing on August 13th of that year as the Berlin Wall was being erected to separate East and West Berlin. Each summer since that time, visitors to the fairgrounds at the intersection of Clayallee and Argentinische Allee in Berlin-Dahlem have strolled the U.S. Main Street and enjoyed a typical American carnival midway with more than 100 rides and games. Food vendors offer such traditional American fare as hot dogs and hamburgers, and beverage stalls sell beer and wine imported from the United States. Activities include daily bingo games in the casino and a pageant naming Mr. and Miss German-American Volksfest. History and cultural exhibits are also presented, with each year's festival highlighting a unique theme, such as a particular state or region within the United States. Past themes have showcased New Orleans, Louisiana, and the Mississippi riverboat culture of the 19th century, the quaint New England charm of autumn in Massachusetts, and the trend-setting southern California style of Los Angeles. Other exhibits draw attention to modern or historic events that have strengthened German-American relations, such as the Berlin Airlift of 1948.

More than 500,000 people attend the Volksfest each year, enjoying a continuous program of musical entertainment that ranges from country music and rock-n-roll to Motown soul and Memphis blues.

CONTACTS:
Hans Purwin KG
Riemerstrasse 11
Berlin 13507 Germany
www.deutsch-amerikanisches-volksfest.de/e-start.htm

♦ 1023 ♦ **German-Speaking Community, Feast Day of the**
November 15

Each of the autonomous regions of Belgium observes its own feast day. Of the three linguistic communities that make up Belgium's population—the Flemish, French, and German—the German-speaking is the least populous. Most individuals of this community reside in a tiny enclave of the Walloon Region that is a separate political entity within the Belgian federal system. This day is an occasion for German speakers to celebrate their ethnic heritage and political autonomy. Feast days in other regions of Belgium include FEAST DAY OF THE FLEMISH COMMUNITY, FEAST DAY OF THE FRENCH COMMUNITY, IRIS FEST, and WALLOON REGIONAL DAY.

Feast Day of the German-Speaking Community was pronounced by parliamentary decree on October 1, 1990, the same day that leaders decided on the German community's emblem and flag. To mark the occasion, regional flags are hung from public buildings in the German-speaking region as well as at locations outside the region with affiliations to the German-speaking community. This holiday falls on the same date as the KING'S BIRTHDAY, a celebration of Leopold I (1790–1865) that has special relevance for the German-speaking community.

CONTACTS:
Belgian Embassy in Washington, D.C.
Belgium Embassy
3330 Garfield St. N.W.
Washington, D.C. 20008
202-333-6900
www.diplobel.us

♦ 1024 ♦ **German Unification Day**
October 3

Unity Day celebrates the reunification of East and West Germany that took place on October 3, 1990. In setting the date of the official reunification, West German Chancellor Helmut Kohl wanted to honor the historic events of November 1989, in which the government of East Germany resigned and thousands of citizens scaled the Berlin Wall and began to demolish it. He did not want to overshadow other important November observances, however, such as ALL SOULS' DAY on November 2 and KRISTALLNACHT on November 9-10. He instead chose October 3, because the German Meteorological Association informed him that, on average, the best weather in Germany occurs on that day.

German Unity Day is observed with speeches, marches, and public events, including the government's official Unity Day celebration street festival, which draws about 300,000 people annually. Each year the location changes so that the celebration rotates among all of the German states.

CONTACTS:
German Embassy
4645 Reservoir Rd. N.W.
Washington, D.C. 20007
202-298-4000; fax: 202-298-4249
www.germany-info.org

♦ 1025 ♦ **Gettysburg Civil War Heritage Days**
First week in July

The Battle of Gettysburg on July 1-3, 1863, marked a turning point in the American Civil War. It was here that General Robert E. LEE'S Confederate army of 75,000 men and the 97,000-man Northern army of General George G. Meade met by chance when a Confederate brigade sent there for supplies observed a forward column of Meade's cavalry. The ensuing battle did not end the war, nor did it attain any major military goals for either the North or the South. But the Confederate army was turned back, and it never recovered from its losses. With 51,000 casualties and 5,000 dead horses, the Battle of Gettysburg ranks as the bloodiest battle in American history.

Every year since 1983 the anniversary of the battle has been commemorated at the Gettysburg National Military Park. Civil War reenactment groups in authentic uniforms, carrying 19th-century weapons of the type used in the battle, demonstrate infantry tactics and drill, cavalry drill, and soldiers' occupations and pastimes. There are also band concerts, a Civil War battle reenactment, lectures by nationally known historians, and a Civil War collectors' show featuring antique arms and uniforms, documents, books, photographs, and personal effects from pre-1865 American military history.

CONTACTS:
Gettysburg National Military Park
1195 Baltimore Pike, Ste. 100
Gettysburg, PA 17325
717-334-1124; fax: 717-334-1891
www.nps.gov

Gettysburg Official Web Site
89 Steinwehr Ave.
Gettysburg, PA 17325
717-334-2100; fax: 717-334-6905
www.gettysburg.com

♦ 1026 ♦ **Gettysburg Day**
July 1

The Battle of Gettysburg, which began on July 1, 1863, was a turning point in the Civil War. Under the leadership of General Robert E. LEE, Confederate soldiers were advancing toward Harrisburg, Pennsylvania, when they encountered General George G. Meade's Union forces. On the third day of the battle, Lee ordered his men to attack the center of the Union line in an action that later came to be known as Pickett's Charge. But Meade had anticipated just such a strategy, and the rebels were forced to retreat to Virginia. The toll of missing, wounded, and dead was more than 23,000 for the North and 28,000 for the South.

On the 50th anniversary of the battle, Civil War veterans reenacted Pickett's Charge. There continued to be major observances at the Gettysburg battlefield on all the major anniversaries, although the 75th (in 1938) was the last in which surviving Civil War veterans actually participated. The annual observation takes place throughout the week of July 1 and includes speeches by distinguished guests, a military band concert, and a parade with floats illustrating historic events (*see* GETTYSBURG CIVIL WAR HERITAGE DAYS).

CONTACTS:
Gettysburg National Military Park
1195 Baltimore Pike, Ste. 100
Gettysburg, PA 17325
717-334-1124; fax: 717-334-1891
www.nps.gov

Gettysburg Official Web Site
89 Steinwehr Ave.
Gettysburg, PA 17325
717-334-2100; fax: 717-334-6905
www.gettysburg.com

SOURCES:
AmerBkDays-2000, p. 492
AnnivHol-2000, p. 111

♦ 1027 ♦ Ghana Farmers' Day
First Friday in December

Much of Ghana's national economy revolves around agriculture, so it is only appropriate that this African country reserves a date to honor its farmers and provide them a day off from their labors. The national administration also uses the occasion to announce its agricultural plans and development policies for the next year.

In 1985 the Provisional National Defense Council, which then constituted Ghana's administration, established the holiday in response to a drought three years before that had imposed serious burdens on farmers and agricultural production. Ghanaian leaders wished to highlight the farmers' struggles and convey their plans to revitalize the agricultural industry. That year's festivities were held in Osino in the Eastern Region, which was most affected by the drought. Similarly, subsequent celebrations have convened in the regions of the country most affected by harvest-time conditions like drought or flooding.

An important component of the day is the awards ceremony, which is held on the regional and the national levels. Judges who have followed farmers' achievements throughout the year bestow prizes for excellence in such categories as husbandry practices, ecological awareness, use of new technology, and contributions to the local community.

CONTACTS:
Embassy of Ghana
3512 International Dr. N.W.
Washington, D.C. 20008
202-686-4520; fax: 202-686-4527

♦ 1028 ♦ Ghana Republic Day
July 1

Ghana's Republic Day celebration is one of the most striking in West Africa, due to the fact that the popular attire includes the brightly colored cloth known as the *kenti*. Although at one time each tribe's kenti had a distinctive pattern, weave, and color combination, today most are orange or yellow with a hexagonal pattern. Men wear it draped over one shoulder and around the waist, while women may wear it as a long skirt.

July 1 is the day on which Ghana became an independent republic in 1960. The people also celebrate March 6 as Independence Day—the day in 1957 when British rule ended and Ghana became the first state in the British Commonwealth to be governed by black Africans.

CONTACTS:
Embassy of Ghana
3512 International Dr. N.W.
Washington, D.C. 20008
202-686-4520; fax: 202-686-4527
www.ghanaembassy.org

SOURCES:
AnnivHol-2000, pp. 40, 110
NatlHolWrld-1968, p. 100

♦ 1029 ♦ Ghanafest
Last Saturday of July

Ghanafest is a one-day, annual event held on the last Saturday of July and sponsored by the Ghana Club of Chicago and other ethnic associations representing Ghanians in the Chicago area. It attracts about 20,000 participants each year to Chicago's Washington Park. The festival celebrates the history and culture of that west African nation and recognizes the special bond of unity between Ghana and the United States.

Begun in 1987 as the Ga-Dangme HOMOWO Festival of Thanksgiving, Ghanafest acquired its current name in 1990. The festival includes a Ghanian Durbar, or gathering of the royal court. Chiefs, queens, and elders of the traditional council participate in a royal procession, and Ghanian and American officials and guests give speeches. Entertainers from Ghana perform in a variety of musical styles, and marketplace vendors offer wares ranging from textiles, fine art, and jewelry to foods, including fried fish, Jollof-rice, and okro-soup. The occasion is also used to give community appreciation and achievement awards to notable attendees.

CONTACTS:
Ghana National Council of Metropolitan Chicago
4433 N. Ravenswood Ave.
Chicago, IL 60640
773-561-5498; fax: 773-271-0335
www.ghananationalcouncil.org/ghanafest.htm

SOURCES:
AAH-2007, p. 183

♦ 1030 ♦ **Ghanta Karna (Gathyamuga)**
July-August; 14th day of waning half of Hindu month of Sravana

This day commemorates the death of Ghanta Karna, or "Bell Ears," a demon with jingling bells in his ears so that he'd never have to hear the name of Vishnu. In Hindu mythology he caused death and destruction wherever he went, until a god in the form of a frog persuaded him to leap into a well, after which the people clubbed him to death and dragged his body to the river to be cremated.

Also known as the **Festival of Boys** because young boys play a primary role in the celebration of Ghanta Karna's death, this day is observed in Nepal by erecting effigies at various crossroads and making passers-by pay a toll. After they've spent the day collecting tolls and preparing for the Ghanta Karna funeral, the boys tie up the effigy with a rope and throw it in the river. Sometimes the effigy is set on fire before being thrown in the water. Young girls hang tiny dolls on the effigy of Ghanta Karna to protect themselves from the monster.

Children also sell iron rings on this day and use the money to buy candy. It is believed that those who have iron nails in the lintels of their homes or are wearing an iron ring will be protected from evil spirits in the coming year.

CONTACTS:
Kantipur Online
Subidhanagar, Tinkune
Kathmandu, BA 8559 Nepal
977-1-4480100; fax: 977-1-4470178
www.kantipuronline.com

SOURCES:
BkHolWrld-1986, Aug 23
FolkWrldHol-1999, p. 464

♦ 1031 ♦ **Giant Lantern Festival**
December 23-24

This festival is a highlight of CHRISTMAS in the Philippines. In San Fernando, Pampanga, giant lanterns of colored paper and *capiz* shells, some 12 feet in diameter, are lit and carried in a parade. The event attracts crowds of people from Manila and nearby provinces.

CONTACTS:
Philippine Tourism Center
556 Fifth Ave.
New York, NY 10036
212-575-7915; fax: 212-302-6759
www.wowphilippines.com.ph

SOURCES:
EncyChristmas-2003, p. 604

♦ 1032 ♦ **Giants, Festival of the (Belgium)**
Fourth weekend in August

In many French and Belgian towns, people carry giants—towering figures representing various biblical, historical, or legendary characters—through the streets in their religious and other festival processions.

One of Belgium's more distinctive and colorful pageants, held in Ath (or Aat), highlights the "Marriage of the Giants." The origins of the festival are a little vague, but the giants—Goliath and his bride, strong-man Samson, a warrior named Ambiorix, and several others—are supposed to date from the mid-15th-century Procession of St. Julien. Other figures were added by local guilds over the years, and today the procession is known as **Les Vêpres de Gouyasse**, because it portrays the marriage of Goliath.

The giants, 20-foot-tall figures made of wicker and cloth, are paraded through the streets; men are underneath the figures and see where they're going by peering out through peepholes. Goliath wears a helmet and breastplate, his bride has orange blossoms in her hair, Samson carries a broken column. After they lumber through the streets to the Church of St. Julien, Goliath and his lady are married.

Along with the giants is the legendary horse, Bayard, purported to be able to change size according to the size of his rider. The medieval story has it that four brothers, the sons of Aymon, were carried by the mighty steed Bayard as they fled the wrath of Charlemagne. The horse and its riders were tracked to a high cliff above the Meuse River; the horse gave a tremendous leap and carried the riders to safety across the river. The replica of the horse weighs about three-quarters of a ton and is propelled by a dozen men while four boys ride on its back.

Besides the procession, the day is marked by the shooting of muskets, revelry, eating, drinking, and dancing.

CONTACTS:
Belgian Tourist Office
220 E. 42nd St., Ste. 3402
New York, NY 10017
212-758-8130; fax: 212-355-7675
www.visitbelgium.com

SOURCES:
FestWestEur-1958, p. 16

♦ 1033 ♦ **Giants, Festival of the (Fête des Géants)**
Begins on the Sunday following July 5

The huge figures that are often carried in procession through the streets of France used to be made of wicker supported by a light wooden frame, but their modern counterparts are usually made of plastic.

For three days and nights during the Fête des Géants in Douai, France, the figure of Gayant is carried through the streets to the accompaniment of drums and church bells. About 25 feet tall and wearing a military uniform, Gayant is followed by his wife, Marie, who is 20 feet high and always dressed in the latest fashion. Then come their three children—Jacquot, Fillion, and the baby, Binbin. The giants leave their home on Rue de Lambres and go to the town hall to salute the mayor, after which they continue on to the Place D'Armes and take part in the carnival festivities.

Another famous procession of the giants takes place in the city of Lille on WHIT-MONDAY, when more than 100 of these fabulous figures are carried through the streets of the town.

CONTACTS:
Douai Tourist Office
70 Place d'Armes
Douai, 59500 France
33-3-2788-2679; fax: 33-3-2799-3878
www.ville-douai.fr

SOURCES:
BkFestHolWrld-1970, p. 65

♦ 1034 ♦ Gibraltar National Day
September 10

The Rock of Gibraltar is a peninsula located on the southern tip of Spain. On September 10, 1967, the people of Gibraltar participated in a national referendum and rejected the option for their small territory to pass under Spanish control. Instead, the Rock of Gibraltar remained a British territory with an arrangement of local sovereignty. Since 1967, Gibraltarians have commemorated the referendum date with celebrations coordinated by the Ministry of Culture.

In recent years, Gibraltar National Day has become an event to foster pride and has extended into Gibraltar National Week. Events leading up to the momentous day are held at different venues and include dance performances, military band concerts, and a governor's parade.

On National Day, people typically dress in the national colors of red and white. A popular tradition is the ceremonial release of 30,000 red and white balloons, each of which represents an individual living on the rock.

CONTACTS:
Gibraltar Tourist Board
www.gibraltar.gi/home

Government of Gibraltar / Ministry for Heritage, Culture, Youth & Sport
310 Main St.
Gibraltar

♦ 1035 ♦ Gift of the Waters Pageant
First full weekend in August

The tract of land now known as Hot Springs State Park in Thermopolis, Wyoming, originally belonged to the Shoshone and Arapaho Indians. They sold it to the United States in 1886, receiving about $60,000 worth of cattle and food supplies in return. Within the boundaries of the land were several hot mineral springs known for their healing powers. In 1889 the Wyoming State Legislature established the site as a park, stating that one-quarter of the water from the main spring—known as Big Spring, the largest hot mineral spring in the world—was to be set aside for public use. There has been a free bathhouse there since 1902.

The highlight of the event known as the Gift of the Waters Pageant is the reenactment of the signing of the treaty deeding the mineral springs to the people of Wyoming. The role of Washakie, chief of the Shoshones, was originally played by Chief Washakie's son, and later by his great-grandson.

CONTACTS:
Thermopolis Chamber of Commerce
220 Park St.
P.O. Box 768
Thermopolis, WY 82443
877-864-3192 or 307-864-3192; fax: 307-864-3128
www.thermopolis.com

SOURCES:
GdUSFest-1984, p. 217

♦ 1036 ♦ Giglio Feast
About two weeks ending July 16

The feast days of Our Lady of Mount Carmel (July 16) and St. Paulinus (June 22) are celebrated together by Italian Americans at the parish of Shrine Church of Our Lady of Mount Carmel in Brooklyn, New York. St. Paulinus (d. 431) was an architect in Nola, Italy, near Naples, who gave himself up to marauders so that a widow's son could be free. In the end, St. Paulinus secured the freedom of all the citizens who had been captured and placed into servitude.

For about two weeks leading up to July 16, there are daily masses and other religious devotions, parties, games, and stands offering Italian sausage, pizza, seafood, and other foods.

The highlights of the festival are the two processions of the giglio (Italian for "lilies"), a huge tower about six stories high and decorated with lilies. On Giglio Sunday, usually the Sunday after July 4, the statue of St. Paulinus is placed atop the giglio and paraded through the parish streets accompanied by a marching band and the singing of the Giglio Song ("O' Giglio 'e Paradiso"). A large boat is also carried to represent the boat that brought St. Paulinus and other freed slaves back home. The procession ends at the church, where there is a special Giglio mass. Afterwards, people retake the streets for the lifting and rotating of the giglio—a tricky feat for the 100 or more men who maneuver the three- or four-ton structure.

On July 16 it all happens again, this time with the giglio carrying the statue of Our Lady of Mount Carmel. One of the notable events of the intervening days is the children's giglio, in which children under 16 do their own parading and lifting with much smaller and lighter structures.

See also LILY FESTIVAL; OUR LADY OF CARMEL, FEAST OF

CONTACTS:
Shrine Church of Our Lady of Mount Carmel
275 N. 8th St.
Brooklyn, NY 11211
718-384-0223; fax: 718-384-5838
www.olmcfeast.com

SOURCES:
FolkAmerHol-1999, p. 302

♦ 1037 ♦ Gilroy Garlic Festival
Last full weekend in July

This event is a celebration of garlic in the California town, located in Santa Clara County, that calls itself the Garlic Capital of the World. The claim is made because 90 percent of America's garlic is grown and processed in the area. Humorist Will ROGERS once described Gilroy as "the only town in America where you can marinate a steak by hanging it on the clothesline."

The highlight of the festival is Gourmet Alley with dozens of food booths that use eight tons of garlic in preparing various garlic-flavored dishes, including garlic ice cream. Other events are a Great Garlic Cook-off and Recipe Contest, arts and crafts exhibits, musical entertainment, and a barn dance.

CONTACTS:
Gilroy Garlic Festival Association Inc.
7473 Monterey St.
P.O. Box 2311
Gilroy, CA 95020
408-842-1625
www.gilroygarlicfestival.com

♦ 1038 ♦ **Ginem**
December

The Bagobo are a Malay people who live in southeastern Mindanao in the Philippines. In December each year, they observe a ceremony known as the Ginem to thank the spirits for domestic and military successes, to ward off illness, and to drive off the *buso*, a class of demons feared by the Bagobo because they eat the flesh of the dead. At one time the Bagobo went on a skull raid before the Ginem, tying the skulls to ceremonial poles. Today the poles, without skulls, are decorated and carried into the *datu's*, or chief's, house. A chicken is sacrificed, and offerings of clothes and knives are made in the hope that the spirits will grant a good harvest and health. There is feasting, dancing, and singing until dawn. In areas where the ceremony lasts more than one day, the feasting continues.

SOURCES:
DictFolkMyth-1984, p. 454

♦ 1039 ♦ **Ginseng Festival**
September 5-7

This festival is a celebration of ginseng in Fusong, a county in the Changbai Mountains of China and the largest ginseng grower in the country. The twisted roots of the ginseng, an herb, have for centuries been considered a cure for many ills as well as an aphrodisiac. The people of Fusong have traditionally celebrated the ginseng harvest, and in 1987 the government officially set aside three days for both a festival and a trade fair of ginseng products. The festival features performances of yangko, dragon, and lion dances; story-telling parties with a ginseng theme; art and photo exhibits; and a fireworks display. The trade fair has exhibits not only of ginseng products but also of Chinese medicines and local crafts.

CONTACTS:
China National Tourist Office
370 Lexington Ave., Ste. 912
New York, NY 10118
888-760-8218 or 212-760-8218; fax: 212-760-8809
www.cnto.org

♦ 1040 ♦ **Gioco del Ponte**
Last Sunday in June

The *Gioco del Ponte*, or "Battle for the Bridge," in Pisa, Tuscany, Italy, goes back to the 13th century. Following a medieval procession, two teams in full medieval costume take part in a traditional competition which involves a reversal of the usual tug-of-war. About 20 or 30 men from each team line up behind a mechanism on rails and push. The first team to make a "goal" on the opposing side wins; the winner is determined by the best of six matches, or a draw match if both teams win three.

CONTACTS:
Tourist Consortium of the Pisa Area
P.O. Box 215
Pisa, 56100 Italy
39-50-8302-53; fax: 39-50-8302-43
www.pisae.it/Inglese/index_old.php

♦ 1041 ♦ **Gion Matsuri**
July 17

Gion Matsuri is the best-known festival in Japan and the biggest in Kyoto. It began in the year 869 when hundreds of people died in an epidemic that swept through Kyoto. The head priest of the Gion Shrine, now called the Yasaka Shrine, mounted 66 spears on a portable shrine, took it to the emperor's garden, and the pestilence ended. In gratitude to the gods, the priest led a procession in the streets. Except for the period of the Onin War (1467-77), which destroyed the city, the procession has been held ever since.

There are events related to the festival throughout July but the main event is the parade of elaborate, carefully preserved floats on July 17. There are 29 *hoko* ("spears") floats and 22 smaller *yama* ("mountains") floats. The immense hoko weigh as much as 10 tons and can be 30 feet tall; they look like wonderfully ornate towers on wheels. They are decorated with Chinese and Japanese paintings and even with French Gobelin tapestries imported during the 17th and 18th centuries. Just under their lacquered roofs musicians play flutes and drums. From the rooftops of the floats two men toss straw good-luck favors to the crowds. The hoko roll slowly on their big wooden wheels, pulled with ropes by parade participants.

Yama floats weigh only about a ton, and are carried on long poles by teams of men. Life-sized dolls on platforms atop each float represent characters in the story the float depicts.

The towns of Hakata (Fukuoka Prefecture), Narita (Chiba Prefecture), and Takayama (Gifu Prefecture) have imitated the Kyoto celebration and now have their own "Gion" festivals.

See also AOI MATSURI; HAKATA GION YAMAGASA; JIDAI MATSURI

CONTACTS:
Japan Information Network, Japan Center for Intercultural
  Communications
2-7-7 Hirakawacho
Chiyodaku
Tokyo, 102-0093 Japan
81-3-3263-5041; fax: 81-3-3230-4107
home.jcic.or.jp

SOURCES:
AnnivHol-2000, p. 119
BkHolWrld-1986, Jul 17
JapanFest-1965, p. 44

♦ 1042 ♦ Girl Scout Day
March 12

This observance marks the anniversary of the founding of the American Girl Scouts by Juliette Gordon Low (1860-1927) in Savannah, Ga., in 1912. The day is the focal point of Girl Scout Week, which begins on the Sunday before March 12 and is observed by Girl Scout troops nationwide in various ways—with community service projects, anniversary parties, and plays. The 80th anniversary in 1992 was celebrated with various events, including the kick-off of a national service project on the environment.

CONTACTS:
Girl Scouts of the USA
420 Fifth Ave.
New York, NY 10018
800-478-7248 or 212-852-8000; fax: 212-852-6509
www.girlscouts.org

SOURCES:
AmerBkDays-2000, p. 195
AnnivHol-2000, p. 43
DictDays-1988, p. 47

♦ 1043 ♦ Gita Jayanti
November-December; 11th day of waxing half of Hindu month of Margasirsa

The birthday of the *Bhagavad Gita*—a Sanskrit poem relating a dialogue between Lord Krishna and Arjuna found in the Hindu epic *Mahabharata*—is celebrated by reading and reciting passages from the *Gita* and by holding discussions on its philosophical aspects. This is also a day on which Hindus fast, worship Krishna, and resolve to put more effort into their study of the *Gita*. Why is this day considered the birthday of the *Gita*? Some texts assert that on the 11th day of the waxing half of Margasirsa, Lord Krishna taught Arjuna the sacred lore of the *Gita* on the battlefield of Kurukshetra, and thus made available to the entire human race the poem often referred to as the "Song Celestial."

SOURCES:
DictWrldRel-1989, p. 96
RelHolCal-2004, p. 180

♦ 1044 ♦ Glorious Twelfth
August 12

August 12 is the legal opening of grouse season in Scotland. If the 12th falls on a Sunday, **Grouse Day** is the following day. Because grouse-shooting has always played such a central role in the life of Scottish gentlemen, the occasion is referred to as the Glorious Twelfth and is observed as a social event by Scots around the world.

SOURCES:
DictDay-1988, pp. 48, 51, 103
OxYear-1999, p. 330

♦ 1045 ♦ Glyndebourne Festival Opera
May-August

Now considered one of the most prestigious opera festivals in the world, the Glyndebourne Festival was founded in 1934 by music lover John Christie and his wife, Audrey Mildmay, who was an opera singer. They built an opera house on the grounds of their Elizabethan estate in Glyndebourne, about 54 miles south of London, and formed an opera company. In the beginning, Christie wanted to stage only Wagnerian operas, but his wife and some of the musicians who helped him put the festival together eventually persuaded him that the emphasis should be on the operas of MOZART. The repertoire expanded even further after Christie's death in 1962, when his son George took over. During the current 11-week season, several full-length operas are presented, at least one of which is by Mozart.

The Glyndebourne Festival has a reputation for spotting and showcasing young talent. It was here that Birgit Nilsson performed in 1951, Joan Sutherland in 1956, and Luciano Pavarotti in 1964. The London Philharmonic Orchestra has been the main ensemble since 1964, and the chorus consists of young British singers who are often selected to sing major roles. The performances start in the late afternoon, and opera-goers are encouraged to bring a picnic dinner so they can eat outdoors and enjoy the grounds during the 85-minute intermission.

CONTACTS:
Glyndebourne Productions Ltd.
Glyndebourne
Lewes, East Sussex BN8 5UU United Kingdom
44-12-7381-2321; fax: 44-12-7381-2783
www.glyndebourne.com

SOURCES:
GdWrldFest-1985, p. 92
MusFestEurBrit-1980, p. 54

♦ 1046 ♦ Goddess of Mercy, Birthday of the
March-April, 19th day of third lunar month; October-November, 19th day of 10th lunar month

The birthday of the Goddess of Mercy is a celebration of Kuan Yin, the *Bodhisattva* ("Buddha-to-be") of infinite compassion and mercy. One of the most beloved of Buddhist deities, he or she is accepted not only by Buddhists but also by Japanese, Chinese, and Koreans. This deity has been depicted as both masculine and feminine and sometimes as transcending sexual identity (with soft body contours but also a moustache).

The *Lotus Sutra*, or scripture, says Avalokitesvara (the deity's Sanskrit name, meaning "the lord who looks in every direction") is able to assume whatever form is needed to relieve suffering. He/she exemplifies the compassion of the enlightened and is known in Tibet as *Spyan-ras gzigs,* "with a pitying look." Kuan Yin, the Chinese name, means "regarder of sounds," or "of the voices of the suffering." The Japanese word for the deity is pronounced "Kannon."

Women especially celebrate Kuan Yin. In Malaysia, hundreds of devotees bearing joss sticks, fresh fruit, flowers, and sweet cakes gather twice a year at temples dedicated to Kuan Yin in Kuala Lumpur and Penang to pray for her benevolence. (She is feminine there and in China, Korea, and Japan.) At the old temple at Jalan Pitt, Penang, puppet shows are staged in celebration of her. In Hong Kong, Kuan Yin is honored on the 19th day of the sixth lunar month at Pak Sha Wan in Hebe Haven.

See also SANJA MATSURI

CONTACTS:
Malaysian Tourism Promotion Board
818 W. 7th St., Ste. 970
Los Angeles, CA 90017
800-336-6842 or 213-689-9702; fax: 213-689-1530
www.tourismmalaysiausa.com

SOURCES:
DictWrldRel-1989, p. 79
EncyRel-1987, vol. 2, p. 552

♦ 1047 ♦ Going to the Fields (Veldgang)
Between April 27 and May 21; Monday before Ascension Thursday

On Rogation Monday (*see* ROGATION DAYS), the inhabitants of the eastern Netherlands village of Mekkelhorst form a procession to the fields to ask God's blessing on all growing things. With the women and girls walking two abreast at the front of the procession, they follow the boundaries of the parish, stopping briefly at an ancient boundary oak and then proceeding to the fields to kneel before a crucifix and pray for a prosperous harvest.

Rogationtide processions like this one are believed to stem from an ancient Roman tradition. The ROBIGALIA is one example of a spring ritual designed to promote the growth of the newly sown crops and to head off diseases that might harm them. Another ancient Roman tradition was to have young maidens visit the fields at the end of May to drive out winter.

SOURCES:
FestWestEur-1958, p. 132
SeasFeast-1961, p. 220

♦ 1048 ♦ Gokarna Aunsi
Between August and September; during the waning half of the Hindu month of Bhadrapada

A Hindu festival unique to Nepal, Gokarna Aunsi honors fathers living and dead. Also known as **Kuse Aunsi**, it is celebrated during Bhadrapada, a lunar month in the Hindu calendar. It takes place during the month's dark fortnight, placing it sometime between August or early September.

In Nepalese culture, fathers are highly regarded as the pillars of the family and the community, so the festival has a significant place among religious days. Children with living

fathers show their appreciation by giving presents and sweets. After the presentation of gifts, it is customary for sons to touch their fathers' feet with their foreheads, while daughters will touch their hands. This tender gesture is known as "looking upon father's face."

Those whose fathers are deceased also pay tribute. One noteworthy ceremony takes place at the Gokarneswor Mahadeva shrine of Gokarna, a village located just east of Nepal's capital, Kathmandu. The shrine has special significance for Hindus because they believe it was the dwelling site of Shiva, who is attributed with having special affinity with the souls of dead.

CONTACTS:
Nepal Tourism Board
Tourist Service Center
Bhirkuti Mandap
Kathmandu, Nepal
www.welcomenepal.com

SOURCES:
FolkWrldHol-1999, p. 513
RelHolCal-2004, p. 173

♦ 1049 ♦ Gold Discovery Days
Third weekend in July

This five-day festival celebrates the beauty of the Black Hills and the discovery of gold on July 27, 1874, near the present-day city of Custer, South Dakota. The scientific expedition led by General George Custer confirmed the growing speculation about gold in the area and opened the way for a steady influx of eager prospectors. The festival includes a street fair, hot air balloon rally, golf tournament, and musical productions. But the highlight of the event is the Paha Sapa Pageant which recreates this important era in South Dakota's history.

Part one of the pageant depicts the *Paha Sapa,* or sacred land of the Sioux Indians. Part two portrays the lure of gold and the coming of Custer's expedition. In part three the Sioux display their rich cultural heritage by performing ancient ceremonial dances. At the end of the pageant, the entire cast—many of whom have participated since they were children—reappear in special costumes to create a "living flag" of the United States.

CONTACTS:
Custer Chamber of Commerce
615 Washington St.
P.O. Box 5018
Custer, SD 57730
800-992-9818 or 605-673-2244; fax: 605-673-3726
www.custersd.com

♦ 1050 ♦ Gold Star Mother's Day
Last Sunday in September

Since 1936 the last Sunday in September has been designated by the U.S. Congress as Gold Star Mother's Day in the United States, honoring the mothers of U.S. service men and women who have died at war. The Gold Star mothers' group was founded in the aftermath of World War I by Grace Darling Siebold, whose son George had been killed in an air battle over France in 1918. She found solace in volunteering at a hospital for wounded veterans and in meeting with the mothers of other soldiers who were killed in the war. The group, officially the American Gold Star Mothers, incorporated itself in Washington, D.C., in 1928 with 25 founding members. The organization took its name from the customary symbol used to denote a family member killed in action during the First World War. Families with active service personnel hung banners in their windows with blue stars signaling the number of family members who were in service. If one was killed, the blue star was replaced by a gold star.

As of 2008, the group counted nearly 1,000 mothers among its membership. Each year Gold Star Mother's Day is commemorated during several ceremonies in the nation's capital, including flower and wreath laying services at the Vietnam Veterans Memorial Wall and the Tomb of the Unknowns in Arlington National Cemetery. The American Gold Star Mothers' national convention coincides with Gold Star Mother's Day, and includes a banquet and a reception for veterans at the organization's headquarters in Washington, D.C.

CONTACTS:
American Gold Star Mothers, Inc.
2128 Leroy Pl. N.W.
Washington, D.C. 20008
202-265-0991; fax: 202-265-6963
www.goldstarmoms.com

SOURCES:
PatHols-2006, p. 254

◆ 1051 ◆ Golden Chariot and Battle of the Lumecon, Procession of the
June

Held on a Sunday in June in Mons, Belgium, this event commemorates the delivery of the town from the plague in 1349. In the morning, a golden chariot carrying a reliquary of St. Waudru is drawn by white horses through the city, followed by clerics and girls dressed in brocades and lace. In the afternoon, ST. GEORGE, mounted on a steed, fights the dragon (the *lumecon*), a terrible-tailed beast called Doudou. The battle represents the triumph of good over evil. Before the fight starts, spectators sing the "Song of the Doudou" while carillons ring. Much boisterous merrymaking and feasting culminates in the evening with a pageant presented by 2,000 actors, musicians, and singers.

CONTACTS:
Belgian Tourist Office
220 E. 42nd St., Ste. 3402
New York, NY 10017
212-758-8130; fax: 212-355-7675
www.visitbelgium.com

◆ 1052 ◆ Golden Days
Third week in July

Golden Days is a celebration in Fairbanks, Alaska, of the discovery of gold here on July 22, 1902, and the Gold Rush days

that followed. This is the largest summertime event in Alaska. Its 10 days of activities include "Fairbanks in Bloom," billed as the farthest-north flower show, a rubber ducky race, beard and hairy-leg contests, drag races, a golf tournament, concerts, and a grand parade.

There's also a Felix Pedro look-alike contest. Felix Pedrone (remembered as Felix Pedro) was the Italian immigrant who first found gold on a creek near what is now Fairbanks.

CONTACTS:
Fairbanks Convention and Visitors Bureau
550 First Ave.
Fairbanks, AK 99701
800-327-5774 or 907-456-5774; fax: 907-452-2867
www.explorefairbanks.com

◆ 1053 ◆ Golden Orpheus
June

Named after the Greek god of song and poetry who, according to legend, lived in the Balkan and Rhodope mountains, the Bulgarian popular music competition known as Golden Orpheus is held every summer in Slanchev Bryag (meaning "Sunny Beach"), a resort town on the Black Sea. Musicians from more than 60 countries compete in every category of popular music, including synthesizer, soul, big band, and pop. A prize is given for the best pop song by a Bulgarian composer, and there is an international competition for singers and instrumentalists. World-renowned conductors, directors, and musicologists serve as the jury for the 10-day festival.

CONTACTS:
Bulgarian Travel Information
National Tourism Promotion and Information Agency
1, Sveta Nedelia Sq.
Sofia, 1040 Bulgaria
359-2-933-58-45; fax: 359-2-989-69-39
www.bulgariatravel.org/eng/index.php

SOURCES:
GdWrldFest-1985, p. 27

◆ 1054 ◆ Golden Shears World Shearing and Wool-handling Championships
Late February or March

The Golden Shears World Shearing and Wool-Handling Championships take place every year in late February or early March in Masterton, New Zealand. Participants with all levels of experience compete in shearing, wool handling, and wool pressing as individuals or in teams. There is also a triathlon event. As many as 120 competitors can take part in a single event. This can require more than 700 sheep, as uniform in size as possible. For the competitors, speed, skill, and style are all important in this fiercely competitive activity, which is keenly followed by fans in New Zealand, Australia, and beyond.

The first Shearing World Championships took place in March 1961 at the War Memorial Stadium in Masterton. It was so popular that the local army was called in to control the crowds. Within a few years, seats for the contest were being sold out 12 months in advance. The event's success inspired other communities in New Zealand and other countries to sponsor local shearing contests, and the level of physicality and technique at the championship grew higher. By the late 1980s, competitive shearing and wool handling had become an established, if unorthodox, athletic event.

CONTACTS:
Golden Shears International Shearing Society
Shear Discovery Centre
12 Dixon St.
P.O. Box 311
Masterton, New Zealand
www.goldenshears.co.nz/index.htm

♦ 1055 ♦ Golden Spike Anniversary
May 10

This reenactment of the completion of America's transcontinental railroad on May 10, 1869, at Promontory Summit, Utah, has been held since 1952. It is supposed to be historically accurate, but differs from accounts of the time, which greatly varied because the crowds kept the members of the press from actually seeing the ceremony. Complicating efforts to reconstruct events, some reporters wrote their stories days before the event occurred.

The building of the transcontinental railroad was a prodigious feat. It was started in 1863, with the Central Pacific working eastward from Sacramento and the Union Pacific laying tracks westward from Omaha. The Central Pacific crews faced the rugged Sierras almost immediately, and also had to have every rail, spike, and locomotive shipped around Cape Horn. Union Pacific had easier terrain, but its crews were harassed by Indians. The Union Pacific crews were Irish, German, and Italian immigrants, Civil War veterans, and ex-slaves. California's labor pool had been drained by the gold rush, so the railroad imported 10,000 Chinese who became the backbone of the labor force.

Today, preliminary events start at 10 A.M., and at 12:30 P.M. two trains—the Central Pacific's "Jupiter" and Union Pacific's "119" (reproductions of the original locomotives that were present in 1869)—steam from opposite directions on the track and meet at the site of the ceremony where men in period dress speak. Then the Golden Spike and three other spikes are tapped into a special railroad tie; at 12:47 an ordinary iron "last spike" is driven into the last tie to connect the railroads and the message "D-O-N-E" is sent by ham radio to the California State Railway Museum in Sacramento. Originally the message "D-O-N-E" was telegraphed (along lines strung beside the railroad) to San Francisco and Philadelphia. There is then much noise of train whistles, bands playing, and people shouting and hurrahing. A second reenactment is performed at 2 P.M.

There were four ceremonial spikes at the original ceremony. One was the famous Golden Spike; it was engraved on the top, "The Last Spike," and on one side, "May God continue the unity of our Country as the Railroad unites the two great Oceans of the World." That spike was made by San Francis-

co jewelers from $350 worth of gold supplied by David Hewes, a contractor friend of Central Pacific President Leland Stanford.

The other spikes were a second gold spike, not engraved, a silver spike from Nevada, and an iron spike from Arizona that was clad in silver and topped with gold.

There was also a polished laurel-wood tie for the ceremonial last tie. Four holes had been augured in it, and the ceremonial spikes were tapped into the holes. (Nobody tried to drive a soft gold spike into a hardwood tie.) The engraved Golden Spike and the silver spike are in the possession of Stanford University, and the iron spike from Arizona belongs to the Smithsonian Institution. The second gold spike and the hardwood tie have been lost, probably during the San Francisco earthquake of 1906. The spikes used in the reenactments are replicas.

CONTACTS:
Utah Office of Tourism, Council Hall
300 N. State St.
Salt Lake City, UT 84114
800-200-1160 or 801-538-1030
www.utah.com

Golden Spike National Historic Site
National Park Service
P.O. Box 897
Brigham City, UT 84302
435-471-2209; fax: 435-471-2341
www.nps.gov

SOURCES:
AmerBkDays-2000, p. 354
AnnivHol-2000, p. 80

♦ 1056 ♦ Good Friday
Between March 20 and April 23; Friday before Easter

There are several theories as to why the day commemorating Jesus' crucifixion is called "Good" Friday. Some scholars think it's a corruption of "God's Friday," while others interpret "good" in the sense of "observed as holy," or to signify that the act of the Crucifixion is central to the Christian view of salvation. It is called **Great Friday** by Orthodox Christians, but it's not surprising that the Friday before EASTER is sometimes referred to as **Black Friday** or **Sorrowful Friday**.

This day has been in the Christian calendar even longer than Easter. And although it was neglected for a long time by Protestant churches, Good Friday has again come into almost universal observance by Christians. From noon to three o'clock many western Christian churches in the U.S. hold the *Tre Ore* (Italian for "three hours," referring to the last three hours Jesus hung on the cross), a service based on the last seven things Jesus said on the cross. Many churches also observe the day by reenacting the procession to the cross as in the ritual of the Stations of the Cross.

In every Orthodox church, the *Epitaphios*, a gold-embroidered pall representing the body of Christ, is laid on a special platform, which is smothered in flowers. During the evening service, the platform is carried out of the church in a procession. The faithful follow, carrying lighted candles and chanting hymns. At squares and crossroads, the procession stops for a prayer by the priest.

Long Friday is another name for Good Friday. In Norway, this day is called **Langfredag**; in Finland, **Pitkäperjantai** (or Long Friday) because it was a day of suffering for Christ.

See also PLEUREUSES, CEREMONY OF

CONTACTS:
Orthodox Church in America
P.O. Box 675
Syosset, NY 11791
516-922-0550; fax: 516-922-0954
www.oca.org

SOURCES:
AmerBkDays-2000, p. 237
BkFest-1937, pp. 6, 16, 30, 41, 56, 70, 86, 96, 103, 112, 121, 147, 167, 184, 211, 227, 249, 259, 275, 291, 300, 309, 330, 338
DaysCustFaith-1957, p. 107
DictFolkMyth-1984, pp. 181, 961, 1072
EncyEaster-2002, p. 234
EncyRel-1987, vol. 3, p. 439
FestSaintDays-1915, p. 62
FestWestEur-1958, pp. 8, 93, 107, 152, 212
FolkAmerHol-1999, p. 168
FolkWrldHol-1999, p. 224
OxYear-1999, p. 618
RelHolCal-2004, pp. 93, 120
SaintFestCh-1904, p. 160

♦ 1057 ♦ **Good Friday (Belgium) (Goede Vrijdag)**
Between March 20 and April 23; Friday before Easter

Belgian churches are draped in black on GOOD FRIDAY, in memory of Jesus' suffering on the cross, and a general air of sadness prevails in the cities and towns. In rural villages, women often wear mourning on this day. In the afternoon, many attend the three-hour Passion service at the local church.

In Veurne, there is a pilgrims' procession that stops before each of the 18 Stations of the Cross, built there in 1680, to pray and sing hymns. The distance between the different stations is said to correspond to the number of steps (5,751) taken by Christ as he went from Jerusalem to Mount Calvary. The original Stations of the Cross were sites associated with Christ's Passion in Jerusalem and the surrounding area. Pictures or carvings of the Stations of the Cross can often be seen on the walls of Roman Catholic churches.

CONTACTS:
Belgian Tourist Office
220 E. 42nd St., Ste. 3402
New York, NY 10017
212-758-8130; fax: 212-355-7675
www.visitbelgium.com

SOURCES:
BkFest-1937, p. 41
BkFestHolWrld-1970, p. 54
FestWestEur-1958, p. 8

♦ 1058 ♦ **Good Friday (Bermuda)**
Between March 20 and April 23; Friday before Easter

The custom of flying kites on GOOD FRIDAY in Bermuda dates back to the 19th century, when a teacher who was having difficulty explaining to his students how Jesus ascended into heaven took them to the highest hill on the island and launched a kite bearing an image of Jesus. When he ran out of string, he cut the line and let the kite fly out of sight. It has been an island tradition since that time for children to fly kites on Good Friday.

Breakfast on EASTER is another Bermudian tradition. It consists of salted cod that has been soaked overnight and then boiled the next day with potatoes. It is served with an olive oil and mayonnaise topping, and sliced bananas on the side.

CONTACTS:
Bermuda Department of Tourism
675 Third Ave., Fl. 20
New York, NY 10017
800-223-6106 or 212-818-9800; fax: 212-983-5289
www.bermudatourism.com

SOURCES:
BkHolWrld-1986, Apr 10
FolkWrldHol-1999, p. 226

♦ 1059 ♦ **Good Friday (England)**
Between March 20 and April 23; Friday before Easter

The Friday before EASTER has often been regarded as a day of ill omen by those in rural areas. In England, bread baked on GOOD FRIDAY was marked with a cross to keep the Devil away, and there was a superstition that hanging a "hot cross bun" in the house on this day would protect it from bad luck in the coming year. Sometimes Good Friday buns or cakes remained hanging on a rack or in a wire basket for years afterward, gathering dust and growing black with mold. A piece of Good Friday cake was thought to be especially good for ill cows.

Other Good Friday superstitions include the belief that breaking a piece of crockery on Good Friday would bring good luck because the sharp point would penetrate Judas Iscariot's body. In rural areas, boys often hunted squirrels on this day, because according to legend, Judas was turned into a squirrel.

SOURCES:
BkFest-1937, p. 56
EncyEaster-2002, p. 178
FestSaintDays-1915, p. 63
FolkWrldHol-1999, p. 241

♦ 1060 ♦ **Good Friday (Italy)**
Between March 20 and April 23; Friday before Easter

Folk processions with realistic images of the dead Jesus displayed on platforms are common in Italian towns and villages on GOOD FRIDAY. Sometimes the platforms are accompanied by cloaked and hooded worshippers, or by large candles carried aloft on long spiked poles. Funereal music and figures of the grieving Mary and angels holding stained graveclothes accompany the procession. Other objects symbolic of the Passion include the cross, the crown of thorns, and the spear. In the afternoon, there is a church service known as *l'agonia*.

At Santa Croce and other churches in Florence, a custom known as "Thrashing Judas Iscariot" traditionally has been observed on Good Friday. Young boys bring long willow rods tied with colored ribbons to church and at a certain point in the service, they beat the benches loudly with the branches.

CONTACTS:
Italian Government Tourist Board
630 Fifth Ave., Ste. 1565
New York, NY 10111
212-245-5618; fax: 212-586-9249
www.italiantourism.com

SOURCES:
BkFest-1937, p. 184
EncyEaster-2002, p. 313
FestSaintDays-1915, p. 64
FestWestEur-1958, p. 93

♦ 1061 ♦ **Good Friday (Mexico) (Viernes Santo)**
Between March 20 and April 23; Friday before Easter

GOOD FRIDAY is a very somber day in Mexico. The churches are often darkened and draped in black. The religious processions that take place on this day represent the funeral that Jesus never had. An effigy of the dead Christ, stained with blood and wearing a crown of thorns, is carried in a glass coffin through the streets. The highlight of these processions is when the statue of Mary, also draped in black, meets the effigy of her crucified son.

The funereal atmosphere is maintained throughout the day. Running, shouting, or using profanity is discouraged, in reverence for the Lord. The mood of those attending church services is very much that of friends and neighbors paying a condolence call on the members of a bereaved family.

See also PASSION PLAY AT TZINTZUNTZAN

SOURCES:
BkFest-1937, p. 227
EncyEaster-2002, pp. 240, 406
FolkWrldHol-1999, p. 235

♦ 1062 ♦ **Good Friday (Poland) (Wielki Piatek)**
Between March 20 and April 23; Friday before Easter

People fast on dry bread and roasted potatoes from GOOD FRIDAY until EASTER Sunday in Poland, but housewives often spend **Great Friday** or **Holy Friday** kneading and rolling out the dough for elaborate Easter cakes. Egg-decorating is also part of the preparations for Easter, and there are three different techniques for decorating eggs: (1) *malowanki* are eggs painted in solid colors with natural substances, such as vegetable skins, roots, or grains; (2) *pisanki* are eggs that are batiked in traditional designs, usually animal or geometrical figures that have been handed down from generation to generation; and (3) *skrobanki* are eggs dyed in solid colors upon which the outlines of birds, flowers, and animals are scratched with a pointed instrument.

In Krakow and other large cities, going from church to church on Good Friday to view the replicas of Jesus' body that are on display traditionally is considered to be an important social event.

See also EASTER IN THE UKRAINE

SOURCES:
BkFest-1937, p. 259
EncyEaster-2002, p. 500

♦ 1063 ♦ **Good Friday (Spain)**
Between March 20 and April 23; Friday before Easter

The religious processions that take place on GOOD FRIDAY in Spain are among the most impressive and elaborate in the world. They are made up of huge *pasos*, or floats, illustrating different scenes in the Passion story and carried by members of various organizations or trade guilds. The pasos are so heavy that it can take 25 or 30 bearers to carry one, and the procession must halt frequently so they can rest.

In Seville, the Good Friday procession dates back to the Middle Ages and includes more than 100 pasos, many of which are elaborate works of art in themselves, with platforms made out of real silver and figures wearing robes embroidered in gold. Among the more outstanding pasos are those portraying the Agony in the Garden, Christ Bearing the Cross, the Crucifixion, and the Descent from the Cross. They are carried by black-robed penitents through the streets of Seville, followed by cross-bearers, uniformed civic leaders, and clergy in magnificent robes.

CONTACTS:
Tourist Office of Spain
666 Fifth Ave., 35th Fl.
New York, NY 10103
212-265-8822; fax: 212-265-8864
www.okspain.org

SOURCES:
BkFest-1937, p. 300
BkFestHolWrld-1970, p. 54
EncyEaster-2002, pp. 240, 565

♦ 1064 ♦ **Goombay!**
Last weekend in August

Goombay! is a celebration of African and Caribbean heritage, culture, and arts held during the last weekend of August at Eagle and Market Streets in Asheville, N.C. A free event sponsored by the Young Men's Institute Cultural Center, Inc., the festival has been held each year since 1982. "Goombay" is a Bantu word that refers both to a goatskin drum and to the music played on it; the word is associated with festivals that commemorate the emancipation of slaves in the British territories of the Caribbean in 1834.

Activities are scheduled over three days and include dance and stilt performances, as well as entertainers in a variety of musical styles, such as reggae, R&B, jazz, and Afro-fusion. In addition, festivalgoers may take part in children's games, mask making, demonstrations of traditional crafts, or, for a fee, participate in African percussion lessons with a master drummer. Food is available at the "Isle of Delight Café," which features Caribbean cuisine.

CONTACTS:
YMI Cultural Center
39 S. Market St.
Asheville, NC 28801
828-252-4614; fax: 828-257-4539
www.ymicc.org

Asheville Convention & Visitors Bureau
151 Haywood St.
Asheville, NC 28802
828-258-6103
www.exploreasheville.com

SOURCES:
AAH-2007, p. 186

♦ 1065 ♦ **Gorilla Naming Ceremony (Kwita Izina)**
Late June

In Kinyarwandan, a language spoken primarily in Rwanda, *Kwita Izina* means "to give a name." The phrase refers to a long-standing ceremony for naming newborn Rwandan babies. In the 21st century, the tradition has extended to naming newborn mountain gorillas. What was once a humble ceremony among park rangers and wildlife conservationists has become an annual international event.

The Rwanda Office of Tourism and National Parks (ORTPN) launched the first gorilla naming ceremony in 2005 as part of a larger effort to monitor gorillas in Rwanda's jungles and to raise awareness about the various factors that threaten the animals and their habitat.

The ceremony, which since 2007 has been known officially as **Kwita Izina**, is a jubilant affair that includes traditional Rwandan dance and music. Past ceremonies have featured the naming of between 10 and 30 gorillas. Each animal is publicly named by a notable figure from Rwanda or another country—typically a conservationist, successful business person, or international celebrity. A fundraising gala dinner often accompanies the Kwita Izina to raise additional funds for gorilla conservation campaigns.

CONTACTS:
Rwanda Office of Tourism and National Parks
Rwanda Tourism Board
Boulevard de la Révolution n°1
P.O. Box 905
Kigali, Rwanda

250-576514; fax: 250-576515
www.rwandatourism.com

♦ 1066 ♦ **Goschenhoppen Historians' Folk Festival**
Second Friday and Saturday of August

The Goschenhoppen region of Pennsylvania, in what is now Montgomery County, was settled in the early 18th century by Mennonite, Schwenkfeldian, Lutheran, Reformed, and Catholic farmers and artisans, most of whom were German immigrants. It remains one of the oldest and most "authentic" Pennsylvania German communities in America. The Goschenhoppen Historians, a group founded in 1963 to study and preserve the culture of the Pennsylvania German, also known as the Pennsylvania Dutch, and related groups, hold an annual Folk Festival at Goschenhoppen Park in East Greenville every summer to educate the public about life in this area during the 18th and 19th centuries and to preserve the traditional skills of the Pennsylvania German people.

Since 1966, when the first Folk Festival was held, the Historians have made every effort to keep the festival as educational and as non-commercial as possible. One of the most interesting aspects is the participation of schoolchildren, who are recruited as apprentices or helpers for the craft demonstrators at the festival. By actively participating in the demonstrations, young people learn traditional skills that might otherwise die out. These include blacksmithing, fishnet making, pewtering, gunsmithing, chair caning, rope making, weaving, and thatch and tile roofing. The Historians also operate a folk life museum and country store.

See also KUTZTOWN FESTIVAL

CONTACTS:
Goschenhoppen Historians Inc.
Red Men's Hall
P.O. Box 476
Green Lane, PA 18054
610-367-8286
www.goschenhoppen.org

Library of Congress
101 Independence Ave. S.E.
Washington, DC 20540
202-707-5000; fax: 202-707-8366
www.loc.gov

♦ 1067 ♦ **Grand Canyon Music Festival**
September

Since 1983, the Grand Canyon National Park has hosted a three-week series of nine concerts of chamber music that promotes music education in the rural and underserved communities near the park. The event began when musicians Robert Bonfiglio and Clare Hoffman, who were hiking at the park, were asked to play a concert for a retiring park ranger. With community and business support, the event has grown to its present scope.

The concerts take place in the Shrine of the Ages on the South Rim of the Grand Canyon National Park and at the Heard Museum, Scottsdale Community College, and on area Indian reservations. The festival has attracted such award-winning composers as John Corigliano, William Bolcom, and Paul Moravec, and concerts are broadcast on National Public Radio. In 2007, the musical groups participating included Trio Solisti, the Calder Quartet, and the string quartet ETHEL. Since 2001, the festival has also sponsored the Native American Composer Apprentice Project to train young composers to write for string quartets.

CONTACTS:
Grand Canyon Music Festival
800-997-8285
www.grandcanyonmusicfest.org

♦ 1068 ♦ Grand Haven Coast Guard Festival
July-August

To honor the men and women who serve in the United States Coast Guard, the port city of Grand Haven, Mich., hosts an annual week-long festival. Grand Haven has been nicknamed "Coast Guard City USA." It is the site of a Coast Guard Sector Field Office that covers the eastern shore of Lake Michigan.

The Grand Haven Coast Guard Festival includes the National United States Coast Guard Memorial Service at Escanaba Park, which remembers those who have given their lives to protect and serve the United States. The park is named in honor of the USCG cutter *Escanaba*, which was torpedoed while engaged in convey escort duty in the North Atlantic during World War II. A total of 101 crew members lost in the tragedy had been stationed in Grand Haven.

Other events include a Kids Parade, a Parade of Ships, free tours of several Coast Guard vessels, live music, a carnival, a Coast Guard retirees' dinner, and the Grand Parade featuring 120 floats.

CONTACTS:
Grand Haven Coast Guard Festival
113 N. Second St.
Grand Haven, MI 49417
888-207-2434 or 616-846-5940; fax: 616-846-2509
www.coastguardfest.org

♦ 1069 ♦ Grand Magal of Shaykh Amadou Bamba
18th day of the Islamic month of Safar

The Grand Magal (or great pilgrimage) of Shaykh Amadou Bamba takes place in Touba, Senegal, on the feast day of Shaykh Amadou Bamba. The Shaykh, who lived from 1850 to 1927, was the country's most revered marabout, or Islamic saint. The pilgrimage is celebrated on the anniversary of the date he was forced by French authorities to depart for a seven-year exile abroad. A charismatic spiritual leader who rejected violence and war, Shaykh Bamba attracted such a large following that the French feared he would challenge their rule. After being allowed to return to Senegal in 1902, he was ordered by the French into a second exile in 1903, this time for four years in Mauritania. In later years, he founded a Sufi order called Mouride (derived from the Arabic word

for "student") and began building the Touba mosque, where he was entombed after his death a year later.

Between one and three million pilgrims attend the Grand Magal each year. Among them are members of the Mouride Brotherhood, which is still run by Shaykh Bamba's descendants. Each year, the current head of the Brotherhood addresses the crowd. Pilgrims seek spiritual guidance from Brotherhood leaders, in addition to offering prayers at the Shaykh's tomb. Once their religious duties are complete, devotees partake of the wares of thousands of vendors who sell food, drink, religious tokens, and crafts on the streets of the city.

CONTACTS:
Senegal Tourism Office
350 5th Ave.
New York, NY 10118
212-279-1953; fax: 212-279-1958
www.senegal-tourism.com

Embassy of Senegal
2112 Wyoming Ave. N.W.
Washington, DC 20008
202-234-0540; fax: 202-332-6315

SOURCES:
UndIslam-2004, p. 397

♦ 1070 ♦ Grand National
First Saturday in April

Grand National is the world-famous steeplechase run at the Aintree Racecourse in Liverpool, England. It was started in 1839 by William Lynn, owner of the Waterloo Hotel in Liverpool, as a means of attracting hotel patrons. The first races were at Maghull just outside Liverpool, but the course was moved to Aintree in 1864 and remained unchanged until 1961 when a railing was erected to keep spectators off the course. The next change was in 1990 when the slope at the infamously hazardous Becher's Brook jump was modified because so many horses had been killed there.

The course is four and one-half miles long and has 16 bush fences, of which 14 are jumped twice. The fences average 5'3" high. All have ditches either on the take-off or landing side. The race is limited now to 40 starters, and usually there is a full field. Of the starters, rarely do as many as half finish, and sometimes only as few as three or four. Horses have to qualify by winning three other set races in England, although any horse that wins the MARYLAND HUNT CUP is automatically eligible to run.

Probably the greatest horse to run the Grand National was Red Rum, a big, strong horse that won in 1973, 1974, and 1977. In 1973, Red Rum set a record for the fastest time—9 minutes, 1.90 seconds.

The race became widely known to the general public with the 1944 movie *National Velvet*, based on the 1935 bestseller by Enid Bagnold. It starred Mickey Rooney, playing an ex-jockey, and Elizabeth Taylor as Velvet Brown, the girl who trains "The Pi" for the Grand National steeplechase. When the jockey scheduled to ride proves unsuitable, Velvet cuts her hair and rides to victory herself, but is disqualified when it's discovered she's a girl. Only men could ride originally, but today women are eligible.

CONTACTS:
Aintree Racecourse
Ormskirk Rd., Aintree
Liverpool, L9 5AS United Kingdom
44-15-1523-2600; fax: 44-15-1522-2920
www.aintree.co.uk

SOURCES:
DictDays-1988, p. 50

◆ 1071 ◆ Grand Prix
March to November

Formerly part of the international racing series that includes the Monaco Grand Prix, the first U.S. Grand Prix was held in 1959 at Sebring, Florida. From 1961 to 1980 it was held at Watkins Glen, N.Y., followed by Detroit (1982-88) and then Phoenix (1989-91). In 1991, however, the racing committee rejected the Phoenix site, and the Grand Prix was not held in the U.S. again until 2000, when it found a new home at the Indianapolis Motor Speedway. The race takes place in September on a new 2.606-mile course contructed at the Speedway.

Points won in this race count toward the World Championship of Drivers. More than 15 Grand Prix races are held yearly in countries around the world; the season runs from March to November.

Like other Grand Prix races, the race at Indianapolis is for Formula One race cars, which are generally smaller and more maneuverable than the cars used in speedway racing. Engine size, fuel, and other specifications are strictly controlled by the Féderation Internationale de l'Automobile (FIA).

CONTACTS:
Federation Internationale de l'Automobile
8 Place de la Concorde
Paris, 75008 France
33-1-4312-4455; fax: 33-1-4312-4466
www.fia.com

U.S. Grand Prix at Indianapolis
Indianapolis Motor Speedway
4790 W. 16th St.
Indianapolis, IN 46222
800-822-4639 or 317-492-6700
my.brickyard.com

◆ 1072 ◆ Grande, Fiesta
December 24-26

Around Christmas time, thousands of Chilean pilgrims gather to honor the Virgen del Rosario (Virgin of the Rosary), patron saint of miners. The ceremonies take place in the copper-mining town of Andacollo, situated in the Andes mountains. The centerpiece of the festival is a famous three-foot wooden statue of the Virgin that is housed in Andacollo's basilica.

The festival pre-dates the founding of Andacollo in 1891. According to legend, an indigenous man found the statue of the Virgin, which is ascribed with magical powers, in the hills of Peru. The relic later found a permanent shrine in the basilica and thereafter became a sacred pilgrimage site.

The festival's main proceedings take place on December 26, during which a religious dance is performed in indigenous costume. Nearby, cockfighting and horseracing attract participants as alterative secular activities.

Andacollo also hosts a separate celebration, Fiesta Chica, which takes place on the first Sunday of October and coincides with the Festival of the Rosary. During that ceremony, the venerated statue is transported from the nearby Temple Antiguo to the basilica in a procession that also features indigenous dances.

CONTACTS:
Embassy of Chile to the United States of America
1732 Massachusetts Ave. N.W.
Washington, D.C. 20036
202-785-1746; fax: 202-887-5579
www.chile-usa.org

◆ 1073 ◆ Grandfather Mountain Highland Games and Gathering of Scottish Clans
Second full weekend in July

This largest and best-known Scottish event in America, held since 1956 on Grandfather Mountain near Linville, N.C., opens with a torchlight ceremony at MacRae Meadows at dusk on Thursday. On Friday athletic and other activities begin and in the evening there's a Celtic Jam, followed by a *ceilidh*, or concert of Scottish folk music. On Saturday a 26.2-mile Mountain Marathon climbs a net elevation of 1,000 feet. Competitions are held throughout the day for Highland dancing, piping, drumming, Scottish fiddling, track and field events, and other athletic events. Entertainment includes sheep-herding demonstrations and performances by pipe bands and Scottish performing artists. Another ceilidh, the Tartan Ball, and a Scottish country dance round out the day. Sunday opens with a worship service, followed by more competitions and entertainment, including the colorful Parade of Tartans and the tug of war between the clans.

One of the founders, Donald F. MacDonald, modeled the event after the Braemar Highland Gathering, thus the Grandfather Mountain Games are often referred to as **America's Braemar**.

See also Alma Highland Festival and Games; Highland Games; and Virginia Scottish Games

CONTACTS:
Grandfather Mountain Highland Games
P.O. Box 1095
Linville, NC 28646
828-733-1333; fax: 828-733-0092
www.gmhg.org

♦ 1074 ♦ Grandparents' Day
September, first Sunday after Labor Day

Grandparents' Day is a far more recent invention than MOTHER'S DAY or FATHER'S DAY. It was fostered by Marion McQuade, and a presidential proclamation on September 6, 1979, made it official. It is observed throughout the United States on the first Sunday after LABOR DAY, except in Massachusetts, where it is observed on the first Sunday in October.

There are a number of ways in which grandparents can be honored and their day celebrated. One is to invite real or "adopted" grandparents to school for the day, where they participate in their grandchildren's classes or special assembly programs. Gift giving is not as widespread on this day as it is on Mother's Day or Father's Day.

See also BABIN DEN

SOURCES:
AnnivHol-2000, p. 164
DictDays-1988, p. 50

♦ 1075 ♦ Grant's (Bill) Bluegrass Festival
Early August

The oldest and largest bluegrass festival west of the Mississippi is held for five days near Hugo, Okla. The festival began in 1969, organized by Bill Grant as an extension of jam sessions in his home. Attendance the first year was less than 1,000; now more than 20,000 show up. There are band and instrument contests for all ages, non-stop entertainment from 10 A.M. until midnight each day, and jam sessions at all hours.

CONTACTS:
Bill Grant's Bluegrass Festival
301 E. Jackson
Hugo, OK 74743
580-326-5063; fax: 580-317-9388
www.grantsbluegrass.com

SOURCES:
MusFestAmer-1990, p. 248

♦ 1076 ♦ Grape Festival
September, Labor Day weekend

The highlight of the Grape Festival held each year in Nauvoo, Illinois, is the historical pageant known as the **Wedding of the Wine and Cheese**. It tells the story of a young French boy who left his unfinished lunch in a limestone cave to keep it cool and then forgot to pick it up. He returned months later and discovered that the bread had grown moldy and spread through the cheese, creating the first blue-veined Roquefort cheese.

In the pageant there is a marriage ceremony celebrating the union of cheese and wine in which a magistrate reads the marriage contract, places it between the wine (carried by the bride) and the cheese (carried by the groom), and circles all three with a wooden hoop symbolizing the wedding ring. The festival also includes parades, a grape stomp, and historical tours.

In the late 1840s, Nauvoo was occupied by French and German Icarians, members of a socialist sect whose creed, "From each according to his ability and to each according to his need," derived from the social-economic philosophy of Karl Marx. The Icarians brought wine-making to the area, and several of their original wine cellars are still used to make the blue cheese that this festival has celebrated for over 50 years. A similar festival is held in Roquefort, France.

CONTACTS:
Nauvoo Tourism Office
1295 Mulholland St.
P.O. Box 500
Nauvoo, IL 62354
877-628-8661 or 217-453-6648; fax: 217-453-2032
www.beautifulnauvoo.com

SOURCES:
GdUSFest-1984, p. 49

♦ 1077 ♦ Grasmere Sports
Late August

This annual event in England's Lake District began in the 1800s to encourage Cumberland and Westmorland wrestling, but it has since expanded to include other traditional Lake District sports. The wrestling competitors stand chest to chest and lock arms behind each other's back. The aim of this subtle form of combat is to throw the opponent to the ground—a goal that many wrestlers struggle all day to achieve while other events are going on elsewhere.

Fell running (a *fell* is a highland plateau), another traditional sport, is an all-out race to the top of the nearest mountain and back. Hound trailing, which reflects the Lake District's importance as a center for fox hunting, is done on foot with packs of hounds who run across the fells after their prey.

Up until 1974, when Cumberland and Westmorland were combined to form Cumbria County, competition between the two rival counties had been fierce.

CONTACTS:
Grasmere Lakeland Sports and Show
Stock Ln., Ambleside, Grasmere
Cumbria, LA22 9SL United Kingdom
44-15-3943-2127
ww.grasmeresportsandshow.co.uk

♦ 1078 ♦ Graveyard Cleaning and Decoration Day
Between May and early September

In some Southern states—particularly Texas, Kentucky, and Tennessee—a day in summer is set aside for honoring the dead and maintaining the local cemetery. Sometimes called **Grave Day**, MEMORIAL DAY, **Decoration Day**, or **Memory Day**, it is a time for families and neighbors to get together, sharing "dinner-on-the-ground" or picnic suppers and listening to sermons. In Pleasant Grove, Kentucky, Grave Day originated as a peace-making ceremony after the Civil War had split Hardin County into two opposing factions.

Graveyard Cleaning Day is often held in July, but it may be observed any time from late May until early September. There usually isn't any connection to official Memorial Day celebrations; the date is a matter of local choice and convenience. In New Orleans, for example, it is customary to whitewash the tombs on ALL SAINTS' DAY. All of these observations, however, harken back to the ancient Roman festival known as the PARENTALIA, an uncharacteristically somber occasion on which people decorated the graves of the deceased with flowers and left food in the cemeteries to sustain the spirits of the dead.

SOURCES:
FolkAmerHol-1999, p. 326

♦ 1079 ♦ **Great American Brass Band Festival**
Mid-June

This weekend re-creation of the golden age of brass bands in America is held at Centre College in Danville, Ky. About a dozen bands from throughout the U.S. and Canada play Sousa march music, ragtime, and jazz in the New Orleans funeral-march style. A highlight is a band playing over-the-shoulder instruments of the Civil War period; the music blew to the rear of the band so it could be heard by the troops marching behind. The festival begins with a hot-air balloon race, and music then continues through the weekend.

CONTACTS:
Great American Brass Band Festival
P.O. Box 429
Danville, KY 40423
800-755-0076 or 859-236-7794; fax: 859-236-9134
www.gabbf.com

♦ 1080 ♦ **Great American Duck Race**
Fourth weekend in August

This uniquely American event started in 1980 in Deming, New Mexico, just to make a little whoopee. Up to 80 live ducks race for cash prizes in an eight-lane chute. There are races that include politicians' heats and a media heat. Other events in the week preceding the duck races are a parade, a lawnmower race, dances, hot-air balloons, an arts and crafts exhibit, an outhouse race, a chili cookoff, a pageant of people dressed like ducks, and a duck contest in which ducks are dressed like people. Race participants come from several states; spectators now number about 20,000, almost double the population of Deming.

Because one duck race a year is not enough, organizers began holding Great American Duck Race II, the Winter Games, over the third weekend in February in 2001. This race is held indoors at the Southwestern New Mexico State Fairgrounds.

CONTACTS:
Great American Duck Race of Deming Inc.
209 S. Diamond
Deming, NM 88030
888-345-1125 or 505-544-0469; fax: 505-544-0774
www.demingduckrace.com

♦ 1081 ♦ **Great American Smokeout**
Third Thursday in November

It was the *Surgeon General's Report on Smoking and Health* that first gave impetus to grassroots efforts to discourage the smoking of cigarettes. As far back as 1971, the town of Randolph, Massachusetts, had asked its residents to give up tobacco for a day. In 1974 the editor of the *Monticello Times* in Minnesota led the first mass movement by smokers to give up cigarettes, calling it "D-Day" for "Don't Smoke." The idea spread quickly throughout Minnesota and skipped west to California in 1977, where it became known as the Great American Smokeout. The following year it was observed nationwide for the first time, under the sponsorship of the American Cancer Society.

The Smokeout focuses attention not only on cigarette smokers but, more recently, on smokeless tobacco users as well. Activities are generally light-hearted rallies, parades, obstacle courses, contests, skits, parties, etc.—all designed to keep smokers away from their cigarettes for an entire day, in the hope that they will continue the effort on their own.

The Cancer Society encourages nonsmokers to "adopt" smokers on this day and support them as they go through withdrawal from nicotine—a drug that is said to be as addictive as heroin. Schools are particularly active in observing the Smokeout, teaching young people that the easiest way to avoid the health problems associated with smoking is never to start. Businesses, hospitals, and other organizations also sponsor programs and activities designed to increase public awareness of the hazards to which both smokers and those who breathe their smoke are exposed—particularly lung cancer.

In recent years, millions of people have quit for the day, and many of them do not return to the habit.

CONTACTS:
American Cancer Society
1180 Ave. of the Americas
New York, NY 10036
800-227-2345 or 212-382-2169; fax: 212-719-0193
www.cancer.org

♦ 1082 ♦ **Great Backyard Bird Count**
Mid-February

The Great Backyard Bird Count takes place every year over four days in mid-February throughout the United States and Canada. Volunteers of all ages and experience, known as "citizen scientists," spend at least 15 minutes counting birds from any location—their home, a park, or a schoolyard. Then they report the number of birds and species they have seen via the Internet. This gives scientists a real-time portrait of which birds are where in North America. The event was launched in 1998 by the National Audubon Society and the Cornell University Ornithology Lab. In 2007, participants submitted more than 80,000 checklists, reporting 11 million birds of 616 different species. The web site of the Great Backyard Bird Count allows participants to track data, get tips on identifying birds, and enter count-related contests.

CONTACTS:
Great Backyard Bird Count
National Audubon Society
700 Broadway
New York, NY 10003
212-979-3000; fax: 212-979-3188
www.audubon.org
www.birdsource.org/gbbc

Cornell Lab of Ornithology
159 Sapsucker Woods Rd.
Ithaca, NY 14850
800-843-2473 or 607-254-2473
www.birds.cornell.edu

♦ 1083 ♦ **Great Battle of Hansan Festival (Hansan Daecheop)**
August

The Great Battle of Hansan Festival is held annually in Tongyeong-si, Gyeongsangnam-do, South Korea, for four days in August. This colorful and eventful celebration marks the stunning victory of Admiral Yi Sun-sin over the Japanese navy at the Battle of Hansan during the Imjin War (1592-1598).

A re-enactment of the battle in the waters off Tongyeong is the undisputed highlight of the event, but dozens of associated activities are also held in this commemoration of Korea's most revered national hero. They include a commemorative parade; performances of music, dance, and drama; art exhibitions; and lectures. Tongyeong, which some refer to as the "Naples of Asia," is a port city renowned for its beautiful setting and vibrant arts scene. The festival has taken place since the 1960s.

CONTACTS:
Great Battle of Hansan Festival
27-1 Docheon-dong
Tongyeong-si, Gyeongsangnam-do 650-110 South Korea
www.hsdf.or.kr/en/index.php

Korea National Tourism Organization
737 N. Michigan Ave., Ste. 910
Chicago, IL 60611
800-868-7567 or 312-981-1717; fax: 312-981-1721
english.visitkorea.or.kr/enu/index.kto

♦ 1084 ♦ **Great Circus Parade**
Mid-July

The Great Circus Parade in Milwaukee, Wisconsin, is a re-creation of a 19th-century circus street pageant. Featuring more than 60 historic circus wagons, 700 horses, wild animals in cages, and hundreds of musicians, clowns, and costumed participants, this annual procession begins with the loading of the half-mile-long circus train at the Circus World Museum in Baraboo. Horses are used to load the flatcars according to traditional circus methods, and the train then embarks on a three-day, 382-mile journey through Wisconsin, arriving in Milwaukee after making several stops at communities in the central and eastern part of the state.

The parade follows a three-mile route through downtown Milwaukee. The wagons are part of the Circus World Museum's collection of historic wagons and show vehicles, many of which have undergone extensive restoration. A display of circus wagons and performances under the Big Top can be seen at Milwaukee's Veterans' Park, which is transformed into the Great Circus Parade Showgrounds for the week of festivities in mid-July.

CONTACTS:
Circus World Museum
550 Water St., Hwy. 113
Baraboo, WI 53913
866-693-1500 or 608-356-8341; fax: 608-356-1800
www.circusparade.com

♦ 1085 ♦ **Great Falls Ski Club Mannequin Jump**
Saturday in early April

In the zany sport of mannequin jumping, contestants build a mannequin—which could represent anything from Sponge Bob Square Pants to a Ninja Turtle—and send it flying off a 15-foot ski jump. The audience just marvels and laughs. Hundreds of spectators come to watch the mannequins fly—and often self-destruct on the way down.

The Great Falls Ski Club Mannequin Jump, which the organizers call "the strangest ski jumping contest on the planet," is held on the first Saturday in April at the Showdown Ski Area in Showdown, Mont. This annual contest has been held since 1995. In addition to the main event, the day's activities feature children's diversions, photography, comedy, and a wide variety of winter sports, including downhill skiing, snowshoeing, snowboarding, and snowmobiling.

CONTACTS:
Showdown Ski Area
2850 Hwy. 89
Neihart, MT 59465
406-236-5522 or 800-433-0022
russell.visitmt.com/listings/9199.htm

♦ 1086 ♦ **Great Locomotive Chase Festival**
First weekend in October

This three-day celebration in Adairsville, Ga., commemorates the storied Civil War locomotive chase that led to the execution of six Union soldiers by the Confederates.

The chase came on April 12, 1862 (the one-year anniversary of the Confederate attack on Fort Sumter), after the Yankee spy, James J. Andrews, stole the Confederate engine named "The General," along with three boxcars and the tender. His plan was to burn the rail bridges between Atlanta and Chattanooga, in order to cut Confederate supply lines.

Andrews swiped the locomotive at Big Shanty (Kennesaw), Georgia, and roared off, stopping to cut telegraph wires and tear up tracks. In due time William A. Fuller, conductor of "The General," who had been having breakfast when his train was stolen, realized something was missing and set off in a handcar with Anthony Murphy. In Adairsville, they boarded the locomotive "Texas," and barreled after "The General" and Andrews, who was trying to reach the bridge at Resaca so he could burn it. The drivers of "The General" kept throwing things on the track to derail the "Texas," but the "Texas" kept in pursuit.

Finally, the Yankee raiders were out of fuel and had nothing left to throw on the track; arriving in Ringgold, Andrews ordered his men to jump and run. They did, but all were apprehended. Andrews and six others were tried and hanged; others were taken as prisoners until being exchanged, and later they received medals from the Union army. The Confederates won the accolades of the Army of the Confederacy.

In 1927, Buster Keaton made the movie *The General* based on the chase, and in 1956, a Disney movie, *The Great Locomotive Chase*, later retitled *Andrews' Raiders*, retold the old story.

Events of the festival include showings of the locomotive-chase movies, a grand parade, beauty pageants, fireworks, and gospel singing. There are also such contests as three-legged races, a marshmallow-spitting contest, a bean-bag toss, a balloon toss, and a tug of war. Attendance is estimated at more than 10,000.

CONTACTS:
Cartersville-Bartow County Convention & Visitors Bureau
P.O. Box 200397
Cartersville, GA 30120
800-733-2280 or 770-385-1357
www.notatlanta.org

♦ 1087 ♦ Great Montana Sheep Drive
August 31

Called "The World's Largest Small Town Parade," the Great Montana Sheep Drive is similar to the annual Running of the Bulls in Pamplona, Spain.

The event, founded in 1989, features hundreds of Montana-bred sheep herded down the six blocks of Main Street in downtown Reed Point, Mont. In a parody of the Spanish bull event, a handful of Reed Point volunteers dressed in black berets and red sashes run ahead of the sheep. There is also a parade, with historic covered wagons and re-enactors dressed in period costumes of the Old West, a log-cutting contest, a shoot-out between two gunfighters, carnival games, and an evening street dance. The lighthearted event has raised money for community projects in the small town (with a population of 185), including a new fire truck and the refurbishing of the town library. Some 12,000 people attend the annual event, making Reed Point one of Montana's largest towns on the weekend of the sheep drive.

CONTACTS:
Reed Point Community Club
P.O. Box 402
Reed Point, MT 59069
406-326-2315

♦ 1088 ♦ Great Moonbuggy Race
April

The Great Moonbuggy Race is held every April in Huntsville, Ala., by the National Aeronautics and Space Administration (NASA). The race challenges university and high school stu-

dents, in teams of six, to design, assemble, and test-drive a human-powered vehicle suitable for driving on the moon. Teams must carry the unassembled vehicle components to the race starting-point in a container similar in size to those used for the original Lunar Roving Vehicles. The teams must assemble their buggies. Then two team members, a male and a female, drive them over a half-mile-long course that simulates lunar terrain, complete with "craters," "rocks," "lava" ridges, and more. Teams are allowed two runs of the course. Their lowest time is added to the vehicle-assembly time for their final score. Prizes are awarded to the three fastest teams in both the university and high-school categories: cash and a trophy to the first-place winners, and plaques to the others. There are special prizes for most unique and most improved vehicle, a rookie award, and a system safety award. Typically about 50 schools take part in all, from about 15 states, and from as far away as Puerto Rico and Germany.

The Great Moonbuggy Race got its start in 1994 to commemorate the 25th anniversary of the Apollo 11 lunar landing. The NASA designers of the Lunar Roving Vehicle used by Apollo astronauts were the inspiration for the race. Eight college teams competed the first year, and the race was expanded to include high school teams in 1996.

CONTACTS:
National Aeronautics and Space Administration, Public
  Communications and Inquiries Management Office
NASA Headquarters, Ste. 5K39
Washington, D.C. 20546-0001
202-358-0001; fax: 202-358-3469
www.nasa.gov.home/index.html

♦ 1089 ♦ Great Sami Winter Fair
Begins first Thursday in February

The Lapps, or Samis as many prefer to be called, are a nomadic people of ancient origin who still make their living keeping reindeer herds in the northernmost regions of Norway, Sweden, and Finland, and on the Kola Peninsula of the former Soviet Union. They started holding the Winter Fair, or Market, in Jokkmokk, Sweden, more than 400 years ago, and have continued to hold it in February because this is the time of year when they bring their reindeer to this area. The four-day event draws many visitors who are curious about Sami culture. It includes the marking of the reindeer, reindeer roundup demonstrations, folk music and dance, films, lectures, and the sale of special Sami foods and handicrafts. In 2004 the market celebrated its 400th anniversary.

CONTACTS:
Jokkmokk Tourist Information
P.O. Box 124
Jokkmokk, 962 23 Sweden
46-971-222-50; fax: 46-971-222-59
www.turism.jokkmokk.se/en.aspx

SOURCES:
GdWrldFest-1985, p. 168

♦ 1090 ♦ Great Schooner Race
First week in July

The Great Schooner Race is held off the shore of Rockland, Maine. Since 1977 the race has featured schooners from the Maine Windjammer Association and a number of other large sailing ships—usually 25 to 30 in all. The race begins at Isleboro Island and ends in Rockland, where the boats parade through Penobscot Bay.

CONTACTS:
Maine Windjammer Association
251 Jefferson St. MS06
Waldoboro, ME 04572
800-807-9463 or 207-374-2993; fax: 207-374-2952
www.sailmainecoast.com

♦ 1091 ♦ **Great Wardmote of the Woodmen of Arden**
First week in August

The Great Wardmote, an archery contest organized much the same way it was in medieval times, takes place during the first week in August. It is held in the village of Meriden, which stands in the middle of the once-vast Forest of Arden and claims to be the geographical center of England. Meetings were traditionally held here to discuss the rights and duties of the foresters. In 1785 the various groups of woodmen joined together into one company, the Woodmen of Arden. Today its 80 members attend their annual four-day meeting in August wearing 18th-century dress, including green hats, green coats with gilt buttons, and white trousers.

The woodmen shoot with six-foot bows made of yew and arrows marked with a stamp that denotes their weight in silver. This medieval convention reflects a time when archery was of crucial importance in battle and shooting practice was mandatory in most towns.

CONTACTS:
Visit Britain
551 Fifth Ave., Ste. 701, 17th Fl.
New York, NY 10176
800-462-2748 or 212-986-2266; fax: 212-986-1188
www.visitbritain.us

SOURCES:
EngCustUse-1941, p. 134
FolkCal-1930, p. 159
YrFest-1972, p. 57

♦ 1092 ♦ **Great World Theatre**
June-September (2000, 2007, ...)

Performed every several years in Einsiedeln, Switzerland, the play known as **El Gran Teatro del Mundo** (Great World Theatre) is the work of Pedro Calderón de la Barca, a 17th-century Spanish dramatist and master of the *auto sacramental,* a type of religious drama in which allegory is used to explain the mysteries of Christianity. In *El Gran Teatre del Mundo,* six representatives of humanity, from beggar to king, face life's challenges and must account for their actions on Judgment Day. The play is performed in German before the facade of a Benedictine monastery and church with a cast of more than 500 townspeople. After the show, the director invites most of the cast to a Eucharistic banquet—with the exception of the Rich Man, who is sent to hell.

CONTACTS:
Einsiedeln Tourism Information
Hauptstrasse 85
Einsiedeln, 8840 Switzerland
41-55-418-4488; fax: 41-55-418-4480

SOURCES:
FestEur-1961, p. 155
IntlThFolk-1979, p. 350

♦ 1093 ♦ **Greece Independence Day**
March 25

This national holiday in Greece celebrates the anniversary of the country's proclamation of independence in 1821 after four centuries of Turkish occupation. The war that followed went on until 1829, when finally the Turkish sultan recognized the independence of Greece. The day is marked with church services and military parades—an especially impressive parade is held in Athens. Greek communities in other parts of the world also observe the day. In New York City, Greece Independence Day is celebrated on the Sunday nearest to March 25 with a parade up Fifth Avenue.

CONTACTS:
Embassy of Greece
2217 Massachusetts Ave. N.W.
Washington, D.C. 20008
202-939-1300; fax: 202-939-1324
www.greekembassy.org

SOURCES:
AmerBkDays-2000, p. 230
AnnivHol-2000, p. 50
DictDays-1988, p. 50
NatlHolWrld-1968, p. 39

♦ 1094 ♦ **Greek Cypriot National Day**
April 1

This holiday marks the anniversary of the 1955 start of the Greek Cypriot liberation struggle against British colonial forces. The Greek community in Cyprus waged a guerilla campaign against the British in order to gain union with Greece. The Turkish community, which preferred an alliance with Turkey, also took up arms, complicating the struggle.

Greek Cypriot National Day is celebrated in South Cyprus, which is the Greek partitioned part of the island. Almost all public services and most private shops are closed. The holiday is often celebrated with parades in city streets, along with music, dancing and flag waving.

CONTACTS:
Embassy of the Republic of Cyprus
2211 R. St. N.W.
Washington, D.C. 02008
202-462-5772 or 202-462-0873; fax: 202-483-6710
www.cyprusembassy.net/home

♦ 1095 ♦ Green Festivals
Usually in spring and fall

The largest green consumer show in the United States, Green Festivals brings individuals, businesses, and investors together to generate eco-friendly strategies for sustainable living. The festivals take place in four U.S. cities—San Francisco, Seattle, Chicago, Washington, D.C.—typically in the spring or fall. The events are jointly organized by Global Exchange, a human rights organization, and Co-Op America, an organization committed to social justice and environmental sustainability. Event co-sponsors include a number of non-profits, publications, and other media enterprises.

The first Green Festival was staged in San Francisco, Calif., in 2004, and its success has led to the replication of the event in the other cities. Organizers describe the events as "parties with a purpose." Their offerings are typical of a tradeshow—guest speakers, panel discussions, workshops, career sessions, and commercial exhibitions. Supplementing the festival are various forms of entertainment including films, live music, and organic cuisine.

The capacity of the festivals has grown dramatically since the inaugural year. In 2007, there were more than 200 guest speaker presentations and 400 green business exhibitions in each city. Combined attendance at all four locations reached 100,000.

Festival directors take pride in visibly demonstrating a commitment to ecological responsibility by reusing, recycling, or composting 96% of the waste generated at the show. Admission discounts are also available to attendees who arrive by bicycle instead of by car—a simple incentive to reduce carbon emissions at the event.

CONTACTS:
Green Festivals
www.greenfestivals.org

♦ 1096 ♦ Green George Festival
April 23

Observed on St. George's Day, April 23, by Romany people (also known as gypsies) in Transylvania, the Green George Festival is a tree-spirit festival in which folkloric beliefs play a major role. A young willow is cut down, decorated with flowers and leaves, and set up in a central place where everyone can see it. Pregnant women may leave a piece of clothing under the tree; if a leaf falls on it by the next morning, they'll have an easy delivery. Sick or elderly people spit on the tree three times, praying for long life and good health.

On April 24, an old custom is for a boy dressed in green leaves and flowers to take three iron nails that have spent three days and three nights in running water, hammer them into the willow, pull them out, and throw them back into the stream. In the evening, Green George appears as a leaf-clad puppet who is also thrown into the stream.

Green George is believed to be a variation on the medieval English Jack in the Green. A relic of European tree worship,

Jack in the Green is associated with Pentecost and other celebrations of spring. On May Day in England, he appeared as a boy (typically a chimneysweep) encased in a framework of lath and hoops covered with ivy and holly and wearing a high headdress of leaves.

SOURCES:
DictFolkMyth-1984, pp. 534, 954

♦ 1097 ♦ Green River Rendezvous
Second weekend in July

A reenactment in Pinedale, Wyo., of the days when mountain men, Indians, and traders came together to transact business, trade, drink, holler, and celebrate. The first rendezvous, or gathering, of trappers was held on the Green River, near the present Wyoming-Utah border. After trading posts were established, the rendezvous became less important. The last of these colorful gatherings was held in 1840. A two-hour pageant recreating these rendezvous has been presented by the Sublette County Historical Society since 1936. Celebrations are held over three days, and other events include black-powder shoots and barbecues.

The trappers, traders, and explorers who came to be known as mountain men were a distinctive breed who numbered in their ranks the legendary Jim Bridger, the scout and Indian agent Kit Carson, and William Sublette, who established the area's first trading post. They were satisfying the demand for fur and especially for beaver; the beaver hat was supreme in the world of fashion at the start of the 19th century.

Besides trapping beaver, they also planted the American claim to much of the territory of the American West. For most of the year, they trapped on the tributaries of the Green River, but for several weeks each summer when there was no beaver trapping, they came out of the wilderness and met at a rendezvous site. Trade goods—blankets, coffee, sugar, gunpowder, and cheap whiskey—were brought from Missouri by pack animals and trade wagons, and the trappers brought their beaver skins.

It was a time for more than trading: on one occasion Jim Bridger rode around in a suit of armor that had been brought to him from Scotland. The rendezvous brought together a concentration of explorers and frontiersmen and provided a stepping stone for the settlers who followed. The rendezvous and the era of the mountain men came to an end in the 1840s when the whims of fashion shifted from beaver hats to silk hats, and the race for beaver furs was over.

See also Mountain Man Rendezvous

CONTACTS:
Sublette County Historical Society
c/o Museum of the Mountain Man
P.O. Box 909
Pinedale, WY 82941
877-686-6266 or 307-367-4101; fax: 307-367-6768

SOURCES:
GdUSFest-1984, p. 216

◆ 1098 ◆ Greenery Day
April 29

This day formerly observed the birthday of Emperor Hirohito of Japan (1901-1989), who was the world's longest ruling monarch. His reign included the attempted military conquest of Asia, the attack on the United States at Pearl Harbor, and his country's defeat after the U.S. dropped atomic bombs on Hiroshima and Nagasaki. He also oversaw Japan's post-war resurgence to a position of economic strength and influence. Hirohito renounced his divinity in 1946 and became a symbolic head of state in Japan's new parliamentary democracy.

Today this day is celebrated as Greenery Day—**Midori-no-Hi**—with parades featuring elaborate floats, paper lanterns, traditional Japanese costumes, and fireworks. Popular places from which to observe the festivities in Tokyo include Tokyo Tower, the highest structure in the city, and Shiba Park. People also mark the day by planting trees and other activities centered around the appreciation of nature.

Greenery Day begins **Golden Week**, which also includes Japan Constitution Memorial Day (May 3) and Kodomo-no-Hi (Children's Day, May 5). It is a popular time for people to take vacations and enjoy the spring weather.

CONTACTS:
Japan Information Network, Japan Center for Intercultural
  Communications
2-7-7 Hirakawacho
Chiyodaku
Tokyo, 102-0093 Japan
81-3-3263-5041; fax: 81-3-3230-4107
home.jcic.or.jp/en/index-e.html

SOURCES:
AnnivHol-2000, p. 70
BkFest-1937, p. 198
NatlHolWrld-1968, p. 52

◆ 1099 ◆ Greenland National Day
June 21

The people of Greenland celebrate National Day on June 21, the longest day of the year. They call the holiday *Ullortuneq* in Greenlandic, which means "the longest day." They celebrate the occasion with communal picnics, shows, and many cultural activities. Since Greenland's current flag was formally instituted on June 21, 1985, they also honor the national flag on this day.

CONTACTS:
Nuuk Tourism
Hans Egedesvej 29
P.O. Box 1615
Nuuk, 3900 Greenland
299-32-27-00; fax: 299-32-27-10
www.nuuk-tourism.gl

◆ 1100 ◆ Greenville Treaty Camporee
Usually a weekend in May in odd-numbered years

On June 16, 1795, General Anthony Wayne and representative chiefs of the Allied Tribes of the Northwest Territory met at Fort Greenville to light a ceremonial council fire and work out the terms of a treaty that would open the Northwest Territory to white settlers. The council fire was not allowed to go out until the treaty was finally signed on August 3.

Today, Boy Scouts from Ohio and other parts of the Midwest meet on a weekend nearest in May during odd-numbered years at Greenville City Park to commemorate the treaty. The Miami Valley Council sponsors the weekend, which attracts more than 1,000 Scouts. There are exhibitions of Boy Scout skills, games, competitions, and demonstrations.

CONTACTS:
Miami Valley Council of Boy Scouts
4999 Northcutt Pl.
P.O. Box 13057
Dayton, OH 45413
937-278-4825; fax: 937-278-9002
www.mvcbsa.com

SOURCES:
AmerFestGd-1956, p. 120

◆ 1101 ◆ Greenwood (Chester) Day
First Saturday in December

Chester Greenwood (1858-1937) made his first pair of "ear protectors" when he was 15 years old. He was granted a patent in 1877 and established an entirely new industry in his hometown of Farmington, Maine, where he continued to refine the design and manufacture of what we now know as earmuffs. By 1918 he was making 216,000 pairs a year, and by 1932 checks and plaids were added to the standard black velvet covering.

Although Greenwood was involved in a number of other business ventures in Farmington and was granted his last patent—for a tempered steel lawn rake—only a few months before he died, it is for his ear protectors that he is primarily remembered. Farmington residents celebrate Chester Greenwood Day on the first Saturday in December (Greenwood was born on December 4) with a parade, flag-raising ceremony, and a foot race. Everyone is encouraged to wear earmuffs for the festivities, including pets.

CONTACTS:
Farmington Chamber of Commerce
407 Wilton Rd.
Farmington, ME 04938
207-778-4215; fax: 207-778-2438
www.farmingtonchamber.org

◆ 1102 ◆ Grenada Independence Day
February 7

This is a national holiday commemorating Grenada's independence from Britain on this day in 1974. Britain had held the island since the 18th century, when France ceded it under the Treaty of Paris.

CONTACTS:
Embassy of Grenada
1701 New Hampshire Ave. N.W.

Washington, D.C. 20009
202-265-2561; fax: 202-265-2468
www.grenadaembassyusa.org

SOURCES:
AnnivHol-2000, p. 23

♦ 1103 ♦ Grenada Thanksgiving Day
October 25

On October 25, 1983, the U.S. and other Caribbean forces invaded Grenada to destabilize the Communist regime that had overthrown the government of Sir Eric Gairy in 1979. Democratic elections were held in December 1984. October 25 is observed as Thanksgiving Day, a public holiday in Grenada.

CONTACTS:
Embassy of Grenada
1701 New Hampshire Ave. N.W.
Washington, D.C. 20009
202-265-2561; fax: 202-265-2468
www.grenadaembassyusa.org

♦ 1104 ♦ Grey Cup Day
Late November

The best teams from the Eastern and Western Conferences of the Canadian Football League play against each other in an annual event similar to the SUPER BOWL in the United States. It is called Grey Cup Day after the trophy that is awarded to the winning team—a cup donated by former Canadian Governor-General Earl Grey in 1909.

Parties are held throughout the country so that fans can get together to watch the big game on television. In sports and social clubs, it is not uncommon to set up two televisions so that rival supporters can each watch their own team. Like its American counterpart, the Super Bowl, the Grey Cup is an occasion for widespread drinking and rowdiness.

CONTACTS:
Canadian Football League
50 Wellington St., E 3rd Fl.
Toronto, ON M5E 1C8 Canada
416-322-9650; fax: 416-322-9651
www.cfl.ca

SOURCES:
DictDays-1988, p. 50

♦ 1105 ♦ Groppenfasnacht (Fish Carnival)
Between March 1 and April 4; Laetare Sunday
(three weeks before Easter)

This Lenten celebration in the village of Ermatingen, Thurgau Canton, Switzerland, takes its name from the *Gropp*, a fish a few inches long caught only in the Ermatingen area. The event dates to the time when fishermen celebrated the breaking up of the ice in the spring because they could return to catching fish. A committee of villagers organizes a procession in which children dress as frogs and dwarfs and follow

a float that carries a huge Gropp, while men march along carrying antique fishing implements.

CONTACTS:
Groppenkomitee Ermatingen
Hauptstrasse 64
Ermatingen, 8272 Switzerland
41-71-664-1144; fax: 41-71-664-2758
www.groppenfasnacht.ch

♦ 1106 ♦ Grotto Day
August 5; July 25

In England during the late 18th and early 19th centuries, oysters were not considered the rare delicacy they are today and were, in fact, one of the common staples of fishermen's diets. The large number of oysters eaten at that time meant there were lots of shells around. On ST. JAMES'S DAY, which was observed on August 5 before the Gregorian, or New Style, Calendar came into use and on July 25 thereafter, children used the shells to construct small decorative grottoes. Perhaps these were to represent the shrine of St. James in Spain. Sometimes the children begged for pennies as a reward for their efforts. Most of this grotto-building took place in London, and the custom continued right up to the 1950s. St. James the Great was one of the Apostles and brother to ST. JOHN THE EVANGELIST, and the scallop shell was his emblem.

SOURCES:
DictDays-1988, pp. 50, 85
OxYear-1999, pp. 307, 323

♦ 1107 ♦ Groundhog Day
February 2

There was a medieval superstition that all hibernating animals—not just groundhogs—came out of their caves and dens on CANDLEMAS to check on the weather. If they could see their shadows, it meant that winter would go on for another six weeks and they could go back to sleep. A cloudy day meant that spring was just around the corner. It was the early German settlers known as the Pennsylvania Dutch who attached this superstition to the groundhog. In Germany it was the badger, and in England, France, and Canada it was the bear who was believed to make similar predictions about the weather.

The most famous forecaster in the United States is Punxsutawney Phil, a legendary groundhog in north-central Pennsylvania believed to be nearly a century old. Members of the Punxsutawney Groundhog Club, along with thousands of other people, trek up to Phil's burrow on Gobbler's Knob on February 2 and get the news directly from him. (They also capture the event on film, which is available for viewing from a link on their web site.) Unfortunately, weather researchers have determined that over the years the groundhog has been correct only 28 percent of the time.

Numerous events take place in Punxsutawney over the days surrounding February 2, including group hikes, parties, live entertainment, fireworks, a winter carnival, and the showing of *Groundhog Day*, the 1993 movie starring Bill Murray.

CONTACTS:
Punxsutawney Groundhog Club
c/o Punxsutawney Chamber of Commerce
124 W. Mahoning St.
Punxsutawney, PA 15767
814-938-7700; fax: 814-938-4303
www.groundhog.org

SOURCES:
AmerBkDays-2000, p. 110
BkFestHolWrld-1970, p. 29
DaysCustFaith-1957, p. 45
DictDays-1988, p. 51
FolkAmerHol-1999, p. 67
OxYear-1999, p. 64

♦ 1108 ♦ **Gualterianas, Festas**
Four days beginning the first Sunday in August

The **Festivals of St. Walter** take place in Guimarães, the 12th-century capital of Portugal. The celebrations, which date back to 1452, include magnificent processions, fireworks, animal fairs, and displays of food and merchandise. Music, ranging from brass bands to modern jazz, can be heard all over the town.

St. Walter (or São Gualter), the town's patron, is represented by an image of a young Franciscan monk who stands in the nave of Senhor dos Passos (Our Lord of the Way of the Cross), the blue-and-white-tiled church that overlooks the town's public garden.

During a Sunday night procession known as the *Procissão Gualteriana*, the image of the saint is carried from the church through the decorated streets of Guimarães while thousands of spectators gather to watch. The procession is followed by a night of fireworks, folk dancing in regional costume, and great activity at the shooting galleries and sideshows that line the streets. The festival culminates on Wednesday with the *Marcha Gualteriana*, a midnight procession of 12 allegorical floats.

CONTACTS:
Portuguese National Tourist Office
590 Fifth Ave., 4th Fl.
New York, NY 10036
800-767-8842 or 212-354-4403; fax: 212-764-6137
www.visitportugal.com

SOURCES:
FestWestEur-1958, p. 181

♦ 1109 ♦ **Guardian Angels Day**
October 2

As early as the ninth century, a day was set aside to honor angels in general and the archangel Michael in particular. This was September 29, the Feast of St. Michael and All Angels or MICHAELMAS. But some people, believing that a particular angel is assigned to watch over each human being,

wanted to honor their own personal protectors or guardian angels. A feast in their honor observed in 16th-century Spain was extended to the whole church by Pope Paul V in 1608, and in 1672 Pope Clement X set October 2 as the universal day for the festival.

SOURCES:
DaysCustFaith-1957, p. 249
OxYear-1999, p. 400
RelHolCal-2004, p. 101

♦ 1110 ♦ **Guatemala Army Day**
June 30

Guatemala's Liberal Revolution, which called for the end of the dictatorship of Vicente Cerna, culminated with a revolt in Guatemala City on June 30, 1871. The coup paved the way for a successful 12-year era under President Justo Rufino Barrios, a leader of the revolution who implemented extensive agrarian reforms as Guatemala's head of state.

Originally known as **Revolution Day**, the anniversary of the 1871 revolt became **Día del Ejército** (Army Day), an official holiday recognizing the service of the armed forces. Typical of most traditional military celebrations, Army Day has been marked over the years by annual parades, usually in Guatemala City, featuring processions of various battalions and divisions.

At the turn of the 21st century, a popular movement grew to force an end to Army Day celebrations. Guatemalan activists began holding a rival event in Guatemala City called the March for Remembrance in honor of the thousands of civilians killed by the repressive military leadership during the country's civil war between 1960 and 1996. The 2007 parade and accompanying protests spawned violence in the streets, and the ongoing campaign of resistance compelled the government to cancel the official parade the following year.

CONTACTS:
Embassy of Guatemala
2220 R St. N.W.
Washington, D.C. 20008
202-745-4952; fax: 202-745-1908
www.guatemala-embassy.org

SOURCES:
AnnivHol-2000, p. 108

♦ 1111 ♦ **Guatemala Independence Day**
September 15

This is the day on which Guatemala won its independence from Spain in 1821. Four other countries also declared their independence on September 15, 1821: COSTA RICA, EL SALVADOR, HONDURAS, and NICARAGUA.

It is a public holiday during which the buildings in Guatemala City are draped in blue-and-white bunting, and there are parades with schoolchildren marching to the music of military bands. A popular holiday pastime is watching *La Conquista* (The Conquest), a traditional dance where the dancers, in wooden masks and red wigs, reenact the conquest of the Mayan Indians by the Spanish soldier Pedro de Alvarado. The Mayan civilization, which had flourished in Guatemala since 2500 B.C.E., began to decline after 900 C.E. Alvarado, the red-haired Spanish conquistador, began subjugating their descendants in 1523.

CONTACTS:
Embassy of Guatemala
2220 R St. N.W.
Washington, D.C. 20008
202-745-4952; fax: 202-745-1908
www.guatemala-embassy.org

SOURCES:
AnnivHol-2000, p. 155
NatlHolWrld-1968, p. 167

♦ 1112 ♦ **Guatemala Revolution Day**
October 20

Like another national holiday, GUATEMALA ARMY DAY, this holiday commemorates a historic transfer of Guatemalan power. On October 20, 1944, university students and military leaders aligned to overthrow the dictator Jorge Ubico. Guatemalans fondly remember the replacement government and its executive leader, Juan José Arévalo, who implemented a series of successful labor and agrarian reforms. Arévalo's presidency and that of his successor, Jacobo Arbenz Guzmán, marked a period of political freedom known as 10 Years of Spring.

Music and fireworks mark the day's lively celebrations, the grandest of which are held in the Plaza Mayor in Guatemala City. It is also common on this day for activists to exercise their free speech, a human right that Arévalo championed, and to stage political demonstrations. Some protests draw thousands of people and extend into the next day.

CONTACTS:
Embassy Guatemala
2220 R St. N.W.
Washington, D.C. 20008
202-745-4952; fax: 202-745-1908
www.guatemala-embassy.org

♦ 1113 ♦ **Guavaween**
Last Saturday of October

Guavaween is a parade and block party with a Latin flavor in Ybor City, a two-square-mile area in Tampa, Fla. Ybor City grew around the cigar factory established in 1886 by Cuban Vicente Martínez Ybor. From the steps of the factory, José Martí (1853-1895), sometimes called the George Washington of Cuba, exhorted the cigar workers to take up arms against Spain.

The area still has a Latin flavor, and Guavaween is an event to celebrate the culture and have a good time. The "guava" stands for the tropical American fruit, while the "ween" alludes to the festival's resemblance to HALLOWEEN, also observed around this time of year. The parade, with 20 to 50 bands, is led by a woman portraying the mythical "Mama

Guava" doing the "Mama Guava Stumble." Many paraders wear costumes lampooning national figures. After the early evening parade, there is partying until the wee hours. Attendance is about 150,000.

CONTACTS:
Ybor City Chamber of Commerce
1800 E. 9th Ave.
Tampa, FL 33605
813-248-3712; fax: 813-247-1764
www.ybor.org

♦ 1114 ♦ **Gudi Padva**
March-April; first day of the waxing half of the Hindu month of Caitra

Gudi Padva marks the beginning of the civil year among Hindus, particularly in the states of Maharashtra, Andhra Pradesh, and Karnataka in central India. The actual New Year (*see* VAISAKH), which begins on the first day of Vaisakha (April-May) is not the same as the beginning of the civil year, which begins on the new moon day of the preceding month, Caitra.

Hindus observe this day by erecting a pole from which hangs a silk banner (a *gudi*) or a piece of women's clothing and a drinking pot. This pole is displayed by sticking it out a window or tying it to the roof or a nearby tree. There are a number of legends associated with the pole, but it generally serves as a good luck symbol.

Other customs associated with this day are visiting friends, bathing, and eating leaves from the *nim* tree, which is believed to bring protection against illness, since this tree has a holy connection with SITALA, the smallpox goddess.

SOURCES:
CelebFestIndia-1994, p. 45
HinduRelYr-1921, p. 42
RelHolCal-2004, p. 184

♦ 1115 ♦ **Guelaguetza, La**
Two consecutive Mondays after July 16

Also known as **Los Lunes del Cerro,** or **Mondays of the Hill,** this huge dance festival is held in the city of Oaxaca, Oaxaca State, Mexico, on the two Mondays after July 16. Costumed dancers from different *oaxaquena* groups perform in a hilltop arena built exclusively for this event. Seats for the nationally televised festival are expensive, and many of the visiting dance groups must stay in local missions. Although the event is now geared mostly to tourists, it represents a unique opportunity to see regional dances from all the Mexican states.

Guelaguetza comes from the Zapotec language and means "the greatest of courtesies." It refers to the traditional way people exchanged gifts: helping each other build houses, tend to fields, assist with births and deaths. The name became linked with the Mondays of the Hill fiestas in the 20th century. Since the 1930s local craftspeople would give gifts they made to guests assembled for the dances, and in 1951 the event became known as La Guelaguetza. In 1974 the state built a special amphitheater to hold the growing numbers of people attending what is now one of the most popular folk festivals in Mexico.

CONTACTS:
Mexico State Tourism
Urawa No. 100
Toluca, 50150 Mexico
52-722-212-5998; fax: 52-722-212-1633
www.spanish-mexico.com

Mexico Tourism Board
21 E. 63rd St., Fl. 3
New York, NY 10021
800-446-3942 or 212-821-0314; fax: 212-821-0367
www.visitmexico.com

SOURCES:
FiestaTime-1965, p. 117
IntlThFolk-1979, p. 274

♦ 1116 ♦ **Guinea-Bissau and Cape Verde National Heroes' Day**
January 20

Citizens of Guinea-Bissau and Cape Verde have great reverence for Amílcar Cabral (1921–1973), a nationalist leader who was assassinated before he could see his native Guinea-Bissau and nearby Cape Verde achieve independence from Portugal. The two countries, which collaborated in an independence campaign begun in the 1950s, settled on January 20 as their National Heroes' Day because it falls on the anniversary of Cabral's murder. That tragic event further stirred the fire of the liberation movement, and the country became independent in 1974.

A public holiday in Guinea-Bissau and Cape Verde, National Heroes' Day commemorates the legacies of Cabral and other freedom fighters. In years past, the government has issued stamps and bank notes with Cabral's image on National Heroes' Day. Leftist associations in West Africa and throughout the world have observed the day by holding symposiums on the writings and political theories of Cabral.

CONTACTS:
Cape Verde Embassy
3415 Massachusetts Ave. N.W.
Washington, D.C. 20007
202-965-6820; fax: 202-965-1207

Guinea-Bissau Embassy
1511 K St. N.W., Ste. 519
Washington, DC 20005
202-347-3950; fax: 202-347-3954

SOURCES:
AnnivHol-2000, p. 12

♦ 1117 ♦ **Guinea-Bissau Independence Day**
September 24

After more than 500 years of Portuguese rule, Guinea-Bissau (formerly known as Portuguese Guinea) declared itself an independent republic on September 24, 1973. The U.S. recognized it as such on September 10, 1974, and Portugal followed suit the same day.

September 24 is a national holiday in Guinea-Bissau.

CONTACTS:
Embassy of Guinea-Bissau
15929 Yukon Ln.
Washington, D.C. 20005
301-947-3958; fax: 202-347-3954

SOURCES:
AnnivHol-2000, p. 159

♦ 1118 ♦ **Guinea Independence Day**
October 2

Guinea became an independent republic on this day in 1958, after having been a French colony since the late 19th century.

Independence Day is a national holiday celebrated all over the country with parades, dances, and sports competitions, especially in the capital city of Conakry.

CONTACTS:
Embassy of Guinea
2112 Leroy Pl. N.W.
Washington, D.C. 20008
202-986-4300; fax: 202-986-4800

SOURCES:
AnnivHol-2000, p. 166
NatlHolWrld-1968, p. 185

♦ 1119 ♦ **Guinea Second Republic Day**
April 3

Guinea Second Republic Day commemorates an event from recent history. Guinea was ruled by a dictatorship led by Sekou Touré, who ruled the small West African nation for over 25 years (1958-1984). After Toure's death, there was a bloodless coup on April 3, 1984. That coup ushered in what many Guineans refer to as the Second Republic, led by former lieutenant Lansana Conté. A military government assumed control of the county until 1993, the year Conté was elected president. His popularity has dwindled over the years, as has enthusiasm for the annual celebration of the historic transfer of power.

The observation of Second Republic Day is largely orchestrated by the government. In honor of the coup's 24th anniversary in 2008, Conté and Guinean prime minister Lansana Kouyate were guests of honor at a wreath-laying ceremony at a martyrs' memorial located in the center of Conakry, the capital city. They also used the occasion to announce the launching of the web site of the Guinea Radio and Television (RTG), a state-run enterprise considered by many to be the government's mouthpiece.

CONTACTS:
Guinea Embassy
2112 Leroy Pl. N.W.
Washington, D.C. 20008
202-483-9420; fax: 202-483-8688

♦ 1120 ♦ **Guru Arjan, Martyrdom of**
May-June; during the Sikh month of Jaith

Guru Arjan (1563-1606) was the fifth of the ten Sikh gurus and the first to be martyred. He became guru in 1581 and is known for many achievements—among them the building of the Golden Temple in the city of Amritsar and compiling the *Adi Granth*, the "First Collection" of Sikh sacred scripture.

Because Guru Arjan was a threat to his power, Jehangir, the emperor of the Mughal Empire, arrested him. Tradition has it that Arjun was tortured to death by being boiled alive while sitting on a burning hot plate. Although he accepted his death peacefully, Arjan left instructions for his successor, Har Gobind, to permit the Sikhs to take up arms to protect the innocent.

People commemorate Guru Arjan's martyrdom by visiting *gurdwaras*, places of worship, for special services. In India, where the weather is exceptionally hot at this time of year, it is traditional for Sikhs to make drinks available to every passerby—a reminder that part of Guru Arjan's torture before his death was being deprived of water.

SOURCES:
RelHolCal-2004, p. 204
SikhFest-1989, p.14

♦ 1121 ♦ **Guru Gobind Singh, Birthday of**
December-January; during the Sikh month of Pausa (Poh)

Born in 1666, Guru Gobind Singh was the last of the ten Sikh gurus. His father, GURU TEGH BAHADUR, was the ninth guru. He is best known for establishing the *Khalsa*, the spiritual brotherhood devoted to defending Sikhism. Guru Gobind Singh is also remembered for his teachings, which include the ideas that living with love, charity, and integrity was more important than observing religious rituals and that men and women are equal.

Guru Gobind Singh was the last guru because, instead of appointing a human successor, he believed that the *Granth Sahib*, the Sikh scriptures, should serve as an eternal Guru to the Sikh community (see GURU GRANTH SAHIB, INSTALLATION OF). His birthday is celebrated by Sikhs in India and around the world with festivities similar to those marking the birthday of Guru Nanak (see GURU PARAB). They include a three-day-long, continuous reading of the *Guru Granth Sahib*, processions, and the singing of sacred songs. Sporting contests and other games are also popular. Many Sikhs go on pilgrimage to the Golden Temple at Amritsar (see GURU ARJAN, MARTYRDOM OF) and to the shrine marking the site of Gobind Singh's birth, Takht Patna Sahib.

SOURCES:
EncyRel-1987, vol. 13, p. 331
RelHolCal-2004, p. 205
SikhFest-1989, p. 22

♦ 1122 ♦ **Guru Granth Sahib, Installation of the**
September-October; during the Sikh month of Asun

GURU GOBIND SINGH, the last of the ten Sikh gurus or spiritual leaders, did not choose a human successor before he died in 1708. Instead, he called his followers together and told them that in the future, the *Adi Granth*, or Sikh scriptures, would serve as Guru. The *Adi Granth* was renamed the Guru Granth Sahib and was installed as the 11th and perpetual Guru to the Sikhs.

The anniversary of the installation of the Guru Granth Sahib is observed with ceremonies in the *gurdwaras*, or houses of worship. These often include readings, the singing of hymns, lectures, and the serving of free meals. A continuous reading of the entire Guru Granth Sahib, which is 1,430 pages long and takes approximately three days to read, may also be conducted. The anniversary of the installation is also a popular day for Sikhs to rededicate themselves to their faith.

SOURCES:
RelHolCal-2004, p. 204
SikhFest-1989, p. 26

♦ 1123 ♦ **Guru Har Krishan, Birthday of**
June-July; during the Sikh month of Har

Har Krishan (1656-64) was the eighth of the ten Sikh gurus or prophets on whose teaching the religion is based. He is often referred to as the "Child Guru" because he was only five years old when he succeeded his father, Guru Har Rai, who died in 1661. Har Krishan himself died of smallpox at the age of eight, so he remained a child throughout his brief time as guru.

The anniversary of his birth is celebrated by Sikhs around the world with special services in the *gurdwaras* (houses of worship) and with readings from the GURU GRANTH SAHIB, the Sikh scriptures.

SOURCES:
RelHolCal-2004, p. 204

♦ 1124 ♦ **Guru Parab**
October-November; full moon day of Hindu month of Kartika

Guru Nanak (1469-1539), was the founder of the Sikh Dharma faith (Sikhism), which was based on a belief in one god and on the rejection of idolatry and caste distinctions. In Pakistan at Nanak's birthplace, Talwandi (now Nankana Sahib, near Lahore, Pakistan), there is a shrine and a holy tank where thousands of Sikhs congregate on this day for a huge fair and festival. Here and at Sikh shrines everywhere, the holy scripture, GURU GRANTH SAHIB, is read continuously and recited on Nanak's birthday. Food is distributed, and processions are common.

Nanak was followed by nine other gurus, under whom Sikhism gradually developed. Other Guru Parabs commemorate these later leaders. For example, the Guru Parab in honor of GURU GOBIND SINGH (1666-1708) is observed during the month of Pausa (December-January).

CONTACTS:
Ministry of Tourism, Government of India
Rm. No 123, Transport Bhawan, No. 1, Parliament St.
New Delhi, Delhi 110 001 India
91-11-23715084; fax: 91-11-23715084
www.tourisminindia.com

SOURCES:
RelHolCal-2004, p. 203
SikhFest-1989, p. 10

♦ 1125 ♦ Guru Purnima
June-July; full moon day of Hindu month of Asadha

In Hinduism, a guru is a personal teacher or guide who has already attained spiritual insight. The tutorial approach to religious instruction has always been emphasized in India, and in ancient times it was the guru who personally transmitted his knowledge of the Vedas, sacred Hindu books, to his student. The student often lived at the home of his guru and looked up to him with devotion.

Guru Purnima, or **Asadha Purnima,** is the day set aside for the veneration of the guru. In ancient times, when students were educated in ashrams and gurukuls, this was the day they would honor their teachers, pay their fees, and give them presents. It was customary to fast on this day and to seek the guru's blessing.

This day is also known as **Vyasa Purnima** after Rishi Vyasa (ca. fifth century B.C.E.), a famous guru who is said to have compiled the four Vedas, the *Mahabharata,* and the Puranas, a series of 18 epics dealing with creation and the gods in the form of fables, legends, and tales.

SOURCES:
CelebFestIndia-1994, p. 62
RelHolCal-2004, p. 171

♦ 1126 ♦ Guru Ram Das, Birthday of
September-October; during the Sikh month of Asun

Ram Das (1534-1581) was the fourth of the ten Sikh gurus and the son-in-law of Amar Das, the third guru. After he was chosen to succeed his father-in-law, his name was changed from Bhai Jetha to Ram Das, which means "God's Servant." His birthday is celebrated during the month of Asun (September-October) in Sikh *gurdwaras,* or houses of worship, with prayers, the singing of hymns, and with readings from the GURU GRANTH SAHIB, the Sikh holy scriptures.

SOURCES:
RelHolCal-2004, p. 204

♦ 1127 ♦ Guru Tegh Bahadur, Martyrdom of
November-December; during the Sikh month of Magar

Tegh Bahadur (1621-1675) was the ninth of the ten Sikh gurus, or spiritual teachers. His son, GURU GOBIND SINGH, was the last human guru. When Tegh Bahadur was 43 years old, he was installed as guru. The tyrant Aurangzeb was the Muslim emperor of India at the time, and his goal was to make everyone in his domain Muslim. Then, as now, most people living in India were Hindu, though there were also small populations of Sikhs, Jains, and other religious groups. Under Aurangzeb's rule, everyone was forced to convert to Islam under threat of death.

At the behest of a group of Hindu priests, Tegh Bahadur went to Delhi in November 1675 to meet with Aurangzeb, who put him in prison. Legend has it that before Tegh Bahadur was beheaded (since he would not convert to Islam), he wrote a message which read, "I gave my head but not my faith." Guru Tegh Bahadur is remembered for giving his life to preserve the integrity of the Sikh religion.

Sikhs everywhere observe his martyrdom with religious processions and pilgrimages at *gurdwaras,* or houses of worship, with a special devotion to him, and especially at the site of his martyrdom in Delhi where the Gurdwara Sisganj temple was built.

SOURCES:
RelHolCal-2004, p. 204
SikhFest-1989, p. 18

♦ 1128 ♦ Gustavus Adolphus Day (Gustaf Adolfsdagen)
November 6

Gustavus Adolphus (1594-1632) was the king of Sweden (1611-32) who laid the foundations of the modern Swedish state and turned the country into a major European power. By resolving the long-standing constitutional struggle between the crown and the aristocracy, he was able to achieve sweeping reforms in the fields of administrative organization, economic development, and particularly education. Among other things, he created the *Gymnasia* in 1620, which provided for secondary education in Sweden, and gave the University of Uppsala the financial support it needed to flourish.

King Gustav II was killed during the Thirty Years' War while leading a cavalry charge at the Battle of Lützen on November 6, 1632, turning a tactical victory into a national tragedy for the Swedes. The anniversary of his death is observed throughout Sweden with patriotic demonstrations—particularly in Skansen, Stockholm's outdoor museum. Enormous bonfires are built on Reindeer Mountain and processions of students carry lighted torches through the museum grounds.

SOURCES:
BkFest-1937, p. 312

♦ 1129 ♦ Guthrie (Woody) Folk Festival
Week of July 14

Fans of folk icon Woody Guthrie (1912–1967) mark his legacy with an annual music festival in his birthplace of

Okehmah, Okla. The event is held on the weekend nearest his birthday, July 14.

The festival, introduced in 1998, is a recently created tradition. For the inaugural festival Okemah was treated to performances by folk stars Billy Bragg and Guthrie's son, Arlo Guthrie, as well as to the dedication of a full-body bronze statue of the legend that stands along the town's main street.

Organizing the festival is the Woody Guthrie Coalition, which shares Guthrie's egalitarian vision to bring music to people by maintaining a free admission policy, even for folk music stars like Jackson Browne, Pete Seeger, and the Kingston Trio. Typically, the only concert that charges admission is for raising the festival's funds. This benefit show is usually held at the Crystal Theatre, a venue where Guthrie had performed as a child.

Many music fans stay until the end of the weekend for the final Sunday performance. This concert, called the Hoot for Huntington's, raises money to treat the disease that took Guthrie's life.

CONTACTS:
Woody Guthrie Folk Festival
Woody Guthrie Coalition, Inc.
P.O. Box 661
Okemah, OK 74859
479-466-7380
www.woodyguthrie.com/main2.htm

♦ 1130 ♦ Guyana Independence Day
May 26

This public holiday marks Guyana's independence from Britain on this day in 1966.

Republic Day, or *Mashramani,* is another national holiday, commemorating February 23, 1970, when Guyana became a republic.

CONTACTS:
Guyana Tourism Authority
National Exhibition Ctr.
Sophia
Georgetown, Guyana
592-219-0094; fax: 592-219-0093
www.guyana-tourism.com

♦ 1131 ♦ Gwangiu Kimchi Festival
October or November

The city of Gwangiu in South Korea holds an annual event to celebrate the nation's favorite condiment, kimchi. A fermented, pickled cabbage, kimchi is produced in the autumn in quantities to last through the winter.

The event, which typically runs from Wednesday to Sunday, celebrates everything kimchi. Visitors can learn about the history and different varieties of kimchi on video and through live demonstrations, sample freshly made kimchi, and purchase many types to try at home. The beloved pickle is also the subject of exhibitions about its history, globalization, and

manufacture. There are competitions for the best kimchi and the best dish to eat with it. Novices can try their hand at making their own kimchi during a hands-on workshop. In addition to the food-related array of activities, the event treats participants to performances of music and dance ranging from traditional Korean to that of many other nations. Although kimchi has been a feature of Korean cuisine for thousands of years, the festival was launched in the last decade by the city of Gwangiu, which is known for its rich culinary tradition.

CONTACTS:
Korea National Tourism Organization
737 N. Michigan Ave., Ste. 910
Chicago, IL 60611
800-868-7567 or 312-981-1717; fax: 312-981-1721
english.visitkorea.or.kr

♦ 1132 ♦ Gyangzê Horse-Racing Festival
Four days in May-June

Masked and costumed dancers and traditional operas dominate the first day of this Tibetan festival. They are performed in the courtyard of the Kumbum, known for its 112 chapels and multi-tiered *stupas* or monuments. But the next three days are devoted to sporting events on horseback, the Tibetans being renowned for their horsemanship. Archers on horseback shoot at targets while riding at full gallop, and some events involve riding yaks instead of horses.

The festival commemorates the highest (in terms of altitude) battle in history, which took place between the Tibetans and the invading British troops in 1903. The British, under the command of Sir Francis Younghusband, slaughtered 600 Tibetans at Guru before moving on to Gyangzê. He then marched into the capital, Lhasa, and forced the acceptance of a trade treaty with the DALAI LAMA, Tibet's ruler.

CONTACTS:
China Tibet Information Center
3/F A2 Building (Rongfeng 2008) BLK 8
305 Guang An Men Wai St.
Beijing, Xuanwu District 100055 China
86-10-5833-6057
eng.tibet.cn

SOURCES:
WildPlanet-1995, p. 295

♦ 1133 ♦ Gynaecocratia
January 8

The Greek title of this observance is a word that means female rule or government. This stab at feminist revolt is of long tradition in northern Greece, where it is common for women to do all the household work and for most men to take life easy in cafes.

Today in the villages of Komotini, Xanthi, Kilkis, and Serres, that standard is reversed for a day when Gynaecocratia is celebrated. The women gather in village cafes to socialize, while the men stay at home cleaning house, tending the babies, and generally looking after household tasks. At dusk, the men join their wives in celebrations.

SOURCES:
OxYear-1999, p. 29

H

♦ 1134 ♦ **Hadaka Matsuri (Naked Festival)**
January or February, depending on location

Hadaka Matsuri—which means, literally, "naked festival"—is a Shinto tradition observed all over Japan, usually not long after NEW YEAR'S DAY or OSHOGATSU. The young men who participate are naked except for traditional white loincloths known as *fundoshi* or *mawashi*. At the ringing of the temple bell, large numbers of them attempt to climb up a thick rope suspended from the temple ceiling. Because the first to reach the top will have good fortune in the coming year, there is often a good deal of jockeying for position on the rope.

Sometimes the participants in Hadaka Matsuri immerse themselves in a river beforehand to purify themselves. Occasionally several semi-naked young men will carry a *mikoshi*, or portable shrine, in the form of a horse, rice bale, or sake barrel into the river with them.

CONTACTS:
Japan National Tourist Organization
1 Rockefeller Pl., Ste. 1250
New York, NY 10020
212-757-5640; fax: 212-307-6754
www.japantravelinfo.com

SOURCES:
IllFestJapan-1993, p. 18

♦ 1135 ♦ **Haile Selassie's Birthday**
July 23

Haile Selassie I (1892-1975), emperor of Ethiopia from 1930 to 1974, was born Tafari Makonnen; he became Prince (or *Ras*) Tafari in 1916. Among the Jamaicans known as Rastafarians, Selassie was believed to be the Messiah, and Ethiopia was identified with heaven. Rastafarian theology and political belief was based on the superiority of the black man and the repatriation of black people to Ethiopia.

Ethiopians still celebrate Haile Selassie's birthday. During the years of his reign as emperor, Selassie would stand on the balcony of his palace in Addis Ababa and greet the thousands of well-wishers who gathered there on his birthday.

See also ETHIOPIA NATIONAL DAY and HAILE SELASSIE'S CORONATION DAY

SOURCES:
NatlHolWrld-1968, p. 123

♦ 1136 ♦ **Haile Selassie's Coronation Day**
November

The Rastafarians (or Ras Tafarians), members of a political-religious movement among the black population of Jamaica, worship Haile Selassie I, "Might of the Trinity." His original name was Tafari Makonnen (1892-1975), and he was emperor of Ethiopia under the name *Ras* (meaning "Prince") Tafari. Rastafarians consider the Ethiopian emperor the Messiah and son of God, and the champion of their race. Their beliefs, which combine political militancy and religious mysticism, include taboos on funerals, second-hand clothing, physical contact with whites, the eating of pork, and all magic and witchcraft.

The Rastafarians' most important celebration is the anniversary of Haile Selassie's Coronation Day, which occurred on November 2, 1930. The dedication of babies to Ras Tafari, recitations, and singing are typically part of the celebrations on this day.

SOURCES:
DictWrldRel-1989, p. 601

♦ 1137 ♦ **Haiti Ancestors' Day**
January 2

Haitians devote the first two days of the calendar year to commemorating the nation's past along with celebrating the new year. The Independence Day festivities that occur on the first day of the year continue into **Jour des Aieux** (Ancestors' Day), an occasion for remembering the founders of Haiti and the individuals who sacrificed their lives during the independence struggle of the early 19th century. The tributes that are held on Ancestors' Day in Haiti and in immigrant communities in major U.S. cities are testimony to the emphasis that Haitian culture places on remembering the country's forefathers.

A large meal often accompanies the day's festivities. Military processions, a common event on Independence Day, may also take place on Ancestors' Day. In years past, particularly during the reign of President Francois Duvalier (1971–1986), the executive leader used this day to deliver radio and television speeches to the nation.

CONTACTS:
Embassy of the Republic of Haiti
2311 Massachusetts Ave. N.W.
Washington, D.C. 20008
202-332-4090; fax: 202-745-7215
www.haiti.org

SOURCES:
AnnivHol-2000, p. 3

◆ 1138 ◆ Haiti Anniversary of the Death of Jean-Jacques Dessalines
October 17

A former slave, Jean-Jacques Dessalines (ca. 1758–Oct. 17, 1806) played a pivotal role under the command of Toussaint L'Ouverture in the Haitian struggle for independence from France. Following the creation of an independent Haiti, Dessalines ruled Haiti as Emperor Jacques I for two years before he was assassinated in a coup. It is Dessalines' legacy as a freedom fighter and a founding father—rather than his autocratic reign as emperor—that Haitians remember on this official holiday commemorating the anniversary of his death.

Haitians observe the holiday by participating in street parades in the capital city of Port-au-Prince and other cities. Port-au-Prince staged a grand celebration in 2006 to mark the 200th anniversary of Dessalines' assassination, during which President René Préval made an appearance for ceremonies. In a town 100 miles north of the capital, actors portrayed slaves in a historical re-enactment to remember the early plight of Dessalines and his fellow citizens.

In New York City, which is home to tens of thousands of Haitian immigrants, October 17 is also observed with cultural performances and presentations on Dessalines and Haitian history. The Haitian Lawyers Leadership Network, a U.S.–based political advocacy group, marked the bicentennial of Dessalines' death by holding events throughout the month of October.

CONTACTS:
Embassy of the Republic of Haiti
2311 Massachusetts Ave. N.W.
Washington, D.C. 20008
202-332-4090; fax: 202-745-7215
www.haiti.org

SOURCES:
AnnivHol-2000, p. 174

◆ 1139 ◆ Haiti Battle of Vertières' Day
November 18

This official public holiday memorializes the last battle for Haitian independence on November 18, 1803, in which Hait-

ian rebels defeated the French colonialists. The victory at Vertières, near the present-day port city of Cap-Haitien, signified the end of a long freedom struggle that stretched out over two major phases. Less than two months after the battle, Haiti became the first black independent republic.

The day was formerly known as **Army Day** or **Armed Forces Day**, and military ceremonies were once the main event. Army parades were staged along the Champs des Mars in the capital city of Port-au-Prince and on the lawn of the National Palace. However, when President Jean-Bertrand Aristide abolished a Haitian army notorious for its brutality in the early 1990s, festival officials phased the armed forces out of the public ceremonies.

The Battle of Vertières Day in 2003 marked the bicentennial anniversary of the victory over the French. In Cap-Haitien, standing before the monument of the Heroes of the Battle of Vertières, President Aristide gave a stirring speech honoring the victorious soldiers.

CONTACTS:
Embassy of the Republic of Haiti
2311 Massachusetts Ave. N.W.
Washington, D.C. 20008
202-332-4090; fax: 202-745-7215
www.haiti.org

SOURCES:
AnnivHol-2000, p. 193

◆ 1140 ◆ Haiti Flag and University Day
May 18

An inscription on the Haitian flag's coat of arms reads: "L'Union fait la force" (Unity Makes Strong). National unity is a primary theme of Flag and University Day, which is an independence celebration as well as an occasion to recognize the country's educational system.

For over a century, the celebration was devoted solely to the national emblem. Flag Day became an annual celebration shortly after Catherine Flon sewed the first red and blue flag in 1803, a year before Haiti won its independence from France. Under instructions from Jean-Jacques Dessalines, Haiti's first ruler, Flon used the template of the French flag's tri-color scheme but removed the white stripe. The remaining blue and red stripes symbolized the black and mulatto citizens who made up Haiti's majority population.

The government incorporated University Day as part of the celebration in 1919. Dantes Bellegarde, then minister of public instruction, advocated for the day because he believed that the sanctity of the educational system was being threatened by the U.S. occupation of Haiti that had begun in 1915.

Haitians wave flags throughout the day's parades and fairs, which take place throughout Haiti as well as in New York and Miami, two cities with large Haitian communities. People also attend presentations by experts on the country's flag and Haitian history.

CONTACTS:
Embassy of the Republic of Haiti
2311 Massachusetts Ave. N.W.
Washington, D.C. 20008
202-332-4090; fax: 202-745-7215
www.haiti.org

♦ 1141 ♦ Haiti Independence Day
January 1

The people of Haiti celebrate both NEW YEAR'S DAY and Independence Day on January 1, the day on which they declared their independence from the French in 1804. Thousands of people assemble in the capital city of Port-au-Prince to see the parades and to visit the National Palace on the Champs de Mars. They set off fireworks, dance in the streets, and sing the national anthem, which honors their founder, Jean-Jacques Dessalines, the hero of the anti-French revolt.

According to Haitian custom, whatever happens to someone on January 1 is indicative of what will happen to them during the coming year, motivating even the poorest people to make an effort to put on new clothes, to visit their friends, and to give and receive gifts in the hope that these efforts will be rewarded in the coming year.

CONTACTS:
Embassy of the Republic of Haiti
2311 Massachusetts Ave. N.W.
Washington, D.C. 20008
202-332-4090; fax: 202-745-7215
www.haiti.org

SOURCES:
FestWrld: Haiti-1999, p. 20
FolkWrldHol-1999, p. 3
NatlHolWrld-1968, p. 6

♦ 1142 ♦ Hakata Dontaku
May 3-4

The largest festival in Japan, Hakata Dontaku is held in Fukuoka City (Fukuoka Prefecture) during Golden Week, the first week in May. This festival attracts more than two million spectators every year because Golden Week is a national holiday encompassing Children's Day (*see* KODOMO-NO-HI), GREENERY DAY, JAPANESE NATIONAL FOUNDATION DAY and JAPAN CONSTITUTION MEMORIAL DAY.

The festival originated in the Muromachi Period (1333-1568) as a procession of the merchants of Hakata, an old section of Fukuoka City, paying their new year visit to the *daimyo*, or feudal lord. The name of the holiday curiously is thought to have derived from the Dutch word *Zondag*, meaning "Sunday," which was broadened to mean "holiday," and corrupted into *Dontaku*.

The festival highlight is a three-hour parade with legendary gods on horseback, floats, and musicians playing *samisens* (a three-stringed instrument similar to a guitar), flutes, and drums.

CONTACTS:
Japan Information Network, Japan Center for Intercultural
  Communications
2-7-7 Hirakawacho
Chiyodaku
Tokyo, 102-0093 Japan
81-3-3263-5041; fax: 81-3-3230-4107
home.jcic.or.jp

SOURCES:
JapanFest-1965, p. 147

♦ 1143 ♦ Hakata Gion Yamagasa
July 1-15

The GION MATSURI at Kyoto is the model for several other Gion festivals in Japan, and the largest of these is the Gion Yamagasa Festival at Fukuoka. The festival involves townspeople on both sides as well as the creators of the famous Hakata dolls. The elaborate floats for which the festival is famous are called *yamagasa*, and beautiful new dolls are made for them each year.

The festival begins on July 1, when participants purify themselves by collecting sand from the seashore. They put the sand in boxes which are slung beneath the yamagasa. The men wear headbands, *happi* coats, and traditional Japanese loincloths. The highlight of the festival occurs on the morning of July 15, when the Oiyama race is held. This is a five-kilometer race in which teams of 28 men run while carrying yamagasa weighing about a ton. Traditional Noh dramas are performed at the Kushida Shrine in Fukuoka.

CONTACTS:
Fukuoka Convention and Visitors Bureau
1-10-1 Tenjin Chuo-ku
Fukuoka, 810-0001 Japan
81-9-2733-5050; fax: 81-9-2733-5055
www.welcome-fukuoka.or.jp/lang/english/index.html

SOURCES:
IllFestJapan-1993, p. 82
JapanFest-1965, p. 162

♦ 1144 ♦ Hala Festival
Mid to late February

The Hala Festival has been held in Kuwait every year since 1999 to celebrate the coming of spring and to promote Arab culture and the local economy. The festival begins with an opening carnival and parade, culminating in a lavish fireworks display that draws up to 250,000 people. Over the course of the subsequent two weeks, visitors are able to enjoy such features as performances of music from around the Middle East, exhibitions of calligraphy and cars, sporting events, and religious events. There are also many activities for children. Shopping is a focal point of the festival, with more than 100 local merchants taking part in prize drawings and special offers, including the sale of millions of retail-discount coupons to festival-goers. The city is swathed in lights, mirroring the bright flowers that bloom on the desert to herald the start of spring.

CONTACTS:
Kuwait-Embassy
2490 Tilden St. N.W.
Washington, D.C. 20008
202-966-0702; fax: 202-966-0517

◆ 1145 ◆ Halashashti
August-September; sixth day of waning half of Hindu month of Bhadrapada

This Hindu festival is often referred to as **Balarama Shashti**, after Krishna's older brother, Balarama, who was born on this day. Balarama's weapon was a plough, so it is also the day on which farmers in India worship the *hala*, or plough. They apply powdered rice and turmeric to the plough's iron blade and decorate it with flowers. A small piece of ground is sanctified and plastered with cow dung, then a small pool of water is dug in the middle and branches of plum, fig, and other fruit trees are planted there. Some women fast all day in the belief that it will ensure happiness, prosperity, and longevity to their sons. When the fast is broken in the evening, there is a great feast and celebration.

SOURCES:
FolkWrldHol-1999, p. 514
RelHolCal-2004, p. 147

◆ 1146 ◆ Halcyon Days
December 14-28

The ancient Greeks called the seven days preceding and the seven days following the WINTER SOLSTICE the "Halcyon Days." According to one legend, the halcyon bird, or kingfisher, nested during this period. Because she built her nest on the water, the gods granted her a respite from storms and high seas so that she could hatch and rear her young.

But Greek mythology has it that Halcyone (or Alcyone), Ceyx's wife and one of Aeolus's daughters, drowned herself when she learned her husband had drowned. The gods took pity on her and transformed them both into kingfishers, and Zeus commanded the seas to be still during these days. Thus it was considered a period when sailors could navigate in safety.

Today, the expression "halcyon days" has come to mean a period of tranquillity, often used as a nostalgic reference to times past.

SOURCES:
BkDays-1864, vol. II, p. 726
DictFolkMyth-1984, p. 475
OxYear-1999, p. 499

◆ 1147 ◆ Half Moon Bay Art and Pumpkin Festival
October, weekend after Columbus Day

This festival, highlighted by a Great Pumpkin Weigh-Off, has been held since 1971 in Half Moon Bay, Calif. The weigh-off winner gets $5 per pound for the heaviest pumpkin; winning pumpkins have weighed in excess of 900 pounds. Other festival features are a Great Pumpkin Parade, arts and crafts, food concessions selling pumpkin bread, pumpkin crepes, pumpkin ice cream, and pumpkin strudel, and entertainment that includes live music, puppet shows, magicians, jugglers, clowns, and professional pumpkin carvers. There are competitions in pumpkin carving and pie eating.

Pumpkins have been grown in the Half Moon Bay area for decades but were used for cattle feed until the 1920s when two farmer brothers decided to try them as human food. That began a surge in pumpkin popularity. The pumpkin festival has also surged; attendance is estimated at 300,000.

CONTACTS:
Miramar Events
P.O. Box 27
El Granada, CA 94018
650-726-3491; fax: 650-726-5181
www.miramarevents.com

◆ 1148 ◆ Halifax Day
April 12

Also known as **Halifax Resolves Day**, **Halifax Resolutions Day**, **Halifax Independence Day**, or **Halifax Resolutions of Independence Day**, this is the day on which, in the spring of 1776, North Carolina's delegates to the Second Continental Congress were given permission to join with representatives from other colonies in declaring their independence from British rule. As the first official sanction of separation from Great Britain, the Halifax Resolutions helped lay the groundwork for the American Revolution.

Halifax Day observances take place in Halifax with reenactments and living history camps.

CONTACTS:
Halifax County Convention and Visitors Bureau
260 Premier Blvd.
Roanoke Rapids, NC 27839
800-522-4282 or 252-583-7191
www.visithalifax.com

Library of Congress
101 Independence Ave. S.E.
Washington, DC 20540
202-707-5000; fax: 202-707-2076
www.loc.gov

SOURCES:
AmerBkDays-2000, p. 280
AnnivHol-2000, p. 61
DictDays-1988, p. 54

◆ 1149 ◆ Halloween
October 31

Halloween has its ultimate origins in the ancient Celtic harvest festival, SAMHAIN, a time when people believed that the spirits of the dead roamed the earth. Irish settlers brought their Halloween customs—which included bobbing for apples and lighting jack-o'-lanterns—to America in the 1840s.

In the United States children go from house to house in costume—often dressed as ghosts, skeletons, or vampires—on

Halloween saying, "Trick or treat!" Though for the most part the threat is in jest, the "trick" part of the children's cry carries the implication that if they don't receive a treat, the children will subject that house to some kind of prank, such as marking its windows with a bar of soap or throwing eggs at it. Most receive treats in the form of candy or money. But Halloween parties and parades are popular with adults as well.

Because nuts were a favorite means of foretelling the future on this night, **All Hallows' Eve** in England became known as **Nutcrack Night**. Other British names for the day include **Bob Apple Night**, **Duck** (or **Dookie**) **Apple Night**, **Crab Apple Night**, **Thump-the-door Night**, and, in Wales, Apple and Candle Night. In the United States it is sometimes referred to as **Trick or Treat Night**.

See also Mischief Night

CONTACTS:
American Folklife Center, Library of Congress
Thomas Jefferson Bldg., Rm. LJG49
101 Independence Ave. S.E.
Washington, D.C. 20540
202-707-5510; fax: 202-707-2076
www.loc.gov

SOURCES:
AmerBkDays-2000, p. 741
BkDays-1864, vol. II, p. 519
BkFest-1937, p. 60
BkHolWrld-1986, Oct 31
DaysCustFaith-1957, p. 280
DictFolkMyth-1984, pp. 181, 869, 961
FestSaintDays-1915, p. 191
FolkAmerHol-1999, p. 427
FolkWrldHol-1999, p. 604
OxYear-1999, p. 436
RelHolCal-2004, p. 275
SaintFestCh-1904, p. 468

♦ 1150 ♦ **Halloween (Ireland)**
October 31

In Ireland, Halloween is observed with traditional foods and customs that are largely based on superstitions or folk beliefs. One of the dishes served is known as *colcannon*, or *callcannon*. It consists of mashed potatoes, parsnips, and chopped onions. A ring, a thimble, a small china doll, and a coin are mixed in, and the one who finds the ring will be married within a year. The one who finds the doll will have children, the one who finds the coin will be wealthy, and the one who finds the thimble will never marry. *Barmbrack*—a cake made with a ring concealed inside—is a variation on the same theme. Whoever gets the ring in his or her slice will be the first to marry. Sometimes there is a nut inside, and the one who finds the nut will marry a widow or widower. If the kernel of the nut is shriveled, the finder will never marry.

Nuts have traditionally played a role in Halloween celebrations in the British Isles. In England, Halloween is known as **Nutcrack Night**. In Ireland, a popular superstition involved putting three nuts on the hearth and naming them after lovers. If one of the nuts cracked or jumped, that lover would

be unfaithful; if it began to burn, it meant that he was interested. If a girl named one of the nuts after herself and it burned together with the nut named after her lover, it meant that they would be married.

The jack-o'-lantern, according to the Irish, was the invention of a man named Jack who was too greedy to get into heaven and couldn't get into hell because he had tricked the devil. The devil threw him a lighted coal from hell instead, and Jack stuck it in the turnip he was eating. According to the legend, he used it to light his way as he wandered the earth looking for a final resting place.

SOURCES:
AmerBkDays-2000, p. 742
BkDays-1864, vol. II, p. 519
BkHolWrld-1986, Oct 31
FestSaintDays-1915, p. 194
FolkWrldHol-1999, p. 604
OxYear-1999, p. 436

♦ 1151 ♦ **Halloween (Isle of Man)**
October 31

In the early part of this century, Halloween was referred to as **Thump-the-Door Night** on the Isle of Man because boys would gather outside the house of someone they didn't like and bombard the door with turnips or cabbages until the inhabitants gave them some money to make them go away—much like the trick-or-treating that goes on in the United States. As might be expected, the game occasionally got out of control, provoking complaints and sometimes legal action. Eventually it fell out of favor.

Halloween is commonly called **Hollantide** on the Isle of Man because there was a time when it marked the beginning of the church year. This was based on the Celtic custom of beginning the year in November instead of in January.

SOURCES:
DictDays-1988, p. 120
FestSaintDays-1915, p. 196
OxYear-1999, p. 460

♦ 1152 ♦ **Halloween (New Orleans, Louisiana)**
October 31

Halloween is a spooky and macabre celebration in New Orleans, La., when costumed revelers parade up and down Bourbon Street and actors dressed as legendary characters are on the streets to narrate their grisly histories. The sheriff's Haunted House in City Park is a standard feature, and a Ghost Train rolls through the park while costumed police officers jump out of bushes to spook the riders. The Voodoo Museum usually offers a special Halloween ritual in which people may see voodoo rites. Walking tours take visitors to such haunts as Le Pretre House, where a Turkish sultan and his five wives were murdered one night in 1792; it is said that their ghosts still have noisy parties.

On a more solemn note, the St. Louis Cathedral holds vigil services on Halloween, and several masses on All Saints'

DAY. On the afternoon of that day, the archbishop leaves the cathedral for St. Louis Cemetery No. 1 to bless the newly scrubbed and decorated tombs.

CONTACTS:
New Orleans Metropolitan Convention and Visitors Bureau
2020 St. Charles Ave.
New Orleans, LA 70130
800-672-6124 or 504-566-5011; fax: 504-566-5046
www.neworleanscvb.com

♦ 1153 ♦ Halloween (Scotland)
October 31

Many of the traditional customs associated with HALLOWEEN in Scotland are described in the famous poem of that name by the Scottish poet Robert BURNS, although not all of them are still observed. "Pulling the kail" referred to the custom of sending boys and girls out into the garden (or kailyard) blindfolded. They were instructed to pull up the first plant they encountered and bring it into the house, where its size, shape, and texture would reveal the appearance and disposition of the finder's future husband or wife. It was also believed that by eating an apple in front of a mirror, a young woman could see the reflection of her future mate peering over her shoulder.

Another custom referred to by Burns was known as "The Three Dishes," or *Luggies*. One was filled with clean water, one with dirty water, and one remained empty. They were arranged on the hearth, and as people were led into the room blindfolded, they would dip their fingers into one of the bowls. Choosing the clean water indicated that one would marry a maiden (or bachelor); the dirty water indicated marriage to a widow (or widower). The empty dish meant that the person was destined never to marry.

"Dipping the shift" was another popular superstition regarding marital prospects. If someone dipped a shirt-sleeve in a south-running stream and hung it up by the fire to dry, the apparition of the person's future mate would come in to turn the sleeve.

Superstition surrounded death as well as marriage. It was customary on Halloween for each member of the family to put a stone in the fire and mark a circle around it. When the fire went out, the ashes were raked over the stones. If one of the stones was found out of place the next morning, it means that the person to whom it belonged would die within the year.

SOURCES:
AmerBkDays-2000, p. 742
BkDays-1864, vol. II, p. 520
FestSaintDays-1915, p. 193
OxYear-1999, p. 436

♦ 1154 ♦ Haloa
Late December or early January

The Haloa was an ancient Greek festival in honor of Demeter and Dionysus. It took place in Eleusis near the time of the WINTER SOLSTICE. The Haloa is believed to have been an attempt to restore the earth's lost fertility and also, in years when it was obvious that the crops were not growing well, to reverse the course of nature and assist the weak shoots in surviving the winter months.

Only women attended the Haloa. Although there are many theories about what went on there, most involve lewd jokes and games, and uninhibited discussions about sex and illicit love. The celebrants carried sexual organs made out of clay, and pastries made to resemble sex organs were set out on the table. It was believed that such obscene behavior encouraged fertility, and it makes sense in view of the fact that the Haloa was held at a time of year when the fields were frozen and the growth of crops was at a temporary standstill. By manipulating sexual and agricultural symbols, by feasting and carrying on, the women attempted to "warm up" the earth and stimulate its dormant fertility.

SOURCES:
AtticFest-1981, p. 104
DictFolkMyth-1984, p. 867
NewCentClassHandbk-1962, p. 513

♦ 1155 ♦ Hambletonian Harness Racing Classic
First Saturday in August

Harness racing's most prestigious race for three-year-old trotters, the Hambletonian is a test of both speed and stamina. Currently held at the Meadowlands Racetrack in East Rutherford, New Jersey, the race dates back to 1926. It is always held on the first Saturday in August and is preceded by a week of other races with purses in the $500,000 range. The purse for the one-mile Hambletonian race is $1.2 million, and the winner usually goes on to take a divisional title.

CONTACTS:
The Hambletonian Society
109 S. Main St., Ste.18
Cranbury, NJ 08512
609-371-2211; fax: 609-371-8890
www.hambletonian.org

♦ 1156 ♦ Hana Matsuri (Flower Festival)
April 8

Hana Matsuri is a celebration of the Buddha's birthday, observed in Buddhist temples throughout Japan, where it is known as **Kambutsue**. The highlight of the celebration is a ritual known as *kambutsue* ("ceremony of 'baptizing' the Buddha"), in which a tiny bronze statue of the Buddha, standing in an open lotus flower, is anointed with sweet tea. People use a small bamboo ladle to pour the tea, made of hydrangea leaves, over the head of the statue. The custom is supposed to date from the seventh century, when perfume was used, as well as tea. Festivities often include a procession of children carrying flowers.

See also VESAK

CONTACTS:
Japan Information Network, Japan Center for Intercultural
    Communications
2-7-7 Hirakawacho

Chiyodaku
Tokyo, 102-0093 Japan
81-3-3263-5041; fax: 81-3-3230-4107
home.jcic.or.jp

SOURCES:
BkFestHolWrld-1970, p. 76
JapanFest-1965, p. 62

◆ 1157 ◆ Hanagasa Odori
Varies

One of the largest festivals in the Tohoku region of Japan, Hanagasa Odori is held in Yamagata on August 5-7. Thousands of dancers holding *hanagasa*, which are hats made out of bamboo or rush and decorated with flowers, dance through the city while spectators cheer them on. The rhythmic pulse of the hanagasa songs keeps the dancers moving together as they march down the city streets yelling "Yassho! Makasho!" and twirling their hats to the left, right, up, and down.

The Hanagasa Festival held in Kyoto on October 9 features a procession of people holding large umbrellas decorated with flowers, but the overall effect is similar.

CONTACTS:
The Yamagata Tourism Information Center
1-1-1, Kajo Central
Jonan-machi
Yamagata, 990-8580 Japan
81-2-3647-2333; fax: 81-2-3646-6333
www.yamagatakanko.com/english/index.html

SOURCES:
IllFestJapan-1993, p. 100
JapanFest-1965, p. 195

◆ 1158 ◆ Hanami
March-April

The word *hana* means "flower" in Japanese, and *hanami* means "flower viewing." However, appreciation of the cherry blossom in Japan is almost a religion, and therefore hanami has come to refer specifically to cherry blossoms. The pink-and-white blooms last for about two weeks, and during that time people swarm to the parks to picnic, play games, tell stories, and dance. Often companies organize hanami parties for their employees. The season usually starts at the end of March in Kyushu, in early April in the Tokyo area, and in late April in the north of Japan. The most famous viewing place is Yoshinoyama near Nara, where it is said 1,000 trees can be seen at a glance.

See also CHERRY BLOSSOM FESTIVAL

CONTACTS:
Japan Information Network, Japan Center for Intercultural
  Communications
2-7-7 Hirakawacho
Chiyodaku
Tokyo, 102-0093 Japan
81-3-3263-5041; fax: 81-3-3230-4107
home.jcic.or.jp

Nara Prefectural Government
30 Nobori-oji-cho
Nara, 630-8501 Japan
81-7-4222-1101; fax: 81-7-4227-4473
www.pref.nara.jp

SOURCES:
BkFestHolWrld-1970, p. 89
FolkWrldHol-1999, p. 264
JapanFest-1965, p. 99

◆ 1159 ◆ Handsel Monday
*First Monday of the year; first Monday after
January 12*

A secular holiday, Handsel Monday was important among the rural people of Scotland. "Handsel" was something given as a token of good luck, particularly at the beginning of something; the modern house-warming gift would be a good example. Thus Handsel Monday was an occasion for gift giving at the start of the new year, and it remained a Scottish tradition from the 14th until the 19th century. Eventually it was replaced by BOXING DAY, and the custom of giving farm laborers and public servants some extra money or a small gift on this day continues.

Because Handsel Monday was so widely celebrated among the rural population, many Scottish peasants celebrated **Auld Handsel Monday** on the first Monday after January 12, reflecting their reluctance to shift from the Old Style, or Julian, calendar to the New Style, or Gregorian, calendar.

SOURCES:
BkDays-1864, vol. I, p. 52
DictDays-1988, p. 54
DictFolkMyth-1984, p. 478
OxYear-1999, p. 650

◆ 1160 ◆ Handy (W. C.) Music Festival
July or August

The W.C. Handy Music Festival honors the "Father of the Blues" in the Alabama Quad-Cities of Florence, Muscle Shoals, Sheffield, and Tuscumbia in the northwestern part of the state known as Muscle Shoals.

William Christopher Handy, the son and grandson of ministers, was born in 1873 in Florence, took an early interest in music, and went on to become a prolific composer, performer, orchestra leader, and music publisher despite his father's ministerial influence. In 1911, he wrote an election campaign song for Mayor Edward H. "Boss" Crump of Memphis, Tenn., that became known as the "Memphis Blues" and was one of the works that made him famous. Others included the classic "St. Louis Blues," "Beale Street Blues," and "Careless Love."

Handy, working in the period of transition from ragtime to jazz, fused elements of black folk music with ragtime to create distinctive blues pieces. He also organized a publishing firm, issued anthologies of black spirituals and blues and studies of American black musicians, and wrote an autobiography, *Father of the Blues*, published in 1941. He expressed his philosophy with these words: "Life is like this old trumpet of mine. If you don't put something into it, you don't get nothing out." When Handy died in 1958, a Harlem minister said, "Gabriel now has an understudy."

The festival celebrates not only Handy's musical heritage but also the musical roots of spirituals and jazz. Opening ceremonies are at the W. C. Handy Home & Museum, a log cabin housing Handy's collected papers and memorabilia. His piano and trumpet are on display.

Throughout the festival there is music by nationally known musicians night and day, street dancing, a foot race, folk art exhibits, and music workshops. Events are held in such non-traditional locations as ball fields, parks, and nursing homes, and concerts are performed in the church where Handy's father and grandfather served as pastor, and in restaurants and clubs. The small community of Muscle Shoals, where several events are held, is known in music circles for having given birth to the "Muscle Shoals Sound" through a recording studio that was set up in 1965. Artists as varied as Aretha Franklin, Peggy Lee, Liza Minnelli, Bob Seger, and the Rolling Stones have recorded here.

CONTACTS:
W. C. Handy Music Festival
217 E. Tuscaloosa St.
Florence, AL 35630
256-766-7642; fax: 256-766-7549
www.wchandymusicfestival.org

SOURCES:
AAH-2007, p. 422

♦ 1161 ♦ **Han'gul Day**
October 9

This day commemorates the invention of the Korean alphabet by scholars under the direction of King Sejong of the Yi Dynasty in 1446.

The Han'gul system consists of 14 consonants and 10 vowels. The symbols for consonants are formed with curved or angled lines; the symbols for vowels are composed of vertical or horizonal straight lines with short lines on either side. Although Sejong made Han'gul the official writing system for the Korean language, it was not used by scholars or upper-class Koreans until after 1945, when Japanese rule came to an end and the influence of Confucianism and Chinese culture waned.

The reign of Sejong (1418-50) was a golden age in Korea, producing—besides the alphabet—the encyclopedic codification of medical knowledge and the development of new fonts of type for printing. (The technique of movable-type printing was developed in Korea in 1234, two hundred years before Johannes Gutenberg's invention in Germany.)

The day is celebrated with Confucian rituals and Choson-period court dances performed at Yongnung, the king's tomb, in Yoju, Kyonggi. Yoju also stages the King Sejong Cultural Festival, which is part of a three-day Grand Cultural Festival, with chanting and processions at Shilluksa Temple, farmers' dances, games such as tug of war, and a lantern parade. In some areas, there are calligraphy contests for both children and adults.

Ceremonies are also held at the King Sejong Memorial Center near Seoul.

CONTACTS:
Korea National Tourism Organization
2 Executive Dr., Ste. 750
Fort Lee, NJ 07024
800-868-7567 or 201-585-0909; fax: 201-585-9041
www.kntoamerica.com

SOURCES:
BkHolWrld-1986, Oct 9
FolkWrldHol-1999, p. 594

♦ 1162 ♦ **Hanukkah (Chanukah)**
Between November 25 and December 26; from Kislev 25 to Tevet 2

Hanukkah commemorates the successful rebellion of the Jews against the Syrians in the Maccabean War of 162 B.C.E., but the military associations of this festival are played down. What is really being celebrated is the survival of Judaism. After the Jews' victory, they ritually cleansed and rededicated the Temple, then relit the menorah ("perpetual lamp"); hence one of the other names for this celebration, the **Feast of Dedication** (Hanukkah means "dedication" in Hebrew). The story is told that although there was only enough consecrated oil to keep the lamp burning for one day and it would take eight days to get more, the small bottle of oil miraculously lasted for the entire eight days. It is for this reason that Hanukkah is also known as the **Feast of Lights**.

Jewish families today celebrate this holiday by lighting a special Hanukkah menorah, a candelabrum with holders for eight candles, one for each day of celebration, plus a ninth, the shammash, "server," used to light the others. One candle is lit on the first night, two on the second, three on the third, through to the eighth night when all are lit. A special prayer is recited during the lighting, and while the candles burn it is a time for songs and games, including the four-sided toy called the dreidel. Other customs include the giving of gifts, especially to children, and decorating the home—something like the CHRISTMAS celebrations in Christian homes around this same time of year.

CONTACTS:
Union of Orthodox Jewish Congregations of America
11 Broadway
New York, NY 10004
212-563-4000; fax: 212-564-9058
www.ou.org

Jewish Community Online
Renaissance Media
29200 Northwestern Hwy., Ste. 110
Southfield, MI 48034
248-354-6060
www.jewish.com

SOURCES:
AmerBkDays-2000, p. 846

BkFest-1937, p. 205
BkFestHolWrld-1970, p. 134
BkHolWrld-1986, Dec 10
DaysCustFaith-1957, p. 326
DictFolkMyth-1984, p. 479
DictWrldRel-1989, pp. 155, 293
EncyChristmas-2003, p. 323
FolkAmerHol-1999, p. 480
FolkWrldHol-1999, p. 684
HolSymbols-2009, p. 339
OxYear-1999, p. 726
RelHolCal-2004, p. 56

◆ 1163 ◆ Hanuman Jayanti
March-April; Hindu month of Caitra

Hanuman, the Monkey God and a central figure in the great Hindu epic, the *Ramayana*, helped Rama rescue his wife Sita from the demon Ravana; for this Rama decreed the two always be worshipped together. He is revered by Hindus all over India in the form of a monkey with a red face who stands erect like a human. His birth anniversary is observed in the month of Caitra with celibacy, fasting, and reading the *Hanuman-Chalisa*. Hindus visit his temples, of which there are many, to offer prayers on this day and to re-paint his image with vermilion.

SOURCES:
DictWrldRel-1989, p. 294
FolkWrldHol-1999, p. 257
RelHolCal-2004, p. 186

◆ 1164 ◆ Harbin Ice and Snow Festival
January 5-February 4

This extravaganza of ice sculptures takes place in the port city of Harbin, the second largest city of northeast China, located in Heilongjiang Province. The sculptures, using themes of ancient legends and stories and modern historic events, depict pavilions, towers, temples, and mythic animals and persons. Located in Zhaolin Park, they shimmer in the sun by day, and at night are illuminated in a rainbow of colors. Theatrical events, art exhibitions, and a photo exhibition mark festival time, and wedding ceremonies are often scheduled at this time in the ice-filled park.

CONTACTS:
China National Tourist Office
370 Lexington Ave., Ste. 912
New York, NY 10118
888-760-8218 or 212-760-8218; fax: 212-760-8809
www.cnto.org

◆ 1165 ◆ Hard Crab Derby, National
September, Labor Day weekend

The first **Hard Crab Derby** was held in 1947. A local newspaper editor dumped a few hard-shell crabs into a circle on Main Street in Crisfield, Maryland. The crab that scurried to an outer circle first was declared the winner, and its owner was awarded a trophy. There doesn't seem to have been any motivation for the race other than the wish to compete with the other derbies that had already been established for horses, automobiles, etc.

Today the National Hard Crab Derby attracts hundred of entries. The Governor's Cup Race, in which entries representing the 50 states compete, takes place on the Saturday of LABOR DAY weekend. There is also a boat-docking contest, a crab-picking contest, and a crab-cooking contest. Parades, beauty contests, concerts, a carnival, and arts and crafts exhibits complete the three-day festival.

CONTACTS:
Crisfield Area Chamber of Commerce
906 W. Main St.
P.O. Box 292
Crisfield, MD 21817
800-782-3913 or 410-968-2500; fax: 410-968-0524
www.crisfieldchamber.com

◆ 1166 ◆ Hari-Kuyo (Festival of Broken Needles)
February 8 or December 8

Hari-Kuyo is a requiem service for needles held throughout Japan. The ceremony of laying needles to rest harkens back to at least the fourth century C.E. Today the services are attended not only by tailors and dressmakers but also by people who sew at home. Traditionally, a shrine is set up in the Shinto style, with a sacred rope and strips of white paper suspended over a three-tiered altar. On the top tier are offerings of cake and fruit, on the second tier there is a pan of tofu, and the bottom tier is for placing scissors and thimbles. The tofu is the important ingredient; people insert their broken or bent needles in it while offering prayers of thanks to the needles for their years of service. In the Buddhist service, special sutras are recited for the repose of the needles. Afterwards, the needles are wrapped in paper and laid to rest in the sea.

A hari-kuyo is held in Kyoto at the Buddhist Temple Horinji on Dec. 8, and in Tokyo one is held at Asakusa Kannon Temple on Feb. 8.

CONTACTS:
Kyoto City Tourism & Culture Information
233-5 Daimon-ji-cho, Atarashimachi-dori
Oike-sagaru, Nakagyo-ku
Kyoto, 604-8315 Japan
81-7-5811-6388; fax: 81-7-5813-3250
www.kyotoguide.com

Tokyo Convention & Visitors Bureau
Kasuga Business Center Bldg. 10F
1-15-15 Nishikata
Bunkyo-ku
Tokyo, 113-0024 Japan
81-3-5840-8892; fax: 81-3-5840-8895
www.tcvb.or.jp/en/index_en.htm

◆ 1167 ◆ Harlem Week
August

Sponsored by the Greater Harlem Chamber of Commerce, Harlem Week is the largest cultural festival in the United States. Participation in Harlem Week and its associated events is estimated to exceed two million people. The festival honors the unique history and importance of the Harlem neighborhood in New York City. This area was the site of an important flourishing in African-American culture known as the Harlem Renaissance during the early 20th century. The Harlem Renaissance marked the emergence of African Americans into the mainstream of the nation's art, music, literature, and culture while simultaneously proclaiming the unique vitality and character of the African-American experience.

When it originated in 1974, Harlem Week was conceived as a single day's celebration of the area's cultural contributions, and sought to revitalize interest in and recognition of the neighborhood's important past. Though the activities have expanded to encompass a wide range of sports, music, and educational events, Harlem Day remains the most important and event-filled day of the month-long celebration. A street fair, including performance stages, marketplace booths, and food vendors, is located on West 135th Street, and the rich musical heritage of the area is commemorated in numerous performances featuring swing, jazz, Latin, gospel, hip hop, reggae, R&B, and blues music. In addition, the festival includes history tours, fashion shows, an all-star basketball game, a youth tennis tournament, a college fair, a health fair, a children's festival, a senior citizens' party, and an auto show.

CONTACTS:
Harlem Week
200A W. 136th St.
New York, NY 10030
212-862-7200; fax: 212-862-8745
harlemweek.harlemdiscover.com

SOURCES:
AAH-2007, 203

◆ 1168 ◆ Harvest Home Festival
Autumn

Many countries celebrate the end of the summer harvest or the "ingathering" of the crops with a special feast. What became known in England as Harvest Home, or **Harvest Thanksgiving**, was called the **Kirn** in Scotland (from the churn of cream usually presented on the occasion), and probably derived from the ancient LAMMAS celebrations. Eventually it gave rise to the **Harvest Festival** in Canada and THANKSGIVING in the United States.

The autumn harvest feast was usually served in a barn, a tent, or outdoors and was preceded by a church service. Although the earliest harvest feasts were served by a farmer or landowner to his laborers, eventually one big feast for the entire parish became the norm.

See also SZÜRET

SOURCES:
AmerBkDays-2000, p. 795
AnnivHol-2000, p. 160
BkDays-1864, vol. II, p. 376
DictFolkMyth-1984, p. 484
OxYear-1999, p. 651
SaintFestCh-1904, p. 424

◆ 1169 ◆ Harvest Moon Days
Full moon nearest September 23

Harvest Moon Days refers to the period of the full moon that falls closest to the AUTUMNAL EQUINOX, around September 23. This is traditionally a time for countries in the Northern Hemisphere to hold their annual harvest festivals.

See also HARVEST HOME FESTIVAL

SOURCES:
AnnivHol-2000, p. 148

◆ 1170 ◆ Hatch Chile Festival
September, Labor Day weekend

This event pays tribute to the green chili (as it is more commonly spelled outside of New Mexico), New Mexico's state vegetable. The small town of Hatch is the center of the chili-growing industry in the southwestern part of the state. At festival time, the aroma of freshly harvested chilis permeates the town, and a marvelous variety of chilis in all forms can be purchased: fresh green chilis—from the mildest to the hottest, dried red chilis in ornamental braids called *ristras*, red chili powder, chili bread, chili salsa, chili jelly, chili wine, and chili con carne. Besides food, the festival features the crowning of a Green Chile Queen, a skeet shoot, a fiddling contest, a cook-off, and a ristra-making contest.

CONTACTS:
Hatch Chamber of Commerce
P.O. Box 38
Hatch, NM 87937
505-267-5050
www.hatchchilefest.com

◆ 1171 ◆ Hatfield and McCoy Reunion Festival and Marathon
Three-day weekend in early June

The Hatfield and McCoy Reunion Festival and Marathon are held annually on a three-day weekend in early June in Pikeville, Ky.; Matewan, W.Va.; and Williamson, W.Va. Events take place in all three locations. The festival commemorates a family feud that has entered American lore and has become synonymous with bitter, irresolvable conflict. The feud involved two families who lived on the Tug Fork, a tributary of the Big Sandy River: the Hatfields on the West Virginia side and the McCoys on the Kentucky side. The fight, which ran from 1878 to 1891, apparently began over property rights, was fueled by a love affair between two members of the opposing families, escalated into multiple murders, and eventually necessitated two governors summoning state militia to maintain the peace. In 2003, descendants of both families signed a truce in Pikeville, but they actually had agreed to stop fighting more than a century before.

Centerpieces of the Hatfield and McCoy Reunion Festival are a marathon and half-marathon (motto: "no feudin', just runnin'"), as well as a three-town, all-terrain-vehicle ride. Other highlights include a tug-of-war across the Tug Fork, involving descendants of the feuding clans; a live, dramatic reenactment of scenes from the world's most famous family fight; and an annual feud-site motorcycle ride. In all three towns, live entertainment, tours of Hatfield-McCoy landmarks, activities such as a cornbread contest and pancake breakfast, arts and crafts, and dancing are offered. More than 300 runners typically take part in the running races, and thousands throng the area for the marathon and festival, which launched in 2000.

CONTACTS:
Tug Valley Road Runners Club
P.O. Box 321
Hardy, KY 41531
606-625-5092
www.hatfieldmccoymarathon.com/festival.cfm

♦ 1172 ♦ **Haxey Hood Game**
January 6

This centuries-old tradition in Haxey, Lincolnshire, England, can be traced back more than 600 years, when Lady Mowbray, whose husband owned a large portion of the parish of Haxey, lost her hood to a sudden gust of wind and 13 local men struggled gallantly to retrieve it. She showed her appreciation by staging an annual reenactment of the event, which is believed by some to be the origin of rugby, an English sport that combines soccer with American football.

The game known as **Throwing the Hood**, which takes place on OLD CHRISTMAS DAY (January 6) each year, involves a Lord (who acts as umpire and master of ceremonies), 13 Plough-Boggins (presumably named for the way the original 13 men turned up the soil in their efforts to capture the hood), a Fool, and as many others as care to participate.

After several warm-up rounds with sham hoods, the real contest begins. The participants wrestle over a piece of leather stuffed with straw, coins, and other fillings. The winners carry it back to their village pub, where a victory celebration takes place. Later, the Boggins go from house to house, singing and collecting money for the celebration.

CONTACTS:
Scunthorpe Tourist Information Centre
Scunthorpe Central Library
Carlton St.
Scunthorpe, DN15 6TX United Kingdom
44-17-2486-0161; fax: 44-17-2485-9737
www.visitnorthlincolnshire.com

SOURCES:
OxYear-1999, p. 25

♦ 1173 ♦ **Hay-on-Wye Festival of Literature**
Late May to early June

This celebration of words and language has been held in Hay-on-Wye, Wales, since 1988. It offers 10 days of comedy, theater, and musical performances in addition to conversations, debates, lectures, interviews, and readings by poets and fiction writers. The festival regularly features some of the most widely known Welsh, Irish, English, European, and

American writers in the world, including Margaret Atwood, Doris Lessing, John Mortimer, William Golding, Anthony Hecht, Joseph Heller, and Jan Morris. Musical performances have included the Welsh National Opera Male Choir and the English Shakespeare Company.

A series of master classes in poetry, short story, and television screenwriting has recently been established for young writers attending the festival whose poems or stories have been published or whose plays have been produced. The master classes include a week of intensive work under the supervision of such renowned writers as Joseph Brodsky, who won the NOBEL PRIZE for Literature in 1980, and the famous Welsh poet and short-story writer Leslie Norris.

CONTACTS:
Hay Festival
The Drill Hall
25 Lion St.
Hay-on-Wye, HR3 5AD United Kingdom
44-87-0990-1299; fax: 44-14-9782-1066
www.hayfestival.co.uk

Hay-on-Wye Tourist Information Bureau
Oxford Rd.
Hay-on-Wye
Herefordshire, Wales HR3 5DG United Kingdom
44-14-9782-0144
www.hay-on-wye.com

♦ 1174 ♦ **Heidi Festival**
Mid-June

The town of New Glarus, Wisconsin, has celebrated the annual Heidi Festival since the 1960s. Founded in 1845 by immigrants from the Swiss canton of Glaurus, the town of New Glarus, Wisconsin, continued to attract Swiss immigrants over the years. Today it celebrates its cultural heritage in its yearly VOLKSFEST and Heidi Festival. The Heidi Festival revolves around four performances of *Heidi*, Johanna Spyri's well-known play about a young Swiss shepherdess. The festival also includes opportunities to enjoy Swiss music, food, and dancing.

CONTACTS:
New Glarus Chamber of Commerce
418 Railroad St.
New Glarus, WI 53574
800-527-6838 or 608-527-2095; fax: 608-527-4991
www.swisstown.com

♦ 1175 ♦ **Helsinki Festival**
Late August to early September

The largest cultural event in the Nordic countries is the Helsinki Festival. It grew out of Sibelius Weeks, established in 1951 to honor Finland's most famous composer, Jean Sibelius (*see also* SIBELIUS FESTIVAL). But when the first official Helsinki Festival was held in 1967, it expanded its programming to include music from all periods—rock, jazz, opera, symphonic music, and chamber works—as well as theater, ballet, circus, and art and photo exhibitions.

Among the many musical events is what is known as the Festival Informal, a series where artists and visitors meet informally for "relaxed performances." Events are held in the city's parks and arcades as well as in the modern Finlandia Hall and and the Finnish National Theatre and Opera.

Ensembles that have performed at the 18-day festival include the Helsinki Philharmonic Orchestra, the Royal Philharmonic Orchestra of London, the Moscow Chamber Opera, the Beaux Arts Trio, the Alvin Ailey American Dance Theater, the Groteska Puppet Theatre of Kracow, the Tientsin Acrobat Company of China, and the Ballet Nacional de Cuba.

CONTACTS:
Helsinki Festival
Lasipalatsi, Mannerheimintie 22-24
Helsinki, 00100 Finland
358-9-6126-5100; fax: 358-9-6126-5161
www.helsinginjuhlaviikot.fi/index.php?&lang=en_GB

SOURCES:
GdWrldFest-1985, p. 75
IntlThFolk-1979, p. 94
MusFestEurBrit-1980, p. 66

♦ 1176 ♦ **Helston Flora Day**
May 8

According to legend, there was a large stone that at one time blocked off the entrance to hell. One night Satan tried to steal the stone. But on his way through Cornwall, England, he was intercepted by the Archangel Michael, who forced him to drop the stone and flee. The town where he dropped it was called Helston (from Hellstone, or stone of hell), and for many years a large block of granite sat in the yard of a tavern there.

The people of Helston continue to celebrate the Archangel's victory, although no one is quite sure why this celebration has been called "Furry Day." It may derive from the Gaelic word *fer* meaning "a fair," or from the Latin *feriae,* meaning "festival." Some think it's a corruption of "Flora's Day," a reference to the original Roman goddess of flowers (*see* FLORALIA). In any case, today the event is known as Helston Flora Day.

The day's festivities include the "Furry dance," which is performed in the streets by men in top hats and women in fancy dresses, and a trip to the woods in search of flowers and leaves. The original rock has long since been broken up into building stones and used for local construction. Flora Day is held on May 8 except in years when the 8th falls on a Sunday or Monday, in which case it is moved to the previous Saturday.

CONTACTS:
Helston Tourist Information Centre
79 Meneage St.
Helston, Cornwall TR13 8RB United Kingdom
44-13-2656-5431; fax: 44-13-2657-2803

SOURCES:
BkFest-1937, p. 58
BkHolWrld-1986, May 8
DaysCustFaith-1957, p. 120
DictDays-1988, p. 45
DictFolkMyth-1984, p. 204
OxYear-1999, p. 200

♦ 1177 ♦ **Hemingway (Ernest) Days Festival**
Week including July 21

This week-long celebration of Ernest Hemingway (1899-1961), the American novelist and short-story writer, is held in Key West, Fla. The festival has been held since 1980 during the week of Hemingway's birthday, July 21. Hemingway made his home in Key West at one time, and his novel, *To Have and Have Not* (1937), is set there. He was awarded the Pulitzer Prize in fiction in 1953 for his short heroic novel about an old Cuban fisherman, *The Old Man and the Sea,* and he received the Nobel Prize for Literature in 1954.

A short-story competition, with a first-place prize of $1,000, drew a total of 981 submissions in 2000. Lorian Hemingway, the writer's granddaughter and a writer herself, is the coordinator of the story contest.

Other events include a street fair, a Hemingway look-alike contest, a fishing tournament, an arm-wrestling competition, and a party and concert at the Hemingway Home and Museum.

CONTACTS:
Florida Keys Tourism Council
1201 White St., Ste. 103
Key West, FL 33040
800-771-5397 or 305-292-1880; fax: 305-294-1699
www.fla-keys.com

Hemingway Home and Museum
907 Whitehead St.
Key West, FL 33040
305-294-1136
hemingwayhome.com

SOURCES:
AmerBkDays-2000, p. 539

♦ 1178 ♦ **Hemis Festival**
Usually in June or July

This three-day Buddhist festival takes place at the Hemis Gompa in the mountainous region of Ladakh in northern India. This is the largest *gompa* (monastery) in Ladakh and has gold statues, huge stone monuments of Buddha called *stupas* that are studded with precious stones, and an impressive collection of *thangkas,* or big scroll religious paintings.

The festival celebrates the birthday of Guru Padmasambhava, the Indian Buddhist mystic who introduced Tantric Buddhism to Tibet in the eighth century. Tradition says he was a native of Swat (now in Pakistan), an area noted for magicians. Tradition also says he brought on an earthquake in Tibet to get rid of the demons who were delaying the building of a monastery.

The festival attracts people from throughout the mountain areas of Ladakh and Tibet—Muslims and Hindus as well as Buddhists, all dressed in their most colorful clothes. A fair springs up, with stalls selling confections, gems, and crafts.

The highlight of the festival is the Devil Dance of the monks (*see also* MYSTERY PLAY OF TIBET). Demon dancers are costumed as satyrs, many-eyed monsters, fierce tigers, or skeletons, while lamas portraying saints wear miters and opulent silks and carry pastoral crooks. These good lamas, ringing bells and swinging censers, scatter the bad lamas, as they all swirl about to the music of cymbals, drums, and 10-foot-long trumpets. The dance is a morality play, a battle between good and evil spirits, and also expresses the idea that a person's helpless soul can be comforted only by a lama's exorcisms.

CONTACTS:
Jammu and Kashmir Government
Directorate of Information
Opposite Pratap Pk.
Srinagar, Jammu & Kashmir 190 001 India
91-194-2452294; fax: 91-194-2452227
www.jammukashmir.nic.in

SOURCES:
RelHolCal-2004, p. 220

◆ 1179 ◆ Henley Royal Regatta
Five days in early July

The international rowing competition known as the Henley Regatta was first held in 1839. The long, straight, nearly two-mile stretch of the Thames River about 35 miles west of London made Henley an ideal location for oarsmen to compete—in fact, it was the site of the Olympic rowing competition in both 1908 and 1948, when London hosted the OLYMPIC GAMES. The races became known as "royal" in 1851, when Prince Albert became the first member of the royal family to patronize the event.

The five-day Regatta's many events include races for eight-oared, four-oared, and pair-oared boats as well as sculling races for quadruple, double, and single sculls. The course takes six to seven minutes to row, and there are often two races taking place simultaneously. Although only male oarsmen were allowed to compete for 154 years, an open women's event was introduced in 1993. The so-called "Women's Henley," held annually a few weeks before the Royal Regatta, has grown rapidly in popularity.

In addition to being a world-class rowing competition for oarsmen from a dozen countries and more than 60 colleges and universities, the Henley Royal Regatta is also a huge lawn party attended by nearly half a million spectators. The hub of social interaction during Regatta week is the Stewards' Enclosure, an exclusive spectators' area located near the end of the course. Parties also take place in tents called "chalets," set up along the banks of the river, as well as in the parking lot, where people serve impressive meals from their cars.

The men traditionally dress in straw hats and rowing blazers and neckties, whose colors indicate what school, college, or club they once rowed for. The women put on their finest summer dresses and hats; short skirts, culottes, or slacks of any kind are forbidden.

CONTACTS:
Henley Royal Regatta
Henley-on-Thames
Oxfordshire, RG9 2LY United Kingdom
44-14-9157-2153; fax: 44-14-9157-5509
www.hrr.co.uk

◆ 1180 ◆ Heritage Holidays
Mid-October

The Heritage Holidays are a five-day celebration of the history of Rome, Ga., which, like its Italian namesake, was built on seven hills. There is also a bronze replica of the Capitoline Wolf outside City Hall. This Roman statue depicting a she-wolf nursing the legendary founders of Rome—Romulus and Remus—was given to the town in 1929 by Benito Mussolini.

Heritage Holidays, however, looks back to different times: it features a re-creation of the famous ride of John Wisdom, who has been called the Paul Revere of the South. During the Civil War, Rome was important to the Confederacy as a rail and manufacturing center. Wisdom, a native of the city who was living in Alabama, was delivering mail when he heard that Yankee soldiers were headed for his hometown. He rode the 67 miles to Rome in 11 hours, wearing out five horses and a mule. The men of Rome set up two old cannons, and the Yanks decided the town seemed too heavily fortified. They surrendered to a smaller Confederate force following them.

Features of the heritage days are a wagon train, parades, riverboat rides, concerts, and a major arts and crafts fair.

CONTACTS:
Greater Rome Convention and Visitors Bureau
601 Broad St.
P.O. Box 1433
Rome, GA 30162
800-444-1834 or 706-236-4400; fax: 706-236-4405
www.romega.us

◆ 1181 ◆ Hermit, Feast of the
September 1

Juan Maria de Castellano is known as a saint among the Hispanic Americans of Hot Springs, New Mexico. He lived in a cave on a mountain peak for three years and slept on the ground. According to legend, he was responsible for a number of miraculous feats, not the least of which was producing water from a rock that had the power to cure blindness and other ills. Once when he had 12 men visit him, the very small amount of food he prepared was sufficient to feed all of them for an entire day.

In the 1930s, the members of the Asociacion de Santa Maria de Guadalupe met twice a year on Hermit's Peak. The second and more important of the two meetings was held on September 1, which came to be known as the Feast of the Hermit. People brought picnics, and some built little huts where they could spend the night. Some came to be cured, while others worked on repairing the fences and clearing the trails. They lit huge bonfires and prayed for the holy man who, like Moses, had caused water to flow from a rock and who, like Jesus, had satisfied the hunger of multitudes.

SOURCES:
FolkAmerHol-1999, p. 356

◆ 1182 ◆ Heurigen Parties
November

ST. MARTIN'S DAY, November 11, is the traditional time when wine taverns in Austria offer the first new wines of the year. Wine feasts called Heurigen parties abound in these taverns throughout the country and are scheduled according to an official *Heurigenkalender*. Traditional foods served with the new wine include sausage, cheese, and bread. Many taverns also stage operettas and other shows for the season.

CONTACTS:
Vienna Tourist Board
Albertinaplatz Maysedergasse
Vienna, A-1025 Austria
43-1-2455-5; fax: 43-1-2455-5666
www.wien.info

SOURCES:
BkFestHolWorld-1970, p. 121
FestEur-1961, p. 15

◆ 1183 ◆ Hi Matsuri (Fire Festival)
October 22

Early on the evening of October 22, people light bonfires along the narrow street leading to the Kuramadera Shrine in Kurama, a village in the mountains north of Kyoto, Japan. The bonfires are made with gigantic roots brought in from the nearby forest. Fire is a purifying element, according to Shinto teachings, and the village and its inhabitants are believed to be protected from accidents on this particular night.

Soon after dusk, people light torches: even babies, under the watchful eyes of their parents, are allowed to carry tiny torches made out of twigs. Young men carry large torches, sometimes so large it takes several men to keep them upright. As they walk through the streets, everyone chants rhythmically, "Sai-rei! Sai-ryo!" ("Festival, good festival"). Sometimes a marcher lets a heavy torch fall, and people try to catch one of the falling sparks because they believe it will bring them good luck.

Around midnight the torches begin to die down and the villagers grow quiet. Everyone gathers around either side of the stairway that takes one to the shrine. The entrance to the stairway has been barred with a rope, which a Shinto priest now cuts. Two groups of strong men carry the two elaborately decorated *mikoshi* or palanquins in which the *kami* or gods are believed to reside when they visit the earth. They take them down the stairway to the outskirts of the village and set them down. Everyone bids farewell to the kami, who must return to their spirit home.

Although no one knows exactly how the Fire Festival originated, some believe it was at one time a test of virility or an initiation rite conducted when a boy reached manhood. Another theory is that it originated in the custom of lighting fires called *mukaebi* to guide gods or spirits from the other world on their visits to earth.

CONTACTS:
Kyoto City Tourism & Culture Information
233-5 Daimon-ji-cho, Atarashimachi-dori
Oike-sagaru, Nakagyo-ku
Kyoto, 604-8315 Japan

81-7-5811-6388; fax: 81-7-5813-3250
www.kyotoguide.com

SOURCES:
IllFestJapan-1993, p. 148
JapanFest-1965, pp. 14, 201
YrJapanFest-1974, p. 25

◆ 1184 ◆ Hidrellez Festival
May 6

The Hidrellez Festival is observed in Turkey every May 6. It is marked as the day that two prophets, Hizir and Ilyas, met each other on Earth, and the holiday also is known as **Ruz-I Hizir** (day of Hizir). The word Hidrellez is a fusing of the two names. The festival is a joyous celebration of the coming of spring. The customs associated with it probably derive from various eastern Mediterranean traditions, including Mesopotamian, Anatolian, and pre-Islamic central-Asian Turkish. All of these cultures have numerous, age-old rituals and ceremonies associated with the renewal and rebirth of spring. Many Turks believe that Hizir drank the water of life and is immortal, and that he is able to bestow people with health, happiness, and abundance. He is a symbol of new life, and in some parts of Turkey, people offer sacrifices and votive offerings "for the sake of Hizir" to make their prayers and wishes come true.

People prepare for Hidrellez by thoroughly cleaning their homes, because they believe that Hizir will not visit houses that are not clean. They also purchase fresh new clothes and shoes to wear for the Hidrellez Festival, and prepare special food, such as fresh lamb or lamb's liver. On Hidrellez night, people leave purses and pantries open and put out food bowls, in the belief that Hizir will bring abundance to the homes he visits. If they desire a house or vineyard, they will make a little model of what they want so that Hizir will help them obtain it. Throughout Turkey at Hidrellez time, people perform various ceremonies to improve or to test their luck, believing that fortunes improve with the reawakening of nature in springtime. Such ceremonies typically are carried out in leafy, green places or near sources of water.

CONTACTS:
Republic of Turkey Ministry of Culture and Tourism
Ataturk Bulvari No: 29
06050 Opera
Ankara, Turkey
www.kultur.gov.tr

SOURCES:
HolSymbols-2009, p. 355
UndIslam-2004, p. 377

◆ 1185 ◆ Higan
*Week including March 20 or 21 and week
including September 23 or 24*

Higan is a week of Buddhist services observed in Japan at the spring and autumn equinoxes (*see* SHUNBUN-NO-HI and AUTUMNAL EQUINOX) when day and night are of equal length.

Both equinoxes have been national holidays since the Meiji Period (1868-1912). Before World War II, they were known as *koreisai*, "festivals of the Imperial ancestors." After the war, when the national holidays were renamed, they became simply spring equinox and autumn equinox.

Higan is the seven-day period surrounding the equinoxes. It means the "other shore," and refers to the spirits of the dead reaching Nirvana after crossing the river of existence. Thus Higan is a celebration of the spiritual move from the world of suffering to the world of enlightenment and is a time for remembering the dead, visiting, cleaning, and decorating their graves, and reciting *sutras*, Buddhist prayers. *O-hagi*, rice balls covered with sweet bean paste, and sushi are offered. It is traditional not to eat meat during this period. Emperor Heizei instituted the celebration in 806 C.E., when he ordered a week-long reading of a certain sutra for the occasion.

In Okinawa it is a home thanksgiving festival. Barley (*omugi*) or barley cakes with brown sugar are eaten with prayers for good fortune.

SOURCES:
FolkWrldHol-1999, p. 565
HolSymbols-2009, p. 357
JapanFest-1965, p. 190

♦ 1186 ♦ Highland Games
Dates vary

Originally impromptu athletic competitions carried out in the Scottish Highlands as part of a clan gathering, Highland games are now held all over the world, usually under the auspices of a local Caledonian society. Although the Jacobites put an end to the clan assemblies in 1745, the tradition of the games survived, and the first of the modern gatherings was held 90 years later at Braemar (*see* BRAEMAR HIGHLAND GATHERING). Today there are about 40 major gatherings in Scotland alone, as well as in Tauranga, New Zealand, and in several American communities such as Goshen, Connecticut, and Alexandria, Virginia, where there is a strong Anglo-Scottish presence.

Events at most Highland gatherings include flat and hurdle races, long and high jumps, pole vaulting, throwing the hammer, and tossing the weight (a round stone ball). A unique Highland event is tossing the caber, a tapered fir pole that must be thrown so that it turns end over end and comes to rest with the small end pointing away from the thrower. Competitors who toss the weight or the caber must wear a traditional Scottish kilt. There are also competitions in bagpipe music and Highland dancing.

See also ALMA HIGHLAND FESTIVAL AND GAMES; GRANDFATHER MOUNTAIN HIGHLAND GAMES AND GATHERING OF SCOTTISH CLANS; and VIRGINIA SCOTTISH GAMES

CONTACTS:
Scottish Tourist Board
23 Ravelston Terr.
Edinburgh, Scotland EH43EU United Kingdom
44-13-1332-2433; fax: 44-13-1315-4545
www.visitscotland.com

SOURCES:
AnnivHol-2000, p. 147

♦ 1187 ♦ Hilaria
March 25

The ancient Romans celebrated the festival of Hilaria for Cybele, the "mother of the gods," and Attis each year on March 25. According to one legend, Cybele fell in love with a human man named Attis. When Attis's attention later strayed to a woman, Cybele made him go insane. He killed himself, after which flowers grew from his blood and his body became a tree. The day of Hilaria, observing this resurrection of sorts, was celebrated with much merry-making and feasting.

SOURCES:
DaysCustFaith-1957, p. 89
DictRomRel-1996, p. 101
EncyEaster-2002, p. 267
FestSaintDays-1915, p. 50

♦ 1188 ♦ Hill Cumorah Pageant
Begins on the third weekend in July

Billed as the largest outdoor pageant in the United States, the Hill Cumorah Pageant is based on the Bible and the *Book of Mormon* and is presented by the Church of Jesus Christ of Latter-Day Saints (popularly called Mormons) in Palmyra, New York, for nine consecutive evenings (excluding Sunday and Monday) beginning on the third weekend in July.

The drama tells the story of the people who lived on the North American continent between 600 B.C.E. and 421 C.E., and how Christ taught these ancient Americans his gospel after his resurrection in Jerusalem. Presented on seven stages, each showing of the pageant can accommodate an audience of 15,000. More than 500 people participate in the pageant on a volunteer basis. Some impressive features of the pageant include water curtains that are used during the "vision" scenes and an erupting volcano.

Hill Cumorah is believed to be the site where, in 1823, the angel Moroni instructed Joseph Smith, the first prophet of the Mormon Church, to look for the secret records, written upon gold plates, that told about the ancient inhabitants of North America—American Indians that the Mormons believe were descended from the Israelites via the tribe of Joseph. Smith was told that the plates were hidden in a hill named Cumorah, located between Palmyra and Manchester, New York. But it was nearly four years before Moroni gave Smith permission to remove the plates and begin their translation. They would eventually be published as the *Book of Mormon* in 1830.

CONTACTS:
Hill Cumorah Visitors' Center
603 State Route 21
Palmyra, NY 14522
315-597-5851; fax: 315-597-0165
www.hillcumorah.com

SOURCES:
GdUSFest-1984, p. 129
RelHolCal-2004, p. 127

♦ 1189 ♦ Hina Matsuri (Doll Festival)
March 3

Hina Matsuri is a festival for girls, celebrated in homes throughout Japan since the Edo Period (1600-1867), when doll making became a highly skilled craft.

A set of 10 to 15 dolls (or *hina*), usually unmatched family heirlooms from various generations, is displayed on a stand covered with red cloth, the stand having at least three and up to seven steps. Dressed in elaborate antique silk costumes, the dolls represent the emperor and empress, ladies-in-waiting, court ministers, musicians, and servants. Replicas of ornate furnishings are part of the display, as are miniature dishes of foods offered to the emperor and empress. People visit each other's homes to admire the dolls.

In parts of Tottori Prefecture, girls make boats of straw, place a pair of paper dolls in them with rice cakes and, after displaying them with the other hina, set them afloat on the Mochigase River. This custom supposedly dates back to ancient times when dolls were used as talismans to exorcize evil; a paper doll cast into a river signified the washing away of human misfortune.

CONTACTS:
Japan Information Network, Japan Center for Intercultural
  Communications
2-7-7 Hirakawacho
Chiyodaku
Tokyo, 102-0093 Japan
81-3-3263-5041; fax: 81-3-3230-4107
home.jcic.or.jp

SOURCES:
BkFest-1937, p. 196
BkFestHolWrld-1970, p. 72
BkHolWrld-1986, Mar 3
DictFolkMyth-1984, p. 540
FolkAmerHol-1999, p. 126
FolkWrldHol-1999, p. 200
HolSymbols-2009, p. 360
JapanFest-1965, p. 72

♦ 1190 ♦ Hippokrateia Festival
August

This festival is a celebration of Hippocrates, the "Great Physician," on Kos, the Greek island where he was born in about 460 B.C.E. A number of ancient manuscripts bear the name of Hippocrates; the best known of these is the *Aphorisms*, a collection of short discussions on the nature of illness, its diagnosis, prognosis, and treatment. The Hippocratic oath, an ethical code attributed to Hippocrates, is still used in graduation ceremonies at many medical schools. In it, the physician pledges to refrain from causing harm and to live an exemplary personal and professional life.

Throughout antiquity, Kos attracted the sick and infirm who came for healing at the Shrine of Asclepius, the god of medicine. Today the island is a popular resort, featuring fine beaches, the ruins of Roman baths, a Greek theater, and a museum with a huge statue of Hippocrates. The festival includes performances of ancient drama, concerts, a flower show, and a reenactment of the Hippocratic oath.

CONTACTS:
Greek National Tourist Organization
645 Fifth Ave., 9th Fl.
New York, NY 10022
212-421-5777; fax: 212-826-6940
www.greektourism.com

SOURCES:
EncyRel-1987, vol. 6, p. 367

♦ 1191 ♦ Hiroshima Peace Ceremony
August 6

This ceremony has been held each year since 1947 at the Peace Memorial Park in Hiroshima, Japan, in memory of the victims of the atomic bomb that devastated the city in 1945. (The day was Aug. 5 in the United States, Aug. 6 in Japan.) It was the first time in history that a weapon of such destruction had been used. The American B-29 Superfortress *Enola Gay* carried the bomb, called "Little Boy." The day is sometimes called **Atomic Bomb Day**, but this refers more accurately to the anniversary of the first atomic bomb test on July 16, 1945, at Alamogordo Air Base in New Mexico.

In announcing the bombing, President Harry S. Truman said, "The force from which the sun draws its power has been loosed against those who brought war to the Far East." The immediate death toll was 60,000, at least 75,000 more were injured, and the bomb wiped out more than four square miles—60 percent of the city. One man on the mission described its explosion as a bright, blinding flash followed by a "black cloud of boiling dust" and above it white smoke that "climbed like a mushroom to 20,000 feet." Three days later, on Aug. 9, a second A-bomb, called "Fat Man," was dropped on Nagasaki, razing the center of the city and killing 39,000. On Aug. 15, Japan surrendered, ending World War II.

The peace ceremony is held in the evening, when the city's citizens set thousands of lighted lanterns adrift on the Ota River and prayers are offered for world peace. Other memorial services are also held throughout the world at this time.

CONTACTS:
Hiroshima Peace Memorial Museum
1-2 Nakajimama-cho, Naka-Ku
Hiroshima, 730-0811 Japan
81-8-2242-7798; fax: 81-8-2247-2464
www.pef.city.hiroshima.jp/top_e.html

SOURCES:
AmerBkDays-2000, p. 564
AnnivHol-2000, p. 134
DictDays-1988, p. 56
HolSymbols-2009, p. 363

♦ 1192 ♦ Hispanic Heritage Month
September 15-October 15

Since 1989, National Hispanic Heritage Month has been celebrated in the United States from September 15 until October

15. Issued as a presidential proclamation each year, this period of time includes such important Hispanic anniversaries as the independence days of Costa Rica, El Salvador, Guatemala, Honduras, and Nicaragua on September 15, Mexico's Festival of Independence on September 16, and Columbus Day, or Day of the Race, around October 12.

The activities that take place during the month, particularly in cities with large Hispanic populations, focus on how Latinos have made the United States a richer and more interesting place to live. They include performances by Latino musical groups, lectures about Hispanic life, and special awards presentations to Latinos who have made significant achievements in business, education, or the arts. In Washington, D.C., Hispanic members of Congress and other political leaders sponsor an annual dinner at which awards are presented.

CONTACTS:
PBS Teacher Source
2100 Crystal Dr.
Arlington, VA 22202
703-739-5000; fax: 703-739-8495
www.pbs.org
Hispanic Heritage Awards Foundation
2600 Virginia Ave. N.W., Ste. 406
Washington, DC 20037
202-861-9797; fax: 202-861-9799
www.hispanicheritageawards.org

SOURCES:
LatinoLife-1995, p. 39

♦ 1193 ♦ Historical Regatta
First Sunday in September

Regattas have been a tradition in Italy for more than seven centuries, and this one in Venice is widely known as one of the most beautiful in the world. It marks the return of Caterina Cornaro (1454-1510), the last queen of Cyprus, to Venice. Originally from a noble Venetian family, Caterina's marriage to James II of Lusignan was arranged by leaders in Venice in an effort to claim Cyprus as Venetian territory. It worked, and in 1489 the dethroned Caterina returned to her homeland to a welcome of regattas and celebrations.

For sheer splendor, the Historical Regatta ranks with the Palio of Siena. It begins with a procession of historical boats, all decorated and strewn with flowers, down the Grand Canal, which is itself decked with flags, banners, and tapestries for the occasion. Leading the procession is the "Machina," a vessel of baroque style with oars, elaborate carvings, and golden sculptures, which serves as a grandstand and carries officials and local dignitaries. Then there are various competitions: for young people, for women, and for small gondolas with two oars and crews in 16th-century costume. The races arouse intense enthusiasm among the spectators, and by the end of the regatta, all of the canals are crowded with boatloads of revelers.

CONTACTS:
Veneto Tourism Office
Palazzo Sceriman
Cannaregio, Venezia 30121 Italy

39-41-2792-602; fax: 39-41-2792-697
www.veneto.to/portal/faces/public/guest?portal:com

SOURCES:
FestEur-1961, p. 121

♦ 1194 ♦ Hitachi Furyumono
Early April

This Japanese festival, held in the city of Hitachi in Ibaraki Prefecture, features puppets known as *furyumono*. They perform on huge floats, some nearly 50 feet high, with five tiers. The front part of the float is concealed by large stage doors, which open to the left and right like extended wings to reveal the puppets performing their plays—usually less complicated retellings of dramas from the Edo Period (1603-1867). The puppeteers must lie down while operating the puppets so that the audience won't be able to see them. A single float may carry as many as 25 puppeteers, along with a seven- or eight-piece orchestra.

The rear part of each float is built to resemble a huge rock. Simpler puppet shows illustrating fables and nursery tales are performed here. The puppetry is part of the annual Cherry Blossom Festival in Hitachi.

CONTACTS:
Japan National Tourist Organization
1 Rockefeller Pl., Ste. 1250
New York, NY 10020
212-757-5640; fax: 212-307-6754
www.japantravelinfo.com

SOURCES:
IllFestJapan-1993, p. 60

♦ 1195 ♦ Hmong New Year
December to January

The Hmong people of Laos mark a 10-day celebration of the New Year to give thanks to spirits and ancestors, as well as to rejoice in a new beginning. They mark the occasion by wearing silk clothing in bright shades of red, green, and white along with ornate silver jewelry. Music is central to the celebration, with tunes played on such traditional instruments as the teun flute and Hmong-style khene pipe. Other traditional activities of the Hmong in Laos include leaf-blowing, ox-fighting, spinning-top competitions, cross-bow demonstrations, and Makkhon, a ceremony that involves young people tossing a ball made of cotton cloth back and forth.

CONTACTS:
Lao National Tourism Administration
Tourism Marketing and Promotion Dept.
P.O. Box 3556
Lane Xang Ave.
Hatsady Village, Chanthabouly District, Ventiane Capital Lao PDR
www.tourismlaos.gov.la

♦ 1196 ♦ Ho Chi Minh's Birthday
May 19

Ho Chi Minh was born on May 19, 1890. Often referred to as the "father of modern Vietnam," Ho Chi Minh spearheaded the Vietnamese people's revolt against French and Japanese occupation. In 1954, after the French and Japanese left, the United States entered the scene, and it was during this struggle that Ho Chi Minh died in 1969. It was another six years before North and South Vietnam united into the Socialist Republic of Vietnam.

On Ho Chi Minh's birthday each year people hold parades in cities, carrying posters depicting him. Many women wear the *ao dai*, traditional Vietnamese dress. Speeches about Ho Chi Minh generally follow the parades.

CONTACTS:
Socialist Republic of Vietnam Embassy
1233 20th St. N.W., Ste. 400
Washington, D.C. 20036
202-861-0737; fax: 202-861-0917
www.vietnamembassy-usa.org

SOURCES:
FestWrld: Viet-1997, p. 21

◆ 1197 ◆ Hobart Cup Day
On or near January 26

There are a number of famous horse races in Australia each year that are observed as holidays in the states where they take place. Hobart Cup Day is a holiday in Southern Tasmania; it is run in Hobart around AUSTRALIA DAY, January 26. Northern Tasmania observes Launceston Cup Day a month later. In South Australia, Adelaide Cup Day is celebrated in May. And the MELBOURNE CUP, the country's richest handicap race, is held on the first Tuesday in November.

CONTACTS:
Hobart City Council
16 Elizabeth St.
P.O. Box 503
Hobart, TAS 7001 Australia
61-3-6238-2711; fax: 61-3-6238-2186
www.hobartcity.com.au

SOURCES:
DictDays-1988, p. 75

◆ 1198 ◆ Hobart Royal Regatta
February

The **Royal Hobart Regatta** is a two-day aquatic carnival that includes sailing, rowing, and swimming events as well as fireworks and parades. It is a holiday in Tasmania, Australia, and is held on the Derwent River sometime in early February during Australia's summer season. Hobart is the capital of Tasmania, Australia's southernmost state.

A similar holiday in northern Tasmania is observed on the first Monday in November and is called **Recreation Day**.

CONTACTS:
Hobart City Council
16 Elizabeth St.

P.O. Box 503
Hobart, TAS 7001 Australia
61-3-6238-2711; fax: 61-3-6238-2186
www.hobartcity.com.au

SOURCES:
DictDays-1988, pp. 56, 95

◆ 1199 ◆ Hobo Convention
One week in mid-August

The small, rural town of Britt, Iowa (population 2,000), seems an unlikely location for a convention of hobos—the unwashed but colorful riders of America's empty boxcars—but for a week each summer its residents play host to this diminishing segment of the population. From across the nation the hobos come to Britt, where they receive free food, sleeping accommodations in empty boxcars, and the adoration of more than 20,000 visitors who want to find out what a hobo's life is really like.

There is a parade, an arts fair, carnival rides, races, and music. But the real action centers on the hobo camp set up by festival organizers on the outskirts of town, where visitors can hear the life stories of these men who have chosen to travel the country unencumbered by family or property.

The hobos are quick to distinguish themselves from tramps and bums. As one explains, "A hobo wants to wander, but he always works for his meals … a tramp wanders, but never does any work; a bum just drinks and wanders." The first Hobo Convention was held in Britt in 1900, and during the 1930s the event attracted hundreds of hobos. But their ranks are thinning, and today the town is lucky if 30 or 40 real hobos show up.

CONTACTS:
Britt Chamber of Commerce
P.O. Box 63
Britt, IA 50423
641-843-3867
www.brittchamberofcommerce.com

◆ 1200 ◆ Hocktide
Between April 5 and May 9; second Monday and Tuesday after Easter

Also known as **Hock Days**, the second Monday and Tuesday after EASTER in England was in medieval times—and in Hungerford, Berkshire, till the present day—associated with collecting dues or rents and money for the church, particularly in rural areas.

There were a number of traditional methods for demanding money, most of them light-hearted rather than threatening. For example, people were often tied up with ropes and had to pay for their release, giving rise to the name **Binding Tuesday**. Or rope might be stretched across the road to stop passersby, who would then have to pay before they were allowed to continue.

In parts of Berkshire, two "Tutti men" in top hats and morning coats—a "tutti" being a small bouquet of flowers—would go from house to house carrying a "tutti pole" decorated with flowers and ribbons. There was also an orange scatterer who threw oranges to the men, old women, and children to keep them busy while the Tutti men went from house to house demanding both money and a kiss from the lady of the house.

In Yorkshire, children were still celebrating **Kissing Day** as recently as the 1950s—widely believed to have derived from hocktide customs.

Hocktide was also one of the QUARTER DAYS.

CONTACTS:
Hungerford Chamber of Commerce
Church St.
Hungerford, RG17 0JG United kingdom
44-77-6761-0721
www.hungerford.org.uk

SOURCES:
BkFest-1937, pp. 16, 57
DictDays-1988, pp. 11, 55, 56, 122
EncyEaster-2002, p. 271
FestSaintDays-1915, p. 91
FolkWrldHol-1992, p. 208
OxYear-1999, p. 625

♦ 1201 ♦ **Hogbetsotso Festival**
On and around the first Saturday in November

The week-long Hogbetsotso festival commemorates the migration of the Anlo-speaking Ewes, an ethnic group on the eastern coast of Ghana, from the ancient walled city of Notsie in present-day northern Togo to their current home in Ghana. According to legend, the Anlo-Ewes escaped the wicked chief, Ago-Koli, by walking backwards amidst dancing and drumming to war songs. Each year the Anlo-Ewes hold the Hogbetsotso festival, or "Festival of the Exodus," to remember their journey and the brave leaders who guided them.

The Anlo-Ewes begin the observance of Hogbetsotso with a period of peacemaking, during which any outstanding problems are resolved. They perform a ceremony to purify the traditional stool that is an important fixture in Ghanaian culture, and they clean their villages by sweeping and burning garbage. The festival culminates with a grand durbar, or reception, of chiefs and their people, which takes place on the first Saturday of November in Anloga. At the durbar, the chiefs wear bright ceremonial clothing and sit in state, while citizens pay them tribute. The entire festival period is marked by singing, dancing and merry-making. Born of age-old oral legend, the Hogbetsotso festival has been celebrated for generations.

CONTACTS:
Ghana Ministry of Tourism and Diaspora Relations
P.O. Box 4386
Accra, Ghana
www.touringghana.com/default.asp

♦ 1202 ♦ **Hogmanay**
December 31

In Scotland and the northern part of England, the last day of the year is known as Hogmanay. There are a number of the-

ories as to where the name comes from—one of them being that it derives from the ancient Scandinavian name for the night preceding the feast of YULE, *Hoggu-nott* or *Hogg-night*. Another is that it comes from the French expression, *Au gui l'an neuf* ("New Year's gift" or "the last day of the year").

Scottish children, often wearing a sheet doubled up in front to form a huge pocket, used to call at the homes of the wealthy on this day and ask for their traditional gift of an oatmeal cake. They would call out, "Hogmanay!" and recite traditional rhymes or sing songs in return for which they'd be given their cakes to take home. It is for this reason that December 31 was also referred to as **Cake Day**.

Today Hogmanay is celebrated much as is NEW YEAR'S EVE around the rest of the Western world, with street and house parties. Such fire ceremonies as torchlight processions and lighting New Year's fires are popular traditions as well.

See also FIRST-FOOT DAY

SOURCES:
BkDays-1864, vol. II, p. 788
BkFest-1937, p. 63
BkHolWrld-1986, Dec 31
DictDays-1988, pp. 56, 81, 84
DictFolkMyth-1984, pp. 181, 499, 791
EncyChristmas-2003, p. 328
FolkWrldHol-1999, p. 779
OxYear-1999, p. 541

♦ 1203 ♦ **Hola Mohalla**
February-March

Hola Mohalla is a three-day Sikh festival celebrated in Anandpur Sahib, Punjab, India, on the day after HOLI, the colorful water-tossing springtime festival. Mock battles with ancient weapons are staged, and there are also exhibitions of traditional martial arts like archery and fencing. The important Sikh prophet, GURU GOBIND SINGH, started this fair sometime between 1680 and 1700.

CONTACTS:
Ministry of Tourism, Government of India
Rm. No 123, Transport Bhawan, No. 1, Parliament St.
New Delhi, Delhi 110 001 India
91-11-23715084; fax: 91-11-23715084
www.tourisminindia.com

Punjab Tourism Development Corp.
SCO 183-184
Sector 8-C
Chandigarh, Punjab 160 018 India
91-172-781138; fax: 91-172-548828
punjabgovt.nic.in/TOURISM/ContactAddresses.htm

SOURCES:
RelHolCal-2004, p. 203
SikhFest-1989, p. 38

♦ 1204 ♦ **Holetown Festival**
Begins in mid-February

The British were not the first European settlers to establish themselves on the Caribbean island of Barbados, but they were the first to remain permanently after they settled in February 1627. The Holetown Festival, which takes place in the historic town of the same name, marks the approximate date of English settlement. A weeklong celebration of history and culture, the festival has been an annual event since 1977.

The opening celebrations are held at the Holetown Monument, which commemorates the settlers' landing. Over the course of the week there are fashion shows, beauty contests, exhibitions, folksongs, an antique car parade, and a carnival at the festival fairgrounds.

Festival organizers ensure that music is integral to the celebration and that a balance exists between the old and the new, the indigenous and the Western. Along with music concerts showcasing authentic Caribbean music and dancing, there are traditional hymns, folksongs, a music festival at the historic St. James Church, and a concert by the Royal Barbados Police Band, in existence since 1889.

CONTACTS:
Barbados Tourism Authority
800 2nd Ave., # 2
New York, NY 10017
212-986-6516
www.visitbarbados.org

SOURCES:
AnnivHol-2000, p. 29

♦ 1205 ♦ Holi
February-March; 14th day of waxing half of Hindu month of Phalguna

Holi is a colorful and boisterous Hindu spring festival in India, also known as the **Festival of Colors**. This is a time of shedding inhibitions: People smear each other with red and yellow powder and shower each other with colored water shot from bamboo blowpipes or water pistols. Restrictions of caste, sex, age, and personal differences are ignored. *Bhang,* an intoxicating drink made from the same plant that produces marijuana, is imbibed, and revelry reigns.

The name of the festival derives from the name of the wicked Holika. According to legend, an evil king had a good son, Prince Prahlad, who was sent by the gods to deliver the land from the king's cruelty. Holika, the king's sister, decided to kill the prince with fire. Believing she was immune to fire, she held the child in her lap and sat in flames. But Lord Krishna stepped in to save Prahlad, and Holika was left in the fire and burned to death. On the night before the festival, images of Holika are burned on huge bonfires, drums pound, horns blow, and people whoop.

Another tale, related to the practice of water-throwing, is that the small monkey god Hanuman (*see* HANUMAN JAYANTI) one day managed to swallow the sun. People were sad to live in darkness, and other gods suggested they rub color on one another and laugh. They mixed the color in water and squirted each other, and Hanuman thought this was so funny he gave a great laugh, and the sun flew out of his mouth.

There is also the story that the Mongol Emperor Akbar thought everyone would look equal if covered with color, and he therefore ordained the holiday to unite the castes.

The celebrations differ from city to city. In Mathura, Lord Krishna's legendary birthplace, there are especially exuberant processions with songs and music. In the villages of Nandgaon and Barsnar, once homes of Krishna and his beloved Radha, the celebrations are spread over 16 days. And in Besant, people set up a 25-foot pole called a *chir* to begin the celebrations and burn it at the end of the festival.

In Bangladesh the festival is called **Dol-Jatra,** the **Swing Festival,** because a Krishna doll is kept in a swinging cradle, or *dol.* In Nepal it is called **Rung Khelna,** "playing with color." They build a three-tiered, 25-foot high umbrella and at its base people light joss sticks, and place flowers and red powder. Instead of squirting water, they drop water-filled balloons from upper windows.

In Suriname it is **Holi Phagwa** and also the **Hindu New Year**.

CONTACTS:
Ministry of Tourism, Government of India
Rm. No 123, Transport Bhawan, No. 1, Parliament St.
New Delhi, Delhi 110 001 India
91-11-23715084; fax: 91-11-23715084
www.tourisminindia.com

SOURCES:
BkFest-1937, p. 163
BkFestHolWrld-1970, p. 8
BkHolWrld-1986, Mar 27
DictFolkMyth-1984, pp. 500, 591, 941
FolkWrldHol-1999, p. 186
HolSymbols-2009, p. 372
RelHolCal-2004, p. 183

♦ 1206 ♦ Holland Festival
June

Holland (the Netherlands) didn't really have a single composer who could be honored by a festival in a specific city or town—such as the MOZART Festival in Salzburg, Austria (*see* SALZBURG FESTIVAL), or Germany's Wagner Festival in BAYREUTH. Instead, it was decided in 1947 to have a single festival focused on three major cities—Amsterdam, Rotterdam, and the Hague/Scheveningen—that would cover a wide range of artistic and cultural activities and at the same time draw top international artists to the Netherlands.

Nowadays the festival is centered in Amsterdam and lasts 23 days in June with nearly 150 programs. The festival offers not only performances of orchestral and choral works but opera, ballet, contemporary music, dance, theater, and film as well.

In recent years the Holland Festival has been connected with the Amsterdam Roots Festival, which began in 1998 and also takes place during the month of June, and concentrates on world culture. The 2000 festival featured 65 musical and dance performances from artists from more than 30 nationalities.

CONTACTS:
Holland Festival
Kleine-Gartmanplantsoen 21

Amsterdam, 1017 RP Netherlands
31-20-530-7110; fax: 31-20-530-7119
hollandfestival.nl

SOURCES:
GdWrldFest-1985, p. 141
IntlThFolk-1979, p. 283
MusFestEurBrit-1980, p. 124
MusFestWrld-1963, p. 193

◆ 1207 ◆ Hollerin' Contest, National
Third Saturday in June

Many years ago, the residents of Spivey's Corner, North Carolina, communicated with each other by calling out their greetings, warnings, and cries of distress. They also hollered for their cows, pigs, and dogs to come in. After modern technology supplanted this primitive mode of communication, a local citizen named Ermon Godwin, Jr., decided in 1969 to revive the custom of hollering by holding a day-long competition on the third Saturday in June each year. In addition to the hollering contests for people of both sexes and all ages, the event includes a pole climb, conch shell-blowing and fox horn-blowing contests, and a watermelon carry. Winners of the competition have demonstrated their skills on nationwide television. Some of the hollerin' can be heard on the contest's web site.

CONTACTS:
Spivey's Corner Volunteer Fire Department
P.O. Box 1242
Dunn, NC 28335
910-567-2600
www.hollerincontest.com

SOURCES:
GdUSFest-1985, p. 133

◆ 1208 ◆ Holmenkollen Day
Week including second Sunday in March

The **Holmenkollen International Ski Meet** is a week-long Norwegian winter festival held at Holmenkollen Hill outside Oslo. It is the main winter sports event of the year and it covers all types of skiing—cross-country racing and jumping as well as downhill and slalom. The world's best skiers meet here to compete for highly coveted prizes.

The high point of the festival comes on Holmenkollen Day, when over a hundred thousand spectators, headed by the king and the royal family, gather at the famous Holmenkollen Hill to watch the ski-jumping event, which has been held here since 1892. Competitors swoop down the 184-foot jump, and the one who soars the farthest wins the coveted King's Cup.

CONTACTS:
Skiforeningen
Kongevn 5
Oslo, N-0787 Norway
47-2292-3200; fax: 47-2292-3250
www.skiforeningen.no/english

SOURCES:
AnnivHol-2000, p. 54

◆ 1209 ◆ Holocaust Memorial Day
Between April 8 and May 6; Nisan 27

Holocaust Memorial Day, or **Yom ha-Shoah,** was established by Israel's Knesset (parliament) as a memorial to the six million Jews slaughtered by the Nazis between 1933 and 1945. It is observed on the 27th day of the month of Nisan, the day on which Allied troops liberated the first Nazi concentration camp at Buchenwald, Germany, in 1945. It is a commemoration that is observed by many non-Jewish people around the world.

CONTACTS:
U.S. Holocaust Memorial Museum
100 Raoul Wallenberg Pl. S.W.
Washington, D.C. 20024
202-488-0400; fax: 202-861-0520
www.ushmm.org

SOURCES:
AnnivHol-2000, p. 60
DictWrldRel-1989, pp. 325, 392
RelHolCal-2004, p. 51

◆ 1210 ◆ Holy Blood, Procession of the
Between April 30 and June 3; Ascension Day

This procession is a major religious event in Bruges, Belgium, to venerate the Holy Blood of Christ that was brought back from the Second Crusade by Thierry d'Alsace, count of Flanders.

Thierry's bravery in Jerusalem in the battles against the Saracens was legendary. As a reward for his courage, King Baudouin entrusted the count with a vial of a few drops of blood supposed to have come from Christ's wounds and collected from under the cross by Joseph of Arimathea. When Thierry returned to Bruges on April 7, 1150, there was a great celebration: flowers were strewn in the streets, people waved the banners of the city trades, city dignitaries welcomed the heroic count, and the Holy Reliquary was taken in solemn procession to the Chapel of St. Basile.

The present procession commemorates that original one, although it was not a regular celebration until 1820. Today, the activities begin at 11 A.M. with a pontifical mass in the cathedral. The procession gets under way at 3 P.M., lasts about an hour and a half, and closes with a blessing by the bishop.

As the celebration gets under way, every church bell peals in this usually quiet city. Through living tableaux, the procession tells the story of the Bible from the fall of Adam and Eve, on through Abraham and Moses and to the New Testament stories of St. John the Baptist, the birth of Jesus, the Last Supper, and the Crucifixion on Calvary. Some dozen groups also depict the triumphant return of Thierry d'Alsace to Bruges. When the procession has returned to Burg Square, where it began, the bishop of Bruges lifts the relic of the Holy Blood and blesses the crowd. Visitors come to Bruges from all over the world for the procession.

See also San Gennaro, Feast of

CONTACTS:
Belgian Tourist Office
220 E. 42nd St., Ste. 3402
New York, NY 10017
212-758-8130; fax: 212-355-7675
www.visitbelgium.com

SOURCES:
BkFest-1937, p. 42
BkHolWrld-1986, May 21
FestWestEur-1958, p. 11
GdWrldFest-1985, p. 19

◆ 1211 ◆ Holy Family, Feast of the
Sunday after January 6, Epiphany

In the Roman Catholic Church the Holy Family—Jesus, Mary and Joseph—is thought to provide the perfect example of what the family relationship should be like. But it was not until the 17th century that the Holy Family was venerated as a family, and the feast itself was not officially instituted until 1921. Its popularity spread rapidly, and it is now celebrated by Roman Catholics all over the world. Each of the three members of the sacred household at Nazareth are also honored as individuals on their own feast days.

SOURCES:
DaysCustFaith-1957, p. 37
RelHolCal-2004, p. 89

◆ 1212 ◆ Holy Ghost, Feast of the
March-July

Holy Ghost Season, or **Altura Do Espírito Santo**, has been celebrated in the Azores, Portugal, since the late 15th century. There are actually two types of celebration: the *bodo*, "banquet," and the *função*, "function." Bodos are held in rural *Impérios*—lavishly decorated buildings that are vacant all year except during the festival. The bodo is a large-scale public festival that includes a mass; a children's procession; the ceremonial distribution of meat, bread, and wine; and a number of other activities including an auction, singing competitions, and bullfights.

The função is a small-scale celebration held in private homes. It represents the payment of a personal promise to the Holy Ghost and consists of a series of ritual exchange events, culminating in the coronation of an emperor, the distribution of gifts to the poor, and a communal meal.

Although Holy Ghost season falls primarily between EASTER and TRINITY SUNDAY, urban Impérios have extended the season to July so the same festival props—such as crowns, flags, and other costly items—can be shared among the various regions. Although observation of the feast has nearly disappeared in continental Portugal, it has been carried to Brazil, Canada, Bermuda, and the United States by Portuguese immigrants.

The Holy Ghost celebrations are based on the story of Queen Isabel of Portugal, who loved the poor and pleaded with God to help her starving people. When two ships laden with cat-tle and grain miraculously appeared in a Portuguese harbor, the Queen served a banquet to the poor and continued this yearly ceremony as an expression of gratitude to God.

See also DIVINE HOLY SPIRIT, FESTIVAL OF THE

CONTACTS:
Portuguese National Tourist Office
590 Fifth Ave., 4th Fl.
New York, NY 10036
800-767-8842 or 212-354-4403; fax: 212-764-6137
www.visitportugal.com

Library of Congress
101 Independence Ave. S.E.
Washington, DC 20540
202-707-5000; fax: 202-707-8366
www.loc.gov

SOURCES:
FolkWrldHol-1999, p. 333
GdUSFest-1984, pp. 88, 156
IntlThFolk-1979, p. 311

◆ 1213 ◆ Holy Innocents' Day
December 28

Also known as **Innocents' Day** or **Childermas**, this day commemorates the massacre of all the male children two years and under in Bethlehem as ordered by King Herod, who hoped that the infant Jesus would be among them. Not surprisingly, this day has long been regarded as unlucky—particularly for getting married or undertaking any important task. Edward IV of England went so far as to change the day of his coronation when he realized it would fall on December 28.

In ancient times, the "Massacre of the Innocents" was reenacted by whipping the younger members of a family. But over the years the tables turned, and in some countries it has become a day when children play pranks on their elders. In Mexico, Childermas is the equivalent of APRIL FOOL'S DAY.

SOURCES:
AmerBkDays-2000, p. 860
BkDays-1864, vol. II, pp. 776, 777
BkFest-1937, pp. 49, 63, 175, 223, 234, 347
DictFolkMyth-1984, pp. 218, 525, 950, 951, 1018
EncyChristmas-2003, p. 339
FestSaintDays-1915, pp. 252, 255
FestWestEur-1958, pp. 20, 84
FolkAmerHol-1999, p. 543
FolkWrldHol-1999, p. 771
IndianAmer-1989, pp. 291, 315
OxYear-1999, p. 536

◆ 1214 ◆ Holy Innocents' Day (Belgium) (Allerkinderendag)
December 28

HOLY INNOCENTS' DAY is the traditional anniversary of the slaughter of Bethlehem's male children by King Herod, who hoped that the infant Jesus would be among them. According to legend, two of the murdered children were buried in the Convent of Saint Gerard in the province of Namur, Belgium.

Many Belgian children turn the tables on their elders each year on December 28 by locking them up. Early in the morning, they collect all the keys in the house, so that whenever an unsuspecting adult enters a closet or room, they can lock the door behind him or her and demand a ransom—usually spending money, candy, a toy, or fruit. The innocent person who is being held for ransom is called a "sugar uncle" or "sugar aunt."

The tricks played by children on Holy Innocents' Day have been compared to the pranks that children in the United States and elsewhere play on APRIL FOOLS' DAY.

SOURCES:
BkFest-1937, p. 49
EncyChristmas-2003, p. 341
FestWestEur-1958, p. 20

♦ 1215 ♦ **Holy Prophet and the Martyrdom of Imam Hasan, Death Anniversary of the**
28th day of the Islamic month of Safar

On the Islamic calendar, the anniversaries of the deaths of the prophet Muhammad and his grandson, Hasan, are held on the same date. As a successor of the first imam, Ali, Hasan is an important figure among Shi'ite Muslims, particularly the sect known as the Twelvers. His death by poisoning is an especially mournful chapter in Islamic history. This holiday is observed in Shi'ite communities of the Middle East and is an official holiday in Iran, a country with a large Shi'ite majority.

Many followers convene special meetings in houses or mosques called *rawda-khanis* to mourn for these two figures. The ceremony is led by a rawda-khan, a person skilled at reciting the narratives of Islam.

Major ceremonies are also take place in Mashhad, a holy city in Iran. Caravans of mourners known as *azadars* arrive from across Iran and from different countries to pay their respects to the Prophet and Hasan.

CONTACTS:
Iran's Ministry of Foreign Affairs
Imam Khomeini Sq.
Tehran, Iran

♦ 1216 ♦ **Holy Queen Isabel, Festival of the**
Biennially in July

Queen Isabel of Portugal, born in 1271, is best known for the "miracle of the roses." When her husband, who was unsympathetic to his wife's frequent errands of mercy for the poor and afflicted, demanded to know what she was carrying in the folds of her robe, she told him it was roses, even though she was concealing bread for the hungry. When she opened her robe for him to inspect, the loaves of bread had been transformed into roses. She was beatified by Pope Leo X in 1516 and canonized by Urban VIII in 1625.

Historically, Queen Isabel was a strong advocate for peace in the tumultuous times in which she lived. When her husband, Dom Diniz, died in 1325, she retired to the convent of Santa Clara in Coimbra, Portugal, which she had founded. As the patroness of Coimbra, Queen Isabel is honored in early July in even-numbered years with a week of festivities that include religious processions, fireworks, speeches, concerts, and popular amusements.

CONTACTS:
Portuguese National Tourist Office
590 Fifth Ave., 4th Fl.
New York, NY 10036
800-767-8842 or 212-354-4403; fax: 212-764-6137
www.visitportugal.com

SOURCES:
FestWestEur-1958, p. 170

♦ 1217 ♦ **Holy Saturday**
Between March 21 and April 24 in the West and between April 3 and May 7 in the East; the day before Easter

The Saturday before EASTER Sunday, also called **Easter Even**, is the last day of HOLY WEEK and brings the season of LENT to a close. In the early church, this was the major day for baptisms. Many churches, especially those of the Anglican Communion, still hold large baptismal services on Holy Saturday. It is also known as the **Vigil of Easter** in reference to the fact that Jesus' followers spent this day, after his crucifixion on GOOD FRIDAY, waiting. The Easter, or Paschal, Vigil, the principal celebration of Easter, is traditionally observed the night of Holy Saturday in many churches today. Another name for this day is the **Descent into Hell**, because it commemorates Jesus' descent into and victory over hell.

Slavic Orthodox Christians bring baskets of food to the church for the Blessing of the Pascha (Easter) Baskets on Holy Saturday. The baskets are filled with the foods from which people have abstained during the Lenten fast and which will be part of the Pascha feast. For many inhabitants of Mexican descent in Los Angeles, California, Holy Saturday is the day for a colorful ceremony known as the Blessing of the Animals, which takes place at the Old Plaza Church near Olvera Street.

CONTACTS:
Christian Resource Institute
4712 N. Hammond
Warr Acres, OK 73122
405-789-0449
www.cresourcei.org

El Pueblo de Los Angeles Historical Monument
845 N. Alameda St.
Los Angeles, CA 90012
213-680-2525
www.olvera-street.com

Orthodox Church in America
P.O. Box 675
Syosset, NY 11791
516-922-0550; fax: 516-922-0954
www.oca.org

SOURCES:
AmerBkDays-2000, p. 238
BkFest-1937, pp. 24, 41, 70, 87, 96, 148, 168, 184, 211, 227, 260, 275, 292, 301, 339

BkHolWrld-1986, Apr 11
DictFolkMyth-1984, p. 258
EncyEaster-2002, p. 284
EncyRel-1987, vol. 3, p. 439
FestWestEur-1958, pp. 9, 60, 94, 108
FolkAmerHol-1999, p. 172
FolkWrldHol-1999, p. 224
IndianAmer-1989, p. 274
OxYear-1999, p. 620
SaintFestCh-1904, p. 161

◆ 1218 ◆ Holy Saturday (Mexico) (Sábado de Gloria)
Between March 21 and April 24; day before Easter

In Mexico, HOLY SATURDAY is observed by burning effigies of Judas Iscariot, the disciple who betrayed Jesus to the religious authorities for 30 pieces of silver. Street vendors sell the papier-mâché effigies, which range from one to five feet in height and make Judas look as ugly as possible. The effigies designed for children are stuffed with candies and hung in the patios of private houses. Other effigies are suspended over the streets or hung from lampposts. All have firecrackers attached, which are ignited as soon as the Mass of Glory is over. As the effigies explode, kids jostle one another in an attempt to retrieve the candies and trinkets that are hidden inside.

The church bells, which have been silent since the Wednesday before EASTER, ring on Holy Saturday, and there are folk beliefs associated with the ringing of the bells. For example, it is believed that plants or hair trimmed while the bells are ringing will grow back faster. Children are often smacked on the legs so that they'll grow taller.

See also BURNING OF JUDAS

CONTACTS:
Mexico Tourism Board
21 E. 63rd St., Fl. 3
New York, NY 10021
800-446-3942 or 212-821-0314; fax: 212-821-0367
www.visitmexico.com

SOURCES:
BkFest-1937, p. 227
BkHolWrld-1986, Apr 11
EncyEaster-2002, p. 406
FolkWrldHol-1999, p. 235

◆ 1219 ◆ Holy Thursday
Between April 30 and June 3; 40 days after Easter

Holy Thursday usually refers to MAUNDY THURSDAY, but in parts of rural England, it traditionally refers to ASCENSION DAY, the day on which Jesus Christ ascended into heaven. The English custom of "well dressing," which may have had its roots in a pagan festival, became associated with Holy Thursday in 1615. There was a severe drought in Derbyshire that year and most of the wells and streams dried up. The only wells that still had water were at Tissington, where people came to get water for their livestock. From that time onward, a special thanksgiving service was held there on Ascension Day, and Tissington became known as "the village of holy wells."

The well-dressing ceremony developed into a full-fledged festival in the 19th century. After delivering his sermon, the priest leads a procession to the wells, which are nearly hidden by screens of fresh flowers fastened to wooden frames. There follows a simple ceremony at each well, asking God to bless and keep the waters pure.

CONTACTS:
Ashbourne Tourist Information Centre
13 Market Place
Ashbourne, Derbyshire DE6 1EU United Kingdom
44-13-3534-3666; fax: 44-13-3530-0638
www.ashbourne-town.com

Tissington Hall
Tissington
Ashbourne, DE6 1RA United Kingdom
44-13-3535-2200
www.tissington-hall.com

SOURCES:
BkDays-1864, vol. I, p. 595
DaysCustFaith-1957, p. 135
EncyEaster-2002, p. 13
SaintFestCh-1904, p. 231

◆ 1220 ◆ Holy Week
Between March 15 and April 18 in the West and between March 28 and May 1 in the East; the week preceding Easter

Holy Week, the seven days beginning with PALM SUNDAY that precede EASTER, is the most solemn week in the Christian year. It includes MAUNDY THURSDAY, GOOD FRIDAY, and HOLY SATURDAY. The Germans call Holy Week **Still Week** or **Silent Week**, and some Americans call it **Passion Week**, although the season known as Passiontide actually refers to the preceding week.

Passion Sunday or CARLING SUNDAY is the fifth Sunday in LENT (the Sunday *before* Palm Sunday), but since Holy Week was also referred to as Passion Week, this apparently led to the identification of Palm Sunday with Passion Sunday. Since 1970 the Roman Catholic Church has considered the two names to be synonymous, although in 1956 the two Sundays were designated the First Sunday and Second Sunday of the Passion. Another name for the fifth Sunday in Lent is Judica Sunday, from the Introit for the day.

See also PRISONERS, FEAST OF THE; SEMANA SANTA IN GUATEMALA

CONTACTS:
Orthodox Church in America
P.O. Box 675
Syosset, NY 11791
516-922-0550; fax: 516-922-0954
www.oca.org

SOURCES:
BkFest-1937, pp. 69, 274
BkFestHolWrld-1970, pp. 51, 53, 54
DaysCustFaith-1957, pp. 103, 106
DictFolkMyth-1984, pp. 1063, 1171

EncyEaster-2002, p. 294
EncyRel-1987, vol. 3, p. 439
FestSaintDays-1915, p. 67
FestWestEur-1958, pp. 164, 192
FolkWrldHol-1999, p. 224
GdWrldFest-1985, p. 65
IntlThFolk-1979, p. 276
OxYear-1999, p. 615

◆ 1221 ◆ Holy Week (Czech Republic)
Between March 15 and April 18; the week
preceding Easter

In the Czech Republic, each day of HOLY WEEK is associated with traditional customs that combine pagan rituals with those commemorating the death and resurrection of Jesus Christ. The first day of the week, PALM SUNDAY, also known as Flower Sunday, commemorates the arrival of Jesus in Jerusalem. On this day priests bless branches, flowers, and wood that have been brought to church by the congregation. Czech farmers make crosses from the blessed materials and place the crosses in their fields in hopes of a bountiful harvest.

During Holy Week, Czechs undertake spring-cleaning of their homes and may even paint them in an effort to refresh their surroundings after the winter. Chimneys are swept and furniture and bedding aired outside. *Škaredá streda* (Ugly Wednesday) is also known as Spy Wednesday in reference to the tradition that it was the day on which Judas Iscariot betrayed Jesus to the Roman authorities. Thursday of Holy Week, known as Holy Thursday or MAUNDY THURSDAY in the English-speaking world, is called *Zelený ctvrtek* (Green Thursday) in the Czech Republic. On this day Czechs traditionally eat a meal featuring green herbs and vegetables. In the past, children would be sent outside in the morning to bathe in a stream or river, then return home to eat *jidasky,* a pastry shaped into a rope. The braided form of this cake refers to the noose and symbolizes the hanging death of Judas. Spreading jidasky or another bread with honey was believed to offer protection from snakebites throughout the year, and bread with honey was also tossed into wells to assure that they would not run dry during the coming year. Church bells are silenced on Green Thursday and replaced in villages by noise-makers such as wooden rattles. On GOOD FRIDAY Czech custom calls for wading across a stream barelegged in order to assure good health. In addition, the weather on this day is believed to portend the weather for the rest of the year.

Saturday of Holy Week is known as White Saturday in the Czech Republic and is considered a lucky day to sow seeds. The day concludes with an Easter Vigil religious service and the return of church bells. Preparations for Easter include decorating eggs (*kraslice*) using a variety of methods to create intricate, colorful designs. Typically, the egg white and yolk are removed before the egg is colored. Techniques for applying color include wax-resistance, painting, and scratching the designs onto dyed shells. Boys and young men weave wands from willow branches and decorate them with ribbons. On Easter Monday they use the whips to symbolically spank girls to promote their good health. In return the girls give them a decorated or chocolate egg.

CONTACTS:
Embassy of the Czech Republic
3900 Spring of Freedom St. N.W.
Washington, D.C. 20008
202-274-9100; fax: 202-966-8540
www.mzv.cz/wwwo/?zu=washington

SOURCES:
EncyEaster-2002, p. 73

◆ 1222 ◆ Holy Week (Haiti)
Between March 15 and April 18; the week
preceding Easter

HOLY WEEK in Haiti is signaled by the appearance of "Monsieur Judas" effigies made out of sawdust and rags. Early in the week these symbolic figures are honored as Jesus' apostles and treasured guests. When Jesus' death is affirmed on GOOD FRIDAY, however, the effigies disappear—usually hidden by someone in a ravine or cane field just outside town.

On Saturday morning everyone starts hunting for Judas, swinging machetes, knives, and clubs as they shout, "Qui bo' li?" (Where is he?). The search often becomes quite frenzied and every time a Judas is found, the attackers slice him to bits. By midday the remains of these effigies litter the ground. This ritual reenactment of Jesus' betrayal by Judas involves Haitians of all ages and reflects the overall tone of Holy Week celebrations, which are more secular than spiritual.

CONTACTS:
Embassy of the Republic of Haiti
2311 Massachusetts Ave. N.W.
Washington, D.C. 20008
202-332-4090; fax: 202-745-7215
www.haiti.org

SOURCES:
FiestaTime-1965, p. 79

◆ 1223 ◆ Holy Week (Mexico)
Between March 15 and April 18; the week
preceding Easter

Although many dramatizations of the events of HOLY WEEK, or **Semana Santa**, take place throughout Mexico, the Passion plays performed in the towns of Taxco, Malinalco, Tzintzuntzan, and Iztapalapa are among the most elaborate. In Malinalco, everyone in town participates in the drama, with the wealthier men taking the parts of Roman soldiers (because they own horses) and less wealthy members of the community representing the Christians, who have no horses but wear brightly colored satin costumes. The young girls are dressed as angels, complete with wings that sparkle in the sunlight.

In Tzintzuntzan, the PASSION PLAY starts at 12:00 P.M. on MAUNDY THURSDAY and doesn't end until midnight on GOOD FRIDAY. The play takes place outdoors, in a grove of olive trees near the church, and is known for the professionalism of its actors. The Iztapalapa pageant takes place during Holy Week, and there are several locations throughout the town where scenes are presented. It is best known for its elaborate costumes.

Mexicans are also known for the effigies of Judas that are displayed in the streets on HOLY SATURDAY. Although some of these papier-mâché effigies represent clowns, cowboys, devils, and pirates, the majority portray unpopular politicians or other citizens who have fallen out of public favor.

CONTACTS:
Mexico Tourism Board
21 E. 63rd St., Fl. 3
New York, NY 10021
800-446-3942 or 212-821-0314; fax: 212-821-0367
www.visitmexico.com

SOURCES:
EncyEaster-2002, p. 406
FiestaTime-1965, pp. 77, 79

♦ 1224 ♦ Holy Week (Panama)
*Between March 15 and April 18; the week
preceding Easter*

In Panama, HOLY WEEK is marked by the appearance of devil dancers who wear headdresses that resemble animals' heads and tails made from bells. They visit small villages on HOLY SATURDAY to get rid of evil spirits for the coming year. In larger towns, they participate in public, staged combat with festival participants in angel costumes. Although the devil can be seen as a biblical character, the purifying rites performed by the devil dancers in rural areas probably originate in indigenous traditions.

CONTACTS:
Embassy of Panama
2862 McGill Terr. N.W.
Washington, D.C. 20008
202-483-1407; fax: 202-483-8413
www.embassyofpanama.org

SOURCES:
FiestaTime-1965, p. 82

♦ 1225 ♦ Holy Week (Philippines)
*Between March 15 and April 18; the week
preceding Easter*

Colorful Passion plays take place throughout LENT in the Philippines (*see* MORIONES FESTIVAL). PALM SUNDAY religious services focus on the joy of Jesus' entry into Jerusalem, and include the blessing of palm branches. Some people visit as many churches as possible on MAUNDY THURSDAY, in a custom known as *visita iglesia* (visit church). Retelling or singing the Passion story is also popular on this day. On GOOD FRIDAY devout Filipinos watch Passion plays, take part in a devotional meditation known as the Stations of the Cross, or participate in public processions of penitents. In some of these, people whip themselves; in others a few people each year will have themselves crucified.

A custom known as *Salubong,* the meeting of the resurrected Jesus and his mother, takes place on EASTER Sunday morning. A religious statue representing Jesus and another representing the Blessed Virgin Mary are taken to the opposite ends of

town. People line up behind one or the other image and begin a procession towards a centrally located church. When the two images meet, a children's choir begin to sing, the veil covering Mary's eyes falls away, and a flock of doves is released. Afterwards the images are returned to the church and people attend Easter Sunday mass.

CONTACTS:
Philippine Tourism Center
556 Fifth Ave.
New York, NY 10036
212-575-7915; fax: 212-302-6759
www.wowphilippines.com.ph

SOURCES:
EncyEaster-2002, p. 491
FestWrld: Phil-1999, p. 12

♦ 1226 ♦ Holy Week (Portugal) (Semana Santa)
*Between March 15 and April 18; the week
preceding Easter*

There are exhibits in the churches and street processions illustrating scenes from the Passion of Christ throughout HOLY WEEK in Portugal. In the city of Guimarães, the church of *Senhor dos Passos* shows a different Passion tableau each day of Holy Week. The processions are usually attended by bands of *anjinhos,* or children dressed as angels, with crowns on their heads and fluffy wings attached to their shoulders. The figures of Jesus, which have real hair, eyelashes, and crystal tears, are elaborately dressed in purple velvet robes. The clergy's vestments are also purple, and worshippers watching the procession throw violets at the image of the suffering Jesus.

CONTACTS:
Portuguese National Tourist Office
590 Fifth Ave., 4th Fl.
New York, NY 10036
800-767-8842 or 212-354-4403; fax: 212-764-6137
www.visitportugal.com

SOURCES:
FestWestEur-1958, p. 164

♦ 1227 ♦ Homage to Cuauhtemoc (Homenaje a Cuauhtemoc)
August

Cuauhtemoc, the last Aztec emperor, is honored each year with a festival held in front of his statue on the Paseo de la Reforma in Mexico City. After the story of his life and his struggle against the Spaniards has been recited in Spanish and native Indian languages, groups of Conchero dancers perform the dances for which they are renowned. Wearing feathered headdresses trimmed with mirrors and beads and carrying pictures of Christ or various saints, they represent the blending of Indian and Spanish cultures. Most Conchero groups have 50 to 100 dancers, and each dances in his own rhythm and to his own accompaniment. The tempo increases gradually until it reaches a sudden climax, followed by a moment of silence.

Cuauhtemoc is admired for his "bold and intimate acceptance of death," in the words of the Mexican poet Octavio Paz. Paz says that the entry of the Spanish into Mexico precipitated the extinction of the Aztec culture.

CONTACTS:
Mexico Tourism Board
21 E. 63rd St., Fl. 3
New York, NY 10021
800-446-3942 or 212-821-0314; fax: 212-821-0367
www.visitmexico.com

SOURCES:
IntlThFolk-1979, p. 273

♦ 1228 ♦ **Homeless Persons' Remembrance Day, National**
On or around December 21

Since 1990, the National Coalition for the Homeless and the National Health Care for the Homeless Council have sponsored National Homeless Persons' Remembrance Day to bring attention to the plight of the nation's homeless population and to encourage the public to act on their behalf.

Local groups across the country are encouraged first to determine the number of homeless persons in their community who died in the previous year and then arrange a ceremony to remember them. Candlelight marches, vigils, graveside services, plays and performances, religious services, and public policy advocacy are the suggested ways of remembering. Some groups have read publicly a list of names of the deceased. Because media attention to such issues increases during the holiday season in December, National Homeless Persons' Remembrance Day was in part created to garner a public forum for this issue, and local groups are encouraged to seek out and work with their local media outlets to publicize the event.

CONTACTS:
National Coalition for the Homeless
2201 P St. N.W.
Washington, D.C. 20037
202-462-4822; fax: 202-462-4823

♦ 1229 ♦ **Homowo**
Between August and September

Homowo is a harvest festival of thanks to the gods of the Ga (or Gan) people as well as the mark of the new year. *Homowo* means "starved gods," and the festival commemorates the good harvest the Ga were given in ancient times. This harvest came after the famine they endured while traveling to their present home in Ghana.

The festival begins on Thursday and those who have moved away are called *Soobii*, "Thursday people," because that's the day they arrive home for the festival. The following day is the yam festival and the day of twins. All twins who are dressed in white are specially treated all day. Each day there are processions, songs, and dancing until the great day arrives: Homowo, or the **Hunger-Hooting Festival** and open house.

Most homes have enough food in them for a week during the festival. Fish are abundant in Ghana at this time of year, and palm-nut soup, *kpokpoi*, or *ko*, round out the traditional menu. Ko is a kind of grits made with unleavened corn dough and palm oil. The chiefs and elders sprinkle the ko everywhere people have been buried, then go to the prison and personally feed the warders. The following day they visit friends and relatives, reconciling and exchanging New Year's greetings.

CONTACTS:
Ghana Tourist Board
P.O. Box 3106
Accra, Ghana
233-21-222153; fax: 233-21-244611
www.ghana.gov.gh

SOURCES:
BkHolWrld-1986, Aug 1
FestGhana-1970, p. 52
FolkWrldHol-1999, p. 528

♦ 1230 ♦ **Homstrom**
First Sunday in February

Homstrom is a Swiss festival celebrating the end of winter. In many ways, it is reminiscent of the February 1 mid-winter festival observed by the ancient Celts, known as IMBOLC. One tradition associated with the day is the burning of a straw man who symbolizes Old Man Winter. It is occasionally observed by Swiss-American communities on the first Sunday in February.

CONTACTS:
Switzerland Tourism
Swiss Ctr., 608 Fifth Ave.
New York, NY 10020
877-794-8037 or 212-757-5944; fax: 212-262-6116
www.myswitzerland.com

SOURCES:
RelHolCal-2004, p. 271

♦ 1231 ♦ **Honduras Independence Day**
September 15

Honduras joined four other Central American countries—COSTA RICA, EL SALVADOR, GUATEMALA, and NICARAGUA—in declaring independence from Spain on September 15, 1821. Independence Day is a national holiday and festivities are especially colorful in the capital city of Tegucigalpa.

CONTACTS:
Embassy of Honduras
3007 Tilden St. N.W.
Washington, D.C. 20008
202-966-7702; fax: 202-966-9751
www.hondurasemb.org

SOURCES:
AnnivHol-2000, p. 155
NatlHolWrld-1968, p. 169

♦ 1232 ♦ **Honduras Soldiers' Day**
October 3

This celebration is held on the birthday of Francisco Morazán (1792–1842), a highly revered Honduran general and statesman. Along with serving as the head of state of his own country, he was also a three-time president of the Central American Federation, a short-lived republic composed of several present-day countries of that region. Morazán's achievements as a military leader in various liberation struggles led the Honduran government to designate his birthday as the official date to honor the country's soldiers.

The day's main celebration is a military parade that takes place in Tegucigalpa, Honduras's capital city. The procession features the service members of every branch of the armed forces, along with dozens of tanks and artillery carriers. The 1997 celebration featured an air display by military helicopters and jet aircraft.

CONTACTS:
Honduran Embassy
3007 Tilden St. N.W.
Washington, D.C. 20008
202-966-7702; fax: 202-966-9751

SOURCES:
AnnivHol-2000, p. 167

♦ 1233 ♦ **Hong Kong Arts Festival**
Three to four weeks over February and March

This annual celebration of the arts in Hong Kong has been held since 1972. Artists from around the world appear for a diverse program that includes opera, orchestral concerts, chamber music, jazz, dance, film, theater, and exhibits. The 1992 program scheduled a presentation of the opera *Tosca* with an international cast, as well as a performance of the 400-year-old Kunju Opera, the oldest surviving form of theater in China, by the Shanghai Kunju Opera Troupe. The 2001 schedule included a production of a full-length Cantonese opera based on the classic novel *The Romance of the Three Kingdoms*, a performance by Yo-Yo Ma and the Silk Road Ensemble, and a Lithuanian production of *Hamlet*.

CONTACTS:
Hong Kong Arts Festival Society Ltd.
12/F Rm., 1205, 2 Harbour Rd.
Wanchai, Hong Kong
852-2824-3555; fax: 852-2824-3798
www.hk.artsfestival.org

SOURCES:
GdWrldFest-1985, p. 105
IntlThFolk-1979, p. 198

♦ 1234 ♦ **Hong Kong Special Administrative Region Establishment Day**
July 1

Formerly an occupied territory of the United Kingdom, Hong Kong became a Special Administrative Region (SAR) of China on July 1, 1997. The day is reserved for official celebrations of Hong Kong and its unique "one country, two systems" arrangement with its mainland ally.

Large crowds observe the anniversary by turning out for an official flag-raising ceremony displaying the emblems of Hong Kong and the People's Republic of China. There is also a parade featuring traditional drumming performances and dragon dance troupes. For the 10th anniversary in 2007, the regional government coordinated a series of events, including a ceremony that swore in Hong Kong's new chief executive, Donald Tsang.

An alternative tradition has developed since the transfer of power in 1997. Dissenters mark the occasion by holding a massive march in which they protest against the Chinese government with demands that it commit to democratic practices like universal suffrage and the protection of freedom of speech. In response to the passage of a controversial national security law by Hong Kong in September 2002, an estimated 500,000 people marched on July 1 in protest from Victoria Park in Causeway Bay to the government headquarters in Hong Kong's Central district.

CONTACTS:
Hong Kong Tourism Board
115 E. 54th St., 2/F
New York, NY 10022-4512
212-421-3382; fax: 212-421-8428

♦ 1235 ♦ **Hooverfest**
August

Hooverfest celebrates the August 10, 1874, birthday of former President Herbert Hoover. The event is hosted by the Herbert Hoover Presidential Library Association of West Branch, Iowa. Hooverfest includes arts and crafts, stage shows, live musical entertainment, a memorial service, and fireworks. The Hoover Presidential Library is situated on a national historic site that includes Hoover's birthplace, his burial site, the library housing the official papers of his administration, and a Quaker meeting house.

A special Hooverball tournament is also held during Hooverfest. Hooverball was invented by White House physician Joel T. Boone as a way to help President Hoover stay fit. The game combines elements from tennis, volleyball, and medicine ball. It is played on a 66-foot by 30-foot court with a volleyball net and either a four-pound or six-pound medicine ball. Teams of two to four players compete against each other. Scoring is the same as in tennis. The game is credited with helping Hoover keep his weight under control. Once popular with the White House staff even after Hoover left office, the game has become less popular in recent years.

CONTACTS:
Herbert Hoover Presidential Library Association
P.O. Box 696
West Branch, IA 52358-0696
800-828-0475; fax: 319-643-2391
www.hooverassociation.org/hooverfest.html

♦ 1236 ♦ **Hope Watermelon Festival**
Second weekend in August

Best known as the birthplace of U.S. President Bill Clinton, Hope, Ark., is also "Home of the World's Largest Watermelons" and hosts the only watermelon festival featuring giant watermelons.

They are indeed large. Hope watermelon growers have been competing to grow the biggest since the 1920s. In 1925, Hugh Laseter created a sensation with a record 136-pounder that was exhibited for a few days and then sent to President Calvin Coolidge. The watermelons kept getting bigger. The 1928 champion was 144¾ pounds and was sent to the Rexall Corp. in Boston, Mass., where it "created quite a bit of excitement," according to old accounts.

The first 200-pound melon was grown in 1979 by Ivan Bright and his son Lloyd; seeds from it went for $8 each. That melon broke a 44-year record held by O. D. Middlebrooks, who had grown a 195-pound melon. (It was sent to actor Dick Powell.) In 1985, Lloyd Bright's 10-year-old son Jason produced a 260-pound watermelon that was recorded in the *1992 Guinness Book of World Records*. These melons attain their great size because of the quality of the soil, an early greenhouse start, and careful pruning. Hope farmers also grow average-size watermelons, weighing 30 to 40 pounds.

The Hope Watermelon Festival originated in 1926, lapsed with hard times, was revived in 1977, and has been held annually ever since with attendance at about 50,000. There has been nationwide television and press coverage because of the colossal melons. This is a festival of real down-home Americana: ice cream socials, a big fish fry, softball, a dog show, arm wrestling, arts and crafts booths, musical entertainment, antique car and engine shows, and hot air balloon rides.

The watermelon events include a watermelon toss, a melon-decorating competition, a melon-eating contest, a melon-seed-spitting contest, and a melon-judging and auction. While he was governor of Arkansas, Mr. Clinton visited the festival to compete in the Watermelon 5K Run.

CONTACTS:
Hope-Hempstead County Chamber of Commerce
101 W. 2nd St.
P.O. Box 250
Hope, AR 71802
870-777-3640; fax: 870-722-6154
www.hopechamberofcommerce.com

♦ 1237 ♦ Hopi Flute Ceremony
Every other year for nine days in mid-August

Like the HOPI SNAKE DANCE, the Flute Ceremony takes place over a nine-day period in the summer on the mesas of northeastern Arizona, where the Hopi Indians live. The two events take place on an alternating basis, with the Snake Dance occurring one year and the Flute Ceremony the next. The purpose of the latter is to encourage rainfall and promote the growth of corn, which is the primary food of the Hopi nation.

The Flute Ceremony takes place in the ancestral rooms of the Flute clan. It begins with a procession into the pueblo led by the clan's chief, who is followed by the Flute boy in his white ceremonial kilt, with a Flute girl on either side wearing feathers in their hair and two white blankets, one of which serves as a skirt.

Many of the rites involved in the Flute Ceremony are actually pantomimes of what the Hopis want their gods to do. For example, the priest may scatter meal on the ground or around the flute altar in imitation of falling rain. Pouring water into the bowl that sits in front of the altar from the six cardinal directions of the world (north, south, east, west, up, down) shows the gods that the priest wants them to send rain from six different directions. Blowing clouds of smoke on the altar shows that he wants rain clouds to appear. And a bullroarer, an instrument that makes a whizzing sound when swung in circles overhead, is used to imitate the sound of thunder.

CONTACTS:
Hopi Cultural Center
P.O. Box 67
Second Mesa, AZ 86043
928-734-2401; fax: 928-734-6651
www.hopiculturalcenter.com

SOURCES:
EncyNatAmerRel-2001, p. 91
EndurHarv-1995, p. 302

♦ 1238 ♦ Hopi Snake Dance
Every other year in August

The Snake Dance is the grand finale of ceremonies to pray for rain, held by individual Hopi tribes in Arizona every two years. Hopis believe their ancestors originated in an underworld, and that their gods and the spirits of ancestors live there. They call snakes their brothers, and trust that the snakes will carry their prayers to the Rainmakers beneath the earth. Thus the Hopi dancers carry snakes in their mouths to impart prayers to them.

The ceremonies, conducted by the Snake and Antelope fraternities, last 16 days. On the 11th day preparations start for the Snake Dance. For four days, snake priests go out from their village to gather snakes. On the 15th day, a race is run, signifying rain gods bringing water to the village. Then the Antelopes build a *kisi*, a shallow pit covered with a board, to represent the entrance to the underworld. At sunset on the 15th day, the Snake and Antelope dancers dance around the plaza, stamping on the kisi board and shaking rattles to simulate the sounds of thunder and rain. The Antelope priest dances with green vines around his neck and in his mouth—just as the Snake priests will later do with snakes.

The last day starts with a footrace to honor the snakes. The snakes are washed and deposited in the kisi. The Snake priests dance around the kisi. Each is accompanied by two other priests: one holding a snake whip and one whose function will be to catch the snake when it's dropped. Then each priest takes a snake and carries it first in his hands and then in his mouth. The whipper dances behind him with his left arm around the dancer's neck and calms the snake by stroking it with a feathered wand. After four dances around the plaza, the priests throw the snakes to the catchers. A priest draws a circle on the ground, the catchers throw the snakes in the circle, the Snake priests grab handfuls of them and run with them to turn them loose in the desert.

The HOPI FLUTE CEREMONY takes place in alternate years.

CONTACTS:
Hopi Cultural Center
P.O. Box 67
Second Mesa, AZ 86043
520-734-2401; fax: 520-734-6651
www.hopiculturalcenter.com

Video of Hopi Snake Dance in 1913, Library of Congress
101 Independence Ave. S.E.
Washington, DC 20540
202-707-5510; fax: 202-707-2076
www.loc.gov

SOURCES:
BkHolWrld-1986, Aug 22
DictFolkMyth-1984, p. 1030
EncyNatAmerRel-2001, p. 276
EncyRel-1987, vol. 10, p. 520
EndurHarv-1995, p. 302
HolSymbols-2009, p. 383
RelHolCal-2004, p. 258

♦ 1239 ♦ **Hora at Prislop**
Second Sunday in August

The Hora is a dancing festival held at Mount Prislop at the Transylvania-Moldavia border in Romania. The dancers of the hora carry big rings that symbolize the friendship of the people of the regions of Moldavia, Maramures, and Transylvania. The top artistic groups gather at Prislop Pass to present a parade in colorful folk costumes and then a program of songs and dances, ending with the lively peasant horas. Typical food dishes of the area are served and folk art is on display.

CONTACTS:
Romanian National Tourist Office
355 Lexington Ave., 19th Fl.
New York, NY 10017
212-545-8484; fax: 212-545-8484
www.romaniatourism.com

SOURCES:
GdWrldFest-1985, p. 157
IntlThFolk-1979, p. 317

♦ 1240 ♦ **Hordad, Feast of**
May, September, October; sixth day of Hordad,
the third Zoroastrian month

This is considered a "sacred name day" in the Zoroastrian calendar because the same *yazata* or spiritual being, Hordad, rules the day of the week as well as the month. Hordad is a lesser deity who stands for wholeness or perfection; also known as Khordad, this spiritual being shares her name with the third month and the sixth day of the week.

The Zoroastrian calendar has 12 months of 30 days each, plus five extra days at the end of the year. Because of discrepancies in the calendars used by widely separated Zoroastrian communities around the world, there are now three different calendars in use, and the Feast of Hordad can fall either in May, September, or October, according to the Gregorian calendar.

There are about 100,000 followers of Zoroastrianism today, and most of them live in northwestern India or Iran. Smaller communities exist in Pakistan, Sri Lanka, Canada, the U.S., England, and Australia.

SOURCES:
RelHolCal-2004, p. 67

♦ 1241 ♦ **Horn Dance**
Monday following first Sunday after September 4

The ancient Horn Dance, believed by many to have originated in Norman times or before, is performed at Abbots Bromley, a small village in Staffordshire, England, as part of the **Wakes Monday** celebration each year. Wakes Monday, the day after the first Sunday following September 4, was at one time part of the Old St. BARTHOLOMEW FAIR. But the Horn Dance is all that remains of the original three-day festival. Although some believe it was once an ancient fertility dance, the Horn Dance probably had something to do with hunting rights and customs in nearby Needwood Forest.

A dozen local men, ranging in age from 12 to more than 50, dress in 16th-century foresters' costumes. Six of them carry reindeer antlers mounted on short wooden sticks. There is also a Hobby Horse, a man playing Robin Hood, a man dressed as a woman who plays the role of Maid Marian, a Fool carrying an inflated bladder on a stick, and a young archer who snaps his bow in time with the music—originally provided by a pipe and tabor but nowadays by a concertina and a triangle.

Beginning at the parish church, the men dance their way around the parish boundaries, stopping to perform at homes and farms along the way. The six deermen, three of whom carry white antlers and three black, take turns "charging" each other while the Hobby Horse prances, the Fool shakes his bladder at the spectators, and Maid Marian takes up a collection. The dancing is over by evening, when everyone adjourns to the local pub or goes home to eat Wakes Cakes, "fair rock candy"—sugar-coated sticks of candy—and brandy snap cookies.

CONTACTS:
Abbots Bromley Parish Council
Village Hall
Abbots Bromley, Staffordshire DE13 8AF United Kingdom
44-18-8950-0660
www.abbotsbromley.com

SOURCES:
DictFolkMyth-1984, pp. 3, 947

♦ 1242 ♦ **Hortobágy Bridge Fair and International**
Equestrian Festival
July

This annual event is a showcase of Hungary's fine horses and riders on the Hortobágy, part of the Great Plain of Hungary. The festival also celebrates the famous nine-arched bridge, built in 1833, that crosses the Hortobágy River and is the longest stone bridge in the country.

The Hortobágy National Park is 150 square kilometers in the grassy *puszta* ("prairie") of the Great Plain near the historic city of Debrecen. During the Turkish occupation that began in the 14th century the area was depopulated, and in the 18th century it was used for breeding horses, cattle, and sheep. The equestrian fair is held outside the city and features the famed Lipizzaner horses (from Austrian stock) in dressage exhibitions, the *csikós* (Hungarian cowboy) in colorful embroidered riding costume, carriage parades, pulling contests for draft horses, and other equestrian events. There are also crafts fairs and a peasant market.

CONTACTS:
Hungarian National Tourist Office
350 Fifth Ave., Ste. 7107
New York, NY 10118
212-695-1221; fax: 212-695-0809
www.gotohungary.com

♦ 1243 ♦ **Hosay Festival**
10th day of Islamic month of Muharram

To Muslims in the Eastern Hemisphere, the **Hussein Festival** is a solemn occasion commemorating the massacre of Hussein and his brother Hassan, grandsons of the prophet Muhammad, on the 10th day of the month of Muharram in 680 (*see* ASHURA). But in Trinidad and Tobago, where the Hosay (or Hussein) Festival was first celebrated in 1884, the traditional procession of mourning has been mixed with various European, African, and Indian rituals to form a unique celebration.

The most popular processions are held in the towns of St. James, Curepe, Tunapuna, Couva, and Cedros. The festival usually begins the evening of Muharram 9 with a solemn procession of flags symbolizing the beginning of the battle of Kerbela, in which Hussein and Hassan were killed. On the second day dancers wearing *tadjahs*—small minaretted tombs made of bamboo, colored tissue, tinfoil, crepe paper, mirrors, and coconut leis—parade through the streets to the accompaniment of African drummers in a ritual that is reminiscent of CARNIVAL (*see* TRINIDAD AND TOBAGO CARNIVAL).

The highlight of the festival occurs on the third night, when the large tadjahs, some of which are six feet tall, are carried through the streets. There are also two moons, representing Hussein and his brother, carried by specially trained dancers. These large crescent-shaped structures are studded with sharp blades and carried on the dancers' shoulders. At midnight, the two moons engage in a ritual embrace to a chorus of cheers from the onlookers.

CONTACTS:
Trinidad and Tobago Tourism Development Authority
National Library Bldg., Hart and Abercromby St.
Port of Spain, Trinidad and Tobago

868-623-6962; fax: 868-625-6096
www.nalis.gov.tt

SOURCES:
FolkWrldHol-1999, p. 435

♦ 1244 ♦ **Hoshana Rabbah**
Between September 27 and October 24; Tishri 21

On each of the first six days of the Jewish SUKKOT festival, a single stanza of the *Hoshanat* litany is recited (except on the Sabbath) and the congregation circles the reader's platform carrying the four species: a palm branch, citron, three myrtle twigs, and two willow branches, all gathered into a bouquet. But on the seventh day, known as the **Great Hoshana**, the congregation makes seven circuits around the altar, after which the four species are laid down and a bunch of five willow branches is picked up and beaten on the ground three times to symbolize humanity's dependence on rain.

Because Hoshana Rabbah is considered the last possible day on which one can seek forgiveness for the sins of the preceding year, the morning service on this day is very solemn. According to Jewish tradition, on YOM KIPPUR God seals the Book of Life and thus each individual's fate for the coming year. Yom Kippur falls on the 10th day of Tishri.

But since the Middle Ages, Hoshana Rabbah has been regarded as an extension of the deadline for Divine judgment. According to an old Jewish folk belief, notes fell from Heaven on this day informing people of how they had been judged. The traditional Yiddish greeting, *a gute kvitl*, "May you receive a good note," reflects this belief. There is also a popular superstition claiming that a man who doesn't see his shadow on this night is fated to die in the coming year.

SOURCES:
DaysCustFaith-1957, p. 272
OxYear-1999, p. 726

♦ 1245 ♦ **Hospital Week, National**
Week including May 12

Although Florence Nightingale (1820-1910), the famous nurse and public health activist, spent most of her life in England, it is in the United States that the anniversary of her birth has been celebrated since 1921 as National Hospital Day.

Originally a day set aside in honor of the woman who made nursing a respectable profession and who revolutionized the way hospitals were run, the May 12 observance was expanded to a week-long event in 1953 so that hospitals could use it to plan and implement more extensive public information programs.

Currently sponsored by the American Hospital Association, National Hospital Week provides an opportunity to recognize employee achievements, to educate the community about the services hospitals offer, and to keep the public up to date on technological advances in the health care field.

In 19th-century England, it was customary for each community to designate a **Hospital Saturday** and a **Hospital Sunday**—a time to collect money for local hospitals both on the streets and in the churches. Hospital Saturday later became ALEXANDRA ROSE DAY.

CONTACTS:
American Hospital Association
1 N. Franklin
Chicago, IL 60606
312-422-3000; fax: 645-722-4796
www.aha.org

SOURCES:
AmerBkDays-2000, p. 360
AnnivHol-2000, p. 81
DictDays-1988, p. 58

♦ 1246 ♦ **Hostos Day**
January 11

Eugenio Maria de Hostos (1839-1903) was a Puerto Rican philosopher and patriot who became a leader of the opposition to Spanish colonial rule in the 19th century. He campaigned for the education of women in Brazil, and his books on law and education triggered reforms in other Latin American countries. He even sponsored the first railroad between Chile and Argentina, across the Andes Mountains. The anniversary of his birth is observed as a public holiday in Puerto Rico on the second Monday in January.

CONTACTS:
Puerto Rico Tourism Company
135 W. 50th St. 22nd Fl.
New York, NY 10020
800-223-6530 or 212-586-6262; fax: 212-586-1212
www.gotopuertorico.com

SOURCES:
AnnivHol-2000, p. 8
BkHolWrld-1986, Jan 11

♦ 1247 ♦ **Hot Air Balloon Classic**
Early August

The **National Balloon Classic** takes place over about a week in early August from a launch field just outside Indianola, Iowa. When the event was first held in 1970, only 11 balloonists participated, but in 2001 there were close to 100 pilots and as many as 250,000 spectators. There are several flights or "tasks" involved in each race, designed to test the pilot's skill in handling his or her balloon. New tasks are added regularly to make the sport more demanding. As a result of the races, Indianola has come to be known as the Balloon Capital of the nation. The city is also the home of the National Balloon Museum.

CONTACTS:
Hot Air Balloon Classic
P.O. Box 346
Indianola, IA 50125
800-359-4692 or 515-961-8415
www.nationalballoonclassic.com

SOURCES:
GdUSFest-1984, p. 58

♦ 1248 ♦ **Houses and Gardens, Festival of**
March-April

One of the nation's oldest and most prestigious house tours is held from mid-March to mid-April in Charleston, S.C. This 300-year-old city has been bombarded by land and sea, devastated by an earthquake, and battered by hurricanes, but it remains a place known for splendid wrought-iron embellished architecture. The port city has 73 pre-Revolutionary buildings, 136 late-18th-century structures, and 600 others built before the 1840s. Among the more interesting areas is Cabbage Row, the model for Catfish Row in DuBose Heyward's novel *Porgy,* on which George Gershwin's opera *Porgy and Bess* was based.

More than 100 homes and gardens, full of blooming azaleas and camellias, are usually included in the festival, which dates from 1947. It features both afternoon and evening candlelight tours, and special candlelight galas with music and wine.

CONTACTS:
Historic Charleston Foundation
40 E. Bay St.
P.O. Box 1120
Charleston, SC 29401
843-723-1623; fax: 843-577-2067
www.historiccharleston.org

SOURCES:
GdUSFest-1984, p. 168

♦ 1249 ♦ **Houston Livestock Show & Rodeo**
Mid-February to early March

The nation's largest livestock show, with more than 35,000 entries, is held in the famous Astrodome of Houston, Tex. The show is a reminder of the 19th-century days when Houston's shipping trade was based on timber, cotton, and cattle. Things get under way with a downtown parade, and the agenda then includes top celebrity entertainers, pig races, and a chili cookoff.

The 2003 rodeo took place in the new Reliant Stadium, whose construction began in 2000.

CONTACTS:
Houston Livestock Show and Rodeo
Reliant Ctr., 8334 Fannin St.
P.O. Box 20070
Houston, TX 77054
832-667-1000; fax: 832-667-1134
www.rodeohouston.com

♦ 1250 ♦ **Howl! Festival**
September 5-9

In honor of Beat poet Allen Ginsberg's famous poem "Howl," which was the focus of an obscenity trial in the

1950s, the East Village and Lower East Side of New York City celebrate their own roles in the development of the American counter culture.

Created by local entrepreneur Philip Hartman in 2002 and centered on Tompkins Square Park, the five-day event includes dance, film, theatre, art, poetry, performance, and a host of other artistic activities. In addition, local clubs, restaurants, art galleries, and other venues participate in the celebration. In 2007, the event also included the Carl Solomon Book Expo, named after the Beat writer who was the inspiration for "Howl" and who is credited with getting the first novels of William Burroughs and Jack Kerouac published. Earlier festivals included the Charlie Parker Jazz Festival and the Allen Ginsberg Poetry Festival. The event ends with a parade down St. Marks Place.

CONTACTS:
Federation of East Village Artists
151 First Ave. , Ste. 88
New York, NY 10003
212-673-5433; fax: 212-505-3098
www.howlfestival.com/index.php

♦ 1251 ♦ **Human Towers of Valls**
June 24

On St. John's Day in the city of Valls in the Catalan region of Spain, a touring acrobatic company, or *comparsa,* presents the **Xiquets de Valls**, or "human towers of Valls." The acrobats form human towers or pyramids with four to six men at the base and one or more children at the top. The towers can extend to eight times a man's height, and they are formed to the musical accompaniment of the *gralla,* or native oboe. There is a point during the performance at which the children on top salute, the music ceases, and the entire structure stands immobile for several seconds before collapsing gracefully to the ground.

The companies also create human towers on St. Ursula's Day, October 22, and other fiestas.

CONTACTS:
Valls Office of Tourism
C/ de la Cort, 61
Catalonia, Valls 43800 Spain
34-977-612-530; fax: 34-977-612-872
www.costadaurada.org/d1/index.php?idioma=EN_EN

SOURCES:
FestWestEur-1958, p. 200

♦ 1252 ♦ **Humor and Satire Festival, International**
June, during odd-numbered years

Gabrovo, Bulgaria, may seem an unlikely place for the only festival in the world devoted to humor. This town, founded by a blacksmith in the 14th century, has a longstanding reputation for stinginess, and many jokes are told about the length to which its inhabitants will go to avoid spending money. The first humor festival was held there in 1967 in hopes of attracting tourism to the area. Now it is a 10-day

event that features a procession of people dressed as their favorite comic figure, a parade of satiric floats, and competitions to see who can get the best laugh. More than a thousand participants from 50 countries—mostly cartoonists, filmmakers, sculptors, artists, and performers specializing in humor and satire—take part in the festival each odd-numbered year, which attracts more than 10,000 spectators.

CONTACTS:
House of Humor and Satire
68, Bryanska St.
P.O. Box 104
Gabrovo, 5300 Bulgaria
359-66-27229; fax: 359-66-26989

SOURCES:
GdWrldFest-1985, p. 26

♦ 1253 ♦ **Hungary Republic Day**
October 23

Republic Day and the 1956 Revolution Anniversary are celebrated on October 23 and originally commemorated the 1956 uprising against Soviet control. On October 23, 1989, in honor of the previous revolution, Hungarians established a new republic, amending the constitution to allow multiparty politics, public assembly, and create separation of power in the government.

CONTACTS:
Hungarian Ministry for Foreign Affairs
Bem rakpart 47
Budapest, H-1027 Hungary
36-1-458-1000; fax: 38-1-212-5918
www.mfa.gov.hu/kum/en/bal

♦ 1254 ♦ **Hungary Revolution and Independence Day**
March 15

On March 15, Hungarians observe the anniversary of the beginning of the revolution in 1848 against the Habsburg monarchy. The revolutionaries called for the creation of a nation-state with freedom of the press and an independent parliamentary government. In 1989, celebrations were open for the first time since the Soviet invasion, and took place all over the country.

CONTACTS:
Hungarian Ministry for Foreign Affairs
Bem rakpart 47
Budapest, H-1027 Hungary
36-1-458-1000; fax: 38-1-212-5918
www.mfa.gov.hu/kum/en/bal

♦ 1255 ♦ **Hunters' Moon, Feast of the**
Second weekend in October

October was traditionally the time when the *voyageurs,* or traders, came to Fort Ouiatenon (in what is now Lafayette, Indiana) to trade their goods, gossip with the local French settlers, and generally relax and enjoy themselves before setting out on their next journey. Ouiatenon was home not only to the Ouiatenon Indian tribe but also to a number of French families from Canada. The Feast of the Hunter's Moon attempts to reenact as accurately as possible the events that took place there during the mid-18th century.

The two-day festival, which was first held in 1968, begins with the arrival of the voyageurs by canoe on the Wabash River. Events include Indian chants, French folk songs, demonstrations of traditional crafts, and the cooking of typical French and Indian foods over an open fire.

CONTACTS:
Tippecanoe County Historical Association
1001 South St.
Lafayette, IN 47901
765-476-8411; fax: 765-476-8414
www.tcha.mus.in.us

SOURCES:
GdUSFest-1985, p. 53

♦ 1256 ♦ **Hurling the Silver Ball**
Monday following February 3

St. Ia (or Eia or Ives) is the patron saint of St. Ives, Cornwall. She was one of a group of Celtic missionary saints believed to have reached the southwestern tip of England miraculously by crossing the Irish Sea in a millstone boat. They made a safe landing at the place where St. Ives now stands, and there are parishes and churches throughout Cornwall named after them.

St. Ives celebrates **Feast Monday**, near the Feast of St. Ia on February 3, by playing an ancient game known as hurling. In this case the ball is made of cork encased in silver, which is believed to be very old and is kept in the town clerk's office during the year.

The mayor begins the game by tossing the silver ball against the side of the parish church, which is dedicated to St. Ia. Children then take over, tossing the ball back and forth in what might be described as a kind of "hand football." The game stops promptly at 12 noon, and whoever has the ball in his or her possession at that time receives a cash prize or a medal. The festivities continue in the afternoon with more sporting events, and there is a municipal ball in the evening.

CONTACTS:
Town of St. Ives
St. Ives Town Council
The Guildhall, Street an Pol
St. Ives, Cornwall TR26 2DS United Kingdom
44-17-3679-7840
www.cornwall.gov.uk

SOURCES:
YrbookEngFest-1954, p. 34
YrFest-1972, p. 123

♦ 1257 ♦ **Hurricane Supplication Day**
Fourth Monday in July

Observed in the U.S. Virgin Islands—St. Croix, St. Thomas, and St. John—Hurricane Supplication Day marks the beginning of the hurricane season. Special church services are held to pray for safety from the storms that ravage these and other Caribbean islands. The custom probably dates back to the "rogation" ceremonies which began in fifth-century England—from the word *rogare*, meaning "to beg or supplicate." Rogations usually followed a frightening series of storms, earthquakes, or other natural disasters, although sometimes they took place annually on the ROGATION DAYS that preceded ASCENSION DAY.

At the end of the hurricane season in October there is a **Hurricane Thanksgiving Day**. Church services are held on the third Monday in October so that the islanders can give thanks for being spared the destruction of a major storm.

CONTACTS:
United States Virgin Islands, Chamber of Commerce
P.O. Box 324
Charlotte Amalie, VI 00804
340-776-0100; fax: 340-776-0588
www.usvichamber.com

SOURCES:
AnnivHol-2000, pp. 126, 181
BkFestHolWrld-1970, p. 125
BkHolWrld-1986, Oct 18
FolkAmerHol-1999, pp. 319, 423

♦ 1258 ♦ **Hurston (Zora Neale) Festival of the Arts and Humanities**
Late January to early February

The Zora Neale Hurston Festival of the Arts and Humanities (also known as the **Zora! Festival**) is an eight-day, multi-disciplinary event held every year in late January to early February in Eatonville, Fla. Zora Neale Hurston was an acclaimed novelist, short-story writer, and playwright. She was also a respected folklorist and anthropologist who devoted herself to preserving the culture of African Americans in the South. She grew up in Eatonville, noted as the oldest incorporated African-American municipality in the United States.

The Zora! Festival was launched in 1990 to showcase her life and work, as well as to celebrate her hometown and the cultural contributions that people of African descent have made to the United States and the world. It features a three-day street festival of the arts, the first day of which is a special education day for school children. The street festival also showcases performances by nationally known acts. During the week prior to the street festival, art exhibits, literary readings, academic presentations, conferences, and lectures, many of them free of charge, are devoted to Hurston and African-American arts in general.

CONTACTS:
Zora! Festival
227 W. Kennedy Blvd.
Eatonville, FL 32751
407-647-3131; fax: 407-539-2192

SOURCES:
AAH-2007, p. 437

♦ 1259 ♦ **Hus (Jan) Day**
July 6

Jan Hus Day is celebrated in the Czech Republic to commemorate Jan Hus, an early 15th century Czech priest, theologian, and reformer. Hus was a critic of the Catholic Church's activities during the reign of King Wenceslas IV. Many clergymen had obtained positions of power in the royal administration and had accumulated wealth and property. Hus advocated the idea of a poor Church that limited itself to Biblical teachings and spiritual affairs. Hus was summoned to the ecclesiastical Council of Constance in 1414. When he refused to recant his teachings, Hus was excommunicated and burnt at the stake on July 6, 1415. Over the centuries, Hus has become a symbol of Czech independence and courage.

Jan Hus Day is a national holiday in the Czech Republic. A wreath is placed on his monument in Old Town Square in Prague, and the national flag is flown at all public places.

CONTACTS:
Embassy of the Czech Republic
3900 Spring of Freedom St. N.W.
Washington, D.C. 20008
202-274-9100; fax: 202-966-8540
www.mzv.cz/wwwo/?zu=washington

I

♦ 1260 ♦ I Madonnari Italian Street Painting Festival
May, Memorial Day weekend

This festival celebrating the ancient Italian tradition of street painting was brought to Santa Barbara, Calif., in 1987. Some 200 professional and amateur artists create chalk "paintings"—both reproductions of old masters and original designs—on the Old Mission courtyard. Artist Kurt Wenner has been known for his *trompe l'oeil* paintings in which he transforms sidewalks into fountains or chasms. In 1988, his *Dies Irae*, or "Day of Wrath," was a maelstrom of struggling bodies. He used 200 sticks of chalk for *Dies Irae*.

In Italy in the 17th century, vagabond artists created sidewalk works of chalk art. Because they often painted the Madonna, they were known as *madonnari*. Artists still follow the tradition in the Italian village of Grazie di Curtatone, and Santa Barbara's "I Madonnari" is considered the village's sister festival. Another sister festival is held at San Luis Obispo Mission on the last weekend in April. The art works, masterful as they are, are gone in a week's time.

CONTACTS:
Santa Barbara Festival Office, Children's Creative Project
3970 La Colina Rd. Ste. 9
Santa Barbara, CA 93110
805-964-4710; fax: 805-563-1103
www.imadonnarifestival.com

♦ 1261 ♦ Ibu Afo Festival
On or near March 20

The Igbo people of Nigeria celebrate their New Year's Eve around March 20 with a solemn ceremony marking the end of the old year and heralding the arrival of the new. The council of elders who fix the annual calendar determine the exact hour at which the year will end. When it arrives, a wailing noise signals the departing year, and children rush into their houses, lock the doors to avoid being carried away by the old year as it leaves, and bang on the doors to add to the din. As soon as the wailing dies down, the doors are thrown open and everyone greets the new year with spontaneous applause.

CONTACTS:
Embassy of the Federal Republic of Nigeria
3519 International Ct. N.W.
Washington, D.C. 20008
202-986-8400; fax: 202-775-1385
www.nigeriaembassyusa.org

SOURCES:
BkHolWrld-1986, Mar 18
FolkWrldHol-1999, p. 213

♦ 1262 ♦ Ice Worm Festival
First full weekend in February

This zany mid-winter festival celebrates the emergence of the ice worm in Cordova, Alaska, where the winters are long and dark and give rise to thoughts of things like ice worms. The highlight of the three-day festival is the procession of a 150-foot-long ice worm (it has a dragon's head) followed by 500 or so paraders. Other events include variety shows, ski events, a survival-suit race, a beauty pageant, music, and dances.

The celebration began in 1961 as a way to shake off the winter blahs, and the legend was born then that an ice worm hibernates during the winter in the Cordova Glacier but starts to hatch or wake up in early February. The worm has gained international fame, and the festival draws great crowds of people.

CONTACTS:
Cordova Chamber of Commerce
P.O. Box 99
404 First St.
Cordova, AK 99574
907-424-7260; fax: 907-424-7259
www.cordovachamber.com

SOURCES:
BkFestHolWrld-1970, p. 31
GdUSFest-1984, p. 8

♦ 1263 ♦ Iceland Independence Day
June 17

Iceland was proclaimed an independent republic on June 17, 1944. Sometimes referred to as **National Day**, the anniversary of this event is also the birthday of Jón Sigurdsson, the nation's 19th-century leader. A varied program of parades, speeches, sporting competitions, outdoor concerts and shows, and amusements culminates in the evening with dancing in the streets of Reykjavik and other towns.

Another National Day was December 1, the anniversary of the 1918 treaty recognizing Iceland as an independent state under the Danish crown. This is now largely a student celebration.

CONTACTS:
Icelandic Tourist Board
655 Third Ave., Ste. 1810
New York, NY 10017
212-885-9700; fax: 212-885-9710
www.goiceland.org

SOURCES:
AnnivHol-2000, p. 101
NatlHolWrld-1968, p. 85

♦ 1264 ♦ Icelandic Festival
First weekend in August

The Icelandic Festival, or **Islendingadagurinn**, held in Gimli, Manitoba, each year is one of the oldest ethnic festivals in Canada, dating back to 1890. The Icelandic settlers who emigrated to Canada after their homes in Iceland were destroyed by volcanic eruptions in 1875 wanted to do something to preserve their heritage and customs, and the current festival continues to reflect this interest in Icelandic culture. The events include choral singing and cultural and artistic displays. Participants dress in native Icelandic costumes and eat traditional foods such as smoked lamb and *skyr,* which is similar to yogurt. In recent years a film festival and sporting events have been added to the more traditional offerings.

CONTACTS:
Icelandic Festival
107-94 First Ave.
Gimli, MB R0C 1B1 Canada
204-642-7417
www.icelandicfestival.com

SOURCES:
GdWrldFest-1985, p. 33
IntlThFolk-1979, p. 63

♦ 1265 ♦ Id al-Adha (Feast of Sacrifice; Eid)
10th through 12th days of Islamic month of Dhu al-Hijjah

This most important feast of the Muslim calendar is the concluding rite of those performing the Hajj or PILGRIMAGE TO MECCA. It is also known as **Id al-Kabir**, the **Great Feast.**

For those not on pilgrimage, Id al-Adha is a three-day festival celebrating Ibrahim's (Abraham's) willingness to obey Allah by killing his son, believed by Muslims to be Ishmael, and not Isaac as written in the Old Testament. Muslims consider Ishmael to be the forefather of the Arabs. According to the Qur'an, Ibrahim had an ax poised over the boy when a

voice from Heaven told him to stop. He was allowed to sacrifice a ram instead. Many Muslim families reenact this show of faith by sacrificing a cow, a ram, or a lamb on this day, using a portion of it for the family feast and donating one- or two-thirds to the poor.

In Turkey this day is called the **Kurban** "sacrificial" **Bayram.** In northern central Africa it is called **Tabaski.** It is an official public holiday in numerous African countries and elsewhere around the world.

See also SALLAH FESTIVAL

SOURCES:
BkFest-1937, p. 238
BkFestHolWrld-1970, p. 80
BkHolWrld-1986, Aug 28
ConEncyIslam-1991, p. 178
DictWrldRel-1989, pp. 290, 569
EncyRel-1987, vol. 7, p. 456, vol. 15, p. 458
FestWrld: Saudi-1999, p. 20
FestWrld: Turkey-1999, p. 16
FolkWrldHol-1999, p. 153
HolSymbols-2009, p. 391
MuhFest-1988, p. 34
OxYear-1999, p. 734
RelHolCal-2004, p. 149
UndIslam-2004, p. 363

♦ 1266 ♦ Id al-Fitr (Eid)
First day of Islamic month of Shawwal

Also known as the **Feast of Fast-Breaking**, or the **Lesser Feast**, Id al-Fitr marks the end of the month-long fast of RAMADAN and the beginning of a three-day feast. It is the second most important Islamic holiday after ID AL-ADHA.

The Id prayer is performed by the whole community at an outdoor prayer ground (*musalla*) or mosque. Then people put on new clothes, children are given presents, and everyone visits relatives and friends. It is the time when everyone asks pardon for all the wrongs of the past year. Village squares have carnival rides, puppet shows, and candy vendors.

It is called **Lebaran** or **Hari Raya** by Indonesians, Thais, and Malaysians. In Turkey, where it is called the **Candy Festival**, or **Seker Bayrami**, this is the day on which children are given candy or money wrapped in handkerchiefs. In Pakistan the special treat associated with this day is *saween*, a spaghetti cooked in milk and sugar, and sprinkled with almonds, pistachios, and dates.

In Malaya, where it is called Hari Raya, they hold open houses. It is the new custom to have one's non-Muslim friends visit to foster more understanding between different religious groups. Muslims in turn will visit Chinese friends during LUNAR NEW YEAR, Hindus during DEWALI, and Christians at CHRISTMAS.

In West Africa, a Mande feast of the virgins has been added to this feast. In western Guinea, young men and women parade all night with floats of animals and boats, singing and dancing; small children sing for presents.

SOURCES:
AmerBkDays-2000, p. 871
BkFest-1937, p. 238
BkFestHolWrld-1970, pp. 80, 113
BkHolWrld-1986, Jun 27
ConEncyIslam-1991, p. 178
DictWrldRel-1989, p. 597
EncyRel-1987, vol. 7, p. 456, vol. 13, p. 91
FestWrld: Saudi-1999, p. 12
FestWrld: Turkey-1999, p. 8
FolkWrldHol-1999, p. 791
HolSymbols-2009, p. 394
MuhFest-1988, p. 63
OxYear-1999, p. 733
RelHolCal-2004, p. 148
UndIslam-2004, pp. 297, 315

◆ 1267 ◆ Id al-Fitr (Nigeria)
First day of the Islamic month of Shawwal

Among Nigerian Muslims Id al-Fitr—the feast concluding the month-long RAMADAN fast—begins with a procession to the emir's palace. People wear new, festive clothes for the event. The emir is the chief or head of state, and as he sits on his throne, beautifully adorned horses and riders honor him with a *sallah*—a traditional, and dramatic, way of showing respect. One by one, each horseman gallops toward the emir at full tilt and halts only at the last possible moment, then the horseman salutes. The emir's own bodyguards are the last to honor him in this unnerving way. After the sallah is over, the feasting and merrymaking starts. Ox-taming—a special form of bullfighting—is a popular entertainment.

The Islamic religion came to Nigeria around the 11th century with Arabs who crossed the Sahara Desert to trade.

See also SALLAH FESTIVAL

CONTACTS:
Embassy of the Federal Republic of Nigeria
3519 International Ct. N.W.
Washington, D.C. 20008
202-986-8400; fax: 202-775-1385
www.nigeriaembassyusa.org

SOURCES:
FestWrld: Nigeria-1998, p. 20

◆ 1268 ◆ Idaho International Dance and Music Festival
Midsummer

Every summer Brigham Young University-Idaho, located in Rexburg, invites dancers from different continents to perform folk dance and music. For community leaders and for the university's arts enthusiasts, the Idaho International Dance & Music Festival is a great opportunity to promote tourism and participate in meaningful cultural exchange.

The university dance directors who founded the festival drew their inspiration from a folk dance tour of Europe they completed in 1983. They envisioned an opportunity to hold a dance event in Rexburg that would attract performers from all over the world. The inaugural festival took place in 1986,

and since then the diversity of the team rosters has been notable. Between 1986 and 2006, 172 teams performed from over 55 countries. In recent years, the nearby town of Hurley has become a second site of the festival; its version takes place within a week or two of the Rexburg festival.

Opening Ceremonies kick off the festival. Over the course of a week about 10 teams representing different countries perform. Attendees have the opportunity to learn from the visiting dance teams in classes covering various cultures and styles of dance.

CONTACTS:
Rexburg Chamber of Commerce
420 W. 4th S.
Rexburg, ID 83440
208-356-5700 or 208-356-5799
www.rexcc.com

◆ 1269 ◆ Idaho Regatta
Last weekend in June

This full-throttle three-day event is held on the Snake River at Burley, Idaho. Burley's population of 9,000 is doubled for the regatta, which is a qualifying race for the American Power Boat Association Western Divisional Championship. A hundred speedboats in 11 inboard limited classes compete for a share of $35,000 in cash prizes—and a mink coat. The regatta has been held since the 1970s, and each year, a coat has been donated as a prize by Lee Moyle, one of the founders of the regatta, and an owner of the Don and Lee Moyle Mink Farm. Boats are entered from throughout the country. They include seven-liter, hydroplanes, super-stock, pro-stock, KRR flat-bottoms, Comp Jets, and stock hydros.

CONTACTS:
Mini-Cassia Chamber of Commere
1177 7th St.
P.O. Box 640
Heyburn, ID 83336
208-679-4793; fax: 208-679-4794
www.minicassiachamber.com

◆ 1270 ◆ Idaho Spud Day
Third Saturday in September

Spud Day is a celebration of the potato in Shelley, Idaho. The potato has come to be thought of as *the* crop of Idaho, but the state actually has a number of other important crops: wheat, hay, oats, barley, beans, peas, sugar beets, and fruits. Nonetheless, the spud gets the hurrahs with a festival that began in 1927 and includes a parade, potato-picking and tug-of-war contests, and, of course, potatoes fried, baked, scalloped, mashed, etc. Five thousand free baked potatoes are given to visitors.

CONTACTS:
City of Shelley
City Hall
101 S. Emerson Ave.
Shelley, ID 83274
208-357-3390; fax: 208-357-3998
www.shelley.govoffice.com

◆ 1271 ◆ Ides
Various

In the ancient Roman calendar, the ides fell on the 15th day of March, May, July, and October, and on the 13th day of the other months. The Roman emperor Julius Caesar was assassinated on the Ides of March in 44 B.C.E., and Shakespeare's famous reference to this day in his play *Julius Caesar*— "Beware the Ides of March"—is probably the best-known use of the term.

The ancient Romans specified a particular day in the month by relating it to the next calends, ides, or nones. For example, "six days before the Ides of June" meant June 8, since the ides in June fell on the 13th.

Calends, sometimes spelled "kalends," refers to the first day of the month, from which the days of the preceding months were counted backward. The order of the days in each month were publicly proclaimed on the calends. For example, "the sixth of the calends of April" meant March 27, or the sixth day before the first day of April (counting April 1 as the first day.)

The Greeks didn't use the term, which is why the phrase "on (or at) the Greek calends" is a synonym for "never." Occasionally, calends was used to mean Settlement Day, since the first of the month was usually the day on which debts were settled.

The nones fell on the ninth day before the ides. In March, May, July, and October, the nones occurred on the seventh of the month because the ides fell on the 15th. In all the other months, the nones occurred on the fifth or 13th days.

SOURCES:
AnnivHol-2000, p. 44
DictDays-1988, p. 18
DictRomRel-1996, p. 104
FestRom-1981, p. 42
OxYear-1999, p. 118

◆ 1272 ◆ Iditarod Trail Sled Dog Race
Early March

The Iditarod is the world's longest and toughest sled dog race, across the state of Alaska from Anchorage on the south-central coast to Nome on the Bering Sea just south of the Arctic Circle. It commemorates a 650-mile mid-winter emergency run to take serum from Nenana to Nome during the 1925 diphtheria epidemic. The race, which began in 1973, follows an old frozen-river mail route and is named for a deserted mining town along the way.

About 70 teams compete each year, and the winner is acclaimed the world's best long-distance dog musher. In 1985, Libby Riddles, age 28, was the first woman to win the race, coming in three hours ahead of the second-place finisher. It took her 18 days. Susan Butcher won in 1986, and again in 1987, 1988, and 1990. In 1991, Rick Swenson battled a howling blizzard on the last leg to win and become the first five-time winner (1977, 1979, 1981, 1982). His prize money was $50,000 out of the $250,000 purse. The 1992 winner, Martin Buser, set a record time of 10 days, 19 hours, and 17 min-

utes. Buser set a new record of 8 days, 22 hours, and 46 minutes when he took his fourth win in 2002.

Mushers draw lots for starting position at a banquet held in Anchorage a couple of days before the race. Each musher, with a team of anywhere from 8 to 18 dogs, can expect to face 30-foot snowdrifts and winds of up to 60 miles an hour.

A number of events are clustered around the running of the race. At Wasilla, near Anchorage, Iditarod Days are held on the beginning weekend of the race and feature softball, golf on ice, fireworks, and snow sculptures. Anchorage stages an International Ice Carving Competition that weekend, with ice carvers from around the world creating their cold images in the city's Town Square. At Nome, the Bering Sea Ice Golf Classic, a six-hole golf tournament, is played on the frozen Bering Sea during the second week of the race.

Various organizations have campaigned against the Iditarod and other sled dog races because of the risks to the dogs and alleged mistreatment. Iditarod organizers provide each dog with a physical examination before the race, yet, according to newspaper reports, it is not unusual for at least one dog each year to die from exhaustion or injuries sustained during the race.

CONTACTS:
Iditarod Trail Committee, Inc.
P.O. Box 870800
Wasilla, AK 99687
907-376-5155; fax: 907-373-6998
www.iditarod.com

People for the Ethical Treatment of Animals
501 Front St.
Norfolk, VA 23510
757-622-7382; fax: 757-622-0457
www.peta.org

SOURCES:
BkHolWrld-1986, Mar 24
HolSymbols-2009, p. 398

◆ 1273 ◆ Idlewild Jazz Festival
Third Saturday in July

Sponsored by the nonprofit Idlewild Foundation, the Idlewild Jazz Festival is a one-day, outdoor event. It recalls the Jazz Age flourishing of Idlewild, Mich., a resort area in the northwestern part of the state. Known as the "Black Eden" during its heyday in the mid-20th century, Idlewild was a favorite vacation destination for African Americans from such Midwestern cities as Chicago and Detroit. With nearly 25,000 visitors each summer, the area grew to include entertainment venues such as the Flamingo and Paradise jazz clubs, where luminaries including Louis Armstrong, Sarah Vaughan, Sammy Davis Jr., and Count Basie performed during the 1950s.

The festival was conceived in 2002 as a means of paying tribute to that heritage and offering a new generation a connection with the past. The festival takes place in a wooded, lakeside setting on Williams Island and includes a program of music that begins at noon and runs well into the night. In addition, related activities include an art fair, marketplace, and writers' workshop. Food vendors offer refreshments ranging from Jamaican specialties and fish to barbecued wings.

CONTACTS:
Idlewild Foundation
1150 Griswold, Ste. 2100
Detroit, MI 48226
313-965-0505
www.idlewildjazzfest.com

Idlewild African-American Chamber of Commerce
P.O. Box 435
Idlewild, MI 49642
800-745-2611
www.iaacc.com

SOURCES:
AAH-2007, p. 223

♦ 1274 ♦ Iduna and Summer Finding
Vernal Equinox; around March 21 in the northern hemisphere and around September 23 in the southern hemisphere

Northern European pagan traditions placed great importance on the official advent of spring known as the vernal equinox. Iduna and Summer Finding, which today are observed by Wiccans and Neo-pagans, are two festivals that celebrate the time of the year in which daylight "overcomes" the night. While they are distinct festivals, both traditions share metaphorical imagery along with the same date.

In Norse mythology, Iduna is the goddess of spring and the keeper of apples of immortality. Her story mirrors that of the Greek goddess Persephone, in which a contriving god abducts her and takes her magical fruit away. She eventually returns, but in the form of a quail, symbolizing the return of the bird from its winter roost. Similarly, Summer Finding focuses on a tradition in which the year's first spotting of a bird or a flower marks the "finding" of the warm season. In some old traditions, whoever discovered the first bird marked the spot with a pole, which is afterwards decorated with flowers.

Among Wiccan and Neo-pagan followers, Summer Finding or Iduna is less commonly observed than Ostara, the equinox festival celebrating the spring goddess of the same name.

SOURCES:
RelHolCal-2004, p. 271

♦ 1275 ♦ Igbi
Sunday nearest February 5

Because February 5 is the day that the sun, it is hoped, will shine for the first time of the year on the village of Khora, and then on Shaitli in the Dagestan region of Russia, the Tsezy (Didoitsy) people celebrate this event marking the middle of winter with a festival known as Igbi.

The name comes from the plural of the Tsezian word *ig*—a ring-shaped bread similar to a bagel—and the baking of these ritual breads plays a central role in the celebration,

which involves a number of masked and costumed characters playing traditional roles. Six *botsi*, or wolves, carrying wooden swords go from house to house collecting the igbi that the women have been baking in preparation for their arrival. The bagels are strung on a long pole known as the *giri*, and those who fail to cooperate are hit with the swords or have their shoes filled with wet snow and ice.

The children get up early on this day, which is now observed on the Sunday nearest February 5 so they don't have to miss school, and go through the village collecting the igbi that have been made especially for them.

Igbi is also a day of reckoning. All through the year the young organizers of the feast have kept notes of the good and bad deeds of the villagers. Now after all the igbi have been collected, there is a ceremony in the center of the village in which the *kvidili*—a traditional figure wearing an animal-skin mask resembling no known animal; lately it looks like a horse with horns and a big mouth like a crocodile—reads out the names of those who have committed a transgression (such as public drunkenness) during the year.

The unlucky ones are dragged to the river and immersed up to their knees through a hole in the ice. Those who are congratulated for their good deeds are handed an ig. At the end of the festival, the kvidili is symbolically slain with a wooden sword.

SOURCES:
FolkWrldHol-1999, p. 122

♦ 1276 ♦ Imam Ali's Birthday
13th day of the Islamic month of Rajab

Ali ibn Abu Talib was the cousin and son-in-law of the prophet Muhammad. He ruled the Rashidun Empire from 656 to 661. Due to sectarian differences in Islam, he is known variously as the fourth caliph by Sunni Muslims and the first imam by Shi'ite Muslims.

To pay tribute to Ali's special role in the Shi'ite succession, followers have always honored the anniversary of his birth date. The holiday is widely observed in countries with large Shi'ite populations, such as Iraq and Iran. Najaf, the Iraqi city where the imam is laid to rest, is a well-known commemoration site. Throughout the year, the city welcomes Shi'ite pilgrims from Iraq and beyond.

In Iran, Ali's birthday was designated an official holiday during the reign of Nasiru al-Din Shah, in the late 19th century. Today, sermons, speeches, and other events commemorating the imam's birth are overseen by the country's Ministry of Culture and Religious Guidance.

CONTACTS:
Iran's Ministry of Foreign Affairs
Imam Khomeini Sq.
Tehran, Iran

♦ 1277 ♦ Imam Ali's Martyrdom, Anniversary of
21st day of the Islamic month of Ramadan

Shi'ite Muslims show great reverence toward Ali ibn Abu Talib, the cousin and son-in-law of the prophet Muhammad. As Muhammad's direct descendant, they have conferred distinction on Ali as the first imam. Ali's reign lasted from 656 to 661, the year in which members of a sect known as the Kharijites carried out his assassination, which according to Shi'ite accounts occurred on Ramadan 19. Ali suffered from the stabbing for two days before he died.

Most Shi'ites believe that Ali's tomb lies in Najaf, a present-day city in Iraq. During the year, the Imam Ali Mosque in Najaf attracts pilgrims from throughout Iraq, Iran, and other countries. On his death anniversary, the city's population swells to as many as two million people as pilgrims gather around the imam's holy shrine to pray and mourn.

In addition to observing the death anniversary, some followers observe the date on which Ali was stabbed. It is customary for followers to maintain a round-the-clock vigil to observe the interval between the imam's stabbing and his death.

CONTACTS:
Iran's Ministry of Foreign Affairs
Imam Khomeini Sq.
Tehran, Iran

♦ 1278 ♦ Imam Sadiq's Martyrdom, Anniversary of
25th day of the Islamic month of Shawwal

Historical accounts differ over the birth year of Ja'far al-Sadiq (699?–765), the sixth Shi'ite imam and founder of an expansion of Islamic *shari'ah* law known as *fiqh*. Records are more certain, however, about the date of his murder, which was believed to be at the hands of the Abbasid ruler al-Mansur. Followers mourn and offer condolences to one another on the death anniversary of this spiritual leader and renowned scholar. It is a public holiday in Iran and is observed in countries with Shi'ite populations.

Many followers observe al-Sadiq's death as they observe other martyr days—with religious processions of mourning and a special meeting called the *rawda-khani*. Convened in houses or mosques, these ceremonies feature *rawda-khans*, individuals who are skilled at reciting Islamic narratives. The retelling of the imam's demise by poisoning often elicits weeping from the audience and other strong expressions of grief.

CONTACTS:
Iran's Ministry of Foreign Affairs
Imam Khomeini Sq.
Tehran, Iran

♦ 1279 ♦ Imbolc (Imbolg)
February 1

One of the "Greater Sabbats" during the Wiccan year, Imbolc celebrates the coming of spring and the recovery of the Earth Goddess after giving birth to the Sun God at YULE. "Wicca" is the name used by many believers in modern Neopagan witchcraft because it doesn't carry the stigma that the terms "witch" or "pagan" carry.

The Greater Sabbats (or Sabbaths) take place four times a year, at the CROSS-QUARTER DAYS of February 1, May 1, August 1, and November 1. In ancient days, some of these were huge get-togethers that involved dancing, singing, and feasting which went on all night. Revolving around the changing of the seasons and the breeding of animals, they served as a way to give thanks for the bounties of the earth. Other names for Imbolc include the **Feast of Pan**, **Feast of Torches**, **Feast of Waxing Lights**, and **Oimelc**.

See also BELTANE; LAMMAS; ST. BRIDGET'S DAY; SAMHAIN

SOURCES:
RelHolCal-2004, p. 270

♦ 1280 ♦ Immaculate Conception, Feast of the
December 8

Theological controversy surrounded this festival for centuries, though popular celebration of it dates to at least the eighth century. The argument hinged on the meaning of the word "immaculate," which in this context refers to the belief that Jesus' mother Mary was conceived without original sin, the basic inclination toward wrongdoing that originates from the sin of Adam. Many leading theologians, including St. Thomas Aquinas, questioned the Immaculate Conception.

Although for many years it remained open for debate, in 1854 Pope Pius IX proclaimed it to be an essential dogma of the Roman Catholic Church, and since that time the Feast of the Immaculate Conception has celebrated God's choice of Mary to give birth to His Son. This is also a pious belief held by many Anglicans.

In Guam, this is a legal holiday also known as **Our Lady of Camarin Day**, commemorating a statute of Mary that a fisherman found floating off the coast. It is observed on the fourth Thursday in November.

CONTACTS:
The Mary Page
Marian Library/International Marian Research Institute
University of Dayton
Dayton, OH 45469
www.udayton.edu

Guam Visitors Bureau
1301 Marina Village Pkwy., Ste. 210
Alameda, CA 94501
800-873-4826 or 510-865-0366; fax: 510-865-5165
www.visitguam.org

SOURCES:
AmerBkDays-2000, p. 818
BkFest-1937, pp. 190, 271
BkFestHolWrld-1970, p. 131
BkHolWrld-1986, Dec 8
DaysCustFaith-1957, p. 308
DictWrldRel-1989, p. 338
FolkWrldHol-1999, p. 694
OxYear-1999, p. 490
RelHolCal-2004, p. 85
SaintFestCh-1904, p. 14

♦ 1281 ♦ **Immaculate Conception, Feast of the (Argentina)**
December 8

Although a number of special fiestas are held in Argentina on December 8, the Feast of the IMMACULATE CONCEPTION of the Virgin Mary, the celebration held in Catamarca stands out. It focuses on the Virgen del Valle, an image of the Virgin Mary that was found in a nearby cave in 1620. Her broad, dark face and narrow eyes marked the Virgen as clearly the product of an indigenous artist.

Every town and hamlet in Catamarca province and in several neighboring provinces has its own replica of the statue, and all bring their images to the provincial capital of San Fernando del Valle de Catamarca for the December 8 procession. Some pilgrims make the journey on foot, which means that they must set out in November to get there on time. Many wear special costumes, and almost everyone also brings brightly hued pennants and flags. They make music with indigenous instruments along the way. When they reach Catamarca, they participate in many of the competitive games associated with the fiesta. The climax of the festival is the procession in which the original image of the Virgen del Valle is escorted through the streets of town while spectators throw white handkerchiefs in the air.

CONTACTS:
National Secretariat of Tourism, Tourist Information Centers
Av. Santa Fe 883
Buenos Aires, C1059ABC Argentina
54-11-4312-2232; fax: 54-11-4302-7816
www.turismo.gov.ar/eng/menu.htm

SOURCES:
FiestaTime-1965, p. 177

♦ 1282 ♦ **Immaculate Conception, Feast of the (Malta)**
December 8

The Republic of Malta is a small country in the central Mediterranean that consists of seven islands. The Maltese Islands have a strong Catholic population that celebrates a wide variety of festivities throughout the religious year.

Maltese families tend to be quite close-knit, and the holidays are a time to strengthen the sense of community and reinforce family bonds. The Maltese people are proud of their religion and parishes, and they go to great lengths to organize and prepare for the celebration day.

Each year many countries, including Malta, celebrate the Feast of the Immaculate Conception on December 8. It is a public holiday set aside to commemorate the birth of the virgin Mary, who is known to the Maltese as "Our Lady without sin." In Malta, this day is one of the feast days celebrated by many Catholics. Feast days are a big part of life on the islands. However, the most important events to all villages are their individual *festas*—celebrations with fireworks, decorated streets, and carts throughout the villages selling many different foods, including traditional sweets

and delicacies such as Maltese nougat—honoring their parish patron saint.

CONTACTS:
Malta Tourism Authority
Auberge D'Italie
Merchants St.
Valetta VLT 1170 Malta
www.visitmalta.com

♦ 1283 ♦ **Immaculate Conception, Feast of the (Mexico)**
December 8

The Feast of the IMMACULATE CONCEPTION of the Virgin Mary is an important day throughout Latin America, but it is especially significant in the Mexican town of San Juan de los Lagos in Jalisco State, where the celebration begins several days in advance. The town's inhabitants temporarily rename the streets where the festival will occur. On Calle de Alegria (Joy Street), for example, there are puppet shows, side shows, games of chance, food stands, and musical performances. On Calle del Azúcar (Sugar Street), all kinds of sweets are sold, including the highly prized *alfajor*, which is a candy made from honey and nuts. And on Calle de las Pieles (Street of Hides), there are exhibitions of animal skins and beautifully made leather goods for sale.

On the morning of December 8, the 11-inch image of the Virgin Mary leaves the local church, carried by priests on a silver litter. Later that afternoon festival organizers put two silver cups on the altar. In one there are scraps of paper bearing the names of devout community members, while the other cup contains blank pieces of paper—with one exception that says "Fiesta de Nuestra Senora de San Juan." Papers are removed two at a time, one from each cup, and the person whose name matches up with the name of the fiesta is in charge of the celebration the following year. Gun shots and ringing bells accompany this news, for it is considered a great honor to be chosen.

CONTACTS:
Jalisco State Tourism Institution
Moreles No. 102
Plaza Tapata
Guadalajara, Jalisco Mexico
52-215-679-9610

SOURCES:
FiestaTime-1965, p. 173

♦ 1284 ♦ **Immaculate Heart of Mary, Feast of the**
May-June; second Saturday following the second Sunday after Pentecost

It was St. John Eudes who initiated the worship of the Holy Heart of Mary in 1648 by composing a Mass and Office, although the feast failed to be approved by the Congregation of Rites in 1669. Repeated requests over the years for official recognition of the feast were reinforced in 1917 when the Virgin Mary appeared at Fátima, Portugal, and expressed her wish that the devotion be established so that Russia would be saved.

On October 31, 1942, the 25th anniversary of the appearance at Fátima, Pope Pius XII consecrated the entire human race to the Immaculate Heart of Mary, and two years later, a feast under that name was established for August 22, octave of the Feast of the IMMACULATE CONCEPTION. (*See also* OUR LADY OF FÁTIMA DAY.) It was moved to its present date in 1969. Roman Catholics observe this day in honor of Mary and to obtain her intercession for world peace and the practice of virtue.

CONTACTS:
The Mary Page
Marian Library/International Marian Research Institute
University of Dayton
Dayton, OH 45469
937-229-4214; fax: 937-229-4258
www.udayton.edu

SOURCES:
RelHolCal-2004, p. 97

♦ 1285 ♦ Impruneta, Festa del
Late October

The fair held at Impruneta, outside Florence, Italy, is one of the largest and noisiest of the autumn harvest festivals held all over Tuscany in October.

For weeks before the festival begins, the walls of Florence are covered with posters announcing when the fair will be held. Dating back three centuries, the *festa* originally celebrated the figure of the Virgin Mary which was believed to have been painted by St. Luke. But now it is primarily a celebration of the harvest and a last opportunity before winter to indulge in the area's special foods and the wines of the Elsa and Pesa valleys.

Chickens, pigeons, and suckling pigs are roasted on spits, and there are tables heaped with home-cured hams and loaves of country-style bread. Other foods associated with the fair include the paper-thin anise cookies known as *brigidini* and almond toffee, which is boiled in iron cauldrons.

CONTACTS:
Italian Government Tourist Board
630 Fifth Ave., Ste. 1565
New York, NY 10111
212-245-5618; fax: 212-586-9249
www.italiantourism.com

♦ 1286 ♦ ImPulsTanz: Vienna International Dance Festival
Early July to early August

Originally a festival with an exclusive focus on instruction, ImPulsTanz: Vienna International Dance Festival has become one of the premiere contemporary dance showcases in Europe. The event boasts more than 40 productions and draws over 30,000 attendees.

In 1984, Vienna cultural manager Karl Regenburger and choreographer Ismael Ivo began collaborating to create a dance festival. Their aim was to increase exposure for Austria's contemporary dance scene. For the first four years a handful of instructors offered about 20 workshops in a given festival. By 1988, organizers had added performance pieces to the program. In the years following capacity grew to offer scholarships and career development programs for festival participants. Today instruction is available to dancers of all levels.

In 2008 festival organizers made plans for a 25th anniversary festival with new productions as well as a retrospective by choreographers who had been with ImPulsTanz since its inception.

CONTACTS:
ImPulsTanz
Museumstraᵃe 5/21
A-1070
Vienna, Austria
www.impulstanz.com/en

♦ 1287 ♦ Inauguration Day
January 20

From 1789 until 1933, the day on which the newly elected president of the United States began his term of office was March 4—now known as **Old Inauguration Day**. The day was changed to January 20 when the 20th Amendment to the Constitution was passed in 1933. When Inauguration Day falls on a Sunday, the oath of office is administered privately, but the public ceremonies are usually postponed until the following day.

The swearing-in of the president had been held on the East Portico of the Capitol building since Andrew JACKSON'S 1829 inauguration. Former president Ronald Reagan changed the site for his inauguration in 1981. Since then, the swearing-in has been held on the West Terrace of the Capitol. This site, which faces out onto the Mall where thousands gather for the event, affords greater visibility for spectators. Reagan reportedly also liked the symbolism of the president facing west, out toward the rest of the country.

At noontime, the chief justice of the United States Supreme Court administers the oath of office to the president, who then delivers an Inaugural Address. This is followed by a colorful Inauguration Parade through the streets of Washington, D.C.

Inauguration festivities are usually somewhat more modest when a president is elected for a second term or when a change in the presidency does not involve a change in the ruling political party.

In the evening inaugural balls are held in a number of different locations, and the president and the first lady try to make a brief appearance at each of them. William Henry Harrison was the first American president to dance at his own inaugural ball, but the exertion proved too much for him. Already suffering from his exposure to the stormy weather during his record-breaking inaugural address (one hour and 45 minutes), he later developed pneumonia and died within a month.

CONTACTS:
Library of Congress
101 Independence Ave. S.E.

Washington, D.C. 20540
202-707-5000; fax: 202-707-8366
www.loc.gov

SOURCES:
AmerBkDays-2000, p. 76
AnnivHol-2000, p. 12
DictDays-1988, p. 59
PatHols-2006, p. 92

♦ 1288 ♦ **Inconfidência Week**
Week including April 21

The *Inconfidência* was a colonial uprising for Brazilian independence from Portugal at the end of the 18th century (*see also* BRAZIL INDEPENDENCE DAY). It is celebrated during the week of April 21 by paying tribute to Joaquim José da Silva Xavier—also known as **Tiradentes** ("tooth-puller") because of his dentistry practice—who became a martyr for independence when the uprising was put down and he was executed.

The Inconfidência Week festivities include performances by orchestras, bands and choirs, and athletic competitions. The city of Ouro Preto is honorarily restored to its former position as state capital of Minas Gerais during the festival.

CONTACTS:
Brazilian Embassy
3006 Massachusetts Ave. N.W.
Washington, D.C. 20008
202-238-2700; fax: 202-238-2827
www.brasilemb.org

SOURCES:
AnnivHol-2000, p. 65
NatlHolWrld-1968, p. 159

♦ 1289 ♦ **Independence of Cartagena City Day**
Mid-November

On November 11, 1811, Cartagena, Colombia, declared its independence from Spain. The holiday is officially celebrated in Colombia on the Monday closest to November 11. However, festivals and street fairs traditionally take place for days around the actual holiday. There are many parades, including the large and colorful parade through the city of Cartagena, which ends at Plaza Trinidad, where the independence of the city was declared. The culmination of the festivities is the National Beauty Contest, when Miss Colombia is chosen from winners of local beauty pageants around the country.

CONTACTS:
Embassy of Colombia
2118 Leroy Pl. N.W.
Washington, D.C. 20008
202-387-8338; fax: 202-232-8643
www.colombiaemb.org

♦ 1290 ♦ **India Republic Day**
January 26

This holiday is an important national festival in India celebrating the day in 1950 when India's ties with Britain were severed and the country became a fully independent republic. The holiday is marked with parades and much celebration in all the state capitals, but the celebration in Delhi is especially grand. There is a mammoth parade with military units, floats from each state, dancers and musicians, and fly-overs. The festivities in Delhi actually last for about a week, with special events of all sorts in auditoriums and hotels. Special festivities took place during the year 2000, when India celebrated its 50th anniversary as an independent republic.

England's Queen Victoria had been proclaimed Empress of India in 1877, and it wasn't until 1947 that India won its long fight for freedom. The India Independence Act was passed by the British Parliament in July 1947, and by August 15 the Muslim nation of Pakistan and the Hindu nation of India had become independent dominions. Lord Mountbatten served as governor-general during the transition period. When a new constitution came into effect in 1950 his governor-generalship ended, and India stood fully independent. Independence Day on Aug. 15 is also a national holiday, but is observed chiefly with speech-making and none of the grandeur of Republic Day.

CONTACTS:
Embassy of India
2107 Massachusetts Ave. N.W.
Washington, D.C. 20008
202-939-7000; fax: 202-265-4351
www.indianembassy.org

SOURCES:
AnnivHol-2000, pp. 15, 136
GdWrldFest-1985, p. 111
IntlThFolk-1979, p. 205
NatlHolWrld-1968, p. 18

♦ 1291 ♦ **Indian Arrival Day**
May 30

The people of Trinidad and Tobago observe May 30 as Indian Arrival Day. This holiday honors the nation's citizens of Indian descent and acknowledges their contribution to the social and cultural landscape of Trinidad and Tobago. In particular, it recalls the arrival of the first boats from India in 1845. The boats brought poor people who were made to work as indentured servants, thereby filling the need for cheap labor created by the emancipation of the nation's African slaves in 1838.

The holiday grew out of an observance organized by Indian social activists in 1977, who used the festival to counter anti-Indian prejudice and to encourage ethnic pride in Trinidad's citizens of Indian descent. It was later adopted as a national observance. Today the holiday is celebrated with reenactments of the arrival of the first ships bringing Indians to Trinidad, parades honoring the history of the nation's Indian citizens and their festivals, and various cultural events.

CONTACTS:
Ministry of Tourism, Trinidad and Tobago Government
51-55 Frederick St.
Port of Spain, Trinidad and Tobago
868-624-1403; fax: 868-625-0437
www.tourism.gov.tt

National Library and Information System Authority of Trinidad and Tobago
National Library Bldg., Hart and Abercromby St.
Port of Spain, Trinidad and Tobago
868-623-6962; fax: 868-625-6096
library2.nalis.gov.tt

♦ 1292 ♦ Indian Market
Third weekend in August

This showplace for traditional and contemporary Indian art is held on the Plaza of Santa Fe, N.M. The market is the oldest and largest juried competition among Indian artists. It originated as part of the 1922 Fiesta de SANTA FE and continued and grew out of concern that the art forms of the Indian pueblos (villages) were disappearing.

Today more than 800 Indians enter the competition, largely from the 19 New Mexico pueblos and the Apache, Navajo, Hopi, and Ute tribes of the Southwest. Besides the booths of art works, there are numerous food booths, offering such Indian specialties as green chile on fried bread. Indian dances are performed at the courtyard of the Palace of the Governors. A poster-signing ceremony and a benefit art auction precede the market days.

CONTACTS:
Southwest Association for Indian Arts Inc.
P.O. Box 969
Santa Fe, NM 87504
505-983-5220; fax: 505-983-7647
www.swaia.org

SOURCES:
GdUSFest-1984, p. 119

♦ 1293 ♦ Indianapolis 500
May, Sunday of Memorial Day weekend

The "Greatest Spectacle in Racing," popularly known as the **Indy 500**, is actually the culmination of a month-long event. It begins the first week in May with the Mayor's Breakfast and parade around the Indianapolis Motor Speedway, the two-and-a-half-mile oval track on which the race takes place. Then there are qualifying races to determine who will participate in the final **Indianapolis 500 Mile Race**, which is held on the Sunday before MEMORIAL DAY.

On the day before the big race, there is a 500 Festival Memorial Parade that draws more than 300,000 spectators to the streets of downtown Indianapolis and features floats, musical groups, and celebrities. The race itself, which has been held in Indianapolis since 1911, regularly attracts about 400,000 spectators to the 559-acre speedway, in addition to 4,000 media people and a nationwide television audience. The Indy 500 is said to be the largest one-day sporting event in the world.

The official track qualifying record belongs to Arie Luyendyk, whose one-lap speed in 1996 was 237.498 mph. He also holds the record for the fastest time to complete the 500-mile race, set in 1990 when he clocked in at 2:40:58.

The Indy racing car is fueled with a blend of fuels (such as methanol and nitromethane) and usually powered by a turbo-charged engine. Officially, the Indy 500 is a testing-ground for devices that will eventually be used in passenger cars. The annual race has been credited with such automotive improvements as the rearview mirror, balloon tires, and ethyl gasoline.

CONTACTS:
Indy Racing League
4565 W. 16th St.
Indianapolis, IN 46222
317-484-6526; fax: 317-484-6525
www.indycar.com

SOURCES:
AmerBkDays-2000, p. 389
GdUSFest-1984, p. 52
HolSymbols-2009, p. 406

♦ 1294 ♦ Indonesia Independence Day
August 17

Indonesia had been a Dutch colony for 300 years when a group of revolutionaries declared independence on August 17, 1945. Indonesians endured four more years of struggle before their independence was formally granted by QUEEN JULIANA of the Netherlands.

This national holiday is celebrated throughout Indonesia with parades, athletic events, and a multitude of cultural and performing arts festivals.

CONTACTS:
Indonesian Embassy
2020 Massachusetts Ave. N.W.
Washington, D.C. 20036
202-775-5200; fax: 202-775-5365
www.embassyofindonesia.org

SOURCES:
AnnivHol-2000, p. 138
IntlThFolk-1979, p. 227
NatlHolWrld-1968, p. 147

♦ 1295 ♦ Indra Jatra
September-October; end of Hindu month of Bhadrapada to early in the Hindu month of Asvina

Indra Jatra is the most important festival of Nepal, combining homage to a god with an appearance by a living goddess. The festival, lasting for eight days, is a time to honor the recently deceased and to pay homage to the Hindu god Indra and his mother Dagini so they will bless the coming harvests. It furthermore commemorates the day in 1768, during an Indra Jatra (*jatra* means "festival"), that Prithwi Narayan Shah (1730-1775) conquered the Katmandu Valley and unified Nepal.

Legend says that Indra, the god of rain and ruler of heaven, once visited the Katmandu Valley in human form to pick flowers for his mother. The people caught him stealing flowers. Dagini, the mother, came down and promised to spread dew over the crops and to take those who had died in the past year back to heaven with her. The people then released Indra and they have celebrated the occasion ever since.

Before the ceremonies start, a 50-foot tree is cut, sanctified, and dragged to the Hanuman Dhoka Palace in Katmandu. It represents Shiva's *lingam*, the phallic symbol of his creative powers, and shows he's come to the valley. As the pole is erected, bands play and cannons boom. Images of Indra, usually as a captive, are displayed, and sacrifices of goats and roosters are offered.

Three gold chariots are assembled in Basantpur Square, outside the home of the Kumari, the living goddess and vestal virgin. She is a young girl who was selected to be a goddess when she was about three years old, and she will be replaced by another girl when she begins to menstruate. This indicates she is human.

Two boys playing the roles of the gods GANESH and Bhairab emerge from the Kumari's house to be attendants to the goddess. Then the goddess herself appears in public for the first time, walking on a carpet so her feet don't touch the ground. The crowds go wild. The king bows to the Kumari, and the procession moves off to the palace where it stops in front of the 12-foot mask of the Bhairab. This is the fearsome form of Shiva in Nepal and is displayed only at this time. The Kumari greets the image and rice beer pours from its mouth. Those who catch a drop of the beer are blessed, but even more are those who catch one of the tiny live fish in the beer.

In the following days the procession moves from place to place around Kathmandu. Masked dancers perform every night at the Hanuman Dhoka square dramatizing each of the earthly incarnations of Vishnu. On the final day of the festival the great pole is carried to the river.

CONTACTS:
Nepal Tourism Board, Tourist Service Center
Bhrikuti Mandap
P.O. Box 11018
Kathmandu, Nepal
977-1-4256909; fax: 977-1-4256910
www.welcomenepal.com

SOURCES:
FolkWrldHol-1999, p. 515
HolSymbols-2009, p. 408

♦ 1296 ♦ Interceltique, Festival
First Friday in August until second Sunday in August

Created in 1971, the Festival Interceltique (**Interceltic Festival**) brings together traditional and contemporary expressions of Celtic culture and arts. Approximately 4,500 singers, instrumentalists, visual artists, dancers, professors, and filmmakers—drawn from the traditionally Celtic lands—take part in the event. These lands include Ireland, Scotland, Wales, Cornwall, Galicia (Spain), Asturias (Spain), and Brittany (France). Participants also come from Canada, the Unit-

ed States, and Australia. The festival takes place in Lorient, a town in Brittany, France. It begins on the first Friday in August and lasts until the second Sunday of August. About 350,000 spectators attend the festival annually. Festival organizers hope not only to promote the vitality of Celtic culture, but also to make its artistic contributions known to the rest of the world.

CONTACTS:
Interceltic Festival of Lorient
2 rue Paul Bert
Lorient, Brittany 56100 France
33-2-9721-2429
www.festival-interceltique.com/index_en.php

♦ 1297 ♦ Inti Raymi Fiesta
June 24

The **Inti Raymi Festival**, also known as the **Inti Raymi Pageant**, **Sun Festival**, or **Feast of the Sun**, is an ancient WINTER SOLSTICE festival celebrated by the Incas in Peru on June 24. Their ancient empire at one time extended along the Pacific coast of South America from the northern border of modern Ecuador to the Río Maule in central Chile. The Incas believed that their land lay at the center of the earth. They honored Inti Raymi, their sun god, at the foot of La Marca Hills, not far from where the actual equator is now known to be. Their religion embraces both Christian and Indian elements, and they still believe that the sun and moon have god-like powers.

The original Inti Raymi celebration involved animal sacrifices performed by the shaman or priest at the top of the hill of La Marca when the sun reached its zenith at the solstice. Today the main celebration takes place in Cuzco, the 12th-century Incan capital, where there is a special procession and mock sacrifice to the sun, followed by a week-long celebration involving folkloric dances, tours of archeological ruins, and regional arts and crafts displays. Bonfires are still lit in the Andes Mountains to celebrate the rebirth of the sun, and people burn their old clothes as a way of marking the end of the harvest cycle.

CONTACTS:
Commission for the Promotion of Peru
Calle Uno Oeste No. 50, piso 13th
Urb. Corpac
Lima, 27 Peru
51-14-224-3131; fax: 51-1-224-7134
www.promperu.gob.pe

SOURCES:
AnnivHol-2000, p. 105
DictFolkMyth-1984, pp. 526, 1032, 1055
FiestaTime-1965, p. 104
GdWrldFest-1985, p. 149

♦ 1298 ♦ Iowa State Fair
11 days ending third Sunday in August

One of America's foremost state fairs, celebrating agriculture and featuring a life-sized cow sculpted out of 600 pounds of sweet butter, is held for 11 days at the fairgrounds in Des

Moines, Iowa. Attracting close to a million people each year, the fair is famous for having inspired the Phil Stong novel, *State Fair,* and three movies based on the novel. Will ROGERS starred in the first movie. The second and third were musicals by Rodgers and Hammerstein and included the now-standard songs "It Might as Well Be Spring" and "It's a Grand Night for Singing."

The fair is also famous for its cow made out of butter. The breed represented varies from year to year. It's kept in a display case cooled to 40 degrees. The most frequently asked question at the fair information booth is, "Where's the butter cow?" (Answer: in the Agriculture Building.)

Sheep are an important feature at the fair, reflecting the fact that Iowa has more sheep farms than any other state. Sheepshearing contests are popular; champions can shear a sheep in 90 seconds. The big boar contest is also popular; the winning animal always weighs in at more than half a ton. There are other competitions as well: checker playing, horseshoe pitching, fiddling, and rolling-pin throwing.

The first Iowa state fair was held in 1854. Memorable moments in the intervening years include the spectacular crash of two trains, one labeled Roosevelt and the other Hoover, which were throttled up at opposite ends of a track. They roared down on each other, crashed, and exploded. The year was 1932, when the presidential candidates were Herbert Hoover and Franklin D. ROOSEVELT.

The fair underwent a period of rapid change between 1880 and 1930, expanding to encompass such activities as horse and auto racing, biplane stunt-flying, high-diving horses, and auto-to-airplane transfers. The American aviator Charles Lindbergh visited the fair in 1927, soon after his triumphant nonstop solo flight across the Atlantic.

CONTACTS:
Iowa State Fair
P.O. Box 57130
Des Moines, IA 50317
515-262-3111; fax: 515-262-6906
www.iowastatefair.com

♦ 1299 ♦ **Iqbal (Muhammad), Birthday of**
November 9

In Pakistan, November 9 has been declared a national holiday to celebrate the birthday of Dr. Allama Muhammad Iqbal, a famous Pakistani poet and philosopher.

Iqbal was born in the city of Sialkot in the Punjab province of Pakistan on November 9, 1877. He was an educated man. In college, he studied English literature, philosophy, and Arabic. While in college, he discovered Urdu poetry, and some of his poems were published in 1901. Soon afterward, he gained recognition as a rising star in Urdu literature. He earned a masters degree in philosophy and served as a lecturer in history, philosophy, and political science.

Iqbal spent time in Europe for graduate studies and then taught in England and Germany. During this time, he wrote and lectured on Islamic subjects that helped him gain recog-

nition in literary circles. Iqbal returned to India in 1908 and practiced law until 1934, when his deteriorating health forced him to give up his practice. He died in 1938. His tomb is in Lahore, the capital of the Pakistani province of Punjab.

To honor Iqbal, Pakistan has declared November 9 a national holiday. On this day, a number of functions are held to honor the great poet. Many educational institutions sponsor programs that showcase his life and achievements. In addition to the main function at Iqbal's tomb, the National Museum of Pakistan in Karachi exhibits Iqbal's personal belongings, including his costumes, books, and publications.

CONTACTS:
Iqbal Academy Pakistan
Government of Pakistan, Ministry of Culture
6th Fl., Academy Block
Aiwan-e-Iqbal Complex
Lahore, Islamic Republic of Pakistan
www.allamaiqbal.com

♦ 1300 ♦ **Iran Islamic Republic Day**
Farvardin 12

Most Iranians welcomed Ayatollah Ruhollah Khomeini's campaign to overthrow Mohammad Reza Shah Pahlavi and install a new theocratic government. Millions greeted him in February 1979, when he returned from 15 years of exile. By the end of the following month, the country was prepared to participate on a national referendum to establish an Islamic Republic based on a new constitution. A large majority voted in favor of the measure on March 30 and 31, leading Khomeini to declare on April 1: "This day of Farvardin 12, the first day of God's government, is to be one of our foremost religious and national festivals."

Iranians congregate throughout the country to celebrate Republic Day, also known as **National Day**. Past celebrations have included an address by the Iranian president. The largest public gathering takes place in Revolution Square, located in the capital city of Tehran. Thousands wave the national flag and some performers play music with traditional instruments.

The Iranian calendar differs slightly from the Gregorian calendar, which means the date of commemoration also does not line up with its Gregorian counterpart.

CONTACTS:
Iran's Ministry of Foreign Affairs
Imam Khomeini Sq.
Tehran, Iran

SOURCES:
AnnivHol-2000, p. 55

♦ 1301 ♦ **Iran Petroleum Nationalization Anniversary**
Esfand 29

Under the leadership of Prime Minister Mohammed Mossadegh, Iran claimed control of its lucrative oil industry by passing a nationalization law on March 15, 1951. Western countries responded two years later by backing favored leader Mohammad Reza Shah Pahlavi in his successful overthrow of Mossadegh. These events further stirred animosity in Iran against Western countries and fed the nationalist sentiment surrounding the observance of this special anniversary.

Celebrations of this event, also known as the **National Day of Oil**, take place in Iran and in Iranian communities abroad. Past activities have included television shows paying tribute to the 1951 legislation and conferences that focus on oil nationalization as well as Iran's present-day foreign policy.

Because the Iranian calendar differs slightly from the Gregorian calendar, the present-day commemoration falls a few days after March 15.

CONTACTS:
Iran's Ministry of Foreign Affairs
Imam Khomeini Sq.
Tehran, Iran

SOURCES:
AnnivHol-2000, p. 47

◆ 1302 ◆ Iran Victory Day of the Iranian Revolution
February 11

Few world events during the late 20th century were as pivotal as the Iranian Revolution of 1979, also known as the Islamic Revolution. Ayatollah Ruhollah Khomeini overthrew Shah Mohammad Reza Pahlavi, signaling the end of a 2,500-year era in which autocratic monarchs ruled Iran, formerly Persia. It also marked the rise of Islamic fundamentalism during those years. Iranians celebrate the coup's anniversary and also commemorate the 10 days that led up to Victory Day.

On February 1, 1979, Khomeini returned to Iran to claim power after spending 15 years in exile. To memorialize the historic moment, a helicopter drops flowers on the ayatollah's tomb, in the Behesht-e Zahra cemetery south of the capital city of Tehran. Then, for the next 10 days, people attend film screenings, music performances, and exhibitions inspired by the revolution.

The celebration on February 11, known as the "Dawn of God" (Yaum Allah), usually entails a mass rally and military parade in Tehran.

CONTACTS:
Iran's Ministry of Foreign Affairs
Imam Khomeini Sq.
Tehran, Iran

SOURCES:
AnnivHol-2000, p. 25

◆ 1303 ◆ Iris Fest (Fete de l'Iris)
First weekend of May

Each of the autonomous regions of Belgium observes its own feast day. The Brussels-Capital Region's celebration, called

Iris Fest (Fete de l'Iris), is held during the first weekend of May. Feast days in other regions of Belgium include FEAST DAY OF THE FLEMISH COMMUNITY, FEAST DAY OF THE FRENCH COMMUNITY, FEAST DAY OF THE GERMAN-SPEAKING COMMUNITY, and WALLOON REGIONAL DAY.

Iris Fest is a relatively new festival, as the Brussels-Capital Region only came into existence following the federalization of Belgium in 1989. The festival's main symbol, the iris plant, has been the region's official emblem since 1991.

Many of the weekend's proceedings are held in the city's central square, the Place du Grand Sablon. An established popular act will perform a concert in the square on Saturday, and live jazz concerts are held on Sunday.

On Sunday, the more event-filled of the two days, the Brussels Parliament opens its doors to the public for tours and classical music performances. For La rue en fête, a colorful festival event held throughout Brussels' streets, people gather for parades, theater, and games for kids.

CONTACTS:
Belgium Embassy
3330 Garfield St. N.W.
Washington, D.C. 20008
202-333-6900; fax: 202-333-3079
www.diplobel.us

◆ 1304 ◆ Ironman Triathlon Championships
Saturday nearest the full moon in October

This extraordinarily grueling international athletic contest has been held since 1978 in Kailua-Kona on Hawaii Island. It consists of a 2.4-mile swim, a 112-mile bicycle race, and, for the final leg, a standard 26.2-mile marathon run. Close to 2,000 stout-hearted men and women participate, preceding the races with a Thursday night party in which they stoke up on carbohydrates. Originally, contestants swam, biked, and ran for the fun and challenge of the event, but cash prizes are now awarded at a banquet the day after the triathlon.

The event is scheduled for the Saturday nearest the full moon in October so that more beach is exposed at low tide, and there is more light from the moon at night. This is the original, but no longer the toughest such contest: double ironmen now challenge triathletes.

CONTACTS:
World Triathlon Corporation
43309 US. Hwy. 19 N.
Tarpon Springs, FL 34689
727-942-4767; fax: 727-942-1987
www.ironman.com

◆ 1305 ◆ Iroquois Midwinter Festival
January

This festival is the traditional midwinter ceremony of the Iroquois Indians in Canada and the United States, which also serves to usher in the new year. The ceremonies are dedicated to giving thanks to the Master of Life, or Creator, and also include prayers to Handsome Lake (Ganio'dai'io, 1735-1815), founder of the Iroquois Longhouse religion. The festival lasts eight or nine days. The first few days are concerned with conducting older traditional ceremonies, including the confession and renewal of each person, various other healing and purifying rites, and the False Face dance. The sacrifice of a white dog used to be part of the festival, but this practice has been abandoned. Out of the many ceremonies in the Iroquois tradition, Handsome Lake especially encouraged the Feather Dance, the Thanksgiving Dance, the Personal Chant, and the Bowl Game—known as "the four sacred rituals." The second half of the festival is devoted to fulfilling these.

SOURCES:
BkHolWrld-1986, Jan 10
DictFolkMyth-1984, p. 835
EncyNatAmerRel-2001, p. 182
EncyRel-1987, vol. 7, p. 284
FolkAmerHol-1999, p. 43

♦ 1306 ♦ Irrigation Festival
First full weekend in May

The Irrigation Festival is the oldest continuous festival in Washington, held since 1896 in Sequim. Originally known as "May Days," the festival celebrated the opening of the first ditch to bring water from the Dungeness River to the arid Sequim prairie. In the early days there were horse races, dancing, a keg of beer hidden in the brush, and tables loaded with food. After a few years, Maypole dances with girls in frilly dresses were a big attraction. The first queen of MAY DAY was chosen in 1908; the first parade was held in 1918; the first queen's float was built in 1948; and a descendant of a pioneer family has been honored as the festival's Grand Pioneer since 1960.

Today, thousands come for a week of activities: a grand parade, a loggers' show, a high school operetta, crafts and flower exhibits, dances, music, and the Ditchwalkers Clam and Spaghetti Dinner.

CONTACTS:
Sequim-Dungeness Chamber of Commerce
1192 E. Washington St.
P.O. Box 907
Sequim, WA 98382
800-737-8462 or 360-683-6197; fax: 360-683-6349
www.sequimchamber.com

♦ 1307 ♦ Islamic Festival
May (odd-numbered years)

Mértola, Portugal, is the site of an Islamic Festival that takes place over four days in May in odd-numbered years. The event celebrates the cultures and peoples of northern Africa and features a wide array of Arab photography, art, cinema, handicrafts, dance, and theater. Seminars cover a variety of subjects, from language to cuisine. Most events are held in the historic town center, which takes on the feel of a "souk," or Arabic market or bazaar. The event is organized by the town council, with the aim of uniting the Portuguese, Spanish, and Islamic cultures that converge in the town's rich his-

tory. Thousands of visitors flock to the festival, which launched in 2001.

CONTACTS:
Portuguese National Tourist Office
590 5th Ave., 4th Fl.
New York, NY 10036
800-767-8842 or 646-723-0200; fax: 212-764-6137
www.visitportugal.com

♦ 1308 ♦ Islamic New Year
First day of the Islamic month of Muharram

The Islamic New Year occurs on the first day of Muharram, the first month in the Islamic calendar. Muharram is one of four especially holy months for Muslims, along with Dhu al-Qadah, Dhu al-Hijjah (when the PILGRIMAGE TO MECCA takes place), and Rajab (when LAYLAT AL-MIRAJ is celebrated). The name of the month means "sacred."

The first day of Muharram commemorates the flight of the Prophet Muhammad from Mecca, where he had experienced hostility toward his teachings, to Medina in 622, which is considered year one in the Muslim calendar. Muhammad's journey, known as the Hijra, is an important milestone in Islamic history, because it brought the religion to more people. Muhammad was welcomed in Medina and soon had many followers.

Devout Muslims observe New Year's Day by going to mosque to worship and listen to stories about Muhammad and early Muslims. Muslims traditionally make resolutions on this day to live more strongly in accord with the teachings of Islam. Some people may exchange gifts, but this is not a popular custom.

SOURCES:
ConEncyIslam-1991, p. 285
MusFest-1987, p. 43
RelHolCal-2004, pp. 143, 144

♦ 1309 ♦ Israel Festival
May-June

This three-week festival, founded in 1961, is primarily dedicated to Israeli arts and culture, although guest conductors and performers from other countries are featured as well. There are symphony and choral concerts, opera, ballet and modern dance, theater, jazz, folklore, films, and art exhibitions at several locations in Jerusalem.

The Israel Philharmonic Orchestra has performed with guest conductors like Zubin Mehta and Leonard Bernstein, and Israeli dance groups offer both traditional and modern programs. Pablo CASALS and Isaac Stern have played there, Rudolf Nureyev and Merce Cunningham have danced at the festival, and Sir John Gielgud has read Shakespeare there.

CONTACTS:
Municipality of Jerusalem
Public Relations and Information Unit
1 Safra Sq.
Jerusalem, 91007 Israel

972-2-629-5981; fax: 972-2-629-6910
www.jerusalem.muni.il/jer_main/defaultnew.a

SOURCES:
GdWrldFest-1985, p. 115
IntlThFolk-1979, p. 238
MusFestWrld-1963, p. 259

◆ **1310** ◆ **Israel Independence Day**
Between April 16 and May 14; Iyyar 5

Known in Hebrew as **Yom ha-Atzma'ut**, this day commemorates the proclamation of independence by Palestinian Jews and the establishment of a provisional government in Israel on May 14, 1948 (5 Iyyar 5708 on the Jewish calendar).

It is observed with parties, performances, and military parades as well as religious rituals, which include the reading of Psalms. In the United States, Jews celebrate Israel Independence Day by attending concerts, films, parades, Israeli fairs, and other public events. An Israeli Day Parade is held in New York City, but it doesn't always take place on the fifth day of Iyyar.

A popular custom on this day for Israelis is to walk at least a short distance somewhere in the country where they have never walked before.

CONTACTS:
Israel Ministry of Foreign Affairs
9 Yitzhak Rabin Blvd.
Kiryat Ben-Gurion
Jerusalem, 91035 Israel
972-2-530-3111; fax: 972-2-530-3367
www.israel-mfa.gov.il

Israel Tribute Committee Inc.
520 Eighth Ave., 15th Fl.
New York, NY 10018
646-472-5388; fax: 212-399-9198

SOURCES:
AnnivHol-2000, p. 229
NatlHolWrld-1968, p. 60

◆ **1311** ◆ **Istanbul Festivals, International**
Varies

Since the first **International Istanbul Festival** was held in 1973, the Istanbul Foundation for Culture and the Arts has used this event to bridge the cultures of East and West and to promote Turkey's rich cultural heritage.

The original festival has now branched out into four annual festivals and one biennial one: the International Istanbul Film Festival, held in April, the International Istanbul Theatre Festival in May-June, the International Istanbul Music Festival over June and July, and the International Istanbul Jazz Festival in July. The International Istanbul Biennial is held from September to November during odd-numbered years and features contemporary visual art.

CONTACTS:
Istanbul Foundation for Culture & the Arts

Istiklal Cad. No.: 146
34435 Beyoglu
Istanbul, 80070 Turkey
90-212-334-0700; fax: 90-212-334-0716
www.iksv.org/english

SOURCES:
GdWrldFest-1985, p. 180
IntlThFolk-1979, p. 369

◆ **1312** ◆ **Isthmian Games**
First month of spring

The Isthmian Games were athletic competitions held in ancient times at Corinth in Greece. They were held during alternate years beginning in 581 B.C.E., with contests in various events, including gymnastics, horse racing, and poetry (the last was open to both men and women). The prize was a crown of celery.

There are differing stories as to the origin of the games; one legend says they were founded by Theseus after he killed the robber chief Sinis. The games were one of the four great national Greek festivals, the others being the OLYMPIC, PYTHIAN, and NEMEAN games. The Isthmian games were especially popular because they offered more amusements than the other three festivals.

SOURCES:
OxClassDict-1970, p. 556

◆ **1313** ◆ **Itabashi Suwa Jinja Ta-Asobi**
January or February

The rice crop is crucial to the Japanese, and various rituals are observed to please the *kami*, or god, who is ultimately responsible for a good harvest. These rice-growing rituals can be traced back to ancient times, although the significance of some has been long forgotten. Since spring begins to emerge in January, signalling the nearness of the new planting season, people perform traditional rituals for a good crop. It is not uncommon to see offerings in rice paddies, usually consisting of charms affixed to plants believed to give good luck, such as pine, chestnut, and bamboo during January. The most popular time to observe these rituals is between January 11 and the night of the full moon.

The festival known as Itabashi Suwa Jinja Ta-Asobi, held at the Suwa Shrine in Tokyo, began as a thanksgiving ritual to the god of the rice paddies (*Ta-no-kami*) in return for the granting of a plentiful harvest. There is also a *mikoshi* parade—mikoshi are the portable shrines or palanquins identified with the gods during their visits to earth—singing, and food. One area is set aside for the performance of traditional dances, which include a rice-planting dance, a weeding dance, a chasing-away-the-bird dance, and a fertility dance. At the end of the festival, a big bonfire is lighted and huge drums are played.

CONTACTS:
Association for Itabashi International Communications
Itabashi City Hall

2-66-1 Itabashi-ku
Tokyo, 173-8501 Japan
81-3-3579-2015; fax: 81-3-3579-4211
www.city.itabashi.tokyo.jp/c_kurashi/005/005929.ht

SOURCES:
JapanFest-1965, pp. 92, 119

♦ 1314 ♦ **Italian Festival**
May, Memorial Day weekend

This event is a weekend festival in McAlester, Okla., in Pittsburgh County, a coal-rich area that drew miners of Italian heritage in the 1880s. The town began as a tent store owned by J. J. McAlester, who discovered and mined the coal here. He was later lieutenant governor of the state. The descendants of the Italian miners celebrate their heritage with folk music, dances, costumes, arts and crafts, and, of course, food, lots of it: 12,000 meatballs, 6,000 sausages, and 200 gallons of spaghetti and sauce.

CONTACTS:
McAlester Italian Festival Foundation Inc.
P.O. Box 1212
McAlester, OK 74502
918-302-8866; fax: 918-423-8824
www.italianfestival.org

♦ 1315 ♦ **Italian Heritage Parade**
Sunday closest to October 12

Since 1869, the city of San Francisco has hosted the annual Italian Heritage Parade, one of the oldest such events in the United States. Originally begun as a way to honor the Italian-American community in San Francisco, the parade has grown to celebrate the October 12 birthday of Christopher Columbus as well.

The parade and many of the related festivities take place in the heavily Italian North Beach area of San Francisco. After services at the Church of Saints Peter and Paul, the parade wends its way from Fisherman's Wharf down Columbus Avenue to Washington Square Park. Floats and marching bands from local community organizations make up the procession. Every year, young girls are chosen from the community to serve as Queen Isabella and her court, named after the Spanish queen who financed Columbus's historic expedition. Dressed in elaborate period costumes, the queen and her court preside over Columbus Day ceremonies throughout the city. The Italian Heritage Parade draws some 400,000 spectators each year.

CONTACTS:
Italian Heritage Parade
415-703-9888
www.sfcolumbusday.org

♦ 1316 ♦ **Italy Liberation Day**
April 25

Liberation Day is a national holiday commemorating the Allied invasion of Italy in 1943 that led to the overthrow of Mussolini's Fascist rule during World War II.

CONTACTS:
Italian Government Tourist Board
630 Fifth Ave., Ste. 1565
New York, NY 10111
212-245-5618; fax: 212-586-9249
www.italiantourism.com

SOURCES:
AnnivHol-2000, p. 68

♦ 1317 ♦ **Itul**
December

This highly regarded ritual is a ceremonial dance performed by the Kuba people who live in the Democratic Republic of Congo (formerly Zaire). It takes place on an infrequent basis, not only because the costs and preparation involved are so extensive but also because it can only be held with the king's authorization; the only sponsors (and funders) may be the children of a king.

An Itul performed for a king is held in the dance area of the palace and is considered more refined because the king's wives are professional dancers and singers. If the Itul is open to the public, it takes place in the plaza in front of the palace. Although it is usually held in December, the dates can vary.

The preparations can take up to several months, but the dance itself lasts only a few hours. The villain's role is danced by someone dressed as an animal, and the plot on which the dance is based combines both traditional episodes and those that have been adapted to whatever animal is chosen.

The dance is performed in two parts over two consecutive days. The first part mourns the destruction caused by the enemy-animal, and the second part deals with its capture and killing. There is a chorus of women kneeling in the center who perform the songs and provide a rhythmical accompaniment by beating calabashes or gourd drums on the ground. The dancers move counterclockwise around the chorus, and the king watches the spectacle from a special shelter set off to one side.

The Itul is considered so important that once the word spreads that the ceremony is taking place, Kuba people from all over rush to attend it. It is revived from time to time by kings who fear that their traditional power is being threatened by modern secular life.

CONTACTS:
Embassy of the Democratic Republic of Congo
1800 New Hampshire Ave. N.W.
Washington, D.C. 20009
202-234-7691; fax: 202-234-2609
kinshasa.usembassy.gov

SOURCES:
FolkWrldHol-1999, p. 692

◆ 1318 ◆ **Ivy Day**
October 6

October 6 is the anniversary of the death of Charles Stewart Parnell (1846-1891), the famous Irish statesman and leader of the Home Rule Party. He entered the House of Commons when he was only 29 and quickly established a reputation for hostility to England and all things English. He became a hero to the Irish poor, many of whom would try to touch his clothes or kiss his hands and knees when he walked through a crowd.

Parnell fell out of public favor somewhat when he became involved in a divorce case in 1890, and the trauma of rejection by so many of his countrypeople is thought to have contributed to his early death in 1891. But he is a symbol of Irish pride and independence, and his name appears frequently in Irish literature, particularly the poetry of William Butler Yeats and the short story in James Joyce's *Dubliners* called "Ivy Day in the Committee Room."

It is somewhat ironic that the sprig of green ivy traditionally worn on this day—chosen by Parnell himself as an emblem—is a color he apparently intensely disliked.

SOURCES:
DictDays-1988, p. 60

◆ 1319 ◆ **Iyomante Matsuri (Bear Festival)**
January-February

Among the Ainu people of the northernmost islands of Japan, especially on Hokkaido, the baiting and killing of a young bear was not considered a brutal act but a ritual send-off to the spirit world. The "divine" cub was ceremoniously fed and cared for, then killed and arranged with fetishes. Some of his own cooked meat and a dish of his own blood, along with cakes and dried fish, were laid before him. He was supposed to bring these gifts to his parents when he arrived in heaven. After a time, Ainu belief has it, he would be reincarnated and return to earth as another cub.

CONTACTS:
Ainu Museum
2-3-4 Wakakusa-cho
Siraoi, Hokkaido 059-0902 Japan
81-1-4482-3914
www.ainu-museum.or.jp/english/english.html

SOURCES:
EncyRel-1987, vol. 1, p. 160; vol. 2, p. 86
FolkWrldHol-1999, p. 681
JapanFest-1965, p. 207

◆ 1320 ◆ **Izumo-taisha Jinzaisai**
Late October to early November; 10th lunar month

According to Shinto belief, the gods from all over Japan assemble during the tenth lunar month at the Izumo-taisha Shrine in Taisha-machi, Shimané Prefecture. Local people have dubbed this month *Kamiarizuki*, or "the month when the gods are present." Of course, elsewhere in Japan it is called *Kannazuki*, or "the month when the gods are absent." Numerous rituals honoring the gods take place, including a formal greeting at the beach and a ceremonial procession to the shrine.

CONTACTS:
Japan National Tourist Organization
1 Rockefeller Pl., Ste. 1250
New York, NY 10020
212-757-5640; fax: 212-307-6754
www.jnto.go.jp

SOURCES:
IllFestJapan-1993, p. 119

J

♦ 1321 ♦ Jackalope Days
Mid to late June

Three days of celebration in Douglas, Wyo., honor the jackalope, an elusive animal that is a cross between a jackrabbit and an antelope (according to the legends of Converse County). The jackalope might be mistaken for a large rabbit except for its antlers, and it might be identified as a small deer, except for its rabbit-like shape.

The jackalope was first seen in 1829 by Roy Ball, a trapper, who was denounced as a liar. Some people still doubt its existence, despite the evidence of numerous stuffed heads on barroom walls. The jackalope is rarely seen because it is a shy animal and comes out of hiding only for breeding with the commonly seen and hornless females, called does, which look like ordinary rabbits. But it breeds only during electrical storms, at the precise moment of the flash when most people are not out wandering around. A 10-foot replica of a jackalope in Centennial Jackalope Square in Douglas attests to the cultural importance of this critter.

Events of Jackalope Days include a downtown carnival, rodeos, a street dance, a parade, the crowning of a rodeo queen, and sports competitions.

CONTACTS:
Douglas Chamber of Commerce
121 Brownfield Rd.
Douglas, WY 82633
877-937-4996 or 307-358-2950; fax: 307-358-2972
www.jackalope.org

♦ 1322 ♦ Jackson's (Andrew) Birthday
March 15

Andrew Jackson (1767-1845), the seventh president of the United States (1829-37), became a national hero during the War of 1812 when he successfully fought the British at New Orleans. Jackson's heroic performance came despite the fact that he was so sick he could barely stand without assistance, and no one knew that a peace treaty had been signed two weeks earlier. His soldiers thought he was as "tough as hickory," resulting in his nickname, "Old Hickory." The anniversary of his birth is a special observance in Tennessee, and the president of the United States usually brings or sends a wreath to be placed on Jackson's grave in the garden at his home, The Hermitage, near Nashville.

Other tributes paid to Jackson during this week include radio speeches and newspaper editorials, school essay contests, and Jackson Day dinners sponsored by the Democratic party, of which he is considered one of the founders. Sometimes these celebrations are held on January 8, BATTLE OF NEW ORLEANS DAY. In Virginia, Jackson's birthday is celebrated in January along with those of Martin Luther KING, Jr. and Robert E. LEE.

CONTACTS:
The Hermitage
4580 Rachel's Ln.
Nashville, TN 37076
615-889-2941; fax: 615-889-9909
www.thehermitage.com

SOURCES:
AmerBkDays-2000, p. 201

♦ 1323 ♦ Jacob's Ladder
May (Main Festival), December (Winter Weekend Festival)

Jacob's Ladder Folk Festival takes place every year over three days in May in Israel at Nof Ginosar on Lake Kinneret. Founded in 1978, the festival is a lively musical and social event that showcases a wide range of folk-music styles, from bluegrass to country rock, from world music to blues, Renaissance, and Irish fiddle music. In 2004, the organizers added an annual indoor festival that takes place over a winter weekend in a hotel in Nof Ginosar. Both events offer, in addition to music, such additional activities as storytelling, dancing, juggling, yoga, tai chi, tractor and trailer tours, swimming, arts and crafts, food booths, and children's shows. Festivalgoers in May can camp on-site.

The festival was founded by three members of Kibbutz Machanayim who had settled in Israel from England and the United States in the 1960s. The festival grew out of a monthly folk club that kibbutz members launched in order to perform and listen to the folk and protest songs they had known in their home countries. About 700 fans attended the first festival, held on the grounds of the kibbutz. After numerous moves and significant growth, the festival now draws prominent musicians from Israel and around the world.

CONTACTS:
Jacob's Ladder Festival
Mishol Nimron 2
Katzrin 12900 Israel
www.jlfestival.com/index.asp

Israel Tourist Office
800 2nd Ave.
New York, NY 10017
888-774-7723 or 212-499-5600; fax: 212-499-5645
goisrael.com

♦ 1324 ♦ Jacob's Pillow Dance Festival
June-August

The second oldest dance festival in the United States (after the Bennington Dance Festival), the Jacob's Pillow Dance Festival takes place for 10 weeks every summer at the historic Ted Shawn Theatre near Lenox, Massachusetts.

Edwin Myers ("Ted") Shawn was an innovative modern dancer and cofounder, with his wife Ruth St. Denis, of Denishawn, the first American modern dance company. In 1933, at his farm named Jacob's Pillow, he founded the Jacob's Pillow Dance Festival as a summer residence and theater for his male dancers. After the group disbanded, Shawn turned Jacob's Pillow into a dance center of international importance—a place where not only ballet but modern and ethnic dance could be presented. Top dancers from all over the world give regular performances throughout the summer to packed houses.

CONTACTS:
Jacob's Pillow Dance Festival
358 George Carter Rd.
P.O. Box 287
Becket, MA 01223
413-243-9919; fax: 413-243-4744
www.jacobspillow.org

SOURCES:
GdUSFest-1984, p. 85

♦ 1325 ♦ Jamaica Festival
Late July through first Monday in August

Originally called the **Independence Festival of Jamaica** because it ended on the first Monday in August, JAMAICA INDEPENDENCE DAY, the two- to three-week-long event now known as the **Jamaica National Festival of the Arts** emphasizes the cultural roots, conservation, and revival of traditional art forms by ethnic groups—particularly folk music, folk dances, and folk games of African origin—as well as nurturing contemporary arts.

Competitions to determine who will perform at the festival begin early in the year at the local level. After regional and national competitions are held, the best in each category are

selected to participate in the final festival programs, which include fine art, photo, and culinary exhibits, music, dance, concerts, plays, and literary readings. The festival has been held in Kingston, Montego Bay, and elsewhere on the island since 1963. A film festival was added in 1977.

CONTACTS:
Jamaica Cultural Development Commission
3 Phoenix Ave.
Kingston, 10 Jamaica
876-926-5726
www.jcdc.org.jm

SOURCES:
GdWrldFest-1985, p. 121

♦ 1326 ♦ Jamaica Independence Day
First Monday in August

The island of Jamaica became an independent nation with loose ties to the British Commonwealth on August 6, 1962. Before that it had been a founding member of the Federation of the West Indies, a group of Caribbean islands that formed a unit within the Commonwealth of Nations. Allegiance to the British gradually gave way to the emergence of a national identity, and the federation was dissolved.

A public holiday throughout the island, Independence Day is celebrated with a grand parade, traditional music and dancing, arts and crafts exhibits, and agricultural and other events as part of the JAMAICA FESTIVAL.

CONTACTS:
Jamaica Cultural Development Commission
3 Phoenix Ave.
Kingston, 10 Jamaica
876-926-5726
www.jcdc.org.jm

SOURCES:
AnnivHol-2000, p. 145
NatlHolWrld-1968, p. 136

♦ 1327 ♦ Jamaica National Heroes Day
Third Monday of October

In Kingston, Jamaica, National Heroes Park contains a series of statues devoted to key figures in the country's history, including independence leader Alexander Bustamente and pan-African crusader Marcus Garvey. As a way to honor the figures commemorated in this park, the Jamaican government has established National Heroes Day. The holiday officially replaced the celebration for Queen Elizabeth's birthday, although she still receives military honors during ceremonies.

The first group of national heroes was designated in 1965, the year of the centenary celebration of the 1865 Morant Bay Rebellion, a pivotal moment in the quest for independence from Great Britain. The first commemoration took place in 1968. As more heroes were added to the official list over subsequent years, National Heroes Day expanded to become **National Heritage Week**.

A typical ceremony held on the Monday that concludes Heritage Week is the National Heroes Day salute. Local parishes all over the island hold award ceremonies to honor community figures, while at National Heroes Park a main ceremony takes place that features a speech by a national leader, typically the prime minister.

CONTACTS:
Jamaica Cultural Development Commission
3 Phoenix Ave.
Kingston, 10 Jamaica
www.jcdc.org.jm/performing_arts.htm

◆ 1328 ◆ Jamestown Day
May 13

Jamestown, Virginia, is the site of the first permanent English settlement in America. A group of 104 settlers sponsored by the London Company (sometimes called the Virginia Company) disembarked about 50 miles from the mouth of the James River on May 13, 1607, and spent a difficult few years fighting famine and disease. Eventually they initiated the tobacco trade that allowed Virginia to become economically self-sufficient. Jamestown also established the first representative government on the continent, brought the first African slaves to the colonies, and built America's first Anglican (Episcopal) church.

On the Sunday nearest May 13, which is officially known as Jamestown Day, a commemorative service is held at the historic site of the original settlement. There are speeches, readings, and choral selections; addresses by British and American officials; and a procession to the Memorial Cross, which marks the town's earliest cemetery, followed by a wreath-laying ceremony.

Organizers are planning special events for the 400th anniversary in 2007.

CONTACTS:
Jamestown-Yorktown Foundation
P.O. Box 1607
Williamsburg, VA 23187
888-593-4682 or 757-253-4838; fax: 757-253-5299
www.historyisfun.org

Colonial National Historic Park
National Park Service
P.O. Box 210
Yorktown, VA 23690
757-898-2410; fax: 757-898-6346
www.nps.gov

Virtual Jamestown
University of Virginia
Virginia Center for Digital History
Charlottesville, VA 22904
www.virtualjamestown.org

SOURCES:
AmerBkDays-2000, p. 361
AnnivHol-2000, p. 82

◆ 1329 ◆ Jamhuri (Kenya Independence Day)
December 12

The biggest of the national holidays in Kenya, Jamhuri is observed to commemorate the full independence of Kenya from the British in 1963. A year later, the country became a republic with Jomo Kenyatta (c. 1894-1978) the first president. The day is celebrated nationwide but with special events in Nairobi—speeches by the president and other officials, parades, fireworks, and *ngomas* (dances) performed in public plazas.

CONTACTS:
Embassy of the Republic of Kenya
2249 R St. N.W.
Washington, D.C. 20008
202-387-6101; fax: 202-462-3829
www.kenyaembassy.com

SOURCES:
AnnivHol-2000, p. 206
NatlHolWrld-1968, p. 226

◆ 1330 ◆ Jammolpur Ceremony
May

Among the tribe known as the Saora in the hills of eastern India, May is the time for the **Blessing of the Seeds** or Jammolpur ceremony, named for Jammolsum, the god of seed.

Farmers bring some of the seed they will be planting soon to an altar set up for the purpose of blessing the seeds. The altar is placed next to a wall painting a priest has completed that morning. Each element in the painting has a symbolic meaning and power; for example, including birds, deer, and porcupines ensures that these animals will stay away from the young crops. It is common for the Saoras to paint such pictures, which they often do to please a particular god or a deceased ancestor who is giving them trouble. It is also held that the painter is given dreams the night before showing him what to paint.

During the ceremony the priest recites an ancient story and sacrifices a chicken, which is later cooked and eaten. He then pours some wine on the altar and sprinkles some seeds there as well, all the while appealing to the god and ancestors for a good growing season. After the ceremony, the blessed seeds are distributed among the farmers, who take them home and mix them in with the seeds they will sow. At harvest time another ceremony, called ROGONADUR, is held.

CONTACTS:
India Tourist Office
1270 Ave. of the Americas, Ste. 1808, 18th Fl.
New York, NY 10020
800-953-9399 or 212-586-4901; fax: 212-582-3274
www.incredibleindia.org

SOURCES:
CelebNature-1969, p. 113

◆ 1331 ◆ Jamshed Navaroz (Jamshed Navroz)
March, July, August; first day of Frawardin, the first Zoroastrian month

The **Zoroastrian New Year** is observed at the VERNAL EQUINOX among the Parsis in India, who are the descendants of the original Zoroastrian immigrants from Iran (formerly Persia). It is traditional for men to dress in white, while women wear colored clothing. Ritual bathing, worship, and the exchange of gifts are part of the celebration. This festival is celebrated in July by the Kadmi sect's calendar and in August by the Shahenshai sect's calendar.

See also NAWRUZ

CONTACTS:
Ministry of Tourism, Government of India
Rm. No 123, Transport Bhawan, No. 1, Parliament St.
New Delhi, Delhi 110 001 India
91-11-23715084; fax: 91-11-23715084
www.tourisminindia.com

SOURCES:
RelHolCal-2004, p. 66

♦ 1332 ♦ **Janaki Navami**
    April-May; ninth day of waxing half of Hindu month of Vaisakha

Sita, heroine of the Hindu epic poem *Ramayana,* is supposed to have sprung on this day from a furrow in a field plowed by King Janaka. He named her Sita, which means "furrow of the earth," and raised her as his own child. She was actually the goddess Lakshmi, sent to the earth to bring about the destruction of Ravana and other demons. Many Hindus believe that Sita represents the ideal Indian woman as an embodiment of self-sacrifice, purity, tenderness, fidelity, conjugal affection, and other virtues. Some believe that she appeared in King Janaka's field on the eighth day of the waning half of Phalguna (February-March), and fast on that day instead of the ninth day of Vaisakha.

SOURCES:
DictWrldRel-1989, p. 695
RelHolCal-2004, p. 168

♦ 1333 ♦ **Janmashtami (Krishnastami; Krishna's Birthday)**
    August-September; new moon day of Hindu month of Bhadrapada

One of the most important Hindu festivals, Janmashtami celebrates the birthday of Lord Krishna, the eighth incarnation of Vishnu and the hero of both rich and poor. Throughout India it is a fast day until the new moon is sighted. Then there are ceremonies and prayers at temples dedicated to Krishna. Rituals include bathing the statue of the infant Krishna and then placing his image in a silver cradle with playthings.

In Mathura, Uttar Pradesh, where Krishna was born, there are performances of Krishna Lila, the folk dramas depicting scenes from Krishna's life. In the state of Tamil Nadu, oiled poles called *ureyadi* are set up, a pot of money is tied to the top, and boys dressed as Krishna try to shinny up the pole and win the prize while spectators squirt water at them.

In Maharashtra, where the festival is known as *Govinda*, pots containing money and curds and butter are suspended high over streets. Boys form human pyramids climbing on each others' shoulders to try to break the pot. These climbing games reflect stories of Krishna, who as a boy loved milk and butter so much they had to be kept out of his reach.

In Nepal, a religious fast is observed on Krishnastami, and Krishna's temple at Lalitpur is visited by pilgrims. People parade in a procession around the town and display pictures of Krishna.

Numerous rich legends tell of Krishna's life. He is supposed to have been adored as a child for his mischievous pranks—tricking people out of their freshly churned butter or stealing the clothes of the cow maidens, called *gopis*, while they bathed in the river. Later, he used his flute to lure the gopis to amorous dalliances. He also defeated the 100-headed serpent Kaliya by dancing it into submission. Paintings, sculpture, and classical dances depict the many episodes of his life. Portraits of him as a child often show him dancing joyously and holding a ball of butter in his hands. Most often he is shown as the divine lover, playing the flute and surrounded by adoring women.

CONTACTS:
Ministry of Tourism, Government of India
Rm. No 123, Transport Bhawan, No. 1, Parliament St.
New Delhi, Delhi 110 001 India
91-11-23715084; fax: 91-11-23715084
www.tourisminindia.com

Uttar Pradesh Tourism Department, Directorate of Tourism
Rajarshi Purshottam Das Tandon Paryatan Bhavan
Vipin Khand, Gomti Nagar
Lucknow, Uttar Pradesh C-13 India
91-522-2308916; fax: 91-522-2308937
www.up-tourism.com

SOURCES:
BkFest-1937, p. 160
BkHolWrld-1986, Aug 26
DictFolkMyth-1984, pp. 590, 924
DictWrldRel-1989, p. 304
EncyRel-1987, vol. 4, p. 454
FolkWrldHol-1999, p. 516
HolSymbols-2009, p. 423
RelHolCal-2004, p. 174

♦ 1334 ♦ **Japan Constitution Memorial Day**
    May 3

Constitution Memorial Day, or **Kempo Kinen-Bi**, is observed as a national holiday on May 3 and commemorates the adoption of the democratic constitution in 1947. The holiday is part of **Golden Week**, which includes Children's Day, KODOMO-NO-HI, on May 3, and GREENERY DAY, April 29.

CONTACTS:
Japan Information Network, Japan Center for Intercultural
  Communications
2-7-7 Hirakawacho
Chiyodaku
Tokyo, 102-0093 Japan
81-3-3263-5041; fax: 81-3-3230-4107
home.jcic.or.jp/en/index-e.html

SOURCES:
AnnivHol-2000, p. 76

◆ 1335 ◆ **Japan Marine Day**
Third Monday in July

What began in Japan as a celebration of an emperor's historic sea voyage has broadened to become a day of awareness for marine environmental issues. A national holiday, Marine Day (or in Japanese, *Umi no hi*) was established in 1991 by several organizations devoted to ocean conservation. The event's original name was **Marine Commemoration Day**.

This holiday was established in 1941 to mark the return of Meiji the Great (1852–1912), Japan's 122nd emperor, from the northern island of Hokkaido in 1876. The vessel that transported the emperor on the historic voyage, the *Meiji-Maru*, has been preserved as a national treasure and is open for public viewing on Marine Day. Special lectures on other historic ships have been presented at the Tokyo University of Mercantile Marine in conjunction with Marine Day festivities.

With the festival's new focus on marine environmental issues, organizations take advantage of the day to raise awareness by scheduling seaside cleanups and other special events. For Japanese schoolchildren, Marine Day also marks the beginning of their summer vacation.

CONTACTS:
Japan Information Network, Japan Center for Intercultural
  Communications
web-japan.org/kidsweb/explore/calendar/july/marineday.html

◆ 1336 ◆ **Japan National Foundation Day**
February 11

The nationwide holiday known as **Kenkoku Kinen-no-Hi** commemorates the accession to the throne of Jimmu Tenno, Japan's first human emperor, in the year 660 B.C.E. He was believed to be a direct descendant of the gods and is credited with founding the Japanese empire. In fact, this day was originally known as **Empire Day** back in 1872, when the Japanese government first established it as a national holiday. It was abandoned after World War II, then brought back as National Foundation Day in 1966.

It is observed throughout Japan with fireworks and speeches on Japan's position in the world. One of the most elaborate celebrations takes place in Tokyo, where special rites are performed at the Imperial Sanctuary. The emperor and empress, the prime minister, and other high officials attend the ceremony.

CONTACTS:
Japan Information Network, Japan Center for Intercultural
  Communications
2-7-7 Hirakawacho
Chiyodaku
Tokyo, 102-0093 Japan
81-3-3263-5041; fax: 81-3-3230-4107
home.jcic.or.jp/en/index-e.html

SOURCES:
AnnivHol-2000, p. 25
BkFest-1937, p. 196
DictWrldRel-1989, p. 382

◆ 1337 ◆ **Japanese Emperor's Birthday**
December 23

This is a national holiday in Japan honoring the birth of Emperor Akihito (b. 1933). He and his family typically appear on the Imperial Palace balcony to greet visitors, who are invited to enter the grounds on this day.

CONTACTS:
Japan Information Network, Japan Center for Intercultural
  Communications
2-7-7 Hirakawacho
Chiyodaku
Tokyo, 102-0093 Japan
81-3-3263-5041; fax: 81-3-3230-4107
home.jcic.or.jp/en/index-e.html

◆ 1338 ◆ **Jayuya Festival of Indian Lore**
Mid-November

The **Jayuya Indian Festival** was started in 1969, when new traces of the Taino Indian culture were discovered in and around Jayuya, Puerto Rico. The town of Jayuya was once a center of Taino Indian activity, and many Taino stone carvings can still be seen in nearby caves, even though the tribe itself is extinct. The annual festival is held in mid-November and is timed to coincide with the anniversary of the first sighting of Puerto Rico by COLUMBUS on November 19, 1493.

Festival events include Indian ceremonies and dances as well as concerts featuring *fotutos* (conch shells) as instruments. There is a ceremonial Taino ball game that resembles soccer, and a village (*yukayeque*) of thatched-roof huts that enables visitors to see how the Indians lived. Visitors can attend lectures on the Taino language and customs or take a tour of the caves containing the Indian drawings.

Although Indian arts and crafts are on sale and there are kiosks serving food typical of the island's indigenous population, the Jayuya Indian Festival also has a serious scholarly purpose, which is to educate people about the Taino culture and to encourage more research in this area. Awards are presented each year at the festival to those who have done scholarly work on Puerto Rico's pre-Columbian cultures.

CONTACTS:
Puerto Rico Tourism Company
666 Fifth Ave., 15th Fl.
New York, NY 10103
800-866-7827 or 212-586-6262; fax: 212-586-1212
www.gotopuertorico.com

SOURCES:
GdUSFest-1984, p. 219

◆ 1339 ◆ **Jazzkaar Festival**
Late April

The Jazzkaar Festival is a 10-day celebration of jazz music held annually in late April in Tallinn, Estonia. Begun in 1990, Jazzkaar culminates the country's observance of international Jazz Appreciation Month and is the largest music festival devoted exclusively to jazz music in the Baltic region of northern Europe. Concerts and associated events are organized and overseen by the Jazzkaar Friends Society.

Performers represent a broad range of jazz variations, including Latin and Middle Eastern traditions, fusion, world beat, and American standards. Over the years more than 3,000 musicians from 40 countries have performed at the festival, and headlining acts in 2008 hailed from Australia, Benin, Brazil, Canada, Iceland, Israel, Spain, Sweden, and the United States, among other countries. The program also showcases numerous musicians from the host country, Estonia. Concerts take place in a range of venues throughout Tallinn, including clubs, cafes, museums, churches, and theaters. In addition to scheduled performances, additional program events include music competitions, student recitals, lectures, workshops, and special programming on national radio and television. Informal jam sessions often occur at the performance venues after hours and continue late into the night.

CONTACTS:
Jazzkaar
Gonsiori 21
Tallinn 10147 Estonia
www.jazzkaar.ee/eng

♦ 1340 ♦ Jefferson's (Thomas) Birthday
April 13

Unique among American presidents, Thomas Jefferson (1743-1826) was not only a statesman but a scholar, linguist, writer, philosopher, political theorist, architect, engineer, and farmer. In Europe, he was praised as the foremost American thinker of his time. In the United States, he is remembered primarily as the author in 1776 of the Declaration of Independence. After retiring from government service, Jefferson founded the University of Virginia, which opened in 1825. He died on July 4, 1826, the 50th anniversary of the signing of the Declaration of Independence.

As one of the founders of the Democratic party, along with Andrew JACKSON, he has been honored since 1936 by the Democratic National Committee, which often sponsors official dinners in various locations across the country known as "Jefferson-Jackson Day Dinners." Sometimes these dinners are held on January 8, the anniversary of the BATTLE OF NEW ORLEANS.

At the University of Virginia at Charlottesville, April 13 was observed for many years as **Founder's Day**, but in 1975 the date was shifted to early fall. There is a formal academic procession, after which an address is given by a nationally known figure. This is also the day on which the Thomas Jefferson Award is give to a leading member of the university community.

A birthday commemoration is held each year at Monticello, Jefferson's home in Virginia, as well as at the Jefferson Memorial on the Mall in Washington, D.C.

CONTACTS:
Monticello
The Thomas Jefferson Foundation

P.O. Box 316
Charlottesville, VA 22902
434-984-9800
www.monticello.org

Library of Congress
101 Independence Ave. S.E.
Washington, DC 20540
202-707-5000; fax: 202-707-8366
www.loc.gov

Thomas Jefferson Memorial
National Park Service
900 Ohio Dr. S.W.
Washington, DC 20024
202-426-6841
www.nps.gov

SOURCES:
AmerBkDays-2000, p. 280
AnnivHol-2000, p. 62

♦ 1341 ♦ Jerash Festival of Culture and Art
Late July to early August

Jordan's Queen Noor (Lisa Najeb Halaby, b. 1951) played an important role in establishing the visual and performing arts festival that is now held in Jerash every summer. Since 1981 visitors have come to the 2,000-year-old ruins where a Greco-Roman city once stood to hear Jordanian music, to see folkloric dances performed by Jordanian and other Arab groups, and to watch Arab plays and puppet shows. Queen Noor opens the nine-day festival by lighting a symbolic flame in the city forum.

In addition to the music, dance, and theater events, the Jerash Festival also includes an Arab book fair, with titles in both Arabic and English, sponsored by the Jordan Department of Libraries, Documentation, and National Archives.

CONTACTS:
Embassy of the Hashemite Kingdom of Jordan
3504 International Dr. N.W.
Washington, D.C. 20008
202-966-2664; fax: 202-966-3110
www.jordanembassyus.org

SOURCES:
GdWrldFest-1985, p. 125

♦ 1342 ♦ Jeshn (Afghan Independence Day)
August 19

Jeshn is a celebration of Afghanistan's independence from British control that has been observed throughout the country but with special ceremonies in Kabul. The Treaty of Rawalpindi, signed on August 8, 1919, gave Afghanistan the right to conduct its own foreign affairs. It was the formal conclusion of the brief Third Anglo-Afghan War, which actually ended in May 1919, but August is a slack agricultural period in Afghanistan and therefore a time when more people can celebrate a holiday.

The holiday has been observed with parades, dancing, games, music, and speeches by government figures.

Often the period of Jeshn has been used for major policy announcements. In 1959, one of the more significant events of modern Afghanistan occurred during Jeshn. Prime Minister Mohammad Daoud and other ministers and cabinet and royal family members appeared on the reviewing stand with their wives and daughters exposing their faces. This was a highly dramatic event; until then, women in public always wore the *burka* (an ankle-length tent-like gown and veil that totally covers the head and face, with only a mesh slit to see through). This marked the beginning of abolishing the required burka, and for years afterward most urban upper-class women went about without a veil.

This all changed in 1996 when the fundamentalist Islamic movement, Taliban, took over most of the country and required women to again wear the burka and severely restricted their movements outside the home, forcing most urban westernized Afghan women to give up their careers and education. The Taliban controlled Afghanistan until 2001, when United States and allied forces ousted the Taliban as part of the war against terrorism.

Despite the unsettled conditions in Afghanistan, Independence Day has continued to be observed.

CONTACTS:
Embassy of Afghanistan
2341 Wyoming Ave. N.W.
Washington, D.C. 20008
202-483-6410; fax: 202-483-6488
www.embassyofafghanistan.org

SOURCES:
AnnivHol-2000, p. 138
NatlHolWrld-1968, p. 71

♦ 1343 ♦ Jewish Cultural Festival
June

The ten-day Jewish Culture Festival takes place each year in Cracow, Poland. Centered in the former Jewish district of Kazimierz, the festival offers a wide array of cultural, historical, religious, and culinary events related to Jewish culture, particularly that of the Jews of Poland and Eastern Europe. Lectures, book launches, klezmer-band performances, folk-dancing lessons, and photographic exhibitions are all among the festival's many rich offerings. Festival participants and spectators come from around the world to visit the festival, which has grown significantly since its launch as an annual event in 1994 (prior to that it had occurred on a less regular schedule since 1988).

The aim of the festival organizers, the Jewish Cultural Festival Society, is to pay tribute to and sustain interest in a way of life that once thrived in Poland but has nearly disappeared since World War II. Before the war, the Jewish population of Poland was 3.5 million, but it was decimated by the Holocaust. Today there are only 10,000 self-described Jews living in Poland.

CONTACTS:
Jewish Cultural Festival Society
ul. Józefa 36

Kraków 31-056
Poland
www.jewishfestival.pl

Poland National Tourist Office
5 Marine View Plaza, Ste. 208
Hoboken, NJ 07030
201-420-9910; fax: 201-584-9153
polandtour.org

♦ 1344 ♦ Jhapan Festival (Manasa Festival)
Mid-August; last day of Hindu month of Sravana

Not for the snake-phobic, *Jhampanias,* or snake charmers, gather in the city of Vishnupur, West Bengal State, India, every August for one of the region's most notable annual festivals. Accompanying them, of course, are snakes of all kinds of local varieties, especially dangerous cobras. Jhampanias train their snakes to perform tricks with them, which attendees can observe to their hearts' content. The patron goddess of snakes is Manasa, a daughter of Shiva, and the festival attracts many who follow her cult.

CONTACTS:
India Tourist Office
1270 Ave. of the Americas, Ste. 1808, 18th Fl.
New York, NY 10020
800-953-9399 or 212-586-4901; fax: 212-582-3274
www.indiatouristoffice.org

SOURCES:
DictHindu-1977, p. 177
WildPlanet-1995, p. 253

♦ 1345 ♦ Jhulan Yatra
Between July and August; 17 days preceding the full moon of Sravana

A Hindu festival honoring Lord Jagannatha, Jhulan Yatra is observed in Orissa, a state in India's eastern region, and Bengal, a region shared by India and its eastern neighbor, Bangladesh.

Lord Jagannatha, which is an expression of the deity Krishna, is the reason for music, dancing, and merriment during Jhulan Yatra (also spelled **Jhulan Latra**). This festival takes place over 17 days preceding the full moon of Sravana, a month of the Hindu calendar that falls sometime between July and August. The celebration, which culminates with the full-moon day, takes place ahead of Janmashtami, the festival marking Krishna's birth. Several towns and cities hold official celebrations, but the grandest of them takes place at the Temple of Jagannath in the Orissa town of Puri.

Jhulan Yatra means "swing festival" in Hindi, a reference to the ornately decorated contraption that is specially built to hold the idols of Jagannath and his lover, Radha. Over the course of several nights during the festival, people gather at nighttime to perform songs and dances before the idols. This ritual, known as the *raslila,* dramatizes scenes from Krishna's life. During the festival, people will also visit temples, where they can obtain forgiveness for sins and pray for wealth and prosperity.

CONTACTS:
Orissa Department of Tourism
Paryatan Bhawan
Museum Campus
Bhubaneswar, Orissa 751014 India
www.orissatourism.gov.in

SOURCES:
RelHolCal-2004, p. 173

♦ 1346 ♦ Jidai Matsuri (Festival of the Ages)
October 22

Jidai Matsuri is one of the three great festivals of Kyoto, Japan, and also one of the more recent, commemorating the founding of the city as capital in the year 794. A procession of more than 2,000 picturesquely costumed people depict the epochs or ages in Kyoto's history. They parade from the Imperial Palace to the Heian Shrine, which was built in the 18th century as a dedication to the emperors who established Kyoto (then called Heian-kyo) as the capital. The capital was moved in 1868 to Tokyo, and the festival stems from that time. Among the paraders is one representing Gen. Toyotomi Hideyoshi, a patron of the arts under whom Kyoto flourished. He reunified the country after a period of civil war in the Azuchi-Momoyama Period (1573-1600). Wearing full armor, he reenacts an official visit to the emperor.

See also AOI MATSURI and GION MATSURI

CONTACTS:
Japan Information Network, Japan Center for Intercultural
   Communications
2-7-7 Hirakawacho
Chiyodaku
Tokyo, 102-0093 Japan
81-3-3263-5041; fax: 81-3-3230-4107
home.jcic.or.jp/en/index-e.html

Kyoto Prefectural Representative Office
1221 Avenue of the Americas
McGraw-Hill Bldg., 42nd Fl.
New York, NY 10020
212-997-6466; fax: 212-302-1581
www.pref.kyoto.jp

SOURCES:
AnnivHol-2000, p. 176
JapanFest-1965, p. 37

♦ 1347 ♦ Jizo Ennichi
24th day of each month

Tradition calls for Japanese Buddhists to honor Kshitigarba Jizo on the 24th day of each month with a ritual known as Jizo Ennichi.

Kshitigarba Jizo is a Bodhisattva, or "Buddha-to-be," who is highly regarded by Buddhists in Japan as well as in China, where he is known as Ti-t'sang.

Among Japanese Buddhists, Kshitigarba is known for helping children, women in labor, and the wicked. He is also believed to participate in ushering in the souls of the faithful when they die. He is frequently shown in monk's robes, holding a

staff with six rings in his right hand (symbolizing the six dimensions of existence in the realm of desire) and an orb or pearl in his left hand whose symbolic meaning is not known. His statue is most often found outside temples, where he can guide both the dead and the living. Shrines in his honor are set up along roadsides, since he protects travelers as well.

SOURCES:
DictWrldRel-1989, p. 418

♦ 1348 ♦ Jodlerfests (Yodeling Festivals)
Summer (end of May through September)

Regional festivals of the art of yodeling are held in the summer months throughout the northern German region of Switzerland. Every two years a national Jodlerfest is held. In 1991, it was in Engelberg and brought together not only yodelers from all over the country but also about 150 players of the Alphorn, a 10- to 15-foot wooden horn with a haunting sound.

The regular annual festivals are held outdoors and feature yodeling clubs, and sometimes soloists, who usually yodel without musical accompaniment. The themes of the songs are related to the mountains, the cows, and the herdsman's life and loves.

Technically, yodeling is a type of singing in which high falsetto and low chest notes alternate. It is supposed to have originated in Switzerland as a way for Alpine cowherds to call from meadow to meadow or to urge on their cows. However, yodeling is also found in other mountain areas in China and North and South America, and among the Aboriginal people of Australia as well as various ethnic groups in Africa.

CONTACTS:
Switzerland Tourism
Swiss Ctr., 608 Fifth Ave.
New York, NY 10020
877-794-8037 or 212-757-5944; fax: 212-262-6116
www.myswitzerland.com

♦ 1349 ♦ Johnson (Samuel) Commemoration
Saturday following September 18

Samuel Johnson, the English lexicographer, writer, critic, and conversationalist known popularly as Dr. Johnson, was born on this day in 1709. His hometown of Lichfield commemorates its most famous citizen by laying a laurel wreath at the foot of his statue, after which the cathedral choir sings religious songs and intones Dr. Johnson's final prayer while standing on the steps of his birth house. In the evening, there is a candlelight supper based on Dr. Johnson's favorite meal: steak-and-kidney pudding with mushrooms or mutton, with apple tarts and cream for dessert. The guests are served ale and hot punch by people dressed in costumes of the 18th century.

On this same day in Uttoxeter, 18 miles away, the story of Samuel Johnson's quarrel with his father is told to the town's assembled schoolchildren. Michael Johnson, the writer's father, sold books from a stall in the Uttoxeter market, and

Samuel's rejection of his father's request for help in manning the stall caused a breach between them that was never healed. After his father's death, Samuel decided that the best way to punish himself for his unforgivable behavior was to stand hatless for hours in pouring rain in the exact location where his father's business had once stood.

The 19th-century American novelist Nathaniel Hawthorne, on a visit to the area, found out the children growing up there did not know the story. Ever since that time, it has been recited to them in the marketplace on this day. Afterwards, one of them lays a wreath on the memorial plaque that marks the place where Dr. Johnson made his penance.

CONTACTS:
Samuel Johnson Birthplace Museum
Breadmarket St.
Lichfield, Staffordshire WS13 6LG United Kingdom
44-15-4326-4972
www.lichfield.gov.uk

SOURCES:
EngCustUse-1941, p. 107
YrFest-1972, p. 71

◆ 1350 ◆ **Jonquil Festival**
First weekend in March

This three-day (Friday through Sunday) festival allows participants to enjoy about 10,000 jonquils in Old Washington Historic State Park in the town of Washington, Ark. The first of these jonquils and daffodils were planted by pioneer families who came here along the Southwest Trail that ran from Missouri to Texas. Washington was the home of the state government after Union troops took Little Rock, Ark., during the Civil War. It is also where James Black, a blacksmith, forged the original Bowie knife for James Bowie in the 1830s.

This festival focuses on the history of Washington; the Pioneer Washington Restoration Foundation, established in 1958, has restored buildings that recreate the period of the early 1800s. Tours are given of these historic buildings. Other events are folk music concerts, food vendors selling funnel cakes (round, greasy, flat cakes made by pouring dough through a funnel onto a grid and sprinkled with powdered sugar) as well as hot dogs and lemonade, an arts and crafts show, blacksmithing, and a special worship service on Sunday morning. The festival attracts about 60,000 visitors.

CONTACTS:
Hope-Hempstead County Chamber of Commerce
P.O. Box 250
Hope, AR 71802
870-777-3640; fax: 870-722-6154
www.hopemelonfest.com

◆ 1351 ◆ **Jordan Independence Day**
May 25

A treaty signed on this day in 1946 established the constitutional monarchy of the Hashemite Kingdom of Jordan and secured the nation's independence from Great Britain.

Parades through the capital city of Amman mark the celebrations of this national holiday.

CONTACTS:
Jordan Embassy
3504 International Dr. N.W.
Washington, D.C. 20008
202-966-2664; fax: 202-966-3110
www.jordanembassyus.org

SOURCES:
AnnivHol-2000, p. 87
NatlHolWrld-1968, p. 69

◆ 1352 ◆ **Jordbruksdagarna**
Last full weekend in September

The town of Bishop Hill, Ill., was founded in 1846 by a group of Swedes fleeing religious persecution in the Old World. Their leader, Erik Jansson, sailed across the Atlantic with 1,200 followers, crossed the Great Lakes on steamers, and walked 150 miles to form the colony named with the English translation of Jansson's birthplace in Sweden. Cholera took its toll on the settlers, but their biggest setback was Jansson's murder in 1850. Without his leadership, the colony entered a period of rapid decline and, since it was bypassed by the main railroad line, time stood still there for about a century. As a result, many of the historic buildings remained undisturbed, and in 1984 Bishop Hill was designated a National Historic Landmark.

Many of the descendants of the original colonists still live in Bishop Hill or nearby towns, and they continue to celebrate a number of traditional Swedish holidays. One of these is Jordbruksdagarna, or **Agricultural Days**, a two-day celebration featuring harvest demonstrations, 19th-century crafts and children's games, and ample servings of Colony Stew. The residents of Bishop Hill also celebrate Lucia Nights (*see* St. Lucy's Day), when young women dressed as "Lucias" serve refreshments in the shops and museums.

CONTACTS:
Bishop Hill State Historic Site
P.O. Box 104
Bishop Hill, IL 61419
309-927-3345
www.bishophill.com

◆ 1353 ◆ **Jorvik Viking Festival**
Mid-February

During the centuries of Viking rule in Europe, York (formerly Jorvik) was a major outpost of the British Isles. The Jorvik Viking Festival, a weeklong festival established in 1985, honors the English city's historical legacy as well as the ethnic heritage of the many Scandinavians who travel to York to participate in the famous re-enactments.

The highlight of the festival is the re-enactment of the Battle of Stamford Bridge, a clash in 1066 between the Normans and the Saxons that marked the end of Viking rule in England. Although the battle actually occurred outside the city, the re-enactment takes place in the Eye of York, a circular grassed area in front of York Castle. Leading up to this main event, the actors perform battle drills and training routines.

Activities of a less violent nature include shopping in a Viking market, the traditional burning of a Viking boat, sword forging demonstrations, and cultural events centered on old Scandinavian tales, dances, and songs.

CONTACTS:
JORVIK Viking Centre
Coppergate
York YO1 9WT United Kingdom
www.jorvik-viking-centre.co.uk

♦ 1354 ♦ Joust of the Quintain
Second weekend in September

In the 17th century a tournament known as the Joust of the Quintain was held in Foligno, Perugia, Italy, to commemorate both the equestrian exercises of the early Roman legionnaires and the Joust of the Ring that was popular throughout Europe during the Middle Ages. The tournament was revived in 1946, adhering as closely as possible to the original rules.

The celebration begins on the evening of the second Saturday in September, when the townspeople gather to hear the First Magistrate announce the event. Early Sunday morning there is a parade of people in Renaissance dress, accompanied by musicians and dancers. Ten "knights" representing the city's 10 districts compete on horseback in the actual tournament, which involves galloping past the statue of Mars and trying to remove the ring in its outstretched hand by spearing it with the tip of a lance. The winner receives an ornamental cloak, and a torchlight parade concludes the day's events.

CONTACTS:
Italian Government Tourist Board
630 5th Ave., Ste. 1565
New York, NY 10111
212-245-5618; fax: 212-586-9249
www.italiantourism.com

SOURCES:
IntlThFolk-1979, p. 243

♦ 1355 ♦ Joust of the Saracens
June and September

The most famous of the Italian jousting festivals, **La Giostra del Saracino** originated during the Crusades (11th-13th centuries), when it was used as a form of propaganda to support the fight to recover the Holy Land from the Muslims. Eight knights representing the four quarters of Arezzo, where the festival takes place, march to the piazza, where an effigy of a Moor or Saracen (i.e., Muslim) has been set up. The effigy is armed with a heavy flail and a shield, which the knights must try to hit in the center with their lances without being touched by the flail. The winner is rewarded with a golden lance on behalf of his district.

CONTACTS:
Associazione Sbandieratori di Arezzo
Piazza Grande, 35

Arezzo, Tuscany 52100 Italy
39-575-2185; fax: 39-575-2185-7
www.etr.it

SOURCES:
FestEur-1961, p. 119

♦ 1356 ♦ Jousting the Bear
March 10

Although jousting normally involves two knights charging each other on horseback with lances, the custom has been changed somewhat in Pistoia, Italy, where **La Giostra dell' Orso** is held in March each year. Twelve horsemen representing the town's four districts join in a procession to the Cathedral Square, each accompanied by a group of costumed attendants. They compete against each other in pairs, racing at a gallop toward the effigies of two bears holding targets in their outstretched paws. Points are won by hitting the targets, and the most successful knight is proclaimed Knight of the Golden Spur of Pistoia.

CONTACTS:
Italian Government Tourist Board
630 Fifth Ave., Ste. 1565
New York, NY 10111
212-245-5618; fax: 212-586-9249
www.italiantourism.com

♦ 1357 ♦ Jousting Tournament
Third Saturday in June and second Sunday in October

Sponsored by the National Jousting Hall of Fame and held since 1823 in Mount Solon, Va., this tournament for "knights" on horseback is reputed to be America's oldest continuous sporting event. The tourney, recalling the knights of old, is held at the Natural Chimneys Regional Park, where rock formations resemble castle towers.

Jousting contestants gallop full-tilt down an 80-yard course as they try to spear and pluck with their lances three steel rings from crossbars; this exercise is called "running at the ring." The rings are as small as ¼" in diameter.

Jousting has been practiced in the United States since the 17th century. Tournaments are also held in Maryland, South Carolina, Virginia, and West Virginia, but the Virginia spectacle is the oldest and the most prestigious. Accompanied by parties, these are high social points of the year. About 150 jousters run at the rings at the Mount Solon tournaments.

CONTACTS:
National Jousting Association
P.O. Box 14
Mount Solon, VA 22843
888-336-1861 or 434-983-2989
www.nationaljousting.com

♦ 1358 ♦ Jubilee Days Festival
Labor Day weekend

Founded in 1948, Jubilee Days began as a celebration of the harvest and of God's blessings on the community. It has since become a celebration of the unique heritage of Zion, Illinois.

The town was founded in 1901 by the reverend John Alexander Dowie, organizer of the Christian Catholic Church. Wanting to create a city ruled by God, Dowie bought some 6,000 acres of land north of Chicago and founded Zion. All residents were given a 1,100 year lease on the land (Dowie assumed that Christ would return within 100 years and his 1,000 year reign would follow that) and shared in the community's profits. In 1905 Dowie suffered a stroke and was unable to oversee further construction of the new city. He died in 1907 and was succeeded by Wilbur Glenn Voliva. The 2007 festival included an arts and crafts festival, a 5k run, a mayor's prayer breakfast, a Zion queen's pageant, a Civil War reenactment, and a 100-plus unit parade.

CONTACTS:
City of Zion
2828 Sheridan Rd.
Zion, IL 60099
847-746-4000
www.cityofzion.com

◆ 1359 ◆ Juhannus (Midsummer Day)
Saturday between June 20 and June 26

Juhannus is a celebration in Finland of the SUMMER SOLSTICE and of the feast of St. John. Like a medieval holiday, people celebrate at the lake shores where they build bonfires and dance all night. Since this is near the longest day of the year, special late performances are held at open-air theaters in many towns. There are also dances at hotels.

Many customs are remnants of pagan times. In earlier times, the bonfire was supposed to reveal the future. Birch tree branches are brought into the homes to insure future happiness. Even buses and office buildings are adorned with birch branches. On the Aland Islands, tall poles are decorated with flowers and leaves, and supper tables are decorated with birch and garlands of flowers. The church made the festival ST. JOHN'S DAY, but the celebration has more pagan overtones than Christian ones.

As Finland's Flag Day, Juhannus is also a national holiday.

CONTACTS:
Ministry of Foreign Affairs of Finland
Department for Communication and Culture
P.O. Box 176
Helsinki, 00161 Finland
358-9-1600-5; fax: 358-9-1605-5901
www.virtual.finland.fi

SOURCES:
FolkWrldHol-1999, p. 392

◆ 1360 ◆ Juliana's (Queen) Birthday
April 30

Juliana Louise Emma Marie Wilhelmina, born on this day in 1909, was queen of the Netherlands from 1948 until 1980,

when she voluntarily abdicated in favor of her oldest daughter, Beatrix (b. 1938). Although she aroused controversy from time to time—especially by employing a faith healer in the 1950s and by letting two of her four daughters marry foreigners, she was a popular monarch whose birthday is still celebrated throughout the Netherlands with parades, fun fairs, and decorations honoring the queens of the House of Orange. Queen Juliana died on March 20, 2004, but her birthday remains a national holiday.

CONTACTS:
Netherlands Government Information Service
P.O. Box 20009
Hague, 2500 EA Netherlands
31-70-356-4000
www.netherlands.info/Introduction.html

Noordeinde Palace
P.O. Box 30412
Hague, 2500 GK Netherlands
31-70-356-4000; fax: 31-70 356 4683
www.koninklijkhuis.nl/english

SOURCES:
AnnivHol-2000, p. 71
NatlHolWrld-1968, p. 54

◆ 1361 ◆ Juneteenth
June 19

Although President Abraham LINCOLN signed the EMANCIPATION Proclamation on January 1, 1863, it wasn't until two years later that the word reached the slaves in Texas. General Gordon Granger arrived in Galveston on June 19, 1865, with the intention of forcing the slave owners there to release their slaves, and the day has been celebrated since that time in eastern Texas, Louisiana, southwestern Arkansas, Oklahoma, and other parts of the Deep South under the nickname "Juneteenth."

Observed primarily in African-American communities, Juneteenth festivities usually include parades, picnics, and baseball games. Although Juneteenth observances can be found as far west as California, many blacks who originally came from east Texas and surrounding areas choose to return home on the weekend nearest the 19th of June.

CONTACTS:
National Juneteenth Museum
2632 N. Charles St.
P.O. Box 7228
Baltimore, MD 21218
410-467-2724
www.juneteenth.com

Juneteenth.com
P.O. Box 871750
New Orleans, LA 70187
504-245-7800
www.juneteenth.com

SOURCES:
AAH-2007, p. 250
AnnivHol-2000, p. 102
BkHolWrld-1986, Jun 19
DictDays-1988, p. 36

FolkAmerHol-1999, p. 261
HolSymbols-2009, p. 428
PatHols-2006, p. 109

♦ 1362 ♦ Junkanoo Festival
December 26; January 1

The **Junkanoo Parade and Festival**, held in Nassau's native quarter, combines elements of MARDI GRAS, mummer's parades, and ancient African tribal rituals. It is held on December 26, BOXING DAY, and January 1, NEW YEAR'S DAY. Masqueraded marchers wearing colorful headpieces and costumes that have taken months to prepare dance to the beat of an Afro-Bahamian rhythm called Goombay, which refers to all Bahamian secular music.

The music is played by a variety of unusual native instruments, including goat skin drums, lignum vitae sticks, pebble-filled "shak-shaks," and steel drums. The name comes from a number of sources. Historically, it referred to the drumbeats and rhythms of Africa, which were brought to the Bahamas by slaves. The term was used during jump-in dances, when the drummer would shout "Gimbey!" at the beginning of each dance. The Ibo tribes in West Africa have a drum they call *Gamby*, from which the name "goombay" probably derived.

The Junkanoo parade, which begins at two o'clock in the morning and continues until sunrise, is followed by the judging of costumes and awarding of prizes. There are Junkanoo parades in Freeport and the Family of Out Islands as well.

In Belize and parts of Guatemala the Junkanoo masqueraders dance from house to house. Their wire-screen masks are painted white or pink, have staring eyes, red lips, black eyebrows, and thin moustaches for men; they are accompanied by two drums and a women's chorus.

In Jamaica, Junkanoo is featured also at political rallies and Independence Day celebrations. There are "root" and "fancy dress" troupes, the latter being more sedate. Their procession contains courtiers; a king and queen preceded by a flower girl; Sailor Boy who uses a whip to keep the audience in line; Babu, an East Indian cowboy with a long cattle prod; and Pitchy Patchy, the latter three being more boisterous than the courtiers. The "root" Junkanoo parade features Amerindians and Warriors, the former dancing with a throbbing rhythm and more body movement; Belly Woman who shakes her belly in time with the music; and Cowhead and other animal characters who butt the crowd. "Root" Junkanoo is usually found in remote villages far from large towns or cities.

There are a number of theories as to where the name "Junkanoo" came from. One is that the festival was started by a West African named Jananin Canno, or from a folkloric figure known in the West Indies, John or Johnny Canoe. Another is that it comes from the French expression *gens inconnus*, or "unknown people," which would seem to refer to the masked dancers.

See also YANCUNÚ, FIESTA DEL

CONTACTS:
Bahamas Tourism Office
60 E. 42nd St., Ste. 1850
New York, NY 10165
212-758-2777; fax: 212-753-6531
www.bahamas.com

SOURCES:
AAH-2007, p. 258
DictFolkMyth-1984, p. 554
EncyChristmas-2003, p. 387
FolkWrldHol-1999, p. 765
GdWrldFest-1985, p. 16
HolSymbols-2009, p. 426

♦ 1363 ♦ Juno Caprotina, Festival of
July 7

Juno was the ancient Roman goddess of women and marriage, identified with the Greek goddess Hera. As the highest deity in the Roman pantheon next to Jupiter, her brother and husband, she ruled all aspects of women's lives, including sexuality and childbirth, and served as a kind of guardian angel for women. Along with Jupiter and Minerva, she shared a temple on the Capitoline Hill in Rome; together they were known as the Capitoline Triad. This temple contained Juno's sacred geese, whose cackling, according to Plutarch, saved Rome from the Gauls in 390 B.C.E.

The two most important festivals in honor of Juno were the Juno Caprotina (or **Nonae Caprotinae**) and the MATRONALIA. The former was held under a wild fig tree in the Campus Martius, or Field of Mars, a floodplain of the Tiber River. The kalends or first day of every month were sacred to Juno, and she was also associated with the ancient ceremony of announcing at the new moon the date of the nones (*see* IDES).

The month of June, named after the goddess Juno, is still considered the most popular month for getting married.

SOURCES:
AmerBkDays-2000, p. 491
DictRomRel-1996, p. 164
FestRom-1981, p. 161
OxClassDict-1970, p. 569
OxYear-1999, p. 285

♦ 1364 ♦ Just for Laughs Festival
Late July

Every July, Montreal hosts one of the largest comedy festivals in the world. The Just for Laughs Festival, also known as the **Montreal International Comedy Festival**, is a time for comedy fans to catch the best acts and for aspiring comedians to make a foray into the industry.

Two Canadians, Gilbert Rozon and Andy Nulman, founded the festival in 1983 as a small French-language show (called **Juste pour rire**) comprised of only two nights. In 1985, the organizers opened the stage to English-speaking comedians, paving the way for newcomers like *Tonight Show* host Jay Leno and sitcom star Jerry Seinfeld to launch their careers. In the subsequent years, the organizers extended Just for

Laughs to 12 days and added a film component to the festival. A TV deal was also inked to attract millions of international viewers.

Today there are more than 1,300 shows and performances, featuring all kinds of comedy as well as juggling and performance art, but the gala shows at Montreal's St. Denis Theatre are always the main event.

CONTACTS:
Just for Laughs
2101 St-Laurent Blvd.
Montreal, QC H2X 2T5 Canada
www.justforlaughs.ca

SOURCES:
AnnivHol-2000, p. 126

♦ 1365 ♦ Jutajaiset Folklore Festival
Late June, including midsummer's eve

The Jutajaiset Folklore Festival is a 10-day cultural fair held each year in late June in Lapland, the artic region of northern Finland. Jutajaiset celebrates midsummer, a period during which the region—known as the "land of the midnight sun"—experiences 24-hour daylight.

Since beginning in 1972, the festival has been sponsored by the youth folklore society Lapin Nuorison Liitto, first in Sodankylä until 1994 and afterwards in Rovaniemi. It showcases the unique culture of the Sami people of Lapland, with educational programs, local artists, dancers, and musicians. In addition, the festival presents performers from throughout the world, including Estonia, India, Mexico, Russia, and Slovakia. Food and refreshments are available on site.

CONTACTS:
Jutajaiset
Rovakatu 26 A 19
FI-96200 Rovaniemi Finland
www.jutajaiset.fi

♦ 1366 ♦ Juturnalia
January 11

According to Virgil, Juturna is the sister of Turnus, king of the Rutuli. In return for her virginity, Jupiter gave her immortality. Afterwards she was turned into a fountain of the same name near the Numicus, the river where Aeneas' dead body was found. The waters from this fountain were used in sacrifices, particularly those in honor of the Roman goddess Vesta, and were believed to have curative powers. On January 11, a festival in honor of Juturna was observed by men working on aqueducts and wells. She was also celebrated at the VULCANALIA on August 23 as a protectress against fire.

SOURCES:
ClassDict-1984, p. 312
DictFolkMyth-1984, p. 564
DictRomRel-1996, p. 126
FestRom-1981, p. 64
OxYear-1999, p. 31

♦ 1367 ♦ Juul, Feast of
December 21 or 22

The Feast of Juul was a pre-Christian festival observed in Scandinavia at the time of the WINTER SOLSTICE. Fires were lit to symbolize the heat, light, and life-giving properties of the returning sun. A YULE (or Juul) log was brought in with great ceremony and burned on the hearth in honor of the Scandinavian god, Thor. A piece of the log was kept as both a token of good luck and as kindling for the following year's log.

In England and in many parts of Germany, France, and other European countries, the Yule log was burned until nothing but ash remained; then the ashes were collected and either strewn on the fields as fertilizer every night until TWELFTH NIGHT or kept as a charm and useful medicine. French peasants believed that if the ashes were kept under the bed, they would protect the house against thunder and lightning, as well as prevent chilblains on the heels during the winter.

The present-day custom of lighting a Yule log at CHRISTMAS is believed to have originated in the bonfires associated with the Feast of Juul.

SOURCES:
DaysCustFaith-1957, p. 352
EncyChristmas-2003, p. 843
RoundYr-1950, p. 196
StoryWrldHol-1924, p. 312

♦ 1368 ♦ Juvenalia
Three days in June

During the Juvenalia festival each year in Krakow, Poland, the students of Jagiellonian University take over the city for three days. After the mayor hands over the keys to the city, they dress up in costumes and masks and parade through the streets making fun of anything they choose. This celebration goes back to a medieval tradition, when new students at the university had to pay a tax to older ones as part of their ritual entry into college life—much like the "hazing" that goes on in fraternities and sororities at American colleges.

CONTACTS:
Polish National Tourist Office
5 Marine View Plz.
Hoboken, NJ 07030
201-420-9910; fax: 201-584-9153
www.polandtour.org

SOURCES:
BkHolWrld-1986, Jun 4

♦ 1369 ♦ JVC Jazz Festival
Mid-August

Known for many years as the **Newport Jazz Festival**, this event was moved to New York in 1972 and later returned to Newport, Rhode Island, as the JVC Jazz Festival. One of the most important jazz festivals in the world, it features legendary jazz performers as well as up-and-coming new stars and some of the most outstanding big bands, jazz combos, and instrumental and vocal soloists in the country. Dizzy Gillespie, Woody Herman, Ella Fitzgerald, Miles Davis, and Sarah Vaughan have performed there, as have Wynton Marsalis and Spyro Gyra. The first evening's event is usually held at the Newport Casino in the International Tennis Hall of Fame. Subsequent concerts during the three-day festival are held outdoors in Fort Adams State Park, where visitors are encouraged to picnic and relax on the lawn as they listen.

Festival Productions also sponsors JVC Jazz Festivals in other cities worldwide from spring through autumn.

CONTACTS:
Festival Network
Pier 35-The Embarcadero, Ste. 201
San Francisco, CA 94133
415-503-9914
www.festivalnetwork.com

SOURCES:
MusFestAmer-1990, p. 200

♦ 1370 ♦ **Jyestha Ashtami**
May-June; eighth day of waxing half of Hindu month of Jyestha

This Hindu festival is celebrated at the shrine of Khir Bhawani in Tullamula, Jammu and Kashmir, in honor of their patron goddess, called Ragnya Devi. Pilgrims come from all over to assemble at the shrine, offer prayers and worship at the foot of the goddess, and sing hymns and songs in her praise. *Khir* (rice boiled in milk) is prepared on this day as a food offering. The marble shrine, located about 25 kilometers from Srinagar, India, overlooks a pool formed by spring waters known for their changing colors. Hundreds of Kashmiri Hindus visit the shrine daily.

CONTACTS:
Jammu and Kashmir Government
Directorate of Information
Opposite Pratap Pk.
Srinagar, Jammu & Kashmir 190 001 India
91-194-2452294; fax: 91-194-2452227
www.jammukashmir.nic.in

SOURCES:
RelHolCal-2004, p. 169

♦ 1371 ♦ **Jyvaskyla Arts Festival**
July

This cultural festival in Finland was started in 1955 by three well-known figures in the music world: Professor Timo Makinen, composer Seppo Nummi, and Professor Paivo Oksala. It has now expanded beyond musical events to include film, theater, art exhibits, and seminars designed to promote understanding among different national and ethnic traditions. In the past, the festival has included a summer Academy of Chamber Music and performances by world-renowned chamber music groups such as the Bartok Quartet and the London Early Music Group. Festival events are held throughout the city in local churches, museums, theaters, and parks.

CONTACTS:
Jyvaskyla Regional Tourist Services
Asemakatu 6
Jyvaskyla, 40100 Finland
358-14-6249-03; fax: 358-14-2143-93
www.jyvaskyla.fi/lang

SOURCES:
GdWrldFest-1985, p. 76
IntlThFolk-1979, p. 95

K

♦ 1372 ♦ **Kaamatan Festival**
May 30-31

Kaamatan is a festival and public holiday in Labuan Territory and the state of Sabah in Malaysia. The festival is celebrated by the Kadazan or Dusun people (also known as the Kadazandusun), the largest indigenous ethnic group in Sabah, which lies on the northern tip of Borneo. Originally headhunters, they were the first native group in Borneo to use the plow. Irrigated (not flooded) rice is their principal crop, and the harvest is a ritual dedicated to the *Bambaazon*, or rice spirit. If the harvest has been good, this is a thanksgiving, and if it has been poor, the ritual is an appeasement of the spirit. The Kadazans believe that spirits reside in natural objects, and rituals are conducted by shamanist priestesses. Besides the solemn aspects of the festival, there is much merrymaking and free flowing of rice wine. This festival is celebrated during most of the month of May throughout the region with carnivals, special exhibits, sports competitions, a beauty pageant and a regatta, all leading up to the rituals on May 30-31 in Penampang.

CONTACTS:
Sabah Tourism Board
Mail Bag 112
88993 Kota Kinabalu
Sabah, Malaysia
www.sabahtourism.com/en

Kadazandusun Cultural Association
Hongkod Koisaan, Km. 7
Penampang Rd. WDT 39
Sabah, Malaysia
6088-713-696; fax: 6088-713-350
www.kdca.org.my

♦ 1373 ♦ **Kakadu Mahbilil Festival**
Early September

The one-day Mahbilil Festival is both a celebration of Australia's indigenous culture and a vehicle for promoting tourism in the Northern Territory. Formerly known as the **Wind Festival**, its festivities take place at Lake Jabiru, located within Kakadu National Park. The national park, a World Heritage Site, adjoins Arnhem Land, which historians conjecture may have been the first territory inhabited by the Aboriginal people.

Aboriginal leaders of Kakadu, who jointly manage the park, invite visitors to join them in celebrating a culture that reaches back 50,000 years. A festival highlight is the Magpie Goose cooking competition, in which contestants show off their best recipes and prepare their meals over a coal fire. Other activities include traditional dancing, market stalls, and live music by local indigenous bands. The festival's 20th anniversary in 2006 featured fireworks, fire twirling displays, and a film festival presenting the works of local young artists.

CONTACTS:
Kakadu National Park
Lake Jabiru
Civil Dr.
Jabiru, Northern Territory 0886 Australia
www.travelnt.com

♦ 1374 ♦ **Kalakshetra Arts Festival**
December-January

The Kalakshetra Foundation, in Tiruvanmiyur in the Tamil Nadu state capital of Chennai, is one of India's outstanding cultural institutions. It was founded in 1936 and directed for many years by Rukmini Devi Arundale, an Indian woman who married an Englishman and devoted herself to the rejuvenation of Indian dance, music, sculpture, and crafts. Rukmini Devi is also known for choreographing 25 dance-dramas, a traditional Indian art form.

The Kalakshetra Arts Festival, which has been held annually for eight days in December-January since 1951, takes place at the Foundation's College of Fine Arts, a school that specializes in teaching the *Bharatanatyam* and other traditional styles of Indian dance. There are folk dance performances, vocal and instrumental recitals, and of course the famous dance-dramas choreographed by Rukmini Devi and based on themes from *puranas,* or Hindu epics.

CONTACTS:
Kalakshetra Foundation
Central Office
Tiruvanmiyur
Chennai, Tamil Nadu 600 041 India
91-44-24524057; fax: 91-44-24524359
www.kalakshetra.in

SOURCES:
IntlThFolk-1979, p. 215

◆ 1375 ◆ **Kalevala Day**
February 28

The *Kalevala* is Finland's national epic poem, researched and transcribed by Dr. Elias Lönnrot (1802-1835). Lönnrot and his assistants traveled throughout the country, asking people to tell them whatever they could remember about the folklore surrounding Kalevala, the "Land of Heroes." On February 28, 1835, after years of research, Lönnrot signed the preface to the first edition of the poem. Its more than 20,000 verses brought to life the adventures of such characters as the warrior Lemminkäinen and the blacksmith Ilmarinen, who played a part in the creation of the world when he forged the "lids of heaven." This event marked a turning point in Finnish literature; up to this point, little had been written in the Finnish language. Lönnrot is honored with parades and concerts on this day.

CONTACTS:
Finnish Literature Society
Hallituskatu 1
P.O. Box 259
Helsinki, 00171 Finland
358-20-1131-231; fax: 358-9-1312-3220
www.finlit.fi/index.php?lang=eng

SOURCES:
AnnivHol-2000, p. 34
BkFest-1937, p. 111
BkHolWrld-1986, Feb 28

◆ 1376 ◆ **Kali Puja**
Between September and October; new moon day of Kartika

In the region of Bengal, which encompasses eastern India and Bangladesh, many Hindus regularly honor Kali, an earth goddess of fearsome appearance and a symbol of fertility. Special temples devoted to Kali are located in Dhaka, Bangladesh; Kolkatta and Dakshineswar in India; and other locations throughout the region. During the year believers conduct daily *pujas* (devotional prayers) to Kali, but one particular new-moon day of the year is set aside for a special Kali Puja. This new-moon day, or *amavasya*, takes place during Kartika, the seventh Bengali month falling between October and November. Kali Puja also coincides with Dewali, a well-known celebration observed by Hindus, Sikhs, and Jains in India and other countries.

Kali, like other Hindu deities, assumes many forms. In paintings and sculpture she most commonly bears a dark and violent demeanor and is depicted standing on the chest of her husband, Shiva. (According to Hindu legend, Shiva prostrated himself before Kali in an attempt to pacify her during a killing rampage.) The goddess's fearsomeness is also the source of her strength, which is why during Kali Puja believers make appeals for her protection from harm and ask her to destroy various evils.

Unlike with other festivals, believers will worship Kali at night. Typically, people gather around elaborate *pandals* (shrines) to the goddess around 9 P.M. Priests will then lead a ceremony, which may involve prayers and sacrifices of animals such as goats, sheep, or buffaloes. Worship may continue until as late as 1 A.M. or 2 A.M.

CONTACTS:
Bangladesh Parjatan Corporation, National Tourism Organization
233 Airport Rd.
Tejgaon
Dhaka 1215 Bangladesh
www.bangladeshtourism.gov.bd

◆ 1377 ◆ **Kallemooi**
Between May 10 and June 13; Saturday before Pentecost

Observed in the North Coast Islands of the Netherlands, the custom known as Kallemooi represents the fishermen's welcome to spring. A tall pole with a transverse arm near the top is erected in the center of the village. A live cock—usually one that has been "borrowed" from a nearby farm—is suspended in a basket from the apex of the crosspiece. An empty bottle is hung from either arm of the structure, which is decorated at the top with the Dutch flag, a green branch, and a placard bearing the word "Kallemooi." For three days and three nights before PENTECOST, or Whitsunday, people feast, make merry, and play Whitsun games. After the fun is over, the rooster is released and returned to its owner.

There has been much speculation about the origin of the word Kallemooi. Some say it can be translated as "calling the May," while others claim it is derived from the word *kalemei*, meaning a "tree without branches" or a bare tree. During the festival, a special drink known as "Kallemooi bitters" is served by all the local inns.

CONTACTS:
Netherlands Board of Tourism & Conventions
355 Lexington Ave., 19th Fl.
New York, NY 10017
888-464-6552 or 212-370-7360; fax: 212-370-9507
us.holland.com

SOURCES:
FestWestEur-1958, p. 134

◆ 1378 ◆ **Kamakura Matsuri (Snow Hut Festival)**
February 15-17

Kamakura Matsuri is held in northern Japan in the Akita Prefecture, at the time of year when there is usually deep snow on the ground. The original purpose of the festival was to offer prayers for a good rice crop to Suijin-sama, the water god.

In Yokote and other towns of the region, children build *Kamakura*, snow houses about six feet in diameter resembling Eskimo igloos. They furnish the huts with tatami mats and a wooden altar dedicated to Suijin-sama and have parties in them, while families gather to drink sweet sake and eat rice cakes and fruits. The rice cakes are made in the shape of cranes and turtles, traditional symbols of longevity, and of dogs called *inukko,* thought to guard against devils.

A similar Kamakura Festival is held in Tokamachi in Niigata Prefecture on Jan. 14.

CONTACTS:
Akita City Hall
1-1-1 Sanno
Akita, 010-0951 Japan
81-1-8863-2033; fax: 81-1-8866-2278
www.pref.akita.jp/e

SOURCES:
BkHolWrld-1986, Feb 15
FolkWrldHol-1999, p. 177

♦ 1379 ♦ **Kamehameha (King) Celebration**
Second Monday in June

A state holiday in Hawaii to celebrate the reign of the island state's first king, this celebration is the only public holiday in the United States that honors royalty.

King Kamehameha I, known as "the Great" (1758?-1819), was the son of a high chief. At his birth it was prophesied that he would defeat all his rivals. He originally was named Paiea, which means "soft-shelled crab." When he grew to manhood he took the name Kamehameha, meaning "the very lonely one" or "the one set apart." By 1810 he had united all the Hawaiian islands and until his death was the undisputed ruler. He promulgated the *mamalahoe kanawai,* or "law of the splintered paddle," which protected the common people from the brutality of powerful chiefs, and he outlawed human sacrifice. He made a fortune for his people with a government monopoly on the sandalwood trade. After his death, he was succeeded by his son, Kamehameha II.

Celebrations extend over much of the month of June. Leis (Hawaiian floral necklaces) are draped on the king's statue across from Iolani Palace, formerly the home of Hawaii's monarchs and now the state capitol in Honolulu, and there is another lei-draping at Kapaau, North Kohala. A floral parade travels from downtown Honolulu to Waikiki; it features a young man who depicts the king wearing a replica of the golden amo-feather cloak and Grecian-style helmet (the originals are kept in Honolulu's Bernice P. Bishop Museum and are displayed on this day). The parade also includes floats and princesses on horseback wearing the *pa'u,* satin riding dresses in the color of their island home. Other events include demonstrations of arts and crafts, a competition of chants and hulas, and a luau, or Hawaiian cookout.

CONTACTS:
King Kamehameha Celebration Commission
355 N. King St.
Honolulu, HI 96817
808-586-0333; fax: 808-586-0335
www.state.hi.us

Library of Congress
101 Independence Ave. S.E.
Washington, DC 20540
202-707-5000; fax: 202-707-8366
www.loc.gov

SOURCES:
AmerBkDays-2000, p. 438
AnnivHol-2000, p. 99
DictDays-1988, p. 63
GdUSFest-1984, p. 44

♦ 1380 ♦ **Kapila Shashti**
August-September; every 60 years during the Hindu month of Bhadrapada

According to Hindu astronomers, Kapila Shashti takes place about every 60 years, when several astronomical events coincide during the day.

There is a myth that explains why Kapila Shashti occurs so rarely. It is said that when the sage Narada, who had always been celibate, decided he wanted to have female companionship, he asked the god Krishna, who had 16,008 wives, if he could marry one of them. Krishna asked only that Narada choose a wife who was not in anyone else's company. Since all of them were busy enjoying the company of others, Narada went to bathe in the Ganges River. When he walked out of the river, he discovered that he had been transformed into a woman. He (now "she") married a hermit and had 60 sons, which left her so exhausted that she begged Vishnu to return her to a man. This Krishna granted, but after Narada was a man again, the sons wailed for their mother to feed them. To quiet the turmoil Vishnu granted each son dominion over one year. Each year of the cycle is named after one of Narada's sons. Thus, the cycle is 60 years long. The last day of the cycle is Kapila Shashti, the day when Krishna turned Narada back into a man.

SOURCES:
HinduRelCustManners-1960, p. 145
HinduRelYr-1921, p. 36

♦ 1381 ♦ **Karneval in Cologne**
November 11 until Ash Wednesday

Pre-Lenten activities are especially festive in Cologne, Germany. The celebration begins officially on the 11th day of the 11th month at 11:11 P.M., when CARNIVAL societies throughout Germany begin their public activities with singers submitting their latest songs and speakers telling funny tales. The date was originally the end of a fasting period ordered by the church.

During the period from early January until the beginning of LENT, the festival calendar is filled with 300 costume balls, performances of original songs and humorous speeches, and numerous smaller affairs sponsored by such special interest groups as skittle clubs and a rabbit breeders' association. The humorous talks began in 1829, and today audiences clap hands in a slow rhythm to show their approval and whistle to express their disapproval.

These events lead up to the final "crazy days" (*Tolle Tage*) just before ASH WEDNESDAY. During this time, the Lord Mayor of Cologne receives the Triumvirate of Carnival—Prince Carnival, the Cologne Virgin (who, according to tradition, is played by a man), and the Cologne Peasant. The prince represents the prince of joy, the peasant the valor of the men of the town, and the virgin the purity of the city of Cologne, whose city walls the enemy never breached. The prince gets the keys to the city and rules the city until Carnival ends.

On *Weiberfastnacht*, or "Women's Carnival," the Thursday before Ash Wednesday, women take control and cut off the ties of any men within reach. This is revenge—women were excluded from Karneval in the 19th century. On Sunday, there are school and suburban parades.

ROSE MONDAY is the day of Carnival's mammoth parade with decorated floats, giant figures, and bands. Police from surrounding districts are on duty and join the crowds in singing and dancing.

On SHROVE TUESDAY, there are more parades, and crowds cheer the prince and his attendants. That evening, the Carnival season ends with a ball in Gürzenich Hall, the city's 15th-century festival hall. The prince returns the keys of the city, and normalcy is back. On Ash Wednesday, people traditionally eat a fish dinner, and so the restraint of Lent begins.

See also FASCHING

CONTACTS:
City of Cologne Tourist Office
Unter Fettenhennen 19
Koln (Am Dom), 50667 Germany
49-22-130-40-0; fax: 49-22-130-40-10
www.koeln.de/en/index.html

SOURCES:
EncyEaster-2002, p. 222

◆ 1382 ◆ Kartika Purnima
October-November; full moon day of Hindu month of Kartika

Hindus celebrate Kartika Purnima in honor of the day when God incarnated himself as the Matsya Avatar in fish form. According to Hindu mythology, the purpose of this incarnation was to save Vavaswata, the seventh Manu and progenitor of the human race, from destruction by a deluge. Good deeds done on this day are believed to earn high religious merit. Bathing in the Ganges or in other holy water is considered to be of special religious significance. Hindus spend the day fasting, meditating, and performing charitable acts.

It is also believed the Shankara killed the demon Tripurasura on this day, for which he is also called the Tripurari. Shiva is worshipped on this occasion, and giving a bull (Shiva's mount) as a gift to a Brahman is considered to be an appropriate and significant act. For this reason, it is common to hold cattle fairs on this day.

SOURCES:
RelHolCal-2004, p. 178

◆ 1383 ◆ Kartika Snan
October-November; Hindu month of Kartika

The Hindu months of Vaisakha (April-May), Kartika (October-November), and Magha (January-February) are regarded as especially sacred and therefore the most suitable for acts of piety. Throughout the month of Kartika, Hindus bathe in a sacred river, stream, pond, or well early in the morning. On the sacred rivers, such as the Ganges and the Yamuna in India, a month-long bathing festival is held. People set up tents on the riverbank for this purpose, have regular morning baths, eat only a single meal each day, and spend their time in prayer, meditation, and other acts of devotion.

Hindu women in villages and towns get up early in the morning and visit the sacred streams in groups, singing hymns. After their baths, they visit the nearby temples. They also fast and hang lamps in small baskets around their houses or on the tops of the bamboo along the river. These lamps are kept burning throughout the month. The women also worship the Tulsi plant, which is considered sacred and is cultivated in homes and temples. When Tulsi leaves are put into any water, it becomes as holy as water from the Ganges. Tulsi leaves offered to Vishnu during the month of Kartika are said to please him more than the gift of a thousand cows.

SOURCES:
RelHolCal-2004, p. 177

◆ 1384 ◆ Kartini Day
April 21

Kartini Day is an Indonesian holiday commemorating the birth in 1879 of Raden Ajeng Kartini, one of the country's national heroes and a pioneer in the emancipation of Indonesian women. Throughout Indonesia women wear their national dress to symbolize their unity, and the nation enjoys parades, lectures, and various school activities.

Lady Kartini, the daughter of a Javanese nobleman who worked for the Dutch colonial administration, was exposed to Western ideas when she attended a Dutch school. When she had to withdraw from school because she was of noble birth, she corresponded with Dutch friends telling of her concern both for the plight of Indonesians under colonial rule and for the restricted lives of Indonesian women. She married in 1903 and began a fight for the right of women to be educated and against the unwritten but all-pervading Javanese law, *Adat*.

She died in 1904 at the age of 25, after the birth of her first child. Her letters were published in 1911 under the title, *Door duisternis tot licht* ("Through Darkness into Light"), and created support for the Kartini Foundation, which opened the first girls' school in Java in 1916.

CONTACTS:
Indonesian Embassy
2020 Massachusetts Ave. N.W.
Washington, D.C. 20036
202-775-5200; fax: 202-775-5365
www.embassyofindonesia.org

SOURCES:
BkHolWrld-1986, Apr 21

◆ 1385 ◆ Karwachoth
October-November; fourth day of waning half of Hindu month of Kartika

Observed by married women in Hindu families, the Karwachoth festival is a day-long fast in honor of the Hindu god Shiva and goddess Parvati, whom they hope will bring prosperity and long life to their husbands. It is also a time for mothers to bless their married daughters and present them with gifts. Virgins and widows are not allowed to participate in the celebrations, which begin at dawn when the women bathe and put on new clothes. The day is devoted to worshipping Shiva and Parvati, and the fast is broken at night when the moon rises.

See also SAVITRI-VRATA

SOURCES:
FolkWrldHol-1999, p. 623
RelHolCal-2004, p. 178

◆ 1386 ◆ Kasone Festival of Watering the Banyan Tree
Mid-April to May; full moon day of Burmese month of Kasone

The most important of the 12 Burmese festivals of the months, **Kasone Full Moon Day**—sometimes known as **Buddha Day**—celebrates the birth and the enlightenment of the Buddha at the foot of the banyan tree. Buddhists in Myanmar (Burma) gather at monasteries and precept halls to practice meditation, to make charitable donations, and to observe the precepts of Buddhism. Another ritual associated with this day is the pouring of water, both individually and collectively, to celebrate the preservation of the banyan tree. Because Kasone is a hot, dry month, fish are often transferred from streams, ponds, and tanks to places where there is more water.

CONTACTS:
Embassy of the Union of Myanmar
2300 S St. N.W.
Washington, D.C. 20008
202-332-3344; fax: 202-332-4351
www.mewashingtondc.com

SOURCES:
FolkWrldHol-1999, p. 184

◆ 1387 ◆ Kasuga Matsuri
March 13

The Kasuga Shrine in Nara is one of the most beautiful and ancient in Japan. Every year on March 13 a festival is held there with elaborate ceremonies and performances that recall the shrine's heyday. The *hiki-uma* horse ceremony, where a sacred horse is led in procession through the streets, and the elegant *Yamato-mai* dance performed by Shinto women are reminiscent of the culture and customs of the Nara and Heian Eras. Construction of the Kasuga Shrine was started during the Nara period (710-784) and was completed in the first years of the Heian period (794-1185).

CONTACTS:
Japan Information Network, Japan Center for Intercultural Communications
2-7-7 Hirakawacho
Chiyodaku
Tokyo, 102-0093 Japan
81-3-3263-5041; fax: 81-3-3230-4107
home.jcic.or.jp/en/index-e.html

SOURCES:
IllFestJapan-1993, p. 30
JapanFest-1965, p. 132

◆ 1388 ◆ Kataklysmos, Feast of (Festival of the Flood)
Between May 10 and June 13; coincides with Christian Pentecost

This religious and popular festival is celebrated only on Cyprus, with its roots in both the Bible and Greek mythology. The Greek word *kataklysmos,* meaning "flood," refers to the Bible's story in the book of Genesis, and a Greek creation story.

In Genesis 6:5-9:1, God decided all humankind was corrupt and that he would bring a flood to destroy all life—except for Noah, his wife, their sons and their sons' wives, and male and female specimens of every beast and fowl. Noah built an ark for this menagerie, and they all lived on it while it rained for 40 days and 40 nights, eventually landing, it is thought, on Mt. Ararat. (*See also* ASHURA.) When the flood ended, God told Noah and his family to be fruitful and replenish the earth.

In the Greek story, Zeus decided to destroy the earth because of human wickedness. Floods covered the earth, leaving only a spot of dry land on top of Mt. Parnassus. After it had rained nine days and nine nights, a great wooden chest drifted to the spot. Within it were Deucalion, the son of Prometheus, and his wife Pyrrha. Prometheus, knowing the flood was coming, had told his son to build the chest and embark in it.

Coming down from the mountain into a dead world, Deucalion and Pyrrha heard a voice telling them to "cast behind you the bones of your mother." They realized the earth was the mother, and stones her bones. They began to throw the stones, and the stones took human shape. They were called Stone People, and rescued the earth from desolation.

Biblical scholars have suggested that the flood described in Genesis is based on the one from ancient Mesopotamian literature, especially in the Gilgamesh Epic, whose hero is called Ut-Napishtim. In this story, the gods bring on the flood because mankind is so noisy they cannot sleep. After the flood, Ut-Napishtim is made a god.

The Kataklysmos festivities, held in seaside towns, usually last from Saturday through Monday. They include games, folk dancing, boat races, swimming competitions, feasting, and the singing of *tchattista*, improvised verses sung in competition. Everyone joins in throwing water at each other, which symbolizes the purification of body and soul. Larnaca is especially known for its celebration of Kataklysmos, and other festivals are held in Limassol, Paphos, Polis, Agia Napa, and Paralimni.

CONTACTS:
Cyprus Tourism Organization
13 E. 40th St.
New York, NY 10016
212-683-5280; fax: 212-683-5282
www.visitcyprus.com

SOURCES:
BkHolWrld-1986, Jun 8
FolkWrldHol-1999, p. 386
IntlThFolk-1979, p. 86

◆ 1389 ◆ **Kataragama Festival**
June-July; 10 days and nights prior to full moon day of Hindu month of Asadha

Kataragama is considered one of the 16 holiest pilgrimage sites in Sri Lanka and is venerated not only by Hindus but by Buddhists and even Muslims. There is a shrine there dedicated to SKANDA, the Hindu god of war, and his consort Valli. Their union is commemorated by taking the god's *yantra,* or icon, from his temple to the temple dedicated to Valli at the opposite end of the town square. It is carried on the back of an elephant to the accompaniment of conch shells and the clamor of thousands of pilgrims, both Hindu and Buddhist, who gather in Kataragama to watch and to undergo penances.

The climax of the festival is the fire-walking ceremony, where devotees walk across a bed of red-hot embers without burning their feet. Other pilgrims walk on shoes with interior spikes, pull carts with lines attached to hooks in their flesh, or dance until they are completely exhausted.

The festival, which is also known as the **Perahära,** concludes at the exact hour of the full moon with a water-cutting ceremony. The priest, along with Skanda's yantra, is lowered into the river. He draws a mandala in the riverbed with a sword and then bathes the god's image. After this symbolic exercise, the pilgrims plunge themselves into the sacred stream in the belief that it will wash away their sins.

CONTACTS:
Kataragama Devotees Trust of Sri Lanka
c/o Living Heritage Trust of Sri Lanka
Nuala, Koslanda
Badulla, Sri Lanka
94-11-69-8255
www.kataragama.org

SOURCES:
DictWrldRel-1989, p. 569
IntlThFolk-1979, p. 345
RelFestSriLank-1982, p. 302

◆ 1390 ◆ **Kattestoet (Festival of the Cats)**
Second Sunday in May; parade every three years (2009, 2012, 2015 . . .)

A peculiar celebration to commemorate an event involving cats, Kattestoet is held in Ieper (Ypres), West Flanders, Belgium. There are different stories about how the festival began. One story says that in 962, Baudoin III, count of Flanders, threw several live cats from his castle tower to show

that he wasn't awed by cats. The animals had historically been worshipped as creatures related to witches, and Baudoin, a recent Christian convert, was demonstrating that he didn't believe in such pagan ideas.

Another story is that cats in great numbers were needed in the Middle Ages to battle mice and rats. The Cloth Hall, where yearly sales of cloth and garments were held, attracted mice, and cats were set free to devour the mice. But once the sales were over, the rodent problem disappeared and there was a cat problem. The solution seemed to be to hurl the live cats from the belfry.

In the celebration today, about 2,000 people, dressed as cats, witches, and giants, march in a parade to the tune of bagpipes. Floats depict the history of the town and of feline figures—Puss in Boots, the Egyptian cat-headed goddess Bast, and others. The climax of the celebration comes when a jester throws toy witches and stuffed cloth cats from the town belfry.

CONTACTS:
Dienst Toerisme
Grote Markt 34
Ypres, B 8900 Belgium
32-57-23-92-20; fax: 32-57-239-275
www.ieper.be/ieper_en.aspx?SGREF=10587

SOURCES:
BkHolWrld-1986, May 12
GdWrldFest-1985, p. 21
HolSymbols-2009, p. 438

◆ 1391 ◆ **Kaustinen Folk Music Festival**
Third week in July

Scandinavia's largest international festival of folk music and dance, Finland's Kaustinen Folk Music Festival was founded in 1968 to preserve Finnish folk music, dance, and art. Only Finnish amateur groups participated in the beginning, but in recent years the festival has included performances by groups from Japan, Greenland, Canada, the United States, and other foreign countries. There are scheduled performances in local banquet halls as well as impromptu sidewalk jam sessions and open air competitions among musicians and dancers. Special events include the Kaustinen Cavalcade, a display of local musicians' talents, and a grand folk music parade.

CONTACTS:
Kansantaiteenkeskus-Folk Arts Centre
PL 11
Kaustinen, 69601 Finland
358-6-0207-2911; fax: 358-6-0207-2912
www.kaustinen.net/index.asp?main=3

SOURCES:
GdWrldFest-1985, p. 77
IntlThFolk-1979, p. 95

◆ 1392 ◆ **Kawagoé Matsuri**
Every two years on October 14-15

Only during the Kawagoé Matsuri can festivalgoers view the enormous, elaborate floats of old Edo (the old name for

Tokyo). This is because there are now so many telephone and power lines crisscrossing the streets of Japanese cities that it has become almost impossible for these large floats to participate in parades. Instead, the *mikoshi*, or portable shrines, are often used.

The *hon-matsuri*, or full festival, is held every other year. More than 20 richly decorated parade floats, thought to be reproductions of floats from Tokyo's Kanda-jinja Shrine, are carried through the streets of Kawagoé. In the evening, the floats come together and bump into one another in the center of town—a ceremony known as *Hikkawasé*. *Hyashi* bands—which play traditional Japanese music on the flute, drum, *shamisen* (three-stringed lute), and other instruments—also spar with one another musically, trying their best to interrupt the others' rhythm.

CONTACTS:
Kawagoe City Tourist Bureau
39-19 Wakita Honcho
Kawagoe, Saitama 350-1123 Japan
81-4-9224-8811
www.city.kawagoe.saitama.jp/icity/browser?ActionCo

SOURCES:
IllFestJapan-1993, p. 117

♦ 1393 ♦ **Kazakhstan National Days**
Various

The central Asian nation of Kazakhstan celebrates a number of important holidays. These include NEW YEAR'S DAY (January 1-2), International WOMEN'S DAY (March 8), Nauryz Meiramy, or NAWRUZ (March 22), Unity of the Kazakh People Day (May 1), Victory Day (May 9), Constitution of the Republic of Kazakhstan Day (August 30, 1995), Republic Day (October 25, 1991), and Independence Day (December 16, 1991).

CONTACTS:
Embassy of Kazakhstan
1401 16th St. N.W.
Washington, D.C. 20036
202-232-5488; fax: 202-232-5845
www.kazakhembus.com

♦ 1394 ♦ **Keaw Yed Wakes Festival**
Sunday of or following August 24

Keaw Yed means "cow's head" in Lancastrian dialect, and *Wakes* refers to the annual feast held in Westhoughton, Lancashire, on the Sunday of or following ST. BARTHOLOMEW'S DAY, August 24 (*see* BARTHOLOMEW FAIR).

Dating back more than 400 years, the Wakes started out as a religious festival featuring a grand rushbearing procession in which a cart filled with new rushes, to replace those used in the church pews, moved through the town, ending up at the church where special services were held. After the sermon, the children were given "rush money" to spend at the fair.

But over time, the rushbearing ceremony faded and the festival became primarily an opportunity for merrymaking. (*See also* RUSHBEARING FESTIVAL.) The foods traditionally served at

the festival included pork pasties and frumenty (also called furmenty or furmety), a porridge made from boiled wheat seasoned with sugar, cinnamon, and raisins.

There have been several attempts to explain the association of the cow's head with the Wakes. One story says that some of the town's wealthier citizens donated a cow to be publicly roasted and distributed to the poor. But rivalry between two factions in town led to a brawl, and the cow's head went to the victors, who were then referred to as "Keaw Yeds" by their rivals.

SOURCES:
YrbookEngFest-1954, p. 114

♦ 1395 ♦ **Keene Pumpkin Festival**
October

Every year since 1991, the town of Keene, N.H., has held the Pumpkin Festival, in which tens of thousands of carved and lit pumpkins are displayed on scaffolding. In 2007, a total of 25,644 pumpkins were displayed.

Scaffolding standing some 50 feet high is set up on Gilbo Avenue, Railroad Square, and Main Street in downtown Keene. The scaffolding is arranged as walls and as four massive towers. Pumpkins are carved and displayed in rows on the scaffolding. Local businesses often have a number of pumpkins carved to spell out an advertising slogan. Community groups will carve out mottos. Individuals carve faces or names. In the evening, candles are lit within each pumpkin to form great flickering orange walls that light up the crowds.

Related activities include the largest children's costume parade in New England, a pumpkin pie eating contest, and a pumpkin seed spitting contest. The town set a world record in 1992 for having the most jack-o-lanterns lit at the same time and place. The event is sponsored by Center Stage Cheshire County, a nonprofit organization that aims to keep downtown Keene vibrant and thriving.

CONTACTS:
Center Stage
39 Central Sq. #305
Keene, NH 03431
603-358-5344; fax: 603-358-6531
www.pumpkinfestival.org

♦ 1396 ♦ **Keiro-no-Hi (Respect-for-the-Aged Day)**
September 15

Keiro-no-Hi is a national holiday in Japan set aside as a day to honor the elderly. At community centers entertainments are held and the guests are given small keepsakes and gifts of food—for example, rice cakes dyed red and white, the traditional Japanese colors of happiness.

CONTACTS:
Japan Information Network, Japan Center for Intercultural
  Communications
2-7-7 Hirakawacho
Chiyodaku

Tokyo, 102-0093 Japan
81-3-3263-5041; fax: 81-3-3230-4107
home.jcic.or.jp/en/index-e.html

SOURCES:
AnnivHol-2000, p. 155
FolkWrldHol-1999, p. 558

♦ 1397 ♦ Keller (Helen) Festival
Last weekend in June

A three-day festival in Tuscumbia, Ala., to honor Helen Keller and her remarkable life. Born in Tuscumbia in 1880, she was left blind, deaf, and mute by illness at the age of 19 months. After Helen's parents appealed to Alexander Graham Bell for help in educating the child, 20-year-old Anne Mansfield Sullivan, partially blind and a graduate of the Perkins School for the Blind in Boston, arrived and taught the child by pressing objects and a manual alphabet into Helen's palm. Helen learned to read and write and later graduated cum laude from Radcliffe College. She became widely known for her writings, and toured the world to promote opportunities for other blind and deaf persons. Samuel L. Clemens (Mark Twain) was so moved by her spirit that he likened Miss Keller to St. Joan of Arc.

Festival events include art exhibits, stage shows, musical entertainment, sports tournaments, a parade, and historic tours. At Miss Keller's birthplace, Ivy Green, visitors can see the pump at which Helen learned her first word, "water." The house contains a library of Braille books, a Braille typewriter, and other mementos.

The Miracle Worker, the play by William Gibson about Helen Keller and Anne Sullivan, has been presented since 1962 on Friday and Saturday nights in late June and July on the grounds of Ivy Green. The play opened in New York in 1959, won the Pulitzer Prize in 1960, and was made into a movie in 1962.

CONTACTS:
Colbert County Tourism & Convention Bureau
719 U.S. Hwy. 72 W.
P.O. Box 740425
Tuscumbia, AL 35674
800-344-0783 or 256-383-0783
www.colbertcountytourism.org

♦ 1398 ♦ Kelly (Emmett) Clown Festival
First weekend in May

Houston, Missouri, is the hometown of Emmett Kelly, who was the world's most famous clown. Kelly was born on December 9, 1898, in Sedan, Kansas, but his Irish father moved the family to a farm near Houston when he was six years old. Kelly developed an interest in cartooning, and by the time he left Houston to seek work in Kansas City at the age of 19, he had gained a reputation as an entertainer with his "chalk talk" act, which involved telling a story while sketching on paper with colored chalk.

Best known for his role as "Weary Willie," a sad-faced tramp dressed in tattered clothes who was originally one of his car-

toon characters, Kelly worked for a number of circuses and in 1952 made his motion picture debut in *The Greatest Show on Earth.* He died in Sarasota, Florida, on March 28, 1979—opening day for the Ringling Bros. and Barnum & Bailey Circus in New York.

Houston's Emmett Kelly Clown Festival began in 1988 and is timed to coincide with the opening of the circus season in May. Among the 700 or 800 clowns who participate in the two-day festival are Emmett Kelly's son (Emmett Kelly, Jr.) and grandson (Joseph Kelly), both of whom continue the "Weary Willie" tradition. In addition to the clown parade and performances of clown stunts and skits, there are a number of "chalk talk" storytelling events.

CONTACTS:
Houston Area Chamber of Commerce
810 S. Sam Houston Blvd.
P.O. Box 374
Houston, MO 65483
417-967-2220; fax: 417-967-2178

♦ 1399 ♦ Kenka Matsuri (Roughhouse Festival)
October 14-15

The Kenka Matsuri (Roughhouse Festival) or **Nada Festival** takes place in October in Shirahama, a suburb of the city of Himeji, Japan. Thousands flock to the shrine where the festival is held, first paying their respects to the *kami*, or gods, and then settling in for the entertainment: a procession of *mikoshi*—portable shrines or palanquins that are elaborately carved and decorated, and that can weigh as much as a thousand pounds. The roughhousing starts as teams of mikoshi-bearers jostle each other for position in the procession to the Matsubara Hachiman Shrine. Once they reach the shrine, the palanquin-bearers spin their heavy burden, tilt it to one side, raise it up high in the air, and let it crash to the ground—difficult maneuvers designed to thrill the crowd and win the kami's approval.

The festival ends when the kami are ready to depart for their spirit home. The mikoshi engage in a final battle in an open field, where thousands of cheering spectators take sides and and egg them on. Festival officials eventually call a halt to the mayhem, and the battered mikoshi are returned to the shrine, where they will be repaired and stored until the next year's festival.

See also Yaya Matsuri

CONTACTS:
Hyogo Tourism Association
Hyogo Prefectural Government Bldg. No.1
5-10-1 Shimoyamate-dori, Chuo-ku, Kobe
Hyogo, 650-8567 Japan
81-7-8361-7661; fax: 81-7-8361-7662
www.hyogo-tourism.jp/english/index.html

SOURCES:
YrJapanFest-1974, p. 13

♦ 1400 ♦ Kent State Memorial Day
May 4

When students at Kent State University in Ohio decided to hold a rally to protest the incursion of U.S. military forces into Cambodia during the Vietnam War, no one thought it would end in a national tragedy or that it would mark a turning point in public opinion about the war. But when the Ohio National Guard started firing indiscriminately at the crowd, four Kent State students were killed and nine were wounded—one of whom was paralyzed from the waist down. The next year, three students were convicted on rioting charges, but the eight guardsmen involved in the tragic incident were never tried. A lawsuit brought by the parents of the slain and wounded students ended in an out-of-court settlement.

A candlelight vigil takes place at the Kent State campus every year on May 4, the anniversary of the 1970 shootings. It begins at midnight on May 3, when a candlelight procession winds its way around the campus and stops in a parking lot near the university's Prentice Hall. There, for the next 12 hours, rotating teams of sentinels stand in the places where Allison Krause, Sandy Scheuer, Bill Schroeder, and Jeff Miller were killed. The vigil is coordinated by the May 4 Task Force, a group led by a Kent State graduate and dedicated to promoting campus awareness and preventing a repetition of the violence.

Although the university refused to discuss the tragedy for 10 years after it occurred, nowadays it is commemorated openly—to the point where the May 4 Memorial is featured prominently in the college catalog and a course is offered on "May 4th and Its Aftermath." There are four permanent scholarships named for the dead.

CONTACTS:
Kent State University
108 Michael Schwartz Ctr.
P.O. Box 5190
Kent, OH 44242
330-672-3000; fax: 330-672-4836
www.kent.edu

SOURCES:
AnnivHol-2000, p. 77

◆ 1401 ◆ Kentucky Derby
First Saturday in May

The Kentucky Derby is the greatest and most glamorous horse race in America, run since 1875 in Louisville, Ky. Also known as the **Run for the Roses** because of the garland of roses draped on the winning horse, it is a one-and-one-quarter-mile race for three-year-old thoroughbreds and is the first race in the Triple Crown; the others are the PREAKNESS and the BELMONT STAKES. The site of the race is hallowed Churchill Downs, the track known for its twin spires, built in 1895.

The race is usually run in slightly over two minutes, but in 1964, Northern Dancer was the first to win the Derby in two minutes flat. In 1973, the great Secretariat, fondly known as Big Red, won in 1:59 2/5. That was the only time the Derby was raced in less than two minutes until Monarchos clocked in at 1:59.97 in 2001. Ridden by Ron Turcotte, Secretariat then went on to take the Triple Crown, exploding from the pack to win the Belmont by an unprecedented 31 lengths.

The Derby took its name from the English horse race that was started in 1780 by the 12th Earl of Derby, and Kentuckians hoped to duplicate the social panache of the Epsom Derby (*see* DERBY DAY). They did, in a different way. The Derby became Louisville's major social occasion of the year; women to this day wear their most stylish hats to the racetrack, and there are numerous lavish Derby breakfasts and parties.

Traditional food includes Kentucky ham and beaten biscuits. And, of course, the Derby wouldn't be the Derby without mint juleps, the bourbon-and-mint drink served in cold silver julep cups or in special iced commemorative glasses at the track. Parties are not confined to Louisville; throughout the country and the world, Derby parties are held to watch the race on television. Stephen FOSTER's "My Old Kentucky Home," the official state song, is played as the horses parade to the post, and spectators in Louisville and far away stand and sing and (sometimes) dab their eyes.

Attendance at Churchill Downs is usually 120,000 to 130,000 people—most of them watching what they can from the infield and a select few, often including royalty, from Millionaires Row high in the clubhouse.

Derby Day is the finale of the 10-day Kentucky Derby Festival—a series of events that include a sternwheel steamboat race on the Ohio River, a Pegasus parade, fireworks, concerts, and a coronation ball.

CONTACTS:
Kentucky Derby Festival
1001 S. Third St.
Louisville, KY 40203
502-584-6383
www.kdf.org

Churchill Downs
700 Central Ave.
Louisville, KY 40208
502-636-4400; fax: 502-636-4554
www.kentuckyderby.com

SOURCES:
AmerBkDays-2000, p. 338
AnnivHol-2000, p. 93
FolkAmerHol-1999, p. 222
GdUSFest-1984, p. 63
HolSymbols-2009, p. 441

◆ 1402 ◆ Kenya Madaraka Day
June 1

The Republic of Kenya, on the eastern coast of Africa, is surrounded by Somalia, Ethiopia, Sudan, Uganda, and Tanzania. In the mid-1800s, British settlers arrived in East Africa. They eventually established the East African Protectorate in 1895, which promoted European settlement in some of the most fertile parts of Kenya, forcing the native Kenyans from their land. In some areas, especially in the arid northern half of the country, there were few British settlers.

Even before Kenya was officially made a British colony in 1920, European settlers were allowed to participate in government. However, Africans were prohibited from direct political participation until 1944, at which time a few appointed (but not elected) African representatives were allowed to sit in the legislature.

Between 1952 and 1959, Kenyans began to rebel against British colonial rule and its land policies. This rebellion took place almost exclusively in the highlands of central Kenya, which were home to the Kikuyu people. Detention camps and restricted villages were established to contain the Kikuyu insurgents. Tens of thousands of Kikuyu died in these areas and in the fighting, compared to approximately 650 British deaths.

Following the rebellions, Africans were given many more opportunities to participate in politics. The first elections to elect Africans to the Legislative Council took place in 1957. On June 1, 1963, Kenya became a self-governing country when Jomo Kenyatta, an ethnic Kikuyu and head of the Kenya African National Union (KANU), became the first prime minister. On December 12, 1963, Kenya became an independent nation. One year later, on December 12, 1964, Kenya became a republic, with Kenyatta serving as the president. Kenyans honor their first president by celebrating KENYATTA DAY every year on October 20.

June 1 is a public holiday in Kenya. The day is set aside to commemorate the day that Kenya became a self-ruling nation. On this day, the main event takes place at Nyayo Stadium in Nairobi. The President addresses the nation, and the uniformed military, singers, and traditional dancers from around the country provide entertainment for the crowds.

The day is full of festive activities, including family picnics and games in the public parks. Many people take this opportunity to go back to their hometowns for the occasion, and often a big meal of goat or chicken is prepared for the special day. Retail business in Nairobi is slower on this day, while public transportation to up-country areas is heavier than normal.

CONTACTS:
Ministry of Tourism and Wildlife Office
Utalii House, Off Uhuru Highway
P.O. Box 30027
Nairobi, Kenya
www.tourism.go.ke

◆ 1403 ◆ Kenya Moi Day
October 10

The Republic of Kenya is on the eastern coast of Africa. It is surrounded by Somalia, Ethiopia, Sudan, Uganda, and Tanzania. British settlers arrived in East Africa in the mid-1800s and eventually promoted European settlement in some of the most fertile parts of Kenya, forcing native Kenyans from their land.

Kenya was officially made a British colony in 1920. European settlers were allowed to participate in government, while Africans were not allowed to participate directly in the political arena.

After many years, Africans were given opportunities to participate in politics. The first elections to elect Africans to the Legislative Council took place in 1957. On June 1, 1963, Kenya became a self-ruling country, and then it became an independent country on December 12 of that same year. Kenya's first president was Jomo Kenyatta, an ethnic Kikuyu and head of the Kenya African National Union (KANU). Kenyans honor their first president by celebrating KENYATTA DAY every year on October 20.

When Kenyatta died in August 1978, Vice President Daniel arap Moi became interim president. By October of that year, Moi was elected head of KANU and designated its sole nominee for the presidential election, formally making him president.

Moi was very popular among the people of Kenya. His leadership style involved touring the country and talking with the people everywhere. He emphasized a philosophy of peace, love, and unity then known as Nyayo. This was very different from Kenyatta's imperial style of governing behind closed doors.

Moi won national elections in 1992 and 1997, but his presidency has been marred by controversy, with accusations of election fraud, corruption, and human rights violations. Moi was constitutionally barred from running in the 2002 presidential elections. At this time, he chose to retire. He remains very popular with the Kenyan people and continues to have some behind-the-scenes influence in Kenyan politics.

October 10 is a national holiday in Kenya. The day has been set aside to honor Moi, the county's second president. Moi Day has been celebrated every year since the 10th day of the 10th month, 10 years after the inauguration of Moi as the second president of Kenya. On this day, political speeches are made, and the people of Kenya take the day off work to relax or enjoy sporting events.

CONTACTS:
Ministry of Tourism and Wildlife Office
Utalii House, Off Uhuru Highway
P.O. Box 30027
Nairobi, Kenya
www.tourism.go.ke

◆ 1404 ◆ Kenya Skydive Boogie
November

Every November, the skies over Diani in Kenya bloom with colorful parachutes during the three-week-long Skydive Boogie, a major event that typically attracts dozens of divers from at least 15 countries. They include members of skydiving clubs and specialist skydive formation teams, as well as novices who may choose a tandem jump for their first skydiving experience. Participants appreciate the excellent weather, wind, and logistical conditions at Diani: because it is located at sea level, divers can experience a full one-minute accelerated free fall from 14,000 feet, compared with the average free-fall duration of 30 seconds. Divers land directly on the beach outside their hotel, and after a short rest, can climb back aboard a plane at Ukunda airstrip, 10 minutes away.

With such convenient logistics, some participants have been able to fit up to 19 dives in a single day. The Boogie was launched in 1989 by Harro Trempeneau of Kenya Skydivers, the group that still organizes it.

CONTACTS:
Kenya Tourist Office
2249 R St. N.W.
Washington, D.C. 20008
202-387-6101
www.magicalkenya.com

◆ 1405 ◆ Kenyatta Day
October 20

The Republic of Kenya is on the eastern coast of Africa. It is surrounded by Somalia, Ethiopia, Sudan, Uganda, and Tanzania. British settlers arrived in East Africa in the mid-1800s and eventually promoted European settlement in some of the most fertile parts of Kenya, forcing the native Kenyans from their land.

Kenya was officially made a British colony in 1920. European settlers were allowed to participate in government, while Africans were not allowed to directly participate in the political arena.

Between 1952 and 1959, Kenyans rebelled against British colonial rule and its land policies. One of the people involved in those rebellions was Jomo Kenyatta, who became the nation's first president. Following the rebellions, Africans were given many more opportunities to participate in politics. The first elections to elect Africans to the Legislative Council took place in 1957. On June 1, 1963, Kenya became a self-ruling country, and then it became an independent country on December 12 of that same year. Kenya's first president was Jomo Kenyatta, an ethnic Kikuyu and head of the Kenya African National Union (KANU).

During his time as president, Kenyatta saw Kenya join the United Nations, promoted education and private enterprise, helped modernize the nation through government-financed technical training and new job opportunities, created trade agreements with neighboring states, and passionately opposed Communism at a time when many newly emerging post-colonial African nations were accepting financing from Russia, China, and Cuba for "freedom struggles." Under Kenyatta's leadership, Kenya grew to be a stable nation, even though there was chaos and civil war in other parts of Africa. This attracted foreign investment in Kenya.

Kenyatta faced criticism, too. He was accused of being too close to Britain, favoring his native Kikuyu tribe, and favoring friends and family when land was granted for development.

Kenyatta died on August 22, 1978, and was succeeded by then Vice President Daniel arap Moi. Kenya celebrates MOI DAY every year on October 10 to honor their second president.

In Kenya, October 20 is a national holiday called Kenyatta Day. It was on this day in 1952 that Kenyatta was arrested and sentenced to seven years in prison with hard labor. He was accused of being involved with the Mau Mau movement, a group that fought against British rule. It was later found that Kenyatta had not been involved with the group.

On Kenyatta Day, a ceremony takes place at Nyayo Stadium in Nairobi. The president addresses the nation and inspects the guard of honor. The ceremony includes a military parade, and singers and traditional dancers from around the country provide entertainment for the crowds.

CONTACTS:
Ministry of Tourism and Wildlife Office
Utalii House, Off Uhuru Highway
P.O. Box 30027
Nairobi, Kenya
www.tourism.go.ke

◆ 1406 ◆ Keretkun Festival
Late autumn

The Chukchi people of northeastern Siberia hold a two- or three-day celebration in late autumn known as the Keretkun Festival, in honor of the "owner" of all the sea animals on which they depend for their livelihood. The purpose of the festival is to symbolically return all the animals that had been killed during the hunting season to the sea, thus replenishing the resource that had been plundered. Objects used in the celebration include a special net made out of reindeer tendons, painted oars, statues of birds, and a small wooden image of Keretkun, which is burned at the end of the festival.

A similar festival is held by the Koryak people, another group that depends upon sea animals for survival. The **Seal Festival** is held at the end of the hunting season in November, and the participants plead with the animals they've killed to return to the sea and let themselves be caught again next year. The dead animals are represented by stylized likenesses made out of seaweed.

CONTACTS:
Russian Travel Information Office
224 W. 30th St., Ste. 701
New York, NY 10001
877-221-7120 or 646-473-2233; fax: 646-473-2205
www.russia-travel.com

SOURCES:
FolkWrldHol-1999, pp. 631, 626

◆ 1407 ◆ Keukenhof Flower Show
Late March-late May

The world's largest flower show takes place in Lisse, South Holland, Netherlands, at the Keukenhof, a former 15th-century estate and hunting lodge that has been turned into a park dotted with lakes. As many as five or six million bulbs blossom here between late March and the end of May, either in hothouses or in the flowerbeds that border the ponds and fountains. There is a museum in Lisse devoted to the history and cultivation of bulbs, and young girls (*meisjes*) in 15th-century dress sell guidebooks to help acquaint visitors with the 800 varieties of tulips, hyacinths, and daffodils that fill the 70-acre park with color. Thousands of people flock to the gardens each spring, although some prefer to view the bulbs from the windows of the Leyden-Haarlem train.

CONTACTS:
Keukenhof
Stationsweg 166a
Lisse, 2161 AM Netherlands
31-252-465-555; fax: 31-252-465-565
www.keukenhof.nl/nm/english.html

SOURCES:
GdWrldFest-1985, p. 142

♦ 1408 ♦ **Kewpiesta**
Third weekend in April

The Kewpie doll, which was very popular in the 1920s and 1930s, was the creation of Rose O'Neill, a writer, artist, and sculptor from the Ozark region of Missouri. Modeled on her baby brother, the kewpie doll had a pointed tuft of hair at the top of the head.

The annual four-day event known as Kewpiesta is held in Branson, about 10 miles south of O'Neill's homestead. Planned and sponsored by members of the National Rose O'Neill Club, the festival includes tours of O'Neill's birthplace, a Kewpie doll look-alike contest, and special displays in store windows. It is held in April, which is the month during which O'Neill died in 1944 as well as the start of the tourist season in the Ozarks.

CONTACTS:
International Rose O'Neill Club Foundation
2013 Ridgeway Dr.
Denison, IA 51442
www.irocf.org

SOURCES:
GdUSFest-1984, p. 104

♦ 1409 ♦ **Khamis al-Amwat**
Between March 26 and April 29; Thursday after Easter

Also known as **Dead Remembrance Thursday**, the observation of this day by Muslims was instituted by Saladin the Magnificent (1137-1193) to offset the widespread celebration in Jordan of EASTER by the Christians and of PASSOVER by the Jews. It is a day to pay respects at burial grounds and offer dyed eggs to children. Before World War II, it became a three-day holiday, which included **Ziyarit al-Nabi Musi,** a visit to the shrine of Moses, or simply **al-Ziyara,** "the Visit."

In Jerusalem on Saturday of HOLY WEEK (*see* HOLY SATURDAY), Muslims hold the feast of Nebi Mousa for the same reason. Peasants from the countryside arrive in great numbers and go to the mosque near the Dome of the Rock. Old green war banners are unfurled and there is a parade to the shrine of Moses near the Dead Sea which can last for several hours.

CONTACTS:
Jordan Embassy
3504 International Dr. N.W.
Washington, D.C. 20008
202-966-2664; fax: 202-966-3110
www.jordanembassyus.org

SOURCES:
FolkWrldHol-1999, p. 234

♦ 1410 ♦ **Khordad 15 Revolt, Anniversary of the**
Khordad 15

Mohammad Reza Shah Pahlavi was the monarch of Iran from 1941 to 1979. During his reign, on June 5, 1963, the government arrested Ayatollah Ruhollah Khomeini, an event that proved to be pivotal in building support for the resistance against the Shah and his Western-supported regime.

The authorities had apprehended Khomeini two days after he delivered an incendiary speech to Islamic students at a *madrassa.* In several towns throughout Iran, large numbers of citizens turned out to demonstrate against the government upon hearing news of Khomeini's arrest. The country was in a state of upheaval for six days, and thus was born the Movement of Khordad 15, named after the Iranian calendar date on which the ayatollah was arrested.

Demonstrations continued on the anniversary of the arrest for 15 years leading up to Khomeini's rise to power. In 1975, one fateful rally held in Khomeini's hometown of Qom was crushed by the Iranian army, resulting in the deaths of many protesters.

In February 1979, millions greeted Khomeini when he returned from 15 years of exile. By the end of the following month, Iranians passed a national referendum to establish an Islamic Republic based on a new constitution. The Shah was removed from power, and Khomeini installed a theocratic government.

Protests became less common after 1979, since Khomeini successfully had fulfilled the mission of the Khordad 15 movement. In the years following the ayatollah's death in 1989, which occurred on Khordad 14, the elaborate memorials for the revered leader began overshadowing the observances of the anniversary the following day.

CONTACTS:
Iran's Ministry of Foreign Affairs
Imam Khomeini Sq.
Tehran, Iran

♦ 1411 ♦ **Khordad Sal**
March, July, August; sixth day of Frawardin, the first Zoroastrian month

The Parsis of India, descendants of the original Zoroastrian immigrants from Iran (formerly Persia), celebrate the birthday of their founder on this day. Zoroaster (or Zarathushtra, c. 1200 B.C.E.) was a Persian prophet and religious reformer whose ideas combined both monotheism and dualism in the worship of Ahura Mazda, the Wise Lord, and his evil opponent, Ahriman. The largest group of Zoroastrians today can be found in India, where they are known as Parsis (or Parsees), although there are still isolated groups of Zoroastrians in Iran.

Zoroaster's birth is observed in March by the Fasli sect, in July by the Kadmi sect, and in August by the Shahenshai sect.

See also FARVARDEGAN DAYS

SOURCES:
AnnivHol-2000, p. 48
FolkWrldHol-1999, p. 518

◆ 1412 ◆ Kiamichi Owa-Chito (Festival of the Forest)
Third weekend in June

A celebration of southeastern Oklahoma's forestry industry and of the culture of the Choctaw Indians of the area, Kiamichi Owa-Chito is held in Beavers Bend Resort Park near Broken Bow. Shortleaf and loblolly pines are abundant in the region, which is the heart of Oklahoma's timberland. The mistletoe, Oklahoma's state flower, also flourishes here. The Forest Heritage Center in the park has exhibits that include petrified logs, tools of the forestry industry, and dioramas.

Sporting events of the festival include canoe races, archery, and log birling (log rolling). Other activities range from contests in turkey and owl calling and a spelling bee to art and photography exhibits and musical entertainment—gospel singing, fiddling, and bluegrass.

CONTACTS:
Beavers Bend Resort Park
P.O. Box 10
Broken Bow, OK 74728
580-494-6179
www.beaversbend.com

Broken Bow Chamber of Commerce
113 W. Martin Luther King
Broken Bow, OK 74728
800-528-7337 or 580-584-3393; fax: 580-584-7698
www.brokenbowchamber.com

SOURCES:
GdUSFest-1984, p. 144

◆ 1413 ◆ Kiddies' Carnival
Between January and March; the week before Carnival

The country of Trinidad and Tobago, located in the West Indies, offers a CARNIVAL celebration for children that mirrors the famous parades for adults. The week before Carnival begins children march in a big parade of their own. The children themselves choose a theme (such as "Arabian Nights") and, with the help of adult family members, create costumes that illustrate their theme. Dressed in beautiful costumes the children sing and dance their way down the streets, moving

to Calypso music or doing the "jump-up," a popular Trinidadian dance.

CONTACTS:
National Library and Information System Authority of Trinidad and Tobago
National Library Bldg., Hart and Abercromby St.
Port-of-Spain, Trinidad and Tobago
868-623-6962; fax: 868-625-6096
www.nalis.gov.tt

SOURCES:
BkHolWrld-1986, Feb 19

◆ 1414 ◆ Kiel Week
Last full week in June

Kiel Week is an international sailing regatta in Kiel, Germany, at which the world's leading yachters compete. Craft of all sorts—sail, motor, and muscle-powered—race on the waters of the Kiel Fjord. Kiel, once the chief naval port of Germany, is a center of inshore and deep-sea fishing, and was host for the sailing races of the 1972 OLYMPIC GAMES.

Kiel Week began in 1882 with 20 yachts. Today there are well over 1,000 yachts competing in three classes of races—international, Olympic, and offshore regattas—as well as more than 1,000 events ranging from talks by international political leaders to such cultural events as art exhibits, theater, and music.

CONTACTS:
Sporthafen Kiel GmbH
Dusternbrooker Weg 2D sternbrooker Weg 2
Kiel, 24105 Germany
49-431-579-59-60; fax: 49-431-579-59-697
www.kieler-woche.de/eng/englishdefault.php

SOURCES:
IntlThFolk-1979, p. 142

◆ 1415 ◆ Khomeini (Ayatollah), Death Anniversary of
Khordad 14

An estimated 6 to 11 million people gathered for the funeral of Ayatollah Ruhollah Khomeini, who had led as Supreme Leader of Iran from 1979 until his death on June 3, 1989. Observances of his death anniversary today do not draw as many participants as did his funeral. But the **Heart-Rending Departure of the Great Leader of the Islamic Republic of Iran**, as the celebration is officially known, is still widely commemorated throughout the country. The event draws thousands of foreigners to the Khomeini mausoleum, a massive structure near Tehran that has become an established pilgrimage site for Shi'ite Muslims.

As with many Shi'ite holidays of mourning, the anniversary of Khomeini's death is marked by dramatic expressions of grief. Many people display black flags and carry posters of the ayatollah. Along with visiting the leader's mausoleum, people will also spend the day in Khomein, the village of his birth, and in Qom, the holy city where he received his Islamic training.

In 2008, Iran held a special five-day celebration that included speeches by Ayatollah Ali Khamenei and the country's president, Mahmoud Ahmadinejad.

The Iranian calendar differs slightly from the Gregorian calendar, which means the date of commemoration also does not line up exactly with its Gregorian counterpart.

CONTACTS:
Iran's Ministry of Foreign Affairs
Imam Khomeini Sq.
Tehran, Iran

SOURCES:
AnnivHol-2000, p. 95
CultureCustomsIran-2006, p. 180

♦ 1416 ♦ Kilkenny Arts Festival
Mid-August

Kilkenny Arts Festival, one of Ireland's oldest and largest international arts festivals, is held annually over 10 days in August in the medieval town of Kilkenny in southeast Ireland. A group of classical music enthusiasts founded the festival in 1974. It now presents an extensive program of music, including classical, jazz, world and traditional styles, as well as theatre, dance, visual art, literature, film, and young people's events. In addition, the festival features lively street performances. The non-profit Kilkenny Arts Festival is dedicated to presenting leading Irish artists, as well as international artists who would not otherwise be seen in Ireland. Drawn by the festival's reputation for innovation and high standards, about 80,000 visitors partake of the festival each year.

CONTACTS:
Kilkenny Arts Festival
9/10 Abbey Business Centre
Abbey St.
Kilkenny, Ireland
www.kilkennyarts.ie/events/index.php

Irish Tourist Board
345 Park Ave.
New York, NY 10154
800-669-9967 or 212-418-0800; fax: 212-371-9052
www.tourismireland.com

♦ 1417 ♦ Killing the Pigs, Festival of
September

In rural areas of Estonia, the Festival of Killing the Pigs traditionally has been celebrated sometime in September. Each village has a few men who are skilled in time-honored methods of slaughtering animals and preparing the meat. On the day of the festival, the women prepare a meal of pork, vodka, and "blood bread"—flour mixed with the animal's blood that is boiled, and then often fried, before it is eaten. After the meal is over, neighbors get together and spend the evening singing and dancing.

SOURCES:
BkFest-1937, p. 106

♦ 1418 ♦ Kim Il-Sung, Birthday of
April 15

The birthday of the late North Korean leader Kim Il-Sung on April 15, 1912, is marked as a public holiday throughout North Korea (official name: Democratic People's Republic of Korea). The holiday is known as the **Day of the Sun**. All over the country, people lay floral wreaths and baskets before the hundreds of statues that commemorate Kim. The main observances take place in the capital city Pyongyang, where officials of numerous organizations and citizens lay flowers at one of the nation's grandest monuments to Kim, located on Mansu Hill.

The late leader's birthday celebration often coincides with the Araring Festival, named after a famous Korean folk song. During the renowned mass games of the festival, up to 100,000 participants take part in various large-scale synchronized dance and gymnastics displays in Pyongyang's 150,000-seat May Day stadium. Tens of thousands of well-trained school children create an effect close to animation in the stadium's stands by flashing colored flashcards in intricately timed routines.

Kim Il-Sung ruled North Korea from 1945 until his death in 1994. Known in his country as the "Great Leader," he is proclaimed in the national constitution as the "eternal president." The current leader of North Korea is his son, Kim Jong-Il. Both men are publicly adulated under the "cult of personality" that was part of Kim Il-Sung's distinctive political philosophy. Today, North Korea is a Communist country with a repressive government.

CONTACTS:
Permanent Representative of the Democratic People's Republic of
    Korea to the United Nations
820 Second Ave.
New York, NY 10017
212-972-3105; fax: 212-972-3154
www.korea-dpr.com

♦ 1419 ♦ Kim Jong-Il, Birthday of
February 16-17

The birth date of North Korean leader Kim Jong-Il (February 16, 1941) is marked with a two-day public holiday observed throughout the country. Large-scale public celebrations—including mass gymnastics displays, musical performances, fireworks, and military demonstrations—are centered in the capital city of Pyongyang. Smaller-scale displays take place in towns and villages throughout North Korea (official name: Democratic People's Republic of Korea). Special horticultural exhibitions feature the Kimjongilia, a flower cultivated to bloom around Kim's birthday. In a country with food and energy shortages, the government also often marks Kim's birthday by allotting North Koreans extra food or electricity.

The Kims have ruled the country since 1945, when Kim Jong-Il's father, Kim Il-Sung, took control of the northern half of the Korean Peninsula. His son was designated his successor in 1980. When the father, Kim Il Sung, died 1994, the son, Kim Jong-Il, became the country's leader. His official title is chairman of the national defense commission, but he is proclaimed in his country as the "sun of the 21st century." Both he and his father are publicly adulated under the "cult of personality" that was part of Kim Il-Sung's distinctive political philosophy. Today, North Korea is a Communist country with a repressive government.

CONTACTS:
Permanent Representative of the Democratic People's Republic of
  Korea to the United Nations
820 Second Ave.
New York, NY 10017
212-972-3105; fax: 212-972-3154
www.korea-dpr.com

◆ 1420 ◆ **Kinderzeche (Children's Party)**
Third full week in July

Kinderzeche is a festival in Dinkelsbühl, Bavaria, Germany, to honor the children who saved the town during the Thirty Years' War of 1618-48. In 1632, according to legend, the Swedish commander, a Colonel Sperreuth, threatened destruction of the town (which endured eight sieges during the war). The town council was debating its response, when a gatekeeper's daughter named Lore proposed gathering a group of children together to appeal to Sperreuth. The council agreed to let her try. As the Swedish troops rode into town, the children sang, and Lore with her small band of children appeared before the commander, knelt, and asked his mercy. The commander's heart softened; he spared the town, and told the citizens, "Children are the rescuers of Dinkelsbühl. Always remember the debt of thanks you owe them."

The celebration today is a reenactment of the event, with participants (most of them Dinkelsbühl residents) in the costume of 17th-century town councilors and soldiers. Highlights of the festival include the parade of the Dinkelsbühl Boys' Band and a performance of a medieval sword dance, in which dancers stand on top of a pedestal of crossed blades. About 300,000 visitors attend the festival.

Dinkelsbühl is about 20 miles from Rothenburg-on-the-Tauber, Germany, which also commemorates an event of the Thirty Years' War with the MEISTERTRUNK PAGEANT.

CONTACTS:
Dinkelsbuhl Touristik Service
Marktplatz
Dinkelsbuhl, D-91550 Germany
49-9851-902-40; fax: 49-9851-552-61-9
www.dinkelsbuehl.de/ISY/index.php?PHPSESSID=cedad8

SOURCES:
BkHolWrld-1986, Jul 16
IntlThFolk-1979, p. 137

◆ 1421 ◆ **King (Martin Luther, Jr.), Birthday**
Federal holiday: third Monday in January;
birthday: January 15

In 1955 Rosa Parks, a black seamstress in Montgomery, Alabama, refused to obey a bus driver's order to give up her seat to a white male passenger. She was fined $14 for her defiance of the Jim Crow (segregationist) law that required blacks to sit in the rear of buses, and if the bus were crowded, to give up their seat to a white passenger. The incident led to a citywide bus boycott and raised its leader, the young black Baptist minister Dr. Martin Luther King, Jr., to national prominence.

King went on to establish the Southern Christian Leadership Conference, to win the Nobel Peace Prize, and to play an active role in the civil rights movement of the 1960s. He was in Memphis, Tennessee, on April 4, 1968, organizing a strike of the city's predominantly black sanitation workers, when he was shot to death at the age of 39 by James Earl Ray.

Martin Luther King Day is a federal holiday, the only one that honors a person who was not a president; federal government offices are closed on that day. It has become a focal point for recognition of African-American history and the American civil rights movement led by Dr. King. It is also a legal holiday in all 50 states, since New Hampshire signed its King holiday legislation into law in 1999. In Alabama it became **Martin Luther King and Robert E. Lee's Birthday**, observed on the third Monday in January. The same day in Virginia is called **Lee-Jackson-King Day**, combining Dr. King's birthday with those of Robert E. Lee and Andrew "Stonewall" Jackson (*see also* LEE DAY, ROBERT E. and JACKSON'S BIRTHDAY, ANDREW). In schools, the day is often observed with special lessons and assembly programs dealing with Dr. King's life and work.

See also BRIDGE CROSSING JUBILEE

CONTACTS:
The Martin Luther King, Jr. Center for Nonviolent Social Change,
  Inc.
449 Auburn Ave. N.E.
Atlanta, GA 30312
404-526-8900
www.thekingcenter.com

Library of Congress
101 Independence Ave. S.E.
Washington, DC 20540
202-707-5000; fax: 202-707-8366
www.loc.gov

SOURCES:
AAH-2007, p. 298
AmerBkDays-2000, pp. 72, 254
AnnivHol-2000, p. 9
BkHolWrld-1986, Jan 15
DictDays-1988, p. 73
DictWrldRel-1989, p. 407
HolSymbols-2009, p. 541
PatHols-2006, p. 185
RelHolCal-2004, p. 90

◆ 1422 ◆ **King (Martin Luther, Jr.) Drum Major for Justice Parade, Battle of the Bands & Drum Line Extravaganza, National**
Monday in mid-January

The National Martin Luther King Jr. Drum Major for Justice Parade, Battle of the Bands & Drum Line Extravaganza is a celebration held annually in St. Petersburg, Fla., on the BIRTH-

DAY OF MARTIN LUTHER KING JR. federal holiday. The event is organized by the Martin Luther King Jr. Holiday & Legacy Association Inc. and led by Sevell Carescale Brown III, whose original idea gave rise to the celebration. Through a grand pageant showcasing the talents of black college students, Brown sought to honor Dr. King's legacy as a "drum major for justice" while encouraging young people to aspire to higher education. The first parade was held on January 20, 1986, the year that Dr. King's birthday was first commemorated as a federal holiday.

To participate in the parade and competition, marching bands travel from historically black colleges and universities throughout the South, including Alabama, Arkansas, Georgia, Mississippi, North Carolina, South Carolina, and Texas. Among the participants are Bethune Cookman University, Florida A & M University, Morehouse College, and the 300-member Historically Black Colleges & Universities All-Star Band, with members drawn from several schools. The parade, which begins at the intersection of Third Avenue South and Dr. Martin Luther King Jr. Street, travels 1.3 miles to South Vinoy Park and is attended by approximately 100,000 spectators. Following the parade, a high-energy band competition gets underway at Tropicana Field Dome Stadium. Scholarships are available to participating band members, and an awards banquet is held on the Friday preceding the parade.

CONTACTS:
Martin Luther King, Jr. Holiday & Legacy Association, Inc.
P.O. Box 12732
St. Petersburg, FL 33733
727-327-6555
www.mlknationalparade.org

♦ 1423 ♦ Kingdom Days
Last weekend in June

This annual festival in Fulton, Missouri, was based on a Civil War confrontation between a Union general and the local militia. On July 28, 1861, there was a battle near Calwood that left 19 dead and 76 wounded. In an effort to spare Callaway County any further bloodshed, Colonel Jefferson Jones sent a letter to General John B. Henderson, commander of the Union military forces in northeastern Missouri. Jones requested that the county be left alone to conduct its own business and to control its own destiny. Henderson, perhaps fearing stiff resistance, agreed to the truce and signed the treaty that designated Callaway County a "kingdom," separate from both the U.S. and the Confederacy. No shots were fired, no one was injured, and the disagreements between the two military units were settled peacefully.

This event was only one of the historic reenactments that took place during the Kingdom Days festival. Others were more humorous, such as the "shotgun" Civil War-era wedding in 1991. Other events have included a parade, bed races, a "baby derby" in which babies up to 18 months old crawl 10 feet to the finish line, a hot air balloon rally, and a pig-kissing contest.

CONTACTS:
Kingdom of Callaway Chamber of Commerce
409 Court St.

Fulton, MO 65251
800-257-3554 or 573-642-3055; fax: 573-642-5182
www.callawaychamber.com

♦ 1424 ♦ King's Birthday (Belgium)
November 15

King Leopold I (1790-1865) of Belgium was named after ST. LEOPOLD, whose feast is celebrated on this day. He was the first leader of Belgium after it achieved independence from the Netherlands in 1831, and reigned until his death. Also known as **Dynasty Day**, or **Fête de la Dynastie**, the day is a major observance particularly among Belgium's German-speaking community.

CONTACTS:
Embassy of Belgium
3330 Garfield St. N.W.
Washington, D.C. 20008
202-333-6900; fax: 202-338-4960
www.diplobel.org

SOURCES:
AnnivHol-2000, p. 191

♦ 1425 ♦ King's Birthday (Denmark)
March 11

Though no longer observed, the birthday of Frederick IX of Denmark (1899-1972) was a national holiday in that country, marked by patriotic speeches and parades. Soldiers in uniform would march down the main street of Copenhagen, the capital, accompanied by military bands. This was also an occasion for singing Denmark's two national anthems, "Kong Kristian Stod Ved Hojen Mast" ("King Kristian Stood Beside the Lofty Mast") and "Der Er Et Yndigt Land" ("This Is a Lovely Land"). The words of the former were written by Johannes Ewald and translated into English by the well-known American poet, Henry Wadsworth Longfellow.

Frederick IX became king of Denmark in 1947 and ruled until his death in 1972. He is remembered for the encouragement he gave to the Danish resistance movement against the German occupation during World War II. In fact, from 1943-45 he was imprisoned by the Germans along with his father, Christian X.

Frederick's daughter, Margrethe, is the current queen of Denmark (*see* Queen MARGRETHE'S BIRTHDAY).

CONTACTS:
Embassy of Denmark
3200 Whitehaven St. N.W.
Washington, D.C. 20008
202-234-4300; fax: 202-328-1470
www.ambwashington.um.dk

SOURCES:
NatlHolWrld-1968, p. 32

♦ 1426 ♦ King's Birthday (Lesotho)
July 17

Veneration for royalty is still customary for the Basotho, the majority group living in the Kingdom of Lesotho. As recently as 1993, the monarch of Lesotho, a tiny country enclosed within South Africa, had full executive power. Accordingly, the birthday of monarch King Letsie III is a momentous occasion.

Born in 1963, King Letsie is the son of King Moshoeshoe II, who became Lesotho's first monarch after the country gained full independence from Great Britain in 1966. Letsie briefly claimed rule between 1990 and 1995, the years when Moshoeshoe II was in exile. With his father's death in 1996, Letsie permanently inherited the throne, although by this stage a newly introduced constitution had demoted Lesotho's status to "living symbol of national unity," which essentially meant he no longer possessed executive or legislative powers.

Many citizens honor the king on his birthday by attending his parade, at which he appears in regal attire and is usually accompanied by his wife, Queen Masenate Mohato Seeiso. In 2003, the royal family announced that in the years to come the official festivities will change location each year to ensure that more residents of the country's ten districts can enjoy greater participation in the celebration.

CONTACTS:
Royal Palace Secretariat
P.O. Box 527
Maseru Lesotho
www.lesotho.gov.ls/king

SOURCES:
AnnivHol-2000, p. 119

♦ 1427 ♦ **King's Birthday (Nepal)**
July 8

The king's birthday is a national public holiday in Nepal, celebrated with a grand parade, song and dance troupes, and fireworks in Kathmandu.

King Gyanendra Bir Bikram Shah took the throne on June 4, 2001, after King Birendra and seven other members of the royal family were tragically shot and killed by Crown Prince Dipendra, acting under the influence of drugs and alcohol. Dipendra also shot himself and he died three days later.

The date of this holiday changes with each king. King Birendra's birthday was December 28. The current king's birthday is July 8.

CONTACTS:
Embassy of Nepal
2131 Leroy Pl. N.W.
Washington, D.C. 20008
202-667-4550; fax: 202-667-5534
www.nepalembassyusa.org

♦ 1428 ♦ **King's Birthday (Thailand)**
December 5

This national holiday celebrates the birthday of Thailand's King Bhumibol Adulyadej (b. 1927), who has been the large-ly symbolic chief of state since 1950. Bangkok blooms with decorations, which are especially lavish in the area of the floodlit Grand Palace. Full dress ceremonies, including a Trooping of the Colors by Thailand's elite Royal Guards, are performed at the palace.

CONTACTS:
The Golden Jubilee Network
Thailand
www.kanchanapisek.or.th/index.en.html

Thai Embassy
1024 Wisconsin Ave. N.W., Ste. 401
Washington, DC 20007
202-944-3600; fax: 202-944-3611
www.thaiembdc.org

SOURCES:
NatlHolWrld-1968, p. 219

♦ 1429 ♦ **Kingsburg Swedish Festival**
Third weekend in May

This festival pays tribute to the Swedish heritage of Kingsburg, Calif. The event began in 1924 as a luncheon to commemorate the midsummer celebration of the harvest in Sweden. Today it's a full-fledged festival running from Thursday through Sunday of the third weekend in May and attracts about 25,000 visitors. Traditional Swedish costumes are worn, and Swedish food is eaten—Swedish pancakes, Swedish pea soup, a smorgasbord. Events include a Parade of Trolls, raising of the May Pole, folk dancing, arts and crafts displays, a horse trot, and live entertainment.

CONTACTS:
Kingsburg District Chamber of Commerce
1475 Draper St.
Kingsburg, CA 93631
559-897-1111; fax: 559-897-4621
www.kingsburgchamberofcommerce.com

♦ 1430 ♦ **Kiplingcotes Derby**
Third Thursday in March

The Kiplingcotes Derby, which is run along the Wolds Way in Yorkshire, England, on the third Thursday in March, dates back more than 450 years, making it the longest-running "flat race" (as opposed to the steeplechase, which involves jumping over obstacles) in England. The route along which the horses run measures four miles in length and cuts through five different parishes, supposedly following an ancient Roman road. It begins near South Dalton and finishes near Kiplingcotes Farm in the parish of Middleton-on-the-Wolds.

The minimum weight that every rider must achieve is 10 stone (140 lbs.), and they are weighed beforehand to weed out cheaters who may have filled their pockets with heavy pieces of metal. The entrance fee paid by each competitor will be awarded to the second-place finisher while the winner takes home the interest on the shares of stock provided in 1618 by the district's landowners to finance the race in future years. It is never a large sum, however, and the prestige of winning is worth more than the actual prize money.

One year, when no riders had signed up for the race, officials took a cart-horse around the track rather than interrupt the centuries-old custom. In addition, in 2001 the race was cancelled due to the outbreak of foot and mouth disease throughout England; however, one rider ceremoniously rode the course.

CONTACTS:
Yorkshire Tourist Board
312 Tadcaster Rd.
York, Yorkshire YO24 1GS United Kingdom
44-19-0470-7961; fax: 44-19-0470-1414
www.yorkshire.com

SOURCES:
YrFest-1972, p. 131

♦ 1431 ♦ **Kiribati Gospel Day (National Church Day)**
July 10

The Republic of Kiribati is a group of 33 coral islands in the central Pacific Ocean, about 2,500 miles southwest of Hawaii. The islands of Kiribati are divided into three groups: the Gilbert Islands, the Phoenix Islands, and the Line Islands. Of the 33 islands, 21 are inhabited. Approximately 90% of the population lives on the Gilbert Islands; only one of the Phoenix Islands (Kanton Island) and three of the Line Islands are permanently inhabited.

European settlers began arriving in Kiribati in the 1800s. In 1892, the Gilbert Islands agreed to become a British protectorate. They became part of a British colony (along with the Ellice Islands and Banaba) in 1916. Over the next 20 years, the Line and Phoenix Islands were incorporated. The republic gained independence from the United Kingdom on July 12, 1979.

Included among the European settlers were missionaries from various denominations. Today, the predominant religions in Kiribati are Roman Catholic (52%) and Protestant (40%). Other religions include Seventh-Day Adventist, Muslim, Baha'i, Latter-day Saints, and Church of God.

On Gospel day, the Roman Catholic and Protestant churches host a celebration that is usually held at the Bairiki National Stadium in the capital, South Tarawa. A combined service is conducted by one of the heads of the two churches. Following the service, the people celebrate in the *maneaba* (center of the village) with local dances, choir, and religious songs performed by different groups from the two churches.

CONTACTS:
Kiribati National Tourism Office
Ministry of Communication, Transport & Tourism Development
P.O. Box 487
Betio, Tarawa Republic of Kiribati
www.visit-kiribati.com

♦ 1432 ♦ **Kiribati Independence Day**
July 12

This island group in the middle of the Pacific Ocean was known as the Gilbert Islands until its independence from Britain on July 12, 1979. Independence Day is observed as a national holiday.

CONTACTS:
Consulate of the Republic of Kiribati
95 Nakolo Pl. Rm. 265
Honolulu, HI 96819
808-834-6775; fax: 808-834-7604

♦ 1433 ♦ **Kiribati National Health Day**
Mid-April

The Republic of Kiribati (pronounced Kiribas) is a group of 33 coral islands in the central Pacific Ocean, about 2,500 miles southwest of Hawaii. The islands of Kiribati are divided into three groups: the Gilbert Islands, the Phoenix Islands, and the Line Islands. All of the islands, except for Banaba in the Gilbert Islands, are atolls (ring-shaped islands with central lagoons). The capital of Kiribati is Tarawa, an atoll in the Gilbert Islands.

Most of the Kiribati atolls are just over 19 feet above sea level and surrounded by barrier reefs. This makes an ideal setting for fishing, snorkeling, scuba diving, swimming, and other water sports.

There are few natural resources found throughout Kiribati. The country's agricultural products include copra (dried coconut meat from which coconut oil is extracted), taro, breadfruit, sweet potatoes, and other vegetables. The main industries are fishing, handicrafts, and tourism. World War II battle sites, game fishing, and ecotourism are some of the more popular attractions.

Every year, the people of Kiribati celebrate National Health Day. It is a public holiday set aside to encourage people to live a healthy lifestyle. This includes not only being active, but also taking time to relax. The Health Department coordinates several sports competitions throughout the day, including soccer, volleyball, softball, boxing, basketball, and cycling. In addition, most people take time to relax and enjoy their hobbies.

CONTACTS:
Kiribati National Tourism Office
Ministry of Communication, Transport & Tourism Development
P.O. Box 487
Betio, Tarawa Republic of Kiribati
www.visit-kiribati.com

♦ 1434 ♦ **Kiribati World Teachers' Day**
October 6

The Republic of Kiribati is a group of 33 coral islands in the central Pacific Ocean, about 2,500 miles southwest of Hawaii.

European settlers began arriving in Kiribati in the 1800s. In 1892, the Gilbert Islands agreed to become a British protectorate. They became part of a British colony (along with the Ellice Islands and Banaba) in 1916. Over the next 20 years, the Line and Phoenix Islands were incorporated. The republic gained independence from the United Kingdom on July 12,

1979. Today, the official language in Kiribati is English. The main languages are English, Gilbertese, and Austronesian.

The constitution of Kiribati requires children between the ages of 6 and 15 years old to attend school. Primary school includes grades 1 through 6, and Junior Secondary School (JSS) includes grades 7 through 9. Once students complete JSS, they may choose to continue on to secondary schools or to pursue vocational or technical careers. Students must successfully complete secondary school in order to attend a higher education institution.

Kiribati joined the United Nations Educational, Scientific, and Cultural Organization (UNESCO) on October 24, 1989. By September 2006, Kiribati had 14 schools participating in UNESCO's Associated Schools Project Network (ASPnet), a network of schools dedicated to promoting quality education.

To show their respect and appreciation for teachers in Kiribati, October 6 has been declared World Teachers' Day. It is a national holiday set aside to acknowledge that teachers contribute greatly to the development of the country's most important resource—people. On World Teacher's Day, the activities include local dancing, singing, and sporting events. Also, the Kiribati Teachers College in Tarawa is open to the public, allowing people to visit the school and learn more about it.

CONTACTS:
Kiribati National Tourism Office
Ministry of Communication, Transport & Tourism Development
P.O. Box 487
Betio, Tarawa Republic of Kiribati
www.visit-kiribati.com

♦ 1435 ♦ **Kiribati Youth Day**
August 7

The Republic of Kiribati is a group of 33 coral islands in the central Pacific Ocean, about 2,500 miles southwest of Hawaii. The islands of Kiribati are divided into three groups: the Gilbert Islands, the Phoenix Islands, and the Line Islands. All of the islands, except for Banaba in the Gilbert Islands, are atolls (ring-shaped islands with central lagoons). Most of the Kiribati atolls are just over 19 feet above sea level and surrounded by barrier reefs. This makes an ideal setting for fishing, snorkeling, scuba diving, swimming, and other water sports.

The constitution of Kiribati requires children between the ages of 6 and 15 years old to attend school. Primary school includes grades 1 through 6, and Junior Secondary School (JSS) includes grades 7 through 9. Once students complete JSS, they may choose to continue on to secondary schools or to pursue vocational or technical careers. Students must successfully complete secondary school in order to attend a higher education institution.

August 7 in Kiribati has been declared Youth Day. The purpose of this national holiday is to promote healthy lifestyles among the youth in Kiribati. Like HEALTH DAY in Kiribati, some of the main events of the day center on sports competitions—soccer, volleyball, boxing, tennis, basketball, and other traditional games such as local wrestling and more. For those youths not participating in the sporting events, there are also local dancing and singing competitions. Youth from the different districts and islands in Kiribati compete in these various events. Afterwards, a youth beauty pageant is held.

CONTACTS:
Kiribati National Tourism Office
Ministry of Communication, Transport & Tourism Development
P.O. Box 487
Betio, Tarawa Republic of Kiribati
www.visit-kiribati.com

♦ 1436 ♦ **Kiwanis Kids' Day**
Fourth Saturday in September

The National Kids' Day Foundation and Kiwanis International first came up with the idea of setting aside a day to focus on children and their welfare in 1949. Kiwanis International eventually assumed responsibility for the program and re-named it Kiwanis Kids' Day.

On the fourth Saturday in September, local Kiwanis clubs sponsor activities designed to show the community's appreciation of and pride in its children. The actual program for the day varies from one club to the next, but some of the more popular activities include parades, picnics and field days, theater parties, free admission programs, poster contests, fishing derbies, talent shows, and youth recognition banquets. The idea is to show youngsters that they are an important part of the community and that the community wants them to be good citizens.

CONTACTS:
Kiwanis International Foundation
3636 Woodview Trace
Indianapolis, IN 46268
800-549-2647 or 317-217-6254; fax: 317-471-8323
kif.kiwanis.org

SOURCES:
DictDays-1988, p. 63

♦ 1437 ♦ **Klo Dance**
Autumn

A harvest celebration among the Baoulé people of Côte d'Ivoire (Ivory Coast) in western Africa, the *klo* dance takes place during the fall harvest season and is similar to HALLOWEEN in the United States. Groups of young boys dressed from head to toe in strips of palm leaves go from house to house, dancing to the accompaniment of sticks beaten together. They ask for "treats"—yams, manioc, or peanuts—and sing a song of thanks if they are given any. But if they are refused, their "trick" is to sing teasing songs and to scold the woman of the house for being stingy. Afterward, the boys take their treats into the bush to eat them.

SOURCES:
FolkWrldHol-1999, p. 531

♦ 1438 ♦ Klondike Days Exposition
Late July

For 10 days in late July every year since 1962, the city of Edmonton, Alberta, Canada, has commemorated the Gold Rush of 1898 and its impact on what was originally a small agricultural town. People dress up in Klondike costumes—long dresses, stockings, and lace-up boots for the women, frontier wear for the men. A two-hour parade through the city's downtown area kicks off the festivities, followed by a band competition at Clark Stadium. There is a gold-panning competition at the Chilkoot Gold Mine and chuckwagon racing. Gambling at a Klondike-style casino is a popular diversion. Klondike garden parties and pancake breakfasts are held throughout the city, which was once the starting point for the overland trip to the Yukon.

CONTACTS:
Edmonton's Capital EX
c/o Northlands Pk.
P.O. Box 1480
Edmonton, AL T5J 2N5 Canada
403-471-7210; fax: 403-471-8176
www.capitalex.ca

SOURCES:
GdWrldFest-1985, p. 30

♦ 1439 ♦ Klondike Gold Discovery Day
Third weekend in August

On August 17, 1896, George Washington Carmack discovered gold at Bonanza Creek in northwestern Canada's Yukon Territory. His discovery triggered a huge gold rush and an enormous influx of American miners and traders. More than 30,000 poured into the Klondike region over the next couple of years, sparking the formation of Dawson and the construction of the Yukon narrow-gage railway. But the Klondike boom was short-lived, and by 1900 most of the miners had given up and were replaced by companies using mechanical mining techniques. To this day, mining remains the area's most important industry.

Also known as **Discovery Day**, this important event in Canada's history is observed as a public holiday in the Yukon. The city of Dawson celebrates with various special events, including a parade, musical entertainment, bathtub races, and, of course, panning for gold.

CONTACTS:
Tourism Yukon
Government of Yukon
P.O. Box 2703
Whitehorse, YT Y1A 2C6 Canada
867-667 5340; fax: 867-667 3546
www.travelyukon.com

SOURCES:
AnnivHol-2000, p. 138

♦ 1440 ♦ Klondike International Outhouse Race
September, Sunday of Labor Day weekend

First held in 1977, the Klondike International Outhouse Race takes place annually in the gold rush city of Dawson in Canada's Yukon Territory. A serious athletic event for some—and an opportunity for less serious competitors to indulge in what can only be described as "bathroom humor"—the race involves four-person teams, each pulling an outhouse on wheels. Many of the teams compete in outrageous costumes and cover their outhouses with appropriate graffiti or equip them with such modern-day comforts as telephones and carpeted seats.

There are two basic types of competitors: the serious runners, who train rigorously for the event and are sent off in the first heat of the three-kilometer race; and those who never make it any further than the first bar on the course, or who reach the finish line from the wrong direction. There are awards for the best dressed as well as the fastest, and the grand trophy is a wooden outhouse with an engraved plaque.

CONTACTS:
Klondike Visitors Association
P.O. Box 389C
Dawson City, YT Y0B 1G0 Canada
867-993-5575; fax: 867-993-6415
www.dawsoncity.ca

♦ 1441 ♦ Knabenschiessen
Second weekend in September

The Knabenschiessen is a marksmanship contest in Zurich, Switzerland, for boys and girls aged 12 to 17. The custom dates to the 17th century when all boys were required to practice their shooting during summer holidays. The final rifle match was a kind of examination. Today, the rifles used are like those that are issued in the army. Prizes are awarded, and the winner is named King, or Queen, of the Marksmen. A huge amusement park is set up for the Knabenschiessen, and there is a parade and market.

CONTACTS:
Zurich Tourism
Stampfenbachstrasse 52, Postfach
Zurich, 8021 Switzerland
41-44-215-4000; fax: 41-44-215-4080
www.zuerich.com/en/welcome.cfm

♦ 1442 ♦ Kneeling Sunday
Between May 24 and June 27; 50 days after Easter

In Orthodox Christianity, PENTECOST (or Whitsunday) is known as Kneeling Sunday. After the liturgy, the congregation kneels while the priest makes three invocations, one of which is a prayer for the repose of the dead. In some rural parts of Greece, the worshippers place flowers from their gardens on the ground in front of them as they kneel, and they burn candles to light the way for the souls of the departed. Sometimes they cover their eyes with rose petals, believing that if their eyes are open when the souls of their loved ones pass by, they will be recognized, and the grief that accompanies this recognition will make it impossible for the soul to leave the earth.

SOURCES:
BkFestHolWrld-1970, p. 66
OxYear-1999, p. 645

♦ 1443 ♦ **Kodomo-no-Hi (Children's Day)**
May 5

Kodomo-no-Hi is a national holiday in Japan that was known as BOYS' DAY from the ninth century, but became a day for both boys and girls in 1948. Today the day is observed largely with family picnics, but some still practice the old custom of flying wind socks in the shape of carp, a common Japanese food fish. Households with sons erect tall bamboo poles outside the home and attach streamers in the shape of carp for each son. The carp supposedly represents the strength, courage, and determination shown in its upstream journeys. The festivities are part of **Golden Week**, which also includes GREENERY DAY (April 29) and JAPAN CONSTITUTION MEMORIAL DAY (May 3).

CONTACTS:
Japan Information Network, Japan Center for Intercultural
 Communication
2-7-7 Hirakawacho
Chiyodaku
Tokyo, 102-0093 Japan
81-3-3263-5041; fax: 81-3-3230-4107
home.jcic.or.jp/en/index-e.html

SOURCES:
BkFest-1937, p. 199
BkFestHolWrld-1970, p. 93
BkHolWrld-1986, May 5
DictFolkMyth-1984, p. 540
FolkAmerHol-1999, p. 220
FolkWrldHol-1999, p. 330

♦ 1444 ♦ **Kojagara**
*September-October; full moon day of Hindu
month of Asvina*

The word "Kojagara" is a combination of two terms, *Kah* and *jagara*, which means "who is awake?" This is what the goddess Lakshmi says when she descends to the earth on the night of the full moon in the month of Asvina. She blesses all those who are awake with wealth and prosperity, so the festivities go on all night. Kojagara is a harvest festival and is celebrated throughout India.

There is a folk tale about a king who fell into dire financial straits. When his queen observed the fast and night vigil in honor of Lakshmi, the goddess of wealth, their fortunes were reversed and prosperity returned to them.

CONTACTS:
India Tourist Office
1270 Ave. of the Americas, Ste. 1808, 18th Fl.
New York, NY 10020
800-953-9399 or 212-586-4901; fax: 212-582-3274
www.indiatouristoffice.org

SOURCES:
RelHolCal-2004, p. 176

♦ 1445 ♦ **Kokila Vrata**
*Every 20 years, on the full moon day of the
intercalary month when it falls in the Hindu
month of Asadha*

A *kokil* is a cuckoo, and this day, which honors Sati, the wife of Shiva, is known as Kokila Vrata because Sati is believed to have once been changed into a cuckoo as a punishment.

According to Hindu mythology, Sati's father, Daksha, agreed to her marriage to Shiva only reluctantly. Daksha hosted a religious feast one day and excluded the couple. Sati appeared at the feast anyway, and soon involved her father in a quarrel over his refusal to accept Shiva as his son-in-law. In anger and vengeance Sati leaped into the sacrificial fire where she burned to death. Since this was considered a sin, she returned to life as a cuckoo in order to make reparation.

Hindus observe Kokila Vrata by eating only one meal per day during the month. They fast entirely on the last day of the month. People also may worship a live cuckoo or an image of one.

SOURCES:
HinduRelCustManners-1960, p. 145
HinduRelYr-1921, p. 117

♦ 1446 ♦ **Koledouvane**
December 24-25

Koledouvane is the ritual singing of CHRISTMAS carols that takes place in Bulgaria each year on December 24 and 25. The *koledari*, or "carol singers," go from house to house and wish people good health and prosperity. Although their dress and ornaments differ from region to region, the *koledarka*, a long oak stick covered with elaborate carving, is a traditional accessory.

A similar ritual, called *Sourvakari*, is carried out on NEW YEAR'S DAY. Those who go from house to house wishing people a Happy New Year carry a decorated dogwood twig, which they use to tap people on the back as they deliver their good wishes. The near coincidence of the two customs can probably be explained by the switch from the Julian to the Gregorian calendar. They have survived as separate celebrations, even though they are closely related in meaning.

SOURCES:
BkFest-1937, p. 73
EncyChristmas-2003, p. 92
FolkWrldHol-1999, p. 720

♦ 1447 ♦ **Kopenfahrt (Barrel Parade)**
*Between February 3 and March 9; Shrove
Tuesday*

The **Kope Festival** on SHROVE TUESDAY has been observed by the salt miners of Lüneburg, Lower Saxony, Germany, since the 15th century. Originally the *Kope*, a wooden barrel filled with stones, was dragged through the narrow streets of the town by *Salzjunker*, or young journeymen salters, on horseback. They were followed by a long procession of local officials, salt mine laborers, and townspeople.

Today the **Kope Procession** has become a folk, rather than a historical, event. As the riders attempt to guide the Kope through the streets, trumpeters blast their instruments as loudly as possible in an attempt to unnerve the horses. Once the Kope is brought to the mouth of the salt mine, it is set on a huge pile of wood and burned. Following the bonfire is a ceremony initiating the Salzjunker into the Guild of Master Salters.

Some believe that the Kopenfahrt bonfire was originally a pagan ceremony symbolizing the sun god's triumph over the forces of darkness. In any case, the festival was revived in 1950 and is now a regular part of the old mining town's annual CARNIVAL celebration.

CONTACTS:
German National Tourist Office
122 E. 42nd St. 20th Fl., Ste. 2000
New York, NY 10168
800-651-7010 or 212-661-7200; fax: 212-661-7174
www.cometogermany.com

SOURCES:
FestWestEur-1958, p. 56

♦ 1448 ♦ **Korea Liberation Day**
August 15

This Korean holiday commemorates the surrender of Japan to the Allies in 1945, liberating Korea from Japan's 35-year occupation. The day also commemorates the formal proclamation of the Republic of Korea in South Korea in 1948, but it is a national holiday in both Koreas.

See also SAMIL-JOL

CONTACTS:
Embassy of the Republic of Korea
2320 Massachusetts Ave. N.W.
Washington, D.C. 20008
202-939-5663; fax: 202-342-1597
www.dynamic-korea.com

SOURCES:
AnnivHol-2000, p. 137
NatlHolWrld-1968, p. 144

♦ 1449 ♦ **Korea National Foundation Day**
October 3

This national holiday in the Republic of Korea (South Korea), also known as **Tangun Day** and **Gaecheon-jeol**, commemorates the legendary founding of the Korean nation in 2333 B.C.E. by Tangun.

Prince Hwan-ung left heaven to rule earth from Mt. T'aebaek. In his kingdom were a bear and a tiger who wished to become humans. Hwan-ung told them that if they remained in a cave for 100 days eating nothing but mugwort and garlic, they would become like people. The tiger got bored, but the bear lasted it out and became a beautiful woman. She and Hwan-ung bore a son called Tangun Wanggom, meaning

Sandalwood King. When he grew up, he built his own city at the present site of P'yongyang (now the capital of North Korea) and called his new kingdom Choson, meaning "morning freshness" or "morning calm." The book *Samguk Yusa*, written in 1289, records this story. The myth is important in that it links the Korean people with a heavenly origin.

The holiday is celebrated with ceremonies at the ancient rock altar of Tangun, on the summit of Mt. Mani on Kanghwa Island, about 25 miles west of Seoul.

CONTACTS:
Embassy of the Republic of Korea
2320 Massachusetts Ave. N.W.
Washington, D.C. 20008
202-939-5663; fax: 202-342-1597
www.dynamic-korea.com

SOURCES:
AnnCustKorea-1983, p. 145
AnnivHol-2000, p. 167

♦ 1450 ♦ **Korean War Veterans Armistice Day, National**
July 27

July 1998 marked the 45th anniversary of the signing of the treaty that ended the Korean War, which lasted from 1950 through 1953. To mark the anniversary, President Bill Clinton proclaimed July 27 a national day of recognition to commemorate the more than 37,000 U.S. service personnel who lost their lives during the war. In doing so, the president called "upon all Americans to observe this day with appropriate ceremonies and activities that honor and give thanks to our distinguished Korean War veterans."

Since that time, National Korean War Veterans Armistice Day has been celebrated each July in community memorial services throughout the country and with speeches and a wreath-laying ceremony at the Korean War Veterans Memorial on the Mall in Washington, D.C. The ceremonies in the nation's capital have attracted as many as 5,000 participants and have included such dignitaries as Ambassador Lee Tae Sik of the Republic of Korea and U.S. Vice President Dick Cheney. As directed by the president's proclamation, U.S. flags are flown at half-staff on July 27th in remembrance of the U.S. personnel who lost their lives during the 37 months of combat in Korea.

CONTACTS:
Korean War Veterans Memorial
National Park Service
900 Ohio Dr. S.W.
Washington, D.C. 20024
202-426-6841
www.nps.gov/kowa

SOURCES:
PatHols, pp. 253-54

♦ 1451 ♦ **Kristallnacht (Crystal Night)**
November 9-10

A 17-year-old Jew named Herschel Grynszpan assassinated the third secretary at the German embassy in Paris on

November 7, 1938, to avenge the expulsion of his parents and 15,000 other Polish Jews to German concentration camps. His act gave the German Nazis the excuse they had been looking for to conduct a *pogrom,* or "organized massacre." Crystal Night, or **Night of the Broken Glass**, gets its name from the shattered glass that littered the streets two nights later, when the windows of Jewish-owned shops and homes were systematically smashed throughout Leipzig and other German and Austrian cities in a frenzy of destruction that resulted in the arrest and deportation of about 30,000 Jews.

Crystal Night marked the beginning of the Nazis' plan to rob the Jews of their possessions and to force them out of their homes and neighborhoods. Although the so-called "Final Solution" (to kill all European Jews) had not been publicly suggested at this point, the Nazis' actions on this night left little doubt as to what the fate of German Jews would be if war broke out. Today Jews everywhere observe the anniversary of this infamous event by holding special memorial services.

In Germany, Kristallnacht coincides with the anniversary of another famous, if very recent, event: the breaching of the Berlin Wall in 1989. The coincidence of the two observances is seen by many as symbolic of the conflicts of German history.

CONTACTS:
Simon Wiesenthal Center's Museum of Tolerance
Multimedia Learning Center Online
9760 W. Pico Blvd.
Los Angeles, CA 90035
800-900-9036 or 310-553-9036; fax: 310-553-4521
motlc.wiesenthal.org

United States Holocaust Memorial Museum
100 Raoul Wallenberg Pl. S.W.
Washington, DC 20024
202-488-0400
www.ushmm.org

SOURCES:
AnnivHol-2000, p. 188
DictWrldRel-1989, p. 202
HolSymbols-2009, p. 453

♦ 1452 ♦ Ksamavani
September; first day of the waning half of Asvina

Jainism, a religion that originated in ancient India, advocates peaceful coexistence. Forgiveness is thus regarded as a sacred act and is foundational to spiritual health. In the spirit similar to that of PARYUSHANA, a better known Jain festival, Ksamavani invites believers to ask for and receive forgiveness. It takes place in India and in Jain communities abroad during the lunar month of Asvina, which falls between September and October.

On Ksamavani, every member of the Jain community approaches family members, neighbors, colleagues, and co-workers and asks them for forgiveness for harms done. The other person can be anyone, irrespective of his or her social standing, and the offenses could be committed knowingly or unknowingly. The ritual is intended to help repair severed ties and relations. It is also a required act for anyone looking

to attain the ultimate goal of nirvana, the term for the liberation of the soul.

CONTACTS:
Ministry of External Affairs
Government of India
South Block
New Delhi, 110011 India
www.mea.gov.in

SOURCES:
RelHolCal-2004, p. 196

♦ 1453 ♦ 'Ksan Celebrations
Friday evenings in July and August

Dances and accompanying songs are performed by the 'Ksan, or Gitxsan, Indians in a longhouse in the Indian Village in Hazelton, British Columbia, Canada. They are generally a celebration of the important things of life, such as breathing and being at one with the cosmos.

The dances are said to go back to pre-history; they were revived in 1958, and the 'Ksan dancers have since performed in New York City, San Francisco, Seattle, Kansas City, Missouri, and even Australia.

Box-shaped skin drums provide the beat for the dances. Songs, besides being about cosmic events, are sometimes songs of marriage, songs of divorce, or what are known as "happy heart songs" about almost anything. Performers must be *Git 'Ksan,* meaning "People of the 'Ksan" (named after the nearby Skeena River).

Because the homeland of the Git 'Ksan is far inland, it was overlooked by the Spaniards and Russians who explored the coast in the 1700s, and fur traders didn't stay here because the climate is too humid for good fur. As a result, the 'Ksan culture has been maintained without outside influences.

CONTACTS:
Ksan Historical Village and Museum
P.O. Box 326
Hazelton, BC V0J 1Y0 Canada
250-842-5544; fax: 250-842-6533
www.ksan.org

♦ 1454 ♦ Kuhio (Prince) Day
Monday on or near March 26

Prince Jonah Kuhio Kalanianaole (1871-1921) was a young man when the Hawaiian monarchy was overthrown in 1893. As a member of the royal family, he fought for the restoration of the monarchy and spent a year as a political prisoner. He lived abroad for a number of years after his release, but eventually returned to his native land and was elected as the first delegate to represent the Territory of Hawaii in the U.S. Congress in 1903. He was reelected and served 10 consecutive terms until his death in 1921.

Because he worked so hard to preserve the old Hawaiian customs and traditions and to take care of the dwindling number of Hawaiian natives, Prince Kuhio has been revered by his people. His birthday is commemorated on the island of

Kauai, where he was born, with a week-long Prince Kuhio Festival during the latter part of March. The festival pays tribute to him by featuring such traditional Hawaiian events as outrigger canoe races, hula dancing, and performances of Hawaiian music.

CONTACTS:
Hawaii Visitors and Convention Bureau
2270 Kalakaua Ave., Ste. 801
Honolulu, HI 96815
800-464-2924 or 808-923-1811; fax: 808-924-0290
www.hvcb.org

SOURCES:
AmerBkDays-2000, p. 236
AnnivHol-2000, p. 51
BkHolWrld-1986, Mar 26

♦ 1455 ♦ Kumbh Mela (Pitcher Fair)
Every 12 years on a date calculated by astrologers (2013, 2025, 2037...)

The Kumbh Mela involves mass immersion rituals by Hindus near the city of Allahabad (the ancient holy city of Prayag) in the north-central state of Uttar Pradesh, India. Millions of pilgrims gather to bathe at the confluence of the Ganges and Yamuna rivers, which is also where the mythical river of enlightenment, the Saraswati, flows. The bathers wash away the sins of their past lives and pray to escape the cycle of reincarnation. *Sadhus*, or holy men, carry images of deities to the river for immersion, and the most ascetic sadhus, naked except for loincloths, their faces and bodies smeared with ashes, go in procession to the waters, escorting images borne on palanquins. The Ganges is not only a sacred river but is the source of all sacred waters. The junction of the three rivers at Allahabad is called the *sangam* and is considered by some the holiest place in India.

The *mela* (fair) is thought to be the largest periodic gathering of human beings in the world; a vast tent city appears, temporary water and power lines are installed, and 10 pontoon bridges are laid across the Ganges. Movies of Hindu gods and heroes are shown from the backs of trucks, and plays recounting Hindu mythology are performed. Merchants lay out all manner of goods.

The story behind the mela is that Hindu gods and *asuras*, or demons, fought for a *kumbh*, or pitcher, carrying *amrit*, the nectar of immortality. The god who seized the kumbh stopped at Prayag, Hardwar, Nasik, and Ujjain on his way to paradise. The journey took 12 days (which are longer than earthly days), and therefore the mela follows a 12-year cycle.

A purification bathing ceremony called the *Magh Mela* is also held each spring in Allahabad. It is India's biggest yearly religious bathing festival. Although the Magh Mela attracts a million people, more or less, the Kumbh Mela dwarfs it!

See also GANGA DUSSEHRA

CONTACTS:
Uttar Pradesh Tourism Department, Directorate of Tourism
Rajarshi Purshottam Das Tandon Paryatan Bhavan
Vipin Khand, Gomti Nagar

Lucknow, Uttar Pradesh C-13 India
91-522-2308916; fax: 91-522-2308937
www.up-tourism.com

Ministry of Tourism, Government of India
Rm. No 123, Transport Bhawan, No. 1, Parliament St.
New Delhi, Delhi 110 001 India
91-11-23715084; fax: 91-11-23715084
www.tourisminindia.com

SOURCES:
DictWrldRel-1989, p. 305
HolSymbols-2009, p. 456
RelHolCal-2004, p. 186

♦ 1456 ♦ Kunta Kinte Heritage Festival
Last weekend in September

The Kunta Kinte Heritage Festival is a two-day event held at the Anne Arundel County Fairgrounds in Crownsville, Md., that celebrates the heritage and culture of African Americans. The festival, which draws about 8,000 visitors annually, is named in honor of Kunta Kinte, a Gambian youth who was forced into slavery in the United States during the late 18th century. His descendant, Alex Haley, listened to family stories he heard from his grandmother and became inspired. He researched his family history and published it in 1976 in the worldwide bestseller *Roots*.

First held in 1987, the Kunta Kinte Heritage Festival was conceived as an opportunity both to celebrate the contributions of African Americans to American culture and to educate younger generations about their history. The festival is held on the last weekend of September each year to reflect Kinte's arrival on the slave ship *Lord Ligonier* at the Annapolis port on September 29, 1767. Music and entertainment range from African dancers to Caribbean steel drum bands, jazz bands, gospel choirs, and hip hop acts. Family activities are emphasized, including games, storytelling, instrument-making, and mask-decorating. A Family Education Tent also offers exhibits and information on a variety of education, career, and health topics as well as information on social groups and political action organizations.

CONTACTS:
Kunta Kinte Celebrations, Inc.
P.O. Box 314
Arnold, MD 21012-0314
410-349-0338; fax: 509.561.8274
www.kuntakinte.org

Kunta Kinte-Alex Haley Foundation Inc.
31 Old Solomons Island Rd., Ste. 102
Annapolis, MD 21401
410-841-6920; fax: 410-841-6505
www.kintehaley.org

SOURCES:
AAH-2007, p. 261

♦ 1457 ♦ Ku-omboka
Usually February or March

Ku-omboka, which means "getting out of the water," is a floodtime festival observed by the Lozi people of Zambia.

When the Zambezi River begins its annual flooding of the Barotzé flood plains, thousands of boats and canoes, led by the chief on his royal barge, make their way to higher ground. When the Lozi reach their new seasonal home at Limulunga, they celebrate with singing and dancing. In July, when the floods have receded, they return to the lowlands.

CONTACTS:
Zambia National Tourist Board
Lusaka Sq., Cairo Rd.
P.O. Box 30017
Lusaka, Zambia
260-1-229087; fax: 260-1-225174
www.zambiatourism.com

SOURCES:
BkHolWrld-1986, Feb 18
FolkWrldHol-1999, p. 192
GdWrldFest-1985, p. 188

♦ 1458 ♦ **Kupalo Festival**
June 24; Midsummer's day and night

A Ukrainian and Russian festival also called **Ivan Kupalo**, dating back to pagan days, Kupalo traditionally is celebrated by young unmarried men and women and boys and girls. The festival takes its name from the god of summer and fertility: Kupalo sleeps in the winter and each spring awakens and shakes the tree he's been under, making the seeds fall as a sign of the year's harvest. During the day and night of the celebration, boys and girls decorate a sapling tree with flowers, seeds, and fruit, call it Kupalo, and dance and sing special songs to please this image of the god.

In other events of the day, young women gather flowers to make a wreath that is tossed into a river; the spot where the wreath reaches the shore indicates the family the girl will marry into. Another custom for girls is to make an effigy of Marena, the goddess of cold, death, and winter. After singing special songs, they burn or drown the effigy to cut the goddess's power over the coming winter; winters in Ukraine are very harsh.

Young men sometimes go into the forest to look for a special fern that only blooms (according to the legend) on the night of MIDSUMMER. They take with them a special cloth, white powder, and a knife. If they find the fern and are strong enough to ward off the enticements of wood nymphs, they draw a circle with the white powder and sit and wait for the fern to bloom. When it does, they cut the blossom with the knife and put the flower in the special cloth. They must never, ever, tell anyone they have found the fern, or they will lose the luck and power it gives. The people's rationale behind this story is that it explains why some people have more talent and luck than others.

The celebrations to a greater or lesser degree are popular in both Ukraine and among Ukrainians in the United States.

CONTACTS:
Ukrainian Embassy
3350 M St. N.W.
Washington, D.C. 20007

202-333-0606; fax: 202-333-0817
www.mfa.gov.ua

♦ 1459 ♦ **Kurijmoj**
September-October through mid-January

Kurijmoj is a four-month CHRISTMAS celebration lasting from late September or early October through mid-January in the tropical Marshall Islands. For these Marshallese people, this is the Christmas season. December 25 itself is called *ronoul lalim raan,* "The Twenty-Fifth Day." Preparations begin in March or April, after EASTER. Kurijmoj is celebrated by people who had been living on the atoll of Enewetak in the Marshall Islands and were forced to move from their homes to the atoll of Wujlan in 1947 so that the U.S. could test atomic bombs on their islands. They were able to return 33 years later.

People begin forming singing and dancing groups called *jepta* and practice together in early October. The jepta groups compete with each other in church at ADVENT with songs, dances, jokes, food, and a "money tree" constructed like a piñata, and again on the Sunday nearest NEW YEAR'S DAY. Each group chooses a theme which often has a biblical foundation, such as the birth of Jesus, the Gospel word, or God's plan. The "money tree" is really more like a parade float, decorated on the outside according to the group's theme and filled on the inside with gifts for the minister of the church. Nowadays the dances resemble a mixture of hula-style dances and Japanese bon dances.

Games are also played during this holiday. In *karate,* the women in a jepta play at being Japanese warriers and loot a men's jepta. In *kalbuuj,* the men of one jepta capture and "arrest" the women of another jepta and confine them to a "jail" the men have created from women's cooking and sleeping houses in the town until the women agree they are well-treated and have no reason to leave. Before the relocation, kalbuuj was a regular game, but since the people have returned to Enewetak, it has been attempted only a few times because the women were traditionally captured after returning from gathering fronds from which to make various handicrafts for the festival. After their return, the plants were not large enough to produce good fronds, so the women's pretext for leaving the town was gone.

The feast on Christmas Day is the largest of the year, with roasted pig, coconuts, rice, bread, fried doughnuts, and *bwiro,* a special treat made from breadfruit. After a short church service at 6 A.M., people divide up the food baskets they have worked hard to prepare and exchange them with each other. By 10 A.M. the jeptas are assembling at the church to perform and compete with each other, dressed up in new clothes, often wearing leis of flowers in their hair and around their necks and other accessories, which are promptly seized by spectators as well as by members of competing jeptas (though people are left wearing at least minimal clothing), who in turn adorn the jepta members with sprays of perfume. Each jepta performs up to 20 songs, so this is a day-long event.

SOURCES:
EncyChristmas-2003, p. 459

♦ 1460 ♦ **Kuta Karnival**
September

One of the most important annual festivals in Indonesia, the nine-day Kuta Karnival has been held in Bali since 2002. Similar to the CARNIVAL and MARDI GRAS events found in other countries, the Kuta Karnival is a time when all the usual rules of behavior are set aside.

For several nights during the Kuta Karnival, the streets of Bali are crowded with people eating and drinking. Among the festivities is a parade with floats, antique cars, a Chinese dragon, and hundreds of traditional Balinese dancers dressed in colorful costumes. Because Bali has long been a popular destination for surfers from around the world, there are also a number of surfing competitions during the carnival for competitors of all age groups. There are swimming, beach volleyball, and skateboarding contests, a wide range of live music performances, cabaret shows, and children's events, including clowns, craft making, balloons, and games. Sporting events include matches sponsored by the World Boxing Association and the World Women's Tennis organizations.

CONTACTS:
Embassy of Indonesia
2020 Massachusetts Ave. N.W.
Washington, D.C. 20036
202-775-5200; fax: 202-775-5365
www.embassyofindonesia.org

♦ 1461 ♦ **Kutztown Festival**
Week including 4th of July

The **Pennsylvania Dutch Folk Festival** in Kutztown, Pennsylvania, is an annual celebration of Pennsylvania Dutch foods, crafts, and customs. Although many people identify the "Pennsylvania Dutch" with the Amish people, the Mennonites, or with the Holland Dutch, the name actually came from the Yankee pronunciation of *deutsch,* meaning "German." But the Pennsylvania Dutch are not simply transplanted Germans, either. Their folk culture is peculiarly American, and they encompass a number of national and religious groups.

The Kutztown Festival acquaints visitors with all aspects of Pennsylvania Dutch culture. There are special foods—such as apple butter, *rivvel* soup (rivvels are like dumplings), and the fruit pies which the Pennsylvania Dutch claim to have originated. Traditional artisans featured at the fair include tinsmiths, weavers, pretzel-makers, candlemakers, cigarmakers, potters, and quilters.

There are reenactments of a Pennsylvania Dutch funeral feast and demonstrations of *nipsi*—a complicated game that involves batting a piece of wood and then "bidding" the number of hops that the opposing team will require to get from where the wood landed back to home base. There is even a seminar on Pennsylvania Dutch cooking. One of the fair's most interesting figures is the *Fraktur* painter, who illuminates birth and baptismal records and book plates with bright colors and flowing scrollwork.

CONTACTS:
Kutztown PA-German Festival
P.O. Box 306
Kutztown, PA 19530
888-674-6136
www.kutztownfestival.com

SOURCES:
AmerBkDays-2000, p. 484
GdUSFest-1984, p. 158

♦ 1462 ♦ **Kuwait Liberation Day**
February 26

After Iraqi President Saddam Hussein's troops invaded Kuwait on August 2, 1990, several countries in the United Nations formed a military coalition—including troops and equipment from the U.S., France, and Britain, and financial assistance from West Germany and Japan—to force them out. Five days later, the first U.S. forces arrived in Saudi Arabia. Operation Desert Storm began on January 17, 1991, and for five weeks, U.S. and British air forces relentlessly bombed Baghdad. This was followed by four days of a ground war which resulted in Hussein's troops leaving Kuwait.

February 26 is a national holiday in Kuwait celebrating the end of Iraq's military presence in Kuwait.

CONTACTS:
Kuwait Cultural Office
3500 International Dr. N.W.
Washington, D.C. 20008
202-364-2100; fax: 202-363-8394
www.kuwaitculture.com

SOURCES:
AnnivHol-2000, p. 32

♦ 1463 ♦ **Kuwait National Day**
February 25

This national holiday commemorates Kuwait's independence from Britain in 1961. Though internally governed by the Sabah family, Britain had handled its foreign affairs since 1899.

CONTACTS:
Kuwait Cultural Office
3500 International Dr. N.W.
Washington, D.C. 20008
202-364-2100; fax: 202-363-8394
www.kuwaitculture.com

SOURCES:
AnnivHol-2000, p. 32

♦ 1464 ♦ **Kuwana Ishitori Matsuri**
July 10-12

The Kuwana Ishitori Matsuri, or **Collect Stones Festival**, commemorates the days when many stones had to be transported by cart to build a shrine. There is a procession of floats, adorned with beautiful cloth, tapestries, and lanterns, through the town of Kuwana, Japan, on July 10, to represent the means by which the rocks were once transported. At midnight the floats all meet at the local shrine, and then each float goes back to the locale it came from. On July 11, there is a presentation of stones at the shrine, followed by a series of processions that lasts till nightime the following day. Then people assemble near the floats, watch the lighting of the float lanterns, and listen to the crashing drum music that fills the air.

CONTACTS:
Japan National Tourist Organization
1 Rockefeller Pl., Ste. 1250
New York, NY 10020
212-757-5640; fax: 212-307-6754
www.jnto.go.jp

SOURCES:
JapanFest-1965, p. 165

♦ 1465 ♦ Kwafie Festival
November-January

The Kwafie Festival is celebrated in Dormaa Ahenkro, Berekum, and Nsuatre in the Brong Ahafo Region of Ghana to commemorate the bringing of fire to the area, said to have been accomplished by ancestors who emigrated to this region long ago. The celebration lasts about three days and can occur in either November, December, or January. In Dormaa Ahenkro the festival begins with an evening torchlight procession from the palace to the house where the sacred stools are kept. The ancestors are worshipped with libations, then the procession returns to the palace. The next morning everyone gathers at the palace where the chief presides over the "laying of logs," or *Nkukuato*, in which lower-level officials bring in logs on their shoulders to give the chief. The highest ranking official chooses three logs to begin the fire, which is then used for cooking a ritual meal.

Later in the day an even grander procession carries the ancestral stools to a nearby body of water for ritual purification. Other sacred ceremonies are also performed. Then the final day of the festival is marked by joyous dancing, music, and feasts on the palace grounds.

CONTACTS:
Ghana Embassy
3512 International Dr. N.W.
Washington, D.C. 20008
202-686-4520; fax: 202-686-4527
www.ghanaembassy.org

SOURCES:
FestGhana-1970, p. 70

♦ 1466 ♦ Kwakiutl Midwinter Ceremony
November through February

The Kwakiutl are one of the Indian tribes who inhabit the northwestern coast of the United States, stretching from northern California to southeastern Alaska. They believe that long ago, before their people even existed, powerful supernatural animals—including bears, wolves, seals, ravens, bees, owls, and killer whales—held dominion over the world. These beings endowed early humans, who were the ancestors of today's Kwakiutl, with a measure of that power.

During their winter ceremonial season, the Kwakiutl acknowledge and reaffirm their connection with the supernatural world by performing sacred dance dramas, or *tseka*. The performers dress in strips of cedar bark and wear masks elaborately designed to invoke the spirits of their supernatural forebears. The dances themselves illustrate characters and incidents from Kwakiutl mythology.

CONTACTS:
Kwakiutl Nation
Fort Rupert Reserve
P.O. Box 1440
Port Hardy, BC V0N 2P0 Canada
250-949-6012; fax: 250-949-6066
www.kwakiutl.ca

Smithsonian Institution
P.O. Box 37012
Washington, DC 20013
202-633-1000
www.si.edu

SOURCES:
EncyNatAmerRel-2001, p. 333
EndurHarv-1995, p. 140
RelHolCal-2004, p. 254

♦ 1467 ♦ Kwanzaa
December 26-January 1

An African-American celebration of family and black culture, Kwanzaa is thought to be observed by five million Americans and perhaps 10 million others in Africa, Canada, the Caribbean, and parts of Europe. The holiday was created in 1966 by Maulana Karenga, chairman of the Black Studies Department at California State University in Long Beach.

In Swahili, Kwanzaa means "first fruits of the harvest," and first-fruit practices common throughout Africa were adapted by Karenga for the celebration.

Each day of the seven-day festival is dedicated to one of seven principles: *umoja* (unity), *kujichagulia* (self-determination), *ujima* (collective work and responsibility), *ujamaa* (cooperative economics), *nia* (purpose), *kuumba* (creativity), and *imani* (faith).

Families gather in the evenings to discuss the principle of the day, and then light a black, red, or green candle and place it in a seven-branched candleholder called a *kinara* to symbolize giving light and life to the principle. On the evening of Dec. 31, families join with other members of the community for a feast called the *karamu*. Decorations are in the red, black, and green that symbolize Africa, and both adults and children wear African garments.

Increasingly, colleges and museums are holding Kwanzaa events during some of the days. For example, in Chicago, an African Market is held on Dec. 28 by the Ujamma Family, a black self-help group. In New York City, the American Museum of Natural History celebrates Kwanzaa with an African Marketplace, poetry, folktales, and music.

CONTACTS:
Kwanzaa, African American Cultural Center
3018 W. 48th St.
Los Angeles, CA 90043
323-299-6124; fax: 323-299-0261
www.officialkwanzaawebsite.org

SOURCES:
AAH-2007, p. 268
AmerBkDays-2000, p. 857
AnnivHol-2000, p. 214
EncyChristmas-2003, p. 416
FolkWrldHol-1999, p. 767
HolSymbols-2009, p. 464
OxYear-1999, p. 535

♦ 1468 ♦ **Kyokusui-no-En**
April 29; first Sunday in March

In ancient Japan high-ranking people entertained themselves with a custom called Kyokusui. They filled a lacquer wine cup with *sake* (rice wine) and placed it in a stream. Participants sitting on a bank downstream tried to write a five-line poem before the sake reached them. They would then snatch the cup out of the stream and drink the sake.

The poems were written on a strip of thick paper known as a *tanzaku*. Most of the poems were *waka*, which is a traditional form in Japanese poetry. It has five lines with a total of 31 syllables: five syllables in the first line, seven in the second, five in the third, and seven in the fourth and fifth lines (5-7-5-7-7).

Kyokusui-no-En is a reenactment of this ancient pastime held April 29 in Kyoto. A similar ceremony is performed in Fukuoka on the first Sunday in March.

CONTACTS:
Kyoto Prefectural Tourism Office
Japan External Trade Organization
1221 Avenue of the Americas, 42nd Fl.
New York, NY 10020
212-997-6466; fax: 212-302-1581
www.pref.kyoto.jp

ACROS Fukuoka Foundation
1-1 Tenjin 1-chome
Fukuoka 2F
Chuo Ku, 810-0001 Japan
81-9-2725-9100
www.acros.or.jp

SOURCES:
IllFestJapan-1993, p. 33

♦ 1469 ♦ **Kyrgyz Independence Day**
August 31

Kyrgyzstan declared independence from the Soviet Union on August 31, 1991, along with other central Asian republics as the Soviet empire crumbled. Located along the famed Silk Road, the trade route connecting the eastern and western parts of Eurasia, the country is mostly mountainous, part of the Tien-Shan, or Celestial Mountains. Independence Day is a national public holiday in the Kyrgyz Republic.

CONTACTS:
Kyrgyz Embassy
2360 Massachusetts Ave. N.W.
Washington, D.C. 20008
202-449-9822; fax: 202-449-9823
www.kgembassy.org

L

♦ 1470 ♦ **La Paz Day**
July 16

Bolivia was officially established as an independent country on August 6, 1825, an event now commemorated each year on BOLIVIA INDEPENDENCE DAY. The capital city of La Paz, however, celebrates its own Independence Day on July 16. The holiday commemorates the date in 1809 when Pedro Domingo Murillo led a revolt of *mestizos*, or those of mixed European and South American heritage, against the Spanish authorities. Murillo's uprising was the second against the Spanish in the space of a few months. Murillo declared Upper Peru, as Bolivia as then known, to be an independent state, but 16 years of struggle were necessary to make his declaration a reality. July 16 is now a municipal holiday in La Paz, and the day is celebrated with parades, concerts, fireworks, and dances.

CONTACTS:
Bolivian Embassy
3014 Massachusetts Ave. N.W.
Washington, D.C. 20008
www.bolivia-usa.com

♦ 1471 ♦ **Labor Day**
First Monday in September

Although workers' holidays had been observed since the days of the medieval trade guilds, laborers in the United States didn't have a holiday of their own until 1882. This was the year when Peter J. McGuire, a New York City carpenter and labor union leader, and Matthew Maguire, a machinist from Paterson, N.J., suggested to the Central Labor Union of New York that a celebration be held in honor of the American worker. Some 10,000 New Yorkers paraded in Union Square, New York, on September 5 of that year—a date specifically chosen by McGuire to fill the long gap between the FOURTH OF JULY and THANKSGIVING.

The first Labor Day observance was confined to New York City, but the idea of setting aside a day to honor workers spread quickly, and by 1895 Labor Day events were taking place across the nation. Oregon, in 1887, was the first state to make it a legal holiday, and in 1894 President Grover Cleveland signed a bill making it a national holiday. The holiday's association with trade unions has declined, but it remains important as the day that marks the end of the summer season for schoolchildren and as an opportunity for friends and families to get together for picnics and sporting events.

Labour Day is celebrated in England and Europe on May 1. In Australia, where it is called EIGHT HOUR DAY, it is celebrated at different times in different states, and commemorates the struggle for a shorter working day. In Antigua and Barbuda, Labor Day is observed on May 6; in the Bahamas, it's June 7; in Bermuda, Sept. 2; in Jamaica, May 23; and in Trinidad and Tobago, June 19. Labor Day is observed on the first Monday in September throughout the United States, in Canada, and in Puerto Rico. In Japan, November 23 is **Labor Thanksgiving Day**, or **Kinro Kansha-no-Hi**, a legal holiday set aside to honor working people and productivity.

CONTACTS:
U.S. Department of Labor
Office of Public Affairs
200 Constitution Ave. N.W.
Washington, D.C. 20210
877-889-5627
www.dol.gov

Library of Congress
101 Independence Ave. S.E.
Washington, DC 20540
202-707-5000; fax: 202-707-8366
www.loc.gov

AFL-CIO
815 16th St. N.W.
Washington, DC 20006
202-637-5000; fax: 202-637-5058
www.aflcio.org

SOURCES:
AmerBkDays-2000, p. 632
AnnivHol-2000, pp. 163, 195
BkFest-1937, p. 18
BkHolWrld-1986, Sep 7
DaysCustFaith-1957, p. 248
DictDays-1988, p. 65
FolkAmerHol-1999, p. 358
HolSymbols-2009, p. 469
PatHols-2006, p. 175

♦ 1472 ♦ **LaborFest**
July 5 through July 31

LaborFest is a cultural and arts festival centered in San Francisco, Calif., that advances workers' rights and commemorates the achievements of the labor movement of the early 20th century. The festival comprises a three-week program of free and paid-admission events, including book and poetry readings, issue-centered discussion forums, an international film festival, music and theater performances, and historical tours and presentations. Held annually since 1994, LaborFest promotes solidarity among workers and includes performers, films, and presenters from around the world.

The festival begins each year on July 5th, the anniversary of "Bloody Thursday," when two union workers were killed by police while supporting a strike by longshoremen and maritime workers on the San Francisco docks in 1934. The deaths on that day catalyzed workers throughout the city to walk off their jobs in what became known as the General Strike of 1934. At LaborFest, boat, bus, walking, and bike tours visit historic sites related to the strike and the history of organized labor in San Francisco. On July 31, the last night of the festival, a closing party is held, featuring a music concert celebrating working-class life.

CONTACTS:
LaborFest
P.O. Box 40983
San Francisco, CA 94140
415-642-8066
www.laborfest.net

SOURCES:
PatHols-2006, p. 181

♦ 1473 ♦ **Lac Long Quan Festival**
Six days in late March-early April

This six-day festival, held in the Vietnamese village of Binh Minh, honors the legendary king Lac Long Quan. According to tradition his wife, Au Co, "hatched" (in the sense of laying an egg) 100 people, who ended up populating what is now the Ha Tay Province.

During the festival people celebrate their ancestors with offerings of fruit and flowers paraded by young women accompanied by folk musicians, then elders bestow blessings on the offerings. Although Lac Long Quan and Au Co are the focus of the proceedings, Buddha is also included and considered a special guest.

CONTACTS:
Vietnam National Administration of Tourism
80 Quan Su Rd.
Hanoi, Vietnam
84-4-942-1061; fax: 84-4-826-3956
www.vietnamtourism.com/e_pages/news/index.a

SOURCES:
WildPlanet-1995, p. 405

♦ 1474 ♦ **Ladouvane**
December 31; June 24

Ladouvane, or the **Singing to Rings**, is a Bulgarian fertility ritual. Traditionally, young girls drop their rings, together with oats and barley (symbols of fertility), into a cauldron of spring water. The rings are tied with a red thread to a bunch of ivy, crane's bill, basil, or some other perennial plant, and the cauldron is left out overnight. Ritual dances are performed around the cauldron and the girls' fortunes are told.

In western Bulgaria, the Central Balkan Range, and along the Danube River, Ladouvane is observed on NEW YEAR'S EVE. In the rest of the country, it is observed on MIDSUMMER DAY.

CONTACTS:
Embassy of the Republic of Bulgaria
1621 22nd St. N.W.
Washington, D.C. 20008
202-387-0174; fax: 202-234-7973
www.bulgaria-embassy.org

♦ 1475 ♦ **Lady Day**
March 25

Lady Day is the name in England for the Feast of the ANNUNCIATION. This day was originally called **Our Lady Day**, a name that applied to three other days relating to the Virgin Mary: the IMMACULATE CONCEPTION (December 8), the NATIVITY OF THE BLESSED VIRGIN MARY (September 8), and the ASSUMPTION OF THE BLESSED VIRGIN MARY (August 15). It commemorates the archangel Gabriel's announcement to Mary that she would give birth to Jesus, and is often referred to simply as The Annunciation. Lady Day is one of the QUARTER DAYS in England and Ireland when rents are paid and tenants change houses. In France it is called **Nôtre Dame de Mars** ("Our Lady of March").

SOURCES:
AnnivHol-2000, p. 51
BkDays-1864, vol. I, p. 417
DaysCustFaith-1957, p. 86
DictDays-1988, pp. 4, 85, 93
FestSaintDays-1915, p. 59
FolkWrldHol-1999, p. 223

♦ 1476 ♦ **Lady Day among Samis**
March 25

In the Sami region of Finland, villages such as Inari and Enontekio celebrate a festival on LADY DAY that usually occurs within the EASTER season. Sami people travel from remote homesteads to participate in a special church service, which is typically succeeded by such outdoor activities as lasso-throwing and skijoring, a sport in which skiers are pulled by reindeer over a frozen lake. Because the festival draws everyone together, March 25 is also a popular time for weddings.

SOURCES:
BkFestHolWrld-1970, p. 62

♦ 1477 ♦ **Lag ba-Omer**
18th day of the Jewish month of Iyyar, or the 33rd day of the 50 days that separate Passover and Shavuot

The name of this Jewish holiday means "thirty-three omer," an *omer* being a sheaf of barley or wheat. In the biblical book of Leviticus, the people were commanded by Jehovah to make an offering of a sheaf of barley on each of the 50 days between PASSOVER and SHAVUOT. After the evening service, the number of the day was solemnly announced, and in time this ceremony came to be known as "the counting of the omer."

Why the 33rd day of this period was singled out may have something to do with an ancient pagan festival of the forest that was celebrated at this same time. Another story claims that the plague that had been decimating the students of Rabbi Akiba in the second century suddenly and miraculously stopped on this day. In any case, the mid-harvest festival of Lag ba-Omer represents a break in the otherwise solemn season between Passover and Shavuot.

SOURCES:
BkFest-1937, p. 207
DaysCustFaith-1957, p. 137
DictWrldRel-1989, p. 567
FolkWrldHol-1999, p. 323
OxYear-1999, p. 728
RelHolCal-2004, p. 52

◆ 1478 ◆ **Lajkonik**
Between May 21 and June 24; first Thursday after Corpus Christi

The most popular folk festival in Krakow, Poland, Lajkonik (or the **Horse Festival**) has lost touch with its medieval roots, but is believed to commemorate the horseman who carried the news of the Tartar defeat during the 13th-century Tartar invasions. A group of 18 costumed people gathers in the courtyard of the Norbertine Monastery in a suburb of Krakow. They include a standard-bearer in the traditional dress of a Polish nobleman, a small band of musicians, and a bearded horseman in oriental costume riding a richly draped but rather small wooden hobby-horse. This is the Lajkonik, originally called the Horse or the "Zwierzyniec Horse," named for the town where the monastery is located, and now the unofficial symbol of Krakow.

After performing a ceremonial dance for the vicar and the nuns, the procession leaves the monastery and moves in the direction of the city. The horseman collects money from the crowds lining the streets, tapping each donor with his rod to bring them good luck; they then join the procession. Eventually the parade ends up in the market square for the climax of the ritual. The city officials greet the horseman in front of the town hall. He dances for the assembled dignitaries and receives from them a sack of money and a glass of wine, which he consumes after toasting the well-being of the city.

The festival was first sponsored by the guild that furnished wood to Krakow and the salt mines. In the past the actors came from the Boatman congregation who, since the Middle Ages, have floated timber down the Vistula River to Krakow. Now they tend to be Krakow factory workers.

CONTACTS:
Polish National Tourist Office

5 Marine View Pl., Ste. 208
Hoboken, NJ 07030
201-420-9910; fax: 201-584-9153
www.poland.travel

SOURCES:
BkFest-1937, p. 262
FolkWrldHol-1999, p. 352

◆ 1479 ◆ **Lakshmi Puja**
September-October; Hindu month of Asvina

The annual festival in honor of the Hindu goddess Lakshmi is held in the autumn, when Hindus of all castes ask for her blessings. Lights shine from every house, and no one sleeps during the celebrations.

Lakshmi is traditionally associated with wealth, prosperity, and good luck. In later Hindu literature, she appears as the dutiful wife of the god Vishnu and is typically portrayed massaging his feet while he rests on the cosmic serpent, Shesa. She remains a popular Hindu goddess to this day in India, where she is a special patron of shopkeepers.

See also TIHAR

SOURCES:
DictHindu-1977, p. 160
DictWrldRel-1989, p. 280

◆ 1480 ◆ **Lammas**
August 1

Possibly one of the four great pagan festivals of Britain—the LUGNASADH—Lammas was known as the **Gule of August** in the Middle Ages. It celebrated the harvest, and was the forerunner of the THANKSGIVING celebrated in the United States and Canada. In medieval England, loaves made from the first ripe grain were blessed in the church on this day—the word *lammas* being a short form of "loaf mass." Lammas Day is similar in original intent to the Jewish Feast of Weeks, also called SHAVUOT or PENTECOST, which came at the end of the PASSOVER grain harvest. A 15th-century suggestion was that the name derived from "lamb" and "mass," and was the time when a feudal tribute of lambs was paid.

In the Scottish Highlands, people used to sprinkle their cows and the floors of their houses with menstrual blood, which they believed was especially potent against evil on this day. It was also one of the QUARTER DAYS in Scotland, when tenants brought in the first new grain to their landlords.

Along with CANDLEMAS, WALPURGIS NIGHT, and HALLOWEEN, Lammas is an important day in Neopagan calendars.

A phrase used from the 16th to the 19th century, "at Latter Lammas Day," meant "never."

SOURCES:
BkDays-1864, vol. II, p. 154
DaysCustFaith-1957, p. 199
DictDays-1988, pp. 51, 66
DictFolkMyth-1984, pp. 601, 961

FestSaintDays-1915, p. 163
FolkWrldHol-1999, p. 484
OxYear-1999, p. 315
RelHolCal-2004, p. 273
SaintFestCh-1904, p. 349

♦ 1481 ♦ Lammas Fair
July

Although it is no longer the important trade fair it was at one time, the Lammas Fair is still held for three days every July in Exeter, England. The opening ceremonies, which date back to medieval times, include a procession from the guildhall by two sergeants carrying a blue-and-white pole decorated with flowers and ribbons, from which a large stuffed white glove is suspended. At noon, the sergeants march to the four ancient gates of the city and proclaim the fair open before returning to the guildhall, where the mayor announces the event.

The custom of displaying a glove to open the fair dates back to ancient Saxon times, when permission to hold a market or fair had to be obtained first from a local judge and then ratified by the king, who sent one of his gloves as a token of his approval. It was reinstituted in 1939, after having been discontinued for a number of years.

CONTACTS:
Exeter City Council
Civic Ct., Paris St.
Exeter, Devon EX1 1JN United Kingdom
44-13-9227-7888; fax: 44-13-9226-5265
www.exeter.gov.uk

SOURCES:
EngCustUse-1941, p. 93
YrbookEngFest-1954, p. 98
YrFest-1972, p. 166

♦ 1482 ♦ Lamp Nights (Kandil Geceleri, Candle Feasts)
Five nights on the Muslim calendar: the 12th of Rabi al-Awwal; first of Rajab; 27th of Rajab; 15th of Shaban; and 27th of Ramadan

Turkish Muslims keep mosques lit all night five times a year in order to commemorate five religious festivals associated with events in the life of the prophet Muhammad: MAWLID-AL-NABI, the Birthday of the Prophet Muhammad (12th of Rabi al-Awwal); the Conception of the Prophet Muhammad (1st of Rajab); LAYLAT-AL-MIRAJ, the Prophet Muhammad's Night Journey and Ascent (27th of Rajab); LAYLAT AL-BARA'AH, the Night of Forgiveness (15th of Shaban); and LAYLAT AL-QADR, the Night of Power (27th of Ramadan). As a whole, these commemorative evenings are known as **Kandil Geceleri**. Kandil means "candle," and the name translates as **Candle Feasts** or Lamp Nights.

On these special nights, Turkish Muslims believe that a special holiness prevails. They attend prayer services at the mosque and engage in such devotional activities as reciting poems or singing songs about the Prophet Muhammad. Ring-shaped sesame-seed biscuits known as *Kandil Simidi* are associated with Lamp Nights, as are *Lokma*, fritters drenched in sweet syrup. In past generations, young people paid visits to their elders on Lamp Nights as a sign of respect, though in recent times a phone call is considered by many to be sufficient.

The custom of Lamp Nights dates to the 16th century, when Sultan Selim II ordered that lamps or candles be placed in mosque minarets to announce the five special holy days. On Lamp Nights in modern times, mosques are brightly illuminated with electric lights, including garlands of bulbs looped between minarets. Some strict Muslims dislike the displays, believing that they imitate the Orthodox Christian practice of displaying lights at Christmastime to mark the birth of Christ.

CONTACTS:
Turkish Tourist Office
2525 Massachusetts Ave. N.W.
Washington, D.C. 20008
202-612-6800; fax: 202-319-7446
www.tourismturkey.org

Turkey Embassy
2525 Massachusetts Ave. N.W.
Washington, DC 02008
202-612-6700; fax: 202-612-6744
www.turkey.org

SOURCES:
UndIslam-2004, pp. 280, 379

♦ 1483 ♦ Land Diving
April and May

On Pentecost Island in Vanuatu, a nation consisting of 80 islands in the southwest Pacific that has been independent since 1980, land diving, or **Nagol**, is a centuries-old fertility ritual that is the precursor of what is known in the United States as "bungee jumping." Tree branches, trunks, and vines from the forest are used to create a tower—about 85 feet tall—while the yams are being harvested in April and May.

Facing a test of resolve and courage, island men and boys ascend the tower with liana vines they have personally selected for strength and accurate length. One end of each vine is tied to the ankle and the other to the tower. Before jumping, the diver gives voice to his innermost thoughts, so that the entire crowd may hear what could be his last words, should he not survive the fall. After the diver leaps off the tower, the vines stretch nearly to the ground and the diver ducks his head out of the way and lets his shoulders touch the land—just barely—to symbolically fertilize the earth for the next year's yam crop. During the ritual, the entire village assembles under the tower to dance, sing, and encourage the divers.

Although land diving originated as an agricultural ritual, today it is also a tourist attraction and source of income for villagers in the southern part of the island, who charge a high entry fee for visitors wishing to take photographs or shoot videos.

CONTACTS:
PROMOCOM Ltd.
P.O. Box 1163
Port Vila, Vanuatu

678-267-18; fax: 678-267-18
www.vanuatutourism.com

SOURCES:
WildPlanet-1995, p. 443

♦ 1484 ♦ **Landing of d'Iberville**
Last weekend in April

This event is a commemoration of the landing in 1699 of Pierre LeMoyne d'Iberville at a spot on Biloxi Bay that is now Ocean Springs, Miss. The arrival of d'Iberville and 200 colonists established the Louisiana Colony for King Louis XIV of France; the territory stretched from the Appalachians to the Rocky Mountains and from Canada to the Gulf of Mexico. D'Iberville built Fort Maurepas here, the first significant structure erected by Europeans on the Gulf Coast.

A replica of the fort is the backdrop for the reenactment of the landing. This pageant boasts a costumed cast representing both the notables of d'Iberville's fleet as well as the welcoming Biloxi Indians. The part of d'Iberville is always played by a celebrity, usually from the political world. However, in 1984, Col. Stuart A. Roosa, an Apollo 14 astronaut, played the explorer. In the reenactment, d'Iberville with his officers debarks and wades ashore, plants a cross in the sand, and claims the land for Louis XIV. The Indians, at first wary, invite the French to their village to smoke a peace pipe. The reenactment was first staged in 1939.

The celebration begins on Friday night with a covered dish supper at the civic center. On Saturday night, there is a formal-dress historic ball and pageant, with the presentation of d'Iberville, his officers, and the Cassette Girls. These were young orphan women who had been taught by Catholic nuns in Paris; they made the long trip to the Gulf Coast to become the brides of the men settled in the territory. They were called Cassette Girls because of the cases each carried that contained their trousseaus. The reenactment takes place on Sunday and is followed by a grand parade. There are also exhibits and street and food fairs.

CONTACTS:
Ocean Springs Chamber Mainstreet Visitors Center
1000 Washington Ave.
P.O. Box 187
Ocean Springs, MS 39564
228-875-4424; fax: 228-875-0332
www.oceanspringschamber.com

♦ 1485 ♦ **Landsgemeinde**
Last Sunday of April

Landsgemeinde is an open-air meeting to conduct cantonal business, held once a year in Appenzell, in the canton of Appenzell Inner-Rhoden in Switzerland. At the meeting, citizens vote on representatives for cantonal offices and on budget and tax proposals. Voting is by raised hands.

The assembly is a tradition that dates back to the very early days of the Swiss state. Women may wear richly embroidered national costumes, and men swords. Other districts in central and eastern Switzerland also have these assemblies, each with distinct customs. In Stans, for example, the blowing of a horn signals the time to walk to the meeting place outside the town; the horn is a reminder of the ancient call to battle.

Landsgemeinde has echos in the town meetings of the United States (*see* TOWN MEETING DAY).

CONTACTS:
Cantonal Administration Canton AI
Marktgasse 2
Appenzell, 9050 Switzerland
41-71-788-9327; fax: 41-71-788-9339
www.ai.ch/en

♦ 1486 ♦ **Landshut Wedding**
Late June to late July, every four years (2009, 2013, 2017 . . .)

This pageant in Landshut, Bavaria, Germany, recreates a lavish 15th-century wedding—that of Duke George the Rich of Bavaria and Princess Hedwig from Poland, which took place in 1475. There were 10,000 guests, and records state that they ate 333 oxen, 275 fat pigs, 40 calves, and 12,000 geese.

Today the festivities are spread over three weeks, with the wedding reenactments on weekends—a play and dances on Saturdays; the historical wedding procession, followed by a concert, on Sundays. During the week, historical dances are performed, and some 2,000 residents dressed as medieval burghers roam the streets. There are also jesters parading, armored knights on horseback, and wandering minstrels.

CONTACTS:
Die Forderer e.V. Landshut
Spiegelgasse 208
Landshut, D-84028 Germany
49-871-229-18; fax: 49-871-274-65-3
www.landshuter-hochzeit.de/welcome.htm

SOURCES:
GdWrldFest-1985, p. 85

♦ 1487 ♦ **Lanimer Festival**
Week in early June

The people of Lanark, Scotland, dedicate an entire week to inspecting and celebrating the boundary stones that enclose the territory gifted to them by King David I of Scotland in the 12th century. This week-long event, known as the Lanimer Festival, features public decorations, a parade of civic officials, marching bands, and a series of tableaux. Because people carrying birch branches march in the procession, it is also known as **The Birks**.

A standard-bearer, selected each year by the town council, starts off the second, midday procession. The procession passes by each of the boundary stones, stopping occasionally for sports and horse races. The days' activities close with the town clerk's pronouncement that the boundaries remain in good condition, and a 900-year-old bell rings in celebration.

CONTACTS:
South Lanarkshire Council
Almada St.
Hamilton, South Lanarkshire ML3 0AA United Kingdom
44-84-5740-6080; fax: 44-84-5304-0022
www.lanark.org.uk, www.southlanarkshire.gov.uk

SOURCES:
YrFest-1972, p. 45

♦ 1488 ♦ Lantern Festival (Korea)
Eighth day of the fourth lunar month

In Korea, Buddha's birthday is observed on the evening of the eighth day of the fourth lunar month and is known as *Deungseog* or "lantern evening." A couple of days beforehand, some households hang a lantern-holder, a pole decorated with a pheasant's tail feather (or branch of pine) and colorful strips of silk. Then, on the evening of the eighth, they hang one lantern for each person in the family and light them. Tradition holds that the more brilliant the household can make its lantern display, the luckier it will be.

Although many types of lanterns are used, some of the most popular resemble a tortoise, duck, ship, drum, lotus flower, heron, carp, watermelon, or sun and moon.

Monks began the custom of hanging lanterns for Buddha's birthday during the middle of the Silla dynasty (seventh-eighth century). As Confucianism took stronger hold during the Yi dynasty (1392-1910), it fell into decline. Later in the 20th century many Koreans revived the tradition, though nowadays it is not as widespread. Still, temples all over South Korea hold celebrations in honor of the Buddha on this day with elaborate lantern displays, particularly in Seoul, where there are festivals at major temples with special religious services, other spiritual activities, games, crafts, and a huge lantern parade.

See also VESAK

CONTACTS:
The Korea Herald
3rd-5th Fl., 1-17, Jeong-dong
P.O. Box 6479, Jung-gu
Seoul, Korea
82-2-727-0205; fax: 82-2-727-0670
www.koreaherald.co.kr

SOURCES:
AnnCustKorea-1983, p. 97
FestWrld: SouthKorea-1998, p. 12
FolkWrldHol-1999, p. 305

♦ 1489 ♦ Lantern Festival (Yuan Hsiao Chieh)
January-February; 15th day of first lunar month,
fourth day of first lunar month in Tibet

The Lantern Festival is a festival of lights that ends the LUNAR NEW YEAR, or Chinese New Year, celebrations and marks the first full moon of the new lunar year.

In China, it's traditional for merchants to hang paper lanterns outside their shops for several days before the full-moon day.

On the night of the festival, the streets are bright with both lanterns and streamers, and people go out in throngs to see the displays. The most popular lanterns are cut-outs of running horses that revolve with the heat of the candles that light them. Other customs include eating round, stuffed dumplings and solving "lantern riddles"—riddles that are written on pieces of paper and stuck to the lanterns. In many areas, children parade with lanterns of all shapes and sizes. It's also thought to be a good night for young women to find husbands. In Penang, Malaysia, single women in their best dresses stroll along the city's promenade, and some parade in decorated cars followed by musicians.

Tibetan Buddhists celebrate the day as MONLAM, or Prayer Festival, and in Lhasa, the butter sculptures of the monks are famous (*see* BUTTER SCULPTURE FESTIVAL). In China's Gansu Province, the Lhabuleng Monastery is the site of sculptured butter flowers made by the lamas and hung in front of the main scripture hall. On the day before the full moon, a dance is performed by about 30 masked lamas to the music of drums, horns, and cymbals. The protagonists are the God of Death and his concubines; they dance with others who are dressed as skeletons, horned stags, and yaks.

In 1990, the Taipei Lantern Festival was first held in Taiwan's capital city. It's held at the Chiang Kai-shek Memorial Hall and features high-tech lanterns with mechanical animation, dry-ice "smoke," and laser beams. In recent years, theme lanterns were modeled after the Chinese zodiacal animals for those years. Sculptor Yuyu Yang has produced elaborate structures for the festival, including a dragon that was 40 feet high with a skin of a stainless-steel grid and 1,200 interior light bulbs that shone through to make it look like a gigantic hand-made paper lantern. Laser beams shot from the dragon's eyes, and red-colored smoke spewed from the mouth. Another year, he created three 33-foot-high goats made of acrylic tubes with colored lights shining from the inside.

The festival also offers musical and folk art performances, a procession of religious and folk floats, and troupes of performers entertaining with martial arts demonstrations, stilt-walking, and acrobatics.

In Hong Kong, anyone who has had a son during the year brings a lantern to the Ancestral Hall, where the men gather for a meal.

The Lantern Festival is supposed to have originated with the emperors of China's Han dynasty (206 B.C.E.-221 C.E.), who paid tribute to the universe on that night. Because the ceremony was held in the evening, lanterns were used to illuminate the palace. The Han rulers imposed a year-round curfew on their subjects, but on this night the curfew was lifted, and the people, carrying their own simple lanterns, went forth to view the fancy lanterns of the palace.

Another legend holds that the festival originated because a maid of honor (named Yuan Xiao, also the name of the sweet dumpling of this day) in the emperor's household longed to see her parents during the days of the Spring Festival. The resourceful Dongfang Shuo decided to help her. He spread the rumor that the god of fire was going to burn down the city of Chang-an. The city was thrown into a panic. Dongfang Shuo, summoned by the emperor, advised him to have everyone leave the palace and also to order that lanterns be hung in every street and every building. In this way, the god of fire would think the city was already burning. The emperor followed the advice, and Yuan Xiao took the opportunity to see her family. There have been lanterns ever since.

CONTACTS:
Hong Kong Tourism Board
115 E. 54th St. 2/F
New York, NY 10022
212-421-3382; fax: 212-421-8428
www.discoverhongkong.com

Taiwan Government Information Office
4201 Wisconsin Ave. N.W.
Washington, DC 20016
202-895-1850; fax: 202-362-6144
www.gio.gov.tw

SOURCES:
BkFestHolWrld-1970, p. 9
BkHolWrld-1986, Feb 27
DictFolkMyth-1984, p. 603
EncyRel-1987, vol. 3, p. 325
FolkWrldHol-1999, p. 91
GdWrldFest-1985, p. 63
HolSymbols-2009, p. 479
RelHolCal-2004, p. 231

◆ 1490 ◆ Lantern Night at Bryn Mawr College
Mid-November

Traditions help build a feeling of community at Bryn Mawr, a women's college near Philadelphia, Pennsylvania, where the induction ceremony of Lantern Night has welcomed freshwomen since the late 1880s. The ceremony takes place in the courtyard of the Cloisters, a quadrangle with a pond at the center. The first-year students process into the courtyard, and the sophomores place candlelit lanterns behind each one. Upperclass women sing a hymn in ancient Greek to the goddess of wisdom, Athena, and freshwomen respond in kind. The ceremony in the Cloisters is followed by a step-sing, in which the students of all classes gather together for fellowship and the singing of lighthearted songs outside of Taylor Hall, on the administration building's steps.

CONTACTS:
Bryn Mawr College
101 N. Merion Ave.
Bryn Mawr, PA 19010
610-526-5000; fax: 610-526-7471
www.brynmawr.edu

SOURCES:
FolkAmerHol-1999, p. 415

◆ 1491 ◆ Lanterns Festival
End of Islamic month of Ramadan

A trader known as Daddy Maggay introduced the custom of parading with lanterns in Freetown, Sierra Leone, during the 1930s. The original lanterns were simple hand-held paper boxes, lit from within and mounted on sticks. They were carried through the streets of Freetown in celebration of the 26th day of RAMADAN, also known as the **Day of Light** or **Lai-Lai-Tu-Gadri**, when the Qur'an was sent to earth by Allah (*see* LAYLAT AL-QADR).

As the years passed, the celebration—and the lanterns—grew larger. Heavy boots, originally worn as protection from the crowds, came to be used to produce drum-like rhythmical beats on the paved streets since some Muslims discourage using drums. Maggay's group was called *bobo*, the name for their distinctive beat. Neighborhood rivalries, based on competition in lantern building, often erupted in violence.

By the 1950s the Young Men's Muslim Association had taken over the festival in hopes of reducing the violence through better organization. The lanterns—which by that time were elaborate float-like structures illuminated from within and drawn by eight-man teams or motor vehicles—were divided into three categories for judging: Group A for ships; Group B for animals and people; and Group C for miscellaneous secular subjects. Prizes were awarded to the top three winners in each group, based on creativity and building technique.

CONTACTS:
Sierra Leone Embassy
1701 19th St. N.W.
Washington, D.C. 20009
202-939-9261; fax: 202-483-1793
www.embassyofsierraleone.org

SOURCES:
FolkWrldHol-1999, p. 676

◆ 1492 ◆ Larentalia
December 23

In ancient Rome, the *lares* were the beneficient spirits of household and family. Along with the *penates* (the gods of the storeroom) and the *manes* (spirits of the dead), they were worshipped privately within the home. Eventually they came to be identified with the spirits of the deceased. Each household had its own *lar*, to whom a prayer was addressed every morning and for whom special offerings were made at family festivals.

During the Larentalia, observed on December 23, offerings were made to the dead, especially at the shrine of Acca Larentia, the nurse of Romulus and Remus, the legendary founders of Rome. A sacrifice was offered on the spot where Acca Larentia was said to have disappeared.

See also COMPITALIA; FERALIA; PARENTALIA

SOURCES:
DictFolkMyth-1984, p. 604
FestRom-1981, p. 210
NewCentClassHandbk-1962, p. 625
OxYear-1999, p. 508

◆ 1493 ◆ Last Great Day
October; Tishri 22

A one-day festival observed by the United Church of God, the Last Great Day immediately follows the Feast of Tabernacles in the seventh month of Tishri, the Hebrew calendar. The Feast of Tabernacles and the Last Great Day are Holy Days that represent for believers the final steps of God's plan for the fate of the world and his people. As prescribed by the United Church of God, which is a Christian sect, believers observe all seven of the Holy Days. For the Last Great Day, they are invited to meditate on the eternal life that awaits God's loyal followers.

The Last Great Day is described in the Book of Revelation as a scene proceeding a 1,000-year-long reign of Christ. Standing before a "great white throne and him who was seated on it," the dead are told whether they have been ordained a life in heaven or if they will suffer eternal damnation in the Lake of Fire. The day has a corollary in the Old Testament's Book of Leviticus, which contains a description of a final day of a series of feasts during which people continuously present God their offerings.

CONTACTS:
United Church of God
P.O. Box 541027
Cincinnati, OH 45254-1027
513-576-9796; fax: 513-576-9795
www.ucg.org

SOURCES:
RelHolCal-2004, p. 133

♦ 1494 ♦ Latin Festival (Feriae Latinae)
April

The Latin Festival was held in Rome for more than a thousand years, making it one of the longest-lived Roman festivals. The original **Feriae Latinae** was held by a group of ancient Latin tribes, who lived a simple pastoral life and worshiped Jupiter on the Alban Mount, about 13 miles outside Rome. All wars came to a halt for the observance. There was a sacrifice of a young white cow who had never been yoked as well as a ritual pouring of milk rather than wine, since the grape had not yet been introduced into Italy. After the sacrifice to Jupiter, the meat of the cow was used for a communal meal. A curious sight accompanied the ritual—little dolls or puppets made to look like people, called *oscilla*, bobbed from tree branches. Some have suggested these may have been symbolic of human sacrifice in earlier times, but others assert they were probably a kind of good-luck emblem.

By the period of the later Republic, the Romans had taken over the ceremony and they commemorated the early Latin peoples, most of whose settlements had by then disappeared. The Latin Festival was normally held in April, before military activities for the year got underway. A temple to Jupiter was built on the site in the sixth century B.C.E. and Romans would gather at the temple Jupiter to participate in the traditional libation and animal sacrifice. Afterward, feasting and games went on for two days.

SOURCES:
BkFairs-1939, p. 59

DictRomRel-1996, p. 77
FestRom-1981, p. 111
RomFest-1925, p. 95

♦ 1495 ♦ Latina, Fiesta
October

The Fiesta Latina takes place on one Saturday every October in Asheville, N.C. A celebration of Latino culture and community, it features Latino music, dance, food, and arts and crafts. It also provides opportunities for local businesses, organizations, and public-health agencies to reach the local Latino community with informational displays and services.

The festival began in 1999, when an Asheville museum sponsored a textile exhibition by Latin-American artists. Officials at the Asheville Latin Americans for Advancement Society decided to use the exhibit as a launch pad for a broader event to reflect many aspects of Latino culture. The event is now affiliated with the Young Men's Institute Cultural Center, a long-standing African-American socio-cultural institution in Asheville.

CONTACTS:
Young Men's Institute Cultural Center
39 S. Market St.
Asheville, NC 28801
828-252-4614; fax: 828-257-4539
www.ymicc.org/fiesta_latina

♦ 1496 ♦ Latter-Day Saints, Founding of the Church of
April 6

April 6, 1830, is the day on which Joseph Smith formally established the Church of Jesus Christ of the Latter-Day Saints (also known as Mormons) in Fayette, New York. Three years later the anniversary of the Church's founding was celebrated for the first time, with a meeting of about 80 people on the Big Blue River in Jackson County, Missouri. After that, there were no "birthday" celebrations until 1837, when a general conference was held to conduct church business and to observe the anniversary. Eventually the idea of holding an annual conference became an established custom, and it was always scheduled to encompass the April 6 founding date.

CONTACTS:
Church of Jesus Christ of Latter-Day Saints
50 N.E. Temple St.
Salt Lake City, UT 84150
801-240-1000; fax: 801-240-1187
www.lds.org

SOURCES:
AmerBkDays-2000, p. 260
DaysCustFaith-1957, p. 94
DictWrldRel-1989, p. 423
FolkAmerHol-1999, p. 196
RelHolCal-2004, p. 126

♦ 1497 ♦ Latvia Independence Day
November 18

Independence Day marks Latvia's declaration of independence from German and Russian occupation on November 18, 1918. The country remained independent until World War II, when it was absorbed by the Soviet Union. Like the other Baltic republics, Latvia proclaimed its independence from Soviet Russia in 1991, on August 21.

CONTACTS:
Embassy of Latvia
2306 Massachusetts Ave. N.W.
Washington, D.C. 20008
202-328-2840; fax: 202-328-2860
www.latvia-usa.org

◆ 1498 ◆ Law Day
May 1

It was the American Bar Association that persuaded President Dwight D. Eisenhower in 1958 to set aside a special day to commemorate the role of law in the United States and to remind people of the contrast between democratic government under the law and the tyranny of Communism. But it wasn't until 1961 that a joint resolution of Congress designated May 1 as Law Day, and President John F. Kennedy asked Americans to display the flag and observe the occasion with appropriate programs—typically mock trials, courthouse tours, special radio and television programs, library exhibits, and essay contests. Most Law Day exercises today are sponsored by the American Bar Association in cooperation with state and local bar associations.

The first of May was previously known as LOYALTY DAY, another attempt to play up the virtues of democracy and to cast Communism in a negative light. It is no coincidence that in the former U.S.S.R., MAY DAY was the great holiday for massive military reviews and other demonstrations of armed power.

CONTACTS:
American Bar Association
321 N. Clark St.
Chicago, IL 60610
800-285-2221 or 312-988-5522; fax: 312-988-5568
www.abanet.org

SOURCES:
AmerBkDays-2000, p. 337
AnnivHol-2000, p. 74
DictDays-1988, p. 67

◆ 1499 ◆ Laylat al-Bara'ah (Shab-Barat)
Eve of the 15th day of the Islamic month of Shaban

This holy day is known as Laylat al-Bara'ah ("Night of Forgiveness") in Arabic and SHAB-BARAT in Persian. Followers observe the date by holding a vigil throughout the night. They congregate at the local mosque to pray, read the Qur'an, and set off fireworks. Like other Islamic traditions, the festival reflects the common elements as well as the differences between the religion's Shi'ite and Sunni sects.

Sunnis regard the holiday exclusively as a night in which one's fate for the upcoming year is determined. According to Sunni lore, every individual's destiny is recorded on a corresponding leaf on the Tree of Life. When Allah shakes this tree on the 15th of Shaban, he fixes the next year's course of events.

Simultaneous to observing these destiny traditions of Laylat al-Bara'ah, Shi'ites also celebrate the BIRTHDAY OF THE TWELFTH IMAM, a figure of paramount importance in the Shi'ite faith who is expected to redeem the world upon his second coming.

SOURCES:
AnnivHol-2000, p. 234
RelHolCal-2004, p. 147
UndIslam-2004, p. 291

◆ 1500 ◆ Laylat al-Miraj
27th day of the Islamic month of Rajab

Laylat al-Miraj commemorates the ascent of the Prophet Muhammad into heaven. One night during the 10th year of his prophecy, the angel Gabriel woke Muhammad and traveled with him to Jerusalem on the winged horse, Burak. There he prayed at the site of the Temple of Solomon with the Prophets Abraham, Moses, Jesus, and others. Then, carried by Gabriel, he rose to heaven from the rock of the Temple Mount, where the Dome of the Rock sanctuary now stands. Allah instructed him regarding the five daily prayers that all Muslims must observe. Muslims today celebrate the evening of the 27th day of Rajab with special prayers. This day is also known as the **Night Journey**, or the **Ascent**.

SOURCES:
AnnivHol-2000, p. 234
BkHolWrld-1986, Apr 29
ConEncyIslam-1991, p. 301
FolkWrldHol-1999, p. 648
HolSymbols-2009, p. 488
RelHolCal-2004, p. 488
UndIslam-2004, p. 283

◆ 1501 ◆ Laylat al-Qadr
One of the last 10 days of Islamic month of Ramadan

Laylat al-Qadr commemorates the night in 610 during which Allah revealed the entire Qur'an (Muslim holy book) to Muhammad. It was then that the angel Gabriel first spoke to him, and was thus the beginning of his mission. These revelations continued throughout the remainder of his life. Children begin studying the Qur'an when they are very young, and they celebrate when they've read all 114 chapters for the first time. Many adults try to memorize the entire Qur'an. The common belief that this day occurred on the 26th or 27th of Ramadan has no Islamic base. It seems to have originated in Manicheism where the death of Mani is celebrated on the 27th of the fasting month. This day is also known as the **Night of Power** or **Night of Destiny**.

See also LANTERNS FESTIVAL

SOURCES:
AnnivHol-2000, p. 235
BkHolWrld-1986, Jun 23
ConEncyIslam-1991, p. 243
DictWrldRel-1989, p. 661
FolkWrldHol-1999, p. 678
HolSymbols-2009, p. 492
UndIslam-2004, p. 339

♦ 1502 ♦ Laytown Strand Races
June

A carnival atmosphere pervades the Laytown Strand Races, a unique horse race run on a beach track by the Irish Sea in Laytown, County Meath, Ireland. Horses, owners, trainers, and bookmakers mingle with horse-lovers, racing fans, party-goers, sun worshippers, and food and beverage vendors on the beach as the tide recedes and the races begin.

CONTACTS:
Meath Tourism Ltd.
Ashbourne Civic Offices, Killegland St.
Ashbourne, County Meath, Ireland
353-18-358022; fax: 353-1-8358120

SOURCES:
WildPlanet-1995, p. 56

♦ 1503 ♦ Lazarus Saturday
Between March 27 and April 30; Saturday before Palm Sunday

In Russia and in all Eastern Orthodox churches, the Saturday before PALM SUNDAY (or Willow Sunday) is set aside to honor Lazarus, whom Jesus raised from the dead. Pussywillows are blessed at the evening service in the Russian Orthodox Church, and the branches are distributed to the worshippers, who take them home and display them above their icons. It was an ancient folk custom for people to beat their children with willow branches—not so much to punish them as to ensure that they would grow up tall and resilient like the willow tree.

On this day in Greece, Romania, and the former Yugoslavia, one custom is for groups of children to carry willow branches from house to house and sing songs and act out the story of Jesus raising Lazarus from the dead. In return, they receive gifts of fruit and candy. They believe the resurrection of Lazarus is symbolic of the renewal of spring, which is why the *Lazarouvane* (the celebration of ST. LAZARUS'S DAY in Bulgaria) focuses on fertility and marriage.

CONTACTS:
Orthodox Church in America
P.O. Box 675
Syosset, NY 11791
516-922-0550; fax: 516-922-0954
www.oca.org

SOURCES:
BkFest-1937, pp. 290, 337
EncyEaster-2002, p. 343
FolkWrldHol-1999, p. 170
OxYear-1999, pp. 502, 643

♦ 1504 ♦ Le Mans Motor Race
June

The motor racing circuit in the city of Le Mans, capital of the Sarthe department of France, has been the scene of important races since 1914, although it wasn't until 1923 that the first 24-hour sports car race for which the course is now famous was held. Over the years the **Le Mans 24-Hour Grand Prix d'Endurance** has had a significant impact on the development of sports cars for racing, resulting in some prototype sports cars that are not far behind Formula I racing cars in terms of power and speed. The original course was rough and dusty, with a lap distance of just under 11 miles. Eventually the road surface was improved, the corners were eased, and the lap distance was reduced to just over eight miles. Part of the course is still a French highway, now flanked by permanent concrete stands for spectators and the pits, where refueling and repairs are done. A serious accident at Le Mans in 1955, in which a French driver and 85 spectators died, led to a number of course improvements.

The all-night racing at Le Mans is a favorite spectacle for motor racing fans. One of the major attractions is the opportunity to watch what goes on in the pits. Although most Grand Prix races can now be run without refueling or tire changing, the highly efficient work of the teams' mechanics still plays an important part in long-duration races like the one at Le Mans.

CONTACTS:
Automobile Club de l'Ouest
Circuit des 24 Heures
Le Mans, 72019 France
33-2-4340-2424; fax: 33-2-4340-2415
www.lemans.org/accueil/index_gb.html

♦ 1505 ♦ Leaders of the Bulgarian National Revival Day (National Enlighteners Day)
November 1

Bulgaria's native culture is rich and ancient, but at one time, it seemed in danger of being lost forever. Bulgaria was under the rule of the Ottoman Empire for almost five centuries, and the Empire's Turkish authorities suppressed any expression of unity or national pride by the Bulgarian people. Bulgaria had poor schools and no other institutions in place to protect and preserve its heritage. Under such conditions, the country's traditional culture could not thrive.

That situation underwent a dramatic reversal during the period known as the Bulgarian National Revival. This cultural renaissance began in the 18th century and is divided into three stages: the early period, including the 18th century and the early part of the 19th century; the middle period, lasting from roughly the 1820s until the Crimean War, which ended in 1856; and the late period, dating from the Crimean War until Bulgaria's liberation from the Ottoman Empire in 1878, as a result of the Russo-Turkish War.

During the Revival, a number of well-educated Bulgarians made a conscious effort to awaken feelings of pride and unity among their countrymen, in part because they felt that such feelings were necessary if Bulgaria were ever to regain its freedom from Ottoman rule. They did this by working to develop Bulgarian literature that would call to mind past glories and hopes for a better future. They worked to establish modern schools, and within a few decades, 1,500 primary schools were in operation throughout the country. This, in turn, allowed more young Bulgarians to further their educations at the great universities of Europe and Russia. Within a short while, the country had a well-educated elite, which took control of the arts and newspapers in Bulgaria.

National pride and unity were greatly reinforced by these efforts, which are credited with paving the way to successful opposition to Ottoman rule. On November 1, Bulgaria celebrates a national holiday to honor and remember those visionaries who did so much to establish a sense of national pride and to lay the foundation for Bulgarian liberation. The holiday was declared official in 1922, but was suspended in 1945 after Bulgaria came under Communist rule, as part of the former Soviet Union. After the dissolution of the Soviet Union, celebration was resumed in 1990 and made official again in 1995.

Across Bulgaria, Leaders of the Bulgarian National Revival Day (sometimes called **National Enlighteners Day**) is an occasion to pay tribute to all those committed to culture and education. It is traditionally a day to give awards to outstanding teachers, actors, and artists of all sorts. Since the 1930s, it has been a tradition in cities and towns throughout the country to hold parades honoring students and teachers. In the capital city of Sofia, the parade progresses beneath huge portraits of those leaders who nourished Bulgaria's cultural rebirth.

CONTACTS:
Bulgarian Embassy
1621 22nd St. N.W.
Washington, D.C. 20008
202-387-0174 or 202-299-0273; fax: 202-234-7973
www.bulgaria-embassy.org

♦ 1506 ♦ Leap Year Day
February 29

The earth actually takes longer than 365 days to complete its trip around the sun—five hours, 48 minutes, and 45 seconds longer, to be precise. To accommodate this discrepancy, an extra day is added to the Gregorian calendar at the end of February every four years (but not in "century" years unless evenly divisible by 400, e.g., 1600 and 2000, but not 1700). The year in which this occurs is called Leap Year, probably because the English courts did not always recognize February 29, and the date was often "leaped over" in the records. There's an old tradition that women could propose marriage to men during Leap Year. The men had to pay a forfeit if they refused. It is for this reason that February 29 is sometimes referred to as **Ladies' Day** or **Bachelors' Day**. Leap Year Day is also **St. Oswald's Day,** named after the 10th-century archbishop of York, who died on February 29, 992.

See also SADIE HAWKINS DAY

CONTACTS:
U.S. Naval Observatory
Astronomical Applications Dept.
3450 Massachusetts Ave. N.W.
Washington, D.C. 20392
202-762-1617; fax: 202-762-1612
aa.usno.navy.mil

SOURCES:
AmerBkDays-2000, p. 170
BkHolWrld-1986, Feb 29
DaysCustFaith-1957, p. 59
DictDays-1988, pp. 8, 67
FolkAmerHol-1999, p. 86
OxYear-1999, pp. 96, 678

♦ 1507 ♦ Lebanon National Day
November 22

Also known as **Independence Day**, this national holiday commemorates Lebanon's independence from France on this day in 1943.

CONTACTS:
Lebanese Embassy
2560 28th St. N.W.
Washington, D.C. 20008
202-939-6300; fax: 202-939-6324
www.lebanonembassyus.org

SOURCES:
AnnivHol-2000, p. 195
NatlHolWrld-1968, p. 209

♦ 1508 ♦ Lebanon Resistance and Liberation Day
May 25

A recently established tradition in Lebanon, this day celebrates the end of Israel's 22-year-long military occupation, which occurred in 2000. That year Israel completed its withdrawal from the country's southern region. Immediately after, the cabinet under Lebanese prime minister Salim al-Hoss declared the public holiday on May 25.

Conferences, rallies, and speeches commemorating the anniversary are commonplace, particularly in southern Lebanon, the region most directly affected by Israel's intervention. In 2000, tens of thousands rejoiced over the retreat of the Israeli defense forces by swarming around public locales in the former war zone. Many displaced individuals were able to return after spending years away from their home communities. The anniversary's political significance has endured for the Lebanese, particularly in view of the renewed combat between Israel and Hezbollah paramilitary forces in 2006.

Resistance and Liberation Day can also be an occasion to turn public attention to the country's ongoing reconstruction efforts. Such was the case for the 2007 anniversary, when Lebanese leaders marked the day by announcing the reopening of the Zahrani bridge, an important road link destroyed in a July 2006 Israeli air strike.

CONTACTS:
Friends of Lebanon

12 Berry Lane
Rickmansworth
Hertfordshire WD3 7HQ United Kingdom
www.friendsoflebanon.org

Embassy of Lebanon
2560 28th St. N.W.
Washington, DC 20008
202-939-6300; fax: 202-939-6324

◆ 1509 ◆ Lee (Ann) Birthday
February 29

Ann Lee (1736-1784) was a leader in the religious movement known as the Shakers. She left England in 1774 to establish Shaker communities throughout New England and New York state, as well as in Kentucky, Ohio, and Indiana. "Mother Ann," as she was known to her followers, believed that sexual desire was the original sin and people must be celibate in order to be closer to God. Shaker communities were known for their inventions (which include the flat broom and the clothespin), their architecture, and their furniture design as well as their commitment to celibacy, communal ownership of property, prayer, and separation from the world. They were pioneers in scientific stock breeding, crop rotation, and food preservation. The only active Shaker community that remains today is at Sabbathday Lake in Poland Spring, Maine.

Since there are less than a dozen Shakers alive, Ann Lee's birthday is no longer celebrated on a large scale, but there are numerous events commemorating the history of the Shaker movement that take place at several sites and museums devoted to Shakerism.

CONTACTS:
United Society of Shakers
707 Shaker Rd.
New Gloucester, ME 04260
207-926-4597; fax: 207-926-3559
www.maineshakers.com

SOURCES:
AmerBkDays-2000, p. 171
AnnivHol-2000, p. 34
DictWrldRel-1989, p. 674
EncyRel-1987, vol. 8, p. 491

◆ 1510 ◆ Lee (Robert E.) Day
Third Monday in January

The Confederate General Robert Edward Lee was born on January 19, 1807. He was in charge of the military and naval forces of Virginia during the Civil War, building a reputation as a brilliant military strategist and a man who inspired great loyalty among his troops. By the time he was appointed general-in-chief of all the Confederate armies, the South's defeat was imminent. Lee's subsequent surrender to General Ulysses S. Grant at the Appomattox Court House in 1865 marked the end of the war (*see* APPOMATTOX DAY).

In 1889 Georgia became the first state to make Lee's birthday a legal holiday. Other states observing Lee's birthday each year include Alabama, Arkansas, Kentucky, and Mississippi. Texas observes Lee's birthday as **Confederate Heroes Day**.

CONTACTS:
National Park Service
George Washington Memorial Parkway
Turkey Run Park
McLean, VA 22101
703-235-1530
www.nps.gov

Stratford Hall Plantation
Birthplace of Robert E. Lee
485 Great House Rd.
Stratford, VA 22558
804-493-8038
www.stratfordhall.org

SOURCES:
AmerBkDays-2000, pp. 68, 77
AnnivHol-2000, p. 11
DictDays-1988, pp. 73, 96

◆ 1511 ◆ Lei Day
May 1

This is a celebration of Hawaii's state symbol of friendship. In 1928 Mrs. John T. Warren came up with the slogan, "Lei Day is May Day," and the holiday has been held there ever since. The events of the day include state-wide lei competitions. Leis are garlands made of flower blossoms, seeds, leaves, ferns, and pods. There is the crowning of a Lei Queen in Honolulu, and assorted exhibits and hula performances. The queen's coronation is accompanied by chanting and the blowing of conch shells.

On the day after the celebration, leis from the state-wide competitions are ceremoniously placed on the graves of Hawaii's royalty at the Royal Mausoleum in Nuuanu Valley.

CONTACTS:
Hawaii Visitors Bureau
2270 Kalakaua Ave., 8th Fl.
Honolulu, HI 96815
800-464-2924 or 808-923-1811; fax: 808-924-0290
www.gohawaii.com & www.hvcb.org

SOURCES:
AmerBkDays-2000, p. 337
AnnivHol-2000, p. 75
DictDays-1988, p. 67

◆ 1512 ◆ Leiden Day
October 3

In 1573 the Dutch city of Leiden (or Leyden) was besieged by the Spaniards. Thousands were dying from disease and hunger, but when a group of desperate citizens pleaded with the Burgomaster to surrender, he replied that he had sworn to keep the city safe and that it was better to die of starvation than shame. His stubbornness heartened the people, and finally the river dikes were cut so that the Dutch army could sail in over the flooded fields and save the city. A statue of the heroic Burgomaster, Adrian van der Werff, was later erected in Leiden's Church of Saint Pancras.

According to legend, the first person to emerge from the besieged city on October 3 was a young orphan boy. In the deserted Spanish camp, he discovered a huge pot of stew that was still hot. He summoned the townspeople, who enjoyed their first hot meal in several months. Known as *Hutspot met Klapstuk,* the mixture of meat and vegetables is still served on this day, along with bread and herring.

CONTACTS:
VVV Tourist Office
Stationsweg 2D
P.O. Box 100
Leiden, 2312 AV Netherlands
31-71-516-1211; fax: 31-71-516-1227
www.hollandrijnland.nl

SOURCES:
BkFest-1937, p. 244
BkHolWrld-1986, Oct 3
FestWestEur-1958, p. 139

♦ 1513 ♦ **Leif Erikson Day**
October 9

The Viking explorer known as Leif the Lucky or Leif Erikson (because he was the son of Eric the Red) sailed westward from Greenland somewhere around the year 1000 and discovered a place he named Vinland after the wild grapes that grew there. No one really knows where Vinland was, but some historians believe that Erikson landed in North America 488 years before COLUMBUS sailed into the New World. The only evidence that this may have happened are a few Viking relics found in Rhode Island, Minnesota, and Ontario. In 1960, the site of a Norse settlement was discovered at L'Anse aux Meadows, at the northern tip of Newfoundland. The site dates from about the year 1000, but it has not been definitively linked to Leif Erikson's explorations.

Because the date and place of Erikson's "discovery" of North America were uncertain, members of the Leif Erikson Association arbitrarily chose October 9 to commemorate this event—perhaps because the first organized group of Norwegian emigrants landed in America on October 9, 1825. But it wasn't until 1964 that President Lyndon B. Johnson proclaimed this as Leif Erikson Day.

States with large Norwegian-American populations—such as Washington, Minnesota, Wisconsin, and New York—often hold observances on this day, as do members of the Sons of Norway, the Leif Erikson Society, and other Norwegian-American organizations. October 9 is a commemorative day in Iceland and Norway as well.

CONTACTS:
Icelandic Embassy
1156 15th St. N.W., Ste. 1200
Washington, D.C. 20005
202-265-6653; fax: 202-265-6656
www.iceland.org

SOURCES:
AmerBkDays-2000, p. 698
AnnivHol-2000, p. 170
FolkAmerHol-1999, p. 417

♦ 1514 ♦ **Lemon Festival**
Late January through mid-February

Since the 1930s the town of Menton, France, has celebrated its annual Lemon Festival for three weeks beginning in late January or February. Festival organizers expect about 300,000 people to visit the town during the festival in order to enjoy the parades—featuring larger-than-life-sized figurines made entirely of citrus fruit, a specialty of the region—and other activities. Performances of local folk music and dance also take place during the festival. In addition, visitors may stroll by scenes from famous stories reconstructed out of citrus fruits and displayed in one of the city's parks. The Lemon Festival coincides with another important local event, the Orchid Festival. Those who attend this exhibit of orchid specimens may also sample regional foods and view the work of local artists.

CONTACTS:
Menton Tourist Office
8, Ave. Boyer BP
Menton, 06506 France
33-4-9241-7676; fax: 33-4-9241-7678
www.menton.fr/rubrique.php3?id_rubrique=33

♦ 1515 ♦ **Lemuralia**
May 9, 11, 15

In ancient Rome the *lemures* were the ghosts of the family's dead, who were considered to be troublesome and therefore had to be exorcized on a regular basis. The lemures were generally equated with larvae or evil spirits, although some people believed that the lemures included the *lares,* or "good spirits," as well (*see* LARENTALIA).

The Lemuralia or **Lemuria** was a yearly festival held on the ninth, 11th, and 15th of May to get rid of the lemures. Supposedly introduced by Romulus, the legendary founder of Rome, after he killed his twin brother Remus, this festival was originally called the **Remuria**. Participants walked barefoot, cleansed their hands three times, and threw black beans behind them nine times to appease the spirits of the dead. On the third day of the festival, a merchants' festival was held to ensure a prosperous year for business. The period during which the Lemuralia was held—the entire month of May—was considered to be an unlucky time for marriages.

SOURCES:
AmerBkDays-2000, p. 333
DictFolkMyth-1984, pp. 123, 613
DictRomRel-1996, p. 131
FestRom-1981, p. 118
FestSaintDays-1915, p. 110
OxYear-1999, p. 201

♦ 1516 ♦ **Lent**
Begins between February 4 and March 10 in West and between February 15 and March 21 in East; 40-day period, beginning on Ash Wednesday in the West and on the Monday seven weeks before Easter in the East; ends on Easter eve, Holy Saturday

Self-denial during a period of intense religious devotion has been a long-standing tradition in both the Eastern and Western churches. In the early days, Christians prepared for EASTER with a strict fast only from GOOD FRIDAY until Easter morning. It wasn't until the ninth century that the Lenten season, called the **Great Lent** in the East to differentiate it from the ADVENT fast called Little Lent, was fixed at 40 days (with Sundays omitted)—perhaps reflecting the biblical importance attached to the number 40: Moses had gone without food for 40 days on Mt. Sinai, the children of Israel had wandered for 40 years with little sustenance, ELIJAH had fasted 40 days, and so did Jesus, between his baptism and the beginning of his ministry.

In the Western church further extensions led to a no-longer-existing "pre-Lent" season, with its Sundays called Septuagesima (roughly 70 days before Easter), Sexagesima (60), and Quinquagesima (50)—all preceding the first Sunday of Lent, QUADRAGESIMA (40).

The first day of Orthodox Lent is called Clean Monday.

For centuries the Lenten season has been observed with certain periods of strict fasting, and with abstinence from meat, and in the East, also from dairy products, wine, and olive oil, as well as giving up something—a favorite food or other worldly pleasure—for the 40 days of Lent. Celebrations such as CARNIVAL and MARDI GRAS offered Christians their last opportunities to indulge before the rigorous Lenten restrictions.

See also ASH WEDNESDAY; CHEESE SUNDAY; MOTHERING SUNDAY; SHROVE MONDAY; SHROVE TUESDAY

CONTACTS:
Christian Resource Institute
4712 N. Hammond
Warr Acres, OK 73122
405-789-0449
www.cresourcei.org

Orthodox Church in America
P.O. Box 675
Syosset, NY 11791
516-922-0550; fax: 516-922-0954
www.oca.org

SOURCES:
BkFest-1937, pp. 68, 308
DaysCustFaith-1957, p. 65
DictFolkMyth-1984, pp. 181, 212, 851
DictWrldRel-1989, pp. 154, 175, 425
EncyEaster-2002, p. 346
EncyRel-1987, vol. 3, p. 440
FestWestEur-1958, p. 211
FolkWrldHol-1999, p. 162
HolSymbols-2009, p. 505
IndianAmer-1989, p. 273
OxYear-1999, p. 608
RelHolCal-2004, pp. 91, 118
SaintFestCh-1904, p. 115

♦ 1517 ♦ **Leonhardiritt (St. Leonard's Ride)**
November 6 or nearest weekend

Also called **Leonhardifahrt**, this is a celebration of St. Leonhard, the patron saint of horses and cattle, observed in vari-

ous towns of Bavaria, Germany. Traditionally, processions of elaborately harnessed horses draw decorated wagons to the local church. Some people also bring their cattle to be blessed. A contest of whip-cracking often follows the procession. Among the towns where Leonard's Ride is held are Bad Tölz, Rottenbuch, Bad Füssing, Waldkirchen, and Murnau. November 6 is the name-day of the saint and the traditional day of the procession, but some towns now hold their rides on a weekend near that date.

CONTACTS:
Bayern Tourismus Marketing GmbH
Leopoldstr 146
Munich, 80804 Germany
49-89-212-39-70; fax: 49-89-212-39-799
www.bayern.by/en/index.html

SOURCES:
BkFest-1937, p. 138
BkHolWrld-1986, Nov 6
FestWestEur-1958, p. 75

♦ 1518 ♦ **Lesotho Independence Day**
October 4

Formerly Basutoland, the Kingdom of Lesotho was formally granted its independence from Great Britain on this day in 1966. It had been a British colony since the 1860s.

Before the flag-changing ceremonies at midnight to symbolize Lesotho's new autonomy, a colorful procession took place as King MOSHOESHOE II (b. 1938) paraded in full regalia leading 100 chiefs into the capital city of Maseru.

CONTACTS:
Lesotho Embassy
2511 Massachusetts Ave. N.W.
Washington, D.C. 20008
202-797-5533; fax: 202-234-6815
www.lesothoemb-usa.gov.ls

SOURCES:
AnnivHol-2000, p. 167
NatlHolWrld-1968, p. 186

♦ 1519 ♦ **Lewis and Clark Festival**
June

This five-day festival commemorates the Lewis and Clark expedition, an early exploration of the vast wilderness of what is now the northwestern United States. The expedition was sponsored by the U.S. government and led by President Thomas JEFFERSON's secretary Meriwether Lewis (1774-1809) and U.S. Army officer William Clark (1770-1838).

Lewis and Clark covered a total of about 8,000 miles. Starting near St. Louis in May 1804, they journeyed up the Missouri River, across the Rocky Mountains, and along the Columbia and other rivers to the Pacific coast. They returned to St. Louis in September 1806 with maps of their route and the surrounding regions; specimens and descriptions of plant, animal, and mineral resources; and information about the native peoples of the West. The success of the expedition enabled the United States to claim the Oregon region, which included what are now the states of Oregon, Washington, and Idaho.

The Lewis and Clark Festival in Great Falls, Montana, celebrates the expedition's stay there in 1805. Giant Springs Heritage State Park is the site of living history reenactments and encampments, where visitors can experience what daily life was like in the early 19th century, watch interpretive demonstrations, and eat typical expedition fare. The festival also features lectures at the Lewis and Clark Interpretive Center, exhibits, seminars, tours of historic sites, float trips, nature hikes, and a treasure hunt.

CONTACTS:
Lewis and Clark Festival
4201 Giant Springs Rd.
P.O. Box 2848
Great Falls, MT 59403
406-452-5661; fax: 406-453-6157
lewisandclark.state.mt.us

◆ 1520 ◆ Li Ch'un
February 4 or 5

Li Ch'un is Chinese for "spring is here." This is one of 24 days in the Chinese calendar marking a change of season. The celebration of spring in some places has involved a procession of local dignitaries, dancers, singers, and musicians. Some of these carried a platform holding an ox and his driver made of paper. Each year the Chinese almanac, the *T'ung Shu*, gives specific instructions about the most auspicious colors to use in creating the ox and driver.

People also traditionally mount a post with feathers outside their homes. The sight of feathers floating in the breeze means that spring has officially arrived.

SOURCES:
AnnivHol-2000, p. 21
BkFestHolWrld-1970, p. 91
DictFolkMyth-1984, pp. 225, 618

◆ 1521 ◆ Liberalia
March 17

Liber and Libera were ancient Roman fertility deities, worshipped along with Ceres. The triad of Ceres, Liber, and Libera was identified with the Greek deities Demeter, Dionysus, and Persephone. At the festival held in honor of Liber and Libera on March 17, young Roman boys who had come of age wore the *toga virilis* for the first time. In the ancient Italian town of Lavinium, a whole month was consecrated to Liber. The various rituals carried out during this time were designed to ensure the growth of newly planted seeds.

See also CEREALIA

SOURCES:
DictFolkMyth-1984, p. 618
FestRom-1981, p. 91
NewCentClassHandbk-1962, p. 641
OxYear-1999, p. 122

◆ 1522 ◆ Liberia Armed Forces Day
February 11

On this day, Liberians honor the soldiers of the country's armed forces. Festivities often include regiment parades and a public address from the Liberian president or the commander-in-chief. Since the day's first observance in 1957, the holiday has evoked mixed memories for Liberians, as the army has been linked with the chaos that plagued the country at the end of the 20th century.

Unlike many of its African neighbors, Liberia steered clear of military coups during the relatively peaceful years under President W. V. S. Tubman (1944–71). However, the army did help carry out the repressive policies of the dictators who succeeded Tubman. Between 1989 and 2003, during two consecutive civil wars, Liberians suffered numerous atrocities by soldiers, as well as by rebel fighters.

For a short period following the war, this holiday received no fanfare because the country's implosion left Liberians with no army to honor. In 2007, however, the defense ministry introduced a newly restructured contingent, which paraded through the main streets of the capital city, Monrovia, before hundreds of attendees.

CONTACTS:
Liberia Ministry of Information, Cultural Affairs and Tourism
  (MICAT)
110 United Nations Dr.
P.O. Box 10-9021
Capitol Hill, 1000
Monrovia, Liberia
www.micat.gov.lr

◆ 1523 ◆ Liberia Flag Day
August 24

The Liberian flag bears a striking resemblance to the American flag, a visual reminder of the historically close ties between this West African country and the United States. Eleven horizontal stripes—six red and five white—represent the signers of the Liberian Declaration of Independence, while the single white star that sits in the flag's upper left corner signifies Liberia's former position as the sole free black state in Africa.

Flag Day, a patriotic day paying homage to Liberia's national emblem, is an official public holiday. Citizens and public buildings display their flags, and parades often feature schoolchildren and military units. The holiday was first observed in an 1847 convention, when the founding fathers approved the flag's design along with establishing the new republic.

CONTACTS:
Liberia Ministry of Information, Cultural Affairs and Tourism
  (MICAT)
110 United Nations Dr.
P.O. Box 10-9021
Capitol Hill, 1000
Monrovia, Liberia
www.micat.gov.lr

SOURCES:
AnnivHol-2000, p. 140
NatlHolWrld-1968, p. 124

♦ 1524 ♦ **Liberia Independence Day**
July 26

This especially important Liberian holiday is celebrated with a parade, a party for the diplomatic corps in Monrovia, and a grand ball in the evening. Similar events are held throughout the country. The day commemorates the signing of the Declaration of Independence in 1847 by the various settlements of the country, establishing the first independent black republic in Africa.

The nation that is now Liberia was settled in the early 1800s by freed American slaves under the auspices of the American Colonization Society. The capital city, Monrovia, is named after U.S. President James Monroe. The first settlers arrived on Providence Island in 1822. Other settlers followed, and they united in 1838. After independence, elections were held, and Joseph Jenkins Roberts was elected the first president in January 1848.

CONTACTS:
Liberian Embassy
5201 16th St. N.W.
Washington, D.C. 20011
202-723-0437; fax: 202-723-0436
www.embassyofliberia.org

SOURCES:
AnnivHol-2000, p. 123
NatlHolWrld-1968 p. 124

♦ 1525 ♦ **Liberia National Redemption Day**
April 12

On April 12, 1980, 13 soldiers stormed Liberia's executive mansion, killing President William R. Tolbert and 26 other government leaders. Shortly after the massacre, 13 cabinet members were publicly executed. The soldiers were led by Samuel Kanyon Doe, a member of the ethnic Krahn tribe who immediately declared himself president of Liberia and set up a military regime called the People's Redemption Council. He also declared that in the coming years April 12 would be National Redemption Day.

Doe associated his regime with *redemption* because he believed that as a member of Liberia's long-repressed indigenous majority, he would lead a restructuring of the country's power base. His rule, however, was not the welcome change that many anticipated. Instead, his regime was marred by corruption and severe political abuses from April 1980 until his death on September 9, 1990.

For Doe's political opponents, National Redemption Day was a time to memorialize the many individuals who were killed during that tragic month in 1980. Today, many Liberians observe the anniversary by remembering the slain.

CONTACTS:
Liberia Ministry of Information, Cultural Affairs and Tourism
  (MICAT)

110 United Nations Dr.
P.O. Box 10-9021
Capitol Hill, 1000
Monrovia, Liberia
www.micat.gov.lr

♦ 1526 ♦ **Liberia National Unification Day**
May 14

This annual observance draws attention to one of the most pressing issues facing Liberians throughout their history: the animosity between the Americo-Liberian elite and the indigenous majority. Under the leadership of President William V. S. Tubman, who led from 1944 to 1971, the divide between these two groups was diminished. In his inaugural address, Tubman introduced his National Unification Policy, which featured among other things an extension of the vote to women and to the country's indigenous people. The official anniversary, sometimes referred to as **Unification and Integration Day**, emerged as a means to draw support for the policy.

The day reminds Liberians to remember what they hold in common and not to dwell on how they diverge. While the friction between Americo-Liberians and indigenous has abated throughout history, a general focus on national unity is still an urgent current issue for this oft-divided country, devastated by two consecutive civil wars between 1989 and 2003.

CONTACTS:
Liberia Ministry of Information, Cultural Affairs and Tourism
  (MICAT)
110 United Nations Dr.
P.O. Box 10-9021
Capitol Hill, 1000
Monrovia, Liberia
www.micat.gov.lr

♦ 1527 ♦ **Liberian Fast and Prayer Day**
2nd Friday in April

Liberians reserve Fast and Prayer Day for collective reflection and self-discipline. The observance of the day is not mandatory since the constitution provides for freedom of religion. Nonetheless, many believe this national observance is in keeping with the spiritual convictions of Liberia's founding fathers. As President W. V. S. Tubman stated in an address commemorating a national fast, the country was established on a "deep and well-founded belief and trust in God through prayer."

The day historically has been observed by Christians, as Liberian Muslims more commonly dedicate the Islamic month of Ramadan to fasting and prayer. While officially the observance spans only 24 hours, the time of fasting and prayer can extend to an entire week. In addition, certain circumstances may prompt a spiritual leader to call for a special week of prayer separate from the one that is held annually. In February 1966, under President Tubman's direction, the country prayed in accordance with the dying wishes of Reverend J. D. K. Baker of the Protestant Episcopal Church. His hope, according to Tubman, was for citizens to pray "for the peace, security and safety of the Liberian State and for the peace and brotherhood of mankind throughout the world."

CONTACTS:
Liberia Ministry of Information, Cultural Affairs and Tourism
  (MICAT)
110 United Nations Dr.
P.O. Box 10-9021
Capitol Hill, 1000
Monrovia, Liberia
www.micat.gov.lr

SOURCES:
AnnivHol-2000, p. 71

♦ 1528 ♦ Liberian President W. V. S. Tubman's Birthday
November 29

The influence of William V. S. Tubman (1895-1971), Liberia's president for 27 continuous years, was so great that his birthday was established an official holiday while he still held office. The national legislature declared the holiday in response to a citizens' appeal made in 1952. Decades after his death, Liberians still celebrate the national hero's birthday, also known as **Goodwill Day**.

Tubman was a popular leader for a number of reasons. Born in Harper, he was the first president not to claim allegiance to the elite power center of Monrovia, a fact that endeared him to the country's indigenous majority. His Unification Policy extended the vote to women and to indigenous people. Perhaps his greatest political achievement, however, was his Open Door policy, which attracted much-needed foreign investment to Liberia.

The most elaborate festivities for Tubman's birthday have always taken place in his native city, Harper, where activities may extend for three days. One Tubman Birthday tradition that has endured for decades is the Queen Rally. This beauty pageant also doubles as a fund-raiser, in which contestants representing civic groups compete for money prizes, which are awarded for public works projects.

CONTACTS:
Liberia Ministry of Information, Cultural Affairs and Tourism
  (MICAT)
110 United Nations Dr.
P.O. Box 10-9021
Capitol Hill, 1000
Monrovia, Liberia
www.micat.gov.lr

♦ 1529 ♦ Libya Day of Arafa
Ninth day of Dhu al-Hijjah, the 12th month of the Islamic lunar calendar

The Islamic nation of Libya recognizes the Day of Arafa as a public holiday. **Waqf al Arafa** (translated as Day of Arafa, Day of Arafat, or **Day of Repentance**) is an Islamic religious observation marked by prayer, fasting, and penitence. One of the five pillars of Islam is the requirement that every able-bodied Muslim make a pilgrimage to Mecca, a city in Saudi Arabia, at least once during his or her lifetime if financially possible. This journey is known as Hajj, the annual PILGRIMAGE TO MECCA that occurs during Dhu-al-Hijjah, the 12th and last month of the Islamic calendar.

The ninth day of Dhu-al-Hijjah is known as the Day of Arafa. On this holy day those conducting Hajj gather on the Plain of Arafat and nearby Mount Arafat—a granite hill east of Mecca also referred to as the Mountain of Mercy—where the prophet Muhammad delivered his final sermon. The pilgrims' experience on the Plain of Arafat is often cited as the height of the annual journey to Mecca and this time spent in prayer and reflection is that which validates a Muslim's participation in Hajj. Many Libyan Muslims and those in other countries fast, perform acts of devotion, and pray for forgiveness of their sins on this day. The observation of Day of Arafa begins at dawn and ceases at sunset. The following day marks the major Muslim festival ID-AL-ADHA.

CONTACTS:
Embassy of the Libyan Arab Jamahiriya
2600 Virginia Ave. N.W., Ste. 705
Washington, D.C. 20037
202-944-9601; fax: 202-944-9606
www.libyanbureau-dc.org

American Muslim Council
1212 New York Ave., Ste. 525
Washington, DC 20005
202-789-2262

♦ 1530 ♦ Libya Declaration of Jamahiriya Day (Declaration of the People's Authority Day)
March 2

On March 2, Libyans celebrate Declaration of Jamahiriya Day, also known as **Declaration of the People's Authority Day**. In observance of this public holiday, schools and businesses are closed throughout the country. Citizens attend speeches and rallies in honor of the founding of the Jamahiriya, which has no official translation. The term, which is derived from the Arab word for republic, roughly means "state of the masses," "people's authority," or "people's power."

The term Jamahiriya was created by Libyan leader Colonel Muammar Qaddafi, who defined it as a "state run by the people without a government" and characterized it as a political advancement for all humankind. This political philosophy is sometimes termed the Third Universal Theory and is an amalgamation of socialism and Islam. On September 1, 1969, Qaddafi staged a coup d'état, overthrowing the Libyan monarchy and establishing a socialist, Islamic republic. Upon taking power he changed the name of the country to the Socialist People's Libyan Arab Jamahiriya. In theory, under Jamahiriya, Libya would be ruled by the people themselves through local councils. In practice, however, Libya is governed by an authoritarian state.

CONTACTS:
Embassy of the Libyan Arab Jamahiriya
2600 Virginia Ave. N.W., Ste. 705

Washington, D.C. 20037
202-944-9601; fax: 202-944-9606
www.libyanbureau-dc.org

♦ 1531 ♦ Libya Revolution Day
September 1

This national holiday commemorates the revolution, led by Col. Muammar Qaddafi (b. 1938), that ousted King Idris I (Muhammad Idris el-Senussi, 1890-1983), who had ruled since 1952, and established a republic known as the People's Arab Jamahiriyah on this day in 1969.

CONTACTS:
Libyan Mission to the U.N.
309 E. 48 St.
New York, NY 10017
212-752-5775; fax: 212-593-4787
www.libyanmission-un.org

♦ 1532 ♦ Lighting of the National Christmas Tree
December

On a selected night in December, the president of the United States lights the national Christmas tree at the northern end of the Ellipse in Washington, D.C., to the accompaniment of orchestral and choral music. The lighting ceremony marks the beginning of the two-week **Pageant of Peace**, a huge holiday celebration in the nation's capital that includes seasonal music, caroling, 50 state Christmas trees, and a burning YULE log.

CONTACTS:
President's Park (White House), White House Visitor Center
White House Liaison
1450 Pennsylvania Ave. N.W.
Washington, D.C. 20242
800-877-8339 or 202-208-1631; fax: 202-208-1643
www.nps.gov/whho/index.htm

SOURCES:
EncyChristmas-2003, p. 527
GdUSFest-1984, p. 205

♦ 1533 ♦ Lights, Festival of
Mid-November to January

The biggest event of the year in Niagara Falls, New York, is its Festival of Lights, which is held for about eight weeks during the CHRISTMAS holiday season. The falls themselves are illuminated, as are displays throughout the town featuring more than 200 life-sized storybook characters in dozens of animated scenes. There is an arts and crafts show, a toy train collectors' show, a boat show, a doll show, and magic shows. There are also numerous sports tournaments. Musical events include performances by internationally known singers, gospel choirs, bell choirs, steel drum bands, jazz groups, and blues bands. During the festival more than half a million lights adorn the city, which was the site of the world's first commercial hydroelectric plant in 1895.

CONTACTS:
Niagara Falls Tourism

5400 Robinson St.
Niagara Falls, ON L2G 2A6 Canada
905-356-6061; fax: 905-356-5567
www.niagarafallstourism.com

♦ 1534 ♦ Lights, Festival of (Ganden Ngamcho)
November-December; 25th day of 10th Tibetan lunar month

This Tibetan Buddhist festival commemorates the birth and death of Tsongkhapa (1357-1419), a saintly scholar, teacher, and reformer of the monasteries, who enforced strict monastic rules. In 1408 he instituted the Great Prayer, a New Year rededication of Tibet to Buddhism; it was celebrated without interruption until 1959 when the Chinese invaded Tibet. He formulated a doctrine that became the basis of the Gelug (meaning "virtuous") sect of Buddhism. It became the predominant sect of Tibet, and Tsongkhapa's successors became the DALAI LAMAS, the rulers of Tibet.

During the festival, thousands of butter lamps (dishes of liquid clarified butter called *ghee,* with wicks floating in them) are lit on the roofs and window sills of homes and on temple altars. At this time people seek spiritual merit by visiting the temples.

CONTACTS:
Office of Tibet
Tibet House, 1 Culworth St.
London, NW8 7AF United Kingdom
44-20-7722-5378; fax: 44-20-7722-0362
www.tibet.com

SOURCES:
FolkWrldHol-1999, p. 618

♦ 1535 ♦ Lilac Festival
Ten days in May

The annual Lilac Festival in Rochester, New York, celebrates the abundance of lilacs in the city's Highland Park. Horticulturalist John Dunbar began the garden with 20 varieties of the flowering shrub in 1892. The festival began six years later as a one-day event for people to enjoy the recently adorned park. Frederick Law Olmstead, who also designed Central Park in New York City, finished the development of Highland Park.

Today this is a ten-day festival during which visitors admire more than 1,200 lilac bushes of more than 500 varieties. In addition to viewing the flowers, visitors to the Lilac Festival can also sample a wide array of international foods and enjoy concerts, art shows, and other free festival events.

CONTACTS:
Greater Rochester Visitors Association Inc.
45 E. Ave., Ste. 400
Rochester, NY 14604
800-677-7282 or 585-546-8484; fax: 585-232-4822
www.lilacfestival.com

♦ 1536 ♦ Lily Festival (Festa dei Giglio)
Begins June 22

The week-long Lily Festival in Nola, Napoli, Italy, honors San Paolino (St. Paulinus), the town's patron saint. Legend has it that the festival began in the fourth century as a "welcome home" celebration when Paolino, who had placed himself in slavery to release a local widow's son, returned from Africa. Eight tradesmen representing the town greeted him by strewing flowers at his feet.

Eventually the eight tradesmen were represented by sticks covered in lilies, and over the years the lily sticks (*gigli* in Italian) grew longer and more ornate. Today they are from 75 feet to nearly 100 feet high. Since they weigh about 50 tons, it takes 40 men to carry each one. After a traditional blessing is given, the crowd throws flowers into the air and begins a costumed procession that meanders through the narrow streets of the town, led by a boat carrying a statue of San Paolino and featuring the eight huge gigli, each of which is surrounded by its own symphony orchestra.

See also GIGLIO FEAST

CONTACTS:
Italian Government Tourist Board
630 Fifth Ave., Ste. 1565
New York, NY 10111
212-245-5618; fax: 212-586-9249
www.italiantourism.com

SOURCES:
BkHolWrld-1986, Jun 28
DaysCustFaith-1957, p. 150
GdWrldFest-1985, p. 118

♦ 1537 ♦ **Lim Festival**
January-February; 13th day of first lunar month

The Lim Festival is an alternating-song contest, held in the commune of Lung Giang, about 18 miles from Hanoi, in the Bac Ninh Province of Vietnam. This is a courtship event, in which girls and boys of different villages carry on a singing courtship dialogue. The singers take part in what is a vocal contest with set rules; one melody, for example, can only be used for two verses of the song, and therefore there is considerable improvising. The storylines of the songs tell of daily events. Young men and women practice them while they are at work in the rice fields or fishing. There is also a weaving competition for young women.

Other Lim Festivals takes place in other villages in the province with processions and games such as human chess and wrestling.

CONTACTS:
Vietnam National Administration of Tourism
80 Quan Su Rd.
Hanoi, Vietnam
84-4-942-1061; fax: 84-4-826-3956
www.vietnamtourism.com/e_pages/news/index.a

♦ 1538 ♦ **Limassol Wine Festival**
Early September

This event is an annual celebration of the wine of Cyprus, lasting nearly two weeks and held in the Municipal Gardens of Limassol, the center of the wine-making industry. Wineries there compete to create the most original and decorative booths, and every evening pour out from barrels free samples of their wine. People sitting at picnic tables may watch exhibits of traditional wine pressing. There are also musical, theatrical, and dance performances.

CONTACTS:
Limassol Municipality
23 Arch Kyprianou St.
Lemesos, 3036 Cyprus
357-5-25-884-300; fax: 357-5-25-365-497
www.limassolmunicipal.com.cy/index_en.html

SOURCES:
GdWrldFest-1985, p. 67
IntlThFolk-1979, p. 82

♦ 1539 ♦ **Lincoln's (Abraham) Birthday**
February 12

Abraham Lincoln, the 16th president of the United States, also called the Great Emancipator, the Rail Splitter, and Honest Abe, was born on Feb. 12, 1809. President throughout the Civil War, he is known for his struggle to preserve the union, his issuance of the EMANCIPATION PROCLAMATION, and his assassination less than two weeks after the Confederate surrender at Appomattox Court House in 1865 (*see* APPOMATTOX DAY).

A wreath-laying ceremony and reading of the Gettysburg Address at the Lincoln Memorial in Washington D.C., are traditional on Feb. 12. Because the Republican party reveres Lincoln as its first president, Republicans commonly hold Lincoln Day fundraising dinners, as the Democrats hold JACKSON Day dinners.

Lincoln's actual birthday, Feb. 12, is a legal holiday in 11 states: California, Connecticut, Illinois, Indiana, Iowa, Kentucky, Michigan, Missouri, New Jersey, New York, and West Virginia. In most other states, Lincoln's and George Washington's birthdays are combined for a legal holiday on the third Monday in February called either PRESIDENTS' DAY or Washington-Lincoln Day.

CONTACTS:
Lincoln Memorial
National Park Service
900 Ohio Dr., S.W.
Washington, D.C. 20024
202-426-6841
www.nps.gov

Library of Congress
101 Independence Ave. S.E.
Washington, DC 20540
202-707-5000; fax: 202-707-8366
www.loc.gov

SOURCES:
AmerBkDays-2000, pp. 134, 283
AnnivHol-2000, p. 26
BkFest-1937, p. 15
BkHolWrld-1986, Feb 12

DictDays-1988, p. 68
HolSymbols-2009, p. 511

◆ 1540 ◆ Lindenfest
Second weekend in July

A 600-year-old linden tree in Geisenheim, Germany, is the center of this annual festival celebrating the new wine. As the oldest town in the Rhineland region, Geisenheim is renowned for its vineyards, and during the **Linden Tree Festival** people come from all over the world to taste the wine, visit the vineyards, and make pilgrimages to Marienthal, a Franciscan shrine in a nearby wooded valley. The ancient linden tree is decorated with lights for the three-day festival, and folk dancing and feasting take place beneath its branches.

CONTACTS:
Rheingau-Taunus Information
An der Basilika 11 a
Oestrich-Winkel, 65375 Germany
49-6723-995-50; fax: 49-6723-995-55-5
www.rheingau-taunus-info.de

SOURCES:
FestWestEur-1958, p. 68

◆ 1541 ◆ Lismore Lantern Parade
June 21

Observed during the winter solstice (June 21 in the southern hemisphere), the Lismore Lantern Parade in New South Wales, Australia, is a relatively new festival honoring an ancient seasonal observance. In 1994 leaders in Lismore established the parade in hopes of revitalizing the town's declining business district. Festival founders selected the longest night of the year to honor the cycles of the seasons, and they selected the lantern as the central motif because they recognized it as a common symbol of hope among a number of cultures.

Every year around Easter, Lismore community groups begin preparing for the parade, offering workshops to construct the parade's original artwork. Volunteers travel from all over southeastern Australia to help make lanterns, costumes, and puppets. The parade is accompanied by other festivities, including a Carnival Dance, music shows, and street theater.

Attendance has grown dramatically since 1994, from a few hundred people to over 25,000, some of whom come from overseas.

CONTACTS:
Lismore Lantern Parade
P.O. Box 1394
Lismore, New South Wales 2480 Australia
www.lismorelanternparade.com.au

◆ 1542 ◆ Literacy Day, International
September 8

Established by the UNITED NATIONS to encourage universal literacy, this day has been observed since 1966 by all coun-

tries and organizations that are part of the United Nations system. It was a direct outgrowth of the World Conference of Ministers of Education in Tehran, Iran, which first called for the eradication of illiteracy throughout the world. Observances are sponsored primarily by UNESCO (United Nations Educational, Scientific, and Cultural Organization) and include the awarding of special literacy prizes.

Prizes are also awarded by the International Reading Association and the Japanese publisher Shoichi Noma to literacy programs that have made a significant difference. For example, in 1984 the Noma Prize was given to the Bazhong District in the People's Republic of China, where the literacy rate had been raised from 10 percent to 90 percent over a 35-year period.

CONTACTS:
United Nations,Education Sector, Division of Basic Education
Literacy and Adult Education Section
7, Place de Fontenoy
Paris, 75352 France
33-1-4568-4669
www.unesco.org

SOURCES:
AnnivHol-2000, p. 152
BkHolWrld-1986, Sep 8

◆ 1543 ◆ Lithuania Independence Day
February 16

This is a national holiday in Lithuania marking the declaration of independence from Austrian, Prussian, and Russian occupation on February 16, 1918.

Today the anniversary is celebrated with festivals and fireworks, particularly in the capital city of Vilnius.

CONTACTS:
Lithuanian Embassy
2300 Clarendon Blvd., Ste. 302
Arlington, VA 22201
202-234-5860; fax: 202-328-0466
www.ltembassyus.org

SOURCES:
AnnivHol-2000, p. 28

◆ 1544 ◆ Lithuania Restoration of Statehood Day
March 11

Lithuania had been independent for only 12 years when the Soviets occupied the country in 1940. The people voted for self-rule in February 1990, and the new democratically elected parliament declared independence from the U.S.S.R. on March 11, 1990. Beginning the next month, the Soviet Union began an economic blockade against Lithuania and eventually resorted to violence against people holding vigil around the capital buildings on January 13, 1991. Outrage from around the world stopped the attack. Within a year the influence of perestroika (Mikhail Gorbachev's social reform policies) and independence movements in the other Soviet states brought about the disintegration of the Soviet Union.

Restoration of Statehood Day is an official holiday in Lithuania.

CONTACTS:
Lithuanian Embassy
2300 Clarendon Blvd., Ste. 302
Arlington, VA 20009
202-234-5860; fax: 202-328-0466
www.ltembassyus.org

SOURCES:
AnnivHol-2000, p. 42

♦ 1545 ♦ Lithuania State Day (Coronation of King Mindaugas)
July 6

Lithuania State Day is a national holiday observed on July 6. On this day, Lithuanians honor the coronation of Mindaugas, who became the first and only king of a unified Lithuania in 1253, bringing the Baltic people together under his leadership. In 2003 Lithuanians celebrated the 750th anniversary of his crowning with a series of cultural activities, including operas, folk music concerts, folk dance performances, parades, and festivals.

Mindaugas founded the first independent Lithuanian state in 1240. Fearing that Lithuania would be unable to withstand attacks from neighboring groups, Mindaugas sought help from the Teutonic Knights, a religious military order that had established power in the southeastern Baltic region. In gratitude for their support, Mindaugas became a Roman Catholic in 1251. He is generally credited with bringing Christianity to the country for the first time, although the people of the Baltic region eventually rebelled against their compulsory Christian conversion, and many returned to pagan beliefs following his assassination in 1263.

CONTACTS:
Lithuanian Embassy
2622 16th St. N.W.
Washington, D.C. 20009
202-234-5860; fax: 202-328-0466
www.ltembassyus.org

♦ 1546 ♦ Little Big Horn Days
Weekend nearest June 25

This festival is a commemoration in Hardin, Mont., of the Old West and particularly of the most famous Indian-U.S. cavalry battle in history, Custer's Last Stand. An hour-long reenactment of that battle, known as the Battle of Little Big Horn, is staged each night of the three-day festival near the actual site of the original battle, which occurred June 25, 1876.

The battle reenactment is performed by more than 200 Indian and cavalry riders. Among them are descendants of the Indian scouts who rode with Colonel George Armstrong Custer, who led more than 200 men to battle and to death. The pageant is based on the notes and outline prepared by Joe Medicine Crow, a tribal historian, and was originally sponsored by the Crow Agency, administrator of the Crow

Reservation. The first presentation of the drama was in 1964. It continued for a number of years before lapsing and then being restored to life in 1990.

Other events of the weekend are a historical symposium, a street dance, a Scandinavian dinner, and a parade.

CONTACTS:
Hardin Area Chamber of Commerce and Agriculture
10 Railway St.
P.O. Box 446
Hardin, MT 59034
406-665-1672; fax: 406-665-3577
www.custerslaststand.org

SOURCES:
AmerBkDays-2000, p. 474

♦ 1547 ♦ Little League World Series
Late August

Little League baseball began in 1939 with only three teams. It was incorporated under a bill signed into law by President Lyndon B. Johnson in 1964. Ten years later the law was amended to allow girls to join Little League teams. It is now played by over 2.5 million boys and girls between the ages of nine and twelve in 48 countries. The field is a smaller version of the regulation baseball diamond, with bases 60 feet apart and a pitching distance of 46 feet.

Every year in August the Little League World Series is held at Howard J. Lamade Field in Williamsport, Pennsylvania, location of the International Headquarters of Little League Baseball and home of the Little League Museum. First-round games are held on Monday, Tuesday, and Wednesday, with every team guaranteed a minimum of three games. Those who advance to the championship game end up playing as many as five games. The U.S. and International Championships are on Thursday, and Friday remains an open date, in case of rain. The series finale is played on Saturday.

World Series games are also held in August for Junior League Baseball (ages 13-14), Senior League (ages 14-16), and Big League (ages 16-18).

CONTACTS:
Little League Baseball
539 U.S. Route 15 Hwy.
P.O. Box 3485
Williamsport, PA 17701
570-326-1921; fax: 570-326-1074
www.littleleague.org

♦ 1548 ♦ Living Chess Game (La Partita a Scácchi Viventi)
Second weekend in September in even-numbered years

Every two years the main piazza in Marostica, Italy, is transformed into a giant chessboard. More than 500 townspeople wearing elaborate medieval costumes portray chessmen and act out a living game: knights in shining armor ride real horses, castles roll by on wheels, and black and white queens and kings march from square to square to meet their destinies. Thousands of spectators watch from bleachers, cheering loudly when a castle is lost and moaning when there is an impending checkmate. The local players begin rehearsing in March for the two-and-a-half hour performances. Some start out as pawns and over the years work their way up to become knights, kings, and queens.

The basis for the game is an incident that took place in 1454, when Lionora, the daughter of the lord of the castle, was being courted by two rivals. They challenged each other to a deadly duel but were persuaded to engage in a game of chess instead. Even today, the moves in the game are spoken in an ancient dialect, including the final *scácco matto!* (checkmate).

CONTACTS:
Pro Marostica
P.zza Castello 1, Marostica
Vicenza, 36063 Italy
39-424-7212-7; fax: 39-424-7280-0
www.marosticascacchi.it

◆ 1549 ◆ **Llama Ch'uyay**
July 31

The Llama Ch'uyay in Sonqo, Bolivia, near La Paz, is the ritual in which llamas are made to drink a "medicine." The llamas are gathered together in a corral and, one at a time, they are forced to drink bottles of *hampi*, a concoction made from *chicha* and *trago* (two kinds of liquor), sugar, barley mash, soup broth, and special herbs. A large male may consume more than five bottles, while baby llamas usually drink only half a bottle. Three bottles is considered a normal dose. After the animals drink their medicine, they are decorated with colored tassels made out of yarn. After the feeding, people may also toss more chicha onto the animals. A similar ritual is performed for horses on July 25, the feast of Santiago (*see* ST. JAMES'S DAY).

SOURCES:
FolkWrldHol-1999, p. 481

◆ 1550 ◆ **Lochristi Begonia Festival**
Last weekend in August

A colorful celebration of the national flower of Belgium, held in Lochristi (six miles from Ghent), where 30 to 33 million flowering tubers are produced each year on more than 400 acres. For the festival, residents create enormous three-dimensional floral tableaux for a parade of flower-decked floats. These depict a different theme each year—for example, the world's favorite fairy tales. Besides the tableaux, arrangements of millions of yellow, red, orange, and white blossoms on beds of sand turn the town's main street into a carpet of flowered pictures. Other events are band concerts and tours to the begonia fields.

The tuberous begonia was originally a tropical plant. It takes its name from Michel Bégon, a French amateur botanist who was an administrator in the West Indies at the time of Louis XIV. The plant reached England in 1777, and Belgium began cultivating the begonia in the middle of the 19th century.

Because the commercial value of the begonias comes from their tubers, or underground stems, the farmers of Lochristi discarded the blossoms before the festival was begun in 1946 and put them to good use.

CONTACTS:
Belgian National Tourist Office
220 E. 42nd St., Ste. 3402
New York, NY 10017
212-758-8130; fax: 212-355-7675
www.visitbelgium.com

SOURCES:
GdWrldFest-1985, p. 21

◆ 1551 ◆ **Lohri**
Around January 14; during Hindu month of Magha

Lohri is a traditional seasonal festival in India celebrating winter's end and the returning prominence of the sun to the Northern Hemisphere. Among Hindus and Sikhs Lohri is a particularly special occasion for families who have had a baby during the previous year; families may celebrate with a feast and family members and friends often give gifts to the new child. This is also a traditional day for young unmarried Sikh women to pray for a good marriage, which custom is said to derive from the association of a 16th-century matchmaker named Dulla Bhutti with Lohri. Another old tradition is for children to go door to door singing for candy from the neighbors, not unlike HALLOWEEN in the United States.

Throughout India Lohri today is widely celebrated at night with bonfires and dancing. People eat seasonal nuts and candies and also throw them into the fire.

See also MAGH SANKRANTI

CONTACTS:
Ministry of Tourism, Government of India
Rm. No 123, Transport Bhawan, No. 1, Parliament St.
New Delhi, Delhi 110 001 India
91-11-23715084; fax: 91-11-23715084
www.tourisminindia.com

SOURCES:
CelebFestIndia-1994, p. 36
RelHolCal-2004, p. 204
SikhFest-1989, p. 44

◆ 1552 ◆ **Loi Krathong**
October-November; full moon night of 12th lunar month

Loi Krathong is an ancient festival held under a full moon throughout Thailand, considered to be the loveliest of the country's festivals. After sunset, people make their way to the water to launch small lotus-shaped banana-leaf or paper boats, each holding a lighted candle, a flower, joss sticks, and a small coin. Loi means "to float" and Krathong is a "leaf cup" or "bowl."

There are several legends linked to the origins of this festival. One holds that the festival began about 700 years ago when

King Ramakhamhaeng of Sukhothai, the first Thai capital, was making a pilgrimage on the river from temple to temple. One of his wives wanted to please both the king and the Lord Buddha, so she created a paper lantern resembling a lotus flower (which symbolizes the flowering of the human spirit), put a candle in it, and set it afloat. The king was so delighted he decreed that his subjects should follow this custom on one night of the year. Fittingly, the ruins of Sukhothai are the backdrop on the night of Loi Krathong for celebrations that include displays of lighted candles, fireworks, folk dancing, and a spectacular sound-and-light presentation.

A second legend traces the festival to the more ancient practice of propitiating the Mother of Water, Me Khongkha. The aim is to thank Me Khongkha and wash away the sins of the past year. The coins in the lotus cups are meant as tokens to ask forgiveness for thoughtless ways.

In yet another story, the festival celebrates the lotus blossoms that sprang up when the Buddha took his first baby steps.

A similar celebration is held in Washington, D.C., at the reflecting pool near the Lincoln Memorial. Dinner and participation are by paid ticket, but anyone passing can watch the adult, child, and teen dances and the exhibition of martial arts; and after dark, the floating candles.

CONTACTS:
Tourism Authority of Thailand
611 N. Larchmont Blvd., Fl. 2
Los Angeles, CA 90004
800-842-4526 or 323-962-9574; fax: 323-461-9834
www.thai-la.net

SOURCES:
BkHolWrld-1986, Nov 17
FolkWrldHol-1999, p. 666
GdWrldFest-1985, p. 173

♦ 1553 ♦ **London, Festival of the City of**
June-July

First held in 1963, the Festival of the City of London was designed to show off the historic "square mile" in the heart of the city. The churches, cathedrals, halls, and other landmarks in this area have served as the setting for the festival's concerts, operas, and theater productions ever since. An open-air production of Gilbert and Sullivan's *Yeoman of the Guard,* staged in the Tower of London to commemorate its 900th anniversary during the festival's first year, has since become a regular event.

Concerts are given by both British and international artists, orchestras, and chamber music groups. There are band concerts, dance recitals, prose and poetry readings, art and photographic exhibits, and a series of ethnic cultural events. Street theater and traveling miracle plays round out the festival's offerings.

CONTACTS:
City of London Festival
12-14 Mason's Ave.
London, EC2V 5BB United Kingdom

44-20-7796-4949; fax: 44-20-7796-4959
www.colf.org

SOURCES:
GdWrldFest-1985, p. 94
IntlThFolk-1979, p. 163

♦ 1554 ♦ **London Bridge Days**
Last week in October

Given its location, this is one of the stranger and more unexpected festivals in all of the United States. Held in Lake Havasu City in the Arizona desert, the festival is a week-long celebration of all things English and of the London Bridge that spans a channel of the Colorado River. This London Bridge was built in 1831 to span the River Thames in London, England. Opening festivities at the time included a banquet held on the bridge and a balloon ascending from it. Like its predecessor mentioned in the nursery rhyme, which was completed in 1209, this bridge was falling down until Robert P. McCulloch, Sr., of the McCulloch Oil Corp., bought 10,000 tons of the granite facing blocks, transported them from foggy Londontown to sunny Arizona, rebuilt the bridge stone by stone, and dedicated it on Oct. 10, 1971. The Bridge Days are a commemoration of that re-opening.

A replica of an English village next to the bridge is the center of festival activities. There are English costume contests, a parade, a ball, musical entertainment, arts and crafts exhibits, a "quit-rent" ceremony (*see* PAYMENT OF QUIT RENT), and a Renaissance Festival. Lake Havasu City is a planned community and resort on the banks of Lake Havasu, which is fed by the Colorado River and impounded by the Parker Dam.

CONTACTS:
Lake Havasu Tourism Bureau
314 London Bridge Rd.
Lake Havasu City, AZ 86403
928-453-3444; fax: 928-453-3344
www.golakehavasu.com

SOURCES:
GdUSFest-1985, p. 11

♦ 1555 ♦ **Long (Huey P.) Day**
August 30

Huey Long was the colorful and often controversial governor of Louisiana from 1928 until 1932. Although he was impeached only a year after he'd been elected, he refused to yield the governorship to his lieutenant governor, a political enemy, and held on to the office until someone he liked better was elected. By then he'd been elected to the U.S. Senate, where he took what many considered to be an extreme stand on the redistribution of wealth, and openly rebelled against the administration of Franklin D. ROO-SEVELT, a fellow Democrat.

In 1934-35 Long reorganized the Louisiana state government and set up what amounted to a dictatorship for himself. He exercised direct control over the judiciary, the police, fire-fighters, schoolteachers, election officials, and tax assessors while still serving as a U.S. Senator. As he was leaving the state capitol building on September 8, 1935, he was shot and killed by Dr. Carl Weiss, the son-in-law of one of his many political enemies.

Despite his controversial political activities, Long was revered by the rural people of the state, who supported his Share-Our-Wealth Society promising a minimum income for every American family. His birthday, August 30, is a special observance in Louisiana which the governor can declare a legal holiday. It has been observed since 1937.

CONTACTS:
Louisiana Secretary of State, Archives Department
3851 Essen Ln.
P.O. Box 94125
Baton Rouge, LA 70804
225-922-1000; fax: 225-922-0433
www.sec.state.la.us

SOURCES:
AmerBkDays-2000, p. 616
AnnivHol-2000, p. 144
DictDays-1988, p. 58
OxYear-1999, p. 351

♦ 1556 ♦ **Looking Glass Powwow**
August

This powwow, held by the Nez Perce Indians each August in Kamiah, Idaho, celebrates the memory of Chief Looking Glass, who was killed in the Nez Perce War of 1877. Nez Perce (meaning "pierced nose" and pronounced NEZ-purse) is the name given by the French to a number of tribes that practiced the custom of nose-piercing. The term is used now to designate the main tribe of the Shahaptian Indians who, however, never pierced their noses.

Other major annual powwows of the Nez Perce are the Mata'Lyma Powwow and Root Feast in Kamiah the third weekend in May with traditional dancing, and the CHIEF JOSEPH and Warriors Memorial Powwow the third weekend in June in Lapwai.

CONTACTS:
Nez Perce Tribal Executive Committee
P.O. Box 305
Lapwai, ID 83540
208-843-2253; fax: 208-843-7354
www.nezperce.org

SOURCES:
IndianAmer-1989, p. 126

♦ 1557 ♦ **Lord Mayor's Show**
Second Saturday in November

The second Friday in November is **Lord Mayor's Day** in London, the day on which the city's Lord Mayor is admitted to office. The following day is the Lord Mayor's Show, a series of civic ceremonies that culminate in a parade to the Law Courts held since 1215. At one time the Lord Mayor rode on horseback or traveled by state barge along the Thames, but

today he rides from Guildhall to the Law Courts in a scarlet and gold coach drawn by six matched horses. This is the only time the mayoral coach is used; the rest of the time it is kept in the Museum of London.

Accompanying the coach is an honor guard of musketeers and pikemen in period dress, as well as many bands and numerous floats decorated to reflect the interests or profession of the new Lord Mayor. This colorful pageant dates back to the 13th century, when King John gave the citizens of London a charter stating that the Mayor was to be elected on September 29 and that he was to present himself either to the King or to the Royal Justices to be officially installed.

See also ELECTION OF THE LORD MAYOR OF LONDON

CONTACTS:
Corporation of London
Guildhall
P.O. Box 270
London, EC2P 2EJ United Kingdom
44-20-7332-1548
www.lordmayorsshow.org

SOURCES:
AnnivHol-2000, p. 199
BkDays-1864, vol. II, p. 561
BkHolWrld-1986, Nov 12
DictDays-1988, p. 69
OxYear-1999, pp. 433, 439, 652

♦ 1558 ♦ **Los Isleños Fiesta**
Late March

The Los Isleños Fiesta is held annually on a weekend in late March in Saint Bernard, La., near New Orleans, to celebrate the culture and heritage of "los isleños." This is the name given to more than 2,000 immigrants from the Canary Islands in Spain to Louisiana, and their descendants. The original settlers were sent to Louisiana from 1778 to 1783 to populate and defend the area, and many of them lived in St. Bernard.

The festival features visitors from the Canary Islands, who perform folk music and dances. Craftsmen and women are on hand to demonstrate traditional isleños crafts. Other activities include a children's area, heritage events, a mini-museum, and ethnic food and drink. In a reflection of more recent settlers to St. Bernard, the festival also includes an Irish-Italian-Isleños parade. The year 2007 marked the 31st anniversary of the celebration.

CONTACTS:
Los Isleños Heritage and Cultural Society
1357 Bayou Rd.
St. Bernard, LA 70085
504-682-0862; fax: 504-682-0862

♦ 1559 ♦ **Losar**
December-January; first day of first Tibetan lunar month

Losar is the new year in Tibet, according to the Tibetan calendar, which is in use throughout the Himalayan region; the date is determined by Tibetan astrologers in Dharmsala, India.

Before the new year, bad memories from the old year must be chased away, so houses are whitewashed and thoroughly cleaned. A little of the dirt collected is thrown away at a crossroads where spirits might dwell. A special dish called *guthuk* is prepared; in it are dumplings holding omens: a pebble promises life as durable as a diamond; cayenne pepper suggests a temperamental personality; a piece of charcoal would mean the recipient has a black heart. On the last day of the old year, monks conduct ceremonies to drive out evil spirits and negative forces. In one such ritual, the monks, in grotesque masks and wigs and exotic robes, perform a dance in which they portray the struggle between good and evil (*see* MYSTERY PLAY OF TIBET).

On the first day of the year, people arise early to place water and offerings on their household shrines. In the three days of the celebration, much special food and drink is prepared. This is a time of hospitality and merrymaking, with feasts, dances, and archery competitions.

Tibet was invaded by the Chinese in 1949, and the DALAI LAMA, the spiritual and political head of Tibet, has been in exile since 1959. Much of the Tibetan culture has been suppressed, but festivals are still observed in a modest way in Tibet and by Tibetans in exile.

Tibetan exiles in India celebrate Losar by flocking to the temple in Dharmsala where the Dalai Lama lives. On the second day of the new year, he blesses people by touching their heads and giving them a piece of red-and-white string. People tie the blessed string around their necks as a protection from illness.

In Bodhnath, on the eastern side of Kathmandu, Nepal, crowds of Tibetan refugees visit the *stupa* there to watch lamas perform rites. Copper horns are blown, there are masked dances, and a portrait of the Dalai Lama is displayed.

CONTACTS:
Office of Tibet
Tibet House, 1 Culworth St.
London, NW8 7AF United Kingdom
44-20-7722-5378; fax: 44-20-7722-0362
www.tibet.com

SOURCES:
BkHolWrld-1986, Feb 23
DictFolkMyth-1984, p. 777
EncyRel-1987, vol. 2, p. 552
FolkWrldHol-1999, p. 78
RelHolCal-2004, p. 217

♦ 1560 ♦ **Lotus, Birthday of the**
24th day of sixth lunar month

The lotus flower is one of the great symbols of Buddhism. In fact, Buddha is often depicted standing on a lotus flower. This flower, which begins its life in mud under water, push-

es up to the surface and rests on top. For this reason the lotus represents life as well as transcendence.

The Birthday of the Lotus is observed at the time of year when lotuses bloom, and people flock to Beijing to see them in its moats and ponds—much as they do in Japan and in Washington, D.C., during cherry blossom time (*see* CHERRY BLOSSOM FESTIVAL). Special lanes for rowboats are cut through the thick layer of lotus blossoms that cover the lakes of the Winter Palace in Beijing.

CONTACTS:
China National Tourist Office
350 Fifth Ave., Ste. 6413
New York, NY 10118
212-760-9700; fax: 212-760-8809
www.cnto.org

SOURCES:
EncyRel-1987, vol. 9, p. 28
FolkWrldHol-1999, p. 417

♦ 1561 ♦ **Louisiana Shrimp and Petroleum Festival**
September, Labor Day weekend

This festival combines a celebration of an old industry and a newer one in Morgan City, La., which once called itself the Jumbo Shrimp Capital of the World. In 1947, oil was discovered offshore, and it was decided to combine the tribute to shrimp with a tribute to oil.

The celebration was originally known as the **Shrimp Festival and Blessing of the Fleet**. It began in 1937 as a revival of the Italian custom of blessing fishing fleets before they set out to sea, but from the first it also included boat races, a dance, a boat parade, and free boiled shrimp. After the world's first commercial offshore well was drilled in the Gulf of Mexico below Morgan City, the shrimp industry was outstripped in economic importance by the petroleum industry, and petroleum seeped into the festival. The highlight, though, is still the Blessing of the Fleet and a water parade, with hundreds of boats taking part. Other events of this festival, one of the state's premier affairs, are fireworks, an outdoor Roman Catholic mass, arts and crafts displays, Cajun culinary treats, musical performances, and the coronation of the festival King and Queen.

CONTACTS:
Louisiana Shrimp and Petroleum Festival and Fair Association
P.O. Box 103
Morgan City, LA 70381
504-385-0703; fax: 504-384-4628
www.shrimp-petrofest.org

SOURCES:
GdUSFest-1984, p. 67

♦ 1562 ♦ **Louisiana Sugar Cane Festival**
Last weekend in September

The Sugar Cane Festival pays tribute to this important crop in New Iberia, La., which lies on the Bayou Teche. The Teche country is known as the "Sugar Bowl of Louisiana." The festival, which began in 1937 and now is participated in by 13 of the 17 sugar-producing parishes of the area, begins on Friday with a Farmers' Day. Highlights of the day are agriculture, homemaking and livestock shows, and a boat parade down Bayou Teche. On Saturday, there's a children's parade and the crowning of Queen Sugar at a ball, and on Sunday, the new Queen Sugar and King Sucrose reign over a parade. Other features are a blessing of the crops and a *fais-do-do*, a dance party.

CONTACTS:
Iberia Parish Convention and Visitors Bureau
2513 Hwy. 14
New Iberia, LA 70560
888-942-3742 or 337-365-1540; fax: 337-367-3791
www.iberiatravel.com

♦ 1563 ♦ Low Sunday
Between March 29 and May 2; Sunday after Easter

The Sunday following the "high" feast of EASTER, it is also known as **Quasimodo Sunday**, **Close Sunday**, or **Low Easterday**. "Low" probably refers to the lack of high ritual used on Easter, and not to the low attendance usual on this day. The name Quasimodo Sunday comes from the Introit of the mass which is said on this day. In Latin it begins with the phrase *Quasi modo geniti infantes*—"As newborn babes...." The famous character Quasimodo in Victor Hugo's novel, *The Hunchback of Notre Dame*, is said to have been found abandoned on this day, which marks the close of Easter week.

SOURCES:
DictDays-1988, pp. 21, 70, 93
EncyEaster-2002, p. 360
FestSaintDays-1915, p. 92
OxYear-1999, p. 626
RelHolCal-2004, p. 94

♦ 1564 ♦ Loyalty Day
May 1

The U.S. Veterans of Foreign Wars designated the first day of May as Loyalty Day in 1947. The intention was to direct attention away from the Communist Party in the United States, which was using U.S. MAY DAY rallies to promote its doctrines and sign up new members. The idea caught on, and soon Loyalty Day was being celebrated throughout the country with parades, school programs, patriotic exercises, and speeches on the importance of showing loyalty to the United States. In Delaware, for example, Loyalty Day was marked by a special ceremony at Cooch's Bridge, where the Stars and Stripes were first displayed in battle. And in New York City, the Loyalty Day parade routinely attracted tens of thousands of participants.

Dissent over American intervention in Vietnam eventually eroded the popularity of Loyalty Day, and in 1968 only a few thousand marchers turned out for the traditional parades in Manhattan and Brooklyn, while 87,000 people participated in the Vietnam peace march in Central Park. Loyalty Day was later replaced by LAW DAY.

SOURCES:
AmerBkDays-2000, p. 337
AnnivHol-2000, p. 74

♦ 1565 ♦ Lu Pan, Birthday of
June-July; 13th day of sixth lunar month

This holiday commemorates the birth of the Taoist patron saint of carpenters and builders. Said to have been born in 507 B.C.E., Lu Pan, a versatile inventor, is sometimes called the Chinese Leonardo da Vinci. In Hong Kong, people in the construction industry observe the day with celebratory banquets to give thanks for their good fortune in the past year and to pray for better fortune in the year to come. They also pay their respects at noon at the Lu Pan Temple in Kennedy Town.

Lu Pan, an architect, engineer, and inventor, is credited with inventing the drill, plane, shovel, saw, lock, and ladder. His wife is said to have invented the umbrella. Because his inventions are indispensable to building, it is common practice at the start of major construction projects for employees to have feasts, burn incense, and offer prayers to Lu Pan so that he may protect them and the construction work from disaster.

SOURCES:
BkHolWrld-1986, Jul 18

♦ 1566 ♦ Lucerne International Festival of Music
Mid-August to mid-September

The first **Lucerne Festival** was held in 1938, when Arturo Toscanini (1867-1957) was persuaded by the city of Lucerne, Switzerland, to conduct a concert at the Tribschen estate, formerly the home of composer Richard Wagner and recently turned into the Wagner Museum.

Because cultural life in Switzerland was not interrupted by World War II, the festival was able to attract many famous conductors and performers who were war refugees. In addition to Toscanini, other well-known participants in the early days of the festival include Bruno Walter (1876-1962), Vladimir Horowitz (1903-1989), Fritz Busch (1890-1951), Artur Schnabel (1882-1951), Pablo CASALS (1876-1973), Herbert von Karajan (1908-1989), and Rudolf Serkin (1903-1991).

Ernest Ansermet (1883-1969), Fritz Busch, and Bruno Walter formed the Swiss Festival Orchestra in 1943, and it has been the festival's mainstay ever since. Comprised of the best musicians in Switzerland who come together specifically for the Lucerne Festival and cannot be heard elsewhere, the orchestra is joined by other national groups—among them the Lucerne Festival Choir, the Lucerne Festival Strings, and the Lucerne Vocal Soloists—as well as internationally known orchestras from other countries. The program offers a balance of symphonic and chamber music as well as master classes, young artists' matinees, and a concert for seniors and persons with disabilities. The Millennium prompted festival organizers to choose music around special themes: "Myths" for 1999's festival, "Metamorphosis" for the 2000 festival, and "Creation" for 2001.

CONTACTS:
Lucerne Festival
Hirschmattstrasse 13
Luzern, 6002 Switzerland
41-41-226-4400; fax: 41-41-226-4460
www.e.lucernefestival.ch

SOURCES:
GdWrldFest-1985, p. 169
MusFestEurBrit-1980, p. 141
MusFestWrld-1963, p. 207

♦ 1567 ♦ **Ludi**
Various

Ludi was the word used for public games in ancient Rome. These were holidays devoted to rest and pleasure. The **Ludi Megalenses** were held every year from April 4-10 from 191 B.C.E. onwards in honor of Cybele, the Roman Mother Goddess, whose image had been brought to Rome in 204 B.C.E. (*see* MEGALESIA). The **Megalensian Games** were followed by the **Ludi Ceriales** in honor of Ceres, the ancient goddess of cereals, from April 12-19 (*see* CEREALIA). Then came the **Ludi Florales** in honor of Flora, the goddess of flowers, from April 27-May 3 (*see* FLORALIA). The Ludi Florales were followed by a period of hard work in the fields, and the next games didn't occur for seven weeks. The **Ludi Apollinares**, or APOLLONIAN GAMES, held in honor of Apollo, went on from July 6-13. The **Ludi Romani**, or ROMAN GAMES, instituted in 366 B.C.E., lasted from September 4-19. And the **Ludi Plebei**, or PLEBEIAN GAMES, which were first held somewhere between 220 and 216 B.C.E., took place November 4-17.

All in all, there were 59 days devoted to these traditional games in the Roman calendar before the time of Sulla, who became dictator of the Roman Republic in 82 B.C.E. They were considered to be the *dies nefasti*—days on which all civil and judicial business must be suspended for fear of offending the gods.

SOURCES:
DictRomRel-1996, p. 134
FestRom-1981, p. 40
OxYear-1999, pp. 291, 447

♦ 1568 ♦ **Lughnasadh**
August 1 or a nearby Sunday

The Lughnasadh was a pre-Christian festival in Ireland associated with the ancient Celtic god Lugh. Occurring at the beginning of the harvest season, the Lughnasadh was a time for gathering berries and other early fruits of the season. Many of the hilltop sites where people came to pick berries were later taken over by the Roman Catholic Church and turned into pilgrimage sites. This is the case in County Mayo, where on the last Sunday in July thousands of pilgrims still climb to the summit of "the Reek," or Croagh Patrick, Ireland's holiest mountain. That day is known as REEK SUNDAY, and a series of masses are held in a small oratory on the top of Croagh Patrick. This is where St. Patrick is said to have spent the 40 days of LENT, and it was from this mountaintop that he is said to have driven all the venomous serpents into

the ocean, thus explaining why there are no snakes in Ireland. Lughnasadh was also a popular time to hold fairs. Today it is observed by many Neopagan groups.

See also CROM DUBH SUNDAY; ST. PATRICK'S DAY; TAILTE FAIR

SOURCES:
DictFolkMyth-1984, pp. 202, 652
FestSaintDays-1915, p. 165
FolkWrldHol-1999, p. 485
OxYear-1999, p. 274

♦ 1569 ♦ **Luilak**
Between May 9 and June 12; Saturday before Pentecost

Luilak, or **Lazybones Day**, is a youth festival celebrated in Zaandam, Haarlem, Amsterdam, and other towns in the western Netherlands. The celebration begins at four o'clock in the morning on the Saturday before PENTECOST, when groups of young people awaken their neighbors by whistling, banging on pots and pans, and ringing doorbells. Any boys or girls who refuse to get up and join the noise-making are referred to as *Luilak*, or "Lazybones," a name that is said to have originated in 1672 when a watchman named Piet Lak fell asleep while French invaders entered the country. Thereafter he was referred to as *Luie-Lak*, "Lazy Lak." In many parts of the country *Luilakbollen*, or "Lazybones Cakes," traditionally baked in the shape of fat double rolls and served with syrup, are a specialty of the season.

Children celebrate Luilak by making little wagons, often shaped like boots and decorated with branches and thistles, known as *luilakken*. Pulling the wagons over the cobblestone streets can generate enough friction to set the wheels smoking. The children then either watch while their luilakken go up in flames or else dump them in the canals.

In Haarlem, Luilak marks the opening of the celebrated Whitsun flower market in the Grote Markt at midnight (*see* MERCHANTS' FLOWER MARKET).

SOURCES:
BkFest-1937, p. 243
BkFestHolWrld-1970, p. 66
FestWestEur-1958, p. 134
FolkWrldHol-1999, p. 341

♦ 1570 ♦ **Lumberjack World Championships**
Last weekend in July

At the turn of the century Hayward, Wisconsin, was one of the most active logging towns in the northern United States. Nowadays Hayward is known primarily as the site of the largest lumberjack competition in the country. Lumberjacks and logrollers from New Zealand, Australia, Canada, England, and the United States come to Hayward to compete in one- and two-man buck sawing, power sawing, a variety of chopping events, and the speed climbing contest, where loggers climb up and down a 90-foot fir pole in less than 30 seconds. There is also a lumberjack relay race, with teams consisting of one speed climber, one "river pig" (logroller), two-man crosscut saw partners, and one standing-cut chopper.

The three-day event takes place at the end of July in the Lumberjack Bowl, a large bay of Lake Hayward that was once used as a giant holding pond for the North Wisconsin Lumber Company and is now used for the World Logrolling Championships. The sport of "birling" or logrolling originated in New England and then moved west. Lumberjacks in overalls, woolen shirts, and high boots learned to maneuver a floating carpet of logs, using their pike poles to break up log jams. A working skill soon became a pastime and then a sporting event. Today's competitors dress in shorts and t-shirts or bathing suits and wear special birling shoes. Competitors stand on a floating log and try to roll each other off balance and into the water.

CONTACTS:
Lumberjack World Championships
P.O. Box 666
Hayward, WI 54843
715-634-2484; fax: 715-934-2359
www.lumberjackworldchampionships.com

SOURCES:
GdUSFest-1984, p. 211

♦ 1571 ♦ **Lunar New Year**
Between January 21 and February 19; first day of first lunar month

The Lunar New Year has certain variations from country to country, but they all include offerings to the household god(s), housecleaning and new clothes, a large banquet, ancestor worship, and firecrackers.

It is the most important and the longest of all Chinese festivals, celebrated by Chinese communities throughout the world. The festival, believed to date back to prehistory, marks the beginning of the new lunar cycle. It is also called the **Spring Festival**, since it falls between the WINTER SOLSTICE and VERNAL EQUINOX. It is the day when everyone becomes one year older—age is calculated by the year not the date of birth.

Activities begin in the 12th month, as people prepare food, clean their houses, settle debts, and buy new clothes. They also paste red papers with auspicious writings on the doors and windows of their homes.

On the 24th day of the 12th month, each Kitchen God leaves earth to report to the Jade Emperor in heaven on the activities of each family during the past year. To send their Kitchen God on his way, households burn paper money and joss sticks and give him offerings of wine. To make sure that his words to the Jade Emperor are sweet, they also offer *tang kwa,* a dumpling that finds its way into the mouths of eager children.

The eve of the new year is the high point of the festival when family members return home to honor their ancestors and enjoy a great feast. The food that is served has symbolic meaning. Abalone, for example, promises abundance; bean sprouts, prosperity; oysters, good business.

This is also a night of colossal noise; firecrackers explode and rockets whistle to frighten away devils. An old legend says that the lunar festival dates from the times when a wild beast (a *nihn;* also the Cantonese word for "year") appeared at the end of winter to devour many villagers. After the people discovered that the beast feared bright lights, the color red, and noise, they protected themselves on the last day of the year by lighting up their houses, painting objects red, banging drums and gongs, and exploding bamboo "crackers." The explosions go on till dawn, and continue sporadically for the next two weeks.

In Hong Kong, it is traditional after the feast to visit the flower markets. Flowers also have symbolic meaning, and gardeners try to ensure that peach and plum trees, which signify good luck, bloom on New Year's Day.

On the first day of the new year, household doors are thrown open to let good luck enter. Families go out to visit friends and worship at temples. Words are carefully watched to avoid saying anything that might signify death, sickness, or poverty. Scissors and knives aren't used for fear of "cutting" the good fortune, and brooms aren't used either, lest they sweep away good luck. Dragon and lion dances are performed, with 50 or more people supporting long paper dragons. There are acrobatic demonstrations and much beating of gongs and clashing of cymbals.

An ancient custom is giving little red packets of money (called *hung-pao* or *lai see*) to children and employees or service-people. The red signifies good fortune, and red is everywhere at this time.

On the third day of the holiday, families stay home, because it's supposed to be a time of bad luck. On the fourth day, local deities return to earth after a stay in heaven and are welcomed back with firecrackers and the burning of spirit money. According to legend, the seventh day is the anniversary of the creation of mankind, and the ninth day is the birthday of the Jade Emperor, the supreme Taoist deity. He is honored, not surprisingly, with firecrackers.

In most Asian countries, people return to work after the fourth or fifth day of celebration. In Taiwan, New Year's Eve, New Year's Day, and the two days following are public holidays, and all government offices, most businesses, restaurants, and stores are closed. The closings may continue for eight days.

By the 13th and 14th days, shops hang out lanterns for the Yuen Siu or LANTERN FESTIVAL, the day of the first full moon of the new year and the conclusion of the celebration.

In Chinese, the lunar new year is known as **Ch'un Chieh,** or "Spring Festival." It was formerly called **Yuan Tan,** "the first morning," but the name was changed when the Gregorian calendar was officially adopted by the Republic of China in 1912. To differentiate the Chinese new year from the Western new year, January 1 was designated *Yuan Tan.* Today in China and in other eastern nations, January 1 is a public holiday, but the Spring Festival is the much grander celebration.

Celebrations vary from country to country and region to region. In some towns in the countryside of Yunnan province in China, for example, an opera is performed by farmers. The Chinese communities in San Francisco and New York City are especially known for their exuberant and ear-splitting celebrations. In China, celebrations were banned from the onset of the Cultural Revolution in 1966 until 1980 when dragons and lions once again appeared on the streets.

In Vietnam, where the holiday is called TET, the ancestors are believed to return to heaven on the fourth day, and everyone has to return to work. On the seventh day, the *Cay Nev* is removed from the front of the home. This is a high bamboo pole that was set up on the last day of the old year. On its top are red paper with inscriptions, wind chimes, a square of woven bamboo to stop evil spirits from entering, and a small basket with betel and areca nuts for the good spirits.

In Taiwan it is called **Sang-Sin**. Small horses and palanquins are cut from yellow paper and burned to serve as conveyances for the Kitchen God.

The New Year's feast is first laid before the ancestor shrine. About seven o'clock, after the ancestors have eaten, the food is gathered up, reheated, and eaten by the family. The greater the amount of food placed before the shrine, the greater will be the reward for the new year.

After the banquet, oranges are stacked in fives before the ancestor tablets and household gods. A dragon-bedecked red cloth is hung before the altar. The dragon is the spirit of rain and abundance, and the oranges are an invitation to the gods to share the family's feasting.

In Korea **Je-sok**, or **Je-ya**, is the name for New Year's Eve. Torches are lit in every part of the home, and everyone sits up all night to "defend the New Year" from evil spirits. In modern Seoul the church bells are rung 33 times at midnight. While the foods may vary, everyone, rich and poor alike, has *duggook* soup, made from rice and containing pheasant, chicken, meat, pinenuts, and chestnuts.

Many games are played. Among the most unusual is girls seesawing. In early times Korean men stopped some of the sterner sports and forbade women to have any outdoor exercises. Korean girls then took to using a seesaw behind their garden walls. But they do it standing up—so as to get a possible glimpse of their boyfriends, as they fly up and down.

In Okinawa's villages there is the custom of new water for **Shogatsu**, the new year. About five o'clock in the morning youngsters bring a teapot of fresh water to the homes of their relatives. There a cupful is placed on the Buddhist god shelf, or the fire god's shelf in the kitchen, and the first pot of tea is made from it.

See also LOSAR, NARCISSUS FESTIVAL, and SOL

CONTACTS:
Hong Kong Tourism Board
115 E. 54th St. 2/F
New York, NY 10022
212-421-3382; fax: 212-421-8428
www.discoverhongkong.com

Taiwan Government Information Office
4201 Wisconsin Ave. N.W.
Washington, DC 20016
202-895-1850; fax: 202-362-6144
www.gio.gov.tw

SOURCES:
AmerBkDays-2000, p. 124
BkFest-1937, pp. 75, 77
DictFolkMyth-1984, pp. 224, 626, 706, 790
EncyRel-1987, vol. 3, pp. 293, 324
FolkAmerHol-1999, p. 46
FolkWrldHol-1999, p. 57
GdWrldFest-1985, p. 62
IntlThFolk-1979, p. 197
OxYear-1999, pp. 700, 704
RelHolCal-2004, pp. 216, 230

♦ 1572 ♦ **Lupercalia**
February 15

This was an ancient Roman festival during which worshippers gathered at a grotto on the Palatine Hill in Rome called the Lupercal, where Rome's legendary founders, Romulus and Remus, had been suckled by a wolf. The sacrifice of goats and dogs to the Roman deities Lupercus and Faunus was part of the ceremony. Luperci (priests of Lupercus) dressed in goatskins and, smeared with the sacrificial blood, would run about striking women with thongs of goat skin. This was thought to assure them of fertility and an easy delivery. The name for these thongs—*februa*—meant "means of purification" and eventually gave the month of February its name. There is some reason to believe that the Lupercalia was a forerunner of modern VALENTINE'S DAY customs. Part of the ceremony involved putting girls' names in a box and letting boys draw them out, thus pairing them off until the next Lupercalia.

SOURCES:
AmerBkDays-2000, p. 106
BkHolWrld-1986, Feb 14
DaysCustFaith-1957, p. 54
DictDays-1988, p. 70
DictRomRel-1996, p. 136
FestRom-1981, p. 76
FestSaintDays-1915, p. 34
OxYear-1999, p. 80

♦ 1573 ♦ **Luxembourg National Day**
June 23

This public holiday is also known as **Grand Duke Day,** since it is the birthday of Jean (b. 1921), the Grand Duke of Luxembourg. It is also the day on which the country celebrates its independence. Although formerly ruled by the Netherlands and Belgium, the grand duchy raised its own flag for the first time in 1890. It remained politically neutral until after its liberation from the Germans at the end of World War II, when it joined the North Atlantic Treaty Organization.

On the eve of the national holiday, Dudelange hosts a torchlight procession, and the castle at Wiltz hosts a fête in the courtyard. In Esch-sur-Alzette, there are athletic competitions and other festivities. Fireworks, parades, special religious services, public concerts, and dancing comprise the elaborate celebration in the capital city of Luxembourg.

On National Day people assemble in the capital, not only to celebrate their independence but also to observe the official birthday of the Grand Duke, who succeeded his mother, the Grand Duchess Charlotte, in 1964. Although Luxembourg covers less than a thousand square miles, the people there identify strongly with their country and speak their own language, known as Luxembourgeois.

CONTACTS:
Luxembourg National Tourist Office
17 Beekman Pl.
New York, NY 10022
212-935-8888; fax: 212-935-5896
www.luxembourgnyc.org

SOURCES:
AnnivHol-2000, p. 104
NatlHolWrld-1968, p. 88

M

♦ 1574 ♦ **Maafa Commemoration**
Third week in September

The Maafa Commemoration is an annual week-long remembrance of the Transatlantic Slave Trade and the experience of Middle Passage. The word Maafa, a Kiswahili word meaning catastrophe, is increasingly being applied to those historical events.

The commemoration, held at the St. Paul Community Baptist Church in Brooklyn, N.Y., centers around a dramatic presentation put on by the church's drama ministry. "The Maafa Suite ... A Healing Journey" depicts the history of African Americans, from Africa to the Jim Crow South. As many as 100 performers in music, dance, and theatre contribute to "The Maafa Suite." The work's creators describe it as a transformative psychodrama that aims to educate and heal the collective memory of African Americans. It is open to the public by paid ticket. Other events during the week include lectures, worship services, Maafa museum tours, a Garden of Gethsemane sweat lodge, and special activities for senior citizens and young people, many of them free of charge. The commemoration first took place in 1995. The play has toured to other African-American churches in the United States, and many churches have created their own Maafa commemorations.

CONTACTS:
St. Paul Community Baptist Church Maafa Resource Center
859 Hendrix St.
Brooklyn, NY 11207
718-257-2884; fax: 718-257-1965
www.themaafa.com

♦ 1575 ♦ **Mabon**
Autumnal (Fall) Equinox, September 22 or 23 in the northern hemisphere

Archaeological findings of prehistoric cultures in the British Isles reveal that important festivals observed the year's equinoxes and solstices. In ancient history, Celtic peoples observed these days as the four QUARTER DAYS: OSTARA (VERNAL EQUINOX), Litha (SUMMER SOLSTICE), YULE (WINTER SOLSTICE), and Mabon (AUTUMNAL EQUINOX). Today, Wiccans and Neo-pagans, who draw many traditions from Celtic culture,

retain the Mabon tradition. Some communities refer to the day simply as "autumn harvest" or "autumn *sabbat.*"

According to Welsh legend, Mabon was a magical youth renowned for his hunting skills. His mother held him captive in a cave, but the warrior Culhwch, with the aid of several animals of the forest, came to the boy's rescue. For many present-day believers, Culhwch's search for Mabon symbolizes everyone's search for the inner child.

Typical Wiccan and Neo-pagan celebrations of Mabon, which take place throughout the world, are circle ceremonies that recognize various harvest themes. A ceremonial site—often an altar—will be decorated with items like corn, apples, wine, or black and white candles (the light and dark colors represent the equinox). Participants may tell stories, light candles, chant, dance, or recite invocations.

CONTACTS:
Pagan Federation
BM Box 7097
London WC1N 3XX United Kingdom
www.paganfed.demon.co.uk

SOURCES:
RelHolCal-2004, p. 275

♦ 1576 ♦ **MacArthur (Douglas) Day**
January 26

Douglas MacArthur (1880-1964), five-star general and supreme commander of the Allied forces in the Southwest Pacific during World War II, was born on this day in Little Rock, Arkansas. Although MacArthur retired from the U.S. Army in 1937, he was recalled to active duty in July 1941. Promoted to general in December 1944, he was appointed commander of all U.S. army forces in the Pacific four months later. After the U.S. dropped an atomic bomb on Hiroshima on August 6, 1945, it was MacArthur who supervised the surrender ceremony in Tokyo. As commander of the Allied occupation of Japan from 1945-51, MacArthur directed the demobilization of Japanese military forces and the drafting of a new constitution.

Many people felt that MacArthur was imperious and egotistical, while to others he appeared warm, courageous, and even humble. Everyone seemed to agree that he possessed superior intelligence and a rare ability to command. His birthday is observed in his home state of Arkansas, where he is widely remembered as one of the state's most famous sons.

SOURCES:
AmerBkDays-2000, p. 88
AnnivHol-2000, p. 15

◆ 1577 ◆ Macedonian Ilinden (St. Elijah's Uprising Day)
August 2

August 2 is an official holiday in Macedonia commemorating the nation's first modern statehood. In 1903, Macedonian Christian nationalists led a rebellion against the Turkish Ottoman Empire. The rebels staged an uprising on August 2 of that year, a date that also marked the Christian feast day of Ilinden, or the prophet Elijah's ascension into heaven. During the uprising, approximately 30,000 Macedonian fighters waged war against 300,000 Turkish troops, declaring Macedonian independence upon liberating the town of Kruševo and establishing the Kruševo Republic. The republic didn't last, however; the nationalists were crushed by the Turks in November 1903 after months of intense violence.

Still, the Ilinden uprising has become a cultural cornerstone in the mythology of modern Macedonia and is acknowledged as an important precursor to the establishment of the present-day Republic of Macedonia. In 2003, Macedonians celebrated the 100th anniversary of the Ilinden uprising with commemorative coins, memorial services, a wide range of art and history exhibitions, and literary works that pay tribute to this memorable date in the Macedonian struggle for freedom and justice.

CONTACTS:
Macedonian Embassy
2129 Wyoming Ave. N.W.
Washington, D.C. 20008
202-667-0501; fax: 202-667-2131
www.macedonianembassy.org

◆ 1578 ◆ Macedonian Independence Day
September 8

Macedonians celebrate their country's sovereignty on September 8. A former Yugoslav republic, Macedonia became independent in fall 1991 upon the breakup of the Socialist Federal Republic of Yugoslavia. Prior to that point, the long-standing independence movement in Macedonia was gaining renewed momentum after a buildup of nationalistic sentiment encouraged by local artists and intellectuals. On January 25, 1991, the Assembly of the Republic of Macedonia passed a resolution demanding federal reconfiguration and naming itself the sole power in the country. On August 23 of that year the assembly drafted a new constitution, which guaranteed sovereignty, democracy, human rights, and the rule of law. Macedonia declared its independence after a referendum held on September 8, 1991, in which 95% of participants voted for an independent Macedonia. After considerable debate, the constitution was accepted on November 17, 1991.

CONTACTS:
Macedonian Embassy
2129 Wyoming Ave. N.W.
Washington, D.C. 20008
202-667-0501; fax: 202-667-2131
www.macedonianembassy.org

◆ 1579 ◆ Macedonian National Uprising Day (Day of Macedonian Uprising in 1941; Macedonian Revolution Day)
October 11

October 11 marks the anniversary of the beginning of the Macedonian people's uprising against fascism during World War II. This holiday is observed through formal ceremonies at which the prime minister and other dignitaries deliver addresses acknowledging the significance of this revolt to the spirit of Macedonian independence. In conjunction with this holiday, the Macedonian Parliament recognizes accomplishments in the areas of science, culture, art, and journalism through the "October 11" life achievement awards.

During the Second World War, the Axis powers controlled the Kingdom of Yugoslavia, of which Macedonia was part. On October 11, 1941, the people of Macedonia began to organize and mount an armed insurrection against their Bulgarian and Italian occupiers with an attack on the local Axis-power headquarters in the city of Prilep, located in the Vardar region of Macedonia. Partisans staged a simultaneous uprising against the fascists in the city of Kumanovo. The October 11 rebellion launched the war for liberation from fascist occupation, which coincided with the rise of the communist movement in Macedonia.

CONTACTS:
Macedonian Embassy
2129 Wyoming Ave. N.W.
Washington, D.C. 20008
202-667-0501; fax: 202-667-2131
www.macedonianembassy.org

◆ 1580 ◆ Macker (Gus) Basketball
January-October; varies according to host city

This 3-on-3 basketball tournament—and party—takes place on the streets of more than 70 cities across the United States. The **Gus Macker 3-on-3 Basketball Tournament** grew out of a low-wager backyard competition when, in 1974, Scott McNeal assembled 17 friends at his parents' house in the western Michigan city of Lowell, near Grand Rapids, to play a basketball tournament with six teams of three people each.

Apparently realizing that this kind of event could have larger popular appeal, McNeal adopted the moniker "Gus Macker" and began holding Macker tournaments once a year in Belding, Michigan. National media attention from the likes of *Sports Illustrated* and ABC's "Wide World of Sports" sparked inquiries from communities around the country, and in 1987 McNeal began taking the Macker on tour.

In 1992 the Macker was honored by the Basketball Hall of Fame as the Official 3-on-3 Tournament. Indoor Mackers were introduced in 1994 so that the games could proceed during winter months in northern cities. Several Canadian cities have begun to participate as well.

The Macker is notable for its stringent guidelines for having a positive, family-oriented event and its insistence on donating proceeds to local charities. By 2009, the organization estimated that since its inception in 1987, approximately $15 million had been raised for local charities.

CONTACTS:
Macker Basketball LLC
812 Industrial Park Dr.
Greenville, MI 48838
616-754-0373; fax: 616-754-0884
www.macker.com

♦ 1581 ♦ Macon Cherry Blossom Festival
Mid-March

This festival celebrates the blooming (traditional date of full bloom is March 23) of the Yoshino cherry trees in Macon, Ga., which calls itself the Cherry Blossom Capital of the World. Cherry trees in Macon date back to 1952, when William A. Fickling discovered a mystery tree on his lawn. It was identified as a Yoshino flowering cherry, a native of Japan. Fickling learned to propagate the trees, and began giving them to the community; today Macon has 170,000 Yoshino cherry trees given by the Fickling family—30 times more than the number in Washington, D.C. The festival honors Fickling, known as "Johnny Cherry seed," and has as its themes love and international friendship.

The 10-day celebration, started in 1982, includes the 10-mile Cherry Blossom Trail, and now offers about 250 activities. Among the events are parades, aircraft displays and fly-ins, a fashion show, fireworks, concerts, a bed race, a lantern-lighting ceremony, and the fire department's Pink Pancake Breakfast. Macon has many antebellum mansions spared by Gen. William T. Sherman on his Civil War march to the sea, so there are several house and garden tours.

The city continues donating trees: about 15,000 are given to area residents for planting each spring.

See also CHERRY BLOSSOM FESTIVAL

CONTACTS:
Macon Cherry Blossom Festival
794 Cherry St.
Macon, GA 31201
478-751-7429; fax: 478-751-7408
www.cherryblossom.com

♦ 1582 ♦ Madagascar Independence Day
June 26

This national holiday commemorates Madagascar's independence from France on this day in 1960. **Republic Day** is another public holiday in Madagascar, held on December 30, the day the new constitution went into effect. The country became a republic in 1975.

CONTACTS:
Madagascar Embassy
2374 Massachusetts Ave. N.W.
Washington, D.C. 20008
202-265-5525; fax: 202-265-3034
www.madagascar-consulate.org

SOURCES:
AnnivHol-2000, p. 106
NatlHolWrld-1968, p. 89

♦ 1583 ♦ Madagascar Martyrs' Day
(Commemoration Day, Insurrection Day)
March 29

Madagascar Martyrs' Day, also known as **Commemoration Day** or **Insurrection Day**, officially memorializes those who died in the Revolt of 1947 against the French. Madagascar had been a French colony since 1896 and then was named an overseas territory within the French Union in the 1946 constitution. Although the French constitution accorded the people of Madagascar full citizenship, its assimilationist policies contradicted the goal of independence for Madagascar. Consequently, Malagasy nationalists formed a movement for autonomy from France.

On March 29, 1947, the people staged a nationalist uprising against colonial forces that eventually spread to one-third of the island. After months of fighting and the arrival of additional troops from France, the colonial army was able to regain control of the island. Casualties from the conflict were reported as high as 80,000 and as low as 8,000, depending on the source. French military courts tried the leaders of the revolt and executed 20. According to some reports, other court hearings resulted in 5,000 to 6,000 convictions with a range of penalties from imprisonment to capital punishment. On March 29 the Malagasy government and people remember those patriots who sacrificed their lives in this rebellion for their country's freedom.

CONTACTS:
Madagascar Embassy
2374 Massachusetts Ave. N.W.
Washington, D.C. 20008
202-265-5525
www.embassy.org/madagascar

♦ 1584 ♦ Madara Kijinsai (Demon-God Event)
April 17

According to an old Japanese legend, when the 14th-century Rakuhoji Temple in Yamatomura burned down, the demon god Madara summoned a number of demons and rebuilt the temple in seven days. Then the demons danced around a bonfire to celebrate their accomplishment and to express their hopes for the temple's future success.

Today, men dress up like demons and, on horseback, climb the 145 stairs to the Rakuhoji Temple. There are also demon dances to commemorate those who saved the temple from oblivion. Since the event takes place in April when the cherry trees are in bloom, many spectators come to Yamatomura not just to see the Demon-God Event but also to view the blossoming trees.

CONTACTS:
Japan National Tourist Organization
1 Rockefeller Pl., Ste. 1250
New York, NY 10020
212-757-5640; fax: 212-307-6754
www.jnto.go.jp

SOURCES:
JapanFest-1965, p. 141

◆ 1585 ◆ Madeleine, Fête de la
July 22

The **Magdalene Festival** is observed in St. Baume, a forested region of Provence, France, on the anniversary of the death of Mary Magdalene. An unfounded ninth-century legend has it that she set out from Palestine in a small boat and miraculously arrived on the shores of Provence. Wandering eastward from Les Saintes-Maries-de-la-Mer, she came to *la fôret de la Baume*, "the forest of the cave," a grotto where she spent 33 years living on wild roots and berries doing penance for her sins.

Thousands of pilgrims have visited *la Sainte Baume*, the holy cave, since the 13th century. Although July 22 is the most popular pilgrimage date, the shrine is visited throughout the year. At one time a journey to the grotto was considered especially important for engaged couples, who went there to ensure a fruitful marriage. More recently, young girls have scrambled up the wooded hillside to ask for the Magdalene's help in finding a husband.

CONTACTS:
French Government Tourist Office
825 Third Ave., Fl. 29
New York, NY 10022
514-288-1904; fax: 212-838-7855
www.franceguide.com

SOURCES:
AnnivHol-2000, p. 121
FestWestEur-1958, p. 45

◆ 1586 ◆ MadFest Juggling Festival
Usually second or third weekend of January

Since 1962, the Madison Area Jugglers have welcomed fellow jugglers every year to their headquarters at the University of Wisconsin in Madison. The MadFest Juggling Festival's reputation has been bolstered by the success of the Madison Area Jugglers' world champion passing team, The Mad 5.

The festival is an occasion for jugglers at all levels to share the tricks of the trade and watch world-class performers. The festivities are also open to unicycling, yo-yoing, and other forms of object manipulation. Beginning in 2006, the Wisconsin State Yo-Yo Contest was added to the festival's proceedings.

The festival usually takes place from Thursday to Saturday. Throughout the festival there is open juggling, during which the jugglers show up at the university's field house to practice or just mingle with other jugglers. Saturday night is reserved for the MadFest Juggling Extravaganza at the Wisconsin Union Theater, where special guest jugglers perform along with other musical and comedy acts.

CONTACTS:
Madison Area Jugglers
716 Langdon St.
Madison, WI 53706
608-263-2400
www.madjugglers.com/madfest

◆ 1587 ◆ Madison County Covered Bridge Festival
Second weekend in October

The Madison County Covered Bridge Festival takes place annually on the second weekend in October in and around Winterset, Iowa. The town is located in Madison County, noted for its historic wooden covered bridges. These structures became world-famous with the success of the best-selling 1992 novel, *The Bridges of Madison County*, by Robert James Waller, and the subsequent film of the same name. The festival, which pre-dates the book and movie, was launched in 1970.

The Covered Bridge Festival celebrates not just Madison County's vintage bridges, but all things old-fashioned. In addition to bridge tours, the weekend's festivities include demonstrations of such traditional activities as sheep shearing, wool spinning, and soap making. The non-stop entertainment includes barbershop quartets, square dancers, and cloggers, plus quilts and antiques are on display. Children are invited to take part in a spelling bee championship, and a parade of antique cars is a highlight of the weekend.

CONTACTS:
Madison County Chamber of Commerce
73 Jefferson St.
Winterset, IA 50273
515-462-1185; fax: 515-462-1393
www.madisoncounty.com/bridge_fest.html

◆ 1588 ◆ Magellan (Ferdinand) Day
March 6

The island of Guam, largest and southernmost of the Mariana Islands in the Pacific Ocean, about 3,000 miles west of Hawaii, was found on this date in 1521 by the Portuguese navigator Ferdinand Magellan. He named the island Ladrones, meaning "thieves," because of the way, according to Magellan, the inhabitants behaved. The island was formally claimed by Spain in 1565, and was later ceded to the United States as a prize at the end of the Spanish-American War. Today, Guam is the site of major U.S. military installations.

Guamanians celebrate their island's founding with an official holiday on the first Monday in March with fiestas and sailboating. This day is also known as **Discovery Day**.

CONTACTS:
Guam Visitors Bureau
1301 Marina Village Pkwy., Ste. 210
Alameda, CA 94501
800-873-4826 or 510-865-0366; fax: 510-865-5165
www.visitguam.org

SOURCES:
AnnivHol-2000, p. 54

◆ 1589 ◆ Magh Sankranti
Usually around January 14; Hindu month of Magha

In celebration of the sun's movement back toward the Northern Hemisphere, people in Nepal visit holy bathing spots during this festival in the Hindu month of Magha. Some actually bathe in the shallow water, but the weather is usually quite chilly and most are content to splash water on their hands and faces and sprinkle it on their heads. People also spend the day sitting in the sun, massaging each other with mustard oil, which is also used by mothers to bless their children. Foods traditionally served on this day include *khichari,* a mixture of rice and lentils; sesame seeds; sweet potatoes; spinach; and home-made wine and beer. Traditional gifts for the priests are a bundle of wood and a clay fire pot.

This holiday is also celebrated all over India, where it is called **Makar Sankranti** or, in some parts of India, LOHRI.

CONTACTS:
Ministry of Tourism, Government of India
Rm. No 123, Transport Bhavan, No. 1, Parliament St.
New Delhi, Delhi 110 001 India
91-11-23715084; fax: 91-11-23715084
www.tourisminindia.com

SOURCES:
CelebFestIndia-1994, p. 35
FolkWrldHol-1999, p. 35
RelHolCal-2004, p. 181

◆ 1590 ◆ Magha Puja (Maka Buja, Full Moon Day)
March-April; full moon night of third lunar month

This important Buddhist holy day is celebrated in India, Laos (as **Makha Bouxa**), and Thailand, where it is a national holiday. The day commemorates the occasion when 1,250 followers ordained by the Buddha arrived by coincidence at Veluvan Monastery in Rajagriha, Bihar, India, to hear him lay down monastic regulations and predict his own death and entry with Nirvana in three months' time. On this day there are sermons in the temples throughout the day, and monks spend the day chanting. The people perform acts of merit-making, such as offering food to monks and freeing captive birds and fish. After sunset, monks lead followers in walking three times around the chapels of monasteries. Each person carries flowers, glowing incense, and a lighted candle in homage to the Buddha. In Laos, the ceremonies are especially colorful at Vientiane and at the Khmer ruins of Wat Ph near Champasak.

SOURCES:
BkHolWrld-1986, Mar 6
EncyRel-1987, vol. 2, p. 551
FolkWrldHol-1999, p. 105
RelHolCal-2004, p. 218

◆ 1591 ◆ Magha Purnima
January-February; full moon day of Hindu month of Magha

Like KARTIKA PURNIMA, this is a Hindu bathing festival. Magha is considered to be one of the four most sacred months, and Hindus believe that bathing in the Ganges on this day is a great purifying act. When they cannot get to the Ganges, they bathe in the sea or in any holy stream, river, or tank (a pool or pond used to store water). Great bathing festivals are held at various places along the banks of the Yamuna, Sarayu, Narmad, and other holy rivers, and people walk for miles to have a bath. There is a large tank that is considered holy at Kumbhkonam, near Madras, which is also a popular destination since Hindus believe that on this particular day, the Ganges flows into the tank.

Magha Purnima is a day for fasting and charities. Early in the morning, libations are offered to dead ancestors, while donations of food, clothes, and money are given to the poor. Then Brahmans are fed and given *dan-dakshina* (offerings) according to one's means and capacity.

SOURCES:
RelHolCal-2004, p. 182

◆ 1592 ◆ Maghi
January-February; during Sikh month of Magh

GURU GOBIND SINGH and his Khalsa, a defense militia of "soldier-saints" he formed, were attacked by the Mughal army at Anandpur. It is said that 40 of his close followers let fear get the best of them and ran away, but they later repented and joined the Guru at Muktsar. There they gave their lives in the Battle of Muktsar in December 1705—an act of self-sacrifice that enabled them to achieve liberation from the cycle of rebirth.

Maghi is a day for honoring these men, who are now known as the Forty Immortals. Sikhs in India and elsewhere observe the holiday by visiting their local *gurdwara* (house of worship) and listening to the recitation of sacred hymns. The observance is particularly solemn at Muktsar in Punjab State, India, where the slaughter occurred.

CONTACTS:
Punjab Tourism Development Corp.
SCO-183-184
Sector 8-C
Chandigarh, Punjab 160 018 India
91-172-781138; fax: 91-172-548828
punjabgovt.nic.in/TOURISM/ContactAddresses.htm

SOURCES:
RelHolCal-2004, p. 205
SikhFest-1989, p. 43

◆ 1593 ◆ **Magna Carta Day**
June 15

The Magna Carta was the "great charter" of English liberties, which the tyrannical King John I was forced by the English nobility to sign on June 15, 1215. Although this day does not appear in the official calendar of any church, it is a day of great religious significance throughout the English-speaking world. One of the 48 personal rights and liberties guaranteed by the Magna Carta was freedom of worship; in fact, the opening words of the document were, "The Church of England shall be free."

The Magna Carta is regarded as one of the most important documents in the history of political and human freedom. Although it may seem remote to Americans, who sometimes take freedom for granted, for the English this date marks the first time that the basic belief in the value of the individual was recognized by the ruling government.

CONTACTS:
British Library
96 Euston Rd.
St. Pancras
London, NW1 2DB United Kingdom
44-87-0444-1500
www.bl.uk

National Archives and Records Administration
Magna Carta online
700 Pennsylvania Ave. N.W.
Washington, DC 20408
866-272-6272 or 301-713-6800
www.archives.gov

SOURCES:
AnnivHol-2000, p. 101
DaysCustFaith-1957, p. 148
OxYear-1999, p. 250
RelHolCal-2004, p. 97

◆ 1594 ◆ **Mahamastakabhishekha (Grand Head-Anointing Ceremony)**
March-April; every 10-15 years during the Jain month of Caitra

The huge image of Bahubali (also known as Gomateshwara), who was the son of the first Jaina *tirthankara* (spiritual guide), was sculpted out of rock at Shravanabelagola in the District of Hassan, Karnataka State, India, and dedicated on March 13, 981. The image of Bahubali, which at 57 feet stands higher than the Colossus of Rhodes, honors a Jaina ascetic who gave up his kingdom and renounced the world after a conflict with his brother, who was the crown prince, made him realize how selfish and acquisitive people really were.

The Grand Head-Anointing Ceremony, as the event is known, only takes place when a certain conjunction, a coincidence of astrological events, occurs—every 10-15 years. Huge numbers of Jaina devotees attend the ceremony. Special scaffolding is set up behind the statue to hold Jaina monks and priests, who pour 1,008 pots of holy liquid—consisting of water, coconuts, plantains, *ghee* (clarified butter), sugar, almonds, dates, poppy seeds, milk, curds, sandal-

wood, gold foil, silver foil, and precious gems and coins—over its head. Attendees shout in devotion as the statue is ritually bathed.

CONTACTS:
Karnataka Tourism
Khanija Bhavan, No. 49, 2nd Fl., Race Course Rd.
Bengalooru, Karnataka 560 001 India
91-80-22352828; fax: 91-80-22352626
www.karnatakatourism.org

SOURCES:
FestIndia-1987, p. 116

◆ 1595 ◆ **Mahavira Jayanti**
March-April; 13th day of waxing half of Hindu month of Caitra

A major Jain festival in India, Mahavira Jayanti is dedicated to Vardhamana (6th century B.C.E.), who came to be known as Mahavira, meaning "great hero" of the Jains. The festival celebrates his birthday, and is marked with prayers, fasting, and recitations. The holiday is observed with special fanfare by eastern Indians at Pawapuri in the state of Bihar, where Mahavira was born near the modern town of Patna. Another large celebration is held at the Parasnatha temple in Calcutta.

Mahavira, a contemporary of the Buddha, is regarded by the Jains as the 24th and last in a series of *Tirthankaras,* or enlightened teachers or "ford-makers," and present-day Jainism is traced to his life and teachings. For 12½ years, he was an ascetic, wandering about, begging for food, and wearing little. Then he found enlightenment, became a *Jina,* meaning "conqueror," and a Tirthankara. He taught for 30 years before he died. Jainism today continues to be an ascetic religion, practiced by about 3.5 million people. They reject any action that could harm a living being, and some, therefore, wear masks over their mouths to prevent the chance of breathing in and thus killing an insect. Jains, with a strong literary tradition, have played an important role in conserving the writings of non-Jain Hindu authors.

See also Dewali

CONTACTS:
Ministry of Tourism, Government of India
Rm. No 123, Transport Bhawan, No. 1, Parliament St.
New Delhi, Delhi 110 001 India
91-11-23715084; fax: 91-11-23715084
www.tourisminindia.com

SOURCES:
DictWrldRel-1989, p. 451
EncyRel-1987, vol. 9, p. 128
FolkWrldHol-1999, p. 258
OxDictWrldRel-1997, p. 602
RelHolCal-2004, p. 195

◆ 1596 ◆ **Maidens' Fair on Mount Gaina**
Third Sunday in July

The Maidens' Fair is a major folk festival held at Mount Gaina in Transylvania, Romania. It was originally a marriage fair, where young men came to choose their future wives, but is now an opportunity for people to display their talents in handicrafts, costume making, singing, and dancing. Thousands of people gather for the events of the fair, which include dance competitions and concerts by folk bands and singers. Other aspects of the festival are feasts and bonfires, and the chanting of satirical verses during certain folk dances.

CONTACTS:
Romanian National Tourist Office
355 Lexington Ave., Fl. 19
New York, NY 10016
212-545-8484; fax: 212-251-0429
www.romaniatourism.com

♦ 1597 ♦ Maidyarem (Maidhyairya; Mid-Year or Winter Feast)
December-January, May, June; 16th-20th days of Dae, the 10th Zoroastrian month

Maidyarem is the fifth of the six great seasonal feasts, known as *gahambars*, of the Zoroastrian religion. It was traditionally celebrated at a point in the agricultural year when, due to extreme cold, all work came to a halt. The name comes from the word *airya*, which means "rest."

The six gahambars were typically joyous festivals that included such activities as special rituals and prayers, and the sharing of food. Although they lasted five days, the fifth day was the only one spent in actual celebration; the other four were for preparation and anticipation of the day's feasting, when families or neighborhoods would get together. These seasonal feasts were designed to give those who worked from dawn to dusk on farms a respite from their labors. Today, with so many Zoroastrians living in urban areas, the importance of the gahambars has diminished.

The Zoroastrian calendar has 12 months of 30 days each, plus five extra days at the end of the year. Because of discrepancies in the calendars used by widely separated Zoroastrian communities around the world, there are now three different calendars in use, and Maidyarem can fall either in December-January, May, or June according to the Gregorian calendar.

There are only about 100,000 followers of Zoroastrianism today, and most of them live in northwestern India or Iran. Smaller communities exist in Pakistan, Sri Lanka, Canada, the U.S., England, and Australia.

SOURCES:
RelHolCal-2004, p. 69

♦ 1598 ♦ Maidyoshahem (Maidhyoishema; Mid-Summer Feast)
June-July, October-November, November-December; 11th-15th days of Tir, the fourth Zoroastrian month

This festival is the second of the six great seasonal festivals, known as *gahambars*, of the Zoroastrian religion. Each of the six gahambars correlates with a phase of agricultural produc-

tion and honors one of the six things created by God: sky, water, earth, plants, animals, and humankind. Maidyoshahem was linked to the creation of the waters.

Traditionally, the gahambars were joyous festivals that lasted five days and provided farm workers with a much-needed respite from their labors. The first four days were spent in preparation for the feasting that took place on the fifth day. Today, however, so many Zoroastrians live in urban areas that the importance of the gahambars has diminished somewhat.

The Zoroastrian calendar has 12 months of 30 days each, plus five extra days at the end of the year. Because of discrepancies in the calendars used by widely separated Zoroastrian communities around the world, there are now three different calendars in use, and Maidyoshahem can fall either in June-July, October-November, or November-December, according to the Gregorian calendar.

See also TIRAGAN

SOURCES:
RelHolCal-2004, p. 67

♦ 1599 ♦ Maidyozarem (Maidhyoizaremaya; Mid-Spring Feast)
April-May, September, October; 11th-15th days of Ardwahist, the second Zoroastrian month

Maidyozarem is the first of the six great seasonal feasts, known as *gahambars*, of the Zoroastrian religion. It is observed from the 41st to the 45th day after NAWRUZ or New Year's Day. Each of the six gahambars correlates with a phase of agricultural production and honors one of the six things created by God: sky, water, earth, plants, animals, and humankind. Maidyozarem—which means "mid-spring"—is linked to the creation of the sky, and the spiritual being associated with this festival is Shahrewar, who presides over metals and minerals and is represented by the consecrated implements used to tend the sacred fire in Zoroastrian temples.

Traditionally, the gahambars were joyous festivals that lasted five days and provided farm workers with a much-needed respite from their labors. The first four days were spent in preparation for the feasting that took place on the fifth day. Today, however, so many Zoroastrians live in urban areas that the importance of the gahambars has diminished somewhat.

The Zoroastrian calendar has 12 months of 30 days each, plus five extra days at the end of the year. Because of discrepancies in the calendars used by widely separated Zoroastrian communities around the world, there are now three different calendars in use, and Maidyozarem can fall either in April-May, early September, or early October, according to the Gregorian calendar.

SOURCES:
RelHolCal-2004, p. 66

♦ 1600 ♦ Maifest
Third weekend in May

The original Maifest in Hermann, Missouri, was a children's festival founded in 1874. The festival was revived in 1952 as a German ethnic festival for people of all ages. Held the third weekend in May, the festival offers German folklore, songs, music, and food in celebration of the arrival of spring. Black beer, cheese, sausage, crackers, and bratwurst are served, and there are band concerts and musical shows.

CONTACTS:
Hermann Area Chamber of Commerce
312 Market St.
Hermann, MO 65041
800-932-8687 or 573-486-2313
www.hermannmo.info

SOURCES:
GdUSFest-1984, p. 105

♦ 1601 ♦ **Maimona (Maimuna)**
Between March 28 and April 25; day after Passover

Jews in North Africa commemorate the philosopher and rabbi, Moses Maimonides (1135 or 1138-1204), on the evening of the last day of PASSOVER and the day that follows. Since the news of Maimonides's death in 1204 reached many Jews during Passover, they were not able to mourn his passing, as custom would normally dictate, by eating bread and an egg. So they postponed it until the following day.

In Libya on this day, each family member receives the *maimona* (from an Arabic word meaning "good fortune")—a small loaf of bread with an egg baked inside, which they eat with slices of lamb.

In Morocco, people dress up or wear costumes. Special displays of food are arranged on tables, including pitchers of milk and bowls of flour with eggs, broad green beans, stalks of wheat, and dates. Surrounding the bowls are honey, fruit, nuts, cookies, lettuce, wine, and a type of pancake known as *muflita*. After going to the synagogue, people stop to bless their friends and sample the refreshments at each home. A lettuce leaf, representing prosperous crops, is dipped in honey, symbolizing sweetness, and given to each guest. Wherever possible, people dip their feet in streams, rivers, or the sea.

SOURCES:
DictWrldRel-1989, p. 494
FolkWrldHol-1999, p. 287

♦ 1602 ♦ **Maine Lobster Festival**
Five days including first weekend in August

Claiming to be the "Original Lobster Festival," the event known as the Maine Lobster Festival has been held in the fishing port of Rockland since 1948. The festival's emphasis is on marine foods and exhibits, with special events such as lobster crate- and trap-hauling races, a Maine cooking contest, the crowning of a Maine Sea Goddess, and a lobster-eating competition. There is also musical entertainment and a big parade, featuring the Sea Goddess, Sea Princesses, and King Neptune and his court.

Although many towns in Maine hold annual lobster festivals, some have gone bankrupt by offering visitors all the lobster they can eat for a ridiculously low price. Although the prices have gone up, the lure of an inexpensive lobster meal remains one of the primary reasons people attend these festivals. At the Rockland festival, the price of the lobster meal is based on the current market price. But the lobster is fresh, and it is steamed in the world's largest lobster cooker.

CONTACTS:
Maine Lobster Festival
P.O. Box 552
Rockland, ME 04841
800-562-2529 or 207-596-0376; fax: 207-354-0128
www.mainelobsterfestival.com

SOURCES:
GdUSFest-1984, p. 78

♦ 1603 ♦ *Maine* **Memorial Day**
February 15

The American battleship *Maine,* which had been sent to Cuba to rescue any Americans who might be endangered by the Cubans' unrest under Spanish rule, was blown up while sitting at anchor in Havana harbor on February 15, 1898. Many in the United States assumed that the Spanish were responsible for the ship's destruction, since American sympathies were clearly with the Cubans. But despite the fact that 260 men died, the question of responsibility for the explosion was never really settled. The Spanish-American War was declared in April, and "Remember the *Maine!*" is the slogan that has been associated with it ever since.

February 15 was observed for many years by the U.S. Navy and by Spanish-American War veterans' associations in Havana and the United States. Some naval units still participate in local observances. This day is sometimes called **Battleship Day** or **Spanish-American War Memorial Day**.

Special observances marked the 100th anniversary of the battleship's destruction in 1998 at Key West, Florida, the ship's last port-of-call before heading to Havana.

CONTACTS:
Library of Congress
101 Independence Ave. S.E.
Washington, D.C. 20540
202-707-5000; fax: 202-707-8366
www.loc.gov

Department of the Navy
Naval Historical Center, Washington Navy Yard
805 Kidder Breese S.E.
Washington, DC 20374
202-433-2210; fax: 202-433-2729
www.history.navy.mil

SOURCES:
AmerBkDays-2000, p. 144
AnnivHol-2000, p. 28
DictDays-1988, p. 10

♦ 1604 ♦ **Making Happiness Festival**
Ninth and 10th days of first lunar month

Some villages in Taiwan observe the **Tso-Fu Festival**, or "making happiness" festival, soon after the LUNAR NEW YEAR. This observance honors the gods as well as women who have borne sons during the past year. On the ninth, village leaders round up images of gods from homes and shrines and head a procession to the temple, which includes musicians as well as people carrying banners and banging gongs. Once there, the new mothers make special offerings of "new-male cakes" called *hsin-ting ping*, while everyone else gives other sacrifices. The next day a special feast is held for the village leaders, the elderly, and the mothers, who now hand out new-male cakes to everyone except other new mothers. The festival concludes with the collection of the images of the gods from the temple and their return to their regular homes.

SOURCES:
FolkWrldHol-1999, p. 85

◆ 1605 ◆ Malawi Freedom Day
June 14

Malawi Freedom Day is a public holiday celebrating the end of the corrupt totalitarian regime that ruled the country for nearly three decades. In 1966, two years after becoming an autonomous nation free from the British government, the African country of Malawi established a new constitution and became a single-party state. Dr. Hastings Kamuzu Banda, leader of the conservative Malawi Congress Party (MCP), became the nation's first president. In 1971, Banda was declared president for life, a position he retained until the 1990s with the help of the paramilitary wing of the MCP.

In 1993, however, growing domestic unrest and pressure from church leaders and the international community forced Banda to allow a public referendum. The Malawian people were asked to decide between continued one-party rule and a multiparty democracy. On June 14, 63% of voters opted to end one-party rule and Banda's regime in favor of democratic leadership. National elections were conducted on May 17, 1994, and the United Democratic Front candidate Bakili Muluzu won the presidency.

CONTACTS:
Malawi Embassy
2408 Massachusetts Ave. N.W.
Washington, D.C. 20008
202-797-1007

SOURCES:
AnnivHol-2000, p. 100

◆ 1606 ◆ Malawi Martyrs' Day
March 3

March 3 is celebrated each year as a national holiday in Malawi honoring the political heroes who gave their lives in the struggle against British colonialism. Malawians often attend church services on March 3 and offer prayers for departed freedom fighters. In addition, Radio Malawi plays tribute music to remember those martyred during the 1959 crisis in Central Africa.

For most of the 19th century, the African nation of Malawi (formerly called Nyasaland) was a British colony. Beginning in the early- to mid-20th century, however, the country's indigenous people began attempts to achieve independence from British rule. During the 1950s, Britain united Malawi with the Federation of Northern and Southern Rhodesia (now known as Zambia and Zimbabwe), a venture that led to widespread resentment of colonial domination. In response, in an effort to attain independence, Malawians formed their own political parties and plotted violent retaliations and acts of sabotage. On March 3, 1959, British forces declared a state of emergency and orchestrated Operation Sunrise, arresting prominent Malawian nationalists and other dissidents. Fury over the arrests of these resistance leaders precipitated the deaths of more than 20 demonstrators. In total, 51 were killed, over 1,300 were detained, and many more were wounded during the state of emergency, which lasted until 1960.

CONTACTS:
Malawi Embassy
2408 Massachusetts Ave. N.W.
Washington, D.C. 20008
202-797-1007

◆ 1607 ◆ Malawi Republic Day
July 6

Also known as **National Day,** this holiday commemorates Malawi's independence from Britain on this day in 1966. The area had been known as Nyasaland. At midnight on July 5-6, 1966, 40,000 people cheered the changing of the flag at Central Stadium, ushering in Malawi's autonomy.

Today ceremonies and prayer services are held at stadiums in Blantyre, Mzuzu, or the capital city of Lilongwe.

CONTACTS:
Malawi Embassy
2408 Massachusetts Ave. N.W.
Washington, D.C. 20008
202-797-1007; fax: 202-265-0976

SOURCES:
AnnivHol-2000, p. 113
NatlHolWrld-1968, p. 111

◆ 1608 ◆ Malaysia Birthday of SPB Yang di-Pertuan Agong
June 2

Malaysia practices a system of government based on a constitutional monarchy and parliamentary democracy. The head of state is the king, also known as Seri Paduka Baginda (SPB) Yang di-Pertuan Agong. Although the term king is used, this is not a hereditary position. The SPB Yang di-Pertuan Agong is also the highest commander of the Malaysian armed forces. The federal head of government is the prime minister.

The SPB Yang di-Pertuan Agong is one of three bodies that make up the Malaysian Parliament. The other two are the Senate (Dewan Negara) and the House of Representatives

(Dewan Rakyat). The Yang di-Pertuan Agong is elected to a five-year term. According to the Malaysian Constitution, only the Conference of Rulers has the power to elect and appoint the Yang di-Pertuan Agong. The Conference of Rulers is a council comprised of state rulers who deliberate on questions of national policy and other important matters.

Every year, June 2 is set aside as a national holiday in Malaysia to celebrate the birthday of the current and past SPB Yang di-Pertuan Agongs.

CONTACTS:
Resource Center, Parliament of Malaysia
Parliament Bldg.
50680 Kuala Lumpur, Malaysia
www.parlimen.gov.my

♦ 1609 ♦ Malcolm X's Birthday
May 19

Malcolm X, whose original name was Malcolm Little (1925-1965), was an outspoken leader in the black nationalist movement of the 1960s. He converted to the Muslim faith while serving time in prison for burglary, and upon his release began touring the country on behalf of the Nation of Islam, led by Elijah Muhammad. In 1964 he was suspended from the sect and started his own religious organization. But hostility between Malcolm's followers and the rival Black Muslims escalated. He was assassinated at a rally in Harlem shortly after his PILGRIMAGE TO MECCA.

Because during most of his career Malcolm X advocated violence (for self-protection) and had a reputation for fanaticism and racism, his leadership was rejected by most other civil rights leaders of his day. But, as reflected in his *The Autobiography of Malcolm X, as Told to Alex Haley*, his pilgrimage to Mecca changed his outlook. After performing the pilgrimage rites, Malcolm composed and sent a letter back home. It read, in part: "For the past week, I have been utterly speechless and spellbound by the graciousness I see displayed all around me by people *of all colors*.... There were tens of thousands of pilgrims ... from blue-eyed blonds to black-skinned Africans. But we were all participating in the same ritual, displaying a spirit of unity and brotherhood that my experiences in America had led me to believe never could exist between the white and the non-white."

His birthday, May 19, is still observed in most major American cities with a large African-American population.

SOURCES:
AAH-2007, p. 279
AmerBkDays-2000, p. 374

♦ 1610 ♦ Maldives Embraced Islam Day
Varies

The Republic of Maldives is an island nation comprised of approximately 1,190 islands in the Indian Ocean. In 1153, Maldives converted from Buddhism to Islam. The main events and festivals in Maldives follow the Muslim calendar.

Children receive religious education both at home and in school, and all children learn the Arabic alphabet. According to legend, the country converted to Islam as follows:

Long ago, Rannamaari, an evil sea-demon, came out from the sea once a month and threatened to destroy everything unless a virgin was sacrificed. Every month the people of the island chose a young girl by lot and left her alone in a small temple as a sacrifice.

One day, a young man named Yousuf Shamsuddin-al Tabrezi arrived on the island. He stayed in the house of a poor couple in Malé. When the daughter of the house was selected for the next sacrifice, Yousuf decided to disguise himself as a girl and take her place in the temple. He went to the temple that night and continuously recited the Holy Quran. The demon came that night, but as it got closer to the temple, it heard the words of the Quran and turned away.

When the islanders went to check on Yousuf in the morning, they were amazed to find him alive and still reciting the Quran. He told them that it was the powers of the Holy Quran that had saved him. He called upon the king to embrace Islam so that the island could be free from the wrath of the demon. The King took his advice and converted to Islam and ordered all of his subjects to do the same.

CONTACTS:
Ministry of Legal Reform, Information and Arts
Rehendhihigun
960-333-4333; fax: 960-333-4334
www.maldivesinfo.gov.mv

♦ 1611 ♦ Maldives Independence Day
July 26

This group of islands in the Indian Ocean had been under British control since 1887 until its full independence on this day in 1965. Independence Day is a national holiday in Maldives.

Maldives became a republic on November 11, 1968, an event commemorated with another national holiday, **Republic Day**. Festivities are held for two days, including November 11.

CONTACTS:
Maldives Mission to the U.N.
820 Second Ave., Ste. 800C
New York, NY 10017
212-599-6194; fax: 212-661-6405
www.maldivesmission-ny.com

SOURCES:
NatlHolWrld-1968, p. 126

♦ 1612 ♦ Maldives National Day
First day of Rabi-al-Awwal, the third month in the Islamic calendar

The Republic of Maldives is an island nation comprised of approximately 1,190 islands in the Indian Ocean. The people of the islands had easy access to precious cowry shells (historically used as currency and in jewelry) and ambergris (a substance produced in the digestive system of sperm whales and used in perfumes). These valuable resources attracted the attention of Portuguese explorers. In 1558, the Portuguese attacked the Maldives islands, killed the country's sultan, and established their own rule. For the next 15 years, the Portuguese ruled the country, despite the islanders' wishes for its former leadership. Among other rules, the Portuguese tried to force Christianity on the Maldivians, who were an Islamic people.

In 1573, a Maldivian named Muhammad Thakurufaanu and his brothers killed the Portuguese leader Andreas Andre and recaptured the island of Malé. Thakurufaanu served as sultan for 12 years, during which time he formed an army, introduced coins, and improved trade and religious observances. His dynasty lasted for the next 132 years.

Today, Maldives celebrates National Day to commemorate the historic event in which Thakurufaanu overthrew the Portuguese rulers. Celebrations on this holiday, which falls on the first day of Rabi-al-Awwal (the third month in the Islamic calendar), consist of parades and root marches in the streets of Malé and other islands.

CONTACTS:
Ministry of Legal Reform, Information and Arts
Rehendhihigun
960-333-4333; fax: 960-333-4334
www.maldivesinfo.gov.mv

♦ 1613 ♦ **Mali Independence Day**
September 22

Mali gained its independence from France on September 22, 1960. As a colony since the 1890s, it was known as French Sudan. In ancient and medieval times Mali had a prominent role in a series of illustrious empires that spanned western Africa.

Also known as **Republic Day**, this is an important national holiday in Mali.

CONTACTS:
Mali Embassy
2130 R St. N.W.
Washington, D.C. 20008
202-332-2249; fax: 202-332-6603
www.maliembassy.us

SOURCES:
AnnivHol-2000, p. 158
NatlHolWrld-1968, p. 177

♦ 1614 ♦ **Mallard Ceremony**
January 14 every 100 years (2001, 2101, 2201, 2301...)

The **Mallard Feast** or **Mallard Day** ceremony held once every 100 years at All Souls College in Oxford commemorates the college's founding in 1438. Henry Chichele, archbishop of Canterbury at the time, wanted to establish a college at Oxford in memory of those who had perished in the

wars between England and France. While he was considering where such a college might be located, he had a dream that when the foundations were being dug, a fattened mallard was found stuck in the drain or sewer. He decided to heed the omen and, when the digging began at the location specified in his dream, a huge mallard was indeed found—a sure sign that his college would flourish.

Although no one is sure exactly when the first commemoration of this event was held, the ceremony itself has remained unchanged. The Fellows of the college nominate the Lord of the Mallard. He in turn appoints six officers, who march before him carrying white staves and wearing medals with the image of the mallard engraved on them. When the Lord is seated in his chair, the officers carry him around the quadrangle three times and sing a traditional song. After that, they climb up to the college roof in a torchlight procession and sing the song again, loudly enough for most of the town to hear. Eventually they retire to their common rooms to drink wine and continue their merrymaking.

CONTACTS:
Oxford University, All Souls College
Mallard Society
Oxford, OX1 4AL United Kingdom
44-18-6527-9379; fax: 44-18-6527-9299
www.all-souls.ox.ac.uk

SOURCES:
BkDays-1864, vol. I, p. 113
OxYear-1999, p. 35

♦ 1615 ♦ **Malta Freedom Day**
March 31

The Republic of Malta is a small country in the central Mediterranean that consists of seven islands. In 1814, Malta became a crown colony of the British empire. Under British rule, the Maltese Islands helped the Allies during World War I. Hundreds of Maltese served as soldiers in the British regiments, and Malta allowed the British to use its dockyard and hospitals. Thousands of sick and wounded soldiers were brought to Malta for treatment, thereby earning the country the title of the "Nurse of the Mediterranean."

Malta also played an important role during World War II. The bravery its people showed during the war led to the country being awarded the George Cross, which is now displayed on its flag. On September 21, 1964, Malta was granted independence from Britain. On December 13 of that same year, Malta became a republic within the Commonwealth, with the President as head of state.

Although Malta gained independence in 1964, the British armed forces did not completely leave until March 31, 1979. It was at that time that the Maltese Prime Minister, Dom Mintoff, demanded that the British either pay a higher rent for their bases or withdraw. This freed Malta of foreign military occupation for the first time in history.

In Malta, Freedom Day is a public holiday that commemorates the day the last of the British military left the Maltese

Islands. On this holiday, a ceremony is held at the War Memorial in Floriana. The main events of the day take place around the Freedom Day Monument in Vittoriosa. In the afternoon, a competitive regatta is held in Grand Harbour, where food and drink booths are set up along the harbor. The participants compete in traditional Maltese boats called *id-dgħajsa Maltija*.

CONTACTS:
Malta Tourism Authority
Auberge D'Italie
Merchants St.
Valetta VLT 1170 Malta
www.visitmalta.com

◆ 1616 ◆ Malta Independence Day
September 21

Malta Independence Day is a nationwide celebration of Malta's independence, achieved on this day in 1964. Malta was under the control of various political entities from its earliest days. In the early 19th century, the Maltese acknowledged Great Britain's sovereignty, but through the years various constitutions were in force, and in the 20th century, self-government was repeatedly granted and suspended. Malta's heroic stand against the Axis in World War II won a declaration that self-government would be restored at the end of the war, and indeed self-government under another constitution was granted in 1947. It was revoked in 1959, restored in 1962, and independence was finally granted in 1964. Ten years later, on Dec. 13, 1974, Malta became a republic—December 13 is a national holiday and horse races at Marsa commemorate that event.

Independence Day is celebrated with parades and festivities throughout the country.

See also VICTORY DAY

CONTACTS:
Malta National Tourist Office
65 Broadway, Ste. 823
New York, NY 10006
212-430-3799; fax: 425-795-3425
www.visitmalta.com

SOURCES:
AnnivHol-2000, pp. 158, 207
NatlHolWrld-1968, p. 176

◆ 1617 ◆ Malta Republic Day
December 13

The Republic of Malta is a small country in the central Mediterranean that consists of seven islands. In 1814, as part of the Treaty of Paris, Malta became a crown colony of the British empire. The colony was used as a shipping waystation and fleet headquarters. Because of its close proximity to the Suez Canal, it was considered to be a very important outpost to the British territories in India.

On September 21, 1964, Malta was granted its independence from Britain. According to its 1964 constitution, Queen Elizabeth II would initially serve as the supreme leader of Malta, with a Governor-General serving as executive authority on her behalf. On December 13, 1974, Malta became a republic within the Commonwealth, with the President as head of state.

To commemorate the day the country became a republic, December 13 has been declared Republic Day in Malta. On this day, a big feast is held and Malta's National Anthem is played and/or sung at the end of all masses. In addition, the President of Malta presents national awards, namely the Order of Merit and *Gieh ir-Repubblika*. These awards inspire a sense of patriotism, as they are awarded as a token of appreciation for those who honor their country through their achievements and service to their community.

Although Malta gained independence in 1964, the British armed forces did not completely leave until March 31, 1979. This was the first time in Malta's history that the country was free of foreign military. To commemorate this day, the people of Malta celebrate FREEDOM DAY.

CONTACTS:
Malta Tourism Authority
Auberge D'Italie
Merchants St.
Valetta VLT 1170 Malta
www.visitmalta.com

◆ 1618 ◆ Malta Sette Guigno (Commemoration of Uprising of June 7, 1919)
June 7

The Republic of Malta is a small country in the central Mediterranean that consists of seven islands. In 1798 Napoleon Bonaparte invaded Malta and took power. The people of Malta did not want to be under French rule, so the country asked the British to help compel the French to leave. In 1799, the British Navy forced the French to withdraw. The Treaty of Paris, signed on May 30, 1814, made Malta a crown colony of the British empire.

Under British rule, the Maltese Islands helped the Allies during World War I. Hundreds of Maltese served as soldiers in the British regiments, and the country allowed the British to use its dockyard and hospitals. Thousands of sick and wounded soldiers were brought to Malta, thereby earning the country the title of the "Nurse of the Mediterranean."

Although the war brought jobs to the country, the wages were relatively low. Many Maltese found it hard to make ends meet. The high cost of living created serious problems for many Maltese. These factors and others prompted riots in Valletta on June 7, 1919. During the riots, four Maltese were killed by British troops. The victims included Guzeppi Bajada, Manwel Attard, Wenzu Dyer, and Karmenu Abela. This tragic event became known as the Sette Guigno Riots.

The 1919 riots impelled the country to establish the first responsible government in Malta in 1921. It was the first time Maltese citizens could elect Maltese members of Parliament.

Today, Malta recognizes the anniversary of the riots as a national holiday. Every year on June 7, Malta holds a commemorative ceremony at Palace Square in Valletta, in front of the House of Representatives. Bouquets of flowers are placed on the monument of the Sette Guigno victims at Addolorata (Our Lady of Sorrows) cemetery. The commemorative celebration also includes marches by the Police Corps and the playing of the national anthem L-Innu Malti, and a moment of silence in memory of the four fallen men.

CONTACTS:
Malta Council for Culture and the Arts
230 Republic St.
Valletta CMR 02 Malta
www.maltaculture.com

◆ 1619 ◆ Mamuralia
March 14

According to one Roman myth, Mamurius was a smith who was run out of the city because the shields he had made for the Roman soldiers failed to protect them when they were substituted for the sacred shield that had fallen from heaven. Another explanation for the ceremonies held on this day is that Mamurius, whose name was a variation of Mars, represented the old year, which had to be driven away on the day preceding the first full moon of the new Roman year. In any case, the rite that took place on March 14 involved leading a man wearing only animal skins through the streets of Rome. He was pursued and beaten with long white rods until he was driven out of the city.

The Mamuralia was unusual in that no other Roman festival occurred on an even-numbered day. One explanation is that the festival was originally held on the IDES of March, but was moved back a day so that people could attend both the horseraces known as the EQUIRRIA and the ANNA PARENNA FESTIVAL held on March 15.

SOURCES:
FestRom-1981, p. 89
OxYear-1999, p. 117
RomFest-1925, p. 44

◆ 1620 ◆ Mandi Safar
During Islamic month of Safar

Mandi Safar is a Muslim bathing festival unique to Malaysia. This holiday, which is observed during the month of Safar, was originally believed to commemorate the last time Muhammad was able to bathe before his death. Muslims wearing bright colors visited beaches for a religious cleansing of the body and soul with water. There is no mention of the rite in the Qur'an (the Muslim holy book), and orthodox Muslims consider it nothing more than a picnic. It continues as a merry holiday. The best-known gathering places are the beaches of Tanjong Kling, near Malacca, and of Penang.

CONTACTS:
Malaysian Tourism Promotion Board
818 W. 7th St., Ste. 970
Los Angeles, CA 90017

800-336-6842 or 213-689-9702; fax: 213-689-1530
www.tourismmalaysiausa.com

SOURCES:
BkHolWrld-1986, Aug 7

◆ 1621 ◆ Manger Yam
November 25

Like the NEW YAM FESTIVALS held in some African countries, Manger Yam is a harvest celebration of the yam crop observed in Haiti, a country mainly comprised of descendants of slaves from west Africa. Because Haitians, too, depend upon the yam crop, they hold the Manger Yam, named after the French *manger,* which means "to eat."

It is considered taboo to eat any of the new yams before the festival for fear of falling ill or bringing ruin to the yam crop. This is also an occasion on which families reunite to celebrate together. In Voodoo, or more properly, Vodoun, belief, it is very important for people to maintain relationships with the dead, as well as with each other and the gods, so the deceased are included in the Manger Yam as well as in other ceremonies and festivals.

In the Voodoo service, the priest or priestess leads prayers to the dead and to the gods and offers the first yams to them. After the ceremony, people feast on yam dishes and enjoy music and dancing.

CONTACTS:
Haitian Embassy
2311 Massachusetts Ave. N.W.
Washington, D.C. 20008
202-332-4090; fax: 202-745-7215
www.haiti.org

SOURCES:
FestWrld: Haiti-1999, p. 7
FiestaTime-1965, p. 171

◆ 1622 ◆ Mani Rimdu
Usually November

This Tibetan Buddhist festival is held at the Tengboche *gompa* (monastery) in Solu Khumbu district high in the Himalayas of Nepal. Merely getting there requires at least a six-day hike in the mountains. But the scenery—which includes Mt. Everest and several lower but equally impressive peaks—is magnificent for those who make it.

Mani Rimdu is a thousand-year-old Buddhist epic that is re-enacted in the courtyard of the monastery. It takes place under a full moon, and begins when masked dancers enter the courtyard in silence. The same re-enactment takes place at the Thami monastery in May or June, although festival organizers in both locations recently have started requesting that foreigners who want to witness the event pay a fee.

CONTACTS:
Nepal Tourism Board, Tourist Service Center
Bhrikuti Mandap
P.O. Box 11018

Kathmandu, Nepal
977-1-4256909; fax: 977-1-4256910
www.welcomenepal.com

Tengboche Monastery Development Project
Tengboche Monastery
Khumbu, Nepal
www.tengboche.org

SOURCES:
WildPlanet-1995, p. 276

♦ 1623 ♦ **ManiganSes—Festival internationale des arts de la marionette**
Mid-September, held biennially

Canada's only international puppet festival, ManiganSes—Festival internationale des arts de la marionette, brings together puppet artists from various Canadian provinces and other world regions to the Quebec region of Saguenay. More than a dozen companies representing nearly every continent put on performances for local residents and puppetry enthusiasts from all over.

The festival was called World Puppet Week when it was first held in 1990. Along with setting up performances, event organizers offered workshops and exhibitions and provided networking opportunities, components that remain part of the six-day festival today.

During the 1990s, the festival attracted the general population with entertaining outdoor shows featuring giant puppets. In 2006, the festival adopted its present name, and moved its date from its traditional slot in July to September so that it would held in conjunction with an autumn cultural festival held in the Saguenay-Lac-Saint-Jean region. Many of the 51 performances that took place that year were staged at an outdoor venue, the Parc de la Riviere-aux-Sables, in the town of JonquiFre.

CONTACTS:
ManiganSes
3865, rue du Roi-Georges
C.P. 503
JonquiFre, QC G7X 7W3 Canada
www.maniganses.com

♦ 1624 ♦ **Manitoba Sunflower Festival**
Last weekend in July

The Mennonites were members of an evangelical Protestant sect that originated in Europe in the 16th century and was named for Menno Simon, a Dutch priest. They began emigrating to North America in the late 17th century and lived primarily as farmers, retaining their German language. A number of Russian Mennonites settled in Manitoba, Canada, where their heritage is still celebrated in the towns along the so-called Mennonite Trail.

Because the Mennonites were the first to extract the oil from sunflower plants, the city of Altona in southern Manitoba has chosen to honor its Mennonite heritage with an annual **Sunflower Festival** during the last weekend in July. Since 1965

the festival has attempted to revive the Mennonite culture by offering performances of "low German" humor and by serving a number of Mennonite foods such as *schmaunfat, veriniki, pluma moose, borscht,* and *rollkuchen.* A special sunflower ice cream is made especially for the festival. Less "authentic" activities include the Great Ping Pong Ball Drop, motorcross races, pancake breakfasts, and a huge farmers' market.

CONTACTS:
Town of Altona
111 Centre St.
Altona, MB R0G 0B0 Canada
204-324-6468; fax: 204-324-1550
www.townofaltona.com

♦ 1625 ♦ **Manly Man Festival and Spam Cook-Off, National**
Father's Day weekend (June)

In 1991 in Roslyn, Wash., a group of male camping buddies got together to create the National Manly Man Festival and Spam Cook-Off. This spoof event displays the alleged manliness of those who attend. Now organized by the Order of the Manly Men, which claims 1,000 members nationwide, the event includes such manly activities as eating bugs, bucking bellies together in greeting, and preparing and eating a variety of Spam-related foods. Spam chowder and Spam quiche are two of the favorites. Those who enter the Spam cook-off can win trophies donated by the Hormel Corp., maker of the canned meat product.

In addition to the Spam-related activities, there is also a parade of manly vehicles down Roslyn's main street (women can participate providing their vehicle is "manly" enough), a tool-belt competition, a softball game, and the selection of the Spam queen, who qualifies based on submitting a 100-word essay. Those men who attend the National Manly Man Festival receive an official membership card, a beer mug, and a certificate proving their manliness. Honorary Order of the Manly Men memberships have been granted to actors Kurt Russell and Bruce Willis, Governor Arnold Schwarzenegger, and former football coach Mike Ditka.

CONTACTS:
Order of the Manly Men
8207 Steilacoom Blvd. S.W.
Tacoma, WA 98498
253-581-7657

♦ 1626 ♦ **Maralal Camel Derby**
August

The Maralal Camel Derby takes place annually over three days in August in Maralal, Kenya, located about 180 miles north of Nairobi in the country's Northern Region. First held in 1990, it welcomes entrants from all over the world, who compete against Kenyan champions in professional and amateur races. The professional camel races are regarded by many as a serious international sport. The race course runs through desert areas with conditions presenting varying levels of difficulty. Camels are available for hire (handlers optional) to anyone who wants to saddle up and take part.

In addition to the camel races, other competitive events include donkey rides for children and bicycle races of 18 miles and 26 miles. Also featured are colorful displays of local dancing. The spectacular festival, organized by Yares Safaris, draws visitors from around the globe, but it has a serious side. The camel races are intended to create awareness of the rapid desertification of Kenya and the benefits that camels can bring to desert inhabitants.

CONTACTS:
Kenya Tourist Office
2249 R St. N.W.
Washington, D.C. 20008
202-387-6101
www.magicalkenya.com

◆ 1627 ◆ Marbles Tournament, National
Late June

The annual National Marbles Tournament began in 1922, when Macy's Department Store in Philadelphia sponsored a promotional tournament. The Scripps-Howard Newspapers sponsored the event until 1955, when the city of Wildwood, New Jersey, and a group of volunteers interested in preserving the game decided to sponsor the event jointly. Traditionally held for five days near the end of June in this New Jersey seaside resort town, the tournament features a competition among champions selected in elimination contests throughout the country. The national boy and girl champions each receive a trophy and a plaque as well as a $2,000 scholarship.

Although there are many games that can be played with marbles—such as Potsies, Poison, Passout, Chassies, Puggy, Black Snake, and Old Boiler (reportedly a favorite with Abraham LINCOLN)—the game played in the national tournament is called Ringer. It is played by placing 13 marbles in the form of a cross in a 10-foot circle. The marbles inside the circle are called "migs" or "miggles." Players alternate shots using a "shooter" or "taw," and the winner is the first one to shoot seven miggles out of the ring.

CONTACTS:
Greater Wildwood Chamber of Commerce
3306 Pacific Ave.
Wildwood, NJ 08260
609-729-4000; fax: 609-729-4003
www.gwcoc.com

◆ 1628 ◆ Mardi Gras
February-March; two weeks before Ash Wednesday

The most flamboyant of Mardi Gras (from the French for "fat Tuesday") celebrations in North America culminates in a riot of parades and throngs of laughing, drinking, dancing people in the streets of New Orleans, La.

The Mardi Gras celebrations symbolize New Orleans, "The City that Care Forgot," to most people. The festivities actual-

ly start on Jan. 6 (EPIPHANY) with a series of private balls. The tempo picks up in the last two weeks of the Carnival season, when the streets ring with 30 separate parades organized by committees called *krewes*. The parades consist of marching jazz bands and lavishly decorated two-story floats carrying the costumed and masked krewe royalty who toss "throws" to pleading spectators; these are beads or bonbons or the coveted Mardi Gras doubloons. Each of the parades has 15 to 20 floats, all decorated to express a certain theme.

Two of the biggest and most elaborate parades, the Krewe of Endymion and the Bacchus parade, take place on the weekend before Mardi Gras. On the day of Mardi Gras, designated the "Day of Un-Rule," the traditional parades spotlight Rex, King of Carnival and Monarch of Merriment, in the morning, and Comus, God of Revelry, by torchlight at night. On that same evening the private balls of Rex and Comus are held. At midnight, the madness of Carnival ends, and LENT begins, and a million or so spectators and participants face sobriety.

New Orleans had its first organized Mardi Gras parade in 1857. It consisted of two floats and was presented by the first Carnival society, the Mistick Krewe of Comus, its name alluding to John Milton's masque, *Comus*. The parade was apparently well received; it was one of the first local institutions revived after the Civil War.

Mardi Gras in New Orleans is the best known, but not the oldest Mardi Gras. A two-week pre-Lenten celebration in Mobile, Ala., stands alone as the oldest celebration of Mardi Gras in the country. It was first observed in 1703 by the French who had founded the port city the year before. When the Spanish occupied Mobile in 1780, they moved it to the eve of the TWELFTH NIGHT of CHRISTMAS and paraded in grotesque costumes and masks. The celebrations were suspended during the Civil War, but were revived in 1866 by Joe Cain, a town clerk who togged himself out as an Indian chief and rode through the streets in a charcoal wagon. The old Mardi Gras societies reappeared, and new ones evolved.

Today a different mystic society parades each evening in the two weeks before Lent, and balls are held that are open to everyone. Mardi Gras itself, the day before ASH WEDNESDAY, is a legal holiday in the state of Louisiana.

Galveston, Texas, has a 12-day period of whoop-de-do leading up to the actual day of **Fat Tuesday** in this barrier-island city of Texas. About 200,000 spectators are attracted to the Mardi Gras festival, which was first held here in 1867. Though it died out at the turn of the century, it was revived in 1985. Growing bigger every year, this celebration features masked balls, royal coronations, Cajun dances, jazz performances, and, of course, numerous parades with dramatic floats.

See also CARNIVAL and SHROVE TUESDAY

CONTACTS:
New Orleans Metropolitan Convention and Visitors Bureau
2020 St. Charles Ave.
New Orleans, LA 70130
800-672-6124 or 504-566-5011; fax: 504-566-5046
www.neworleanscvb.com

Mobile Convention and Visitors Corporation
1 S. Water St.
P.O. Box 204
Mobile, AL 36602
800-566-2453 or 251-208-2000; fax: 251-208-2060
www.mobile.org

Mardi Gras Galveston official site
Galveston Island Convention and Visitors Bureau
Visitor Information Center
Galveston, TX 77550
888-425-4753
mardigrasgalveston.com

SOURCES:
AmerBkDays-2000, p. 128
BkFestHolWrld-1970, p. 32
DictFolkMyth-1984, p. 193
EncyEaster-2002, p. 364
FolkAmerHol-1999, p. 88
GdUSFest-1984, p. 5
RelHolCal-2004, p. 91

♦ 1629 ♦ **Mardi Gras (France)**
Between February 3 and March 9; Tuesday before Ash Wednesday

MARDI GRAS (Fat Tuesday) is the last day of CARNIVAL, the three-day period of uninhibited celebration that precedes LENT. The festivities in France are particularly colorful in southern cities like Cannes, Menton, and Grasse, all in Alpes-Maritimes department, where people go out in the streets in costume and indulge in all sorts of noisy pranks, such as tooting tin horns and pelting passersby with confetti and flowers. Each town, in fact, has its own *bataille de fleurs* (battle of flowers) right before Lent, with people in flower-decked cars and floats driving for hours along the streets and boulevards, throwing flowers at each other.

One of the great celebrations of Europe is the carnival at Nice, where grotesque, caricatured figures parade down the Avenue de la Gare—among them giant cabbages and carrots, gnomes, devils on horseback, nymphs, and fairies. King Carnival, dressed in striped hose and a slashed doublet, leads the parade from his throne on a float draped with purple velvet. On the night of Mardi Gras, the King Carnival effigy is burned at the stake.

In Paris and some other French cities, butchers observe Carnival with the fête of the *Boeuf Gras,* or Fat Ox. An ox decked with garlands of greenery, flowers, and ribbons is led through the streets in procession, followed by a triumphal cart bearing a young boy known as the "King of the Butchers." The crowd pays tribute to him by blowing horns and throwing confetti, flowers, and sweets.

See also NICE CARNAVAL

CONTACTS:
French Government Tourist Office
444 Madison Ave., Fl. 20
New York, NY 10022
800-391-4909 or 212-838-7800; fax: 212-838-7855
www.franceguide.com

SOURCES:
BkFest-1937, p. 120
BkFestHolWrld-1970, p. 33
FestWestEur-1958, p. 34

♦ 1630 ♦ **Margrethe's (Queen) Birthday**
April 16

The birthday of Queen Margrethe II (b. 1940) is observed in the capital city of Copenhagen, where people congregate in the courtyard of Amalienborg, the royal palace. Carrying small Danish flags, children cheer and sing for the Queen, refusing to go home until she comes out to greet them. She often appears on the balcony at lunchtime and makes a speech, which is followed by a changing of the Royal Guard in its scarlet dress uniforms.

CONTACTS:
Embassy of Denmark
3200 Whitehaven St. N.W.
Washington, D.C. 20008
202-234-4300; fax: 202-328-1470
www.ambwashington.um.dk

SOURCES:
AnnivHol-2000, p. 63
BkHolWrld-1986, Apr 16

♦ 1631 ♦ **Marian Days**
First weekend of August

In 1975 the Congregation of the Mother Co-Redemptrix, a Vietnamese religious order, established a new campus in Carthage, Mo. The order's priests and brothers were among tens of thousands of Vietnamese citizens who came to the United States to escape the turmoil of the Vietnam War (1959–1975). Many Vietnamese Catholics believed their safe passage to America was the result of the Virgin Mary's intervention. Marian Days, which the small town of Carthage has hosted since 1977, is a time for Vietnamese Catholics to honor the Mother of Jesus and recognize the protection she offered to refugees.

Despite its small size, Carthage somehow manages to handle the influx of more than 70,000 visitors for the summer celebration. Attendees come from all over the country; some stay in nearby hotels, and others camp on the grounds of the Catholic order's 28-acre campus or in residents' backyards. A festival area is arranged before the weekend for church groups to erect food tents and various displays.

The weekend's events, which include daily Masses, penance ceremonies, benedictions, and religious lectures, lead up to the Saturday celebration, which consists of a parade for the Virgin Mary as well as a fireworks and balloon ceremony. The weekend closes with a final mass that is recited in Vietnamese and translated into English.

CONTACTS:
Congregation of the Mother Co-Redemptrix
1900 Grand Ave.
Carthage, MO 64836
417-358-7787
www.dongcong.org

♦ 1632 ♦ **Marino Wine Festival**
First weekend in October

The Italian town of Marino is located in the area southeast of Rome known as the Castelli Romani, after the numerous castles, palaces, and Renaissance villas that dot the landscape. Marino is known as a wine town, and there are about a hundred *cantine*—small, nondescript taverns where tourists and residents can buy the local wine, which is often siphoned from a large vat and poured into an empty mineral water bottle, for a very low price. It's not surprising, then, that during the town's wine festival in early October the new grape harvest is celebrated by letting the previous year's wine gush freely from the Moors Fountain. Crowds of Romans eager to escape the city descend upon Marino with jugs, bottles, and thermoses to fill. The wine is free for the taking and is the perfect accompaniment to a *porchetta* sandwich, the filling made by slowly roasting pig over a woodfire with fresh garlic, rosemary, and olive oil.

CONTACTS:
Italian Government Tourist Board
630 Fifth Ave., Ste. 1565
New York, NY 10111
212-245-5618; fax: 212-586-9249
www.italiantourism.com

♦ 1633 ♦ **Marion County Ham Days**
Last full weekend in September

This event is a weekend celebration of the famous Kentucky smoked ham, held in Lebanon (Marion County), Ky., since 1970. The affair started with a simple country ham breakfast served to about 300 people on the street; now about 50,000 folks show up. Breakfast (ham cured in Marion County, eggs, biscuits with local honey, fried apples) is still served on Saturday and Sunday, but there is more: a "Pigasus Parade" with more than 100 floats, a Pokey Pig 5-kilometer run, a crafts and antiques show, a hog-calling contest, a hay-bale toss, and a hot air balloon race.

CONTACTS:
Lebanon-Marion County Chamber of Commerce
239 N. Spalding Ave., Ste. 201
Lebanon, KY 40033
270-692-9594; fax: 270-692-2661
www.hamdays.com

♦ 1634 ♦ **Mariposa Folk Festival**
First weekend in July

This three-day folk music festival is the oldest in Canada, where it has served as a model for many smaller festivals. Since 1961 the festival has presented a broad spectrum of folk music—from Kentucky blues to Indian chanting—by performers from all over Canada, the United States, Britain, Africa, and Australia. The events are held on the grounds of Tudhope Park in Orillia, Ontario, about 60 miles north of Toronto.

The Mariposa Festival helped pioneer the workshop concept, emphasizing the importance of establishing a dialogue between the artist and the audience. In addition to the workshops hosted by festival musicians, there is a "folk-play" area where a family can work with a particular performer, who shares his or her special talents with both children and their parents.

CONTACTS:
Mariposa Folk Foundation
37 Mississaga St., W.
P.O. Box 383
Orillia, ON L3V 3A5 Canada
705-326-3655; fax: 705-326-3655
www.mariposafolk.com

SOURCES:
IntlThFolk-1979, p. 74
MusFestAmer-1990, p. 232

♦ 1635 ♦ **Maritime Day, National**
May 22

The day chosen to commemorate the contribution of American commercial shipping is, appropriately, the day on which the *Savannah* left its home port in Georgia in 1819 to attempt the first steam-propelled crossing of the Atlantic. So unusual was it to see a steam-powered vessel in those days that when the *Savannah* passed the naval station at Cape Clear, Ireland, the authorities thought she was on fire and quickly dispatched a royal cutter to assist her. In reality, the *Savannah* was equipped with sails and only relied on her engines for about 90 hours of the journey.

It was President Franklin D. Roosevelt who first proclaimed May 22 as National Maritime Day in 1933. Since that time observations of this day have grown in popularity, particularly in American port cities. Ships are opened to the public, maritime art and essay contests are held, and parades and band concerts are common. Environmentalists sometimes take advantage of the attention focused on the country's maritime heritage on this day to draw attention to pollution and deterioration of maritime environments, particularly in large commercial ports like New York City.

CONTACTS:
U.S. Maritime Service Veterans
P.O. Box 2361
Berkeley, CA 94702
www.usmm.org

Maritime Administration
U.S. Dept. of Transportation
400 Seventh Ave. S.W.
Washington, DC 20590
800-996-2723 or 202-366-5807
www.marad.dot.gov

SOURCES:
AmerBkDays-2000, p. 380
AnnivHol-2000, p. 85

♦ 1636 ♦ **Marlboro Music Festival**
Mid-July to mid-August

It was the noted violinist Adolf Busch who came up with the idea of establishing a summer community for musicians that would free them from the pressures and restrictions of concert life. Every summer since 1951, a group of artists from all over the world has gathered in Marlboro, Vermont, to exchange musical ideas. The Marlboro Music School, which holds an eight-week session each summer, is primarily a place where students or those who are just starting out on their professional careers can study contemporary and classical chamber music.

During the five-week festival, the general public has an opportunity to hear the results of their collaborations. But the primary emphasis at Marlboro is on rehearsing the works that the participants themselves have selected, rather than on performing them for the public.

Although many noted musicians have been associated with Marlboro, perhaps the best known is Pablo CASALS, the world-famous cellist who conducted the Marlboro Festival Orchestra and taught master classes there from 1960 to 1973.

CONTACTS:
Marlboro Music Festival
1616 Walnut St., Ste. 1600
Philadelphia, PA 19103
215-569-4690; fax: 215-569-9497
www.marlboromusic.org

Marlboro Music Festival
P.O. Box K
Marlboro, VT 05344
802-254-2394; fax: 802-254-4307
www.marlboromusic.org

SOURCES:
MusFestAmer-1990, p. 142

♦ 1637 ♦ **Marley's (Bob) Birthday**
Week of February 6

A week-long Bob Marley Birthday celebration takes place every year over the course of the week of his birth date (February 6, 1945). Events center in and around the Bob Marley museum in Kingston, Jamaica. The museum is located at 56 Hope Road, where Marley lived during the 1970s and recorded many of the reggae-music albums for which he is famous. The celebration typically encompasses such events as symposia on Marley's life and work, films, lectures, learning activities for children, and of course a series of concerts celebrating Marley's music. In the past, Marley's four sons have performed to benefit Ghetto Youths, a charity that two of Marley's sons founded to help young artists get started in the music business.

The birthday celebration is sponsored by Tuff Gong Records International, the landmark Caribbean record company founded by Marley in 1965, which also runs the Bob Marley Foundation. Since Marley's death in 1981, the birthday celebration has grown in momentum, and it now draws hundreds of fans to his hometown.

CONTACTS:
Tuff Gong International/Bob Marley Foundation
350 Fifth Ave., Ste. 5101
New York, NY 10118

212-563-5173; fax: 212-594-1594
www.bobmarley-foundation.com/t31.html

Jamaica Tourist Board
1320 S. Dixie Hwy., Ste. 1101
Coral Gables, FL 33146
800-233-4582 or 305-665-0557; fax: 305-666-7239
www.jamaicatravel.com

♦ 1638 ♦ **Maroon Festival**
January 6

When Jamaica was a Spanish territory in the 16th century, African slaves were brought in to work the plantations. The Spanish, disappointed by the lack of gold on the island, eventually left and the former slaves fled to the mountains. During the 17th and 18th centuries, the island's British inhabitants were often harassed or attacked by the descendants of these well-armed and organized fugitive slaves, who were called Maroons (having been marooned or deserted by their owners). By 1738 the Maroons had been given permission to settle in the northern part of the island.

The annual Maroon Festival is held at Accompong on January 6, and commemorates the 1759 signing of the peace treaty with the English and establishment of the town of Accompong. It is celebrated with traditional dancing and singing, maroon feasts and ceremonies, the blowing of the *abeng*, and the playing of maroon drums.

CONTACTS:
Jamaica Tourist Board
801 Second Ave., Fl. 20
New York, NY 10017
800-233-4582 or 212-856-9727; fax: 212-856-9730
www.jamaicatravel.com

♦ 1639 ♦ **Marrakech Popular Arts Festival**
Mid-July

The annual five-day national festival of popular arts is held in Marrakech, Morocco, every July. It showcases folk singers, dancers, theater troupes, fortune-tellers, fire-swallowers, and snake charmers from all over Morocco, as well as a variety or artists and entertainers from Europe, Asia, and South America, including China, Peru, and Ukraine. Performances take place at outdoor venues all over the city, with the major events centered in the ruins of the 16-century Badi Palace or the Djemma el Fna (main town square). Launched in the mid-1960s, the festival is one of the longest-running of its kind.

CONTACTS:
Morocco National Tourist Office
20 E. 46th St., Ste. 1201
New York, NY 10017
212-557-2520; fax: 212-949-8148
www.visitmorocco.org

♦ 1640 ♦ **Marriage Fair**
September

This mass engagement and marriage *moussem*, or "festival," is held in the remote village of Imilchil in the Atlas Mountains of Morocco. As many as 30,000 people of the Ait Hadiddou tribe, a Berber clan, gather for the three days of the moussem. Also known as the **Fiancée Festival**, this is a combined trade fair and pageant of public courtship, instant engagement, and the immediate exchange of marriage vows. The festival solves the problem of meeting a mate in a society where isolation is the norm: the men spend half a year moving with their flocks to upland pastures, while the women stay in the villages, planting crops and weaving rugs.

Families and their herds of sheep and donkeys stream onto the Imilchil plateau at dawn of the first day. They sell or barter their wool, meat, grain, and vegetables, while tradesmen set up tents of pottery, rugs, and tools. Musicians beat tambourines, games are played, and acrobats perform. The center of their Islam-influenced devotions is the tomb of the holy man Sidi Mohammed el Merheni. It's not certain when he lived but it's known that the marriages he blessed were happy.

The courtship proceeds with women wearing a peaked headdress and striped wool capes over white dresses. Their eyes are outlined with kohl and their cheeks are rouged. The prospective grooms, wearing white robes and turbans, weave in pairs through the clusters of brides-to-be. A man speaks to a woman, the woman nods assent, and if the family approves, the couple will enter the wedding tent to seek approval from a representative of the Ministry of Justice in Rabat. Brides who have not been previously married will leave the moussem with their fathers, and be welcomed by their grooms' families with a feast later in the year. Women who are divorcées or widows will go directly to live with their husbands. (Ait Hadiddou women are free to divorce and remarry.)

When a woman consents to marriage, she tells her suitor, "You have captured my liver." The Ait Hadiddou consider the liver to be the soul of love because it aids digestion and well-being.

CONTACTS:
Moroccan National Tourist Office
20 E. 46th St., Ste. 1201
New York, NY 10017
212-557-2520; fax: 212-949-8148

♦ 1641 ♦ Marshall Islands Constitution Day
May 1

In 1943, during World War II, the Allied forces—the United States, Britain, France, Union of Soviet Socialist Republics (USSR), Australia, Belgium, Brazil, Canada, China, Denmark, Greece, Netherlands, New Zealand, Norway, Poland, South Africa, and Yugoslavia—invaded the Marshall Islands. By 1944, the Allied forces occupied the Marshall Islands. At the end of World War II, the United States was given effective power in the Marshall Islands. Throughout their occupation, the United States conducted nuclear weapons testing on the islands (*see also* Marshall Islands Memorial and Nuclear Victims Day).

On May 1, 1979, the Marshall Islands constitution was signed, establishing it as a self-governing country. In 1982,

the Marshall Islands officially changed its name to the Republic of the Marshall Islands.

Constitution Day is a public holiday in the Marshall Islands. On this day of celebration, people gather together for a parade to commemorate their independence. Also as part of the celebration, field-day contests are held between all private and public schools, entities within the community itself, and more. Some of these contests include basketball, women's softball, men's baseball, volleyball, soccer, tug-of-war, and various track-and-field events.

CONTACTS:
Embassy of the Republic of the Marshall Islands
2433 Massachusetts Ave. N.W.
Washington, D.C. 20008
202-234-5414; fax: 202-232-3236
www.rmiembassyus.org

♦ 1642 ♦ Marshall Islands Fishermen's Day
First Friday in July

In the Marshall Islands, Fishermen's Day is a public holiday that is sponsored by the Marshalls Billfish Club. During the Fishermen's Day contest, competing fishermen go out into the ocean and attempt to catch the most, the biggest, or the heaviest fish in any of several categories. Because the boats often leave between 5:30 and 6:00 A.M., competitors usually register the evening before the actual contest day. The fishing often lasts as late as 5:00 P.M., at which time the fish are weighed and measured.

The Marshall Islands is well known to have some of the best sport-fishing conditions in the world. In 1981, four friends, Tom Micheals, Wally Milne, Ramsey Reimers, and Ronnie Reimers, founded the Marshalls Billfish Club so that they could be invited to compete in the Hawaiian Invitational Billfish Tournament (HIBT) championship in Kona, Hawaii. During their first time competing in this tournament, the Marshalls Billfish Club won with a 711-pound marlin caught by Ramsey Reimers. That fish remains in the top ten for that competition.

The win at the 1981 HIBT inspired the four friends to set up an annual tournament in the Marshall Islands every July. They recruited many volunteers to help plan and run the very first tournament in July 1982. The Marshall Islands government endorsed the club, local businesses made contributions, and several off-island supporters also contributed to the event. Since then, the event has become a national holiday and a source of enjoyment to hundreds of people each year.

The Marshalls Billfish Club now has a Board of Directors, consisting of seven elected directors and four appointed positions (President, Vice President, Director, and Secretary). There are now over 200 members in the club.

CONTACTS:
Marshall Islands Visitors Authority
P.O. Box 5
Majuro 96960 Marshall Islands
www.visitmarshallislands.com

Marshalls Billfish Club
P.O. Box 1139
Majuro, MH 96960 Republic of the Marshall Islands
www.billfishclub.com

♦ 1643 ♦ Marshall Islands Gospel Day
First Friday in December

Gospel Day in the Marshall Islands is similar to THANKSGIV-ING day in the United States. The only difference between the two countries' celebrations is that the Marshallese people attend church on this day to commemorate the first missionaries who brought the light of God to the Marshall Islands.

Today, most Marshallese are Protestants. In general, the Marshallese people are very religious. In the Republic of the Marshall Islands, Sundays are set aside for rest and relaxation and attending church services.

The largest church in the Marshall Islands is the United Church of Christ; however, many other Protestant denominations have churches in the Marshall Islands, including Assembly of God, Baptist, and Seventh Day Adventists. In addition, the Catholic Church has established a strong presence in the islands. And more recently, the Church of Latter-day Saints has also become established.

CONTACTS:
Embassy of the Republic of the Marshall Islands
2433 Massachusetts Ave. N.W.
Washington, D.C. 20008
202-234-5414; fax: 202-232-3236
www.rmiembassyus.org

♦ 1644 ♦ Marshall Islands Lutok Kobban Alele
Last week of September

The inhabitants of Micronesia's Marshall Islands have long kept a tradition centered on the *alele*, a soft-sided basket handmade from the native pandanus plant. This treasured item contains a family's most valuable possessions, and according to Marshallese custom, passes through generations in the trust of the family's eldest female.

The phrase "Lutok Kobban Alele" means pour out the valuable contents of the basket. The event of the same name is a weeklong festival that honors the basket as a national symbol and celebrates Marshallese culture in general. The inaugural festival was held in 1986, the year that the Marshall Islands ended a long era under U.S. administration. In years past, the festival has been sponsored by the Marshall Islands Alele Museum.

Festivities conclude with an official ceremony on MANIT DAY, a public holiday observed on the last Friday of September. Activities take place in the capital city of Marjuro and include performances by Marshallese singers and dancers, feasts promoting local foods, traditional storytelling, and demonstrations of basket weaving and cooking.

CONTACTS:
Alele Museum

P.O. Box 629
Majuro, MH 96960 Marshall Islands
members.tripod.com/~alelemuseum/Index.html

♦ 1645 ♦ Marshall Islands Manit Day (Marshall Islands Custom Day)
Last Friday in September

Cultural values and customs in the Marshall Islands are known as *manit*. Manit Day is part of the annual cultural festival LUTOK KOBBAN ALELE, which is the last week of September. The purpose of Lutok Kobban Alele is to promote and preserve the Marshallese culture.

The Manit Day celebration takes place near the Alele Museum, Library, and National Archive, which displays exclusive and original artifacts of the Marshall Islands. On Manit Day, people from the general public can set up a booth outside the museum to sell their handicrafts, food, drinks, etc. Many Marshallese handicrafts are known for their high quality and use of natural products. Woven baskets, fans, hats, wall hangings, purses, mats, coasters, and Marshallese stick charts are made from such raw materials as coconut, pandana leaves, and likajir shells. Popular Marshallese products also include such coconut oil products as hand soaps and laundry detergents. These products are good for the skin, but they do not harm the environment.

As part of the celebration, children from all of the public schools have the opportunity to perform dances, sing songs, perform skits, or tell folklore stories. In addition, some local traditional contest games, including coconut husking and basket weaving, are often conducted.

CONTACTS:
Embassy of the Republic of the Marshall Islands
2433 Massachusetts Ave. N.W.
Washington, D.C. 20008
202-234-5414; fax: 202-232-3236
www.rmiembassyus.org

Marshall Islands Visitors Authority
P.O. Box 5
Majuro, 96960 Republic of the Marshall Islands
www.visitmarshallislands.com

♦ 1646 ♦ Marshall Islands Memorial and Nuclear Victims Day
March 1

The Republic of the Marshall Islands is comprised of 29 atolls in the North Pacific Ocean. An atoll is a group of coral islands that form a ring around a shallow lagoon.

After World War II, the United States occupied the Marshall Islands for several decades. In 1946, the United States began a nuclear testing program in the Marshall Islands to test post-World War II nuclear weapons.

In 1954, the United States detonated Bravo, the most powerful hydrogen bomb ever tested by the United States, on Bikini atoll. The fallout radiation from the test forced the evacuation of Marshallese and U.S. military personnel on four of the atolls. Many of the people exposed to the radiation began to experience nausea, vomiting, and itching skin and eyes. Those who were most heavily exposed suffered skin burns and later hair loss. The U.S. Atomic Energy Commission issued a statement to the press calling Bravo a "routine atomic test" and stating that some Americans and Marshallese were "unexpectedly exposed to some radioactivity. There were no burns. All were reported well."

Throughout the remainder of the 1950s, the U.S. government declared the islands safe for rehabitation and returned the islanders to their homes. The U.S. government gave the islanders money and set up trust funds to compensate for the damages, and nuclear testing continued. By 1963, the first thyroid tumors began to appear among those who had been exposed to the Bravo test, and U.S. doctors noticed a higher than normal incidence of growth retardation among young islanders. In 1969, the Atomic Energy Commission stated, "There's virtually no radiation left and we can find no discernible effect on either plant or animal life."

By the mid-1970s, it became clear that the damage was much more extensive than originally reported. Throughout the 1980s and 1990s, the U.S. government set up trust funds for the Marshallese residents and paid the victims millions of dollars in total.

On Memorial and Nuclear Victims Day, Marshallese people from the four atolls that were affected by the bomb and fallout gather to pray and commemorate their atolls and those who were killed during the bomb testing.

CONTACTS:
Embassy of the Republic of the Marshall Islands
2433 Massachusetts Ave. N.W.
Washington, D.C. 20008
202-234-5414; fax: 202-232-3236
www.rmiembassyus.org

Alele Museum, Library and National Archives
P.O. Box 629
Majuro, 96960 Republic of the Marshall Islands
members.tripod.com/~alelemuseum/Index.html

♦ 1647 ♦ **Marshall Islands President's Day**
November 17

The Republic of the Marshall Islands has designated November 17 as President's Day, a day to remember the nation's first president, Amata Kabua. Kabua started his career as a school teacher and rose to become paramount chief of the Island of Majuro and head of state of the Marshall Islands. He served five terms as president of the Marshall Islands, beginning in 1979 when the country became independent and continuing until his death in 1996.

There are no organized activities or events on this day.

CONTACTS:
Embassy of the Republic of the Marshall Islands
2433 Massachusetts Ave. N.W.
Washington, D.C. 20008
202-234-5414; fax: 202-232-3236
www.rmiembassyus.org

♦ 1648 ♦ **Martenitza**
March 1

Every year on March 1, people in Bulgaria present each other with *martenitzas*—two joined tassels of red-and-white woolen thread resembling a simple CHRISTMAS decoration symbolizing health and happiness. The custom originated with the ancient Thracians, and the first martenitzas had silver or gold coins attached to them. Today it is most widespread in Bulgaria, although the Martenitza is also celebrated in southern Romania, Albania, Greece, and Cyprus.

The rites are varied. In some regions, women dress completely in red on this day. In northeastern Bulgaria, the lady of the house traditionally tosses a red cloth over a fruit tree, or spreads a red woolen cloth on the fields for fertility. In stockbreeding areas, a red-and-white thread is tied to the cattle. Bulgaria is the only country where this particular fertility custom seems to have survived. In Greece the "March" is tied to the wrist or big toe of children to protect them from the March sun. They remove it when they see the first swallow or stork, signs of springtime. On Cyprus it is hoped that one's skin will be as red (healthy) as the string. In Canada, Bulgarian-Macedonians throw the string out for the first robins to use in their nests.

See also DRYMIAIS

SOURCES:
FolkWrldHol-1999, p. 197

♦ 1649 ♦ **Martinmas**
November 11

This is the feast day of St. Martin of Tours (c. 316-397), one of the most popular saints of the Middle Ages. It is said that when he heard that he had been elected bishop of Tours, he hid himself in a barn. A squawking goose gave away his hiding place, and the day is still celebrated with roast goose dinners. Another popular legend involves St. Martin's cloak, which he divided with his sword, giving half to a shivering beggar.

In Germany and northern Europe, Roman Catholics commemorate St. Martin while Protestants commemorate Martin Luther's baptismal day (*see* MARTINSFEST).

For rural people, Martinmas comes at a happy time of year: the crops are in, the animals have been slaughtered, the new wine is ready, and the hard work of summer and autumn is over. It's no surprise, then, that St. Martin is the patron saint of tavern keepers, wine-growers, and drunkards. There is a good deal of weather lore associated with this day. Spells of mild autumn weather that Americans refer to as "Indian summer" are called "St. Martin's summer" or "a Martinmas summer" in Europe and England. It was once a QUARTER DAY. Nowadays, in England, this day is more remembered as Armistice Day (*see* VETERANS DAY).

In Belgium, where it is called **Sint Maartens Dag**, St. Martin's Day is a favorite holiday among children. Like ST. NICHOLAS, St. Martin visits them on the feast day eve bringing them gifts. On November 11 apples and nuts are tossed into children's rooms while they stand with their faces turned to the wall. *Gauffres*, little waffle cakes, are particularly popular on St. Martin's Day.

This day is also an important festival in the Netherlands. There it is known as **Beggar's Day**, and boys and girls serenade their neighbors and beg for goodies. In many towns the children light a bonfire and dance and shout around it. Then they march in processions with lanterns made from scooped-out turnips, carrots, or beets.

In other European countries, St. Martin's Day is regarded as a time to give thanks for the harvest and is often observed with feasting. Goose is the traditional meal. In Sweden, November 11 is known as **Martin's Goose Day** (**Marten Gas**). In France, *mal de Saint Martin* (St. Martin's sickness) is the name given to the upset stomach that often follows overindulgence. There is also an impressive ceremony at St. Martin's shrine in Tours on this day.

See also HUERIGEN PARTIES; QUADRILLES OF SAN MARTIN; ST. MARTIN'S DAY IN PORTUGAL

CONTACTS:
General Council of Indre-et-Loire
Place the prefecture
Tours, 37927 France
33-2-4731-4731; fax: 33-2-4731-4271
www.cg37.fr

SOURCES:
BkDays-1864, vol. II, p. 567
BkFest-1937, p. 107
DaysCustFaith-1957, p. 286
DictFolkMyth-1984, p. 682
EncyChristmas-2003, p. 463
FestSaintDays-1915, p. 204
FestWestEur-1958, pp. 18, 27, 48, 101, 140, 185, 216
FolkWrldHol-1999, p. 650
OxYear-1999, pp. 456, 457
SaintFestCh-1904, p. 481

♦ 1650 ♦ Martinmas (Ireland)
November 11

There are a number of superstitions and folk beliefs associated with MARTINMAS in Ireland. One is that you must have roast goose for dinner or risk eating no more goose in the coming year. (According to legend, when St. Martin heard that he had been elected Bishop of Tours, he hid himself in a barn but was given away by a squawking goose.) In any case, it is traditional to kill a sheep, lamb, kid, pig, calf, or cow on St. Martin's Eve and eat the meat on **St. Martin's Day**, after sprinkling the animal's blood in the four corners of the house as well as on the walls, threshold, and floor. A dot of blood is even smeared on the forehead of each family member in the belief that it will protect them from evil for one year. The shedding of blood may also be a survival of the time when animals were killed right before winter because it was difficult to find fodder.

On the Aran Islands off the western coast of Ireland, there is a legend that when St. Martin stopped at the house of a poor woman and asked for something to eat, she sacrificed her child because she had no meat to offer him. But when he left the house, the woman found her child still asleep in his cradle. Aran Islanders sacrifice an animal on Martinmas in memory of this miracle, and feed roast cock or goose to any beggar who comes to the door on November 11.

Fishermen in Ireland will not go fishing on Martinmas, believing that if they do, they will meet a horseman riding over the sea, followed by a terrible storm. It is also considered bad luck to turn a wheel of any kind—car, mill, or spinning—on this day.

SOURCES:
BkDays-1864, vol. II, p. 568
DaysCustFaith-1957, p. 287
DictFolkMyth-1984, p. 682
FolkWrldHol-1999, p. 651

♦ 1651 ♦ Martinsfest
November 10-11

Martin's Festival in Germany honors both St. Martin of Tours (*see* MARTINMAS and ST. MARTIN'S DAY IN PORTUGAL) and Martin Luther (1483-1546), the German theologian and leader of the Protestant REFORMATION.

In Düsseldorf, a man dressed as St. Martin rides through the streets followed by hundreds of children. Many carry lanterns made from hollowed-out pumpkins. It is thought that the rites associated with St. Martin's Day may have originated as an early thanksgiving festival in honor of Freya, the ancient German goddess of plenty.

While German Roman Catholics honor St. Martin on this day, Protestants honor Martin Luther, who was born on November 10, 1483, and baptized on the 11th. In Erfurt, where Martin Luther attended the university, there is a procession of children carrying lanterns. This ends in the plaza in front of the cathedral and the Severi Church. With their lanterns the children form the "Luther rose," or the escutcheon of Martin Luther.

CONTACTS:
Tourist Association Duesseldorf
Breite St. 69
Duesseldorf, 40213 Germany
49-211-172-02-0; fax: 49-211-161-07-1
www.duesseldorf-tourismus.de/default_en.php?PHPSES

Tourist Information Erfurt
Weimarische St. 45
Erfurt, D-99084 Germany
49-361-664-00; fax: 49-361-664-02-90
www.erfurt-tourist-info.de

SOURCES:
AnnivHol-2000, p. 188
BkFest-1937, p. 138
BkFestHolWrld-1970, p. 122
DictWrldRel-1989, pp. 440, 606
FestWestEur-1958, p. 77
OxYear-1999, p. 456

♦ 1652 ♦ Martyrdom of Joseph and Hyrum Smith
June 27

Members of the Church of Jesus Christ of Latter-Day Saints, also known as Mormons, commemorate the day on which their founder, Joseph Smith, and his brother, Hyrum, were murdered in the city jail in Carthage, Illinois, in 1844. Joseph Smith had announced his candidacy for the U.S. presidency earlier that year, and he had been attacked by a group of Mormon dissenters for his political ambition and his alleged polygamy: There is evidence that he may have married as many as 50 wives, although he acknowledged only his first.

As the mayor of Nauvoo, Ill., Smith saw to it that the press used to print the opposition newspaper was destroyed. Threats of mob violence followed, and Smith and his brother were eventually jailed on charges of treason. Although the brothers had been promised protection by the governor, a mob of men with blackened faces stormed the jail on June 27 and killed them, thus elevating them to the status of martyrs.

CONTACTS:
Church of Jesus Christ of Latter-Day Saints
50 N.E. Temple St.
Salt Lake City, UT 84150
801-240-1000; fax: 801-240-1534
www.lds.org

Joseph Smith Historic Visitor Center
P.O. Box 338
Nauvoo, IL 62354
217-453-2246
www.cofchrist.org

SOURCES:
AmerBkDays-2000, p. 847
DictWrldRel-1989, p. 424
RelHolCal-2004, p. 127

♦ 1653 ♦ **Martyrs' Day (Lebanon)**
May 6

Martyrs' Day has been observed as a public holiday since 1970 to honor the fallen heroes of Arab nationalism. The date, May 6, was selected to commemorate the 21 Arab intellectuals who were hanged on that date in 1916 in Beirut, Lebanon, and Damascus, Syria, by an official of the occupying Ottoman Empire.

On Martyrs' Day, ceremonies of public commemoration are led by government officials in Beirut at Martyrs' Square, named in honor of the murdered nationalists. Officials and citizens also lay wreaths at martyrs' monuments in Beirut and throughout the country.

CONTACTS:
Embassy of Lebanon
2560 28th St. N.W.
Washington, D.C. 20008
202-939-6300; fax: 202-939-6324
www.lebanonembassyus.org/index.html

♦ 1654 ♦ **Martyrs of North America, Feast of the**
October 19

The **Feast of the North American Martyrs** commemorates the death of eight priests who were killed by the Iroquois,

mortal enemies of the Huron Indians, with whom the priests had been working for 34 years. There was a great deal of missionary activity being carried out in what is now Canada and upstate New York during the 1600s, and many of the devoted missionaries who worked among the Indians in the area extending from Nova Scotia to the Great Lakes met with torture and often cruel death. The eight who are remembered on this day are St. Rene Goupil (1608-1642), St. Isaac Jogues (1607-1646), St. John Lalonde (d. 1646), and their companions, French Jesuits who died in 1649. They were canonized together in 1930, and a shrine built for them at Auriesville, New York, holds a novena (a traditional Roman Catholic ritual of prayer lasting nine days) each year over nine days including October 19.

CONTACTS:
National Shrine of North American Martyrs
136 Shrine Rd.
Auriesville, NY 12016
518-853-3033
www.martyrshrine.org

SOURCES:
AmerBkDays-2000, p. 718
AnnivHol-2000, p. 175
DaysCustFaith-1957, p. 242

♦ 1655 ♦ **Marya**
July-August; third day of waning half of Hindu month of Sravana

When Gautama sat down under the Bo tree to await Enlightenment, Mara, the Buddhist Lord of the Senses and satanic tempter, tried a number of strategies to divert him from his goal. Disguised as a messenger, Mara brought the news that one of Gautama's rivals had usurped his family's throne. Then he scared away the other gods who had gathered to honor the future Buddha by causing a storm of rain, rocks, and ashes to fall. Finally, he sent his three daughters, representing thirst, desire, and delight, to seduce Gautama—all to no avail.

In the city of Patan, Nepal, a procession on this day commemorates the Buddha's triumph over Mara's temptations. A procession of 3,000 to 4,000 people, carrying gifts—usually butter lamps—for Lord Buddha, moves through the city from shrine to shrine. Some wear masks and others play traditional Nepalese musical instruments. The devil dancers and maskwearers in the parade often pretend to scare the children who line the streets by suddenly jumping out at them.

CONTACTS:
Embassy of Nepal
2131 Leroy Pl. N.W.
Washington, D.C. 20008
202-667-4550; fax: 202-667-5534
www.nepalembassyusa.org

SOURCES:
FolkWrldHol-1999, p. 470

♦ 1656 ♦ **Maryland Day**
March 25

Maryland Day, or **Founder's Day**, commemorates the landing of the first colonists there in 1634, and the first Roman Catholic Mass they celebrated. Named after Henrietta Maria, the consort of King Charles I (1600-1649) of England, Maryland was the first proprietary colony on the American mainland. George Calvert, Lord Baltimore (1580?-1632), was appointed by the king as proprietor, and as a Catholic he hoped to establish a refuge for other Catholics who had been persecuted in Anglican England. He was succeeded as head of the colony by his son, Cecilius Calvert (1605-1675), the second Lord Baltimore, who brought 200 more colonists over from England.

CONTACTS:
Maryland State Archives
Maryland Manual On-Line
350 Rowe Blvd.
Annapolis, MD 21401
800-235-4045 or 410-260-6400; fax: 410-974-3895
www.mdarchives.state.md.us

Maryland Secretary of State
State House
Annapolis, MD 21401
888-874-0013 or 410-974-5521; fax: 410-974-5190
www.sos.state.md.us

SOURCES:
AmerBkDays-2000, p. 231
AnnivHol-2000, p. 50
DictDays-1988, p. 74

♦ 1657 ♦ **Maryland Hunt Cup**
Last Saturday in April

A steeplechase that has been run in Maryland since 1894, the Hunt Cup is considered the premier such horse race in America and one of the toughest steeplechases in the world. It's a timber race: the jumps are over stout post-and-rail fences rather than hedges as in the English GRAND NATIONAL. Since 1922, it has always been held in Glyndon, the locale of the Green Spring Valley Hounds, a hunt club. The course is four miles long and has 22 fences, none of which is jumped twice. The highest fence is the 16th at 4'10", while the most spectacular, causing the most spills, is the 4'6" third fence, near the beginning of the race before the horses are well warmed up.

The first race was held to settle a dispute between two hunt clubs, Green Spring Valley Hounds and the Elkridge Hunt, over which had the better fox-hunting horses. Originally only for club members, the race was opened to all comers in 1903, and a rivalry between Pennsylvania and Maryland horses began and still endures.

At the first race, a silver cup and $100 were awarded to the winner. Today there is still a cup, but the purse has grown to $65,000. Memorable horses have been Mountain Dew, a three-time winner in the 1960s; Jay Trump, also a three-time winner in the 1960s and the winner of the English Grand National in 1965; and Ben Nevis, twice a winner, who took seven seconds off the course record in 1978. Ben Nevis, who also won the English Grand National, was a small horse but a spectacular athlete.

The Hunt Cup was originally only for men, but women were allowed to enter in the late 1970s, and in 1980 Joy Slater was the first woman to take the prize.

Tailgate parties are held before the race, and a hunt ball after it is attended by riders, trainers, jockeys, owners, and members of the two local hunt clubs. It's considered the social event of the season.

CONTACTS:
Maryland Office of Tourism Development
217 E. Redwood St., Fl. 9
Baltimore, MD 21202
866-639-3526 or 410-767-6288; fax: 410-333-6643
www.mdisfun.org

♦ 1658 ♦ **Maryland Seafood Festival**
September

The Maryland Seafood Festival has been held since the 1960s. This three-day festival held in early September features the preparation and sale of seafood dishes, especially Maryland regional favorites. Many children's and family activities are available, such as beach bingo, face painting, and a beach volleyball contest. Local restaurants participate in a Crab Soup Cookoff. The festival takes place at Sandy Point State Park in Annapolis, Maryland. It coincides with the annual "Save the Bay Day," sponsored by the Chesapeake Bay Foundation.

CONTACTS:
Maryland Seafood Festival
1100 E. College Pkwy., Sandy Point State Pk.
Annapolis, MD 21409
410-268-7682
www.mdseafoodfestival.com

♦ 1659 ♦ **Marymass Festival**
Second and third weeks in August

The Marymass Festival is famous for its horse races, believed to be the oldest in Europe. It is named after Mary, the mother of Jesus and is held near August 15, the Feast of the ASSUMPTION. But it also honors Mary (1542-1587), queen of Scots, who is said to have visited Irvine and enjoyed the festivities in 1563. In addition to the horse races, there is a parade, the crowning of a Marymass queen, fireworks, and other events.

CONTACTS:
Irvine Carters Society
86 Montgomery St.
Irvine, Scotland KA12 8PW United Kingdom
44-12-9427-5515
www.marymass.org

♦ 1660 ♦ **Marzas**
February 28-March 1

On the last night of February and the first of March in Spain, young *marceros,* or March serenaders, wander through the streets singing songs to their girlfriends and asking for donations of food and sweets to celebrate the arrival of spring. The term *marzas* refers both to the traditional songs they sing and to the gifts they receive. Although the songs themselves vary, they always mention the month of March and the coming of spring, leading many to believe that the tradition has its roots in pagan rituals celebrating the passing of winter.

SOURCES:
DictFolkMyth-1984, p. 1063

♦ 1661 ♦ **Marzenna Day**
Saturday or Sunday nearest March 21

A festival day along the Vistula River in Poland, Marzenna Day is a spring ritual particularly enjoyed by young people. A *Marzenna* is a straw doll about three or four feet tall and dressed in rags, a striped shirt, a hat, and lots of ribbons. On this day near the first day of spring (*see* VERNAL EQUINOX), the townspeople, dressed in costume, accompany the Marzenna to the river and throw her in. Not only is this act a final farewell to winter, but it also recalls an old legend about a young man whose faith in one god was so great that he was able to save a girl who was about to be sacrificed to appease the gods of storms and floods. After the doll is thrown into the water, the people welcome spring with singing and dancing.

SOURCES:
AnnivHol-2000, p. 48
BkHolWrld-1986, Mar 23

♦ 1662 ♦ **Masi Magham**
February-March; full moon day of the Hindu month of Magha

The Masi Magham festival is observed every 12 years during the full moon of the Hindu month of Magha, although a smaller festival takes place annually. Hindus flock to Kumbakonam in southern India to bathe in the Maha-Magha tank, where the waters of nine holy rivers are said to be mixed: the Ganges, the Yumma, the Godavari, the Saraswati, the Narmada, the Cauvery, the Kumari, the Payoshni, and the Sarayu. Bathing in the sacred tank (or pool) purifies them of their sins.

The Masi Magham festival is also a time for gift-giving, particularly in support of charitable institutions. One way of measuring the size of one's gift to the poor is to give one's weight in gold, a custom known as *Tulabhara.* Sometimes the gold collected in this way is used to renovate the 16 temples that have been built over the years near the site of the sacred tank.

In Malaysia, the Masi Magham is a two-day festival celebrated by the Chettiyar (a Tamil merchant caste) community in Malacca. The image of Subramanya, a Hindu god, is taken in procession to the temple known as Sannasi Malai Kovil, formerly the home of a famous ascetic who had the power to heal. Oratorical contests are held and dramas are staged at the temple, and at the end of the day, the statue is taken back through the streets of Malacca to Poyyatha Vinayagar Kovil, where it remains for another year.

CONTACTS:
Tamil Nadu Tourism
Tourism Complex, No. 2 Wallajah Rd.

Chennai, Tamil Nadu 600 002 India
91-44-25383333; fax: 91-44-25381567
www.tamilnadutourism.org

Malaysian Tourism Promotion Board
818 W. Seventh St., Ste. 970
Los Angeles, CA 90017
800-336-6842 or 213-689-9702; fax: 213-689-1530
www.tourismmalaysiausa.com

SOURCES:
BkFestHolWrld-1970, p. 91
FolkWrldHol-1999, p. 189

♦ 1663 ♦ **Maskal**
September 27

Maskal ia a Christian festival in Ethiopia to commemorate the finding of the True Cross, the cross on which Christ was crucified. (*Maskal* means "cross.") The celebration comes at the end of the rainy season in the Ethiopian spring, when fields are blooming with yellow flowers known as the maskal flowers. In communities throughout the nation, a tall pole called a *demara* is set up and topped with a cross. Families place smaller demaras against the big one, and in the evening they are made into a huge bonfire. Religious ceremonies are performed around the bonfire, with songs and dancing. The ashes of the burned-out fire are considered holy, so the people place the powder of the ashes on their foreheads.

See also EXALTATION OF THE CROSS

CONTACTS:
Ethiopian Embassy
3506 International Dr. N.W.
Washington, D.C. 20008
202-364-1200; fax: 202-587-0195
www.ethiopianembassy.org

Ethiopian Tourism Commission
P.O. Box 2183
Addis Ababa, Ethiopia
251-1-517-470; fax: 251-1-517-533
www.tourismethiopia.org

SOURCES:
AnnivHol-2000, p. 161
BkHolWrld-1986, Sep 27
FolkWrldHol-1999, p. 569
GdWrldFest-1985, p. 75

♦ 1664 ♦ **Masters Golf Tournament**
First full week in April

Known to golf fans everywhere as **The Masters**, this annual tournament has been held at the exclusive Augusta National Golf Club in Georgia since it was first started there in 1934 by Bobby Jones, who designed the course. It has long been associated with names like Ben Hogan, Sam Snead, Arnold Palmer, and Jack Nicklaus. Former U.S. President Dwight Eisenhower often played the course and stayed in a cottage to the left of the 10th tee that is still called "Ike's Cottage."

The qualifying rounds are held on Thursday and Friday of the four-day tournament, and the top 44 finishers participate in the final round. The top 24 finishers are automatically invited back the next year and do not have to qualify again. In addition to the cash prize, the winner of the tournament, which has been referred to as "golf's rite of spring," receives a trophy and a green blazer. Each year on the Tuesday night before the tournament, there is a Champions Dinner attended by past winners and hosted by the defending champion—all of them wearing their distinctive green jackets.

It wasn't until September 1990 that the Augusta National Golf Club admitted its first black member, Ron Townsend, president of the Gannett Television Group. Had the Club refused to admit a black man, it is likely that the Masters would no longer have been held there, since the PGA (Professional Golfers' Association) now has rules forbidding discriminatory membership practices.

Seven years later, Tiger Woods, an African-American player, broke a 32-year tournament record and became golf's newest sensation.

CONTACTS:
Augusta National, Inc.
2604 Washington Rd.
Augusta, GA 30904
706-667-6000
www.masters.org

Augusta Metropolitan Convention and Visitors Bureau
1450 Greene St., Ste. 110
P.O. Box 1331
Augusta, GA 30901
800-726-0243 or 706-823-6600; fax: 706-823-6609
www.augustaga.org

SOURCES:
HolSymbols-2009, p. 553

♦ 1665 ♦ **Matralia**
June 11

The Matralia was an ancient Roman festival in honor of Mater Matuta, who is often confused with the Greek dawn goddess, Leucothea. Modern authorities describe Mater Matuta, who has no mythology but whose cult was widespread in ancient times, as a goddess of the dawn's light and of childbirth—the dawn being a lucky time to give birth. She was also a deity of matrons, and only matrons and freeborn women were allowed to participate in the festival held at her shrine in the round temple known as the Forum Boarium.

Not much is known about what went on during the Matralia, but it appears that only the wife of a first marriage was allowed to decorate the image of the goddess. No female slaves were allowed in the temple—except for one, who was driven out after being slapped on the face. The women offered prayers primarily on behalf of their nieces and nephews; their own children were considered to be of secondary importance. They made offerings of flowers and often arrived at the temple carrying their relatives' children in their arms.

SOURCES:
ClassDict-1984, p. 360

DictFolkMyth-1984, p. 693
FestRom-1981, p. 150
OxYear-1999, p. 244
RomFest-1925, p. 154

♦ 1666 ♦ **Matriculation, Feast of the**
February

The Feast of the Matriculation is a noisy and lighthearted celebration for university students in Italy. It is observed in various university cities, but the festivities are especially lively in Padua, where everyone in town as well as students from other parts of the country participate. The students march through the streets of Padua in noisy groups wearing the many-colored hats of their respective colleges. They all congregate at the famous Caffé Pedrocchi, where the celebration continues. Although no one is exactly sure what gave rise to this feast, it is apparently a very old tradition.

CONTACTS:
Italian Government Tourist Board
630 Fifth Ave., Ste. 1565
New York, NY 10111
212-245-5618; fax: 212-586-9249
www.italiantourism.com

SOURCES:
FestEur-1961, p. 114

♦ 1667 ♦ **Matrimonial Tea Party**
Between May 11 and June 14; Whit-Monday, Monday after Pentecost

Known locally as **Goûter Matrimonial** or **Déjeuner Matrimonial**, the Matrimonial Tea party that takes place on WHIT-MONDAY every year in écaussinnes-Lalaing in Belgium is an opportunity for young, unmarried women to entertain eligible bachelors. The first Matrimonial was organized by a young man named Marcel Tricot early in the 20th century.

At 9 o'clock in the morning, the visiting unmarried men, who must appear in full bridegrooms' dress and wear a symbolic cup on their lapels, are greeted at the town hall and invited to write their names in an official guest book. Then there are receptions, speeches by local officials, sightseeing tours, band concerts, and plenty of opportunity for the bachelors to walk through the streets, which are decorated with streamers, pennants, and humorous poems appropriate to the occasion.

At three in the afternoon the annual tea is announced. One of the young women welcomes the bachelors in the name of all of the "old maids" in écaussinnes-Lalaing. The "tea" consists of coffee, beer, and locally made sweets, and it is followed by folk dancing and merrymaking that continues for most of the night. No statistics are available concerning the success of the event in terms of matchmaking.

CONTACTS:
Belgian National Tourist Office
220 E. 42nd St., Ste. 3402
New York, NY 10017
212-758-8130; fax: 212-355-7675
www.visitbelgium.com

SOURCES:
FestEur-1961, p. 23
FestWestEur-1958, p. 12

◆ 1668 ◆ Matronalia
March 1

Also known as the **Matronales Feriae,** the Matronalia was an ancient Roman festival in honor of Juno, the goddess of women. It was observed on March 1, the day on which her temple was dedicated. The cult of Juno was established by the king of the Sabines, Titus Tatius, and the Matronalia celebrated not only the sacredness of marriage as an institution but the peace that followed the first marriages that took place between Roman men and Sabine women.

It was customary for married women to form a procession to Juno's temple, where offerings were made to the goddess. At home, women received gifts from their husbands on this day and held feasts for their female slaves. They also prayed for marital peace and harmony.

SOURCES:
FestRom-1981, p. 85
OxClassDict-1970, p. 569
OxYear-1999, p. 102

◆ 1669 ◆ Matsu, Birthday of
23rd day of third lunar month

This holiday celebrates the birthday of the Chinese deity Matsu (or Ma-cho or Mazu), the Goddess of the Sea who is venerated by fishermen for protecting them from storms and disasters at sea. People pay homage to her on her birthday at the Meizhou Mazu Temple on Meishou Island, Fujian Province, China, on Taiwan, and in other Chinese communities.

One Chinese legend says that the goddess was born in about 960 and, because she never cried in the first month of her life, was named Lin Moniang, *moniang* meaning "quiet girl." She began to read when she was eight, studied Buddhist and Taoist scriptures, became a believer in Buddhism at 10, studied magic arts when she was 12, and at 28 achieved nirvana and became a goddess. She is worshipped because she is believed to have performed many miracles during her life. Courts in successive dynasties issued decrees to honor her with such titles as "Holy Princess" and "Holy Mother."

In Taiwan, the story is that Matsu, a girl from Hokkien Province in China, took up the fishing trade to support her mother after her fisherman father died. One day she died at sea, and because of her filial devotion, she came to be worshipped as a deity. During World War II, when American planes started to bomb Taiwan, many women prayed to Matsu, and it is said that some women saw a girl dressed in red holding out a red cloth to catch the falling bombs.

She is known as A-Ma, or the Mother Goddess, on Macao. The legend there says A-Ma was a beautiful young woman whose presence on a Canton-bound ship saved it from disaster. All the other ships in the fleet, whose rich owners had refused to give her passage, were destroyed in a storm.

Whatever the story, people whose lives depend on the sea visit the goddess' temples on her birthday.

On Taiwan, the most famous celebration site is the Chaotien Temple in Peikang. Built in 1694, it is Taiwan's oldest, biggest, and richest Matsu temple. A carnival-like atmosphere prevails during the **Matsu Festival,** with watermelon stalls, cotton candy stalls, and sling-shot ranges set up along roadsides. There are parades of the goddess and other gods through village streets, where altars bearing sacrifices of food and incense have been set up. Hundreds of thousands of people pour out of buses and arrive on foot at Peikang. Many of them make pilgrimages from the town of Tachia about 60 miles north, spending a week visiting about 16 Matsu temples along the route. Peikang becomes so crowded it's hard to move, and the firecrackers are deafening. It has been estimated that 75 percent of all firecrackers manufactured on Taiwan are exploded in Peikang during the Matsu Festival; afterwards the remnants of the firecrackers lie two inches deep on the streets.

See also TIN HAU FESTIVAL

CONTACTS:
Taiwan Government Information Office
4201 Wisconsin Ave. N.W.
Washington, D.C. 20016
202-895-1850; fax: 202-362-6144
www.gio.gov.tw

SOURCES:
FolkWrldHol-1999, p. 255

◆ 1670 ◆ Maundy Thursday
Between March 19 and April 22 in West and between April 1 and May 5 in East; Thursday before Easter

Also known as **Green Thursday** in Germany from the practice of giving a green branch to penitents as a sign that their penance was completed; **Shere** or **Sheer Thursday,** meaning "free from guilt"; **Paschal Thursday, Passion Thursday,** or **Holy Thursday,** it is the day preceding GOOD FRIDAY.

It commemorates Jesus' institution of the Eucharist during the Last Supper, celebrated by Christians since the middle of the fourth century. The practice of ceremonial footwashing in imitation of Jesus, who washed his disciples' feet before the Last Supper as a sign and example of humility and love, has been largely discontinued in Protestant churches. However, the Roman Catholic Church and the Anglican Communion still celebrate the rites of Maundy Thursday, which may include handing out special coins known as "Maundy money" to the aged and the poor, instead of footwashing. Also on this day, the sacramental Holy Oils, or chrism, are blessed.

The name "Maundy" probably comes from the Latin *mandatum,* or "commandment," referring to Jesus' words after he washed the feet of his disciples: "A new commandment I give unto you, that you love one another as I have loved you" (John 13:34).

SOURCES:
AmerBkDays-2000, p. 235
BkDays-1864, vol. I, p. 411

BkFest-1937, pp. 56, 183, 227, 329
DaysCustFaith-1957, p. 106
DictFolkMyth-1984, pp. 694, 1163
EncyEaster-2002, p. 386
FestSaintDays-1915, p. 61
FestWestEur-1958, pp. 8, 60, 93, 212
FolkAmerHol-1999, p. 167
FolkWrldHol-1999, p. 244
OxYear-1999, p. 617
SaintFestCh-1904, p. 158

♦ 1671 ♦ Mauni Amavasya
January-February; 15th day of waning half of Hindu month of Magha

Complete silence is observed on the day known to Hindus as Mauni Amavasya. Because bathing during Magha, one of the most sacred Hindu months, is considered to be a purifying act, many Hindus camp out along the banks of the Ganges River throughout the month and bathe daily in the sacred river. But the bathing and fasting end with the observance of Mauni Amavasya, a day for worshipping Lord Vishnu and circumambulating the peepal (a type of ficus) tree, which is mentioned in the *Bhagavad Gita* and is regarded as holy.

For many Hindus, the celebration takes place at Prayag, a well-known pilgrimage center where the Ganges, Yamuna, and Saraswati rivers flow together. Some live here for a full month, practicing rituals and ceremonial sacrifices known as *Kalpa-Vas*. Religious discourses and services are held daily, and the worshippers who come here eat only one meal a day or confine their diet to fruit and milk.

SOURCES:
RelHolCal-2004, p. 183

♦ 1672 ♦ Mauritania Independence Day
November 28

This national holiday commemorates Mauritania's independence from France on November 28, 1960, after more than 50 years under French rule.

CONTACTS:
Mauritania Embassy
2129 Leroy Pl. N.W.
Washington, D.C. 20008
202-232-5700; fax: 202-319-2623
www.mauritaniaembassy.us

SOURCES:
AnnivHol-2000, p. 197
NatlHolWrld-1968, p. 211

♦ 1673 ♦ Mauritius Independence Day
March 12

This national holiday commemorates the day in 1968 when Mauritius gained independence from Britain, after being under its rule since the early 19th century.

CONTACTS:
Mauritius Tourism Promotion Authority

Air Mauritius Centre, Fl. 11
5, President John Kennedy St.
Port-Louis, Mauritius
230-210-1545; fax: 230-212-5142
www.mauritius.net

SOURCES:
AnnivHol-2000, p. 43

♦ 1674 ♦ Maverick Sunday Concerts
Sundays from July to early September

Hervey White, a novelist, poet and architect, purchased a piece of farmland he named "Maverick" just outside of Woodstock, New York, around the turn of the century. Within a few years, White had built a "music chapel" there and organized a Sunday afternoon concert series designed to give professional orchestral musicians an opportunity to play chamber music during the off-season. The series was under way by 1916, making the Maverick Sunday Concerts the oldest continuous chamber music series in the United States.

The concerts, which take place on Sunday afternoons from July to early September, are held in an unusual rustic concert hall made of locally cut and milled oak, pine, and chestnut. There are 56 paned windows in the front gable, a huge porch along one side, and seating for an audience of 400. The programming runs the gamut from traditional music for quintets, quartets, trios, and duos to the very latest contemporary compositions. Many of the works performed there in the past were composed by Alexander Semmier, who directed the Maverick concerts from 1954 to 1969. There have also been world premieres by noted Hudson Valley composers and performances by the Tokyo String Quartet, the Dorian Woodwind Quintet, the Beaux Arts Quartet, the Manhattan String Quartet, and the Cremona Arts Trio.

CONTACTS:
Maverick Concerts
P.O. Box 9
Woodstock, NY 12498
845-679-8217
www.maverickconcerts.org

SOURCES:
MusFestAmer-1990, p. 103

♦ 1675 ♦ Mawlid al-Nabi (Maulid al-Nabi; Prophet's Birthday)
12th day of the Islamic month of Rabial-Awwal

Mawlid al-Nabi celebrates the birth of Muhammad, the founder of Islam. Born in Mecca around 570, he was a shepherd and a trader who began to receive revelations from God when he was 40 years old. Over the next 23 years he not only established a religion but brought an unprecedented political unity to Arab tribes. Muhammad's birth began to be observed as a public holiday about the 12th century, except by conservative sects such as the Wahhabis who do not celebrate any human. They believe that to do so would detract from the worship of God. It is celebrated with the recitation of litanies in mosques, and with firecrackers and gift-giving throughout the Middle East and countries with prominent Muslim populations. In Burkina Faso and parts of Ghana the holiday is called DAMBA and in Indonesia, SEKATEN. The Prophet's birthday is a legal holiday in more than 30 countries around the world.

SOURCES:
AnnivHol-2000, p. 234
BkFest-1937, p. 237
BkFestHolWrld-1970, p. 79
BkHolWrld-1986, Dec 3
ConEncyIslam-1991, p. 263
DictWrldRel-1989, pp. 365, 348, 468, 498
FolkWrldHol-1999, p. 561
HolSymbols-2009, p. 561
OxYear-1999, p. 732
RelHolCal-2004, p. 145
UndIslam-2004, p. 275

♦ 1676 ♦ May Day
May 1

Many of the customs associated with the first day of May may come from the old Roman FLORALIA, or festival of flowers. These include the gathering of branches and flowers on MAY DAY EVE or early May Day morning, the choosing and crowning of a May Queen, and dancing around a bush, tree, or decorated pole, the maypole. The sports and festivities that are held on this day symbolize the rebirth of nature as well as human fertility. In fact, the ritual drinking and dancing around the maypole in colonial America so horrified the Pilgrim Fathers that they outlawed the practice and punished the offenders. This is probably why May Day has remained a relatively quiet affair in this country.

In Communist countries, May Day has been transformed into a holiday for workers, marked by parades that are an occasion for displaying military strength. The May Day Parade in Red Square, Moscow, has long been a spectacular example, though less so in recent years with the dissolution of the Soviet Union and the resulting relaxation of Cold War tensions. Perhaps in reaction to such displays, Americans instituted LOYALTY DAY and LAW DAY on this same date. In Great Britain, May 1 is LABOR DAY. More than 50 other countries also celebrate Labor Day in honor of workers on May 1.

See also VAPPU

SOURCES:
AmerBkDays-2000, p. 334
BkDays-1864, vol. I, p. 570
BkFest-1937, pp. 17, 58, 88, 113, 122, 186, 261, 278, 310
DaysCustFaith-1957, p. 115
DictFolkMyth-1984, pp. 129, 202, 203, 534, 695, 750, 866, 946, 1064
EncyEaster-2002, p. 397
FestSaintDays-1915, pp. 102, 105, 109
FestWestEur-1958, p. 37
FolkAmerHol-1999, p. 205
FolkWrldHol-1999, p. 315
OxYear-1999, p. 184

♦ 1677 ♦ May Day (Czech Republic) (Prvého Máje)
May 1

The traditional maypole associated with MAY DAY in western Europe, the United States, and elsewhere plays a central role in the celebration of May 1 in the former Czechoslovakia (now the countries of the Czech Republic and Slovak Republic). On May Day Eve, boys traditionally plant maypoles underneath their girlfriends' windows, so that the girls will wake up and see them first thing in the morning. In some villages, it is customary to raise a maypole beneath the window of the most popular girl in town. The maypole is said to represent the girl's life; the taller it is, the longer she will live. Sometimes it is a small tree, decorated with ribbons and colored eggshells.

Bands give concerts in village squares on May Day, and musicians go from house to house, singing. As a traditional spring festival, May Day has been a time for Czechs and Slovaks to sing, dance, and take pleasure in the beauty of the season.

See also MAY DAY EVE IN THE CZECH REPUBLIC

SOURCES:
BkFest-1937, p. 88

♦ 1678 ♦ May Day (France)
May 1

In France the celebration of MAY DAY is inextricably linked to flowers. It is considered good luck to wear lilies-of-the-valley on this day, and it is believed that any wishes made while wearing the flowers are bound to come true. Sometimes sprays of pressed lilies are sent to distant friends and loved ones. In southern France the flower vendors sell lilies-of-the-valley on every street corner.

The **First of May** has political overtones in France as well, and it is a public holiday officially observed as LABOR DAY. Political demonstrations, speeches, and parades are common on this day—similar to May Day celebrations in England, Russia, and other countries.

CONTACTS:
French Government Tourist Office
444 Madison Ave., Fl. 20
New York, NY 10022
800-391-4909 or 212-838-7800; fax: 212-838-7855
www.franceguide.com

SOURCES:
BkDays-1864, vol. I, p. 579
BkFest-1937, p. 122
BkFestHolWrld-1970, p. 85
DictFolkMyth-1984, p. 696
FestWestEur-1958, p. 37
FolkWrldHol-1999, p. 315

♦ 1679 ♦ May Day (Scandinavia)
May 1

In Scandinavia, the celebration of MAY DAY actually begins on April 30, WALPURGIS NIGHT. But the big event of the day is a mock battle between summer and winter, usually represented by two husky young men. Summer always wins, and winter is buried in effigy.

In the Swedish university town of Uppsala, students wearing white caps gather together to hear songs and speeches. Huge bonfires, also associated with Walpurgis Night, are popular in many areas of Sweden. Political speeches, parades of labor organizations, and public demonstrations take place on May 1 as well.

There is a superstition in Norway, dating back to pre-Christian times, about hearing the cuckoo's first call in spring: If the call comes from the south, the year will be good; if it is heard from the north, one will become ill or die in the coming year; if it comes from the west, one will be successful; and if it comes from the east, one will be lucky in love. For this reason, traditional Norwegian calendars show a bird perched in a tree on the mark for May 1.

SOURCES:
BkFest-1937, p. 310
DaysCustFaith-1957, p. 116
FolkWrldHol-1999, pp. 317, 318

♦ 1680 ♦ **May Day (Spain)**
May 1

Many Spanish MAY DAY customs are believed to have pagan origins (*see* FLORALIA). At the end of April, young people (in some villages, only bachelors) choose a tall pine tree to use as a maypole and set it up in the plaza. They decorate it with ribbons, beads, and eggshells, and as they dance around it they sing May songs. The ceremonies around the tree continue for several days, and on the last day of the month the tree is sold to raise money for refreshments or a dinner.

La Maya refers to both the girls who take part in the May Day celebrations and to the May Queen. It is traditional for a group of boys and girls to choose a queen, sit her on a couch or chair, and dance around her on May Day. They sing love songs, or *coplas,* in which they ask for food and money from everyone who passes by, and then use the contributions for a feast or banquet.

In some areas, the May Queen has been replaced by a *Cruz de Mayo,* or May cross. An altar is set up with candles, a white cloth, and a cross decorated with flowers and ribbons. There is dancing around the altar and requests for food and money. Sometimes young girls carry the wooden May crosses through the streets, asking for contributions. It is possible that this custom resulted from the confusion of May Day with the Feast of the Holy Cross, formerly observed by the Roman Catholic Church on May 3 (*see* EXALTATION OF THE CROSS), and still observed by Catholics in Latin America (*see* DÍA DE LA SANTA CRUZ)

CONTACTS:
Tourist Office of Spain
666 Fifth Ave., Fl. 35
New York, NY 10103
212-265-8822; fax: 212-265-8864
www.okspain.org

SOURCES:
DictFolkMyth-1984, p. 1064
FolkWrldHol-1999, p. 318

♦ 1681 ♦ **May Day Eve (Czech Republic)**
April 30

According to an old Czech superstition, witches try to enter people's homes on the eve of MAY DAY and do them harm. At one time it was customary to sprinkle sand or grass on the doorstep, in the belief that the witches had to count the grains or blades before entering the house. Now the "Burning of the Witches" ceremony is observed in some parts of the country by building bonfires on the mountain tops. Brooms that have been dipped in pitch are plunged into the fire and then held aloft like torches.

In Postupice, a town in the Bohemian region, a Maypole and Burning of the Witches Festival is held April 30-May 1 every year. The young men put up a maypole, decorated with ribbons and colored wreaths, in the village square on the afternoon of April 30. The next day, both men and women dress up in peasant costumes, weaving the ribbons in and out as they dance around the maypole and celebrate the coming of spring. The burning of the witches takes place afterward, when the villagers throw their broomsticks into the bonfire and burn the witches in effigy. People gather around the bonfire to drink brandy or beer and roast sausages as they watch the witches burn.

SOURCES:
BkFest-1937, p. 88
GdWrldFest-1985, p. 68

♦ 1682 ♦ **May Day Eve (Ireland)**
April 30

According to Irish legend, the fairy people fight among themselves on the eve of MAY DAY. Every seven years, the combat is especially intense, for they compete with one another for the crops, taking the best ears of wheat, barley, and oats as their prize. By mixing the barley with dew gathered from a mountain top at midnight, they make a strong liquor. One drink is believed to set them dancing for 24 hours without pausing to rest.

The custom of celebrating May Day Eve with bonfires or with a May bush decorated with candles can be traced back to the pagan feast of BELTANE, which marked the summer's beginning. In Ireland, a horse's skull was often burned in the bonfire. On November Eve (October 31) in County Cork, a procession led by a man called "The White Mare," who was dressed in a white robe and carried a symbolic horse's head, went from house to house soliciting contributions of money and food. Because fairies and the spirits of the dead were believed to roam around on this night, food was left out to ward off their mischief.

SOURCES:
AmerBkDays-2000, p. 335
DictFolkMyth-1984, p. 202
EncyEaster-2002, p. 403
FolkWrldHol-1999, p. 303
OxYear-1999, p. 179

♦ 1683 ♦ **May Day Eve (Italy)**
April 30

In Modena, Italy, if tradition is followed, the boys of the town sing May songs under the village windows on the eve of MAY DAY. A talented musician is often asked to sing to the sweethearts of the others, and the boys compete with one another to see who can compose the most persuasive lyrics. On the Sunday following, it is customary for the boys to appear with empty baskets at the houses they have serenaded. The families fill the baskets with things to eat.

May Day itself, or *Calendimaggio*, bears little resemblance to the original pagan spring festival once celebrated in ancient Rome. Modern-day Italians attend horse races, fireworks exhibitions, and various types of competitions and lotteries which are held throughout the country on May 1.

SOURCES:
BkFest-1937, p. 186

♦ 1684 ♦ **May Day Eve (Switzerland)**
(Maitag Vorabend)
April 30

Certain villages in the Seeland and Burgdorf regions of the canton of Bern in Switzerland still observe the ancient custom of planting the *Maitannli*, or May pine tree. Boys from the village steal into the forest after dark on May Day Eve, April 30, and cut down small pine trees, which they deck with flowers and ribbons and plant under their sweethearts' bedroom windows, at the front gate, or occasionally on the roof. The young man who plants the symbolic tree is usually welcomed and entertained by the girl and her family. Girls who have a reputation for being arrogant or unpopular sometimes find a grotesque straw puppet in place of the traditional Maitannli.

SOURCES:
AmerBkDays-2000, p. 335
BkFest-1937, p. 318

♦ 1685 ♦ **May Festival, International**
May

Germany's second oldest music festival (after the BAYREUTH FESTIVAL) is the **Wiesbaden May Festival**, founded in 1896. Kaiser Wilhelm II came to Wiesbaden, which is about 26 miles west of Frankfurt, to officiate at the grand opening.

The month-long festival offers eight or nine full-length operas performed in the original language, symphonic concerts, ballet, drama, experimental theater, and mime. Most of the festival events are held in the rococo-style Hessian State Theater, the Kleines Haus (a small auditorium for plays), and the Kurhaus (for symphonic concerts). Among the world-renowned groups that have been invited to perform at the festival are the Netherlands Dance Theatre, Japan's Red Buddha Theatre, the Salzburg Marionettes, the Hamburg State Opera, the Berlin State Opera, the Zurich Opera, the Welsh Philharmonic Orchestra Cardiff, and the Greek National Ballet.

CONTACTS:
Internationale Maifestspiele in Wiesbaden
Hessisches Staatstheater Wiesbaden
Christian-Zair-St. 3

Wiesbaden, Hesse 65189 Germany
49-611-132-32-5
www.staatstheater-wiesbaden.de

SOURCES:
GdWrldFest-1985, p. 87
IntlThFolk-1979, p. 151
MusFestEurBrit-1980, p. 106

♦ 1686 ♦ **Mayberry Days**
Last full weekend in September

This annual event celebrates "The Andy Griffith Show," a weekly television comedy show about the adventures of a small-town sheriff in a fictional town called Mayberry that was produced from 1960 to 1968 and remains on the air in syndication. The festival was first held in 1990 in actor Andy Griffith's home town of Mount Airy, North Carolina, to celebrate the show's 30th anniversary. Since that time it has grown into a three-day event that attracts fans of the show from all over the United States and Canada.

Highlights of the festival include concerts by the Doug Dillard Band (Doug Dillard appeared on the show as one of the Darling boys, a mountain family that visited Mayberry), a "Sheriff's Choice" golf tournament, and Colonel Tim's Talent Time, which is modeled after the talent show that takes place in one of the program's episodes. There is also a parade, a Mayberry trivia contest, a pie-eating contest, a barbecue cook-off, and a silent auction. Actors associated with the show are often special guests at the festival, and watching reruns of old shows is a favorite activity.

CONTACTS:
Surry Arts Council
218 Rockford St.
Mt. Airy, NC 27030
800-286-6193 or 336-786-7998; fax: 336-786-9822
www.surryarts.org

♦ 1687 ♦ **Mayfest, International**
May

International Mayfest is a five-day celebration of the arts—performing, visual, and literary—held in Tulsa, Okla. One of the largest festivals in the state, the event features a juried art fair and theatrical presentations. In the past, these varied works have been staged: *Three Penny Opera*, *Our Town*, and *Revenge of the Space Pandas*. There is also a variety of musical entertainment and ethnic foods from all corners of the globe.

CONTACTS:
Tulsa Convention and Visitors Bureau
321 S. Boston Ave., Ste. 101
Tulsa, OK 74103
918-582-6435
www.tulsamayfest.org

♦ 1688 ♦ **Mayoring Day**
May

In England, this is the day on which the new mayor of a town or borough parades through the streets. If it takes place on a Sunday, it is often called **Mayor's Sunday** and is celebrated with a church service. In Rye, Sussex, the old tradition of the "hot-penny scramble" is carried out on this day. The new mayor throws hot pennies to the children, who then scramble to pick them up. This custom probably dates back to the time when Rye minted its own coins, and they were distributed while still hot from the molds.

CONTACTS:
Rye Tourist Information Centre
Rye Heritage Ct.
Strand Quay
Rye, East Sussex TN31 7AY United Kingdom
44-17-9722-6696; fax: 44-17-9722-3460
www.visitrye.co.uk

SOURCES:
DictDays-1988, p. 75

♦ 1689 ♦ Maytime Festival, International
Last weekend in May

A festival center since the 12th century, the city of Dundalk in County Louth, Ireland, is the home of the International Maytime Festival and also of the International Amateur Theatre Association. It is the festival's aim to improve amateur theater standards and to bring together outstanding amateur theater groups from all over the world. Over 200 events are presented each year in the Dundalk Town Hall auditorium. There are also a number of "fringe" events, such as a children's afternoon theater and a lunchtime theater, that are presented in other locations.

Amateur theater groups wishing to participate in the International Maytime Festival are judged on the basis of their work by the International Amateur Theatre Association's center in their own country. Theater groups from throughout the British Isles, the United States, and eastern Europe have appeared at the festival in recent years.

CONTACTS:
Dundalk Chamber of Commerce
20 Upper Williamsons Mall
Francis St.
Dundalk, Ireland
353-42-9336343; fax: 353-42-9332085
www.dundalkprofile.ie

Irish Centre of International Amateur Theatre Association
46 Thomas St.
P.O. Box 3094
Dublin, 8 Ireland
353-1-4530369; fax: 353-1-4530369
homepage.eircom.net/~iatairl

SOURCES:
IntlThFolk-1979, p. 233

♦ 1690 ♦ McClure Bean Soup Festival
Second Tuesday through Saturday in September

When a group of Civil War veterans met on the second floor of the Joseph Peters Blacksmith Shop in Bannerville, Pennsyl-vania, in 1883 to organize a Grand Army of the Republic Post, they probably had no idea that their actions might some day lead to a bean soup festival. But when they served a special bean soup at their first meeting, it was such a hit that they eventually invited the public to a "real Civil War bean soup dinner" in 1891. Today, thousands of gallons of bean soup are prepared in 35-gallon kettles, 16 of which can be heated simultaneously over a special battery of wood-fire furnaces set up for the occasion. The cooks, all of whom wear Civil War uniforms, take turns stirring the soup with wooden ladles for 180-minute shifts.

As the Civil War veterans died out, their sons took over the festival, which is now held at the Henry K. Ritter Camp #65 Sons of the Union War Veterans. It takes place for two full days and five nights, usually a Tuesday through Saturday in September, and includes political speeches, exhibits, parades, nightly entertainment, and amusement rides. The recipe for the soup is based on the original Civil War recipe, and it is served to over 70,000 people.

CONTACTS:
McClure Bean Soup Festival
P.O. Box 8
McClure, PA 17841
800-338-7389
www.mcclurebeansoup.com

SOURCES:
GdUSFest-1984, p. 159

♦ 1691 ♦ Mecklenburg Independence Day
May 20

The citizens of Mecklenburg County, North Carolina, would like to think that their ancestors were the first to call for independence from the British when they adopted the Mecklenburg Declaration of Independence on May 20, 1775. But historians now believe that the resolutions calling for independence that had been sent to the Second Continental Congress in Philadelphia were never actually presented there.

Even though the Mecklenburg patriots may not have been the first to declare their independence from British rule, their actions represent an important step on the road to the American Revolution.

CONTACTS:
Mecklenburg Historical Association
P.O. Box 35032
Charlotte, NC 28235
www.meckdec.org

Library of Congress
101 Independence Ave. S.E.
Washington, DC 20540
202-707-5000; fax: 202-707-8366
www.loc.gov

SOURCES:
AmerBkDays-2000, p. 378
AnnivHol-2000, p. 84
DictDays-1988, p. 75

◆ 1692 ◆ Medora Musical
June-September, Labor Day

Theodore ("Teddy") Roosevelt, the 26th president of the United States, spent two years ranching in the Dakota Territory as a young man. When the Spanish-American War was declared in 1898, Roosevelt resigned his position as assistant secretary of the Navy under President William McKinley and organized the First Volunteer Cavalry, nicknamed the "Rough Riders," and took them to Cuba. His colorful exploits, particularly in the Battle of Santiago, made him a national hero.

Every night from mid-June through LABOR DAY in Medora, North Dakota, there is a musical extravaganza known as the Medora Musical—a patriotic song-and-dance salute to Teddy Roosevelt and his Rough Riders. The musical is performed in a natural amphitheater featuring an outdoor escalator to get people to their seats. The colorful buttes and ravines of the Badlands form a dramatic backdrop for the Broadway-class variety show.

CONTACTS:
Theodore Roosevelt Medora Foundation
P.O. Box 198
Medora, ND 58645
800-633-6721 or 701-623-4444; fax: 701-623-4494
www.medora.com

◆ 1693 ◆ Meenakshi Kalyanam (Chitrai Festival)
*Between March and May; during Hindu months
of Caitra or Vaisakha*

The marriage of the goddess Meenakshi, an incarnation of Parvati, and Lord Sundereswarar (also known as Lord Shiva), is celebrated in Madurai, Tamil Nadu, India. The rituals are observed at the Meenakshi Temple, one of the biggest temple complexes in India, most of it built between the 12th and 18th centuries. There is a huge procession, with chariots carrying the temple images, dressed in special robes and jewels, through the streets. The people, in celebrating the marriage of the deities, also commemorate their own marriages. This festival is also celebrated in Malaysia, where it is known as PANGUNI UTTIRAM.

CONTACTS:
Tamil Nadu Tourism
Tourism Complex, No. 2 Wallajah Rd.
Chennai, Tamil Nadu 600 002 India
91-44-25383333; fax: 91-44-25381567
www.tamilnadutourism.org

SOURCES:
BkHolWrld-1986, May 10
DictWrldRel-1989, pp. 482, 570
RelHolCal-2004, p. 185

◆ 1694 ◆ Megalesia
April 4

The cult of the Phrygian goddess Cybele (also known as Kybele, the Great Mother or Magna Mater; *see also* BONA DEA

and OPALIA) was established in Rome on this day in 204 B.C.E., when her image was installed in the temple of Victory on the Palatine Hill. Eventually her own temple was built on the same hill, but April 4 continued to be set aside as a commemoration of the foreign goddess' arrival in Rome.

Her festival was given a Greek name, the Megalesia, and in the beginning, no Roman citizens were allowed to take part in it. But over time it spread to the streets of Rome, where Cybele's image was carried in a chariot drawn by lions with her castrated priests leaping and gashing themselves in a frenzy of devotion. The procession went from the Palatine to the Circus, where games known as LUDI and plays known as *ludi megalenses* were held. The task of keeping the festival under Phrygian control—and within the bounds of propriety—eventually proved to be difficult, and the Megalesia became little more than a holiday celebrated in honor of the Magna Mater.

SOURCES:
AmerBkDays-2000, p. 246
DictRomRel-1996, p. 150
EncyRel-1987, vol. 4, p. 186
FestRom-1981, p. 97
NewCentClassHandbk-1962, p. 689
OxYear-1999, pp. 147, 152
SeasFeast-1961, p. 185

◆ 1695 ◆ Meiji Setsu
November 3

This day was formerly observed as the birthday of the Emperor Meiji (1852-1912), who ruled Japan from 1868 until his death. Meiji Tenno abolished feudalism, raised the people's standard of living, and secured Japan's reputation as a great world power. It was during his reign that Japan made rapid progress toward becoming a modern nation by using Western institutions, technology, and learning as its model. It was during this period that a constitution was adopted, a parliament was convened, civil and criminal laws were codified, and an educational system was established. Railways were built, and electric lights and telephones were put into use.

Today, November 3 is still a national holiday, but it is known as BUNKA-NO-HI, or Culture Day.

CONTACTS:
Japan National Tourist Organization
1 Rockefeller Pl., Ste. 1250
New York, NY 10020
212-757-5640; fax: 212-307-6754
www.jnto.go.jp

SOURCES:
BkFest-1937, p. 200
JapanFest-1965, pp. 204, 217

◆ 1696 ◆ Meistertrunk Pageant (Master Draught Pageant)
Between May 8 and June 11; Pentecost

This celebration in the medieval town of Rothenburg-on-the-Tauber, Germany, commemorates a gargantuan drinking feat in 1631. The pageant is staged for four days ending on WHIT-MONDAY, and the play itself, *Meistertrunk,* is also performed on various occasions during the summer. The best known of the Bavarian history plays, *Meistertrunk* dramatizes a chronicled event of the Thirty Years' War: the town was threatened with destruction by Imperial troops led by the famed general, Johann Tserclaes Tilly. The general saw the state wine beaker and decided to play a game with the town's life at stake. If a council member could drink off the entire beaker of wine—about a gallon—in one draught, Tilly promised to spare the town. Burgomaster George Nusch accepted the challenge and emptied the beaker in one mighty gulp and the town was saved.

The play is performed out of doors with the entire town a stage. Tilly's troops are camped outside the city walls, and in the market square costumed children plead with the general. The same beaker that Nusch drained in 1631 is used in the reenactment.

A parade precedes the play, and the "Shepherds' Dance" is performed after it in the market square. The dance, dating to 1516, is in honor of St. Wolfgang, the patron saint of shepherds, and recalls the time a member of the shepherds' guild raced from his pastures to warn the city of the approach of an enemy.

CONTACTS:
Meistertrunk Managing Committee
Jagerstrasse 4
Rothenburg ob der Tauber, 91541 Germany
49-9861-529-2; fax: 49-9861-876-65
www.meistertrunk.de

Shepherd's Dance Exhibition at Rothenburg
011-49-160-7615249
www.schaefertanzrothenburg.de

SOURCES:
FestWestEur-1958, p. 66
GdWrldFest-1985, p. 87

♦ 1697 ♦ **Meitlisonntag**
Second Sunday in January

In the Seetal district of Aargau, Switzerland, the girls of Meisterschwanden and Fahrwangen hold a procession on the second Sunday in January known as Meitlisonntag, "Girls' Sunday." They dress in historical uniforms and stage a military parade before an all-female General Staff. The custom dates from the Villmergen War of 1712, a conflict in which the women of Meisterschwanden and Fahrwangen played a vital role in achieving victory. The military procession is followed by a popular festival.

CONTACTS:
Switzerland Tourism
Swiss Ctr., 608 Fifth Ave.
New York, NY 10020
877-794-8037 or 212-757-5944; fax: 212-262-6116
www.myswitzerland.com

SOURCES:
AnnivHol-2000, p. 18

♦ 1698 ♦ **Melbourne Cup Day**
First Tuesday in November

The only public holiday in the world dedicated to a horse race, Melbourne Cup Day has been observed in Melbourne, Victoria, Australia, since the first Cup race was held there in 1867. The event actually features seven races, including the grueling handicap race of just under two miles, which is run by some 20 thoroughbreds for a purse worth $4 million. The story of Phar Lap, the legendary New Zealand thoroughbred who won the Cup in 1930 after nearly being shot by unscrupulous gamblers, was made into a movie—*Far Lap* (1984), directed by Simon Wincer—that made the Cup an event familiar to people all over the world.

Cup Day is not only a legal holiday in the state of Victoria, but is observed throughout the world in offices where Australians work. For those who attend, it is a particularly glamorous event. The champagne flows, huge sums of money are wagered, and the women wear lavish hats while the men turn out in grey top hats and dark morning suits. There are similar races held in other Australian states (*see* HOBART CUP DAY), but the Melbourne Cup is still the number one classic of the Australian horseracing circuit.

A six-week festival, known as the **Spring Racing Carnival**, leads up to the big day and lasts well into November.

CONTACTS:
Victoria Racing Club
400 Epson Rd.
Flemington, VIC 3031 Australia
61-3-0072-7575
www.vrc.net.au

Australian Cultural Network
Department of Communications, Information Technology, and the
  Arts, Australian Government
P.O. Box 2154
Canberra City, ACT 2601 Australia
61-2-6271-1000; fax: 61-2-6271-1901
www.acn.net.au

SOURCES:
AnnivHol-2000, p. 198
DictDays-1988, p. 75

♦ 1699 ♦ **Melbourne International Comedy
Festival**
Late March to mid-April

The Melbourne International Comedy Festival is Australia's largest annual cultural event, featuring as many as 230 different shows and drawing as many as 400,000 attendees. The festival was founded in 1987 by two comedians, Barry Humphries and Peter Cook.

For three and a half weeks, Melbourne becomes a comedy metropolis, with many activities taking place at the city's Town Hall. The main event in festivals past has been the Opening Night Gala, which features an all-star lineup.

Along with enjoying standup comedy, festival attendees also check out theatre events, street performance, and short films.

Comedians who stand out from the rest of the pack receive official awards at the end of the festival.

Every year festival planners maintain a strong focus on fostering new comedic talents. In the months preceding the big event, competitions are held throughout Australia to determine who will perform at the main stage in Melbourne. Comedians of nearly all ages are welcomed: there is a Class Clown contest for youths between ages 9 and 17 in addition to the Raw Comedy open-mic competition for adult artists.

CONTACTS:
Melbourne International Comedy Festival
P.O. Box 341
Fitzroy
Victoria 3065 Australia
www.comedyfestival.com.au

♦ 1700 ♦ **Memorial Day**
Last Monday in May

Memorial Day is a legal holiday, formerly known as **Decoration Day**, proclaimed annually by the president to honor U.S. citizens who have died in war. Since 1950, by congressional request, the day is also set aside to pray for permanent peace.

Both religious services and patriotic parades mark the day's celebrations. In the national official observance, a wreath is placed on the Tomb of the Unknown Soldier in Arlington National Cemetery in Virginia. One of the more moving observances is at the Gettysburg National Cemetery in Pennsylvania, where schoolchildren scatter flowers over the graves of unknown soldiers of the Civil War.

The association of poppies with fallen soldiers was popularized by the poet John McCrae, who wrote the lines "In Flanders fields the poppies blow/Between the crosses, row on row." Flanders was the site of heavy fighting during World War I, and for many who wrote about it later, the poppy came to symbolize both the beauty of the landscape and the blood that was shed there. Poppies are sold by veterans' organizations around the holiday.

The practice of decorating graves of war dead began before the close of the Civil War. However, an officially set day was established in 1868 when Gen. John A. Logan, commander-in-chief of the Grand Army of the Republic, issued an order naming May 30 as a day for "strewing with flowers or otherwise decorating the graves of comrades who died in defense of their country during the late rebellion." The day became known as Decoration Day, but as it was extended to include the dead of all wars, it took the name Memorial Day.

CONTACTS:
Gettysburg National Military Park
1195 Baltimore Pike, Ste. 100
Gettysburg, PA 17325
717-334-1124; fax: 717-334-1891
www.nps.gov

Arlington National Cemetery
214 McNair Rd.
Arlington, VA 22211
703-607-8000; fax: 703-607-8583
www.arlingtoncemetery.org

Library of Congress
101 Independence Ave. S.E.
Washington, DC 20540
202-707-5000; fax: 202-707-8366
www.loc.gov

SOURCES:
AmerBkDays-2000, p. 403
AnnivHol-2000, p. 91
BkHolWrld-1986, May 30
DaysCustFaith-1957, p. 132
DictDays-1988, p. 30
FolkAmerHol-1999, p. 234
HolSymbols-2009, p. 571
OxYear-1999, p. 228
PatHols-2006, p. 207

♦ 1701 ♦ **Memorial Day Luminaria at Fredericksburg National Cemetery**
Saturday in late May

Memorial Day Luminaria at Fredericksburg National Cemetery was created to honor those "who have given their lives for their country." Each year on the Saturday closest to Memorial Day, hundreds of volunteers from the Commonwealth Girl Scout Council and the Boy Scouts of America set, light, and maintain candles on the graves of more than 15,300 U.S. soldiers who are buried in Fredericksburg National Cemetery. Graves receiving luminaria include thousands of those who died during the Civil War in addition to several hundred burials from other periods in American history.

The vigil, which was first held in 1996, runs from 8:00 PM to 11:00 PM, and includes walking tours of the Marye's Heights gravesite and "Taps" performed each half hour. The cemetery remains open until all the luminarias have gone out. Between 3,000 and 6,000 visitors take part in this event each year.

CONTACTS:
Fredericksburg and Spotsylvania National Military Park
120 Chatham Lane
Fredericksburg, VA 22405
540-654-5532; fax: 540-371-1907
www.nps.gov/frsp/index.htm

SOURCES:
PatHols-2006, p. 215

♦ 1702 ♦ **Memphis in May International Festival**
May

This month-long festival in Memphis, Tenn., focuses on a different nation's culture each year, with exhibitions, lectures, films, performing arts presentations, sporting events, and student exchange programs.

Beginning on the first weekend in May, the festival opens with the Beale Street Music Festival—Beale Street being "the birthplace of the blues." The second festival weekend features a salute to the year's honored country with special exhibits and events showcasing the music, food, art, and dance of the country. The third weekend is an international barbecue competition, dubbed the "Superbowl of Swine," and the fourth weekend is the Great Southern Food Festival, including music and storytelling.

Festival events take place at Memphis's riverfront park, museums, botanical gardens, galleries, hospitals, theaters, shopping malls, and universities. The festival ends with the Sunset Symphony playing a concert of music from the featured country and then for the finale, Tchaikovsky's *1812 Overture*, complete with live cannons and an impressive display of fireworks.

CONTACTS:
Memphis in May International Festival
88 Union Ave., Ste. 301
Memphis, TN 38103
901-525-4611; fax: 901-525-4686
www.memphisinmay.org

SOURCES:
GdUSFest-1984, p. 176

♦ 1703 ♦ **Menuhin Festival**
Mid-July through early September

The fashionable resort town of Gstaad, Switzerland, is the setting for an annual summer music festival founded in 1956 by the world-renowned violinist Yehudi Menuhin (b. 1916). Menuhin's name and status have attracted internationally known soloists, orchestras, and chamber music groups to the festival—among them the Zurich Chamber Orchestra, the Chamber Music Ensemble of the Academy of St. Martin-in-the-Fields, and the Zurich Collegium Musicum. Students from the Menuhin School in London and the International Menuhin Music Academy in Gstaad are also invited to perform at least one concert each season. Menuhin's sister, Hepzibah, and son, Jeremy, have performed as soloists at the festival.

Although the emphasis is usually on chamber music and solo recitals, large orchestral pieces are occasionally performed as well. Chamber music concerts are given in the cone-roofed chapel at Saanen.

CONTACTS:
Menuhin Festival Gstaad
Postfach 65
Gstaad, 3780 Switzerland
41-33-748-8338; fax: 41-33-748-8339
www.menuhinfestivalgstaad.ch

SOURCES:
MusFestEurBrit-1980, p. 143

♦ 1704 ♦ **Mercè, Festa de la**
September

Nearly 400 events celebrate the patron saint of Barcelona, La Madonna de la Mercè, each year for a few days including September 24. In years past, the Madonna's feast was observed with religious processions, but these days the processions are augmented by the city's liveliest party of the year with fireworks, street art, live music and dancing, acrobats forming human towers, and sporting events.

CONTACTS:
Barcelona City Council
Placa Sant Jaume 2
Barcelona, 08002 Spain
34-934-027-000
www.bcn.cat/english/ihome.htm

♦ 1705 ♦ **Merchants' Flower Market**
Between May 10 and June 13; the seventh Sunday after Easter

Whitsunday, or PENTECOST, in the Dutch city of Haarlem is the day on which the famous flower market opens in the *Grote Markt* (Great Market). Flower merchants arrive in the afternoon or early evening to set up displays of their flowers on tables and carts. When all the flowers have been arranged, the lights are turned off. As midnight approaches, the market square fills with people. As the bells begin to ring in the steeple of St. Bavo's Church, floodlights go on and thousands of tulips, daffodils, irises, and geraniums appear as if by magic. The festival continues all night until eight o'clock in the morning, with dancing to the sound of barrel organs. People buy herring, pastries, and ice cream from food vendors as well as flowers to place in their windows or on their dining-room tables in celebration of Whitsuntide.

See also LUILAK

CONTACTS:
Netherlands Board of Tourism & Conventions
355 Lexington Ave., 19th Fl.
New York, NY 10017
888-464-6552 or 212-370-7360; fax: 212-370-9507
us.holland.com

SOURCES:
BkFestHolWrld-1970, p. 65
FestWestEur-1958, p. 135

♦ 1706 ♦ **Merdeka Day**
August 31

Merdeka Day is a national holiday in Malaysia to commemorate its *merdeka*, or independence, from the British in 1957. Parts of Malaysia were under the rule of various foreign powers for centuries, but by the 1920s all the states eventually comprising Malaysia were ruled by Britain. The Federation of Malaya was founded in 1957 and Malaysia was formed in 1963.

The streets of towns and cities are decorated on this day, and there are numerous parades, exhibitions, and stage shows.

CONTACTS:
Malaysian Tourism Promotion Board
818 W. 7th St., Ste. 970
Los Angeles, CA 90017
800-336-6842 or 213-689-9702; fax: 213-689-1530
www.tourismmalaysiausa.com

SOURCES:
AnnivHol-2000, p. 144
GdWrldFest-1985, p. 131
IntlThFolk-1979, p. 267

◆ 1707 ◆ **Merengue Festival (Festival de Merengue)**
Last week in July-first week in August

The merengue is a lively Caribbean dance that originated in Haiti and the Dominican Republic. Its main characteristic is a limping side-step, and it corresponds to the rumba of Cuba or the samba of Brazil.

The world's most famous merengue festival takes place in Santa Domingo, the Dominican Republic's capital city, where outdoor stages are set up along the city's waterfront, and top bands play merengue music while couples swirl and shake to the fast-paced, pulsating rhythms.

In addition to watching the performances and competitions among merengue dancers, festivalgoers can enjoy the music of DJs and bands on the street, imbibe rum and beer, and eat the signature pork sandwiches, *chimichurris*.

CONTACTS:
Dominican Republic Tourism Office
136 E. 57th St., Ste. 803
New York, NY 10022
888-374-6361 or 212-588-1012; fax: 212-588-1015
www.godominicanrepublic.com

SOURCES:
WildPlanet-1995, p. 510

◆ 1708 ◆ **Merrie Monarch Festival**
March-April; week after Easter

The Merrie Monarch Festival is a week of festivities in Hilo honoring Hawaii's King David Kalakaua (1836-1891), who reigned from 1874 to 1891, and gave the United States exclusive rights to maintain a naval station at PEARL HARBOR. The week's events, starting on EASTER, close with the world's largest hula competition on the last three nights. The top hula schools (*hula halau*) compete in ancient and modern hula.

CONTACTS:
Big Island Visitors Bureau
250 Keawe St.
Hilo, HI 96720
808-961-5797; fax: 808-961-2126
www.merriemonarchlive.com

◆ 1709 ◆ **Meskwaki Powwow**
Mid-August

The Meskwaki Powwow is held annually on the second weekend of August at the home of the Meskwaki Tribal Nation in Tama, Iowa. It is Iowa's only all-Indian powwow, held at the only Native American settlement in the state. Traditional dancing is at the heart of the event. Featured performers in colorful tribal regalia execute such ceremonial dances as the Victory Dance, which honors soldiers and veterans, and the Buffalo Dance, which reaches back to the tribe's days as active hunters. Among the other dozen or so showcased dances are the Friendship Dance, War Dance, and Pipe Dance. The event also offers arts and crafts and special exhibits. All are welcome to attend.

The annual Meskwaki Powwow has been held since 1913. It grew from the tribe's Green Corn Dance, which accompanied the harvesting of crops each year. From 1902 to 1912, the Meskwaki nation held "field days," a week-long festival of dancing, horse-racing, and games that did not accompany a harvest. In 1912, the Meskwaki chief asked a group of men to plan the following year's field days. In 1913, the event, now called a powwow, was held at the same location it occupies today. More social than spiritual, the present-day powwow still is a reaffirmation of hope, kinship, and friendship, according to tribe members.

CONTACTS:
Meskwaki Tribal Nation
Sac and Fox of the Mississippi in Iowa
349 Meskwaki Rd.
Tama, IA 52339
641-484-4678 or 800-944-9503; fax: 641-484-4321
www.meskwaki.com

◆ 1710 ◆ **Messiah Festival**
March-April; eight days during Easter week

The first Messiah Festival in Lindsborg, Kansas, was held in 1882 by a group of Swedish immigrants under the leadership of Dr. and Mrs. Carl Swensson. Using the voices of local townspeople, the Swenssons established what is now known as the Bethany Oratorio Society, a group of 400 singers that includes faculty and students from Bethany College and a 50-member symphony orchestra. Other groups that perform at the annual festival include the Bethany College Choir and the Bethany Community Symphony Orchestra.

The program consists primarily of choral works, oratorios, and solo recitals, often by guest soloists such as Barbara Hocher, D'Anna Fortunato, Ronald Corrado, and Susan von Reichenback. All concerts are held at the college's Presser Auditorium. Lindsborg's Messiah Festival is often referred to as the "Oberammergau of the Plains." (*See also* OBERAMMERGAU PASSION PLAY.)

CONTACTS:
Bethany College
421 N. First St.
Lindsborg, KS 67456
785-227-3311; fax: 785-227-2004
www.bethanylb.edu

SOURCES:
MusFestAmer-1990, p. 61

◆ 1711 ◆ **Mevlana, Festival of**
Mid-December

This nine-day festival is held in Konya, Turkey, the home of the religious sect known as the Mevlevi. Sometimes referred to as the "Order of the Whirling Dervishes" for the prominent role that ritual dance plays in their weekly observance of *sama* (congregational music), the sect was founded in the 13th century by Mevlana Celaleddin Rumi, one of Turkey's greatest poets and mystics. Their practices were banned in the early part of the 20th century, but in 1954 Konya was given permission to revive the ritual dances. For nine days each year in December, the dervishes dance to the accompaniment of chanting and the music of flute, zither, and drums. Their turning and whirling motions are supposed to represent communion with the Divine.

The Mevlana Festival also offers lectures on the Mevlevis and special exhibits of art that date back to the 11th century.

CONTACTS:
Turkish Embassy
2525 Massachusetts Ave. N.W.
Washington, D.C. 20008
202-612-6700; fax: 202-612-6744
www.turkishembassy.org

SOURCES:
DictWrldRel-1989, p. 632
FestWrld: Turkey-1999, p. 12
GdWrldFest-1985, p. 181
UndIslam-2004, p. 403

♦ 1712 ♦ Mexico Festival of Independence
September 15-16

The **Fiesta Patrias** celebrates the anniversary of Mexico's independence. Although the festival itself goes on for the greater part of a week, it comes to a dramatic climax at 11 o'clock on the night of September 15 in Mexico City as crowds of merrymakers wait for the president to appear on the balcony of the National Palace and proclaim the famous *Grito de Dolores* ("cry of Dolores")—the "call to freedom" that the priest Miguel Hidalgo y Costilla (1753-1811) of the town of Dolores used to rouse the peasant population to fight for their independence in 1810. The people respond by cheering *Viva México!* and shooting off pistols and fireworks.

The Festival of Independence is celebrated in smaller communities throughout Mexico in much the same way, with the local mayor reciting the *Grito de Dolores* at precisely 11 o'clock.

The following day is Independence Day, which is celebrated with fireworks, the ringing of cathedral bells, and a huge military parade. One of the big events on Independence Day is the drawing for the National Lottery. Tickets are inexpensive, and the winner becomes an instant millionaire. Almost everyone watches the drawing on television or listens to the radio to see who wins.

CONTACTS:
Mexico Tourism Board
21 E. 63rd St., Fl. 3
New York, NY 10021
800-446-3942 or 212-821-0314; fax: 212-821-0367
www.visitmexico.com

SOURCES:
AnnivHol-2000, p. 155
BkFest-1937, p. 229
GdWrldFest-1985, p. 135
NatlHolWrld-1968, p. 172

♦ 1713 ♦ Meyboom
August 9

One of the oldest folk traditions in Belgium, Meyboom is an amalgamation of Belgian folklore, patron-saint celebration, and traditional neighborhood rivalry. In 2008, the people of Belgium observed the 700th anniversary of the festival. As in centuries past, the event was marked with a procession of giant puppets and the planting of a *meyboom* (Dutch for "may tree").

The legend is told by a local fraternity known as the Brotherhood of Saint-Laurent's Companions. In 1213 a wedding party was attacked by marauders from the village of Leuven, located about 20 miles east of the capital city, Brussels. A group of archers came to the victims' rescue, and in reward, the duke gave them permission to plant a maypole on the eve of their patron saint's feastday, St. Laurent. The first celebration took place in 1208.

Today, in keeping with tradition established by the Brotherhood, a young tree is planted on the corner of Rue des Sables and Rue du Marais in Brussels. Before the official planting, a throng of merrymakers gathers for the tree's presentation at Place des Sablons. Then a procession of trumpeters and costumed giants accompanies the tree to its final destination. Time is of the essence, since according to custom, if the *meyboom* is not planted by 5:00 P.M. the city will be cursed and the good fortune destined for the locals will be transferred instead to the people of Leuven.

CONTACTS:
Companions of St. Laurence
Rue au Beurre 42
Brussels 1000 Belgium
www.meyboom.be

♦ 1714 ♦ Miami/Bahamas Goombay Festival
Early June

The Miami/Bahamas Goombay Festival is held over two days in early June each year in Coconut Grove, Fla. It was founded to commemorate the cultural and historical influence of South Florida's first black residents: the workers and craftsmen who arrived in Miami in the early 1800s to build the first hotel in Coconut Grove.

Launching in 1976, the free festival celebrates the music, art, culture, and heritage of the Bahamas and of multi-ethnic Miami with a parade, performances, ethnic food, and a variety of basketball and music activities. The event is named for the traditional music of the Bahamas, which blends African and colonial European influences. Goombay, which means "rhythm" in the Bantu language, is also the name for the goatskin drum that provides the beat for this type of Bahamian music. The festival, which was established as a non-profit organization by William R. Rolle and nine other activists, now draws about 300,000 participants to its colorful attractions.

CONTACTS:
Miami/Bahamas Goombay Festival in Coconut Grove, Inc.
P.O. Box 330052
Miami, FL 33133
800-891-7811; fax: 954-442-0427
www.goombayfestivalcoconutgrove.com/index.html

♦ 1715 ♦ Mi-Carême
Between March 8 and April 11; fourth Sunday in Lent

This break from the strictness of LENT has traditionally been observed in France, Belgium, and various islands of the French West Indies—including Guadeloupe, St. Barthélemy, and Martinique. In Paris, it is customarily celebrated with the **Fête des Blanchisseuses**, or laundresses, who choose a queen from each of the various metropolitan districts. The district queens and the queen of queens chosen by them ride through the streets on a float, followed by their costumed courtiers and ladies-in-waiting. Then there is a colorful ball for the washerwomen that night.

In Belgium, **Mid-Lent** or **Half-Vasten** is the day when someone dresses up as the Count of Mid-Lent and distributes gifts to children.

CONTACTS:
French Government Tourist Office
444 Madison Ave., 16th Fl.
New York, NY 10022
800-391-4909 or 212-838-7800; fax: 212-838-7855
www.franceguide.com

SOURCES:
BkFest-1937, pp. 40, 121
FestSaintDays-1915, p. 52
FestWestEur-1958, p. 35

♦ 1716 ♦ Michaelmas
September 29 in the West; November 8 in the East

The **Feast of the Archangel Michael**, or the **Day of St. Michael and All Angels**, is a traditional feast day in the Roman Catholic, Anglican Communion, and Orthodox churches. The cult of ST. MICHAEL, traditionally regarded as the leader of the heavenly host of angels, probably originated in the East, then spread to the West by the fifth century. The Roman Catholic feast honors the archangels Michael, Gabriel, and Raphael, while in the East and the Anglican communion, Michael and all the angels are honored.

Churches dedicated to Michael can be found in Asia and throughout coastal Europe, usually in places where Michael is reputed to have saved the community from the threat of a monster or giant. The ninth-century abbey Mont St. Michel, off the coast of Normandy, France, once held the shield worn by Michael in his fight against the dragon.

There is an old saying that if you eat goose on Michaelmas you won't have to worry about money for a year. When tenants paid their rent on this day (see QUARTER DAYS), it was customary to include "one goose fit for the lord's dinner." Feasting on goose dinners is still part of the Michaelmas tradition, particularly in Ireland.

SOURCES:
BkDays-1864, vol. II, p. 387
BkFest-1937, p. 153
DaysCustFaith-1957, p. 242
DictFolkMyth-1984, pp. 504, 716

FestSaintDays-1915, p. 180
FestWestEur-1958, p. 155
FolkWrldHol-1999, p. 571
OxYear-1999, pp. 391, 392, 410
RelHolCal-2004, p. 101
SaintFestCh-1904, p. 428

♦ 1717 ♦ Michaelmas (Norway)
September 29

In Norway, **Mikkelsmesse** is the time of year when cows and goats are herded down from the mountain farms, or *saeters*, to the valley homesteads. Almost all farms of any importance have saeters, which are similar to summer camps and are normally operated by women. Cattle and other animals are put out to pasture in the lush mountain meadows, and, traditionally, the girls—usually the eldest daughters of the family—milk and tend the animals and make butter, goat's cheese, and other dairy products for sale or for use on the farms throughout the winter. When the girls return to their family homes in late September with their tubs of butter and well-fed animals wearing garlands of flowers, it is an occasion for dancing, singing, and feasting.

SOURCES:
FestWestEur-1958, p. 155

♦ 1718 ♦ Michigan Brown Trout Festival
Third through fourth weekend in July

You don't have to be a professional charter captain or even a local fisherman to participate in the Michigan Brown Trout Festival, which has been held in Alpena on the shores of Lake Huron since 1975. The main event is the two-day Super Tournament, which pits boat against boat. Cash prizes are awarded to those who catch the largest fish (by weight) in each of five divisions—brown trout, salmon, lake trout, steelhead, and walleye—each day and over the course of the week-long festival.

Tens of thousands of people come to Alpena to enjoy not only the fishing competitions but the sailboat races, entertainment, and other festival events. The lucky person who catches Big Brownie, a specially tagged brown trout, during the festival wins a $50,000 savings bond. But the luck that is familiar to fishermen everywhere has plagued those attending the festival as well: no one has ever collected.

Michigan is also home to the National Trout Festival, which dates back to 1933. About 40,000 fishermen and visitors come to the small town of Kalkaska, which has 275 miles of trout streams and 85 lakes stocked with brown, brook, rainbow, and lake trout. This festival is timed to coincide with the opening of trout season, which is the last Saturday in April throughout Michigan.

CONTACTS:
Michigan Brown Trout Festival
c/o Community Development Bldg.
235 W. Chisholm St.
Alpena, MI 49707
989-255-5397
www.alpenami-browntrout.com

Kalkaska Area Chamber of Commerce
353 S. Cedar
P.O. Box 291
Kalkaska, MI 49646
231-258-9103; fax: 231-258-6155
www.kalkaskami.com

♦ 1719 ♦ **Michigan Renaissance Festival**
August-September for seven consecutive weekends

Visitors who walk through the turreted gates of the annual Renaissance Festival in Holly, Michigan, are made to feel as if they're stepping back into the 16th century. The festival has a permanent, 200-acre site which is set up to resemble a European village. Festival activities, which are designed to entertain and educate, include theater, games, and equestrian events as well as displays and demonstrations of Renaissance crafts and cooking. The entire event, which takes place over seven consecutive weekends beginning in mid-August, is based on the theme of a harvest celebration in which visitors are encouraged to participate. They can try their hand at archery or dueling, sample roasted turkey drumsticks, observe the arts of glassblowing, pewter casting, and blacksmithing, and witness a Tournament of Chivalry in which costumed knights on horseback joust on the gaming field.

The popularity of Renaissance festivals began with their introduction in California during the 1960s. Such events are now held in Detroit, Minneapolis, Kansas City, Kansas, and Largo and Sarasota, Florida, and in many other cities across the country. Attendance at the Holly festival has grown to more than 150,000 since it was first held in 1980.

CONTACTS:
Michigan Renaissance Festival
12600 Dixie Hwy.
Holly, MI 48442
800-601-4848 or 248-634-5552; fax: 248-634-7590
www.michrenfest.com

♦ 1720 ♦ **Mid-Autumn Festival**
Full moon nearest September 15; 15th day of eighth lunar month

This festival to honor the moon goddess is a national holiday in China and a day celebrated throughout the Far East and in Asian communities all over the world. It is also known as the **Moon Cake Festival**. In Korea, it is called **Hangawi** or CHUSEOK; in Vietnam **Trung Thursday**; in Hong Kong **Chung Ch'iu**; and in Taiwan **Tiong-chhiu Choeh**.

Family reunions are traditional on this day, giving it some resemblance to the American THANKSGIVING. People travel long distances to be together for exchanging presents, feasting, and eating moon cakes. The ingredients of the cakes and the celebration vary according to the region.

In Taiwan, people have picnics and climb mountains to have a better view of the moon. Besides eating moon cakes, people eat pomeloes, a sweet local fruit. The Chinese word for pomelo sounds like the Chinese word for "blessing," so this is considered an especially good time to indulge in pomeloes. It's also a time for lovers to tryst.

In Malaysia, Vietnam, and other areas, it is a children's festival. They parade through the streets on the night of the festival with candle-lit paper lanterns, some of them white and round like the moon, others like all sorts of animals. Dancers parade with dragons made of paper and cloth, and firecrackers are lit after the parades. In Hong Kong children also carry paper lanterns, and many people spend the evening on the beaches watching the moon and the many bonfires that are lit on this night.

In Suzhou, China, a celebration is held in the Museum of Chinese Drama and Opera, with spectators seated at small porcelain tables where they eat moon cakes, drink jasmine tea, and watch a program of Chinese classical music, ballad-singing, acrobatics, and comic scenes from operas.

In Japan, the custom of *tsukimi*, or "moon-viewing," is observed at the same time as the Chinese festival—at the time of the full moon nearest September 15. People set up a table facing the horizon where the moon will rise, and place offerings on the table to the spirit of the moon. These would include a vase holding the seven grasses of autumn, cooked vegetables, and *tsukimi dango*, moon-viewing dumplings made of rice flour. Moon-viewing festivals are held at Hyakkaen Garden, Mukojima, Tokyo, and on Osawa at Daikakuji Temple in Kyoto, where the moon is watched from boats with dragons on their bows.

There are 20 to 30 varieties of moon cakes, which in their roundness are symbolic of family unity. Some are made of lotus seed paste, some of red bean paste, some with mixed nuts, and some have a duck egg in the center. In some regions, the moon cakes are crusty, while in others they are flaky.

There are also varying versions of the origins of the festival, which is thought to go back to the ninth century. One version has it that the Chinese, looking at the dark side of the full moon, saw a hare or rabbit, which was able to make a potion for immortality. The festival was the rabbit's birthday, and people sold rabbits on the streets. Moon cakes were made to feed the rabbits. Another version says that the day marks the overthrow of the Mongol overlords in ancient China; the moon cakes supposedly hid secret messages planning the overthrow.

The more accepted version is that the day is a harvest festival at a time when the moon is brightest. At this time of year, as the weather gets colder, people want a day to rest and enjoy life.

CONTACTS:
Hong Kong Tourism Board
115 E. 54th St. 2/F
New York, NY 10022
212-421-3382; fax: 212-421-8428
www.discoverhongkong.com

Taiwan Government Information Office
4201 Wisconsin Ave. N.W.
Washington, DC 20016
202-895-1850; fax: 202-362-6144
www.gio.gov.tw

SOURCES:
BkFest-1937, p. 81
BkFestHolWrld-1970, p. 115
BkHolWrld-1986, Sep 16
DictFolkMyth-1984, pp. 191, 225, 231
EncyRel-1987, vol. 3, p. 326
FolkWrldHol-1999, p. 504
GdWrldFest-1985, p. 158
HolSymbols-2009, p. 578
IntlThFolk-1979, p. 198
OxYear-1999, p. 703

♦ 1721 ♦ Mid-Autumn Festival (Singapore)
Full moon nearest September 15

The MID-AUTUMN FESTIVAL, sometimes known as the **Mooncake Festival**, is observed by Chinese communities around the world. In Singapore, the mooncakes served during the festival recall a 14th-century uprising against the Mongols, when word of the revolt was spread by concealing the message in cakes that were then smuggled out to compatriots. Today the cakes are often sold along with lanterns and are filled with either a sweet bean paste or with melon and lotus seeds, and may be flavored with orange peels, egg yolks, or other spices. On the night of the Mid-Autumn Festival, children all over Singapore have parades so they can show off their lighted lanterns. There are also lantern-making contests, Chinese costume-making competitions, lion and dragon dances, and concerts.

CONTACTS:
National Heritage Board of Singapore
140 Hill St., 03-02 MITA Bldg.
Singapore, 179369 Singapore
65-6338-0000
www.nhb.gov.sg

SOURCES:
GdWrldFest-1985, p. 158

♦ 1722 ♦ Middfest International
Three days in late September-early October

Middletown, Ohio, is home to the annual festival of international culture known as Middfest. Designed to promote world understanding, friendship, and peace, the festival highlights the culture of a different country each year. Performers, artists, and dignitaries from the featured country come to Middletown and stay with local families. During the week preceding the three-day festival, they perform in nearby communities, give talks, and demonstrate their art and skills.

Countries that have been invited to participate since the festival's inception in 1981 include Luxembourg, Mexico, Egypt, Brazil, Japan, Switzerland, Canada, Italy, India, and Ireland. Included in the celebration are museum-quality exhibits, ethnic dances, and menus from all over the world. Lectures, workshops, films, and special interest activities are also scheduled throughout Middfest weekend.

CONTACTS:
Middfest International
One Donham Pl.

Middletown, OH 45042
513-425-7707; fax: 513-425-7921
www.middfestinternational.org

♦ 1723 ♦ Midimu Ceremony
June-October

The Midimu ceremony is a masked dance ritual celebrating the end of the three-year initiation period for Makonde boys and girls. Although the Makonde originally lived in Malawi, Zambia, and Zimbabwe, they have migrated to Tanzania and Mozambique as well. During the dry season, which occurs between June and October, a group of the men inform their families that they must take a long trip. There is a public farewell ceremony, and then they disappear for 10 to 15 days. During this time they go from one village to the next and perform the masked dances of the Midimu ceremony, visiting the house of each new initiate and, after portraying various mythical stories in dance, receive honey, meat, jewelry, and occasionally money in return.

The Midimu ceremony always begins at night during the time when the moon moves from the quarter to the half phase. It usually follows a happy event—such as a successful hunt, a good haul of fish, or a bountiful harvest.

SOURCES:
FolkWrldHol-1999, p. 548

♦ 1724 ♦ Mid-Lent (Italy)
Between March 8 and April 7; fourth Sunday in Lent

In Italy **Mezza Quaresima**, or Mid-Lent, is a day of respite from the otherwise severe restrictions of LENT. Parties, dances, and street celebrations take place throughout the country, and many feature effigies of *Quaresima* that resemble a lean, witch-like old hag—in stark contrast to the fat man who represents CARNIVAL.

In Abruzzi, according to custom, the effigy of Quaresima is pierced with seven feathers and suspended on a rope stretched across the street. On each Saturday in Lent the villagers pluck out one feather to signify the end of one of the seven weeks of the Lenten season.

CONTACTS:
Italian Government Tourist Board
630 Fifth Ave., Ste. 1565
New York, NY 10111
212-245-5618; fax: 212-586-9249
www.italiantourism.com

SOURCES:
FestSaintDays-1915, p. 52
FestWestEur-1958, p. 92

♦ 1725 ♦ Midnight Sun Festival
June 21

The Midnight Sun Festival is a celebration of the SUMMER SOLSTICE in Nome, Alaska, where the sun shines for better than 22 hours a day in the peak of summer. In Nome, the longest day of the year is feted on two days with a street dance, blanket toss, barbecue, Monte Carlo night (gambling), Eskimo dances, a parade, and a mock bank hold-up and jail. A river raft race has been held at midnight on June 21 since the 1960s. Various homemade rafts paddle down a one- to two-mile course on the Nome River, and the winning team claims a fur-lined honey bucket, which is passed on from year to year. A softball tournament, with about 20 men's and women's teams competing for trophies, precedes the day of the solstice. Games start at about 10 P.M.

Various places in Alaska celebrate the midnight sun in various ways: Skagway throws a dance, and at Tok in 1990, the Frigid Poets Society began the practice of climbing a mountain to watch the sun not set.

In Fairbanks, a midnight baseball game is played without artificial lights. The home team, Fairbanks Goldpanners (the name recalls the gold-rush days of early Fairbanks), is reputed to be one of the best semi-pro teams in the nation. The solstice is also marked with department store sales. On the day before the baseball game, there is a Midnight Sun Run, a 10-kilometer race attracting local and national runners, with refreshments and entertainment at the finish.

This excessive activity at midnight may be at least partly explained by the function of the pineal gland. In humans, this pinecone-shaped gland is thought to produce the hormone melatonin that circulates through the body and triggers two reactions—drowsiness and reduced sex drive. Light inhibits melatonin production and thus makes it easier to do with less sleep when the sun shines. Hence, baseball games at midnight. (It is also a fact that 72 percent of Alaska babies are conceived between May and September.)

CONTACTS:
Fairbanks Convention and Visitors Bureau
550 First Ave.
Fairbanks, AK 99701
800-327-5774 or 907-456-5774; fax: 907-452-2867
www.explorefairbanks.com

Nome Convention and Visitors Bureau
P.O. Box 240 H-P
Nome, AK 99762
907-443-6624; fax: 907-443-5832
www.nomealaska.org

♦ 1726 ♦ Midnight Sun Intertribal Powwow
July

Since 2001, the Midnight Sun Intertribal Powwow has been held in Fairbanks, Ala. Drawing together members of many tribes from across North America, the powwow is designed to bring together the diverse Native American traditions found in Alaska. Besides the native Athabascan and Eskimo tribes in Alaska, members of other tribes from across the United States and Canada have also moved to the state. Making these tribal members aware of each others' traditions and finding common ground among them all is the primary goal of the powwow. Bringing these traditions to the attention of the general public in a favorable light is another goal.

The Midnight Sun Intertribal Powwow begins with a blessing of the grounds. Entertainment includes dance groups from several tribal traditions and drum groups playing native music. Some dancing events are open to visitors. Booths sell foods, native crafts, and costumes. The last event of the powwow is the release of an eagle into the air.

CONTACTS:
Fairbanks Arts Association
P.O. Box 80034
Fairbanks, AK 99708
907-456-2245
www.midnightsunpowwow.net

♦ 1727 ♦ Midsummer Day
June 24, or nearest Friday

This ancient pagan festival of the SUMMER SOLSTICE, originally kept on June 21, is celebrated in Europe and Scandinavian countries in much the same way as BELTANE was celebrated in Ireland. Bonfires are still lit in some places on **Midsummer Eve** as a way of driving out evil and renewing reproductive powers. At one time it was believed that all natural waters had medicinal powers on this day, and people bathed in streams and rivers to cure their illnesses. Midsummer Day is also sacred to lovers. Shakespeare's romantic comedy, *A Midsummer Night's Dream*, reflects the traditional spirit associated with this festival.

The Swedish begin their **Midsommar** celebration on the Friday before Midsummer Eve and continue through Sunday. Every town and village sets up a maypole, or *Majstang*, which is decorated with flowers, leaves, and flags. In Rattvik, Sweden, on Lake Siljan, the festivities are held on a pier. The province of Dalarna, where some of Sweden's oldest wooden cottages have been preserved, is a popular place to spend the Midsommar festival weekend.

The Swedes call Midsommar "the day that never ends," because the sun doesn't begin to set until 10:00 P.M. and it rises again at 2:00 A.M. In areas of Norway and Sweden that lie above the Arctic Circle, the sun shines brightly 24 hours a day for six weeks.

When June 24 was designated ST. JOHN'S DAY by the Christian Church, the fires that had been associated with the pagan festival were reinterpreted to symbolize St. John, whom the Lord had once called "a burning and shining light." But the pre-Christian elements surrounding Midsummer Day never really disappeared, and the Feast of St. John has long been associated with solstitial rites. This day is also one of the official QUARTER DAYS in England.

In Estonia, St. John's Eve is a national holiday known as **Voidupuha**, or **Victory Day**, commemorating the 1919 Battle of Vonnu in which Estonia regained control from Baltic-German rule; because celebrations extend into the night, the next day, June 24, is also a public holiday.

See also CALINDA DANCE; INTI RAYMI FESTIVAL; JUHANNUS; KUPALO FESTIVAL; ST. HANS FESTIVAL

CONTACTS:
Estonian Ministry of Foreign Affairs, Press and Information
    Department
Islandi valjak 1
Tallinn, 15049 Estonia
372-6-317-000; fax: 372-6-317-099
www.vm.ee

SOURCES:
AmerBkDays-2000, pp. 470, 474
BkDays-1864, vol. I, p. 814
BkFest-1937, pp. 32, 59, 125, 136, 213, 220
DaysCustFaith-1957, p. 151
DictFolkMyth-1984, pp. 105, 157, 168, 202, 203, 253, 486, 606, 629, 723,
    747, 754, 789, 866, 871, 930, 961, 966, 1032, 1172
FestWestEur-1958, pp. 13, 27, 43, 68, 153, 167, 199, 235
FolkWrldHol-1999, p. 392
OxYear-1999, p. 259
SaintFestCh-1904, p. 301

♦ 1728 ♦ Mihr, Festival of
February

The Church of Armenia, proud of its ancient lineage and determined to retain its national character, has made it a point to keep a number of pagan ceremonies alive by investing them with Christian significance. This seems to be the case with the Festival of Mihr, the ancient god of fire. This pagan spring festival was originally observed by lighting fires in Mihr's honor in the marketplace, and by lighting a lantern that burned throughout the year in the temple. When Christianity was introduced in Armenia early in the third century, fires were lit on this day in the church courtyards, and people danced around them or jumped through the flames.

The modern-day Armenian celebration of the Presentation of Christ in the Temple or CANDLEMAS retains many elements of the pagan Festival of Mihr.

SOURCES:
BkFest-1937, p. 23

♦ 1729 ♦ Mihragan
*February, March, October; 16th day of Mihr, the
    seventh Zoroastrian month*

Mihragan probably was adapted from the ancient Persian Feast of MITHRA. The 16th of Mihr is considered a "sacred name day" because both the day and the month share the name of the Zoroastrian spiritual being or *yazata* known as Mihr (or Meher, or sometimes Mithra), who presides over justice and who is traditionally identified with the sun. In the Zoroastrian religion, name-day feasts are cerebrated with special religious services which may be performed in a fire temple, a meeting hall, or a private home by either priests or laypeople.

Mihragan is the festival of the AUTUMNAL EQUINOX, and as such, it should occur exactly six months after the festival of the VERNAL EQUINOX, JAMSHED NAVAROZ, which falls on the first day of the first Zoroastrian month. Because the month is Mihr, it was thought to be more appropriate to celebrate the festival on the day—in this case, the 16th—that bears the same name as the month.

Mihragan is also associated with a legendary ancient event—the day on which the heroic Faridun ascended the throne of Persia after killing the mythical evil ruler Zohak.

The Zoroastrian calendar has 12 months of 30 days each, plus five extra days at the end of the year. Because of discrepancies in the calendars used by widely separated Zoroastrian communities around the world, there are now three different calendars in use, and Mihragan can fall either in February, March, or October according to the Gregorian calendar.

There are only about 100,000 followers of Zoroastrianism today, and most of them live in northwestern India or Iran. Smaller communities exist in Pakistan, Sri Lanka, Canada, the U.S., England, and Australia.

SOURCES:
RelHolCal-2004, p. 68

♦ 1730 ♦ Milan Trade Fair
April

The Milan Trade Fair was originally started in 1920 to allow Italy and other European countries to display their products. It grew into a 10-day event in April hosting 35,000 manufacturers from 110 countries, 25 of whom had their own pavilions. Although the trade fair is a boost for Milan's economy, the city was chosen primarily because of its geographical proximity to the rest of Europe. Today the center hosts more than 70 shows year round. There are also buildings devoted to the products of the various regions of Italy, with displays of leathercrafts, jewelry, textiles, graphic arts, fashions, and ceramics.

CONTACTS:
Fiera Milano SpA
Piazzale Giulio Cesare
Milano, Lombardy 20145 Italy
39-2-4997-7816; fax: 39-2-4997-7963
www.fieramilano.it

SOURCES:
GdWrldFest-1985, p. 117

♦ 1731 ♦ Mille Miglia
May

The three-day endurance rally in Italy for vintage racing cars known as the Mille Miglia, or **Thousand Miles**, began in 1927 as an all-out race, and it took about 20 hours to cover the course. By 1938, the roads had improved to the point where it took only about 12 hours, and the all-time record of 10 hours, seven minutes, 48 seconds was set in 1955. This meant that the driver had to average nearly 100 miles per hour on roads that drivers normally would hesitate to traverse at 40. A tragic accident in 1957, in which one of the racers, his navigator, and 11 spectators were killed, led to a ban against racing on public roads and brought the Mille Miglia to an abrupt halt.

The event was reorganized in 1977 with different rules. Although it still features vintage racing cars from the 1920s through the 1950s and the same roads, drivers are given three days—rather than 10 hours—to cover the thousand miles. Driving in ordinary traffic, the competitors have to average a set number of miles per hour on 34 timed sections of the course, 19 of which are driven over particularly challenging and scenic stretches of road.

The route begins in Brescia, goes east to Verona, and then southeast to Ferrera, where the drivers spend the night. Early the next morning they leave for Ravenna, follow the coast to Rimini, and then head into the mountains, where they must cover some of the most serpentine and beautiful roads in the world. The drivers spend the second night in Rome and on the third day make a 12-hour dash back to Brescia via Viterbo, Siena, Florence, and Bologna.

CONTACTS:
MAC Events S.r.l
Corso Torino
Genova, 16199 Italy
39-10-5531-767; fax: 39-10-8630-021
www.1000miglia.eu/inglese/home.html

♦ 1732 ♦ **Min, Festival of**
Autumn

Min was an ancient Egyptian god, often identified with Amun and Horus. As the god of fertility and rain, he was frequently represented holding a thunderbolt. Ancient Egyptians also associated Min with a bull, in which form he was also believed to be present at the annual harvest festival held in his honor. There were processions at the temple in Luxor, where the god also may have been offered lettuce, considered an aphrodesiac.

SOURCES:
Festivals-1981, p. 9
HarvFestWrld-1995, p. 33

♦ 1733 ♦ **Minehead Hobby Horse Parade**
April 30-May 1

In England and Wales, hobby horses have been a part of celebrations welcoming spring as far back as anyone can remember. In the waterfront town of Minehead, Somerset, the "sailors' horse" has a boat-shaped frame 7-10 feet long, which is carried on the shoulders of a man whose body is concealed by a canvas curtain that hangs to the ground. His head is covered by a painted tin mask and a tall dunce cap. Through a slit in the canvas, he can reach out his hand for contributions from spectators. Hundreds of rainbow-colored ribbons stream from the top of the horse, fluttering in the wind as he cavorts about town to the accompaniment of a drum and an accordion. Most of the money that is collected by the hobby horse and his companions is spent in the local pub afterwards, although some of it is supposed to go to charitable causes.

On MAY DAY Eve the horse sets out promptly at midnight, ending up at Whitecross (a crossroads to the west of town, the former site of a maypole) on May Day morning. Later in the afternoon the group goes to the nearby village of Dunster and pays its respects to the lord of the local castle. The hobby horse performs again in the square at Dunster that evening.

A similar ceremony is held in Padstow, Cornwall, where "Old 'Obby 'Oss" is a ferocious-looking monster with snapping jaws and sharp teeth. During the dance that represents the culmination of the Padstow ceremony, the horse goes through a ritualistic death and rebirth—an indication, perhaps, of the ceremony's roots in ancient fertility rites driving out winter and welcoming spring.

CONTACTS:
Minehead Tourist Information Centre
17 Friday St.
Minehead, Somerset TA24 5DJ United Kingdom
44-84-5345-2465; fax: 44-16-4370-7166

Padstow Tourist Information Centre
North Quay
Padstow, Cornwall PL28 8AF United Kingdom
44-18-4153-3449; fax: 44-18-4153-2356
home.freeuk.net

SOURCES:
BkHolWrld-1986, May 2
OxYear-1999, p. 188
YrbookEngFest-1954, pp. 48, 51

♦ 1734 ♦ **Minneapolis Aquatennial Festival**
Ten days, including the third full week in July

The Aquatennial Festival takes place in Minneapolis, one of America's coldest cities, during the one time of the year it's most likely to be warm and rain-free, according to meteorologists. It is not only a celebration of summer but of the region's many rivers and lakes. Of the nearly 50 events in the festival, one of the most popular is the Milk Carton Boat Race, a competition for vessels made entirely from milk cartons. In 1993, the largest-ever boat was entered—a 100-foot, 25,000-milk carton vessel resembling an aircraft carrier with a "cargo" of nearly 150 people, honoring veterans of Operation Desert Storm.

First held in 1940, the Aquatennial Festival also features such events as the evening Torchlight Parade and the Grande Day Parade, a sand castle competition, a sailing regatta, a triathlon, and a fireworks display. More than 800,000 people attend the 10-day annual festival.

CONTACTS:
Minneapolis Downtown Council
81 S. 9th St., Ste. 260
Minneapolis, MN 55402
612-338-3807; fax: 612-338-0634
www.aquatennial.org
www.downtownmpls.com

SOURCES:
FunAlsoRises-1998, p. 159

♦ 1735 ♦ **Miramichi Folk Song Festival**
August

Miramichi, a timber port along the St. Lawrence River in Canada, also refers to a type of ballad or narrative song associated with Canadian lumber camps. Miramichi became the newest city in the province of New Brunswick when in 1995 the towns of Newcastle and Chatham, as well as several area villages, combined to incorporate one city. The Miramichi Folk Song Festival, held over three to five days in August, is devoted entirely to songs and ballads in the miramichi "come all ye" style that tell stories of adventure, tragedy, and romance. While most of the songs are performed without accompaniment, they are often followed by tunes played on the fiddle, mouth organ, accordion, or guitar. There are also step-dancing and tap-dancing contests.

Founded in 1958, the festival features local folk singers and musicians as well as groups from all over Canada and the United States.

CONTACTS:
Miramichi Folk Song Festival Inc.
P.O. Box 13
Miramichi, NB E1V 3M2 Canada
506-623-2150; fax: 506-623-2261
www.miramichifolksongfestival.com

SOURCES:
GdWrldFest-1985, p. 38
IntlThFolk-1979, p. 65

♦ 1736 ♦ Misa de Gallo
December 16-24

Misa de Gallo is the start of the CHRISTMAS season in the Philippines, blending Christian tradition with the harvest thanksgiving of the ancient Filipinos.

As the first cockcrows are heard at dawn on Dec. 16, bells of the Roman Catholic churches ring, brass bands parade through towns, children fire small bamboo cannons, and skyrockets burst—all to awaken people for the Misa de Gallo, called **Cock's Mass** in English and **Simbang Gabi** in Tagalog. Each morning of the festival families walk to churches for mass at dawn. Then, on Dec. 24, there is a midnight mass. After the services, people congregate in food stalls that have been set up around church patios or go home for traditional breakfasts of rice cakes and ginger tea or cocoa.

Legend says the Cock's Mass started in the 1700s when a Spanish priest thought that blending native custom with Catholic ritual would help spread the faith. Filipinos had long celebrated good harvests with festivals of thanksgiving, and the priest called the farmers together at harvest time to thank God for good fortune and to pray for a good harvest in the coming year.

SOURCES:
AnnivHol-2000, p. 209
BkFestHolWrld-1970, pp. 144, 154
EncyChristmas-2003, p. 501
FolkWrldHol-1999, p. 703
GdWrldFest-1985, p. 151
IntlThFolk-1979, p. 289

♦ 1737 ♦ Mischief Night
November 4

The idea of letting children have a "lawless night" originated in England, and was often celebrated on MAY DAY EVE (April 30) or on HALLOWEEN. But in the mid-17th century, when GUY FAWKES DAY (November 5) became a national holiday, Guy Fawkes Eve became the most popular night for mischief in England, Australia, and New Zealand, where it is sometimes called **Mischievous Night** or **Danger Night**.

SOURCES:
AnnivHol-2000, p. 186
BkHolWrld-1986, Nov 4
DictDays-1988, pp. 26, 77

♦ 1738 ♦ Misisi Beer Feast
October; Twamo

The ritual harvest feast known as the **Misisi** takes place in Uganda after the millet harvest each year. The Sebei people make a beer out of the *misisi* ("grain that is left on the ground") after the millet stalks have been gathered and placed in granaries. Misisi also refers to the cobs of maize that are too small to be worth storing. In addition to beer, the feast includes maize meal, steamed plantains, and a bullock, ram, or chickens.

A special group of close relatives is invited to the feast, and the host's father (or some other elder) pours the beer from a libation gourd or *mwendet* and offers it to a friend, saying, "Please accept this beer; I am still alive and let us enjoy it together." Libations are poured with the right hand, inside the house or *kraal*, naming the host's father, brothers, mother, mother's brothers, grandparents, father-in-law, brothers-in-law, and all deceased members of the clan who still have living descendants. Libations are poured for the evil spirits with the left hand, outside the kraal, naming deceased relatives who are jealous because they never had children, or those who cursed them in life.

The Misisi Beer Feast is usually held during the month called Twamo, which is around the same time as the month of October. Mukutanik, an adaptation of Misisi, is held at CHRISTMAS. In areas of Uganda where the millet ripens sooner, it is held earlier.

SOURCES:
FolkWrldHol-1999, p. 549

♦ 1739 ♦ Miss America Pageant
September

What began in 1921 as an attempt by the Business Men's League of Atlantic City, New Jersey, to keep tourists in town after LABOR DAY has developed into an American institution. The week-long event that begins when the winners of the 50 state pageants arrive on Monday includes evening gown, swimsuit, and talent competitions; a parade along Atlantic City's famous boardwalk; and, on Saturday evening, final judging of the 10 semifinalists and five finalists, culminating in the crowning of the new Miss America shortly before midnight. Bert Parks, who hosted the pageant on television for 25 years, was renowned for his patented rendition of "There She Goes," the song that is traditionally sung as the new Miss America walks down the runway in Convention Hall for the first time. In addition to a year of travel and lucrative personal appearances, the winner receives a $50,000 scholarship.

The Miss America Pageant has had its ups and downs over the years—notably the 1968 protests by members of the women's liberation movement, who lit a symbolic fire in a trashcan and threw in a brassiere, some fashion magazines, and makeup—giving rise to the labeling of feminists as "bra-burners." Vanessa Williams, the first African American to win the pageant, was also the first to be dethroned when it was revealed in July of 1984 that she had once posed nude for *Penthouse* magazine. But many former Miss Americas have gone on to achieve successful careers as models, actresses, or television personalities, or in public service—among them Phyllis George (Miss America 1971), Mary Ann Mobley (1959), and Bess Myerson (1945).

CONTACTS:
The Miss America Organization
222 New Rd., Ste. 700
Linwood, NJ 08221
609-653-8700; fax: 609-653-8740
www.missamerica.org

SOURCES:
AmerBkDays-2000, p. 633
HolSymbols-2009, p. 589

♦ 1740 ♦ **Mithra, Feast of**
January, February, September; first day of Mihr, the seventh Zoroastrian month

This is a lesser feast celebrated on the first day of the seventh month by Zoroastrians, who are followers of the Persian prophet, Zoroaster (also known as Zarathushtra, believed to have lived around 1200 B.C.E.). Because there are only about 100,000 Zororastrians in the world and their communities are often widely separated, they actually use three different calendars: the Fasli, the Shahanshahi, and the Kadmi calendars, which means that their festivals have three different dates according to the Gregorian calendar. The Feast of Mithra coincides with the AUTUMNAL EQUINOX in the Fasli calendar.

Mithra is an alternate name for the spiritual being Mihr, who is charged with overseeing contracts and fair dealing. Mithra is also responsible for avenging people who have broken contracts or who have not dealt fairly with one another. Some scholars believe that he is the basis for the Roman god by the same name.

Of the modern-day followers of Zoroastrianism, most live in northwestern India (where they are known as Parsis) or Iran. Smaller communities exist in Pakistan, Sri Lanka, Canada, the U.S., England, and Australia.

See also MIHRAGAN

SOURCES:
RelHolCal-2004, p. 67

♦ 1741 ♦ **Miwok Acorn Festival**
Usually weekend after fourth Friday of September

This is an annual two-day event of the Miwok (which means "people") Indians, held at the Indian Grinding Rock State Historic Park near Sacramento, Calif. The park was a gathering place for Indians for thousands of years until Europeans settled there in 1848 at the time of the Gold Rush. This is an ancient harvest festival, largely religious, with ceremonial rites and traditional dances. It celebrates the acorn, just as Indians in the east have harvest festivals for the turkey, and in the south and southwest for corn. Acorns were a staple of the California Indians' diet, and were ground to make soup and meal for bread.

CONTACTS:
Federated Indians of the Graton Rancheria
6400 Redwood Dr., Ste. 300
Rohnert Park, CA 94928
707-566-2288; fax: 707-566-2291
www.coastmiwok.com, www.nps.gov

SOURCES:
IndianAmer-1989, p. 346

♦ 1742 ♦ **Mnarja (Imnarja; Feast of St. Peter and St. Paul)**
June 29

Mnarja is the principal folk festival of Malta and a public holiday there, thought to have been originally a harvest festival. It is held in Buskett Gardens, a park with extensive vineyards and orange and lemon orchards not far from Mdina, Malta's medieval capital. The name of the festival is a corruption of the Italian *luminaria,* meaning "illumination," since in long-ago times, the bastions around Mdina were illuminated by bonfires for the event. At one time, Mnarja was such a popular and important feast that a husband traditionally promised his bride on their wedding day that he would take her to Buskett on Mnarja Day every year.

Festivities begin on the eve of Mnarja with an agricultural show that continues through the next morning and folk-singing (*ghana*) and folk-music competitions. The traditional food of the evening is fried rabbit. On the following day, bareback horse and donkey races bring the feast to an end. The winners receive *paljj,* "embroidered banners," which they donate to their town church.

See also ST. PAUL'S SHIPWRECK, FEAST OF; STS. PETER AND PAUL DAY

CONTACTS:
Malta National Tourist Office
65 Broadway, Ste. 823
New York, NY 10006
212-430-3799; fax: 425-795-3425
www.visitmalta.com

SOURCES:
AnnivHol-2000, p. 108
FolkWrldHol-1999, p. 408

♦ 1743 ♦ **Mobile International Festival**
November

Founded in 1982, the Mobile International Festival is meant to share the many cultures of the Mobile, Ala., community with the public.

The festival begins with an opening ceremony and a parade of flags. The Mobile Civic Center houses native dancers, costumes, crafts, musical concerts, acrobats, martial arts, puppet theatre, art gallery, and cuisine from such countries as Japan, Korea, Ireland, Kenya, China, Greece, Panama, Indonesia, Mexico, Nepal, and India. Visitors are given a "passport" when they enter the festival and collect a stamp as they visit each country's cultural exhibit. In 2006, the Mobile International Festival received an Arts in Education grant from the Alabama State Council on the Arts to present a program about the Yoruba culture of West Africa in five Mobile County elementary schools. The 2007 theme for the festival was "Landmarks around the World."

CONTACTS:
Mobile International Festival
2900 Dauphin St.
Mobile, AL 36606
251-470-7730
www.mobileinternationalfestival.org

♦ 1744 ♦ **Mobile-Phone Throwing World Championship**
Last week in August

The Mobile-Phone Throwing World Championship takes place during the last week of August in Savonlinna, Finland. The light-hearted event offers several categories for men, women, and teams: original, which is based only on the distance of throw and requires a traditional "over the shoulder" toss; freestyle, with no age limits, based on the distance of the throw, style, aesthetics, and creative choreography; and juniors, which requires an "over the shoulder" throw, but is limited to children 12 years old and under. Contest organizers provide contestants with mobile phones to throw in the World Championship. They include a variety of brands and models, and all are fitted with batteries. First-place winners get a new mobile phone.

The competition was created in part to highlight Finland's vital role in developing mobile-phone technology. Direct-dial car phones were introduced in Finland in 1971, and as early as 1981, Finland and its Nordic neighbors Sweden, Norway, and Denmark had access to a public mobile telephone network. Since the inaugural Mobile-Phone Throwing World Championship in 2000, several European countries—including Norway, Switzerland, and Germany—have introduced their own national championships.

CONTACTS:
Savonlinna Congress & Festivals
Linnankatu 9
Savonlinna 57130 Finland
www.savonlinnafestivals.com/en_index

♦ 1745 ♦ **Mochi N o Matsuri**
Eighth day of 12th lunar month

The **Rice Cake Festival** is a minor public holiday native to Okinawa. The rice cakes, called *mochi* or *muchi*, are red or white and cylindrical, about four inches long and one inch in diameter. They are wrapped in the leaf of the *sannin* plant or in sugar cane leaves. On the morning of the eighth day of the 12th lunar month, the cakes are placed on a special shelf while prayers are said. Then they are served to guests or hung by string around the room.

SOURCES:
FolkWrldHol-1999, p. 785

♦ 1746 ♦ **Mohawk Trail Concerts**
Weekends in July

The Mohawk Trail is a stretch of 67 miles along Route 2 from Greenfield in northern Massachusetts to the New York boundary. It was originally an Indian path, then a route for covered wagons and stagecoaches. Nowadays it is favored by tourists, particularly during the New England fall foliage season.

The Mohawk Trail Concerts began in 1970 as a series of chamber music performances by musicians who spent the summer in and around Charlemont, a rural area 120 miles northwest of Boston. One of the founding musicians, violinist-composer Arnold Black (1923-2000), eventually became the artistic director for what evolved into a weekend concert series that now extends through the month of July, with other special concerts throughout the year. Performances are given in the Federated Church of Charlemont, where the audiences hear both well-known musicians and young artists in a varied program of classical, contemporary, jazz, and folk music.

CONTACTS:
Mohawk Trail Concerts
75 Bridge St.
Shelburne Falls, MA 01370
888-682-6873 or 413-625-9511
www.mohawktrailconcerts.org

SOURCES:
MusFestAmer-1990, p. 77

♦ 1747 ♦ **Mohegan Homecoming**
Third weekend in August

The Mohegan Homecoming, which takes place in Uncasville, Connecticut, on the third weekend in August each year, is a modern festival that has evolved from the pre-Columbian thanksgiving ceremony held by the Indians to thank their creator for the corn harvest. Up until 1941 the Mohegans held a Green Corn Festival, also known as the Wigwam Festival, but later the event was billed as a "homecoming"—a time for Mohegan Indians living in all parts of the world to come home and renew their roots. It is an opportunity to conduct tribal business, such as the installation of new chieftains and medicine women, and to update one another on tribal matters. Foods served at the festival include succotash, clam chowder, and other New England specialties; other events include traditional dancing, storytelling, and arts and crafts displays.

CONTACTS:
The Mohegan Tribe
5 Crow Hill Rd.
Uncasville, CT 06382
860-862-6100
www.mohegan.nsn.us

◆ 1748 ◆ Moldova Independence Day
August 27

The Republic of Moldova is situated between Romania and Ukraine, and it has often by occupied by surrounding nations. In 1359, the Moldovan feudal state was formed. In 1812, the Russian-Turkish Peace Treaty was signed. In accordance with the treaty, the Russian empire annexed the eastern part of Moldova, making it a Russian province. In 1918, the country united with Romania. This unity lasted till 1940, when the Soviet Union annexed the country. Moldova functioned as a territorial entity within the Soviet Union until the late 20th century.

On August 27, 1991, the Republic of Moldova became an independent and sovereign state. To commemorate this momentous occasion, the country celebrates Independence Day every year on August 27. As part of the celebrations, the Moldovan President addresses the people of the country with a festive speech. Public concerts, fairs, and outdoor activities are held in Chisinau, the capital of Moldova, and in other cities around the country. On August 27, 2001, the first military parade was held in Chisinau to celebrate the first 10 years of the country's independence.

CONTACTS:
Republic of Moldova
MD-2012 Chisinau
22 Str. Pushkin, 5th Fl.
Moldova
www.moldova.md/en

◆ 1749 ◆ Moldova Memorial Easter (Moldova Grave-Visiting Day)
Monday after Easter Monday

The most prevalent religion in Moldova is Christianity; in fact, almost half of the population belongs to the Eastern Orthodox Church. The two most important religious holidays in Moldova are Christmas and Easter. The day of Orthodox Easter changes from year to year, falling on the first Sunday after the first new moon following the day of the spring equinox. A six-week fast precedes the holiday, and the traditional foods served on Easter are similar to those served on Christmas.

In Moldova, the Easter celebration lasts two days—Easter Sunday and Easter Monday, which is the official public holiday. One week after Easter Monday is Memorial Easter. On this day, people visit and take care of the graves of their deceased relatives.

CONTACTS:
Ministry of Culture and Tourism
Piata Marii Adunari 1
MD-2033, mun

Chisinau Republica Moldova
www.turism.md/eng

◆ 1750 ◆ Moldovan Language Day
August 31

Limba Noastra, or **Our Language Day**, is a public holiday in Moldova, which is the official name of the former Moldavian Soviet Socialist Republic, a historic region of northeastern Romania. On August 31, 1989, Moldova became the first Soviet republic to pass a law declaring its language, Moldovan, to be the official language of the republic. The language law also formally proclaimed that Moldovan and Romanian were the same. The Soviets had insisted that Moldovan was a different language from Romanian in order to promote the idea that Moldova and Romania were separate nations.

Second in importance only to MOLDOVA INDEPENDENCE DAY on August 27, Language Day is celebrated with ceremonies at the burial sites of individuals linked to the struggle for cultural rights of Romanians, especially Romanian poets and writers.

CONTACTS:
Moldovan Embassy
2101 S. St. N.W.
Washington, D.C. 20008
202-667-1130; fax: 202-667-1204
www.embassyrm.org

◆ 1751 ◆ Mollyockett Day
Third Saturday in July

Mollyockett was a Pequawket Indian who lived among the early settlers of western Maine. Born between 1730 and 1740, she lived in the area now known as Bethel after 1770 and made frequent trips throughout the Androscoggin Valley and into northern New Hampshire, Vermont, and Quebec. She was known as an "Indian doctress" who treated the white settlers of New England as well. One of her most famous patients was the infant Hannibal Hamlin, whom she found near death and cured with warm cow's milk. He grew up to become Abraham LINCOLN's vice president. Mollyockett was also known as a storyteller, famous for her tales of buried Indian treasure.

The local festival that is currently known as Mollyockett Day in Bethel, Maine, started out in the 1950s as a fundraising event for families in need of assistance. In 1970 the name was changed in honor of the Indian woman whose generosity and self-reliance have become legendary. The festival includes a parade, foot races, rubber ducky race, and Maine lobsters.

CONTACTS:
Bethel Area Chamber of Commerce
8 Station Pl.
P.O. Box 1247
Bethel, ME 04217
800-442-5826 or 207-824-2282; fax: 207-824-7123
www.bethelmaine.com

◆ 1752 ◆ Monaco Grand Prix
May

One of the last true road circuits, the Monaco GRAND PRIX winds through the streets of Monte Carlo, along the harbor, and through a tunnel. It is a Formula One motor race, which refers to very specific rules governing the car's weight, maximum number of cylinders, fuel, and engine cylinder capacity. First run in 1929, the Monaco Grand Prix has a lap distance of 1.95 miles with an unusually high number of corners, which demand constant gear-changes and maximum concentration from the drivers. In 1955 an Italian car skidded and ended up in the harbor, underscoring the dangerous and unusual nature of this race.

Formula One cars are single-seaters, although prior to the 1920s the mechanic rode in the car as well. The engine is located in the rear, and the driver, protected by special clothing, a crash helmet, and goggles, steers with a very small wheel from a reclining position, to reduce air drag to a minimum. Grand Prix races are held all over the world and are approximately 200 miles in length. But most are now run on specially constructed courses designed to simulate road conditions.

CONTACTS:
Monaco Government Tourist Office
565 Fifth Ave.
New York, NY 10017
800-753-9696 or 212-286-3330; fax: 212-286-9890
www.visitmonaco.com

SOURCES:
GdWrldFest-1985, p. 137

♦ 1753 ♦ Monkey God, Birthday of the
September

This holiday is a celebration by Chinese Taoists of Tai Seng Yeh, the popular Monkey God, who sneaked into heaven and acquired miraculous powers; he is thought to cure the sick and absolve the hopeless. He is the godfather of many Chinese children.

In Singapore, Taoist mediums go into a trance to let the god's spirit enter their bodies; then, possessed, they howl and slash themselves with knives, and scrawl symbols on scraps of paper that are grabbed by devotees. There are also puppet shows and Chinese street opera performances at Chinese temples.

CONTACTS:
Singapore Tourism Board
1156 Ave. of the Americas, Ste. 702
New York, NY 10036
212-302-4861; fax: 212-302-4801
www.visitsingapore.com

SOURCES:
BkHolWrld-1986, Sep 17
FolkWrldHol-1999, p. 510
GdWrldFest-1985, p. 158

♦ 1754 ♦ Monkey Party
November-December

Yongyuth Kijwattananuson first offered this banquet to the long-tailed macaque monkeys who live in the city of Lop Buri, Thailand, in 1988 to thank them for making his hotel so attractive to visitors. It has since become an institution, especially for the hundreds of monkeys who normally spend their time begging and stealing food from townspeople and tourists. Dozens of chefs prepare numerous dishes featuring fruit and vegetables on tables covered with red tablecloths and then wait for the monkeys to overcome their fear of the spectators, loudspeakers, and media people who assemble to cover the event. Once they realize it's safe, the monkeys eventually approach the tables to feast on the offerings, playing and throwing food in the process. According to local legend, some of the monkeys can be seen disembarking from trains the morning of the event, though it is more likely that the majority, at least, are local inhabitants.

CONTACTS:
Yongyuth Kijwattananuson
Lopburi Inn and Resort
114 Phaholyothin Road, T. Tasala
Maung, Lopburi, 15000 Thailand
662-643-1191; fax: 66-36-614795
www.lopburiinnresort.co.th

Tourism Authority of Thailand
611 N. Larchmont Blvd., 1st Fl.
Los Angeles, CA 90004
800-842-4526 or 323-461-9814; fax: 323-461-9834
www.tourismthailand.org

SOURCES:
WildPlanet-1995, p. 400

♦ 1755 ♦ Monlam (Prayer Festival)
Usually February; 4th-25th days of first Tibetan lunar month

The greatest festival in Tibet follows the Tibetan New Year (LOSAR) celebrations, and commemorates the miraculous powers of Buddha. The two-week festival was started in the 14th century by Tsongkhapa, the great reformist monk, to ensure that the new year would be successful and prosperous. It is a time to attend examinations of and make offerings to monks, to light butter lamps, and above all to socialize, get the latest news, and watch sports events such as wrestling, archery, and horse racing. On the 15th day celebrants throng to Lhasa's famous Jokhang temple, where monks have created enormous butter sculptures. (*See* BUTTER SCULPTURE FESTIVAL.) A procession around the Barkor, the old city of Lhasa, carries a statue of Maitreya, the future Buddha.

When the Chinese denounced religious observances in 1959, the festival died. It was revived again in 1986, and has been observed since, although not with the grandeur of earlier days.

CONTACTS:
Office of Tibet
Tibet House, 1 Culworth St.
London, NW8 7AF United Kingdom
44-20-7722-5378; fax: 44-20-7722-0362
www.tibet.com

SOURCES:
BkHolWrld-1986, Mar 9

FolkWrldHol-1999, p. 82
RelHolCal-2004, p. 217

◆ 1756 ◆ **Monterey Jazz Festival**
Third or fourth weekend in September

This festival is a three-day celebration of jazz held since 1958 outside Monterey, Calif., at the Monterey Fairgrounds, where seven stages accommodate dozens of acts and 40,000 fans. Jimmy Lyons, a West Coast disc jockey, is credited with starting the first festival, and since then it has attracted top jazz artists. Among the many who have appeared are Dizzy Gillespie, Woody Herman, Thelonius Monk, Gerry Mulligan, Odetta, and Pee Wee Russell. The festival has boasted a number of world premieres: Duke Ellington's *Suite Thursday*, Lalo Schifrin's *Gillespiana*, and Charles Mingus's *Meditations on Monterey* are a few of them.

The atmosphere is jazzy and cosmopolitan. Booths outside the arena sell food for every taste, from sweet-potato pies to tacos to beef teriyaki.

CONTACTS:
Monterey Jazz Festival
P.O. Box Jazz
Monterey, CA 93942
925-275-9255; fax: 831-373-0244
www.montereyjazzfestival.org

SOURCES:
GdUSFest-1984, p. 21
MusFestAmer-1990, p. 184

◆ 1757 ◆ **Montreal Jazz Festival**
Last weekend in June through first week in July

What has been called the most important cultural event in Canada and the largest jazz festival in the world, the **Festival International de Jazz de Montréal** has attracted some of the greatest names in jazz—including Miles Davis, Pat Metheny, Ray Charles, and Dizzy Gillespie. More than a million people come to the festival, about one-fourth of them from outside Montreal. Although the first festival in 1980 featured only about 20 performances, the 1995 event had 2,000 artists performing in 400 concerts.

Montreal's streets are closed for the 11 days of the festival to make room for the outdoor performances, which take place rain or shine, and represent a mix of traditional, modern, and innovative jazz.

CONTACTS:
Festival International de Jazz de Montreal
400, de Maisonneuve W Blvd., 9th Fl.
Montreal, QC H3A 1L4 Canada
514-523-3378; fax: 514-525-8033
www.montrealjazzfest.com/Fijm2008/accueil_e

◆ 1758 ◆ **Montreux International Jazz Festival**
July

The most widely known jazz festival in Europe is held in Montreux, Switzerland, for about two weeks in July. There are big band, blues, country and western, jazz rock, folk jazz, and avant garde jazz concerts, most of which are held inside the Convention Centre's Stravinski Auditorium and Miles Davis Hall. Other concerts and jam sessions are held on the terrace and in the gardens of the Casino and on boats cruising Lake Leman. Most of the bands, combos, and soloists who have appeared at Montreux are American: Oscar Peterson, Dizzy Gillespie, Ella Fitzgerald, Count Basie, Miles Davis, Ray Charles, and Buddy Rich, to name just a few. Attention is also paid to up-and-coming talent, sometimes from countries as far away as Japan and Brazil. The Montreux Festival has been an annual event since 1967 and inspired the DETROIT INTERNATIONAL JAZZ FESTIVAL, a sister jazz festival held every year over LABOR DAY weekend in Detroit, Michigan.

CONTACTS:
Montreux Jazz Festival
CP 126 Sentier de Collonge 3
Montreux-Territet, 1820 Switzerland
41-21-966-4444; fax: 41-21-966-4433
www.montreuxjazz.com/news/index_en.aspx

Detroit International Jazz Festival
660 Woodward Ave., Ste. 13
Detroit, MI 48226
313-879-1144; fax: 313-879-1145
www.detroitjazzfest.com

SOURCES:
GdWrldFest-1985, p. 170
MusFestEurBrit-1980, p. 145

◆ 1759 ◆ **Moon Day**
July 20

The first man to walk on the moon was American astronaut Neil Armstrong. On July 20, 1969, he and his fellow astronaut, Edwin E. "Buzz" Aldrin, left the command module *Columbia* and landed the lunar module *Eagle* on the moon's Sea of Tranquillity. Armstrong's first words as he stepped out on the lunar surface were heard by an estimated 600 million television viewers around the world: "That's one small step for a man, one giant leap for mankind."

Air Force Lieutenant Colonel Michael Collins, pilot of the *Columbia,* continued to circle the moon for the 21½ hours during which Armstrong and Aldrin conducted their experiments. The information they collected about the moon's soil, terrain, and atmospheric conditions made an enormous contribution to knowledge of the universe and future space exploration. The Apollo 11 mission was completed eight years after President John F. Kennedy told Congress he believed that the United States could put a man on the moon before the decade ended.

CONTACTS:
NASA Public Communications Office
NASA Headquarters, Ste. 5K39
Washington, D.C. 20546
202-358-0001; fax: 202-358-3469
www.nasa.gov

SOURCES:
AmerBkDays-2000, p. 536
AnnivHol-2000, p. 120

♦ 1760 ♦ Moore (Billy) Days
Third weekend in October

Billy Moore Days celebrate the pioneer who established a stage stop, general store, and saloon in what became Avondale, Ariz. Avondale and the other Tri-City towns of Goodyear and Litchfield Park commemorate Billy Moore with a carnival, arts and crafts fair, golf tournament, burro races, car show, a street dance, and a 100-unit parade in which assorted politicians and the Arizona Maid of Cotton take part. The celebration has been held since 1954.

Billy Moore's story is surrounded by legend. He is supposed to have belonged to the gang of guerrillas led by William Clarke Quantrill, but historians think he was a young blacksmith with the gang, not one of the pillagers. Whatever he was, he was exiled by the governor of Missouri for his part in the Quantrill gang, and he headed out for Arizona Territory in 1867. Before setting up business, he either had a run-in with an outlaw or was attacked by Apaches; in any event, he was seriously injured, and a Yaqui Indian woman who later became his wife nursed him back to health.

In the late 1880s Moore bought 280 acres of land at the stage stop known as Coldwater for 25 cents an acre under the Desert Lands Act of 1877. He became a justice of the peace and was postmaster at the Coldwater station until 1905, when the post office was moved to a different location because liquor and the mail were being distributed from the same station in violation of the law. Billy Moore died in 1934 at the age of 92.

CONTACTS:
Southwest Valley Chamber of Commerce
289 N. Litchfield Rd.
Goodyear, AZ 85338
623-932-2260; fax: 623-932-9057
www.southwestvalleychamber.org

♦ 1761 ♦ Moors and Christians Fiesta
April 22-24

Moors and Christians fiestas are celebrated throughout the year all over Spain to commemorate various battles between the two groups. But it is the **Fiesta of Alcoy** in the province of Alicante that is one of the most colorful. Coinciding with the feast day of ST. GEORGE on April 23, the fiesta commemorates the victory of the Christians over the Moorish leader al-Azraq in 1276.

The three-day event begins on the morning of April 22 with the ceremonial entry of the Christians, symbolizing the forces that assembled to defend the town of Alcoy in the 13th century. The Moors arrive in the afternoon, dressed in exotic Oriental costumes. On April 23 the relic of St. George is carried in procession from his temple to the parish Church of Santa Maria, where a mass is sung. On the third day the battle is reenacted and an apparition of St. George appears on the battlements of the castle.

In the 15th, 16th, and 17th centuries, fiestas of Moors and Christians were danced. It is believed that this type of celebration eventually crossed the sea to England and became the familiar Morris dance.

CONTACTS:
Tourist Office of Spain
666 Fifth Ave., Fl. 35
New York, NY 10103
212-265-8822; fax: 212-265-8864
www.okspain.org

SOURCES:
HolSymbols-2009, p. 598
IntlThFolk-1979, p. 332

♦ 1762 ♦ Moose Dropping Festival
Second weekend in July

When the snow melts on Denali (Mount McKinley) during the Alaskan summer, the citizens of nearby Talkeetna start gathering moose droppings in preparation for their annual July festival. Varnished moose droppings are turned into jewelry and other decorative and useful objects. Some droppings are also put aside for such festival events as the Moose Nugget Toss, where participants throw them at a target resembling a moose. The Mountain Mother Contest is another festival highlight. These supermoms show what they're capable of by mastering a number of feats within a short time period, such as carrying a baby doll and grocery bags across a river, changing diapers, splitting wood, and baking a pie.

CONTACTS:
Moose Dropping Festival
c/o Talkeetna Historical Society
P.O. Box 76
Talkeetna, AK 99676
907-733-2487; fax: 907-733-2484
www.talkeetnahistoricalsociety.org

SOURCES:
WildPlanet-1995, p. 616

♦ 1763 ♦ Moravian Music Festival
Mid-June for one week in odd-numbered years

When the Moravian Church established its first American communities in the 18th century, the settlers continued to nurture their musical heritage in worship as well as in daily life—virtually interchangeable for the Moravians, for whom music was an essential component of life. As such, singing, playing instruments, and composing music were second nature to most Moravians.

Thor Johnson, the son of a Moravian minister, helped 20th-century America rediscover Moravian music when he conducted the first Early American Moravian Music Festival in Bethlehem, Pennsylvania, in 1950. Later that decade, the Moravian Music Foundation was established in North Carolina to preserve and publish the music in the archives of the Moravian Church in America.

What is now known as the Moravian Music Festival is held every two years, in cities within the northern and southern provinces of the Moravian Church in America. The archives managed by the Moravian Music Foundation provide the choral, orchestral, and chamber music performed at the festival. In addition to concerts and recitals, the festival presents seminars and workshops.

CONTACTS:
Moravian Music Foundation
Southern Music Archives, Research Library and Main Office
457 S. Church St.
Winston-Salem, NC 27101
336-725-0651; fax: 336-725-4514
www.moravianmusic.org

SOURCES:
MusFestAmer-1990, p. 119

♦ 1764 ♦ Moreska Sword Dance
July 29; July-August

The Moreska Sword Dance is a ritual dance of medieval knights that has been performed every July 29 for centuries. The dance takes place in Korcula, the main town of the island of Korcula off the coast of the former Yugoslavia (now within Croatia), in honor of the town's patron saint, Theodore. The dance-cum-pageant, with many clashes of steel, symbolizes the battle against the Turks when Korcula was under the control of the kings of Bosnia in the late 14th century.

A spirited and athletic dance, it also has been performed in other parts of Europe. There is historical evidence, for example, that the Moreska, whose name is derived from the Spanish word for "Moorish," was danced in 1156 in Lerida, Spain, to portray the expulsion of the Moors from Aragon. Originally performed only on July 29, it is now presented within the six-week **Festival of Sword Dances** running through July and August, though the grandest performance is still on the 29th. Korcula has hosted the festival since 1997 to celebrate and preserve the 400-year-old tradition of sword dancing.

From the 15th century, Korcula was under the control, successively, of Venice, Austria, France, Britain, again Austria, and Italy, until being ceded to Yugoslavia after World War I. It was under Italian occupation in World War II and liberated by Yugoslavian partisans in 1944-45. Marco Polo is supposed to have been born on Korcula.

See also MOORS AND CHRISTIANS FIESTA

CONTACTS:
Korcula Tourist Office
Grad bb
Korcula, 20260 Croatia
385-20 710-610; fax: 385-20-710-611
www.korcula.net

SOURCES:
IntlThFolk-1979, p. 390

♦ 1765 ♦ Morija Arts and Cultural Festival
Two events; one in April and one in October

The legacy of European colonialism and other historic forces have inhibited the indigenous culture of the Kingdom of Lesotho, an enclave within South Africa. The primary objective of the Morija Arts and Cultural Festival, promoted as the country's premier annual cultural event, is to revive the cultural life of the Sotho people. Additionally, the festival boosts tourism and the sale of traditional African crafts.

Established in 1999, the festival takes place in a large village of Morija in the Maseru district. It is coordinated by Morija Museum & Archives, with financial support from the Royal Family, the Lesotho government, and various churches, private donors, and nongovernmental organizations.

Originally held in October, the three-day festival was moved to April in 2008. Its agenda has remained consistent with past celebrations and has included cultural exhibits, night concerts, and workshops for various artists and performers. A second festival component, the Morija Festival Cultural Competitions, was added in 2007 and was held over two days in early October. The competitions serve to increase the participation of Sotho youth, a special priority for Morija Museum & Archives. Various primary and high school groups, as well as community cultural groups, compete in the areas of traditional dance, instrumental performance, and drama and poetry.

CONTACTS:
Morija Museum & Archives
P.O. Box 12
Morija 190 Lesotho
www.morijafest.com

♦ 1766 ♦ Moriones Festival
Begins between March 15 and April 18; Holy Week

One of the more popular and colorful of the many Passion plays—folk dramas that retell the story of Jesus' arrest, trial, and crucifixion—is performed before EASTER in the Philippines. Held on the island-province of Marinduque with participants wearing masks and costumes of Roman soldiers, Moriones tells the story of the legendary Roman soldier, Longinus, who is said to have been blind in one eye. As he pierced the side of the crucified Jesus, a drop of the blood cured his blindness. The first thing he saw with both eyes was Christ's passage to heaven. According to the legend Longinus announced this good news. The Roman warriors, however, wanted to stop this report and captured him.

Many local men take part in the Marinduque play, performing the roles of Roman soldiers. They wear large wooden masks covered with black beards and painted with enormous black eyes, open mouths, and pink flesh. The masks disguise their identities, as their participation serves as an act of humble religious devotion rather than an attempt to garner public recognition. Longinus escapes from the Roman soldiers three times in the Marinduque Passion play, but cannot evade capture on the fourth attempt. The Roman soldiers lead Longinus to a scaffold, but he continues to declare his faith in Christ. The Moriones cut his head off and carry it through town, while bringing his body along on a stretcher.

CONTACTS:
Philippines Department of Tourism
556 Fifth Ave.
New York, NY 10036
212-575-7915; fax: 212-302-6759
www.tourism.gov.ph

SOURCES:
EncyEaster-2002, p. 491
FestWrld: Phil-1999, p. 12
GdWrldFest-1985, p. 152
IntlThFolk-1979, p. 289

♦ 1767 ♦ **Mormon Pioneer Day**
July 24

After their founder, Joseph Smith, was murdered in 1844, the Mormons—members of the Church of Jesus Christ of Latter-Day Saints—moved westward from their settlement in Nauvoo, Illinois, under the leadership of Brigham YOUNG. When Young surveyed the Salt Lake Valley on July 24, 1847, he proclaimed, "This is the right place." Thousands of Mormon pioneers followed him over the next two decades, many of them pushing their belongings in handcarts.

The original 40-acre plot with log houses where the Mormons settled is the modern Salt Lake City, and the day on which Young chose the site is celebrated not only in Utah but in surrounding states with significant Mormon populations, such as Idaho, Arizona, Nevada, Wyoming, and California. Other states observe their own **Pioneer Day** at different times of the year.

CONTACTS:
Utah Office of Tourism, Council Hall
300 N. State St.
Salt Lake City, UT 84114
800-200-1160 or 801-538-1030
www.utah.com

SOURCES:
AmerBkDays-2000, p. 542
AnnivHol-2000, p. 122
DictDays-1988, p. 89
FolkAmerHol-1999, p. 304

♦ 1768 ♦ **Morocco Independence Day**
November 18

Independence Day, also known as **Fete de l'Independence**, is a national holiday commemorating Morocco's independence from France on November 18, 1927; a secret treaty in 1904 had divided Morocco between France and Spain.

Throne Day, March 3, was also a public holiday, commemorating the anniversary of King Hassan II's accession in 1961. When King Hassan II died in 1999, his son, Mohammed VI

(b. 1963), became king, and now it is his birthday on August 21 that is celebrated, along with July 30, his coronation day.

Other public holidays in Morocco include: August 20, the anniversary of the king's and people's revolution, and November 6, the anniversary of the Green March in 1975. In order to claim the Western Sahara for Morocco, more than 300,000 Moroccans marched into the territory, which the Spanish still controlled; Spanish troops left the area by early 1976.

CONTACTS:
Moroccan National Tourist Office
20 E. 46th St., Ste. 1201
New York, NY 10017
212-557-2520; fax: 212-949-8148

SOURCES:
AnnivHol-2000, p. 193
NatlHolWrld-1968, p. 30

♦ 1769 ♦ **Moro-Moro Play**
April or May

The term *moro-moro* refers to a type of folk drama performed in villages throughout the Philippines, usually during fiestas. Although each village's moro-moro is a little different in terms of treatment, all are full of romance and melodrama, and the highpoint is always a battle between Muslims and Christians. Local people write the script, which is in verse, and some performances include quite elaborate scenery and costumes. Music and dance are also part of the production.

One of the most notable moro-moros is held in San Dionisio in Rizal Province, where the drama is performed in the church and the village square every spring, usually in April or May.

See also MOORS AND CHRISTIANS FIESTA

CONTACTS:
Philippine Tourism Center
556 Fifth Ave.
New York, NY 10036
212-575-7915; fax: 212-302-6759
www.philippinetourism.us

SOURCES:
IntlThFolk-1979, p. 290

♦ 1770 ♦ **Morris Rattlesnake Roundup**
Second weekend in June

In 1956, when the first **Rattlesnake Roundup** was held in Morris, Pennsylvania, more than 400 of the poisonous snakes were caught and sold to leather craftsmen and zoos. But their numbers have dwindled since that time, and the trend has been toward the protection of endangered species—even poisonous ones. Now only about 25 to 35 snakes are found each year, and by law they must be returned to the wild. The roundup is sponsored by the local fire department and about 80 hunters participate, catching the snakes with tongs and forked sticks. Most of the snakes are 30"-45" long.

CONTACTS:
Wellsboro Area Chamber of Commerce
P.O. Box 733
Wellsboro, PA 16901
570-724-1926; fax: 570-724-5084
www.wellsboropa.com

◆ 1771 ◆ Moshoeshoe's Day
March 11

Moshoeshoe (also called **Mshweshwe** or **Moshesh**, and pronounced mow-SHOO-shoo; c. 1790-1870) was a leader in South Africa who organized a group of tribes to fight the Zulu warlord, Shaka. He called his followers the Basotho (or Basuto) people, and although they succeeded in fending off the Zulu, they were eventually drawn into a war with the Europeans who started settling their territory. Moshoeshoe and the Basotho retreated into the mountains, and from this position they were able to keep the European invaders at bay. In 1868 the Basotho nation became a British protectorate known as Basutoland, and in 1966 it became the independent kingdom of Lesotho within the British Commonwealth (*see* LESOTHO INDEPENDENCE DAY).

The Basotho people continue to honor their founder on this day with a solomn wreath-laying ceremony in the capital city of Maseru, along with sporting events and traditional music and dancing.

CONTACTS:
Lesotho Government
Ministry of Communications
P.O. Box 36
Maseru, Lesotho
266-22-323-86
www.lesotho.gov.ls

SOURCES:
AnnivHol-2000, p. 42
BkHolWrld-1986, Mar 12

◆ 1772 ◆ Most Precious Blood, Feast of the
Formerly July 1

In the Roman Catholic Church, July was the month of the Most Precious Blood—referring to the blood of Jesus, which ever since the time of the Last Supper has been regarded by Christians as possessing redemptive power. But it wasn't until 1849 that a specific day was chosen for general observance of this festival. At that time Pope Pius IX was forced into exile while Rome was under attack by the French. One of his companions, who happened to be a general officer of the Fathers of the Most Precious Blood, tried to convince the Pope to promise that if he regained his papal lands he would establish this festival as a universal observance. The Pope, of course, said he didn't want to bargain with God, but that he would extend the festival to the whole church anyway. Since he reached this decision on the day before the first Sunday in July, it was originally the first Sunday that was dedicated to the Most Precious Blood. But Pius X moved the feast to the first day of July. In 1969 it was suppressed altogether and is no longer on the church calendar.

SOURCES:
DaysCustFaith-1957, p. 166
RelHolCal-2004, p. 99

◆ 1773 ◆ Mothering Sunday
March-April; fourth Sunday in Lent

It was the custom in 17th-century England for Christians to pay their respects on the fourth Sunday in LENT to the "Mother Church" where they had been baptized. Also known as **Misers**, or **Mid-Lent**, **Sunday,** this day usually included a visit to one's parents—to "go a-mothering," as it was called back then. It was common practice to bring a cake or trinket for the mother of the family. In England the favorite gift was the simnel cake, a saffron-flavored fruitcake topped with almond paste.

In the Roman Catholic Church and the Anglican Communion, the fourth Sunday in Lent is known as **Laetare Sunday**. The Introit of the Mass begins with the word "Rejoice" (*laetare* in Latin), marking a slight respite in the solemn Lenten season, hence the terms Mid-Lent Sunday and **Refreshment Sunday**. Priests may wear rose-colored vestments to mass, instead of the usual purple for Lent, so the day is also called **Rose Sunday**. Also on this day the pope blesses the Golden Rose, an ornament resembling a spray of roses, symbolizing spiritual joy.

SOURCES:
BkDays-1864, vol. I, p. 335
BkFest-1937, p. 55
DaysCustFaith-1957, p. 89
DictDays-1988, pp. 76, 78, 95, 112
DictFolkMyth-1984, pp. 752, 1013
EncyEaster-2002, p. 334
FestSaintDays-1915, p. 50
FolkWrldHol-1999, p. 168
OxYear-1999, p. 612
RelHolCal-2004, p. 92
SaintFestCh-1904, p. 143

◆ 1774 ◆ Mother-in-Law Day
Fourth Sunday in October

Modeled on the celebration of MOTHER'S DAY and FATHER'S DAY, **Mother-in-Law's Day** was first celebrated on March 5, 1934, in Amarillo, Texas, where it was initiated by the editor of the local newspaper. The observance was later moved to the fourth Sunday in October.

Mothers-in-law have never enjoyed the widespread respect and devotion that mothers have received over the years, and the rising divorce rate has given the whole concept of in-laws a less permanent place in the national imagination. This may be part of the reason why Mother-in-Law Day has failed to catch on like Mother's Day, Father's Day, and even GRANDPARENTS' DAY. But many people feel that mothers-in-law deserve a special day of their own, if for no other reason than for their good humor in enduring the many jokes that have been told about them.

SOURCES:
AnnivHol-2000, p. 182

♦ 1775 ♦ **Mother's Day**
Second Sunday in May

The setting aside of a day each year to honor mothers was the suggestion of Anna M. Jarvis of Philadelphia, Pennsylvania, whose own mother had died on May 9, 1906. She held a memorial service and asked those attending to wear white carnations—a gesture that soon became a tradition. By 1914 President Woodrow Wilson had proclaimed a national day in honor of mothers, and some people still wear carnations on the second Sunday in May—pink or red for mothers who are living and white for those who have died.

Sometimes Mother's Day is confused with MOTHERING SUNDAY, an English holiday that falls on the fourth Sunday in LENT. But Mother's Day is now observed in England as well, and the traditions associated with Mothering Sunday have been largely forgotten. A number of Protestant churches have designated this day as the **Festival of the Christian Home**.

See also CHILDREN'S DAY

SOURCES:
AmerBkDays-2000, p. 353
AnnivHol-2000, p. 92
BkHolWrld-1986, May 14
DaysCustFaith-1957, p. 133
DictDays-1988, p. 78
FolkAmerHol-1999, p. 229

♦ 1776 ♦ **Mothman Festival**
September

In 1966 the first sightings of a creature that came to be known as Mothman were first reported in the small town of Point Pleasant, W.Va., Mothman was said to have two glowing red eyes, large wings, and a height of six or seven feet. Witnesses reported him flying along the dark roads around town, especially near the old weapons plant where the government stored explosives during World War II. The story soon caught national attention. As the stories of Mothman died down, reports of UFO sightings, of animal mutilations, and of mysterious "men in black" began circulating. The collapse of the nearby Silver Bridge in December 1967, in which 46 cars fell into the Ohio River, was also thought to be connected with the odd events. Since then, Point Pleasant has become, like Roswell, N.Mex., one of the leading sites for those who investigate strange phenomena.

Since 2001 the Mothman Museum of Point Pleasant has sponsored the Mothman Festival. Those interested in the Mothman phenomena and in such paranormal topics as ghosts and UFOs gather in the town. Merchandise booths are set up along the town's main streets, and posters, books, T-shirts, and a host of other products are available. Music concerts are also held along the river.

CONTACTS:
Mothman Museum
411 Main St.
Point Pleasant, WV 25550
www.mothmanlives.com

♦ 1777 ♦ **Motorcycle Week (Bike Week)**
First week in March

Bike Week is the largest motorcycle meet in the world, held for 10 days in Daytona Beach, Fla. The event began in 1937, as an outgrowth of automobile races. These had been started years earlier on Daytona's Ormond Beach by Henry Ford, who had a mansion and was testing cars there. It was suspended for a few years during World War II, but the 50th anniversary was celebrated in 1991, with half a million people attending.

The highlight of the week is the Daytona 200 race, which attracts competitors from all over the world and is considered one of the most prestigious motorcycle road races in the world. Other race events include a three-hour U.S. Endurance Championship race and vintage motorcycle races on Classics Day. The events take place in the Daytona Beach Municipal Stadium, with a quarter-mile banked oval track, and on the Daytona International Speedway.

Motorcyclists come from around the world, and most bring their motorcycles with them. A popular feature of the week is a mammoth parade of over 5,000 motorcycles. Parade watchers include large contingents of elderly people, some of whom hold signs saying "Grandmothers Love Biking" and other slogans. Concerts and trade shows are held throughout the week.

CONTACTS:
Official Bike Week Headquarters
Daytona Beach Halifax Area Chamber of Commerce
126 E. Orange Ave.
Daytona Beach, FL 32114
386-225-0981; fax: 904-258-5104
www.daytonachamber.com

♦ 1778 ♦ **Mount Cameroon Race**
Last Sunday in January

The annual "mad race" requires athletes to run up and down Mt. Cameroon (13,353 ft.) in the central African country of Cameroon. The race is the most difficult in Africa; the course is so steep that runners have to carry poles, and temperatures can vary from a humid 80 degrees F. at the start of the race to freezing at the summit. On the night before the race, local people make sacrifices to appease the mountain spirits. Thousands of spectators watch the race, in which about 250 runners usually participate; the winner's time can be under four hours.

CONTACTS:
Cameroon Embassy
2349 Massachusetts Ave. N.W.
Washington, D.C. 20008
202-265-8790; fax: 202-387-3826
www.ambacam-usa.org

♦ 1779 ♦ **Mount Ceahlau Feast**
Second Sunday in August

A folk event that has ancient roots, the Mount Ceahlau Feast is held at Durau, Romania, at the foot of Mount Ceahlau. The mountain was considered sacred to the Dacians, the ancestors of the present Romanians, and was the scene of their annual celebrations. In those days, people climbed to the summit to greet the sun with religious ceremonies and feasts. Today there are demonstrations of such sports as wrestling and foot racing, and exhibits and sales of folk art.

CONTACTS:
Romanian National Tourist Office
355 Lexington Ave., Fl. 19
New York, NY 10017
212-545-8484; fax: 212-545-8484
www.romaniatourism.com

♦ 1780 ♦ **Mount Fuji Climbing Season, End of**
On or near August 26

Climbing Mount Fuji is such a popular sport in Japan that the climbing season has a formal opening and closing. It begins on July 1, when the six most popular routes for the journey up the mountain are opened for the summer, and ends with a fire festival in the city of Fujiyoshida on or near the evening of August 26. Huge torches more than 10 feet high and several feet in circumference are set up along the streets, and families pile up firewood in front of their houses. At about 5 P.M., two portable shrines are brought down from the mountain and carried through the main street of Fujiyoshida. About an hour later, all the torches and family bonfires are lit simultaneously. The flames continue long past midnight, and thousands of spectators flock to the town to witness the spectacle.

CONTACTS:
City of Fujiyoshida
1842 Shimoyoshida Fujiyoshida-shi
Yamanashi-ken
Fujiyoshida, 403-8601 Japan
81-5-5522-1111; fax: 81-5-5522-0703
www.city.fujiyoshida.yamanashi.jp/div/english/html

SOURCES:
BkFestHolWrld-1970, p. 110

♦ 1781 ♦ **Mount Hagen Show**
Late August

This gathering, known as a sing-sing, in Papua New Guinea provides an opportunity for outsiders to experience the ceremonial drumming, dancing, and other displays of tribal culture of hundreds of Western Highland clans. Performers wear their traditional tribal garb, often with body paint and an elaborate headdress made of feathers. The annual Mount Hagen show, staged more for tourists than for the locals, includes a competition that encourages decorative costumes and wild dancing to the accompaniment of nonstop drumming. Ritualistic sing-sings performed by individual tribes are also held throughout the highlands, but these are more private ceremonies.

CONTACTS:
Papua New Guinea Tourism Promotion Authority in USA
5000 Birch St., Ste. 3000
Newport Beach, CA 92660
949-752-5440; fax: 949-476-3741
www.pngtourism.org.pg

SOURCES:
WildPlanet-1995, p. 438

♦ 1782 ♦ **Mount Isa Rodeo and Mardi Gras**
August

For three days in August, Mount Isa, a city in the outback of Queensland, hosts Australia's largest rodeo in grand style. Begun in 1959 by three of the city's Rotary Clubs, the rodeo has contributed more than $2.5 million to worthy organizations over the years, and the event has involved the entire community. Among the offerings are the Rodeo Mardi Gras, with a Friday night parade of floats through the central business district; an annual "Best Dressed Premises" contest during the week leading up to the rodeo, in which businesses decorate their premises in a rodeo theme and encourage their staffs to wear rodeo-style costumes; and a fairground on blocked-off city streets in central Mount Isa, with carnival rides, entertainment, and food from Friday afternoon until early Saturday morning.

As for the main event, the rodeo attracts competitors from all over the world, with more than $200,000 in prize money available. Individual events include bull riding, saddle and bareback bronc riding, steer wrestling, team roping, and rope and tie.

CONTACTS:
Isa Rotary Rodeo Inc.
Buchanan Park Events Complex, Cnr George & Sutton St.
P.O. Box 353
Mount Isa, QLD 4825 Australia
61-7-4743-2706; fax: 61-7-4743-8435
www.isarodeo.com.au

SOURCES:
WildPlanet-1995, p. 425

♦ 1783 ♦ **Mountain Man Rendezvous**
September, Labor Day weekend

The Mountain Man Rendezvous is a celebration of 19th-century history at Fort Bridger, Wyo. This town was founded in 1842 as a trading post by mountain men Jim Bridger and Louis Vasquez. It was established as a stronghold by Mormons in 1853, and taken over by the U.S. Army in 1959. In the great westward migration, streams of wagon trains passed through Fort Bridger for points west.

The Mountain Man Rendezvous began in 1973 and today attracts about 45,000 visitors over four days. The days of 1820-40 are reenacted with people in calico and buckskins, furs and feathers. A teepee village is set up where campers wear clothing of the period, and there is a traders' row where replicas of pre-1840 items are for sale. Other activities include competitions in tomahawk throwing and archery, costume and cooking contests, black-powder shoots, and Indian tribal dances.

See also GREEN RIVER RENDEZVOUS

CONTACTS:
Fort Bridger Historical Association
P.O. Box 112

Fort Bridger, WY 82933
307-782-3842
www.fortbridgerhistorical.org

♦ 1784 ♦ Mountain State Forest Festival
Last weekend in September through first week in October

This festival is an eight-day celebration of the timber industry—one of West Virginia's biggest industries—in the small town of Elkins. The 60th annual festival was held in 1996, but the event actually has its origins in the 1930 three-day "fall homecoming" held to call attention to the area's scenic attractions. The festival was suspended during World War II. Today attendance tops 100,000.

A highlight of the festival is the crowning of Queen Silvia, who wears an elaborate embroidered velvet gown. Usually the governor crowns the queen, but in 1936, President Franklin D. ROOSEVELT did the honors. After his address, a pageant was presented that was based on the ancient Egyptian myth of creation.

Events today salute the timber industry but also include non-timber events. Hence, there are forestry and wood-products exhibits and lumberjack contests along with a horseshoe tournament, live musical entertainment, a motorcycle race, arts and crafts exhibits, and a mammoth buckwheat cake and sausage feed. Buckwheat cakes are a local favorite. There are additionally several parades, including a fireman's parade with antique and modern fire equipment.

CONTACTS:
Mountain State Forest Festival
P.O. Box 388
Elkins, WV 26241
304-636-1824
www.forestfestival.com

SOURCES:
GdUSFest-1984, p. 209

♦ 1785 ♦ Moving Day
May 1; May 25

The idea of packing up one's belongings and changing residences on a particular day has been a tradition in many countries. In 19th-century America, May 1st was the normal day for the inhabitants of Boston and New York to change their place of residence, since leases normally expired on this day.

In Scotland, it was called **Flitting Day** and took place on May 25. The decision of whether to "sit or flit" was up to the tenant, but "flitting" seemed to be more common. On Flitting Day they had to vacate their houses by noon, which often meant a great upheaval for the family during the preceding day or two. But apparently the novelty value of flitting outweighed the boredom of sitting. In some parts of Scotland, this occurs on May 1, and is also called **Term Day.**

In Norway, Moving Day or **Flyttedag** takes place sometime during the autumn months. But rather than being a day for

changing residences, it is a day when servants searching for employment flock to the larger towns and cities dressed in the costumes of their native villages. Sometimes they ride in small carts or wagons, piled high with painted trunks or bundles of clothing and other possessions. While city residents take advantage of this opportunity to interview their help for the coming year, the servants seeking employment often try to sell their produce, farm animals, and handicrafts on the street.

SOURCES:
BkDays-1864, vol. I, p. 679
BkFest-1937, p. 252
DictDays-1988, p. 42
FestWestEur-1958, p. 155
FolkWrldHol-1999, p. 320

♦ 1786 ♦ Moxie Festival
Second weekend in July

Moxie, originally a nerve tonic, was invented in 1876 by Dr. Augustine Thompson of Union, Maine. In 1884 it became a carbonated beverage whose main ingredient was gentian root. The Moxie Festival in Lisbon, Maine, began as an autograph session for Frank Potter, the author of *The Moxie Mystique*, in 1982. Within a few years the event had grown to include a pancake breakfast, parade, car show, craft fair, chicken barbecue, and firemen's muster.

Although Moxie is no longer widely available, those who remember it describe it as a kind of precursor to Coca Cola. The drink can still be found in Maine, where it is quite popular. About 10,000 people attend the festival each year.

CONTACTS:
Town of Lisbon
300 Lisbon St.
Lisbon, ME 04250
207-353-3000; fax: 207-353-3007
www.moxiefestival.com

♦ 1787 ♦ Mozambique Independence Day
June 25

This national holiday commemorates Mozambique's independence from Portugal, attained on this day in 1975 after 10 years of warfare and nearly half a century of Portuguese rule.

CONTACTS:
Embassy of the Republic of Mozambique
1525 New Hampshire Ave. N.W.
Washington, D.C. 20036
202-293-7146; fax: 202-835-0245
www.embamoc-usa.org

SOURCES:
AnnivHol-2000, p. 106

♦ 1788 ♦ Mozambique Lusaka Agreement Day
September 7

In December 1992, Zambia's Ministry of Tourism convened wildlife law enforcement officers from eight eastern and southern African countries in Lusaka, Zambia. The purpose of this meeting was to discuss ways to stop the illegal trade of wild plants and animals from these countries. During this meeting, the group developed the Lusaka Agreement on Co-operative Enforcement Operations Directed at Illegal Trade in Wild Fauna and Flora.

Following this initial meeting, several working group meetings were held among members of the Convention on International Trade in Endangered Species of Wild Fauna and Flora (CITES), Interpol, and U.S. Fish & Wildlife Service, as well as London University lawyers for the Foundation for International Environment Law Development (FIELD). The Lusaka Agreement was formally adopted on September 8, 1994, and the agreement took effect on December 10, 1996.

There are currently six parties to the agreement: The Republics of Congo (Brazzaville), Kenya, Tanzania, Uganda, Zambia, and the Kingdom of Lesotho. The Republics of South Africa, Ethiopia, and the Kingdom of Swaziland are signatories.

As part of the agreement, the Lusaka Agreement Task Force was launched on June 1, 1999. This permanent inter-governmental task force was set up to coordinate activities in and among the states affected by the Lusaka Agreement. The task force is responsible for conducting investigations into violations of national laws involving the illegal trade of wild fauna and flora. The headquarters for the Lusaka Agreement Task Force is located in Nairobi, Kenya.

To show support for this important agreement, September 7 has been declared Lusaka Agreement Day in Mozambique. It is a public holiday throughout the country.

CONTACTS:
Lusaka Agreement Task Force
The Director
Lusaka Agreement Task Force
P.O. Box 3533-00506
Nairobi, Kenya
www.lusakaagreement.org

♦ 1789 ♦ **Mozambique Peace Day**
October 4

The United States Institute of Peace (USIP) is an independent, nonpartisan, national institution that was established in 1985. It is funded by the United States Congress to help prevent and resolve violent international conflicts, promote post-conflict stability and development, and increase conflict management capacity, tools, and intellectual capital worldwide.

To accomplish these goals, the Institute shares its knowledge, skills, and resources with others and directly engages in peace-building efforts around the world. The Institute is comprised of experts from the government, military, non-governmental organizations (NGOs), academia, and the private sector. In addition, the Institute partners with non-profit organizations, academic institutions, government agencies, international organizations, and the military. The USIP played an instrumental role in brokering the peace in Mozambique.

On October 4, 1992, after approximately 15 years of armed conflict throughout the Republic of Mozambique, Joaquim Alberto Chissano, President of the Republic of Mozambique, signed the Mozambique General Peace Agreement in Rome, Italy. The signing of this agreement essentially put an end to the country's civil war.

To commemorate this day, the Republic of Mozambique has declared October 4 as Peace Day.

CONTACTS:
United States Institute of Peace
1200 17th St. N.W.
Washington, D.C. 20036
202-457-1700 or 202-429-6063
www.usip.org

♦ 1790 ♦ **Mozart (Wolfgang Amadeus), Birthday of**
January 27

Wolfgang Amadeus Mozart was born in Salzburg, Austria, on this day in 1756 and died only 35 years later, on December 5, 1791. An extraordinarily precocious child, he began performing at the age of three and was composing by the age of five. Mozart represents the high point of the late 18th-century Viennese Classical style, and his achievements in composing operas, chamber music, symphonies, and piano concerti have earned him a reputation as one of the greatest musical geniuses of all time.

Mozart's birthday is observed by musical societies all over the world, who often give concerts of his music on this day. The city of his birth also honors him every summer with the SALZBURG FESTIVAL—which has become so closely identified with him that it is often referred to as "The Mozart Festival"—and at the end of January with MOZART WEEK.

CONTACTS:
Austrian National Tourist Office
120 W. 45th St.
P.O. Box 1142
New York, NY 10036
212-944-6880; fax: 212-730-4568
www.austria.info

SOURCES:
AnnivHol-2000, p. 15

♦ 1791 ♦ **Mozart Festival (Mozartfest)**
June-July

The only time Wolfgang Amadeus Mozart (1756-1791) spent in Würzburg was when he stopped there for some coffee while traveling between Salzburg and Frankfurt, but the German city has hosted a Mozart Festival in early summer each year since 1922, with the exception of a nine-year interruption during and after World War II. Daily concerts of Mozart's symphonies, concertos, sonatas, motets, sacred vocal works, and operas are performed from early June to early July, with little repetition due to the vast number of such works.

Würzburg's churches, palaces, and fortresses often serve as locations for the concerts, the most impressive being Prince

Bishop's Residence, considered one of Europe's most stunning baroque palaces. Mozart's *Eine kleine Nachtmusik* is performed on Saturday evenings in the torchlit garden of the Residence, while indoor concerts are given in the elaborate baroque *Kaisersaal* (Imperial Hall), which has a ceiling fresco painted by Giovanni Tiepolo (1696-1770), the great Italian artist.

Musical groups that have performed at past festivals include the Würzburg Philharmonic Orchestra, the Bambert Symphony Orchestra, the Prague Chamber Orchestra, and the Amadeus Quartet.

CONTACTS:
Mozartfest-Kartenburo
Haus zum Falken, Marktplatz 9
Wurzburg, 97070 Germany
49-931-372-33-6; fax: 49-931-373-93-9
www.mozartfest.de

SOURCES:
MusFestEurBrit-1980, p. 102

◆ 1792 ◆ Mozart Week (Mozartwoche)
Last week in January

Wolfgang Amadeus Mozart was born on January 27, 1756. Every January since 1956, his birthday has been celebrated by the people of Salzburg, Austria, where he was born, with a music festival devoted entirely to his works. Along with his chamber music and symphonies, Mozart's operas are often given in concert form. The festival also prides itself on presenting many of his lesser known works, which are seldom performed elsewhere.

The principle ensembles for the festival are the Vienna Philharmonic Orchestra and the Mozarteum Orchestra, under the leadership of both native and guest conductors. The concerts are given in a number of sites associated with Mozart's life, including the Mozarteum Building, St. Peter's Church, the Salzburg Cathedral, and even Mozart's home.

Organizers plan a huge celebration in 2006 for Mozart's 250th birthday anniversary.

CONTACTS:
International Mozarteum Foundation
Schwartzstrasse 26
Salzburg, A-5020 Austria
43-662-8894-00; fax: 43-662-8894-036
www.mozarteum.at/default.asp?SID=91570907013577&de

General Secretariat Mozart
Chiemseegasse 6
Salzburg, A-5020 Austria
43-662-8042-2006; fax: 43-662-8042-2861
www.linie3.com/m2k6/e

Salzburg City Tourist Office
Auerspergstrasse 6
Salzburg, A-5020 Austria
43-662-8898-70; fax: 43-662-8898-732
www2.salzburg.info

SOURCES:
MusFestEurBrit-1980, p. 22

◆ 1793 ◆ Mule Days
May, Memorial Day weekend

A raucous salute in Bishop, Calif., to that workhorse of the ages, the mule. Bishop is an outfitting point for pack trips and lies between California's two highest mountain ranges. The entire region depends on mules to transport people and gear into the High Sierra.

Mule Days was started in 1969 by mule-packers who wanted to have a good time and initiate their summer packing season. Now about 50,000 people show up in Bishop (population 3,500) for the Thursday-through-Monday celebration.

A highlight is the Saturday morning 250-unit parade, billed as the world's largest non-motorized parade. It includes pack strings from local pack stations and national parks, a sheep-drawn wagon, llamas (used for sheepherding), and a rider on a Brahma steer. The pack loads demonstrate how mules haul such various necessities as machinery, wood, and outhouses into remote areas. Other events include mule-shoeing contests and such muleback cowboy events as steer roping and barrel racing. The weekend's wildest events are "packers' scrambles," where about 50 packers scramble to catch mules, pack and saddle them, and race away with horses and cattle. About 40 horses, two dozen cattle, and 80 mules raise the dust in the arena during the scrambles.

Draft horses and miniature horses also put in appearances, and there are mule shows and sales, western art, barbecues, and country dances. Motels are booked solid a year in advance. Ronald Reagan attended Mule Days in 1974 when he was California's governor.

Mules are the sterile progeny of male asses or donkeys and mares (female horses). The rarer offspring of male horses and female donkeys are called hinneys. Mules have been beasts of burden for at least 3,000 years.

CONTACTS:
Bishop Mule Days Celebration
1141 N. Main St.
Bishop, CA 93514
760-872-4263; fax: 760-872-2328
www.muledays.org

SOURCES:
GdUSFest-1984, p. 15

◆ 1794 ◆ Mulid of Shaykh Yusuf Abu el-Haggag (Moulid of Abu el-Haggag)
Two weeks prior to the beginning of the Muslim observance of Ramadan

The Mulid of Shaykh Yusuf Abu el-Haggag celebrates the patron shaykh of Luxor, Egypt, with a two-day street festival that draws Muslims and visitors alike. It takes place two weeks prior to the start of Ramadan in the ninth month of the Islamic lunar calendar. The festival highlight is the procession of large boats, an Islamic symbol for the journey toward spiritual enlightenment, through the city's labyrinthine streets. Entertainment includes tahtib, or a stick fight accompanied by beating drums, horse races, dance, and music.

The shaykh, though born in Damascus, is highly honored in Luxor, where he established a spiritual retreat, or *zawiyah*.

CONTACTS:
Tour Egypt
20-95-382215 or 20-95-383294
www.luxorguide.com

SOURCES:
UndIslam-2004, p. 389

♦ 1795 ♦ **Munich Opera Festival**
July

Although Munich, Germany, may be best known for its OKTOBERFEST, it is also the home of one of the world's great opera festivals. The focus is on three composers who were associated with the city in some way: Richard Strauss (1864-1949), who was born there; Richard Wagner (1813-1883), some of whose operas premiered there; and Wolfgang Amadeus MOZART (1756-1791), some of whose operas were first performed in the rococo Residenz Theater, a former royal palace. But other operas have been staged there as well, particularly those by Gaetano Donizetti (1797-1848), Gioacchino Rossini (1792-1868), Ruggero Leoncavallo (1858-1919), Pietro Mascagni (1863-1945), and other Italian composers. About 16 operas are normally presented during the month-long festival, along with one or two ballets and a few recitals.

Most of the operas are staged in the Nationaltheater, home of the Bavarian State Opera. Some of the events take place in the Cuvilliés-Theater, a horseshoe-shaped rococo theater that was destroyed in World War II and then rebuilt according to its original plan. There is an hour-long intermission to allow patrons time to eat dinner.

CONTACTS:
Munich Opera Festival
Bavarian State Opera
Max-Joseph-Platz 2
Munich, D-80539 Germany
49-89-218-50-1; fax: 49-89-218-51-133
www.muenchner-opern-festspiele.de/233-UmVkU1lTX0Nv

SOURCES:
GdWrldFest-1985, p. 85
MusFestEurBrit-1980, p. 103

♦ 1796 ♦ **Muñoz-Rivera Day**
July 17

Luis Muñoz-Rivera was born on this day in 1859 in Barranquitas, Puerto Rico. A statesman, journalist, and patriot who devoted his life to the cause of Puerto Rican independence, Muñoz-Rivera was instrumental in obtaining Puerto Rico's charter of home rule from Spain in 1897 and served as secretary of state and later president of the first autonomist cabinet. However, when the United States put an end to his country's short-lived experiment with home rule, Muñoz-Rivera resigned. He eventually went to live in the U.S., where he continued to advocate Puerto Rican independence by publishing a magazine to acquaint North Americans with the plight of his homeland. He died in 1910 just before the passage of the Jones Bill, which gave Puerto Rico a large measure of self-government.

Muñoz-Rivera's birthday is a public holiday in Puerto Rico. His hometown of Barranquitas holds a three-day crafts fair every July that is timed to coincide with the birthday anniversary celebration. The fair tries to keep traditional skills and crafts alive by passing them on to the young.

CONTACTS:
Puerto Rico Tourism Company
135 W. 50th St., 22nd Fl.
New York, NY 10020
800-223-6530 or 212-586-6262; fax: 212-586-1212
www.gotopuertorico.com

Library of Congress
101 Independence Ave. S.E.
Washington, DC 20540
202-707-5000; fax: 202-707-8366
www.loc.gov

SOURCES:
AnnivHol-2000, p. 119
GdUSFest-1984, p. 218

♦ 1797 ♦ **Muscat Festival**
January to February

Muscat Festival has been sponsored annually since 1998 by the municipal government of Muscat, Oman. It takes place over several weeks in late January and early February. The festival is a showcase of Oman's traditional Arabian arts and culture, with a wide array of performances, exhibitions, sports, and children's activities, as well as such modern spectacles as a Formula 2 powerboat championship race. Over the course of the festival, which takes place at indoor and outdoor venues all over the city, as many as three million people take part.

CONTACTS:
Muscat Festival
www.muscat-festival.com

Oman Embassy
2535 Belmont Rd. N.W.
Washington, DC 02008
202-387-1980; fax: 202-745-4933

♦ 1798 ♦ **Mushroom Festival**
First weekend in May

Richmond, Missouri, isn't the only town that claims to be the "Mushroom Capital of the World." Kennett Square, Pennsylvania, and Stover, Missouri, share this distinction as well. But Richmond is known for its highly prized morel mushrooms, which resemble a deeply pitted or folded cone-like sponge at the top of a hollow stem. The highlight of the annual Mushroom Festival, which has been held in Richmond since 1980, is the Big Morel Contest. Other events include a parade, crafts, a carnival, mushroom eating, and much more. Mushroom hunters flock to the town's wooded areas in search of the morel, known as the "Golden Fleece of mushrooms" because it is hard to find and has never been successfully cultivated.

Widespread morel hunting during the festival has necessitated an informal code of ethics among hunters. The rules include asking permission to hunt on privately owned lands, avoiding damage to the delicate fungi by inadvertently "stomping" small morels concealed by leaves, and dividing the day's booty with one's fellow "morellers." Above all, the hunters must refrain from revealing where they found their prize-winning specimens.

CONTACTS:
Richmond Chamber of Commerce
107 N. Thornton
Richmond, MO 64085
816-776-6916; fax: 816-776-6917
cofcommerce.home.mchsi.com

♦ 1799 ♦ Music and Dance Festival, International
June-July

One of the most important music and dance festivals in Europe, the festival in Granada, Spain, celebrated its 50th year in 2001. It features an array of international orchestras and performers in settings of incomparable grandeur, such as the Alhambra (a 14th-century palace built for the Moorish kings), the adjoining Renaissance palace of Charles V, and the theater of the Generalife Gardens.

CONTACTS:
Festival Internacional de Música y Danza de Granada
Corral del Carbon, Calle Mariana Pineda s/n
Granada, 18009 Spain
34-958-221-844; fax: 34-958-220-691
www.granadafestival.org/index.asp

SOURCES:
GdWrldFest-1985, p. 162
IntlThFolk-1979, p. 337
MusFestEurBrit-1980, p. 136
MusFestWrld-1963, p. 165

♦ 1800 ♦ Mut l-ard
May 17

This is believed to be the first day of summer in Morocco, and the word *mut l-ard* means "death of the earth." Various rituals performed on this day by different tribes are designed to ward off evil and danger. For example, it is believed that rising at dawn and taking a bath will strengthen the body, and there is a taboo against sleeping, which is believed to result in a loss of courage. A special dish made from barley, fresh milk or buttermilk, and the root of a plant called *bûzeffur* is prepared and eaten on this day in the belief that it will make the people strong and ward off evil. In some areas it is believed that a husband's affections will waver on this day, and that the wife should therefore make herself as attractive as possible by using cosmetics.

SOURCES:
FolkWrldHol-1999, p. 359

♦ 1801 ♦ Myanmar Armed Forces Day
March 27

The Union of Myanmar, known as Burma until 1989, is in southeast Asia. It is bordered by China, Laos, Thailand, Bangladesh, and India.

Throughout most of the 1800s, Burma was ruled by the British. In 1819, the British invaded Burma and took over parts of the country. By 1886, they had control over the entire country and made it a province of India, which was also under British control.

In 1930 a Burman named Saya San led a major armed rebellion against the British. San was executed by the British, but he inspired other Burmese to demand independence.

Aung San, an outspoken student leader, continued the fight for Burma's independence. He was eventually arrested, but he escaped to China, where he collaborated with the Japanese. The Japanese promised San that if he helped to overthrow the British, they would make Burma an independent nation. San helped the Japanese oust the British, and the Japanese ruled Burma from 1942 until 1945. By then it had become clear to San that the Japanese had no intention of handing Burma back to its people. On March 27, 1945, he helped the World War II Allied forces remove the Japanese from power.

Today, Myanmar celebrates Armed Forces Day on March 27 to commemorate the day that Aung San rebelled against the Japanese. The day is celebrated with a military parade and fireworks. Since 1989, the Tatmadaw, the Myanmar military, has made it a tradition to pardon several prisoners on Armed Forces Day.

CONTACTS:
Myanmar Tourism Promotion Board
Marketing Committee
c/o Traders Hotel
Level 3, Business Centre
223 Sule Pagoda Rd.
Yangon, Myanmar
www.myanmar-tourism.com

♦ 1802 ♦ Myanmar Independence Day
January 4

The southeast Asian country of Burma, renamed Myanmar in 1989 by its military government, was under the control of the British for more than a century. During World War II, the Japanese captured Burma and created a puppet state, which came to an end when the Japanese were driven out at the end of the war in 1945. The Burmese people were unwilling to return to British rule, and when they were given their independence on January 4, 1948, they refused to join the British Commonwealth.

The capital, Yangon (formerly Rangoon), is decorated for the Independence Day festivities. Most of the people dress in their national costume, which consists of an *aingyi* (blouse or shirt) and a *longyi* (skirt). Women draw the longyi to one side, fold it back to the opposite side, and tuck it in at the waist, while men tie theirs in front. The Burmese are unusual in that they have kept their national dress longer than most other southeast Asian countries. Although men often wear regular Western shirts, on Independence Day they're more likely to put on their collarless Burmese shirts. A dish known as *pan-thay khowse* (noodles and chicken) is traditionally served on this day, as is *nga sak kin* (curried fish balls). The preferred beverage is tea.

CONTACTS:
Embassy of the Union of Myanmar
2300 S St. N.W.
Washington, D.C. 20008
202-332-3344; fax: 202-332-4351
www.mewashingtondc.com

SOURCES:
AnnivHol-2000, p. 4
NatlHolWrld-1968, p. 12

♦ 1803 ♦ **Myanmar Martyrs' Day**
July 19

The Union of Myanmar, known as Burma until 1989, is bordered by China, Laos, Thailand, Bangladesh, and India.

Throughout most of the 1800s, Burma was ruled by the British. Under British rule, the Burmese people were considered second-class citizens. Over time, this led to discontent among the Asian population, and they began to organize independence movements. Toward the turn of the century, in an effort to appease the Burmese citizens, the British gave them a bit more autonomy. However, this was not enough to satisfy the Burmese. In 1930, a Burmese man named Saya San led an armed rebellion against the British. San was executed by the British, but he served as an inspiration to other Burmese.

Aung San, a student at Rangoon University, was an outspoken proponent of Burmese independence. He collaborated with the Japanese to overthrow the British empire. The Japanese promised San that if he helped to overthrow the British, they would make Burma an independent nation. With San's help, the Japanese succeeded in removing the British from power in 1942. The Japanese then ruled Burma, but it soon became clear to San that the Japanese had no intention of handing Burma back to its people. He sided with the Allies during World War II, and on March 27, 1945, he helped them remove the Japanese from power.

The British granted Burma its independence in 1947. On July 13, 1947, Aung San gave his last public speech. In this speech, he urged his fellow Burmese to mend their ways and be more disciplined. On July 19, 1947, Aung San and six of his cabinet members, including his older brother, were assassinated during an Executive Council meeting. His political adversary, U Saw, was found guilty of participating in the assassinations and was later executed for his part in the killings.

July 19 has been declared Martyr's Day, a national holiday on which the people of Myanmar remember their slain leader Aung San. On this day, the country holds a moment of

silence, and a ceremony is held as family members of Aung San and the other assassinated cabinet members lay wreaths on their tombs.

Unfortunately, the promise of an independent nation was short-lived. Burma was initially a democratic republic until 1962, when General Ne Win led a military coup d'etat. Since that time, the country has been ruled by a military government. In 1990, multi-party elections were held and the main opposition won a landslide victory, but the repressive military junta refused to hand over power. The United States has refused to recognize the name Myanmar, which has been used since 1989 by the military government, and continues to use the nation's previous name, Burma.

Today, Aung San's daughter, Aung San Suu Kyi, has followed her father's lead. She is very involved in the political struggle for human rights and has called for a democratic government. She has been placed under house arrest several times. While under house arrest, she was awarded several awards for democracy and human rights, including the Nobel Peace Prize in 1991.

CONTACTS:
Myanmar Tourism Promotion Board
Marketing Committee
c/o Traders Hotel
Level 3, Business Centre
223 Sule Pagoda Rd.
Yangon Myanmar
www.myanmar-tourism.com

♦ 1804 ♦ **Myanmar Peasants' Day**
March 2

The Union of Myanmar, known as Burma until 1989, is in southeast Asia. It is bordered by China, Laos, Thailand, Bangladesh, and India. The population consists of 135 ethnic groups.

In the 1800s, Burma was conquered by Great Britain, which made it a province of India (also under British control). In the 1900s, Burma first became a self-governing colony then became independent in 1948. The country was initially a democratic republic until 1962, when General Ne Win led a military coup d'etat. Since that time, the country has been ruled by a military government. In 1990, multi-party elections were held and the main opposition won a landslide victory, but the repressive military junta refused to hand over power. The United States has refused to recognize the name Myanmar, which has been used since 1989 by the military government, and continues to use the nation's previous name, Burma.

The predominant industry in Myanmar is agriculture. At one point, Myanmar was the biggest exporter of rice in Asia, but now their line of agricultural products is more diverse— beans, peas, black matpe, maize, sesame and by products, Niger seeds, various spices (coriander, dry ginger, turmeric, red chili, onions, and more), timber, and rattan.

The country could not support these agricultural activities without the peasant workers. To show their appreciation for the peasants' contribution to Myanmar society, the country has declared March 2 Peasants' Day. It is a national holiday.

It was also on this day in 1962 that Burmese General Ne Win led the military coup. The country holds parades on this day to honor him.

CONTACTS:
Myanmar Tourism Promotion Board
Marketing Committee
c/o Traders Hotel
Level 3, Business Centre
223 Sule Pagoda Rd.
Yangon Myanmar
www.myanmar-tourism.com

♦ 1805 ♦ Myanmar Union Day
February 12

The Union of Myanmar, also known as Burma, has declared February 12 a national holiday. Union Day commemorates the day in 1947 that Bogyoke Aung San, a Burmese nationalist leader, helped to unify all of Burma.

When Britain annexed Burma in 1886, the country was not unified: central Burma was inhabited by Burmese people, while the outlying areas were inhabited by ethnic minorities. The British continued to govern Burma into the 20th century. In the 1930s, Aung San led student protests, causing the British government to imprison him. He fled to Japan in 1940, returning in 1941 with the invading Japanese as head of the Burma Independence Army (BIA). He later served as minister of defense in the puppet government headed by Ba Maw. Aung San became disillusioned with the Japanese and handed the BIA over to the Allies in 1945.

Aung San helped establish the Anti-Fascist People's Freedom League (AFPFL), the Burmese political organization that led the struggle for Burma's independence from Great Britain. He emerged after the World War II as de facto prime minister of British Burma and negotiated the agreement that won Burma its independence. On February 12, 1947, Aung San and leaders from national groups across the country signed the "Panglong Agreement." That action unified Burma and demanded that the British government restore independence to all of Burma. But Aung San did not live to see it: he was assassinated on July 19, 1947, before the country officially became independent on January 4, 1948.

Five days before Union Day, an annual relay of the Union flag begins. A ceremony to mark the start of the relay is held at City Hall. The flag is carried through 45 townships before arriving at People's Square on Pyay Road for a Union Day ceremony.

CONTACTS:
Myanmar Tourism Promotion Board
Marketing Committee
c/o Traders Hotel
Level 3, Business Centre
223 Sule Pagoda Rd.
Yangon Myanmar
www.myanmar-tourism.com

♦ 1806 ♦ Mystery Play (Elche)
August 14-15

El Misterio d'Elx, or the Mystery Play of Elche, is a medieval drama about the death and assumption of the Virgin Mary that takes place in August on the Feast of the ASSUMPTION in Elche, a town in Valencia, Spain. The first part of the play is performed on August 14, the day before the feast, and it deals with the death of the Virgin and the ascension of her soul to heaven on a throne, or *araceli*, carried by five angels. In the second part, performed on August 15, the Virgin is buried and the Gate of Heaven opens. The araceli descends a second time and takes the Virgin away. She is crowned at the heavenly portal while organ music plays, bells ring, and firecrackers explode.

The mystery play is performed from a raised platform in the sanctuary of the Church of La Merced. It is considered by many to be one of Spain's greatest religious dramatic survivals, and it is believed to date back to the early 13th century.

CONTACTS:
Valencia Tourist Office
Communitat Valenciana, Aptdo. de Correos 48
Burjassot, 46100 Spain
34-902-123-212; fax: 34-902-220-211
www.comunitat-valenciana.com

SOURCES:
FestEur-1961, p. 141
FestWestEur-1958, p. 203
SpanFiestas-1968, p. 164

♦ 1807 ♦ Mystery Play (Tibet)
January-February; last day of Tibetan year

Originally performed by a devil-dancing cult to drive out the old year along with its demons and human enemies, this annual dramatic presentation was known to Tibetans as the **Dance of the Red-Tiger Devil** and to Europeans as the **Pageant of the Lamas** or the Mystery Play of Tibet. Under Buddhist influence, it was seen as symbolizing the triumph of the Indian missionary monks, led by Padmasambhava (*see also* HEMIS FESTIVAL and PARO TSHECHU), over pagan devils, and more recently, it has been changed to represent the assassination of Lang-darma, the king who tried to rid Tibet of Lamaism. Despite its many transformations over the years, however, the play continues to retain the devil-dancing features of its earliest form.

It is performed on the last day of the year in the courtyards of Buddhist temples or monasteries and continues for two days. A group of priests in black miters is confronted by one group of demons after another, which they manage to exorcize. On the second day, a dough effigy representing the enemies of Tibet and Lamaism is dismembered and disemboweled. Pieces of the effigy are thrown to the audience, who eat them or keep them to use as talismans. The play is followed by a burnt offering and a procession.

See also LOSAR

CONTACTS:
Office of Tibet
Tibet House, 1 Culworth St.
London, NW8 7AF United Kingdom
44-20-7722-5378; fax: 44-20-7722-0362
www.tibet.com

SOURCES:
DictFolkMyth-1984, p. 777

N

♦ 1808 ♦ NAACP Image Awards
Early March

The NAACP Image Awards is an annual event held in March at a gala ceremony in Los Angeles that is broadcast during prime time on the Fox Television Network. The awards are presented by the National Association for the Advancement of Colored People, the long-established American civil rights organization. The awards recognize exceptional performances and achievements in the arts by people of color. They also honor outstanding champions of social justice. The 36 award categories include music, television, motion pictures, and literature, in addition to such honorary awards as the Chairman's Award, the President's Award, and the Image Awards Hall of Fame. Past winners form a roll call of exceptional achievers, from Stevie Wonder to Barak Obama.

The awards were established by the Beverly Hills/Hollywood branch of the NAACP in 1967, at the peak of civil-rights activism in the United States. Troubled by the generally negative portrayal of the black experience in popular media, the chapter founded the awards to honor the best actors, writers, producers, and directors of color, and to recognize those in the entertainment industry who supported them. The NAACP has long been involved in the struggle for greater and more positive representation of African Americans in popular media, beginning with a protest of the 1915 film *Birth of a Nation*, by D.W. Griffiths.

CONTACTS:
NAACP Image Awards
4929 Wilshire Blvd., Ste. 310
Los Angeles, CA 90010
323-938-5268; fax: 323-938-5045
www.naacpimageawards.net/main.html

SOURCES:
AAH-2007, p. 325

♦ 1809 ♦ Naadam
July 11-13

This Mongolian festival, sometimes spelled **Nadaam**, spotlights three major sports events. Its history goes back to the 13th century when Marco Polo described a gathering of 10,000 white horses. Mongolian chieftains, after meeting for parleys, competed in horse racing, archery, and wrestling, the "three manly games" for a Mongolian. Later, the fairs included women and were held in July or August when the pastures were lush and the horses well-fed.

Today Naadam is held from July 11 (Revolution Day, a legal holiday in Mongolia) to July 13 in provinces throughout the country. The chief Naadam is in the stadium in Ulaanbaatar, the capital. In Inner Mongolia (the Inner Mongolia Autonomous Region of China), Naadam is celebrated on July 20-26 on the Gogantala Pasture and at Lake Salim in the prefecture of Xinjiang. Other Naadams are held as people desire.

The fairs bring together the nomadic people who pitch a city of *yurts* or *gers*, felt tents. Wrestling is usually the first event; at Ulaanbaatar, several hundred participants make a grand entrance in special tight-fitting costumes that leave the chest bare, proving the wrestler is male, though today wrestlers often wear only tight shorts and boots. A legend has it that long ago many men were once defeated by a woman, thus the costume had to expose the chest. Titles awarded to top wrestlers are Falcon, Elephant, Lion, and Titan, and their prizes are silk scarves and horses.

The second sport is archery, a sport of great antiquity—sixth-century Mongols hunted hares with bows and arrows while riding at full speed. Modern contests are both on foot and horseback.

The last of the traditional sporting events is horse racing. In the national Naadam, the featured race is for children from around the ages of 6-10 who cover cross-country courses ranging from 5 to 30 kilometers. When night falls, a bowed stringed instrument called a *matouqin* is played, and people sit by their yurts talking, dancing, and drinking aromatic butter tea and *kumys*, a drink made of fermented mare's milk.

CONTACTS:
Mongolian Tourist Board
State Administrative Bldg.-14
Sambuu St.-11
Ulaanbaatar-38, 210628 Mongolia
976-11-318-493; fax: 976-11-318-492
www.mongoliatourism.gov.mn

United Nations Office in Mongolia
12 United Nations St.

P.O. Box 46/1009
Ulaanbaatar, 210646 Mongolia
976-11-327870; fax: 976-11-324683
www.un-mongolia.mn

SOURCES:
AnnivHol-2000, p. 115
FestWrld: Mongolia-1999, p. 20
FolkWrldHol-1999, p. 432
HolSymbols-2009, p. 605

♦ 1810 ♦ **Naag Panchami**
July-August; waxing half of Hindu month of Sravana

A Hindu festival celebrated throughout India and Nepal, dedicated to the sacred serpent, Ananta, on whose coils Vishnu rested while he was creating the universe. According to Hindu belief, snakes can bring wealth and rain, and unhappy ones can cause a home to collapse. Therefore milk and flowers are offered to snakes, especially cobras; snake deities; or painted snake images at shrines. Because snakes are also worn by Shiva, hundreds of snakes are released at the Shiva temples in Ujjain, Madhya Pradesh, where Shiva lived after destroying a demon, and in Varanasi, Uttar Pradesh, considered the religious capital of the Hindu faith. In Jodhpur, Rajasthan, huge cloth *naags*, or cobras, are displayed.

CONTACTS:
India Tourist Office
1270 Avenue of the Americas, Ste. 1808
New York, NY 10020
800-953-9399 or 212-586-4901; fax: 212-582-3274
www.indiatouristoffice.org

Nepal Embassy
2131 Leroy Pl. N.W.
Washington, DC 20008
202-667-4550; fax: 202-667-5534
www.nepalembassyusa.org

SOURCES:
BkFest-1937, p. 159
BkHolWrld-1986, Aug 8
CelebFestIndia-1994, p. 64
DictFolkMyth-1984, pp. 671, 921
DictWrldRel-1989, p. 431
FolkWrldHol-1999, p. 471
RelHolCal-2004, p. 171

♦ 1811 ♦ **Nabanna**
November to December; during the Hindu month of Agrahayana (Margasirsa)

The harvest festival of Nabanna (sometimes spelled **Navanna**) is a very popular ceremony among the Hindu rice growers of Bangladesh and West Bengal, India. It typically honors the Goddess Lakshmi, who symbolizes wealth and fertility, and takes place during Agrahayana, a Bangla month that falls between November and December.

According to folk custom, a community cannot enjoy the new rice crop until Lakshmi is first offered *nabanna* ("new food" or "new rice" in Bangla). Farmers will cut and husk a

special variety of rice and typically offer it prepared as rice porridge. In some cases, ancestral spirits and local deities are also the intended recipients of the offering. Other customs during the festival include greeting the moon with lamps, giving children gifts and sweetened milk, and offering rice and other types of food to crows. According to folklore, the flight patterns of the birds that pick up the food can foretell a community's fortunes.

The celebration in the capital, Dhaka, differs from those in agricultural regions, as residents employ the holiday to make a political statement and reassert Bangladesh's cultural independence from Pakistan.

CONTACTS:
Bangladesh Parjatan Corporation, National Tourism Organization
233 Airport Rd.
Tejgaon
Dhaka 1215 Bangladesh
www.bangladeshtourism.gov.bd

♦ 1812 ♦ **Nabekamuri Matsuri (Pan-on-Head Festival)**
May 8

The Nabekamuri or Pan-on-Head Festival held in Sakata at the Chikuma Shrine is one of the most unusual of all Japanese festivals. Its roots can be traced back to a time when a previously married woman arrived in Sakata balancing a pan on her head, perhaps to signify her domestic history. Today, about a dozen children march in a parade through town, wearing enormous papier-mâché pans on their heads that are tied under their chins. Other parade participants include lion dancers, people wearing Noh play costumes, flutists, and young girls carrying sacred mirrors.

CONTACTS:
Japan National Tourist Organization
1 Rockefeller Pl., Ste. 1250
New York, NY 10020
212-757-5640; fax: 212-307-6754
www.jnto.go.jp

SOURCES:
JapanFest-1965, p. 148

♦ 1813 ♦ **Nagoya City Festival**
October

An annual secular festival in Nagoya, Aichi Prefecture, Japan, started by the city's merchants in 1955 to give thanks for their prosperity. It features a parade of about 700 participants depicting historical figures in period costume, among them Oda Nobunaga, Toyotomi Hideyoshi, and Tokugawa Ieyasu, the three feudal warlords who unified the country at the end of the 16th century.

CONTACTS:
Nagoya Convention and Visitors Bureau
Nagoya Chamber of Commerce and Industry, Bldg. 11F
10-19, Sakae 2-Chome, Naka-ku
Nagoya, 460-0008 Japan
81-5-2201-5972; fax: 81-5-2201-5785
www.ncvb.or.jp/en/contents

♦ 1814 ♦ **Namahage Festival**
February 13-15 or weekend including second Sunday in February

A *namahage* is a man dressed as a demon, wearing a grotesque mask and cape made of straw, and carrying a wooden pail and a wooden kitchen knife. Namahages traditionally appear on New Year's Eve at residents' homes to warn children and new wives not to be lazy (*see* OMISOKA). In 1964 the city of Oga adapted what was originally, and still is, a community event that occurs in people's homes into a public festival that welcomes tourists. The Shinzan Shrine is the site for the festivities, also known as the **Namahage Sedo Matsuri** or the **Demon Mask Festival**. In the dark, tens of people disguised as namahage parade down from the mountains and head to the shrine for music and dancing. As early as the 12th century, priests at the shrine would make a fire and pray as they baked rice cakes for the namahage. Today a bonfire and rice cakes still await the arrival of the namahage.

CONTACTS:
Akita City Hall
1-1-1 Sanno
Akita, Akita Prefecture 010-0951 Japan
81-1-8866-2033; fax: 81-1-8866-2278
www.pref.akita.jp/e

SOURCES:
IllFestJapan-1993, p. 132
JapanFest-1965, p. 210

♦ 1815 ♦ **Namibia Heroes Day**
August 26

The Republic of Namibia, formerly South West Africa, is the 31st largest country in the world. There are 13 named regions in Namibia.

For over 100 years, Namibia was under oppressive occupation—first by the Germans, starting in 1884, and then by the Afrikaners of South Africa, starting in 1920. During both the German and South African occupations, the Namibian people lost rights to their land, minerals, and resources. Many were forced to work as indentured laborers or work on white-owned farms.

In 1946, the United Nations declared Namibia a trust territory, giving the country rights of self-determination, but South Africa was not willing to give up control. As the apartheid system of segregation spread across South Africa, Namibia was also affected. In 1966, the United Nations officially dissolved South Africa's authority over Namibia, but South Africa ignored this action and continued to rule Namibia.

August 26, 1966, marked the start of nearly 30 years of violence in Namibia. On this day, the South West Africa People's Organization (SWAPO) attacked a group of forces from the South African Colonial Apartheid regime at Ongulumbashe. For the next 24 years, the People's Liberation Army of Namibia (PLAN) and the South African Colonial Apartheid regime were at war. On March 21, 1990, Namibia officially gained independence from South Africa.

To honor those who lost their lives fighting for national freedom, Namibia has designated August 26 as Heroes' Day. On this day, thousands of Namibians gather at Ongulumbashe to celebrate. During this full day of celebration, representatives from all 13 regions give performances and cultural presentations, including traditional praise songs and dances. In addition, there is a re-enactment of the battle of Ongulumbashe, which concludes with the raising of the Namibian flag in the same manner as the real fighters did after each triumph during the war.

In Namibia's capital city of Windhoek, the Heroes' Acre national monument was erected to honor the freedom fighters.

CONTACTS:
Republic of Namibia
www.grnnet.gov.na

Namibia-1on1.com
www.namibia-1on1.com

♦ 1816 ♦ **Nanakusa Matsuri (Seven Herbs or Grasses Festival)**
January 7

A Japanese ceremony dating back to the ninth century, also called **Wakana-setsu** or **"Festival of Young Herbs,"** or **Jinjitsu** **"Man Day"** because it occurs on the zodiacal day for "man." After an offering to the clan deity in the morning, participants partake of *nanakusa gayu*, a rice gruel seasoned with seven different herbs that is said to have been served for its medicinal value to the young prince of the Emperor Saga (ruled 810-824). The herbs are shepherd's-purse, chickweed, parsley, cottonweed, radish, as well as herbs known as *hotoke-no-za* and *aona* in Japanese.

SOURCES:
DictFolkMyth-1984, p. 540
FolkWrldHol-1999, p. 83

♦ 1817 ♦ **Napa Valley Mustard Festival**
February and March

Since 1994, the Napa Valley Mustard Festival has been held in the Napa Valley of northern California. It is held in winter, when the wild mustard plant is in bloom. During this time, the wild mustard plant transforms the dormant vineyards of the region into rolling yellow and green expanses.

The Napa Valley region, known for its vineyards, began the festival to bring tourists to the area during the off season. It has since grown to be a regional celebration of the area's arts, food, and culture. The six-week long festival features art and photography contests, special gourmet dining events, a jazz concert, a marketplace at COPIA: The American Center for Wine, Food and the Arts featuring foods and mustards from around the world, the World-Wide Mustard Competition Awards Ceremony, and Napa Valley Chefs' Mustard Recipe Competition. The World-Wide Mustard Competition has 19 categories ranging from sweet-hot to classic Dijon. More than 500 restaurants, wineries, and food companies participate in the festival.

CONTACTS:
Napa Valley Mustard Festival
P.O. Box 3603
Yountville, CA 94599
707-944-1133
www.mustardfestival.org

♦ 1818 ♦ **Napoleon's Day**
May 5

Napoleon Bonaparte, emperor of France from 1804-15, is one of the most celebrated individuals in European history and still has many admirers in France. Often referred to as "Le Corse" (from Corsica, where he was born) or "Le Petit Caporal" (the little corporal) for his short stature, Napoleon is best known for the zeal with which he pursued the military expansion of France and for his reforms, which left a lasting mark on the judicial, financial, administrative, and educational institutions of not only France, but much of western Europe.

After finally abdicating in favor of his son on June 22, 1815, Napoleon was exiled to the island of St. Helena in the southern Atlantic with a small group of followers. He died there on May 5, 1821, at the age of only 51. But his legend grew, and in 1840 his remains were taken from St. Helena back to Paris, where a magnificent funeral was held. He was finally entombed under the gold-plated dome of the Church of Saint-Louis, one of the buildings in the compound of the Hôtel des Invalides, where his descendants and admirers still congregate on May 5 each year to attend a commemorative mass.

See also CAPE VINCENT FRENCH FESTIVAL

CONTACTS:
Paris Convention and Visitors Bureau
25 rue des Pyramides
Paris, 75001 France
33-8-9268-3000; fax: 33-1-4952-5300
en.parisinfo.com

Napoleon Foundation
148 Blvd. Haussmann
Paris, 75008 France
33-1-5643-4600; fax: 33-1-5643-4601
www.napoleon.org

SOURCES:
AnnivHol-2000, p. 77

♦ 1819 ♦ **Narak Chaturdashi**
October-November; 14th day of waning half of Hindu month of Kartika

The day after DHAN TERAS is celebrated by Hindus as Narak Chaturdashi. It is dedicated to Yama, the god of Naraka, or Hell. Bathing at dawn on this day is considered essential; in fact, those who bathe after the sun has risen risk losing their religious merit. After bathing, Hindus offer libations to Yama three times in the hope that he will spare them the tortures of hell. A fast is observed and in the evening, lamps are lit in Yama's honor.

SOURCES:
RelHolCal-2004, p. 179

♦ 1820 ♦ **Narcissus Festival**
January or February

A celebration in Honolulu, Hawaii, to usher in the Chinese or LUNAR NEW YEAR. There are a queen pageant and a coronation ball, Chinese cooking demonstrations, food booths, and arts and crafts exhibits. A parade features lion dances and fireworks. The first Narcissus Festival was held in 1950, narcissus blossoms being chosen as a symbol of hope that Chinese culture would have a renaissance in Hawaii.

CONTACTS:
Chinese Chamber of Commerce of Hawaii
70 N. King St., Ste. 202
Honolulu, HI 96817
808-533-3181; fax: 808-533-3184
www.chinesechamber.com

SOURCES:
BkFestHolWrld-1970, p. 26
GdUSFest-1984, p. 42

♦ 1821 ♦ **Nariyal Purnima (Coconut Day)**
July-August; full moon day of the Hindu month of Sravana

Nariyal (or Narali) Purnima, Coconut Day, is celebrated by Hindus in western India in the union territory of Daman and Diu, on India's west coast, and in the nearby state of Maharashtra at the end of the monsoon season. This is the time of year when the fishing and water-trade season begins again, and, in thanks, people gather at the shores and throw coconuts into the Arabian Sea as offerings to Varuna, the sea god. Why coconuts? For one thing, because the nut of the coconut appears to have three eyes, it is associated with the god Shiva, who is represented as having three eyes. For another, coconut kernals are a standard offering to the gods. Finally, many consider breaking a coconut to bring good luck to any new venture, such as the beginning of the trade season.

SOURCES:
DictFolkMyth-1984, p. 240
DictHindu-1977, p. 323
HinduRelCustManners-1960, p. 148
HinduRelYr-1921, p. 48
RelHolCal-2004, p. 172

♦ 1822 ♦ **Narsimha Jayanti**
April-May; 14th day of waxing half of Hindu month of Vaisakha

According to Hindu mythology, this is the day on which Vishnu appeared as the Narsimha, or Man-Lion, to free the world from the demon king, Hiranyakasipu. The king, who had forbidden the worship of anyone but himself, was very annoyed to discover that his own son, Prahlada, was an ardent devotee of Vishnu. He tortured Prahlada in an attempt to convert him, but the child remained unmoved in his devotion. Then the king tried to kill Prahlada by having him trampled by elephants and thrown off precipices, but again without success. Eventually Hiranyakasipu became so enraged that he rushed to kill Prahlada with his own sword, asking the child, "Where is your savior?" It was at this moment that Vishnu stepped from behind a nearby pillar in the form of Narsimha—half-lion, half-man—and tore the king to pieces.

On this day, Hindus fast, meditate, and pray for the spiritual fortitude of Prahlada. Sometimes they demonstrate the depth of their devotion by giving cows, grain, gold, robes, and other goods to the poor and the Brahmans as acts of charity.

SOURCES:
RelHolCal-2004, p. 169

♦ 1823 ♦ NASA Day of Remembrance
Last Thursday of January

To commemorate and honor those who have died in America's space program, NASA established the Day of Remembrance in 2004. The day particularly focuses on those astronauts who died in three NASA space tragedies: the three astronauts who died in the *Apollo 1* fire on January 27, 1967 (Roger Chafee, Gus Grissom, and Ed White); the seven astronauts who died in the Shuttle *Challenger* disaster of January 28, 1986 (Gregory B. Jarvis, Christa McAuliffe Ronald E. McNair, Ellison S. Onizuka, Judith A. Resnik, Francis R. Scobee, and Michael J. Smith); and the seven astronauts who died in the Shuttle *Columbia* tragedy of February 1, 2003 (Micahel P. Anderson, David Brown, Kalpana Chawla, Laurel Salton Clark, Rick D. Husband, William C. McCool, and Ilan Ramon). The day also remembers those NASA employees who died in training accidents, car crashes, and maintenance accidents, including the helicopter crew who perished while engaged in the Columbia debris recovery effort.

NASA headquarters in Washington, D.C., observes the day with remarks by a number of high-ranking officials and astronauts and a roll call of all those who have died. The event is broadcast by closed-circuit television to NASA facilities throughout the world. At Cape Canaveral in Florida, a minute of silence is observed at noon. Flags at all NASA facilities are flown at half-staff.

CONTACTS:
National Aeronautics and Space Administration
Ste. 5K39
NASA Headquarters
Washington, D.C. 20546-0001
202-358-0001; fax: 202-358-3469
www.nasa.gov

♦ 1824 ♦ Natal Day in Nova Scotia
First Monday in August

Several of Canada's provinces observe a holiday on the first Monday in August. In Halifax, the capital of Nova Scotia, and throughout the province, this day is known as Natal Day in celebration of the municipality's birthday. Its official name is **Alexander Keith's Natal Day**, in recognition of the prominent local brewer and politician who lived in the 19th century. The holiday's main organizer is the Halifax Regional Municipality.

In 1895, local leaders made plans for an official celebration to mark the arrival of the railway, slated for August of that year. In response to the news that the tracks had not yet been completed, the leaders decided to keep the date but alter the celebration to remember the municipality's birthday instead.

Family activities take place during the few days leading up to Natal Day. In Halifax there is a concert and a fireworks show at Angus L. Macdonald Bridge in the harbor. Dartmouth, a neighbor city, has in past years hosted its own fireworks show at Lake Banook Cove. It also hosts the Dartmouth Natal Day Road Race, a running competition held since 1907.

CONTACTS:
Alexander Keith's Natal Day Festival
Halifax-Dartmouth Natal Day Steering Committee
P.O. Box 1749
Halifax, NS B3J 3A5 Canada
www.natalday.org

SOURCES:
AnnivHol-2000, p. 145

♦ 1825 ♦ Natchez Spring and Fall Pilgrimages
March-April and October

These events, held since 1932 in Natchez, Miss., attract about 75,000 people to tour the county's antebellum houses. Women in hoop skirts welcome visitors to the mansions and their gardens of azaleas, camellias, olive trees, and boxwood hedges.

Natchez, situated on 200-foot bluffs overlooking the Mississippi River, was named for the Natchez Indians. It was founded by the French in 1716, and was the first European settlement on the river. It had a golden era in the 60 years after Mississippi became a territory in 1798. The town was an important river port, and wealthy citizens had vast plantations and built magnificent homes. Thirty-one of these, some owned by descendants of the original families, are open for the spring tours. They include such spectacular homes as Longwood, the largest octagonal house remaining in the United States, and Auburn, an imposing mansion with a free-standing stairway to the second floor.

Besides the tours, there are candlelight dinners in Magnolia Hall, a mansion that houses a costume museum, and presentations four times a week of the "Confederate Pageant," a lavish musical with local performers in costume presenting vignettes of the Old South. "Southern Road to Freedom," presented by the Holy Family Choir, is a musical tribute to the struggles and victories of African Americans in Natchez from colonial days to the present, and is performed three times a week.

During the celebration in October, there is another mansion tour. During the three-week Natchez Fall Pilgrimage there are 18 homes open to tours.

CONTACTS:
Natchez Pilgrimage Tours
640 S. Canal St.
P.O. Box 347
Natchez, MS 39121
800-647-6742 or 601-446-6631; fax: 601-446-8687
www.natchezpilgrimage.com

SOURCES:
GdUSFest-1984, p. 101

◆ 1826 ◆ Natchitoches Christmas Festival
Late November through New Year's Eve

Named after a Native American tribe, Natchitoches (pronounced *Nack-a-tish*) is the oldest permanent settlement in the Louisiana Purchase Territory. It is also home to one of the oldest community-based holiday celebrations in the country. Since 1927, both townspeople and visitors have made the festival a fixture in their holiday routine.

The Natchitoches Christmas Festival keeps families entertained for over six weeks. The Festival of Lights, held the weekend before Thanksgiving, opens the season with a brilliant display of Christmas lights in the Downtown Historic District. Natchitoches coordinates with Shreveport-Bossier City, Louisiana, and six Texas cities to join together a Trail of Lights that stretches between all the municipalities.

The Christmas Festival, which draws more than 100,000 people, is the premier event of the festival season. The Christmas Festival is observed with a parade, an assortment of river bank booths, arts and crafts, and a traditional fireworks show over Cane River Lake. The fireworks tradition dates as far back as the late 1930s.

The festivities continue up until the New Year's Eve celebration, with guided tours of holiday homes, nightly excursions by streetcar or carriages, and additional fireworks shows that are held each Saturday evening.

CONTACTS:
Natchitoches Convention and Visitor's Bureau
781 Front St.
Natchitoches, LA 71457
800-259-1714; fax: 318-352-2415
www.christmasfestival.com

◆ 1827 ◆ Nations, Festival of (Minnesota)
First weekend in May

Minnesota's largest ethnic celebration, the Festival of Nations takes place in St. Paul, a city of great ethnic diversity. Nearly 100 different ethnic groups (up from 65 in the 1980s) participate in this event, which has been presented by the International Institute of Minnesota since 1932 and features costumes, folk craft demonstrations, and cultural exhibits. Folk dance and music performances run continuously and showcase performers from Greece, Egypt, Ireland, Polynesia, Norway, Ecuador, Armenia, and many other countries.

Food is one of the festival's main attractions. Past offerings have included sausage with kraut (Czech), falafel sandwiches (Palestinian), beef pita pockets (Oromo people of Ethiopia and Kenya), spinach pie (Egyptian), choux a la creme (French strawberry cream puff), and syrnyk (Ukrainian cheesecake). Visitors who are thirsty can find mango milk shakes (Indian), green tea (Japanese), and egg coffee (Finnish). Sidewalk cafes serve authentic food from more than four dozen countries.

CONTACTS:
International Institute of Minnesota
1694 Como Ave.
St. Paul, MN 55108
651-647-0191; fax: 651-647-9268
www.iimn.org

SOURCES:
GdUSFest-1984, p. 97

◆ 1828 ◆ Nations, Festival of (Montana)
Eight days beginning first Saturday in August

A celebration of the multi-ethnic heritage of Red Lodge, Mont. In its early days, Red Lodge was a coal-mining town where miners who came from a number of European nations established their own communities. This festival began in 1950 to honor the different ethnic traditions. Today there is dancing, singing, and eating. Special foods are served by representatives of England, Scotland, Ireland, Wales, Germany, Finland, the Scandinavian countries, Italy, and the several nationalities that made up the former Yugoslavia. Eight days of events wind up with an All Nations Parade followed by a street dance.

CONTACTS:
Red Lodge Area Chamber of Commerce
601 N. Broadway
P.O. Box 988
Red Lodge, MT 59068
888-281-0625 or 406-446-1718
www.redlodgechamber.org

SOURCES:
GdUSFest-1984, p. 108

◆ 1829 ◆ Native American Ceremonies in June at Devils Tower
June

Devils Tower is an 867-foot-tall rock formation located in northeast Wyoming. For centuries, it has been the sacred site of Native American religious and cultural ceremonies. These include vision quests, sweat-lodge rites, prayer offerings, pipe ceremonies and the group ritual known as the Sun Dance. The Lakota Sioux, Cheyenne, Eastern Shoshone, Crow and Kiowa are among more than 20 Native American tribes that honor Devils Tower as a holy place and a vital cultural resource. In more recent times, Devils Tower also has become a popular site for tourists and for rock climbers.

June is an especially active and significant month for Native American ceremonies at Devils Tower because of the occurrence of the summer solstice. On June 21, various tribes hold private and sacred services at the tower's base. As a result, in

1995 the U.S. National Park Service, which maintains the tower as a national monument, asked climbers to refrain voluntarily from visiting during June in order not to disrupt religious ceremonies. In 1996, the Park Service also banned guided tours during June. Though these moves were controversial, with at least one law suit filed in response, many climbers respect the voluntary ban. Park officials have noted a decrease of up to 85 percent of normal climbing activity in June.

CONTACTS:
Devils Tower National Monument
P.O. Box 10
Devils Tower, WY 82714
307-467-5283; fax: 307-467-5350
www.nps.gov/archive/deto/home.htm

♦ 1830 ♦ **Native American Music Awards (Nammys)**
October 4

Begun in 1998, the Native American Music Awards (nicknamed the **Nammys**) honor the best musicians and composers in the Native American and aboriginal music fields. Sponsored by the Native American Music Association, the Nammys promote Native American music by bringing it to the attention of a national audience.

The Nammys honor some 30 categories of music, ranging from Artist of the Year and Best Female Artist to Flutist of the Year and Best Pow Wow Recording. Some of the categories are specific to traditional Native American music. Other categories are more general, covering Native American artists who perform rock, jazz, or New Age music. Some 200 recordings are typically evaluated for the awards. The awards show, which takes place at a casino, has been broadcast on satellite television.

The Native American Music Association also maintains the world's largest archive of Native American music, containing 7,000 recordings. It promotes the hiring and training of Native Americans in the music and performance industries and presents musical concerts throughout the United States.

CONTACTS:
Native American Music Association
511 Avenue of the Americas, # 371
New York, NY 10011
212-228-8300; fax: 646-688-6883
www.nativeamericanmusicawards.com/index.cfm

♦ 1831 ♦ **Native Islander Gullah Celebration**
February

The Native Islander Gullah Celebration takes place annually over four weekends in February on Hilton Head Island, S.C. The event showcases the rich history and heritage of the island's Gullahs, the name for people of African origin inhabiting the islands and coastal areas of the southeastern United States. The word also refers to the language of these people, a rich mix of English and various African languages. The event was founded in 1996 to promote economic opportunities for minority business owners in Hilton Head and to boost tourism to the area, as well as to highlight Gullah arts, crafts, food, and history.

Entertainment at the celebration includes storytelling, traditional gospel music, African dance, and popular R&B and jazz. An expo provides demonstrations in such traditional arts and crafts as sweet-grass basket-making, indigo dying techniques, African "long-strip" quilting, and weaving fish nets. Other events include film and theatrical presentations and literary celebrations, with an emphasis on the vivid folklore, superstitions, and oral traditions of the Gullahs. A cultural symposium sponsors panel discussions of the Gullah language and culture.

CONTACTS:
Hilton Head Island Gullah Celebration
P.O. Box 23452
Hilton Head, SC 29925
843-689-9314 or 877-650-0676
www.gullahcelebration.com

Native Business and Community Affairs Association, Inc.
21 Cardinal Rd., Ste. 105
Hilton Head Island, SC 29926
843-689-9314

♦ 1832 ♦ **Nativity of the Blessed Virgin Mary, Feast of the**
September 8

Only three births are celebrated in the whole Christian calendar: the Virgin Mary's, St. John's on June 24, (ST. JOHN'S DAY), and Jesus Christ's on December 25 (CHRISTMAS). Although it is not known where the September 8 date of Mary's birth originated, it seems to have been established by the end of the seventh century. In the Coptic and Abyssinian churches, the first day of every month is celebrated as the birthday of the Virgin Mary.

There are a number of legends describing the Virgin Mary's birth. Most early works of art show Mary and her mother, Anne, surrounded by elaborate furnishings and ancient Hebrew decorations, with a choir of angels hovering overhead. There are more festivals in honor of Mary than of any other saint—among them the Feasts of the IMMACULATE CONCEPTION the ANNUNCIATION, the Purification or CANDLEMAS, and the VISITATION.

In Malta there is a regatta in the capital, Valletta, in celebration of the defeat of the Turks by the Knights of St. John of Jerusalem on this day in 1565, and the end of the Axis siege in 1943 (*see* VICTORY DAY).

In northern Europe, the **Feast of the Nativity of Our Lady** functioned as a traditional harvest festival—a time to give thanks to Mary for the bounty of the fields and to ask her to protect the crops until they were harvested. Native Americans in the United States often observe September 8 with traditional Indian harvest dances in Mary's honor, following mass in the local Roman Catholic mission church.

CONTACTS:
The Mary Page
Marian Library/International Marian Research Institute

University of Dayton
Dayton, OH 45469
937-229-4214; fax: 937-229-4258
www.udayton.edu

Malta National Tourist Organization
65 Broadway, Ste. 823
New York, NY 10006
212-430-3799; fax: 425-795-3425
www.visitmalta.com

SOURCES:
DaysCustFaith-1957, p. 232
FestWestEur-1958, p. 70
FolkWrldHol-1999, p. 553
IndianAmer-1989, pp. 289, 301
OxYear-1999, p. 365
RelHolCal-2004, p. 100
SaintFestCh-1904, p. 400

♦ 1833 ♦ Nativity of the Blessed Virgin Mary, Feast of the (Germany)
September 8

Farmers of the Black Forest region of Germany customarily bring their horses to St. Märgen on this day to be blessed by the local priest. The horses wear traditional harnesses with well-polished brass, which are decorated with flowers. Streamers of ribbon are woven into their manes and tails. Both the farmers and their wives may wear the traditional costumes of the Black Forest valley.

Long known as the center of a famous horse-breeding area, St. Märgen is especially noted for the sturdy horses that work the neighboring farms. September 8, the Feast of the NATIVITY OF THE BLESSED VIRGIN MARY, is known in the Black Forest region as **Pferdeweihe**, or the **Blessing of Horses**.

SOURCES:
FestWestEur-1958, p. 70

♦ 1834 ♦ Nativity of the Blessed Virgin Mary, Feast of the (Peru)
September 8

The Feast of the NATIVITY OF THE BLESSED VIRGIN MARY is widely celebrated in Peru, with festivities often beginning on September 1 and lasting for more than a week. It is one of only three birthdays observed by the Roman Catholic Church, the others being CHRISTMAS and John the Baptist's birthday (*see* ST. JOHN'S DAY).

Several towns in the Mantaro Valley of the Huancayo area hold large fiestas in honor of the Virgen of Cocharcas in the days surrounding September 8. In the village of Sapallango, for example, the festival includes a dance reenactment of the death of an Incan ruler, fireworks, and bullfights. Other Peruvian areas that celebrate the Virgin's nativity include Cuzco, Chumbivilcas, Cajamarca, and Loreto.

CONTACTS:
Commission for the Promotion of Peru
Calle Uno Oeste No. 50, piso 13th
Urb. Corpac

Lima, 27 Peru
51-1-4224-3131; fax: 51-1-224-7134
www.promperu.gob.pe

SOURCES:
FiestaTime-1965, p. 137

♦ 1835 ♦ Nativity of the Theotokos
September 8

The Greek word *theotokos* means "god-bearer," or "mother of God." The feast known as the **Nativity of Our Most Holy Lady, the Theotokos** (or simply as the Nativity of the Theotokos) is observed in Orthodox Christian churches on September 8. Western Christian churches celebrate the feast on the same day, but call it the NATIVITY OF THE BLESSED VIRGIN MARY.

The feast of Mary's nativity is believed to have originated in the East, probably in Syria or Palestine, some centuries ago. It was already a major celebration in Jerusalem by the end of the fifth century, and by the seventh century it had become established in the Roman liturgy. By the 11th century, the observation of this feast had spread throughout the Christian world.

Mary was declared to be *Theotokos* as a result of the Council of Ephesus, held in 431. A major item on the Council's agenda was the theological controversy over Mary: Was she the mother of the incarnate Son of God, or had she given birth to a human being who was later united to the Son of God? The Council condemned the latter viewpoint as heretical.

CONTACTS:
Greek Orthodox Archdiocese of Australia
242 Cleveland St.
Redfern, NSW 2016 Australia
61-2-9698-5066; fax: 61-2-9698-536
www.greekorthodox.org.au

♦ 1836 ♦ Nauru Independence Day
January 31

This island in the Pacific Ocean gained independence from Great Britain on January 31, 1968. It had been governed by Australia. Independence Day is a national holiday in Nauru.

CONTACTS:
Nauru, Permanent Mission to the U.N.
800 Second Ave., Ste. 400D
New York, NY 10017
212-937-0074; fax: 212-937-0079
www.un.int

SOURCES:
NatlHolWrld-1968, p. 19

♦ 1837 ♦ Navajo Mountain Chant
Nine days at the end of winter

Among the Navajo Indians of Arizona, the nine-day Mountain Chant marks a transition in the seasons. It takes place in late winter, at the end of the thunderstorms but before the spring winds arrive. The chant is also considered a healing ceremony, performed not only for individuals who are sick but to restore order and balance in human relationships.

The Mountain Chant is based on a legend that chronicles the adventures of Dsilyi Neyani, the eldest son of a wandering Navajo family. He is captured by the Utes while hunting one day, but he manages to escape. During his long journey to rejoin his family, he encounters many hazards and learns a great deal about magic and ceremonial acts—rituals that play an important role in the Mountain Chant. He is gone so long that when he finally returns, his family is now the size of a tribe and relaying his adventures to them takes several days. The rituals he brings back are so compelling that messengers are immediately dispatched to find more witnesses to what he has learned.

The Chant consists of four ceremonies, all based on the same legend. Perhaps the most moving ceremony takes place on the final day, when the medicine man emerges from the lodge or hogan at sunset and begins to chant, while a circle of evergreens eight to ten feet tall—each concealing a man holding the tree—moves to create a circular enclosure with a bonfire in the center. The bonfire is lit, and later in the evening dancers whose bodies are covered in white clay (to protect their skin from the heat) rush into the circle and perform.

CONTACTS:
Navajo Tourism Department
P.O. Box 663
Window Rock, AZ 86515
928-810-8501; fax: 928-810-8500
www.discovernavajo.com

SOURCES:
DancingGods-1931, p. 208
HolSymbols-2009, p. 615

♦ 1838 ♦ **Navajo Nation Fair at Window Rock**
Early September

The Navajo Nation Fair at Window Rock is a five-day gala billed as the "World's Largest American Indian Fair," held in Window Rock, Ariz., the capital of the Navajo Nation. More than 100,000 visitors attend the fair, which dates back to 1947. It features a parade through the Window Rock area and a rodeo with more than 900 cowboys and cowgirls from eight different Indian rodeo associations. Other events include horse races, an inter-tribal powwow, a Miss Navajo Nation competition, an Indian fry-bread contest, a baby contest, country and western dances, Indian song and dance competitions, and agricultural and livestock exhibits. Arts and crafts exhibits are also part of Navajo fairs: the Navajos are famous for turquoise and silver jewelry, sand paintings, and woven rugs. The art of weaving was taught to Navajo women, their lore says, by Spider Woman, one of the Holy People from the underworld.

The Navajo Reservation covers 17.5 million acres and is the largest in the United States.

See also SHIPROCK NAVAJO NATION FAIR

CONTACTS:
Navajo Nation Fair Office
P.O. Box 2370
Window Rock, AZ 86515
928-871-6647; fax: 928-871-6637
www.navajonationfair.com

SOURCES:
AmerBkDays-2000, p. 640
AnnivHol-2000, p. 164
IndianAmer-1989, p. 289

♦ 1839 ♦ **Navajo Night Chant**
Nine days in late fall or early winter

The nine-night ceremony known as the Night Chant or the Nightway (Yei Bei Chei) is believed to date from around 1000 B.C.E., when it was first performed by the Indians who lived in Canyon de Chelly (now eastern Arizona). It is considered to be the most sacred of all Navajo ceremonies and one of the most difficult to learn, because it involves memorizing many songs, prayers, and the complicated designs used in sand paintings. Like the NAVAJO MOUNTAIN CHANT, the Night Chant is basically a healing ritual, designed both to cure people who are sick and to restore the order and balance of human relationships within the Navajo universe.

The Night Chant begins when the medicine man—a combination doctor-priest who has learned the intricate and detailed practices that are essential to the chant—emerges from the lodge leading the dancers, who represent the gods. The medicine man intones a long healing prayer for those who are sick and performs several other ritual acts. Then the dancers begin. The chant itself is performed without variation and has a hypnotic effect on the listeners.

CONTACTS:
Navajo Tourism Department
P.O. Box 663
Window Rock, AZ 86515
928-810-8501; fax: 928-810-8500
www.discovernavajo.com

SOURCES:
DancingGods-1931, p. 233
EncyNatAmerRel-2001, p. 202
HolSymbols-2009, p. 619

♦ 1840 ♦ **Nawruz (Naw roz; No Ruz; New Year)**
Beginning about March 21 for 13 days

The first day of spring (*nawruz* means "new day") celebrated by all religious groups in Iran and Afghanistan. In India, it is celebrated by the Parsis as JAMSHED NAVAROZ. The holiday is pre-Islamic, a legacy of Zoroastrian Persia. It is also called **Ras al-Am**. In Afghanistan it is celebrated as **Nauruz**; in Kashmir as **Nav Roz**; and in Turkmenistan, it's **Novrus Bairam**. Nawruz is also celebrated in Kazakhstan, Kyrgyzstan, Uzbekistan, and Azerbaijan.

The origins of Nawruz are obscure, but it is generally thought to have been a pastoral festival marking the change from winter to summer. Legends have grown up around the holiday. In Afghanistan, where it is also **Farmer's Day**, an ugly old woman named Ajuzak is thought to roam around when Nawruz begins. If it rains on Nawruz, she is washing her hair and the spring plantings will thrive. The Achaemenid kings (559 B.C.E.-330 B.C.E.) are known to have celebrated Nawruz, probably with gift-giving. Farmers decorate their cows and come into the city for an annual agricultural fair with prizes. Betting on kite flying is a sport for later in the day.

A special event, *jandah bala kardan* ("raising of the standard"), is held on Nawruz at the tomb of Hazrat Ali in Mazar-i-Sharif in northern Afghanistan. The *jandah,* or standard, is raised in the courtyard of the shrine, and stays there for 40 days. Thousands visit the shrine to touch the staff to gain merit, and the sick and crippled touch it hoping for cures. The standard comes down at a time when a distinct kind of red tulip blooms and then soon fades; at this time, people visit friends and wish each other long lives and many children.

Buzkashi, the national game of Afghanistan, is usually played on Nawruz, especially in Mazar-i-Sharif. *Buzkashi* means "goat-grabbing," and the object of the game is for a team of horse riders to grab the carcass of a goat placed in a pit, carry it around a goal post, and put it back in the pit. The game is supposed to have developed on the plains of Mongolia and Central Asia, sometimes using a prisoner-of-war instead of a goat; now a dead calf is usually used. It's a ferocious game occasionally producing fatalities; there are several hundred horsemen (*chapandaz*) on each team, and they gallop at breakneck speed, lashing at horses and each other with special buzkashi whips.

Special Afghan dishes on Nawruz are *samanak,* a dessert made of wheat and sugar, and *haft-mewah* ("seven fruits")—a compote of walnuts, almonds, pistachio nuts, red and green raisins, dried apricots, and a fruit called *sanjet.*

In Iran, Nawruz is an event lasting 13 days, during which people wear new clothes, give gifts, and visit friends and relatives. Banquet tables traditionally hold seven foods starting with the letter S. Plates with sprouting wheat symbolize fertility, as do eggs, which are colored. Other symbols on the table are a mirror, candlesticks, and a bowl of water with a green leaf in it. The 13th day after No Ruz is Sizdah-Bedar or "13th day out" and everyone picnics in the country or on rugs in city parks. The idea is to get out of their houses, taking any bad luck with them.

For the Baha'i, the day also marks the end of the 19-day fast, from March 2-20, when Baha'i abstain from food and drink from sunrise to sunset as a reminder that one's true nature is spiritual rather than material.

See also AYYAM-I-HA

SOURCES:
BkFestHolWrld-1970, p. 7
BkHolWrld-1986, Mar 21
DictFolkMyth-1984, p. 869
EncyEaster-2002, p. 418
FolkWrldHol-1999, p. 218
HolSymbols-2009, p. 623

◆ 1841 ◆ Nawruz (Kazakhstan)
Around March 21

The people of Kazakhstan celebrate NAWRUZ around the time of the VERNAL EQUINOX. This holiday, rendered Nauryz in Kazakhstan, celebrates the start of the new year and is the most festive of all the nation's holidays. Indeed Kazakhs sometimes call it *Ulys Kuni,* meaning "the first day of the new year," or *Ulystyn uly kuni,* "the great day of the people."

Special activities take place to commemorate the occasion, including horse races, games, and all kinds of merrymaking. People dress in their best clothing, prepare large and tasty meals, exchange well-wishes and congratulations, and visit friends and family. Since the activities that take place on Nauryz are thought to foretell one's fortune for the year, people try to include an abundance of food and other good things in their celebrations.

The main meal takes place around noon, and is introduced and concluded by the mullah's recitation of, a prayer honoring the ancestors. At the end of the feast, the oldest male blesses all those present so that they may prosper in the year to come. The number seven is considered a lucky number for this festival. It represents the seven days of the week. In the course of the celebrations, elderly men will be presented with seven cups of a special festival beverage called *nauryz-kozhe.* The beverage is itself made from seven grades of seven different kinds of grain.

CONTACTS:
Permanent Mission of the Republic of Kazakhstan to the United Nations
866 United Nations Plz., Ste. 586
New York, NY 10017
212-230-1900; fax: 212-230-1172
www.un.int/kazakhstan

◆ 1842 ◆ Ncwala
December or January; actual date determined by astrologers

The most sacred of the national ceremonies of the independent kingdom of Swaziland, the Ncwala is the "first fruits festival." Held at the Royal Kraal (residence) at Ludzidzini outside the capital of Mbabane, it is a six-day ritualized festival of song, dance, folklore, and martial display, focusing on the king as the source of fertility and the symbol of power and unity.

In what is known as the "little iNcwala," representatives from the Bemanti people, having journeyed to the shores of the Indian Ocean in the neighboring country of Mozambique to gather foam from the water, return to the Kraal and the celebrating begins. Then, unmarried young men go out to the countryside to collect branches of the lusekwane shrub (a kind of acacia) which will be used in the bonfire at the end of the festival.

During the main ceremony, warriors dance and chant to persuade the king (who has secluded himself) to return to his people. He finally appears wearing a black-plumed headdress, dances the king's dance and eats part of a pumpkin, paving the way for all to enjoy the harvest. On the last day people feed a bonfire with bedding and other items from the old year, a cleansing for a fresh start to the new agricultural year.

CONTACTS:
Swaziland Ministry of Tourism
Income Tax Bldg., 2nd Fl.
P.O. Box 2652
Mbabane, Swaziland
268-404-4556; fax: 268-404-5415
www.gov.sz

SOURCES:
BkHolWrld-1986, Dec 22
FolkWrldHol-1999, p. 546

♦ 1843 ♦ **N'cwala**
February 24

In 1835 the Ngoni tribe, an offshoot of the Zulus, left South Africa and moved into what is now the country of Zambia. The festival known as N'cwala celebrates the tribe's satisfaction with its environs since that time and also marks the beginning of the harvest. This is a festival of thanksgiving and people congregate in the village of Mutenguleni, including the paramount chief, where the celebration takes place on February 24. Groups of dancers display their skills for the paramount chief, who traditionally chooses one group as having outdone the others, which is no small feat, given that Ngoni dancers are renowned throughout the region. The chief is also responsible for being the first to sample the season's new foods and blessing it for the people.

CONTACTS:
Zambia National Tourist Board
Lusaka Sq., Cairo Rd.
P.O. Box 30017
Lusaka, Zambia
260-1-229087; fax: 260-1-225174
www.zambiatourism.com

SOURCES:
CelebFestCarnFeast-1997, p. 12
WildPlanet-1995, p. 212

♦ 1844 ♦ **NEBRASKAland DAYS**
12 days in mid-June

This celebration of Nebraska's Western heritage is held in North Platte, the home of Colonel William "Buffalo Bill" Cody. This famous buffalo hunter, U.S. Army scout, and Indian fighter eventually became a touring showman, organizing his first Wild West exhibition in 1883. His stars included Annie OAKLEY and Chief Sitting Bull. Since 1965 the NEBRASKAland DAYS celebration has honored North Platte's most famous citizen by bestowing the Buffalo Bill Award on a well-known Western film star. Past winners have included Andy Devine, Gene Autry, Henry Fonda, Slim Pickens, and Wilford Brimley.

Other highlights of the festival include the Buffalo Bill Rodeo; the Frontier Review, which tells the story of the West

in song and dance; entertainment by top country and western performers; a parade; and a Chuckwagon Pork Breakfast.

CONTACTS:
NEBRASKAland DAYS
509 E. 4th
P.O. Box 706
North Platte, NE 69103
888-313-5606 or 308-532-7939; fax: 308-532-3789
www.nebraskalanddays.com

♦ 1845 ♦ **Nebuta Matsuri**
August 2-7

Nebuta Matsuri, the main festival of Aomori Prefecture in Japan, features processions of huge, elaborately painted papier-mâché figures called *nebuta.* The festival supposedly originated when Sakanoue-no-Tamuramaro (758-811) was sent here to put down a rebellion. He won by raising dummy soldiers along the skyline, making the enemy think his army was bigger than it was.

Today in the capital city of Aomori, the nebuta figures, up to 49 feet wide and 26 feet high, depict ferociously scowling samurai warriors. Illuminated from within by candles, they glow as they are carried through the streets at nightfall. Spectators wear hats made of flowers and dance in the streets.

A similar but smaller festival is held in Hirosaki Aug. 1-7. Here, the nebuta are fan-shaped and depict warriors on one side and beautiful women on the other.

CONTACTS:
Aomori Tourism and Convention Association, Aomori Nebuta
    Excutive Committee
4F, Aomoriken-Shoko-Kaikan
2-2-17 Hashimoto, Aomori-shi
Aomori, 030-0823 Japan
81-1-7723-7211; fax: 81-1-7723-7215
www.nebuta.jp

Aomori City Office
22-5 chuo 1 chome
Aomori, 030-0822 Japan
81-1-7734-1111
www.city.aomori.aomori.jp

Japan Information Network, Japan Center for Intercultural
    Communications
2-7-7 Hirakawacho
Chiyodaku
Tokyo, 102-0093 Japan
81-3-3263-5041; fax: 81-3-3230-4107
home.jcic.or.jp

SOURCES:
JapanFest-1965, p. 174

♦ 1846 ♦ **Neighbor Day**
Sunday before Memorial Day weekend

In 1993, following a local hate crime incident between teenagers that left one dead and another in jail, the town of Westerly, R.I., instituted Neighbor Day to promote the idea that all citizens should "Love Thy Neighbor as Thyself."

Citizens of Westerly celebrate Neighbor Day by getting to know better other people in their community. Town officials and local business leaders sponsor and host social gatherings to foster interactions between residents. Private individuals host open houses for their neighbors and friends. Friendly contacts via mail, email, or telephone are also encouraged.

The concept of a Neighbor Day has been promoted by Westerly and adopted in several other cities: Providence, R.I., celebrates a National Neighborhood Day, while Seattle, Wash., celebrates a Neighbor Appreciation Day.

CONTACTS:
Town Clerk, Town Hall
45 Broad St.
Westerly, RI 02891
fax: 401-348-2571
www.neighbordayworldwide.com

♦ 1847 ♦ **Nemean Games**
Probably August

Ancient Greek games, one of four ancient Greek festivals involving games, held every second year in the sanctuary of Zeus in the valley of Nemea in the northeastern part of the Greek Peloponnesus. Little is known of these games before 573 B.C.E. Legend says they may have been originated by Hercules after he slew the lion of Nemea—one of his 12 labors. He killed the lion by driving it into a cave and strangling it. The games consisted of gymnastic, equestrian, and musical contests. Winners were crowned with a garland of wild celery.

See also ISTHMIAN GAMES; PYTHIAN GAMES; and OLYMPIC GAMES

SOURCES:
ClassDict-1984, p. 399
GdAnctWrld-1986, p. 427
OxClassDict-1970, p. 726

♦ 1848 ♦ **Nemoralia**
August 13

The Nemoralia was an ancient Roman festival in honor of the goddess Diana held at Nemi, in the territory of Aricia about 16 miles southeast of Rome. As the goddess of the hunt, Diana presided over the forests of Aricia. There was a grove, or *nemus,* there that adjoined a famous shrine dedicated to the goddess, and her priest was known as *rex nemorensis,* or "king of the grove." By custom, the rex nemorensis was a runaway slave who attained his royal office by murdering his predecessor.

Diana was worshipped throughout Rome and Latium (now western Italy) on August 13, the day on which her temple on the Aventine Hill had been dedicated by Servius Tullius. But her most famous cult was in Aricia, where the Nemoralia was observed to protect the vines and the fruit trees as well as to celebrate Diana's power. Some experts believe that the Christian Feast of the Dormition, or ASSUMPTION on August 15, eventually incorporated the harvest-blessing element of the ancient Nemoralia. It is still common in some parts of the

Orthodox Christian Church for worshippers to make offerings of new wheat and cakes to the Theotokos on that day.

SOURCES:
ClassDict-1984, p. 400
DictRomRel-1996, p. 60
EncyRel-1987, vol. 4, p. 349
FestRom-1981, p. 173
FestSaintDays-1915, p. 173
GdAnctWrld-1986, pp. 64, 427
OxYear-1999, p. 331
RomFest-1925, p. 198

♦ 1849 ♦ **Nenana Ice Classic**
Late February

Alaska's oldest tradition, a legal game that allows people to bet on when the massive ice cover on the Tanana River will break up. The Classic is kicked off in late February in Nenana (which has a population of about 570) with a winter carnival known as Tripod Days. At this time, a 1,500-pound spruce tripod is set into the ice of the Tanana River with a rope leading to a watchtower and clock. Two to three months later when the ice starts to move, a siren will sound, and when the tripod has moved 100 feet downstream, a meat cleaver stops the hands of the clock. This becomes the official time of the breakup. This setup of tripod, tower, clock, and cleaver has been the same since 1936 and has never failed.

Throughout Alaska, people place $2.50 bets in red gas cans with their predictions on the month, day, and hour of the ice's breakup. In early April, Nenana residents collect and sort the tickets. The earliest breakup ever recorded was April 20, 1940, at 3:27 A.M., and the latest May 20, 1964, at 11:41 A.M.

Wagering on the Nenana River ice began informally in 1906 when Jimmy Duke, owner of a roadhouse on the banks of the Tanana, started wagering with his chum Adolph "Two Cord" Nelson on the breakup day. In 1913, railroad engineers surveying the site for a bridge got in on the betting, and a pool started. In 1917, they started keeping records, and that year has been marked as the first official year of the Nenana Ice Classic. Now it's part of Alaskan lore, and the red betting cans are sometimes called the first spring flower. In 1990, 152,000 tickets were sold, and after deductions for taxes and expenses, the purse was $138,000. In 2000 the jackpot was worth a record-breaking $335,000.

CONTACTS:
Nenana Ice Classic
P.O. Box 272
Nenana, AK 99760
907-832-5446; fax: 907-832-5888
www.nenanaakiceclassic.com

♦ 1850 ♦ **Nepal Democracy Day**
February 18

Also known as **Rashtriya Prajatantra Divas**, this holiday commemorates the introduction of a democratic system of government in Nepal, which had been ruled by the Rana family since the mid-19th century.

Two other national holidays in Nepal are Unity Day, January 11—celebrating the unification of the various principalities into one country more than 200 years ago—and Constitution Day, November 8—observing the adoption of a new Nepalese constitution in 1990.

CONTACTS:
Embassy of Nepal
2131 Leroy Pl. N.W.
Washington, D.C. 20008
202-667-4550; fax: 202-667-5534
www.nepalembassyusa.org

SOURCES:
AnnivHol-2000, pp. 7, 29
NatlHolWrld-1968, p. 26

♦ 1851 ♦ **Neri-Kuyo**
August 16, every three years (2011, 2014…)

A Buddhist ceremony held every three years at Joshinji Temple in Tokyo, Japan, to celebrate the coming to earth of the Bodhisattvas. They are Buddhas-to-be who have undertaken a quest for enlightenment and have vowed to save all beings before they attain Buddhahood.

One of the best-known vows taken by a Bodhisattva is this:

Living beings are countless—
I vow to save them all.
Passions are inextinguishable—
I vow to extinguish them all.
Dharma truths are measureless—
I vow to master them all.
The Buddha-way is unexcelled—
I vow to attain it.

For the Neri-Kuyo in Tokyo, a curved wooden bridge is erected between two of the temple buildings, and local people dressed as Amitabha Buddha and 24 other Bodhisattvas file slowly across the bridge and back again. Wearing golden masks and haloes and fanned by attendants, they repeat this ceremony three times a day.

CONTACTS:
Japan National Tourist Organization
1 Rockefeller Pl., Ste. 1250
New York, NY 10020
212-757-5640; fax: 212-307-6754
www.jnto.go.jp

SOURCES:
DictWrldRel-1989, p. 112

♦ 1852 ♦ **Netherlands Military Tattoo**
September

The Netherlands Military Tattoo takes place every year over five days in September in Ahoy Rotterdam, the Netherlands. It is one of the biggest and best-known displays of military drumming, bag piping, band music, and precision marching in Europe. Drawing on long-standing military tradition, the Netherlands Military Tattoo has been performed for the public since 1978. The ticketed event takes place in an indoor arena.

The word tattoo derives from the Dutch phrase *Doe den tap toe*(literal translation: 'Turn off the taps'), because drummers used to be sent out into Dutch garrison towns at curfew to remind tavern keepers to turn off the beer taps so soldiers would return to barracks.

CONTACTS:
Stichting Nationale Taptoe
van Brederodekazerne
Postbus 10151
GC Vught 5260 The Netherlands
www.nationaletaptoe.nl

Netherlands Board of Tourism
355 Lexington Ave., 19th Fl.
New York, NY 10017
888-464-6552 or 212-370-7360; fax: 212-370-9507
holland.com

♦ 1853 ♦ **Nevis Tea Meeting**
Full moon night in summer

The pageant known as the **Tea Meeting** held on the island of Nevis in the West Indies probably developed from church fund-raising events in the 19th century. The characters include a King, his Queen, and their court. The King and Queen sit on a stage while costumed members of the audience get up and perform for them—singing, dancing, reciting poetry, or giving a speech. Tea (or some other hot drink) is served and ceremonial fruit, cakes, and kisses from the King and Queen are auctioned off. Then the King and Queen and their court give ironic speeches, followed by more audience acts. If there is enough participation from the audience, the pageant can go on all night. It is common for scoffers in the back of the room to make loud and obscene comments throughout the performance.

CONTACTS:
St. Kitts-Nevis Tourism Office
8720 Georgia Ave., Ste. 905
Silver Spring, MD 20910
877-533-1555 or 301-587-1555; fax: 301-587-0647

SOURCES:
FolkWrldHol-1999, p. 479

♦ 1854 ♦ **New Brunswick Day**
First Monday in August

Like several other Canadian provinces, New Brunswick has made the first Monday of August a provincial holiday. The official day, which legislation enacted in 1976, seeks to boost tourism to New Brunswick as well as shine a spotlight on local heritage. The site of the official celebration rotates each year.

The New Brunswick Department of Tourism, Recreation and Heritage organizes the heritage activities leading up to Monday, which typically entail flag-raising ceremonies, speeches by dignitaries, and live entertainment. In 1990, the department initiated a new tradition, the awarding of the New Brunswick Day Merit Award. This honor is bestowed on local citizens for their efforts in one of six categories: art and culture, business, community leadership, environment, sport and recreation, and volunteer services.

CONTACTS:
New Brunswick Day Celebration Committee
New Brunswick Provincial Capital Commission
103 Church St.
Fredericton, NB E3B 4C8 Canada
fetenbday.gnb.ca

♦ 1855 ♦ **New Church Day**
June 19

New Church Day refers to the Church of the New Jerusalem, founded in London in the late 18th century by the disciples of Emanuel Swedenborg, the Swedish scientist, philosopher, and theologian. In 1817, the General Convention of the New Jerusalem in the U.S.A. was founded in Philadelphia.

Swedenborg's followers believe that in 1757 there was a great judgment in the spiritual world, and that as a result the evil spirits were separated from the good and a new heaven was established. At that time Jesus called his apostles together and told them to preach the new doctrines in the new heaven, just as he had told them to do 16 centuries earlier on earth. All of this took place on June 19 and 20. June 19 is also the date on which Swedenborg's disciples met in 1770 to organize the Church of the New Jerusalem. Every year on this day members of the New Church, called Swedenborgians, meet to conduct important church business and to commemorate the church's founding.

CONTACTS:
New Church/General Church of the New Jerusalem
P.O. Box 743
Bryn Athyn, PA 19009
877-411-4673 or 215-914-4911
www.newchurch.org

SOURCES:
DaysCustFaith-1957, p. 148
DictWrldRel-1989, p. 728
RelHolCal-2004, pp. 129, 130

♦ 1856 ♦ **New Deal Festival**
Mid-July, one Saturday

The New Deal Festival celebrates the heritage of Arthurdale, W.Va., as the first of about 100 "New Deal" communities established during the Great Depression by President Franklin D. Roosevelt. In 1934 and 1935, the federal government resettled 165 disadvantaged families from nearby coal-mining communities to the 1,000-acre site that was named Arthurdale after its original owner, Richard Arthur. Families were settled in new homes with amenities then unusual for rural dwellers, such as electricity and indoor plumbing. They were encouraged to be self-sufficient by growing food and raising animals, and soon the town had established its own church, post office, and high school.

Such planned towns were a cherished project of First Lady Eleanor Roosevelt, and she visited Arthurdale many times to

distribute high school diplomas or Christmas gifts to residents. In 1985, residents established a heritage non-profit organization to purchase land and restore historic buildings to preserve the unique history of the community. They began to mark the town's founding and to celebrate its legacy with the New Deal Festival.

The festival features educational events, such as museum tours, lectures, and book signings. A mountain crafts and antique sale is held, and there are demonstrations of such skills as weaving and blacksmithing. Participants can enjoy live music and story-telling, an antique tractor and car display, and an appearance by "Eleanor Roosevelt," played by an actress.

CONTACTS:
Arthurdale Heritage, Inc.
P.O. Box 850
Arthurdale, WV 26520
304-864-3959
www.arthurdaleheritage.org

♦ 1857 ♦ **New England Folk Festival**
Third weekend in April

The first New England Folk Festival was held in 1944, and for 25 years it was held in different locations throughout New England. Now its permanent home is in Natick, Massachusetts, and all of the festival's events are held in and around Natick High School. The emphasis is on folk dancing: Morris dancing teams from all over the country perform at the festival, and there are square and contra dances, folk dance workshops, and many other events for folk dance enthusiasts. There are also instrumental jam sessions, national food booths, and displays of ethnic crafts, such as Ukrainian EASTER eggs and colored scrimshaw.

The festival is unusual in that those who attend are encouraged to participate by bringing along their musical instruments and joining in any impromptu or scheduled jam sessions or workshops. Attendees are also encouraged to dance with any group they choose.

CONTACTS:
New England Folk Festival Association
1770 Massachusetts Ave.
P.O. Box 282
Cambridge, MA 02140
781-662-6710; fax: 781-662-6730
www.neffa.org

SOURCES:
MusFestAmer-1990, p. 224

♦ 1858 ♦ **New Fire Ceremony**
Every 52 years

Among the ancient Aztec people of what is now Mexico, the year was divided into 18 months of 20 days each, plus a five-day "unlucky" period. There was also a ritualistic period of 260 days, which was composed of 13 months with 20 named days in each month. When one cycle was superimposed on the other, it resulted in a "century" of 52 years. Although festivals were observed each month, the most impressive and important occurred at the end of the 52-year cycle, when people feared that the world would be destroyed. It was known as the New Fire Ceremony because the old altar fire was extinguished and a new one was lit, symbolizing the new lease on life that the dawn of a new cycle represented.

Just before dusk on the day of the ceremony, all fires in the Valley of Mexico were put out. Huge crowds of people followed their priests from Mexico City to a temple several miles away on the Hill of the Star. Because the hill permitted them to view the heavens in all directions, it was here that the priests waited for a celestial sign telling them that the world would end or that a new century would begin. If the constellation known as the Pleiades passed the zenith, life would continue as it had. But if it failed to do so, the sun and stars would be changed into wild beasts who would fall to the earth and devour all the people, after which an earthquake would complete the destruction.

As soon as the heavenly signal received a favorable interpretation, burning torches were carried by runners throughout the valley to relight the fires in each house.

SOURCES:
DictFolkMyth-1984, p. 713
EncyRel-1987, vol. 2, p. 27

♦ 1859 ♦ **New Jersey Offshore Grand Prix**
August

Formerly known as the **Benihana Grand Prix Power Boat Regatta** and before that as the **Hennessy Grand Prix**, this race is not only one of the largest offshore power boat races in the country but a festival as well, with a beauty pageant, band concerts, and fireworks taking place at the popular beach resort of Point Pleasant. The race runs along the Atlantic coast of New Jersey attracting more than 250,000 spectators to the state's beaches.

When the regatta was first held in 1964, it covered a 265-mile course around Long Island. But it was eventually moved to the Jersey shore, where there were more open beaches and clear waterways. In addition to the large number of onshore spectators, about 3,000 power boats watch the race from the water.

CONTACTS:
New Jersey Offshore Powerboat Racing Association
Offshore Beach
Point Pleasant Beach, NJ 08742
732-583-8502
www.njoffshore.com

SOURCES:
GdUSFest-1984, p. 119

♦ 1860 ♦ **New Orleans Jazz and Heritage Festival**
Late April to early May

A 10-day feast for the ears, the eyes, and the stomach held in New Orleans, Louisiana. The festival's forerunner was the

New Orleans International Jazz Fest organized in 1968 to celebrate the city's 250th anniversary. Among the jazz greats on hand were Louis Armstrong and Duke Ellington. After it disbanded, George Wein, the founder of the famed Newport Jazz Festival (*see* JVC JAZZ FESTIVAL), urged the initiation of a festival to celebrate the regional culture of New Orleans, and in 1970 it was underway. A high spot in the festival was the evening when Eubie Blake, then 95 years old, was honored as a ragtime and jazz pioneer; he played several of his own tunes, including "I'm Just Wild About Harry" and "Memories of You."

Today it brings together thousands of musicians, artisans, and cooks who do their thing for more than half a million visitors. The concerts feature not only traditional and contemporary jazz, but also other music forms developed in New Orleans: ragtime, country, Cajun, zydeco, gospel, folk, and Latin. Food tents serve a multitude of indigenous foods, such as jambalaya, andouille, crawfish bisque, gumbo, frog legs, and so on. Hundreds of artisans also display their crafts.

CONTACTS:
New Orleans Jazz & Heritage Festival & Foundation
336 Camp St., Ste. 250
New Orleans, LA 70130
504-410-4100
www.nojazzfest.com

SOURCES:
GdUSFest-1984, p. 71
MusFestAmer-1990, p. 194

♦ 1861 ♦ **New Yam Festival**
End of June

Celebrated by almost every ethnic group in Nigeria, the New Yam Festival is observed annually at the end of June. It is considered taboo to eat the new yam before this festival. The high priest sacrifices a goat and pours its blood over a symbol representing the god of the harvest. Then the carcass is cooked and a soup is made from it, while the yams are boiled and pounded to make *foofoo*. After the priest has prayed for a better harvest in the coming year, he declares the feast open by eating the pounded yam and the soup. Then everyone joins in, and there is dancing, drinking, and merrymaking. After the festival is over, new yam may be eaten by anyone in the community.

Among the Igbo people, the yam crop is considered sacred, and anyone who steals yam is banished. This is because the original yam is believed to have grown out of the flesh of two children who had been sacrificed so that the other Igbo children wouldn't starve. At the New Yam Festival, each household places four or eight new yams on the ground and cuts small pieces off the head and the tail. The yams are then cooked with palm oil and chicken, and the meal is considered to be a symbolic reenactment of the original sacrifice.

Among the Yoruba people, where the New Yam Festival is known as **Eje**, the celebration is more elaborate. It takes place over two days and consists of purification rites, presentation rites, divining rites, and thanksgiving rites. In one divination rite, a recently harvested yam is divided into two parts. They are thrown on the ground, and if one lands face up and the other face down, this is considered a positive sign for the life of the community and the success of crops in the coming year. If both fall face down or face up, problems lie ahead.

CONTACTS:
Embassy of the Federal Republic of Nigeria
3519 International Ct. N.W.
Washington, D.C. 20008
202-986-8400; fax: 202-775-1385
www.nigeriaembassyusa.org

SOURCES:
FolkWrldHol-1999, p. 536

♦ 1862 ♦ **New Year for Trees**
Around December 23

Today, several groups in Great Britain and Ireland practice what they believe to be ancient Druidism. They hold Druidic festivals at the beginning of spring, summer, autumn and winter. They observe December 23 as the New Year for Trees, because it falls right after the WINTER SOLSTICE, which marks the rebirth of the sun and the start of a new year according to the tree calendar.

See also TU BISHVAT

SOURCES:
RelHolCal-2004, p. 270

♦ 1863 ♦ **New Year's Day**
January 1

Celebrating the first day of the year on the first day of January is a relatively modern practice. Although the Romans began marking the beginning of their civil year on January 1, the traditional springtime opening of the growing season and time for major military campaigns still held on as the popular New Year celebration.

William the Conqueror decreed that the New Year commence on January 1, but practice in England was still variable. Even after the Gregorian calendar was adopted by all Roman Catholic countries in 1582, Great Britain and the English colonies in America continued to begin the year on March 25 in accordance with the old Julian calendar. It wasn't until 1752 that Britain and its possessions adopted the New Style (Gregorian) calendar and accepted January 1 as the beginning of the year.

New Year's Day is a public holiday in the U.S. and in many other countries, and is traditionally a day for receiving visitors and recovering from NEW YEAR'S EVE festivities. A favorite pastime in the United States is watching football games on television—especially the ROSE BOWL game in Pasadena, California, the COTTON BOWL in Dallas, Texas, the SUGAR BOWL in New Orleans, Louisiana, and the ORANGE BOWL in Miami, Florida. A number of parades are also televised on New Year's Day, one of the most famous being the Mummers' Parade in Philadelphia, Pennsylvania. New Year's

is a time for making resolutions for the coming year—promises that are loudly proclaimed and then often forgotten.

See also HOGMANAY; LUNAR NEW YEAR; OSHOGATSU; ST. BASIL, FEAST OF; SOL

SOURCES:
AmerBkDays-2000, pp. 2, 248
BkDays-1864, vol. I, p. 27
BkFest-1937, pp. 3, 14, 22, 29, 37, 51, 65, 77, 84, 94, 101, 110, 118, 131, 143, 157, 165, 178, 194, 203, 210, 218, 236, 240, 248, 266, 273, 288, 297, 307, 316, 326, 335
DaysCustFaith-1957, pp. 17, 355
DictFolkMyth-1984, pp. 181, 790, 791, 950, 1063
EncyChristmas-2003, pp. 509, 549
FestSaintDays-1915, pp. 1, 2, 4, 7
FestWestEur-1958, pp. 3, 22, 32, 54, 87, 105, 121, 150, 160, 188, 210, 225
FolkAmerHol-1999, p. 1
FolkWrldHol-1999, p. 1
OxYear-1999, p. 6

♦ 1864 ♦ **New Year's Day (Denmark) (Nytaarsdag)**
January 1

In towns and cities throughout Denmark, the New Year marks the beginning of one of the most important social seasons in the calendar. Men and women attend church services and later call on relatives and friends to wish them a Happy New Year. These social calls only last about a half hour, but they go on for almost two weeks. Wine and small cookies are usually served during these visits.

Young people usher in the New Year by banging loudly on their friends' doors and throwing pieces of broken pottery that they have collected during the year against the sides of their houses.

CONTACTS:
Embassy of Denmark
3200 Whitehaven St. N.W.
Washington, D.C. 20008
202-234-4300; fax: 202-328-1470
www.ambwashington.um.dk

SOURCES:
BkFest-1937, p. 94
BkFestHolWrld-1970, p. 2
EncyChristmas-2003, p. 194
FestWestEur-1958, p. 22

♦ 1865 ♦ **New Year's Day (France)**
January 1

Known as **Le Jour de l'An** or **Le Jour des étrennes** for the gifts that are exchanged on this day, NEW YEAR'S DAY in France is a time for family reunions, visits, and greeting cards or letters. Tradespeople traditionally send their errand boys or girls to deliver gifts to their patrons. The baker, for example, might send a *brioche,* while the butcher might send a chicken and the dairyman some eggs. Those who deliver the gifts are usually given wine or money. Servants and clerks often receive an extra month's pay as a New Year's gift, while family and friends give each other chocolates, flowers, preserved fruit, and *marrons glacés,* or candied chestnuts.

In the afternoon, men pay social calls on their women friends and young people visit their elders. In the evening, a formal dinner is usually held at the home of the family's eldest member. Since relatives come from far and wide to attend these reunions, they are usually very large and festive affairs.

SOURCES:
BkFest-1937, p. 188
EncyChristmas-2003, p. 265
FestWestEur-1958, p. 32
FolkWrldHol-1999, p. 2

◆ 1866 ◆ New Year's Day (Germany)
January 1

According to German folk tradition, **Neujahr** is a time of new beginnings, and the first day of the year must be lived as you hope to live during the next 12 months. Housewives put forth an extra effort to make sure their homes are in order, and everyone wears new clothes. People avoid unpleasant tasks and try not to spend money, although they often jingle the coins in their pockets for good luck. People exchange greeting cards, but the giving of gifts is confined to those who have served the family throughout the year—for example, the mail carrier, janitor, and cleaning person.

SOURCES:
BkFest-1937, p. 131
BkFestHolWrld-1970, p. 3
FestWestEur-1958, p. 54

◆ 1867 ◆ New Year's Day (Lithuania)
January 1

Lithuanians have nicknamed New Year's Eve "Little Christmas Eve," because the holidays are celebrated in comparable ways. After eating dinner people sit up to welcome the start of the new year. Like Christmas Eve, New Year's Eve furnishes Lithuanians with an important opportunity for fortune telling. Many New Year's Eve superstitions taught young men and women a wide variety of charms that would reveal something of their future mates.

People watch the weather on New Year's Day carefully, as it is believed to predict the weather for the coming year. Human activities are also viewed as indicators of future events. People try to smile and be kind to one another, as this means that they can expect the same throughout the year. People hope to hear good news when they rise on New Year's Day. The first piece of news they hear, whether good or bad, reveals the kind of news they will receive in the year to come.

SOURCES:
EncyChristmas-2003, p. 432

◆ 1868 ◆ New Year's Day (Malta)
January 1

The Republic of Malta is a small country in the central Mediterranean that consists of seven islands. The Maltese Islands have a strong Catholic population that celebrates a wide variety of events throughout the religious year. Religious holidays are widely celebrated in Malta. Most Maltese families are very close-knit, and the holidays are a time to strengthen the sense of community and reinforce family bonds.

In Malta, the arrival of the New Year is celebrated on both a secular level and a religious level. Starting on New Year's Eve, most Maltese celebrate by going out for dinner and/or attending a party to ring in the New Year. For New Year's Day, most Maltese celebrate on a secular level by going out for lunch or organizing family lunches. On a religious level, many Maltese celebrate the Feast of Mary Mother of God. Across the country, religious new year celebrations are held in churches and chapels. Practicing Catholics in Malta are expected to observe the Feast of Mary Mother of God by attending mass on this day.

CONTACTS:
Malta Tourism Authority
Auberge D'Italie
Merchants St.
Valetta VLT 1170 Malta
www.visitmalta.com

◆ 1869 ◆ New Year's Day (Netherlands) (Nieuwjaarsdag)
January 1

The first day of the New Year in the Netherlands is spent eating holiday cakes, breads, and waffles, visiting friends, and drinking *slemp*, a traditional New Year's hot beverage made with milk, tea, sugar, and spices. Traditional baked specialties include *knijpertjes*, or "clothespins," which have been popular since the Middle Ages, and a long decorative loaf known as *duivekater*. These and other holiday cakes and pastries are served with slemp, which was originally sold to skaters from stalls on the ice-covered canals.

In Zeeland, Overijssel, and other areas, boys go from house to house ringing bells and wishing people a Happy New Year. Sometimes they bang on a homemade drum called a *rommelpot*, or "rumble pot," and beg for pennies. It is possible that the rommelpot was originally intended to frighten away evil spirits at the start of the New Year.

SOURCES:
BkFest-1937, p. 240
FestWestEur-1958, p. 121

◆ 1870 ◆ New Year's Day (Portugal) (Ano Novo)
January 1

In Portugal, the New Year begins with special church services. Afterward, friends and relatives visit each other's houses, greeting each other with "Boas Festas" (Happy Holidays) and exchanging good wishes. In addition, people often make promises about how they will live their lives in the coming year.

In northern Portugal, children go through the neighborhood singing old songs called *janeiras* ("January songs"), which are thought to bring luck in the coming year. Sometimes a band of local musicians will go through the streets, stopping to play a special selection when they pass the house of someone they know.

There are many traditions and folk beliefs concerning NEW YEAR'S DAY. People tend to mind their manners, believing that how they conduct themselves on this day foreshadows their behavior for the coming year. If they should pay off a debt on New Year's Day, they are likely to end up paying for the next 12 months. It is the custom in Portugal on NEW YEAR'S EVE to choose 12 grapes from a bunch, and to eat them one after another just as the clock strikes 12, offering New Year's wishes to everyone in the room. This act is supposed to guarantee happiness in the coming year.

SOURCES:
BkFest-1937, p. 266
BkFestHolWrld-1970, pp. 3, 5
FestWestEur-1958, p. 160

♦ 1871 ♦ **New Year's Day (Romania) (Anul Nou)**
January 1

Children welcome the New Year in Romania with an ancient fertility rite called *samanatul*, or "sowing." They stuff their pockets with corn and go from house to house, throwing corn at people and greeting them with wishes for a long life. In some parts of Romania, the *sorcova*—a stick to which flowers are tied—is used instead of corn. The flowers are from twigs plucked on ST. ANDREW'S EVE and forced into blossom by CHRISTMAS. Rather than throwing corn at people, the children brush their faces lightly with the sorcova. This custom may be a survival from ancient Roman times, when people saluted one another with laurel branches.

Romanians also celebrate NEW YEAR'S DAY by exchanging gifts. Servants, the poor, and the young often receive gifts of money.

SOURCES:
BkFest-1937, p. 273

♦ 1872 ♦ **New Year's Day (Russia)**
January 1

Under the Communist system NEW YEAR'S DAY largely replaced CHRISTMAS as the major winter festival in the former Soviet Union (*see* RUSSIAN WINTER FESTIVAL). Since the dissolution of the Soviet Union, however, this, or NEW YEAR'S EVE, is still the day on which Grandfather Frost visits and brings gifts for children. Within the walls of Moscow's Kremlin, there was a huge party at the Palace of Congresses attended by as many as 50,000 children. Entertainment at the party included the arrival of *D'yed Moroz*, or Grandfather Frost, wearing a white beard, red robe, and a hat trimmed in white fur and riding a Sputnik-drawn sleigh or some other outlandish vehicle. There were also troops of folk dancers, magicians, clowns, and tumblers who performed for the children. Older Muscovites celebrated New Year's by attending dances at schools, clubs, the-aters, and union halls. Outside of Moscow, the same festivities took place on a more modest scale.

Caviar, smoked fish, roast meats, and other treats were served in honor of the holiday. Among the many cakes and sweets served were *babka*, a yeast coffee cake made in a round pan, and *kulich*, a fancy fruitbread of Ukrainian origin made in three tiers to symbolize the Trinity.

SOURCES:
BkFest-1937, p. 288
EncyChristmas-2003, p. 653
FolkWrldHol-1999, p. 5

♦ 1873 ♦ **New Year's Day (Switzerland) (Neujahrstag)**
January 1

The Swiss celebrate NEW YEAR'S DAY with amateur dramatic performances, visits with friends, and feasting on roast goose with chestnut stuffing, New Year's bread, and *birewegge*, or pear pie, which looks like a shiny loaf of bread and has a rich filling of pears and raisins. Goose necks filled with ground giblets, seasoning, and other ingredients are a favorite delicacy when sliced thin and served as a between-meal snack. Although the holiday is generally a quiet one, children often hide on New Year's morning, startling their parents when they jump out to give them New Year's greetings.

According to Swiss folklore, the first day of January is full of omens and predictions. A red sky, for example, signifies storms, fire, and war in the coming year. Meeting a woman the first thing on New Year's Day is thought to bring bad luck, while encountering a man or a child is looked upon as a good sign.

SOURCES:
BkFest-1937, p. 316
FestWestEur-1958, p. 225

♦ 1874 ♦ **New Year's Eve**
December 31

The last day of the year is usually greeted with mixed emotions—joy and anticipation on the one hand, melancholy and regret on the other. Some celebrate by attending midnight church services, while others congregate in public places like Times Square in New York City, or Trafalgar Square in London, Glasgow's George Square or Edinburgh's Iron Kirk to count down the closing seconds of the old year. In the United States, people congregate at parties, some lasting all night, and many people spend New Year's Eve in front of the television watching other people celebrate. In recent years, celebrations in time zones all over the world have also been televised, so viewers can celebrate several times in one night, if they wish.

In Scotland, December 31 is known as **Old Year's Night**, or HOGMANAY. Although there are a number of theories about the derivation of the name, the tradition it refers to involves handing out pieces of oat-cake to poor children, who go from door to door calling out "Hogmanay!" In the United States, the Scottish song "Auld Lang Syne," with lyrics by poet Robert Burns, is sung at almost every New Year's Eve celebration, while in London, the Scots at St. Paul's Churchyard toast and sing.

In Denmark the New Year is "shot in" with a thunderous explosion of fireworks, rockets, and Chinese pistols. In some villages, young people play pranks such as those done on Halloween in the United States.

Iceland has bonfires to clean up trash and elf dances, because elves are believed to be about on this night and might want to stop and rest on their way.

Neapolitans believe it brings luck to throw pots and dishes out the windows at midnight.

On the last two days of the year in Japan, a fire watch is implemented to prepare for the New Year, their most important holiday. Young men gather into groups then go to separate parts of the towns. They carry a clapper which they sound every few yards, crying out, "take care with fire."

Armenian families spend the night at home feasting. During the celebration, the neighbors, one at a time, lower a basket of presents down the chimney, then it is the recipients' turn to go to their neighbors.

Romanian boys used to go around to their neighbors with a *plugusorul*, a little plough, which may be a remnant of the Roman Opalia, the festival to the goddess of abundance, Ops. Later they changed to a homemade drum that sounds like a bull, which is what pulls the plough through the meadow. They ring cow bells and crack whips and recite hundreds of verses of their country story at the top of their lungs.

See also First Night; Ladouvane; Omisoka

SOURCES:
AmerBkDays-2000, p. 868
BkDays-1864, vol. II, p. 787
BkFest-1937, pp. 63, 99, 117, 306, 335
DaysCustFaith-1957, p. 325
DictFolkMyth-1984, pp. 12, 842, 1100
EncyChristmas-2003, pp. 549, 755
FestSaintDays-1915, p. 256
FestWestEur-1958, pp. 21, 30, 84, 149, 159, 187, 209, 242
FolkAmerHol-1999, p. 1
FolkWrldHol-1999, p. 773
GdWrldFest-1985, p. 168
OxYear-1999, p. 542

♦ 1875 ♦ New Year's Eve (Brazil)
December 31

One of the most exotic New Year's Eve celebrations in the world takes place along the beaches of Brazil—particularly Copacabana Beach in Rio de Janeiro, where thousands of followers of Candomblé, a religion practiced in Brazil, meet to pay homage to the ocean goddess, Yemanjá (or Iemanjá). Dressed in white and carrying fresh flowers, candles, and *cachaça* (sugarcane alcohol), they flock to the beach around 10

o'clock and lay out tablecloths surrounded by candles and covered with gifts for the goddess. Animal sacrifices are not uncommon.

The ceremony reaches its peak at midnight, when fireworks go off and people rush into the water—shrieking, sobbing, or singing—carrying their flowers and gifts for Yemanjá. If the waves carry their gifts out to sea, it means that the goddess was satisfied and they can go home happy. It is considered an ill omen if the ocean throws back their gifts.

CONTACTS:
RIOTUR - City of Rio de Janeiro Tourism Authority
Piazza Pio X, 119 / 9th Ctr.
Rio de Janeiro, 20040-020 Brazil
55-21-2271-7000; fax: 55-21-2223-4871
www.riodejaneiro-turismo.com.br/pt

♦ 1876 ♦ New Year's Eve (Ecuador)
December 31

Many Ecuadorians celebrate the Old Year, *Año Viejo*, on December 31 by stuffing an old shirt and pair of pants with straw and sewing them together to make an effigy of a man. With a hat on his head, a pipe in his mouth, and a cane in his hand, the scarecrow figure sits in a chair in front of the house, sometimes under an arch made of cypress branches. Someone draws up a mock "last will and testament" listing various family members' faults that must be done away with. At midnight, or earlier if there are small children in the house, someone reads the will aloud and everyone makes jokes about its contents. Then the straw figure is lit with a match, and the faults of the Old Year go up in flames. Sometimes the old man's "widow" goes from house to house, dressed in black and begging for contributions to charity.

After the straw men have burned and the widows have come in from the streets, everyone sits down to enjoy the spiced foods typically served on this night. The most popular is a crisp fried pastry in the shape of a doughnut, which is dipped into a brown sugar syrup.

SOURCES:
BkFestHolWrld-1970, p. 16
BkHolWrld-1986, Dec 31

♦ 1877 ♦ New Year's Eve (Germany) (Silvesterabend)
December 31

In different areas of Germany, it is considered lucky to eat certain foods on the last night of the old year. Carp is served frequently, not only in homes but in fashionable city restaurants. Another favorite is *Silvesterabend* punch, a hot drink made from red wine flavored with cinnamon and sugar. *Feuerzangenbowle*, or "fire tongs punch," has special cones of sugar, soaked in liquor, suspended over the punch bowl. When they are set aflame, the alcoholic sugar drips into the hot wine below. In Baden, a special dried pea soup is considered to bring good luck when served on New Year's Eve. Along the lower Rhine, "little New Year" yeast cookies are baked in the form of spiral wreaths, pretzels, or circles. Everyone leaves a bit of each food served on his or her plate until after midnight in the belief that it will ensure a well-stocked pantry in the coming year.

According to ancient Germanic folk belief, the only way to drive out demons, devils, and other evil spirits on the last night of the year is by making noise. Grown men can be seen riding hobby horses up and down the streets of German villages on New Year's Eve at midnight, and *Buttenmandl* ("Little Butten Men"), who are peasants dressed in straw clothing and deerskin animal masks, ring bells and drag clanking chains through the streets in an effort to drive out evil spirits.

In the Bavarian Alps, shooting parties are still popular. Sometimes members of shooting societies will climb a mountain and shoot off 500 or more old mortars in unison. (*See* CHRISTMAS SHOOTING.)

In the Bavarian town of Oberammergau, a "star singer" carrying a large illuminated star on a long pole leads a New Year's Eve procession that lasts for several hours (*see also* EPIPHANY IN GERMANY). He sings a song that summarizes the events of the past year and extends good wishes for the year to come, accompanied by members of the Passion Play orchestra (*see also* OBERAMMERGAU PASSION PLAY).

New Year's pranks are common in Germany, such as chocolates with mustard inside, sugar lumps with spiders inside, and firework dogs that produce a string of black, sausage-like material when burned. Among young people, "lead-pouring" parties are popular. They drop a little melted lead into a bowl of cold water and read each other's fortunes by interpreting the shapes the metal assumes.

SOURCES:
EncyChristmas-2003, p. 282
FestWestEur-1958, p. 84
FolkWrldHol-1999, p. 774

♦ 1878 ♦ **New Year's Eve (Spain)**
December 31

In Spain, it is customary for families to gather on NEW YEAR'S EVE in small groups to celebrate the coming of the New Year. Shortly before midnight, bags or bunches of grapes are distributed. When midnight arrives, everyone eats one grape for each stroke of the clock. Eating all 12 grapes before the clock is finished striking ensures good luck in the New Year. The grapes are usually washed down with muscatel wine. So firmly entrenched is the grape-eating custom that in theaters and cinemas, the show is often interrupted at midnight on New Year's Eve so that the audience can eat the grapes and drink the wine they've brought with them.

NEW YEAR'S DAY is spent visiting family and friends, feasting, and exchanging cards and gifts. Eating and drinking well on this day is believed to guarantee an abundance of food and drink in the coming year.

SOURCES:
BkFest-1937, p. 297

DictFolkMyth-1984, p. 1063
EncyChristmas-2003, p. 733
FestWestEur-1958, p. 188
FolkWrldHol-1999, p. 6

♦ 1879 ♦ **New Year's Parade of Firemen (Dezome-shiki)**
January 6

Each year on January 6, the Tokyo Fire Department hosts a parade of vehicles and a display of ladder stunts to remind citizens of the dangers of fire and to pray for a safe year. The event dates from the Edo Period (17th through 19th centuries), when great fires struck several times. The New Year's Parade of Firemen originated then, with firemen praying in front of the shrine of Ueno Toshogu for a safe, fire-free year ahead. In those days, the main fire-fighting technique was to tear down the buildings near the source of the fire to prevent it from spreading. Ladders were indispensable tools, because the firefighters had to climb the roofs of the buildings, and they needed great agility and strength to scale the ladders.

The highlight of the present-day Parade of Firemen hearkens back to this tradition, as men dressed as firemen from the Edo period perform circus-like acrobatic stunts on bamboo ladders. In addition to the ladder displays, the event features large-scale fire-fighting and emergency drills, and a parade of more than 100 fire engines and helicopters. Similar events are held on January 6 throughout Japan, but the Tokyo event is considered the most spectacular.

CONTACTS:
Japan National Tourist Organization
515 S. Figueroa St., Ste. 1470
Los Angeles, CA 90071
213-623-1952; fax: 213-623-6301
www.jnto.go.jp/eng/index.html

♦ 1880 ♦ **New York City Marathon**
First Sunday in November

The New York City Marathon began in 1970 as a race four times around Central Park. But in 1976, Fred Lebow and the New York Road Runners Club, the world's largest running club and the race's sponsor, decided to get corporate support, invite top runners from all over the world, and to run the course through all five New York boroughs.

Unlike the BOSTON MARATHON, which is run primarily through the countryside and small towns, the New York course is urban, beginning at the tollbooth plaza at the end of the Verrazano-Narrows Bridge on Staten Island and progressing across the bridge through Brooklyn, Queens, Manhattan, and the Bronx before finishing in Manhattan's Central Park.

About 30,000 runners compete in the race, and over a million New Yorkers turn out to watch. In addition to cash prizes ranging from $65,000 for the first-place finishers to $7,500 for fifth place, thousands more in bonuses are handed out each year.

The marathon has had a positive effect on New York City's public image, which has suffered because of its high crime rate and frequent clashes between ethnic groups. The runners who compete regularly in New York say that the crowds are enthusiastic and friendly, and city dwellers look upon it as a time to forget racial and ethnic differences and cheer the runners on.

Like most things in New York City, its marathon is amazing. Rosie Ruiz, well known for being disqualified for cheating in the Boston Marathon, was thrown out in New York for taking the subway to the finish line.

Then there's race organizer Fred Lebow: although an avid runner he had never run New York until he was struck by brain cancer. Then in 1992, the cancer in remission, this 60-year-old Romanian-born escapee from the Holocaust finally ran the 26.2 mile course. His companion on his heroic run was his good friend and nine-time New York winner, Grete Waitz of Norway. Lebow's time: 5 hours 32 minutes 34 seconds.

In 1992 Australian-born Lisa Ondieki set a new women's course record of 2:24:40 and won a $30,000 bonus in addition to the standard $20,000 purse and Mercedes-Benz automobile. Willie Mtolo, a 28-year-old Zulu from South Africa, won his first major international marathon in 1992. This was a special victory for him since he had been unable to compete outside his homeland until that year: South African athletes had suffered a 21-year political embargo. Mtolo's time: 2 hours 9 minutes 29 seconds.

In the 2000 race, runners came from more than 150 countries, and over 100 contenders competed in the Marathon's first official wheelchair and handcycle division. Several scheduled runners were lost in the 2001 terrorist attack on the World Trade Center, and some relatives and friends signed up to run in their places. The Road Runners Club dedicated the 2001 Marathon to the victims of the attacks.

CONTACTS:
New York Road Runners Club
9 E 89th St.
New York, NY 10128
877-697-7786 or 212-860-4455
www.nyrrc.org

♦ 1881 ♦ **New Zealand Festival**
Late February to early March during even-numbered years

For three weeks every two years, artists, writers, and performers from all over the world come to Wellington, New Zealand, to showcase their talents in music, dance, theater, opera, literature, and the visual arts. The New Zealand Festival offers everything from Afro-Cuban dance music to the Viennese opera of Richard Strauss, from classical ballet to cutting-edge theater, and much more. The *New Zealand Post* Writers and Readers Week also takes place within the festival. In addition, the festival highlights the work of contemporary Maori and other indigenous artists.

CONTACTS:
NZ International Arts Festival
Press House, 82 Willis St.

P.O. Box 10-113
Wellington, New Zealand
64-4-473-0149; fax: 64-4-471-1164
www.nzfestival.nzpost.co.nz

SOURCES:
WildPlanet-1995, p. 431

♦ 1882 ♦ **New Zealand National Agricultural Fieldays**
Second week of June

The largest agricultural show in New Zealand takes place for three days during the second week in June in Hamilton, and attracts visitors from more than 40 countries. There are exhibits covering every type of rural activity, demonstrations of how to use the latest farm equipment, and contests in such areas as hay-baling, wire-fencing, tractor-driving, and helicopter log-lifting.

Other agricultural shows in New Zealand include the Agricultural and Pastoral Show at Auckland in late November and the Canterbury Agricultural and Pastoral Show in mid-November. In a country that in 1990 had more than 60 million sheep and only 3.3 million people, these regional agricultural shows attract the kind of audience that is usually associated with major athletic competitions.

See also ROYAL SHOWS

CONTACTS:
New Zealand National Agricultural Fieldays
P.O. Box 3015
Hamilton, 3240 New Zealand
64-7-843-4499; fax: 64-7-843-8572
www.fieldays.co.nz

SOURCES:
BkHolWrld-1986, Jun 9

♦ 1883 ♦ **Newfoundland Discovery Day**
Monday nearest June 24

Newfoundland distinguishes itself from several other Canadian provinces by celebrating its provincial holiday on a different calendar date. Most Canadian provinces and territories observe the holiday on the first Monday of August, but Newfoundlanders have selected June 24 because that historic date marks Italian explorer John Cabot's discovery of the region in 1497.

In 1997 Newfoundland celebrated the 500th anniversary of Cabot's landfall. A modern-day replica of the explorer's ship, the *Matthew,* was built, and sailors reenacted the historic journey from Bristol, England, to Newfoundland. Thousands of people gathered in the town of Bonavista at the site where historians conjecture Cabot landed. There they welcomed the ship at the end of its seven-week voyage. Among the dignitaries who attended were England's Queen Elizabeth and Prince Philip along with Newfoundland premier Brian Tobin.

CONTACTS:
Government of Newfoundland and Labrador
Communications Branch

10th Fl., East Block
Confederation Bldg.
St. John's, NL A1B 4J6 Canada
www.gov.nl.ca

SOURCES:
AnnivHol-2000, p. 293

♦ 1884 ♦ **Newport Harbor Christmas Boat Parade**
December 17-23

Newport Harbor Christmas Boat Parade is a week-long nightly parade of boats at Newport Beach, Calif. The area has one of the largest concentrations of pleasure craft in the world—more than 9,000 boats are docked at the harbor. More than 150 boats of all kinds, wildly decorated with lights that depict Santa Claus, snowmen, snowflakes, and other symbols of winter, join the parade. Some boats carry huge inflated figures (an enormous Grinch in an engineer's cap appeared in 1990) and many play music. The vessels range from rowboats to tugs to elegant yachts.

The floating parades actually started in 1908 as a FOURTH OF JULY spectacular. (The Fourth parades are no more.) John Scarpa, a real-estate broker was trying to sell some property, and to promote it he lit up a gondola and eight canoes with Japanese lanterns and paraded around the harbor. This developed into the **Illuminated Water Parade**, and was a highlight of the Fourth for years. In 1946, the city got a barge, put a tree and carolers on it, and towed it around the harbor, and that began the current December parades. They are considered the "granddaddy" of water parades, the biggest in the nation. About a million spectators watch them during the festival's seven days.

CONTACTS:
Newport Beach Chamber of Commerce
1470 Jamboree Rd.
Newport Beach, CA 92660
949-729-4400; fax: 949-729-4417
www.newportbeach.com

♦ 1885 ♦ **Newport Music Festival**
Two weeks in mid-July

In 1969 the Metropolitan Opera in New York City decided to establish its summer home in Newport, Rhode Island. The fog and humidity, however, played havoc with the artists' delicate instruments, and it quickly became apparent that Newport wasn't the place for outdoor opera. But the grand rooms of its famed waterfront mansions provided an ideal setting for chamber music. Using members of the Metropolitan Opera Orchestra, the festival in its infancy paved the way for the "Romantic revival," which soon spread worldwide.

The Newport Music Festival still offers music of the Romantic era (1825-1900) but in recent years it has expanded its offerings and now presents a wide spectrum of composers and performers. Dozens of world premieres of forgotten or lost minor masterpieces by well-known composers, such as the four-handed *Andante Cantabile* by Claude Debussy (1862-1918), have taken place here, as have the North American

debuts of many now-famous international and American artists, such as the young Dimitris Sgouros. More than 60 concerts are presented during the two-week festival, which has developed a reputation for programs so rare and varied that they draw music-lovers from thousands of miles away.

CONTACTS:
Newport Music Festival
P.O. Box 3300
Newport, RI 02840
401-846-1133; fax: 401-849-1857
www.newportmusic.org

SOURCES:
GdUSFest-1984, p. 167
MusFestAmer-1990, p. 134

♦ 1886 ♦ **Newport to Bermuda Race**
June in even-numbered years

One of the oldest sailing races in the international calendar, the race from Newport, Rhode Island, to Bermuda was initiated by Thomas Fleming Day, editor and founder of *Rudder* magazine. At the time, most existing ocean races were for yachts of more than 100 feet, and Day wanted to see a race for smaller yachts (less than 40 feet overall). The first such race, in 1904, was run from Brooklyn, New York, to Marblehead, Massachusetts, a distance of 330 nautical miles. The following year it went from Brooklyn to Hampton Roads, Virginia (250 miles). In 1906, the finish was in Bermuda.

The Bermuda races died out in 1910, but they were revived in 1923 under the sponsorship of the Cruising Club of America (CCA). Since 1924 the race has been sailed biennially in June. The starting point was moved from New London, Connecticut, to Montauk, Long Island. But now the race is run from Narragansett Bay off Newport to St. David's Head, Bermuda—a distance of 635 nautical miles. Sponsored jointly by the CCA and the Royal Bermuda Yacht Club, the Newport to Bermuda Race is now part of the Onion Patch trophy series, which consists of this and three local, unnamed races.

CONTACTS:
Bermuda Race Organizing Committee
580 Thames St., Ste. 418
Newport, RI 02840
772-584-1055; fax: 401-537-9155
www.bermudarace.com

♦ 1887 ♦ **Ngan Duan Sib (Tenth Lunar Month Festival)**
September-October; 10th lunar month

In the city of Nakhon Si Thammarat in Thailand, a festival is held during the tenth lunar month to feed the ghosts of ancestors for their annual visit among the living. Buddhist tradition holds that they reside in hell and because of sins they committed when they were alive, these spirits have very small mouths, which makes them constantly hungry. So during the Tenth Lunar Month Festival people try to placate the unworldly visitors with gifts and food designed to fit into tiny mouths.

A major event is a parade of food to the temple. Floats carry gifts and foods resembling such objects as clothing, coins, games, and boats—everything the spirits will need, including transportation back to their home. A popular sweet is called *la*, a toffee-like cookie or candy made from rice flour, brown palm sugar, and egg yolks thin enough to fit in the ghosts' small mouths. Tables are set up on the temple's front grounds to hold the food when the parade arrives. After allowing the ghosts a few minutes with the food, children are permitted to sample the treats.

It is traditional for children, and men, to dress up as ghosts and skeletons during the festival and prowl around, menacing people and begging for money—much like the trick-or-treating that goes on in the United States at HALLOWEEN.

CONTACTS:
Tourism Authority of Thailand
611 N. Larchmont Blvd., 1st Fl.
Los Angeles, CA 90004
800-842-4526 or 323-461-9814; fax: 323-461-9834
www.tourismthailand.org

SOURCES:
FestWrld: Thailand-1998, p. 20

♦ 1888 ♦ **Nganja, Feast of**
April

A harvest custom in Angola, the Feast of Nganja is primarily celebrated by children. On a day in April, when the harvest is ripe, they go out to their family fields and gather some fresh corn. In small groups they go to the woods, where they build campfires and roast their corn on the cob. But the real excitement of the feast lies in the game that is played while the corn is being cooked. Without warning, a child from one group may jump up and steal the corn from another. The robbing and plundering is good-natured, although there are always a few children who end up with no corn at all.

A similar children's feast held in Angola during the harvest months of February, March, and April is known as the Feast of Okambondondo. This all-night celebration is held indoors, with the girls doing all the cooking and the meal itself being served in the kitchen just before dawn.

SOURCES:
FolkWrldHol-1999, p. 521

♦ 1889 ♦ **Ngmayem Festival**
March; in some areas October

The Ngmayem Festival is a harvest celebration that takes place in March in Manya Krobo in southeastern Ghana. The festival has been held annually since 1944 to foster tribal unity, but it commemorates the end of a famine that occurred hundred of years ago.

The festival derives its name from the historic importance of *ngma*, or millet, to the survival of the tribe, though that grain now is cultivated mainly for ritual purposes. Traditional foods associated with Ngmayem include mashed yam, palm

soup, roasted corn, and meal. Festivities and rites are planned throughout the harvest month, and these may include dances, marriages, naming ceremonies, and other rituals designed to strengthen relationships and allegiances within the tribe. Events during the main festival week include blessings, cleansing ceremonies, thanksgiving services, visitation of royal tombs, and commemoration of ancestors. Festivalgoers dress in colorful attire and adorn themselves with beads.

Krobo leaders also conduct a *durbar*, or court reception, in which tribe members meet with chiefs to discuss the government and administration of the group and to hear updates on development projects and political issues affecting the people, such as water rights and border disputes. Beginning in the 2000s, a Ngmayem Festival was also celebrated annually in October in Dodowa to celebrate the harvest, foster tribal unity, and educate younger generations about their history.

CONTACTS:
National Commission on Culture
1 Gamal Abdul Nasser Ave.
Private Mail Bag
Ministries Post Office
Accra, Ghana
www.ghanaculture.gov.gh

♦ 1890 ♦ **Ngoc Son Temple Festival**
Autumn

The Ngoc Son Temple sits on a little island in Hoan Kiem Lake in Hanoi, the capital of Vietnam. The lake is named after a 500-year-old legend. It was said that a divine tortoise lived in the lake. When China ruled Vietnam, the tortoise gave a warrior named Le Loi a sword with sacred powers. This Le Loi wielded to liberate Vietnam, eventually becoming Emperor Le Thai To. Later he went out on the lake to give the sword back to the tortoise, who took it, then disappeared into the lake's depths—thus, the lake's name means "Lake of the Restored Sword."

The Ngoc Son, meaning "Jade Mound," Temple honors three Vietnamese saints—a doctor, La To, a writer, Van Xuong, and a martial artist, Quan Vu—and one patriotic hero, Tran Hung Dao. The annual festival commemorates these ancestors with a procession from Hanoi which crosses a bridge to the temple. Some play traditional instruments along the way. At the temple a special worship service is held, then everyone enjoys a feast.

CONTACTS:
Vietnam National Administration of Tourism
80 Quan Su Rd.
Hanoi, Vietnam
84-4-942-1061; fax: 84-4-826-3956
www.vietnamtourism.com/e_pages/news/index.a

SOURCES:
FestWrld: Viet-1997, p. 16

♦ 1891 ♦ **Ngondo Festival**
November-December

For the majority of the Sawa, an ethnic group composed of various coastal peoples of Cameroon, guidance comes from the Jengu water spirits. The annual Ngondo Festival is a special occasion for Sawa chiefs to petition these spirits for prophecies and warnings and to communicate those messages to a gathered assembly. The event, which lasts a few weeks, takes place on the banks of the Wouri River in the country's most populous city, Douala. Various cultural activities accompany the discernment process of the festival.

It is possible for the Sawa to receive the same message twice. Such was the case with the 2007 festival, when chiefs announced for the second year in a row that Sawa sons and daughters should focus more intently on joint and constructive action.

Sawa chiefs deliver their messages at the water feast that officially closes the Ngondo Festival. Activities preceding the water feast include traditional wrestling competitions, art exhibitions, choral singing, round table conferences, a trade fair, a canoe race, and a Miss Ngondo pageant.

CONTACTS:
Embassy of the Republic of Cameroon
2349 Massachusetts Ave. N.W.
Washington, D.C. 20036
202-265-8790; fax: 202-387-3826
www.ambacam-usa.org

♦ 1892 ♦ Nguillatun
Usually March

The Mapuche Indians live in southern Chile and west central Argentina, particularly in the province of Neuquén. The name *Mapuche* means "people of the earth." The autumn harvest usually comes in March and for the Mapuche, this is a time to say special prayers to give thanks and ask for fertility and protection from floods, droughts, and other disasters. A special *nguillatun* (gee-ya-TOON), or prayer ceremony, is held at harvest time and is led by a *machi*, a religious leader who is usually a woman. People apply blue and white paint to their faces—colors which are considered spiritually positive. For two to four days the Mapuche pray, sing, dance and feast.

CONTACTS:
Embassy of Chile
1732 Massachusetts Ave. N.W.
Washington, D.C. 20036
202-785-1746; fax: 202-887-5579
www.chile-usa.org

SOURCES:
EncyRel-1987, vol. 9, p. 186
FestWrld: Chile-1998, p. 24

♦ 1893 ♦ Nicaragua Battle of San Jacinto Day
September 14

In Nicaragua, the month of September is full of celebratory activities across the country to commemorate the 1856 battle at Hacienda San Jacinto and Nicaraguan independence.

Starting on September 1, people hang the Nicaraguan flag around their homes, and the Central American Patrimonial Festivities begin. An inaugural ceremony at the Plaza de los Honores del Palacio Presidencial kicks off the week-long festival during which school marching bands from across the country combine music and choreography to compete against bands from other schools. The final contest is held at the National Stadium in Managua, where the groups compete in front of judges for the title of best musical group in the country.

Also during the month of September, a burning torch is carried through Central America, from Guatemala to Costa Rica. It is passed from hand to hand by the best students and other outstanding individuals from each municipality. Each person carries the torch for no more than 100 meters. The total run is 387 kilometers and involves more than 8,000 students. When the torch reaches the National Cultural Palace, the president kicks off folkloric events that occur throughout the day. On September 13, the national flag is hung at all schools and the national anthem is broadcast in across the country.

September 14 is a national holiday dedicated to the anniversary of the independence of Central America and the battle at San Jacinto. Starting at 7:30 in the morning, the president awards the Presidential Medallion to the best students and teachers from around the country at the Plaza de la Fé Juan Pablo Segundo. Marching bands from 100 schools in the capital (approximately 15,000 students) and bands from the National Army and the Police participate in a parade that day.

The celebrations conclude on September 15 with the reading of the Act of Independence of Central America in all state schools throughout Nicaragua.

CONTACTS:
Embassy of Nicaragua
1627 New Hampshire Ave. N.W.
Washington, D.C. 20009
202-939-6570; fax: 202-939-6542

♦ 1894 ♦ Nicaragua Independence Day
September 15

Nicaragua shares its Independence Day with four other Central American countries—COSTA RICA, EL SALVADOR, GUATEMALA, and HONDURAS—all of which declared their independence from Spain on September 15, 1821. There is a parade in the capital city of Managua, and the president and other public officials give speeches. Nicaraguans also celebrate Independence Day by attending cockfights and bullfights. But unlike bullfights in other countries, the Nicaraguan matador does not kill the bull. Instead, he tries to mount it and ride it rodeo-style.

CONTACTS:
Embassy of Nicaragua
1627 New Hampshire Ave. N.W.
Washington, D.C. 20009
202-939-6570; fax: 202-939-6542

SOURCES:
AnnivHol-2000, p. 155
NatlHolWrld-1968, p. 170

◆ 1895 ◆ **Nice Carnaval**
January-February; three weekends before Shrove Tuesday

Dating back to the late 13th century and deriving, some believe, from ancient rites of spring, the CARNIVAL celebration in Nice, France, is one of the Mediterranean resort town's most picturesque spectacles. It actually begins about three weeks before SHROVE TUESDAY with the arrival of King Carnival. The next two Saturdays and Sundays are filled with processions, confetti battles, and masked balls. The processions of floats, each accompanied by marchers or riders on horseback wearing elaborate costumes, draw large crowds. There are also parades of "big heads," large heads representing various personages made of pasteboard, and huge panels of light illustrating the year's theme decorate the Place Messena, the carnival grounds in the heart of Nice. During the last five days before Shrove Tuesday, a grand *charivari*, or street party, ensues with roving musicians, singers, and actors mingling with onlookers. On Shrove Tuesday, King Carnival is burnt in a bonfire on the shore and fireworks close out the long pre-Lenten celebration.

Flowers play an important role in the Nice Carnaval, for it is in the south of France that the flowers for French perfume are grown. During the festivities, there are several afternoons devoted to *Bataille de Fleurs*, Parades of Flowers, consisting of some 20 floats, all meticulously decorated with 4,000-5,000 fresh flowers.

CONTACTS:
Nice Convention and Visitors Bureau
BP 4079
Nice, 06302 France
33-8-9270-7407; fax: 33-4-9214-4649
www.nicetourisme.com/GB/som.html

SOURCES:
BkFest-1937, p. 120
BkFestHolWrld-1970, p. 33
BkHolWrld-1986, Feb 20
DictFolkMyth-1984, p. 192
EncyRel-1987, vol. 3, p. 101
FestWestEur-1958, p. 34

◆ 1896 ◆ **Nicodemus Emancipation and Homecoming Celebration**
Last weekend in July

The Nicodemus Emancipation and Homecoming Celebration is held annually the last weekend in July to celebrate the abolishment of slavery in the United States. It also celebrates Nicodemus, an all-black town in northwest Kansas that was settled by former slaves fleeing the south in 1877 after the post-Civil War Reconstruction period had ended. The town was named after a legendary slave who reportedly bought his own freedom. The town is the only still-living all-black community west of the Mississippi founded by former slaves. Originally settled by 350 freed slaves, it now has a permanent population of about 40 people. The town, which comprises five historic buildings, was declared a National Historic Site in 1998. Only one building is open to visitors.

The Emancipation and Homecoming Celebration has taken place every year since 1878. The event includes such attractions as a parade, a fashion show, military displays, and descendants' program, which draws relatives of the original town settlers from across the country.

CONTACTS:
Nicodemus National Historic Site
304 Washington Ave.
Nicodemus, KS 67625-3015
785-839-4233 or 785-839-4321; fax: 785-839-4325
www.nps.gov/nico/home.htm

SOURCES:
AAH-2007, p. 355

◆ 1897 ◆ **Niger Republic Day**
December 18

On August 3, 1960, Niger gained full independence from France, after having been a colony since 1922. Niger had voted to become a republic on December 18, 1958. August 3 is a national holiday celebrating Independence Day, while December 18 is Republic Day.

CONTACTS:
Embassy of the Republic of Niger
2204 R St. N.W.
Washington, D.C. 20008
202-483-4224; fax: 202-483-3169
www.nigerembassyusa.org

SOURCES:
AnnivHol-2000, pp. 130, 210
NatlHolWrld-1968, p. 228

◆ 1898 ◆ **Nigeria National Day**
October 1

Also known as **Independence Day**, this national holiday commemorates the autonomy of Nigeria that officially began October 1, 1960, after being under British control since 1900. Nigeria became a federal republic with a new constitution on October 1, 1963. In 1966 some military officers staged a coup and ruled until other army officers overthrew them in 1975. Civilian rule was restored on the anniversary of freedom, October 1, 1979. The city of Lagos was the capital until 1986, when the government center moved to Abuja.

CONTACTS:
Embassy of the Federal Republic of Nigeria
3519 International Ct. N.W.
Washington, D.C. 20008
202-986-8400; fax: 202-775-1385
www.nigeriaembassyusa.org

SOURCES:
AnnivHol-2000, p. 165
NatlHolWrld-1968, p. 183

◆ 1899 ◆ **Night of the Radishes**
December 23

Night of the Radishes is a festival that dates from the 19th century that combines art, agriculture, and religion. It is held in the *zócalo*, or main square, in Oaxaca, Mexico, 300 miles south of Mexico City. The radish made its first appearance here during the Spanish colonial period, and in commemoration Oaxaqueños carve them into elaborate shapes and display them on **La Noche de Ratanos**. The radishes, the same red-skinned, white-fleshed roots commonly eaten in salads, grow to yam-size here and are each uniquely shaped by growing through the rocky soil.

Indian families harvest these vegetables, combine and sculpt them into elaborate forms depicting biblical scenes, especially the nativity of Jesus. Historical and Aztec themes are also represented. After the awarding of cash prizes and ribbons, a fireworks display caps the night.

During the festival and throughout the CHRISTMAS season, another custom is observed: people buy small pottery bowls filled with sweet fried dough called *buñuelos*. After they eat the dough, they fling the bowl violently to the ground. The walks become thick with pottery shards.

CONTACTS:
Mexico Tourism Board
21 E. 63rd St., Fl. 3
New York, NY 10021
800-446-3942 or 212-821-0314; fax: 212-821-0367
www.visitmexico.com

SOURCES:
BkHolWrld-1986, Dec 23
IntlThFolk-1979, p. 274

♦ 1900 ♦ **Night Watch**
July 13

La Retraite aux Flambeaux, or the Night Watch, is a half-holiday in France that is celebrated on the eve of BASTILLE DAY. The lights in Paris are darkened in remembrance of the day in 1789 when the Bastille fell. Colorful processions of soldiers, patriotic bands, and people bearing torches and Chinese lanterns march through the streets, followed by crowds of spectators. The procession usually ends at the home of a prominent citizen, who offers the torch- and lantern-bearers something to drink.

CONTACTS:
French Government Tourist Office
444 Madison Ave., 16th Fl.
New York, NY 10022
800-391-4909 or 212-838-7800; fax: 212-838-7855
www.francetourism.com

SOURCES:
AnnivHol-2000, p. 117
BkFest-1937, p. 125

♦ 1901 ♦ **Niman Festival**
July

The Niman, or **Going Home Ceremony**, takes place in the Hopi Indian pueblos of northeastern Arizona. After entering the pueblos in February, the *katchinas,* ancestral spirits imper-

sonated by men wearing elaborate masks, leave again in July. During the six months when they are present in the pueblo (*see* POWAMÛ CEREMONY), the katchinas appear in a series of dances, of which the Niman is the last. For the Going Home Ceremony, up to 75 dancers representing katchinas spend an entire day singing and dancing. They give bows, arrows, and other gifts to the boys and katchina dolls to the girls before returning to their mountain homes.

CONTACTS:
Hopi Cultural Center
P.O. Box 67
Second Mesa, AZ 86043
520-734-2401; fax: 520-734-6651
www.hopiculturalcenter.com

Carnegie Museum of Natural History
4400 Forbes Ave.
Pittsburgh, PA 15213
412-622-3131; fax: 412-622-3274
www.carnegiemnh.org

SOURCES:
BkHolWrld-1986, Jul 26, 178
DictFolkMyth-1984, pp. 566, 793
EncyNatAmerRel-2001, p. 202
EncyRel-1987, vol. 10, p. 520

♦ 1902 ♦ **Nine Imperial Gods, Festival of the**
First nine days of ninth lunar month

As celebrated today in Singapore, the Festival of the Nine Imperial Gods derives from an ancient Chinese cleansing ritual. The festival begins with a procession to a body of water. There a Taoist priest prays for the spirits of the Gods to enter an urn of burning incense. The procession then carries the urn to a temple, where worshippers can bring offerings. Outside the Tou Mu Kong temple, near Kangkar, Singapore, people are informed of the Gods' presence by the raising of nine oil lamps dangling from a bamboo pole. Worshippers enter the temple by crossing a specially constructed bridge. By crossing the bridge, devotees trust that they are cleansed of all evil from the previous year.

Chinese operas known as *wayang* shows—some of which take two or more days to complete—are often performed during the nine days of the festival.

On the ninth day, a final procession takes the urn back to the water's edge, where it is placed in a small boat to carry the Gods back to the heavens.

CONTACTS:
Singapore Tourism Board
1156 Ave. of the Americas, Ste. 702
New York, NY 10036
212-302-4861; fax: 212-302-4801
www.visitsingapore.com

SOURCES:
FolkWrldHol-1999, p. 578

♦ 1903 ♦ **Nino Fidencio Festival**
October

In 1938, a local healer named El Nino Fidencio was allegedly murdered in the northeast Mexican town of Espinazo. Rumors spread that doctors, jealous of his healing abilities, had killed him.

Born Jose Fidencio Sintora Constantino in 1890, Fidencio displayed an early talent for herbal remedies. Soon, people from nearby towns would journey to Espinazo to see the *curandero*, or mystical healer, and be cured. In 1928, radical Mexican president Plutarco Elias Calles came to Espinazo to arrest the healer Fidencio for practicing medicine without a license. But Fidencio is said to have cured the president and his ailing daughter, which brought him and his healing miracles to national attention. Upon his death in 1938, rumors spread that Fidencio had been murdered. Detractors claim that Fidencio was an alcoholic who drank himself to an early death.

For a week each October, thousands of pilgrims flock to Espinazo to place flowers at the tomb of El Nino Fidencio and hold spontaneous rituals involving sacred songs, herbs, and various oils and potions. Those afflicted with disease bathe themselves in a small pond near the tomb that is said to contain healing waters. These rituals draw on Catholic ceremony as well as ancient Aztec beliefs and peasant folklore. Again drawing on Catholic teachings, pilgrims call Fidencio "El Guadalupano," or the son of the Virgin of Guadalupe, a Mexican saint. Despite warnings from the Catholic Church to stay away from this heretical pilgrimage, thousands of otherwise devoutly Catholic Mexicans come to remember the legendary village healer.

◆ 1904 ◆ Nippy Lug Day
Between February 6 and March 12; Friday following Shrove Tuesday

A "lug" at one time referred to the ear-flap of a man's cap, but in Scotland and northern England it became a synonym for the ear itself. In 19th-century Scotland, schoolchildren called their teachers "nip-lugs" because they often pulled their pupils' ears as a disciplinary measure. In Westmorland, England, it was traditional at one time for children to pinch each other's ears on the Friday following SHROVE TUESDAY, giving rise to the name Nippy Lug Day.

SOURCES:
DictDays-1988, p. 82

◆ 1905 ◆ Nirjala Ekadashi
May-June; 11th day of waxing half of Hindu month of Jyestha

Of the 24 EKADASHI or 11th-day fasts observed during the course of the Hindu year, Nirjala Ekadashi is one of the more important. No food or even water is taken on this day, which is an act of extreme devotion since the month of Jyestha is very hot. Both men and women observe a strict fast and offer *puja* (worship) to Vishnu to ensure happiness and forgiveness of their sins. *Panchamrata* is prepared by mixing together milk, ghee (clarified butter), curds, honey, and sugar. It is then offered to the image of Vishnu, which has been draped

in rich clothing and jewels, with a fan placed beside it. Hindus meditate on Vishnu as the Lord of the Universe and worship the deity with flowers, lamps, water, and incense.

Some Hindus believe that faithful observance of the fast and other rituals on Nirjala Ekadashi ensures happiness, salvation, longevity, and prosperity. Those who can afford to do so give clothes, grains, umbrellas, fans, and pitchers filled with water to the Brahmans.

SOURCES:
RelHolCal-2004, p. 170

◆ 1906 ◆ Nisei Week
Early August

Nisei Week is an annual Japanese-American festival in the Little Tokyo area of Los Angeles, Calif. Little Tokyo is the social, cultural, and economic center for the Japanese and Nisei community of southern California. The Nisei are people of Japanese descent born and raised in the United States. Held since 1934, this week-long festival features a parade, a carnival, Japanese folk dancing, celebrity appearances, and a prince and princess pageant. There are special exhibits of bonsai, flower arranging, doll making, tea ceremonies, and other Japanese arts. Sports competitions and demonstrations include jiu-jitsu and karate. Attendance is about 50,000.

CONTACTS:
Nisei Week Foundation
244 S. San Pedro St., Ste. 303
Los Angeles, CA 90012
213-687-7193; fax: 213-687-6510
www.niseiweek.org

◆ 1907 ◆ Niue Peniamina Gospel Day
Fourth Friday in October

Niue is a tropical island northeast of New Zealand that is approximately 269 square meters in size, with a population of approximately 1,500 people. It is one of the world's smallest self-governing states. Although the country was annexed to New Zealand in 1901, it gained sovereignty in 1974. The country still uses the New Zealand currency today.

Niue is believed to have been settled between 400 and 1100 CE by people from Samoa, Tonga, and the Cook Islands. Captain James Cook discovered the island in 1774 but met much resistance from the Niuans.

Niue Peniamina Gospel Day derives from the nation's conversion to Christianity. In 1830, John Williams, of the London Missionary Society, traveled to Niue, determined to convert the islanders to Christianity. He kidnapped two local boys named Niumaga and Uea to try to educate and convert them. Several months later, the boys returned to Niue, but the Niuans no longer accepted them. The islanders eventually killed Uea and his father.

Niumaga continued to face rejection by his fellow Niuans, so he and his friend, Peniamina Nukai, left for Samoa. Peniamina worked as a servant for Dr. George Turner, a famous missionary. While working for Dr. Turner, Peniamina learned to read and write, and he converted to Christianity.

On October 26, 1846, Peniamina returned to Niue, bringing with him his Christian beliefs and ideals. He preached to his fellow islanders and began to convert many to Christianity.

Today, Niue remains a deeply Christian country. Sunday is truly a day of rest; as a result most businesses are closed, and very few activities are conducted on Sunday. For example, fishing, diving and boating are not allowed on Sundays.

Every year, on the fourth Friday of October, Niuans observe Peniamina Gospel Day as a national holiday to celebrate the day that Peniamina brought Christianity to the island.

CONTACTS:
Niue Tourism Office
Commercial Centre
P.O. Box 42
Alofi, Niue Island
www.niueisland.com

♦ 1908 ♦ Nizhni Novgorod
Varies

The great medieval fair held at Nizhni Novgorod, Russia, began in the 16th century at the monastery of St. Macarius, a popular place of pilgrimage. It grew so large that the little town of Makaraev could barely accommodate it, and when it burned to the ground in 1816, it was relocated to a new town that had been built expressly to house it. The new city was located on the sandy plains where the Oka and Volga rivers flower together, making it an ideal spot for international trade. It was called Nizhni Novgorod or "Lower New City."

Nizhni Novgorod was largely a barter fair and entirely a market of direct trade, where no merchant placed orders for goods he could not inspect. Everything sold was displayed there, including cloth, furs, hides, cotton, iron, and half-wild horses. Although the height of the fair was in August, caravans and sailboats began to arrive in June. The bishop of the Russian Orthodox Church officially opened the fair with a solemn service on July 15th, but the real fair couldn't begin until the tea boats arrived, having sailed up the Volga River at the end of their 7,000-mile journey from China. Once the price of tea was determined, the prices of all the other goods was set and the trading began in earnest. This usually occurred during the first few days of August.

More than 200,000 traders took up residence in Nizhni Novgorod for the duration of the fair, and they spent most of their time smoking and drinking tea and making verbal agreements that they sealed with a handshake. By 1900, the fair was doing business worth more than $100 million a year. But during several periods—the Revolution in 1917, civil wars, and periods of famine—desperate Russians from nearby cities went down to the deserted fair and dismantled the stone and brick buildings to get at their wooden window and door frames, which they burned to stay warm.

The Soviet government under Lenin reopened the fair in 1923, but seven years later the Stalin regime abolished all 18,000 Russian fairs because they were not a part of the Kremlin-controlled trade program. The fairgrounds reopened in 1991 after the collapse of the Soviet Union. It has been modernized and now hosts major exhibition events year-round.

CONTACTS:
Russian Embassy
2650 Wisconsin Ave. N.W.
Washington, D.C. 20007
202-298-5700; fax: 202-298-5735
www.russianembassy.org

SOURCES:
BkFairs-1939, p. 188

♦ 1909 ♦ Nobel Prize Ceremony
December 10

Nobel Prizes are awarded each year to people, regardless of nationality, deemed by committees to have made the most significant practical efforts toward the well-being of the human race. In his will, the Swedish inventor Alfred Nobel (1833-1896) directed that the income from his $9 million estate be used to fund five annual prizes for the most important discoveries or inventions in the fields of physics, chemistry, and physiology or medicine; for the most distinguished literary work of an idealistic nature; and for the most effective work in the interest of international peace. The first Nobel Prizes were awarded in 1901, but a sixth prize—in economics—was added in 1969.

Prize winners receive the awards, each worth a little over $1 million, at a special ceremony in Stockholm, Sweden, on December 10, the anniversary of Alfred Nobel's death in 1896. The peace prize is awarded in Oslo, Norway.

CONTACTS:
The Nobel Foundation
Sturegatan 14
P.O. Box 5232
Stockholm, SE-102 45 Sweden
46-8-663-0920; fax: 46-8-660-38-47
www.nobelprize.org

SOURCES:
FestEur-1961, p. 150

♦ 1910 ♦ Noel Night
First Saturday in December

Noel Night is a community holiday celebration that takes place on the first Saturday of December in the University Cultural Center area of Detroit, Mich. The area encompasses such institutions as Wayne State University, museums devoted to art, science, history, and African-American history, and numerous churches, restaurants, and shops. The event area extends from Ferry Street to Willis Street on the north and south and from St. Antoine to Cass Avenue on the east and west, including the main thoroughfare Woodward Avenue, which is closed to automobile traffic during the festival.

Held annually since 1973, Noel Night offers dozens of unique holiday displays and activities, including horse-drawn carriage rides, a living nativity scene, musical and comedy performances, holiday lighting, and an ice sculpture competition. A community sing-a-long led by the Salvation Army Band concludes the festivities, which take place between 5:00 P.M. and 9:30 P.M. Restaurants and street vendors offer holiday foods and refreshments, including soups, roasted almonds, and hot chocolate, and museums offer free admission during the festival.

CONTACTS:
University Cultural Center Association
4735 Cass
Detroit, MI 48201
313-577-5088
www.detroitmidtown.com/05

♦ 1911 ♦ **Nomaoi Matsuri (Horse Festival)**
July 23-25

Eight villages take part in the Horse Festival held in Hara-machi, Japan, in July. Hibarino moor provides the open space where men on horseback wearing ancient armor and helmets reenact a military muster that was originally organized by a former lord of the fief. Other festival events that take place on the moor include the breaking of wild horses, horse races, and games, while in town there is a procession of men and their horses and a parade of shrine floats.

CONTACTS:
Haramachi City
2-27 Motomachi, Haramachi-shi
Fukushima-ken, 960-8035 Japan
81-2-4422-2111; fax: 81-2-4424-5214
www.city.minamisoma.lg.jp

SOURCES:
JapanFest-1965, p. 165

♦ 1912 ♦ **Nombre de Jesús**
February 1-15

The two-week fair known as Nombre de Jesús takes place in the village of San Pedro Nonualco in El Salvador. The celebration centers on two images of the Christ Child—one with blond hair and blue eyes, and the other with black hair and black eyes—which are sent from the nearby town of Cojute-peque. The light-complexioned Christ Child is the best-loved image, and people cover it with money and gifts as it passes. The major-domo of the fiesta is usually the fortunate one who gets to keep this image in his house during the two weeks.

People do traditional dances in a circle around the veiled figure of the blond infant—an activity that Catholic priests have tried, unsuccessfully, to discourage. Although many different local foods are served, a favorite is the dove-shaped candy called *chancaca*, made of ground corn and sugar, that young men traditionally present to their sweethearts.

CONTACTS:
Embassy of El Salvador
1400 16th St. N.W., Ste. 100
Washington, D.C. 20036
202-265-9671; fax: 202-232-3763
www.elsalvador.org

SOURCES:
FiestaTime-1965, p. 29

♦ 1913 ♦ **Nordic Fest**
Last full weekend in July

The Nordic Fest held annually in Decorah, Iowa, prides itself on preserving the area's Norwegian heritage without resorting to commercialism. From Friday night through Sunday of the last full weekend in July, the festival offers arts and crafts displays, dances, lectures, concerts, sporting events, and museum visits. Both the Norwegian-American Museum and the Porter House Museum are open to visitors, and there is a walking tour of the Home of the Trolls—a troll being the Norwegian version of the pixie or elf. The festival begins with a parade and Norse Fire Celebration, and the events that follow are all designed to highlight a particular aspect of Decorah's Norwegian heritage. Scandinavian dancers perform, Norse plays are put on for the children, and special Norwegian and English church services are held.

The festival has been held annually in Decorah since 1967. The Luther College Women's Club had sponsored a Scandinavian Festival Day since 1936, and eventually it was expanded to the present three-day event.

CONTACTS:
Nordic Fest
507 W. Water St.
P.O. Box 364
Decorah, IA 52101
800-382-3378 or 563-382-3990
www.nordicfest.com

SOURCES:
GdUSFest-1984, p. 55

♦ 1914 ♦ **Norsk Høstfest**
Second week in October

All five Scandinavian countries—Denmark, Finland, Iceland, Norway, and Sweden—are represented at the annual Scandinavian heritage festival known as Norsk Høstfest that has been held in Minot, North Dakota, since 1978. The festival includes performances by top entertainers, one of whom is selected by the previous year's ticketholders as the "People's Choice" and many of whom are either Scandinavian or Americans of Scandinavian descent. There are also Swedish accordion players, Scandinavian folk dancers, and Lakota flute players, who perform at the Høstfest complex on North Dakota's state fairgrounds in Minot. The complex includes five stages, 40 food booths, and dozens of demonstration areas for craftsmen and artisans—among them the highly skilled *rosemalers*, or "folk painters." The Viking Age Club sets up an authentic encampment to show how the North Plains Scandinavian settlers lived.

Food is a big part of the five-day festival, which features traditional Scandinavian delicacies. More than 60,000 visitors come to Minot to sample Swedish sweet bread, *søt suppe* (fruit soup), *potet klub* (potato dumpling), Icelandic cake, *rømmergrøt* ("red porridge," a rhubarb pudding), Danish kringle (pretzel-shaped cookie), *lefse* (a thin, potato cake spread with butter and cinnamon and folded over), and *lutefisk* (cod soaked in lye and then boiled). A similar Scandinavian festival, the Hjemkomst Festival, is held in June in Fargo.

CONTACTS:
Norsk Hostfest Association
P.O. Box 1347
Minot, ND 58702
701-852-2368; fax: 701-838-7873
www.hostfest.com

♦ 1915 ♦ North American Indian Days
Second week in July

One of the largest gatherings of United States and Canadian Indian tribes, held in Browning, Montana, the hub of the Blackfeet Indian Reservation in the northwest mountains of the state. The powwow grounds fill up with teepees for four festive days of traditional Indian dancing, games, and sporting events. There are also exhibits of arts and crafts—beadwork, quill and feather work, moccasins and other leather goods.

CONTACTS:
Blackfeet Nation
P.O. Box 850
Browning, MT 59417
406-338-7521; fax: 406-338-7530
www.blackfeetnation.com

SOURCES:
IndianAmer-1989, p. 23

♦ 1916 ♦ North American International Auto Show
Last two weeks in January

The North American International Auto Show (NAIAS) is an automobile exhibition held each year in Detroit, Mich., which is known as the Motor City. In addition to presenting cars that will be available to consumers in the upcoming model year, each year dozens of concept vehicles that have never been seen in North America or in the world are unveiled during the show.

The NAIAS is one of the oldest and largest automobile exhibitions in the world. It began in 1907 when the Detroit Auto Dealers Association formed and decided to showcase their offerings to the public. It has been held nearly every year since then, with the exception of several years during and after World War II.

The Detroit Auto Show began as a gathering in a riverside park and moved to various locations throughout the City of Detroit, finally locating in its current setting at Cobo Center in downtown Detroit in 1965. It has been called NAIAS since 1989, a name change that reflects the participation of automobile manufacturers from around the world. The show runs annually during the final two weeks in January, with the first week reserved for media and industry insiders and the second week open to the public. Since 1976 a black-tie charity ball has taken place on the eve of the public opening of the show. The 2008 show included 119 exhibits and was attended by more than 700,000 public spectators, 37,000 industry insiders, 15,000 charity preview guests, and 6,300 journalists from 63 countries.

CONTACTS:
North American International Auto Show
1900 W. Big Beaver
Troy, MI 48084
248-643-0250; fax: 248-637-0784
www.naias.com

Cobo Center
One Washington Blvd.
Detroit, MI 48226
313-877-8777 or 313-877-8111
www.cobocenter.com

♦ 1917 ♦ North American Solar Challenge
July

A biannual competition in which participants design, build, and race solar-powered cars in a cross-country event. The cars entered in the race (called "rayce" due to the solar-powered vehicles used) are designed and built by teams of engineering students from about 20 American and Canadian universities. The purpose of the event is "to promote and celebrate educational excellence and engineering creativity."

Originally begun as Sunrayce USA in 1990 and organized by General Motors, the race was renamed the American Solar Challenge in 2001 and the North American Solar Challenge in 2005. When the Department of Energy withdrew its support, the 2007 race was cancelled. The event is now sponsored by Toyota and the Crowder College MARET Center. The 2008 race will run some 2,500 miles from Dallas, Texas, to Calgary, Alberta, Canada, while the previous race, in 2005, went from Chicago to Los Angeles. While on the road, each solar-powered car is accompanied by a safety vehicle sporting rooftop hazard flashers; each solar caravan is accompanied by an official observer to keep contestants apprised of possible road problems ahead. The North American Solar Challenge is the longest solar-powered car race in the world.

CONTACTS:
North American Solar Challenge
601 Laclede Ave.
Neosho, MO 64850
417-455-5666; fax: 417-455-5669
www.americansolarchallenge.org

♦ 1918 ♦ North American Wife-Carrying Championship
October

The North American Wife-Carrying Championship began in 2000. The WIFE-CARRYING WORLD CHAMPIONSHIP, held in

Sonkajärvi, Finland, inspired contest organizers in Maine to develop a North American competition. The American competition takes place at the Sunday River Ski Resort in Bethel, Maine. As in the world championship, a man may carry a woman other than his wife. Penalties apply for dropping one's "wife." The couple who completes the course in the shortest length of time wins. The course measures 278 yards and includes two 39" hurdles, sand, grass, sharp turns, and a waist-deep pond. Winners fly to Finland to represent North America in the world championship.

CONTACTS:
Sunday River Ski Resort
P.O. Box 4500
Newry, ME 04216
207-824-3000; fax: 207-824-5110
www.sundayriver.com

♦ 1919 ♦ North Korea Victory Day
July 27

Victory Day marks the end of the Korean War, the three-year conflict between North Korea (official name: Democratic People's Republic of Korea), which was backed by the U.S.S.R. and China, and South Korea (official name: Republic of Korea), which was supported by the United Nations and United States. On July 27, 1953, the opponents signed an armistice that formally ended the war. The document ended overt hostilities, but it was not a permanent peace treaty between the nations. North and South Korea remain separate entities and occupy essentially the same territory they did when the war began. The border zone known as the demilitarized zone (DMZ) is heavily guarded on both sides, including almost 40,000 U.S. troops on the south side. Today, North Korea (official name: Democratic People's Republic of Korea) is a Communist country with a repressive government.

Victory Day is a public holiday observed throughout North Korea. Officials and citizens mark the occasion by laying wreaths and flowers at military cemeteries and monuments nationwide. In the capital city, Pyongyang, public celebrations can include displays by military personnel, dance performances, and youth oratorical events. In addition, officials take part in public wreath- and flower-laying ceremonies at national monuments in the city.

CONTACTS:
Permanent Representative of the Democratic People's Republic of
  Korea to the United Nations
820 Second Ave.
New York, NY 10017
212-972-3105; fax: 212-972-3154
www.korea-dpr.com

♦ 1920 ♦ North Pole Winter Carnival
Early March

The North Pole Winter Carnival is a weekend celebration of winter in North Pole, Alaska, a suburb of Fairbanks. North Pole was named by Con Miller, a man who bought a Fairbanks trading post in 1949. When he cleaned it out, he found a Santa Claus suit and started wearing it on trips to the interior to buy furs and sell supplies. A few years later he built a new trading post southeast of Fairbanks, called it Santa Claus House, and named the town around it North Pole. The town now has a government and a post office. It also has the Winter Carnival which features the North Pole Championship Sled Dog Race, a dog weight-pulling contest, carnival rides and games, food booths, crafts bazaars, and live entertainment.

CONTACTS:
City of North Pole
125 Snowman Ln.
North Pole, AK 99705
907-488-2281; fax: 907-488-3002
www.northpolealaska.com

♦ 1921 ♦ Northern Games
July

A showcase for traditional Inuit and Indian sports and culture, the Northern Games are held in the Northwest Territories of Canada in July each year. They feature traditional dances, drumming competitions, arts and crafts displays, and the "Good Woman" Contest, which gives Northern women a chance to demonstrate their skill in such areas as animal skinning and bannock baking. The games are held in Inuvik and draw competitors from Alaska, Yukon Territory, and Labrador as well.

CONTACTS:
Town of Inuvik
Tourism Department
P.O. Box 1160
Inuvik, NT X0E 0T0 Canada
867-777-8600; fax: 867-777-8601
www.inuvik.ca

SOURCES:
GdWrldFest-1985, p. 42

♦ 1922 ♦ Northwest Folklife Festival
May, Memorial Day weekend

The Northwest Folklife Festival is an international four-day event started in 1972 in Seattle, Wash., that draws performers and artisans from Washington, Oregon, Idaho, Alaska, and the Canadian province of British Columbia. The emphasis is on amateur performers and ethnicity with some 100 countries represented. Events include music and dance on 17 stages; demonstrations by artisans of such skills as leather tanning, boatbuilding, blacksmithing, and broom making; and an International Food Village that offers food from more than 30 nations.

The festival spans the MEMORIAL DAY weekend, starting on Friday and winding up on Monday.

CONTACTS:
Northwest Folklife
158 Thomas St., Ste. 32
Seattle, WA 98109
206-684-7300; fax: 206-684-7190
www.nwfolklife.org

SOURCES:
MusFestAmer-1990, p. 230

♦ 1923 ♦ Norway Constitution Day (Syttende Mai)
May 17

May 17, 1814, marks both Norway's declaration of independence from Sweden and the day on which its constitution was signed. At that time, however, the king of Sweden still ruled Norway, and true independence didn't come until 1905, when the union with Sweden was dissolved and Norway chose its own king. Nevertheless, this day remains the great spring festival in Norway, and today it is celebrated primarily by young people.

The children's procession in Oslo, the capital city, is the largest of many school parades throughout the country. Marching behind their school bands and banners, the children pass under the balcony of the Royal Palace in salute to the king. Students who are about to graduate from secondary school and enter college cheer and spin their tasseled caps in the air on bamboo canes. In the afternoon, many neighborhoods have celebrations of their own so that children who are too young to participate in the school parades may march near their homes. Everyone joins in the procession, waving Norwegian flags, leading dogs, and pushing baby carriages. Eventually they congregate in the town square to listen to patriotic speeches and play games.

May 17 has been celebrated since the 1820s and is sometimes referred to as **Norway's National Day** or **Norway's Liberation Day**.

See also Syttende Mai Fest

CONTACTS:
Norwegian Ministry of Foreign Affairs
7 Juni-plassen/Victoria Terrasse
P.O. Box 8114
Oslo, N-0032 Norway
47-2224-3600; fax: 47-2224-9580, 47-2224-9581
www.regjeringen.no/en.html?id=4

SOURCES:
AmerBkDays-2000, p. 372
AnnivHol-2000, p. 83
BkHolWrld-1986, May 17
NatlHolWrld-1968, p. 64
OxYear-1999, p. 210

♦ 1924 ♦ Nuestra Señora de Itatí
July 16

The town of Itatí is situated on the banks of Argentina's Paraná River. Two days before the well-known festival of Neustra Señora de Itatí, which is held on July 16, thousands of pilgrims begin to arrive from San Luis de Palmar in a seemingly endless procession of people on horseback, in carts, and on foot, carrying flags and an image of St. Louis. Festival goers arrive from all over Argentina as well, not only to honor Nuestra Señora but to enjoy the nightly festivities of drinking and games of chance.

Worship services take place on the 16th in the huge basilica that guards the copper statue of the Virgin, which is more than 24 feet high. Pilgrims even ascend up into the statue until their heads reach the Virgin's crown.

CONTACTS:
National Secretariat of Tourism, Tourist Information Centers
Av. Santa Fe 883
Buenos Aires, C1059ABC Argentina
54-11-4312-2232; fax: 54-11-4302-7816
www.turismo.gov.ar/eng/menu.htm

SOURCES:
FiestaTime-1965, p. 113

♦ 1925 ♦ Nuestra Senora de Peñafrancia, Feast of
Third week of September

A grand fiesta devoted to Our Lady of Peñafrancia, held in Naga City on the Bicol peninsula in the Philippines. Some 200 years ago a Spanish official attributed the recovery of his ill daughter to the lady and built a shrine to her in Naga City, starting the devotion to her that has lasted into the present.

This is the biggest festival of the Bicol region; it starts with a nine-day novena at the Naga Cathedral. A procession then carries the image of the Virgin to a pagoda on a festooned barge, which is surrounded by a flotilla of smaller boats. The people on the smaller boats chant prayers and hymns as they proceed along the river. Meanwhile, on the shore, pilgrims from other Bicol provinces kneel and pray as the barge passes by. When the water-borne pagoda has finished its journey, there are shouts of "Viva la virgen!" and the image is taken back to its shrine.

CONTACTS:
Philippine Tourism Center
556 Fifth Ave.
New York, NY 10036
212-575-7915; fax: 212-302-6759
www.philippinetourism.us

♦ 1926 ♦ Nuits de Fourvière
Late June to early September

The city of Lyon, France, was called "Lugdunum" in Roman times, and the city's old Roman theater, the Théâtre Romain de Fourvière, is still used for public performances. This large outdoor arena seats 3,000 people and is the principal venue in a summer festival known as the Nuits de Fourvière, or Nights of Fourvière. This festival includes music, ballet, and theater events. Musical performances range from opera and symphonic music, to world and pop music. The Nuits de Fourvière begins in June and ends in September, though most of the performances take place in July.

CONTACTS:
Les Nuits de Fourviere
1 Rue Cleberg
Lyon, 69005 France
33-4-7257-1540; fax: 33-4-7257-1549
www.nuits-de-fourviere.org

♦ 1927 ♦ **Nunavut Day**
July 9

In relation to Canada's other provincial holidays, Nunavut Day is a new observance because the territory of Nunavut is itself new. Canada's northernmost territory was established on July 9, 1993, through a land claim signed by the national government and the Inuit of the Nunavut Settlement Area. Territory leaders first designated Nunavut Day on April 1, but in 1999 they settled on the present date to commemorate the historic land agreement, which conferred self-governing powers to the territory.

Most of the day's activities take place in Nunavut's hub and capital city, Iqaluit. Festivities include barbeques, parades, traditional Inuit games, and feasts featuring local cuisine of caribou, walrus, and arctic char. In recent years, the day's program has also included organized tournaments of cribbage, checkers, and Scrabble.

CONTACTS:
Government of Nunavut
Directorate
P.O. Box 1000
Station 700
Iqualuit, NU X0A 0H0 Canada
www.gov.nu.ca

♦ 1928 ♦ **Nusardil**
Seventh Sunday after Pentecost (June)

Assyrian Christians celebrate Nusardil to commemorate the church's baptism ceremony. But the origins of the ceremony are said to date to pre-Christian times. Assyrian pagans worshipped gods of fire, air, and water. Sprinkling water on the path of a pagan religious procession was a common practice meant to show respect. When St. Thomas converted the Assyrians to Christianity in the first century C.E., he resorted to a mass baptism because of the many people involved. His splashing of water on a crowd of people, combined with the earlier pagan tradition, led to the current practice.

Traditionally, Nusardil participants splash or spill water on each other in a ritualistic way. Even those not associated with the celebration may get splashed for fun. Today, children also use squirt guns or similar devices to spray water on each other and on their elders. While the ceremony has its serious side, it is also a lighthearted occasion. Assyrian churches in America will often have a picnic on Nusardil. Food and a variety of outdoor games are combined with the water splashing ceremony.

CONTACTS:
Assyrian Church of the East
P.O. Box 621
Fairfield, New South Wales 2165 Australia
www.assyrianchurch.com.au

♦ 1929 ♦ **Nuuk Snow Festival**
Third weekend in March

In 1994 the town of Nuuk, Greenland, held its first snow-sculpture festival. It has since become an annual event, sched-uled for the third weekend in March. It attracts contestants from all over Greenland, as well as from Canada, the United States, Sweden, Norway, Finland, and Denmark. Festival organizers give each team of sculptors a compressed block of snow. The teams then set to work, transforming the square block into an amazing variety of shapes. Their efforts are displayed in a sculpture park that is illuminated at night, creating beautiful lights and shadows on the sculptures. Prizes for the best sculptures are awarded on the fourth day of the festival.

CONTACTS:
Nuuk Tourism
P.O. Box 199
Nuuk, DK-3900 Greenland
299-32-27-00; fax: 299-32-27-10
www.snow.gl/database.asp?lang=eng

♦ 1930 ♦ **Nyambinyambi**
Spring

The annual planting festival called the **Rain-Calling Ceremony**, or Nyambinyambi, is observed by the Kwangali people of Namibia, who believe that the land must be cleansed before the rain can fall and the fields can be planted. The chief sends his grandson out to cut down a tree, which is erected at the entrance gate to the village. The people lay their planting tools, seeds, pumpkins, and hunting weapons at the base of the tree and pray to the god known as Karunga, or Kalunga, to bring them a plentiful harvest and a good hunting season. In the Songhay's region of Niger, this is called **Genji Bi Hori**, "Black Spirit Festival." They also pray that rain will fall soon after the ceremony, which is believed to rid the country of bad luck.

The Songhay rain-bringing ceremony is held at the end of the hot dry season. Known as **Yenaandi** ("the act of cooling off") or the **Rain Dance**, it is usually held on a Thursday, the *Tooru* ("gods") sacred day, and is addressed to the four principal Tooru deities: Dongo, the god of thunder; Cirey, the god of lightning; Moussa Nyori, the god of clouds and wind; and Hausakoy, the god of blacksmithing.

CONTACTS:
Embassy of the Republic of Niger
2204 R St. N.W.
Washington, D.C. 20008
202-483-4224; fax: 202-483-3169
www.nigerembassyusa.org

SOURCES:
FolkWrldHol-1999, p. 273

♦ 1931 ♦ **Nyepi**
March

The people of Bali in Indonesia celebrate the VERNAL EQUINOX and the New Year by driving the devils out of the villages and then observing a day of stillness, known as Nyepi or Njepi. It is believed that when spring arrives and the rainy season ends, the Lord of Hell, Yama, sweeps the devils out of Hades. The devils then fall on Bali, making it necessary to purify the entire island.

First the evil spirits are lured out of their hiding places with an elaborate offering of food, drink, money, and household utensils. Samples of every seed and fruit and of every animal used as food are all laid out in an eight-point star representing the Rose of the Winds. Then the evil spirits are driven out of the village by the strong incantations and curses of the priests, and by the people who run through the streets with their faces and bodies painted, lighting firecrackers, carrying torches, beating the trees and the ground, and banging drums, tin cans, and anything else they can find to make noise to drive the demons away. Animal sacrifices play an important role in the ceremony, because blood is believed to cleanse the impure earth.

The following day, Nyepi, marks the start of the New Year and the arrival of spring. It is observed with the suspension of all activity: no cooking or fires, no sexual intercourse, and no work of any kind are permitted.

CONTACTS:
Indonesian Embassy
2020 Massachusetts Ave. N.W.
Washington, D.C. 20036
202-775-5200; fax: 202-775-5365
www.embassyofindonesia.org

SOURCES:
FolkWrldHol-1999, p. 216
HolSymbols-2009, p. 640

O

♦ 1932 ♦ Oakley (Annie) Festival
First weekend in August

The legendary markswoman known as Annie Oakley was born Phoebe Ann Moses near Willow Dell, Ohio, on August 13, 1860. Her father died when she was very young, and Annie learned to shoot game for her family with her father's rifle. At the age of 15 she was invited to participate in a shooting match in Cincinnati with Frank Butler, a champion marksman. She won the match and married Butler a year later. Together they toured the country with their shooting act, "Butler and Oakley," and in 1884 they joined Buffalo Bill's Wild West Show. They performed with the show throughout Europe and the United States for 17 years, including a command performance for Queen Victoria during her Jubilee year (1887). Annie and Frank returned to Ohio in the 1920s to be near their family and friends. She died in Greenville on November 3, 1926, and he died 18 days later.

The Annie Oakley Festival in Greenville commemorates "Little Miss Sure Shot" (as she was dubbed by the great Sioux Indian chief, Sitting Bull) with shooting and sports competitions and demonstrations of hide tanning, knife throwing, bead working, and other activities associated with the Old West. There is a tour of Annie Oakley's gravesite and a Miss Annie Oakley Shooting Contest for young girls. A highlight of the festival is the Annie Oakley Days Parade.

CONTACTS:
Darke County Visitors Bureau
537 S. Broadway, Ste. 203
Greenville, OH 45331
800-504-2995 or 937-548-5158; fax: 937-548-2385
www.visitdarkecounty.org

SOURCES:
AmerBkDays-2000, p. 585

♦ 1933 ♦ Oath Monday
July

A centuries-old custom in Ulm, Germany, that combines politics and pageantry. Each year in July, the bürgermeister, or mayor, gives a policy speech in the market square, listens to the public discussions, and then, after the ringing of a bell, takes an oath swearing to stand "for rich and poor" in all matters "of the public weal."

Events then shift to the Danube River and a waterborne parade called the *Nabada*. Rafts and boats are decorated with tableaux of papier-mâché figures that satirize local and regional politics. With them are floating bands and private boats. Later, back on land, a medieval pageant is presented.

The oath-taking began in 1397 when the city was on the verge of bankruptcy. The nobles, who had been running the city, agreed to sit down with representatives of the guilds—groups of merchants and craftsmen. At the close of the negotiations, the guilds had a majority on the city council, the citizens had the right to a hearing before major city decisions were made, and the Solemn Oath was established, ending the privileges of the aristocracy.

CONTACTS:
Tourist-Information Centre Ulm
Münsterplatz 50
Ulm, Baden-Wrttemburg 89073 Germany
49-731-161-28-30; fax: 49-731-161-16-41
www.tourismus.ulm.de/kurzinfos/gb-u_ulm.pdf

♦ 1934 ♦ Oberammergau Passion Play
May through October, once every decade in years ending in zero

The most famous of Passion plays, held since the 17th century in the small woodcarving village of Oberammergau, Germany, in the Bavarian Alps.

The play, depicting the story of Christ's suffering, crucifixion, and resurrection, is presented in six hours by a cast of about 2,000. All performers are villagers, and the 600 with speaking parts are required to have been born in Oberammergau. The role of Mary is traditionally played by an unmarried woman. Close to half a million people attend the productions, which are staged in an open-air theater seating 5,000.

Legend says that the play was first performed in 1634 in fulfillment of a vow. The plague was sweeping Europe, and the Oberammergau elders swore to God that they would reenact the Passion of Christ if he would spare the remaining villagers; already a fifth of the population had been lost. The plague passed by, and the play has been performed since then (shifting to decennial years in 1700), except in 1870 during the Franco-Prussian War and during World War II. In modern times, the play has aroused protests that the 1860 text had anti-Semitic overtones. Director Christian Stückl and assistant director Otto Huber revised the text and music for the 2000 Passion Play in response to those concerns.

CONTACTS:
Oberammergau Tourismus
Eugen-Papst-St. 9a
Oberammergau, D-82487 Germany
49-8822-922-74-0; fax: 49-8822-922-74-5
www.oberammergau.de/ot_e/index.htm

SOURCES:
EncyEaster-2002, p. 458
GdWrldFest-1985, p. 86
IntlThFolk-1979, p. 146

♦ 1935 ♦ **Obon Festival**
July 13-15; August 13-15

Also called the **Bon Festival** or **Festival of the Dead**, this is the time when the dead revisit the earth, according to Japanese Buddhist belief. Throughout Japan, in either July or August, depending on the area, religious rites and family reunions are held in memory of the dead.

On the first evening of the festival, small bonfires are lit outside homes to welcome the spirits of ancestors. A meal, usually vegetables, rice cakes, and fruit, is set out for the spirits, and for two days they are spoken to as though they were present. On the final day (July 15 or Aug. 15), farewell dumplings are prepared, and another bonfire is lit outside the house to guide the spirits back. The climax is the *Bon-Odori*, "dance of rejoicing," folk dances held in every town by the light of paper lanterns, to comfort the souls of the dead. Some Bon-Odori dances are especially famous—one being the **Awa Odori** of Tokushima, which is accompanied by puppet shows and groups of musicians parading night and day.

At midnight some families gather the leftover rice cakes and food and take them to the waterfront. They are placed in a two- or three-foot-long boat made of rice straw with a rice straw sail; a lit paper lantern is on the bow and burning joss sticks at the stern. The breeze carries the boats, sustaining the spirits on their outward trip.

Obon celebrations are also held in Japanese communities throughout the world. About 500 people usually take part in the Bon-Odori in Chicago in July, and there are noted celebrations in several California cities.

CONTACTS:
Japan Information Network, Japan Center for Intercultural
   Communications
2-7-7 Hirakawacho
Chiyodaku
Tokyo, 102-0093 Japan
81-3-3263-5041; fax: 81-3-3230-4107
home.jcic.or.jp/en/index-e.html

SOURCES:
BkFest-1937, pp. 80, 200
BkHolWrld, Jul 13
DictFolkMyth-1984, pp. 154, 155, 541, 542, 730, 812, 1051
DictWrldRel-1989, pp. 31, 135, 374
EncyRel-1987, vol. 2, p. 553
FolkAmerHol-1999, p. 294
FolkWrldHol-1999, p. 457
IntlThFolk-1979, p. 261
RelHolCal-2004, p. 220

♦ 1936 ♦ **Obzinky**
Late August or early September

There are two harvest celebrations in the Czech and Slovak Republics. One of them, known as **Posviceni**, is the church consecration of the harvest. The other, Obzinky, is a secular festival where the field workers celebrate the end of the harvest by making a wreath out of corn, ears of wheat or rye, and wildflowers. Sometimes the wreath is placed on the head of a pretty young girl, and sometimes it is placed in a wagon along with decorated rakes and scythes and pulled in procession to the home of the landowner. The laborers present the wreath and congratulate their employer on a good harvest, after which they are invited to participate in dancing and feasting at the farm owner's expense. Foods served at the feast traditionally include roast pig, roast goose, and *Kolace*—square cakes filled with plum jam or a stuffing made from sweetened cheese or poppy seed. Beer and *slivovice*, a prune liquor, accompany the food.

The woman who binds the last sheaf is known as the *Baba* ("old woman") in some areas. In others, the Baba is a doll made from the last sheaf of grain and decorated with ribbons and flowers. Like the wreath, the Baba is carried in procession to the landlord's home, where it occupies a place of honor until the next harvest.

A similar harvest festival, known as the **Nubaigai**, is held in Lithuania. Here, too, a Baba is borne in procession to the farm; sometimes the worker who bound the last sheaf is wrapped up in it. But the harvest wreath is carried on a plate covered with a white linen cloth, and as the procession advances, the reapers sing an old song about how they rescued the crop from a huge bison that tried to devour it.

SOURCES:
BkFest-1937, p. 90
FolkWrldHol-1999, p. 525

♦ 1937 ♦ **Ochi Day**
October 28

Ochi Day is a national holiday in Greece related to the word *ochi*, which means "no." (Ochi can also be spelled *oxi*; it is pronounced "O-hee," with a gutteral h-sound.) This holiday commemorates the day during World War II when Greeks said ochi to an attempted incursion ordered by Italy's fascist dictator, Benito Mussolini.

On the morning of October 28, in 1940, the Italian ambassador to Greece called on Gen. Ioannis Metaxas, the self-appointed prime minister, to demand that Italian troops be allowed to occupy certain strategic areas in Greece. Metaxas curtly responded, "Ochi." The Italians invaded, but were routed by the Greeks.

Ochi Day is observed in Greece with military and school parades; it is also a public holiday celebrated in Cyprus with parades.

CONTACTS:
Embassy of Greece
2217 Massachusetts Ave. N.W.
Washington, D.C. 20008
202-939-1300; fax: 202-939-1324
www.greekembassy.org

SOURCES:
AnnivHol-2000, p. 179

♦ 1938 ♦ Octave of Our Lady, Consoler of the Afflicted
April-May; third through fifth Sundays after Easter

The **Octave of Notre Dame la Consolatrice des Affligés** or **Our Lady of Luxembourg** is observed in Luxembourg beginning on the third Sunday after EASTER and lasting from eight to 15 days. Since 1666, when Luxembourg-Ville was dedicated to the patronage of Mary the Consolatrice and the keys of the city were entrusted to her statue in the cathedral, she has been regarded as the capital city's protector, and her festival is the country's most outstanding religious celebration. Colorful banners are hung across the streets, and the route of the procession is lined with fir trees. Brass bands, Boy Scouts, Girl Guides, school and church groups, and small children dressed as priests, bishops, and cardinals start the procession, scattering rose petals. The image of the Virgin follows, dressed in dark blue velvet embroidered with gold and jewels. The symbolic key of Luxembourg-Ville hangs from one of her wrists.

According to legend, the statue was discovered in a hollow oak in 1624 by some Jesuit students. They took it to the Jesuit college church (now the cathedral) and placed it on the altar. That night the figure vanished mysteriously and was later found in the oak. The same thing occurred a second time, at which point the church fathers realized that the Virgin wished to remain outside the fortress walls. They built a tiny chapel for the image in 1625, which became a pilgrimage center. The chapel was destroyed in the French Revolution, but the image was miraculously saved and eventually installed in the cathedral's main altar. When NAPOLEON I made his triumphal entry into the fortress after the Revolution, a little girl officially presented him with the keys on a crimson cushion. "Take them back," he told her. "They are in good hands."

CONTACTS:
Luxembourg National Tourist Office
17 Beekman Pl.
New York, NY 10022
212-935-8888; fax: 212-935-5896
www.visitluxembourg.com

SOURCES:
FestWestEur-1958, p. 109

♦ 1939 ♦ October Feasts
October

The October Feasts have been held every year in the city of Guadalajara in the state of Jalisco, Mexico, since 1965. Throughout the month residents and visitors enjoy a variety of cultural events that celebrate local and international culture, including opera, jazz and other musical performances, art exhibits, folk dances, ballet, theater, and food. Attendees can also find amusement park rides, bungee jumping, and a haunted house billed as "one of the largest in Latin America."

CONTACTS:
Guadalajara Tourism Bureau
Monumento Los Arcos
Av. Vallarta 2641
Col. Arcos Vallarta, 44110 Mexico
52-3616-9150; fax: 52-3616-9150
vive.guadalajara.gob.mx/indexi.asp

♦ 1940 ♦ October Horse Sacrifice
October 15

In ancient Rome, a chariot race was held in the Field of Mars on October 15. After the race was over, the right-hand horse of the winning chariot was killed as a sacrifice to Mars. The head was cut off first, and there was a fight between the inhabitants of two different quarters of the city to see who could seize the head and place it in a designated spot. As soon as the tail was cut off, it was rushed to the king's hearth so that the blood would fall on the hearth. The rest of the blood was preserved until April 21, when it was mixed with other blood in a special ceremony and given to shepherds to burn, since they believed that the smoke would purify their flocks (*see* PARILIA).

The symbolic elements of the October Horse Sacrifice—the race, the choice of the right-hand horse, the blood, the hearth, and the necklace of loaves that was hung around the horse's head—all have strong associations with fertility. Although the horse sacrifice may have started out as a fertility rite, it later became a martial one.

SOURCES:
DictFolkMyth-1984, p. 811
DictRomRel-1996, p. 168
FestRom-1981, p. 193
OxYear-1999, p. 415

♦ 1941 ♦ October War of Liberation Anniversary
October 6

In Syria, the anniversary of the Arab-Israeli War of 1973 is celebrated on October 6, the day the hostilities started with a surprise attack by Syrian and Egyptian forces that caught the Israelis off guard during the Jewish fast of YOM KIPPUR. Although the Arab armies were turned back, they inflicted heavy casualties on Israel and reclaimed some of the land they had lost in the Six-Day War. Also known as **Tishrin**—after the month of October in which the war started—the celebration tends to play up the Arab soldiers' role in the war with special television broadcasts glorifying the conflict, art exhibits, plays, films, concerts, rallies, and wreath-laying ceremonies. No mention is made of the fact that 6,000 Syrians died in the conflict, or that Israeli troops reached the outskirts of Damascus.

In Egypt, October 6 is Armed Forces Day, commemorating the Egyptians' role in the October War. Anwar Sadat, the hero of that war, was assassinated on October 6, 1981, while viewing the Armed Forces Day parade.

See also ARMED FORCES DAY (EGYPT)

CONTACTS:
Embassy of Syria
2215 Wyoming Ave. N.W.
Washington, D.C. 20008
202-232-6313; fax: 202-234-9548
www.syrianembassy.us

♦ 1942 ♦ **Odalan (Temple's Birthday)**
Various

Hindus in Bali, an island in Indonesia, celebrate the birthday of their local temple every 210 days. Odalans commemorate the anniversary of a temple's consecration. Because the Balinese Pawukon calendar is 210 days long, this happens roughly every seven months according to the Gregorian calendar. Most often, odalans last about three days, though the festivities can go on for a week or more.

Before an odalan, people are busy preparing food and other offerings and decorating the temple. An odalan consists of worship services, presentations of such offerings as food, money, and flowers in the temple, and special anointings. After religious services, there are huge feasts, music and dancing, and puppet plays.

CONTACTS:
Indonesian Embassy
2020 Massachusetts Ave. N.W.
Washington, D.C. 20036
202-775-5200; fax: 202-775-5365
www.embassyofindonesia.org

SOURCES:
FestWrld: Indonesia-1997, p. 12
IntlThFolk-1979, p. 220

♦ 1943 ♦ **Odo Festival**
December-August, biannually

The Odo festival marks the return of the dead (*odo*) to visit the living in the northern Igbo villages of Nigeria. Lasting in some places from December until August, the festival has three distinct stages: the arrival of the odo, their stay with the living, and their departure. The first stage is observed with ritual celebrations and festivities welcoming the returning spirits of the dead. Then there is a stretch of six or more months during which the spirits of the dead interact with their living relatives and visit their ancestral homes. Their final departure is a very emotional affair (*see* AWURU ODO FESTIVAL), since they will not return for two more years.

Odo plays, featuring certain stock characters identified by their costumes and the manner in which they interact with the audience, are usually performed at the return and staying stages of the odo journey. Most of the roles are played by men, while the women function as chorus members and sometimes as spectators. The performers wear costumes traditionally made from plant fiber, leaves, beads, and feathers, although more durable cloth costumes are becoming more common in contemporary Odo plays. A musical accompaniment, featuring xylophones, drums, and rattles, is known as *obilenu* music, meaning "that which lies above."

CONTACTS:
Embassy of the Federal Republic of Nigeria
3519 International Ct. N.W.
Washington, D.C. 20008
202-986-8400; fax: 202-775-1385
www.nigeriaembassyusa.org

SOURCES:
FolkWrldHol-1999, p. 682

♦ 1944 ♦ **Odunde Festival**
Early June

The Odunde Festival takes place annually on the streets of south Philadelphia over the second weekend in June. Odunde means "Happy New Year" in the language of the Yoruba people of Nigeria. A celebration of the African new year, the Odunde Festival centers on a vibrant procession to the Schuylkill River, where participants make offerings of flowers and fruit to the River Goddess Oshun. Oshun is one of 401 orishas, similar to Christian saints, revered in the Yoruba religion, Ifa. Drumming, singing, incantations, and prayers accompany the procession and offerings. All are welcome to take part in the parade and ceremonies.

The festival also features a wealth of entertainment, from rap to fashion shows to tap dancing to African dance. African-centered food, crafts, clothing, and jewelry are on offer. The festival also has incorporated such events as a reception for ambassadors and an African business symposium. Founded in 1975 with a $100 grant, the popular, free festival welcomes as many as 500,000 participants over its three days.

CONTACTS:
Odunde, Inc.
P.O. Box 21748
Philadelphia, PA 19146
215-732-8510; fax: 215-732-8508
www.odundeinc.org

SOURCES:
AAH-2007, p. 361
HolSymbols-2009, p. 652

♦ 1945 ♦ **Odwira**
September

Odwira is a celebration of national identity by the Akan or Asante people of Ghana, once known as the Gold Coast. The festival originated centuries ago as a time for people to assemble after the yam harvest, and was inaccurately called the Yam Festival by non-Africans.

The kingdom of Ashanti, which is now the region of Ashanti, became rich and powerful in the late 1600s under its first ruler, Asantahene ("King") Osei Tutu. He is believed to have initiated the festival with the additional purpose of reinforcing the loyalty of the subjugated chiefs. The nation he built up withstood the British until 1901. He built a palace at Kumasi, and to further strengthen the nation, he and a priest, Okomfo Anokye, introduced the legendary Golden Stool. Supposed to have been brought down from heaven, it was thought to enshrine the nation's soul and became a symbol of the bond between all Ashanti people. Tutu also set down laws for life and religion. Much of this culture still survives.

During Odwira, the national identity is reinforced with purification ceremonies: a priest in each town prepares a purification bundle of certain tree branches and shoots, and in the evening carries it out of town and buries it. The Golden Stool is carried in a procession and placed on a throne without touching the ground. Huge umbrellas to protect participants from the sun add to the color of the procession. Drums and horns provide music.

CONTACTS:
Ministry of Tourism & Diasporan Relations, Ghana Tourist Board
P.O. Box 4386
Accra, Ghana
233-21-222153; fax: 233-21-244611
www.touringghana.com

SOURCES:
BkHolWrld-1986, Sep 19
EncyRel-1987, vol. 1, p. 167
FolkWrldHol-1999, p. 526
HolSymbols-2009, p. 654

♦ 1946 ♦ **Ohio River Sternwheel Festival**
September, weekend after Labor Day

A sternwheeler is a boat propelled by a paddle wheel at the stern or rear of the vessel. At one time they were a common sight along the Ohio River, although many have fallen into decay or have been turned into floating restaurants.

The riverfront town of Marietta, Ohio, is home to two of the sternwheelers that remain in working order and is the site of an annual Sternwheel Festival celebrating the heyday of the riverboat during the 19th century. Anywhere from 25 to 30 sternwheelers arrive in Marietta during the first week in September for the festival, which begins on the Friday after LABOR DAY.

Outdoor concerts, calliope music, entertainment by singers and dancers, and the crowning of Queen Genevieve of the River take place on Saturday, and on Sunday there are sternwheel races. Two of the largest and best-known sternwheelers, the *Delta Queen* and the *River Queen*, participate in the festival every year.

CONTACTS:
Ohio River Sternwheel Festival
121 Putnam St., Ste. 110

P.O. Box 2109
Marietta, OH 45750
800-288-2577 or 740-373-5178
www.ohioriversternwheelfestival.org, www.mariettao

♦ 1947 ♦ **Oklahoma Day**
April 22

After forcing the Indians to move west of the Mississippi River during the early decades of the 19th century, Congress set aside a vast area including all of what is now Oklahoma and called it the Indian Territory, telling them the land would be theirs forever. But eventually the U.S. government reneged on its policy in response to pressure from railroad companies and land-hungry homesteaders. Part of the Indian Territory was opened to white settlement by allowing "land runs," in which homesteaders raced across the border to stake their claim to 160-acre plots offered free of charge. Those who managed to sneak across the line before the official opening were called "sooners," which is how Oklahoma came to be nicknamed "the Sooner State." The land run of April 22, 1889, paved the way for the organization of the Oklahoma Territory in 1890, and for Oklahoma's statehood in 1907.

Also known as **Oklahoma 89ers Day**, the celebrations on April 22 focus on the town of Guthrie, the site of the original land office about 80 miles from the starting border. In 1915, the "89ers," as the original participants came to be called, reenacted the land rush, and each year Guthrie observes its anniversary with an 89ers festival. Elsewhere in Oklahoma, the day is celebrated with parades, rodeos, and events based on the land rush theme.

See also CHEROKEE STRIP DAY

CONTACTS:
Oklahoma Historical Society
2401 N. Laird Ave.
Oklahoma City, OK 73105
800-288-2577 or 405-521-2491; fax: 405-521-2492
www.ok-history.mus.ok.us

Guthrie Chamber of Commerce
212 W. Oklahoma Ave.
Guthrie, OK 73044
405-282-1947; fax: 405-282-5389
www.guthrieok.com

SOURCES:
AmerBkDays-2000, p. 304

♦ 1948 ♦ **Oklahoma Historical Day**
October 10

The early history of Oklahoma is replete with stories about a French family named Chouteau. Major Jean Pierre Chouteau and his half-brother, René Auguste, monopolized the fur trade with the Indians, and in 1796 Chouteau established the first permanent non-Indian settlement within the boundaries of what is now Oklahoma when he built a cabin to serve as a headquarters and trading post in Salina. Chouteau's birthday, October 10, became a legal holiday known as Oklahoma

Historical Day in 1939, and a major annual celebration, also called **Chouteau Day**, is held in Salina each year, though it is no longer a state holiday.

CONTACTS:
Salina Chamber of Commerce
900 N. Saltwell St.
Salina, OK 74365
918-434-8181

SOURCES:
AmerBkDays-2000, p. 699
AnnivHol-2000, p. 171

♦ 1949 ♦ **Okmulgee Pecan Festival**
Third weekend in June

The Okmulgee Pecan Festival is a nutty festival in Okmulgee, Okla., that made the *Guinness Book of World Records* in 1988 for the world's largest pecan pie. The pie had a diameter of 40 feet, and it weighed about 16½ tons. Even with the help of the culinary arts department of the Oklahoma State University Technical Branch in Okmulgee, this was an enormous task. So in 1990 the big event was a pecan cookie with a diameter of 32 feet and a weight of 7,500 pounds. That was a bit of a chore, too. In 1991, it was decided to keep it simple and celebrate with the "World's Largest Pecan Cookie and Ice Cream Party." More than 15,000 cookies and 5,000 single servings of vanilla ice cream were served.

Okmulgee, a name that means "bubbling waters" in the Creek language, is the capital of the Creek Nation. It is also an area that raises a lot of pecans; some 600 acres near Okmulgee are devoted to growing pecans. The festival began in 1984 and has been voted one of the top 10 festivals in the state. Besides large pecan concoctions, it offers a carnival, a pecan bake-off, a pie-throwing booth, arm-wrestling contests, the crowning of a Pecan Prince and Princess, and a turtle race.

CONTACTS:
Okmulgee Tourism
208 W. 6th St.
Okmulgee, OK 74447
918-758-1015; fax: 918-758-0968
www.okmulgeetourism.com

♦ 1950 ♦ **Okpesi Festival**
September

The Igbo people of Nigeria believe that failure to perform this annual rite will bring bad luck not only to the individual but to the entire community. It must be carried out by every male child whose father has died, for it is a ceremony in honor of the Igbo ancestors, or *ndioki*. Also known as **Itensi**, the ritual begins with a blood sacrifice of cocks, after which the blood is spread on wooden altars built specifically for the purpose. The sacrifice is followed by a feast during which communion is achieved both among the living and between the living and the dead.

See also ODO FESTIVAL

SOURCES:
FolkWrldHol-1999, p. 552

♦ 1951 ♦ **Oktoberfest**
Late September through early October

The first Oktoberfest was held on October 12, 1810, in honor of the marriage of Crown Prince Ludwig of Bavaria to Princess Therese von Saxony-Hildburghausen. Since that time it has become, above all else, a celebration of German beer. The Lord Mayor of Munich, Germany, opens the first barrel, and the 16-day festival begins. Both citizens and tourists flock to this event, which is marked by folk costume parades in which brewery horses draw floats and decorated beer wagons through the streets. Oktoberfest celebrations modeled on the German festival are also held in cities throughout the United States.

CONTACTS:
Munich Tourist Office
Sendlinger St. 1
Munich, D-80331 Germany
49-89-233-96-500; fax: 49-89-233-30-233
www.muenchen.de/home/60093/Homepage.html

SOURCES:
AnnivHol-2000, p. 182
BkFest-1937, p. 137
BkHolWrld-1986, Sep 21
FestWestEur-1958, p. 72
GdWrldFest-1985, p. 86

♦ 1952 ♦ **Okunchi Matsuri**
October 7-9

Regarded as among the most unusual festivals in Japan, the Okunchi Festival in Nagasaki dates back to the 17th century, when many Chinese lived in the city and when both Dutch and Chinese traders regularly anchored their ships there. For many years, the ruling shogun of Japan barred foreigners from other Japanese ports, and the few Dutch and Chinese ships that were allowed to stop in Nagasaki were the country's only point of contact with the non-Japanese world. The Okunchi Festival pays tribute to these traders by presenting both a Dutch dance and a Chinese dragon dance, along with processions, street fairs, and other entertainment.

The Dutch and Chinese dances are performed in an open area at the beginning of the many stairs that go to the Suwa Shrine. Civic authorities and priests view the ceremony from the stairs, while the rest of the audience sits on risers flanking the performance area. Two young women execute the Dutch dance, one of whom wears a false mustache and plays the part of a man. The two dancers bend at the waist, exchange coy smiles, and flirt with each other, to the amusement of the crowd. The Chinese dance features four dragons made out of cloth stretched over flexible frames. Each dragon conceals about a dozen dancers, who help it "dance" with snakelike motions by maneuvering the black rods attached to its body. The dragon dance reenacts the legendary battle between darkness, symbolized by the dragon, and light, symbolized by the sun—a golden globe atop a long pole. Needless to say, the sun always wins.

In addition to the dances, the Okunchi Festival also features the traditional procession of the *mikoshi*—the ornate palanquin on which the local deity is believed to descend for a ride as it is carried through the streets. The festival ends when the empty mikoshi returns to the shrine after the god has departed.

A similar Okunchi Festival is held at the end of October in Karatsu in Saga Prefecture.

CONTACTS:
Japan National Tourist Organization
1 Rockefeller Pl., Ste. 1250
New York, NY 10020
212-757-5640; fax: 212-307-6754
www.jnto.go.jp

SOURCES:
IllFestJapan-1993, p. 114
JapanFest-1965, pp. 194, 202
YrJapanFest-1974, p. 43

♦ 1953 ♦ **Old Christmas Day**
January 6 or 7

In addition to being the Feast of the EPIPHANY, January 6 is known as Old Christmas Day. When England and Scotland switched over from the Julian to the Gregorian calendar in 1752, 11 days were dropped to make up for the calendar discrepancy that had accumulated with the use of the Julian calendar. In all subsequent years, CHRISTMAS arrived 11 days early. Many people, especially in rural areas, had trouble accepting the loss of these 11 days, and continued to recognize the holidays of the Julian calendar as Old Christmas, Old CANDLEMAS, Old MIDSUMMER DAY, etc. Russians and Ukrainians celebrate this holiday on January 7.

See also CHRISTMAS (RUSSIAN ORTHODOX)

SOURCES:
EncyChristmas-2003, p. 579
FolkWrldHol-1999, p. 26

♦ 1954 ♦ **Old Fiddler's Convention**
Second week in August

A five-day concert in the small town of Galax, Va., the Old Fiddler's Convention spotlights old-time music in an outdoor setting. The convention was organized in 1935 as a fundraising event by members of Moose Lodge No. 733 and was dedicated to "keeping alive the memories and sentiments of days gone by." About 25,000 people now attend.

Hundreds of contestants take part, competing for cash prizes and trophies in categories that include guitar, mandolin, dulcimer, dobro, clawhammer and bluegrass banjo, clog or flatfoot dancing, and folk singing.

CONTACTS:
Old Fiddler's Convention

1114 E. Stuart Dr.
P.O. Box 655
Galax, VA 24333
276-236-8541
www.oldfiddlersconvention.com

SOURCES:
MusFestAmer-1990, p. 252

♦ 1955 ♦ **Old Pecos Bull and Corn Dance**
August 2

On the **Feast of Porcingula** (named after the shrine of their patron saint, Santa Maria de los Angeles, in Portiuncula, Italy), Indians at the Jemez Pueblo in New Mexico hold a celebration that combines both traditional Indian and Roman Catholic elements. On August 1, the day before the feast, six Indian priests wearing white shirts and trousers with red headbands and sashes come out of the ceremonial kiva and circle the plaza, chanting. Then the dancers are summoned to the kiva to prepare for the next day's corn dance.

On August 2, a mass is sung in honor of Santa Maria de los Angeles, after which the priest of Jemez accompanies her image to the shrine that has been set up for her in the plaza. The Pecos "bull," named after the people who were forced to abandon the Pecos Pueblo in favor of Jemez in 1838, is really a dancer carrying a framework that resembles a bull. Throughout the two days of the festival, the bull is prodded with sticks and tormented in mock bullfights. The men and boys who play the role of matador are less than flattering in their imitations of white men, which usually draw laughs from the spectators. There is a feast for the bull and the bullfighters, and after that the corn dance is performed before Santa Maria's shrine.

CONTACTS:
Department of Tourism Jemez Pueblo
7413 Hwy. 4
P.O. Box 100
Jemez Pueblo, NM 87024
877-733-5687 or 505-834-7235; fax: 505-834-2221
www.jemezpueblo.org

SOURCES:
IndianAmer-1989, p. 300

♦ 1956 ♦ **Old Saybrook Torchlight Parade and Muster**
Second Saturday night in December

In 1970 the Colonial Saybrook Fifes and Drums, under the leadership of Bill Reid, revived the tradition of a CHRISTMAS torchlight parade. In early December each year, in colonial America, the village militia would muster with their fifes and drums and march to the town green carrying torches and lanterns. When they heard the fifes and drums pass, the townspeople would follow behind the militia, also carrying torches and lanterns, to the green where a community meeting and carol sing would take place. It is thought that the event originally commemorated ADVENT.

Old Saybrook, Connecticut (population 10,000), is located at the mouth of the Connecticut River on Long Island Sound and was settled in 1635. It is the only community in the United States that is known to have revived this tradition.

The modern-day procession follows the traditional ritual with no less than 58 fife and drum corps from as far away as Virginia, New Jersey, and New York made up of 35 people per unit on average, plus support groups. The corps are sometimes led by Santa Claus himself and the marchers often augment their colonial-style costumes with seasonal decorations. For example, Christmas lights sparkle on tricornered hats, and silver tinsel hangs from flintlock rifles. The fifes and drums play not only colonial martial music but also the joyous and peaceful songs of Christmas. Citizens of the town and thousands of visitors join the march carrying torches and lanterns to the town green for a community carol sing led by the high school band.

CONTACTS:
Old Saybrook Chamber of Commerce
1 Main St.
P.O. Box 625
Old Saybrook, CT 06475
860-388-3266
www.oldsaybrookchamber.com

♦ 1957 ♦ **Old Silvester**
December 31, January 13

The custom known as **Silvesterklausen** in the small town of Urnäsch in Appenzell Outer Rhoden Canton, Switzerland, is performed both on December 31, *New* Silvester Day (ST. SYLVESTER'S DAY), and on January 13, or *Old* Silvester Day. (The two dates reflect the change from the Julian, or Old Style, calendar to the Gregorian, or New Style, calendar in 1582.)

The men of the village, wearing masks, costumes, and heavy harnesses with bells, traditionally walk in groups from house to house—or, in the surrounding countryside, from one farm to the next—singing wordless yodels. The friends and neighbors who receive them offer them a drink before they move on to the next house. The yodelers are usually so well disguised that their neighbors don't recognize them.

SOURCES:
EncyChristmas-2003, p. 690
FestWestEur-1958, p. 242
FolkWrldHol-1999, p. 34
GdWrldFest-1985, p. 168

♦ 1958 ♦ **Old Spanish Days**
Early August

This five-day fiesta held in Santa Barbara, California, in early August draws heavily on the area's Spanish-American and Mexican-American heritage. The celebration begins with the Fiesta Pequeña, or "Little Festival," on the steps of the Santa Barbara Mission, the 10th of the 21 Spanish missions built in California by Fray Junípero Serra and his successors. The opening ceremonies include Spanish and Mexican songs and

dances, the traditional fiesta blessing, and the introduction of ST. BARBARA, who is portrayed by a local citizen. The next few days are filled with flamenco guitarists, Mexican folklore dancers, and other performances at the Lobero Theatre, the site of the first Old Spanish Days festival in 1924.

The highlight of the week is the historical parade, featuring floats that depict various episodes in Santa Barbara's history, marching bands and precision drill teams, costumed flower girls, and horses in ornate silver trappings. Other popular events include the children's parade and the rodeo and stock horse show.

CONTACTS:
Old Spanish Days-Fiesta
129 Castillo St.
P.O. Box 21557
Santa Barbara, CA 93121
805-962-8101; fax: 805-962-9943
www.oldspanishdays-fiesta.org

♦ 1959 ♦ **Older Persons, International Day of**
October 1

The UNITED NATIONS General Assembly decided to set aside October 1 as International Day for the Elderly in 1990 (later designated as the International Day of Older Persons), at which time it asked its member nations to contribute to the Trust Fund for Ageing, which supports projects in developing countries that benefit the elderly.

By designating a day when governments are supposed to focus on what they can do to provide for the elderly, the U.N. hopes not only to forestall problems related to the aging of the population but to focus attention on the promise that a maturing population holds for social, economic, cultural, and spiritual undertakings. The United Nations also set aside the year 1999 as the International Year of Older Persons.

CONTACTS:
United Nations, Department of Public Information
Rm. S-1070L J, K, L
New York, NY 10017
212-963-6842; fax: 212-963-6914
www.un.org

♦ 1960 ♦ **Old-Time Country Music Contest and Festival, National**
September, week before Labor Day

Created by Bob Everhart as part of America's bicentennial celebration in 1976, the National Old-Time Country Music Contest and Festival in Avoca, Iowa, is now the largest gathering of public domain music-makers and listeners in the United States.

Sponsored by the National Traditional Country Music Association, the festival's purpose is to preserve the music that, in Everhart's words, has been "prostituted, violated, diluted, and in many instances altered so dramatically that it is no longer recognizable as a traditional American art form." There are more than 30 competitions in such varied musical genres as ragtime, polka, Cajun, mountain, folk, cowboy, Western, swing, yodeling, and gospel. The festival also includes songwriting contests and the National Bluegrass Band Championships. Non-musical events include storytelling and cowboy poetry contests and arts and crafts displays.

CONTACTS:
National Traditional Country Music Association
P.O. Box 492
Anita, IA 50020
405-521-2491

♦ 1961 ♦ Oldtime Fiddlers' Contest and Festival, National
Third full week in June

The National Oldtime Fiddlers' Contest and Festival is a major musical event in the United States, held for a full week in Weiser, Idaho, where fiddling was first heard in 1863. A way station was established that year at Weiser, and people traveling through in covered wagons stopped for rest and recreational fiddling. In 1914, the first fiddling contest was held, but interest petered out until 1953 when Blaine Stubblefield, a fiddle fan and member of the local chamber of commerce, initiated a fiddling competition. In 1963, in conjunction with Idaho's Centennial, the competition officially became the National Oldtime Fiddlers' Contest.

Awards are given for the national champion in several categories; this is big-time fiddling, with contestants having won their spot through competitions in other states. Besides music, there is a fiddlers parade, street dancing, and singalongs; another attraction is the National Fiddlers' Hall of Fame here. Attendance is about 10,000.

CONTACTS:
National Oldtime Fiddlers' Contest and Festival
115 W. Idaho
Weiser, ID 83672
208-414-0255; fax: 208-414-0256
www.fiddlecontest.com

SOURCES:
GdUSFest-1984, p. 45
MusFestAmer-1990, p. 241

♦ 1962 ♦ Ole Time Fiddlers and Bluegrass Festival
May, Memorial Day Weekend

A festival for genuinely old-time fiddlers, the Ole Time Fiddlers and Bluegrass Festival is held at Fiddler's Grove Campground in Union Grove, N.C. The festival was organized in 1970 by Harper A. Van Hoy as a serious musical venture, and admission is limited to 5,000 people to attract those who want to hear what Van Hoy has called the "purest mountain music this side of the Mississippi."

A special contest category is for fiddlers who must meet these criteria: they are over 55 years old, have had no formal musical training, and have learned from fiddlers older than themselves. There are competitions for all the major instruments of traditional American music, including autoharp,

banjo, fiddle, harmonica, and mandolin. Workshops are conducted for most of the instruments played in competition, as well as in shape-note singing, storytelling, clog dancing, and children's folk music. Additionally, there are arts and crafts and food.

CONTACTS:
Fiddler's Grove Inc.
P.O. Box 364
Sherrills Ford, NC 28673
828-478-3735
www.fiddlersgrove.com

SOURCES:
MusFestAmer-1990, p. 246

♦ 1963 ♦ Olney White Squirrel Count
October

The community of Olney, Ill., boasts a population of rare white squirrels. It is believed that the animals first appeared in the area just after the American Civil War. For many years, the city in southern Illinois has been concerned with preserving the squirrels. Ordinances prohibit cats and dogs, the squirrels' natural enemies, from running loose. Feeding stations have been set up in residential neighborhoods where the squirrel population is high. Laws give the squirrels the right-of-way on city streets, while residents are fined if they try to leave town with one of the animals.

Every year an official count is done to determine how the white squirrel population is surviving. No actual count as such is conducted. Rather, professors from nearby Central College, with the help of volunteers, try to gauge whether the number of animals is increasing or decreasing and whether any migration is taking place. The numbers have varied over the years. Most observers tend to believe that the white squirrel population has increased not only in the town of Olney, but in the surrounding countryside as well. The annual count was brought to national attention in 2002 during the 100-Year White Squirrel Celebration. In addition to the annual count, the event included a parade, a 5K race, the dedication of a statue to the white squirrel, and an official blessing of the animal.

CONTACTS:
City of Olney
300 S. Whittle Ave.
Olney, IL 62450
618-395-7302; fax: 618-395-7304
www.ci.olney.il.us/Visitors/WhiteSquirrel.htm

♦ 1964 ♦ Olympic Games
Winter Games every four years (2010, 2014, 2018…); Summer Games every four years (2012, 2016, 2020…)

The world's oldest sports spectacular, the first known Olympiad was held in 776 B.C.E. in Olympia, Greece. It is believed the festivals began before 1400 B.C.E. The modern games, which until recently were held roughly every four years in different countries, were revived in 1896 by Baron

Pierre de Coubertin of France. Those 1896 summer games took place in Athens, with 13 nations sending about 300 male athletes to compete in 42 events and 10 different sports. Now nearly 200 nations send thousands of male and female athletes to the Olympics, and hundreds of millions watch the events on television. Some winter sports were included in early years of the modern Olympics, but the Winter Games as a separate event didn't begin until 1924.

In ancient Greece, four national religious festivals—the Olympic Games, the Pᴙᴛʜɪᴀɴ Gᴀᴍᴇs, the Nᴇᴍᴇᴀɴ Gᴀᴍᴇs, and the Iꜱᴛʜᴍɪᴀɴ Gᴀᴍᴇs—were major events; the Olympic Games, honoring Zeus, were especially famous. Records tell of Olympic Games every four years from 776 B.C.E. to 217 C.E. when, with Greece under Roman domination, the games had lost their religious purpose and the athletes vied only for money. They were abolished by the Roman emperor, Theodosius I. It is generally believed, however, that the festival consisted not only of sporting contests, but of the presentation of offerings to Zeus and other gods. At first, these were simple foot races; later the long jump, discus- and javelin-throwing, wrestling, boxing, *pancratium* (a ferocious combination of boxing and wrestling), and chariot racing were added. Poets and dramatists also presented works. The games opened with trumpet fanfares and closed with a banquet.

Modern Olympics comprise Summer Games, held in a large city, and Winter Games, held at a resort. Since 1994, the games are still on a four-year cycle, but two years apart: Winter Games in 2002, 2006, 2010, etc., and Summer Games in 2000, 2004, 2008, etc. There are 28 approved sports for the Summer Games. The Winter Games consist of seven approved sports.

Today, the opening ceremonies highlight a parade of the athletes led by those from Greece, in honor of the original Games, followed by the athletes from the other nations, in alphabetical order according to the spelling in the country's language; the host country enters last.

After the Games are declared open, the dramatic lighting of the Olympic flame occurs. A cross-country relay runner carries a torch first lit in Olympia, and ignites the flame that burns for the 15-16 days of the games. Thousands of runners, representing each country between Greece and the host country, take part in the four-week torch relay. This is followed by a spectacular production of fireworks, strobe lights, fly-overs, music, dance, and assorted entertainment.

The Winter Games of 1992, held in Albertville, France, were historic in their reflection of dramatic political changes. The Soviet Union had broken up in August 1991, and athletes from five former Soviet republics competed as representatives of the Commonwealth of Independent States or United Team, and the Olympic flag, not that of the U.S.S.R., was raised for the winners.

The first- and second-place medals are both made of silver but the first place has a wash of gold; the third-place medal is bronze.

The Olympics are supposed to be nonpolitical but have been marked (and marred) by politics. In 1936, Adolf Hitler, who called blacks an inferior race, opened the Olympics in Berlin, Germany, as a propaganda show. It was thus a great triumph for humanity when Jesse Owens, a black man from Ohio State University, won four gold (first place) medals. He won the 100- and 200-meter dashes and the running broad jump, and was on the winning 400-meter relay team. Hitler ducked out of the stadium so he wouldn't have to congratulate Owens.

In 1972, the Games in Munich, Germany, were struck with horror when 11 Israeli athletes were killed by Arab terrorists.

The 1980 Games were opened in Moscow by Communist Party chairman Leonid I. Brezhnev, but athletes from the United States, Canada, West Germany, Japan and 50 other countries didn't participate. Their countries boycotted the event in protest of the Soviet invasion of Afghanistan. Terrorism again struck the Games in Atlanta in 1996.

Prominent Olympics participants have included:

Jim Thorpe, an American Indian and one of the greatest all-round athletes of all time, won gold medals for the decathlon and pentathlon in 1912. The following year, he was stripped of the medals when an investigation showed he had played semiprofessional baseball. He died in 1953, and the medals were restored to his family in 1982.

Paavo Nurmi, known as the "Flying Finn," won nine gold medals in long-distance running in three Olympics—in 1920, 1924, and 1928. On an extremely hot day at the Paris Summer Games in 1924, Nurmi set Olympic records in the 1,500-meter and 5,000-meter runs. Two days later, he won the 10,000-meter cross-country race. In 1928, he set a record for the one-hour run, covering 11 miles and 1,648 yards. His 1924 wins were considered the greatest individual performance in the history of track and field.

The Norwegian skater Sonja Henie won three gold medals—in 1928, 1932, and 1936. In 1924, at the age of 11, she was the youngest Olympian contestant ever (she finished last that year). She thrilled crowds by incorporating balletic moves into what had been standard skating exercises.

Emil Zatopek, a Czech long-distance runner, won three gold medals in 1952 and set Olympic records for the 5,000- and 10,000-meter races and for the marathon.

Jean-Claude Killy, known as "Le Superman" in his native France, won three gold medals in Alpine ski events at Grenoble, France, in 1968.

Mark Spitz, a swimmer from California, became the first athlete to win seven gold medals in a single Olympics (1972). He set world records in four individual men's events, and won the remaining medals in team events. These teams also set world records. Spitz, 22 at the time, was so popular for a while that his photo was a pinup poster.

Michael Phelps turned in an even more spectacular performance. At the 2004 Olympics he won six gold medals, but that was just the warm up. In 2008, he set a new record by winning eight gold medals—in the 100- and 200-meter butterfly; the 200-meter freestyle; the 200- and 400-meter individual medley; the 4x100-meter medley relay; and the 4x100- and 4x200-meter freestyle relay. He set new world records in seven of those events, all but the 100-meter butterfly. In total, Phelps has won 14 Olympic gold medals and two bronze medals, for an awe-inspiring 16 medals in just two Olympic appearances.

See also CULTURAL OLYMPIAD

CONTACTS:
International Olympic Committee
Chateau de Vidy
Lausanne, 1007 Switzerland
41-21-621-6111; fax: 41-21-621-6216
www.olympic.org

Olympic Museum
1, Quai d'Ouchy
Lausanne, 1001 Switzerland
41-21-621-6511; fax: 41-21-621-6512
www.museum.olympic.org

SOURCES:
BkHolWrld-1986, Aug 5
HolSymbols-2009, p. 662

♦ 1965 ♦ Omak Stampede and Suicide Race
Second weekend in August

The Omak Stampede and Suicide Race includes three days of professional rodeo in Omak, Wash. What makes this different from other rodeos is the World Famous Suicide Race which was featured on the 1980s television program, "Ripley's Believe It or Not." This is a terrifying hoof-thundering gallop by 15-20 mounted horses down an almost vertical hill, across the Okanogan River, and then into the rodeo arena. Four of these races are held, one after each rodeo performance.

The rodeos top off a week of activities which include Indian ceremonies, dances, and stick games, a type of gambling, at an Indian teepee village. (Much of the town of Omak is on the Colville Indian Reservation; the name Omak comes from the Indian word *omache,* meaning "good medicine.") Other events are a Not Quite White Water Raft Race, a western art show, a grand parade, a kiddies' parade, and dances. Attendance is 20,000 to 30,000.

Animal rights activists have protested the race because of the extreme danger to the horses. Since 1983, at least 15 horses have died in the race or been euthanized after injuries sustained in the race.

CONTACTS:
Omak Stampede
P.O. Box 2028
Omak, WA 98841
800-933-6625 or 509-826-1983
www.omakstampede.org

The Progressive Animal Welfare Society
15305 44th Ave. W.
P.O. Box 1037
Lynnwood, WA 98087
425-787-2500; fax: 425-742-5711
www.paws.org

♦ 1966 ♦ Oman National Day
November 18-19

This holiday in Oman observes the birthday of Sultan Qaboos Bin Said (b. 1940) on November 18, but festive events continue through the 19th as well. His accession to the throne took place on July 23, 1970. National Day events include parades, pageantry, an equestrian show, a marine festival, fireworks, and, every five years, an elaborate military show.

CONTACTS:
Embassy of the Sultanate of Oman
2535 Belmont Rd. N.W.
Washington, D.C. 20008
202-387-1980; fax: 202-745-4933
www.omani.info

♦ 1967 ♦ Ombashira Matsuri
Early April to mid-May, every six years

This ceremony, which takes place in Suwa, Japan, and represents a symbolic rebuilding of the Suwa-taisha Shrine, has four parts. The first is called *Yamadashi,* "taking the tree from the forest," a spirited event in which many people participate in cutting down a large fir tree, known as *ombashira.* The second part is *Satobiki,* "parading it through the streets." Men dressed as *daimyo,* or feudal lords, march in this parade, singing special woodcutters' folk songs known as *min'yo.* In the third part of the ceremony, known as *Kawawatashi,* the tree is carried across the river. In the festival's grand finale, called *Hikitaté,* the log is planted upright at a corner of the four shrines by tying ropes to the top and pulling it until it is vertical.

This event takes place once in six years, in the Year of the Monkey and the Year of the Tiger. Because felling the tree and transporting it to the shrine is a long process, the festival begins in early April and ends in the middle of May.

CONTACTS:
Japan National Tourist Organization
1 Rockefeller Pl., Ste. 1250
New York, NY 10020
212-757-5640; fax: 212-307-6754
www.jnto.go.jp

SOURCES:
IllFestJapan-1993, p. 42

♦ 1968 ♦ Omisoka
December 31

New Year's Eve in Japan is observed by settling financial accounts (*kake*), eating a special noodle dish known as *okake,* which is hot soup over noodles, and taking a hot bath followed by a well-earned rest. Widely celebrated on December 31, Omisoka marks the end of the preparations for New Year's celebrations, which go on for the next three days. It is a popular time for visitors to drop in to exchange New Year's greetings over cups of hot sake and decorated *mochi* cakes.

The city of Ashikaga, 50 miles north of Tokyo, is the site of the 1,200-year-old Saishoji temple, headquarters for the Akutai

Matsuri, the "naughty festival," or "festival of abusive language." On New Year's Eve there, participants walk (or take a bus) up a dark mountain road led by a man blowing a *horagai*, a shell that is supposed to fend off bad tidings. Some carry lanterns and wear cardboard hats bearing the picture of Bishamonten, one of the seven gods of fortune in Japanese Buddhism. The Saishoji temple was built in honor of this god.

The festival originated more than 200 years ago so repressed workers could let off steam; therefore, this is not simply a midnight stroll. Those hiking toward the temple atop the 1,000-foot-high hill scream curses into the night. They curse politicians, teachers, bad grades, low pay, and any other complaints of modern daily life in Japan. They release pent-up frustrations with words they ordinarily would not say directly to anyone. *Bakayaro* is one of the words most frequently heard. It means, roughly, "you idiot."

After the 40-minute walk the crowd storms into the temple, the bell is rung, prayers are offered, and the cursing continues. But when the new year arrives at midnight, the curses end and more typical celebration begins. Then the celebrants turn to another unique ceremony: when the priest calls the name of each worshipper, the individual kneels with a wide red lacquer bowl at his or her lips. Sake is then poured onto the person's forehead, runs across his or her face, into the bowl and is consumed. All this occurs while the priest reads the worshipper's personal wishes for the new year to the pounding of a taiko drum. This ceremony is supposed to ensure that happiness will flow in the new year.

On Omisoka, people wearing kimonos fill the streets as they go to visit shrines. But millions watch the "Red and White Song Contest" on TV. This marathon song festival, first organized in 1950, has become an indispensable ritual of the New Year. The show, lasting up to four hours, usually has 50 performers, 25 on each team. The Red team is comprised of women, the White team men. When the performances are over, the audience and a panel of judges decide which team won. Typical past performances include an orchestra playing Mozart and a group singing Okinawan folk music; a bit less typical was a female singer in a gown of feathers that made her look like a bird; as she finished her song she flapped her arms and flew away, suspended by a wire.

The TV show ends shortly before midnight in time for an older tradition: the tolling of the great bells in Buddhist temples at midnight. Priests strike the bells 108 times, a reminder of the 108 human frailties or sins in Buddhist belief. By the end of the 108 strokes of the bell, the impure desires of the old year have been driven away.

An ancient folk ritual of a very different sort is observed on the Oga Peninsula, Akita Prefecture, on New Year's Eve. Young men play the part of hairy devils called NAMAHAGE, dressing in grotesque red and blue masks and straw cloaks. They stomp through the streets shouting, "Any wicked people about?" and then pound on people's doorways, the idea being to frighten children and newly married women so that they won't be lazy. After being admitted to a home, they sit down for rice cakes, first scaring the wits out of children with stories of what will happen to them if they are naughty.

See also OSHOGATSU

CONTACTS:
Japan Information Network, Japan Center for Intercultural
  Communication
2-7-7 Hirakawacho
Chiyodaku
Tokyo, 102-0093 Japan
81-3-3263-5041; fax: 81-3-3230-4107
home.jcic.or.jp

Broadcasting Culture Research Institute, Japan Broadcasting
  Corporation
Atago-Mori Tower 16F, 2-5-1 Atago
Minato-ku
Tokyo, 105-6216 Japan
81-3-5400-6800; fax: 81-3-3436-5880
www.nhk.or.jp/nhkworld

Ashikaga Tourist Association
3-6-4 Ise-cho
Ashikaga, Tochigi 326-0053 Japan
81-2-8443-3000; fax: 81-2-8420-2159
www.city.ashikaga.tochigi.jp

SOURCES:
BkFest-1937, p. 201
FolkWrldHol-1999, p. 775

♦ 1969 ♦ **Omizutori Matsuri (Water-Drawing
            Festival)**
March 1-14

Omizutori Matsuri is marked by religious rites, officially called **Shuni-e**, that have been observed for 12 centuries at the Buddhist Todaiji Temple in the city of Nara, Nara Prefecture, Japan. During this period of meditative rituals, the drone of recited sutras and the sound of blowing conchs echo from the temple. The high point comes on March 12, when young monks on the gallery of the temple brandish burning pine-branch torches, shaking off burning pieces. Spectators below try to catch the sparks, believing they have magic power against evil.

At 2 A.M. on March 13, the ceremony of drawing water is observed to the accompaniment of ancient music. Buckets are carried to a well, and the first water of the year is drawn and offered to the Buddha. Then the monks perform a final dramatic fire dance to the beating of drums.

For many Japanese, the Omizutori signals the start of spring.

CONTACTS:
Nara City Information Network
Nara City Hall Tourism Information Ctr.
1-1-1 Nijo Oji Minami
Nara, 630-8012 Japan
81-7-4222-3900; fax: 81-7-4234-1111
www.city.nara.nara.jp

SOURCES:
AnnivHol-2000, p. 43
RelHolCal-2004, p. 217

♦ 1970 ♦ **Ommegang**
First Thursday in July and the previous Tuesday

A medieval pageant presented on the Grand-Place of Brussels, Belgium, and one of the country's most popular attractions. The pageant in its present form dates only from 1930, the year of the centenary of Belgium, but it is a reenactment of the Ommegang of 1549. And that Ommegang had gone back at least to 1359, when it was first recorded.

The word *ommegang* is from the Flemish words *omme* ("around") and *gang* ("march"), and was a word used for processions around monuments. The present Brussels Ommegang is linked to the story of Béatrice Soetkens.

The year was 1348. Béatrice, a poor but honest woman, was told by the Virgin Mary to go to Antwerp to get a miracle-making statue. Béatrice ordered her husband to start rowing his boat to take her to Antwerp, and there she was able to get the statue, despite the interference of the sexton. On the way back to Brussels, her husband, exhausted, had to stop rowing, but the drifting boat safely arrived in Brussels at a spot where archers practiced. A church was built there, and every year the statue was carried around under the protection of the "Grand Serment," the Archery Guild.

That was the start of the Ommegang. At first wholly religious, in time profane elements were mingled. The royal princes were admirers of the Ommegang, and details of the 1549 Ommegang are known through the works of Juan Christobal Calvete de Estrelle, the chronicler of Philippe II, son of Charles V. The 1549 Ommegang was dedicated to Charles.

The Ommegang disappeared after 1810, but has been the same since its 1930 revival. It is preceded by strolling musicians, followed by a parade of people representing the magistrate and various city officials; the court of Marie of Hungary, with pages, ladies-in-waiting, and a hunting group of dogs and falcons; and the Court of Charles V, with mounted knights bearing banners. Many of those representing the court figures are descendants of the original noble families.

Then the actual procession takes place, led by the Knight of Peace and the Theban trumpets. Participants include trade groups with floats, archers and crossbowmen, and stilt walkers and groups of dancers and Gilles (clowns) dancing around symbolic animals: the legendary horse Bayard and the four sons of Aymon [*see* GIANTS, FESTIVAL OF THE (BELGIUM)] surrounded by eagles, a pelican, unicorn, dragon, lion, and serpent.

CONTACTS:
Ommegang-Brussels Events
180 Rue des Tanneurs
Brussels, B 1000 Belgium
32-2-512-19-61; fax: 32-2-502-6835
www.ommegang.be

SOURCES:
BkHolWrld-1986, Jul 2

♦ 1971 ♦ **Onam**
August-September; four days during Hindu month of Bhadrapada

A harvest festival and a celebration of ancient King Mahabali in the state of Kerala in India. This is Kerala's biggest festival,

lasting 10 days and featuring dancing, feasting, and displays of elaborately designed carpets of flowers. It's famous for the races of the so-called snake boats held at Champakulam, Aranmulai, and Kottayam. The boats are designed in all shapes—with beaks or kite tails—and have crews of up to 100 men who row to the rhythm of drums and cymbals.

The festival honors King Mahabali, who was sent into exile in the nether world when gods grew jealous of him. He's allowed to return to his people once a year, and the boat races, cleaned homes, carpets of flowers, clapping dances by girls, and other events are the welcome for him.

CONTACTS:
Ministry of Tourism, Government of India
Rm. No 123, Transport Bhavan, No. 1, Parliament St.
New Delhi, Delhi 110 001 India
91-11-23715084; fax: 91-11-23715084
www.tourisminindia.com

Kerala Department of Tourism
Park View
Thiruvananthapuram, Kerala, 695 033 India
91-471-232-1132; fax: 91-471-2322279
www.keralatourism.org

SOURCES:
BkHolWrld-1986, Sep 15
GdWrldFest-1985, p. 111
RelHolCal-2004, p. 173

♦ 1972 ♦ **Onwasato Festival**
August

Observed by the Igbo people of Nigeria, the Onwasato Festival marks the beginning of the harvest season and is celebrated by feasting on the new crops, particularly yams. The highlight of the festival is the thanksgiving ritual in which the senior member of each family kills a fowl in the *Obu* (the father's sitting-house), sprinkles the blood on the *Okpensi* (the family symbol), and gives thanks to the family's ancestors. The feathers are then removed and scattered on the threshold of the compound—a sign that the people have forsaken all evil for the coming season. Of all the many fowl that are killed, one is roasted and set aside, while the others are used for the first day's feasting. On the second day of the festival, all the members of the extended family meet in the senior member's Obu and share the fowl that has been set aside in a ritual known as the "handing round of fowl," or *Inya Okuku.*

SOURCES:
FolkWrldHol-1999, p. 536

♦ 1973 ♦ **O'odham Tash Fair and All-Indian Rodeo**
Mid-February

The O'odham Tash Fair and All-Indian Rodeo is held every year over a four-day weekend in mid-February in Casa Grande, Ariz. One of the largest Native-American festivals in the United States, it draws dozens of tribes to take part in a celebration of native peoples. Events include an all-Indian rodeo, ceremonial dance displays, and a juried arts and crafts competition, as well as a parade, a rodeo-queen's pageant, and co-ed softball tournaments. All are welcome to come watch the events. The fair celebrated its 40th anniversary in 2007.

CONTACTS:
O'odham Tash Nation
P.O. Box 11165
Casa Grande, AZ 85230-1165
520-836-4723 or 800-916-1515; fax: 520-426-1731
www.oodhamtash.freeservers.com/index.html

◆ 1974 ◆ Opal Festival
March-April, Easter weekend

The South Australian town of Coober Pedy is known for its opal mines, producing about 70 percent of the world's opals. In the early 20th century, newcomers to the area—explorers, miners, construction workers, soldiers returning from World War I—built underground dugouts in which to live because of the harsh environment of the outback, with its excessive heat and minimal water supply. Thus, the town came to be called "kupa piti" or "white man in a hole" by the aboriginal people.

Celebrated over EASTER weekend, Coober Pedy's annual Opal Festival includes such competitive events as the mine rescue demonstration, stein holding competition, beer belly contest, tug-of-war, tossing the sausage, triathlons for men and women, games and races for children, football, and the multicultural dance and singing competition. While the fun begins on Thursday night with the festival cabaret, Saturday is the main day, kicking off with a morning street parade featuring a marching band, mining equipment, and floats and culminating in a fireworks display and a dance at night. Throughout the festival, the opal walk leads festivalgoers from shop to shop to view rare and beautiful specimens, and dugout tours are available. There are also displays of local handicrafts, along with food and drink tents, stage acts, aboriginal dancing, and music.

CONTACTS:
Coober Pedy Opal Festival
Hutchison St.
P.O. Box 425
Coober Pedy, SA 5723 Australia
61-8-8672-5298; fax: 61-8-8672-5699
www.cooberpedy.sa.gov.au

SOURCES:
WildPlanet-1995, p. 420

◆ 1975 ◆ Opalia
December 19

The ancient Roman fertility goddess Ops was known by several different names—among them Rhea, Cybele, BONA DEA, Magna Mater (*see* MEGALESIA), Thya, and Tellus. She married Saturn and was the mother of Jupiter, and was usually portrayed as a matron, with a loaf of bread in her left hand and her right hand opened as if offering assistance. There were actually two festivals in her honor. The Opalia was observed on December 19, when it is believed that a sacrifice to Ops

was made in the temple of Saturn. On August 25, the Opiconsivia, the sacrifice took place in the Regia or king's house.

Not much is known about what actually took place during the Opalia. There is even some disagreement as to whether Ops was the wife of Saturn or the wife of Consus. The fact that the Opalia was held four days after the CONSUALIA on December 15, and that the Opiconsivia was held four days after the festival in honor of Consus on August 21 has been used to support the theory that Ops was actually the wife of Consus. In any case, it appears that women played an important role in the festival. Because Ops was a fertility goddess, she was often invoked by touching the earth.

SOURCES:
ClassDict-1984, p. 424
DictFolkMyth-1984, p. 825
DictRomRel-1996, p. 169
FestRom-1981, pp. 180, 207
OxYear-1999, pp. 345, 503
RomFest-1925, pp. 212, 273

◆ 1976 ◆ Open Marathon, International
Mid-October

The International Open Marathon is a modern-day marathon in Greece run by male and female athletes of all ages. The race retraces the course of the Greek soldier, Pheidippides, who ran from the battlefield at Marathon to Athens to bring news of the Athenian victory over the Persians, a distance of about 25 miles. The starting line today is in the village of Marathon and the finish line is at the Olympic Stadium in the heart of Athens.

A mound in Marathon marks the grave of 192 Athenian soldiers killed in the 490 B.C.E. victory.

CONTACTS:
Greek National Tourist Organization
645 Fifth Ave., 9th Fl.
New York, NY 10022
212-421-5777; fax: 212-826-6940
www.visitgreece.gr

◆ 1977 ◆ Opening of the Underground Caves Day (Te Kauki Nanganga')
November 20

The end of World War II is marked annually by the people of Butaritari Island (northern islands of the independent republic of Kiribati, located in the Central Pacific Ocean). Each year, they open the caves that were built to shelter them during WWII. Accompanied by a celebration, the event takes place on the anniversary of the day the caves initially were opened after the war ended in 1945.

Traditionally, the people of Butaritari would gather in the maneaba (meeting house), and older citizens would share their stories and experiences of the struggle between U.S Marines and Japanese soldiers for control of the island. The event's main activities take place in Ukiangang village on

Butaritari Island, featuring singing, dancing, feasting, and indoor and outdoor games.

CONTACTS:
Kiribati National Tourism Office
Ministry of Communication, Transport and Tourism Development
P.O. Box 487
Betio
Tarawa Republic of Kiribati
www.visit-kiribati.com

♦ 1978 ♦ **Orange Bowl Game**
January 1

One of the older post-season college football games, first played in 1935, in which the two top teams meet at the 75,521-seat LandShark Stadium in Miami, Florida, to play for the national championship every four years. Top teams also contend during the years in which the national championship is determined in one of the other three bowl cities—Pasadena, California's Rose Bowl, New Orleans, Louisiana's Sugar Bowl, and Phoenix, Arizona's Fiesta Bowl—which alternately host the biggest college football game of the year.

The game is preceded by a New Year's Eve Orange Bowl Parade along Biscayne Boulevard. A parade more on the satirical side is the King Mango Strut held each year near Jan. 1 in Coconut Grove, Florida.

CONTACTS:
Orange Bowl Committee
703 Waterford Way, Ste. 590
Miami, FL 33126
305-341-4700; fax: 305-341-4750
www.orangebowl.org

SOURCES:
AmerBkDays-2000, p. 12

♦ 1979 ♦ **Orange Day (Orangemen's Day)**
July 12

Sometimes referred to simply as **The Twelfth** or **The Glorious Twelfth**, this is the anniversary of the Battle of Boyne, which took place in Ireland on July 1, 1690, when the old Julian calendar was still in use. Ireland was under English rule at the time, and the trouble began when James II, who was Roman Catholic, was deposed in 1668 and his throne was given to William of Orange, a Protestant. Each side raised an army of about 30,000 men, and the two clashed on the banks of the Boyne River. The Protestants won a decisive victory, but that was hardly the end of the conflict. The Catholics formed underground societies designed to restore the line of James, and the Protestants countered by forming the Orange Order, committed to maintaining the link with Protestant England. As Irishmen left Ireland and England for the New World, lodges of Orangemen were formed in Canada and the United States, where Orange Day is still observed by Protestant Irish.

SOURCES:
AnnivHol-2000, p. 116
DaysCustFaith-1957, p. 178

DictDays-1988, p. 84
OxYear-1999, pp. 291, 330

♦ 1980 ♦ **Oregon Dune Mushers' Mail Run**
March; dates vary according to the tide schedules

The Oregon Dune Mushers' Mail Run takes place every year, with teams of 4 to 12 dogs in different class groups completing a 75-mile course between North Bend and Florence, Ore. Traveling through the Oregon Dunes National Recreation Area, about 15-20 teams take two to three days to complete the run. It is non-competitive, designed only to test the endurance of the dogs and their "mushers," who ride in wheeled carts.

The event commemorates early American history, when the strength of humans and animals, and their mutual co-operation, were essential to the settling of the United States. The course, which runs along the Pacific coast on roads, trails, and over huge sand dunes, also harkens back to the days before 1914, when a railway tunnel finally was completed in the Gardiner area of Oregon. Prior to that date, beaches commonly were used as highways. Even today, the beach area between the low-tide mark and the mean high-tide mark is under the jurisdiction of Oregon's highway system.

The Oregon Dune Mushers' Mail Run was conceived in 1977 by dog musher Jim Tofflemire after he ran the famous 1,200-mile-long Iditarod Trail Sled Dog Race from Anchorage to Nome, Alaska. He had struggled to raise the funds for the race, and he wanted to help others raise money while also experiencing the unique mushing conditions on the Oregon coast. In keeping with his original vision, the Oregon run includes a distinctive fund-raising element. Each musher carries three commemorative stamped envelopes and is required to have the stamps cancelled in the three communities that the race course passes through: North Bend, Lakeside, and Florence. The envelopes then are sold as a fundraiser to benefit the Oregon Dune Mushers. The organization often uses the proceeds to send mushers to the Iditarod Race.

CONTACTS:
Oregon Dune Mushers
P.O. Box 841
North Bend, OR 97459
541-677-8393 or 888-726-3386
www.oregondunemushers.com

♦ 1981 ♦ **Original Gullah Festival**
May, the weekend before Memorial Day

The Original Gullah Festival is held annually in Beaufort, S.C., on the weekend before Memorial Day. Founded in 1986, its aim is to promote awareness of local customs and culture through the arts. The three-day event features such entertainment as jazz, blues, reggae, and gospel musicians; storytelling and dance performances; arts and crafts displays; museum exhibits; and a variety of food vendors.

The term Gullah, or Geechee, is used to refer to the African-American people and culture descended from slaves brought from Africa to the coastal region of South Carolina and the

Georgia Low Country. Because of its relative geographic isolation in island communities, Gullah culture retained distinctly African and Caribbean features, including traditional foods, crafts, folk beliefs, and language.

The Original Gullah Festival was founded by Rosalie Pazant, her three daughters, and a family friend, inspired by a discussion of the "good old days" of celebrating Memorial Day in the African-American community. Pazant is still president of the board of directors that organizes and oversees the event, along with an executive committee. From 35 people at the first festival, the attendance has expanded to as many as 70,000 over the festival's three days.

CONTACTS:
Gullah Festival of South Carolina, Inc.
P.O. Box 83
Beaufort, SC 29901

♦ 1982 ♦ Osaka International Festival
April

Founded in 1958 as a meeting place for Eastern and Western cultures, the Osaka International Festival presents classical music performed by orchestras, chamber ensembles, and solo artists from Japan and other countries. The program also includes dance, drama, and opera, with performances given in the 2,709-seat Osaka Festival Hall, one of the largest and most modern in the Far East. The Comedie Française, Vienna Burgtheater, and Théâtre de France Renaud-Barrault have performed there, as have the New York City Ballet, the Alwin Nikolais Dance Theatre, and the Ballet Aztlan de Mexico.

Every Osaka Festival features classical Japanese Noh dance-dramas and Kabuki theatrical performances. The Bunraku Puppet Theatre also presents traditional Japanese dramas using dolls that are two-thirds human size. The two-week festival is scheduled to take place in April, which is cherry-blossom time in Osaka.

CONTACTS:
Japan National Tourist Organization
1 Rockefeller Pl., Ste. 1250
New York, NY 10020
212-757-5640; fax: 212-307-6754
www.jnto.go.jp

SOURCES:
GdWrldFest-1985, p. 124
IntlThFolk-1979, p. 258
MusFestWrld-1963, p. 264

♦ 1983 ♦ Oshogatsu (New Year's Day)
January 1

This is the "festival of festivals" in Japan, also known as **Ganjitsu**, actually celebrated for several days. Government offices, banks, museums and most businesses are closed from NEW YEAR'S DAY, a national holiday, through January 3.

From the middle of December, streets are decorated with pine and plum branches, bamboo stalks, and ropes festooned with paper. Traditional home decorations are small pine trees with bamboo stems attached, which are placed on either side of the front entrance to represent longevity and constancy. For weeks before New Year's, people clean house and purchase new clothes for the children; this is also a time for exchanging gifts, sending greeting cards, and paying off personal debts.

On New Year's Day, it's traditional to pray at the household altar and to eat special foods, for example, steamed rice that has been pounded into small, round, gooey cakes called *mochi*. Herring roe is eaten for fertility, black beans for health, dried chestnuts for success, and porgy and prawns are omens of happiness.

Business resumes on Jan. 4, and the holiday period is over on Jan. 7 when decorations come down as part of the festival of NANAKUSA MATSURI.

See also HADAKA MATSURI; OMISOKA; UTAKAI HAJIME

SOURCES:
BkFest-1937, p. 194
BkFestHolWrld-1970, pp. 2, 14
DictFolkMyth-1984, pp. 181, 540, 730, 790, 871
DictWrldRel-1989, p. 374
EncyRel-1987, vol. 2, p. 553
FolkWrldHol-1999, p. 63
RelHolCal-2004, p. 216

♦ 1984 ♦ Osorezan Taisai
July 20-24

Mt. Osoré, located on the Shimokita Peninsula in the north of Honshu, Japan, is a spiritual center for many Japanese. It is known as a place where departed souls congregate. During the Osorezan Taisai Festival, or **Osorezanrei Grand Festival**, people flock to the mountain at Mutsu City, Aomori Prefecture, where psychics endeavor to summon the spirits of the dead by chanting. The priests who cross the weathered slopes of the mountain in procession add to the festival's grim and ghostly atmosphere.

CONTACTS:
Aomori Prefectural Government
1-1-40 Nagashima
Aomori, Aomori Prefecture 030-8570 Japan
81-1-7722-1111; fax: 81-1-7773-2691
www.pref.aomori.lg.jp/en

SOURCES:
IllFestJapan-1993, p. 145

♦ 1985 ♦ Ostara
Around March 22

Ostara, which coincides with the VERNAL EQUINOX, is one of the four pagan QUARTER DAYS, along with Litha (SUMMER SOLSTICE), Mabon (AUTUMNAL EQUINOX), and YULE. It is observed by those who follow Wicca (modern witchcraft) and Neopaganism by lighting fires to commemorate the return of light in the spring and to honor the god and goddess.

Also known as Eostre or Alban Eilir, Ostara is also regarded as a time of fertility and conception. In some Wiccan traditions, it is marked as the time when the goddess conceives the god's child, which will be born at the Winter Solstice.

SOURCES:
RelHolCal-2004, p. 271

♦ 1986 ♦ **Otsa Festival**
Between August and November

The Ekperi people of eastern Nigeria celebrate the annual three-day Otsa Festival to purify their land and promote community solidarity. Masquerade plays are held in which primarily male members of the community wear masks and colorful costumes. Women play the role of "mother" to each play, accepting donations to pay for masks and costumes required for the performance.

While the masquerades vary from village to village and borrow elements from other villages as well as from neighboring tribes, certain key factors seem to be common throughout the region. On Otsa eve, a giant figure named Umese, wearing a mask and clad in locally woven cloth, goes from house to house. This giant dances and sings and collects donations to pay for the coming masquerades. The first of the Otsa day masquerades is performed by young boys who wear ragged cloth masks and costumes that have been created by the village's elderly men. These costumes are said to contain "medication" that will protect the boys from harm and, in a larger sense, protect the village as well. Later masquerades feature performers dancing and wearing masks made from cloth or carved wood. Some performers dance on behalf of certain segments of the community, such as the hunters, and their headdress will reflect these concerns. A dancer performing on behalf of the village's children, for example, may wear toy dolls. Several new performances are added each year while others are dropped or revised. Some 30 masquerades are usually performed during the Otsa Festival.

CONTACTS:
Embassy of the Federal Republic of Nigeria
3519 International Ct. N.W.
Washington, D.C. 20008
202-986-8400; fax: 202-775-1385
www.nigeriaembassyusa.org/index.html

♦ 1987 ♦ **Our Lady Aparecida, Festival of**
October

Brazil's patron saint, the Virgin Mary *Aparecida* ("she who has appeared"), is honored with a 10-day festival in the city near São Paulo that bears her name. Legend has it that after a poor day's catch, fishermen cast their nets into the Paraiba do Sul River and pulled up a small statue of the Virgin Mary, carved out of black wood. When they cast their nets again, they came up full of fish. This was the first miracle attributed to the saint, and the city of Aparecida with its beautiful church built to house the statue is now the destination of many pilgrimages.

Nossa Senhora de Aparecida is celebrated during the month of October, but the 12th is a legal public holiday in Brazil to honor the saint.

CONTACTS:
Brazilian Embassy
3006 Massachusetts Ave. N.W.
Washington, D.C. 20008
202-238-2700; fax: 202-238-2827
www.brasilemb.org

♦ 1988 ♦ **Our Lady of Carmel, Feast of**
July 16

Our Lady of Carmel (the *Madonna del Carmine*) is the patroness of the city of Naples, Italy. Her festival is celebrated with dancing, singing, and magnificent fireworks displays. Brightly decorated wax replicas of human body parts used to be sold at booths near the church, and people suffering from various physical ailments appealed to the Madonna to restore their health by offering her these replicas of the diseased portions of their bodies.

Her feast is also observed by Italian Americans in the United States. For example, it is part of the elaborate Giglio Feast celebrated in Brooklyn, New York.

See also Tirana, La

CONTACTS:
Italian Government Tourist Board
630 Fifth Ave., Ste. 1565
New York, NY 10111
212-245-5618; fax: 212-586-9249
www.italiantourism.com

SOURCES:
BkFest-1937, p. 188

♦ 1989 ♦ **Our Lady of Fátima Day**
July 13

This Portuguese holiday commemorates the appearance of the Virgin Mary to three children, aged 7 to 10, from the village of Fátima in 1917. The first appearance to the dos Santos children—Lucia, and her cousins, Jacinta and Francisco—took place on May 13, 1917, when they saw what they thought was lightning and a lady appeared to them from the top of a nearby tree. No one really took their story seriously, however, until the same thing began to occur on the 13th of every month. Each time the children went to see the Virgin, they were accompanied by an increasingly large crowd of adults. She appeared to them for the last time on October 13, in the presence of about 70,000 onlookers, when she revealed she was Our Lady of the Rosary. She told them to recite the rosary daily, and asked that a church be built for her.

Eventually the cult of Our Lady of Fátima spread, a basilica was built, and pilgrimages to the isolated shrine became common. Two great pilgrimages take place each year on May 13 and October 13, with smaller groups making their way to Fátima around the 13th day of each month in between. July

13 is considered Our Lady of Fátima Day because it was two months after the Virgin's first appearance that a large number of adults witnessed the same miracle: the sun seemed to dance, tremble, and finally fall. It took 20 years for the event to be investigated, authenticated, and the cult granted acceptance by the Pope.

CONTACTS:
Leiria Fatima Tourism Region
Jardim Luis de Camoes Apartado 1115
Leiria, 2401-801 Portugal
351-244-848-770; fax: 351-244-848-779
www.rt-leiriafatima.pt/site/frontoffice/default.as

SOURCES:
AnnivHol-2000, p. 117
DaysCustFaith-1957, p. 179
DictWrldRel-1989, p. 254
FestWestEur-1958, p. 161
OxYear-1999, p. 206

♦ 1990 ♦ **Our Lady of Guadalupe, Feast of (United States)**
December 12

The Feast of OUR LADY OF GUADALUPE is celebrated by Roman Catholics in the southwestern United States, where the Spanish influence is still strong. At the pueblo just north of Taos, New Mexico, there is an impressive torchlight procession on December 12. At the Jemez Pueblo, *matachines* (clowns or buffoons) perform a variety of Indian ceremonial dances. At churches and plazas throughout New Mexico, Texas, and Arizona, such traditional Indian dances as the arc and arrow, gourd, braid, feather, palm, owl, and snake dances are performed on this day.

Several masses are held on this day at Our Lady of Guadalupe Church in San Diego, California, where the *mañanitas*, or "good morning song," is sung to the Virgin Mary, and *mariachis*, strolling musicians, perform in the Virgin's honor.

CONTACTS:
Indian Pueblo Cultural Center
2401 12th St. N.W.
Albuquerque, NM 87104
866-855-7902 or 505-843-7270; fax: 505-842-6959
www.indianpueblo.org

Our Lady of Guadalupe Church
1770 Kearney Ave.
San Diego, CA 92113
619-233-3838; fax: 619-233-3252
www.diocese-sdiego.org

SOURCES:
FolkAmerHol-1999, p. 490
IndianAmer-1989, pp. 300, 303

♦ 1991 ♦ **Our Lady of Guadalupe, Fiesta of**
December 12

Nuestra Señora de Guadalupe is the patron saint of Mexico, and on December 12 thousands of pilgrims flock to her shrine at the famous Church of Guadalupe outside Mexico City. On the evening of December 11 crowds have already gathered for mariachi-led singing and special ceremonies at midnight, which are carried on national television.

This great religious festival commemorates the appearance of the Virgin Mary on Tepeyac hill just north of present-day Mexico City. According to legend, she identified herself to an Indian convert named Juan Diego in the early morning of December 9, 1531, and told him to tell the bishop to build her a shrine there. When the bishop refused to believe the story, the Virgin filled Diego's homespun blanket with Castillian roses, which did not normally grow in Mexico, as proof of his vision. When Juan opened the blanket to show the bishop the roses, they had vanished. In their place was an image of Mary on the blanket. It soon adorned the newly built shrine and has hung there for four centuries without any apparent deterioration or fading of colors.

The story of Juan Diego and the Virgin is reenacted in a puppet show each year, and relics of Our Lady of Guadalupe are sold in the streets. It is said that only the French shrine at Lourdes and the one at Fátima attract as many pilgrims (*see* OUR LADY OF FÁTIMA DAY and OUR LADY OF LOURDES, FEAST OF).

She is the patron saint of Peruvian students, and of all of Central and South America. In El Salvador, it is called *Día del Indio* ("Day of the Indian").

In 1990, Pope John Paul II beatified Juan Diego, a necessary step on the way to sainthood.

CONTACTS:
Mexico Tourism Board
21 E. 63rd St., Fl. 3
New York, NY 10021
800-446-3942 or 212-821-0314; fax: 212-821-0367
www.visitmexico.com

SOURCES:
BkFest-1937, p. 232
DaysCustFaith-1957, p. 311
DictFolkMyth-1984, p. 258
DictWrldRel-1989, p. 569
FolkAmerHol-1999, p. 490
FolkWrldHol-1999, p. 698
IndianAmer-1989, pp. 290, 300, 303
IntlThFolk-1979, p. 272
OxYear-1999, p. 496

♦ 1992 ♦ **Our Lady of Lourdes, Feast of**
February 11

The Feast of Our Lady of Lourdes commemorates the first of 18 appearances of the Virgin Mary to a 14-year-old French peasant girl, Bernadette Soubirous. The young girl's visions occurred between February 11 and July 16, 1858, near the town of Lourdes. The Virgin led her to a nearby grotto, and the miraculous spring that appeared there has been associated ever since with the power to heal.

Pilgrimages to the grotto were authorized in 1862, and the Feast of Our Lady of Lourdes was extended to the entire

Roman Catholic Church in 1907. Some five million people a year make the pilgrimage to Lourdes, making it one of the world's major pilgrimage sites. Many of them are sick, and the cures they report are reviewed by a special medical bureau. As of 1976, the Church had accepted only 63 of these cures as miraculous.

CONTACTS:
Sanctuary of Our Lady of Lourdes
1 Ave., Monseigneur Theas
Lourdes, 65108 France
33-5-6242-7878; fax: 33-5-6242-7877
www.lourdes-france.com/index.php?lang=en

SOURCES:
AnnivHol-2000, p. 25
BkHolWrld-1986, Feb 11
DaysCustFaith-1957, p. 50
DictWrldRel-1989, p. 439
OxYear-1999, pp. 73, 158

♦ 1993 ♦ Our Lady of Nazaré Festival
September 8-18

Nazaré has been called "the most picturesque town in Portugal," and thousands of tourists flock here every summer to paint, film, and photograph the quaint fishing village. The Church of Our Lady of Nazareth was built near the place where the Virgin Mary is said to have saved the life of Fuas Roupinho, who was pursuing a white deer when a sudden sea mist arose and caused him to lose his bearings. The Virgin halted his horse in its tracks—a hoof-print is still visible—and, as the mist cleared, Roupinho discovered that he was on the brink of a cliff, 300 feet above the ocean. Today the town is built on two levels, the lower one extending along the beach. A pilgrimage chapel overlooks the town from the upper level.

The name *Nazaré* comes from a statue of the Virgin brought back here from Nazareth, the childhood home of Jesus, by a monk in the fourth century. The annual 10-day festival that takes place in the town's main square begins on September 8, the anniversary of the miracle, and includes bullfights, musical concerts, and folk dancing.

Some of the best and most dangerous fishing in all of Portugal goes on here. Fishermen have to negotiate a treacherous barrier reef with a difficult swell that often capsizes entire boats with their crews. Therefore, the Nazaré fishermen, who carry the Virgin's statue on their shoulders in three festive processions, are the focus of the event.

CONTACTS:
Leiria Fatima Tourism Region
Jardim Luis de Camoes Apartado 1115
Leiria, 2401-801 Portugal
351-244-848-770; fax: 351-244-848-779
www.rt-leiriafatima.pt/site/frontoffice/default.as

SOURCES:
FestWestEur-1958, p. 184

♦ 1994 ♦ Our Lady of Solitude, Fiesta of
December 18

The **Virgen de la Soledad**, or Our Lady of Solitude, is the patroness of the state of Oaxaca, Mexico. According to legend, she first appeared in the city in 1543 when a man leading 12 burros arrived in town one night and discovered the next morning that there was a 13th among them. The mysterious animal passed away almost instantaneously, and when the man opened the huge chest it was carrying he discovered an almost life-sized image of the Virgin. A church was built on the site, which was discovered to lie over an immense deposit of silver, and the sealed entrance to the mine can still be seen to the right of the main aisle. Legend has it that the priest used to descend into the mine when it was dark and carry out silver through a tunnel that led to the church.

Preparations for the fiesta begin several days before December 18, when carnival rides and food and gambling booths are set up in the vicinity of the church. For several evenings there are *calendas,* processions of men and women carrying colored paper lanterns illuminated by candles and poles topped with figures of birds, boats, and other objects made out of flowers, leaves, or colored paper. There are also floats with various themes and huge papier-mâché caricatures of well-known individuals.

Thousands of pilgrims come from all over the state of Oaxaca to see the Virgin, who is dressed in velvet and satin gowns and who wears an emerald-and-diamond-studded crown for the fiesta. Despite her elegant attire, however, she is the patron saint of Mexican sailors, and a folktale holds that she often disappears from her niche at night and comes back at daybreak wet with drops of sea water.

CONTACTS:
Mexico Tourism Board
21 E. 63rd St., Fl. 3
New York, NY 10021
800-446-3942 or 212-821-0314; fax: 212-821-0367
www.visitmexico.com

SOURCES:
FiestaTime-1965, p. 182

♦ 1995 ♦ Our Lady of Sorrows Festival
Friday, Saturday, and Sunday closest to August 20

The pilgrimage to the church of Our Lady of Sorrows, or **Nossa Senhora da Agonia**, in Viana do Castelo, Portugal, is one of the country's most colorful religious festivals. Sometimes called the **Pardon of Our Lady of Sorrows**, it includes a procession in which the image of the Virgin Mary is carried over flower-strewn streets. Participants also enjoy fireworks on the River Lima, a parade of carnival giants and dwarfs, bullfights, and regional singing and folk dancing.

CONTACTS:
Avenida Cabo Verde
Parque Empresarial Praia Norte, Lote 18
Viana do Castelo, 4900-350 Portugal
351-258-839-150; fax: 351-258-839-159
www.festas-agonia.com

SOURCES:
IntlThFolk-1979, p. 314

◆ 1996 ◆ **Our Lady of the Angels, Feast of**
August 2

Our Lady of the Angels or **Nuestra Señora de los Angeles** is the patron saint of Costa Rica. Although her feast day, August 2, is observed throughout the country, the celebration focuses on Cartago, where the black stone said to bear her image is housed in the basilica that was erected on the spot where she is said to have appeared more than 300 years ago to a poor Indian girl who was gathering firewood.

On August 2 each year the small black stone image of the Virgin rides through the streets in a religious procession from the basilica to the church of St. Nicholas, where it remains until the first Saturday of September. The entire route of the procession is decorated with carpets of flowers and colored sand, and there are floats depicting various religious scenes and events. At one time many worshippers used to follow the procession dressed as Indians with strange designs painted on their faces. Although they claimed that they were fulfilling a special vow to the Virgin, church authorities prohibited the practice in 1958 because it was regarded as pagan superstition. Instead, penitents must follow the route of the procession in bare feet while balancing heavy stones on their heads or shoulders.

CONTACTS:
Embassy of Costa Rica
2114 S St. N.W.
Washington, D.C. 20008
202-234-2945; fax: 202-265-4795
www.costarica-embassy.org

SOURCES:
FiestaTime-1965, p. 127

◆ 1997 ◆ **Our Lady of the Good Death Festival**
Begins on the Friday nearest August 15

The state of Bahia in northeastern Brazil is largely populated by Afro-Brazilians, descendants of the estimated 3.5 million slaves brought to the country during the transatlantic slave trade. Among this segment is a well-known Afro-Catholic group called *Irmandade da Boa Morte*(Sisterhood of Good Death), founded in 1823 by freed female slaves living in the town of Cachoeira. A major celebration observed by the sisterhood is the Our Lady of the Good Death Festival, a unique version of the FEAST OF THE ASSUMPTION OF THE BLESSED VIRGIN MARY. Intermixed with the feast's Catholic traditions are the sisterhood's expressions of Candomblé, a separate religion with origins in the Yoruban culture of West Africa.

Over three days, the several dozen women who constitute the sisterhood hold mass and processions dramatizing Mary's death. It is a time of mourning as well as celebration for Mary's ascension into heaven, upon which she becomes *Nossa Senhora da Gloria*(Our Lady of Glory).

One way the sisters depart from Catholic festival observance is by worshiping Orishás, which are Yoruban spirits that represent major forces of nature. There are also performances of the samba de roda (ring samba). These non-Catholic expres-

sions of the festival and other Candomblé practices have attracted criticism from Brazilian church leaders.

CONTACTS:
Bahia Tourism Authority
Ave. Simon Bolivar S/N
Centro de Convenções da Bahia-1Piso
Salvador, Bahia CEP 41750-230 Brazil
www.bahia.com.br

◆ 1998 ◆ **Our Lady of the Rock, Festival of**
Every Sunday in October

The church of **Nossa Señora da Penha**, Our Lady of the Rock, rises up from a 300-foot-high granite boulder on the outskirts of Rio de Janeiro, Brazil. A number of legends accounts for the church's unusual location, one of which is that a man sleeping at the foot of the boulder was rescued from being eaten by a crocodile by the Virgin's miraculous intervention.

Pilgrims travel to the church every Sunday during the month of October. Some climb the 365 stone steps that have been carved out of the granite entirely on their knees because they have made a pledge to the Virgin, while others carry huge candles and wax images of body parts that she has cured. The large square at the base of the rock is filled with stalls selling food and drink with which the pilgrims can refresh themselves. Ferris wheels, carousels, games, and fireworks enliven the festivities. In the city of Rio De Janeiro, the festival is considered second in importance only to CARNIVAL.

Local people say that a man once caught his foot on the top step and tumbled back down the steps. Assuming that the strange downward progression represented the fulfillment of a promise made to the Virgin, the other pilgrims politely moved to the side as he passed by.

CONTACTS:
Brazilian Embassy
3006 Massachusetts Ave. N.W.
Washington, D.C. 20008
202-238-2700; fax: 202-238-2827
www.brasilemb.org

SOURCES:
FiestaTime-1965, p. 160

◆ 1999 ◆ **Ouray Ice Festival**
January

The Ouray Ice Festival is an ice-climbing competition and exposition held annually in January in Ouray, Colo. In addition to the main contest, which tests ice-climbers' skill and speed, competitions are held for such feats as axe-throwing and tight-rope walking across a gorge. Also on offer are manufacturers' displays of specialty equipment, film and slide-show presentations, and a climbing wall for children. Anyone can register to compete.

The first Ouray Ice Festival was held in January 1996, promoted by Jeff Lowe, an ice-climbing pioneer.

CONTACTS:
Ouray Ice Festival
P.O. Box 1058
Ouray, CO 81427
970-325-4288; fax: 970-325-4288
www.ourayicefestival.com/index.php

♦ 2000 ♦ **Outback Festival**
September in odd-numbered years

In 1895 A. B. "Banjo" Patterson wrote "Waltzing Matilda," the song that is most closely identified with the Australian outback. The song was based on an incident that occurred at Dogworth Station near Winton, Queensland, and it was in Winton that the ballad was first sung in public. Today Winton is host to the biennial Outback Festival, which celebrates Australia's pioneer traditions. There are parades, picnics, historic tours, safaris, rodeos, sheep-shearing and whip-cracking demonstrations, pigeon races, and sports competitions at the festival, which is held in September, at the end of the Australian winter.

The Bronze Swagman Award is presented at the festival for the best "bush verse"—similar to COWBOY POETRY in the United States. Entries are accepted from all over the world, but the poems must be written in English and must portray an "Australian Bush" theme.

CONTACTS:
Outback Festival Inc.
P.O. Box 24
Winton, QLD 4735 Australia
61-7-4657-1277; fax: 61-7-4657-1558
www.outbackfestival.org

SOURCES:
IntlThFolk-1979, p. 19

♦ 2001 ♦ **Ovoo Worship Festival**
June

Although the date varies by location, the Ovoo Worship Festival takes place in rural areas throughout Mongolia during the month of June. Ovoos are shrines at which individuals can make offerings for safe journeys or economic well-being. They are constructed out of rocks, tree branches, leaves, and other materials to form a kind of pyramid shape. Inside may be some kind of representation of God. Small towns and villages pay homage at the ovoos in June and hold festivals featuring Buddhist prayers, special food, and horse races. The people also usher in the growing season as they honor the ovoos, praying for a fruitful harvest.

CONTACTS:
Embassy of Mongolia
2833 M St. N.W.
Washington, D.C. 20007
202-333-7117; fax: 202-298-9227
www.mongolianembassy.us

SOURCES:
WildPlanet-1995, p. 332

♦ 2002 ♦ **Ox Cart Festival**
Second weekend of February

In Thailand, oxen are conventionally used for plowing rice paddies. But for one weekend in February, they become race animals in a famous competition set in the central region's Phetchaburi Province. A tradition that dates back to the reign of King Rama V (1868–1910), the Ox Cart Festival celebrates an agricultural custom and is an opportunity for Thai officials to promote tourism in Phetchaburi Province and the rest of the country.

According to tradition, rice farmers of Amphoe Ban Laem, a village in Phetchaburi, would mark the end of the harvest season by harnessing oxen to unused carts and racing them for a distance of nearly 1,000 feet. It was, and still is, an occasion for gambling between ox owners and spectators. Wagers typically center around bottles of *lao khao*, a strong form of rice whisky. Once only a local phenomenon, the competition grew in popularity until King Rama V decided to hold races at Bangkok's Royal Palace, where thousands of people attended. Soon after, it became part of the capital's celebrations to mark the Thai New Year.

The Ox Cart Festival has been an official annual event in Phetchaburi Province since 1998. There are multiple races staged throughout the province, but the best known takes place in Amphoe Ban Laem.

CONTACTS:
Tourism Authority of Thailand
Central Region Office 2
Saeng Chuto Rd.
Kanchanaburi, Amphoe Muang 71000 Thailand
www.tourismthailand.org

♦ 2003 ♦ **Ozark Folk Festival**
Second weekend in October

The Ozark Folk Festival in Eureka Springs, Ark., was first held in 1948 to preserve the music and folklore of the Ozarks. For two or three days, musicians, mostly nonprofessional, gather to play mountain music on fiddles, banjos, jackass jawbones, harmonicas, dulcimers, and other non-electrified instruments. Only traditional Ozark music is allowed, and that means it must be at least 70 years old. Some of the music dates back to Elizabethan times. Also on the menu are performances by jig, clog, and square-dance groups, crafts displays, and a Festival Queen contest.

Eureka Springs, about 50 miles north of Fayetteville, is the oldest health spa in the Ozarks, and the winding streets and houses are much the same as they were in the 1880s.

CONTACTS:
Eureka Springs Advertising & Promotions Commission
P.O. Box 522
Eureka Springs, AR 72632
866-566-9387 or 479-253-7333; fax: 479-363-9380
www.eurekasprings.org

SOURCES:
MusFestAmer-1990, p. 218

P

◆ 2004 ◆ Pacific Northwest Festival
August

Most opera companies shy away from Richard Wagner's *Der Ring des Nibelungen* because of the technical difficulties involved in staging the work and because it is assumed that only audiences in Wagner's native Germany will have the stamina to sit through the entire four-opera cycle. But in 1975, the Seattle Opera proved not only that the *Ring* could be staged, but that it could draw huge audiences. Under the direction of Glenn Ross, the Seattle Opera started its annual Wagner festival, performing the uncut *Ring* cycle in German the first week and in English the second week with an augmented orchestra. All operas are performed in the Seattle Opera House, which had been remodeled for the 1962 World's Fair.

Some of the world's finest Wagnerian performers have participated in the Pacific Northwest Festival over the years, among them Herbert Becker, Ingrid Bjoner, Philip Booth, Ute Vinzing, Paul Crook, and Malcolm Rivers. When General Director Speight Jenkins decided in 1985 to stage an entirely new production of *Die Walkure*, one of the operas in the *Ring* cycle, he was booed for his innovative approach by those who preferred the more traditional production.

See also Bayreuth Festival and Ravello Music Festival

CONTACTS:
Seattle Opera
1020 John St.
P.O. Box 9248
Seattle, WA 98109
800-426-1619 or 206-389-7600; fax: 206-389-7651
www.seattleopera.org

◆ 2005 ◆ Pack Monday Fair
Monday following October 10

The Pack Monday Fair, which used to be called St. Michael's Fair because it is held on the Monday following Old Michaelmas Day, is held in Sherborne, England. It begins shortly after midnight on Sunday, when a band of young people lock arms and march through the streets of Sherborne blowing bugles, horns, and whistles, and banging metal pots, tea-trays, and garbage can lids together. Locals call this noise-making brigade "Teddy Roe's Band," a tradition that has persisted for several centuries even though town authorities have tried to stamp it out.

The people of Sherborne say that a man named Teddy Roe once served as the chief mason involved in the reconstruction of the Sherborne Abbey Church. A fire that took place in the late 15th century destroyed much of the church. The workers who rebuilt the church completed the fan-vaulting in 1490. Legend has it that when the workers finished they "packed" the instruments of their trade and paraded in triumph through the main avenues of town, led by Teddy Roe. Another explanation asserts that Teddy Roe had no connection with the abbey, but that he came to Sherborne later and revived the ancient tradition of the Pack Monday Fair, which had lapsed. Yet another theory is that banging on pots and pans originated in the pagan custom of making loud noises to frighten away evil spirits.

CONTACTS:
Sherborne Tourist Information Centre
3 Tilton Ct., Digby Rd.
Sherborne, Dorset DT9 3NL United Kingdom
44-19-3581-5341; fax: 44-19-3581-7210
www.sherbornetown.com

SOURCES:
EngCustUse-1941, p. 94
YrbookEngFest-1954, p. 147
YrFest-1972, p. 171

◆ 2006 ◆ Paczki Day
Thursday before Lent in Poland; Tuesday before Lent in the United States

Paczki Day is a day in early to mid February in Poland and the United States on which a rich, jelly- or crème-filled doughnut is traditionally eaten in anticipation of the 40 days of fasting required during the religious season of Lent. In Poland, the observance of Paczki Day is known as *Thusty Czwartek,* or Fat Thursday; in the United States, Polish-Americans celebrate Paczki Day on Fat Tuesday, the day before Ash Wednesday, which signals the beginning of Lent. Since at least the Middle Ages, consuming butter or lard was prohibited during the observance of Lent in Poland. In the final days before the fast began, households traditionally used up their stores of these products by preparing rich foods such as cakes and pastries. Paczki are made of dense, rich dough that is deep-fried and may be filled with fruit-flavored jam or crème; they are often glazed or coated with powdered sugar.

In the United States, areas with large Polish-American populations—such as Chicago, Cleveland, and Detroit—have widely adopted the custom of eating paczki in the days prior to the start of Lent, with many Polish neighborhoods taking on a festival atmosphere as patrons flock to ethnic bakeries for authentic paczki. In the largely Polish-American community of Hamtramck, Michigan, free, continuous entertainment is provided throughout the day, an annual paczki-eating contest is held, and radio stations broadcast live from the scene. Throughout the community, bars open as early as 7:00 AM on Paczki Day and offer traditional Polish cuisine, including pierogi, golumpki, and kielbasa; in addition, many serve specialty items including "paczki shots" or liquor-filled paczki.

CONTACTS:
Embassy of The Republic of Poland
2640 16th St. N.W.
Washington, D.C. 20009
202-234-3800
www.washington.polemb.net

City of Hamtramck, Michigan
3401 Evaline
Hamtramck, MI 48212
313-876-7700
www.hamtramck.us/events/pages/paczki.php

SOURCES:
EncyEaster-2002, p. 426

♦ 2007 ♦ Pafos Aphrodite Festival Cyprus
Late August-early September

The Pafos Aphrodite Festival Cyprus is held each year at the medieval Castle Square in Pafos, Cyprus. Cyprus is an island nation whose cultural heritage dates back more than 9,000 years, taking in Greek temples, Roman art, and artifacts from numerous other periods. The festival was established by various organizations in the Pafos district in the hope of establishing and promoting the locality as a center of high-profile cultural events. In 1998, the government granted annual funding for the Pafos Aphrodite Festival Cyprus.

The first show, performed in 1999, was Verdi's *Aida*. Ensuing years have seen the performance of *La Traviata, Rigoletto, Tosca, Zorba the Greek*, and *Turnadot*. Each year, the performance is subtitled in English and Greek.

CONTACTS:
Pafos Aphrodite Festival Cyprus
25th March St.
P.O. Box 60032
8100 Pafos, Cyprus

♦ 2008 ♦ Pageant of the Golden Tree
Every five years, two days in late August

The Pageant of the Golden Tree, which is celebrated in the historic town of Bruges, Belgium, has been an official celebration of national history and local tradition since 1958. The tradition behind the festival dates back to medieval times. In 1468, a pageant was held commemorating the wedding of Princess Margareth of York and Charles the Bold, Duke of Burgundy and Count of Flanders. The central emblem of the tournament was a Golden Tree, which stood in the center of the market square where jousting knights competed for a prize horse.

The festival is held on two consecutive nights. The main event, which is performed for thousands of Belgians and tourists, is the dramatization of the historic pageant, including the grand entrance of the wedding party and the medieval tournament. In addition to these performances, as many as 2,000 actors representing about 100 groups parade through the streets of Bruges on floats, accompanied by giant puppets.

The celebration that took place in 2002 marked a modernization of the event. Bruges leaders, taking advantage of the city's European Union-designated status as a Cultural Capital, shed light on the region's modern history, in particular the period during which local magistrates and guilds gained more power under the ruling sovereigns.

CONTACTS:
Royal Committee for Bruges Initiative
BarriFrestraat 55
8200 St. Michael
Bruges Belgium
www.comitevoorinitiatief.be/activiteiten/2007/goudenboom/index EN.html

♦ 2009 ♦ Paine (Thomas) Day
January 29

Thomas Paine (1737-1809) was a propagandist and humanitarian whose influential pamphlet, *Common Sense*, is credited with persuading the American colonies to declare their independence from Great Britain. Six months after the publication of *Common Sense* in January 1776, the Declaration of Independence was signed. While Paine was serving in George WASHINGTON's army during the Revolutionary War, he wrote his inspirational tract, *The Crisis*, whose opening line was the famous, "These are the times that try men's souls."

On the Sunday nearest January 29, Paine's birthday, he is honored by members of the Thomas Paine National Historical Association in New Rochelle, New York. They lay a wreath at his monument in the Thomas Paine Memorial Museum, which houses some of his letters and personal effects. The museum is located on Paine's former farmland, and the cottage in which he lived is only a short walk away. This day is also known as **Common Sense Day**, to encourage the use of good sense in protecting the rights of all people.

CONTACTS:
Thomas Paine National Historical Association
983 North Ave.
New Rochelle, NY 10804

914-632-5376
www.thomaspaine.org

SOURCES:
AmerBkDays-2000, pp. 51, 98
AnnivHol-2000, p. 16

♦ 2010 ♦ **Paitishahem (Patishahya; Feast of Bringing in the Harvest)**
January, February, September; 26th-30th days of Shahrewar, the sixth Zoroastrian month

Paitishahem is the third of the six great seasonal feasts, known as *gahambars*, of the Zoroastrian religion. Each of the six gahambars correlated with a phase of agricultural production—in this case, bringing in the harvest—and honored one of the six things created by God: sky, water, earth, plants, animals, and humankind.

Traditionally, the gahambars were joyous festivals that lasted five days and provided farm workers with a much-needed respite from their labors. The first four days were spent in preparation for the feasting that took place on the fifth day. Today, however, so many Zoroastrians live in urban areas that the importance of the gahambars has diminished somewhat.

The Zoroastrian calendar has 12 months of 30 days each, plus five extra days at the end of the year. Because of discrepancies in the calendars used by widely separated Zoroastrian communities around the world, there are now three different calendars in use, and Paitishahem can fall either in January, February, or September according to the Gregorian calendar.

There are only about 100,000 followers of Zoroaster (also known as Zarathushtra, believed to have lived around 1200 B.C.E.) today, and most of them live in northwestern India or Iran. Smaller communities exist in Pakistan, Sri Lanka, Canada, the U.S., England, and Australia.

SOURCES:
RelHolCal-2004, p. 67

♦ 2011 ♦ **Pakistan Day**
March 23

This national holiday is also known as **Republic Day,** and is the anniversary of a 1940 resolution calling for a Muslim country for Muslim Indians. On the same day in 1956, Pakistan became an Islamic republic within the British Commonwealth.

Pakistan Day is celebrated with parades and fairs.

CONTACTS:
Embassy of Pakistan
3517 International Ct. N.W.
Washington, D.C. 20008
202-243-6500; fax: 202-686-1544
www.embassyofpakistanusa.org

SOURCES:
AnnivHol-2000, p. 49
NatlHolWrld-1968, p. 37

♦ 2012 ♦ **Pakistan Independence Day**
August 14

On this day in 1947, Pakistan gained independence from Britain. Pakistan had been part of the immense British colony of India since the 18th century.

Independence Day is a national holiday observed in much the same way as PAKISTAN DAY.

CONTACTS:
Embassy of Pakistan
3517 International Ct. N.W.
Washington, D.C. 20008
202-243-6500; fax: 202-686-1544
www.embassyofpakistanusa.org

SOURCES:
AnnivHol-2000, p. 136
NatlHolWrld-1968, p. 37

♦ 2013 ♦ **Pakistan Kashmir Solidarity Day**
February 5

On February 5, 1990, Pakistanis protested against Indian rule in an armed uprising. Nawaz Sharif, who was the main opposition leader and the chief minister of Punjab at that time, put advertisements in newspapers calling for a nationwide strike on February 5 to enable the people "to pray for God's help for the success of jihad in Kashmir." More than 80,000 Kashmiris lost their lives during the demonstrations.

Pakistan People's Party Government leader Benazir Bhutto responded by declaring the day a public holiday, naming it Kashmir Solidarity Day. It is a national holiday, so government offices, banks, schools, and colleges are closed for the day. Along many of the major roads in the capital city, banners are displayed to show Pakistan's solidarity with the Kashmirs.

On Kashmir Solidarity Day across the country and in Pakistan-occupied Kashmir, a five-minute period of silence is observed to remember those who were killed during the uprising, and politicians around the country lead prayers of tribute. In addition, every province plans their own events, including rallies or processions, seminars, and speeches.

During a speech on Kashmir Solidarity Day in 2007, President Musharraf stressed the importance of restoring peace in the region. He said, "Our children should never again live in fear or mistrust, but should be nurtured in an environment where honor, dignity, and freedom of all is assured." He paid tribute to those who lost their lives to uphold the ideals of freedom and liberty. And to honor their memory, he pledged "to spare no efforts in our quest to win back to Kashmir its lost glory and to make it a citadel of peace and harmony."

♦ 2014 ♦ **Palau Independence Day**
October 1

The Republic of Palau is a small island nation in the southern Pacific Ocean, near the Philippines, Indonesia, and Papua

New Guinea. For the last 4,000 years, Palau has been settled by people from various countries. Originally, migrants from Indonesia settled in Palau. In the 18th century, the British had a more prominent presence. In the 19th century, the Spanish influence dominated the country. After the Spanish-American War, Spain sold Palau to Germany in 1899.

In 1914, the Treaty of Versailles gave Japan control over Palau. Under Japanese rule, the Palauan culture shifted the economy from a level of subsistence to a market economy, and individual property ownership became more common.

In 1947, after World War II, Palau became one of six island districts that became part of the Trust Territory of the Pacific Islands that were to be administered by the United States. As part of its mandate, the United States was to improve Palau's infrastructure and educational system so that it could eventually become a self-sufficient nation.

Palau approved a new constitution in 1981, and then signed a Compact of Free Association with the United States in 1982. The Compact went into effect on October 1, 1994, making Palau an independent nation.

Palau has dedicated this day as a national holiday. Palau Independence Day is the most celebrated holiday of the year. On this day, the nation celebrates events that include cultural feasts and symposiums.

CONTACTS:
Palau Visitors Authority
P.O. Box 256
Koror 96940 Republic of Palau
www.visit-palau.com

♦ 2015 ♦ **Palio, Festival of the**
July 2, August 16

The **Palio of the Contrade** is a horse race that has been held twice a year in Siena, Tuscany, Italy, since the 13th century. The race features Siena's 17 *contrade*, or "ward organizations." In the Middle Ages these were rival military companies, but they are now social clubs. In each race, 10 of Siena's 17 contrade compete, hiring a professional jockey and selecting his attendants. The 10 contrade that will participate are determined by a drawing. Each contrade also has its own animal symbol, flag, color, museum, church, and motto. In medieval costume and with banners flying, the riders form a procession that carries the *Palio*, painted silk standards, through the city streets.

The race itself is run in the city's main square, the Piazza del Campo. There is intense rivalry, distrust, cheating, fixing, and bribery and frequent fights. The jockeys ride bareback, each holding a whip, which he can use on his opponents' horses as well as on his own. Riders for the finalist contrade race three times around the Piazza, and the winning contrade receives the Palio to hang on its church until the next festival. Revelry and merrymaking continue until dawn, and the winning jockey is honored with a victory dinner.

The second big race, held on August 16, is known as **Madonna del Voto Day**, in honor of the Virgin Mary.

CONTACTS:
Comune of Siena, The Public Relations Office
Piazza del Campo, 7
Siena, 53100 Italy
39-577-292230
www.comune.siena.it

Siena Tourist Information
Piazza del Campo, 56
Siena, 53100 Italy
39-577-280551; fax: 39-577-2810-41
www.italiantourism.com

SOURCES:
AnnivHol-2000, p. 111
BkFest-1937, p. 187
BkHolWrld-1986, Aug 16
FestWestEur-1958, p. 98
GdWrldFest-1985, p. 119
OxYear-1999, pp. 277, 335

♦ 2016 ♦ **Palio of the Goose and River Festival**
June 28-29

In the Middle Ages the Leap of the Goose was a test of swimming skill for the local boatmen in Pavia, Lombardy, Italy. Now it is a combined rowing and swimming relay race held at the end of June each year. Competitors leap from a raft at the end of the race and try to reach a goose suspended in air. Geese apparently played an important part in the city's history, acting as sentries when Pavia was besieged by the Gauls. In the procession through the streets of Pavia that precedes the competition, live geese are carried in cages.

There is also a Tournament of the Towers in which teams of six men from each of the city's nine wards try to knock down each other's wooden towers in a mock battle. A final battle involves the Beccaria Tower, which can only be approached by gangplanks. The winners set the tower on fire.

CONTACTS:
Italian Government Tourist Board
630 Fifth Ave., Ste. 1565
New York, NY 10111
212-245-5618; fax: 212-586-9249
www.italiantourism.com

♦ 2017 ♦ **Palm Sunday**
Between March 15 and April 18 in the West and between March 28 and May 1 in the East; the Sunday before Easter

During the Jewish PASSOVER celebration, Jesus rode into Jerusalem and was given a hero's welcome by the people, who had heard of his miracles and regarded him as the leader who would deliver them from the domination of the Roman Empire. They carried palm branches, a traditional symbol of victory, and spread them in the streets before him, shouting "Hosanna, glory to God" (John 12:12,13). Palms are still used in church services on this day, which is the beginning of HOLY WEEK, and Jesus' triumphal entry into Jerusalem is often reenacted with a procession—the most impressive being the one in Rome, where the pope, carried in ST. PETER'S CHAIR, blesses the palms.

At the beginning or end of the service, the palms are distributed to the congregation. In some countries, where palms are not available, branches of other trees—particularly pussy willow, olive, box, yew, and spruce—are used. They are later hung up in houses for good luck, buried to preserve crops, or used to decorate graves. Other names for this day include **Passion Sunday**, Fig Sunday, **Willow Sunday**, **Branch Sunday**, **Blossom Sunday,** and, in France, **Rameaux.**

SOURCES:
AmerBkDays-2000, p. 225
BkDays-1864, vol. I, p. 395
BkFest-1937, pp. 183, 300, 337
DaysCustFaith-1957, p. 104
DictFolkMyth-1984, pp. 181, 841, 954, 1171
EncyEaster-2002, p. 431
EncyRel-1987, vol. 3, p. 441
FestSaintDays-1915, p. 54
FestWestEur-1958, pp. 59, 92, 107, 125, 163, 192
FolkAmerHol-1999, p. 167
FolkWrldHol-1999, p. 172
OxYear-1999, p. 616
RelHolCal-2004, pp. 93, 120

♦ 2018 ♦ **Palm Sunday (Austria)**
Between March 15 and April 18; the Sunday before Easter

Palm Sunday commemorates Jesus' entry into Jerusalem, where he was greeted by people waving palm branches. In Austria and the Bavarian region of Germany, farmers make *Palmbuschen* by attaching holly leaves, willow boughs, and cedar twigs to the tops of long poles. After the Palmbuschen have been blessed in the local church, the farmers set them up in their fields or barns to ward off illness, to protect their crops from hail and drought, and to preserve their families from other disasters. The Palmbuschen are kept there throughout the year.

See also Palm Sunday (Germany)

SOURCES:
BkHolWrld-1986, Apr 5
EncyEaster-2002, p. 437
FestWestEur-1958, p. 59

♦ 2019 ♦ **Palm Sunday (Finland)**
Between March 15 and April 18; the Sunday before Easter

Instead of the traditional palm branches used in Palm Sunday observances elsewhere, birch branches are used in rural areas of Finland. Children may gather the branches or willow switches in the woods and decorate them with paper flowers and cloth streamers. According to custom, on the Saturday or Sunday before Easter, known as **Willowswitch Saturday** and **Willowswitch Sunday**, they go from house to house and spank the woman of the house lightly while reciting a Finnish refrain wishing her good health. The woman then uses a switch on her livestock in the same way. The switches are eventually collected and saved, to be used again the first

time the cattle are driven to pasture in the new year. The children return on Easter to receive a treat.

Pussywillow or birch branches are also used to foretell the arrival of spring. Once they are cut, the days are counted until the buds on the branches open; this is how many weeks it will take for the trees in the forest to bud.

SOURCES:
BkFest-1937, p. 112
EncyEaster-2002, pp. 203, 440
FolkWrldHol-1999, p. 229

♦ 2020 ♦ **Palm Sunday (Germany) (Palmsonntag)**
Between March 15 and April 18; the Sunday before Easter

Although Palm Sunday customs vary from one part of Germany to the next, all celebrate the resurgence of life as symbolized by the arrival of spring. In the Black Forest, people decorate tall poles with pussywillows, heart or cross motifs, and long multicolored ribbon streamers. They set the decorated poles up in front of their houses and later carry them in procession to the local church, where they are blessed by the priest.

In Bavaria, branches from 12 different kinds of wood are cut, then bent and fastened to long poles in a semicircular shape and decorated with glass beads to resemble glittering trees. The trees are carried in procession to the church, blessed by the priest, and then set up in the farmers' fields to protect the crops and ensure a bountiful harvest.

One of the more unusual Palm Sunday customs in Germany is the *Palm Esel*, or wooden Palm Donkey, symbolic of the ass upon which Jesus entered Jerusalem. This survival of an ancient folk custom is carried to the village church. People believe that if they touch the Palm Donkey, they will share in the blessing that emanated from the humble ass that once carried Jesus.

See also Palm Sunday (Austria)

SOURCES:
EncyEaster-2002, pp. 227, 437
FestWestEur-1958, p. 59

♦ 2021 ♦ **Palm Sunday (Italy) (Domenica delle Palme)**
Between March 15 and April 18; the Sunday before Easter

On Palm Sunday, the piazzas in front of most small Italian churches are filled with people dressed in spring clothes and vendors selling olive and palm branches. The olive branches are often gilded or painted silver, and the palms are braided into crosses and decorated with roses, lilies, or other flowers. After the palms have been blessed in the church, they are often exchanged as a peace offering or sign of reconciliation between those who have quarreled. In Rapallo, a center for the silk industry, silkworms' eggs are taken to church on Palm Sunday to be blessed.

The most impressive Palm Sunday observance, however, takes place in Rome. The pope, carried in St. Peter's Chair on the shoulders of eight men, comes out of St. Peter's Basilica to bless the palms. After the service, the golden palms are distributed among the clergy and the olive branches are distributed to the congregation. Then the thousands of worshippers who have gathered in St. Peter's Square march through the basilica and around the portico, emerging from one door and re-entering through another to symbolize the entry of Jesus into Jerusalem. The procession eventually makes its way to the high altar, where mass is said. Some of the palm branches are saved and later burned to make the next year's Ash Wednesday ashes. The rest are given to the people to take home, where they are treasured as protection against evil, particularly lightning and storms.

CONTACTS:
Italian Government Tourist Board
630 Fifth Ave., Ste. 1565
New York, NY 10111
212-245-5618; fax: 212-586-9249
www.italiantourism.com

SOURCES:
BkFest-1937, p. 183
BkFestHolWrld-1970, p. 50
DaysCustFaith-1957, p. 104
FestSaintDays-1915, p. 55
FestWestEur-1958, p. 92

♦ 2022 ♦ Palm Sunday (Netherlands) (PalmZondag)
Between March 15 and April 18; the Sunday before Easter

The *Palmpaas*, or "Easter palm," in the Netherlands is a stick between 18" and 54" long to which a hoop has been attached. The hoop is covered with boxwood and decorated with colored paper flags, eggshells, sugar rings, oranges, raisins, figs, chocolate eggs, and small cakes. There are figures of swans or cocks on top that are made out of baked dough. Sometimes there are contests for the most elaborate Palmpaas. Children in rural areas of the Netherlands go from one farm to the next with their Palmpaas, singing nonsense verses in which they ask for Easter eggs, sometimes for use in the popular Easter sport of *eiertikken*, or egg tapping.

With its egg and bird decorations, it seems likely that the Palmpaas was originally a fertility symbol that represented the arrival of spring in the village and the resurgence of life after winter. In some Roman Catholic areas, the Palmpaas are blessed by the local priest and then saved as protection against lightning and sore throats during the coming year.

SOURCES:
EncyEaster-2002, p. 439
FestWestEur-1958, p. 125
FolkWrldHol-1999, p. 173

♦ 2023 ♦ Palm Sunday (United States)
Between March 15 and April 18; the Sunday before Easter

Programs of sacred music are performed in many American towns and cities on Palm Sunday. They are often sponsored by and held in churches, but may be part of the musical community's regular concert series. These programs usually begin on or before Palm Sunday and may continue throughout Holy Week. Some of the more popular pieces performed at these concerts include Bach's *St. John Passion* or *St. Matthew Passion*, Handel's *Messiah*, Gounod's *La Rédemption*, Haydn's *Seven Last Words*, Beethoven's *Christ on the Mount of Olives*, and Sir John Stainer's *Crucifixion*. Bethany College's Messiah Festival in Lindsborg, Kansas, has been held during Holy Week for over 100 years.

In addition to musical performances, plays or pageants dealing with Holy Week themes are often performed on Palm Sunday as well. The same group that performs the Black Hills Passion Play in South Dakota all summer for many years portrayed the last seven days in the life of Christ during Holy Week at an amphitheater near Lake Wales, Florida.

In St. Augustine, Florida, the Blessing of the Fishing and Shrimp Fleet takes place on Palm Sunday. Shrimp trawlers and other fishing boats, as well as many privately owned vessels, circle past the City Yacht Pier to receive the local priest's blessing.

Many people place the palm branches that have been blessed in the churches on Palm Sunday behind religious pictures and statues in homes, stores, and restaurants.

CONTACTS:
St. Augustine, Ponte Vedra & The Beaches Visitors & Convention Bureau
88 Riberia St., Ste. 400
St. Augustine, FL 32084
800-653-2489 or 904-829-1711; fax: 904-829-6149
www.getaway4florida.com

♦ 2024 ♦ Pan American Day
April 14

April 14, 1890, is the day on which the First International Conference of American States adopted a resolution forming what is now known as the Organization of American States (OAS). The original member countries include Argentina, Bolivia, Brazil, Chile, Colombia, Costa Rica, Cuba, the Dominican Republic, Ecuador, El Salvador, Guatemala, Haiti, Honduras, Mexico, Nicaragua, Panama, Paraguay, Peru, the United States, Uruguay, and Venezuela. Since 1967, 14 more countries have joined: Barbados, Trinidad and Tobago, Jamaica, Grenada, Suriname, Dominica, St. Lucia, Antigua and Barbuda, St. Vincent and the Grenadines, the Bahamas, St. Kitts and Nevis, Canada, Belize, and Guyana.

The purpose of the OAS, which has remained basically unchanged since that time, is to strengthen peace and security in the Western Hemisphere by promoting understanding among the various countries of North, Central, and South America. The International Union of American Republics (now called the Pan American Union)—the central permanent agency and general secretariat of the OAS—designated

April 14 as Pan American Day in 1930, and it was first observed the following year.

Although each member country holds its own celebration, it is at the Pan American Union building in Washington, D.C., that one of the largest observances takes place. Students from all over the Western Hemisphere travel to Washington where, against a backdrop of flags in the courtyard of the House of the Americas, they perform a program of folk songs and dances. Ceremonies are also held in Miami and in other cities with large populations from Latin American countries.

CONTACTS:
Organization of American States
17th St. & Constitution Ave. N.W.
Washington, D.C. 20006
202-458-3000; fax: 202-458-6421
www.oas.org

SOURCES:
AmerBkDays-2000, p. 284
AnnivHol-2000, p. 62
BkHolWrld-1986, Apr 14
DictDays-1988, p. 87

♦ 2025 ♦ **Panama Independence Days**
November 3; November 28

Panama celebrates two Independence Days: November 28, the anniversary of freedom from Spain, and November 3, the anniversary of independence from Colombia. Both are national holidays. After gaining independence from Spain on November 28, 1821, Panama joined the Republic of Greater Colombia. For 50 years, Panama struggled for complete autonomy. In 1903, Colombia and Panama disagreed on whether to let the U.S. build a canal at Panama. With U.S. backing, Panama broke away on November 3, 1903, and the canal was built.

November 3 is celebrated with parades and fireworks in Panama City.

CONTACTS:
Panama Embassy
2862 McGill Terr. N.W.
Washington, D.C. 20008
202-483-1407; fax: 202-483-8413
www.embassyofpanama.org

SOURCES:
AnnivHol-2000, pp. 185, 197
NatlHolWrld-1968, p. 200

♦ 2026 ♦ **Panathenaea**
July or August

Panathenaea is the most important of the ancient Greek festivals, celebrated in Athens in honor of Athena, the patron goddess of that city. The lesser festival was held every year, and the Great Panathenaea every fourth year much more elaborately. The date was the 28th of the Attic month of Hecatombaeon (July or August).

In the yearly celebrations, there were musical and athletic contests, animal sacrifices, and a procession. The procession of the Great Panathenaea was an especially grand affair and is pictured on a frieze of the Parthenon. The *peplus*, a garment with an embroidered depiction of the battle of the gods and the giants, was rigged like a sail on a ship with wheels and carried through the city to the Acropolis. The procession included priests leading a train of animals that would be sacrificed, maidens carrying sacrificial implements, warriors, old men with olive branches, and horses. The festival ended with the sacrifice of oxen and a banquet.

SOURCES:
ClassDict-1984, p. 440
DictFolkMyth-1984, p. 88
NewCentClassHandbk-1962, p. 809
OxClassDict-1970, p. 774

♦ 2027 ♦ **Pancake Day**
Between February 3 and March 9; Shrove Tuesday

For the people of Olney, England, and Liberal, Kansas, Pancake Day is more than another name for SHROVE TUESDAY. The old custom of making pancakes on the Tuesday preceding ASH WEDNESDAY has survived in the form of a Pancake Race. Ladies of both towns run a 450-yard course, flipping pancakes as they go. Participants must wear a skirt, an apron, and a headscarf, and must toss their pancakes in the air three times as they run. The winner of the Kansas race is announced by a transatlantic phone call to Olney immediately after it is over.

The Olney race dates back to 1445. According to the legend, a housewife who was making pancakes heard the bell summoning her to church and was in such a hurry that she ran along the road with the frying pan still in her hand. The Liberal, Kansas, race has been run since 1950. It only lasts about a minute, but it draws a good deal of media attention and is followed by pancake-eating contests, a parade, and children's races.

CONTACTS:
International Pancake Day Inc.
P.O. Box 665
Liberal, KS 67905
620-626-1320; fax: 620-624-9639
www.pancakeday.net

Town of Olney, The Olney Centre
High St.
Olney, Buckinghamshire MK46 4EF United Kingdom
44-12-3471-1679; fax: 44-12-3424-1107
www.olneytowncouncil.co.uk

SOURCES:
BkHolWrld-1986, Feb 25
DictDays-1988, p. 87
DictFolkMyth-1984, p. 842
EncyEaster-2002, p. 442
GdWrldFest-1985, p. 96
OxYear-1999, p. 607

♦ 2028 ♦ **Panchadaan**
August-September, third day of waning half of Hindu month of Bhadrapada; July-August, eighth day of waxing half of Hindu month of Sravana

The **Alms Giving Festival** in Nepal is based on the Dangatha chapter of the *Kapidawdan*, an ancient Buddhist text, stating that those who donate food and clothing to beggars on this day will be blessed with seven great gifts: health, happiness, longevity, wisdom, wealth, fame, and children. All Buddhists, rich or poor, go from door to door in large groups begging for alms. They are usually well received in Nepalese homes—even non-Buddhist people give food or money to the Buddhist beggars on this day.

In Patan and elsewhere in Nepal, Panchadaan is observed on the eighth day of the waxing half of Sravana. In Kathmandu and Bhadgaon, it is observed on the third day of the waning half of Bhadrapada.

SOURCES:
FolkWrldHol-1999, p. 519

♦ 2029 ♦ **Panguni Uttiram (Panguni Uthiram)**
March-April; 10 days including full moon day of Hindu month of Caitra

The full moon day of Caitra is the day on which the Hindu god Shiva married the goddess Meenakshi at Madura, Indonesia. The 10-day Hindu festival that follows also celebrates the marriage of Subramanya to Theivanai, adopted daughter of Indra.

Panguni Uttiram is a popular festival in Malaysia, where the worship of Subramanya is widespread. There are fairs on the temple grounds and processions in which Hindu gods and goddesses are carried through the streets in chariots. In Kuala Lumpur, Subramanya and his consort are taken from the Sentul temple in an elaborately decorated chariot through the city streets. Free meals are served throughout the day to visitors. At Bukit Mertajam, a fire-walking ceremony is held on this day.

In India, this festival is known as MEENAKSHI KALYANAM.

CONTACTS:
Malaysian Tourism Promotion Board
818 W. 7th St., Ste. 970
Los Angeles, CA 90017
800-336-6842 or 213-689-9702; fax: 213-689-1530
www.tourism.gov.my

SOURCES:
FolkWrldHol-1999, p. 259

♦ 2030 ♦ **Papa Festival**
January

According to tradition, Okomfo Anokye, the founder of the Ashanti nation in Ghana used the following method for choosing a location for the capital city: he planted two trees and decided to establish the seat of government at whichever site's tree grew. The tree planted at Kumasi flourished, thus Kumasi is the capital of the Ashanti Region. The other tree, planted at Kumawu, died. Still, each year in January the people of Kumawu remember their past.

The festival is named for the local god and begins with a procession of ancestral stools, or thrones, to a nearby river, where they are cleansed. Then a bonfire is lit and burns all night. The next morning, the chief makes an offering to all the chiefs who have passed on. Finally, a procession takes the chief, carried in a palanquin, to the site where the legendary tree was planted for the ritual slaughtering of a cow or bull. Later, there is a scramble of young men to cut a piece of the meat. Those who attempt to do so are often beaten back with whips and branches, but those who succeed in escaping with their portion are regarded with admiration, especially by the young women in the crowd of spectators.

CONTACTS:
Embassy of Ghana
3512 International Dr. N.W.
Washington, D.C. 20008
202-686-4520; fax: 202-686-4527
www.ghanaembassy.org

SOURCES:
FestGhana-1970, p. 48

♦ 2031 ♦ **Papua New Guinea Independence Day**
September 16

This national holiday celebrates Papua New Guinea's independence on this day in 1975. In the late 19th century Germany laid claim to the northeastern section of the island, while Britain ruled the southeastern section. Britain left its section to Australia in 1902, which occupied the German area in 1914, and eventually administered the whole area until independence, though it is still part of the British Commonwealth.

In 2000, Papua New Guinea celebrated its silver jubilee (25th) anniversary of independence with a flag-raising ceremony, a parade, and musical and dance performances in the capital city, Port Moresby.

CONTACTS:
Embassy of Papua New Guinea
1779 Massachusetts Ave. N.W., Ste. 805
Washington, D.C. 20036
202-745-3680; fax: 202-745-3679
www.pngembassy.org

♦ 2032 ♦ **Parada del Sol**
Late February

In 1951 the town of Scottsdale, Ariz., began an annual Sunshine Festival. The event featured a parade through the downtown that led to the city park for a family barbeque. In 1954, the newly-formed Scottsdale Jaycees took over the event and renamed it the Parada del Sol.

Wanting to use the Parada del Sol to highlight Scottsdale's Old West heritage, the Jaycees adopted the slogan "The West's Most Western Town" to promote the event. They added western-style staged gunfights and holdups to the festival. In 1956 a Professional Rodeo Cowboys Association-sanctioned rodeo was added. Over the years, the rodeo has been held at different sites around Scottsdale, including the Scottsdale Stadium and the Rawhide Western Town. It is now located at the Equidome Arena at WestWorld in north Scottsdale.

Since 1959 the Parada del Sol has begun with the Hashknife Pony Express run from the town of Holbrook to Scottsdale, the only pony express service still officially authorized by the U.S. Postal Service. This delivery is followed by the two-mile parade itself, held on a Saturday, which features 150 floats and some 1,000 horses. The parade ends in Old Town, where spectators can go for a block party with food, drinks, games, live music, and pony rides for the children. The three-day rodeo begins on the following Friday.

CONTACTS:
Scottsdale Jaycees Parada del Sol
P.O. Box 292
Scottsdale, AZ 85252
480-990-3179
www.scottsdalejaycees.org/paradadelsol

♦ 2033 ♦ Paraguay Independence Day
May 14 and 15

Paraguayans set aside two days to celebrate their independence from Spain, which they won on May 14, 1811, after a bloodless revolution led by Dr. José Gaspar Rodríguez Francia (1766-1840). Dr. Francia was also instrumental in the design of Paraguay's flag, which is the only national flag in the world that is different on both sides.

The most elaborate Independence Day parade is in the capital, Asunción. People may wear traditional clothes as they stroll down the streets: for the men, fancy shirts, broad-brimmed straw hats, ponchos, a *faja* (sash) around the waist, and full trousers known as *bombachas*; for the women, blouses with lace inserts and brightly colored embroidery, full skirts with many layers of petticoats underneath, and a *rebozo* or shawl similar to the Spanish mantilla. *Sopa Paraguay,* a traditional Independence Day dish, is served on this day because it is only on special occasions that the poor can afford to buy the eggs and cheese that go into the soup.

CONTACTS:
Embassy of Paraguay
2400 Massachusetts Ave. N.W.
Washington, D.C. 20008
202-483-6960; fax: 202-234-4508
www.embaparusa.gov.py

SOURCES:
AnnivHol-2000, p. 82
NatlHolWrld-1968, p. 62

♦ 2034 ♦ Pardon of Nossa Senhora dos Remédios
Early September

Both religious and secular activities play a part in the Pardon of Nossa Senhora dos Remédios, a pilgrimage to the Sanctuary of Our Lady of the Remedies in Lamego, Portugal, a small town known for its port wine and smoked ham. Great numbers of pilgrims climb the monumental staircase up to the baroque church, but the highlight of the festival is the tri-umphal procession on the last day, in which thousands of country people in local costume participate. There is also a battle of flowers, a folklore festival, fireworks, sports contests, and handicraft exhibitions.

CONTACTS:
Portuguese National Tourist Office
590 Fifth Ave., 4th Fl.
New York, NY 10036
800-767-8842 or 212-354-4403; fax: 212-764-6137
www.visitportugal.com

SOURCES:
IntlThFolk-1979, p. 308

♦ 2035 ♦ Pardon of Ste. Anne d'Auray
Last weekend in July

In the 17th century in Brittany, the story goes, St. Anne, mother of the Virgin Mary, appeared to a peasant named Yves (or Yvon) and told him that she wanted to see her ruined chapel rebuilt. Yves reported this to his bishop, who at first refused to believe him, but eventually changed his mind. Soon afterward, a broken image of St. Anne was found in a field nearby, and people started making contributions so that the effigy could be enshrined. A church was built in Auray and soon it became a place of pilgrimage for believers all over France.

The **Pardon of St. Anne** remains one of Brittany's most picturesque festivals. On their knees, 20,000 devout Roman Catholics mount the *Scala Santa,* the sacred stairway leading to the chapel containing St. Anne's statue. Many Bretons attending the festival wear the ornate headdresses and embroidered costumes for which their province is famous. They come to pay homage to St. Anne and pray she will grant their requests.

CONTACTS:
Association of Shrine Towns of France
Office of Tourism, rue Jean-Marie Vianney
Ars-On-Formans, 01480 France
33-4-7408-1076; fax: 33-4-7408-1542
www.villes-sanctuaires.com/anglais/index.htm

SOURCES:
BkFest-1937, p. 126
BkHolWrld-1986, Jul 25
FestWestEur-1958, p. 46
FolkWrldHol-1999, p. 450

♦ 2036 ♦ Parentalia
February 13

This was an ancient Roman festival held in honor of the *manes,* or souls of the dead—in particular, deceased relatives. It began a season for remembering the dead, which ended with the Feralia on February 21. This week was a quiet, serious occasion, without the rowdiness that characterized other Roman festivals. Everything, including the temples, closed down, and people decorated graves with flowers and left food—sometimes elaborate banquets—in the cemeteries in the belief that it would be eaten by the spirits of the deceased.

February 22 was devoted to forgiveness and the restoration of friendships broken during the preceding year.

SOURCES:
DaysCustFaith-1957, p. 53
DictFolkMyth-1984, p. 673
DictRomRel-1996, p. 174
FestRom-1981, p. 74
FestSaintDays-1915, p. 31
OxYear-1999, p. 75

♦ 2037 ♦ **Parilia (Palilia)**
April 21

This ancient Roman festival was held in honor of Pales, the protector of shepherds and their flocks—although some say it was named after *pario,* meaning "to bear or increase." Pales was sometimes regarded as male, and therefore similar to Pan or Faunus, and sometimes as female, and therefore related to Vesta, or Anna Parenna (*see* ANNA PARENNA FESTIVAL). In any case, the Parilia was a pastoral rite that was observed not only in rural areas but also in Rome, where it coincided with the city's founding in 753 B.C.E. In fact, it is believed that Romulus, one of the legendary founders of Rome, played a significant role in the cleansing and renewal rituals associated with the Parilia.

Although no sacrifices were offered, lustrations (purifying ceremonies) were carried out with fire and smoke. The blood that had been preserved from the OCTOBER HORSE SACRIFICE six months earlier was burned, as were bean shells and the ashes of the cattle sacrificed at the CEREALIA. The stables were purified with smoke and swept out with brooms. There were also offerings to Pales of cheese, boiled wine, and millet cakes. In rural areas, heaps of straw were set ablaze, and shepherds and their flocks had to pass over or through them three times. The festival ended with a huge open-air feast.

SOURCES:
AmerBkDays-2000, p. 246
ClassDict-1984, p. 437
DictFolkMyth-1984, p. 845
DictRomRel-1996, p. 175
FestRom-1981, p. 103
OxYear-1999, p. 164

♦ 2038 ♦ **Paris Air and Space Show**
June in odd-numbered years

The biennial **Salons Internationaux de l'Aéronautique et de l'Espace** is held at Le Bourget Airport just outside of Paris—the airfield where Charles Lindbergh landed after his historic nonstop flight from New York in 1927. It attracts more than half a million visitors who come to see exhibits of aircraft, launching and ground equipment, missile propulsion units, navigational aids, anti-aircraft detection devices, and other aeronautic equipment.

On the last day of the 11-day event there is a special flying demonstration that has occasionally been marred by spectacular crashes. In 1989, for example, a Soviet MiG-29 flying only 580 feet above the ground in a maneuver designed to display its slow-speed handling suddenly plummeted earthward, burying its needle-shaped nose eight feet into the rain-softened turf before bursting into flames. The pilot was fortunate enough to have ejected in time and sustained only minor injuries.

The 39th biennial Paris Air Show was held in 1991, just a few months after the Persian Gulf War, and a worldwide recession had threatened to scuttle the event. But the role played by high technology aircraft in the Allied victory over Saddam Hussein attracted a record number of exhibitors—approximately 1,700 from 38 countries—and spectators. The 1999 show hosted 1,895 exhibitors from 41 countries and more than 250,000 visitors.

CONTACTS:
Salons Internationaux de l'Aeronautique et de l'Espace
4 rue Galilee
Paris, 75116 France
33-1-5323-3341

SOURCES:
GdWrldFest-1985, p. 81

♦ 2039 ♦ **Paris Autumn Festival (Festival d'Automne)**
Mid-September through late December

The Autumn Festival marks the return of Parisians from their August holidays and the start of the city's cultural season. When it was founded in 1972, the festival incorporated two existing events—Semaines Musicales Internationales and the Festival of International Dance—with theater and art exhibitions. It now encompasses film, photography, and other contemporary arts on an international scale.

Most of the theater presentations are experimental in some way, and they have included productions by Richard Foreman's Ontological Hysteric Theatre from the United States, Peter Stein's Schaubuhne am Halleschen Ufer from West Berlin, Denmark's Odin Teatret, Poland's Teatr Cricot 2, and Taganka Theatre from the former U.S.S.R.

Composers whose works have been performed there include Pierre Boulez, György Ligeti, John Cage, and Iannis Zenakis. Martha Graham's, Merce Cunningham's, and Maurice Béjart's dance companies have performed at the festival, as have the New York Philharmonic, the London Sinfonietta, and the Orchestre de Paris. Events are held in numerous locations throughout Paris, among them the Pompidou Center, the Théâtre de Chaillot, and the Théâtre des Champs Elysées.

CONTACTS:
Festival d'Automne a Paris
156, rue de Rivoli
Paris, 75001 France
33-1-5345-1700; fax: 33-1-5345-1701
www.festival-automne.com/newmain_index.php

SOURCES:
IntlThFolk-1979, p. 116
MusFestEurBrit-1980, p. 86

♦ 2040 ♦ **Parker (Charlie) Jazz Festival**
Last weekend in August

The Charlie Parker Jazz Festival is a free event sponsored by the City Parks Foundation in New York City. Held annually since 1993, the event comprises two concerts held over a weekend in late August to commemorate Parker's birthday, August 29, 1920. Known to jazz followers as "Yardbird" or more simply "Bird," Parker was one of the most innovative and influential jazz saxophonists of the 20th century. His works are particularly noted for their complexity and virtuoso improvisation, which continue to attract critical admiration more than 50 years after his death in 1955.

The festival concerts take place at Marcus Garvey Park in Harlem and Tompkins Square Park in the East Village, neighborhoods in which Parker lived and worked. About 7,000 people attended the festival's 15th anniversary performances in 2007, which featured such artists as vocalist Abbey Lincoln, drummer Chico Hamilton, pianist Marc Cary, and trumpeter Maurice Brown.

CONTACTS:
City Parks Foundation
Charlie Parker Jazz Festival
830 Fifth Ave., Room 280
New York, NY 10021
212-360-1399
www.cityparksfoundation.org

SOURCES:
AAH-2007, p. 93

♦ 2041 ♦ **Paro Tsechu**
Early spring on a date set by the lamas, or 10th-15th days of second lunar month

One of the most popular festivals of Bhutan, a principality northeast of India in the Himalayas, is held in the town of Paro. (*Tsechus* means "tenth day" and relates to the birth of the Buddha. It is used as "festival" is used in English.)

The Paro festival is held over five days to commemorate the life and deeds of Padmasambhava [*see also* MYSTERY PLAY OF (TIBET)]. Known in Bhutan as Guru Rinpoche, he was a mystic who lived in the eighth century and brought Buddhism to Bhutan from Tibet.

The purpose of this festival is to exorcize evil influences and to ensure good fortune in the coming year. The highlight of Paro events comes before dawn on the last day when a huge appliqued scroll known as the *Thongdrel* is unfurled from the top of the wall of the *Dzong* (the monastery and district center). It is displayed to onlookers in the courtyard until just before the first rays of the sun touch it. The Thongdrel is said to have the power to confer blessings and provide respite from the cycle of existence. It is a type of *thangka* (a religious scroll of any size) and is so big that it covers the three-story wall of the Dzong, and it depicts the life of the Guru Rinpoche, his various peaceful manifestations, and his consorts.

Dressed in their best clothes, people bring dried yak meat and *churra*, a puffed rice dish, to the Dzong and watch

masked dancers. A series of dances, called *cham*, are performed for the festival. One of these, the Black Hat Dance, tells of the victory over a Tibetan king who tried to wipe out Buddhism; those who watch the dance are supposed to receive great spiritual blessings. The Dance of the Four Stags commemorates the vanquishing of the god of the wind by Guru Rinpoche. The god rode on a stag, and the guru commandeered the stag as his own mount. Another dance, the Deer Dance, tells the story of Guru Rinpoche teaching Buddhism while traveling through the country on the back of a deer. The dances are performed by monks who play the roles of deities, heroes, and animals dressed in brilliantly colored silks and brocades. They wear carved wooden or papier mâché masks symbolizing the figure they portray.

The dances are accompanied by the music of drums, bells, gongs, conch-shell trumpets, and horns. Some horns are so long that they touch the ground.

Other activities include folk dancing and singing and lewd performances by clowns called *atsaras*. Many of the dances and performances are typical of Tibetan Buddhist traditions also observed in Tibet and the Ladakh area of India.

CONTACTS:
Far Fung Places L.L.C.
1914 Fell St.
San Francisco, CA 94117
415-386-8306; fax: 415-386-8104
www.farfungplaces.com
www.kingdomofbhutan.com

SOURCES:
BkHolWrld-1986, Apr 20
HolSymbols-2009, p. 692

♦ 2042 ♦ **Parshurama Jayanti**
April-May; third day of waxing half of Hindu month of Vaisakha

According to Hindu mythology, it was Parashurama (Rama with an Ax) who destroyed the evil Kshatriya kings and princes 21 times, including the thousand-armed warrior, Arjuna. His birthday, Parashurama Jayanti, is therefore observed with fasting, austerities, and prayer. It is also a day to worship Lord Vishnu, of whom Parashurama is believed to be the sixth incarnation. To Hindus, Parashurama represents filial obedience, austerity, power, and brahmanic ideals.

Parashurama's story is told in the *Mahabharata* and in the Puranas, or Hindu epics. He also appears in the *Ramayana*, where he challenges Ramachandra, the seventh avatar or incarnation of Vishnu, to a test of strength. When it becomes apparent that he is losing, Parashurama pays homage to Ramachandra and retires to the Himalayas. The Malabar region on the southwest coast of India is believed to have been founded by Parashurama.

SOURCES:
DictFolkMyth-1984, p. 844
RelHolCal-2004, p. 168

◆ 2043 ◆ **Parshva, Birthday of**
December-January; 10th day of the waning half of the Jain month of Pausa

Parshva was the 23rd Jina or Tirthankara (spiritual guide) of Jainism. He lived during the ninth century B.C.E., for about 100 years, according to legend. He became a wandering ascetic when he was 30 years old and later founded what is considered the original white-clad (Svetambara) monks in the Jaina tradition. His birth is celebrated by Jains on the 10th day of the waning half of Pausa (December-January), particularly in Bihar and West Bengal, where he gained a large following.

The parents of MAHAVIRA (6th century B.C.E.), the 24th Tirthankara and "Great Hero" of the Jain religion, were adherents of Parshva's spiritual teachings. Although Mahavira is much better known, Jains believe that he did not found a new religion so much as provide guidance for a tradition that had already been established.

SOURCES:
OxDictWrldRel-1997, p. 737
RelHolCal-2004, p. 195

◆ 2044 ◆ **Partridge Day**
September 1

This is traditionally the day on which the partridge-hunting season opens in England. Just as Grouse Day in Scotland (*see* GLORIOUS TWELFTH) was often referred to as St. Grouse's Day, Partridge Day was sometimes called **St. Partridge's Day**.

SOURCES:
DictDays-1988, p. 87

◆ 2045 ◆ **Paryushana**
August-September; Hindu month of Bhadrapada

Like most other Jaina festivals, the Paryushana festival is observed by focusing on the 10 cardinal virtues: forgiveness, charity, simplicity, contentment, truthfulness, self-restraint, fasting, detachment, humility, and continence. Believers ask those whom they may have offended to forgive them, and friendships that have lapsed during the year are restored.

The Paryushana festival is observed all over India in the month of Bhadrapada (August-September), but on different dates. The Svetambara Jainas observe it for eight days, and then the ten-day celebration of the Digambara Jainas begins.

SOURCES:
FolkWrldHol-1999, p. 520
OxDictWrldRel-1997, p. 737
RelHolCal-2004, p. 195

◆ 2046 ◆ **Pascua Florida Day**
On or near April 2

Although no one knows for certain the date on which Ponce de León (1460-1521) landed at Florida in 1513, it is widely believed that he first stepped ashore somewhere between St. Augustine and the mouth of the St. Johns River on April 2. He named the land Pascua Florida because it was Eastertime. *Pascua* is a Spanish word meaning "Easter," and *Florida* means "flowering" or "full of flowers." (In Scotland and northern England, another name for EASTER was Pasch Day; among Orthodox Christians it is called Pascha.)

The Florida state legislature designated April 2 **Florida State Day** in 1953, but when it falls on a Saturday or Sunday, the holiday is observed on the preceding Friday or the following Monday. The week ending on April 2 is known as Pascua Florida Week, a time when both school children and adults are encouraged to attend special programs devoted to the area's discovery and history.

SOURCES:
AnnivHol-2000, p. 56
DictDays-1988, p. 87

◆ 2047 ◆ **Passion Play at Tzintzuntzan**
Between March 19 and April 22; Thursday and Friday before Easter

The *Penitentes*, or penitents, are a lay brotherhood of religious flagellants. In Mexico on GOOD FRIDAY, they often participate in Passion plays dramatizing the events of the closing days in the life of Jesus. One of the most complete and colorful Passion plays is the one staged in Tzintzuntzan in the state of Michoacán. Performed in an olive grove near the church, the play begins at noon on the Thursday preceding EASTER with a representation of the Last Supper and continues until midnight on Good Friday. The penitents wear black loincloths and face-coverings, lashing their own bare backs and wearing chains that bite into the flesh of their ankles. They carry heavy crosses in imitation of Jesus. In Passion plays elsewhere in Mexico, the penitents hold bundles of cacti on their shoulders while candles burn into the palms of their hands.

CONTACTS:
Mexico Tourism Board
21 E. 63rd St., Fl. 3
New York, NY 10021
800-446-3942 or 212-821-0314; fax: 212-821-0367
www.visitmexico.com

SOURCES:
DictFolkMyth-1984, p. 851
IntlThFolk-1979, p. 277

◆ 2048 ◆ **Passover**
Begins between March 27 and April 24; Nisan 15-21 (or 22)

Also known as **Pesah**, **Pesach**, or the **Feast of Unleavened Bread**, Passover is an eight-day celebration (seven days in Israel and by Reform Jews) of the deliverance of the Jews from slavery in Egypt. It is one of the three PILGRIM FESTIVALS (*see also* SHAVUOT and SUKKOT). According to the book of Exodus, when Pharaoh refused to let Moses lead the Jews out of Egypt, God sent a number of plagues—including locusts, fire, and hailstones—but Pharaoh still was unmoved. A 10th and final plague, during which the Angel of Death was sent to kill the Egyptians' first-born sons, finally persuaded Pharaoh to relent. All the Jews had been instructed to sacrifice a lamb and sprinkle the blood on their doorposts so that the Angel would "pass over" and spare their sons.

Jewish families today eat a ceremonial dinner called the *Seder* at which they retell the story of the Exodus from Egypt and eat various symbolic foods—including meat of the paschal lamb, bitter herbs (recalling the harsh life of slavery) and wine (symbolizing the fruitfulness of the earth). The *matzoh*, a flat, unleavened bread, is meant to symbolize the haste with which the Jews left: they didn't have time to let their bread rise before baking it. In strictly religious Jewish homes today, all foods made with leavening are prohibited during this season.

See also FIRSTBORN, FAST OF THE

CONTACTS:
Union of Orthodox Jewish Congregations of America
11 Broadway
New York, NY 10004
212-563-4000; fax: 212-564-9058
www.ou.org

SOURCES:
AmerBkDays-2000, pp. 239, 299
BkFest-1937, p. 207
BkFestHolWrld-1970, pp. 52, 63
BkHolWrld-1986, Apr 4
DaysCustFaith-1957, p. 112
DictWrldRel-1989, pp. 155, 390, 560, 668
EncyEaster-2002, p. 464
FolkAmerHol-1999, p. 160
FolkWrldHol-1999, p. 283
HolSymbols-2009, p. 696
OxYear-1999, p. 727
RelHolCal-2004, p. 50

♦ 2049 ♦ **Patriot Day (September 11 Day)**
September 11

Patriot Day in the United States commemorates the anniversary of the terrorist attacks that took place on September 11, 2001, in New York City, N.Y.; Washington, D.C.; and in the skies above Shanksville, Penn. On that day, hijackers associated with the al Qaeda terrorist organization commandeered four commercial airliners and planned to intentionally crash them into several sites. They flew two of the planes into the Twin Towers of the World Trade Center in lower Manhattan and one into the Pentagon in the nation's capital. The fourth plane, which was believed to be headed either to the White House or to the U.S. Capitol, crashed in a field in rural Pennsylvania after passengers on the plane figured out the hijackers' intentions and resisted them.

As designated by an act of Congress in December 2001, each year the president proclaims a day of national observance in memory of the more than 2,700 people who lost their lives in the attacks. Throughout the nation, flags are flown at half-staff and a moment of silence is observed at 8:46 A.M. Eastern time, the exact moment the first plane flew into the North Tower of the World Trade Center.

Observances take place at each of the three sites of attack. In New York, the site of the greatest loss of life, a memorial service takes place during the morning of September 11 each year; moments of silence are observed at the exact times that the planes crashed into the towers and that the towers collapsed. Surviving family members recite the names of the deceased. On the evening of September 11, a light display known as the Tribute in Light fills the sky with beams of light in the space formerly taken up by the World Trade Center towers. In Washington, D.C., victims of the attacks are remembered at a public wreath-laying ceremony in Arlington National Cemetery as well as a private ceremony at the Pentagon for family and friends of those who died. In Shanksville, Pennsylvania, a memorial service is also held near the crash site of United Airlines Flight 93, the only hijacked aircraft that did not reach its intended target. The ceremony in Pennsylvania includes tolling of the bells and reading a list of victims.

In addition to the services planned at the sites of the attacks, memorial tributes are held throughout the United States, particularly at state and municipal government buildings, public safety offices, and fire stations. These events typically include patriotic remarks, observance of moments of silence, and wreath-laying ceremonies.

CONTACTS:
Office of the Mayor
City Hall
New York, NY 10007
212-639-9675; fax: 212-788-2460
nyc.gov

Flight 93 National Memorial
National Park Service
109 W. Main St., Ste. 104
Somerset, PA 15501-2035
814-443-4557; fax: 814-443-2180
www.nps.gov/flni

Arlington National Cemetery
Arlington, VA 22211
703-607-8000
www.arlingtoncemetery.org

SOURCES:
PatHols-2006, p. 227

♦ 2050 ♦ **Patriots' Day**
Third Monday in April

The battles of Lexington and Concord, Massachusetts, marked the beginning of the American Revolution on April 19, 1775. This is a legal holiday in Massachusetts and Maine. Although no one really knows who fired the first shot on the Lexington green—"the shot heard 'round the world," in the words of Ralph Waldo Emerson—the British proceeded from Lexington to Concord, where there was a second bloody confrontation at North Bridge.

Residents of Maine and Massachusetts have observed Patriots' Day since the 18th century with costume parades, flag-raising ceremonies, and reenactments of the battles and the famous rides of Paul Revere and William Dawes, who were sent to warn their comrades in Concord of the British troops' approach. The BOSTON MARATHON, one of the most famous of the world's marathon races, is run each year on Patriots' Day. Sometimes this day is referred to as **Lexington Day** or **Battles of Lexington and Concord Day**.

CONTACTS:
Library of Congress
101 Independence Ave. S.E.
Washington, D.C. 20540
202-707-5510; fax: 202-707-2076
www.loc.gov

Lexington Chamber of Commerce
1875 Massachusetts Ave.
Lexington, MA 02420
781-862-2480; fax: 781-862-5995
www.lexingtonchamber.org

Concord Chamber of Commerce
15 Walden St., Ste. 7
Concord, MA 01742
978-369-3120; fax: 978-369-1515
www.concordchamberofcommerce.org

SOURCES:
AmerBkDays-2000, p. 292
AnnivHol-2000, p. 64
DictDays-1988, pp. 68, 88

♦ 2051 ♦ **Paul Bunyan Show**
First full weekend in October

Paul Bunyan is the mythical hero of lumberjacks in the United States, and many tall tales have been passed down about his adventures with Babe the Blue Ox and Johnny Inkslinger. Among other things, these tales describe how he created Puget Sound and the Grand Canyon, and how his hotcake griddle was so large that it had to be greased by men using sides of bacon for skates. The first Bunyan stories were published in 1910, and within 15 years he had become a national legend.

Since 1952 the **Paul Bunyan Festival,** sponsored jointly by the Ohio Forestry Association and Hocking College in Nelsonville (which grants a degree in forestry) has focused on wood products and forestry conservation. It is the lumber industry's opportunity to familiarize visitors with the journey wood takes from the forest to finished products and an opportunity for both professional and student lumberjacks to test their skills in chopping and sawing. Teams of draft horses compete in a log-skidding contest—an operation that is performed today by heavy machines—and turn-of-the-century steam logging equipment is on display. Billed as the largest live forestry exposition in the East, the show gives visitors an opportunity to see both traditional and modern logging techniques in action.

CONTACTS:
Hocking College
3301 Hocking Pkwy.
Nelsonville, OH 45764
877-462-5464 or 740-753-3591; fax: 740-753-7065
www.hocking.edu

Ohio Forestry Association Inc.
746 Morrison Rd.
Columbus, OH 43230

888-388-7337 or 614-497-9580; fax: 614-497-9581
www.ohioforest.org

♦ 2052 ♦ **Payment of Quit Rent**
September 29

One of London's oldest and most unusual events, the annual Payment of Quit Rent, takes place at the Royal Courts of Justice on MICHAELMAS, September 29. The ceremony symbolizes the city of London's payment to the Crown for two parcels of land: the first, known as The Forge, is thought to have been the old tournament ground for the Knights of the Templars, who rented it in 1235 for an annual payment of horseshoes and nails. The second, a piece of land in Shropshire known as The Moors, came into the city's possession during the reign of Henry VIII and was rented from the Crown for an annual payment of a bill-hook and a hatchet.

During the first part of the ceremony, the City Solicitor counts out six huge horseshoes from Flemish war horses and 61 nails. He gives them to the Queen's Remembrancer, who keeps them in his office until the following year. During the second part, the City Solicitor demonstrates how sharp the blades of the bill-hook and hatchet are by cutting up a bundle of twigs. These, too, are presented to the Queen's Remembrancer, who is dressed in his wig and ceremonial robes.

CONTACTS:
Visit Britain
551 Fifth Ave., Ste. 701
New York, NY 10176
800-462-2748 or 212-850-0330; fax: 212-986-1188
www.visitbritain.com/us

SOURCES:
YrbookEngFest-1954, p. 137

♦ 2053 ♦ **Payson Rodeo**
Third weekend in August

The Payson Rodeo is a rodeo, parade, and general Wild West three-day weekend in the cowboy-and-cattle country of Payson, Ariz. The first Payson rodeo was held in 1885, and it's been held ever since with no interruptions, not even for war, making it the world's oldest continuous Professional Rodeo Cowboys Association rodeo. Events of the weekend include the parade with floats, dancers, and cowboys, country music, a chili cookout, and arts and crafts. Total attendance is usually about 30,000.

CONTACTS:
Rim Country Regional Chamber of Commerce
100 W. Main St.
P.O. Box 1380
Payson, AZ 85547
800-672-9766 or 928-474-4515; fax: 928-474-8812
www.rimcountrychamber.com

♦ 2054 ♦ **Peace, International Day of**
September

The day of the opening session of the UNITED NATIONS General Assembly, and a day proclaimed by the U.N. to promote the ideals of peace. The first official observance of the day was in September 1982.

At the United Nations the day is marked with a special message by the secretary-general, who then rings the Japanese Peace Bell and invites people throughout the world to reflect on the meaning of peace.

Special events are organized in various countries, and in the United States the mayors of a number of cities issue proclamations for the day.

CONTACTS:
United Nations, Department of Public Information
Rm. S-1070L J, K, L
New York, NY 10017
212-963-6842; fax: 212-963-6914
www.un.org

♦ 2055 ♦ Peanut Festival, National
Mid-October

The National Peanut Festival is a nine-day festival in Dothan, Ala., honoring the peanut, a multimillion-dollar crop in Alabama. A highlight is the Goober Parade, for which the streets are paved with peanuts by a giant cement mixer that moves along the line of march throwing out a ton of peanuts, while parade watchers scramble for them. It is said the parade attracts as many as 200,000 spectators. Other events include the selection of Peanut Farmer of the Year, a cooking contest of peanut dishes, crafts exhibits, fireworks, a beauty pageant, and live entertainment.

The festival began in 1938, was discontinued during World War II, and resumed in 1947. Revenues from the festival help the economy not only of Dothan but of neighboring areas of Florida and Georgia. Plains, Ga., the home of peanut farmer and former President Jimmy Carter, is just over the state border.

The peanut and its potential became nationally if not internationally known because of the work of George Washington Carver, who in 1896 became head of agricultural research at Tuskegee Institute in Tuskegee, Ala. His research program ultimately developed 300 derivative products from peanuts, including cheese, flour, inks, dyes, soap, and cosmetics. The research was crucial to the South's economy; the peanut crop freed farmers of their dependence on cotton, which depleted the soil and could be wiped out by boll weevils. When Carver arrived in Tuskegee, the peanut was not recognized as a crop; within the next 50 years, it became the South's second largest cash crop after cotton. Carver was the guest of honor at the first Peanut Festival in 1938.

CONTACTS:
National Peanut Festival Association Inc.
5622 Hwy. 231 S.
Dothan, AL 36301
334-793-4323; fax: 334-793-3247
www.nationalpeanutfestival.com

SOURCES:
GdUSFest-1984, p. 4

♦ 2056 ♦ Pearl Harbor Day
December 7

Pearl Harbor Day marks the anniversary of the Japanese raid on Pearl Harbor in 1941, bringing the United States into World War II and widening the European war to the Pacific.

The bombing, which began at 7:55 A.M. Hawaiian time on a Sunday morning, lasted little more than an hour but devastated the American military base on the island of Oahu in the Hawaiian Islands. Nearly all the ships of the U.S. Pacific Fleet were anchored there side by side, and most were damaged or destroyed; half the bombers at the army's Hickam Field were destroyed. The battleship USS *Arizona* sank, and 1,177 sailors and Marines went down with the ship, which became their tomb. In all, the attack claimed more than 3,000 casualties— 2,403 killed and 1,178 wounded.

On the following day, President Franklin D. ROOSEVELT addressed a solemn Congress to ask for a declaration of war. His opening unforgettable words: "Yesterday, December 7, 1941—a date which will live in infamy—the United States of America was suddenly and deliberately attacked by naval and air forces of the Empire of Japan." War was declared immediately with only one opposing vote, that by Rep. Jeannette Rankin of Montana.

In the months that followed, the slogan "Remember Pearl Harbor" swept America, and radio stations repeatedly played the song of the same name with these lyrics:

Let's remember Pearl Harbor, as we go to meet the foe,
Let's remember Pearl Harbor, as we did the Alamo.
We will always remember, how they died for liberty,
Let's remember Pearl Harbor, and go on to victory.

Many states proclaim a Pearl Harbor Remembrance Day, and each year, services are held on December 7 at the *Arizona* Memorial in Pearl Harbor. The marble memorial, built over the sunken USS *Arizona* and dedicated in 1962, was designed by architect Albert Preis, a resident of Honolulu who was an Austrian citizen in 1941 and was interned as an enemy alien.

In 1991, on the 50th anniversary of the attack, commemorations were held over several days in Hawaii.

The observances began on Dec. 4, designated as Hawaii Remembrance Day. Ceremonies recalled the death of civilians in downtown Pearl Harbor. One of them was Nancy Masako Arakaki, a nine-year-old Japanese-American girl killed when anti-aircraft shells fell on her Japanese-language school.

On Dec. 5, Survivors Day, families of those present in Pearl Harbor in 1941 attended ceremonies at the *Arizona* Memorial. Franklin Van Valkenburgh, the commanding officer of the USS *Arizona*, was among those remembered; he posthumously won the Medal of Honor for his heroism aboard ship.

Dec. 6 was a Day of Reflection, intended to focus on the gains since the war rather than on the losses of the day.

On Pearl Harbor Day itself, former President George Bush, who received the Distinguished Flying Cross for heroism as a

Navy pilot in the Pacific during World War II, spoke at ceremonies beginning at 7:55 a.m. at the *Arizona* Memorial. Other dignitaries were all Americans; no foreign representatives were invited, out of political prudence. Other events included a parade, a flyover by jet fighters, an outdoor concert by the Honolulu Symphony presenting the premiere of *Pearl Harbor Overture: Time of Remembrance* by John Duffy, and a wreath-laying service at the National Memorial Cemetery of the Pacific in the Punchbowl overlooking Honolulu. And finally, at sunset on Pearl Harbor Day, survivors and their families gathered at the Arizona Visitors Center for a final service to honor those who died aboard the battleship in 1941.

CONTACTS:
Library of Congress
101 Independence Ave. S.E.
Washington, D.C. 20540
202-707-5510; fax: 202-707-2076
www.loc.gov

USS Arizona Memorial
National Park Service
1 Arizona Memorial Pl.
Honolulu, HI 96818
808-422-0561; fax: 808-483-8608
www.nps.gov

Naval Historical Center
805 Kidder Breese S.E.
Washington Navy Yard, Bldg. 76
Washington, DC 20374
202-433-4882; fax: 202-433-8200
www.history.navy.mil

SOURCES:
AmerBkDays-2000, p. 816
AnnivHol-2000, p. 204
PatHols-2006, p. 219

♦ 2057 ♦ **Pendleton Round-Up and Happy Canyon**
Mid-September

One of the best-known rodeos in the West, held since 1910 in the small ranch town of Pendleton, Ore. The home of internationally known saddle makers, Pendleton is also the heart of Oregon's wheat-producing region. The week-long round-up started as a celebration of the end of the wheat harvest. Happy Canyon was inaugurated four years later when two local men decided the entertainment at a local fair was of poor quality and too expensive. The Happy Canyon shows at first depicted historical episodes and evolved into the present-day Happy Canyon Pageant, a presentation by Northwest Indian tribes that features a teepee encampment and ceremonial dancing. Nowadays, each day of the rodeo begins with a cowboy breakfast (ham, eggs, flapjacks) at Stillman Park and ends with the pageant.

In between, the rodeo features the standard competitions approved by the Professional Rodeo Cowboys Association—bronco riding, bareback riding, Brahma bull riding, steer wrestling, and calf and steer roping. Additionally, there are wild horse and stagecoach races and wild-cow milking.

CONTACTS:
Pendleton Round-Up and Happy Canyon Association

1205 S.W. Court Ave.
P.O. Box 609
Pendleton, OR 97801
800-457-6336 or 541-276-2553; fax: 541-276-9776
www.pendletonroundup.com

♦ 2058 ♦ **Penitents, Procession of the (Belgium)**
Last Sunday in July

The Procession of the Penitents is a religious procession in Veurne (or Furnes), West Flanders, Belgium. Penitents in coarse robes and hoods walk barefoot through town, many carrying heavy wooden crosses. The procession, to the sound of drumbeats, is interspersed with scenes depicting biblical events. In some, costumed people dramatize Old and New Testament characters. In others there are carved wooden figures on platforms. At the end of the procession, bishops parade carrying the Sacred Host; and as the Sacrament passes, spectators quietly kneel. After the procession is over there is a *kermess*, or fair, in the marketplace. The celebration traditionally draws large crowds.

Two legends account for the origins of the procession. One says that it dates back to 1099 when crusader Count Robert II of Flanders returned from Jerusalem with a fragment of the True Cross. The other traces it to 1644 when townsfolk carried crosses in a reenactment of the last walk of Jesus before his crucifixion. The procession was to seek intercession against the plague and an outbreak of war between the Spanish and French.

CONTACTS:
Tourist Office of Veurne
Grote Markt 27
Veurne, B 8630 Belgium
32-58-33-05-31; fax: 32-58-33-05-96
tourism.veurne.be/home/2263/default_tourism

SOURCES:
BkHolWrld-1986, Jul 27
FestWestEur-1958, p. 14

♦ 2059 ♦ **Penitents, Procession of the (Spain)**
Between May 3-June 6; the week preceding Pentecost

During the week before PENTECOST on the Spanish side of the Pyrénées near the French border, a procession of penitents, covered from head to toe in black except for their eyes, makes its way from the village of Burgos to the Abbey of Roncesvalles. With heavy wooden crosses tied to their backs, they struggle up the steep two-mile path that leads to the abbey, chanting a doleful *Miserere*. After attending mass there, the penitents make their confessions without removing the black hoods that hide their faces.

Since the penitents come from five surrounding villages, each parish performs its own penitential march over a five-day period. According to legend, the procession originated as an act of penance among 23 families seeking atonement for the sins they had committed during the year.

CONTACTS:
Orreaga-Roncesvalles Tourist Office
Antiguo Molino
Roncesvalles, Spain
34-948-760-301; fax: 34-948-76-03-01

SOURCES:
FestSaintDays-1915, p. 112
FestWestEur-1958, p. 196

♦ 2060 ♦ Pennsylvania Day
On or near October 24

The state of Pennsylvania was named for William Penn, who was born in London on October 24, 1644. As a young man he joined the Quakers, who were at that time considered a radical religious group, and eventually he used his inheritance from his father to establish a Quaker colony in the New World. He put a great deal of thought and planning into how his colony would be governed, and insisted that the colonists treat the Indians with respect. The colony thrived, its population growing from about 1,000 in 1682 to more than 12,000 seven years later.

Pennsylvanians have always held large celebrations on major anniversaries of Penn's birth, and in 1932 the governor proclaimed October 24 as **William Penn Commemoration Day**, or simply **Penn Day**. This day was also commemorated with a special pageant held in Jordans, Buckinghamshire, England, where Penn and his family are buried. Since that time celebrations have tended to be local rather than statewide. In recent decades, the week of October 24 has been celebrated as **Pennsylvania Week**.

Any observation using his name would undoubtedly have made William Penn turn over in his grave, as he was outspoken in his opposition to the practice of naming streets, cities, states, or anything else after people.

CONTACTS:
Pennsylvania Historical and Museum Commission
State Museum Bldg., 30 North St.
Harrisburg, PA 17120
717-787-3362; fax: 717-783-9924
www.portal.state.pa.us

SOURCES:
AmerBkDays-2000, p. 709
BkDays-1864, vol. II, p. 60
DictDays-1988, p. 91
DictWrldRel-1989, p. 564

♦ 2061 ♦ Pennsylvania Dutch Folk Festival
First week in July

The Pennsylvania Dutch Folk Festival has been held since the 1950s. The festival, which began in Kutztown, Pennsylvania, has been forced to search for a new location in recent years, landing in Schuykill and then in Adamstown. The festival offers demonstrations of traditional Pennsylvania Dutch crafts, such as quilting, folk music and dancing, Pennsylvania Dutch foods, an old-fashioned country auction, a recre-

ation of daily life in a traditional Pennsylvania Dutch community, children's activities, and more.

CONTACTS:
Kutztown Pa-German Festival
P.O. Box 306
Kutztown, PA 19530
888-674-6136
www.kutztownfestival.com

♦ 2062 ♦ Pentecost
Between May 10 and June 13 in West and between May 24 and June 27 in East; seventh Sunday after Easter

As recorded in the New Testament in Acts 2, it was on the 50th day after Easter that the Apostles were praying together and the Holy Spirit descended on them in the form of tongues of fire. They received the "gift of tongues"—the ability to speak in other languages—and immediately began to preach about Jesus Christ to the Jews from all over the world who had flocked to Jerusalem for the Feast of Shavuot. (Pentecost, from the Greek word meaning "fiftieth," is also one of the names for the second of the three Jewish Pilgrim Festivals.) Christian Pentecost thus became not only a commemoration of the Holy Spirit's visit, but also the birth of the Christian Church. It was on roughly this same day, centuries earlier, that Moses received the Ten Commandments on Mt. Sinai and the Jewish religious community got its start.

The English call it **White Sunday**, or **Whitsunday**, after the white garments worn on Pentecost by the newly baptized. Although it is not certain when Pentecost began to be observed by Christians, it may have been as early as the first century. The period beginning with the Saturday before Whitsunday and ending the following Saturday is known as **Whitsuntide**, or in modern times simply as **Whitsun**.

Whitsunday has been linked to pagan spring rites, such as the English custom of Morris dancing and the drinking of "Whitsun ale." In Scotland, Whitsunday was one of the Quarter Days. In Estonia and Finland, eggs are dyed as at Easter because their hens don't lay until this time. In Germany it is called **Pfingsten**, and pink and red peonies, called *Pfingstrosen*, or "Whitsun roses," are the symbols along with birch trees. Some churches lower a carved dove into the congregation and call this "swinging the Holy Ghost." Cattle are decorated and an overdressed person is said to be "dressed like a Whitsun ox." A holdover pagan game is called "hunting the green man," or *Laubmannchen*—a young man dressed in leaves and moss hides, and children hunt for him.

See also Kneeling Sunday; Pinkster Day

CONTACTS:
Christian Resource Institute
4801 N.W. 62nd St.
Oklahoma City, OK 73122
801-497-0946
www.cresourcei.org

Orthodox Church in America
6850 N. Hempstead Turnpike

P.O. Box 675
Syosset, NY 11791
516-922-0550; fax: 516-922-0954
www.oca.org

SOURCES:
AmerBkDays-2000, p. 371
BkDays-1864, vol. I, p. 629
BkFest-1937, pp. 97, 135, 244, 268
DaysCustFaith-1957, pp. 161, 354
DictFolkMyth-1984, pp. 629, 750, 1127, 1175, 1176
EncyEaster-2002, p. 479
EncyRel-1987, vol. 3, p. 440
FestSaintDays-1915, p. 118
FestWestEur-1958, pp. 26, 42, 65, 153, 165, 215, 233
FolkAmerHol-1999, p. 245
FolkWrldHol-1999, p. 339
OxYear-1999, p. 631
RelHolCal-2004, pp. 96, 122
SaintFestCh-1904, p. 245

♦ 2063 ♦ People's Army of North Korea, Founding of the
April 25

The founding of the People's Army of North Korea (official name: Democratic People's Republic of Korea) in 1932 is marked every year with a national public holiday. The main celebration takes place in the capital city of Pyongyang and includes oratorical meetings, where various officials praise the army's exploits. Public displays can also include parades, gun-salutes, fireworks, choruses, dance displays, and drum-beating.

According to the country's official government news agency (Central Korean News Agency of the Democratic People's Republic of Korea), the year 2007 marked the 75th anniversary of the army's founding. While many sources list February 8, 1948, as the army's official start-date, other sources note that earlier versions of the army launched in the 1930s. The North Korean government apparently observes 1932 as the date of the army's founding. Despite the nation's small size, the People's Army of North Korea rates among the top five largest armies in the world, noted the U.S. Department of State in 2007, with an estimated 1.21 million armed personnel.

CONTACTS:
Permanent Representative of the Democratic People's Republic of
   Korea to the United Nations
820 Second Ave.
New York, NY 10017
212-972-3105; fax: 212-972-3154
www.korea-dpr.com

♦ 2064 ♦ Peppercorn Ceremony
Day near April 23

This ceremony has been a tradition on the island of Bermuda since 1816, when a lease to the State House in St. George (the seat of Bermuda's government from 1620-1815) was granted to the mayor, aldermen, and common council of St. George in trust by the members of the Masonic Lodge for the annual rent of one peppercorn. The date for the annual rent payment was originally December 27, the feast of ST. JOHN THE EVANGELIST, but it was changed to the most suitable day nearest April 23, ST. GEORGE'S DAY, in honor of the patron saint for whom the town is named.

On the day of the Peppercorn Ceremony, the governor of Bermuda arrives at the State House with great pomp in a horse-drawn carriage, is welcomed by the mayor of St. George, and receives a key to the State House for the purpose of holding a meeting of Her Majesty's Executive Council, which upholds the conditions of the lease. The rent of one peppercorn is delivered on a velvet pillow and members of the Executive Council proceed to the State House for their meeting.

The old State House building, with mortar made of turtle oil and lime, was constructed in 1619 and is believed to be the first stone building in Bermuda. Until the capital was moved to Hamilton in 1815, Parliament met there. Bermuda's Parliament is the third oldest in the world (after Iceland and England).

CONTACTS:
Bermuda Department of Tourism
675 3rd Ave., 20th Fl.
New York, NY 10017
800-223-6106 or 212-818-9800; fax: 212-983-5289
www.bermudatourism.com

SOURCES:
AnnivHol-2000, p. 67

♦ 2065 ♦ Perchtenlauf
January 6

The Perchtenlauf in Austria is usually held on EPIPHANY, but in some areas it is celebrated at a later date. The *Perchten* are old masks, usually of witches and fearsome animals, that have been handed down from generation to generation. People wearing the masks run through the village beating drums, ringing bells, singing, shouting, and making as much noise as possible to scare winter away—an ancient custom that can be traced back to pre-Christian times. Another tradition associated with the Perchtenlauf is the cracking of whips—again, an attempt to drive out winter.

Dancing also plays a part in the celebration. The *Perchtentanz* takes place when the procession of masked figures stops in the main square of the village and everyone begins to dance wildly, making even more noise than before. The Perchten dances of Imst and Thaur in Tirol are particularly well known for their brightly colored old masks. Another notable Perchten pageant takes place in the Gastein Valley village of Bad Gastein in the state of Salzburg.

See also EPIPHANY (GERMANY)

CONTACTS:
Austrian National Tourist Office
120 W. 45th St.
P.O. Box 1142
New York, NY 10036

212-944-6880; fax: 212-730-4568
www.austria.info

SOURCES:
DictFolkMyth-1984, p. 346

♦ 2066 ♦ Perseids
Visibility peaks around August 10-12

Meteors, also called shooting stars or falling stars, are seen as streaks of light in the sky that result when a small chunk of stony or metallic matter enters the Earth's atmosphere and vaporizes. A meteor shower occurs when a number of meteors enters the Earth's atmosphere at approximately the same time and place. The shower's name is usually derived from the constellation (or a star within it) from which the shower appears to originate.

Since the year 36 C.E. there have been records of an annual meteor shower known as the Perseids (because it appears to originate in the constellation Perseus) that is most observable during the nights of August 10-12. Observers everywhere except the South Pole can see as many as 60 meteors an hour streak across the sky on what is often referred to as the **Night of the Shooting Stars**.

CONTACTS:
American Meteor Society
44017 Woodland Ct.
Callahan, FL 32011
904-879-2646
www.amsmeteors.org

SOURCES:
BkHolWrld-1986, Aug 11

♦ 2067 ♦ Perth International Arts Festival
January-February

Originally designed as a program of cultural entertainment for students attending evening and summer classes at the University of Western Australia, the Perth International Arts Festival has grown into one of Australia's major arts festivals. It offers drama, dance, music, opera, films, art exhibits, children's programs, and even sporting events at locations throughout the city.

Although the focus is on Australian performing artists, international groups appear there on a regular basis, including England's Chichester Festival Theatre Company, the National Theater of the Deaf from the United States, Spain's Madrid Flamenco Company, and the Stratford National Theatre of Canada.

Plays performed at the festival range from the classics to contemporary works by Australian and English dramatists. The month-long festival also features open-air folk music concerts and dancing, street theater, parades, improvisations, and other dramatic performances.

CONTACTS:
Perth International Arts Festival
M418, 3 Crawley Ave., University of Western Australia

Crawley, WA 6009 Australia
61-8-6488-2000; fax: 61-8-6488-8555
www.perthfestival.com.au

SOURCES:
GdWrldFest-1985, p. 10
IntlThFolk-1979, p. 29

♦ 2068 ♦ Peru Battle of Angamos
October 8

The War of the Pacific (1879-1883), also known as the Saltpeter War, began when Chile and Bolivia fought for control of a portion of the Atacama Desert, which was full of valuable minerals.

On October 8, 1879, the Chilean Navy captured Peru's ironclad steam-propelled warship, the *Huáscar*, and killed the captain, Admiral Miguel Grau. After this battle, the Peruvians lost their momentum against the Chilean forces. Chile gained control over the seas and was thus able to invade Peru and Bolivia.

October 8 is a national holiday in Peru. This day is set aside to remember the lost Battle of Angamos. On this day, military and civil parades are held, and celebrations are held to honor the heroic deeds of Admiral Miguel Grau and his role in the Battle of Angamos.

CONTACTS:
Embassy of the United States
Avenida La Encalada cdra. 17 s/n
Lima 33 Peru
lima.usembassy.gov

♦ 2069 ♦ Peru Independence Day
July 28-29

Peru had been a colony of Spain for nearly 300 years when Simon Bolívar (1783-1830), along with José SAN MARTÍN (1778-1850), led the Battle of Ayacucho in 1824 that resulted in the end of Spanish rule of Bolivia and Peru. San Martín had declared independence on July 28, 1821, but Peru's sovereignty was not secured until Bolívar's forces defeated the Spanish at Ayacucho. Bolívar then became the ruler of Peru (*see also* BOLIVIA INDEPENDENCE DAY).

Celebrated all over Peru, Independence Day is a public holiday. In the south, festivities also take place on July 25, ST. JAMES'S DAY.

CONTACTS:
Commission for the Promotion of Peru
Calle Uno Oeste No. 50, piso 13th
Urb. Corpac
Lima, 27 Peru
51-1-4224-3131; fax: 51-1-224-7134
www.promperu.gob.pe

SOURCES:
AnnivHol-2000, p. 124
NatlHolWorld-1968, p. 127

◆ 2070 ◆ Peyote Dance (Híkuli Dance)
January

To the Tarahumara (who call themselves Rarámuri) and Huichol Indians of northern Mexico, peyote, or *híkuli,* is the mescal button, derived from the tops of a cactus plant and used as a stimulant or hallucinogen during religious ceremonies. In October and November, they head for eastern Chihuahua to gather peyote. The peyote will be used in January in the dance that follows the deer hunt, because peyote is identified with deer. The dancers paint symbolic designs, such as corn, squash, and fruit, on their faces. They ingest peyote to induce a supernatural state and to encourage the growth of crops. The dance is characterized by sudden jumping and twisting movements; the beat is set by rubbing deer bones together or shaking deer-hoof rattles.

SOURCES:
DictFolkMyth-1984, p. 861

◆ 2071 ◆ Pffiferdaj
First Sunday in September

An Alsatian festival of medieval origin, Pffiferdaj—also known as the **Day of the Strolling Fiddlers,** or **Fiddlers' Festival**—is celebrated in the city of Ribeauvillé, France, an area widely known for its wines. In the Middle Ages the Ribeaupierre family started a musicians' union here, and every September the musicians of Alsace gathered to pay homage to the lord of Ribeaupierre by forming a procession to the church of Notre Dame du Dusenbach.

Today the custom continues. Wine flows freely from the fountain in front of the town hall, and a procession of fiddlers and other musicians, often playing old instruments, makes its way through the town. Their costumes and floats recall life in the Middle Ages.

CONTACTS:
Ribeauville & Riquewihr Tourist Office
1 Grand'Rue
P.O. Box 90067
Ribeauville, 68153 France
33-3-8973-2323; fax: 33-3-8973-2329
www.ribeauville-riquewihr.com/client/index.php?ids

SOURCES:
BkHolWrld-1986, Sep 9

◆ 2072 ◆ Phagwa
Full moon day in March

The Hindu festival of Phagwa celebrates the VERNAL EQUINOX and the start of the Hindu New Year (*see* VAISAKH). In Trinidad and Tobago, a Carnival spirit has gradually pervaded the festivities, which now combine both secular and religious elements and are no longer confined to Hindus. The celebration includes bonfires (to symbolize the destruction of Holika, the evil sister of King Hiranya Kashipu; *see also* HOLI) and Chowtal-singing competitions, which mix religious and secular music and are heavily influenced by calypso. The spraying of *Abeer* powder, a red vegetable dye made into a bright fuchsia liquid, gives everyone's hair and skin a tie-dyed effect.

Band competitions, similar to those held at Carnival (*see* TRINIDAD AND TOBAGO CARNIVAL), are held at several locations throughout the island. There are also reenactments of the legend of Holika, complete with oriental costumes, crowns, jewelry, and flowers.

CONTACTS:
National Library and Information System Authority of Trinidad
   and Tobago
National Library Bldg., Hart and Abercromby St.
Port-of-Spain, Trinidad and Tobago
868-623-6962; fax: 868-625-6096
www.nalis.gov.tt

◆ 2073 ◆ Phchum Ben
September or October

The 15-day period also known as **Prachum-Ben** in Cambodia is dedicated to rituals for the dead. It occurs during the rainy season when skies are usually overcast, and the darkness seems an appropriate time for Yama, God of the Underworld, to let the souls of the dead visit their families. The traditional offering to the dead consists of *ben*—special cakes made of glutinous rice mixed with coconut milk and other ingredients—arranged on a platter around a centerpiece and placed on a pedestal. Sometimes the rice is formed into a cone called *bay bettbor,* with flags, flowers, and joss sticks used to decorate the top. During this time a monk says prayers at the tombs of the dead.

SOURCES:
FolkWrldHol-1999, p. 502

◆ 2074 ◆ Philippines Independence Day
June 12

As a result of the Spanish-American War, the United States became involved in the Filipino struggle for independence at the end of the 19th century. The Americans called back Emilio Aguinaldo (1869-1964), the exiled rebel leader, and helped him bring centuries of Spanish rule to an end. Aguinaldo declared the islands independent on June 12, 1898. But the U.S. acquired the Philippines after signing the Treaty of Paris in 1899, and it wasn't until July 4, 1946, that the islands were granted full independence.

For many years, Filipinos set aside July 4 to celebrate their own independence and to acknowledge their longstanding ties to the United States. But in 1962, President Diosdada Macapagal changed the date to June 12, the anniversary of Aguinaldo's initial declaration of independence from Spain. The U.S. ambassador often speaks at Independence Day ceremonies in Manila, which include a military parade and the pealing of church bells. After the official ceremonies are over, Filipinos devote the remainder of the day to recreation. There are games and athletic competitions, fireworks displays, and Independence Day balls. In Hawaii, which has a large Filipino population, there are often Filipino fiestas celebrating Philippine heritage.

CONTACTS:
Philippine Information Agency
MMIO, PIA Bldg., Visayas Ave.
Quezon City, Philippines
63-2-929-4521
www.pia.gov.ph

SOURCES:
AmerBkDays-2000, p. 441
AnnivHol-2000, p. 99
NatlHolWrld-1968, p. 83

◆ 2075 ◆ Phra Buddha Bat Fair
February-March

This annual festival takes place at the Phra Buddha Bat or Phra Phutthabat temple (the Shrine of the Holy Footprint), a hill temple in Saraburi, Thailand, where the Holy Footprint of the Buddha is enshrined. This is one of the most sacred places in Thailand, and pilgrims throng here during the festival to pay homage. The festival features performances of folk music and a handicraft bazaar.

CONTACTS:
Tourism Authority of Thailand
611 N. Larchmont Blvd., 1st Fl.
Los Angeles, CA 90004
800-842-4526 or 323-461-9814; fax: 323-461-9834
www.tourismthailand.org

◆ 2076 ◆ Pickett (Bill) Invitational Rodeo
Various weekends from February through November

The Bill Pickett Invitational Rodeo, in operation since 1984, is a series of rodeo competitions in the United States that features the nation's only touring black rodeo. The event is named in honor of Bill Pickett (1870-1932), the first African American selected to the Rodeo Hall of Fame in Oklahoma City, Okla.

The tour begins in February in Memphis, Tenn., and draws more than 100,000 annually. During the regular season, cowboys and cowgirls compete in weekend events in cities throughout the country. Events include bareback riding, barrel racing, bull riding, calf roping, steer undecorating, and bulldogging. Bulldogging, also known as steer wrestling, is an event created by the rodeo's namesake, who performed in the famous 101 Ranch Wild West Show with "Buffalo Bill" Cody, Will Rogers, and Tom Mix. A timed event, it features a cowboy on horseback racing a 600- to 700-pound bull, grabbing onto its horns, jumping out of his saddle, and wrestling the bull to the ground—all within a few seconds.

The top 10 finishers in each event at the end of the season in September are invited to compete in the championship rodeo held in November in Las Vegas, Nev. The championship festivities include a number of social and sporting events, with a formal reception for the participants and a golf tournament.

CONTACTS:
Bill Pickett Invitational Rodeo
P.O. Box 39163

Denver, CO 80239-1163
303-373-1246; fax: 303-373-2747
www.billpickettrodeo.com

SOURCES:
AAH-2007, p. 54

◆ 2077 ◆ Pickle Festival
Third weekend in August

The small town of Linwood, Michigan, is a center for pickle growing and processing. Since 1977 it has hosted a three-day festival in honor of its native product. Because so many local residents grow their own cucumbers and develop their own pickling recipes, there is a pickle-canning contest. Another popular event is the pickle-eating contest. Competitors are timed to see how long it takes them to unwrap and eat a pickle. The first one who is able to whistle afterward wins.

CONTACTS:
Bay City Convention & Visitors Bureau
901 Saginaw St.
Bay City, MI 48708
888-229-8696 or 989-893-1222; fax: 989-893-7016
www.tourbaycitymi.org

◆ 2078 ◆ Pied Piper Open Air Theater
Sundays, mid-May through mid-September

A dramatization of the legend of the Pied Piper of Hamelin, presented on an open-air stage in Hamelin (or Hameln), Germany.

According to the legend, in 1284 Hamelin was infested with rats. A stranger appeared, wearing an outlandishly colored (pied) coat, and he promised to free the town of its plague of vermin if they would pay him a set sum of money. The town agreed, and the piper began playing his pipes, and all the rats and mice came out of the houses and gathered around the piper. He led them to the Weser River, walked into it, and they followed him and were drowned. But the citizens refused to pay the piper. He left, angry. On June 26, he returned, dressed as a hunter and wearing a red hat. He played his pipes, and this time children followed him. He led 130 children out of the town and to the Koppenberg hill where they disappeared—forever. Only two children remained behind. One was blind, and couldn't see where the children went, and one was mute.

Research tends to discredit the legend. One theory is that the ratcatcher was Nicholas of Cologne, who led thousands of German children on the disastrous Children's Crusade in 1212. Another holds that the story stemmed from the arrival of a labor agent who lured many young men to Bohemia with the promise of good wages.

Fortunately, the people of Hamelin don't let research get in the way of a good story. Today, the children of Hamelin are the principal performers in the play, and their number is limited to 130 in keeping with the legend.

Robert Browning, the English poet who wrote the poem "The Pied Piper of Hamelin" to amuse a sick child, described the vermin this way:

Rats!
They fought the dogs and killed the cats,
And bit the babies in the cradles,
And ate the cheeses out of the vats,
And licked the soup from the cooks' own ladles…

When the piper arrived and began to play, Browning wrote,

…out of the houses the rats came tumbling.
Great rats, small rats, lean rats, brawny rats,
Brown rats, black rats, gray rats, tawny rats . . .
Brothers, sisters, husbands, wives—
Followed the Piper for their lives.

And then when the piper led the children off to Koppenberg, a portal opened wide, the piper and the children entered, and—

When all were in to the very last,
The door in the mountainside shut fast.

CONTACTS:
Hameln Marketing and Tourismus GmbH
Deisterallee 1
Hameln, D-31785 Germany
49-5151-957-82-3; fax: 49-5151-957-84-0
www.hameln.com

♦ 2079 ♦ Piedigrotta, Festival of
September 7-9

Held in Naples, Italy, for three days in September, the Festival of Piedigrotta is known primarily for its noise and gaiety. According to one legend, it commemorates the destruction in 44 C.E. of a site that had formerly been the scene of pagan orgies, and the building of a chapel in its place. A second explanation is that the chapel was built in 1356 after the Blessed Virgin Mary had appeared to a priest, a nun, and a man named Peter and ordered its construction. In any case, the festival is a particularly joyful one, with processions, fireworks, and some very unusual puppet shows. Visitors to Naples during festival time discover that it is almost impossible to get any sleep.

CONTACTS:
Italian Government Tourist Board
630 Fifth Ave., Ste. 1565
New York, NY 10111
212-245-5618; fax: 212-586-9249
www.italiantourism.com

SOURCES:
FestEur-1961, p. 121

♦ 2080 ♦ Pig Festivals
Various

For the Bundi people of Papua New Guinea, the Pig Festival is an event of enormous importance that encompasses dozens of social ceremonies and political events. Among other things, it is a time when tribe members must settle their debts, and it provides opportunities to trade goods. Marriage ceremonies, initiation ceremonies, bride-price payments, menstruation and courtship ceremonies also take place during the period of the Pig Festival. The *kanam*, a Bundi dance performance that represents the animals and birds that live in the forest, is frequently performed at pig festivals.

CONTACTS:
Embassy of Papua New Guinea
1779 Massachusetts Ave. N.W., Ste. 805
Washington, D.C. 20036
202-745-3680; fax: 202-745-3679
www.pngembassy.org

SOURCES:
FolkWrldHol-1999, p. 542

♦ 2081 ♦ Pig's Face Feast
Sunday following September 14

A number of explanations have been offered for the custom of eating pig's face, or pork-chop, sandwiches on the Sunday following Holy Cross Day (September 14; *see* EXALTATION OF THE CROSS) in the Cotswold village of Avening, England. One involves the love of Matilda of Flanders (d. 1083), who later became the wife of William the Conqueror, for Brittric, Lord of Gloucester. When Brittric refused to reciprocate, Matilda married William and then, as Queen, ordered Brittric's imprisonment and, eventually, his death. She later repented and built a church at the place where Brittric had once ruled as lord of the manor. The church was completed on September 14, Holy Cross Day, and the Queen is said to have held a boar's head dedication feast. The wild boars were so delicious that the people of Avening continued to celebrate their church dedication by eating the same meat. Another legend says that the feast commemorates the slaying of a troublesome wild boar, which took place on or around this date.

Today there is an evening anniversary service in Holy Cross Church at Avening, after which the villagers participate in an 11th-century banquet headed by Queen Matilda and other historic characters in period costume. Pork sandwiches are also served in the local pubs.

CONTACTS:
Holy Cross Church, Avening Parish Council
28 Partridge Way
Avening, Gloucestershire GL7 1BQ United Kingdom
44-12-8565-6139
www.avening-pc.gov.uk

SOURCES:
DictDays-1988, p. 89
YrbookEngFest-1954, p. 128

♦ 2082 ♦ Pike Festival, National
May

The National Pike Festival (also known as the National Road Festival) is literally the "world's longest festival"—90 miles of events along Route 40 in southwestern Pennsylvania and parts of West Virginia and Ohio. The original section of the road (or "pike," as in turnpike road) from Baltimore to Cumberland, Maryland, was Thomas JEFFERSON's idea in 1806. The section between Cumberland and Wheeling, West Virginia, was the first road to receive federal funding in 1811.

Since 1974 the festival has commemorated America's first transportation link from the East to the western frontier. It was originally designed as a Bicentennial event in Pennsylvania, but the idea caught on quickly, and towns along Route 40 in nearby states were eager to add their own events.

The festival begins on a weekend in mid-May as locales from western Maryland through southwestern Pennsylvania and eastern Ohio celebrate "the road that made the nation." Wagon trains originating from all parts travel along the route known as the National Road. When they set up camp for the night, there are bonfires and other entertainment to which the public is invited. Inns, taverns, toll-houses, and other historic buildings along the route host tours and special ceremonies.

CONTACTS:
National Road Heritage Corridor
65 W. Main St., 2nd Fl.
Uniontown, PA 15401
724-437-9877; fax: 724-437-6550
www.nationalroadpa.org

◆ 2083 ◆ **Pilgrim Festivals**
Various

The ancient Israelites were expected to celebrate three pilgrim festivals: PASSOVER, SHAVUOT, and SUKKOT. They are referred to in Hebrew as the *shalosh regalim*, "three (foot) pilgrimages," because the Bible commanded that they be observed "in the place the Lord your God will choose." Adult males over the age of 13 traditionally made a pilgrimage to Jerusalem on these three occasions. But after the Temple there was destroyed, the law requiring pilgrimages lapsed. The obligation to rejoice on the three pilgrim festivals—by eating meat, drinking wine, and wearing new clothes—continued.

Today, Jews come from all over the world to spend these festivals in Jerusalem. But now they tend to be sorrowful voyages, made for the purpose of mourning the destruction of the Temple. It is for this reason that Jews traditionally gather at the Wailing Wall—the only remaining retaining wall of the Temple Mount, site of the First and Second Temples, built during the first century B.C.E. in the reign of Herod.

CONTACTS:
Israel Ministry of Tourism
800 Second Ave.
New York, NY 10017
888-774-7723 or 212-499-5660; fax: 212-499-5665
www.goisrael.com

◆ 2084 ◆ **Pilgrim Progress Pageant**
Every Friday during August

It was on Plymouth Rock in what is now Plymouth, Massachusetts, that the Pilgrims landed in December 1620 to found their first permanent settlement north of Virginia. More than half of the 102 people who sailed on the *Mayflower* to the New World died of exposure, illness, and hunger by the end of the first winter.

An annual series of parades is organized by the General Society of Mayflower Descendants. Each Friday in August at 6:00 P.M., a group of men, women, and children dressed as Pilgrims form a procession up Leyden Street to the site of the former Fort-Meetinghouse on Burial Hill, now the Church of the Pilgrimage on Main Street. When they reach the site of the old fort, they reenact the church service that was held by the survivors at the end of that first winter in 1621. The pageant has been held every August since 1921 and also takes place on THANKSGIVING Day.

CONTACTS:
Destination Plymouth
170 Water St., Ste. 10C
Plymouth, MA 02360
508-747-7533; fax: 508-747-7535
www.visit-plymouth.com

SOURCES:
GdUSFest-1984, p. 88

◆ 2085 ◆ **Pilgrim Thanksgiving Day (Plymouth, Massachusetts)**
Last Thursday in November

Ten thousand visitors flock to Plymouth, Massachusetts, on THANKSGIVING Day to watch the annual procession from Plymouth Rock to the First Parish Church, where the congregation sings the same psalms sung by the original Pilgrims more than three and a half centuries ago. Each marcher represents one of the men, women, and children who survived the 1620 trip from England aboard the *Mayflower* to form the settlement known as Plimoth Plantation.

The modern-day Plimoth Plantation is a living-history village that recreates Pilgrim life in 1627. Costumed actors and historians carry out many of the same activities performed by the original Pilgrims, such as sheep-shearing, building houses, planting crops, weeding gardens, and cooking. Each November Plimoth offers a variety of programs as well as period dining that features original Thanksgiving Day foods.

CONTACTS:
Plimoth Plantation
137 Warren Ave.
P.O. Box 1620
Plymouth, MA 02360
508-746-1622
www.plimoth.org

SOURCES:
AmerBkDays-2000, p. 795
GdUSFest-1984, p. 89

◆ 2086 ◆ **Pilgrimage of Our Lady of Valme**
Each Sunday in October

The Romería (pilgrimage) of Our Lady of Valme involves a cross-country pilgrimage. The image of Our Lady of Valme is kept in the parish church of Dos Hermanas, but on this day she is carried in an elaborate procession to the shrine of Valme, on a hill overlooking Seville, Spain. Legend has it that King Ferdinand III stopped here on his way to free Seville from the Moors. He prayed to the Virgin Mary, "*valme*" (bless me), and promised a sanctuary for her if he was successful.

Accompanied by children in carriages, decorated floats, local men on horseback carrying silver maces, and Andalusian cavaliers and their ladies in regional dress, the cart bearing the statue of the Virgin Mary dressed in a blue velvet cloak is drawn by oxen with gilded horns and garlands of flowers around their necks. The pilgrims walk behind, and there is laughter, hand-clapping, and singing with tambourine accompaniment. Every so often fireworks are set off so the pilgrims in Valme can judge the progress of the procession.

It takes about three hours to reach the sanctuary, then the cavaliers open the gates, everyone rushes inside, the statue is carried in at shoulder height, and the mass begins. Afterwards, there is dancing, singing, and drinking until sunset, when the image is escorted back to Dos Hermanas.

CONTACTS:
Dos Hermanas Municipality
Plaza de la Constitucion
Dos Hermanas, 41700 Spain
34-954-919-500; fax: 34-954-919-525

SOURCES:
FolkWrldHol-1999, p. 596

♦ 2087 ♦ **Pilgrimage of Saut d'Eau**
July 16

Although it falls at the same time as a church holiday honoring OUR LADY OF CARMEL, the pilgrimage to the church in Ville-Bonheur, Haiti, combines both Christian and Voodoo beliefs. There is a sacred grove just outside Ville-Bonheur where, according to legend, the Virgin Mary once appeared on top of a palm tree. When people started neglecting the local church and worshipping the palm tree instead, the priest ordered it chopped down. Since no one wanted to kill the tree, the priest did it himself. Then he found people coming to pay honor to the roots, so he had those ripped out. Shortly thereafter the priest suffered a stroke and died. The people interpreted his death as a sign of the correctness of the vision.

The pilgrimage to this holy place, known as Saut d'Eau (waterfall), involves following a steep, winding trail and walking along a pebbly stream-bed for several hundred yards. Pilgrims eventually reach a place where two waterfalls tumble from a precipice more than 100 feet high—a kind of natural cathedral where rainbows are common in the mist that rises from the falls. This is the home of Damballah-wedo and other African deities who play a part in the Haitian religious practice known as Voodoo, or Vodoun.

Some worshipers tie colored cords, which they have purchased as offerings to the African *loa* (deities), to the sacred trees at the foot of the falls, while others bathe in the water. The pilgrims gather up a small bit of dirt from the base of the trees and carry it home in their handkerchiefs. These same pilgrims can be seen later in the day paying their respects to the Virgin in the local church—further evidence of the way in which this pilgrimage has brought together Christian and Voodoo beliefs.

CONTACTS:
Embassy of the Republic of Haiti
2311 Massachusetts Ave. N.W.
Washington, D.C. 20008
202-332-4090; fax: 202-745-7215
www.haiti.org

SOURCES:
FestWrld: Haiti-1999, p. 15
FiestaTime-1965, p. 114

♦ 2088 ♦ **Pilgrimage of the Dew**
May-June; Friday before Pentecost to Tuesday following

This colorful procession, known as the **Romería del Rocío**, or Pilgrimage of the Dew, begins during the week preceding Whitsunday, or PENTECOST, in towns and villages of Andalusia, Spain. The pilgrims' destination is the church of El Rocío in Almonte, Huelva, where a small statue of the Virgin known as *La Blanca Paloma* ("the White Dove") resides. They travel in two-wheeled, white-hooded farm carts, drawn by oxen wearing bells, flowers, and ribbon streamers. Some of the carts are set up as moving shrines to the Virgin, and the pilgrims themselves are dressed in regional costumes.

On Pentecost, the pilgrims file past the church of El Rocío and pay homage to La Blanca Paloma. There are fireworks at midnight, followed by dancing and singing until dawn. On Monday, the image of the Virgin is carried in solemn procession through the streets of Almonte. Being chosen to bear the statue on one's shoulders is considered a special privilege, eagerly sought by those who wish to receive special indulgence during the coming year. The procession is accompanied by the chanting of priests and the shouts of the pilgrims, who call out "Viva la Blanca Paloma!" as they wend their way through the town.

CONTACTS:
Oficina de Turismo Huelva
Avda. de Alemania 12
Huelva, 21001 Spain
34-959-257-403; fax: 34-959-257-403
www.andalucia.org

SOURCES:
FestWestEur-1958, p. 196

♦ 2089 ♦ **Pilgrimage to Chalma**
January 1-5

Chalma is a small Mexican town located in a deep canyon. Five hundred years ago, the Aztecs made pilgrimages to a

580

nearby cave, where they brought offerings of flowers and incense to a stone idol known as Otzocteotl, God of the Caves. After the Spanish conquest of Mexico, two Augustinian missionaries attempted to convert the people to Christianity but failed. Finally they brought a large cross made of wood to the cave, hoping to erect it in place of the idol. But when they entered, they found the stone image smashed to pieces and, in the place where it stood, a life-sized crucifix. As the local people learned of this remarkable occurrence, they were quickly converted to Christianity.

The cave became such a popular place of pilgrimage that in 1683, the image of Christ, known as the Señor de Chalma, was moved to the altar of a church that had just been built to house it. This is where pilgrims from all over Mexico come during the first five days of January to ask the Señor's blessing for the coming year and to express their gratitude for the favors he has granted them in the year that has just ended. Pilgrimages also take place in February, August, September, and often during HOLY WEEK and at CHRISTMAS.

CONTACTS:
Mexico Tourism Board
21 E. 63rd St., Fl. 3
New York, NY 10021
800-446-3942 or 212-821-0314; fax: 212-821-0367
www.visitmexico.com

SOURCES:
FiestaTime-1965, p. 3

♦ 2090 ♦ **Pilgrimage to Mecca (Hajj)**
Eighth-13th days of Islamic month of Dhu al-Hijjah

At least once in a lifetime, every Muslim man or woman (if she is accompanied by a male protector) with the means and the opportunity to do so is expected to make a pilgrimage to Mecca, the city in Saudi Arabia where Muhammad was born. It is one of the "five pillars" (fundamental duties) of Islam, and must be performed during the special pilgrimage season. The Qur'an (Muslim holy book) says the founder of this pilgrimage was Abraham.

The pilgrims wear two sheets of seamless white cloth and perform elaborate rites at the Grand Mosque of Mecca and in the immediate vicinity, which require about six days to complete. The focal point is the Kaaba, a 15-foot high stone structure that stands in the center court of the Grand Mosque of Mecca. In one corner of the court is the Black Stone, believed to have been brought by the angel Gabriel to Moses when he was rebuilding the Kaaba. It is a symbol of eternity because of its durability and is not worshipped, but is rather a sanctuary consecrated to God, and toward which all Muslim prayers are oriented.

Among the stages of the pilgrimage are walking around the Kaaba seven times, sacrificing a ram, ox, or camel, gathering at the Mount of Mercy and "standing before God" from noon to sunset, and throwing pebbles at three pillars at Mina, which represent Satan's tempting Abraham not to sacrifice his son. (*See* ID AL-ADHA.)

It is not uncommon for two million or more Muslims to participate in the pilgrimage, which has forced Saudi Arabia and other countries to explore new methods for freezing, preserving, and distributing the meat that is produced by so many sacrifices. The huge crowds have also challenged Saudi authorities as hundreds of people have been killed during stampedes in recent years.

At the end of the pilgrimage, it is customary to visit the tomb of Muhammad at Medina before returning home. Returning pilgrims, wearing the green scarf of the Hajj, are met by family and friends who have rented taxis and decorated them with palm branches and the families' best rugs. The pilgrim's house has been decorated with palm-leaf arches, and sometimes outlined with lights. In Kurdish and Egyptian villages, the doorways will also have designs suggesting the journey. Then a feast and party finish the welcome home.

CONTACTS:
Saudi Arabian Embassy
601 New Hampshire Ave. N.W.
Washington, D.C. 20037
202-337-4076; fax: 202-944-5983
www.saudiembassy.net

Saudi Arabian Ministry of Pilgrimage
Omar Bin Al-Khatab St.
Riyadh, 11183 Saudi Arabia
966-1-402-2200; fax: 966-1-402-2555
www.moe.gov.sa/openshare/englishcon

SOURCES:
BkHolWrld-1986, Aug 27
ConEncyIslam-1991, p. 313
DictWrldRel-1989, pp. 290, 569
FolkWrldHol-1999, p. 153
HolSymbols-2009, p. 321
OxYear-1999, p. 733
UndIslam-2004, p. 345

♦ 2091 ♦ **Pilgrimage to Moulay Idriss**
Late August or September

The most important *moussem*, or "festival," in Morocco is held in the holy city of Moulay Idriss. Moulay Idriss I was the eighth-century imam (Muslim prayer leader) who united the Berbers and founded the city of Fez and the first dynasty of Morocco; he is supposed to have had 500 wives, 1,000 children, and 12,000 horses. His burial place is the white Mausoleum of Moulay Idriss. The town named for him grew up around the tomb after his death.

This moussem lasts several weeks and alternates between prayers and celebrations. A feature is the *fantasia*, a great charge of horses and costumed riders who fire their rifles into the air and perform equestrian stunts as they gallop. There are also bazaars and singing and dancing.

CONTACTS:
Moroccan National Tourist Office
20 E. 46th St., Ste. 1201
New York, NY 10017
212-557-2520; fax: 212-949-8148
www.visitmorocco.org

♦ 2092 ♦ Pilgrimage to Qoyllur Riti
May-June

Although CORPUS CHRISTI processions are common, the pilgrimage to Qoyllur Riti in Peru is unique. The journey involves a dangerous climb up a glacier near Cuzco to honor an apparition of Jesus that was witnessed there in 1780, although it is believed that a related custom took place there before the arrival of Christianity. It is sometimes called the Star Snow Festival (*Qoyllur* means "star") because it takes place at a time when the constellation known as the Pleiades first becomes visible in the night sky.

The pilgrimage is one of the biggest celebrations of the year, and the festivities go on for nearly two-and-a-half weeks. On Wednesday morning, ringing church bells rouse townspeople by 4 A.M. They rise and begin to sweep streets, construct fruit stands, and make ready temporary altars in anticipation of the procession. In the outlying parishes, images of the saints are prepared for their entrance into Cuzco. While men bear the images in turns, women tote beverages and food in their wraps. All of these smaller processions arrive around 11 o'clock at Cuzco at the church of Santa Clara, where they do honor to the Virgin of Bethlehem, who is the guardian of Cuzco.

The big procession forms the next day, with everyone wearing the native dress of his or her region. Those who make it to the top of the glacier, which is 16,000 feet above sea level, erect a cross, recite prayers, and light candles. The mountain is said to be a home for the spirits of those who have committed mortal sins. But the climb is also believed to strengthen the pilgrims, many of whom are young men, making them more able to avoid falling under the influence of harmful powers. On the journey down the mountain, the pilgrims often carry blocks of ice, which some regard as possessing the power to heal the sick. Many others water their fields with the melted ice in the belief that it is holy water.

CONTACTS:
Commission for the Promotion of Peru
Calle Uno Oeste No. 50, piso 13th
Urb. Corpac
Lima, 27 Peru
51-1-4224-3131; fax: 51-1-224-7134
www.promperu.gob.pe

SOURCES:
CelebCustRitWrld-1996, p. 161
FestWrld: Peru-1998, p. 16
FiestaTime-1965, p. 107

♦ 2093 ♦ Pilgrimage to Shrine of Father Laval
September 9

An annual pilgrimage by thousands of people of all faiths to the shrine of Roman Catholic priest Père Jacques Désiré Laval in Port Louis, Mauritius. Father Laval came to Mauritius in 1841 and devoted himself to the spiritual improvement of the emancipated slaves until his death in 1864. The pilgrimage is held on the day of his death. It originated on the day the priest was buried, when more than 30,000 weeping people followed his bier as he was taken for burial opposite the Ste. Croix Church. A monument to him has since been erected there. Many masses are celebrated at the shrine on the memorial day, starting early in the morning. A vigil ends the day. Miracles of healing are attributed to Father Laval, who was beatified in 1979 in Rome by Pope John Paul II.

CONTACTS:
Mauritius Tourism Promotion Authority
Air Mauritius Centre, 11th Fl.
5, President John Kennedy St.
Port Louis, Mauritius
230-210-1545; fax: 230-212-5142
www.mauritius.net

♦ 2094 ♦ Pilgrimage to Souvenance
Early April

Every Easter for over 200 years, hundreds of devotees of voodoo journey to the Haitian village of Souvenance to visit a holy temple. The village, some 90 miles north of the capital city of Port-au-Prince, was founded by freed slaves from the West African country of Dahomey, now called Benin, and is considered to be a direct link to the ancients. The village temple is one of the most important sites of the voodoo religion.

During the five-day ceremony, devotees dress in white and wearing white scarves wrapped around their heads. The ceremony includes drumming, dancing, chanting, and sacrificing such animals as bulls, rams, and goats. The sacrificed animals, with slit throats, are passed among the believers so that the blood soaks the white garments they wear. Some believers hold the dead animals above themselves so that the blood drips down onto their heads. The sacrifices are devoted to the warrior god Ogoun. Worshippers dance throughout the night, imbibing rum and cane liquor and ingesting various herbs. The loas, or gods, are believed to take possession of some of the worshippers during the service. Voodoo is one of three state-recognized religions in Haiti, and some two thirds of the population is said to participate in its rites.

CONTACTS:
Embassy of the Republic of Haiti
2311 Massachusetts Ave. N.W.
Washington, D.C. 20008
202-332-4090; fax: 202-745-7215
www.haiti.org

♦ 2095 ♦ Pilgrimage to the Tomb of Sunan Bayat
21st day of the Javanese month of Mulud

Islamic Pilgrims flock to the tomb of the Sufi saint, Sunan Bayat, in Tembayat, Java, Indonesia, each year on the anniversary of his birth. This type of birthday pilgrimage is known as a "mulid," or anniversary, festival. Sunan Bayat was a 16th-century non-Muslim king who gave up his wealth and privilege in order to pray, preach, and meditate. Many Indonesians consider Sunan Bayat to be one of the nine Sufi saints who converted the people of the island of Java to Islam. Others count him as an honorary tenth member of the exalted group.

Pilgrims visit his mountain-top tomb year-round, but the mulid pilgrimage is considered to be especially auspicious for pilgrims. The last leg of the pilgrims' journey begins in a modern parking lot at the foot of the staircase leading up the mountain. Here visitors can use modern facilities for the ritual washing that is required before formal prayers can be offered. Visitors also must buy a ticket to gain entry to the burial compound. They then ascend to the tomb up a winding staircase, where small stalls along the way offer food, drink, and religious tokens.

Once at the tomb, pilgrims rely on an attendant, seated in the antechamber, who prays on their behalf, alternating prayers with a recitation of the first chapter of the Islamic Holy Book, the Koran, in Arabic. As they enter the pitch darkness of the tomb itself, pilgrims often lay flowers at the graves of Sunan Bayat and his two wives, who are buried on either side of him. According to local custom, new buds will appear suddenly on the flower stalks as a sign that the saint is willing to answer a pilgrim's prayers. Because many Javanese Muslims believe that a saint's *barakah*—or grace—is strongest in the evening, they visit late and remain at the burial complex until at least midnight. Others pay extra money to sleep on the site in order to best absorb Sunan Bayat's *barakah.*

CONTACTS:
Embassy of Indonesia
2020 Massachusetts Ave. N.W.
Washington, D.C. 20036
202-775-5200; fax: 202-775-5365
www.embassyofindonesia.org

Lao National Tourism Administration
Tourism Marketing and Promotion Dept.
P.O. Box 3556
Lane Xang Ave.
Hatsady Village, Chanthabouly District, Ventiane Capital Lao PDR
www.tourismlaos.gov.la

SOURCES:
UndIslam-2004, p. 393

♦ 2096 ♦ Pine Battle of Vinuesa
August 14-16

The Pine Battle or *Pinochada* of Vinuesa in the province of Soria, Spain, takes place in an area where the nobility once built a number of hunting lodges and where King Juan I located his main residence in the 14th century. The town of Vinuesa stands at the opening of a valley and is cradled on both sides by hills studded with pine trees. Tradition dictates that Juan II had the pines planted as a gift memorializing the pleasant times he had there hunting with his father.

On August 14, two tall pine trees are erected at the entrance to the village and in the main square. There is a ceremony in the church that evening at which the mayor's wife makes an offering to Our Lady of the Pine, an image of the Virgin that is attached to a pine trunk in a recess above the altar.

On the morning of August 15, two fraternities representing the town's two patrons, Our Lady and SAN ROQUE, join in a procession to the church. There they perform a *revolteo,* a flag-twirling ceremony which takes place at many festivals in Spain. Later that afternoon there is a procession to a nearby field, where ceremonial dances are performed and there is another revolteo. The second day of the festival ends with a twilight procession featuring an image of the Virgin that is a replica of the 11th-century original.

On the final day of the festival, there is a ceremonial mock battle in which the women of Vinuesa attack the men with pine branches. The explanation for this is that centuries ago, when an image of the Virgin was found between two pine trees near the boundary between Vinuesa and Covaleda, a quarrel broke out over who would get to keep the image. After several hours of fighting, the men of Vinuesa asked for reinforcements, and their wives arrived to help them. The women tore branches from the pine trees and used them to strike their opponents in the eyes, thus winning the battle for Vinuesa.

SOURCES:
SpanFiestas-1968, p. 160

♦ 2097 ♦ Pinkster Day
Between May 10 and June 13; 50 days after Easter

When PENTECOST (Whitsunday) became part of the Christian calendar in northern Europe, the name underwent numerous transformations. In Germany it became *Pfingsten,* and the Dutch called it *Pinkster.* When the Dutch settled in New York, they called the feast of Pentecost "Pinkster Day."

By the beginning of the 19th century, Albany had become a center for this celebration, which took place on Capitol, or "Pinkster," Hill and consisted of a week-long carnival dominated by the city's African-American population. It is said that their African-inspired dancing and music horrified the staid Dutch settlers, and by 1811 Pinkster Day had been legally prohibited by the New York state legislature.

SOURCES:
AAH-2007, p. 381
BkFest-1937, p. 244
DaysCustFaith-1957, p. 162
DictDays-1988, p. 89
FolkAmerHol-1999, p. 245

♦ 2098 ♦ Pirates Week
Last week in October

Pirates Week is a Cayman Islands festival celebrating the history of Grand Cayman, at one time a favorite haunt for pirates and buccaneers. The entire island is transformed into a pirate encampment for the week-long festival. There is a mock invasion of George Town, parades, pageants, and the trial of the pirates. Everyone dresses up in costumes, and the singing, dancing, and food fairs that are held throughout the island all revolve around a pirate theme.

The Cayman Islands—from the Spanish *caimán,* meaning "alligator"—were apparently unoccupied when first sighted by Columbus in 1503. Although frequented by Spanish, English, and French ships, they were not claimed by anyone until they were ceded to the British in 1670 and settlers started arriving. Before long, the islands' remote location made them an ideal stopover for pirates.

CONTACTS:
Pirates Week Administration
10 Shedden Rd.
P.O. Box 51
Grand Cayman, KY1-1101 Cayman Islands
345-949-5859; fax: 345-949-5449
www.piratesweekfestival.com

SOURCES:
GdWrldFest-1985, p. 61

♦ 2099 ♦ **Pitra Visarjana Amavasya**
September-October; waning half of Hindu month of Asvina

During this two-week festival in India, no male family member is allowed to shave, nor is it permissible to cut hair, pare nails, or wear new clothes. It is a time for honoring ancestors by making special offerings of food and water, especially *khir*, or rice boiled in milk. Brahmans (priests, members of the highest Hindu caste) are often invited to partake of these special foods in the belief that they will ensure that the offerings reach the souls of departed family members. It is usually the eldest son or senior member of the family who performs the rituals associated with this festival.

SOURCES:
BkFest-1937, p. 160
FolkWrldHol-1999, p. 587
RelHolCal-2004, p. 177

♦ 2100 ♦ **Plague Sunday**
Last Sunday in August

When the plague reached the village of Eyam, Derbyshire, England, in 1665, about three-fifths of the town's population was wiped out. But under the leadership of Vicar William Mompesson, the villagers displayed both courage and selflessness, voluntarily isolating themselves from other villages in the parish and requesting that their food and medical supplies be dropped off at a point outside the village. The disease eventually became so virulent that the vicar had to hold open-air services for his dwindling congregation in a place up in the hills known as Cucklet Dell.

Every year on the last Sunday in August, a procession of clergy, standard bearers, choir members, and musicians forms at Eyam's parish church and slowly proceeds up the road leading toward the Dell. Hundreds of villagers, tourists, hikers, cyclists, and parents with baby carriages fall in behind them, finding seats on the grassy slopes of the Dell's natural amphitheater. A simple sermon pays tribute to the plague victims and the 74 villagers who survived.

CONTACTS:
Exam Church

Parish Office, Church St.
Eyam, Hope Valley S32 5QU United Kingdom
44-14-3363-0930; fax: 44-14-3363-0930
www.spanglefish.com

SOURCES:
DictDays-1988, p. 89
YrbookEngFest-1954, p. 116

♦ 2101 ♦ **Planting the Penny Hedge**
Between April 29 and June 2; eve of Ascension Day

The Penny Hedge—"penny" meaning penance—is a fence of interlaced stakes and boughs that is built along the water's edge at Boyes Staith, near Whitby, England. It is set up early in the morning on the eve of Ascension Day and should be sturdy enough to survive three tides.

According to the local legend, in 1159 three noblemen were out hunting a wild boar. When the animal took refuge in a hermitage occupied by a monk from Whitby Abbey, the holy man closed his door and refused to release it. The hunters were so angry that they beat the monk with their staves to the point of death. When the abbot of Whitby arrived on the scene, he decided that the hunters should receive a heavy punishment, but the dying monk convinced him otherwise. Instead, the abbot ordered them to build a hedge every year on the shore of Whitby Harbor while the bailiff blew a horn, announced a summary of their offences, and shouted, "Out on ye!" The first hedge was set up in 1160.

Today the story of the crime is no longer recited during the performance of the task, nor is the hedge still built by the descendants of the murderers. It is usually the harbor master himself who continues the tradition by building the hedge, while church and civil dignitaries, along with townspeople and visitors, look on.

CONTACTS:
Whitby Tourist Information Centre
Langborne Rd.
Whitby, North Yorkshire YO21 1YN United Kingdom
44-19-4760-2674

SOURCES:
EngCustUse-1941, p. 62
YrbookEngFest-1954, p. 224
YrFest-1972, p. 33

♦ 2102 ♦ **Plebeian Games (Ludi Plebeii)**
November 4-17

The Roman leader Flaminus is thought to have instituted the Plebeian Games in 220 B.C.E. They originally may have been held in the Circus Flaminius, which he built. Later, they may have moved to the Circus Maximus, a huge open arena between the Palatine and Aventine hills. The Games were dedicated to Jupiter, one of whose feast days was November 13. The Games themselves took place from November 15-17 and included horse and chariot races and contests that involved running, boxing and wrestling. The first nine days of the festival (November 4-12) were devoted to theatrical performances.

See also APOLLONIAN GAMES; LUDI; ROMAN GAMES

SOURCES:
FestRom-1981, p. 196
RomFest-1925, p. 252

♦ 2103 ♦ **Pleureuses, Ceremony of**
Between March 20 and April 23; Friday before Easter

This GOOD FRIDAY ceremony takes place at the Church of Romont in Switzerland. Held since the 15th century, the ceremony begins with a reading from the Bible of the Passion of Christ (the last seven days of his life). The congregation then begins its procession through the village streets. The weepers or mourners (the *Pleureuses*) are veiled in black attire resembling nuns' habits, and walk slowly behind a young girl portraying the Virgin Mary. She walks behind a penitent wearing a black hood and carrying a large cross. The mourners carry the symbols of the Passion on scarlet cushions: a crown of thorns, a whip, nails, a hammer, tongs, and St. Veronica's shroud (Veronica was a woman in the crowd who, as Christ passed her carrying the cross, wiped his face and his image was, according to legend, imprinted on the cloth). During the procession, the town resounds with chants and prayers.

CONTACTS:
Romont Tourism Office
Rue de Chateau 112
Romont, 1680 Switzerland
41-26-651-9055; fax: 41-26-651-9059
www.romont.ch

♦ 2104 ♦ **Plough Monday**
January, first Monday after Epiphany

This ancient rustic English holiday, also called **Fool Plough** or **Fond Plough**, or **Fond Pleeaf**, survived into the late 1800s. It is thought to have started in the days of the medieval Roman Catholic Church, when farmers, or ploughmen, kept candles called plough-lights burning in churches before the images of saints.

Once a year, on the Monday after EPIPHANY (before ploughing begins), or sometimes at the end of LENT (to celebrate the end of ploughing), they gathered in villages to ask for money to pay for the plough-lights. The Reformation of the 16th century ended this homage to saints, but not the day's celebration as a time to return to labor after the CHRISTMAS festivities.

By the 19th century, the day was observed with music, dancing, processions, and collecting money through trick-or-treat type means. "The Bessy"—a man dressed up to look ridiculous in women's clothing—and "The Fool," wearing animal skins or a fur cap and tail, solicited money from door to door so they could buy food and drink for their merrymaking. The ploughmen dragged a beribboned plough from house to house, shouting "God speed the plough," and if a home owner failed to make a contribution, they ploughed up his front yard. The money collected was spent not on plough-lights but on ale in the public houses.

The custom of blessing the plough on the prior day, Plough Sunday, was still observed in some areas in the 20th century.

SOURCES:
BkDays-1864, vol. I, p. 94
DaysCustFaith-1957, p. 38
DictDays-1988, p. 90
DictFolkMyth-1984, pp. 138, 410
EncyChristmas-2003, p. 610
FestSaintDays-1915, p. 19
FolkWrldHol-1999, p. 24
OxYear-1999, p. 601
RelHolCal-2004, p. 89
SaintFestCh-1904, p. 63

♦ 2105 ♦ **Poetry Festival of Medellín, International**
June-July

One of the largest poetry events in the world, the International Poetry Festival of Medellín is more than a typical gathering of poets and critics. Since its inception in 1991, the festival has been a politically charged platform for artists and intellectuals to demand more peaceful government policies for Medellín and the rest of Colombia, which has been long ravaged by political violence. Because of the festival's dissident stance, the Colombian government has refused to offer financial support, although outside funding has come from several European countries.

The International Poetry Festival in Medellín was founded as a means to promote creativity and artistic consciousness amidst the brutality of the country's long-running drug wars. The festival's organizers, The Prometeo Art and Poetry Corporation, formed that group after launching a poetry publication called Prometeo. Their aim was to use poetry to restore and renew their country's social fabric and to mobilize people to improve society..

The festival was an immediate success and grew quickly, now taking place over eight days. Poets from South America and around the world give free recitals in public parks, university theatres, prisons, schools, and libraries. The events attracting the largest audiences are the opening reading and the closing ceremony, which typically draw several thousand people. Residents of the city and visitors from far and wide flock to the festival to join in the intense enthusiasm and creative energy that are hallmarks of the event.

Between 1991 and 2007, the festival featured a cumulative total of 820 poets from 142 countries and indigenous nations. Among the festival's major political initiatives were the first Global Conference on Poetry for Peace, held in 2003, and a special 2007 meeting of the newly formed National Congress of Art and Poetry for Peace in Colombia, made up of more than 100 artists, poets, journalists, and intellectuals.

CONTACTS:
Corporation of Art and Poetry Prometeo:
Transversal 39 A
No. 72-52
Medellin Colombia
www.festivaldepoesiademedellin.org

Colombia - Embassy
2118 Leroy Pl. N.W.
Washington, DC 20008
202-387-8338; fax: 202-232-8643
www.colombiaemb.org

♦ 2106 ♦ Poetry Month, National
April

Established by the Academy of American Poets in 1996, National Poetry Month centers attention on the contributions and accomplishments of American poets. Activities during the month-long event, which is celebrated primarily by educational institutions, libraries, bookstores, and nonprofit organizations throughout the United States and Canada, include poetry readings, poetry festivals, displays and exhibits, workshops, and other events designed to help Americans of all ages learn more about poetry and its place in our contemporary culture.

CONTACTS:
Academy of American Poets
584 Broadway, Ste. 604
New York, NY 10012
212-274-0343; fax: 212-274-9427
www.poets.org

♦ 2107 ♦ Polar Bear Swim Day
January 1

Since 1920, a group of hardy swimmers has celebrated NEW YEAR'S DAY by plunging into the frigid waters of Vancouver's English Bay. As crazy as it sounds, the custom has spread to the United States, where chapters of the American Polar Bear Club have established themselves in a number of states known for their cold winter weather. In Sheboygan, Wisconsin, more than 300 daring swimmers—many of them in costume—brave the ice floes of Lake Michigan to take their New Year's Day swim. About 3,000 to 4,000 spectators stay bundled up on the beach and watch. The Sheboygan event has gradually expanded into a day-long festival, with a brat-fry, a costume contest, and live entertainment.

CONTACTS:
Greater Vancouver Convention and Visitors Bureau
200 Burrard St., Ste. 210
Vancouver, BC V6C 3L6 Canada
604-682-2222; fax: 604-682-1717
www.tourismvancouver.com

Sheboygan County Convention and Visitors Bureau
712 Riverfront Dr., Ste. 101
Sheboygan, WI 53081
800-457-9497 or 920-457-9491; fax: 920-457-6269
www.sheboygan.org

SOURCES:
AnnivHol-2000, p. 3

♦ 2108 ♦ Polish Constitution Day
May 3

May 3, known in Poland as **Swieto Trzeciego Maja**, is a patriotic legal holiday honoring the nation's first constitution,

adopted in 1791. It introduced fundamental changes in the way Poland was governed, based on the ideas of the French Revolution, and represented an attempt to preserve the country's independence. Although the May 3rd Constitution (as it was called) represented a great advance for the Polish people, it also aroused the anxieties of neighboring countries and eventually led to the Second Partition two years later.

CONTACTS:
Embassy of The Republic of Poland
2640 16th St. N.W.
Washington, D.C. 20009
202-234-3800; fax: 202-328-6271
www.washington.polemb.net

SOURCES:
AnnivHol-2000, p. 76
BkFest-1937, p. 261

♦ 2109 ♦ Polish Independence Day
November 11

This national holiday commemorates the re-creation of the state of Poland at the end of World War I. On November 11, 1918, Poland was granted independence after having been partitioned under the rule of Prussia, Austria, and Russia for more than 100 years. After the Soviet system took over the country, the holiday was abolished. But in 1989, after the Communist government fell, Independence Day was once again a national holiday.

See also POLISH SOLIDARITY DAY

CONTACTS:
Embassy of The Republic of Poland
2460 16th St. N.W.
Washington, D.C. 20009
202-234-3800; fax: 202-328-6271
www.washington.polemb.net

SOURCES:
AnnivHol-2000, p. 189

♦ 2110 ♦ Polish Liberation Day
July 22; January 17

July 22 is the anniversary of the day on which the KRN (National Home Council) established the Polish Committee of National Liberation (PKWN) in 1944, the first people's government in the country's thousand-year history. The PKWN manifesto issued on this date proclaimed that its first priorities were complete liberation from the Nazis and the freeing of ancient Polish lands on the Baltic Sea and Odra River, as well as the democratization of the country.

In the city of Warsaw, January 17 is observed as Liberation Day. It was on this day in 1945 that the city was freed from Nazi oppression by Soviet troops. Special ceremonies are held at the Monument to the Unknown Soldier in Warsaw's Victory Square.

SOURCES:
NatlHolWrld-1968, p. 121

♦ 2111 ♦ **Polish Solidarity Day**
August 31

This marks the day in 1980 when the Polish labor union Solidarnosc (Solidarity) was formed at the Lenin Shipyards in Gdansk. Under the leadership of Lech Walesa, an electrician at the shipyard, 17,000 workers had staged a strike earlier in the year to protest rising food prices. An agreement was finally reached between the Gdansk strikers and the Polish Communist government, allowing free unions to be formed, independent of the Communist Party.

Solidarity was formally founded on September 22 and consisted of about 50 labor unions. But when the union stepped up its demands, staging a series of controlled strikes throughout 1981 to pressure the government for free elections and economic reforms, Premier Wojciech Jaruzelski was subjected to even greater pressure from the Soviet Union to put a stop to the group's activities. On December 13, 1981, martial law was declared, the fledgling union's legal status was terminated, and Walesa was put under arrest. He was released in November 1982, and martial law was lifted six months later.

After almost a decade of struggle, Solidarity was finally granted legal status on April 17, 1989, clearing the way for the downfall of the Polish Communist Party. The Polish labor union's successful struggle marked the beginning of similar changes in other Communist-bloc countries in Europe, many of whom overthrew their Communist leaders and took the first steps toward establishing more democratic forms of government. Solidarity's founding is celebrated not only in Poland but by Polish Americans in the United States, with demonstrations and programs in support of Polish workers.

CONTACTS:
Solidarnosc
ul. Waly Piastowski 24
Gdansk, 80-855 Poland
48-58-308-42-32; fax: 48-58-308-44-82
www.solidarnosc.org.pl

SOURCES:
AnnivHol-2000, p. 144

♦ 2112 ♦ **Polka Festival, National**
May, Memorial Day weekend

The National Polka Festival takes place in Ennis, Texas, on Memorial Day Weekend. Founded in 1966, this festival attracts 50,000 people to Ennis for a Saturday and Sunday filled with Czech music, food, folk dance, folk costumes, and crafts. A Saturday morning parade composed of floats, marching bands, clowns, groups of kids, seniors, and representatives from civic organizations kicks off the event. The town's four halls, all with spacious dance floors, host bands at various times throughout the day. On Sunday morning visitors may attend a Polka mass.

CONTACTS:
Ennis Convention and Visitors Bureau
002 E. Ennis Ave.

Ennis, TX 75119
888-366-4748 or 972-878-4748; fax: 972-875-1018
www.nationalpolkafestival.com

♦ 2113 ♦ **Pongal**
Mid-January

A colorful four-day harvest and thanksgiving celebration in southern India, Pongal honors the sun, the earth, and the cow. It is called Pongal in the state of Tamil Nadu; **Karnataka** in Andhra Pradesh; and **Makara Sankranti** in Gujarat.

The first day is called Bhogi Pongal and is for cleaning everything in the house. On the second day, freshly harvested rice and *jaggery* ('palm sugar') are put to boil in new pots. When the mixture bubbles, people cry out, "Pongal!" ('It boils.') The rice is offered to Surya, the sun, before people taste it themselves, thus the second day is called Surya Pongal. On the third day, called Mattu Pongal (Festival of the Cow), village cows and oxen are bathed, decorated with garlands of bells, beads, and leaves, and worshipped.

On the fourth day, known as Kanyapongal, the festival of Jallikattu takes place in villages near Madurai in Tamil Nadu as well as in Andhra Pradesh. Bundles containing money are tied to the sharpened horns of bulls. The animals are paraded around the village and then stampeded. Young men who are brave enough try to snatch the money from the bulls' horns.

In Ahmedabad in the state of Gujarat, the celebration is a time of competitive kite-flying, and is termed the **International Kite Festival**. The skies are filled with kites, and kite makers come from other cities to make their multicolored kites in all shapes. As darkness falls, the battle of the kites ends, and new kites soar aloft, each with its own paper lamp, so that the sky is filled with flickering lights.

CONTACTS:
Tamil Nadu Tourism
Tourism Complex, No. 2 Wallajah Rd.
Chennai, Tamil Nadu 600 002 India
91-44-25383333; fax: 91-44-25381567
www.tamilnadutourism.org

Ministry of Tourism, Government of India
Rm. No 123, Transport Bhawan, No. 1, Parliament St.
New Delhi, Delhi 110 001 India
91-11-23715084; fax: 91-11-23715084
www.tourisminindia.com

SOURCES:
AnnivHol-2000, p. 9
BkHolWrld-1986, Jan 14
EncyRel-1987, vol. 4, p. 409
FolkWrldHol-1999, p. 98
OxYear-1999, p. 721
RelHolCal-2004, p. 181

♦ 2114 ♦ **Pooram**
April-May; Hindu month of Vaisakha

One of the most spectacular festivals of southern India, this is a celebration in Trichur (or Thrissur), Kerala, dedicated to

Lord Shiva. People fast on the first day of the festival and the rest of the days are devoted to fairs, processions, and fireworks displays. The highlight of the pageantry comes when an image of the deity Vadakkunathan is taken from the temple and carried in a procession of temple elephants ornately decorated with gold-plated mail. The Brahmans riding them hold colorful ceremonial umbrellas and whisks of yak hair and peacock feathers. The elephants lumber through the pagoda-shaped gateway of the Vadakkunathan temple and into the village while drummers beat and pipers trill. Fireworks light the skies until dawn.

CONTACTS:
Department of Tourism, Government of Kerala
Park View
Thiruvananthapuram, Kerala 695 033 India
91-471-2321132; fax: 91-471-2322279
www.keralatourism.org

♦ 2115 ♦ Pori International Jazz Festival
Mid-July

Pori, Finland, is 150 miles northwest of Helsinki—far enough north to guarantee 19 hours of daylight during the summer jazz festival that has been held there since 1966. It offers up to 10 major concerts and numerous smaller concerts as well as jam sessions, films, a children's program, and many informal musical events in the city's cafes, restaurants, jazz clubs, and art galleries. All styles of jazz—from traditional to contemporary, dixieland, blues, and swing—are represented. Performers at past festivals have included Herbie Hancock, Chuck Mangione, Ornette Coleman, Dizzy Gillespie, Sonny Rollins, and B.B. King as well as Scandinavian jazz artists. The major concerts are held in an outdoor amphitheater on Kirjurinluoto Island, a natural park in the heart of the city. There are also lectures, films, and exhibitions on jazz and its influence.

CONTACTS:
Pori Jazz Office
Pori Jazz 66 ry, Pohjoisranta 11 D
Pori, 28100 Finland
358-2-6262-200; fax: 358-2-6262-225
www.porijazz.fi

SOURCES:
GdWrldFest-1985, p. 77
MusFestEurBrit-1980, p. 69

♦ 2116 ♦ Portland Rose Festival
June

The Portland Rose Festival is a month-long salute to the rose in Portland, Ore., and certainly one of the sweetest-smelling festivals anywhere.

The "City of Roses" has been putting on a rose festival since 1907 and claims now to produce the biggest celebration of the rose in the world. To justify such a claim, the festival offers more than 60 events. These include an air show, musical concerts, fireworks, the Portland Arts Festival, tours and cruises on visiting U.S. and Canadian Navy ships, and boat and Indy-class car races.

The salute starts with the coronation of the Rose Queen, and continues with parade after parade, including a starlight parade, called the second largest lighted parade in the United States, the largest children's parade, and the climax—a grand floral parade, with dozens of rose-bedecked floats. On the final days of the festival, the Portland Rose Society stages the Rose Show, the oldest and largest rose show in the country, with about 20,000 individual blossoms exhibited.

Portland is thought to have started its life as a rose city in the early 19th century, when traders brought with them seeds of the wild rose of England. It flourished as the Oregon Sweet Briar. Settlers brought more roses, and then in 1888, Mrs. Henry L. Pittock held a rose show in her front yard, and that evolved into today's festival.

The parade is one of two major floral parades in the country, the other being the better known Tournament of Roses in Pasadena, Calif., every New Year's Day.

CONTACTS:
Portland Rose Festival Foundation
5603 S.W. Hood Ave.
Portland, OR 97239
503-227-2681; fax: 503-227-6603
www.rosefestival.org

SOURCES:
AmerBkDays-2000, p. 421
GdUSFest-1984, p. 151

♦ 2117 ♦ Portugal Liberation Day
April 25

Liberation Day, or **Liberty Day**, is a public holiday commemorating the military coup on this day in 1974 that removed Marcello Caetano (1906-1980) from power, reflecting the opposition of many Portuguese to their government's military policies and wars in Africa.

CONTACTS:
Embassy of Portugal
2125 Kalorama Rd. N.W.
Washington, D.C. 20008
202-328-8610; fax: 202-462-3726
www.visitportugal.com

SOURCES:
AnnivHol-2000, p. 68

♦ 2118 ♦ Portugal National Day
June 10

Also known as **Camões Memorial Day** and **Portugal Day**, this national holiday observes the death anniversary of Luis Vas de Camões (1524-1580), Portugal's national poet. His epic work, *The Lusiads* (1572), was based on the voyage to India of Portuguese explorer Vasco de Gama.

This national holiday is observed with patriotic speeches, games, and costumed citizens in the capital city of Lisbon.

CONTACTS:
Embassy of Portugal

2125 Kalorama Rd. N.W.
Washington, D.C. 20008
202-328-8610; fax: 202-462-3726
www.visitportugal.com

SOURCES:
AnnivHol-2000, p. 98
NatlHolWrld-1968, p. 82

◆ 2119 ◆ **Portugal Republic Day**
October 5

This national holiday commemorates the establishment of the Portuguese Republic on this day in 1910, which ended over two centuries of the monarchical rule of the Portuguese royal family, the House of Braganca.

CONTACTS:
Embassy of Portugal
2125 Kalorama Rd. N.W.
Washington, D.C. 20008
202-328-8610; fax: 202-462-3726
www.visitportugal.com

SOURCES:
AnnivHol-2000, p. 168

◆ 2120 ◆ **Portugal Restoration of Independence Day**
December 1

This public holiday commemorates the restoration of Portugal's independence from Spain on December 1, 1640. Philip II (1527-1598) of Spain assumed control of Portugal in 1580 upon the death of Henry, prince of Portugal, and the "Spanish captivity" lasted for 60 years. Revolution began in Lisbon, and in 1640, the Portuguese dethroned Philip IV (1605-1665; grandson of Philip II) and reclaimed independence for Portugal.

CONTACTS:
Embassy of Portugal
2125 Kalorama Rd. N.W.
Washington, D.C. 20008
202-328-8610; fax: 202-462-3726
www.visitportugal.com

SOURCES:
AnnivHol-2000, p. 200

◆ 2121 ◆ **Posadas**
December 16-24

This nine-day CHRISTMAS celebration in Mexico commemorates the journey Mary and Joseph (the parents of Jesus) took from Nazareth to Bethlehem. Reenacting the couple's search for shelter (*posada* in Spanish) in which the infant Jesus might be born, a group of "pilgrims" will knock on someone's door and ask the owner to let them in. Although they may initially be refused, the master of the house finally invites them to enter, and the Posadas party begins. The children are blindfolded and given a chance to break the *piñata* (a clay or papier-mâché animal that hangs from the ceiling and is filled with candy and toys) by swinging at it with a

stick. The posadas are repeated for nine evenings, the last occurring on CHRISTMAS EVE.

The MISA DE GALLO, or Mass of the Cock (so-called because it's held so early in the day), ends after midnight, and then there are fireworks and, in some towns, a special parade with floats and *tableaux vivants* representing biblical scenes.

In small Mexican villages, there is often a procession led by two children bearing images of Joseph and Mary riding a burro. The adult members of the group carry lighted tapers and sing the Litany of the Virgin as they approach each house. There is also a famous Posadas celebration on Olvera Street in Los Angeles.

CONTACTS:
Mexico Tourism Board
21 E. 63rd St., Fl. 3
New York, NY 10021
800-446-3942 or 212-821-0314; fax: 212-821-0367
www.visitmexico.com

Olvera Street
El Pueblo De Los Angeles Historic Park
845 N. Alameda St.
Los Angeles, CA 90012
213-680-2525
www.olvera-street.com

SOURCES:
BkFest-1937, p. 232
BkFestHolWrld-1970, pp. 137, 155
BkHolWrld-1986, Dec 16
EncyChristmas-2003, p. 624
FolkAmerHol-1999, p. 496
FolkWrldHol-1999, p. 743
RelHolCal-2004, p. 85

◆ 2122 ◆ **Poson**
May-June; full moon day of Hindu month of Jyestha

This festival, also called **Dhamma Vijaya** and **Full Moon Day**, celebrates the bringing of Buddhism to Sri Lanka (formerly Ceylon). It is second in importance only to VESAK. The story of this day is that King Devanampiya Tissa was chasing a deer in the forest of Mihintale when someone called out his name. He looked up and saw a figure in a saffron-colored robe standing on a rock with six companions. The robed figure was the holy patron of Sri Lanka, Arahat Mahinda, the son of Emperor Asoka of India, who was a convert to Buddhism from Hinduism. He had sent his son and companions as missionaries to Ceylon in about 251 B.C.E. Mahinda converted King Devanampiya Tissa and the royal family, and they in turn converted the common people. Mahinda, who propagated the faith through works of practical benevolence, died in about 204 B.C.E.

While the holiday is celebrated throughout Sri Lanka, the major ceremonies are at the ancient cities of Anuradhapura and Mihintale. There, historical events involving Mahinda are reenacted, streets and buildings are decorated and illuminated, and temples are crowded. In Mihintale people climb to the rock where Arahat Mahinda delivered his first sermon to the king. An important part of the festival is paying homage to the branch of the Bodhi Tree brought to Sri Lanka by Mahinda's sister, SANGHAMITA. This is the tree that Gautama sat under until he received enlightenment and became the Buddha.

CONTACTS:
Sri Lanka Tourist Board
111 Wood Ave. S., Ste. 323
Edison, NJ 08820
732-516-9800; fax: 732-452-0087
www.srilankatourism.org

SOURCES:
EncyRel-1987, vol. 2, p. 551; vol. 4, p. 318

♦ 2123 ♦ **Potato Blossom Festival**
July

Founded in 1937 to celebrate Maine's primary food crop, the potato, this festival is held the third weekend in July in Fort Fairfield, Maine, when the potato blossoms are in bloom. Fort Fairfield is the nation's largest potato producer. From 1937 to 1960, the festival was held in a series of towns in northern Maine before Fort Fairfield was officially chosen as the permanent site.

Potato-related events include the Jr. Miss Potato Blossom Pageant, a potato recipe contest, a potato picking contest, and mashed potato wrestling. Other events include musical concerts, bicycle races, a household pet show, an antique farm equipment show, a human chess game, a tractor pull, a two-hour parade, and fireworks. In 1950, the Potato Blossom Festival sponsored the first marathon race to be held in the state of Maine.

CONTACTS:
Fort Fairfield Chamber of Commerce
18 Community Center Dr.
Fort Fairfield, ME 04742
207-472-3802; fax: 207-472-3810
fortcc.org

♦ 2124 ♦ **Potato Days**
October

In Norway during the fall potato harvest, it was customary to give children a week off school to help in the fields. Norwegian farmers would put in a request for a certain number of children and feed them during their week of employment. Although this arrangement is no longer as common as it was up until the 1950s, children still help harvest the potatoes on their families' farms, and the traditional fall vacation is still known as the potato vacation, or *potetserie*.

A similar arrangement can be found in the United States, especially in states where there are many small farms producing a single crop. In northern Maine, children also harvest potatoes, and in Vermont some schools give their students time off to help pick apples.

SOURCES:
BkHolWrld-1986, Oct 28
FolkWrldHol-1999, p. 542

♦ 2125 ♦ **Powamû Ceremony**
February

The Hopi Indians believe that for six months of the year ancestral spirits called the *katchinas* leave their mountain homes and visit the tribe, bringing health to the people and rain for their crops. The Hopi who live at the Walpi Pueblo in northeastern Arizona celebrate the entry of the Sky Father (also known as the Sun God) into the pueblo in February by dramatizing the event in a ceremony known as Powamû. The Sky Father, represented by a man wearing a circular mask surrounded by feathers and horsehair with a curved beak in the middle, is led into the pueblo from the east at sunrise. There he visits the house and *kiva* (underground chamber used for religious and other ceremonies) of the chief, performing certain ceremonial rites and exchanging symbolic gifts.

A similar sequence of events is performed in July during the NIMAN FESTIVAL. At this time, the Sky Father is ushered out of the pueblo. In the intervening months, it is assumed that he remains in the village or nearby, making public appearances in masked dances from time to time.

CONTACTS:
Hopi Cultural Center
P.O. Box 67
Second Mesa, AZ 86043
928-734-2401; fax: 928-734-6651
www.hopiculturalcenter.com

SOURCES:
DictFolkMyth-1984, pp. 123, 566, 883
EncyNatAmerRel-2001, p. 229
EncyRel-1987, vol. 10, p. 520
FolkAmerHol-1999, p. 72

♦ 2126 ♦ **Prague Kolache Festival**
First Saturday in May

The Prague Kolache Festival is held every year on the first Saturday in May in Prague, Okla. The event celebrates the rich Czech heritage of the city's founding families, who settled in the area around the turn of the last century. The event is named after a Czech pastry that consists of a sweet roll with a fruit center. The first Kolache Festival took place in 1951, as a dress rehearsal for a celebration of the town's 50th birthday in 1952. The popular event carried on annually through 1955, when a 10-year lapse occurred. It has now been held consistently since 1965.

The festival draws as many as 30,000 people to a town of just 2,500 residents. Organizers estimate that 50,000 kolaches are consumed each year. A contest for the best homemade kolache, bread, and wine is a highlight of the festival. It also features an arts-and-crafts show, amusement-park-style carnival, and parade showcasing antique tractors and colorful Czech folk clothing. A variety of free entertainment, ethnic food and drink, and Czech dancing and costume competitions round out the day. Topping it off is the crowning of the Kolache Festival "royalty." By custom, the newly crowned queen opens the evening's popular polka street dance, which carries on until 10:00 that night.

CONTACTS:
Prague Kolache Festival
405-567-4866
www.praguekolachefestival.com/index.htm

Prague Chamber of Commerce
1023 Jim Thorpe Blvd.
P.O. Box 111
Prague, OK 74864
405-567-2616
www.praguechamber.org/index.htm

♦ 2127 ♦ Prague Spring International Music Festival
Three weeks in May

When the Prague Spring International Music Festival was organized in 1946, the Czech Philharmonic Orchestra was celebrating its 50th year and was given a prominent place on the program that first year. But orchestras, musical ensembles, and performing artists from around the world participate in this three-week festival, which presents symphonic, chamber and vocal music; jazz; opera; musical theater; and world premieres of Czech and other contemporary composers. The festival always opens with the symphonic poems of Czech composer Bedrich Smetana (1824-1884), *Ma Vlast* (My Country), and concludes with Ludwig van Beethoven's (1770-1827) Ninth Symphony. In addition, the Prague Spring Competition, founded one year after the festival itself, showcases the instrumental talents of young musicians.

CONTACTS:
Prazskejaro o.p.s.
Hellichova 18
Prague, 118 00 Czech Republic
420-2-5731-1921; fax: 420-2-5731-3725
www.festival.cz/en/rubrika.php?id_rubrika=25

SOURCES:
MusFestEurBrit-1980, p. 35
MusFestWrld-1963, p. 198
WildPlanet-1995, p. 125

♦ 2128 ♦ Prayer for Christian Unity, Week of
January 18-25

The Week of Prayer for Christian Unity, as organized by the World Council of Churches, dates back to 1964. Calls for Christian unity and efforts to bring Christians of various denominations together in worship can be traced back at least 200 years earlier, however. In 1908, the Rev. Paul Watson proposed a week-long observance dedicated to Christian unity to be scheduled between the feasts of St. Peter's Chair (January 18) and St. Paul (January 25), the two great leaders of the first Christians. The World Council of Churches maintains these dates. Each year an inter-denominational committee selects a scriptural theme and prepares the outlines of a worship service for each day of the Week of Prayer. Individual congregations are free to use the material as is, or vary it to suit local practices and traditions.

CONTACTS:
World Council of Churches
150 route de Ferney

P.O. Box 2100
Geneva, 1211 Switzerland
41-22-791-6111; fax: 41-22-791-0361
www2.wcc-coe.org

♦ 2129 ♦ Preakness Stakes
Third Saturday in May

The 10-day **Preakness Festival** or **Maryland Preakness Celebration** culminates in the running of the Preakness Stakes, the "middle jewel of the Triple Crown" of horseracing—the other two being the Kentucky Derby and the Belmont Stakes. Held at Baltimore's Pimlico Race Course, the Preakness was first run on May 27, 1873. The festival leading up to the race features recreational, sporting, and cultural events—including hot air balloons, a 5K run, and a parade.

CONTACTS:
Maryland Jockey Club
Pimlico Race Course
5201 Park Heights Ave.
Baltimore, MD 21215
800-638-1859 or 410-542-9400
www.marylandracing.com

Preakness Celebration Inc.
401 E. Pratt St., Ste. 311
Baltimore, MD 21202
410-578-4451; fax: 410-837-3042
www.preaknesscelebration.com

SOURCES:
GdUSFest-1984, p. 81

♦ 2130 ♦ Premio Lo Nuestro Latin Music Awards
February

Since 1989, the Univision television network has been awarding the Premios Lo Nuestro Latin Music Awards. Some 35 categories of music and performance are honored. It is the oldest such awards program in the United States.

The televised awards ceremony features live performances by nominated musical acts along with music videos. Journalists and media celebrities from throughout Latin America come to the event. Among those artists who have won the awards are Ricky Martin, Gloria Estefan, Jennifer Lopez, Aventura, and Ivy Queen. While originating from the United States, the Premio Lo Nuestro Latin Music Awards program is broadcast throughout Latin America.

CONTACTS:
Univision
9405 N.W. 41st St.
Miami, FL 33178-2301
305-471-3900; fax: 305-471-4065
www.univision.com

♦ 2131 ♦ Presentation of the Blessed Virgin Mary, Feast of the
November 21

The Feast of the Presentation of the Blessed Virgin Mary was first celebrated by the Greeks in about the eighth century and was not adopted by the Roman Catholic Church until the later Middle Ages; no one is quite sure when this festival was first introduced. As related in the apocryphal Book of James, it commemorates the presentation of the three-year-old Mary in the Temple to consecrate her to the service of God. Many have confused this festival with the Feast of the Presentation of Christ in the Temple, otherwise known as CANDLEMAS.

CONTACTS:
The Mary Page
Marian Library/International Marian Research Institute
University of Dayton
Dayton, OH 45469
937-229-4214; fax: 937-229-4258

SOURCES:
FolkWrldHol-1999, p. 659
OxYear-1999, p. 469
RelHolCal-2004, p. 105
SaintFestCh-1904, p. 493

◆ 2132 ◆ Preservation of the Ozone Layer, International Day for the
September 16

In 1994, the UNITED NATIONS established September 16 as International Day for the Preservation of the Ozone Layer. The date honors the September 16, 1987, signing of the Montreal Protocol on Substances that Deplete the Ozone Layer. Nations may observe the day with activities that support the aims of the Protocol.

CONTACTS:
United Nations, Department of Public Information
Rm. S-1070L J, K, L
New York, NY 10017
212-963-6842; fax: 212-963-6914
www.un.org

◆ 2133 ◆ Presidents' Day
Third Monday in February

The passage of Public Law 90-363 in 1968, also known as the "Monday Holiday Law," changed the observance of WASHINGTON'S BIRTHDAY from February 22 to the third Monday in February. Because it occurs so soon after LINCOLN'S BIRTHDAY, many states—such as Hawaii, Minnesota, Nebraska, Wisconsin, and Wyoming—combine the two holidays and call it Presidents' Day or **Washington-Lincoln Day**. Some regard it as a day to honor all former presidents of the United States.

See also Appendix

SOURCES:
AmerBkDays-2000, p. 149
AnnivHol-2000, p. 34
DictDays-1988, p. 91
PatHols-2006, p. 265

◆ 2134 ◆ Pretzel Sunday
Between March 8 and April 7; fourth Sunday in Lent

On **Bretzelsonndeg** in Luxembourg, it is the custom for boys to present their sweethearts with decorated pretzel-cakes. If a girl wants to encourage the boy, she reciprocates with a decorated egg on EASTER Sunday. If the pretzel-cake is large, the egg must be large also; a small cake warrants a small egg.

The custom is reversed during LEAP YEAR, when girls give cakes to boys on Pretzel Sunday, and boys return the favor with eggs at Easter. Married couples often participate in the exchange of cakes and eggs as well.

SOURCES:
FestWestEur-1958, p. 106

◆ 2135 ◆ Primrose Day
April 19

Benjamin Disraeli, Earl of Beaconsfield, novelist, and twice prime minister of England, died on this day in 1881. When he was buried in the family vault at Hughenden Manor, near High Wycombe, Queen Victoria came to lay a wreath of primroses, thought to be his favorite flower, on his grave. Two years later the Primrose League was formed to support the principles of Conservatism which Disraeli had championed. The organization's influence ebbed after World War I, but Primrose Day is remembered in honor of Disraeli and his contribution to the Conservative cause.

SOURCES:
DictDays-1988, p. 91
OxYear-1999, p. 163

◆ 2136 ◆ Prince's Birthday in Liechtenstein
August 15

The Prince's Birthday is a national holiday in Liechtenstein. This 60-square-mile country (population around 32,000) gets almost 25 percent of its revenue from selling postage stamps. The country is a constitutional monarchy headed by Prince Franz Joseph II, who turned over actual power to his son, Hans-Adam (b. 1945), in 1984. It was founded at the end of the 17th century when Johann Adam von Liechtenstein, a wealthy Austrian prince, bought land in the Rhine valley from two bankrupt counts. In 1719, he obtained an imperial deed creating the country. That date is considered the official birth of the nation. Members of the Liechtenstein family have ruled the country ever since.

Franz Joseph II was born on Aug. 16, 1905, but his birthday is celebrated on Aug. 15, the day of the Feast of the ASSUMPTION. Celebrations take place in the capital city of Vaduz. People come from the countryside for the festivities which include an open house at the prince's home and castle, Schloss Vaduz, dancing in the streets, special food in the cafes, and fireworks in the evening.

CONTACTS:
Princely House of Liechtenstein
Furstenhaus von Liechtenstein
Schloss Vadux
Vaduz, 9490 Liechtenstain
423-2381-280; fax: 423-238-1281
www.fuerstenhaus.li/en

♦ 2137 ♦ Prinsjesdag
Third Tuesday in September

The state opening of Parliament in the Netherlands takes place on the third Tuesday in September at the 13th-century Ridderzaal, or Knights' Hall, in The Hague. Queen Beatrix rides to Parliament in a golden coach drawn by eight horses. She is received by the two houses of Parliament—the Upper House and the Lower House, corresponding to the Senate and the House of Representatives in the United States—to whom she addresses her speech outlining the government's intended majority program for the coming year.

A similar ceremony is observed in Great Britain (*see* STATE OPENING OF PARLIAMENT).

CONTACTS:
Government Information Service
P.O. Box 20001
Hague, 2500 EA Netherlands
31-70-356-4000; fax: 31-70-356-4683
www.koninklijkhuis.nl/english

♦ 2138 ♦ Prisoners, Feast of the
Between March 15 and April 18; Tuesday before Easter

Popayán, Colombia, is famous for the beauty of its HOLY WEEK celebrations, which include the traditional blessing of the palms on PALM SUNDAY and a procession between rows of waving palm branches. But one of the more unusual ceremonies held during this week is called the Feast of the Prisoners.

A procession of litters covered with plates and bowls of food and cases of soft drinks arrives at the local prison on Tuesday afternoon, accompanied by government officials, the archbishop in ceremonial garb, and schoolgirls with more things to eat. The prisoners are gathered in the courtyard to listen to various addresses. One of them who is approaching the end of his sentence is selected to sit, guarded and manacled, at a special table. He symbolizes Barrabas, the man in the biblical EASTER story whom the crowd clamored to free instead of Jesus. As people walk by the chosen prisoner they deposit gifts of food or money for him to retrieve when he is set free at the end of the day. That night there is a candlelight procession in which large decorated litters depict scenes from the Passion of Christ or bear images of the saints.

Although no one knows how far back Popayán's Holy Week traditions extend, historical records indicate that Easter ceremonies were being held there in 1558.

CONTACTS:
Embassy of Colombia
2118 Leroy Pl. N.W.
Washington, D.C. 20008
202-387-8338; fax: 202-232-8643
www.colombiaemb.org

SOURCES:
EncyEaster-2002, p. 64
FiestaTime-1965, p. 74

♦ 2139 ♦ Puccini Festival
Every June-August

The Puccini Festival is held annually each summer in Torre del Lago in Tuscany, Italy, to honor and celebrate Giacomo Puccini (1858-1924), the Italian composer of such beloved operas as *La Boheme* and *Madame Butterfly.* Over the course of each summer from June through August, the festival presents distinguished and often innovative productions of Puccini's works. More than 40,000 music lovers attend ticketed festival concerts and operas each summer. The productions take place in an open-air theatre close to the Villa Mausoleum, where Puccini lived and worked. In addition to musical performances, such collateral events as talks and art exhibitions having to do with Puccini's life and work are held throughout the area all summer.

The festival was founded in 1930 by Giovacchino Forzano, a playwright and librettist, and Pietro Mascagri, a friend from Puccini's school days. Shortly before he died, Puccini had written in a letter to Forzano of his desire to "listen to one of my operas in the open air." Six years after the maestro's death, his friend honored his wish by mounting a production of *La Boheme* on the lakeshore in front of Puccini's house, on a provisional stage built on piles in the lake. The festival has thrived ever since. In 1966, the performances moved to a large amphitheatre on reclaimed land near the lake harbor. In 2008, the festival plans to open a modern new 3,200-seat open-air theatre that will be the centerpiece of a cultural park celebrating Puccini and his achievements.

CONTACTS:
Fondazione Festival Pucciniano
Piazzale Belvedere Puccini 4
Torre de Lago Puccini (LU) 55048 Italy
www.puccinifestival.it

Italian Government Travel Office
630 5th Ave., Ste. 1565
New York, NY 10111
212-245-5027; fax: 212-586-9249
www.italiantourism.com

♦ 2140 ♦ Puck Fair
August 10-12

A traditional gathering that dates back hundreds of years, Puck Fair is a three-day event held in Killorglin in County Kerry, Ireland. A large male goat is decorated with ribbons and paraded through the streets on the first day, which is known as Gathering Day. The goat, known as King Puck, presides over the fair from his "throne," an enclosure on a three-story platform in the town square. The main event of the second day, known as Puck's Fair Day, is a livestock show. On the third day, known as Scattering Day or Children's Day, King Puck is led out of town to the accompaniment of traditional Irish music. People come from all over Europe and the United States to attend the fair.

CONTACTS:
Puck Fair Ltd.
Sean Scoil - School Rd.
Killorglin, County Kerry Ireland

353-66-9762366; fax: 353-66-9762366
www.puckfair.ie

SOURCES:
FolkWrldHol-1999, p. 493

♦ 2141 ♦ Puerto Rico Constitution Day
July 25

Puerto Rico Constitution Day is the anniversary of the day on which Puerto Rico changed from a territory to a commonwealth and adopted its new constitution in 1952. Sometimes referred to as **Commonwealth Day**, July 25 is a legal holiday throughout the island. It is celebrated with parades, speeches, fireworks, and parties.

The most interesting thing about the relationship between Puerto Rico and the United States is its voluntary nature. Under the commonwealth arrangement, islanders elect a governor and a legislature as well as a resident commissioner who is sent—with a voice but not a vote—to the U.S. Congress in Washington, D.C. The relationship remains permanent for as along as both parties agree to it, but it can be changed at any time by mutual consent. The reason Puerto Rico became a commonwealth rather than an independent republic or a state is that the election of 1948 failed to produce a majority vote in favor of either of these alternatives.

CONTACTS:
Puerto Rico Tourism Company
666 Fifth Ave., 15th Fl.
New York, NY 10103
800-866-7827 or 212-586-6262; fax: 212-586-1212
www.gotopuertorico.com

SOURCES:
AmerBkDays-2000, p. 543
AnnivHol-2000, p. 123

♦ 2142 ♦ Pulaski Day
October 11; first Sunday in October

Count Casimir Pulaski was already a seasoned fighter for the cause of independence when he first arrived in America in 1777 to help General George WASHINGTON and the Continental Army overthrow the British. While still a teenager he had fought to preserve the independence of his native Poland, and when he was forced to flee his country he ended up in Paris. There he met Benjamin FRANKLIN and Silas Deane, who were impressed by his military background and arranged for him to join the American revolutionaries.

Although he was put in charge of the mounted units and given the title Commander of the Horse, Pulaski had trouble maintaining his soldiers' respect. He spoke no English and was unwilling to take orders from anyone, including Washington. Eventually he resigned from the army and raised an independent cavalry corps, continuing his fight for the colonies' independence. It was on October 11, 1779, that the Polish count died while trying to free Savannah, Georgia, from British control.

The president of the United States proclaims October 11 as Pulaski Day each year, and it is observed with parades and patriotic exercises in communities in Georgia, Indiana, Nebraska, and Wisconsin. The biggest Pulaski Day parade takes place in New York City on the first Sunday in October, when more than 100,000 Polish Americans march up Fifth Avenue.

CONTACTS:
General Pulaski Memorial Parade Committee Inc
295 Greenwich St., Ste. 353
New York, NY 10007
212-254-1180
www.pulaskiparade.org

SOURCES:
AmerBkDays-2000, p. 184
AnnivHol-2000, pp. 39, 171

♦ 2143 ♦ Punjabi American Festival
May

Since 1994, the Punjabi American Heritage Society has sponsored the annual Punjabi American Festival in Yuba City, Calif. The event is meant to celebrate the Punjabi culture of Northern India and to introduce young Punjabi-Americans to their heritage. Many Punjabi immigrants have settled in the Yuba City area of California. The festival is the largest of its kind in North America.

The Punjabi American Festival is a day-long event held at the Yuba-Sutter Fairgrounds in Yuba City. It begins with the playing of the National Anthem, followed by children reciting a Punjabi prayer. Featured are Bhangra dance groups, which contain both male and female dancers in colorful costumes performing songs and intricate dances. Traditionally, Bhangra dances are performed to celebrate harvest time. There are also other ethnic folk dancers and musical performers, Punjabi comedy skits, arts and crafts, movies, children's games, and over 50 booths selling traditional foods, clothing, and jewelry. Over 300 children participate in the stage performances. A number of prominent Punjabis from across the country are also honored by the Punjabi American heritage Society during the festival. The money raised is used towards cultural projects in the Yuba City community.

CONTACTS:
Punjabi American Heritage Society
P.O. Box 621
Yuba City, CA 95992
www.punjabiamericanheritagesociety.org

♦ 2144 ♦ Punkin Chunkin World Championship
October-November

A celebration held the first weekend after Halloween in Sussex County, Del., since 1986, the Punkin Chunkin World Championship involves shooting pumpkins as far as possible using homemade catapults, trebuchets, slingshots, or pneumatic air cannons. No prizes are offered except for bragging rights.

There are various levels of competition based on the type of machine used and the age of participants. Pumpkins are weighed beforehand, the competing teams are given three minutes to prepare and load their machines, and then each team in turn is given the chance to launch their projectile. Each team gets the best of three shots. Judges on ATVs ride out in the field to mark and measure the distance each pumpkin traveled. Pumpkins that break apart in midair are considered "pie" and are disqualified. The 2007 event was held in a farm field near Bridgeville, Del. Punkin Chunkin festivals are said to have spread to some 50 other locations across America.

CONTACTS:
World Championship Punkin Chunkin Association
P.O. Box 217
Nassau, DE 19969
www.punkinchunkin.com/main.htm

♦ 2145 ♦ Punky (Punkie) Night
Last Thursday in October

In the English village of Hinton St. George, Somerset, it is traditional for both children and adults to walk through town carrying "punkies," or lanterns made from carved-out mangel-wurzels, or mangolds (a variety of beet), with candles in them. Some say that the custom originated when parish women made crude vegetable lanterns to guide their husbands home after a long evening at the local pub. October 28 was traditionally the date for the Chiselborough Fair, and it was not uncommon for the men to drink too much and get lost in the fields on their way home.

Although this custom is observed in other English towns, the celebration at Hinton St. George is by far the best established. There is a procession of children carrying punkies through the streets, begging for money, and singing the "punky song." A prize is given out for the best carved punky. There is no evidence that the name "punky" came from "pumpkin," but the custom is very similar to what takes place on HALLOWEEN in the United States, where carved, candlelit pumpkins are displayed in windows and on doorsteps.

SOURCES:
DictDays-1988, p. 92
FolkWrldHol-1999, p. 603
OxYear-1999, p. 394

♦ 2146 ♦ Puppeteers, Festival of
Early July

The art of making and performing with puppets has enjoyed a resurgence in the decades since World War II—particularly in the Czech Republic, where puppet ensembles proliferated after 1945. Every summer since 1951, a nationwide festival of puppeteers has been held in Chrudim. Puppeteers from other countries are often invited to participate in the festival.

In addition to the performances of puppet theaters, there are discussions and seminars on the art of puppetry.

Other international puppet festivals have been held in Barcelona, Spain; Braunschweig, Germany; Bielski-Biala, Poland; Bialystok, Poland; Bochum, Germany; and Washington, D.C.

CONTACTS:
City of Chrudim
The Old Town Hall, The Ressel Sq. 1
Chrudim, 53701 Czech Republic
420-469-645-821; fax: 420-469-645-821
www.chrudim-city.cz/index.asp?ll=en

SOURCES:
IntlThFolk-1979, p. 88

♦ 2147 ♦ Purim
Between February 25 and March 25; Adar 14

Six hundred years before the Christian era, most Jews were slaves in Persia. The Persian prime minister Haman, who generally hated Jews and particularly hated a proud Jew named Mordechai, persuaded King Ahasuerus (Xerxes I) to let him destroy the empire's entire Jewish population. Haman cast lots (*pur* is Akkadian for "lot") to find out which day would be the most auspicious for his evil plan, and the lots told him that things would go especially well on the 14th of Adar. This is why Purim is also called **The Feast of Lots**.

The king did not realize that his own wife, Esther, was Jewish, and that Mordechai was her cousin, until she pleaded with him to spare her people. Haman was hanged, and his position as prime minister was given to Mordechai.

Ahasuerus granted the Jews an extra day to vanquish Haman's supporters, so the rabbis decreed that in Jerusalem and other walled cities, Purim should be celebrated on 15 Adar and called *Purim Shushan*, Hebrew for "Susa," the Persian capital. In leap year, the 14th (or 15th in Jerusalem) Adar is known as *Purim Katan*, "the lesser Purim."

The Old Testament Book of Esther is read aloud in synagogues on the eve and morning of Purim, and listeners drown out every mention of Haman's name by jeering and stamping their feet. Purim is also a time for sharing food with friends and for charity to the poor.

See also PURIMS, SPECIAL

CONTACTS:
Union of Orthodox Jewish Congregations of America
11 Broadway
New York, NY 10004
212-563-4000; fax: 212-564-9058
www.ou.org

Union for Reform Judaism
633 Third Ave.
New York, NY 10017
212-650-4000
www.urj.org

SOURCES:
AmerBkDays-2000, p. 226
BkFest-1937, p. 206
DaysCustFaith-1957, p. 68
DictFolkMyth-1984, p. 477
DictWrldRel-1989, pp. 155, 588
EncyRel-1987, vol. 4, p. 438

FolkAmerHol-1999, p. 112
FolkWrldHol-1999, p. 180
HolSymbols-2009, p. 733
OxYear-1999, p. 727
RelHolCal-2004, p. 57

♦ 2148 ♦ Purims, Special
Various

Just as Jews throughout the world celebrate their escape from the evil plot of the Persian prime minister Haman (*see* PURIM), many individual Jewish communities commemorate their deliverance from specific calamities by observing their own Purims. The **Padua Purim**, for example, observed on 11 Sivan, celebrates Jews' deliverance from a major fire in Padua, Italy, in 1795. The **Baghdad Purim**, observed on 11 Av, celebrates the conquest of Baghdad by the Arabs and the defeat of the Persians. The **Snow Purim**, observed on 24 Tevet, celebrates the major snowstorm in Tunis that caused extensive damage and injury elsewhere but left the Jewish quarter of the city untouched. And the **Hitler Purim**, observed in Casablanca, Morocco, on 2 Kislev, commemorates the city's escape from German domination during World War II.

CONTACTS:
Union of Orthodox Jewish Congregations of America
11 Broadway
New York, NY 10004
212-563-4000; fax: 212-564-9058
www.ou.org

SOURCES:
RelHolCal-2004, p. 57

♦ 2149 ♦ Purple Heart Day
August 7

Purple Heart Day is observed in the United States and commemorates the establishment in 1782 of the Badge of Military Merit, an award created by George Washington to honor soldiers for their distinguished action in battle. The Purple Heart was not used after the Revolutionary War, but was restored in 1932 as an honor for those who have been wounded or killed in battle.

On August 7 throughout the country, local chapters of the Military Order of the Purple Heart sponsor services to remember and honor medal recipients from their communities. Taking place in a variety of locations, including parks, cemeteries, and state capitols, these ceremonies often feature prayers, military music, reminiscences by award recipients, and speeches by government and military officials. In some communities a picnic or potluck follows. Services are also scheduled at the National Purple Heart Hall of Honor in New Windsor, N.Y. The Hall of Honor opened in 2006 and is dedicated to collecting and preserving the stories of those who have earned a Purple Heart medal. It is located on the site of Washington's last encampment and the site where the first modern recipients of the Purple Heart were awarded their medals in 1932.

CONTACTS:
Military Order of the Purple Heart Service Foundation

P.O. Box 49
Annandale, VA 22003
703-354-2140; fax: 703-642-2054
www.purpleheart.org

National Purple Heart Hall of Honor
P.O. Box 207
374 Temple Hill Rd.
Vails Gate, NY 12584-0207
877-284-6667 or 845-561-1765; fax: 845-569-0382
thepurpleheart.com

SOURCES:
PatHols-2006, p. 254

♦ 2150 ♦ Pushkar Mela
October-November; full moon day of Hindu month of Kartika

Pushkar Mela is a camel fair and one of the best known of the Hindu religious fairs of India. It is held at Pushkar, the place where it is said a lotus flower slipped out of Lord Brahma's hands. Water sprang up where the petals fell and created the holy waters of Pushkar Lake. A temple to Brahma on the shore of the lake is one of the few temples in India dedicated to Brahma. Pushkar is in the state of Rajasthan, a vast desert area dotted with oases and populated with wild black camels.

The commercial side of the fair features the sale of about 10,000 camels. Sheep, goats, horses, and donkeys are also sold there. Countless stalls offer such camel accouterments as saddles and blankets embellished with mirrors, bangles, brass utensils, and brass-studded belts. Camel races are a highlight. In the "camel rush" people jump onto camels, and the camel that holds the most people wins a prize.

On the night of the full moon (*Kartika Purnima*), devotees bathe in the waters of the lake and then make offerings of coconut and rice at the Brahma temple.

CONTACTS:
Department of Tourism, Art & Culture, Government of Rajasthan
Govt. Hostel Campus
Paryatan Bhawan, M.I. Rd.
Jaipur, Rajasthan 302 001 India
91-141-5110595; fax: 91-141-5110591
www.rajasthantourism.gov.in

SOURCES:
BkHolWrld-1986, Oct 21
GdWrldFest-1985, p. 112

♦ 2151 ♦ Putrada Ekadashi
July-August; 11th day of waxing half of Hindu month of Sravana

The Hindu EKADASHI, or 11th-day fast known as Putrada Ekadashi, is observed primarily by parents who want to produce a son. A fast is observed, Vishnu is worshipped and meditated upon, and the Brahmans are fed and presented with robes and money. Fasting and piety on this day are believed to ensure the conception of a boy, especially for those who sleep in the same room where Vishnu has been worshipped.

Would-be parents are also expected to observe the Ekadashi that falls in the waning half of the month of Sravana. It is known as **Kamada Ekadashi**, or the Wish-Fulfilling Ekadashi.

SOURCES:
RelHolCal-2004, p. 172

♦ 2152 ♦ **Pythian Games**
Every four years in August

The Pythian Games were ancient Greek games considered next in importance to the OLYMPIC GAMES. From 586 B.C.E.,

they were held every four years on the plain near Delphi. Competitions in instrumental music, singing, drama, and recitations in verse and prose were primary, but there were also athletic and equestrian contests modeled on those at Olympia. The prize was a crown of bay leaves.

See also ISTHMIAN GAMES, NEMEAN GAMES, OLYMPIC GAMES

SOURCES:
DictFolkMyth-1984, p. 67
NewCentClassHandbk-1962, p. 956
OxClassDict-1970, p. 904

Q

♦ 2153 ♦ **Qatar Independence Day**
September 3

This national holiday celebrates Qatar's full independence from Britain on this day in 1971.

CONTACTS:
Embassy of State of Qatar
2555 M St. N.W.
Washington, D.C. 20037
202-274-1600; fax: 202-237-0061
www.qatarembassy.net

SOURCES:
AnnivHol-2000, p. 149

♦ 2154 ♦ **Qiantang River Tidal Bore Watching Festival, International**
18th day of the eighth lunar month

The rare phenomenon known as the tidal bore, in which a tidal wave roars up a river, has always attracted thousands of spectators. Scientists have designated the massive wave that travels up the Qiantang River in China's eastern region the world's largest tidal bore. More than 300,000 people gather for this natural wonder during the autumn full moon, on a day when the gravitational pull on the water is greatest.

Yanguan Town in Haining, Hangzhou, is the best place to watch the tidal event and thus has become the host site of the festival. It coincides with the Mid-Autumn Festival (or Moon Cake Festival), a holiday celebrated throughout the Far East. Festivalgoers in Haining practice the old custom of eating moon cakes, a staple pastry of the Mid-Autumn Festival.

The Qiantang waves have been recorded as high as 30 feet. Some attendees decide to watch from a close distance, which has resulted in drownings during years when the tide is especially strong. One popular safe vantage point is the multi-storied Liuhe Pagoda, an ancient famous structure located near the river.

CONTACTS:
China National Tourist Office
350 Fifth Ave., Ste. 6413
New York, NY 10018

212-760-8218; fax: 212-760-8809
www.cnto.org

♦ 2155 ♦ **Qing Ming Festival (Ching Ming Festival)**
Fourth or fifth day of third lunar month

The Qing Ming Festival is a day for Chinese throughout the world to honor their dead. *Qing Ming* means "clear and bright," and refers to the weather at this time of year. It is a Confucian festival that dates back to the Han Dynasty (206 B.C.E. to 221 C.E.), and it is now a Chinese national holiday. It is computed as 105 days after the Winter Solstice, Tong-ji.

The day is observed in the countryside with visits to ancestral graves to sweep, wash, repair, and paint them. Offerings of food, wine, incense, and flowers are made, firecrackers are set off, and paper money is burned at the graveside, so that the ancestors will have funds to spend in the afterworld. (The Chinese traditional belief is that the afterlife is quite similar to this life, and that the dead live a little below ground in the Yellow Springs region.)

In ancient China, people spent Qing Ming playing Chinese football and flying kites. Today, they picnic and gather for family meals. In the cities, though, it has been changed to a day of patriotism with placement of memorial wreaths only to Chinese revolution heroes in a few state-run public cemeteries.

The day is also called **Cold Food Day** (in Korea, **Han Sik-il**; in Taiwan, **Han Shih**) because, according to an ancient legend, it was taboo to cook the day before.

In Taiwan, yellow paper strips about 3 x 2 inches, are stuck in the ground of the grave, as is shingling. This symbolically maintains the home of one's ancestors. Then the prayers and food offerings are done.

See also Thanh-Minh and Ullambana

CONTACTS:
Hong Kong Tourism Board
115 E. 54th St., Fl. 2
New York, NY 10022
212-421-3382; fax: 212-421-8428
www.discoverhongkong.com

Taiwan Government Information Office
4201 Wisconsin Ave. N.W.
Washington, DC 20016
202-895-1800; fax: 202-362-6144
www.gio.gov.tw

SOURCES:
BkFestHolWrld-1970, p. 87
BkHolWrld-1986, Apr 6
DictFolkMyth-1984, pp. 225, 228, 478, 789
EncyRel-1987, vol. 3, pp. 293, 325
FolkWrldHol-1999, p. 279
HolSymbols-2009, p. 120
OxYear-1999, p. 705
RelHolCal-2004, p. 232

♦ 2156 ♦ **Quadragesima Sunday**
Between February 8 and March 14; first Sunday in Lent in West

The name for the first Sunday in LENT is derived from the Latin word meaning "fortieth." The first Sunday of the Lenten season is 40 days before EASTER. The other "numbered" Sundays, all before Lent, are Quinquagesima ("fiftieth"), Sexagesima ("sixtieth"), and Septuagesima ("seventieth"). These are reckoned by an approximate number of days before Easter; only Quadrigesima is close to the actual count. These names, as well as "Pre-Lent," are no longer used, the calendar now referring to the number of Sundays after EPIPHANY, e.g. first Sunday after Epiphany, second Sunday after Epiphany, and so on until ASH WEDNESDAY, then, first Sunday in Lent.

SOURCES:
DictDays-1988, p. 93
EncyEaster-2002, pp. 19, 349, 350
FestWestEur-1958, p. 8
OxYear-1999, pp. 42, 43, 602, 605, 612
RelHolCal-2004, p. 92
SaintFestCh-1904, p. 97

♦ 2157 ♦ **Quadrilles of San Martin**
November 11

Every year on San Martin's Day (*see* MARTINMAS), the Quadrilles of St. Martin—often described as an "equestrian ballet"—have been held in the old Colombian town named after the saint. Forty-eight expert riders, all male and mounted on Creole horses, divide into four groups and take their places at the four corners of the town's large square.

Each group of riders is dressed to represent a different ethnic group that has played a part in Colombia's past: The Moors (Arabs) wear turbans and white, Oriental-looking robes and carry scimitars; the Spaniards wear black riding jackets, white breeches, tall boots, and cowboy hats and carry sabers; the Blacks wear exotic African headgear and animal skins and carry long machetes; and the Indians wear feather headdresses, breastplates, and elaborate necklaces and are armed with bows and arrows.

The performances reenact various events in Colombia's history, including the battles between the Spanish and the Moors and the wars of independence waged against Spain. Although the acts themselves are carefully staged, they often involve improvisation requiring fast riding and split-second timing.

After the Quadrilles are over, residents and visitors gather in the square's open-air cafes to drink *aguardiente*, the local anise-flavored liquor, to eat *ternara a la llanera*, or barbecued baby beef, and to watch the fireworks displays that are set off over the city. Participation in the Quadrilles is an honor that is handed down from one generation to the next among the city's oldest families.

See also MOORS AND CHRISTIANS FIESTA

CONTACTS:
Embassy of Colombia
2118 Leroy Pl. N.W.
Washington, D.C. 20008
202-387-8338; fax: 202-232-8643
www.colombiaemb.org

SOURCES:
GdWrldFest-1985, p. 65

♦ 2158 ♦ **Quarter Days**
Various

The four traditional quarter days in England, Northern Ireland, and Wales are LADY DAY (March 15), MIDSUMMER DAY (June 24), MICHAELMAS (September 29), and CHRISTMAS Day (December 25). They mark off the four quarters of the year and the times at which rents and other payments are due. It was also customary to move into or out of a house on a quarter day.

In Scotland the quarter days are CANDLEMAS (February 2), PENTECOST (or Whitsunday, the seventh Sunday after Easter), LAMMAS (August 1), and MARTINMAS (November 11).

See also CROSS-QUARTER DAYS

SOURCES:
DictDays-1988, pp. 18, 66, 73, 75, 93, 131
DictFolkMyth-1984, p. 601
FestSaintDays-1915, pp. 163, 166, 204
OxYear-1999, pp. 521, 588
RelHolCal-2004, p. 268

♦ 2159 ♦ **Quartier d'été**
Mid-July to mid-August

From mid-July to mid-August the city of Paris, France, hosts an outdoor arts festival, featuring more than 200 performances and 450 guest artists. Events take place in concert halls, gardens, parks, squares, and alongside the city's monuments. The menu of events includes music, dance, theater, film, and circus performances, as well as storytelling and visual arts exhibits. The festival began in 1990.

CONTACTS:
Paris Convention and Visitors Bureau
25, rue des Pyramides
Paris, 75001 France
33-8-9268-3000; fax: 33-1-4952-5300
en.parisinfo.com

♦ 2160 ♦ Quebec City Festival of Sacred Music
October-November

The Quebec City Festival of Sacred Music includes all musical forms, as long as they are spiritually inspired. This open-minded policy has resulted in festival programs featuring such diverse style as gospel, Negro spirituals, Gregorian chants, Celtic music, and throat singing.

The event's founder, local Quebec City priest Mario Dufour, believed that sacred music was so beautiful and spiritually edifying that a festival should be organized around it. He also envisioned that the music genre could connect with enthusiasts over many religious and linguistic boundaries. His own St. Roch Church was the suggested venue for the inaugural festival held in 1997, which at that time was the first of its kind in North America. The church has hosted the 11-day event ever since.

Over the years, world-renowned international performers have been selected for the program, and the event has become an established part of the Quebec City's cultural calendar.

CONTACTS:
Quebec Festival of Sacred Music
SS20-109
Dalhousie St.
Quebec City, QC G1K 4B9 Canada
www.festivalmusiquesacree.ca

♦ 2161 ♦ Quebec Winter Carnival
Late January to mid-February

Winter carnivals are common throughout Canada, but the celebration of winter that has been held since the mid-1950s in Quebec City ranks among the great carnivals of the world. It begins with the Queen's Ball at the Château Frontenac, a hotel resembling a huge medieval castle in the center of the city, and a parade of illuminated floats.

The International Ice Sculpture Contest, featuring artists from several northern countries, is held at Place Carnaval. More than 40,000 tons of snow are trucked in to construct a large snow castle, which is illuminated at night and which serves as a mock jail for those who fail to remain smiling throughout the celebration. Bonhomme Carnaval, the festival's seven-foot-high snowman mascot dressed in a red cap and traditional sash, roams the streets teasing children and looking for people to lock up in the Ice Palace. The festival drink is caribou, a blend of white alcohol and red wine.

An unusual festival event is the hazardous race of steel-bottomed boats on the semi-frozen St. Lawrence River. Each boat has a team of five, and its members must maneuver around ice floes and occasionally drag their boats over large patches of ice.

An interesting feature of this festival is the way it is financed. A principal source of income for the Carnaval Association is the candle, or "bougie," sale. People who buy the bougies increase the chances that their representative "duchess" (and there are a number of duchesses chosen from all over Quebec) will be selected as Carnaval Queen. They also get a chance to participate in a giant lottery. More than 10,000 people participate in the sale and distribution of candles on "Bougie Night."

CONTACTS:
Carnaval de Quebec
290 rue Joly
Quebec, QC G1L 1N8 Canada
418-626-3716; fax: 418-626-7252
www.carnaval.qc.ca

SOURCES:
FolkWrldHol-1999, p. 138
GdWrldFest-1985, p. 56

♦ 2162 ♦ Quecholli
280th day of the Aztec year; end of 14th month

Mixcoatl was the Aztec god of the chase, also known as the Cloud Serpent. He had deer or rabbit characteristics, was identified with the morning star, and, as one of the four creators of the world, made fire from sticks just before the creation of man. The festival in his honor, known as Quecholli, was observed with a ceremonial hunt. According to the civil cycle of the Aztec calendar—which consisted of 18 months of 20 days each, plus five unlucky days—Quecholli was celebrated at the end of the 14th month. This was also the day on which weapons were made.

SOURCES:
DictFolkMyth-1984, p. 734

♦ 2163 ♦ Queen's Birthday (Thailand)
August 12

Queen's Birthday is a nationwide celebration in Thailand of the birthday of Her Majesty Queen Sirikit (b. 1932). Throughout the country, buildings are decorated to honor the queen, but the most splendid are in Bangkok, where buildings and streets are brilliant with colored lights.

CONTACTS:
Government Public Relations Department
Rama VI Rd.
Soi 30
Bangkok, 10400 Thailand
66-2-618-2373; fax: 66-2-618-2358
thailand.prd.go.th/index.php

SOURCES:
AnnivHol-2000, p. 135

♦ 2164 ♦ Queen's Day (England)
November 17

This is the day on which Queen Elizabeth I ascended to the throne in 1558 upon the death of her sister, Queen Mary I. Often referred to as the Virgin Queen because she never married, Elizabeth reigned for 44 years—a period that came to be known as the Elizabethan Age because it marked England's rise as a major European power in commerce, politics, and the arts.

The anniversary of her coronation was celebrated for more than 300 years after her reign ended, primarily as a holiday for those working in government offices. After the Gunpowder Plot was exposed in 1605, two years following Elizabeth's death, the day was marked by anti-papal demonstrations, which included burning the pope in effigy. **Queen Elizabeth's Day** eventually merged with the celebration of GUY FAWKES DAY.

CONTACTS:
The British Monarchy Official Web Site
Buckingham Palace
London, SW1A 1AA United Kingdom
44-20-7930-4832
www.royal.gov.uk

SOURCES:
AnnivHol-2000, p. 192
DictDays-1988, p. 93
OxYear-1999, p. 466

♦ 2165 ♦ Queenship of Mary
August 22

Mary, the mother of Jesus, was identified with the title of "Queen" at least as early as the 13th century. Artists often depicted her as wearing a crown or being crowned as she was received into heaven. When Pope Pius XII solemnly defined the dogma of the ASSUMPTION of Mary in 1950, he stated that she was raised body and soul to heaven, "to shine resplendent as Queen at the right hand of her Son."

On October 11, 1954, during the Marian year that marked the centenary of the proclamation of the dogma of the IMMACULATE CONCEPTION of Mary, Pope Pius XII established the feast of the Queenship of Mary on May 31. After the Second Vatican Council, the feast (classified as an obligatory memorial) was changed to August 22 so that it would follow the Feast of the Assumption on August 15.

SOURCES:
AnnivHol-2000, p. 140
ChristYr-1991, p. 99

OxYear-1999, p. 342
RelHolCal-2004, p. 99

♦ 2166 ♦ Quintaine, La
Second Sunday in November

St. Leonard, the patron saint of prisoners, is honored each year in the French town of St.-Léonard-de-Noblat by a ceremony in which 30 men carry the *quintaine*, a three-foot-high box painted to resemble a prison, to the church to be blessed. Afterward they mount it on a post and strike it with mallets as they gallop by on horseback. Fragments of the smashed quintaine are said to bring good luck and to make hens lay eggs.

CONTACTS:
Saint-Leonard-de-Noblat Tourism Office
Place du Champs de Mars
Sainte Leonard-de-Noblat, 87400 France
33-5-5556-2506; fax: 33-5-5556-3697
www.tourisme.fr/recherche/e_index.htm

SOURCES:
BkHolWrld-1986, Nov 8

♦ 2167 ♦ Quirinalia
February 17

Quirinus was an ancient Roman deity who closely resembled Mars, the god of war. His name is associated with that of the Quirinal, one of the seven hills on which Rome was built and the site of an ancient Sabine settlement that was the seat of his cult. Eventually Quirinus was identified with Romulus, one of the legendary founders of Rome, and his festival on February 17, the Quirinalia, coincided with the date on which Romulus was believed to have been deified. This festival was also associated with the advent of spring warfare, when the shields and weapons of the army, which had been purified and retired for the winter, were brought out. The temple dedicated to Quirinus on the hill known as the Quirinal was one of the oldest in Rome.

SOURCES:
AmerBkDays-2000, p. 174
DictFolkMyth-1984, p. 916
FestRom-1981, p. 78
OxYear-1999, p. 81

R

◆ 2168 ◆ Räben-Chilbi
Second Saturday in November

Every year on the second Saturday in November, the town of Richterswil, a picturesque town on Lake Zurich in Switzerland, celebrates a holiday named Räben-Chilbi. This holiday centers on a very common vegetable—the turnip.

Räben-Chilbi is the largest turnip festival in Europe. On this day, school classes and clubs prepare for the "Räbeliechtli" procession, for which displays made from carved turnips lit with candles make their way around town. Approximately 26 tons of turnips and 50,000 candles are used each year. This statistic earned the festival a place in the *Guinness Book of Records* in 1998.

The whole town is also decorated for the occasion. The carved turnips are on display in the windows of the homes and buildings along the route. In addition, a wide variety of music and entertainment are part of the celebrations.

CONTACTS:
Switzerland Tourism
Tödistrasse 7
CH-8002
Zurich Switzerland
www.myswitzerland.com

◆ 2169 ◆ Race of the Ceri
May 15

The Race of the Ceri (Candles) held in Gubbio, Umbria, Italy, every May 15 is thought by some to have originated in pre-Christian times because its date coincides with the IDES of May in the pagan calendar, but the better-founded explanation is that it commemorates the city's patron, St. Ubaldo Baldassini (d. 1160). The candles for which the event is named were originally made of wax but are now heavy, tower-like wooden structures reinforced with iron bands. These are taken in procession to the Piazza dei Consoli, where the teams of bearers who carry them pause to rest. Then, upon a signal, the bearers run with the candles up to the top of Mount Ingino, where they are offered to St. Ubaldo, whose feast is observed the following day.

CONTACTS:
Italian Government Tourist Board
630 Fifth Ave., Ste. 1565
New York, NY 10111
212-245-5618; fax: 212-586-9249
www.italiantourism.com

SOURCES:
FestEur-1961, p. 117

◆ 2170 ◆ Race Relations Sunday
Sunday nearest February 12

This day is observed on the Sunday nearest Abraham LINCOLN'S BIRTHDAY because of the role he played in freeing the slaves during the Civil War. Up until 1965 it was sponsored by the National Council of Churches, but since that time, sponsorship has been taken over by individual denominations within the National Council. A number of Roman Catholic groups observe Race Relations Sunday as well, and some Jewish organizations observe it on the preceding Sabbath. Although it was originally conceived in 1924 as an opportunity to focus on improving relations among all races, the longstanding racial conflict between whites and African Americans in the United States has made this the focal point in recent decades.

There are a number of other observances dealing with race relations at this same time in February. The NAACP (National Association for the Advancement of Colored People) was established on Lincoln's Birthday in 1909, and members of this organization combine the observance of Race Relations Sunday with their organization's founding and with the birthday of the black abolitionist and early human rights activist Frederick Douglass on February 7, 1817.

SOURCES:
DaysCustFaith-1957, p. 60

◆ 2171 ◆ Race Unity Day
Second Sunday in June

Race Unity Day is observed worldwide by Baha'is and others with meetings and discussions. The day was begun in 1957 by the Baha'i National Spiritual Assembly in the United States, with the purpose of focusing attention on racial prejudice.

The Baha'is see racism as a major barrier to peace, and teach that there must be universal recognition of the oneness of all humans to achieve peace.

CONTACTS:
Baha'i National Center
1233 Central St.
Evanston, IL 60201
800-228-6483 or 847-869-9039; fax: 847-733-3578
www.us.bahai.org

SOURCES:
AnnivHol-2000, p. 109
ConEncyBahai-2000, p. 286
RelHolCal-2004, p. 155

◆ 2172 ◆ Radha Ashtami
August-September; eighth day of waning half of Hindu month of Bhadrapada

This Hindu holiday celebrates the birth of Radha, who was the mistress of the god Krishna during the period of his life when he lived among the cowherds of Vrindavana. Although she was the wife of another *gopa* (cowherd), she was the best-loved of Krishna's consorts and his constant companion. Some Hindus believe that Radha is a symbol of the human soul drawn to the ineffable god Krishna, or the pure, divine love to which the fickle, human love returns.

Images of Radha are bathed on this day and then dressed and ornamented before being offered food and worship. Hindus bathe in the early morning and fast all day to show their devotion to Radha.

SOURCES:
RelHolCal-2004, p. 175

◆ 2173 ◆ Radunitsa
Ninth day after Eastern Orthodox Easter, which is the first Sunday after the first full moon on or following the vernal equinox

The Slavic peoples of Eastern Europe observe Radunitsa as an Orthodox Christian holiday. This day of remembrance for the dead arrives nine days after Easter. In Belarus, a country that sits on Russia's western border, Radunitsa is a state holiday.

The holiday's origins are not Christian but pagan, thus dating back to ancient times. Many pagan believers of the region once devoted the day to ritual wailing and left gifts of eggs on the graves of the deceased. During the middle ages, churches tried to suppress this tradition's observance, but in subsequent centuries the church adopted the pagan customs into the Easter rites. The dyed eggs left for the dead, for instance, have evolved to symbolize Christ's surfacing from the tomb.

The spirit of Radunitsa is joyful in the midst of mourning. (In Slavic languages, *Radunitsa*and its variations mean "Joy Day.") Believers anticipate that the dead will triumph over

death as Christ did following his crucifixion. Eating paschal (Easter) foods is a popular way to celebrate. Congregations will gather to eat eggs as well as pancakes, grains like *kutya*or *kulichi,* and a type of gingerbread called *prianiki.*

CONTACTS:
Embassy of Belarus
1619 New Hampshire Ave. N.W.
Washington, D.C. 20009
202-986-1604; fax: 202-986-1805
www.belarusembassy.org

Orthodox Church in America
P.O. Box 675
Syosset, NY 11791-0675
516-922-0550; fax: 516-922-0954
www.oca.org

◆ 2174 ◆ RAGBRAI
Last full week in July

A bicycle ride (not race) across the state of Iowa, RAGBRAI is billed as the oldest, longest, and largest bicycle-touring event in the nation and possibly the world. The sponsor from the start has been the *Des Moines Register,* and RAGBRAI stands for **Register's Annual Great Bicycle Ride Across Iowa.** The field is limited to 8,500, and participants are chosen through a drawing.

The ride began in 1973 when Don Kaul, a *Register* columnist who worked out of Washington, D.C., was challenged by another columnist, John Karras, to bicycle across the state to learn about Iowa. The challenge was accepted, and both decided to ride. Karras wrote an article telling about the plan and inviting readers to go along: at the start of the race, there were 300 riders, and 115 rode the distance. One of these was 83-year-old Clarence Pickard, who rode a woman's bike from border to border.

The ride was intended as a one-time event, but interest was such that it continued the next year, and the next, when it got the RAGBRAI name. The route is different each year but always runs from west to east. Distances average 471 miles; the longest was the 540 miles of RAGBRAI XIII in 1985. According to tradition, riders dip their rear tires in the Missouri River at the start of the tour and seven days later dip their front tires in the Mississippi River when they finish. Multi-day touring rides have been organized in other states since RAGBRAI started.

CONTACTS:
RAGBRAI
715 Locust St.
P.O. Box 622
Des Moines, IA 50303
800-474-3342 or 515-284-8282; fax: 515-284-8138
www.ragbrai.org

SOURCES:
AnnivHol-2000, p. 127

◆ 2175 ◆ Raid on Redding Ridge
First weekend in June

Held at Putnam Memorial State Park, reenactors portray the British invasion of Connecticut in 1777. Other activities include encampments of both British and American soldiers, artillery demonstrations, infantry drills, and crafts of the Revolutionary period. Spectators are kept a safe distance away, but they are encouraged to observe and ask questions.

CONTACTS:
Putnam Memorial State Park
Rte. 58
Redding, CT 06896
203-938-2285
www.putnampark.org

♦ 2176 ♦ **Rainforest World Music Festival**
July/August

Musicians and music enthusiasts from all over the world gather on the large island of Borneo, Malaysia, to celebrate indigenous culture and artistic diversity at the Rainforest World Music Festival. This three-day event features a diverse group of performers hailing from various islands of the Malaysian archipelago, neighboring countries of Southeast Asia, and around the world.

The festival is organized by the Malaysia Tourist Board and takes place at the Sarawak Cultural Village, an ethnic-themed park situated in Borneo's jungle. Since 1997, the program has featured a balance of cultural education and entertaining performances. Both the festival and the village attract tourists who are engaged in indigenous customs and expressions and may already be familiar with such exotic instruments as the boat lute, jaw harp, and nose flute.

Over the years events have been organized in conjunction with the music festival, including the Folk Art Forum, which addresses issues of cultural exchange and economic sustainability for folk artists, and the Rainforest World Craft Bazaar, inaugurated in 2008 as an opportunity for indigenous peoples to sell their wares and demonstrate their various skills as craftspeople.

CONTACTS:
Sarawak Tourism Board
6th & 7th Fl.
Yayasan Sarawak Bldg.
Jalan Masjid
Kuching, Sarawak 93400 Malaysia
www.sarawaktourism.com

♦ 2177 ♦ **Raksha Bandhan**
July-August; full moon day of Hindu month of Sravana

This day, sometimes also referred to as **Brother and Sister Day**, is celebrated in some parts of India by brothers and sisters to reaffirm their bonds of affection, as well as to perform a ritual of protection. A sister ties a bracelet, made of colorful threads and amulets, called a *rakhi* on her brother's wrists. The brother in turn may give his sister gifts—a piece of jewelry or money—while promising to protect her.

In Nepal it is a festival for both Hindus and Buddhists, for which they may even attend each others' temples. The Brahmins put the golden threads around everyone's wrist; it is worn until DEWALI.

CONTACTS:
Ministry of Tourism, Government of India
Rm. No 123, Transport Bhawan, No. 1, Parliament St.
New Delhi, Delhi 110 001 India
91-11-23715084; fax: 91-11-23715084
www.tourisminindia.com

SOURCES:
BkFest-1937, p. 159
BkHolWrld-1986, Nov 3
EncyRel-1987, vol. 6, p. 362; vol. 15, p. 480
FolkWrldHol-1999, p. 466
RelHolCal-2004, p. 172

♦ 2178 ♦ **Rally Day**
Late September or early October

In liturgical Protestant churches, Rally Day marks the beginning of the church calendar year. It typically occurs at the end of September or the beginning of October. Although not all Protestant churches observe this day, the customs associated with it include giving Bibles to children, promoting children from one Sunday school grade to the next, welcoming new members into the church, and making a formal presentation of church goals for the coming year.

SOURCES:
RelHolCal-2004, p. 101

♦ 2179 ♦ **Ram Roasting Fair**
May-June; Tuesday after Pentecost

The town of Kingsteignton in Devonshire, England, observes an annual custom every year on Whit-Tuesday (*see* WHIT-MONDAY) that is said to date back to pre-Christian times, when the village suffered from lack of water. The people prayed to their gods for help, and almost immediately a new spring rose in a meadow nearby. The spring, known as Fair Water, never ran dry, even during the hottest of summers. A live ram was slaughtered as a thanksgiving offering.

After Christianity arrived in Devonshire, a live lamb was carried through the streets on Whit-Monday in a cart covered with lilacs and laburnum, and everyone who met it was asked to contribute something toward the cost of the next day's ceremony. On Tuesday, the ram was killed and roasted whole, and slices of the meat were sold cheaply to the poor.

Today, the people of Kingsteignton still observe the annual ram roasting—usually a deer roasting, because rams are more costly and harder to come by. Local butchers in long white coats turn the spit over a huge log fire, while the crowds amuse themselves with sports and MAY DAY festivities. In the evening, the deer is cut up and distributed to the holders of lucky numbers, since there is not enough meat for everyone.

CONTACTS:
Visit Britain
551 Fifth Ave., Ste. 701
New York, NY 10176
800-462-2748 or 212-850-0330; fax: 212-986-1188
www.visitbritain.com

SOURCES:
EngCustUse-1941, p. 8
YrbookEngFest-1954, p. 241
YrFest-1972, p. 40

♦ 2180 ♦ **Rama Leela Festival**
September-October; near the 10th day of waxing half of Hindu month of Asvina

The Hindu festival of Dussehra (*see* DURGA PUJA), observed on the 10th day of the waxing half of Asvina, celebrates the victory of the legendary hero Rama over the demon Ravana. The Rama Leela (or Ramalila) is a cycle of pageant plays based on the Hindu epic, *Ramayana,* which details the life and heroic deeds of Rama. Around the time of Dussehra, therefore, the Rama Leela is performed in towns and cities through northern India—most notably at Agra, Allahabad, Rama Nagar, and Varanasi. The performances last between seven and 31 days, during which the *Ramayana* is constantly recited to the accompaniment of music.

Perhaps the most important of these performances takes place for 31 days in Rama Nagar, where the scenes are enacted at various set locales in the form of processions depicting various scenes from the *Ramayana.*

CONTACTS:
Directorate of Tourism, Uttar Pradesh
Rajarshi Purshottam Das Tandon Paryatan Bhavan
C-13, Vipin Khand, Gomti Nagar
Lucknow, Uttar Pradesh C-13 India
91-522-2308916; fax: 91-522-2308937
www.up-tourism.com

SOURCES:
IntlThFolk-1979, p. 216
RelHolCal-2004, p. 176

♦ 2181 ♦ **Ramadan**
Ninth month of the Islamic year

The month of Ramadan traditionally begins with the actual sighting of the new moon, marking the start of the ninth month in the Islamic lunar calendar. Authorities in Saudi Arabia are relied upon for this official sighting. With the exception of children, the sick, and the very old, devout Muslims abstain from food, drink, smoking, sex, and gambling from sunrise to sunset during this period.

This holiest season in the Islamic year commemorates the time when the Qur'an, the Islamic holy book, is said to have been revealed to Muhammad. This occurred on LAYLAT AL-QADR, one of the last 10 nights of the month. Fasting during the month of Ramadan is one of the Five Pillars (fundamental religious duties) of Islam. It is a time for self-examination and increased religious devotion—similar to the Jewish period from ROSH HASHANAH to YOM KIPPUR and the Christian LENT.

Many West Africans have a two-day carnival, similar to SHROVE TUESDAY, before Ramadan starts.

Because it is based on the Islamic lunar calendar, which does not use intercalated days to stay aligned with the solar calendar's seasons, Ramadan moves through the year, occurring in each of the seasons over time.

The **Fast of Ramadan** ends when the new moon is again sighted and the new lunar month begins. It is followed by the ID AL-FITR, Festival of Breaking Fast, which lasts for three days and is marked by feasting and the exchange of gifts.

SOURCES:
AmerBkDays-2000, p. 870
AnnivHol-2000, p. 234
BkFest-1937, p. 238
BkFestHolWrld-1970, pp. 80, 112
BkHolWrld-1986, May 29
ConEncyIslam-1991, p. 329
DictDays-1988, p. 94
DictWrldRel-1989, pp. 65, 365, 597, 661
FolkWrldHol-1999, p. 668
HolSymbols-2009, p. 752
OxYear-1999, p. 733
RelHolCal-2004, p. 147
UndIslam-2004, pp. 297, 315

♦ 2182 ♦ **Ramanavami (Ram Navami)**
March-April; ninth day of waxing half of Hindu month of Caitra

The Hindu festival of Ramanavami celebrates the birth of Rama, who was the first son of King Dasaratha of Ayodhya. According to Hindu belief, the god Vishnu was incarnated in 10 different human forms, of which Rama was the seventh. He and his wife, Sita, are venerated by Hindus as the ideal man and wife. Because Rama is the hero of the great religious epic poem, the *Ramayana,* Hindus observe his birthday by reciting stories from it. They also flock to temples, such as that in Ayodhya in Uttar Pradesh, where the image of Rama is enshrined, and chant prayers, repeating his name as they strive to free themselves from the cycle of birth and death.

CONTACTS:
Directorate of Tourism, Uttar Pradesh
Rajarshi Purshottam Das Tandon Paryatan Bhavan
C-13, Vipin Khand, Gomti Nagar
Lucknow, Uttar Pradesh C-13 India
91-522-2308916; fax: 91-522-2308937
www.up-tourism.com

SOURCES:
BkFest-1937, p. 164
BkHolWrld-1986, Apr 18
DictFolkMyth-1984, p. 923
DictWrldRel-1989, pp. 304, 597
FolkWrldHol-1999, p. 260
RelHolCal-2004, p. 185

♦ 2183 ♦ **Ramayana Ballet**
Full moon nights from May to October

The most spectacular dance-drama on the island of Java, Indonesia, is held on an open-air stage at the Prambanan Temple near Yogyakarta. The ballet is a contemporary abbreviated version of the Hindu epic, the *Ramayana*, unfolding over the four nights to tell the story of Prince Rama banished from his country to wander for years in the wilderness. More than 100 dancers and players in *gamelans* (percussive orchestras) present spectacles of monkey armies, giants on stilts, and clashing battles. The rich carvings—lions and *Ramayana* scenes—of the Prambanan temple complex in the background are spotlighted by the moon.

CONTACTS:
Yogyakarta Tourist Information Centre
Tourist Information Center, Jl. Malioboro 14
Yogyakarta, 55213 Indonesia
62-274-62811

SOURCES:
GdWrldFest-1985, p. 113
IntlThFolk-1979, p. 225

♦ 2184 ♦ **Rand Show**
March-April; during the Easter season

Also known as the **Rand Easter Show**, the Rand Show was founded in 1895. This South African industrial, commercial, and agricultural show is similar to what a huge state fair is like in the United States. The Rand Show was sponsored by the Witwatersrand Agricultural Society, but has been owned by Kagiso Media since 1999. It is considered to be the most important event of its kind in South Africa. It features agricultural, industrial, and livestock exhibitions, equestrian shows, live entertainment, and an amusement park. The most popular feature is the consumer goods display. Hundreds of thousands of people attend the Rand Show each year, which is held at the Expo Centre in Johannesburg.

CONTACTS:
Kagiso Exhibitions & Events
1st Fl., Block D, Crownwood Office Pk.
P.O. Box X383
Johannesburg, South Africa
27-11-661-4000; fax: 27-11-496-3880
www.randshow.co.za

SOURCES:
GdWrldFest-1985, p. 160

♦ 2185 ♦ **Rara (Ra-Ra)**
February-April; weekends in Lent

In Haiti the celebration of CARNIVAL is known as Rara for the groups of people who come down from the hills to dance in processions on the weekends throughout LENT and particularly during EASTER week. It begins by calling on Legba, who appears as Carrefour, the guardian of thresholds and crossroads.

Each Rara band consists of a musical group, a band chief, a queen with attendants, a women's choir, and vendors selling food. The group's leader often dresses like a jester and twirls

a long baton known as a *jonc*. On SHROVE TUESDAY night, the Rara bands perform a Bruler Carnival in which they carry out the ritual burning of various carnival objects then make a cross on their forehead with the ashes. Rara has deep ties with Voodoo and its resemblance to other Carnival celebrations is largely superficial.

See also CARNIVAL LAMAYOTE

CONTACTS:
Embassy of the Republic of Haiti
2311 Massachusetts Ave. N.W.
Washington, D.C. 20008
202-332-4090; fax: 202-745-7215
www.haiti.org

SOURCES:
BkHolWrld-1986, Apr 9
FestWrld: Haiti-1999, p. 11
FolkWrldHol-1999, p. 139
RelHolCal-2004, p. 284

♦ 2186 ♦ **Rasa Leela Festival**
August-September; Hindu month ofBhadrapada

JANMASHTAMI is the birthday of Krishna, the eighth incarnation of the Hindu god Vishnu, which is observed on the new moon day of the month of Bhadrapada. In the city of Mathura in Uttar Pradesh, an important center of Indian art and the birthplace of Krishna, a month-long festival is held during Bhadrapada. The Rasa Leela play cycle, a traditional operatic ballet based on the Krishna legend, is performed throughout the month. In other Indian cities, such as Manipur, the festival has been shortened. The Rasa Leela (or Ras-Lila) Festival takes its name from the *ras*, or dance, of Krishna, the divine flute-player, and his consort, Radha.

CONTACTS:
Directorate of Tourism, Uttar Pradesh
Rajarshi Purshottam Das Tandon Paryatan Bhavan
C-13, Vipin Khand, Gomti Nagar
Lucknow, Uttar Pradesh C-13 India
91-522-2308916; fax: 91-522-2308937
www.up-tourism.com

SOURCES:
DictFolkMyth-1984, p. 924
EncyRel-1987, vol. 4, p. 455

♦ 2187 ♦ **Rath Yatra**
June-July; second day of waxing half of Hindu month of Asadha

Rath Yatra is an outpouring of tens of thousands of pilgrims to honor Jagannath, Lord of the Universe, in Puri in the state of Orissa, India. Jagannath, worshipped primarily in Orissa, is a form of Krishna (though the term applies also to Vishnu), and the Jagannath Temple in Puri is one of the largest Hindu temples in the country.

During the festival, wooden images of Jagannath, his brother, Balbhadra, and his sister, Subhadra, are taken in procession in three huge chariots or carts that look like temples and are called *raths*. They go from the Jagannath Temple to be bathed at Gundicha Mandir, a temple about a mile away; the gods are installed there for a week before being brought back to the Jagannath Temple. This is such a popular festival because all castes are considered equal, and everyone has to eat the food prepared by low caste men at the shrine.

The main chariot has a striped yellow-and-orange canopy 45 feet high with 16 wheels, each seven feet in diameter. It is occupied by scores of riders and pulled by thousands of devotees. Because the moving chariot becomes an inexorable force that could crush anything in its path, the name of the god entered the English language as "**Juggernaut**."

The festival is also known as the **Jagannath Festival**, or **Car Festival**. Others are held in Varanasi, Uttar Pradesh State, in Mahesh, a suburb of Calcutta, West Bengal State, and other areas, but the most impressive Rath Yatra is at Puri.

CONTACTS:
Department of Tourism, Government of Orissa
Paryatan Bhawan, Museum Campus
Bhubaneswar, Orissa 751 014 India
91-674-2432177; fax: 91-674-430887
www.orissatourism.gov.in

SOURCES:
BkHolWrld-1986, Jul 12
DictFolkMyth-1984, p. 537
DictWrldRel-1989, pp. 304, 368
RelHolCal-2004, p. 170

♦ 2188 ♦ **Ratification Day**
January 14

Most people associate the end of the Revolutionary War with the surrender of Lord Cornwallis at YORKTOWN, Virginia, in 1781. But it was almost two years later that the Treaty of Paris was signed. It then had to be ratified by the Continental Congress and returned to England within six months. As members of the Congress arrived in Annapolis, Maryland, to ratify the treaty, it became apparent that they needed delegates from two more states to constitute a quorum. With prodding from Thomas JEFFERSON, the delegates from Connecticut finally arrived, and South Carolina Congressman Richard Beresford was dragged from his sickbed in a Philadelphia hotel room. Once everyone was assembled, the treaty was quickly ratified on January 14, 1784, and the American Revolution was officially ended. But it was still too late to get it back to England by the March deadline, since an ocean crossing took at least two months. Fortunately, Britain was willing to forgive the delay.

The Old Senate Chamber in Maryland's historic State House at Annapolis has been preserved exactly as it was when the ratification took place. On January 14, the same type of flag that was displayed in 1784—with 12 stars in a circle and the 13th in the center—flies over the State House and many other buildings in Annapolis. The ceremony that takes place inside varies from year to year, but it often revolves around a particular aspect of the original event. One year, for example, the original Treaty of Paris was put on display in the rotunda.

CONTACTS:
Library of Congress
101 Independence Ave. S.E.
Washington, D.C. 20540
202-707-5000; fax: 202-707-2076
www.loc.gov

SOURCES:
AnnivHol-2000, p. 9

♦ 2189 ♦ **Rato (Red) Machhendranath**
April-May; Hindu month of Vaisakha

The chariot procession known as Rato (Red) Machhendranath is the biggest event in Patan, Nepal. The festival honors Machhendranath, the god of rain and plenty, who is worshipped by both Hindus and Buddhists in different incarnations, and has shrines at both Patan and in the village of Bungamati, a few miles south of Patan. The festival, held when the monsoon season is approaching, is a plea for plentiful rain.

The image of the god, a carved piece of red-painted wood, is taken from the shrine in the Pulchowk area at the start of the festivities and paraded around the city in several stages on a wheeled chariot. The chariot is a huge wooden wagon that is towed by hundreds of devotees. Finally, after a month of being hauled about, the chariot is dismantled, and the image is conveyed to Bungamati to spend six months at the temple there.

A similar but shorter festival, the Sweta (or White) Machhendranath, is held in Kathmandu in March or April. The image of the god is taken from the temple at Kel Tole, placed on a chariot and pulled from one historic location to another. When it arrives in the south of the city, the chariot is taken apart, and the image is returned to its starting place.

CONTACTS:
Nepal Tourism Board, Tourist Service Center
Bhrikuti Mandap
P.O. Box 11018
Kathmandu, Nepal
977-1-4256909; fax: 977-1-4256910
www.welcomenepal.com

SOURCES:
GdWrldFest-1985, p. 138

♦ 2190 ♦ **Rat's Wedding Day**
19th day of first lunar month

The Rat's Wedding Day is observed in some Chinese households on the 19th day of the first lunar month. It is customary to go to bed early so that the rats have plenty of time to enjoy themselves. Food is left out for them in the hope that it will dissuade the more ravenous rodents from disturbing the householder's kitchen. If a very large rat takes up residence in a house, it is regarded as the "Money Rat" and is treated well on this day, for its arrival indicates that the householder will prosper.

SOURCES:
FolkWrldHol-1999, p. 97
OxYear-1999, p. 700

♦ 2191 ♦ **Ravello Music Festival**
Mid-July

When German composer Richard Wagner (1813-1883) visited the famous Villa Rufolo in 1880 in Ravello, Italy, he was so impressed by its beauty that he used it as the setting for *Parsifal*, his final opera. Fifty years after his death, the residents of Ravello held a commemorative concert at the Villa, and 20 years later, in 1953, another commemorative concert of Wagnerian music was given. Since then the concerts have been held annually. They last about a week and focus entirely on music composed by Wagner, by composers who influenced (or were influenced by) him, and by composers with whom he had some connection. Most take place in the gardens of the 13th-century Villa Rufolo, the church of Santa Maria Gradillo, and the park, with its view of the Bay of Naples.

See also BAYREUTH FESTIVAL and PACIFIC NORTHWEST FESTIVAL

CONTACTS:
Ravello Concert Society
Via Trinita, 3
Ravello, Salerno 84010 Italy
39-89-858-149; fax: 39-89-8582-49
www.ravelloarts.org

SOURCES:
MusFestEurBrit-1980, p. 116

♦ 2192 ♦ **Ravinia Festival**
June-September

Chicago's 12-week festival of classical music, theater, and dance takes place in Highland Park, one of the city's northern suburbs. Although today the festival can boast performances by some of the world's most distinguished conductors, soloists, symphony orchestras, and dance companies, its history since 1904 has been punctuated by periodic financial crises and, in the 1940s, a fire that destroyed the Ravinia Park pavilion. But since that time the festival has rebounded, expanding to include pop, jazz, and folk music as well as several weeks of theater performances. Nearly half a million people attend the festival each year.

CONTACTS:
Ravinia Festival
P.O. Box 896
Highland Park, IL 60035
847-266-5100; fax: 847-266-0641
www.ravinia.org

SOURCES:
GdUSFest-1984, p. 48
MusFestAmer-1990, p. 56
MusFestWrld-1963, p. 292

♦ 2193 ♦ **Reconciliation, Day of**
December 16

The South African legal holiday known as the Day of Reconciliation was established on December 16, 1838, in commemoration of the victory of the Voortrekkers over Dingane (also spelled Dingaan) and the Zulus. It was formerly called Day of the Covenant. The "covenant" it refers to is the vow that Andries Pretorius (1798-1853) and the Voortrekkers made with God as they prepared for the Battle of Blood River: that if they were victorious, the day would be observed as a Sabbath and a church would be built in gratitude.

The original name for this holiday was **Dingaan's Day**. Then it was called **Day of the Vow** during apartheid. After South Africa renounced apartheid and held its first democratic election in 1994, the day remained a legal holiday but acquired a new name to reflect its new focus—promoting national unity and healing.

CONTACTS:
South African Government Online
Information Centre
Private Bag X745
Pretoria, 0001 South Africa
www.gov.za

Truth and Reconciliation Commission
Old Mutual Bldg., 9th Fl.
106 Adderley St.
Cape Town, 8001 South Africa
27-21-424-5161; fax: 27-21-424-5225
www.truth.org.za

SOURCES:
AnnivHol-2000, p. 209
DictDays-1988, p. 28

♦ 2194 ♦ **Reconciliation Week, National**
May 27-June 3

Australia sets aside the week between May 27 and June 3 to honor the culture and history of its Aborigines and Torres Strait Islanders and to promote reconciliation and forgiveness for the treatment that these indigenous peoples have suffered at the hands of white Australians. Since it was first held in 1996, National Reconciliation Week has featured various activities designed to promote understanding between indigenous and non-indigenous Australians, such as the People's Walk for Reconciliation across the Sydney Harbor Bridge in 2000.

The starting and ending dates of the commemoration are important anniversaries: On May 27, 1967, 90 percent of Australians voted to eliminate parts of their country's constitution that were discriminatory against indigenous Australians, and on June 3, 1992, the High Court of Australia ruled on the Eddie Mabo case, acknowledging the rights of indigenous Australians by rejecting the idea that Australia had been uninhabited until the first British settlers arrived.

Since 1998, this week-long celebration has encompassed National Sorry Day on May 28. An inquiry into the forcible removal of Aboriginal and Torres Strait Island children from their families led to a recommendation that a formal day of apology be declared, offering the community an opportunity to get involved in activities acknowledging the impact of the policy of forcible removal on these people. Australians are encouraged to sign local "Sorry Books" or to register their apologies electronically.

CONTACTS:
Australia's Culture and Recreation Portal
Department of Environment, Water, Heritage and the Arts,
 Australian Government
P.O. Box 787
Canberra, ACT 2601 Australia
61-2-6271-1000; fax: 61-2-6271-1901
www.acn.net.au

Reconciliation Australia
Old Parliament House
King George Terr.
Parkes, ACT 2600 Australia
61-2-6273-9200; fax: 61-2-6273-9201
www.reconciliation.org.au

♦ 2195 ♦ **Red Earth Native American Cultural Festival**
Second weekend in June

One of the largest such events in the country, the Red Earth Native American Cultural Festival is held in Oklahoma City and draws participants from more than 150 American Indian tribes. The three-day festival features arts and crafts, dancing, and parades.

The name Oklahoma means "red people," being derived from two Choctaw words, *okla*, meaning "people," and *humma*, meaning "red." There are 35 tribes with tribal councils now living in Oklahoma. Their population is more than 175,000, the second largest of any state in the nation.

CONTACTS:
Red Earth Inc.
2100 N.W. 52nd St.
Oklahoma City, OK 73111
405-427-5228; fax: 405-427-8079
www.redearth.org

♦ 2196 ♦ **Red Flannel Festival**
First Saturday of October

During a cold winter in 1936, flannel shirt merchants in Cedar Springs, Mich., stumbled upon an opportunity to boost the sales of their warm garments. In response to an editorial written by Cedar Springs' local press, a national news story showed appreciation for red flannel longjohns. The welcome press helped elicit numerous orders from all over the country, and the town's subsequent windfall gave birth to a celebration of local industry known as the Red Flannel Festival, first held in 1939.

With the closure of the Red Flannel Factory in 1994, the fates of the local business and the festival were in jeopardy. But local business women kept red flannel production going, and dedicated volunteers managed to preserve the festival tradition.

The event, also called **Red Festival Day**, has its share of distinctive traditions. Scheer's Lumberjack Show celebrates Michigan's lumber legacy, featuring demonstrations by real lumberjacks who chop wood, speed-climb trees, and throw axes. The Keystope Kops, the icon of the festival, circulate the crowd to "arrest" offenders who do not wear the obligatory red.

Other festivities include a Prince and Princess Contest, a grand parade, a 5K run and walk, and a window decorating contest, in which contestants conjure up their best red flannel displays. Two other established traditions, the Horseshow Throwing Contest and the Red Flannel Queen Scholarship Pageant, date back to the inaugural festival.

CONTACTS:
Red Flannel Festival
21 E. Maple St.
P.O. Box 43
Cedar Springs, MI 49319
616-696-2662
www.redflannelday.com

♦ 2197 ♦ **Red Waistcoat Festival**
First or second weekend in July

The **Festa do Colete Encarnado**, or Red Waistcoat Festival, celebrates the *campionos*—the cowboys who watch over the bulls in the pasturelands of the Ribatejo in Portugal, and who traditionally wear red vests, green stocking caps, blue or black trousers, and red sashes. Supposedly the best bulls for bullfighting are those that have been allowed to roam freely in the vast, rich pastures for which this part of the country is famous, and bullfights play a big part in the festival. But unlike bullfighting elsewhere, no one gets hurt and it's against Portuguese law to kill the bull.

A highlight of the festival is the traditional running of the bulls through the streets of Vila Franca de Xira, which is about 20 miles from Lisbon. In addition to bullfighting, there are folk dances, fireworks, and various competitions for the campionos, including the Ribatejan fandango, a competitive dance for men only.

CONTACTS:
Portuguese National Tourist Office
590 Fifth Ave., 4th Fl.
New York, NY 10036
800-767-8842 or 212-354-4403; fax: 212-764-6137
www.visitportugal.com

SOURCES:
FestWestEur-1958, p. 180
GdWrldFest-1985, p. 156
IntlThFolk-1979, p. 314

♦ 2198 ♦ **Redentore, Festa del**
Third Sunday in July

Festa del Redentore, or **Feast of the Redeemer**, is celebrated in Venice, Italy—one of only two remaining provincial religious festivals surviving in Venice. (The other is at the church of the Salute on the Grand Canal, which commemorates deliverance from the plague, but is more religious in nature.)

It also marks the end of the plague in the late 16th century, when the people of Venice dedicated a church on Guidecca Island to Jesus the Redeemer and vowed to visit it every year. They continue to keep their promise by building a bridge of boats across the Guidecca and Grand canals, across which worshippers can walk back and forth during the celebration.

At dawn, the boats all go out to the Lido to watch the sun rise over the Adriatic Sea. During the festival the cafes, shops, canals, and the church are decorated with lights. When the bridge of boats closes at around nine o'clock, a fireworks display begins.

Services inside the Church of the Redentore, which include masses commemorating the redeeming power of Jesus, are quite solemn in comparison to what is going on outside—a festival that has been described as the "Venetian Bacchanal."

CONTACTS:
Italian Government Tourist Board
630 Fifth Ave., Ste. 1565
New York, NY 10111
212-245-5618; fax: 212-586-9249
www.italiantourism.com

SOURCES:
BkHolWrld-1986, Jul 19
GdWrldFest-1985, p. 120

♦ 2199 ♦ **Reed Dance**
Late August or early September

The Reed Dance is the culmination of a week-long coming-of-age ceremony for young girls in Swaziland. They gather in the royal city of Lobamba and spend several days along the riverbank gathering reeds for the Queen Mother. They use the reeds to rebuild the screens that surround the Queen Mother's *kraal*, or enclosure. The Reed Dance is performed for the Queen Mother near the end of the ceremony, when the girls, dressed in bead skirts and beautiful jewelry, perform complicated steps done in perfect time, tossing reeds high into the air. Since the Reed Dance, also known as **Umhlanga**, is not a sacred ceremony, visitors are welcome to watch.

CONTACTS:
Swaziland Ministry of Tourism
Income Tax Bldg., 2nd Fl.
P.O. Box 2652
Mbabane, Swaziland
268-404-4556; fax: 268-404-5415
www.gov.sz

SOURCES:
BkHolWrld-1986, Aug 21
FolkWrldHol-1999, p. 501

♦ 2200 ♦ **Reek Sunday**
Last Sunday in July

In County Mayo, thousands of pilgrims climb Croagh Patrick on the last Sunday in July to pray on the spot where Ireland's patron saint, St. Patrick, is believed to have started his ministry. Those wishing to maximize the arduousness of the journey ascend the 2,510-foot mountain, known locally as the Reek, in bare feet and at night. The traditional time to begin the ascent is midnight and the climb takes about three hours. There are stopping points along the way where pilgrims pray before continuing. Many visit the small chapel at the top where masses are celebrated.

Croagh Patrick has been a pilgrimage site since at least the 12th century and possibly as far back as the seventh century.

See also Crom Dubh Sunday

CONTACTS:
Westport Tourist Office
The Mall
James St.
Westport, County Mayo Ireland
353-98-25711; fax: 353-98-26709
www.visitmayo.com

Croagh Patrick Information Centre
Teach na Miasa
Murrisk, County Mayo Ireland
353-98-64114; fax: 353-98-64115
www.croagh-patrick.com

SOURCES:
FolkWrldHol-1999, p. 485
RelHolCal-2004, p. 99

♦ 2201 ♦ **Reformation Day**
October 31

When Martin Luther (1483-1546), a German monk and religious reformer, nailed his 95 "theses" (or propositions) to the church door in Wittenberg on October 31, 1517, his only intention was to voice his opinions about certain practices and customs in the Roman Catholic Church, in the hope that someone would engage him in a public debate.

Instead, so many people agreed with his ideas that they spread throughout western Europe and touched off a religious revolt known as the Reformation. As a result, many Christians broke their centuries-old connection with the Roman Catholic Church and established independent churches of their own, prime among them being the Lutheran Church.

October 31 is observed by most Protestant denominations as Reformation Day, and the preceding Sunday is known as **Reformation Sunday**. In Germany, the day is sometimes referred to as **Luther's Theses Day**.

See also Martinsfest

CONTACTS:
Concordia Theological Seminary
6600 N. Clinton St.
Fort Wayne, IN 46825
260-452-2100; fax: 260-452-2121
www.ctsfw.edu

SOURCES:
BkFest-1937, p. 106
DaysCustFaith-1957, p. 277
DictWrldRel-1989, p. 606
OxYear-1999, p. 434
RelHolCal-2004, p. 105

♦ 2202 ♦ **Regatta of the Great Maritime Republics**
Late May

The great maritime republics of Italy for which this event is named are Pisa, Genoa, Amalfi, and Venice. Although they no longer enjoy the wealth and power of medieval days, since 1956 the four cities have commemorated their former greatness with a friendly battle to rule the seas. The location rotates among the cities each year. Before the regatta begins, there is an elaborate parade with people dressed in period costume. Then the longboats—which were blessed by then Bishop Angelo Roncalli before he became Pope John XXIII—decorated to represent each of the republics take off on a 2,000-meter race.

CONTACTS:
Municipality of Pisa
Tourism Office, Via C. Cammeo 2
Pisa, 56100 Italy
39-50-8302-53; fax: 39-50-8302-43
www.comune.pisa.it/english

♦ 2203 ♦ **Reggae Sumfest**
July

The largest reggae event in the world, Reggae Sumfest, takes place each July in Montego Bay, Jamaica. The annual festival features the world's best-known reggae performers as well as salespeople hawking such island specialties as curried goat, bammy and fish, sugarcane, and jelly coconut. This is one of the world's premier musical events, attracting up to 50,000 people.

Reggae originated as the music of the Jamaican poor, reflecting social discontent and the Rastafarian movement. Jamaican-born reggae star Bob Marley, who died of brain cancer at the age of 36, transformed the island-bred music into an international craze. He is venerated in Jamaica much as ELVIS Presley is in the United States, and his former house and studio in Kingston, called Tuff Gong, is still a center for some of the more serious reggae music being produced today.

CONTACTS:
Summerfest Productions
Montego Bay, Ste. 1,
P.O. Box 1178
St. James, Jamaica
876-953-2933; fax: 876-953-8295
www.reggaesumfest.com

♦ 2204 ♦ **Reindeer Driving Competition**
Late March

The Sami people who live in the northern parts of the Scandinavian countries round up their herds of reindeer between December and March every year to count, sort, slaughter, and mark their animals in much the same way that cattle and sheep are rounded up in the United States and elsewhere. Round-ups usually last from one to three days and often include athletic competitions. In late March in Inari, Finland, men and women compete on cross-country skis as they try to herd 100 reindeer over a 3¼-mile course. The fastest time wins the competition.

CONTACTS:
Northern Lapland Tourism
Saariselante 1

Saariselka, 99830 Finland
358-16-6684-02; fax: 358-16-6684-03
www.saariselka.fi/index.php?la=en

SOURCES:
BkHolWrld-1986, Mar 15

♦ 2205 ♦ **Repudiation Day**
November 23

The Stamp Act of 1765 forced the American colonies to pay a tax on various official documents and publications, such as legal papers, liquor permits, lawyers' licenses, and school diplomas. The tax on newspapers and pamphlets was particularly burdensome, as it was based on the number of printed sheets and advertisements in each publication. The tax had to be paid in British pounds sterling, which made it even more expensive. In defiance of the new law, the court of Frederick County, Maryland, declared that it would carry on its business without the tax stamps required by the Act. In March 1766, the Act was rescinded by Parliament.

The date on which the Stamp Act was repudiated, November 23, has been observed for many years as a half-holiday in Frederick County to commemorate this courageous act. It has been customary for the Daughters of the American Revolution (DAR) to meet in the courthouse on this day and to listen while the clerk of the circuit court reads the original 1765 decision.

SOURCES:
AnnivHol-2000, p. 195
DictDays-1988, p. 95

♦ 2206 ♦ **Restoration of Independence of the Republic of Latvia**
May 4

The Restoration of Independence of the Republic of Latvia from the USSR is marked as a national public holiday in Latvia every May 4. On that date in 1990, Latvia's Supreme Court re-declared the country a free democratic parliamentary republic. Following a transitional period, full independence was attained on August 21, 1991.

Prior to World War I, present-day Latvia was divided into several provinces ruled by the Russian Empire. After the upheaval of the First World War, Latvian pro-independence forces joined together to create a provisional parliament, the Latvian People's Council. On November 18, 1918, the group proclaimed Latvia an independent and democratic republic. The country celebrates every November 18 as LATVIA INDEPENDENCE DAY, a national holiday. Since 1920, Latvia has been acknowledged continuously by other countries as an independent state, despite occupations by Nazi Germany from 1941 to 1945, and by the Soviet Union from 1940 to 1941 and 1945 to 1991. After Latvia's Supreme Court re-declared the country a free republic on May 4, 1990, its *de facto* independence was restored on August 21, 1991.

CONTACTS:
Embassy of Latvia

2306 Massachusetts Ave. N.W.
Washington, D.C. 20008
202-328-2840; fax: 202-328-2860
www.latvia-usa.org

♦ 2207 ♦ Return Day
November, the Thursday after Election Day

In the early 19th century, the rural residents of Sussex County, Delaware, had to travel all the way to Georgetown, the county seat, to cast their ballots on ELECTION DAY. The roads were rough, the weather was often bad, and many of the men were uneasy about leaving their families behind.

In 1828, the General Assembly adopted new election laws establishing polling places in the "hundreds," as the political subdivisions of the county were called (probably referring to the early English "group of 100 hides," the number of land units necessary to support one peasant family). While this spared voters from having to travel, they had no way of finding out the results of the election because there were no county newspapers. The tabulations were rushed to Georgetown by couriers, and the results were read two days later from the courthouse steps. Many of the farmers in the surrounding areas would take a day off and travel to Georgetown with their families to hear the announcement and to join in the festivities, which included cockfights, band concerts, and open-air markets. The winning candidates were often carried around the town green in an impromptu victory celebration.

Of course, there is no longer any need to wait two days to hear election results (with the notable exception of the 2000 election). But the residents of Georgetown continue the tradition, which includes a formal announcement of the results on the Thursday after the Presidential Election Day. There are parades, picnics, military displays, and, of course, politicking. Both the winners and the losers circulate among their supporters. Street vendors sell roast oxen, which has been cooked on a spit, and there is a parade down Market Street reminiscent of the days when farmers would arrive in town in their wagons and ox-drawn carts.

CONTACTS:
Georgetown Historical Society
108 E. Main St.
Georgetown, MA 01833
978-352-2208
www.georgetownhistoricalsociety.com

SOURCES:
FolkAmerHol-1999, p. 443

♦ 2208 ♦ Reversing Current, Festival of the (Water Festival; Bonn Om Tuk)
Late October or November

The Festival of the Reversing Current is a festival and national holiday to celebrate a natural phenomenon in Cambodia. Tonle Sap, a lake, is connected to the Mekong River by the Tonle Sap River, which normally flows south from the lake. But during the rainy season, from mid-May to mid-October, the flood-swollen Mekong backs up and flows backward through the Tonle Sap River into the lake. The depth of the lake jumps from seven feet to 35 feet, and the total surface quadruples. The normal southward flow returns when the dry season starts. Because of the phenomenon, the Tonle Sap lake is an extremely rich source of freshwater fish.

The festival, held at the time when the Tonle Sap returns to its normal direction, is a time of fireworks, merrymaking and races of pirogues, or long canoes, at Phnom Penh.

CONTACTS:
Phnom Penh Municipality
3 Quai Sisovath
Phnom Penh, 12206 Cambodia
855-23-723-949; fax: 855-23-466-043
www.phnompenh.gov.kh/english/introduction.h

SOURCES:
Revolution Days*See under* individual countries

♦ 2209 ♦ Reykjavik Arts Festival (Listahátí í Reykjavík)
Late May to early June in even-numbered years

Originally called the **North Atlantic Festival**, this nearly three-week-long festival highlights the performing and visual arts. Vladimir Ashkenazy, the famous pianist and an Icelandic citizen, founded the festival with Ivar Eskeland, former director of the Nordic House in Reykjavik. While Eskeland was primarily interested in establishing a Nordic arts festival, Ashkenazy wanted it to be international in scope. The two men combined their goals, and the first festival was held in 1970.

Since that time the festival has seen performances by violinist Yehudi MENUHIN, flutist James Galway, conductor André Previn, bassist Boris Christoff, and the London Sinfonietta. Artists and companies from Austria, Denmark, Germany, France, Greenland, Norway, Sweden, and the United States have also performed there. The festival is well attended not only by local people but by tourists as well.

CONTACTS:
Reykjavik Arts Festival
Laekjargata 3b
P.O. Box 88
Reykjavik, 121 Iceland
354-561-2444; fax: 354-562-2350
artfest.is/default.asp?lang_id=en

SOURCES:
GdWrldFest-1985, p. 108
IntlThFolk-1979, p. 201

♦ 2210 ♦ Rhode Island Independence Day
May 4

Rhode Island was the first and only state to declare its independence from England entirely on its own. Relations between the colony and its British rulers had deteriorated rapidly after the 1772 incident in which Rhode Island colonists boarded and burned the British revenue cutter, the *Gaspee*, which had been patrolling the coastal waters in search of local smugglers (*see* GASPEE DAYS). On May 4, 1776, both houses of the General Assembly renounced the colony's allegiance to Great Britain—a full two months before the rest of the colonies followed suit on July 4 (*see* FOURTH OF JULY).

Rhode Islanders celebrate this event during May, which is Rhode Island Heritage Month, with flag-raising ceremonies, cannon salutes, and parades of local patriotic, veterans', and scouting organizations.

SOURCES:
AmerBkDays-2000, p. 341
AnnivHol-2000, p. 76

♦ 2211 ♦ Rice-Planting Festival at Osaka
June 14

There are many rituals associated with the growing of rice in Japanese farming communities. June marks the beginning of the rainy season, and transplanting usually takes place during June and July. In many rural celebrations, young women in costume perform rituals including planting seedlings while singing rice-planting songs to the accompaniment of pipes and drums. Sometimes women light fires of rice straw and pray to the rice god. Shinto priests are often asked to offer prayers for a good harvest season.

On June 14 in Osaka, thousands congregate to observe a group of young kimono-clad women plant rice and sing in the sacred fields near the Sumiyoshi Shrine. Working rhythmically to the music, the young women appear to be participating in a dance rather than the hard work of planting.

CONTACTS:
Osaka Convention and Tourism Bureau
5F Resona Semba Bldg.
4-4-21, Minamisemba, Chuo-ku
Osaka, 542-0081 Japan
81-6-6282-5911; fax: 81-6-6282-5914
www.octb.jp/english

SOURCES:
BkHolWrld-1986, Jun 7
JapanFest-1965, pp. 92, 158

♦ 2212 ♦ Richmond Fossil Festival
First weekend of May, held biennially

The Australian town of Richmond, located in northwest Queensland, celebrates its archaeological treasures every two years at its Kronosaurus Korner and Richmond Marine Fossil Museum. The festival is also a celebration of the town's outback identity, with a number of traditional community events including a loader pull, a rodeo, and a rock-throwing competition. It has been observed since 2002.

Scheduled events on the opening day, Friday, include a fossil-finding expedition, a school concert, and the rodeo. Saturday focuses on Kronosaurus Korner, the site of a parade, novelty events, and the famous physical contest known as the World Champion Moonrock Throwing Competition, which challenges men to heave a rock weighing over 59 pounds.

On Sunday, festivalgoers attend the Show and Shine Car Show. On Monday, the festival closes with more archaeological activities including "fossicking" (sifting for fossils) and a fossil preparation workshop.

CONTACTS:
Richmond Shire Council
50 Goldring St.
Richmond, Queensland 4822 Australia
www.richmond.qld.gov.au

♦ 2213 ♦ Ridvan, Feast of
April 21-May 2

The Feast of Ridvan is a Baha'i celebration to commemorate a 12-day period in 1863. That's when the Baha'i founder, BAHA'U'LLAH (which means "Glory of God"), made the declaration that he was God's messenger for this age—the one foreseen by the Bab to be a prophet of the same rank as Abraham, Moses, Jesus, Muhammad, Buddha, Krishna, and Zoroaster. The first, ninth, and 12th days of the period are holy days when work is suspended. The celebration starts at sunset, April 20, the eve of Ridvan.

When he made his declaration, Baha'u'llah was staying outside Baghdad, Iraq, at a garden he called *Ridvan,* meaning "Paradise." On the first day, he declared his manifestation to his family and close associates. On the ninth day other followers joined him, and the declaration of his station became public knowledge. On the 12th day, he left the garden.

Nineteen years earlier, the Bab had prophesied that one greater than he would come (*see* BAB, DECLARATION OF THE); Baha'u'llah's proclamation stated that he was the "promised one." He set forth the form of the Baha'i religion, teaching the unity of all religions and the unity and brotherhood of all mankind. He wrote more than 100 works of sacred literature.

CONTACTS:
Baha'i National Center
1233 Central St.
Evanston, IL 60201
800-228-6483 or 847-733-3559; fax: 847-733-3578
www.us.bahai.org

SOURCES:
AnnivHol-2000, p. 64
ConEncyBahai-2000, p. 296
DictWrldRel-1989, pp. 87, 89
OxYear-1999, p. 694
RelHolCal-2004, p. 155

♦ 2214 ♦ Riley (James Whitcomb) Festival
Begins first Thursday in October

James Whitcomb Riley (1849-1916), a poet best known for his nostalgic dialect verse, is honored in his hometown of Greenfield, Indiana, with a three-day festival held around his birthday on October 7 each year. Most of the events are held near the Riley Birthplace Museum, the house where the poet spent his childhood, although there are poetry contests, programs in the local schools, and parades through the streets of downtown Greenfield as well.

The festival was started in 1911 by Minnie Belle Mitchell, an author who wanted schools and literary clubs to observe the poet's birthday. The governor of Indiana proclaimed October 7 as **Riley Day** soon afterward, and Riley attended the celebration in 1912, finding himself smothered in bouquets of flowers as his car paraded down the street.

Today Riley is best remembered for such poems as "When the Frost is on the Punkin," "The Raggedy Man," and "Little Orphan Annie," which later inspired both the Raggedy Ann and Andy dolls as well as the Orphan Annie comic strip, which was successfully brought to Broadway as the musical *Annie*.

CONTACTS:
Riley Festival
312 E. Main St., Ste. C
Greenfield, IN 46140
317-462-2141; fax: 317-467-1449
www.rileyfestival.com

SOURCES:
AmerBkDays-2000, p. 694
GdUSFest-1984, p. 51

♦ 2215 ♦ **Risabha's Nirvana and Mauni Amavasya**
January-February; 14th and 15th day of the
waning half of the Hindu month of Magha

Jains, a religious minority who are most heavily concentrated in India, honor 24 spiritual guides named Tirthankaras. Foremost among these divine beings is the original Tirthankara, Risabha. According to Jain tradition, Risabha lived 600,000 years ago. He is credited with establishing the first Indian emperor and instituting fundamental social conventions for humans. Jains in India and other countries celebrate Risabha's Nirvana and Mauni Amavasya over two days in Magha, a Jain lunar month that falls between January and February.

Jains revere Tirthankaras for attaining nirvana, a state of total liberation from an endless cycle of birth and death. On the Nirvana day of Risabha, known in southern India as **Jinara-tri**, believers remember their spiritual guide's liberation at Mount Kailash, a mythic site of the Himalayas range in Tibet known to Jains as Ashtapada. They typically observe the day with processions.

Mauni Amavasya takes place on the next day, and for Svetambara Jains, the religion's dominant sect, it is a time for silent reflection.

CONTACTS:
Ministry of External Affairs
Government of India
South Block
New Delhi 110011 India
www.mea.gov.in

SOURCES:
RelHolCal-2004, p. 195

♦ 2216 ♦ **Rishi Panchami**
August-September; fifth day of waxing half of
Hindu month of Bhadrapada

Hindus devote the day of Rishi Panchami to the Sapta Rishis, also known as the seven seers or mental sons of Brahma: Bhrigu, Pulastya, Kratu, Pulaha, Marichi, Atri, and Vasistha. An earthenware or copper pitcher filled with water is placed on an altar sanctified with cow dung. The seven seers are then worshipped with betel leaf, flowers, camphor, and lamps. Only fruits are eaten on this day.

Rishi Panchami is primarily a women's festival, but men may observe it for the well-being and happiness of their wives. Devi Arundhati, the wife of Rishi Vasistha and a model of conjugal excellence, is also worshipped on this day.

SOURCES:
RelHolCal-2004, p. 174

♦ 2217 ♦ **River Kwai Bridge Week**
Last week in November

River Kwai Bridge Week in Kanchanaburi, Thailand, commemorates World War II's infamous Death Railway and the River Kwai (Khwae Noi) Bridge. Between 1942 and 1945, more than 16,000 Allied prisoners of war and 49,000 impressed Asian laborers were forced by the Japanese to build a railway through the jungle from Bangkok, Thailand, into Burma (now Myanmar), and it is said that one person died for every railway tie on the track. At the Kanchanaburi War Cemetery, commemorative services are held every April 25 for the 6,982 American, Australian, British, and Dutch prisoners of war buried there.

The bridge became known as a symbol of the horrors and futilities of war through the novel, *The Bridge Over the River Kwai*, by Pierre Boulle and the 1957 movie based on it, *The Bridge on the River Kwai*. During the week-long events, the reconstructed bridge (it was bombed during the war) is the setting for sound-and-light presentations, and there are also historical exhibitions and rides on World War II-era trains.

CONTACTS:
Tourism Authority of Thailand
611 N. Larchmont Blvd., 1st Fl.
Los Angeles, CA 90004
800-842-4526 or 323-461-9814; fax: 323-461-9834
www.tourismthailand.org

♦ 2218 ♦ **River to Reef Festival**
First Sunday in October

"Celebrating Our Way of Life" is the theme of the River to Reef Festival held in the town of Mackay, located on the eastern coast of Australia in Queensland. The celebration's name refers to the two natural landmarks of Mackay: the Pioneer River and one of the country's most popular tropical destinations, the Great Barrier Reef.

The celebration, which has taken place since 2005, offers food, dance, music, and other activities typically found at a family festival. Most events are held at the main stage, located alongside the Pioneer River. Children are treated to a concert that kicks off with a procession by a colorful "river serpent." Rock bands square off in a competition that includes a performance of an original song having a "River to Reef" theme. Other activities include a fashion show, a culinary competition, a show featuring fire-twirling performances, a riverside carnival, and a boat show.

CONTACTS:
Mackay City Council
P.O. Box 1410
Mackay, Queensland QLD 4740 Australia
www.mackay.qld.gov.au

◆ 2219 ◆ Rizal Day
December 30

A national holiday in the Philippines, Rizal Day commemorates the execution of the national hero, Dr. José Rizal, on this day in 1896. Flags fly at half-staff throughout the country, and special rites are led by the president at the 500-foot obelisk that is the Rizal Monument in Manila.

Rizal, born in 1861 in the Philippines, was a doctor who studied medicine in Spain, France, and Germany. He was also a botanist, educator, man of letters, and inspiration for the Philippine nationalist movement. Writing from Europe and denouncing the corrupt ruling of the Philippines by Spanish friars, he became known as a leader of the Philippine reform movement.

He wrote the novel, *Noli me tangere* (1886; *The Lost Eden*, 1961), for which the Spanish administration deported him shortly after he had returned to the Philippines in 1887. He again returned to the Philippines in 1892 and founded a non-violent reform movement, as a result of which he was exiled to the Philippine island of Mindanao, where he established a school and hospital.

Rizal had no direct role in the nationalist insurrection; nevertheless, he was arrested, tried for sedition, and executed by a firing squad. On the eve of his execution, he wrote the poem "Mi Ultimo Adiós," meaning "My Last Farewell." The poem, in the original Spanish and translated into other languages, is transcribed on a marble slab near the Rizal Monument.

CONTACTS:
Philippine Tourism Center
556 Fifth Ave.
New York, NY 10036
212-575-7915; fax: 212-302-6759
www.philippinetourism.us

SOURCES:
AnnivHol-2000, p. 215

◆ 2220 ◆ Road Building
April

In areas of Nigeria where the Igbo live, especially Mbaise, there is a festival in April known as **Emume Ibo Uzo**, or Road Building. It is a time for everyone in the community to get together and maintain the major thoroughfares by clearing and leveling them. This festival was particularly important in the days before government-sponsored road building became common.

SOURCES:
FolkWrldHol-1999, p. 266

◆ 2221 ◆ Roberts's (Joseph Jenkins) Birthday
March 15

Joseph Jenkins Roberts (1809–1876), Liberia's first and seventh president, led the movement for an independent Liberia, established in 1848. Along with being a celebration of the forefather's birth, this day (also known as **J. J. Roberts Day**) is an occasion to pay homage to Liberia's historical role as Africa's oldest republic.

Born a free man in Norfolk, Virginia, Roberts moved to Liberia, which was originally a colony, in 1829, part of a group of former slaves and slave descendants organized by the American Colonization Society. As lieutenant-governor and then governor of the colony, Roberts led Liberia through its transition into a sovereign republic.

In many respects, Roberts's birthday stands apart from other holidays that recognize Liberian notables because he was a member of the established Americo-Liberian elite, a group historically criticized for wielding control over the country's indigenous population for more than a century.

CONTACTS:
Liberia Ministry of Information, Cultural Affairs and Tourism (MICAT)
110 United Nations Dr.
P.O. Box 10-9021
Capitol Hill, 1000
Monrovia, Liberia
www.micat.gov.lr

SOURCES:
AnnivHol-2000, p. 44

◆ 2222 ◆ Robigalia
April 25

The ancient Romans knew how much damage certain fungi could do to their crops, but they attributed these diseases to the wrath of the gods. Robigus was the Roman god who personified such blights, and the annual festival known as the Robigalia was designed to placate him. It was believed that prayers and sacrifices made on this day, April 25, would head off the mildew, rust, wilt, and other blights that so often devastated their crops.

SOURCES:
AmerBkDays-2000, p. 247
DictFolkMyth-1984, p. 916
DictRomRel-1996, p. 192
FestRom-1981, p. 108
OxYear-1999, p. 171

◆ 2223 ◆ Robin Hood Festival in Nottinghamshire, England
Week in late July to early August

The Robin Hood Festival takes place for one week in late July to early August every year in Sherwood Forest, an ancient woodland in Nottinghamshire, England. The event celebrates the life and times of one of the most popular outlaws in the world: Robin Hood. Activities and entertainment include children's theater, strolling players, jesters, jousting, and music. There are demonstrations in such aged arts as falconry and long-bow-shooting, and a medieval market offers a variety of goods. As many as 75,000 visitors take part in the week's activities. The festival is free, with nominal charges for some performances and activities. It has taken place every year since 1975.

Robin Hood is a legendary figure who is portrayed as a romantic medieval bowman who lived as an outlaw in Sherwood Forest, outsmarting and stealing from the wealthy to help the poor and oppressed. Whether or not Robin Hood was based on a real person is a question debated by historians to this day. While several possible candidates have been identified, there is no conclusive evidence pointing to a single man. Some historians believe that the Robin Hood myth may have originated in the pre-Christian belief in a nature spirit or god of the forest.

CONTACTS:
Sherwood Forest Country Park
Sherwood Forest Visitor Centre
Edwinstowe
Edwinstowe, Nottinghamshire NG21 9HN UK
www.nottinghamshire.gov.uk/robinhoodfestival

♦ 2224 ♦ Robin Hood Festival in Sherwood, Oregon
Mid-July; Friday and Saturday

The Robin Hood Festival has taken place in Sherwood, Ore., every year since just after World War II. At that point in the town's history, the economy was slow, and local core businesses were threatened by a new commercial area at Highway 99 called Six Corners. Inspired by the need to help, and also by the re-release of the classic 1938 film *The Adventures of Robin Hood,* Sherwood's civic leaders decided to capitalize on the legend connected to their town's name. Initially, a group of World War II veterans in Robin Hood costumes made appearances at movie theaters where the film was showing. They were so popular that they were invited back, and soon they were invited to appear at various festivals in the Portland area. It eventually led to the creation of the popular Sherwood event.

The Robin Hood Festival features a parade, a knighting ceremony, live music, comedy, and dancing. Each year a Maid Marian is crowned. Food and plenty of community spirit round out the event.

CONTACTS:
Robin Hood Festival
P.O. Box 496
Sherwood, OR 97140
503-625-4233
www.robinhoodfestival.com

♦ 2225 ♦ Robinson (Jackie) Day
April 15

Jackie Robinson Day is celebrated throughout Major League Baseball (MLB) in honor of Jackie Robinson, the first African American to play professional baseball in the MLB. In the first half of the 20th century, baseball was segregated. Robinson and other African Americans played in the Negro Leagues, but discrimination prevented them from playing in the MLB. On April 15, 1947, Robinson played his first professional game for the Brooklyn Dodgers. In addition to breaking the color barrier, he went on to be named Rookie of the Year and later the National League's Most Valuable Player. A six-time All-Star, he was elected in 1962 to the Baseball Hall of Fame in Cooperstown, New York.

To commemorate Robinson's achievements, activities are planned each year at all MLB stadiums on April 15th, or the date closest to that on which a baseball game is scheduled. Home teams coordinate activities for the tribute, which may include pregame award presentations, special guests throwing the first pitch, prizes for fans in attendance, and appearances by other legendary baseball stars. Jackie Robinson Day has been celebrated each year since 2004, with Robinson's widow, Rachel, and other family members taking part in the annual ceremonies. To honor Robinson in 2007, many players donned special jerseys emblazoned with the number 42, which was Robinson's number and which was permanently retired from baseball in 1997 on the 50th anniversary of his first game as a Dodger.

CONTACTS:
Jackie Robinson Day
Major League Baseball
c/o MLB Advanced Media, L.P.
75 Ninth Ave., 5th Fl.
New York, NY 10011
mlb.mlb.com/mlb/events/jrd/index_07.jsp

Jackie Robinson Foundation
One Hudson Sq.
75 Varick St., 2nd Fl.
New York, NY 10013-1917
212-290-8600; fax: 212-290-8081
www.jackierobinson.org

SOURCES:
AAH-2007, p. 233

♦ 2226 ♦ Robots at Play
August

Robots at Play is an international festival of robotics, intended to promote the understanding, use, and enjoyment of robots in everyday life. The festival, held in Denmark, includes exhibits of robots at work; areas where visitors can play games with robot opponents, dance with robots, and otherwise interact with them; art featuring robots; robot films; and a professional conference on robotics. There is a robot-building competition for children, an area featuring robots built from scrap material, and a designer's competition with a prize of 75,000 DK, sponsored by the Fionia Bank.

The designers' competition encourages entrants to combine robotic function, good design, and artistry. In 2006, the first year of the competition, the top prize was taken by Huggable, a robotic teddy bear designed by Dan Stiehl and Cynthia Breazeal, a team from the Massachusetts Institute of Technology. Huggable was designed to mimic the attributes of a companion animal such as a cat or dog in order to provide the therapeutic benefits that real animals have been shown to provide to the elderly and infirm. In 2007, the prize was won by the team of Hideki Kozima, from Japan, and Marek Michalowski, from the United States, for their robot Keepon. A small unit with a soft, rubbery skin, Keepon featured cameras in its eyes and a microphone in its nose. It was designed to interact with young children and aid in the study of their nonverbal play.

CONTACTS:
Robots at Play
Louise Skovborg Just, Project Manager
Robocluster
Forskerparken 10
DK-5230, Odense M Denmark
www.robocluster.dk

Henrik Hautop Lund
Chairman, Robots at Play
Maersk Mc-Kinney Moller Institute
University of Southern Denmark, Campusvej 55
DK-5230, Odense M, Denmark
www.robotsatplay.dk

♦ 2227 ♦ **Rock Ness**
Weekend in early June

The shores of the world-famous Loch Ness outside Inverness, Scotland, is the site of this summer music festival featuring acts from the diverse genres of electronic, dance, and rock. Despite its remote location in the Scottish Highlands, the event still draws as many as 35,000 music fans.

The first Rock Ness took place on June 24, 2006, with a bill favoring electronic acts. A successful attendance draw inspired organizers to extend the event to a full weekend the following year. Exposure for the event increased again in 2008 when performances were televised for the first time on Channel 4, a major British network. That year organizers also featured a more diverse program, with the dance acts performing on Saturday and the rock bands playing on Sunday.

Keeping in practice with similar multiple-day events, Rock Ness concert-goers typically stay in campsites located on the festival grounds. In addition to the music, other attractions in past years have been the Bollywood Cocktail Bar and the Big Love Inflatable Church, which performed an actual wedding ceremony in 2008.

CONTACTS:
Rock Ness
www.rockness.co.uk

♦ 2228 ♦ **Rodgers (Jimmie) Festival**
May

This country music festival in Meridian, Miss., salutes the life and music of Jimmie Rodgers on the anniversary of his death

on May 26, 1933. Rodgers was born in Meridian in 1897 and left school at 14 to work on the Mississippi and Ohio Railroad; later, during his singing career, he was known as the "Singing Brakeman." He learned to play the guitar and banjo, and learned the blues from black railroad workers. Mr. Rodgers's music blended blues with the sounds of country, work, hobo, and cowboy songs. In 1925, because tuberculosis prevented him from working any longer for the railroad, he became a performer, and quickly a best-selling recording artist.

Today he is considered the Father of Country Music. Among his recordings that had a lasting influence on popular singers were "Blue Yodel No. 1," "Brakeman's Blues," and "My Time Ain't Long." The Jimmie Rodgers Memorial and Museum in Meridian has exhibits of his guitar, concert clothing, and railroad equipment he used.

The week-long festival highlights top musical stars and features a talent contest and a beauty contest.

CONTACTS:
Jimmie Rodgers Foundation
P.O. Box 2170
Meridian, MS 39302
888-868-7720 or 601-482-8001
www.jimmierodgers.com

♦ 2229 ♦ **Rogation Days**
Between April 30 and June 3; Monday, Tuesday, and Wednesday preceding Ascension Day

Since medieval times, the three days before ASCENSION DAY (called HOLY THURSDAY in Great Britain) have been known as Rogation Days (from *rogare*, "to pray"). Both the Roman Catholic and Protestant churches set them aside as days of abstinence and prayer, especially for the harvest.

In many churches in the United States **Rogation Sunday**, the fifth Sunday after EASTER, has been known as **Rural Life Sunday** or **Soil Stewardship Sunday** since 1929—a day when the religious aspects of agricultural life are emphasized. It is also known as **Cantate Sunday** because the Latin Mass for this day begins with the first words of Psalm 98, *Cantate Domino,* "Sing to the Lord."

The Rogation Days also had a secular meaning at one time in England, where they were called **Gang Days** or **Gange Days**—from the Saxon word *gangen,* meaning "to go." There was a custom of walking the parish boundaries during the three days before Holy Thursday (Ascension Day), the procession consisting of the priests and prelates of the church and a select number of men from the parish. Later, these Rogation Days were set aside for special local celebrations. In 19th-century Dorsetshire, for example, a local festival called the Bezant was held each year on Rogation Monday.

SOURCES:
AmerBkDays-2000, p. 339
BkDays-1864, vol. I, p. 582
DaysCustFaith-1957, p. 135
DictDays-1988, pp. 19, 46, 96
EncyEaster-2002, p. 532
FestSaintDays-1915, p. 99

FolkWrldHol-1999, p. 336
OxYear-1999, p. 628
RelHolCal-2004, p. 95
SaintFestCh-1904, p. 227

♦ 2230 ♦ Rogers (Roy) Festival
First weekend in June

With his wife Dale Evans, Roy Rogers was one of America's best-known singing cowboys. The couple starred in a popular television series, "The Roy Rogers Show," which ran from 1951 to 1957, and featured his horse, Trigger, and dog, Bullet.

Since 1984, Rogers has been honored in his hometown of Portsmouth, Ohio, with an annual festival sponsored by the Roy Rogers-Dale Evans Collectors Association. The four-day event includes displays of Roy Rogers memorabilia, tours of Roy Rogers's boyhood home, and special performances by old-time Western stars such as the late Lash LaRue, "King of the Bullwhip." There are showings of Roy Rogers's films and television programs, and Western memorabilia collectors set up booths to sell and exchange their wares.

Proceeds from the annual event go into a Roy Rogers Scholarship Fund that pays for a needy student to attend Shawnee State University in Portsmouth. Rogers's son, Roy (Dusty) Rogers, Jr., a cowboy singer in his own right, often attends the festival.

CONTACTS:
Roy Rogers - Dale Evans Collectors Association
P.O. Box 1166
Portsmouth, OH 45662
740-353-0900
www.royrogersfestival.org

♦ 2231 ♦ Rogers (Will) Day
November 4

The birthday of America's "cowboy philosopher" is observed in Oklahoma, where he was born on November 4, 1879, when it was still the Indian Territory (*see* OKLAHOMA DAY). After his first appearance as a vaudeville entertainer in 1905 at Madison Square Garden, he developed a widespread reputation as a humorist. He went on to become a writer, a radio performer, and a motion-picture star, best loved for his gum-chewing, homespun image.

Will Rogers died in a plane crash on August 15, 1935, while flying with the well-known aviator, Wiley Post. A monument to the two men was erected at the site of the crash near Point Barrow, Alaska. Rogers's birthday was first observed in 1947, with a celebration at the Will Rogers Memorial near the town of Claremore where he was born. Beneath the statue of Rogers at the memorial is printed the statement for which he is best remembered: "I never met a man I didn't like."

CONTACTS:
Will Rogers Museum
1720 W. Will Rogers Blvd.
P.O. Box 157

Claremore, OK 74017
800-324-9455 or 918-341-0719; fax: 918-343-8119
www.willrogers.com

SOURCES:
AmerBkDays-2000, p. 752

♦ 2232 ♦ Rogonadur
December-January

The Saora people, who live in the hills of eastern India and worship their own gods rather than those of the Hindus, celebrate a harvest festival in December or January known as Rogonadur, which refers to a type of bean known as the red gram. The festival, which lasts several days, is preceded by a religious ceremony a week or so before, in which the priest makes an offering of new gram to the gods and appeals to them to visit for the festival.

Bunches of fresh gram decorate village homes and shrines for the celebration, which includes dancing and music at each shrine. In the mornings people make private offerings of gram to the gods in their homes before heading outside to start the communal festivities. After a few days, the priest holds a concluding ceremony, makes a final offering, then dismisses the gods.

See also JAMMOLPUR CEREMONY

SOURCES:
CelebNature-1969, p. 116

♦ 2233 ♦ Roman Games (Ludi Romani)
September 4-19

Like the PLEBEIAN GAMES, the Roman Games were held in honor of Jupiter. They date back to the dedication of the temple to Jupiter on the Capitoline hill on September 13, 509 B.C.E., making them the most ancient of the ancient Roman games. Originally a one-day event, by the time of Caesar the Games lasted a full 15 days.

A grand procession to the Circus Maximus, a huge arena just outside Rome, signalled the beginning of the festival. Along with the athletes, the procession included charioteers, dancers, musicians playing flutes and lyres, men dressed in goatskins to look like satyrs, images of the gods, and the animals who were to be sacrificed came last.

Events included boxing, running, and wrestling contests, occasional mock battles, and two- and four-horse chariot races. Sometimes the drivers were accompanied by partners on foot, who, after a chariot crossed the finish line, had to race each other back to the other end of the arena to decide the entire contest.

See also APOLLONIAN GAMES; LUDI

SOURCES:
DictRomRel-1996, p. 134
FestRom-1981, p. 183

♦ 2234 ♦ Romania National Day
December 1

The national holiday of Romania has been celebrated since 1990, after the fall of Romanian Communist Party head Nicolae Ceausescu, with military parades, speeches and a holiday from work. This day marks the unification in 1918 of Romania and Transylvania and the formation of the Romanian state within its present-day boundaries. Romania's full independence had been recognized in 1878, but Transylvania had remained outside the new state. On December 1, a Romanian assembly passed the resolution of unity celebrated on National Day.

CONTACTS:
Romanian Embassy
1607 23rd St. N.W.
Washington, D.C. 20008
202-232-3694; fax: 202-232-4748
www.roembus.org

SOURCES:
AnnivHol-2000, p. 201

♦ 2235 ♦ Rondo Days Celebration
Third week of July

The Rondo Days Celebration launched in 1983 as a showcase for the rich African-American culture and heritage of the Rondo community in St. Paul, Minn. Rondo, the city's vibrant, predominantly black neighborhood, was destroyed and its people displaced in the 1960s by the construction of the I-94 freeway. Recreating the energy and spirit of Rondo and bringing together former residents and other Minnesotans and visitors was the inspiration for the celebration's founders, Marvin "Roger" Anderson and Floyd Smaller. The celebration is now run by a non-profit organization.

The event takes place during the third week of July in St. Paul. A celebration of multi-cultural food, art, music, and activities, it now draws up to 35,000 visitors a year. Other highlights include a community parade, a free dinner honoring the community's senior citizens, and a five-kilometer fun walk and run. There also is an annual, hotly contested drillteam competition drawing squads from across the country.

CONTACTS:
Rondo Ave. Inc.
651-646-6597
www.rondoaveinc.org

♦ 2236 ♦ Roosevelt (Franklin D.) Day
January 30

Franklin Delano Roosevelt (1882-1945) was the 32nd president of the United States and the only one elected to four terms of office. He fell ill from polio in 1921, but regained partial use of his legs. His administration extended from the darkest days of the Great Depression to the Japanese attack on Pearl Harbor. He never lived to see the final Allied victory at the end of World War II, however; he was stricken with a massive cerebral hemorrhage and died at the Little White House in Warm Springs, Georgia, on April 12, 1945.

Roosevelt's birthday is observed by family members, friends, and representatives of various organizations at his home at Hyde Park, New York. The ceremony begins at 11:00 A.M., when a color guard from the U.S. Military Academy at West Point marches into the rose garden where the President is buried and takes its place before his grave. Wreaths are laid, and a family member places cut flowers on the grave. The superintendent of the military academy presents the "President's Wreath," a prayer is offered, and the event concludes with three volleys from a ceremonial firing squad.

CONTACTS:
Franklin D. Roosevelt National Historic Site
National Park Service
4097 Albany Post Rd.
Hyde Park, NY 12538
800-337-8474 or 845-229-9115; fax: 845-229-0739

SOURCES:
AmerBkDays-2000, p. 100
AnnivHol-2000, p. 17
DictDays-1988, p. 44

♦ 2237 ♦ Roots Festival
May or June during even-numbered years

The first Roots Festival took place in the west African country of the Gambia in 1996. The event derives its name from African-American writer Alex Haley's book *Roots*, in which he traces his ancestry back to the Gambian village of Juffureh. Sponsored by Gambia's Department of State for Tourism and Culture, the Roots Festival aims to memorialize the enslavement and transportation of millions of Africans. It also serves to build bridges between the African diaspora and the people of the Gambia, in order to celebrate and strengthen African cultural identity and to encourage trade and business ties. The festival includes music and dance performances, plays, tours of African cultural sites, opportunities to participate in Gambian rite of passage rituals, a beauty contest, a fashion show, and a seminar on business opportunities in Gambia. This biennial festival takes place in even-numbered years in the capital city of Banjul.

CONTACTS:
Gambia Tourism Authority
Kololi
P.O. Box 4085
Bakau, Gambia
220-446-2491; fax: 220-446-2487
www.visitthegambia.gm

♦ 2238 ♦ Ropotine (Repotini)
Between April 7 and May 18; third Tuesday after Easter

This Romanian festival is celebrated exclusively by women, who take advantage of this day to turn the tables on their husbands. It is the one day of the year when women are the masters: they feast all day, and they can punish men for any slights they may have suffered. Traditionally, women get together and make household utensils out of straw and clay, particularly a shallow baking dish for bread, known as the *tzesturi*, used to bake rolls and cakes which they hand out to children and the poor "to keep away wars."

SOURCES:
FolkWrldHol-1999, p. 253

♦ 2239 ♦ **Rosary, Festival of the**
First Sunday in October

The rosary is a string of beads used by Roman Catholics to count a ritual series of prayers consisting of 15 paternosters ("Our Fathers," also known as the Lord's Prayer), and 150 *Ave Marias*, or "Hail Marys." The rosary is divided into 15 decades—each decade containing one paternoster marked by a large bead and 10 Ave Marias marked by 10 smaller beads. As the prayers are recited, the beads are passed through the fingers, making it easier to keep track of the sequence.

The festival, observed on the first Sunday in October, was established by Pope Pius V under the name of Santa Maria de Victoria (St. Mary of Victory). But the name was changed by Gregory XIII to Festival of the Rosary. Among the events for which the faithful in the former Yugoslavia give thanks on this day is the victory of Prince Eugene over the Turks at Belgrade in 1716.

SOURCES:
BkDays-1864, vol. II, p. 402
DictWrldRel-1989, p. 630
OxYear-1999, p. 406
SaintFestCh-1904, p. 438

♦ 2240 ♦ **Rose Bowl Game**
January 1

The Rose Bowl Game is the oldest and best known of the post-season college football bowl games, held in Pasadena, Calif., the home of the TOURNAMENT OF ROSES. The first Rose Bowl game was played in 1902 between Michigan and Stanford; the Michigan Wolverines, coached by Fielding H. "Hurry Up" Yost, demolished the Indians, 49-0. Yost was known for his "point-a-minute" teams, and the Michigan 11 had racked up 550 points in 11 winning games, unscored on and untied, before the bowl encounter. Willie Heston, one of the great all-time backs, led the team to victory.

Football gave way to chariot races after that first game, but football came back to stay in 1916. Among the notable highlights in the years since then was the wrong-way run in 1929. The University of California was playing Georgia Tech. Roy Riegels, the center and captain of California's Golden Bears, picked up a Tech fumble, started toward the Tech goal line, and then, facing a troop of Tech defenders, cut across the field and started toward his own goal line, 60 yards away. Players on both sides gaped. Finally Benny Lom, a Bears halfback, ran after Riegels and grabbed him at the three-yard line. Tech players bounced him back to the one. California

tried a punt, but it was blocked and the ball rolled out of the end zone. The officials declared a safety, and Georgia Tech won the contest by one point.

From 1947 to 1998 the Rose Bowl brought together the champions of the Midwest Big Ten and Pac Ten (Pacific Ten) Conferences; since 1999, the top two ranked teams in any conference have played here. Numerous other bowl games have come along since 1902: the ORANGE BOWL in Miami, the SUGAR BOWL in New Orleans, and the COTTON BOWL in Dallas started games in the mid-1930s, and by the 1980s there were 16 bowl games in late December or on NEW YEAR'S DAY.

CONTACTS:
Tournament of Roses
391 S. Orange Grove Blvd.
Pasadena, CA 91184
626-449-4100; fax: 626-449-9066
www.tournamentofroses.com

SOURCES:
AmerBkDays-2000, p. 12
BkFestHolWrld-1970, p. 3
BkHolWrld-1986, Jan 1
DictDays-1988, p. 97
EncyChristmas-2003, p. 258
FolkAmerHol-1999, p. 9

♦ 2241 ♦ **Rose Festival**
May-June

According to legend, a Persian trader brought rose bush cuttings to the Balkans hundreds of years ago to provide attar for his lady's perfume. Bulgaria still supplies 90 percent of the world's rose attar, and roses are raised for food and medicinal purposes as well.

The 10-day festival that celebrates Bulgaria's role in the cultivation and export of roses is held in Kazanlak, a small town in what is known as the Valley of the Roses. It begins with a procession of farmers and young people dressed in native costume and carrying baskets for the ritual picking of the rose petals. Even the queen of the pageant is selected not for her beauty but for her rose-picking ability. After she is crowned, she leads a long chain dance into Kazanlak, where her arrival is the signal to begin the Parade of Roses. Rose-decorated floats, costumed paraders, and folk dancers follow a route that winds through all the nearby towns. Afterward, there are picnics featuring Bulgarian foods. Folk dance and song programs complete the festival activities.

The Rose Festival is always held in late May and early June, the blooming season for roses. It takes 3,300 pounds of rose petals to make two pounds of rose attar.

CONTACTS:
Embassy of the Republic of Bulgaria
1621 22nd St. N.W.
Washington, D.C. 20008
202-387-0174; fax: 202-234-7973
www.bulgaria-embassy.org

SOURCES:
GdWrldFest-1985, p. 27

♦ 2242 ♦ Rose Monday
Between February 2 and March 8; Monday before Lent

Germany is famous for its CARNIVAL celebrations, which reach a climax on Rose Monday, the day before SHROVE TUESDAY. More than 400 Carnival balls are held in Munich alone, and Rose Monday celebrations are held in Cologne, Düsseldorf, Mainz, Münster, and Berlin as well. In addition to balls and parades, which take place in small towns as well as the cities, the day is observed by singing songs, often with haunting tunes, that have been composed especially for Carnival.

Because it is the last time for hi-jinks before LENT, **Rosenmontag** is characterized by a free-for-all atmosphere in which the normal rules of behavior are relaxed. It is not uncommon, for example, for people to go up to strangers on the street and kiss them.

The German name for the day, *Rosen Montag*, or "Roses Monday," is a mispronunciation of the original name *Rasen Montag*, meaning "rushing Monday" or "live-it-up Monday."

CONTACTS:
German Information Center
4645 Reservoir Rd. N.W.
Washington, D.C. 20007
202-471-5532; fax: 202-471-5526
www.germany.info

SOURCES:
BkFest-1937, p. 132
DictFolkMyth-1984, pp. 192, 370, 977, 1082
EncyEaster-2002, p. 224
FestWestEur-1958, pp. 55, 56
FolkWrldHol-1999, p. 134
RelHolCal-2004, p. 91

♦ 2243 ♦ Rose of Tralee Beauty Contest
Last full weekend in August

The village of Tralee in County Kerry is famous for a festival that is unique in Ireland: the annual beauty contest for the "Rose of Tralee." Held during a long weekend in late August, the festivities begin with the playing of a harp by a woman belonging to a Kerry family in which harp-playing has been a traditional occupation for generations. There are also horse races and competitions in singing, dancing, and storytelling, but it is the beauty contest that draws the most attention. Contestants come from Ireland, Britain, the United States, and even Australia, although the winner must be of Kerry descent.

"The Rose of Tralee," a popular Irish ballad, was written by William Pembroke Mulchinock, who lived just outside the village of Tralee and fell in love with a girl who was a servant in one of the nearby houses. To put a stop to the relationship, his family sent him to India, where he served as a soldier for three years. He returned to Tralee just in time to see the funeral procession of the girl he loved, who had died of a broken heart. In the public park just outside of Tralee there is a memorial to the ill-fated lovers.

CONTACTS:
Rose of Tralee
Ashe Memorial Hall, Denny St.
Tralee, County Kerry Ireland
353-66-7121322; fax: 353-66-7122654
www.roseoftralee.ie

SOURCES:
GdWrldFest-1985, p. 114
IntlThFolk-1979, p. 236

♦ 2244 ♦ Rosh Hashanah
Between September 6 and October 4; Tishri 1 and 2

Rosh Hashanah marks the beginning of the **Jewish New Year** and the first two of the 10 High Holy Days (*see* TESHUVAH) that conclude with YOM KIPPUR, the Day of Atonement. Unlike the secular NEW YEAR'S DAY observance, this is a solemn season during which each person is subject to review and judgment for the coming year. It is a time of prayer and penitence, and is sometimes called the **Day of Remembrance** or the **Day of Blowing the Shofar**. The story of Abraham is read in the synagogue, and the blowing of the *shofar* ("ram's horn") serves as a reminder that although Abraham, in obedience to God, was willing to sacrifice his son, Isaac, God allowed him to sacrifice a ram instead. The plaintive sound of the shofar is also a call to penitence.

Orthodox Ashkenazim (Jews whose ancestors came from northern Europe) observe the ceremony of Tashlikh, a symbolic throwing of one's sins into a body of water, on the first day of Rosh Hashanah; Kurds jump into the water; kabbalists shake their garments to "free" themselves from sin. All debts from the past year are supposed to be settled before Rosh Hashanah, and many Jews ask forgiveness from friends and family for any slights or transgressions of the concluding year.

Jews celebrate the New Year by eating a special rounded loaf of challah bread, symbolic of the continuity of life, as well as apples dipped in honey, symbols of sweetness and health.

CONTACTS:
Union for Reform Judaism
633 Third Ave.
New York, NY 10017
212-650-4000; fax: 212-650-4169
www.urj.org

Union of Orthodox Jewish Congregations of America
11 Broadway
New York, NY 10004
212-563-4000; fax: 212-564-9058
www.ou.org

SOURCES:
AmerBkDays-2000, p. 683
BkFest-1937, p. 203
BkHolWrld-1986, Sep 18
DaysCustFaith-1957, pp. 244, 331, 337
DictDays-1988, pp. 27, 56, 97, 134
DictFolkMyth-1984, p. 1009
DictWrldRel-1989, pp. 155, 390, 630
FolkAmerHol-1999, p. 397
FolkWrldHol-1999, p. 554

HolSymbols-2009, p. 773
OxYear-1999, p. 726
RelHolCal-2004, p. 53

♦ 2245 ♦ Roswell UFO Festival
Early July

Around July 4, 1947, a UFO (unidentified flying object) allegedly crashed near Roswell, a farming and ranching community in southeastern New Mexico. According to some reports, the bodies of four aliens were found at a site around 30 miles from Roswell. Mack Brazel worked on a ranch southeast of Corona, New Mexico, where he found strange debris on July 5. The next day he went to Roswell to show it to the Chaves County sheriff, who in turn passed the information along to officials at Roswell Army Air Field (RAAF). An investigation was begun and a press release about the crash was released by the RAAF. The headline in the July 8 *Roswell Daily Record* read, "RAAF Captures Flying Saucer on Ranch in Roswell Region." But the Army-Air Force changed its story the next day, claiming that the debris was from a weather balloon.

The "Roswell Incident" has remained a subject of controversy for years. In September 1994 the Air Force produced a report which asserted that the recovered object was in fact a spy balloon flown as part of the then-top-secret Project Mogul. On the 50th anniversary of the event in 1997 the Air Force issued a report designed to put continuing rumors about a cover-up to rest. That report claimed the retrieved bodies were actually crash-test dummies (even though such experiments did not begin until 1953).

The town of Roswell celebrates its reputation as the UFO capital of the United States with a week-long festival in early July, which has been officially designated as "Alien Month." Activities include a UFO parade, an alien puppet show, concerts, and special exhibits. The UFO Museum and Research Center invites UFO experts from around the world to speak at the festival, which combines traditional FOURTH OF JULY barbecues and fireworks with serious discussion of UFO reports.

CONTACTS:
Roswell Chamber of Commerce
131 W. 2nd St.
P.O. Box 70
Roswell, NM 88201
877-849-7679 or 505-623-5695; fax: 505-624-6870
www.roswellnm.org

♦ 2246 ♦ Rousa, Feast of
Between April 29 and June 2; the 25th day after Easter

In parts of Greece, the **Feast of Mid-Pentecost**, which occurs on the 25th day after EASTER, is called the Feast of Rousa (or Rosa). On this day, a special ceremony is performed to ward off scarlatina, or scarlet fever. The children bake rolls out of flour, butter, honey, sesame oil, and other ingredients which they have collected from their neighbors. Along with other foods, these are eaten at a children's banquet, which is followed by singing and dancing. Central to the ceremony, however, is the baking of special ring-shaped cakes, which can only be made by a girl whose name is unique in the neighborhood and which must be baked in a specially built oven.

After the banquet is over, these ring-shaped cakes are divided among the children and hung up to dry. If any of the children who participated in the feast come down with scarlet fever or any similar disease, a piece of the cake is pounded and sprinkled over their skin, which has already been smeared with molten sugar, honey, or sesame oil. This is believed to be an infallible cure.

While the name of this feast is widely believed to come from the crimson rash that accompanies scarlet fever, it may also be a remnant of the old Roman festival known as Rosalia, or Feast of the Roses.

SOURCES:
FolkWrldHol-1999, p. 252

♦ 2247 ♦ Rousalii
May-June; Pentecost or Trinity Sunday, Sunday after Pentecost

In Romania, PENTECOST or the week after, including TRINITY SUNDAY, is the time when the Rousalii, the three daughters of an emperor who were ill-treated during their lives on earth and later became goddesses, set out to cause misery and mischief wherever they could. Traditional Romanian belief holds that during the period from Trinity Sunday to ST. PETER'S DAY (June 29), the Rousalii roam over the earth, causing high winds and storms. People may be caught up in whirlwinds, or children may be snatched from the arms of their mothers if they venture outdoors or travel any distance from home.

On the eve of Rousalii, it is traditional to place a twig of wormwood under your pillow. Because medicinal herbs supposedly lose their potency for several weeks after Rousalii, it is considered unwise to gather any herbs from the fields until at least nine weeks have passed.

SOURCES:
EncyRel-1987, vol. 4, p. 216
FolkWrldHol-1999, p. 343

♦ 2248 ♦ Route 66 Festival
Summer

Known as the "Mother Road" and "America's Main Street," Route 66 once carried travelers across the southern part of the United States for over 2,400 miles, passing through some of Arizona and New Mexico's most scenic areas. But when Interstate 40 was built in the 1960s, Route 66 was bypassed, causing great economic hardship to the communities—some of them Native American—that depended on the highway for their livelihood. Entire towns were boarded up, and miles of the road bed were replaced with cornfields.

The movement to "Save Historic Route 66" by promoting heritage tourism along the historic highway began in the late

1960s and has been going on ever since. Route 66 festivals have been held in several towns and cities located along the old highway, particularly Landergin, Texas, Albuquerque, New Mexico, and Clinton, Oklahoma, where the Route 66 Museum is located. They feature such events as lectures by authors who have written books about the highway, the showing of films involving Route 66, photographic and art exhibits, and music by such well-known performers as the late Bobby Troup, best remembered for his hit song, "Get Your Kicks on Route 66."

The Route 66 National Diamond Jubilee was celebrated in Albuquerque July 20-22, 2001. It was the site of the annual Steinbeck Awards Dinner, at which an award is presented to an individual who has made a significant contribution to preserving Route 66.

CONTACTS:
New Mexico Route 66 Association
1415 Central Ave. N.E.
Albuquerque, NM 87106
505-852-2995
www.rt66nm.org

Oklahoma Historical Society
2401 N. Laird Ave.
Oklahoma City, OK 73105
800-288-2577 or 405-521-2491; fax: 405-521-2492
www.ok-history.mus.ok.us

♦ 2249 ♦ Royal Ascot
Mid-June

The racecourse on Ascot Heath in Berkshire, England, is the site of a world-famous horse race also called the **Royal Meeting**, that was initiated in 1711 by Queen Anne. The Royal Ascot race meeting goes on for four days in June each year and culminates in the event known as the **Ascot Gold Cup**, a race that is nearly two miles long for horses more than three years old. Although the Gold Cup race was established in 1807, the original cup was stolen 100 years later.

A major social and fashion event as well as a sporting one, the Royal Ascot race is usually attended by the British sovereign and receives widespread media coverage. It has even given its name to a type of broad neck-scarf traditionally worn by well-dressed English gentlemen at the races.

CONTACTS:
Ascot Racecourse
Ascot
Berkshire, SL5 7JX United Kingdom
44-87-0727-8765; fax: 44-87-0460-1248
www.ascot.co.uk

♦ 2250 ♦ Royal Brunei Armed Forces Day
May 31

The formation of the Royal Brunei Armed Forces took place on May 31, 1961. Brunei had been a British protectorate since 1888, dependent on the British armed forces for its defense. In 1961, some 60 Brunei recruits began training as part of a transition period toward complete independence for the

country, which occurred in 1984. The Royal Brunei Armed Forces maintain close ties with the British military forces, as well as those of Malaysia and Singapore. They also regularly cooperate in exercises with the armed forces of New Zealand, Australia, and the United States.

The formation of the Royal Brunei Armed Forces is commemorated each year. Around the country, there may be parades and military displays put on by various units of the armed forces. In the capital city of Bandar Seri Begawan, the occasion is usually commemorated at the Taman Haji Sir Omar Ali Saifuddien in the city center. Events include a military parade and such military demonstrations as parachuting exhibitions or mock battles. In 2007, the Royal Brunei Armed Forces marked the anniversary by giving special presents to those children who were celebrating their first birthday on that day. The children were given special souvenirs of the occasion, and bank accounts were opened in their names.

CONTACTS:
Brunei Tourism
Ministry of Industry and Primary Resources
Jalan Menteri Besar
Bandar Seri Begawan BB3910, Brunei Darussalam
www.tourismbrunei.com

♦ 2251 ♦ Royal Easter Show
March-April; one week during the Easter holiday

The largest and best-attended of the Australian agricultural fairs, the Royal Easter Show was first held in 1822 as a way of promoting the country's agricultural industry and helping people sell their products. Now it attracts more than a million visitors each year and has expanded to include sports competitions, fashion and flower shows, and celebrity performances, in addition to the usual agricultural and industrial exhibits.

The show was held at the Moore Park Showground in Sydney every year from 1882 to 1997, although it was canceled during the 1919 influenza epidemic and during World War II, when the showground was occupied by the Australian army. Sponsored by the Royal Agricultural Society of New South Wales, the Royal Easter Show has been held since 1998 at the Sydney Showground at Homebush Bay and attracts more than 600 exhibitors each year and is similar to some of the larger American state fairs, such as the Iowa State Fair and the Eastern States Exposition.

See also Royal Shows

CONTACTS:
Royal Agricultural Society of New South Wales
1 Showground Rd., Sydney Olympic Pk.
Homebush Bay, NSW 2127 Australia
61-2-9704-1111; fax: 61-2-9704-1122
www.eastershow.com.au

SOURCES:
GdWrldFest-1985, p. 6

♦ 2252 ♦ Royal Ploughing Ceremony
Early May

The Royal Ploughing Ceremony is an ancient Brahman ritual held on a large field near the Grand Palace in Bangkok, Thailand. It celebrates the official start of the annual rice-planting season and is believed to ensure an abundant rice crop. The king presides over the rituals, in which the participants wear scarlet and gold costumes and oxen wear bells.

The Brahmans are a small Hindu group in Thailand, numbering only a few thousand families, but they have considerable influence. Royal and official ceremonies are almost always performed by them. The national calendar is prepared by Brahmans and the royal astrologers. Brahman rites blend with those of Buddhism, the dominant Thai religion.

CONTACTS:
Tourism Authority of Thailand
611 N. Larchmont Blvd., 1st Fl.
Los Angeles, CA 90004
800-842-4526 or 323-461-9814; fax: 323-461-9834
www.tourismthailand.org

♦ 2253 ♦ Royal Shows
April, July, August, September, October

More than 500 agricultural shows are held in Australia each year, but the annual Royal Shows, held in each of the state capitals, are famous for their outstanding livestock, agricultural, and industrial exhibits as well as their competitive events. More than four and one-half million people visit the **Royals** each year.

The **Royal Queensland Show**, noted for its unusual display of tropical plants and flowers from all over the state of Queensland, is held in August. The **Hobart Royal Show** is held in mid-October. The **Royal Melbourne Show,** the **Royal Adelaide Show**, and the **Perth Royal Show** are held in September. The ROYAL EASTER SHOW, held at Sydney's 71-acre show grounds in early to mid-April, is the most popular of the country's Royal Shows. All of the Royals feature attractions such as sheepdog trials, wood chopping, and tree-felling contests, and the uniquely Australian camp drafts—an unusual rodeo event in which cattle are driven over a course that tests both horse and rider.

Other agricultural shows include **Alice Springs Show, Tennant Creek Show, Katherine Show**, and **Darwin Show**—all observed in the Northern Territory during the month of July.

CONTACTS:
Australian Tourist Commission
2049 Century Park E., Ste. 1920
Los Angeles, CA 90067
310-229-4870; fax: 310-552-1215
www.australia.com

SOURCES:
DictDays-1988, p. 56

♦ 2254 ♦ Ruhr Festival
May-June

Germany's Ruhr Valley is known as a coal-mining and industrial center, and the annual cultural festival celebrated in Recklinghausen continues to reflect the needs and issues of the area. The festival grew out of an informal arrangement in 1946 between the artists of the Hamburg State Opera and the people of the mining town of Recklinghausen. In return for desperately needed coal to keep their theater's heating system from freezing, performers from Hamburg would go to Recklinghausen to perform their plays and operas. A new theater was built there in 1965 with the motto, "Coal I Gave for Art—Art I Gave for Coal."

The vast majority of the people who attend the festival's theater productions, concerts, and exhibitions are industrial workers, and the local trade unions lend their financial support. Events at the Ruhr Festival often address an economic or industrial theme, and there are scientific and political seminars covering new technological developments and their implications for working people.

CONTACTS:
Nordrhein-Westfalen Tourismus e.V.
Worringer St. 22
Cologne, D-50668 Germany
49-221-179-45-0; fax: 49-221-179-45-17
www.nrw-tourism.com

SOURCES:
IntlThFolk-1979, p. 148

♦ 2255 ♦ Rukmini Ashtami
December-January; eighth day of waning half of Hindu month of Pausa

Vaishnavite Hindus believe that Rukmini, Lord Krishna's primary wife and queen, was born on this day. According to the *Harivansha Purana*, she fell in love with Krishna but was already betrothed to Shishupala, king of Chedi. As she was going to the temple on her wedding day, Krishna carried her off in his chariot. They were pursued by Shishupala and Rukmin, her brother, but Krishna defeated them and eventually married her.

The fast known as Rukmini Ashtami is observed by women, both married and unmarried. Rukmini, Krishna, and Pradyumna, their son, are worshipped. A Brahman priest is also fed and given *dan-dakshina*, or charitable gifts, on this day. Many middle-class Hindus believe that observance of this fast ensures conjugal happiness and prosperity, and that it will help them find good husbands for unmarried girls.

SOURCES:
RelHolCal-2004, p. 180

♦ 2256 ♦ Rumi Festival
September to early October

Each September, the Rifa Ma'rufi Order of America, the American branch of an established Sufi Muslim order, sponsors a festival to honor the 13th-century poet and Sufi Islamic mystic Jelaluddin al-Rumi. Held in Chapel Hill and Carrboro, North Carolina, the event attracts hundreds of people to readings of the poets work, Rumi-related lectures, and performances of the music and dance for which the order are renowned. For devotees, music and dance are channels to spiritual ecstasy. Its members are best known in the West as "whirling dervishes" because of their dance rituals that involve spinning in place for extended periods of time.

The Rumi Festival, which spans several days, is held in September (often running into early October) to honor Rumi's birth month and to mark the re-birth of his popularity in the United States and abroad. It was inspired by the famous URS OF JELALUDDIN AL-RUMI, or Whirling Dervish Festival, held every December in Konya, Turkey. The American festival launched in 1997. It is hosted by the Rifai Ma'rufi Order of America, with participation and support from the University of North Carolina Seminar for Comparative Islamic Studies.

CONTACTS:
Rifai Ma'rufi Order of America
P.O. Box 202
Chapel Hill, NC 27149

Carolina Center for the Study of the Middle East and Muslim
  Civilizations
3025 FedEx Global Education Center
301 Pittsboro St.
CB# 7582
Chapel Hill, NC 27599-7582
919-843-0129; fax: 919-843-2102
www.unc.edu/mideast/index.shtml

♦ 2257 ♦ Runeberg (Johan Ludvig), Birthday of
February 5

Johan Ludvig Runeberg (1804-1877) is widely regarded as Finland's greatest poet. His work embodied the patriotic spirit of his countrymen and, because it was written in Swedish, exerted a great influence on Swedish literature as well. One of his poems, "Vårtland" ("Our Country"), became the Finnish national anthem.

Schools throughout Finland are closed on Runeberg's birthday. Busts and pictures of him are displayed in shop windows, particularly in Helsinki, with rows of white candles placed in the foreground. A special ceremony is observed at Runeberg's monument in the Esplanade, where his statue is decorated with garlands of pine and spruce, suspended between four huge torches. Students lay wreaths of flowers at the foot of the monument and sing the national anthem. At night the torches are lit, and lighted candles burn in the windows of houses and apartments.

CONTACTS:
Ministry of Foreign Affairs of Finland
Department for Communication and Culture
P.O. Box 176
Helsinki, 00161 Finland
358-9-1600-5; fax: 358-9-1341-5901
www.virtual.finland.fi

SOURCES:
BkFest-1937, p. 110

♦ 2258 ♦ Running of the Bulls in Mexico
Sunday following August 15

The running of the bulls that takes place on the Sunday following the Feast of the ASSUMPTION in Huamantla, Tlaxcala, Mexico, is considered to be far more dangerous than the famous running of the bulls in Pamplona, Spain, during the SAN FERMIN FESTIVAL. This is because the bulls are released from cages in nine different locations, making it almost impossible for those who are trying to outrun the bulls to anticipate the direction from which they are coming or the path that they are likely to follow through the maze of streets that lead to the arena. In Pamplona, the bulls are all released in one location, and they follow a well-known route to the bullring.

This particular running of the bulls dates back to the time when the Spanish conquistadores first brought cattle to Mexico, and the custom of running the bulls through the streets of Huamantla was observed every year until it began to fade around 1700. A group of local people revived the tradition in the 1920s as part of the **Assumption Fiesta**.

CONTACTS:
Tlaxcala Tourist Office
Avenida Juarez esq. Lardizabal
Tlaxcala, 90000 Mexico
52-246-465-0900
www.tlaxcala.gob.mx

SOURCES:
GdWrldFest-1985, p. 135

♦ 2259 ♦ Rushbearing Festival
Saturday nearest August 5

The custom of rushbearing in England dates back more than 1,000 years, perhaps to an ancient Roman harvest festival. Young girls would cover the floor of the parish church with rushes and fasten elaborate flower garlands to the walls. After the invention of floor coverings eliminated the need for rushes, the original ceremony gradually evolved into a flower festival, similar to MAY DAY celebrations, with sports, folk dancing, and floral processions.

Modern-day rushbearing ceremonies still take place in Great Musgrave, Ambleside, Grasmere, and Warcop in Westmorland, although Grasmere claims to be the only community where the rushbearing tradition has remained unbroken since ancient times. The poet William Wordsworth was largely responsible for keeping the custom alive there during the early 19th century. He and his sister, Dorothy, lived at Dove Cottage in Grasmere from 1799 until 1808.

Most rushbearing festivals begin with a procession of children carrying flower garlands and wood-framed bearings with rushes woven into traditional designs and ecclesiastical emblems. When they reach the parish church, they scatter rushes over the floor and arrange the garlands and bearings around the altar and against the church walls. There is a religious service, after which the entire village participates in sports, Maypole dancing, and other festivities. Most rushbearing events take place in July and August, often on the Saturday nearest ST. ANNE'S DAY (July 26) or St. Oswald's Day (August 5).

CONTACTS:
Grasmere Tourist Information Centre
Red Bank Rd.
Grasmere, Cumbria LA22 9SW United Kingdom
44-15-3943-5245; fax: 44-15-3943-5057

SOURCES:
FolkCal-1930, p. 164
OxYear-1999, p. 301
YrbookEngFest-1954, pp. 95, 101, 108

♦ 2260 ♦ **Russell (C. M.) Auction**
Third weekend in March

The C. M. Russell Auction features an art auction, a celebration of western artist Charles M. Russell, and a western-style good time in Great Falls, Mont., where Charley Russell had his home and studio. The affair began in 1969 to raise money for the C. M. Russell (as he signed his paintings) Museum, which was then just getting started. Events include seminars, dance demonstrations by the Blackfeet Indians, an exhibit of paintings and sculpture of western artists and an auction of their works, and a Quick Draw, in which artists have 30 minutes to draw any subject they want. Their quick draws are then auctioned. There is also a chuckwagon brunch and a Charley Russell Birthday Party (he was born March 19, 1864, and died in 1926).

Charley Russell, a cowboy artist who was also the author of a collection of stories and sketches, *Trails Plowed Under,* depicted the early days of cowpunchers and Indians in Montana and Wyoming. In an introduction to *Trails Plowed Under,* Will ROGERS wrote that there will never be "the Real Cowboy, Painter and Man, combined that old Charley was." Charley Russell wrote about himself: "I am an illustrator. There are lots better ones, but some worse." His paintings now are coveted by collectors and worth millions.

CONTACTS:
C. M. Russell Museum
400 13th St. N.
Great Falls, MT 59401
406-727-8787; fax: 406-727-2402
www.cmrussell.org

♦ 2261 ♦ **Russian Winter Festival**
December 25-January 5

The Russian Winter Festival is a festival of arts and a time of holiday partying largely in Moscow, Russia, and somewhat less grandly in other cities of the former Soviet Union. In Moscow, there are circuses, performances of Russian fables for children, and other special theatrical presentations as well as traditional outdoor parties with troika (sled) rides, folk games, and dancing around fir trees. On NEW YEAR'S EVE, children wait for gifts from "Grandfather Frost"—who wears a red robe and black boots and has a white beard—and his helper, Snow Girl.

In the past, Grandfather Frost was associated with CHRISTMAS, but religious holidays were stamped out after the 1917 Revolution. After the dissolution of the Soviet Union in 1991,

people began to openly revive old traditions, and Grandfather Frost may again become a Christmas figure, though Santa Claus has also become popular in Russia.

CONTACTS:
Russian Travel Information Office
224 W. 30th St., Ste. 701
New York, NY 10001
877-221-7120 or 646-473-2233; fax: 646-473-2205
www.russia-travel.com

SOURCES:
AnnivHol-2000, p. 213
EncyChristmas-2003, p. 653
GdWrldFest-1985, p. 183
IntlThFolk-1979, p. 375

♦ 2262 ♦ **Rwanda Independence Day**
July 1

This national holiday celebrates Rwanda's independence from Belgium on July 1, 1962, after nearly 50 years of Belgian rule.

CONTACTS:
Rwanda Embassy
1714 New Hampshire Ave. N.W.
Washington, D.C. 20009
202-232-2882; fax: 202-232-4544
www.rwandaembassy.org

SOURCES:
AnnivHol-2000, p. 110
NatlHolWrld-1968, p. 102

♦ 2263 ♦ **Rwanda Liberation Day**
July 4

The Republic of Rwanda is a landlocked country in central Africa. It is bordered by Uganda, Tanzania, Burundi, and the Democratic Republic of Congo.

Rwanda's original inhabitants were the Tutsi and Hutu people. The country was ruled by Tutsi kings until the Europeans began arriving in 1894. Rwanda became a German colony in 1899, but the Belgian military from Zaire took control of the country in 1915. After World War I, Rwanda became a mandate territory of the League of Nations under the administration of Belgium.

The Belgian rulers established discriminatory practices throughout the country, leading the Batutsi king and his chiefs to form the Union Nationale Rwandaise (UNAR), a political party that demanded independence. In response, the Belgian authorities created another party called Parmehutu. In 1959, under the Belgian supervision, the Parmehutu began the massacre of hundreds of thousands of Batutsi. On July 1, 1962, the United Nations terminated the Belgian trusteeship and granted full independence to Rwanda.

On July 5, 1973, Major General Juvenal Habyarimana led the military and took power. He dissolved the National Assembly and the Parmehutu Party and abolished all political activity. In December 1978, Rwandans overwhelmingly endorsed a new constitution and elected Habyarimana as president. He was re-elected in 1983 and again in 1988. In response to public pressure for political reform, President Habyarimana announced in 1990 his plans to transform Rwanda's one-party state into a multi-party democracy. Later that year, Rwandan exiles, primarily ethnic Tutsis, formed the Rwandan Patriotic Front (RPF) and invaded Rwanda. A cease-fire took effect on July 31, 1992.

On April 6, 1994, an airplane carrying President Habyarimana and the President of Burundi was shot down, and both presidents were killed. The Rwandan Army and militia groups immediately began rounding up and killing all Tutsis and moderate Hutus throughout the country. As many as 800,000 Tutsis and moderate Hutus had been killed by July. On July 4, 1994, the RPF took over Kigali, and the war ended on July 16. This is now known as the Rwandan genocide.

Today, Rwandans across the country celebrate the anniversary of their liberation on July 4. The main celebrations take place at Amahoro Stadium in Kigali. Delegations from Ethiopia, the Democratic Republic of Congo, Burundi, Uganda, South Africa, Tanzania, and Zimbabwe attend the colorful ceremony that includes a military parade, music, dancing, and recitals. The president addresses the nation, calling on the people to reflect on the past tragedies of Rwanda and the successes that have been made since 1994 to rebuild and develop the country. The celebrations in Kigali also include an official state reception and a football game between Rwanda and Uganda. Similar ceremonies are held around the country to mark Liberation Day.

CONTACTS:
Republic of Rwanda Ministry of Commerce, Industry, Investment
  Promotion, Tourism & Cooperatives
www.minicom.gov.rw

♦ 2264 ♦ **Rwanda National Heroes' Day**
February 1

The Republic of Rwanda is a landlocked country in central Africa, bordered by Uganda, Tanzania, Burundi, and the Democratic Republic of Congo. Rwandans celebrate Heroes' Day on February 1. National celebrations take place starting early in the morning with the laying of wreaths at the Heroes' Cemetery at Remera, Kigali, by the president, officials of the government, and the families of the country's heroes.

National Heroes' Day commemorates events that occurred after April 6, 1994, when Rwandan President Juvenal Habyarimana and the president of Burundi were killed when their airplane was shot down. After that, the Rwandan military began to systematically kill all Tutsis and moderate Hutus. Local officials and government-sponsored radio stations called on ordinary citizens to kill their Tutsi neighbors. Hundreds of thousands of Tutsi and moderate Hutus were killed. This is now known as the Rwandan genocide. Victims of this genocide are remembered on Heroes' Day.

During the Rwandan genocide, rebels surrounded the Nyange Secondary School and asked the students to identify the Tutsi students. When a group of students refused to do this, the rebels killed them. This heroic act is also remembered on National Heroes' Day. Wreaths are laid at Nyange in memory of students who stood against the rebel forces. The national Heroes' Day celebration at Nyange features songs, dances, and poems praising the virtues and good example of the national heroes. The people are reminded of the great value in service to the country that the national heroes have shown those who are still alive.

CONTACTS:
Republic of Rwanda Ministry of Commerce, Industry, Investment
  Promotion, Tourism & Cooperatives
www.minicom.gov.rw

S

♦ 2265 ♦ Saba Saba Day
July 7

July 7 marks the day when the ruling party of Tanzania, known as TANU (Tanganyika African National Union), was formed in 1954. The TANU Creed is based on the principles of socialism as set forth in the TANU Constitution. Also known as **Saba Saba Peasants' Day** or **Industrial Day**, it is officially celebrated in a different region of the country each year with traditional dances, sports, processions, rallies, and fairs.

Tanzania, perhaps best known as the home of Mount Kilimanjaro, was formed in 1964 when Tanganyika merged with Zanzibar.

CONTACTS:
Embassy of the United Republic of Tanzania
2139 R St. N.W.
Washington, D.C. 20008
202-939-6125; fax: 202-797-7408
www.tanzaniaembassy-us.org

SOURCES:
AnnivHol-2000, p. 114

♦ 2266 ♦ Sabantui
Spring

Sabantui, or the **Festival of the Plow**, was originally an agricultural celebration of the planting season. The date is now set each year by the president of the Republic of Tatarstan. The festival is held in Kazan on the Volga River. The events include climbing a greased pole to reach a cock in a cage on top and "smashing the crocks," a variation of Pin-the-Tail-on-the-Donkey in which a blindfolded player who has been spun around several times tries to break open crockery pieces that contain prizes. There are also wrestling matches, foot and horse races, and lots of music and food.

Sabantui is also celebrated by Tatars living in Belarus. People of Tatar ancestry in Turkey observe Tepresh in June, a similar festival marking the end of the planting season.

CONTACTS:
Tatarstan Department of Foreign Affairs
Kazan, Tatarstan 420014 Russia

7-843-232-7552; fax: 7-843-232-7088
www.tatar.ru

SOURCES:
BkHolWrld-1986, Jun 25
FestWrld: Russia-1997, p. 24
FolkWrldHol-1999, p. 406

♦ 2267 ♦ Sabbat
Eight times a year, on the solstices, equinoxes, and Cross-Quarter Days

The eight Sabbats are the major holidays celebrated by members of the various Neopagan religions that have flourished in the United States since the mid-1960s. Although normally observed on the VERNAL EQUINOX, SUMMER SOLSTICE, AUTUMNAL EQUINOX, WINTER SOLSTICE, and CROSS-QUARTER DAYS (February 1, May 1, August 1, and November 1), the Sabbats may sometimes be displaced from their traditional dates in order to fall closer to that of a specific Neopagan festival.

Since 1970, the outdoor celebration of Sabbats in the United States has increased in popularity on both the local and national levels. Although local gatherings may attract a few hundred people, there is now an annual cycle of festivals—approximately one for each Sabbat in each major region of the United States—that is regularly attended by thousands of Neopagan adherents. The Sabbat ritual typically combines drama, poetry, music, costume, and dance.

SOURCES:
RelHolCal-2004, p. 268

♦ 2268 ♦ Sabbath of Rabbi Isaac Mayer Wise
Last Sabbath in March

Isaac Mayer Wise (1819-1900), a prominent American rabbi, is generally considered the pioneer of Reform Judaism in America. In 1875 he founded the Hebrew Union College in Cincinnati for the training of rabbis and was its president until his death. Wise also helped organize the Union of American Hebrew Congregations in 1873 and the Central Conference of American Rabbis in 1889.

Reform Judaism began in Germany during the European Age of Enlightenment in the 18th century, when some Jews were struggling to reconcile their traditional beliefs with modern thought and learning. Reform Jews abandoned many ancient ceremonial traditions and stressed ethical teachings over ritualistic observance. Rabbi Wise was the leader who brought these reforms to the United States. Adherents to Reform Judaism honor both the birth and death of Rabbi Wise on the last Sabbath in the month of March.

CONTACTS:
Union for Reform Judaism
633 Third Ave.
New York, NY 10017
212-650-4000; fax: 212-650-4169
www.urj.org

SOURCES:
RelHolCal-2004, p. 57

♦ 2269 ♦ Sacaea
Five days, including the vernal equinox, March 21 or 22

Sacaea was an ancient five-day Babylonian New Year festival associated with Anaitis, the Syrian war goddess identified with the Greek goddess Athena. It was characterized by drunkenness and licentious behavior as well as a reversal of the usual customs and relationships. Slaves ruled their masters throughout the festival, and a mock king was selected from among the criminals. After being feasted and honored for five days, the mock king was executed, thereby serving as a surrogate for the real king, who was supposed to die each new year when a new king was born.

The festival was instituted by Cyrus, king of the Persians, when he marched against the Sacae, or people of Scythia. In order to detain the enemy, he set out tables laden with delicacies to which they were unaccustomed. While they lingered over the food, he was able to destroy them.

SOURCES:
ClassDict-1984, p. 43

♦ 2270 ♦ Sacred Heart of Jesus, Feast of the
Between May 22 and June 25; Friday after Corpus Christi

The Feast of the Sacred Heart of Jesus is a solemnity (meaning a festival of the greatest importance) in the Roman Catholic Church celebrated on the Friday after Corpus Christi. It is devoted to the symbol of Jesus' love for all humanity and is a significant holiday in Colombia.

SOURCES:
DictWrldRel-1989, p. 637
OxYear-1999, p. 635
RelHolCal-2004, p. 96
SaintFestCh-1904, p. 273

♦ 2271 ♦ Sadie Hawkins Day
Usually first Saturday in November

Sadie Hawkins Day was created as a day when spinsters can legitimately chase bachelors; if caught, the men are obliged to marry their pursuers. Artist Al Capp invented the unpretty but hopeful Sadie Hawkins and her day in his comic strip, *L'il Abner,* some time in the 1930s. In the following decades, Sadie Hawkins Days, usually featuring dances to which males were invited by females, were popular on school campuses. Celebrations are rarer now.

Capp's long-running *L'il Abner,* named for its good-looking but not-too-bright hero, injected the hillbilly characters of Dogpatch into American culture.

SOURCES:
AnnivHol-2000, p. 199
DictDays-1988, p. 100

♦ 2272 ♦ Safari Rally
July

The Safari Rally, a grueling weekend auto race, takes place on a 2,550-mile circuit over unpaved roads. Starting outside Nairobi, Kenya, the route is considered the toughest in the world; the roads climb in and out of the Great Rift Valley, and there are severe changes in climate. Furthermore, it's the rainy season when the race is held, and the roads can turn into virtual swamps. There are usually about 100 entrants, and fewer than 10 to 20 finish.

The rally began as part of the celebrations marking the coronation of QUEEN ELIZABETH II in 1953 and was called the **Coronation Rally**. It generated such interest that it was continued and renamed the **East African Safari,** with Kenya, Uganda, and Tanzania on the route. Since 1974, it has been confined to Kenya. Nairobi gets rally fever at this time of year. The city is hung with flags, and cars sprayed to look like rally cars zoom around the streets. Thousands of spectators watch the race at various points along the route.

CONTACTS:
Embassy of the Republic of Kenya
2249 R St. N.W.
Washington, D.C. 20008
202-387-6101; fax: 202-462-3829
www.kenyaembassy.com

SOURCES:
GdWrldFest-1985, p. 126

♦ 2273 ♦ Saffron Rose Festival
Last Sunday in October

Saffron, the world's most expensive spice, is harvested from the stigmas of the autumn-flowering *Crocus sativus*. Much of the world's saffron comes from Spain's La Mancha region, and it is used to flavor French bouillabaisse, Spanish paella, cakes, breads, cookies, and the cuisines of East India, the Middle East, and North Africa. It takes 35,000 flowers to produce one pound.

The Saffron Rose Festival held in the town of Consuegra each year celebrates this exotic crop, which must be harvested by hand so that the valuable stigmas are not crumpled. Hosted by a national television personality, the celebrations include parades and contests, traditional folk dancing, and the crowning of a pageant queen. Costumed characters from CERVANTES's 17th-century novel, *Don Quixote*, stroll among the crowds who flock to Consuegra for the fiesta.

CONTACTS:
Tourist Office of Spain
666 Fifth Ave., 35th Fl.
New York, NY 10103
212-265-8822; fax: 212-265-8864
www.okspain.org

♦ 2274 ♦ **Sahara National Festival**
November or December

The Tunisian city of Douz is considered the gateway to the Sahara Desert. It is also the site of the annual Sahara National Festival, when nomads and Bedouins from all over the country gather to compete in camel races and to perform traditional music. There is also a poetry contest, a traditional wedding ceremony, and greyhound racing. The time of the week-long festival—which celebrates the date harvest—varies according to the weather, but usually takes place in November or December. A date marketplace is set up during the festival, usually on a Thursday, and fresh dates as well as *lagmi* (the juice of the date palm, fermented in the sun) are sold. Other items for sale at the market, which draws as many tourists as tribesmen, include camels, incense, ebony, rugs, desert flowers, caftans, and Berber tapestries.

CONTACTS:
Embassy of Tunisia
1515 Massachusetts Ave. N.W.
Washington, D.C. 20005
202-862-1850; fax: 202-862-1858

SOURCES:
GdWrldFest-1985, p. 178

♦ 2275 ♦ **Saigon Liberation Day**
April 30

In the mid-20th century, Vietnam was divided into two separate nations. Civil war broke out between North Vietnam, which was allied with the communist regime in China, and South Vietnam, which was allied with the French and the United States. On April 30, 1975, the Vietnam War officially came to an end as communist North Vietnamese tanks rolled onto the grounds of the Presidential Palace in the South Vietnamese capital city of Saigon. The war was a victory for the communist forces and a defeat for the American military. U.S. armed forces were forced out of the country, while the democratic government of South Vietnam was removed from power.

To mark the anniversary of their military victory, the Vietnamese hold celebrations throughout the month of April. The capture of each major city or region by North Vietnamese forces during that month is celebrated locally on the day it happened. The celebrations culminate on April 30th,

when the entire nation celebrates the final victory in Saigon (now named Ho Chi Minh City).

In Ho Chi Minh City, there are military parades featuring marching bands and Vietnam War veterans. Costumed dancers reenact the shooting down of American warplanes. Fireworks are shot off to mark the hour when the South Vietnamese government officially surrendered. The president and other high-ranking officials normally give speeches from the nation's capital in Hanoi. In 2005, the government released some 7,500 political prisoners as part of an amnesty to mark the occasion.

CONTACTS:
Embassy of the Socialist Republic of Vietnam
1233 20th St. N.W., Ste. 400
Washington, D.C. 20036
202-861-0737; fax: 202-861-0917
www.vietnamembassy-usa.org

♦ 2276 ♦ **Saigusa Matsuri**
June 17

For hundreds of years the citizens of Nara, Japan, have searched the surrounding mountains for lilies, gathering them each summer in preparation for the **Lily Festival** at the Isagawa Shrine. The lilies are placed in a Shinto shrine where seven ladies wearing white robes perform a blessing ceremony over them, and a Shinto priest carries a large bundle of the flowers to the altar as an offering. Then the seven women perform a special dance in which they wave lily stalks in a motion designed to ward off the problems brought on by the wet weather typical this time of year. Afterwards, the lilies are mounted on a float and taken out in a procession through the streets of Nara, where it is believed that they will purify the air.

CONTACTS:
Nara City Information Network
Nara City Hall Tourism Information Ctr.
1-1-1 Nijo Oji Minami
Nara, 630-8012 Japan
81-7-4222-3900; fax: 81-7-4234-1111
www.city.nara.nara.jp/b_hp/english/index.htm

SOURCES:
BkHolWrld-1986, Jun 17
RelHolCal-2004, p. 243

♦ 2277 ♦ **Saintes Festival of Ancient Music**
Mid-July

Saintes, an ancient Roman city about 16 miles inland from the Atlantic coast of southwest France, is the setting for a week-long festival of medieval and Renaissance music in July. Concerts are held in some of the town's most famous sites, including Abbaye aux Dames, built in the 11th century, and St. Eutrope Church, with its ancient Roman crypts.

Although the artists who perform there are not always as well known as those who perform at the Festival of International Contemporary Arts, which takes place at the same time only 40 miles away in La Rochelle, performers at Saintes have included the Ensemble Vocal and Instrumental of Nantes, the Ensemble Polyphonique de Paris, and Le Collectif de Musique Ancienne de Paris. For music lovers whose tastes span the centuries, the combination of the two festivals is ideal.

CONTACTS:
Saintes Tourism Office
Ville Musso, 62, cours National - BP 96
Saintes, Charente-Maritime, 17103 France
33-5-4674-2382; fax: 33-5-4692-1701
www.ot-saintes.fr/gbsainteshistorique.htm

SOURCES:
MusFestEurBrit-1980, p. 89

◆ 2278 ◆ Saints, Doctors, Missionaries, and Martyrs Day
November 8

Since the Reformation the Church of England has not added saints to its calendar. Although there have certainly been many candidates for sainthood over the past 450 years, and many martyrs who have given their lives as foreign missionaries, the Church of England has not canonized them, although a few are commemorated on special days. Instead, since 1928 it has set aside November 8, exactly one week after ALL SAINTS' DAY, to commemorate "the unnamed saints of the nation."

See also ST. CHARLES DAY

SOURCES:
AnnivHol-2000, p. 187
DaysCustFaith-1957, p. 284
RelHolCal-2004, p. 105

◆ 2279 ◆ Sakata Chauth
January-February; fourth day of the waning half of the Hindu month of Magha

Hindu men and women fast on this day in honor of GANESH, the Hindu god of wisdom with the head of an elephant, because it is believed to be the day of his birth. After being bathed first thing in the morning, the statue of Ganesh is worshipped with sweets and balls made of *jaggery* (a coarse, dark sugar made from palm trees) and sesame seeds. When the moon rises the fast is broken, and the moon god is worshipped and offered water. The day-long fast observed on Sakata Chauth is believed to ensure wisdom, a trouble-free life, and prosperity.

SOURCES:
DictHindu-1977, p. 91
RelHolCal-2004, p. 183

◆ 2280 ◆ Sallah (Salah) Festival
10th day of Islamic month of Dhual-Hijjah

ID AL-ADHA is an occasion of much pomp and ceremony in Nigeria, where it is also known as the **Durbar Festival**. This is the culmination of the Muslim PILGRIMAGE TO MECCA and a day of communal prayer. People throng together in their best

regalia. Processions of nobles on horseback are led by the emir to the prayer grounds. After a prayer service, the emir, dressed in white and carrying the historic sword of Katsina, is seated in state on a platform. Groups of men take turns galloping up, reining in so their horses rear up at the last moment, and salute the emir. He raises the sword in response. Later, there is entertainment by musicians, acrobats, jesters, and dancers. Niger and some other African countries also celebrate the day with elaborate festivities.

See also ID AL-FITR (NIGERIA)

CONTACTS:
Embassy of the Federal Republic of Nigeria
3519 International Ct. N.W.
Washington, D.C. 20008
202-986-8400; fax: 202-775-1385
www.nigeriaembassyusa.org

Niger Embassy
2204 R St. N.W.
Washington, DC 20008
202-483-4224; fax: 202-483-3169
www.nigerembassyusa.org

◆ 2281 ◆ Salvation Army Founder's Day
April 10

April 10 is the day on which William Booth (1829-1912), founder of the international religious and charitable movement known as the Salvation Army, was born in Nottingham, England. His work as a pawnbroker in London acquainted Booth with all forms of human misery and economic suffering, and his conversion to Methodism led to a career as a Methodist lay preacher and eventually as an independent evangelist.

With the help of his wife, Catherine Mumford, he established the East London Revival Society, which soon became known as the Christian Mission and later the Salvation Army, characterized by its military ranks, uniforms, flags, bands, and regulation books. Booth's work encompassed social reform as well as religious conversion, and he set up children's and maternity homes, food and shelter stations, and agencies for helping discharged criminals. The Salvation Army expanded to the United States in 1880, and today it has outposts in more than 80 countries.

Although Booth's birthday is observed to varying degrees at Salvation Army outposts around the world, a major celebration was held on the organization's centennial in 1965. In the United States, there were open houses at Salvation Army institutions, special commemorative religious services, and other anniversary events. In London, a centennial congress was held in the Royal Albert Hall. The Salvation Army regards 1865 as the year of its founding because on July 2 that year, William Booth first preached at an open-air meeting in London's East End, a slum district notorious for its poverty and crime rate.

CONTACTS:
Salvation Army
101 Queen Victoria St.

London, EC4P 4EP United Kingdom
44-20-7332-0101; fax: 44-20-7236-4981
www.salvationarmy.org

Salvation Army National Headquarters
615 Slaters Ln.
P.O. Box 269
Alexandria, VA 22313
800-728-7825 or 703-684-5500; fax: 703-684-3478
www.salvationarmyusa.org

SOURCES:
AmerBkDays-2000, p. 269
AnnivHol-2000, p. 60
DictWrldRel-1989, p. 646
EncyRel-1987, vol. 2, p. 289
RelHolCal-2004, p. 95

♦ 2282 ♦ Salzburg Festival
July-August

Although the city of Salzburg, Austria, did little to honor its most famous native son during his lifetime, it has been making up for the oversight ever since. The Salzburg Festival is so closely identified with Wolfgang Amadeus MOZART (1756-1791) that it is often referred to simply as the **Mozart Festival**. Although it features musical events by a wide variety of composers and performances by internationally celebrated musicians, conductors, singers and instrumentalists, the festival has always paid special homage to Mozart—especially so in 1991 during the Mozart bicentennial celebration.

The festival takes place at the end of July and through most of August at different venues throughout the city. Most of the operatic and large orchestral pieces are performed in the Festspielhaus, while other performances take place in the Landestheater. Chamber music concerts are usually given in the hall of the Mozarteum, and the Residenz is the scene for serenade concerts held by candlelight. Visits to Mozart's birthplace at Getreidegasse 9 are especially popular during the festival.

CONTACTS:
Salzburg Festival
Herbert von Karajan Platz 11
Postfach 140
Salzburg, A-5010 Austria
43-662-80455-00; fax: 43-662-80455-55
www.salzburgerfestspiele.at/Home/DASPROGRAMM/KARTE

SOURCES:
GdWrldFest-1985, p. 13
IntlThFolk-1979, p. 39
MusFestEurBrit-1980, p. 25
MusFestWrld-1963, p. 79

♦ 2283 ♦ Samhain (Samain)
November 1

This ancient Celtic harvest festival was celebrated at the beginning of winter. According to Celtic folklore, this was the day when the souls of the dead and other supernatural entities gathered and would have access to the human realm—thus giving rise to the fears about ghosts and goblins that we now associate with HALLOWEEN, or Samhain Eve.

SOURCES:
AmerBkDays-2000, p. 741
BkHolWrld-1986, Oct 31, Nov 1
DictFolkMyth-1984, pp. 202, 968
FestSaintDays-1915, p. 191
FolkWrldHol-1999, p. 604
OxYear-1999, p. 441
RelHolCal-2004, p. 275

♦ 2284 ♦ Sàmi Easter Festival
March to April, depending on the date of Easter

The Sàmi Easter Festival takes place annually during Easter week in Kautokeino, Norway. The Sàmi people are the indigenous people of the northernmost Nordic regions, including northern Norway. Festival activities include tours by reindeer-drawn sleigh, ice fishing, and snowmobiling. There are art exhibitions and several concerts, with some featuring traditional yoik, as well as modern music of the Samis. The festival is also host to the annual reindeer-racing world-cup race. A highlight of the event is an outdoor drive-in cinema for snowmobiles, known as the Ice Cinema. A film festival runs every year in conjunction with the Sàmi festival, with a variety of films on offer for viewing indoors or out. The main festival launched in 1972, with the film festival debuting in 1997.

CONTACTS:
Saami Easterfest
www.saami-easterfestival.org/index.html

Norwegian Tourist Board
P.O. Box 4649
Grand Central Station
New York, NY 10163
212-885-9700; fax: 212-885-9710
www.visitnorway.com

♦ 2285 ♦ Sàmi National Holiday
February 6

The Sàmi people (formerly known as Lapplanders) are indigenous to the arctic area of the Nordic countries, including Norway, Sweden, Finland, and Russia. Many Sàmi make a living in reindeer husbandry and fishing. Nature is very important to the Sàmi.

The Sàmi have not always had an easy life in Norway. At the end of the 1800s, the Norwegian government implemented policies of Norwegianization, which required everyone to conform to the Norwegian way of life. Schools were not allowed to teach Sàmi language or culture. However, attitudes changed by the mid-1950s, and Norwegian authorities recognized the importance of maintaining the Sàmi culture. Since then, policies have been modified to reflect these changing attitudes, and Norway now embraces the Sàmi language, traditions, and culture.

February 6 is recognized as Sàmi National Holiday in Norway, Sweden, Finland, and Russia. This day is full of activities that celebrate the Sàmi culture. Sàmi National Holiday was first celebrated in 1993 and has become a popular event and a time for the indigenous Sàmi people to celebrate their cultural identity.

CONTACTS:
Royal Norwegian Embassy in Washington
2720 34th St. N.W.
Washington, D.C. 20008
202-333-6000; fax: 202-337-0870
www.norway.org/embassy

♦ 2286 ♦ Samil-jol (Independence Movement Day)
March 1

The Korean national holiday Samil-jol celebrates the anniversary of the independence demonstrations in 1919 protesting the Japanese occupation. (*Samil* means 'three-one,' signifying third month, first day.) Japan had taken over Korea in 1910, depriving Koreans of many of their freedoms. The March 1 movement was a turning point; an estimated two million people took to the streets in peaceful demonstrations, and a declaration of independence was read at a rally in Seoul. The demonstrations were met with thousands of arrests, and close to 23,000 Koreans were killed or wounded. Independence leaders formed a provisional government abroad, and there were major anti-Japanese rallies in the 1920s, but independence didn't come until 1945 with Japan's surrender and the end of World War II. The day is marked with the reading of the 1919 Declaration of Independence at Pagoda Park in Seoul.

See also KOREA LIBERATION DAY

CONTACTS:
Embassy of the Republic of Korea
2320 Massachusetts Ave. N.W.
Washington, D.C. 20008
202-939-5663; fax: 202-342-1597
www.dynamic-korea.com

SOURCES:
AnnivHol-2000, p. 36

♦ 2287 ♦ Samoa Independence Day
June 1

Samoa (called Western Samoa until 1997) gained independence from New Zealand on January 1, 1962. Because the rainy season in Samoa comes in January, however, celebrations are held in June on the first day of the month.

CONTACTS:
Permanent Mission of Samoa to the UN
800 Second Ave., Ste. 400 J
New York, NY 10017
212-599-6196; fax: 212-599-0797

SOURCES:
NatlHolWrld-1968, p. 9

♦ 2288 ♦ San Antonio, Fiesta
Ten days including April 21

The Fiesta San Antonio is a 10-day extravaganza of events held since 1901 in San Antonio, Tex., including SAN JACINTO DAY, April 21. The fiesta celebrates the 1836 Battle of San Jacinto that won Texas' independence from Mexico, and is much more than a simple independence celebration. The distinctive highlight of the fiesta is the Battle of Flowers Parade alongside the ALAMO. Merrymakers originally pelted each other with flowers, but now people crush *cascarones,* decorated eggshells filled with confetti, on each others' heads. Another focal event is "A Night in Old San Antonio," which actually goes on for four nights, bringing thousands into La Villita—"the little town," the earliest residential area of the city, now restored—for block dancing and more than 200 booths selling all kinds of ethnic foods. Some 150 other events include concerts, flower and fashion shows, sporting events, art fairs, a *charreada* (Mexican rodeo), dances and pageants with people in lavish costume, torchlit floats in the Fiesta Flambeau Parade, and decorated barges in the San Antonio River Parade.

CONTACTS:
Fiesta San Antonio Commission
2611 Broadway
San Antonio, TX 78215
877-723-4378 or 210-227-5191; fax: 210-227-1139
www.fiesta-sa.org

Library of Congress
101 Independence Ave. S.E.
Washington, DC 20540
202-707-5510; fax: 202-707-2076
www.loc.gov

SOURCES:
GdUSFest-1984, p. 186

♦ 2289 ♦ San Blas, Fiesta of
February 3

San Blas is the patron saint of Paraguay, and his feast day, February 3, is observed throughout the country. Asunción and other large cities host religious processions, and the smaller villages often have bullfights on this day. Flowers, ribbons, and paper money (attached to the tail) adorn the bull. Because this event is a humorous commentary on bullfighting rather than a real bullfight, the goal is not to kill the bull. Instead, bullfighters try to grab hold of the bull and remove the money from its tail without getting hurt.

See also ST. BLAISE'S DAY

CONTACTS:
Embassy of Paraguay
2400 Massachusetts Ave. N.W.
Washington, D.C. 20008
202-483-6960; fax: 202-234-4508
www.embaparusa.gov.py

SOURCES:
FiestaTime-1965, p. 30

♦ 2290 ♦ San Estevan, Feast of
September 2

The Feast of San Estevan is a harvest dance and annual feast day in the Indian pueblo of Acoma in New Mexico. Acoma is a cluster of adobes atop a barren mesa 367 feet above a valley. It was established in the 12th century and is the oldest continuously inhabited community in America. Only about 50 people now live there year-round, but Acoma people from nearby villages return for feast days and celebrations.

The mesa is dominated by the mission church of San Estevan del Rey, which was completed in 1640 under the direction of Friar Juan Ramirez. All the building materials, including massive logs for the roof, had to be carried from the valley below. Supposedly Friar Juan had gained both the confidence of the Acoma people and access to the mesa by saving an infant from a fall off the mesa's edge. His delivery of the child back to the mother was considered a miracle.

A mass and procession begin the feast day. The statue of the patron saint, ST. STEPHEN (San Estevan in Spanish) is taken from the church to the plaza where the dances are performed from 9:00 A.M. to 5:00 P.M. There are 15 or so different dances—Bear, Butterfly, and Rainbow are some of them.

Acoma also has two rooster pulls, one in June and one in July. These are religious sacrificial ceremonies, during which prayers are offered for rain, for persons who need help, and for the country. Animal rights activists have protested the sacrificial aspect of these rites.

CONTACTS:
Indian Pueblo Cultural Center
2401 12th St. N.W.
Albuquerque, NM 87104
866-855-7902 or 505-843-7270
www.indianpueblo.org

SOURCES:
IndianAmer-1989, pp. 288, 294
RelHolCal-2004, p. 100

♦ 2291 ♦ **San Fermin Festival**
July 6-14

The festivities surrounding this well-known festival in Pamplona, Spain, honoring the city's bishop, begin with a rocket fired from the balcony of the town hall. Bands of *txistularis* (a Basque word pronounced chees-too-LAH-rees)—with dancers, drummers, and *txistu* players (a musical instrument like a flute)—and bagpipers march through the town and its suburbs playing songs announcing the "running of the bulls," an event that has taken place here for 400 years. Each morning, young men, dressed in typical Basque costumes, risk their lives running through the streets of Pamplona ahead of the bulls being run to the bullring where the bullfights will be held. Perhaps the best-known portrayal of this scene occurs in Ernest Hemingway's novel, *The Sun Also Rises*.

CONTACTS:
Pamplona Tourist Office
c/Hilarion Eslava 1
Pamplona, 31001 Spain
34-948-206-540; fax: 34-948-207034

SOURCES:
AnnivHol-2000, p. 114
BkHolWrld-1986, Jul 7
FestWestEur-1958, p. 201
GdWrldFest-1985, p. 163

♦ 2292 ♦ **San Francisco, Fiesta of**
September 26-October 4

In Quibdó, Colombia, the Fiesta of San Francisco is one of the biggest celebrations of the year. The town is divided into eight sections, and each is responsible for putting up its own decorations and altars in preparation for the procession on October 4, which is the highlight of the festival. But several days of sports—which include boxing, horse-racing, cycling, and pig-catching contests—precede this. The streets are filled with people dressed up as devils, savages, and various animals, and there are dancing and fireworks every night. Mock bullfights are held with *vacalocas* (crazy cows), which are wooden cows or bulls with flaming horns.

On the final day, there is an afternoon procession in which everyone—the local police, schoolchildren, religious organizations, and members of the general public—accompany the statue of ST. FRANCIS as it is carried through the streets of Quibdó.

CONTACTS:
Embassy of Colombia
2118 Leroy Pl. N.W.
Washington, D.C. 20008
202-387-8338; fax: 202-232-8643
www.colombiaemb.org

SOURCES:
FiestaTime-1965, p. 154

♦ 2293 ♦ **San Francisco's Day (Lima, Peru)**
August 4 and October 4

On Santo Domingo's Day, August 4, and again on St. Francis's (San Francisco's) Day on October 4, there is a fiesta in Lima where the two saints and their churches exchange greetings. A procession sets out from each church, complete with its own music, major-domo, and image of the saint carried on a litter. The two groups meet in the plaza under a decorated triumphal arch, at which point the litters are lowered in commemoration of the historical meeting between the two men, who died only five years apart in the 13th century. Church bells ring and fireworks are set off, with elaborate banquets to follow at the monasteries of the saint whose day is being celebrated.

See also ST. FRANCIS OF ASSISI, FEAST OF

CONTACTS:
Commission for the Promotion of Peru
Calle Uno Oeste No. 50, piso 13th
Urb. Corpac
Lima, 27 Peru
51-1-4224-3131; fax: 51-1-224-7134
www.promperu.gob.pe

SOURCES:
BkFestHolWrld-1970, p. 111

♦ 2294 ♦ San Gennaro, Feast of
September 19

San Gennaro, or St. Januarius, fourth-century bishop of Benevento, is the patron saint of Naples, Italy. According to legend, he survived being thrown into a fiery furnace and then a den of wild beasts, but was eventually beheaded during the reign of Diocletian. His body was brought to Naples, along with a vial containing some of his blood. The congealed blood, preserved since that time in the Cathedral of San Gennaro, is claimed to liquefy on the anniversary of his death each year—an event that has drawn crowds to Naples since 1389.

Scientists have recently come up with a possible explanation for the phenomenon: certain substances, including some types of mayonnaise, are normally thick gels that can be liquefied instantly by shaking or stirring. Left standing, such liquids soon revert to gels. The answer may never be known because, to date, the Roman Catholic Church has forbidden opening the vial and analyzing its chemical nature.

The Society of San Gennaro in New York City's "Little Italy" section began holding a San Gennaro festival on Mulberry Street in 1925. Since 1996, however, the festival has been organized by the Figli (Children) of San Gennaro, an organization within the Archdiocese of New York City. The 11-day event attracts nearly two million spectators. It includes processions carrying a statue of St. Januarius from the shrine at Most Precious Blood Church as well as a street fair. One of the goals of the event is to find a mate for the festival queen, who more often than not has married within two years after her festival reign. Proceeds from the festival go to low-income schools and parishes on the city's Lower East Side. In 2001, the festival was cancelled due to the nearby terrorist attacks of September 11. Instead, the church held a memorial service followed by a candlelight procession of the statue of the saint.

See also HOLY BLOOD, PROCESSION OF THE

CONTACTS:
Italian Government Tourist Board
630 Fifth Ave., Ste. 1565
New York, NY 10111
212-245-5618; fax: 212-586-9249
www.italiantourism.com

Figli di San Gennaro Inc.
109 Mulberry St.
New York, NY 10002
212-226-6427
www.sangennaro.org

SOURCES:
AnnivHol-2000, p. 157
DaysCustFaith-1957, p. 238
FolkAmerHol-1999, p. 390
GdUSFest-1984, p. 125
OxYear-1999, p. 379

♦ 2295 ♦ San Geronimo Feast Day
September 29-30

San Geronimo Feast Day is the feast day for St. Jerome, the patron saint of Taos Pueblo, probably the best known of the 19 Indian pueblos (villages) in New Mexico. For 1,000 years, the Tiwa-speaking Taos Indians have lived at or near the present pueblo. In the 1540s Spanish soldiers arrived, thinking they had discovered one of the lost cities of gold. The gold-brown adobe, multi-story structures are the largest existing pueblo structures of their kind in the U.S., unchanged from the way they looked to the Spaniards, and are still the home of about 1,500 residents.

The feast day commences on the evening of Sept. 29 with a sundown dance, followed by vespers in the San Geronimo Mission. On the following day, there are foot races in the morning, and in the afternoon, frightening looking "clowns" with black-and-white body paint and wearing black-and-white costumes climb a pole; the act has secret religious significance to the Taos. An Indian trade fair offers Indian crafts and foods for sale.

The Taos Pueblo is also known for its CHRISTMAS celebrations, lasting from Christmas Eve through Dec. 29. On CHRISTMAS EVE, there is a pine torch procession from the church through the plaza, and on Christmas Day, the Deer Dance is often performed.

CONTACTS:
Taos Pueblo
P.O. Box 1846
Taos, NM 87571
505-758-1028
www.taospueblo.com

SOURCES:
IndianAmer-1989, pp. 289, 319

♦ 2296 ♦ San Ildefonso Firelight Dances
January 22-23

These late January festivities mark a highlight in the ceremonial year at San Ildefonso Pueblo near Santa Fe, New Mexico. January 23 is the pueblo's feast day, celebrated with a special church service and dances, such as the Buffalo, Comanche, and Deer dances. The dances are a way of paying respect and giving thanks for the animals on which people depend for food and other materials. On the evening before, there are bonfires and a firelight procession.

CONTACTS:
Indian Pueblo Cultural Center
2401 12th St. N.W.
Albuquerque, NM 87104
866-855-7902 or 505-843-7270
www.indianpueblo.org

SOURCES:
EndurHarv-1995, p. 137

♦ 2297 ♦ San Isidro in Peru, Fiesta of
First two weeks in May

ST. ISIDORE is the patron saint of agriculture, and in the agricultural community of Moche, Peru, the celebration of his festival (May 15) lasts throughout the first two weeks in May. Every night during this period the image of San Isidro, garbed in simple clothes and a hat woven from straw, spends the night at a different farm. The image is placed on an outdoor altar decorated with whatever fruits and vegetables that particular farm produces, and there is considerable competition among the farmers to exceed each other in setting up these altars. After the saint leaves, the altar is taken down and the fruit is distributed among neighbors and guests. A band escorts the saint to the home of his next host.

The saint is returned to the church in Moche on the afternoon of May 14. The straw hat is removed and a silver one put in its place, along with a velvet cape embroidered with gold, in preparation for the procession on May 15. On the nights of May 14 and 15, devil dancers wearing horned masks roam the countryside, taking from small farms whatever they can lay their hands on. Because they are known as the "devils of San Isidro," their deeds go unpunished.

CONTACTS:
Commission for the Promotion of Peru
Calle Uno Oeste No. 50, piso 13th
Urb. Corpac
Lima, 27 Peru
51-1-4224-3131; fax: 51-1-224-7134
www.promperu.gob.pe

SOURCES:
FiestaTime-1965, p. 93

♦ 2298 ♦ **San Isidro of Seville, Feast of**
April 4

St. Isidro or Isidore (c. 560-636) was born in Cartagena, Spain, and eventually became bishop of Seville, a post formerly held by his older brother, St. Leander. St. Isidro is known for creating schools throughout the country and, especially, his writing of the *Etymologies*, an encyclopedic treatment of all kinds of subjects ranging from mathematics to theology. His feast day is celebrated not only in Spain, but in many Latin American countries as well.

In Río Frío, Colombia, April occurs in autumn and is typically very dry. On San Isidro's feast day, April 4, townspeople process the saint's image around the streets and hope that he will help bring some much-needed rain. The procession traditionally takes two steps forward, then one step backward, and so on, with the idea that if it drags out long enough, some rain may fall before the festivities end. If no rain falls, the people who had been singing praises to St. Isidro during the procession may well begin to insult and swear at him.

CONTACTS:
Embassy of Colombia
2118 Leroy Pl. N.W.
Washington, D.C. 20008
202-387-8338; fax: 202-232-8643
www.colombiaemb.org

SOURCES:
FolkWrldHol-1999, p. 278

♦ 2299 ♦ **San Isidro the Farmer, Feast of**
May 15

The **Feast of St. Isidore the Ploughman** is celebrated in Madrid, Spain, with eight days of bullfighting at the Plaza de Toros, colorful parades, and many artistic, cultural, and sporting events. Street vendors sell pictures of the saint, small glass or pottery bells believed to ward off harm from thunder and lightning, and whistle-stemmed glass roses, which provide a noisy accompaniment to the feasting and dancing that go on.

San Isidro (c. 1070-1130) is the patron saint of Madrid and also of farmers. He worked on a farm outside Madrid. According to legend, one day, as his master was spying on him to see how hard he was working, an angel and a yoke of white oxen appeared at Isidro's side. He was canonized in 1622, and local farmers still attend a special mass on his feast day, May 15. The Festival of San Isidro is celebrated in other Spanish towns as well, particularly León and Alicante.

San Isidro is also the patron saint of Saipan, capital of the Northern Mariana Islands in the western Pacific Ocean near Guam. While dance groups practice, men form hunting and fishing parties to provide food, and youth organizations clean and prepare the festival site. The fiesta begins at the end of a novena (nine days of prayers and special religious services). It features games of skill and traditional dances with prizes for the winners, and a great variety of foods.

Philippine towns and villages also commemorate St. Isidro. In Quezon Province, ornaments made from rice meal dyed in bright colors, called *kiping*, are attached to the fronts of houses. Townspeople and the priest parade through town and when that's over, the kiping are eaten.

See also CARABAO FESTIVAL and ST. ISIDORE, FESTIVAL OF

CONTACTS:
Madrid Municipal Office of Tourist Information
Plaza Mayor 3
Madrid, 28013 Spain
34-91-366-5477

Marianas Visitors Authority
P.O. Box 500861
Saipan, Northern Mariyanas 96950 Commonwealth of the Northern Mariana Islands
670-664-3200; fax: 670-664-3237

Philippine Tourism Center
556 Fifth Ave.
New York, NY 10036
212-575-7915; fax: 212-302-6759
www.wowphilippines.com.ph

SOURCES:
BkFest-1937, p. 302
FestWestEur-1958, p. 195
FolkWrldHol-1999, p. 357
GdWrldFest-1985, p. 153
IntlThFolk-1979, p. 272
OxYear-1999, p. 208

♦ 2300 ♦ **San Jacinto Day**
April 21

Fresh from his March 1836 victory at the Battle of the ALAMO, General Antonio López de Santa Anna (1795?-1876) of Mexico proceeded eastward until he encountered the Texan army general, Samuel Houston (1793-1863), at a place called San Jacinto, about 22 miles east of the present-day city of Houston. Raising the now familiar cry of "Remember the Alamo!" Houston's 900 soldiers defeated the Mexican force of nearly 1,600 in a battle that lasted only 18 minutes. Santa Anna was taken prisoner and forced to sign a treaty pledging his help in securing independence for Texas, which was annexed by the United States in 1845.

A legal holiday in Texas, San Jacinto Day is celebrated throughout the state but particularly in San Antonio, where the highpoint of the 10-day SAN ANTONIO FIESTA is the huge Battle of Flowers parade winding through miles of the city's downtown streets.

CONTACTS:
Texas State Historical Association, University of Texas at Austin
1 University Station D0901
Austin, TX 78712
512-471-1525; fax: 512-471-1551
www.tsha.utexas.edu

San Jacinto Battleground State Historical Park Complex
Texas Parks and Wildlife Dept.
3523 Hwy. 134
LaPorte, TX 77571
281-479-2431
www.tpwd.state.tx.us

SOURCES:
AmerBkDays-2000, p. 300
AnnivHol-2000, p. 65
DaysCustFaith-1957, p. 97
DictDays-1988, p. 108
HolSymbols-2009, p. 795

♦ 2301 ♦ San José Day Festival
March 19 and September 19

The San José Day Festival at Laguna Pueblo, about 45 miles west of Albuquerque, New Mexico, used to take place only on ST. JOSEPH'S DAY, March 19. But today it is also celebrated on September 19, when freshly harvested crops can be sold and festivities enjoyed in the summer weather.

The fiesta's events reflect both traditional Laguna events and the Roman Catholic influence common to the pueblos. There are Catholic masses and processions honoring St. Joseph as well as traditional Laguna dancing. Attendees, including other native peoples, can also enjoy a carnival with rides, numerous food stands, and sporting events. One of the largest draws is the annual All-Indian Baseball Tournament in September; Laguna boasts five semi-pro baseball teams.

CONTACTS:
Indian Pueblo Cultural Center
2401 12th St. N.W.
Albuquerque, NM 87104
866-855-7902 or 505-843-7270
www.indianpueblo.org

SOURCES:
FolkAmerHol-1999, p. 383

♦ 2302 ♦ San Juan and San Pedro Festivals
June 24; June 29

The celebrations of ST. JOHN'S DAY (June 24) and ST. PETER'S DAY (June 29) in Tobatí, Paraguay, have much in common. Both have a religious element, with special masses, and a traditional folk element, with a game called *Toro Candil*. In this game, someone plays the toro, or bull, by wearing a hide-covered frame with a bull's skull attached to the front and chasing everyone around. His horns are wrapped with rags drenched with kerosene and set on fire, so that when darkness falls and he chases spectators through the streets, the flaming horns make the game more exciting.

Other costumed characters who play a part in the game include a *ñandú guazú* (a rhea, which is similar to an ostrich) and men playing Guaycurú Indians dressed in rags with faces painted black. The ñandú—actually a child inside a small leaf-covered cage—follows the bull around, and pesters him. The Guaycurú chase women around and threaten to abduct them. Other participants in the festival carry blazing torches and menace women—a remnant, perhaps, of the ancient festivals observed on June 24 with bonfires and the practice of walking barefoot over live coals (*see also* MIDSUMMER DAY).

CONTACTS:
Embassy of Paraguay
2400 Massachusetts Ave. N.W.
Washington, D.C. 20008
202-483-6960; fax: 202-234-4508
www.embaparusa.gov.py

SOURCES:
FiestaTime-1965, p. 101
FolkWrldHol-1999, p. 408

♦ 2303 ♦ San Juan de Dios, Fiesta of
March 7-8

San Juan de Dios (St. John of God) was born in Portugal in 1495. He was a soldier for Spain for some years, but after his troop was disbanded in 1536, he took up a life as a shepherd. John underwent a period of emotional and spiritual difficulty when he was around 40. With the assistance of a priest, he found some stability and decided to devote his life to God, eventually establishing a house in Granada for the sick and the poor. John fell ill after rescuing a man who was in danger of drowning in a flood, and he died in 1550 when he was 55. A religious order, the Brothers Hospitallers, was founded in his honor, and thereafter he was known as John of God and the patron saint of hospitals.

In Puno, Peru, San Juan de Dios is celebrated with a two-day fiesta. On March 7, llamas bring in dry wood for bonfires in a parade with flute and drum music, and in the evening bonfires blaze. The next day, St. John of God's feast day, a procession takes the saint's image through the streets of Puno, and dancers and musicians create a festive atmosphere around the church.

CONTACTS:
Commission for the Promotion of Peru
Calle Uno Oeste No. 50, piso 13th
Urb. Corpac

Lima, 27 Peru
51-1-4224-3131; fax: 51-1-224-7134
www.promperu.gob.pe

SOURCES:
FiestaTime-1965, p. 56
OxDictSaints-1987, p. 234
SaintsFestCh-1904, p. 127

♦ 2304 ♦ San Juan Pueblo Feast Day
June 24

San Juan Pueblo Feast Day is a day to honor St. John the Baptist, the patron saint of the San Juan Pueblo, near Espanola, New Mexico. The pueblo, where the first New Mexican capital was founded by the Spaniards in 1598, is headquarters today for the Eight Northern Indian Pueblos Council.

The San Juan feast day observations, like those of other New Mexican pueblos, combines Roman Catholic ritual with traditional Indian ceremonies.

The celebration begins on the evening of June 23 with vespers and mass in the Church of St. John the Baptist. After the services, St. John's statue is carried to a shrine prepared for it in the pueblo's plaza. This procession is followed by a one-mile run in which anyone can participate; a "sing" by the pueblo war chiefs, or officers; a procession of singers and runners; and two Buffalo dances, each presented by two men and one woman wearing buffalo costumes.

The actual feast day begins with a mass, and is followed by an assortment of dances, which usually include Buffalo, Comanche, and Green Corn (harvest) dances. Men beat drums and chant as the dancers, arrayed in long lines and wearing body paint and elaborate costumes with feathers and beads, move slowly and rhythmically to the beat. Vendors sell jewelry, crafts, and assorted souvenirs, and a carnival with a ferris wheel and carousel is also part of the celebration.

See also ST. JOHN'S DAY

CONTACTS:
Ohkay Owingeh Pueblo
P.O. Box 1099
San Juan Pueblo, NM 87566
505-852-4400; fax: 505-852-4820

SOURCES:
IndianAmer-1989, pp. 286, 312

♦ 2305 ♦ San Lorenzo, Día de
August 10

St. Laurence of Rome was a deacon under Pope Sixtus II in the third century. According to legend, St. Laurence was cooked alive on a gridiron, a few days after the pope was martyred. In the midst of his torture, it is said he suggested that his tormentors turn him over to ensure that he would be well-roasted. His feast day is August 10.

As the patron saint of Zinacantan, Chiapas State, Mexico, San Lorenzo is honored with a five-day festival that takes place

August 7-11 each year. The highlight is a procession, interrupted periodically by a dance performed by the *Capitanes*. Each dancer holds one foot out in front while hopping on the other foot for a time, then they shift so that the opposite foot is held out. Thousands attend the festival, which includes a huge open market and a fireworks display.

CONTACTS:
Mexico Tourism Board
21 E. 63rd St., Fl. 3
New York, NY 10021
800-446-3942 or 212-821-0314; fax: 212-821-0367
www.visitmexico.com

SOURCES:
AnnivHol-2000, p. 134
DaysCustFaith-1957, p. 204
FolkWrldHol-1999, p. 492
SaintFestCh-1904, p. 361

♦ 2306 ♦ San Marino Anniversary of the Arengo
March 25

The Republic of San Marino, a landlocked nation surrounded by Italy, is the smallest republic in the world. It is also the oldest existing state in Europe.

The Arengo was the first form of government in the Republic of San Marino. Under this form of government, all of the patriarchs assembled to decide on important matters dealing with public life in San Marino. This was workable while the population of San Marino was small. But as the population continued to grow, they needed a new means of governing the country.

In 1243, the first two Consuls, the Captains Regent, were elected to office for a period of six months. Every six months, new Captains Regent were appointed. From that point, the Arengo did not meet as an assembly of Patriarchs until March 25, 1906. By then, it was much different from its original form and purpose. The Arengo was still part of community life and met twice a year, in April and October. When new regents were elected, every patriarch could send petitions and requests of public interest to the Grand and General Council.

The Arengo still exists today. Twice a year, the citizens of San Marino can send requests of public interest to the Grand and General Council through their regents. Within one month the regents must decide whether the requests will be discussed in the Council.

March 25 in San Marino is a national holiday that commemorates the Arengo of 1906, which marked the birth of a Parliament elected directly by the people. On this day, all of the military corps appear in full-dress uniform in front of Palazzo Begni. A laurel wreath is placed on the monument to the Fallen, and the ceremony continues with a mass in the Basilica to thank the founder saint. All of the corps participate in a parade through the streets of the old town center.

CONTACTS:
Republic of San Marino State Office of Tourism
www.visitsanmarino.com

♦ 2307 ♦ San Marino Investiture of New Captains Regent
April 1 and October 1

The Republic of San Marino, a landlocked nation surrounded by Italy, is the smallest republic in the world. It is also the oldest existing state in Europe.

The first form of government in San Marino was the Arengo. Under this form of government, all of the patriarchs assembled to decide on important matters dealing with public life in San Marino. This was workable while the population of San Marino was small. But as the population continued to grow, they needed a new means of governing the country.

In 1243, the first two Consuls, the Captains Regent, were elected to office for a period of six months. Every six months, new Captains Regent were appointed. This form of rule has continued to date.

Every April 1 and October 1, the Heads of State are installed in office in a traditional ceremony that follows the centuries-old protocol.

According to the rules, the ceremony begins at 9.45 A.M. with a flag-raising ceremony in Piazza della Libertà, by the Guard of Honour of the Great and General Council, the Militia, and the Military Band. Between 10:00 A.M. and 1:00 P.M., the Captains Regent, the Authorities, and the Diplomatic and Consular Corps, dressed in traditional costumes, are escorted by the Military Corps in a parade that winds along the narrow streets of the old town center. After a ceremony at Palazzo Valloni and in the Basilica del Santo, they meet again in the Government Building, where the exchange of powers takes place between the Captains Regent who have just terminated their mission and the new Captains Regent who are about to guide the republic for the next six months. These ceremonies are open to the public. In fact, the public and visitors to the country are encouraged to witness these time-honored ceremonies.

An important part of this ceremony is when the Official Speaker makes a speech relating to major problems or issues of international importance.

CONTACTS:
Republic of San Marino State Office of Tourism
www.visitsanmarino.com

♦ 2308 ♦ San Marino Liberation Day (Feast Day of Saint Agatha)
February 5

The Republic of San Marino, a landlocked nation surrounded by Italy, is the smallest republic in the world. It is also the oldest existing state in Europe.

Republic of San Marino was twice occupied by military forces, but only for a few months each time: in 1503 by Cesare Borgia, known as Valentino, and in 1739 by Cardinal Giulio Alberoni. Freedom from Borgia came after the tyrant died, while in the case of Cardinal Alberoni, civil disobedience was used to protest against this abuse of power.

In 1739, Cardinal Alberoni invaded San Marino and occupied the country. For the next several months, the people of San Marino protested the occupation and appealed to the Vatican. Clandestine messages were sent to obtain justice from the Pope. The Pope recognized the rights of San Marino and on February 5, 1740, he restored the country's independence.

Today, San Marino celebrates Liberation Day on February 5 to mark the anniversary of the liberation of San Marino. As part of the celebration, there is a public procession from the city of Borgo Maggiore to the capital city of San Marino proper. In addition, various civic celebrations take place throughout the day.

February 5 in San Marino is also dedicated to Saint Agatha, the "co-patron" of the city. Special services are held on this day. In San Marino, Saint Agatha is second only to Saint Marinus, the legendary stone-mason and philosopher who is said to have founded the original city of San Marino.

CONTACTS:
Republic of San Marino State Office of Tourism
www.visitsanmarino.com

♦ 2309 ♦ San Martín Day
Monday after August 17

This national holiday in Argentina honors José Francisco de San Martín, who died on this day in 1850.

Spain had ruled what is now Argentina, as well as nearly all the rest of South and Central America, since the 16th century. Born in 1778 in a town called Yapeyú, San Martín, formerly a soldier in the Spanish army in Europe, came home in 1812 to fight in the revolution against Spain. He led forces across the Andes—an unprecedented accomplishment—to defeat the Spanish in Chile and Peru. The victories he led assured independence from Spain for much of the region.

After passing the torch to Simon Bolívar, another famous South American revolutionary leader (*see also* BOLIVIA INDEPENDENCE DAY), San Martín resigned in 1822. He left Argentina in 1824, and lived out his life in exile in France.

CONTACTS:
Embassy of Argentina
1600 New Hampshire Ave. N.W.
Washington, D.C. 20009
202-238-6401; fax: 202-332-3171
www.embassyofargentina.us

SOURCES:
AnnivHol-2000, p. 137

♦ 2310 ♦ San Miguel, Fiesta de
September 29

On ST. MICHAEL'S DAY in Taypi, La Paz Department, Bolivia, there is a fiesta that demonstrates the importance of both maintaining and crossing the boundaries that exist between communities. Two dance groups—one from Taypi and the other from Ranikera, about three hours walking distance away—meet in the town square for religious ceremonies and dance performances. Both groups perform at the same time, but do so as individual units, without mingling with the other group. They also maintain their boundaries while eating and resting, each group at one far end of the square. Five communal meals are served, with dancing in between, while spectators from other nearby towns observe the proceedings without entering the festival space.

CONTACTS:
Embassy of Bolivia
3014 Massachusetts Ave. N.W.
Washington, D.C. 20008
202-483-4410; fax: 202-328-3712
www.bolivia-usa.org

SOURCES:
FolkWrldHol-1999, p. 571

♦ 2311 ♦ **San Pedro International Costa Maya Festival**
July or August

Ambergris Caye is the largest island of Belize and a major historical site of the Mayan empire, a vast pre-Colombian civilization that extended from Honduras to Mexico. It is also the site of the San Pedro International Costa Maya Festival, an annual event that celebrates the region's Mayan heritage and entices tourists from around the world. Performing at the festival are dancers, musicians, and other entertainers who represent the five countries of the Mundo Maya (Maya World): Mexico, Belize, Guatemala, Honduras, and El Salvador.

The festival began after several leaders of a Belizean chamber of commerce were inspired by a Honduran cultural celebration in 1991. They decided to launch their own party the following year. They set up the festivities in San Pedro Town, the main hub on Amergris Caye. The event's original name was the International Sea & Air Festival, a reference to the aircraft and sea vessels that attendees used to travel to the festivities.

Today, the weeklong festival is considered the biggest in Belize. The opening night is devoted to the Reina de la Costa Maya (Queen of the Mayan Coast), a beauty pageant that has been held since 1996. Each successive night is devoted to highlighting a different Mundo Maya country. Performers from all countries gather for Sunday's grand finale show.

Musicians perform a wide range of music including reggae, salsa, merengue, and traditional Maya. Dancing often accompanies the music performances and enhances the display of traditional culture.

CONTACTS:
Belize Tourism Board
P.O. Box 325
64 Regent St.
Belize City Belize
www.goambergriscaye.com/fest.html

♦ 2312 ♦ **San Roque, Fiesta of**
Week beginning the first Sunday in September

San Roque is the patron saint of Tarija, Bolivia, whose natives, known as *chapacos*, are a mixture of Spaniards and Tomata Indians.

The townspeople wear their best and most colorful clothes—and decorate their dogs—for the fiesta in San Roque's honor that begins on the first Sunday in September. There are processions of the saint's image, which has also been brightly adorned, throughout the week which go through the streets, stopping at the hospital and area churches. Participants in the processions include dancers, singers, musicians, and people who've made personal vows.

The celebration of San Roque is said to go back to colonial times, when a plague devastated the city. After the Spanish colonists prayed to San Roque, the disease reportedly subsided, thus the people began an annual fiesta in thanksgiving.

CONTACTS:
Embassy of Bolivia
3014 Massachusetts Ave. N.W.
Washington, D.C. 20008
202-483-4410; fax: 202-328-3712
www.bolivia-usa.org

SOURCES:
FiestaTime-1965, p. 140

♦ 2313 ♦ **Sandburg Days Festival**
Three days in April

This festival honors Carl Sandburg (1878-1967), a Pulitzer Prize-winning American poet and biographer of Abraham LINCOLN. It is sponsored by the Carl Sandburg Historic Site Association, located at the home where Sandburg was born in Galesburg, Illinois. Literary, history, sporting, theatrical, musical, and children's events are held at the Sandburg house, Knox College, and other venues in Galesburg during the three-day festival, as well as a golf tournament and a folk concert.

As a poet, Sandburg is best known for writing about American cities, particularly Chicago, and for incorporating American folklore in his poems. He also published a highly acclaimed autobiography, *Always the Young Strangers* (1953), which described his boyhood in Galesburg.

CONTACTS:
Carl Sandburg Historic Site Association
313 E. Third St.
Galesburg, IL 61401
309-342-2361
www.sandburg.org

Galesburg Area Convention and Visitors Bureau
2163 E. Main St.
Galesburg, IL 61401
309-343-2485; fax: 309-343-2521
www.visitgalesburg.com

♦ 2314 ♦ **Sandcastle Competition**
Usually July

The Sandcastle Competition is a cash-prize arts competition in the most ephemeral of media, sand and water, held since

1981 in Imperial Beach, Calif. Close to 250,000 spectators come for the parade, the food booths, the fireworks, the band concert—and the sand-castle building. This is no child's play; about 400 amateur and professional contestants compete for cash prizes totaling more than $20,000. Professionals make money building huge sand castles in malls and hotels.

There are specific rules regarding the construction of the castles: no adhesives can be used, but water spray rigs are allowed to keep the art works from drying out and blowing away; teams can number up to 10, but no substitutions are permitted.

In the past, the sand sculptures have represented assorted animals from the nearby San Diego Zoo, including hippos, lions, elephants, and creatures of the sea. One "castle" was a sand sofa with a sand man seated on it, a sand dog by his side, a sand television set, and a sand beer can. The sculpting is always scheduled for a Sunday, and by Sunday night the elaborate works of art, some 14 feet long, are lost to high tide.

The date of the festival is set through checking oceanographic tide tables to make sure the sculpting happens on a day when the tide is lower than normal. Events preceding the Sunday competition are a casual-dress Sandcastle Ball on Friday night, a community breakfast, parade, children's sand-sculpting contest, art exhibits, and fireworks. On Sunday, there's nothing but sculpting and live music.

CONTACTS:
The U.S. Open Sandcastle Committee Inc.
P.O. Box 476
Imperial Beach, CA 91933
619-424-6663

♦ 2315 ♦ **Sanghamita Day**
May-June; full moon day of Hindu month of Jyestha

Observed by Buddhists in Sri Lanka (formerly Ceylon), this day celebrates the arrival of Sanghamita, daughter of Emperor Asoka of India, in 288 B.C.E. According to legend, Buddhism was first brought to Sri Lanka by a group of missionaries led by Mahinda, Asoka's son. Mahinda later sent for his sister, Sanghamita, who arrived with a branch from the Bodhi tree at Gaya, sacred to Buddhists as the tree under which the Buddha was sitting when he attained Enlightenment. The sapling was planted in the royal city of Anuradhapura, where Sanghamita founded an order of nuns. Buddhists still make pilgrimages to the city on this day to see what is believed to be the oldest documented tree in the world.

See also POSON

CONTACTS:
Sri Lanka Tourist Board
111 Wood Ave. S., Ste. 323
Edison, NJ 08820
732-516-9800; fax: 732-452-0087
www.srilankatourism.org

SOURCES:
BkHolWrld-1986, Dec 2

♦ 2316 ♦ **Sango Festival**
Early November

Sango has an extremely prominent cult among the Oyo people of Nigeria. Because Sango, a former Oyo ruler, is identified with thunder and lightning, the festival held in his honor takes place toward the end of the rainy season in early November and features various ceremonies connected with rain magic.

On the first day of the seven-day festival, women form a procession to the river, where they sink a hollow calabash gourd filled with special medicines to mark the beginning of the dry season. The *Timi*, or king, meets the worshippers at a place near the river, accompanied by drummers, trumpeters, and a huge crowd of onlookers. The women of the palace put on a special musical performance praising all the tribe's rulers throughout its history.

The remainder of the week is devoted to similar performances of music and dance before the Timi, although their real purpose is to please and entertain the god Sango. The main performer each day dances in a self-induced trance-like state, during which it is believed that he speaks with the voice of Sango and is impervious to pain. The festival concludes on the seventh day with a procession of fire in which a worshipper carries a large pot containing a sacred flame that brings blessings to all parts of the village.

CONTACTS:
Embassy of the Federal Republic of Nigeria
3519 International Ct. N.W.
Washington, D.C. 20008
202-986-8400; fax: 202-775-1385
www.nigeriaembassyusa.org

SOURCES:
FolkWrldHol-1999, p. 624

♦ 2317 ♦ **Sanja Matsuri (Three Shrines Festival)**
Weekend near May 18

One of the most spectacular festivals in Tokyo, Japan, Sanja Matsuri honors Kannon, the GODDESS OF MERCY (known as Kuan Yin in Chinese), and three fishermen brothers who founded the Asakusa Kannon Temple in the 14th century. *Sanja* means "three shrines," and, according to legend, after the brothers discovered a statue of Kannon in the Sumida River, their spirits were enshrined in three places. The festival has been held each year since the late 1800s on a weekend near May 18. Activities are focused on the Asakusa Temple and Tokyo's "Shitamachi," or downtown area.

More than 100 portable shrines called *mikoshi*, which weigh up to two tons and are surmounted by gold phoenixes, are paraded through the streets to the gates of the temple. Carrying them are men in *happi* coats—the traditional short laborers' jackets—worn to advertise their districts. There are also priests on horseback, musicians playing "sanja-bayashi" festival music, and dancers in traditional costume. On Sunday, various dances are performed.

CONTACTS:
Tokyo Convention & Visitors Bureau
Kasuga Business Center Bldg. 10F, 1-15-15 Nishikata
Bunkyo-ku
Tokyo, 113-0024 Japan
81-3-5840-8892; fax: 81-3-5840-8895
www.tcvb.or.jp/en/index_en.htm

SOURCES:
IllFestJapan-1993, p. 56
JapanFest-1965, p. 152

♦ 2318 ♦ Sanno Matsuri
Every two years in June

Held in Tokyo at the Hié Shrine, the Sanno Matsuri is held every two years, alternating with the Kanda Matsuri at the Kanda Shrine. During the Edo era (1603-1867) when Japan was ruled by the shogun, this festival was attended by the shogun himself. More than 40 festival floats were paraded through the streets, although today only three *mikoshi* (portable shrines) are seen.

People in special holiday outfits jam into the shrine complex. On June 15, the shrine's mikoshi and gilded lions' heads are brought out for the main parade, along with the *dashi* (festival floats or carts) sent by each of the surrounding districts. They are accompanied by about 400 participants dressed in costumes of the Heian Era (9th-12th centuries). The *miko*, shrine maidens, perform *kagura*—sacred dance and music in honor of the gods.

A good-luck ceremony associated with the Sanno Matsuri is known as the *Chi-no-Wa Shinji*. It involves passing—twice to the left and once to the right—through a big circle woven together with *chigaya* (a kind of grass) attached to a frame made of bamboo.

CONTACTS:
Tokyo Convention & Visitors Bureau
Kasuga Business Center Bldg. 10F, 1-15-15 Nishikata
Bunkyo-ku
Tokyo, 113-0024 Japan
81-3-5840-8892; fax: 81-3-5840-8895
www.tcvb.or.jp/en/index_en.htm

SOURCES:
IllFestJapan-1993, p. 72
JapanFest-1965, p. 159

♦ 2319 ♦ Sant' Efisio, Festival of
May 1-4

Although nearly every town and village in Sardinia, Italy, has its own festival, one of the most important is the **Sagra di Sant' Efisio** at Cagliari, which commemorates the martyrdom of a third-century Roman general who was converted to Christianity and was credited with saving the town from the plague. In early May a procession accompanies a statue of St. Efisio, Sardinia's patron saint, through the streets of Cagliari to the church of Pula, the town where he suffered martyrdom. Three days later the statue returns to Cagliari. Several thousand pilgrims on foot, in carts, or on horseback, wearing costumes that date from the 17th century and earlier, take part in the procession, which culminates in a parade down Cagliari's main avenue that is said to rival the parade on ST. PATRICK'S DAY in New York City.

CONTACTS:
Italian Government Tourist Board
630 Fifth Ave., Ste. 1565
New York, NY 10111
212-245-5618; fax: 212-586-9249
www.italiantourism.com

SOURCES:
IntlThFolk-1979, p. 241

♦ 2320 ♦ Santa Fe, Fiesta de
September, weekend after Labor Day

The Fiesta de Santa Fe is a religious and secular festival said (without much argument) to be the oldest such event in the country. It dates to 1712 and recalls the early history of Santa Fe, New Mexico.

The Spanish *conquistadores* were ousted from Santa Fe in 1680 in a revolt by the Pueblo Indians. Led by Don Diego de Vargas, the Spanish peacefully regained control in 1693. Vargas had promised to honor *La Conquistadora*, the small statue of the Virgin Mary that is now enshrined in St. Francis Cathedral, if she granted them success. The first procession was held in 1712 to fulfill that promise.

The festivities start the Thursday night after LABOR DAY with the burning of Zozobra, or Old Man Gloom, a 50-foot-high fabric and wood effigy whose yearly immolation began in 1926. Thousands watch and shout "Burn him!" when the effigy groans and asks for mercy. Fireworks announce the end of Gloom. The next morning there is a mass. Then comes the grand procession: Vargas and the fiesta queen, *la reina*, lead the way on horseback to the town plaza, escorted by the *Caballeros de Vargas*, Vargas's guards or manservants, who are also on horseback.

Afterwards, spectators make their way to the plaza for the start of three days of dancing, street fairs, a grand ball, and a parade with floats satirizing local politicians. The fiesta ends Sunday night with a mass of thanksgiving and a candlelight procession to the Cross of Martyrs overlooking Santa Fe.

CONTACTS:
Santa Fe Fiesta Council Inc.
P.O. Box 4516
Santa Fe, NM 87502
505-988-7575
www.santafefiesta.org

SOURCES:
AmerBkDays-2000, p. 624

♦ 2321 ♦ Santa Fe Chamber Music Festival
July-August

This festival in Santa Fe, New Mexico, started in 1973 and has since produced a range of musical programs from the baroque to the modern. The festival began impressively: the acclaimed cellist Pablo CASALS (1876-1973) was the first honorary president, and artist Georgia O'Keeffe (1887-1986) produced the first of her now-famous posters and program covers. Fourteen artists presented six Sunday concerts that first year; now dozens of musicians of international acclaim take part. Youth concerts, open rehearsals, in-state tours to Indian reservations and small communities, out-of-state tours, and National Public Radio broadcasts have expanded the audiences.

Santa Fe, with its ancient tri-ethnic culture, has a great roster of historic buildings, and from time to time they serve as concert halls. For instance, chamber music concerts have been presented in the Romanesque Cathedral of St. Francis, built in 1869; the Palace of the Governors, in continuous use since 1610; and the 18th-century Santuario de Nuestra Señora de Guadalupe, where altar bells rather than dimming lights signal the end of intermissions.

CONTACTS:
Santa Fe Chamber Music Festival
P.O. Box 2227
Santa Fe, NM 87504
888-221-9836 or 505-983-2075; fax: 505-986-0251
www.santafechambermusic.org

SOURCES:
GdUSFest-1984, p. 121
MusFestAmer-1990, p. 95

♦ 2322 ♦ Santa Fe Opera Festival
End of June through August

The internationally acclaimed Santa Fe Opera Festival began in 1957 and survived the burning of the opera house in 1967. It is now staged in an open-air opera "house" atop a mesa outside Santa Fe, New Mexico, that was renovated from 1996 to 1998.

The Gala Opening Celebration includes an Opera Ball to benefit apprentice programs for young artists, and, on opening night, a festive reception, tailgate parties (with tablecloths and caviar and people in formal dress) and, after the performance, waltzing for the entire audience.

CONTACTS:
Santa Fe Opera
P.O. Box 2408
Santa Fe, NM 87504
800-280-4654 or 505-986-5955; fax: 505-995-3030
www.santafeopera.org

SOURCES:
GdUSFest-1984, p. 121
MusFestAmer-1990, p. 172
MusFestWrld-1963, p. 273

♦ 2323 ♦ Santa Inés, Fiesta of
Week preceding the Sunday nearest January 21

The Mayas of Yucatán, Mexico, celebrate this fiesta in the town of Dzitas, which is located near the well-known Chichén Itzá ruins. The preparation of foods for the fiesta, especially the grinding of the maize for the cakes known as *arepas*, takes place on the Wednesday preceding the Sunday nearest January 21, which is the most important day. Some of these cakes are consumed right away by the *cargadores*, as the men in charge of the fiesta are known, and some are offered to visitors, whom villagers expect will donate funds toward the cost of the festival.

The highlight of the Santa Inés Fiesta is an organized Mayan dance known as a *jarana*. A thatched enclosure is built especially for the dance, which is performed by Maya young people. Dancing couples face one another, the men with their hands in back of them and the women lifting their skirts just a bit. The dance floor may hold more than 200 pairs of dancers at a time, and the jarana is considered a good opportunity to meet young people of the opposite sex.

On the final Sunday another ritual, called the pig's head dance, is held to transfer authority to those who will organize the following year's fiesta. Some of the dancers carry roasted pigs' heads decorated with colored paper flags. At the end of the dance, each new cargador receives one of the pig heads from his predecessor, a symbol of the authority and responsibility that has been conferred on him.

CONTACTS:
Mexico Tourism Board
21 E. 63rd St., Fl. 3
New York, NY 10021
800-446-3942 or 212-821-0314; fax: 212-821-0367
www.visitmexico.com

SOURCES:
FiestaTime-1965, p. 17

♦ 2324 ♦ Santa Isobel, Fiesta of
July 4

Santa Isobel is the great fiesta of the Yaqui Indians of southern Arizona and Mexico, observed on July 4. It features the coyote dance—a ceremonial dance performed for soldiers, chiefs, and pueblo officials who have died, as well as at certain specific fiestas. Three men, each wearing the head and hide of a coyote and holding a bow which they strike with a piece of cane, perform a slow step in a crouching position, stamping the ground with the flat of their feet to the accompaniment of a water drum. All night long the dancers advance toward and retreat from the drum, their motions mimicking those of a coyote. Just before dawn, a plate of meat is placed in front of each of the dancers. Each man picks the meat up in his teeth, just as a coyote would, and delivers it to the drum.

CONTACTS:
Pascua Yaqui Tribe
7474 S. Camino de Oeste
Tucson, AZ 85757
520-883-5000; fax: 520-883-5014
www.pascuayaqui-nsn.gov

SOURCES:
DictFolkMyth-1984, p. 258

♦ 2325 ♦ Santa Rita, Fiesta of
May 22

It is said that when St. Rita was a child, she wanted to become a nun, but she ended up marrying to please her parents. Her husband turned out to be abusive, unfaithful, and, about 20 years into their marriage, was involved in some activity that got him murdered. Rita then fulfilled her childhood dream and joined a nunnery at Cascia, Italy. Her ministry as a nun focused on caring for the ill and troubled until she died of tuberculosis in 1447.

Villagers in Apastepeque, San Vicente Department, El Salvador, celebrate Santa Rita's feast day, May 22, with a dance-drama called the Dance of the *Tunco de Monte*, or Wild Pig. This is an Indian dance going back to pre-Christian times and is popular among Indians all over El Salvador. One person dresses in pig skins and pretends to be a pig, while other dancers portray various other stock characters. They enact the chasing and, finally, killing of the pig. At the concluding "feast" the hunter who has caught the pig alternates between praying to Santa Rita for the welfare of the village and cracking jokes.

CONTACTS:
Embassy of El Salvador
1400 16th St. N.W., Ste. 100
Washington, D.C. 20036
202-265-9671; fax: 202-232-3763
www.elsalvador.org

SOURCES:
FiestaTime-1965, p. 94
OxDictSaints-1987, p. 370

♦ 2326 ♦ Santa Rosalia Fishermen's Festival
September, weekend after Labor Day

St. Rosalia is the patron saint of Palermo, and Sicilian Americans living in Monterey, California, observe a two-day festival in her honor in the hope that she will protect their fishermen at sea and provide an abundant catch.

The Santa Rosalia Fishermen's Festival dates prior to World War II, when a statue of the saint was taken in procession from San Carlos Church to fishermen's wharf. A blessing of the fleet followed, and the statue of Santa Rosalia was returned to the church for a concluding religious ceremony. By the early 1950s, however, the festival had expanded to include fireworks, parades, water events, contests, and colorful fishing nets decorating the streets of downtown Monterey.

Today the festival also celebrates Italian heritage with a traditional bocci ball competition, Italian music and food, and an arts and crafts fair.

CONTACTS:
Monterey County Convention & Visitors Bureau
P.O. Box 1770
Monterey, CA 93942
877-666-8373 or 831-649-6544
www.montereyinfo.org

SOURCES:
FolkAmerHol-1999, p. 394

♦ 2327 ♦ Santamaría (Juan) Day
Mid-April

Juan Santamaría is remembered as a national hero in Costa Rica. The country had been threatened in 1856 by William Walker, an American imperialist who planned to use his mercenary army to conquer Central America and use its citizens for slave labor. Walker had already taken control of Nicaragua and organized a similar invasion of Costa Rica.

Santamaría, a 19-year-old drummer boy from the town of Alajeula, was part of the makeshift militia that fought Walker's forces. On April 11, 1856, Santamaría volunteered for a dangerous assignment. There are conflicting stories about his actions, which either set fire to Walker's fort or his ammunitions store. In any event, Santamaría was killed in the process, and Walker's forces were eventually repelled.

Juan Santamaría Day is actually a week-long festival of parades, concerts, dancing, and marching bands throughout the country, with the biggest celebrations in Alajuela. The official holiday, when schools, government offices, and businesses are closed, is usually on April 11, the anniversary of Santamaría's death. But the official date has been changed in recent years. If April 11 occurs during Easter week or on a weekend, the national holiday is celebrated on the closest Monday.

CONTACTS:
Embassy of Costa Rica
2114 S St. N.W.
Washington, D.C. 20008
202-234-2945 or 202-234-2946; fax: 202-265-4795
www.costarica-embassy.org

♦ 2328 ♦ Santander International Festival of Music and Dance
July-August

Santander, a resort town in northern Spain on the Atlantic coast, is not only a popular summer vacation destination but also the home of an international music and dance festival that has been held there since 1951. The month-long festival offers symphonic, choral, and chamber music; recitals; classical and Spanish dance; and jazz. Although the programs are chosen more for their broad appeal than for their adventurousness, some of the great international ensembles of the world have performed at Santander. Events are held at the Festival Palace of Cantabria, which opened in 1991 opposite the Bay of Santander, as well as at various churches, monuments, and historic sites around the city.

CONTACTS:
Santander International Festival
Gamazo, s/n.
Santander, 39004 Spain
34-942-210-508; fax: 34-942-314-767
www.festival-int-santander.org

SOURCES:
GdWrldFest-1985, p. 163
IntlThFolk-1979, p. 341
MusFestEurBrit-1980, p. 137
MusFestWrld-1963, p. 169

♦ 2329 ♦ Santo Toribio Fiesta
April 27

According to legend, St. Toribio arrived in La Villa de Macate, Peru, at a time when the stream that had supplied the town with water had gone dry. The inhabitants were about to prepare to move elsewhere when St. Toribio knocked his staff against the rocks that surrounded the spring three times, releasing a torrent of water.

On April 27, there is a fiesta held in La Villa de Macate where this miracle is reenacted. After a procession in which the saint's image is carried to the place where the miracle occurred, the priest strikes the same rock three times with a staff, and the water, which has been temporarily diverted, again floods the streambed.

CONTACTS:
Commission for the Promotion of Peru
Calle Uno Oeste No. 50, piso 13th
Urb. Corpac
Lima, 27 Peru
51-1-4224-3131; fax: 51-1-224-7134
www.promperu.gob.pe

SOURCES:
FiestaTime-1965, p. 62

♦ 2330 ♦ Santon Fair
December

Santons are the small, colored clay figures that appear in crèches throughout France at CHRISTMAS. Thousands of people come from all over to purchase their santons at the Santon Fair, which takes place during the month of December in Marseilles. In addition to the usual biblical figures, a number of local figures, garbed in traditional Provençal clothing, can be purchased at the fair. They are made by local families who have passed down the molds and models from generation to generation since the 17th century.

SOURCES:
BkFestHolWrld-1970, p. 128
EncyChristmas-2003, pp. 264, 544

♦ 2331 ♦ São Tomé and Principe National Independence Day
July 12

On this day in 1975, São Tomé and Principe gained official independence from Portugal and became a democratic republic. July 12 is a national holiday in São Tomé and Principe.

CONTACTS:
Permanent Mission of Sao Tome and Principe to the UN
400 Park Ave., 7th Fl.
New York, NY 10168
212-317-0533; fax: 212-317-0580

♦ 2332 ♦ Sapporo Snow Festival (Yuki Matsuri)
February 5-11 (or February 6-12 if February 11 falls on a Saturday or Sunday)

An exuberant celebration of snow and ice held since 1950 in Sapporo, the capital city of the Japanese island of Hokkaido. In 1974, the first international Snow Statue Contest was held. The week's activities feature a colorful parade and competitive events in winter sports. What particularly draws more than two million tourists, though, is the display of colossal ice sculptures along the main street and snow statues in Odori Park.

Because of the shortage of snow in the festival area, thousands of tons of snow are trucked in from the suburbs. The sculptures are spectacular—intricately carved and often several stories high. About three weeks before the festival the work begins: a wooden frame is built and packed with snow; after the snow has hardened the frame is removed and the carving begins. A different theme is chosen each year for the sculptures.

CONTACTS:
Sapporo Snow Festival
Tourism Department
2F City Hall N1, Kita 1 Nishi 2
Sapporo, 060-0001 Japan
81-1-1211-2376
www.snowfes.com/english/index.html

SOURCES:
AnnivHol-2000, p. 34
BkHolWrld-1986, Feb 6
JapanFest-1965, p. 125

♦ 2333 ♦ Sarasota Circus Festival and Parade
January

Colossal! Spectacular! The Sarasota Circus Festival and Parade is a non-stop circus early in the year in the capital of the circus world, Sarasota, Fla. The festival has included a parade in downtown Sarasota. Events include shows of magic, juggling, clowning, dog stunts, knife throwing, and various other acts all day long. In addition, there are outdoor "thrill shows"—performers on high sway poles, on high wires, and on motorcycles on high wires. And there are displays of miniature circuses, arts and crafts, and a circus art and photography show.

Sarasota was put on the circus map in 1927 when John Ringling, one of the founding Ringling brothers, decided to make Sarasota the winter headquarters for the Ringling Bros. and Barnum & Bailey Circus. They moved in 1960 to nearby Venice, but Sarasota was by then established as a circus mecca, and many circus people now make their year-round homes there. Furthermore, the city is home to the Circus Hall of Fame and the Ringling Museum of the Circus. John Ringling's palatial home, Ca d'Zan, completed in 1925, can be seen there, along with the John and Mabel Ringling Museum of Art, which has a fine collection of the art work of Peter Paul Rubens.

CONTACTS:
Circus Sarasota
8251 15th St. E., Ste. B
Sarasota, FL 34243
941-355-9335; fax: 941-355-7978
www.circussarasota.org

♦ 2334 ♦ **Saratoga Festival**
June-August

The Saratoga Performing Arts Center in Saratoga Springs, New York, is the summer home of the New York City Ballet, the Philadelphia Orchestra, and the Spa Summer Theater. The festival held there every summer includes not only performances by these groups, but also a four-week summer school program for talented high school students interested in dance, orchestra and jazz studies, and theater. Ballet and orchestral performances take place in a partially enclosed amphitheater, and visitors often arrive a few hours early to picnic on the grass and enjoy the spacious grounds of the Saratoga Spa State Park, where the center is located.

The Saratoga Festival has seen a number of world premieres, among them the 1976 premiere of Gian Carlo Menotti's first symphony (*see* SPOLETO FESTIVAL USA) and the 1974 world premiere of the ballet, *Coppelia*. The summer theater performs both classical and contemporary plays in the center's 500-seat theater.

CONTACTS:
Saratoga Performing Arts Center
108 Ave. of The Pines
Saratoga Springs, NY 12866
518-587-3330; fax: 518-584-0809
www.spac.org

SOURCES:
GdUSFest-1984, p. 130
MusFestAmer-1990, p. 110

♦ 2335 ♦ **Sasquatch! Music Festival**
Memorial Day Weekend

Since 2002, fans of independent rock music have converged on central Washington for the Sasquatch! Music Festival, a three-day outdoor music festival in May. This event, which offers a serene view of the Columbia River gorge, is a welcome change from the dirt and the grime of many outdoor concert settings. The Gorge Ampitheatre has achieved acclaimed status as one of North America's premiere outdoor venues.

The Sasquatch! lineup usually features about two dozen bands, performing on the three stages of the Gorge Ampitheatre. Bands not on the main bill perform on the Yeti Stage and the Wookie Stage. At the Sasquatch Mainstage, fans have the option of milling in the front or catching the music further back on the grassy hillside. The festival's organic approach and eco-friendly policy is bolstered by its purchase of carbon offsets.

CONTACTS:
Adam Zacks / Seattle Theatre Group
911 Pine St.
Seattle, WA 98101
206-467-5510; fax: 206-315-8066
www.sasquatchfestival.com

♦ 2336 ♦ **Sata-Häme Accordion Festival**
Early July

Every summer, the Finnish town of Ikaalinen draws accordion players from all over Europe and as far away as South America to the Sata-Häme Accordion Festival. During festival week, they perform in the Finnish Folk Musician Championships and the finals of the Gold and Silver Accordion competitions. For some 30 years, festival goers have also enjoyed the free outdoor concerts held on Lake Kyrösjärvi, in the parks of Wanha Kauppala, and around the town. Accordion lessons and workshops are also offered.

CONTACTS:
Sata-Hame Accordion Festival
PL 33 Valtakatu 7
Ikaalinen, 39501 Finland
358-3-4400-224; fax: 358-3-4501-264
en.satahamesoi.fi/index

SOURCES:
WildPlanet-1995, p. 26

♦ 2337 ♦ **Satchmo SummerFest**
Early August

The Satchmo SummerFest is a celebration of the music and legacy of jazz musician Louis "Satchmo" Armstrong, who was born in New Orleans, La., on August 4, 1901. The four-day weekend festival takes place in early August in the city's French quarter. It started in 2001 as a commemoration of the centenary of the beloved performer's birth, and was such a success that it was adopted as an annual event by French Quarter Festivals, Inc.

At the center of the festival is jazz music performed on three stages devoted, respectively, to traditional jazz, contemporary jazz, and brass bands. Participants also honor Armstrong with an annual exhibit of art on a Satchmo theme, with awards for outstanding entries. There are speakers' seminars on the history of music, jazz exhibits, a children's stage, and a jazz-themed Catholic mass. Also featured is a "Satchmo Strut" through New Orleans' live music district, and plenty of New-Orleans-style food, including a red-beans-and-rice luncheon.

CONTACTS:
French Quarter Festivals, Inc.
400 N. Peters St., Ste. 205
New Orleans, LA 70130
504-522-5730 or 800-673-5725; fax: 504-522-5711
www.fqfi.org

SOURCES:
AAH-2007, p. 393

♦ 2338 ♦ **Saturnalia**
December 17-23

This ancient Roman WINTER SOLSTICE festival began on December 17 and lasted for seven days. It was held in honor of Saturn, the father of the gods, and was characterized by the suspension of discipline and reversal of the usual order. Grudges and quarrels were forgotten; businesses, courts, and schools closed down; wars were interrupted or postponed;

slaves were served by their masters; and masquerading or change of dress between the sexes often occurred. It was traditional to offer gifts of imitation fruit (a symbol of fertility), dolls (symbolic of the custom of human sacrifice), and candles (reminiscent of the bonfires traditionally associated with pagan solstice celebrations).

Households would select a mock king to preside over the festivities, which were characterized by various kinds of excesses—giving rise to the modern use of the term *saturnalian*, meaning "a period of unrestrained license and revelry."

SOURCES:
AmerBkDays-2000, p. 804
BkDays-1864, vol. II, p. 745
DaysCustFaith-1957, p. 315
DictFolkMyth-1984, pp. 941, 974
DictWrldRel-1989, p. 182
EncyChristmas-2003, p. 711
EncyRel-1987, vol. 3, p. 98
FestRom-1981, p. 205
FestSaintDays-1915, p. 232
OxYear-1999, p. 501
RelHolCal-2004, p. 270
SaintFestCh-1904, p. 36

♦ 2339 ♦ Saturnalia Roman Festival
Second Sunday in January

The winter solstice celebration of Saturnalia, once a festive observance throughout the Roman Empire, was eventually subsumed by the celebration of Christmas. In the small Welsh village of Llanwrtyd Wells, located in an area that still features Roman structures and artifacts, residents devote a weekend to this long-forgotten holiday honoring the god Saturn.

Llanwrtyd Wells, which prides itself as the "wacky festival capital of the world," takes a tongue-in-cheek approach to the observance, which is organized to draw tourists as well as relive Roman culture. The festival's gladiator chariot race, for example, accompanies a winter beer festival and features mountain bikes towing barrels instead of proper horse-drawn chariots.

This event and others attract attendees dressed in the requisite togas and laurel hats. Festival goers remain in costume for the Saturnalia Ramble, a marked walk through the Welsh countryside along old Roman roads. To enhance the celebration, local pubs and restaurants offer Roman-themed food.

CONTACTS:
Green Events Ltd.
Tourist Information Centre
01591-610666
www.green-events.co.uk

♦ 2340 ♦ Saudi Arabia National Heritage and Folk Culture Festival (Janadriyah Festival)
Two weeks in February/March

Janadriyah, a town located outside Riyadh, Saudi Arabia, is the site of an annual camel race every year that dates back to

the early 1970s. The event attracted the country's traditionalists because it exemplified the older customs of Saudi Arabia, a country whose steps at modernization have been a source of national concern in recent decades.

Seeking to promote the traditional nature of this event and other customs, Saudi Arabian Crown Prince Abdullah ibn Abd al-Aziz and the National Guard established the National Heritage and Folk Culture Festival in 1985. The camel race remains the central event of this annual two-week festival, popularly called the **Janadriyah Festival**, but other activities promoting time-honored expressions and practices round out the program. Classical forms of poetry, dance, theater, and music are all featured, as well as exhibitions of traditional crafts.

About 3,000 camels and their jockeys compete in the big race before a large crowd, which typically includes Saudi Arabia's reigning monarch. Nearby the site of the race stands a permanent "heritage" village, where artisans like carpenters, blacksmiths, metalsmiths, and cobblers demonstrate their crafts. The village usually features a *beit sha'ar*, a Bedouin tent that offers spectators a vivid picture of nomad life.

Each night ends with nightly readings of poetry, lectures on Arabic literature, and music and dance performances by troupes from throughout the Arabian Peninsula.

CONTACTS:
Saudi Arabia Embassy
601 New Hampshire Ave. N.W.
Washington, D.C. 20037
202-337-4076; fax: 202-944-5983
www.saudiembassy.net

♦ 2341 ♦ Savitri-Vrata (Savitri Vow)
May-June; 13th day of waning half of Hindu month of Jyestha

Savitri-Vrata is observed by Hindu women in honor of the legendary princess Savitri. She loved her husband, Satyavan, so much that she refused to leave him when he died, eventually persuading Yama, King of Death, to give him back. Women whose husbands are alive spend the day fasting and praying, anointing their husbands' foreheads with sandalwood paste, and showering them with gifts of food and flowers. Women whose husbands have died beg to be delivered from the miseries of widowhood in a future existence. The *vrata*, or vow, is a ritual practice observed by Hindu women for a period of 14 years to obtain their wish.

See also KARWACHOTH

SOURCES:
BkFest-1937, p. 158
FolkWrldHol-1999, p. 380
RelHolCal-2004, p. 170

♦ 2342 ♦ Savonlinna Opera Festival
Early July to early August

The Savonlinna Opera Festival is a month-long music festival in Savonlinna, Finland. Considered one of Europe's most important musical events, it began in 1967 with a performance of Beethoven's *Fidelio*. In 1992, for its 25th anniversary, *Fidelio* was presented again, as well as George and Ira Gershwin's *Porgy and Bess*, produced by Opera Ebony of New York and conducted by Estonian maestro Eri Klas.

The main site of the festival is the Olavinlinna Castle, the best-preserved medieval fortress in Finland. It was built in 1475 and named by Swedes and Finns on the lookout for raiding Russian armies.

CONTACTS:
Savonlinna Opera Festival Office
Olavinkatu 27
Savonlinna, 57130 Finland
358-15-4767-50; fax: 358-15-4767-540
www.operafestival.fi/In_English.iw3

SOURCES:
GdWrldFest-1985, p. 78
MusFestEurBrit-1980, p. 70

♦ 2343 ♦ Schäferlauf
August 24 or the following weekend

ST. BARTHOLOMEW'S DAY is celebrated in Markgröningen and other towns in the Swabia district of Germany with a barefoot race among shepherds and shepherdesses of the Black Forest. The first known race in Markgröningen was in 1445. Today in Markgröningen, an international music festival is held the weekend before the race. Children of active shepherds still race barefoot, and the winning shepherd and shepherdess are given a sheep or a large mutton roast. After the race there are other pastoral activities, such as a shepherds' dance and a water-carriers' race in which contestants must balance a pail of water on their heads and pour it into a tub at the finish line.

CONTACTS:
City of Markgroningen
Stadt Markgroningen, Marktplatz 1
Markgroningen, 71706 Germany
49-7145-130; fax: 49-7145-131-31
www.markgroeningen.de

SOURCES:
BkHolWrld-1986, Aug 24
FestWestEur-1958, p. 69

♦ 2344 ♦ Schemenlauf
Between January 26 and March 3; week preceding Ash Wednesday

The Schemenlauf, or **Running of the Spectres**, takes place during the CARNIVAL season at Imst, Austria, in the Tirolean Alps. The roots of this traditional Austrian celebration can be traced back to the Middle Ages, when people believed that the densely wooded mountain slopes were populated by good and evil spirits with the power to prevent or promote the growth of seeds in the ground. To ward off the evil spirits, they resorted to mummery and wore frightening masks (*see* PERCHTENLAUF) as they danced through the village mak-

ing as much noise as they could. Originally the festival may have been a way of welcoming spring.

Only men are allowed to participate in the Schemenlauf at Imst. About 400 *Schemen* ("spectres") join the procession, often stopping to invite spectators to join them in the traditional circular dance. Visitors come from all over the world to see this colorful festival, which is followed by a night of revelry reminiscent of MARDI GRAS celebrations elsewhere.

CONTACTS:
Tourismusverband Imst-Gurgltal
Johannesplatz 4
Imst, A-6460 Austria
43-5412-6910-0; fax: 43-5412-6910-8
www.imst.at

SOURCES:
BkFest-1937, p. 29

♦ 2345 ♦ Schubertiade
Mid-June

When Austrian composer Franz Schubert (1797-1828) participated in concerts put on for a small group of friends and fans, these intimate gatherings became known as "Schubertiads." Since 1976, the festival in honor of Schubert's music known as Schubertiade has attempted to recreate this tradition. Under the artistic direction of Hermann Prey, who retired as artistic director in 1984, a 10-year cycle of Schubert's symphonies, songs, and piano concertos has been planned in the exact order in which they were composed, with chamber music, choral music, and operas performed in between. Since 1984, however, the program has also included works by composers other than Schubert.

Initially the concerts were given at the Palace of Hohenems in Hohenems, Austria, with the Alps rising in the background. During the 1990s the festival moved to Feldkirch, and now the Schubertiade is held in the village of Schwarzenberg at the Angelika-Kauffmann-Saal, a beautiful timber-framed hall, at the Kleine Dorfsaal next door, and at the Hotel Post in the neighboring village of Bezau.

A number of ensembles known for their interpretations of Schubert's work have participated in the festival, including the Brandeis Quartet, the Franz Schubert Quartet, the Amadeus Quartet, and the Vienna Philharmonic Orchestra.

CONTACTS:
Schubertiade GmbH
Villa Rosenthal, Schweizer Strasse 1
Postfach 100
Hohenems, A-6845 Austria
43-5576-7209-1; fax: 43-5576-7545-0
www.schubertiade.at/Schubertiade/f_news.2.h

SOURCES:
MusFestEurBrit-1980, p. 27

♦ 2346 ♦ Schützenfest (Marksmen's Festival)
July

This event in Germany is a tradition going back 400 years. There are a number of marksmen's festivals held during the summer months. The biggest of these, in Hannover, is held for 10 days at the beginning of July and attracts about 200,000 spectators. It features merry-go-rounds, other carnival rides, and food booths, many serving sausage. The fair is highlighted by Europe's longest festival procession. There are marksmen's brass-and-pipe bands, paraders in folk costumes, floats, and horse-drawn carriages. Other notable marksmen's festivals are in Düsseldorf in July and in Biberach in Baden-Württemberg in June or July. The Biberach festival has been celebrated every year since 1649 and features a procession of more than 1,000 costumed children.

CONTACTS:
Hannover Tourismus Service
Ernst-August-Platz 8
Hannover, D-30159 Germany
49-511-123-45-111; fax: 49-511-123-45-112
www.hannover.de/english/index.html

SOURCES:
AnnivHol-2000, p. 126
FestWestEur-1958, p. 74

♦ 2347 ♦ **Schutzengelfest (Festival of the Guardian Angel)**
Second Sunday in July

Schutzengelfest is a religious and social occasion in northern Switzerland observed since the 17th century. Its setting is the *Wildkirchli*, or "chapel in the wild," a cave in the Alpstein mountain range in the Appenzell Innerrhoden Canton. A Capuchin monk decided in 1621 that the cave, which is now renowned for prehistoric finds, was an ideal place for a mountain worship service. In 1679, Paulus Ulmann, a priest in nearby Appenzell, set up a foundation to ensure that services would continue.

The festival starts at 10 A.M. when a priest or monk from Appenzell conducts the worship service. Then, a yodelers' choir gives a festive concert, and participants start walking to the villages of Ebenalp or Aescher for feasting and dancing.

CONTACTS:
Switzerland Tourism
Swiss Ctr., 608 Fifth Ave.
New York, NY 10020
877-794-8037 or 212-757-5944; fax: 212-262-6116
www.myswitzerland.com

♦ 2348 ♦ **Schwenkfelder Thanksgiving (Gedaechtnisz Tag)**
September 24

The Schwenkfelders who now live in Pennsylvania Dutch country are the descendants of a small Protestant sect that sprang up in Germany around the time of the Reformation. They were followers of Caspar Schwenkfeld (1489-1561), a Silesian Reformation theologian who founded the movement called "Reformation by the Middle Way." He and his followers separated themselves from orthodox Protestant circles and formed the small societies and brotherhoods that still survive in the United States as the Schwenkfelder Church, or "Confessors of the Glory of Christ."

In 1733, a handful of Schwenkfelder's followers arrived in Philadelphia, and a second group emigrated from Germany on September 22, 1734. The next day they swore their allegiance to the British king, then they spent the following day, September 24, expressing their gratitude to God for having delivered them from persecution. In the Pennsylvania Dutch counties where Schwenkfelders still live, this day is observed as a special THANKSGIVING Day.

CONTACTS:
Central Schwenkfelder Church
Valley Forge Rd.
P.O. Box 67
Worcestor, PA 19490
610-584-4480; fax: 610-584-5761
www.centralschwenkfelder.com

SOURCES:
AnnivHol-2000, p. 160
DaysCustFaith-1957, p. 241

♦ 2349 ♦ **Sea, Festival of the (Seamen's Day, Sjomannadagur)**
First weekend in June

The Festival of the Sea is based on the Icelandic tradition of Seamen's Day, an occasion to honor all who make their living from the sea. It takes place annually, primarily in the city of Reykjavík, but also in fishing towns and villages nationwide.

Traditionally, fishermen compete during the festival in swimming and rowing races and other tests of strength, including the popular tug-of-war. However, the festival has been modernized in recent years, and now includes numerous cultural activities, parades, arts-and-crafts activities for kids, food fairs (featuring sea food in particular), and sailing competitions. In addition, newer residents of Iceland are given the opportunity to share the cultures of their homelands. Tourists come from far and wide to participate in the fun and to view boats and ships as they rest in the harbors.

CONTACTS:
Tourist Board of Iceland
P.O. Box 4649
Grand Central Station
New York, NY 10163
213-885-9700; fax: 212-885-9710
www.goscandinavia.com

♦ 2350 ♦ **Sea Islands Black Heritage Festival**
Mid-August

The Sea Islands Black Heritage Festival is a cultural festival held annually at Epworth by the Sea in St. Simons Island, Ga. The festival celebrates the local Gullah heritage and provides a means of preserving and promoting African culture in the diaspora.

The term Gullah, or Geechee, is used to refer to the African-American people and culture descended from slaves brought

650

from Africa to the coastal region of South Carolina and the Georgia Low Country. Because of its relative geographic isolation in island communities, Gullah culture retained distinctly African and Caribbean features, including traditional foods, crafts, folk beliefs, and language.

Sponsored by A Project for Cultural Affairs (APCA), the Sea Islands Black Heritage Festival takes place on a weekend in mid-August and showcases Gullah/Geechee culture through storytelling, music, art, and such crafts as basket weaving, quilting, and preserve making. An opening night party is held on Friday night, and on Sunday visitors may tour sites connected with local black history. A special Children's Corner offers family activities throughout the weekend, including games, storytelling, crafts, and drumming.

CONTACTS:
Sea Islands Black Heritage Festival
116 Odum Lane
St. Simons Island, GA 31522
912-230-2834 or 912-230-2831; fax: 912-638-5579
www.seaislandsblackheritagefestival.com

♦ 2351 ♦ **Sea Music Festival**
Second weekend in June

The only event of its kind in the Western Hemisphere, the annual Sea Music Festival takes place during the second weekend in June at Mystic Seaport Museum in Mystic, Connecticut. Since 1980 the ships and exhibits representing a 19th-century maritime village along the Mystic River have been the backdrop for more than 40 musicians and chantey (pronounced SHANT-ee) singers from around the world. The festival, attracting about 10,000 visitors, is a tribute to the music that has been an integral part of shipboard life since the 16th century.

The festival offers performances of chanteys, or sailors' work songs, as well as "forebitters"—songs sung for entertainment. Most of the lyrics and melodies are of British or Irish origin, although many incorporate American fiddle tunes, African-American minstrel ditties, older ballads, and the popular music of the time. Chanteys helped the sailor maintain the rhythm of a tedious job. In fact, it was considered bad luck to sing a chantey when no work was being done.

The event features daytime and evening concerts Thursday through Sunday, symposia, workshops, and a dance. There is also a special preview concert for museum members that highlights a well-known performer each year.

CONTACTS:
Mystic Seaport-Museum of America and the Sea
75 Greenmanville Ave.
P.O. Box 6000
Mystic, CT 06355
888-973-2767 or 860-572-5315
www.mysticseaport.org

♦ 2352 ♦ **Sea Offering Ceremonies**
Varies

Offering ceremonies are an important practice in some Javanese religious groups. These ceremonies are often conducted by fishermen in coastal towns at various times of the year as their way of giving thanks to the sea god for their livelihood and of asking for his protection during the coming year.

In some places the Sea Offering Ceremony coincides with a major Muslim holiday. At Klidang Beach in Central Java, for example, it is held as part of ID AL-FITR. In Malang, East Java, it coincides with MAWLID AL-NABI, the Prophet Muhammad's birthday observance.

The offering ceremony held every August in Tegal, Central Java, is in many ways characteristic. There is a feast and a puppet show the night before the ceremony. In the morning, the fishermen bring their offerings down to the beach. A convoy of decorated boats sets out to sea, and the offerings—which often include food, flowers, or a bull's head—are thrown into the water.

CONTACTS:
Central Java Provincial Tourism Office
Jl. Madukoro Blok BB, 1-D Komplek PRPP
Semarang
Central Java, 50144 Indonesia
62-24-760-8570; fax: 62-24-760-8573

East Java Government Tourism Service
Jl. Wisata Menanggal
Surabaya
East Java, Indonesia
62-31-853-1814; fax: 62-31-853-1822
www.eastjava.com

SOURCES:
IntlThFolk-1979, p. 223

♦ 2353 ♦ **Seafair**
July-August

Seafair is an annual summer festival for residents of and visitors to the Greater Puget Sound region of northwest Washington state. The three-week festival features more than 40 educational, cultural, and sporting events, most of which are water-related. It begins with the Pirates' Landing at Alki Beach in West Seattle and includes concerts, a torchlight parade, hydroplane races on Lake Washington, and Bon Odori (Japanese folk dancing) performances (*see also* OBON FESTIVAL). Local businesspeople are honored by being named Commodores, and scholarships are awarded to the festival Queen and Sea Princesses. Seafair claims to be one of the largest festivals in the United States, attracting more than 54 million visitors annually.

CONTACTS:
Seafair
2200 Sixth Ave., Ste. 400
Seattle, WA 98121
206-728-0123; fax: 206-728-9506
www.seafair.com

SOURCES:
GdUSFest-1984, p. 208

♦ 2354 ♦ **Seagull-Calling Contest**
First Saturday in May

The annual Seagull-Calling Contest is held at Marina Park in Port Orchard, Wash., on the first Saturday in May. Contestants of all ages can vie for the title of "Best Seagull Caller in the Country." There are solo, duet, trio, and group categories. Prizes are also awarded for such categories as the most seagulls lured, best costume, most authentic call, and cutest call. Baiting is permitted, so many of contestants bring such delicacies as greasy French fries to lure the gulls. Bribing the judges is not only allowed, it is encouraged. The event is free of charge, and usually draws between 40-50 contestants and many onlookers.

Conceived as a one-off publicity stunt for the centennial of Port Orchard in 1986, the contest has become a beloved event, much covered by national television programs.

CONTACTS:
Port Orchard Chamber of Commerce
1014 Bay St., No. 8
Port Orchard, WA 98336
360-876-3505 or 800-982-8139; fax: 360-895-1920

♦ 2355 ♦ **Sealing the Frost**
Early April

The Cuchumatan Indians of Santa Eulalia in northern Guatemala hold a rather risky ceremony every year early in the planting season. The town of Santa Eulalia is perched high in the mountains and the Indians traditionally believe that the cold frost resides in a crack over the edge of a cliff outside town. In order to protect the new crops from a late frost, the religious leaders in town lead a procession to the cliff. They tie a rope around the waist of one of the leaders and lower him over the edge where he fills in the crack with cement to keep the frost in.

SOURCES:
BkHolWrld-1986, Apr 8
FiestaTime-1965, p. 61

♦ 2356 ♦ **Sebring 12-Hour Race**
March

The **International Grand Prix Sports Car 12-Hour Endurance Race** held every year in March ranks with the INDIANAPOLIS 500 and LE MANS as one of the three great auto races in the world. Held in Sebring, Florida, since 1950, the event draws nearly 100,000 spectators and has featured such world-renowned drivers as Mario Andretti, Juan Fangio of Argentina, and Stirling Moss of England.

CONTACTS:
Sebring International Raceway
113 Midway Dr.
Sebring, FL 33870
800-626-7223 or 863-655-1442; fax: 863-655-1777
www.sebringraceway.com

SOURCES:
GdUSFest-1984, p. 36

♦ 2357 ♦ **Sechseläuten**
Third Monday of April and preceding Sunday

This colorful springtime festival in Zurich, Switzerland, ushers in spring by exploding the *Böögg* ("snowman"), the symbol of winter. *Sechseläuten* means the "six-o'clock ringing," and the present custom stems from the 14th-century practice of ringing the cathedral bells at six in the evening (instead of wintertime seven) to proclaim the earlier end of the spring and summer work day. The first ringing of the six o'clock bell was a good excuse for a celebration.

Festivities begin with a children's parade on Sunday, with the children in historical costumes and accompanied by the Böögg, which is stuffed with cotton wadding and firecrackers. On Monday, members of the guilds (formerly, associations of craftsmen, but now social groups) parade through the flag-festooned city in medieval costumes, accompanied by bands. Everyone converges at Sechseläutenplatz on the shore of Lake Zurich at six that evening, the bells ring, groups on horseback gallop around the Böögg to the music of a hunting march, and then the Böögg explodes and burns. Torchlight parades go on into the night, and feasts are held at guild halls.

CONTACTS:
Zurich Tourism
Stampfenbachstrasse 52, Postfach
Zurich, 8021 Switzerland
41-44-215-4000; fax: 41-44-215-4080
www.zuerich.com/en/welcome.cfm

SOURCES:
AnnivHol-2000, p. 71
BkFest-1937, p. 317
BkHolWrld-1986, Apr 19
FestWestEur-1958, p. 227

♦ 2358 ♦ **Seged**
November; 29th day of eighth lunar month

Seged is a religious festival of unclear origin observed only by Ethiopian Jews known as the Falashas or the Beta Israel. It begins with a procession up a hill to the place where the ritual will be held. The participants wear clean, preferably white, clothes with colored fringe, symbolic of the state of purity in which they have kept themselves by avoiding sexual intercourse and bodily contact with non-Falashas for seven days. The priests, who lead the procession, sing prayers and carry the *Orit* (the Jewish scriptures in Geez—an ancient local language—written on parchment) and other holy books wrapped in colored cloth. Everyone who climbs the hill carries a stone, which is placed on an already existing circular wall marking the holy area where the Orit will be placed.

The ceremony itself includes a commemoration of the dead, where those who wish to honor their deceased relatives place a seed of grain on the stone wall for each relative and say a special prayer. There are also readings from the Orit and donations of money to the priests. After the service is over, the procession moves back down the hill to the prayerhouse, where food for the communal meal—usually *indjära* (bread), *kay wot* (meat stew), and *t'alla* (beer)—is distributed. The remainder of the day is spent in non-religious festivities, especially singing and dancing to the music of *masänqos* (one-stringed bowed lutes).

SOURCES:
FolkWrldHol-1999, p. 627

♦ 2359 ♦ **Seijin-no-Hi (Adults Day; Coming-of-Age Day)**
Second Monday in January

This national holiday in Japan honors those who reached their 20th birthday (voting age) in the previous year. Gatherings, usually with speakers, are held in community centers where the honorees show off their new adult finery. A traditional archery contest is held on this day at Sanjusangendo Temple in Kyoto, with people from throughout Japan participating. Until 2000, Seijin-no-Hi was observed on January 15, but now it is celebrated on the second Monday in January.

CONTACTS:
Japan Information Network, Japan Center for Intercultural
   Communications
2-7-7 Hirakawacho
Chiyodaku
Tokyo, 102-0093 Japan
81-3-3263-5041; fax: 81-3-3230-4107
home.jcic.or.jp/en/index-e.html

SOURCES:
AnnivHol-2000, p. 9
FolkWrldHol-1999, p. 37

♦ 2360 ♦ **Sekaten**
12th day of the Muslim month of Rabial-Awwal

The Prophet Muhammad's birthday, MAWLID AL-NABI, is a public holiday in Indonesia and is celebrated with the festival of Sekaten on the island of Java. Religious ceremonies, including recitations from the Qur'an, the Muslim holy book, coexist with traditional Javanese dances and music.

In the city of Yogyakarta, a procession of *gamelan* musical instruments begins at the palace, or *keraton*, and parades to the Great Mosque. A gamelon is a group of mostly percussion instruments, such as gongs, drums, and xylophones, that comprise an Indonesian orchestra. Gamelans are stored in the palace, but come out for this festive occasion to provide music for worshippers and spectators. Javanese dances and shadow puppet plays are also performed on Sekaten.

CONTACTS:
Indonesian Embassy
2020 Massachusetts Ave. N.W.
Washington, D.C. 20036
202-775-5200; fax: 202-775-5365
www.embassyofindonesia.org

SOURCES:
FestWrld: Indonesia-1997, p. 8

♦ 2361 ♦ **Semana Criolla (Gaucho Festival)**
Between March 15 and April 18; during Holy Week

Gauchos—Latin American cowboys—are highly revered in Uruguay, where for more than 150 years they fought the Indians and ruled the plains. Semana Criolla, a three-week festival that pays tribute to gauchos, coincides with the observance of HOLY WEEK. In the Prado, a park in Montevideo, men in typical gaucho dress—high boots, baggy pants, ponchos, and cowboy hats—compete against each other in horsemanship, lassoing, and bronco-busting, much like a rodeo in the western United States.

The bronco-busting is the highlight of the gaucho festival, and contestants come from all over the country to undergo a screening process designed to select the best applicants for the competitions. There is as much emphasis on elegant costumes and beautiful saddles as there is on the skills involved, and occasionally female gauchos make a name for themselves by appearing in this event.

CONTACTS:
Uruguay Tourist Bureau
1077 Ponce de Leon Blvd.
Coral Gables, FL 33134
877-878-4829 or 305-443-9764; fax: 305-443-7802
www.turismo.gub.uy

SOURCES:
FiestaTime-1965, p. 68

♦ 2362 ♦ **Semana Santa (Guatemala)**
Between March 15 and April 18; Palm Sunday to Easter

Semana Santa, or HOLY WEEK, is without doubt the biggest occasion of the year in Antigua, the old colonial capital of Guatemala, and one of the largest EASTER celebrations in the New World. Thousands of tourists and believers come to the city to witness this massive display of religious theater. The entire Passion play, beginning with Jesus' entry into Jerusalem on PALM SUNDAY and ending with his Resurrection on Easter, is reenacted in the streets of Antigua—complete with armor-clad Roman soldiers on horseback, who charge through the town early on GOOD FRIDAY looking for Jesus. Men in purple robes and accompanied by Roman soldiers take turns carrying *andas* ("floats") through the streets.

CONTACTS:
Guatemala Tourist Commission
299 Alhambra Cir., Ste. 510
Coral Gables, FL 33134
888-464-8281 or 305-442-0651; fax: 305-442-1013
www.visitguatemala.com

SOURCES:
EncyEaster-2002, p. 257
FiestaTime-1965, p. 76
FolkWrldHol-1999, p. 232

♦ 2363 ♦ **Semik**
May-June; seventh Thursday after Easter

In pre-revolutionary Russia, Semik—from *semy*, meaning "the seventh"—took place on the seventh Thursday after EASTER and was observed primarily by young girls. They would go to the woods and pick birch branches, decorating them with ribbons and wreaths. Then they would throw the wreaths into the nearest brook or river. If the wreath stayed on the surface, it meant that they would be married in a year, but if it sank, it meant that they would remain single—or, if married, would soon be widowed. In some areas the wreaths were hung on trees, and as long as they remained there, the girls would have good fortune. Another custom associated with the Semik was the performance of traditional songs and dances by young girls and boys in the forest, often around a decorated birch tree.

In pagan times, the Semik was the feast of a wood god, celebrated at the time of year when the new leaves first appeared on the trees. Since it was the young girls who spent most of their time in the forest picking berries and mushrooms while the women worked in the fields, it is likely that the wreaths hung on the trees were at one time an offering to the wood god.

See also WIANKI FESTIVAL OF WREATHS

SOURCES:
FolkWrldHol-1999, p. 350
OxYear-1999, p. 645

♦ **2364** ♦ **Sending the Winter Dress**
October-November; first day of 10th lunar month

This is the day on which the Chinese send winter clothes to their dead ancestors. They are not real items of clothing but paper replicas. People display the paper clothes in their homes before wrapping them up and addressing them. That done, families proceed to the graves of their departed ones and burn the packages.

This is one of three annual occasions in remembrance of ancestors who have passed on; the other two are CHUNG YEUNG and QING MING.

SOURCES:
FolkWrldHol-1999, p. 617

♦ **2365** ♦ **Senegal Independence Day**
April 4

For many years, Senegal was controlled by various European powers, and France gradually began gaining control over the area in the 17th century. On April 4, 1960, Senegal won its independence from France. Today, April 4 is a national holiday celebrated all over the country, but festivities are particularly grand in the capital city of Dakar.

CONTACTS:
Senegal Tourism Office
350 5th Ave.
New York, NY 10118
212-695-9630; fax: 212-695-9658
www.senegal-tourism.com

Embassy of Senegal
2112 Wyoming Ave. N.W.
Washington, DC 20008
202-234-0540; fax: 202-332-6315

SOURCES:
AnnivHol-2000, p. 57
NatlHolWrld-1968, p. 46

♦ **2366** ♦ **Senj International Summer Carnival**
August

Carnival events are most traditionally held in early spring, in conjunction with LENT, but the masquarade and party spirit of the Carnival are transplanted to early August each year on the eastern shore of the Adriatic Sea. There, in the city of Senj, Croatia, the Senj International Summer Carnival has been held since 1967. Revelers from around the world come to attend the four-day event. Likewise, while many of the parade participants are drawn from local talent, many come from other nations, including Sweden, Austria, and Italy. The festivities reach their height on Saturday, when the main Carnival procession, made up of about 3,000 costumed revelers, makes its way through the streets of Senj, watched by crowds numbering as many as 25,000 people.

CONTACTS:
Senj Tourist Board
Stara Cesta 2
53270 Senj, Croatia
www.tz-senj.hr

Croatian Embassy
2342 Massachusetts Ave. N.W.
Washington, DC 20008
202-588-5899; fax: 202-588-8936
www.croatiaemb.org

♦ **2367** ♦ **Señor de los Milagros**
October 18-28

A religious brotherhood affiliated with the church of Las Nazarenas in Lima, Peru, has maintained an annual devotional procession that began in the 17th century. This devotion centers on a painting of Christ, known as Señor de los Milagros, or Lord of the Miracles. The artist of the painting was an Angolan man brought to Peru as a slave in the 1600s. He lived on a plantation in the Pachacamilla area of Lima and there painted the image of the crucified, brown-skinned Jesus on a wall. This wall painting survived several attempts to erase it and at least one earthquake, in 1746. For these reasons, area Roman Catholics believed it to be an unusual image of Christ that required protection and special attention.

Many men are required to carry the two-ton litter upon which rests the portion of the wall with the painting of Señor de los Milagros. Held between October 18-28, the procession attracts thousands of people, making it one of the most well attended processions in South America. This time of year is sometimes referred to as Purple Spring, because October is springtime in Peru and because nearly everyone dresses in purple for the occasion.

Along the route—which starts at the church of Las Nazarenas and winds its way through the streets of Lima until it reaches the church of La Merced—food stands offer numerous delicacies, especially the traditional favorite sweet, *Tur-*

ron de Doña Pepa. The throngs of people who visit Lima in October for the Señor de los Milagros can also attend a series of bullfights at the Plaza de Acho.

CONTACTS:
Commission for the Promotion of Peru
Calle Uno Oeste No. 50, piso 13th
Urb. Corpac
Lima, 27 Peru
51-1-4224-3131; fax: 51-1-224-7134
www.promperu.gob.pe

SOURCES:
BkFestHolWrld-1970, p. 95
FestWrld: Peru-1998, p. 24
FiestaTime-1965, p. 157

♦ 2368 ♦ **Señor de los Temblores Procession**
Monday before Easter

There is a legend in Peru that early in the 17th century, some men from the port city of Callao discovered an unusual box while out fishing. The shape of the floating box led them to believe that a crucifix might be concealed within, and they brought news of their discovery to Lima church authorities. The church authorities wanted the box brought to them, but it was so heavy that no one was able to lift it. When they resolved to have the box taken to Ayacucho, the box also became mysteriously heavy. But when someone suggested it be sent to Cuzco, the box suddenly lightened—which all present interpreted as a sign that the image in the box desired to go there.

Shortly after it was installed in a chapel of the unfinished cathedral in Cuzco, the city was hit by the terrible earthquake of 1650. The earth shook for three days, and it didn't stop until the crucifix was taken from the undamaged church and carried into the streets. Thereafter, it was called el Señor de los Temblores (Lord of the Earthquakes), and the people believed that it protected Cuzco from earthquakes for almost 300 years.

To commemorate this event, the Quechua Indians of Cuzco take the Lord of the Earthquakes out in procession every year on the Monday before EASTER. Before it leaves the church, however, it is carefully dusted and dressed in white, lace-trimmed panties, which are then covered first with a white loincloth and then with a black velvet one. The statue wears no clothes on its arms or chest, although it wears a curly wig topped by a gold crown. It is carried in the procession by 30 men bearing a heavy litter made of solid silver, and Quechua Indians carrying lighted candles lay down a "carpet" of red flower petals for the Señor to pass over. With church officials bringing up the rear, the procession stops at various churches throughout the city, where the litter enters the church. Few brave a look directly into the Señor's face, as tradition holds that a single glance from the statue indicates that one will die in the year to come.

Although Cuzco suffered a serious earthquake in 1941, the Indians maintain faith in the image's power to protect them.

CONTACTS:
Commission for the Promotion of Peru

Calle Uno Oeste No. 50, piso 13th
Urb. Corpac
Lima, 27 Peru
51-1-4224-3131; fax: 51-1-224-7134
www.promperu.gob.pe

SOURCES:
FiestaTime-1965, p. 64

♦ 2369 ♦ **Serbia Statehood Day of the Republic**
February 15

The Republic of Serbia is a landlocked nation in central and southeastern Europe. For over 300 years, starting in 1459, Serbia was under the control of Turkish Ottoman rule. Because the Serbian people were being oppressed by the Ottoman sultans, many migrated to other parts of the Balkan Peninsula.

On February 15, 1804, Serbian patriot Djordje Petrovic Karadjordje led an uprising against the Ottoman to gain independence. This uprising lasted over nine years, but in the end the Ottoman remained in control. A second uprising, led by Milos Obrenovic, occurred in 1815 and lasted two years. The second uprising was successful, and Serbia formally gained independence from the Ottoman Empire in 1829.

In 2001, the Serbian Parliament declared February 15 a state holiday to commemorate the day in 1804 that the first Serbian uprising against the Turks began. A ceremony is held in Orasac to celebrate the first Serbian uprising and constitution (signed in 1835), which led to the creation of the modern Serbian state. The main celebrations include festive concerts, film and theater premiers, exhibitions, and many other events.

♦ 2370 ♦ **Serreta, Festa da**
September 8-15

The Festa da Serreta that has been held annually since 1932 in Gustine, California, is based on a similar festival held on the island of Terceira in the Azores, from which many of Gustine's residents emigrated. It is held in honor of *Nossa Senhora dos Milagres*, "Our Lady of Miracles," for whom a 16th-century priest built a small chapel in the Azorean village of Serreta.

The week-long festival attracts thousands of visitors. Highlights include the *Bodo do Leite* ("Banquet of Milk") fresh-drawn from the cows as is the practice in the Azores. There are also *cantorías ao desafio* (extemporaneous song contests), which draw contestants from all over California and even some Azoreans.

The image of *Nossa Senhora* is carried in a procession from the church to a portable chapel, or *capela*, that is brought out specifically for use on this occasion. A group of women sit in the chapel and watch over the donations of money that are left there. Another festival event is the traditional bullfight, which takes place in a rectangular arena. The bull is held by a long rope, his horns are padded, and the men do not so much fight him as play with him.

CONTACTS:
Our Lady of Miracles Church
307 Linden Ave.
Gustine, CA 95322
209-854-6692

Portuguese National Tourist Office
590 Fifth Ave., 4th Fl.
New York, NY 10036
800-767-8842 or 212-354-4403; fax: 212-764-6137
www.visitportugal.com

SOURCES:
FolkAmerHol-1999, p. 376

♦ 2371 ♦ Seton (Mother) Day
December 1

The Company of the Daughters of Charity, a community of Catholic women ministering to the "poorest of the poor," was founded in France in 1633 by St. Vincent de Paul and Louise de Marillac. In 1809 an American woman, Elizabeth Ann Bayley Seton (1774-1821), modeled her Emmitsburg, Maryland-based community after the French Daughters, which she called the American Sisters of Charity. The French and American congregations united in 1850 and formed an international community of women serving the poor worldwide.

On September 14, 1975, Mother Seton, as she is known to her followers, became the first American-born saint to be canonized by the Roman Catholic Church. The Sisters of Charity of St. Vincent de Paul continue to observe December 1 as the anniversary of the founding of their order. Many also observe January 4, the day she died, as her feast day (*see* St. Elizabeth Ann Seton, Feast of).

CONTACTS:
Sisters of Charity Federation
6301 Riverdale Ave.
Bronx, NY 10471
718-549-9200
www.sisters-of-charity.org

SOURCES:
RelHolCal-2004, p. 84

♦ 2372 ♦ Setsubun (Bean-Throwing Festival)
·   *February 3 or 4*

Setsubun is a ceremony observed in all major temples throughout Japan to mark the last day of winter according to the lunar calendar. People throng temple grounds where the priests or stars such as actors and sumo wrestlers throw dried beans to the crowd who shout, "Fortune in, goblins out!" Some people also decorate their doorways with sardine heads, because the evil spirits don't like their smell. Beans caught at the temple are brought home to drive out evil there.

CONTACTS:
Japan Information Network, Japan Center for Intercultural
  Communications
2-7-7 Hirakawacho
Chiyodaku
Tokyo, 102-0093 Japan

81-3-3263-5041; fax: 81-3-3230-4107
home.jcic.or.jp/en/index-e.html

SOURCES:
AnnivHol-2000, p. 19
BkFest-1937, p. 196
BkHolWrld-1986, Feb 3
DictFolkMyth-1984, p. 541
FolkWrldHol-1999, p. 111

♦ 2373 ♦ Seven Sisters Festival
July-August; seventh day of seventh lunar month

The Seven Sisters Festival is a celebration for would-be lovers, observed in China, Korea, Taiwan, and Hong Kong. It is based on an ancient Chinese legend and is also known as the **Maiden's Festival**, **Double Seventh**, **Chhit Sek**, and Chilseog. In the legend, an orphaned cowherd is forced from his home by his elder brother and sister-in-law, who give him only a broken-down cart, an ox, and a tiny piece of land. The ox, called Elder Brother the Ox, takes pity on the cowherd, and tells him that on a certain day seven girls will visit earth from heaven to bathe in a nearby river. If the young man steals the clothes of any one of the girls, she will marry him.

The cowherd steals the clothes of the Seventh Maiden. They fall in love, marry, and live happily for three years, when she is ordered back to heaven by the gods. When the cowherd dies, he becomes immortal, but the Queen Mother of the Western Heaven keeps the two apart by drawing a line across the sky—the Silver River, or Milky Way. They can cross this only once a year, on the seventh day of the seventh month, on a bridge formed by thousands of magpies.

On the sixth day of the seventh month, unmarried men pay homage to the cowherd, and on the seventh day, young unmarried women make offerings of combs, mirrors, paper flowers, and powder puffs to the Seventh Maiden. The festival is celebrated chiefly at home, but in Hong Kong young women also visit Lover's Rock on Bowen Road on Hong Kong Island to burn *joss* ('incense') sticks, lay offerings at the rock, and consult soothsayers.

See also Tanabata

CONTACTS:
Hong Kong Tourism Board
115 E. 54th St. 2nd Fl.
New York, NY 10022
212-421-3382; fax: 212-421-8428
www.discoverhongkong.com

SOURCES:
BkFest-1937, p. 79
BkHolWrld-1986, Aug 10
DictFolkMyth-1984, p. 216
EncyRel-1987, vol. 3, p. 326
FolkWrldHol-1999, p. 452
OxYear-1999, p. 702

♦ 2374 ♦ Seville Fair
April

Over the past century, the Seville Fair, also known as the **April Fair**, has developed into one of Spain's major spectacles. Originally a market for livestock, the fair with its multi-colored tents, wreaths, and paper lanterns now transforms the city of Seville. The singing, dancing, and drinking go on for a week, and a sense of joyousness pervades the city. The week's activities include a parade of riders and a number of bullfights held in the Plaza de la Maestranza (equestrian parade ground)—now considered the "cathedral" of bullfighting.

CONTACTS:
Consorcio de Turismo
Edificio Laredo Pza
San Francisco, 19 4
Seville, 41004 Spain
34-954-592-915; fax: 34-954-595-295
www.turismo.sevilla.org/paginas_en/portada.asp

SOURCES:
AnnivHol-2000, p. 67
FestWestEur-1958, p. 194
GdWrldFest-1985, p. 163
HolSymbols-2009, p. 808
IntlThFolk-1979, p. 342

♦ 2375 ♦ Seward's Day
Last Monday in March

When William Henry Seward, secretary of state for President Andrew Johnson, signed the treaty authorizing the purchase of Alaska from Czarist Russia for $7 million on March 30, 1867, most Americans thought he was crazy. They called it "Seward's folly," "Seward's icebox," and "Johnson's polar bear garden." But public opinion quickly changed when gold was discovered in the region.

Since that time, Alaska's natural resources have paid back the initial investment many times over. Its natural gas, coal, and oil reserves, in addition to its seafood and lumber industries, have proved to be far more valuable than its gold. Unfortunately, Seward did not live to see his foresight commemorated as a legal holiday in the state of Alaska. The purchase of Alaska is now widely regarded as the crowning achievement of both William Seward and President Johnson. (*See* ALASKA DAY.)

CONTACTS:
Library of Congress
101 Independence Ave. S.E.
Washington, D.C. 20540
202-707-5000; fax: 202-707-2076
www.loc.gov

SOURCES:
AmerBkDays-2000, p. 243
AnnivHol-2000, p. 54
BkHolWrld-1986, Mar 30
DictDays-1988, p. 109

♦ 2376 ♦ Seychelles Independence Day
June 29

Also known as **Republic Day**, Seychelles Independence Day is a national holiday that commemorates Seychelles' transi-

tion to an independent republic on this day in 1976. It had been a British colony since 1903. Before that, it was a dependency of Mauritius, which was ruled by France.

When Seychelles became independent, the people had a three-month-long party.

CONTACTS:
Republic of Seychelles to the UN
800 Second Ave., Ste. 400C
New York, NY 10017
212-972-1785; fax: 212-972-1786

SOURCES:
AnnivHol-2000, p. 108

♦ 2377 ♦ Seychelles Liberation Day
June 5

Less than a year after gaining independence (see above), a coup overthrew the government. Two major political parties had developed in Seychelles, the Seychelles Democratic Party (SDP) and the Seychelles People's United Party (SPUP). James Mancham, the leader of the SDP party, which won the majority vote, became president, and France Albert Rene became prime minister. Rene's supporters led the overthrow and ousted Mancham on June 5, 1977, an event commemorated as a public holiday on Liberation Day.

CONTACTS:
Republic of Seychelles to the UN
800 Second Ave., Ste. 400C
New York, NY 10017
212-972-1785; fax: 212-972-1786

♦ 2378 ♦ Seychelles National Day
June 18

The Republic of Seychelles comprises 115 islands in the western Indian Ocean. Seychelles was first settled by the French in 1770 and remained in French hands until Napoleon was defeated at Waterloo. In 1814, Seychelles was ceded to Britain under the Treaty of Paris.

Under the British rule, the population of Seychelles doubled, and important estates that produced coconut, food crops, cotton, and sugar cane were established.

Seychelles gained independence from Britain in 1976 and became a republic within the commonwealth. The republic was under single party rule until December 4, 1991, when President France Albert René announced a return to the multiparty system of government. On June 18, 1993, a new constitution was approved, and the first multiparty presidential and legislative elections were held in July. President René won that election and served as president until 2006.

June 18th is known as National Day in Seychelles. This national holiday commemorates the implementation of a multiparty democracy. On this day, thousands of people attend celebratory events that include parades, a flower show, music, and a presidential speech.

CONTACTS:
Seychelles Tourism Board
P.O. Box 1262
Victoria, Mahé Seychelles
www.seychelles.travel

◆ 2379 ◆ Shab-Barat
14th day of Islamic month of Sha'ban

Shab-Barat (or **Shab-i-Barat, Shaaban**) is a time when Muslims—particularly those in India and Pakistan—ask Allah to forgive the people they know who have died. They often spend the night in mosques praying and reading the Qur'an, and they visit graveyards to pray for the souls of their friends and ancestors. They also celebrate Allah's mercy by setting off fireworks, illuminating the outsides of their mosques, and giving food to the poor.

Also known as **Laylat al-Bara'ah**, or the **Night of Forgiveness**, Shab-Barat is a time of intense prayer in preparing for RAMADAN, for it is believed that this is the night on which God fixes the destinies of humans for the coming year and sins are absolved.

SOURCES:
BkHolWrld-1986, May 13
FolkWrldHol-1999, p. 661
HolSymbols-2009, p. 483
OxYear-1999, p. 733
RelHolCal-2004, p. 147
UndIslam-2004, p. 291

◆ 2380 ◆ Shad Festival
Last full weekend in April

Since 1981, the city of Lambertville, N.J., has celebrated the Shad Festival, honoring the annual return of the shad fish to the Delaware River to spawn. Because of water pollution in the area many years ago, the shad—also called river herring—were almost wiped out. But a major cleanup of area pollution brought the commercial fish back to the region. The festival also promotes the preservation of the environment and of the Delaware River ecosystem.

The two-day street festival features an arts show, cooking demonstrations, and live music concerts. Local nonprofit and community volunteer organizations use the event as a fundraiser by selling food and other items. A poster auction raises money for college scholarships for local students. There are also demonstrations of how the local fishing community catches shad with nets. The Shad Festival has won the Governor's Conference on Tourism Best Event Award three times.

CONTACTS:
Lambertville Area Chamber of Commerce
60 Wilson St.
Lambertville, NJ 08530
609-397-0055
www.lambertville.org

◆ 2381 ◆ Shah Abdul Latif Death Festival
14th-16th days of Islamic month of Safar

This festival commermorates the death of poet-musician Shah Abdul Latif (1689-1752) at Bhit Shah, Sindh, Pakistan. He was one of the most beloved of Pakistan's mystic Sufi poet-musicians who founded a music tradition based on popular themes and using folk melodies. He was the author of the *Risalo*, the best-known collection of romantic poetry in the Sindhi language; its heroes and heroines have become symbols of the oppression of Sindh by foreign occupiers.

At Latif's *urs*, or "death festival," a huge fair takes place outside the poet's shrine. There are wrestling matches (a popular entertainment in Sindh), a circus, theater, and numerous food and souvenir booths. Inside the shrine the atmosphere is quiet, and there is devotional singing by well-known Sindh groups. The main event of the urs is a concert at which the annual Latif Award is presented to the best performers.

CONTACTS:
Sindh Department of Tourism
114-115, Block C
Sea Breeze Pl., Shahrah-e-Faisal
Karachi, Karachi Pakistan
92-6064-7788530; fax: 92-6064-7782706
www.sindh.gov.pk

Culture and Tourism Department, Government of Sindh
Sindh Secretariat
Karachi, Sindh Pakistan
92-21-0590607; fax: 92-21-9212060
www.sindh.gov.pk

◆ 2382 ◆ Shaheed Day
February 21

Shaheed or **Shahid Day** is a national day of mourning in Bangladesh. Before becoming an autonomous country in 1971 (*see* BANGLADESH INDEPENDENCE DAY), this land had been East Pakistan ever since all of India gained independence from Britain in 1947. As East Pakistan, the country was poorer and less powerful than West Pakistan (now Pakistan), where the central government was. East Pakistan paid its taxes to West Pakistan, which gave East Pakistan little economic support in return. In addition, West Pakistan wanted to make its language, Urdu, the only official language of both Pakistans. Most of the people in East Pakistan spoke Bengali (some of the Indian region of Bengal became East Pakistan in 1947), and they were strongly opposed to the restriction of the use of their language in government and commerce.

In 1952 university students held protests which erupted in violence. Lives were lost, and as a memorial, people form a procession from the Azimpur graveyard on February 21 each year.

CONTACTS:
Embassy of Bangladesh
3510 International Dr. N.W.
Washington, D.C. 20008
202-244-0183; fax: 202-244-2771
www.bangladoot.org

SOURCES:
AnnivHol-2000, p. 30

♦ 2383 ♦ Shahi Durbar
Last week in February

The annual fair known as Shahi Durbar takes place in the town of Sibi in the Baluchistan Province of Pakistan. The event goes back to the 15th century when it centered around a gathering of tribal elders (*durbar* means "royal gathering"), and it is still an occasion for local politicians to speechify and debate each other. But it also features an agricultural fair, a handicraft market, and numerous sporting events, including horse racing, tent pegging, wrestling, and cockfighting. Relatively few foreigners come to the fair, but it represents a unique opportunity to observe the traditional customs and costumes of the tribal people of Baluchistan.

CONTACTS:
Pakistan Tourist Development Corp.
22-A , Saeed Plaza
Blue Area, Jinnah Ave.
Islamabad, 44000 Pakistan
92-51-920-3772; fax: 92-51-920-4027
www.tourism.gov.pk

SOURCES:
WildPlanet-1995, p. 279

♦ 2384 ♦ Shahrewar, Feast of
January, August, December; fourth day of
Shahrewar, the sixth Zoroastrian month

The Feast of Shahrewar is one of the "sacred name days" in the Zoroastrian religion, where the day and the month share the name of the same *yazata* or spiritual being—in this case, Shahrewar, who represents Desirable (or Benevolent) Dominion and who presides over metals and minerals. Because there are actually three different Zoroastrian calendars in use by widely separated Zoroastrian communities, the Feast of Shahrewar occurs in either January, August, or December.

Among the followers of Persian prophet Zoroaster (also known as Zarathushtra, believed to have lived around 1200 B.C.E.), a name-day feast is observed with religious ceremonies in fire temples, meeting halls, or private homes.

There are only about 100,000 followers of Zoroastrianism today, and most of them live in northwestern India or Iran. Smaller communities exist in Pakistan, Sri Lanka, Canada, the U.S., England, and Australia.

SOURCES:
RelHolCal-2004, p. 67

♦ 2385 ♦ Shaker Festivals
Various

Shakers are members of the United Society of Believers in Christ's Second Appearing, a celibate sect founded in 1747 in England. The Society, an offshoot of the Quakers, adopted ritual practices such as shaking, shouting, dancing, whirling, and singing in tongues, hence the nickname "Shakers." Communal settlements were established in the United States by Shaker leader Ann LEE, an Englishwoman known to her followers as Mother Ann and thought to be the first of the Believers to experience the constant indwelling of the spirit of Christ. She came to America in 1774 and founded the first Shaker church in what is now Watervliet, New York. The Shaker movement later spread throughout New England, Kentucky, Ohio, and Indiana. It reached its peak in the 1840s with a total membership of about 6,000. By 1905 the movement counted only 1,000 adherents. Today less than a dozen Shakers remain, living together in a small community at Sabbathday Lake, Maine.

The simple lines of Shaker furniture and other crafts strongly influenced American furniture design. What's more, craftspeople from these inventive communities designed the first screw propeller, rotary harrow, clothespin, and other items.

A number of Shaker festivals take place at Shaker museums and historic villages across the country. In South Union, Kentucky, the Shaker Museum hosts "Civil War Days" in mid-August, a two-day recreation of life in South Union's Shaker community during the Civil War. In late September the Museum sponsors "Harvest Day," an event that allows visitors to experience a day in a Shaker community around harvest time in the 1870s.

The Shaker Village of Pleasant Hill, Kentucky, holds a "Day of Releasement" in late July, in which visitors experience life in a Shaker community on a day off from work. They also celebrate a "Shaker Fourth" on the FOURTH OF JULY, recreating a typical Shaker Independence Day. Various Shaker villages and museums honor Mother Ann Day on August 5, in which they celebrate the life of Shaker leader Ann Lee.

CONTACTS:
Shaker Museum
P.O. Box 30
South Union, KY 42283
800-811-8379 or 270-542-4167; fax: 270-542-7558
www.shakermuseum.com

Sabbathday Lake Shaker Village Museum
707 Shaker Rd.
New Gloucester, ME 04260
207-926-4597
www.shaker.lib.me.us

Shaker Heritage Society
1848 Shaker Meeting House, Albany-Shaker Rd.
Albany, NY 12211
518-456-7890; fax: 518-452-7348
www.crisny.org

♦ 2386 ♦ Shakespeare's (William) Birthday
April 23

No one really knows the exact date of William Shakespeare's birth, although he was baptized on April 26, 1564, and died on April 23, 1616. April 23 is also ST. GEORGE'S DAY, and this may be why it was decided to observe the birth of England's greatest poet and dramatist on the feast day of England's patron saint. Special pageants are held at Stratford-upon-Avon in Warwickshire, where Shakespeare was born and where thousands of tourists go each year to see his plays performed.

CONTACTS:
Stratford-upon-Avon Tourist Information Center
Bridgefoot
Stratford-upon-Avon, Warwickshire CV37 6GW United Kingdom
44-17-8929-3127; fax: 44-17-8929-5262
www.stratford-upon-avon.co.uk

The Shakespeare Centre
Henley St.
Stratford-upon-Avon, Warwickshire CV37 6QW United Kingdom
44-17-8920-4016; fax: 44-17-8926-3138
www.shakespeare.org.uk

SOURCES:
AmerBkDays-2000, p. 308
BkDays-1864, vol. I, p. 542
DictDays-1988, p. 109

♦ 2387 ♦ Shalako Ceremonial
Late November or early December

One of the most impressive of the Pueblo Indian dances, the Shalako Ceremonial is held at the Zuni Pueblo in southwestern New Mexico. In this ceremony of all-night dancing and chants, houses are blessed, the dead are commemorated, and prayers are offered for good health and good weather in the coming year. The dance features towering masked figures with beaks who represent messengers from the rainmakers. They make clacking noises as they approach designated houses, and once inside the houses, they remove their masks, chant, and share food. Other figures taking part in the ceremonial are rain gods, warriors carrying whips, and the fire god, who is depicted by a young boy. The dancing goes on all through the cold night. The following morning, there are foot races.

CONTACTS:
Indian Pueblo Cultural Center
2401 12th St. N.W.
Albuquerque, NM 87104
866-855-7902 or 505-843-7270
www.indianpueblo.org

SOURCES:
DictFolkMyth-1984, pp. 566, 589, 1001
EncyNatAmerRel-2001, p. 264
IndianAmer-1989, pp. 290, 321
RelHolCal-2004, p. 253

♦ 2388 ♦ Sham el-Nessim
Between April 5 and May 9; Monday after Coptic Easter

A national holiday and folk festival in Egypt, the Sham el-Nessim has been observed for thousands of years as a day to smell the breezes and celebrate spring. *Nessim* means "zephyr," the spring breeze, and *sham* means "to breathe in." While the date is set by the Coptic calendar, the holiday is now a non-religious national holiday observed by everyone as a family affair.

Traditionally, people pack picnics to have outings along the Nile River or in parks. Certain food is specified for the occasion: the main dish is *fessikh,* a kind of salted fish, and it's also traditional to have *mouloukhiya* (stuffed vine leaves) and eggs with decorated, colored shells. The foods are believed to prevent disease, and the eggs symbolize life. Vast numbers of fish are eaten in Cairo on Sham al-Nessim.

Other traditions call for placing freshly cut flowers at doors and windows, and putting a clove of garlic at the head of each bed to prevent boredom and fatigue for those who lie there.

At the time of the pharaohs, spring was celebrated with gifts of lotus flowers to wives or loved ones, and families enjoyed river outings on flower-decorated barges and *feluccas* (small sailing vessels).

CONTACTS:
State Information Service, Egypt Ministry of Information
3 Al Estad Al Bahary St.
Nasr City, Cairo Egypt
20-2261-7304; fax: 20-2261-7308
www.sis.gov.eg/En

SOURCES:
BkFestHolWrld-1970, p. 74
BkHolWrld-1986, Apr 28
FolkWrldHol-1999, p. 215

♦ 2389 ♦ Shankaracharya Jayanti
April-May; fifth or 10th day of waxing half of Hindu month of Vaisakha

Although he is believed to have lived between 788 and 820, Hindu tradition says that Adi Shankaracharya, one of India's greatest saint-philosophers, flourished in 200 B.C.E. He revived Brahmanism and raised Vedanta philosophy to new heights, producing a number of original philosophical works and commentaries on the Upanishads, Vedanta Sutras, and the *Bhagavad Gita.* Shankaracharya also composed many popular hymns, worked numerous miracles, and urged Hindus to devote themselves to God in all of his many forms and incarnations.

Shankaracharya's birthday, known as Shankaracharya Jayanti, is celebrated on the fifth day of Vaisakha in southern India and on the 10th day in northern India. It is usually spent fasting, meditating, and studying Shankaracharya's works.

SOURCES:
RelHolCal-2004, p. 168

♦ 2390 ♦ Sharad Purnima
September-October; full moon day of Hindu month of Asvina

Hindus devote this day to the moon god, Hari. In the belief that *amrit* (elixir) is showered on the earth by moonbeams, they prepare *khir* (milk thickened with rice and mixed with sugar) on this day and offer it to Hari amid the ringing of bells and chanting of hymns. The mixture is left out in the moonshine all night so that it may absorb the amrit falling from the moon. The resulting khir is believe to possess special qualities. In the evening, the moon god is worshipped and offered food. The next morning, the specially prepared khir is given to the devotees.

SOURCES:
RelHolCal-2004, p. 176

♦ 2391 ♦ Shavuot (Shabuoth)
Between May 16 and June 13; Sivan 6-7

Shavuot ("weeks") is the second of the three PILGRIM FESTI-VALS (*see also* PASSOVER and SUKKOT). It follows Passover by 50 days and is also known in English as *Pentecost* from the Greek word meaning "fiftieth" (like the Christian PENTECOST, which comes 50 days after EASTER). It is also called the **Feast of Weeks** or **Feast of the Harvest**, because it originally marked the end of the seven weeks of the Passover barley harvest and the beginning of the wheat harvest. At one time, all adult male Jews were expected to bring their first *omer*, or "sheaf," of barley to the Temple in Jerusalem as a thanksgiving offering. Today dairy dishes are associated with Shavuot, particularly cheese blintzes.

After the period of Jewish slavery in Egypt, Shavuot took on a new meaning: it celebrated Moses' return from the top of Mt. Sinai with the two stone tablets containing the Ten Commandments, the most fundamental laws of the Jewish faith, and is therefore also known as the **Festival of the Giving of the Law**. Orthodox and Conservative Jews in the Diaspora celebrate two days of Shavuot as full holidays, while Reform Jews and those living in Israel observe only the first day.

See also LAG BA-OMER

CONTACTS:
Union of Orthodox Jewish Congregations of America
11 Broadway
New York, NY 10004
212-563-4000; fax: 212-564-9058
www.ou.org

SOURCES:
AmerBkDays-2000, pp. 371, 435
BkFest-1937, p. 208
BkFestHolWrld-1970, p. 70
BkHolWrld-1986, May 25
DaysCustFaith-1957, pp. 137, 159, 161
DictWrldRel-1989, pp. 155, 390, 564, 678
FestSaintDays-1915, p. 119
FolkAmerHol-1999, p. 243
FolkWrldHol-1999, p. 382
HolSymbols-2009, p. 816
OxYear-1999, p. 728
RelHolCal-2004, p. 52

♦ 2392 ♦ Sheboygan Bratwurst Days
First weekend in August

Sheboygan Bratwurst Days is a celebration in Sheboygan, Wis., that is scented with the smoke from 3,000 to 4,000 bratwursts being grilled. Sheboygan, billing itself the "Bratwurst Capital of the World," or alternatively, the "Wurst City of the World," is the home of several large sausage factories that ship bratwurst around the country and of numerous smaller markets that make tons of brat. (*Brat*, incidentally, rhymes with *cot*, not *cat*.)

The celebration's main event is a parade led by a 13-foot-tall balloon Bavarian figure in lederhosen who is known as the *Bratmeister*, or "sausage master." In 1991, a highlight of the parade was a float carrying giant twin brats—two 130-pound brats on a hard roll made from 40 pounds of dough.

The point of the festival is to eat brats, and the smell of them cooking on outdoor grills permeates the city. There are a brat-and-pancake breakfast and a brat-eating contest. Other events include band concerts, a magic show, wrestling matches, competitions for children, and a stumpf-fiddle contest. The stumpf fiddle is an instrument combining bells, springs, BB-filled pie plates, wood blocks, and taxi horns on a wooden pole with a rubber ball at the bottom.

Germans settled in Sheboygan in the 1830s and 1840s and immediately began making sausage. In 1953, to celebrate the city's 100th birthday, a Bratwurst Day was held in August. The mayor's proclamation noted that the city "has achieved national fame and recognition for the exclusive manufacture of a special kind of roasting sausage . . ."

The celebration was canceled in 1966 because it had become too rowdy. In 1978, Bratwurst Days came back for the city's 125th anniversary. Today the festival attracts about 50,000 people.

CONTACTS:
Sheboygan Jaycees
P.O. Box 561
Sheboygan, WI 53082
920-803-8980
www.sheboyganjaycees.com

♦ 2393 ♦ Sheelah's Day
March 18

Even the Irish aren't exactly sure who Sheelah was. Some say she was St. Patrick's wife; some say his mother. But one thing that they all seem to agree on is how this day should be celebrated: by drinking whiskey. The shamrock worn on ST. PATRICK'S DAY is supposed to be worn on the following day as well, until it is "drowned" in the last glass of the evening. If someone should drop his shamrock into his glass and drink it before the "drowning ceremony" takes place, he has no choice but to get a fresh shamrock and another glass.

SOURCES:
AnnivHol-2000, p. 47
DaysCustFaith-1957, p. 81
DictDays-1988, p. 110

♦ 2394 ♦ Shellfish Gathering (Shiohi-gari)
April 4

April 4 is approximately the date on which the tide is usually at its lowest in Japan. Families dress in brightly colored clothing and gather in coastal areas where the shellfish are known to be plentiful. They go out in boats decorated with red and white bunting and wait until the tide goes out and strands them on the bottom. Then they dig for clams, which they often cook and eat on the spot for lunch. Fishermen living nearby are more than willing to supplement their efforts, selling clams from their own stock to those whose digging has been unsuccessful. Most people buy a bag of shellfish to take home as well. The maritime police are usually kept busy rescuing those who go out too far and are caught by the incoming tide.

SOURCES:
BkFestHolWrld-1970, p. 76

♦ 2395 ♦ **Shembe Festival**
First day in July to the last Sunday

The Shembe Festival, named for Isaiah Shembe (c. 1870-1935), the sect's founder, is one of three annual festivals observed by the Nazareth Baptist Church (Church of the Ama Nazaretha). It takes place at the Ematabetulu village near Inanda, South Africa. The other two are the October festival, observed at Judia near Ginginglovu, and the January festival observed on Inhlangakazi Mountain. All aspects of worship, ritual, dress, and festivals were established by Shembe in 1911. The church's beliefs are a mixture of pagan, Old Testament, and Christian ideas.

The **July Festival** is the most popular of the three, and church members come from all over South Africa to attend it. Some live in temporary encampments for the festival, which begins on the first day of July and ends on the last Sunday. Throughout this period there are alternate days of dancing and rest. The sacred dancing that takes place on the final Sunday usually draws large numbers of spectators. Other activities during the festival include sermons by a variety of preachers, testimonies by church members, and prayer for the sick.

The men and women dance separately, and their costumes vary considerably. The two male groups of dancers, for example, are the Njobo and the Iscotch. The Njobo, who are mostly older men, wear traditional Zulu dress, as do the female groups. But the younger male dancers of the Iscotch group wear a long white smock with a tasseled hem over a black pleated kilt, a white pith helmet, black army boots with black-and-white football socks, and a light green tie bearing icons of the prophet Shembe and other church leaders.

The dances, which can last an entire day, involve rows of 50 or more dancers, each of which takes its turn at the front and then gradually works its way to the back, allowing those who tire to leave the group without being noticed.

CONTACTS:
South African Tourism Board
500 Fifth Ave., Ste. 2040, 20th Fl.
New York, NY 10110
800-822-5368 or 212-730-2929; fax: 212-764-1980
www.southafrica.net

SOURCES:
AnnivHol-2000, p. 126
FolkWrldHol-1999, p. 422
GdWrldFest-1985, p. 159

♦ 2396 ♦ **Shemini Atzeret**
Between September 27 and October 25; Tishri 22

Shemini Atzeret, or "eighth day of solemn assembly," is actually the eighth day of the festival of SUKKOT, but it is celebrated as a separate holiday dedicated to the love of God. The second day of Shemini Atzeret is known as SIMHAT TORAH and is also celebrated separately by Orthodox and Conservative Jews. Most Reform Jews celebrate Shemini Atzeret concurrently with Simhat Torah.

In ancient times, prayers for rain were recited on this day—a practice that is still part of Orthodox services. It is also one of four Jewish holidays on which the *Yizkor*, or memorial rite for the dead, is observed. The other three are YOM KIPPUR, the second day of SHAVUOT, and the last day of PASSOVER.

CONTACTS:
Union of Orthodox Jewish Congregations of America
11 Broadway
New York, NY 10004
212-563-4000; fax: 212-564-9058
www.ou.org

SOURCES:
AmerBkDays-2000, p. 710
AnnivHol-2000, p. 228

♦ 2397 ♦ **Shenandoah Apple Blossom Festival**
Early May

This four-day celebration of the apple orchards of Virginia's Shenandoah Valley is held in Winchester, the state's apple center. The festival was inaugurated in 1924 to publicize the area's historic, scenic, and industrial assets. Its motto was: "The bounties of nature are the gift of God." Winchester was settled in 1732, and George Washington, an early landlord in the area, required each tenant to plant four acres of apples.

The festival comes when the orchards are in bloom. About 250,000 people visit to enjoy the pink and white blossoms and the special events, including the coronation of Queen Shenandoah, a title once held by Luci Baines Johnson, former President Lyndon B. Johnson's youngest daughter. The 2001 Queen was Tyne Vance, granddaughter of former President Gerald R. Ford. Other attractions are parades, concerts and band competitions, a circus, and fireworks.

CONTACTS:
Shenandoah Apple Blossom Festival Inc.
135 N. Cameron St.
Winchester, VA 22601
800-230-2139 or 540-662-3863
www.thebloom.com

SOURCES:
AmerBkDays-2000, p. 332
GdUSFest-1984, p. 202

♦ 2398 ♦ **Shepherd's Fair**
Two weeks beginning the third or fourth Sunday in August

Also known as the **Schueberfouer** or **Schuebermesse**, the Shepherd's Fair held in Luxembourg City at the end of August every year dates back to 1340, when it was founded by John the Blind, count of Luxembourg and king of Bohemia. Originally a market for the wool and sheep merchants of medieval Europe, the Shepherd's Fair has shifted its focus over the years. Today it is geared toward entertainment rather than commerce, with carousels, food stands, and candy booths everywhere. Practically the only remnant of the original fair is the *Marche des Moutons*, (March of the Sheep), a parade of sheep decorated with ribbons and led by shepherds in folkloric costumes, accompanied by a band playing an ancient tune known as the *Hammelsmarsch*, or "Sheeps' March."

CONTACTS:
Luxembourg National Tourist Office
17 Beekman Pl.
New York, NY 10022
212-935-8888; fax: 212-935-5896
www.visitluxembourg.com

SOURCES:
FestEur-1961, p. 81
GdWrldFest-1985, p. 129

♦ 2399 ♦ **Shichi-Go-San (Seven-Five-Three Festival)**
November 15

Shichi-Go-San is an ancient Japanese celebration that marks the special ages of seven, five, and three. It has long been traditional for families to take girls aged seven, boys of five, and all three-year-olds, dressed in their finest, to the neighborhood Shinto shrine where their birth is recorded. There they are purified, and the priest prays to the tutelary deity for their healthy growth. At the end the priest gives each child two little packages: one containing cakes in the form of Shinto emblems (mirror, sword, and jewel), and the other holding sacred rice to be mixed with the evening meal. Afterwards, there are often parties for the children, and customarily they are given a special pink hard candy, called "thousand-year candy," to symbolize hopes for a long life. Because Nov. 15 is not a legal holiday, families now observe the ceremony on the Sunday nearest that date.

Legend says that the custom started because parents believed their children's mischievousness was caused by little worms that somehow entered their bodies. The visits to the shrines were to pray that the mischief-making worms would depart. A more likely story is that the festival began in the days when children often died young, and parents gave thanks for those who survived.

CONTACTS:
Japan Information Network, Japan Center for Intercultural
  Communications
2-7-7 Hirakawacho
Chiyodaku
Tokyo, 102-0093 Japan
81-3-3263-5041; fax: 81-3-3230-4107
home.jcic.or.jp/en/index-e.html

SOURCES:
AnnivHol-2000, p. 192
BkHolWrld-1986, Nov 15
FolkWrldHol-1999, p. 654

♦ 2400 ♦ **Shick-Shack Day (Shik-Shak Day, Shicsack Day, Shig-Shag Day)**
May 29

The *Oxford English Dictionary* suggests that this day takes its name from a corruption of *shitsack*, a derogatory term for the Nonconformists, Protestants who did not follow the doctrines and practices of the established Church of England. It was later applied to those who did not wear the traditional sprig of oak on May 29, or **Royal Oak Day**—the birthday of Charles II and the day in 1660 on which he made his triumphal entry into London as king after a 12-year interregnum.

The association of Charles II (1630-1685) and the oak tree dates back to 1651 when, after being defeated by Oliver CROMWELL in battle, legend has it he took refuge from his pursuers in an oak tree behind a house known as Boscobel. *Shick-shack* has since become synonymous with the oak-apple or sprig of oak itself, and May 29 is celebrated—particularly in rural areas of England—in memory of the restoration of King Charles and his preservation in the Royal Oak. Also called **Oak Apple Day**, **Oak Ball Day**, **Bobby Ack Day**, **Yack Bob Day**, **Restoration Day**, or **Nettle Day**.

SOURCES:
AnnivHol-2000, p. 90
BkDays-1864, vol. I, p. 696
DictDays-1988, pp. 14, 81, 83, 96, 98, 110, 134
FolkWrldHol-1999, p. 364
OxYear-1999, p. 225

♦ 2401 ♦ **Shilla (Silla) Cultural Festival**
October in even-numbered years

The Shilla Cultural Festival is an exuberant three-day festival, one of Korea's biggest and most impressive, to celebrate the country's ancient Shilla Kingdom. The celebrations are held in Kyongju, the capital of the Shilla Kingdom, and throughout the Kyongju Valley, where there is a great treasure of historic buildings: the Sokkuram Grotto, one of Asia's finest Buddhist shrines with a granite dome; Ch'omsongdae, a seventh-century bottle-shaped stone structure that is the world's earliest known extant observatory; royal tombs; palaces; and pleasure pavilions. The Shilla Kingdom in the southeastern portion of what is now Korea flourished from 57 B.C.E. to 935 C.E., and defeated two rival kingdoms, unifying all three in 676. The Unified Shilla Period is considered a golden age of Buddhist arts and especially of granite Buddhist sculpture.

The festival features concerts, wrestling matches, Buddhist pagoda dancing, games and contests, and lavish processions with elaborate floats.

CONTACTS:
Korea National Tourism Organization
1 Executive Dr., Ste. 100
Fort Lee, NJ 07024
201-585-0909; fax: 201-585-9041

♦ 2402 ♦ **Shinbyu**
September 2

Shinbyu is a Burmese Buddhist initiation ceremony for boys. According to traditional beliefs held by many Buddhists, every person should enter a monastery for a time in order to deepen their understanding of the Buddhist religion. This is what the Shinbyu ceremony is about. Parents dress their sons in robes and fancy headdresses that resemble the costume that the Buddha wore before he renounced his life as a prince. The boys ride white horses through the streets in parade and enjoy a sumptuous banquet provided by their parents. Afterwards the boys go to the temple, where their heads are shaved and they enter into the monastic life for a period of time that typically lasts from three days to three months.

SOURCES:
BkHolWrld-1986, Sep 2
RelHolCal-2004, p. 221

♦ 2403 ♦ **Shinju Matsuri Festival**
Late August-early September

The Shinju Matsuri Festival, also known as the **Festival of the Pearl**, is a 10-day celebration of the multicultural heritage of Broome, a tourist town in Western Australia. In the late 1800s, a wealth of pearls was discovered in the region, drawing fortune seekers from Japan, Malaysia, China, and Europe. In celebrating Shinju Matsuri, held annually since 1970, Broome relives those glorious boon days and celebrates the town's distinct ethnic heritage.

During the festival, Broome's Chinatown district is the site of a float parade as well as the waking of Sammy, a Chinese festival dragon. There are also tributes to the town's pearling history, a Mardi Gras festival, a Carnival of Nations, Dragon Boat Races, traditional and contemporary art exhibits, and a Gala Ball. A fireworks ceremony closes the week's festivities.

CONTACTS:
Shinju Matsuri Events Managers – Goolarri Media Enterprises
P.O. Box 2708
Broome, Western Australia 6725 Australia
www.shinjumatsuri.com

♦ 2404 ♦ **Shinnecock Powwow**
September, Labor Day weekend

The Shinnecock Indians, like many other Native Americans, host a major powwow over the long LABOR DAY weekend. People travel from all over the United States, and beyond, to attend. The Shinnecock Powwow has been held for more than 50 years. Events include arts, crafts, music, storytelling, and, of course, dancing competitions.

The Shinneock Indians are part of the Algonquian nation of Indians. "Shinnecock" means "those who live where the land flattens." A good portion of their 500-acre reservation is tidal marshland. The Shinnecock have been known as whalers and fishermen, and many of the foods served at the powwow reflect their historical links to the sea.

CONTACTS:
Shinnecock Indian Nation Tribal Office
P.O. Box 5006

Southampton, NY 11969
631-283-6143; fax: 631-822-1270
www.shinnecocknation.com

SOURCES:
EndurHarv-1995, p. 2

♦ 2405 ♦ **Shinran-Shonin Day**
May-June

Shinran-Shonin (1173-1262) was a Japanese Buddhist monk and a disciple of Honen, the founder of the Pure Land sect of Buddhism in Japan. Although Shinran did not wish to oppose his teacher by founding a new denomination, he did strive to clarify how the principles of Pure Land Buddhism were constituted, and the school of Buddhism he founded is therefore known as the "True Pure Land School," or Jodo Shin-shu.

Shinran thought that people achieved salvation through faith rather than through religious practices. Therefore, he disagreed with the celibacy and hardships imposed by monastic Buddhism. Although Shinran was not the first Buddhist monk to marry, his marriage signified the point in history where Japan began to turn in the direction of lay Buddhism. Shinran-Shonin Day is observed in May or June by Japanese Pure Land Buddhists.

SOURCES:
OxDictWrldRel-1997, p. 891
WrldBuddhism-1984, p. 223

♦ 2406 ♦ **Shiprock Navajo Nation Fair**
Usually first weekend of October

Also known as the **Northern Navajo Fair**, this fair began in 1924 and is considered the oldest and most traditional of Navajo fairs. It is a harvest fair held in Shiprock, New Mexico, the largest populated community of the Navajo Nation.

The fair coincides with the conclusion of an ancient healing ceremony, the NAVAJO NIGHT CHANT. This is a nine-day chant known as the *Yei Bei Chei,* and is a complex ritual usually conducted after the first frost. Parts of the ceremony may be witnessed by the public. Among the more colorful public rituals are *Two Yei's Come* and the grand finale in which sacred masked dancers begin a dance late Saturday night and continue into the pre-dawn.

After watching the healing ceremony, spectators go on to other events of the fair such as an all-Indian rodeo, an intertribal powwow, a livestock show, a carnival, the Miss Northern Navajo Pageant, Indian arts and crafts exhibits, and a Saturday morning parade.

See also NAVAJO NATION FAIR AT WINDOW ROCK

CONTACTS:
Navajo Tourism Department
P.O. Box 663
Window Rock, AZ 86515
928-810-8501; fax: 928-810-8500
www.discovernavajo.com

SOURCES:
AmerBkDays-2000, p. 640
IndianAmer-1989, p. 269
RelHolCal-2004, p. 259

♦ 2407 ♦ Shishi Odori (Deer Dance)
Various

The Shishi Odori or **Deer Dance** of Japan's Ehime Prefecture dates back to the early 17th century. Young boys wearing deer masks with antlers beat small drums known as *kodaiko* and act out a search for the female deer who tries to conceal herself. At the Uwatsuhiko Shrine at Uwajima, the *Yatsushishi-odori,* or Eight Deers Dance, performed in late October, is particularly graceful and is one of the highlights of the autumn festivals held in the Ehime Prefecture.

A Shishi Odori is also held at Hananomaki in Iwate Prefecture. Eight men wearing deer masks perform a sunlight, moonlight, and starlight dance; a measured, ceremonial dance; and a dance that tells the story of a deer's life. This kind of dancing is usually performed during the month of March, but only at the request of visitors.

CONTACTS:
Japan National Tourist Organization
1 Rockefeller Pl., Ste. 1250
New York, NY 10020
212-757-5640; fax: 212-307-6754
www.jnto.go.jp

Iwate Prefectural Government
Public Relations and Communication Division
10-1 Uchimaru
Morioka, Iwate 020-8570 Japan
81-1-9629-5336; fax: 81-1-9629-5339
www.pref.iwate.jp/~hp0312/seikatsu-sodan/en/index

SOURCES:
IllFestJapan-1993, p. 118
JapanFest-1965, p. 133

♦ 2408 ♦ Shivaratri
February-March; 14th day of waning half of Hindu month of Phalguna

A Hindu holiday observed throughout India and Nepal. Legend says that on this night Lord Shiva, the great god of destruction (who is also the restorer), danced the Tandav, his celestial dance of Creation, Preservation, and Destruction. Hindu devotees of Shiva eat only once on the day before this "Night of Shiva," and then fast and tell stories about him. In India, pilgrims throng the Shiva shrines in Chidambaram (Tamil Nadu), Kalahasti (Andhra Pradesh), and Varanasi (Uttar Pradesh), where special celebrations are held. Mandi in Himachal Pradesh becomes one big party. Devotees carry deities on temple chariots, and there are folk dances and folk music.

Hundreds of thousands make the pilgrimage to Pashupatinath Temple in Kathmandu, Nepal, for worship, feasting, and ritual bathing in the holy Bagmati River.

In Port Louis, Mauritius, wooden arches covered with flowers are carried to Grand Bassin, to get water from the holy lake to wash the symbols of Shiva.

CONTACTS:
Ministry of Tourism, Government of India
Rm. No 123, Transport Bhawan, No. 1, Parliament St.
New Delhi, Delhi 110 001 India
91-11-23715084; fax: 91-11-23715084
www.tourisminindia.com

Nepal Tourism Board, Tourist Service Center
Bhrikuti Mandap
P.O. Box 11018
Kathmandu, Nepal
977-1-4256909; fax: 977-1-4256910
www.welcomenepal.com

SOURCES:
BkHolWrld-1986, Mar 10
FolkWrldHol-1999, p. 190
RelHolCal-2004, p. 184

♦ 2409 ♦ Shrimp Festival, National
Second weekend in October

A waterside festival held for four days in Gulf Shores, Ala., drawing crowds estimated at 200,000. This festival began in this shrimping and resort area in 1971 as a one-day event to liven things up after LABOR DAY. The big event was a shrimp-cooking contest, and shrimp dishes have been in the forefront since. About 30 percent of the food vendors' fare includes shrimp, with lots of jambalaya and kabobs. Also on the menu are such dishes as shark and Greek foods including seafood gyros (pronounced YEER-ohs). Events of the festival include a children's art village, an air show, live musical entertainment, and arts and crafts displays.

CONTACTS:
Alabama Gulf Coast Area Chamber of Commerce
3150 Gulf Shores Pkwy.
P.O. Box 3869
Gulf Shores, AL 36547
251-968-6904; fax: 251-968-5332
www.alagulfcoastchamber.com

♦ 2410 ♦ Shrove Monday
Between February 2 and March 8; Monday before Ash Wednesday

Many countries celebrate Shrove Monday as well as SHROVE TUESDAY, both days marking a time of preparation for LENT. It is often a day for eating pastry, as the butter and eggs in the house must all be used up before Lent. In Greece it is known as **Clean Monday** and is observed by holding picnics at which Lenten foods are served. In Iceland, the Monday before Lent is known as **Bun Day**. The significance of the name is twofold: It is a day for striking people on the buttocks with a stick before they get out of bed as well as a day for eating sweet buns with whipped cream. The latter custom is believed to have been introduced by Danish and Norwegian bakers who emigrated to Iceland during the late 19th century.

SOURCES:
EncyEaster-2002, p. 61
FolkWrldHol-1999, p. 127

♦ 2411 ♦ **Shrove Tuesday**
Between February 3 and March 9; day before Ash Wednesday

There are a number of names in the West for the last day before the long fast of LENT. The French call it MARDI GRAS (meaning "Fat Tuesday"), because it was traditionally a time to use up all the milk, butter, and eggs left in the kitchen. These ingredients often went into pancakes, which is why the English call it PANCAKE DAY and still celebrate it with games and races that involve tossing pancakes in the air.

Other names include **Shuttlecock** (or **Football**) **Day**, after sports associated with this day; **Doughnut Day**; **Bannock** (or **Bannocky**) **Day** (a bannock being the Scottish equivalent of a pancake), and **Fastingong** (meaning "approaching a time of fast"). The name "Shrove Tuesday" is derived from the Christian custom of confessing sins and being "shriven" (i.e., absolved) just before Lent.

In northern Sweden, people eat a meat stew. In the south, they eat Shrove Tuesday buns called *semlor*, made with cardamom, filled with almond paste, and topped with whipped cream.

No matter what its name, the day before ASH WEDNESDAY has long been a time for excessive eating and merrymaking. The Mardi Gras parade in New Orleans is typical of the masquerades and dancing in the streets that take place in many countries on this day as people prepare for the long Lenten fast.

See also CARNIVAL; CHEESE SUNDAY; CHEESE WEEK; FASCHING; FASTENS-EEN

SOURCES:
AmerBkDays-2000, p. 128
EncyEaster-2002, p. 561
OxYear-1999, p. 606

♦ 2412 ♦ **Shrove Tuesday (Bohemia)**
Between February 3 and March 9; day before Ash Wednesday

In the Bohemian region of the Czech Republic, a mummer known as the "Oats Goat" traditionally is led from house to house on SHROVE TUESDAY. He dances with the women of the house, and in return they feed him and give him money. Like the Fastnachtsbär (or Shrovetide Bear) in parts of Germany, the Oats Goat is dressed in straw and wears horns on his head. He is associated with fertility; at one time it was widely believed that dancing with the Fastnachtsbär ensured the growth of crops.

SOURCES:
DictFolkMyth-1984, pp. 370, 807

♦ 2413 ♦ **Shrove Tuesday (Estonia)**
Between February 3 and March 9; day before Ash Wednesday

Schools are closed in Estonia on the last day before LENT, known as **Vastla Päev**, and children often spend the entire day sledding. At night, their mothers serve a traditional SHROVE TUESDAY soup, which is made from pigs' feet boiled with dried peas or lima beans. After dinner, the children play with the *vuriluu kont*, or the bones left over from the pigs' feet soup. A hole is drilled in each bone and a doubled rope is inserted through the hole. When the contrivance is manipulated in a certain way it causes a terrific rattle, which delights the children and is a traditional way to end the day's celebration.

SOURCES:
BkFest-1937, p. 102

♦ 2414 ♦ **Shrove Tuesday (Finland)**
Between February 3 and March 9; day before Ash Wednesday

Children in Finland often spend SHROVE TUESDAY, a school holiday, sledding and enjoying other outdoor sports. According to an old folk saying, the better the coasting and the longer the hills one rides on **Laskiaispäivä**, the more bountiful the coming harvest will be. A typical Finnish meal on this day would include pea soup and *blini*, or rich pancakes, served with caviar and *smetana*, a kind of sour milk. A typical dessert consists of wheat buns filled with almond paste, placed in deep dishes, and eaten with hot milk.

There are many folk beliefs surrounding Shrove Tuesday. At one time, women would not spin on this day, believing that if they did, no flax would grow the following summer. Men refrained from planing wood, the common wisdom being that if farm animals walked on the chips made by the planes, their feet would become swollen and sore.

SOURCES:
BkFest-1937, p. 111

♦ 2415 ♦ **Shrove Tuesday (Netherlands)**
Between February 3 and March 9; day before Ash Wednesday

The day preceding the Lenten fast is known as **Vastenavond** (Fast Eve) in the Netherlands, where it is a time for feasting and merrymaking. In the provinces of Limburg and Brabant, it is customary to eat pancakes and *oliebollen*, or rich fried cakes with currants, raisins, and apples added. Brabant specializes in *worstebrood*, a special kind of bread that appears ordinary on the outside but is filled with spiced sausage meat.

In the southern part of the country, the CARNIVAL season lasts for three days, beginning on the Sunday before ASH WEDNESDAY. In other areas, the celebration is confined to one day. The farmers of Schouwen-en-Duiveland, on the island of Zeeland, still observe the old Vastenavond custom of gathering at the village green with their horses in the afternoon. The animals are carefully groomed and decorated with paper roses. The men ride their horses down to the beach, making sure the animals get their feet wet. The leader of the procession toots on a horn. It is possible that this custom originated in an ancient spring purification rite, when blowing horns was believed to drive away evil spirits and getting wet was a symbolic act of cleansing.

SOURCES:
BkFest-1937, p. 241
FestWestEur-1958, p. 124
FolkAmerHol-1999, p. 102

♦ 2416 ♦ **Shrove Tuesday (Pennsylvania Dutch)**
Between February 3 and March 9; day before Ash Wednesday

Among the Pennsylvania Dutch, work is taboo on SHROVE TUESDAY, just as it is on other religious holidays. There is an old superstition that if a woman sews on Shrove Tuesday, she will prevent her hens from laying their eggs. Some believe that sewing on this day means that the house will be visited by snakes during the spring and summer.

A special kind of cake or doughnut known as a *fasnacht* is eaten on this day. Rectangular with a slit down the middle, it is often soaked with molasses and then dunked in saffron tea. Sometimes the fasnachts were crumbled and fed to the chickens in the belief that it would prevent the hawks from snatching the chicks in the spring. Another old custom associated with Shrove Tuesday is "barring out," or locking the teacher out of the local school. In many areas, CHRISTMAS is barring-out day.

SOURCES:
EncyChristmas-2000, p. 35
FolkAmerHol-1999, p. 100

♦ 2417 ♦ **Shrovetide (Norway) (Fastelavn)**
Between February 3 and March 9; Sunday before Ash Wednesday

Formerly observed on the Monday before ASH WEDNESDAY, Fastelavn, or **Shrove Sunday**, is a holiday that Norwegian children anticipate eagerly. They rise at dawn and, armed with *fastelavnsris* (decorated birch or evergreen branches), they go from room to room and strike with their branches anyone who is still in bed. The children receive a hot cross bun for every victim they spank.

The fastelavnsris can be quite elaborate, often decorated with tinsel and paper streamers or brightly colored paper roses. Sometimes a doll with stiff, full skirts is tied to the topmost branch. The curious custom of switching with branches may be traced to an ancient pagan rite heralding the fruitfulness of spring.

SOURCES:
BkFest-1937, p. 249
FestWestEur-1958, p. 151

♦ 2418 ♦ **Shunbun-no-Hi (Vernal Equinox Day)**
March 21

In Japan, where the VERNAL EQUINOX is a national holiday, the entire week during which the equinox occurs is called HIGAN,

which means "other shore." According to Buddhist belief, a river divides this world and the next; it is only by crossing the river, which entails resisting temptation's powerful currents, that one attains enlightenment.

The observance of Vernal Equinox Day began during the reign of seventh-century Prince Shotoku. It became a national holiday during the Meiji period. Visiting the family cemetery is a popular activity on this day, and people tend to regard it as a happy event. Although no meat is served during the week, *o-hagi*, soft rice balls covered with sweetened bean paste, are popular, as is rice and vegetables with a vinegar-based sauce. Shunbun-no-Hi is a day set aside to honor nature and to show respect for growing things.

CONTACTS:
Japan Information Network, Japan Center for Intercultural
  Communications
2-7-7 Hirakawacho
Chiyodaku
Tokyo, 102-0093 Japan
81-3-3263-5041; fax: 81-3-3230-4107
home.jcic.or.jp/en/index-e.html

SOURCES:
JapanFest-1965, p. 133

♦ 2419 ♦ **Shwedagon Pagoda Festival**
February-March; full moon day of the Burmese month of Tabaung

The people of Myanmar (formerly Burma) celebrate their local pagodas or temples on the full moon day in the month of Tabaung (February-March in the Gregorian calendar). Visitors to the pagoda take the opportunity to make offerings and to pray. Many people construct a pagoda out of sand, a custom thought to bring good luck.

The largest celebration is held at the Shwedagon Pagoda in Yangon (formerly Rangoon), the capital city of Myanmar. This ancient temple, which is more than 2,500 years old, is 300 feet tall and has a dome covered in gold and precious jewels. People selling flowers, incense, and little gold Buddhas line the steps leading to the pagoda, hoping to sell their wares to people who want to leave an offering at the shrine. Souvenirs, in the form of papier-mâché dolls, hand-woven baskets, cloth and pottery, are for sale in the bamboo stalls clustered at the foot of the pagoda.

The dome of the Shwedagon Pagoda, with its two tons of gold and more than 5,000 diamonds, glitters so brightly that it can often be seen by airplanes flying overhead.

CONTACTS:
Embassy of the Union of Myanmar
2300 S St. N.W.
Washington, D.C. 20008
202-332-3344; fax: 202-332-4351
www.mewashingtondc.com

SOURCES:
CelebSouthAsia-1996

♦ 2420 ♦ **Siaosi Tupou I (King) Day**
December 4

Located in the Pacific Ocean some 1,250 miles north of New Zealand, the island nation of Tonga consists of about 150 islands, 36 of which are inhabited, with a population of about 120,000. King George Tupou I, also known by his Tongan name of King Siaosi Tupou I, was the first king of the Pacific island nation. He took on the title on December 4, 1845, and the date is a Tongan national holiday.

Born into the extensive royalty of Tonga, Tupou wanted to be named king at an early age. But he was not recognized by the chiefs because he came from the small island of Ha'apai. Tupou resorted to military engagement to secure the cooperation of some chiefs. A series of political maneuvers over some 15 years, including earning the backing of local missionaries by promising to spread Christianity in the region, eventually made the ambitious Tupou to be legally named king of all the Tongan islands.

Tupuo's rule was marked by a number of landmark events. He abolished serfdom and introduced the nation's first written laws. He opened the country's first parliament and introduced its first constitution. He also forbade the purchase of Tongan land by foreigners, hoping in this way to stop what he saw as the exploitation of his people. Tupou ruled as king in a constitutional monarchy with legally-defined powers until his death in 1893.

Tonga honors King Tupou I for establishing much about their country, both good and bad, that still distinguishes it today.

CONTACTS:
General Consulate of Tonga in San Francisco
360 Post St., Ste. 604
San Francisco, CA 94108
415-781-0365; fax: 415-781-3964

♦ 2421 ♦ **Sibelius Festival**
First two weeks in October

Jean Sibelius (1865-1957) was a Finnish composer known for his seven symphonies and many symphonic poems for orchestra. Most of the symphonic poems are based on the *Kalevala*, Finland's national epic poem. But his most famous work is *Finlandia*, which was first performed in Helsinki in 1900. Because it expressed so much national pride and patriotism, the work became the anthem of the Finnish independence movement, and for many years the Russians refused to allow its performance.

From 1951 to 1965 Helsinki hosted Sibelius Weeks as an annual musical tribute to the composer; after 1965 the festival expanded to become the HELSINKI FESTIVAL. Today an annual Sibelius Festival is held in the town of Järvenpää during the first two weeks in October.

CONTACTS:
Jarvenpaa Tourist Information Office
Jarvenpa-talo
Hallintokatu, 04400 Finland

358-9-2719-2718; fax: 358-9-2711-199
www.jarvenpaa.fi/sivu/index.tmpl?sivu_id=13

SOURCES:
FestEur-1961, p. 30
MusFestWrld-1963, p. 188

♦ 2422 ♦ **Sierra Leone Independence Day**
April 27

This national holiday celebrates the day Sierra Leone became independent from Britain in 1961.

Independence Day festivities are especially elaborate in the capital city of Freetown.

CONTACTS:
Embassy of Sierra Leone
1701 19th St. N.W.
Washington, D.C. 20009
202-939-9261; fax: 202-483-1793
www.embassyofsierraleone.org

SOURCES:
NatlHolWrld-1968, p. 109

♦ 2423 ♦ **Sihanouk's (King) Birthday (Former King's Birthday and King Sihamoni Coronation Day)**
October 29-October 31

The celebration of former Norodom Sihanouk's birthday on October 31 has been combined with the October 29 anniversary of the coronation of his son, King Norodom Sihamoni. Sihanouk abdicated in favor of his son in 2004. This national holiday is also known as **Former King's Birthday** and **King Sihamoni Coronation Day**.

The three-day celebration is centered in Phnom Penh, around the Royal Palace. People from all over the country come to the capital city to watch parades, partake in cultural events, and see the elaborate fireworks display along the riverbank near the palace.

CONTACTS:
Royal Embassy of Cambodia
4530 16th St. N.W.
Washington, D.C. 20011
202-726-7742 or 202-726-8268; fax: 202-726-8381
www.embassyofcambodia.org

Tourism of Cambodia
262 Monivong Blvd.
Khan Daun Penh
Phnom Penh, Cambodia
www.tourismcambodia.com

♦ 2424 ♦ **Silent Days**
Begins between March 19 and April 22; Thursday, Friday, and Saturday before Easter

The last three days of HOLY WEEK—MAUNDY THURSDAY, GOOD FRIDAY, and HOLY SATURDAY—were at one time referred to as the **Swidages**, from an Old English word meaning "to be silent." From this came Silent Days or **Still Days**—three days during which the church bells in England remained silent. The bells were rung again at the EASTER Vigil service.

SOURCES:
DictDays-1988, p. 111
EncyEaster-2002, p. 609

◆ 2425 ◆ "Silent Night, Holy Night" Celebration
December 24

The world's best known Christmas carol, "Silent Night, Holy Night," was written and composed by Franz Gruber and Father Josef Mohr. The carol was first performed on CHRISTMAS EVE, 1818, at St. Nickola Church in Oberndorf, Austria. This event is commemorated in Oberndorf, Hallein, Wagrain, Salzburg, and other towns in the state of Salzburg by holding a candlelight procession on December 24. Everyone sings the carol as they march to the church and again when they are inside. It is usually sung in various languages to honor the many nations where the birth of the Christ child is celebrated.

CONTACTS:
Silent Night Association
Stille-Nacht-Platz 7, Untersbergstrasse 25
Oberndorf
Salzburg, A-5110 Austria
43-6272-4225-39; fax: 43-6272-4225-14
English Version is not available

SOURCES:
EncyChristmas-2003, p. 144
GdWrldFest-1985, p. 12

◆ 2426 ◆ Simadan Festival
February-April

Simadan is a folk festival celebrating the sorghum harvest on the island of Bonaire in the Netherlands Antilles. Sorghum is a cereal grass, and it was at one time a staple for the island's natives. Farm owners, known as *kunuku,* enlist the aid of their friends, family, and neighbors to harvest the crop. To give thanks for the assistance and the abundant harvest, they hold a Simadan consisting of traditional food, song, and dance.

Foods served at the festival include goat soup, *funchi* (similar to finely textured grits), *giambo* (okra soup), *repa* (sorghum-based pancakes), and *boontji kunuku* (beans). The music features back-and-forth singing from one group to another accompanied by such instruments as the guitar, marimba, *bari* (drum), *karko* (conchshell), and triangle. Hand-clapping also drives the rhythm. The *wapa,* a Simadan dance, involves rows of dancers moving and interacting with each other to a steady beat.

In the past, Bonaireans stored their food in the *Mangasina di Rey,* or Storehouse of the King, located in the village of Rincon. At the height of the harvest season, the kunuku would make a thanksgiving offering of sorghum seed, which would be blessed by the priest and stored in the Mangasina di Rey. This took place during EASTER and was known as Simadan di Pastor. This particular festival continues to be celebrated in Rincon and Nikiboko.

CONTACTS:
Bonaire Government Tourist Office, Adams Unlimited
80 Broad St., 32nd Fl., Ste. 3202
New York, NY 10004
800-266-2473 or 212-956-5912; fax: 212-956-5913
www.tourismbonaire.com

◆ 2427 ◆ Simbra Oilor (Sheep Counting)
May

Simbra (or Sambra) Oilor is a rural folk festival held in parts of Romania, including Transylvania and Banat. In May people herd sheep to the mountains for summer grazing. But before they leave, on the morning of Simbra Oilor all the sheep are milked in order to estimate how much cheese each will produce. This cheese will then be paid throughout the summer to those who own the sheep. Afterwards, there is a community potluck feast.

In some places a similar festival is held in the fall when the sheep are brought back down from the mountains.

CONTACTS:
Romanian National Tourist Office
355 Lexington Ave., 19th Fl.
New York, NY 10017
212-545-8484; fax: 212-251-0429
www.romaniatourism.com

SOURCES:
FoodFestDanube-1969, p. 243

◆ 2428 ◆ Simhat Torah
Between September 28 and October 26; Tishri 22 or 23

This Jewish holiday, which follows SUKKOT, celebrates the annual completion of the public reading of the Torah, or the first five books of the Bible, and the beginning of a new reading cycle. The hand-lettered scrolls of the Torah are removed from the Ark (a box-like container) and paraded around the synagogue—and sometimes through the streets—amidst singing and dancing. Simhat Torah means "rejoicing in the law," which is as good a description as any of what takes place on this day. To be chosen as the Bridegroom of the Law—to read the final verses of the last book, Deuteronomy—or the Bridegroom of the Beginning—to read the opening verses of the first book, Genesis—is considered a great honor.

In Israel and among Reform Jews, this festival is observed on the 22nd day of Tishri, concurrently with SHEMINI ATZERET; all other Jews celebrate it separately on the 23rd day. Israelis also hold a second *hakkafot* ("procession around the synagogue") on the night after Simhat Torah, frequently accompanied by bands and choirs.

Simhat Torah customs have varied from country to country. In Afghanistan all the scrolls are taken out of their Arks and heaped in a pyramid almost to the synagogue's roof. In Cochin, China, a carpet was laid on the courtyard flagstones, coconut oil lamps were heaped in a pyramid in front of the synagogue entrance, and the scrolls of the Law carried around the outside of the synagogue. One synagogue in Calcutta, India, has 50 scrolls, and the women go from scroll to scroll, kissing them. At the end of the holiday a Simhat Torah ball is held and a beauty queen chosen. Young Yemeni children are taken to the synagogue for the first time on this holiday.

In southern France, two mourners stand on either side of the reader, crying bitterly as the death of Moses is related. The Bridegrooms of the Law in Holland are escorted home in a torchlight parade accompanied by music. A crown from one of the Torah scrolls was placed on the head of every reader in medieval Spain, and in some places in eastern Europe, the reader wore a large paper hat decorated with bells and feathers.

CONTACTS:
Union for Reform Judaism
633 Third Ave.
New York, NY 10017
212-650-4000; fax: 212-650-4169
www.urj.org

Union of Orthodox Jewish Congregations of America
11 Broadway
New York, NY 10004
212-563-4000; fax: 212-564-9058
www.ou.org

SOURCES:
AmerBkDays-2000, p. 710
BkFest-1937, p. 204
BkHolWrld-1986, Oct 11
DictWrldRel-1989, pp. 155, 693
FolkAmerHol-1999, p. 407
FolkWrldHol-1999, p. 592
HolSymbols-2009, p. 834
OxYear-1999, p. 726

♦ 2429 ♦ **Sinai Liberation Day**
April 25

This legal holiday in Egypt commemorates the final withdrawal of Israeli troops on this date in 1982 under the 1978 Camp David agreement between Egypt and Israel to return the Sinai Peninsula to Egypt.

CONTACTS:
State Information Service, Egypt Ministry of Information
3 Al Estad Al Bahary St.
Nasr City, Cairo Egypt
20-2261-7304; fax: 20-2261-7308
www.sis.gov.eg/En

SOURCES:
AnnivHol-2000, p. 68

♦ 2430 ♦ **Singapore National Day**
August 9

Singapore National Day is a public holiday in Singapore to commemorate its independence. Singapore was the administrative seat for the Straits Settlements, a British crown colony, from 1867 until it was occupied by Japan in World War II. It was restored to Britain in 1945, became a part of Malaysia in 1963, and became independent in 1965. The hol-

iday is celebrated with a spectacular parade, cultural dances, and fireworks.

CONTACTS:
Singapore Embassy
3501 International Dr. N.W.
Washington, D.C. 20008
202-537-3100; fax: 202-537-0876
www.mfa.gov.sg

Singapore Infomap
Ministry of Information, Communications and the Arts
Singapore, Singapore
app.www.sg

SOURCES:
AnnivHol-2000, p. 133
GdWrldFest-1985, p. 159

♦ 2431 ♦ **Sinhala Avurudu**
April 13 or 14

Sinhala Avurudu, or New Year, is celebrated in Sri Lanka (formerly Ceylon) as a non-religious festival by both Sinhalese and Tamils. The exact hour of the new year is determined by astrologers, and often the new year does not begin when the old year ends. The few hours between the new and old year are known as the *nona gathe* ("neutral period"), and all activities, including eating and drinking, must stop for that time.

In the villages the new year traditionally begins with lighting a fire in the kitchen and wearing new clothes. The color of these clothes is determined by an almanac. The ceremonies reach a climax with an anointing ceremony. Oil is mixed with an herbal paste and a family elder rubs this oil on the heads of all the family members as they sit with a white cloth under their feet. The holiday is also a day of public festivities, including sports, games, dancing, and special dinners.

CONTACTS:
Sri Lanka Tourist Board
111 Wood Ave. S, Ste. 323
Edison, NJ 08820
732-516-9800; fax: 732-452-0087
www.srilankatourism.org

SOURCES:
GdWrldFest-1985, p. 165
IntlThFolk-1979, p. 345

♦ 2432 ♦ **Sinjska Alka**
First weekend in August

Sinjska Alka is a day of jousting on horseback in the small town of Sinj, near Split in Croatia. The festival commemorates a victory of a peasant army over the Turks in 1715, even though the 60,000 Turks outnumbered the Sinj warriors by three to one. The annual tournament was supposedly instituted soon after the 1715 victory.

On this day, young men who have trained throughout the year ride horses headlong down the steep 140-yard run and try to spear an iron ring, or *alka*, suspended from a rope about nine feet off the ground. The ring has a diameter of six inches and within it is another two-inch ring. The jouster who most successfully spears the rings in three tries is the winner and receives a sash and silver medal. The band plays a triumphal march and shots are fired for all top scorers.

Before the contest, there is a ceremonial procession through the streets. The contestants march through Sinj accompanied by their mace bearers and shield bearers wearing 18th-century costumes decorated with gold and silver.

CONTACTS:
Sinj Tourist Information Office
Vrlicka 50
Sinj, 21 230 Croatia
385-21-826-352; fax: 385-21-826-352
www.tzsinj.hr

Alka Tournament of Sinj
Chivalric Association of Alkars
Sinj, Croatia
www.alka.hr

SOURCES:
IntlThFolk-1979, p. 403

♦ 2433 ♦ **Sinulog Festival**
Third weekend in January

The Sinulog Festival takes place on the island of Cebu in the Philippines, held at the same time as the frenzied ATI-ATIHAN FESTIVAL in Kalibo and the more sedate DINAGYANG in Iloilo City. The word *sinulog* is derived from the rootword *sulog*, meaning "river current"; the dancing of the festival is thought to flow like a river.

The festival celebrates both early Cebuano culture and the history of the Christianization of Cebu, combining the pageantry of early years with today's Christian ritual. An image of Cebu's patron saint, the Santo Niño ("the Holy Child," Jesus), is carried in a procession along the streets, while drums beat in the ritual for a bountiful harvest and revelers dance in the streets.

CONTACTS:
Philippine Tourism Center
556 Fifth Ave.
New York, NY 10036
212-575-7915; fax: 212-302-6759
www.philippinetourism.us

♦ 2434 ♦ **Sioux Sun Dance**
Late June

Although many North American Indian tribes hold ritual dances in honor of the sun and its life-giving powers, the Sioux were known to hold one of the most spectacular. Usually performed during the SUMMER SOLSTICE, preparations for the dance included the cutting and raising of a tree that would be considered a visible connection between the heavens and earth, and the setting up of teepees in a circle to represent the cosmos.

Participants abstained from food and drink during the dance itself, which lasted from one to four days, and decorated

their bodies in the symbolic colors of red (sunset), blue (sky), yellow (lightning), white (light), and black (night). They wore deerskin loincloths, wristlets and anklets made out of rabbit fur, and carried an eagle-wing bone whistle in their mouths. The dance often involved self-laceration or hanging themselves from the tree-pole with their feet barely touching the ground. Sometimes the dancers fell unconscious or tore themselves loose, which was considered evidence that they'd had a visionary experience. After the dance, they were allowed to have a steam bath, food, and water.

See also ARAPAHO SUN DANCE; SOUTHERN UTE TRIBAL SUN DANCE

SOURCES:
DictFolkMyth-1984, p. 1088
EncyNatAmerRel-2001, p. 291
EncyRel-1987, vol. 14, p. 143

♦ 2435 ♦ **Sitala Ashtami**
March-April; eighth day of the waxing half of the Hindu month of Caitra

Sitala Ashtami is a Hindu festival honoring Sitala, goddess of smallpox. She is named for the chill typically experienced during high fever. She is believed to have the power to protect people from smallpox and to give people smallpox, and her blessings are invoked for protection against the disease.

On this day, Hindu women visit the nearest Sitala shrine in the morning, offering the goddess rice, homemade sweets, cooked food, and holy water mixed with milk. In some places colorful fairs are held near Sitala's shrines, and there is merry-making, dancing, feasting, and the buying and selling of wares.

SOURCES:
DictHindu-1977, p. 278
RelHolCal-2004, p. 185

♦ 2436 ♦ **Sithinakha**
May-June; sixth day of waxing half of Hindu month of Jyestha

This is the birthday of the Hindu god Kumara, also known as SKANDA, the god of war and son of Shiva. Kumara has six heads because he was nursed by the karttikas—six women who, as stars, comprise the Pleiades. For this reason he is also called *Karttikeya*, "son of Karttikas." The six heads also represent the six senses (including extrasensory perception). He has a large following under the name *Subrahmanya*, meaning "dear to the Brahmanas."

Most Hindus observe this day with a ritual purification bath followed by processions to the temples to honor Kumara. It is also considered a good opportunity to clean out wells and tanks, because the snake gods are off worshipping on this day and it's safe to enter their habitats.

In Nepal, eight different kinds of cakes, made from eight different grains, are offered to Kumara on his birthday, and for this reason Sithinakha is sometimes referred to as the **Cake Festival**. Lotus-shaped windmills are often set on rooftops at this time, to symbolize the end of bad times and the onset of holier days.

SOURCES:
FolkWrldHol-1999, p. 379

♦ 2437 ♦ **Sitka Summer Music Festival**
First three weeks in June

The Sitka Summer Music Festival is a series of concerts featuring internationally known musicians, held during the first three weeks in June in Sitka, Alaska. Chamber music concerts are held on Tuesdays, Fridays, and Saturdays, and there are programs ranging from classical to pop. The concerts are given in the Centennial Building auditorium, which has a wall of glass behind the stage. Since the nights are light in June, the audience can look at mountains, eagles, water, and mist while listening to the music. Violin virtuoso Paul Rosenthal founded the festival in 1972, producing the first musical event with four other musicians, and going on to emphasize a repertoire of 18th- and 19th-century classics.

CONTACTS:
Sitka Summer Music Festival
P.O. Box 201988
Anchorage, AK 99520
907-277-4852; fax: 907-277-4842
www.sitkamusicfestival.org

SOURCES:
MusFestAmer-1990, p. 22

♦ 2438 ♦ **Sjomannadagur (Seaman's Day)**
First Sunday in June

Sjomannadagur is a day honoring the role that fishing and fishermen have played in Icelandic history, celebrated in the coastal towns and cities of Iceland. Sailors take the day off, and the Seaman's Union sponsors many events. These include competitions in rowing and swimming, tugs-of-war, and sea rescue competitions. On the more solemn side, medals are awarded for rescue operations of the past year. Most celebrations begin with a church service and a trip to the local cemetery to honor sailors lost at sea. Afterward there are children's parades, dances, outdoor cookouts, and bonfires in the evening. The proceeds from the day's events throughout the country go to the national fund that supports old seamen's homes.

CONTACTS:
Icelandic Tourist Board
655 Third Ave., Ste. 1810
New York, NY 10017
212-885-9700; fax: 212-885-9710
www.icelandtouristboard.com

SOURCES:
AnnivHol-2000, p. 109

♦ 2439 ♦ **Skanda Sashti**
October-November; six days beginning the sixth day of the waxing half of the Tamil month of Aippasi (Hindu month of Asadha)

Skanda is a son of Shiva. He is also known as Subrahmanya, especially in southern India. According to Hindu mythology, Shiva cast his seed into fire, where it was afterwards received by the river goddess Ganga (the Ganges River), who "gave birth" to Skanda. She hid him among the rushes on the bank of the river, where he was found by the six *karttikas* (the Pleiades) and raised by them, for which reason he has six heads and is often referred to as Skanda-Karttikeya. He was born for the purpose of destroying Taraka, a demon whom the gods particularly wanted to get rid of. The festival known as Skanda Sashti celebrates Taraka's defeat.

The focus of the celebration is the six holy places in southern India associated with Skanda, especially in the state of Tamil Nadu. Thousands of Hindus gather at each of these temples to sing hymns, chant psalms, and dramatize scenes from the god's life. Hindus believe that observing this festival ensures success, prosperity, happiness, and peace.

See also SITHINAKHA

CONTACTS:
Arulmigu Subramanya Swami Temple
Tiruchendur, Tamil Nadu 628 215 India
91-4639-42221
www.tiruchendur.org

SOURCES:
DictHindu-1977, p. 281
RelHolCal-2004, p. 177

♦ 2440 ♦ **Skipjack Races and Land Festival**
September, Labor Day weekend

A skipjack is a kind of sail-powered fishing boat popular in the 19th century. Around the turn of the 20th century over 1,000 skipjacks worked the waters off Deal Island, Maryland. By 1960, only 40 remained. It was then that local enthusiasts revived the skipjack races, which dated back to 1871 but had only been organized in 1921. The revived races have continued since 1960, scheduled for LABOR DAY weekend. People from all over the state come to Deal Island harbor on that weekend, to cheer on the skippers of these traditional craft and to honor the contribution that the fishing industry has made to the region's history.

CONTACTS:
Skipjack Races
Deal Island-Chance Lions Club
P.O. Box 158
Deal Island, MD 21821
410-784-2785
www.webauthority.net/lions.htm

Somerset County Tourism
P.O. Box 243
Princess Anne, MD 21853
800-521-9189 or 410-651-2968; fax: 410-968-2501
www.visitsomerset.com

♦ 2441 ♦ **Slovak Republic Independence Day**
January 1

On January 1, 1993, the Slovak Republic peacefully split off from the Czech Republic and became an independent country. Other national holidays include Constitution Day, commemorating the ratification of the Slovak Republic's constitution on September 1, 1992; National Uprising Day, August 29, observing Slovakia's battle against Nazi Germany in 1944; and July 5, Sts. Cyril and Methodius Day.

CONTACTS:
Embassy of the Slovak Republic
3523 International Ct. N.W.
Washington, D.C. 20008
202-237-1054; fax: 202-237-6438
www.slovakembassy-us.org

♦ 2442 ♦ **Slovenia National Day**
June 25

Slovenia declared its independence from Yugoslavia on June 25, 1991, after elections in 1990 showed that 88% of the people wished to secede from Yugoslavia. Previously, Slovenia, which is a little smaller than New Jersey, was part of the Austria-Hungarian kingdom. It joined with Serbia, Croatia, and Montenegro at the end of World War I, and this federation was called Yugoslavia after 1929.

CONTACTS:
Embassy of the Republic of Slovenia
2410 California St.
Washington, D.C. 20008
202-386-6601; fax: 202-386-6633
www.washington.embassy.si

♦ 2443 ♦ **Smithsonian Kite Festival**
Late March

The Kite Festival held on the Mall in Washington, D.C., every spring is co-sponsored by the Smithsonian Resident Associate Program and the National Air and Space Museum. First held in 1966, the festival was started by Dr. Paul Garber, a kite fancier and historian emeritus of the National Air and Space Museum. Until his death in 1992, Dr. Garber served as master of ceremonies for the festivities.

A major focus of the annual festival is the competition for hand-made kites, which must be capable of flying at a minimum altitude of 100 feet for at least one minute. Kites are judged on the basis of appearance (design, craftsmanship, beauty) as well as on performance (takeoff, climb, angle, recovery). Trophies are awarded in many categories—for example, airplane, bird figure, box-kite, spacecraft, and delta—and age groups. Participants come from all regions of the United States as well as several foreign countries. Immediately following the kite display program, a kite-building workshop is held for members of the Smithsonian Resident Associate Program.

CONTACTS:
The Smithsonian Associates
1100 Jefferson Dr. S.W.
P.O. Box 23293
Washington, D.C. 20560

202-357-3030; fax: 202-786-2034
www.smithsonianassociates.org

♦ 2444 ♦ **Smithville Fiddlers Jamboree and Crafts Festival**
Weekend near July 4

Acclaimed enough to have been the subject of an hour-long documentary on national television, the Fiddlers Jamboree and Crafts Festival held every year on a weekend near the Fourth of July in Smithville, Tennessee, celebrates the style of country music popularly known as bluegrass. Musical competitions are held in 24 different categories, including fiddle, banjo, mandolin, guitar, dulcimer, harmonica, folk singing, gospel singing, buck dancing, and clog dancing.

There are also musical performances, both formal and impromptu, as well as more than 200 booths where working artists and craftspeople display their work. Most of the events are held on a stage set up in front of the DeKalb County Courthouse. The highlight of the festival is a head-to-head contest between the best of the fiddlers. The winner receives a cash prize and the Berry C. Williams Memorial Trophy, named after the festival's founder.

CONTACTS:
Smithville Fiddlers Jamboree and Crafts Festival
P.O. Box 83
Smithville, TN 37166
615-597-8500
www.smithvillefiddlersjamboree.net

SOURCES:
GdUSFest-1984, p. 179

♦ 2445 ♦ **Snan Yatra**
May-June; full moon day of Hindu month of Jyestha

This Hindu bathing festival is held in Puri, Orissa, India. Images of the gods Jagannath, Balbhadra, Subhadra, and Sudarshan are brought in a grand procession to the bathing platform for their ceremonial baths. As mantras from the Vedas, or Hindu sacred writings, are recited, consecrated water is poured over the deities. Then they are dressed in ceremonial robes before going into seclusion for 15 days. For Hindus, this is an occasion for rejoicing and merrymaking.

CONTACTS:
Department of Tourism, Government of Orissa
Paryatan Bhawan, Museum Campus
Bhubaneswar, Orissa 751 014 India
91-674-2432177; fax: 91-674-430887
www.orissatourism.gov.in

SOURCES:
RelHolCal-2004, p. 170

♦ 2446 ♦ **So Joo Festival: The Eve of St. John's Feast Day**
June 23

June 23, the eve of the Feast of St. John the Baptist, is celebrated each year in Porto, Portugal, with a curious ritual. Festival-goers tap each other on the head with plastic hammers or leeks. Some say the gesture indicates romantic interest, others claim it brings good luck to the recipient. The custom can be traced to the 19th century, when long-stemmed garlic flowers were used in mid-summer games, and in turn, to pagan times. Indeed, the fireworks, music, all-night dancing, and colorful processions that feature on St. John's Eve are more closely allied to pagan summer solstice rituals than religious observances. A large amount of wine is drunk, and grilled sardines are consumed. The festival is also known as "So Joo," which is an anglicized form of the Portuguese words for Saint John.

CONTACTS:
Porto City Council Tourist Office
Rua Clube dos Feniaos, 25
Porto 4000-172 Portugal
www.portoturismo.pt

♦ 2447 ♦ Sofia Music Weeks
May-June

Sofia, Bulgaria, is one of Europe's oldest cities and thus an appropriate site for an international classical music festival. For the three weeks of this festival, the capital city's most stately concert halls—including Bulgaria Hall and the National Palace of Culture—open their doors to opera companies, ballet companies, symphonies, orchestras, and other artists. The festival also includes an educational component for classical music students.

The festival first took place in 1971 and expanded throughout that decade. By 1982 it had earned a membership in the European Festivals Association. Although all international performers are welcomed and appreciated, festival organizers ensure representation for national artists. Past years have featured the Sofia Philharmonic, Sofia Opera, Bulgarian Radio Symphony Orchestra and Mixed Choir, and Sofia Soloists Chamber Ensemble. Music selections will often celebrate great native composers.

Beyond the performances, the festival program offers symposiums on music theory, photograph exhibitions, screenings of filmed operas, and master classes for young musicians and singers.

CONTACTS:
National Palace of Culture
1 Bulgaria Sq.
Sofia 1414 Bulgaria
www.worldnn.com/pp/smw/index.html

♦ 2448 ♦ Sokjon-Taeje Memorial Rites
Second and eighth lunar months

The Sokjon-Taeje (or Seokjeon-Daeje) Memorial Rites began centuries ago in China to commemorate the contributions of ethical philosopher CONFUCIUS. The Rites are no longer held in China, but they continue to be observed twice a year, in the spring and in the autumn, at the important Songgyungwan University in Seoul, South Korea. Confucianism has had a deep and lasting impact on Korean culture. Among other things, Confucius taught respect for one's elders and those in authority, which is a legacy Koreans hold to today.

Students participate in the somber ceremony, which includes offerings of food and wine to Confucius, traditional dances and costumes, and poem recitations.

SOURCES:
FestWrld: SouthKorea-1998, p. 24

♦ 2449 ♦ Sol
January-February; first day of first lunar month; January 1-2

One of the biggest holidays of the year in Korea, Sol, or LUNAR NEW YEAR, is celebrated largely by rural people and is a two-day national holiday. January 1 and 2, also national holidays, are celebrated more by residents of cities. On Sol, tradition calls for families to gather in their best clothes and for children to bow to parents and grandparents to reaffirm family ties. A soup made of rice dumplings called *duggook* is always served, and it is customary to play *yut*, a game played with wooden blocks and a game board. Young girls see-saw standing up. During early Confucianism, women were not allowed any outdoor exercises. See-sawing this way bounced them above their enclosing walls, and they could see their boyfriends. This made see-sawing a love sport and not exercise. It is still very popular.

CONTACTS:
Korea National Tourism Organization
2 Executive Dr., Ste. 750
Fort Lee, NJ 07024
800-868-7567 or 201-585-0909; fax: 201-585-9041
www.kntoamerica.com

SOURCES:
AnnCustKorea-1983, p. 19
FolkWrldHol-1999, p. 72

♦ 2450 ♦ Solidarity with the Palestinian People, International Day of
November 29

In 1977, the General Assembly of the UNITED NATIONS declared November 29 International Day of Solidarity with the Palestinian People. On December 1, 2000, the Assembly reaffirmed the U.N.'s responsibility to work towards the peaceful creation of a Palestinian homeland and lauded those countries that observed the International Day of Solidarity with the Palestinian People.

CONTACTS:
United Nations, Department of Public Information
Rm. S-1070L J, K, L
New York, NY 10017
212-963-6842; fax: 212-963-6914
www.un.org

◆ 2451 ◆ Solomon Islands Independence Day
July 7

The Solomon Islands in the southwest Pacific gained independence from Britain on this day in 1978. They had been under British control since 1900. Independence Day is a national holiday throughout the islands.

CONTACTS:
Permanent Mission of Solomon Islands to the UN
800 Second Ave., Ste. 400 L
New York, NY 10017
212-599-6192; fax: 212-661-8925

◆ 2452 ◆ Somalia Independence Day
July 1

Somalia became an independant, unified country on July 1, 1960. In colonial times, Somalia was divided up between Britain and Italy. The northern part of the region was British Somaliland, and other areas belonged to Italy. June 26 is the anniversary of independence of British Somaliland from Britain in 1960, while July 1, 1960, is the day the former Italian Somaliland became independent from Italy. On July 1, 1960, both areas were united as the Republic of Somalia.

Since a government overthrow in 1991, however, the country has disintegrated into the Republic of Somaliland and the Republic of Puntland, neither of which is recognized by what is left of the Republic of Somalia, represented by the transitional national government established in October 2000.

SOURCES:
NatlHolWrld-1968, p. 103

◆ 2453 ◆ Song of Hiawatha Pageant
Last two weekends in July and first weekend in August

Pipestone, Minnesota, was named for the soft red stone used by the Native American Dakota tribe to make their ceremonial pipes. The Dakotas believe that their tribe originated here, and that the stone was colored by the blood of their ancestors.

On weekends in late July and early August each year, the story of Hiawatha (Haionhwat'ha, fl. c.1570)—the chief of the Onondaga tribe immortalized in Henry Wadsworth Longfellow's poem, "Song of Hiawatha"—is told in symbolic pantomime with traditional Indian music and dances. The audience watches the performance from the opposite side of a quiet reflecting pool that lies at the bottom of the pipestone quarry where the pageant is held.

The Great Spirit appears at the top of the cliff, where he shows his children the pink stone and makes a calumet or peace pipe. With the last whiff on his pipe, the Great Spirit disappears in a cloud of smoke. The Three Maidens, who once guarded the place where the Great Spirit lived, can be seen in the form of three huge boulders. The pageant ends with the death of Hiawatha and his departure on a "long and distant journey."

CONTACTS:
Hiawatha Club
P.O. Box 1
Pipestone, MN 56164
800-430-4126 or 507-825-3316; fax: 507-825-3317
www.pipestoneminnesota.com

◆ 2454 ◆ Songkran
Around April 12-15 (when the Sun enters Aries)

Songkran is the traditional NEW YEAR in Thailand and a public holiday. The celebration actually lasts for three days in mid-April, and takes the form of religious ceremonies as well as public festivities. Merit-making ceremonies are held at Buddhist temples, water is sprinkled on Buddhist images, and captive birds and fish are freed. Water-splashing on the streets is also a part of the festivities, especially among young people. The young do not splash older people, but instead sprinkle water on their hands or feet to honor them.

The celebration is held with special élan in Chiang Mai with beauty contests, parades, dancing, and, of course, water splashing.

See also WATER-SPLASHING FESTIVAL

CONTACTS:
Tourism Authority of Thailand
611 N. Larchmont Blvd., 1st Fl.
Los Angeles, CA 90004
800-842-4526 or 323-461-9814; fax: 323-461-9834
www.tourismthailand.org

SOURCES:
AnnivHol-2000, p. 61
BkFestHolWrld-1970, p. 11
BkHolWrld-1986, Apr 13
EncyRel-1987, vol. 2, p. 553
FolkWrldHol-1999, p. 294
GdWrldFest-1985, p. 174
RelHolCal-2004, p. 219

◆ 2455 ◆ Soul Saturdays (Saturday of Souls)
Dates vary with most in February through May

Soul Saturdays are a series of Saturdays set aside in the liturgical calendar of Eastern and Greek Orthodox Catholic Churches for the remembrance of those who have died. These days occur on designated Saturdays before and during the seasons of LENT and EASTER: the first two are observed on the two Saturdays before Lent begins, the third Saturday of Souls coincides with the first Saturday of Lent, and the fourth Soul Saturday takes place on the Saturday before PENTECOST, the close of the Easter season.

Saturday holds special significance in the religious calendar as the day on which the crucified Jesus lay dead in the tomb before his resurrection. On each Soul Saturday a special service is held where prayers are offered in memory of those who have died and a list of the names of the dead is recited. Participants attending the services prepare *kollyva,* a dish made of sweetened, boiled wheat kernels, raisins, almonds, and pomegranate seeds that is traditionally associated with funerals and memorial services in Greece and Eastern Europe. In addition to attending religious services, participants often visit the graves of departed family members on Soul Saturdays, to clean and decorate the burial sites.

CONTACTS:
Greek Orthodox Archdiocese of America
8 East 79th St.
New York, NY 10075
212-570-3500; fax: 212-570-3569
www.goarch.org

Orthodox Church in America
P.O. Box 675
Syosset, NY 11791-0675
516-922-0550; fax: 516-922-0954
www.oca.org

SOURCES:
EncyEaster-2002, pp. 564-65

♦ 2456 ♦ **Sound Symposium**
July in even-numbered years

The Sound Symposium is an international music and arts festival held every two years in St. John's, Newfoundland, Canada. The symposium features an eclectic mix of artists whose work involves the innovative or masterful manipulation of sound, and hopes to inspire rising artists to explore new avenues in music, performance art, and the visual arts.

Performances take place in a variety of locales, from concert halls to the streets, and from old army bunkers to the beach. They include dance, theater, performance art, gallery exhibitions, and all kinds of music. Participants may sample new expressions in jazz, electronic music, percussion, rock and roll, classical, folk music, experimental music, world music, improvisational music, and experiments with newly invented instruments. The musicians who participate in the "Harbor Symphony," for example, board boats and play compositions written for the various whistles and horns on board. Symposium participants may also join workshops led by the guest artists.

CONTACTS:
Sound Symposium
P.O. Box 23232
St. John's, NL A1B 4J9 Canada
709-753-4630; fax: 709-753-4630
www.soundsymposium.com

♦ 2457 ♦ **South Africa Freedom Day**
April 27

In 1652, the Dutch East India Trading Company set up a station in Cape Town, South Africa, to service passing ships. After that, European pioneers began to colonize South Africa. In 1657, colonial authorities started giving land to the European settlers. As more Europeans arrived and built their farms, the need for land and labor grew. The settlers began spreading into other areas, and they brought people from East Africa and Madagascar to serve as slaves.

By the mid-1700s, even though there were more slaves than European colonists in South Africa, the white colonists continued to maintain power and authority. Throughout South Africa the minority white population practiced apartheid, an official policy of segregation that involved discrimination against non-white citizens in political, legal, and economic matters. Black South Africans faced stifling discrimination in all areas of their lives. Intense pressure from other countries forced the South African government to put an end to the practice of apartheid. In February 1990, South African President Frederik Willem de Klerk ended apartheid in the county.

On April 27, 1994, the Republic of South Africa held its first democratic elections. The African National Congress (ANC), an important black organization formed to fight for the freedom and rights of all black citizens, won the election. The new ANC-led government began the reconstruction and development of the country and its institutions, bringing with it socio-economic change that improved the lives of all South Africans, especially the poor.

Every year, the Republic of South Africa celebrates Freedom Day, a public holiday that commemorates the anniversary of the historic day in 1994. Special cultural events and exhibitions are held in various venues around Cape Town, the legislative capital of South Africa, and other locations around the country.

CONTACTS:
South Africa Government
Cape Town, Western Cape South Africa
www.info.gov.za

♦ 2458 ♦ **South Africa Heritage Day**
September 24

On September 24, 1995, the Republic of South Africa celebrated its first Heritage Day. The day was declared a national holiday by the first democratically elected government of South Africa, which was elected on April 27, 1994. According to the Department of Arts, Culture, Science and Technology, the word heritage is defined as "that which we inherit: the sum total of wild life and scenic parks, sites of scientific or historical importance, national monuments, historic buildings, works of art, literature and music, oral traditions and museum collections together with their documentation." To help South Africans celebrate their heritage, this day has been set aside to recognize all aspects of South African culture, including creative expression, historical inheritance, language, food, and the land in which they live.

During his speech on Heritage Day in 1996, President Nelson Mandela said, "When our first democratically elected government decided to make Heritage Day one of our national days, we did so because we knew that our rich and varied cultural heritage has a profound power to help build our new nation.

We did so knowing that the struggles against the injustice and inequities of the past are part of our national identity; they are part of our culture. We knew that, if indeed our nation has to rise like the proverbial phoenix from the ashes of division and conflict, we had to acknowledge those whose selfless efforts and talents were dedicated to this goal of non-racial democracy."

The government of the Republic of South Africa determines a theme for each year's celebrations. That first Heritage Day celebration in 1995 focused on composer Enoch Sontonga, the creator of a hymn that was adopted as the national anthem, His gravesite was declared a national monument, and his music was highlighted.

CONTACTS:
South Africa Government
Cape Town, Western Cape South Africa
www.info.gov.za

♦ 2459 ♦ South Africa National Arts Festival (Grahamstown Festival)
Late June through early July

Grahamstown, South Africa, is the site for what is purportedly the world's largest arts festival after Britain's Edinburgh Arts Festival. Since the inaugural festival in 1974, this small city in the Eastern Cape has increasingly drawn more people for the 11-day National Arts Festival (also known as the **Grahamstown Festival**), and has expanded its number of shows from 60 to more than 500. Organized by the Grahamstown Foundation, the festival takes both South African and international entrants.

The festival program manages an even balance of sophisticated and popular entertainment. Performances cross the spectrum from opera, cabaret, and jazz to stand-up comedy and folk music. The Fringe Festival, which in some years has featured up to 200 performances, attracts fans of more unconventional art.

The festival's largest theater venue is the 1820 Settlers National Monument. Smaller productions, which include those on the festival's fringe program, take place in any of the town's available public halls or large rooms.

Grahamstown has also gained a reputation for the enormous street market that materializes during the festival and bolsters the region's economy. Traders come from all over the Eastern Cape and set up stands in public parks and market squares to sell homemade and manufactured products.

CONTACTS:
National Arts Festival
P.O. Box 304
Grahamstown 6140 South Africa
www.nafest.co.za

♦ 2460 ♦ South Africa Republic Day
May 31

A referendum held in South Africa on October 6, 1960, narrowly approved the formation of the Republic of South Africa, although "colored" voters were excluded as part of the country's long-standing policy of racial segregation known as apartheid. The closeness of the vote—52.14 percent in favor, 47.42 percent opposed—reflected the mixed feelings of both the Afrikaners and the British settlers, although the former generally supported the idea.

The Union of South Africa became the Republic of South Africa on May 31, 1961, thus severing its long-standing ties to the old British Empire.

Also on this date in 1902 the Boer War ended. The Treaty of Vereeniging was signed by representatives of the South African Republic and the Orange Free State who had been waging war with Great Britain since October 12, 1899. Eight years later, the Union of South Africa was inaugurated, uniting the Cape of Good Hope, Natal, the Transvaal, and the Orange Free State.

CONTACTS:
South African History Online
8th Fl., Charter House, 179 Bosman St.
P.O. Box 29204
Sunnyside, Pretoria Central 0001 South Africa
27-12-323-5522; fax: 27-12-326-2037
www.sahistory.org.za

SOURCES:
AnnivHol-2000, p. 90
DictDays-1988, pp. 95, 124
NatlHolWrld-1968, p. 72

♦ 2461 ♦ South Africa Women's Day
August 9

On August 9, 1956, a protest march was held at the Union Buildings in Pretoria, South Africa, the country's main government offices. Approximately 20,000 women participated in a peaceful march to protest against policies that restricted the rights of African women. These policies were intended to "tighten up control of movement of African women to town, registration of their service contracts, and a compulsory medical examination for all African women town-dwellers." They were protesting in part against pass laws, which governed the movement of all blacks, with special restrictions for women. The law required all black women to carry passes, which were special identification documents to show that they were allowed to enter areas that were for white people only.

The Federation of South African Women (established in 1954 to set up a broad-based women's organization) staged the protest march to challenge the idea that "a woman's place is in the kitchen." When the women arrived at the Union Buildings, they carried petitions signed by more than 100,000 people to give to J.G. Strijdom, the prime minister. Then they sang a freedom song composed specifically for the march:

Wathint' abafazi, Strijdom!
Wathint' imbokodo uzo kufa!

(Now you have touched the women, Strijdom!
You have struck a rock! You will be crushed!)

This song has come to represent the women's movement in South Africa.

Every year, on August 9, people gather at the Victoria & Alfred Waterfront Amphitheatre in Cape Town to celebrate National Women's Day. South African men, women, and children celebrate the achievements of women—not only from South Africa but also from all over the world. This day is celebrated to remind people of the contributions and achievements women have made to society and for women's rights, and to acknowledge the difficulties and prejudices many women still face.

Leading up to National Women's Day is the annual Women in Focus program, workshops that are intended to enlighten, inform, and entertain women with a series of innovative and celebratory programs.

CONTACTS:
South Africa Government
Cape Town, Western Cape South Africa
www.info.gov.za

V&A Waterfront Head Office
Portswood Close
Portswood Ridge
Victoria & Alfred Waterfront
Cape Town, Western Cape South Africa
www.waterfront.co.za

♦ 2462 ♦ South Africa Youth Day
June 16

Throughout the history of South Africa, black citizens have suffered from segregation and oppression by the white leaders. In 1953, the South African government passed the Bantu Education Act, which included provisions for the establishment of a Black Education Department in the Department of Native Affairs to develop a curriculum that addressed the "nature and requirements of the black people." The aim of this curriculum was to provide black South Africans with an education that would give them only the skills necessary to serve their own people or to work in labor-intensive jobs under whites. Blacks were not to receive an education that would lead them to seek positions they would not be allowed to hold in society. The Bantu Education Act also declared that Afrikaans, a Dutch dialect, was to be used on an equal basis with English in secondary schools.

By 1975, black students began to fight against their lower-class status. They started to protest not only the fact that Afrikaans was a mandatory part of their education, but also the segregated schools and universities, poor facilities, overcrowded classrooms, and poorly trained teachers.

On June 16, 1976, more than 20,000 students from Soweto began a protest march. Police were called to the scene, and violent riots broke out. These riots lasted eight months, during which time approximately 700 people, many of them youths, were killed.

June 16 has been set aside as Youth Day (previously known as Soweto Day), a public holiday across the Republic of South Africa, to commemorate the day the protests began and to honor the youth who lost their lives during the riots.

Ceremonies, parades, and historic exhibitions are part of the celebrations across South Africa.

CONTACTS:
South Africa Government
Cape Town, Western Cape South Africa
www.info.gov.za

♦ 2463 ♦ South Carolina Peach Festival
Mid-July

The South Carolina Peach Festival is a 10-day festival in Gaffney, S.C., to salute the state's peach industry. Events of the festival include a parade, beauty pageants, country music concerts, and peach desserts. Gaffney's year-round tribute to the peach is the eye-catching "peachoid," a one-million-gallon water tank in the shape and color of a peach with a great metal leaf hanging over it.

CONTACTS:
South Carolina Peach Festival Inc.
225 S. Limestone St.
P.O. Box 549
Gaffney, SC 29340
864-489-5721
www.scpeachfestival.org

♦ 2464 ♦ South Korea Constitution Day
June 17

Constitution Day, July 17, is observed as a national holiday in South Korea on the anniversary of the date that the country's constitution was declared in 1948. It was declared a public holiday in October 1948. Apart from the display of flags in public places, citizens and officials do little to formally celebrate the occasion, although events such as marathons are often held on the day. Following a restructuring of the South Korean public sector work force to adhere to a 40-hour work week, Constitution Day will no longer be a free day for workers as of 2008; however, it still will be observed as a day of commemoration.

The entire Korean peninsula (i.e., present-day North and South Korea) was under the control of Japan from 1910 until the end of World War II. When Japan surrendered in August 1945, the U.S.S.R. took control of the northern half of the peninsula, while the southern half came under control of the United States. Despite attempts to unify the two regions, by 1948 it was clear that their sharp political differences made reunification impossible. South Korea held its first democratic elections and selected members for the National Assembly before the national constitution was proclaimed on July 17. On August 15, 1948, the Republic of Korea was established in the south with Syngman Rhee as the first President. Less than a month later, the Democratic People's Republic of Korea, under the leadership of then-Premier Kim Il-Sung, was founded in the North.

CONTACTS:
Embassy of the Republic of Korea in the United States of America
2450 Massachusetts Ave. N.W.
Washington, DC 20008

202-939-5600; fax: 202-342-1597
www.dynamic-korea.com

♦ 2465 ♦ South Korea Memorial Day
June 6

South Korea (official name: Republic of Korea) has designated June 6 as a national holiday to honor soldiers and civilians who sacrificed their lives for their country during the Korean War, 1950-1953.The main ceremony of remembrance is held at the National Cemetery in the capital city, Seoul.

Throughout the country, officials and citizens pray and lay flowers at the graves of the war dead. Citizens display the flag of South Korea, which is called Tae-guk-gi, on the front doors of their homes to commemorate the civilians and soldiers who died in war. Memorial Day was declared a public holiday on April 19, 1956.

CONTACTS:
Embassy of the Republic of Korea in the United States of
   America, Washington, DC 20008
2450 Massachusetts Ave. N.W.
Washington, D.C. 20008
202-939-5600; fax: 202-342-1597
www.dynamic-korea.com

♦ 2466 ♦ Southern 500
November

The Southern 500 is the oldest southern stock-car race, held in Darlington, S.C., since 1950. The race, which draws about 80,000 spectators, is one of the four so-called crown jewels in the NASCAR (National Association for Stock Car Auto Racing) Sprint Cup circuit and is considered the forerunner of those races. The others are the DAYTONA 500 (in Florida), the WINSTON 500 (Talladega, Ala.), and the COCA-COLA 600 (Charlotte, N.C.).

The first of the southern super speedways, the Darlington track was promoted and built by Harold Brasington, a sometime racing driver, and a group of Darlington citizens. The track was built on land owned by Sherman J. Ramsey, a farmer, and he insisted that his minnow pond not be disturbed. So the track had to skirt around it. Sports writers dubbed the oddly configured raceway the "Lady in Black," supposedly because it was fickle with drivers, like a mysterious woman. The winner of the first race in 1950 was Johnny Mantz.

CONTACTS:
Darlington Raceway
1301 Harry Byrd Hwy.
Darlington, SC 29540
866-459-7223 or 843-395-8499
www.darlingtonraceway.com

National Association for Stock Car Auto Racing
1801 W. International Speedway Blvd.
Daytona Beach, FL 32115
386-253-0611; fax: 386-681-4041
www.nascar.com

SOURCES:
FolkAmerHol-1999, p. 363

♦ 2467 ♦ Southern Ute Tribal Sun Dance
Mid-July

The Southern Ute Tribal Sun Dance is a ritual ceremony of ancient origin held by the Southern Ute Indians in Ignacio, Colo., often on the Sunday and Monday after the FOURTH OF JULY. The dancers who perform the ceremony are chosen from those who dream dreams and see visions, and they fast for four days before the dancing. While the public is allowed to attend, dress must be circumspect, and women are not allowed who are "on their moon," that is, having their menstrual period.

The Sun Dance was at one time performed by most Plains tribes, and usually involved self-torture. The Utes, however, did not practice this.

See also ARAPAHO SUN DANCE; SIOUX SUN DANCE

CONTACTS:
Southern Ute Tribal Council
P.O. Box 737
Ignacio, CO 81137
970-563-0100; fax: 970-563-0396
www.southern-ute.nsn.us

SOURCES:
EncyRel-1987, vol. 14, p. 143
IndianAmer-1989, pp. 121, 360

♦ 2468 ♦ Southwestern Exposition Livestock Show & Rodeo
Last two weeks of January

This event is the oldest continuously running livestock show in the United States, held since 1896 in Fort Worth, Tex. The exposition calls to mind Fort Worth's past when it was considered the capital of the southwestern cattle empire, and stockyards ringed the city. The world's first indoor rodeo was featured here in 1918.

Events of the exposition include a parade, horse shows, a midway, big-name entertainers, and $600,000 in show premiums and rodeo purses. The more than 17,000 head of livestock include beef and dairy cattle, sheep, swine, goats, horses, donkeys, mules, pigeons, poultry, sheepdogs, and llamas. The latter have been found to be more effective against coyotes than guns, dogs, electric fences, or chemical repellants. About 500 of them guard sheep in the Rocky Mountain region.

CONTACTS:
Southwestern Exposition Livestock Show and Rodeo
Will Rogers Memorial Center & Facilities
3400 Crestline Rd.
Fort Worth, TX 76101
817-877-2400; fax: 817-877-2499
www.fwssr.com

♦ 2469 ♦ Soyaluna (Hopi Soyal Ceremony)
December 22

The Hopi Indians traditionally believed that at the time of the WINTER SOLSTICE, the sun had traveled as far from the earth as he ever did. Only the most powerful humans could persuade the sun to turn around and come back to the pueblo. The purpose of Soyaluna, which is still held among the Hopi who live on the mesas of Arizona, is to prevent the disappearance of the sun at the time of year when the days are at their shortest.

The main ceremony takes place in the *kiva*, a large, circular underground room that can only be entered by climbing down a ladder through a hole in the ceiling. Hopi priests prepare the kiva by scattering cornmeal around the floor. On the west wall of the kiva, a stack of corn serves as an altar, surrounded by stalks and husks. Each family has given some corn to make the altar. At the solstice, everyone assembles in the kiva for rituals designed to bring the sun back for another agricultural year.

CONTACTS:
Hopi Cultural Center
P.O. Box 67
Second Mesa, AZ 86043
928-734-2401; fax: 928-734-6651
www.hopiculturalcenter.com

SOURCES:
DictFolkMyth-1984, p. 1058
EncyNatAmerRel-2001, p. 280
EndurHarv-1995, p. 111
RelHolCal-2004, p. 253

♦ 2470 ♦ **Spamarama**
April or May

Spamarama is an annual salute to Spam, the canned lunch meat, that has been held in Austin, Texas, since 1978. Spamarama—"the official pandemonious potted pork party"—includes the Spam Cook-Off in which chefs vie to offer the best presentation of Spam, the Spam Jam (live musical entertainment), and the Spam-Alympics (events include a Spam relay race, a Spamburger-eating contest, and a Spam toss). The festival, which is also a charity event, has no association with Hormel Foods Corp., the company that produces the canned meat.

Hormel's main office is located in Austin, Minnesota, where the Spam Museum opened in September 2001.

CONTACTS:
Spamarama
9027 Northgate Blvd., Ste. 101
Austin, TX 78758
512-834-1827; fax: 512-834-9504
www.spamarama.org

♦ 2471 ♦ **Special Olympics**
February and June-July

The Special Olympics is an international program of year-round sports training and athletic competition for more than one million children and adults with mental retardation. It was founded by Eunice Kennedy Shriver, who organized the first International Special Olympics Summer Games at Soldier Field in Chicago in 1968. Five years earlier, Shriver had started a day camp for people with mental retardation, and

she quickly saw that they were far more capable in sports and physical activities that many experts thought.

Today, athletes from 160 countries participate in local, national, and international competitions in 26 summer and winter sports, such as basketball, cycling, gymnastics, soccer, floor hockey, alpine skiing, figure skating, and aquatics. There are Special Olympics chapters in all 50 states of the U.S., and about 25,000 communities have Special Olympics programs. The Special Olympics World Summer Games are held every four years in early summer (June-July) and the Special Olympics World Winter Games are held every four years in February. The president of the United States often attends the opening ceremonies, during which the Special Olympic Cauldron is lit.

CONTACTS:
Special Olympics International
1133 19th St. N.W.
Washington, D.C. 20036
202-628-3630; fax: 202-824-0200
www.specialolympics.org

♦ 2472 ♦ **Spendarmad, Feast of**
February, June, July; fifth day of Spendarmad, the 12th Zoroastrian month

The Feast of Spendarmad is one of the "sacred name days" in the Zoroastrian religion, where the day and the month share the name of the same *yazata*, or spiritual being—in this case, Spendarmad, who represents Holy Devotion and who presides over the earth. In the past, the Feast of Spendarmad was also a special feast for women, whose husbands would give them presents on this day. Such gift giving is still a part of the festival in some areas, but the practice is no longer widespread.

Among the followers of Zoroaster (also known as Zarathushtra, believed to have lived around 1200 B.C.E.), the Persian prophet, a name-day feast is an occasion for religious ceremonies which can be performed in a fire temple, meeting hall, or private home. Because there are actually three different Zoroastrian calendars in use by widely separated Zoroastrian communities, the Feast of Spendarmad occurs either in February, June, or July in the Gregorian calendar.

There are only about 100,000 followers of Zoroastrianism today, and most of them live in northwestern India or Iran. Smaller communities exist in Pakistan, Sri Lanka, Canada, the U.S., England, and Australia.

SOURCES:
RelHolCal-2004, p. 69

♦ 2473 ♦ **Spiedie Fest and Balloon Rally**
Early August

The Spiedie Fest and Balloon Rally takes place annually in Otsiningo Park in Binghampton, N.Y., over three days in early August. The Spiedie Fest began in 1983 when a few families got together to decide who had the best recipe for *spiedie*—a regional delicacy of Italian descent. It consists of small pieces of marinated meat that are skewered and grilled, then served on Italian bread or a roll with fresh marinade on top. In 1985, the families decided to move the cooking contest to a local park and to feature five hot-air balloons, as well as a children's area. The aim was a community event that was fun, safe, and inexpensive. Recently, more than 100,000 have attended each festival, which now incorporates one of the leading hot-air balloon rallies in the United States. Besides bolstering local pride, the event benefits the community, with all profits going to charities in local Broome County.

The centerpieces of the festival are five balloon launches (weather permitting) at dawn and dusk, and the spiedie cooking contest. Other highlights are an antique car display, a craft show featuring more than 200 vendors, a sand volleyball tournament, and a five-kilometer run/walk. There also are live music acts, a variety of food, and celebrity appearances.

CONTACTS:
Spiedie Fest Balloon Rally Expo, Inc.
P.O. Box 275
Westview Station
Binghampton, NY 13905-0275
607-765-6604; fax: 607-729-2062

♦ 2474 ♦ **Spirit Burying**
January-February; second to 15th days of the first lunar month

Spirit burying, or *Mae-gwi*, is a new year custom common in rural areas of Korea. Farmers form bands and process around the village, visiting each home. In some areas the farmers wear masks and costumes and perform a traditional drama; in others they march around banging gongs and playing other musical instruments. Each household rewards the band with food, drink, or money. Any money collected is then put into a general community fund. Traditional belief has it that such activity will subdue evil spirits and provide for the village's protection in the coming year.

See also SOL; TAEBORUM

SOURCES:
AnnCustKorea-1983, p. 58

♦ 2475 ♦ **Spiritual Baptist (Shouters) Liberation Day**
March 30

The people of Trinidad and Tobago observe March 30 as Spiritual Baptist (Shouters) Liberation Day. This national holiday, instituted in 1996, honors an African-American religious sect once outlawed in Trinidad and Tobago. The Spiritual Baptists originally came to the islands as former American slaves, who had fought for the British in the Revolutionary War. Their style of worship combined African and American Baptist beliefs and practices. Services include bell ringing, shouting, and high-volume singing and chanting. The colonial government of Trinidad and Tobago accused the Spiritual Baptists of disturbing the peace. In 1917, the government for-

bade the group (nicknamed the "Shouters") from practicing their religion. This law was overturned in 1951. The recently established national holiday honors the Spiritual Baptists' long struggle against religious persecution. It is observed with speeches and religious services.

CONTACTS:
Ministry of Tourism, Trinidad and Tobago Government
51-55 Frederick St.
Port of Spain, Trinidad and Tobago
868-624-1403; fax: 868-625-0437
www.gov.tt

♦ 2476 ♦ **Spock Days/Galaxyfest**
Second weekend of June

Vulcan, a town located in the Canadian province of Alberta, has an inadvertent yet auspicious connection with the highly successful Star Trek franchise: it has the same name as the species to which the character Dr. Spock belongs. Since 1991 the annual celebration now known as Spock Days/Galaxyfest has boosted tourism and brought into town fans eager for another celebration of the cult phenomenon that has been spawned by the Star Trek movies and TV shows.

There are two structures in Vulcan that build upon the town's Star Trek connection: the replica of the famous starship U.S.S. *Enterprise*, which stands at the town's main entrance, and the Vulcan Tourism and Trek Station, which opened to the public in 1998 and is the base of operations for Spock Days/Galaxyfest.

Initial there were two festivals: the VulCon, the original celebration, and the Spockdays Rodeo that was added later. In 2002 the events were combined to take place over one long weekend. Typically, events include a costume contest, a Klingon-inspired stunt-game competition, a Galaxy Awards Banquet, and appearances by cast members from Star Trek shows.

CONTACTS:
Vulcan Tourism
115 Centre St. E.
P.O. Box 1161
Vulcan, AL T0L 2B0 Canada
www.town.vulcan.ab.ca/events/galaxyfest.html

♦ 2477 ♦ **Spoken Word Festival, Calgary International**
March-April

The Calgary Spoken Word Society was created in 2003 by poet Sheri-D Wilson to promote spoken word poetry locally, provincially, nationally, and internationally, through performance and education. The Society sponsored the first annual Calgary International Spoken Word Festival in 2004. A rousing success, it consisted of four events featuring artists from across Canada. Each year since the event has expanded, with more artists and more events. Today, the festival includes more than a dozen events featuring a wide range of voices and viewpoints.

In addition, the Spoken Word Society has created other events throughout the year to promote spoken word poetry. In 2005, it launched the monthly Calgary Poetry Slam, which gives up-and-coming poets the opportunity to perform. Also in 2005, the Society created the Word Travels program, which places poets in Calgary area high schools. This program presents an innovative approach to literacy, using the accessibility of Spoken Word to introduce students to the world of literature, speak to students in their own language, and give them the voice to speak in their own. A recent innovation of the Spoken Word Society is the Poetry Postcard Project, in which local poets were invited to share their work on a series of 9 x 4 inch postcards as a way of marking summer and travel.

CONTACTS:
Calgary International Spoken Word Festival
403-686-4292
www.calgaryspokenwordfestival.com

◆ 2478 ◆ Spoleto Festival USA
May-June

Pulitzer Prize-winning composer Gian Carlo Menotti founded the **Festival of Two Worlds** in Spoleto, Italy, in 1958, and brought it to Charleston, South Carolina, under the name **Spoleto USA** in 1977. The annual 17-day international arts festival focuses on new works and productions, and routinely offers more than 100 events in opera, chamber music, symphonic concerts, theater, dance, and art. In recent years, the festival has also offered jazz and other newer musical performances.

CONTACTS:
Spoleto Festival USA
P.O. Box 157
Charleston, SC 29402
843-579-3100; fax: 843-723-6383
www.spoletousa.org

SOURCES:
GdUSFest-1984, p. 169
GdWrldFest-1985, p. 120
IntlThFolk-1979, p. 248
MusFestAmer-1990, p. 136

◆ 2479 ◆ Spring Break
February-April

Spring Break is an annual celebration of spring—and of school vacations—by an estimated two million college students who whoop it up, sunbathe, party, drink, dance, and listen to loud music.

From the early 1950s until 1985, Fort Lauderdale, Fla., was a prime destination. In 1960 the movie, *Where the Boys Are* (based on the Glendon Swarthout novel of the same name), featuring Connie Francis, George Hamilton, and Yvette Mimieux, was all about spring break. It gave Fort Lauderdale great national exposure. But the hordes of students got to be too much; by 1985, 350,000 people took over the city for six weeks and tied up not just traffic but the legal system. Fort Lauderdale started clamping down, and now only about 20,000 students visit.

Popular destinations today include Panama City Beach, Fla., Daytona Beach, Fla., South Padre Island, Tex., Palm Springs, Calif., the Bahamas, Jamaica, and Mexico. To lure the spring breakers, various towns and resorts spend millions of dollars and offer an abundance of free activities, including beach sports, concerts, movie premieres, and contests.

CONTACTS:
Cancun Convention & Visitors Bureau
Cancun Center, 1st. Flr., Blvd. Kukulcan
Hotel Zone
Cancun, Q.Roo 77500 Mexico
52-998-881-2745; fax: 52-998-881-2774
cancun.travel/en

South Padre Island Convention & Visitors Bureau
600 Padre Blvd.
South Padre Island, TX 78597
800-767-2373 or 956-761-3000; fax: 956-761-3024
www.sopadre.com

Panama City Beach Convention & Visitors Bureau
16000 Front Beach Rd.
Panama City, FL 32403
800-722-3224 or 850-233-5070
www.thebeachloversbeach.com

SOURCES:
Spring Equinox *See* **Vernal Equinox**

◆ 2480 ◆ Spring of Culture
March

The first Arab state to discover oil, the Persian Gulf country of Bahrain has enjoyed dramatic economic development since the first half of the 20th century. In recent decades, government organizations have worked toward making its national arts program as robust as its oil industry. The Spring of Culture Festival, held every March in the capital city of Manama, helps fulfill this cultural mission and promotes tourism to the country. The festival is organized by the Sector of Culture and Heritage with the support of the Economic Development Board.

Thanks to its reputation as a meeting place between the East and the West, Spring of Culture is able to attract performers from all over the world. The festival was first held in 2006. In its first few years, the proceedings sometimes continued into April to overlap with the internationally known Bahrain Formula One Grand Prix, also held in Manama.

National, regional, and international artists converge on Manama to perform poetry readings, music, theater, and dance. Experts also present lectures and hold workshops. A survey of past performers illustrates the diversity of the performers: over the years the event has featured a Lebanese musician, a Senegalese singer, an Algerian-French thinker, and a Japanese drumming troupe.

CONTACTS:
Economic Development Board of Bahrain
P.O. Box 11299

Manama Kingdom of Bahrain
www.bahrainedb.com

◆ 2481 ◆ Springtime Festival
Begins between March 11 and April 15; four successive Thursdays before Orthodox Easter

Celebrated by people of all religious faiths, the Springtime Festival is a regional celebration throughout the Bekáa (or Beqaa) Valley in eastern Lebanon. It takes place during LENT, on four successive Thursdays preceding the Eastern Orthodox EASTER.

The first Thursday, known as Thursday-of-the-Animals, is a day of rest for domestic working animals, whose heads are decorated with a spot of henna, which is symbolic of blood and life. On the following Thursday, known as Thursday-of-the-Plants, young children and unmarried girls wash themselves in water scented with crushed flowers. Next is Thursday-of-the-Dead, a day for visiting the graves of family and friends. Last is Thursday-of-the-Jumping, or Day of the Jumping, when people living in the mountains come down by the thousands to the plains to join in the festival activities. They visit the tomb of Noah, which is outside Zahle, and then the shrine of the Wadi Zaour, a locally popular Muslim saint, in Anjar, a town that was an Armenian refugee village in the 1940s. There they receive blessings for good health. Eventually everyone returns to the villages, where there is dancing in the streets and even on the mosque grounds.

SOURCES:
FolkWrldHol-1999, p. 164

◆ 2482 ◆ Spy Wednesday
Between March 19 and April 22; Wednesday before Easter

The Wednesday before EASTER Sunday is the day on which the disciple Judas Iscariot made the deal to betray Jesus. In order to arrest Jesus without exciting the populace, Judas led the Jewish priests to the Garden of Gethsemane, near Jerusalem, where Jesus had gone at night to pray with the other 11 disciples after the Last Supper (*see* MAUNDY THURSDAY). Judas identified Jesus by kissing him and addressing him as "Master." For this he was paid 30 pieces of silver, the price of a slave in the Old Testament.

The name "Spy Wednesday" is said to be of Irish origin, although the Bible never refers to Judas as a spy. His surname, Iscariot, is believed by some to be a corruption of the Latin *sicarius*, meaning "murderer" or "assassin."

SOURCES:
DaysCustFaith-1957, p. 106
DictDays-1988, p. 113
EncyEaster-2002, p. 574

◆ 2483 ◆ Sri Lanka National Day
February 4

The former British colony of Ceylon changed its name in 1972 to Sri Lanka, which means "Blessed Isle." Sri Lankans commemorate the granting of their independence from Great Britain on February 4, 1948, with public gatherings throughout the island and special services in the temples, churches, and mosques. There are also parades, folk dances, processions, and national games.

CONTACTS:
Sri Lankan Embassy
2148 Wyoming Ave. N.W.
Washington, D.C. 20008
202-483-4025; fax: 202-232-7181
www.slembassyusa.org

SOURCES:
AnnivHol-2000, p. 21
IntlThFolk-1979, p. 345
NatlHolWrld-1968, p. 22

◆ 2484 ◆ St. Agatha Festival
February 3-5

Sant' Agata is especially revered in Catania, Sicily, where her relics are preserved in a silver casket. The beautiful young Sicilian virgin was put to death in the third century because she refused to yield to the advances of a Roman prefect. Among the tortures she is said to have endured was having her breasts cut off, and to this day she is the patron saint of nursing mothers and women suffering from diseases of the breast.

On February 3, 4 and 5 each year, a silver bust of St. Agatha wearing a jewel-encrusted crown is carried in procession from the cathedral to Catania's various churches. Included in the procession are the *ceri*, huge wooden replicas of candlesticks which are carved with episodes from the saint's martyrdom. The streets are lined with streamers and flowers, and illuminated by strings of colored lights after dark. The festival ends with a fireworks display in the piazza.

CONTACTS:
Regione Siciliana, Regional Council for Tourism, Communications and Transport
Via Emanuele Notarbartolo, 9
Palermo, Sicily 90141 Italy
39-91-6968-201; fax: 39-91-6968-135
www.regione.sicilia.it

SOURCES:
AnnivHol-2000, p. 22
FestSaintDays-1915, p. 32
FestWestEur-1958, p. 90
OxYear-1999, p. 68

◆ 2485 ◆ St. Agnes's Eve
January 20

The eve of St. Agnes's Day (January 21) has long been associated with various superstitions about how young girls might discover the identity of their future husbands. According to one such belief, a girl who went to bed without any supper on this night would dream of the man she was to marry. John

Keats used this legend as the basis for his well-known poem, "The Eve of St. Agnes," in which a young maid dreams of her lover and wakes to find him standing at her bedside.

St. Agnes herself was martyred sometime during the fourth century, when she may have been only 12 or 13 years old, because she had consecrated herself to Christ and refused to marry. She was later named the patron saint of young virgins. In art St. Agnes is often represented with a lamb or sometimes with a dove with a ring in its beak.

SOURCES:
BkDays-1864, vol. I, p. 140
BkFest-1937, p. 180
BkHolWrld-1986, Jan 21
DaysCustFaith-1957, p. 28
DictDays-1988, p. 100
DictFolkMyth-1984, p. 28
FestSaintDays-1915, p. 20
OxYear-1999, p. 44
SaintFestCh-1904, p. 75

♦ 2486 ♦ St. Alban's Day
June 22

St. Alban is the first and best known of all the English saints and martyrs. He was a soldier living as a pagan in the town of Verulamium, probably during the third century, when a Christian priest named Amphibalus, pursued by Roman persecutors, begged for refuge in his house. Alban took him in and was soon converted by him and baptized. When he could conceal Amphibalus no longer, Alban changed clothes with him and gave himself up as the priest. The deception was soon discovered, however, and Alban was brought before the governor, condemned, and beheaded.

There are a number of legends concerning St. Alban's execution. One is that when the crowd that gathered to watch the beheading was too large to get across the small bridge leading to the execution place, St. Alban said a prayer and caused the waters to divide. Another is that when he asked for a drink of water, a spring gushed forth from the ground in front of him. Supposedly, the soldier who was appointed to kill St. Alban refused to do so, and was beheaded along with the saint.

A shrine was later erected in Verulamium, and the town was renamed St. Albans. The cathedral hosts a festival each year on a weekend near St. Alban's Day, when pilgrims gather for special services, a procession, and other events.

CONTACTS:
Cathedral & Abbey Church of St Alban
St. Albans, Hertfordshire AL1 1BY United Kingdom
44-17-2786-0780; fax: 44-17-2785-0944
www.stalbanscathedral.org.uk

SOURCES:
BkDays-1864, vol. I, p. 808
DaysCustFaith-1957, p. 149
OxYear-1999, p. 257

♦ 2487 ♦ St. Andrew's Day
November 30

St. Andrew, the brother of ST. PETER, was the first apostle called by Jesus, but he is primarily known today as the patron saint of Scotland, though he was also chosen to be patron saint of Russia. According to the apocryphal and unreliable Acts of St. Andrew, he went to Greece, and having converted the proconsul's wife there, he was condemned to be crucified. Fastened to an X-shaped cross by cords rather than nails, he eventually died of thirst and starvation.

St. Andrew's association with Scotland didn't come about until four centuries after his death, when some of his relics were brought there. Although there are a number of churches throughout England and Scotland that bear St. Andrew's name, many associate it with the famous St. Andrew's golf course near Dundee. Some Scots continue the custom of wearing a "St. Andrew's cross" on November 30, which consists of blue and white ribbons shaped like the letter X. The tradition for this form of a cross began no earlier than the 13th century.

This is also a major feast in Lapland and a time for weddings and meeting new people.

SOURCES:
BkDays-1864, vol. II, p. 635
BkFest-1937, pp. 62, 174
DaysCustFaith-1957, p. 296
DictFolkMyth-1984, p. 55
FestSaintDays-1915, p. 216
FolkWrldHol-1999, p. 663
OxYear-1999, p. 479

♦ 2488 ♦ St. Andrew's Eve (Noc Swietego Andreja)
November 29

The eve of ST. ANDREW'S DAY is a special night for young Polish girls who want to find husbands. They play *Andrzejki*, or "Andrew's games," a kind of fortune telling. Young girls break off dry branches from cherry trees, place them in wet sand, and tend them carefully for the next few weeks. If the branch blooms by CHRISTMAS, it is believed that they will marry within the year. Pouring liquid wax into cold water is another popular method of foretelling their romantic futures. The shapes into which the wax hardens often provide clues with which they can read their fate. The boys try to foretell their own futures on St. Catherine's Eve (*see also* ST. CATHERINE'S DAY, November 25).

The patron saint of both Russia and Scotland, St. Andrew's name means "manly" or "courageous," making him an appropriate target for the appeals of young girls seeking lovers. Andrzejki are popular among Polish Americans as well, where they include peeling apples to see what letter the apple peel seems to form when thrown over the peeler's left shoulder.

Austrian peasant women also forced fruit tree branches, but they brought them to Christmas mass and believed they gave them the ability to see all the witches in the congregation.

SOURCES:
FolkAmerHol-1999, p. 448
OxYear-1999, p. 478

♦ 2489 ♦ **St. Anne's Day**
July 26

In 1650, a group of Breton sailors built a tiny frame church at the place where the town of Beaupré, Quebec, Canada, now stands. They wanted to honor of St. Anne, the traditional name for the mother of the Virgin Mary and wife of Joachim or St. Joseph (the apostle James names her in his Letter). The sailors had been caught in a vicious storm at sea and vowed that if St. Anne would save them, they would build her a sanctuary at the spot where their feet first touched land. In 1658, the people of the village built a new and larger church, and it was then that the first of St. Anne de Beaupré's miraculous cures took place, when a local man suffering from rheumatism came to the church and walked away in perfect health. Since that time thousands of cures have been reported at the Basilica of Sainte Anne de Beaupré, which has been called the "Lourdes of the New World" after the famous shrine in France.

St. Anne is the patron saint of Canada. The pilgrimage to her shrine in Beaupré is one of the major pilgrimages on the North American continent. Romanies from Canada and the United States also arrive to celebrate Santana ("St. Anna"). They camp on the church property, prepare a *slava* feast of special foods for and prayers to St. Anne, and visit their families (*see* Pardon of Ste. Anne D'Auray).

SOURCES:
AnnivHol-2000, p. 123
DaysCustFaith-1957, p. 192
FolkWrldHol-1999, p. 449
OxYear-1999, p. 308

♦ 2490 ♦ **St. Anthony of Padua, Feast of**
June 13

St. Anthony of Padua (1195-1231) is the patron saint of people who lose things and of children. He has also become, like St. Francis of Assisi, a patron saint of animals. In the days before automobiles, people in Rome sent their horses and mules to St. Anthony's Church to be blessed on this day. The Feast of St. Anthony is also celebrated by many Puerto Rican communities, as well as by American Indians in the southwestern United States. In New Mexico, for instance, traditional Indian dances are held on **San Antonio's Day** in the pueblos at Taos, San Juan, Santa Clara, San Ildefonso, Sandia, Cochiti, and elsewhere.

One of the most outstanding celebrations is held in New York City's Greenwich Village. St. Anthony's Shrine Church on West Houston and Sullivan Streets, in the heart of one of the original Little Italy sections of New York, boasts the oldest Italian Roman Catholic congregation in the city and is the site of a 10-day festival that combines religious observance and the carnival atmosphere of a street fair. Masses are held all day on June 13, and a procession bearing the statue of St. Anthony through the streets begins at seven o'clock that evening. Thousands of people are drawn to the festival, which extends from the weekend before the actual feast day through the weekend following it.

In the village of El Pinar, Granada, Spain, a novena ends with the Rosary on St. Anthony's Eve. Then a fiesta begins with a parade of huge papier-mâché heads of historical and imaginary characters (called *gigantes* "giants" and *cabezudos* "big-heads"), on 10-foot-tall wire frames and dressed in long robes. This parade is accompanied by a band playing *pasodobles* (a quick, light march often played at bullfights). Boys toss firecrackers, small children hide in terror, fireworks are set off, street dancing begins, and carnival booths are set up. On the 13th, the parade begins at 9 A.M. After a noon High Mass, the statue of St. Anthony is paraded through the village for three hours. The band plays and pairs of men in two lines dance the *jota* (a complex dance using the rhythm of boot-heels and castanets). When the dancers tire, they are replaced by eager onlookers. At their return to the church, they block the door to keep St. Anthony from going in so the dancing can go on. Parishioners lay money at the feet of the statue for the support of the church for the coming year.

St. Anthony of Padua was born in Lisbon, Portugal, in 1195, and is the patron saint of Portugal. The festivities held here in his honor begin on the evening of June 12 with an impressive display of *marchas*, walking groups of singers and musicians, who parade along the Avenida da Liberdade. The celebration continues the next day with more processions and traditional folk dancing.

Throughout the month of June, children in Lisbon prepare altars in the saint's honor, covering boxes and tables with white paper and decorating them with candles and pictures of St. Anthony. They beg "a little penny for San António" from passersby, but the money—once used to restore the church of San António da Sé after its destruction by an earthquake in 1755—is now put toward a children's feast.

Because he is considered the matchmaker saint, St. Anthony's Eve is a time when young people write letters asking António for help in finding a mate. Another custom of the day is for a young man to present the girl he hopes to marry with a pot of basil concealing a verse or love letter.

CONTACTS:
The Shrine Church of Saint Anthony of Padua
154 Sullivan St.
New York, NY 10012
212-777-2755; fax: 212-673-6684
www.stanthonynyc.org

SOURCES:
AmerBkDays-2000, p. 443
BkFest-1937, p. 187
DaysCustFaith-1957, p. 144
DictWrldRel-1989, p. 42
EncyRel-1987, vol. 1, p. 306
FestWestEur-1958, p. 166
FolkAmerHol-1999, p. 252
FolkWrldHol-1999, p. 387
IndianAmer-1989, pp. 286, 288, 301, 303, 306, 309, 312, 315, 319

♦ 2491 ♦ **St. Anthony the Abbot, Feast of**
January 17

St. Anthony the Abbot was one of the earliest saints, and, if St. Athanasius's biography of him is correct, Anthony lived more than 100 years (251-356). Living as a hermit, Anthony nonetheless attracted disciples and ventured out occasionally to become involved in the doctrinal controversies of his day. Eventually he came to be regarded as a healer of animals as well as of people. The order of Hospitallers of St. Anthony, founded during the 12th century, endeavored to keep animals in good health by hanging bells around their necks. His feast day is celebrated in Mexico and other parts of Latin America by bringing household pets and livestock into the churchyard, where the local priest blesses them with holy water. All the animals are carefully groomed and often decorated with ribbons and fresh flowers.

In some Latin American cities, the **Blessing of the Animals** takes place on a different day—often on HOLY SATURDAY, the day before EASTER. Hispanic people and others in the United States often celebrate the Blessing of the Animals on this day as well. In Los Angeles, the procession of animals to Our Lady of the Angels Church follows a cobblestone path that was laid by Mexican settlers more than 200 years ago.

SOURCES:
AnnivHol-2000, p. 10
BkFest-1937, pp. 225, 298
FestWestEur-1958, pp. 189, 226
OxYear-1999, p. 39
RelHolCal-2004, p. 89

♦ 2492 ♦ St. Augustine of Hippo, Feast of
August 28

St. Augustine's career as a Christian got off to a slow start. The son of a pagan father and a Christian mother, he spent most of his youth in dissipation and promiscuity. He was 32 years old when he converted to Christianity in 386 after undergoing conflicts within himself on how he was living and what he believed; hearing St. Ambrose preach was said to have influenced him as well. A few years later he became bishop of Hippo in North Africa. For the next 40 years he was a teacher, writer, preacher, and theologian who exerted a profound influence on the development of Christian doctrine. He is best known for his spiritual autobiography, the *Confessions*, which detail the excesses of his youth, his career as a teacher of rhetoric, his years as a believer in Manicheism and Platonism, and his belated conversion to Christianity. It is primarily for his writings that he is known as the patron saint of theologians and scholars and one of the "Four Latin Fathers" of the Christian Church.

St. Augustine also typifies the Christian who has been converted slowly, as exemplified by his well-known prayer, "O God, make me pure—but not yet." When a company of Spanish soldiers landed on the coast of Florida on St. Augustine's Day in 1565, they named the U.S.'s oldest European community after him.

SOURCES:
AmerBkDays-2000, p. 614
AnnivHol-2000, p. 143
DaysCustFaith-1957, p. 221

DictWrldRel-1989, p. 77
EncyRel-1987, vol. 1, p. 520
OxYear-1999, p. 348
SaintFestCh-1904, p. 384

♦ 2493 ♦ St. Barbara's Day
December 4

Scholars doubt that St. Barbara existed as more than a legend that emerged during the second century. The story is that her father locked her away in a tower to prevent her from ever marrying. When she became a Christian he tried to kill her, then turned her in to the pagan authorities. Then he was killed by a bolt of lightning.

In parts of France, Germany, and Syria, St. Barbara's Day is considered the beginning of the CHRISTMAS season. In southern France, especially in Provence, it is customary to set out dishes holding grains of wheat soaked in water on sunny window sills. There is a folk belief that if the "St. Barbara's grain" grows quickly, it means a good year for crops. But if it withers and dies, the crops will be ruined. On CHRISTMAS EVE, the grain is placed near the crèche as a symbol of the coming harvest. There is a similar custom in Germany and the Czech and Slovak republics, where cherry branches are placed in water and tended carefully in the hope that they will bloom on Christmas Eve. In Syria, St. Barbara's Day is for feasting and bringing food to the poor.

In Poland, St. Barbara's Day is associated with weather prophecies. If it rains, it will be cold and icy on Christmas Day; if it's cold and icy, Christmas will be rainy.

SOURCES:
BkFest-1937, p. 128
DaysCustFaith-1957, p. 305
DictFolkMyth-1984, p. 950
EncyChristmas-2003, p. 657
FestWestEur-1958, p. 49
FolkAmerHol-1999, p. 484
FolkWrldHol-1999, p. 685
OxYear-1999, p. 485

♦ 2494 ♦ St. Barnabas's Day
June 11

Before England adopted the Gregorian calendar in 1752, June 11 was the day of the SUMMER SOLSTICE. In addition to being the longest day of the year, it was also St. Barnabas's Day (or **Barnaby Day**), and this association gave rise to the old English jingle, "Barnaby bright, Barnaby bright, the longest day and the shortest night." It was customary on this day for the priests and clerks in the Church of England to wear garlands of roses and to decorate the church with them. Other names for this day were **Long Barnaby** and **Barnaby Bright**.

SOURCES:
BkDays-1864, vol. I, p. 769
DaysCustFaith-1957, p. 143
DictDays-1988, pp. 9, 69, 100
OxYear-1999, p. 245

♦ 2495 ♦ St. Bartholomew's Day
August 24

St. Bartholomew is the patron saint of beekeepers and honey-makers, and for this reason it was traditional in England for the honey crop to be gathered on August 24. Since the main ingredient in mead—an ancient alcoholic drink that is still made in some parts of England today—is honey, the Blessing of the Mead is also observed on St. Bartholomew's Day.

In ancient Rome, mead was offered to the gods of love and fertility. Although few people today still believe that drinking mead will help a marriage produce children, the drink is still believed to have curative powers.

In St. Mount's Bay, Cornwall, a special ceremony is held by the Almoner of the Worshipful Company of Mead Makers. It begins with a church service, and then the participants move to the Mead Hall, where the Almoner, who is also the vicar of the parish, blesses the mead that has been fermenting for two years and pours it into a special cup. The mead can then be moved to a storage vat. In the past, mead was traditionally drunk from a bowl, known as a mazer, made from birds-eye maple with a silver rim.

See also BARTHOLOMEW FAIR; SCHÄFERLAUF; STOURBRIDGE FAIR

CONTACTS:
Visit Britain
551 Fifth Ave., Ste. 701
New York, NY 10176
800-462-2748 or 212-850-0330; fax: 212-986-1188
www.visitbritain.com/us

SOURCES:
AmerBkDays-2000, p. 606
YrbookEngFest-1954, p. 113
YrFest-1972, p. 61

♦ 2496 ♦ St. Basil, Feast of
January 1

NEW YEAR'S DAY and the feast day for Agios Vasilis (St. Basil) are one and the same in Greece and Cyprus, and for all Orthodox Christians. Celebrations begin on NEW YEAR'S EVE when Agios Vasilis is believed to visit each house, blessing the people and their belongings and animals, and bringing presents to the children. Nowadays, the parish priest goes around and blesses the homes of his flock.

On New Year's Day, a cake called the *Vassilopita*, or "St. Basil's bread," is ceremoniously sliced, according to varying traditions going back to Byzantine times. Usually the first slice is cut for Jesus Christ, the next is for the house, and the following for absent family members. A coin has been baked in the cake, and the person finding the coin will be the luckiest member of the family that year.

St. Basil was a monk and church father who left many influential writings, including a defense of the study of pagan writings by Christians. He was born about the year 329 and was declared a saint soon after his death on Jan. 1 of the year 379 in Caesarea (in present-day Israel).

SOURCES:
BkFest-1937, pp. 3, 143, 273, 288
BkFestHolWrld-1970, p. 4
DictWrldRel-1989, p. 93
EncyChristmas-2003, p. 660
EncyRel-1987, vol. 2, p. 78
FolkWrldHol-1999, p. 12
OxYear-1999, p. 6

♦ 2497 ♦ St. Blaise's Day
February 3

The association of St. Blaise (or **Blase,** or **Blasius**) with the blessing of throats can be traced to a number of sources. According to one story, as he was being led to his own execution in 316, he miraculously cured a child who was suffering from a throat infection. Another story has it that he saved the life of a boy who was choking on a fishbone. In any case, St. Blaise, since the sixth century in the East, has been the patron saint of people who suffer from throat afflictions, and celebrations on this day in the Roman Catholic Church often include the blessing of throats by the priest. In Paraguay, the religious services are followed by a holiday festival (*see* SAN BLAS, FIESTA OF).

Among the many tortures said to have been suffered by this saint was having his body torn by iron combs similar to those used at one time by wool-combers in England. St. Blaise thus became the patron saint of wool-combers as well, and his feast day has traditionally been celebrated in English towns where the woolen industry is important.

In Spain they bake small loaves, called *tortas de San Blas* ("San Blas's loaves") or *panecillos del santo* ("little breads of the saint"). They are blessed during mass, and each child eats a bit to prevent him or her from choking during the year.

SOURCES:
BkDays-1864, vol. I, p. 219
DaysCustFaith-1957, p. 46
DictDays-1988, p. 100
FestSaintDays-1915, p. 31
FolkAmerHol-1999, p. 70
FolkWrldHol-1999, p. 121
OxYear-1999, pp. 65, 74

♦ 2498 ♦ St. Brendan's Day
May 16

St. Brendan, who lived in the sixth century, is one of the most popular Irish saints. In addition to founding a number of monasteries, including the one at Clonfert in Galway, Ireland, he was alleged to be the author of *Navigatio Brendani*, the story of his journey with a crew of four monks to a land across the ocean (the tale, however, is thought to have been written in the 10th century). No one, including St. Brendan himself, knew exactly where he had been when he returned, but a number of legends concerning the journey developed over the centuries—one of which claims that he actually reached the American continent.

In 1977, an Irishman named Tim Severin built a boat out of leather like the one described in *Navigatio* and set out to follow St. Brendan's instructions. After 50 days at sea, he ended up in Newfoundland, giving credence to the theory that St. Brendan reached America 1,000 years before Columbus.

SOURCES:
AnnivHol-2000, p. 83
BkHolWrld-1986, May 16
DaysCustFaith-1957, p. 124
OxYear-1999, p. 210

◆ 2499 ◆ St. Bridget's Day
February 1

St. Bridget (or **Brigid**, or **Bride**) is the female patron saint of Ireland. She has also been identified with an ancient pagan goddess. Her feast day, February 1, was traditionally the first day of spring and of the new year in rural Ireland because it marked the start of the agricultural season. Legends about Bridget associate her with abundance and fertility; her cows, for example, allegedly gave milk up to three times a day. She is credited with an almost endless number of miracles and was buried in the same church at Downpatrick where the bodies of St. Patrick and St. Columba lie. She lived during the sixth century and probably established the first Irish convent, around which the city of Kildare eventually grew.

Many old customs and folk beliefs are associated with St. Bridget's feast day. For example, people would not perform any work on this day that involved turning or twisting, or that required the use of a wheel. It was also customary on the eve of the saint's day for the oldest daughter of the family to bring a bundle of rushes to the door. Playing the role of St. Bridget, she would distribute the rushes among the family members, who would make crosses from them and, after the crosses were sprinkled with holy water, hang them throughout the house. Because St. Bridget is said to have woven the first cloth in Ireland, a cloth known as the *Brat Bhride,* or "Bridget's cloak," was left outside on the steps, and during the night it was believed to acquire special healing powers.

The custom of having women propose marriage to men during Leap Year can also be traced to St. Bridget. As legend has it, she complained to St. Patrick about the fact that men always took the initiative and persuaded him to grant women the right to do so during one year out of every four. Then Bridget proposed to Patrick, who turned her down but softened his refusal by giving her a kiss and a silk gown.

SOURCES:
BkDays-1864, vol. I, p. 206
BkFest-1937, p. 53
DaysCustFaith-1957, p. 43
DictFolkMyth-1984, pp. 165, 966
FestSaintDays-1915, p. 24
FolkWrldHol-1999, p. 109
OxDictSaints-1987, p. 62
OxYear-1999, pp. 57, 60
SaintFestCh-1904, p. 89

◆ 2500 ◆ St. Catherine's Day
November 25 (suppressed in 1969 in the Roman Catholic Church)

St. Catherine is now thought to have been a folkloric figure rather than a historical person; for that reason, her feast day is no longer observed in the Roman Catholic Church calendar. According to apocryphal writings, St. Catherine of Alexandria was sentenced to death by Emperor Maxentius for her extraordinary success in converting people to Christianity in the fourth century. He placed her in a torture machine that consisted of wheels armed with sharp spikes so that she would be torn to pieces as the wheels revolved. She was saved from this grim fate by divine intervention, but then the Emperor had her beheaded. The "Catherine Wheel" in England today is a type of firework that revolves in pinwheel fashion. In the United States, the "cartwheels" performed regularly by aspiring gymnasts repeat the motion of St. Catherine on the wheel of torture.

In 18th-century England, young women in the textile districts engaged in merry-making or "catherning" on this day, which is sometimes referred to as **Cathern Day**. As the patron saint of old maids, St. Catherine is still celebrated in France by unmarried women under 25, especially those employed in the millinery and dressmaking industries. They wear "Catherine bonnets" on November 25—homemade creations of paper and ribbon. The French expression *coiffer Sainte Catherine* (to don St. Catherine's bonnet), is used to warn girls that they are likely to become spinsters.

SOURCES:
BkFest-1937, p. 128
DaysCustFaith-1957, p. 295
DictDays-1988, pp. 19, 101
DictFolkMyth-1984, pp. 197, 1168
FestSaintDays-1915, pp. 213, 215
FestWestEur-1958, p. 48
FolkWrldHol-1999, p. 662
OxYear-1999, p. 474

◆ 2501 ◆ St. Catherine's Day (Estonia)
November 25

Estonian folklorists believe that the customs associated with Kadripäev, or St. Catherine's Day in Estonia, may date back to pre-Christian times. The holiday is strongly associated with women and their traditional activities, such as herding. People dress up in light-colored clothing, symbolizing winter's snow, and visit their neighbors, singing songs and offering blessings for the family's sheep and other herd animals. In return householders offer them cloth, wool, or food. An old superstition connected with the day forbade such activities as shearing and weaving, and sometimes knitting and sewing, as a means of protecting the sheep. Estonians associate Kadripäev with the arrival of winter.

CONTACTS:
Estonian Institute
Suur-Karja 14
P.O. Box 3469
Tallinn, 10506 Estonia
372-6-314-355; fax: 372-6-314-356
www.einst.ee

◆ 2502 ◆ **St. Cecilia's Day**
November 22

Not much can be said with confidence about St. Cecilia's life. According to her apocryphal acts, which date from the fifth century, she was a Roman from a noble family who was put to death in the second or third century for her Christian beliefs. How she became the patron saint of music and musicians is not exactly known, but according to legend she played the harp so beautifully that an angel left heaven to come down and listen to her. In any case, the Academy of Music in Rome accepted her as its patron when it was established in 1584.

In 1683, a musical society was formed in London especially for the celebration of St. Cecilia's Day. It held a festival each year at which a special ode was sung. The poet John Dryden composed his "Ode for St. Cecilia's Day" in 1687 for this purpose. By the end of the 17th century it was customary to hold concerts on November 22 in St. Cecilia's honor—a practice which has faded over the years, but there are still many choirs and musical societies that bear her name.

SOURCES:
AnnivHol-2000, p. 195
BkDays-1864, vol. II, p. 604
DaysCustFaith-1957, p. 293
DictDays-1988, p. 101
FolkAmerHol-1999, p. 447
OxYear-1999, p. 470
SaintFestCh-1904, p. 494

◆ 2503 ◆ **St. Charlemagne's Day**
January 28

Charlemagne wasn't actually a saint at all; he was an emperor and the first ruler of the Holy Roman Empire, crowned in 800 by Pope Leo III. But because of his great interest in education, French college students refer to him as a saint and a hero. Although he was never able to read and write himself, Charlemagne, whose name means "Charles the Great," founded the University of Paris. In fact, his reign was marked by a huge cultural revival, including significant advances in scholarship, literature, and philosophy.

St. Charlemagne's Day is still celebrated by college students in France, who hold champagne breakfasts at which professors and top students recite poems and give speeches.

SOURCES:
AnnivHol-2000, p. 15
DaysCustFaith-1957, p. 34
EncyRel-1987, vol. 3, p. 225

◆ 2504 ◆ **St. Charles's Day**
January 30

Charles I, crowned king of England in 1625, was illegally executed on Jan. 30, 1649, primarily for defending the Anglican Church. His body was secretly buried in Windsor Castle. He was widely acclaimed as a martyr. A royal decree ordered a special service on this day to be in the Book of Common

Prayer from 1662 to 1859. It also ordered it to be a day of national fasting. The anniversary of this event is commemorated by the Society of Charles the Martyr with an annual service at the site of his execution in Whitehall, London. St. Charles is the only post-Reformation figure to be honored in this way by the Church of England.

See also Saints, Doctors, Missionaries and Martyrs Day

CONTACTS:
Society of King Charles the Martyr
22 Tyning Rd.
Winsley, Wiltshire BA15 2JJ United Kingdom
44-12-2586-2965
www.skcm.org

SOURCES:
AnnivHol-2000, p. 17
BkDays-1864, vol. I, p. 189
DaysCustFaith-1957, p. 35
DictDays-1988, p. 19
OxYear-1999, p. 54
SaintFestCh-1904, p. 87

◆ 2505 ◆ **St. Christopher's Day**
May 9 in the East and July 25 in the West

The lack of reliable information about St. Christopher's life led the Roman Catholic Church to lessen the significance of his feast in its universal calendar in 1969. But he is still widely venerated—especially by travelers, of whom he is the patron saint. According to the most popular legend, Christopher became a ferryman, carrying people across a river on his strong shoulders while using his staff for balance. One day he carried a small child across, but the weight was so overwhelming that he almost didn't make it to the other side. When he did, the child revealed himself as Christ, explaining his great weight by saying, "With me thou hast borne the sins of the world." The name Christopher means "Christ-bearer."

St. Christopher's Day is observed by members of the Christopher movement in the United States, whose mission is to encourage individual responsibility and positive action. Founded by a member of the Roman Catholic Maryknoll order, the movement has its headquarters in New York City and embraces people of other denominations as well.

In Nesquehoning, Pennsylvania, St. Christopher's Day is the occasion for the **Blessing of the Cars**. The custom began in 1933, when the pastor of Our Lady of Mount Carmel Church started blessing automobiles on the feast day of the patron saint of travelers because he himself had been involved in three serious car accidents. Sometimes it takes an entire week to bless all the cars that arrive in Nesquehoning from throughout Pennsylvania and other nearby states. In recent years other Catholic churches in the area have taken up the custom and perform their own blessing ceremonies. (*See also* St. Frances of Rome, Feast of.)

CONTACTS:
The Christophers
5 Hanover Sq., 11th Fl.
New York, NY 10004

888-298-4050 or 212-759-4050; fax: 212-838-5073
www.christophers.org

SOURCES:
AnnivHol-2000, p. 122
BkDays-1864, vol. II, p. 122
BkHolWrld-1986, Jun 14
DaysCustFaith-1957, p. 190
FestSaintDays-1915, p. 156
FolkAmerHol-1999, p. 318
OxYear-1999, p. 306

◆ 2506 ◆ St. Clare of Assisi, Feast of
August 11

There were a number of women who joined the Second Order of St. Francis, but the first and most famous was St. Clare (c. 1194-1253). The daughter of a wealthy and noble family, she heard St. Francis preach about his rule of poverty and penance and, at the age of 18, left home to dedicate herself to the Franciscan way of life. She was joined 16 days later by her sister, Agnes. Other women, referred to as the Poor Ladies, were eventually drawn to the hard life that Clare had chosen, and the religious order that she and Francis founded is known today as the Poor Clares (*see also* ST. FRANCIS OF ASSISI, FEAST DAY OF).

Clare outlived Francis, who died in 1226, by 27 years. Although she was ill and confined to her bed for most of this time, she was a tireless proponent of the so-called "Primitive Rule," which calls for perpetual fasting except on Sundays and CHRISTMAS. In addition to their vows of poverty, chastity, and obedience, the Poor Clares also take a vow of enclosure, which means that they never leave the convent.

Clare died in 1253 and was canonized on August 12, 1255. Her feast day, which was observed for centuries by Roman Catholics and some Episcopalians, was eventually moved to August 11, the date of her death according to the revised Roman Catholic calendar and some other calendars.

SOURCES:
AnnivHol-2000, p. 134
OxYear-1999, p. 329

◆ 2507 ◆ St. Columba's Day
June 9

Along with ST. BRIDGET and ST. PATRICK, St. Columba (c. 521-597), also known as **Colm Cille**, **Columeille**, or **Columcille**, is a patron saint of Ireland. Although he led an exemplary life, traveling all over Ireland to set up churches, schools, and monasteries, he is chiefly remembered for his self-imposed exile to the island of Iona off the Scottish coast.

According to legend, Columba felt that he was responsible for the battle of Cuildremne, where 3,000 men were killed, and resolved to atone for his actions by winning 3,000 souls for Christ. He landed at Iona on the eve of PENTECOST, and proceeded to found a monastery and school from which he and his disciples preached the gospel throughout Scotland. Although he had been forbidden to see his native country

again, he returned several years later, allegedly blindfolded, to save the poets of Ireland, who were about to be expelled because they had grown so arrogant and overbearing.

St. Columba is also associated with the story of how the robin got its red breast. When Columba asked the robin who landed on his window sill to sing him a song, the robin sang the story of the crucifixion and how he had pulled the thorns out of Christ's forehead and, in doing so, had been covered with his blood.

SOURCES:
AnnivHol-2000, p. 97
DaysCustFaith-1957, p. 142
OxYear-1999, p. 242

◆ 2508 ◆ St. Crispin's Day
October 25

According to legend, Crispin and his brother Crispinian traveled from Rome to the French town of Soissons, where they preached and earned a living as shoemakers, offering shoes to the poor at a very low price and using leather provided by angels. The people of Soissons built a church in their honor in the sixth century, and since that time they have been known as the patron saints of shoemakers and other workers in leather. People who wore shoes that were too tight were said to be "in St. Crispin's prison."

This is also the day on which the French and English armies fought the battle of Agincourt in the middle period of the Hundred Years War (1415). The association between the feast day and the battle is so strong that writers sometimes use "St. Crispin's Day" as an expression meaning "a time of battle" or "a time to fight." This day is also called the **Feast of Crispian**, **St. Crispian's Day**, **Crispin's Day**, **Crispin Crispian**, and the **Day of Crispin Crispianus**.

SOURCES:
BkDays-1864, vol. II, p. 492
BkHolWrld-1986, Oct 25
DaysCustFaith-1957, p. 267
DictDays-1988, p. 101
DictFolkMyth-1984, p. 261
FestSaintDays-1915, p. 188
FolkWrldHol-1999, p. 600
OxYear-1999, p. 427

◆ 2509 ◆ St. David's Day
March 1

The patron saint of Wales, St. David was a sixth-century priest who founded an austere religious order and many monasteries and churches, and eventually became primate of South Wales. His day is observed not only by the people of Wales but by Welsh groups all over the world. There are large communities of Welsh throughout the United States—particularly in Pennsylvania, Ohio, Wisconsin, and Florida—who celebrate St. David's Day with performances of choral singing, for which the Welsh are noted (*see also* EISTEDDFOD). The St. David's Society of New York holds an annual banquet on March 1, and the Welsh Society of

Philadelphia, which was established in 1802, celebrates with eating, drinking, and songs.

The leek, Wales' national symbol, is often worn on St. David's Day. According to legend, when St. David was leading his people to victory against the Saxons, he commanded them to wear leeks in their hats to avoid being confused with the enemy. In the United States, the daffodil has replaced the leek.

CONTACTS:
Welsh Society of Philadelphia
325 Kerwood Rd.
P.O. Box 7287
Wayne, PA 19087
610-256-3030
www.welsh-society-phila.org

SOURCES:
AmerBkDays-2000, p. 178
BkDays-1864, vol. I, p. 315
BkHolWrld-1986, Mar 1
DaysCustFaith-1957, p. 70
DictFolkMyth-1984, p. 612
FestSaintDays-1915, p. 37
FolkAmerHol-1999, p. 124
FolkWrldHol-1999, p. 199
OxYear-1999, pp. 103, 104

◆ 2510 ◆ **St. Demetrius's Day**
October 26 in the East and October 8 in the West

St. Demetrius is the patron saint of Salonika (Thessalonike) in northeastern Greece, near where he was martyred, perhaps during the fourth century. His feast day marks the beginning of winter for farmers, and a spell of warm weather after October 26 is often called "the little summer" or "the summer of St. Demetrius." It is a day for opening and tasting the season's new wines. St. Demetrius is also the patron saint of soldiers.

October 26 is also the anniversary of the liberation of Salonika from the Turks in 1912.

SOURCES:
AnnivHol-2000, p. 178
DictFolkMyth-1984, p. 867
FolkWrldHol-1999, p. 601
GdWrldFest-1985, p. 103
IntlThFolk-1979, p. 196
OxYear-1999, p. 430

◆ 2511 ◆ **St. Denis's Day**
October 9

Also known as St. Dionysius, St. Denis is the patron saint of France. According to legend, Pope Clement sent him to what is now France to establish the Church there, during the reign of Emperor Decius (249-251), but the pagans who greeted him did not treat him well. When he came to Paris as their first bishop, they threw him to the wild beasts, but the beasts licked his feet. Then they put him in a fiery furnace, but he emerged unharmed. The most widely repeated legend is that they beheaded him on Martyr's Hill—the place now known as Montmartre in Paris—but he miraculously picked up his

head and carried it for two miles before expiring at the site where the Church of St. Denis was later built.

Denis has also been identified with St. Dionysius the Areopagite, legendarily portrayed as a convert of ST. PAUL.

SOURCES:
DaysCustFaith-1957, p. 253
OxYear-1999, p. 408
SaintFestCh-1904, p. 443

◆ 2512 ◆ **St. Dismas's Day**
March 25; second Sunday in October

According to the Bible, two thieves were crucified with Jesus. The one on his right, traditionally called Dismas, repented and was promised, "Today thou shalt be with me in Paradise" (Luke 23:43). He is therefore the patron saint of persons condemned to death. In the United States, the National Catholic Prison Chaplains' Association, by special permission from Rome, observes the second Sunday in October as **Good Thief Sunday** and holds masses in American prisons in honor of St. Dismas. March 25 is also the Feast of the ANNUNCIATION.

SOURCES:
AnnivHol-2000, p. 50
DaysCustFaith-1957, p. 88
DictDays-1988, pp. 33, 49
EncyEaster-2002, p. 245
OxYear-1999, p. 133
RelHolCal-2004, p. 92

◆ 2513 ◆ **St. Dunstan's Day**
May 19

St. Dunstan (c. 909-988) was the archbishop of Canterbury. According to legend, St. Dunstan was such a good man that Satan felt his activities had to be watched all the time. One day, when Dunstan was working at the monastery forge, he looked up and saw the devil peering at him through the window. He quickly pulled the red-hot tongs from the coals and grabbed the devil's nose with them, refusing to let go until he promised not to tempt him any more. Howling in pain, Satan ran and dipped his nose in nearby Tunbridge Wells to cool it off, which is why the water there is sulphurous. St. Dunstan is buried in Canterbury Cathedral. He is the patron saint of blacksmiths, jewelers, and locksmiths.

SOURCES:
AnnivHol-2000, p. 84
BkDays-1864, vol. I, p. 653
DaysCustFaith-1957, p. 126
OxYear-1999, pp. 210, 212

◆ 2514 ◆ **St. Dymphna's Day**
May 15

According to legend, St. Dymphna (or Dimpna) was the daughter of a seventh-century Irish king. She fled with her priest to Geel, Belgium, to escape her pagan father's demand for an incestuous marriage. There she was found by the king, who killed her and the priest.

St. Dymphna came to be known as the patron saint of the insane, and for centuries mental patients were brought to the site of her relics in Geel, where the townsfolk looked after them. An infirmary was eventually built next to the Church of St. Dymphna, and by 1852 Geel was placed under state medical supervision.

Today there is a large, well-equipped sanatorium for the mentally ill in Geel, known throughout the world for its "boarding out" system, which allows harmless mental patients to be cared for as paying guests in the homes of local citizens. On May 15 special church services are held and a religious procession moves through the streets carrying a stone from St. Dymphna's alleged tomb—a relic that at one time was applied to patients as part of their therapy.

CONTACTS:
Geel Tourist Office
Market 33
Geel, B 2440 Belgium
32-14-57-09-50; fax: 32-14-59-15-57
www.visitbelgium.com

SOURCES:
AnnivHol-2000, p. 82
BkFest-1937, p. 42
DaysCustFaith-1957, p. 123
FestWestEur-1958, p. 11
OxYear-1999, p. 208

♦ 2515 ♦ **St. Elizabeth Ann Seton, Feast of**
January 4

The first native-born American to be declared a saint, Elizabeth Ann Seton (1774-1821) was canonized in 1975. She was the founder of the first religious community for women in the United States, the American Sisters of Charity, and she was responsible for laying the foundations of the American Catholic school system. She also established orphan asylums, the forerunners of the modern foundling homes and child-care centers run today by the Sisters of Charity.

Special services commemorating Elizabeth Ann Seton's death on January 4, 1821, are held on major anniversaries at the Chapel of St. Joseph's Provincial House of the Daughters of Charity in Emmitsburg, Maryland, the headquarters for her order of nuns, and at Trinity Episcopal Church in New York City, of which she was a member before her conversion to Roman Catholicism in 1805. More than 100,000 people attended her canonization ceremony at St. Peter's Basilica in Rome. On that same day, over 35,000 pilgrims flocked to Emmitsburg, where six masses were said in honor of the new saint.

See also SETON (MOTHER) DAY

CONTACTS:
The National Shrine of Saint Elizabeth Ann Seton
333 S. Seton Ave.
Emmitsburg, MD 21727
301-447-6606; fax: 301-447-6061
www.emmitsburg.net

Trinity Episcopal Church
74 Trinity Pl.
New York, NY 10006
212-602-0800
www.trinitywallstreet.org

SOURCES:
AmerBkDays-2000, p. 19
AnnivHol-2000, p. 3

♦ 2516 ♦ **St. Elmo's Day**
June 2

The day that is known as St. Elmo's Day is actually **St. Erasmus's Day**, in honor of a third-century Italian bishop who is thought to have suffered martyrdom around the year 304. Erasmus was a patron saint of sailors and was especially popular in the 13th century. He is often referred to as Elmo, a variation of Erasmus.

Sometimes at sea on stormy nights, sailors will see a pale, brushlike spray of electricity at the top of the mast. In the Middle Ages, they believed that these fires were the souls of the departed, rising to glory through the intercession of St. Elmo. Such an electrical display is still referred to as "St. Elmo's Fire."

SOURCES:
DaysCustFaith-1957, p. 140
OxYear-1999, p. 235

♦ 2517 ♦ **St. Evermaire, Game of**
May 1

The **Spel van Sint Evermarus**, or the Game of St. Evermaire, is a dramatic reenactment of the slaying of eight pilgrims in Rousson (Rutten), Belgium, on their way to the Holy Land in 699. After spending the night at a farmhouse, the story goes, the saint and his seven companions were murdered by a robber.

This event is portrayed by the townspeople of Rousson, Belgium, each year on the first day of May in the meadow near the Chapel of St. Evermaire. Following a procession around the casket believed to contain the saint's bones, costumed villagers representing St. Evermaire and his companions are attacked by 50 "brigands" riding heavy farm horses and led by Hacco, the legendary assailant. By the end of the drama, the saint and the seven pilgrims lie dead.

Although the event was not commemorated for 200 years after its occurrence, the inhabitants of Rousson have faithfully presented their play for the past 10 centuries.

CONTACTS:
Belgian National Tourist Office
220 E. 42nd St., Ste. 3402
New York, NY 10017
212-758-8130; fax: 212-355-7675
www.visitbelgium.com

SOURCES:
FestWestEur-1958, p. 9

♦ 2518 ♦ **St. Frances Cabrini, Feast of**
December 22; November 13

The first American citizen to be proclaimed a saint of the Roman Catholic Church, Francesca Xavier Cabrini (1850-1917) was born in Italy. After serving as a nurse and a teacher in her native country, and seeing the miserable conditions under which so many orphans lived, she became a nun and was appointed superior of the orphanage at Codogno. Known thereafter as Mother Cabrini, she founded the Missionary Sisters of the Sacred Heart in 1880 and established a number of other schools and orphanages. Nine years later she and six of her nuns landed in New York, where they had been sent to help the Italian immigrants. She went on to establish orphanages, schools, and hospitals in many American cities, as well as in Europe and South America. She was canonized on July 7, 1946, and her feast day is December 22.

St. Frances Cabrini's feast day is commemorated in many places, but particularly at Mother Cabrini High School in New York City, in whose chapel she is buried. November 13, the day on which she was beatified, is also observed at every establishment of the Missionary Sisters of the Sacred Heart.

CONTACTS:
Missionary Sisters of the Sacred Heart of Jesus
610 King of Prussia Rd.
Radnor, PA 19087
610-902-1039
www.mothercabrini.com

SOURCES:
AmerBkDays-2000, p. 526
OxYear-1999, p. 507

♦ 2519 ♦ **St. Frances of Rome, Feast of**
March 9

St. Frances of Rome (1384-1440), also known as Francesca Romana or Frances the Roman, was a model for housewives and widows. In her 40 years of marriage to Lorenzo Ponziano, it is said there was never the slightest dispute or misunderstanding between them. Despite the death of her children, her husband's banishment, and the confiscation of their estates, she continued to nurse the sick, care for the poor, and settle disputes wherever she went.

Eventually she founded a society of women who pledged to offer themselves to God and to serve the poor. Known at first as the Oblates of Mary, they were afterwards called the Oblates of Tor de Specchi, after the building in which they were housed. When she died, St. Frances's body was removed to Santa Maria Nuova in Rome, which is now known as the church of Santa Francesca Romana. She is the patron saint of widows.

St. Frances's feast day is observed on March 9, the date on which she died. Because she is also the patron saint of motorists—although no clear reason for this is given—it is customary for Italian drivers to flock to the Colosseum in Rome for the blessing of their cars. Crowds also visit Tor de Specchi and Casa degli Esercizi Pii (formerly her home, the

Palazzo Ponziano), whose rooms are opened to the public on this day.

See also ST. CHRISTOPHER'S DAY

CONTACTS:
Italian Government Tourist Board
630 Fifth Ave., Ste. 1565
New York, NY 10111
212-245-5618; fax: 212-586-9249
www.italiantourism.com

SOURCES:
OxYear-1999, p. 111

♦ 2520 ♦ **St. Francis of Assisi, Feast of**
October 3-4

The most important festival of the Franciscan calendar in Assisi, Italy, the feast of St. Francis (1181-1226) commemorates the saint's transition from this life to the afterlife. For two days the entire town is illuminated by oil lamps burning consecrated oil brought from a different Italian town each year. A parchment in St. Francis's handwriting, believed to be the saint's deathbed blessing to his follower, Brother Leo, is taken to the top of the Santa Maria degli Angeli basilica—built in the 16th century around St. Francis's humble hermitage known as the *Porciúncula*—and the people are blessed by the pope's representative (*see* FORGIVENESS, FEAST OF).

In the United States, it is not uncommon for people to bring their pets to church to be blessed on St. Francis's feast day, because of his love for animals as expressed in his *Canticle of Creatures*.

See also ST. ANTHONY THE ABBOT and SAN FRANCISCO

CONTACTS:
Italian Government Tourist Board
630 Fifth Ave., Ste. 1565
New York, NY 10111
212-245-5618; fax: 212-586-9249
www.italiantourism.com

SOURCES:
BkFestHolWrld-1970, p. 111
BkHolWrld-1986, Oct 4
DaysCustFaith-1957, p. 251
DictWrldRel-1989, p. 266
FolkAmerHol-1999, p. 413
IndianAmer-1989, pp. 257, 289, 302
OxYear-1999, p. 402

♦ 2521 ♦ **St. Gabriel, Feast of**
Around December 28

St. Gabriel is one of the most popular Ethiopian Orthodox saints and believed to intercede on behalf of those who pray to him more than other saints. Thousands of Orthodox Christians, Muslims, Greeks, Armenians, and tribal people make a pilgrimage on his feast day to Kullubi, Ethiopia. Many carry boulders on their backs in a show of piety, and women often carry babies named after the saint to the local church's baptismal font, as St. Gabriel has a reputation for granting the requests of women who wish to become pregnant.

Most of the pilgrims set up campsites and usually listen to High Mass over loudspeakers, since the church at Kullubi is very small.

CONTACTS:
Ethiopian Tourism Commission
P.O. Box 2183
Addis Ababa, Ethiopia
251-1-517-470; fax: 251-1-517-533
www.tourismethiopia.org

SOURCES:
WildPlanet-1995, p. 182

♦ 2522 ♦ **St. Gens, Festival of (La Fête de St. Gens)**
*Sunday following May 15; first weekend in
September*

St. Gens, patron saint of the fever-afflicted, was born in Monteux, France, which he is said to have saved from a great drought in the 12th century. He is honored twice annually in his native Provence: first, at Monteux on the Sunday following May 15, and again, at Beaucet, on the first Saturday and Sunday in September. The ceremonies held on both occasions are similar, consisting of a procession with the saint's image, prayers for the sick, and supplications for rain.

According to legend, St. Gens retired to a desert place near Mont Ventoux, where he worked the land with a team of oxen. One day a wolf attacked and ate one of the oxen. St. Gens made the wolf pay by hitching him with the remaining ox and forcing him to plow the land.

CONTACTS:
Monteux Tourist Center
Parc du Chateau d'Eau
Monteux, 84170 France
33-4-9066-9718; fax: 33-4-9066-9719

SOURCES:
FestWestEur-1958, p. 37

♦ 2523 ♦ **St. George's Day**
April 23; November 23

Nothing much is known for certain about St. George, but the patron saint of England is popularly known in medieval legend for slaying a vicious dragon that was besieging a town in Cappadocia. After being fed two sheep a day, they became scarce and people had to be given instead—beginning with the king's daughter. She was on her way to the dragon's den to be sacrificed when she met St. George, who insisted on fighting the dragon and, according to another legend, eventually stunned it with his spear. Making a leash out of the princess's sash, he let her lead the monster back to the city like a pet dog. When the people saw what had happened, they were converted to Christianity. To this day, St. George is often depicted with a dragon.

St. George's Day, sometimes referred to as **Georgemas,** has been observed as a religious feast as well as a holiday since the 13th century. In the United States, there are St. George's societies in Philadelphia, New York City, Charleston, S.C., and Baltimore, Maryland, dedicated to charitable causes that hold annual dinners on this day.

St. George's Day is celebrated on November 23 as a national holiday in the Republic of Georgia. A festival is held at the cathedral of Mtskheta, the old capital and religious center of Georgia.

See also Georgiritt; Golden Chariot and Battle of the Lumecon, Procession of the; St. George's Day in Bulgaria; St. George's Day in Syria

CONTACTS:
Georgian Embassy
2209 Massachusetts Ave. N.W.
Washington, D.C. 20008
202-387-2390; fax: 202-387-0864
embassy.mfa.gov.ge

SOURCES:
AmerBkDays-2000, p. 308
BkDays-1864, vol. I, p. 539
BkFest-1937, pp. 58, 104, 169, 330
DaysCustFaith-1957, pp. 98, 287
DictDays-1988, pp. 46, 102
FestSaintDays-1915, p. 93
FestWestEur-1958, pp. 63, 231
FolkWrldHol-1999, p. 299
OxYear-1999, p. 166

♦ 2524 ♦ **St. George's Day (Bulgaria)**
May 6

St. George's Day, or **Gergiovden,** is one of the most important celebrations in Bulgaria. It marks the start of the stock-breeding season. The sheep are turned out to graze on the eve of this day because the dew is believed to have curative powers. Special foods are served the following day, traditional songs are sung, and both livestock and their pens are decorated with blossoming willow twigs.

Traditional rural Bulgarian belief holds that someone who is born on this day is blessed with wisdom and beauty. In some areas a lamb is slaughtered, and the door sill is smeared with its blood to protect the house from witches, illness, and other forms of bad luck.

SOURCES:
AnnivHol-2000, p. 78
BkFest-1937, p. 71

♦ 2525 ♦ **St. George's Day (Syria) (Id Mar Jurjus)**
April 23

In Syria, where he is known as Mar Jurjus, St. George is honored not only by Christians but by Muslims, who know him as al-Khidr and at one time identified him with the prophet Elijah. There are shrines dedicated to St. George throughout the country, and several monasteries mark sites where the saint is said to have revealed himself. One of the most important is the monastery at Humeira, near Tripoli, Syria, where both Christians and Muslims from all over Syria attend a folk festival each year on ST. GEORGE'S DAY, April 23.

CONTACTS:
Embassy of Syria
2215 Wyoming Ave. N.W.
Washington, D.C. 20008
202-232-6313; fax: 202-234-9548
www.syrianembassy.us

SOURCES:
BkFest-1937, p. 330
BkFestHolWrld-1970, p. 81

♦ 2526 ♦ **St. Giles Fair**
Monday and Tuesday after the Sunday following
September 1

The St. Giles Fair, held in Oxford, England, dates back even further than Oxford University. It is the only one remaining of the five great fairs once held in Oxford, and it still occupies its original site on St. Giles Street.

When it started more than 800 years ago, St. Giles was an important trade fair. Today it features sports and popular amusements, including "dodge-em" cars, swing-boats, and gaily painted "roundabouts" (rotaries). Booths sell holiday foods and other merchandise, and visitors flock to the fair from throughout Oxfordshire and the surrounding counties.

St. Giles serves as the patron of the physically disabled, and according to legend the fair was situated outside the walls of the city because townsfolk did not want lame people and beggars to enter the city. The St. Giles Fair is held on the Monday and Tuesday after the Sunday following his feast day, which is September 1.

CONTACTS:
St. Giles' Church
10 Woodstock Rd.
Oxford, OX2 6HT United Kingdom
44-18-6531-1198
www.st-giles-church.org

SOURCES:
BkFairs-1939, p. 165
YrbookEngFest-1954, p. 119
YrFest-1972, p. 170

♦ 2527 ♦ **St. Gregory's Day**
March 12

St. Gregory was a sixth-century monk who became a pope. He is said to have invented the Gregorian chant. Popular legend attributes many acts of kindness to St. Gregory. One is that he freed frogs from the ice of early spring. Another is that he loved beggars and fed them at his own table with food served on golden plates.

St. Gregory is also the patron saint of schoolchildren and scholars. In Belgium, schoolchildren rise early on March 12 and

parade through the streets dressed as "little soldiers of St. Gregory." They carry a big basket for gifts and are accompanied by a noisy drummer. One of them is dressed as Pope Gregory in gaudy vestments and a gold paper crown. The young girls in the procession wear big shoulder bows that resemble the wings of a butterfly. They march from house to house, pausing at each door to sing a song and to ask for treats.

The procession always includes a group of angels, because the legend says that when Gregory was walking through the slave market at Rome, he saw a group of handsome young English youths. Upon learning their nationality, he exclaimed, "Were they but Christians, they would truly be *angeli* [angels], not *Angli* [Anglo-Saxons]!"

SOURCES:
FestWestEur-1958, p. 5
OxYear-1999, p. 114

♦ 2528 ♦ **St. Gudula's Day**
January 8

St. Gudula (or Gudule) is the patron saint of Brussels, Belgium. According to legend, Satan was so envious of her piety and influence among the people that he often tried to extinguish her lantern as she returned from midnight mass. But as she prayed for help, an angel would re-light the candle.

She died in 712, and her relics were moved to Brussels in 978. Since 1047 they have remained in the church of St. Michael, thereafter named the Cathedral of St. Gudula. Her feast day is observed with great solemnity in Brussels, particularly at the cathedral that bears her name.

SOURCES:
BkDays-1864, vol. I, p. 73
BkFest-1937, p. 38
FestWestEur-1958, p. 4
SaintFestCh-1904, p. 58

♦ 2529 ♦ **St. Hans Festival**
June 24

Like other MIDSUMMER DAY celebrations, the St. Hans (St. John) Festival in Norway combines both pagan and Christian customs. This festival was originally held in honor of the sun god, for the ancients believed that the sun's change of course at the SUMMER SOLSTICE was an important event. The gates of the upper and lower worlds stood wide open at this time, and supernatural beings such as trolls and goblins roamed the earth.

After Christianity was introduced, the Norwegian midsummer festival was linked to the birth of John the Baptist (*see* ST. JOHN'S DAY), and it became known as **Sankt Hans Dag**, or **St. John's Day**. But some of the ancient customs and superstitions surrounding Midsummer Day have persisted. Only a century ago it was still common for Norwegians to hide their pokers and to carve a cross on their broomsticks as a way of warding off witches who might otherwise use these household items for transportation. The present-day custom of decorating with birch boughs also has its roots in ancient times, when the foliage was considered a symbol of the life force that awakens in Nature in the spring and early summer.

The festival of St. Hans is still celebrated in Norway much as it has been for hundreds of years. On *Jonsok*, or St. John's Eve, Norwegians who live near the fjords head out in their boats, which are decorated with green boughs and flowers, to get the best possible view of the St. John's bonfires on the mountains.

CONTACTS:
Innovation Norway-Tourism
655 Third Ave., Ste. 1810
New York, NY 10017
212-885-9700; fax: 212-885-9710
www.innovasjonnorge.no

SOURCES:
FestWestEur-1958, p. 153
FolkWrldHol-1999, p. 397

♦ 2530 ♦ St. Herman Pilgrimage
August 9 and two adjoining days

The St. Herman Pilgrimage takes place for three days on and near August 9 on Kodiak Island and nearby Spruce Island in Alaska. The pilgrimage marks the anniversary of the canonization of St. Herman by the Russian Orthodox Church in 1970. It is attended by the church's clergy and faithful Christians from Alaska, the lower 48 states, and often from other countries. The event includes services at the Holy Resurrection Cathedral in Kodiak, as well as a boat trip to Spruce Island, where St. Herman lived as a hermit in the first half of the 19th century, lovingly serving the native people and God. At Spruce Island, divine services take place at the chapel of Ss. Sergius & Herman, which was founded by St. Herman himself. Pilgrims may drink from a spring thought to be invested by St. Herman with miracle-working properties. They also pray at the remains of St. Herman, where the saint's hat and his cross and chain are displayed. In Kodiak, other pilgrimage activities include tea with the bishop and a grand banquet. Also on offer are educational talks and displays.

Saint Herman was born in Russia in 1756. As a hermetic monk, he was asked in 1793 to join a mission to North America. The group traveled to Kodiak Island to spread the news of Christianity to the native Aleut people. Eventually Herman moved to Spruce Island, where he prayed, fasted, built a chapel, and devoted himself to serving the people. His deep spirituality and healing powers led to his glorification as a saint in 1970. The first canonized American saint, Herman was also known as the Wonder Worker of Alaska.

CONTACTS:
Russian Orthodox Diocese of Alaska
P.O. Box 210569
Anchorage, AK 99521-0569
907-279-0025; fax: 907-279-9748

♦ 2531 ♦ St. Hilary's Day
January 13 or 14

St. Hilary of Poitiers (c. 315-c. 367) was a French theologian who, as bishop of Poitiers, defended the divinity of Christ against Arianism, which affirmed that Christ was not truly divine because He was a "created" being. The so-called "Hilary term," beginning in January at Oxford and Dublin universities, is named after him. At one time the phrase also referred to a term or session of the High Court of Justice in England. According to tradition St. Hilary's Day—observed on January 13 by Anglicans but on January 14 by Roman Catholics—is the coldest day of the year.

SOURCES:
DictDays-1988, p. 103
OxYear-1999, p. 33

♦ 2532 ♦ St. Hubert de Liège, Feast of
November 3

St. Hubert (d. 727) is the patron saint of hunters, dogs, and victims of rabies. His feast day is especially honored at the church named for him in the little town of St. Hubert, Luxembourg Province, Belgium, on the first weekend in November. People who live in the Forest of Ardennes bring their dogs to the church to be blessed, and St. Hubert's Mass marks the official opening of the hunting season. In some places special loaves of bread are brought to the mass to be blessed, after which everyone eats a piece and feeds the rest to their dogs, horses, and other domestic animals to ward off rabies.

According to legend, St. Hubert was once more interested in hunting than he was in observing church festivals. But on GOOD FRIDAY one year, while he was hunting, he saw a young white stag with a crucifix between its antlers. The vision was so powerful that he changed his ways, became a monk, and was eventually made bishop of Liège. The site of this event is marked by a chapel about five miles from St. Hubert.

Thousands of pilgrims visit St. Hubert's shrine at the Church of St. Hubert each year. Among the artifacts there are his hunting horn and mantle, supposedly given to him by the Virgin Mary—a thread of which, when placed on a small cut on the forehead, is supposed to cure people who suffer from rabies. His relics are enshrined at the cathedral in Liège.

CONTACTS:
St. Hubert Tourist Information Office
12 Rue Saint Gilles
St. Hubert, B 6870 Belgium
32-61-61-30-10; fax: 32-61-61-54-44
www.saint-hubert-tourisme.be

SOURCES:
AnnivHol-2000, p. 185
BkFest-1937, p. 46
DaysCustFaith-1957, p. 283
FestWestEur-1958, pp. 17, 118
FolkWrldHol-1999, p. 643
SaintFestCh-1904, p. 473

♦ 2533 ♦ St. Ignatius Loyola, Feast of
July 31

St. Ignatius Loyola (1491-1556) founded the Society of Jesus, the Roman Catholic religious order whose members are known as Jesuits. Now the largest single religious order in the world, the Jesuits are known for their work in education, which St. Ignatius believed was one of the best ways to help people. In the United States, which currently has more Jesuits than any other country, they train hundreds of thousands of high school, college, and university students every year. St. Ignatius is the patron saint of retreats and those who attend retreats.

The Feast of St. Ignatius is celebrated by Jesuits everywhere, but particularly in the Basque region of Spain where he was born. The largest Basque community in North America, located in Boise, Idaho, holds its annual **St. Ignatius Loyola Picnic** on the last weekend in July—an event often referred to as the **Basque Festival**. Every five years (2000, 2005, etc.) Boise's Basque Organization holds Jaialdi ("Big Festival"), the International Basque Cultural Festival, which features Basque music, dancing, food, sports, and more. (*See also* BASQUE FESTIVAL, NATIONAL.) The first Basques settled in the United States in 1865.

CONTACTS:
Basque Museum and Cultural Center
611 Grove St.
Boise, ID 83702
208-343-2671; fax: 208-336-4801
www.basquemuseum.com

SOURCES:
BkDays-1864, vol. II, p. 148
BkHolWrld-1986, Jul 31
DictWrldRel-1989, p. 336
OxYear-1999, p. 312

♦ 2534 ♦ **St. Isidore, Festival of**
Mid-May

Although indigenous fertility rites were outlawed when Mexico was conquered by the Spaniards and converted to Catholicism, a few pre-Hispanic festivities have survived—often overlaid with Christian meaning. One of these is the Festival of St. Isidore in Metepec, where farmers honor their patron saint around the time of his feast day, May 15. The men dress up as women and accompany their plows and oxen, which have been decorated with flowers, in a procession to the fields.

In Acapantzingo, Morelos State, there is a sowing festival in mid-May that includes a folk play and ritual dances, while in Matamoros, Tamaulipas State, there is a procession in honor of St. Isidore followed by dances that depict the events of the Spanish conquest.

See also SAN ISIDRO IN PERU, FIESTA OF; SAN ISIDRO THE FARMER, FEAST OF

CONTACTS:
Mexico Tourism Board
21 E. 63rd St., Fl. 3
New York, NY 10021
800-446-3942 or 212-821-0314; fax: 212-821-0367
www.visitmexico.com

SOURCES:
IntlThFolk-1979, p. 272

♦ 2535 ♦ **St. James's Day**
July 25 in the Western Church; April 30 in the Eastern Church

The Apostle James the Great (d. 44) was martyred by Herod. Also known as Santiago, he is the patron saint of Spain. His feast day is celebrated in the Western Church on July 25, the anniversary of the day on which, according to Spanish tradition, his body was miraculously discovered in Compostela, Spain, after being buried there for 800 years. A church was built on the site, which later became the town of Santiago de Compostela, once a place of pilgrimage second only to Jerusalem and Rome. St. James's Day is still celebrated in Compostela with a weeklong festival that features a mock burning of the 12th-century cathedral and an elaborate fireworks display.

The Indian pueblos of New Mexico, which were the target of early Spanish missionary efforts, also observe St. James's Day. At the **Fiestas de Santiago y Santa Ana**, held annually in the Taos Pueblo on July 25 and 26 (or the nearest weekend), the corn dance is performed in honor of both St. James and ST. ANNE, the mother of the Virgin Mary, whose feast day follows Santiago Day. Ritual dances also take place in the Santa Ana, Laguna, and Cochiti pueblos. At Acoma Pueblo, Santiago's Day is celebrated by holding a rooster pull.

In Loíza, Puerto Rico, the **Fiesta of St. James the Apostle** or **Fiesta de Santiago Apóstol** is the biggest celebration of the year. It focuses on three images of the saint—the *Santiago de los Muchachos* (St. James of the Children), the *Santiago de los Hombres* (St. James of the Men), and the *Santiago de las Mujeres* (St. James of the Women)—which are carried from the homes of the *mantenedoras* (keepers) who have kept guard over them all year to a place near the sea known as *Las Carreras*, "the racetracks."

Santiago de los Hombres begins the procession, stopping in front of the house where another saint is kept. This second image joins the first and the procession continues until all three end up at Las Carreras, where the traditional ceremony of racing with the flags of the saints takes place. Farm workers and fishermen dress in traditional costumes and perform music and dances of African origin. St. James's Day is also a popular choice for baptisms and marriages.

His feast day in the Eastern Church is April 30.

CONTACTS:
Puerto Rico Tourism Company
666 Fifth Ave., Fl. 15
New York, NY 10103
800-866-7827 or 212-586-6262; fax: 212-586-1212
www.gotopuertorico.com

Galicia Consellería de Cultura, Communicacion Social e Turismo
Pavillon de Galicia-San Lazaro
Santiago de Compostela, 15703 Spain
34-981-572-004
www.xacobeo.es

Library of Congress
101 Independence Ave. S.E.
Washington, DC 20540
202-707-5510; fax: 202-707-2076
www.loc.gov

SOURCES:
DaysCustFaith-1957, p. 189
DictFolkMyth-1984, pp. 963, 971, 1063, 1111
FestSaintDays-1915, p. 152
FestWestEur-1958, p. 202
FolkAmerHol-1999, p. 313
FolkWrldHol-1999, p. 448
IndianAmer-1989, pp. 287, 309, 319
OxYear-1999, pp. 306, 307

♦ 2536 ♦ **St. Joan of Arc, Feast Day of**
May 30; May 9

The second patron saint of France (the first is ST. DENIS) and one of the best known of all the saints, Joan of Arc—whom the French refer to as Jeanne d'Arc, the "Maid of Orleans," for the role she played in saving the city of Orleans from the British in the 15th century—was a young, pious peasant girl from the village of Domremy. In 1428 she heard voices she identified as ST. MICHAEL, ST. CATHERINE, and St. Margaret telling her to help the dauphin, Charles VII, recover his kingdom from the British. Her mission was accomplished within 15 months, but Joan was captured by the king's enemies, tried for witchcraft and heresy, and burned at the stake in Rouen on May 30, 1431.

St. Joan's Day is celebrated on May 30 everywhere except in the city of New Orleans, Louisiana, where she is honored on May 9, the day after the anniversary of her dramatic rescue of the French city for which New Orleans was named. In France, the **Fête de Jeanne d'Arc** is observed with special ceremonies in Rouen and Orleans, where the streets are decorated with banners, garlands, and portraits of the teenage girl who was canonized in 1920, five centuries after she led the French forces to victory and brought about the coronation of Charles VII at Reims.

CONTACTS:
Rouen Tourism Office
25 Place de cathédrale
Rouen, 76000 France
33-2-3208-3240; fax: 33-2-3208-3244
www.rouentourisme.com

SOURCES:
AnnivHol-2000, p. 90
BkFest-1937, p. 123
BkHolWrld-1986, May 11
DaysCustFaith-1957, p. 130
DictWrldRel-1989, p. 383
EncyRel-1987, vol. 8, p. 96
OxYear-1999, p. 226

♦ 2537 ♦ **St. John Lateran, Feast of the Dedication of**
November 9

This Roman Catholic observance commemorates Pope Sylvester's consecration of the Basilica of the Most Holy Savior, commonly known as St. John Lateran, in Rome on November 9, 324. Churches as they are known today—that is, buildings set apart as places of worship—did not exist for the first two centuries of the Christian era; believers gathered in each other's homes. Thus, the pope's public dedication of this church at the beginning of the fourth century was a first in Christianity and merited a special celebration.

St. John Lateran began as the mansion of a wealthy Roman family named Laterani until it was given to the Christians, serving as the residence of popes for a thousand years. The home was built around a great hall, and this hall became the church. It was called a "basilica," a word that originally described an oblong hall, rounded at one or both ends, where public assemblies were held. A baptistry was added and dedicated to St. John the Baptist, and since the 12th century, the church has been known as St. John Lateran.

SOURCES:
DaysCustFaith-1957, p. 285
RelHolCal-2004, p. 105

♦ 2538 ♦ **St. John the Baptist, Martyrdom of**
August 29

St. John the Baptist was beheaded by King Herod because he had denounced Herod's marriage to Herodias, the wife of his half-brother Philip (Luke 3:19, 20), an illegal union according to Jewish law. Herodias' daughter by a former marriage, by legend called Salome, pleased Herod so much with her dancing that he swore to give her whatever she wanted. At her mother's urging she asked for the head of John the Baptist on a platter (Matthew 14:3-12). Herod, grief-stricken over having let himself be maneuvered into killing a good and innocent man, later had the head concealed within the palace walls to spare it any further indignities. It remained there until after the discovery of the holy cross by St. Helena, an event which drew many pilgrims to Jerusalem. Two of them found the head after St. John appeared to them in a vision.

The Martyrdom of St. John the Baptist—also known as the **Feast of the Beheading** in the Eastern Orthodox Church—has been celebrated by Christians since the fourth century. The observance started at Sebaste (Samaria), where the Baptist was believed to have been buried.

See also EXALTATION OF THE CROSS; ST. JOHN'S DAY

SOURCES:
DaysCustFaith-1957, p. 152
OxYear-1999, p. 349

♦ 2539 ♦ **St. John the Evangelist's Day**
December 27

John the Evangelist, also called **St. John the Divine**, was thought to be not only the youngest of the Apostles but the longest-lived, dying peacefully of natural causes at an advanced age. Although he escaped actual martyrdom, St. John endured considerable persecution and suffering for his beliefs. He is said to have drunk poison to prove his faith (so he is the patron saint of protection against poison), been cast into a cauldron of boiling oil, and at one point banished to the lonely Greek island of Patmos, where he worked among the criminals in the mines. He remained healthy, vigorous, and miraculously unharmed throughout these trials and returned to Ephesus where it is believed he wrote the Gospel according to John. He is also believed to be the author of the New Testament Book of Revelation, though many scholars disagree.

See also ST. STEPHEN'S DAY

SOURCES:
AmerBkDays-2000, p. 858
BkDays-1864, vol. II, p. 771
DaysCustFaith-1957, p. 323
EncyChristmas-2003, p. 665
FolkWrldHol-1999, p. 770
OxYear-1999, p. 535

◆ 2540 ◆ St. John's Day
June 24

It is unusual for a saint's day to commemorate his birth rather than his death, but John the Baptist (d. c. 29) and the Virgin Mary are the exceptions here. (*See* NATIVITY OF THE BLESSED VIRGIN MARY, FEAST OF THE). Roman Catholics, Eastern Orthodox Christians, Anglicans, and Lutherans honor St. John on the anniversary of his birth; the Roman Catholic and Orthodox churches commemorate his death as well, on August 29 (*see* ST. JOHN THE BAPTIST, MARTYRDOM OF).

John was the cousin of Jesus, born in their old age to Zechariah and Elizabeth, a kinswoman of the Virgin Mary. John was the one chosen to prepare the way for the Messiah. It is a pious belief of many that he was sanctified—that is, freed from original sin—in his mother's womb when she was visited by Mary. (*See* VISITATION, FEAST OF THE.) He lived as a hermit in the wilderness on a diet of honey and locusts until it was time to begin his public ministry. He preached repentance of sins and baptized many, including Jesus (*see* EPIPHANY). He denounced King Herod and his second wife, Herodias, and it was she who vowed revenge for John's condemnation of her marriage, and who had her daughter, Salome, demand the Baptist's head on a platter.

Many St. John's Day customs date from pre-Christian times, when June 24 was celebrated as MIDSUMMER DAY. Celebrations in some areas still bear the hallmarks of the old pagan SUMMER SOLSTICE rites, such as bonfires, dancing, and decorating with flowers. For the French in Canada, the **Feast of the Nativity of St. John the Baptist** is one of the biggest celebrations of the year, especially in Quebec. The **San Juan Fiesta** in New York City takes place on the Sunday nearest June 24 and is the year's most important festival for Hispanic Americans.

St. John's Day (**Día de San Juan**) is a major holiday throughout Mexico. As the patron saint of waters, St. John is honored by decorating fountains and wells and by bathing in local streams and rivers. The bathing begins at midnight—often to the accompaniment of village bands—and it is customary for spectators to throw flowers among the bathers. In Mexico City and other urban centers, the celebration takes place in

fashionable bath-houses rather than rivers, where there are diving and swimming contests as well. Street vendors sell small mules made out of cornhusks, decorated with flowers and filled with sugar cane and candy.

A family of yellow-flowered plants, commonly called St.-John's-wort, is used by voodoo conjurors and folk medicine practitioners to ward off evil spirits and ensure good luck. In the southern United States, all species of the plant are called John the Conqueror root, or "John de Conker," and all parts of it are used: the root, leaves, petals, and stems. The plant's imagery is often mentioned in African-American folklore and blues music.

The leaves, and often the petals, contain oil and pigment-filled glands that appear as reddish spots when held to the light. According to legend, these spots are John the Baptist's blood, and the plant is most potent if rituals are performed on his birthday.

See also SAN JUAN AND SAN PEDRO FESTIVALS; SAN JUAN PUEBLO FEAST DAY; ST. HANS FESTIVAL

SOURCES:
AmerBkDays-2000, p. 473
BkDays-1864, vol. I, p. 814
BkFest-1937, p. 229
BkFestHolWrld-1970, p. 98
BkHolWrld-1986, Jun 24
DaysCustFaith-1957, pp. 151, 222
DictFolkMyth-1984, pp. 1063, 1082
DictWrldRel-1989, p. 384
FestSaintDays-1915, p. 140
FolkAmerHol-1999, p. 264
IndianAmer-1989, pp. 287, 296, 312, 319
OxYear-1999, p. 263

◆ 2541 ◆ St. John's Day (Guatemala)
June 24

Día de San Juan or ST. JOHN'S DAY has been observed by some Guatemalan Indians, especially those in Camotan, Chiquimula Department, and San Juan Sacatepéquez, Guatemala Department, with a traditional dance known as *Los Gigantes* (The Giants). It is based on a story from the Popol Vuh, the sacred book of the Quiché Mayan Indians, but it also incorporates two events from the Bible: the beheading of St. John the Baptist and David's struggle against Goliath. The dancers wear red, blue, yellow and white costumes; these colors symbolize the four directions of the compass. Some dancers also wear veils, which refers to an ancient belief that at one time the sun and moon had faces that were veiled. Using their swords, dancers outline the path the sun takes when it rises and sets in both the opening and closing sequences of the dance.

CONTACTS:
Embassy of Guatemala
2220 R St. N.W.
Washington, D.C. 20008
202-745-4952; fax: 202-745-1908
www.guatemalaembassy.org

SOURCES:
FiestaTime-1965, p. 103

♦ 2542 ♦ St. John's Day (Portugal)
June 24

Both ST. JOHN'S DAY and St. John's Eve (*see also* MIDSUMMER DAY) are widely celebrated in Portugal with parades, pageants, bullfights, fireworks, and other popular amusements. Many of the traditional rites connected with fire, water, and love are still observed here as well. Young people dance around bonfires and couples often leap over these fires, holding hands. Mothers sometimes hold their children over the burning embers, and cattle and flocks are driven through the ashes—all to take advantage of the curative powers of St. John's fires. Similar traditions focus on water, which on St. John's Eve is supposed to possess great healing power.

One of the most interesting St. John's Day celebrations takes place in Braga and is known as the *Dança de Rei David*, or Dance of King David. The role of King David is always performed by a member of a certain family living near Braga, and the dance itself probably dates back to medieval times. The King is dressed in a tall crown and voluminous cape. Ten shepherds or courtiers who accompany him wear velvet coats in brilliant colors and turban-style hats. Shepherds play ancient tunes on their fiddles, flutes, and triangles. As they parade through town this group stops frequently to perform the ritualistic Dance of King David.

CONTACTS:
Portuguese National Tourist Office
590 Fifth Ave., 4th Fl.
New York, NY 10036
800-767-8842 or 212-354-4403; fax: 212-764-6137
www.visitportugal.com

SOURCES:
DictFolkMyth-1984, p. 1082

♦ 2543 ♦ St. John's Day (Puerto Rico)
June 24

Wading or bathing in the water on ST. JOHN'S DAY is a tradition that many see as symbolic of John the Baptist baptizing Jesus. In Puerto Rico, **San Juan Day** is observed by gathering at the beaches to eat, dance, drink, build bonfires, and bathe in the Caribbean. At midnight, revelers take a swim in the ocean, a tradition based on the biblical scene in which John, the cousin of Jesus, baptizes him. Over the years, the religious significance of the event has been overshadowed, and today bathing in the water is believed to bring good luck in the coming year.

The annual St. John the Baptist Day parade in Camden, New Jersey, has been going on since the 1950s, not long after the first Puerto Ricans began migrating there to take jobs in the Campbell Soup factory. Billed as the only organized parade in the city, the event is eagerly anticipated by the area's thousands of Hispanic Americans, many of whom line the parade route from Cooper and Second Streets to Wiggins Park along the waterfront. There is a competition for the best float and a steady procession of salsa dancers, folk dancers, and beauty queens. The parade marks the culmination of a week of festivities—including a banquet, art exhibits, and a flag-raising ceremony—that honor the area's Hispanics.

In Hartford, Connecticut, a San Juan Bautista Festival has been held on the Saturday nearest June 24 since 1979. Sponsored by the San Juan Center, Inc., it includes Puerto Rican food and entertainment, particularly bands that play Puerto Rican music and use traditional instruments of the homeland. Although the Hartford festival is designed to give the area's Puerto Rican population an opportunity to celebrate their heritage, it draws many other people as well.

CONTACTS:
Puerto Rico Tourism Company
666 Fifth Ave., 15th Fl.
New York, NY 10103
800-866-7827 or 212-586-6262; fax: 212-586-1212
www.gotopuertorico.com

SOURCES:
AnnivHol-2000, p. 105
FolkAmerHol-1999, p. 268

♦ 2544 ♦ St. John's Eve (Denmark)
June 23

Known in Denmark as **Sankt Hans Aften**, St. John's Eve occurs near the longest day of the year and therefore is an occasion for national rejoicing. Huge bonfires, often topped with tar barrels or other flammable materials, light up the night sky for miles around. Sometimes an effigy of a witch, perhaps a pagan symbol of winter or death, is thrown on the fire. Along the coast, fires are built on the beach or shore. People go out in their boats to watch them burn and to sing romantic songs. Sometimes there are speeches, singing games, dances, and fireworks as well.

Midsummer Eve is also a popular time for Danes to leave their year-round homes and go to vacation cottages on the coast.

CONTACTS:
Embassy of Denmark
3200 Whitehaven St. N.W.
Washington, D.C. 20008
202-234-4300; fax: 202-328-1470
www.ambwashington.um.dk

SOURCES:
BkFestHolWrld-1970, p. 101
FestWestEur-1958, p. 27

♦ 2545 ♦ St. John's Eve (France) (La Vielle de la Saint Jean)
June 23

The custom of lighting bonfires on the eve of ST. JOHN'S DAY has been said to originate with the ancient Druids, who built fires at the SUMMER SOLSTICE in honor of the sun god. Bonfires are still an important part of the festivities on St. John's Eve in France, where participants contribute something to burn. Traditionally, the village priest often lights the fire and leads the townspeople in the singing of hymns and the chanting of prayers.

In upper Brittany, St. John's fires are built around tall poles, which are set on the hilltops. A boy named Jean or a girl named Jeanne provides a bouquet or wreath for the pole and kindles the fire. Then the young people sing and dance around it while it burns. Sometimes the fire is replaced by a burning torch thrown skyward or by a wagon wheel covered with straw, set ablaze, and rolled downhill.

At sea, Breton fishermen traditionally put old clothing in a barrel, hoist it up the mainmast, and set it afire so that other ships in the fishing fleet can share the celebration.

There are many folk beliefs associated with St. John's Eve. One is that strewing the ashes from the St. John's fires over the fields will bring a good harvest. Another is that leaping over the dying embers guarantees that the crops will grow as high as the jumper can jump. In the sheep-raising Jura district, shepherds drive their flower-decked animals in a procession and later nail the flower wreaths to their stable doors as a protection against the forces of evil.

CONTACTS:
French Government Tourist Office
444 Madison Ave., 16th Fl.
New York, NY 10022
800-391-4909 or 212-838-7800; fax: 212-838-7855
www.francetourism.com

SOURCES:
BkFest-1937, p. 125
FestWestEur-1958, p. 43
FolkWrldHol-1999, p. 393

♦ 2546 ♦ **St. John's Eve (Germany)**
(Johannisnacht)
June 23

The SUMMER SOLSTICE, or *Sommersonnenwende,* in Germany is observed by lighting the *Johannisfeuer,* or St. John's fire. Young boys often try to leap through the flames, and young lovers join hands and try to jump over the fire together in the belief that if they succeed, they will never be parted. Cattle driven through the bonfire's ashes are believed to be safe from danger and disease in the coming year.

According to German folklore, the water spirits demanded a human victim on MIDSUMMER DAY. But contrary to the danger this implies, people often went out and bathed on St. John's Eve in streams or rivers to cure disease and strengthen their legs. In the Thuringia region, wreaths were hung on the doors because it was believed that St. John the Baptist walked through the streets on this night, and that he would bow to any door with a wreath on it.

SOURCES:
BkFest-1937, p. 136
DictFolkMyth-1984, p. 723
FestWestEur-1958, p. 68
FolkWrldHol-1999, p. 394

♦ 2547 ♦ **St. John's Eve (Greece)**
June 23

A custom still practiced in some rural Greek villages on ST. JOHN'S DAY is a procession of young boys and girls escorting the *Kalinitsa,* the girl considered the most beautiful in the neighborhood. On St. John's Eve, the young people gather at the Kalinitsa's house and dress her up as a bride, with a veil and a garland of flowers around her neck. The procession itself is led by a young boy holding a rod. He is followed by the Kalinitsa, who is in turn followed by four "ladies in waiting" and a little girl holding a parasol over the Kalinitsa's head. Other girls and boys accompany them, and they go around the village singing a song about drawing water for the sweet basil. If they should encounter a procession from another neighborhood at a crossroad, the parasols are lowered over the Kalinitsas' faces so they won't set eyes on each other. On the following day, June 24, the children gather at the Kalinitsa's house for a party.

Another old Greek custom, known as the *Erma,* is for two people who have chosen each other for friends to plant some seeds in a basket and raise them in darkness a few weeks before St. John's Day. On St. John's Eve they exchange plants and pledge their friendship by shaking hands three times over a fire.

SOURCES:
BkFestHolWrld-1970, p. 99
FestSaintDays-1915, p. 146

♦ 2548 ♦ **St. John's Eve (Ireland)**
June 23

The Irish still celebrate St. John's Eve with bonfires, dancing, omens, and prayers. People build fires on the hillsides and feed the flames with fragrant boughs. As the fires burn low, both old and young people customarily join hands and jump over the embers in the belief that it will bring an abundant harvest. Young Irish girls used to drop melted lead into water on St. John's Eve. They would then look for clues about their future in whatever shape the lead assumed.

According to Irish folklore, the soul leaves the body on this night and wanders about until it reaches the place where death will eventually strike. This belief was so widespread at one time that people routinely sat up all night on St. John's Eve to keep their souls from making the trip.

SOURCES:
BkDays-1864, vol. I, p. 815
BkFest-1937, p. 59
OxYear-1999, p. 259

♦ 2549 ♦ **St. John's Eve (Spain)**
June 23

La Víspera de San Juan in Spain is dedicated to water and fire. Fireworks displays are common and *bogueras,* or bonfires, are lit in the city of Alicante, as well as villages, hilltops, and fields. In the Pyrénées, folk beliefs surround the bonfires and their charred remains, which are considered protection from thunderstorms. Cinders from the fires can also be mixed with the newly sown crops or put in the garden to ensure rapid growth. In other places people believe that cabbages planted on St. John's Eve will come up within 24 hours, and that beans will be ready by St. Peter's Day, six days later. Folkloric beliefs also focus on water. Walking through the dew or bathing in the sea on this day is believed to promote beauty and health.

Young girls traditionally believe that San Juan will help them see into their future. By placing a bowl of water outside the window and breaking an egg into it at midnight on St. John's Eve, they try to read their destiny in the shape the egg assumes. Similarly, pouring melted lead into a bowl of water at noon gives clues as to what kind of man they will marry.

In the province of Asturias, a dance known as the *corri-corri* is performed on St. John's Day by six women with one man pursuing them. The sexual motif of the dance links it to the fertility rites associated with Midsummer Day in ancient times. In the Basque region, men perform the *bordón-danza*, or sword dance, in two facing lines, wearing white shirts and breeches, red sashes and berets, and carrying long sticks in place of the traditional swords. The fact that this dance is performed most commonly on St. John's Day suggests a connection with ancient Summer Solstice rites.

Pastry shops in Spain sell special cakes shaped like the letter J on St. John's Eve, which may be decorated with pink sugar roses and elaborate scrolls.

CONTACTS:
Valencia Tourist Office
Communitat Valenciana, Aptdo. de Correos 48
Burjassot, 46100 Spain
34-902-123-212; fax: 34-902-220-211
www.comunitat-valenciana.com

SOURCES:
DictFolkMyth-1984, pp. 157, 253
FestWestEur-1958, p. 199
FolkWrldHol-1999, p. 399

♦ 2550 ♦ **St. John's Eve and Day (Latvia)**
(Jans vakars)
June 23-24

The three-day Midsummer festival known as **Ligo Svetki** is Latvia's greatest feast of the year. It begins on St. John's Eve, when boys and girls meet in the village squares. The boys chase the girls and, in accordance with an ancient custom, beat them with cattail switches. Then the young people gather flowers, herbs, and grasses to make wreaths that will be used in ceremonies the following day.

They also practice *Ligo* songs, which are based on the traditional Latvian *daina*, a short, unrhymed song in which epic and lyric elements are mixed. Sometimes the songs take the form of singing contests in praise or blame of the various men in town who are named Janis (or John): One group of singers praises a certain Janis for the prosperity of his farm

and livestock, while another points out that his garden is full of weeds, his barnyard is littered with rubbish, and his servants are lazy. These songs serve as a reminder to everyone that their homes must be ready for the guests who will arrive on the following night—the boys and girls who arrive armed with their wreaths and place them on the heads of Janis and his wife.

As in many other countries, lighting bonfires is a tradition in Latvia on St. John's Night. Young people jump over the fires in the belief that it will ensure a good harvest. Others wave Ligo torches and perform typical Latvian folk dances, such as the *Trisparu deja*, the *Jandalins*, the *Ackups*, and the *Sudmalinas*. In some Latvian towns, arches made from birch branches and wildflowers are placed in front of the houses, and the ceremonies associated with the Ligo feast are performed beneath these fragrant canopies.

SOURCES:
BkFest-1937, pp. 213, 214
DictFolkMyth-1984, p. 606
FolkWrldHol-1999, p. 395

♦ 2551 ♦ **St. Joseph the Worker, Feast of**
May 1

A public holiday in Malta, celebrated with festivities throughout the country. In Valletta, a highlight of the mass conducted by the archbishop in St. John's Cathedral is the blessing of the tools and products of laborers and craftsmen.

St. Joseph, the husband of the Virgin Mary, was a carpenter who taught Jesus his craft. He is the patron saint of workers, laborers, carpenters, cabinetmakers, and joiners. In 1955, Pope Pius XII established the Feast of St. Joseph the Worker on May 1 as a counter-celebration to the Communists' May Day celebrations honoring workers.

CONTACTS:
Malta National Tourist Office
65 Broadway, Ste. 823
New York, NY 10006
212-430-3799; fax: 425-795-3425
www.visitmalta.com

♦ 2552 ♦ **St. Joseph's Day**
March 12-19

The feast of the foster-father of Jesus, known as **Dia de San Giuseppe**, is widely observed in Italy as a day of feasting and sharing with the poor, of whom he is the patron saint. Villages prepare a "table of St. Joseph" by contributing money, candles, flowers, or food. Then they invite three guests of honor—representing Jesus, Mary, and Joseph—to join in their feast, as well as others representing the 12 Apostles. They also invite the orphans, widows, beggars, and poor people of the village to eat with them. The food is blessed by the village priest and by the child chosen to represent Jesus; then it is passed from one person to the next. The **Feast of St. Joseph** is celebrated by Italians in the United States and in other countries as well.

In Valencia, Spain, it is a week-long festival called **Fallas de San Jose (Bonfires of St. Joseph)**. It has its roots in medieval times when, on St. Joseph's Eve, the carpenters' guild made a huge bonfire out of the wood shavings that had accumulated over the winter to honor the carpenter patron saint, St. Joseph. This act marked the end of winter and was the last night on which candles and amps would have to be lighted. In fact, the carpenters often burned the *parot*, or wooden candelabrum, in front of their shops.

Nowadays the parots have become *fallas*, or huge floats of intricate scenes made of wood and papier-mâché, satirizing everything from the high cost of living to political personalities. On St. Joseph's Eve, March 18, the fallas parade through the streets. At midnight on March 19, the celebration ends with the spectacular ceremony known as the *crema*, when all the fallas are set on fire. One *Ninot*, or "doll," from each falla is chosen, and before the fire the best one is selected and preserved in a special museum. Another highlight is the *crida*, which consists of a series of public announcements made from the Torres de Serrano by the Queen of the Fallas and the city mayor. The festival is said to reflect the happy and satirical nature of the Valencians.

See also SAN JOSÉ DAY FESTIVAL and SWALLOWS OF SAN JUAN CAPISTRANO

CONTACTS:
Italian Government Tourist Board
630 Fifth Ave., Ste. 1565
New York, NY 10111
212-245-5618; fax: 212-586-9249
www.italiantourism.com

Valencia Tourist Bureau
Aptdo. de Correos 48
Burjassot
Valencia, 46100 Spain
34-963-649-506; fax: 34-963-649-507
www.comunitatvalenciana.com

Fallera Central Board
Av. Plata 117
Valencia, 46006 Spain
34-963-525-478; fax: 34-963-521-730
www.fallasfromvalencia.com

SOURCES:
BkFest-1937, pp. 181, 299
BkHolWrld-1986, Mar 19
DaysCustFaith-1957 p. 82
FestWestEur-1958, p. 90
FolkAmerHol-1999, p. 142
FolkWrldHol-1999, p. 209
GdUSFest-1984, p. 72
NatlHolWrld-1968, p. 36
OxYear-1999, p. 126

♦ 2553 ♦ St. Jude's Day
October 28

Because St. Jude is believed to have been martyred with St. Simon in Persia, where they had gone to preach Christianity, their feast is celebrated jointly on October 28, thought to be the date on which their relics were moved to old St. Peter's

basilica. Aside from the fact that they were both apostles, little is known about Simon and Jude. The New Testament refers to "Judas, not Iscariot" to distinguish Jude the Apostle from the Judas who betrayed Jesus.

Since St. Jude is the patron saint of hopeless causes, the saint day is observed particularly by students, who often ask for his help on exams. St. Jude and St. Joseph traditionally are the most important saints to Roman Catholics in Buffalo, New York, where people buy St. Jude medals to help them win over impossible odds or achieve the unachievable.

SOURCES:
AnnivHol-2000, p. 179
ChristYr-1991, p. 113
DaysCustFaith-1957, p. 269
FolkAmerHol-1999, p. 424
OxYear-1999, p. 432

♦ 2554 ♦ St. Kitts and Nevis Independence Day
September 19

Saint Kitts and Nevis is officially called the Federation of Saint Kitts and Nevis. An island nation in the West Indies in the Leeward Islands, it consists of the islands of Saint Kitts, Nevis, and Sombrero. Most of the people on these islands are descendants of Africans who were originally brought to the islands as slaves.

In 1493, Christopher Columbus landed on Saint Kitts and named the island Saint Christopher, after his patron saint. During this same voyage, Columbus also landed on Nevis. It wasn't until 1623 that English colonists began to settle on Saint Christopher's Island. At that time, the English shortened its name to Saint Kitts Island. In 1628, English colonists began to settle on Nevis. For the next 100 years, the British and French formed a rivalry for control over the islands. In 1782, the British took permanent control over the islands.

The islands, along with nearby Anguilla, were united in 1882. They joined the West Indies Federation in 1958 and remained in that association until its dissolution in 1962. Saint Kitts, Nevis, and Anguilla became a self-governing state of the United Kingdom in 1967. Anguilla seceded in 1980, and Saint Kitts and Nevis gained independence on September 19, 1983.

Every year, the people of Saint Kitts and Nevis celebrate Independence Day on September 19. Various celebrations take place across the islands on this day, including a cultural program of dance, live music, local food, and traditional displays.

CONTACTS:
St Kitts Tourism Authority
Pelican Mall
Bay Rd.
Basseterre
Saint Kitts and Nevis
www.stkittstourism.kn

♦ 2555 ♦ St. Kitts and Nevis National Heroes Day
September 17

Saint Kitts and Nevis is officially called the Federation of Saint Kitts and Nevis. An island nation in the West Indies in the Leeward Islands, it consists of the islands of Saint Kitts, Nevis, and Sombrero. Most of the people on these islands are descendants of Africans who were originally brought to the islands as slaves.

In 1493, Christopher Columbus landed on Saint Kitts and named the island Saint Christopher, after his patron saint. During this same voyage, Columbus also landed on Nevis. It wasn't until 1623 that English colonists began to settle on Saint Christopher's Island. At that time, the English shortened its name to Saint Kitts Island. In 1628, English colonists began to settle on Nevis. For the next 100 years, the British and French formed a rivalry for control over the islands. In 1782, the British took permanent control over the islands.

The islands, along with nearby Anguilla, were united in 1882. They joined the West Indies Federation in 1958 and remained in that association until its dissolution in 1962. Saint Kitts, Nevis, and Anguilla became a self-governing state of the United Kingdom in 1967. Anguilla seceded in 1980, and Saint Kitts and Nevis gained independence on September 19, 1983.

In 1998, the Saint Kitts and Nevis federal Parliament passed the National Honours Act. Through this act, various awards and acknowledgements were established, including a National Heroes Day. On this day, the country honors those who have distinguished themselves for the good of the islands. The first National Heroes Day was celebrated on September 16, 1998. The first National Hero was the late Robert L. Bradshaw, the first Premier of the Associated State of Saint Kitts, Nevis, and Anguilla.

CONTACTS:
St Kitts Tourism Authority
Pelican Mall
Bay Rd.
Basseterre
Saint Kitts and Nevis
www.stkittstourism.kn

Embassy of St. Kitts and Nevis
3216 New Mexico Ave. N.W.
Washington, DC 20016
202-686-2636
www.stkittsnevis.org

♦ 2556 ♦ **St. Knut's Day**
January 13

Tjugondag Knut, or St. Knut's Day, marks the end of the Yuletide season in Sweden. King Canute (or Knut) ruled Denmark, England, and Norway in the 11th century; his feast day is January 13. Rather than letting the holidays fade quietly, Swedish families throughout the country hold parties to celebrate the final lighting (and subsequent dismantling) of the CHRISTMAS tree. After letting the children eat the cookies and candies used to decorate the tree, and after packing the ornaments away in their boxes, it is customary to hurl the tree through an open window.

In Norway, January 13 is known as **Tyvendedagen**, or **Twentieth Day**, since it is the 20th day after Christmas. It is observed in much the same way, with parties and the dismantling of the Christmas tree. But instead of throwing the tree out the window, it is customarily chopped up and burned in the fireplace.

SOURCES:
BkFest-1937, p. 308
BkHolWrld-1986, Jan 13
EncyChristmas-2003, p. 667
FestWestEur-1958, pp. 151, 211
FolkWrldHol-1999, p. 33
OxYear-1999, p. 34

♦ 2557 ♦ **St. Lazarus's Day**
Between March 27 and April 30; Saturday before Palm Sunday

In Bulgaria, St. Lazarus's Day (**Lazarouvane** or **Lazarovden**) is the great Slavic festival of youth and fertility and doesn't have much to do with Lazarus himself. The day takes its name from a series of ritual games and songs studied in advance by young girls during LENT. Although there are many versions of the ritual, they all have a common focus, which is the "coming out" of girls who are ready to be married. Particular attention is paid to dress, which usually involves colorful traditional costumes and heavy jewelry. In former times, the people of Bulgaria believed that the more elaborate the rituals devoted to marriage, the better the chances for happiness, long life, and a house full of children.

See also LAZARUS SATURDAY

SOURCES:
FolkWrldHol-1999, p. 170
OxYear-1999, p. 502

♦ 2558 ♦ **St. Leopold's Day**
November 15

St. Leopold (1073-1136), the patron saint of Austria, was buried in the abbey he had established in Klosterneuburg, Lower Austria. His feast day is observed there with the ceremony known as **Fasselrutschen**, or the **Slide of the Great Cask**, in the abbey's wine cellar. Participants climb the narrow staircase that leads to the top of the cask, which was sculpted by a famous Viennese woodcarver and holds 12,000 gallons of wine, and then slide down its smooth surface to a padded platform at its base. The faster the trip down, according to tradition, the better luck the person will have in the coming year.

St. Leopold's Day is also known as **Gaense Tag**, or **Goose Day**, because the traditional evening meal served on this day is roast goose. Mid-November marks the beginning of the new wine season, and all over Austria there are wine-drinking picnics and parties around this day, known as HEURIGEN PARTIES.

CONTACTS:
Tourismusverein Klosterneuburg

Niedermarkt 4, Bahnhof Kierling / Bahnsteig 1
Klosterneuburg, A-3400 Austria
43-2243-3203-8; fax: 43-2243-2677-3
tvs.reps.at/info/index-english.html

SOURCES:
AnnivHol-2000, p. 191
BkFest-1937, p. 33
OxYear-1999, p. 464

♦ 2559 ♦ **St. Lucia Independence Day**
February 22

The West Indies island of St. Lucia celebrates its national independence holiday on February 22. On that day in 1979 the country gained full independence from Britain. St. Lucia had been a British colony since 1814.

CONTACTS:
St. Lucia Tourist Board
800 Second Ave., 9th Fl.
New York, NY 10017
800-456-3984 or 212-867-2950; fax: 212-867-2795
www.stlucia.org

♦ 2560 ♦ **St. Lucy's Day**
December 13

According to tradition, St. Lucy, or Santa Lucia, was born in Syracuse, Sicily, in the third or fourth century. She was endowed with a fatal beauty that eventually attracted the unwanted attentions of a pagan nobleman, to whom she was betrothed against her will. She is the patron saint of the blind because in an attempt to end the affair, she supposedly cut out her eyes, which her suitor claimed "haunted him day and night." But God restored her eyes as a reward for her sacrifice. She was then probably killed by a sword thrust through her throat. Because of this she is the patron saint for protection from throat infections.

St. Lucy allegedly blinded herself on the shortest, darkest day of the year (*see* WINTER SOLSTICE), and she later became a symbol of the preciousness of light. Her day is widely celebrated in Sweden as **Luciadagen**, which marks the official beginning of the CHRISTMAS season. Lucy means "light," and to the sun-starved inhabitants of Scandinavia, she often appears in a shining white robe crowned by a radiant halo.

It is traditional to observe Luciadagen by dressing the oldest daughter in the family in a white robe tied with a crimson sash. Candles are set into her crown, which is covered with lingonberry leaves. The younger girls are also dressed in white and given haloes of glittering tinsel. The boys—called *Starngossar*, or Star Boys—wear white robes and tall cone-shaped hats, made of silver paper, and carry star-topped scepters.

The "Lucia Bride" with her crown of burning candles, followed by the Star Boys, younger girls, and dancing children, called *tomten*, or "gnomes," wakens each member of the household on the morning of December 13 with a tray of coffee and special saffron buns or ginger cookies.

Although this is a family celebration, the Lucia tradition nowadays is observed in schools, offices, and hotels as well. Specially chosen Lucias and their attendants visit hospitals to cheer up the sick and elderly. The largest public celebration in Sweden takes place in Stockholm, where hundreds of girls compete for the title of "Stockholm Lucia."

From Sweden the Lucy celebrations spread to Finland, Norway, and Denmark. Swedish immigrants brought St. Lucy's Day to the United States, and the Swedish customs survive in Swedish-American communities throughout the country.

In Rockford, Illinois, for example, the St. Lucy's Day program is staged by the Swedish Historical Society at the Erlander Home Museum. The young woman chosen as Lucia on this day has to meet certain criteria, such as participation in Swedish classes, contributions to Swedish culture, or membership in one of Rockford's many Swedish societies.

At Bethany College in Lindsborg, Kansas, freshmen in the women's dormitories traditionally are awakened at three o'clock in the morning by a white-clad Lucia bearing coffee and baked goods. St. Lucy's Day is also observed by Swedish Americans in Minneapolis-St. Paul, Seattle, Chicago, and San Diego.

CONTACTS:
Skansen Museum
P.O. Box 27807
Stockholm, S-11593 Sweden
46-8-442-8000

Erlander Home Museum
404 S. Third St.
Rockford, IL 61104
815-963-5559
www.swedishhistorical.org

SOURCES:
BkDays-1864, vol. II, p. 687
BkFest-1937, pp. 191, 312
BkFestHolWrld-1970, pp. 132, 133
DaysCustFaith-1957, p. 313
EncyChristmas-2003, p. 668
FestWestEur-1958, pp. 101, 217
FolkAmerHol-1999, p. 494
FolkWrldHol-1999, p. 699
GdWrldFest-1985, p. 166
OxYear-1999, p. 497
RelHolCal-2004, p. 85
SaintFestCh-1904, p. 20

♦ 2561 ♦ **St. Marinus Day**
September 3

This is the official foundation day of the Republic of San Marino, a landlocked area of less than 30 square miles on the Adriatic side of central Italy. The oldest independent country in Europe, San Marino takes its name from St. Marinus, who lived in the fourth century. According to legend, he was a deacon and stonemason working on an aqueduct one day when a woman wrongly identified him as the husband who had deserted her. She pursued him into the mountains, where he barricaded himself in a cave until she eventually gave up. He spent the rest of his life on Monte Titano as a hermit. The present-day city of San Marino was built on the site where his original hermitage was believed to be.

CONTACTS:
San Marino Tourism Office
Ufficio del Turismo
Contrade Omagnano, 47890 Repubblica di San Marino (RSM)
378-0549-882998; fax: 378-0549-882575
www.visitsanmarino.com

SOURCES:
AnnivHol-2000, p. 149
OxYear-1999, p. 359

♦ 2562 ♦ **St. Mark, Fair of (Feria de San Marcos)**
Mid-April to early May

The Fair of St. Mark, which is held annually for nearly a month in Aguascalientes, dates back to the early 17th century and remains one of Mexico's most famous fiestas. It is primarily a showcase for the country's more than 200 forms of ritual and folk dance, each of which has its own meaning, mythology, history, and pageantry. There are also commercial and art exhibits, cockfights, bullfights, sports competitions, parades, and a battle of flowers. The wandering musicians known as *mariachis* give concerts, and regional folk dance groups from all over Mexico perform in the San Marcos Garden.

CONTACTS:
Mexico Tourism Board
21 E. 63rd St., Fl. 3
New York, NY 10021
800-446-3942 or 212-821-0314; fax: 212-821-0367
www.visitmexico.com

SOURCES:
IntlThFolk-1979, p. 267

♦ 2563 ♦ **St. Mark's Day**
April 25

Although he is often assumed to be one of the Apostles, Mark was much too young at the time to be more than a follower of Jesus. He is known primarily as the author of one of the four Gospels, which biblical scholars believe is based on what he learned from his close friend and traveling companion, ST. PETER. St. Mark the Evangelist is also associated with Venice, Italy, where the church bearing his name was built over the place where his relics were taken in 815.

In England, it was believed that if you kept a vigil on the church porch from 11 o'clock on St. Mark's Eve until one o'clock in the morning, you would see the ghosts of all those who would die in the coming year as they walked up the path and entered the church. Young girls believed that if they left a flower on the church porch during the day and returned for it at midnight, they would see a wedding procession, including an apparition of their future husband, as they walked home. Because it involved an all-night vigil, St. Mark's Day eventually came to be associated with various forms of licentious behavior, which is why the parochial cler-

gy in the Middle Ages decided that the day should be one of abstinence.

SOURCES:
AmerBkDays-2000, p. 314
BkDays-1864, vol. I, p. 549
DaysCustFaith-1957, p. 101
DictDays-1988, p. 104
FestSaintDays-1915, p. 98
OxYear-1999, pp. 170, 172

♦ 2564 ♦ **St. Mark's Day (Hungary)**
April 25

In Hungary, St. Mark's Day is also known as **Buza-Szentelo** or the **Blessing of the Wheat**, during which people follow their priest or minister in a procession to the wheat fields where the crop is blessed. They return to the village carrying spears of the blessed wheat, which some believe has healing powers. The fields are again blessed when harvesting begins on June 29, STS. PETER AND PAUL DAY.

SOURCES:
BkFest-1937, p. 169
FolkWrldHol-1999, p. 302

♦ 2565 ♦ **St. Maron's Day**
February 9

St. Maron (also spelled *St. Maroun*), the patron saint of Lebanon, was a monk who died in 410 C.E. After his death his disciples, the forefathers of the Maronite Christian sect, migrated from the Monastery of St. Maron in Syria to Mount Lebanon, where a large segment of Maronite Christians are settled today.

The **Feast of St. Maron**, as it is known in Lebanon, does not have the cultural significance for its citizens that it had in past eras, a change in great part due to the country's changing demographics along religious lines. Today Maronites only make up one-quarter of the Lebanese population (between one-half and one million). Many Lebanese Christians immigrated to North and South America, Europe, and Australia to escape the conditions of a long civil waged between 1975 and 1991.

In Lebanon and abroad, the most common ceremony of the feast day is the Maronite liturgy, which is a distinctive blend of Catholic doctrine, Arabic music, and singing in Syriac-Aramaic, a classical language that was spoken by Jesus.

CONTACTS:
Eparchy of Saint Maron of Brooklyn
109 Remsen St.
Brooklyn, NY 11201
718-237-9913; fax: 718-243-0444
www.stmaron.org

SOURCES:
AnnivHol-2000, p. 24

◆ 2566 ◆ St. Martha, Coffin Fiesta of
July 29

St. Martha was the sister of Mary and Lazarus who pleaded with Jesus to bring her dead brother back to life. Jesus did so, and because Martha played such an important role in this story, folk beliefs often assign her the power of granting miraculous cures.

In San Xosé de Ribarteme, in the province of Pontevedra in the region of Galicia, Spain, near the northern border of Portugal, the *ofrecidos*—people who have made a vow to St. Martha—lie in open coffins during a procession that takes place after High Mass on St. Martha's feast day. Most of the ofrecidos are women, but there are always a few men as well. They hire the coffins from the church, usually because they themselves or a member of their family has recently been cured by St. Martha's intervention. Most wear coarse net tunics called *mortajas* (shrouds) to indicate that they represent the "living dead."

SOURCES:
SpanFiestas-1968, p. 154

◆ 2567 ◆ St. Martha's Day
Last weekend in June

Martha was the sister of Mary and of Lazarus, whom Jesus raised from the dead (*see also* LAZARUS SATURDAY and ST. LAZARUS'S DAY). She is best known for her role in the Lord's visit to the house she shared with her two siblings in Bethany. While Mary sat and listened to their guest, Martha was busy serving and cleaning up. When she complained, Jesus told her that what Mary was doing was just as important as housework. For this reason, Martha is known as the patroness of housewives, cooks, and laundresses.

Martha's second, and legendary, claim to fame is that she killed a dragon who was ravaging the Provençal countryside, hiding on the wooded banks of the Rhone and periodically feeding on flocks and men. She overcame the beast by sprinkling holy water on him, then she bound him with her belt and led him into town, where the townspeople stoned him to death. A church was built on the site of this alleged event in what is now known as Tarasçon in Provence, France.

Every year on the last weekend in June a procession takes place there that commemorates St. Martha's power. In the first procession, eight men representing those devoured by the dragon walk next to its spiked body and manipulate the tail and jaws, which snap at the crowd of spectators. In the second procession, the dragon trots along behind a young girl representing St. Martha. Traditionally, she is dressed in white and leads the dragon leashed on her crimson ribbon belt.

See also STES. MARIES, FÊTE DES

CONTACTS:
Tourist Office
16 Blvd. Itam
Tarascon, 13150 France

33-4-9091-0352; fax: 33-4-9091-2296
www.tarascon.org

SOURCES:
AnnivHol-2000, p. 124
DaysCustFaith-1957, p. 194
FestWestEur-1958, p. 44
OxYear-1999, p. 311
SaintFestCh-1904, p. 345

◆ 2568 ◆ St. Martin's Carnival
February-March; Tuesday of Carnival week

The highlight of CARNIVAL celebrations in the village of Huixquilucan, Mexico, is a mock battle between two local churches. In the church of St. Martin, an image of the saint on horseback is given a new suit and sombrero each year. Across town, in the church of San Juan, a humble statue of the Virgin Mary appears in a pink dress and white veil and crown. According to local legend, St. Martin mounts his horse nightly and goes to visit the Virgin at San Juan church. Members of the San Juan church resent the implications of this legend and insist that their Virgin would not accept any male visitor at night, whether saint or ordinary mortal.

The argument comes to a head on Tuesday of Carnival week, when the two churches battle each other late in the afternoon. Both sides use firecrackers, rotten eggs, eggshells filled with paint, and even sticks and stones as weapons, and the battle continues for a couple of hours. Finally, the authorities call a halt to the event, and both sides claim victory.

CONTACTS:
Mexico Tourism Board
21 E. 63rd St., Fl. 3
New York, NY 10021
800-446-3942 or 212-821-0314; fax: 212-821-0367
www.visitmexico.com

SOURCES:
BkFestHolWrld-1970, p. 36

◆ 2569 ◆ St. Martin's Day (Portugal)
November 11

In many European countries, the celebration of St. Martin's Day is associated with slaughtering animals, and Portugal is no exception. On the **Feast of São Martinho** people roast chestnuts, drink red Portuguese wine, and butcher a pig. There is a St. Martin's Day Fair at Golegã, in Ribatejo, that features a famous horse show at which some of the country's finest thoroughbreds are displayed. Another well-known St. Martin's Day Fair is held at Penafiel, in Trás-os-Montes. The parades and celebrations that are held in towns and villages throughout Portugal on this day are usually more secular than Christian in flavor.

See also MARTINMAS

CONTACTS:
Portuguese National Tourist Office
590 Fifth Ave., 4th Fl.
New York, NY 10036

800-767-8842 or 212-354-4403; fax: 212-764-6137
www.visitportugal.com

SOURCES:
FestWestEur-1958, p. 185
FolkWrldHol-1999, p. 651

♦ 2570 ♦ **St. Martin's Eve (Estonia) (Mardi Päev)**
November 10

Traditionally, children in Estonia go from door to door at dusk on St. Martin's Eve in much the same way that American children trick-or-treat on HALLOWEEN. Their refrain is, "Please let us in because Mardi's fingers and toes are cold," and if they are not welcomed into the house and given treats, they retaliate by singing rude and uncomplimentary songs. Usually they're ushered into the kitchen, where such delicacies as apples, nuts, cookies, and raisin bread are handed out. Turnips—one of the few winter vegetables in Estonia—are another prized gift, as is *viljandi kama,* a kind of meal comprised of 15 different grains and dried vegetables mixed with sour milk, sugar, and cream that is regarded as a special treat. Well-to-do families give children bags of viljandi kama on Martin's Day to show how prosperous they are.

CONTACTS:
Estonian Ministry of Foreign Affairs, Press and Information
  Department
Islandi valjak 1
Tallinn, 15049 Estonia
372-6-317-000; fax: 372-6-317-099
www.vm.ee

SOURCES:
BkFest-1937, p. 107

♦ 2571 ♦ **St. Mary's County Oyster Festival**
Third weekend in October

Oyster festivals are common in areas where the oyster industry has survived. But the festival that has been held at the start of the oyster season in Leonardtown, Maryland, since 1967 has a special significance for those skilled in the fine art of oyster shucking. The highlight of the October festival is the National Oyster Shucking Championship to see who can open the most oysters as quickly and neatly as possible. The winner of this contest goes on to compete in the GALWAY OYSTER FESTIVAL in Ireland the following year.

The season's new oysters are served in every imaginable way: raw on the half-shell with sauce, steamed, fried, and stewed in a broth. The two-day festival also offers cooking demonstations and live musical entertainment.

CONTACTS:
St. Mary's County Oyster Festival
P.O. Box 653
Leonardtown, MD 20650
301-475-4200; fax: 301-475-4414
www.usoysterfest.com

SOURCES:
GdUSFest-1985, p. 83

♦ 2572 ♦ **St. Matthias's Day**
February 24

The story of how St. Matthias was elected to replace Judas Iscariot as one of the 12 apostles after Judas committed suicide can be found in the Bible's Book of Acts (1:15-26). It was Peter who declared that the number of apostles should be restored to 12, and the choice of who would succeed Judas was made by casting lots. Two men were nominated—Matthias and Joseph—and the lot fell upon Matthias.

There is no historical record of Matthias's deeds or death. His fame rests almost entirely upon the fact that he took the betrayer Judas' place, although legend claims that he was stoned and beheaded in Ethiopia in 64 C.E.

SOURCES:
DaysCustFaith-1957, p. 58
RelHolCal-2004, p. 92
SaintsFestCh-1904, p. 114

♦ 2573 ♦ **St. Médardus's Day**
June 8

St. Médardus, or Médard, who lived from about 470 to 560, was the bishop of Vermandois, Noyon, and Tournai in France. Because he was the patron saint of farmers and good weather, he has come to play a role in weather lore similar to that of the English ST. SWITHIN. In Belgium he is known as the rain saint, and there is an old folk rhyme that says, "If it rains on St. Médard's Day, it will rain for 40 days."

SOURCES:
BkFest-1937, p. 43
FestWestEur-1958, p. 13
FolkAmerHol-1999, p. 251
OxYear-1999, p. 241

♦ 2574 ♦ **St. Mennas's Day**
November 11

There are actually two different saints by the name of Mennas. One was born in Egypt and enlisted in the Roman army. He hid in a mountain cave in Phrygia to avoid persecution, but then boldly entered the arena at Cotyaeum and proclaimed that he was a Christian—an act of courage for which he was beheaded in 295. The second St. Mennas was a Greek from Asia Minor who became a hermit in the Abruzzi region of Italy and died in the sixth century.

In Greece, St. Mennas's Day is observed by shepherds. Because he has the power to reveal where lost or stolen objects lie, his name is invoked by shepherds who have lost their sheep, or who wish to protect their flocks from wolves. Shepherds' wives refrain from using scissors on St. Mennas's Day. Instead, they wind a thread around the points of the scissors—a symbolic action designed to keep the jaws of wolves closed and the mouths of the village gossips shut. St. Mennas's Day is also regarded as the beginning of the winter season.

SOURCES:
BkFestHolWrld-1970, p. 124

FolkWrldHol-1999, p. 653
OxYear-1999, p. 457

♦ 2575 ♦ **St. Michael's Day**
September 29 in the West and November 8 in the East; first Sunday in October

Coming at the end of the harvest season, St. Michael's Day has traditionally been a day for giving thanks and for celebrating the end of the season of hard work in the fields.

In Finland **Mikkelin Paiva** is observed on the first Sunday in October. In the countryside, servants are hired and next year's labor contracts signed. The harvesters celebrate the end of their labors on Saturday night by holding candlelight dances. The observation of Mikkelin Paiva replaced an earlier festival known as **Kekri**, which was celebrated by each landowner as soon as his crops were safely in the barns. The "Kekri" (spirits of the dead) were rewarded with a feast for their help with the farm work. The Kekri festival was probably a remnant of some form of ancestor worship.

In Ethiopia, where St. Michael's Day is observed on November 8, people attend services at any churches consecrated to *Mika'el*. The celebrations include chanting and dancing by the clergy, and a procession carrying the holy ark, or *tabot*, out of the church and then, later in the day, returning it. The services are followed by singing and dancing, an occasion for young men to possibly find a bride.

See also MICHAELMAS; SAN MIGUEL, FIESTA DE; TIMQAT; TURA MICHELE FAIR

CONTACTS:
Embassy of Ethiopia
3506 International Dr. N.W.
Washington, D.C. 20008
202-364-1200; fax: 202-587-0195
www.ethiopianembassy.org

SOURCES:
BkHolWrld-1986, Sep 29
DaysCustFaith-1958, p. 242
DictFolkMyth-1984, pp. 203, 504, 716
FestWestEur-1958, p. 71
FolkAmerHol-1999, p. 446
FolkWrldHol-1999, pp. 571, 588, 649

♦ 2576 ♦ **St. Modesto's Day**
December 18

St. Modesto is the patron saint of farmers in Greece. His feast day is celebrated with various rituals in honor of farm animals. Sometimes a special mass is said for the cattle. In Lemnos, *kollyva* (cooked wheat berries) and holy water are mixed with their fodder, while in Lesbos, the holy water is sprinkled on the fields to ward off locusts and disease. For horses and oxen, December 18 is a day of rest.

The Eastern Orthodox Church reserves this day to commemorate St. Modestus, who was patriarch of Jerusalem from 631 to 634. He had been abbot of St. Theodosius's Monastery in the desert of Judah, and was administrator of Jerusalem dur-

ing the captivity of St. Zacharias in Persia. Modestus is known for a sermon he preached on the bodily ASSUMPTION of the Virgin Mary into heaven.

SOURCES:
FolkWrldHol-1999, p. 706
OxYear-1999, p. 503

♦ 2577 ♦ **St. Nichiren's Pardon, Festival of**
September 11-13

At the Botamochi Temple in Kamakura, Japan, this festival honors St. Nichiren (1222-1282), considered to be Japan's most fervent Buddhist priest. Born the son of a poor fisherman, Nichiren established Kamakura as the homebase for his extensive and energetic missionary efforts. But the energy and self-confidence with which he devoted himself to political and social events soon aroused the distrust of the government and other Buddhist sects. He was banished to the peninsula of Izu in 1261, but later pardoned. This only increased his attacks on the other sects and he was finally exiled to the island of Sado in the Sea of Japan in 1271. After four years there, he returned and spent the rest of his life on Mount Minobu, now the site of the main Nichiren temple. Nichiren spent the remainder of his life teaching the monks of his sect and continuing his missionary work.

Today there are several million Nichiren Buddhists. The Festival of St. Nichiren's Pardon is observed by members of the Nichiren sect with massive demonstrations and the loud chanting of prayers attributed to Nichiren, accompanied by the beating of drums. At Kamakura, people make offerings of *botamochi*, rice balls covered with sweet bean paste, in his honor.

SOURCES:
JapanFest-1965, p. 187
WrldBuddhism-1984, p. 225

♦ 2578 ♦ **St. Nicholas's Day**
December 6

Very little is known about St. Nicholas's life, except that in the fourth century he was the bishop of Myra in what is now Turkey. One of the legends surrounding him is that he saved three sisters from being forced into prostitution by their poverty-stricken father by throwing three bags of gold into their room, thus providing each of them with a dowry. This may be the source of St. Nicholas's association with gift giving.

On December 6 in the Netherlands, St. Nicholas, or *Sinterklass*, still rides into town on a white horse, dressed in his red bishop's robes and preceded by "Black Peter," a Satanic figure in Moorish costume who beats the bad children with a switch while rewarding the good children with candy and gifts. He is the patron saint of sailors, and churches dedicated to him are often built so they can be seen off the coast as landmarks.

The American Santa Claus, a corruption of "St. Nicholas," is a cross between the original St. Nicholas and the British "Father Christmas." The political cartoonist Thomas Nast created a Santa Claus dressed in furs and looking more like

King Cole—an image that grew fatter and merrier over the years, until he became the uniquely American figure that adorns thousands of cards, decorations, and homes throughout the CHRISTMAS season. Although Americans open their gifts on Christmas or CHRISTMAS EVE, in the Netherlands, Switzerland, Germany, and some other European countries, gifts are still exchanged on December 5, St. Nicholas's Eve, or December 6, St. Nicholas's Day.

CONTACTS:
Netherlands Board of Tourism & Conventions
355 Lexington Ave., 19th Fl.
New York, NY 10017
888-464-6552 or 212-370-7360; fax: 212-370-9507
us.holland.com

SOURCES:
AmerBkDays-2000, p. 814
BkDays-1864, vol. II, p. 661
BkFest-1937, pp. 34, 48, 129, 190, 245
DaysCustFaith-1957, p. 306
EncyChristmas-2003, pp. 674, 680
FestSaintDays-1915, p. 219
FestWestEur-1958, pp. 19, 49, 81, 118, 144
FolkAmerHol-1999, p. 485
FolkWrldHol-1999, p. 686
OxYear-1999, p. 486
SaintFestCh-1904, p. 11

♦ 2579 ♦ **St. Nicholas's Day (Greece)**
December 6

As the patron saint of ships and seamen, St. Nicholas is very important to the Greeks, so many of whom have traditionally made their living at sea. Many Greek ships, from the smallest fishing boat to the largest commercial vessel, carry an icon of the saint on board. Seamen honor St. Nicholas on his feast day, which falls at a time of year when storms grow more frequent, by burning a light before this icon and saying prayers for the safety of their boat or ship.

SOURCES:
BkFest-1937, p. 154
BkFestHolWorld-1970, p. 130

♦ 2580 ♦ **St. Nicholas's Day (Italy)**
May 7-8

The **Festa di San Nicola** is celebrated in Italy on May 7 and 8, the anniversary of the transfer of the saint's relics by a group of 11th-century sailors from Bari, who risked their lives to rescue St. Nicholas's body from Muslims who threatened to desecrate his tomb at Myra in Asia Minor. This is the same St. Nicholas who is associated with CHRISTMAS and the giving of gifts to children. Therefore he is the patron saint of children.

Thousands of pilgrims come to the Basilica of San Nicola in Bari, Puglia, to worship at the saint's tomb and to ask for his help. Nicholas is also the patron saint of sailors. There is a procession on this day in which a group of Barese sailors take the saint's image down to the water, where it is placed on a flower-decked boat and taken out to sea. Hundreds of small craft carrying pilgrims and fishermen accompany the vessel,

and at night the statue is returned to its place of honor on the altar of San Nicola's crypt.

CONTACTS:
Assessorato al Turismo Regione Puglia
Via Bozzi 45C
Bari, Puglia 70122 Italy
39-80-5401-111
www.pugliaturismo.com/Inglese

SOURCES:
BkDays-1864, vol. II, p. 663
BkFest-1937, p. 190
EncyChristmas-2003, p. 684
FeastSaintDays-1915, p. 224
FestWestEur-1958, p. 96

♦ 2581 ♦ **St. Olav's Day**
July 29

The feast day of St. Olav (995-1030), also known as **Olsok,** was at one time observed throughout Norway, although today the primary celebration takes place in Trondheim. It commemorates the death of Olav Haraldsson—the second King Olav—at the Battle of Stiklestad in the year 1030. By 1070, work had begun on Nidaros Cathedral, which was erected over King Olav's grave and drew crowds of pilgrims during the annual Olsok days throughout the Middle Ages. Although it is said that King Olav did not display many saintly qualities during his reign (1015-28), he was responsible for introducing Christianity, and legend has embellished his reputation over the years, so that today he is also considered the champion of national independence.

St. Olav is the patron saint of Norway, and his name is identified with the highest Norwegian civilian decoration. The anniversary of his death is still marked by religious services, fireworks, and public merry-making. Every year the battle in which he died is reenacted by a large and colorful cast, occasionally drawing a well-known actor such as Liv Ullman, during the **St. Olav Festival** in Trondheim.

In the Faroe Islands, this is known as **Olavsoka,** or "St. Olav's Wake," a national holiday. Parliament opens on the 29th, but the festivities—that include dancing, rock concerts, sports events, speeches, drinking, a parade of members of *Logting* (parliament) to the church for a sermon then back for the opening session—begin the night before and continue into the early hours of the 30th.

CONTACTS:
St. Olav Festival at Trondheim
P.O. Box 2045
Dronningens gt. 1B
Trondheim, N-7410 Norway
47-7384-1450; fax: 47-7384-1451
www.olavsfestdagene.no/en

Faroe Islands Tourist Board
P.O. Box 118
Torshavn, Faroe Islands FO-110 Denmark
45-3558-00; fax: 45-3558-01
www.visit-faroeislands.com/?Language=EN

SOURCES:
AnnivHol-2000, p. 124
BkHolWrld-1986, Jul 29
FestWestEur-1958, p. 154
FolkWrldHol-1999, p. 451
OxYear-1999, p. 311

◆ 2582 ◆ St. Patrick's Day
March 17

The patron saint of Ireland, St. Patrick, was born about 390 in Roman Britain—scholars disagree as to exactly where—and died around 461. His grandfather was a Christian priest, and his father a deacon and an official of the Roman Empire in Britain. He is said to have been kidnapped at the age of 16 by Irish raiders and sold into slavery in Ireland; he escaped after six years, and received his religious training in continental monasteries. After being consecrated a bishop, he returned to Ireland about 432 as a missionary. The association of St. Patrick with the shamrock stems from his supposed use of its three-part leaf to explain the concept of the Holy Trinity to his largely uneducated listeners (*see* TRINITY SUNDAY).

St. Patrick's Purgatory has been a famed site of pilgrimage since the early 13th century. It is on Station Island in Lough Derg in County Donegal where St. Patrick had a vision promising that all who came to the sanctuary in penitence and faith would receive an indulgence for their sins. Additionally, if their faith remained strong, they would be allowed a glimpse of the tortures of the damned and the joys of the redeemed.

The **Feast of St. Patrick** is celebrated by Roman Catholics, the Anglican Communion, and Lutherans on March 17. The day is also popularly celebrated, particularly in the U.S., by "the wearing of the green," with many people of Irish and other extractions wearing some item of green clothing. Parties featuring corned beef and cabbage, and even the drinking of beer dyed green with food coloring are also part of this celebration of Irish heritage.

The St. Patrick's Day Parade in New York City, which dates back to 1762, is the largest in the United States and a major event for Irish Americans. More than 125,000 marchers participate, stopping at St. Patrick's Cathedral on Fifth Avenue for the blessing of the archbishop of New York. In Boston the St. Patrick's Day Parade goes back even farther, to 1737. In fact, during the siege of Boston which forced the British evacuation on March 17, 1776, General George WASHINGTON used "Boston" as the day's secret password and "St. Patrick" as the appropriate response (*see* EVACUATION DAY).

See also REEK SUNDAY and ST. PATRICK'S DAY PARADE IN SAVANNAH

CONTACTS:
Library of Congress
101 Independence Ave. S.E.
Washington, D.C. 20540
202-707-5000; fax: 202-707-8366
www.loc.gov

SOURCES:
AmerBkDays-2000, p. 210

BkDays-1864, vol. I, p. 382
BkFest-1937, pp. 15, 55
BkHolWrld-1986, Mar 17
DaysCustFaith-1957, p. 78
DictWrldRel-1989, p. 563
FestSaintDays-1915, p. 38
FolkAmerHol-1999, p. 137
FolkWrldHol-1999, p. 207
OxYear-1999, p. 122
RelHolCal-2004, p. 92

◆ 2583 ◆ St. Patrick's Day (Ireland)
March 17

The observation of ST. PATRICK'S DAY is universal but traditionally less frenzied in Ireland than it is in the United States. Instead of the massive parades, rowdy parties, and commercialism of U.S. celebrations, many Irish spend the day attending Mass, wearing sprigs of real shamrock, and hailing each other with the traditional St. Patrick's Day greeting: "Beannacht na feile Padraig oraibh"—"May the blessings of St. Patrick be with you." Since 1996, however, Dublin has hosted a colorful St. Patrick's Festival. It lasts four days and features musical performances, street theater, fireworks, and a grand parade.

Because it falls during LENT, St. Patrick's Day is anticipated as a reprieve from the deprivations of the period preceding EASTER. It is a time when children can gorge themselves on sweets and adults can indulge in a pint at the local pub. A traditional St. Patrick's Day dinner usually includes colcannon—a dish made of mashed potatoes, butter, onions, and kale.

CONTACTS:
St. Patrick's Festival
St. Stephen's Green House
Earlsfort Terr.
Dublin, 2 Ireland
353-1-6763205; fax: 353-1-6763208
www.stpatricksday.ie

SOURCES:
BkFest-1937, p. 55
BkFestHolWrld-1970, p. 74
BkHolWrld-1986, Mar 17
DaysCustFaith-1957, p. 81
FolkAmerHol-1999, p. 137
FolkWrldHol-1999, p. 207
NatlHolWrld-1968, p. 34

◆ 2584 ◆ St. Patrick's Day Encampment
Weekend nearest March 17

The winter of 1779-80 was a time of discouragement and despair for the Continental Army. General George WASHINGTON set up camp in Morristown, New Jersey, that year so he could rest and reassemble his men. The soldiers' winter routine was bleak and monotonous. There was so much work to be done that they did not even celebrate CHRISTMAS. General Washington did, however, grant his men a holiday on March 17, ST. PATRICK'S DAY. A good portion of the American army was Irish, and political changes taking place in Ireland at the time found a sympathetic following among the American revolutionaries.

The St. Patrick's Day Encampment of 1780 is reenacted each year at the Jockey Hollow Encampment Area in Morristown. Between 30 and 40 men and their camp followers set up camp for the weekend and perform more or less the same chores and activities that Washington's men performed, although the trend toward milder winters has robbed the event of some of its authenticity. The original March 17 encampment was not the first St. Patrick's Day celebration in America; the first celebration took place in Boston in 1737.

CONTACTS:
Morristown National Historic Park
30 Washington Pl.
Morristown, NJ 07960
973-539-2016; fax: 973-285-5021

♦ 2585 ♦ **St. Patrick's Day Parade (Savannah, Georgia)**
March 17

One of the oldest and biggest parades in the country, held since 1824 in Savannah, Ga., a city with a long Irish history. The oldest Irish society in the United States, the Hibernian Society, was formed in Savannah in 1812 by 13 Irish Protestants. The next year they held a private procession that was a forerunner to the present St. Paddy's parade. The first public procession is recorded in 1824, and public parades have been held ever since. There have been only six lapses of this parade: for wars, sympathy for the Irish Revolution, and for an unrecorded reason. The first floats appeared in 1875; according to reports of the time, one carried two women representing Ireland and America, and another had 32 women for the 32 counties of Ireland.

Today the parade, which follows a route through the city's historic district, comprises between 200 and 300 separate units, including family groups, commercial floats, Georgia and out-of-state high school bands, and military bands and marching units. The day begins with mass at the Cathedral of St. John the Baptist. Members of the Fenian Society of Savannah, formed in 1973, start things off with a members' breakfast of green grits before they form a marching unit. The other main activity is eating. The fare is predominately green—grits, beer, doughnuts, etc. Crowds are estimated at anywhere from 300,000 to 500,000.

See also ST. PATRICK'S DAY

CONTACTS:
St. Patrick's Day Parade Committee
5 W. Liberty St.
P.O. Box 9224
Savannah, GA 31412
912-233-4804; fax: 912-233-8244
www.savannahsaintpatricksday.com

♦ 2586 ♦ **St. Paul, Feast of the Conversion of**
January 25

Saul of Tarsus, a highly educated, devout Jew, was converted to Christianity on the road to Damascus not long after the death of Jesus Christ. Later he was known as Paul and through his life, his teachings, and his writings became the most influential leader in the history of the church. According to tradition, he was beheaded during Nero's persecution of Christians about the year 67.

At St. Paul's Chapel in New York City, the oldest church building in Manhattan, the path through the graveyard that is routinely used as a shortcut between Broadway and Fulton Street is closed for 48 hours, beginning on the eve of the Feast of the Conversion of St. Paul.

At one time the weather on this day was linked to predictions about the coming year. Fair weather on St. Paul's Day was said to presage a prosperous year; snow or rain an unproductive one. Clouds meant that many cattle would die, and a windy day was said to be the forerunner of war.

In memory of Sts. Paul and Peter, the World Council of Churches sponsors the Week of PRAYER FOR CHRISTIAN UNITY, which begins on January 18, the feast of ST. PETER'S CHAIR, and ends on January 25.

See also STS. PETER AND PAUL DAY

SOURCES:
AmerBkDays-2000, p. 87
BkDays-1864, vol. I, p. 157
BkFest-1937, p. 52
DaysCustFaith-1957, pp. 30, 155
DictDays-1988, p. 105
DictWrldRel-1989, p. 563
FestSaintDays-1915, p. 22
OxYear-1999, pp. 47, 48
SaintFestCh-1904, p. 80

♦ 2587 ♦ **St. Paul Winter Carnival**
Last week of January to first week of February

This 10-day winter festival was established in 1886 in response to a newspaper story from the East that described St. Paul, Minnesota, as "another Siberia, unfit for human habitation." A group of local businessmen set out to publicize the area's winter attractions, and the first winter carnival featured an Ice Palace in St. Paul's Central Park constructed by a Montreal contractor.

Since that time, an entire legend has developed about the founding of St. Paul. This legend is reenacted each year. The main players are Boreas, King of the Winds, the Queen of the Snows, and the fire god, Vulcanus, who storms the Ice Palace but is persuaded by the Queen to submit to Boreas and let the people enjoy their carnival celebration.

Highlights include ice golf, skating, skiing, and sled dog races, softball on ice, ice carving and snow sculpture contests, and a parade featuring antique sleighs and cutters.

CONTACTS:
St. Paul Festival & Heritage Foundation
429 Landmark Ctr., 75 W. 5th St.
St. Paul, MN 55102

651-223-4700; fax: 651-223-4707
www.winter-carnival.com

SOURCES:
GdUSFest-1984, p. 98

♦ 2588 ♦ **St. Paul's Shipwreck, Feast of**
February 10

This feast is a commemoration in Malta of the shipwreck of St. Paul on the island in 60 C.E., an event told about in the New Testament. Paul, the story says, was being taken as a prisoner aboard ship to Rome where he was to stand trial. When storms drove the ship aground, Paul escaped and was welcomed by the "barbarous people" (meaning they were not Greco-Romans). According to legend, he got their attention when a snake bit him on the hand but did him no harm, and he then healed people of diseases. Paul stayed for three months in Malta, converting the people to Christianity (Acts 27:1-28:11). Paul is the patron saint of Malta and snakebite victims.

The day is a public holiday, and is observed with family gatherings and religious ceremonies and processions.

See also MNARJA

CONTACTS:
Malta National Tourist Office
65 Broadway, Ste. 823
New York, NY 10006
212-430-3799; fax: 425-795-3425
www.visitmalta.com

SOURCES:
FolkWrldHol-1999, p. 124

♦ 2589 ♦ **St. Peter's Chair, Festival of**
January 18

In ancient times it was the custom in many dioceses for Roman Catholics to observe the anniversary of the date on which the diocese first received a bishop. Perhaps the only remaining observance of this type takes place at the Vatican in Rome, where St. Peter is honored as bishop of Rome and the first pope. The current pope, wearing his triple crown and vestments of gold cloth, is carried in his chair of state on this day in a spectacular procession up the nave of St. Peter's Basilica. He is deposited behind the altar on a richly decorated throne that enshrines the plain wooden chair on which St. Peter is believed to have sat. The ceremony dates back to at least 720 and is regarded as one of the most magnificent ecclesiastical observances to be held at St. Peter's.

CONTACTS:
Italian Government Tourist Board
630 Fifth Ave., Ste. 1565
New York, NY 10111
212-245-5618; fax: 212-586-9249
www.italiantourism.com

SOURCES:
BkDays-1864, vol. I, p. 130
DaysCustFaith-1957, p. 24

OxYear-1999, p. 41
SaintFestCh-1904, p. 71

♦ 2590 ♦ **St. Peter's Day (Belgium)**
June 29

Sint Pieter (as he is called in Belgium), who walked across the water to reach Jesus, is honored each year on June 29 by Belgian fishermen, mariners, and others who are exposed to the dangers of the sea. The **Blessing of the Sea** ceremony is performed at Blankenberge and other seaport towns in West Flanders near the saint's day. After a special church service is held, a procession of clergy, church dignitaries, and seamen carry votive offerings, flowers, and garlands down to the shore. Then the priests board the boats and go out to bless the waves.

Although the custom has died out in all but a few rural areas, the building of bonfires is traditional on St. Peter's Day in Belgium. Years ago, children trundled wheelbarrows from one farm to the next in search of wood for St. Peter's fires. As the flames grew higher and higher, the children danced in a ring around the bonfire. People still light candles on this night and say the rosary in commemoration of St. Peter.

See also STS. PETER AND PAUL DAY

CONTACTS:
Westtour v.z.w.
Toerisme Brugge - Zeebrugge
P.O. Box 744
Bruges, B 8000 Belgium
32-50-44-46-46; fax: 32-50-44-46-45
www.westtoer.be

SOURCES:
BkFest-1937, p. 44
BkFestHolWrld-1970, p. 102
FestWestEur-1958, p. 14

♦ 2591 ♦ **St. Peter's Fiesta**
Weekend nearest June 29

Honoring the patron saint of fishermen, **St. Peter's Day** is celebrated in fishing villages and ports all over the world. Perhaps the largest American celebration takes place in Gloucester, Massachusetts, where St. Peter's Fiesta has been celebrated by the Italian-American fishing community for several decades. The life-sized statue of St. Peter donated by an Italian-American fishing captain in 1926 provided a focal point for the celebration, and the Sunday morning procession carrying this statue from the St. Peter's Club to an outdoor altar erected on the waterfront is still the highlight of the two-day festival. The mass that follows is usually celebrated by a visiting bishop or cardinal, who also officiates at the Blessing of the Fleet that afternoon.

Other festival events include seine boat (formerly used to haul in the catch) races and a "greasy-pole" contest in which competitors try to retrieve a red flag from the end of a well-greased pole suspended over the water.

The 2000 film *The Perfect Storm* dramatized the dangers Gloucester fishermen face.

CONTACTS:
St. Peter's Fiesta Committee
P.O. Box 3105
Gloucester, MA 01930
978-283-5243
www.stpetersfiesta.org

SOURCES:
BkFestHolWrld-1970, p. 102

♦ 2592 ♦ **St. Placidus Festival**
July 11

Sankt Placidusfest is a religious procession held on July 11 at Disentis, Switzerland, in honor of St. Placidus, who was murdered near the Benedictine abbey that he and St. Sigisbert helped establish there in 614. A wealthy landowner, Placidus donated the land for the abbey, joined the religious order as a monk, and was later beheaded for defending the abbey's ecclesiastical rights.

Every year the relics of St. Placidus and St. Sigisbert are carried in a solemn procession from the abbey to the parish church and back through the village to the abbey. Traditionally, during the ceremonies, parishioners in colorful folk costumes chant the old, and very long, "Song of St. Placidus."

CONTACTS:
Switzerland Tourism
Swiss Ctr., 608 Fifth Ave.
New York, NY 10020
877-794-8037 or 212-757-5944; fax: 212-262-6116
www.myswitzerland.com

SOURCES:
BkFest-1937, p. 320
FestWestEur-1958, p. 236

♦ 2593 ♦ **St. Polycarp's Day**
February 23 (formerly January 26)

St. Polycarp (c. 69-c. 155) was a disciple of St. JOHN THE EVANGELIST and one of the earliest fathers of the Christian Church. He became bishop of Smyrna in 96 and, when the persecution of Christians was ordered by Roman Emperor Marcus Aurelius, he was condemned to be burned at the stake. But according to legend, the fire formed an arch over his head and his body was left unharmed. When a spear was plunged into his heart, so much blood poured out that it quenched the flames. He finally succumbed, although the date of his martyrdom has been questioned, with some asserting it took place sometime between 166 and 169. That would have made him an astonishing 120 years old. Scholars believe there are good reasons for the original date of 155, however, which would have made him 86 when he was martyred.

Polycarp's friends and fellow Christians got together afterward to discuss how they might best carry on his memory. In fact, it was the martyrdom of St. Polycarp that gave rise to one of Christianity's richest traditions: the annual commemoration of the anniversary of a saint's death, a practice that didn't become universal until the third century. The earliest of these observances consisted of a memorial banquet, but by the fourth century they included a vigil service followed by celebration of the Eucharist.

SOURCES:
AnnivHol-2000, p. 31
DaysCustFaith-1957, p. 33
DictWrldRel-1989, p. 463
OxYear-1999, p. 89
SaintFestCh-1904, p. 81

♦ 2594 ♦ **St. Rocco's Celebration (Rokovo)**
August

St. Rocco's Celebration, or **Rokovo** as it is also known, has its roots in the feast day of St. Rocco. This saint, sometimes referred to as Rok, is the patron saint of the Catholic parish in the town of Virovitica, Croatia. Rocco was born into a noble family in France in c. 1295. Orphaned at an early age, he was taken in by a wealthy uncle, but eventually took a vow of poverty and began the life of a religious pilgrim. Bubonic plague was prevalent at the time, and Rocco is said to have miraculously healed many sufferers by praying for them.

His feast day, August 16, is the center of the St. Rocco's Celebration, although the celebration goes on for two or three weeks in total. The festival was first held in 1992, and in that year, August 16 was also designated the Day of the Town of Virovitica. The events, which are jointly organized by the Town of Virovitica and its Tourist Board, include music and dance performances, sports competitions, and art and historical exhibitions.

CONTACTS:
Virovitica Tourist Board
Trg kralja Tomislava 1, p.p. 49
33000 Virovitica, Croatia

Croatian National Tourist Board
Iblerov trg 10/IV
10000 Zagreb, Croatia
www.croatia.hr

♦ 2595 ♦ **St. Roch's Day**
August 16

Also known as Roque or Rock, St. Roch (c. 1295-c. 1327) was a Frenchman who went on a pilgrimage to Rome. The plague struck while he was there, and, legend has it, he spent his time healing the afflicted by miraculous means. Eventually he contracted the disease himself and retreated to a forest to die alone. But his faithful dog brought him food every day, and he recovered enough to return to his home in Montpelier. He had changed so much, however, that no one recognized him. He was arrested as a spy and died in prison.

Known as the patron saint of the sick and the plague-stricken, St. Roch is honored annually throughout Italy. In Florence there is a flower festival that includes a 14th-century historical costume parade, races, and competitions. In Realmonte, Sicily, the saint's poverty is recalled with a procession of people dressed in rags who carry a shabby picture of the saint.

In Spain, SAN ROQUE festivals are held every August around A Coruña Province. They feature traditional dances of farmers and seamen and processions in honor of St. Roch.

CONTACTS:
Italian Government Tourist Board
630 Fifth Ave., Ste. 1565
New York, NY 10111
212-245-5618; fax: 212-586-9249
www.italiantourism.com

Coruna Tourist Office
Darsena de La Marina, s/n
A Coruna, 15001 Spain
34-981-221-822
www.coruna.es

SOURCES:
BkFest-1937, p. 188
DictDays-1988, p. 106
IntlThFolk-1979, p. 334
OxYear-1999, p. 336

♦ 2596 ♦ **St. Rose of Lima's Day**
August 30

St. Rose was the first canonized saint of the Americas, born in Lima, Peru, in 1586. She is the patron saint of Central and South America and the Philippines. When her parents tried to persuade her to marry, she began a self-imposed exile in the summerhouse in the yard, where she lived as a Dominican nun and inflicted severe penances on herself. She died in 1617 and was canonized in 1671.

On her feast day a candlelight procession takes place from her shrine in the church of Santo Domingo to the cathedral. Adults wear purple robes, while children wear white ones. People sing religious hymns as they accompany the rose-covered image to the cathedral. St. Rose's Day is a public holiday throughout Peru.

CONTACTS:
Commission for the Promotion of Peru
Calle Uno Oeste No. 50, piso 13th
Urb. Corpac
Lima, 27 Peru
51-1-4224-3131; fax: 51-1-224-7134
www.promperu.gob.pe

SOURCES:
AnnivHol-2000, p. 144
BkHolWrld-1986, Aug 30
OxYear-1999, p. 342
SaintFestCh-1904, p. 388

♦ 2597 ♦ **St. Sarkis's Day**
January 21

In Armenia St. Sarkis is associated with predictions about love and romance. It is customary for young lovers to put out crumbs for birds and watch to see which way the birds fly off, for it is believed that their future spouse will come from the same direction. It is also traditional to leave some *pokhint*—a dish made of flour, butter, and honey—outside the door on St. Sarkis's Day. According to legend, when St. Sarkis

was battling the Georgians, the roasted wheat in his pocket miraculously turned into pokhint.

SOURCES:
FolkWrldHol-1999, p. 43

♦ 2598 ♦ **St. Sava's Day**
January 14 in the West and December 5 in the East

St. Sava (1174–c. 1235) was a Serbian noble of the Nemanya dynasty who renounced his right to the throne and chose instead to become a monk. While his brother was crowned king, Sava became archbishop of Serbia and the cultural and spiritual leader of his people. He was the founder of the Serbian Orthodox Church and played a central role in education and the beginnings of medieval Serbian literature.

As the patron saint of the former Yugoslavia, St. Sava, or Sveti Sava, is commemorated on the anniversary of his death with special church services, speeches, and choral singing. Schoolchildren sing, dance, and recite poems in his honor.

SOURCES:
BkFest-1937, p. 336
OxYear-1999, p. 51

♦ 2599 ♦ **St. Sebastian's Day**
January 20

St. Sebastian is known as the patron saint of archers for reasons that are all too obvious: legend has it that when his two brothers were imprisoned for being Christians, he went to visit them and to encourage them to stand by their faith, converting many of the other prisoners and their visitors in the process. His actions drew attention to his own beliefs, however, and he was condemned to die by being tied to a stake and shot with arrows until his body resembled a pincushion. When a Christian woman came to claim his body for burial, she discovered that he was still alive and nursed him back to health. Undaunted, he confronted his persecutors again. This time they succeeded in killing him, and his body was thrown into the great sewer of Rome in 288. All that is known with reasonable surety is that Sebastian lived, was an early martyr, and was buried on the Appian Way in Rome.

In Zinacantán, Chiapas State, Mexico, there is a nine-day celebration in honor of St. Sebastian, extending from January 17 to January 25, that marks the transfer of authority from the Big Alcalde (or chief magistrate) to his successor. At the end of the festival, the outgoing Big Alcalde is escorted with his articles of office to the house of the incoming Big Alcalde. There is an elaborate ritual during which he hands over an image of San Sebastian and other symbols of his authority. The festival also features a jousting pantomime, dancing to the rhythm of a special drum, two feasts, and a mock healing ceremony. The connection between the **Día de San Sebastián** festivities and the martyrdom of St. Sebastian, however, remains obscure.

People in the city of Rio de Janeiro, Brazil, also celebrate the feast day of their patron saint with church services, colorful religious processions, and other festivities.

See also EL POCHÓ DANCE-DRAMA

CONTACTS:
Mexico Tourism Board
21 E. 63rd St., Fl. 3
New York, NY 10021
800-446-3942 or 212-821-0314; fax: 212-821-0367
www.visitmexico.com

Rio de Janeiro Tourism Authority
Rua da Assembleia, 10-9 Fl.
Downtown
Rio de Janeiro, 20119-900 Brazil
55-21-2217-7575; fax: 55-21-2531-1272
www.riodejaneiro-turismo.com.br

SOURCES:
AnnivHol-2000, p. 12
DaysCustFaith-1957, p. 27
FolkWrldHol-1999, p. 41
OxYear-1999, p. 43

♦ 2600 ♦ **St. Spyridon (Spiridion) Day**
December 12 in the East and December 14 in the West

St. Spyridon is the patron saint of Corfu, Zakynthos, and Kephalonia; these are among the Ionian Islands located off the western coast of Greece. Although he was born a shepherd in Cyprus, he became bishop of Tremithus and was renowned for his rustic simplicity. He supposedly attended the Nicene Council (325) and defended the Apostolic faith against the Arians. After his death in c. 348, his relics were brought from Cyprus to Constantinople and then to Corfu in 1456. Every year a sacred relic of the saint, dressed in costly vestments, is carried through the streets on his feast day. Colorful folk festivities complete the day-long celebration. This day is celebrated on December 14 in the Roman Catholic Church.

CONTACTS:
Greek National Tourist Organization
645 Fifth Ave., 9th Fl.
New York, NY 10022
212-421-5777; fax: 212-826-6940
www.visitgreece.gr

Tourism Directorate of Corfu
Rizospaston Vouleuton & Iakovou Polyla
Kerkyra, 49100 Greece
30-26610-37520; fax: 30-26610-30298
www.gnto.gr/?langID=2

SOURCES:
BkFest-1937, p. 154
FolkWrldHol-1999, p. 701

♦ 2601 ♦ **St. Stephen's Day**
December 26

On this day in c. 35, St. Stephen became the first Christian martyr. The New Testament book of Acts records that Stephen was chosen by the Apostles as one of the first seven deacons of the church in Jerusalem. He was later denounced as a blasphemer by the Sanhedrin, the Jewish council in ancient Palestine, and stoned to death. St. Stephen is the patron saint of bricklayers.

December 26, 27, and 28, otherwise known respectively as St. Stephen's Day, ST. JOHN THE EVANGELIST'S DAY, and HOLY INNOCENTS' DAY, are considered examples of the three different degrees of martyrdom. St. Stephen's death is an example of the highest class of martyrdom—that is to say, both in will and in deed. St. John the Evangelist, who showed that he was ready to die for Christ but was prevented from actually doing so, exemplifies martyrdom in will, but not in deed. And the children who lost their lives in the slaughter of the Innocents provide an example of the martyrdom in deed but not in will.

In many countries, St. Stephen's Day is celebrated as an extra Christmas holiday. In England, it is known as BOXING DAY. In Austria, priests bless the horses because St. Stephen is their patron. In Poland tossing rice at each other symbolizes blessings and recalls Stephen's stoning. And in Ireland, boys with blackened faces carrying a paper wren, go about begging and "hunting the wren." The hunting of the wren is most likely a carryover from an old belief that the robin, symbolizing the NEW YEAR, killed the wren, symbolizing the Old, at the turning of the year.

See also SAN ESTEVAN, FEAST OF

CONTACTS:
Dingle Peninsula Tourism
Comharchumann Turasoireachta Chorca Dhuibhne
Dingle, County Kerry Ireland
353-66-9151188; fax: 353-66-9151991
www.dingle-peninsula.ie

SOURCES:
BkDays-1864, vol. II, p. 763
BkFest-1937, p. 35
DaysCustFaith-1957, p. 321
DictFolkMyth-1984, p. 950
EncyChristmas-2003, p. 686
FestSaintDays-1915, p. 249
FestWestEur-1958, p. 104
FolkAmerHol-1999, p. 540
FolkWrldHol-1999, p. 768
OxYear-1999, p. 532
SaintFestCh-1904, p. 40

♦ 2602 ♦ **St. Stephen's Day (Hungary)**
August 20

Hungary celebrates three national days, according to a 1991 state mandate. The founding of Hungary is commemorated on August 20, which is also the feast day of the founder of the country, St. Stephen of Hungary (c. 975-1038). He assumed the kingship in 1000 and worked to unite the various clans into a single Christian state. In 1950 the day was changed to Constitution Day by the communist regime, but since 1990, it has again celebrated St. Stephen.

CONTACTS:
Ministry for Foreign Affairs of the Republic of Hungary
Bem rkp. 47 1027 Budapest, Bem rakpart 47
Budapest, H-1027 Hungary

36-1-458-1000; fax: 36-1-212-5918
www.mfa.gov.hu/kum/en/bal

SOURCES:
OxYear-1999, p. 340

◆ 2603 ◆ **St. Swithin's Day**
July 15

When Swithin, the bishop of Winchester, England, died in 862, he was buried according to his wish, outside the cathedral in the churchyard, in a place where the rain from the eaves poured down. Whether this request was prompted by humility on his part or a wish to feel "the sweet rain of heaven" on his grave, it was reversed after his canonization, when clerical authorities tried to move his remains to a site within the church. According to legend, the heavens opened and there was a heavy rainfall—a show of the saint's displeasure that made it impossible to remove his body. This led to the popular belief that if it rains on St. Swithin's Day it will rain for 40 days; but if it is fair, it will be dry for 40 days. Swithin is the patron saint of rain, both for and against it.

SOURCES:
BkDays-1864, vol. II, p. 61
BkFest-1937, p. 60
DaysCustFaith-1957, p. 181
DictDays-1988, p. 106
FestSaintDays-1915, p. 150
FolkAmerHol-1999, p. 298
FolkWrldHol-1999, p. 443
OxYear-1999, pp. 278, 294
SaintFestCh-1904, p. 328

◆ 2604 ◆ **St. Sylvester's Day**
December 31

St. Sylvester (d. 335) was pope in the year 325, when Emperor Constantine declared that the pagan religion of Rome was abolished and that Christianity would henceforth be the official religion of the Empire. Although it is unclear exactly what role, if any, St. Sylvester played in this important event, he is always given at least some of the credit for stamping out paganism.

Because St. Sylvester's Day is also NEW YEAR'S EVE, it is celebrated in Switzerland by lighting bonfires in the mountains and ringing church bells to signal the passing of the old year and the beginning of the new. It is a day for rising early, and the last to get out of bed or to reach school are greeted with shouts of "Sylvester!" In some Swiss villages, grain is threshed on specially constructed platforms to ensure a plentiful harvest in the coming year (*see also* OLD SILVESTER).

St. Sylvester's Eve is celebrated in Austria, Hungary, and Germany. It is not uncommon in restaurants and cafes for the owner to set a pig loose at midnight. Everyone tries to touch the pig because it is considered a symbol of good luck. In private homes, a marzipan pig may be hung from the ceiling and touched at midnight.

SOURCES:
AmerBkDays-2000, p. 868
BkFest-1937, pp. 36, 49, 141, 176, 323, 347
BkHolWrld-1986, Jan 13
DaysCustFaith-1957, p. 325
DictDays-1988, pp. 23, 36, 125
EncyChristmas-2003, p. 690
FestWestEur-1958, pp. 21, 84, 242
FolkWrldHol-1999, p. 780
OxYear-1999, p. 540
SaintFestCh-1904, p. 48

◆ 2605 ◆ **St. Sylvester's Day (Madeira)**
December 31

In many European countries, December 31, in addition to NEW YEAR'S EVE, is also the observance of ST. SYLVESTER'S DAY, the feast day of Pope Sylvester (314-335). In Madeira, a group of eight Portuguese islands off the northwest coast of Africa, one of the world's most impressive fireworks displays takes place on the evening of this day, which is known as the Great Festival of St. Sylvester. The noise of the fireworks resounds over the Bay of Funchal, the islands' capital, where oceanliners make a special stop so that passengers can watch the celebrations.

CONTACTS:
Portuguese National Tourist Office
590 Fifth Ave., 4th Fl.
New York, NY 10036
800-767-8842 or 212-354-4403; fax: 212-764-6137
www.visitportugal.com

SOURCES:
FestEur-1961, p. 135

◆ 2606 ◆ **St. Tammany's Day**
May 1

During the Revolutionary War, the American troops were amused by the fact that the "Redcoats" (i.e., the British) had a patron saint: ST. GEORGE, who had a reputation for protecting English soldiers. So they decided to adopt a patron saint of their own, and chose for the purpose a disreputable 17th-century Delaware Indian chief named Tammanend. They dubbed him "St. Tammany" or "St. Tamina," chose May 1 for his festival, and celebrated the day with pompous and ridiculous ceremonies.

After the revolution Tammany Societies were eventually formed in many cities and towns, representing middle-class opposition to the power of the aristocratic Federalist Party. In the early 19th century the Society of Tammany became identified with the Democratic party. But the society's tendency to dole out gifts to the poor and to bribe political leaders—among them the notorious "Boss" Tweed of New York City—made the name "Tammany Hall" (the building in which the organization had its headquarters in New York City) synonymous with urban political corruption.

SOURCES:
DaysCustFaith-1957, p. 122
FolkAmerHol-1999, p. 211
OxYear-1999, p. 193

♦ 2607 ♦ St. Teresa's Day
October 15

St. Teresa of Ávila (1515-1582) was a Spanish Carmelite nun and reformer who recognized that the discipline in convents had relaxed to the point where they were little more than social clubs. In 1562, amidst intense opposition, she withdrew from the big convent she had entered in 1535 and established a small house with only 13 members known as the Reformed, or Discalced, Carmelites. Teresa's nuns devoted themselves to a rigorous way of life that had been largely forgotten in most monastic orders. They never left the convent, they maintained almost perpetual silence, they lived in austere poverty, and, as a symbol of their humility, they wore sandals instead of shoes—thus the designation "discalced," which means "barefoot." Before she died, Teresa had established 17 such communities. She was canonized by Pope Gregory XV in 1622.

Every year in Ávila, Spain, there is a huge celebration in honor of St. Teresa on October 15. The day is filled with religious services, parades, dances, games, and feasts, and the streets are decorated with banners and flowers. St. Teresa of Ávila is often colloquially referred to as "Big St. Teresa" to distinguish her from St. Teresa of Lisieux, a 19th-century Carmelite nun and author.

CONTACTS:
Tourist Office of Spain
666 Fifth Ave., 35th Fl.
New York, NY 10103
212-265-8822; fax: 212-265-8864
www.okspain.org

SOURCES:
AnnivHol-2000, p. 172
DaysCustFaith-1957, p. 259
DictWrldRel-1989, p. 753
OxYear-1999, p. 415
SaintFestCh-1904, p. 450

♦ 2608 ♦ St. Thomas's Day
December 21 by Malabar Christians and
Anglicans; July 3 by Roman Catholics; October 6
in the East

St. Thomas the Apostle was dubbed "Doubting Thomas" because, after the Resurrection, the other Apostles told him that they had seen Jesus, and he wouldn't believe them until he had touched Jesus' wounds himself. When the Apostles left Jerusalem to preach to the people of other nations, as Jesus had instructed them to do, tradition says Thomas traveled eastward toward India. In Kerala, the smallest state in India, the Malabar Christians (or Christians of St. Thomas) claim St. Thomas as the founder of their church. For them his feast day is a major celebration. Thomas is the patron saint of India and Pakistan.

In December Mayan Indians in Chichicastenago, Guatemala, honor the sun god they worshipped long before they became Christians with a dangerous ritual known as the *palo voladore*, or "flying pole dance." Three men climb to the top of a 50-foot pole. As one of them beats a drum and plays a flute, the other two wind a long rope attached to the pole around one

foot and jump. If they land on their feet, it is believed that the sun god will be pleased and that the days will start getting longer—a safe bet in view of the fact that St. Thomas's Day coincides with the WINTER SOLSTICE.

CONTACTS:
Catholic Archbishop's House Trichur
East Fort
Thrissur, Kerala 680 005 India
91-487-2333325; fax: 91-487-2338204
www.archdioceseoftrichur.com

Guatemala Tourist Commission
7th Avenue 1-17 Zone 4, Civic Ctr.
Guatemala City, Guatemala
502-331-3333; fax: 502-331-8893
www.guatemala.travel.com.gt

SOURCES:
BkDays-1864, vol. II, p. 723
BkFest-1937, p. 246
BkHolWrld-1986, Dec 21
DaysCustFaith-1957, p. 317
EncyChristmas-2003, pp. 225, 692
FestSaintDays-1915, p. 224
FolkWrldHol-1999, p. 708
OxYear-1999, pp. 279, 506

♦ 2609 ♦ St. Thorlak's Day
December 23

Thorlak Thorhalli (1133-1193) was born in Iceland and, after being educated abroad, returned there to become bishop of Skalholt in 1177 or 1178. He was canonized by the Icelandic parliament five years after his death, even though the Roman Catholic Church has never officially confirmed the cult. His day traditionally marks the climax of CHRISTMAS preparations for Icelanders. It is associated with housecleaning and clothes washing, as well as the preparation of special foods. The *hangiket*, or smoked mutton, for Christmas was usually cooked on this day, and in the western fjords, the ammonia-like smell of skate hash cooked on St. Thorlak's Day is still considered a harbinger of the holiday season.

SOURCES:
EncyChristmas-2003, p. 350
FolkWrldHol-1999, p. 713
OxYear-1999, p. 509

♦ 2610 ♦ St. Tryphon's Day (Montenegro and Bulgaria) (Trifon Zarezan)
February 1 or February 14 (varies)

The patron saint of gardeners, St. Tryphon is believed to have been born in Phrygia and was put to death by the Roman emperor Diocletian in about 250. Today, he is a popular figure among vine growers in Bulgaria and Montenegro. It is thus appropriate in those countries that St. Tryphon's Day, or **Trifon Zarezan**, coincides with the beginning of the pruning season in February. Roman Catholics living in other countries observe the saint's day on November 10.

Accompanying the saint's day in Bulgaria and Montenegro is a secular tradition that has developed in the vineyard districts. Seeking a blessing from the saint, growers will sprinkle wine on their vineyards before commencing an evening celebration of feasting and drinking.

Celebrations of a more somber nature take place in the Catholic and Orthodox churches of the two countries. One of the most widely attended ceremonies takes place in the Montenegrin city of Kotor at the Cathedral of St. Tryphon, built in the 12th century in honor of the saint.

See also VINEGROWER'S DAY

CONTACTS:
United States Embassy in Montenegro
Ljubljanska bb
Podgorica 81000 Montenegro
382-81-225-417; fax: 382-81-241-358
podgorica.usembassy.gov

◆ 2611 ◆ **St. Urho's Day**
March 16

St. Urho, whose name in Finnish means "hero," is credited with banishing a plague of grasshoppers that was threatening Finland's grape arbors. His legend in the United States was popularized in the 1950s, largely through the efforts of Professor Sulo Havumaki of Bemidji State University in Minnesota. After being celebrated as a "joke holiday" for several years in the Menahga-Sebeka area, the idea spread to other states with large Finnish populations.

The actual celebrations, which are largely confined to Finnish communities, include wearing St. Urho's official colors—Nile green and royal purple—drinking grape juice, and chanting St. Urho's famous words, "Grasshopper, grasshopper, go away," in Finnish. In some areas there is a ceremonial "changing of the guard"—in this case, two makeshift guards carrying pitchforks or chainsaws (to cut down the giant grasshoppers) who meet and exchange clothing, including humorous or unusual undergarments.

The similarities between this day and St. PATRICK'S DAY, observed on March 17, can hardly be overlooked. St. Patrick, who is believed to have driven the snakes out of Ireland, is widely regarded as a rival to St. Urho and his grasshoppers. There is some evidence that native Finns who have visited friends and relatives in the U.S. are taking the St. Urho's celebration back to Finland with them.

CONTACTS:
Menahga Civic & Commerce
P.O. Box C
Menahga, MN 56464
218-564-4557; fax: 218-564-4612
www.cityofmenahga.com

SOURCES:
AnnivHol-2000, p. 45
OxYear-1999, p. 121

◆ 2612 ◆ **St. Vaclav's Day**
September 28

Also known as **St. Wenceslas** (c. 907-929), St. Vaclav was a Bohemian prince who became the patron saint of the former Czechoslovakia. He was raised a Christian and eventually took over the government, encouraging the work of German missionaries who were trying to Christianize Bohemia. His zeal antagonized his non-Christian opponents, his brother among them, and he was eventually murdered by his brother or his brother's supporters. A few years later, his remains were transferred to the Church of St. Vitus in Prague, which became a popular pilgrimage site in the medieval period.

St. Vaclav's Day is a holiday throughout the Czech Republic. The virtues of "Good King Wenceslas" have been memorialized by the popular 19th-century Christmas carol of that name, though it rests on no historical basis.

SOURCES:
AnnivHol-2000, p. 161
BkFest-1937, p. 90
DictWrldRel-1989, p. 803
EncyChristmas-2003, p. 808
OxYear-1999, p. 391

◆ 2613 ◆ **St. Vincent and the Grenadines Independence and Thanksgiving Day**
October 27

A group of islands in the West Indies, St. Vincent and the Grenadines gained independence from Britain on October 27, 1979, and citizens celebrate their freedom with this national holiday.

CONTACTS:
St. Vincent and the Grenadines: St. Vincent/The Grenadines
   Tourist Office
801 Second Ave., 21st Fl.
New York, NY 10017
800-729-1726 or 212-687-4981; fax: 212-949-5946
www.svgtourism.com

SOURCES:
AnnivHol-2000, p. 178

◆ 2614 ◆ **St. Vincent and the Grenadines National Heroes Day**
March 14

St. Vincent and the Grenadines is a nation comprised of a group of more than 30 islands, with St. Vincent being the largest of the islands. St. Vincent and the Grenadines are part of the Windward Islands in the Caribbean Sea.

Every March, the country celebrates Heroes and Heritage month. Throughout the month, the country learns about and remembers the past by holding cultural events and Indigenous People's Day celebrations. Many Vincentians make an annual pilgrimage to the Grenadine island of Balliceaux to pay homage to the fallen indigenous people, many of whom were later exiled to the region that became Belize and other parts of Central America.

March 14 is National Heroes Day. On this day, the country honors their national hero, Chief Joseph Chatoyer. He led the nation in preventing the Europeans from colonizing the islands. On March 14, 1795, Chatoyer was killed by British troops at Dorsetshire Hill. A monument honoring Chatoyer stands on this spot. As part of the Heroes Day celebration, a wreath-laying ceremony is held at the obelisk at Dorsetshire Hill.

CONTACTS:
St. Vincent and the Grenadines Ministry of Tourism and Culture
Cruise Ship Terminal
Harbour Quay
Kingstown, St. Vincent & The Grenadines
www.svgtourism.com

St. Vincent Ministry of Tourism and Culture (United States office)
Second Ave., 21st Fl.
New York, NY 10017
800-729-1726 or 212-687-4981; fax: 212-949-5946

♦ 2615 ♦ **St. Vincent's Day**
January 22

São Vicente is the patron saint of Lisbon, Portugal. St. Vincent of Saragossa was a deacon who was arrested along with Bishop Valerius. While Valerius was banished, Vincent was tortured and martyred in Spain under Diocletian's authority around the year 304. According to legend, his body was thrown to be devoured by vultures, but it was defended by a raven. Then his body was cast into the sea, but it came to shore and was buried.

St. Vincent's feast day is January 22. In Lisbon, people celebrate St. Vincent's Day with processions and prayers. But in the surrounding rural areas, there are a number of folk traditions associated with this day. Farmers believe that by carrying a resin torch to the top of a high hill on January 22, they can predict what the coming harvest will be like. If the wind extinguishes the flame, the crops will be abundant; if the torch continues to burn, a poor growing season lies ahead.

CONTACTS:
Portuguese National Tourist Office
590 Fifth Ave., 4th Fl.
New York, NY 10036
800-767-8842 or 212-354-4403; fax: 212-764-6137
www.visitportugal.com

SOURCES:
FestWestEur-1958, p. 161
OxYear-1999, p. 45

♦ 2616 ♦ **St. Vitus's Day**
June 15

According to legend, St. Vitus was raised as a Christian by his nurse and his foster father. All three suffered persecution and were eventually put to death for their beliefs around 303, when Vitus was still a young boy. A chapel was later built in his honor at Ulm, Germany, and it was believed that anyone who danced before his shrine there on June 15, St. Vitus's Day, would be assured of good health in the coming year.

Whether the motions of the enthusiastic dancers resembled the symptoms of those suffering from any of the diseases known as chorea, or whether people who suffered from disorders of the nervous system were often miraculously cured at the shrine is not known for certain, but chorea is commonly referred to as "St. Vitus's dance" for the violent motions that accompany the disease. St. Vitus is the patron saint not only of those suffering from epilepsy and other disorders of the nervous system, but of actors and dancers as well.

SOURCES:
DaysCustFaith-1957, p. 145
OxYear-1999, p. 250
SaintFestCh-1904, p. 290

♦ 2617 ♦ **Stanford Antigua Sailing Week**
April-May

The island nation of Antigua and Barbuda is famous for stiff easterly trade winds, which are ideal for sailing. Thus, it is little wonder that Antigua is the site of a major international sailing event. Organized by the Antigua Hotels and Tourist Association, the Stanford Antigua Sailing Week runs from late April into May and draws racing fans and yachting enthusiasts from all over the world.

The first Antigua Sailing Week took place in 1968, when yacht broker Desmond Nicholson and Antiguan hotel owner Howard Hulford recruited a total of 17 boats to participate in a three-day event. Since then the regatta has expanded to include as many as 1,500 sailors and 200 yachts of various sizes that compete in 16 different classes. Nearly every day of Sailing Week, yachts face off in courses of various distances and orientations toward the wind.

The competition took the name Stanford Antigua Sailing Week when the international financial company became its main sponsor in 2007, the same year the yachting community celebrated the competition's 40th anniversary.

CONTACTS:
Stanford Antigua Sailing Week
P.O. Box W2005
St. John's Antigua, W.I.
www.sailingweek.com

♦ 2618 ♦ **Stånga Games**
Four days including second weekend of July

The Stånga Games, often referred to as the "Gotlandic Olympics," have been held on Gotland Island in the Baltic Sea since 1924. They are the Swedish equivalent of Scotland's BRAEMAR HIGHLAND GATHERING, with competitive games and sports played the way they were in Viking times (late 700s to 1100 C.E.). Ancient square-and-border-ball is a popular team event in which the ball is hit with the hand or kicked with the foot, and teams must try to gain as much of their opponents' ground as possible. The Gotlandic pole-throwing contest is much like "tossing the caber" in Scotland. Another game, the Stone, is similar to horseshoes. It uses two stones, one made of stone and one of metal, which the players throw with the object of landing them as near as possible to the post. In the Gotlandic pentathlon, the participants compete in five events: a run, a game similar to the Stone, a high jump, pole throwing, and Cumberland wrestling. Other games include kick astride, hook the bottom, rule the roast, tug-of-pole, and breaking the ox.

CONTACTS:
Traditional Gutnic Sports Association
Neptungatan 4
Visby, S-621 41 Sweden
46-498-207-067; fax: 46-498-215-474

SOURCES:
WildPlanet-1995, p. 104

♦ 2619 ♦ **Stanton (Elizabeth Cady) Day**
November 12

Elizabeth Cady Stanton (1815-1902) was a pioneer in the struggle for women's rights. After graduating from the Troy Female Academy (now known as the Emma Willard School), one of the first schools devoted to providing better education for women, she married journalist and abolitionist Henry Brewster Stanton—although she carefully omitted the word "obey" from their wedding ceremony.

With a group of other women, she helped organize the first women's rights convention, held at Seneca Falls, New York, in 1848. This is where Stanton drew up her famous bill of rights for women, which included the first formal demand for women's suffrage in the United States. But it was her partnership with Susan B. ANTHONY, beginning in 1851, that galvanized the women's rights movement. Together they organized the National Woman Suffrage Association, planned suffrage campaigns, spoke out in favor of liberal divorce laws, and fought for political, legal, and industrial equality for women. Stanton died, however, 18 years before the 19th Amendment to the Constitution, granting women the right to vote, became law in 1920.

Governor Herbert Lehman of New York declared November 12 Elizabeth Cady Stanton Day in 1941. Stanton's birthday has long been observed by women's rights groups throughout the United States, particularly the National Organization for Women (NOW).

CONTACTS:
Library of Congress
101 Independence Ave. S.E.
Washington, D.C. 20540
202-707-5510; fax: 202-707-2076
www.loc.gov

Women's Rights National Historic Park
National Park Service
136 Fall St.
Seneca Falls, NY 13148
315-568-2991; fax: 315-568-2141
www.nps.gov

Public Broadcasting Service
1320 Braddock Pl.
Alexandria, VA 22314
703-739-5000
www.pbs.org

SOURCES:
AmerBkDays-2000, p. 767
AnnivHol-2000, p. 190

♦ 2620 ♦ **Star Festival**
January-February; 18th day of Chinese lunar year

In traditional Chinese belief, gods have great influence on people's lives and reside on the stars and planets. When LUNAR NEW YEAR is over, therefore, a day is set aside for men and boys to worship the Star Gods. Women are traditionally forbidden to participate in the ceremony, which consists of setting up a small table or altar in the courtyard of the house with a very simple food offering—usually sweetened rice balls. Two pictures are placed on the altar, one of the Star Gods and another of the cyclical signs associated with them. Inside a sealed envelope is a chart of lucky and unlucky stars. The father of the household prays to whichever star was associated with his birthday, then lights special lamps, made of red and yellow paper and filled with perfumed oil, that have been arranged around the altar. They burn out quickly, then each son of the house goes to the altar to relight three of the lamps in order to honor his star. If their flames burn brightly, it means he will have good luck in the coming year.

SOURCES:
BkFestHolWrld-1970, p. 25

♦ 2621 ♦ **State Fair of Texas**
Late September through the beginning of October

Not surprisingly, the State Fair of Texas is one of the nation's biggest state fairs, claiming more than three million visitors to the 200-acre Fair Park in Dallas. The fair began in 1887, and in 1952 Big Tex, its symbol of bigness, arrived. Big Tex is a 52-foot-tall cowboy with a 30-foot chest and 7'8" biceps, wearing a five-foot-high, 75-gallon cowboy hat. The cowboy stands in the middle of the fairgrounds booming out welcomes and announcements. The skeleton of the cowboy was built in 1949 to be the world's tallest Santa Claus for a CHRISTMAS celebration in Kerens, Tex. It was sold to the State Fair, and Dallas artist Jack Bridges used baling wire and papier-mâché to create the cowboy that debuted in 1952. The following year, a motor was installed to move the cowboy's jaw in sync with a voice mechanism, and Big Tex has been booming ever since. Among fair events are a college football game, concerts, and parades.

CONTACTS:
State Fair of Texas
3921 Martin Luther King Blvd.
P.O. Box 150009
Dallas, TX 75210
214-565-9931; fax: 214-421-8710
www.bigtex.com

SOURCES:
GdUSFest-1984, p. 181

♦ 2622 ♦ **State Opening of Parliament**
Early November

This colorful British ritual is observed at the beginning of November when the members of Parliament return after the long summer recess. Crowds assemble in the streets of Westminster, an inner borough of Greater London, in hopes of catching a glimpse of the Queen as she arrives in her horse-drawn coach, dressed in royal robes of state and escorted by the Household Cavalry. The Queen is not allowed to enter the House of Commons because she is not a commoner, so after being met by the Lord Chancellor she is led straight to the House of Lords. Seated on a magnificent throne and surrounded by various church and state officials in their robes, she reads aloud the speech that has been written for her by members of the government outlining their plans for the coming session.

An interesting tradition that accompanies the opening of Parliament is the searching of the cellars of both Houses. This goes back to 1605, when GUY FAWKES and his accomplices tried to blow the Houses up.

CONTACTS:
United Kingdom Parliament, Parliamentary Education Unit
Room 604, Norman Shaw Bldg.
London, SW1A 2TT United Kingdom
44-20-7219-3074; fax: 44-20-7219-2570
www.parliament.uk

The British Monarchy Official Web Site
Buckingham Palace
London, SW1A 1AA United Kingdom
44-20-7930-4832
www.royal.gov.uk

SOURCES:
AnnivHol-2000, p. 199

♦ 2623 ♦ Ste. Genevieve, Jour de Fête à (Days of Celebration)
Second full weekend in August

Ste. Genevieve became the first permanent settlement in the state of Missouri when the French arrived in 1725. At one time it rivaled St. Louis in size and importance, and the town still prides itself on its authentic 18th- and 19th-century architecture.

The annual Jour de Fête that has been held in mid-August each year since 1965 not only celebrates the area's French heritage but is a German and Spanish festival as well. Historic homes dating back to 1770 are opened to the public, people dress in colonial costumes, and arts and crafts are on display.

CONTACTS:
Ste. Genevieve Chamber of Commerce
251 Market St.
Ste. Genevieve, MO 63670
573-883-3686; fax: 573-883-7092
www.saintegenevieve.org

Library of Congress
101 Independence Ave. S.E.
Washington, DC 20540
202-707-5510; fax: 202-707-2076
www.loc.gov

SOURCES:
GdUSFest-1984, p. 106

♦ 2624 ♦ Steinbeck (John) Festival
First week in August

Salinas, California, birthplace of famous American author John Steinbeck (1902-1968), has hosted a yearly literary festival in his honor since 1980. Steinbeck, who was awarded the NOBEL PRIZE for literature in 1962, wrote extensively about the people, places, and social conditions of his homeland in California's central coastal region. The festival gives Steinbeck fans an opportunity to visit many of the places that formed Steinbeck's worldview and inspired his works. The four-day event features lectures on aspects of Steinbeck's work and life, tours, performances of plays and screenings of movies based on Steinbeck's stories, and a book fair. The festival also sponsors a short story contest, the winner of which receives a cash prize of $1,000.

CONTACTS:
National Steinbeck Center
1 Main St.
Salinas, CA 93901
831-796-3833; fax: 831-796-3828
www.steinbeck.org

♦ 2625 ♦ Stes. Maries, Fête des
May 24-25

According to a French legend, St. Sarah, patron saint of gypsies, was the Egyptian handmaid of Sts. Mary Jacoby and Mary Salome, and all three were shipwrecked off the Provençal coast of France. The three holy women supposedly died in the small Provençal village of Les Saintes Maries-de-la-Mer, where their remains are said to be preserved in the 15th-century church of Les Saintes-Maries. The relics of St. Sarah are deeply venerated by the Romanies, or gypsies, of southern France, who try to worship at her shrine at least once during their lives.

The highlight of the service held at the church during the **Festival of the Holy Maries** occurs when the flower-decked reliquary of the Maries is lowered slowly through a trap door in the ceiling. On the second day of the festival, there is a procession down to the sea for the blessing of the painted wooden vessel known as the "Bark of the Saints." The bark holds a silver urn which is believed to contain some of the bones of the saints. Thousands of devout pilgrims make the journey to Les Saintes Maries-de-la-Mer each year.

CONTACTS:
Saintes-Maries-de-la-Mer Office of Tourism
5 Av. Van Gogh
P.O. Box 16
Saintes-Maries de la Mer, 13460 France
33-4-9097-8255; fax: 33-4-9097-7115
www.saintesmaries.com/us/index.php

SOURCES:
AnnivHol-2000, p. 87
BkFest-1937, p. 123
DictFolkMyth-1984, p. 954
FestWestEur-1958, p. 38
FolkWrldHol-1999, p. 361

♦ 2626 ♦ **Steuben (Baron Friedrich) Day**
September 17

Baron Friedrich Wilhelm Ludolf Gerhard Augustus von Steuben (1730-1794) was an experienced Prussian soldier who came to America in 1777 and volunteered to serve in the Continental army without rank or pay. He was sent to join General George WASHINGTON at Valley Forge, where he trained Washington's men in the intricacies of military drill, earning himself the sobriquet "Drill Master of the American Revolution." Steuben led one of Washington's divisions at the Battle of YORKTOWN, and his experience in siege warfare helped the American troops achieve the victory that soon brought the Revolutionary War to an end. In gratitude for his contributions, he was granted American citizenship and given a large piece of land in the Mohawk Valley and a yearly pension.

Steuben's birthday, September 17, was first celebrated by members of the Steuben Society of America, an organization founded in 1919 by U.S. citizens of German descent. The Society now has branches in many states, which observe the anniversary with patriotic exercises. At Valley Forge State Park in Pennsylvania, there is a Steuben birthday celebration featuring German music and speeches at the monument to him erected in 1915. There are also Steuben Day parades in New York City, Philadelphia, and Chicago on or near the Prussian hero's birthday.

CONTACTS:
Steuben Society of America
6705 Fresh Pond Rd.
Ridgewood, NY 11385
718-381-0900; fax: 718-628-4874
www.steubensociety.org

Steuben Day Observance Association of Philadelphia and
    Vicinity, Inc.
8601 Roosevelt Blvd.
Philadelphia, PA 19152
215-332-3400; fax: 215-332-6050
www.steubenparade.com

SOURCES:
AmerBkDays-2000, p. 652

♦ 2627 ♦ **Stewardship Sunday**
Second Sunday in November

This is the day on which many churches in the United States and Canada begin their campaign for financial support in the coming year. The term "stewardship" refers to Christian and Jewish teaching that all creation belongs to God and that each man and woman is an agent or steward to whom God's property is entrusted for a while. On this Sunday each year, churches appeal to their members' sense of responsibility as stewards of the money God has entrusted to them.

SOURCES:
DaysCustFaith-1957, p. 300

♦ 2628 ♦ **Stickdance**
Spring

Observed by the Athabascan Indians of Alaska, Stickdance is a week of ceremonies to grieve for the dead. The ancient ceremony, usually held long after the deaths of those memorialized, is now observed only in two villages on the Yukon River—Kaltag and Nulato.

Each evening of the ceremony, people go to the community hall with traditional foods—moose, salmon, beaver, rabbit, ptarmigan (a kind of grouse)—for a meal called a *potlatch*. After the meal, the women stand in a circle, swaying and chanting traditional songs for the dead. The hall becomes more crowded each night. On Friday night, as the women dance in a circle, the men carry in a tall spruce tree stripped of branches and wrapped in ribbons. The tree is erected in the center of the room and wolf and fox furs are draped on it. The people then dance around it and chant continuously through the night. In the morning, the men tear the furs and ribbons from the stick and carry it away to the Yukon River, where they break it into pieces and throw the pieces on the river's ice.

On Saturday night, people representing the dead are ritually dressed in special clothes. Somberly, they leave the hall and go to the river where they shake the spirits from their clothing. On their return to the hall, the mood becomes festive; gifts are exchanged and a night of celebration begins. The following morning the people who have represented the dead walk through the village shaking hands with people, sharing food and drink, and saying farewell.

Stickdance is held at irregular intervals, since it takes months or longer to prepare for it. People must choose those who will represent the dead being honored and make their clothes, and they must also save up to buy gifts.

The Athabascans, who may have descended from bands who crossed from Asia, have lived in Alaska longer than the Eskimos have and speak a language that is in the same family as that spoken by Navajos and Apaches.

SOURCES:
EncyNatAmerRel-2001, p. 286

♦ 2629 ♦ **Stiftungsfest**
Last weekend in August

Appropriately enough, Minnesota's oldest continuous festival is held in the town of Norwood-Young America. Loosely translated as "founders' day," Stiftungsfest was created in 1861 by the Young America Pioneer Maennerchor (men's choir) as a way of bringing the music of old Germany to the new world. Well-known bands and singing groups from Germany as well as local groups perform during the three-day event, which includes a traditional German beer garden, a Heritage Tent showcasing German arts and crafts, and a Grand Parade.

CONTACTS:
Stiftungsfest Committee
P.O. Box 133
Norwood Young America, MN 55397
952-467-1812; fax: 952-467-3571
www.stiftungsfest.org

♦ 2630 ♦ Stir-Up Sunday
November-December; Sunday before Advent

The collect for the Sunday preceding ADVENT in the Church of England begins, "Stir up, we beseech Thee, O Lord, the wills of thy faithful people." But the other "stirring up" that takes place on this day is more literal: the stirring of the batter for the traditional CHRISTMAS pudding, which must be prepared weeks in advance. It is customary for each member of the family to take turns stirring the pudding with a wooden spoon (symbolic of Jesus' crib), which is thought to bring good luck. The stirring is done clockwise, with eyes closed, and the stirrer makes a wish.

SOURCES:
BkHolWrld-1986, Nov 22
DictDays-1988, p. 114
EncyChristmas-2003, p. 741
FolkWrldHol-1999, p. 679
OxYear-1999, pp. 500, 636

♦ 2631 ♦ Stockton Asparagus Festival
Last weekend in April

This two-day celebration takes place in Stockton, Calif., the heart of the region that claims to be the "Asparagus Capital of the Nation." In fact, California accounts for about 90 percent of the fresh-market asparagus production in the country, and most of that asparagus comes from Stockton's San Joaquin Delta region.

The festival began in 1986 to promote the asparagus and it now draws 80,000 spectators to the region's various events. These include about 50 food booths in Asparagus Alley, a wine-tasting booth, a fun run (some runners wear asparagus spears in their headbands), a car show of some 200 antique and classic cars, arts and crafts, live entertainment, and children's activities.

There's also a recipe contest; among the past winning entries are enchiladas and lasagna made, of course, with asparagus. Other popular asparagus dishes served include asparaberry shortcake (it is said the asparagus gives a nutmeg flavor to the strawberries), asparagus-and-beef sandwiches, and asparagus bisque.

The festival is also a time to promulgate information about the asparagus. Fair-goers learn that asparagus is a source of vitamins A and C; the first trainload of asparagus was sent east from California in 1900; the Greeks and Romans used asparagus as a medicine for bee stings, dropsy, and toothache, and also as an aphrodisiac.

CONTACTS:
Stockton Asparagus Festival
311 E. Main St., Ste. 204
Stockton, CA 95202
209-644-3740; fax: 209-644-3755
www.asparagusfest.com

♦ 2632 ♦ Stonewall Rebellion, Anniversary of the
June 27

The Stonewall Inn was a gay bar in New York City's Greenwich Village that was raided by the police on June 27, 1969. Police frequently monitored the bar and undertook occasional raids in the past, but on that Friday night, the encounter turned explosive. As the outraged crowd threw stones and bottles, the police retaliated by aiming a fire hose against it. Eventually, more police arrived and subdued what had turned into a riot.

Today, the Stonewall Rebellion is regarded as a turning point in the history of the gay rights movement. It is commemorated in New York, Philadelphia, and other U.S. cities with parades, memorial services for those who have died of AIDS, and other activities designed to draw attention to the ways in which homosexuals have been discriminated against.

CONTACTS:
Stonewall Veterans Association
70-A Greenwich Ave., Ste. 120
New York, NY 10011
212-627-1969; fax: 212-374-6348
www.stonewallvets.org

SOURCES:
FolkWrldHol-1999, p. 271

♦ 2633 ♦ Store Bededag
Between April 18 and May 21; fourth Friday after Easter

A public holiday in Denmark, Store Bededag is a nationwide day of prayer which has been observed since the 18th century, when King Christian VII's prime minister, Count Johann Friedrich Struensee, decided that one great day of prayer should replace the numerous penitential days observed by the Evangelical Lutheran Church, the state church.

The eve of **Common Prayer Day** is announced by the ringing of church bells. In former times, it was customary for Copenhagen burghers to greet the spring by putting on new clothes and strolling around the city ramparts. Then they went home and ate *varme hveder,* a small square wheat bread, served hot. Today, people still dress in their spring finery and eat the traditional bread, but now they walk along the famous Langelinie, the boulevard that faces Copenhagen's waterfront.

CONTACTS:
Embassy of Denmark
3200 Whitehaven St. N.W.
Washington, D.C. 20008
202-234-4300; fax: 202-328-1470
www.ambwashington.um.dk

SOURCES:
FestWestEur-1958, p. 25

♦ 2634 ♦ Storytelling Festival, National
First weekend in October

A three-day festival in Jonesborough, Tenn., the National Storytelling Festival was started in 1973 to revive the ancient folk art of storytelling. The popularity of storytelling seemed to be dying, replaced by radio, television, and movies. The first festival was the idea of Jimmy Neil Smith, a Jonesborough schoolteacher who became executive director of the festival's sponsor, the National Association for the Preservation and Perpetuation of Storytelling (now known as the Storytelling Foundation International), which was formed in 1975 and is headquartered in Jonesborough. That first event drew about 60 people. At first, people sat on bales of hay, then the festival moved to kitchens and parlors and porches, and finally into the large tents that are used now. The festival has inspired scores of similar events around the country as well as college courses in storytelling.

About 6,000 people now attend to listen to storytellers relate ghost stories, sacred stories, ballads, tall tales, myths, legends, and fairy tales. Restaurants set up food booths, and a resource tent provides tapes and other material. The 20th-anniversary celebration in 1992 brought together more than 80 storytellers who had all appeared at previous festivals. A highlight was a special ghost-story concert by tellers of supernatural tales.

See also TELLABRATION and YUKON INTERNATIONAL STORYTELLING FESTIVAL

CONTACTS:
International Storytelling Center
116 W. Main St.
Jonesborough, TN 37659
800-952-8392 or 423-753-2171; fax: 423-913-8219
www.storytellingfestival.net

SOURCES:
GdUSFest-1984, p. 174

♦ 2635 ♦ **Stourbridge Fair**
Began August 24 for three weeks

In the 17th century the Stourbridge Fair, held at Stourbridge (or Sturbridge) near Cambridge, was England's chief place of exchange. It was established around 1200 as a benefit for the local lepers' hospital, and it was put on by the town and Cambridge University beginning on ST. BARTHOLOMEW'S DAY, August 24, and continuing for about three weeks. It was held at Duddery Square, where all the cloth and clothing shops were located. Merchants and wholesalers could buy everything from Italian silks to furs from the Baltics and linen from Flanders. Those who attended the fair would bring home souvenirs known as "fairings"—originally relics or images of saints, but later trinkets of all sorts or gingerbread in the shape of hobby-horses covered with gilt. The fair was held for the last time in 1855.

Although there were other amusements for fairgoers, including rope dancing and puppet shows, those who wanted to see the greatest entertainers of England and Europe would go to London for the BARTHOLOMEW FAIR, which was held at this same time of year.

SOURCES:
BkFair-1939, p. 170
YrFest-1972, p. 162

♦ 2636 ♦ **Stratford Festival**
April-November

What started in Stratford, Ontario, in 1953 as a six-week Shakespearean drama festival under the artistic leadership of Alec Guinness and Irene Worth has since expanded into a 26-week event drawing an audience of half a million people. All of Shakespeare's plays have been performed here over the years, as well as works by Sophocles (c. 496-406 B.C.E.), Henrik Ibsen (1828-1906), Jean-Baptiste Molière (1622-1673), Anton Chekhov (1860-1904), Richard Sheridan (1751-1816), Samuel Beckett (1906-1989), and a number of Canadian playwrights. The festival's repertory company, known as the Stratford Company, goes on tour during the months when the festival is not in session.

CONTACTS:
Stratford Festival
55 Queen St.
P.O. Box 520
Stratford, ON K1A 1J5 Canada
519-271-4040
www.stratfordfestival.ca

SOURCES:
GdWrldFest-1985, p. 52
IntlThFolk-1979, p. 73
MusFestAmer-1990, p. 161

♦ 2637 ♦ **Strawberry Festival**
June

The Strawberry Festival is one of several annual festivals held by Iroquois Indians. At Tonawanda, N.Y., the people congregate in their longhouse to hear a lengthy recitation of the words of Handsome Lake (Ganio "Día Io," 1735-1815). In 1799 this Seneca prophet delivered a message calling for cooperative farming, abstention from hard drink, abandonment of witchcraft and magic, the prohibition of abortion, and other instructions. This is the basis of today's Longhouse religion.

Following the recitations and speeches are ceremonial dances accompanied by chants and the pounding of turtle-shell rattles. Lunch follows, with a strawberry drink and winding up with strawberry shortcake. The Iroquois say, "You will eat strawberries when you die," because strawberries line the road to heaven.

Other traditional Iroquois celebrations include the IROQUOIS MIDWINTER FESTIVAL, a Maple Dance held when maple syrup and sugar are made, a Planting Festival, and the Green Corn Dance, at which the principal dish is succotash, made not just with corn and lima beans but also with squash and venison or beef.

CONTACTS:
Tonawanda Band of Seneca
7027 Meadville Rd.
Basom, NY 14013
716-542-4244; fax: 716-542-4008

SOURCES:
DictWorldRel-1989, p. 533
EncyNatAmerRel-2001, p. 289
EncyRel-1987, vol. 6, p. 191

♦ 2638 ♦ **Struga Poetry Evenings**
Mid-June

The annual international poetry festival known as Struga Poetry Evenings was launched in 1962 with a series of readings by Macedonian poets in honor of Konstantin and Dimitar Miladinov, brothers born in the early 19th century. Both were known as great writers, teachers, and intellectuals, and many consider Konstantin Miladinov to be the founder of modern Macedonian poetry. The Struga festival opens each year with his poem "Longing for the South."

The festival takes place over five days in late August, drawing about 20 Macedonian and 30 international poets, who take part in readings and symposia. The festival also typically features an art exhibit, workshops in poetry-related subjects, and leisure activities. A festival centerpiece is the international poetry reading, Meridians, held after the opening ceremony. The presentation of special awards are always highlights of the festival. The Miladinov Brothers Award acknowledges the best poetry book by a Macedonian author in the period between two festivals, and the Struga Bridges Award, presented jointly by the festival and UNESCO, recognizes the best debut poetry book by an author of any country. A festival jury also selects one poet as the Gold Wreath Award winner, who presides as laureate over the festival.

CONTACTS:
Struga Poetry Evenings
P.O. Box 109
Struga 6330 Republic of Macedonia
www.svp.org.mk

Macedonia - Embassy
1101 30th St. N.W., Ste. 302
Washington, DC 20007
202-337-3063; fax: 202-337-3093

♦ 2639 ♦ **Sts. Cosmas and Damian Day**
September 27

Legend has Cosmas (also Cosme or Cosmo) and Damian as twin brothers from Syria who were brought up in the Christian faith and who devoted their lives to medicine. As doctors they refused payment for their services, instead asking those who benefited from their healing to believe in Christ. What can be reasonably asserted is that they probably lived and were martyred in Syria during or before the fifth century.

In Brazil, the feast of Cosmas and Damian is celebrated on September 27 and it is traditional to give candy to children, since the saints are patrons of children. Yoruban mythology, which lives on through African Brazilians, tells of another set of holy twins, who are often associated with Cosmas and Damian.

SOURCES:
AnnivHol-2000, p. 161
BkFest-1937, p. 151
BkHolWrld-1986, Sep 27
OxYear-1999, p. 389

♦ 2640 ♦ **Sts. Peter and Paul Day**
June 29

It is said that St. Peter and St. Paul were both martyred on June 29, and for this reason their names have been linked in various observances around the world. In Malta, the feast of St. Peter and St. Paul is a harvest festival known as Mnarja. In Peru, the **Día de San Pedro y San Pablo** is celebrated in fishing villages because St. Peter is the patron saint of fishermen. Processions of decorated boats carrying an image of the saint are common, and sometimes a special floating altar is set up, with decorations made out of shells and seaweed.

In Valparaíso, Chile, this sort of procession has been going on since 1682.

In Trinidad fishermen first go out to catch fish to give to the poor and as they return, the Anglican priest blesses them and the sea. Then the partying begins. After the priest leaves, bongo and bele dances are done to honor St. Peter.

CONTACTS:
Commission for the Promotion of Peru
Calle Uno Oeste No. 50, piso 13th
Urb. Corpac
Lima, 27 Peru
51-1-4224-3131
www.promperu.gob.pe

Chilean Tourism Board
Providencia Ave., 2nd Fl.
Santiago, 1550 Chile
56-2-731-8419; fax: 56-2-236-1417
www.visit-chile.org/index.php?lang=eng

Tourism and Industrial Development Company (Trinidad and Tobago) Ltd.
29 Tenth Ave.
Barataria1, Trinidad and Tobago
868-675-70347; fax: 868-638-7962
www.tdc.co.tt

SOURCES:
AmerBkDays-2000, p. 488
BkFest-1937, pp. 7, 151, 171, 294, 331
DaysCustFaith-1957, p. 155
DictWrldRel-1989, pp. 563, 566
FestWestEur-1958, p. 14
FolkWrldHol-1999, p. 408
OxYear-1999, pp. 269, 270
SaintFestCh-1904, p. 308

♦ 2641 ♦ **Students' Fight for Freedom and Democracy, Day of (Struggle for Freedom and Democracy Day, World Students' Day)**
November 17

In 1939, Nazi troops invaded Czechoslovakia and took over the country, installing a dictatorship. Student-led demonstrations against the occupation in late October and early November 1939 led to the death of several students, most notably, Jan Opletal of Charles University in Prague. On November 17, the day Opletal was to be buried, more protests were held. Nazi troops subsequently executed nine student leaders, closed all universities, and sent many students to a concentration camp.

November 17 became a date of national recognition for Czechs after World War II. The date took on greater significance on November 17, 1989, when Czech students gathered 50 years after the original protest, this time to demonstrate against the communist regime. This marked the beginning of the so-called Velvet Revolution to reestablish a democratic government.

The Day of Students' Fight for Freedom and Democracy is a national holiday in the Czech Republic. People gather and light candles near a "V for Victory" memorial plaque on National Avenue in Prague. Ribbons in the national colors of red, blue, and white are often worn. Music associated with the 1989 protest is played, and the national flag is flown in all public places.

CONTACTS:
Embassy of the Czech Republic
3900 Spring of Freedom St. N.W.
Washington, D.C. 02008
202-274-9100; fax: 202-966-8540
www.mzv.cz

♦ 2642 ♦ Sturgis Motorcycle Rally
First Monday of August through following
Sunday

A mammoth yearly rally of 250,000 or so motorcyclists in small Sturgis, S.D. (population 7,000), formerly called the **Black Hills Motorcycle Classic**. There are races, merrymaking, band music, and usually some misbehavior, including arrests for drunken driving. There tend to be numerous accidents with injuries, and sometimes, fatalities. Motorcycle drag racing runs eight days, and other official events include bike shows, a swap meet, monster truck races, Tough Man and Tough Woman Contests (the titles determined by fights in which biting and kicking but not much else are forbidden), and a fireworks show. The rally also includes unofficial events, especially weddings; bikers find it romantic to get married during the rally, and 100 or more couples get married there every year.

The rally began in 1938 when Clarence (Pappy) Hoel, a local motorcycle dealer, invited some fellow bikers to a get-together. His wife, Pearl, made hot dogs, potato salad, and iced tea for the crew. The rally has been held ever since, except for two years during World War II, and has become part of biker lore.

CONTACTS:
City of Sturgis Rally Dept.
1040 2nd St., Ste. 201
Sturgis, SD 57785
605-720-0800; fax: 605-720-0801
www.sturgismotorcyclerally.com

♦ 2643 ♦ Styrian Autumn (Steirischer Herbst)
October-November

Dedicated to the avant-garde in music, drama, literature, and the fine arts, this month-long festival in Austria celebrates spontaneity and experimentation. Founded in 1968, its goal is to remove the barrier between the producers and con-

sumers of culture by presenting world premieres of plays, operas, and musical works by contemporary artists, workshops and symposia on 20th-century composers, exhibitions of contemporary art, and a variety of fringe events that include circus acts and multimedia shows. Ticket prices are purposely kept low, and many festival events are offered free of charge. There are also interdisciplinary symposia. The festival takes its name from the province of Styria, whose capital city, Graz, is where the work of Austria's modernists is performed and displayed.

CONTACTS:
Steirischer Herbst Festivalbu ro
Sackstrasse 17
Graz, A-8010 Austria
43-316-823-007-61; fax: 43-316-823-007-77
www.steirischerherbst.at

SOURCES:
GdWrldFest-1985, p. 12
IntlThFolk-1979, p. 33
MusFestEurBrit-1980, p. 28

♦ 2644 ♦ Sudan Independence Day
January 1

Sudan became an independent republic on NEW YEAR'S DAY in 1956, after having been a joint British-Egyptian territory since 1899.

Independence Day is celebrated as a national holiday with elaborate festivities in the capital city of Khartoum.

CONTACTS:
Embassy of the Republic of Sudan
2210 Massachusetts Ave.
Washington, D.C. 20008
202-338-8565; fax: 202-667-2406
www.sudanembassy.org

SOURCES:
AnnivHol-2000, p. 1
NatlHolWrld-1968, p. 10

♦ 2645 ♦ Sugar Ball Show (Sugar-Coated Haws Festival)
16th through 18th days of first lunar month

This temple festival is held at the Haiyunan Buddhist convent of Sifang District in Qingdao, Shandong Province, China. Set for the day of the first spring tide, this festival has been held since the convent was built in the 17th century near the end of the Ming Dynasty. Originally fishermen observed this time to pray for safety and a good harvest. Now sugar balls, also called *haws*—yams, oranges, and dates dipped in hot syrup and then cooled until crisp—colorfully displayed on long skewers, are specialties of the fair. About 200,000 people attend the show.

♦ 2646 ♦ Sugar Bowl Classic
January 1

New Orleans, Louisiana, has been host to football and lots of hoopla since the Sugar Bowl originated there in 1935. That first game took place in the depths of the Great Depression, and since then the Sugar Bowl has survived many difficulties, including a World War and a devastating hurricane.

The first Sugar Bowl took place in 1935 between Tulane University's Green Wave, unbeaten in the South, and Temple University's Owls, the only unbeaten team in the North. The Green Wave and the Owls waged an exciting contest in which Tulane overcame a 14-point deficit to win, 20-14. Since then, the annual event has included a berth for the Southeastern Conference champion. Alabama has won the most games with eight wins (many with legendary coach Bear Bryant), and Louisiana State is right behind them with seven wins. In 2009, the Sugar Bowl celebrated its 75th anniversary with a Legends Luncheon event that welcomed 42 former coaches and Most Valuable Players back to New Orleans. In the 75th annual Sugar Bowl, Utah trounced Alabama, 31-17.

The Sugar Bowl has been played in New Orleans every year except 2006 when, for the only time in the history of the game, it was played away from the city. This was soon after the devastating Hurricane Katrina, which killed hundreds of people and destroyed thousands of homes and businesses. The New Orleans Superdome was left standing, but badly damaged. So in 2006, the Sugar Bowl staff moved to Georgia and put on the game in the Georgia Dome. The game moved back to New Orleans the following year.

CONTACTS:
Allstate Sugar Bowl
1500 Sugar Bowl Dr.
New Orleans, LA 70112
504-828-2440; fax: 504-828-2441
www.allstatesugarbowl.com

SOURCES:
AmerBkDays-2000, p. 12
BkFestHolWrld-1970, p. 3
GdUSFest-1984, p. 73

♦ 2647 ♦ **Sukkot (Sukkoth, Succoth)**
    Begins between September 20 and October 18;
    Tishri 15-21

After their escape from slavery in Egypt, the Jews wandered in the desert for 40 years under the leadership of Moses. For much of the time they lived in huts, or *sukkot,* made of wooden frames covered with branches or hay. The festival of Sukkot, also known as the **Feast of Tabernacles** or the **Feast of Booths,** commemorates this period in Jewish history. It is also one of the PILGRIM FESTIVALS (*see also* PASSOVER and SHAVUOT).

The traditional way of observing Sukkot was to build a small booth or tabernacle and live in it during the seven-day festival. Nowadays Orthodox congregations build a *sukkah* in the synagogue, while Reform Jews make miniature models of the ancient huts and use them as centerpieces on the family table. Although linked to the Exodus from Egypt, Sukkot also celebrates the fall harvest and is sometimes referred to as the **Feast of the Ingathering.**

A major part of the festival is the four species: a palm branch, citron, three myrtle twigs, and two willow branches. These are tied together and waved at different points in the service, to "rejoice before the Lord."

Like other Jewish holidays, Sukkot begins at sundown on the preceding evening. The seventh day of Sukkot is known as HOSHANA RABBAH and is the last possible day on which one can seek and obtain forgiveness for the sins of the previous year—an extension of the YOM KIPPUR or the Day of Atonement. The eighth day of Sukkot is known as SHEMINI ATZERET, and the day after that is called SIMHAT TORAH, which is now celebrated as a separate holiday by Orthodox and Conservative Jews.

CONTACTS:
Union for Reform Judaism
633 Third Ave.
New York, NY 10017
212-650-4000; fax: 212-650-4169
www.urj.org

Union of Orthodox Jewish Congregations of America
11 Broadway
New York, NY 10004
212-563-4000; fax: 212-564-9058
www.ou.org

SOURCES:
AmerBkDays-2000, p. 710
BkFest-1937, p. 204
BkFestHolWrld-1970, pp. 118, 123
BkHolWrld-1986, Oct 1
DaysCustFaith-1957, p. 270
DictWrldRel-1989, pp. 155, 390, 723
FolkAmerHol-1999, p. 403
FolkWrldHol-1999, p. 567
HolSymbols-2009, p. 910
OxYear-1999, p. 726
RelHolCal-2004 p. 55

♦ 2648 ♦ **Sumamao, Fiesta de**
    December 26

The Argentine ritual drama known as *sumamao,* which means "beautiful river," is named after the location in which it is traditionally performed—near the Rio Dulce. It used to take place in a deserted chapel near the river, but nowadays it is sponsored by a ranch owner, who sets up a small altar on his property.

On San Esteban's (ST. STEPHEN'S) Day, December 26, an avenue of *arcos,* or arches—made from trees that have been stripped of their branches except for a tuft on top and tied together by cords hung with *ichas* (cakes in the form of puppets)—leads up to the altar. The drama begins at dawn with trumpets and fireworks, followed by a slow procession of men on horseback through the arches. The rest of the drama unfolds throughout the day, culminating in the demolition of the arcos and the eating of the ichas. A fiesta concludes the celebration.

The sumamao is primarily an agricultural ritual aimed at winning the favor of the gods by offering sacrifices and exorcizing evil spirits. Social dances—including the *zamba,* the *gato,* and the *chacarera*—have replaced the orgiastic behavior that followed the ritual in ancient times.

CONTACTS:
National Secretariat of Tourism, Tourist Information Centers
Av. Santa Fe 883
Buenos Aires, C1059ABC Argentina
54-11-4312-2232; fax: 54-11-4302-7816
www.turismo.gov.ar/eng/menu.htm

SOURCES:
DictFolkMyth-1984, p. 1086

♦ 2649 ♦ Suminuri Matsuri
January 15

Suminuri Matsuri is a New Year tradition observed for more than half a millennium in a district of Matsunoyama, Niigata Prefecture, Japan. People adorn their homes and streets with decorations made of paper, tree branches, and bamboo for OSHOGATSU, New Year's Day. After the holiday they take down the decorations and burn them, keeping the ashes for the Suminuri Festival. People take their ashes outside and mix them with some snow, then rub the concoction on each other's faces for luck in the new year.

CONTACTS:
Niigata Prefectural Government
Tourism Division, 4-1 Shinko-cho
Niigata, 950-8570 Japan
81-2-5280-5968; fax: 81-2-5283-4345
www.pref.niigata.jp/seisaku/kokusai/english

SOURCES:
IllFestJapan-1993, p. 142

♦ 2650 ♦ Summer Festival
July 4

There is something for everybody on the FOURTH OF JULY in Owensboro, Ky. A highlight has been the "Anything That Goes and Floats Race," in which contestants must have a vehicle that gets them to the Ohio River and then floats them for a decent distance on the river. Vehicles that have made it into the water include bicycles attached to a canoe, a skateboard tied to a plastic raft, and large pontoons powered by bicycles on land and paddlewheels in the water.

Other events include musical entertainment, sporting events, and, of course, fireworks.

CONTACTS:
Owensboro-Daviess County Convention & Visitors Bureau
215 E. Second St.
Owensboro, KY 42303
800-489-1131 or 270-926-1100; fax: 270-926-1161
www.visitowensboro.com

♦ 2651 ♦ Summer Solstice
June 21-22 (Northern Hemisphere); December 21-22 (Southern Hemisphere)

There are times during the year, respectively in each hemisphere, when the sun is at its furthest point from the equator. It reaches its northernmost point around June 21, which is the longest day of the year for those living north of the equator,

and its southernmost point around December 22, which is the longest day for those living in the Southern Hemisphere. The summer solstice marks the first day of the summer season—the word *solstice* is from the Latin word, *solstitium*, meaning "sun-stopping," since the point at which the sun appears to rise and set stops and reverses direction after this day.

Although it was very common to celebrate the summer solstice in ancient times, modern American observations are comparatively rare. But there are a number of solstice observances held by New Age and Neopagan groups throughout the United States.

See also CAPAC RAYMI; DOAN NGU; DRUIDS' SUMMER SOLSTICE CEREMONY; MIDNIGHT SUN FESTIVAL; MIDSUMMER DAY; YSYAKH

SOURCES:
AmerBkDays-2000, p. 462
BkFest-1937, p. 136
DictDays-1988, pp. 69, 114
DictFolkMyth-1984, p. 1032
FestSaintDays-1915, p. 4
FestWestEur-1958, p. 68

♦ 2652 ♦ Sun Fun Festival
First week in June

Sun Fun Festival is a beach festival at Myrtle Beach, S.C., to celebrate the state's Grand Strand, a 60-mile stretch of white-sand ocean beach. Myrtle Beach is the central city on the strand and so the fitting place for this five-day celebration that includes an air show, beauty pageants, beach games, music and dance performances, and a sandcastle-building contest. The record for the world's longest sandcastle was set here in 1990—the castle measured 10½ miles long. As many as 200,000 people attend.

CONTACTS:
Myrtle Beach Area Chamber of Commerce
1200 N. Oak St.
P.O. Box 2115
Myrtle Beach, SC 29578
800-356-3016 or 843-626-7444; fax: 843-448-3010
www.myrtlebeachinfo.com

SOURCES:
GdUSFest-1984, p. 171

♦ 2653 ♦ Sun Pageant Day
January-March

It is not uncommon for towns in the northern part of Norway to observe **Solday**, or **Sun Day**, when the sun reappears at the end of January or in early February. In Narvik, Nordland County, for example, Sun Pageant Day is celebrated in early February.

The sun's reappearance is particularly welcome for the people of Rjukan, Telemark County, which is nestled so deeply in a narrow valley that the sun doesn't shine there from early October to mid-March.

Although the date of the Sun Pageant in Rjukan varies from year to year, it always entails weeks of preparation. The town square is decorated with tall ice columns topped by flaming torches. At one end there is a throne on a raised wooden platform for the "Prince of the Sun," who leads a procession of costumed figures into the square and officially begins the celebration. The eating, singing, folk dancing, and fireworks continue for most of the day and night.

CONTACTS:
Telemark Tourist Information Office
P.O. Box 3133
Handelstorget
Skien, N-3707 Norway
47-3590-0030; fax: 47-3590-0021

SOURCES:
AnnivHol-2000, p. 24
BkHolWrld-1986, Jan 31

♦ 2654 ♦ Sun Yat-sen, Birthday of
November 12

Sun Yat-sen (1866-1925) was the leader of the Chinese Nationalist Party (Kuomintang). He served as the first provisional president of the Republic of China (1911-12) and later as its de facto ruler (1923-25). Because he possessed an exceptionally broad knowledge of the West and developed a grand plan for China's industrialization, he is known as "the father of modern China."

Sun Yat-sen's birthday is a holiday in Taiwan. The anniversary of his death, March 12, is observed as Arbor Day in Taiwan.

See also DOUBLE TENTH DAY

CONTACTS:
Taiwan Government Information Office
4201 Wisconsin Ave. N.W.
Washington, D.C. 20016
202-895-1853; fax: 202-362-6144
www.gio.gov.tw

SOURCES:
AnnivHol-2000, p. 190

♦ 2655 ♦ Sundance Film Festival
Ten days in mid-January

Originally held in Salt Lake City and known as the United States Film Festival, since 1984 the Sundance Film Festival has been organized by the Sundance Institute, founded by actor and director Robert Redford. It is an internationally recognized showcase for independent films, many of which would not ordinarily be seen by distributors and studios. Although most are American, Canadian and other foreign films are also screened during the 10-day festival, held in Park City, Utah, every January. The highlight of the festival is the American Independent Dramatic and Documentary Competition, where new American independent films are given their premieres. Judges for the competition have included well-known directors, screenwriters, and film critics.

Many emerging independent filmmakers now look to the Sundance Film Festival as their first opportunity to present their films before an audience. Filmgoers and the entertainment industry look to the Festival for the discovery of new talent and as a champion of films that challenge audiences and expand the boundaries of the art of filmmaking.

CONTACTS:
Sundance Institute
1825 Three Kings Dr.
P.O. Box 684429
Park City, UT 84060
435-658-3456; fax: 435-658-3457
www.sundance.org

♦ 2656 ♦ Sunday of Orthodoxy
First Sunday of Lent in the Christian Orthodox calendar

The first Sunday of Lent in the Christian Orthodox church commemorates the victory in the eighth century of the Orthodox over the iconoclasts, who denounced the use of icons and destroyed them. On this day, worshippers hear readings from the Syndicon, a text that declares the suitability of using icons in prayer and worship both public and private.

See also SUNDAY OF ST. GREGORY PALAMAS, SUNDAY OF THE HOLY CROSS, and SUNDAY OF ST. JOHN CLIMACOS

CONTACTS:
Orthodox Church in America
P.O. Box 675
Syosset, NY 11791-0675
516-922-0550; fax: 516-922-0954
www.oca.org

♦ 2657 ♦ Sunday of St. Gregory Palamas
Second Sunday of Lent in the Christian Orthodox calendar

The Christian Orthodox church dedicates the second Sunday in Lent to St. Gregory Palamas, who was born in Constatinople around 1296 C.E. Along with several members of his family, he entered a monastery on Mt. Athos after the death of his father. Gregory believed that, although God ultimately is unknowable, humanity can experience God's power through the Christian sacraments and mystical experience, both of which are possible only through the Incarnation of Christ. Gregory believed that a dedicated focus on the son of God can open believers' hearts and minds to God's work in their own lives.

See also SUNDAY OF ORTHODOXY; SUNDAY OF THE HOLY CROSS; and SUNDAY OF ST. JOHN CLIMACOS

CONTACTS:
Orthodox Church in America
P.O. Box 675
Syosset, NY 11791-0675
516-922-0550; fax: 516-922-0954
www.oca.org

♦ 2658 ♦ **Sunday of St. John Climacos**
Fourth Sunday in Lent in the Orthodox Christian calendar

Orthodox Christians dedicate the fourth Sunday of Lent to St. John Climacos, born in Syria in 525 C.E. Although surnamed Scholasticas, St. John often is called "Climacos," meaning "of the ladder." This refers to his most important holy writing, The Ladder of Divine Ascent, which details in 30 parts, or steps, all the Christian virtues. Employing many parables and historical touches drawn from monastic life, it is considered by many to be a cornerstone of literature of spiritual struggle and growth.

St. John was well educated, but chose to abandon scholarship for spirituality. John went to Mt. Sinai, which was known for its holy monks, to find a teacher. Under the guidance of a monk named Martyrius, he practiced Christian virtues. After his mentor's death, John retreated into isolation for 20 years, where he studied the lives of the saints and became one of the most learned men of the Church. At age 70, John was persuaded to become leader of a group of monks. His guidance was so effective and renowned that the pope, St. Gregory the Great, gave him a large sum of money for the hospital of Sinai, where many pilgrims stayed. After only four years in the leadership position, John returned to his hermit's life of spiritual contemplation.

See also SUNDAY OF ORTHODOXY; SUNDAY OF ST. GREGORY PALAMAS; and SUNDAY OF THE HOLY CROSS

CONTACTS:
Orthodox Church in America
P.O. Box 675
Syosset, NY 11791
516-922-0550; fax: 516-922-0954
www.oca.org

♦ 2659 ♦ **Sunday of St. Mary of Egypt**
Fifth Sunday of Great Lent under the Orthodox moveable cycle, and also on April 1 under the fixed Orthodox cycle

The Sunday of St. Mary of Egypt is celebrated by Orthodox Christians on the fifth Sunday of Great Lent and also on April 1. St. Mary was a sinful, lustful woman who repented and became devout. She is seen as the least worthy person, but through God's mercy she became a treasure chosen by God. Among stories told about St. Mary, there is a tale of the time she attempted to enter a church in Jerusalem, but was driven back by an unseen force, although her companions entered without delay. This prompted Mary to open her heart and to pray to the mother of Jesus, the Virgin Mary. After she begged forgiveness, she again attempted to enter the holy place, and found that the same sort of force that previously had prevented her entry now propelled her forward. Mary of Egypt is also said to have retired to the desert to live as a hermit, having received a divine message to do so. Not long before she died, she encountered St. Zosimas of Palestine, a venerable monk who gave her a mantle to wear and who related her

story to the faithful. St. Mary of Egypt is revered as a patron saint of penitent women.

On the fifth Sunday of Great Lent, St. Mary of Egypt is the subject of sermons during the Divine Liturgy. On this day, Orthodox priests typically bless dried fruit after the services.

CONTACTS:
Orthodox Church in America
P.O. Box 675
Syosset, NY 11791
516-922-0550; fax: 516-922-0954
www.oca.org

SOURCES:
RelHolCal-2004, p. 119

♦ 2660 ♦ **Sunday of the Holy Cross**
Third Sunday of Lent under the Christian Orthodox calendar

On the third Sunday of Lent in the Orthodox Christian faith, believers are exhorted to contemplate the cross upon which Christ was crucified. It is day of extensive fasting and deep prayer. Meditation on the Holy Cross calls upon believers to consider their own mortality, but more importantly, to consider Christ in his passion and subsequent resurrection.

See also SUNDAY OF ORTHODOXY; SUNDAY OF ST. GREGORY PALAMAS; and SUNDAY OF ST. JOHN CLIMACOS

CONTACTS:
Orthodox Church in America
P.O. Box 675
Syosset, NY 11791
516-922-0550; fax: 516-922-0954
www.oca.org

♦ 2661 ♦ **Sunday School Day**
First Sunday in May

In the Polynesian kingdom of Tonga, a group of islands whose inhabitants are primarily Methodist, the first Sunday in May is known as **Faka Me**, or Sunday School Day. The children rise early and bathe in the sea, after which they put on the new clothes that their mothers have made: *valas*, or kilts, for the boys and new dresses for the girls. Then they all go to church, where the youngest children sing a hymn or recite a verse of scripture in front of the congregation and the older children present biblical dramas.

At the feast that always follows a church service, the children sit on mats spread on the ground. A variety of Polynesian specialties—including roast pig, lobster, chicken, and fish steamed in coconut milk, and potato-like vegetables called *ufi*—are served to the children by the adults on long trays made of woven coconut fronds known as *volas*. The parents stand behind their children and fan them to keep them cool as they eat.

Sunday School Day is observed in various ways by Protestant children in other countries as well.

See also WHITE SUNDAY

SOURCES:
FolkWrldHol-1999, p. 311

♦ 2662 ♦ **Sundiata, Festival**
Third weekend in February

Held each year since 1981, the Festival Sundiata is a celebration of African-American heritage, culture, arts, and history held at Seattle Center in Seattle, Wash., during the third weekend of February. Admission to the festival is free, and events are spread over four days, from Thursday through the Monday holiday celebrating WASHINGTON'S BIRTHDAY. Festival Sundiata draws approximately 50,000 participants from the Pacific Northwest.

The fair is named in honor of Sundiata Keita, a historic king of the Mali Empire in West Africa, whose 13th-century reign is remembered as a time of great cultural and economic achievement. Organized by the Sundiata African American Cultural Association, the festival emphasizes entertainment, art, and education. Activities include music, percussion, and dance performances, lectures, storytelling, cooking demonstrations, and interactive craft exhibits, such as mask making. Festival Sundiata also features an art exhibition showcasing black artists in various media, including painting, sculpture, textiles, photography, and multimedia, which remains open to the public during the week following the festival.

CONTACTS:
Sundiata African American Cultural Association
P.O. Box 24723
Seattle, WA 98124
206-329-8086
www.festivalsundiata.org

SOURCES:
AAH-2007, p. 153

♦ 2663 ♦ **Super Bowl Sunday**
Usually last Sunday in January

The day of the championship game of the National Football League, which marks the culmination of the American professional football season. The game is played at a preselected site, always either a warm-weather city or one with a covered stadium. The contestants are the winners from each of the league's two divisions, the American Football Conference and the National Football Conference.

The first game was played on Jan. 15, 1967, in the Los Angeles Coliseum; the Green Bay Packers beat the Kansas City Chiefs by a score of 35-10. Since then, the games have been identified by Roman numerals (e.g., Super Bowl II in 1968), and, in keeping with this pretension, are surrounded by hoopla reminiscent of Roman imperial excess. Fans vie for Super Bowl tickets, and corporations woo clients with lavish Super Bowl trips.

Nationwide, the day is celebrated with at-home parties to watch the game on television, and many, many people watch: about 40 million viewers in the U.S. out of about 800 million around the world tune in to the Super Bowl. At sports bars, fans gather to watch wall-sized television screens, drink beer, and cheer.

CONTACTS:
National Football League
280 Park Ave.
New York, NY 10017
212-450-2000; fax: 212-681-7599
www.nfl.com

SOURCES:
HolSymbols-2009, p. 923

♦ 2664 ♦ **Superman Celebration**
June

Since 1978 the town of Metropolis, Ill., celebrates the popular D.C. Comics hero Superman with an annual event. According to his comic book adventures, Superman lives in the city of "Metropolis," which is usually taken to be New York. But Metropolis, Illinois, argues otherwise and celebrates the character as a hometown boy. A 15-foot bronze statue of the character stands in the town's Superman Square.

The four-day Superman Celebration features appearances by artists and writers who create the Superman comic books and actors from various television series, including the 1950s Superman series and the more recent "Smallville" series, which chronicles the adventures of Superman as a boy. An outdoor film festival includes documentaries about the superhero and screenings of his movies and television programs. In addition, a comics art gallery, a Jeopardy-style quiz game featuring Superman trivia questions, a Superdog contest, a superhero parade, and live music round out the festivities. The town's Super Museum, housing the world's largest collection of Superman-related items, hosts a memorabilia auction and dinner.

CONTACTS:
Superman Celebration
800-949-5740
www.supermancelebration.net

Super Museum
517 Market St.
Metropolis, IL 62960
618-524-5518
supermuseum.weebly.com

♦ 2665 ♦ **Suriname Independence Day**
November 25

Suriname had been under Dutch control for more than 200 years when it gained independence on this day in 1975, which is observed as a national holiday.

CONTACTS:
Embassy of the Republic of Suriname
4301 Connecticut Ave. N.W., Ste. 460
Washington, D.C. 20008
202-244-7488; fax: 202-244-5878
www.surinameembassy.org

SOURCES:
AnnivHol-2000, p. 196

♦ 2666 ♦ Surya Sashti
*October-November; sixth day of the waxing half
of the Hindu month of Kartika*

The observance of Surya Sashti includes a three-day fast for married Hindu women with children. They must abstain even from drinking water, and yet they must make offerings of food and water as they worship Surya, the sun god, and keep an all-night vigil.

On the following day, women bathe before sunrise, worship the rising sun, and break their fast. Brahmans, who are members of the highest Hindu class, are fed and given gifts on this day. Hindu women believe that by keeping the fast and observing the festival's other rules, they will be guaranteed good health, longevity, and the happiness of their children and husbands.

SOURCES:
DictHindu-1977, p. 291
RelHolCal-2004, p. 178

♦ 2667 ♦ Susuharai (Soot Sweeping)
December 13

In Japan, many people choose to give their houses a thorough cleaning at year's end. Worn or broken furniture and utensils and items that have been lost are replaced. New *tatami* mats, which are the thick straw mats on which people sit and sleep, are brought in, and damage to the paper sliding doors in traditional Japanese houses is repaired. In some areas, it is customary to tie pounded rice cakes (*mochi-bana*, "rice-cake flowers") to the branches of willow trees as an offering to the gods. Friends and co-workers may also throw "year-end forgetting parties" known as *bonen-kai*.

SOURCES:
JapanFest-1965, p. 208

♦ 2668 ♦ Svenskarnas Dag
Fourth Sunday in June

One of the largest festivals in the United States celebrating the traditions of a specific ethnic group, Svenskarnas Dag honors the Swedish heritage of the people of Minneapolis, Minnesota, and the longest day of the year. When the festival first started in 1934 it was observed in August, but in 1941 the day was changed to the fourth Sunday in June so that it would coincide with midsummer observances in Sweden (*see* MIDSUMMER DAY).

Held in Minnehaha Park in Minneapolis, the festival includes a band concert, Swedish folk dancing, choral group performances, and the crowning of a Midsummer Queen. A national celebrity of Swedish descent is often asked to officiate at this one-day event, which attracts more than 100,000 visitors each year.

CONTACTS:
Svenskarnas Dag Committee
P.O. Box 23469
Richfield, MN 55423
612-825-8808
www.svenskarnasdag.com

SOURCES:
GdUSFest-1984, p. 97

♦ 2669 ♦ Svetitskhovloba
July 13 and October 14

Built in the 11th century, the Svetitskhoveli Cathedral is located in the historical town of Mtskheta in Georgia. It is one of the principal worship sites of the Georgian Orthodox faith and the place where many local monarchs have been crowned and laid to rest. It has also inspired a major Georgian Orthodox holiday, Svetitskhovloba, which is celebrated two days of the year.

Svetitskhovloba pays homage to this cathedral, whose name means "Life Giving Pillar," as well as to the relic that it is believed to hold: the cloak of Christ, or as believers call it, the "Tunic of God." During the holiday, Christians gather for collective prayer in the cathedral and to remember the Twelve Apostles. Then, for the day's main ceremony, pilgrims from Georgia and other nearby countries congregate for a mass baptism at the junction of the Aragvi and Kura rivers. Children as well as adults are baptized.

The first observance of the year, on July 13, arrives the day after the Georgian celebration of STS. PETER AND PAUL DAY. The second observance, on October 14, is also known as **Mtskhetoba** (Day of Mtskheta).

CONTACTS:
Patriarchate of Georgia
#1 Erekle II's Sq.
Tbilisi, Georgia

Republic of Georgia Embassy
1615 New Hampshire Ave. N.W., Ste. 300
Washington, DC 20009
202-387-2390; fax: 202-393-4537

♦ 2670 ♦ Swallow, Procession of the
March 1

The Procession of the Swallow takes place in Greece on March 1 as a celebration of the arrival of spring. Children go from house to house in pairs, carrying a rod from which a basket full of ivy leaves is hung. At the end of the rod is an effigy of a bird made of wood with tiny bells around its neck. This is the "swallow," the traditional harbinger of spring.

As they proceed through the village, the children sing "swallow songs" that go back more than 2,000 years. The woman of the house takes a few ivy leaves from the basket and places them in her hen's nest in the hope that they will encourage the hen to produce more eggs. The children receive a few eggs in return, and they move on to the next house. The ivy, which is green all year round, is symbolic of growth and fertility, and it is believed to have the power to bring good health to hens and other animals.

SOURCES:
BkFestHolWrld-1970, p. 71
DictFolkMyth-1984, p. 1091

◆ 2671 ◆ Swallows of San Juan Capistrano
March 19 and October 23

San Juan Capistrano was the name of a mission built on the Pacific Coast by Father Junipero Serra in 1777. Even after the buildings collapsed in an earthquake 35 years later, thousands of swallows continued to nest in the ruins of the church. Local people noticed that the swallows tended to fly south on October 23, the death anniversary of St. John of Capistrano, and returned on March 19, ST. JOSEPH'S DAY.

Beginning in 1940, the sentimental love song "When the Swallows Come Back to Capistrano" (words and music by Leon René) was recorded by a variety of artists. This brought attention to the event and media attention further made it known. A Swallow Festival is held each year at the mission in San Juan Capistrano near Los Angeles, California, around the time of the birds' return. Also known as the **Fiesta de las Golondrinas**, it features what is billed as the largest non-motorized parade in the country. In addition to the Swallow Festival, the Mission hosts various cultural and historic events throughout the year.

CONTACTS:
Mission San Juan Capistrano
26801 Ortega Hwy.
San Juan Capistrano, CA 92675
949-234-1300; fax: 949-481-9895
www.missionsjc.com

SOURCES:
AnnivHol-2000, pp. 47, 177
BkHolWrld-1986, Oct 23
DictDays-1988, p. 116
FolkAmerHol-1999, p. 146

◆ 2672 ◆ Swan Upping
Third week in July

The tradition of marking newborn swans goes back six centuries, to a time when most of the swans on England's public waters were owned by the queen. Later the members of two livery companies (trade guilds), the Company of Dyers and the Company of Vintners, were given the right to keep swans on the Thames River between London and Henley.

Every year since 1363, the Queen's swan master and the swan wardens of the two livery companies row up the Thames, starting at Blackfriars in the center of London and continuing upstream to Abingdon, and "up" all the swan families into the boats, where they are marked with identification numbers. There are very specific rules governing how ownership is decided, and the six boats, each flying a large silk flag as they row up the river, form a procession that has changed little over the centuries.

CONTACTS:
The British Monarchy Official Web Site
Buckingham Palace
London, SW1A 1AA United Kingdom
44-20-7930-4832
www.royal.gov.uk

SOURCES:
BkHolWrld-1986, Jul 21
GdWrldFest-1985, p. 95

◆ 2673 ◆ Swaziland Independence Day
September 6

Independence Day is a national holiday in Swaziland. On this day in 1968, Swaziland became self-governing after having been ruled by Britain since 1903. This national holiday was also known as **Somhlolo Day** or **Sobhuza Day**, named after Sobhuza II (1899-1982), king of Swaziland from 1921 until his death. In 1973, he disregarded the constitution passed upon independence and assumed supreme power.

CONTACTS:
The Embassy of the Kingdom of Swaziland
1712 New Hampshire Ave. N.W.
Washington, D.C. 20009
202-234-5002; fax: 202-234-8254
www.swazilandembassyus.com

SOURCES:
AnnivHol-2000, p. 150

◆ 2674 ◆ Swedish Flag Day
June 6

Constitution and Flag Day commemorates the adoption of the Swedish constitution on June 6, 1809, and the ascension of Gustavus I to the throne on June 6, 1523. It is observed throughout Sweden with patriotic meetings, parades, and the raising of flags. In Stockholm the main celebration takes place at the Stadium, where the Swedish national anthem is sung by a chorus of several thousand voices, and King Carl XVI Gustav awards flags to various schools, sports clubs, and other organizations. In the evening the celebration continues at Skansen, the oldest open-air museum in Europe.

CONTACTS:
Swedish Institute
Sverigehuset
Hamngatan/Kungstradgarden, P.O. Box 7434
Stockholm, SE-103 91 Sweden
46-8-453-7800; fax: 46-8-20-7248
www.si.se

◆ 2675 ◆ Swedish Homage Festival
Second weekend in October in odd-numbered years

Svensk Hyllningsfest, or the Swedish Homage Festival, is a biennial event held for three days during the second week in October in Lindsborg, Kansas. It honors the Swedish pioneers who first settled the area and celebrates the heritage of Lindsborg's Swedish-American population. More than

50,000 people attend the festival, which started in 1941 and is now held only in odd-numbered years.

Events include a parade; Swedish folk dancing, singing, and band music; Swedish arts and crafts displays; and a huge *smörgasbord,* or hot and cold buffet.

CONTACTS:
Svensk Hyllningsfest
P.O. Box 323
Lindsborg, KS 67456
www.svenskhyllningsfest.org

SOURCES:
GdUSFest-1984, p. 61

♦ 2676 ♦ **Sweetest Day**
Third Saturday in October

More than 40 years ago, a man from Cleveland came up with the idea of showing the city's orphans and shut-ins that they hadn't been forgotten by distributing small gifts to them on a Saturday in October. Over the years, other Clevelanders took up the idea of spreading cheer not only to the underprivileged but to everyone. The celebration of what came to be called Sweetest Day soon spread to Detroit and other American cities.

This holiday is unusual in that it is not based on any one group's religious beliefs or on a family relationship. Because it falls midway between FATHER'S DAY and CHRISTMAS, however, it has come to be regarded as a merchandising opportunity. Although it is still supposed to be an occasion to remember others with a kind act, a word of encouragement, or a long-overdue letter, local merchants in cities where Sweetest Day is observed usually get together and promote the day as a time to purchase gifts.

SOURCES:
AnnivHol-2000, p. 182
HolSymbols-2009, p. 927

♦ 2677 ♦ **Sweetwater Rattlesnake Round-Up**
Second weekend in March

Billed "The World's Largest Rattlesnake Round-Up," this is one of several rattlesnake round-ups in Texas. It was started in 1958 by ranchers in Sweetwater to thin out the snakes plaguing them and their livestock, and now the average annual catch is 12,000 pounds of Western Diamondback Rattlesnake. Some 30,000 spectators watch the goings-on.

The round-up is sponsored by the Sweetwater Jaycees, who stress the focus on safety (hunters are governed by state hunting laws) and the benefits of the round-up. The round-up supports various Jaycee charitable causes.

The weekend events include snake-handling demonstrations and the awarding of prizes for the most pounds and the biggest snake. There are also a Miss Snake Charmer Queen Contest, a parade, rattlesnake dances with country bands, and a rattlesnake meat-eating contest. A cook shack fries and serves more than 4,000 pounds of rattlesnake meat each year.

Other Texas rattlesnake round-ups are held from February through April in Cleburne, Brownwood, Big Spring, San Angelo, Jacksboro, Gainesville, and Freer. A number of other southern states also have rattlesnake round-ups.

In recent years, state departments of natural resources and conservation organizations have warned of the health risks of eating rattlesnakes caught at round-ups. In addition, the Humane Society has condemned the cruelty to snakes during these events and argues that rattlesnakes actually present relatively little danger to livestock—and that holding roundups increases the chances that humans will be bitten.

CONTACTS:
Sweetwater Chamber of Commerce
810 E. Broadway
Sweetwater, TX 79556
800-658-6757 or 325-235-5488
www.sweetwatertexas.org

Humane Society of the United States, Department of
    Philanthropy
2100 L St. N.W.
Washington, DC 20037
800-808-7858 or 301-258-3130; fax: 301-548-7700
www.hsus.org

SOURCES:
FolkAmerHol-1999, p. 122

♦ 2678 ♦ **Swiss National Day**
August 1

A nationwide celebration of the Swiss Confederation, observed with torchlight processions, fireworks, shooting contests, and folkloric events. The day commemorates the occasion in 1291 when representatives of the three original cantons of Schwyz, Uri, and Unterwalden met on the Rutli meadow and swore an oath of alliance and mutual defense to lay the foundations of the Confederation.

In 1991, yearlong 700th-anniversary festivities set different themes for the different language areas. A celebration of the Federal Pact of 1291 was the theme for the German-speaking region; a Four Cultures Festival, demonstrating cultural diversity, for the French-speaking region; and a Festival of Solidarity, illustrating Switzerland's role in the international community, in the Romansh- and Italian-speaking areas.

CONTACTS:
Embassy of Switzerland
2900 Cathedral Ave. N.W.
Washington, D.C. 20008
202-745-7900; fax: 202-387-2564
www.swissemb.org

SOURCES:
AnnivHol-2000, p. 128
FestWestEur-1958, p. 224
NatlHolWrld-1968, p. 132

♦ 2679 ♦ **Syria Martyrs' Day**
May 6

In 1916, a meeting of Arab intellectuals in Paris called for the liberation of all Arab countries from Turkish rule. In response, Turkish Sultan Abdul Hamid appointed Jamal Pasha the governor of Damascus. Jamal Pasha ordered mass arrests of dissidents. When a group of Syrian nationalists refused to renounce their views, they were hanged in al-Murjeh square in Damascus on May 6, 1916. The executions sparked Arab resistance throughout the Ottoman Empire. An Arab army led by Sharif Hussein of Mecca soon defeated the Turks. The Ottoman Empire collapsed at the end of World War I.

To commemorate the heroic event, the Syrian president lays a wreath at the martyrs' monument at Qasyoun Mountain. The president hosts a banquet in the evening for the children of the Syrian martyrs. The day is celebrated with fireworks, parades, military air shows, and speeches.

CONTACTS:
Embassy of the Syrian Arab Republic in the USA
2215 Wyoming Ave. N.W.
Washington, D.C. 20008
202-232-6313
www.syrianembassy.us

♦ 2680 ♦ **Syria National Day**
April 17

This national holiday commemorates the withdrawal of French troops on this day in 1946, when Syria proclaimed its independence after more than 20 years of French occupation. It is also known as **Independence Day** and **Evacuation Day**.

CONTACTS:
Embassy of Syria
2215 Wyoming Ave. N.W.
Washington, D.C. 20008
202-232-6313; fax: 202-234-9548
www.syrianembassy.us

SOURCES:
AnnivHol-2000, p. 63
NatlHolWrld-1968, p. 48

♦ 2681 ♦ **Syttende Mai Fest**
Weekend nearest May 17

Norway Constitution Day is celebrated each year by descendants of Norwegian immigrants who first settled in Spring Grove, Minnesota. The town, incorporated in 1889, was the first Norse settlement in Minnesota, and the Norwegian language can still be heard in the town's streets and cafes. The Syttende Mai Fest offers ethnic foods, folk music and costumes, a show of traditional Norwegian arts and crafts, and a grand parade led by the "King of Trolls." Young children dressed as creatures known as *Nisse* roam the streets during the festival, wearing green caps and playing tricks on people. Unlike the trolls, who thrive on darkness and are known for making things go wrong, the Nisse bring luck and help out

with household tasks. During the festival, the store windows often feature displays with trolls or Nisse peeking out.

Other Minnesota towns celebrating Syttende Mai with special festivities include Hendricks, Milan, Wahkon, and Willmar. Syttende Mai is celebrated by Norwegian communities in other states as well. The celebration in Stoughton, Wisconsin, takes place on the weekend nearest May 17 and features folk dancing, a Norwegian smorgasbord, and demonstrations of *rosemaling* (painted or carved floral designs) and *hardanger* (a form of pulled thread embroidery).

CONTACTS:
City of Spring Grove
118 1st Ave. N.W.
Spring Grove, MN 55974
507-498-5221
www.springgrovemn.com

Stoughton Chamber of Commerce
532 E. Main St.
Stoughton, WI 53589
888-873-7912 or 608-873-7912; fax: 608-873-7743
www.stoughtonwi.com

♦ 2682 ♦ **Szüret**
Late October

Since wine is the national drink of the Hungarian people, the Szüret, or **Grape Gathering**, is a time for great celebration. In fact, many peasant marriages take place after this yearly festival. As they have done since ancient times, the grape gatherers make an enormous "bouquet" out of grapes and two men carry it on a pole in procession to the vineyard owner's home, accompanied by musicians, clowns, and young girls dressed in white wearing flower wreaths on their heads. When they reach their destination, they hang the cluster of grapes from the ceiling and accept the vineyard owner's invitation to join in the feasting and dancing.

A traditional game known as "robber" is often played during the festival, either as the grapes are being gathered or during the dancing that takes place later. While several men guard the bouquet of grapes, the others try to steal the fruit off the vines. Anyone who gets caught is dragged before a mock judge and forced to pay a penalty—usually by performing a song, a solo dance, or a pantomime while his companions make fun of him.

CONTACTS:
Hungarian National Tourist Office
350 Fifth Ave., Ste. 7107
New York, NY 10118
212-695-1221; fax: 212-695-0809
www.gotohungary.com

SOURCES:
BkFest-1937, p. 173
FolkWrldHol-1999, p. 530

T

♦ 2683 ♦ Ta Mo's Day
Fifth day of 10th lunar month

Ta Mo (or Bodhidharma) was a sixth-century Indian monk who founded the Ch'an school of Buddhism in China, known in Japan as Zen Buddhism. Information about his historical existence is quite sketchy. But he is said to have believed that the Law of Buddha could only be understood through contemplation, without the aid of books or rituals. According to legend, he spent nine years meditating in front of a cave wall, during which time his legs fell off. The Japanese, to whom he is known as DARUMA, have a legless doll, constructed in such a way that no matter how it is placed on the ground, it always returns to a sitting position.

There is another legend that Ta Mo cut off his eyelids in a fit of anger after falling asleep during meditation. When they fell to the ground, his eyelids took root and grew up as the first tea plant. This legend is the basis for the practice among Zen monks of drinking tea to stay awake during meditation. Members of the Ch'an (or Zen) sect of Buddhism observe the fifth day of the 10th month as Ta Mo's Day. People in Japan customarily give Daruma dolls to those who have worked hard to achieve a goal.

SOURCES:
DictFolkMyth-1984, p. 1102
DictWrldRel-1989, p. 111
EncyRel-1987, vol. 2, p. 263
RelHolCal-2004, p. 221

♦ 2684 ♦ Ta'anit Esther (Fast of Esther)
Between February 13 and March 13; Adar 13

The **Fast of Esther** commemorates the three days that Queen Esther fasted before petitioning her husband, King Ahasuerus (Xerxes I) of Persia, to spare the Jews of her country from destruction by Haman, the Persian prime minister, in the sixth century B.C.E. (*See* PURIM.)

Ordinarily observed on the 13th day of the Jewish month of Adar, Ta'anit Esther is observed on the preceding Thursday (Adar 11) when Adar 13 falls on the Sabbath.

This date was originally a minor festival commemorating Judah Maccabee's defeat of the Syrian general Nicanor, known as the "Day of Nicanor." In time it gave way to the present Fast of Esther.

CONTACTS:
Union of Orthodox Jewish Congregations of America
11 Broadway
New York, NY 10004
212-563-4000; fax: 212-564-9058
www.ou.org

SOURCES:
AnnivHol-2000, p. 229

♦ 2685 ♦ Tabuleiros Festival (Festa dos Tabuleiros)
Four days in mid-July every third year

The town of Tomar in Portugal has been celebrating the Tabuleiros ("headdresses") Festival for 600 years as a way of expressing gratitude for the harvest and charity for the poor. The highlight of the festival is the procession through town of hundreds of girls in traditional headdresses selected from Tomar and the surrounding communities.

The foundation of the headdress, which weighs about 33 pounds and must be at least as tall as the girl who carries it, is a round basket covered with a linen cloth. An elaborate framework of bamboo sticks and wires holds up 30 small loaves of bread arranged in five rows. Flowers made of colored paper disguise the wires and the entire structure is topped with a white dove or Maltese cross. The priest blesses the bread, and the girls keep their tabuleiros for the entire year to ward off sickness. This is also a time for making donations to the poor and the afflicted.

CONTACTS:
Portuguese National Tourist Office
590 Fifth Ave., 4th Fl.
New York, NY 10036
800-767-8842 or 212-354-4403; fax: 212-764-6137
www.visitportugal.com

SOURCES:
BkHolWrld-1986, Jul 8
FestWestEur-1958, p. 171
IntlThFolk-1979, p. 313

♦ 2686 ♦ Taeborum (Daeboreum)
February; 15th day of the first lunar month

Taeborum marks the first full moon of the LUNAR NEW YEAR in Korea (*see* SOL) and is at least as important as that holiday. Many customs and games are traditional on this day, which is also sometimes called the Great Fifteenth. The Fifteenth, or Full Moon Day, marks the end of the New Year season in Korea and is regarded as the final opportunity to ensure good luck for the coming year. It is considered lucky on this day for people to routinely repeat their actions nine times—particularly children, who compete with each other to see how many "lucky nines" they can achieve before the day is over.

It is common to celebrate the Great Fifteenth with kite flying and kite fighting, which is done by covering the strings with glass dust and then crossing them so that they rub together as they fly. The string held by the more skillfully manipulated kite eventually cuts through the string of the less successful kite, sending it crashing to the ground.

Another popular sport on this day is the tug-of-war. In some areas, an entire town or county is divided into two opposing teams. It is widely believed that the winners will bring in a plentiful crop and will be protected from disease in the coming year.

See also BRIDGE WALKING; BURNING THE MOON HOUSE; SPIRIT BURYING; TORCH FIGHT

CONTACTS:
Korea Foundation
10-11F, Diplomatic Center Bldg., 2558 Nambusunhwanno,
   Seocho-gu
P.O. Box 227
Seoul, 137-863 South Korea
82-2-3463-5600; fax: 82-2-3463-6075
www.koreana.or.kr

SOURCES:
AnnCustKorea-1983, pp. 53, 69
FolkWrldHol-1999, p. 88

♦ 2687 ♦ Tagore (Rabindranath), Birthday of
May 7

This date commemorates the birth of Rabindranath Tagore (1861-1941), the great poet, philosopher, social reformer, dramatist, and musician of Calcutta, India. Born into a family of painters, writers, and musicians, Tagore possessed talents for all those creative professions. In 1913, he was the first non-European to win the NOBEL PRIZE for literature. The Tagore family has been important in India's cultural history from the 19th century and is especially revered in Calcutta. Rabindranath Tagore's birthday is celebrated with a festival of his poetry, plays, music, and dance dramas. There are discussions at schools and universities of his ideas on education and philosophy, and screenings of films based on Tagore's short stories and novels made by filmmaker and Calcutta native, Satyajit Ray.

CONTACTS:
India Tourist Office

1270 Avenue of the Americas, Ste. 1808, 18th Fl.
New York, NY 10020
800-953-9399 or 212-586-4901; fax: 212-582-3274
www.indiatouristoffice.org

Ministry of Tourism, Government of India
Rm. No 123, Transport Bhawan, No. 1, Parliament St.
New Delhi, Delhi 110 001 India
91-11-23715084
www.tourisminindia.com

SOURCES:
AnnivHol-2000, p. 78

♦ 2688 ♦ Taiiku-no-Hi
October 10

Taiiku-no-Hi, or **Health-Sports Day**, is a national legal holiday in Japan set aside to promote good physical and emotional health through athletic activity. Since 1966 it has been observed on the anniversary of the first day of the OLYMPIC GAMES held in Tokyo in 1964.

SOURCES:
AnnivHol-2000, p. 170

♦ 2689 ♦ Tailte Fair (Teltown Fair)
Mid-July to mid-August

Tailte was the foster mother of Lugh, an ancient Celtic god and patron of fairs. The Tailte (or Teltown) Fair, held in ancient Ireland for more than 2,000 years, was an early harvest festival in which the first fruits of the harvest were sacrificed to the spirit of Tailte, who was further honored by funeral games. Each chieftain brought his best athletes—runners, jumpers, spear throwers, and horsemen—as well as his harpists and poets and storytellers, who competed like the athletes for prizes of gold rings and jeweled ornaments. The Tailteann Games, as they were known, were last held in 1169, and the Irish have since revived them. The fair itself lasted until 1806.

See also LUGHNASADH

SOURCES:
BkFair-1939, p. 159

♦ 2690 ♦ Taiwan Armed Forces Day
September 3

Founded in 1955, Armed Forces Day in Taiwan honors that country's military and celebrates their victory over the Japanese in World War II. Called in Taiwan the War of Resistance, that struggle actually began before World War II when Japan invaded the Chinese mainland.

The day is marked by military parades featuring special units chosen for their precision and outstanding performance. A troop-cheering by the onlookers is also part of the celebration, as are educational activities covering the history of the war period and the role played by the Taiwanese military in defeating the enemy. A speech is delivered by the national defense minister in which he honors those soldiers who fought in the War of Resistance and their surviving families. The day is also marked by the members of the armed forces having a rare day off from work.

CONTACTS:
Taipei Economic and Cultural Representative Office in the United States
4201 Wisconsin Ave. N.W.
Washington, D.C. 20016
202-895-1850; fax: 202-362-6144
www.taiwanembassy.org/us/mp.asp?mp=12

♦ 2691 ♦ **Taiwan Peace Memorial Day**
February 28

Following the end of World War II, the island of Taiwan won independence from Japan, and the Chinese Nationalist government officially took over the island. On February 28, 1947, misunderstandings between the new government and the native residents led to an uprising that was brutally suppressed. A period known as the White Terror ensued, in which thousands of Taiwanese were killed or imprisoned. For years, the period was never discussed in public, and official textbooks did not mention it. But in 1995, President Lee Teng-hui made a formal apology for the incident. Since then, other steps have been taken to heal the wounds. The February 28 Incident Memorial Foundation was founded to compensate victims and their families and to restore the good names of those who were wrongly accused.

February 28 has been named Peace Memorial Day and is marked by memorial services for the victims, concerts, art exhibitions, and group runs. Taiwan's president attends a ceremony in which he rings a ceremonial bell, bows to the victims' families, and hands them a certificate acknowledging that they are guilty of no crime. The day is also referred to as "228 Memorial Day" in reference to the original date of the 28th day of the second month: 2/28.

CONTACTS:
Embassy, The Republic of China on Taiwan
4201 Wisconsin Ave. N.W.
Washington, D.C. 20016
202-895-1800; fax: 202-966-0825

♦ 2692 ♦ **Tajikistan Day of National Unity**
June 27

On June 27, 1997, a treaty was signed between Islamic rebels and the Russian-backed Tajikistan government, bringing to an end a bloody five-year-long civil war. The day is remembered as the Day of National Unity.

To mark the one-year anniversary of the treaty, 100 members of the rebel group United Tajik Opposition were officially sworn in as members of the Tajik Army. On the Day of National Unity in 2007, the Tajik parliament passed a law granting amnesty to all rebels who had fought against the government, provided they had not committed murder, rape, human or drug trafficking, or terrorism. Some 2,000 prison inmates were released under the new law. The 2007 com-

memoration also marked the opening of 11 new buildings in the city of Dushanbe.

CONTACTS:
Tajikistan Embassy in the U.S.
1005 New Hampshire Ave.
Washington, D.C. 20037
202-223-6090; fax: 202-223-6091
www.tjus.org

♦ 2693 ♦ **Tajikistan Independence Day**
September 9

On September 9, 1991, Tajikistan officially declared its independence from the distintegrating Soviet Union. Independence Day is celebrated with parades, solomn services, theatrical events and pageantry. July 22 is another national holiday, celebrating the Tajik language.

CONTACTS:
The Embassy of the Republic of Tajikistan
1005 New Hampshire Ave. N.W.
Washington, D.C. 20037
202-223-6090; fax: 202-223-6091
www.tjus.org

♦ 2694 ♦ **Takayama Matsuri**
April 14-15 and October 9-10

Held twice a year in Japan, in the spring and the autumn, the Takayama Festival is famous for its elaborately decorated *yatai*, festival floats. These were first used at Kyoto's GION MATSURI, and later appeared in other parts of the country. Twelve of these floats appear at the April festival, held at Takayama's Hié Shrine, and 11 participate in the October festival at the Sakuragaoka-hachimangu Shrine. They are so highly decorated—with beautiful fabrics, lacquered wood, and patterned metals—that they are often referred to as "Yomeimon in motion," a reference to the famous gate at the Toshogu Shrine in Nikko. Some yatai feature performances of *kabuki*, puppet plays, often performed by cleverly designed mechanical marionettes.

A highlight of the festival is the parade of metal gongs known as *tokeigaku*, which produce a unique kind of folk music. There is also a *Shishi-mai*, or Lion Dance, originally used by Japanese farmers to ward off wild boars and other animals that threatened their crops.

CONTACTS:
Japan National Tourist Organization
1 Rockefeller Pl., Ste. 1250
New York, NY 10020
212-757-5640; fax: 212-307-6754
www.jnto.go.jp

Hida Tourist Information Office
Showa-machi, 1-chome
Takayama, Gifu Prefecture 506-0053 Japan
81-5-7732-5328
www.hida.jp/english/index.htm

SOURCES:
IllFestJapan-1993, p. 38

◆ 2695 ◆ Take Our Daughters to Work Day
Fourth Thursday in April

Sponsored by the Ms. Foundation for Women since 1993, this is a day dedicated to girls between the ages of nine and 15, who are encouraged to go to work with their parents, grandparents, or other adults in their lives. The purpose is to support girls' development and to help them stay focused on their future during adolescence. Spending a day at work with an adult, it is hoped, will increase girls' interest in planning their own education and careers, and will inspire educators, employers, and parents to redress the inequalities in job opportunities for women.

CONTACTS:
Ms. Foundation for Women
120 Wall St. 33rd Fl.
New York, NY 10005
212-742-2300; fax: 212-742-1653
www.ms.foundation.org

◆ 2696 ◆ Také-no-Nobori
Sunday near July 15

The origins of this rain festival go back to 1504, a year in which there was no rain all summer in what is now the Nagano Prefecture of Japan. Villagers appealed to their god and were rewarded with three days of rain in a row. Thankful, they made an offering to the god of two especially fine pieces of cloth, sufficient to make two kimonos.

Today people in Uedo City continue this tradition each year on a Sunday near July 15. People trek up to the shrine on Mount Ogamidake and offer pieces of homemade cloth to the god.

CONTACTS:
City of Uedo, Convention Bureau
1-11-16, Ote
Ueda-shi, Nagano Prefecture 386-8601 Japan
81-2-6822-4100; fax: 81-2-6822-6023
www.city.ueda.nagano.jp/hp/English/index.html

SOURCES:
IllFestJapan-1993, p. 103
JapanFest-1965, p. 167

◆ 2697 ◆ Tako-Age (Kite Flying)
April, May, June

Kite-flying battles are a favorite sport in Japan, and numerous kite festivals take place in the spring. In the battles, the object is to cut down other kites by means of skillful maneuvering; broken glass embedded in the kite lines also helps.

The kite festivals of Nagasaki are held in April and May, with teams of as many as 20 people controlling colossal kites up to 25' x 30' in size.

In Hamamatsu in Shizuoka Prefecture, a kite festival is held on the beach May 3-5. It is thought to have originated in the mid-16th century when the lord of one of the fiefdoms celebrated the birth of a son by flying a giant kite. It is the biggest event now in the western region of the prefecture, with more than 1,000 kites sparring in the sky. Other festival events include parades of 50 floats in the evenings.

In Shirone in Niigata Prefecture, two teams on opposite banks of the Nakanokuchi River wage kite battles in mid-June. This festival supposedly dates back some 300 years when the people of one village accidentally crashed a huge kite onto a neighboring village.

CONTACTS:
Hamamatsu City
Tourism Information Center
165-16 Sunayama-cho, JR Hamamatsu Station
Hamamatsu, 430-0926 Japan
81-5-3452-1634; fax: 81-5-3413-5920
www.city.hamamatsu.shizuoka.jp/hamaEng/index.htm

Niigata Visitors and Convention Bureau
1-613-69 Hakusan-ur
Kaikan 2nd Fl., Chuo-ku
Niigata, 950-1101 Japan
81-2-5265-8000; fax: 81-2-5266-3357
www.nvcb.or.jp/en

Japan Kite Association
1-12-10 Nihonbashi
Chuoh-ku
Tokyo, 103-0027 Japan
81-3-3275-2704; fax: 81-3-3273-0575
www.tako.gr.jp/eng/index_e.html

SOURCES:
AnnivHol-2000, p. 56
GdWrldFest-1985, p. 122

◆ 2698 ◆ Tam Kung Festival
May; eighth day of fourth lunar month

A celebration of the birthday of the god Tam Kung is held at the Tam Kung Temple in Shau Kei Wan on Hong Kong Island. Like TIN HAU, Tam Kung is a popular deity among fisherfolk. He is a Taoist child-god, whose powers were apparent when he was only 12 years old. His greatest gift was controlling the weather, but he could also heal the sick and predict the future. Residents of the Shau Kei Wan area believe he saved many lives during an outbreak of cholera in 1967. His birthday is marked with a grand procession, Cantonese opera, and lion and dragon dances.

CONTACTS:
Hong Kong Tourism Board
115 E. 54th St., 2nd Fl.
New York, NY 10022
212-421-3382; fax: 212-421-8428
www.discoverhongkong.com

◆ 2699 ◆ Tammuz, Fast of the 17th of (Shivah Asar be-Tammuz)
Between June 17 and July 24; Tammuz 17

The **Fast of Tammuz** commemorates the breaching of the walls of Jerusalem in 586 B.C.E., when the Babylonians conquered Judah, destroyed the Temple, and carried most of the Jewish population off into slavery. But this destruction had a happy ending: after 70 years the people returned and rebuilt the Temple. Then the Roman army breached the walls of Jerusalem in the year 70 C.E., dooming both the city and its Temple for the second time. This time the destruction and the scattering of the people—known as the Diaspora—had a far more tragic finality. Jews remain scattered over the face of the earth to this day. Other sad events associated with this day are the shattering of the first Tablets of the Law by Moses, and the collapse of the sacrificial system caused by the Roman invasion in 70 C.E.

The Fast of Tammuz begins THREE WEEKS of mourning lasting until TISHA BE-AV.

See also ASARAH BE-TEVET

CONTACTS:
Union of Orthodox Jewish Congregations of America
11 Broadway
New York, NY 10004
212-563-4000; fax: 212-564-9058
www.ou.org

SOURCES:
DaysCustFaith-1957, p. 159
DictWrldRel-1989, p. 155
OxYear-1999, p. 728

♦ 2700 ♦ **Tanabata (Star Festival)**
July 7, August 6-8

This Japanese festival is based on a Chinese legend of parted lovers who are identified with two of the brightest stars in the night sky. In the legend, Vega, representing a weaver-princess, is permitted by the king to marry the simple cowherd, Altair. But after they marry, the princess neglects her weaving and the herdsman forgets his cows, so the king separates them, making them live on opposite sides of the River of Heaven, as the Milky Way is known in Japan. On the seventh day of the seventh month, the lovers are able to meet when a flock of magpies makes a bridge across the river. If it's rainy, the lovers have to wait another year.

The festival is observed throughout Japan, with people hanging colorful strips of paper on bamboo branches outside their homes. It is an especially colorful occasion in Sendai (Miyagi Prefecture), where it occurs a month later, on August 6-8. The whole city is decked out with paper streamers and works of origami, the Japanese art of paper folding.

See also CHILSEOG; SEVEN SISTERS FESTIVAL

CONTACTS:
Japan Information Network, Japan Center for Intercultural
  Communications
2-7-7 Hirakawacho
Chiyodaku
Tokyo, 102-0093 Japan
81-3-3263-5041; fax: 81-3-3230-4107
home.jcic.or.jp

Council for Sendai International Commercial Port Development
16-12, Honcho 2-chome
Aoba-ku
Sendai, 980-8414 Japan

81-2-2265-8181; fax: 81-2-2217-1551
www.sendaicci.or.jp

SOURCES:
AnnivHol-2000, p. 239
BkFest-1937, p. 199
BkHolWrld-1986, Jul 7
DictFolkMyth-1984, p. 540
FolkWrldHol-1999, p. 453

♦ 2701 ♦ **Tangata Manu (Birdman Ceremony)**
Spring

Sometime around the 14th century, different groups on Easter Island, also known as Rapanui, were at war with each other, perhaps over a lack of food caused by a mini ice age. Some scholars theorize that the islanders began the Tangata Manu, or *Manutara*, as a way of resolving their conflicts.

Each tribal chief would select a young man to compete with representatives from other tribes in an egg hunt. Each man swam to a nearby island in search of the first egg laid by a seabird known as a tern. This process could take as long as a month. The chief of the first one to swim back with the egg was called the "birdman" for the year.

Carvings of the Birdman—represented as a bird-headed man whose hand grasps an egg—can be found all over Easter Island.

CONTACTS:
Embassy of Chile
1732 Massachusetts Ave. N.W.
Washington, D.C. 20036
202-785-1746; fax: 202-887-5579
www.chile-usa.org

SOURCES:
FestWrld: Chile-1998, p. 12

♦ 2702 ♦ **Tanglewood Music Festival**
July-August

Tanglewood is a 210-acre estate donated in 1937 by Mrs. Gorham Brooks. Located in the Berkshire Mountains of western Massachusetts, it is the summer home of the Boston Symphony Orchestra. What was originally known as the Berkshire Festival started in 1936 and in 1940 became part of the Berkshire Music Center, now the Tanglewood Music Center, where advanced American and foreign musicians come to study and perform for nine weeks each summer.

The festival includes concerts by the Boston Symphony and the Berkshire Music Center Orchestra as well as chamber music, jazz, choral and vocal concerts, and music theater productions. In early August there is a Festival of Contemporary Music that focuses on new works, some of which have been specially commissioned for the festival.

The grounds at Tanglewood open about two hours prior to the concerts so people can picnic on the lawns. More than 350,000 people come to Tanglewood over the course of the festival each summer.

CONTACTS:
Boston Symphony Orchestra
297 W. St.
Boston, MA 01240
888-266-1200 or 413-637-1600; fax: 413-637-5227
www.bso.org

SOURCES:
GdUSFest-1984, p. 86
MusFestAmer-1990, p. 81
MusFestWrld-1963, p. 280

♦ 2703 ♦ Tango Festival
Late February-early March

Historians say tango evolved as a dance form in Buenos Aires, Argentina, toward the end of the 19th century. It is thus fitting that the city would host a festival devoted to the dance. Since 1999, the Tango Festival has invited aficionados to immerse themselves in the step routines of this romantic art form.

Dance performances are the centerpiece of the festival, which is popular among natives as well as tourists. Typically, on the last Friday of February a performance at *La Selección Nacional de Tango* will launch the festival; then, for the next nine days events are held at multiple locations, including concert halls, clubs, and *barrios.*

The festival does not restrict itself to dance performances, however. Past festivals have featured original musical pieces performed by musical troupes from neighboring countries as well as from Europe. There are also photo exhibits, classes, and a trade fair offering tango records, books, and clothing and accessories.

CONTACTS:
Tangodata
Teatro General San Martín
1530 Corrientes Ave.
8th Fl.
Buenos Aires Argentina
www.tangodata.gov.ar/ingles

♦ 2704 ♦ Tango-no-Sekku (Boys' Day Festival)
May 5

The Boys' Day Festival in Japan dates back to the Tokugawa period (1603-1867). For centuries, Japanese farmers had frightened off harmful insects by hanging brightly colored banners and scary figurines in their fields. These later came to resemble warriors and rather than being placed in the fields, they were kept in the house to encourage young boys to imitate samurai warriors' courage—a practice approved by that era's rulers. In the latter part of the 18th century, people decided that the indoor display wasn't enough, and they started flying tubular wind-socks in the form of carp from poles outside their houses. To commemorate the old days, however, families set up tiers of shelves bearing figures of warriors and their equipment—armor, helmets, swords, etc. These miniature figures were treasured and kept for the festival from one year to the next.

The celebration, since 1945, of KODOMO-NO-HI, or Children's Day, was intended to replace Tango-no-Sekku. But in fact, many of the activities associated with May 5—which include sumo wrestling, *kendo* (fencing with bamboo staves), and climbing competitions—tend to focus on boys.

SOURCES:
JapanFest-1965, p. 69

♦ 2705 ♦ Tano Festival (Dano-nal; Swing Day)
May-June; fifth day of fifth lunar month

An ancient spring agricultural festival in Korea, the Tano Festival started as a planting ritual and a time to pray for a good harvest. It falls in the farming season between the planting of rice seedlings and their transplanting to the paddy fields. With the lunar SOL or New Year's Day and MID-AUTUMN FESTIVAL, it is one of the country's three great festivals on the lunar calendar. Festivities in the countryside include swinging contests for girls: swings are suspended from tall poles or bridges, and the girls, sometimes in pairs, try to ring a bell with their feet as they swing. Boys and men sometimes compete in this, but usually they take part in *ssirum*, native Korean wrestling, a sport that can be dated to 400 C.E. Today ssirum matches are nationally televised.

In the usually sleepy east coast town of Kangnung, the festival goes on for nearly a week. Activities include a mask dance-drama of ancient tradition and shaman *kut*, ritualistic ceremonies combining theatrics with music and dance.

The ceremonies are performed by a shaman, or *mudang*, a priestess who is able to appease spirits to prevent natural disasters. The mudang is also a talented performer with supernatural powers when in a trance. A long-lived indigenous shamanistic faith of uncertain origin involves the worship of spirits and demons who reside in natural objects—rocks, mountains, trees, and so on. Shamanists also believe the dead have souls, and that the mudangs can mediate between the living and the departed.

Korea is nominally more than 70 percent Buddhist and more than 15 percent Christian, but it actively remains about 90 percent shamanist.

CONTACTS:
Korea Foundation
10-11F, Diplomatic Center Bldg., 2558 Nambusunhwanno,
   Seocho-gu
Seoul, 137-863 Korea
82-2-3463-5684; fax: 82-2-3463-6086
www.koreana.or.kr

Gangwon-do Tourist Office
15 Pongui-dong
Chunchon-shi
Kangwon-do, Gangwon 200-700 Korea
82-33-254-2011; fax: 82-33-249-4018
eng.gwd.go.kr/page/main.html

SOURCES:
BkHolWrld-1986, Jun 16
FolkWrldHol-1999, p. 374
HolSymbols-2009, p. 933

♦ 2706 ♦ **Tanzania Independence Day**
December 9

Tanzania Independence Day is a celebration of independence from the British in 1961 of Tanganyika, which merged with Zanzibar in 1964 to become Tanzania. The day is a national holiday celebrated with parades, youth leagues marching before the president at the stadium in Dar es Salaam, school games, cultural dances, and aerobatics by the air force.

CONTACTS:
Embassy of the United Republic of Tanzania
2139 R St. N.W.
Washington, D.C. 20008
202-939-6125; fax: 202-797-7408
www.tanzaniaembassy-us.org

SOURCES:
AnnivHol-2000, p. 205
NatlHolWrld-1968, p. 222

♦ 2707 ♦ **Tanzania Union Day**
April 26

On April 26, 1964, the East African countries of Tanganyika and Zanzibar merged to form the United Republic of Tanzania. Union Day celebrates this merger.

In the city of Dar es Salaam, speeches and a parade mark Union Day. Dignitaries from nearby countries join Tanzanian government officials in these festivities.

In 2004, to mark Union Day, Tanzanian president Benjamin Mkapa pardoned nearly 4,500 prisoners who had been sentenced for minor crimes or who had less than three years to serve of a longer sentence.

CONTACTS:
Embassy of the United Republic of Tanzania
2139 R St. N.W.
Washington, D.C. 20008
202-939-6125 or 202-884-1080; fax: 202-797-7408
www.tanzaniaembassy-us.org

♦ 2708 ♦ **Tarantula Fest and Barbecue**
First Saturday of October

The tarantula mating season begins in mid-August and lasts through early November, and northern California's Henry W. Coe State Park sees plenty of the spiders crossing its roads during this time of year. Park rangers view the mass exodus as a great opportunity to hold a festival and a barbecue complete with typical fare as well as tarantula cookies and suckers.

The bolder attendees of the festival go for the tarantula-handling. Some even muster the courage to pose for pictures as the spiders crawl on their faces (this particular breed of tarantula is docile and its venom is virtually harmless). Plenty of other proceedings accompany the main event. The Tarantulas, the park's jug music "house band," usually perform. There are also displays of non-native tarantulas, merchandise for sale, and a raffle. The park's visitor center also opens up for people to learn more about tarantulas and the

park, which covers 87,000 acres, making it the largest state park in northern California.

CONTACTS:
Henry W. Coe State Park
9000 East Dunne Ave.
Morgan Hill, CA 95037
408-779-2728; fax: 408-778-5749
www.coepark.org/tfest.html

♦ 2709 ♦ **Tarnetar Mela**
August-September; three days in the Hindu month of Bhadrapada

This famous fair is held in Tarnetar, a small town in India's Gujarat State. People from area tribes wear their most exquisite clothes for the three-day event, particularly young unmarried people, since the fair is mainly an occasion for them to find spouses. Young men carry magnificently decorated *chhatris* (umbrellas)—a sight for which the fair is renowned—to signal their availability to young women. The Trinetreshwar, or temple of Shiva, provides the grounds for the fair, which abound in food stalls, craft and cattle exhibits, sporting events, and lots of dancing.

Adding to the prospective matrimonial atmosphere is the traditional belief that connects Tarnetar with the marriage between Draupadi and Arjuna, the warrior-hero of the Hindu epics, the *Mahabarata* and the *Bhagavad Gita.*

CONTACTS:
Gujarat Tourism Corporation
Nigam Bhavan
Sector 16
Gandhinagar, Gujarat 382 016 India
91-79-3222029; fax: 91-79-3222189

SOURCES:
WildPlanet-1995, p. 255

♦ 2710 ♦ **Tartu Hanseatic Days**
Late June-July

Tartu, Estonia, is an ancient city first mentioned in written works in the year 1030. Situated on the Baltic Sea, it was one of the influential cities belonging to the Hanseatic League, a powerful group of allied cities during the Middle Ages that controlled trade on the Baltic, and to some extent the North Sea as well. At the time, Tartu was an important meeting place for tradesmen from Germany, Sweden, Russia, and other lands. In 1986, the Hanseatic Days celebration was established to preserve this aspect of Tartu's heritage. It has since become one of the most important cultural events in all of Estonia.

During Hanseatic Days, those attending the festivities have ample opportunity to learn about life in medieval times. Festival staff members dress in period costume and carry out a variety of authentic activities. Agricultural practices and skilled trades are demonstrated. There are processions, cultural programs, knights tournaments, concerts, and exhibitions of folk art and handcrafts. Entertainment is also provided by wandering jesters, dance and musical companies, circus performers, and street theater groups. Performances by symphonies and choirs are also common at this time. Special events are organized for children, and there is a rowing race held on the Emajogi River, which runs through Tartu.

In addition to celebrating the past, Hanseatic Days is a time for representatives of the Hanseatic cities to come together and look to the present and future. In seminars and conferences, attendees meet to discuss ways to create strong partnerships and use the Hanseatic alliance in the years to come.

CONTACTS:
Tartu Tourist Information Center
Raekoja plats 14
Tartu, Estonia
www.visittartu.com

♦ 2711 ♦ **Taste of Chicago**
*10 days extending from the last week of June
through the first week of July*

Taste of Chicago is the largest food festival in the United States and one of the most popular tourist attractions in Illinois. Begun as a one-day celebration of Chicago's diverse cuisine in 1980, the Taste of Chicago quickly grew into a 10-day food and entertainment spectacle that attracts more than 3.5 million visitors each year. The first Taste festival was held in a three-block area of Michigan Avenue on July 4, 1980. However, with attendance more than triple the anticipated 75,000 visitors, the festival relocated the following year to nearby Grant Park on the Lake Michigan waterfront. In addition to extending the length of the festival from one day to 10, organizers also expanded the number of vendor restaurants to 70 and offered a full range of local and national music acts to entertain festivalgoers. Over the years additional entertainment and education programs were added, including cooking classes, family-themed crafts, fitness demonstrations, and world culture exhibits.

While the Taste of Chicago extends from late June into early July, the most popular day to attend is July 3, when a schedule of celebrity music performers culminates in a spectacular municipal fireworks display over Lake Michigan.

CONTACTS:
Taste of Chicago
Mayor's Office of Special Events
121 N. LaSalle St., Rm. 806
Chicago, IL 60602
312-744-3315; fax: 312-744-8523
www.tasteofchicago.us

SOURCES:
PatHols-2006, p. 169

♦ 2712 ♦ **Tater Days**
First weekend and Monday in April

Considered the oldest trade day in the U.S., Tater Days is now a celebration of the sweet potato in Benton, Ky. The event started in 1843 when sweet potatoes were a staple crop of the area. Today the "tater" is honored with a parade, flea market, gospel music, arts and crafts exhibits, and a Miss Tater Day contest. Most of the food served is some kind of sweet potato concoction.

CONTACTS:
Marshall County Tourist Commission
93 Carroll Rd.
Benton, KY 42025
800-467-7145 or 270-527-3128; fax: 270-527-9193
www.kentuckylake.org

SOURCES:
AnnivHol-2000, p. 72

♦ 2713 ♦ **Ta'u Fo'ou**
January 1

New Year's Day in Tonga, a Polynesian island kingdom in the South Pacific, is reminiscent of CHRISTMAS EVE celebrations in the United States and western Europe, when carolers go from house to house singing Christmas songs. But because the new year arrives in the middle of the Southern Hemisphere's summer, when schoolchildren are on holiday and the weather is warm, the caroling custom has a cultural twist. Boys and girls go from house to house singing hymns, rounds, and other songs that they have created specifically for the occasion. Instead of offering them hot chocolate or coffee, their friends and neighbors show their appreciation by offering fruit or cool drinks. Sometimes the children will be given a piece of *tapa*, Polynesian bark cloth.

SOURCES:
FolkWrldHol-1999, p. 7

♦ 2714 ♦ **Taungbyon Spirit Festival**
Eight days before the full moon in August

Part circus, part multinational marketplace, the Spirit Festival in Taungbyon, Myanmar, commemorates the Brother Lords, two brothers who lived in the 11th century. Condemned to die for their laziness, the brothers were recognized as spirit-gods after their deaths. The festival includes folk dramas, ceremonial dances, and opportunities to gamble and socialize. Images reflecting the pre-Buddhist animist traditions of the Burmese people are daubed with ceremonial oils and taken through the streets in procession. Shamans (intermediaries between the natural and the spirit worlds) hold many assemblies during the fair.

CONTACTS:
Embassy of the Union of Myanmar
2300 S St. N.W.
Washington, D.C. 20008
202-332-3344; fax: 202-332-4351
www.mewashingtondc.com

SOURCES:
WildPlanet-1995, p. 374

♦ 2715 ♦ **Tazaungdaing**
*October-November; full moon day of Burmese
month of Tazaungmone*

The Tazaungdaing festival was observed in Burma (now officially called Myanmar) even before the spread of Buddhism. It was held in honor of the God of Lights, and it marked the awakening of the Hindu god Vishnu from his long sleep. Burmese Buddhists later attached their own religious significance to the festival, saying that this was the night that Siddhartha's mother, sensing that her son was about to discard the royal robes of his birth and put on the robes of the monkhood, spent the entire night weaving the traditional yellow robes for him. To commemorate her achievement, a weaving contest is held at the Shwe Dagon Pagoda in Rangoon (now called Yangon). Another festival activity is the offering of *Kathin* robes to the Buddhist monks to replace the soiled robes they have worn throughout the rainy season. This offering ceremony begins on the first waning day of THADINGYUT and continues until the full moon night of Tazaungmone.

The Tazaungdaing festival is celebrated by sending up fire balloons and lighting multicolored lanterns, especially at the Sulamani Pagoda in Tavatimsa. Sometimes called the **Tawadeintha Festival**, this day commemorates the return of Gautama Buddha from his visit to heavenly Tawadeintha to visit his mother's reincarnated spirit. Holy men with lit candles illuminated his path back to earth.

CONTACTS:
Embassy of the Union of Myanmar
2300 S St. N.W.
Washington, D.C. 20008
202-332-3344; fax: 202-332-4351
www.mewashingtondc.com

SOURCES:
BkHolWrld-1986, Nov 19
EncyRel-1987, vol. 2, p. 552
FolkWrldHol-1999, p. 781

♦ 2716 ♦ Taziyeh
Ninth day of Islamic month of Muharram

For Shi'ite Muslims, the martyrdom of the Prophet Muhammad's grandson, Hussein, is one of the more critical events in Islamic history. In 680 C.E., Hussein and a small group of Shi'ite supporters clashed with Sunnis in Karbala, a city in present-day Iraq, and were killed. The Shi'ite holiday of ASHURA commemorates Hussein's death and the days leading up to it. The 10 days make up the initial days of Muharram, the first month of the Islamic year.

Iranian Shi'ites mark the eve of Ashura by celebrating Taziyeh, which is named after the passion play of the same name. Performances of *taziyeh* are common in Iraq, Pakistan, and India, as well as in Iran, but only in Iran has the tradition developed into a formal holiday. The word *taziyeh* means "consolation" and signifies the blessing that performers are believed to receive by imitating the sacred events that befell the prophet's family. Sometimes the shows coincide with religious processions.

After experiencing its heyday in the 19th century, *taziyeh* performances dropped off since they were written off as a folk custom for the lower classes. During the Iranian Revolution in 1979, clerics re-authorized the tradition and *taziyeh* experienced a resurgence, with more elaborate productions and greater attendance numbers.

CONTACTS:
Iran's Ministry of Foreign Affairs
Imam Khomeini Sq.
Tehran, Iran

SOURCES:
CultureCustomsIran-2006, p.184
RelHolCal-2004, p. 144

♦ 2717 ♦ Teachers' Day in the Czech Republic
March 28

March 28 is the birthday of Jan Amos Komensky (1592-1670; his name is also rendered John Comenius), a noted educational reformer and theologian in the former Czechoslovakia. Komensky was the first person to write an illustrated textbook for children. Published in 1658, it was pocket-sized and used for teaching Latin words. Komensky was also a proponent of compulsory education who pointed out the state's obligation to provide kindergarten training and schooling. It has been traditional for children to honor him on Teachers' Day, or **Komensky Day**, by bringing flowers and gifts to their teachers. The day is also observed with lectures, music, and educational activities.

SOURCES:
BkFest-1937, p. 85
BkHolWrld-1986, Mar 28

♦ 2718 ♦ Teej (Tij; Green Teej)
July-August; third day of waxing half of Hindu month of Sravana

Teej is a way to welcome the monsoon, the season when the wind from the Indian Ocean brings heavy rainfall. The festival is celebrated especially in the dry, desert-like state of Rajasthan in northwestern India. Because the monsoon augurs good crops and fertility, this is also a celebration for women and is dedicated to the Hindu goddess, Parvati, consort of Lord Shiva and patron goddess of women. On this day, she is supposed to have been reunited with Shiva.

On Teej women traditionally paint delicate designs on their hands and feet with henna. Specially decorated swings are hung from trees in every village, and women swing on them and sing songs in praise of Parvati. Married women go to their parents' home and receive gifts of clothes and jewelry. There are also local fairs and processions carrying the image of the goddess.

In Jaipur, the capital of Rajasthan, women dressed in their finest go out to the main temple with flowers and brass vessels filled with water to worship the goddess and sing her praise. A palanquin carrying an image of Parvati is carried through the streets in a procession of decorated elephants, camels, horses, chariots, dancers, and musicians.

On this day in Kathmandu, Nepal, Hindu women visit Pashupatinath Temple to worship Shiva and Parvati. Ritual bathing in the sacred Bagmati River is supposed to wash away the sins of the past year.

CONTACTS:
Department of Tourism , Art & Culture, Government of Rajasthan
Govt. Hostel Campus, Paryatan Bhawan, M.I. Rd.
Jaipur, Rajasthan 302 001 India
91-141-25110595; fax: 91-141-25110591
www.rajasthan.gov.in

Nepal Embassy
2131 Leroy Pl. N.W.
Washington, DC 20008
202-667-4550; fax: 202-667-5534
www.nepalembassyusa.org

SOURCES:
BkHolWrld-1986, Aug 6
FestIndia-1987, p. 38
FolkWrldHol-1999, p. 473
HolSymbols-2009, p. 937
RelHolCal-2004, p. 171

♦ 2719 ♦ **Tejano Conjunto Festival**
Mid-May

Conjunto music originated in the late 19th century in southern Texas, where the mingling of Germanic and Mexican cultures produced a unique folk music. The German settlers introduced the accordian, to which the Mexicanos added the Spanish bajo sexto guitar for a new kind of music. "Tejano" refers to conjunto music as it is played in Texas, which differs from the "Norteño" conjunto played in northern Mexico.

The Tejano Conjunto Festival held for five days in mid-May every year in San Antonio, Texas, is the largest festival of its kind in the world. Since 1982 it has featured some of the best Tejano conjunto artists performing traditional, popular, and progressive conjunto music. The festival also includes an induction ceremony for the Conjunto Music Hall of Fame, a poster contest, art exhibits, a silent auction, and awards presentations held at San Antonio's Guadalupe Theater and Rosedale Park.

CONTACTS:
Guadalupe Cultural Arts Center
1300 Guadalupe St.
San Antonio, TX 78207
210-271-3151; fax: 210-271-3480
www.guadalupeculturalarts.org

SOURCES:
LatinoLife-1995, p. 35
WildPlanet-1995, p. 609

♦ 2720 ♦ **Tekakwitha (Kateri) Feast Day**
July 14

The first Native American to be beatified, Kateri Tekakwitha (1656–1680) is a venerated figure among both Catholics and Native Americans as well as the patroness of ecology and the environment. Catholic churches—in particular those named

after her or based in places connected to her legacy—hold mass on her feast day, during which congregants may offer prayers to God through her intercession.

Known as the "Lily of the Mohawk," Tekakwitha was born in upstate New York to a Christian Algonquin mother and a non-Christian Mohawk father. She was baptized in 1656. Acutely aware that her newfound faith did not make her popular with her village, she moved to a Christian community near Montreal, Canada. Up until her death at the age of 24, she devoted herself to prayer, fasting, and service. Witnesses at her deathbed reported that her facial scars, left by a bout with smallpox, suddenly disappeared after she died. Her legacy has inspired a campaign for her sainthood. In 1980 Pope John Paul II declared her "Blessed"—the last designation made by the Church before someone officially becomes a saint.

Among the North American churches and shrines sites that have noteworthy feast day celebrations are the National Kateri Shrine in Fonda, New York, where she had her first encounter with Christianity; and the Kateri Center at the Saint Francis-Xavier Mission at Kahnawake, Quebec, where she lived following her conversion.

CONTACTS:
National Shrine of Blessed Kateri Tekakwitha
P.O. Box 627
Fonda, NY
www.katerishrine.com

Kateri Tekakwitha Center
St. Francis Xavier Mission
P.O. Box 70
Kahnawake, QC Canada

♦ 2721 ♦ **Tell (Wilhelm) Festival**
September, Labor Day weekend

New Glarus, Wisconsin, was settled by a group of Swiss immigrants in 1845 and is still referred to as "Little Switzerland." It is the location of several annual events designed to draw attention to the area's Swiss heritage. These include the Heidi Festival in June and the Volksfest in August. But one of the most popular is the Wilhelm Tell Pageant that has been performed each year on Labor Day weekend since 1938.

The highlight of the William Tell story, of course, is the famous "apple scene" where the imprisoned patriot is given a chance at freedom if he can shoot an apple off his son's head. The play includes performances by the famous New Glarus yodelers and the costumed usherettes, who perform Swiss folk dances. The play is given in Swiss-German on Sunday afternoon and in English on Saturday and Monday. The pageant weekend includes dancing on the green, Swiss singing, and other traditional Swiss forms of entertainment.

See also William Tell Play

CONTACTS:
New Glarus Chamber of Commerce
418 Railroad St.
New Glarus, WI 53574
800-527-6838 or 608-527-2095; fax: 608-527-4991
www.swisstown.com

♦ 2722 ♦ Tell (William) Play
Thursdays and Saturdays from late June to early September

The Swiss legendary hero William Tell symbolized the struggle for individual and political freedom. When he defied the Austrian authorities, he was forced to shoot an apple off his son's head in order to gain his freedom. He was later arrested for threatening the governor's life, saved the same governor's life en route to prison, escaped, and ultimately killed the governor in an ambush. These events supposedly inspired the Swiss people to rebel against Austrian rule.

Although there is no hard evidence to support William Tell's existence, the story of his test as a marksman has passed into folklore. German dramatist J. C. Friedrich von Schiller (1759-1805) wrote a play about Tell in 1804. Set in the environs of Altdorf, the legendary site of the apple-shooting incident, Schiller's play has been performed at an open-air theater in Interlaken, Switzerland, since 1912.

See also WILHELM TELL FESTIVAL

CONTACTS:
Tell-Freilichtspiele
Postfach
Interlaken, 3800 Switzerland
41-33-822-3722; fax: 41-33-822-5722
www.tellspiele.ch/e/fakten

♦ 2723 ♦ Tellabration
Third weekend in November

A nationwide night of storytelling, Tellabration was started in 1988 by storyteller J. G. ("Paw-Paw") Pinkerton. The event began with storytelling going on in six communities in Connecticut. The next year, Texas and Missouri also had Tellabrations, and by 1991, storytelling on this night was happening in 72 communities in 27 states, as well as in locations in Bermuda and Canada. Eventually, the length of Tellabrations extended to a weekend. In 1999 people held Tellabrations in 42 states and 14 countries. Proceeds of the event go toward developing the archives of Storytelling Foundation International (formerly the National Association for the Preservation and Perpetuation of Storytelling) in Jonesborough, Tenn.

Pinkerton originated the event as a way to encourage storytelling for adults, feeling that storytelling keeps culture alive. He grew up in a small Texas town listening to family stories—especially those told by his grandfather who had herded cattle in the early days of Texas. Pinkerton became a mining executive and, after retiring in 1988, devoted his time to promoting storytelling from his Connecticut home.

See also STORYTELLING FESTIVAL, NATIONAL and YUKON INTERNATIONAL STORYTELLING FESTIVAL

CONTACTS:
National Storytelling Network
132 Boone St., Ste. 5
Jonesborough, TN 37659
800-525-4514 or 423-913-8201; fax: 423-753-9331
www.storynet.org

♦ 2724 ♦ Telluride Film Festival
September, Labor Day weekend

A three-day celebration of the silver screen in Telluride, Colo., the Telluride Film Festival features free outdoor showings in Elks Park with the audience bundled in blankets and sleeping bags. The festival attracts celebrity film makers, actors, and film scholars from all over the globe for national and international premieres and viewings of experimental filmmaking, retrospectives, and tributes.

CONTACTS:
Telluride Film Festival
800 Jones S.
Berkeley, CA 94710
510-665-9494; fax: 510-665-9589
www.telluridefilmfestival.org

SOURCES:
GdUSFest-1984, p. 28

♦ 2725 ♦ Telluride Hang Gliding Festival
Second week in June

The largest hang gliding event in the country is held in Telluride, Colo., the small mountain resort that began life as a mining town and is known today as the "festival capital of the Rockies." Top hang gliders from throughout the world come here to soar and spin above Town Park. On the last day of the six-day event, in the competition for the World Acrobatic Championship, fliers skid, loop, somersault, and pirouette from the heights of the ski mountain, trailing colored smoke from their wingtips.

CONTACTS:
Telluride Colorado Visitor Guide, Telluride Publishing
P.O. Box 964
Telluride, CO 81435
800-431-7111 or 970-728-4245; fax: 970-728-4302
www.telluridevisitorguide.com

♦ 2726 ♦ Telluride Jazz Festival
First weekend in August

This festival consists of three days of jazz in Telluride, Colo. Top artists produce jazz of all schools—traditional, Chicago, blues, big band, and Latin. The music happens both indoors—at the historic Sherman Opera House and at various pubs—and outdoors at the Town Park Pavilion. The festival began in 1977.

Telluride also boasts a three-day Bluegrass and Country Music Festival in late June, and a Chamber Music Festival held during two weekends in August. A special feature of that festival is the gourmet dessert concert, when fancy treats are served with the music, and the concert closes with a classical jam session.

CONTACTS:
Telluride Society for Jazz
P.O. Box 2132
Telluride, CO 81435

970-728-7009; fax: 970-728-5834
www.telluridejazz.com

Telluride Bluegrass Festival
P.O. Box 769
Lyons, CO 80540
800-624-2422 or 303-823-0848; fax: 303-823-0849
www.bluegrass.com

Telluride Chamber Music Association
P.O. Box 115
Telluride, CO 81435
970-728-8686; fax: 970-369-1351
www.telluride.com

SOURCES:
MusFestAmer-1990, p. 190

♦ 2727 ♦ **Ten Days on the Island**
Late March-early April, biennially

Every two years, arts enthusiasts travel to Tasmania, an island off the southern coast of Australia, for Ten Days on the Island. First launched in 2001, this biennial festival celebrates island culture and showcases local and international art in all major forms: dance, theatre, music, opera, film, and literature. The festival's organizer, Tasmania's Department of Tourism, Arts and the Environment, markets the festival with the double aim of drawing tourists and boosting employment for local artists and arts practitioners.

There are on average 200 ticketed and free performances and exhibitions, held at roughly 40 locations in the island's capital, Hobart, and throughout the state of Tasmania. Estimates of past events have counted 160,000 attendants. The festival has drawn more international artists over the years, and in 2007, it began offering regional tours of theater productions.

CONTACTS:
Ten Days on the Island
Level 5
147 Macquarie St. Hobart
G.P.O. Box 1403
Hobart, Tasmania 7001 Australia
www.tendaysontheisland.org

Tasmania Department of Tourism, Arts and the Environment
Head Office
Level 8, 22 Elizabeth St.
Hobart, Tasmania 7000 Australia
www.dtae.tas.gov.au

♦ 2728 ♦ **Tenjin Matsuri**
July 24-25

The Tenjin Festival in Japan honors the scholar and statesman Sugawara Michizane (845-903), who was deified as Tenjin after his death and regarded as the god of literature. The festival began about 950 C.E. as a purification rite. Today, the Tenjin Festival opens at the Temmangu Shrine with the beating of the *Moyooshi Daiko*, a drum about five feet in diameter. It lies flat in a cart and is struck by several men, known as *Ganji*, wearing tall peaked red hats. Other participants in the procession do everything in their power to prevent the drummers from drumming. They remove the platform on

which the drum sits and tilt it in every direction, but the drummers keep striking it furiously. The drum-cart is followed by a masked figure on horseback who represents Sarutahiko, the deity who led all the other gods to Japan. There are Lion Dancers to drive away evil spirits, costumed children, and various carts and palanquins carrying local dignitaries and the mayor of Osaka.

Most important is the *mikoshi*—the heavy, ornately decorated portable shrine in which the soul of Tenjin is believed to reside. In the evening, the parade moves to the river, with numerous barges and boats carrying glowing lanterns, while bonfires illuminate the banks. Fireworks mark the end of the festival, and the barges are towed back up the river so that the sacred objects can be returned to the shrine by morning.

CONTACTS:
Osaka Convention and Tourism Bureau
5F Resona Semba Bldg.
4-4-21, Minamisemba, Chuo-Ku
Osaka, 542-0081 Japan
81-6-6282-5911; fax: 81-6-6282-5914

SOURCES:
HolSymbols-2009, p. 940
IllFestJapan-1993, p. 88
JapanFest-1965, pp. 25, 172

♦ 2729 ♦ **Tennessee Walking Horse National Celebration**
August-September, 11 days ending the Saturday before Labor Day

This festival features 11 days and nights of pageantry and competition for more than 2,000 Tennessee Walking Horses in Shelbyville, Tenn., the "Walking Horse Capital of the World." The horses compete for more than $650,000 in prizes and the title of World Grand Champion. The celebration is the nation's largest horse show in terms of spectators (close to 250,000 fans come to this town of 13,000) and the second largest in numbers of entered horses.

The blood lines of the Tennessee Walking Horse are traced back to the Thoroughbred, the Standardbred, the Morgan, and the American Saddle Horse. It was bred pure in the early days of Tennessee for the threefold purpose of riding, driving, and general farm work. Today, it's a pleasure mount and a show horse with distinctive high-stepping gaits.

The three natural gaits of the Tennessee Walker are the flatfoot walk, the running walk, and the canter. The flat-foot walk, the slowest, is a diagonally opposed movement of the feet. The running walk starts like the flat-foot walk and, as speed increases, the hind foot overstrides the front track. It is the only gait of a horse where the forefoot strikes the ground a mere instant before the hindfoot. The canter is a rhythmic motion known as the "rocking-chair" movement.

The Shelbyville celebration began in 1939, at the initiative of horse owner Henry Davis of Wartrace, Tenn., who thought his county should celebrate its most important asset. The celebration has been held ever since without interruption.

Besides the horse shows, the celebration features an equestrian trade fair, horse sales, an arts-and-crafts festival, and America's largest barn decoration competition. The barns and stalls are elegantly decorated with brass lanterns, chandeliers, fine art, rugs, and expensive furnishings.

CONTACTS:
Tennessee Walking Horse National Celebration
P.O. Box 1010
Shelbyville, TN 37162
931-684-5915; fax: 931-684-5949
www.twhnc.com

SOURCES:
GdUSFest-1984, p. 179

♦ 2730 ♦ **Terlingua Chili Cookoff**
First full weekend in November

The Terlingua Chili Cookoff is a contest of chili chefs held in Terlingua, Tex., an abandoned mining town near the Big Bend desert area in the southwestern part of the state. More than 200 cooks from as many as 30 states and occasionally from foreign countries show up to prepare the official state dish, and thousands of spectators drive or fly in. Humorists Wick Fowler and H. Allen Smith staged the first cookoff in 1967, deciding to locate it in the hot desert because it was a contest for a hot dish. It has become such an institution that the number of entrants has to be kept down by earning points at preliminary cookoffs, especially the CHILYMPIAD.

CONTACTS:
Chili Appreciation Society International
1516 Prairie Dr.
El Paso, TX 79925
915-772-2379
www.chili.org

♦ 2731 ♦ **Terminalia**
February 23

In ancient Rome, February 23 marked the end of the year and was therefore an appropriate time to honor Terminus, the god of boundaries and landmarks. The terminus, or boundary stone marking the outer limits of Rome, stood between the fifth and sixth milestones on the road to Laurentum. During the observance of the Terminalia, property owners would gather there—or at the boundary stones that marked their private lands—to place garlands around the stone and offer sacrifices. Afterward there would be singing and socializing among family members and servants.

Ceremonies that involve marking boundaries are common in England and Scotland as well (*see* ASCENSION DAY and COMMON RIDINGS DAY).

SOURCES:
DictFolkMyth-1984, pp. 129, 493, 1106
DictRomRel-1996, p. 221
FestRom-1981, p. 79
OxYear-1999, p. 89

♦ 2732 ♦ **Teshuvah**
September-October; during the month of Tishri between Rosh Hashanah and Yom Kippur

The ten days between ROSH HASHANAH and YOM KIPPUR are known to Jews as Aseret Yemey Tushuvah, or **Ten Days of Penitence**. They are a time for reflection, introspection, and repentance, during which people apologize to one another for any wrongs they may have committed during the previous year. The Hebrew word *teshuvah* means "turning." According to tradition, an unfavorable verdict about one's behavior may be changed by repentance and charity. Each day the famous prayer of confession, which begins "Our Father, our King," is recited at the service in the temple.

In Palestine, pilgrimages are made during this period to the tomb of Rachel and other sacred burial places, as well as to the graves of relatives. In other countries, it is customary to visit the local cemetery. No weddings or banquets may be held during these days, and scholarly Jews spend their time reading and studying the sacred books.

The atmosphere during this time is not one of sadness but of thoughtfulness and kindness. Jews often greet one another by saying, *Gemar Hatimah Tovah*, which means, "May the final verdict be favorable."

CONTACTS:
Union of Orthodox Jewish Congregations of America
11 Broadway
New York, NY 10004
212-563-4000; fax: 212-564-9058
www.ou.org

♦ 2733 ♦ **Tet**
January-February; first to seventh days of first lunar month

The Vietnamese New Year, Tet, is an abbreviation for **Tet Nguyen Dan**, meaning "first day." This is the most important festival of the year, signifying both the beginning of the year and of spring. It's also seen as a precursor of everything that will happen in the coming year, and for that reason, efforts are made to start the year properly with family reunions, paying homage to ancestors, and wiping out debts.

At the start of the festival, the Spirit of the Hearth goes to the abode of the Emperor of Jade to report on family members. The spirit should be in a good frame of mind, so a tree is built of bamboo and red paper to ward off evil spirits. At midnight the New Year and the return of the Spirit of the Hearth are welcomed with firecrackers, gongs, and drums. The festival then continues for a week, with special events on each day. A favorite food of the festival is *banh chung*, which is made of sticky rice, yellow beans, pig fat, and spices wrapped in leaves and boiled for half a day.

Tet became known worldwide in 1968 for the Tet Offensive of the Vietnam War. The LUNAR NEW YEAR truce was shattered on Jan. 31 with attacks by North Vietnam and the National Liberation Front against more than 100 South Vietnamese cities. The United States embassy in Saigon was attacked and parts of it held by the Viet Cong for six hours; the headquarters of U.S. Gen. William Westmoreland at Tan Son Nhut Airport outside Saigon was also attacked. The city of Hue was captured. The attacks were repulsed, and the U.S. and South Vietnam claimed victory. But television viewers had seen the ferocity of the attack and the flight of Saigon residents, and the offensive led to increased movements in the United States to end the war.

CONTACTS:
Vietnam National Administration of Tourism
80 Quan Su Rd.
Hanoi, Vietnam
84-4-942-1061; fax: 84-4-826-3956
www.vietnamtourism.com/e_pages/news/index.a

SOURCES:
AnnivHol-2000, p. 239
FolkAmerHol-1999, p. 61
FolkWrldHol-1999, p. 76
HolSymbols-2009, p. 948
RelHolCal-2004, p. 230

♦ 2734 ♦ Texas Citrus Fiesta
Third full weekend in January

An annual festival held in Mission, Tex., the Texas Citrus Fiesta salutes the Texas citrus industry and, especially, the Texas Ruby Red Grapefruit. Mission, in the Rio Grande Valley, was founded by the Catholic Missionary Society of the Oblate Fathers, who built a mission here in 1824. They also are credited as the first community to plant citrus fruit in the region, which is now famous for the Ruby Red Grapefruit.

Among the events of the fiesta are a style show featuring garments made of Rio Grande Valley agricultural products: dried orange peel, seeds, and onion skins are used in creating costumes that range from ballgowns to bikinis. Other events include parades, the coronation of a Citrus Queen, arts and crafts, and food and games.

CONTACTS:
Texas Citrus Fiesta
1420 Kika De La Garza Loop Mission
Mission, TX 78572
956-585-9724; fax: 956-585-9728
www.texascitrusfiesta.net

♦ 2735 ♦ Texas Folklife Festival
Early June

Often described as "the largest block party in Texas," the Texas Folklife Festival was founded in 1972 by O. T. Baker, exhibits manager at the Institute of Texan Cultures, as a celebration of the state's ethnic cultures and pioneer heritage. There are demonstrations of the crafts, work skills, costumes, foods, and customs of about 40 different ethnic groups living in Texas today. Visitors can learn how to make a cowhide chair, for example, or the proper way to pickle olives. There have been lessons in Swiss yodeling, splitting shingles, and blacksmithing, as well as musical performances by German oompah bands, Czech accordionists, and Dutch singers. The four-

day festival is sponsored by the Institute of Texan Cultures and is held at HemisFair Park in downtown San Antonio.

CONTACTS:
UTSA's Institute of Texan Cultures
801 S. Bowie St.
San Antonio, TX 78205
210-458-2330; fax: 210-458-2205
www.texancultures.utsa.edu

SOURCES:
GdUSFest-1984, p. 187
MusFestAmer-1990, p. 229

♦ 2736 ♦ Texas Independence Day
March 2

A legal holiday in Texas, March 2 commemorates both the convention at Washington-on-the-Brazos held on this day in 1836, when delegates prepared for the separation of Texas from Mexico, and the birthday of Sam Houston (1793-1863), who led the Texans to victory over the Mexicans in the battle of SAN JACINTO. The convention formed an interim government, drew up a constitution, and made Sam Houston commander-in-chief of the Texan military forces. But their work was interrupted by the invading Mexican army. It wasn't until the following month that the Republic of Texas forced the issue of independence at the battle of San Jacinto. Texas is the only state to celebrate independence from a country other than England.

March 2 is also known as **Sam Houston Day** and **Texas Flag Day**, although these are "special observance days" rather than legal holidays. This period in Texas history, beginning with the Washington-on-the-Brazos convention and ending with Sam Houston's decisive victory at San Jacinto, is celebrated each year during "Texas Week."

CONTACTS:
Washington-on-the-Brazos State Historical Park
P.O. Box 305
Washington, TX 77880
888-273-6426 or 936-878-2214
www.tpwd.state.tx.us

Texas State Historical Association
1 University Station D0901
Austin, TX 78712
512-471-1525; fax: 512-471-1551
www.tsha.utexas.edu

SOURCES:
AmerBkDays-2000, p. 177
AnnivHol-2000, p. 37
DictDays-1988, p. 118

♦ 2737 ♦ Texas Rose Festival
Third week in October

An annual tribute to roses in Tyler, Tex., center of the region that produces more than a third of the field-grown roses in the United States. Tyler's Municipal Rose Garden, one of the largest rose gardens in the country, covers 14 acres and has some 30,000 rose bushes, representing more than 400 varieties. They blossom among pines, fountains, gazebos, and archways, peaking in May but continuing through October. The five-day festival features the coronation of a Rose Queen, a rose show, a parade of floats decorated with roses, and tours of the rose gardens. There are also arts and crafts shows, a square-dance festival, and a symphony concert.

CONTACTS:
Texas Rose Festival Association
P.O. Box 8224
Tyler, TX 75711
903-597-3130; fax: 903-597-3031
www.texasrosefestival.com

Tyler Rose Museum
420 Rose Park Dr.
Tyler, TX 75702
903-597-3130; fax: 903-597-3031
www.texasrosefestival.com

♦ 2738 ♦ **Thadingyut**
September-October; full moon of Thadingyut

For Buddhists, the period that begins with the full moon day of the 11th lunar month and continues until the full moon day of the 12th lunar month marks the end of the Buddhist Lent and the beginning of the *Kathin*, or pilgrimage season. Also known as **Robe Offering Month**, this is a time when Buddhists make pilgrimages to various temples, bringing food and gifts—particularly new robes—to the monks. In Myanmar (formerly Burma), Thadingyut is the day on which the Buddha completed his preaching of the *Abhidhamma*, or "philosophy," and it is sometimes referred to as **Abhidhamma Day**. In Laos, it is called **Boun Ok Vatsa**, or the **Festival of the Waters**, as it is a popular time for pirogue (canoe) races. In Thailand, it is called **Tod Kathin**—the *kathin* being a wooden frame on which scraps of cloth were stretched before being sewn together to make into robes.

See also TAZAUNGDAING; WASO

SOURCES:
BkHolWrld-1986, Jul 23, Sep 22, Oct 20, Oct 27, Oct 29
FolkWrldHol-1999, p. 615

♦ 2739 ♦ **Thailand Constitution Day**
December 10

In 1932 Thailand's absolute monarchy was replaced with a constitutional monarchy. King Rama VII oversaw the transfer of power. Under the newly instituted constitution of that time, the monarchy remained in place and the king was designated the head of state, head of the armed forces, upholder of all religions, and sacred and inviolable in his person.

In practice, however, while the monarchy is still held in esteem by the people, real power in Thailand has often been held by the military. Reflecting the country's volatile politics, Thailand has had a series of 18 constitutions or charters since 1932, the latest one being adopted in 2007. All of them have allowed for a constitutional monarchy with greater or lesser power. Celebrations on Constitution Day involve the people

thanking the monarchy for granting them a chance to take part in running the country.

CONTACTS:
Royal Thai Embassy
1024 Wisconsin Ave. N.W.
Washington, D.C. 20007
202-338-9700
www.thaiembdc.org

♦ 2740 ♦ **Thailand Coronation Day**
May 5

On May 5, 1950, King Bhumibol Adulyadej was crowned Rama IX of Thailand, the ninth king of the Chakri dynasty. Ever since, the day has been celebrated as Coronation Day in Thailand.

The celebration begins on May 3 with Buddhist monks holding a service at the Amarindra Vinichai Hall in the Grand Palace. A high monk delivers a sermon and scriptures are read in honor of the Chakri family ancestors. On May 4th, the Chief of Brahmin priests reads out the official proclamation of Coronation Day. In the evening, Buddhist priests perform a chanting ceremony. On May 5, the Buddhist monks are given a feast and the king wears his full regalia. At noon, the Royal Thai Army and Navy each give a 21-gun salute. Later in the day, the king awards medals and decorations to those citizens who have done outstanding services for the state.

CONTACTS:
Royal Thai Embassy
1024 Wisconsin Ave. N.W.
Washington, D.C. 20007
202-338-9700
www.thaiembdc.org

♦ 2741 ♦ **Thaipusam (Thai Poosam)**
January-February; three to 12 days in Hindu month of Magha

Thaipusam is a dramatic Hindu festival celebrated in India, Malaysia, Sri Lanka, Singapore, South Africa, Mauritius, and elsewhere. The day marks the birthday and victory of the Hindu god Subramaniam, also known as Lord Murugar, over the demons, and is a time of penance and consecration to the god, usually involving self-mortification in a test of mind over pain.

In Malaysia, the festival is a public holiday in the states of Perak, Penang, and Selangor. In Georgetown, Penang, a statue of Subramaniam—covered with gold, silver, diamonds, and emeralds—is taken from the Sri Mariamman temple along with his consorts, Valli and Theivanai, and placed in a silver chariot. Then begins a grand procession to his tomb in the Batu Caves, near the capital city of Kuala Lumpur, where the statue is carried up 272 steep steps, and placed beside the permanent statue kept there. The next day about 200,000 people begin to pay homage, while movies, carousels, and other entertainments are provided for their amusement.

The most intense form of penance and devotion is the carrying of *kavadee*—a wooden arch on a wooden platform—which the Tamil people of Mauritius practice in a unique way—much more elaborately and solemnly than in other countries. Devotees, both male and female, abstain from meat and sex during the sacred 10 days before the festival. Each day they go to the temple (*kovil*) to make offerings, and in Port Louis, at Arulmigu Sockalingam Meenaatchee Amman Kovil, Murugar and his two consorts are decorated differently each day to depict episodes in the deity's life.

On the eve of the celebration, devotees prepare their kavadees and decorate them with flowers, paper, and peacock feathers. They may be built in other shapes, such as a peacock or temple, but the arch is most common. The next morning, priests pour cow milk into two brass pots and tie them to the sides of each kavadee. Fruits, or *jagger* (a coarse, brown sugar made from the East Indian palm tree), may also be placed on the platform. Then religious ceremonies are performed at the shrines to put the bearers in a trance. When ready, penitents have their upper bodies pierced symmetrically with *vels*, the sacred lance given to Lord Subramaniam by his mother, Parvati; some also have skewers driven through their cheeks, foreheads, or tongues.

The procession then begins, with the devotees carrying the kavadees on their shoulders. Some penitents draw a small chariot by means of chains fixed to hooks dug into their sides; some walk to the temple on sandals studded with nails. Groups of young men and women follow, singing rhythmic songs. Each region may have 40 to 100 kavadees, but in places like Port Louis there may be 600 to 800. At the temple, the kavadee is dismounted, the needles and skewers removed by the priest, and the milk in the pots—which has stayed pure—is poured over the deity from head to foot. The penitents then go out and join the crowds.

Some believe carrying the kavadee washes away sins through self-inflicted suffering; others say the kavadee symbolizes the triumph of good over evil.

In Durban, South Africa, these rites last 12 days and are also performed during Chitray Massum in April-May.

CONTACTS:
Malaysian Tourism Promotion Board
818 W. 7th St., Ste. 970
Los Angeles, CA 90017
800-336-6842 or 213-689-9702; fax: 213-689-1530
www.visitmalaysia.com

Mauritius Tourism Promotion Authority
Air Mauritius Centre, Fl. 11
5, President John Kennedy Street
Port Louis, Mauritius
230-210-1545; fax: 230-212-5142
www.mauritius.net

SOURCES:
FolkWrldHol-1999, p. 100
GdWrldFest-1985, p. 132
HolSymbols-2009, p. 948

♦ 2742 ♦ **Thanh-Minh**
Fifth day of third lunar month

Thanh-Minh (which means "pure and bright") in Vietnam is a day to commemorate the dead. Families brings flowers, food, incense, and other offerings to the graves of deceased relatives. Sometimes they visit the graves a few days in advance to prepare for Thanh-Minh by raking or sweeping the surrounding area and painting the tombs.

See also QING MING FESTIVAL

SOURCES:
FolkWrldHol-1999, p. 254

♦ 2743 ♦ **Thanksgiving**
Fourth Thursday in November (U.S.); second Monday in October (Canada)

The Pilgrim settlers of New England were not the first to set aside a day for expressing their gratitude to God for the harvest. The Greeks and the Romans paid tribute to their agricultural goddesses, the Anglo-Saxons celebrated LAMMAS and HARVEST HOME FESTIVAL, and the Jews have their eight-day SUKKOT, or Feast of Tabernacles. The first American Thanksgiving was entirely religious, and took place on December 4, 1619, when a group of 38 English settlers arrived at Berkeley Plantation on the James River. Their charter decreed that their day of arrival be celebrated yearly as a day of thanksgiving to God.

But most Americans think of the first "official" Thanksgiving as being the one that took place at Plymouth Colony in October 1621, a year after the Pilgrims first landed on the New England coast. They were joined in their three-day feast by Massasoit, the chief of the Wampanoag Indians, and about 90 of his fellow tribesmen.

The Episcopal Church and many states declared Thanksgiving holidays, but it wasn't until 1863 that President Abraham LINCOLN proclaimed the last Thursday in November as a national day to give thanks. Each year thereafter, for 75 years, the president proclaimed the same day to be celebrated. In 1939, however, President Franklin D. ROOSEVELT moved it one week earlier to allow more time for Christmas shopping. Finally, Congress ruled that the fourth Thursday of November would be the legal federal holiday of Thanksgiving after 1941. Canadians celebrate their Thanksgiving on the second Monday in October.

Today Thanksgiving is a time for family reunions and traditions, most of which center around the preparation of an elaborate meal featuring turkey and a dozen or so accompanying dishes. Although some people go to special church services on Thanksgiving day, far more line the streets of Philadelphia, Detroit, and New York City, where huge parades are held. In many places Santa Claus arrives in town on this day, and the widespread sales that begin in department stores the next day mark the start of the CHRISTMAS shopping season.

See also PILGRIM THANKSGIVING DAY; SCHWENKFELDER THANKS-GIVING

CONTACTS:
Library of Congress
101 Independence Ave. S.E.
Washington, D.C. 20540
202-707-5510; fax: 202-707-2076
www.loc.gov

Canadian Heritage
25 Eddy St.
Gatineau, QC K1A 0M5 Canada
819-997-0055
www.pch.gc.ca/index_e.cfm

SOURCES:
AmerBkDays-2000, pp. 462, 794
BkDays-1864, vol. II, p. 614
BkFest-1937, pp. 13, 19
BkFestHolWrld-1970, pp. 118, 124
BkHolWrld-1986, Nov 27
DaysCustFaith-1957, p. 300
EncyChristmas-2003, p. 443
FolkAmerHol-1999, p. 449
GdUSFest-1984, p. 89
HolSymbols-2009, p. 951
OxYear-1999, p. 654
PatHols-2006, p. 237
RelHolCal-2004, p. 106

♦ 2744 ♦ **Thargelia**
May-June

This ancient Greek festival was celebrated in Athens on the sixth and seventh days of the ancient Greek month of Thargelion (which fell sometime between late May and early June) to honor Apollo. In addition to offerings of first fruits, or the first bread from the new wheat, it was customary to select two condemned criminals (either two men or a man and a woman) to act as scapegoats for community guilt. First they were led through the city and then driven out and banished. If circumstances warranted a greater sacrifice, they were killed—either thrown into the sea or burned on a pyre. On the second day of the festival there was an offering of thanksgiving, a procession, and the official registration ceremony for individuals who had been adopted.

SOURCES:
DictFolkMyth-1984, p. 67
NewCentClassHandbk-1962, p. 1069
OxClassDict-1970, p. 1051

♦ 2745 ♦ **That Luang Festival**
Full moon in November

This annual weeklong festival takes place in Vientiane, the capital city of Laos, at the time of the full moon. The festival is centered in and around That Luang Stupa, the country's most sacred Buddhist temple, which is the National Symbol of Laos. During the festival, hundreds of monks from all over the country gather to chant, pray, and accept alms and gifts of flowers and food from local people. Buddhists consider giving to the monks beneficial, and they give willingly, without accepting thanks. The monks, for their part, share their takings with the poor of the city.

On the evening of the full moon, the monks take part in a sacred procession. This is capped off by a grand fireworks display and revelry through the night in which entire families take part. Dancing, music, drinking, and eating go on far into the night. During the day, an international trade fair takes place in the city that showcases tourism in Laos and other countries in the region. Vendors selling goods and trinkets on the streets add to a carnival-like atmosphere.

CONTACTS:
Embassy of Lao People's Democratic Republic
2222 S St. N.W.
Washington, D.C. 20008
202-332-6416; fax: 202-332-4923
www.laoembassy.com
Org2All

♦ 2746 ♦ **Thay Pagoda Festival**
March-April

This Vietnamese festival, which varies in length, is held in honor of Buddhist monk Dao Hanh, who lived during the Ly Dynasty (1009-1225 C.E.). Dao Hanh was said to have invented what is known as *mua roi can*, "water puppetry," an activity that plays an important part in the festival. The puppet shows take place on the pond in front of the pagoda. The puppeteers stand mostly underwater behind a curtain in order to control the puppets' actions on a stage on the water's surface.

In addition to water puppet performances, the festival features firecracker competitions, folk singing, rowing contests, and mountain-climbing events. It is held in the village of Thay (or Thuy Khe village) in the Quoc Oai District of Ha Tay Province.

CONTACTS:
Vietnam National Administration of Tourism
80 Quan Su Rd.
Hanoi, Vietnam
84-4-942-1061; fax: 84-4-826-3956
www.vietnamtourism.com/e_pages/news/index.a

SOURCES:
WildPlanet-1995, p. 406

♦ 2747 ♦ **Thesmophoria**
Late October or early November; three days during ancient Greek month of Pyanopsion

Thesmophoria was an ancient Greek festival held in honor of Demeter Thesmophoros, the goddess of the harvest and fertility and the protectress of marriage; it is unclear whether this festival was named after the goddess or vice versa. It was celebrated by women, perhaps only married women, and lasted three days, between the 11th and the 13th (some say between the 14th and the 16th) of the month of Pyanopsion (which fell between October and November), at the time of the autumn sowing of the new crops.

According to Greek mythology, Demeter's daughter, Kore, was gathering flowers near Eleusis one day when she was abducted by Pluto, god of the underworld, and taken away to his subterranean kingdom. By lowering pigs into chasms in the earth, the women commemorated the abduction of Kore. Some of the women had to enter the underground chambers themselves and bring up the putrefied remains of the pigs that had been cast there the year before. The rotten flesh was placed on altars and mixed with seed corn, which was then sown in the fields as a kind of magical fertilizer to ensure a good crop. The women fasted on the second day, and on the third they celebrated the magic of fertility in the animal as well as the plant kingdoms.

In Athens and other Greek cities, the women who celebrated the Thesmophoria dressed in white robes and observed a period of strict chastity for several days before and during the ceremony. They would strew their beds with herbs that were supposed to ward off venereal diseases and sit on the ground to promote the fertility of the corn that had just been sown. Although the festival itself was taken very seriously, it was not uncommon for the women to joke among themselves, as if in doing so they could cheer the goddess Demeter, who suffered greatly over the loss of her daughter.

The Romans had a similar festival in honor of Ceres, called the CEREALIA.

SOURCES:
AtticFest-1981, p. 70
ClassDict-1984, p. 625
DictFolkMyth-1984, pp. 867, 870, 1108
EncyRel-1987, vol. 14, p. 481
NewCentClassHandbk-1962, p. 1086
OxClassDict-1970, p. 1062
SeasFeast-1961, p. 135

◆ 2748 ◆ **Thimithi Fire-Walking Ceremony**
October-November; during the Tamil month of Aipasi

The Thimithi Fire-Walking Ceremony takes place in Singapore's Sri Mariamman Temple during the Tamil month of Aipasi (which corresponds to the Hindu month of Kartika; Tamil people hail from southern India). This Tamil Hindu observance is part of a two-month festival in which various scenes from the great Hindu epic, the *Mahabharata,* are reenacted by devotees and the epic itself is read aloud in installments.

During the Thimithi Fire-Walking Ceremony followers of the goddess Draupadi—who plays a major role in the *Mahabharata*—walk across a bed of red-hot coals. This observance begins at 2:00 A.M. in the Sri Srinivasa Perumal Temple. The fire walking takes place more than 12 hours later, at 5:00 P.M. The Padukalam (Battle Field) ceremony, based on a battle scene from the *Mahabharata,* takes place before the fire-walking event. The *Mahabharata* tells that after an 18-day-long war Draupadi volunteered to walk on hot coals in order to demonstrate her purity.

Today's worshippers do so to show their faith in the goddess. They begin by making offerings at Draupadi's shrine. Then they receive bracelets of yellow string, in which a piece of turmeric and a sprig of margosa leaves are entwined. In addi-

tion they are prepared for their ordeal with three whip lashes across the wrist. Then they form a procession leading to the Sri Mariamman Temple, where the bed of hot coals awaits them. After crossing the coals, devotees splash through a pit of milk, set up as a means of soothing the skin on their feet. Local historians trace the Thimithi Fire-Walking Ceremony at this temple to the 1840s.

CONTACTS:
Hindu Endowments Board
397 Serangoon Rd.
Singapore, 218123 Singapore
65-6296-3469
www.heb.gov.sg

◆ 2749 ◆ **Thimphu Tsechu**
September-October

Thimphu Tsechu is a three-day festival of religious ceremonies and costumed dances held in Thimphu, the capital city of Bhutan. *Tsechu* means "tenth day" and is used in much the same way as "festival" is used in English. Many of the dances performed at the tsechu are designed to teach lessons about how one's behavior on earth affects the afterlife, while others are believed to influence the actions of the spirits or to purify sacred ground.

Perhaps the most famous and exotic of the *cham* dances performed at the festival is the Dance of the Drummers from Dametsi, thought to have been introduced by a saint who lived in the 16th century. The dance represents the vision of the heavenly castle of Guru Rinpoche, which the saint saw in a dream. It is performed by 12 men who wear animal masks and yellow skirts. They bang on beautifully adorned drums to celebrate the victory of Mahayana Buddhism. They jump about and execute complex patterns, which symbolize the playful antics of the gods and spirits of the afterlife.

CONTACTS:
Bhutan Tourism Corporation Ltd.
P.O. Box 159
Thimphu, Bhutan
975-322647; fax: 975-23392
www.kingdomofbhutan.com

SOURCES:
WildPlanet-1995, p. 224

◆ 2750 ◆ **Thingyan**
Mid-April; during Burmese month of Tagu

The three-day feast of the New Year in Burma (now officially called Myanmar) is also known as the **Water Festival** because of the custom of throwing or squirting water on others. The festival has been traditional for centuries; King Narathihapate (1254-1287) built enclosed corridors running from his palace to the banks of the Irrawaddy River; inside them he and his courtiers reveled in water throwing.

During the celebration, pots of clear cold water are offered to monks at monasteries to wash or sprinkle images of Buddha. Everyone else gets drenched; young men and women roam the streets dousing everybody with buckets of water or turning hoses on them. On the final day, the traditional Burmese New Year, birds and fish are set free, and young people wash the hair of their elders. The water-splashing custom originated with the idea that through this ritual the bad luck and sins of the old year were washed away. Now splashing people is more a frolicsome thing to do and also a way of cooling off. This is the hottest time of year in Burma, and temperatures can sizzle above 100 degrees.

See also LUNAR NEW YEAR and SONGKRAN

CONTACTS:
Embassy of the Union of Myanmar
2300 S St. N.W.
Washington, D.C. 20008
202-332-3344; fax: 202-332-4351
www.mewashingtondc.com

SOURCES:
BkHolWrld-1986, Apr 13
DictFolkMyth-1984, pp. 913, 1108
FolkWrldHol-1999, p. 291

♦ 2751 ♦ **Third Prince, Birthday of the**
April-May; eighth and ninth days of fourth lunar month

This Chinese Taoist festival honors the Third Prince, a miracle-working child-god who rides on the wheels of wind and fire. In Singapore, Chinese mediums in trances dance, slash themselves with spiked maces and swords, and write charms on yellow paper with blood from their tongues. There is also a street procession of stilt-walkers, dragon dancers, and Chinese musicians.

CONTACTS:
Singapore Tourism Board
1156 Ave. of the Americas, Ste. 702
New York, NY 10036
212-302-4861; fax: 212-302-4801
www.visitsingapore.com

♦ 2752 ♦ **Thjodhatid**
First weekend in August

Thjodhatid is a three-day "people's feast" celebrated in the Vestmannaeyjar area (or Westmann Islands) of Iceland. The festival commemorates the granting of Iceland's constitution on July 1, 1874, which permitted the nation, long under the control of Denmark, to handle its own domestic affairs. Because of foul weather, the island people of Vestmannaeyjar weren't able to attend the mainland celebration, so they held their own festival at home a month later. They've been holding this month-late celebration ever since.

Most of the festivities take place in Herjólfsdalur on Heimaey Island. Enormous bonfires are built, and there are sporting events, dancing, singing, and eating and drinking. People come from the mainland for this event, so the island is filled with campers.

CONTACTS:
Vestmannaeyjar Tourist Information Center
Vestmannabraut 38
Vestmannaeyjar, 900 Iceland
354-481-1271; fax: 354-481-1572

♦ 2753 ♦ **Thorrablót (Thorri Banquet)**
February

Thorrablóts, which are held in February in towns throughout Iceland, are midwinter feasts featuring traditional Icelandic foods and beverages that may be repugnant to visitors with nonadventurous taste buds. The fare includes *hákarl* (a gamey shark); ram's testicles; *lundi* (broiled puffin birds); *blódmör* (sheep's blood pudding); and seal and whale meat. Dessert may be more palatable for non-natives: *skyr*, made from curd and dried wild crowberries. The locals wash everything down with a schnapps nicknamed "black death." Live music and dancing accompanies the feasting.

CONTACTS:
Icelandic Tourist Board
655 Third Ave., Ste. 1810
New York, NY 10017
212-885-9700; fax: 212-885-9710
www.goiceland.org

SOURCES:
WildPlanet-1995, p. 48

♦ 2754 ♦ **Three Archbishops, Day of the**
January 30

In Greece during the 11th century there was a popular controversy over which of the three fourth-century archbishops—Basil the Great, Gregory the Theologian, or John Chrysostom—was the greatest saint of the Greek Orthodox Church. In 1081 Bishop John of Galatia resolved the problem by reporting that the three saints had appeared to him in a vision to say that they were all equal in the eyes of God. Their equality is celebrated on this day, which is also known as the **Holiday of the Three Hierarchs**. In Greek schools special exercises are held in honor of the three, who supported the classical Greek tradition at a time when many early Christians were opposed to all non-Christian literature.

SOURCES:
BkHolWrld-1986, Jan 30

♦ 2755 ♦ **Three Choirs Festival**
Third full week in August

One of Europe's oldest continuing music festivals, the Three Choirs Festival alternates among the three English cathedral cities of Gloucester, Worcester, and Hereford. The festival traditionally opens at the host cathedral with a performance by a choir and orchestra. Concerts during the rest of the week-long event take place either in the cathedral or in local theaters and historic homes.

Records show that the festival was founded before 1719, and that it was held, as it is now, in succession at the three cathedrals. In the early days of the festival, it was customary for two or more wealthy patrons—called stewards—to underwrite the cost of the event. Today, subscribers to the festivals are still referred to as stewards, and money collected at the doors of the cathedral following a performance still benefits the Charity for the Relief of Widows and Orphans of Clergy, which has been affiliated with the festival since 1724.

CONTACTS:
Three Choirs Festival Association
Community House
7C College Green
Gloucester, GL1 2LX United Kingdom
44-14-5252-9819
www.3choirs.org

SOURCES:
GdWrldFest-1985, p. 91
MusFestEurBrit-1980, p. 61
MusFestWrld-1963, p. 27

♦ 2756 ♦ Three Kings Day in Indian Pueblos
January 6

Three Kings Day in Indian Pueblos is the day for the installation of new officers and governors at most of the 19 Indian pueblos in New Mexico. The inaugural day begins with a church ceremony during which four walking canes, the symbols of authority, are passed on to the new governor. The governor is honored with a dance, which starts in mid-morning and is usually some form of an animal dance—often the EAGLE, Elk, Buffalo, and Deer dances. Spirited and animated, they are considered a form of prayer. Each dance is very different from the others, and the same dance differs from pueblo to pueblo, although certain aspects are similar. In the Deer Dance, for example, dancers "walk" holding two sticks that represent their forelegs. They wear elaborate costumes and antler headdresses.

New Mexico's 19 pueblos are: Acoma, Cochiti, Isleta, Jemez, Laguna, Nambe, Picuris, Pojoaque, Sandia, San Felipe, San Ildefonso, San Juan, Santa Ana, Santa Clara, Santo Domingo, Taos, Tesuque, Zia, and Zuni. Each of them celebrates its saint's feast day as well as other occasions with dances and ceremonies that are an expression of thanksgiving, prayer, renewal, and harmony with nature. Many dances tell stories, legends, or history. Besides the feast days and Three Kings Day (EPIPHANY), most pueblos observe these other major holidays: NEW YEAR'S DAY, EASTER, and CHRISTMAS, which is often celebrated for two to five days.

CONTACTS:
Indian Pueblo Cultural Center
2401 12th St. N.W.
Albuquerque, NM 87104
866-855-7902 or 505-843-7270; fax: 505-842-6959
www.indianpueblo.org

SOURCES:
DictFolkMyth-1984, pp. 346, 571
FolkAmerHol-1999, p. 30
IndianAmer-1989, pp. 285, 306

♦ 2757 ♦ Three Weeks
Begins between June 17 and July 24 and ends between July 17 and August 14; from Tammuz 17 until Av 9

The 17th of Tammuz, also known as **Shivah Asar be-Tammuz**, marks the day on which the walls of Jerusalem were breached by the Babylonians under Nebuchadnezzar (*see also* ASARAH BE-TEVET). The three-week period between this day and the ninth of Av (*see* TISHA BE-AV) is known in Hebrew as the period **Bén ha-Metsarim**, in reference to Lamentations 1:3, which describes the city of Jerusalem as having been overtaken by her persecutors "between the straits."

Because this period is associated with the destruction of the Temple, it is a time of mourning for the Jewish people. As the days draw closer to the ninth of Av, the signs of mourning increase in severity. Although there are differences between Ashkenazi and Sephardic customs, the restrictions include not shaving or cutting one's hair, not wearing new clothes, nor eating fruit for the first time in season. Beginning with the first day of Av, the Ashkenazi custom is not to eat any meat nor drink any wine until after Tisha be-Av, while Sephardim refrain from meat and wine beginning with the Sunday preceding the ninth of Av. On Tisha be-Av itself, it is not permitted to eat or drink, to wear leather shoes, to anoint with oil, to wash (except where required), or to engage in sexual relations. On each of the three Sabbaths during the Three Weeks, a special prophetic passage of the Old Testament, known as a *haftarah*, is read.

CONTACTS:
Union of Orthodox Jewish Congregations of America
11 Broadway
New York, NY 10004
212-563-4000; fax: 212-564-9058
www.ou.org

SOURCES:
DaysCustFaith-1957, p. 159
DictWrldRel-1989, p. 155
RelHolCal-2004, p. 52

♦ 2758 ♦ Tiananmen Square Anniversary
June 4

Each year thousands of people in Hong Kong, China, gather on June 4 to commemorate the anniversary of the Tiananmen Square massacre with a candlelight vigil. On that same date in 1989, Chinese government tanks rolled into Beijing's Tiananmen Square killing hundreds of demonstrators calling for democratic reforms in China and injuring 10,000 more. The Chinese government has suppressed similar commemorative efforts in other Chinese cities, but since Hong Kong was a British colony until 1997, the tradition of the candlelight vigil took hold there. Since 1997 the Chinese government has discouraged the Hong Kong commemorations and pressured foreign news correspondents not to cover the yearly event. Organizers say the number of participants has been shrinking with each passing year. In the year 2002 about 45,000 people attended the vigil.

CONTACTS:
Beijing Municipal People's Government
2 Zhengyi Rd.
East Town District
Beijing City, 100744 China
86-10-6519-2335
www.ebeijing.gov.cn

♦ 2759 ♦ **Tichborne Dole**
March 25

The custom of handing out a dole, or allotment of flour, to the village poor in Alresford, Hampshire, England, dates back to the 12th or 13th century. Lady Mabella Tichborne, who was on her deathbed at the time, begged her husband to grant her enough land to provide an annual bounty of bread to the poor, who were suffering from a recent failure of the wheat crop. Her husband, in a less charitable frame of mind, snatched a blazing log from the fire and said that his wife could have as much land as she was able to crawl across before the flames died out. Although she had been bedridden for years, Lady Mabella had her servants carry her to the fields bordering the Tichborne estate and miraculously managed to crawl across 23 acres. With her dying breath, she proclaimed that if her heirs should ever fail to honor the bequest, the family name would die out.

On March 25, or Lady Day, each year, villagers in need of assistance gather at the porch of Tichborne House to claim their portion of the gift: a gallon of flour for adults, half as much for children. The fields across which Lady Mabella dragged herself are still known as "The Crawls."

CONTACTS:
Hampshire County Council Information Centre
Mottisfont Ct.
High St.
Winchester, Hampshire SO23 8ZB United Kingdom
44-19-6287-0500; fax: 44-19-6286-4621
www.hants.gov.uk

St. Gregory's Church
The Presbytery
Martin St.
Bishops Waltham, Hampshire SO32 1DN United Kingdom
44-14-8989-5889
www.saint-gregorys.org.uk

SOURCES:
AnnivHol-2000, p. 51
FolkCal-1930, p. 28
OxYear-1999, p. 134
YrbookEngFest-1954, p. 41

♦ 2760 ♦ **Tihar**
October-November; waning half of Hindu month of Kartika

Tihar is a five-day Hindu festival in Nepal that honors different animals on successive days. The third day of the festival, Lakshmi Puja, dedicated to the goddess of wealth, is known throughout India as Dewali.

On the first day of the festival, offerings of rice are made to crows, thought to be sent by Yama, the god of death, as his "messengers of death." The second day honors dogs, since in the afterworld dogs will guide departed souls across the river of the dead. Dogs are fed special food and adorned with flowers. Cows are honored on the morning of the third day; they, too, receive garlands and often their horns are painted gold and silver.

The third day is the most important day of the festival, when Lakshmi will come to visit every home that is suitably lit for her. Consequently, as evening falls, tiny candles and butter lamps flicker in homes throughout the country.

The fourth day is a day for honoring oxen and bullocks, and it also marks the start of the new year for the Newari people of the Kathmandu Valley. On the fifth day, known as Bhai Tika, brothers and sisters meet and place *tikas* (dots of red sandalwood paste, considered emblems of good luck) on each other's foreheads. The brothers give their sisters gifts, and the sisters give sweets and delicacies to their brothers and pray to Yama for their brothers' long life. This custom celebrates the legendary occasion when a girl pleaded so eloquently with Yama to spare her young brother from an early death that he relented and the boy lived.

CONTACTS:
Nepal Tourism Board, Tourist Service Center
Bhrikuti Mandap
P.O. Box 11018
Kathmandu, Nepal
977-1-4256909; fax: 977-1-4256910
www.welcomenepal.com

SOURCES:
FolkWrldHol-1999, p. 622
HolSymbols-2009, p. 959

♦ 2761 ♦ **Time Observance Day**
June 10

Emperor Tenchi (or Tenji) of Japan (626-671) is credited with making the first water clock, a device that measured time by the amount of water leaking out of a vessel. Because keeping track of time was not standard practice in the seventh century, the Japanese honor their 38th emperor on June 10, the day on which he first ordered the hour to be announced by sounding temple bells and drums.

The **Rokoku Festival**, or **Water Clock Festival**, is held on this day at the Omi Jingu Shrine in the city of Otsu, Shiga Prefecture, where the emperor's water clock is housed.

While placing so much emphasis on keeping track of the time may sound odd to Americans, it is important to remember that the Japanese were traditionally lax in such matters, often failing to announce the time when a meeting or function would begin because it depended on the readiness of the person in charge.

SOURCES:
BkFestHolWrld-1970, p. 97

♦ 2762 ♦ **Timor-Leste Anniversary of the Indonesian Invasion**
December 7

During Indonesia's 24-year occupation of its smaller neighbor, East Timor, the Timorese began commemorating historical dates, including the anniversary of the invasion of Indonesian forces on December 7, 1975. The arrival of the Indonesians initiated a period of occupation in which about 200,000 Timorese were killed. Today, in the Democratic Republic of Timor-Leste (internationally recognized since 2002), this anniversary remains an occasion to mourn those who were killed and to seek redress for crimes committed during the occupation.

Beginning in 1976, the year Indonesia annexed the nation then known as East Timor, the Timorese established a tradition of gathering in the capital, Dili, to commemorate the anniversary of the invasion and stage a public protest over Indonesia's actions. Candlelight vigils and commemorative church services also became common throughout the country and around the world. An historic demonstration took place on the 20th anniversary in 1995, when 112 East Timorese and supporters temporarily occupied Russian and Dutch embassies in Jakarta, the capital of Indonesia.

In the years since Timor-Leste achieved independence, human rights and other political groups have marked milestone anniversaries of the invasion by continuing to demand justice for the occupation's victims.

CONTACTS:
Embassy of the Democratic Republic of Timor Leste
4201 Connecticut Ave. N.W., Ste. 504
Washington, D.C. 20008
202-966-3202; fax: 202-966-3205

♦ 2763 ♦ **Timor-Leste Proclamation of Independence Day**
November 28

After the East Timorese declared independence from Portugal on November 28, 1975, it took over two decades to fulfill the promise of freedom. Their plans were foiled by neighboring Indonesia, which carried out its own occupation of its neighbor between 1975 and 1999. A second date, EAST TIMOR INDEPENDENCE DAY, was established when the Democratic Republic of Timor-Leste, as it is officially known, finally became a free state on May 2, 2002.

Observances for the November 28 anniversary honor the veterans of the independence movement. State leaders and other dignitaries usually participate in a parade, and the president of the country often bestows medals of honor to distinguish individuals who fought for the country's freedom.

CONTACTS:
Embassy of the Democratic Republic of Timor Leste
4201 Connecticut Ave. N.W., Ste. 504
Washington, D.C. 20008
202-966-3202; fax: 202-966-3205

SOURCES:
AnnivHol-2000, p. 197

♦ 2764 ♦ **Timor Santa Cruz Massacre Day (National Youth Day)**
November 12

The Santa Cruz Massacre Day (**National Youth Day**) remains among the most significant anniversaries for veterans of the Timorese independence movement, which was active during the Indonesian occupation between 1975 and 1999. In 1991, 271 protesters—many of them students—disappeared or were killed at the Santa Cruz cemetery in the Timor-Leste capital, Dili. That massacre sparked international outrage and kept the spotlight on the Indonesian occupation until it ended in 1999.

Before Indonesia withdrew forces, the anniversary of the Santa Cruz Massacre inspired several political protests, in towns and cities of Timor-Leste and among sympathetic communities throughout the world. In 1994, on the third anniversary, a group of Timorese activists scaled the fence of the U.S. embassy in Jakarta, Indonesia, to request political asylum.

The tone of the day was and remains mournful. During the occupation years, Timorese often lit candles, and it was often an occasion for public figures to rally the people. On the fifth anniversary of the massacre, NOBEL Peace Prize–winner José Ramos-Horta called on Timorese to begin a new phase of their campaign for self-determination.

CONTACTS:
Embassy of the Democratic Republic of Timor Leste
4201 Connecticut Ave. N.W., Ste. 504
Washington, D.C. 20008
202-966-3202; fax: 202-966-3205

♦ 2765 ♦ **Timqat (Timkat)**
January 19-20

Because the Ethiopian CHRISTMAS, called GANNA, falls on January 7, EPIPHANY (Timqat) is celebrated on January 19. Timqat celebrates the baptism of Jesus in the Jordan River. It begins at sunset on Epiphany Eve, when people dress in white and go to their local church. From the church they form a procession with the *tabot*, or holy ark, in which the ancient Israelites put the Tablets of the Law, or Torah, the first five books of the Old Testament. Ethiopians do not believe it was lost, but that it is now preserved in the Cathedral of Axum in Ethiopia (each Ethiopian Orthodox church has a blessed replica of the tabot as well). They accompany it to a lake, stream, or pond. It is placed in a tent, where it is guarded all night while the clergy and villagers sing, dance, and eat until the baptismal service the following morning. At dawn the clergy bless the water and sprinkle it on the heads of those who wish to renew their Christian vows. Then the procession, again bearing the tabot, returns to the church. The festivities continue until the following day, January 20 or the Feast of St. Michael.

Ethiopian religious processions are characterized by the priests' richly colored ceremonial robes, fringed, embroidered umbrellas, and elaborately decorated crosses. The national sport of *guks* is often played at Timqat. Warriors with shields of hippopotamus hide, wearing lion-mane capes and headdresses ride on caparisoned horses and try to strike each other with thrown bamboo lances.

CONTACTS:
Embassy of Ethiopia
3506 International Dr. N.W.
Washington, D.C. 20008
202-364-1200; fax: 202-587-0195
www.ethiopianembassy.org

Ethiopian Tourism Commission
P.O. Box 2183
Addis Ababa, Ethiopia
251-1-517-470; fax: 251-1-517-533
www.tourismethiopia.org

SOURCES:
BkFestHolWrld-1970, p. 23
EncyChristmas-2003, p. 758
FolkWrldHol-1999, p. 39

♦ 2766 ♦ Tin Hau Festival
23rd day of third lunar month

This birthday festival in Hong Kong celebrates Tin Hau, queen of Heaven and goddess of the sea. Also known as Tien-hou or Matsu, she is one of the most popular deities in Hong Kong; there are about 24 Tin Hau temples throughout the territory, and fishermen often have shrines to her on their boats. Her story dates back many centuries. It is said that she was born with mystical powers in a fishing village in Fukien Province, and that as a young girl she saved her two brothers from drowning during a storm. Today she is revered for her ability to calm the waves and to guarantee bountiful catches, and for her protection from shipwrecks and sickness.

The festivities include parades, performances of Chinese opera, and the sailing of hundreds of junks and sampans, decked out with colorful streamers, through Hong Kong's waterways to the temples. The temple in Joss House Bay is especially known for its festival, which attracts thousands of fisherfolk. The original temple was built southwest of the present temple in 1012 by two brothers who said their lives were saved by the statue of Tin Hau that they clutched when they were shipwrecked. A typhoon destroyed that temple, and descendants of the brothers built another one on the present site in 1266.

See also MATSU, BIRTHDAY OF

CONTACTS:
Hong Kong Tourism Board
115 E. 54th St., 2nd Fl.
New York, NY 10022
212-421-3382; fax: 212-421-8428
www.discoverhongkong.com

♦ 2767 ♦ Tiragan
July, November, December; 13th day of Tir, the fourth Zoroastrian month

Tiragan is a Zoroastrian celebration in honor of Tishtrya, a deity identified with rain as well as Sirius, the Dog Star. It is held during the *gahambar* or seasonal feast of MAIDYOSHAHEM, also known as the Mid-Summer Feast. The followers of Persian prophet Zoroaster (also known as Zarathushtra, believed to have lived around 1200 B.C.E.), believe that dogs belong to the good part of creation and that they serve as helpers to mankind. Dogs are also thought to possess the ability to see spiritual beings. Much like the celebration of HOLI in India and of SONGKRAN in Thailand, the festival's activities include splashing people with water.

The 13th day of Tir is also associated with a legendary event during the reign of King Minochiher, when a dispute about the boundary between Iran and Turan (a region in what is now southeastern Iran) was decided by the throwing of an arrow (tir) by an archer named Erekhsha.

There are only about 100,000 followers of Zoroastrianism today, and most of them live in northwestern India or Iran. Smaller communities exist in Pakistan, Sri Lanka, Canada, the U.S., England, and Australia.

SOURCES:
RelHolCal-2004, p. 67

♦ 2768 ♦ Tirana, La
About a week, including July 16

Each July tens of thousands of pilgrims set up camp in the small village of La Tirana, in the Tarapacá region of northern Chile. July 16 is the feast day of the Virgen del Carmen and the highlight of the festival (*see also* OUR LADY OF CARMEL). On that day there is a colorful, musical procession of images of the Virgen and Jesus around the village accompanied by more than 100 dance groups in elaborate costumes. Dancers who attend the festival practice traditional Andean dances all year round for the event, and many view their dancing as an act of devotion to the Virgen. During the rest of the time people wander the markets that have sprung up, worship at the chapel that houses the image of the Virgen, and participate in masses and other religious activities organized by the Diocese of Iquique.

CONTACTS:
Embassy of Chile
1732 Massachusetts Ave. N.W.
Washington, D.C. 20036
202-785-1746; fax: 202-887-5579
www.chile-usa.org

SOURCES:
FestWrld: Chile-1998, p. 8

♦ 2769 ♦ Tirupati Festival
August-September; about nine days during Hindu month of Bhadrapada

Tirupati, Andhra Pradesh, India, is considered an essential pilgrimage center for every devout Hindu. The shrine there, one of the richest temples in the world, is situated on the seven Tirumala hills. Since Tirupati is the seat of Lord Venkteshwara, a manifestation of Lord Vishnu, Venkteshwara is also known as the "Lord of the Seven Hills." The grand festival, called *Bhramotsavam*, is held at Tirupati during the month of Bhadrapada for about nine days, during which Hindus gather to seek Lord Venkteshwara's blessings for material and spiritual gains.

Hindus who make a pilgrimage to Tirupati during the festival in the month of Bhadrapada often shave their hair off as a votive offering. Parents bring very young children there to perform their first tonsure (the act of clipping the hair) at the feet of the image of Lord Venkteshwara.

CONTACTS:
Tirumala Tirupati Devasthanams Temple Administration
TTD Administrative Bldg.
K.T. Rd.
Tirupati, Andhra Pradesh 517 501 India
91-85-7431777; fax: 91-85-7430358
www.ttdsevaonline.com

Ministry of Tourism, Government of India
Rm. No 123, Transport Bhawan, No. 1, Parliament St.
New Delhi, Delhi 110 001 India
91-11-23715084; fax: 91-11-23715084
www.tourisminindia.com

SOURCES:
RelHolCal-2004, p. 173

♦ 2770 ♦ **Tisha be-Av**
Between July 17 and August 14; Av 9

The Jewish **Fast of Av** is a period of fasting, lamentation, and prayer in memory of the destruction of both the First and Second Temples in Jerusalem. When the Babylonians under Nebuchadnezzar destroyed the First Temple in 586 B.C.E., the Jews rebuilt it, but continued the fast day. Then the Second Temple was destroyed by the Romans under Titus, who burned it down in 70 C.E., and a long period of exile began for the Jews.

The Fast of Av begins at sunset the previous day and lasts for more than 24 hours. The nine days from the beginning of the month of Av through Tisha be-Av mark a period of intense mourning for the various disasters and tragedies that have befallen the Jewish people throughout history.

See also ASARAH BE-TEVET and THREE WEEKS

CONTACTS:
Union of Orthodox Jewish Congregations of America
11 Broadway
New York, NY 10004
212-563-4000; fax: 212-564-9058
www.ou.org

SOURCES:
AnnivHol-2000, p. 229
BkFest-1937, p. 209
BkHolWrld-1986, Aug 4
DaysCustFaith-1957, p. 197
FolkWrldHol-1999, p. 446
OxYear-1999, p. 728
RelHolCal-2004, p. 53

♦ 2771 ♦ **Tivoli Gardens Season**
Mid-April to late September

Tivoli Gardens is a renowned entertainment center that has been a summer attraction in the middle of Copenhagen, Denmark, since 1843. There are orchestral, jazz, and rock concerts; ballet; and Italian pantomimes featuring Pantaloon, Columbine, and Harlequin performed with the original musical scores. Another favorite entertainment is the Tivoli Guards, a band comprised of youngsters dressed in uniforms similar to those worn by the Royal Guard. At night the gardens dazzle with laser light shows and fireworks.

CONTACTS:
Tivoli Gardens
Tivoli A/S, 3 Vesterbrogade
P.O. Box 233
Copenhagen V, DK-1630 Denmark
45-33-15-10-01
www.tivoligardens.com

SOURCES:
FestEur-1961, p. 27
MusFestEurBrit-1980, p. 41

♦ 2772 ♦ *To Kill a Mockingbird* **Annual Production**
April-May

A two-act dramatization of Harper Lee's novel *To Kill a Mockingbird* is presented over several weekends each spring at the courthouse in Lee's hometown, Monroeville, Ala. Presented by amateur players from the community, the production draws hundreds of fans of the Pulitzer-Prize-winning novel, published in 1960.

The first act generally is performed outdoors, with the action moving into the historic 1903 courtroom for Act Two. Members of the audience are chosen to portray the jury in one of the play's climactic scenes. The courthouse setting is highly prized, because it inspired the set created for the trial scenes in the popular 1962 film version of *To Kill a Mockingbird*. The movie starred Gregory Peck as Atticus Finch, the principled attorney fighting racism in 1930s Alabama.

Lee, who never wrote another book, still lives in Monroeville, but is said never to have attended the production based on her masterpiece. Monroeville began hosting performances in 1990, and it has transformed the town into a destination for tourists. Paid tickets to the performances sell out quickly in advance.

CONTACTS:
Monroe County Heritage Museums
P.O. Box 1637
31 N. Alabama Ave.
Monroeville, AL 36461
251-575-7433
www.frontiernet.net/~mchm/index.htm

♦ 2773 ♦ **Togo Independence Day**
April 27

Togo became independent on this day in 1960, after being under French control from the end of World War I. Independence Day is a national holiday in Togo.

CONTACTS:
The Republic of Togo
2208 Massachusetts Ave. N.W.
Washington, D.C. 20008
202-234-4212; fax: 202-232-3190

SOURCES:
AnnivHol-2000, p. 69
NatlHolWrld-1968, p. 51

♦ 2774 ♦ Togo National Liberation Day
January 13

On January 13, 1967, Togo president Nicolas Grunitzky, of mixed Kabye, Ewe, and Polish heritage, was overthrown by Gnassingbé Eyadema, who remained president of Togo until 2005. He was succeeded by his son Faure Gnassingbé. Bowing to both internal and international pressure, Faure Gnassingbé agreed to step down and hold a general election. He won that election and has ruled, despite opposition, as president. National Liberation Day celebrates the accession to power of his father, Gnassingbé Eyadema.

To celebrate National Liberation Day, the Togo military joins with civilian bands to mount several colorful parades down the Boulevard du Mono in the city of Lomé. Dissident groups have long opposed the celebrations, noting that January 13, 1963, saw the assassination of the nation's first president, Sylvanus Olympio. Because of the conflicting events that have happened on the same day in Togo history, President Gnassingbé in 2005 took a step toward appeasing his critics by publicly calling Sylvanus Olympio the true father of Togo's independence. In 2008, he called for an end to the public celebrations on National Liberation Day. The army would celebrate the day quietly on their own military bases, while the civilian population was urged to pray for national reconciliation.

CONTACTS:
Embassy of the Republic of Togo in the USA
2208 Massachusetts Ave. N.W.
Washington, D.C. 20008
202-234-4212

♦ 2775 ♦ Tohono O'odham Nation Rodeo
Three days in February

The Tohono O'odham Nation Rodeo has been a tradition for more than 60 years. Thousands of visitors come to Sells, Arizona, for the event each year for three days of rodeo and festivities in February. Dancers from tribes nationwide recreate ceremonial dances designed to bring rain, cure illness, or prepare for war, while Native American cowboys and cowgirls compete for $40,000 in prize money in such events as bareback riding, saddle bronc riding, bull riding, calf roping, steer wrestling, and barrel racing. Craft shows highlight the work of local Tohono O'odham and Pima artists and craftspeople, along with Maricopa pottery and baskets and Hopi kachina dolls.

The Tohono O'odham Nation, which in 1986 changed its name from Papago (meaning "Bean People") to Tohono

O'odham (which means "Desert People"), have lived in the desert regions of what is now Arizona and Mexico for centuries. They are renowned for their ability to grow food in the desert, and the festival features lots of traditional Indian foods, including fry bread and barbecue.

CONTACTS:
Tohono O'odham Nation
P.O. Box 837
Sells, AZ 85634
520-383-2028; fax: 520-383-3379
www.tonation-nsn.gov

SOURCES:
EndurHarv-1995, p. 159
WildPlanet-1995, p. 607

♦ 2776 ♦ Toji (Winter Solstice)
December 22

The earliest mention of Winter Solstice celebrations in Japan dates back at least to 725 C.E. and comes from records left by Emperor Shomu. It is an especially happy time for farmers, because it marks the time of year when the days begin to grow longer and the sun nearer. Many of the customs associated with Toji are still observed in rural areas; they include enjoying citrus baths, eating foods made from pumpkins (which is believed to bring good luck), and offering gifts to one's ancestors. Servants and workers are often given a day off, and many shrines sponsor bonfires.

SOURCES:
JapanFest-1965, p. 209

♦ 2777 ♦ Tok Race of Champions Dog Sled Race
Late March

The last race of the Alaska dog-mushing season, held since 1954 in Tok, which claims to be the Dog Capital of Alaska. Mushers from Alaska, Canada, and the lower 48 states participate in six-dog, eight-dog and open-class events for cash prizes.

Tok, a trade center for nearby Athabascan Indian villages, is also a center for dog breeding, training, and mushing. It's not quite certain where the name of the town came from; some say it derives from a native word meaning "peace crossing," and others believe the village was originally called Tokyo and shortened to Tok during World War II.

CONTACTS:
Tok Dog Mushers Association
P.O. Box 45
Tok, AK 99780
907-883-5313
www.tokdogmushers.org

♦ 2778 ♦ Tolling the Devil's Knell
December 24

To celebrate the birth of Christ and the death of the Devil, All Saints Minster Church in Dewsbury, Yorkshire, rings its bell the same number of times as the number of the year (for example, 2,000 times in 2000) on CHRISTMAS EVE. The tolling starts at 11:00 P.M., stops during the church service from midnight to 12:45, and is then resumed until the years have been tolled away. The custom has been going on for almost 700 years, although there was an interruption in the early 19th century and again during World War II, when all bell-ringing was banned except to signal enemy invasion.

Although no one seems to remember exactly how the custom started, there is a legend that says Sir Thomas Soothill donated the tenor bell to the parish church as a penance for murdering a young boy servant and then trying to conceal his body. The bell has been called "Black Tom of Soothill" since the 13th century, and **Tolling Black Tom** is supposed to keep the parish safe from the Devil for another 12 months.

CONTACTS:
All Saints Minster Church
Rishworth Rd.
Dewsbury, West Yorkshire WF12 8DD United Kingdom
44-19-2445-7057; fax: 44-19-2443-9547

SOURCES:
EncyChristmas-2003, p. 198

♦ 2779 ♦ **Tom Sawyer Days, National**
Week of July 4

Sponsored by the Hannibal, Missouri, Jaycees, the National Tom Sawyer Days celebration began in 1956 with a Tom Sawyer Fence Painting Contest and a Tom and Becky competition. Three years later, all of the events relating to the fictional character originally created by Mark Twain in his 1876 novel were combined with the traditional FOURTH OF JULY celebration in Hannibal, and Independence Day was officially proclaimed "Tom Sawyer Day." In 1961 it became a national event, and today the festival spans five days and includes a number of unique competitions.

Contestants for the fence-painting competition, who must be 10 to 13 years old, come primarily from the 10 states bordering the Mississippi River. They are judged on the authenticity of their costumes (which must be based on details from Mark Twain's book), the speed with which they can whitewash a four-by-five-foot section of fence, and the quality of their work.

The Frog Jump Competition is another of the festival's highlights, drawing up to 300 children and their pet frogs, each of whom is allowed three jumps. Competitors for the Tom and Becky competition must be eighth graders living in Hannibal, and the winners serve as goodwill ambassadors for the year.

See also CALAVERAS COUNTY FAIR AND FROG JUMPING JUBILEE

CONTACTS:
Hannibal Jaycees
137 Jaycee Dr.
Hannibal, MO 63401
573-221-3231; fax: 573-221-6999
www.hannibaljaycees.org

♦ 2780 ♦ **Tomatina (Tomato Battle)**
Last week in August

Regardless of which legend one believes, what began in 1945 as a few tossed tomatoes as a show of disdain for the repressive Franco regime—or during a feud among friends—or by a fan unhappy with a musician's performance—has developed into full-fledged tomato warfare in Buñol, Valencia, Spain, during the last week in August. La Tomatina also happens to coincide with the town's patron saint festival, and while the tomato battle itself takes place on a Wednesday, the festivities last for a week.

Residents prepare for the impending food fight by protecting their storefronts and homes with plastic, donning special clothing, and imbibing alcohol. Thousands of pounds of tomatoes are trucked into town and dropped off at the Plaza del Pueblo, Buñol's main square, and the light-hearted battle commences. Although anyone is fair game when it comes to choosing a target, La Tomatina offers a good opportunity for males and females to meet and flirt with each other. This community-sanctioned tomato bath leaves both the festivalgoers and the streets covered with pulp, seeds, and juice, but after the cleanup, celebrants continue to enjoy the festival's fireworks, parades, food, and music.

CONTACTS:
The Institute of Tourism of Spain (Instituto de Turismo de Espana)
Jose Lazaro Galdiano, 6
Madrid, 28071 Spain
34-913-433-500
www.latomatina.es

SOURCES:
WildPlanet-1995, p. 100

♦ 2781 ♦ **Tonga Emancipation Day**
June 4

June 4 is a national holiday in the Kingdom of Tonga, celebrating its full independence from Britain. Located in the Pacific Ocean some 1,250 miles north of New Zealand, the island nation of Tonga consists of about 150 islands, 36 of which are inhabited. With a population of about 120,000, Tonga is ruled by a royal family that goes back to 1831.

On June 4, 1863, King George Tupuo I abolished the system of serfdom in the island nation of Tonga. The historic occasion is remembered on Emancipation Day, which is celebrated just after the conclusion of the annual three-day Ha'apai Festival. The Ha'apai Festival begins on Tonga's outer islands and ends on Lifuka Island on June 4th. Both the festival and Emancipation Day are marked with feasts and dancing.

CONTACTS:
General Consulate of Tonga in San Francisco
360 Post St., Ste. 604
San Francisco, CA 94108
415-781-0365

♦ 2782 ♦ **Tonga Heilala Festival**
Week of July 4

Located in the Pacific Ocean some 1,250 miles north of New Zealand, the island nation of Tonga consists of about 150 islands, 36 of which are inhabited. With a population of about 120,000, Tonga is ruled by a royal family that goes back to 1831.

The Heilala Festival celebrates the flowering of the heilala, Tonga's national flower. But for many years, the Heilala Festival also coincided with the birthday celebrations for Tonga's King George Tupou IV. Since the king's death in 2006, the festival now includes the birthday of Crown Prince Tupouto'a Lavaka.

The weeklong Heilala Festival features a host of events, including a Miss Heilala Pageant, parades of floats, processions, and music festivals. The streets of Tongatapu are covered with colorful flowered arches, while decorative lights illuminate the Royal Tomb at Mala'ekula and the Royal Palace. Among the live entertainment is the dance group Lakalaka from Vavau, which features some 1,000 dancers. In addition to food, drinks, and live music, there are also traditional crafts on display. A night-time torch-lighting ceremony, named Tupakapakanava, involves a group of participants carrying flaming torches of dry reeds along the northern coastline of Tongatapu. The evenings often end with gatherings around beach bonfires.

CONTACTS:
General Consulate of Tonga in San Francisco
360 Post St. , Ste. 604
San Francisco, CA 94108
415-781-0365

♦ 2783 ♦ **Tonga National Day**
November 4

On November 4, 1875, King George Tupou I gave his consent to the constitution of the new nation of Tonga. Celebrated for many years as **Tonga Constitution Day**, the government of Tonga in 2006 renamed the holiday Tonga National Day and pronounced it an occasion to celebrate the country's heritage as a whole.

Located in the Pacific Ocean some 1,250 miles north of New Zealand, the island nation of Tonga consists of about 150 islands, 36 of which are inhabited. With a population of about 120,000, Tonga is ruled by a royal family that goes back to 1831. King George Tupou I conquered the islands that now make up Tonga and granted his people a constitution guaranteeing their rights in 1875. His great-grandson, King George Tupou II, signed a treaty of friendship with England in 1900 that made Tonga a protected state. Tonga achieved complete independence in 1970 and became a member of the United Nations in 1999.

CONTACTS:
General Consulate of Tonga in San Francisco
360 Post St. , Ste. 604
San Francisco, CA 94108
415-781-0365

♦ 2784 ♦ **Tono Matsuri**
September 14-15

This autumn festival in Japan, observed in the hope that it will bring a good harvest, provides an excellent display of traditional Japanese arts. There is a SHISHI ODORI dance, performed to the accompaniment of taiko drums; *Taué-odori*, a rice-planting dance; *kagura* (sacred music and dance) performances; and *Yabusamé* (horseback archery) demonstrations. There is also a children's parade, called *Chigo-gyoretsu*. A distinctive genre of festival music, known as *Nambu-bayashi*, is performed on the grounds of the Tonogo-hachi-mangu Shrine in Tono.

CONTACTS:
Japan National Tourist Organization
1 Rockefeller Pl., Ste. 1250
New York, NY 10020
212-757-5640; fax: 212-307-6754
www.japantravelinfo.com

SOURCES:
IllFestJapan-1993, p. 108

♦ 2785 ♦ **Torch Festival**
24th through 26th days of sixth lunar month

The Torch Festival is a traditional holiday of many of the Yi people in Yunnan and Sichuan Provinces in China. Revelers dress in fine clothes, and the girls are especially colorful in embroidered gowns and headdresses of all colors. Celebrations begin with the sound of firecrackers, followed by folk dancing, athletic contests in such sports as pole-climbing and wrestling, and a bullfight. At night, huge bonfires are lit, dancers whirl around them, and a parade of people carrying torches brightens the night.

CONTACTS:
Yunnan Tourism Information Center
4th Floor, Yunnan Zhijian Bldg.
76 E Dongfeng Rd.
Kunming, Yunnan Province 650051 China
86-871-3210-972; fax: 86-871-3120-740
www.yunnantourism.net

♦ 2786 ♦ **Torch Fight**
February; 15th day of the first lunar month

Torch fights are still popular in some rural areas in Korea to celebrate the first full moon of the LUNAR NEW YEAR (SOL). Neighboring farming villages form their own teams and fight each other with torches made of burning bundles of straw. Young men and boys do the fighting, and the number of torches they use depends on the number of people in their families. A hill is usually the designated battleground, and the torch-bearers gather there and wait for the full moon to rise, at which point a gong signals the beginning of the battle.

The fighting consists of members of each team rushing their opponents, brandishing their lit torches. While no one usually gets hurt in this game, participants generally go home with singed hair and clothing.

See also TAEBORUM

CONTACTS:
Korea National Tourism Organization
2 Executive Dr., Ste. 100
Fort Lee, NJ 07024
800-868-7567 or 201-585-0909; fax: 201-585-9041
www.kntoamerica.com

SOURCES:
AnnCustKorea-1983, p. 61
FestWrld: SouthKorea-1998, p. 11

♦ 2787 ♦ Tori-no-ichi (Rooster Festival)
November

The **Rooster Festival** in Japan takes its name from the mythological rooster who helped bring the sun god out from hiding in a cave, and the bird became a symbol of material well-being. Many members of the Shinto sect who observe this festival are wealthy merchants and speculators, and the bamboo rakes that can be seen everywhere at this time are called *kumade.* People carry these rakes, usually decorated with good-luck emblems and the smiling face of the laughing goddess Okame, because they represent the power to pull toward them anything they desire. Some of the rakes are small enough to be worn in a woman's hair, while others are so large and heavily decorated that it takes several men to carry them through the streets. Sometimes, signs advertising restaurants or shops are hung from them and used throughout the year.

CONTACTS:
Japan Information Network, Japan Center for Intercultural
  Communications
2-7-7 Hirakawacho
Chiyodaku
Tokyo, 102-0093 Japan
81-3-3263-5041; fax: 81-3-3230-4107
home.jcic.or.jp

Asakusa Umaimono-kai (Association of Restaurants and Shops)
  Japan
www.asakusa-umai.ne.jp

♦ 2788 ♦ Toronto Caribana (Toronto Caribbean Carnival)
Summer; varies

Since 1967, Toronto, Canada, has hosted a multi-week summer festival called Caribana, also known as the **Toronto Caribbean Carnival**. The festival was originally created as a community heritage project for Canada's Centennial year. It is the largest Caribbean festival in North America, bringing in more than one million people each year.

Caribana is a Trinidad-style carnival that includes music, dance, food, and costumes from Jamaica, Guyana, the Bahamas, Brazil, and other cultures represented in Toronto. The main event of the festival is the mile-long Caribana Parade, which is one of the largest in North America. The parade participants dress in brilliant costumes, and dozens of trucks fill the parade route all day, carrying artists giving live performances in soca, calypso, steel pan, reggae, and salsa.

In addition to the parade, main events include a two-day Olympic Island Caribbean Arts Festival, a calypso competition, a Caribana king and queen pageant, parties, Caribbean food, outdoor concerts, music, and dance. These events are intended to celebrate the community's heritage and culture.

This festival is similar to Calgary's annual CARIFEST celebration.

CONTACTS:
Festival Management Committee
1470 Don Mills Rd., Ste. 305
Toronto, ON M3B 2X9 Canada
www.caribanafestival.com

Caribana (Tourist Info)
4-2880 Queen St. E., Ste. 123
Brampton, ON L6S 6H4 Canada
www.caribanatoronto.com

♦ 2789 ♦ Toronto International Film Festival
First week of September

Second in size only to the Cannes Film Festival in France, the Toronto International Film Festival is considered one of the world's most prestigious artistic events. As such, it features some of the year's most anticipated films, attracts leading stars in the movie business, and serves as a major networking and educational opportunity for industry professionals.

Established by the Toronto International Film Festival Group, the festival was first held in 1976. From its inception, the event intended to attract worldwide attention yet simultaneously promote the domestic film industry. Today, people attend several showcases of Canadian-made films.

Festival organizers pride themselves on creating a public festival, which means film submissions from all over are accepted and screenings are open to the public as well as to the media and the film industry. The Toronto International Film Festival Group reports that it handles more than 300,000 public and industry admissions. From this group of films, Toronto theaters host screenings of over 300 films, representing about 50 different countries.

In spite of its lasting reputation for highlighting independent and international cinema, the festival has attracted attention and controversy since the 1990s for the submissions from Hollywood and the grand film marketing campaigns that promote them.

CONTACTS:
Toronto International Film Festival Group
2 Carlton St.
Toronto, ON MSB 1J3 Canada
www.torontointernationalfilmfestival.ca

SOURCES:
AnnivHol-2000, p. 163

♦ 2790 ♦ Torta dei Fieschi
August 14

When Count Fieschi of Lavagna in Genoa, Italy, was married in 1240, he invited his guests—and everyone else in town—to share a cake that was more than 30 feet high. The citizens of Lavagna haven't forgotten his generosity, and each year they celebrate the event on August 14. Dressed in costumes, they parade to the town square, where they pin to their clothes a piece of paper (blue for men, white for women) on which a word is written. When they find someone wearing the same word, the couple is given a piece of "Fieschi's cake."

CONTACTS:
Italian Government Tourist Board
630 Fifth Ave., Ste. 1565
New York, NY 10111
212-245-5618; fax: 212-586-9249
www.italiantourism.com

SOURCES:
BkHolWrld-1986, Aug 14

♦ 2791 ♦ Toshogu Haru-No-Taisai (Great Spring Festival of the Toshogu Shrine)
May 17-18

This festival—also known as the **Sennin Gyoretsu**, or **Procession of 1,000 People**—provides the most spectacular display of ancient samurai costumes and weaponry in Japan. The Toshogu Shrine, in Nikko, Tochigi Prefecture, was built in 1617 to house the mausoleum of Tokugawa Ieyasu (1543-1616), the first of the Tokugawa shoguns. The festival originated in honor of the reburial of Ieyasu in the new mausoleum.

On the first day of the festival, dignitaries and members of the Tokugawa family make offerings to the deities of the shrine. Also on this day, warriors on horseback shoot at targets with bows and arrows. On the morning of May 18 more than 1,000 people take part in the procession from Toshogu to Futarasan Shrine, including hundreds of samurai warriors with armor, helmets, and weaponry. Also marching are priests with flags; men with stuffed hawks representing huntsmen; men in fox masks to honor the fox spirits that protect the shrine; and musicians with drums and bells.

CONTACTS:
Tochigi Prefecture
1-1-20 Hanawada
Utsunomiya, Tochigi 320-8501 Japan
81-2-8623-3165; fax: 81-2-8623-2199
www.pref.tochigi.jp/intro/gaikokugo/english/englis

SOURCES:
GdWrldFest-1985, p. 123
JapanFest-1965, p. 33

♦ 2792 ♦ Tour de France
July

The Tour de France is the world's greatest bicycle race and also the annual sports event with the most viewers—an estimated one billion who watch television coverage beamed around the world and 14.6 million who stand by the roadside.

The tour, started in 1903, takes place mostly in France and Belgium, but also visits Spain, Italy, Germany, and Switzerland. It is divided into 21 timed stages, or legs, over three weeks, and has become a French national obsession. The newspaper sports columnist Red Smith once wrote that "an army from Mars could invade France, the government could fall, and even the recipe for sauce Béarnaise be lost, but if it happened during the Tour de France nobody would notice."

The route and distance of the tour is different each year, averaging 3,500 kilometers (about 2,100 miles, or the distance from Chicago to Los Angeles). It always includes strenuous mountain passes and a finale in Paris. The number of riders is limited to 180, and the rider with the lowest cumulative time for all stages is the winner. There have been four five-time winners: Jacques Anquetil (1957, 1961-64), Eddy Merckx (1969-72, 1974), Bernard Hinault (1978, 1979, 1981, 1982, 1985), and Miguel Indurain from Spain (1991-95). Merckx, a Belgian who seemed almost immune to pain, is considered the all-time greatest cycler. He competed in 1,800 races and won 525 of them. In 1986, Greg LeMond was the first American to win the tour. He was nearly killed in a 1987 hunting accident, and endured accidents and operations during the next two years, but came back to win the tour in 1989 and again in 1990. American and former Olympian Lance Armstrong narrowly survived cancer diagnosed in 1996 and went on to win the Tour from 1999 to 2005—the first person to win seven times.

The first tour in 1903 was organized as a publicity stunt by Henri Desgranges, bicyclist and publisher of the cycling magazine *L'Auto.* On July 1, 1903, 60 bikers started from the Alarm Clock Café on the outskirts of Paris, and three weeks later Maurice Garin was the winner, and the tour was born. In 1984, the Tour Feminin, a special women's race, was added to the tour, and is now a stage race of about 1,000 kilometers, run concurrently with the final two weeks of the men's tour. The first winner was an American, Marianne Martin.

CONTACTS:
Amaury Sport Organisation
2 rue Rouget de Lisle
Issy-Les-Moulineaux
Paris, 92130 France
33-1-4133-1400
www.aso.fr/index_us.html

SOURCES:
BkHolWrld-1986, Jul 5
HolSymbols-2009, p. 975

♦ 2793 ♦ Tournament of Roses (Rose Parade)
January 1

The Rose Parade is one of the world's most elaborate and most photographed parades, held every New Year's Day in Pasadena, Calif. The parade is made up of about 50 floats elaborately decorated—and completely covered—with roses, orchids, chrysanthemums, and other blossoms that portray the year's theme. Additionally there are more than 20 bands, 200 horses and costumed riders, a grand marshal, a Rose Queen, and the Queen's princesses. The parade is five and one-half miles long, attracts about one million spectators along the route and picks up about 350 million television viewers around the world.

The first festival, called the Battle of Flowers, was held on Jan. 1, 1890, under the auspices of the Valley Hunt Club. The man responsible was Charles Frederick Holder, a naturalist and teacher of zoology. He had seen battles of the flowers on the French Riviera (*see* MARDI GRAS IN FRANCE), and figured California could do something similar; his suggestion resulted in a parade of decorated carriages and buggies followed by amateur athletic events. The parade evolved gradually. Floral floats were introduced, and in 1902 the morning parade was capped by a football game, which was replaced in following years by chariot races. In 1916, football came back, and the ROSE BOWL GAME is now traditionally associated with the parade.

In 1992, the theme of the tournament was "Voyages of Discovery," and it kicked off the Columbus Quincentennial. Co-grand marshals were Cristobal Colon, a descendant of Christopher COLUMBUS, and Colorado Rep. Ben Nighthorse Campbell, a Cheyenne chief.

CONTACTS:
Tournament of Roses
391 S. Orange Grove Blvd.
Pasadena, CA 91184
626-449-4100; fax: 626-449-9066
www.tournamentofroses.com

SOURCES:
AmerBkDays-2000, p. 12
AnnivHol-2000, p. 3
EncyChristmas-2003, p. 258
FolkAmerHol-1999, p. 9

♦ 2794 ♦ **Town Meeting Day**
First Tuesday of March

An official state holiday in Vermont, this is the day on which nearly every town elects its officers, approves budgets, and deals with other civic issues in a daylong public meeting of the voters. It more or less coincides with the anniversary of Vermont's admission to the Union on March 4, 1791 (*see* Appendix). Vermonters pride themselves on their active participation in these meetings, which often include heated debates on issues of local importance.

SOURCES:
AnnivHol-2000, p. 54
DictDays-1988, p. 121

♦ 2795 ♦ **Trafalgar Day**
October 21

This is the anniversary of the famous naval battle fought by the British off Cape Trafalgar, Spain, in 1805. The British navy, under the command of Viscount Horatio Nelson (1758-1805), defeated the combined French and Spanish fleets, thus eliminating the threat of NAPOLEON's invasion of England. The victory that cost Lord Nelson his life was commemorated by the column erected in his honor in London's Trafalgar Square. Ceremonies on Trafalgar Day, or **Nelson Day**,

include a naval parade from London's Mall to Trafalgar Square, where a brief service is held and wreaths are placed at the foot of Nelson's Column.

CONTACTS:
Official Nelson Commemorations Committee, National Maritime
    Museum
Park Row
Greenwich
London, SE10 9NF United Kingdom
44-20-8312-6637; fax: 44-20-8312-6722, 44-20-8312-6646
www.nmm.ac.uk

Royal Naval Museum
HM Naval Base (PP66)
Portsmouth, Hampshire PO1 3NH United Kingdom
44-23-9272-7562; fax: 44-23-9272-7575
www.royalnavalmuseum.org

SOURCES:
AnnivHol-2000, p. 175
DictDays-1988, p. 121

♦ 2796 ♦ **Transfer Day**
Last Monday in March

On March 31, 1917, the U.S. government formally purchased the Virgin Islands from Denmark for the sum of $25 million—about $295 an acre. Located about 34 miles east of Puerto Rico, the U.S. Virgin Islands consist of about 50 small islets and cays in addition to the three large islands of St. Thomas, St. John, and St. Croix. The United States purchased them primarily for their strategic importance, and they are still considered a vital key to the defense of the Panama Canal Zone and the Caribbean.

Transfer Day is usually observed with a parade and other public festivities. There was a major celebration in 1967, 50 years after the transfer took place, with events that underscored Danish-American friendship and a reenactment of the original transfer ceremony of 1917. The climax of the year-long semi-centennial celebration came when the governors of all 50 states as well as Guam, Puerto Rico, and American Samoa landed in St. Thomas for the 59th National Governors' Conference. Danish-American Week was observed at the same time.

CONTACTS:
The Library of Congress
101 Independence Ave. S.E.
Washington, D.C. 20540
202-707-5000; fax: 202-707-8366
www.loc.gov

SOURCES:
AmerBkDays-2000, p. 244
AnnivHol-2000, p. 53

♦ 2797 ♦ **Transfiguration, Feast of the**
August 6

As described in the first three Gospels, when Jesus' ministry was coming to an end, he took his three closest disciples—Peter, James, and John—to a mountaintop to pray. While he was praying, his face shone like the sun and his garments became glistening white. Moses (symbolizing the Law) and ELIJAH (symbolizing the prophets) appeared and began talking with him, testifying to his Messiahship. Then a bright cloud came over them, and a voice from within the cloud said, "This is my beloved Son, with whom I am well pleased; listen to him." The disciples were awestruck and fell to the ground. When they raised their heads, they saw only Jesus (Matthew 17).

Observance of this feast began in the Eastern church as early as the fourth century, but it was not introduced in the Western church until 1457. It is observed by Roman Catholics, Orthodox Christians, Lutherans, and Anglicans; most Protestants stopped observing it at the time of the REFORMATION. The mountaintop on which the Transfiguration took place is traditionally believed to be Mount Tabor, a few miles east of Nazareth in Galilee. However, many scholars believe it was Mount Hermon, or even the Mount of Olives.

SOURCES:
DaysCustFaith-1957, p. 201
FolkWrldHol-1999, p. 490
OxYear-1999, p. 324
RelHolCal-2004, p. 99
SaintFestCh-1904, p. 358

♦ 2798 ♦ Transpac Race
Begins early July in odd-numbered years

It was in 1906, the year of the great San Francisco earthquake, that the first yacht race across the Pacific was held. Because of the earthquake, only three yachts participated, ranging in length from 48 feet to 115 feet overall. The course was from Los Angeles to Honolulu.

The Transpac Race was originally held in even-numbered years, with a long break between 1912 and 1923, and another interruption, after the Japanese attack on Pearl Harbor, between 1941 and 1947. It is currently held in odd-numbered years and is sponsored by the Transpacific Yacht Club.

The finish can be close: in the 1965 race, with 55 yachts participating, there were fewer than 100 yards between the first two finishers as they struggled up the Molokai Channel. One had lost her main boom and the other's boom was badly damaged.

CONTACTS:
Transpacific Yacht Club
430 Catalina Dr.
San Pedro, CA 92663
949-646-5129; fax: 949-646-0089
www.transpacificyc.org

♦ 2799 ♦ Trial of Louis Riel
July-August

Louis Riel (1844-1885) was the leader of the métis, Canadians of mixed French and Indian ancestry. He became their champion in the struggle for Canadian unification during the late 19th century and was twice elected to the House of Commons but

never seated. He became a U.S. citizen in 1883, but returned to Canada two years later to lead the North-West Rebellion. Defeated, he was eventually tried for treason, convicted, and hanged at Regina, Saskatchewan, on November 16, 1885.

The transcripts of Riel's five-day trial are the basis for a full-length courtroom drama that is performed in July and August in Regina. Riel's life and death are seen today as symbolic of the problems between French and English Canadians.

CONTACTS:
Tourism Regina
Hwy. 1 E
P.O. Box 3355
Regina, SK S4P 3H1 Canada
306-789-5099; fax: 306-789-3171
www.tourismregina.com

Library and Archives Canada
395 Wellington St.
Ottawa, ON K1A ON4 Canada
613-996-5115
www.collectionscanada.gc.ca/index-e.html

SOURCES:
IntlThFolk-1979, p. 77

♦ 2800 ♦ Tribeca Film Festival
April

The Tribeca Film Festival was founded in 2002 in response to the terrorist attacks on the World Trade Center on September 11, 2001. In the wake of the attacks, one section of New York City—the Lower Manhattan neighborhood of Tribeca, located near the World Trade Center site—had suffered significant financial losses. The festival's founders—actor Robert De Niro, film producer Jane Rosenthal, and philanthropist Craig Hatkoff—believed a festival devoted to music, culture, and independent film would restore Lower Manhattan as a major center for filmmaking and would generate opportunities for artists in the independent film world.

Spanning a week in April, the Tribeca Festival showcases movies at various theaters in Tribeca and throughout Manhattan. Juries decide on the best films in competitions in the categories of documentary, feature, and short film. In addition to the film screenings, there are also panel talks, music performances, and workshops for aspiring filmmakers.

In its initial years the festival fulfilled its goals to promote Tribeca and bolster the film industry. The event has recorded up to 1 million attendees and has featured more than 200 films. In 2006, the film festival entered into a partnership with Tropfest, the world's largest short film festival held in Australia. The following year, Tropfest@Tribeca was established as a freestanding festival that is held in September.

CONTACTS:
Tribeca Cinemas
54 Varick St.
New York, NY 10013
212-941-2001
www.tribecafilmfestival.org

◆ 2801 ◆ Tribute of the Three Cows
July 13

This unusual event takes place on the Pierre St. Martin, located in the Pyrénées Mountains between Spain and France, on July 13 every year. Representatives of the French Pyrenean valley of Barétous and those of the Spanish Pyrenean valley of Roncal meet at the summit at 10 o'clock in the morning and pile their hands on top of each other's in a show of friendship. Then the French hand over three cows, which must be healthy two-year-olds. The Spaniards prepare a banquet afterward, which is cooked over fires made from wood that is hauled up the mountain by mules.

This tribute was imposed by treaty in 1375, when the two valleys were at war with each other, and the Roncal cowmen emerged as the victors. Such local treaties were often made without the consent of the national governments, and a number of them are still adhered to. But the annual Tribute of the Three Cows is by far the most unusual and picturesque.

CONTACTS:
French Government Tourist Office
444 Madison Ave., Fl. 16
New York, NY 10022
800-391-4909 or 212-838-7800; fax: 212-838-7855
www.francetourism.com

Tourist Office of Spain
666 Fifth Ave., Fl. 35
New York, NY 10103
212-265-8822; fax: 212-265-8864
www.okspain.org

SOURCES:
SpanFiestas-1968, p. 137

◆ 2802 ◆ Trigo, Fiesta Nacional del (National Wheat Festival)
February

For more than 40 years the city of Leones in Córdoba Province, Argentina, has held an annual tribute to farmers and the wheat harvest. A blessing of the new wheat takes place at a special morning mass. Young women vie to be selected as the Wheat Queen. There is a parade of floats and farm vehicles, and prizes for the finest wheat.

CONTACTS:
National Secretariat of Tourism, Tourist Information Centers
Av. Santa Fe 883
Buenos Aires, C1059ABC Argentina
54-11-4312-2232; fax: 54-11-4302-7816
www.turismo.gov.ar/eng/menu.htm

SOURCES:
FiestaTime-1965, p. 57

◆ 2803 ◆ Trinidad and Tobago Carnival
Between February 2 and March 8; Monday and Tuesday before Ash Wednesday

One of the most spectacular and frenzied CARNIVAL celebrations before LENT, the Trinidad and Tobago Carnival is a non-stop 48-hour festival in which almost everyone on the island participates. It started out in the late 19th century as a high-spirited but relatively sedate celebration involving a torch-light procession in blackface called *canboulay*—from *cannes brulées*, or "burned cane"—patterned after the procession of slaves on their way to fight fires in the cane fields. There was also music in the streets and masked dancing, although slaves were not permitted to wear masks. With the emancipation of the slaves, Carnival became a free-for-all with raucous music and displays of near-nudity. The government tried to crack down on the celebrations, but in 1881 there were canboulay riots in which 38 policemen were injured. After that, a law was passed that forbade parading before six o'clock in the morning on Carnival Monday. That moment is still known as *jouvé* (possibly from *jour ouvert*, or "daybreak").

Today the main events are the two carnival day parades, which involve 25 to 30 costumed bands, each with about 2,500 marchers and its own king and queen. There is a calypso competition in which steel bands and calypso composers vie for the title of "Calypso Monarch." Few get any sleep during the two-day celebration, and the event ends with the *las lap*, which is a wild, uninhibited dance in the streets.

CONTACTS:
National Library and Information System Authority of Trinidad and Tobago
National Library Bldg., Hart and Abercromby Streets
Port-of-Spain, Trinidad, West Indies
868-623-6962; fax: 868-625-6096
www.nalis.gov.tt

SOURCES:
EncyEaster-2002, p. 610
FolkWrldHol-1999, p. 148
GdWrldFest-1985, p. 175

◆ 2804 ◆ Trinidad and Tobago Emancipation Day
August 1

Since 1985, August 1 has been celebrated in Trinidad and Tobago as Emancipation Day, rather than COLUMBUS Discovery Day, as in former years. Slavery was abolished in 1833 throughout the British Empire, and eventually slaves in the colony of Trinidad and Tobago were freed. The day begins with an all-night vigil and includes religious services, cultural events, processions past historic landmarks, addresses by dignitaries, and an evening of shows with a torchlight procession to the National Stadium.

CONTACTS:
National Library and Information System Authority of Trinidad and Tobago
National Library Bldg., Hart and Abercromby St.
Port-of-Spain, Trinidad and Tobago
868-623-6962; fax: 868-625-6096
www.nalis.gov.tt

Ministry of Tourism, Trinidad and Tobago Government
51-55 Frederick St.
Port-of-Spain, Trinidad and Tobago
868-624-1403; fax: 868-625-0437
www.tourism.gov.tt

SOURCES:
AnnivHol-2000, p. 128

◆ 2805 ◆ Trinidad and Tobago Independence Day
August 31

After being subjected to British rule since 1802, Trinidad and Tobago became an independent commonwealth state on this day in 1962.

This national holiday is celebrated amid a Carnival atmosphere, with an elaborate military parade accompanied by calypsos at the Queen's Park Savannah. Religious services are varied to accommodate the Yoruba Orisha, Hindu, Muslim, Baptist, and other faiths represented in the citizenry. Later in the day, awards are presented at the National Awards Ceremony to those who have notably served their country.

CONTACTS:
National Library and Information System Authority of Trinidad
   and Tobago
National Library Bldg., Hart and Abercromby St.
Port-of-Spain, Trinidad and Tobago
868-623-6962; fax: 868-625-6096
www.nalis.gov.tt

Ministry of Tourism, Trinidad and Tobago Government
51-55 Frederick St.
Port-of-Spain, Trinidad and Tobago
868-624-1403; fax: 868-625-0437
www.tourism.gov.tt

SOURCES:
AnnivHol-2000, p. 149
NatlHolWrld-1968, p. 152

◆ 2806 ◆ Trinidad and Tobago Republic Day
September 24

The country of Trinidad and Tobago consists of two islands in the Caribbean just northeast of Venezuela. The islands became British colonies during the 19th century and in 1889 were joined into one colony. On August 31, 1962, Trinidad and Tobago gained independence from England. On August 1, 1976, the nation became a republic. To mark the occasion, September 1—the date when the nation's first parliament met—has become Republic Day. The holiday was removed from the calendar from 1999 to 2002 to make room for SPIRITUAL BAPTIST (SHOUTERS) LIBERATION DAY. But it returned in 2002 and remains today.

Republic Day is normally celebrated with a parade and other festivities, including dances and feasts. The Royal Oak Derby, Trinidad and Tobago's most important horse race, is normally run on this day as well. The nation's president always gives a speech stressing that being a republic means that all citizens are to assume responsibility for their own actions as the price of freedom.

CONTACTS:
Embassy of Trinidad and Tobago
1708 Massachusetts Ave. N.W.
Washington, D.C. 20036-1975

202-467-6490 or 202-467-6493; fax: 202-785-3130
www.ttembassy.cjb.net

◆ 2807 ◆ Trinity Sunday
Between May 17 and June 20; first Sunday after Pentecost in the West and Monday after Pentecost in the East

Trinity Sunday differs from other days in the Christian calendar in that it is not associated with a particular saint or historic event. Instead, it is a day that celebrates the central dogma of Christian theology: that the One God exists as three persons with one substance—as the Father, the Son, and the Holy Spirit. The idea of a festival in honor of the Trinity was first introduced by Stephen, bishop of Liège, Belgium, in the 10th century. But it took several more centuries for a feast in honor of so abstract a concept to find its way into the church calendar. It became popular in England perhaps because of the consecration of Thomas à Becket on that day in 1162, but it wasn't until 1334 that it became a universal observance decreed by Pope John XXII. The day after Trinity is sometimes referred to as Trinity Monday.

Tradition has it that ST. PATRICK of Ireland used a shamrock as a symbol of the "three-in-one," triune God.

SOURCES:
DaysCustFaith-1957, p. 164
DictWrldRel-1989, p. 768
FestSaintDays-1915, p. 128
OxYear-1999, p. 633
RelHolCal-2004, p. 96
SaintFestCh-1904, p. 256

◆ 2808 ◆ Triple Crown Pack Burro Races
July-August

Every year, three races of pack burros and human runners take place in the Colorado Rocky Mountains. The first leg of the triple crown starts in Fairplay and is held the last weekend in July. The second leg, the first weekend in August, starts in Leadville. The final race is two weeks later in Buena Vista.

The first organized pack burro races were held in 1949 along a route over Mosquito Pass between Leadville and Fairplay; in 1979, the Buena Vista race became the final leg of the triple crown. The races cover from 15 to 30 miles over 13,500-foot mountain passes, sometimes in snow, and generally take the 20 to 25 entrants three to four hours. Women run a different, shorter course than men. Contestants can't ride their burros, but must run alongside them. (They can and frequently do push the animals.) Winners of individual races get cash prizes; the total purse at Buena Vista is $5,020. The men's winner at Leadville gets $1,200.

The word *burro* is Spanish and means "donkey." The history of these animals in the West goes back to the Gold Rush days of the 1800s when pack burros carried great loads of machinery and supplies to mining camps. Pack burro racing is thought to have started in those times.

The race days are surrounded by a variety of activities and are now major events in the small Colorado towns. In Buena Vista, for example, there are duck races, storytellers, and gold panning. Fairplay has llama races, and Leadville holds contests in mine drilling events. There's also a triple crown outhouse race; each town in the burro triple crown stages an outhouse race, with definite rules (e.g., one member of the outhouse team must sit in the outhouse during the race wearing colored underwear and/or a bathrobe).

CONTACTS:
Leadville Boom Days Committee
P.O. Box 596
Leadville, CO 80461
719-486-1900
www.leadvilleboomdays.com

South Park Chamber of Commerce
P.O. Box 312
Fairplay, CO 80440
719-836-3410
www.southparkchamber.com

Buena Vista Area Chamber of Commerce
343 Hwy. 24 S.
P.O. Box 2021
Buena Vista, CO 81211
719-395-6612
www.buenavistacolorado.org

♦ 2809 ♦ Trois Glorieuses
Third weekend in November

The **Three Glorious Days** to which the name of this French wine festival refers occur in November in Côte d'Or Department, Burgundy, in eastern France. The festival is observed in three different wine-producing centers. On the first day, at the Château of Clos Vougeot, the Confrerie des Chevaliers du Tastevin put on their red robes and square toques (a type of soft hat popular in the 16th century) to receive their new members—the *tastevin* is a small silver cup used to taste wines. This event is followed by a pig dinner during which hundreds of bottles of wine are uncorked. The second day of the festival takes place at Beaune, where a wine auction is held at the Hospice de Beaune, whose cellars are open to the public. On the third and final day in Meursault, everyone who has taken part in the work of the wine harvest is invited to a huge banquet. There is folk dancing and merrymaking as the festival draws to a close.

The Confrérie des Chevaliers du Tastevin was formed in 1934 to put the French wine industry back on its feet after a number of disastrous vintage failures. They hold a series of wine-tasters' banquets throughout Burgundy, but the most elaborate ones are part of this three-day festival.

CONTACTS:
Confrerie des Chevaliers du Tastevin
Chateau du Clos Vougeot
Vougeot, 21640 France
33-3-8062-8609; fax: 33-3-8062-8275
www.tastevin-bourgogne.com

Burgundy Tourism Department
Conseil Regional
P.O. Box 1602

Dijon, Burgundy 21035 France
33-3-8028-0280; fax: 33-3-8028-0300
www.burgundy-tourism.com

SOURCES:
GdWrldFest-1985, p. 80

♦ 2810 ♦ Trumpets, Feast of
September; Tishri 1

The first day of Tishri, the seventh month of the Hebrew calendar, has religious significance for Jewish people and two sects of Christianity: Seventh-Day Adventists and the United Church of God. The day has different meanings for these groups. Jewish people celebrate the beginning of Tishri, which falls sometime between September and October, as Rosh Hashanah. The Christian group knows the holiday as the Feast of Trumpets. The day's significance is revealed in the biblical book of Revelation, in which a prophecy states that a seventh or "last" trumpet will announce the second coming of Jesus Christ, who will deliver the followers of God in heaven.

The Feast of Trumpets is the fourth of the seven Holy Days whose observance is central to the faith of the United Church of God. These days prefigure God's plan for creation, which he has revealed in the context of a spiritual harvest. The Days, also known as Feasts, are explained in detail in the Book of Leviticus, which recounts God's instructions to Moses about how to celebrate the feasts.

CONTACTS:
United Church of God
P.O. Box 541027
Cincinnati, OH 45254-1027
513-576-9796; fax: 513-576-9795
www.ucg.org

General Conference of Seventh-Day Adventists
12501 Old Columbia Pike
Silver Spring, MD 20904
301-608-6000
www.adventist.org

SOURCES:
RelHolCal-2004, p. 133

♦ 2811 ♦ Tsagaan Sar (Mongolian New Year)
Between end of January and beginning of March

The New Year in Mongolia is determined by a lunar calendar and marks the beginning of spring. People generally celebrate for three days with lots of visiting, feasting, music, and sporting events. *Tsagaan Sar* means "white month," a reference to the milk and other dairy foods which become more plentiful in the spring.

People begin getting ready for the holiday about a month ahead of time, making repairs to and cleaning living quarters and sheds, preparing food in advance, and buying or fashioning gifts. The night before New Year's Day is *Bituun*, the occasion for parties to say goodbye to the old year.

After the New Year has begun, people often wear new clothes and spend at least a couple of days paying brief visits to family members, friends and neighbors, giving a small, inexpensive gift to each, then returning home to be themselves the recipients of visitors and gifts. Many *gers*, the tents in which Mongolian nomads live, resound with music played on traditional string instruments and overflow with special festive foods and drinks during the holiday.

CONTACTS:
Embassy of Mongolia
2833 M St. N.W.
Washington, D.C. 20007
202-333-7117; fax: 202-298-9227
www.mongolianembassy.us

Mongolia Today (online magazine)
www.mongoliatoday.com

SOURCES:
FestWrld: Mongolia-1999, p. 12

♦ 2812 ♦ **Tsunahiki Matsuri**
June

The tug-of-war is a traditional way to pray for a plentiful harvest throughout Japan and it is a popular event around the country. Several annual tugs-of-war take place in Okinawa Prefecture, and the one in Yonabaru, which is said to be about 400 years old, is one of the more famous. Thousands of people take part, dividing themselves into the East and West teams. Each team parades half of the rope, which can be three to five feet thick, to the beach, where they are connected by wooden poles, and then tugged on furiously by both sides until a winner is proclaimed.

See also UNDERWATER TUG-OF-WAR FESTIVAL

CONTACTS:
Okinawa Convention and Visitors Bureau
1831-1 Oroku
Naha, Okinawa 901-0152 Japan
81-9-8898-3000; fax: 81-9-8898-2202
www.ocvb.or.jp/index.php

SOURCES:
CustCultOkinawa-1959, p. 113

♦ 2813 ♦ **Tsurugaoka Hachiman Shrine Matsuri**
September 14-16

After the opening ceremonies are held on September 14, the annual celebration at the Tsurugaoka Hachiman shrine in Kamakura, Japan, begins on the 15th with a parade of three *mikoshi*, portable shrines to which the spirits of the gods are believed to descend during the festival. But the highlight occurs the following day, when the Yabusame takes place. It features three men on horseback in hunting clothes called *karishozoku*, which date from the Kamakura Era (1192-1333) and feature wide-brimmed, high-crowned hats with chin straps and elaborate kimono-style robes. The horsemen, all of whom are top-rated archers, ride down a straight track about 850 feet long near the shrine's entrance. Three targets are set

up along the route, and the archers shoot their arrows at them while travelling at a high rate of speed.

In feudal times, Yabusame was an arrow-shooting game in which samurai warriors, under the guise of being contestants, showed off their battle skills. Today it is primarily a form of entertainment.

CONTACTS:
Japan National Tourist Organization
1 Rockefeller Pl., Ste. 1250
New York, NY 10020
212-757-5640; fax: 212-307-6754
www.japantravelinfo.com

SOURCES:
IllFestJapan-1993, p. 110
JapanFest-1965, p. 189

♦ 2814 ♦ **Tu Bishvat (Bi-Shevat; B'Shevat; Hamishah Asar Bishevat)**
Between January 16 and February 13; Shevat 15

Tu Bishvat, also known as **New Year for Trees**, is a minor Jewish festival similar to ARBOR DAY. It is first referred to in the late Second Temple period (515 B.C.E.-20 C.E.), when it was the cut-off date for levying the tithe on the produce of fruit trees. When Jewish colonists returned to Palestine during the 1930s, they reclaimed the barren land by planting trees wherever they could. It became customary to plant a tree for every newborn child: a cedar for a boy and a cypress or pine for a girl.

Today the children of Israel celebrate Tu Bishvat with tree planting and outdoor games. In other countries, Jews observe the festival by eating fruit that grows in the Jewish homeland—such as oranges, figs, dates, raisins, pomegranates, and especially almonds, the first tree to bloom in Israel's spring.

CONTACTS:
Union for Reform Judaism
633 Third Ave.
New York, NY 10017
212-650-4000; fax: 212-650-4169
www.urj.org

Union of Orthodox Jewish Congregations of America
11 Broadway
New York, NY 10004
212-563-4000; fax: 212-564-9058
www.ou.org

SOURCES:
BkFest-1937, p. 206
BkFestHolWrld-1970, p. 18
BkHolWrld-1986, Jan 29
DaysCustFaith-1957, p. 40
FolkWrldHol-1999, p. 50
OxYear-1999, p. 727
RelHolCal-2004, p. 56

♦ 2815 ♦ **Tuan Wu (Double Fifth)**
May-June; fifth day of fifth lunar month

The Double Fifth holiday is celebrated throughout China but is most popular south of the Yangtze River. It is also a festive holiday in Taiwan, Hong Kong, and among Chinese Americans. One reason why dragon boat races are often held on this day is that dragon boats are believed to offer protection against disease, particularly for the paddlers. Another reason is that Ch'ü Yüan (c. 343-c. 289 B.C.E.), a renowned minister of the Ch'u kingdom and a famous poet, threw himself into the Mi Lo River on the fifth day of the fifth month. When the people heard about his suicide, they all jumped into their boats and paddled out to save him, but it was too late. So they wrapped rice in bamboo leaves or stuffed it into sections of bamboo tube and floated it on the river to provide sustenance for his spirit. It is traditional to prepare and eat sticky rice dumplings known as *zong ze* or *tzung tzu* on this day in honor of the drowned poet Ch'ü Yüan.

Charms made from chunks of incense are used to ward off the so-called "five poisonous things"—which vary in different parts of China depending upon the climate and the local animal life. In Taiwan, for example, the five poisonous things are wall-lizards, toads, centipedes, spiders, and snakes. The charms are made in the shape of these harmful creatures, and sometimes small cakes resembling the creatures are eaten on this day.

Another custom associated with the Double Fifth is the placing of mugwort plants in the doorposts of each house. These branches are supposed to frighten evil spirits away and preserve those living in the house from summer diseases. Those who take a bath at noon on the fifth day of the fifth month are believed to be immune from illness for one year.

See also DRAGON BOAT FESTIVAL

SOURCES:
AnnivHol-2000, p. 239
BkFest-1937, p. 79
BkHolWrld-1986, Jun 18
DictFolkMyth-1984, pp. 206, 1130, 1185
EncyRel-1987, vol. 3, p. 326
FolkAmerHol-1999, p. 221
FolkWrldHol-1999, p. 369

♦ 2816 ♦ **Tubman (Harriet) Annual Pilgrimage**
Memorial Day weekend

The Harriet Tubman Annual Pilgrimage is held every Memorial Day weekend at her gravesite and former home in Auburn, N.Y. In addition to a ceremony at Tubman's grave, there are commemorative activities, including a banquet. Many of the activities take place on the 30-acre site of her residence. The site also contains other historic buildings, such as the home for aged people that Tubman established and where she herself received care before her death at age 93.

Harriet Tubman was an African-American abolitionist and humanitarian born in 1820. A former slave, she is most famous for leading hundreds of slaves to freedom via the "Underground Railroad," a network of abolitionists and safe houses. This heroic accomplishment led to her being defined as the "Moses of her People." After the abolition of slavery,

Tubman worked tirelessly to help the poor, the elderly, and freed slaves, and to further the rights of women.

CONTACTS:
Harriet Tubman Home
180 South St.
Auburn, NY 13201
315-252-2081
www.nyhistory.com/harriettubman/resources.htm

SOURCES:
AAH-2007, p. 206

♦ 2817 ♦ **Tucson International Mariachi Conference**
Last week in April

Mariachi is traditional Mexican folk music with vocal, instrumental, and dance components. A small group of musicians typically sing and play some combination of the following instruments—guitar, *vihuela* (a small guitar-like instrument), *guitarrón* (a larger bass-like instrument), violin, and trumpet. Mariachi music also lends itself to the rhythmic *zapateado* dance, where the performers' boot heels act as percussion instruments.

Since the early 1980s, Mexican music enthusiasts have gathered in Arizona every April for the five-day Tucson International Mariachi Conference. Attendees take part in cultural workshops geared toward young people, enjoy performances by top mariachi bands, and join in the fun at the Fiesta de Garibaldi, an outdoor street festival offering food, arts and crafts, dance, and music.

CONTACTS:
La Frontera Tucson International Mariachi Conference
P.O. Box 3035
Tucson, AZ 85702
520-838-3908; fax: 520-792-9854
www.tucsonmariachi.org

SOURCES:
LatinoLife-1995, p. 34

♦ 2818 ♦ **Tucson Meet Yourself Festival**
Second weekend in October

The annual folk and ethnic festival known as Tucson Meet Yourself has been held in Tucson, Arizona, since 1974. Designed to promote southern Arizona's wide mix of cultures—which includes Mexican-, Czechoslovakian-, Italian-, German-, and Indian-American groups—the festival features formal presentations of traditional music and dance, demonstrations by folk artists and craftspeople, and workshops in which various experts on ethnic customs and traditions hold informal discussions, give lessons, and organize games.

Food, however, is the festival's primary attraction. Dozens of food booths, each operated by a non-profit organization identified with a specific cultural heritage and elaborately decorated to represent elements of "the old country," are set up throughout the park in which the event is held. Although American-Indian and Mexican-American specialties predominate, the booths have featured Irish, Finnish, Hungarian, Ukrainian, Greek, Armenian, Vietnamese, Japanese, Sri Lankan, and many other ethnic dishes, giving the festival the well-earned nickname of "Tucson Eat Yourself."

CONTACTS:
Tucson Meet Yourself
349 W. 31st St.
Tucson, AZ 85733
520-792-4806
www.tucsonmeetyourself.org

♦ 2819 ♦ Tulip Time
Second weekend in May

When a group of high school students in Pella, Iowa, staged an operetta called *Tulip Time in Pella* in 1935, the only tulips growing in the town were in wooden pots. But the musical performance gave the local chamber of commerce an idea for promoting the town's Dutch heritage. They hired tulip specialists from the Netherlands to teach them how to plant and care for tulips. Then they planted thousands of bulbs and got the local historical society started preserving the town's Dutch buildings and heirlooms.

Today Pella (named "city of refuge" by the first Dutch immigrants, who were fleeing religious intolerance in their homeland) has been renovated to resemble a typical village in the Netherlands. During the festival, townspeople dress in Dutch provincial costumes and engage in such activities as street scrubbing, authentic Dutch dancing and folk music, and tours of the formal tulip gardens. One of these gardens features a Dutch windmill and a pond shaped like a wooden shoe.

Unlike most local festivals, Tulip Time is not a commercial event. There are no souvenir stands or food booths, although the local shops, museums, and restaurants offer a wide variety of Dutch specialties. Many of the events take place at the Tulip Torne, a tower with twin pylons more than 65 feet high that was built as a memorial to the early Dutch settlers.

CONTACTS:
Pella Historical Village
507 Franklin Ave.
Pella, IA 50219
641-628-4311; fax: 641-628-9192
www.pellatuliptime.com

SOURCES:
GdWrldFest-1985, p. 59

♦ 2820 ♦ Tulsa Indian Arts Festival
First weekend in February

The Tulsa Indian Arts Festival features exhibitions of the work of Native American fine artists, dancing, music, auctions, storytelling, and such foods as corn soup, meat pies, and fry bread. Artists also provide educational demonstrations for the many schoolchildren who often attend. People from more than 60 tribes live in Oklahoma, whose name comes from the Choctaw meaning "red people."

CONTACTS:
Tulsa Indian Arts Festival
Greenwood Cultural Center
322 N. Greenwood
Tulsa, OK 74120
918-749-6073; fax: 918-749-6389
www.tulsaindianartfest.com

SOURCES:
EndurHarv-1995, p. 167

♦ 2821 ♦ Tulsidas Jayanti (Birthday of Tulsidas)
July-August; seventh day of the waxing half of the Hindu month of Sravana

The Indian poet Tulsidas (1532?-1623) is best known for his retelling of the epic *Ramayana* in Hindi, the language of the common people. Another work, *Ramcaritmanas* ("The Holy Lake of the Deeds of Rama"), has been so influential that it is often referred to as "the Bible of North India." In fact, he and his works are so greatly revered that tradition regards him as a reincarnation of Valmiki, the legendary author of the *Ramayana.*

Tulsidas wrote that he was the son of a brahman, a member of the highest Hindu caste, but his parents didn't want to keep him because of the astrological interpretation of the planets and stars dominant at the time of his birth. Therefore they turned Tulsidas over to a Hindu holy man who raised him. Tulsidas went on to marry a woman with whom he was very much in love. Apparently, at some point she told him, "If you loved Rama half as much as you love this perishable body, your sorrows would be over," which is credited with awakening his devotion to Rama and changing the course of his life.

Many Hindus believe that Tulsidas died on the same day that he was born. They spend this day fasting and performing works of charity. Reading and reciting the *Ramayana* is another popular activity, as are discussions, lectures, seminars, and symposia on his life and works.

SOURCES:
DictWrldRel-1989, p. 770
EncyRel-1987, vol. 15, p. 81
OxDictWrldRel-1997, p. 995
RelHolCal-2004, p. 172

♦ 2822 ♦ Tunisia Independence Day
March 20

Independence Day is a public holiday commemorating a treaty signed on this day in 1956 that formally recognized Tunisia's independence from France. It had been a French colony since the 1880s.

CONTACTS:
Embassy of Tunisia
1515 Massachusetts Ave. N.W.
Washington, D.C. 20005
202-862-1850; fax: 202-862-1858
www.tunisia.or.jp

SOURCES:
AnnivHol-2000, p. 47

♦ 2823 ♦ Tunisia New Era Day (Ben Ali's Accession to Power)
November 7

On November 7, 1987, Zine El Abidine Ben Ali assumed control of Tunisia, becoming the nation's second president. He argued that the country's first president, Habib Bourguiba, was in bad health. Muslim fundamentalists had taken advantage of the situation to engage in terrorist actions against the state. Bourguiba, too, had been in power for 30 years under a one-party government that had strayed from its democratic ideals. Tunisia New Era Day celebrates the accession of Ben Ali to power.

Ben Ali claims to have made great strides in safeguarding the freedoms and human rights of his people. On New Era Day in 2007, he announced a number of measures designed to promote democracy and the rule of law. These included lowering the voting age from 20 to 18, allocating at least 30 percent of the candidate slots within his own Constitutional Democratic Rally party to women, and allowing opposition political groups greater access to the media. But Muslim parties are still not recognized, and Ben Ali has been accused of using excessive police force against political opponents.

CONTACTS:
Embassy of Tunisia
1515 Massachusetts Ave. N.W.
Washington, D.C. 20005
202-862-1850; fax: 202-862-1858

♦ 2824 ♦ Tunisia Republic Day
July 25

This public holiday in Tunisia is held on the anniversary of the vote to abolish monarchical rule and found the republic on July 25, 1957.

CONTACTS:
Embassy of Tunisia
1515 Massachusetts Ave. N.W.
Washington, D.C. 20005
202-862-1850; fax: 202-862-1858

SOURCES:
AnnivHol-2000, p. 123

♦ 2825 ♦ Tura Michele Fair (Augsburg Day)
September 29

On ST. MICHAEL'S DAY in Augsburg, Bavaria, there is an annual autumn fair that attracts visitors from all over Germany. One of the fair's chief attractions is the hourly appearance of figures representing the Archangel Michael and the Devil that are built into the foundation of Perlach Turm, or Tower, called *Tura* in local dialect. The slender structure, 225 feet high, standing next to Peter's Kirche (church) was originally a watch tower, but it was heightened in 1615 and converted into a belfry. Whenever the tower bell strikes on St. Michael's Day, the armor-clad figure of the Archangel appears and stabs with his pointed spear at the Devil writhing at his feet.

Although the figures were destroyed during World War II, they were later replaced. For over four centuries spectators have gathered around the Tura to watch the symbolic drama reenacted on St. Michael's Day.

CONTACTS:
Augsburg Tourist Information
Schiessgrabenstrasse 14
Augsburg, 86150 Germany
49-821-502-07-0; fax: 49-821-502-07-45
www.regio-augsburg.de

SOURCES:
FestWestEur-1958, p. 71

♦ 2826 ♦ Turkey National Sovereignty and Children's Day
April 23

This festival was started in 1920 by Mustafa Kemal Atatürk, the founder of the Turkish Republic, who recognized how important children were to his country's future and dedicated this day to them. On this national public holiday, Atatürk is honored with special services in Ankara, Turkey's capital city, at the monument built for him. Afterwards a children's program takes place in which children from around the world wear festive traditional costumes and dance and sing. In Istanbul, a similar celebration is held in the national soccer stadium.

Environmental scouts, similar to Boy Scouts in the United States, often observe this day by planting trees.

CONTACTS:
Embassy of the Republic of Turkey
2525 Massachusetts Ave. N.W.
Washington, D.C. 20008
202-612-6700; fax: 202-612-6744
www.turkishembassy.org

SOURCES:
AnnivHol-2000, p. 66
FestWrld: Turkey-1999, p. 20

♦ 2827 ♦ Turkey Republic Day
October 29

The Turkish Republic was founded by Mustafa Kemal Atatürk in 1923 after the fall of the Ottoman Empire. Kemal was named the first president on October 29, a full republican constitution was adopted the following April, and all members of the Ottoman dynasty were expelled from the country. Although Islam remained the state religion for several years, this clause was eventually removed from the constitution and in April 1928, Turkey became a purely secular state.

The public celebration, which lasts for two days, includes parades, music, torchlight processions, and other festivities in honor of the founding of the republic. The largest parades are held in Ankara and Istanbul.

CONTACTS:
Embassy of the Republic of Turkey
2525 Massachusetts Ave. N.W.
Washington, D.C. 20008
202-612-6700; fax: 202-612-6744
www.turkishembassy.org

SOURCES:
AnnivHol-2000, p. 179
IntlThFolk-1979, p. 373
NatlHolWrld-1968, p. 194

♦ 2828 ♦ Turkey Victory Day
August 30

Turkey Victory Day honors the founder of modern Turkey, Mustafa Kemal Atatürk, and the military victory over the Greeks in 1922. In 1923, Turkey was established as an independent republic. The holiday is a celebration of the nation's military, the republic Atatürk founded, and the spirit of the Turkish people to resist tyranny and rule by outsiders.

Victory Day is celebrated throughout Turkey and on the island of Cyprus. The primary celebration is held at Atatürk's Mausoleum in the city of Ankara. Leading military officials visit the tomb to lay a ceremonial wreath. Veterans come from all over Turkey to attend the event. Wreaths are also placed on various statues of Atatürk found throughout the city. A ceremony including military and governmental officials is then held at the Atatürk Culture Center. Military leaders later retire to the General Staff headquarters to greet dignitaries from the country's major political parties, parliamentary and judicial officials, and the prime minister. A ceremony is also held at the War Academy in Istanbul, while marches are held in major cities across the country.

CONTACTS:
Embassy of the Republic of Turkey
2525 Massachusetts Ave. N.W.
Washington, D.C. 20008
202-612-6700; fax: 202-612-6744
www.turkishembassy.org

♦ 2829 ♦ Turkish Wrestling Championships
July

Yagli gures, or "grease wrestling," is Turkey's most popular sport. An annual wrestling tournament has been held in July at Kirkpinar, near the Turkish-Greek border, for more than six centuries. The competitors cover their bodies and their leather knee breeches with oil, making it extremely difficult to get a grip on one's opponent. Although the Turks have proved their superiority at wrestling at many OLYMPIC GAMES, this national form of the sport requires exceptional skill and strength training.

CONTACTS:
Ministry of Culture
Ataturk Bulvan No. 29, Opera
Ankara, 6050 Turkey
90-312-309-08-50; fax: 90-312-312-64-73
www.kultur.gov.tr/EN

SOURCES:
FestEur-1961, p. 161
FestWrld: Turkey-1999, p. 24
IntlThFolk-1979, p. 368
WildPlanet-1995, p. 171

♦ 2830 ♦ Turkmenistan Independence Day
October 27-28

This national holiday commemorates Turkmenistan's independence from the U.S.S.R. on October 27, 1991. Turkmenistan and other republics were gradually able to establish their own autonomous states due to the relaxation of Soviet rule influenced by the policy of perestroika. When the Soviet Union ceased to exist in December 1991, their independence was assured.

CONTACTS:
Embassy of Turkmenistan
2207 Massachusetts Ave. N.W.
Washington, D.C. 20008
202-588-1500; fax: 202-280-1003
www.turkmenistanembassy.org

♦ 2831 ♦ Turkmenistan National Days
Various

The newly independent (1991) nation of Turkmenistan celebrates a large number of national holidays honoring Turkmen arts, popular culture, religion, civics, and history. Memory Day (January 12) commemorates the Turkmen tribesmen massacred by Russian Imperial troops at the Battle of Goek-Tepe in 1881. On May 9, Victory Day, the nation memorializes the end of World War II (1945). Remembrance Day (October 6) recalls those who died in the earthquake that devasted the country in 1948. Neutrality Day (December 1) promotes the government's official policy of neutrality in international affairs, while Good Neighborliness Day (December 7) publicizes Turkmenistan's intent to be a good neighbor to other countries. Turkmen Bakhsi Day (July 14) pays tribute to Bakhsi, the ancient literary genre of oral epics still popular in Turkmenistan. Horse Day (April 27) celebrates Turkmenistan's outstanding horses and the cultural tradition of horse breeding. The nation's fine oriental carpets and the women who weave them are praised on Carpet Day (May 25).

Other national holidays include NEW YEAR'S DAY (January 1), RAMADAN (moveable), National Flag Day (February 19), International WOMEN'S DAY (March 8), Novruz-Bairam, or NAWRUZ (March 21), A Drop of Water Is a Grain of Gold Day (April 6), Revival and Unity Day (May 18), Holiday of the poetry of Magtymguli (May 19), Kurban-Bairam (ID AL-ADHA; moveable), Day of Election of the First President (June 21), Turkmen Melon Holiday (July 10), Student Youth Day (November 17), and Harvest Holiday/Bread Day (November 30).

CONTACTS:
Embassy of Turkmenistan
2207 Massachusetts Ave. N.W.
Washington, D.C. 20008
202-588-1500; fax: 202-280-1003
www.turkmenistanembassy.org

♦ 2832 ♦ **Turon**
December; the week after Christmas

A Polish peasant festival observed in the week following CHRISTMAS, Turon may be a remnant of an ancient festival in honor of the winter god Radegast. *Turon* is a Polish word for "bull" or "ox." People wear several different animal disguises as they go from house to house singing carols and receiving food and drink from their neighbors in return. Other traditional costumes worn in the celebration represent a wolf, a bear, and a goat. The original turon symbolized frost, consuming vegetation with its huge mouth.

SOURCES:
DictFolkMyth-1984, p. 1132

♦ 2833 ♦ **Turtle Days**
Mid-June

The origins of this unusual festival, held in Churubusco, Indiana, can be traced back to 1948, when a farmer named Gale Harris spotted a huge turtle one day while patching his roof. Since the lakes around town were known as prime turtle-breeding grounds, the turtle's appearance was not surprising. But its apparent size was—four or five feet wide and six feet long, according to Harris and others who glimpsed it. Harris tried every way he could think of to capture the monster, but the turtle always managed to escape. Finally he went to the lengths of pumping water out of the lake, but just as there remained only about an acre of water in the lake, Harris got appendicitis. By the time he recovered from surgery, it had rained, ruining the dams and refilling the lake.

The town decided to capitalize on all the publicity it had received—newspapers around the country had been reporting on the search for the turtle, now dubbed Oscar, "the Beast of 'Busco'"—and organize a community festival. The first Turtle Days festival was held in 1950. Now held annually in mid-June, the event features a parade with a turtle float, booths selling turtle soup, and turtle races.

CONTACTS:
Churubusco Chamber of Commerce
P.O. Box 83
Churubusco, IN 46723
260-693-9810
www.churubuscochamber.org

SOURCES:
FolkAmerHol-1999, p. 300

♦ 2834 ♦ **Turtle Independence Day**
July 4

Since 1989, the Mauna Lani Resort in Hawaii has taken in baby Hawaiian green sea turtles from the Sea Life Park Hawaii by Dolphin Discovery in Oahu, Hawaii. Staffers raise the turtles in salt water ponds located on the resort hotel's grounds until they reach maturity and can be released into the wild. Baby turtles are only a few inches across, while mature turtles must be between 18 and 24 inches across. Every Fourth of July, a Turtle Independence Day is held in

which turtles old enough and large enough to live in the ocean are brought down to the hotel's beach and let go. The hotel estimates that they have raised and released 125 turtles since the program began.

Because it is observed on the island of Hawaii, Turtle Independence Day serves as a way to promote a species native to the state. It is also an opportunity for families to learn more about the creatures. In addition to the release of the mature turtles, which is open to the public, the hotel also has entertainment, games, canoe rides, and educational displays for the children during the event.

CONTACTS:
Mauna Lani Resort
68-1400 Mauna Lani Dr.
Kohala Coast, HI 96743
808-885-6622

♦ 2835 ♦ **Tuvalu Independence Day**
October 1

Independence Day is the only national celebration in Tuvalu. The nation of Tuvalu consists of nine islands in the South Pacific with a total surface area of 10 square miles. Settled by Polynesian people some 3,000 years ago, Tuvalu came to the attention of the larger world in the 19th century when the British colonized the islands. Called the Elice Islands by the British, they played a crucial role during World War II as a key airbase in the fight against Japan. Achieving independence in 1978, the islands renamed themselves Tuvalu, which means "eight islands," a reference to the eight out of nine islands which have been inhabited for centuries.

Independence Day is marked in the capital city of Funafuti with an official government flag raising ceremony followed by a parade of policemen and schoolchildren. Similar events are held in smaller communities throughout the country. In addition to several days of feasting and dance, the Independence Day Sports Festival is held, in which citizens enjoy a number of sporting competitions.

CONTACTS:
Tuvalu Permanent Mission to the UN
800 2nd Ave, Ste. 400-D
New York, NY 10017
212-490-0534; fax: 212-808-4975

♦ 2836 ♦ **Twelfth Imam, Birthday of the**
15th day of the Islamic month of Shaban

Among Shi'ite Muslims, Muhammad al-Mahdi holds distinction as a direct descendant of the prophet Muhammad and the 12th and last imam. More important, followers believe he achieved immortality during his earthly life in the late ninth century, and that after a long departure, he will return as the savior of the world.

Iran, a country with the largest Shi'ite population, holds birthday celebrations in various towns and cities. Typical festivities include picnics, firework displays, and outdoor concerts. Qom, considered the holiest of Iranian cities next to

Mashhad, is a popular celebration site. Many worshippers visit the Jamkaran Mosque, located on the city's outskirts. According to local belief, Imam Mahdi delivered a prophecy in 974 locating his eventual return at this mosque site. A tradition has emerged in which visitors to the mosque leave their wishes and personal requests for the imam.

CONTACTS:
Iran's Ministry of Foreign Affairs
Imam Khomeini Sq.
Tehran, Iran

♦ 2837 ♦ Twelfth Night
January 5-6

The evening before EPIPHANY is called **Epiphany Eve**, or Twelfth Night, and it traditionally marks the end of the CHRISTMAS season, also called **Twelfthtide** in England. Since **Twelfth Day** is January 6, there is some confusion over exactly when Twelfth Night occurs, and it is often observed on the night of Epiphany rather than the night before.

Twelfth Night is an occasion for merrymaking, as reflected in Shakespeare's comedy, *Twelfth Night*. Celebrations reflect ancient WINTER SOLSTICE rites encouraging the rebirth of the New Year and also the Magis' visit to the Christ child.

Pageants held on this night typically include fantastic masked figures, costumed musicians, and traditional dances, such as the Abbots Bromley Antler Dance, or HORN DANCE, in England. Customarily, the Twelfth Night cake is sliced and served and the man who gets the hidden bean and the woman the pea are the king ("King of the Bean" or "Lord of Misrule") and queen for the festivities.

SOURCES:
AmerBkDays-2000, p. 23
BkDays-1864, vol. I, pp. 55, 58
BkFest-1937, pp. 51, 119
DictDays-1988, p. 123
DictFolkMyth-1984, pp. 114, 137, 689, 856
EncyChristmas-2003, p. 760
FestSaintDays-1915, p. 14
FestWestEur-1958, p. 123
FolkAmerHol-1999, p. 27
FolkWrldHol-1999, p. 22
OxYear-1999, pp. 19, 23, 40

♦ 2838 ♦ Twins Days Festival
First full weekend in August

The Twins Days Festival, which takes place every year in Twinsburg, Ohio, began in 1976 as part of the town's bicentennial celebration. Since then it has become an international event, drawing twins from as far away as Japan and Nigeria. It is listed in the *Guinness Book of World Records* as the World's Largest Annual Gathering of Twins. The festival now draws nearly 3,000 sets of twins.

Events include the "Double Take Parade," Twins Talent Show, panel discussions, a golf tournament, and contests for the twins (and triplets) who look most alike and least alike, the youngest twins, those who have traveled the farthest, etc.

About a third of the sets of twins who come to the festival are not identical, and participants are assured they do not have to come dressed alike, although many choose to do so. Individuals who have lost a twin are encouraged to come as well. A similar event, known as Twin-O-Rama, is held in mid-July in Cassville, Wisconsin.

CONTACTS:
Twins Days Festival Committee
9825 Ravenna Rd.
Twinsburg, OH 44087
330-425-3652; fax: 330-425-7280
www.twinsdays.org

♦ 2839 ♦ Tynwald Ceremony
July 5

The Isle of Man, located off the coast of England in the Irish Sea, was once the property of the Vikings. It was here that they established their custom of holding an open-air court for the settling of disputes and the passing of laws. They held their "Thing," or tribal parliament, in an open space, usually near a hill or mound, because they feared the magic associated with roofed buildings and wanted everyone to have easy access to the meeting.

Today, the Tynwald Ceremony—whose name comes from the Norse *Thing vollr,* meaning a fenced open parliament—is held at St. John's on Tynwald Hill. According to local lore, this hill contains soil from each of the Isle of Man's 17 ancient parishes. The ceremony takes place on July 5, which is Old MIDSUMMER DAY, when the Lieutenant-Governor of the Isle of Man exits a special service at St. John's Chapel and is accompanied to the hill by church and state officials. The chief justice reads a brief summary of every bill that has been passed during the year—first in English, and then in Manx, the old language of the island. This formality, once concluded, symbolizes the fact that the inhabitants of the Isle of Man have acknowledged the acts of the British Parliament and have incorporated them into the laws of their land.

CONTACTS:
Office of the Clerk of Tynwald, The Parliament of the Isle of Man
  Tynwald
Legislative Bldg.
Douglas
Isle of Man, IM1 3PW British Isles
44-16-24-685500; fax: 44-1624-685504
www.tynwald.org.im

SOURCES:
EngCustUse-1941, p. 120
FestEur-1961, p. 80
FolkCal-1930, p. 148
YrFest-1972, p. 51

♦ 2840 ♦ Tyre Festival
Late July-early August

Tyre, located in southern Lebanon, is an ancient Phoenician city and a UNESCO World Heritage Site that dates back to the third millennium B.C.E. In recent decades, the historic city has also been traumatized by conflict between extremist elements and the Israeli Defense Forces. Organizers eager to bring joy to a city populace long plagued by bombs and the climate of war established the Tyre Festival in 1996, a summer celebration of Lebanese culture and music.

The festival is held at Tyre's Al-Bass archaeological site, which features large Roman ruins of a necropolis (ancient cemetery) and a stadium. Local and international artists perform at the festival. Past programs have included concerts by solo vocalists, choirs, and Arabic orchestras; dance performances; marionette shows; and music concerts featuring a traditional stringed instrument called the *oud*.

CONTACTS:
Lebanon Ministry of Tourism
550 Central Bank St.
Ministry Bldg.
Beirut, Lebanon
www.tyrefestival.com

U

♦ 2841 ♦ **Uesugi Matsuri**
April 29-May 3

This Japanese festival, held in Yonezawa, commemorates the illustrious warrior Uesugi Kenshin (1530-1578), known for his strong principles and for staying away from women all his life. He fought battles in the hopes of becoming emperor of Japan, but he became ill and died while leading an assault on Kyoto. Uesugi Kenshin is also remembered for his role in a series of five battles, fought on a triangular island in the middle of the Matsukawa river, known as the Battles of Kawanakajima. It was here that he faced his arch-enemy Takeda Shingen, the ruler of a neighboring state. Both men passed away due to natural causes before either accomplished a conclusive victory.

The Uesugi Matsuri commemorates the warrior and his soldiers with mock battles and various costumed events, as well as a *Musha Gyoretsu*, a parade of warriors of the Sengoku (Warring States) Era.

CONTACTS:
The Yamagata Tourism Information Center
1-1-1, Kajo Central
Jonan-machi
Yamagata, 990-8580 Japan
81-2-3647-2333; fax: 81-2-3646-6333
www.yamagatakanko.com/english

SOURCES:
IllFestJapan-1993, p. 44

♦ 2842 ♦ **Uganda Independence Day**
October 9

This national holiday commemorates Uganda's independence from Britain on this day in 1962, after 70 years of British rule. Uganda became a republic in 1963 on its one-year independence anniversary.

CONTACTS:
Embassy of the Republic of Uganda
5911 16th St. N.W.
Washington, D.C. 20011
202-726-7100; fax: 202-726-1727
www.ugandaembassy.com

SOURCES:
AnnivHol-2000, p. 170
NatlHolWrld-1968, p. 187

♦ 2843 ♦ **Uganda Liberation Day**
January 26

Uganda has had a troubled history in the recent past, with European colonization followed by political and military unrest, several coups, and a succession of rulers, including the ruthless dictator Idi Amin. Uganda Liberation Day marks the events of January 26, 1986, when the military junta was overthrown by the National Resistance Army following a five-year civil war. Yoweri Kaguta Museveni assumed the presidency at that time. His reign has been marked by relative stability and economic growth, although marred by his intervention in the civil war in the Democratic Republic of the Congo. Museveni also faces a rebel movement in northern Uganda.

On the evening before celebration of Uganda Liberation Day, fireworks are exploded over the capital city of Kampala. The next day, a parade involving all branches of the Uganda military is held either at the Kololo Independence grounds or at the Kololo airfield, just outside Kampala. The country's president presides over the occasion. In 2004, the vice president of North Korea and an emissary from Libya were present at the celebration. Ugandan schoolchildren are normally bussed in for the day. Other festivities include a bull roast on the grounds of Makerere University. Throughout the country, the general public marks the day with sporting events and hearty feasts.

CONTACTS:
Embassy of the Republic of Uganda
5911 16th St. N.W.
Washington, D.C. 20011
202-726-7100; fax: 202-726-1727
www.ugandaembassy.com

♦ 2844 ♦ **Uganda Martyrs Day**
June 3

On June 3, 1886, the country of Uganda's first Christian converts were executed in the town of Namugongo. Then known as Buganda, the country had just begun attracting the attention of Catholic and Anglican missionaries. Sons of many of the region's leading families had converted to Christianity. The king of Buganda, Mwanga II, saw this conversion as a sign of treachery against his authority. He arrested 45 of the young Christian men and had them brought to him at Namugongo. When the converts refused to renounce their faith, they were burned alive on a funeral pyre.

To commemorate the event, Christian pilgrims from all over Uganda journey to Namugongo and the town's Anglican church. In 2003, an estimated 800,000 pilgrims participated in the event. Uganda's vice-president and other high-ranking officials also attended.

During the reign of Uganda's dictator Idi Amin, a Muslim, another massacre of the 19th century was also commemorated. Amin was angered that a massacre of some 70 Muslims in 1857 had never been honored or officially remembered, so he had a small mosque erected across the road from the Anglican church in Namugongo. Amin was ousted from power in 1979 before he could complete a planned larger mosque. Soldiers of his successor, Obote II, reportedly slaughtered pigs on the site, desecrating the land and rendering it unsuitable for Muslim religious activities.

CONTACTS:
Embassy of the Republic of Uganda
5911 16th St. N.W.
Washington, D.C. 20011
202-726-7100; fax: 202-726-1727
www.ugandaembassy.com

♦ 2845 ♦ Uganda National Heroes Day
June 9

Uganda National Heroes Day honors all those who sacrificed themselves to better the lives of the Ugandan people. Unfortunately, the holiday is one of the most divisive days in the Ugandan year. What constitutes a hero, and who specifically should be honored, are matters of debate in the country. Many of the heroes officially recognized by the government are fallen soldiers who died during Uganda's civil war in the 1980s. But the scars of that war, and the memories of crimes committed by both sides against the Ugandan people, are still in evidence today. There is no widespread agreement as to which of that war's fallen should be honored.

Some citizens have argued for remembering less controversial heroes, such as the Ugandan doctor who detected a deadly Ebola outbreak before it spread.

CONTACTS:
Embassy of the Republic of Uganda
5911 16th St. N.W.
Washington, D.C. 20011
202-726-7100; fax: 202-726-1727
www.ugandaembassy.com

♦ 2846 ♦ Uhola Festival
Varies

Observed by the Dakarkari people in Nigeria, the Uhola Festival is preceded by a housecleaning period during which the villages, the shrines, and the surrounding hills are cleaned up and put in order. This time is dominated by the drinking of local beer, called *m'kya*. The *Yadato*—boys and girls from wealthy families—go into seclusion for a four-week period prior to the Uhola, where they are properly fed and fattened, and encouraged to rest up for the celebration.

On the first day of the festival, the Yadato must dance in front of the chiefs' palace and present the chiefs with Uhola gifts. The celebration then moves to the village square, where they continue to dance and sing songs satirizing prostitutes, unmarried pregnant girls, irresponsible men—even political figures. The highlight of the second day of the festival is the wrestling contest, which also takes place in the village square. Sometimes the Dakarkari wrestle against other tribes, and the victor in each match receives a prize from the chief. The wrestling, prize giving, and speeches continue for about four more days, until the priest declares that the festival is over.

Only girls who are engaged to be married are allowed to participate in the Uhola. Their future husbands must have completed their *golmo*—a period of farm labor in lieu of paying for their brides. After the Uhola, the girls move into their prospective husbands' homes, while new boys go into golmo.

CONTACTS:
Embassy of the Federal Republic of Nigeria
3519 International Ct. N.W.
Washington, D.C. 20036
202-986-8400; fax: 202-775-1385
www.nigeriaembassyusa.org

SOURCES:
FolkWrldHol-1999, p. 536

♦ 2847 ♦ Ukraine Constitution Day
June 28

On June 28, 1996, the country of Ukraine adopted a new constitution. Having gained independence in 1991 following the collapse of the Soviet Union, Ukraine began working on drafting a new constitution. Five years of work were required before the final document was written and approved by the country's parliament. The constitution created a democratic form of government that guarantees human rights and freedoms for its citizens under the rule of law.

Since it is a fairly new holiday, traditions have not yet been established to celebrate the day. In Kiev, popular Ukrainian musicians and singers give concerts in Maidan Nezalezhnosty Square. In 2007, Ukrainian President Victor Yushchenko attended ceremonies at the Taras Shevchenko Opera House in Kiev.

CONTACTS:
Embassy of Ukraine
3350 M St. N.W.
Washington, D.C. 20007
202-333-0606; fax: 202-333-0817
www.mfa.gov.ua/usa/en

♦ 2848 ♦ **Ukraine Independence Day**
August 24

On this day in 1991, just after a failed coup in Moscow, Ukraine declared its independence from the U.S.S.R. On December 1, 1991, 90 percent of the people voted for independence.

CONTACTS:
Embassy of Ukraine
3350 M St. N.W.
Washington, D.C. 20007
202-333-0606; fax: 202-333-0817
www.mfa.gov.ua

♦ 2849 ♦ **Ukraine Unification Day (National Reunification Day)**
January 22

On January 22, 1919, the Ukrainian People's Republic and the West Ukrainian People's Republic merged into a single nation. In a ceremony held in the city of Kiev, the two separate nations agreed to become the nation of Ukraine.

The Ukrainian People's Republic had been formed in January 1918 from Ukrainian land that had formerly been part of Russia. The West Ukrainian People's Republic was created in 1918 from land that had formerly been part of the Austro-Hungarian Empire. This was the first time that the Ukrainian people had established a single nation out of all the territory they occupied.

The day became an official holiday in 1999. In 2008, Ukrainian president Victor Yushchenko proposed that the holiday be renamed **National Reunification Day**. The day was remembered in 1987 when hundreds of thousands of people joined hands in a 550-kilometer long human chain stretching from the capital city of Kiev to the city of Lviv in western Ukraine.

CONTACTS:
Embassy of Ukraine
3350 M St. N.W.
Washington, D.C. 20007
202-333-0606; fax: 202-333-0817
www.mfa.gov.ua/usa/en

♦ 2850 ♦ **Ukrainian Harvest Festivals**
Varies; usually mid-October

Ukrainian harvest festivals have some elements in common with state and county fairs in the United States: stalls where farmers display their best produce of the season for prizes, games, and entertainment. In the great farming regions of Ukraine, known as "the breadbasket of Europe," harvest festivals have been celebrated for millennia. It is traditional to bake loaves of bread at harvest time with decorative images suggestive of the new crops, such as stalks of wheat.

Modern festivals often feature a parade to the fairgrounds, such sporting competitions as tugs-of-war, sack jumping, soccer, volleyball, and basketball, and musical, dance, and comedic performances.

Ukraine is also known for the *hopak*, a dance in which men hold their arms out, crouch down close to the floor and shoot their legs out in quick movements. This dance is said to have originated as a Ukrainian military exercise.

SOURCES:
FestWrld: Ukraine-1998, p. 20

♦ 2851 ♦ **Ullambana (Hungry Ghosts Festival; All Souls' Feast)**
July-August; full moon or 15th day of seventh lunar month

A Buddhist and Taoist festival probably dating back to the sixth century and CONFUCIUS, Ullambana is observed in China as well as throughout the rest of eastern Asia. A legend attaches to this feast's origins: a Buddhist monk named Moggallana sought to save his mother from hell, where she went after her death because of her greed. The Buddha proposed that Moggallana and his fellow monks offer money, apparel, and food on behalf of all the souls he would encounter there. Moggallana did as the Buddha suggested and so rescued his mother. Because it illustrated the Chinese virtue of honoring one's parents, Ullambana became the best-loved Buddhist festival in China, and from there it spread to Japan, Korea, and other east Asian countries.

It is believed that during this month the souls of the dead are released from purgatory to roam the earth. In Taiwan the day is called "opening of the gates of Hell." This makes it a dangerous time to travel, get married, or move to a new house.

Unhappy and hungry spirits—those who died without descendants to look after them or who had no proper funeral (because they were killed in a plane crash, for example)—may cause trouble and therefore must be placated with offerings. So people burn paper replicas of material possessions like automobiles, furniture, clothing, and paper money ("ghost money") believing that this frees these things for the spirits' use. Joss sticks are burned, and offerings of food are placed on tables outside people's homes. Prayers are said at all Chinese temples and at Chinese shops and homes, and *wayang* (Chinese street opera) and puppet shows are performed on open-air stages.

Families in Vietnam remember the souls of the dead by visiting their graves. It is known as **Yue Lan**, **Vu Lan Day**, **Day of the Dead**, and **Trung Nguyen**. The festival, the second most important of the year after TET, is observed throughout the country in Buddhist temples and homes and offices. To remember the dead, families perform the *dan chay*, an offering of incense at graves. An altar at home is prepared with two levels—one for Buddha with offerings of incense, fruit, and rice, and one for departed relatives with rice soup, fruit, and meat. It is considered best if offerings include the *tan sinh*, three kinds of creatures—fish, meat, and shrimp—and the *ngu qua*, five kinds of fruit. Money and clothes made of votive papers are also burned at this time.

CONTACTS:
Consulate General of Vietnam

1700 California St., Ste. 430
San Francisco, CA 94109
415-922-1707; fax: 415-922-1848
www.vietnamconsulate-ca.org

Taiwan Government Information Office
4201 Wisconsin Ave. N.W.
Washington, DC 20016
202-895-1850; fax: 202-362-6144
www.gio.gov.tw

Hong Kong Tourism Board
115 E. 54th St. 2/F
New York, NY 10022
212-421-3382; fax: 212-421-8428
www.discoverhongkong.com

SOURCES:
AnnivHol-2000, p. 239
BkHolWrld-1986, Aug 18
DictFolkMyth-1984, pp. 225, 1051
DictWrldRel-1989, pp. 135, 581
EncyRel-1987, vol. 3, pp. 293, 326
FolkWrldHol-1999, p. 461
OxYear-1999, p. 702
RelHolCal-2004, p. 233
WrldBuddhism-1984, p. 209

♦ 2852 ♦ Ullr Fest
Late January to early February

A winter festival in Breckenridge, Colo., this celebration recognizes Ullr, the Norse god of winter and a stepson of Thor. Highlights are a parade, skiing and other sporting events, and a snow sculpture championship.

CONTACTS:
Breckenridge Resort Chamber
311 S. Ridge St.
P.O. Box 1909
Breckenridge, CO 80424
888-251-2417 or 970-453-2913; fax: 970-453-7238
www.gobreck.com

SOURCES:
DictFolkMyth-1984, p. 1148

♦ 2853 ♦ Umoja Karamu
Fourth Sunday in November

The African-American holiday of Umoja Karamu, which means "unity feast" in Kiswahili, celebrates family members' commitment to one another. Established in 1971 by Brother Edward Sims, Jr., the feast was observed on the fourth Sunday in November, a date set by the Temple of the Black Messiah in Washington, D.C. African-American churches and families in several states continue to celebrate the festival, although it is not as widely observed as KWANZAA.

Five periods of African-American life, each symbolized by a particular color, provide the framework for the Umoja Karamu ceremony: 1) the family in Africa, before slavery in America (black); 2) the enslaved family in America (white); 3) the family freed from slavery (red); 4) the family struggling for true liberation (green); 5) the family anticipating the future

(orange or gold). Narratives, music, and foods relating to each period are part of the ceremony.

SOURCES:
AfrAmerHol-1991, p. 63
AAH-2007, p. 411

♦ 2854 ♦ Underwater Tug-of-War Festival
January 15

It's not the POLAR BEAR SWIM, but the annual tug-of-war in Mihama, Fukui Prefecture, does involve people jumping into cold waters in the middle of winter. This is a ritual connected with the local Shinto shrine. Legend has it that a huge snake once menaced the waters of Hiruga Lake, which opens out into the Sea of Japan. The people drove the snake away by taking a huge rope, bigger than the snake, into the water. Today, young men struggle in a tug-of-war while standing in the lake. The rope symbolizes the snake, and the tug-of-war continues until the rope is pulled apart or cut in two. The event also serves as a ritual appealing for a good fishing season.

CONTACTS:
Fukui Prefecture
3-17-1 ote fukui-shi fukui-pref
Tsuruga, 910-8580 Japan
81-7-7032-1111
www.pref.fukui.lg.jp/english

♦ 2855 ♦ United Arab Emirates National Day
December 2

This national holiday commemorates the December 2, 1971, expiration of a British treaty that inhibited self-rule for the sheikhdoms on the Persian Gulf in the eastern Arabian peninsula, and the union of seven of the sheikhdoms in the former Trucial States to become the United Arab Emirates. The Emirates' major cities celebrate National Day December 2-3.

CONTACTS:
Embassy of United Arab Emirates
3522 International Ct. N.W., Ste. 400
Washington, D.C. 20008
202-243-2400; fax: 202-243-2432
www.uae-embassy.org

SOURCES:
AnnivHol-2000, p. 201

♦ 2856 ♦ United Nations Day
October 24

The international peacekeeping organization known as the United Nations was formally established on October 24, 1945, in the wake of World War II. Representatives from the United States, Great Britain, the Soviet Union, and China first met in August and September of 1944 at the Dumbarton Oaks estate in Washington, D.C., to discuss the problems involved in creating such an agency, and the results of their talks became the basis for the United Nations Charter that was ratified the following year. Although it has not always been successful in maintaining world peace, the U.N. has served as an important international forum for the handling of conflicts in the Middle East, Korea, Somalia, the former Yugoslavia, and other troubled areas.

Each member nation observes October 24, and in some places the entire week is known as **United Nations Week**. In the United States, events taking place on this day include parades, international fairs, and dinners featuring foods from different countries. It is also common to hold debates and discussions designed to acquaint the public with the U.N.'s functions. Schools frequently observe United Nations Day by holding folk festivals that teach students the music, songs, and dances of different countries, or by organizing special programs focusing on their geography, products, government, and culture.

CONTACTS:
United Nations, Global Teaching and Learning Project
United Nations HQ, Rm. 931-B
New York, NY 10017
212-963-8589; fax: 212-963-3358
www.un.org

SOURCES:
AmerBkDays-2000, p. 728
AnnivHol-2000, p. 177
BkHolWrld-1986, Oct 24
DictDays-1988, p. 124

♦ 2857 ♦ **United States Air and Trade Show**
Third weekend in July

Dayton, Ohio, has been a center for aeronautical research and development ever since two of its local residents, Orville and Wilbur WRIGHT, created the first successful flying machine in their bicycle shop and tested their invention just a few miles outside of town.

Dayton began celebrating its heritage as "the birthplace of aviation" by staging informal air shows shortly after the turn of the century, and by the early 1970s, the **Dayton Air Fair** was a regular annual event consisting of flying demonstrations and aircraft displays. By 1988 it was called the **Dayton Air and Trade Show**, reflecting a growing emphasis on the commercial aspects of the aviation and aerospace industry. It was renamed the United States Air and Trade Show in 1990, when it became an international exposition, and through the 1990s the trade show was held biennially. The trade show was not held in 2001-2003, however, and its future is uncertain.

Every year, the third weekend in July is devoted to the air show, which features bi-planes, gliders, helicopters, and jets flown by some of the most famous names in the field of aviation.

Visitors and participants can also visit the United States Air Force Museum, the National Aviation Hall of Fame, the restored Wright Brothers Cycle Shop, and Wright-Patterson Air Force Base, which continues to play a major role in the development of aerospace technology.

CONTACTS:
Dayton Air Show

3800 A Wright Dr.
Vandalia, OH 45377
937-898-5901; fax: 937-898-5121
www.usats.org

♦ 2858 ♦ **United States Open Championship in Golf**
Four days ending the third Sunday in June

The **U.S. Open**, conducted by the United States Golf Association, is the oldest golf tournament in North America, and was first held in 1895. More than 6,000 professional and amateur golfers vie for only 156 available places. Unlike the MASTERS, which is an invitational tournament, the U.S. Open is for anyone good enough to survive the qualifying rounds.

Rather than being played on the same course each year, its location changes. It is traditionally played on the nation's best courses, such as Merion in Philadelphia, Oakland Hills in Birmingham, Mich., Baltusrol in Union County, N.J., Winged Foot in Mamaroneck, N.Y., and Pebble Beach on the Monterey Peninsula of California. Since the 1930s, it has been the U.S.G.A.'s practice every 10 to 15 years to take the Open back to certain courses that have demonstrated they can produce a rigorous test for the world's top golfers. The tournament itself takes four days. There is a qualifying round followed by three days of 18 holes each, for a total of 72 holes.

The U.S. Open is one of the most difficult golf championships to win. Its list of champions includes Bobby Jones, Walter Hagen, Gene Sarazen, Ben Hogan, Arnold Palmer, Jack Nicklaus, Lee Trevino, Tom Watson, and Tiger Woods. The 1913 tournament, which was won by an unknown 20-year-old store clerk named Francis Ouimet, is considered to have marked the transformation of golf in America from an elite game to a public pastime.

CONTACTS:
United States Golf Association
P.O. Box 708
Far Hills, NJ 07931
908-234-2300; fax: 908-234-9687
www.usopen.com

♦ 2859 ♦ **United States Open Tennis**
September

The **U.S. Open** is the final tournament in the four events that make up the Grand Slam of tennis. (The others are the AUSTRALIAN OPEN, the FRENCH OPEN and WIMBLEDON.) Also known as the **U.S. Championships**, the games are played on hard courts at Flushing Meadows Park in Queens, N.Y. They had been played from 1915 to 1978 in Forest Hills, also in Queens. Separate amateur and professional open championships were held in 1968 and 1969, and the tournament became exclusively an open in 1970.

The U.S. National Lawn Tennis Association was established in 1881, and the first official U.S. National Championship was played under its auspices that year in Newport, R.I. The first women's championship was played in 1887. The golden age at Forest Hills is considered to have been the 1920s when

William T. "Big Bill" Tilden II dominated the game. He was U.S. Open champion seven times: 1920-25 and 1929. Other seven-time winners were Richard Sears (1881-87) and William Larned (1901, 1902, 1907-11). Jimmy Connors took the title five times (1974, 1976, 1978, 1982, 1983). In the women's championships, Molla Bjurstedt Mallory is the all-time champ; she won eight times (1915-18, 1920-22, 1926). Helen Wills Moody won seven times (1923-25, 1927-29, 1931). "Little Poker Face," as she was called, also won eight Wimbledons and four French Opens.

Ranking near the top of the excitement scale were the wins in the U.S. Championships that sewed up the Grand Slam championship. In 1938, Don Budge was the first to win all four Grand Slam titles. The feat wasn't equaled until 1962 when Rod Laver won all four. Then he did it again in 1969. In 1953, Californian Maureen Connolly became the first woman to sweep the Grand Slam titles. Known as "Little Mo," she had won her first U.S. Championship at the age of 16 in 1951. A horse-riding accident in 1954 cut her career short, and she died in 1969. Women who have won all Grand Slam titles since then are Margaret Smith Court in 1970 and Steffi Graf in 1988.

CONTACTS:
United States Tennis Association
70 W. Red Oak Ln.
White Plains, NY 80604
914-696-7000; fax: 914-696-7234
www.usta.com

♦ 2860 ♦ United Tribes International Powwow
Early September over four days

The United Tribes International Powwow takes place every year over a four-day weekend in early September at United Tribes Technical College in Bismarck, N.Dak. The event typically draws 20,000 to see more than 1,500 drummers and dancers representing about 70 Native-American tribes. Contests are held for all age groups in singing, dancing, and drumming. Other festival events include a parade, a softball tournament, arts and crafts, and a national Miss Indians pageant for contestants between the ages of 17 and 26. The event also hosts such visiting cultural performers as a Maori dance troupe from New Zealand.

The powwow is affiliated with United Tribes Technical College, which was founded in 1969 to serve the academic and cultural requirements of American-Indian students and their families. The powwow launched the same year. A non-alcohol event, the powwow is open to all. Free camping is available at the site. The winner of many awards, the powwow is considered a premier cultural event of North Dakota.

CONTACTS:
United Tribes Technical College
3315 University Dr.
Bismarck, ND 58504
701-255-3285
www.unitedtribespowwow.com

♦ 2861 ♦ Universal Prayer Day (Dzam Ling Chi Sang)
Usually June or July; 14th to 16th days of fifth Tibetan lunar month

Universal Prayer Day is a Tibetan Buddhist festival and a time for spiritual cleansing. During this time, people hang prayer flags on tree tops, burn juniper twigs, and build bonfires to worship the Buddha and local gods. Fire in the Tibetan culture is symbolic of cleansing. Family picnics are also common during the festival.

This is also the time of the once-a-year display of the famous giant *thangkas*, scroll paintings, at Tashilhunpo Monastery in Shigatse, Tibet. Tashilhunpo (which means "heap of glory"), the seat of the Panchen Lamas, once had more than 4,000 monks. But the monastery was disbanded by the Chinese in 1960, and only a few hundred monks remain.

At this time, three huge thangkas with images of the Buddha are displayed for three days on a nine-story wall on the monastery grounds. Thangkas, which are made in all sizes, were first known in Tibet in the 10th century, and were used in monastery schools as teaching devices. They were always consecrated before they were hung.

Panchen Lamas came into being in the 17th century when the fifth Dalai Lama gave the title *panchen*, meaning "great scholar," to his beloved tutor. The tutor was then found to be the reincarnation of Amitabha, the Buddha of infinite light, and subsequent Panchen Lamas are new incarnations. As with Dalai Lamas, when a Panchen Lama dies, a search is conducted for an infant boy who is the new incarnation.

See also DALAI LAMA, BIRTHDAY OF THE

CONTACTS:
Office of Tibet
Tibet House, 1 Culworth St.
London, NW8 7AF United Kingdom
44-20-7722-5378; fax: 44-20-7722-0362
www.tibet.com

♦ 2862 ♦ University of Pennsylvania Relay Carnival
Seven days, beginning on the Sunday before the last weekend in April

The **Penn Relays** is the oldest and largest track and field event in the United States. The first relay meet held on the campus of the University of Pennsylvania in Philadelphia was on April 21, 1895, but even back then the tents and the festival atmosphere contributed to its reputation as a carnival rather than just a series of races. Since that time, the Penn Relays have served as a springboard for athletes who later went on to win OLYMPIC medals—such as Carl Lewis, Joan Benoit, Edwin Moses, and Frank Shorter. It is also a breeding ground for rising track and field stars, with more than 700 high school teams and 180 college teams participating.

The event begins on the Sunday before the last weekend in April (unless that day is EASTER, in which case the Relays begin a week earlier) with a 20-kilometer road race. There is a heptathlon and a decathlon on Tuesday and Wednesday, and the rest of the week is filled with walk, sprint, distance, and field events for athletes of all ages and abilities—including Special Olympians (*see also* SPECIAL OLYMPICS). More than 70,000 spectators are drawn to the event, which receives wide press coverage.

CONTACTS:
Penn Relays Office
219 S. 33rd St.
Philadelphia, PA 19104
215-898-6145; fax: 215-573-2797
www.thepennrelays.com

♦ 2863 ♦ Up-Helly-Aa
Last Tuesday in January

This ancient fire festival is observed by people of Lerwick in the Shetland Islands. In pre-Christian times their Norse ancestors welcomed the return of the sun god with YULE, a 24-day period of feasting, storytelling, and bonfires. The last night of the festival was called Up-Helly-Aa, or "End of the Holy Days."

Today a group known as the Guizers builds a 31-foot model of a Viking longship, complete with a dragon's head and many oars, in honor of those Viking invaders who decided to remain in Scotland. On the night of Up-Helly-Aa, the Guizers dress in Norse costumes and helmets and carry the boat to a large open field. There they throw lit torches into the ship and burn it.

Up-helly-Aa originally referred to EPIPHANY, or January 6—the day when the Yuletide holidays came to an end. The shifting of the date to the end of January probably reflects the change from the Julian to the Gregorian calendar in 1752. This day is also referred to as **Uphaliday, Uphelya, Up-Helly-Day, Uphalie Day,** or **Uphalimass.**

CONTACTS:
Shetland Islands Tourism
Market Cross
Lerwick, Shetland ZE1 0LU United Kingdom
44-87-0199-9440; fax: 44-19-5046-0807
www.visitshetland.com

SOURCES:
AnnivHol-2000, p. 18
BkHolWrld-1986, Jan 28
DictDays-1988, p. 124
EncyChristmas-2003, p. 776
FolkWrldHol-1999, p. 48
RelHolCal-2004, p. 270

♦ 2864 ♦ Urini Nal (Children's Day)
May 5

Urini Nal has been a national holiday in South Korea since 1975. Schools are closed and parks are packed with children. Events of the day may include wrestling and martial arts exhibitions, dancing, and the presentation of puppet shows and plays. Cake shops give away rice cake favors. The holiday is intended to forge the bonds of family life.

SOURCES:
AnnivHol-2000, p. 78

♦ 2865 ♦ Urs Ajmer Sharif
First through sixth days of the Islamic month of Rajab

This is the *urs,* death anniversary, of the Sufi saint Khwaja Muin al-Din Muhammad Chishti (or Moinuddin Muhammad Chishti, 1142-1236), who founded a major Sufi order in India. His tomb, known as the Dargah, is located in Ajmer, Rajasthan, India, considered by many South Asian Muslims to be the most important PILGRIMAGE site next to Mecca.

The saint is often referred to as Gharib Nawaz, meaning "protector of the poor," because he spent much of his life in service to the less fortunate. He also had a great love of devotional music, believing it had the potential to enhance one's spirituality. Such songs, called *qawwali,* are sung during his death festival. Chishti is said to have retreated into solitude six days before he died, thus his urs is celebrated not only on the anniversary of his death, but also on the preceding five days.

In addition to special religious services, offerings, prayers, and other ceremonies, a huge fair takes over the town of Ajmer during the urs. Vendors sell food and religious items, and some of the finest poets of the Urdu language gather to provide readings.

CONTACTS:
Government of Rajasthan, Department of Tourism Art & Culture
  Govt. Hostel Campus
Paryatan Bhawan, M.I. Rd.
Jaipur, Rajasthan 302 001 India
91-141-5110595; fax: 91-141-5110591
www.rajasthantourism.gov.in

SOURCES:
EncyRel-1987, vol. 14, p. 348
OxDictWrldRel-1997, p. 213
WildPlanet-1995, p. 241

♦ 2866 ♦ Urs of Baba Farid Shakar Ganj
Fifth, sixth, and seventh days of the Islamic month of Muharram

Urs of Baba Farid Shakar Ganj is marked every year to commemorate the death anniversary of the great Punjabi poet and Sufi Muslim saint, Baba Farid Shakar Ganj, born in 1188 C.E. He is known as the first Punjabi saint and the father of Punjabi culture. On his death anniversary, pilgrims from around the world visit his shrine-like tomb, or *mazar,* in Pakpattan, Pakistan. On this occasion, Bahashti Darwaza (Paradise Door), made of silver and overlaid with gold flowers, is opened to allow thousands of devotees to pass through over the course of the three-day occasion. The anniversary also is marked with folk music and ecstatic dancing by the faithful. This commemoration has taken place every year for more than 750 years.

CONTACTS:
Pakistan Tourism Development Corporation
22-A
Saeed Plaza, Blue Area
Jinnah Ave.
Islamabad, 44000 Pakistan

SOURCES:
UndIslam-2004, p. 392

◆ 2867 ◆ Urs of Jelaluddin al-Rumi (Whirling Dervish Festival)
Week leading up to December 17

Each year up to a million people flood Konya, Turkey, on the anniversary of the death of the poet and Sufi Islamic mystic Jelaluddin al-Rumi. The prolific and influential poet was born in 1207 in what is now Afghanistan. After spending most of his life in present-day Turkey, he died there in 1273. Rumi's teachings are the basis for the Sufi Muslim order known as Mevlevi in Turkish and Malawi in Arabic. The order uses music and dance to experience spiritual ecstasy, and its members are most commonly known as "whirling dervishes" because of their dance rituals that involve spinning in place for extended periods of time.

During the week leading up to December 17, lights bejewel the town of Konya, shop keepers offer special merchandise, and thousands of visitors arrive to partake of exhibits and lectures related to Rumi and the Mevlevi order. Festivalgoers also visit Rumi's tomb, situated in an extensive Mevlevi complex, which comprises one of Turkey's most-visited museums. The climax of the festival week takes place on December 17, when Mevlevis perform their whirling dance wearing costumes that feature white trousers, a full white overskirt, and tall cylindrical hats. Each of these items represents an aspect of the dancer's ego, which is symbolically overcome during the dance by the performer's spirit ascending to love and truth. Before the dance, Rumi's poems are recited and prayers offered. The dance occurs in seven parts, each of which has a particular meaning. The whirling, which is said to mirror the circular movements of creation, from an atom's particles to the planets' orbits, occurs in the fifth section. Muslims and non-Muslims alike attend the striking, world-renowned display. It inspired the RUMI FESTIVAL, held annually in North Carolina to honor the beloved poet and his teachings.

CONTACTS:
Turkish Tourist Office
2525 Massachusetts Ave. N.W.
Washington, D.C. 20008
202-612-6800; fax: 202-319-7446
www.tourismturkey.org

Turkey Embassy
2525 Massachusetts Ave. N.W.
Washington, DC 02008
202-612-6700; fax: 202-612-6744
www.turkey.org

SOURCES:
UndIslam-2004, p. 400

◆ 2868 ◆ Uruguay Constitution Oath Taking Day
July 18

The country of Uruguay adopted its first constitution on July 18, 1830, shortly after becoming an independent country in 1928. Although it adopted other constitutions in 1917, 1934, 1952, and 1967, the 1830 version laid the groundwork upon which all later versions have relied. The 1830 constitution, modeled after the American and French constitutions, created executive, legislative, and judicial branches of government. The legislative branch consists of a senate and a house of representatives. Later constitutions checked the powers of the president and provided for a separation of church and state. Constitutional amendments adopted in 1976 strengthened the political powers of the country's military.

To commemorate the adoption of Uruguay's first constitution, speeches are given by government officials and a parade featuring a military band, mounted cavalry, and soldiers is held in the capital city of Montevideo.

CONTACTS:
Embassy of Uruguay in the United States
1913 I St. N.W.
Washington, D.C. 20006
202-331-1313; fax: 202-331-8142
www.uruwashi.org

◆ 2869 ◆ Uruguay Independence Day
August 25

This national holiday commemorates the declaration of independence from Portuguese rule on this day in 1825. By 1828, Uruguay was officially autonomous.

Patriotic ceremonies are held in the capital city of Montevideo, with speeches and the singing of the national anthem.

CONTACTS:
Embassy of Uruguay
1913 I St. N.W.
Washington, D.C. 20006
202-331-1313; fax: 202-331-8142
www.uruwashi.org

SOURCES:
AnnivHol-2000, p. 141
NatlHolWrld-1968, p. 150

◆ 2870 ◆ Utah Arts Festival
Late June

The Utah Arts Festival was founded in 1977 in Salt Lake City and is now a five-day event held on stages and in the streets, plazas, and galleries. Hundreds of booths are set up for regional foods and for exhibits of sculpture, painting, pottery, folk arts, and photography. In a Children's Art Yard, stories are told of Utah's mining days and natural history. Live performances of contemporary, jazz, bluegrass, folk, and salsa music as well as dance, theater, symphony, and opera performances are presented on three stages.

CONTACTS:
Utah Arts Festival Foundation
230 S. 500 West, Ste. 120
Salt Lake City, UT 84101
801-322-2428; fax: 801-363-8681
www.uaf.org

SOURCES:
GdUSFest-1984, p. 191
MusFestAmer-1990, p. 141

♦ 2871 ♦ **Utakai Hajime (Imperial Poem-Reading Ceremony)**
Mid-January

Utakai Hajime, the Imperial Poem-Reading Ceremony, is a centuries-old New Year's tradition in Japan. The first historical reference to this custom dates back to 1267. The ceremony took place off and on over the years, but has been a regular annual event since 1879. It takes place in the Matsunoma Stateroom at the Imperial Palace in Tokyo and is attended by the emperor, empress, other members of the imperial family, judges, and guests. Many people, including people outside Japan, write poems for this annual competition and the chance to read one's winning poem in this company. In January 2000, a Japanese high school student won the honor for the second year in a row, the youngest winner ever.

The initial poetry readings are those composed by members of the public, followed by those by the royal family, ending with the poem written by the emperor, which is read five times. The poems are traditionally written in *tanka* style. These are traditional short poems of only five lines and 31 syllables: the first line has five syllables, the second has seven, the third has five, and the last two lines each have seven.

CONTACTS:
Japan Echo (bimonthly journal)
2-2-1 Uchisaiwai-cho, Nippon Press Ctr. Bldg.
Chiyoda-ku
Tokyo, 100-0011 Japan
81-3-3519-3511; fax: 81-3-3519-3519
www.japanecho.co.jp

SOURCES:
BkFestHolWrld-1970, p. 27

♦ 2872 ♦ **Ute Bear Dance**
May, Memorial Day weekend

An ancient ceremony of the Southern Ute Indians, the Ute Bear Dance is now held on the Sunday and Monday of MEMORIAL DAY weekend in Ignacio, Colo. Originally the ritual was held in late February or early March, at the time when bears awaken from their hibernation. It stemmed from the belief that the Utes were descended from bears, and the dance served both to help the bears coming out of hibernation and to gain power from them, since bears were believed to cure sickness and to communicate with people in the Spirit World.

Today the dance is largely a social occasion, and is what is called a women's dance, since the women ask the men to dance. This practice is rooted in the habits of bears: supposedly the female bear wakes first and then chases the male bear. In earlier days, two bears—a man and woman wearing bearskins, with red paint around their mouths to suggest the bloody ferocity of the bears—romped around a corral, the female chasing the male, and both responding ferociously toward anyone who might laugh. In the present-day dance, lines of women and men advance toward each other, gradually dancing in pairs. The dancing goes on until sunset, when there is a feast.

CONTACTS:
Southern Ute Tribal Council
P.O. Box 737
Ignacio, CO 81137
970-563-0100; fax: 970-563-0396
www.southern-ute.nsn.us

SOURCES:
EncyNatAmerRel-2001, p. 15
HolSymbols-2009, p. 992
IndianAmer-1989, p. 121

♦ 2873 ♦ **Uzbekistan Constitution Day**
December 8

On December 8, 1992, the new constitution of Uzbekistan was signed, creating a democratic system of government for the newly-independent country.

Uzbekistan was created in 1924 by the communist government of the Soviet Union. The traditional boundaries of Central Asia were redefined under the communists to make nationalistic or ethnic opposition to the central government more difficult. Uzbekistan remained a part of the Soviet Union until the collapse of the communist regime, becoming an independent nation in 1991.

On Constitution Day, the country's president usually broadcasts a message of greeting to the Uzbekistan people in which he reiterates the democratic ideals of the constitution and outlines what steps the government has taken to ensure those ideals are carried out.

On Constitution Day in 2007, the Uzbekistan senate passed a law liberalizing criminal punishments. Under this new law, women, young people under the age of 18, men over 60, and foreign citizens who have been arrested for a first crime will no longer be imprisoned. Prison sentences for nonviolent crimes were also reduced.

CONTACTS:
Embassy of Uzbekistan to the United States
1746 Massachusetts Ave.
Washington, D.C. 20036-1903
202-887-5300; fax: 202-293-6804
www.uzbekistan.org

♦ 2874 ♦ **Uzbekistan Independence Day**
September 1

The Republic of Uzbekistan was one of the central Asian republics of the former Soviet Union until 1991, when it and other republics declared their independence from the U.S.S.R. Independence Day, September 1, is celebrated throughout the country with parties, music, and exhibits.

CONTACTS:
Embassy of Uzbekistan
1746 Massachusetts Ave. N.W.
Washington, D.C. 20036-1903
202-887-5300; fax: 202-293-6804
www.uzbekistan.org

V

◆ 2875 ◆ Vaisakh
April-May; first day of Hindu month of Vaisakha

Vaisakh is the Hindu New Year and a harvest festival, celebrated primarily in northern India and Bangladesh with temple worship, ritual bathing in rivers, and a New Year's fair. For Sikhs, it is their most important holy day.

In Malaysia and India, especially in the Indian state of Punjab, where the gospel of the Sikhs began, Vaisakh (also spelled **Baisakh**) is particularly significant. On this day in 1689 GURU GOBIND SINGH chose the five leaders (called the *Panch Pyare*, or "Beloved Five") who formed the Khalsa, the militant fraternity of the Sikhs. There the holiday is celebrated in the temples, with a 48-hour reading of the GURU GRANTH SAHIB (the Sikh holy book), prayers, hymns, and sermons. Castelessness, an important Sikh principle, is emphasized by everyone eating and sitting together. Afterwards, there is feasting and dancing of the *bhangra*, a popular and athletic folk dance for men, depicting the entire farming year.

In the Indian state of Kerala, the festival is known as **Vishu**. Activities include fireworks and what is called *Vishu Kani*, a display of grain, fruits, flowers, gold, new cloth, and money, which is supposed to ensure a prosperous year.

The festival is called **Bohag Bihu** in Assam, and there it is celebrated for a week with music, folk dances, and community feasting. Traditions include decorating cattle, smearing them with turmeric, and giving them brown sugar and eggplant to eat. Also during this time, there is a day on which young people look for marriage partners. The girls wear beautiful scarves, and the boys look for the most lovely orchids; they present these to each other and then dance.

CONTACTS:
Punjab Tourism Development Corp.
SCO-183-184
Sector 8-C
Chandigarh, Punjab 160 018 India
91-172-781138; fax: 91-172-548828
punjabgovt.nic.in/TOURISM/ContactAddresses.htm

SOURCES:
AnnivHol-2000, p. 61
BkFest-1937, p. 157

DictFolkMyth-1984, p. 790
FolkWrldHol-1999, p. 306
HolSymbols-2009, p. 997
RelHolCal-2004, pp. 167, 203

◆ 2876 ◆ Vaitarani
November-December; 11th day of the waning half of the Hindu month of Margashirsha

Vaitarani is the river that, according to Hindu belief, runs between the earth and the underworld, which the dead must cross to reach the realm of Yama, who is the ruler and judge of the dead. It plays much the same role in Hindu mythology that the River Styx plays in Greek mythology. Because this river is said to be filled with all kinds of filth, blood, and moral offenses, Hindus believe that it can only be crossed with the aid of a cow. It is for this reason that cows are given in charity to Brahmans where there is a death in the community.

On the day known as Vaitarani, devout Hindus observe a fast and other prescribed rituals. In the evening they worship a black cow, who is bathed in fragrant water and has sandal paste applied to her horns. Brahmans are given gifts of food, clothes, and a cow made out of gold or silver.

SOURCES:
DictHindu-1977, p. 318
RelHolCal-2004, p. 180

◆ 2877 ◆ Valdemar (King) Day
June 15

According to legend, Danish King Valdemar II set out to conquer the pagan Estonians and convert them to Christianity. During the night of June 15, 1219, the Estonians made a surprise attack on the Danish camp. As he raised his arms toward heaven to pray for help, the Danish archbishop discovered that as long as he could hold his arms up, the Danes were able to push back the enemy. But when they dropped from weariness, the Estonians gained ground. Eventually a red banner with a white cross floated down from the sky and, as the archbishop caught it, he heard a voice from the clouds say that the Danes would win if they raised this banner before their enemies. A messenger took the banner to King Valdemar, and the Danes won the battle.

Schools, sports organizations, and Boy Scout troops in Denmark often hold pageants on June 15, also known as **Flag Day**, in which they reenact the story of the *Dannebrog* (the Danish flag) and King Valdemar. The red and white flag can be seen flying everywhere on this day in honor of its miraculous first appearance.

CONTACTS:
Embassy of Denmark
3200 Whitehaven St. N.W.
Washington, D.C. 20008
202-234-4300; fax: 202-328-1470
www.ambwashington.um.dk

SOURCES:
AnnivHol-2000, p. 101

♦ 2878 ♦ **Valentine's Day**
February 14

St. Valentine is believed to have been a Roman priest who was martyred on this day around 270. How he became the patron saint of lovers remains a mystery, but one theory is that the Church used the day of St. Valentine's martyrdom in an attempt to Christianize the old Roman LUPERCALIA, a pagan festival held around the middle of February. Part of the ancient ceremony entailed putting girls' names in a box and letting the boys draw them out. Couples would thus be paired off until the following year. The Church substituted saints' names for girls' names, in the hope that the participant would model his life after the saint whose name he drew. But by the 16th century, it was once again girls' names that ended up in the box. Eventually the custom of sending anonymous cards or messages to those one admired became the accepted way of celebrating **St. Valentine's Day**.

Valentine's Day has been the occasion for such events as underwater weddings and "kiss-ins" and "hug-ins"—in 1999, about 3,000 couples in Belarus attempted to set a new world record for the largest kiss-in (previously held by 1,600 couples in Spain); in 2002 more than 1,000 students and teachers at a South African high school went for the world's biggest hug-in.

SOURCES:
AmerBkDays-2000, p. 139
BkDays-1864, vol. I, p. 255
BkFest-1937, p. 15
DaysCustFaith-1957, p. 54
DictFolkMyth-1984, p. 866
FestSaintDays-1915, p. 34
FolkAmerHol-1999, p. 76
FolkWrldHol-1999, p. 174
OxYear-1999, pp. 76, 77
SaintFestCh-1904, p. 103

♦ 2879 ♦ **Valley of the Moon Vintage Festival**
Last full weekend in September

Valley of the Moon Vintage Festival is California's oldest wine festival, held since the late 1890s in Sonoma, the cradle of the state's wine industry. Located in Sonoma Valley, which Jack London made famous as the "Valley of the Moon," the city was founded in 1835 by Gen. Mariano Guadalupe Vallejo. In 1846, the Northwest became part of the United States, and, on June 14 of that year, American settlers invaded Sonoma, captured Vallejo and his Mexican garrison, and raised an improvised Bear Flag to proclaim California a republic. On July 9, the flag was replaced by the Stars and Stripes.

In the 1850s, Hungarian nobleman Count Agoston Haraszthy planted thousands of cuttings from European grape vines to establish the Buena Vista Winery, now the state's oldest premium winery, becoming the father of California's wine industry. In 1863, a double wedding united the two prominent wine-making families—the Vallejos and the Haraszthys.

The three-day festival focuses on this history, presenting reenactments of the 1846 Bear Flag Revolt and of the double wedding. There are also wine tastings, parades, live music, a blessing of the grapes, a firemen's water fight, and grape stomps.

CONTACTS:
Valley of the Moon Vintage Festival
P.O. Box 652
Sonoma, CA 95476
707-996-2109

♦ 2880 ♦ **Valmiki Jayanti**
September-October; full moon day of the Hindu month of Asvina

This festival celebrates the birthday of the poet Valmiki, whom Hindus believe to be the author of the epic poem *Ramayana*. A contemporary of Rama, the hero of the *Ramayana*, Valmiki himself is represented as taking part in some of the scenes he relates. No one knows for certain when the poem was written; estimates range from 500 to 300 B.C.E., with portions added between 300 B.C.E. and 200 C.E.

On Valmiki's birthday, people make processions and carry his portrait through the main streets of towns and villages. Members of the disadvantaged Indian classes pay particular homage to Valmiki, from whom they claim they are descended.

SOURCES:
DictHindu-1977, p. 246
RelHolCal-2004, p. 176

♦ 2881 ♦ **Vaman Dwadashi**
August-September; 12th day of Bhadrapada

According to Hindu belief, the god Vishnu turned himself into a dwarf, Vamana, to trick Bali, who conquered and ruled the kingdom of Indra, into giving up some of his domain. This story appears in the Hindu epic, the *Ramayana*. Devout Hindus worship both Vishnu and Bali with a fast beginning on the 11th day of Bhadrapada and keeping an all-night vigil. Offerings and mantras are made to an image of Vamana. On the 12th, Hindus rise at dawn, bathe, continue to worship the image of Vamana, then, finally, break their fast with a festive meal. It is primarily women who observe this day, and they often invite a young Brahman boy to the celebration—a boy to represent the short height of Vamana, and a Brahman because it is believed that good fortune will come to those who give alms to Brahmans. Thus the boy is given such gifts as shoes and an umbrella.

SOURCES:
DictHindu-1977, p. 321
HinduRelCustManners-1960, p. 149
HinduRelYr-1921, p. 77

♦ 2882 ♦ **Vandalia Gathering**
May, Memorial Day weekend

A folk festival held on the state capitol grounds in Charleston, W.Va., the Vandalia Gathering serves to exhibit the best of the state's traditional arts, music, dance, crafts, and food. Events include music by fiddlers, banjo players, and lap-dulcimer players, clogging, craft demonstrations, liars' contests, storytelling, and an exhibition of quilts made by West Virginia's top quilters. Held since 1976, the festival attracts about 35,000 people.

See also WEST VIRGINIA DAY

CONTACTS:
WV Division of Culture and History, The Cultural Center
Capitol Complex, 1900 Kanawha Blvd., E.
Charleston, WV 25305
304-558-0220; fax: 304-558-2779
www.wvculture.org

♦ 2883 ♦ **Vanuatu Custom Chiefs Day**
March 5

Among the 83 islands that compose the island nation of Vanuatu are many that have rejected European influence and instead prefer to live according to their traditional customs. While customs vary widely throughout the islands, village life, subsistence farming, a belief in magic, and rule by chiefs are common.

In 1977 a National Council of Chiefs was set up by the government to advise and propose ways to ensure the preservation of traditional ways of life through Vanuatu. These tribal chiefs are honored on March 5 of each year, which is a public holiday. Celebratory activities on this day include sporting events, carnivals, agricultural fairs, and arts festivals.

CONTACTS:
Vanuatu Tourism Office—North America
995 Holly Ct.
Monteagle, TN 37356
931-924-5253; fax: 931-924-1866
www.vanuatutourism.com

♦ 2884 ♦ **Vanuatu Father Walter Lini Day**
February 21

A former Anglican priest, Father Walter Lini became the first prime minister of the newly independent country of Vanuatu in 1980. His term in office was marked by tensions with several larger countries, including France and the United States. Lini strongly opposed French atom bomb testing in the Pacific and supported the independence movement in the French colony of New Caledonia. He also called for a reduced American naval presence in the region and resisted efforts of foreigners to develop or invest in Vanuatu. After establishing relations with Libya, Cuba, and Vietnam, Lini also pushed for what he called "Melanesian socialism"—a system based on the traditional Polynesian idea that a people's land is owned in common. Lini left office in 1991 and passed away in 1999.

Despite those who remember him for his authoritarian ways, Lini is honored on February 21 as the father of Vanuatu's independence. To mark the 25th anniversary of the country's independence, the 2005 celebration of Father Walter Lini Day included a special remembrance service at the Tagabe Anglican Church with President Kalkot Matas Kelekele attending. Prime minister Ham Lini, Walter Lini's brother, presided over a ceremony in which a floral wreath was placed on the late priest's grave.

CONTACTS:
Vanuatu Tourism Office—North America
995 Holly Ct.
Monteagle, TN 37356
931-924-5253; fax: 931-924-1866
www.vanuatutourism.com

♦ 2885 ♦ **Vanuatu Independence Day**
July 31

The most important national holiday in Vanuatu, Independence Day is celebrated throughout the country. It marks the end of colonial rule by the French and British. This archipelago of 83 islands is located about 1,000 miles northeast of Australia.

The first Europeans to visit Vanuatu were Spanish explorers in 1605, but it was the French who established the first permanent settlements in the 1850s. By the early 1900s, the islands were ruled under a joint French-British agreement. In the 1960s, secessionist ideas began to spread throughout the island chain, and in May 1980 an insurrection in Tanna brought the matter to the forefront. Self-rule came to Vanuatu in July of that same year. Father Walter Lini, a former Anglican priest, became the country's first prime minister.

The largest Independence Day celebrations take place in the capital city of Port Vila. A number of sporting events are held, as well as canoe and yacht races in the harbor. A military parade takes place in Independence Park. Dancing takes place and aerobics groups from throughout Vanuatu perform, and a string band competition is held.

CONTACTS:
Vanuatu Tourism Office—North America
995 Holly Ct.
Monteagle, TN 37356
931-924-5253; fax: 931-924-1866
www.vanuatutourism.com

♦ 2886 ♦ Vanuatu Unity Day
November 29

The nation of Vanuatu is an archipelago of 83 islands, 113 languages, and a host of different tribal groups. To celebrate the unification of differing groups into one nation, Unity Day was established on November 29. On that day in 1977, unrest in the islands, then under French-British administration, caused a great loss of life. Such internal division is something that present-day Vanuatu citizens do not want to see repeated.

To celebrate this day, representatives from all of Vanuatu's peoples come to the capital city of Port Vila. High chiefs from all the islands attend the festivities, which include performances by native dancers in their traditional dress and a parade. Music concerts and sporting events are also part of the celebration. Ordinary citizens usually observe the day with picnics or by camping. In 2004 President Kalkot Mataskelekele asked that church leaders spend an hour or two that day in special prayer for national unity.

CONTACTS:
Vanuatu Tourism Office—North America
995 Holly Ct.
Monteagle, TN 37356
931-924-5253; fax: 931-924-1866
www.vanuatutourism.com

♦ 2887 ♦ Vappu
May 1

Vappu is a national holiday and celebration of the coming of spring in Finland. This traditional festival rejoicing the end of the long northern winter is also LABOR DAY, and factories that are said to "never close" do close on May 1 and CHRISTMAS Day.

For students (and even gray-bearded former students), the "anything goes" celebration begins at midnight on the eve of MAY DAY, called Vapunaatto, when they wear white student caps and indulge in anything not indecent or criminal. It's traditional in Helsinki for students to wade across the moat that surrounds the statue of Havis Amanda, a mermaid, and place their caps on her head. There are balloons, streamers, horns, and masks everywhere, and few get much sleep. On May Day itself, the students lead processions through the streets of Helsinki, and then enjoy carnivals and concerts. Workers in most provincial towns generally gather in more solemn fashion to celebrate with speeches and parades.

CONTACTS:
Virtual Finland
Ministry of Foreign Affairs of Finland, Department for
  Communication and Culture
P.O. Box 176
Helsinki, 00161 Finland
358-9-1600-5; fax: 358-9-1605-5901
www.virtual.finland.fi

SOURCES:
BkFest-1937, p. 113

♦ 2888 ♦ Vaqueros, Fiesta de los
Last full week in February

Fiesta de los Vaqueros is a weeklong event in Tucson, Ariz., featuring the "world's longest non-motorized parade" and the largest outdoor midwinter rodeo in the United States. The fiesta starts with the parade—a two-mile-long procession of more than 200 entries, including such old horse-drawn vehicles as buckboards, surreys (with or without the fringe on top), western stagecoaches, and Conestoga wagons. The first parade was in 1925; now about 200,000 people line the parade route.

The eight days of rodeo include the standard events as well as daily Mutton Bustin' contests. In these, four- to six-year-olds test their riding skills on sheep. There are also demonstrations by Appaloosa trick stallions and by the Quadrille de Mujeres, a women's precision-riding team.

CONTACTS:
Tucson Rodeo Grounds
4823 S. 6th Ave.
Tucson, AZ 85702
800-964-5662 or 520-294-1280; fax: 520-294-1379
www.tucsonrodeoparade.com

♦ 2889 ♦ Vasaloppet
Late February to first Sunday in March

The biggest cross-country ski race in the world takes place in Sweden on the first Sunday in March each year. The course begins on the border between Norway and Sweden, in a huge frozen field outside the village of Sälen, and ends 54 miles away in the Swedish town of Mora. The race was named for a young Swedish nobleman, Gustav Vasa, who persuaded the people of Mora to help him drive out the Danes in 1520. He later ruled the country for almost 40 years as King Gustavus I.

More than 8,000 men compete in the annual race, which for even the strongest skier takes over five hours to complete. Because they consider this to be a test of their manhood, many Swedish men celebrate their 50th birthdays by entering the race. More than 325,000 have officially completed the Vasaloppet since the race became a national ski festival in 1922. Numerous other ski events take place over the last week in February leading up to the main Vasaloppet race.

CONTACTS:
Vasaloppet Mora
Vasaloppets Hus
Mora, Kopparberg Province SE-792 32 Sweden
46-250-392-00; fax: 46-250-392-50
www.vasaloppet.se

SOURCES:
BkHolWrld-1986, Mar 7

♦ 2890 ♦ Vasant Panchami (Basant Panchami)
January-February; fifth day of waxing half of Hindu month of Magha

Vasant Panchami is a festival of spring, celebrated throughout India among Hindus and Sikhs at the end of January or in early February. People wear bright yellow clothes, the color of the mustard flower that heralds the onset of spring, and mark the day with music, dancing, and kite-flying.

In Shantiniketan, West Bengal, the festival is celebrated with special lavishness in honor of Sarasvati, the Hindu goddess of learning and the arts. Her images are taken in procession to rivers to be bathed, and books and pens are placed at her shrine.

Many five-year-old Sikh children begin attending school for the first time on this day because Sikhs believe it a sacred time for children to begin their education.

In recent years, many young people observe Vasant Panchami (also spelled **Basant Panchami**) by exchanging tokens of affection, similar to VALENTINE'S DAY in the United States.

CONTACTS:
Department of Tourism, Government of West Bengal
2, Brabourne Road
Kolkata, West Bengal 700 001 India
91-33-22258134; fax: 91-33-22254565
www.wbtourism.com

SOURCES:
BkHolWrld-1986, Feb 16
OxYear-1999, p. 720
RelHolCal-2004, p. 182
SikhFest-1989, p. 41

♦ 2891 ♦ Vatsa (Ho Khao Slak)
June-July to October-November; full moon of Asadha to the full moon of Karttika

Vatsa, also known as **Ho Khao Slak**, is the Laotian observance of WASO or the Buddhist Rains Retreat. It begins later in the year than the traditional season observed in many other Buddhist communities, and the customs associated with it are also slightly different in Laos. But it is still a three- or four-month period when Buddhist monks must stay in one place in retreat rather than remain on the move.

People draw the name of a monk in the local monastery and bring him a gift of food, flowers, or one of the eight essential items that Buddhist monks are permitted to own (a robe, an alms bowl, a belt, a razor, a needle, a filter with which to strain water, a staff, and a toothpick). Parents often give toys and candy to their children as well. At the end of the festival, boat races are held on the rivers at Vientiane, Luang Phabang, and Savannakhet.

SOURCES:
RelHolCal-2004, p. 221
WrldBuddhism-1984, p. 57

♦ 2892 ♦ Vegetarian Festival
September-October; first nine days of ninth lunar month

The Vegetarian Festival is an annual nine-day affair observed on the island of Phuket off southwestern Thailand by resi-dents of Chinese ancestry. During the nine days, observers eat only vegetarian foods. The festival begins with a parade in which devotees wear white, and continues with ceremonies at temples, performances of special feats by ascetics, and acts of self-mortification—walking on hot coals, piercing the skin, and so on. The festival celebrates the beginning of the month called "Taoist Lent," when devout Chinese abstain from meat. It is thought, however, that the self-mortification acts are derived from the Hindu festival of THAIPUSAM.

CONTACTS:
Tourism Authority of Thailand
611 N. Larchmont Blvd., 1st Fl.
Los Angeles, CA 90004
800-842-4526 or 323-461-9814; fax: 323-461-9834
www.tourismthailand.org

♦ 2893 ♦ Vendimia, Fiesta de la
Second week in September

Spain is famous for its sherry, and some of the best sherry comes from the southwestern part of the country, in a district known as Jerez de la Frontera. This is said to be one of the few remaining places where the juice of the grapes is extracted by trampling them in huge wooden vats, or *lagares.* Although most people think this is done with bare feet, the participants actually wear specially designed hobnail boots.

In mid-September Jerez de la Frontera holds its **Grape Harvest Festival**, or Fiesta de la Vendimia, which includes flamenco dancing, *cante jondo* singing (a distinctive and deeply moving variety of Spanish gypsy song), and bullfighting. There is also an official "blessing of the grapes" and the season's first wine before the statue of San Ginés de la Jara, the patron saint of the region's winegrowers. The blessing is part of a colorful pageant held at the Collegiate Church of Santa Maria. All of the events that take place during the festival pay tribute in one way or another to wine sherry, the area's most famous product.

CONTACTS:
Jerez Tourist Information Office
Alameda Cristina, s/n
Jerez de la Frontera, Spain
34-956-149-863
www.turismojerez.com

SOURCES:
DictFolkMyth-1984, p. 483
FestWestEur-1958, p. 204
GdWrldFest-1985, p. 161

♦ 2894 ♦ Venezuela Battle of Carabobo Day
June 24

The Battle of Carabobo was fought in Venezuela on June 24, 1821, between the Spanish, led by Field Marshal Miguel de La Torre, and the Venezuelan freedom fighters, led by Simón Bolívar. It was fought some 30 kilometers from the town of Valencia in Venezuela. The battle was one-sided; Bolívar's men suffered only one casualty for every 15 inflicted on the Spanish. Irish, Welsh, and English volunteers fought on Bolívar's side, comprising the British Legion. Their victory led to the independence of Venezuela. The day is sometimes celebrated in Venezuela as Army Day.

At the site of the battle is the Alley of Glory, along which a number of low pillars hold busts of the soldiers who fought in the battle. The alley leads to the Triumphal Arch, which features two female figures representing peace and victory. Below the arch is the tomb of the unknown soldier, guarded by two soldiers wearing uniforms from the time of Bolívar.

The Battle of Carabobo Day is marked by a military parade in Carabobo. The 2006 parade featured some 100,000 active duty and reserve troops, 170 tanks, 29 planes, and 500 military horses. In 2005, fearing a possible assassination attempt, Venezuelan president Hugo Chavez had changed the site of the parade to the military academy in the capital city of Caracas.

CONTACTS:
Embassy of the Bolivarian Republic of Venezuela in the United
   States
1099 30th St. N.W.
Washington, D.C. 20007
202-342-2214; fax: 202-342-6820
www.embavenez-us.org

♦ 2895 ♦ **Venezuela Independence Day**
July 5; April 19

Revolutionary struggle against Spanish rule began in Venezuela in 1810. On July 5, 1811, a group of citizens in Caracas became the first in South America to proclaim a formal declaration of independence from Spain. Forces led by Simón Bolívar assured independence in 1821.

April 19 is another national holiday, known as both Declaration of Independence Day and Day of the Indian.

CONTACTS:
Venezuelan Consular Office
1099 30th St. N.W.
Washington, D.C. 20007
202-342-2214; fax: 202-342-6820
www.embavenez-us.org

SOURCES:
AnnivHol-2000, pp. 64, 113
NatlHolWrld-1968, p. 109

♦ 2896 ♦ **Verdur Rock**
Last weekend of June

Verdur Rock, a music festival held in the French-speaking region of Belgium known as Wallonia, offers amateur rock bands a rare shot at playing before a large audience. As many as 10,000 gather for the free one-day event at the Verdur Theater, an open-air venue standing on top of the historic citadel of Namur. The festival was founded in 1985 and is coordinated by the Youth Service de la Ville de Namur.

Over the years organizers have negotiated a balance between established international and Belgian performers and the "Young Talents," local French-speaking bands who earn

stage slots by beating out other competitors. Concert performers include past Verdur Rock winners and the victor of the Cégep Rock contest, a sister festival held in Montreal, Canada, also catering to amateur acts.

CONTACTS:
Youth Service
Esplanade de l'Hôtel de Ville
B-5000
Namur, Wallonia Belgium
www.verdur-rock.be

♦ 2897 ♦ **Vermont Maple Festival**
Last weekend in April

Vermont is the official maple capital of the world, and the maple festival held there each spring is really a statewide celebration. Maple sugaring—the process of tapping maple trees, gathering the sap, and boiling it in the sugarhouse to produce syrup—was a main source of income for the early settlers in Vermont as well as their main source of sweets. The sugaring industry flourished until World War II, when the number of producers dropped sharply. In the 1940s, 1950s, and 1960s, the growing emphasis on dairy farming resulted in the suspension of many sugaring operations. Although there has been a resurgence of interest in recent years, mild winters have taken their toll on the maple sugar crop because cold nights are needed to make the sap flow.

Since 1968 the three-day festival in St. Albans has promoted Vermont maple products through educational exhibits, sugaring equipment displays, essay contests, syrup competitions, maple cooking contests, and a parade. In addition to maple syrup, the festival gives visitors an opportunity to sample maple cream, maple candy, and maple sugar on snow.

CONTACTS:
Vermont Maple Festival
P.O. Box 255
St. Albans, VT 05478
802-524-5800
www.vtmaplefestival.org

SOURCES:
GdUSFest-1984, p. 195

♦ 2898 ♦ **Vernal Equinox**
March 21 or 22

The vernal equinox, Latin for "of spring" and "equal night," is one of the two occasions during the year when the sun crosses the equator, and the days and nights everywhere are nearly of equal length. It marks the beginning of spring in the Northern Hemisphere and the beginning of autumn in the Southern Hemisphere.

See also AUTUMNAL EQUINOX; HIGAN; NYEPI; SHUNBUN-NO-HI

CONTACTS:
Lab for Particles and Fields
Code 672
Goddard Space Flight Center
Greenbelt, MD 20771

301-286-0447
www-istp.gsfc.nasa.gov

The Royal Observatory Greenwich, National Maritime Museum
Greenwich Park
Greenwich, Greater London SE10 9NF United Kingdom
44-20-8312-6565; fax: 44-20-8312-6632
www.nmm.ac.uk

SOURCES:
AmerBkDays-2000, p. 222
BkDays-1864, vol. II, p. 364
DictDays-1988, p. 37
DictFolkMyth-1984, p. 1105
FolkWrldHol-1999, p. 215

♦ 2899 ♦ **Vernal Equinox (Chichén Itzá)**
    March 21

Chichén Itzá, located on Mexico's Yucatán Peninsula, is one of the country's biggest and best preserved Mayan ruins. Every year on the VERNAL EQUINOX, the angle of the sunlight hitting the enormous El Castillo pyramid creates a shadow that gives the illusion of a snake slithering down its side. The Mayans believed that this was Kukulcán, the feathered snake god known to the Aztecs as Quetzalcoatl.

Researchers were not aware of the annual awakening of the serpent god until 30 to 40 years ago, but since that time tourists have converged on the site on March 21—although the serpent can be seen up to four days before or after the equinox. Visitors enjoy folk dancers, musicians, and poets while they wait for the moment of the serpent's appearance, when the hours of sunlight equal the hours of darkness. Although the serpent can also be seen at the AUTUMNAL EQUINOX in September, this is during the rainy season and cloudy weather often spoils the effect.

CONTACTS:
Yucatan State Tourism Office
Calle 59 No. 514 POR 66 y 64
Centro C.P., 97000 Mexico
52-999-924-9389; fax: 52-999-928-6547

SOURCES:
WildPlanet-1995, p. 536

♦ 2900 ♦ **Verrazano (Giovanni da) Day**
    April 17

Observed in New York state, Verrazano Day commemorates the discovery of New York Harbor by the Italian navigator Giovanni da Verrazano on April 17, 1524. With the backing of King Francis I of France, Verrazano sailed his ship *La Dauphine* to the New World, reaching the Carolina coast in March 1524 and then sailing northward, exploring the eastern coast of North America. In addition to discovering the present-day site of New York City's harbor, he also discovered Block Island and Narragansett Bay in what is now Rhode Island, plus 32 islands off the coast of Maine, including Monhegan. Verrazano was the first European explorer to name newly discovered sites in North America after persons and places in the Old World.

In naming the Verrazano-Narrows Bridge, New York gave Verrazano official recognition. Spanning New York Harbor from Brooklyn to Staten Island, the 4,260-foot suspension bridge, built between 1959 and 1964, succeeded the Golden Gate Bridge in San Francisco as the world's longest suspension bridge until the Humber Bridge was completed in 1981 in Kingston upon Hull, England. Upon its completion in 1998, Japan's Akashi-Kaikyo Bridge took over the title with a span of over 6,500 feet.

SOURCES:
AnnivHol-2000, p. 63

♦ 2901 ♦ **Vesak (Wesak; Buddha's Birthday)**
    April-May; full moon of Hindu month of
    Vaisakha; April 8

This is the holiest of Buddhist holy days, celebrating the Buddha's birth, enlightenment, and death, or attaining of Nirvana. While these anniversaries are observed in all Buddhist countries, they are not always celebrated on the same day. In Theravada Buddhist countries, all three anniversaries are marked on the full moon of Vaisakha. In Japan and other Mahayana Buddhist countries, the three anniversaries are usually observed on separate days—the birth on April 8, the enlightenment on December 8, and the death on February 15.

Vesak is a public holiday in many countries, including Thailand, Indonesia, Korea, and Singapore.

This celebration differs from country to country, but generally activities are centered on the Buddhist temples, where people gather to listen to sermons by monks. In the evening, there are candlelit processions around the temples. Homes are also decorated with paper lanterns and oil lamps. Because it's considered important to practice the virtues of kindness to all living things, it's traditional in some countries to free caged birds on this day. In some areas, booths are set up along streets to dispense food. In Burma (Myanmar), people water the Bodhi tree with blessed water and chant prayers around it (*see* KASONE FESTIVAL OF WATERING THE BANYAN TREE).

The Buddha was born as a prince, Siddhartha Gautama, at Lumbini in present-day Nepal, an isolated spot near the border with India, and Lumbini is one of the most sacred pilgrimage destinations for Buddhists, especially on Vesak. A stone pillar erected in 250 B.C.E. by the Indian emperor Asoka designates the birthplace, and a brick temple contains carvings depicting the birth. Another center of celebrations in Nepal is the Swayambhunath temple, built about 2,000 years ago. On this day it is constantly circled by a procession of pilgrims. The lamas in colorful silk robes dance around the *stupa* (temple) while musicians play. On this day each year, the stupa's collection of rare *thangkas* (embroidered religious scrolls) and mandalas (geometrical and astrological representations of the world) is shown on the southern wall of the stupa courtyard.

Sarnath, Uttar Pradesh, India, is the place where the Buddha preached his first sermon, and a big fair and a procession of relics of the Buddha highlight the day there. Bodh Gaya (or Buddh Gaya) in the state of Bihar is also the site of special celebrations. It was here that Siddhartha Gautama sat under the Bodhi tree, attained enlightenment, and became known as the Buddha, meaning the "Enlightened One."

Gautama was born about 563 B.C.E. into a regal family and was brought up in great luxury. At the age of 29, distressed by the misery of mankind, he renounced his princely life and his wife and infant son to become a wandering ascetic and to search for a path that would give relief from suffering. For six years he practiced severe austerities, eating little. But he realized that self-mortification wasn't leading him to what he sought. One morning, sitting in deep meditation, under a ficus tree now called the Bodhi tree, he achieved enlightenment, or awakening. This was at Bodh Gaya in about 528 B.C.E., when Gautama was 35 years old. In the years that followed, he laid down rules of ethics (see MAGHA PUJA) and condemned the caste system. He taught that the aim of religion is to free oneself of worldly fetters in order to attain enlightenment, or Nirvana, a condition of freedom from sorrow and selfish desire. The Buddha trained large numbers of disciples to continue his work. He died in about 483 B.C.E.

From its start in northern India, Buddhism spread throughout Asia. The religion grew especially after Asoka, the first great emperor of India, adopted it as his religion in the third century B.C.E. and traveled about preaching and building hospitals and monasteries. He also sent his son, Mahinda, to preach the tenets of Buddhism in Sri Lanka (see POSON). The Buddhism practiced in Southeast Asia is the oldest form of the religion, known as Theravada Buddhism, or "The Way of the Elders." As Buddhism went north, into Nepal, Bhutan, Tibet, China, Korea, and then Japan, it took a different form called Mahayana Buddhism, or "The Great Vehicle."

Vesak, or **Wesak**, is also known as **Waisak** (Indonesia), **Wisakha Bucha** (Thailand), **Buddha Jayanti** (Nepal and India), **Phat Dan Day** (Vietnam), **Buddha Purnima** (India), **Kambutsu-e** or HANA MATSURI (Japan), **Full Moon of Kason** (Myanmar), **Vixakha Bouxa** (Laos) and sometimes the **Feast of the Lanterns**.

See also BUN BANG FAI and SONGKRAN

SOURCES:
BkFestHolWrld-1970, pp. 76, 78
BkHolWrld-1986, May 26
DictWrldRel-1989, pp. 121, 135
EncyRel-1987, vol. 2, p. 548, vol. 3, p. 325
FolkAmerHol-1999, p. 198
FolkWrldHol-1999, pp. 305, 308
HolSymbols-2009, p. 1020
IntlThFolk-1979, p. 345
RelHolCal-2004, pp. 170, 218

♦ 2902 ♦ **Veterans Day**
November 11; second Sunday in November in Great Britain

On November 11, 1918, the armistice between the Allied and Central Powers that halted the fighting in World War I was signed in Marshal Ferdinand Foch's railroad car in the forest of Compiègne, France. In the United States, the name **Armistice Day** was changed to Veterans Day in 1954 to honor those who have served their country in other wars as well.

In Great Britain, Canada, and France, it is dedicated primarily to those who died in either of the world wars. The British, Australians, and Canadians call it **Remembrance Day**. In England it is also known as **Poppy Day** for the red paper flowers sold by the British Legion to benefit veterans. In the U.S. veterans groups sell poppies on MEMORIAL DAY.

An attempt in 1971 to make Veterans Day conform to the "Monday Holiday Law" by scheduling it on the fourth Monday in October triggered widespread resistance, and seven years later it was moved back to the traditional November 11 date. In many places the 11th day of the 11th month is celebrated by observing a two-minute silence at 11:00 in the morning, the hour at which the hostilities ceased.

CONTACTS:
U.S. Department of Veterans Affairs
1722 I St. N.W.
Washington, D.C. 20421
800-827-1000
www.va.gov

Australian War Memorial
P.O. Box 345
Canberra, ACT 2601 Australia
61-2-6243-4211; fax: 61-2-6243-4325
www.awm.gov.au

Veterans Affairs Canada
Canada Remembers Division
97 Queen St., Rm. 329, Dominion Bldg.
Charlottetown, PE C1A 8M9 Canada
902-566-8075; fax: 902-566-8501
www.vac-acc.gc.ca/general

SOURCES:
AmerBkDays-2000, p. 764
BkFest-1937, p. 19
BkHolWrld-1986, Nov 11
DaysCustFaith-1957, p. 287
DictDays-1988, pp. 5, 125
DictFolkMyth-1984, p. 976
HolSymbols-2009, p. 1023
OxYear-1999, p. 458
PatHols-2006, p. 249

♦ 2903 ♦ **Veterans Day (Emporia, Kansas)**
November 11 and the preceding week

Veterans Day was founded in Emporia, Kansas, on November 11, 1953, and that city commemorates the holiday with a special program of events each year. For decades, November 11 was observed in the United States as Armistice Day, the anniversary of the end of World War I. But in 1953 the City of Emporia created a special program to honor all veterans, not just those from the 1914 to 1918 era. The idea attracted notice and gained support among lawmakers in other states and in the U.S. Congress, which passed a bill changing the name of the federal holiday the following year.

In recognition of its unique role in defining Veterans Day, Emporia celebrates the holiday with 10 days of special events, including museum exhibits, running and walking races, essay and poster contests, discussion panels, war films, luncheons, entertainment, and memorial luminaria. Sponsored by the Emporia Chamber of Commerce and Convention & Visitors Bureau, most events are free and open to the public. In addition to a blood drive, the Veterans Administration Health Center collects personal care items and clothing to be delivered to inpatient and outpatient programs for veterans in need. On the Saturday preceding the Veterans Day federal holiday, a parade sponsored by the Veterans of Foreign Wars (VFW) is held on Commercial Street in downtown Emporia, and a memorial service follows. Veterans Day concludes with a free dinner for all veterans at a local restaurant.

CONTACTS:
Emporia Chamber of Commerce and Convention & Visitors
  Bureau
719 Commercial
P.O. Box 703
Emporia, KS 66801
800-279-3730 or 620-342-1803; fax: 620-342-3223
www.emporiakschamber.org

SOURCES:
PatHols-2006, p. 259

♦ 2904 ♦ **Veterans Homecoming (Branson, Missouri)**
November 5 through 11

Veterans Homecoming in Branson, Missouri, is the largest Veterans Day commemoration in the United States, with more than 50,000 veterans and their families attending annually. Events extend over the week before November 11, and include special entertainment performances, lectures, social receptions, reenactments, and military memorials. The Branson Veterans Task Force, which organizes the celebration, maintains a headquarters at Branson's Celebration Hall, where veterans and active duty personnel can receive a free lunch daily throughout the week. Special tributes to veterans take place throughout the town, including the world's largest flying American flag, a salute to the troops on the showboat *Branson Belle*, and candlelight memorials remembering those who lost their lives in war. Each day "Reveille" and "Retreat" signal the beginning and the end of the day's activities, and throughout the week visitors enjoy free performances by military bands and drill teams. On Veterans Day a parade sponsored by the American Legion proceeds through downtown Branson. Throughout the week special discounts are given to veterans at various dining and retail establishments as well as museums, shows, and hotels.

CONTACTS:
Branson Veterans Task Force
P.O. Box 128
Branson, MO 65615
417-337-8387; fax: 417-334-7894
bransonveterans.com

Branson/Lakes Area Chamber of Commerce/CVB
P.O. Box 1897

Branson, MO 65615
800-296-0463
www.explorebranson.com

SOURCES:
PatHols-2006, p. 260

♦ 2905 ♦ **Veterans Pow Wow**
Early November

The annual Veterans Pow Wow in Topeka, Kans., honors service veterans and active-duty U.S. service personnel on a date close to Veterans Day in early November. Hosted since 2001 by the Awi Akta District of the Northern Cherokee Nation of the Old Louisiana Territory, the event was held at Washburn University before moving to the Gage Park Zoo Shelter House in 2007.

The Pow Wow uses traditional Native American dancing and drumming. It includes a color guard from the local community and a special tribute to a veteran from among tribe members. Dancers and musicians in formal regalia participate in a drum circle and gourd dancing; all drums are welcome. The event, which includes Native American craft and food vendors, is attended by about 400 people.

CONTACTS:
Awi Akta District of the Northern Cherokee Nation of the Old
  Louisiana Territory
4327 S.W. 17th Terr.
Topeka, KS 66604
785-266-8248
awiakta.org

SOURCES:
PatHols-2006, p. 259

♦ 2906 ♦ **Victory Day (Our Lady of Victories Day)**
September 8

This national holiday in Malta celebrates the lifting of two sieges:

In 1565, the Hospitallers, or the Knights of the Order of St. John of Jerusalem, with 6,000-9,000 men, held Malta against a four-month siege by some 29,000 Ottoman Turks. The onslaught left half the knights dead, but the Turks didn't fare well either—the knights used the heads of Turkish captives as cannonballs, and the defeat of the Turks humbled the Ottoman Empire. (Malta was under the control of the knights, a religious and military order of the Roman Catholic Church dedicated to tending the sick and poor and warring against Muslims, from 1530 until June 1798, when NAPOLEON took possession of the island.)

During World War II, the island fought off Axis powers (Germany and Italy) despite three years of severe air bombardment. In April 1942, air-raid alerts averaged about 10 a day; the ruins included the Royal Opera House in Valletta, destroyed by a German bomb. British Prime Minister Winston Churchill called Malta "our only unsinkable aircraft carrier."

On April 15, 1942, England's King George VI awarded the island of Malta the George Cross, Britain's highest decoration for civilian gallantry, to "honour her brave people … to bear witness to a heroism and devotion which will long be famous in history." This was the first time a medal was conferred on any part of the commonwealth. At this time, Britain also declared that self-government would be restored at the end of hostilities.

The holiday is celebrated with parades, fireworks, and a colorful regatta and boat races in the Grand Harbour at Valletta. A highlight of the boat races is that of the *dgnajsas*, oared taxi boats with painted designs. They are thought to date back to Phoenician times (800 B.C.E.).

See also MALTA INDEPENDENCE DAY

CONTACTS:
Malta National Tourist Office
65 Broadway, Ste. 823
New York, NY 10006
212-430-3799; fax: 425-795-3425
www.visitmalta.com

SOURCES:
AnnivHol-2000, p. 151

♦ 2907 ♦ **Victory Day (Russia)**
May 9

Victory Day is a national public holiday in the Russian Federation. It celebrates the defeat of Nazism and the end of World War II on European soil. On this day people remember the 27 million Russian civilians and soldiers who perished during the war. Each year on May 9 people crowd Moscow's Red Square for solemn rites of remembrance—one minute of silence and cannon or gun salutes—as well as traditional musical and dance performances. Veterans may attend wearing their uniforms and medals. Many leave flowers at memorials and graves. TV stations often air films about World War II.

CONTACTS:
Embassy of the Russian Federation
2650 Wisconsin Ave. N.W.
Washington, D.C. 20007
202-298-5700; fax: 202-298-5735
www.russianembassy.org

SOURCES:
AnnivHol-2000, p. 79
FestWrld: Russia-1997, p. 13

♦ 2908 ♦ **Vidalia Onion Festival**
Last weekend in April to early May

There are no tears during this tribute to Georgia's state vegetable, the sweet Vidalia onion, which is said to be burp-free, good for digestion, *and* tearless. The festival is held in Vidalia (nearby Glenville has a rival onion festival, usually a week earlier) at the height of the harvest season, which extends from mid-April to early June.

This onion is an interesting vegetable, officially the F-1 hybrid yellow granex, a round white onion with a yellow skin. Local folks hail it as the "world's sweetest onion," and, in fact, it has a sugar content of 12.5 percent, making it as sweet as a Valencia orange. If the seed is planted anywhere but Georgia, however, it becomes a normal sharp-tasting onion, probably due to the soil. Therefore, the name Vidalia may be given only to onions grown throughout 13 Georgia counties and parts of seven other counties (by act of the state legislature and federal directive).

According to a local story, Vidalia onions have been known since 1931, when a farmer discovered the onions didn't make him cry and so got a premium price for them even during the Depression. But they didn't become widely known until Delbert Bland of Bland Farms, a big onion producer, started a marketing campaign and mail-order onion business in 1984. In 1990, the sweet-onion business in Georgia amounted to about $35 million.

The celebration of the onion includes standard festival fare—music, a street dance, a fishing rodeo and expo, and a fun run. It also has a competition for Miss Vidalia Onion (a beautiful high school or college woman). Other beauty pageant winners are Miss Vidalia Onion Seed (ages 3-5), Miss Vidalia Onion Sprout (ages 6-9), Miss Spring Onion (ages 10-12), and Miss Junior Vidalia Onion (ages 13-16). Finally, there are onion-eating contests, and a Vidalia Onion Cook-Off, which produces cakes, breads, and muffins made with onions.

CONTACTS:
Vidalia Area Convention and Visitors Bureau
100 Vidalia Sweet Onion Dr., Ste. A
Vidalia, GA 30474
912-538-8687; fax: 912-538-1466
www.vidaliaarea.com

♦ 2909 ♦ **Vienna Festival**
May-June

This six-week festival, founded in 1951, regularly attracts more than a million people to the city of Vienna, Austria. There are hundreds of performances of music, opera, ballet, and drama by some of the best-known Austrian and foreign companies in the world—including the Royal Shakespeare Company, the Merce Cunningham Dance Company, the Martha Graham Dance Company, the Noh Theater of Japan, and the Malegot Ballet of St. Petersburg.

Like the EDINBURGH INTERNATIONAL FESTIVAL, the Vienna Festival also includes many "fringe" events offered by independent theater, dance, and musical groups.

CONTACTS:
Vienna Festival Service
Lehargasse 11
Vienna, A-1060 Austria
43-1-5892-222; fax: 43-1-5892-249
www.festwochen.at

SOURCES:
GdWrldFest-1985, p. 14
IntlThFolk-1979, p. 42

MusFestEurBrit-1980, p. 29
MusFestWrld-1963, p. 87

♦ 2910 ♦ Vietnam Ancestors Death Anniversary
10th day of the third lunar month (April)

Traditionally, Vietnamese families will remember the death of an ancestor on the anniversary of his or her death. Family members gather for the festive occasion to enjoy a banquet. It is customary to include at least one member of each generation of the family, even if this involves traveling a great distance. Foods include personal favorites of the deceased as well as chicken, a prized meat in Vietnam. In central Vietnam, it is customary to make stuffed rice flour balls. Special anniversary desserts are also prepared, desserts which are made only during this event. Because of the time and effort involved, wealthier families often hire caterers to prepare the food.

The deceased ancestor is thought to return for a visit on this day. He or she is ritually greeted at the beginning of the occasion. In addition to the banquet, offerings are made on the family altar and incense sticks are burned in honor the ancestor as well as the *cong*, or "God of the Home." The *Thanh hoang*, or "God of the Village," is also honored.

Until recently, the Ancestors Death Anniversary was observed only on the actual day of the death. But the Vietnamese government standardized the celebration to an annual observance to be held on the 10th day of the third lunar month, which occurs in April.

CONTACTS:
Embassy of the Socialist Republic of Vietnam
1233 20th St. N.W., Ste. 400
Washington, D.C. 20036
202-861-0737; fax: 202-861-0917
www.vietnamembassy-usa.org

♦ 2911 ♦ Vietnam National Day
September 2

The Socialist Republic of Vietnam observes its declaration of independence from France as a national holiday. On this day in 1945 Ho Chi Minh (1890-1969) proclaimed the establishment of the Democratic Republic of Vietnam. To celebrate Vietnam's national holiday, people gather in major cities, including Hanoi, for speeches, parades, fireworks, and other festivities.

CONTACTS:
Embassy of the Socialist Republic of Vietnam
1233 20th St. N.W., Ste. 400
Washington, D.C. 20036
202-861-0737; fax: 202-861-0917
www.vietnamembassy-usa.org

SOURCES:
AnnivHol-2000, p. 149
NatlHolWrld-1968, p. 156

♦ 2912 ♦ Vietnam Veterans Memorial Anniversary
November 11

The Vietnam Veterans Memorial Anniversary commemorates the dedication of the Vietnam Veterans Memorial in Washington, D.C., on November 13, 1982. Known commonly as "The Wall," the black granite Memorial is set within Constitution Gardens on Constitution Avenue between 21st and 23rd Streets. It lists the names of 58,256 U.S. service personnel who were killed while serving in Vietnam between 1957 and 1975.

Development and construction of the Memorial was overseen by the Vietnam Veterans Memorial Fund, Inc., a private organization that raised money for the project through donations and held an open competition for design proposals. The winning design was submitted by Maya Lin, a native of Ohio who was a student at Yale University at the time her design was chosen. In 1984 the Vietnam Veterans Memorial was brought under the oversight of the National Park Service.

Each year on Veterans Day, the anniversary of the Memorial's dedication is celebrated with a special ceremony, including speakers and a military color guard. As many as 10,000 veterans, family, and friends have gathered to participate in the Veterans Day observance. In 2007, the 25th anniversary of the Memorial, a special program included speeches by General Colin Powell and representatives of veterans' and family service organizations, including the American Gold Star Mothers, Gold Star Wives, and others. Musicians performed patriotic hymns and "Taps," and representatives of the armed services and family groups placed memorial wreaths.

CONTACTS:
Vietnam Veterans Memorial Wall
National Park Service
900 Ohio Dr. S.W.
Washington, D.C. 20024
202-426-6841
www.nps.gov/vive

SOURCES:
PatHols-2006, p. 254

♦ 2913 ♦ Vignerons, Fête des (Winegrowers' Festival)
August, approximately every 20-25 years

Held only five times during each of the 19th and 20th centuries in Vevey, Switzerland, the Fête des Vignerons is a pageant of music, dance, and song depicting the passage of the seasons in winegrowing country and honoring the most talented workers in the vineyards. It lasts more than two weeks and has a cast of thousands, drawn from the local population. The pageant takes place in an open-air theater, specially constructed each time the festival is held, with Lake Geneva and the mountains beyond as a backdrop. The festival was last held in 1999.

CONTACTS:
Confrerie des Vignerons
Rue du Chateau 2
Vevey, 1800 Switzerland
41-21-923-8705; fax: 41-21-923-8706
www.fetedesvignerons.ch

SOURCES:
FestEur-1961, p. 158
IntlThFolk-1979, p. 355

♦ 2914 ♦ Viking Festival
Mid-June

The annual Viking festival has been held since 2000 in the town of Hafnarfjordur, Iceland. During the festival, held near the summer solstice in mid-June, Viking-culture enthusiasts from around the world display reconstructions of Viking garb, handicraft, and traditions, ranging from weddings to sword and archery fights. The festival typically draws about 150 "Vikings" from Iceland and many foreign countries. They include hand-picked woodcarvers, stone carvers, other craftsmen, storytellers, and show fighters. In addition to Viking displays, the festival offers its thousands of spectators and visitors a market; live music, dance, and drama; guided walks; and art exhibitions.

CONTACTS:
Hafnarfjörour Information Centre
Strandgata 6
ID 590169-7579
Hafnarfjordur 220 Iceland
www.hafnarfjordur.is/bright_days

Tourist Board of Iceland
P.O. Box 4649
Grand Central Station
New York, NY 10163
213-885-9700; fax: 212-885-9710
www.goscandinavia.com

♦ 2915 ♦ Viña del Mar International Song Festival
Third week in February

The seaport of Viña del Mar in Valparaiso, Chile, is one of South America's most popular attractions and also the site of one of the continent's biggest music events, the Viña del Mar International Song Festival **(Festival Internacional de la Canción de Viña del Mar)**. The weeklong festival attracts thousands of people, including many tourists, and is broadcast in 21 countries.

An annual event established in 1960, the festival takes place at an outdoor amphitheatre called the Quinta Vergara. From its inception, the festival has held a song competition that traditionally features performers from about 10 Spanish-speaking countries. There is also a program featuring folk musicians and an international show that includes English-speaking as well as Latin performers.

CONTACTS:
Chilean Tourism Board
Providencia Ave., 2nd Fl.
Santiago
Santiago, 1550 Chile
www.sernatur.cl

♦ 2916 ♦ Vinalia
April 23, August 19

There were two ancient Roman festivals that were sacred to Venus and known as the Vinalia. The first, observed on April 23, was called the **Vinalia Priora**; the second, on August 19, was the **Vinalia Rustica**. Both festivals, it seems, were originally sacred to Jupiter. But after the worship of Venus was introduced into Rome in the second century B.C.E., its popularity spread so quickly that the older association with Jupiter gradually faded.

April 23 was probably the day on which the wineskins were first opened, the new wine having been brought into Rome just a few days earlier. Libations from the newly opened skins were made to Jupiter (later Venus, who was a deity of gardens and therefore of vineyards as well). After the libation, the wine was tasted. Winegrowers were warned not to bring the new wine into the city until the Vinalia had been proclaimed on the *nones,* or the ninth day before the IDES of the month.

There is some confusion about what went on at the August festival. Some believe that this—not April 23—was the day on which the new wine was brought into Rome. Others say that the Vinalia Rustica was a rite designed to protect the vintage that would follow from disease, storms, and other harmful influences.

SOURCES:
FestRom-1981, pp. 106, 177
OxYear-1999, pp. 166, 338
RomFest-1925, p. 85

♦ 2917 ♦ Vincy Carnival
Late June to early July

Carnival festivities take place on the Caribbean island of St. Vincent from late June to early July. Touring musical groups, led by one or two "maskers" who act as leaders, are a primary feature of the celebrations. The leaders are usually dressed as traditional characters—among them the Devil, Wild Indian, Bold Robber, and the hump-backed Bruise-ee-Back. Each group may perform a song written for the occasion by its leader, and usually acts out some kind of violent argument that will amuse or scare the onlookers and persuade them to donate some money. The songs are mocking or even slanderous in nature, and usually concern an individual or event associated with a particular locale. The band members typically dress in costumes based on that of their leader, but sometimes they merely blacken their faces, dab crude slogans and faces onto their white t-shirts and pants, and wear *washikongs* (tennis shoes) and strangely constructed hats.

CONTACTS:
St. Vincent and the Grenadines Tourist Information Office
801 Second Ave., 21st Fl.
New York, NY 10017
800-729-1726 or 212-687-4981; fax: 212-949-5946
www.svgtourism.com

SOURCES:
FolkWrldHol-1999, p. 146

♦ 2918 ♦ **Vinegar Festival, International**
Mid-June Saturday

The International Vinegar Festival, a celebration of the sour liquid condiment, takes place every year on one Saturday in mid-June in Roslyn, S.Dak. The family-friendly day features a parade, live entertainment, cooking demonstrations, a handicrafts market, and food vendors. Participants can enjoy such activities as a vinegar-tasting party and making crafts from vinegar bottles. A centerpiece of the festival is billed as the "mother of all vinegar contests," with vinegars from around the globe presented for judging to a panel of chefs.

The festival was launched in 2000 as a means to help the tiny town of Roslyn stay economically vibrant. A committee called CARE (Committee for the Advancement of Roslyn and Eden) sought a niche to draw visitors, and they found it thanks to a local writer named Lawrence Diggs, also known as "Vinegar Man." A food scientist, he is a collector of vinegars and the author of *Vinegar: Appreciating, Making, and Enjoying Vinegar*. He helped to found a vinegar museum in Roslyn, housed in a building donated by the city, which has been featured by such prestigious food journals as *Bon Appetit* and *Gourmet*.

CONTACTS:
Vinegar Man
P.O. Box 201
Roslyn, SD 57261
877-486-0075

Vinegar Connoisseurs International
104 W. Carlton Ave.
Roslyn, SD 57261
800-342-4519

♦ 2919 ♦ **Vinegrower's Day**
February 14

This pre-harvest vineyard festival in Bulgaria involves pruning the vines and sprinkling them with wine. Ritual songs and dances are performed in hopes of a plentiful grape harvest. In some areas, a "Vine King" is crowned with a wreath of twigs from the vineyards. Everyone treats him with great respect, for it is believed that fertility depends on the King's happiness.

Participation in the **Trifon Zarezan** festivities is something that both locals and foreign tourists look forward to. Visits to well-known Bulgarian vineyards are organized, the vines are pruned, and guests are given an opportunity to sample the local wine and foods.

See also ST. TRYPHON'S DAY

CONTACTS:
National Information and Advertising Center
1 St. Sofia Str.
Sofia, 1000 Bulgaria
359-2-987-9778; fax: 359-2-987-9778
www.mi.government.bg/eng/index.html

SOURCES:
AnnivHol-2000, p. 27

♦ 2920 ♦ **Vintage Computer Festivals**
First weekend of November

By offering a huge display of old computer hardware, software, and ephemera, Vintage Computer Festivals provide to the public a hands-on perspective on the computer revolution, as well as the simple pleasure of playing with old computers. The success of the main festival, which is held in California's Silicon Valley, has spawned regional festivals in New England and Europe. The first European version of the festival took place in 2000, and the first East Coast version was held the following year.

Computer collector Sellam Ismail founded the festival with a mission to network with collectors and advance research on the history of the computer. At the first festival, in 1997, collectors exchanged stories, traded equipment, listened to talks by established industry figures, and attended workshops on vintage computer collecting. This basic format of the event has not changed, even as the festival has expanded.

In addition to the main exhibit and the speaker presentations, there is a side event known as the Vintage Computer Film Festival, which screens films on vintage computing as well as technological development.

CONTACTS:
Vintage Computer Festival
2442 Research Dr.
Livermore, CA 94550
925-294-5900
www.vintage.org

♦ 2921 ♦ **Vintners' Procession**
Thursday after July 4

The Worshipful Company of Vintners (Winemakers) of the city of London holds its annual procession on the Thursday following July 4, the Feast of the Translation of St. Martin. Starting at 5:30 P.M., they walk from the Vintners' Hall in Upper Thames Street to the church of St. James, Garlickhythe. Two wine porters, dressed in top hats and white smocks and carrying birch brooms, lead the procession, sweeping the road of any "foulness" so that Company officials don't slip or soil their fur and velvet robes—the type of event that occurred more often in 1205, when a court order decreed that the roads be swept first and that the Master, Wardens, and Brethren be provided with herbal nosegays to sniff so they wouldn't be offended by any "noxious flavours or other ill vapours."

The Company of Vintners was once one of the wealthiest and most influential of London's ancient guilds or livery companies. Today it has the right to export and import all spirits from and to the Port of London, or anywhere within a three-mile limit.

CONTACTS:
Worshipful Company of Vintners
Vintners' Hall, Upper Thames St.
London, EC4V 3BG United Kingdom
44-20-7236-1863; fax: 44-20-7236-8177
www.vintnershall.co.uk

SOURCES:
EngCustUse-1941, p. 115
FolkCal-1930, p. 151
YrbookEngFest-1954, p. 94
YrFest-1972, p. 150

♦ 2922 ♦ **Virgen de Los Angeles Day**
August 2

Costa Rica honors its patron saint, La Virgen de los Angeles (also known as La Negrita), on this national holiday. La Negrita is a statue of the Virgin Mary with Baby Jesus in her arms. The statue is carved in dark wood, which is how La Negrita ("little dark one") earned its name. The statue is housed in the Basilica Virgen de Los Angeles in Cartago, next to a small stream. Many Costa Ricans believe both the statue and the stream have curative powers. A legend about the statue dates back to August 2, 1635, when a local woman found the statue in the woods and took it more than once to her home, but the statue kept returning to the spot where she first saw it.

People from all over the country come to Cartago on August 2 to celebrate the mass at the Basilica, pray to Little Negrita, and collect water from the stream. Many pilgrims come on foot, after journeys of several days. Celebrations of the holiday include street fairs, live music, and feasts throughout Costa Rica.

CONTACTS:
Embassy of Costa Rica
2114 S St. N.W.
Washington, D.C. 20008
202-234-2945 or 202-234-2946; fax: 202-265-4795
www.costarica-embassy.org

♦ 2923 ♦ **Virgin of the Pillar, Feast of the**
October 12

According to an ancient legend, the Virgin Mary appeared to Santiago, or St. James the Apostle, when he was in Saragossa (Zaragoza), Aragón, Spain. She spoke to him from the top of a pillar, which he interpreted as a sign that he should build a chapel where the column stood. *Nuestra Señora del Pilar* has since become a major pilgrimage center.

The Feast of the Virgin of the Pillar is observed with special masses and processions in honor of *La Virgen*. The *Gigantes*—giant cardboard and canvas figures concealing the men who dance behind them—are brought out especially for the occasion. Often representing Spanish kings and queens or famous literary and historical figures, they can be 20- to 30-feet tall. The *cabezudos*, or "big heads," on the other hand, are grotesque puppets with huge heads which are meant to poke fun at certain professions or personalities. Also characteristic of the festival are *jota* contests in which Aragon's regional folk dance is performed to the accompaniment of guitars, mandolins, and lutes.

See also St. James's Day

CONTACTS:
Zaragoza Tourist Board

Plaza de Ntra. Sra. Del Pilar, s/n.
Zaragoza, Spain
34-976-201-200; fax: 34-976-721-281
www.zaragoza.es

SOURCES:
DictWrldRel-1989, p. 569
FestWestEur-1958, p. 205
IntlThFolk-1979, p. 344
OxYear-1999, p. 412

♦ 2924 ♦ **Virginia Scottish Games**
Fourth weekend in July

Alexandria, Virginia, was founded by Scotsmen in 1749 and named for Scottish merchant John Alexander. The city celebrates its Scottish heritage with a two-day Celtic country fair featuring bagpipe bands, world-class athletes, Celtic dancers, a national fiddling championship, and an international harp competition.

One of the most colorful attractions is the Highland dancing, which involves hundreds of competitors ranging in age from preschoolers to adults. The highlight of the athletic contests is the caber toss, which is part of a seven-event competition known as the Highland Heptathlon. These contests trace their origins to the ancient HIGHLAND GAMES of northern Scotland, where military chiefs demonstrated their strength at annual clan gatherings.

See also ALMA HIGHLAND FESTIVAL AND GAMES; GRANDFATHER MOUNTAIN HIGHLAND GAMES AND GATHERING OF SCOTTISH CLANS

CONTACTS:
Virginia Scottish Games Association
3700 W. Braddock Rd.
P.O. Box 1338
Alexandria, VA 22313
703-912-1943
www.vascottishgames.org

♦ 2925 ♦ **Visitation, Feast of the**
May 31

On this day Christian churches in the West commemorate the Virgin Mary's visit to her cousin Elizabeth. After learning that she was to be the mother of Jesus, Mary went into the mountains of Judea to see her cousin, the barren wife of Zechariah, who had conceived a son who would come to be known as John the Baptist. According to the Gospel of Luke, Elizabeth's baby "leaped in her womb" (1:41) at the sound of Mary's voice. It was at this moment, according to the belief of some Roman Catholics, that John the Baptist was cleansed from original sin and filled with heavenly grace. Mary stayed with Elizabeth for three months and returned home just before John was born.

See also St. John's Day

CONTACTS:
Marian Library/International Marian Research Institute
University of Dayton

Dayton, OH 45469
937-229-4214; fax: 937-229-4258
www.udayton.edu

SOURCES:
AnnivHol-2000, p. 90
BkDays-1864, vol. II, p. 11
BkFest-1937, p. 187
DaysCustFaith-1957, p. 168
EncyChristmas-2003, p. 471
RelHolCal-2004, p. 96
SaintFestCh-1904, p. 315

♦ 2926 ♦ **Visvakarma Puja**
August-September; end of Hindu month of Bhadrapada

Dedicated to Visvakarma, the patron god of all Hindu artisans, the **Festival of Tools** is a workers' holiday in India dedicated to each individual's most important tool or instrument. A pitcher representing the god is set in a place of honor in every home and shop, and before it the people lay their most important tool. Students might place one of their schoolbooks there, musicians would place the instrument they play, artists would put their favorite brushes before the pitcher, tailors their scissors, gardeners their rakes, fishermen their nets, etc. A candle is lit in front of the pitcher, and sometimes incense is burned or scented water is sprinkled over the tool. Workers give thanks for their tools and implore Visvakarma's help in plying their trade.

After this ceremony is over, people gather in parks or public places and spend the rest of the day with games and feasting.

CONTACTS:
Department of Tourism, Government of West Bengal
2, Brabourne Road
Kolkata, West Bengal 700 001 India
91-33-22258134; fax: 91-33-22254565
www.wbtourism.com

♦ 2927 ♦ **V-J Day (Victory over Japan Day)**
August 14

V-J Day commemorates the anniversary of Japan's surrender to the Allies in 1945, ending World War II. The atomic bombs dropped on Hiroshima on Aug. 6 and Nagasaki on Aug. 9, and the Soviet Union's invasion of Manchuria in the previous week made the surrender inevitable. The announcement of the surrender by President Harry S. Truman set off street celebrations from coast to coast in the United States. In New York City, Times Square was jammed with people embracing and dancing. In Naples, Italy, the Andrews Sisters had just finished singing "Don't Sit Under the Apple Tree" to U.S. troops when Maxine Andrews was given a slip of paper and read the news; joyous bedlam ensued.

The official end of the war didn't come until Sept. 2, when Gen. Douglas MacArthur accepted the Japanese surrender from Gen. Yoshijiro Umezu aboard the USS *Missouri* in Tokyo Bay. He said, "Today the guns are silent. A great tragedy has

ended.… The holy mission has been completed." President Truman declared Sept. 2 as official V-J Day.

V-J Day is a legal holiday only in the state of Rhode Island, where it is called Victory Day. In Connecticut, the tiny village of Moosup (a section of the town of Plainfield) claims to have the only V-J Day parade in the country. Sponsored by the local American Legion post, it began small in 1961 and now features more than 200 units—marching bands, floats, civic groups, color guards, and Gold Star Mothers (women who lost a son or daughter in war)—and attracts some 10,000 spectators.

CONTACTS:
National Archives and Records Administration
700 Pennsylvania Ave. N.W.
Washington, D.C. 20408
800-234-8861 or 301-837-1850; fax: 301-837-0319
www.archives.gov

Naval Historical Center
805 Kidder Breese S.E.
Washington Navy Yard, Bldg. 76
Washington, DC 20374
202-433-4882; fax: 202-433-8200
www.history.navy.mil

American Legion Post No. 91
66 Prospect St.
Moosup, CT 06354
860-564-8005

SOURCES:
AmerBkDays-2000, p. 585
AnnivHol-2000, p. 136
DictDays-1988, p. 126

♦ 2928 ♦ **Vlöggelen**
Between March 22 and April 25; Easter Sunday and Monday

As practiced in the eastern Netherlands village of Ootmarsum, the Vlöggelen, or **Winging Ceremony**, is believed to be the remnant of an ancient spring fertility rite. It is a ritualistic dance through the narrow cobbled streets led by eight unmarried men, linked to form a human chain that advances slowly, "like birds on the wing." The dancers enter the front doors of shops, inns, farmhouses, and barns, emerging through the back doors to the melody of an old EASTER hymn with so many verses that the dancers must read the words pinned to the back of the person in front of them. Later, the men fetch firewood for a huge bonfire that night. In recent years, the tradition has drawn criticism from the Dutch Council of Christians and Jews, because the lyrics of the song blame the Jews for Jesus' death.

See also EASTER MONDAY IN THE NETHERLANDS

SOURCES:
FestWestEur-1958, p. 130

♦ 2929 ♦ **Vohuman, Feast of**
January, May, June; second day of Vohuman, the 11th Zoroastrian month

The Feast of Vohuman is one of the "sacred name days" in the Zoroastrian religion, where the day and the month share the name of the same *yazata*, or spiritual being—in this case, Vohuman, who represents Good Mind (or Good Thought) and who presides over animals. Because there are actually three different Zoroastrian calendars in use by widely separated Zoroastrian communities, the Feast of Vohuman occurs either in January, May, or June.

Among the followers of Persian prophet Zoroaster (also known as Zarathushtra, believed to have lived around 1200 B.C.E.), a name-day feast is an occasion for religious services which can be performed in a fire temple, meeting hall, or private home.

There are about 100,000 followers of Zoroastrianism today, and most of them live in northwestern India or Iran. Smaller communities exist in Pakistan, Sri Lanka, Canada, the U.S., England, and Australia.

SOURCES:
RelHolCal-2004, p. 69

♦ 2930 ♦ **Volksfest**
First Sunday in August

Founded in 1845 by immigrants from the Swiss canton of Glaurus, the town of New Glarus, Wisconsin, continued to attract Swiss immigrants over the years. Today it celebrates this cultural heritage in its yearly Volksfest and HEIDI FESTIVAL. The Volksfest Festival honors SWISS NATIONAL DAY, which takes place on August 1. The citizens of New Glarus have switched the day of their observance to the first Sunday in August, however. Festivities take place in Tell Shooting Park, one-half mile north of town. They include performances of Swiss music by various choral groups, yodeling, *thalerschwingen* and accordion music, Swiss folk dancing, and flag throwing. Frequently a representative from the Swiss Embassy or Swiss government will attend as an honored speaker.

CONTACTS:
New Glarus Chamber of Commerce
418 Railroad St.
New Glarus, WI 53574
800-527-6838 or 608-527-2095; fax: 608-527-4991
www.swisstown.com

♦ 2931 ♦ **Volunteer Day for Economic and Social Development, International**
December 5

In 1985 the UNITED NATIONS established December 5 as International Volunteer Day for Economic and Social Development. The Assembly hoped that in so doing, it would draw favorable attention to the contribution made by these volunteers, and thus inspire more people to serve the world community as volunteers.

CONTACTS:
United Nations, Department of Public Information
Rm. S-1070L J, K, L

New York, NY 10017
212-963-6842; fax: 212-963-6914
www.un.org

♦ 2932 ♦ **Voodoo Music Experience**
Late October

The Voodoo Music Experience is an annual music festival that takes place in New Orleans, La., over a three-day weekend in late October. The event debuted in 1999 with the aim of showcasing the verve and diversity of New Orleans' renowned music scene, as well as bringing famed acts to the city. More than 120 musicians performed at the event in 2007.

Performers are grouped into three categories: "Le Ritual" for established musicians; "Le Flambeau" for artists who reflect New Orleans' musical history and traditions; and "Le Carnival" for musicians and performance artists from New Orleans' underground art and bohemian scene. Rage Against the Machine, Red Hot Chili Peppers, Plain White Ts, Dr. John, the Neville Brothers, and Ratty Scurvics Singularity are all among past Voodoo Music Experience performers. Up to 93,000 fans attend each festival.

CONTACTS:
Voodoo Music Experience
www.voodoomusicfest.com

♦ 2933 ♦ **Vulcanalia (Volcanalia)**
August 23

Vulcan was the ancient Roman god of volcanic or destructive fire—not to be confused with the Greek god Hephaestus, who was the god of the blacksmith's forge and therefore a kindly fire god. In offering sacrifices to Vulcan, it was customary to burn the whole victim—usually a calf or a boar—rather than reserving a part of the animal, as was common when worshipping other gods.

The Vulcanalia, or festival in honor of Vulcan, was held on August 23, right at the time of year when forest fires might be expected and when the stored grain was in danger of burning. For this reason Vulcan's cult was very prominent at Ostia, where Rome's grain was stored. At the Vulcanalia, which was observed in Egypt, in Athens, and in Rome, the priest or flamen Volcanis performed a sacrifice, and the heads of families burned small fish they had caught in the Tiber River.

It was the Emperor Augustus who divided the city of Rome into small districts to facilitate fire fighting, and who was honored as Volcanus Quietus Augustus.

SOURCES:
AmerBkDays-2000, p. 555
ClassDict-1984, p. 665
DictFolkMyth-1984, p. 1163
DictRomRel-1996, p. 242
FestRom-1981, p. 178
OxYear-1999, p. 342

W

◆ 2934 ◆ Waila Festival
Late May

Since 1989, the Arizona Historical Society has sponsored the annual Waila Festival in Tucson, Ariz. Waila (pronounced Why-la) is a native music of the Tohono O'odham Indian tribe of southern Arizona. Waila uses such instruments as the accordion, alto saxophone, guitars, and drums. Similar to the Polish polka or Scottish folk dances, waila is a lively, danceable music. The event celebrates the 100-year-old musical form, promotes local groups playing the music, and brings the traditions and culture of the Tohono O'odham tribe to the attention of a wider public.

The Waila Festival is held on the grounds of the University of Arizona. Four waila bands perform and the spectators spread out blankets and lawn chairs to enjoy the music. Dancing is encouraged. Traditional foods like tepary beans, squash, corn soup, and cholla buds are for sale.

CONTACTS:
Arizona Historical Society
Tucson Main Museum
949 E. Second St.
Tucson, AZ 85719
520-628-5774
www.arizonahistoricalsociety.org

◆ 2935 ◆ Waitangi Day
February 6

A national public holiday in New Zealand, February 6 commemorates the signing of the 1840 Treaty of Waitangi, in which the Maori natives agreed to coexist peacefully with the European settlers. Although it was first declared a national day of commemoration in 1960, Waitangi Day was not observed as a public holiday outside the North Island until it became **New Zealand Day** in 1973. It was observed as such until 1976, when it again became known as Waitangi Day.

The town of Waitangi is located on the Bay of Islands at the northern end of the North Island, and the day on which the treaty was signed is observed there by the Royal New Zealand Navy and the Maoris each year.

Because of continued discrimination against them, some Maoris protested the occasion during the 1980s. In 1988 the New Zealand government cancelled the national commemoration ceremonies and has attempted to reorganize the observance in later years. But the protests continued through the 1990s and early 2000s.

CONTACTS:
Ministry for Culture and Heritage
History and Heritage Units
P.O. Box 5364
Wellington, New Zealand
61-4-471-4027; fax: 61-4-499-4490
www.nzhistory.net.nz

The Ministry of Tourism, Government of New Zealand
Level 7, MED Bldg., 33 Bowen St.
P.O. Box 5640
Wellington, New Zealand
64-4-498-7440; fax: 64-4-498-7445
www.govt.nz

Waitangi Tribunal
Level 3, 110 Featherston St.
P.O. Box 5022
Wellington Central, New Zealand
64-4-914-3000; fax: 64-4-914-3001
www.waitangi-tribunal.govt.nz

SOURCES:
AnnivHol-2000, p. 22
DictDays-1988, p. 127
NatlHolWrld-1968, p. 24

◆ 2936 ◆ Wakakusayama Yaki (Mount Wakakusa Fire Festival)
January 15

This event, held near the Japanese city of Nara, is, along with DAIMONJI OKURIBI, one of the ancient capital's most thrilling spectacles. It takes place on Mt. Wakakusa, a series of three smooth, round hills just over 1,000 feet high located east of the city. Fireworks are ignited, and at six o'clock in the evening, priests from the temples of Todai-ji and Kofuku-ji set fire to the dry grass on the slopes. The whole mountain turns into a flaming beacon that lights up the night sky and can be seen for miles.

Also known as the **Mt. Wakakusa Dead Grass-Burning Event**, the festival commemorates the historic burning of the hill 10 centuries ago during a friendly disagreement about the boundaries of the two major temples and a shrine in Nara. Kofuku-ji's five-story pagoda, built in the 8th century, is the second highest in all of Japan. The silhouette of this temple, seen against the fires on Mt. Wakakusa, is one of Japan's best-known images.

CONTACTS:
Nara Prefectural Government
30 Nobori-oji-cho
Nara, 630-8501 Japan
81-7-4222-1101; fax: 81-7-4227-4473
www.pref.nara.jp

SOURCES:
IllFestJapan-1993, p. 14
JapanFest-1965, p. 121

♦ 2937 ♦ Walking Days
May-June, Whit-Monday week

Throughout Lancashire and Yorkshire, England, Walking Days are an important feature of community life. Each town or village has its own parade of children from schools and churches of all denominations. Traffic is held up, the shops are closed, and thousands of spectators come from all the surrounding towns to watch the procession, which can take more than three hours to pass. The children are often dressed in white, and the girls wear veils or wreaths and carry bouquets of flowers. In Manchester, the procession takes place on WHIT-MONDAY, while other communities usually celebrate their Walking Days on the following Friday or Sunday.

This northern English custom may have originated with the traditional "Club Walks," which were ceremonial walks to church made by various social and other groups. In Warrington, Lancashire, Walking Day is June 28—the traditional date of the Newtown and Latchford Heath Races. It was the rector of Warrington who initiated the custom in 1835 to publicize a negative aspect of the horse races: the fact that parents who lost money on the horses often brought poverty upon their children.

SOURCES:
EngCustUse-1941, p. 64
YrbookEngFest-1954, p. 239
YrFest-1972, p. 50

♦ 2938 ♦ Wall Street Rat Race
May

This unusual 2.5-mile race features Wall Street runners who don business suits instead of fitness gear, pump cellular phones and briefcases instead of hand weights, and follow a route that takes them through the heart of New York City's financial district. Both individual runners and teams participate, and prizes are awarded not only to the top three male and female finishers but also to the runner wearing the "zaniest costume." Since 1987 the Carey Wall Street Rat Race, coordinated by the New York Runners Club and spon-

sored by Carey Limousine, has raised money for Very Special Arts (VSA), an international nonprofit organization that serves children and adults with disabilities. VSA offers programs in visual arts, drama, dance, music, and creative writing through schools, cultural institutions, health and rehabilitation organizations, and associations for people with disabilities.

CONTACTS:
New York Road Runners Club
9 E. 89th St.
New York, NY 10128
212-860-4455; fax: 212-369-4704
www.nyrrc.org

♦ 2939 ♦ Walloon Regional Day
Third Sunday in September

Each of the autonomous regions of Belgium observes its own feast day. September is a month of celebration for Belgium's Walloon Region. In addition to the local traditional festivities, Walloon Regional Day takes place on the third Sunday of the month, and the FEAST DAY OF THE FRENCH COMMUNITY is held in Wallonia during September. Feast days in other regions of Belgium include FEAST DAY OF THE FLEMISH COMMUNITY, FEAST DAY OF THE GERMAN-SPEAKING COMMUNITY, and IRIS FEST.

Established as a federal state in 1993, Wallonia is Belgium's largest region, making up 55 percent of the country's territory. Yet Walloon Regional Day is a new celebration that is not as popular or as commonly observed as the more established regional days. The main festivities take place in the regional capital, Nemur.

CONTACTS:
Belgium Embassy
3330 Garfield St. N.W.
Washington, D.C. 20008
202-333-6900; fax: 202-333-3079
www.diplobel.us

♦ 2940 ♦ Walpurgis Night (Walpurgisnacht)
April 30

People who lived in the Harz Mountains of Germany believed for many centuries that witches rode across the sky on the eve of St. Walpurga's Day to hold a coven on Brocken Mountain. To frighten them off, they rang church bells, banged pots and pans, and lit torches topped with hemlock, rosemary, and juniper. The legend of Walpurgis Night is still celebrated in Germany, Austria, and Scandinavia with bonfires and other festivities designed to welcome spring by warding off demons, disaster, and darkness, particularly the towns of Schierke-am-Brocken, Blankenburg, Elend, and Bad Suderode in the German state of Saxony-Anhalt.

St. Walpurga (or Walburga) was an eighth-century English nun who later became a German abbess. She is the patron saint against dog bites and rabies. On the eve of May 1 her remains were moved from Heidenheim to Eichstätt, Germany, where her shrine became a popular place of pilgrimage. Legend has it that the rocks at Eichstätt give off a miraculous oil possessing curative powers. She is the saint who is also associated with protection against magic.

CONTACTS:
German National Tourist Office
122 E. 42nd St., 20th Fl., Ste. 2000
New York, NY 10168
800-651-7010 or 212-661-7200; fax: 212-661-7174
www.germany-tourism.de

SOURCES:
AmerBkDays-2000, p. 332
BkFest-1937, p. 310
DaysCustFaith-1957, p. 102
DictDays-1988, p. 128
DictFolkMyth-1984, pp. 114, 425, 961, 1165
EncyEaster-2002, p. 631
FestWestEur-1958, pp. 25, 214
FolkAmerHol-1999, p. 203
FolkWrldHol-1999, p. 304
OxYear-1999, pp. 94, 178
RelHolCal-2004, p. 271

♦ 2941 ♦ **Wampanoag Powwow**
Weekend nearest July 4

It was Massasoit, chief of the Wampanoag Indians, who made a peace treaty with the Pilgrims who settled at Plymouth, Massachusetts, in 1620. Most of the tribe was later wiped out in what was known as King Philip's War, but the survivors fled to Martha's Vineyard and Nantucket, or joined the Cape Cod Indians who had remained neutral in the struggle.

For centuries Wampanoag Indians have held annual powwows during the summertime, which have been opportunities for tribal members to reunite in one place for feasts and traditional ceremonies and other activities. Today, more than 1,000 Wampanoag Indians live in Mashpee, Massachusetts, and hold their annual powwow over the FOURTH OF JULY weekend. One traditional game played is known as "fireball." It is similar to soccer but is played with a flaming ball. Fireball is a "medicine game"; men who participate believe that the bruises, burns, and other wounds they suffer during the game will relieve a loved one's illness.

CONTACTS:
Mashpee Wampanoag Tribal Council Inc.
483 Great Neck Rd. S
P.O. Box 1048
Mashpee, MA 02649
508-477-0208; fax: 508-477-1218
www.mashpeewampanoagtribe.com

SOURCES:
EndurHarv-1995, p. 272
HolSymbols-2009, p. 1029

♦ 2942 ♦ **Wangala (Hundred Drums Festival)**
November, after harvest

A festival that lasts several days and celebrates the harvest, Wangala is held in the Garo Hills of the state of Meghalaya in northeastern India. It involves a ceremony led by the village

priest, climaxing in a dance to the sound of 100 drums and the music of gongs, flutes, and trumpets.

CONTACTS:
The Directorate of Tourism, Government of Meghalaya
3rd Secretariat, Nokrek Bldg.
Lower Lachaumiere
Shillong, Meghalaya 793 001 India
91-364-2500736; fax: 91-364-2226054
www.megtourism.gov.in

♦ 2943 ♦ **Waratambar**
August

Waratambar is observed by members of the Christian population of Papua New Guinea, who comprise more than half of the country's four million people. It is a day for giving thanks to the Lord for what Christianity has done for people throughout the world. Farmers and their families take time off work to participate in the celebration, which focuses on singing and dancing. The songs express an appreciation of and closeness to nature and all creatures; the dances dramatize tribal wars. Costumes worn by the dancers are traditionally handmade—of ferns, moss, leaves, flowers, and other natural materials.

Waratambar is observed on different days in August in different provinces. In New Ireland, the date is August 24.

CONTACTS:
Embassy of Papua New Guinea
1779 Massachusetts Ave. N.W., Ste. 805
Washington, D.C. 20036
202-745-3680; fax: 202-745-3679
www.pngembassy.org

SOURCES:
FolkWrldHol-1999, p. 499

♦ 2944 ♦ **Warei Taisai**
July 22-24

This Japanese festival is held in Uwajima in late July. Hundreds of ships dock in the harbor, all decorated with flags. In town, there is the parade of the *Ushioni*, a creature that looks like a combination of a whale and a dragon that is carried through the streets by 15 to 20 young people.

Another festival highlight is the *Hashiri-komi* ceremony, a procession of young people carrying portable shrines called *mikoshi* into the sea while rockets explode all around them. The Warei Tasai festival dates back to the 18th century and is the highlight of the summer festival season in Ehime Prefecture.

CONTACTS:
Japan National Tourist Organization
1 Rockefeller Pl., Ste. 1250
New York, NY 10020
212-757-5640; fax: 212-307-6754
www.japantravelinfo.com

SOURCES:
IllFestJapan-1993, p. 87

♦ 2945 ♦ Warri Festival, National
October-November

Warri, the national board game of Antigua and Barbuda, stirs up enough devotion to warrant an annual competition. Antiguans inherited this board game from their West African slave ancestors, who played it on Caribbean sugar plantations in the 19th century. Despite attempts by slave owners to phase the game out, the tradition survived into the present age and eventually penetrated the arena of international competition.

The game consists of a thick wooden board with 12 pockets containing pieces or counters called *nickars.* These pieces typically are identical shells that can be found on Antigua's beaches.

The game can be played with two or more players. Using arithmetic skill, a Warri player beats his or her opposition by capturing 25 counters.

Competition at the National Warri Festival is organized into several classes, including the Masters, Seniors, Juniors, and the Novice Division. There are also open competitions for women and schools. Antiguans, who take pride in their national game, are perennial favorites to win the competition.

CONTACTS:
Antigua Hotels & Tourists Association
Island House, New Gates St.
P.O. Box 454
St. John's Antigua, W.I
www.antigua-barbuda.org

♦ 2946 ♦ Warsaw Autumn Festival
September

Officially called the **International Festival of Contemporary Music**, the Warsaw Autumn Festival's offerings in its early years were more conservative than the name would seem to indicate. Today more experimental music and world premieres are performed along with classical standbys of the 20th century.

Established in 1956 by a group of Polish composers who wanted to bring other East European as well as West European countries together, the festival has presented the work of Luciano Berio, Michael Tippett, Krzysztof Pendericki, Witold Lutoslawski, and other 20th-century composers.

The concerts, which continue for about 10 days in September, are held in the National Philharmonic building, the Royal Castle, and other venues around the city. Orchestras that have performed in these locations include the Scottish National Orchestra of Glasgow, the Tokyo Metropolitan Symphony Orchestra, the Polish Chamber Orchestra, and the National Philharmonic Orchestra and Choir of Warsaw.

CONTACTS:
Warsaw Autumn Festival
Rynek Starego Miasta 27
Warsaw, 00-272 Poland
48-22-831-060; fax: 48-22-831-0607
www.warszawska-jesien.art.pl

SOURCES:
GdWrldFest-1985, p. 154
IntlThFolk-1979, p. 298
MusFestEurBrit-1980, p. 130
MusFestWrld-1963, p. 254

♦ 2947 ♦ Washington State Apple Blossom Festival
May

The oldest blossom festival in the United States, this event has been held annually in Wenatchee, Washington, since 1920 (with the exception of the World War II years). It began with a suggestion from Mrs. E. Wagner, a Wenatchee resident who wanted to see something similar to the celebration held in her native New Zealand when the apple orchards were in bloom. Originally called **Blossom Days**, the event grew in size and popularity until it reached its current status as an 11-day festival drawing up to 100,000 spectators.

In 1947 the name of the festival was officially changed from the **Wenatchee Apple Blossom Festival** to its present name, although it continues to be held in Wenatchee, the "Apple Capital of the World." In addition to seeing the Wenatchee Valley orchards in full bloom, the events include parades, a foodfest, a marching band competition, and sporting events. In 1967 the Aomori Apple Blossom Festival in Japan became Wenatchee's "sister festival," and the two towns have exchanged visitors a number of times.

CONTACTS:
Washington State Apple Blossom Festival
2 S. Chelan Ave., Ste. A
P.O. Box 2836
Wenatchee, WA 98801
509-662-3616; fax: 509-665-0347
www.appleblossom.org

SOURCES:
AmerBkDays-2000, p. 326
BkFestHolWrld-1970, p. 89

♦ 2948 ♦ Washington's (George) Birthday
February 22; observed third Monday in February

George Washington's birthday was not always celebrated in the United States as widely as it is today. The date itself was in question for a while, since the Gregorian calendar was adopted in England during Washington's lifetime and this shifted his birthday from February 11 to February 22 (*see* OLD CHRISTMAS DAY). Then there was a period when Washington's association with the Federalist party made the Antifederalists (or Jeffersonian Republicans) uncomfortable, and they put a damper on any official celebrations. It wasn't until Washington's death in 1799 that such feelings disappeared and he was regarded as a national hero.

As commander-in-chief of the Continental Army during the American Revolution and as the first president of the United States, George Washington looms large in American literature and legend. By the centennial of his birth in 1832, celebrations were firmly established, and his name had been given not only to the nation's capital, but to a state and more than 20 cities and towns. The federal government combined Washington's birthday with that of another famous American president, Abraham LINCOLN as PRESIDENTS' DAY, observed on the third Monday in February.

At his death in 1799 Washington was a lieutenant general, then the highest military rank in the United States. That same year Congress had established the nation's highest military title, General of the Armies of the United States, intending it for him, but he didn't live to receive it. Subsequently, he was outranked by many U.S. Army officers, so in 1976 Congress finally granted it to him. He is now the senior general officer on Army rolls; General John J. Pershing is the only other officer to have been so honored—he received it in September 1919 for his work during World War I.

See also WASHINGTON'S BIRTHDAY CELEBRATION IN ALEXANDRIA, VIRGINIA and WASHINGTON'S BIRTHDAY CELEBRATION IN LOS DOS LAREDOS

CONTACTS:
Library of Congress
101 Independence Ave. S.E.
Washington, D.C. 20540
202-707-5000; fax: 202-707-8366
www.loc.gov

SOURCES:
AmerBkDays-2000, p. 155
BkDays-1864, vol. I, p. 284
BkHolWrld-1986, Feb 22
GdUSFest-1984, p. 198
OxYear-1999, p. 87
PatHols-2006, p. 265

◆ 2949 ◆ Washington's (George) Birthday Celebration (Alexandria, Virginia)
Third Monday in February and preceding weekend

Every year, Alexandria, Va., hosts an array of activities devoted to George Washington, including the nation's largest parade honoring the Father of Our Country. Alexandria calls itself Washington's hometown; he kept a townhouse there, was one of the city's original surveyors, organized the Friendship Fire Company, and was a vestryman of Christ Church Parish and Charter Master of Masonic Lodge No. 22. A reminder of the president's association with the Masons is the George Washington Masonic National Memorial, a 333-foot-tall replica of the ancient lighthouse in Alexandria, Egypt.

Celebrations of Washington's birthday have been held in Alexandria since the president's lifetime. The first parade to honor him was in 1798, when he came from his Mt. Vernon home to review the troops in front of Gadsby's Tavern.

The present-day festivities get off to an elegant start over the weekend with a banquet followed by the George Washington Birthnight Ball in Gadsby's Tavern, a duplication of the birthday-eve parties held in Washington's lifetime. People wear 18th-century dress, and the banquet toasts to Washington are usually delivered by people who are prominent in current

events and who reflect Washington's military background. In 1991, former chairman of the U.S. Joint Chiefs of Staff Gen. Colin Powell (later Secretary of State under President George W. Bush) proposed the toast. His name and face became widely known during the Persian Gulf War of 1991.

On Monday is the big parade. It lasts two hours and usually draws about 75,000 spectators. George and Martha Washington are depicted, along with other colonial personages. The paraders include a number of Scottish bagpipe groups (the city was founded by Scots), Masonic units, equestrian groups, color guards, fife and drum corps, and horse-drawn carriages.

See also WASHINGTON'S BIRTHDAY

CONTACTS:
George Washington Birthday Celebration Committee
1108 Jefferson St.
Alexandria, VA 22314
703-991-4474; fax: 703-991-4474
www.washingtonbirthday.net

SOURCES:
GdUSFest-1984, p. 198

◆ 2950 ◆ Washington's (George) Birthday Celebration (Los Dos Laredos)
First half of February

This is a two-week celebration in honor of George Washington, held since 1898 by Laredo, Tex., and its sister city on the other side of the Mexican border, Nuevo Laredo. The two Laredos (*los dos Laredos* in Spanish) are linked by history and by three bridges across the Rio Grande. Founded by the Spanish in 1755, Laredo has been under seven different national flags. Both cities also celebrate Mexico's Independence Day during Expomex in September (*see also* MEXICO FESTIVAL OF INDEPENDENCE).

Washington's birthday events include dances, fireworks, mariachi music, a fun run, a jalapeno-eating contest, and parades with lavishly decorated floats.

CONTACTS:
Washington's Birthday Celebration Association
1819 E. Hillside Rd.
Laredo, TX 78041
956-722-0589; fax: 956-722-5528
www.wbcalaredo.org

◆ 2951 ◆ Waso (Buddhist Rains Retreat)
June-July to September-October; full moon of Buddhist month of Waso to full moon of Buddhist month of Thadingyut

Waso is a three-month period when monks remain in monasteries to study and meditate. At other times of the year, monks wander the countryside, but this is the time of monsoons in Southeast Asia, and the Buddha chose this period for retreat and prayer so they wouldn't walk across fields and damage young rice plants. However, even in China,

Japan, and Korea—countries that don't have monsoons—the Waso is observed. It is also known as the **Buddhist Lent**. In Cambodia and India it is called **Vassa** or **Vossa**. In Burma (now Myanmar) and Thailand it is called **Phansa**, **Waso**, **Wasa**, or **Wazo Full Moon Day**; and in Laos, Vatsa.

The months are considered a time of restraint and abstinence. Weddings are not celebrated, and people try to avoid moving to new homes. Many young men enter the priesthood just for the retreat period, and therefore many ordinations take place. The new young monks have their heads shaved and washed with saffron, and they are given yellow robes. Many lay people attend the monasteries for instruction.

The day just prior to the retreat commemorates the Buddha's first sermon to his five disciples, 49 days after his enlightenment.

In Thailand, the start of the retreat, called Khao Phansa, is observed in the northeastern city of Ubon Ratchathani with the Candle Festival, in which beeswax candles carved in the shapes of birds and other figures, several yards high, are paraded and then presented to the temples. In many places, a beeswax candle is lit at the beginning of Waso and kept burning throughout the period. In Saraburi, people offer flowers and incense to monks who walk to the hilltop Shrine of the Holy Footprint where they present the offerings as tribute (*see also* Phra Buddha Bat Fair). It is traditional everywhere for people to bring food and other necessities to the monasteries.

The end of this period, called **Ok-Barnsa**, or **Full Moon Day of Thadingyut**, is a time of thanksgiving to the monks, and also, according to legend, the time when the Buddha returned to earth after visiting his mother in heaven and preaching to her for three months. During the month of celebration (known as **Kathin**), lay people present monks with new robes and other items for the coming year.

Boat races are held on the rivers in Laos at Vientiane, Luang Phabang and Savannakhet, and in Thailand at numerous places. A special ceremony takes place in Bangkok when elaborate golden royal barges, rowed by oarsmen in scarlet, proceed to Wat Arun (the Temple of Dawn), where the king presents robes to the monks.

At Sakon Nakhon in northeastern Thailand, people build temples and shrines from beeswax and parade them through the streets to present them at temples. After the presentations, there are regattas and general festivities.

In Myanmar, a Festival of Lights called the **Tassaung Daing** or Tazaungdaing Festival is held at this time, when the moon is full. Homes are lit with paper lanterns, and all-night performances are staged by dancers, comedians, and musicians. A major event of the festival is an all-night weaving contest at the Shwe Dagon pagoda in Rangoon (officially called Yangon); young unmarried women spend the night weaving robes, and at dawn they are offered to images of the Buddha at the pagoda. Similar weaving competitions are held throughout the country.

See also Thadingyut

CONTACTS:
Tourism Authority of Thailand
0611 N. Larchmont Blvd., 1st Fl.
Los Angeles, CA 90004
800-842-4526 or 323-461-9814; fax: 323-461-9834
www.tourismthailand.org

SOURCES:
BkHolWrld-1986, Jul 23, Sep 22, Oct 20, Oct 29
EncyRel-1987, vol. 2, p. 551
FolkWrldHol-1999, p. 412
HolSymbols-2009, p. 1033
RelHolCal-2004, p. 220

♦ 2952 ♦ **Watch Night (Bolden, Georgia)**
December 31

Watch Night services are held every New Year's Eve at 10:00 P.M. at Mt. Calvary Baptist Church in the village of Eulonia, near Bolden, Ga. The heart of the event is a "ring-shout" performance by the McIntosh County Shouters. Call-and-response singing, counter-clockwise dance movements, and interlocking rhythms created with hand-clapping and stick beating on the wooden floor are key elements of the ring-shout, which has indisputable roots in African tradition. The ring-shout was written about by outsiders as early as 1845, but many believed it had died out until this church's group of performers came to light in 1980. The McIntosh County Shouters have since been featured in concerts, on television, and on a CD. The Watch Night service is open to all.

Watch Night is a solemn yet joyful Christian vigil on the last night of the year in which hymns, testimonies, and prayers are shared. Because the Emancipation Proclamation freeing slaves in the United States went into effect at midnight on January 1, 1863, African Americans have invested the occasion with added significance. Some even refer to Watch Night as Freedom's Eve.

SOURCES:
AAH-2007, pp. 413, 416
HolSymbols-2009, p. 1036

♦ 2953 ♦ **Watch Night Service**
December 31

The custom of holding a "Watch Night" service on New Year's Eve was started in America by St. George's Methodist Church in Philadelphia in 1770. The custom has since been adopted by a number of denominations throughout the country. Methodists, Presbyterians, and others gather in their churches on the night of December 31. A five-minute period of silence is observed right before midnight, when a hymn of praise is sung.

Sometimes New Year's Eve is referred to as **Watch Night**, a time for people to gather and celebrate as they see the old year out and the new year in.

CONTACTS:
St. George's Methodist Church and Methodist Museum
235 N. 4th St.
Philadelphia, PA 19106

215-925-7788; fax: 215-925-7788
www.historicstgeorges.org

SOURCES:
AAH-2007, pp. 413, 416
DaysCustFaith-1957, p. 325
DictDays-1988, p. 129
EncyChristmas-2003, p. 803
HolSymbols-2009, p. 1036

♦ 2954 ♦ Water-Drawing Festival
Begins between September 20 and October 18; night following the first day of Sukkot and each night of the festival thereafter

The name of this ancient Jewish festival comes from Isaiah 12:3, which says, "Therefore with joy shall ye draw water out of the wells of salvation." The water-drawing ceremony, also known as **Simhat bet ha-Sho'evah**, was a matter of dispute between Pharisees, who regarded it as an oral tradition handed down from Sinai, and the Sadducees, who saw no basis for it and often showed outright contempt for the entire ritual. The more the Sadducees opposed it, the more emphasis the Pharisees placed on the water libation, which was considered a particularly joyful occasion and was performed in the temple on the night following the first day of SUKKOT and then on each remaining night of the festival. Huge bonfires were lit throughout Jerusalem and the people stayed up dancing and singing for most of the night, often dozing off on each other's shoulders.

There have been attempts to revive the water-drawing festival in a more modern form, primarily among Israel's contemporary *kibbutzim*, or agricultural communities.

CONTACTS:
Union of Orthodox Jewish Congregations of America
11 Broadway
New York, NY 10004
212-563-4000; fax: 212-564-9058
www.ou.org

♦ 2955 ♦ Water-Splashing Festival (Dai New Year)
Mid-April

The Dai people of southwestern Yunnan Province of China celebrate the birthday of Buddha (*see* VESAK) and the new year in the middle of April with the Water-Splashing Festival. In tropical Xishuangbanna, a land of elephants and golden-haired monkeys, the celebration begins with dragon-boat races and fireworks displays. On the second day, people visit Buddhist temples. The third day, which is New Year's Day, is the high point. Dressed in colorful local costumes, people carry buckets and pans of water to the temple to bathe the Buddha, and they then splash water at each other. The water symbolizes happiness and good health. It washes away the demons of the past year and welcomes in a new year of good harvests, better livestock, and increased prosperity.

CONTACTS:
Yunnan Tourism Information Center
4th Floor, Yunnan Zhijian Bldg.

76 E. Dongfeng Rd.
Kunming, Yunnan Province 650051 China
86-871-3210-972; fax: 86-871-3120-740
www.yunnantourism.com

SOURCES:
WildPlanet-1995, p. 301

♦ 2956 ♦ Watermelon-Eating and Seed-Spitting Contest
Second Sunday in September

The only event of its kind sanctioned by the United States Department of Agriculture, the Watermelon-Eating and Seed-Spitting Contest held since 1965 in Pardeeville, Wisconsin, is attended by up to 9,000 people—eaters, spitters, and spectators. It takes eight people an entire day to cut up the 4,500-5,000 watermelons used in the contest. This festival also includes a watermelon volleyball competition, watermelon carving and growing contests, a parade, and a T-shirt design contest. But it is the eating and spitting contests that most people come to see.

Tongue-in-cheek rules for the spitting contest are strictly enforced: professional tobacco spitters are not eligible; denture wearers must abide by the judge's decision if their teeth go further than the seed; and no one is allowed to propel their seeds through a pipe, tube, or other hollow object. There is a team spitting competition, a couples' spitting competition, and separate competitions for men and women.

CONTACTS:
Pardeeville Watermelon Festival
Chandler Pk.
Pardeeville, WI 53954
608-429-3214

♦ 2957 ♦ Watermelon Thump
Last full weekend in June

This is a celebration of the watermelon harvest in Luling, Tex. The chief watermelon-related events are watermelon judging, a watermelon auction, watermelon-eating competitions, and watermelon seed-spitting contests leading to a Championship Seed Spit-Off. Among other activities are a parade, a carnival, and the coronation of the Watermelon Thump Queen.

CONTACTS:
Watermelon Thump
421 E. Davis St.
P.O. Box 710
Luling, TX 78648
830-875-3214; fax: 830-875-2082
www.watermelonthump.com

♦ 2958 ♦ Watts Festival
August

The Watts Festival is held every August over a three-day weekend in Los Angeles. The event began in 1966 as a celebration of African-American cultural awareness, community pride, and political consciousness in the wake of the riots that took place over six days in the Watts area of the city in 1965. It also was founded as a commemoration of the 34 people who died in the disturbance. The Watts Festival is now billed as one of the longest-running African-American cultural celebrations in the United States.

The festival features 16 distinct programs: an art exhibit, business exhibits, a carnival, a children's village, community forums, concerts, food and drink concessions, a fashion show, a film festival, the Goodwill Ambassador Scholarship, a performing arts stage, a senior citizens' pavilion, social service agencies, a "Spirit of Watts" tour, a sports village, and a custom car, bike, and van show. The concerts are a highlight of the festival, and such world-class performers as Stevie Wonder, James Brown, and Nancy Wilson have volunteered their talents to the Watts Summer Festival.

CONTACTS:
Watts Summer Festival, Inc.
944 W. 53rd St.
Los Angeles, CA 90037
323-789-7304; fax: 323-789-5652

SOURCES:
AAH-2007, p. 418

♦ 2959 ♦ **Wayne Chicken Show**
Second Saturday in July

This lighthearted one-day event takes place in Wayne, Nebraska, a town that is known primarily as a pork capital. But, as one of the festival's organizers admits, "We didn't want to make fun of pigs," and since there were some egg-processing plants and chicken farms in the area who were willing to contribute to the cause, the Wayne Chicken Show was "hatched" in 1981. Billed as an "eggszotic eggstravaganza," up to 15,000 people witness competitions in rooster crowing, chicken flying, egg dropping and catching, and a national cluck-off whose winner has appeared on the Tonight Show. There are prizes for the oddest egg, the most beautiful beak, and the best chicken legs on a human. The eggs and chefs for the free "omelette feed" are donated by egg producers in the area.

CONTACTS:
Wayne Chamber of Commerce
108 W. 3rd St.
Wayne, NE 68787
402-375-2240; fax: 402-375-2246
www.chickenshow.com

♦ 2960 ♦ **WCSH Sidewalk Art Festival**
Saturday in late August

The WCSH 6 Sidewalk Art Festival is held every year on a Saturday in late August in Portland, Maine. More than 300 artists typically display their work at the outdoor event, which draws thousands of visitors to the festival area. The exhibit is juried, with cash prizes for first, second, and third place. For the fourth prize, the WCSH 6 Purchase Prize, cash is awarded, plus the winning art work becomes part of the permanent art collection of the festival sponsor, local televi-

sion station WCSH 6. August 2007 marked the 42nd anniversary of the festival. Its organizers bill it as the largest and oldest one-day art show in northern New England.

CONTACTS:
WCSH 6
www.wcsh6.com/life/community/events/art_festival

♦ 2961 ♦ **Wedding Festivities (Galicnik, Macedonia)**
July 12

It was common practice at one time in the former Yugoslavia for men to leave their villages or even to emigrate in search of higher paying work. On a specific day they would all return to their villages and mass wedding celebrations would be held. Galicnik is one of the last strongholds of this ancient custom, and on St. Peter's Day each year a multiple wedding feast is held. It begins on St. Peter's Eve with a torchlight procession of brides to three fountains where water is drawn for a purification ceremony. The most interesting feature of the wedding ceremony itself is that brides, bridegrooms, and guests knock their heads together. The first night of the marriage is spent in a complicated hide-and-seek game and the newlyweds do not sleep together. There is a great feast on the second day and that night the marriages are consummated.

Because the village of Galicnik is cut off from the rest of the world by snow for much of the winter, it is transformed during the summer, when many former residents and tourists come for the July 12 wedding festivities. Similar village wedding ceremonies are held in the Slovenian towns of Ljubljana (end of July) and Bled (mid-August).

CONTACTS:
Macedonia Ministry of Culture
Ilinden bb
Skopje, Macedonia 01000
389-314-7147; fax: 389-311-3014
www.culture.in.mk

SOURCES:
IntlThFolk-1979, p. 388

♦ 2962 ♦ **Week of Solidarity with the Peoples of Non-Self-Governing Territories**
Begins May 25

In 1999 the General Assembly of the United Nations asked the special committee on decolonization to honor the week beginning May 25 as the Week of Solidarity with the Peoples of Non-Self-Governing Territories. In 1972 the United Nations established this same week as the Week of Solidarity with the Colonial Peoples of Southern Africa and Guinea (Bissau) and Cape Verde Fighting For Freedom, Independence and Equal Rights. They chose May 25 as the starting date since it had already been established as AFRICAN LIBERATION DAY.

CONTACTS:
United Nations, Department of Public Information
Rm. S-1070L

New York, NY 10017
212-963-6842; fax: 212-963-6914
www.un.org

♦ 2963 ♦ West Virginia Day
June 20

West Virginia Day is a state holiday in West Virginia to celebrate its joining the Union in 1863 as the 35th state. The creation of the state was a result of the Civil War. The settlers of western Virginia defied the state's vote to secede from the Union, and President LINCOLN justified the "secession" of West Virginia from Virginia as a war act. He proclaimed its statehood in April of 1863 and on June 20 West Virginia formally entered the Union as an anti-slave state. The western Virginians' movement for independence from Virginia had actually started long before the Civil War; as early as 1776, western Virginians had the idea of establishing a separate colony called Vandalia, named for Queen Charlotte, wife of British King George III, who believed herself to be a descendant of the Vandals of early Europe.

The day is marked with ceremonies at the state capitol in Charleston and at the West Virginia Independence Hall in Wheeling. It was there that the conventions were held to declare West Virginia's independence from Virginia.

CONTACTS:
The Cultural Center
1900 Kanawha Blvd., E.
Charleston, WV 25305
304-558-0220; fax: 304-588-2779
www.wvculture.org

West Virginia Division of Tourism
90 MacCorkle Ave. S.W.
South Charleston, WV 25303
800-225-5982 or 304-558-2200; fax: 304-558-2459
www.wvtourism.com

SOURCES:
AmerBkDays-2000, p. 460
AnnivHol-2000, p. 103
DictDays-1988, p. 130

♦ 2964 ♦ West Virginia Italian Heritage Festival
September, Labor Day weekend

This three-day street festival in Clarksburg, W.Va., celebrates Italian culture. The festival began in 1979 and attracts from 175,000 to 200,000 visitors for tastes of food, music, dance, crafts, and sports. A queen, known as Regina Maria, reigns over the festivities. Distinctively Italian events are a bocci tournament, a homemade wine contest, a pasta cookoff (prizes for the best red sauce and best white sauce) for both professional and amateur cooks, and Italian religious observances. There are also strolling musicians, organ grinders, and puppeteers.

About 40 percent of Clarksburg's population is of Italian descent. Italians came here around the turn of the century for plentiful coal-mining jobs and it is said the mountains are reminiscent of those in northern Italy.

CONTACTS:
West Virginia Italian Heritage Festival
340 W. Main St.
P.O. Box 1632
Clarksburg, WV 26302
304-622-7314; fax: 304-622-5727
www.wvihf.com

♦ 2965 ♦ West Virginia Strawberry Festival
Usually late May or early June

A long-standing, good-tasting tradition in Buckhannon, W.Va., the center of a strawberry-growing region. The festival began in 1936, was suspended during World War II, and celebrated its 50th anniversary in 1991 with a block-long strawberry shortcake. Visitors, who numbered about 100,000, got free samples.

The festival focuses on what can be done culinarily to the strawberry: there are pancake breakfasts with strawberry jam, strawberry syrup, and fresh strawberries. There's a strawberry recipe contest, with recipes for such delights as strawberry cakes, pies, and cookies, kiwi-and-strawberry pizza, chicken glazed with strawberries, and strawberry stirring sticks (take drinking straws and fill with strawberries). The festival includes the coronation of a king and queen, a Strawberry Party Gras (a street festival of music and dancing), strawberry auctions, the sweetest strawberry tasting contest, an antique car show, and contests and parades.

CONTACTS:
The West Virginia Strawberry Festival Association Inc.
P.O. Box 117
Buckhannon, WV 26201
304-472-9036; fax: 304-472-9037
www.wvstrawberryfestival.com

♦ 2966 ♦ Western Stock Show, National
Mid-January

The National Western Stock Show is the world's largest livestock exhibition and the show of shows in Denver, Colo. This is a 16-day trade show for the ranching industry, drawing visitors from throughout the U.S. as well as Mexico and Canada. On view at the stock show are more than 20,000 Hereford, Angus, Simmental, Shorthorn, and Longhorn cattle. Plus Arabian, Morgan, draft, miniature and quarter horses, and ewes, llamas, and yaks. Transactions in the millions of dollars are daily events; the livestock auctions as a matter of course can bring six figures for a single bull.

There are also daily rodeos, with more than 1,000 professional cowboys and cowgirls taking part in calf roping, bull and bronco riding, steer wrestling, and barrel racing. Sheepshearing contests, displays for children, exhibits and sales of livestock supplies, and exhibitions of Western paintings are other features.

More than half a million people attend, among them ranchers wearing belt buckles with diamonds and boots with the value of diamonds.

CONTACTS:
National Western Stock Show
4655 Humboldt St.
Denver, CO 80216
303-297-1166; fax: 303-292-1708
www.nationalwestern.com

SOURCES:
GdUSFest-1984, p. 26

♦ 2967 ♦ **Wexford Festival Opera**
Late October

The Wexford Festival Opera is best known for its staging of obscure or seldom-heard operas from the 17th to the 20th centuries. Held in a small seaport community in the southeastern corner of Ireland since 1951, the festival has based its success on its choice of rare operas and relatively unknown singers, many of whom have later become quite famous.

Three operas are staged during the two-week festival in Wexford's Georgian-style Theatre Royal, built in 1832. Some of the unusual operas presented there include Bedrich Smetana's *The Two Widows*, Joseph Haydn's *Il Monde della Luna*, and Francesco Cavalli's *Eritrea*, which had not been performed since 1652.

The festival also features choral and symphonic concerts and a fireworks display.

CONTACTS:
Wexford Opera
Theatre Royal, High St.
Wexford, Ireland
353-53-9122400; fax: 353-53-9122144
www.wexfordopera.com

SOURCES:
GdWrldFest-1985, p. 115
MusFestEurBrit-1980, p. 111

♦ 2968 ♦ **Whale Festivals (Alaska)**
Various

Gray whales are native to the northern Pacific Ocean. They spend their summers in the Bering Sea but migrate every year to the waters off the coast of Mexico, where female whales give birth to their young. Since the whales prefer to hug the coast as they make their long journey, they are often visible to those living in seaside towns. Several towns along the migration route have begun to celebrate the whales' yearly appearances by hosting whale festivals. Other whale species also make this yearly migration, and are sometimes seen in coastal waters as well.

In Alaska, the towns of Sitka and Kodiak both hold whale festivals. Kodiak's Whalefest takes place in April, as the whales pass by on their way to their summer feeding grounds. Besides watching the whales—which can be done on land—festivalgoers can attend lectures, films, storytelling and children's events, radio talk shows, crafts workshops, art exhibits, and more.

The Sitka festival takes place in November. Sitka festivalgoers most commonly spot humpback whales, but also catch glimpses of gray whales, orca (killer) whales, dall, and harbor porpoises. Festival organizers coordinate a program of whale-watching tours, special presentations by marine biologists, and performances by Native and Russian dance troupes.

CONTACTS:
Sitka Whale Fest
P.O. Box 6004
Sitka, AK 99835
907-747-7964; fax: 907-747-7194
www.sitkawhalefest.org

Kodiak Whalefest
P.O. Box 1903
Kodiak, AK 99615
907-486-3737

♦ 2969 ♦ **Whale Festivals (California)**
March

Several whale festivals take place in the state of California. Gray whales are native to the northern Pacific Ocean. They spend their summers in the Bering Sea but migrate every year to the waters off the coast of Mexico, where female whales give birth to their young. Since the whales prefer to hug the coast as they make their long journey, they are often visible to those living in seaside towns. Several towns along the migration route have begun to celebrate the whales' yearly appearances by hosting whale festivals.

Santa Barbara's festival occurs in March, when gray whales pass by on their way north to Alaska and the Bering Sea. In addition to whale-watching opportunities, the festival also includes a street fair, complete with live music, dance, and other forms of entertainment, lectures, a rubber duck race, storytelling, displays of art and crafts, and information about whales.

Dana Point, California, also holds its Festival of Whales on two consecutive weekends in March. This event features a street fair, musical entertainment, an art show, educational events and presentations, and a parade.

The neighboring northern California towns of Mendocino and Fort Bragg hold their whale festivals on consecutive weekends in March. Their celebrations include whale-watching cruises, wine tasting, seafood chowder tasting, nature walks, and visits to the Cabrillo Point lighthouse.

CONTACTS:
Santa Barbara Whale Festival
P.O. Box 40834
Santa Barbara, CA 93140
805-897-3187

Dana Point Festival of Whales
34675 Golden Lantern
Dana Point, CA 92629
888-440-4309 or 949-472-7888
www.dpfestivalofwhales.com

Fort Bragg-Medocino Coast Chamber of Commerce
332 N. Main St.

P.O. Box 1141
Fort Bragg, CA 95437
800-726-2780 or 707-961-6300; fax: 707-964-2056
www.mendocinocoast.com

◆ 2970 ◆ Wheat Harvest (Transylvania)
Late summer

In Transylvania, a region of Romania that was at one time part of Hungary, the gathering of the wheat harvest in late summer reflects traditional customs that have been largely supplanted by modern agricultural methods elsewhere. Here the owner of a farm must still rely on friends and neighbors to gather the crops. When the last sheaf is harvested, a wreath made of wheat and wild flowers is taken to the farmer's house by young girls in traditional dress. The other farm laborers lie in wait for the procession and carry out a mock ambush by drenching everyone in water. When the landowner first appears in the harvest field, the harvesters tie him up and demand a ransom for his release.

When the procession arrives at the landowner's house, poems in his honor are recited. The wreath is hung in a special place where it will remain until the next harvest. There is a feast for everyone, followed by dancing to the music of a gypsy band. A special delicacy associated with the harvest feast is gingerbread cookies. In fact, elaborately shaped and decorated gingerbread cookies are considered a part of the region's folk art tradition.

SOURCES:
FolkWrldHol-1999, p. 530

◆ 2971 ◆ Wheat Harvest Festival (Provins, France)
Last weekend of August

The small village of Provins in north-central France celebrates its wheat harvest at the end of the summer. On the last Saturday and Sunday of August, villagers decorate their homes and shops with wheat and wildflowers. There are also exhibits of antique farming tools and parades featuring harvest floats pulled by tractors. The villagers reenact ancient rituals involving wheat and perform demonstrations of how the grain is separated, ground, and baked to make bread.

CONTACTS:
Provins Tourism Office
Chemin de Villecran
P.O. Box 44
Provens, 77482 France
33-1-6460-2626; fax: 33-1-6460-1197
www.provins.net/anglais/default.htm

◆ 2972 ◆ Whe'wahchee (He'dewachi; Dance of Thanksgiving)
August

Whe'wahchee is the annual dance and celebration of the Omaha Indian tribe of Nebraska, held on the Omaha Reservation in northeastern Nebraska. The ceremonies take place near a pole, usually made out of a cottonwood or willow tree, which represents numerous sacred beliefs.

The 188th dance was held in 1991, making this the oldest powwow in the United States. LEWIS AND CLARK encountered the Omahas in 1803 and mentioned the **Omaha Dance of Thanksgiving** in their journal.

CONTACTS:
Omaha Tribe of Nebraska
P.O. Box 368
Macy, NE 68039
402-837-5391; fax: 402-837-5308
www.indianaffairs.state.ne.us

SOURCES:
EncyNatAmerRel-2001, p. 119

◆ 2973 ◆ Whistlers Convention, International
Third week in April

This convocation of whistlers in Louisburg, N.C., is highlighted by whistlers' contests for children, teenagers, and adults. Held since 1974, it grew out of a folk festival.

The convention features a school for whistlers and a concert in which the performer is usually someone who can both sing and whistle. On the Sunday after the contest, whistlers whistle at church services and on Monday give demonstrations in schools.

The grand champion in 1992 was Sean Lomax of Murrieta, Calif., who whistled the First Movement of Beethoven's Fifth Symphony and a selection from Bizet's *Carmen*. This is serious whistling.

This convention isn't a big event, but it is the only one in the United States, and in 1992 it attracted people from 10 states and three Canadian provinces. In addition, Masaaki Moku, a whistler from Osaka, Japan, was there; he whistled the Japanese national anthem for the contest audience.

CONTACTS:
Franklin County Arts Council
P.O. Box 758
Louisburg, NC 27549
919-496-1191
www.whistlingiwc.com

◆ 2974 ◆ White Nights
June

This celebration marks the time of year in St. Petersburg (formerly Leningrad), Russia, when the nights are so short that the sky appears white, or light grey, and twilight lasts only 30 or 40 minutes. The city, with its many buildings painted in pastel shades of lavender, green, pink, and yellow, has a particularly beautiful charm during the white nights. The city is full of various cultural events to celebrate this summer twilight. The Mariinsky Theatre presents a special program of ballets, operas, and symphonic concerts. In addition, there is a chamber music festival and an international jazz festival.

CONTACTS:
St. Petersburg City Administration
Smolny
St. Petersburg, 191060 Russia
eng.gov.spb.ru

Mariinsky Theatre
1, Teatralnaya Sq.
St. Petersburg, 190000 Russia
7-812-326-4141; fax: 7-812-314-1744
www.tickets.mariinsky.ru

SOURCES:
GdWrldFest-1985, p. 182
IntlThFolk-1979, p. 373

♦ 2975 ♦ **White Nights**
The days before, during, and after the full moon,
generally the 13th, 14th, and 15th of each month

According to suggestions in Islamic folklore, the days before, during, and after a full moon are likely to be especially blessed or lucky. On these dates, the skies are bathed in the silvery light of the full or nearly full moon, making the nights "white." In the Islamic calendar, months begin on the first day of the new moon and last for 29 or 30 days; therefore, the White Nights generally occur on the 13th, 14th, and 15th of each month.

Many Muslims worldwide consider the White Nights a good time to observe optional fast days. Shia Muslim officials recommend extra prayers on White Nights that fall during the months of Rajab, Shaban, and Ramadan. Some believe that special blessings will come to those who observe this teaching.

CONTACTS:
Islamic Society of North America
6555 S. 750 East
Plainfield, IN 46168
317-839-8157; fax: 317-839-1840
www.isna.net

SOURCES:
UndIslam-2004, pp. 381, 440

♦ 2976 ♦ **White Sunday**
Second Sunday in October

This is a special day celebrated in the Christian churches of both American Samoa and the country of Samoa to honor children. Each child dresses in white and wears a crown of white frangipani blossoms. The children line up and walk to church, carrying banners and singing hymns, while their parents wait for them inside. Instead of the usual sermon, the children present short dramatizations of Bible stories such as the good Samaritan, Noah's ark, and the prodigal son. After the performance is over, the children return to their homes, where their parents serve them a feast that includes roast pig, bananas, taro, coconuts, and cakes. They are allowed to eat all they want, and in a reversal of the usual custom, **Lotu-A-Tamaiti** is the one day of the year when the adults don't sit down to eat first.

See also SUNDAY SCHOOL DAY

SOURCES:
AnnivHol-2000, p. 181
BkHolWrld-1986, Oct 14
FolkWrldHol-1999, p. 590

♦ 2977 ♦ **Whit-Monday (Whitmonday)**
Between May 11 and June 14; Monday after
Pentecost

The day after Whitsunday (PENTECOST) is known as Whit-Monday, and in Great Britain it is also the **Late May Bank Holiday** (*see* BANK HOLIDAY). The week that includes these two holidays, beginning on Whitsunday and ending the following Saturday, is called Whitsuntide.

Until fairly recently, Whit-Monday was one of the major holidays of the year in Pennsylvania Dutch country. In the period from 1835 to just after the Civil War, Whit-Monday was referred to as the "**Dutch Fourth of July**" in Lancaster, Pennsylvania, where rural people came to eat, drink, and be entertained. In Lenhartsville, another Pennsylvania Dutch town, Whit-Monday was known as **Battalion Day**, and it was characterized by music, dancing, and military musters. So much carousing went on that one Pennsylvania newspaper suggested that the name "Whitsuntide" be changed to "Whiskeytide."

See also WALKING DAYS

SOURCES:
BkDays-1864, vol. I, p. 643
BkFest-1937, p. 98
BkFestHolWrld-1970, p. 65
DictDays-1988, p. 131
FestWestEur-1958, pp. 12, 26
OxYear-1999, p. 632

♦ 2978 ♦ **Whole Enchilada Fiesta**
Late September

The Whole Enchilada Fiesta is marked by lots of red chili, lots of corn meal, lots of cheese, and lots of people. This festival in Las Cruces, New Mexico, draws about 100,000 people who scramble to get a taste of the world's biggest enchilada. It's 10 feet long and is made of 750 pounds of stone ground corn for the dough, 75 gallons of red chili sauce, and 175 pounds of cheese. The enchilada is prepared as the climactic Sunday afternoon event: while thousands watch and cheer, giant tortillas are lifted from 175 gallons of bubbling vegetable oil and smothered with the chili sauce and cheese and served. Before this grand moment, there will have been a parade, street dances, arts and crafts exhibits, and a fun run. Las Cruces is the largest business center in southern New Mexico, but its economic foundation is agriculture, and chilis are a big crop.

See also HATCH CHILE FESTIVAL

CONTACTS:
The Whole Enchilada Fiesta
P.O. Box 8248
Las Cruces, NM 88006
505-526-1938
www.enchiladafiesta.com

◆ 2979 ◆ Whuppity Scoorie
March 1

On March 1 every year, Lanark's parish church bell rings exactly at 6 P.M., after a four-month silence. As the bell begins to ring, children in this Scottish town parade three times round the church, dangling pieces of string with paper balls attached at the other end. Then they start striking one another with the paper balls in a play fight. Pennies are then tossed to the ground, which heightens the children's enjoyment as they rush to collect them.

One explanation for the origin of this festival is that it can be traced back to pagan times, when people believed that making a great deal of noise would scare away evil spirits and protect the crops from damage. Another is that an English soldier, who once sought refuge in the church from Scottish defender William Wallace (c. 1270-1305) and his men, had to circle it three times before the doors were opened, crying "Sanctuary!" while Wallace's men pursued him, crying "Up at ye!"—the phrase from which festival's name is believed to have derived.

CONTACTS:
Lanark Tourist Information Centre
Horsemarket
Ladyacre Rd.
Lanark, Scotland ML11 7LQ United Kingdom
44-15-5566-1661; fax: 44-15-5566-1143

SOURCES:
FestEur-1961, p. 77
YrFest-1972, p. 129

◆ 2980 ◆ Wianki Festival of Wreaths
June 23

On St. John's Eve in Poland, young girls traditionally perform a ritual that can be traced back to pagan times. They weave garlands out of wild flowers, put a lit candle in the center, and set them afloat in the nearest stream. If the wreath drifts to shore, it means that the girl will never marry, but if it floats downstream, she will find a husband. If the wreath should sink, it means that the girl will die before the year is out. Since the boy who finds a wreath, according to the superstition, is destined to marry the girl who made it, boys hide in boats along the riverbanks and try to catch their girlfriends' wreaths as they float by.

A variation on this custom, known as the Wianki Festival of Wreaths (*wianki* means "wreath" in Polish), is observed by Polish Americans in Washington, D.C., on this same day every year. The wreaths are made out of fresh greens, the candles are lit at twilight, and they're set afloat in the reflecting pool in front of the Lincoln Memorial. Because there is no current, the wreaths don't drift much at all. But young men gather around the pool anyway, in the hope that the wind will blow their girlfriends' wreaths toward them.

See also MIDSUMMER DAY and SEMIK

CONTACTS:
City of Krakow

ul. Szpitalna 25
Krakow, Poland
48-12-432-0110; fax: 48-12-432-0062
www.krakow.pl/en/?chl=EN

Polish-American Arts Association
P.O. Box 9442
Washington, DC 20016
www.paaa.us

SOURCES:
BkFest-1937, p. 263

◆ 2981 ◆ Wicklow Gardens Festival
May 1 to July 31

In County Wicklow, Ireland, more than 20 private gardens are open to the public in May and June for the Wicklow Gardens Festival. The Wicklow climate is especially conducive to gardening, and the county itself is known as the "Garden of Ireland." The gardens participating in the festival range from the grounds surrounding large, historic houses to cottage gardens. Some of the gardens date back to the 17th century, while others have been planted more recently. Some are open year round. Others are closed to the public except during the festival. Many of the gardens that charge entrance fees during the festival donate the money to local charities.

CONTACTS:
Wicklow County Council
Wicklow Tourist Office
Fitzwilliam Sq.
Wicklow, Ireland
353-404-20155; fax: 353-404-20072
www.wicklow.ie

◆ 2982 ◆ Wife-Carrying World Championships
Early July

The annual Wife-Carrying World Championships have been held in Sonkajärvi, Finland, since the 1990s. The residents of Sonkajärvi trace the idea of wife carrying back to a 19th-century bandit named Rosvo-Ronkainen. In order to join his band, prospective robbers had to prove themselves by running a kind of obstacle course. In those days thieves sometimes did carry off women from rival villages, so local residents combined the two ideas, inventing wife-carrying contests.

Just as in times past, the wife you carry off does not have to be your own. Today's male contestants may carry any woman over the age of 17 who weighs at least 49 kilos (107.8 lbs.). (Lighter contestants can enter if they carry weights that bring them up to 49 kilos.) The course measures 253.5 meters in length and includes one water obstacle and two dry land obstacles. Any contestant that drops his "wife" is fined 15 seconds. The couple that completes the course in the shortest length of time wins. In addition to a medal, the winning couple receives the wife's weight in beer. The contest includes a special division for men who actually carry their own wives.

Only about 30 couples compete in these world championships. These contestants include the winners of the NORTH AMERICAN WIFE-CARRYING CHAMPIONSHIP in Bethel, Maine.

The Wife-Carrying World Championship is sponsored by the Association of Sonkajärvi Entrepreneurs and the local government, and is part of the three-day long Sonkajärvi County Fair, which also includes a beer barrel-rolling contest.

CONTACTS:
Sonkajärvi Eukonkanto Oy
Rutakontie 21
Sonkajärvi, 74300 Finland
358-17-2727-105; fax: 358-17-2727-106
www.sonkajarvi.fi

◆ 2983 ◆ **Wigilia**
December 24

Christians in Poland, like Christians around the world, regard the entire period from CHRISTMAS EVE (December 24) to EPIPHANY (January 6) as part of the CHRISTMAS season. Although their customs and the timing of their specific Christmas celebrations may differ from village to village, it all occurs during these two weeks. *Wigilia* means "to watch" or "keep vigil" in Polish. It takes place on Christmas Eve and commemorates the vigil that the shepherds kept on the night of Christ's birth. But it's very possible that the celebration goes back to pre-Christian times. Showing forgiveness and sharing food were part of the Poles' ancient WINTER SOLSTICE observance, a tradition that can still be seen in what is known as the *Gody*—the days of harmony and goodwill that start with the Wigilia and last until Epiphany, or Three Kings Day.

Because some people still cling to the ancient belief that wandering spirits roam the land during the darkest days of the year, it is not uncommon for Poles to make an extra effort to be hospitable at Christmas time, leaving out a pan of warm water and a bowl of nuts and fruits for any unexpected visitors.

SOURCES:
BkFest-1937, p. 256
BkFestHolWrld-1970, p. 142
EncyChristmas-2003, p. 621
FolkWrldHol-1999, p. 749

◆ 2984 ◆ **Wild Horse Festival (Soma-Nomaioi)**
July 22-25

The Wild Horse Festival, or **Soma-Nomaioi**, takes place annually in Soma City and Minami-Soma City in Fukushima Prefecture in eastern Japan. The festival occurs over four days, July 22-25. It is a historical re-enactment of military exercises that are more than 1,000 years old.

In the event's highlight, on July 24, about 600 mounted samurai warriors in replicas of traditional Japanese armor gallop across the vast Hibarigahara plain and vie for 40 shrine flags propelled into the air by fireworks. On the same day, 12 armored Samurai warriors compete in a 1,000-meter race. Other colorful spectacles include opening ceremonies at three shrines on July 23; a procession on July 24 summoned by conch shell horn and war drums; and the Nomagake ritual on July 25. During the latter event, white-clad wranglers capture horses with their bare hands and offer them at the Odaka Shrine. These military exercises are thought to have

originated in the 10th century, and they have been re-enacted for hundreds of years. Thousands of visitors come to witness the colorful spectacle and amazing equestrian skills.

CONTACTS:
Japan National Tourist Organization
One Rockefeller Plaza
New York, NY 10020
212-757-5640; fax: 212-307-6754
www.japantravelinfo.com

◆ 2985 ◆ **Wilder (Laura Ingalls) Pageant**
July, over three consecutive three-day weekends

The Laura Ingalls Wilder Pageant is held every July over three consecutive three-day weekends in De Smet, S.Dak., where the beloved author came of age in the late 19th century. The pageant features a play based on one of Wilder's autobiographical novels, such as *Little House on the Prairie* or *The Long Winter*. The plays are produced and performed outdoors by about 100 local volunteers on a 30-acre site purchased in 1974 especially for this purpose by the Laura Ingalls Wilder Pageant Society. The site is nestled between the site of the actual Ingalls homestead, the big slough, and Silver Lake—all locations made famous by Wilder's books. Pageant-goers can enjoy a pioneer-themed gift shop and café, as well as music and free wagon rides while they wait for each evening's show to start.

The inspiration for the Laura Ingalls Wilder Pageant was a 1951 radio dramatization of *The Long Winter*, which is set in De Smet. Local people gained permission to turn the radio play into a drama, which they performed for free in 1955 at the town's high-school auditorium. In 1968, a group of De Smet actors revived the play for a summer arts festival. Its success prompted volunteers to launch the Laura Ingalls Wilder Pageant as an outdoor family play to celebrate the life and works of De Smet's hometown author. The Laura Ingalls Wilder Pageant Society, a non-profit organization, was founded in 1973 and the pageant site was purchased a year later. People from all over the world now gather there to celebrate the family values and pioneering spirit captured forever by Wilder's books.

CONTACTS:
Laura Ingalls Wilder Pageant
P.O. Box 154
De Smet, SD 57231
800-776-3594 or 800-880-3383

◆ 2986 ◆ **Wilderness Woman Competition**
First weekend in December

In the midst of Winterfest, celebrated the entire month of December in Talkeetna, Alaska, a tongue-in-cheek competition for unmarried women takes place that pokes fun at the lack of eligible females in this northernmost state. Sponsored by the Talkeetna Bachelor Society, the Wilderness Woman Competition puts single ladies in the driver's seat—of a snowmobile—to snake through an obstacle course. After completing a number of other tasks, including the preparation of food, contestants must bring their homemade snack and a beer to a football-watching bachelor—quite a fantasy in this town at the foot of Mount McKinley where men far outnumber the women. The Bachelor Auction and Ball follow the competition.

CONTACTS:
Talkeetna Chamber of Commerce
P.O. Box 334
Talkeetna, AK 99676
907-733-2330
www.talkeetnachamber.org

SOURCES:
WildPlanet-1995, p. 621

♦ 2987 ♦ **Wildlife Film Festival, International**
Week in mid-April

Since 1978, the world's top wildlife filmmakers and producers have gathered in Missoula, Montana, for eight days every spring to share their ideas, techniques, and products with others in their field and with interested members of the public. Today, about 200 new films are presented for viewing, with a special showing of films for children. There is a wildlife parade as well as workshops and panel discussions at different venues in downtown Missoula, and about 10,000 people attend the annual event.

CONTACTS:
International Wildlife Film Festival
718 S. Higgins Ave.
Missoula, MT 59801
406-728-9380; fax: 406-728-2881
www.wildlifefilms.org

♦ 2988 ♦ **Williams (Roger) Day**
February 5

Roger Williams was the founder of the American Baptist Church. Born in Wales, he arrived in the Massachusetts colony on this day in 1631 and soon found himself in profound disagreement with the local Puritans. The latter admitted no distinction between crime and sin, while Williams contended that the civil authorities only had a right to punish those who had committed a civil offense. The argument led to a court trial in 1635, and soon afterward Williams was banished from the colony. He fled south to what is now called Providence and founded the Rhode Island colony. Under his leadership, the people of Rhode Island were the first to establish a Baptist congregation on American soil (in 1638) and the first to build a community based on this principle of religious liberty.

Baptists in the United States still celebrate the day of his arrival in America. The First Baptist Meeting House in Providence holds its annual Forefathers Service in May, honoring Williams as its founder and often using the 18th-century order of worship.

CONTACTS:
The First Baptist Church in America
75 N. Main St.
Providence, RI 02903

401-454-3418; fax: 401-421-4095
www.fbcia.org

Roger Williams National Memorial, National Park Service
282 N. Main St.
Providence, RI 02903
401-521-7266; fax: 401-521-7239
www.nps.gov

SOURCES:
AmerBkDays-2000, p. 116
AnnivHol-2000, p. 22
DaysCustFaith-1957, p. 47
RelHolCal-2004, p. 90

♦ 2989 ♦ **Williams (Tennessee) New Orleans Literary Festival**
Late March

Admirers of the work of American playwright Tennessee Williams (1911-1983) gather together to celebrate his work—and that of other southern writers—at the Tennessee Williams New Orleans Literary Festival. The five-day event, scheduled in late March, features performances of plays, master classes, literary tours of the city, concerts, a book fair, poetry and prose readings, and a wide variety of lectures and discussions led by scholars, writers, and performers. The festival closes with a tea party, a play, and a "Stella-Shouting Contest," in which festivalgoers compete to imitate Stanley Kowalski's bellowing cry of "Stella!" as performed by actor Marlon Brando in the movie version of Tennessee Williams's play, *A Streetcar Named Desire*.

CONTACTS:
Tennessee Williams/New Orleans Literary Festival
938 Lafayette St., Ste. 514
New Orleans, LA 70113
504-581-1144; fax: 504-283-6922
www.tennesseewilliams.net

♦ 2990 ♦ **Wimbledon**
Late June to early July; six weeks before first Monday in August

The oldest and most prestigious tennis tournament in the world, the **Lawn Tennis Championships** at Wimbledon are held for 13 days each summer, beginning six weeks before the first Monday in August, on the manicured courts of the All England Lawn Tennis and Croquet Club. The first competition in 1877 was supposedly an attempt to raise money to purchase a new roller for the croquet lawns, and it featured only the men's singles event. Today the world's best tennis players compete for both singles and doubles titles that are the most coveted in tennis. The event is watched on television by tennis fans all over the world, many of whom get up at dawn or conduct all-night vigils around their television sets so as not to miss a single match. Members of the English royal family often watch the finals from the Royal Box.

The Centre Court at Wimbledon, where the championships are held, is off-limits to members and everyone except the grounds staff. On the Saturday before the competition begins, four women members of the club play two or three sets to "bruise" the grass and make sure the courts are in good shape.

CONTACTS:
The All England Lawn Tennis and Croquet Club
Church Rd.
Wimbledon
London, SW19 5AE United Kingdom
44-20-8944-1066; fax: 44-20-8947-8752
www.wimbledon.org

♦ 2991 ♦ **Wind Festival**
First day of second lunar month

In the rural districts of Korea's Kyongsang-namdo and Kyongsang-pukto Provinces, a grandmother known as *Yungdeung Mama* comes down from heaven every year on the first day of the second lunar month and returns on the 20th day. If she brings her daughter with her, there is no trouble; but if she brings her daughter-in-law, who is an epileptic, it means that a stormy wind known as *Yungdeung Baram* will wreck ships and ruin the crops. To prevent such devastation, farmers, fishermen, and sailors offer special prayers and sacrifices to Yungdeung Mama and her daughter-in-law. Tempting foods and boiled rice are set out in the kitchen or garden, and little pieces of white paper containing the birthdates of family members are burned for good luck: the higher the ashes fly, the better the luck. Sometimes altars are made out of bamboo branches with pieces of cloth or paper tied to them. Sacrifices are laid under the altars, which remain standing until the 20th day of the month.

SOURCES:
FolkWrldHol-1999, p. 191

♦ 2992 ♦ **Windjammer Days**
Tuesday and Wednesday in late June

The annual Windjammer Days Festival in Boothbay Harbor, Maine, celebrates the U.S. Coast Guard's 200 years of service to coastal Maine. The festival is also a salute to the large sailing merchant ships that once carried trade along the New England coast. The locals claim that this festival, which has been going on since 1963, was the original gathering of "tall ships," although they are for the most part sailing schooners rather than the full-rigged clipper ships and barks that have gathered in New York, Boston, and other port cities for more recent celebrations.

There is an antique boat parade as well as tours of Navy and Coast Guard ships. Band concerts, seafood, and fireworks add to the merrymaking.

In the 19th century the Boothbay region played an active role in the shipping trade, carrying lumber to South America and the West Indies. There was a time when more than a hundred of these coastal vessels might have been seen in Boothbay Harbor, waiting out a spell of bad weather.

CONTACTS:
Boothbay Harbor Region Chamber of Commerce
192 Townsend Ave.
Boothbay Harbor, ME 04538
800-266-8422 or 207-633-2353; fax: 207-633-7448

SOURCES:
GdUSFest-1984, p. 76

♦ 2993 ♦ **Wings 'n Water Festival**
Third weekend in September

This two-day event celebrates the coastal environment of southern New Jersey. It is sponsored by the Wetlands Institute, an organization dedicated to conserving coastal salt marshes and educating the public about marshland ecology. Since 1983 the Institute has held the Wings 'n Water Festival in September every year to raise funds for its various educational and research projects as well as to raise public awareness of the salt marsh by offering activities that relate to its unique environment.

Salt marsh safaris and boat cruises, a decoy and decorative bird-carving show, exhibits of naturalist and maritime art, and a wildlife craft market are among the events. There is also a Black Lab retriever demonstration, musical entertainment featuring traditional American instruments, and various booths serving oysters, clams on the half shell, chowders, "shrimpwiches," Maryland hard-shelled crabs, and Maine lobster. Festival events are held along a 15-mile stretch of the South Jersey coast that includes Avalon, Stone Harbor, and Cape May Court House.

CONTACTS:
Wetlands Institute
1075 Stone Harbor Blvd.
Stone Harbor, NJ 08247
609-368-1211; fax: 609-368-3871
www.wetlandsinstitute.org

♦ 2994 ♦ **Winnipeg Folk Festival**
Second weekend in July

The largest event of its kind in North America, the Winnipeg Folk Festival is essentially a music festival featuring bluegrass, gospel, jazz, Cajun, swing, Celtic, and other performers from Canada and around the world. Held at Birds Hill Park, about 19 miles northeast of Winnipeg, the festival has seen performances by such world-renowned artists as Odetta, Bonnie Raitt, Bruce Cockburn, Pete Seeger, Eric Bogle, Ladysmith Black Mambazo, and Billy Bragg. There are concerts, jam sessions, a juried handicrafts village, children's performances, and folk dancing. The festival was started in 1974 by Mitch Podolak, a veteran in the folk music field, and although it only lasts for three days, it also operates on a year-round basis as a folklore and music center.

CONTACTS:
Winnipeg Folk Festival
203-211 Bannatyne Ave.
Winnipeg, MB R3B 3P2 Canada
204-231-0096; fax: 204-231-0076
www.winnipegfolkfestival.ca

SOURCES:
GdWrldFest-1985, p. 36
MusFestAmer-1990, p. 234

♦ 2995 ♦ **Winston 500**
April

This 500-mile stock-car race is Alabama's biggest sporting event. It's held at the Talladega SuperSpeedway, known as the "World's Fastest Speedway." The Winston 500 is one of the Big Four NASCAR (National Association for Stock Car Auto Racing) events in the Sprint Cup Series (formerly the Winston Cup). The other big events are the DAYTONA 500, the COCA-COLA 600, and the SOUTHERN 500. The Winston is considered the fastest of the four. The winner in Talladega in 1991 was 51-year-old Harry Gant, who had never won two races in a row in his 11 years on the circuit and was the surprise of the season. He won four straight in 1991, beginning with the Southern 500 at Darlington International Raceway in South Carolina. "Age don't have nothing to do with it," Gant said about the streak. His day's work at Talladega driving an average speed of 165.62 miles an hour entitled him to $81,950.

Talladega, which opened in 1969, has 83,200 permanent grandstand seats and each year attracts more than 350,000 spectators.

CONTACTS:
Talladega SuperSpeedway
P.O. Box 777
Talladega, AL 35161
877-462-3342
www.talladegasuperspeedway.com

National Association for Stock Car Auto Racing
1801 W. International Speedway Blvd.
Daytona Beach, FL 32115
386-253-0611; fax: 386-681-4041
www.nascar.com

♦ 2996 ♦ **Winter Festival of Lights**
Early November through late January

A premier light show in Wheeling, W. Va., the Winter Festival of Lights started in 1985 and is now considered a rival of the light show at Niagara Falls (*see* LIGHTS, FESTIVAL OF). More than a million people visit each year to see two million lights on the downtown Victorian buildings, dozens of giant displays, 200 lighted trees, and about 10 miles of drive-by light displays with architectural and landscape lighting designed by world-famous lighting designers. Some 300 acres of the city's Oglebay Park (a former private estate that was left to the city) are covered with animated light displays that depict symbols of HANUKKAH and CHRISTMAS and general winter scenes. There are also nighttime parades and storefront animations.

CONTACTS:
Wheeling Chamber of Commerce
1310 Market St.
Wheeling, WV 26003
304-233-2575; fax: 304-233-1320
www.wheelingchamber.com

Library of Congress
101 Independence Ave. S.E.
Washington, DC 20540
202-707-5510; fax: 202-707-2076
www.loc.gov

♦ 2997 ♦ **Winter Solstice**
June 21-22 (Southern Hemisphere); December 21-22 (Northern Hemisphere)

This is the shortest day of the year, respectively in each hemisphere, when the sun has reached its furthest point from the equator. It also marks the first day of winter.

The winter solstice has played an important role in art, literature, mythology, and religion. There were many pre-Christian seasonal traditions marking the winter solstice, and huge bonfires were an integral part of these ancient solar rites. Although winter was regarded as the season of dormancy, darkness, and cold, the gradual lengthening of the days after the winter solstice brought on a more festive mood. To many peoples this return of the light was cause for celebration that the cycle of nature was continuing.

See also DONGJI; HALOA; INTI RAYMI FIESTA; JUUL, FEAST OF; SOY-ALUNA; TOJI; YULE

CONTACTS:
Lab for Particles and Fields
Code 672, Goddard Space Flight Center
Greenbelt, MD 20771
301-286-0447
www-istp.gsfc.nasa.gov

The Royal Observatory Greenwich
The National Maritime Museum Greenwich
London, SE10 9NF United Kingdom
44-20-8312-6565; fax: 44-20-8312-6632
www.rog.nmm.ac.uk

SOURCES:
AmerBkDays-2000, p. 842
BkFest-1937, p. 82
DictDays-1988, pp. 110, 131
EncyChristmas-2003, p. 828
FestSaintDays-1915, p. 4
FolkWrldHol-1999, p. 710
SaintFestCh-1904, p. 32

♦ 2998 ♦ **Winter Solstice (China)**
December 23

The Chinese honor the god T'ien at the WINTER SOLSTICE. According to tradition, this is the day on which the ancient emperors of China would present themselves before T'ien at the Forbidden City in the capital of Beijing to offer sacrifices. Today, people commemorate the longest night of the year by visiting temples and serving feasts in their homes to honor deceased family members.

The imperial winter solstice ceremonies were closed to all foreigners and almost all Chinese. When the monarchy ended in 1912, the imperial rites were discontinued. Nevertheless, the people of Hong Kong still observe the winter solstice by taking a day off to feast with their families and present offerings to their ancestors.

SOURCES:
FolkWrldHol-1999, p. 710
RelHolCal-2004, p. 235

◆ 2999 ◆ Winterlude
10 days in February

A midwinter civic festival held in Ottawa, Canada, Winterlude is primarily a celebration of winter sports. The Rideau Canal, which has been referred to as "the world's longest skating rink," is nearly eight kilometers (five miles) long and provides an excellent outdoor skating facility. There is also snowshoeing, skiing, curling (a game in which thick heavy stone and iron disks are slid across the ice toward a target), speedskating, dogsled racing, barrel jumping, and tobogganing. For those who prefer not to participate in the many sporting events, there is an elaborate snow sculpture exhibit known as Ice Dream. Nearly half a million people attend the 10-day festival each year.

CONTACTS:
National Capital Commission
202-40 Elgin St.
Ottawa, ON K1P 1C7 Canada
613-239-5555; fax: 613-239-5063
www.canadascapital.gc.ca/bins

SOURCES:
FolkWrldHol-1999, p. 108

◆ 3000 ◆ Wizard of Oz Festival
Third weekend in September

The story of Oz, originally created by author L. Frank Baum in his 1900 children's book *The Wonderful Wizard of Oz*, has become an enduring tale for the ages. In 1939, the classic film *The Wizard of Oz* was released, based on Baum's book. Since 1982, the story has come to life again every September in the town of Chesterton, Ind., as townspeople dress up and portray Dorothy, the Scarecrow, the Tin Man, the Cowardly Lion, Glinda the Good Witch, and other characters. A huge sculpture of the Tin Man overlooks the proceedings from the top of a downtown building. The festival also serves as a reunion site for actors who played the Munchkins in the film—many come every year to meet fans and participate in the annual hour-long Oz Fantasy Parade, Munchkin autograph parties, a Munchkin celebrity dinner and dance, and a Munchkin breakfast.

As if all this were not enough, the festival also has a town crier competition, Auntie Em's pie contest, a juried arts and crafts display, Oz memorabilia collectors' gatherings, and a teddy bear parade and tea party.

CONTACTS:
Duneland Chamber of Commerce
220 Broadway
P.O. Box 2711
Chesterton, IN 46304
219-926-5513; fax: 219-926-7593
www.chestertonchamber.org

◆ 3001 ◆ Wolf Trap Summer Festival Season
May-September

Located just 30 minutes from downtown Washington, D.C., in Vienna, Virginia, Wolf Trap Farm Park for the Performing Arts hosts musical performances on a year-round basis. But Wolf Trap is best known for the Summer Festival Season. Recent seasons have featured productions by the New York City Opera, the National Symphony Orchestra, the Kirov Ballet from Leningrad (now St. Petersburg, Russia), the Bolshoi Ballet, and the Joffrey Ballet as well as performances by Ray Charles, Johnny Cash, John Denver, Willie Nelson, Emmylou Harris, and jazz trumpeter Wynton Marsalis.

Concerts are held in the 6,900-seat Filene Center, about half of which is exposed to the open sky. Many concertgoers bring a picnic supper and dine on the grass. Smaller concerts are held during the festival as well as off-season in the pre-Revolutionary, 350-seat German Barn.

CONTACTS:
Wolf Trap Foundation for the Performing Arts
1645 Trap Rd.
Vienna, VA 22182
877-965-3872 or 703-255-1900
www.wolf-trap.org

SOURCES:
MusFestAmer-1990, p. 149

◆ 3002 ◆ Wolfe (Thomas) Festival
October 3

The Thomas Wolfe Festival is a celebration of the writer's birth in 1900 in Asheville, N.C. The celebrations usually extend several days beyond the actual birthday and include dramatizations of Wolfe's works, the performance of musical compositions based on his writings, workshops conducted by Wolfe scholars, and a walking tour of "Wolfe's Asheville." This includes a visit to Riverside Cemetery, where Wolfe and members of his family, as well as some of the people he fictionalized in his novels, are buried.

The center of the celebration is the Thomas Wolfe Memorial State Historic Site, the boarding house run by his mother, where Thomas Wolfe grew up. It still has the sign dating back to his mother's time hanging over the porch, "Old Kentucky Home." In his famous first novel, *Look Homeward, Angel*, published in 1929, Wolfe fictionalized Asheville as Altamont and called the boarding house "Dixieland."

Other works by Wolfe include *Of Time and the River*, published in 1935, and *The Web and the Rock* and *You Can't Go Home Again*, both published after his death in 1938.

CONTACTS:
Thomas Wolfe Memorial State Historic Site
52 N. Market St.
Asheville, NC 28801
828-253-8304; fax: 828-252-8171
www.wolfememorial.com

◆ 3003 ◆ Women's Day, International
March 8

Not only is this day commemorating women one of the most widely observed holidays of recent origin, but it is unusual in that it began in the United States and was adopted by many other countries, including the former U.S.S.R. and the People's Republic of China. This holiday has its roots in the March 8, 1857, revolt of American women in New York City, protesting conditions in the textile and garment industries, although it wasn't proclaimed a holiday until 1910.

In Great Britain and the United States, International Women's Day is marked by special exhibitions, films, etc., in praise of women. In the former U.S.S.R., women received honors for distinguished service in industry, aviation, agriculture, military service, and other fields of endeavor.

CONTACTS:
United Nations, Global Teaching and Learning Project
United Nations HQ, Rm. 931-B
New York, NY 10017
212-963-8589; fax: 212-963-3358
www.un.org

SOURCES:
AnnivHol-2000, p. 41
BkFest-1937, p. 284
BkFestHolWrld-1970, p. 73
FolkWrldHol-1999, p. 205
OxYear-1999, p. 111

◆ 3004 ◆ Wood (Grant) Art Festival
Second Sunday in June

American artist Grant Wood (1892-1942) is best known for his painting, *American Gothic,* of a dour-looking farmer holding a pitchfork as he stands with his daughter in front of their 19th-century Gothic revival farmhouse. The annual Grant Wood Art Festival in Stone City-Anamosa, Iowa, celebrates the area's heritage as "Grant Wood Country" with juried art exhibits, children's and adults' "Art Happenings," dramatic and musical presentations, and guided bus tours of Stone City.

Born in Anamosa, Wood traveled to Europe several times, where he was exposed to Flemish and German primitive art. But he eventually returned to Iowa to paint the scenes he knew best in the clean-cut, realistic style for which he became famous. He established an art colony in the Stone City valley in 1932-33, and replicas of the colorful ice wagons used as housing by the students and instructors serve as a backdrop for the exhibits of contemporary artists during the festival.

The original *American Gothic*—one of the most widely parodied paintings in the world—is on display at the Chicago Art Institute.

CONTACTS:
Grant Wood Art Festival Inc.
124 E. Main St.
Anamosa, IA 52205
800-280-0773 or 319-462-4267

◆ 3005 ◆ Wood (Henry) Promenade Concerts
Mid-July to mid-September

Popularly known as **The Proms,** the nine-week concert series that has been held in London since 1895 presents solo recitals, operas, symphonies, chamber music, and popular music to enormous audiences. Tens of thousands of listeners tune in to the concerts on their radios or televisions, and 7,000-8,000 crowd into the Royal Albert Hall. The series is named after Henry Wood, a pianist and singing teacher who served as conductor at the Proms for 46 years and who is credited with establishing its first permanent orchestra, introducing young and aspiring musicians to the public, and attracting the primarily youthful crowd that attends the Proms every year. The idea for the series came from France, where "promenade concerts"—in other words, concerts where strolling around and socializing took precedence over listening to the music—were popular.

A highlight of the Proms is "Last Night," which occurs on a Saturday in mid-September. *Fantasia of Sea Songs,* composed by Henry Wood, is a traditional part of the Last Night program, as is a setting of Blake's "Jerusalem" and Elgar's "Pomp and Circumstance." Many festival patrons wear party hats, throw streamers, and chant rhymes similar to those heard at football games as the festival draws to a close.

CONTACTS:
BBC Proms Box Office
Royal Albert Hall, Kensington Gore
London, SW7 2AP United Kingdom
44-20-7589-8212
www.bbc.co.uk

SOURCES:
DictDays-1988, p. 66
MusFestEurBrit-1980, p. 58

◆ 3006 ◆ Wooden Boat Festival
Late June to early July

Since 1977, the Lake Union Wooden Boat Festival has been held each year from late June to early July in Seattle, Wash. The festival runs during the week preceding Independence Day and celebrates the maritime heritage of the Northwest region. Attracting about 10,000 participants each year, the Wooden Boat Festival is sponsored by the Center for Wooden Boats, a "hands-on maritime museum" located at the south end of Lake Union on Valley Street. The Center is dedicated to preserving the traditions and skills of small craft sailing. It maintains a fleet of historic craft, which are available to rent from its livery year-round, though not during the festival. The Wooden Boat Festival includes boatbuilding demonstrations, storytelling, boat rides and races, sailing lessons, safety education, knot tying, and model boat workshops. Food and music add to the festival atmosphere.

CONTACTS:
Center for Wooden Boats
1010 Valley St.
Seattle, WA 98109-4468
206-382-2628; fax: 206-382-2699
www.cwb.org

SOURCES:
PatHols-2006, p. 166

◆ 3007 ◆ Woodward Dream Cruise
Third Saturday in August

Since 1995, the one-day Woodward Dream Cruise has featured a parade of cars driving down a 16-mile stretch of Woodward Avenue in the suburbs just north of Detroit, Mich. Owners of antique cars, muscle cars, custom cars, street rods, and special interest cars participate.

The first Dream Cruise was held in 1995 as a one-time event to raise funds for a children's soccer field. It attracted a crowd of 250,000, more than 10 times the number anticipated. The event proved so popular that it has grown into an annual event and has occurred each year since then, on the third Saturday in August. More than 40,000 classic cars travel the route from 9:00 A.M. to 9:00 P.M. Spectators line up along the sidewalks with folding chairs and blankets to watch the parade of interesting cars.

Car clubs, radio stations, and the automobile industry have taken an active role. Street rods and concept cars from North America and around the world participate in the Dream Cruise, which has developed into a multi-community street festival, with entertainment stages, food and merchandise vendors, parades, and automotive displays. It is arguably the largest one-day auto event in the world.

Woodward Avenue has a long automotive history. The second person to ever drive a car on Woodward Avenue was Henry Ford in 1896. In the 1950s and 1960s, Woodward Avenue was the Detroit area's most popular spot to go "cruising," driving slowly up and down the street to show off your car and to see the cars of others. The Dream Cruise reflects a past era, when youth in the area often "cruised" Woodward Avenue at night, driving muscle cars, visiting drive-in restaurants, looking for friends, or engaging in street races. Because the Dream Cruse particularly celebrates the heyday of the automobile from that time period and Detroit's prominence in the automobile industry, some of those who drive cars in the Woodward Dream Cruise wear 1950s style clothing and play "oldies" rock music from their car radios.

The Woodward Dream Cruise, Inc., is a nonprofit organization that coordinates the efforts of the nine communities involved in the event. Sales of Dream Cruise merchandise raise money for nearly 100 local charities.

The Woodward Dream Cruise has inspired similar cruises in nearby Macomb County, northeast of Detroit. Various "Gratiot Cruises" take place on Gratiot Avenue, another main thoroughfare once known for cruising.

CONTACTS:
Woodward Dream Cruise, Inc.
www.woodwarddreamcruise.com

Ferndale Downtown Development Authority
149 W. Nine Mile Rd.
Ferndale, MI 48220
248-546-1573; fax: 248-591-7034
www.ferndaledreamcruise.com

♦ 3008 ♦ **Workers' Party of North Korea, Founding of the**
October 10

The founding of the ruling Workers' Party of North Korea (official name: Democratic People's Republic of Korea) on October 10, 1945, is marked as a national holiday throughout the country. Some historians cite the party's founding date as June 30, 1949, when the North Korean and South Korean communist parties merged. However, the North Korean government recognizes the earlier date, on which a meeting took place to found the "North Korea Bureau of the Communist Party of Korea."

The main public celebrations of the Founding of the Workers' Party take place in the capital city of Pyongyang. Commemorative dance and song performances, evening galas, and oratorical meetings all can be elements of the holiday observance. Similar speeches and performances also are featured in towns and cities throughout the country.

CONTACTS:
Permanent Representative of the Democratic People's Republic of
   Korea to the United Nations
820 Second Ave.
New York, NY 10017
212-972-3105; fax: 212-972-3154
www.korea-dpr.com

♦ 3009 ♦ **World AIDS Day**
December 1

In order to promote more social tolerance and a greater awareness of HIV (human immunodeficiency virus) and AIDS (acquired immune deficiency syndrome), the World Health Organization (WHO) declared December 1 as World Aids Day in 1988. Every year various global agencies, including the American Association for World Health, take the lead in coordinating this day and in educating people about HIV/AIDS, which has claimed nearly 22 million lives in the 20 years since the first AIDS cases were diagnosed.

In the United States, local communities, organizations, and schools have observed World AIDS Day by displaying sections of the NAMES Project AIDS Memorial Quilt, each square of which represents an individual who has died of AIDS; exhibiting their own artwork focusing on the AIDS crisis; disseminating education and prevention materials; collecting personal care and food items for centers that serve AIDS patients; and holding candlelight memorial services, among many other events.

CONTACTS:
World Health Organization
20 Ave. Appia
Geneva, 1211 Switzerland
41-22-791-2111; fax: 41-22-791-3111
www.who.int

SOURCES:
HolSymbols-2009, p. 1056

♦ 3010 ♦ **World Champion Bathtub Race**
Fourth Sunday of July

In 1967, the British Columbian city of Nanaimo decided to mark its centennial anniversary with a race in its Nanaimo Harbor. Thus was born the International World Championship Bathtub Race, the main event of the four-day Nanaimo Marine Festival.

The 36-mile race features homemade entries that have the shape and design of a tub and run on a boat motor that does not exceed eight horsepower. The original 1967 race featuring the first 200 "tubbers" posed some dangers, convincing organizers of the need for formal rules and safety precautions. Today's racers must follow all guidelines and their craft must meet certain specifications that have been established by the Loyal Nanaimo Bathtub Society.

Nanaimo's businesses participate by having their own "Bathtub Spirit" competition, which involves decorating their workplaces in the Marine Festival theme. Other festival events include a Sail Past on Wheels Fun Parade, a "Kiddies Karnival," and a fireworks show.

CONTACTS:
Loyal Nanaimo Bathtub Society
373 Franklyn St.
Nanaimo, BC V9R 2X5 Canada
www.bathtubbing.com

♦ 3011 ♦ **World Championship Crab Races**
February

This sporting event in Crescent City, Calif., features races of the nine- to 11-inch Dungeness crabs that are caught off this northern California coastal city. The crabs are urged down a four-foot raceway, prizes are awarded, and the winning crab gets a trip back to the harbor for a ceremonious liberation. This is also an eating event: throughout the day about 3,000 pounds of fresh cracked crab are served.

The event began in 1976, but its origins are older. Traditionally, local fishermen returned to port after a day of crabbing and celebrated the catch by racing their liveliest crabs in a chalked circle.

CONTACTS:
Crescent City Chamber Of Commerce.
1001 Front St.
Crescent City, CA 95531
800-343-8300
www.northerncalifornia.net

♦ 3012 ♦ **World Championship Hoop Dance Contest**
Early February

The World Championship Hoop Dance Contest annually draws dancers from around North America to compete in the traditional art of Native-American intertribal hoop dance. Individual performers may use as few as four to as many as 50 hoops, manipulating them to create such designs as globes or butterflies. Each dancer incorporates aspects of his or her distinctive culture into the dance, with emphasis on grace, speed, and athleticism.

The event takes place on the first weekend in February at the Heard Museum in Phoenix, Ariz. Over the course of the two-day event, dancers compete in five age divisions, ranging from under five to 40-plus. They vary in experience from near-beginner to top champions. The contest has been held every year since 1991. Its sponsor, the Heard Museum, specializes in Native American arts and artifacts.

CONTACTS:
Heard Museum
2301 N. Central Ave.
Phoenix, AZ 85004
602-252-8848
www.heard.org

♦ 3013 ♦ **World Creole Music Festival**
Last weekend of October

Creole music, language, and culture are sources of national pride for the island nation of Dominica, as they are for peoples throughout the Caribbean, Latin America, and other regions where Creoles have settled. The World Creole Music Festival is a three-day event showcasing this distinctive music and culture. It is held in Dominica's capital city, Roseau, and other cities on the island during the country's independence celebrations. The festival has become a major tourist event, drawing thousands of visitors from the French Caribbean, North America, and other regions of the world.

The festival has been a great financial boon for Dominica's tourism industry. According to the coordinating organization, the Dominica Festivals Commission, the inaugural festival in 1997 drew 10,000 "paid patrons." By 1999 this total more than doubled. The Commission has also established what it describes as "fringe activities"—Creole in the Park and Zouk on the River—as part of a strategy to stimulate development of local Dominican business communities.

The festival's performers, who are Dominican or travel to the island from other Creole-speaking locations, perhaps have benefited the most from the exposure. The festival has brought attention to a diverse set of musical genres that are directly or indirectly associated with Creole music, including cadence-lypso, zouk, soukous, bouyon, and zydeco.

CONTACTS:
Dominica Festivals Commission
Valley Rd.
Roseau Dominica
www.festivalmusiquecreoledominique.com

♦ 3014 ♦ **World Cup**
June-July, every four years (2010, 2014, 2018,...)

The World Cup is the world series of soccer. Since 1930 (except during World War II), the international championship games have been played every four years, sandwiched between the OLYMPIC GAMES. The series was started under the auspices of the Fédération Internationale de Football Association (FIFA) and is now the best attended sporting event in the world. It's claimed that, including television viewers, more than 30 billion people watched it in 1998.

Soccer is also called football or association football; the word soccer comes from assoc., an abbreviation for "association." It originated in England in the public schools (which are actually more like American private schools), and spread to universities and then into local clubs, attracting more and more working-class players. British sailors took the game to Brazil in the 1870s, and businessmen carried it to Prague and Vienna in the 1880s and 1890s. Belgium and France began an annual series of games in 1903. In 1904, international competition was such that FIFA was formed, and by 1998, it claimed more than 200 member associations in 77 nations. In 1946, the trophy was named the Jules Rimet Cup for the president of FIFA from 1921 to 1954.

From its inception the World Cup has been played on a rotating basis between Europe and the Americas, but in 2002, Korea and Japan co-hosted the World Cup in Asia for the first time.

In 1991, the first women's World Cup Tournament was held and was won by the U.S. It was the first cup ever taken by the United States.

The first World Cup was played in Montevideo, Uruguay, and Uruguay won. Brazil has won the World Cup five times; Italy and Germany have each won three times. Brazil's wins came in 1958, 1962, 1970, 1994, and 2002; the first three happened under the leadership of Edson Arantes do Nascimento, better known as Pelé and sometimes as the *Pérola Negra*, or "Black Pearl." A Brazilian national hero and at the time one of the best-known athletes in the world, the 5'8" Pelé combined kicking strength and accuracy with the knack of anticipating other players' moves. He announced his retirement in 1974 but in 1975 signed a three-year $7 million contract with the New York Cosmos; after leading them to the North American Soccer League championship in 1977, he retired for good.

CONTACTS:
International Federation of Association Football
Strasse 20
P.O. Box 8044
Zurich, 8023 Switzerland
41-43-222-7777; fax: 41-43-222-7878
www.fifa.com

SOURCES:
BkHolWrld-1986, Jul 30
HolSymbols-2009, p. 1058

♦ 3015 ♦ World Day for Water
March 22

In 1992 the UNITED NATIONS declared March 22 World Day for Water. Programs associated with the day draw attention to the ways in which proper water resource management contributes to a nation's economic and social vitality.

CONTACTS:
United Nations, Department of Public Information
Rm. S-1070L
New York, NY 10017
212-963-6842; fax: 212-963-6914
www.un.org

♦ 3016 ♦ World Day of Prayer
First Friday in March

The idea of designating a day for Christians to pray together was suggested in 1887 by the Presbyterian Church in the United States. Today, the observance has spread to other denominations, all of which hold the same service—translated, of course, into the appropriate language—on the first Friday in March. In each community, one church is selected for the service, and throughout the day women of all denominations come and go, each staying as long as she wishes, to take her place in this worldwide chain of prayer.

It is the Church Women United movement that organizes the observance and selects a theme upon which women around the world focus as they join together in prayer. The praying starts as soon as the sun crosses the International Date Line and travels westward around the globe.

CONTACTS:
Church Women United
475 Riverside Dr., Ste. 1626A
New York, NY 10115
800-298-5551 or 212-870-2347; fax: 212-870-2338
www.churchwomen.org

SOURCES:
BkFestHolWrld-1970, p. 47
DaysCustFaith-1957, p. 67
RelHolCal-2004, p. 92

♦ 3017 ♦ World Day to Combat Desertification and Drought
June 17

In 1994 the UNITED NATIONS established World Day to Combat Desertification and Drought on June 17. The date coincides with the June 17, 1994, signing of the Convention to Combat Desertification. Observances draw attention to the need for cooperation between nations in order to stop desertification and respond to drought.

CONTACTS:
United Nations, Department of Public Information
Rm. S-1070L
New York, NY 10017
212-963-6842; fax: 212-963-6914
www.un.org

♦ 3018 ♦ World Development Information Day
October 24

In 1972 the United Nations established World Development Information Day on October 24. The purpose of this observance is to raise awareness about world economic development and the programs devised by the U.N. to promote development. The date was chosen to coincide with UNITED NATIONS DAY and the adoption of the International Development Strategy for the Second United Nations Development Decade.

CONTACTS:
United Nations, Department of Public Information

Rm. S-1070L
New York, NY 10017
212-963-6842; fax: 212-963-6914
www.un.org

♦ 3019 ♦ World Environment Day
June 5

The UNITED NATIONS General Assembly designated June 5 World Environment Day in 1972. The date was chosen because it marked the opening day of the United Nations Conference on the Human Environment in Stockholm, Sweden, which led to the establishment of the United Nations Environment Programme, based in Nairobi, Kenya. The conference was convened again 20 years later, in the hope that nations would recapture the enthusiasm of the 1972 conference and take up the challenge of preserving and enhancing the environment.

The General Assembly urges countries and organizations to mark this day with activities that educate people about threats to the environment and encourage them to strike a balance between development and concern for the earth's future.

CONTACTS:
United Nations
Global Teaching and Learning Project
National Plz., Rm. DCI-552
New York, NY 10017
212-963-8589
www.un.org

United Nations Environment Programme
United Nations Ave., Gigiri
P.O. Box 30552
Nairobi, Kenya
254-2-623-128; fax: 254-2-623-692
www.unep.org

♦ 3020 ♦ World Eskimo-Indian Olympics
Mid-July

The World Eskimo-Indian Olympics is a gathering in Fairbanks, Alaska, of Native people from throughout the state and Canada to participate in three days of games of strength and endurance. Events include the popular blanket toss, which originated in whaling communities as a method of tossing a hunter high enough to sight far-off whales. The tossees are sometimes bounced as high as 28 feet in the air. Also on the program are a sewing competition, a seal-skinning contest, Native dancing, and such events as the knuckle-hop contest, in which contestants get on all fours and hop on their knuckles. The winner is the one who goes the farthest.

CONTACTS:
World Eskimo-Indian Olympics Inc. (aka World Exhibition of
   Indigenous Olympics)
P.O. Box 72433
Fairbanks, AK 99707
907-452-6646; fax: 907-456-2422
www.weio.org

SOURCES:
EndurHarv-1995, p. 288
GdUSFest-1984, p. 9

♦ 3021 ♦ World Food Day
October 16

Proclaimed in 1979 by the conference of the Food and Agriculture Organization (FAO) of the UNITED NATIONS, World Food Day is designed to heighten public awareness of the world food problem and to promote cooperation in the struggle against hunger, malnutrition, and poverty. October 16 is the anniversary of the founding of the FAO in Rome, Italy, in 1945.

CONTACTS:
United Nations Food and Agriculture Organization
Viale delle Terme di Caracalla
Rome, Italy
39-6-2585-2
www.fao.org

United Nations, Department of Public Information
Rm. S-1070L
New York, NY 10017
212-963-6842; fax: 212-963-6914
www.un.org

♦ 3022 ♦ World Invocation Day (Festival of Goodwill)
Spring, during the full moon in Sagittarius

World Invocation Day, also known as the **Festival of Goodwill**, is a holiday observed by the Arcane School and the churches and organizations descended from it. The Arcane School was established by Alice A. Bailey in 1923 as a training school for adult men and women in meditation techniques and the development of spiritual potential.

The focus of this observance is a prayer written by Bailey, known as the Great Invocation, which is recited by people at meetings around the world. This festival is the forerunner of recent examples of "worldwide prayer meetings," such as the Harmonic Convergence in 1988.

CONTACTS:
The Arcane School
120 Wall St., 24th Fl.
New York, NY 10005
212-292-0707; fax: 212-292-0808
www.lucistrust.org

♦ 3023 ♦ World Peace Festival
Saturday in early August

The World Peace Festival is celebrated annually on a Saturday in early August at the World Peace Sanctuary in Amenia, N.Y. Described by its organizers as a day of prayers of peace and gratitude, the festival is devoted to a culture of peace. It celebrates all that unites the world's diverse cultures. The day includes a flag ceremony honoring all the nations of the world and the distinctive heritage of each. In an Interfaith Pavilion, representatives of such faiths as Jain, Muslim, Baha'I, and Native Americans share their traditions. Visitors also can wander a Peace Labyrinth. In addition, the event features live music, children's activities, international food and drink vendors, and not-for-profit booths selling crafts and goods from around the world. The event has been celebrated every year since 1990.

The festival sponsor, the World Peace Prayer Society, is associated with the Department of Public Information at the United Nations. It is non-religious, non-political, and non-profit. It aims to support harmony, peace, and goodwill among all citizens of the world. Anyone is welcome to join the World Peace Prayer Society, via its web site, and admission is free. All that is asked of members is that they take into their hearts and lives the prayer "May peace prevail on earth."

CONTACTS:
World Peace Prayer Society
The World Peace Sanctuary
26 Benton Rd.
Wassaic, NY 12592
845-877-6093; fax: 845-877-6862
www.worldpeace.org

♦ 3024 ♦ **World Population Day**
July 11

World Population Day was established by the Governing Council of the UNITED NATIONS Development Programme to focus public attention on the issue of population growth. Schools, businesses, and organizations around the world are urged to observe July 11 with speeches, programs, and activities that address population issues and encourage people to think of solutions to the health, social, and economic problems associated with population growth. World Population Day is an outgrowth of the Day of Five Billion, which was observed on July 11, 1987, to mark the approximate date when the world's population reached five billion.

The world's population reached 6.06 billion by 2000, and could surpass eight billion by the year 2050, according to U.N. estimates.

CONTACTS:
United Nations, Population Fund
220 E. 42nd St.
New York, NY 10017
212-297-5000; fax: 212-370-0201
www.unfpa.org

♦ 3025 ♦ **World Religion Day**
Third Sunday in January

World Religion Day was initiated in 1950 by the National Spiritual Assembly of the Baha'i faith in the United States. The purpose was to call attention to the harmony of the world's religions and emphasize that the aims of religion are to create unity among people, to ease suffering, and to bring about peace. The day is observed with gatherings in homes, public meetings and panel discussions, and proclamations by government officials.

CONTACTS:
Baha'i National Center
1233 Central St.
Evanston, IL 60201
800-228-6483 or 847-733-3559; fax: 847-733-3578
www.us.bahai.org

SOURCES:
AnnivHol-2000, p. 18
ConEncyBahai-2000, p. 198
RelHolCal-2004, p. 157

♦ 3026 ♦ **World Rock Paper Scissors Championship**
October

Since 2002, the World Rock Paper Scissors (RPS) Society has hosted an annual championship in Toronto, Ontario, Canada, to find the world's best player of the childhood game. The familiar game is usually used to settle everyday disputes between children. It involves displaying one's hand in three positions: as a "rock" (fist), "paper" (flat, palm down), or "scissors" (first two fingers). To determine the winner of each round, the rules are as follows: rock breaks scissors, scissors cut paper, and paper covers rock. The game is sometimes known as **Rochambeau**.

Some 500 game enthusiasts from around the world participate in the championship to win a total of $10,000 in prizes. There are no eligibility requirements to attend or play. A fee of $40 is charged. Two players go against each other with a referee standing by to determine the winner of each match. The original 500 players are whittled down to the last two players, and the outcome of their match determines the champion. The contest takes place at a Toronto bar.

Besides the prize money, champions have appeared as guests on such TV programs as "Late Night with Conan O'Brien" and the "Ellen Degeneres Show." The World Rock Paper Scissors Society claims a history going back to 1842 London and boasts some 2,300 members worldwide. It also sponsors a series of RPS tournaments in other cities around the world.

CONTACTS:
World RPS Society
Trilogy Bldg.
Toronto, ON Canada
www.worldrps.com

♦ 3027 ♦ **World Santa Claus Congress**
Late July

The World Santa Claus Congress is held every July at the Bakken amusement park in Klampenborg, Denmark. The three-day event typically brings together more than 100 Santa Clauses from a more than a dozen countries, including Japan and Venezuela. The Santas, who may attend by invitation only, must submit proof of professional Santa status—for example, a videotape of themselves serving as Santa Claus at a shopping mall. During the congress, the Santas can take professional development courses in such subjects as how to walk like, laugh like, and exude the generous spirit of Santa

Claus. They dance around a Christmas tree and enjoy a traditional Danish Christmas feast of roast pork, cabbage, and rice pudding. By tradition, the Santas also travel by antique fire engines and buses to a nearby beach for an annual dip in the sea. The congress has taken place at Bakken every year since July 1963, when an entertainer at the park invited a group of Danish Santas to a children's party.

CONTACTS:
Bakken
A/S Dyrehavsbakken
Dyrehavevej 62
Klampenborg 2930 Denmark
www.bakken.dk

♦ 3028 ♦ **World Series**
October

Also known as the **Fall Classic**, this best-of-seven-games play-off is between the championship baseball teams of the American and National Leagues. Games are played in the home parks of the participating teams, but the Series is truly a national event. For many it marks the spiritual end of summer and is a uniquely American occasion—like the FOURTH OF JULY.

The first World Series was played in 1903 between the Boston Red Sox and the Pittsburgh Pirates. There was a lapse in 1904, but the Series resumed in 1905 and has been played annually ever since. The seven-game format was adopted in 1922.

Highlights of the Series mirror the symbolism of life that some see in the game itself; they include moments of athletic perfection and of human error, of drama and of scandal.

The scandal came when eight team members of the Chicago White Sox (ever afterwards to be known as the Black Sox) were accused of conspiring with gamblers to lose the 1919 World Series. Star left fielder "Shoeless" Joe Jackson admitted his part in the scandal, and on leaving court one day, heard the plea of a tearful young fan, "Say it ain't so, Joe."

Brooklyn Dodgers catcher Mickey Owen brought groans from fans with an error that has resounded in Series history. He let a ball get away from him—in 1941, in the ninth inning, on the third strike, with the Dodgers ahead of the New York Yankees by one run. The Yankee team revived and went on to win. Fifteen years later, in 1956, Yankee pitcher Don Larsen gave fans a rare thrill when he pitched a perfect game (no hits, no walks, no runners allowed on base) against the Dodgers, beating them 2-0. It remains the only perfect game pitched in a Series. Both these World Series were called Subway Series, because New York City fans could commute by subway from the Dodgers' Ebbets Field in Brooklyn to Yankee Stadium in the Bronx.

Another dramatic moment came in the 1989 Series. On Oct. 17, at 5:04 P.M., while 60,000 fans were waiting for the introduction of the players at San Francisco's Candlestick Park, an earthquake struck and the ballpark swayed. Players and fans were safely evacuated (although 67 people in other parts of the city died in the quake), and 10 days later the Series resumed in the same park. The Oakland Athletics mowed down the San Francisco Giants in four straight games.

CONTACTS:
Office of the Baseball Commissioner
245 Park Ave., 31st Fl.
New York, NY 10167
800-975-3277 or 212-931-7800; fax: 212-949-8636
www.mlb.com

SOURCES:
BkHolWrld-1986, Oct 17
HolSymbols-2009, p. 1064

♦ 3029 ♦ **World Space Week**
October 4-10

In 1999 the UNITED NATIONS designated October 4 through October 10 as World Space Week. The week celebrates the contributions that space science and technology have made to improving life on earth. October 4 was chosen to commemorate the former U.S.S.R.'s October 4, 1957, launch of Sputnik, the first manmade satellite in space. October 10 honors the 1967 signing of the U.N. Treaty on Principles Governing the Activities of States in the Exploration and Use of Outer Space.

CONTACTS:
United Nations, Department of Public Information
Rm. S-1070L
New York, NY 10017
212-963-6842; fax: 212-963-6914
www.un.org

♦ 3030 ♦ **World Wristwrestling Championships**
Second Saturday of October

These competitions are the original world championship matches in wristwrestling, which is similar to but slightly different from armwrestling. The one-day competitions, held in Petaluma, Calif., since 1962, originated in Mike Gilardi's Saloon in 1957. A bank building has now replaced Gilardi's. The excitement generated by the first backroom bar contests led Bill Soberanes, a columnist for the *Petaluma Argus-Courier*, to transform the bar sport into an international championship.

Fifty men entered the first world championship in 1962. The final pairings that year pitted David-and-Goliath contestants Earl Hagerman, at 5'8", and Duane Benedix, 6'4". In four seconds, Hagerman won. There was only one division at that time; now there are several weight divisions for men and women. Contestants number from 250 to 300 with wrestlers coming from as far away as Australia, Germany, and Russia. The event has been viewed by a TV audience of 200 million. Sometimes there are cash prizes; other times there are none. In the past a purse of more than $5,000 has been split among the winning contestants. But medals and trophies are always awarded.

CONTACTS:
Petaluma Visitors Program
210 Lakeville St.

Petaluma, CA 94952
877-273-8258 or 707-769-0429
www.visitpetaluma.com

◆ 3031 ◆ World's Biggest Fish Fry
Last full week in April

A spring festival in Paris, Tenn., the World's Biggest Fish Fry makes use of the catfish in nearby Kentucky Lake. The fish fry began in 1954, and by the next year more than 1,600 pounds of catfish were served. Now, some 13,000 pounds of catfish are cooked, and about 100,000 people show up in this town of 10,000 to eat, fish, and look around.

Events include a car show, arts and crafts exhibits, a two-hour parade and a smaller Small Fry Parade, and the coronation of a Queen of the Tennessee Valley and a Junior King and Queen. In the Fishing Rodeo, prizes are awarded for the biggest bass and biggest crappie, which must be caught in Kentucky Lake using legal sport equipment. Besides fried fish to eat, there are hush puppies, small deep-fat fried corn meal balls; some say these were originally made and tossed to puppies to keep them from begging while meals were being prepared.

CONTACTS:
Paris-Henry County Chamber of Commerce
P.O. Box 8
Paris, TN 38242
800-345-1103 or 731-642-3431; fax: 731-642-3454
www.paris.tn.org

SOURCES:
GdUSFest-1984, p. 178

◆ 3032 ◆ World's Championship Duck-Calling Contest and Wings Over the Prairie Festival
November, Thanksgiving week

This contest is an annual sporting event in Stuttgart, Ark., the "Rice and Duck Capital of the World." The first duck-calling contest was held in 1936 and attracted 17 contestants. The winner that year was Thomas E. Walsh of Mississippi who was awarded a hunting coat valued at $6.60. Today, there are hundreds of participants in the various calling events (including the women's, intermediate, and junior world's championships). The main World's Championship contest is limited to between 50 and 80 callers who have qualified in sanctioned state and regional calling events. These elite duck callers vie for a prize package worth $15,000. This celebration of the waterfowl hunting season is held when the rice fields around Stuttgart have been harvested and the ducks have ample opportunity for feeding. The duck hunting here is billed as the finest in the world.

Ducks are called by blowing a "duck call," a device about the size of a cigar. Originally the callers had to demonstrate four calls—the open-water call, the woods call, the mating call, and the scare call. Now contestants are judged on the hail, or long-distance, call; the mating, or lonesome-duck, call; the feed, or chatter, call; and the comeback call. Judges sit behind a screen so they can't see the contestants. And since 1955, a

"Champion of Champions" contest for former World Champions has been staged every five years.

The related events that have sprung up around the contest have been formalized as the Wings Over the Prairie Festival. Included are fun shoots, an arts and crafts fair, a sportsmen's dinner and dance, a 10K race, children's duck-call clinics, and a duck-gumbo cookoff. In 1957 the Grand Prairie Beauty Pageant debuted in which a Queen Mallard is crowned.

CONTACTS:
Stuttgart Chamber of Commerce
507 S. Main
P.O. Box 1500
Stuttgart, AR 72160
870-673-1602
www.stuttgartarkansas.com

◆ 3033 ◆ World's Largest Salmon Barbecue
Late June or early July

Some 5,000 pounds of salmon are barbecued for close to 5,000 visitors in the city of Fort Bragg on the northern coast of California. Besides salmon freshly caught in local waters and freshly barbecued, the menu offers corn on the cob, salad, hot bread, and ice cream. The feasting is followed by fireworks and dancing. The event is sponsored by the Salmon Restoration Association of California, and proceeds from it help restore the once abundant salmon runs on the rivers of the area.

CONTACTS:
Salmon Restoration Association
P.O. Box 1448
Fort Bragg, CA 95437
707-964-2781
www.salmonrestoration.com

◆ 3034 ◆ Wrangler National Finals Rodeo
Begins first Friday in December

Rodeo's premier event, sometimes called the SUPER BOWL of rodeos, is a 10-day affair that has been held since 1985 in Las Vegas, Nev. The Wrangler National Finals Rodeo, which offered a record $2.45 million in prize money in 1991, is reserved for the top 15 contestants in each of seven events: bareback riding, steer wrestling, team roping, saddle bronc riding, calf roping, women's barrel racing, and bull riding. The winners are considered the world champions in their event. There is also a world all-around champion.

The national finals debuted in 1959 in Dallas, moved to Los Angeles in 1962 and to Oklahoma City in 1965, where it stayed until its move to Las Vegas 20 years later. Attendance is about 85,000.

The rodeo is preceded by the Miss Rodeo America Pageant. Events during the 10 days of rodeo include a Professional Rodeo Cowboys Association convention and trade show, horsemanship competitions, a hoedown, the National Finals Rodeo Christmas Gift Show, cowboy poetry gatherings, style shows, a golf invitational, fashion shows, and dances. The World Champions Awards Banquet is the grand finale.

See also Dodge National Circuit Finals Rodeo

CONTACTS:
Professional Rodeo Cowboys Association
101 Pro Rodeo Dr.
Colorado Springs, CO 80919
719-593-8840; fax: 719-548-4876
www.prorodeo.com

SOURCES:
GdUSFest-1984, p. 146

♦ 3035 ♦ **Wright Brothers Day**
December 17

It was on the morning of December 17, 1903, that Wilbur and Orville Wright became the first men to fly and control a powered heavier-than-air machine. Orville Wright took his turn at piloting on this particular day and his historic 12-second flight (120 feet) near Kitty Hawk, North Carolina, was witnessed by only a handful of observers. It wasn't until the brothers went on to set additional flight records that they received widespread acclaim for their achievements. Their original plane (patented in 1906) can be seen today at the National Air and Space Museum in Washington, D.C.

Although Wright Brothers Day has been observed in one way or another and under various names throughout the United States almost since the flight took place, the more notable observations include the annual Wright Brothers Dinner held in Washington, D.C., by the National Aeronautic Association. Celebrations are also held in North Carolina at Kitty Hawk and in Dayton, Ohio, where the brothers were born and where they opened their first bicycle shop in 1892.

Events on December 17 traditionally include a "flyover" by military aircraft and a special ceremony held at the Wright Brothers National Memorial, a 425-acre area that features a 60-foot granite pylon on top of Kill Devil Hill, where the Wright Brothers' camp was located. The flyover takes place at precisely 10:35 A.M., the time of the original flight in 1903.

A week of special events in 2003 marked the 100th anniversary of the Wright brothers' flight. There were aviation exhibits and programs, air shows and fly-bys, and visiting astronauts. An attempted re-enactment of the original flight, however, was thwarted by bad weather.

CONTACTS:
Wright Brothers National Memorial, National Park Service
1401 National Park Dr.
Manteo, NC 27954
252-441-7430; fax: 252-473-2595
www.nps.gov

National Air and Space Museum, Smithsonian Institution
Independence Ave. at 6th St. S.W.
Washington, DC 20560
202-357-2700
www.nasm.si.edu

First Flight Centennial Foundation
8845 Caratoke Hwy., Harbinger Center, Ste. 4
Point Harbor, NC 27964

252-491-5165; fax: 252-491-5172
www.firstflightcentennial.org

SOURCES:
AmerBkDays-2000, p. 834
AnnivHol-2000, p. 210

♦ 3036 ♦ **Wurstfest (Sausage Festival)**
Begins on the Friday before the first Monday in November

A festival billed as "The Best of the Wurst," Wurstfest is held in the town of New Braunfels, Tex., to celebrate the sausage-making season and recall the town's German heritage. New Braunfels was settled in 1845 by German immigrants led by Prince Carl of Solms-Braunfels, a cousin of Queen Victoria. The prince chose lands along the Comal and Guadalupe rivers, envisioning a castle on the riverbanks. But the rigors of the wilderness proved too much, and he abandoned his castle plans and went home, while those who had followed him were left behind. They were decimated by starvation and disease, but the survivors eventually prospered, finding abundant water and rich soil.

The ten-day "salute to sausage" features polka music, German singing and dancing, arts and crafts, sporting events, a *biergarten*, and German food—especially sausage.

CONTACTS:
Wurstfest Association
P.O. Box 310309
New Braunfels, TX 78131
800-221-4369 or 830-625-9167
www.wurstfest.com

♦ 3037 ♦ **Wuwuchim**
November

Wuwuchim is the new year for the Hopi Indians, observed in northeastern Arizona. This is thought to be the time when *Katchina* spirits emerge from *Shipap*, the underworld, to stay a short time on earth. It is the most important of Hopi rituals because it establishes the rhythms for the year to come. For several days, prayers, songs, and dances for a prosperous and safe new year are led by the priests in the *kivas*, or ceremonial chambers. The men of the tribe dance, wearing embroidered kilts, and priests from the Bear Clan chant about the time of creation. It may also serve as an initiation rite for boys.

CONTACTS:
Hopi Cultural Center
P.O. Box 67
Second Mesa, AZ 86043
520-734-2401; fax: 520-734-6651
www.hopiculturalcenter.com

SOURCES:
DictFolkMyth-1984, p. 1185
EncyNatAmerRel-2001, p. 339
IndianAmer-1989, p. 265
RelHolCal-2004, p. 253

X

♦ 3038 ♦ **Xilonen, Festival of**
Eight days beginning on June 22

This ancient Aztec festival was held in honor of Xilonen, the goddess of maize (corn); she is also known as Chicomecoatl. Like many other Aztec ceremonies, this one involved human sacrifice. Each night unmarried girls formed a procession to a temple carrying young green corn as an offering to the goddess. They wore their hair long and loose, which represented their unmarried status and also may have been suggestive of the long tassles of ripe corn. A slave girl was chosen to represent the goddess and dressed to resemble her. On the last night she was sacrificed in a ceremony for Xilonen.

SOURCES:
CelebNature-1969, p. 137
DictFolkMyth-1984, p. 216
GodsSymbAncMex-1993, p. 60

♦ 3039 ♦ **Xipe Totec, Festival of**
March

Among the Aztec Indians of Mexico, Xipe Totec was a god of war. The observance of his festival, also known as **Tlacax-** ipehualiztli, took place in March according to the Gregorian calendar. Xipe Totec was often referred to as "Our Lord the Flayed One" (or, "the Flayer"), and statues and other images of him show the god wearing a human skin.

The Festival of Xipe Totec was an occasion for Aztec warriors to mimic the god. They killed their prisoners of war, often cutting their hearts out, and removed their skins from their bodies. They would then wear these skins for the entire 20-day month and hold mock battles, after which they would discard the now-rotting skins into caves or bury them.

Many scholars have noticed an agricultural metaphor in this practice—likening the wearing of human skin to the process by which a seed grows inside a rotting hull before emerging as a fresh shoot—but more recent scholarship has tended to discredit any connection between Xipe Totec, the donning of skins, and Aztec agricultural rituals.

SOURCES:
CelebNature-1969, p. 136
GodsSymbAncMex-1993, p. 188

Y

♦ 3040 ♦ **Yale-Harvard Regatta**
Usually during first weekend in June

This famous college crew race has been held since 1865 between arch-rivals Yale and Harvard on the Thames River (pronounced THAYMZ) in New London, Connecticut. The event, which claims to be the oldest crew competition in the country, is timed to coincide with the turning of the tide, either upriver or downriver. It begins with a two-mile freshman race, followed by a two-mile combination race featuring the best rowers from all classes. Then there is a three-mile junior varsity race. But the highlight is the four-mile varsity race.

Prior to World War II, crowds of up to 60,000 used to line the banks of the Thames to watch the race, but nowadays only a third as many come to watch—many of them by boat.

CONTACTS:
Harvard Crew, Harvard University
59 Shepard St.
P.O. Box 157
Cambridge, MA 02138
617-495-1000
www.hcs.harvard.edu/nharvcrew/Website/History/HY

SOURCES:
GdUSFest-1984, p. 30

♦ 3041 ♦ **Yam Festival at Aburi**
September or October

This is an annual harvest festival celebrating the new yam crop and Ntoa, god of the harvest, observed in the town of Aburi in Ghana's Eastern Region. The festival is preceded by a 40-day period of somberness to encourage farmers to continue overseeing the gathering of the harvest. Even funerals are considered inappropriate, although if someone does die during this time, it is customary to sacrifice a sheep to appease the god and then to hold as brief a funeral as possible. It is also forbidden for any new yam to be brought to town before the festival, since no one should enjoy the new crop until it has been presented and offered to Ntoa.

The festival begins in the morning with a purification procession: one man goes to the spring to fill a pot of water; as he carries it through the streets, another man carries a sapling and periodically dips the sapling into the water and sprinkles water along the path while saying a ritual prayer. Later in the day a priest in a white robe emerges from the fetish house, where he has been confined throughout the 40 days, and leads a procession through the town, stopping at certain points to slice three chips off a new yam tuber he carries. It is believed that if two or more of these peelings fall with the skin side down, the year will be full of good fortune. If, however, the peelings fall with the skin side up, it bodes ill for the coming year. An attendant usually makes sure this doesn't happen, though. Then prayers and an offering of palm wine, drinking water, eggs, new yam, and a sheep are made to Ntoa, and a ceremonial feast follows.

See also NEW YAM FESTIVAL

CONTACTS:
Embassy of Ghana
3512 International Dr. N.W.
Washington, D.C. 20008
202-686-4520; fax: 202-686-4527
www.ghanaembassy.org

SOURCES:
FestGhana-1970, p. 28

♦ 3042 ♦ **Yancunú, Fiesta del**
December 25-January 6

The *Baile del Yancunú* takes place in the northern coastal towns of Honduras around CHRISTMAS and EPIPHANY. Its roots lie in African folk traditions rather than in Christianity, however. It is said that performing the dance insures abundance in the coming year. This area of the country is inhabited mainly by Caribs, people who trace their ancestors back to African slaves imported from St. Vincent during the colonial era.

The dancers, all men, wear brightly colored long-sleeved shirts, skirts that resemble kilts, knee-high stockings, and masks made from metallic cloth and paint. Strings of seashells hang from various parts of their bodies, which make a rustling sound as they dance. There are six to 12 dancers in each group and four drummers who strike their instruments with their palms. Members of these groups speak in different dialects, which becomes apparent when they begin to dance, a performance they accompany by singing and yelling. Sometimes the dancers form a circle, with pairs in the center dancing the principal role.

See also JUNKANOO FESTIVAL

CONTACTS:
Embassy of Honduras
3007 Tilden St. N.W.
Washington, D.C. 20008
202-966-7702; fax: 202-966-9751
www.hondurasemb.org

SOURCES:
FiestaTime-1965, p. 187

◆ 3043 ◆ Yarmouth Clam Festival
Third weekend of July

Held in a small town in southern Maine, the Yarmouth Clam Festival has been a New England tradition since 1965. For a few days, the town expands to as much as 15 times its size, receiving nearly 120,000 visitors.

The event is a great introduction to the many methods of clam preparation. Festival goers have their choice of steamed clams, whole fried clams, clam strips, clam cakes, clam chowder, and fried clams in batter, among other traditional festival fare. Along with celebrating Yarmouth's seafood, the festival is also a fundraiser, with proceeds from the seafood booths helping to support over 35 local nonprofit organizations.

Other clam-related activities include clam-shucking contests and It's Clamtastic!, a competition added to the festival in 2006. Taking place on the Thursday before the festival officially opens, the competition invites people to sample and judge seafood platters from local restaurants.

Beyond sampling clams and other seafood, attendees can choose from a number of other activities including rides, games, live music, an antique show, a parade on Friday night, and a fireworks show on Saturday.

CONTACTS:
Yarmouth Chamber of Commerce
162 Main St.
Yarmouth, ME 04096
207-846-3984; fax: 207-846-5419
www.clamfestival.com

◆ 3044 ◆ Yaya Matsuri (Shouting Festival)
February 1-8

Like the KENKA MATSURI (Quarrel Festival) held in Himeji, the Yaya Matsuri held in Owase, Japan, during the first week in February features *mikoshi*, portable shrines, carried through the streets by groups of young men who meet and deliberately crash into each other. The festival takes its name from their shouts—"Yaya! Yaya!"—as they run into one another. Although the origin of this unusual custom is not known, houses located along the route of the procession usually have to put up protective fences to ensure that their property is not damaged.

Several special events, including dances, are held during the weeklong festival. On the last night, there is a ceremony at the Owase Shrine to determine who will participate in the festival the next year.

CONTACTS:
Japan National Tourist Organization
1 Rockefeller Pl., Ste. 1250
New York, NY 10020
212-757-5640; fax: 212-307-6754
www.japantravelinfo.com

SOURCES:
JapanFest-1965, p. 122

◆ 3045 ◆ Yellow Daisy Festival
Second weekend in September

The Yellow Daisy Festival is a tribute to a rare flower, the yellow daisy, or *Viguiera porteri*, that blooms on Stone Mountain near Atlanta, Ga. The flowers, two and one-half feet tall, grow in granite crevices, sprouting in April and not blooming until September, when they give the mountain a golden blanket. They wilt if they are picked and seem to thrive only in the crevices. They were first discovered in 1846 by Pennsylvania missionary Thomas Porter, who sent a specimen to noted botanist Asa Gray for identification. Gray decided it was the *Viguiera* genus, comprising about 60 other species that grow largely in Central America and Mexico. The only other place in the United States the yellow daisy has been identified is California, but there the plant is larger and woodier.

The festival, held since 1969 at Georgia's Stone Mountain Park, offers tours to view the daisy and much more: one of the South's largest arts and crafts shows, live music, and children's activities.

CONTACTS:
Stone Mountain Park
P.O. Box 778
Stone Mountain, GA 30086
800-317-2006 or 770-498-5690
www.stonemountainpark.com

SOURCES:
GdUSFest-1984, p. 40

◆ 3046 ◆ Yemanjá Festival
February 2

Yemanjá is a major festival of the Candomblé religion in the Rio Vermelho district of Salvador, Bahia state, Brazil. *Maes-de-santo* and *filhas-de-santo* (men and women mediums, or followers of the saints) sing and dance from daybreak on, summoning *Yemanjá*, or *Iemanjá* (the goddess of the ocean), to the festival. Offerings are placed in boats and carried down to the sea, where they are set afloat. Thousands of people flock to the coast for the festivities.

See also NEW YEAR'S EVE IN BRAZIL

CONTACTS:
Bahia Tourism Authority

Av. Simon Bolivar S/N
Centro de Convences da Bahia-1dg Pisa
Salvador, Bahia 41750-230 Brazil
55-71-3117-3000; fax: 55-71-3371-0110
www.bahiatursa.ba.gov.br

SOURCES:
EncyRel-1987, vol. 1, p. 104

♦ 3047 ♦ Yemen Independence and National Days
May 22; November 30

Independence Day in Yemen is November 30, a national holiday to commemorate Yemen's independence from the British. It was won on that day in 1967, when evacuation of British soldiers was complete and the leading political group, the National Liberation Front, declared the formation of the independent state of the People's Republic of South Yemen. The British had occupied key portions of the country since the 1830s.

National Day observes the official proclamation of the unification of the Yemen Arab Republic (North Yemen) and the People's Democratic Republic of Yemen (South Yemen) on May 22, 1990. An agreement to a common constitution, government, and economy between both had been signed the day before.

CONTACTS:
Embassy of the Republic of Yemen
2319 Wyoming Ave. N.W.
Washington, D.C. 20037
202-965-4760; fax: 202-337-2017
www.yemenembassy.org

SOURCES:
AnnivHol-2000, pp. 85, 198

♦ 3048 ♦ Yemen Revolution Days
September 26; October 14

Yemen observes two Revolution Days: one commemorates the revolutionary movement that overthrew the monarchy of Imam Muhammad al-Badr on September 26, 1962, and helped pave the way for the creation of the Yemen Arab Republic. Before that could occur, however, British occupation of the area remained another force impeding independence. Revolts against the British then ensued in 1962-63, and by 1967, the British granted Yemen its sovereignty (*see* YEMEN INDEPENDENCE AND NATIONAL DAYS). These revolts are commemorated on October 14.

CONTACTS:
Embassy of the Republic of Yemen
2319 Wyoming Ave. N.W.
Washington, D.C. 20037
202-965-4760; fax: 202-337-2017
www.yemenembassy.org

SOURCES:
AnnivHol-2000, pp. 160, 172

♦ 3049 ♦ Yom ha-Zikkaron
Between April 15 and May 13; Iyyar 4

In Israel, the **Day of Remembrance** honors those who died fighting for the establishment of the Israeli state. It is observed on the day preceding Yom ha-Atzma'ut, or ISRAEL INDEPENDENCE DAY. During Shahavit (the morning service), a candle is lit in memory of fallen soldiers, the ark is opened, and Psalm 9, "Over the death of the son," is recited. This is followed by a prayer for the war dead and other prayers for lost relatives. The service concludes with a reading of Psalm 114.

At the end of the day, sirens are sounded and a few minutes of silence are observed throughout Israel. At sundown, Yom ha-Atzma'ut begins and the mood shifts to one of celebration.

CONTACTS:
Union of Orthodox Jewish Congregations of America
11 Broadway
New York, NY 10004
212-563-4000; fax: 212-564-9058
www.ou.org

♦ 3050 ♦ Yom Kippur
Between September 15 and October 13; Tishri 10

Also known as the **Day of Atonement** or **Yom ha-Din**, the **Day of Judgment**, Yom Kippur is the holiest and most solemn day in the Jewish calendar, and the last of the 10 High Holy Days, or Days of Penitence (*see* TESHUVAH), that begin with ROSH HASHANAH, the Jewish New Year. It is on this day that Jews acknowledge transgressions, repent through confession, then make atonement to God to obtain his forgiveness, with the hope of being inscribed in the Book of Life. It is not uncommon for Jews to spend the entire 24 hours at the synagogue, where five services are held.

Yom Kippur is a strict day of fasting; not even water may be taken from sundown to sundown. It is also a day of reconciliation for those who have done each other harm during the past year and a day of charity toward the less fortunate. It is the only fast day that is not postponed if it falls on the Sabbath.

CONTACTS:
Union for Reform Judaism
633 Third Ave.
New York, NY 10017
212-650-4000; fax: 212-650-4169
www.urj.org

Union of Orthodox Jewish Congregations of America
11 Broadway
New York, NY 10004
212-563-4000; fax: 212-564-9058
www.ou.org

SOURCES:
AmerBkDays-2000, p. 699
BkFest-1937, p. 203
BkFestHolWrld-1970, p. 6
BkHolWrld-1986, Sep 28
DaysCustFaith-1957, p. 246
DictFolkMyth-1984, p. 1009
DictWrldRel-1989, pp. 65, 155, 390, 817
FolkAmerHol-1999, p. 401
FolkWrldHol-1999, p. 559
HolSymbols-2009, p. 1081

OxYear-1999, p. 726
RelHolCal-2004, p. 55

◆ 3051 ◆ Yom Yerushalayim
Between May 9 and June 6; Iyyar 28

Jerusalem Day commemorates the capture and reunification of Jerusalem during the Six-Day War (on 28 Iyyar 5727 on the Jewish calendar—June 7, 1967), after which Israel gained possession of the Old City of Jerusalem, which had been under Jordanian rule, and other Arab lands. It is the most recent addition to the Jewish calendar and is observed primarily in Israel.

Although there are no specific rituals connected with this relatively new holiday, it is common to recite the Hallel (Psalms 115-118), Psalm 107, and the Aleinu, or concluding prayer. Because this day falls during the LAG BA-OMER period—which begins on the second night of PASSOVER and continues through SHAVUOT—the mourning customs traditionally observed during this time are suspended for the day.

CONTACTS:
Union of Orthodox Jewish Congregations of America
11 Broadway
New York, NY 10004
212-563-4000; fax: 212-564-9058
www.ou.org

◆ 3052 ◆ York Festival and Mystery Plays
July during even-numbered years

From 1350 until 1570, a series of "mystery plays"—dramas recounting the story of mankind from the Creation to the Last Judgment—were produced in the city of York, England, on CORPUS CHRISTI by the medieval craft guilds. The event was revived in 1951. Since 1998 the plays have been staged on wagons, as they were in medieval times, which move to different sites within the city as they are performed. The York Early Music Festival, which takes place annually, incorporates the mystery plays into its program during even-numbered years.

CONTACTS:
The National Centre for Early Music, York Early Music
   Foundation
St. Margaret's Church
Off Walmage
York, Y01 9TL United Kingdom
44-19-0463-2220; fax: 44-90-0461-2631
www.ncem.co.uk

SOURCES:
GdWrldFest-1985, p. 97
IntlThFolk-1979, p. 181
MusFestEurBrit-1980, p. 64

◆ 3053 ◆ Yorktown Day
October 19

On October 19, 1781, Lord Cornwallis surrendered his British and German troops to General George WASHINGTON's Allied American and French troops at Yorktown, Virginia. Although the peace treaty recognizing American independence was not ratified until January 14, 1784, the fighting was only sporadic in the intervening two years, and the Battle of Yorktown is widely considered to mark the end of the Revolutionary War.

There has been some sort of patriotic observance of this day since its first anniversary in 1782. But since 1949, Yorktown Day activities have been planned and sponsored by the Yorktown Day Association, composed of representatives from 13 different patriotic and government organizations.

Events held at the Colonial National Historical Park in Yorktown include a commemorative ceremony at the French Cemetery and the placing of a wreath at both the French Monument and the Monument to Alliance and Victory. There are other patriotic exercises, 18th-century tactical demonstrations, a parade of military and civilian units, and musical presentations by fife and drum units from all over the eastern United States. The events are often attended by visiting French dignitaries.

CONTACTS:
Colonial National Historic Park, National Park Service
P.O. Box 210
Yorktown, VA 23690
757-898-2410; fax: 757-898-6346
www.nps.gov

Liberty! Chronicle of the Revolution
Public Broadcasting Service
1320 Braddock Pl.
Alexandria, VA 22314
703-739-5000
www.pbs.org

SOURCES:
AmerBkDays-2000, pp. 60, 722

◆ 3054 ◆ Young's (Brigham) Birthday
June 1

Often referred to as "the American Moses," Brigham Young led thousands of his religious followers across 1,000 miles of wilderness from their Illinois settlement to find refuge in what is now Salt Lake City, Utah. He became the second president of the Church of Jesus Christ of the Latter-day Saints, whose members are also known as Mormons. The anniversary of Young's birth on June 1, 1801, is observed by Mormon churches worldwide, as is July 24, the date on which he arrived in the Salt Lake Valley in 1847 (*see* MORMON PIONEER DAY).

CONTACTS:
Church of Jesus Christ of Latter-day Saints
50 N.E. Temple St.
Salt Lake City, UT 84150
801-240-1000; fax: 801-240-1187
www.lds.org

SOURCES:
EncyRel-1987, vol. 15, p. 539
RelHolCal-2004, p. 126

◆ 3055 ◆ Ysyakh
June 21-22

This is a celebration of the midnight sun, observed in the Yakut region in the northeastern part of Russia on the SUMMER SOLSTICE. In 1992 the Yakut Autonomous Soviet Republic became the Republic of Sakha (the Yakut people's name for themselves) within the Russian Federation.

The festivities include foot races, horse races, and often sled dog and reindeer races. Folk dancing and feasting—primarily on boiled beef and *kumiss*, or fermented mare's milk—complete the celebration, which often goes on all night.

CONTACTS:
Tourist Agency of the Republic of Sakha
5 Oktyabrskaya St.
Yakutsk, Republic of Sakha 677027 Russia
7-401-235-1144; fax: 7-401-235-0897
www.yakutiatravel.com/eng/main.htm

Ministry of Tourism, Republic of Sakha
10 Ordjonikidze St.
Yakutsk, Republic of Sakha 677000 Russia
7-401-234-2328; fax: 7-401-234-2765
www.minpred.ru

SOURCES:
FolkWrldHol-1999, p. 707

◆ 3056 ◆ Yudu Nal
15th day of the sixth lunar month

Yudu, which means "washing one's hair in flowing water," is a tradition that goes back to the Silla period (7th-9th centuries) in Korean history. It has been the custom on this day to go on picnics near a moving body of water, a stream, river, or waterfall, and to bathe and wash one's hair. Folklore has it that doing so will ward off fever and other heat-related ills. In any case, swimming in a cool stream is a refreshing way to beat hot summer weather. In modern times people also call this activity *mulmaji*, "greeting the water."

SOURCES:
AnnCustKorea-1983, p. 117
FolkWrldHol-1999, p. 416

◆ 3057 ◆ Yukigassen Festivals
February and March

Yukigassen contests are organized snowball fights. They take place in several countries, including Japan and Finland. The Mt. ShowaShinzan International Yukigassen takes place in Sobetsu, Hokkaido Prefecture, Japan, each February. The event began in 1988, and consists of matches between two teams of seven players, each armed with 90 snowballs. Teams compete in rounds of plays until one emerges as the overall winner and is awarded a cup.

In 1995 the town of Kemijärvi, Lappi Province, Finland, inspired by its sister city of Sobetsu, began to host its own Yukigassen competition. Its festival, held in March, also attracts competitors from around the world.

CONTACTS:
ShowaShinzan International Yukigassen Executive Committee
Sobetsu Town Office
Aza Takinomachi 245, Sobetsu-cho, Usu-gun
Hokkaido, 052-0101 Japan
81-1-4266-2244; fax: 81-1-4266-7001
www.town.sobetsu.lg.jp

City of Kemijärvi
Kemijärvi City Tourist Office
Kuumaniemenkatu 2 A
Kemijärvi, 98100 Finland
358-16-8783-94; fax: 358-16-8782-91
www.kemijarvi.fi

◆ 3058 ◆ Yukon International Storytelling Festival
First weekend in June

Storytellers have come from all over the world to regale audiences at the Yukon International Storytelling Festival in Whitehorse, Yukon, though a great many come from the polar regions. Located north of the Arctic Circle, the Yukon Territory in northwestern Canada has hosted the festival since 1988. Storytellers and other entertainers perform in three tents over the three-day event. There are also drum dances and other musical and dance performers.

See also STORYTELLING FESTIVAL, NATIONAL and TELLABRATION

CONTACTS:
Yukon International Storytelling Festival
P.O. Box 31722
Whitehorse, YT Y1A 6L3 Canada
867-633-7550; fax: 867-633-3883
www.storytelling.yk.net

SOURCES:
EndurHarv-1995, p. 261

◆ 3059 ◆ Yule
December 22; December 25

Also known as **Alban Arthan**, Yule is one of the "Lesser Sabbats" of the Wiccan year, thought to be a time when ancient believers celebrated the rebirth of the sun god and the lengthening of the days. This took place annually around the time of the WINTER SOLSTICE and lasted for 12 days.

The SABBATS are the eight holy days generally observed in modern witchcraft (Wicca) and Neopaganism. They revolve around the changing of the seasons and agricultural events, and have been celebrated outdoors with feasting, dancing, and performances of poetry, drama, and music. There are four "Greater Sabbats," falling on February 2 (*see* IMBOLC), April 30, July 31, and October 31 (*see* SAMHAIN). The Lesser Sabbats fall on the solstices and equinoxes.

Yule, or **Yule Day**, is also an old Scottish expression for CHRISTMAS day, "Yule," deriving from the old Norse word *jól*, referring to a pre-Christian winter solstice festival. CHRISTMAS EVE is sometimes referred to as "Yule-Even."

See also JUUL, FEAST OF

SOURCES:
BkDays-1864, vol. II, pp. 735, 745
DaysCustFaith-1957, p. 352
EncyChristmas-2003, p. 843
FestSaintDays-1915, pp. 9, 232
OxYear-1999, p. 516
RelHolCal-2004, p. 269
SaintFestCh-1904, p. 40

Z

◆ 3060 ◆ **Zambia Farmers Day**
August 7

Farmers Day celebrates the country of Zambia's agricultural sector, praises their efforts in providing crops to feed the country, and gives them a day to relax from their labors. Governmental officials normally give speeches outlining the advances in the harvest of crops, particularly maize. But average citizens enjoy a variety of sporting events that are held on the Farmers Day weekend. In 2005 Mobil Oil Zambia began sponsoring the Zambia Closed Tennis Championship on Farmers Day. Other events include soccer championships.

CONTACTS:
Embassy of the Republic of Zambia
2419 Massachusetts Ave. N.W.
Washington, D.C. 20008
202-265-9717; fax: 202-265-9718
www.zambiaembassy.org

◆ 3061 ◆ **Zambia Heroes Day**
First Monday in July

In 1964, Zambia won its freedom from England and became an independent nation. Those who fought in that freedom struggle are honored and remembered each year on Heroes Day. The somber day is a public holiday and all Zambians take the day off work.

In 1974 then-president Dr. Kenneth Kaunda presented a gift to the nation to honor its heroes: a statue of a man with no shirt or shoes and defiantly raising a chained hand into the air. Erected in the capital city of Lusaka, the one-and-a-half-ton bronze statue has become the rallying point for any holiday, march, or remembrance in which freedom plays a role. Both government and opposition groups often hold rallies at the statue.

In 2004 Zambian vice-president Nevers Mumba proposed that Heroes Day be refocused to include the members of the Zambian soccer team who died in a plane crash in 1993. Eighteen members of the winning team died when the Zambian Air Force jet they were riding in crashed off the coast of Gabon.

CONTACTS:
Embassy of the Republic of Zambia
2419 Massachusetts Ave. N.W.
Washington, D.C. 20008
202-265-9717; fax: 202-265-9718
www.zambiaembassy.org

◆ 3062 ◆ **Zambia Independence Day**
October 24

On this day in 1964, the British colony of Northern Rhodesia became the independent Republic of Zambia, after decades of nationalist struggle.

For two days, including October 24, celebrations and parades are held all over Zambia, but the most elaborate are in the capital city of Lusaka. Labor and youth organizations march along with the armed forces with dancing and music. Various tribal dances from all over the country are performed in Independence Stadium, and there are gymnastics performances by children. October 24 is also the occasion for the final game of the annual Independence Soccer Trophy.

CONTACTS:
The Embassy of the Republic of Zambia
2419 Massachusetts Ave. N.W.
Washington, D.C. 20008
202-265-9717; fax: 202-265-9718
www.zambiaembassy.org

SOURCES:
AnnivHol-2000, p. 177
GdWrldFest-1985, p. 188
NatlHolWrld-1968, p. 190

◆ 3063 ◆ **Zambia Unity Day**
First Tuesday in July

Because Zambia is composed of several different tribal groups, the founders of the country promoted the idea of national unity as a means to keep the young nation from falling apart. Zambia Unity Day was created to help foster solidarity between the diverse groups that make up the country.

The slogan "One Zambia, One Nation" is used to signify the goal of the holiday. Remembrance speeches on Unity Day stress that people of varying backgrounds and political beliefs had come together to work for Zambian independence. That spirit must be maintained for Zambia to grow in the future.

CONTACTS:
Embassy of the Republic of Zambia
2419 Massachusetts Ave. N.W.
Washington, D.C. 20008
202-265-9717; fax: 202-265-9718
www.zambiaembassy.org

♦ 3064 ♦ Zanzibar Revolution Day
January 12

In December 1963, the African island of Zanzibar won independence from England. A month later, on January 12, 1964, a revolution led by John Okello of the Afro-Shirazi Party overthrew the sultan who ruled Zanzibar. Okello's revolution was bloody. Black citizens of Zanzibar believed that Arab and Indian businessmen, who ran most of the island's commerce, had been unfairly installed by the English colonists. Within the first few days, some 17,000 Arabs and Indians were killed. Many more fled the country, leaving their belongings and businesses to be confiscated by the new government without compensation. Abeid Karume was named president and the country's name changed to the People's Republic of Zanzibar.

Karume began a program of befriending the communist nations of China, East Germany, and the Soviet Union. He accepted their financial aid and technical advisors. The new government seized and nationalized Arab- and Indian-owned businesses and ousted most Europeans from the country. By 1972, Karume's autocratic rule led to widespread dissatisfaction. In April of that year, gunmen assassinated Karume in the Afro-Shirazi Party headquarters. Since his death, Zanzibar (now a semiautonomous part of Tanzania since merging with neighboring Tanganyika) has moved to a more free-market approach to trade, working hard to develop a tourist industry.

Zanzibar Revolution Day marks the occasion of the revolt that installed Karume as president. His son, Amani Karume, is now the island's president. Celebrations are held at the Amaan Stadium and a wreath is officially placed at the gravesite of Abeid Karume.

CONTACTS:
Embassy of The United Republic of Tanzania
2139 R St. N.W.
Washington, D.C. 20008
202-939-6125 or 202-884-1080; fax: 202-797-7408
www.tanzaniaembassy-us.org

♦ 3065 ♦ Zarthastno Diso
April, May, June; 11th day of Dae, the 10th Zoroastrian month

This is the day on which the followers of Zoroaster (or Zarathushtra), the Persian prophet and religious reformer, commemorate their founder's death, at one time believed to have occurred in 551 B.C.E. He is now believed to have lived around 1200 B.C.E. Zoroaster was a figure associated with occult knowledge and the practice of magic on the one hand, and on the other, with the monotheistic concept of God familiar in modern-day Christianity and Judaism. The largest group of his followers are the Parsis of India, although they can also be found in isolated areas of Iran, and elsewhere around the world.

Zoroaster's death is observed in April by the Fasli sect of Zoroastrians, in May by the Kadmi sect, and in June by the Shahenshai sect.

SOURCES:
RelHolCal-2004, p. 69

♦ 3066 ♦ Zimbabwe Defense Forces Day
August 15

To honor the nation's armed forces, Zimbabwe holds a special celebration annually on August 15. Despite the economic problems that plague the African country, including inflation over 400 percent and unemployment of 70 percent, the nation spends enormous amounts of its wealth on military equipment and training for its defense forces. President Robert Mugabe has explained that opposition to Zinbabwe's controversial land reform program, which involves confiscating farm land owned by whites to give to black military veterans, has pushed him to ensure that the country can defend itself from aggressive foreign powers.

To celebrate Zimbabwe Defense Forces Day in 2006, President Robert Mugabe inspected parading troops in a soccer stadium in the capital city. Wearing a green and gold sash and displaying his medals, Mugabe rode through the stadium in an open military vehicle.

CONTACTS:
Embassy of Zimbabwe
1608 New Hampshire Ave. N.W.
Washington, D.C. 20009
202-332-7100; fax: 202-483-9326
www.zimbabwe-embassy.us

♦ 3067 ♦ Zimbabwe Heroes' Day
August 9

To honor those members of the armed forces who gave their lives to defend Zimbabwe, the nation holds an annual day of remembrance for them on August 9.

Celebrations are held at the National Heroes Acre, where fallen heroes are buried, in the capital city of Harare. Families of the dead lay wreaths on the graves. The country's president visits each grave and speaks with the families. Nearby, special stands are installed to seat spectators. Young people march from the center of the city to the site, singing revolutionary songs as they march. A variety of musical groups perform, including church choirs and war veterans' choirs, and schoolchildren recite poems about revolutionary struggle. Dance groups perform traditional *itshomani* and *injukwa* dances.

Similar ceremonies are held throughout the country. In the city of Masvingo, celebrations are held at the Masvingo Provincial Heroes Acre. Drum majorettes, boy soldiers, and war veterans march from the suburb of Pangolin to the memorial site. The president's speech is read to the crowd, and music and dance programs are presented.

CONTACTS:
Embassy of Zimbabwe
1608 New Hampshire Ave. N.W.
Washington, D.C. 20009
202-332-7100; fax: 202-483-9326
www.zimbabwe-embassy.us

♦ 3068 ♦ Zimbabwe Independence Day
April 18

Independence Day is the major holiday in Zimbabwe, which means "stone dwelling" in Bantu. Like much of Africa, the area that is now Zimbabwe was long controlled by Europeans. Cecil Rhodes formed the British South Africa Company in 1889 to colonize the region, and European settlers began arriving in the 1890s. Rhodes's company governed the country until 1922 when the 34,000 European settlers chose to become a self-governing British colony, Southern Rhodesia. In 1923, Southern Rhodesia was annexed by the British Crown.

A fight for independence took place in the 1970s. An independent constitution was written for Zimbabwe in London in 1979. Independence followed on April 18, 1980. The white minority finally consented to multiracial elections in 1980, which Robert Mugabe won in a landslide.

Independence Day is celebrated in every city and district of the nation with political rallies, parades, traditional dances, singing, and fireworks.

CONTACTS:
Embassy of Zimbabwe
1608 New Hampshire Ave. N.W.
Washington, D.C. 20009
202-332-7100; fax: 202-438-9326
www.zimbabwe-embassy.us

SOURCES:
AnnivHol-2000, p. 63

♦ 3069 ♦ Zimbabwe National Unity Day
December 22

Begun in 1997, National Unity Day celebrates the coming together of Zimbabwe's two political parties, the Zanu-PF and PF Zapu (one representing the Shona-speaking and the other the Ndebele-speaking peoples). These two groups had fought together against the colonial government of Rhodesia in the 1970s. Upon independence, however, and the creation of Zimbabwe, the two parties often clashed over the political direction the country should take. Violence erupted between them in the 1980s. Since the merger, the government of Zimbabwe has explained that the move has resulted in a government of unity in which all factions of the population are represented without conflict.

Among the celebrations to mark National Unity Day are a number of sporting events, including a soccer championship in which the winning team receives the Unity Cup. In the city of Masvingo, the general public and leading political figures gather at the Great Zimbabwe National Monuments for a concert featuring a number of popular singers and musicians.

CONTACTS:
Embassy of Zimbabwe
1608 New Hampshire Ave. N.W.
Washington, D.C. 20009
202-332-7100; fax: 202-483-9326
www.zimbabwe-embassy.us

♦ 3070 ♦ Zurich Festival
June-July

Originally called the Zurich May Festival, this international music, dance, and theater festival in Switzerland was founded in 1909 by Alfred Reucker, director at the time of the Zurich Opera House, because the opera season usually ended in April, and singers and actors needed more work. It was patterned after the BAYREUTH FESTIVAL, with the primary emphasis on opera, but since that time it has expanded to include orchestral and chamber music, vocal and instrumental recitals, ballet, and art exhibits.

Past performers at the festival have included the Royal Shakespeare Company, Tokyo's Red Buddha Theatre, the Netherlands Dance Theatre, Belgium's Ballet of the 20th Century, and the Abafumi Company of Uganda. Exhibits in city museums are set up to coincide with the festival, and there are master classes for young musicians.

CONTACTS:
Zurich Tourism
Bahnhofbrucke 1
Postfach
Zurich, 8023 Switzerland
41-44-215-4000; fax: 41-44-215-4044
www.zurichtourism.ch/en/welcome.cfm

Zurich Festival
c/o Opernhaus Zurich
Matthias v. Bausznern, Falkenstrasse 1
Zurich, 8008 Switzerland
41-44-269-9090; fax: 41-44-260-7025
www.zuercher-festspiele.ch/en

SOURCES:
GdWrldFest-1985, p. 172
IntlThFolk-1979, p. 356

♦ 3071 ♦ Zwiebelmarkt (Onion Market)
Fourth Monday in November

Zwiebelmarkt is a great celebration of onions and the principal festival of Bern, the capital of Switzerland, known for its bear pit and mechanical clock that displays a parade of wonderful mechanical figures every hour. The onion market is said to date back to the great fire of 1405, after which farmers of the lake region of Canton Fribourg were given the right to sell their products in Bern because they helped rebuild the city. This story is probably a made-up one, since the first documented mention of onions came in the middle of the 19th century.

Farmers at hundreds of stalls offer for sale more than 100 tons of strings of onions, as well as other winter vegetables and nuts. There is a carnival spirit, with confetti battles, people dressed in disguises, and jesters doing satires of the year's events.

CONTACTS:
Bern Tourism
Amthausgasse 4
P.O. Box 169
Berne, 3000 Switzerland
41-31-328-1212; fax: 41-31-328-1277
www.berninfo.com/en

SOURCES:
AnnivHol-2000, p. 199
FestWestEur-1958, p. 238

♦ 3072 ♦ **Zydeco Music Festival (Southwest Louisiana)**
Early September

The American music known as Zydeco was originally called "La La," which is Creole French for "house dance." The Creoles are the descendants of the original French and Spanish settlers of the Gulf States, particularly Louisiana. It was traditional at one time for the Creole community to help each other with harvest-related work. Once the tasks were com-

pleted, the fun would begin when they celebrated with a La La, using such instruments as the scrubboard (*frottoir*), spoons, fiddle, triangles, and an accordion to create a musical accompaniment.

Later, during hard times, a family might hold a La La on a Saturday night at their home. They would move all the furniture out of a room, charge a small fee to get in, and sell gumbo and beverages. The music played at these informal gatherings was later called "Zydeco"—from *les haricots,* the French word for snapbeans—by Clifton Chenier, a well-known Zydeco musician.

In 1981 a group of Louisiana citizens, concerned that Creole and Zydeco music was disappearing, organized the Southwest Louisiana Zydeco Music Festival. The first Zydeco Festival was held the following year in a farmer's field on the outskirts of Opelousas. Today the festival is sponsored by the Southern Development Foundation and features Creole food along with performances by well-known Zydeco bands.

CONTACTS:
Original Southwest Louisiana Zydeco Music Festival
361 Congress St.
Opelousas, LA 70570
337-942-2392; fax: 337-942-9201
www.zydeco.org

Opelousas Museum and Interpretive Center
315 N. Main St.
Opelousas, LA 70570
337-948-2589; fax: 337-948-2592
www.opelousas.info

Appendices

APPENDIX 1

Glossary of Words Relating to Time

A descriptive listing of words relating to periods of time is included below. Many of the words are adjectives in form, but also are commonly used as nouns, e.g., the bicentennial of the U.S. Constitution. All terms are defined in two separate lists: first by number referred to, then alphabetically.

Listed by Number

diurnal, per diem, quotidian
 daily; of a day

nocturnal
 nightly; of a night

nichthemeron
 a period of 24 hours

semidiurnal
 twice a day

hebdomadal
 weekly; a period of seven days

semiweekly
 twice a week

biweekly
 1. every two weeks
 2. twice a week

fortnightly
 once every two weeks

triweekly
 1. every three weeks
 2. three times a week

novendial
 a period of nine days

monthly, tricenary
 1. relating to a period of one month
 2. thirty days

bimonthly
 1. every two months
 2. twice a month

semimonthly
 twice a month

bimester
 relating to a period of two months

trimester
 relating to a period of three months

trimonthly
 1. every three months
 2. three times a month

biquarterly
 twice every three months

biannual
 twice a year (not necessarily at equally spaced
 intervals)

triannual
 three times a year

semiannual, semiyearly, semestral
 every half year or six-month period

annual, solennial, quotennial, per annum
 yearly; once a year

biennial, biennium, biyearly, diennial
 relating to a period of two years

triennial, triennium
 relating to a period of three years

quadrennial, quadrennium, quadriennial
 relating to a period of four years

quinquennial, quintennial, quinquennium
 relating to a period of five years

sexennial, sextennial
 relating to a period of six years

septenary, septennial, septennium
 relating to a period of seven years

octennial
 relating to a period of eight years

novennial
relating to a period of nine years

decennary, decennial, decennium
relating to a period of 10 years

undecennial
relating to a period of 11 years

duodecennial
relating to a period of 12 years

quindecennial
relating to a period of 15 years

septendecennial
relating to a period of 17 years

vicennial, vigintennial
relating to a period of 20 years

tricennial, trigintennial
relating to a period of 30 years

quinquagenary, semicentennial, semicentenary
relating to a period of 50 years

centenary, centennial, centennium, centurial
relating to a period of 100 years

quasquicentennial
relating to a period of 125 years

sesquicentenary, sesquicentennial
relating to a period of 150 years

bicentenary, bicentennial, bicentennium
relating to a period of 200 years

tercentenary, tricentennial, tercentennial
relating to a period of 300 years

quadricentennial, quatercentennial
relating to a period of 400 years

quincentenary, quincentennial
relating to a period of 500 years

sexcentenary
relating to a period of 600 years

septicentennial
relating to a period of 700 years

antemillennial, premillennial
relating to the period before the millennium

millennial, millennium
relating to a period of 1000 years; 10 centuries

postmillennial
relating to the period after the millennium

sesquimillennium
relating to a period of 1500 years; 15 centuries

bimillenary, bimillennial, bimillennium
relating to a period of 2000 years; 20 centuries

perennial
occurring year after year

plurennial
lasting for many years

aeonial
everlasting

Listed Alphabetically

aeonial
everlasting

annual
yearly; once a year

antemillennial
relating to the period before the millennium

biannual
twice a year (not necessarily at equally spaced intervals)

bicentenary, bicentennial, bicentennium
relating to a period of 200 years

biennial, biennium
relating to a period of two years

bimester
relating to a period of two months

bimillenary, bimillennial, bimillennium
relating to a period of 2000 years; 20 centuries

bimonthly
1. every two months
2. twice a month

biquarterly
twice every three months

biweekly
1. every two weeks
2. twice a week

biyearly
relating to a period of two years

centenary, centennial, centennium, centurial
relating to a period of 100 years

decennary, decennial, decennium
relating to a period of 10 years

diennial
relating to a period of two years

diurnal
daily; of a day

duodecennial
relating to a period of 12 years

fortnightly
once every two weeks

hebdomadal
　　weekly; a period of seven days

millennial, millennium
　　relating to a period of 1000 years; 10 centuries

monthly
　　1. relating to a period of one month
　　2. thirty days

nichthemeron
　　a period of 24 hours

nocturnal
　　nightly; of a night

novendial
　　a period of nine days

novennial
　　relating to a period of nine years

octennial
　　relating to a period of eight years

per annum
　　yearly; once a year

per diem
　　daily; of a day

perennial
　　occurring year after year

plurennial
　　lasting for many years

postmillennial
　　relating to the period after the millennium

premillennial
　　relating to the period before the millennium

quadrennial, quadrennium, quadriennial
　　relating to a period of four years

quadricentennial
　　relating to a period of 400 years

quasquicentennial
　　relating to a period of 125 years

quatercentennial
　　relating to a period of 400 years

quincentenary, quincentennial
　　relating to a period of 500 years

quindecennial
　　relating to a period of 15 years

quinquagenary
　　relating to a period of 50 years

quinquennial, quinquennium, quintennial
　　relating to a period of five years

quotennial
　　yearly; once a year

quotidian
　　daily; of a day

semestral, semiannual
　　every half year or six-month period

semicentenary, semicentennial
　　relating to a period of 50 years

semidiurnal
　　twice a day

semimonthly
　　twice a month

semiweekly
　　twice a week

semiyearly
　　every half year or six-month period

septenary
　　relating to a period of seven years

septendecennial
　　relating to a period of 17 years

septennial, septennium
　　relating to a period of seven years

septicentennial
　　relating to a period of 700 years

sesquicentenary, sesquicentennial
　　relating to a period of 150 years

sesquimillennium
　　relating to a period of 1500 years; 15 centuries

sexcentenary
　　relating to a period of 600 years

sexennial, sextennial
　　relating to a period of six years

solennial
　　yearly; once a year

tercentenary, tercentennial
　　relating to a period of 300 years

triannual
　　three times a year

tricenary
　　1. relating to a period of one month
　　2. thirty days

tricennial
　　relating to a period of 30 years

tricentennial
　　relating to a period of 300 years

triennial, triennium
　　relating to a period of three years

trigintennial
　　relating to a period of 30 years

trimester
    relating to a period of three months

trimonthly
    1. every three months
    2. three times a month

triweekly
    1. every three weeks
    2. three times a week

undecennial
    relating to a period of 11 years

vicennial, vigintennial
    relating to a period of 20 years

APPENDIX 2

Calendars throughout History:
An Overview of Calendar Systems around the World

This section provides information on calendars in various parts of the world and within major religious traditions. Following a general historical overview, these calendars will be discussed in the order in which they were developed or established:

Calendars throughout History: An Overview

The calendar is so ordinary, and yet so important, that one can hardly imagine a time when it did not exist. It is a fundamental commodity of life. Its significance is so great that in some cultures the institution and maintenance of dating systems have sacred status, and they fall under the jurisdiction of religious authorities.

Around the globe, through centuries of human history, a wide range of different calendars have been used to order time in a systematic manner—a need that all human civilizations share. Today, the Western Gregorian calendar serves as an international standard for business and diplomatic purposes. On the world's stage, this is a recent development, and people of various religions, nations, and societies still employ many other calendars to mark the passing of time. The characteristics of these calendars are as diverse as the societies that developed them. All calendars, however, serve the common purpose of enabling people to work together to accomplish specific goals.

In the broadest sense, a calendar consists of the set of rules that a society uses to determine which days are ordinary and which are days are holy, or holidays.

Thousands of years ago, before the beginning of the written historical record, people lived in small tribal societies based on hunting and gathering. Activities were likely coordinated by word of mouth, and time-keeping methods were fairly uncomplicated. People probably used days as indications of time, and perhaps they even recognized periods similar to months through observing changes in the moon's appearance. They would have observed seasonal and annual patterns, but without a formal system of reckoning them. Almost certainly, their needs did not demand anything as complex as a decade or century.

Over the course of time, people began living in agricultural communities with larger populations and diversified work forces. This shift required that people become more interdependent. For example, if farmers and city dwellers were going to conduct business efficiently, they must come to the marketplace at the same time. As a result, the need for a tool to arrange societal events became apparent.

Ancient Egyptians and Babylonians Systematize Their Calendars

The first two cultures that influenced the development of the Western Gregorian calendar were the Babylonians and Egyptians. Both shared similar characteristics—an agricultural base, a large population spread over a significant expanse of land, and a need to gather together at regular intervals to observe religious festivals. The responsibility for forming a central time-reckoning system so that people would know when to arrive at these festivals was placed in the hands of the respective religious communities.

To develop their calendars, both groups followed similar approaches. They divided time into three major divisions—what we now recognize as days, months, and years—and then went about calculating the exact duration of each category. The questions faced by the ancient Babylonians and Egyptians were the same questions all subsequent calendar makers have had to address:

- How long is a day?
- How long is a month?
- How long is a year?

These values may seem obvious to a modern observer, but it took centuries of ongoing observations, measurements, and calculations to set them.

The Day

The basic building block of all calendars is the day. The length of the day is set by the amount of time in which the earth completes one rotation on its axis. During the fifth century B.C.E. (Before Common Era, which is equivalent to the term B.C.), the Babylonians divided this duration of time into 24 segments that we now know as hours. However, because accurate measurement of seconds and even minutes was not possible until the 16th century C.E. (Common Era, equivalent to A.D.), the length of those hours has not always been fixed.

The day was given scientific regularity only with the development of accurate clocks, the demand for which was a byproduct of the interest in maritime navigation that came with the Renaissance.

The Month

A lunar month, the period of a complete cycle of the phases of the moon, lasts approximately 29.5 days, is easy for all to recognize, short enough to be counted without using large numbers, matches closely with the female menstrual cycle and, given its relation to the tidal cycle, also matches the duration of cyclic behavior in some marine animals. Its simplicity and minimal ease of observation (if one discounts cloudy skies) led to its great significance, and it was widely used as the basis for calendars in many cultures. The length of each month varied according to the culture. For example, the Babylonians alternated between 29- and 30-day months, while the Egyptians fixed them at 30 days.

The Seasons and the Year

But the problem inherent in the use of a lunar calendar is that the cycles of the sun, not the moon, determine the seasons, the predictability of which is essential to the success of agriculture. The seasons could be determined by solar observation, either by measuring the cycle of the midday shadow cast by a stick placed vertically in the ground, or by sophisticated astronomical calculations. Either system resulted in a solar year of approximately 365 days, incompatible with the 12 lunar months, each with 29.5 days, that resulted in a 354-day year.

Civilizations attempted to reconcile lunar months with the solar year in varied ways. The most influential ancient effort was that of the Egyptian astronomers. Working from precise mathematical observations and borrowing from Babylonian astronomy, they drew up the Roman calendar that Julius Caesar introduced.

Perhaps the most difficult issue faced by calendar makers was establishing the length of the year. Although measuring a complete cycle of seasons may not seem complicated, it created significant problems for many calendar systems.

Each season in a cycle was marked by weather changes. Some seasons were warm, others cold; some had high levels of precipitation, others low. This cycling of the seasons originally defined the year—a period of time important to agrarian cultures that depended heavily on the ability to predict optimal planting and harvesting times.

Each season contained several new moons or months. The cycling of the moon and the cycling of weather patterns were not synchronized. This led to different systems for measuring a year's length.

Babylonians and Egyptians Disagree

In the fifth century B.C.E., the Babylonians and Egyptians both arrived at a specific number of days in the year, but their conclusions were different. The Babylonians claimed that the year was 360 days long while the Egyptians more accurately estimated the year at 365 days. The discrepancy between the two lengths of the year is puzzling.

One possibility for the difference is that the Babylonians simply miscalculated. This is unlikely, however, in light of their sophisticated astronomical and mathematical systems. Another explanation is that they rounded their figure from 365 to 360 to facilitate the interaction of the year with their base-12 numerical system.

The problem with the Babylonians' five-day omission was that the months would not stay in line with the seasons of the year. Each year the beginning of each month would occur at least five days earlier in relation to the position of the sun. Eventually, the months would be completely dissociated with the seasons in which they originally occurred. To correct this problem, the Babylonians periodically added months to the calendar, a process termed intercalation, which can also be used to add "leap" days or weeks.

The Babylonians were not the only people to face the problem of keeping the months coordinated with the seasons. Even though the Egyptians calculated the length of the year more accurately, they too realized that their determination was not exactly perfect.

The Solar System Affects the Length of the Year

Precise division of a year into months or days is impossible because the seasons, the phases of the moon, and the ever-cycling periods of daylight and nighttime are determined by the earth's relationship to the sun and the moon. The movements of these heavenly bodies do not neatly coincide with the mathematical systems of any human civilization.

The quest to discover the secrets of how the universe fits together has motivated astronomers throughout history. In the second century C.E., Ptolemy, a Greek astronomer, formulated the theory that the earth was the center of the universe and that the sun, stars, moon, and other planets revolved around it. In the 15th century C.E., the Polish astronomer Copernicus advocated the notion that the earth rotated on an axis and, along with the other heavenly bodies in the solar system, revolved around the sun. Shortly after the Copernican assertion, Galileo presented supporting evidence based on observations he had made using his invention, the telescope.

The Gap between the Lunar and Solar Cycles

We now understand that an 11.25-day difference exists between the 354-day lunar cycle on which the months are based and the 365.25-day solar cycle that determines the seasons. Calendar systems have applied three main strategies in their search for a solution to this discrepancy.

The first, called a lunar calendar, ignores the seasons and allows the lunar (moon) cycle to be the basis of the year, as the Islamic calendar does. A second is called a lunisolar calendar. It involves an elaborate system of calculations to add days or months to the lunar year until it coincides with the solar year. The Jewish calendar is one example. The third system, which originated with the Egyptians, is the pure solar calendar. It allows the sun to determine not only the seasons but the length of the months as well.

Chinese Calendar

The Chinese calendar, widely used in Asian countries, is based on the oldest system of time measurement still in use, with its origin believed to be 2953 B.C.E. Part of the reason that the Chinese calendar has survived intact for so long is that, until the middle of the 20th century, the document was considered sacred. Any changes to the calendar were tightly controlled by imperial authorities, and the penalty for illegally tampering with the time-keeping system was death. Until the rise of Communism in China during the 20th century, the official calendar was presented to the emperor, governors, and other dignitaries in an annual ceremony. Since 1912, the Gregorian calendar has been in use for civic purposes.

The Chinese New Year takes place on the new moon nearest to the point that is defined in the West as the 15th degree of the zodiacal sign of Aquarius. Each of 12 months in the Chinese year is 29 or 30 days long and is divided into two parts, each of which is two weeks long. The Chinese calendar, like all lunisolar systems, requires periodic adjustment to keep the lunar and solar cycles integrated, therefore an intercalary month is added when necessary.

The names of each of the 24 two-week periods sometimes correspond to festivals that occur during the period. Beginning with the New Year, which takes place in late January or early February, these periods are known by the following names: Spring Begins (New Year), the Rain Water, the Excited Insects, the Vernal Equinox, the Clear and Bright, the Grain Rains, the Summer Begins, the Grain Fills, the Grain in Ear, the Summer Solstice, the Slight Heat, the Great Heat, the Autumn Begins, the Limit of Heat, the White Dew, the Autumnal Equinox, the Cold Dew, the Hoar Frost Descends, the Winter Begins, the Little Snow, the Heavy Snow, the Winter Solstice, the Little Cold, and the Great Cold.

Calendars of India

Throughout its history, India has used a plethora of calendars and dating systems, which have included two basic types: a civil calendar that changed with each new regime and a religious calendar maintained by the Hindus. Although each geographical region had its own Hindu calendar, most of the calendars shared some elements that they gleaned from a common heritage.

India's Original Calendar

India's first time-reckoning system emerged before 1000 B.C.E. It was based on astronomical observations and consisted of a solar year of 360 days comprising 12 lunar months. The discrepancy between the length of the solar and lunar years was corrected by intercalating a month every 60 months.

In 1200 C.E., the Muslims brought the use of their calendar to India for administrative purposes, and in 1757 the British introduced the Gregorian calendar. Even so, each separate state maintained a calendar that its citizens used in their daily interactions. Throughout India's colonial days, the entrenchment of these local calendars created havoc for the central government because any given date would yield up to six different interpretations throughout the country. The difficulties continued as an indigenous government took control in 1947.

The Saka Era Calendar

When India became a unified and independent nation, the differences among regional calendars included more than 30 methods for determining the beginning of the era, the year, and the month. These variations in the Hindu calendar were the culmination of nearly 3,000 years of history.

In 1952, the Calendar Reform Committee was established and charged with task of devising a unified system that would adhere to modern astronomical calculations and accommodate the calculation of dates for religious festivals. As a result of the committee's work, the National Calendar of India was adopted in 1957.

The National Calendar of India is a 12-month lunisolar calendar with traditional Hindu month names. Some months are 30 days in length; others are 31 days. The year is 365 days long, with an extra day added to the end of the first month every four years (coinciding with leap years in the Gregorian calendar).

The National Calendar of India counts years from the inception of the Saka Era (S.E.)—the spring equinox in 79 C.E. In the year in which it was adopted, the first day of the first month (Caitra) was Caitra 1, 1879 S.E., which corresponded to March 22, 1957 C.E. Using the Gregorian calendar for comparison, the year 1926 in the Saka Era began on March 22, 2004 C.E.

Dates for religious festivals, which depend on lunar and solar movements, are calculated annually by the India Meteorological Department, although regional variations still exist. For administrative purposes, the Indian government currently follows the Gregorian calendar.

Hindu Calendar

Although each geographical region of India has had its own calendar, all are based on an ancient calendar, the earliest time measurement system in India, found in texts thought to date from as early as 1000 B.C. Of the multitudinous regional Hindu calendars, used only for religious holidays, the majority divide an approximate solar year of 360 days into 12 months. Each day is 1/30th of a month, with the intercalation of a leap month every 60 months. Time measurements based on observations of the constellations are used along with the calendar. Each month is divided into two fortnights: *krsna* (waning or dark half) and *sukla* (waxing or bright half). In southern India, the month begins with the new moon. In other parts of the country, the full moon is considered to be the beginning of the month. Many references to the Hindu calendar (depending on the source) are given as follows: month, fortnight (either S=waxing or K=waning), and number of the day in that fortnight, e.g., Rama Navami: Caitra S. 9.

The names of the Hindu months (with variant spellings) are given below, with the Burmese name for the month in brackets:

Caitra or Chaitra [Tagu]: March-April

Vaisakha [Kasone]: April-May

Jyeshta or Jyaistha [Nayhone]: May-June

Ashadha or Asadha [Waso]: June-July

Sravana [Wagaung]: July-August

Bhadrapada [Tawthalin]: August-September

Asvina [Thadingyut]: September-October

Kartika or Karttika [Tazaungmone]: October-November

Margasirsa or Margashirsha [Nadaw]: November-December

Pausa or Pausha [Pyatho]: December-January

Magha [Tabodwei]: January-February

Phalguna [Tabaung]: February-March

Jain Calendar

The Indian calendars generally have lunar months, but the duration of an average year is a sidereal year. The dates of most all the Jain festivals are calculated using such a lunisolar calendar. In northern India, the beginning of the month occurs at the full moon. This means that the first fortnight is waning. People in southern India typically mark the beginning of the month at the new moon and the first fortnight is waxing. Jains begin the new year in the autumn with the Diwali festival commemorating the liberation (achievement of Nirvana) of their founder, Nataputta Mahavira. The Hindu new year generally occurs in the spring; however, in Gujarat, the Hindu new year also starts with Diwali.)

Mahavira's achievement of Nirvana (at his death) in 527 B.C.E. also serves as the epoch for the Jain calendar. Diwali 2004 C.E., for example, begins the year 2531 V.N.S. (Vira Nirvana Samvat).

Cyclical Eras

The Jain concept of how time cycles through progressive and regressive eras also differs from the Hindus'. Jains believe that a complete cycle of time consists of twelve separate units. Of these, six represent deteriorating conditions and six represent improving conditions. The third and fourth units of both half-cycles represent times when neither extreme predominates. Only during these units can the Tirthankaras be born.

Currently, the earth is experiencing the fifth unit in the declining part of the time cycle. Risabha, the first Tirthankara of the current age, is said to have been born during the third unit; Mahavira was born at the close of the fourth. Each of the last two units in the declining half-cycle has a duration of 21,000 years.

The months of the Jain calendar are given below. The names of the Jain months are nearly the same as those of the Hindu months, but the Jain new year begins in Kartika, rather than in Caitra.

Kartika: October-November

Margasira: November-December

Pausa: December-January

Magha: January-February

Phalguna: February-March

Caitra: March-April

Vaisakha: April-May

Jyestha: May-June

Asadha: June-July

Sravana: July-August

Bhadrapada: August-September

Asvina: September-October

Buddhist Calendar

The Buddhist calendar, which originated in India, varies among different geographic locations, as does the Hindu calendar, with which it shares many common elements. Buddhism spread outside India after the Buddha's death in 483 B.C.E. The method for determining the date of the new year is not uniform among Buddhist sects. Theravada Buddhists (those primarily in Sri Lanka, Laos, Burma/Myanmar, Thailand, and Cambodia), using a Hindu calendar as their basis, calculate the months by the moon and the new year by the sun's position in relation to the twelve segments of the heavens, each named for a sign of the zodiac. The solar new year begins when the sun enters Aries, usually between April 13th and 18th. The lunar months alternate between twenty-nine and thirty days in length. The first lunar month is usually sometime in December, except for the Burmese Buddhist calendar, which begins in April (see Hindu Calendar above for Burmese names). Periodically, the seventh month has an intercalary day, and an intercalary month is added every few years. Cambodia, Laos, and Thailand refer to the months by number. Tibetan Buddhists, whose calendar has been heavily influenced by the Chinese calendar, begin their new year at the full moon nearest to the midpoint of Aquarius. Mahayana Buddhists (those primarily in Tibet, Mongolia, China, Korea, and Japan) base their holidays on Buddhist, Chinese, or Gregorian calendars.

Sikh Calendar

The Sikh calendar dates from the religion's inception in the 15th century C.E. It is a lunar calendar that is based on the moon's movement from one zodiac sign into the next rather than on the phase of the moon. The dates of some festivals, however, derive from the phase of the moon. The beginning of a new month is called the Sangrand. It is announced in the Sikh house of worship (gurdwara) but it is not a festival day.

Sikh festivals are marked on a special calendar called the Sikh Gurpurab Calendar. A gurpurab is a date commemorating births, deaths (and martyrdoms), or other important events associated with the lives of the 10 Sikh human *Guru*s or with the Sikh scriptures, the *Guru Granth Sahib*. The Gurpurab Calendar also notes the anniversary dates of historic incidents important to the Sikh faith.

The Sikh Gurpurab Calendar begins with the month of Chait (March/April), showing its inspiration from the Hindu calendar. The Sikh New Year celebration, however, falls on the first day of the second month, Basakh.

The Sikh have used several calendars since their religious tradition began in the 15th century. Over time, the lunar calendar, called the Bikrami calendar, was used predominantly. The Bikrami calendar consisted of 12 months averaging 29.5 days. This yields a year that is approximately 11 days shorter than the solar year. To keep the lunar calendar in line with the solar seasons, the Sikh calendar intercalated an extra lunar month whenever two new moons occur within the same solar month. The 13th lunar month then took the name of the solar month in which it fell. The names of the regular 12 lunar months are listed in the *Guru Granth Sahib*.

The solar component of the Bikrami calendar, however, did not correspond exactly to the natural solar year—every 70 years a discrepancy equal to one day accrued. To resolve this problem, two calendars were developed to accurately match the natural solar year: the Nanakshai Calendar, which is based on Guru Nanak's birth, and the Khalsa Calendar, which is based on the founding of the Khalsa. In 1999 C.E., the Sikhs adopted the Nanakshai Calendar. Although the choice generated some controversy, it is now used to observe all Sikh religious holidays, and has grown increasingly popular, especially among Sikh communities outside India.

The Nanakshai calendar is devised in a manner that maintains consistency with the western Gregorian calendar so that holidays always fall on the same day of the year. It begins with the month of Chait (Chait 1 falls on March 14) and contains five months of 31 days and seven months of 30 days. The last month usually contains 30 days, but in leap years, an extra day is added.

The Nanakshai calendar counts years from Guru Nanak's birth in 1469 C.E. The year 536 Nanakshai began in the year 2004 C.E.

The months of the Nanakshai calendar, along with variant spellings, are given below.

Chait or **Chet**: March-April

Basakh or **Vaisakhi**: April-May

Jaith or **Jeth**: May-June

Har or **Harh**: June-July

Sawan: July-August

Bhadro or **Bhadon**: August-September

Asun or **Asu**: September-October

Katik: October-November

Magar or **Maghar**: November-December

Poh: December-January

Magh: January-February

Phagan or **Phagun**: February-March

Mayan and Aztec Calendars

The Mayan and Aztec civilizations both used what is commonly referred to as the Mesoamerican calendar. This ancient calendar may have derived from the Olmec civilization, which thrived between 1300 and 400 B.C.E. in what is now southeastern Mexico, along the Gulf. The Mesoamerican calendrical system, which probably originated between 1000–900 B.C.E., employed not just one calendar, but a system of two interconnecting calendars: a 260-day calendar and a 365-day calendar. These two calendars ran alongside each other. Every 52 years, a named day from the 260-day calendar would be the same as a named day from the 365-day calendar (there are 18,980 days in 52 years, and 18,980 is the least common multiple of both 365 and 260). This 52-year cycle was observed by both the Mayans and the Aztecs.

Mayan civilization, in what is now southeastern Mexico, Belize, and portions of Guatemala and Honduras, flourished between about 300–900 C.E., a period known as the Classical Mayan era. The Mayans used the 260-day calendar—known as the *tzolkin*—for sacred purposes, and the 365-day solar-based calendar—called the *haab*—for agricultural purposes. The Mayan calendar system employed glyphs, small pictorial inscriptions, to represent such time periods as a day, a month, and a year, as well as to represent specific months of the year and specific days in the months. Each day was named for a god who was thought to be manifest as that day. The days' numbers were written using a combination of dots and bars. The 260-day Mayan calendar was divided into 13 months of 20 named days. The 365-day calendar was divided into 18 months of 20 named days plus a brief month of five days, called *Uayeb*, or "ominous days." The 52-year Mayan cycle is known as the Calendar Round. The 260-day system is thought to be the only one of its kind in the world. Scholars are not certain what the significance of 260 is, though some have noted that the average duration of human pregnancy is approximately 260 days long. In addition, the Mayans had a highly developed knowledge of astronomy, and 260 was a number significant in calculating the appearance of Venus—the planet identified with the Mayan god Kukulcán, known as Quetzalcoatl to the Toltec people, who flourished in Mesoamerica (and dominated the Mayans) from the 10th century to the middle of the 12th century.

Mayans also developed the Long Count, an extensive system of time-reckoning which attempted to encompass the time of the world from its creation to its end. The Mayans are thought to have developed the Long Count between 400 B.C.E. and 100 A.D. From this system, they dated the current creation to have occurred in 3114 B.C.E. (or 3113 B.C.E., by some contemporary calculations). This Long Count, according to some scholars, will end in December 2011 (or 2012).

The Aztecs—they called themselves Mexica—dominated Mesoamerica after the Toltec empire collapsed, from the early 1300s up until the Spanish began colonization in the early 1600s. Like the Mayans, the Aztecs used the 260-day calendar divided into 13 months of 20 days; they called it *tonalpohualli*, or "count of day." Their 365-day calendar also consisted of 18 months of 20 days plus a period of five days, which the Aztecs believed to be unlucky. The Aztecs also named their days after deities, but, unlike the Mayan system, Aztec numerical notation consisted only of dots. Aztecs probably did not use a Long Count. At the end of their 52-year cycle—which they called *xiuhmolpilli*, or "year bundle"—the Aztecs celebrated the new beginning with a great renewal ceremony (see NEW FIRE CEREMONY).

Today, the 365-day civil calendar predominates throughout the region, though some contemporary Mayans also continue to use the 260-day calendar to observe sacred festivals.

Babylonian Calendar

Babylonian, Sumerian, and Assyrian astronomers living in the Mesopotamian Valley hundreds of years B.C.E. developed calendars that would influence the later Roman Julian and Gregorian calendars. These calendars were based on the phases of the moon and were closely related to the religious life of the cultures that developed them. The influence of the Mesopotamian civilizations on the global art of calendar making was far-reaching because many of the techniques they developed were adopted by future societies.

Of the various cultures that thrived in the Mesopotamian valley, the Babylonians seem to have most significantly influenced calendar making. Many details of the evolution of the Babylonian calendar have been lost over the centuries, but it is known that the calendar was lunar in nature, had a system of intercalation, had months divided into seven-day units, and had days with twenty-four hours.

Because these early calendar makers were pioneers in the field, they were among the first to be confronted with the discrepancy between the lunar and solar cycles—a problem that had the potential to render any calendar system ineffective. To reconcile the two natural courses, the Babylonians worked out a schedule whereby an extra month was periodically intercalated. The process of intercalation, termed *iti dirig*, seems to have been rather arbitrary at first, but by 380 B.C.E. a formal system was adopted adding an extra month in the third, sixth, eighth, eleventh, seventeenth, and nineteenth years. Many other cultures, including the Greeks, developed similar intercalation schemes which may have drawn their inspiration from the Babylonian model.

Although the origin of the week has been a subject of much research and debate among scholars since the time of Plutarch (46-119 C.E.), most agree that the Babylonians are the primary source for the week in the Western civil calendar. Many researchers also conclude that the Babylonians devised the week as a part of their religious practices. They have observed that years, months, and days all reflect natural cycles, but the week does not. This observation has led to some questions: Why does the week have seven days? Why are the days named after celestial bodies? Why are the days not arranged according to the order of the planets in the solar system? Many proposed solutions to these quandaries have surfaced over the course of time.

Details of the Babylonian calendar are few, but some are known. It appears that the major festival was the New Year celebration which took place in the spring of the year during the Babylonian month of Nisanu. On the first day of the festival, a ritual marriage was performed between the king and the high priestess, who symbolized the sovereignty of the land. On this day, the Babylonian creation myth (called *Enuma elish* from its opening words, "When on high") was read aloud. On the fifth day, Rites of Atonement were observed. During the Rites the king, as a representative of the people, endured a ritual of abasement to atone for the sins of the people against the gods. On the seventh day, the Festival of the Sun, or spring equinox, took place.

Zoroastrian Calendars

Zoroastrianism originated in Iran. The religion's founder Zoroaster, thought to have lived around 1200 B.C.E., converted a tribal Iranian prince, Vishtaspa. By the time of the Sasanian dynasty (226-651 B.C.E.), Zoroastrianism was the Persian state religion. After the Muslim conquest of Persia in the middle of the seventh century, many Zoroastrians migrated to India, particularly the western state of Gujarat, where they became known as the "Parsi" (meaning "Persian") community.

The Zoroastrian calendar derived from the ancient Babylonian calendar, except that the former's days and months were dedicated to spiritual beings. In the mid-18th century, some Parsis adopted the Iranian calendar and called it the *qadimi* calendar, giving rise to the Zoroastrian sect known as Kadmi. Others remained with the traditional religion and calendar, though it was a month behind the Kadmi calendar, and were referred to as Shenshais, often rendered Shahanshahis. In 1906, the Fasli sect was founded. It advocated the use of a calendar closer to the Gregorian one, in which the new year would always begin at the vernal equinox and which would add an extra day every four years.

All three Zoroastrian calendars have the same twelve 30-day months with five intercalary days called *Gatha* coming at the end of the twelfth month. The differences are in how each reconciles the lunar year with the natural solar year. As a result, a single date on each Zoroastrian calendar corresponds to three different Gregorian dates. For example, in 2002, the first day of the first month (Frawardin 1) fell on March 21 according to the Fasli calendar, on July 22 according to the Kadmi calendar, and on August 21 according to the Shahanshai calendar.

The Zoroastrian month names and approximate English meanings are:

Frawardin or Fravardin (Humanity) March-April*

Ardwahist or Ardibehest (Truth and Righteousness) April-May

Hordad or Khordad (Perfection) May-June

Tir (Sirius, the Dog Star) June-July

Amurdad or Amardad (Immortality) July-August

Shahrewar or Sherever (Benevolent Dominion) August-September

Mihr or Meher (Fair Dealing) September-October

Aban or Avan (Water or Purity) October-November

Adar or Adur (Fire) November-December

Dae or Deh (Creator) December-January

Vohuman or Bahman (Good Mind) January-February

Spendarmad or Aspandarmad (Holy Devotion) February-March

* Gregorian month ranges corresponding to the Fasli calendar

Roman Julian Calendar

Julius Caesar ordered the change of the reformed Roman lunar calendar to a solar-based one in 46 B.C.E. The intercalation of ninety days corrected a growing discrepancy between the seasons and the months in which they had traditionally fallen. Prior to this intercalation, the Roman civic year had come to be about three months "ahead" of the seasons, so spring began in June. The year 46 B.C.E. was assigned 445 days to make the adjustment; it was called *ultimus annus confusionis,* "the last year of the muddled reckoning." The new calendar, based on the Egyptian solar calendar, provided for a year of 365 days with an additional day in February every fourth year. The addition of this leap year and day gives the Julian year an average length of 365.25 days—very close to the actual solar cycle. The Julian calendar (O.S., or Old Style) remained in civic use in the West for more than 1,600 years, is still the basis of the "Old Calendarist" Orthodox Christian liturgical calendar, and is used by all Orthodox Christian churches to determine the date of Easter.

Jewish Calendar

In 358 C.E., Hillel II introduced a permanent calendar based on mathematical and astronomical calculations, eliminating the need for eyewitness sightings of the new moon with which the new month begins. Due to doubts as to when the new moon appeared, biblical law stated that those living outside Israel would observe two days rather than one for each festival, except for Yom Kippur, the Day of Atonement. The Talmud required that this custom continue even after the calendar was formulated. The Jewish era begins with the date of Creation, traditionally set in 3761 B.C.E.

Only slight modifications were made to Hillel's calendar, and it has remained unchanged since the tenth century. A day is reckoned from sundown to sundown, a week contains seven days, a month is either twenty-nine or thirty days long, and a year has twelve lunar months plus about eleven days, or 353, 354, or 355 days. To reconcile the calendar with the annual solar cycle, a thirteenth month of thirty days is intercalated in the third, sixth, eighth, eleventh, fourteenth, seventeenth, and nineteenth years of a nineteen-year cycle; a leap year may contain from 383 to 385 days. The civil calendar begins with the month of Tishri, the first day of which is Rosh Hashanah, the New Year. The cycle of the religious calendar begins on Nisan 15, Passover (Pesach).

The names of the months of the Jewish calendar were borrowed from the Babylonians. The pre-exilic books of the Bible usually refer to the months according to their numerical order, beginning with Tishri, but there are four months mentioned with different names: Nisan/Abib, Iyyar/Ziv, Tishri/Ethanim, and Heshvan/Bul:

Nisan: mid-March to mid-April

Iyyar: mid-April to mid-May

Sivan: mid-May to mid-June

Tammuz: mid-June to mid-July

Av: mid-July to mid-August

Elul: mid-August to mid-September

Tishri: mid-September to mid-October

Heshvan: mid-October to mid-November

Kislev: mid-November to mid-December

Tevet: mid-December to mid-January

Shevat: mid-January to mid-February

Adar: mid-February to mid-March

*The intercalary month of Adar II is inserted before Adar as needed.

Islamic Calendar

The Islamic calendar, called *hijri* or Hegirian, is still strictly lunar-based. Moreover, the *actual* beginning of a month depends on the sighting of the new moon. Traditionally, if the sky is overcast and the new moon is not visible, the previous month runs another thirty days before the new month begins. However, the *practical* beginning of a month is according to astronomical calculations of lunar cycles. The Islamic era begins July 16, 622 C.E., the date of the hegira or flight into exile of the Prophet Muhammad from Mecca to Medina.

There are twelve Islamic lunar months, some of twenty-nine, others of thirty days; these yield 354 days in the Islamic year. The fixed holidays set in the Islamic calendar thus move "backward" about ten days each year in relation to the Gregorian calendar. In roughly thirty-six years, Ramadan, the Islamic holy month of fasting, moves back through the entire solar year. The Islamic day runs from sundown to sundown.

Other calendars were developed in Islamic countries for the sake of agriculture, which depends on a solar calendar. The Coptic calendar, a variation of the Julian, was used until recently, but is now limited primarily to Egypt and the Sudan, countries with large Coptic populations. The Turkish fiscal calendar, also Julian-based, was used in the Ottoman Empire. Nowadays, the Gregorian calendar is followed nearly everywhere for civic purposes, and the Islamic calendar determines only the days of religious observance. Saudi Arabia is one exception, and, at least officially, employs the Islamic calendar as the calendar of reference.

The names of the Islamic months are an ancient reflection of the seasons of the solar year:

Muharram: the sacred month

Safar: the month which is void

Rabi al-Awwal: the first spring

Rabi ath-Thani: the second spring

Jumada-l-Ula: the first month of dryness

Jumada-th-Thaniyyah: the second month of dryness

Rajab: the revered month

Shaban: the month of division

Ramadan: the month of great heat

Shawwal: the month of hunting

Dhu al-Qadah: the month of rest

Dhu al-Hijjah: the month of pilgrimage

Gregorian Calendar

By the late 16th century, the difference between the Julian calendar and the seasons had grown to ten days because the Julian year, averaging 365.25 days, was slightly longer than the actual length of a solar year, which, by modern calculation, is known to be 365.242199 days long. Fixed holy days began to occur in the "wrong" season, both for the church and for farmers, who used certain holy days to determine planting and harvesting. Pope Gregory XIII ordered the reform that deleted ten days from the year 1582; in that year, October 15 was the day after October 5. This change, coupled with the elimination of leap days in "century" years unless evenly divisible by 400 (e.g., 1600, 2000), corrected the calendar so that today only occasional "leap seconds" are needed to keep months and seasons synchronized. At first adopted only in Roman Catholic countries, the Gregorian calendar (N.S., or New Style) gradually came to be accepted throughout the West, and today has become the calendar used by most of the world, at least for business and government.

Christian Liturgical Calendars

Clearly visible within the Christian liturgical calendar are elements of both the Hebrew and Greek time-keeping systems. Most immediately recognizable, however, are the influences of the Jewish calendar. The movable feasts within Christianity, such as Easter and Pentecost, have connections to Hebrew celebrations.

Many branches of Christianity follow similar calendars to mark the holy days of the year. The calendar focuses attention on special incidents in Jesus's life and also provides for the remembrance of many saints and historical events. It includes two types of dates: movable feasts, which are typically established based on their relationship to the Feast of the Resurrection (Easter), and fixed holidays.

Old and New Calendars

Throughout the centuries the Julian Calendar has been in use in both the Christian East and West. The introduction of the Gregorian Calendar fueled the ever-accelerating animosity between the two Churches. Even though many in the East recognized the inadequacies of the Julian Calendar, leading some to go so far as to devise new calendars for themselves, it nevertheless remained in use throughout the Byzantine period and beyond.

With the introduction of the Gregorian Calendar, Pope Gregory tried to convince the Orthodox to adopt it, but the latter refused because it would alter the dating of Easter. Canon 7 of the Council of Nicea (325) set clear regulations for the dating of Easter. To adopt the Gregorian Calendar would mean having Easter coincide with the Jewish Passover, something clearly against the canonical stipulations.

Orthodox Churches continued to use the Julian Calendar until May of 1923 when the Ecumenical Patriarch Meletios IV convened an "Inter-Orthodox Congress" in Constantinople. Not all Orthodox Churches were represented. Though invited, the Churches of Alexandria, Antioch, and Jerusalem did not attend. The Church of Bulgaria was never asked. Only the Orthodox Churches of Cyprus, Greece, Romania, and Serbia participated. Even then, no unanimous decision was reached regarding the calendar of choice. It has been only in recent years that the Churches of Alexandria, Antioch, Constantinople, Cyprus, Greece, Poland, Romania, and, in 1968, Bulgaria, voted to adopt the new Gregorian Calendar. The Churches of Jerusalem, Russia, and Serbia continue to adhere to the old Julian Calendar.

Western Liturgical Calendar

The western Christian liturgical year begins in late November with a season called Advent. Four weeks long, Advent provides a time during which Christians prepare for Jesus's birth. Advent is followed by Christmas and the Christmas season during which Jesus's birth is celebrated. Epiphany, in early January commemorates Jesus's appearance to the Gentiles (non-Jews). Lent is a season of introspection and penance in preparation for Easter. It concludes with Holy Week, when events in the last week of Jesus's life are highlighted. The Easter season begins on Resurrection Sunday and lasts until Ascension Day, commemorating Jesus's ascension into heaven. The season of Pentecost begins with the celebration of the coming of the Holy Spirit. The longest season of the year, Trinity, completes the cycle.

The revised Roman Catholic calendar of 1969 changed some of the days on which certain saints were honored. Once universally honored days became only locally honored. According to Catholic law, followers are obligated to participate in Mass weekly on either a Saturday evening or Sunday morning and on six other days identified as holy days of obligation: Christmas, Solemnity of Mary, Ascension, Assumption of the Blessed Virgin, All Saints Day, and Immaculate Conception.

Orthodox Liturgical Calendars

In the Orthodox Church, two different calendars determine holidays and feast days. One, attributed to the Roman Emperor Julius Caesar, bears his name. The latter emerged in the 16th century as an effort to correct the discrepancy between calendar time and calculated astronomical time. It added 13 days back into the year and was named for Pope Gregory XIII, who commissioned the work.

There are five main elements to the Orthodox liturgical calendar: the daily cycle, the weekly cycle, the Paschal cycle, the cycle of fixed feasts, and the cycle of eight tones.

In contrast to practice in many other Christian Churches of starting the liturgical year with the first Sunday in Advent, the Orthodox liturgical year begins on September 1. In the Ecumenical Patriarchate this is observed as the Day of the Environment, with the role in the salvation of the world of the Theotokos, the mother of God, being emphasized. The Nativity of the Virgin Mary on September 8 and her Dormition on August 15 come at opposite ends of the liturgical year. Other than those included among the twelve great feasts, the other Marian feast day is December 9, the Conception of the Virgin by St. Anne.

March 25, the Annunciation, is another major feast of the Theotokos, but it is also a feast of the Conception of Christ and begins a series of feasts of the Lord. The Nativity of the Lord, as well as the Visit of the Magi, is observed in the Orthodox Church on December 25. The Circumcision of Jesus falls on January 1, the feast of Saint Basil the Great. For the Orthodox Christian, Epiphany, or Theophany as it is sometimes known, is January 6 and commemorates Christ's baptism. The feast of the Transfiguration is held on August 6.

The Paschal cycle begins four weeks before Lent, on the Sunday of the Pharisee and the Publican. Lent itself begins on Pure Monday and ends on Lazarus Saturday, the day before Palm Sunday. The Passion, the Mystical Supper, the Agony, Betrayal, Trial, Sufferings, Death, Burial and Glorious Resurrection, the Assumption into Heaven of the Lord, and the Sending of His Holy Spirit upon the Apostles are all celebrated in the feasts of the Paschal cycle. The cycle ends with Pentecost Sunday, the feast of the Holy Trinity, and the Sunday of All Saints.

In addition to the special feast days of the Lord or of Mary, every day on the Orthodox Calendar commemorates some saint. These may be saints venerated by all of Christendom, Latin Church saints from early centuries, saints particular to a specific locale, or the Righteous, or Dikaios, of the Old Law. Somewhat anachronistically, the Maccabees are commemorated as though they were Christian martyrs. The Maccabees were the family of Mattathias who, in 167 B.C.E., led the Jewish revolt against Antiochus IV Epiphanes. Even some Latin Church saints from after the Great Schism are recognized, and some Latin feasts, such as Corpus Christi, are observed.

In the medieval period of the Church, all music was organized on the basis of a system of eight tones. These tones continue to have not only musical significance but a calendrical significance as well. Beginning the first Sunday after Easter, St. Thomas Sunday, each successive week uses the texts and music of the next of the eight tones for its offices. Each day of the week has its distinctive hymns and verses for each of these eight tones. The book which contains the texts for each day's services for all eight tones is called the Parakletike.

Baha'i Calendar

The Baha'i calendar, called the Badí (meaning "wondrous"), consists of 19 months, each with 19 days. Four intercalary days—called AYYAM-I-HA, the Days of Ha—occur after the 18th month in regular years, while five are inserted in leap years. Nineteen multiplied by 19 equals 361, plus four intercalary days equals 365. But the number 19 was chosen for more than its mathematical convenience. The Baha'i religion's first prophet, Mirza Ali Mohammad (also known as the BAB), devised a calendar for the new religion. He had 18 followers, thus these 19 original Babis are remembered in the calendar's structure.

The 19-Day Feast takes place on the first day of each month and constitutes the regular Baha'i worship gathering. Each Feast follows the same three-part format: prayer, congregational business, and fellowship with a shared meal.

The Baha'i year begins on the vernal equinox, March 21. Baha'i years are numbered. Year 1 was 1844, the year of the Bab's Declaration. Each Baha'i month is named for an attribute of God:

Bahá (Splendor) March 21

Jalál (Glory) April 9

Jamál (Beauty) April 28

Azamat (Grandeur) May 17

Núr (Light) June 5

Rahmat (Mercy) June 24

Kalimát (Words) July 13

Kamál (Perfection) August 1

Asmá (Names) August 20

'Izzat (Might) September 8

Mashiyyat (Will) September 27

'Ilm (Knowledge) October 16

Qudrat (Power) November 4

Qawl (Speech) November 23

Masá'il (Questions) December 12

Sharaf (Honor) December 31

Sultán (Sovereignty) January 19

Mulk (Dominion) February 7

Ayyam-i-Ha (Days of Ha; intercalary days): February 26-March 1 (February 26-March 2 in leap years)

'Alá' (Loftiness) March 2 (month of fasting)

APPENDIX 3

Comparative Table of Calendar Systems

The Gregorian calendar is based on the solar cycle of 365 days per year, while the Jewish, Hindu, and Burmese calendars are based on the lunar cycle of 29.5 days per month. The first day of the lunar months depicted here is typically the day of the new moon. The lunar months can overlap with the Gregorian months near which they fall. This is reflected in the chart below. While the Burmese calendar is essentially identical to the Hindu, the names of the months differ and are thus represented below. An asterisk (*) denotes the months in which the various New Years fall.

Gregorian Calendar	Jewish Calendar	Hindu, Jain, Buddhist and Sikh Calendar	Burmese Calendar
January*	Shevat	Magha	Tabodwei
February			
	Adar	Phalguna	Tabaung
March			
	Nisan	Caitra*	Tagu*
April			
	Iyyar	Vaisakha*	Kasone
May			
	Sivan	Jyeshta	Nayhone
June			
	Tammuz	Ashadha	Waso
July			
	Av	Sravana	Wagaung
August			
	Elul	Bhadrapada	Tawthalin
September			
	Tishri*	Asvina	Thadingyut
October			
	Heshvan	Kartika	Tazaungmone
November			
	Kislev	Margasirsa	Nadaw
December			
	Tevet	Pausa	Pyatho

APPENDIX 4

Phases of the Moon from 2009 to 2020
Given in Eastern Standard Time

Many cultures and religions have attached great importance to the cycles of the moon as visible from their vantage points on Earth. Thus the moon has significantly influenced the development of various calendars around the world throughout history (*see* Appendix 2, **Calendar Systems around the World**). The changing appearance of the moon in its orbit around Earth has inspired peoples to signify events by relating them to phases of the moon and scheduling holy days and festivals accordingly.

The Muslim calendar is strictly based on the moon. Each month begins with the sighting of the new crescent moon in the sky. Thus, the month-long holy fast of Ramadan begins with the new moon and ends with the next new moon when Id al-Fitr celebrates the end of the fast.

In the Christian calendar the most important holiday—Easter—is scheduled after the first full moon after the vernal equinox.

Hindu calendars appoint particular days within the lunar cycle to celebrate numerous holidays. Many are scheduled on particular days counting from the new moon or the full moon of a month. For example, the spring festival of Holi takes place during the waxing phase of the moon in the month of Phalguna—the period of the lunar month during which the moon appears to become fuller. Likewise, many holidays in the Buddhist and Jain calendars—which are based on the Indian calendars—are observed according to the moon's position.

Traditional Chinese holidays are also scheduled according to a calendar that is partly based on the lunar cycle.

Finally, although many Native American tribes observe special occasions according to solar and seasonal changes, some are scheduled with reference to certain phases of the moon, such as the Iroquois Midwinter Festival, which Longhouse followers traditionally hold five days after the first new moon in January.

The table below gives the dates and times of the four major phases of the moon—new, first quarter, half, and full—in U.S. Eastern Standard Time. For ease of reference, an additional table shows civilian equivalents to military time.

Civilian Time – Military Time

12:00 A.M.. – 00:00	08:00 A.M.. – 08:00	04:00 P.M.. – 16:00
01:00 A.M.. – 01:00	09:00 A.M.. – 09:00	05:00 P.M.. – 17:00
02:00 A.M.. – 02:00	10:00 A.M.. – 10:00	06:00 P.M.. – 18:00
03:00 A.M.. – 03:00	11:00 A.M.. – 11:00	07:00 P.M.. – 19:00
04:00 A.M.. – 04:00	12:00 P.M.. – 12:00	08:00 P.M.. – 20:00
05:00 A.M.. – 05:00	01:00 P.M.. – 13:00	09:00 P.M.. – 21:00
06:00 A.M.. – 06:00	02:00 P.M.. – 14:00	10:00 P.M.. – 22:00
07:00 A.M.. – 07:00	03:00 P.M.. – 15:00	11:00 P.M.. – 23:00

Phases of the Moon – 2009			
New Moon ●	**First Quarter** ◖	**Full Moon** ○	**Last Quarter** ◗
	Jan 4 06:56	Jan 10 22:27	Jan 17 21:46
Jan 26 02:55	Feb 2 18:13	Feb 9 09:49	Feb 16 16:37
Feb 24 20:35	Mar 4 02:46	Mar 10 21:38	Mar 18 12:47
Mar 26 11:06	Apr 2 09:34	Apr 9 09:56	Apr 17 08:36
Apr 24 22:23	May 1 15:44	May 8 23:01	May 17 02:26
May 24 07:11	May 30 22:22	Jun 7 13:12	Jun 15 17:15
Jun 22 14:35	Jun 29 06:28	Jul 7 04:21	Jul 15 04:53
Jul 21 21:35	Jul 28 17:00	Aug 5 19:55	Aug 13 13:55
Aug 20 05:01	Aug 27 06:42	Sep 4 11:03	Sep 11 21:16
Sep 18 13:44	Sep 25 23:50	Oct 4 01:10	Oct 11 03:56
Oct 18 00:33	Oct 25 19:42	Nov 2 14:14	Nov 9 10:56
Nov 16 14:14	Nov 24 16:39	Dec 2 02:30	Dec 8 19:13
Dec 16 07:02	Dec 24 12:36	Dec 31 14:13	

Phases of the Moon – 2010			
New Moon ●	**First Quarter** ◖	**Full Moon** ○	**Last Quarter** ◗
			Jan 7 05:40
Jan 15 02:11	Jan 23 05:53	Jan 30 01:18	Feb 5 18:49
Feb 13 21:51	Feb 21 19:42	Feb 28 11:38	Mar 7 10:42
Mar 15 16:01	Mar 23 06:00	Mar 29 21:25	Apr 6 04:37
Apr 14 07:29	Apr 21 13:20	Apr 28 07:18	May 5 23:15
May 13 20:04	May 20 18:43	May 27 18:07	Jun 4 17:13
Jun 12 06:15	Jun 18 23:30	Jun 26 06:30	Jul 4 09:35
Jul 11 14:40	Jul 18 05:11	Jul 25 20:37	Aug 2 23:59
Aug 9 22:08	Aug 16 13:14	Aug 24 12:05	Sep 1 12:22
Sep 8 05:30	Sep 15 00:50	Sep 23 04:17	Sep 30 22:52
Oct 7 13:44	Oct 14 16:27	Oct 22 20:36	Oct 30 07:46
Nov 5 23:52	Nov 13 11:39	Nov 21 12:27	Nov 28 15:36
Dec 5 12:36	Dec 13 08:59	Dec 21 03:13	Dec 27 23:18

Phases of the Moon – 2011

New Moon ●	First Quarter ◑	Full Moon ○	Last Quarter ◑
Jan 4 04:03	Jan 12 06:31	Jan 19 16:21	Jan 26 07:57
Feb 2 21:31	Feb 11 02:18	Feb 18 03:36	Feb 24 18:26
Mar 4 15:46	Mar 12 18:45	Mar 19 13:10	Mar 26 07:07
Apr 3 09:32	Apr 11 07:05	Apr 17 21:44	Apr 24 21:47
May 3 01:51	May 10 15:33	May 17 06:09	May 24 13:52
Jun 1 16:03	Jun 8 21:11	Jun 15 15:13	Jun 23 06:48
Jul 1 03:54	Jul 8 01:29	Jul 15 01:40	Jul 23 00:02
Jul 30 13:40	Aug 6 06:08	Aug 13 13:58	Aug 21 16:55
Aug 28 22:04	Sep 4 12:39	Sep 12 04:27	Sep 20 08:39
Sep 27 06:09	Oct 3 22:15	Oct 11 21:06	Oct 19 22:30
Oct 26 14:56	Nov 2 11:38	Nov 10 15:16	Nov 18 10:09
Nov 25 01:10	Dec 2 04:52	Dec 10 09:36	Dec 17 19:48
Dec 24 13:06			

Phases of the Moon – 2012

New Moon ●	First Quarter ◑	Full Moon ○	Last Quarter ◑
	Jan 1 01:15	Jan 9 02:30	Jan 16 04:08
Jan 23 02:39	Jan 30 23:10	Feb 7 16:54	Feb 14 12:04
Feb 21 17:35	Feb 29 20:22	Mar 8 04:40	Mar 14 20:25
Mar 22 09:37	Mar 30 14:41	Apr 6 14:19	Apr 13 05:50
Apr 21 02:18	Apr 29 04:58	May 5 22:35	May 12 16:47
May 20 18:47	May 28 15:16	Jun 4 06:12	Jun 11 05:41
Jun 19 10:02	Jun 26 22:30	Jul 3 13:52	Jul 10 20:48
Jul 18 23:24	Jul 26 03:56	Aug 1 22:27	Aug 9 13:55
Aug 17 10:54	Aug 24 08:54	Aug 31 08:58	Sep 8 08:15
Sep 15 21:11	Sep 22 14:41	Sep 29 22:19	Oct 8 02:33
Oct 15 07:02	Oct 21 22:32	Oct 29 14:50	Nov 6 19:36
Nov 13 17:08	Nov 20 09:31	Nov 28 09:46	Dec 6 10:32
Dec 13 03:42	Dec 20 00:19	Dec 28 05:21	

Phases of the Moon – 2013			
New Moon ●	**First Quarter** ◑	**Full Moon** ○	**Last Quarter** ◐
			Jan 4 22:58
Jan 11 14:44	Jan 18 18:45	Jan 26 23:38	Feb 3 08:56
Feb 10 02:20	Feb 17 15:31	Feb 25 15:26	Mar 4 16:53
Mar 11 14:51	Mar 19 12:27	Mar 27 04:27	Apr 2 23:37
Apr 10 04:35	Apr 18 07:31	Apr 25 14:57	May 2 06:14
May 9 19:29	May 17 23:35	May 24 23:25	May 31 13:58
Jun 8 10:56	Jun 16 12:24	Jun 23 06:32	Jun 29 23:54
Jul 8 02:14	Jul 15 22:18	Jul 22 13:15	Jul 29 12:43
Aug 6 16:51	Aug 14 05:56	Aug 20 20:45	Sep 5 06:36
Sep 12 12:08	Sep 19 06:13	Sep 26 22:56	Oct 4 19:35
Oct 11 18:02	Oct 18 18:38	Oct 26 18:41	Nov 3 07:50
Nov 10 00:57	Nov 17 10:16	Nov 25 14:28	Dec 2 19:22
Dec 9 10:12	Dec 17 04:28	Dec 25 08:48	

Phases of the Moon – 2014			
New Moon ●	**First Quarter** ◑	**Full Moon** ○	**Last Quarter** ◐
			Jan 1 06:14
Jan 7 22:39	Jan 15 23:52	Jan 24 00:19	Jan 30 16:39
Feb 6 14:22	Feb 14 18:53	Feb 22 12:15	Mar 1 03:00
Mar 8 08:27	Mar 16 12:09	Mar 23 20:46	Mar 30 13:45
Apr 7 03:31	Apr 15 02:42	Apr 22 02:52	Apr 29 01:14
May 6 22:15	May 14 14:16	May 21 07:59	May 28 13:40
Jun 5 15:39	Jun 12 23:11	Jun 19 13:39	Jun 27 03:09
Jul 5 06:59	Jul 12 06:25	Jul 18 21:08	Jul 26 17:42
Aug 3 19:50	Aug 10 13:09	Aug 17 07:26	Aug 25 09:13
Sep 2 06:11	Sep 8 20:38	Sep 15 21:05	Sep 24 01:14
Oct 1 14:33	Oct 8 05:51	Oct 15 14:12	Oct 23 16:57
Oct 30 21:48	Nov 6 17:23	Nov 14 10:16	Nov 22 07:32
Nov 29 05:06	Dec 6 07:27	Dec 14 07:51	Dec 21 20:36
Dec 28 13:31			

Phases of the Moon – 2015

New Moon ●	First Quarter ◐	Full Moon ○	Last Quarter ◑
	Jan 4 23:53	Jan 13 04:47	Jan 20 08:14
Jan 26 23:48	Feb 3 18:09	Feb 11 22:50	Feb 18 18:47
Feb 25 12:14	Mar 5 13:06	Mar 13 12:48	Mar 20 04:36
Mar 27 02:43	Apr 4 07:06	Apr 11 22:44	Apr 18 13:57
Apr 25 18:55	May 3 22:42	May 11 05:36	May 17 23:13
May 25 12:19	Jun 2 11:19	Jun 9 10:42	Jun 16 09:05
Jun 24 06:03	Jul 1 21:20	Jul 8 15:24	Jul 15 20:24
Jul 23 23:04	Jul 31 05:43	Aug 6 21:03	Aug 14 09:54
Aug 22 14:31	Aug 29 13:35	Sep 5 04:54	Sep 13 01:41
Sep 21 03:59	Sep 27 21:50	Oct 4 16:06	Oct 12 19:06
Oct 20 15:31	Oct 27 07:05	Nov 3 07:24	Nov 11 12:47
Nov 19 01:27	Nov 25 17:44	Dec 3 02:40	Dec 11 05:29
Dec 18 10:14	Dec 25 06:11		

Phases of the Moon – 2016

New Moon ●	First Quarter ◐	Full Moon ○	Last Quarter ◑
		Jan 2 00:30	Jan 9 20:30
Jan 16 18:26	Jan 23 20:46	Jan 31 22:28	Feb 8 09:39
Feb 15 02:46	Feb 22 13:20	Mar 1 18:11	Mar 8 20:54
Mar 15 12:03	Mar 23 07:01	Mar 31 10:17	Apr 7 06:24
Apr 13 22:59	Apr 22 00:24	Apr 29 22:29	May 6 14:30
May 13 12:02	May 21 16:15	May 29 07:12	Jun 4 22:00
Jun 12 03:10	Jun 20 06:02	Jun 27 13:19	Jul 4 06:01
Jul 11 19:52	Jul 19 17:57	Jul 26 18:00	Aug 2 15:45
Aug 10 13:21	Aug 18 04:27	Aug 24 22:41	Sep 1 04:03
Sep 9 06:49	Sep 16 14:05	Sep 23 04:56	Sep 30 19:12
Oct 8 23:33	Oct 15 23:23	Oct 22 14:14	Oct 30 12:38
Nov 7 14:51	Nov 14 08:52	Nov 21 03:33	Nov 29 07:18
Dec 7 04:03	Dec 13 19:06	Dec 20 20:56	Dec 29 01:53

Phases of the Moon – 2017			
New Moon ●	**First Quarter** ◑	**Full Moon** ○	**Last Quarter** ◐
Jan 5 14:47	Jan 12 06:34	Jan 19 17:14	Jan 27 19:07
Feb 3 23:19	Feb 10 19:33	Feb 18 14:33	Feb 26 09:58
Mar 5 06:32	Mar 12 09:54	Mar 20 10:58	Mar 27 21:57
Apr 3 13:39	Apr 11 01:08	Apr 19 04:57	Apr 26 07:16
May 2 21:47	May 10 16:43	May 18 19:33	May 25 14:44
Jun 1 07:42	Jun 9 08:10	Jun 17 06:33	Jun 23 21:31
Jun 30 19:51	Jul 8 23:07	Jul 16 14:26	Jul 23 04:46
Jul 30 10:23	Aug 7 13:11	Aug 14 20:15	Aug 21 13:30
Aug 29 03:13	Sep 6 02:03	Sep 13 01:25	Sep 20 00:30
Sep 27 21:54	Oct 5 13:40	Oct 12 07:25	Oct 19 14:12
Oct 27 17:22	Nov 4 00:23	Nov 10 15:37	Nov 18 06:42
Nov 26 12:03	Dec 3 10:47	Dec 10 02:51	Dec 18 01:31
Dec 26 04:20			

Phases of the Moon – 2018			
New Moon ●	**First Quarter** ◑	**Full Moon** ○	**Last Quarter** ◐
	Jan 1 21:24	Jan 8 17:25	Jan 16 21:17
Jan 24 17:20	Jan 31 08:27	Feb 7 10:54	Feb 15 16:05
Feb 23 03:09	Mar 1 19:51	Mar 9 06:20	Mar 17 08:12
Mar 24 10:35	Mar 31 07:37	Apr 8 02:18	Apr 15 20:57
Apr 22 16:46	Apr 29 19:58	May 7 21:09	May 15 06:48
May 21 22:49	May 29 09:20	Jun 6 13:32	Jun 13 14:43
Jun 20 05:51	Jun 27 23:53	Jul 6 02:51	Jul 12 21:48
Jul 19 14:52	Jul 27 15:20	Aug 4 13:18	Aug 11 04:58
Aug 18 02:49	Aug 26 06:56	Sep 2 21:37	Sep 9 13:01
Sep 16 18:15	Sep 24 21:53	Oct 2 04:45	Oct 8 22:47
Oct 16 13:02	Oct 24 11:45	Oct 31 11:40	Nov 7 11:02
Nov 15 09:54	Nov 23 00:39	Nov 29 19:19	Dec 7 02:20
Dec 15 06:49	Dec 22 12:49	Dec 29 04:34	

Phases of the Moon – 2019

New Moon ●	First Quarter ◐	Full Moon ○	Last Quarter ◑
			Jan 5 20:28
Jan 14 01:45	Jan 21 00:16	Jan 27 16:10	Feb 4 16:04
Feb 12 17:26	Feb 19 10:53	Feb 26 06:28	Mar 6 11:04
Mar 14 05:27	Mar 20 20:43	Mar 27 23:10	Apr 5 03:50
Apr 12 14:06	Apr 19 06:12	Apr 26 17:18	May 4 17:45
May 11 20:12	May 18 16:11	May 26 11:33	Jun 3 05:02
Jun 10 00:59	Jun 17 03:31	Jun 25 04:46	Jul 2 14:16
Jul 9 05:55	Jul 16 16:38	Jul 24 20:18	Jul 31 22:12
Aug 7 12:31	Aug 15 07:29	Aug 23 09:56	Aug 30 05:37
Sep 5 22:10	Sep 13 23:33	Sep 21 21:41	Sep 28 13:26
Oct 5 11:47	Oct 13 16:08	Oct 21 07:39	Oct 27 22:38
Nov 4 05:23	Nov 12 08:34	Nov 19 16:11	Nov 26 10:06
Dec 4 01:58	Dec 12 00:12	Dec 18 23:57	Dec 26 00:13

Phases of the Moon – 2020

New Moon ●	First Quarter ◐	Full Moon ○	Last Quarter ◑
Jan 2 23:45	Jan 10 14:21	Jan 17 07:58	Jan 24 16:42
Feb 1 20:42	Feb 9 02:33	Feb 15 17:17	Feb 23 10:32
Mar 2 14:57	Mar 9 12:48	Mar 16 04:34	Mar 24 04:28
Apr 1 05:21	Apr 7 21:35	Apr 14 17:56	Apr 22 21:26
Apr 30 15:38	May 7 05:45	May 14 09:03	May 22 12:39
May 29 22:30	Jun 5 14:12	Jun 13 01:24	Jun 21 01:41
Jun 28 03:16	Jul 4 23:44	Jul 12 18:29	Jul 20 12:33
Jul 27 07:32	Aug 3 10:59	Aug 11 11:45	Aug 18 21:41
Aug 25 12:58	Sep 2 00:22	Sep 10 04:26	Sep 17 06:00
Sep 23 20:55	Oct 1 16:05	Oct 9 19:39	Oct 16 14:31
Oct 23 08:23	Oct 31 09:49	Nov 8 08:46	Nov 15 00:07
Nov 21 23:45	Nov 30 04:30	Dec 7 19:37	Dec 14 11:17
Dec 21 18:41	Dec 29 22:28		

Source: National Aeronautics and Space Administration, NASA Eclipse Web Site, "Phases of the Moon." Available online at http://eclipse.gsfc.nasa.gov/phase/phase2001gmt.html.

Overview of the World's Major Religions

This section provides basic information about the world's major religions, including when and where they originated; founder(s); theological orientation; major sacred texts; denominations and sects; estimated number of adherents around the world; and a listing of the main holidays in chronological order by the religion's calendar.

Bahá'í

When originated: 1844

Where originated: Iran

Founder(s): Mírzá Husayn-'Ali Núrí (Bahá'u'lláh); Siyyid 'Alí-Muhammad (the Báb)

Basic orientation: Monotheistic

Major sacred texts: Kitáb-i-Aqdas (The Most Holy Book), Kitáb-i-Õqán (Book of Certitude), and others written by Mírzá Husayn-'Ali Núrí (Bahá'u'lláh)

Major denominations and sects: none

Approx. number of adherents: 5 million in about 235 countries

Major holidays in order by the religion's calendar:

Mar 21 – Festival of Naw-Rúz
Apr 21 – May 2 – Festival of Ridván
May 23 – Declaration of the Báb
May 29 – Ascension of Bahá'u'lláh
Jun, second Sun – Race Unity Day
Jul 9 – Martyrdom of the Báb
Oct 20 – Birth of the Báb
Nov 12 – Birth of Bahá'u'lláh
Nov 26 – Day of the Covenant
Nov 28 – Ascension of 'Abdu'l-Bahá
Jan, third Sun – Ayyám-i-Há
Mar 2-20 – Nineteenth-Month Fast

Buddhism

When originated: Sixth century B.C.E.

Where originated: India

Founder(s): Siddhartha Gautama, the Buddha

Basic orientation: Other: achieving enlightenment by accepting the four noble truths—1. There is suffering; 2. Suffering results from desire; 3. The way to end suffering is to end desire; 4. The Eightfold Path shows the way to end suffering—and the Eightfold Path: 1. Right view or right understanding; 2. Right thoughts and aspirations; 3. Right speech; 4. Right conduct and action; 5. Right way of life; 6. Right effort; 7. Right mindfulness; 8. Right contemplation.

Major sacred texts: The Sutras

Major denominations and sects: Theraveda, Mahayana, Tibetan, Chinese, Japanese, Zen

Approx. number of adherents: 500 million worldwide, largely in Asia

Major holidays in order by the religion's calendar:

April 8 or full moon day of Vaisakha - Vesak (birthday of the Buddha)
July 6 - Birthday of the Dalai Lama
July-September - Waso
July-August – Ullambana (Hungry Ghosts Festival)

Christianity - Orthodox

When originated: 30s C.E.

Where originated: Palestine

Founder(s): Jesus of Nazareth

Basic orientation: Monotheistic

Major sacred text: The Bible

Major denominations and sects: Adherents fall under the Patriarchs of Constantinople, Alexandria, Antioch, and Jerusalem; additional congregations include Russia, Serbia, Romania, Bulgaria, Georgia, Cyprus, Greece, Poland, Albania, Armenia, Slovakia, the Czech Republic, and Ukraine

Approx. number of adherents: 250 million worldwide

Major holidays in order by the religion's calendar:

September 8 – Nativity of the Virgin Mary
September 14 – Elevation of the Life-giving Cross
November 21 – Presentation of the Virgin Mary in the Temple
December 25 or January 7 – Christmas
January 6 or January 19 – Epiphany
February 2 – Presentation of Christ in the Temple
March 25 – The Annunciation
April or May – Palm Sunday
April or May – Easter
40 days after Easter – The Ascension
50 days after Easter – Pentecost
August 6 – The Transfiguration
August 15 – The Repose, or Dormition, of the Virgin Mary

Christianity - Western

When originated: 30s C.E.

Where originated: Palestine

Founder(s): Jesus of Nazareth

Basic orientation: Monotheistic

Major sacred text: The Bible

Major denominations and sects: Catholicism, Protestantism, Anglican, Episcopalian

Approx. number of adherents: 1.7 billion

Major holidays in order by the religion's calendar:

December 25 – Christmas
January 1 – Feast of the Circumcision/Solemnity of Mary
January 6 – Epiphany
Sunday after Epiphany – Feast of the Holy Family
February 2 – Presentation of Jesus in the Temple
February (40 days before Easter) - Ash Wednesday
March 25 – The Annunciation
March or April – Palm Sunday
March or April – Maundy or Holy Thursday
March or April – Good Friday
March or April – Easter
40 days after Easter – The Ascension
50 days after Easter – Pentecost
1st Sunday after Pentecost – Trinity Sunday
Thursday after Trinity Sunday – Corpus Christi
May or July – Feast of the Visitation
August 6 – Feast of the Transfiguration
August 15 – The Assumption of the Blessed Virgin
September 8 – Feast of the Nativity of the Blessed Virgin
November 1 – All Saints' Day
November 2 All Souls' Day
November 21 – Feast of the Presentation of the Virgin Mary

Confucianism

When originated: Fifth century B.C.E.

Where originated: China

Founder(s): Confucius

Basic orientation: Other: philosophical, ethical system

Major sacred texts: The "Four Books," *Lun-yu* (The Analects), *Ta-hsueh* (The Great Learning), *Chung Yung* (The Doctrine of the Mean), *Meng-tzu* (The Book of Mencius), and the Five Classics: *Shu Ching* (The Book of History), *Shih Ching* (The Book of Odes), *I Ching* (The Book of Changes), *Ch-un Ch'ui* (Spring and Autumn Annals), and *Li Chi* (The Book of Rites)

Major denominations and sects: School of Thought, School of the Mind, School of Practical Learning

Approx. number of adherents: Five million

Major holidays in order by the religion's calendar:

First Sunday in May – Chongmyo Taeje (Royal Shrine Rite)
September 28 – Confucius's Birthday (Teacher's Day)
During second and eighth Chinese lunar months – Sokjon-Taeje Memorial Rites

Hinduism

When originated: 4000 B.C.E.

Where originated: Indus Valley of the Indian subcontinent

Founder(s): none

Basic orientation: Polytheistic – pantheon includes more than 30 million deities

Major sacred texts: The Vedas and the Epics (*Ramayana*, *Mahabharata*, and *Bhagavad Gita*)

Major denominations and sects: Vaishnavas, Saivites, Rama cults, and Krishna cults

Approx. number of adherents: From 500 million to more than one billion worldwide

Major holidays in order by the religion's calendar: There are hundreds of holidays, feasts, and fasts observed by the world's Hindus (*see index for a listing of those included in this volume*); this list includes only a few of the most widely celebrated.

Vaisakha 1 (April-May) – Vaisakh (Hindu New Year)
2nd day of waxing half of Asadha (June-July) – Rath Yatra full moon day of Sravana (July-August) – Raksha Bandhan
7-10 days during waxing half of Bhadrapada (August-September) – Ganesh Chaturthi
New moon day of Bhadrapada (August-September) – Krishna's Birthday/Janmashtami waxing half of Asvina (September-October) – Durga Purga/Dussehra/ Navaratri
15th day of waning half of Kartika (October-November) – Dewali
14th day of waxing half of Phalguna (February-March) – Holi
14th day of waning half of Phalguna (February-March) – Shivaratri
9th day of waxing half of Caitra (March-April) – Ramanavami

Islam

When originated: Seventh century C.E.

Where originated: Arabia

Founder(s): Muhammad

Basic orientation: Monotheistic

Major sacred text: Koran (or Quran)

Major denominations and sects: Sunni, Shia (or Shi'ite), Sufi, Ibadis (or Kharijites)

Approx. number of adherents: One billion worldwide

Major holidays in order by the religion's calendar:

Muharram 1 – Muharram (New Year)
Muharram 10 – Ashura
Rabi al-Awwal 12 – Mawlid al-Nabi (birthday of Muhammad)
Rajab 27 – Laylat al-Miraj
Ramadan 1-30 – Fast of Ramadan
Ramadan 27 – Laylat al-Qadr
Shawwal 1-3 – Id al-Fitr
Dhu al-Hijjah 8-13 – Hajj (Pilgrimage to Mecca)
Dhu al-Hijjah 10-12 Id al-Adha

Jainism

When originated: Sixth century B.C.E.

Where originated: India

Founder(s): Vardhamana Mahavira

Basic orientation: Polytheistic

Major sacred texts: The angas, the Kalpa Sutra

Major denominations and sects: Digambaras, Svetambaras, Sthanakvasis and Terapanthi

Approx. number of adherents: Four million worldwide, most in India

Major holidays in order by the religion's calendar:

15th day of waning half of Kartika (October-November) – Dewali

10th day of waning half of Pausa (December-January) – Birthday of Parshva

13th day of waxing half of Caitra (March-April) – Mahavir Jayanti (Birthday of Mahavira)

month of Asadha (June-July) to month of Bhadrapada (August-September) – Caturmas

during waning half of Bhadrapada (August-September) – Paryushana

Judaism

When originated: 1800 B.C.E.

Where originated: Palestine

Founder(s): Abraham

Basic orientation: Monotheistic

Major sacred texts: The Torah, Mishnah, and Talmud

Major denominations and sects: Orthodox, Reform (or Progressive), Conservative, Hasidism, Zionism, Reconstructionist

Approx. number of adherents: 13 million in nearly 100 countries worldwide, most in Israel and the United States

Major holidays in order by the religion's calendar:

Nisan 14 – Fast of the First-born
Nisan 15-21 (or 22) – Passover
Nisan 16 – Sivan 5 – Counting of the Omer
Nisan 27 – Yom Hashoah (Holocaust Day)
Iyyar 18 – Lag ba-Omer
Sivan 6 – Shavuot
Tammuz 17 – Fast of the Seventeenth of Tammuz
Tammuz 17 – Av 9 – Three Weeks of Mourning
Av 9 – Tisha be-Av
Tishri 1-2 – Rosh Hashanah (New Year)
Tishri 10 – Yom Kippur
Tishri 15-21 – Sukkot (Fast of Tabernacles)
Tishri 22 – Shemini Atzeret
Tishri 23 – Simhat Torah
Kislev 25 to Tevet 2 – Hanukkah
Tevet 10 – Asarah be-Tevet
Shevat 15 – Tu Bishvat
Adar 13 – Ta-anit Esther (Fast of Esther)
Adar 14 – Purim

Shinto

When originated: Sixth century C.E.

Where originated: Japan

Founder(s): none

Basic orientation: Polytheistic

Major sacred texts: *Kojiki*, *Nihongi*, and *Engishiki*

Major denominations and sects: Shrine Shinto, Sect Shinto, Confucian Shinto

Approx. number of adherents: About three million identify Shinto as their primary religion; about 110 million take part in some way; most adherents are in Japan

Representative holidays included in this volume:

January or February – Hadaka Matsuri
June 17 – Saigusa Matsuri
September 17 – Chinkashiki
October 19 – Bettara-Ichi
Late October to early November – Izumo-taisha Jinzaisai
November – Tori-no-ichi

Sikhism

When originated: Fifteenth century C.E.

Where originated: India

Founder(s): Guru Nanak

Basic orientation: Monotheistic

Major sacred texts: Guru Granth Sahib

Major denominations and sects: Nirankari, Namdhari

Approx. number of adherents: 20 million worldwide, most in India

Major holidays in order by the religion's calendar:

Chait 1 (March-April) – Scriptural New Year
Chait 1 (March-April) – Hola Mohalla
Basakh 1 (April-May) – Baisakhi (Birth of the Khalsa)
Basakh 1 (April-May) – Guru Parab (Guru Nanak's Day)
Har 2 (June-July) – Martyrdom of Guru Arjun
Sawan 8 (July-August) - Birthday of Guru Har Krishan
Bhadro 17 (August-September) – Installation of the Guru Granth Sahib
Asun 25 (September-October) – Birthday of Guru Ram Das
Magar 11 (November-December) – Martyrdom of Guru Teg Bahadur
Poh 23 (December-January) – Guru Gobind Singh's Birthday
During month of Magh (January-February) - Maghi

Taoism

When originated: Fifth century B.C.E.

Where originated: China

Founder(s): Lao Tzu

Basic orientation: Polytheistic

Major sacred texts: *Tao-tsang*

Major denominations and sects: Heavenly Masters, Perfect Truth

Approx. number of adherents: 20 million

Major holidays in order by the religion's calendar:

23rd day of third Chinese month (March-April) – Matsu Festival
8th day of fourth Chinese month (April-May) – Tam Kung Festival

8th-9th days of fourth Chinese month (April-May) – Birthday of the Third Prince

13th day of sixth Chinese month (June-July) – Birthday of Lu Pan

Full moon day of seventh Chinese month (July-August) – Festival of Hungry Ghosts

First 9 days of ninth Chinese month (September-October) – Festival of the Nine Imperial Gods

During ninth Chinese month (September-October) – Monkey God Festival

During 12th Chinese month (December-January) – Ta Chiu

Zoroastrianism

When originated: Before 1500 B.C.E.

Where originated: Iran

Founder(s): Zoroastr (Zarathustra)

Basic orientation: Monotheistic

Major sacred texts: The Avesta

Major denominations and sects: None, though adherents follow one of three calendars: Fasli, Shahanshahi, and Qadimi. Each calendar has the same named months, but their Gregorian equivalents vary.

Approx. number of adherents: 150,000-180,000 worldwide

Major holidays in order by the religion's calendar:

Frawardin 1 – Nawruz (New Year)
Frawardin 6 – Khordad Sal
Frawardin 19 – Feast of Frawardin
Ardwahist 3 – Feast of Ardwahist
Ardwahist 11-15 – Maidyozarem
Hordad 6 – Feast of Hordad
Tir 11-15 – Maidyoshahem
Tir 13 – Tiragan
Amurdad 7 – Feast of Amurdad
Shahrewar 4 – Feast of Shahrewar
Shahrewar 26-30 – Paitishahem
Mihr 1 – Feast of Mithra
Mihr 16 – Mihragan
Mihr 26-30 – Ayathrem
Aban 10 – Aban Parab
Adar 9 – Adar Parab
Dae 1, 8, 15, and 23 – Feasts of Dae
Dae 11 – Zarthastno Diso
Dae 16-20 – Maidyarem
Vohuman 2 – Feast of Vohuman
Spendarmad 5 – Feast of Spendarmad
Spendarmad 26-30 – Farvardegan Days

Facts about the U.S. States and Territories

This section lists for each of the 50 states: the date and order of admission to the Union; information about current or past admission day observances, if applicable; state nicknames, mottoes, animals, flowers, and other symbols; reference sources noting the admission day; and web sites and offices to contact for further information. This last item includes governor's offices, secretaries of state, and state libraries. For territories, listed are year of association with the U.S.; nicknames, mottoes, flowers, and other symbols; and web sites and offices to contact.

Alabama

Twenty-second state; admitted on December 14, 1819 (seceded from the Union on January 11, 1861, and was readmitted on June 25, 1868)

Alabama does not observe the anniversary of its admission day, but did hold festivities in 1969 in honor of the 150th, or sesquicentennial, anniversary of statehood. There were historical pageants, a boat parade, formal balls, music, fireworks, and the issuance of a commemorative stamp. The state was named for a southern Indian tribe, possibly a subdivision of the Chickasaws.

State capital: Montgomery
Nicknames: The Heart of Dixie; The Yellowhammer State; The Cotton State
State motto: *Audemus jura nostra defendere* (Latin "We dare maintain our rights")
State agricultural museum: Dothan Landmarks Park
State amphibian: Red Hills Salamander (*Phaeognathus hubrichti Highton*)
State barbecue championship: Demopolis Christmas on the River Barbecue Cook-Off
State bible: The Bible
State bird: Yellowhammer or Common Flicker (*Colaptes auratus*)
State butterfly and mascot: Easter tiger swallowtail
State championship horse show: Alabama State Championship Horse Show
State creed: Alabama's Creed
State folk dance: Square dance
State fish: saltwater: Fighting tarpon (*Tarpon atlanticus*); **freshwater**: Largemouth bass (*Micropterus salmoides*)
State flower: Camellia (*Camellia japonica L.*); **wildflower**: Oak-leaf Hydrangea (*Hydrangea quercifolia Bartr*)
State fossil: Basilosaurus cetoides
State fruit: Blackberry
State game bird: Wild turkey
State gemstone: Star blue quartz
State historic theatre: Alabama Theatre for the Performing Arts
State horse: Racking horse
State horseshoe tournament: Stockton Fall Horseshoe Tournament

State insect: Monarch butterfly (*Danaus plexipuss*)
State mammal: Black bear
State mineral: Hematite (red iron ore)
State nut: Pecan
State outdoor drama: *The Miracle Worker*
State outdoor musical drama: *The Incident at Looney's Tavern*
State quilt: Pine Burr Quilt
State Renaissance faire: Florence Renaissance faire
State reptile: Red-bellied turtle (*Pseudemys alabamensis*)
State rock: Marble
State shell: Johnstone's Junonia (*Scaphella junonia johnstoneae*)
State soil: Bama soil series
State song: "Alabama"
State spirit: Conecuh Ridge Alabama Fine Whiskey
State stone: Marble
State tree: Southern Longleaf Pine (*Pinus palustris Miller*)
State tree fruit: Peach

More about state symbols at:

http://www.archives.state.al.us/kids_emblems/index.html

SOURCES:

AmerBkDays-2000, p. 829
AnnivHol-2000, p. 208

STATE OFFICES:

State web site:
http://www.alabama.gov

Office of the Governor
State Capitol 600 Dexter Ave
Suite N-104
Montgomery, AL 36130
334-242-7100
fax: 334-353-0004
http://www.governor.state.al.us

Secretary of State
PO Box 5616
Montgomery, AL 36103
334-242-7200
fax: 334-242-4993
http://www.sos.state.al.us

Alabama Public Library Service
6030 Monticello Dr
Montgomery, AL 36130
334-213-3900
fax: 334-213-3993
http://www.apls.state.al.us

Archives & History Dept
624 Washington Ave
Montgomery, AL 30130
334-242-4435
fax: 334-240-3433
http://www.archives.state.al.us

Alaska

Forty-ninth state; admitted on January 3, 1959

SEE ALASKA DAY

State capital: Juneau
Nickname: The Last Frontier
State motto: North to the Future
State bird: Willow ptarmigan (*Lagopus lagopus*)
State fish: Chinook (king) salmon (*Oncorhynchus tshawytscha*)
State flower: Forget-me-not (*Myosotis sylvatica* or *M. scorpioides*)
State fossil: Woolly mammoth (*Mammuthus primigenius*)
State gem: Jade
State insect: Four spot skimmer dragonfly
State land mammal: Moose
State marine mammal: Bowhead whale (*Balaena mysticetus*)
State mineral: Gold
State song: "Alaska's Flag"
State sport: Dogteam racing (mushing)
State tree: Sitka spruce (*Picea sitchensis*)

More about state symbols at:

http://www.commerce.state.ak.us/oed/student_info/student.htm

SOURCES:
AmerBkDays-2000, p. 16
AnnivHol-2000, p. 3

STATE OFFICES:
State web site:
http://www.state.ak.us

Office of the Governor
PO Box 110011
Juneau, AK 99811
907-465-3500
fax: 907-465-3532
http://www.gov.state.ak.us

Alaska State Library
PO Box 110571
Juneau, AK 99811
907-465-2910
fax: 907-465-2151
http://www.library.state.ak.us

Arizona

Forty-eighth state; admitted on February 14, 1912

State capital: Phoenix
Nickname: Grand Canyon State
State motto: *Ditat Deus* (Latin "God Enriches")
State amphibian: Arizona tree frog (*Hyla eximia*)
State bird: Cactus wren (*Campylorhynchus brunneicapillus*)
State butterfly: Two-tailed swallowtail
State colors: Federal blue and old gold
State fish: Apache trout (*Salmo apache*)
State flower: Blossom of the saguaro cactus (*Carnegiea gigantea*)
State fossil: Petrified wood
State gem: Turquoise
State mammal: Ringtail (*Bassariscus astutus*)
State neckwear: Bola tie
State reptile: Arizona ridge-nosed rattlesnake (*Crotalus willardi*)
State songs: "Arizona March Song" and "Arizona"
State tree: Palo Verde (*Cercidium floridum*)

More about state symbols at:

http://www.governor.state.az.us/kids/State_Facts.asp
http://www.lib.az.us/museum/symbols.cfm

SOURCES:
AmerBkDays-2000, p. 141
AnnivHol-2000, p. 27

STATE OFFICES:
State web site:
http://www.az.gov

Office of the Governor
1700 W Washington St
Executive Tower 9th Fl
Phoenix, AZ 85007
602-542-4331
fax: 602-542-7601
http://www.governor.state.az.us

Secretary of State
1700 W Washington St
West Wing 7th Fl
Phoenix, AZ 85007
602-542-4285
fax: 602-542-1575
http://www.azsos.gov

Arizona State Library
1700 W Washington St
Rm 200
Phoenix, AZ 85007
602-542-4035
fax: 602-542-4972
http://www.lib.az.us

Arkansas

Twenty-fifth state; admitted on June 15, 1836 (seceded from the Union on May 6, 1861, and was readmitted in June 1868)

The state was named for Ohio Valley Indians' name for the Quapaw Indians who lived in northern Arkansas.

State capital: Little Rock
Nickname: The Natural State
State motto: *Regnat populus* (Latin "The people rule")
State beverage: Milk
State bird: Mockingbird (*Mimus polyglottos*)
State flower: Apple blossom (*Malus sylvestris*)
State folk dance: Square dance
State fruit and vegetable: South Arkansas vine-ripe pink tomato
State gem: Diamond
State insect: Honeybee (*Apis mellifera*)
State mammal: White-tail deer
State mineral: Quartz crystal
State musical instrument: Fiddle
State rock: Bauxite
State songs: "Arkansas," "Arkansas (You Run Deep in Me)," "Oh Arkansas," and "The Arkansas Traveler"
State tree: Pine (*Pinus palustris*)

More about state symbols at:
http://www.soskids.arkansas.gov/k-4-history-state-symbols. html

SOURCES:
AmerBkDays-2000, p. 448
AnnivHol-2000, p. 101

STATE OFFICES:
State web site:
http://www.arkansas.gov

Office of the Governor
State Capitol Bldg
Little Rock, AR 72201
501-682-2345
fax: 501-682-1382
http://www.arkansas.gov/governor

Secretary of State
State Capitol Bldg
Rm 256
Little Rock, AR 72201
501-682-1010
fax: 501-682-3510
http://www.sosweb.state.ar.us

Arkansas State Library
1 Capitol Mall
5th Fl
Little Rock, AR 72201
501-682-1527
fax: 501-682-1529
http://www.asl.lib.ar.us

California

Thirty-first state; admitted on September 9, 1850

City and state offices, banks, and public schools close in California to mark this legal holiday on the first Monday in September. Two organizations—the Native Sons of the Golden West and the Native Daughters of the Golden West—have sponsored annual programs in different locations throughout the state each year. In addition, many communities hold festivities of their own, including parades, music, food, and dancing.

State capital: Sacramento
Nickname: The Golden State
State motto: *Eureka* (Greek "I Have Found It")
State animal: California grizzly bear (*Ursus* (*arctos*) *horribilis*)
State bird: California valley quail (*Callipepla californica*)
State colors: Yale blue and golden yellow
State dance: West Coast swing dance
State fife and drum band: The California Consolidated Drum Band
State fish: South Fork golden trout (*Salmo aguabonita*)
State folk dance: Square dance
State fossil: California saber-toothed cat (*Smilodon californicus*)
State flower: California poppy (*Eschscholtzia californica*)
State gemstone: Benitoite
State gold rush ghost town: Bodie
State grass: Purple needlegrass (*Nassella pulchra*)
State insect: California dog-face butterfly (flying pansy)
State marine fish: Garibaldi
State marine mammal: California gray whale (*Eschrichtius robustus*)
State military museum: The California State Military Museum and Resource Center
State mineral: Native gold
State prehistoric artifact: Chipped stone bear
State reptile: California desert tortoise (*Gopherus agassizii*)
State rock: Serpentine
State silver rush ghost town: Calico
State soil: San Joaquin soil
State song: "I Love You, California"
State tall ship: Californian
State tartan: California State Tartan
State theater: Pasadena Playhouse
State trees: Two species of California redwoods (*Sequoia sempervirens* and *Sequoia gigantea*)

More about the state at:
http://www.learncalifornia.org/doc.asp?ID=678

SOURCES:
AmerBkDays-2000, p. 636
AnnivHol-2000, p. 152

CONTACT:
Native Daughters of the Golden West
543 Baker St.
San Francisco, CA 94117-1405
800-994-6349
415-563-9091
fax: 415-563-5230
http://www.ndgw.org
ndgwgpo@mindspring.com

Native Sons of the Golden West
414 Mason St.
San Francisco, CA 94102
415-392-1223
fax: 415-392-1224
http://www.nsgw.org/sesqui.html
nsgwgp@pacbell.net

STATE OFFICES:
State web site:
http://www.ca.gov

Office of the Governor
State Capitol
1st Fl
Sacramento, CA 95814
916-445-2841
fax: 916-445-4633
http://www.governor.ca.gov

Secretary of State
1500 11th St
Sacramento, CA 95814
916-653-6814
fax: 916-653-4620
http://www.ss.ca.gov

California State Library
914 Capitol Mall
Sacramento, CA 95814
916-654-0261
fax: 916-654-0241
http://www.library.ca.gov

Colorado

Thirty-eighth state; admitted on August 1, 1876

State capital: Denver
Nickname: Centennial State
State motto: *Nil sine Numine* (Latin "Nothing without the Diety")
State animal: Rocky Mountain bighorn sheep (*Ovis canadensis*)
State bird: Lark bunting (*Calamospiza melanocoryus Stejneger*)
State fish: Greenback cutthroat trout (*Oncorhynchus clarki somias*)
State flower: Columbine (*Aguilegia caerules*)
State folk dance: Square dance
State fossil: Stegosaurus
State gem: Aquamarine
State grass: Blue Grama
State insect: Colorado Hairstreak Butterfly (*Hypaurotis cysalus*)
State mineral: Rhodochrosite
State rock: Yule marble
State song: "Where the Columbines Grow" and "Rocky Mountain High"
State tartan: Colorado State Tartan
State tree: Colorado blue spruce (*Picea pungens*)

More about state symbols at:
http://www.colorado.gov/dpa/doit/archives/history/symbemb.htm

SOURCES:
AmerBkDays-2000, p. 555
AnnivHol-2000, p. 128
DictDays-1988, p. 22

STATE OFFICES:
State web site:
http://www.colorado.gov

Office of the Governor
136 State Capitol Bldg
Denver, CO 80203
303-866-2471

fax: 303-866-2003
http://www.colorado.gov/governor

Secretary of State
1700 Broadway
2nd Fl
Denver, CO 80290
303-894-2200
fax: 303-894-4860
http://www.sos.state.co.us

Colorado State Library
201 E Colfax Ave
Rm 309
Denver, CO 80203
303-866-6900
fax: 303-866-6940
http://www.cde.state.co.us/index_library.htm

Connecticut

Fifth state; adopted the U.S. Constitution on January 9, 1788

State capital: Hartford
Nickname: The Constitution State
State motto: *Qui Transtulit Sustinet* (Latin "He Who Transplanted Still Sustains")
State aircraft: Corsair F4U
State animal: Sperm whale (*Physeter macrocephalus*)
State bird: American robin (*Turdus migratorius*)
State cantata: "The Nutmeg"
State composer: Charles Edward Ives (1874-1954)
State fish: American shad
State flagship: *Schooner Amistad*
State flower: Mountain laurel (*Kalmia latifolia*)
State folk dance: Square dance
State fossil: *Eubrontes giganteus*
State hero: Nathan Hale (1755-1776)
State heroine: Prudence Crandall (1803-1890)
State insect: European (praying) mantis (*Mantis religiosa*)
State mineral: Garnet
State shellfish: Eastern oyster (*Crassostrea virginica*)
State ship: *USS Nautilus* (first nuclear-powered submarine)
State song: "Yankee Doodle"
State tartan: Connecticut State Tartan
State tree: Charter oak or white oak (*Quercus alba*)

More about state symbols at:
http://www.kids.ct.gov

SOURCES:
AmerBkDays-2000, p. 41
AnnivHol-2000, p. 7

STATE OFFICES:
State web site:
http://www.ct.gov

Office of the Governor
210 Capitol Ave
Hartford, CT 06106
860-566-4840
fax: 860-524-7395
http://www.ct.gov/governorrell

Secretary of State
210 Capitol Ave

Rm 104
Hartford, CT 06106
860-509-6200
fax: 860-509-6209
http://www.sots.state.ct.us

Connecticut State Library
231 Capitol Ave
Hartford, CT 06106
860-757-6510
fax: 860-757-6503
http://www.cslib.org

Delaware

First state; adopted the U.S. Constitution on December 7, 1787

December 7 is Delaware Day, commemorating the day it became the first state to ratify the Constitution. In 1939, the state legislature decreed that a commission be set up to organize the annual celebration. Since then, the observance has consisted mainly of the singing of patriotic songs, recitations of the Pledge of Allegiance and "Our Heritage," a poem by Herman Hanson, and speeches and readings on the state's history.

State capital: Dover
Nicknames: The First State; The Diamond State; The Blue Hen State
State motto: Liberty and Independence
State beverage: Milk
State bird: Blue Hen
State butterfly: Tiger Swallowtail
State fish: Weakfish (*Cynoscion regalis*)
State flower: Peach blossom (*Prunus persica*)
State fossil: Belemnite
State herb: Sweet golden rod
State insect: Ladybug (*Hippodamia convergens*)
State macroinvertebrate: Stonefly
State marine animal: Horseshoe crab
State mineral: Sillimanite
State soil: Greenwich Loam
State song: "Our Delaware"
State star: Delaware Diamond
State tree: American holly (*Ilex opaca*)

More about state symbols at:
http://www.delaware.gov/egov/portal.nsf/portal
   /aboutfactsandsymbols
http://www.destatemuseums.org/education/Homework/
   statefacts.shtml

SOURCES:
AmerBkDays-2000, p. 815
AnnivHol-2000, p. 203

STATE OFFICES:
State web site:
http://www.delaware.gov

Office of the Governor
150 William Penn St
2nd Fl
Dover, DE 19901
302-577-3210
fax: 302-739-2775
http://www.state.de.us/governor

Secretary of State
401 Federal St
Suite 3
Dover, DE 19901
302-739-4111
fax: 302-739-3811
http://www.state.de.us/sos/sos.shtml

Delaware Div of Libraries
43 S DuPont Hwy
Dover, DE 19901
302-739-4748
fax: 302-739-6787
http://state.lib.de.us/

District of Columbia

Established as a municipal corporation on February 21, 1871

Motto: Justitia omnibus (Latin, "Justice to all")
Flower: American Beauty rose
Tree: Scarlet oak
Bird: Wood thrush

DISTRICT OFFICE:
Government web site:
http://www.dc.gov

Executive Office of the Mayor
1350 Pennsylvania Ave NW
Suite 316
Washington, DC 20004
http://www.dc.gov/index.asp

Florida

Twenty-seventh state; admitted on March 3, 1845 (seceded from the Union on January 10, 1861, and was readmitted on June 25, 1868)

Florida does not hold regular admission day celebrations, but a centennial observance did occur in 1945. A three-cent stamp was issued, schools gave presentations, and there were local exhibits and commemorations. The Library of Congress hosted an exhibit on Florida from March 3 through May 31.

SEE ALSO PASCUA FLORIDA DAY

State capital: Tallahassee
Nicknames: The Sunshine State; Alligator State; Everglades State; Southernmost State; Orange State
State motto: In God We Trust
State animal: Florida panther (*Felis concolor*)
State beverage: Orange juice
State bird: Mockingbird (*Mimus polyglottos*)
State butterfly: Zebra longwing
State fish: **freshwater**: Largemouth bass (*Micropterus salmoides*); **saltwater**: Atlantic sailfish (*Istiophorus platypterus*)
State flower: Orange blossom; **wildflower**: Coreopsis
State gem: Moonstone
State marine mammals: Manatee (*Trichechus manatus*) and porpoise (dolphin) (*Tursiops truncatus*)
State reptile: American alligator (*alligator mississippiensis*)
State shell: Horse conch (*Pleuroploca gigantea*)

State soil: Myakka fine sand
State song: "Old Folks at Home" (also known as "Swanee River")
State stone: Agatized coral
State tree: Sabal palm (*Sabal palmetto*)

More about state symbols at:
http://dhr.dos.state.fl.us/facts/symbols/

SOURCES:
AmerBkDays-2000, p. 181
AnnivHol-2000, p. 38

STATE OFFICES:
State web site:
http://www.myflorida.com

Office of the Governor
State Capitol
Tallahassee, FL 32399
850-488-4441
fax: 850-487-0801
http://www.myflorida.com

Secretary of State
500 S Bronough St
Tallahassee, FL 32399
850-245-6500
fax: 850-245-6125
http://www.dos.state.fl.us

State Library of Florida
500 S Bronough St
Tallahassee, FL 32399
850-245-6600
fax: 850-245-6651
http://dlis.dos.state.fl.us/stlib

Georgia

Fourth state; adopted the U.S. Constitution on January 2, 1788 (seceded from the Union on January 19, 1861, and was readmitted on July 15, 1870)

State capital: Atlanta
Nicknames: The Empire State of the South; The Peach State; The Goober State; The Peachtree State
State motto: Wisdom, Justice, Moderation
State amphibian: green tree frog
State art museum: Georgia Museum of Art
State atlas: Atlas of Georgia
State ballet: Atlanta Ballet
State beef cook off: Shoot the Bull
State bird: Brown thrasher (*Toxostoma rufum*)
State botanical garden: State Botanical Garden of Georgia
State butterfly: Tiger swallowtail (*Papilio glaucus*)
State creed: Georgian's creed
State crop: Peanut
State fish: Largemouth bass (*Micropterus salmoides*)
State flower: Cherokee rose (*Rosa laevigata*); **wildflower**: Azalea (*Rhododendron*)
State folk dance: Square dance
State folk festival: Georgia Folk Festival
State folk life play: *Swamp Gravy*
State fossil: Shark tooth
State fruit: Peach

State game bird: Bobwhite quail
State gem: Quartz
State historic drama: *The Reach of Song*
State insect: Honeybee (*Apis mellifera*)
State marine mammal: Right whale (*Baleana glacialin*)
State mineral: Staurolite
State musical theater: Jekyll Island Musical Theater Festival
State peanut monument: Turner County Peanut Monument
State pork cook off: Slosheye Trail Big Pig Jig
State 'possum: Pogo 'possum
State poultry: "Poultry Capital of the World"
State prepared food: Grits
State railroad museum: Historic Railroad Shops
State reptile: Gopher tortoise
State seashell: Knobbed whelk (*Busycon carica*)
State school: Plains High School
State song: "Georgia on My Mind"
State tartan: Georgia tartan
State theater: Springer Opera House
State transportation history museum: Southeastern Railway Museum
State tree: Live oak (*Quercus virginiana*)
State vegetable: Vidalia sweet onion
State waltz: "Our Georgia"

More about state symbols at:
http://sos.georgia.gov/state_symbols/state_symbols.html

More about the state at:
http://sos.georgia.gov/archives

SOURCES:
AmerBkDays-2000, p. 14
AnnivHol-2000, p. 3

STATE OFFICES:
State web site:
http://www.georgia.gov

Office of the Governor
State Capitol
Rm 203
Atlanta, GA 30334
404-656-1776
fax: 404-657-7332
http://www.gov.state.ga.us

Secretary of State
State Capitol
Rm 214
Atlanta, GA 30334
404-656-2881
fax: 404-656-0513
http://www.sos.state.ga.us

Georgia Public Library Services
1800 Century Pl
Suite 150
Atlanta, GA 30345
404-982-3560
fax: 404-982-3563
http://www.georgialibraries.org

Hawaii

Fiftieth state; admitted on August 21, 1959

Hawaii's admission day anniversary is observed as a state holiday on the third Friday in August every year.

State capital: Honolulu
Nicknames: Aloha State; Paradise of the Pacific; Pineapple State
State motto: *Ua mau ke ea o ka aina i ka pono* (Hawaiian "The Life of the Land Is Perpetuated in Righteousness")
State bird: Nene (pronounced nay-nay) or Hawaiian goose (*Nesochen sandvicensis*)
State fish: Humuhumunukunukuapua'a (not official; rectangular trigger fish, *Rhinecantus aculeatus*)
State flower: Pua aloalo (Yellow hibiscus, *Hibiscus brackenridgei*)
State gem: Black coral
State language: English and Hawaiian
State mammal: Hawaiian monk seal (ilio-holo-i-ka-uaua; *Monachus schauinslandi*)
State marine mammal: Humpback whale
State song: "Hawaii Ponoi"
State tree: Kukui (Candlenut, *Aleurites moluccana*)

More about state symbols at:
http://hawaii.gov/dbedt/info/economic/library/facts/photos

More about the state at:
http://hawaii.gov/dbedt/info/economic/library/facts/state

SOURCES:
AmerBkDays-2000, p. 600
AnnivHol-2000, p. 146

STATE OFFICES:
State web site:
http://www.hawaii.gov

Office of the Governor
415 S Beretania St
State Capitol
Honolulu, HI 96813
808-586-0034
fax: 808-586-0006
http://gov.state.hi.us

Hawaii State Public Library
478 S King St
Honolulu, HI 96813
808-586-3505
http://www.hcc.hawaii.edu/hspls

Idaho

Forty-third state; admitted on July 3, 1890

In 1963, Idaho held a centennial celebration marking the anniversary of its becoming a territory of the United States. From June 27 to July 6, numerous activities were sponsored by more than 165 organizations in the Boise area, including "Old Fashioned Bargain Days," balls, parades, singing, street dancing, fireworks, a rifle shoot, sports events, an art exhibit, rodeo, picnics, a poetry reading, an air show, and a historical pageant presenting memorable episodes from the state's history.

State capital: Boise
Nickname: Gem State
State motto: *Esto perpetua* (Latin "Let it be perpetual")
State bird: Mountain bluebird (*Sialia arctcia*)
State fish: Cutthroat trout (*Salmo clarki*)
State flower: Syringa (*Philadelphus lewisii*)
State folk dance: Square dance
State fossil: Hagerman horse (*Equus simplicidens*)
State fruit: huckleberry (*Vaccinium membranaceum*)
State gem: Star garnet
State horse: Appaloosa
State insect: Monarch butterfly (*Danaus plexippus*)
State raptor: Peregrine falcon (*falco peregrinus*)
State song: "Here We Have Idaho"
State tree: Western white pine (*Pinus monticola pinaceae*)
State vegetable: Potato

More about state symbols at:
http://gov.idaho.gov/fyi/symbols/symbols_index.html

SOURCES:
AmerBkDays-2000, p. 498
AnnivHol-2000, p. 111

STATE OFFICES:
State web site:
http://www.idaho.gov

Office of the Governor
State Capitol Bldg
2nd Fl
Boise, ID 83720
208-334-2100
fax: 208-334-3454
http://gov.idaho.gov

Secretary of State
700 W Jefferson St
Rm 203
Boise, ID 83720
208-334-2300
fax: 208-334-2282
http://www.idsos.state.id.us

Idaho Commission for Libraries
325 W State St
Boise, ID 83702
208-334-2150
fax: 208-334-4016
http://libraries.idaho.gov/

Illinois

Twenty-first state; admitted on December 3, 1818

The 150th, or sesquicentennial, anniversary of Illinois' statehood was celebrated throughout the state during 1968. In December 1967, a year-long exhibit on Illinois history opened at Chicago's Field Museum of Natural History. Miniature replicas of historic rooms—Carl Sandburg's birthplace, Jane Addams's Hull House office, and the Palmer House Hotel's Silver Dollar Barber Shop of 1875—were on display in Carson Pirie Scott department stores. Lincoln's birthday on February 12 was observed with programs commemorating his career in Illinois. On July 4, there was a parade, drama, musical events, fireworks, and speeches at Steeleville. As part of the year-long celebration, the Old State House in Springfield was restored.

State capital: Springfield
Nicknames: Prairie State; Land of Lincoln; Corn State
State motto: State Sovereignty, National Union
State animal: White-tailed deer (*Odocoileus virginianus*)
State amphibian: Eastern tiger salamander
State bird: Cardinal (*Cardinalis cardinalis*)
State dance: Square dance
State fish: Bluegill (*Lepomis macrochirus*)
State flower: Violet (*Viola*)
State fossil: Tully Monster (*Tullimonstrum gregarium*)
State insect: Monarch butterfly (*Danaus plexippus*)
State mineral: Fluorite
State prairie grass: Big bluestem (*Andropogon furcatus*)
State reptile: Painted turtle
State song: "Illinois"
State tree: White oak (*Quercus alba*)

More about state symbols at:
http://www.illinois.gov/facts/symbolsdesc.cfm
http://www.state.il.us/kids/learn/symbols/default.htm

More about the state at:
http://www.illinois.gov/facts/history.cfm

SOURCES:
AmerBkDays-2000, p. 809
AnnivHol-2000, p. 201

STATE OFFICES:
State web site:
http://www.illinois.gov

Office of the Governor
State Capitol Bldg
Rm 207
Springfield, IL 62706
217-782-6830
fax: 217-782-1853
http://www.illinois.gov/gov

Secretary of State
State Capitol Bldg
Rm 213
Springfield, IL 62756
217-782-2201
fax: 217-785-0358
http://www.sos.state.il.us

Illinois State Library
300 S 2nd St
Springfield, IL 62701
217-782-2994
fax: 217-785-4326
http://www.cyberdriveillinois.com/departments/library
  /home.html

Indiana

Nineteenth state; admitted on December 11, 1816

Indiana Day, December 11, is not a legal holiday, but has been observed sporadically since Indiana's General Assembly proclaimed the holiday in February 1925. Schools often hold commemorative programs. The sesquicentennial anniversary

in 1966, however, was marked throughout that year with historical pageants and recreations of such notable events as the signing of the state's constitution.

State capital: Indianapolis
Nickname: Hoosier State
State motto: The Crossroads of America
State bird: Cardinal (*Cardinalis cardinalis*)
State flower: Peony (*Paeonia*)
State language: English
State poem: "Indiana"
State river: Wabash
State song: "On the Banks of the Wabash, Far Away"
State stone: Indiana limestone
State tree: Tulip tree (yellow poplar; *Liriodendron tulipfera*)

More about state symbols at:
http://www.in.gov/history/2522.htm

More about the state at:
http://www.in.gov/about.htm
http://www.in.gov/history/5699.htm

SOURCES:
AmerBkDays-2000, p. 825
AnnivHol-2000, p. 206
DictDays-1988, p. 59

STATE OFFICES:
State web site:
http://www.in.gov

Office of the Governor
State House
200 W Washington St Rm 206
Indianapolis, IN 46204
317-232-4567
fax: 317-232-3443
http://www.in.gov/gov

Secretary of State
State House
200 W Washington St Rm 201
Indianapolis, IN 46204
317-232-6531
fax: 317-233-3283
http://www.in.gov/sos

Indiana State Library
140 N Senate Ave
Indianapolis, IN 46204
317-232-3675
fax: 317-232-3728
http://www.statelib.lib.in.us

Iowa

Twenty-ninth state; admitted on December 28, 1846

State capital: Des Moines
Nicknames: The Hawkeye State; The Corn State
State motto: Our Liberties We Prize, and Our Rights We
  Will Maintain
State bird: Eastern goldfinch (*Carduelis tristis*)
State flower: Wild rose (*Rosa pratincola*)
State song: "The Song of Iowa"
State stone: Geode

State tree: Oak (Quercus)

More about state symbols at:
http://www.legis.state.ia.us/Pubinfo/StateSymbols/
http://www.iowa.gov/state/main/facts.html

More about the state at:
http://www.iowahistory.org/index.html

SOURCES:
AmerBkDays-2000, p. 859
AnnivHol-2000, p. 214

STATE OFFICES:
State web site:
http://www.iowa.gov

Office of the Governor
State Capitol Bldg
Des Moines, IA 50319
515-281-5211
fax: 515-281-6611
http://www.governor.state.ia.us

Secretary of State
321 E 12th St
1st Fl
Des Moines, IA 50319
515-281-5204
fax: 515-242-5953
http://www.sos.state.ia.us

Iowa State Library
112 E Grand Ave
Des Moines, IA 50319
515-281-4105
fax: 515-281-6191
http://www.statelibraryofiowa.org

Kansas

Thirty-fourth state; admitted on January 29, 1861

Kansas Day has been observed since 1877, most often in school programs about the state. The Kansas State Historical Society sponsors celebrations at the Kansas History Center in Topeka.

State capital: Topeka
Nicknames: Sunflower State; Wheat State; Jayhawk State
State motto: *Ad Astra per Aspera* (Latin "To the Stars Through Difficulties")
State amphibian: Barred tiger salamander
State animal: American buffalo or bison (*Bison bison*)
State bird: Western meadowlark (*Sturnella neglecta*)
State flower: Sunflower (*Helianthus annuus*)
State insect: Honeybee (*Apis mellifera*)
State march: "The Kansas March"
State reptile: Ornate box turtle
State song: "Home on the Range"
State tree: Cottonwood (*Populus deltoides*)

More about state symbols at:
http://www.kssos.org/resources/kansaskids_facts.html
http://www.kshs.org/kids/things/symbols/

SOURCES:
AmerBkDays-2000, p. 95
AnnivHol-2000, p. 16

CONTACT:
Kansas State Historical Society
6425 SW Sixth Ave.
Topeka, 66615-1099
785-272-8681
fax: 785-272-8682
TTY: 785-272-8683
http://www.kshs.org/you/ksday.htm

STATE OFFICES:
State web site:
http://www.kansas.gov

Office of the Governor
State Capitol Bldg
2nd Fl
Topeka, KS 66612
785-296-3232
fax: 785-296-7973
http://www.ksgovernor.org

Secretary of State
120 SW 10th Ave
1st Fl
Topeka, KS 66612
785-296-4564
fax: 785-296-4570
http://www.kssos.org

Kansas State Library
300 SW 10th Ave
Capitol Bldg Rm 343N
Topeka, KS 66612
785-296-3296
fax: 785-296-6650
http://skyways.lib.ks.us

Kentucky

Fifteenth state; admitted on June 1, 1792

Admission Day is not regularly observed in Kentucky, although festivities were held on the 100th, 150th, and 175th anniversaries of statehood.

State capital: Frankfort
Nicknames: The Bluegrass State; The Hemp State; The Tobacco State; The Dark and Bloody Ground
State motto: United We Stand, Divided We Fall
State bird: Cardinal (*Cardinalis cardinalis*)
State amphitheater: Iroquois Amphitheater
State arboretum: Bernheim Arboretum and Research Forest
State bluegrass song: "Blue Moon of Kentucky"
State botanical garden: University of Kentucky Arboretum
State bourbon festival: Kentucky Bourbon Festival
State butterfly: Viceroy
State center for celebration of African American heritage: Kentucky Center for African American Heritage
State covered bridge: Switzer covered bridge
State dance: Clogging
State drink: Milk
State fish: Kentucky spotted bass
State flower: Goldenrod (*Solidago nemoralis*)
State fossil: Brachiopod
State fruit: blackberry (***Rubus allegheniensis***)
State gemstone: Fresh water pearl
State honey festival: Clarkson Honeyfest
State horse: Thoroughbred
State language: English

State mineral: Coal
State music: Bluegrass
State musical instrument: Appalachian Dulcimer
State outdoor musical: "The Stephen Foster Story"
State pipe band: Louisville Pipe Band
State rock: Kentucky agate
State science center: Louisville Science Center
State silverware pattern: "Old Kentucky Blue Grass, The Georgetown Pattern"
State song: "My Old Kentucky Home"
State soil: Crider soil series
State steam locomotive: *Old 152*
State theatre pipe organ: Kentucky Theatre's Mighty Wurlitzer
State tree: Tulip Poplar (*Lirodendroan tulipifera*)
State tug-o-war championship: The Fordsville Tug-o-War Championship
State wild game animal species: Gray squirrel (*Sciurus carolinensis*)

More about state symbols at:
http://www.kdla.ky.gov/resources/KYSymbols.htm

SOURCES:
AmerBkDays-2000, p. 411
AnnivHol-2000, p. 94
DictDays-1988, p. 113

STATE OFFICES:
State web site:
http://www.kentucky.gov

Office of the Governor
State Capitol Bldg 700 Capitol Ave
Rm 100
Frankfort, KY 40601
502-564-2611
fax: 502-564-2517
http://governor.ky.gov

Secretary of State
State Capitol Bldg 700 Capitol Ave
Rm 152
Frankfort, KY 40601
502-564-3490
fax: 502-564-5687
http://sos.ky.gov

Kentucky Dept for Libraries & Archives
300 Coffee Tree Rd
Frankfort, KY 40602
502-564-8300
fax: 502-564-5773
http://www.kdla.ky.gov

Louisiana

Eighteenth state; admitted on April 30, 1812 (seceded in 1861 and was readmitted on June 25, 1868)

State capital: Baton Rouge
Nicknames: The Pelican State; The Bayou State; Fisherman's Paradise; Child of the Mississippi; Sugar State
State motto: Union, Justice, and Confidence
State amphibian: Green tree frog (*Hyla cinerea*)
State bird: Brown pelican (*Pelecanus occidentalis*)
State colors: Blue, white, and gold

State crustacean: Crawfish
State dog: Louisiana Catahoula leopard dog
State drink: Milk
State environmental song: "The Gifts of Earth"
State flower: Magnolia (*Magnolia grandiflora*); **wildflower**: Louisiana iris (*Giganticaerulea*)
State fossil: Petrified palm wood
State freshwater fish: White perch (*pomoxis annularis*)
State gem: Agate
State insect: Honeybee (*Apis mellifera*)
State mammal: Louisiana black bear
State march song: "Louisiana My Home Sweet Home"
State musical instrument: Diatonic ("Cajun") accordion
State painting: "Louisiana"
State reptile: Alligator
State songs: "Give Me Louisiana"; "You Are My Sunshine"
State tree: Bald cypress (*Taxodium distichum*)

More about state symbols at:
http://www.sos.louisiana.gov/tabid/217/Default.aspx

More about the state at:
http://doa.louisiana.gov/about_history.htm
http://www.louisianapurchase2003.com

SOURCES:
AmerBkDays-2000, p. 329
AnnivHol-2000, p. 71

STATE OFFICES:
State web site:
http://www.louisiana.gov

Office of the Governor
PO Box 94004
Baton Rouge, LA 70804
225-342-7015
fax: 225-342-7099
http://www.gov.state.la.us

Secretary of State
PO Box 94125
Baton Rouge, LA 70804
225-922-1000
fax: 225-922-0002
http://www.sec.state.la.us

Louisiana State Library
701 N 4th St
Baton Rouge, LA 70821
225-342-4915
fax: 225-219-4725
http://www.state.lib.la.us

Maine

Twenty-third state; admitted on March 15, 1820

State capital: Augusta
Nicknames: The Pine Tree State; The Lumber State; The Border State; The Old Dirigo State
State motto: *Dirigo* (Latin "I lead")
State animal: Moose (*Alces alces*)
State berry: Wild blueberry
State bird: Chickadee (*Parus atricapillus*)
State cat: Maine coon cat

State fish: Landlocked salmon (*Salmo sala Sebago*)
State flower: White pine cone and tassel (*Pinus strobes, Linnaeus*)
State fossil: *Pertica quadrifaria*
State gemstone: Tourmaline
State herb: Wintergreen (*Gaulthoria procumbens*)
State insect: Honeybee (*Apis mellifera*)
State soil: Chesuncook Soil Series
State soft drink: Moxie
State song: "State of Maine Song"
State tree: Eastern white pine (*Pinus strobus*)
State vessel: *Schooner Bowdoin*

More about state symbols at:

http://www.state.me.us/sos/kids/allabout/symbols
/symbols.htm
http://www.maine.gov/legis/senate/statehouse/symbols
/Emblems.htm

SOURCES:

AmerBkDays-2000, p. 204
AnnivHol-2000, p. 44

STATE OFFICES:

State web site:
http://www.maine.gov

Office of the Governor
1 State House Stn
Augusta, ME 04333
207-287-3531
fax: 207-287-1034
http://www.maine.gov/governor

Secretary of State
148 State House Stn
Augusta, ME 04333
207-626-8400
fax: 207-287-8598
http://www.maine.gov/sos/

Maine State Library
64 State House Stn
Augusta, ME 04333
207-287-5600
fax: 207-287-5615
http://www.state.me.us/msl

Maryland

Seventh state; adopted the U.S. Constitution on April 28, 1788

SEE MARYLAND DAY

State capital: Annapolis
Nicknames: The Old Line State; Free State
State motto: *Fatti maschii, parole femine* (Latin "Strong deeds, gentle words")
State bird: Baltimore oriole (*Icterus galbula*)
State boat: Skipjack
State cat: Calico
State crustacean: Maryland blue crab (*Callinectes sapidus*)
State dinosaur: *Astrodon johnstoni*
State dog: Chesapeake Bay retriever
State drink: Milk
State fish: Rockfish (*Morone saxatilis*)

State flower: Black-eyed Susan (*Rudbeckia hirta*)
State folk dance: Square dance
State fossil shell: *Ecphora gardnerae gardnerae*
State gem: Patuxent river stone
State horse: Thoroughbred
State insect: Baltimore checkerspot butterfly (*Euphydryas phaeton*)
State reptile: Diamondback terrapin turtle (*Malaclemys terrapin*)
State song: "Maryland, My Maryland"
State sport: Jousting
State team sport: Lacrosse
State summer theater: Olney Theatre (Montgomery County)
State theater: Center State (Baltimore)
State tree: White oak (*Quercus alba*)

More about state symbols at:

http://www.msa.md.gov/msa/mdmanual/01glance/html
/symbols/00list.html
http://www.mdkidspage.org/StateSymbols.htm

SOURCES:

AmerBkDays-2000, p. 324
AnnivHol-2000, p. 70

STATE OFFICES:

State web site:
http://www.maryland.gov

Office of the Governor
State House
100 State Cir
Annapolis, MD 21401
410-974-3901
fax: 410-974-3275
http://www.gov.state.md.us

Secretary of State
16 Francis St
Jeffery Bldg 1st Fl
Annapolis, MD 21401
410-974-5521
fax: 410-974-5190
http://www.sos.state.md.us

State Archives
350 Rowe Blvd
Annapolis, MD 21401
410-260-6400
fax: 410-974-2525
http://www.mdarchives.state.md.us

Massachusetts

Sixth state; adopted the U.S. Constitution on February 6, 1788

State capital: Boston
Nicknames: The (Old) Bay State; The Old Colony State; The Puritan State; The Baked Bean State; The Pilgrim State
State motto: *Ense petit placidam sub libertate quietem* (Latin "By the sword we seek peace, but peace only under liberty")
Ode of the Commonwealth: "Ode to Massachusetts"
State artist: Norman Rockwell
State author and illustrator: Theodor Geisel
State bean: Baked navy bean

State berry: Cranberry (*Vaccinium macrocarpon*)
State beverage: Cranberry juice
State bird: Black-capped chickadee (*Penthestes atricapillus*)
State blues artist: Taj Mahal (Henry St. Clair Fredericks**)**
State building and monument stone: Granite
State cat: Tabby cat (*Felis familiaris*)
State ceremonial march: "The Road to Boston"
State children's book: *Make Way For Ducklings*
State citizenry: Bay Staters
State colors: Blue, green and cranberry
State cookie: Chocolate chip
State designation of citizens: Bay Staters
State dessert: Boston cream pie
State dog: Boston terrier (*Canis familiaris bostenensis*)
State donut: Boston creme doughnut
State explorer rock: Dighton Rock
State fish: Cod (*Gadus morrhua*)
State flower: Mayflower (also called ground laurel or trailing arbutus, *Epigaea regens*)
State folk dance: Square dance
State folk hero: Johnny Appleseed
State folk song: "Massachusetts"
State fossil: Theropod dinosaur tracks
State game bird: Wild turkey (*Meleagris gallopavo*)
State gem: Rhodonite
State glee club song: "The Great State of Massachusetts"
State heroine: Deborah Sampson (1760-1827; while disguised as a man under the name of Robert Shurtleff, she fought with the Continental Army against the British)
State historical rock: Plymouth Rock
State horse: Morgan horse (*Equus cabullus morganensis*)
State insect: Ladybug (*Hippodamia convergens*)
State inventor: Benjamin Franklin
State Korean war memorial: Korean War Memorial (in Shipyard Park)
State marine mammal: Right whale (*Eubabalena glacialis*)
State MIA/POW memorial: MIA/POW Memorial (Bourne)
State mineral: Babingtonite
State muffin: Corn muffin
State patriotic song: "Massachusetts (Because of You Our Land Is Free)"
State peace statue: Orange Peace Statue
State poem: "Blue Hills of Massachusetts"
State polka song: "Say Hello to Someone from Massachusetts"
State reptile: Garter snake
State rock: Roxbury pudding stone (Roxbury conglomerate)
State shell: New England neptune (*Neptuna lyrata decemcostata*)
State soil: Paxton soil series
State song: "All Hail to Massachusetts"
State sport: Basketball
State Southwest Asia war memorial: Southwest Asia War Memorial
State tartan: Bay State Tartan
State tree: American elm (*Ulmus americana*)
State vessel: *Schooner Ernestina*
State Vietnam War memorial: Vietnam War Memorial

More about state symbols at:
http://www.sec.state.ma.us/cis/cismaf/mf1a.htm

SOURCES:
AmerBkDays-2000, p. 121
AnnivHol-2000, p. 23

STATE OFFICES:
State web site:
http://www.mass.gov

Office of the Governor
State House
Executive Office Rm 360
Boston, MA 02133
617-725-4000
fax: 617-727-9725
http://www.mass.gov/gov

Secretary of the Commonwealth
State House
Rm 337
Boston, MA 02133
617-727-9180
fax: 617-742-4722
http://www.sec.state.ma.us

Massachusetts Board of Library Commissioners
98 N Washington St
Boston, MA 02114
617-725-1860
fax: 617-421-9833
http://mblc.state.ma.us

Michigan

Twenty-sixth state; admitted on January 26, 1837

The anniversary of Michigan's statehood was previously observed as Michigan Day, but is no longer a holiday.

State capital: Lansing
Nicknames: The Great Lakes State; The Wolverine State; Winter Wonderland; the Upper Peninsula is often referred to as the Land of Hiawatha
State motto: *Si quaeris peninsulam amoenam, circumspice* (Latin "If you seek a pleasant peninsula, look about you")
State bird: Robin (*Turdus migratorius*)
State fish: Brook trout (*Salvelinus fontinalis*)
State flower: Apple blossom (*Malus sylvestris*); **wildflower**: Dwarf lake iris (*Iris lacustris*)
State fossil: Mastadon
State game mammal: Whitetailed deer (*Odocoileus virginianus*)
State gem: Greenstone (chlorastrolite)
State reptile: Painted turtle (*Chysemys picta*)
State soil: Kalkaska sand
State song: "My Michigan" (official); "Michigan, My Michigan" (unofficial)
State stone: Petoskey stone (*Hexagonaria pericarnata*)
State tree: White pine (*Pinus strobus*)

More about state symbols at:
http://www.michigan.gov

SOURCES:
AmerBkDays-2000, p. 90
AnnivHol-2000, p. 15

STATE OFFICES:
State web site:
http://www.michigan.gov

Office of the Governor
PO Box 30013
Lansing, MI 48909
517-373-3400
fax: 517-335-6863
http://www.michigan.gov/gov

Secretary of State
430 W Allegan St
4th Fl
Lansing, MI 48918
517-373-2510
fax: 517-241-3442
http://www.michigan.gov/sos

Library of Michigan
702 W Kalamazoo St
PO Box 30007
Lansing, MI 48909
517-573-5504
fax: 517-373-1580
http://www.libofmich.lib.mi.us

Minnesota

Thirty-second state; admitted on May 11, 1858

State capital: St. Paul
Nicknames: North Star State; Gopher State; Bread and Butter State; The Land of 10,000 Lakes
State motto: *L'Etoile du Nord* (French "The North Star")
State bird: Common loon (*Gavia immer*)
State butterfly: Monarch (*Danaus plexippus*)
State drink: Milk
State fish: Walleye (*Stizostedion vitreum*)
State flower: Pink and white lady's slipper (*Cypripedium reginae*)
State fruit: Honeycrisp apple (*Malus pumila* cultivar Honeycrisp)
State gem: Lake Superior agate
State grain: Wild rice or manomin (*Zizania aquatica* or *Zizania palustris*)
State muffin: Blueberry muffin
State mushroom: Morel or sponge mushroom (*Morchella esculenta*)
State photograph: "Grace"
State song: "Hail! Minnesota"
State tree: Norway (red) pine (*Pinus resinosa*)

More about state symbols at:

http://www.sos.state.mn.us/student/symbols.html
http://www.leg.state.mn.us/leg/Symbols.asp

SOURCES:

AmerBkDays-2000, p. 357
AnnivHol-2000, p. 80

STATE OFFICES:

State web site:
http://www.state.mn.us

Office of the Governor
130 State Capitol
75 Rev Dr Martin Luther King Jr Blvd
Saint Paul, MN 55155
651-296-3391
fax: 651-296-2089
http://www.governor.state.mn.us

Secretary of State
60 Empire Dr
Suite 100
Saint Paul, MN 55103
651-296-2803
fax: 651-215-0682
http://www.sos.state.mn.us

Mississippi

Twentieth state; admitted on December 10, 1817 (seceded on January 9, 1861, and was readmitted on February 23, 1870)

No admission day celebrations occur, but in 1917 the state held centennial ceremonies including speeches and music. On the sesquicentennial, or 150th, anniversary in 1967, there were exhibits at the Old Capitol Building museum, and efforts got underway to preserve state historical documents (including appropriating $1,120,000 for building a new archives center).

State capital: Jackson
Nicknames: The Magnolia State; Eagle State; Border-Eagle State; Bayou State; Mud-cat State
State motto: *Virtute et armis* (Latin "By valor and arms")
State beverage: Milk
State bird: Mockingbird (*Mimus polyglottos*)
State butterfly: Spicebush swallowtail (*Papilio troilus*)
State dance: Square dance
State fish: Largemouth or black bass (*Micropterus salmoides*)
State flower: Magnolia blossom (*Magnolia grandiflora*); **wildflower**: Coreopsis
State fossil: Prehistoric whale
State insect: Honeybee (*Apis mellifera*)
State mammal: land: White-tailed deer (*Odocoileus virginianus*); **water**: Bottle-nosed dolphin (*Tursiops truncatus*)
State reptile: Alligator
State shell: Oyster shell (*Crassostrea virginica*)
State song: "Go, Mississippi"
State stone: Petrified wood
State toy: Teddy bear
State tree: Magnolia (*Magnolia grandiflora*)
State waterfowl: Wood duck (*Aix sponsa*)

More about state symbols at:

http://www.its.state.ms.us/et/portal/MSSymbols/symbols.htm
http://www.visitmississippi.org/resources/state_symbols.asp

More about the state at:

http://www.ms.gov/about_ms.jsp

SOURCES:

AmerBkDays-2000, p. 822
AnnivHol-2000, p. 205

STATE OFFICES:

State web site:
http://www.mississippi.gov

Office of the Governor
PO Box 139
Jackson, MS 39205
601-359-3150
fax: 601-359-3741
http://www.governorbarbour.com

Secretary of State
PO Box 136
Jackson, MS 39205
601-359-1350
fax: 601-359-1499
http://www.sos.state.ms.us

Mississippi Library Commission
1221 Ellis Ave
Jackson, MS 39209
601-961-4111
fax: 601-354-4181
http://www.mlc.lib.ms.us

Archives & History Dept
PO Box 571
Jackson, MS 39205
601-576-6850
fax: 601-576-6899
http://www.mdah.state.ms.us

Missouri

Twenty-fourth state; admitted on August 10, 1821

State capital: Jefferson City
Nickname: Show Me State
State motto: *Salus populi suprema lex esto* (Latin "Let the welfare of the people be the supreme law")
State amphibian: American Bullfrog (*Rana catesbeiana*)
State bird: Bluebird (*Sialia sialis*)
State day: Missouri Day, third Wednesday in October
State dinosaur: Hadrosaur or duck-billed (*Hypsibema missouriense)*
State fish: Channel catfish (*Ictalurus punctatus*)
State flower: Hawthorn blossom (*Crataegus*)
State folk dance: Square dance
State fossil: Crinoid (*Delocrinus missouriensis*)
State grape: Norton/Cynthiana grape (*Vitis Aestivalis*)
State horse: Missouri fox trotting horse
State insect: Honeybee (*Apis mellifera*)
State land animal: Missouri mule; **aquatic animal**: Paddlefish
State mineral: Galena
State musical instrument: Fiddle
State rock: Mozarkite (chert or flint rock)
State song: "Missouri Waltz"
State tree: Flowering dogwood (*Cornus florida*)
State tree nut: Eastern black walnut (*Juglans nigra*)

More about state symbols at:

http://www.sos.mo.gov/symbols/

SOURCES:

AmerBkDays-2000, p. 579
AnnivHol-2000, p. 134

STATE OFFICES:

State web site:
http://www.missouri.gov

Office of the Governor
PO Box 720
Jefferson City, MO 65102
573-751-3222
fax: 573-751-1495
http://www.gov.state.mo.us

Secretary of State
PO Box 778
Jefferson City, MO 65102
573-751-4936
fax: 573-526-4903
http://www.sos.state.mo.us

Missouri State Library
600 W Main St
PO Box 387
Jefferson City, MO 65102
573-751-3615
fax: 573-526-1142
http://www.sos.mo.gov/library

Montana

Forty-first state; admitted on November 8, 1889

State capital: Helena
Nicknames: Treasure State; Big Sky Country; Bonanza State; Land of Shining Mountains; Mountain State
State motto: *Oro y Plata* (Spanish "Gold and Silver")
State animal: Grizzly bear (*Ursus (arctos) horribilis*)
State ballad: "Montana Melody"
State bird: Western meadowlark (*Sturnella neglecta*)
State butterfly: Mourning cloak (*Nymphalis antiopa*)
State fish: Black-spotted cutthroat trout (*Salmo clarki*)
State flower: Bitterroot (*Lewisia rediviva*)
State fossil: Duck-billed dinosaur (*Maiasaura peeblesorum*)
State gems: Yogo sapphire; Montana agate
State grass: Bluebunch wheatgrass (*Agropyron spicatum*)
State song: "Montana"
State tree: Ponderosa pine (*Pinus ponderosa*)

More about state symbols at:

http://mhs.mt.gov/education/studentguide/Symbols.asp
http://www.montanakids.com/

SOURCES:

AmerBkDays-2000, p. 762
AnnivHol-2000, p. 187

STATE OFFICES:

State web site:
http://www.mt.gov

Office of the Governor
PO Box 200801
Helena, MT 59620
406-444-3111
fax: 406-444-4151
http://www.governor.mt.gov

Secretary of State
PO Box 202801
Helena, MT 59620
406-444-2034
fax: 406-444-3976
http://www.sos.state.mt.us

Montana State Library
1515 E 6th Ave
PO Box 201800
Helena, MT 59620
406-444-3115
fax: 406-444-0266
http://msl.state.mt.us

Nebraska

Thirty-seventh state; admitted on March 1, 1867

Nebraska's admission day anniversary is marked as State Day. On March 1 every year, state law requires the governor to issue a proclamation about the anniversary and call on citizens to celebrate. Schools may mark the occasion with programs about the state's history. The centennial celebration was held during much of 1967 with festivals, rodeos, pageants, and exhibits.

State capital: Lincoln
Nicknames: Cornhusker State; Tree Planters' State
State motto: Equality Before the Law
State ballad: "A Place Like Nebraska"
State baseball capital: Wakefield
State beverage: milk
State bird: Western meadowlark (*Sturnella neglecta*)
State Christmas tree: Colorado blue spruce (planted near the capital in 1876)
State fish: Channel cutfish (*Ictalurus punctatus*)
State flower: Goldenrod (*Solidago serotina*)
State folk dance: Square dance
State fossil: Mammoth
State gem: Blue agate (blue chalcedony)
State grass: Little bluestem (*Schizachyrium scoparium*), also called "bunch grass" or "beard grass"
State historic baseball capital: St. Paul
State insect: Honeybee (*Apis mellifera*)
State mammal: Whitetail deer (*Odocoileus virginianus*)
State poet laureate: John G. Neihardt
State river: Platte River
State rock: Prairie agate
State slogan: "Battle born"
State soil: Holdrege series (*Typic arguistolls*)
State soft drink: Kool-Aid
State song: "Beautiful Nebraska"
State tartan: Nevada Tartan
State tree: Cottonwood (*Populus deltoides*)
State village of lights: Cody

More about state symbols at:

http://www.nlc.state.ne.us/bestofweb/statesymbols.html

More about the state at:

http://nebraskalegislature.gov/web/public/bluebook

SOURCES:

AmerBkDays-2000, p. 174
AnnivHol-2000, p. 36

STATE OFFICES:

State web site:
http://www.nebraska.gov

Office of the Governor
PO Box 94848
Lincoln, NE 68509
402-471-2244
fax: 402-471-6031
http://gov.nol.org

Secretary of State
PO Box 94608
Lincoln, NE 68509
402-471-2554
fax: 402-471-3237
http://www.sos.state.ne.us

Nebraska State Library
PO Box 98931
Lincoln, NE 68509
402-471-3189
fax: 402-471-1011
http://www.nlc.state.ne.us

Nevada

Thirty-sixth state; admitted on October 31, 1864

Nevada Day is a legal holiday throughout the state observed the last Friday in October, but the most festive celebrations take place in Carson City, where the Admission Day parade has been held since 1938. There are historical Indian pageants, a costume ball, a Miss Nevada crowning, dancing, picnicking, games, and other events. Students have entered a historical essay contest since 1959, and the winners are awarded during the festivities.

State capital: Carson City
Nicknames: Silver State; Sagebrush State; Battle-Born State
State motto: All for Our Country
State animal: Desert bighorn sheep (*Ovis canadensis*)
State artifact: Tule duck
State bird: Mountain bluebird (*Sialia currucoides*)
State colors: Silver and blue
State fish: Lahontan cutthroat trout (*Salmo clarki henshawi*)
State flower: Sagebrush (*Artemisia tridentata*)
State fossil: Ichthyosaur (*Shonisaurus*)
State grass: Indian ricegrass (*Oryzopsis hymenoides*)
State metal: Silver
State precious gemstone: Virgin Valley Black Fire opal
State reptile: Desert tortoise (*Gopherus agassizii*)
State rock: Sandstone
State semi-precious gemstone: Turquoise
State soil: Orovada series
State song: "Home Means Nevada"
State trees: Single-leaf piñon (*Pinus monophylla*) and Bristlecone pine (*Pinus aristata*)

More about state symbols at:

http://www.leg.state.nv.us/General/FACTS.cfm
http://dmla.clan.lib.nv.us/docs/nsla/services/nvfacts.htm

SOURCES:

AmerBkDays-2000, p. 743
AnnivHol-2000, p. 180
DictDays-1988, p. 81

STATE OFFICES:

State web site:
http://www.nv.gov

Office of the Governor
101 N Carson St
Carson City, NV 89701
775-684-5670
fax: 775-684-5683
http://gov.state.nv.us

Secretary of State
101 N Carson St
Suite 3
Carson City, NV 89701
775-684-5708

fax: 775-684-5725
http://sos.state.nv.us

Nevada State Library & Archives
100 N Stewart St
Carson City, NV 89701
775-684-3360
fax: 775-684-3330
http://dmla.clan.lib.nv.us/docs/nsla

New Hampshire

Ninth state; adopted the U.S. Constitution on June 21, 1788

State capital: Concord
Nicknames: The Granite State; The Mother of Rivers;
Switzerland of America; White Mountain State
State motto: Live Free or Die
State amphibian: Spotted newt (*Notophthalmus viridescens*)
State animal: White-tailed deer (*Odocoileus virginianus*)
State bird: Purple finch (*Carpodacus purpureus*)
State butterfly: Karner blue (*Lycaeides melissa*, subspecies
samuelis)
State flower: Purple lilac (*Syringa vulgaris*); **wildflower**:
Pink lady's slipper (*Cypripedium acaule*)
State freshwater fish: Brook trout (*Salvelinus fontinalis*);
saltwater game fish: Striped bass (*Roccus saxatilis*)
State fruit: Pumpkin
State gem: Smoky quartz
State insect: Ladybug (*Hippodamia convergens*)
State mineral: Beryl
State rock: Granite
State song: "Old New Hampshire"
State sport: Skiing
State tartan: New Hampshire tartan
State tree: White birch (*Betula papyrifera*)

More about state symbols at:
http://www.nh.gov/nhinfo/
http://www.gencourt.state.nh.us/senate/misc/kids.html

SOURCES:
AmerBkDays-2000, p. 466
AnnivHol-2000, p. 103

STATE OFFICES:
State web site:
http://www.nh.gov

Office of the Governor
State House
107 N Main St Rm 208
Concord, NH 03301
603-271-2121
fax: 603-271-7680
http://www.nh.gov/governor

Secretary of State
107 N Main St
State House Rm 204
Concord, NH 03301
603-271-3242
fax: 603-271-6316
http://www.sos.nh.gov

New Hampshire State Library
20 Park St

Concord, NH 03301
603-271-2144
fax: 603-271-2205
http://www.nh.gov/nhsl

New Jersey

Third state; adopted the U.S. Constitution on December 18, 1787

State capital: Trenton
Nickname: The Garden State
State motto: Liberty and Prosperity
State animal: Horse (*Equus caballus*)
State bird: Eastern goldfinch (*Carduelis tristis*)
State dance: Square dance
State dinosaur: *Hadrosaurus foulki*
State fish: Brook trout (*Salvelinus fontinalis*)
State flower: Purple violet (*Viola sororia*)
State fruit: Blueberry (*Vaccinium corymbosum*)
State insect: Honeybee (*Apis mellifera*)
State memorial tree: Dogwood (*Cornus florida*)
State shell: Knobbed whelk (*Busycon Caricagmelin*)
State ship: *A.J. Meerwald*
State tree: Red oak (*Quercus borealis maxima*)

More about state symbols at:
http://www.njleg.state.nj.us/kids/index.asp
http://www.state.nj.us/nj/about/facts/

SOURCES:
AmerBkDays-2000, p. 837
AnnivHol-2000, p. 210

STATE OFFICES:
State web site:
http://www.newjersey.gov

Office of the Governor
125 W State St
Box 001
Trenton, NJ 08625
609-292-6000
fax: 609-292-3454
http://www.state.nj.us/governor

Secretary of State
125 W State St
PO Box 300
Trenton, NJ 08625
609-984-1900
fax: 609-292-7665
http://www.state.nj.us/state

New Jersey State Library
185 N State St
PO Box 520
Trenton, NJ 08625
609-292-6200
fax: 609-292-2746
http://www.state.nj.us/statelibrary/njlib.htm

New Mexico

Forty-seventh state; admitted on January 6, 1912

New Mexico does not regularly observe the anniversary of its statehood, but in 1972, the 60th anniversary of its admission to the U.S., a commemoration was held in Santa Fe. There was a reception at the Palace of Governors, where members of the Sociedad Folklórica dressed in costumes of the 1910s.

State capital: Santa Fe
Nickname: Land of Enchantment
State motto: *Crescit Eundo* (Latin "It Grows as It Goes")
State aircraft: Hot air balloon
State amphibian: Mexico spadefoot (*Spea multiplicata*)
State ballad: "Land of Enchantment—New Mexico"
State balloon museum: Anderson-Abruzzo International Balloon Museum
State bilingual song: "New Mexico—Mi Lindo Nuevo Mexico"
State bird: Chaparral bird or roadrunner (*Geococcyx californianus*)
State butterfly: Sandia hairstreak (*Callophrys mcfarlandi*)
State cookie: Bizcochito
State fish: Rio Grande cutthroat trout (*Salmo clerki*)
State flower: Yucca flower (*Yucca glauca*)
State fossil: Coelophysis dinosaur
State gem: Turquoise
State grass: Blue grama (*Bouteloua gracillis*)
State insect: Tarantula hawk wasp (*Pepsis formosa*)
State mammal: Black bear (*Ursus americanus*)
State poem: "A Nuevo Mexico" ("To New Mexico")
State question: "Red or Green?" (refers to which chile one prefers)
State reptile: New Mexico whiptail (*Cnemidophorus neomexianus*)
State slogan: *"Everybody is somebody in New Mexico."*
State songs: "O, Fair New Mexico" and "Asi es Nuevo Mejico"
State tie: Bolo tie
State train: Cumbres & Toltec Railroad
State tree: Piñon or nut pine (*Pinus edulis*)
State vegetables: Chile (*Capsicum annum*) and frijol or pinto bean (*Phaseolus vulgaris*)

More about state symbols at:
http://www.sos.state.nm.us/KidsCorner/index.html

More about the state at:
http://www.newmexicohistory.org/
http://www.newmexico.gov/

SOURCES:
AmerBkDays-2000, p. 29
AnnivHol-2000, p. 5

STATE OFFICES:
State web site:
http://www.state.nm.us

Office of the Governor
State Capitol Bldg
490 Santa Fe Trail Rm 400
Santa Fe, NM 87501
505-827-3000
fax: 505-476-2226
http://www.governor.state.nm.us

Secretary of State
325 Don Gaspar Ave
Suite 300
Santa Fe, NM 87503
505-827-3600
fax: 505-827-8081
http://www.sos.state.nm.us

New Mexico State Library
1209 Camino Carlos Rey
Santa Fe, NM 87507
505-476-9700
http://www.nmstatelibrary.org

New York

Eleventh state; adopted the U.S. Constitution on July 26, 1788

Capital: Albany
Nickname: The Empire State
State motto: *Excelsior* (Latin "Ever upward")
State animal: Beaver (*Castor canadensis*)
State beverage: Milk
State bird: Bluebird (*Sialia sialis*)
State bush: Lilac
State freshwater fish: Brook or speckled trout (*Salvelinus fontinalis*); **saltwater**: Striped bass
State flower: Rose (genus *Rosa*)
State fossil: *Eurypterus remipes* (distant relative of the horseshoe crab)
State fruit: Apple (*Malus sylvestris*)
State gem: Garnet
State insect: Ladybug (*Hippodamia convergens*)
State muffin: Apple muffin
State reptile: Common snapping turtle
State shell: Bay scallop (*Agropecten irradians*)
State tree: Sugar maple (*Acer saccharum*)

More about state symbols at:
http://www.dos.state.ny.us/kids_room/index.html
http://www.dec.ny.gov/education/1887.html

SOURCES:
AmerBkDays-2000, p. 545
AnnivHol-2000, p. 123

STATE OFFICES:
State web site:
http://www.state.ny.us

Office of the Governor
State Capitol
Executive Chamber
Albany, NY 12224
518-474-8390
fax: 518-474-1513
http://www.state.ny.us/governor

Secretary of State
41 State St
Albany, NY 12231
518-474-0050
fax: 518-474-4765
http://www.dos.state.ny.us

New York State Library
Empire State Plaza
Albany, NY 12230
518-474-5355
fax: 518-474-5786
http://www.nysl.nysed.gov

North Carolina

Twelfth state; adopted the U.S. Constitution on November 21, 1789 (joined the Confederacy on May 20, 1861, and was readmitted to the Union on June 25, 1868)

State capital: Raleigh
Nicknames: The Tarheel State; Old North State; Turpentine State
State motto: *Esse quam videri* (Latin "To be rather than to seem")
State beverage: Milk
State bird: Cardinal (*Cardinalis cardinalis*)
State birthplace of traditional pottery: Seagrove area
State blue berry: Blueberry; **red berry**: Strawberry
State boat: Shad boat
State carnivorous plant: Venus flytrap
State Christmas tree: Fraser fir
State colors: Red and blue
State folk dance: Clogging; **popular dance**: Shag
State dog: Plott hound (*Canis familiaris*)
State fish: Channel bass (*Sciaenops ocellatus*)
State flower: Dogwood blossom (*Cornus florida*); **wild-flower**: Carolina lily (*Lilium michauxii*)
State freshwater trout: Southern Appalachian brook trout
State fruit: Scuppernong grape
State gemstone: Emerald
State historical boat: Shad boat
State insect: Honeybee (*Apis mellifera*)
State mammal: Eastern gray squirrel (*Sciurus carolinensis*)
State reptile: Eastern box turtle (*Terrapene carolina*)
State rock: Granite
State shell: Scotch bonnet (*Phalium granulatum*)
State song: "The Old North State"
State tartan: Carolina tartan
State toast: "Tar Heel Toast"
State tree: Pine (*Pinus palustris*)
State vegetable: Sweet potato (*Ipornoea batatas*)

More about state symbols at:
http://www.naturalsciences.org/funstuff/ncsymbols /symbols.html
http://www.secretary.state.nc.us/kidspg/homepage.asp

SOURCES:
AmerBkDays-2000, p. 782
AnnivHol-2000, p. 194

STATE OFFICES:
State web site:
http://www.ncgov.com

Office of the Governor
166 W Jones St
20301 MSC
Raleigh, NC 27699
919-733-5811
fax: 919-733-2120
http://www.governor.state.nc.us

Secretary of State
PO Box 29622
Raleigh, NC 27699
919-807-2005
fax: 919-807-2010
http://www.secstate.state.nc.us

North Carolina State Library
109 E Jones St
Raleigh, NC 27699
919-807-7400
fax: 919-733-8748
http://statelibrary.dcr.state.nc.us

North Dakota

Thirty-ninth state; admitted on November 2, 1889

State capital: Bismarck
Nicknames: Flickertail State; Peace Garden State; Roughrider State
State motto: Liberty and Union, Now and Forever, One and Inseparable
State beverage: Milk
State bird: Western meadowlark (*Sturnella neglecta*)
State dance: Square dance
State fish: Northern pike (*Esox lucius*)
State flower: Wild prairie rose (*Rosa blanda* or *R. arkansana*)
State fossil: Teredo petrified wood
State fruit: Chokecherry (*Prunus virginiana*)
State grass: Western wheatgrass (*Agropyron smithii*)
State honorary equine: Nokota horse
State language: English
State march: "Flickertail March"
State song: "North Dakota Hymn"
State tree: American elm (*Ulmus americana*)

More about state symbols at:
http://www.nd.gov/category.htm?id=75

SOURCES:
AmerBkDays-2000, p. 748
AnnivHol-2000, p. 184

STATE OFFICES:
State web site:
http://www.nd.gov

Office of the Governor
600 E Boulevard Ave
Dept 101
Bismarck, ND 58505
701-328-2200
fax: 701-328-2205
http://governor.state.nd.us

Secretary of State
600 E Boulevard Ave
Dept 108
Bismarck, ND 58505
701-328-2900
fax: 701-328-2992
http://www.nd.gov/sos/

North Dakota State Library
604 East Blvd
Dept 250
Bismarck, ND 58505
701-328-2492
fax: 701-328-2040
http://ndsl.lib.state.nd.us

Ohio

Seventeenth state; admitted on March 1, 1803

State capital: Columbus
Nicknames: Buckeye State; Mother of Presidents; Gateway State
State motto: With God All Things Are Possible
State animal: White-tailed deer (*Odocoileus virginianus*)
State beverage: Tomato juice
State bird: Cardinal (*Cardinalis cardinalis*)
State groundhog: Buckeye Chuck
State flower: Scarlet carnation (*Dianthus caryophyllus*); **wildflower**: Large white trillium (*Trillium grandiflorum*)
State fossil: Trilobite (*Isotelus*)
State gemstone: Ohio flint
State herb capital: Gahanna
State insect: Ladybird beetle (ladybug, *Hippodamia convergens*)
State poetry day: Ohio Poetry Day (third Friday of every October)
State prehistoric monument: Newark earthworks
State reptile: Black racer snake (*Coluber constrictor constrictor*)
State rock song: "Hang on Sloopy"
State song: "Beautiful Ohio"
State tree: Buckeye (*Aesculus glabra*)

More about state symbols at:
http://www.governorsresidence.ohio.gov/children/symbols.aspx
http://oplin.lib.oh.us/ohiodefined/symbols.html

More about the state at:
http://www.ohiohistorycentral.org/

SOURCES:
AmerBkDays-2000, p. 175
AnnivHol-2000, p. 36

STATE OFFICES:
State web site:
http://www.ohio.gov

Office of the Governor
77 S High St
30th Fl
Columbus, OH 43215
614-466-3555
fax: 614-466-9354
http://governor.ohio.gov

Secretary of State
180 E Broad St
16th Fl
Columbus, OH 43215
614-466-2655
fax: 614-644-0649
http://www.sos.state.oh.us

State Library of Ohio
274 E 1st Ave
Columbus, OH 43201
614-644-7061
fax: 614-466-3584
http://winslo.state.oh.us

Oklahoma

Forty-sixth state; admitted on November 16, 1907

Since 1921, November 16 has been designated Oklahoma Statehood Day. It has also been Oklahoma State Flag Day since 1968. In 1957, in honor of the 50th anniversary of statehood, the state legislature decreed the week of November 11-16 to be Oklahoma Week. In 1965, the lawmakers mandated public schools to conduct programs on the state's history and achievements on November 16. Annual observance of Oklahoma Statehood Day began in 1921 under the sponsorship of the Oklahoma Heritage Association, which continues to hold a dinner at the state capital at which notable Oklahomans are inducted into the Oklahoma Hall of Fame. Oklahoma Statehood Day is also observed annually with a ceremony at the Washington Cathedral in the nation's capital.

SEE ALSO OKLAHOMA DAY

State capital: Oklahoma City
Nickname: The Sooner State
State motto: *Labor omnia vincit* (Latin "Labor conquers all things")
State animal: American buffalo (*Bison bison*)
State amphibian: Bullfrog (*Rana catesbeiana*)
State beverage: Milk
State bird: Scissor-tailed flycatcher (*Muscivora forficatus*)
State butterfly: Black swallowtail (*Papilio polyxenes*)
State cartoon character: Gusty
State children's song: "Oklahoma, My Native Land"
State colors: Green and white
State country and western song: "Faded Love"
State crystal: Hourglass Selenite Crystal
State fish: White (sand) bass (*Morone chrysops*)
State floral emblem: Mistletoe (*Phoradendron serotinum*)
State flower: Oklahoma Rose; **wildflower**: Indian blanket (*Gaillardia pulchella*)
State flying mammal: Mexican free-tailed bat
State folk dance: Square dance
State fossil: Saurophaganax Maximus
State fruit: Strawberry
State furbearer: Raccoon
State game animal: White-tailed deer
State game bird: Wild turkey
State grass: Indiangrass (*Sorghastrum nutans*)
State insect: Honeybee (*Apis mellifera*)
State meal: Fried Okra, Squash, Cornbread, Barbeque Pork, Biscuits, Sausage & Gravy, Grits, Corn, Strawberries, Chicken Fried Steak, Black-eyed Peas, and Pecan Pie
State monument: The Golden Driller
State musical instrument: Fiddle
State percussive musical instrument: Drum
State poem: "Howdy Folks"
State reptile: Collared lizard (mountain boomer, *Crotaphytus collaris*)
State rock: Barite rose (rose rock or Cherokee rose)
State soil: Port Silt Loam (*Cumulic haplustolls*)
State song: "Oklahoma!"
State theater: Lynn Riggs Players of Oklahoma, Inc.
State tree: Redbud (*Cercis canadensis*)
State vegetable: Watermelon (*Citrullus lanatus*)
State waltz: "Oklahoma Wind"

More about state symbols at:
http://www.okhistory.org/kids/aboutok.html
http://www.ok.gov/osfdocs/stinfo.html

SOURCES:
AmerBkDays-2000, p. 773
AnnivHol-2000, p. 192

CONTACT:
Oklahoma Heritage Association
201 NW 14th St
Oklahoma City, 73103
888-501-2059
405-235-4458
http://www.oklahomaheritage.com/
oha@telepath.com

STATE OFFICES:
State web site:
http://www.ok.gov

Office of the Governor
State Capitol
Rm 212
Oklahoma City, OK 73105
405-521-2342
fax: 405-521-3353
http://www.governor.state.ok.us

Secretary of State
2300 N Lincoln Blvd
Rm 101
Oklahoma City, OK 73105
405-521-3912
fax: 405-521-3771
http://www.sos.state.ok.us

Oklahoma Dept of Libraries
200 NE 18th St
Oklahoma City, OK 73105
405-521-2502
fax: 405-525-7804
http://www.odl.state.ok.us

Oregon

Thirty-third state; admitted on February 14, 1859

While Admission Day is often commemorated by programs in schools, it is not a legal holiday in Oregon.

State capital: Salem
Nicknames: Beaver State; Pacific Wonderland; Webfoot State
State motto: *Alis volat propiis* (Latin "She flies with her own wings"; motto since 1987); The Union (motto from 1859 to 1987)
State animal: Beaver (*Castor canadensis*)
State beverage: Milk
State bird: Western meadowlark (*Sturnella neglecta*)
State colors: Navy blue and gold
State dance: Square dance
State father: Dr. John McLoughlin (October 19, 1784 – September 3, 1857)
State fish: Chinook salmon (*Oncorhynchus tshawytscha*)
State flower: Oregon grape (*Mahonia aquifolium*)
State fossil: Metasequoia (dawn redwood)
State fruit: Pear (*Pyrus communis*)
State gemstone: Oregon sunstone
State insect: Oregon swallowtail butterfly (*Papilio oregonius*)

State mother: Tabitha Moffatt Brown (May 1, 1780 – May 4, 1858)
State mushroom: Pacific golden chanterelle (*Cantharellus formosus*)
State nut: Hazelnut (*Corylus avellana*)
State rock: Thunderegg (geode)
State seashell: Oregon hairy triton (*Fusitriton oregonensis*)
State song: "Oregon, My Oregon"
State tree: Douglas fir (*Pseudotsuga menziesii*)

More about state symbols at:
http://bluebook.state.or.us/kids/

SOURCES:
AmerBkDays-2000, p. 142
AnnivHol-2000, p. 27

STATE OFFICES:
State web site:
http://www.oregon.gov

Office of the Governor
900 Court St NE
Salem, OR 97301
503-378-3111
fax: 503-378-6827
http://www.governor.state.or.us

Secretary of State
900 Court St NE
Rm 136
Salem, OR 97301
503-986-1500
fax: 503-986-1616
http://www.sos.state.or.us

Oregon State Library
250 Winter NE State Library Bldg
Salem, OR 97301
503-378-4243
fax: 503-588-7119
http://oregon.gov/OSL

Pennsylvania

Second state; adopted the U.S. Constitution on December 12, 1787

State capital: Harrisburg
Nicknames: Keystone State; Quaker State
State motto: Virtue, Liberty, and Independence
State animal: White-tailed deer (*Odocoileus virginianus*)
State beverage: Milk
State dog: Great Dane
State fish: Brook trout (*Salvelinus fontinalis*)
State flagship: *U.S. Brig Niagara*
State flower: Mountain laurel (*Kalmia latifolia*)
State fossil: *Phacops rana*
State game bird: Ruffed grouse or partridge (*Bonasa umbellus*)
State insect: Firefly (*Poturis pennsylvanica*)
State plant: Penngift crownvetch (*Coronilla varia*)
State song: "Pennsylvania"
State tree: Eastern hemlock (*Tsuga canadensis*)

More about state symbols at:
http://www.phmc.state.pa.us/bah/pahist/

SOURCES:
AmerBkDays-2000, p. 827
AnnivHol-2000, p. 207

STATE OFFICES:

State web site:
http://www.state.pa.us

Office of the Governor
225 Main Capitol Bldg
Harrisburg, PA 17120
717-787-2500
fax: 717-772-8284
http://www.governor.state.pa.us

Secretary of the Commonwealth
302 North Office Bldg
Harrisburg, PA 17120
717-787-6458
fax: 717-787-1734
http://www.dos.state.pa.us

Pennsylvania Commonwealth Libraries
333 Market St
Harrisburg, PA 17126
717-787-2646
fax: 717-772-3265
http://www.statelibrary.state.pa.us

Rhode Island

Thirteenth state; adopted the U.S. Constitution on May 29, 1790

State capital: Providence
Nicknames: The Ocean State; Little Rhody; Plantation State
State motto: Hope
State bird: Rhode Island red hen
State drink: Coffee milk
State flower: Violet (*Viola palmata*)
State folk art: Charles I.D. Looff Carousel (Crescent Park Carousel)
State fruit: Rhode Island greening apple
State mineral: Bowenite
State rock: Cumberlandite
State shell: Quahaug (*Mercenaria mercenaria*)
State song: "Rhode Island, It's for Me"
State tall ship and flagship: *USS Providence* (replica)
State tartan: Rhode Island
State tree: Red maple (*Acer rubrum*)
State yacht: *Courageous*

More about state symbols at:
http://www.visitrhodeisland.com/make-plans/for-students/
http://www.ri.gov/facts/factsfigures.php

SOURCES:
AmerBkDays-2000, p. 401
AnnivHol-2000, p. 89

STATE OFFICES:

State web site:
http://www.ri.gov

Office of the Governor
State House
Providence, RI 02903
401-222-2080

fax: 401-273-5729
http://www.governor.state.ri.us

Secretary of State
217 State House
Providence, RI 02903
401-222-2357
fax: 401-222-1356
http://www.state.ri.us

Rhode Island Office of Library & Information Services
1 Capitol Hill
4th Fl
Providence, RI 02908
401-222-2726
fax: 401-222-4195
http://www.olis.state.ri.us

South Carolina

Eighth state; adopted the U.S. Constitution on May 23, 1788 (seceded from the Union in December 1860, and was readmitted on June 25, 1868)

State capital: Columbia
Nicknames: The Palmetto State; The Rice State; The Swamp State; The Iodine State
State mottoes: *Animis opibusque parati* (Latin "Ready in soul and resource"); *Dum spiro spero* (Latin "While I breathe, I hope")
State American folk dance: Square dance
State amphibian: Spotted salamander (*Ambystoma maculatum*)
State animal: White-tailed deer (*Odocoileus virginianus*)
State beverage: Milk
State bird: Carolina wren (*Thryothorus ludovicianus*)
State botanical garden: Botanical Garden at Clemson University
State butterfly: Eastern tiger swallowtail (*Pterourus glaucus*)
State dance: The shag
State dog: Boykin spaniel
State fish: Striped bass (*Morone saxatilis*)
State flower: Carolina (yellow) jessamine (*Gelsemium sempervirens*)
State fruit: Peach
State gem: Amethyst
State grass: Indian grass (*Sorghastrum nutans*)
State hospitality beverage: South Carolina-grown tea
State insect: Carolina mantid, or praying mantis (*Mantis religiosa*)
State music: The spiritual; **popular music**: Beach music
State opera: *Porgy and Bess*
State railroad museum: South Carolina Railroad Museum in Fairfield County
State reptile: Loggerhead turtle (*Caretta caretta*)
State shell: Lettered olive (*Oliva sayana*)
State songs: "Carolina"; "South Carolina on My Mind"
State spider: Carolina wolf spider (*Hogna carolinensis*)
State stone: Blue granite
State tree: Palmetto
State waltz: Richardson Waltz
State wild game bird: Wild turkey (*Meleagris gallopavo*)

More about state symbols at:
http://www.scstatehouse.net/studentpage/

More about the state at:
http://sc.gov/Portal/Category/factsandhistory

SOURCES:
AmerBkDays-2000, p. 383
AnnivHol-2000, p. 86

STATE OFFICES:

State web site:
http://www.sc.gov

Office of the Governor
PO Box 12267
Columbia, SC 29211
803-734-2100
fax: 803-734-5167
http://www.scgovernor.com

Secretary of State
PO Box 11350
Columbia, SC 29211
803-734-2170
fax: 803-734-1661
http://www.scsos.com

South Carolina State Library
PO Box 11469
Columbia, SC 29211
803-734-8666
fax: 803-734-8676
http://www.state.sc.us/scsl

South Dakota

Fortieth state; admitted on November 2, 1889

State capital: Pierre
Nickname: Mount Rushmore State
State motto: Under God the People Rule
State animal: Coyote (*Canis latrans*)
State bird: Ring-necked pheasant (*Phasianus colchicus*)
State dessert: Kuchen
State fish: Walleye (*Stizostedion vitreum*)
State flower: American pasque or May Day flower (*Pulsatilla hisutissima*)
State fossil: Triceratops
State gem: Fairburn agate
State insect: Honeybee (*Apis mellifera*)
State jewelry: Black Hills gold
State mineral: Rose quartz
State soil: Houdek soil
State song: "Hail, South Dakota"
State sport: Rodeo
State tree: Black Hills spruce (*Picea glauca densata*)

More about state symbols at:
http://www.state.sd.us/state/sdsym.htm
http://www.travelsd.com/about/facts.asp

SOURCES:
AmerBkDays-2000, p. 750
AnnivHol-2000, p. 184

STATE OFFICES:

State web site:
http://www.sd.gov/

Office of the Governor
500 E Capitol
Pierre, 57501-5070
605-773-3212
http://www.state.sd.us/governor
sdgov@state.sd.us

Secretary of State
500 E Capitol, Ste 204
Pierre, 57501-5070
605-773-3537
fax: 605-773-6580
http://www.sdsos.gov
sdsos@state.sd.us

State Library
Mercedes MacKay Bldg
800 Governors Dr
Pierre, 57501-2294
800-423-6665
605-773-3131
fax: 773-6962
http://library.sd.gov
library@state.sd.us

Tennessee

Sixteenth state; admitted on June 1, 1796 (seceded on June 8, 1861, and was readmitted on July 24, 1866)

In 1929, the state legislature designated June 1 as Statehood Day in Tennessee.

State capital: Nashville
Nicknames: The Volunteer State; The Big Bend State; The Mother of Southwestern Statesmen
State motto: Agriculture and Commerce
State agricultural insect: Honeybee (*Apis mellifera*)
State amphibian: Tennessee cave salamander (*Gyrinophilu palleucus*)
State animal: Raccoon (*Procyon lotor*)
State aviation hall of fame: Tennessee Aviation Hall of Fame
State bird: Mockingbird (*Mimus polyglottos*)
State butterfly: Zebra swallowtail (*Eurytides marcellus*)
State commercial fish: Channel catfish (*Ictalurus lacustris*); **game fish**: Largemouth bass (*Micropterus salmoides*)
State declamation: "I am Tennessee"
State flower: cultivated: Purple iris (Genus *Iridaceae*); **wild**: Passion flower (*Passiflora incarnata*)
State folk dance: Square dance
State fossil: *Pterotrigonia (Scabrotrigonia) thoracica*
State fruit: Tomato (*Lycopersicon lycopersicum*)
State game bird: Bobwhite quail (*Colinus virginianus*)
State gem: Tennessee pearl
State horse: Tennessee Walking Horse
State insects: Ladybug (*Hippodamia convergens*); firefly (*Photinus pyralls*)
State jamboree and crafts festival: Smithville Fiddlers'-Jamboree and Crafts Festival
State paintings: *Tennessee Treasures; Tennessee Treasures Too*
State poem: "Oh Tennessee, My Tennessee"
State reptile: Eastern box turtle (*Terrapene carolina*)
State rocks: Limestone; agate
State slogan: Tennessee—America at Its Best

State songs: "When It's Iris Time in Tennessee"; "Tennessee Waltz"; "My Homeland, Tennessee"; "My Tennessee"; "Rocky Top"; "Tennessee"; "The Pride of Tennessee"
State tree: Tulip poplar (*Liriodendron tulipifera*)
State wild animal: Raccoon (*Procyon lotor*)

More about state symbols at:
http://tennessee.gov/sos/symbols/

More about the state at:
http://www.state.tn.us/sos/bluebook/

SOURCES:
AmerBkDays-2000, p. 413
AnnivHol-2000, p. 94
DictDays-1988, p. 113

STATE OFFICES:
State web site:
http://www.tennessee.gov

Office of the Governor
State Capitol
1st Fl
Nashville, TN 37243
615-741-2001
fax: 615-532-9711
http://www.tennessee.gov/governor

Secretary of State
State Capitol
1st Fl
Nashville, TN 37243
615-741-2819
fax: 615-532-9547
http://www.state.tn.us/sos

Tennessee State Library & Archives
403 7th Ave N
Nashville, TN 37243
615-741-2764
fax: 615-741-6471
http://state.tn.us/tsla

Texas

Twenty-eighth state; admitted on December 29, 1845 (seceded from the Union on February 1, 1861, and was readmitted on March 30, 1870)

State capital: Austin
Nickname: The Lone Star State
State motto: Friendship
State air force: Commemorative Air Force (formerly Confederate Air Force)
State bird: Mockingbird (*Mimus polyglottos*)
State bread: Pan de campo
State cooking implement: Cast iron dutch oven
State dinosaurs: Brachiosaur sauropod and pleurocoelus
State dish: Chili
State dog breed: Blue Lacy
State epic poem: "Legend of Old Stone Ranch"
State fiber and fabric: Cotton
State fish: Guadalupe bass
State flower: Bluebonnet (*Lupinus subcarnosus, Lupinus texensis and all other varieties*)
State flower song: "Bluebonnets"

State footwear: Cowboy boot
State flying mammal: Mexican free-tailed bat
State folk dance: Square dance
State fruit: Texas red grapefruit
State gem: Texas blue topaz
State gemstone cut: Lone star cut
State grass: Sideoats Grama
State health nut: Pecan
State insect: Monarch butterfly
State large mammal: Longhorn; **small**: Armadillo
State maritime museum: Texas Maritime Museum
State musical instrument: Guitar
State native pepper: Chiltepin
State native shrub: Texas purple sage
State pastries: Sopaipilla; strudel
State pepper: Jalapeno
State petrified stone: Palmwood
State plant: Prickly pear cactus
State plays: *The Lone Star; Texas; Beyond the Sundown; Fandangle*
State precious metal: Silver
State railroad: Texas State Railroad
State reptile: Texas horned lizard
State rodeo drill team: Ghostriders
State song: "Texas, Our Texas"
State sport: Rodeo
State shell: Lightning whelk
State ship: *USS Texas*
State shrub: Crape myrtle
State snack: Tortilla chips and salsa
State tall ship: *Elissa*
State 10K: Texas Round-up 10K
State tartan: Texas Bluebonnet
State tie: Bolo tie
State tree: Pecan (*Carya illinoensis*)
State vegetable: Sweet onion
State vehicle: Chuck wagon

More about state symbols at:
http://www.texasonline.com/portal/tol/en/gov/1/4
http://www.senate.state.tx.us/kids/kids.htm

More about the state at:
http://www.tsl.state.tx.us/ref/abouttx/

SOURCES:
AmerBkDays-2000, p. 867
AnnivHol-2000, p. 215

STATE OFFICES:
State web site:
http://www.texas.gov

Office of the Governor
PO Box 12428
Austin, TX 78711
512-463-2000
fax: 512-463-1849
http://www.governor.state.tx.us

Secretary of State
PO Box 12697
Austin, TX 78711
512-463-5770
fax: 512-475-2761
http://www.sos.state.tx.us

Texas State Library
1201 Brazos
Austin, TX 78701
512-463-5460
fax: 512-463-5436
http://www.tsl.state.tx.us

Utah

Forty-fifth state; admitted on January 4, 1896

State capital: Salt Lake City
Nicknames: Beehive State; Salt Lake State; Crossroads of the West
State motto: Industry
State animal: Rocky Mountain elk (*Cervus canadensis*)
State bird: California gull (*Larus californicus*)
State cooking pot: Dutch oven
State emblem: Beehive
State fish: Bonneville cutthroat trout (*Salmo clarki*)
State flower: Sego lily (*Calochortus nuttallii*)
State folk dance: Square dance
State fossil: Allosaurus
State fruit: Cherry
State gem: Topaz
State grass: Indian ricegrass (*Oryzopsis hymenoides*)
State historic vegetable: Sugar beet
State hymn: "Utah, We Love Thee"
State insect: Honeybee (*Apis mellifera*)
State mineral: Copper
State rock: Coal
State song: "Utah, This Is The Place"
State Star: Dubhe
State tartan: Utah State Tartan
State vegetable: Spanish sweet onion
State tree: Blue spruce (*Picea pungens*)

More about state symbols at:
http://www.utah.gov/about/symbols.html

More about the state at:
http://www.utah.gov/about/
http://pioneer.utah.gov/utah_on_the_web/index.html

SOURCES:
AmerBkDays-2000, p. 21
AnnivHol-2000, p. 4

STATE OFFICES:
State web site:
http://www.utah.gov

Office of the Governor
PO Box 142220
Salt Lake City, UT 84114
801-538-1000
fax: 801-538-1528
http://www.utah.gov/governor

Utah State Library
250 N 1950 West
Suite A
Salt Lake City, UT 84116
801-715-6777
fax: 801-715-6767
http://library.utah.gov

Vermont

Fourteenth state; admitted on March 4, 1791

Town meetings held all over the state on the first Tuesday in March serve in part to commemorate Vermont's Admission Day (*see* TOWN MEETING DAY).

State capital: Montpelier
Nickname: The Green Mountain State
State motto: Freedom and Unity
State animal: Morgan horse
State beverage: Milk
State bird: Hermit thrush (*Hylocichla guttata*)
State butterfly: Monarch butterfly (*Danaus plexippus*)
State fish: **cold water**: Brook trout (*Salvelinus fontinalis*); **warm water**: Walleye (*Stizostedion vitreum vitreum*)
State flower: Red clover (*Trifolium pratense*)
State fossil: White whale (*Delphinapterus leucus*)
State fruit and pie: Apple
State gem: Grossular garnet
State insect: Honeybee (*Apis mellifera*)
State mineral: Talc
State rocks: Marble, granite, and slate
State soil: Tunbridge soil series
State song: "These Green Mountains" designated new state song in 2000; old state song was "Hail, Vermont"
State tree: Sugar maple (*Acer saccharum*)

More about state symbols at:
http://dol.state.vt.us/www_root/000000/html/emblems.html
http://www.sec.state.vt.us/kids/symbols.html

More about the state at:
http://www.sec.state.vt.us/kids/pubs/history_facts_fun.pdf
http://www.sec.state.vt.us/kids/history.html

SOURCES:
AmerBkDays-2000, p. 182
AnnivHol-2000, p. 39

STATE OFFICES:
State web site:
http://www.vermont.gov

Office of the Governor
109 State St
5th Fl
Montpelier, VT 05609
802-828-3333
fax: 802-828-3339
http://www.vermont.gov/governor

Secretary of State
26 Terrace St
Drawer 9
Montpelier, VT 05609
802-828-2363
fax: 802-828-2496
http://www.sec.state.vt.us

Vermont Dept of Libraries
109 State St
Montpelier, VT 05609
802-828-3261
fax: 802-828-2199
http://dol.state.vt.us

Virginia

Tenth state; adopted the U.S. Constitution on June 25, 1788 (seceded from the Union in April 1861, and was readmitted on January 26, 1870)

State capital: Richmond
Nicknames: Old Dominion; Mother of Presidents; Mother of Statesmen
State motto: *Sic semper tyrannis* (Latin "Thus ever to tyrants")
State beverage: Milk
State bat: Virginia big-eared bat (*Corynorhinus (= Plecotus) townsendii virginianus*)
State bird: Cardinal (*Cardinalis cardinalis*)
State boat: Chesapeake Bay Deadrise
State dog: American foxhound
State festival: Virginia Covered Bridge Festival.
State fish: Brook trout (*salvelinus fontinalis*)
State flower: American dogwood (*Cornus florida*)
State folk dance: Square dance
State folklore center: Blue Ridge Institute
State fossil: *Chesapecten jeffersonius* (scallop)
State insect: Tiger swallowtail butterfly (*Papilio glaucus Linne*)
State shell: Oyster shell (*Crassostraea virginica*)
State song: "Carry Me Back to Old Virginia" had been state song since 1940; the state held a contest to choose a new song in 1998, but none has been selected (as of April, 2008)
State tree: American dogwood (*Cornus florida*)

More about state symbols at:

http://www.virginia.org/site/features.asp?FeatureID=138
http://www.virginia.gov/cmsportal2/facts_and_history_4096/facts_4104/trivia_facts.html
http://www.vatc.org/pr/facts/factsymbols.asp

SOURCES:

AmerBkDays-2000, p. 476
AnnivHol-2000, p. 106

STATE OFFICES:

State web site:
http://www.virginia.gov

Office of the Governor
Capitol Bldg
3rd Fl
Richmond, VA 23219
804-786-2211
fax: 804-371-6351
http://www.governor.virginia.gov

Secretary of the Commonwealth
830 E Main St
14th Fl
Richmond, VA 23219
804-786-2441
fax: 804-371-0017
http://www.soc.state.va.us

Library of Virginia
800 E Broad St
Richmond, VA 23219
804-692-3500
fax: 804-692-3594
http://www.lva.lib.va.us

Washington

Forty-second state; admitted on November 11, 1889

Admission Day is observed in Washington by closing public schools (however, schools are expected to hold special patriotic and historic programs on the preceding Friday). Former significant anniversaries of statehood—the 25th, 50th, and 75th—were commemorated with speeches (by President Franklin D. Roosevelt in 1939) and ceremonies.

State capital: Olympia
Nickname: Evergreen State
State motto: *Alki* (unspecified American Indian language "By and By")
State amphibian: Pacific chorus frog (*Pseudacris regilla*)
State arboretum: Washington Park Arboretum
State bird: Willow goldfinch or wild canary (*Spinus tristis salicamans*)
State colors: Green and gold
State dance: Square dance
State fish: Steelhead trout (*Salmo gairdnerii*)
State flower: Coast or pink rhododendron (*Rhododendron macrophyllum*)
State folk song: "Roll on, Columbia, Roll on"
State fossil: Columbian mammoth (*Mammuthus columbi*)
State fruit: Apple (*Malus sylvestris*)
State gem: Petrified wood
State grass: Bluebunch wheatgrass (*Agropyron spicatum*)
State insect: Green darner dragonfly (*Anax junius Drury*)
State marine mammal: Orca (*Orcinus orca*)
State ship: *Lady Washington*
State song: "Washington, My Home"
State tartan: Washington State Tartan
State tree: Western hemlock (*Tsuga heterophylla*)
State vegetable: Walla Walla sweet onion

More about state symbols at:

http://www.leg.wa.gov/Legislature/StateSymbols/
http://www.secstate.wa.gov/seal/symbols.aspx

More about the state at:

http://historylink.org/

SOURCES:

AmerBkDays-2000, p. 766
AnnivHol-2000, p. 189

STATE OFFICES:

State web site:
http://access.wa.gov

Office of the Governor4
302 14th St SW
PO Box 40002
Olympia, WA 98504
360-902-4111
fax: 360-753-4110
http://www.governor.wa.gov

Secretary of State
PO Box 40220
Olympia, WA 98504
360-902-4151
fax: 360-586-5629
http://www.secstate.wa.gov

Washington State Library
6880 Capitol Blvd S
Olympia, WA 98504
360-704-5200
fax: 360-586-7575
http://www.secstate.wa.gov/library

West Virginia

Thirty-fifth state; admitted on June 20, 1863

The centennial celebration took place throughout the state during the year of 1963 with parades, pageants, sporting events, historical exhibits and reenactments, various arts contests, musical events, fireworks, and, on June 20 at the capitol in Charleston, a speech by President John F. Kennedy.

SEE ALSO WEST VIRGINIA DAY

State capital: Charleston
Nickname: The Mountain State
State motto: *Montani Semper Liberi* (Latin "Mountaineers are always free")
State animal: Black bear (*Ursus* (*Euarctos*) *americanus*)
State bird: Cardinal (*Cardinalis cardinalis*)
State butterfly: Monarch
State colors: Old gold and blue
State fish: Brook trout (*Salvelinus fontinalis*)
State flower: Great laurel or Rhodondendron (*Rhododendron maximum*)
State fruit: Golden delicious apple
State gem: Mississippian Fossil Coral (*Lithostrotionella*)
State insect: Honeybee (*Apis mellifera*)
State soil: Monongahela Silt Loam
State songs: "The West Virginia Hills"; "West Virginia, My Home Sweet Home"; "This Is My West Virginia"
State tree: Sugar maple (*Acer saccharum*)

More about state symbols at:
http://www.wvtourism.com/spec.aspx?pgID=77
http://www.legis.state.wv.us/Educational/Kids_Page/kids.html

More about the state at:
http://www.wv.gov/sec.aspx?pgID=27
http://www.wvtourism.com/spec.aspx?pgID=3

SOURCES:
AmerBkDays-2000, p. 460
AnnivHol-2000, p. 103
DictDays-1988, p. 130

STATE OFFICES:
State web site:
http://www.wv.gov

Office of the Governor
State Capitol Bldg
1900 Kanawha Blvd E
Charleston, WV 25305
304-558-2000
fax: 304-342-7025
http://www.wvgov.org

Secretary of State
1900 Kanawha Blvd E
Bldg 1 Suite 157K

Charleston, WV 25305
304-558-6000
fax: 304-558-0900
http://www.wvsos.com

West Virginia Library Commission
1900 Kanawha Blvd E
Charleston, WV 25305
304-558-2041
fax: 304-558-2044
http://www.librarycommission.lib.wv.us

Wisconsin

Thirtieth state; admitted on May 29, 1848

State capital: Madison
Nicknames: Badger State; America's Dairyland; Copper State
State motto: Forward
State animal: Badger (*Taxidea taxus*); **wildlife animal**: White-tailed deer (*Odocoileus virginianus*) **domestic animal**: Dairy cow (*Bos taurus*)
State ballad: "Oh Wisconsin, Land of My Dreams"
State beverage: Milk
State bird: Robin (*Turdus migratorius*)
State dance: Polka
State dog: American water spaniel
State fish: Muskellunge (muskie, *Esox masquinongy Mitchell*)
State flower: Wood violet (*Viola papilionacea*)
State fossil: Trilobite (*Calymene celebra*)
State fruit: Cranberry *(vaccinium macrocarpon)*
State grain: Corn (*Zea mays*)
State insect: Honeybee (*Apis mellifera*)
State mineral: Galena
State rock: Red granite
State soil: Antigo silt loam
State song: "On, Wisconsin!"
State symbol of peace: Mourning dove (*Zenaidura macroura corolinensis linnaus*)
State tree: Sugar maple (*Acer saccharum*)
State waltz: "The Wisconsin Waltz"

More about state symbols at:
http://www.wisconsin.gov/state/core/wisconsin_state _symbols.html
http://dnr.wi.gov/org/caer/ce/eek/nature/state/index.htm

More about the state at:
http://www.wisconsinhistory.org/

SOURCES:
AmerBkDays-2000, p. 400
AnnivHol-2000, p. 89

STATE OFFICES:
State web site:
http://www.wisconsin.gov

Office of the Governor
State Capitol
PO Box 7863
Madison, WI 53707
608-266-1212
fax: 608-267-8983
http://www.wisgov.state.wi.us

Secretary of State
PO Box 7848
Madison, WI 53707
608-266-8888
fax: 608-266-3159
http://www.sos.state.wi.us

Wisconsin Dept of Public Instruction Library Services Div
125 S Webster St
PO Box 7841
Madison, WI 53707
608-266-3390
fax: 608-267-1052
http://www.dpi.state.wi.us/

Wyoming

Forty-fourth state; admitted on July 10, 1890

State capital: Cheyenne
Nicknames: Equality State; Cowboy State; Big Wyoming
State motto: Equal Rights
State bird: Meadowlark (*Sturnella neglecta*)
State coin: Golden dollar
State dinosaur: Triceratops
State fish: Cutthroat trout (*Salmo clerki*)
State flower: Indian paintbrush (*Castilleja linariaefolia*)
State fossil: Knightia
State gemstone: Jade (nephrite)
State icon: Bucking horse
State mammal: Bison (*Bison bison*)
State reptile: Horned toad (*Douglassi brevirostre*)
State song: "Wyoming"
State sport: Rodeo
State tree: Plains cottonwood (*Populus sargentii*)

More about state symbols at:
http://wyoming.gov/wyoinfo.asp
http://wyoming.gov/state/wyoming_news/general/general.asp

More about the state at:
http://wyoming.gov/about.asp

SOURCES:
AmerBkDays-2000, p. 519
AnnivHol-2000, p. 115

STATE OFFICES:
State web site:
http://wyoming.gov

Office of the Governor
State Capitol
200 W 24th St Rm 124
Cheyenne, WY 82202
307-777-7434
fax: 307-632-3909
http://wyoming.gov/governor

Secretary of State
200 W 24th St
Cheyenne, WY 82002
307-777-7378
fax: 307-777-6217
http://soswy.state.wy.us

Wyoming State Library
2301 Capitol Ave

Cheyenne, WY 82002
307-777-6333
fax: 307-777-6289
http://www-wsl.state.wy.us

American Samoa

American Samoa has been a U.S. territory since 1899; its inhabitants are considered U.S. nationals.

Capital: Pago Pago
Motto: *Samoa—Muamua le Atua* (Samoan "Samoa—Let God Be First")
Flower: Paogo (ulafala)
Plant: Ava (kava)
Song: "Amerika Samoa"
Tree: Paogo or pandanus

GOVERNMENT OFFICES:
Government web site:
http://americansamoa.gov

Office of the Governor
Executive Office Bldg
Third Floor, Utulei
Pago Pago, American Samoa 96799
011-684-633-4116
fax: 011-684-633-2269
http://americansamoa.gov/gov_office/gov_office.htm

Department of Local Government
011-684-633-5201
fax: 011-684-633-5590

Feleti Barstow Public Library
997687 Utulei Way
Pago Pago, American Samoa 96799
011-684-633-5816
fax: 011-684-633-5816

Guam

Guam has been a territory of the U.S. since 1898, but has been allowed autonomy in local affairs since 1950; native inhabitants are citizens of the U.S. but cannot vote in U.S. elections.

Capital: Hagatna (Agana)
Nicknames: Tano I'ManChanorro (Land of the Chamorros); Where America's Day Begins; America's Paradise in the Pacific
Bird: Totot (also known as the Mariana fruit dove or love bird; *Ptilinopus roseicapilla*)
Flower: Puti tai nobio or bougainvillea (*bougainvillea spectabilis*)
Hymn: "Guam Hymn" ("Fanohge Chamorro")
Languages: Chamorro; English
Tree: Ifil or Ifit (Intsia bijuga)

GOVERNMENT OFFICES:
Government web site:
http://www.guam.gov

Office of the Governor
Ufisinan Maga'lahi
Executive Chambers
PO Box 2950

Hagatna, Guam 96932
011-671-472-8931
fax: 011-671-477-4826
http://www.guamgovernor.net
governor@mail.gov.gu

Lieutenant Governor
PO Box 2950
Hagatna, Guam 96932
011-671-475-9380
fax: 011-671-47-2007
http://www.guamltgovernor.org
ltgov@mail.gov.gu

Public Library System
Nieves M. Flores Memorial Library
254 Martyr St
Hagatna, Guam 96910
011-671-475-4573
fax: 011-671-477-9777
http://gpls.guam.gov
gpls@gpls.guam.gov

Northern Mariana Islands

In 1947 the U.N. assigned the Islands to the U.S. to administer; in 1978 the Islands became a self-governing commonwealth under U.S. sovereignty; inhabitants became U.S. citizens in 1986, but cannot vote in U.S. elections.

Capital: Saipan (Capitol Hill)
Bird: Marianas Fruit Dove (*Ptilonopus roseicapilla*)
Flower: Plumeria (*Plumeria rubra forma acutifolia*)
Tree: Flame tree (*Delonix regia*)

GOVERNMENT OFFICES:

Office of the Governor
Caller Box 10007
Capital Hill
Saipan, 96950
670-664-2200
fax: 670-664-2211

Joeten-Kiyu Public Library
P.O. Box501092
Saipan, 96950
670-235-4758
fax: 670-235-7322
http://www.cnmilibrary.com/
saipanlib@cnmilibrary.com

Puerto Rico

Puerto Rico became a territory of the U.S. in 1917, and, on July 25, 1952, a commonwealth with autonomous local governmental units; inhabitants have been U.S. citizens since 1917.

See PUERTO RICO CONSTITUTION DAY

Capital: San Juan
Nickname: Island of Enchantment
Motto: *Joannes est nomen ejus* (Spanish "Juan [John] Is His Name")
Animal: El coquí or tree frog (*Francolinus coqui*)
Bird: Reinita
Flower: Maga or Puerto Rico hibiscus (*Thespesia grandiflora*)
Languages: English; Spanish

Song: "La Borinqueña"
Sport: Beisbol or baseball
Tree: Ceiba or silk-cotton or kapok tree (*Ceiba pentandra*)

More about the symbols at:
http://www.gobierno.pr/GPRPortal/Inicio/PuertoRico/Simbolos (Spanish only)
http://www.elboricua.com/FactSheet.html

GOVERNMENT OFFICES:

Government web site:
http://www.gobierno.pr (Spanish only)

Office of the Governor
La Fortaleza
PO Box 9020082
San Juan, 00902-0082
787-721-7000
http://www.fortaleza.gobierno.pr (Spanish only)

State Department
Apartado 9023271
San Juan, Puerto Rico 00902-3271
787-722-2121
http://www.estado.gobierno.pr (Spanish only)

University of Puerto Rico Library System
Rio Piedras Campus
PO Box 23302
San Juan, 00931-3302
787-764-0000
fax: 787-772-1479

U.S. Virgin Islands

The U.S. Virgin Islands were purchased by the U.S. on March 31, 1917; in 1927 native inhabitants were made U.S. citizens.

See TRANSFER DAY

Capital: Charlotte Amalie
Nickname: The American Paradise
Motto: United in Pride and Hope
Bird: Yellow breast (bananaquit; *Coereba flaveola*)
Flower: Yellow cedar or trumpetbush (*Tecoma stans*)
Language (official): English
March: "Virgin Islands March"

More about the symbols at:
http://www.usvitourism.vi/en/pdfs/Visitor_Guide.pdf

More about the territory at:
http://www.usvitourism.vi/

GOVERNMENT OFFICES:

Government web site:
http://www.gov.vi/

Office of the Governor
Government House
21-22 Kongens Gade
Charlotte Amalie
St. Thomas, VI 00802
340-774-0001
fax: 340-693-4374
http://www.governordejongh.com
contact@ governordejongh.com

Division of Libraries, Archives and Museums
20 Dronningens Gade
St. Thomas, 00802
340-774-3407
fax: 340-775-1887

APPENDIX 7

Legal Holidays by State

The following federal public holidays are observed throughout the United States:

Jan 1	New Year's Day
Jan, third Mon	Martin Luther King Jr. Birthday
Feb, third Mon	Presidents' Day
May, last Mon	Memorial Day
Jul 4	Independence Day
Sep, first Mon	Labor Day
Oct, second Mon	Columbus Day
Nov 11	Veterans Day
Nov, fourth Thurs	Thanksgiving Day
Dec 25	Christmas

Listed below are additional legal holidays observed by the various states, the District of Columbia, the Commonwealth of Puerto Rico, and the territories of American Samoa, Guam, Northern Mariana Islands, and the U.S. Virgin Islands. For Christian movable holidays, the range of months during which the day may fall is provided.

Alabama

Jan, third Mon	Martin Luther King Jr. Birthday and Robert E. Lee's Birthday
Feb, third Mon	Washington and Jefferson's Birthdays
Apr, fourth Mon	Confederate Memorial Day
Jun, first Mon	Jefferson Davis's Birthday
Oct, second Mon	Columbus Day and American Indian Heritage Day

Alaska

Mar, last Mon	Seward's Day
Oct 18	Alaska Day

Arizona

Jan, third Mon	Martin Luther King Jr. Birthday and Civil Rights Day
Sep 17	Constitution Commemoration Day

Arkansas

Jan, third Mon	Martin Luther King Jr. Birthday and Robert E. Lee's Birthday
Feb, third Mon	Washington's Birthday and Daisy Gatson Bates Day
Dec 24	Christmas Eve

California

Feb 12	Lincoln's Birthday
Feb, third Mon	Washington's Birthday
Mar 31 (or next Mon)	Cesar Chavez Day
Nov, Fri after Thanksgiving	Day after Thanksgiving

Colorado

None in addition to the standard holidays

Connecticut

Feb 12	Lincoln Day
Feb, third Mon	Washington's Birthday
Mar-Apr: Fri, before Easter	Good Friday

Delaware

Mar-Apr: Fri, before Easter	Good Friday
Nov, Fri after Thanksgiving	Day after Thanksgiving
Nov, every two years	General Election Day as it occurs

District of Columbia

Jan 20	Inauguration Day (in years when a new president is elected)
April 16	DC Emancipation Day

909

Florida

Nov, Fri after Thanksgiving . . . . . .Day after Thanksgiving

Georgia

Apr 26 . . . . .Confederate Memorial Day
Nov, Fri after Thanksgiving . . . . .Robert E. Lee's
                     Birthday (traditionally observed Jan 19)
Dec 26 . . . . .Presidents' Day
                  (traditionally observed Feb, third Mon)

Hawaii

Mar 26 . . . . .Prince Jonah Kuhio Kalanianaole Day
Mar-Apr: Fri before Easter . . . . .Good Friday
Jun 11 . . . . .King Kamehameha I Day
Aug, third Fri . . . . .Statehood Day
Nov, first Tues (even years) . . . . .Election Day

Idaho

None in addition to the standard holidays

Illinois

Feb 12 . . . . .Lincoln's Birthday
Feb, third Mon . . . . .Washington's Birthday
Nov . . . . .General Election Day
Nov, Fri after Thanksgiving . . . . . .Day after Thanksgiving
Dec 24 . . . . .Christmas Eve

Indiana

Presidents' Day not a legal holiday

Mar-Apr: Fri before Easter . . . . .Good Friday
May, first Tues . . . . .Primary Election Day
          (except year following presidential election)
Nov, first Tues . . . . .General Election Day
          (except year following presidential election)
Nov, Fri after Thanksgiving . . . . .Lincoln's Birthday
               (traditionally observed Feb 12)
Dec 26 . . . . .Washington's Birthday
          (traditionally observed Feb, third Mon)

Iowa

Presidents' Day not a legal holiday

Nov, Fri after Thanksgiving . . . . . .Day after Thanksgiving

Kansas

Presidents' Day not observed

Nov, Fri after Thanksgiving . . . . . .Day After Thanksgiving

Kentucky

Jan, dates vary . . . . .New Year's (2 days)
Mar-Apr, Fri before Easter . . . . . . .Good Friday (half day)
Nov . . . . .General Presidential Election
Nov, Fri after Thanksgiving . . . . . .Day after Thanksgiving
Dec, dates vary . . . . .Christmas (2 days)

Louisiana

Jan, second Mon every
four years in Baton Rouge . . . . .Inauguration Day
Feb, day before Ash Wednesday . . . . .Mardi Gras Day
Mar-Apr: Fri before Easter . . . . .Good Friday
Nov (even years) . . . . .Election Day

Maine

Apr, third Mon . . . . .Patriots' Day
Nov, Fri after Thanksgiving . . . . . .Day after Thanksgiving

Maryland

Nov . . . . .Election Day
Nov, Fri after Thanksgiving . . . . . .Day after Thanksgiving

Massachusetts

Apr, third Mon . . . . .Patriots' Day

Michigan

Nov, first Tues (even years) . . . . .Election Day
Nov, Fri after Thanksgiving . . . . . .Day after Thanksgiving
Dec 24 . . . . .Christmas Eve
Dec 31 . . . . .New Year's Eve

Minnesota

None in addition to the standard holidays

Mississippi

Jan, third Mon . . . . .Martin Luther King Jr. Birthday
                  and Robert E. Lee's Birthday
Apr, last Mon . . . . .Confederate Memorial Day
May, last Mon . . . . .Memorial Day
              and Jefferson Davis's Birthday

Missouri

Feb 12 . . . . .Lincoln Day
May 8 . . . . .Harry S. Truman Day

Montana

Nov, first Tues . . . . .General Election Day

Nebraska

Apr, last Fri . . . . .Arbor Day
Nov, Fri after Thanksgiving . . . . . .Day after Thanksgiving

Nevada

Oct, last Fri . . . . .Nevada Day
Nov, Fri after Thanksgiving . . . . .Family Day

New Hampshire

Nov, first Tues (even years) . . . . .Election Day
Nov, Fri after Thanksgiving . . . . . .Day after Thanksgiving

New Jersey

Feb 12 . . . . .Lincoln's Birthday
Feb, third Mon . . . . .Washington's Birthday
Mar-Apr: Fri before Easter . . . . .Good Friday
Nov . . . . .Election Day

New Mexico

None in addition to the standard holidays

New York

Feb 12 . . . . .Lincoln's Birthday
Feb, third Mon . . . . .Washington's Birthday
Nov . . . . .Election Day

North Carolina

Presidents' Day not a legal holiday

Mar-Apr: Fri before Easter . . . . .Good Friday
Nov, Fri after Thanksgiving . . . . . .Day After Thanksgiving
Dec 24 . . . . .Christmas Eve

North Dakota

Mar-Apr: Fri before Easter . . . . .Good Friday

Ohio

None in addition to the standard holidays

Oklahoma

Nov, Fri after Thanksgiving . . . . . .Day after Thanksgiving

Oregon

None in addition to the standard holidays

Pennsylvania

Nov, Fri after Thanksgiving . . . . . .Day after Thanksgiving

Rhode Island

Presidents' Day not a legal holiday

Aug, second Mon . . . . .Victory Day (V-J Day)
Nov . . . . .Election Day

South Carolina

May 10 . . . . .Confederate Memorial Day
Nov, Fri after Thanksgiving . . . . . .Day after Thanksgiving
Dec 26 . . . . .Day after Christmas

South Dakota

Oct, second Mon . . . . .Native Americans' Day

Tennessee

Mar-Apr: Fri before Easter . . . . .Good Friday

Texas

Jan 19 . . . . .Confederate Heroes Day
Mar 2 . . . . .Texas Independence Day
Apr 21 . . . . .San Jacinto Day
Jun 19 . . . . .Emancipation Day (Juneteenth)
Aug 24 . . . . .Lyndon Baines Johnson Day
Nov . . . . .Election Day
Nov, Fri after Thanksgiving . . . . . .Day after Thanksgiving
Dec 24 . . . . .Christmas Eve
Dec 26 . . . . .Day after Christmas

Utah

Jul 24 . . . . .Pioneer Day

Vermont

Mar, first Tues . . . . .Town Meeting Day
Aug 16 . . . . .Bennington Battle Day
Nov, Fri after Thanksgiving . . . . . .Day after Thanksgiving

Virginia

Jan, Fri before third Mon . . . . .Lee-Jackson Day
Oct, second Mon . . . . .Columbus Day
and Yorktown Victory Day
Nov, Fri after Thanksgiving . . . . . .Day after Thanksgiving

Washington

Nov, Fri after Thanksgiving . . . . . .Day after Thanksgiving

West Virginia

Feb, third Mon	Presidents' Day/Washington's Birthday
May, second Tues (even years)	Primary Election Day
Jun 20	West Virginia Day
Nov, first Tues (even years)	Election Day
Nov, Fri after Thanksgiving	Day after Thanksgiving
Dec 24	Christmas Eve (half day)
Dec 31	New Year's Eve (half day)

Wisconsin

Presidents' Day not a legal holiday

Dec 24	Christmas Eve

Wyoming

None in addition to the standard holidays

TERRITORIES

American Samoa

Apr 17	American Samoa Flag Day
Jul 17	Manu'a Day
Dec 31	New Year's Eve

Guam

Presidents' Day and Columbus Day not legal holidays

Jul 21	Liberation Day

Nov 2	All Souls Day
Dec 8	Our Lady of Camarin Day

Northern Mariana Islands

Mar 24	Commonwealth Covenant Day
Mar-Apr: Fri before Easter	Good Friday
Oct, second Mon	Commonwealth Cultural Day
Nov 4	Citizenship Day
Dec 8	Constitution Day

Puerto Rico

Jan 6	Three Kings' Day
Jan, second Mon	Eugenio María de Hostos Day
Mar 22	Emancipation Day
Mar-Apr: Fri before Easter	Good Friday
Apr, third Mon	José de Diego Day
Jul 17	Luis Muñoz Rivera Day
Jul 25	Constitution Day
Jul 27	José Celso Barbosa's Birthday
Nov, first Tuesday	General Election Day
Nov 19	Discovery Day
Dec 24	Christmas Eve (half day)

U.S. Virgin Islands

Jan 6	Three Kings' Day
Mar 31	Transfer Day
Mar-Apr: Thurs before Easter	Holy Thursday
Mar-Apr: Fri before Easter	Good Friday
Mar-Apr: Mon after Easter	Easter Monday
Jul 3	Virgin Islands Emancipation Day
Nov 1	D. Hamilton Jackson Day (Liberty Day)
Dec 26	Christmas Second Day

APPENDIX 8

Tourism Information Sources for the U.S. States and North America

The following includes tourism information sources for the United States, Canada, and Mexico. Within the United States, the list is organized first by state, plus the District of Columbia. Within each state listing, listings are in the following order, although each state may not have all offices:

UNITED STATES

Alabama

Alabama Tourism & Travel Bureau
401 Adams Ave, Ste 126
Montgomery, AL 36104
Phone: 334-242-4169; Fax: 334-242-4554
Toll-free: 800-252-2262
www.touralabama.org

Business Council of Alabama
PO Box 76
Montgomery, AL 36101
Phone: 334-834-6000; Fax: 334-241-5984
Toll-free: 800-665-9647
www.bcatoday.org

Greater Birmingham Convention & Visitors Bureau
2200 9th Ave N
Birmingham, AL 35203
Phone: 205-458-8000; Fax: 205-458-8086
Toll-free: 800-458-8085
www.sweetbirmingham.com

Huntsville/Madison County Convention & Visitor's Bureau
500 Church St
Huntsville, AL 35801
Phone: 256-551-2230; Fax: 256-551-2324
Toll-free: 800-772-2348
www.huntsville.org

Mobile Bay Convention & Visitors Bureau
1 S Water St
Mobile, AL 36602
Phone: 251-208-2000; Fax: 251-208-2060
Toll-free: 800-566-2453
www.mobile.org

Montgomery Area Chamber of Commerce Convention &
  Visitor Bureau
300 Water St
Union Stn

Montgomery, AL 36104
Phone: 334-261-1100; Fax: 334-261-1111
Toll-free: 800-240-9452
www.visitingmontgomery.com

Tuscaloosa Convention & Visitors Bureau
1305 Greensboro Ave
Tuscaloosa, AL 35401
Phone: 205-391-9200; Fax: 205-759-9002
Toll-free: 800-538-8696
www.tcvb.org

Birmingham Regional Chamber of Commerce
505 N 20th St
Suite 200
Birmingham, AL 35203
Phone: 205-324-2100; Fax: 205-324-2560
www.birminghamchamber.com

Chamber of Commerce of Huntsville/Madison County
PO Box 408
Huntsville, AL 35804
Phone: 256-535-2000; Fax: 256-535-2015
www.huntsvillealabamausa.com

Chamber of Commerce of West Alabama
PO Box 020410
Tuscaloosa, AL 35402
Phone: 205-758-7588; Fax: 205-391-0565
www.tuscaloosachamber.com

Mobile Area Chamber of Commerce
451 Government St
Mobile, AL 36602
Phone: 251-433-6951; Fax: 251-432-1143
Toll-free: 800-422-6951
www.mobilechamber.com

Montgomery Area Chamber of Commerce
41 Commerce St
Box 79
Montgomery, AL 36101
Phone: 334-834-5200; Fax: 334-265-4745
www.montgomerychamber.com

Alaska

Alaska Tourism Development Office
PO Box 11801
Juneau, AK 99811
Phone: 907-465-2012; Fax: 907-465-3767
www.commerce.state.ak.us/oed/toubus/home.cfm

Alaska State Chamber of Commerce
217 2nd St
Suite 201
Juneau, AK 99801
Phone: 907-586-2323; Fax: 907-463-5515
www.alaskachamber.com

Anchorage Convention & Visitors Bureau
524 W 4th Ave
Anchorage, AK 99501
Phone: 907-276-4118; Fax: 907-278-5559
Toll-free: 800-478-1255
www.anchorage.net

Fairbanks Convention & Visitors Bureau
550 1st Ave
Fairbanks, AK 99701
Phone: 907-456-5774; Fax: 907-452-2867
Toll-free: 800-327-5774
www.explorefairbanks.com

Juneau Convention & Visitors Bureau
One Sealaska Plaza
Suite 305
Juneau, AK 99801
Phone: 907-586-1737; Fax: 907-586-1449
Toll-free: 800-587-2201
www.traveljuneau.com

Anchorage Chamber of Commerce
1016 W 6th Ave
Suite 303
Anchorage, AK 99501
Phone: 907-272-2401; Fax: 907-272-4117
www.anchoragechamber.org

Fairbanks Chamber of Commerce
800 Cushman St
Suite 114
Fairbanks, AK 99701
Phone: 907-452-1105; Fax: 907-456-6968
www.fairbankschamber.org

Juneau Chamber of Commerce
3100 Channel Dr
Suite 300
Juneau, AK 99801
Phone: 907-463-3488; Fax: 907-463-3489
www.juneauchamber.com

Arizona

Arizona Tourism Office
1110 W Washington St
Suite 155
Phoenix, AZ 85007
Phone: 602-364-3700; Fax: 602-364-3701

Toll-free: 888-520-3434
www.arizonaguide.com

Arizona Chamber of Commerce & Industry
1850 N Central Ave
Suite 1010
Phoenix, AZ 85014
Phone: 602-248-9172; Fax: 602-265-1262
Toll-free: 800-498-6973
www.azchamber.com

Flagstaff Convention & Visitors Bureau
323 W Aspen Ave
Flagstaff, AZ 86001
Phone: 928-779-7611; Fax: 928-556-1305
Toll-free: 800-217-2367
www.flagstaffarizona.org

Greater Phoenix Convention & Visitors Bureau
400 E Van Buren St
1 Arizona Center Suite 600
Phoenix, AZ 85004
Phone: 602-254-6500; Fax: 602-253-4415
Toll-free: 877-225-5749
www.visitphoenix.com

Mesa Convention & Visitors Bureau
120 N Center St
Mesa, AZ 85201
Phone: 480-827-4700; Fax: 480-827-4704
Toll-free: 800-283-6372
www.mesacvb.com

Metropolitan Tucson Convention & Visitors Bureau
100 S Church Ave
Tucson, AZ 85701
Phone: 520-624-1817; Fax: 520-884-7804
Toll-free: 800-638-8350
www.visittucson.org

Scottsdale Convention & Visitors Bureau
4343 N Scottsdale Rd
Suite 170
Scottsdale, AZ 85251
Phone: 480-421-1004; Fax: 480-421-9733
Toll-free: 800-782-1117
www.scottsdalecvb.com

Tempe Convention & Visitors Bureau
51 W 3rd St
Suite 105
Tempe, AZ 85281
Phone: 480-894-8158; Fax: 480-968-8004
Toll-free: 800-283-6734
www.tempecvb.com

Flagstaff Chamber of Commerce
101 W Rt 66
Flagstaff, AZ 86001
Phone: 928-774-4505; Fax: 928-779-1209
www.flagstaffchamber.com

Glendale Chamber of Commerce
PO Box 249
Glendale, AZ 85311
Phone: 623-937-4754; Fax: 623-937-3333

Toll-free: 800-437-8669
www.glendaleazchamber.org

Greater Phoenix Chamber of Commerce
201 N Central Ave
Suite 2700
Phoenix, AZ 85073
Phone: 602-254-5521; Fax: 602-495-8913
www.phoenixchamber.com

Mesa Chamber of Commerce
120 N Center St
Mesa, AZ 85201
Phone: 480-969-1307; Fax: 480-827-0727
www.mesachamber.org

Scottsdale Area Chamber of Commerce
7343 Scottsdale Mall
Scottsdale, AZ 85251
Phone: 480-945-8481; Fax: 480-947-4523
www.scottsdalechamber.com

Tempe Chamber of Commerce
PO Box 28500
Tempe, AZ 85285
Phone: 480-967-7891; Fax: 480-966-5365
www.tempechamber.org

Tucson Metropolitan Chamber of Commerce
465 W St Mary's Rd
Tucson, AZ 85701
Phone: 520-792-2250; Fax: 520-882-5704
www.tucsonchamber.org

Arkansas

Arkansas Parks & Tourism Dept
1 Capitol Mall
Little Rock, AR 72201
Phone: 501-682-7777; Fax: 501-682-1364
Toll-free: 800-628-8725
www.arkansas.com

Arkansas State Chamber of Commerce
410 S Cross St
PO Box 3645
Little Rock, AR 72203
Phone: 501-372-2222; Fax: 501-372-2722
www.statechamber-aia.dina.org

Fort Smith Convention & Visitors Bureau
2 N 'B' St
Fort Smith, AR 72901
Phone: 479-783-8888; Fax: 479-784-2421
Toll-free: 800-637-1477
www.fortsmith.org

Hot Springs Convention & Visitors Bureau
134 Convention Blvd
Hot Springs, AR 71901
Phone: 501-321-2277; Fax: 501-321-2136
Toll-free: 800-543-2284
www.hotsprings.org

Little Rock Convention & Visitors Bureau
426 W Markham St
PO Box 3232
Little Rock, AR 72203
Phone: 501-376-4781; Fax: 501-374-2255
Toll-free: 800-844-4781
www.littlerock.com

Fort Smith Chamber of Commerce
612 Garrison Ave
Fort Smith, AR 72901
Phone: 479-783-6118; Fax: 479-783-6110
www.fschamber.com

Greater Hot Springs Chamber of Commerce
659 Ouachita Ave
Hot Springs, AR 71901
Phone: 501-321-1700; Fax: 501-321-3551
Toll-free: 800-467-4636
www.hotspringschamber.com

Greater Little Rock Chamber of Commerce
1 Chamber Plaza
Little Rock, AR 72201
Phone: 501-374-2001; Fax: 501-374-6018
www.littlerockchamber.com

California

California Travel & Tourism Commission
PO Box 1499
Sacramento, CA 95812
Phone: 916-444-4429; Fax: 916-322-3402
www.visitcalifornia.com

California Chamber of Commerce
PO Box 1736
Sacramento, CA 95812
Phone: 916-444-6670; Fax: 916-325-1272
www.calchamber.com

Anaheim/Orange County Visitor & Convention Bureau
800 W Katella Ave
Anaheim, CA 92802
Phone: 714-765-8888; Fax: 714-991-8963
Toll-free: 888-598-3200
www.anaheimoc.org

Chula Vista Convention & Visitors Bureau
233 4th Ave
Chamber of Commerce Bldg
Chula Vista, CA 91910
Phone: 619-426-2882; Fax: 619-420-1269
www.chulavistaconvis.org

Fresno City & County Convention & Visitors Bureau
848 M St
3rd Fl
Fresno, CA 93721
Phone: 559-445-8300; Fax: 559-445-0122
Toll-free: 800-788-0836
www.fresnocvb.org

Garden Grove Visitors Bureau
12866 Main St

Suite 102
Garden Grove, CA 92840
Phone: 714-638-7950; Fax: 714-636-6672
www.gardengrovechamber.org

Greater Bakersfield Convention & Visitors Bureau
515 Truxtun Ave
Bakersfield, CA 93301
Phone: 661-325-5051; Fax: 661-325-7074
Toll-free: 866-425-7353
www.bakersfieldcvb.org

Huntington Beach Conference & Visitors Bureau
301 Main St
Suite 208
Huntington Beach, CA 92648
Phone: 714-969-3492; Fax: 714-969-5592
surfcityusa.com

Long Beach Convention & Visitors Bureau
1 World Trade Center
Suite 300
Long Beach, CA 90831
Phone: 562-436-3645; Fax: 562-435-5653
Toll-free: 800-452-7829
www.visitlongbeach.com

Los Angeles Convention & Visitors Bureau
333 S Hope St
18th Fl
Los Angeles, CA 90071
Phone: 213-624-7300; Fax: 213-624-9746
Toll-free: 800-228-2452
www.lacvb.com

Modesto Convention & Visitors Bureau
1150 9th St
Suite C
Modesto, CA 95354
Phone: 209-526-5588; Fax: 209-526-5586
Toll-free: 888-640-8467
www.visitmodesto.com

Monterey County Convention & Visitors Bureau
150 Oliver St
PO Box 1770
Monterey, CA 93942
Phone: 831-649-1770; Fax: 831-648-5373
Toll-free: 888-221-1010
www.montereyinfo.org

Oakland Convention & Visitors Bureau
463 11th St
Oakland, CA 94607
Phone: 510-839-9000; Fax: 510-839-5924
www.oaklandcvb.com

Oxnard Convention & Visitors Bureau
200 W 7th St
Oxnard, CA 93030
Phone: 805-385-7545; Fax: 805-385-7571
Toll-free: 800-269-6273
www.oxnardtourism.com

Palm Springs Desert Resorts Convention & Visitors Authority
70-100 Hwy 111

Rancho Mirage, CA 92270
Phone: 760-770-9000; Fax: 760-770-9001
Toll-free: 800-967-3767
www.palmspringsusa.com

Riverside Convention & Visitors Bureau
3750 University Ave
Suite 175
Riverside, CA 92501
Phone: 951-222-4700; Fax: 951-222-4712
Toll-free: 888-913-4636
www.riversidecvb.com

Sacramento Convention & Visitors Bureau
1608 'I' St
Sacramento, CA 95814
Phone: 916-808-7777; Fax: 916-808-7788
Toll-free: 800-292-2334
www.sacramentocvb.org

San Bernardino Convention & Visitors Bureau
201 N 'E' St
Suite 103
San Bernardino, CA 92401
Phone: 909-889-3980; Fax: 909-888-5998
Toll-free: 800-867-8366
san-bernardino.org

San Diego Convention & Visitors Bureau
2215 India St
San Diego, CA 92101
Phone: 619-232-3101; Fax: 619-696-9371
www.sandiego.org

San Francisco Convention & Visitors Bureau
201 3rd St
Suite 900
San Francisco, CA 94103
Phone: 415-974-6900; Fax: 415-227-2602
www.sfvisitor.org

San Jose Convention & Visitors Bureau
408 Almaden Blvd
San Jose, CA 95110
Phone: 408-295-9600; Fax: 408-277-3535
Toll-free: 800-726-5673
www.sanjose.org

Santa Barbara Visitors Bureau & Film Commission
1601 Anacapa St
Santa Barbara, CA 93101
Phone: 805-966-9222; Fax: 805-966-1728
Toll-free: 800-927-4688
www.santabarbaraca.com

Stockton/San Joaquin Convention & Visitors Bureau
445 W Webber Ave
Suite 220
Stockton, CA 95203
Phone: 209-547-2770; Fax: 209-466-5271
www.visitstockton.org

Anaheim Chamber of Commerce
201 E Center St
Anaheim, CA 92805
Phone: 714-758-0222; Fax: 714-758-0468
anaheimchamber.org

Chula Vista Chamber of Commerce
233 4th Ave
Chula Vista, CA 91910
Phone: 619-420-6602; Fax: 619-420-1269
www.chulavistachamber.org

Fremont Chamber of Commerce
39488 Stevenson Pl
Suite 100
Fremont, CA 94539
Phone: 510-795-2244; Fax: 510-795-2240
www.fremontbusiness.com

Fresno Chamber of Commerce
2331 Fresno St
Fresno, CA 93721
Phone: 559-495-4800; Fax: 559-495-4811
www.fresnochamber.com

Garden Grove Chamber of Commerce
12866 Main St
Suite 102
Garden Grove, CA 92840
Phone: 714-638-7950; Fax: 714-636-6672
Toll-free: 800-959-5560
www.gardengrovechamber.org

Glendale Chamber of Commerce
200 S Louise St
Glendale, CA 91205
Phone: 818-240-7870; Fax: 818-240-2872
www.glendalechamber.com

Greater Bakersfield Chamber of Commerce
1725 Eye St
Bakersfield, CA 93301
Phone: 661-327-4421; Fax: 661-327-8751
www.bakersfieldchamber.org

Greater Riverside Chambers of Commerce
3985 University Ave
Riverside, CA 92501
Phone: 951-683-7100; Fax: 951-683-2670
www.riverside-chamber.com

Greater Stockton Chamber of Commerce
445 W Weber Ave
Suite 220
Stockton, CA 95203
Phone: 209-547-2770; Fax: 209-466-5271
www.stocktonchamber.org

Huntington Beach Chamber of Commerce
19891 Beach Blvd
Suite 140
Huntington Beach, CA 92648
Phone: 714-536-8888; Fax: 714-960-7654
www.hbchamber.org

Long Beach Area Chamber of Commerce
1 World Trade Center
Suite 206
Long Beach, CA 90831
Phone: 562-436-1251; Fax: 562-436-7099
www.lbchamber.com

Los Angeles Area Chamber of Commerce
350 S Bixel St
Los Angeles, CA 90017
Phone: 213-580-7500; Fax: 213-580-7511
www.lachamber.org

Modesto Chamber of Commerce
PO Box 844
Modesto, CA 95353
Phone: 209-577-5757; Fax: 209-577-2673
www.modchamber.org

Monterey Peninsula Chamber of Commerce
380 Alvarado St
Monterey, CA 93940
Phone: 831-648-5360; Fax: 831-649-3502
www.mpcc.com

Oakland Metropolitan Chamber of Commerce
475 14th St
Suite 100
Oakland, CA 94612
Phone: 510-874-4800; Fax: 510-839-8817
www.oaklandchamber.com

Oxnard Chamber of Commerce
400 E Esplanade Dr
Suite 302
Oxnard, CA 93036
Phone: 805-983-6118; Fax: 805-604-7331
www.oxnardchamber.org

Palm Springs Chamber of Commerce
190 W Amado Rd
Palm Springs, CA 92262
Phone: 760-325-1577; Fax: 760-325-8549
www.pschamber.org

Sacramento Metro Chamber of Commerce
1 Capital Mall
Suite 300
Sacramento, CA 95814
Phone: 916-552-6800; Fax: 916-443-2672
www.metrochamber.org

San Bernardino Area Chamber of Commerce
PO Box 658
San Bernardino, CA 92402
Phone: 909-885-7515; Fax: 909-384-9979
www.sbachamber.org

San Diego Regional Chamber of Commerce
402 W Broadway
Suite 1000
San Diego, CA 92101
Phone: 619-544-1300
sdchamber.org

San Francisco Chamber of Commerce
235 Montgomery St
12th Fl
San Francisco, CA 94104
Phone: 415-392-4520; Fax: 415-392-0485
www.sfchamber.com

San Jose Silicon Valley Chamber of Commerce
310 S 1st St

San Jose, CA 95113
Phone: 408-291-5250; Fax: 408-286-5019
www.sjchamber.com

Santa Ana Chamber of Commerce
PO Box 205
Santa Ana, CA 92702
Phone: 714-541-5353; Fax: 714-541-2238
www.santaanachamber.com

Santa Barbara Region Chamber of Commerce
924 Anacapa St
Suite 1
Santa Barbara, CA 93101
Phone: 805-965-3023; Fax: 805-966-5954
www.sbchamber.org

Colorado

Colorado Tourism Office
1625 Broadway
Suite 1700
Denver, CO 80202
Phone: 303-892-3885; Fax: 303-892-3848
Toll-free: 800-265-6723
www.colorado.com

Colorado Assn of Commerce & Industry
1600 Broadway
Suite 1000
Denver, CO 80202
Phone: 303-831-7411; Fax: 303-860-1439
www.cochamber.com

Aspen Chamber Resort Assn
425 Rio Grande Pl
Aspen, CO 81611
Phone: 970-925-1940; Fax: 970-920-1173
Toll-free: 800-670-0792
www.aspenchamber.org

Boulder Convention & Visitors Bureau
2440 Pearl St
Boulder, CO 80302
Phone: 303-442-2911; Fax: 303-938-2098
Toll-free: 800-444-0447
www.bouldercoloradousa.com

Colorado Springs Convention & Visitors Bureau
515 S Cascade Ave
Colorado Springs, CO 80903
Phone: 719-635-7506; Fax: 719-635-4968
Toll-free: 800-368-4748
www.experiencecoloradosprings.com

Denver Metro Convention & Visitors Bureau
1555 California St
Suite 300
Denver, CO 80202
Phone: 303-892-1112; Fax: 303-892-1636
Toll-free: 800-234-6257
www.denver.org

Durango Area Tourism Office
111 S Camino del Rio

Durango, CO 81301
Phone: 970-247-3500; Fax: 970-385-7884
Toll-free: 800-525-8855
www.durango.org

Fort Collins Convention & Visitors Bureau
19 Old Town Sq
Suite 137
Fort Collins, CO 80524
Phone: 970-232-3840; Fax: 970-232-3841
Toll-free: 800-274-3678
www.ftcollins.com

Greater Pueblo Chamber of Commerce & Visitors Council
302 N Santa Fe Ave
Pueblo, CO 81003
Phone: 719-542-1704; Fax: 719-542-1624
Toll-free: 800-233-3446
www.pueblo.org

Aspen Chamber Resort Assn
425 Rio Grande Pl
Aspen, CO 81611
Phone: 970-925-1940; Fax: 970-920-1173
Toll-free: 800-670-0792
www.aspenchamber.org

Aurora Chamber of Commerce
562 Sable Blvd
Suite 200
Aurora, CO 80011
Phone: 303-344-1500; Fax: 303-344-1564
www.aurorachamber.org

Boulder Chamber of Commerce
2440 Pearl St
Boulder, CO 80302
Phone: 303-442-1044; Fax: 303-938-8837
www.boulderchamber.com

Colorado Springs Chamber of Commerce
2 N Cascade Ave
Suite 110
Colorado Springs, CO 80903
Phone: 719-635-1551; Fax: 719-635-1571
www.coloradospringschamber.org

Denver Metro Chamber of Commerce
1445 Market St
Denver, CO 80202
Phone: 303-534-8500; Fax: 303-534-3200
www.denverchamber.org

Durango Area Chamber of Commerce
111 S Camino del Rio
PO Box 2587
Durango, CO 81303
Phone: 970-247-0312; Fax: 970-385-7884
Toll-free: 888-414-0835
www.durangobusiness.org

Fort Collins Area Chamber of Commerce
225 S Meldrum St
Fort Collins, CO 80521
Phone: 970-482-3746; Fax: 970-482-3774
www.fcchamber.org

Greater Pueblo Chamber of Commerce
302 N Santa Fe Ave
Pueblo, CO 81003
Phone: 719-542-1704; Fax: 719-542-1624
Toll-free: 800-233-3446
www.pueblochamber.org

Connecticut

Connecticut Commission on Culture & Tourism
755 Main St
1 Financial Plaza
Hartford, CT 06103
Phone: 860-256-2800; Fax: 860-256-2811
www.cultureandtourism.org

Connecticut Tourism Div
505 Hudson St
Hartford, CT 06106
Phone: 860-270-8080; Fax: 860-270-8077
Toll-free: 888-288-4748
www.ctbound.org

Connecticut Business & Industry Assn
350 Church St
Hartford, CT 06103
Phone: 860-244-1900; Fax: 860-278-8562
www.cbia.com

Greater Hartford Convention & Visitors Bureau
31 Pratt St
4th Fl
Hartford, CT 06103
Phone: 860-728-6789; Fax: 860-293-2365
www.enjoyhartford.com

Greater New Haven Convention & Visitors Bureau
169 Orange St
New Haven, CT 06510
Phone: 203-777-8550; Fax: 203-782-7755
Toll-free: 800-332-7829
www.newhavencvb.org

Bridgeport Regional Business Council
10 Middle St
14th Fl
Bridgeport, CT 06604
Phone: 203-335-3800; Fax: 203-366-0105
www.brbc.org

Greater New Haven Chamber of Commerce
900 Chapel St
10th Fl
New Haven, CT 06510
Phone: 203-787-6735; Fax: 203-782-4329
www.gnhcc.com

MetroHartford Alliance
31 Pratt St
Suite 5
Hartford, CT 06103
Phone: 860-525-4451; Fax: 860-293-2592
www.metrohartford.com

Stamford Chamber of Commerce
733 Summer St
Suite 101
Stamford, CT 06901
Phone: 203-359-4761; Fax: 203-363-5069
www.stamfordchamber.com

Delaware

Delaware Tourism Office
99 Kings Hwy
Dover, DE 19901
Phone: 302-739-4271; Fax: 302-739-5749
Toll-free: 866-284-7483
www.visitdelaware.net

Delaware State Chamber of Commerce
PO Box 671
Wilmington, DE 19899
Phone: 302-655-7221; Fax: 302-654-0691
Toll-free: 800-292-9507
www.dscc.com

Greater Wilmington Convention & Visitors Bureau
100 W 10th St
Suite 20
Wilmington, DE 19801
Phone: 302-652-4088; Fax: 302-652-4726
Toll-free: 800-422-1181
www.wilmcvb.org

Kent County Tourism Corp
435 N DuPont Hwy
Dover, DE 19901
Phone: 302-734-1736; Fax: 302-734-0167
Toll-free: 800-233-5368
www.visitdover.com

Rehoboth Beach Convention Center
229 Rehoboth Ave
Rehoboth Beach, DE 19971
Phone: 302-227-4641; Fax: 302-227-4643
cityofrehoboth.com

Central Delaware Economic Development Council
435 N DuPont Hwy
Dover, DE 19901
Phone: 302-678-3028; Fax: 302-678-0189
Toll-free: 800-624-2522
www.cdedc.org

Rehoboth Beach-Dewey Beach Chamber of Commerce
501 Rehoboth Ave
Rehoboth Beach, DE 19971
Phone: 302-227-2233; Fax: 302-227-8351
Toll-free: 800-441-1329
www.beach-fun.com
District of Columbia

District of Columbia Convention & Tourism Corp
901 7th Street NW
4th Fl
Washington, DC 20001
Phone: 202-789-7000; Fax: 202-789-7037
Toll-free: 800-422-8644
www.washington.org

District of Columbia Chamber of Commerce
1213 K St NW
Washington, DC 20005
Phone: 202-347-7201; Fax: 202-638-6762
www.dcchamber.org

US Chamber of Commerce
1615 H St NW
Washington, DC 20062
Phone: 202-659-6000; Fax: 202-463-5836
Toll-free: 800-638-6582
www.uschamber.com

Washington DC Convention & Tourism Corp
901 7th St NW
4th Fl
Washington, DC 20001
Phone: 202-789-7000; Fax: 202-789-7037
Toll-free: 800-422-8644
www.washington.org

Florida

Florida Tourism Commission
661 E Jefferson St
Suite 300
Tallahassee, FL 32301
Phone: 850-488-5607; Fax: 850-224-2938
Toll-free: 888-735-2872
www.visitflorida.com

Florida Chamber of Commerce
136 S Bronough St
Tallahassee, FL 32301
Phone: 850-521-1200; Fax: 850-521-1219
Toll-free: 877-521-1200
www.flchamber.com

Alachua County Visitors & Convention Bureau
30 E University Ave
Gainesville, FL 32601
Phone: 352-374-5231; Fax: 352-338-3213
Toll-free: 866-778-5002
www.visitgainesville.net

Daytona Beach Area Convention & Visitors Bureau
126 E Orange Ave
Daytona Beach, FL 32114
Phone: 386-255-0415; Fax: 386-255-5478
Toll-free: 800-544-0415
www.daytonabeach.com

Greater Fort Lauderdale Convention & Visitors Bureau
100 E Broward Blvd
Suite 200
Fort Lauderdale, FL 33301
Phone: 954-765-4466; Fax: 954-765-4467
Toll-free: 800-356-1662
sunny.org

Greater Miami Convention & Visitors Bureau
701 Brickell Ave
Suite 2700
Miami, FL 33131
Phone: 305-539-3000; Fax: 305-530-5859

Toll-free: 800-933-8448
www.gmcvb.com

Greater Naples Marco Island Everglades Convention &
 Visitors Bureau
3050 N Horseshoe Dr
Suite 218
Naples, FL 34104
Phone: 239-403-2384; Fax: 239-403-2404
Toll-free: 800-688-3600
www.paradisecoast.com

Jacksonville & the Beaches Convention & Visitors Bureau
550 Water St
Suite 1000
Jacksonville, FL 32202
Phone: 904-798-9111; Fax: 904-798-9103
Toll-free: 800-733-2668
www.visitjacksonville.com

Monroe County Tourist Development Council
1201 White St
Suite 102
Key West, FL 33040
Phone: 305-296-1552; Fax: 305-296-0788
Toll-free: 800-648-5510
www.fla-keys.com

Orlando/Orange County Convention & Visitors Bureau
6700 Forum Dr
Suite 100
Orlando, FL 32821
Phone: 407-363-5800; Fax: 407-370-5000
Toll-free: 800-551-0181
www.orlandoinfo.com

Palm Beach County Convention & Visitors Bureau
1555 Palm Beach Lakes Blvd
Suite 800
West Palm Beach, FL 33401
Phone: 561-233-3000; Fax: 561-471-3990
Toll-free: 800-833-5733
www.palmbeachfl.com

Pensacola Convention & Visitors Bureau
1401 E Gregory St
Pensacola, FL 32502
Phone: 850-434-1234; Fax: 850-432-8211
Toll-free: 800-874-1234
www.visitpensacola.com

Saint Johns County Convention & Visitors Bureau
88 Riberia St
Suite 400
Saint Augustine, FL 32084
Phone: 904-829-1711; Fax: 904-829-6149
Toll-free: 800-653-2489
www.oldcity.com

Saint Petersburg/Clearwater Area Convention & Visitors
 Bureau
13805 58th St N
Suite 2-200
Clearwater, FL 33760
Phone: 727-464-7200; Fax: 727-464-7222
Toll-free: 800-345-6710
www.floridasbeach.com

Sarasota Convention & Visitors Bureau
6701 N Tamiami Trail
Sarasota, FL 34236
Phone: 941-957-1877; Fax: 941-951-2956
Toll-free: 800-522-9799
www.sarasotafl.org

Tallahassee Area Convention & Visitors Bureau
106 E Jefferson St
Tallahassee, FL 32301
Phone: 850-606-2305; Fax: 850-606-2301
Toll-free: 800-628-2866
www.seetallahassee.com

Tampa Bay Convention & Visitors Bureau
400 N Tampa St
Suite 2800
Tampa, FL 33602
Phone: 813-223-1111; Fax: 813-229-6616
Toll-free: 800-826-8358
www.visittampabay.com

Chamber of Commerce of the Palm Beaches
401 N Flagler Dr
West Palm Beach, FL 33401
Phone: 561-833-3711; Fax: 561-833-5582
www.palmbeaches.org

Daytona Beach-Halifax Area Chamber of Commerce
126 E Orange Ave
Daytona Beach, FL 32114
Phone: 386-255-0981; Fax: 386-258-5104
www.daytonachamber.com

Gainesville Area Chamber of Commerce
300 E University Ave
Suite 100
Gainesville, FL 32601
Phone: 352-334-7100; Fax: 352-334-7141
www.gainesvillechamber.com

Greater Fort Lauderdale Chamber of Commerce
512 NE 3rd Ave
Fort Lauderdale, FL 33301
Phone: 954-462-6000; Fax: 954-527-8766
www.ftlchamber.com

Greater Miami Chamber of Commerce
1601 Biscayne Blvd
Miami, FL 33132
Phone: 305-350-7700; Fax: 305-374-6902
Toll-free: 888-660-5955
www.greatermiami.com

Greater Sarasota Chamber of Commerce
1945 Fruitville Rd
Sarasota, FL 34236
Phone: 941-955-8187; Fax: 941-366-5621
www.sarasotachamber.org

Greater Tampa Chamber of Commerce
PO Box 420
Tampa, FL 33601
Phone: 813-228-7777; Fax: 813-223-7899
Toll-free: 800-298-2672
www.tampachamber.com

Hialeah Chamber of Commerce & Industries
240 E 1st Ave
Hialeah, FL 33010
Phone: 305-888-7780; Fax: 305-888-7804
www.hialeahchamber.org

Jacksonville Chamber of Commerce
3 Independent Dr
Jacksonville, FL 32202
Phone: 904-366-6600; Fax: 904-632-0617
www.myjaxchamber.com

Key West Chamber of Commerce
402 Wall St
Key West, FL 33040
Phone: 305-294-2587; Fax: 305-294-7806
Toll-free: 800-527-8539
www.keywestchamber.org

Miami Beach Chamber of Commerce
1920 Meridian Ave
3rd Fl
Miami Beach, FL 33139
Phone: 305-672-1270; Fax: 305-538-4336
www.miamibeachchamber.com

Naples Area Chamber of Commerce
2390 Tamiami Trail N
Naples, FL 34103
Phone: 239-262-6141; Fax: 239-435-9910
www.napleschamber.org

Orlando Regional Chamber of Commerce
PO Box 1234
Orlando, FL 32802
Phone: 407-425-1234; Fax: 407-835-2500
www.orlando.org

Pensacola Area Chamber of Commerce
117 W Garden St
Pensacola, FL 32502
Phone: 850-438-4081; Fax: 850-438-6369
www.pensacolachamber.com

Saint Augustine & Saint Johns County Chamber of Commerce
1 Riberia St
Saint Augustine, FL 32084
Phone: 904-829-5681; Fax: 904-829-6477
www.staugustinechamber.com

Saint Petersburg Area Chamber of Commerce
100 2nd Ave N
Suite 150
Saint Petersburg, FL 33701
Phone: 727-821-4069; Fax: 727-895-6326
www.stpete.com

Tallahassee Chamber of Commerce
PO Box 1639
Tallahassee, FL 32302
Phone: 850-224-8116; Fax: 850-561-3860
www.talchamber.com/

Georgia

Georgia Tourism Div
285 Peachtree Center Ave NE
Suite 1000
Atlanta, GA 30303
Phone: 404-656-2000; Fax: 404-651-9063
Toll-free: 800-847-4842
www.georgiaonmymind.org

Georgia Chamber of Commerce
235 Peachtree St NE
Suite 2000
Atlanta, GA 30303
Phone: 404-223-2264; Fax: 404-223-2290
Toll-free: 800-241-2286
www.gachamber.com

Atlanta Convention & Visitors Bureau
233 Peachtree St NE
Suite 100
Atlanta, GA 30303
Phone: 404-521-6600; Fax: 404-584-6331
Toll-free: 800-285-2682
www.atlanta.net

Augusta Metropolitan Convention & Visitors Bureau
1450 Greene St
Suite 110
Augusta, GA 30901
Phone: 706-823-6600; Fax: 706-823-6609
Toll-free: 800-726-0243
www.augustaga.org

Columbus Convention & Visitors Bureau
900 Front Ave
Columbus, GA 31901
Phone: 706-322-1613; Fax: 706-322-0701
Toll-free: 800-999-1613
www.visitcolumbusga.com

Macon-Bibb County Convention/Visitors Bureau
450 ML King Blvd
Macon, GA 31201
Phone: 478-743-3401; Fax: 478-745-2022
Toll-free: 800-768-3401
www.maconga.org

Savannah Area Convention & Visitors Bureau
101 E Bay St
Savannah, GA 31401
Phone: 912-644-6401; Fax: 912-644-6499
Toll-free: 877-728-2662
www.savcvb.com

Augusta Metro Chamber of Commerce
PO Box 1837
Augusta, GA 30903
Phone: 706-821-1300; Fax: 706-821-1330
www.augustagausa.com

Greater Columbus Chamber of Commerce
1200 6th Ave
PO Box 1200
Columbus, GA 31902
Phone: 706-327-1566; Fax: 706-327-7512

Toll-free: 800-360-8552
www.columbusgachamber.com

Greater Macon Chamber of Commerce
305 Coliseum Dr
Macon, GA 31217
Phone: 478-621-2000; Fax: 478-621-2021
www.maconchamber.com

Metro Atlanta Chamber of Commerce
235 Andrew Young International Blvd NW
Atlanta, GA 30303
Phone: 404-880-9000; Fax: 404-586-8464
www.metroatlantachamber.com

Savannah Area Chamber of Commerce
101 E Bay St
Savannah, GA 31401
Phone: 912-644-6400; Fax: 912-644-6499
Toll-free: 877-728-2662
www.savannahchamber.com

Hawaii

Hawaii Business Economic Development & Tourism Dept
PO Box 2359
Honolulu, HI 96804
Phone: 808-586-2355; Fax: 808-586-2377
www.hawaii.gov/dbedt

Hawaii Tourism Authority
1801 Kalakaua Ave
Honolulu, HI 96815
Phone: 808-973-2255; Fax: 808-973-2253
www.hawaii.gov/tourism

Hawaii Chamber of Commerce
1132 Bishop St
Suite 402
Honolulu, HI 96813
Phone: 808-545-4300; Fax: 808-545-4369
Toll-free: 800-464-2924
www.cochawaii.com

Hawaii Visitors & Convention Bureau
2270 Kalakaua Ave
Suite 801
Honolulu, HI 96815
Phone: 808-923-1811; Fax: 808-924-0290
Toll-free: 800-464-2924
www.gohawaii.com

Idaho

Idaho Tourism Development Div
700 W State St
PO Box 83720
Boise, ID 83720
Phone: 208-334-2470; Fax: 208-334-2631
Toll-free: 800-842-5858
www.visitid.org

Idaho Assn of Commerce & Industry
PO Box 389

Boise, ID 83701
Phone: 208-343-1849; Fax: 208-338-5623
www.iaci.org

Boise Convention & Visitors Bureau
312 S 9th St
Suite 100
Boise, ID 83702
Phone: 208-344-7777; Fax: 208-344-6236
Toll-free: 800-635-5240
www.boise.org

Pocatello Convention & Visitors Bureau
324 S Main St
Suite B
Pocatello, ID 83204
Phone: 208-235-7659; Fax: 208-233-1527
Toll-free: 877-922-7659
www.pocatellocvb.com

Boise Metro Chamber of Commerce
PO Box 2368
Boise, ID 83701
Phone: 208-472-5205; Fax: 208-472-5201
www.boisechamber.org

Greater Pocatello Chamber of Commerce
324 S Main St
Pocatello, ID 83204
Phone: 208-233-1525; Fax: 208-233-1527
www.pocatelloidaho.com

Illinois

Illinois Tourism Bureau
100 W Randolph St
Suite 3-400
Chicago, IL 60601
Phone: 312-814-4732; Fax: 312-814-6175
Toll-free: 800-226-6632
www.enjoyillinois.com

Illinois State Chamber of Commerce
311 S Wacker Dr
Suite 1500
Chicago, IL 60606
Phone: 312-983-7100; Fax: 312-983-7101
www.ilchamber.org

Central Illinois Tourism Development Office
700 E Adams St
Springfield, IL 62701
Phone: 217-525-7980; Fax: 217-525-8004
www.visitcentralillinois.com

Champaign County Convention & Visitors Bureau
1817 S Neil St
Suite 201
Champaign, IL 61820
Phone: 217-351-4133; Fax: 217-359-1809
Toll-free: 800-369-6151
www.cucvb.org

Chicago Convention & Tourism Bureau
2301 S Lake Shore Dr

McCormick Complex Lakeside Center
Chicago, IL 60616
Phone: 312-567-8500; Fax: 312-567-8533
www.choosechicago.com

Chicago Office of Tourism
78 E Washington St
4th Fl
Chicago, IL 60602
Phone: 312-744-2400; Fax: 312-744-2359
Toll-free: 877-244-2246
www.877chicago.com/

Peoria Area Convention & Visitors Bureau
456 Fulton St
Suite 300
Peoria, IL 61602
Phone: 309-676-0303; Fax: 309-676-8470
Toll-free: 800-747-0302
www.peoria.org

Rockford Area Convention & Visitors Bureau
102 N Main St
Rockford, IL 61101
Phone: 815-963-8111; Fax: 815-963-4298
Toll-free: 800-521-0849
www.gorockford.com

Springfield Convention & Visitors Bureau
109 N 7th St
Springfield, IL 62701
Phone: 217-789-2360; Fax: 217-544-8711
Toll-free: 800-545-7300
www.visitspringfieldillinois.com

Champaign County Chamber of Commerce
1817 S Neil St
Suite 201
Champaign, IL 61820
Phone: 217-359-1791; Fax: 217-359-1809
www.ccchamber.org

Chicagoland Chamber of Commerce
200 E Randolph St
Suite 2200
Chicago, IL 60601
Phone: 312-494-6700; Fax: 312-494-0660
www.chicagolandchamber.org

Greater Springfield Chamber of Commerce
3 S Old State Capitol Plaza
Springfield, IL 62701
Phone: 217-525-1173; Fax: 217-525-8768
www.gscc.org

Peoria Area Chamber of Commerce
124 SW Adams St
Suite 300
Peoria, IL 61602
Phone: 309-676-0755; Fax: 309-676-7534
www.peoriachamber.org

Rockford Regional Chamber of Commerce
308 W State St
Suite 190
Rockford, IL 61101

Phone: 815-987-8100; Fax: 815-987-8122
www.rockfordchamber.com

Indiana

Indiana Tourism Development Office
1 N Capitol Ave
Suite 100
Indianapolis, IN 46204
Phone: 317-232-8860; Fax: 317-233-6887
Toll-free: 888-365-6946
www.in.gov/enjoyindiana

Indiana State Chamber of Commerce
115 W Washington St Suite 850-S
Indianapolis, IN 46204
Phone: 317-264-3110; Fax: 317-264-6855
www.indianachamber.com

Bloomington/Monroe County Convention & Visitors Bureau
2855 N Walnut St
Bloomington, IN 47404
Phone: 812-334-8900; Fax: 812-334-2344
Toll-free: 800-800-0037
www.visitbloomington.com

Evansville Convention & Visitors Bureau
401 SE Riverside Dr
Evansville, IN 47713
Phone: 812-425-5402; Fax: 812-421-2207
Toll-free: 800-433-3025
www.evansvillecvb.org

Fort Wayne/Allen County Convention & Visitors Bureau
1021 S Calhoun St
Fort Wayne, IN 46802
Phone: 260-424-3700; Fax: 260-424-3914
Toll-free: 800-767-7752
www.visitfortwayne.com

Indianapolis Convention & Visitors Assn
200 S Capitol Ave
1 RCA Dome Suite 100
Indianapolis, IN 46225
Phone: 317-639-4282; Fax: 317-639-5273
Toll-free: 800-323-4639
www.indy.org

South Bend/Mishawaka Convention & Visitors Bureau
401 E Colfax Ave
Suite 310
South Bend, IN 46617
Phone: 574-234-0051; Fax: 574-289-0358
Toll-free: 800-828-7881
www.livethelegends.org

Chamber of Commerce of Saint Joseph County
401 E Colfax Ave
Suite 310
South Bend, IN 46617
Phone: 574-234-0051; Fax: 574-289-0358
www.sjchamber.org

Greater Bloomington Chamber of Commerce
400 W 7th St

Suite 102
Bloomington, IN 47404
Phone: 812-336-6381; Fax: 812-336-0651
www.chamber.bloomington.in.us

Greater Fort Wayne Chamber of Commerce
826 Ewing St
Fort Wayne, IN 46802
Phone: 260-424-1435; Fax: 260-426-7232
www.fwchamber.org

Indianapolis Chamber of Commerce
111 Monument Cir
Suite 1950
Indianapolis, IN 46204
Phone: 317-464-2200; Fax: 317-464-2217
www.indychamber.com

Metropolitan Evansville Chamber of Commerce
100 NW 2nd St
Suite 100
Evansville, IN 47708
Phone: 812-425-8147; Fax: 812-421-5883
www.evansvillechamber.com

Iowa

Iowa Tourism Office
200 E Grand Ave
Des Moines, IA 50309
Phone: 515-242-4705; Fax: 515-242-4718
Toll-free: 888-472-6035
www.traveliowa.com

Iowa Assn of Business & Industry
904 Walnut St
Suite 100
Des Moines, IA 50309
Phone: 515-280-8000; Fax: 515-244-8907
Toll-free: 800-383-4224
www.iowaabi.org

Cedar Rapids Area Convention & Visitors Bureau
119 1st Ave SE
PO Box 5339
Cedar Rapids, IA 52406
Phone: 319-398-5009; Fax: 319-398-5089
Toll-free: 800-735-5557
www.cedar-rapids.com

Dubuque Convention & Visitors Bureau
300 Main St
Suite 200
Dubuque, IA 52001
Phone: 563-557-9200; Fax: 563-557-1591
Toll-free: 800-798-4748

Greater Des Moines Convention & Visitors Bureau
400 Locust St
Suite 265
Des Moines, IA 50309
Phone: 515-286-4960; Fax: 515-244-9757
Toll-free: 800-451-2625
www.seedesmoines.com

Cedar Rapids Area Chamber of Commerce
424 1st Ave NE
Cedar Rapids, IA 52401
Phone: 319-398-5317; Fax: 319-398-5228
www.cedarrapids.org

Dubuque Area Chamber of Commerce
300 Main St
Suite 200
Dubuque, IA 52001
Phone: 563-557-9200; Fax: 563-557-1591
Toll-free: 800-798-4748
www.dubuquechamber.com

Greater Des Moines Partnership
700 Locust St
Suite 100
Des Moines, IA 50309
Phone: 515-286-4950; Fax: 515-286-4974
Toll-free: 800-376-9059
www.desmoinesmetro.com

Kansas

Kansas Travel & Tourism Development Div
1000 SW Jackson St
Suite 100
Topeka, KS 66612
Phone: 785-296-5403; Fax: 785-296-6988
Toll-free: 800-252-6727
www.travelks.org

Kansas Chamber of Commerce & Industry
835 SW Topeka Blvd
Topeka, KS 66612
Phone: 785-357-6321; Fax: 785-357-4732
www.kansaschamber.org

Kansas City Kansas/Wyandotte County Convention &
  Visitors Bureau
727 Minnesota Ave
PO Box 171517
Kansas City, KS 66117
Phone: 913-321-5800; Fax: 913-371-3732
Toll-free: 800-264-1563
www.visitthedot.com

Visit Topeka Inc
1275 SW Topeka Blvd
Topeka, KS 66612
Phone: 785-234-1030; Fax: 785-234-8282
Toll-free: 800-235-1030
www.visittopeka.travel

Wichita Convention & Visitors Bureau
100 S Main St
Suite 100
Wichita, KS 67202
Phone: 316-265-2800; Fax: 316-265-0162
Toll-free: 800-288-9424
www.visitwichita.com

Greater Topeka Chamber of Commerce
120 SE 6th St
Suite 110

Topeka, KS 66603
Phone: 785-234-2644; Fax: 785-234-8656
www.topekachamber.org

Kansas City Kansas Area Chamber of Commerce
PO Box 171337
Kansas City, KS 66117
Phone: 913-371-3070; Fax: 913-371-3732
www.kckchamber.com

Wichita Area Chamber of Commerce
350 W Douglas Ave
Wichita, KS 67202
Phone: 316-265-7771; Fax: 316-265-7502
www.wichitachamber.org

Kentucky

Kentucky Travel Dept
500 Mero St
Suite 2200
Frankfort, KY 40601
Phone: 502-564-4930; Fax: 502-564-5695
Toll-free: 800-225-8747
www.kentuckytourism.com

Kentucky Chamber of Commerce
464 Chenault Rd
Frankfort, KY 40601
Phone: 502-695-4700; Fax: 502-695-6824
www.kychamber.com

Frankfort/Franklin County Tourist & Convention
  Commission
100 Capitol Ave
Frankfort, KY 40601
Phone: 502-875-8687; Fax: 502-227-2604
Toll-free: 800-960-7200
www.frankfortky.org

Lexington Convention & Visitors Bureau
301 E Vine St
Lexington, KY 40507
Phone: 859-233-7299; Fax: 859-254-4555
Toll-free: 800-845-3959
www.visitlex.com

Louisville & Jefferson County Convention & Visitors Bureau
401 W Main St
Suite 2300
Louisville, KY 40202
Phone: 502-584-2121; Fax: 502-584-6697
Toll-free: 800-792-5595
www.gotolouisville.com

Frankfort Area Chamber of Commerce
100 Capitol Ave
Frankfort, KY 40601
Phone: 502-223-8261; Fax: 502-223-5942
www.frankfortky.org

Greater Lexington Chamber of Commerce
330 E Main St
Suite 100
Lexington, KY 40507

Phone: 859-254-4447; Fax: 859-233-3304
www.lexchamber.com

Greater Louisville Inc
614 W Main St
Louisville, KY 40202
Phone: 502-625-0000; Fax: 502-625-0010
Toll-free: 800-500-1066
www.greaterlouisville.com

Louisiana

Louisiana Culture Recreation & Tourism Dept
PO Box 94361
Baton Rouge, LA 70804
Phone: 225-342-8115; Fax: 225-342-3207
www.crt.state.la.us

Louisiana Tourism Office
PO Box 94291
Baton Rouge, LA 70804
Phone: 225-342-8100; Fax: 225-342-8390
www.louisianatravel.com

Louisiana Assn of Business & Industry
3113 Valley Creek Dr
PO Box 80258
Baton Rouge, LA 70898
Phone: 225-928-5388; Fax: 225-929-6054
Toll-free: 888-816-5224
www.labi.org

Baton Rouge Convention & Visitors Bureau
730 North Blvd
Baton Rouge, LA 70802
Phone: 225-383-1825; Fax: 225-346-1253
Toll-free: 800-527-6843
www.visitbatonrouge.com

Jefferson Convention & Visitors Bureau
1221 Elmwood Park Blvd
Suite 300
Jefferson, LA 70123
Phone: 504-731-7083; Fax: 504-731-7089
Toll-free: 877-572-7474
www.gatewaytoneworleans.com

Lafayette Convention & Visitors Commission
1400 NW Evageline Thwy
Lafayette, LA 70501
Phone: 337-232-3737; Fax: 337-232-0161
Toll-free: 800-346-1958
www.lafayettetravel.com

New Orleans Metropolitan Convention & Visitors Bureau
2020 St Charles Ave
New Orleans, LA 70130
Phone: 504-566-5011; Fax: 504-566-5046
Toll-free: 800-672-6124
www.neworleanscvb.com

Shreveport-Bossier Convention & Tourist Bureau
629 Spring St
Shreveport, LA 71101
Phone: 318-222-9391; Fax: 318-222-0056

Toll-free: 800-551-8682
www.shreveport-bossier.org

Bossier Chamber of Commerce
710 Benton Rd
Bossier City, LA 71111
Phone: 318-746-0252; Fax: 318-746-0357
www.bossierchamber.com

Greater Baton Rouge Chamber of Commerce
564 Laurel St
Baton Rouge, LA 70801
Phone: 225-381-7125; Fax: 225-336-4306
www.brchamber.org

Greater Lafayette Chamber of Commerce
804 E St Mary Blvd
Lafayette, LA 70503
Phone: 337-233-2705; Fax: 337-234-8671
www.lafchamber.org

Greater Shreveport Chamber of Commerce
400 Edwards St
Shreveport, LA 71101
Phone: 318-677-2500; Fax: 318-677-2541
Toll-free: 800-448-5432
www.shreveportchamber.org

Jefferson Chamber of Commerce
3421 N Causeway Blvd
Suite 203
Metairie, LA 70002
Phone: 504-835-3880; Fax: 504-835-3828
www.jeffersonchamber.org

New Orleans Chamber of Commerce
1515 Poydras St
Suite 1010
New Orleans, LA 70112
Phone: 504-522-7226; Fax: 504-522-1355
www.neworleanschamber.org

Maine

Maine Tourism Office
59 State House Stn
Augusta, ME 04333
Phone: 207-287-5711; Fax: 207-287-8070
Toll-free: 888-624-6345
www.visitmaine.com

Maine State Chamber of Commerce
7 University Dr
Augusta, ME 04330
Phone: 207-623-4568; Fax: 207-622-7723
www.mainechamber.org

Convention & Visitors Bureau of Greater Portland
245 Commercial St
Portland, ME 04101
Phone: 207-772-5800; Fax: 207-874-9043
www.visitportland.com

Greater Bangor Convention & Visitors Bureau
40 Harlow Pl

Bangor, ME 04401
Phone: 207-947-5205; Fax: 207-942-2146
Toll-free: 800-916-6673
www.bangorcvb.org

Bangor Region Chamber of Commerce
519 Main St
Bangor, ME 04401
Phone: 207-947-0307; Fax: 207-990-1427
www.bangorregion.com

Bar Harbor Chamber of Commerce
93 Cottage St
PO Box 158
Bar Harbor, ME 04609
Phone: 207-288-5103; Fax: 207-288-2565
Toll-free: 888-540-9990
www.barharborinfo.com

Kennebec Valley Chamber of Commerce
21 University Dr
Augusta, ME 04330
Phone: 207-623-4559; Fax: 207-626-9342
www.augustamaine.com

Portland Regional Chamber
60 Pearl St
Portland, ME 04101
Phone: 207-772-2811; Fax: 207-772-1179
www.portlandregion.com

Maryland

Maryland Tourism Development Office
217 E Redwood St
9th Fl
Baltimore, MD 21202
Phone: 410-767-3400; Fax: 410-333-6643
Toll-free: 800-543-1036
www.mdisfun.org

Maryland Chamber of Commerce
60 West St
Suite 100
Annapolis, MD 21401
Phone: 410-269-0642; Fax: 410-269-5247
www.mdchamber.org

Annapolis & Anne Arundel County Conference & Visitors
   Bureau
26 West St
Annapolis, MD 21401
Phone: 410-268-8687; Fax: 410-263-9591
Toll-free: 888-302-2852
www.visit-annapolis.org

Baltimore Area Convention & Visitors Assn
100 Light St
12th Fl
Baltimore, MD 21202
Phone: 410-659-7300; Fax: 410-727-2308
Toll-free: 800-343-3468
www.baltimore.org

Ocean City Convention & Visitors Bureau
4001 Coastal Hwy
Ocean City, MD 21842
Phone: 410-289-8181; Fax: 410-723-8655
Toll-free: 800-626-2326
www.ococean.com

Annapolis & Anne Arundel County Chamber of Commerce
49 Old Solomons Island Rd
Suite 204
Annapolis, MD 21401
Phone: 410-266-3960; Fax: 410-266-8270
www.annapolischamber.com

Baltimore City Chamber of Commerce
312 N ML King Blvd
Baltimore, MD 21201
Phone: 410-837-7101; Fax: 410-837-7104
www.baltimorecitychamber.com

Ocean City Chamber of Commerce
12320 Ocean Gateway
Ocean City, MD 21842
Phone: 410-213-0144; Fax: 410-213-7521
Toll-free: 888-626-3386
www.oceancity.org

Massachusetts

Massachusetts Travel & Tourism Office
10 Park Plaza
Suite 4510
Boston, MA 02116
Phone: 617-973-8500; Fax: 617-973-8525
Toll-free: 800-227-6277
www.mass-vacation.com

New England Council Inc
98 N Washington St
Suite 201
Boston, MA 02114
Phone: 617-723-4009; Fax: 617-723-3943
www.newenglandcouncil.com

Greater Boston Convention & Visitors Bureau
2 Copley Pl
Suite 105
Boston, MA 02116
Phone: 617-536-4100; Fax: 617-424-7664
Toll-free: 888-733-2678
www.bostonusa.com

Greater Springfield Convention & Visitors Bureau
1441 Main St
Suite 136
Springfield, MA 01103
Phone: 413-787-1548; Fax: 413-781-4607
Toll-free: 800-723-1548
www.valleyvisitor.com

Worcester County Convention & Visitors Bureau
30 Worcester Center Blvd
Worcester, MA 01608
Phone: 508-755-7400; Fax: 508-754-2703
Toll-free: 800-231-7557
www.worcester.org

Cape Cod Chamber of Commerce
5 Shoot Flying Hill Road
Centerville, MA 02632
Phone: 508-362-3225; Fax: 508-362-3698
Toll-free: 888-332-2732
www.capecodchamber.org

Greater Boston Chamber of Commerce
75 State St
2nd Fl
Boston, MA 02109
Phone: 617-227-4500; Fax: 617-227-7505
www.bostonchamber.com

Greater Springfield Chamber of Commerce
1441 Main St
Suite 136
Springfield, MA 01103
Phone: 413-787-1555; Fax: 413-731-8530

Worcester Regional Chamber of Commerce
339 Main St
Worcester, MA 01608
Phone: 508-753-2924; Fax: 508-754-8560
www.worcesterchamber.org

Michigan

Michigan Travel Michigan
300 N Washington Sq
Lansing, MI 48913
Phone: 517-373-0670; Fax: 517-373-0059
Toll-free: 888-784-7328
travel.michigan.org

Michigan Chamber of Commerce
600 S Walnut St
Lansing, MI 48933
Phone: 517-371-2100; Fax: 517-371-7224
Toll-free: 800-748-0266
www.michamber.com

Ann Arbor Area Convention & Visitors Bureau
120 W Huron St
Ann Arbor, MI 48104
Phone: 734-995-7281; Fax: 734-995-7283
Toll-free: 800-888-9487
www.annarbor.org

Detroit Metropolitan Convention & Visitors Bureau
211 W Fort St
Suite 1000
Detroit, MI 48226
Phone: 313-202-1800; Fax: 313-202-1808
Toll-free: 800-225-5389
www.visitdetroit.com

Flint Area Convention & Visitors Bureau
316 Water St
Flint, MI 48502
Phone: 810-232-8900; Fax: 810-232-1515
Toll-free: 800-253-5468
flintcommercecenter.com

Grand Rapids/Kent County Convention & Visitors Bureau
171 Monroe Ave NW
Suite 700
Grand Rapids, MI 49503
Phone: 616-459-8287; Fax: 616-459-7291
Toll-free: 800-678-9859
www.visitgrandrapids.org

Greater Lansing Convention & Visitors Bureau
1223 Turner St
Suite 200
Lansing, MI 48906
Phone: 517-487-0077; Fax: 517-487-5151
Toll-free: 800-648-6630
www.lansing.org

Ann Arbor Area Chamber of Commerce
115 W Heron
3rd Fl
Ann Arbor, MI 48104
Phone: 734-665-4433; Fax: 734-665-4191
www.annarborchamber.org

Detroit Regional Chamber
PO Box 33840 1 Woodward Ave
Suite 1900
Detroit, MI 48232
Phone: 313-964-4000; Fax: 313-964-0183
www.detroitchamber.com

Genesee Regional Chamber of Commerce
519 S Saginaw St
Suite 200
Flint, MI 48502
Phone: 810-232-7101; Fax: 810-233-7437
www.thegrcc.org

Grand Rapids Area Chamber of Commerce
111 Pearl St NW
Grand Rapids, MI 49503
Phone: 616-771-0300; Fax: 616-771-0318
www.grandrapids.org

Lansing Regional Chamber of Commerce
300 E Michigan Ave
Suite 300
Lansing, MI 48933
Phone: 517-487-6340; Fax: 517-484-6910
www.lansingchamber.org

Minnesota

Minnesota Tourism Office
121 7th Pl E
Suite 100
Saint Paul, MN 55101
Phone: 651-296-5029
Toll-free: 888-868-7476
www.exploreminnesota.com

Minnesota Chamber of Commerce
400 Robert St N
Suite 1500
Saint Paul, MN 55101
Phone: 651-292-4650; Fax: 651-292-4656

Toll-free: 800-821-2230
www.mnchamber.com

Duluth Convention & Visitors Bureau
21 W Superior St
Suite 100
Duluth, MN 55802
Phone: 218-722-4011; Fax: 218-722-1322
Toll-free: 800-438-5884
www.visitduluth.com

Greater Minneapolis Convention & Visitors Assn
250 Marquette Ave
Suite 1300
Minneapolis, MN 55401
Phone: 612-767-8000; Fax: 612-335-5839
Toll-free: 800-445-7412
www.minneapolis.org

Rochester Convention & Visitors Bureau
111 S Broadway
Suite 301
Rochester, MN 55904
Phone: 507-288-4331; Fax: 507-288-9144
Toll-free: 800-634-8277
www.rochestercvb.org

Saint Paul River Centre Convention & Visitors Authority
175 W Kellogg Blvd
Suite 502
Saint Paul, MN 55102
Phone: 651-265-4900; Fax: 651-265-4999
Toll-free: 800-627-6101
www.stpaulcvb.org

Chamber of Commerce of Fargo Moorhead
202 1st Ave N
Moorhead, MN 56560
Phone: 218-233-1100; Fax: 218-233-1200
www.fmchamber.com

Duluth Area Chamber of Commerce
5 W 1st St
Suite 101
Duluth, MN 55802
Phone: 218-722-5501; Fax: 218-722-3223
www.duluthchamber.com

Minneapolis Regional Chamber of Commerce
81 S 9th St
Suite 200
Minneapolis, MN 55402
Phone: 612-370-9100; Fax: 612-370-9195
www.minneapolischamber.org

Rochester Area Chamber of Commerce
220 S Broadway
Suite 100
Rochester, MN 55904
Phone: 507-288-1122; Fax: 507-282-8960
www.rochestermnchamber.com

Saint Paul Area Chamber of Commerce
401 N Robert St
Suite 150
Saint Paul, MN 55101

Phone: 651-223-5000; Fax: 651-223-5119
www.saintpaulchamber.com

Mississippi

Mississippi Tourism Development Div
PO Box 849
Jackson, MS 39205
Phone: 601-359-3297; Fax: 601-359-5757
Toll-free: 866-733-6477
www.visitmississippi.org

Mississippi Economic Council
PO Box 23276
Jackson, MS 39225
Phone: 601-969-0022; Fax: 601-353-0247
Toll-free: 800-748-7626
www.msmec.com

Metro Jackson Convention & Visitors Bureau
921 N President St
Jackson, MS 39202
Phone: 601-960-1891; Fax: 601-960-1827
Toll-free: 800-354-7695
www.visitjackson.com

Mississippi Gulf Coast Convention & Visitors Bureau
PO Box 6128
Gulfport, MS 39506
Phone: 228-896-6699; Fax: 228-896-6788
Toll-free: 888-467-4853
www.gulfcoast.org

Tupelo Convention & Visitors Bureau
399 E Main St
Tupelo, MS 38804
Phone: 662-841-6521; Fax: 662-841-6558
Toll-free: 800-533-0611
tupelo.net

Area Development Partnership
1 Convention Center Plaza
Hattiesburg, MS 39401
Phone: 601-296-7500; Fax: 601-296-7505
Toll-free: 800-238-4288
www.theadp.com

Greater Jackson Chamber Partnership
PO Box 22548
Jackson, MS 39225
Phone: 601-948-7575; Fax: 601-352-5539
www.metrochamber.com

Mississippi Gulf Coast Chamber of Commerce
11975-E Seaway Rd
Gulfport, MS 39503
Phone: 228-604-0014; Fax: 228-604-0105
www.mscoastchamber.com

Missouri

Missouri Tourism Div
PO Box 1055
Jefferson City, MO 65102

Phone: 573-526-5900; Fax: 573-751-5160
Toll-free: 800-877-1234
www.missouritourism.org

Missouri Chamber of Commerce
PO Box 149
Jefferson City, MO 65102
Phone: 573-634-3511; Fax: 573-634-8855
www.mochamber.org

Branson/Lakes Area Convention & Visitors Bureau
269 State Hwy 248
PO Box 1897
Branson, MO 65615
Phone: 417-334-4136; Fax: 417-334-4139
Toll-free: 800-214-3661
www.bransonchamber.com

Columbia Convention & Visitors Bureau
300 S Providence Rd
Columbia, MO 65203
Phone: 573-875-1231; Fax: 573-443-3986
Toll-free: 800-652-0987
www.visitcolumbiamo.com

Convention & Visitors Bureau of Greater Kansas City
1100 Main St
Suite 2200
Kansas City, MO 64105
Phone: 816-221-5242; Fax: 816-691-3805
Toll-free: 800-767-7700
www.visitkc.com

Jefferson City Convention & Visitors Bureau
213 Adams St
Jefferson City, MO 65101
Phone: 573-632-2820; Fax: 573-638-4892
Toll-free: 800-769-4183
www.visitjeffersoncity.com

Saint Louis Convention & Visitors Commission
1 Metropolitan Sq
Suite 1100
Saint Louis, MO 63102
Phone: 314-421-1023; Fax: 314-421-0039
Toll-free: 800-325-7962
www.explorestlouis.com

Springfield Missouri Convention & Visitors Bureau
815 E Saint Louis St
Springfield, MO 65806
Phone: 417-881-5300; Fax: 417-881-2231
Toll-free: 800-678-8767
www.springfieldmo.org

Branson/Lakes Area Chamber of Commerce
PO Box 1897
Branson, MO 65615
Phone: 417-334-4136; Fax: 417-334-4139
Toll-free: 800-214-3661
www.bransonchamber.com

Columbia Chamber of Commerce
300 S Providence Rd
Columbia, MO 65203
Phone: 573-874-1132; Fax: 573-443-3986
chamber.columbia.mo.us

Greater Kansas City Chamber of Commerce
911 Main St
Suite 2600
Kansas City, MO 64105
Phone: 816-221-2424; Fax: 816-221-7440
www.kcchamber.com

Independence Chamber of Commerce
210 W Truman Rd
Independence, MO 64050
Phone: 816-252-4745; Fax: 816-252-4917
www.independencechamber.com

Jefferson City Area Chamber of Commerce
213 Adams St
Jefferson City, MO 65101
Phone: 573-634-3616; Fax: 573-634-3805
www.jcchamber.org

Saint Louis Regional Commerce & Growth Assn
1 Metropolitan Sq
Suite 1300
Saint Louis, MO 63102
Phone: 314-231-5555; Fax: 314-444-1122
Toll-free: 877-785-7242
www.stlrcga.org

Springfield Area Chamber of Commerce
202 S John Q Hammons Pkwy
Springfield, MO 65806
Phone: 417-862-5567; Fax: 417-862-1611
Toll-free: 800-879-7504
www.springfieldchamber.com

Montana

Montana Promotion Div (Travel Montana)
PO Box 200533
Helena, MT 59620
Phone: 406-444-2654
Toll-free: 800-847-4868
www.visitmt.com

Montana Chamber of Commerce
PO Box 1730
Helena, MT 59624
Phone: 406-442-2405; Fax: 406-442-2409
www.montanachamber.com

Billings Convention & Visitors Bureau
815 S 27th St
PO Box 31177
Billings, MT 59107
Phone: 406-245-4111; Fax: 406-245-7333
Toll-free: 800-735-2635
www.billingscvb.visitmt.com

Helena Convention & Visitors Bureau
225 Cruse Ave
Helena, MT 59601
Phone: 406-447-1530; Fax: 406-447-1532
Toll-free: 800-743-5362
helenacvb.visitmt.com

Billings Area Chamber of Commerce
815 S 27th St
Billings, MT 59101
Phone: 406-245-4111; Fax: 406-245-7333
Toll-free: 800-735-2635

Great Falls Area Chamber of Commerce
710 1st Ave N
Great Falls, MT 59401
Phone: 406-761-4434; Fax: 406-761-6129
Toll-free: 800-735-8535
www.greatfallschamber.org

Helena Area Chamber of Commerce
225 Cruse Ave
Helena, MT 59601
Phone: 406-442-4120; Fax: 406-447-1532
Toll-free: 800-743-5362
www.helenachamber.com

Nebraska

Nebraska Travel & Tourism Div
PO Box 98907
Lincoln, NE 68509
Phone: 402-471-3796; Fax: 402-471-3026
Toll-free: 877-632-7275
www.visitnebraska.org

Nebraska Chamber of Commerce & Industry
PO Box 95128
Lincoln, NE 68509
Phone: 402-474-4422; Fax: 402-474-5681
www.nechamber.com

Greater Omaha Convention & Visitors Bureau
1001 Farnam St
Suite 200
Omaha, NE 68102
Phone: 402-444-4660; Fax: 402-444-4511
Toll-free: 800-332-1819
www.visitomaha.com

Lincoln Convention & Visitors Bureau
1135 M St
3rd Fl
Lincoln, NE 68508
Phone: 402-434-5335; Fax: 402-436-2360
Toll-free: 800-423-8212
www.lincoln.org

Greater Omaha Chamber of Commerce
1301 Harney St
Omaha, NE 68102
Phone: 402-346-5000; Fax: 402-346-7050
www.omahachamber.net

Lincoln Chamber of Commerce
PO Box 83006
Lincoln, NE 68501
Phone: 402-436-2350; Fax: 402-436-2360
www.lcoc.com

Nevada

Nevada Tourism Commission
401 N Carson St
Carson City, NV 89701
Phone: 775-687-4322; Fax: 775-687-6779
Toll-free: 800-237-0774
www.travelnevada.com

Carson City Convention & Visitors Bureau
1900 S Carson St
Suite 100
Carson City, NV 89701
Phone: 775-687-7410; Fax: 775-687-7416
Toll-free: 800-638-2321
www.carson-city.org

Las Vegas Convention & Visitors Authority
3150 S Paradise Rd
Las Vegas, NV 89109
Phone: 702-892-0711; Fax: 702-892-2824
Toll-free: 800-332-5333
www.lvcva.com

Reno-Sparks Convention & Visitors Authority
PO Box 837
Reno, NV 89504
Phone: 775-827-7600; Fax: 775-827-7686
Toll-free: 800-443-1482
www.visitrenotahoe.com

Carson City Area Chamber of Commerce
1900 S Carson St
Suite 200
Carson City, NV 89701
Phone: 775-882-1565; Fax: 775-882-4179
www.carsoncitychamber.com

Las Vegas Chamber of Commerce
3720 Howard Hughes Pkwy
Las Vegas, NV 89169
Phone: 702-735-1616; Fax: 702-735-2011
www.lvchamber.com

New Hampshire

New Hampshire Travel & Tourism Development Office
PO Box 1856
Concord, NH 03302
Phone: 603-271-2665; Fax: 603-271-6870
Toll-free: 800-386-4664
www.visitnh.gov

New Hampshire Business & Industry Assn
122 N Main St
3rd Fl
Concord, NH 03301
Phone: 603-224-5388; Fax: 603-224-2872
www.nhbia.org

Manchester Area Convention & Visitors Bureau
889 Elm St
3rd Fl
Manchester, NH 03101
Phone: 603-666-6600; Fax: 603-626-0910
www.manchestercvb.com

New Hampshire Div of Travel & Tourism Development
172 Pembroke Rd
PO Box 1856
Concord, NH 03302
Phone: 603-271-2666; Fax: 603-271-6870
Toll-free: 800-262-6660
www.visitnh.gov

Greater Concord Chamber of Commerce
40 Commercial St
Concord, NH 03301
Phone: 603-224-2508; Fax: 603-224-8128
www.concordnhchamber.com

Greater Manchester Chamber of Commerce
889 Elm St
Manchester, NH 03101
Phone: 603-666-6600; Fax: 603-626-0910
www.manchester-chamber.org

New Jersey

New Jersey Commerce Economic Growth & Tourism
  Commission
20 W State St
PO Box 820
Trenton, NJ 08625
Phone: 609-777-0885; Fax: 609-777-4097
www.state.nj.us/commerce

New Jersey Travel & Tourism Div
PO Box 820
Trenton, NJ 08625
Phone: 609-777-0885; Fax: 609-633-7418
Toll-free: 800-847-4865
www.state.nj.us/travel

New Jersey State Chamber of Commerce
216 W State St
Trenton, NJ 08608
Phone: 609-989-7888; Fax: 609-989-9696
www.njchamber.com

Atlantic City Convention & Visitors Authority
2314 Pacific Ave
Atlantic City, NJ 08401
Phone: 609-449-7130; Fax: 609-348-3426
Toll-free: 888-228-4748
www.atlanticcitynj.com

Capital Region Convention & Visitors Bureau
1A Quakerbridge Plaza Dr
Mercerville, NJ 08619
Phone: 609-689-9964; Fax: 609-586-9989
www.visitcapitalregion.org

Atlantic City Regional Chamber of Commerce
1125 Atlantic Ave
Suite 105
Atlantic City, NJ 08401
Phone: 609-345-5600; Fax: 609-345-1666
www.atlanticcitychamber.com

Greater Paterson Chamber of Commerce
100 Hamilton Plaza

Suite 1201
Paterson, NJ 07505
Phone: 973-881-7300; Fax: 973-881-8233
www.greaterpatersoncc.org

Hudson County Chamber of Commerce
660 Newark Ave
Suite 220
Jersey City, NJ 07306
Phone: 201-386-0699; Fax: 201-386-8480
www.hudsonchamber.org

Mercer Regional Chamber of Commerce
1A Quakerbridge Plaza Dr
Mercerville, NJ 08619
Phone: 609-689-9960; Fax: 609-586-9989
www.mercerchamber.org

Newark Regional Business Partnership
744 Broad St
26th Fl
Newark, NJ 07102
Phone: 973-522-0099; Fax: 973-824-6587
www.newarkrbp.org

New Mexico

New Mexico Tourism Dept
491 Old Santa Fe Trail
Santa Fe, NM 87503
Phone: 505-827-7400; Fax: 505-827-7402
Toll-free: 800-545-2070
www.newmexico.org

New Mexico Assn of Commerce & Industry
PO Box 9706
Albuquerque, NM 87119
Phone: 505-842-0644; Fax: 505-842-0734
www.aci.nm.org

Albuquerque Convention & Visitors Bureau
20 First Plaza
Suite 601
Albuquerque, NM 87102
Phone: 505-842-9918; Fax: 505-247-9101
Toll-free: 800-733-9918
www.abqcvb.org

Las Cruces Convention & Visitors Bureau
211 N Water St
Las Cruces, NM 88001
Phone: 505-541-2444; Fax: 505-541-2164
Toll-free: 800-343-7827
www.lascrucescvb.org

Santa Fe Convention & Visitors Bureau
60 E San Francisco St
Santa Fe, NM 87501
Phone: 505-955-6200; Fax: 505-955-6222
Toll-free: 800-777-2489
www.santafe.org

Greater Albuquerque Chamber of Commerce
PO Box 25100
Albuquerque, NM 87125

Phone: 505-764-3700; Fax: 505-764-3714
abqchamber.com

Greater Las Cruces Chamber of Commerce
760 W Picacho Ave
Las Cruces, NM 88005
Phone: 505-524-1968; Fax: 505-527-5546
lascruces.org

Santa Fe Chamber of Commerce
8380 Cerrillos Rd
Suite 302
Santa Fe, NM 87507
Phone: 505-988-3279; Fax: 505-984-2205
www.santafechamber.com

New York

New York (State) Tourism Div
PO Box 2603
Albany, NY 12220
Phone: 518-474-4116; Fax: 518-486-6416
Toll-free: 800-225-5697
www.iloveny.com

Business Council of New York State Inc
152 Washington Ave
Albany, NY 12210
Phone: 518-465-7511; Fax: 518-465-4389
Toll-free: 800-358-1202
www.bcnys.org

Albany County Convention & Visitors Bureau
25 Quackenbush Sq
Albany, NY 12207
Phone: 518-434-1217; Fax: 518-434-0887
Toll-free: 800-258-3582
www.albany.org

Greater Buffalo Convention & Visitors Bureau
617 Main St
Suite 200
Buffalo, NY 14203
Phone: 716-852-2356; Fax: 716-852-0131
Toll-free: 800-283-3256
www.visitbuffaloniagara.com

Greater Rochester Visitors Assn
45 East Ave
Suite 400
Rochester, NY 14604
Phone: 585-546-3070; Fax: 585-232-4822
Toll-free: 800-677-7282
www.visitrochester.com

NYC & Co
810 7th Ave
3rd Fl
New York, NY 10019
Phone: 212-484-1200; Fax: 212-484-1222
Toll-free: 800-692-8474
www.nycvisit.com

Syracuse Convention & Visitors Bureau
572 S Salina St

Syracuse, NY 13202
Phone: 315-470-1910; Fax: 315-471-8545
Toll-free: 800-234-4797
www.visitsyracuse.org

Westchester County Office of Tourism
222 Mamaroneck Ave
Suite 100
White Plains, NY 10605
Phone: 914-995-8500; Fax: 914-995-8505
Toll-free: 800-833-9282
www.westchestertourism.com

Albany-Colonie Regional Chamber of Commerce
107 Washington Ave
Albany, NY 12210
Phone: 518-434-1214; Fax: 518-434-1339
www.ac-chamber.org

Buffalo Niagara Partnership
665 Main St
Suite 200
Buffalo, NY 14203
Phone: 716-852-7100; Fax: 716-852-2761
Toll-free: 800-241-0474
www.thepartnership.org

Greater Syracuse Chamber of Commerce
572 S Salina St
Syracuse, NY 13202
Phone: 315-470-1800; Fax: 315-471-8545
www.syracusechamber.com

New York City Partnership & Chamber of Commerce Inc
1 Battery Park Plaza
5th Fl
New York, NY 10004
Phone: 212-493-7500; Fax: 212-344-3344
www.nycp.org

Rochester Business Alliance
150 State St
Rochester, NY 14614
Phone: 585-454-2220; Fax: 585-263-3679
www.rochesterbusinessalliance.com

Yonkers Chamber of Commerce
20 S Broadway
Suite 1205
Yonkers, NY 10701
Phone: 914-963-0332; Fax: 914-963-0455
www.yonkerschamber.com

North Carolina

North Carolina Tourism Div
301 N Wilmington St
Raleigh, NC 27601
Phone: 919-733-4171; Fax: 919-733-8582
Toll-free: 800-847-4862
www.visitnc.com

North Carolina Citizens for Business & Industry
225 Hillsborough St
Suite 460

Raleigh, NC 27603
Phone: 919-836-1400; Fax: 919-836-1425
www.nccbi.org

Asheville Area Convention & Visitors Bureau
36 Montford Ave
PO Box 1010
Asheville, NC 28802
Phone: 828-258-6102; Fax: 828-254-6054
Toll-free: 800-257-5583
www.exploreasheville.com

Charlotte Convention & Visitors Bureau
500 S College St
Suite 300
Charlotte, NC 28202
Phone: 704-334-2282; Fax: 704-342-3972
Toll-free: 800-722-1994
www.charlottecvb.org

Durham Convention & Visitors Bureau
101 E Morgan St
Durham, NC 27701
Phone: 919-687-0288; Fax: 919-683-9555
Toll-free: 800-446-8604
dcvb.durham.nc.us

Greater Raleigh Convention & Visitors Bureau
421 Fayetteville St Mall
Suite 1505
Raleigh, NC 27602
Phone: 919-834-5900; Fax: 919-831-2887
Toll-free: 800-849-8499
www.visitraleigh.com

Greensboro Area Convention & Visitors Bureau
317 S Greene St
Greensboro, NC 27401
Phone: 336-274-2282; Fax: 336-230-1183
Toll-free: 800-344-2282
www.visitgreensboro.com

Winston-Salem Convention & Visitors Bureau
200 Brookstown Ave
Winston-Salem, NC 27101
Phone: 336-728-4200; Fax: 336-728-4220
Toll-free: 800-331-7018
www.wscvb.com

Asheville Area Chamber of Commerce
36 Montford Ave
Asheville, NC 28801
Phone: 828-258-6101; Fax: 828-251-0926
Toll-free: 800-257-1300
www.ashevillechamber.org

Charlotte Chamber of Commerce
PO Box 32785
Charlotte, NC 28232
Phone: 704-378-1300; Fax: 704-374-1903
www.charlottechamber.com

Greater Durham Chamber of Commerce
300 W Morgan St
Suite 1400
Durham, NC 27701

Phone: 919-682-2133; Fax: 919-688-8351
www.durhamchamber.org

Greater Raleigh Chamber of Commerce
PO Box 2978
Raleigh, NC 27602
Phone: 919-664-7000; Fax: 919-664-7099
www.raleighchamber.org

Greater Winston-Salem Chamber of Commerce
PO Box 1408
Winston-Salem, NC 27102
Phone: 336-725-2361; Fax: 336-721-2209
www.winstonsalem.com

Greensboro Area Chamber of Commerce
342 N Elm St
Greensboro, NC 27401
Phone: 336-275-8675; Fax: 336-230-1867
www.greensborochamber.com

North Dakota

North Dakota Tourism Div
604 E Boulevard Ave
Bismarck, ND 58505
Phone: 701-328-2525; Fax: 701-328-4878
Toll-free: 800-435-5663
www.ndtourism.com

Greater North Dakota Assn
PO Box 2639
Bismarck, ND 58502
Phone: 701-222-0929; Fax: 701-222-1611
Toll-free: 800-382-1405
www.gnda.com

Bismarck-Mandan Convention & Visitors Bureau
1600 Burnt Boat Dr
Bismarck, ND 58503
Phone: 701-222-4308; Fax: 701-222-0647
Toll-free: 800-767-3555
www.discoverbismarckmandan.com

Fargo-Moorhead Convention & Visitors Bureau
2001 44th St SW
Fargo, ND 58103
Phone: 701-282-3653; Fax: 701-282-7815
Toll-free: 800-235-7654
www.fargomoorhead.org

Greater Grand Forks Convention & Visitors Bureau
4251 Gateway Dr
Grand Forks, ND 58203
Phone: 701-746-0444; Fax: 701-746-0775
Toll-free: 800-866-4566
www.grandforkscvb.org

Bismarck-Mandan Chamber of Commerce
1640 Burnt Boat Dr
Bismarck, ND 58502
Phone: 701-223-5660; Fax: 701-255-6125
www.bismarckmandan.com

Grand Forks Chamber of Commerce
202 N 3rd St
Grand Forks, ND 58203
Phone: 701-772-7271; Fax: 701-772-9238
www.gfchamber.com

Ohio

Ohio Travel & Tourism Div
PO Box 1001
Columbus, OH 43216
Phone: 614-466-8844; Fax: 614-466-6744
Toll-free: 800-282-5393
www.discoverohio.com

Ohio Chamber of Commerce
230 E Town St
Columbus, OH 43215
Phone: 614-228-4201; Fax: 614-228-6403
Toll-free: 800-622-1893
www.ohiochamber.com

Akron/Summit County Convention & Visitors Bureau
77 E Mill St
Akron, OH 44308
Phone: 330-374-7560; Fax: 330-374-7626
Toll-free: 800-245-4254
www.visitakron-summit.org

Convention & Visitors Bureau of Greater Cleveland
50 Public Sq
Terminal Tower Suite 3100
Cleveland, OH 44113
Phone: 216-621-4110; Fax: 216-621-5967
Toll-free: 800-321-1001
www.travelcleveland.com

Dayton/Montgomery County Convention & Visitors Bureau
1 Chamber Plaza
Suite A
Dayton, OH 45402
Phone: 937-226-8211; Fax: 937-226-8294
Toll-free: 800-221-8235
www.daytoncvb.com

Greater Cincinnati Convention & Visitors Bureau
300 W 6th St
Cincinnati, OH 45202
Phone: 513-621-2142; Fax: 513-621-5020
Toll-free: 800-246-2987
www.cincyusa.com

Greater Columbus Convention & Visitors Bureau
90 N High St
Columbus, OH 43215
Phone: 614-221-6623; Fax: 614-221-5618
Toll-free: 800-354-2657
www.experiencecolumbus.com

Greater Toledo Convention & Visitors Bureau
401 Jefferson Ave
Toledo, OH 43604
Phone: 419-321-6404; Fax: 419-255-7731
Toll-free: 800-243-4667
www.dotoledo.org

Youngstown/Mahoning County Convention & Visitors
  Bureau
21 W Boardsman St
Youngstown, OH 44503
Phone: 330-740-2130; Fax: 330-286-0093
Toll-free: 800-447-8201
www.youngstowncvb.com

Cincinnati USA Regional Chamber
441 Vine St
Suite 300
Cincinnati, OH 45202
Phone: 513-579-3100; Fax: 513-579-3102
www.gccc.com

Dayton Area Chamber of Commerce
1 Chamber Plaza
Suite 200
Dayton, OH 45402
Phone: 937-226-1444; Fax: 937-226-8254
www.daytonchamber.org

Greater Akron Chamber
1 Cascade Plaza
17th Fl
Akron, OH 44308
Phone: 330-376-5550; Fax: 330-379-3164
Toll-free: 800-621-8001
www.greaterakronchamber.org

Greater Cleveland Partnership
50 Public Sq
Suite 200
Cleveland, OH 44113
Phone: 216-621-3300; Fax: 216-621-6013
Toll-free: 800-562-7121
www.gcpartnership.com

Greater Columbus Chamber of Commerce
37 N High St
Columbus, OH 43215
Phone: 614-221-1321; Fax: 614-221-9360
Toll-free: 800-950-1321
www.columbus.org

Toledo Regional Chamber of Commerce
300 Madison Ave
Suite 200
Toledo, OH 43604
Phone: 419-243-8191; Fax: 419-241-8302
www.toledochamber.com

Youngstown Warren Regional Chamber
11 Federal Plaza Center
Suite 1600
Youngstown, OH 44503
Phone: 330-744-2131; Fax: 330-746-0330
www.regionalchamber.com

Oklahoma

Oklahoma Tourism & Recreation Dept
15 N Robinson St
Suite 100
Oklahoma City, OK 73105

Phone: 405-521-2406; Fax: 405-521-3992
Toll-free: 800-652-6552
tourism.state.ok.us

Oklahoma State Chamber
330 NE 10th St
Oklahoma City, OK 73104
Phone: 405-235-3669; Fax: 405-235-3670
Toll-free: 800-364-6465
www.okstatechamber.com

Oklahoma City Convention & Visitors Bureau
189 W Sheridan St
Oklahoma City, OK 73102
Phone: 405-297-8912; Fax: 405-297-8888
Toll-free: 800-225-5652
www.visitokc.com

Tulsa Convention & Visitors Bureau
2 W 2nd St Suite 150
Williams Center Tower II
Tulsa, OK 74103
Phone: 918-585-1201; Fax: 918-592-6244
Toll-free: 800-558-3311
www.visittulsa.com

Greater Oklahoma City Chamber of Commerce
123 Park Ave
Oklahoma City, OK 73102
Phone: 405-297-8900; Fax: 405-297-8916
Toll-free: 800-616-1114
www.okcchamber.com

Tulsa Metro Chamber
2 W 2nd St Suite 150
Williams Center Tower II
Tulsa, OK 74103
Phone: 918-585-1201; Fax: 918-585-8016
www.tulsachamber.com

Oregon

Oregon Tourism Commission
670 Hawthorne Ave SE
Suite 240
Salem, OR 97301
Phone: 503-378-8850
Toll-free: 800-547-7842
www.traveloregon.com

Convention & Visitors Assn of Lane County Oregon
PO Box 10286
Eugene, OR 97440
Phone: 541-484-5307; Fax: 541-343-6335
Toll-free: 800-547-5445
www.visitlanecounty.org

Portland Oregon Visitors Assn
1000 SW Broadway
Suite 2300
Portland, OR 97205
Phone: 503-275-9750; Fax: 503-275-9774
Toll-free: 800-962-3700
www.travelportland.com

Salem Convention & Visitors Assn
1313 Mill St SE
Salem, OR 97301
Phone: 503-581-4325; Fax: 503-581-4540
Toll-free: 800-874-7012
www.travelsalem.com

Eugene Chamber of Commerce
1401 Willamette St
Eugene, OR 97401
Phone: 541-484-1314; Fax: 541-484-4942
www.eugenechamber.com

Portland Business Alliance
200 SW Market St
Suite 1717
Portland, OR 97201
Phone: 503-224-8684; Fax: 503-323-9186
www.portlandalliance.com

Salem Area Chamber of Commerce
1110 Commercial St NE
Salem, OR 97301
Phone: 503-581-1466; Fax: 503-581-0972
www.salemchamber.org

Pennsylvania

Pennsylvania Tourism Office
404 North St
4th Fl
Harrisburg, PA 17120
Phone: 717-720-1301; Fax: 717-787-0687
Toll-free: 800-847-4872
www.visitpa.com

Pennsylvania Chamber of Business & Industry
417 Walnut St
Harrisburg, PA 17101
Phone: 717-255-3252; Fax: 717-255-3298
Toll-free: 800-225-7224
www.pachamber.org

Erie Area Convention & Visitors Bureau
208 E Bayfront Pkwy
Suite 103
Erie, PA 16507
Phone: 814-454-7191; Fax: 814-459-0241
Toll-free: 800-524-3743
www.eriepa.com

Gettysburg Convention & Visitors Bureau
571 Middle St
PO Box 4117
Gettysburg, PA 17325
Phone: 717-334-6274; Fax: 717-334-1166
Toll-free: 800-337-5015
www.gettysburg.com

Greater Pittsburgh Convention & Visitors Bureau
425 6th Ave
30th Fl
Pittsburgh, PA 15219
Phone: 412-281-7711; Fax: 412-644-5512
Toll-free: 800-359-0758
www.visitpittsburgh.com

Hershey-Capital Region Visitors Bureau
112 Market St
4th Fl
Harrisburg, PA 17101
Phone: 717-231-7788; Fax: 717-231-2808
Toll-free: 877-727-8573
www.hersheycapitalregion.com

Lehigh Valley Convention & Visitors Bureau
840 Hamilton St
Suite 200
Allentown, PA 18101
Phone: 610-882-9200; Fax: 610-882-0343
Toll-free: 800-747-0561
www.lehighvalleypa.org

Pennsylvania Dutch Convention & Visitors Bureau
501 Greenfield Rd
Lancaster, PA 17601
Phone: 717-299-8901; Fax: 717-299-0470
Toll-free: 800-723-8824
www.padutchcountry.com

Philadelphia Convention & Visitors Bureau
1700 Market St
Suite 3000
Philadelphia, PA 19103
Phone: 215-636-3300; Fax: 215-636-3327
Toll-free: 800-225-5745
www.pcvb.org

Erie Regional Chamber & Growth Partnership
208 E Bayfront Pkwy
Erie, PA 16507
Phone: 814-454-7191; Fax: 814-459-0241
Toll-free: 800-524-3743
www.eriechamber.com

Gettysburg-Adams County Area Chamber of Commerce
18 Carlisle St
Suite 203
Gettysburg, PA 17325
Phone: 717-334-8151; Fax: 717-334-3368
www.gettysburg-chamber.org

Greater Lehigh Valley Chamber of Commerce
462 W Walnut St
Allentown, PA 18102
Phone: 610-841-5800; Fax: 610-437-4907
www.lehighvalleychamber.org

Greater Philadelphia Chamber of Commerce
200 S Broad St
Suite 700
Philadelphia, PA 19102
Phone: 215-545-1234; Fax: 215-790-3600
www.greaterphilachamber.com

Greater Pittsburgh Chamber of Commerce
425 6th Ave
Suite 1100
Pittsburgh, PA 15219
Phone: 412-392-4500; Fax: 412-392-1040
Toll-free: 800-843-8772
www.pittsburghchamber.com

Greater Scranton Chamber of Commerce
222 Mulberry St
Scranton, PA 18503
Phone: 570-342-7711; Fax: 570-347-6262
www.scrantonchamber.com

Harrisburg Regional Chamber
3211 N Front St
Suite 201
Harrisburg, PA 17110
Phone: 717-232-4099; Fax: 717-232-5184
www.harrisburgregionalchamber.org

Lancaster Chamber of Commerce & Industry
100 S Queen St
PO Box 1558
Lancaster, PA 17608
Phone: 717-397-3531; Fax: 717-293-3159
www.lcci.com

Rhode Island

Rhode Island Tourism Div
1 W Exchange St
Providence, RI 02903
Phone: 401-222-2601; Fax: 401-273-8270
Toll-free: 800-556-2484
visitrhodeisland.com

Rhode Island Economic Development Corp
1 W Exchange St
Providence, RI 02903
Phone: 401-222-2601; Fax: 401-222-2102
www.riedc.com

Newport County Convention & Visitors Bureau
23 America's Cup Ave
Newport, RI 02840
Phone: 401-849-8048; Fax: 401-849-0291
Toll-free: 800-326-6030
www.gonewport.com

Providence Warwick Convention & Visitors Bureau
1 W Exchange St
Providence, RI 02903
Phone: 401-274-1636; Fax: 401-351-2090
Toll-free: 800-233-1636
www.pwcvb.com

Greater Providence Chamber of Commerce
30 Exchange Terr
4th Fl
Providence, RI 02903
Phone: 401-521-5000; Fax: 401-751-2434
www.provchamber.com

Newport County Chamber of Commerce
45 Valley Rd
Middletown, RI 02842
Phone: 401-847-1600; Fax: 401-849-5848
www.newportchamber.com

South Carolina

South Carolina Parks Recreation & Tourism Dept
1205 Pendleton St
Columbia, SC 29201
Phone: 803-734-1650; Fax: 803-734-0133
southcarolinaparks.com

South Carolina Chamber of Commerce
1201 Main St
Suite 1700
Columbia, SC 29201
Phone: 803-799-4601; Fax: 803-779-6043
Toll-free: 800-799-4601
www.scchamber.net

Charleston Area Convention & Visitors Bureau
423 King St
Charleston, SC 29403
Phone: 843-853-8000; Fax: 843-853-0444
Toll-free: 800-868-8118
www.charlestoncvb.com

Columbia Metropolitan Convention & Visitors Bureau
PO Box 15
Columbia, SC 29202
Phone: 803-545-0000; Fax: 803-545-0013
Toll-free: 800-264-4884
www.columbiacvb.com

Greater Greenville Convention & Visitors Bureau
631 S Main St
Suite 301
Greenville, SC 29601
Phone: 864-421-0000; Fax: 864-421-0005
Toll-free: 800-351-7180
www.greatergreenville.com

Hilton Head Island Visitors & Convention Bureau
1 Chamber Dr
PO Box 5647
Hilton Head Island, SC 29938
Phone: 843-785-3673; Fax: 843-785-7110
Toll-free: 800-523-3373
www.hiltonheadisland.org

Myrtle Beach Area Convention Bureau
1200 N Oak St
Myrtle Beach, SC 29577
Phone: 843-626-7444; Fax: 843-448-3010
Toll-free: 800-356-3016
www.myrtlebeachinfo.com

Charleston Metro Chamber of Commerce
2750 Speissegger Dr
Suite 100
North Charleston, SC 29405
Phone: 843-577-2510; Fax: 843-723-4853
www.charlestonchamber.net

Greater Columbia Chamber of Commerce
930 Richland St
Columbia, SC 29201
Phone: 803-733-1110; Fax: 803-733-1149
www.columbiachamber.com

Greater Greenville Chamber of Commerce
24 Cleveland St
Greenville, SC 29601
Phone: 864-242-1050; Fax: 864-282-8509
www.greenvillechamber.org

Hilton Head Island-Bluffton Chamber of Commerce
1 Chamber Dr
Hilton Head Island, SC 29928
Phone: 843-785-3673; Fax: 843-785-7110
Toll-free: 800-523-3373
www.hiltonheadisland.org

Myrtle Beach Area Chamber of Commerce
1200 N Oak St
Myrtle Beach, SC 29577
Phone: 843-626-7444; Fax: 843-626-0009
Toll-free: 800-356-3016
www.myrtlebeachinfo.com/chamber/

South Dakota

South Dakota Tourism Office
711 E Wells Ave
Pierre, SD 57501
Phone: 605-773-3301; Fax: 605-773-3256
Toll-free: 800-732-5682
www.travelsd.com

South Dakota Chamber of Commerce & Industry
108 N Euclid Ave
Pierre, SD 57501
Phone: 605-224-6161; Fax: 605-224-7198
www.sdchamber.biz

Pierre Convention & Visitors Bureau
800 W Dakota Ave
Pierre, SD 57501
Phone: 605-224-7361; Fax: 605-224-6485
Toll-free: 800-962-2034
pierrechamber.com

Rapid City Convention & Visitors Bureau
444 Mt Rushmore Rd N
Rapid City, SD 57701
Phone: 605-343-1744; Fax: 605-348-9217
Toll-free: 800-487-3223
www.rapidcitycvb.com

Sioux Falls Convention & Visitors Bureau
200 N Phillips Ave
Suite 102
Sioux Falls, SD 57104
Phone: 605-336-1620; Fax: 605-336-6499
Toll-free: 800-333-2072
www.siouxfallscvb.com

Pierre Area Chamber of Commerce
800 W Dakota Ave
Pierre, SD 57501
Phone: 605-224-7361; Fax: 605-224-6485
Toll-free: 800-962-2034
pierre.org

Rapid City Area Chamber of Commerce
444 Mt Rushmore Rd N
Rapid City, SD 57701
Phone: 605-343-1744; Fax: 605-343-6550
www.rapidcitychamber.com

Sioux Falls Area Chamber of Commerce
200 N Phillips Ave
Suite 102
Sioux Falls, SD 57104
Phone: 605-336-1620; Fax: 605-336-6499
www.siouxfalls.com

Tennessee

Tennessee Chamber of Commerce & Industry
611 Commerce St
Suite 3030
Nashville, TN 37203
Phone: 615-256-5141; Fax: 615-256-6726
www.tnchamber.org

Chattanooga Area Convention & Visitors Bureau
2 Broad St
Chattanooga, TN 37402
Phone: 423-756-8687; Fax: 423-265-1630
Toll-free: 800-322-3344
www.chattanoogafun.com

Johnson City Convention & Visitors Bureau
603 E Market St
Johnson City, TN 37601
Phone: 423-461-8000; Fax: 423-461-8047
Toll-free: 800-852-3392
www.johnsoncitytn.com

Knoxville Tourism & Sports Corp
301 S Gay St
Knoxville, TN 37902
Phone: 865-523-7263; Fax: 865-673-4400
Toll-free: 866-790-5373
www.knoxville.org

Memphis Convention & Visitors Bureau
47 Union Ave
Memphis, TN 38103
Phone: 901-543-5300; Fax: 901-543-5350
Toll-free: 800-873-6282
www.memphistravel.com

Nashville Convention & Visitors Bureau
211 Commerce St
Suite 100
Nashville, TN 37201
Phone: 615-259-4700; Fax: 615-259-4126
Toll-free: 800-657-6910
www.nashvillecvb.com

Chattanooga Area Chamber of Commerce
811 Broad St
Chattanooga, TN 37402
Phone: 423-756-2121; Fax: 423-267-7242
www.chattanoogachamber.com

Johnson City/Jonesborough/Washington County Chamber
   of Commerce
603 E Market St
Johnson City, TN 37601
Phone: 423-461-8000; Fax: 423-461-8047
Toll-free: 800-852-3392
www.johnsoncitytn.com

Knoxville Area Chamber Partnership
17 Market Sq
Suite 201
Knoxville, TN 37902
Phone: 865-637-4550; Fax: 865-523-2071
www.knoxvillechamber.com

Memphis Regional Chamber of Commerce
22 N Front St
Suite 200
Memphis, TN 38103
Phone: 901-543-3500; Fax: 901-543-3510
www.memphischamber.com

Nashville Chamber of Commerce
211 Commerce St
Suite 100
Nashville, TN 37201
Phone: 615-743-3000; Fax: 615-256-3074
www.nashvillechamber.com

Texas

Texas Tourism Div
PO Box 12728
Austin, TX 78711
Phone: 512-462-9191; Fax: 512-936-0089
Toll-free: 800-888-8839
www.traveltex.com

Texas Assn of Business
1209 Nueces St
Austin, TX 78701
Phone: 512-477-6721; Fax: 512-477-0836
www.tabcc.org

Abilene Convention & Visitors Bureau
1101 N 1st St
Abilene, TX 79601
Phone: 325-676-2556; Fax: 325-676-1630
Toll-free: 800-727-7704
abilenevisitors.com

Amarillo Convention & Visitor Council
1000 S Polk St
PO Box 9480
Amarillo, TX 79105
Phone: 806-374-1497; Fax: 806-373-3909
Toll-free: 800-692-1338
www.visitamarillotx.com

Arlington Convention & Visitors Bureau
1905 E Randol Mill Rd
Arlington, TX 76011
Phone: 817-265-7721; Fax: 817-265-5640
Toll-free: 800-433-5374
www.acvb.org

Austin Convention & Visitors Bureau
301 Congress Ave
Suite 200
Austin, TX 78701
Phone: 512-474-5171; Fax: 512-583-7282
Toll-free: 800-926-2282
www.austintexas.org

Brownsville Convention & Visitors Bureau
PO Box 4697
Brownsville, TX 78523
Phone: 956-546-3721; Fax: 956-546-3972
Toll-free: 800-626-2639
www.brownsville.org

Corpus Christi Convention & Visitors Bureau
1201 N Shoreline Blvd
Corpus Christi, TX 78401
Phone: 361-881-1888; Fax: 361-887-9023
Toll-free: 800-678-6232
www.corpuschristicvb.com

Dallas Convention & Visitors Bureau
325 N Saint Paul St
Suite 700
Dallas, TX 75201
Phone: 214-571-1000; Fax: 214-571-1008
Toll-free: 800-232-5527
www.dallascvb.com

El Paso Convention & Visitors Bureau
1 Civic Center Plaza
El Paso, TX 79901
Phone: 915-534-0600; Fax: 915-534-0687
Toll-free: 800-351-6024
www.elpasocvb.com

Fort Worth Convention & Visitors Bureau
415 Throckmorton St
Fort Worth, TX 76102
Phone: 817-336-8791; Fax: 817-336-3282
Toll-free: 800-433-5747
www.fortworth.com

Garland Convention & Visitors Bureau
200 N 5th St
Garland, TX 75040
Phone: 972-205-2749; Fax: 972-205-2504
www.ci.garland.tx.us

Greater Houston Convention & Visitors Bureau
901 Bagby St
Suite 100
Houston, TX 77002
Phone: 713-437-5200; Fax: 713-227-6336
Toll-free: 800-446-8786
www.visithoustontexas.com

Irving Convention & Visitors Bureau
222 W Las Colinas Blvd
Suite 1550
Irving, TX 75039
Phone: 972-252-7476; Fax: 972-257-3153
Toll-free: 800-247-8464
www.irvingtexas.com

Lubbock Convention & Visitors Bureau
1301 Broadway St
Suite 200
Lubbock, TX 79401
Phone: 806-747-5232; Fax: 806-747-1419
Toll-free: 800-692-4035
www.lubbocklegends.com

Plano Convention & Visitors Bureau
2000 E Spring Creek Pkwy
Plano, TX 75074
Phone: 972-422-0296; Fax: 972-424-0002
Toll-free: 800-817-5266
www.planocvb.com

San Antonio Convention & Visitors Bureau
203 S Saint Marys St
2nd Fl
San Antonio, TX 78205
Phone: 210-207-6700; Fax: 210-207-6768
Toll-free: 800-447-3372
www.sanantoniocvb.com

South Padre Island Convention & Visitors Bureau
600 Padre Blvd
South Padre Island, TX 78597
Phone: 956-761-6433; Fax: 956-761-9462
Toll-free: 800-767-2373
www.sopadre.com

Abilene Chamber of Commerce
174 Cypress St
Suite 200
Abilene, TX 79601
Phone: 325-677-7241; Fax: 325-677-0622
www.abilene.com/chamber

Amarillo Chamber of Commerce
1000 S Polk St
Amarillo, TX 79101
Phone: 806-373-7800; Fax: 806-373-3909
www.amarillo-chamber.org

Arlington Chamber of Commerce
505 E Border St
Arlington, TX 76010
Phone: 817-275-2613; Fax: 817-261-7535
Toll-free: 800-834-3928
www.arlingtontx.com

Brownsville Chamber of Commerce
1600 University Blvd
Brownsville, TX 78520
Phone: 956-542-4341; Fax: 956-504-3348
www.brownsvillechamber.com

Corpus Christi Chamber of Commerce
1201 N Shoreline Blvd
Corpus Christi, TX 78401
Phone: 361-881-1800; Fax: 361-882-4256
www.corpuschristichamber.org

Fort Worth Chamber of Commerce
777 Taylor St
Suite 900
Fort Worth, TX 76102

Phone: 817-336-2491; Fax: 817-877-4034
www.fortworthcoc.org

Garland Chamber of Commerce
914 S Garland Ave
Garland, TX 75040
Phone: 972-272-7551; Fax: 972-276-9261
www.garlandchamber.com

Greater Austin Chamber of Commerce
210 Barton Springs Rd
Suite 400
Austin, TX 78704
Phone: 512-478-9383; Fax: 512-478-6389
Toll-free: 800-856-5602
www.austinchamber.org

Greater Dallas Chamber of Commerce
700 N Pearl St
Suite 1200
Dallas, TX 75201
Phone: 214-746-6600; Fax: 214-746-6799
www.dallaschamber.org

Greater El Paso Chamber of Commerce
10 Civic Center Plaza
El Paso, TX 79901
Phone: 915-534-0500; Fax: 915-534-0510
Toll-free: 800-651-8065
www.elpaso.org

Greater Houston Partnership
1200 Smith St
Suite 700
Houston, TX 77002
Phone: 713-844-3600; Fax: 713-844-0200
www.houston.org

Greater Irving & Las Colinas Chamber of Commerce
5221 N O'Connor Blvd
Suite 100
Irving, TX 75039
Phone: 214-217-8484; Fax: 214-389-2513
www.irvingchamber.com

Greater San Antonio Chamber of Commerce
PO Box 1628
San Antonio, TX 78296
Phone: 210-229-2100; Fax: 210-229-1600
www.sachamber.org

Lubbock Chamber of Commerce
1301 Broadway
Suite 101
Lubbock, TX 79403
Phone: 806-761-7000; Fax: 806-761-7010
Toll-free: 800-321-5822
www.lubbockchamber.com

Plano Chamber of Commerce
1200 E 15th St
Plano, TX 75074
Phone: 972-424-7547; Fax: 972-422-5182
www.planocc.org

Utah

Utah Travel Development Div
300 N State St
Salt Lake City, UT 84114
Phone: 801-538-1900; Fax: 801-538-1399
Toll-free: 800-200-1160
travel.utah.gov

Mountainland Travel Region Office
586 E 800 North
Orem, UT 84097
Phone: 801-229-3800; Fax: 801-229-3801
www.mountainland.org

Ogden/Weber Convention & Visitors Bureau
2501 Wall Ave
Union Stn Suite 201
Ogden, UT 84401
Phone: 801-627-8288; Fax: 801-399-0783
Toll-free: 800-255-8824
www.ogdencvb.org/

Salt Lake Convention & Visitors Bureau
90 S West Temple
Salt Lake City, UT 84101
Phone: 801-521-2822; Fax: 801-355-9323
Toll-free: 800-541-4955
www.visitsaltlake.com

Utah Valley Convention & Visitors Bureau
111 S University Ave
Provo, UT 84601
Phone: 801-851-2100; Fax: 801-851-2109
Toll-free: 800-222-8824
www.utahvalley.org/cvb

Chamber Ogden/Weber
2484 Washington Blvd
Suite 400
Ogden, UT 84401
Phone: 801-621-8300; Fax: 801-392-7609
Toll-free: 866-990-1299
www.echamber.cc

Provo/Orem Chamber of Commerce
51 S University Ave
Suite 215
Provo, UT 84601
Phone: 801-379-2555; Fax: 801-379-2557
thechamber.org

Salt Lake City Chamber of Commerce
175 E 400 South
Suite 600
Salt Lake City, UT 84111
Phone: 801-364-3631; Fax: 801-328-5098
www.saltlakechamber.org

Vermont

Vermont Tourism & Marketing Dept
134 State St
Montpelier, VT 05602
Phone: 802-828-3236; Fax: 802-828-3233

Toll-free: 800-837-6668
www.vermontvacation.com

Vermont Chamber of Commerce
PO Box 37
Montpelier, VT 05601
Phone: 802-223-3443; Fax: 802-223-4257
www.vtchamber.com

Burlington Convention & Visitors Bureau
60 Main St
Suite 100
Burlington, VT 05401
Phone: 802-863-3489; Fax: 802-863-1538
Toll-free: 877-264-3503

Central Vermont Chamber of Commerce
33 Stewart Rd
Berlin, VT 05602
Phone: 802-229-5711; Fax: 802-229-5713
Toll-free: 877-887-3678
www.central-vt.com/chamber/index.html

Lake Champlain Regional Chamber of Commerce
60 Main St
Suite 100
Burlington, VT 05401
Phone: 802-863-3489; Fax: 802-863-1538
Toll-free: 877-686-5253
www.vermont.org

Virginia

Virginia Tourism Corp
901 E Byrd St
Richmond, VA 23219
Phone: 804-786-2051; Fax: 804-786-1919
Toll-free: 800-847-4882
www.vatc.org

Virginia Chamber of Commerce
9 S 5th St
Richmond, VA 23219
Phone: 804-644-1607; Fax: 804-783-6112
Toll-free: 800-477-7682
www.vachamber.com

Alexandria Convention & Visitors Assn
221 King St
Alexandria, VA 22314
Phone: 703-838-4200; Fax: 703-838-4683
Toll-free: 800-388-9119
www.funside.com

Arlington Convention & Visitors Service
1100 N Glebe Rd
Suite 1500
Arlington, VA 22201
Phone: 703-228-0888; Fax: 703-228-0806
Toll-free: 800-296-7996
www.stayarlington.com

Chesapeake Conventions & Tourism Bureau
3815 Bainbridge Blvd
Chesapeake, VA 23324

Phone: 757-502-4898; Fax: 757-502-4883
Toll-free: 888-889-5551
www.visitchesapeake.com

Newport News Tourism Development Office
700 Town Center Dr
Suite 320
Newport News, VA 23606
Phone: 757-926-1400; Fax: 757-926-1441
Toll-free: 888-493-7386
www.newport-news.org

Richmond Metropolitan Convention & Visitors Bureau
401 N 3rd St
Richmond, VA 23219
Phone: 804-782-2777; Fax: 804-780-2577
Toll-free: 800-370-9004
www.richmond.com/visitors

Roanoke Valley Convention & Visitors Bureau
101 Shenandoah Ave NE
Roanoke, VA 24016
Phone: 540-342-6025; Fax: 540-342-7119
Toll-free: 800-635-5535
www.visitroanokeva.com

Virginia Beach Convention & Visitor Bureau
2101 Parks Ave
Suite 500
Virginia Beach, VA 23451
Phone: 757-437-4700; Fax: 757-437-4747
Toll-free: 800-700-7702
www.vbfun.com

Williamsburg Area Convention & Visitors Bureau
421 N Boundary St
Williamsburg, VA 23185
Phone: 757-229-6511; Fax: 757-229-2047
Toll-free: 800-368-6511
www.visitwilliamsburg.com

Alexandria Chamber of Commerce
801 N Fairfax St
Suite 402
Alexandria, VA 22314
Phone: 703-549-1000; Fax: 703-739-3805
www.alexchamber.com

Arlington Chamber of Commerce
2009 14th St N
Suite 111
Arlington, VA 22201
Phone: 703-525-2400; Fax: 703-522-5273
www.arlcc.org

Greater Richmond Chamber of Commerce
600 E Main St
7th Fl
Richmond, VA 23219
Phone: 804-648-1234; Fax: 804-783-9366
www.grcc.com

Hampton Roads Chamber of Commerce
420 Bank St
Norfolk, VA 23510
Phone: 757-622-2312; Fax: 757-622-5563
www.hamptonroadschamber.com

Salem/Roanoke County Chamber of Commerce
611 E Main St
Salem, VA 24153
Phone: 540-387-0267; Fax: 540-387-4110
www.s-rcchamber.org

Virginia Peninsula Chamber of Commerce
21 Enterprise Pkwy
Suite 100
Hampton, VA 23666
Phone: 757-262-2000; Fax: 757-262-2009
Toll-free: 800-556-1822
www.vpcc.org

Williamsburg Area Chamber of Commerce
PO Box 3495
Williamsburg, VA 23185
Phone: 757-229-6511; Fax: 757-229-2047
Toll-free: 800-368-6511
www.williamsburgcc.com

Washington

Washington Tourism Div
PO Box 42525
Olympia, WA 98504
Phone: 360-725-4172; Fax: 360-753-4470
www.experiencewashington.com

Association of Washington Business
PO Box 658
Olympia, WA 98507
Phone: 360-943-1600; Fax: 360-943-5811
Toll-free: 800-521-9325
www.awb.org

Olympia/Thurston County Visitor & Convention Bureau
PO Box 7338
Olympia, WA 98507
Phone: 360-704-7544; Fax: 360-704-7533
Toll-free: 877-704-7500
www.visitolympia.com

Seattle's Convention & Visitors Bureau
1 Convention Pl
701 Pike St Suite 800
Seattle, WA 98101
Phone: 206-461-5800; Fax: 206-461-5855
Toll-free: 866-732-2695
www.visitseattle.org

Southwest Washington Convention & Visitors Bureau
101 E 8th St
Suite 110
Vancouver, WA 98660
Phone: 360-750-1553; Fax: 360-750-1933
Toll-free: 877-600-0800
www.southwestwashington.com

Spokane Convention & Visitors Bureau
201 W Main
Suite 301
Spokane, WA 99201
Phone: 509-747-3230; Fax: 509-623-1297
Toll-free: 888-776-5263
www.visitspokane.com

Tacoma Regional Convention & Visitor Bureau
1119 Pacific Ave
5th Fl
Tacoma, WA 98402
Phone: 253-627-2836; Fax: 253-627-8783
Toll-free: 800-272-2662
www.traveltacoma.com

Greater Seattle Chamber of Commerce
1301 5th Ave
Suite 2500
Seattle, WA 98101
Phone: 206-389-7200; Fax: 206-389-7288
www.seattlechamber.com

Greater Vancouver Chamber of Commerce
1101 Broadway
Suite 100
Vancouver, WA 98660
Phone: 360-694-2588; Fax: 360-693-8279
www.vancouverusa.com

Olympia/Thurston County Chamber of Commerce
809 Legion Way
Olympia, WA 98501
Phone: 360-357-3362; Fax: 360-357-3376
www.thurstonchamber.com

Spokane Regional Chamber of Commerce
801 W Riverside Ave
Suite 100
Spokane, WA 99201
Phone: 509-624-1393; Fax: 509-747-0077
www.spokanechamber.org

Tacoma-Pierce County Chamber of Commerce
950 Pacific Ave
Suite 300
Tacoma, WA 98402
Phone: 253-627-2175; Fax: 253-597-7305
www.tacomachamber.org

West Virginia

West Virginia Tourism Div
2101 Washington St E
Charleston, WV 25305
Phone: 304-558-2200; Fax: 304-558-2956
Toll-free: 800-225-5982
www.state.wv.us/tourism

West Virginia Chamber of Commerce
PO Box 2789
Charleston, WV 25330
Phone: 304-342-1115; Fax: 304-342-1130
www.wvchamber.com

Charleston Convention & Visitors Bureau
200 Civic Center Dr
Charleston, WV 25301
Phone: 304-344-5075; Fax: 304-344-1241
Toll-free: 800-733-5469
www.charlestonwv.com

Greater Morgantown Convention & Visitors Bureau
201 High St
Suite 3
Morgantown, WV 26505
Phone: 304-292-5081; Fax: 304-291-1354
Toll-free: 800-458-7373
www.tourmorgantown.com

Wheeling Convention & Visitors Bureau
1401 Main St
Wheeling, WV 26003
Phone: 304-233-7709; Fax: 304-233-1470
Toll-free: 800-828-3097
www.wheelingcvb.com

Charleston Regional Chamber of Commerce
1116 Smith St
Charleston, WV 25301
Phone: 304-340-4253; Fax: 304-340-4275
www.charlestonwvchamber.org

Morgantown Area Chamber of Commerce
1009 University Ave
Morgantown, WV 26507
Phone: 304-292-3311; Fax: 304-296-6619
Toll-free: 800-618-2525
www.morgantownchamber.com

Wheeling Area Chamber of Commerce
1310 Market St
Wheeling, WV 26003
Phone: 304-233-2575; Fax: 304-233-1320
www.wheelingchamber.com

Wisconsin

Wisconsin Tourism Dept
201 W Washington Ave
2nd Fl
Madison, WI 53707
Phone: 608-266-2161; Fax: 608-266-3403
Toll-free: 800-432-8747
www.travelwisconsin.com

Wisconsin Manufacturers & Commerce
PO Box 352
Madison, WI 53701
Phone: 608-258-3400; Fax: 608-258-3413
www.wmc.org

Greater Madison Convention & Visitors Bureau
615 E Washington Ave
Madison, WI 53703
Phone: 608-255-2537; Fax: 608-258-4950
Toll-free: 800-373-6376
www.visitmadison.com

Greater Milwaukee Convention & Visitors Bureau
101 W Wisconsin Ave
Suite 425
Milwaukee, WI 53203
Phone: 414-273-3950; Fax: 414-273-5596
Toll-free: 800-231-0903
www.milwaukee.org

Packer Country Visitor & Convention Bureau
1901 S Oneida St
Green Bay, WI 54304
Phone: 920-494-9507; Fax: 920-494-9229
Toll-free: 888-867-3342
www.packercountry.com

Greater Madison Chamber of Commerce
PO Box 71
Madison, WI 53701
Phone: 608-256-8348; Fax: 608-256-0333
www.greatermadisonchamber.com

Green Bay Area Chamber of Commerce
400 S Washington St
Green Bay, WI 54301
Phone: 920-437-8704; Fax: 920-437-1024
www.titletown.org

Metropolitan Milwaukee Assn of Commerce
756 N Milwaukee St
Milwaukee, WI 53202
Phone: 414-287-4100; Fax: 414-271-7753
www.mmac.org

Wyoming

Wyoming Tourism Div
214 W 15th St
Cheyenne, WY 82002
Phone: 307-777-2828; Fax: 307-777-2877
Toll-free: 800-225-5996
www.wyomingtourism.org

Casper Area Convention & Visitors Bureau
992 N Poplar St
Casper, WY 82601
Phone: 307-234-5362; Fax: 307-261-9928
Toll-free: 800-852-1889
www.casperwyoming.info

Cheyenne Area Convention & Visitors Bureau
121 W 15th St
Suite 202
Cheyenne, WY 82001
Phone: 307-778-3133; Fax: 307-778-3190
Toll-free: 800-426-5009
www.cheyenne.org

Casper Area Chamber of Commerce
500 N Center St
Casper, WY 82601
Phone: 307-234-5311; Fax: 307-265-2643
Toll-free: 866-234-5311
www.casperwyoming.org

Greater Cheyenne Chamber of Commerce
121 W 15th St
Suite 204
Cheyenne, WY 82001
Phone: 307-638-3388; Fax: 307-778-1407
www.cheyennechamber.org

Jackson Hole Chamber of Commerce
990 W Broadway St

Jackson, WY 83001
Phone: 307-733-3316; Fax: 307-733-5585
www.jacksonholechamber.com

CANADA

Canada Consulate General
550 S Hope St
9th Fl
Los Angeles, CA 90071
Phone: 213-346-2700; Fax: 213-620-8827
www.dfait-maeci.gc.ca/los_angeles/

Canada Embassy
501 Pennsylvania Ave NW
Washington, DC 20001
Phone: 202-682-1740; Fax: 202-682-7726
www.canadianembassy.org

Canada Consulate
200 S Biscayne Blvd
Suite 1600
Miami, FL 33131
Phone: 305-579-1600; Fax: 305-374-6774
geo.international.gc.ca/can-am/miami/

Canada Consulate General
1175 Peachtree St NE
100 Colony Sq Suite 1700
Atlanta, GA 30361
Phone: 404-532-2000; Fax: 404-532-2050
www.dfait-maeci.gc.ca/atlanta/

Canada Consulate General
180 N Stetson Ave
Suite 2400
Chicago, IL 60601
Phone: 312-616-1860; Fax: 312-616-1877
www.dfait-maeci.gc.ca/chicago

Canada Consulate General
3 Copley Pl
Suite 400
Boston, MA 02116
Phone: 617-262-3760; Fax: 617-262-3415
www.dfait-maeci.gc.ca/boston

Canada Consulate General
600 Renaissance Ctr
Suite 1100
Detroit, MI 48243
Phone: 313-567-2340; Fax: 313-567-2164
www.dfait-maeci.gc.ca/detroit

Canada Consulate General
701 4th Ave S
Suite 900
Minneapolis, MN 55415
Phone: 612-332-7486; Fax: 612-332-4061
www.dfait-maeci.gc.ca/minneapolis

Canada Consulate General
3000 HSBC Ctr
Buffalo, NY 14203
Phone: 716-858-9500; Fax: 716-852-2477
www.dfait-maeci.gc.ca/buffalo/

Canada Consulate General
1251 Ave of the Americas
Concourse Level
New York, NY 10020
Phone: 212-596-1628; Fax: 212-596-1790
geo.international.gc.ca/can-am/new_york/

Canada Consulate General
750 N Saint Paul St
Suite 1700
Dallas, TX 75201
Phone: 214-922-9806; Fax: 214-922-9815
www.dfait-maeci.gc.ca/dallas

Canada Consulate General
1501 4th Ave
Suite 600
Seattle, WA 98101
Phone: 206-443-1777; Fax: 206-443-9662
www.dfait-maeci.gc.ca/seattle/

Canada Permanent Mission to the UN
885 2nd Ave
14th Fl
New York, NY 10017
Phone: 212-848-1100; Fax: 212-848-1195
www.un.int/canada

Alberta

Travel Alberta
999 8th St SW
Suite 500
Calgary, AB T2R1J5
Phone: 403-297-2700; Fax: 403-297-5068
Toll-free: 800-252-3782
www.travelalberta.com

Alberta Chambers of Commerce
10025 - 102A Ave Suite 1808
Edmonton Ctr
Edmonton, AB T5J2Z2
Phone: 780-425-4180; Fax: 780-429-1061
www.abchamber.ca

Calgary Chamber of Commerce
100 6th Ave SW
Calgary, AB T2P0P5
Phone: 403-750-0400; Fax: 403-266-3413
www.calgarychamber.com

Edmonton Chamber of Commerce
9990 Jasper Ave
Suite 600
Edmonton, AB T5J1P7
Phone: 780-426-4620; Fax: 780-424-7946
www.edmontonchamber.com

British Columbia

Canadian Tourism Commission
1055 Dunsmuir St Suite 1400
4 Bentall Center Box 49220
Vancouver, BC V7X1L2

Phone: 604-638-8300Toll-free:
www.canadatourisme.com
travel.bc.ca

Canadian Tourism Commission
3697 Quadra St
Victoria, BC V8X1H5
Phone: 866-810-6645; Fax: 866-768-1899
travel.bc.ca

British Columbia Chamber of Commerce
750 W Pender St
Suite 1201
Vancouver, BC V6C2T8
Phone: 604-683-0700; Fax: 604-683-0416
www.bcchamber.org

Greater Victoria Chamber of Commerce
852 Fort St
Suite 100
Victoria, BC V8W1H8
Phone: 250-383-7191; Fax: 250-385-3552
www.victoriachamber.ca

North Vancouver Chamber of Commerce
124 W 1st St
Suite 102
North Vancouver, BC V7M3N3
Phone: 604-987-4488; Fax: 604-987-8272
Toll-free: 877-880-4699
www.nvchamber.bc.ca

Vancouver Board Of Trade
999 Canada Pl
Suite 400
Vancouver, BC V6C3E1
Phone: 604-681-2111; Fax: 604-681-0437
www.vancouver.boardoftrade.com

West Vancouver Chamber of Commerce
1310 Marine Dr
West Vancouver, BC V7T1B5
Phone: 604-926-6614; Fax: 604-926-6436
Toll-free: 888-471-9996
www.westvanchamber.com

Manitoba

Travel Manitoba
155 Carlton St
7th Fl
Winnipeg, MB R3C3H8
Phone: 204-927-7800; Fax: 204-927-7828
Toll-free: 800-665-0040
www.travelmanitoba.com

Manitoba Chamber of Commerce
227 Portage Ave
Winnipeg, MB R3B2A6
Phone: 204-948-0100; Fax: 204-948-0110
www.mbchamber.mb.ca

Winnipeg Chamber of Commerce
259 Portage Ave
Suite 100

Winnipeg, MB R3B2A9
Phone: 204-944-8484; Fax: 204-944-8492
www.winnipeg-chamber.com

New Brunswick

Tourism New Brunswick
26 Roseberry St
PO Box 12345
Campbellton, NB E3N2G4
Phone: 506-789-4982; Fax: 506-789-2044
Toll-free: 800-561-0123
www.tourismnewbrunswick.ca

Atlantic Provinces Chamber of Commerce
236 Saint George St
Suite 21
Moncton, NB E1C1W1
Phone: 506-857-3980; Fax: 506-859-6131
www.apcc.ca

Enterprise Fredericton
570 Queen St
Suite 102
Fredericton, NB E3B6Z6
Phone: 506-444-4686; Fax: 506-444-4649
Toll-free: 800-200-1180
www.gfedc.nb.ca

Fredericton Chamber of Commerce
270 Rockwood Rd
PO Box 275
Fredericton, NB E3B4Y9
Phone: 506-458-8006; Fax: 506-451-1119
www.frederictonchamber.ca

Saint John Board of Trade
40 King St
PO Box 6037
Saint John, NB E2L4R5
Phone: 506-634-8111; Fax: 506-632-2008
www.sjboardoftrade.com

Newfoundland & Labrador

Newfoundland & Labrador Tourism
PO Box 8730
Saint John's, NL A1B4K2
Phone: 709-729-2830; Fax: 709-729-0057
Toll-free: 800-563-6353
www.newfoundlandandlabradortourism.com

Saint John's Board of Trade
PO Box 5127
Saint John's, NL A1C5V5
Phone: 709-726-2961; Fax: 709-726-2003

Nova Scotia

Nova Scotia Dept of Tourism & Culture
1800 Argyle St
Halifax, NS B3J3N8

Phone: 902-424-5000; Fax: 902-424-2668
Toll-free: 800-565-0000
www.NovaScotia.com

Metropolitan Halifax Chamber of Commerce
656 Windmill Rd
Suite 200
Dartmouth, NS B3B1B8
Phone: 902-468-7111; Fax: 902-468-7333
www.halifaxchamber.com

Northwest Territories

NWT Tourism
Box 610
Yellowknife, NT X1A2N5
Phone: 867-873-7200; Fax: 867-873-4059
Toll-free: 800-661-0788
www.explorenwt.com

Northwest Territories Chamber of Commerce
4910 50th St
YK Center PO Box 13
Yellowknife, NT X1A3S5
Phone: 867-920-9505; Fax: 867-873-4174
www.nwtchamber.com

Nunavut

Nunavut Tourism
PO Box 1450
Iqaluit, NU X0A0H0
Phone: 867-979-6551; Fax: 867-979-1261
Toll-free: 800-491-7910
www.nunavuttourism.com

Ontario

Ontario Tourism Marketing Partnership Corp
900 Bay St
Hearst Block 10th Fl
Toronto, ON M7A2E1
Phone: 905-282-1721; Fax: 905-282-7433
Toll-free: 800-668-2746
www.ontariotravel.net

York Region Tourism
17250 Young St
Box 147 4th Fl
Newmarket, ON L3Y6Z1
Phone: 905-883-3442; Fax: 905-895-3482
Toll-free: 888-448-0000
www.yorktourism.com

Canadian Chamber of Commerce
350 Sparks St Delta Office Tower
Suite 501
Ottawa, ON K1R7S8
Phone: 613-238-4000; Fax: 613-238-7643
www.chamber.ca

Canadian Chamber of Commerce Toronto Office
55 University Ave
Suite 901
Toronto, ON M5J2H7
Phone: 416-868-6415; Fax: 416-868-0189
www.chamber.ca

Ontario Chamber of Commerce
180 Dundas St W
Suite 505
Toronto, ON M5G1Z8
Phone: 416-482-5222; Fax: 416-482-5879
occ.on.ca

Ottawa Chamber of Commerce
1701 Woodward Dr
Suite LL-20
Ottawa, ON K2C0R4
Phone: 613-236-3631; Fax: 613-236-7498
www.ottawachamber.ca

Toronto Board of Trade
1 First Canadian Pl
PO Box 60
Toronto, ON M5X1C1
Phone: 416-366-6811; Fax: 416-366-6460
www.bot.com

Upper Ottawa Valley Chamber of Commerce
2 International Dr
Pembroke, ON K8A6W5
Phone: 613-732-1492; Fax: 613-732-5793
www.upperottawavalleychamber.com

Windsor & District Chamber of Commerce
2575 Ouellette Pl
Windsor, ON N8X1L9
Phone: 519-966-3696; Fax: 519-966-0603
www.windsorchamber.org

Prince Edward Island

Prince Edward Island Tourism
PO Box 2000
Charlottetown, PE C1A7N8
Phone: 902-368-4441; Fax: 902-368-4438
Toll-free: 888-734-7529
www.gov.pe.ca

Quebec

Tourisme Quebec
1255 Peel St
Office 100
Montreal, QC H3B4V4
Phone: 514-873-2015; Fax: 514-864-3838
www.tourisme.gouv.qc.ca/anglais/index.html

Board of Trade of Metropolitan Montreal
380 Saint-Antoine St W
Suite 6000
Montreal, QC H2Y3X7
Phone: 514-871-4000; Fax: 514-871-1255
www.btmm.qc.ca

Canadian Chamber of Commerce Montreal Office
1155 University St
Suite 709
Montreal, QC H3B3A7
Phone: 514-866-4334; Fax: 514-866-7296
www.chamber.ca

Chambre de Commerce du Quebec
576 E Saint Catherine St
Suite 200
Montreal, QC H2L2E1
Phone: 514-522-1885; Fax: 514-522-9468
Toll-free: 888-595-8110
www.ccquebec.ca

Chambre de Commerce et d'Industrie du Quebec
  Metropolitain
17 Saint-Louis St
Quebec, QC G1R3Y8
Phone: 418-692-3853; Fax: 418-694-2286
www.ccquebec.ca

Saskatchewan

Tourism Saskatchewan
1922 Park St
Regina, SK S4N7M4
Phone: 306-787-9600; Fax: 306-787-0715
Toll-free: 877-237-2273
www.sasktourism.com

Yukon

Tourism Yukon
PO Box 2703
Whitehorse, YT Y1A2C6
Phone: 867-667-5036; Fax: 867-667-3546
Toll-free: 800-661-0494
www.touryukon.com

Whitehorse Chamber of Commerce
302 Steele St
Suite 101
Whitehorse, YT Y1A2C5
Phone: 867-667-7545; Fax: 867-667-4507
www.whitehorsechamber.com

Yukon Chamber of Commerce
307 Jarvis St
Suite 101
Whitehorse, YT Y1A2H3
Phone: 867-667-2000; Fax: 867-667-2001
www.yukonchamber.com

MEXICO

Mexico Tourism Board
5975 Sunset Dr
Suite 305
Miami, FL 33143
Phone: 786-621-2909; Fax: 786-621-2907
Toll-free: 800-446-3942
www.visitmexico.com

Mexico Tourism Board
225 N Michigan Ave
Suite 1850
Chicago, IL 60601
Phone: 312-228-0517; Fax: 312-228-0515
Toll-free: 800-446-3942
www.visitmexico.com

Mexico Tourism Board
400 Madison Ave
Suite 11-C
New York, NY 10017
Phone: 212-308-2110; Fax: 212-308-9060
Toll-free: 800-446-3942
www.visitmexico.com

Mexico Tourism Board
4507 San Jacinto
Suite 308
Houston, TX 77004
Phone: 713-772-2581; Fax: 713-772-6058
Toll-free: 800-446-3942
www.visitmexico.com

US-Mexico Chamber of Commerce Inter-American Chapter
7001 SW 97th Ave
Miami, FL 33173
Phone: 305-275-1536; Fax: 305-275-1480
www.usmcoc.org

US-Mexico Chamber of Commerce California Pacific
  Chapter
2450 Colorado Ave
Suite 400E
Santa Monica, CA 90404
Phone: 310-586-7901; Fax: 310-586-7800
www.usmcocca.org

US-Mexico Chamber of Commerce
1300 Pennsylvania Ave NW
Suite 0003
Washington, DC 20004
Phone: 202-312-1520; Fax: 202-312-1530
www.usmcoc.org

Mexico Consulate
1201 F Ave
Douglas, AZ 85607
Phone: 520-364-3107; Fax: 520-364-1379

Mexico Consulate
571 N Grand Ave
Nogales, AZ 85621
Phone: 520-287-2521; Fax: 520-287-3175

Mexico Consulate General
1990 W Camelback Rd
Suite 110
Phoenix, AZ 85015
Phone: 602-242-7398; Fax: 602-242-2957
www.sre.gob.mx/phoenix

Mexico Consulate
408 Heber Ave
Calexico, CA 92231
Phone: 760-357-3863; Fax: 760-357-6284

Mexico Consulate
2409 Merced St
Fresno, CA 93721
Phone: 559-233-9770; Fax: 559-233-6156

Mexico Consulate
293 N 'D' St
San Bernardino, CA 92401
Phone: 909-889-9836; Fax: 909-889-8285

Mexico Consulate General
2401 W 6th St
Los Angeles, CA 90057
Phone: 213-351-6800Toll-free:
www.sre.gob.mx/losangeles

Mexico Consulate General
3151 W 5th St
Oxnard, CA 93030
Phone: 805-984-8738; Fax: 805-984-8747
www.consulmexoxnard.com

Mexico Consulate General
1010 8th St
Sacramento, CA 95814
Phone: 916-441-2987; Fax: 916-441-3176
www.mexico.us/consulate.htm

Mexico Consulate General
1549 India St
San Diego, CA 92101
Phone: 619-231-8414Toll-free:
www.sre.gob.mx/sandiego

Mexico Consulate General
532 Folsom St
San Francisco, CA 94105
Phone: 415-392-5554; Fax: 415-495-3971

Mexico Consulate General
540 N 1st St
San Jose, CA 95112
Phone: 408-294-3414; Fax: 408-294-4506
www.consulmexsj.com

Mexico Consulate General
5350 Leesdale Dr
Denver, CO 80246
Phone: 303-331-1110; Fax: 303-331-1872
www.consulmex-denver.com

Mexico Embassy
1911 Pennsylvania Ave NW
Washington, DC 20006
Phone: 202-728-1600; Fax: 202-728-1766
portal.sre.gob.mx/usa

Mexico Consulate
100 W Washington St
Orlando, FL 32801
Phone: 407-422-0514; Fax: 407-422-9633

Mexico Consulate General
5975 SW 72nd St
Suite 101
Miami, FL 33143
Phone: 786-268-4900; Fax: 786-268-4875
www.sre.gob.mx/miami

Mexico Consulate General
2600 Apple Valley Rd
Atlanta, GA 30319
Phone: 404-266-2233; Fax: 404-266-2302
www.consulmexatlanta.org

Mexico Consulate General
204 S Ashland Ave
Chicago, IL 60607
Phone: 312-855-1380Toll-free:
www.consulmexchicago.com

Mexico Consulate
20 Park Plaza
Suite 506
Boston, MA 02116
Phone: 617-426-4942; Fax: 617-695-1957
Toll-free: 800-601-1289
www.sre.gob.mx/boston

Mexico Consulate
645 Griswold Ave
8th Fl
Detroit, MI 48226
Phone: 313-964-4515; Fax: 313-964-4522
www.sre.gob.mx/detroit

Mexico Consulate
1610 4th St NW
Albuquerque, NM 87102
Phone: 505-247-2147; Fax: 505-842-9490
www.users.qwest.net/consulmexalb

Mexico Consulate General
27 E 39th St
New York, NY 10016
Phone: 212-217-6400; Fax: 212-217-6493
www.consulmexny.org

Mexico Consulate
1234 SW Morrison St
Portland, OR 97205
Phone: 503-229-0790; Fax: 503-274-1540
www.sre.gob.mx/portland

Mexico Consulate
111 S Independence Mall E
Bourse Bldg Suite 310
Philadelphia, PA 19106
Phone: 215-922-4262; Fax: 215-923-7281

Mexico Consulate
301 Mexico Blvd
Brownsville, TX 78520
Phone: 956-542-4431; Fax: 956-542-7267
www.sre.gob.mx/brownsville

Mexico Consulate
2398 Spur 239
PO Box 1275
Del Rio, TX 78840
Phone: 830-775-2352; Fax: 830-774-6497

Mexico Consulate
2252 E Garrison St
Eagle Pass, TX 78852
Phone: 830-773-9255; Fax: 830-773-9397

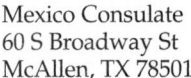

Mexico Consulate
60 S Broadway St
McAllen, TX 78501
Phone: 956-686-0244; Fax: 956-686-4901

Mexico Consulate General
800 Brazos St
Suite 330
Austin, TX 78701
Phone: 512-478-2866; Fax: 512-478-8008
www.sre.gob.mx/austin

Mexico Consulate General
8855 N Stemmons Fwy
Dallas, TX 75247
Phone: 214-252-9250Toll-free:
www.consulmexdallas.com

Mexico Consulate General
910 E San Antonio St
El Paso, TX 79901
Phone: 915-533-3644; Fax: 915-532-7163
www.sre.gob.mx/elpaso

Mexico Consulate General
4506 Carolinas St
Houston, TX 77004

Phone: 713-271-6800; Fax: 713-271-3201
www.sre.gob.mx/houston

Mexico Consulate General
1612 Farragut St
Laredo, TX 78040
Phone: 956-723-0990; Fax: 956-723-1741
www.sre.gob.mx/laredo

Mexico Consulate General
127 Navarro St
San Antonio, TX 78205
Phone: 210-227-9145; Fax: 210-227-9817
www.consulmexsat.org

Mexico Consulate
2132 3rd Ave
Seattle, WA 98121
Phone: 206-448-6819; Fax: 206-448-4771
www.sre.gob.mx/seattle

Mexico Permanent Mission to the UN
2 UN Plaza
28th Fl
New York, NY 10017
Phone: 212-752-0220; Fax: 212-688-8862
www.un.int/mexico

APPENDIX 9

Facts about the U.S. Presidents

This section lists all U.S. presidents in the order in which they held office, their birth dates and places, spouses, death dates and places, burial sites, political parties, nicknames, career highlights, and notable landmarks commemorating them. The diamond symbol (◆) indicates that an entry on a festival celebrating the president appears in the main text.

◆ George Washington

First president (1789-97)

Born Feb 22, 1732, Popes Creek (now Wakefield), Westmoreland County, VA

Married Martha Dandridge Custis, 1759

Died Dec 14, 1799, Mt. Vernon, VA

Buried in family vault, Mt. Vernon, VA

Federalist. "Father of His Country." Fought in French and Indian War. Served in Continental Congress. Commander-in-Chief during Revolutionary War. Bill of Rights passed. Laid cornerstone of Capitol in Washington, DC.

LANDMARKS:

Birth site: George Washington Birthplace National Monument, 1732 Popes Creek Rd., Washington's Birthplace, VA 22443-5115, 804-224-1732; fax: 804-224-2142
http://www.nps.gov/gewa
GEWA_Superintendent@nps.gov

Anderson House Museum, 2118 Massachusetts Ave., N.W., Washington, DC 20008-2810, 202-785-2040; fax: 202-785-0729
http://www.societyofthecincinnati.org
admin@societyofthecincinnati.org

Brandywine Battlefield Park, Box 202, Chadds Ford, PA 19317, 610-459-3342
http://www.ushistory.org/brandywine/brandywine.htm

Deshler-Morris House, 5442 Germantown Ave., Philadelphia, PA 19144, 215-597-7130; fax: 215-861-4950
http://www.nps.gov/demo
http://www.ushistory.org/germantown/lower/deshler.-htm

Dey Mansion, 199 Totowa Rd., Wayne, NJ 07470, 973-696-1776

Federal Hall National Memorial, 26 Wall St., New York, NY 10005, 212-825-6888; fax: 212-825-6874
http://www.nps.gov/feha
MASI_Superintendent@nps.gov

Gadsby's Tavern Museum, 134 N. Royal St., Alexandria, VA 22314, 703-838-4242; fax: 703-838-4270
http://oha.alexandriava.gov/gadsby

George Washington Masonic National Memorial, 101 Callahan Dr., Alexandria, VA 22301, 703-683-2007; fax: 703-519-9270
http://www.gwmemorial.org

Mary Washington House, 1200 Charles St., Fredericksburg, VA 22401, 540-373-1569
http://www.apva.org/marywashingtonhouse
marywashingtonhouse@apva.org

Military Office Museum, Braddock and Cork Sts., Winchester, VA 22601, 540-662-4412
http://www.fortedwards.org/cwffa/gw-off.htm

Morristown National Historical Park, 30 Washington Place, Morristown, NJ 07960-4299, 973-539-2016; fax: 973-285-5021
http://www.nps.gov/morr
MORR_Interpretation@nps.gov

Mount Vernon, 3200 Mount Vernon Memorial Hwy., P.O. Box 110, Mount Vernon, VA 22121, 703-780-2000
http://www.mountvernon.org
info@mountvernon.org

Rockingham State Historic Site, 108 CR 518, Rocky Hill, NJ 08540, 609-683-7132
http://www.rockingham.net

Valley Forge National Historical Park, 1400 N. Louter Line Dr., King of Prussia, PA 19406, 610-783-1077; fax: 610-783-1060
http://www.nps.gov/vafo
VAFO_Superintendent@nps.gov

Washington Monument, National Mall, 900 Ohio Dr., S.W., Washington, DC 20024, 202-426-6841
http://www.nps.gov/wamo
National_Mall@nps.gov

Washington's Headquarters Museum, 140 Virginia Rd., North White Plains, NY 10601, 914-864-7000
http://www.westchestergov.com/parks
mlbmillerhouse@verizon.net

◆ Indicates that an entry on a festival celebrating the president appears in the main text

Washington's Headquarters State Historic Site, 84 Liberty St., Newburgh, NY 12550, 845-562-1195

John Adams

Second president (1797-1801)

Born Oct 30, 1735, Braintree (now Quincy), MA

Married Abigail Smith, 1764

Died Jul 4, 1826, Quincy, MA

Buried at United First Parish Church (Church of the Presidents), 1306 Hancock St., Quincy, MA 02169, 617-773-1290 or 617-773-7499
http://www.ufpc.org
ufpc@ufpc.org

Federalist. "Father of American Independence." Served in Continental Congress. Helped draft and signed Declaration of Independence. Secretary of War. Minister to Great Britain, Netherlands. Vice President. First occupant of White House. Son was sixth president (*see* John Quincy Adams).

LANDMARKS:

Birth site: Adams National Historic Park, 135 Adams St., Quincy, MA 02169, 617-770-1175; fax: 617-472-7562
http://www.nps.gov/adam
ADAM_Visitor_Center@nps.gov

◆ Thomas Jefferson

Third president (1801-09)

Born Apr 13, 1743, Shadwell, Charlottesville, Goochland County (now Albemarle County), VA

Married Martha Wayles Skelton, 1772

Died Jul 4, 1826, Charlottesville, VA

Buried at Monticello, Charlottesville, VA

Democratic-Republican. "Father of the Declaration of Independence." Served in Continental Congress. Drafted Declaration of Independence. Governor of Virginia. Minister to France. Secretary of State. Vice President. Completed Louisiana Purchase.

LANDMARKS:

Birth site: Shadwell, Charlottesville, VA 22902

Jefferson Memorial, 900 Ohio Dr., S.W., Washington, DC 20024-2000, 202-426-6841; fax: 202-426-1844
http://www.nps.gov/thje
National_Mall@nps.gov

Jefferson National Expansion Memorial (Gateway Arch), 11 N. 4th St., St. Louis, MO 63102, 314-655-1700
http://www.nps.gov/jeff
JEFF_Superintendent@nps.gov

Monticello, P.O. Box 316, Charlottesville, VA 22902, 434-984-9800 or 434-984-9822
http://www.monticello.org

Poplar Forest, P.O. Box 419, Forest, VA 24551-0419, 434-525-1806; fax: 434-525-7252

http://www.poplarforest.org

Tuckahoe Plantation, 12601 River Rd., Richmond, VA 23233, 804-784-5736; fax: 804-784-7335
http://www.tuckahoeplantation.com
historictuckahoe@aol.com

James Madison

Fourth president (1809-17)

Born Mar 16, 1751, Port Conway, VA

Married Dolley Dandridge Payne Todd, 1794

Died Jun 28, 1836, Orange County, VA

Buried at Montpelier, Orange County, VA

Democratic-Republican. "Father of the Constitution." Served in Continental Congress. Signed Constitution. U.S. Representative. Secretary of State. Participated in War of 1812. Forced to flee White House when British invaded Washington, DC.

LANDMARKS:

Birth site (marker): Belle Grove, Port Conway, VA

James Madison Museum, 129 Caroline St., Orange, VA 22960-1532, 540-672-1776
http://www.jamesmadisonmus.org
info@jamesmadisonmus.org

Montpelier, 11407 Constitution Hwy., Montpelier Station, VA 22957, 540-672-2728
http://www.montpelier.org

The Octagon, 1799 New York Ave., N.W., Washington, DC 20006, 202-638-3221; fax: 202-626-7420 (houses the American Architectural Foundation)
http://www.archfoundation.org/octagon/about
info@theoctagon.org

James Monroe

Fifth president (1817-25)

Born Apr 28, 1758, Westmoreland County, VA

Married Elizabeth Kortright, 1786

Died Jul 4, 1831, New York, NY

Buried at Marble Cemetery, New York, NY; removed 1858 to Hollywood Cemetery, 412 S. Cherry St., Richmond, VA 23220, 804-648-8501
http://www.hollywoodcemetery.org
Info@hollywoodcemetery.org

Democratic-Republican. "Era of Good Feeling President." Fought in Revolutionary War. Served in Continental Congress. Governor of Virginia. U.S. Senator. Secretary of State. Secretary of War. First inauguration held outdoors. Author of the Monroe Doctrine.

LANDMARKS:

Birth site (marker): Monrovia, State Hwy. V.A. 205 between Oak Grove and Colonial Beach, VA

Ash Lawn-Highland residence, 1000 James Monroe Pkwy., Charlottesville, VA 22902, 434-293-9539; fax: 434-293-8000

◆ Indicates that an entry on a festival celebrating the president appears in the main text

http://www.ashlawnhighland.org
info@ashlawnhighland.org

James Monroe Museum and Memorial Library, 908 Charles St., Fredericksburg, VA 22401-5810, 540-654-1043
http://www.umw.edu/jamesmonroemuseum

Oak Hill residence, Aldie, Loudoun County, VA 22001 (private residence)
http://www.nps.gov/history/nr/travel/journey/oak.htm

John Quincy Adams

Sixth president (1825-29)

Born Jul 11, 1767, Braintree (now Quincy), MA

Married Louisa Catherine Johnson, 1797

Died Feb 23, 1848, Washington, DC

Buried at United First Parish Church, 1306 Hancock St., Quincy, MA 02269, 617-773-1290
http://www.ufpc.org
ufpc@ufpc.org

Democratic-Republican. "Old Man Eloquent." Minister to Great Britain, Netherlands, Russia. U.S. Senator. Secretary of State. U.S. Representative. Father was second president (*see* John Adams).

LANDMARKS:

Birth site: 141 Franklin St., Quincy, MA 02269, 617-773-1177

Adams National Historic Park, 135 Adams St., Quincy, MA 02269, 617-770-1175; fax: 617-472-7562
http://www.nps.gov/adam
ADAM_Visitor_Center@nps.gov

◆ Andrew Jackson

Seventh president (1829-37)

Born Mar 15, 1767, Waxhaw, SC

Married Rachael Donelson Robards, 1791

Died Jun 8, 1845, Nashville, TN

Buried at the Hermitage Estate, 4580 Rachael's Lane, Hermitage, TN 37076, 615-889-2941; fax: 615-889-9909
http://www.thehermitage.com
info@thehermitage.com

Democrat (Democratic-Republican). "Old Hickory." Governor of Florida. U.S. Representative and Senator. Fought against Indians and in War of 1812. First president born in a log cabin.

LANDMARKS:

Birth site (disputed): Andrew Jackson State Park and Museum, 196 Andrew Jackson Park Rd., Lancaster, SC 29720, 803-285-3344
http://www.discovercarolina.com/html/s04history01.html

Birth site (disputed): Andrew Jackson Birthplace Marker, NC 25 (S. Main) at Rehobeth Rd., Waxhaw, NC 28173

McCamie Cabin site marker, Mecklenburg County, NC

Springfield Plantation, Route 1, Box 201, Fayette, MS 39069

Martin Van Buren

Eighth president (1837-41)

Born Dec 5, 1782, Kinderhook, NY

Married Hannah Hoes, 1807

Died Jul 24, 1862, Kinderhook, NY

Buried at Kinderhook Cemetery, Albany Ave., Kinderhook, NY

Democrat (Democratic-Republican). "Sage of Kinderhook." U.S. Senator. Governor of New York. Secretary of State. Vice President. First president born a U.S. citizen.

LANDMARKS:

Birth site (marker): 46 Hudson St., Kinderhook, NY 12106

Lindenwald residence, 1013 Old Post Rd., Kinderhook, NY 12106, 518-758-9689; fax: 518-758-6986
http://www.nps.gov/mava
MAVA_info@nps.gov

William Henry Harrison

Ninth president (1841)

Born Feb 9, 1773, Berkeley, Charles City County, VA

Married Anna Tuthill Symmes, 1795

Died Apr 4, 1841, Washington, DC

Buried at Harrison Tomb State Memorial, Loop Ave., North Bend, OH, 513-941-3744
http://ohsweb.ohiohistory.org/places/sw11

Whig. "Old Tippecanoe." Fought against Indians and in War of 1812. U.S. Representative. U.S. Senator. Died in office, serving shortest term of a president. Grandson was twenty-third president (*see* Benjamin Harrison).

LANDMARKS:

Birth site: Berkeley Plantation, 12602 Harrison Landing Rd., Charles City, VA 23030, 804-829-6018; fax: 804-829-6757
http://www.berkeleyplantation.com

Grouseland, 3 West Scott St., Vincennes, IN 47591, 812-882-2096
http://www.grouselandfoundation.org
grouseland@sbcglobal.net

John Tyler

Tenth president (1841-45)

Born Mar 29, 1790, Greenway, Charles City County, VA

Married Letitia Christian, 1813; Julia Gardiner, 1844

Died Jan 18, 1862, Richmond, VA

Buried at Hollywood Cemetery, 412 S. Cherry St., Richmond, VA 23220, 804-648-8501
http://www.hollywoodcemetery.org
Info@hollywoodcemetery.org

Whig. "Accidental president." U.S. Representative. Governor of Virginia. U.S. Senator. Succeeded presidency upon death of William Henry Harrison. Elected representative to Confederate Congress.

◆ Indicates that an entry on a festival celebrating the president appears in the main text

LANDMARKS:

Birth site: Greenway, Charles City County, VA (private residence)

Sherwood Forest Plantation, 14501 John Tyler Hwy., Charles City, VA 23030, 804-829-5377; fax: 804-829-2947
http://www.sherwoodforest.org

James Knox Polk

Eleventh president (1845-49)

Born Nov 2, 1795, near Pineville, Mecklenburg County, NC

Married Sarah Childress, 1824

Died Jun 15, 1849, Nashville, TN

Buried at Polk Place, Nashville, TN; removed 1893 to State Capitol Grounds, Nashville, TN 37243, 615-741-0830

Democrat. "Napoleon of the Stump." U.S. Representative. Speaker of the House. Governor of Tennessee. First inauguration ceremony relayed by telegraph. Acquired much of western and southwestern U.S.

LANDMARKS:

Birth site: Polk Memorial, Box 475, Pineville, NC 28134, 704-889-7145
http://www.ah.dcr.state.nc.us/sections/hs/polk/polk.htm
polk@ncmail.net

Polk home, 301 W. Seventh St., P.O. Box 741, Columbia, TN 38402, 931-388-2354
http://www.jameskpolk.com
jamespolk@bellsouth.net

Zachary Taylor

Twelfth president (1849-50)

Born Nov 24, 1784, Montebello, Gordonsville, VA

Married Margaret Mackall Smith, 1810

Died Jul 9, 1850, Washington, DC

Buried at Zachary Taylor National Cemetery, 4701 Brownboro Rd., Louisville, KY 40207, 502-893-3852

Whig. "Old Rough and Ready." Fought against Indians and in War of 1812 and Mexican War. Son-in-law was Jefferson Davis. Died in office.

LANDMARKS:

Birth site (marker): Montebello, Gordonsville, VA

Springfield, 5608 Apache Rd., Louisville, KY 40207, 502-897-9990

Millard Fillmore

Thirteenth president (1850-53)

Born Jan 7, 1800, Summerhill, Cayuga County, NY

Married Abigail Powers, 1826; Caroline Carmichael McIntosh, 1858

Died Mar 8, 1874, Buffalo, NY

Buried at Forrest Lawn Cemetery, 1411 Delaware Ave., Buffalo, NY 14209, 716-885-1600

Whig. "His Accidency." U.S. Representative. Succeeded presidency upon death of Zachary Taylor.

LANDMARKS:

Birth site (marker): Fillmore Rd., Summerhill, NY

Birth site (replica): Fillmore Glen State Park, 1686 State Route 38, Moravia, NY 13118, 315-497-0130; fax: 315-497-0128

Childhood home (marker): Carver Rd., New Hope, NY

Millard Fillmore House Museum, 24 Shearer Ave., East Aurora, NY 14052, 716-652-8875

Franklin Pierce

Fourteenth president (1853-57)

Born Nov 23, 1804, Hillsborough (now Hillsboro), NH

Married Jane Means Appleton, 1834

Died Oct 8, 1869, Concord, NH

Buried at Old North Cemetery, North State St., Concord, NH 03301

Democrat. "Young Hickory of the Granite Hills." U.S. Representative. U.S. Senator. Fought in Mexican War.

LANDMARKS:

Birth site: Hillsboro, NH

Pierce Homestead, State Hwy. 31, Box 896, Hillsboro, NH 03244, 603-478-3165
http://www.franklinpierce.ws/homestead/homestead.html

Pierce House (marker), 52 South Main St., Concord, NH 03301

Pierce Manse, 14 Penacook St., Box 425, Concord, NH 03301, 603-225-4555; fax: 603-225-0540
http://www.piercemanse.org

James Buchanan

Fifteenth president (1857-61)

Born Apr 23, 1791, Cove Gap, PA

Died Jun 1, 1868, Lancaster, PA

Buried at Woodward Hill Cemetery, 538 East Strawberry St., Lancaster, PA 17602, 717-295-7220

Democrat. "Bachelor president." Fought in War of 1812. U.S. Representative. Minister to Russia. U.S. Senator. Secretary of State. Minister to Great Britain.

LANDMARKS:

Birth site (marker): Buchanan's Birthplace Historical State Park, c/o Cowans Gap State Park, 6235 Aughwick Rd., Fort Loudon, PA 17224-9801, 717-485-3948
http://www.dcnr.state.pa.us/stateparks/parks/buchanansbirthplace.aspx
cowansgapsp@state.pa.us

♦ Indicates that an entry on a festival celebrating the president appears in the main text

Birth site (cabin): Mercersburg Academy, 300 E. Seminary St., Mercersburg, PA 17236, 717-328-2151

James Buchanan Hotel (marker), 17 N. Main St., Mercersburg, PA 17236, 717-328-3008

Wheatland, 1120 Marietta Ave., Lancaster, PA 17603, 717-392-8721; fax: 717-295-8825
http://www.wheatland.org
director@wheatland.org

◆ Abraham Lincoln

Sixteenth president (1861-65)

Born Feb 12, 1809, Hodgenville, Hardin County (now Larue County), KY

Married Mary Todd, 1842

Died Apr 15, 1865, Washington, DC

Buried at Oak Ridge Cemetery, Springfield, IL

Republican. "Honest Abe." Fought in Blackhawk War. U.S. Representative. U.S. divided by Civil War while president. Issued Emancipation Proclamation. Author of Gettysburg Address. First president assassinated.

LANDMARKS:

Birth site: Lincoln Birthplace National Historic Site, 2995 Lincoln Farm Rd., Hodgenville, KY 42748, 270-358-3137; fax: 270-358-3874
http://www.nps.gov/abli
ABLI_Adminstration@nps.gov

Childhood home: Knob Creek Farm, 7120 Bardstown Rd., Hodgenville, KY 42748, 270-358-3137; fax: 270-358-3874
http://www.nps.gov/abli
ABLI_Administration@nps.gov

Abraham Lincoln Library and Museum, Lincoln Memorial University, 6965 Cumberland Gap Pkwy., Harrogate, TN 37752, 423-869-3611 or 800-325-0900
http://www.lmunet.edu/Museum

Abraham Lincoln Presidential Library, Museum, & Foundation, 112 N. Sixth St., Springfield, IL 62701, 217-782-5764 or 800-610-2094
http://www.alplm.org

Civil War Library and Museum, 1805 Pine St., Philadelphia, PA 19103, 215-735-8196
http://www.netreach.net/~cwlm

Ford's Theatre National Historic Site, Petersen House, 900 Ohio Dr., S.W., Washington, DC 20024, 202-426-6841; fax: 202-426-1845
http://www.nps.gov/foth
NACC_FOTH_Interpretation@nps.gov

Lincoln Boyhood National Memorial, 2916 E. South St., P.O. Box 1816, Lincoln City, IN 47552, 812-937-4541; fax: 812-937-9929
http://www.nps.gov/libo
LIBO_Superintendent@nps.gov

Lincoln College Museum, Lincoln College, 300 Keokuk St., Lincoln, IL 62656, 217-735-5050
http://www.lincolncollege.edu/museum

Lincoln Depot, Monroe St. between Ninth and Tenth Sts., Springfield, IL 62704, 217-492-4241, ext. 221; fax: 217-492-4673
http://www.nps.gov/liho/depot/depot.htm
lincolnhome@nps.gov

Lincoln-Herndon Law Offices State Historic Site, 6th and Adams Sts., Springfield, IL 62701, 217-785-7289
http://www.illinoishistory.gov/hs/Lincoln_herndon.htm

Lincoln Home National Historic Site, 413 S. Eighth St., Springfield, IL 62701-1905, 217-492-4241; fax: 217-492-4673
http://www.nps.gov/liho
liho_information@nps.gov

Lincoln Homestead State Park, 5079 Lincoln Park Rd., Springfield, KY 40069, 859-336-7461
http://parks.ky.gov/findparks/recparks.lh

Lincoln Log Cabin State Historic Site, 400 S. Lincoln Highway Rd., P.O. Box 100, Lerna, IL 62440, 217-345-1845; fax: 217-345-6472
http://www.lincolnlogcabin.org
lincoln_log@ihpa.state.il.us

Lincoln Memorial, 900 Ohio Dr., S.W., Washington, DC 20024, 202-426-6841
http://www.nps.gov/linc
National_Mall@nps.gov

Lincoln Memorial Shrine, 125 W. Vine St., Redlands, CA 92373, 909-798-7632
http://www.lincolnshire.org
archives@akspl.org

Lincoln Monument, 339 Lafayette Ave., Council Bluffs, IA, 712-328-4650 (Council Bluffs Parks, Recreation, and Public Property)
http://parksandrec.councilbluffs-ia.gov/historical.asp?page=9

Lincoln Museum, 66 Lincoln Sq., Hodgenville, KY 42748, 270-358-3163
http://www.lincolnmuseum-ky.org
abe@lincolnmuseum-ky.org

Mount Pulaski Courthouse State Historic Site, 113 S. Washington St., P.O. Box 355, Mount Pulaski, IL 62556, 217-732-3919
http://www.illinoishistory.gov/hs/mount_pulaski.htm

New Salem State Historic Site, 15588 History Ln., Petersburg, IL 62675, 217-632-4000; fax: 217-632-4010
http://www.lincolnsnewsalem.com

Oak Ridge Cemetery, Lincoln's Tomb, 1500 Monument Ave., Springfield, IL 62702, 217-782-2717
http://www.illinoishistory.gov/hs/lincoln_tomb.htm
lincolntomb@springnet1.com

Old State Capitol State Historic Site, 1 Old State Capitol Plaza, Springfield, IL 62701, 217-785-7960
http://www.state.il.us/HPA/ha/old_capitol.htm

Postville Courthouse (replica) State Historic Site, 914 Fifth St., P.O. Box 355, Lincoln, IL 62656, 217-732-8930
http://www.illinoishistory.gov/hs/postville_courthouse.htm

Postville Courthouse, Greenfield Village, 20900 Oakwood Blvd, Dearborn, MI 48124-4088, 313-982-6001; TDD: 313-271-2455
http://www.hfmgv.org

◆ Indicates that an entry on a festival celebrating the president appears in the main text

Andrew Johnson

Seventeenth president (1865-69)

Born Dec 29, 1808, Raleigh, NC

Married Eliza McArdle, 1826

Died Jul 31, 1875, Carter's Station, TN

Buried at Andrew Johnson National Cemetery, Greeneville, TN

Democrat. "Tennessee Tailor." U.S. Representative. Governor of Tennessee. U.S. Senator. Succeeded presidency upon assassination of Abraham Lincoln. First president to be impeached (acquitted).

LANDMARKS:

Birth site: Mordecai Historic Park, 1 Mimosa St., Raleigh, NC 27604, 919-857-4364
http://www.raleigh-nc.org

Andrew Johnson National Site and Cemetery, 121 Monument Ave., Greeneville, TN 37743, 423-639-3711; fax: 423-798-0754
http://www.nps.gov/anjo
ANJO_Superintendent@nps.gov

President Andrew Johnson Museum and Library, 423-636-7348 or 800-729-0256, ext. 5251
http://ajmuseum.tusculum.edu

Ulysses Simpson Grant

Eighteenth president (1869-77)

Born Apr 27, 1822, Point Pleasant, OH

Married Julia Boggs Dent, 1848

Died Jul 23, 1885, Mt. McGregor, NY

Buried at General Grant National Memorial, Riverside Dr. and W. 122nd St., New York, NY 10027, 212-666-1640; fax: 212-932-9631
http://www.nps.gov/gegr
MASI_Superintendent@nps.gov

Republican. "United States Grant." Fought in Mexican War. General in Civil War. Fifteenth Amendment (right of suffrage) ratified.

LANDMARKS:

Birth site: Grant Birthplace Historic Site, 1591 State Rt. 232, Point Pleasant, OH 45153, 513-553-4911
http://www.ohiohistory.org/places/sw08/index.shtml

Childhood home: U.S. Grant Boyhood Home, 219 E. Grant Ave., Georgetown, OH 45121, 937-378-4222
http://www.usgrantboyhoodhome.org
info@usgrantboyhoodhome.org

City Point Unit residence, Petersburg National Battlefield, 1539 Hickory Hill Rd., Petersburg, VA 23803, 804-732-3531; fax: 804-732-0835
http://www.nps.gov/pete
PETE_Superintendent@nps.gov

Grant Cottage State Historic Site, Mt. McGregor, P.O. Box 2294, Wilton, NY 12831, 518-587-8277
http://nysparks.state.ny.us/historic-sites

Grant's "Hardscrabble" Farm, 10501 Gravois Rd., St. Louis, MO 63123, 314-843-1700
http://www.grantsfarm.com

U.S. Grant National Historic Site, 7400 Grant Rd., St. Louis, MO 63123, 314-842-3298; fax: 314-842-1659
http://www.nps.gov/ulsg
ULSG_Site_Manager@nps.gov

U.S. Grant Home, 500 Bouthillier St., P.O. Box 333, Galena, IL 61036, 815-777-3310
http://www.granthome.com
granthome@granthome.com

U.S. Grant House, Michigan State Fair Grounds, 1120 W. State Fair, Detroit, MI 48203, 313-369-8250
http://www.michigan.gov/mistatefair

U.S. Grant Boyhood Public School, 508 S. Water St., Georgetown, OH 45121, 937-378-4222
http://www.usgrantboyhoodhome.org
info@usgrantboyhoodhome.org

Rutherford Birchard Hayes

Nineteenth president (1877-81)

Born Oct 4, 1822, Delaware, OH

Married Lucy Ware Webb, 1852

Died Jan 17, 1893, Fremont, OH

Buried at Spiegel Grove National Historic Landmark, Rutherford B. Hayes Presidential Center, Fremont, OH

Republican. "Dark Horse President." Fought in Civil War. U.S. Representative. Governor of Ohio. Some electoral votes in dispute; election decided by special electoral commission.

LANDMARKS:

Birth site (marker): E. William and Winter St., Delaware, OH

Hayes Home, Hayes Museum, and Spiegel Grove National Historic Landmark, Rutherford B. Hayes Presidential Center, 1337 Hayes Ave., Fremont, OH 43420, 419-332-2081; fax: 419-332-4952
http://www.rbhayes.org

James Abram Garfield

Twentieth president (1881)

Born Nov 19, 1831, Orange (now Moreland Hills), OH

Married Lucretia Rudolph, 1858

Died Sep 19, 1881, Elberon, NJ

Buried at Lake View Cemetery, 12316 Euclid Ave., Cleveland, OH 44106, 216-421-2665
http://www.lakeviewcemetery.com

Republican. "Martyr President." Fought in Civil War. U.S. Representative. Died of wounds 2 1/2 months after being shot by assassin.

LANDMARKS:

Birth site (marker): James A. Garfield Memorial Cabin, Moreland Hills, OH, 440-248-1188; fax: 440-498-9588
http://www.morelandhills.com/historical_2.html

♦ Indicates that an entry on a festival celebrating the president appears in the main text

Lawnfield, President Garfield National Historic Site, 8095 Mentor Ave., Mentor, OH 44060, 440-255-8722; fax: 440-974-2045
http://www.nps.gov/jaga
jaga_interpretation@nps.gov

Chester Alan Arthur

Twenty-first president (1881-85)
Born Oct 5, 1829, Fairfield, VT
Married Ellen Lewis Herndon, 1859
Died Nov 18, 1886, New York, NY
Buried at Albany Rural Cemetery, Cemetery Ave., Menands, NY 12204, 518-463-7017; fax: 518-463-0787
http://www.albanyruralcemetery.org

Republican. "Elegant Arthur." Succeeded presidency upon death of James Garfield.

LANDMARKS:

Childhood home (replica): Chester A. Arthur State Historic Site, Chester Arthur Rd., East Fairfield, VT 05448, 802-933-8362
http://www.historicvermont.org/sites/html/arthur.html

Arthur House, 123 Lexington Ave., New York, NY (private residence; closed to the public)
http://www.nps.gov/history/history/online_books/Presidents/site37.htm

Grover Cleveland

Twenty-second and twenty-fourth president (1885-89; 1893-97)
Born Mar 18, 1837, Caldwell, NJ
Married Francis Folsom, 1886
Died Jun 24, 1908, Princeton, NJ
Buried at Princeton Cemetery, 29 Greenview Ave., Princeton, NJ 08542, 609-924-1369
http://www.princetonol.com/groups/cemetery

Democrat. "Sage of Princeton." Governor of New York. Only president to serve two non-consecutive terms. Only president married in White House.

LANDMARKS:

Birth site: 207 Bloomfield Ave., Caldwell, NJ 07006, 973-226-0001; fax: 973-226-1810
http://www.caldwellnj.com/grover.htm

Childhood home: 109 Academy St., Fayetteville, NY (private residence; closed to the public)

Cleveland House, Cleveland Hill Rd., Tamworth, NH (private residence; closed to the public)

Grover Cleveland Cottage, Deer Park Hotel Rd., Deer Park, MD (private residence; closed to the public)

Westland, 15 Hodge Rd., Princeton, NJ (private residence; closed to the public)
http://www.nps.gov/history/history/online_books/Presidents/site36.htm

Benjamin Harrison

Twenty-third president (1889-93)
Born Aug 20, 1833, North Bend, OH
Married Caroline Lavinia Scott, 1853; Mary Scott Lord Dimmick, 1896
Died Mar 13, 1901, Indianapolis, IN
Buried at Crown Hill Cemetery, 700 W. 38th St., Indianapolis, IN 46208, 317-925-8231
http://www.crownhill.org

Republican. "Centennial President." Served in Civil War. U.S. Senator. Grandfather was ninth president (*see* William Henry Harrison).

LANDMARKS:

Birth site (location): grounds of Harrison Tomb State Memorial, Loop Ave., North Bend, OH, 513-941-3744
http://ohsweb.ohiohistory.org/places/sw11

Benjamin Harrison Home, 1230 N. Delaware St., Indianapolis, IN 46202, 317-631-1888
http://www.presidentbenjaminharrison.org

William McKinley

Twenty-fifth president (1897-1901)
Born Jan 29, 1843, Niles, OH
Married Ida Saxton, 1871
Died Sep 14, 1901, Buffalo, NY
Buried at McKinley National Memorial, Canton, OH

Republican. "Idol of Ohio." Served in Civil War. U.S. Representative. Governor of Ohio. Died of wounds almost two weeks after being shot by assassin.

LANDMARKS:

Birth site: 40 S. Main St., Niles, OH 44446, 330-652-1774

McKinley National Memorial, Presidential Library & Museum, 800 McKinley Monument Dr., N.W., Canton, OH 44708, 330-455-7043; fax: 330-455-1137
http://www.mckinleymuseum.org
info@mckinleymuseum.org

National McKinley Birthplace Memorial Museum and Library, 40 N. Main St., Niles, OH 44446, 330-652-1704; fax: 330-652-5788
http://www.mckinley.lib.oh.us
mckinley@mcklib.org

Saxton-McKinley Home, 331 Market Ave. S., Canton, OH 44702, 330-452-0876

◆ Theodore Roosevelt

Twenty-sixth president (1901-09)
Born Oct 27, 1858, New York, NY
Married Alice Hathaway Lee, 1880; Edith Kermit Carow, 1886
Died Jan 6, 1919, Oyster Bay, NY

◆ Indicates that an entry on a festival celebrating the president appears in the main text

Buried at Youngs Memorial Cemetery, Cove Neck Rd. and East Main St., Oyster Bay, NY
http://www.nps.gov/sahi/youngs.htm

Republican. "Hero of San Juan Hill." Fought in Spanish-American War. Governor of New York. Succeeded presidency upon assassination of William McKinley. Youngest man to become president. Awarded Nobel Peace Prize.

LANDMARKS:

Birth site: 28 E. 20th St., New York, NY 10003, 212-260-1616; fax: 212-677-3587
http://www.nps.gov/thrb
MASI_Superintendent@nps.gov

Sagamore Hill National Historic Site, 20 Sagamore Hill Rd., Oyster Bay, NY 11771, 516-922-4788; fax: 516-922-4792
http://www.nps.gov/sahi
sahi_information@nps.gov

Theodore Roosevelt Inaugural National Historic Site, 641 Delaware Ave., Buffalo, NY 14202, 716-884-0095; fax: 716-884-0330
http://www.nps.gov/thri
THRI_Administration@nps.gov

Theodore Roosevelt Island Park, George Washington Memorial Pkwy., Turkey Run Park, McLean, VA 22101, 703-289-2500
http://www.nps.gov/this
gwmp_superintendent@nps.gov

Theodore Roosevelt National Park, Maltese Cross Cabin, Box 7, Medora, ND 58645-0007, 701-623-4466; fax: 701-623-4840
http://www.nps.gov/thro
THRO_Interpretation@nps.gov

William Howard Taft

Twenty-seventh president (1909-13)

Born Sep 15, 1857, Cincinnati, OH

Married Helen Herron, 1886

Died Mar 8, 1930, Washington, DC

Buried at Arlington National Cemetery, 214 McNair Rd., Arlington, VA 22211, 703-607-8000
http://www.arlingtoncemetery.org/historical_information/william_taft.html

Republican. Solicitor General. Governor-General of Philippines. Secretary of War. First president to throw out baseball on opening day. Sixteenth amendment enacted. Chief Justice of the Supreme Court.

LANDMARKS:

Birth site: William Howard Taft National Historic Site, 2038 Auburn Ave., Cincinnati, OH 45219, 513-684-3262; fax: 513-684-3627
http://www.nps.gov/wiho
WIHO_Interpretation@nps.gov

The Quarry, 1763 E. McMillan St., Cincinnati, OH (private residence)

Woodrow Wilson

Twenty-eighth president (1913-21)

Born Dec 29, 1856, Staunton, VA

Married Ellen Louise Axson, 1885; Edith Bolling Galt, 1915

Died Feb 3, 1924, Washington, DC

Buried at National Cathedral, Massachusetts and Wisconsin Aves., N.W., Washington, DC 20016, 202-537-6200
http://www.cathedral.org/cathedral

Democrat. "Professor." Governor of New Jersey. Held first presidential press conference. Author of Fourteen Points plan. Eighteenth and Nineteenth Amendments enacted. Awarded Nobel Peace Prize.

LANDMARKS:

Birth site: Woodrow Wilson Birthplace and Museum, 18-24 N. Coalter St., P.O. Box 24, Staunton, VA 24402-0024, 540-885-0897; fax: 540-886-9874
http://www.woodrowwilson.org
info@woodrowwilson.org

Early childhood home: 419 Seventh St., Augusta, GA 30901, 706-722-9828
http://www.wilsonboyhoodhome.org

Childhood home: 1705 Hampton St., Columbia, SC 29201, 803-252-7742 (Historic Columbia Foundation)
http://www.historiccolumbia.org/history/wilson.html

Woodrow Wilson House Museum, 2340 S St., N.W., Washington, DC 20008, 202-387-4062; fax: 202-483-1466
http://www.woodrowwilsonhouse.org

Warren Gamaliel Harding

Twenty-ninth president (1921-23)

Born Nov 2, 1865, Blooming Grove (now Corsica), OH

Married Florence Kling De Wolfe, 1891

Died Aug 2, 1923, San Francisco, CA

Buried at Harding Memorial, Vernon Heights Blvd., Marion, OH

Republican. U.S. Senator. First presidential election returns broadcast on radio. Teapot Dome Scandal. Died in office.

LANDMARKS:

Birth site (marker): State Hwy. 97, east of County Rd. 20, Corsica, OH

Harding Home and Museum, 380 Mt. Vernon Ave., Marion, OH 43302, 740-387-9630 or 800-600-6894
http://ohsweb.ohiohistory.org/places/c03/index.shtml

◆ Calvin Coolidge

Thirtieth president (1923-29)

Born Jul 4, 1872, Plymouth Notch, VT

Married Grace Anna Goodhue, 1905

Died Jan 5, 1933, Northampton, MA

Buried at Plymouth Notch Cemetery, Vermont Hwy. 100A, Plymouth Notch, VT 05056, 802-672-3773

◆ Indicates that an entry on a festival celebrating the president appears in the main text

Republican. "Silent Cal." Governor of Massachusetts. Succeeded presidency upon death of Warren Harding. First inaugural speech broadcast on radio.

LANDMARKS:

Birth site: Birthplace & Boyhood Home, 3780 Rte. 100A, P.O. Box 257, Plymouth Notch, VT 05056, 802-672-3773
http://www.historicvermont.org/coolidge/CoolidgeTour.html

The Beeches, 16 Hampton Terrace, Northampton, MA (private residence; closed to the public)

Calvin Coolidge Memorial Room, Forbes Library, 20 West St., Northampton, MA 01060, 413-587-1014
http://www.forbeslibrary.org/coolidge/coolidge.shtml

Memorial Foundation, P.O. Box 97, Plymouth, VT 05056, 802-672-3389; fax: 802-672-3369
http://www.calvin-coolidge.org

Northampton Home, 21 Massasoit St., Northampton, MA (private residence; closed to the public)

◆ Herbert Clark Hoover

Thirty-first president (1929-33)

Born Aug 10, 1874, West Branch, IA

Married Lou Henry, 1899

Died Oct 20, 1964, New York, NY

Buried at Herbert Hoover National Historic Site, West Branch, IA
http://www.nps.gov/heho
HEHO_Interpretation@nps.gov

Republican. "Grand Old Man." Involved in Boxer Rebellion in China. Chairman of Commission for Relief in Belgium. Secretary of Commerce. Wall Street crash (Black Tuesday), 1929.

LANDMARKS:

Birth site: Herbert Hoover National Historic Site, 110 Parkside Dr., P.O. Box 607, West Branch, IA 52358-0607, 319-643-2541; fax: 319-643-5367
http://www.nps.gov/heho
HEHO_Interpretation@nps.gov

Herbert Hoover Academic Bldg., George Fox University, Newberg, OR 97132, 503-538-8383
http://www.georgefox.edu/maps_loca/inter_map/campus-quad/hoover.html

Herbert Hoover Presidential Library and Museum, 210 Parkside Dr., West Branch, IA 52358, 319-643-5301
http://hoover.archives.gov

Hoover Institution on War, Revolution and Peace, 434 Galvez Mall, Stanford University, Palo Alto, CA 94305-6010, 650-723-1754 or 877-HOOVERI (466-8374); fax: 650-723-1687
http://www.hoover.org
horaney@hoover.stanford.edu

Hoover-Minthorn House Museum, 115 S. River St., Newberg, OR 97132, 503-538-6629

Lou Henry Hoover House, Stanford University, 623 Miranda Ave., Palo Alto, CA 94304 (official residence of university president; closed to the public)

Presidential Library Association, P.O. Box 696, West Branch, IA 52358, 319-643-5327; fax: 319-643-2391
http://www.hooverassociation.org
info@hooverassociation.org

Shenandoah Camp Hoover, Shenandoah National Park, VA, 3655 U.S. Highway 211 E., Luray, VA 22835-9036, 540-999-3500; fax: 540-999-3601
http://www.nps.gov/shen
SHEN_Superintendent@nps.gov

◆ Franklin Delano Roosevelt

Thirty-second president (1933-45)

Born Jan 30, 1882, Hyde Park, NY

Married Eleanor Roosevelt, 1905

Died Apr 12, 1945, Warm Springs, GA

Buried at Franklin D. Roosevelt National Historic Site, Hyde Park, NY

Democrat. "F.D.R." Governor of New York. Author of the New Deal. Only four-term president. Died in office.

LANDMARKS:

Birth site: Franklin D. Roosevelt National Historic Site, 4097 Albany Post Rd., Hyde Park, NY 12538, 845-229-9115; fax: 845-229-0739
http://www.nps.gov/hofr
ROVA_webmaster@nps.gov

Franklin D. Roosevelt Library and Museum, 4079 Albany Post Rd., Hyde Park, NY 12538, 845-486-7770
http://www.fdrlibrary.marist.edu
roosevelt.library@nara.gov

Franklin Delano Roosevelt Memorial, 900 Ohio Dr. S.W., Washington, DC 20024, 202-426-6841
http://www.nps.gov/frde
National_Mall@nps.gov

Little White House State Historic Site, 401 Little White House Rd., Warm Springs, GA 31830, 706-655-5870
http://www.gastateparks.org/info/littlewhite

Roosevelt Campobello International Park, P.O. Box 97, Lubec, ME 04652, 506-752-2922; fax: 506-752-6000
http://www.nps.gov/roca
info@fdr.net

◆ Harry S. Truman

Thirty-third president (1945-53)

Born May 10, 1884, Lamar, MO

Married Elizabeth "Bess" Virginia Wallace, 1919

Died Dec 26, 1972, Kansas City, MO

Buried at Harry S. Truman Library and Museum, Independence, MO

Democrat. "Give 'Em Hell Harry." Fought in World War I. U.S. Senator. Succeeded presidency upon death of Franklin

◆ Indicates that an entry on a festival celebrating the president appears in the main text

D. Roosevelt. Authorized use of atomic bomb against Japan. Implemented the Fair Deal.

LANDMARKS:

Birth site: Harry S. Truman Birthplace State Historic Site, 1009 Truman Ave., Lamar, MO 64759, 417-682-2279
http://www.mostateparks.com/trumansite.htm

Childhood home: 909 West Waldo St., Independence, MO (private residence; closed to the public)
http://www.trumanlibrary.org/places/in2.htm

Harry S. Truman Courtroom and Office, Independence Square Courthouse, Main at Maple St., Rm. 109, Independence, MO 64050, 816-881-4431
http://www.jacksongov.org

Harry S. Truman Key West Little White House Museum, 111 Front St., Key West, FL 33040, 305-294-9911; fax: 305-294-9988
http://www.trumanlittlewhitehouse.com

Harry S. Truman Library and Museum, 500 W. U.S. Highway 24, Independence, MO 64050, 816-268-8200 or 800-833-1225; fax: 816-268-8295
http://www.trumanlibrary.org
truman.library@nara.gov

Harry S. Truman National Historic Site, 223 N. Main St., Independence, MO 64050, 816-254-9929; fax: 816-254-4491
http://www.nps.gov/hstr
HSTR_Superintendent@nps.gov

◆ Dwight David Eisenhower

Thirty-fourth president (1953-61)
Born Oct 14, 1890, Denison, TX
Married Marie "Mamie" Geneva Doud, 1916
Died Mar 28, 1969, Washington, DC
Buried at Eisenhower Center, Abilene, KS

Republican. "Ike." General in World War II. Commander of NATO. First televised press conference.

LANDMARKS:

Eisenhower Birthplace State Historical Park, 609 S. Lamar Ave., Denison, TX 75021, 903-465-8908; fax: 903-465-8988
http://www.eisenhowerbirthplace.org
birthplace@glassportal.net

Dwight D. Eisenhower Presidential Library & Museum, 200 S.E. 4th St., Abilene, KS 67410, 785-263-6700 or 877-RING-IKE (746-4453); fax: 785-263-6715
http://www.eisenhower.archives.gov
eisenhower.library@nara.gov

Eisenhower National Historic Site, 250 Eisenhower Farm Dr., Gettysburg, PA 17325, 717-338-9114; fax: 717-338-0821
http://www.nps.gov/eise
eise_site_manager@nps.gov

◆ John Fitzgerald Kennedy

Thirty-fifth president (1961-63)
Born May 29, 1917, Brookline, MA

Married Jacqueline Lee Bouvier, 1953
Died Nov 22, 1963, Dallas, TX
Buried at Arlington National Cemetery, 214 McNair Rd., Arlington, VA 22211, 703-607-8000
http://www.arlingtoncemetery.org/historical_
information/JFK.html

Democrat. "J.F.K." Served in World War II. U.S. Representative. U.S. Senator. First president born in twentieth century. Youngest elected president. Fourth president assassinated.

LANDMARKS:

Birth site: John F. Kennedy National Historic Site, 83 Beals St., Brookline, MA 02446, 617-566-7937; fax: 617-730-9884
http://www.nps.gov/jofi
FRLA_Kennedy_NHS@nps.gov

John F. Kennedy Library and Museum, Columbia Point, Boston, MA 02125, 617-514-1600; TDD: 617-514-1573
http://www.jfklibrary.org

Kennedy Compound, Irving and Merchant Ave., Hyannis Port, MA (private residence; closed to the public)
http://www.nps.gov/history/history/online_books/
presidents/site30.htm

Sixth Floor Museum at Dealey Plaza & Memorial Plaza Marker, 411 Elm St., Dallas, TX 75202-3308, 214-747-6600 or 888-485-4854; fax: 214-747-6662
http://www.jfk.org
jfk@jfk.org

Lyndon Baines Johnson

Thirty-sixth president (1963-69)
Born Aug 27, 1908, near Stonewall, TX
Married Claudia Alta "Lady Bird" Taylor, 1934
Died Jan 22, 1973, San Antonio, TX
Buried at Johnson Family Cemetery, Lyndon B. Johnson National Historic Park, Johnson City, TX
http://www.nps.gov/lyjo/cem.htm

Democrat. "L.B.J." U.S. Representative. Served in World War II. U.S. Senator. Succeeded presidency upon assassination of John F. Kennedy. Author of the "Great Society."

LANDMARKS:

Birth site: Junction School, LBJ Ranch, LBJ Ranch Unit, Lyndon B. Johnson National Historical Park, Johnson City, TX 78636, 830-868-7128; fax: 830-868-7863
http://www.nps.gov/lyjo
http://www.nps.gov/lyjo/bp.htm
http://www.nps.gov/lyjo/junct.htm
LYJO_Superintendent@nps.gov

Childhood home: 9th St. between "F" and "G" Sts., Johnson City, TX 78636
http://www.nps.gov/lyjo/boyhood.htm

Johnson Settlement, Johnson City Unit, Lyndon B. Johnson Historical Park, Johnson City, TX 78636, 830-868-7128; fax: 830-868-7863
http://www.nps.gov/lyjo/settle.htm

◆ Indicates that an entry on a festival celebrating the president appears in the main text

Lyndon Baines Johnson Library and Museum, University of Texas at Austin, 2313 Red River St., Austin, TX 78705, 512-721-0200
http://www.lbjlib.utexas.edu
johnson.library@nara.gov

Lyndon Baines Johnson Memorial Grove on the Potomac, Turkey Run Park, George Washington Memorial Pkwy., McLean, VA 22101, 703-289-2500; fax: 703-289-2598
http://www.nps.gov/lyba
gwmp_superintendent@nps.gov

Lyndon B. Johnson State Historical Park, U.S. 290, P.O. Box 238, Stonewall, TX 78671, 830-644-2252
http://www.tpwd.state.tx.us/park/lbj/lbj.htm

Richard Milhous Nixon

Thirty-seventh president (1969-74)
Born Jan 9, 1913, Yorba Linda, CA
Married Patricia Ryan, 1940
Died Apr 22, 1994, New York, NY
Buried at Richard Nixon Birthplace, Yorba Linda, CA

Republican. Served in World War II. U.S. Representative. U.S. Senator. Vice President. First president to visit communist China. First and only president to resign (Watergate scandal).

LANDMARKS:

Birth site: Nixon Library and Birthplace, 18001 Yorba Linda Blvd., Yorba Linda, CA 92886, 714-993-5075; fax: 714-528-0544
http://www.nixonlibraryfoundation.org

California White House, Del Presidente Ave., San Clemente, CA (private residence; closed to the public)

Nixon Presidential Materials, Staff National Archives at College Park, 8601 Adelphi Rd., College Park, MD 20740, 301-837-3290; fax: 301-837-3202
http://nixon.archives.gov
nixon@nara.gov

Gerald Rudolph Ford

Thirty-eighth president (1974-77)
Born Jul 14, 1913, Omaha, NE
Married Betty Bloomer Warren, 1948
Died Dec 26, 2006, Rancho Mirage, CA
Buried at Gerald R. Ford Museum, Grand Rapids, MI

Republican. Served in World War II. U.S. Representative. First vice president to take office under Twenty-fifth Amendment. Succeeded presidency upon resignation of Richard Nixon. Only president to serve in office without being elected.

LANDMARKS:

Birth site park: 32nd and Woolworth Ave., Omaha, NE 68105, 402-444-5955
http://www.nebraskahistory.org/conserve/brthsite.htm (Nebraska State Historical Society)

Childhood home: 649 Union Ave, S.E., Grand Rapids, MI (private residence; closed to the public)

Family home: 514 Crown View Dr., Alexandria, VA (private residence; closed to the public)

Gerald R. Ford Library, University of Michigan at Ann Arbor, 1000 Beal Ave., Ann Arbor, MI 48109, 734-205-0555; fax: 734-205-0571
http://www.ford.utexas.edu

Gerald R. Ford Museum, 303 Pearl St., N.W., Grand Rapids, MI 49504, 616-254-0400; fax: 616-254-0386
http://www.ford.utexas.edu

Retirement home: Thunderbird Country Club, 40-471 Sand Dune Rd., Rancho Mirage, CA 92270 (private residence; closed to the public)

James Earl Carter

Thirty-ninth president (1977-81)
Born Oct 1, 1924, Plains, GA
Married Rosalynn Smith, 1946

Democrat. "Jimmy." Governor of Georgia. First president to walk from Capitol to White House after inauguration. Camp David accords signed between Israel and Egypt. U.S. embassy staff held hostage in Tehran, Iran.

LANDMARKS:

Birth site: Plains Nursing Center (now the Lillian G. Carter Nursing Center), 225 Hospital St., Plains, GA 31780

Childhood home: Jimmy Carter National Historic Site, 300 N. Bond St., Plains, GA 31780, 229-824-4104; fax: 229-824-3441
http://www.nps.gov/jica

Carter Center, One Copenhill, 453 Freedom Pkwy., Atlanta, GA 30307, 404-420-5100 or 800-550-3560
http://www.cartercenter.org
http://www.jimmycarter.com
carterweb@emory.edu

Jimmy Carter Library & Museum, 441 Freedom Pkwy., Atlanta, GA 30307, 404-865-7100; fax: 404-865-7102
http://www.jimmycarterlibrary.org
carter.library@nara.gov

Retirement home: Woodland Dr., Plains, GA (private residence; closed to the public)

Ronald Wilson Reagan

Fortieth president (1981-89)
Born Feb 6, 1911, Tampico, IL
Married Jane Wyman, 1940, divorced 1949; Nancy Davis, 1952
Died Jun 5, 2004, Los Angeles, CA
Buried at the Ronald Reagan Presidential Library, Simi Valley, CA

Republican. "Great Communicator." Movie actor. Non-combat duty in World War II. Governor of California. Oldest

◆ Indicates that an entry on a festival celebrating the president appears in the main text

president. Only president to be wounded in assassination attempt and survive. Iran-Contra affair.

LANDMARKS:

Birth site: 111 Main St., Tampico, IL 61283, 815-438-2130
http://www.tampicohistoricalsociety.com/citymax.com/
R_Reagan_Birthplace_Museum.html

Childhood home: 816 S. Hennepin Ave., Dixon, IL 61021, 815-288-5176; fax: 815-288-3642
http://www.ronaldreaganhome.com
info@ronaldreaganhome.com

California White House, Rancho del Cielo, 3333 Refugio Canyon, Santa Barbara, CA (home of Young America's Foundation; closed to the public)

Ronald Reagan Presidential Foundation, 40 Presidential Dr., Simi Valley, CA 93065, 805-522-2977; fax: 805-520-9702
http://www.reaganfoundation.org
info@reaganfoundation.org

Ronald Reagan Presidential Library & Museum, 40 Presidential Dr., Simi Valley, CA 93065, 805-577-4000; fax: 805-577-4074
http://www.reaganfoundation.org
Reagan.library@nara.gov

George Herbert Walker Bush

Forty-first president (1989-93)
Born Jun 12, 1924, Milton, MA
Married Barbara Pierce, 1945

Republican. Served in World War II. U.S. Representative. U.N. Ambassador. C.I.A. Director. Vice President. First acting president under Twenty-fifth amendment. Fall of Berlin Wall. Dissolution of Soviet Union. Persian Gulf War.

LANDMARKS:

Birth site: 173 Adams St., Milton, MA 02186 (private residence; closed to the public)

Childhood home: Grove Lane, Greenwich, CT (private residence; closed to the public)

Family summer home: Walker's Point, Kennebunkport, ME (private residence; closed to the public)

George Bush Library, 1000 George Bush Dr. W., Texas A&M University, College Station, TX 77845, 979-691-4000; fax: 979-691-4050
http://bushlibrary.tamu.edu
Reservations.Bush@nara.gov

Bill Clinton

Forty-second president (1993-2001)
Born Aug 19, 1946, Hope, AR
Married Hillary Rodham, 1975

Democrat. Rhodes Scholar. Governor of Arkansas. Proposed national health care plan. North American Free Trade Agree-

ment. Middle East peace accord. Dayton Agreement for peace in Bosnia and Herzegovina. Second president to be impeached (acquitted). First first lady to be elected to the U.S. Senate.

LANDMARKS:

Childhood home: 117 S. Hervey St., Hope, AR

Childhood home: 321 E. 13th St., Hope, AR

Childhood home (marker): 1011 Park Ave., Hot Springs, AR (private residence; closed to the public)

Clinton Birthplace Foundation, P.O. Box 1925, Hope, AR 71801, 870-777-4455
http://www.clintonbirthplace.com
http://www.nps.gov/nr/travel/presidents/bill_clinton
_birthplace.html
clinton@arkansas.net
clintonsbirthplace@sbcglobal.net

Clinton Presidential Center, Foundation, & Library, 1200 President Clinton Ave., Little Rock, AR 72201, 501-370-8000; fax: 501-375-0512
http://www.clintonfoundation.org

George Walker Bush

Forty-third president (2001-2009)
Born Jul 6, 1946, New Haven, CT
Married Laura Welch, 1977

Republican. "George W." Governor of Texas. Son of forty-first president (*see* George Herbert Walker Bush). Presided over historic shift in Senate just after first 100 days. War against terrorism in response to the September 11, 2001, attacks in the United States. Invaded Iraq in 2003. Passed "No Child Left Behind" education bill.

LANDMARKS

Birth site: Childhood home: 1412 West Ohio Ave, Midland, TX 79701, 866-684-4380
http://www.bushchildhoodhome.com
http://www.nps.gov/nr/travel/presidents/george_bush_
home.html

George W. Bush Presidential Center, George W. Bush Foundation, P.O. Box 600610, Dallas, TX 75206, 214-890-9943
http://www.georgewbushlibrary.com
info@georgewbushlibrary.com

Barack Hussein Obama

Forty-fourth president (2009-)
Born Aug 4, 1961, Honolulu, HI
Married Michelle Robinson, 1992

Democrat. Illinois Senator. U.S. Senator. Proposed national health care plan.

◆ Indicates that an entry on a festival celebrating the president appears in the main text

Facts about Countries around the World

This section provides basic information about the independent nations of the world: official name (in English); capital city; internet country code; flag description; national anthem, motto, and symbols (when available); geographical description of location; total area; brief climate description; proper terms for nationality; population numbers; languages spoken; and information on ethnic groups and religions.

Afghanistan

Official name: Islamic Republic of Afghanistan

Capital city: Kabul

Internet country code: .af

Flag description: Three vertical bands of black (hoist), red, and green, with a gold emblem centered on the red band; the emblem features a temple-like structure encircled by a wreath on the left and right and by an inscription above pronouncing the Muslim faith: "There is no God but Allah and Mohammed is his Prophet" and "Allah is Great."

National anthem: "Soroud-e-Melli" (Hymn of the People)

Geographical description: Southern Asia, north and west of Pakistan, east of Iran

Total area: 249,935 sq. mi. (647,500 sq. km.)

Climate: Arid to semiarid; cold winters and hot summers

Nationality: *noun*: Afghan(s); *adjective*: Afghan

Population: 31,889.923 (July 2007 CIA est.)

Ethnic groups: Pashtun 42%, Tajik 27%, Hazara 9%, Uzbek 9%, Aimak 4%, Turkmen 3%, Baloch 2%, other 4%

Languages spoken: Afghan Persian or Dari (official) 50%, Pashto (official) 35%, Turkic languages (primarily Uzbek and Turkmen) 11%, 30 minor languages (primarily Balochi and Pashai) 4%; much bilingualism

Religions: Sunni Muslim 80%, Shi'a Muslim 19%, other 1%

Albania

Official name: Republic of Albania

Capital city: Tirana

Internet country code: .al

Flag description: Red with a black two-headed eagle in the center

National anthem: Himni Flamurit (" The Flag Hymn"; first line in English translation: "United all around the flag")

Geographical description: Southeastern Europe, bordering the Adriatic Sea and Ionian Sea, between Greece in the south and Montenegro and Serbia to the north

Total area: 11,099 sq. mi. (28,748 sq. km.)

Climate: Mild temperate; cool, cloudy, wet winters; hot, clear, dry summers; interior is cooler and wetter

Nationality: *noun*: Albanian(s); *adjective*: Albanian

Population: 3,600,523 (July 2007 CIA est.)

Ethnic groups: Albanian 98.6%, Greeks 1.17%, others (Vlachs, Roma, Serbs, Montenegrins, Macedonians, Balkan Egyptians, and Bulgarians) 0.23%

Languages spoken: Albanian (official), Greek, Vlach, Romani, Slavic dialects

Religions: Muslim 70%, Albanian Orthodox 20%, Roman Catholic 10%

Algeria

Official name: People's Democratic Republic of Algeria

Capital city: Algiers

Internet country code: .dz

Flag description: Two equal vertical bands of green (hoist side) and white; a red, five-pointed star within a red crescent centered over the two-color boundary; the crescent, star, and color green are traditional symbols of Islam (the state religion)

National anthem: "Quassaman," by Moufdi Zakaria

Geographical description: Northern Africa, bordering the Mediterranean Sea, between Morocco and Tunisia

Total area: 919,590 sq. mi. (2,381,740 sq. km.)

Climate: Arid to semiarid; mild, wet winters with hot, dry summers along coast; drier with cold winters and hot summers on high plateau; sirocco is a hot, dust/sand-laden wind especially common in summer

Nationality: *noun*: Algerian(s); *adjective*: Algerian

Population: 33,333,216 (July 2007 CIA est.)

Ethnic groups: Arab-Berber 99%, European less than 1%

Languages spoken: Arabic (official), French, Berber dialects

Religions: Sunni Muslin (state religion) 99%, Christian and Jewish 1%

Andorra

Official name: Principality of Andorra

Capital city: Andorra la Vella

Internet country code: .ad

Flag description: Three equal vertical bands of blue (hoist side), yellow, and red with the national coat of arms centered in the yellow band; the coat of arms features a quartered shield; similar to the flags of Chad and Romania, which do not have a national coat of arms in the center, and the flag of Moldova, which does bear a national emblem

National anthem: "Hymna Andorra" (first line: "El gran Carlemany mon pare dels alarbs me deslliurà"), lyrics by Dr Benlloch, Episcopal Co-Prince of Andorra, music by Father Marfany

National motto: Virtus Unita Fortior

National flower: Grandalla (daffodil family)

Geographical description: Southwestern Europe, between France and Spain

Total area: 180 sq. mi. (468 sq. km.)

Climate: Temperate; snowy, cold winters and warm, dry summers

Nationality: *noun*: Andorran(s); *adjective*: Andorran

Population: 71,822 (July 2007 CIA est.)

Ethnic groups: Spanish 43%, Andorran 33%, Portuguese 11%, French 7%, other 6% (1998 CIA est.)

Languages spoken: Catalan (official), French, Castilian, Portuguese

Religion: Predominantly Roman Catholic

Angola

Official name: Republic of Angola

Capital city: Luanda

Internet country code: .ao

Flag description: Two equal horizontal bands of red (top) and black with a centered yellow emblem consisting of a five-pointed star within half a cogwheel crossed by a machete (in the style of a hammer and sickle)

Geographical description: Southern Africa, bordering the South Atlantic Ocean, between Namibia and Democratic Republic of the Congo

Land area: 481,400 sq. mi. (1,246,700 sq. km.)

Climate: Semiarid in south and along coast to Luanda; north has cool, dry season (May to October) and hot, rainy season (November to April)

Nationality: *noun*: Angolan(s); *adjective*: Angolan

Population: 12,263,596 (July 2007 CIA est.)

Ethnic groups: Ovimbundu 37%, Mbundu 25%, Bakongo 13%, mestico (mixed European and African) 2%, European 1%, other 22%

Languages spoken: Portuguese (official), Umbundu, Kimbundu, Kikongo dialects

Religions: indigenous religions 47%, Roman Catholic 38%, Protestant 15% (1998 country est.)

Antigua and Barbuda

Official name: Antigua and Barbuda

Capital city: St. John's

Internet country code: .ag

Flag description: Red, with an inverted isosceles triangle based on the top edge of the flag; the triangle contains three horizontal bands of black (top), light blue, and white, with a yellow rising sun in the black band

National anthem: "Fair Antigua and Barbuda / We thy sons and daughters stand" (first lines), lyrics by Novelle Hamilton Richards, music by Walter Garnet Picart Chambers

National motto: "Each Endeavouring, All Achieving"

National animal: European Fallow Deer. (Dama dama dama)

National bird: Frigate Bird, Man-o'-War or Weather Bird. (Fregata magnificens L.) **National flower**: Agave, Dagger Log or Batta Log (Barbuda); (Agave karatto Miller)

National fruit: Antigua "Black" Pineapple (Ananas comosus (L.) Merril)

National sea creature: Hawksbill Turtle or 'oxbill. (Eretmochelys imbricata)

National stone: Petrified wood

National tree: Whitewood. (Bucida buceras L.)

Geographical description: Caribbean, islands between the Caribbean Sea and the North Atlantic Ocean, east-southeast of Puerto Rico

Total area: 170 sq. mi. (442 sq. km.); Antigua: 108 sq. mi. (281 sq. km.) and Barbuda: 62 sq. mi. (161 sq. km.)

Climate: Tropical maritime; little seasonal temperature variation

Nationality: *noun*: Antiguan(s), Barbudan(s); *adjective*: Antiguan, Barbudan

Population: 69,481 (July 2007 CIA est.)

Ethnic groups: Black African 91%, mixed African and European 4.4%, European 1.7%, other 2.9%

Languages spoken: English (official), local dialects

Religions: Anglican 25.7%, Seventh Day Adventist 12.3%, Pentecostal 10.6%, Moravian 10.5%, Roman Catholic 10.4%, Methodist 7.9%, Baptist 4.9%, Church of God 4.5%, other Christian 5.4%, other 2%, none or unspecified 5.8%

Argentina

Official name: Argentine Republic

Capital city: Buenos Aires

Internet country code: .ar

Flag description: Three equal horizontal bands of light blue (top), white, and light blue; centered in the white band is a radiant yellow sun with a human face known as the Sun of May

National anthem: "Himno Nacional Argentino" (first lines: Oíd, mortales, el grito sagrado: "¡libertad, libertad, libertad!"), lyrics by Vicente López y Planes, music by Blas Parera

National flower: flower of the ceibo tree (also called seibo, seíbo or bucaré)

Geographical description: Southern South America, bordering the South Atlantic Ocean, between Chile and Uruguay

Total area: 1.1 million sq. mi. (2.8 million sq. km.)

Climate: Mostly temperate; arid in southeast; subantarctic in southwest

Nationality: *noun*: Argentine(s); *adjective*: Argentine

Population: 40,301,927 (July 2007 CIA est.)

Ethnic groups: European (mostly Spanish and Italian) 97%, mestizo (mixed European and Amerindian), Amerindian or other non-white groups 3%

Languages spoken: Spanish (official), English, Italian, German, French

Religions: Nominally Roman Catholic 92% (less than 20% practicing), Protestant 2%, Jewish 2%, other 4%

Armenia

Official name: Republic of Armenia

Capital city: Yerevan

Internet country code: .am

Flag description: Three equal horizontal bands of red (top), blue, and orange

National anthem: "Mer Hayrenik" (Our Fatherland), lyrics by Mikael Nalbandian

Geographical description: Southwestern Asia, east of Turkey

Total area: 11,500 sq. mi. (29,800 sq. km.)

Climate: Highland continental, hot summers, cold winters

Nationality: *noun*: Armenian(s); *adjective*: Armenian

Population: 2,971,650 (July 2007 CIA est.)

Ethnic groups: Armenian 97.9%, Yezidi (Kurd) 1.3%, Russian 0.5%, other 0.3% (2001 census)

Languages spoken: Armenian 97.7%, Yezidi 1%, Russian 0.9%, other 0.4% (2001 census)

Religions: Armenian Apostolic Church 94.7%, other Christian 4%, Yezidi 1.3%

Aruba

Official name: Aruba

Capital city: Oranjestad

Internet country code: .aw

Flag description: Blue, with two narrow, horizontal, yellow stripes across the lower portion and a red four-pointed star outlined in white in the upper hoist-side corner

National anthem: "Aruba Dushi Tera"

Geographical description: Island in the Caribbean Sea, north of Venezuela

Total area: 112 sq. mi. (180 sq. km.)

Climate: Tropical marine; little seasonal temperature variation

Nationality: *noun*: Aruban(s); *adjective*: Aruban

Population: 100,018 (July 2007 CIA est.)

Ethnic groups: Mixed European/Caribbean Amerindian 80%, other 20%

Languages spoken: Dutch (official) 5.8%, Papiamento (Spanish-Portuguese-Dutch-English dialect) 66.3%, Spanish, English

Religions: Roman Catholic 82%, Protestant and other Christian 8%, other (Hindu, Muslim, Confucian, Jewish) 10%

Australia

Official name: Commonwealth of Australia

Capital city: Canberra

Internet country code: .au

Flag description: Blue with the flag of the United Kingdom in the upper hoist-side quadrant and a large seven-pointed star in the lower hoist-side quadrant known as the Commonwealth or Federation Star, representing the federation of the colonies of Australia in 1901; the star depicts one point for each of the six original states and one representing all of Australia's internal and external territories; on the fly half is a representation of the Southern Cross constellation in white with one small five-pointed star and four larger, seven-pointed stars

National anthem: "Advance Australia Fair" by Peter Dodds McCormick

National flower: Golden wattle (*Acacia pycnantha* Benth.)

National gemstone: Opal

Geographical description: Oceania, continent between the Indian Ocean and the South Pacific Ocean

Total area: 3 million sq. mi. (7.7 million sq. km.)

Climate: Generally arid to semiarid; temperate in south and east; tropical in north

Nationality: *noun*: Australian(s); *adjective*: Australian

Population: 20,434,176 (July 2007 CIA est.)

Ethnic groups: European 92%, Asian 7%, Aboriginal and other 1%

Languages spoken: English 79.1%, Chinese 2.1%, Italian 1.9%, other 11.1%, unspecified 5.8%

Religions: Roman Catholic 26.4%, Anglican 20.5%, other Christian 20.5%, Buddhist 1.9%, Muslim 1.5%, other 1.2%, unspecified 12.7%, none 15.3%

Austria

Official name: Republic of Austria

Capital city: Vienna

Internet country code: .at

Flag description: Three equal horizontal bands of red (top), white, and red

National anthem: "Land der Berge " (Land of Mountains), lyrics by Paula von Preradovic, composer uncertain

Geographical description: Central Europe, north of Italy and Slovenia

Total area: 32,369 sq. mi. (83,858 sq. km.)

Climate: Temperate; continental, cloudy; cold winters with frequent rain and some snow in lowlands and snow in mountains; moderate summers with occasional showers

Nationality: *noun*: Austrian(s); *adjective*: Austrian

Population: 8,199,783 (July 2007 CIA est.)

Ethnic groups: Austrians, Croats, Hungarians, Slovenes, Czechs, Slovaks, Roma, Sinti

Languages spoken: German

Religions: Roman Catholic 73.6%, Protestant 4.7%, Muslim 4.2%, other 3.5%, non-denominational 12 %, unknown 3.5%

Azerbaijan

Official name: Republic of Azerbaijan

Capital city: Baku

Internet country code: .az

Flag description: Three equal horizontal bands of blue (top), red, and green; a crescent and eight-pointed star in white are centered in the red band

National anthem: "Azerbaijan, Azerbaijan!" lyrics by Ahmed Javad, music by Useyir Hajibeyov

Geographical description: Southwestern Asia, bordering the Caspian Sea, between Iran and Russia, with a small European portion north of the Caucasus range

Total area: 33,436 sq. mi. (86,600 sq. km.)

Climate: Dry, semiarid steppe

Nationality: *noun*: Azerbaijani(s) or Azeri(s); *adjective*: Azerbaijani or Azeri

Population: 8,120,247 (July 2007 CIA est.)

Ethnic groups: Azeri 90.6%, Dagestani 2.2%, Russian 1.8%, Armenian 1.5%, other 3.9%

Languages spoken: Azerbaijani (Azeri) 90.3%, Lezgi 2.2%, Russian 1.8%, Armenian 1.5%, other and unspecified 4.3%

Religions: Muslim 93.4%, Russian Orthodox 2.5%, Armenian Orthodox 2.3%, other 1.8%

Bahamas

Official name: Commonwealth of The Bahamas

Capital city: Nassau

Internet country code: .bs

Flag description: Three equal horizontal bands of aquamarine (top), gold, and aquamarine, with a black equilateral triangle based on the hoist side

National anthem: "March On Bahamaland" by Timothy Gibson

National motto: "Forward Upward Onward Together"

National bird: Flamingo

National fish: Blue marlin (Makaira nigricans)

National flower: Yellow elder

National song: "God Bless Our Sunny Clime," lyrics by Rev. Philip Rahming, music by Timothy Gibson and Clement Bethel

National tree: Lignum vitae

Geographical description: Caribbean, chain of islands in the North Atlantic Ocean, southeast of Florida, northeast of Cuba

Total area: 5,382 sq. mi. (13,939 sq. km.)

Climate: Tropical marine; moderated by warm waters of Gulf Stream

Nationality: *noun*: Bahamian(s); *adjective*: Bahamian

Population: 305,655 (July 2007 CIA est.)

Ethnic groups: Black African 85%, white European 12%, Asian and Hispanic 3%

Languages spoken: English (official), Creole

Religions: Baptist 35.4%, Anglican 15.1%, Roman Catholic 13.5%, Pentecostal 8.1%, Chuch of God 4.8%, Methodist 4.2%, other Christian 15.2%, none or unspecified 2.9%, other 0.8%

Bahrain

Official name: Kingdom of Bahrain

Capital city: Manama

Internet country code: .bh

Flag description: Red, the traditional color for flags of Persian Gulf states, with a white serrated band (five white points) on the hoist side; the five points represent the five pillars of Islam

National anthem: "Bahrainona, Maleekuna" (first line; English translation: Our Bahrain, our King)

Geographical description: Middle East, archipelago in the Persian Gulf, east of Saudi Arabia

Total area: 274 sq. mi. (727 sq. km.)

Climate: Arid; mild, pleasant winters; very hot, humid summers

Nationality: *noun*: Bahraini(s); *adjective*: Bahraini

Population: 708,573, which includes 235,108m non-nationals (July 2007 CIA est.)

Ethnic groups: Bahraini 63%, Asian 19%, other Arab 10%, Iranian 8%

Languages spoken: Arabic (official), English, Farsi, Urdu

Religions: Citizen population is 98% Muslim (about 70% Shi'a and 30% Sunni), other religious groups among non-national population include Christian, Jewish, Hindu, Baha'is, Buddhists, and Sikhs

Bangladesh

Official name: People's Republic of Bangladesh

Capital city: Dhaka

Internet country code: .bd

Flag description: Green field with a large red disk shifted slightly to the hoist side of center; the red disk represents the rising sun and the sacrifice to achieve independence; the green field symbolizes the lush vegetation of Bangladesh

National anthem: "Amar Sonar Bangla" (My Golden Bengal); (first line in English: My Bengal of gold, I love you), lyrics in Bengali by Rabindranath Tagore, translated by Syed Ali Ahsan

National animal: Royal Bengal tiger

National bird: Doel or magpie robin

National flower: Shapla or water lily

National fruit: Jackfruit (Kathal)

Geographical description: Southern Asia, bordering the Bay of Bengal, between Myanmar (Burma) and India

Total area: 55,813 sq. mi. (147,570 sq. km.)

Climate: Tropical; mild winter (October to March); hot, humid summer (March to June); humid, warm rainy monsoon (June to October)

Nationality: *noun*: Bangladeshi(s); *adjective*: Bangladeshi

Population: 150,448,339 (July 2007 CIA est.)

Ethnic groups: Bengali 98%, non-Bengali Muslims and tribal groups 2%

Languages spoken: Bangla (official; also known as Bengali), English

Religions: Muslim 83%, Hindu 16%, Christian 0.3%, Buddhist 0.6%, other 0.3%

Barbados

Official name: Barbados

Capital city: Bridgetown

Internet country code: .bb

Flag description: Three equal vertical bands of blue (hoist side), gold, and blue with the head of a black trident centered on the gold band; the trident head represents independence and a break with the past (the colonial coat of arms contained a complete trident)

National anthem: "We loyal sons and daughters all" (first line of chorus), lyrics by Irving Burgie, music by C. Van Roland Edwards

National flower: Pride of Barbados (Dwarf Poinciana or Flower Fence; Poinciana pulcherrima linnaeus)

Geographical description: Caribbean, island in the North Atlantic Ocean, northeast of Venezuela

Total area: 166 sq. mi. (431 sq. km.)

Climate: Tropical; rainy season (June to October)

Nationality: *noun*: Barbadian(s) or, informally, Bajan(s); *adjective*: Barbadian; informally, Bajan

Population: 280,946 (July 2007 CIA est.)

Ethnic groups: Black African 90%, white European 4%, Asian and or mixed 6%

Languages spoken: English

Religions: Anglican 40%, Pentecostal 8%, Methodist 7%, other Protestant 12%, Roman Catholic 4%, none 17%, other 12%

Belarus

Official name: Republic of Belarus

Capital city: Minsk

Internet country code: .by

Flag description: Red horizontal band (top) and green horizontal band one-half the width of the red band; a white vertical stripe on the hoist side bears Belarusian national ornamentation in red

National anthem: Lyrics by M. Klimkovich and U. Karyzna, music by N. Sakalouski

Geographical description: Eastern Europe, east of Poland

Total area: 80,100 sq. mi. (207,600 sq. km.)

Climate: Cold winters, cool and moist summers; transitional between continental and maritime

Nationality: *noun*: Belarusian(s); *adjective*: Belarusian

Population: 9,724,723 (July 2007 CIA est.)

Ethnic groups: Belarusian 81.2%, Russian 11.4%, Polish 3.9%, Ukrainian 2.4%, Jewish 0.3%, other 0.8%

Languages spoken: Belarusian and Russian

Religions: Eastern Orthodox 80%, Roman Catholic 14%, Protestant 2%, other (including Autocephalous Orthodox, Jewish, Muslim, and Krishna) 4%

Belgium

Official name: Kingdom of Belgium

Capital city: Brussels

Internet country code: .be

Flag description: Three equal vertical bands of black (hoist side), yellow, and red; the design was based on the flag of France

National anthem: "La Brabançonne"

National motto: French: "L'Union fait la force," Dutch: "Eendracht maakt macht" (Strength lies in unity)

Geographical description: Western Europe, bordering the North Sea, between France and the Netherlands

Total area: 12,566 sq. mi. (32,547 sq. km.)

Climate: Temperate; mild winters, cool summers; rainy, humid, cloudy

Nationality: *noun*: Belgian(s); *adjective*: Belgian

Population: 10,392,226 (July 2007 CIA est.)

Ethnic groups: Fleming 58%, Walloon 31%, mixed or other 11%

Languages spoken: Dutch 60%, French 40%, German less than 1%

Religions: Roman Catholic 75%, others (including Protestant, Jewish, Muslim, Anglican, Greek and Russian Orthodox, and none) 25%

Belize

Official name: Belize

Capital city: Belmopan

Internet country code: .bz

Flag description: Blue with a narrow red stripe along the top and the bottom edges; centered is a large white disk bearing the coat of arms; the coat of arms features a shield flanked by two workers in front of a mahogany tree with the national motto *Sub umbra florero* on a scroll at the bottom, all encircled by a green garland

National anthem: "Land of the Free"

National motto: "Sub Umbra Florero" (Under the shade I flourish)

National animal: Tapir or Mountain Cow (Tapirello Bairdii)

National bird: Keel-Billed Toucan (Ramphastos Solfurantus)

National flower: Black Orchid (Encyclia Cochleatum)

National tree: Mahogany tree (Swietenia Macrophilla)

Geographical description: Central America, bordering the Caribbean Sea, between Guatemala and Mexico

Total area: 8,867 sq. mi. (22,966 sq. km.)

Climate: Tropical; very hot and humid; rainy season (May to November); dry season (February to May)

Nationality: *noun*: Belizean(s); *adjective*: Belizean

Population: 294,385 (July 2007 CIA est.)

Ethnic groups: Mestizo 48.7%, Creole 24.9%, Maya 10.6%, Garifuna 6.1%, other 9.7%

Languages spoken: Spanish 46%, Creole 32.9%, Mayan dialects 8.9%, English (official) 3.9%, Garifuna (Carib) 3.4%, German 3.3%, other 1.4%, unknown 0.2%

Religions: Roman Catholic 49.6%, Pentecostal 7.4%, Anglican 5.3%, Seventh-Day Adventist 5.2%, Mennonite 4.1%, Methodist 3.5%, Jehovah's Witnesses 1.5%, other (including Muslim, Hindu, and Buddhist) 14%, none 9.4%

Benin

Official name: Republic of Benin

Capital city: Porto-Novo is official capital city; Cotonou is the seat of government

Internet country code: .bj

Flag description: Two equal horizontal bands of yellow (top) and red (bottom) with a vertical green band on the hoist side

National anthem: "L'Aube Nouvelle" (The New Dawn)

National motto: "Fraternité - Justice - Travail"

Geographical description: Western Africa, bordering the Bight of Benin, between Nigeria and Togo

Total area: 43,483 sq. mi. (116,622 sq. km.)

Climate: Tropical; hot, humid in south; semiarid in north

Nationality: *noun*: Beninese (singular and plural); *adjective*: Beninese

Population: 8,078,314 (July 2007 CIA est.)

Ethnic groups: Fon and related groups 39.2%, Adja and related groups 15.2%, Yoruba and related groups 12.3%, Bariba and related groups 9.2%, Peulh and related groups 7%, Ottamari and related groups 6.1%, Yoa-Lokpa and related groups 4%, Dendi and related groups 2.5%, other (including Europeans) 1.6%, unspecified 2.9%

Languages spoken: French (official), Fon and Yoruba predominant in the south, Nagot, Bariba, Dendi and other tribal languages in the north

Religions: Roman Catholic 27.1%, Muslim 24.4%, Vodun (Voodoo) 17.3%, Celestial Christian 5%, Methodist 3.2 %, other Christian 7.5%, other traditional local religious groups 6%, other religious groups 1.9%, and none 6.5%

Bermuda

Official name: Bermuda

Capital city: Hamilton

Internet country code: .bm

Flag description: Red, with the flag of the United Kingdom in the upper hoist-side quadrant and the Bermudian coat of arms (white and green shield with a red lion holding a scrolled shield showing the sinking of the ship *Sea Venture* off Bermuda in 1609) centered on the outer half of the flag

Geographical description: North America, group of islands in the North Atlantic Ocean, east of South Carolina (US)

Total area: 22.7 sq. mi. (58.8 sq. km.)

Climate: Subtropical; mild, humid; gales, strong winds common in winter

Nationality: *noun*: Bermudian(s); *adjective*: Bermudian

Population: 66,163 (July 2007 CIA est.)

Ethnic groups: Black African 54.8%, white European 34.1%, mixed 6.4%, other 4.3%, unspecified 0.4%

Languages spoken: English (official)

Religions: Anglican 23%, Roman Catholic 15%, African Methodist Episcopal 11%, Seventh-Day Adventist 7%, Methodist 4%, other Protestant 7%, other 12%, unaffiliated 6%, unspecified 1%, none 14%

Bhutan

Official name: Kingdom of Bhutan

Capital city: Thimphu

Internet country code: .bt

Flag description: Divided diagonally from the lower hoist side corner; the upper triangle is yellow and the lower triangle is orange; centered along the dividing line is a large black and white dragon facing away from the hoist side

National anthem: "In the Kingdom of Druk, where cypresses grow" (first line in English translation)

Geographical description: Southern Asia, between China and India

Total area: 17,953 sq. mi. (46,500 sq. km.)

Climate: Varies; tropical in southern plains; cool winters and hot summers in central valleys; severe winters and cool summers in Himalayas

Nationality: *noun*: Bhutanese (singular and plural); *adjective*: Bhutanese

Population: 634,982 (2006 government est.)

Ethnic groups: Bhote (Drukpa) 50%, ethnic Nepalese (including Lhotsampas) 35%, indigenous or migrant groups 15%

Languages spoken: Dzongka (official), English, Tibetan dialects, Nepalese dialects

Religions: Lamaistic Buddhist (state religion) 75%, Indian- and Nepalese-influenced Hinduism 25%

Bolivia

Official name: Republic of Bolivia

Capital city: La Paz

Internet country code: .bo

Flag description: Three equal horizontal bands of red (top), yellow, and green with the coat of arms centered on the yellow band; similar to the flag of Ghana, which has a large black five-pointed star centered in the yellow band

Geographical description: Central South America, southwest of Brazil

Total area: 425,000 sq. mi. (1.1 million sq. km.)

Climate: Varies with altitude; humid and tropical to cold and semiarid

Nationality: *noun*: Bolivian(s); *adjective*: Bolivian

Population: 9,119,152 (July 2007 CIA est.)

Ethnic groups: Quechua 30%, mestizo (mixed European and Amerindian) 30%, Aymara 25%, European 15%

Languages spoken: Spanish, Quechua, Aymara, Guarani

Religions: Roman Catholic 95%, Evangelical Methodist 5%

Bosnia and Herzegovina

Official name: Bosnia and Herzegovina

Capital city: Sarajevo

Internet country code: .ba

Flag description: A wide medium blue vertical band on the fly side with a yellow isosceles triangle abutting the band and the top of the flag; the remainder of the flag is medium blue with seven full five-pointed white stars and two half stars top and bottom along the hypotenuse of the triangle

National anthem: "Intermeco"

Geographical description: Southeastern Europe, bordering the Adriatic Sea and Croatia

Total area: 19,767 sq. mi. (51,197 sq. km.)

Climate: Hot summers and cold winters; areas of high elevation have short, cool summers and long, severe winters; mild, rainy winters along coast

Nationality: *noun*: Bosnian(s), Herzegovinian(s); *adjective*: Bosnian, Herzegovinian

Population: 4,552,198 (July 2007 CIA est.)

Ethnic groups: Bosniak (formerly Bosnian, associated with religious term Muslim) 48%, Serb 37.1%, Croat 14.3%, other 0.6%

Languages spoken: Bosnian, Croatian, Serbian

Religions: Muslim 40%, Orthodox 31%, Roman Catholic 15%, Protestant 4%, other 10%

Botswana

Official name: Republic of Botswana

Capital city: Gaborone

Internet country code: .bw

Flag description: Light blue with a horizontal white-edged black stripe in the center

National anthem: "Fatshe La Rona" (Our Land)

Geographical description: Southern Africa, north of South Africa

Total area: 224,710 sq. mi. (582,000 sq. km.)

Climate: Semiarid; warm winters and hot summers

Nationality: *noun*: Motswana (singular), Batswana (plural); *adjective*: Motswana (singular), Batswana (plural)

Population: 1,815,508 (July 2007 CIA est.)

Ethnic groups: Tswana (or Setswana) 79%, Kalanga 11%, Basarwa (or "San") 3%, other (including Kgalagadi, Herero, Bayeyi, Hambukush, Khoi, and European) 7%

Languages spoken: Setswana 78.2%, Kalanga 7.9%, Sekgalagadi 2.8%, English (official) 2.1%, other and unspecified 9%

Religions: Christian 71.6%, Badimo 6%, other 1.4%, unspeficied 0.4%, none 20.6%

Brazil

Official name: Federative Republic of Brazil

Capital city: Brasilia

Internet country code: .br

Flag description: Green with a large yellow diamond in the center bearing a blue celestial globe with 27 white five-pointed stars (one for each state and the Federal District) arranged in the same pattern as the night sky over Brazil; the globe has a white equatorial band with the motto *ordem e progresso* (Order and Progress)

National anthem: "Himno Nacianal Brasileiro," lyrics by Joaquim Osório Duque Estrada, music by Francisco Manuel da Silva

National bird: Sabiá or Thrush (Turdus rufiventris)

National flower: Ipê-amarelo - (Tecoma chrysostricha)

Geographical description: Eastern South America, bordering the Atlantic Ocean

Total area: 3,290,000 sq. mi. (8,511,965 sq. km.)

Climate: Mostly tropical, but temperate in south

Nationality: *noun*: Brazilian(s); *adjective*: Brazilian

Population: 190,010,647 (July 2007 CIA est.)

Ethnic groups: White European (including Portuguese, Italian, German, Spanish ancestry) 53.7%, mulatto (mixed white European and black African) 38.5%, black African 6.2%, other (including Japanese, Arab, Amerindian) 0.9%, unspecified 0.7%

Languages spoken: Portuguese, Spanish, English, French

Religions: Roman Catholic 73.6%, Protestant 15.4%, Spiritualist 1.3%, Bantu/Vodun 0.3%, other 1.8%, unspecified 0.2%, none 7.4%

Brunei

Official name: Brunei Darussalam

Capital city: Bandar Seri Begawan

Internet country code: .bn

Flag description: Yellow with two diagonal bands of white (top, almost double width) and black starting from the upper hoist side; the national emblem in red is superimposed at the center; the emblem includes a swallow-tailed flag on top of a winged column within an upturned crescent above a scroll and flanked by two upraised hands

National anthem: "Allah Peliharakan Sultan" (God Bless His Majesty), lyrics by Yura Halim, music by Haji Awang Besar Sagap

National motto: "Always Render Service by God's Guidance"

Geographical description: Southeastern Asia, bordering the South China Sea and Malaysia

Total area: 2,226 sq. mi. (5,765 sq. km.)

Climate: Tropical; hot, humid, rainy

Nationality: *noun*: Bruneian(s); *adjective*: Bruneian

Population: 374,577 (July 2007 CIA est.)

Ethnic groups: Malay 67%, Chinese 15%, indigenous 6%, other 12%

Languages spoken: Malay, English, Chinese

Religions: Muslim (official religion) 67%, Buddhist 13%, Christian 10%, other (including indigenous religions) 10%

Bulgaria

Official name: Republic of Bulgaria

Capital city: Sofia

Internet country code: .bg

Flag description: Three equal horizontal bands of white (top), green, and red

National anthem: "Mila Rodino" (O Motherland Most Dear), based on music and lyrics by Tsvetan Radoslavov

National motto: "Unity Makes Strength"

Geographical description: Southeastern Europe, bordering the Black Sea, between Romania and Turkey

Total area: 42,823 sq. mi. (110,912 sq. km.)

Climate: Temperate; cold, damp winters; hot, dry summers

Nationality: *noun*: Bulgarian(s); *adjective*: Bulgarian

Population: 7,322,858 (July 2007 CIA est.)

Ethnic groups: Bulgarian 83.9%, Turk 9.4%, Roma 4.7%, other (including Macedonian, Armenian, Tatar, and Circassian) 2%

Languages spoken: Bulgarian 84.5%, Turkish 9.6%, Roma 4.1%, other and unspecified 1.8%

Religions: Bulgarian Orthodox 84.5%, Muslim 12.2%, other Christian 1.2%, other 4%

Burkina Faso

Official name: Burkina Faso

Capital city: Ouagadougou

Internet country code: .bf

Flag description: Two equal horizontal bands of red (top) and green with a yellow five-pointed star in the center; uses the popular pan-African colors of Ethiopia

National anthem: "L' Hymne de la Victoire" / "Ditanyè" (Hymn of Victory)

Geographical description: Western Africa, north of Ghana

Total area: 106,000 sq. mi. (274,200 sq. km.)

Climate: Tropical; warm, dry winters; hot, wet summers

Nationality: *noun*: Burkinabe (singular and plural); *adjective*: Burkinabe

Population: 14,326,203 (July 2007 CIA est.)

Ethnic groups: Mossi over 40%, other (including Gurunsi, Senufo, Lobi, Bobo, Mande, and Fulani) about 60%

Languages spoken: French (official), Dioula and other native languages 90%

Religions: Muslim 60%, indigenous religions 24%, Roman Catholic 17%, Protestant 3%

Burma/Myanmar

Official name: Union of Burma/Myanmar

Capital city: Rangoon

Internet country code: .mm

Flag description: Red with a blue rectangle in the upper hoist-side corner bearing 14 white, five-pointed stars encircling a cogwheel containing a stalk of rice; the 14 stars represent the seven administrative divisions and seven states

National anthem: "Kaba Makye" (Our Free Homeland; first line in English translation: "We shall always love Myanmar, Land of our forefathers") by Y. M. B. Saya Tin

Geographical description: Southeastern Asia, bordering the Andaman Sea and the Bay of Bengal, between Bangladesh and Thailand

Total area: 261,228 sq. mi. (676,578 sq. km.)

Climate: Tropical monsoon; cloudy, rainy, hot, humid summers (southwest monsoon, June to September); less cloudy, scant rainfall, mild temperatures, lower humidity during winter (northeast monsoon, December to April)

Nationality: *noun*: Burmese (singular and plural); *adjective*: Burmese

Population: 47,373,958 (July 2007 CIA est.)

Ethnic groups: Burman 68%, Shan 9%, Karen 7%, Rakhine 4%, Chinese 3%, Indian 2%, Mon 2%, other 5%

Languages spoken: Burmese, minority languages

Religions: Buddhist 89%, Muslim 4%, Baptist 3%, Roman Catholic 1%, traditional indigenous 1%, other 2%

Burundi

Official name: Republic of Burundi

Capital city: Bujumbura

Internet country code: .bi

Flag description: Divided by a white diagonal cross into red panels (top and bottom) and green panels (hoist side and fly side) with a white disk superimposed at the center bearing three red six-pointed stars outlined in green arranged in a triangular design (one star above, two stars below)

National anthem: "Burundi Bwacu" (Hymn of Independence)

National motto: Unity-Work-Progress

Geographical description: Central Africa, east of Democratic Republic of the Congo

Total area: 10,747 sq. mi. (27,830 sq. km.)

Climate: Equatorial; high plateau with considerable altitude variation; two wet seasons (February to May and

September to November), and two dry seasons (June to August and December to January)

Nationality: *noun*: Burundian(s); *adjective*: Burundian

Population: 8,390,505 (July 2007 CIA est.)

Ethnic groups: Hutu (Bantu) 85%, Tutsi (Hamitic) 14%, Twa (Pygmy) 1%

Languages spoken: Kirundi (official), French (official), Swahili (along Lake Tanganyika and in the Bujumbura area)

Religions: Roman Catholic 62%, indigenous religions 23%, Muslim 10%, Protestant 5%

Cambodia

Official name: Kingdom of Cambodia

Capital city: Phnom Penh

Internet country code: .kh

Flag description: Three horizontal bands of blue (top), red (double width), and blue with a white three-towered temple representing Angkor Wat outlined in black in the center of the red band; only national flag to incorporate an actual building in its design

National anthem: "Our Country"

National motto: "Nation, Religion, King"

Geographical description: Southeastern Asia, bordering the Gulf of Thailand, between Thailand, Vietnam, and Laos

Total area: 69,900 sq. mi. (181,040 sq. km.)

Climate: Tropical; rainy, monsoon season (May to November); dry season (December to April); little seasonal temperature variation

Nationality: *noun*: Cambodian(s); *adjective*: Cambodian

Population: 13,995,904 (July 2007 CIA est.)

Ethnic groups: Khmer 90%, Vietnamese 5%, Chinese 1%, other 4%

Languages spoken: Khmer (official) 95%, French, English

Religions: Theravada Buddhist 95%, other (Islam, Christian, and indigenous religions) 5%

Cameroon

Official name: Republic of Cameroon

Capital city: Yaounde

Internet country code: .cm

Flag description: Three equal vertical bands of green (hoist side), red, and yellow with a yellow five-pointed star centered in the red band; uses the popular pan-African colors of Ethiopia

National anthem: "Ô Cameroun, berceau de nos ancêtres" (O Cameroon, Thou Cradle of Our Fathers)

Geographical description: Western Africa, bordering the Bight of Biafra, between Equatorial Guinea and Nigeria

Total area: 184,000 sq. mi. (475,000 sq. km.)

Climate: Varies with terrain, from tropical along coast to semiarid and hot in north

Nationality: *noun*: Cameroonian(s); *adjective*: Cameroonian

Population: 18,060,382 (July 2007 CIA est.)

Ethnic groups: Cameroon Highlanders 31%, Equatorial Bantu 19%, Kirdi 11%, Fulani 10%, Northwestern Bantu 8%, Eastern Nigritic 7%, other African 13%, non-African less than 1%

Languages spoken: French (official), English (official), 24 major African language groups

Religions: Indigenous religions 40%, Roman Catholic 20%, Protestant 20%, Muslim 20%

Canada

Official name: Canada

Capital city: Ottawa

Internet country code: .ca

Flag description: Two vertical bands of red (hoist and fly side, half width), with white square between them; an 11-pointed red maple leaf is centered in the white square; the official colors of Canada are red and white

National anthem: "O Canada," English lyrics by Justice Robert Stanley Weir, French lyrics by Adolphe-Basile Routhier, music by Calixa Lavallée

National symbols: maple leaf, maple tree, and beaver

Geographical description: Northern North America, bordering the North Atlantic Ocean on the east, North Pacific Ocean on the west, and the Arctic Ocean on the north, north of the conterminous United States

Total area: 3.8 million sq. mi. (9.9 million sq. km.)

Climate: Varies from temperate in south to subarctic and arctic in north

Nationality: *noun*: Canadian(s); *adjective*: Canadian

Population: 33,390,141 (July 2007 CIA est.)

Ethnic groups: British Isles ancestry 28%, French ancestry 23%, other European 15%, Amerindian 2%, other (Arab, Asian, African) 6%, mixed ancestry 26%

Languages spoken: English (official) 59.3%, French (official) 23.2%, other 17.5%

Religions: Roman Catholic 42.6%, Protestant 23.3%, other Christian 4.4%, Muslim 1.9%, other and unspecified 11.8%, none 16%

Cape Verde

Official name: Republic of Cape Verde

Capital city: Praia

Internet country code: .cv

Flag description: Five unequal horizontal bands; the topmost band of blue - equal to one half the width of the flag - is followed by three bands of white, red, and white, each equal to 1/12 of the width, and a bottom stripe of blue equal to one quarter of the flag width; a circle of 10 yellow five-pointed stars, each representing one of the islands, is centered on the red stripe and positioned 3/8 of the length of the flag from the hoist side

National anthem: "Cântico da Liberdade"

Geographical description: Western Africa, group of islands in the North Atlantic Ocean, west of Senegal

Total area: 1,557 sq. mi. (4,033 sq. km.)

Climate: Temperate; warm, dry summer; precipitation meager and very erratic

Nationality: *noun*: Cape Verdean(s); *adjective*: Cape Verdean

Population: 423,613 (July 2007 CIA est.)

Ethnic groups: Creole (mixed African and Portuguese) 71%, African 28%, European 1%

Languages spoken: Portuguese, Crioulo (Portuguese-West African blend)

Religions: Roman Catholic more than 85%, Protestant less than 15%

Central African Republic

Official name: Central African Republic

Capital city: Bangui

Internet country code: .cf

Flag description: Four equal horizontal bands of blue (top), white, green, and yellow with a vertical red band in center; there is a yellow five-pointed star on the hoist side of the blue band

National anthem: "Le Renaissance" (Rebirth)

Geographical description: Central Africa, north of Democratic Republic of the Congo

Total area: 242,000 sq. mi. (622,983 sq. km.)

Climate: Tropical; hot, dry winters; mild to hot, wet summers

Nationality: noun: Central African(s); adjective: Central African

Population: 4,369,038 (July 2007 CIA est.)

Ethnic groups: Baya 33%, Banda 27%, Sara 10%, Mandja 13%, Mboum 7%, M'baka 4%, Yakoma 4%, other 2%

Languages spoken: Sangho

Religions: Indigenous religions 35%, Roman Catholic 25%, Protestant 25%, Muslim 15%

Chad

Official name: Republic of Chad

Capital city: N'Djamena

Internet country code: .td

Flag description: Three equal vertical bands of blue (hoist side), yellow, and red; design was based on the flag of France

National anthem: "La Tchadienne" (The Chadian)

Geographical description: Central Africa, south of Libya

Total area: 496,000 sq. mi. (1,284,634 sq. km.)

Climate: Tropical in south, desert in north

Nationality: *noun*: Chadian(s); *adjective*: Chadian

Population: 9,885,661 (July 2007 CIA est.)

Ethnic groups: Sara 27.7%, Arab 12.3%, Mayo-Kebbi 11.5%, Kanem-Bornou 9%, Ouaddai 8.7%, Hadjarai 6.7%, Tandjile 6.5%, Gorane 6.3%, Fitri-Batha 4.7%, other 6.4%, unknown 0.3%

Languages spoken: French (official), Arabic (official), Sara (in the south), more than 120 other languages and dialects

Religions: Muslim 53.1%, Roman Catholic 20.1%, Protestant 14.2%, indigenous religions 7.3%, other and unknown 2.2%, none 3.1%

Chile

Official name: Republic of Chile

Capital city: Santiago

Internet country code: .cl

Flag description: Two equal horizontal bands of white (top) and red; there is a blue square the same height as the white band at the hoist-side end of the white band; the square bears a white five-pointed star in the center representing a guide to progress and honor; blue symbolizes the sky, white is for the snow-covered Andes, and red stands for the blood spilled to achieve independence; design was influenced by the United States flag

National anthem: "Cancion Nacionale de Chile" (National Song of Chile; first line: "Puro Chile, es tu cielo azulado"), lyrics by Eusebio Lillo, music by Ramón Carnicer

Geographical description: Southern South America, bordering the South Pacific Ocean, between Argentina and Peru

Total area: 302,778 sq. mi. (756,945 sq. km.)

Climate: Temperate; desert in north; Mediterranean in central region; cool and damp in south

Nationality: *noun*: Chilean(s); *adjective*: Chilean

Population: 16,284,741 (July 2007 CIA est.)

Ethnic groups: Spanish descent and mixed Spanish-Amerindian 95%, Amerindian 3%, other 2%

Languages spoken: Spanish

Religions: Roman Catholic 70%, Evangelical 15.1%, Jehovah's Witness 1.1%, other Christian 1%, other 4.6%, none 8.3%

China

Official name: People's Republic of China

Capital city: Beijing

Internet country code: .cn

Flag description: Red with a large yellow five-pointed star and four smaller yellow five-pointed stars (arranged in a vertical arc toward the middle of the flag) in the upper hoist-side corner

National anthem: March of the Volunteers, lyrics by Tian Han, music by Nie Er

Geographical description: Eastern Asia, bordering the East China Sea, Korea Bay, Yellow Sea, and South China Sea, between North Korea and Vietnam

Total area: 3.7 million sq. mi. (9,596,960 sq. km.)

Climate: Extremely diverse; tropical in south to subarctic in north

Nationality: *noun*: Chinese (singular and plural); *adjective*: Chinese

Population: 1,321,851,888 (July 2007 CIA est.)

Ethnic groups: Han Chinese 91.9%, Zhuang, Uygur, Hui, Yi, Tibetan, Miao, Manchu, Mongol, Buyi, Korean, and other nationalities 8.1%

Languages spoken: Standard Chinese or Mandarin (Putonghua, based on the Beijing dialect), Yue (Cantonese), Wu (Shanghainese), Minbei (Fuzhou), Minnan (Hokkein-Taiwanese), Xiang, Gan, Hakka dialects, and other minority languages

Religions: Daoist (Taoist), Buddhist, Christian 3-4%, Muslim 1-2%; officially atheist

Colombia

Official name: Republic of Colombia

Capital city: Bogota

Internet country code: .co

Flag description: Three horizontal bands of yellow (top, double-width), blue, and red; similar to the flag of Ecuador, which is longer and bears the Ecuadorian coat of arms superimposed in the center

National bird: Condor

National flower: Orchid (Cattleya trianae)

National tree: Wax palm (Ceroxylon quindiuense)

Geographical description: Northern South America, bordering the Caribbean Sea, between Panama and Venezuela, and bordering the North Pacific Ocean, between Ecuador and Panama

Total area: 440,000 sq. mi. (1,138,910 sq. km.)

Climate: Tropical along coast and eastern plains; cooler in highlands

Nationality: *noun*: Colombian(s); *adjective*: Colombian

Population: 44,379,598 (July 2007 CIA est.)

Ethnic groups: Mestizo 58%, white 20%, Afro-Colombian 14%, black 4%, mixed black-Amerindian 3%, Amerindian 1%

Languages spoken: Spanish

Religions: Roman Catholic 90%, other 10%

Comoros

Official name: Union of the Comoros

Capital city: Moroni

Internet country code: .km

Flag description: Four equal horizontal bands of yellow (top), white, red, and blue with a green isosceles triangle based on the hoist; centered within the triangle is a white crescent with the convex side facing the hoist and four white, five-pointed stars placed vertically in a line between the points of the crescent; the horizontal bands and the four stars represent the four main islands of the archipelago - Mwali, Njazidja, Nzwani, and Mahore (Mayotte - territorial collectivity of France, but claimed by Comoros); the crescent, stars, and color green are traditional symbols of Islam

National anthem: "Udzima Wamasiwa" (Union des Óles), lyrics by Said Hachim Sidi Abderemane, music by Kamildine Abdallah et Said Hachim Sidi Abderemane

Geographical description: Southern Africa, group of islands at the northern mouth of the Mozambique Channel, about two-thirds of the way between northern Madagascar and northern Mozambique

Total area: 838 sq. mi. (2,171 sq. km.)

Climate: Tropical marine; rainy season (November to May)

Nationality: *noun*: Comoran(s); *adjective*: Comoran

Population: 711,417 (July 2007 CIA est.)

Ethnic groups: Antalote, Cafre, Makoa, Oimatsaha, Sakalava

Languages spoken: Arabic (official), French (official), Shikomoro (a blend of Swahili and Arabic)

Religions: Sunni Muslim 98%, Roman Catholic 2%

Congo, Democratic Republic of the

Official name: Democratic Republic of the Congo

Capital city: Kinshasa

Internet country code: .cd

Flag description: Sky blue field divided diagonally from the lower hoist corner to upper fly corner by a red stripe bordered by two narrow yellow stripes; a yellow, five-pointed star appears in the upper hoist corner

National anthem: "Debout Congolaise!" (Arise Congolese!)

National motto: *Justice - Paix - Travail* (Justice, Peace, Work)

Geographical description: Central Africa, northeast of Angola

Total area: 905,063 sq. mi. (2,345,410 sq. km.)

Climate: Tropical; hot and humid in equatorial river basin; cooler and drier in southern highlands; cooler and wetter in eastern highlands; north of Equator - wet season (April to October), dry season (December to February); south of Equator - wet season (November to March), dry season (April to October)

Nationality: *noun*: Congolese (singular and plural); *adjective*: Congolese

Population: 65,751,512 (July 2007 CIA est.)

Ethnic groups: More than 200 African ethnic groups; the Bantu family (Mongo, Luba, Kongo) and Mangbetu-Azande (Hamitic) comprise about 45% of the population

Languages spoken: French (official), Lingala, Kingwana (a dialect of Kiswahili or Swahili), Kikongo, Tshiluba

Religions: Roman Catholic 50%, Protestant 20%, Kimbanguist 10%, Muslim 10%, other (including indigenous and syncretic faiths) 10%

Congo, Republic of the

Official name: Republic of the Congo

Capital city: Brazzaville

Internet country code: .cg

Flag description: Divided diagonally from the lower hoist side by a yellow band; the upper triangle (hoist side) is green and the lower triangle is red; uses the popular pan-African colors of Ethiopia

National anthem: "La Congolaise"

Geographical description: Western Africa, bordering the South Atlantic Ocean, between Angola and Gabon

Total area: 132,000 sq. mi. (342,000 sq. km.)

Climate: Tropical; rainy season (March to June); dry season (June to October); persistent high temperatures and humidity; particularly enervating climate astride the Equator

Nationality: *noun*: Congolese (singular and plural); *adjective*: Congolese or Congo

Population: 3,800,610 (July 2007 CIA est.)

Ethnic groups: Kongo 48%, Sangha 20%, M'Bochi 12%, Teke 17%, Europeans and others 3%

Languages spoken: French (official), Lingala, Monokutuba, and Kikongo and other local languages and dialects

Religions: Christian 50%, indigenous religions 48%, Muslim 2%

Costa Rica

Official name: Republic of Costa Rica

Capital city: San Jose

Internet country code: .cr

Flag description: Five horizontal bands of blue (top), white, red (double width), white, and blue, with the coat of arms in a white elliptical disk on the hoist side of the red band; above the coat of arms a light blue ribbon contains the words "America Central" and just below it near the top of the coat of arms is a white ribbon with the words, *Republica Costa Rica*

National anthem: "Noble patria, tu hermosa bandera" (first line: Noble Homeland, Your Beautiful Flag), lyrics by José María Zeledón, music by Manuel María Gutiérrez

National bird: Yiguirro (Turdus grayi)

National flower: Guaria Morada (Cattleya skinneri)

National symbol of work: la carreta costarricense (Costa Rican ox-cart)

National tree: Guanacaste Tree (Enterolobium ciclocarpum)

Geographical description: Central America, bordering both the Caribbean Sea and the North Pacific Ocean, between Nicaragua and Panama

Total area: 19,730 sq. mi. (51,100 sq. km.)

Climate: Tropical and subtropical; dry season (December to April); rainy season (May to November); cooler in highlands

Nationality: *noun*: Costa Rican(s); *adjective*: Costa Rican

Population: 4,133,884 (July 2007 CIA est.)

Ethnic groups: European (including mestizo) 94%, African 3%, Amerindian 1%, Chinese 1%, other 1%

Languages spoken: Spanish (official), Caribbean Creole English dialect

Religions: Roman Catholic 76.3%, Evangelical 13.7%, Jehovah's Witness 1.3%, other Protestant 0.7%, other 4.8%, none 3.2%

Cote d'Ivoire

Official name: Republic of Cote d'Ivoire

Capital city: Yamoussoukro

Internet country code: .ci

Flag description: Three equal vertical bands of orange (hoist side), white, and green; similar to the flag of Ireland, which is longer and has the colors reversed - green (hoist side), white, and orange; also similar to the flag of Italy, which is green (hoist side), white, and red; design was based on the flag of France

National anthem: "L'Abidjanaise" (Song of Abidjan)

Geographical description: Western Africa, bordering the North Atlantic Ocean, between Ghana and Liberia

Total area: 124,500 sq. mi. (322,500 sq. km.)

Climate: Tropical along coast, semiarid in far north; three seasons - warm and dry (November to March), hot and dry (March to May), hot and wet (June to October)

Nationality: *noun*: Ivoirian(s); *adjective*: Ivoirian

Population: 18,013,409 (July 2007 CIA est.)

Ethnic groups: Akan 42.1%, Voltaiques or Gur 17.6%, Northern Mandes 16.5%, Krous 11%, Southern Mandes 10%, other (including 130,000 Lebanese and 14,000 French) 2.8%

Languages spoken: French (official), 60 local dialects with Dioula the most widely spoken

Religions: Muslim 35-40%, indigenous religions 25-40%, Christian 20-30%

Croatia

Official name: Republic of Croatia

Capital city: Zagreb

Internet country code: .hr

Flag description: Three equal horizontal bands of red (top), white, and blue superimposed by the Croatian coat of arms (red-and-white checkered)

National anthem: "Lijepa nasa domovino" (Our Beautiful Homeland), lyrics by Antun Mihanović, music by Josip Runjanin

Geographical description: Southeastern Europe, bordering the Adriatic Sea, between Bosnia and Herzegovina and Slovenia

Total area: 21,831 sq. mi. (56,542 sq. km.)

Climate: Mediterranean and continental; continental climate predominant with hot summers and cold winters; mild winters, dry summers along coast

Nationality: *noun*: Croat(s), Croatian(s); *adjective*: Croatian

Population: 4,493,312 (July 2007 CIA est.)

Ethnic groups: Croat 89.6%, Serb 4.5%. other (including Bosniak, Hungarian, Slovene, Czech, and Roma) 5.9%

Languages spoken: Croatian 96.1%, Serbian 1%, other and undesignated (including Italian, Hungarian, Czech, Slovak, and German) 2.9%

Religions: Roman Catholic 87.8%, Serbian Orthodox 4.4%, other Christian 0.4%, Muslim 1.3%, other and unspecified 0.9%, none 5.2%

Cuba

Official name: Republic of Cuba

Capital city: Havana

Internet country code: .cu

Flag description: Five equal horizontal bands of blue (top, center, and bottom) alternating with white; a red equilateral triangle based on the hoist side bears a white, five-pointed star in the center

National anthem: "La Bayamesa" (The Bayamo Song) by Pedro Figueredo

Geographical description: Caribbean, island between the Caribbean Sea and the North Atlantic Ocean, 150 km south of Key West, Florida

Total area: 44,200 sq. mi. (110,860 sq. km.)

Climate: Tropical; moderated by trade winds; dry season (November to April); rainy season (May to October)

Nationality: *noun*: Cuban(s); *adjective*: Cuban

Population: 11,394,043 (July 2007 CIA est.)

Ethnic groups: Mulatto 51%, European 37%, African 11%, Chinese 1%

Languages spoken: Spanish

Religions: Roman Catholic, Santeria, Protestant, Jehovah's Witness, Jewish

Cyprus

Official name: Republic of Cyprus

Capital city: Nicosia

Internet country code: .cy

Flag description: White with a copper-colored silhouette of the island (the name Cyprus is derived from the Greek word for copper) above two green crossed olive branches in the center of the flag; the branches symbolize the hope for peace and reconciliation between the Greek and Turkish communities

National anthem: "Imnos pros tin Eleftherian" (The Hymn to Liberty)

National plant: Cyprus cyclamen

National tree: Golden oak (Quercus alnifolia)

Geographical description: Middle East, island in the Mediterranean Sea, south of Turkey

Total area: 3,572 sq. mi. (9,251 sq. km.); 3,355 sq. km. Are in Turkish-controlled north Cyprus

Climate: Temperate; Mediterranean with hot, dry summers and cool winters

Nationality: *noun*: Cypriot(s); *adjective*: Cypriot

Population: 788,457 (July 2007 CIA est.); est. 264,000 reside in Turkish-controlled north Cyprus

Ethnic groups: Greek 77%, Turkish 18%, other 5%

Languages spoken: Greek, Turkish, English

Religions: Greek Orthodox 78%, Muslim 18%, other (including Maronite and Armenian Apostolic) 4%

Czech Republic

Official name: Czech Republic

Capital city: Prague

Internet country code: .cz

Flag description: Two equal horizontal bands of white (top) and red with a blue isosceles triangle based on the hoist side (identical to the flag of the former Czechoslovakia)

National anthem: "Kde domov muj?" (Where Is My Home?), lyrics by Josef Kajetán Tyl, music by Frantisek Skroup

National symbols: Lion, eagle, linden tree

Geographical description: Central Europe, southeast of Germany

Total area: 30,450 sq. mi. (78,864 sq. km.)

Climate: Temperate; cool summers; cold, cloudy, humid winters

Nationality: noun: Czech(s); adjective: Czech

Population: 10,228,744 (July 2007 CIA est.)

Ethnic groups: Czech 90.4%, Moravian 3.7%, Slovak 1.9%, other (including Roma, Silesian, Polish, and German) 4%

Languages spoken: Czech 94.9%, Slovak 2%, other 2.3%, unidentified 0.8%

Religions: Roman Catholic 26.8%, Protestant 2.1%, other 3.3%, unspecified 8.8%, unaffiliated 59%

Denmark

Official name: Kingdom of Denmark

Capital city: Copenhagen

Internet country code: .dk

Flag description: Red with a white cross that extends to the edges of the flag; the vertical part of the cross is shifted to the hoist side, and that design element of the Dannebrog (Danish flag) was subsequently adopted by the other Nordic countries of Finland, Iceland, Norway, and Sweden

National anthems: Royal anthem: "Kong Christian stod ved højen mast" (King Christian stood by lofty mast), lyrics by Johannes Ewald, original source of melody is unknown; national anthem: "Der er et yndigt land" (There is a lovely land), lyrics by Adam Oehlenschläger, music by Hans Ernst Krøyer

Geographical description: Northern Europe, bordering the Baltic Sea and the North Sea, on a peninsula north of Germany (Jutland); also includes two major islands (Sjaelland and Fyn)

Total area: 16,639 sq. mi. (43,094 sq. km.)

Climate: Temperate; humid and overcast; mild, windy winters and cool summers

Nationality: *noun*: Dane(s); *adjective*: Danish

Population: 5,468,120 (July 2007 CIA est.)

Ethnic groups: Scandinavian, Inuit, Faroese, German, Turkish, Iranian, Somali

Languages spoken: Danish, English, Faroese, Greenlandic (an Inuit dialect), German

Religions: Evangelical Lutheran 95%, other Christian (including other Protestant and Roman Catholic) 3%, Muslim 2%

Djibouti

Official name: Republic of Djibouti

Capital city: Djibouti

Internet country code: .dj

Flag description: Two equal horizontal bands of light blue (top) and light green with a white isosceles triangle based on the hoist side bearing a red five-pointed star in the center

Geographical description: Eastern Africa, bordering the Gulf of Aden and the Red Sea, between Eritrea and Somalia

Total area: 8,450 sq. mi. (21,883 sq. km.)

Climate: Desert; torrid, dry

Nationality: *noun*: Djiboutian(s); *adjective*: Djiboutian

Population: 496,374 (July 2007 CIA est.)

Ethnic groups: Somali 60%, Afar 35%, other (including French, Arab, Ethiopian, and Italian) 5%

Languages spoken: French (official), Arab (official), Somali, Afar

Religions: Muslim 94%, Christian 6%

Dominica

Official name: Commonwealth of Dominica

Capital city: Roseau

Internet country code: .dm

Flag description: Green, with a centered cross of three equal bands - the vertical part is yellow (hoist side), black, and white and the horizontal part is yellow (top), black, and white; superimposed in the center of the cross is a red disk bearing a sisserou parrot encircled by 10 green five-pointed stars edged in yellow; the 10 stars represent the 10 administrative divisions (parishes)

National anthem: "Isle of beauty, isle of splendour" (first line)

National bird: Sisserou parrot

Geographical description: Caribbean, island between the Caribbean Sea and the North Atlantic Ocean, about one-half of the way from Puerto Rico to Trinidad and Tobago

Total area: 290 sq. mi. (754 sq. km.)

Climate: Tropical; moderated by northeast trade winds; heavy rainfall

Nationality: *noun*: Dominican(s); *adjective*: Dominican

Population: 72,386 (July 2007 CIA est.)

Ethnic groups: African 86.8%, mixed African and European 8.9%, Carib Amerindian 2.9%, white 0.8%, other 0.7%

Languages spoken: English (official), French patois

Religions: Roman Catholic 61.4%, Seventh-Day Adventist 6%, Pentecostal 5.6%, Baptist 4.1%, Methodist 3.7%, Church of God 1.2%, Jehovah's Witness 1.2%, other Christian 7.7%, Rastafarian 1.3%, Other (including Muslim and Baha'i) or unspecified 1.6%, none 6.1%

Dominican Republic

Official name: Dominican Republic

Capital city: Santo Domingo

Internet country code: .do

Flag description: A centered white cross that extends to the edges divides the flag into four rectangles - the top ones are blue (hoist side) and red, and the bottom ones are red (hoist side) and blue; a small coat of arms featuring a shield supported by an olive branch (left) and a palm branch (right) is at the center of the cross; above the shield a blue ribbon displays the motto, *Dios, Patria, Libertad* (God, Fatherland, Liberty), and below the shield, *Republica Dominicana* appears on a red ribbon

National bird: "Cigua Palmera"

National flower: Flor de la Caoba

Geographical description: Caribbean, eastern two-thirds of the island of Hispaniola, between the Caribbean Sea and the North Atlantic Ocean, east of Haiti

Total area: 18,704 sq. mi. (48,442 sq. km.)

Climate: Tropical maritime; little seasonal temperature variation; seasonal variation in rainfall

Nationality: *noun*: Dominican(s); *adjective*: Dominican

Population: 9,365,818 (July 2007 CIA est.)

Ethnic groups: Mixed African and European 73%, European 16%, African 11%

Languages spoken: Spanish

Religions: Roman Catholic 95%, other 5%

Ecuador

Official name: Republic of Ecuador

Capital city: Quito

Internet country code: .ec

Flag description: Three horizontal bands of yellow (top, double width), blue, and red with the coat of arms superimposed at the center of the flag

National anthem: info in Spanish at http://www.presidencia.gov.ec/modulos.asp?id=20

Geographical description: Western South America, bordering the Pacific Ocean at the Equator, between Colombia and Peru

Total area: 106,888 sq. mi. (276,840 sq. km.)

Climate: Tropical along coast, becoming cooler inland at higher elevations; tropical in Amazonian jungle lowlands

Nationality: *noun*: Ecuadorian(s); *adjective*: Ecuadorian

Population: 13,755,680 (July 2007 CIA est.)

Ethnic groups: Mestizo (mixed European and Amerindian) 65%, Amerindian 25%, Spanish and other European 7%, African 3%

Languages spoken: Spanish (official), Quechua and other indigenous languages

Religions: Roman Catholic 95%, other 5%

Egypt

Official name: Arab Republic of Egypt

Capital city: Cairo

Internet country code: .eg

Flag description: Three equal horizontal bands of red (top), white, and black; the national emblem (a gold Eagle of Saladin facing the hoist side with a shield superimposed on its chest above a scroll bearing the name of the country in Arabic) centered in the white band; design is based on the Arab Liberation

National anthem: "My homeland, my homeland, my hallowed land" (first line in English translation), lyrics by Younis al-Qadi, music by Sayed Darwish

Geographical description: Northern Africa, bordering the Mediterranean Sea, between Libya and the Gaza Strip, and the Red Sea north of Sudan, and includes the Asian Sinai Peninsula

Total area: 386,000 sq. mi. (1,001,450 sq. km.)

Climate: Desert; hot, dry summers with moderate winters

Nationality: *noun*: Egyptian(s); *adjective*: Egyptian

Population: 80,335,036 (July 2007 CIA est.)

Ethnic groups: Egyptian 98%, Berber, Nubian, Bedouin, and Beja 1%, Greek, Armenian and other European (primarily Italian and French) 1%

Languages spoken: Arabic (official), English, French

Religions: Muslim (mostly Sunni) 90%, Coptic Christian 9%, other Christian 1%

El Salvador

Official name: Republic of El Salvador

Capital city: San Salvador

Internet country code: .sv

Flag description: Three equal horizontal bands of blue (top), white, and blue with the national coat of arms centered in the white band; the coat of arms features a round emblem encircled by the words *Republica de El Salvador en la America Central*

National anthem: "Saludemos la patria orgullosos" (first line of chorus), lyrics by Juan José Cañas, music by Juan Aberle

National bird: Torogoz or Talapo

National flower: Izote flower

National tree: Maquilishuat

Geographical description: Central America, bordering the North Pacific Ocean, between Guatemala and Honduras

Total area: 8,008 sq. mi. (20,742 sq. km.)

Climate: Tropical; rainy season (May to October); dry season (November to April); tropical on coast; temperate in uplands

Nationality: *noun*: Salvadoran(s); *adjective*: Salvadoran

Population: 6,948,073 (July 2007 CIA est.)

Ethnic groups: Mestizo 90%, European 9%, Amerindian 1%

Languages spoken: Spanish, Nahua

Religions: Roman Catholic about 48%, Protestant 28%, other Christian less than 5%, none 14.6%

Equatorial Guinea

Official name: Republic of Equatorial Guinea

Capital city: Malabo

Internet country code: .gq

Flag description: Three equal horizontal bands of green (top), white, and red with a blue isosceles triangle based on the hoist side and the coat of arms centered in the white band; the coat of arms has six yellow six-pointed stars (representing the mainland and five offshore islands) above a gray shield bearing a silk-cotton tree and below which is a scroll with the motto *Unidad, Paz, Justicia* (Unity, Peace, Justice)

Geographical description: Western Africa, bordering the Bight of Biafra, between Cameroon and Gabon

Total area: 10,827 sq. mi. (28,050 sq. km.)

Climate: Tropical; always hot, humid

Nationality: *noun*: Equatorial Guinean(s) or Equatoguinean(s); *adjective*: Equatorial Guinean or Equatoguinean

Population: 551,201 (July 2007 CIA est.)

Ethnic groups: Fang 85.7%, Bubi 6.5%, Mdowe 3.6%, Annobon 1.6%, Bujeba1.1%, other 1.4%

Languages spoken: Spanish (official) 67.6%, French (official) and others, including Fang and Bubi 32.4%

Religions: Christian 93%, indigenous religions 5%, other (including Muslim and Baha'i) 2%

Eritrea

Official name: State of Eritrea

Capital city: Asmara

Internet country code: .er

Flag description: Red isosceles triangle (based on the hoist side) dividing the flag into two right triangles; the upper triangle is green, the lower one is blue; a gold wreath encircling a gold olive branch is centered on the hoist side of the red triangle

National emblem: Camel

Geographical description: Eastern Africa, bordering the Red Sea, between Djibouti and Sudan

Total area: 48,000 sq. mi. (125,000 sq. km.)

Climate: Hot, dry desert strip along Red Sea coast; cooler and wetter in the central highlands (heaviest rainfall June to September); semiarid in western hills and lowlands

Nationality: *noun*: Eritrean(s); *adjective*: Eritrean

Population: 4,906,585 (July 2007 CIA est.)

Ethnic groups: Tigrigna 50%, Tigre and Kunama 40%, Afar 4%, Saho (Red Sea coast dwellers) 3%, other 3%

Languages spoken: Afar, Arabic, Tigre and Kunama, Tigrigna, other Cushitic languages

Religions: Sunni Muslim 50%, Orthodox Christian 30%, Roman Catholic 13%, other (including Protestant, Seventh-Day Adventist, Jehovah's Witness, Buddhist, Hindu, and Baha'i) less than 5%, indigenous religions 2%

Estonia

Official name: Republic of Estonia

Capital city: Tallinn

Internet country code: .ee

Flag description: Pre-1940 flag restored by Supreme Soviet in May 1990 - three equal horizontal bands of blue (top), black, and white

National anthem: "My Native Land," lyrics by Johann Voldemar Jannsen, music by Fredrik Pacius

National bird: Swallow

National flower: Cornflower

National stone: Limestone

Geographical description: Eastern Europe, bordering the Baltic Sea and Gulf of Finland, between Latvia and Russia

Total area: 17,462 sq. mi. (45,226 sq. km.)

Climate: Maritime, wet, moderate winters, cool summers

Nationality: *noun*: Estonian(s); *adjective*: Estonian

Population: 1,315,912 (July 2007 CIA est.)

Ethnic groups: Estonian 67.9%, Russian 25.6%, Ukrainian 2.1%, Belarusian 1.3%, Finn 0.9%, other 2.2%

Languages spoken: Estonian (official) 67.3%, Russian 29.7%, other 2.3%, unknown 0.7%

Religions: Evangelical Lutheran 13.6%, Orthodox Christian 12.8%, other Christian (including Methodist, Seventh-Day Adventist, Roman Catholic, Pentecostal) 1.4%, unaffiliated 34.1%, other and unspecified 32%, none 6.1%

Ethiopia

Official name: Federal Democratic Republic of Ethiopia

Capital city: Addis Ababa

Internet country code: .et

Flag description: Three equal horizontal bands of green (top), yellow, and red with a yellow pentagram and single yellow rays emanating from the angles between the points on a light blue disk centered on the three bands; Ethiopia is the oldest independent country in Africa, and the three main colors of her flag were so often adopted by other African countries upon independence that they became known as the pan-African colors

Geographical description: Eastern Africa, west of Somalia

Total area: 472,000 sq. mi. (1,127,127 sq. km.)

Climate: Tropical monsoon with wide topographic-induced variation

Nationality: *noun*: Ethiopian(s); *adjective*: Ethiopian

Population: 76,511,887 (July 2007 CIA est.)

Ethnic groups: Oromo 40%, Amhara 25%, Tigre 7%, Somali 6%, Sidama 9%, Gurage 2%, Wolaita 4%, Afar 4%, other 3%

Languages spoken: Amharic (official), Tigrinya, Arabic, Guaragigna, Oromigna, English, Somali

Religions: Ethiopian Orthodox 40%, Sunni Muslim 45-50%, Protestant 5%, remainder affiliate with indigenous religions

Fiji

Official name: Republic of the Fiji Islands

Capital city: Suva

Internet country code: .fj

Flag description: Light blue with the flag of the United Kingdom in the upper hoist-side quadrant and the Fijian shield centered on the outer half of the flag; the shield depicts a yellow lion above a white field quartered by the cross of Saint George featuring stalks of sugarcane, a palm tree, bananas, and a white dove

National anthem: "Meda Dau Doka" (first line in English: "Blessing grant oh God of nations on the isles of Fiji"), lyrics by Michael Francis Alexander Prescott, music from traditional Fijian song

National symbol: Tabua (whale's tooth)

Geographical description: Oceania, island group in the South Pacific Ocean, about two-thirds of the way from Hawaii to New Zealand

Total area: 7,056 sq. mi. (18,376 sq. km.)

Climate: Tropical marine; only slight seasonal temperature variation

Nationality: *noun*: Fiji Islander or Fijian(s); *adjective*: Fiji or Fijian ("Fijian" should only be used to describe a thing or person of indigenous Fijian origin)

Population: 918,675 (July 2007 CIA est.)

Ethnic groups: Fijian 54.8%, Indian 37.4%, other (including European, Chinese, other Pacific Islanders) 7.9%

Languages spoken: English (official), Fijian (official), Hindi

Religions: Methodist 34.5%, Roman Catholic 7.2%, Assembly of God 3.8%, Seventh-Day Adventist 2.6%, other Christian 4.9%, Hindu 34% (Sanatan 25%, Arya Samaj 1.2%, other Hindu 7.8%), Sunni Muslim 4.2%, other Muslim 2.8%, other or unspecified 5.6%, none 0.3%

Finland

Official name: Republic of Finland

Capital city: Helsinki

Internet country code: .fi

Flag description: White with a blue cross extending to the edges of the flag; the vertical part of the cross is shifted to the hoist side in the style of the Dannebrog (Danish flag)

National anthem: "Maamme" (translated from the Swedish "Vårt land" [Our Land]), lyrics by Johan Ludvig Runeberg, music by Fredrik Pacius

National animal: Brown bear (Ursus arctos)

National bird: Whooper swan (Cygnus Cygnus)

National fish: Perch (Perca fluviatilis)

National flower: Lily-of-the-valley (Convallaria majalis)

National rock: Granite

National tree: Birch (Betula pendula)

Geographical description: Northern Europe, bordering the Baltic Sea, Gulf of Bothnia, and Gulf of Finland, between Sweden and Russia

Total area: 130,558 sq. mi. (338,144 sq. km.)

Climate: Cold temperate; potentially subarctic but comparatively mild because of moderating influence of the North Atlantic Current, Baltic Sea, and more than 60,000 lakes

Nationality: *noun*: Finn(s); *adjective*: Finnish

Population: 5,238,460 (July 2007 CIA est.)

Ethnic groups: Finn 93.4%, Swede 5.7%, Russian 0.4%, Estonian 0.2%, Roma 0.2%, Sami 0.1%

Languages spoken: Finnish (official) 92%, Swedish (official) 5.6%, other (including Sami and Russian) 2.4%

Religions: Lutheran Church of Finland 84.2%, Orthodox Church 1.1%, other Christian 1.1%, other 0.1%, none 13.5%

France

Official name: French Republic

Capital city: Paris

Internet country code: .fr (territories' codes are French Guinea .gf, Guadeloupe .gp, Martinique .mq, and Reunion .re)

Flag description: three equal vertical bands of blue (hoist side), white, and red; known as the "Le drapeau tricolore" (French Tricolor), the origin of the flag dates to 1790 and the French Revolution; the official flag for all French dependent areas

National anthem: "La Marseillaise" by Rouget de Lisle

National emblem: Gallic rooster

National motto: "Liberté, Egalité, Fraternité" (Liberty, Equality, Fraternity)

Geographical description: The continental territory is considered "metropolitan France" and is located in western Europe, bordering the Bay of Biscay and English Channel, between Belgium and Spain, southeast of the United Kingdom; bordering the Mediterranean Sea, between Italy and Spain.

Locations of French territories are as follows:

French Guiana: Northern South America, bordering the North Atlantic Ocean, between Brazil and Suriname

Guadeloupe: Caribbean, islands between the Caribbean Sea and the North Atlantic Ocean, southeast of Puerto Rico

Martinique: Caribbean, island between the Caribbean Sea and North Atlantic Ocean, north of Trinidad and Tobago

Reunion: Southern Africa, island in the Indian Ocean, east of Madagascar

Total area: 212,741 sq. mi. (551,000 sq. km.)

Climate: *metropolitan France:* generally cool winters and mild summers, but mild winters and hot summers along the Mediterranean; occasional strong, cold, dry, north-to-northwesterly wind known as mistral

French Guiana: tropical; hot, humid; little seasonal temperature variation

Guadeloupe and Martinique: subtropical tempered by trade winds; moderately high humidity; rainy season (June to October); vulnerable to devastating cyclones (hurricanes) every eight years on average

Reunion: tropical, but temperature moderates with elevation; cool and dry (May to November), hot and rainy (November to April)

Nationality: *noun*: Frenchman(men), Frenchwoman(women); *adjective*: French

Population: Total including territories: 63,718,187; metropolitan France only: 60,876,136 (July 2007 CIA est.)

Ethnic groups: Metropolitan France: Celtic and Latin with Teutonic, Slavic, African, Indochinese, and Basque minorities

Territories: African, European, mixed African and European, East Indian, Chinese, Amerindian

Languages spoken: French 100% (declining dialects and languages in metropolitan France include Provencal, Breton, Alsatian, Corsican, Catalan, Basque, Flemish; French and various Creole patois spoken in territories)

Religions: metropolitan France: Roman Catholic 83-88%, Muslim 5-10%, Protestant 2%, Jewish 1%, unaffiliated 4%; territories: Roman Catholic, Protestant, Hindu, Muslim, Buddhist, and others

Gabon

Official name: Gabonese Republic

Capital city: Libreville

Internet country code: .ga

Flag description: Three equal horizontal bands of green (top), yellow, and blue

National anthem: "La Concorde"

Motto: "Gouvernement du peuple, par le peuple et pour le peuple"

Geographical description: Western Africa, bordering the Atlantic Ocean at the Equator, between Republic of the Congo and Equatorial Guinea

Total area: 103,347 sq. mi. (267,667 sq. km.)

Climate: Tropical; always hot, humid

Nationality: *noun*: Gabonese (singular and plural); *adjective*: Gabonese

Population: 1,454,867 (July 2007 CIA est.)

Ethnic groups: Approximately 40 Bantu tribes, including Fang, Bapounou, Nzebi, and Obamba; about 150,000 expatriates from Europe and elsewhere in Africa

Languages spoken: French (official), Fang, Myene, and other local languages

Religions: Christian 55%-75%, indigenous religions and Muslim less than 1%

The Gambia

Official name: Republic of The Gambia

Capital city: Banjul

Internet country code: .gm

Flag description: Three equal horizontal bands of red (top), blue with white edges, and green

National anthem: "For The Gambia, our homeland" (first line), adapted from the traditional Mandinka song "Foday Kaba Dumbuya"

Geographical description: Western Africa, bordering the North Atlantic Ocean and Senegal

Total area: 4,361 sq. mi. (11,300 sq. km.)

979

Climate: Tropical; hot, rainy season (June to November); cooler, dry season (November to May)

Nationality: *noun*: Gambian(s); *adjective*: Gambian

Population: 1,688,359 (July 2007 CIA est.)

Ethnic groups: Mandinka 42%, Fula 18%, Wolof 16%, Jola 10%, Serahuli 9%, other African 4%, non-African 1%

Languages spoken: English (official), Mandinka, Wolof, Fula, and other indigenous languages

Religions: Muslim 90%, Christian 9%, indigenous religions 1%

Georgia

Official name: Georgia

Capital city: Tbilisi

Internet country code: .ge

Flag description: White rectangle, in its central portion a red cross connecting all four sides of the flag; in each of the four corners is a small red bolnur-katskhuri cross; the five-cross flag appears to date back to the 14th century

National anthem: "Freedom" (translated by Irakli Charkviani), lyrics by David Magradze, music by Zakaria Paliashvili

Geographical description: Southwestern Asia, bordering the Black Sea, between Turkey and Russia

Total area: 26,911 sq. mi. (69,700 sq. km.)

Climate: Warm and pleasant; Mediterranean-like on Black Sea coast

Nationality: noun: Georgian(s); adjective: Georgian

Population: 4,646,003 (July 2007 CIA est.)

Ethnic groups: Georgian 83.8%, Azeri 6.5%, Armenian 5.7%, Russian 1.5%, other 2.5%

Languages spoken: Georgian (official) 71%, Russian 9%, Armenian 7%, Azeri 6%, other 7%; Abkhaz is the official language in the Autonomous Republic of Abkhazia

Religions: Orthodox Christian 83.9%, Muslim 9.9%, Armenian Apostolic 3.9&, Catholic 0.8%, other 0.8%, none 0.7%

Germany

Official name: Federal Republic of Germany

Capital city: Berlin

Internet country code: .de

Flag description: Three equal horizontal bands of black (top), red, and gold

National anthem: Third verse of "Das Lied der Deutschen" by August Heinrich Hoffmann von Fallersleben, sung to Joseph Haydn's "Kaiserhymne"

Geographical description: Central Europe, bordering the Baltic Sea and the North Sea, between the Netherlands and Poland, south of Denmark

Total area: 137,821 sq. mi. (357,000 sq. km.)

Climate: Temperate and marine; cool, cloudy, wet winters and summers; occasional warm mountain (foehn) wind

Nationality: *noun*: German(s); *adjective*: German

Population: 82,400,996 (July 2007 CIA est.)

Ethnic groups: German 91.5%, Turkish 2.4%, other (including Greek, Italian, Polish, Russian, Serbo-Croatian, Spanish) 6.1%

Languages spoken: German

Religions: Protestant 34%, Roman Catholic 34%, Muslim 3.7%, unaffiliated or other 28.3%

Ghana

Official name: Republic of Ghana

Capital city: Accra

Internet country code: .gh

Flag description: Three equal horizontal bands of red (top), yellow, and green with a large black five-pointed star centered in the yellow band; uses the popular pan-African colors of Ethiopia; similar to the flag of Bolivia, which has a coat of arms centered in the yellow band

National anthem: "God bless our homeland Ghana" (first line)

Geographical description: Western Africa, bordering the Gulf of Guinea, between Cote d'Ivoire and Togo

Total area: 92,100 sq. mi. (238,538 sq. km.)

Climate: Tropical; warm and comparatively dry along southeast coast; hot and humid in southwest; hot and dry in north

Nationality: *noun*: Ghanaian(s); *adjective*: Ghanaian

Population: 22,931,299 (July 2007 CIA est.)

Ethnic groups: Akan 45.3%, Mole-Dagbon 15.2%, Ewe 11.7%, Ga-Dangme 7.3%, Guan 4%, Gurma 3.6%, Grusi 2.6%, Mande-Busanga 1%, other tribes 1.4%, other 7.8%

Languages spoken: Asante 14.8%, Ewe 12.7%, Fante 9.9%, Boron (Brong) 4.6%, Dagomba 4.3%, Dangme 4.3%, Dagarte (Dagaba) 3.7%, Akyem 3.4%, Ga 3.4%, Akuapem 2.9%, other 36.1% (includes English [official])

Religions: Pentecostal/Charismatic 24.1%, Protestant 18.6%, Catholic 15.1%, other Christian 11%, Muslim 15.9%, indigenous religions 8.5%, other 0.7%, none 6.1%

Greece

Official name: Hellenic Republic

Capital city: Athens

Internet country code: .gr

Flag description: Nine equal horizontal stripes of blue alternating with white; there is a blue square in the upper hoist-side corner bearing a white cross; the cross symbolizes Greek Orthodoxy, the established religion of the country

National anthem: "Hymn to Freedom" (English translation by Rudyard Kipling), first two verses of poem by Dionysios Solomos, music by Nicholas Mantzaros

Geographical description: Southern Europe, bordering the Aegean Sea, Ionian Sea, and the Mediterranean Sea, between Albania and Turkey

Total area: 51,146 sq. mi. (131,957 sq. km.)

Climate: Temperate; mild, wet winters; hot, dry summers

Nationality: *noun*: Greek(s); *adjective*: Greek

Population: 10,706,290 (July 2007 CIA est.)

Ethnic groups: Greek 93%, other (foreign citizens) 7% (percents represent citizenship, since Greece does not collect data on ethnicity)

Languages spoken: Greek (official) 99%, other (including English, French, Turkish, Albanian) 1%

Religions: Greek Orthodox 98%, Muslim 1.3%, other (including Jewish, Catholic, Protestant and other religions) 0.7%

Grenada

Official name: Grenada

Capital city: Saint George's

Internet country code: .gd

Flag description: A rectangle divided diagonally into yellow triangles (top and bottom) and green triangles (hoist side and outer side), with a red border around the flag; there are seven yellow five-pointed stars with three centered in the top red border, three centered in the bottom red border, and one on a red disk superimposed at the center of the flag; there is also a symbolic nutmeg pod on the hoist-side triangle (Grenada is the world's second-largest producer of nutmeg, after Indonesia); the seven stars represent the seven administrative divisions

National anthem: "Hail! Grenada, land of ours" (first line)

Geographical description: Caribbean, island between the Caribbean Sea and Atlantic Ocean, north of Trinidad and Tobago

Total area: 133 sq. mi. (344 sq. km.)

Climate: Tropical; tempered by northeast trade winds

Nationality: *noun*: Grenadian(s); *adjective*: Grenadian

Population: 89,971 (July 2007 CIA est.)

Ethnic groups: African 82%, mixed African and European 13%, European and East Indian 5%, and trace of Arawak/Carib Amerindian

Languages spoken: English (official), French patois

Religions: Roman Catholic 44%; Anglican 12%; Pentecostal 11%; Seventh-Day Adventist 11%; Methodist, Presbyterian, Church of God, Baptist, and Evangelical more than 2%; Jehovah's Witnesses, Brethren, Baha'i, Hindu, Moravian, Muslim, Rastafarian, and Salvation Army 1% or less; none 4%

Guatemala

Official name: Republic of Guatemala

Capital city: Guatemala City

Internet country code: .gt

Flag description: Three equal vertical bands of light blue (hoist side), white, and light blue with the coat of arms centered in the white band; the coat of arms includes a green and red quetzal (the national bird) and a scroll bearing the inscription *Libertad 15 de Septiembre de 1821* (the original date of independence from Spain) all superimposed on a pair of crossed rifles and a pair of crossed swords and framed by a wreath

National bird: Quetzal

Geographical description: Central America, bordering the North Pacific Ocean, between El Salvador and Mexico, and bordering the Gulf of Honduras (Caribbean Sea) between Honduras and Belize

Total area: 42,042 sq. mi. (108,890 sq. km.)

Climate: Tropical; hot, humid in lowlands; cooler in highlands

Nationality: *noun*: Guatemalan (s); *adjective*: Guatemalan

Population: 12,728,111 (July 2007 CIA est.)

Ethnic groups: Mestizo (mixed Amerindian-Spanish - in local Spanish called *Ladino*) and European 59.4%, K'iche 9.1%, Kaqchikel 8.4%, Mam 7.9%, Q'eqchi 6.3%, other Mayan 8.6%, indigenous non-Mayan 0.2%, other 0.1%

Languages spoken: Spanish 60%, Amerindian languages 40% (23 officially recognized Amerindian languages, including Quiche, Cakchiquel, Kekchi, Mam, Garifuna, and Xinca)

Religions: Roman Catholic, Protestant, indigenous Mayan

Guinea

Official name: Republic of Guinea

Capital city: Conakry

Internet country code: .gn

Flag description: Three equal vertical bands of red (hoist side), yellow, and green; uses the popular pan-African colors of Ethiopia

Geographical description: Western Africa, bordering the North Atlantic Ocean, between Guinea-Bissau and Sierra Leone

Total area: 95,000 sq. mi. (245,860 sq. km.)

Climate: Generally hot and humid; monsoonal-type rainy season (June to November) with southwesterly winds; dry season (December to May) with northeasterly harmattan winds

Nationality: *noun*: Guinean (s); *adjective*: Guinean

Population: 9,947,814 (July 2007 CIA est.)

Ethnic groups: Peuhl 40%, Malinke 30%, Soussou 20%, other ethnic groups 10%

Languages spoken: French (official), local ethnic languages

Religions: Muslim 85%, Christian 8%, indigenous religions 7%

Guinea-Bissau

Official name: Republic of Guinea-Bissau

Capital city: Bissau

Internet country code: .gw

Flag description: Two equal horizontal bands of yellow (top) and green with a vertical red band on the hoist side; there is a black five-pointed star centered in the red band; uses the popular pan-African colors of Ethiopia

National anthem: "Esta é a Nossa Pátria Bem Amada"

National motto: Unidade, Luta, Progress (Union, Fight, Progress)

Geographical description: Western Africa, bordering the North Atlantic Ocean, between Guinea and Senegal

Total area: 13,946 sq. mi. (36,120 sq. km.)

Climate: Tropical; generally hot and humid; monsoonal-type rainy season (June to November) with southwesterly winds; dry season (December to May) with northeasterly harmattan winds

Nationality: *noun*: Guinean(s) or Bissau-Guinean; *adjective*: Guinean or Bissau-Guinean

Population: 1,472,780 (July 2007 CIA est.)

Ethnic groups: African 99% (includes Balanta 30%, Fula 20%, Manjaca 14%, Mandinga 13%, Papel 7%), European and mulatto less than 1%

Languages spoken: Portuguese (official), Crioulo, French, African languages

Religions: Indigenous religions 50%, Muslim 45%, Christian 5%

Guyana

Official name: Cooperative Republic of Guyana

Capital city: Georgetown

Internet country code: .gy

Flag description: Green, with a red isosceles triangle (based on the hoist side) superimposed on a long, yellow arrowhead; there is a narrow, black border between the red and yellow, and a narrow, white border between the yellow and the green

National anthem: "Dear land of Guyana of rivers and plains" (first line)

Geographical description: Northern South America, bordering the North Atlantic Ocean, between Suriname and Venezuela

Total area: 83,000 sq. mi. (214,970 sq. km.)

Climate: Tropical; hot, humid, moderated by northeast trade winds; two rainy seasons (May to August, November to January)

Nationality: *noun*: Guyanese (singular and plural); *adjective*: Guyanese

Population: 769,095 (July 2007 CIA est.)

Ethnic groups: East Indian 43%, African 30%, Amerindian 9%, other (European, Chinese, and mixed) 17%

Languages spoken: English, Amerindian languages (primarily Carib and Arawak), Guyanese Creole, Caribbean Hindustani (a dialect of Hindi), Urdu

Religions: Christian 50%, Hindu 35%, Muslim 10%, other 5%

Haiti

Official name: Republic of Haiti

Capital city: Port-au-Prince

Internet country code: .ht

Flag description: Two equal horizontal bands of blue (top) and red with a centered white rectangle bearing the coat of arms, which contains a palm tree flanked by flags and two cannons above a scroll bearing the motto *L'union fait la force* (Union Makes Strength)

National anthem: "La Dessalinienne," lyrics by Justin Lhérisson, music by Nicolas Geffrard

Geographical description: Caribbean, western one-third of the island of Hispaniola, between the Caribbean Sea and the North Atlantic Ocean, west of the Dominican Republic

Total area: 10,714 sq. mi. (27,750 sq. km.)

Climate: Tropical; semiarid where mountains in east cut off trade winds

Nationality: noun: Haitian(s); adjective: Haitian

Population: 8,706,497 (July 2007 CIA est.)

Ethnic groups: African 95%, European and mixed African and European 5%

Languages spoken: French (official), Creole (official)

Religions: Roman Catholic 80%, Protestant 16% (Baptist 10%, Pentecostal 4%, Adventist 1%, other 1%), none 1%, other 3%; roughly half of the population practices vodun (voodoo)

Honduras

Official name: Republic of Honduras

Capital city: Tegucigalpa

Internet country code: .hn

Flag description: Three equal horizontal bands of blue (top), white, and blue with five blue, five-pointed stars arranged in an X pattern centered in the white band; the stars represent the members of the former Federal Republic of Central America - Costa Rica, El Salvador, Guatemala, Honduras, and Nicaragua

National anthem: "Your flag is a splendor of sky" (first line in English translation); lyrics by Augusto Constancio Coello, music by Carlos Hartling

National flower: Orquid Rhyncholaelya Digviana

Geographical description: Central America, bordering the Caribbean Sea, between Guatemala and Nicaragua and bordering the Gulf of Fonseca (North Pacific Ocean), between El Salvador and Nicaragua

Total area: 43,278 sq. mi. (112,090 sq. km.)

Climate: Subtropical in lowlands, temperate in mountains

Nationality: *noun*: Honduran(s); *adjective*: Honduran

Population: 7,483,763 (July 2007 CIA est.)

Ethnic groups: Mestizo (mixed Amerindian and European) 90%, Amerindian 7%, African 2%, European 1%

Languages spoken: Spanish, Amerindian languages

Religions: Roman Catholic 97%, Protestant 3%

Hong Kong

Official name: Hong Kong Special Administrative Region [of China]

Internet country code: .hk

Flag description: Red with a stylized, white, five-petal bauhinia flower in the center

Geographical description: Eastern Asia, bordering the South China Sea and China

Total area: 426 sq. mi. (1,104 sq. km.)

Climate: Subtropical monsoon; cool and humid in winter, hot and rainy from spring through summer, warm and sunny in fall

Nationality: *noun*: Chinese or Hong Konger; *adjective*: Chinese or Hong Konger

Population: 6,980,412 (July 2007 CIA est.)

Ethnic groups: Chinese 94.9%, Filipino 2.1%, other 3%

Languages spoken: Cantonese (official) 89.2%, other Chinese dialects 6.4%, English (official) 3.2%, other 1.2%

Religions: Indigenous religions 90%, Christian 10%

Hungary

Official name: Republic of Hungary

Capital city: Budapest

Internet country code: .hu

Flag description: Three equal horizontal bands of red (top), white, and green

National anthem: "Himnusz" (first line in English translation: O, my God, the Magyar bless), lyrics by Ferenc Kölcsey, music by Ferenc Erkel

Geographical description: Central Europe, northwest of Romania

Total area: 35,910 sq. mi. (93,030 sq. km.)

Climate: Temperate; cold, cloudy, humid winters; warm summers

Nationality: *noun*: Hungarian(s); *adjective*: Hungarian

Population: 9,956,108 (July 2007 CIA est.)

Ethnic groups: Magyar 89.9%, Roma 4% (est.), German 2.6%, Serb 2%, Slovak 0.8%, Romanian 0.7%

Languages spoken: Magyar 98.2%, other 1.8%

Religions: Roman Catholic 51.9%, Calvinist 15.9%, Lutheran 3%, Greek Catholic 2.6%, other Christian 1%, other or unspecified 11.1%, unaffiliated 14.5%

Iceland

Official name: Republic of Iceland

Capital city: Reykjavik

Internet country code: .is

Flag description: Blue with a red cross outlined in white extending to the edges of the flag; the vertical part of the cross is shifted to the hoist side in the style of the Dannebrog (Danish flag)

National anthem: "Ó, Gu vors lands" (O, God of Our Land), lyrics by Matthías Jochumsson, music by Sveinbjörn Sveinbjörnsson

Geographical description: Northern Europe, island between the Greenland Sea and the North Atlantic Ocean, northwest of the United Kingdom

Total area: 39,600 sq. mi. (103,000 sq. km.)

Climate: Temperate; moderated by North Atlantic Current; mild, windy winters; damp, cool summers

Nationality: *noun*: Icelander(s); *adjective*: Icelandic

Population: 301,931 (July 2007 CIA est.)

Ethnic groups: Homogeneous mixture of descendants of Norwegians and Celts 94%, population of foreign origin 6%

Languages spoken: Icelandic, English, Nordic languages, German widely spoken

Religions: Lutheran Church of Iceland 85.5%, Reykjavik Free Church 2.1%, Roman Catholic Church 2%, Hafnarfjorour Free Church 1.5%, other Christian 2.7%, other or unspecified 3.8%, unaffiliated 2.4%

India

Official name: Republic of India

Capital city: New Delhi

Internet country code: .in

Flag description: Three equal horizontal bands of saffron (subdued orange) (top), white, and green with a blue chakra (24-spoked wheel) centered in the white band

National anthem: "Jana-gana-mana" by Rabindranath Tagore ("Thou art the ruler of the minds of all people," Tagore's translation of first line)

National animal: Tiger (Panthera tigris)

National bird: Indian peacock (Pavo cristatus)

National flower: Lotus (Nelumbo Nucipera Gaertn)

National fruit: Mango

National song: "Vande Mataram" by Bankimchandra Chatterji (first line translated by Sri Aurobindo: "I bow to thee, Mother")

National tree: Indian fig tree or banyan tree (Ficus bengalensis)

Geographical description: Southern Asia, bordering the Arabian Sea and the Bay of Bengal, between Burma and Pakistan

Total area: 1.27 million sq. mi. (3,287,590 sq. km.)

Climate: Varies from tropical monsoon in south to temperate in north

Nationality: *noun*: Indian(s); *adjective*: Indian

Population: 1,129,866,154 (July 2007 CIA est.)

Ethnic groups: Indo-Aryan 72%, Dravidian 25%, Mongoloid and other 3%

Languages spoken: Hindi (official) 30%, English (official) widely spoken, and 14 other official languages: Bengali, Telugu, Marathi, Tamil, Urdu, Gujarati, Malayalam, Kannada, Oriya, Punjabi, Assamese, Kashmiri, Sindhi, and Sanskrit

Religions: Hindu 80.5%, Muslim 13.4%, Christian 2.3%, Sikh 1.9%, other (including Buddhist, Jain, Parsi) 1.8%, unspecified 0.1%

Indonesia

Official name: Republic of Indonesia

Capital city: Jakarta

Internet country code: .id

Flag description: Two equal horizontal bands of red (top) and white; similar to the flag of Monaco, which is shorter; also similar to the flag of Poland, which is white (top) and red

National anthem: "Indonesia Raya" (Great Indonesia) by Wage Rudolf Supratman

Geographical description: Southeastern Asia, archipelago between the Indian Ocean and the Pacific Ocean

Total area: 736,000 sq. mi. (1,919,440 sq. km.)

Climate: Tropical; hot, humid; more moderate in highlands

Nationality: *noun*: Indonesian(s); *adjective*: Indonesian

Population: 234,693,997 (July 2007 CIA est.)

Ethnic groups: Javanese 45%, Sundanese 14%, Madurese 7.5%, coastal Malays 7.5%, others 26%

Languages spoken: Bahasa Indonesia (official, modified form of Malay), English, Dutch, local dialects (the most widely spoken of which is Javanese)

Religions: Muslim 86.1%, Protestant 5.7%, Roman Catholic 3%, Hindu 1.8%, Buddhist, other, or unspecified 3.4%

Iran

Official name: Islamic Republic of Iran

Capital city: Tehran

Internet country code: .ir

Flag description: Three equal horizontal bands of green (top), white, and red; the national emblem (a stylized representation of the word Allah in the shape of a tulip, a symbol of martyrdom) in red is centered in the white band; *Allah Akbar* (God Is Great) in white Arabic script is repeated 11 times along the bottom edge of the green band and 11 times along the top edge of the red band

Geographical description: Middle East, bordering the Gulf of Oman, the Persian Gulf, and the Caspian Sea, between Iraq and Pakistan

Total area: 636,295 sq. mi. (1.648 million sq. km.)

Climate: Mostly arid or semiarid, subtropical along Caspian coast

Nationality: *noun*: Iranian(s); *adjective*: Iranian

Population: 65,397,521 (July 2007 CIA est.)

Ethnic groups: Persian 51%, Azeri 24%, Gilaki and Mazandarani 8%, Kurd 7%, Arab 3%, Lur 2%, Baloch 2%, Turkmen 2%, other 1%

Languages spoken: Persian and Persian dialects 58%, Turkic languages (besides Turkish) 26%, Kurdish 9%, Luri 2%, Balochi 1%, Arabic 1%, Turkish 1%, other 2%

Religions: Muslim 98% (Shi'a 89%, Sunni 9%), other (includes Zoroastrian, Jewish, Christian, and Baha'i) 2%

Iraq

Official name: Republic of Iraq

Capital city: Baghdad

Internet country code: .iq

Flag description: Three equal horizontal bands of red (top), white, and black with three green five-pointed stars in a horizontal line centered in the white band; the phrase

Allahu Akbar (God Is Great) in green Arabic script - *Allahu* to the right of the middle star and *Akbar* to the left of the middle star - was added in January 1991 during the Persian Gulf crisis; similar to the flag of Syria, which has two stars but no script, Yemen, which has a plain white band, and that of Egypt which has a gold Eagle of Saladin centered in the white band; design is based upon the Arab Liberation colors

Geographical description: Middle East, bordering the Persian Gulf, between Iran and Kuwait

Total area: 168,753 sq. mi. (437,072 sq. km.)

Climate: Mostly desert; mild to cool winters with dry, hot, cloudless summers; northern mountainous regions along Iranian and Turkish borders experience cold winters with occasionally heavy snows that melt in early spring, sometimes causing extensive flooding in central and southern Iraq

Nationality: *noun*: Iraqi(s); *adjective*: Iraqi

Population: 27,499,638 (July 2007 CIA est.)

Ethnic groups: Arab 75%-80%, Kurdish 15%-20%, Turkoman, Chaldean, Assyrian, or others less than 5%

Languages spoken: Arabic (official), Kurdish (official in Kurdish regions), Assyrian, Armenian

Religions: Muslim 97% (Shi'a 60%-65%, Sunni 32%-37%), Christian or other 3%

Ireland

Official name: Ireland

Capital city: Dublin

Internet country code: .ie

Flag description: Three equal vertical bands of green (hoist side), white, and orange

National anthem: "The Soldier's Song" by Peadar Kearney

National emblem: Harp

Geographical description: Western Europe, occupying five-sixths of the island of Ireland in the North Atlantic Ocean, west of Great Britain

Total area: 27,136 sq. mi. (70,282 sq. km.)

Climate: Temperate maritime; modified by North Atlantic Current; mild winters, cool summers; consistently humid; overcast about half the time

Nationality: *noun*: Irishman(men), Irishwoman(women), Irish (collective plural); *adjective*: Irish

Population: 4,109,086 (July 2007 CIA est.)

Ethnic groups: Celtic, English

Languages spoken: English (official), Irish (or Gaelic, also official)

Religions: Roman Catholic 88.4%, Church of Ireland 3%, other Christian 1.6%, Muslim, 1%, Jewish 0.1%, other, unspecified, or none 8.35%

Israel

Official name: State of Israel

Capital city: Jerusalem

Internet country code: .il

Flag description: White with a blue hexagram (six-pointed linear star) known as the Magen David (Shield of David) centered between two equal horizontal blue bands near the top and bottom edges of the flag

National anthem: "Hatikva"

National emblem: Menorah

Geographical description: Middle East, bordering the Mediterranean Sea, between Egypt and Lebanon

Total area: 7,850 sq. mi. (20,330 sq. km.)

Climate: Temperate; hot and dry in southern and eastern desert areas

Nationality: *noun*: Israeli(s); *adjective*: Israeli

Population: 6,426,679 (includes about 187,000 Israeli settlers in the West Bank, about 20,000 in the Israeli-occupied Golan Heights, and fewer than 177,000 in East Jerusalem; July 2007 CIA est.)

Ethnic groups: Jewish 76.4% (Israel-born 67.1%, Europe/America-born 22.6%, Africa-born 5.9%, Asia-born 4.2%), non-Jewish (mostly Arab) 23.6%

Languages spoken: Hebrew (official), Arabic (official for Arab minority), English, Russian

Religions: Jewish 76.4%, Muslim 16%, Arab Christians 1.7%, other Christian 0.4%, Druze 1.6%, unspecified 3.9%

Italy

Official name: Italian Republic

Capital city: Rome

Internet country code: .it

Flag description: Three equal vertical bands of green (hoist side), white, and red; inspired by the French flag brought to Italy by Napoleon in 1797

National anthem: "Fratelli d'Italia" (Brothers of Italy), lyrics by Geoffredo Mameli, music by Michele Novaro

Geographical description: Southern Europe, a peninsula extending into the central Mediterranean Sea, northeast of Tunisia

Total area: 116,303 sq. mi. (301,225 sq. km.)

Climate: Predominantly Mediterranean; Alpine in far north; hot, dry in south

Nationality: *noun*: Italian(s); *adjective*: Italian

Population: 58,147,733 (July 2007 CIA est.)

Ethnic groups: Italian (includes small clusters of German-, French-, and Slovene-Italians in the north and Albanian-Italians and Greek-Italians in the south)

Languages spoken: Italian (official), German (parts of Trentino-Alto Adige region are predominantly German speaking), French (small French-speaking minority in Valle d'Aosta region), Slovene (Slovene-speaking minority in the Trieste-Gorizia area)

Religions: Roman Catholic about 90% (about one-third regularly attend services), other 10% (includes longstanding Protestant and Jewish communities and a growing Muslim immigrant community)

Jamaica

Official name: Jamaica

Capital city: Kingston

Internet country code: .jm

Flag description: Diagonal yellow cross divides the flag into four triangles - green (top and bottom) and black (hoist side and outer side)

National anthem: "Eternal Father bless our land" (first line), composed by Hugh Sherlock, Robert Lightbourne, Mapletoft Poulle and Mrs. Poulle

National bird: Doctor-Bird (Trochilus polytmus) or Swallow-Tail Hummingbird

National flower: Lignum Vitae (Guiacum officinale)

National fruit: Ackee (Blighia sapida)

National motto: "Out of Many One People"

National song: "I Pledge My Heart," lyrics by Victor Stafford Reid, sung to tune of "I Vow to Thee My Country"

National tree: Blue Mahoe (Hibiscus elatus)

Geographical description: Caribbean, island in the Caribbean Sea, south of Cuba

Total area: 4,244 sq. mi. (10,991 sq. km.)

Climate: Tropical; hot, humid; temperate interior

Nationality: noun: Jamaican(s); adjective: Jamaican

Population: 2,780,132 (July 2007 CIA est.)

Ethnic groups: African 90.9%, East Indian 1.3%, Chinese 0.2%, European 0.2%, mixed 7.3%, other 0.1%

Languages spoken: English, patois

Religions: Protestant 62.5% (Seventh-Day Adventist 10.8%, Pentecostal 9.5%, Other Church of God 8.3%, Baptist 7.2%, New Testament Church of God 6.3%, Church of God in Jamaica 4.8%, Church of God of Prophecy 4.3%, Anglican 3.6%, other Christian 7.7%), Roman Catholic 2.6%, other (including Rastafarian and Jewish) or unspecified 14.2%, none 20.9%

Japan

Official name: Japan

Capital city: Tokyo

Internet country code: .jp

Flag description: White with a large red disk (representing the sun without rays) in the center

National anthem: "Kimigayo," lyrics from traditional poem of unknown authorship, music by Hayashi Hiromori

Geographical description: Eastern Asia, island chain between the North Pacific Ocean and the Sea of Japan, east of the Korean Peninsula

Total area: 145,902 sq. mi. (377,864 sq. km.)

Climate: Varies from tropical in south to cool temperate in north

Nationality: *noun*: Japanese (singular and plural); *adjective*: Japanese

Population: 127,433,494 (July 2007 CIA est.)

Ethnic groups: Japanese 98.5%, Koreans 0.5%, Chinese 0.4%, other 0.7%

Languages spoken: Japanese

Religions: observe both Shinto and Buddhist 84%, other 16% (including Christian 0.7%)

Jordan

Official name: Hashemite Kingdom of Jordan

Capital city: Amman

Internet country code: .jo

Flag description: Three equal horizontal bands of black (top), representing the Abbassid Caliphate; white, representing the Ummayyad Caliphate; and green, representing the Fatimid Caliphate; a red isosceles triangle on the hoist side, representing the Great Arab Revolt of 1916, and bearing a small white seven-pointed star symbolizing the seven verses of the opening Sura (Al-Fatiha) of the Koran; the seven points on the star represent faith in One God, humanity, national spirit, humility, social justice, virtue, and aspirations; design is based on the Arab Revolt flag of World War I

National anthem: "A-Sha-al Maleek"

Geographical description: Middle East, northwest of Saudi Arabia

Total area: 34,495 sq. mi. (89.342 sq. km.)

Climate: Mostly arid desert; rainy season in west (November to April)

Nationality: *noun*: Jordanian(s); *adjective*: Jordanian

Population: 6,053,193 (July 2007 CIA est.)

Ethnic groups: Arab 98%, Circassian 1%, Armenian 1%

Languages spoken: Arab (official), English

Religions: Sunni Muslim 92%, Christian (majority Greek Orthodox, but some Greek and Roman Catholics, Syrian Orthodox, Coptic Orthodox, Armenian Orthodox, and Protestant denominations) 6%, other (several small Shi'a Muslim and Druze populations) 2%

Kazakhstan

Official name: Republic of Kazakhstan

Capital city: Astana

Internet country code: .kz

Flag description: Sky blue background representing the endless sky and a gold sun with 32 rays soaring above a golden steppe eagle in the center; on the hoist side is a national ornamentation in gold

National anthem: "We are a valiant people, sons of honour" (first line in English translation), lyrics by Muzafar Alimbayev, Kadyr Myrzaliyev, Tumanbai Moldagaliyev and Zhadyra Daribayeva, music by Mukan Tulebayev, Eugeny Brusilovsky and Latif Khamidi

Geographical description: Central Asia, northwest of China; a small portion west of the Ural River in easternmost Europe

Total area: 1.05 million sq. mi. (2.7 million sq. km.)

Climate: Continental, cold winters and hot summers, arid and semiarid

Nationality: *noun*: Kazakhstani(s); *adjective*: Kazakhstani

Population: 15,284,929 (July 2007 CIA est.)

Ethnic groups: Kazakh 55.8%, Russian 28.3%, Ukrainian 3.3%, Uzbek 2.6%, German 1.8%, Uyghur 1.5%, other 5.0%

Languages spoken: Kazakh (Qazaq, state language) 64.4%, Russian (official, used in everyday business, designated the "language of interethnic communication") 95%

Religions: Sunni Muslim 47%, Russian Orthodox 44%, Protestant 2%, other 7%

Kenya

Official name: Republic of Kenya

Capital city: Nairobi

Internet country code: .ke

Flag description: Three equal horizontal bands of black (top), red, and green; the red band is edged in white; a large warrior's shield covering crossed spears is superimposed at the center

National anthem: "Ee Mungu nguvu yetu" (first line in English translation: "O God of all creation")

Geographical description: Eastern Africa, bordering the Indian Ocean, between Somalia and Tanzania

Total area: 224,960 sq. mi. (582,646 sq. km.)

Climate: Varies from tropical along coast to arid in interior

Nationality: *noun*: Kenyan(s); *adjective*: Kenyan

Population: 36,913,721 (July 2007 CIA est.)

Ethnic groups: Kikuyu 22%, Luhya 14%, Luo 13%, Kalenjin 12%, Kamba 11%, Kisii 6%, Meru 6%, other African 15%, non-African (Asian, European, and Arab) 1%

Languages spoken: English (official), Kiswahili (official), numerous indigenous languages

Religions: Protestant 45%, Roman Catholic 33%, Muslim 10%, indigenous religions 10%, other (including Hindu, Sikh, Jewish, Baha'i) 2%

Kiribati

Official name: Republic of Kiribati

Capital city: Tarawa

Internet country code: .ki

Flag description: The upper half is red with a yellow frigate bird flying over a yellow rising sun, and the lower half is blue with three horizontal wavy white stripes to represent the ocean

Geographical description: Oceania, group of 33 coral atolls in the Pacific Ocean, straddling the Equator; the capital Tarawa is about one-half of the way from Hawaii to Australia; note - on 1 January 1995, Kiribati proclaimed that all of its territory lies in the same time zone as its Gilbert Islands group (UTC +12) even though the Phoenix Islands and the Line Islands under its jurisdiction lie on the other side of the International Date Line

Total area: 266 sq. mi. (719 sq. km.)

Climate: Tropical; marine, hot and humid, moderated by trade winds

Nationality: *noun*: I-Kiribati (singular and plural, pronounced ee-keer-ah-bhass); *adjective*: I-Kiribati

Population: 107,817 (July 2007 CIA est.)

Ethnic groups: Micronesian 98.8%, other 1.2%

Languages spoken: English (official), Gilbertese/I-Kiribati

Religions: Roman Catholic 52%, Protestant (Congregational) 40%, other (includes Seventh-Day Adventist, Muslim, Baha'i, Latter-day Saints, Church of God) 8%

Korea, North

Official name: Democratic People's Republic of Korea

Capital city: Pyongyang

Internet country code: .kp

Flag description: Three horizontal bands of blue (top), red (triple width), and blue; the red band is edged in white; on the hoist side of the red band is a white disk with a red five-pointed star

Geographical description: Eastern Asia, northern half of the Korean Peninsula bordering the Korea Bay and the Sea of Japan, between China and South Korea

Total area: 47,000 sq. mi. (120,410 sq. km.)

Climate: Temperate with rainfall concentrated in summer

Nationality: *noun*: Korean(s); *adjective*: Korean

Population: 23,301,725 (July 2007 CIA est.)

Ethnic groups: Korean; small ethnic Chinese and Japanese populations

Languages spoken: Korean

Religions: Buddhism, Confucianism, Shamanism, Chongdogyo, Christian; autonomous religious activities have been virtually nonexistent since 1945

Korea, South

Official name: Republic of Korea

Capital city: Seoul

Internet country code: .kr

Flag description: White with a red (top) and blue yin-yang symbol in the center; there is a different black trigram from the ancient *I Ching* (Book of Changes) in each corner of the white field

National anthem: "Aegukga" (Love the Country)

National flower: Rose of Sharon (Hibiscus Syriacus L.)

Geographical description: Eastern Asia, southern half of the Korean Peninsula bordering the Sea of Japan and the Yellow Sea

Total area: 38,022 sq. mi. (98,477 sq. km.)

Climate: Temperate, with rainfall heavier in summer than winter

Nationality: *noun*: Korean(s); *adjective*: Korean

Population: 49,044,790 (July 2007 CIA est.)

Ethnic groups: Korean; small Chinese minority

Languages spoken: Korean, English

Religions: Christian 26.3% (Protestant 19.7%, Roman Catholic 6.6%), Buddhist 23.2%, other or unknown 1.3%, none 49.3%

Kuwait

Official name: State of Kuwait

Capital city: Kuwait City

Internet country code: .kw

Flag description: Three equal horizontal bands of green (top), white, and red with a black trapezoid based on the hoist side; design, which dates to 1961, based on the Arab revolt flag of World War I

National anthem: "Kuwait, My Country, May you be safe and glorious!" (first line in English translation), lyrics by Meshari Al-Adwani, music by Ibrahim Al-Soula

Geographical description: Middle East, bordering the Persian Gulf, between Iraq and Saudi Arabia

Total area: 6,880 sq. mi. (17,820 sq. km.)

Climate: Dry desert; intensely hot summers; short, cool winters

Nationality: *noun*: Kuwaiti(s); *adjective*: Kuwaiti

Population: 2,505,559 (includes 1,291,354 non-nationals; July 2007 CIA est.)

Ethnic groups: Kuwaiti 45%, other Arab 35%, South Asian 9%, Iranian 4%, other 7%

Languages spoken: Arab (official), English

Religions: Muslim 80% (Sunni 70%, Shi'a 30% among Kuwaiti citizens), other (includes Christian, Hindu, Parsi, Buddhist, Sikh) 20%

Kyrgyzstan

Official name: Kyrgyz Republic

Capital city: Bishkek

Internet country code: .kg

Flag description: Red field with a yellow sun in the center having 40 rays representing the 40 Kyrgyz tribes; on the obverse side the rays run counterclockwise, on the reverse, clockwise; in the center of the sun is a red ring crossed by two sets of three lines, a stylized representation of the roof of the traditional Kyrgyz yurt

Geographical description: Central Asia, west of China

Total area: 77,181 sq. mi. (198,500 sq. km.)

Climate: Dry continental to polar in high Tien Shan; subtropical in southwest (Fergana Valley); temperate in northern foothill zone

Nationality: *noun*: Kyrgyzstani(s); *adjective*: Kyrgyzstani

Population: 5,284,149 (July 2007 CIA est.)

Ethnic groups: Kyrgyz 67%, Uzbek 14%, Russian 11%, Dungan (ethnic Chinese Muslims) 1%, Uygur 1%, Tatars 0.9%, German 0.3%, other 4.8%

Languages spoken: Kyrgyz (official) 64.7%, Uzbek 13.6%, Russian (official) 12.5%, Dungun 1%, other 8.2%

Religions: Muslim 75%, Russian Orthodox 20%, other 5%

Laos

Official name: Lao People's Democratic Republic

Capital city: Vientiane

Internet country code: .la

Flag description: Three horizontal bands of red (top), blue (double width), and red with a large white disk centered in the blue band

National anthem: "Xat Lao"

Geographical description: Southeastern Asia, northeast of Thailand, west of Vietnam

Total area: 91,430 sq. mi. (236,800 sq. km.)

Climate: Tropical monsoon; rainy season (May to November); dry season (December to April)

Nationality: *noun*: Lao(s) or Laotian(s); *adjective*: Lao or Laotian

Population: 6,521,998 (July 2007 CIA est.)

Ethnic groups: More than 40 ethnic groups, broken down descriptively as follows: Lao Loum (lowland) 68%, Lao Theung (upland) 22%, Lao Soung (highland) including the Hmong and the Yao 9%, ethnic Vietnamese/Chinese 1%

Languages spoken: Lao (official), French, English, local languages

Religions: Buddhist 65%, indigenous religions 32.9%, Christian 1.3%, other and unspecified 0.8%

Latvia

Official name: Republic of Latvia

Capital city: Riga

Internet country code: .lv

Flag description: Three horizontal bands of maroon (top), white (half-width), and maroon

National anthem: "Dievs, svētī Latviju!" (God bless Latvia!), by Kārlis Baumanis (better known as Baumaņu Kārlis)

National bird: Baltā cielava or white wagtail (Motacilla alba)

National flower: Pīpene or daisy (Leucanthemum vulgare, earlier also known as Chrysanthemum leucanthemum)

National insect: Two-spot ladybird (Adalia bipunctata)

National river: Daugava, the "river of fate" or "mother of rivers"

National stone: Amber

National trees: Linden, or lime tree (Tilia cordata, Latvian: liepa) and the oak (Quercus robur, Latvian: ozols)

Geographical description: Eastern Europe, bordering the Baltic Sea, between Estonia and Lithuania

Total area: 24,938 sq. mi. (64,589 sq. km.)

Climate: Maritime; wet, moderate winters

Nationality: *noun*: Latvian(s); *adjective*: Latvian

Population: 2,259,810 (July 2007 CIA est.)

Ethnic groups: Latvian 59%, Russian 28.5%, Belarusian 3.8%, Ukrainian 2.5%, Polish 2.4%, other (including Lithuanian) 3.8%

Languages spoken: Latvian (official; also called Lettish) 58.2%, Russian 37.5%, Lithuanian and other 4.3%

Religions: Roman Catholic 22%, Lutheran 20%, Russian Orthodox 15%

Lebanon

Official name: Lebanese Republic

Capital city: Beirut

Internet country code: .lb

Flag description: Three horizontal bands consisting of red (top), white (middle, double width), and red (bottom) with a green cedar tree centered in the white band

National anthem: "An-Nashid Al-Watani Al-Lubnani" (All for the country, for the glory, for the flag), lyrics by Rashid Nakhle, music by Wadih Sabra

Geographical description: Middle East, bordering the Mediterranean Sea, between Israel and Syria

Total area: 4,015 sq. mi. (10,400 sq. km.)

Climate: Mediterranean; mild to cool, wet winters with hot, dry summers; mountains experience heavy winter snows

Nationality: *noun*: Lebanese (singular and plural); *adjective*: Lebanese

Population: 3,925,502 (July 2007 CIA est.)

Ethnic groups: Arab 95%, Armenian 4%, other 1% (*note*: many Christian Lebanese do not identify themselves as Arab but rather as descendents of the ancient Canaanites and prefer to be called Phoenicians).

Languages spoken: Arabic (official), French, English, Armenian

Religions: Muslim (Shi'a, Sunni, Druze, Isma'ilite, Alawite or Nusayri) 59.7%, Christian (Maronite Catholic, Greek Orthodox, Melkite Catholic, Armenian Orthodox, Syrian Catholic, Armenian Catholic, Syrian Orthodox, Roman Catholic, Chaldean, Assyrian, Copt, Protestant) 39%, other 1.3%

Lesotho

Official name: Kingdom of Lesotho

Capital city: Maseru

Internet country code: .ls

Flag description: Three horizontal stripes of blue (top), white, and green in the proportions of 3:4:3; the colors represent rain, peace, and prosperity respectively; centered in the white stripe is a black Basotho hat representing the indigenous people; the flag was unfurled in October 2006 to celebrate 40 years of independence

Geographical description: Southern Africa, an enclave of South Africa

Total area: 11,718 sq. mi. (30,355 sq. km.)

Climate: Temperate; cool to cold, dry winters; hot, wet summers

Nationality: *noun*: Mosotho (singular), Basotho (plural); *adjective*: Basotho

Population: 2,125,262 (July 2007 CIA est.)

Ethnic groups: Sotho 99.7%, Europeans, Asians, and other 0.3%

Languages spoken: Sesotho (southern Sotho; official), English (official), Zulu, Xhosa

Religions: Christian 80%, including Roman Catholic (majority), Lesotho Evangelical, Anglican, other denominations; other religions include Islam, Hindu, indigenous religions

Liberia

Official name: Republic of Liberia

Capital city: Monrovia

Internet country code: .lr

Flag description: Eleven equal horizontal stripes of red (top and bottom) alternating with white; there is a white five-pointed star on a blue square in the upper hoist-side corner; the design was based on the United States flag

National anthem: "All Hail, Liberia Hail!", lyrics by Daniel Bashiel Warner, music by Olmstead Luca

National bird: Pepperbird

Geographical description: Western Africa, bordering the North Atlantic Ocean, between Cote d'Ivoire and Sierra Leone

Total area: 43,000 sq. mi. (111,369 sq. km.)

Climate: Tropical; hot, humid; dry winters with hot days and cool to cold nights; wet, cloudy summers with frequent heavy showers

Nationality: *noun*: Liberian(s); *adjective*: Liberian

Population: 3,195,931 (July 2007 CIA est.)

Ethnic groups: African 95% (including Kpelle, Bassa, Gio, Kru, Grebo, Mano, Krahn, Gola, Gbandi, Loma, Kissi, Vai, Dei, Bella, Mandingo, and Mende), Americo-Liberians 2.5% (descendants of immigrants from the US who had been slaves), Congo People 2.5% (descendants of immigrants from the Caribbean who had been slaves)

Languages spoken: English (official), more than 15 indigenous languages

Religions: Christian 40%, Muslim 20%, indigenous religions 40%

Libya

Official name: Great Socialist People's Libyan Arab Jamahiriya

Capital city: Tripoli

Internet country code: .ly

Flag description: Plain green; green is the traditional color of Islam (the state religion)

Geographical description: Northern Africa, bordering the Mediterranean Sea, between Egypt and Tunisia

Total area: 679,358 sq. mi. (1,759,540 sq. km.)

Climate: Mediterranean along coast; dry, extreme desert interior

Nationality: *noun*: Libyan(s); *adjective*: Libyan

Population: 6,036,914 (July 2007 CIA est.)

Ethnic groups: Berber and Arab 97%, other (including Greeks, Maltese, Italians, Egyptians, Pakistanis, Turks, Indians, and Tunisians) 3%

Languages spoken: Arabic, English, French, Italian

Religions: Sunni Muslim 97%, other 3%

Liechtenstein

Official name: Principality of Liechtenstein

Capital city: Vaduz

Internet country code: .li

Flag description: Two equal horizontal bands of blue (top) and red with a gold crown on the hoist side of the blue band

National anthem: "Oben am jungen Rhein lehnet sich Liechtenstein an Alpenhöhn" (first line), sung to the music of "God Save the King"

Geographical description: Central Europe, between Austria and Switzerland

Total area: 61.7 sq. mi. (160 sq. km.)

Climate: Continental; cold, cloudy winters with frequent snow or rain; cool to moderately warm, cloudy, humid summers

Nationality: *noun*: Liechtensteiner(s); *adjective*: Liechtenstein

Population: 34,247 (July 2007 CIA est.)

Ethnic groups: Alemannic 86%, Italian, Turkish, and other 14%

Languages spoken: German (official), Alemannic dialect

Religions: Roman Catholic 76.2%, Protestant 7%, unknown 10.6%, other 6.2%

Lithuania

Official name: Republic of Lithuania

Capital city: Vilnius

Internet country code: .lt

Flag description: Three equal horizontal bands of yellow (top), green, and red

Geographical description: Eastern Europe, bordering the Baltic Sea, between Latvia and Russia

Total area: 26,080 sq. mi. (65,200 sq. km.)

Climate: Transitional, between maritime and continental; wet, moderate winters and summers

Nationality: *noun*: Lithuanian(s); *adjective*: Lithuanian

Population: 3,575,439 (July 2007 CIA est.)

Ethnic groups: Lithuanian 84.6%, Polish 6.3%, Russian 5.1%, other or unspecified 4%

Languages spoken: Lithuanian (official) 84.6%, Russian, and Polish

Religions: Roman Catholic 79%, Russian Orthodox 4.1%, Protestant (including Lutheran and Evangelical Christian Baptist) 1.9%, other or unspecified 5.5%, none 9.5%

Luxembourg

Official name: Grand Duchy of Luxembourg

Capital city: Luxembourg

Internet country code: .lu

Flag description: Three equal horizontal bands of red (top), white, and light blue; similar to the flag of the Netherlands, which uses a darker blue and is shorter; design was based on the flag of France

National anthem: "Ons Hémécht" (Our Motherland)

National flower: Rose

Geographical description: Western Europe, between France and Germany

Total area: 999 sq. mi. (2,586 sq. km.)

Climate: Modified continental with mild winters, cool summers

Nationality: *noun*: Luxembourger(s); *adjective*: Luxembourg, Luxembourgian, Luxembourgish

Population: 480,222 (July 2007 CIA est.)

Ethnic groups: Celtic base (with French and German blend), Portuguese, Italian, Slavs (from Montenegro, Albania, and Kosovo), Belgians, French, and Germans

Languages spoken: Luxembourgish (national language), German (administrative language), French (administrative language), English

Religions: Roman Catholic 87%, other (includes Protestant, Jewish, and Muslim) 13%

Macau

Official name: Macau Special Administrative Region [of China]

Internet country code: .mo

Flag description: Light green with a lotus flower above a stylized bridge and water in white, beneath an arc of five gold five-pointed stars: one large in center of arc and four smaller

Geographical description: Eastern Asia, bordering the South China Sea and China

Total area: 10.9 sq. mi. (28.2 sq. km.)

Climate: Subtropical; marine with cool winters, warm summers

Nationality: *noun*: Macanese, Chinese (singular and plural); *adjective*: Macanese, Chinese

Population: 456,989 (July 2007 CIA est.)

Ethnic groups: Chinese 95.7%, Macanese (mixed Portuguese and Asian ancestry) 1%, other 3.3%

Languages spoken: Portuguese (official), Cantonese (official), Hokkien, Mandarin, other Chinese dialects

Religions: Buddhist, Roman Catholic

Macedonia

Official name: Republic of Macedonia

Capital city: Skopje

Internet country code: .mk

Flag description: A yellow sun with eight broadening rays extending to the edges of the red field

Geographical description: Southeastern Europe, north of Greece

Total area: 9,928 sq. mi. (25,713 sq. km.)

Climate: Warm, dry summers and autumns; relatively cold winters with heavy snowfall

Nationality: *noun*: Macedonian(s); *adjective*: Macedonian

Population: 2,055,915 (July 2007 CIA est.)

Ethnic groups: Macedonian 64.2%, Albanian 25.2%, Turkish 3.9%, Roma 2.7%, Serb 1.8%, other 2.2%

Languages spoken: Macedonian 66.5%, Albanian 25.1%, Turkish 3.5%, Roma 1.9%, Serbian 1.2%, other 1.8%

Religions: Eastern Orthodox 64.7%, Muslim 33.3%, other Christian 0.37%, other and unspecified 1.63%

Madagascar

Official name: Republic of Madagascar

Capital city: Antananarivo

Internet country code: .mg

Flag description: Two equal horizontal bands of red (top) and green with a vertical white band of the same width on hoist side

National anthem: "Ry Tanindraza nay malala ô" (Oh, Our Beloved Fatherland)

National motto: "Tanindrazana, Fahafahana, Fandrosoana" (Fatherland, Liberty, Progress)

Geographical description: Southern Africa, island in the Indian Ocean, east of Mozambique

Total area: 228,880 sq. mi. (592,800 sq. km.)

Climate: Tropical along coast, temperate inland, arid in south

Nationality: *noun*: Malagasy (singular and plural); *adjective*: Malagasy

Population: 19,448,815 (July 2007 CIA est.)

Ethnic groups: Malayo-Indonesian (Merina and related Betsileo), Cotiers (mixed African, Malayo-Indonesian, and Arab ancestry - Betsimisaraka, Tsimihety, Antaisaka, Sakalava), French, Indian, Creole, Comoran

Languages spoken: Malagasy, French, English

Religions: Indigenous religions 52%, Christian 41%, Muslim 7%

Malawi

Official name: Republic of Malawi

Capital city: Lilongwe

Internet country code: .mw

Flag description: Three equal horizontal bands of black (top), red, and green with a radiant, rising, red sun centered in the black band

Geographical description: Southern Africa, east of Zambia

Total area: 45,747 sq. mi. (118,484 sq. km.)

Climate: Sub-tropical; rainy season (November to May); dry season (May to November)

Nationality: *noun*: Malawian(s); *adjective*: Malawian

Population: 13,603,181 (July 2007 CIA est.)

Ethnic groups: Chewa, Nyanja, Tumbuka, Yao, Lomwe, Sena, Tonga, Ngoni, Ngonde, Asian, European

Languages spoken: English (official), Chichewa (official), regional dialects, i.e., Chitumbuka, Chiyao, Chilomwe

Religions: Protestant 55%, Roman Catholic 20%, Muslim 20%, indigenous beliefs 3%, other 2%.

Malaysia

Official name: Malaysia

Capital city: Kuala Lumpur

Internet country code: .my

Flag description: Fourteen equal horizontal stripes of red (top) alternating with white (bottom); there is a blue rectangle in the upper hoist-side corner bearing a yellow crescent and a yellow 14-pointed star; the crescent and the star are traditional symbols of Islam; the design was based on the flag of the United States

National anthem: "Negaraku" (My Homeland)

National flower: Hibiscus

Geographical description: Southeastern Asia, peninsula bordering Thailand and northern one-third of the island of Borneo, bordering Indonesia, Brunei, and the South China Sea, south of Vietnam

Total area: 127,316 sq. mi. (329,749 sq. km.)

Climate: Tropical; annual southwest (April to October) and northeast (October to February) monsoons

Nationality: *noun*: Malaysian(s); *adjective*: Malaysian

Population: 24,821,286 (July 2007 CIA est.)

Ethnic groups: Malay 50.4%, Chinese 23.7%, indigenous 11%, Indian 7.1%, other 7.8%

Languages spoken: Bahasa Malaysia (official), English, Chinese (Cantonese, Mandarin, Hokkien, Hakka, Hainan, Foochow), Tamil, Telugu, Malayalam, Panjabi, Thai; in East Malaysia there are several indigenous languages, the most widely spoken of which are Iban and Kadazan

Religions: Muslim 60.4%, Buddhist 19.2%, Christian 9.1%, Hindu 6.3%, Confucianism, Taoism, other traditional Chinese religions 2.6%, other or unknown 1.5%, none 0.8%

Maldives

Official name: Republic of Maldives

Capital city: Male

Internet country code: .mv

Flag description: Red with a large green rectangle in the center bearing a vertical white crescent; the closed side of the crescent is on the hoist side of the flag

National flower: Finifenmaa (Pink rose)

National tree: Dhivehi Ruh (Coconut palm)

Geographical description: Southern Asia, group of atolls in the Indian Ocean, south-southwest of India

Total area: 115 sq. mi. (298 sq. km.)

Climate: Tropical; hot, humid; dry, northeast monsoon (November to March); rainy, southwest monsoon (June to August)

Nationality: *noun*: Maldivian(s); *adjective*: Maldivian

Population: 369,031 (July 2007 CIA est.)

Ethnic groups: South Indians, Sinhalese, Arabs

Languages spoken: Maldivian Dhivehi (dialect of Sinhala, script derived from Arabic), English spoken by most government officials

Religions: Sunni Muslim

Mali

Official name: Republic of Mali

Capital city: Bamako

Internet country code: .ml

Flag description: Three equal vertical bands of green (hoist side), yellow, and red; uses the popular pan-African colors of Ethiopia

National anthem: "Le Mali"

National motto: "Un Peuple, un But, une Foi" (One Nation, One Goal, One Faith)

Geographical description: Western Africa, southwest of Algeria

Total area: 474,764 sq. mi. (1,240,278 sq. km.)

Climate: Subtropical to arid; hot and dry (February to June); rainy, humid, and mild (June to November); cool and dry (November to February)

Nationality: *noun*: Malian(s); *adjective*: Malian

Population: 11,995,402 (July 2007 CIA est.)

Ethnic groups: Mande 50% (Bambara, Malinke, Soninke), Peul 17%, Voltaic 12%, Songhai 6%, Tuareg and Moor 10%, other 5%

Languages spoken: French (official), Bambara 80%, numerous African languages

Religions: Muslim 90%, indigenous 6%, Christian 4%

Malta

Official name: Republic of Malta

Capital city: Valletta

Internet country code: .mt

Flag description: Two equal vertical bands of white (hoist side) and red; in the upper hoist-side corner is a representation of the St. George Cross, edged in red

National anthem: "L-Innu Malti" (first line in English: Guard her, O Lord, as ever Thou hast guarded!), lyrics by Dun Karm Psaila, music by Robert Samut

Geographical description: Southern Europe, islands in the Mediterranean Sea, south of Sicily (Italy)

Total area: 122 sq. mi. (316 sq. km.)

Climate: Mediterranean; mild, rainy winters; hot, dry summers

Nationality: *noun*: Maltese (singular and plural); *adjective*: Maltese

Population: 401,880 (July 2007 CIA est.)

Ethnic groups: Maltese (descendants of ancient Carthaginians and Phoenicians, with strong elements of Italian and other Mediterranean stock)

Languages spoken: Maltese (official), English (official)

Religions: Roman Catholic 98%

Marshall Islands

Official name: Republic of the Marshall Islands

Capital city: Majuro

Internet country code: .mh

Flag description: Blue with two stripes radiating from the lower hoist-side corner - orange (top) and white; there is a white star with four large rays and 20 small rays on the hoist side above the two stripes

National anthem: "Forever Marshall Islands" by President Amata Kabua

Geographical description: Oceania, two archipelagic island chains of 29 atolls, each made up of many small islets, and five single islands in the North Pacific Ocean, about one-half of the way from Hawaii to Australia

Total land area: 70 sq. mi. (181 sq. km.)

Climate: Tropical; hot and humid; wet season May to November; islands border typhoon belt

Nationality: *noun*: Marshallese (singular and plural); *adjective*: Marshallese

Population: 61,815 (July 2007 CIA est.)

Ethnic groups: Marshallese 90%, American, Filipino, Chinese, New Zealander, Australian, other Micronesian (FSM), Kiribati, Korean, and Fijian 10%

Languages spoken: Two major Marshallese dialects from Malayo-Polynesian family; English

Religions: Protestant 54.8%, Assembly of God 25.8%, Roman Catholic 8.4%, Bukot nan Jesus 2.8%, Mormon 2.1%, other Christian 3.6%, other 1%, none 1.5%

Mauritania

Official name: Islamic Republic of Mauritania

Capital city: Nouakchott

Internet country code: .mr

Flag description: Green with a yellow five-pointed star above a yellow horizontal crescent; the closed side of the crescent is down; the crescent, star, and color green are traditional symbols of Islam

National anthem: lyrics taken from poem by Baba Ould Cheikh

Geographical description: Northern Africa, bordering the North Atlantic Ocean, between Senegal and Western Sahara

Total area: 419,212 sq. mi. (1,030,070 sq. km.)

Climate: Desert; constantly hot, dry, dusty

Nationality: *noun*: Mauritanian(s); *adjective*: Mauritanian

Population: 3,270,065 (July 2007 CIA est.)

Ethnic groups: Arab-Berber (White Moor), Arab-Berber-Negroid (Black Moor), Haalpulaar, Soninke, Wolof (Black African Mauritanians)

Languages spoken: Arabic (official), Hassaniya (Arabic dialect), French, Pulaar, Wolof, and Soninke

Religions: Muslim 100%

Mauritius

Official name: Republic of Mauritius

Capital city: Port Louis

Internet country code: .mu

Flag description: Four equal horizontal bands of red (top), blue, yellow, and green

National anthem: "Glory to thee, Motherland" (first line), lyrics by Jean Georges Prosper, music by Philippe Gentil

National flower: Trochetia Boutoniana (Boucle d'Oreille)

Geographical description: Southern Africa, island in the Indian Ocean, east of Madagascar

Total area: 720 sq. mi. (1,865 sq. km.)

Climate: Tropical, modified by southeast trade winds; warm, dry winter (May to November); hot, wet, humid summer (November to May)

Nationality: *noun*: Mauritian(s); *adjective*: Mauritian

Population: 1,250,882 (July 2007 CIA est.)

Ethnic groups: Indo-Mauritian 68%, Creole 27%, Sino-Mauritian 3%, Franco-Mauritian 2%

Languages spoken: Creole (common), French, English (official), Hindi, Urdu, Hakka, Bhojpuri

Religions: Hindu 48%, Roman Catholic 23.6%, Muslim 16.6%, other Christian 8.6%, other 2.5%, unspecified 0.3%, none 0.4%

Mexico

Official name: United Mexican States

Capital city: Mexico City

Internet country code: .mx

Flag description: Three equal vertical bands of green (hoist side), white, and red; the coat of arms (an eagle perched on a cactus with a snake in its beak) is centered in the white band

National anthem: "Mexicanos, al grito de Guerra" (Mexicans, at the cry of war - first line of chorus), lyrics by Francisco González Bocanegra, music by Jaime Nunó

Geographical description: Middle America, bordering the Caribbean Sea and the Gulf of Mexico, between Belize and the United States and bordering the North Pacific Ocean, between Guatemala and the United States

Total area: 761,600 sq. mi. (1,972,500 sq. km.)

Climate: Varies from tropical to desert

Nationality: *noun*: Mexican(s); *adjective*: Mexican

Population: 108,700,891 (July 2007 CIA est.)

Ethnic groups: mestizo (Amerindian-Spanish) 60%, Amerindian or predominantly Amerindian 30%, white 9%, other 1%

Languages spoken: Spanish, various Mayan, Nahuatl, and other regional indigenous languages

Religions: Roman Catholic 76.5%, Protestant 6.3% (Pentecostal 1.4%, Jehovah's Witnesses 1.1%, other 3.8%), other 0.3%, unspecified 13.8%, none 3.1%

Micronesia

Official name: Federated States of Micronesia

Capital city: Palikir

Internet country code: .fm

Flag description: Light blue with four white five-pointed stars centered; the stars are arranged in a diamond pattern

National anthem: "Tis here we are pledging with heart and with hands" (first line)

Geographical description: Oceania, island group in the North Pacific Ocean, about three-quarters of the way from Hawaii to Indonesia

Total area: 270 sq. mi. (702 sq. km.)

Climate: Tropical; heavy year-round rainfall, especially in the eastern islands; located on southern edge of the typhoon belt with occasionally severe damage

Nationality: *noun*: Micronesian(s); *adjective*: Micronesian; Chuukese, Kosraen(s), Pohnpeian(s), Yapese

Population: 107,862 (July 2007 CIA est.)

Ethnic groups: Chuukese 48.8%, Pohnpeian 24.2%, Kosraean 6.2%, Yapese 5.2%, Yap outer islands 4.5%, Asian 1.8%, Polynesian 1.5%, other 6.4%, unknown 1.4%

Languages spoken: English (official and common language), Trukese, Pohnpeian, Yapese, Kosrean, Ulithian, Woleaian, Nukuoro, Kapingamarangi

Religions: Roman Catholic 50%, Protestant 47%, other 3%

Moldova

Official name: Republic of Moldova

Capital city: Chisinau (Kishinev; pronounced kee-shee-now)

Internet country code: .md

Flag description: Same color scheme as Romania - three equal vertical bands of blue (hoist side), yellow, and red; emblem in center of flag is of a Roman eagle of gold outlined in black with a red beak and talons carrying a yellow cross in its beak and a green olive branch in its right talons and a yellow scepter in its left talons; on its breast is a shield divided horizontally red over blue with a stylized ox head, star, rose, and crescent all in black-outlined yellow

National anthem: "Limba noastră-i o comoară" (first line), lyrics by Alexei Mateevici, music by Alexandru Cristea

Geographical description: Eastern Europe, northeast of Romania

Total area: 13,000 sq. mi. (33,843 sq. km.)

Climate: Moderate winters, warm summers

Nationality: *noun*: Moldovan(s); *adjective*: Moldovan

Population: 4,320,490 (July 2007 CIA est.)

Ethnic groups: Moldovan/Romanian 78.2%, Ukrainian 8.4%, Russian 5.8%, Gagauz 4.4%, Bulgarian 1.9%, other 1.3%

Languages spoken: Moldovan (official, virtually the same as the Romanian language), Russian, Ukrainian, Gagauz (a Turkish dialect)

Religions: Eastern Orthodox 98%, Jewish 1.5%, Baptist and other 0.5%

Monaco

Official name: Principality of Monaco

Capital city: Monaco

Internet country code: .mc

Flag description: Two equal horizontal bands of red (top) and white; similar to the flag of Indonesia which is longer and the flag of Poland which is white (top) and red

Geographical description: Western Europe, bordering the Mediterranean Sea on the southern coast of France, near the border with Italy

Total area: 0.8 sq. mi. (1.95 sq. km.)

Climate: Mediterranean with mild, wet winters and hot, dry summers

Nationality: *noun*: Monegasque(s) or Monacan(s); *adjective*: Monegasque or Monacan

Population: 32,671 (July 2007 CIA est.)

Ethnic groups: French 47%, Monegasque 16%, Italian 16%, other 21%

Languages spoken: French (official), English, Italian, Monegasque

Religions: Roman Catholic 90%, other 10%

Mongolia

Official name: Mongolia

Capital city: Ulaanbaatar

Internet country code: .mn

Flag description: Three equal, vertical bands of red (hoist side), blue, and red; centered on the hoist-side red band in yellow is the national emblem (*soyombo* - a columnar arrangement of abstract and geometric representation for fire, sun, moon, earth, water, and the yin-yang symbol)

Geographical description: Northern Asia, between China and Russia

Total area: 604,103 sq. mi. (1,566,500 sq. km.)

Climate: Desert; continental (large daily and seasonal temperature ranges)

Nationality: *noun*: Mongolian(s); *adjective*: Mongolian

Population: 2,951,786 (July 2007 CIA est.)

Ethnic groups: Mongol (mostly Khalkha) 85%, Turkic (mostly Kazakh) 7%, Tungusic 4.6%, other (including Chinese and Russian) 3.4%

Languages spoken: Mongolian, Kazakh, Russian, and English

Religions: Tibetan Buddhist Lamaism 94%, Christian, Muslim, Shamanism 6%

Montenegro

Official name: Republic of Montenegro

Capital city: Podgorica

Internet country code: .me

Flag description: A red field bordered by a narrow golden-yellow stripe with the Montenegrin coat of arms centered

Geographical description: Southeastern Europe, between the Adriatic Sea and Serbia

Total area: 5,381 sq. mi. (13,938 sq. km.)

Climate: Mediterranean climate, hot dry summers and autumns and relatively cold winters with heavy snowfalls inland

Nationality: *noun*: Montenegrin(s); *adjective*: Montenegrin

Population: 684,736 (July 2007 CIA est.)

Ethnic groups: Montenegrin 43%, Serbian 31%, Bosniak 8%, Albanian 5%, other (Croat, Roma) 12%

Languages spoken: Serbian (official; Ijekavian dialect), Bosnian, Albanian, Croatian

Religions: Orthodox 74%, Muslim 18%, Roman Catholic 4%

Morocco

Official name: Kingdom of Morocco

Capital city: Rabat

Internet country code: .ma

Flag description: Red with a green pentacle (five-pointed linear star) known as Sulayman's (Solomon's) seal in the center of the flag; red and green are traditional colors in Arab flags, although the use of red is more commonly associated with the Arab states of the Persian gulf; design dates to 1912

National anthem: "Royaume du Maroc: Garde Royale"

National motto: God, The Country, The King

Geographical description: Northern Africa, bordering the North Atlantic Ocean and the Mediterranean Sea, between Algeria and Western Sahara

Total area: 172,413 sq. mi. (446,550 sq. km.)

Climate: Mediterranean, becoming more extreme in the interior

Nationality: *noun*: Moroccan(s); *adjective*: Moroccan

Population: 33,757,175 (July 2007 CIA est.)

Ethnic groups: Arab-Berber 99.1%, other 0.7%, Jewish 0.2%

Languages spoken: Arabic (official), Berber dialects, French often the language of business, government, and diplomacy

Religions: Muslim 98.7%, Christian 1.1%, Jewish 0.2%

Mozambique

Official name: Republic of Mozambique

Capital city: Maputo

Internet country code: .mz

Flag description: Three equal horizontal bands of green (top), black, and yellow with a red isosceles triangle based on the hoist side; the black band is edged in white; centered in the triangle is a yellow five-pointed star bearing a crossed rifle and hoe in black superimposed on an open white book

National anthem: "Moçambique nossa terra gloriosa!" (Mozambique, our Glorious Land - first line of chorus)

Geographical description: Southeastern Africa, bordering the Mozambique Channel, between South Africa and Tanzania

Total area: 309,494 sq. mi. (801,590 sq. km.)

Climate: Tropical to subtropical

Nationality: *noun*: Mozambican(s); *adjective*: Mozambican

Population: 20,905,585 (July 2007 CIA est.)

Ethnic groups: African (Makhuwa, Tsonga, Lomwe, Sena, and others) 99.66%, Europeans 0.06%, Euro-Africans 0.2%, Indians 0.08%

Languages spoken: Emakhuwa 26.1%, Xichangana 11.3%, Portuguese 8.8% (official; spoken by 27% of population as a second language), Elomwe 7.6%, Cisena 6.8%, Echuwabo 5.8%, other Mozambican languages 32%, other foreign languages 0.3%, unspecified 1.3%

Religions: Roman Catholic 23.8%, Muslim 17.8%, Zionist Christian 17.5%, other 17.8%, none 23.1%

Namibia

Official name: Republic of Namibia

Capital city: Windhoek

Internet country code: .na

Flag description: A wide red stripe edged by narrow white stripes divides the flag diagonally from lower hoist corner to upper fly corner; the upper hoist-side triangle is blue and charged with a yellow 12-rayed sunburst; the lower fly-side triangle is green

National anthem: "Namibia Land of the Brave"

National motto: Unity, Liberty, Justice

Geographical description: Southern Africa, bordering the South Atlantic Ocean, between Angola and South Africa

Total area: 320,827 sq. mi. (823,145 sq. km.)

Climate: Desert; hot, dry; rainfall sparse and erratic

Nationality: noun: Namibian(s); adjective: Namibian

Population: 2,055,080 (July 2007 CIA est.)

Ethnic groups: Black 87%; white 6%; mixed race 7%. About 50% of the population belong to Ovambo ethnic group, and 9% to the Kavango ethnic group. Other ethnic groups are: Herero 7%, Damara 7%, Nama 5%, Caprivian 4%, San (Bushmen) 3%, Baster 2%, and Tswana 0.5%.

Languages spoken: English (official) 7%, Afrikaans common language of most of the population and about 60% of the white population, German 32%, indigenous languages (including Oshivambo, Herero, Nama) 1%

Religions: Christian 80% to 90% (at least 50% Lutheran 50%), indigenous religions 10% to 20%

Nauru

Official name: Republic of Nauru

Capital city: no official capital; government offices in Yaren District

Internet country code: .nr

Flag description: Blue with a narrow, horizontal yellow stripe across the center and a large white 12-pointed star below the stripe on the hoist side; the star indicates the country's location in relation to the Equator (the yellow stripe) and the 12 points symbolize the 12 original tribes of Nauru

National anthem: "Nauru bwiema" (Nauru Our Homeland)

Geographical description: Oceania, island in the South Pacific Ocean, south of the Marshall Islands

Total area: 8.1 sq. mi. (21 sq. km.)

Climate: Tropical with a monsoonal pattern; rainy season (November to February)

Nationality: *noun*: Nauruan(s); *adjective*: Nauruan

Population: 13,528 (July 2007 CIA est.)

Ethnic groups: Nauruan 58%, other Pacific Islander 26%, Chinese 8%, European 8%

Languages spoken: Nauruan (official; a distinct Pacific Island language), English widely understood, spoken, and used for most government and commercial purposes

Religions: Protestant 66.7, Roman Catholic 33.3%

Nepal

Official name: Nepal

Capital city: Kathmandu

Internet country code: .np

Flag description: Red with a blue border around the unique shape of two overlapping right triangles; the smaller, upper triangle bears a white stylized moon and the larger, lower triangle bears a white 12-pointed sun

National bird: Impean Pheasant Danfe

National flower: Rhododendron Arboreum (Lali Gurans)

Geographical description: Southern Asia, between China and India

Total area: 56,136 sq. mi. (147,181 sq. km.)

Climate: Varies from cool summers and severe winters in north to subtropical summers and mild winters in south

Nationality: *noun*: Nepalese (singular and plural); *adjective*: Nepalese

Population: 28,901,790 (July 2007 CIA est.)

Ethnic groups: Chhettri 15.5%, Brahman-Hill 12.5%, Magar 7%, Tharu 6.6%, Tamang 5.5%, Newar 5.4%, Muslim 4.2%, Kami 3.9%, Yadav 3.9%, other 32.7%, unspecified 2.8%

Languages spoken: Nepali 47.8%, Maithali 12.1%, Bhojpuri 7.4%, Tharu (Dagaura/Rana) 5.8%, Tamang 5.1%, Newar 3.6%, Magar 3.3%, Awadhi 2.4%, other 10%, unspecified 2.5%

Religions: Hindu 80.6%, Buddhist 10.7%, Muslim 4.2%, Kirant 3.6%, other 0.9%

Netherlands

Official name: Kingdom of the Netherlands

Capital city: Amsterdam

Internet country code: .nl

Flag description: Three equal horizontal bands of red (top), white, and blue; similar to the flag of Luxembourg, which uses a lighter blue and is longer; one of the oldest flags in constant use, originating with William I, Prince of Orange, in the latter half of the 16th century

National anthem: "Wilhelmus"

Geographical description: Western Europe, bordering the North Sea, between Belgium and Germany

Total area: 16,485 sq. mi. (41,526 sq. km.)

Climate: Temperate; marine; cool summers and mild winters

Nationality: *noun*: Dutchman(men), Dutchwoman(women); *adjective*: Dutch

Population: 16,570,613 (July 2007 CIA est.)

Ethnic groups: Dutch 83%, other 17% (of which 9% are non-Western origin, mainly Turks, Moroccans, Antilleans, Surinamese, and Indonesians)

Languages spoken: Dutch, Frisian

Religions: Roman Catholic 31%, Dutch Reformed 13%, Calvinist 7%, Muslim 5.5%, other 2.5%, none 41%

Netherlands Antilles

Official name: Netherlands Antilles

Capital city: Willemstad (on Curacao)

Internet country code: .an

Flag description: White, with a horizontal blue stripe in the center superimposed on a vertical red band, also centered; five white, five-pointed stars are arranged in an oval pattern in the center of the blue band; the five stars represent the five main islands of Bonaire, Curacao, Saba, Sint Eustatius, and Sint Maarten

Geographical description: Caribbean, two island groups in the Caribbean Sea - composed of five islands, Curacao and Bonaire located off the coast of Venezuela, and Sint Maarten, Saba, and St. Eustatius lie east of the United States Virgin Islands

Total area: 597 sq. mi. (960 sq. km.)

Climate: tropical; ameliorated by northeast trade winds

Nationality: *noun*: Dutch Antillean(s); *adjective*: Dutch Antillean

Population: 223,652 (July 2007 CIA est.)

Ethnic groups: Mixed African-Amerindian-European 85%, other 15% (includes Carib Amerindian, European, East Asian) 15%

Languages spoken: Papiamento (a Spanish-Portuguese-Dutch-English dialect) 65,4%, English 15.9%, Dutch 7.3% (official), Spanish 6.1%, Creole 1.6%, other 1.9%, unspecified 1.8%

Religions: Roman Catholic 72%, Pentecostal 4.9%, Protestant 3.5%, Seventh-Day Adventist 3.1%, Methodist 2.9%, Jehovah's Witnesses 1.7%, other Christian 4.2%, Jewish 1.3%, other or unspecified 1.2%, none 5.2%

New Zealand

Official name: New Zealand

Capital city: Wellington

Internet country code: .nz

Flag description: Blue with the flag of the United Kingdom in the upper hoist-side quadrant with four red five-pointed stars edged in white centered in the outer half of the flag; the stars represent the Southern Cross constellation

National anthems: "God Defend New Zealand" and "God Save the Queen"

Geographical description: Oceania, islands in the South Pacific Ocean, southeast of Australia

Total area: 104,440 sq. mi. (270,500 sq. km.)

Climate: Temperate with sharp regional contrasts

Nationality: *noun*: New Zealander(s); *adjective*: New Zealand

Population: 4,115,771 (July 2007 CIA est.)

Ethnic groups: European 77%, Maori 14.6%, other Polynesian Pacific peoples 6.9%, other 1.5%

Languages spoken: English (official), Maori (official), Sign Language (official)

Religions: Anglican 14.9%, Roman Catholic 12.4%, Presbyterian 10.9%, Methodist 2.9%, Pentecostal 1.7%, Baptist 1.3%, other Christian 9.4%, other 3.3%, unspecified 17.2%, none 26%

Nicaragua

Official name: Republic of Nicaragua

Capital city: Managua

Internet country code: .ni

Flag description: Three equal horizontal bands of blue (top), white, and blue with the national coat of arms centered in the white band; the coat of arms features a triangle encircled by the words *Republica de Nicaragua* on the top and *America Central* on the bottom; similar to the flag of El Salvador, which features a round emblem centered in the white band; also similar to the flag of Honduras, which has five blue stars arranged in an X pattern centered in the white band

Geographical description: Central America, bordering both the Caribbean Sea and the North Pacific Ocean, between Costa Rica and Honduras

Total area: 59,998 sq. mi. (129,494 sq. km.)

Climate: Tropical in lowlands, cooler in highlands

Nationality: *noun*: Nicaraguan(s); *adjective*: Nicaraguan

Population: 5,675,356 (July 2007 CIA est.)

Ethnic groups: Mestizo (mixed Amerindian and European) 69%, white 17%, black Jamaican 9%, Amerindian 5%

Languages spoken: Spanish (official) 97.5%, Miskito 1.7%, other 0.8% (English and indigenous languages on Atlantic coast)

Religions: Roman Catholic 72.9%, Evangelical 15.1%, Moravian 1.5%, Episcopal 0.1%, other 1.9%, none 8.5%

Niger

Official name: Republic of Niger

Capital city: Niamey

Internet country code: .ne

Flag description: Three equal horizontal bands of orange (top), white, and green with a small orange disk (representing the sun) centered in the white band

National motto: Fraternity – Work – Progress

Geographical description: Western Africa, southeast of Algeria

Total area: 490,000 sq. mi. (1,267,000 sq. km.)

Climate: Desert; mostly hot, dry, dusty; tropical in extreme south

Nationality: *noun*: Nigerien(s); *adjective*: Nigerien

Population: 12,894,865 (July 2007 CIA est.)

Ethnic groups: Haoussa 55.4%, Djerma Sonrai 21%, Touareg 9.3%, Peuhl 8.5%, Kanouri Manga 4.7%, other 1.2%

Languages spoken: French (official), Hausa, Djerma, Fulfulde, Kanuri, Tamachek, Toubou, Gourmantche, Arabic

Religions: Muslim 85%, other (includes indigenous religions and Christian) 15%

Nigeria

Official name: Federal Republic of Nigeria

Capital city: Abuja

Internet country code: .ng

Flag description: Three equal vertical bands of green (hoist side), white, and green

National motto: "Unity and Faith, Peace and Progress"

Geographical description: Western Africa, bordering the Gulf of Guinea, between Benin and Cameroon

Total area: 356,700 sq. mi. (923,768 sq. km.)

Climate: Varies; equatorial in south, tropical in center, arid in north

Nationality: *noun*: Nigerian(s); *adjective*: Nigerian

Population: 135,031,164 (July 2007 CIA est.)

Ethnic groups: Nigeria, Africa's most populous country, is composed of more than 250 ethnic groups; the following are the most populous and politically influential: Hausa and Fulani 29%, Yoruba 21%, Igbo (Ibo) 18%, Ijaw 10%, Kanuri 4%, Ibibio 3.5%, Tiv 2.5%

Languages spoken: English (official), Hausa, Yoruba, Igbo (Ibo), Fulani

Religions: Muslim 50%, Christian 40%, indigenous religions 10%

Niue

Official name: Niue

Capital city: Alofi

Internet country code: .nu

Flag description: Yellow with the flag of the United Kingdom in the upper hoist-side quadrant; the flag of the

United Kingdom bears five yellow five-pointed stars - a large one on a blue disk in the center and a smaller one on each arm of the bold red cross

Geographical description: Oceania, island in the South Pacific Ocean, east of Tonga

Total area: 100 sq. mi. (260 sq. km.)

Climate: Tropical; modified by southeast trade winds

Nationality: *noun*: Niuean(s); *adjective*: Niuean

Population: 1,492 (July 2007 CIA est.)

Ethnic groups: Niuen 78.2%, Pacific Islander 10.2%, European 4.5%, mixed 3.9%, Asian 0.2%, unspecified 3%

Languages spoken: Niuean, a Polynesian language closely related to Tongan and Samoan; English

Religions: Ekalesia Niue (Niuean Church - a Protestant church closely related to the London Missionary Society) 61.1%, Latter-Day Saints 8.8%, Roman Catholic 7.2%, Jehovah's Witnesses 2.4%, Seventh-Day Adventist 1.4%, other 8.4%, unspecified 8.7%, none 1.9%

Norway

Official name: Kingdom of Norway

Capital city: Oslo

Internet country code: .no

Flag description: Red with a blue cross outlined in white that extends to the edges of the flag; the vertical part of the cross is shifted to the hoist side in the style of the Dannebrog (Danish flag)

Geographical description: Northern Europe, bordering the North Sea and the North Atlantic Ocean, west of Sweden

Total area: 148,725 sq. mi. (385,199 sq. km.)

Climate: Temperate along coast, modified by North Atlantic Current; colder interior with increased precipitation and colder summers; rainy year-round on west coast

Nationality: *noun*: Norwegian(s); *adjective*: Norwegian

Population: 4,627,926 (July 2007 CIA est.)

Ethnic groups: Norwegian (Nordic, Alpine, Baltic); Sami, a racial-cultural minority of 40,000; foreign nationals (415,000) from Nordic and other countries

Languages spoken: Bokmal Norwegian (official), Nynorsk Norwegian (official), small Sami- and Finnish-speaking minorities; note - Sami is official in six municipalities

Religions: Church of Norway 85.7%, Pentecostal 1%, Roman Catholic 1%, other Christian 2.4%, Muslim 1.8%, other 8.1%

Oman

Official name: Sultanate of Oman

Capital city: Muscat

Internet country code: .om

Flag description: Three horizontal bands of white, red, and green of equal width with a broad, vertical red band on the hoist side; the national emblem (a khanjar dagger in its sheath superimposed on two crossed swords in scabbards) in white is centered near the top of the vertical band

Geographical description: Middle East, bordering the Arabian Sea, Gulf of Oman, and Persian Gulf, between Yemen and United Arab Emirates

Total area: 119,498 sq. mi. (309,500 sq. km.)

Climate: Dry desert; hot, humid along coast; hot, dry interior; strong southwest summer monsoon (May to September) in far south

Nationality: *noun*: Omani(s); *adjective*: Omani

Population: 3,204,897 (July 2007 CIA est.)

Ethnic groups: Arab, Baluchi, South Asian (Indian, Pakistani, Sri Lankan, Bangladeshi), East African

Languages spoken: Arabic (official), English, Baluchi, Urdu, Swahili, Hindi and Indian dialects

Religions: Ibadhi Muslim 75%, other (includes Sunni Muslim, Shi'a Muslim, Hindu, Christian) 25%

Pakistan

Official name: Islamic Republic of Pakistan

Capital city: Islamabad

Internet country code: .pk

Flag description: Green with a vertical white band (symbolizing the role of religious minorities) on the hoist side; a large white crescent and star are centered in the green field; the crescent, star, and color green are traditional symbols of Islam

National anthem: Blessed be the sacred Land (first line in English translation), lyrics by Abdul Asar Hafeez Jullundhri, music by Ahmed G. Chagla

National animal: Markhor

National bird: Chakor (Red-legged partridge)

National flower: Jasmine

National poet: Allama Muhammad Iqbal (1877-1938)

National tree: Deodar (Cedrus Deodara)

Geographical description: Southern Asia, bordering the Arabian Sea, between India on the east and Iran and Afghanistan on the west and China in the north

Total area: 310,527 sq. mi. (803,943 sq. km.)

Climate: Mostly hot, dry desert; temperate in northwest; arctic in north

Nationality: *noun*: Pakistani(s); *adjective*: Pakistani

Population: 164,741,924 (July 2007 CIA est.)

Ethnic groups: Punjabi, Sindhi, Pashtun (Pathan), Baloch, Muhajir (immigrants from India at the time of partition and their descendants), Saraiki, and Hazara

Languages spoken: Punjabi 48%, Sindhi 12%, Siraiki (a Punjabi variant) 10%, Pashtu 8%, Urdu (official) 8%, Balochi 3%, Hindko 2%, Brahui 1%, English (official; lingua franca of Pakistani elite and most government ministries), Burushaski and other 8%

Religions: Muslim 97% (Sunni 77%, Shi'a 20%), other (includes Christian and Hindu) 3%

Palau

Official name: Republic of Palau

Capital city: Melekeok

Internet country code: .pw

Flag description: Light blue with a large yellow disk (representing the moon) shifted slightly to the hoist side

National anthem: "Belau Rekid" (Our Palau), composed by Ymesei O. Ezekiel

Geographical description: Oceania, group of islands in the North Pacific Ocean, southeast of the Philippines

Total area: 190 sq. mi. (458 sq. km.)

Climate: Tropical; hot and humid; wet season May to November

Nationality: noun: Palauan(s); adjective: Palauan

Population: 20,842 (July 2007 CIA est.)

Ethnic groups: Palauan (Micronesian with Malayan and Melanesian admixtures) 69.9%, Filipino 15.3%, Chinese 4.9%, other Asian 2.4%, white 1.9%, Carolinian 1.4%, other Micronesian 1.1%, other or unspecified 3.2%

Languages spoken: Palauan 64.7% official in all islands except Sonsoral (Sonsoralese and English are official), Tobi (Tobi and English are official), and Angaur (Angaur, Japanese, and English are official), Filipino 13.5%, English 9.4%, Chinese 5.7%, Carolinian 1.5%, Japanese 1.5%, other Asian 2.3%, other languages 1.5%

Religions: Roman Catholic 41.6%, Protestant 23.3%, Modekngei (indigenous to Palau) 8.8%, Seventh-Day Adventist 5.3%, Jehovah's Witness 0.9%, Latter-Day Saints 0.6%, other 3.1%, unspecified or none 16.4%

Panama

Official name: Republic of Panama

Capital city: Panama City

Internet country code: .pa

Flag description: Divided into four equal rectangles; the top quadrants are white (hoist side) with a blue five-pointed star in the center and plain red; the bottom quadrants are plain blue (hoist side) and white with a red five-pointed star in the center

Geographical description: Central America, bordering both the Caribbean Sea and the North Pacific Ocean, between Colombia and Costa Rica

Total area: 30,193 sq. mi. (78,200 sq. km.)

Climate: Tropical maritime; hot, humid, cloudy; prolonged rainy season (May to January), short dry season (January to May)

Nationality: noun: Panamanian(s); adjective: Panamanian

Population: 3,242,173 (July 2007 CIA est.)

Ethnic groups: Mestizo (mixed African, Amerindian, and European) 70%, Amerindian and mixed (West Indian) 14%, white 10%, Amerindian 6%

Languages spoken: Spanish (official), English 14%

Religions: Roman Catholic 84%, Protestant 15%, other 1%

Papua New Guinea

Official name: Independent State of Papua New Guinea

Capital city: Port Moresby

Internet country code: .pg

Flag description: Divided diagonally from upper hoist-side corner; the upper triangle is red with a soaring yellow bird of paradise centered; the lower triangle is black with five white five-pointed stars of the Southern Cross constellation centered

National anthem: "O Arise All You Sons"

Geographical description: Oceania, group of islands including the eastern half of the island of New Guinea between the Coral Sea and the South Pacific Ocean, east of Indonesia

Total area: 178,710 sq. mi. (462,860 sq. km.)

Climate: Tropical; northwest monsoon (December to March), southeast monsoon (May to October); slight seasonal temperature variation

Nationality: noun: Papua New Guinean(s); adjective: Papua New Guinean

Population: 5,795,887 (July 2007 CIA est.)

Ethnic groups: Melanesian, Papuan, Negrito, Micronesian, Polynesian

Languages spoken: Melanesian Pidgin serves as the lingua franca, English spoken by 1%-2%, Motu spoken in Papua region; more than 800 indigenous languages spoken (over one-tenth of the world's total)

Religions: Indigenous religions 34%, Roman Catholic 22%, Lutheran 16%, Presbyterian/Methodist/London Missionary Society 8%, Anglican 5%, Evangelical Alliance 4%, Seventh-Day Adventist 1%, other Protestant 10%

Paraguay

Official name: Republic of Paraguay

Capital city: Asuncion

Internet country code: .py

Flag description: Three equal horizontal bands of red (top), white, and blue with an emblem centered in the white band; unusual flag in that the emblem is different on each side; the obverse (hoist side at the left) bears the national coat of arms (a yellow five-pointed star within a green wreath capped by the words *Republica del Paraguay*, all within two circles); the reverse (hoist side at the right) bears the seal of the treasury (a yellow lion below a red Cap of Liberty and the words *Paz y Justicia* (Peace and Justice) capped by the words *Republica del Paraguay*, all within two circles)

Geographical description: Central South America, northeast of Argentina

Total area: 157,047 sq. mi. (406,752 sq. km.)

Climate: Subtropical to temperate; substantial rainfall in the eastern portions, becoming semiarid in the far west

Nationality: noun: Paraguayan(s); adjective: Paraguayan

Population: 6,669,086 (July 2007 CIA est.)

Ethnic groups: Mestizo (mixed Spanish and Amerindian) 95%, other 5%

Languages spoken: Spanish (official), Guarani (official)

Religions: Roman Catholic 89.6%, Protestant (including Mennonite and other Christian) 7.3%, other or unspecified 1.9%, none 1.1%

Peru

Official name: Republic of Peru

Capital city: Lima

Internet country code: .pe

Flag description: Three equal vertical bands of red (hoist side), white, and red with the coat of arms centered in the white band; the coat of arms features a shield bearing a vicuna, cinchona tree (the source of quinine), and a yellow cornucopia spilling out gold coins, all framed by a green wreath

National anthem: lyrics by Jose de la Torre Ugarte, music by Jose Bernardo Alcedo

Geographical description: Western South America, bordering the South Pacific Ocean, between Chile and Ecuador

Total area: 496,225 sq. mi. (1,285,220 sq. km.)

Climate: Varies from tropical in east to dry desert in west; temperate to frigid in Andes

Nationality: *noun*: Peruvian(s); *adjective*: Peruvian

Population: 28,674,757 (July 2007 CIA est.)

Ethnic groups: Amerindian 45%, Mestizo (mixed Amerindian and European) 37%, European 15%, African, Japanese, Chinese, and other 3%

Languages spoken: Spanish, Quechua, Aymara, and a large number of Amazonian languages

Religions: Roman Catholic 81%, Seventh Day Adventist 1.4%, other Christian 0.7%, other 0.6%, unspecified or none 16.3%

Philippines

Official name: Republic of the Philippines

Capital city: Manila

Internet country code: .ph

Flag description: Two equal horizontal bands of blue (top; representing peace and justice) and red (representing courage); a white equilateral triangle based on the hoist side represents equality; the center of the triangle displays a yellow sun with eight primary rays, each representing one of the first eight provinces that sought independence from Spain; each corner of the triangle contains a small yellow five-pointed star representing the three major geographical divisions of the country: Luzon, Visayas, and Mindanao; the design of the flag dates to 1897

National anthem: "Lupang Hinirang," music from "Marcha Nacional Filipina" (Philippine National March) by Julian Felipe; lyrics from poem "Filipinas" by Jose Palma

National motto: "Maka-Diyos, Maka-Tao, Makakalikasan At Makabansa."

Geographical description: Southeastern Asia, archipelago between the Philippine Sea and the South China Sea, east of Vietnam

Total area: 117,187 sq. mi. (300,000 sq. km.)

Climate: Tropical marine; northeast monsoon (November to April); southwest monsoon (May to October)

Nationality: *noun*: Filipino(s); *adjective*: Philippine

Population: 91,077,287 (July 2007 CIA est.)

Ethnic groups: Tagalog 28.1%, Cebuano 13.1%, Ilocano 9%, Bisaya/Binisaya 7.6%, Hiligaynon Ilonggo 7.5%, Bikol 6%, Waray 3.4%, other 25.3%

Languages spoken: Filipino (official; based on Tagalog) and English (official); eight major dialects - Tagalog, Cebuano, Ilocano, Hiligaynon or Ilonggo, Bicol, Waray, Pampango, and Pangasinan

Religions: Roman Catholic 80.9%, Muslim 5%, Evangelical 2.8%, Iglesia ni Kristo 2.3%, Aglipayan 2%, other Christian 4.5%, other (including Buddhist) 1.8%, unspecified 0.6%, none 0.1%

Poland

Official name: Republic of Poland

Capital city: Warsaw

Internet country code: .pl

Flag description: Two equal horizontal bands of white (top) and red; similar to the flags of Indonesia and Monaco which are red (top) and white

National anthem: "Mazurek Dabrowskiego" (Dombrowski's Mazurka; informally known in English as "Poland Is Not Yet Lost" or "Poland Has Not Yet Perished")

National emblem: White eagle on a red field

Geographical description: Central Europe, east of Germany

Total area: 120,725 sq. mi. (312,683 sq. km.)

Climate: Temperate with cold, cloudy, moderately severe winters with frequent precipitation; mild summers with frequent showers and thundershowers

Nationality: *noun*: Pole(s); *adjective*: Polish

Population: 38,518,241 (July 2007 CIA est.)

Ethnic groups: Polish 96.7%, German 0.4%, Belarusian 0.1%, Ukrainian 0.1%, other and unspecified 2.7%

Languages spoken: Polish 97.8%, other and unspecified 2.2%

Religions: Roman Catholic 89.8% (about 75% practicing), Eastern Orthodox 1.3%, Protestant 0.3%, other 0.3%, unspecified 8.3%

Portugal

Official name: Portuguese Republic

Capital city: Lisbon

Internet country code: .pt

Flag description: Two vertical bands of green (hoist side, two-fifths) and red (three-fifths) with the Portuguese coat of arms centered on the dividing line

National anthem: "A Portuguesa"

Geographical description: Southwestern Europe, bordering the North Atlantic Ocean, west of Spain

Total area: 35,672 sq. mi. (92,391 sq. km.)

Climate: Maritime temperate; cool and rainy in north, warmer and drier in south

Nationality: *noun*: Portuguese (singular and plural); *adjective*: 10,642,836

Population: 10,642,836 (July 2007 CIA est.)

Ethnic groups: Homogeneous Mediterranean stock with small minority groups from Africa (Angola, Cape Verde, Mozambique), South America (Brazil) and Eastern Europe (Ukraine, Romania).

Languages spoken: Portuguese (official), Mirandese (official - but locally used)

Religions: Roman Catholic 84.5%, other Christian 2.2%, other 0.3%, unknown 9%, none 3.9%

Qatar

Official name: State of Qatar

Capital city: Doha

Internet country code: .qa

Flag description: Maroon with a broad white serrated band (nine white points) on the hoist side

National anthem: "Swearing by God who erected the sky" (first line in English translation)

Geographical description: Middle East, peninsula bordering the Persian Gulf and Saudi Arabia

Total area: 4,427 sq. mi. (11,437 sq. km.)

Climate: Arid; mild, pleasant winters; very hot, humid summers

Nationality: *noun*: Qatari(s); *adjective*: Qatari

Population: 907,229 (July 2007 CIA est.)

Ethnic groups: Arab 40%, Indian 18%, Pakistani 18%, Iranian 10%, other 14%

Languages spoken: Arabic (official), English commonly used as a second language

Religions: Muslim 77.5%, Christian 8.5%, other 14%

Romania

Official name: Romania

Capital city: Bucharest

Internet country code: .ro

Flag description: Three equal vertical bands of blue (hoist side), yellow, and red; the national coat of arms that used to be centered in the yellow band has been removed

National anthem: "Deşteaptă-te Române!" (Awaken Thee, Romanian!)

Geographical description: Southeastern Europe, bordering the Black Sea, between Bulgaria and Ukraine

Total area: 91,699 sq. mi. (237,499 sq. km.)

Climate: Temperate; cold, cloudy winters with frequent snow and fog; sunny summers with frequent showers and thunderstorms

Nationality: *noun*: Romanian(s); *adjective*: Romanian

Population: 22,276,056 (July 2007 CIA est.)

Ethnic groups: Romanian 89.5%, Hungarian 6.6%, Roma 2.5%, Ukrainian 0.3%, German 0.3%, Russian 0.2%, Turkish 0.2%, other 0.4%

Languages spoken: Romanian (official) 91%, Hungarian 6.7%, Romany 1.1%, other 1.2%

Religions: Eastern Orthodox (including all sub-denominations) 86.8%, Protestant (various denominations including

Reformate and Pentecostal) 7.5%, Roman Catholic 4.7%, other (mostly Muslim) and unspecified 0.9%, none 0.1%

Russia

Official name: Russian Federation

Capital city: Moscow

Internet country code: .ru

Flag description: Three equal horizontal bands of white (top), blue, and red

National anthem: lyrics from poem by Sergey Mikhalkov, music by Alexander Alexandrov

National symbol: Two-headed eagle

Geographical description: Northern Asia (the area west of the Urals is considered part of Europe), bordering the Arctic Ocean, between Europe and the North Pacific Ocean

Total area: 6.5 million sq. mi. (17 million sq. km.)

Climate: Ranges from steppes in the south through humid continental in much of European Russia; subarctic in Siberia to tundra climate in the polar north; winters vary from cool along Black Sea coast to frigid in Siberia; summers vary from warm in the steppes to cool along Arctic coast

Nationality: *noun*: Russian(s); *adjective*: Russian

Population: 141,377,752 (July 2007 CIA est.)

Ethnic groups: Russian 79.8%, Tatar 3.8%, Ukrainian 2%, Bashkir 1.2%, Chuvash 1.1%, other or unspecified 12.1%

Languages spoken: Russian, many minority languages

Religions: Russian Orthodox, Islam, Judaism, Roman Catholicism, Protestant, Buddhist

Rwanda

Official name: Republic of Rwanda

Capital city: Kigali

Internet country code: .rw

Flag description: Three horizontal bands of sky blue (top, double width), yellow, and green, with a golden sun with 24 rays near the fly end of the blue band

National anthem: "Rwanda Nziza"

Geographical description: Central Africa, east of Democratic Republic of the Congo

Total area: 10,169 sq. mi. (26,338 sq. km.)

Climate: Temperate; two rainy seasons (February to April, November to January); mild in mountains with frost and snow possible

Nationality: *noun*: Rwandan(s); *adjective*: Rwandan

Population: 9,907,509 (July 2007 CIA est.)

Ethnic groups: Hutu (Bantu) 84%, Tutsi (Hamitic) 15%, Twa (Pygmy) 1%

Languages spoken: Kinyarwanda (official) universal Bantu vernacular, French (official), English (official), Kiswahili (Swahili) used in commercial centers

Religions: Roman Catholic 56.5%, Protestant 26%, Adventist 11.1%, Muslim 4.6%, indigenous religions 0.1%, none 1.7%

Saint Kitts and Nevis

Official name: Federation of Saint Kitts and Nevis

Capital city: Basseterre

Internet country code: .kn

Flag description: Divided diagonally from the lower hoist side by a broad black band bearing two white five-pointed stars; the black band is edged in yellow; the upper triangle is green, the lower triangle is red

National anthem: "O Land of Beauty!" (first line)

National bird: Brown pelican (Pelecanusoccidentalis)

National flower: Poinciana or flamboyant (Delonix regia)

Geographical description: Caribbean, islands in the Caribbean Sea, about one-third of the way from Puerto Rico to Trinidad and Tobago

Total area: St. Kitts 65 sq. mi. (168 sq. km.); Nevis 36 sq. mi. (93 sq. km.)

Climate: Tropical, tempered by constant sea breezes; little seasonal temperature variation; rainy season (May to November)

Nationality: *noun*: Kittitian(s), Nevisian(s); *adjective*: Kittitian, Nevisian

Population: 39,349 (July 2007 CIA est.)

Ethnic groups: Predominantly African ancestry; some British, Portuguese, and Lebanese

Languages spoken: English

Religions: Principally Anglican, with Evangelical Protestant and Roman Catholic minorities

Saint Lucia

Official name: Saint Lucia

Capital city: Castries

Internet country code: .lc

Flag description: Blue, with a gold isosceles triangle below a black arrowhead; the upper edges of the arrowhead have a white border

National anthem: "Sons and daughters of Saint Lucia love the land that gave us birth" (first line)

National bird: Saint Lucia parrot (Amazona versicolor)

National flowers: Rose and Marguerite

National motto: "The Land, The People, The Light"

Geographical description: Caribbean, island between the Caribbean Sea and North Atlantic Ocean, north of Trinidad and Tobago

Total area: 238 sq. mi. (619 sq. km.)

Climate: Tropical, moderated by northeast trade winds; dry season January to April, rainy season May to August

Nationality: *noun*: Saint Lucian(s); *adjective*: Saint Lucian

Population: 170,649 (July 2007 CIA est.)

Ethnic groups: African descent 82.5%, mixed 11.9%, East Indian 2.4%, other or unspecified 3.1%

Languages spoken: English (official), French patois

Religions: Roman Catholic 67.5%, Seventh-Day Adventist 8.5%, Pentecostal 5.7%, Rastafarian 2.1%, Anglican 2%, Evangelical 2%, other Christian 5.1%, other 1.1%, unspecified 1.5%, none 4.5%

Saint Vincent and the Grenadines

Official name: Saint Vincent and the Grenadines

Capital city: Kingstown

Internet country code: .vc

Flag description: Three vertical bands of blue (hoist side), gold (double width), and green; the gold band bears three green diamonds arranged in a V pattern

National anthem: "Saint Vincent, Land so beautiful" (first line)

Geographical description: Caribbean, islands between the Caribbean Sea and North Atlantic Ocean, north of Trinidad and Tobago

Total area: 130 sq. mi. (340 sq. km.)

Climate: Tropical; little seasonal temperature variation; rainy season (May to November)

Nationality: *noun*: Saint Vincentian(s) or Vincentian(s); *adjective*: Saint Vincentian or Vincentian

Population: 118,149 (July 2007 CIA est.)

Ethnic groups: African descent 66%, mixed 19%, East Indian 6%, Carib Amerindian 2%, other 7%

Languages spoken: English, French patois

Religions: Anglican 47%, Methodist 28%, Roman Catholic 13%, other (includes Hindu, Seventh-Day Adventist, other Protestant) 12%

Samoa

Official name: Independent State of Samoa

Capital city: Apia

Internet country code: .ws

Flag description: Red with a blue rectangle in the upper hoist-side quadrant bearing five white five-pointed stars representing the Southern Cross constellation

National anthem: "O le Fua o le Saolotoga o Samoa" (The Banner of Freedom), lyrics and music by Sauni I. Kuresa

National motto: "Faavae i le Atua Samoa" (God Be the Foundation of Samoa)

Geographical description: Oceania, group of islands in the South Pacific Ocean, about one-half of the way from Hawaii to New Zealand

Total area: 1,133 sq. mi. (2,934 sq. km.)

Climate: Tropical; rainy season (November to April), dry season (May to October)

Nationality: *noun*: Samoan(s); *adjective*: Samoan

Population: 214,265 (July 2007 CIA est.)

Ethnic groups: Samoan 92.6%, Euronesians (mixed European and Polynesian) 7%, Europeans 0.4%

Languages spoken: Samoan (Polynesian), English

Religions: Congregationalist 34.8%, Roman Catholic 19.6%, Methodist 15%, Latter-Day Saints 12.7%, Assembly of God 6.6%, Seventh-Day Adventist 3.5%, Worship Centre 1.3%, other Christian 4.5%, other 1.9%, unspecified 0.1%

San Marino

Official name: Republic of San Marino

Capital city: San Marino

Internet country code: .sm

Flag description: Two equal horizontal bands of white (top) and light blue with the national coat of arms superimposed in the center; the coat of arms has a shield (featuring three towers on three peaks) flanked by a wreath, below a crown and above a scroll bearing the word *Libertas* (Liberty)

National anthem: written by Federico Consolo (score only)

Geographical description: Southern Europe, an enclave in central Italy

Total area: 23.6 sq. mi. (61.2 sq. km.)

Climate: Mediterranean; mild to cool winters; warm, sunny summers

Nationality: *noun*: Sammarinese (singular and plural); *adjective*: Sammarinese

Population: 29,615 (July 2007 CIA est.)

Ethnic groups: Sammarinese, Italian

Languages spoken: Italian

Religions: Roman Catholic

São Tomé and Príncipe

Official name: Democratic Republic of São Tomé and Príncipe

Capital city: São Tomé

Internet country code: .st

Flag description: Three horizontal bands of green (top), yellow (double width), and green with two black five-pointed stars placed side by side in the center of the yellow band and a red isosceles triangle based on the hoist side; uses the popular pan-African colors of Ethiopia

Geographical description: Western Africa, islands in the Gulf of Guinea, straddling the Equator, west of Gabon

Total area: 386 sq. mi. (1,001 sq. km.)

Climate: Tropical; hot, humid; one rainy season (October to May)

Nationality: *noun*: Sao Tomean (s); *adjective*: Sao Tomean

Population: 199,579 (July 2007 CIA est.)

Ethnic groups: mestico (mixed African Europeanz), angolares (descendants of Angolan slaves), forros (descendants of freed slaves), servicais (contract laborers from Angola, Mozambique, and Cape Verde), tongas (children of servicais born on the islands), Europeans (primarily Portuguese)

Languages spoken: Portuguese (official)

Religions: Catholic 70.3%, Evangelical 3.4%, New Apostolic 2%, Adventist 1.8%, other 3.1%, none 19.4%

Saudi Arabia

Official name: Kingdom of Saudi Arabia

Capital city: Riyadh

Internet country code: .sa

Flag description: Green, a traditional color in Islamic flags, with the Shahada or Muslim creed in large white Arabic script (translated as "There is no god but God; Muhammad is the Messenger of God") above a white horizontal saber (the tip points to the hoist side); design dates to the early 20th century and is closely associated with the Al Saud family which established the kingdom in 1932

Geographical description: Middle East, bordering the Persian Gulf and the Red Sea, north of Yemen

Total area: 784,233 sq. mi. (1,960,582 sq. km.)

Climate: Harsh, dry desert with great temperature extremes

Nationality: *noun*: Saudi(s); *adjective*: Saudi or Saudi Arabian

Population: 27,601,038 (includes 5,576,076 non-nationals; July 2007 CIA est.)

Ethnic groups: Arab 90%, Afro-Asian 10%

Languages spoken: Arabic

Religions: Muslim 100%

Senegal

Official name: Republic of Senegal

Capital city: Dakar

Internet country code: .sn

Flag description: Three equal vertical bands of green (hoist side), yellow, and red with a small green five-pointed star centered in the yellow band; uses the popular pan-African colors of Ethiopia

Geographical description: Western Africa, bordering the North Atlantic Ocean, between Guinea-Bissau and Mauritania

Total area: 76,000 sq. mi. (196,840 sq. km.)

Climate: Tropical; hot, humid; rainy season (May to November) has strong southeast winds; dry season (December to April) dominated by hot, dry, harmattan wind

Nationality: *noun*: Senegalese (singular and plural); *adjective*: Senegalese

Population: 12,521,851 (July 2007 CIA est.)

Ethnic groups: Wolof 43.3%, Pular 23.8%, Serer 14.7%, Jola 3.7%, Mandinka 3%, Soninke 1.1%, European and Lebanese 1%, other 9.4%

Languages spoken: French (official), Wolof, Pulaar, Serer, Diola, Mandingo, Soninke

Religions: Muslim 94%, Christian (mostly Roman Catholic) 5%, indigenous religions 1%

Serbia

Official name: Republic of Serbia

Capital city: Belgrade

Internet country code: .rs

Flag description: Three equal horizontal stripes of red (top), blue, and white; charged with the coat of arms of Serbia shifted slightly to the hoist side

National anthem: "Boze Pravde" (God of Justice), music by Davorin Jenko and lyrics by Jovan Djordjevic

Geographical description: Southeastern Europe, between Macedonia and Hungary

Total area: 34,116 sq. mi. (88,361 sq. km.)

Climate: In the north, continental climate (cold winters and hot, humid summers with well distributed rainfall); in other parts, continental and Mediterranean climate (relatively cold winters with heavy snowfall and hot, dry summers and autumns)

Nationality: *noun*: Serb(s); *adjective*: Serbian

Population: 10,150,265 (July 2007 CIA est.)

Ethnic groups: Serb 82.9%, Hungarian 3.9%, Romany 1.4%, Yugoslavs 1.1%, Bosniaks 1.8%, Montenegrin 0.9%, other 8%

Languages spoken: Serbian (official) 88.3%, Hungarian 3.8%, Bosniak 1.8%, Romany 1.1%, other 4.1%, unknown 0.9%

Religions: Serbian Orthodox 85%, Roman Catholic 5.5%, Muslim 3.2%, unspecified 2.6%, other, unknown, or atheist 2.6%, Protestant 1.1%

Seychelles

Official name: Republic of Seychelles

Capital city: Victoria

Internet country code: .sc

Flag description: Five oblique bands of blue (hoist side), yellow, red, white, and green (bottom) radiating from the bottom of the hoist side

Geographical description: archipelago in the Indian Ocean, northeast of Madagascar

Total area: 176 sq. mi. (455 sq. km.)

Climate: Tropical marine; humid; cooler season during southeast monsoon (late May to September); warmer season during northwest monsoon (March to May)

Nationality: *noun*: Seychellois (singular and plural); *adjective*: Seychellois

Population: 81,895 (July 2007 CIA est.)

Ethnic groups: Mixed French, African, Indian, Chinese, and Arab

Languages spoken: Creole 91.8%, English 4.9%, other 3.1%, unspecified 0.2%

Religions: Roman Catholic 82.3%, Anglican 6.4%, Seventh-Day Adventist 1.1%, other Christian 3.4%, Hindu 2.1%, Muslim 1.1%, other non-Christian 1.5%, unspecified 1.5%, none 0.6%

Sierra Leone

Official name: Republic of Sierra Leone

Capital city: Freetown

Internet country code: .sl

Flag description: Three equal horizontal bands of light green (top), white, and light blue

Geographical description: Western Africa, bordering the North Atlantic Ocean, between Guinea and Liberia

Total area: 29,925 sq. mi. (71,740 sq. km.)

Climate: Tropical; hot, humid; summer rainy season (May to December); winter dry season (December to April)

Nationality: *noun*: Sierra Leonean(s); *adjective*: Sierra Leonean

Population: 6,144,562 (July 2007 CIA est.)

Ethnic groups: 20 African ethnic groups 90% (Temne 30%, Mende 30%, other 30%), Creole (Krio) 10% (descendants of freed Jamaican slaves who were settled in the Freetown area in the late-18th century), refugees from Liberia's recent civil war, small numbers of Europeans, Lebanese, Pakistanis, and Indians

Languages spoken: English (official, regular use limited to literate minority), Mende (principal vernacular in the south), Temne (principal vernacular in the north), Krio (English-based Creole, spoken by the descendants of freed Jamaican slaves who were settled in the Freetown area, a lingua franca and a first language for 10% of the population but understood by 95%), and several other indigenous languages

Religions: Muslim 60%, Christian and indigenous religions 40%

Singapore

Official name: Republic of Singapore

Capital city: Singapore

Internet country code: .sg

Flag description: Two equal horizontal bands of red (top) and white; near the hoist side of the red band, there is a vertical, white crescent (closed portion is toward the hoist side) partially enclosing five white five-pointed stars arranged in a circle

National anthem: "Majulah Singapura" (Onward Singapore)

National flower: Vanda Miss Joaquim orchid

National symbol: Lion head

Geographical description: Southeastern Asia, islands between Malaysia and Indonesia

Total area: 271 sq. mi. (704 sq. km.)

Climate: Tropical; hot, humid, rainy; two distinct monsoon seasons - Northeastern monsoon (December to March) and Southwestern monsoon (June to September); inter-monsoon - frequent afternoon and early evening thunderstorms

Nationality: *noun*: Singaporean(s); *adjective*: Singapore

Population: 4,553,009 (July 2007 CIA est.)

Ethnic groups: Chinese 76.8%, Malay 13.9%, Indian 7.9%, other 1.4%

Languages spoken: Mandarin 35%, English 23%, Malay 14.1%, Hokkien 11.4%, Cantonese 5.7%, Teochew 4.9%, Tamil 3.2%, other Chinese dialects 1.8%, other 0.9%

Religions: Buddhist 42.5%, Muslim 14.9%, Taoist 8.5%, Hindu 4%, Catholic 4.8%, other Christian 9.8%, other 0.7%, none 14.8%

Slovakia

Official name: Slovak Republic

Capital city: Bratislava

Internet country code: .sk

Flag description: Three equal horizontal bands of white (top), blue, and red superimposed with the coat of arms of Slovakia (consisting of a red shield bordered in white and bearing a white Cross of Lorraine surmounting three blue hills); the coat of arms is centered vertically and off-set slightly to the hoist side

National anthem: "Nad Tatrou sa blyska"

Geographical description: Central Europe, south of Poland

Total area: 18,859 sq. mi. (48,845 sq. km.)

Climate: Temperate; cool summers; cold, cloudy, humid winters

Nationality: *noun*: Slovak(s); *adjective*: Slovak

Population: 5,447,502 (July 2007 CIA est.)

Ethnic groups: Slovak 85.8%, Hungarian 9.7%, Roma 1.7%, Ruthenian/Ukrainian 1%, other and unspecified 1.8%

Languages spoken: Slovak (official) 83.9%, Hungarian 10.7%, Romany 1.8%, Ukrainian 1%, other or unspecified 2.6%

Religions: Roman Catholic 69%, Protestant 9%, Greek Catholic 4%, Orthodox 0.9%, other 0.6%, unknown 3.5%, none 13%

Slovenia

Official name: Republic of Slovenia

Capital city: Ljubljana

Internet country code: .si

Flag description: Three equal horizontal bands of white (top), blue, and red, with the Slovenian seal (a shield with the image of Triglav, Slovenia's highest peak, in white against a blue background at the center; beneath it are two wavy blue lines depicting seas and rivers, and above it are three six-pointed stars arranged in an inverted triangle, which are taken from the coat of arms of the Counts of Celje, the great Slovene dynastic house of the late 14th and early 15th centuries); the seal is in the upper hoist side of the flag centered in the white and blue bands

National anthem: the seventh stanza of France Preseren's poem "Zdravljica" (A Toast), music by Stanko Premrl

Geographical description: Central Europe, eastern Alps bordering the Adriatic Sea, between Austria and Croatia

Total area: 7,906 sq. mi. (20,273 sq. km.)

Climate: Mediterranean climate on the coast, continental climate with mild to hot summers and cold winters in the plateaus and valleys to the east

Nationality: *noun*: Slovene(s); *adjective*: Slovenian

Population: 2,009,245 (July 2007 CIA est.)

Ethnic groups: Slovene 83.1%, Serb 2%, Croat 1.8%, Bosniak 1.1%, other (including Hungarian, Montenegrin, Macedonian, Albanian, Italian, Roma) or unspecified 12%

Languages spoken: Slovenian (official) 91.1%, Serbo-Croatian 4.5%, other or unspecified 4.4%; Hungarian and Italian are spoken in the border regions, and German fluency is common near the Austrian border. Bosnian, Croatian, and Serbian are spoken by a sizable (6% of the population) minority. English is widely understood by business people and students.

Religions: Roman Catholic 57.8%, Muslim 2.4%, Orthodox 2.3%, other Christian 0.9%, unaffiliated 3.5%, other or unspecified 23%, none 10.1%

Solomon Islands

Official name: Solomon Islands

Capital city: Honiara

Internet country code: .sb

Flag description: Divided diagonally by a thin yellow stripe from the lower hoist-side corner; the upper triangle (hoist side) is blue with five white five-pointed stars arranged in an X pattern; the lower triangle is green

Geographical description: Oceania, group of islands in the South Pacific Ocean, east of Papua New Guinea

Total area: 11,599 sq. mi. (27,556 sq. km.); archipelago: 280,000 sq. mi. (725,197 sq. km.)

Climate: Tropical monsoon; few extremes of temperature and weather

Nationality: *noun*: Solomon Islander(s); *adjective*: Solomon Islander

Population: 566,842 (July 2007 CIA est.)

Ethnic groups: Melanesian 93%, Polynesian 4%, Micronesian 1.5%, other 1.5%

Languages spoken: Melanesian pidgin in much of the country is lingua franca; English is official, but spoken by only 1%-2% of the population; 120 indigenous languages

Religions: Anglican Church of Melanesia 32.8%, Roman Catholic 19%, South Seas Evangelical 17%, Seventh-Day Adventist 11.2%, United Church (Methodist) 10.3%, Christian Fellowship Church 2.4%, other Christian 4.4%, other 2.4%, unspecified 0.3%, none 0.2%

Somalia

Official name: Somalia

Capital city: Mogadishu

Internet country code: .so

Flag description: Light blue with a large white five-pointed star in the center; blue field influenced by the flag of the United Nations

Geographical description: Eastern Africa, bordering the Gulf of Aden and the Indian Ocean, east of Ethiopia

Total area: 246,199 sq. mi. (637,657 sq. km.)

Climate: Principally desert; northeast monsoon (December to February), moderate temperatures in north and hot in south; southwest monsoon (May to October), torrid in the north and hot in the south, irregular rainfall, hot and humid periods (tangambili) between monsoons

Nationality: *noun*: Somali(s); *adjective*: Somali

Population: 9,118,773 (this July 2007 CIA estimate was derived from an official census taken in 1975 by the Somali Government; population counting in Somalia is complicated by the large number of nomads and by refugee movements in response to famine and clan warfare)

Ethnic groups: Somali 85%, Bantu and other non-Somali 15% (including 30,000 Arabs)

Languages spoken: Somali (official), Arabic, Italian, English

Religions: Sunni Muslim 99.9%

South Africa

Official name: Republic of South Africa

Capital city: Pretoria

Internet country code: .za

Flag description: Two equal width horizontal bands of red (top) and blue separated by a central green band which splits into a horizontal Y, the arms of which end at the corners of the hoist side; the Y embraces a black isosceles triangle from which the arms are separated by narrow yellow bands; the red and blue bands are separated from the green band and its arms by narrow white stripes

National anthem: A combination of "Nkosi Sikelel' iAfrika" by Enoch Sontonga and "The Call of South Africa" (Die Stem van Suid-Afrika), lyrics by C. J. Langenhoven, music by M. L. de Villiers

National animal: Springbuck/springbok (Antidorcas marsupialis)

National bird: Blue crane (Anthropoides paradisia)

National fish: Galjoen (Coracinus capensis)

National flower: King Protea (Protea cynaroides)

National tree: Real yellowwood (Podocarpus latifolius)

Geographical description: Southern Africa, at the southern tip of the continent of Africa

Total area: 470,462 sq. mi. (1,219,912 sq. km.)

Climate: Mostly semiarid; subtropical along east coast; sunny days, cool nights

Nationality: *noun*: South African(s); *adjective*: South African

Population: 43,997,828 (July 2007 CIA est.)

Ethnic groups: Black African 79%, white 9.6%, colored 8.9%, Indian/Asian 2.5%

Languages spoken: IsiZulu 23.8%, IsiXhosa 17.6%, Afrikaans 13.3%, Sepedi 9.4%, English 8.2%, Setswana 8.2%, Sesotho 7.9%, Xitsonga 4.4%, isiNdebele—all official; other (including siSwati and Tshivenda) 7.2%

Religions: Zion Christian 11.1%, Pentecostal/Charismatic 8.2%, Roman Catholic 7.1%, Methodist 6.8%, Dutch Reformed 6.7%, Anglican 3.8%, Muslim 1.5%, other Christian 36%, other 2.3%, unspecified 1.4%, none 15.1%

Spain

Official name: Kingdom of Spain

Capital city: Madrid

Internet country code: .es

Flag description: Three horizontal bands of red (top), yellow (double width), and red with the national coat of arms on the hoist side of the yellow band; the coat of arms includes the royal seal framed by the Pillars of Hercules, which are the two promontories (Gibraltar and Ceuta) on either side of the eastern end of the Strait of Gibraltar

National anthem: "Grenadier March" or "Royal Spanish March"

Geographical description: Southwestern Europe, bordering the Bay of Biscay, Mediterranean Sea, North Atlantic Ocean, and Pyrenees Mountains, southwest of France

Total area: 194,884 sq. mi. (504,750 sq. km.)

Climate: Temperate; clear, hot summers in interior, more moderate and cloudy along coast; cloudy, cold winters in interior, partly cloudy and cool along coast

Nationality: *noun*: Spaniard(s); *adjective*: Spanish

Population: 40,448,191 (July 2007 CIA est.)

Ethnic groups: Composite of Mediterranean and Nordic groups; distinct ethnic groups within Spain include the Basques, Catalans, and Galicians

Languages spoken: Castilian Spanish (official) 74%, Catalan 17%, Galician 7%, and Basque 2% are official regionally

Religions: Roman Catholic 94%, other (including Protestant and Muslim) 6%

Sri Lanka

Official name: Democratic Socialist Republic of Sri Lanka

Capital city: Colombo

Internet country code: .lk

Flag description: Yellow with two panels; the smaller hoist-side panel has two equal vertical bands of green (hoist side) and orange; the other panel is a large dark red rectangle with a yellow lion holding a sword, and there is a yellow bo leaf in each corner; the yellow field appears as a border around the entire flag and extends between the two panels

National anthem: "Sri Lanka Matha"

National flower: Blue Water Lily (Nymphaea stellata)

Geographical description: Southern Asia, island in the Indian Ocean, south of India

Total area: 25,332 sq. mi. (65,610 sq. km.)

Climate: Tropical monsoon; northeast monsoon (December to March); southwest monsoon (June to October)

Nationality: *noun*: Sri Lankan(s); *adjective*: Sri Lankan

Population: 20,926,315 (July 2007 CIA est.)

Ethnic groups: Sinhalese 74%, Tamil 18%, Burgher (descendants of Dutch and Portuguese colonist) and others 8%

Languages spoken: Sinhala (official and national language) 74%, Tamil (national language) 18%, other 8% (English is commonly used in government and is spoken competently by about 10% of the population)

Religions: Buddhist 69.1%, Muslim 7.6%, Hindu 7.1%, Christian 6.2%, unspecified 10%

Sudan

Official name: Republic of the Sudan

Capital city: Khartoum

Internet country code: .sd

Flag description: Three equal horizontal bands of red (top), white, and black with a green isosceles triangle based on the hoist side

Geographical description: Northern Africa, bordering the Red Sea, between Egypt and Eritrea

Total area: 967,500 sq. mi. (2,505,810 sq. km.)

Climate: tropical in south; arid desert in north; rainy season varies by region (April to November)

Nationality: *noun:* Sudanese (singular and plural); *adjective:* Sudanese

Population: 39,379,358 (July 2007 CIA est.)

Ethnic groups: black 52%, Arab 39%, Beja 6%, foreigners 2%, other 1%

Languages spoken: Arabic (official), Nubian, Ta Bedawie, diverse dialects of Nilotic, Nilo-Hamitic, Sudanic languages, English

Religions: Sunni Muslim 70% (in north), Christian 5% (mostly in south and Khartoum), indigenous religions 25%

Suriname

Official name: Republic of Suriname

Capital city: Paramaribo

Internet country code: .sr

Flag description: Five horizontal bands of green (top, double width), white, red (quadruple width), white, and green (double width); there is a large, yellow, five-pointed star centered in the red band

National anthem: "Rise country men rise" (first line)

National flower: Fajalobi ("passionate love"; orchid)

National motto: Justitia – Pietas – Fides (Justice-Faith-Loyalty)

Geographical description: Northern South America, bordering the North Atlantic Ocean, between French Guiana and Guyana

Total area: 63,037 sq. mi. (163,194 sq. km.)

Climate: Tropical; moderated by trade winds

Nationality: *noun:* Surinamer(s); *adjective:* Surinamese

Population: 470,784 (July 2007 CIA est.)

Ethnic groups: Hindustani (also known locally as "East Indians"; their ancestors emigrated from northern India in the latter part of the 19th century) 37%, Creole (mixed white and black) 31%, Javanese 15%, "Maroons" (their African ancestors were brought to the country in the 17th and 18th centuries as slaves and escaped to the interior) 10%, Amerindian 2%, Chinese 2%, white 1%, other 2%

Languages spoken: Dutch (official), English (widely spoken), Sranang Tongo (Surinamese, sometimes called Taki-Taki, is native language of Creoles and much of the younger population and is lingua franca among others), Caribbean Hindustani (a dialect of Hindi), Javanese

Religions: Hindu 27.4%, Protestant 25.2% (predominantly Moravian), Roman Catholic 22.8%, Muslim 19.6%, indigenous religions 5%

Swaziland

Official name: Kingdom of Swaziland

Capital city: Mbabane

Internet country code: .sz

Flag description: Three horizontal bands of blue (top), red (triple width), and blue; the red band is edged in yellow; centered in the red band is a large black and white shield covering two spears and a staff decorated with feather tassels, all placed horizontally

Geographical description: Southern Africa, between Mozambique and South Africa

Total area: 6,704 sq. mi. (17,363 sq. km.)

Climate: Varies from tropical to near temperate

Nationality: *noun:* Swazi(s); *adjective:* Swazi

Population: 1,133,066 (July 2007 CIA est.)

Ethnic groups: African, overwhelmingly Swazi 97%, European 3%

Languages spoken: English (official, government business conducted in English), siSwati (official)

Religions: Zionist 40% (a blend of Christianity and indigenous ancestral worship), Roman Catholic 20%, Muslim 10%, other (includes Anglican, Bahai, Methodist, Mormon, Jewish) 30%

Sweden

Official name: Kingdom of Sweden

Capital city: Stockholm

Internet country code: .se

Flag description: Blue with a golden yellow cross extending to the edges of the flag; the vertical part of the cross is shifted to the hoist side in the style of the Dannebrog (Danish flag)

National anthem: "Du gamla, Du fria" (Thou ancient, Thou freeborn)

Geographical description: Northern Europe, bordering the Baltic Sea, Gulf of Bothnia, Kattegat, and Skagerrak, between Finland and Norway

Total area: 173,731 sq. mi. (449,964 sq. km.)

Climate: Temperate in south with cold, cloudy winters and cool, partly cloudy summers; subarctic in north

Nationality: *noun:* Swede(s); *adjective:* Swedish

Population: 9,031,088 (July 2007 CIA est.)

Ethnic groups: indigenous population: Swedes with Finnish and Sami minorities; foreign-born or first-generation immigrants include Finns, Iraqis, former Yugoslav nationals, Iranians, Danes, Norwegians, Greeks, Turks

Languages spoken: Swedish, small Sami- and Finnish-speaking minorities

Religions: Lutheran 87%, other (includes Roman Catholic, Orthodox, Baptist, Muslim, Jewish, and Buddhist) 13%

Switzerland

Official name: Swiss Confederation

Capital city: Bern

Internet country code: .ch

Flag description: Red square with a bold, equilateral white cross in the center that does not extend to the edges of the flag

National anthem: "Schweizerpsalm" (Swiss Psalm)

Geographical description: Central Europe, east of France, north of Italy

Total area: 15,941 sq. mi. (41,285 sq. km.)

Climate: Temperate, but varies with altitude; cold, cloudy, rainy/snowy winters; cool to warm, cloudy, humid summers with occasional showers

Nationality: *noun*: Swiss (singular and plural); *adjective*: Swiss

Population: 7,554,661 (July 2007 CIA est.)

Ethnic groups: German 65%, French 18%, Italian 10%, Romansch 1%, other 6%

Languages spoken: German (official) 63.7%, French (official) 20.4%, Italian (official) 6.5%, Serbo-Croatian 1.5%, Albanian 1.3%, Portuguese 1.2%, Spanish 1.1%, English 1%, Romansch (official) 0.5%, other 2.8%

Religions: Roman Catholic 41.8%, Protestant 35.3%, Muslim 4.3%, Orthodox 1.8%, other Christian 0.4%, other 1%, unspecified 4.3%, none 11.1%

Syria

Official name: Syrian Arab Republic

Capital city: Damascus

Internet country code: .sy

Flag description: Three equal horizontal bands of red (top), white, and black, colors associated with the Arab Liberation flag; two small green five-pointed stars in a horizontal line centered in the white band; former flag of the United Arab Republic where the two stars represented the constituent states of Syria and Egypt; similar to the flag of Yemen, which has a plain white band, Iraq, which has three green stars (plus an Arabic inscription) in a horizontal line centered in the white band, and that of Egypt, which has a gold Eagle of Saladin centered in the white band; the current design dates to 1980

Geographical description: Middle East, bordering the Mediterranean Sea, between Lebanon and Turkey

Total area: 71,504 sq. mi. (185,170 sq. km.)

Climate: Mostly desert; hot, dry, sunny summers (June to August) and mild, rainy winters (December to February) along coast; cold weather with snow or sleet periodically in Damascus

Nationality: *noun*: Syrian(s); *adjective*: Syrian

Population: 19,314,747 (July 2007 CIA est.)

Ethnic groups: Arab 90.3%, Kurds 9%, Armenians, Circassians, Turkomans 0.7%

Languages spoken: Arabic (official); Kurdish, Armenian, Aramaic, Circassian widely understood; French, English somewhat understood

Religions: Sunni Muslims 74%, Alawis 12%, Christians 10%, Druze 3%, and small numbers of other Muslim sects, Jews, and Yazidis

Taiwan

Official name: Taiwan

Capital city: Taipei

Internet country code: .tw

Flag description: Red with a dark blue rectangle in the upper hoist-side corner bearing a white sun with 12 triangular rays

National flower: Plum blossom (prunus mei)

Geographical description: Eastern Asia, islands bordering the East China Sea, Philippine Sea, South China Sea, and Taiwan Strait, north of the Philippines, off the southeastern coast of China

Total area: 13,887 sq. mi. (35,967 sq. km.)

Climate: Tropical; marine; rainy season during southwest monsoon (June to August); cloudiness is persistent and extensive all year

Nationality: *noun*: Taiwan(s); *adjective*: Taiwan

Population: 22,858,872 (July 2007 CIA est.)

Ethnic groups: Taiwanese (including Hakka) 84%, mainland Chinese 14%, indigenous 2%

Languages spoken: Mandarin Chinese (official), Taiwanese (Min), Hakka dialects

Religions: mixture of Buddhist and Taoist 93%, Christian 4.5%, other 2.5%

Tajikistan

Official name: Republic of Tajikistan

Capital city: Dushanbe

Internet country code: .tj

Flag description: Three horizontal stripes of red (top), a wider stripe of white, and green; a gold crown surmounted by seven gold five-pointed stars is located in the center of the white stripe

Geographical description: Central Asia, west of China

Total area: 55,251 sq. mi. (143,100 sq. km.)

Climate: Mid-latitude continental, hot summers, mild winters; semiarid to polar in Pamir Mountains

Nationality: *noun*: Tajikistani(s); *adjective*: Tajikistani

Population: 7,076,598 (July 2007 CIA est.)

Ethnic groups: Tajik 79.9%, Uzbek 15.3%, Russian 1.1%, Kyrgyz 1.1%, other 2.6%

Languages spoken: Tajik (official), Russian widely used in government and business

Religions: Sunni Muslim 85%, Shi'a Muslim 5%, other 10%

Tanzania

Official name: United Republic of Tanzania

Capital city: Dar es Salaam

Internet country code: .tz

Flag description: Divided diagonally by a yellow-edged black band from the lower hoist-side corner; the upper triangle (hoist side) is green and the lower triangle is blue

National anthem: "Wimbo Wa Taifa" (God Bless Africa)

National motto: "Uhuru na Umoja" (Freedom and Unity)

National symbol: Uhuru Torch

Geographical description: Eastern Africa, bordering the Indian Ocean, between Kenya and Mozambique

Total area: 378,000 sq. mi. (945,000 sq. km.)

Climate: Varies from tropical along coast to temperate in highlands

Nationality: *noun*: Tanzanian(s), Zanzibari(s); *adjective*: Tanzanian, Zanzibari

Population: 39,384,223 (July 2007 CIA est.)

Ethnic groups: mainland - African 99% (of which 95% are Bantu consisting of more than 130 tribes), other 1% (consisting of Asian, European, and Arab); Zanzibar - Arab, African, mixed Arab and African

Languages spoken: Kiswahili or Swahili (official), Kiunguja (name for Swahili in Zanzibar), English (official, primary language of commerce, administration, and higher education), Arabic (widely spoken in Zanzibar), many local languages

Religions: mainland - Christian 30%, Muslim 35%, indigenous religions 35%; Zanzibar - more than 99% Muslim

Thailand

Official name: Kingdom of Thailand

Capital city: Bangkok

Internet country code: .th

Flag description: Five horizontal bands of red (top), white, blue (double width), white, and red

National animal: Elephant

National architecture: Sala Thai (Thai Pavilion)

National flower: Ratchaphruek (Cassia fistula Linn)

Geographical description: Southeastern Asia, bordering the Andaman Sea and the Gulf of Thailand, southeast of Burma

Total area: 198,114 sq. mi. (513,115 sq. km.)

Climate: Tropical; rainy, warm, cloudy southwest monsoon (mid-May to September); dry, cool northeast monsoon (November to mid-March); southern isthmus always hot and humid

Nationality: *noun*: Thai (singular and plural); *adjective*: Thai

Population: 65,068,149 (July 2007 CIA est.)

Ethnic groups: Thai 75%, Chinese 14%, other 11%

Languages spoken: Thai, English (secondary language of the elite), ethnic and regional dialects

Religions: Buddhist 94.6%, Muslim 4.6%, Christian 0.7%, other (including Hindu, Brahmin) 0.1%

Timor-Leste

Official name: Democratic Republic of Timor-Leste (formerly East Timor)

Capital city: Dili

Internet country code: .tl

Flag description: Red, with a black isosceles triangle (based on the hoist side) superimposed on a slightly longer yellow arrowhead that extends to the center of the flag; there is a white star in the center of the black triangle

National anthem: "Pátria" (Fatherland), lyrics by Francisco Borja da Costa, music by Afonso de Araújo

Geographical description: Southeastern Asia, northwest of Australia in the Lesser Sunda Islands at the eastern end of the Indonesian archipelago; note - Timor-Leste includes the eastern half of the island of Timor, the Oecussi (Ambeno) region on the northwest portion of the island of Timor, and the islands of Pulau Atauro and Pulau Jaco

Total area: 5,794 sq. mi. (15,007 sq. km.)

Climate: Tropical; hot, humid; distinct rainy and dry seasons

Nationality: *noun*: Timorese (singular and plural); *adjective*: Timorese

Population: 1,084,971 (July 2007 CIA est.; *note:* other estimates range as low as 800,000)

Ethnic groups: Austronesian (Malayo-Polynesian), Papuan, small Chinese minority

Languages spoken: Tetum (official), Portuguese (official), Indonesian, English; there are about 16 indigenous languages, including Tetum, Galole, Mambae, and Kemak, which are spoken by significant numbers of people

Religions: Roman Catholic 98%, Muslim 1%, Protestant 1%

Togo

Official name: Togolese Republic

Capital city: Lomé

Internet country code: .tg

Flag description: Five equal horizontal bands of green (top and bottom) alternating with yellow; there is a white five-pointed star on a red square in the upper hoist-side corner; uses the popular pan-African colors of Ethiopia

Geographical description: Western Africa, bordering the Bight of Benin, between Benin and Ghana

Total area: 21,924 sq. mi. (56,785 sq. km.)

Climate: Tropical; hot, humid in south; semiarid in north

Nationality: *noun*: Togolese (singular and plural); *adjective*: Togolese

Population: 5,701,579 (July 2007 CIA est.)

Ethnic groups: African (37 tribes; most prominent are Ewe, Mina, Kabye, Cotocoli, Moba) 99%, European and Syrian-Lebanese less than 1%

Languages spoken: French (official and the language of commerce), Ewe and Mina (the two major African languages in the south), Kabye (sometimes spelled Kabiye) and Dagomba (the two major African languages in the north)

Religions: Christianity, Islam, indigenous religions

Tonga

Official name: Kingdom of Tonga

Capital city: Nuku'alofa

Internet country code: .to

Flag description: Red with a bold red cross on a white rectangle in the upper hoist-side corner

Geographical description: Oceania, archipelago in the South Pacific Ocean, about two-thirds of the way from Hawaii to New Zealand

Total area: 288 sq. mi. (747 sq. km.)

Climate: Tropical; modified by trade winds; warm season (December to May), cool season (May to December)

Nationality: *noun*: Tongan(s); *adjective*: Tongan

Population: 116,921 (July 2007 CIA est.)

Ethnic groups: Tongan 98%, other Polynesian, European

Languages spoken: Tongan, English

Religions: Christian (Free Wesleyan Church claims over 30,000 adherents)

Trinidad and Tobago

Official name: Republic of Trinidad and Tobago

Capital city: Port-of-Spain

Internet country code: .tt

Flag description: Red with a white-edged black diagonal band from the upper hoist side to the lower fly side

National anthem: "Forged from the love of liberty" (first line) by Patrick S. Castagne

National birds: Scarlet Ibis (Tantalus Ruber) and Cocrico (Rufus Tailed Guan)

National flower: Chaconia, called "Wild Poinsettia" or "Pride of Trinidad and Tobago" (of the family Rubianceae)

National motto: "Together We Aspire, Together We Achieve"

National watchwords: Discipline, Production, Tolerance

Geographical description: Caribbean, islands between the Caribbean Sea and the North Atlantic Ocean, northeast of Venezuela

Total area: 1,980 sq. mi. (5,128 sq. km.)

Climate: Tropical; rainy season (June to December)

Nationality: *noun*: Trinidadian(s), Tobagonian(s); *adjective*: Trinidadian, Tobagonian

Population: 1,056,608 (July 2007 CIA est.)

Ethnic groups: Indian (South Asian) 40%, African 37.5%, mixed 20.5%, European 0.6%, Chinese 0.3%, other or unspecified 1.1%, unspecified 0.8%

Languages spoken: English (official), Caribbean Hindustani (a dialect of Hindi), French, Spanish, Chinese

Religions: Roman Catholic 26%, Hindu 22.5%, Anglican 7.8%, Baptist 7.2%, Pentecostal 6.8%, Muslim 5.8%, Seventh-Day Adventist 4%, other Christian 5.8%, other 10.8%, unspecified 1.4%, none 1.9%

Tunisia

Official name: Tunisian Republic

Capital city: Tunis

Internet country code: .tn

Flag description: Red with a white disk in the center bearing a red crescent nearly encircling a red five-pointed star; the crescent and star are traditional symbols of Islam

Geographical description: Northern Africa, bordering the Mediterranean Sea, between Algeria and Libya

Total area: 63,378 sq. mi. (163,610 sq. km.)

Climate: Temperate in north with mild, rainy winters and hot, dry summers; desert in south

Nationality: *noun*: Tunisian(s); *adjective*: Tunisian

Population: 10,276,158 (July 2007 CIA est.)

Ethnic groups: Arab-Berber 98%, European 1%, other 1%

Languages spoken: Arabic (official and one of the languages of commerce), French (commerce)

Religions: Muslim 98%, Christian 1%, Jewish and other 1%

Turkey

Official name: Republic of Turkey

Capital city: Ankara

Internet country code: .tr

Flag description: Red with a vertical white crescent (the closed portion is toward the hoist side) and white five-pointed star centered just outside the crescent opening

National anthem: "Istiklal Marsi" (The Independence March)

Geographical description: Southeastern Europe and southwestern Asia (that portion of Turkey west of the Bosporus is geographically part of Europe), bordering the Black Sea, between Bulgaria and Georgia, and bordering the Aegean Sea and the Mediterranean Sea, between Greece and Syria

Total area: 314,500 sq. mi. (814,578 sq. km.)

Climate: Temperate; hot, dry summers with mild, wet winters; harsher in interior

Nationality: *noun*: Turk(s); *adjective*: Turkish

Population: 71,158,647 (July 2007 CIA est.)

Ethnic groups: Turkish 80%, Kurdish 20% (estimated)

Languages spoken: Turkish (official), Kurdish, Dimli (or Zaza), Azeri, Kabardian, Arabic, Armenian, Greek (*note:* there is also a substantial Gagauz population in the European part of Turkey)

Religions: Muslim (mostly Sunni) 99.8%, other (mostly Christians, Jews, and Baha'i) 0.2%

Turkmenistan

Official name: Turkmenistan

Capital city: Ashgabat (Ashkhabad)

Internet country code: .tm

Flag description: Green field with a vertical red stripe near the hoist side, containing five tribal *guls* (designs used in producing carpets) stacked above two crossed olive branches similar to the olive branches on the United Nations flag; a white crescent moon representing Islam with five white stars representing the regions or *velayats* of Turkmenistan appear in the upper corner of the field just to the fly side of the red stripe

National anthem: "The great creation of Turkmenbashy" (first line in English translation)

Geographical description: Central Asia, bordering the Caspian Sea, between Iran and Kazakhstan

Total area: 303,292 sq. mi. (488,100 sq. km.)

Climate: Subtropical desert

Nationality: *noun*: Turkmen(s); *adjective*: Turkmenistani

Population: 5,097,028 (July 2007 CIA est.)

Ethnic groups: Turkmen 85%, Uzbek 5%, Russian 4%, other 6%

Languages spoken: Turkmen 72%, Russian 12%, Uzbek 9%, other 7%

Religions: Muslim 89%, Eastern Orthodox 9%, unknown 2%

Tuvalu

Official name: Tuvalu

Capital city: Funafuti

Internet country code: .tv

Flag description: Light blue with the flag of the United Kingdom in the upper hoist-side quadrant; the outer half of the flag represents a map of the country with nine yellow five-pointed stars symbolizing the nine islands

Geographical description: Oceania, island group consisting of nine coral atolls in the South Pacific Ocean, about one-half of the way from Hawaii to Australia

Total area: 10 sq. mi. (26 sq. km.)

Climate: Tropical; moderated by easterly trade winds (March to November); westerly gales and heavy rain (November to March)

Nationality: *noun*: Tuvaluan(s); *adjective*: Tuvaluan

Population: 11,992 (July 2007 CIA est.)

Ethnic groups: Polynesian 96%, Micronesian 4%

Languages spoken: Tuvaluan, English, Samoan, Kiribati (on the island of Nui)

Religions: Church of Tuvalu (Congregationalist) 97%, Seventh-Day Adventist 1.4%, Baha'i 1%, other 0.6%

Uganda

Official name: Republic of Uganda

Capital city: Kampala

Internet country code: .ug

Flag description: Six equal horizontal bands of black (top), yellow, red, black, yellow, and red; a white disk is superimposed at the center and depicts a red-crested crane (the national symbol) facing the hoist side

National anthem: "Oh, Uganda! may God uphold thee"

National bird: Crested crane (Regulorum gibbericeps)

National motto: "For God and My Country"

Geographical description: Eastern Africa, west of Kenya

Total area: 93,070 sq. mi. (241,040 sq. km.)

Climate: Tropical; generally rainy with two dry seasons (December to February, June to August); semiarid in northeast

Nationality: *noun*: Ugandan(s); *adjective*: Ugandan

Population: 30,262,610 (July 2007 CIA est.)

Ethnic groups: African 99% (including Baganda 16.9%, Banyakole 9.5%, Basoga 8.4%, Bakiga 6.9%, Iteso 6.4%, Langi 6.1%, Acholi 4.7%, Bagisu 4.6%, Lugbara 4.2%, Bunyoro 2.7%, other African), European, Asian, Arab 1%

Languages spoken: English (official national language, taught in grade schools, used in courts of law and by most newspapers and some radio broadcasts), Ganda or Luganda (most widely used of the Niger-Congo languages, preferred for native language publications in the capital and may be taught in school), other Niger-Congo languages, Nilo-Saharan languages, Swahili, Arabic

Religions: Roman Catholic 41.9%, Protestant 42% (Anglican 35.9%, Pentecostal 4.6%, Seventh-Day Adventist 1.5%), Muslim 12.1%, other 3.1%, none 0.9%

Ukraine

Official name: Ukraine

Capital city: Kyiv (Kiev)

Internet country code: .ua

Flag description: Two equal horizontal bands of azure (top) and golden yellow represent grain fields under a blue sky

National anthem: "Sche ne vmerla Ukrainy i slava i volya" (first line in English translation: The glory and fame of Ukraine are still alive), lyrics by Pavlo Chubynsky, music by Mykhailo Verbytsky

Geographical description: Eastern Europe, bordering the Black Sea, between Poland, Romania, and Moldova in the west and Russia in the east

Total area: 233,000 sq. mi. (603,700 sq. km.)

Climate: Temperate continental; Mediterranean only on the southern Crimean coast; precipitation disproportionately distributed, highest in west and north, lesser in east and southeast; winters vary from cool along the Black Sea to cold farther inland; summers are warm across the greater part of the country, hot in the south

Nationality: *noun*: Ukrainian(s); *adjective*: Ukrainian

Population: 46,299,862 (July 2007 CIA est.)

Ethnic groups: Ukrainian 77.8%, Russian 17.3%, Belarusian 0.6%, Moldovan 0.5%, Crimean Tatar 0.5%, Bulgarian 0.4%, Hungarian 0.3%, Romanian 0.3%, Polish 0.3%, Jewish 0.2%, other 1.8%

Languages spoken: Ukrainian (official) 67%, Russian 24%, other 9% (includes small Romanian-, Polish-, and Hungarian-speaking minorities)

Religions: Ukrainian Orthodox - Kyiv Patriarchate 19%, Orthodox (no particular jurisdiction) 16%, Ukrainian Orthodox - Moscow Patriarchate 9%, Ukrainian Greek

Catholic 6%, Ukrainian Autocephalous Orthodox 1.7%, Protestant, Jewish, none 38%

United Arab Emirates

Official name: United Arab Emirates

Capital city: Abu Dhabi

Internet country code: .ae

Flag description: Three equal horizontal bands of green (top), white, and black with a wider vertical red band on the hoist side

Geographical description: Middle East, bordering the Gulf of Oman and the Persian Gulf, between Oman and Saudi Arabia

Total area: 30,000 sq. mi. (82,880 sq. km.)

Climate: Desert; cooler in eastern mountains

Nationality: *noun*: Emirati(s); *adjective*: Emirati

Population: 4,444,011 (July 2007 CIA est.)

Ethnic groups: Indian, Pakistani, Bangladeshi, Egyptian, Jordanian, Iranian, Filipino, other Arab; only 15-20% of residents are U.A.E. citizens)

Languages spoken: Arabic (official), Persian, English, Hindi, Urdu

Religions: Muslim 96% (Shi'a 16%), other (includes Christian, Hindu) 4%

United Kingdom

Official name: United Kingdom of Great Britain and Northern Ireland (note - Great Britain includes England, Scotland, and Wales)

Capital city: London

Internet country code: .uk

Flag description: Blue field with the red cross of Saint George (patron saint of England) edged in white superimposed on the diagonal red cross of Saint Patrick (patron saint of Ireland), which is superimposed on the diagonal white cross of Saint Andrew (patron saint of Scotland); properly known as the Union Flag, but commonly called the Union Jack; the design and colors (especially the Blue Ensign) have been the basis for a number of other flags including other Commonwealth countries and their constituent states or provinces, and British overseas territories

National anthem: "God Save the Queen"

Geographical description: Western Europe, islands including the northern one-sixth of the island of Ireland between the North Atlantic Ocean and the North Sea, northwest of France

Total area: 93,000 sq. mi. (243,000 sq. km.)

Climate: Temperate; moderated by prevailing southwest winds over the North Atlantic Current; more than one-half of the days are overcast

Nationality: *noun*: Briton(s), British (collective plural); *adjective*: British

Population: 60,776,238 (July 2007 CIA est.)

Ethnic groups: English 83.6%, Scottish 8.6%, Welsh 4.9%, Northern Irish 2.9%, African 2%, Indian 1.8%, Pakistani 1.3%, mixed 1.2%, other 1.6%

Languages spoken: English, Welsh, Irish Gaelic, Scottish Gaelic

Religions: Christian (Anglican, Roman Catholic, Presbyterian, Methodist) 71.6%, Muslim 2.7%, Hindu 1%, other 1.6%, unspecified or none 23.1%

United States

Official name: United States of America

Capital city: Washington, D.C.

Internet country code: .us

Flag description: Thirteen equal horizontal stripes of red (top and bottom) alternating with white; there is a blue rectangle in the upper hoist-side corner bearing 50 small white five-pointed stars arranged in nine offset horizontal rows of six stars (top and bottom) alternating with rows of five stars; the 50 stars represent the 50 states, the 13 stripes represent the 13 original colonies; known as Old Glory; the design and colors have been the basis for a number of other flags, including Chile, Liberia, Malaysia, and Puerto Rico

National anthem: "The Star-Spangled Banner"

National bird: Bald eagle

National mottoes: *E pluribus unum* (Out of Many, One) and "In God We Trust"

Geographical description: North America, bordering both the North Atlantic Ocean and the North Pacific Ocean, between Canada and Mexico

Total area: 3,794,062 sq. mi. (9,826,630 sq. km.)

Climate: Mostly temperate, but tropical in Hawaii and Florida, arctic in Alaska, semiarid in the Great Plains west of the Mississippi River, and arid in the Great Basin of the southwest; low winter temperatures in the northwest are ameliorated occasionally in January and February by warm chinook winds from the eastern slopes of the Rocky Mountains

Nationality: *noun*: American(s); *adjective*: American

Population: 301,139,947 (July 2007 CIA est.)

Ethnic groups: European 81.7%, black 12.9%, Asian 4.2%, Amerindian and Alaska native 1%, native Hawaiian and other Pacific islander 0.2% (*note*: a separate listing for Hispanic is not included because the United States Census Bureau considers Hispanic to mean a person of Latin American descent, including persons of Cuban, Mexican, or Puerto Rican origin, living in the U.S. who may be of any race or ethnic group - white, black, Asian, etc.)

Languages spoken: English 82.1%, Spanish 10.7%, other Indo-European 3.8%, Asian and Pacific island 2.7%, other 0.7%

Religions: Protestant 52%, Roman Catholic 24%, Mormon 2%, Jewish 1%, Muslim 1%, other 10%, none 10%

Uruguay

Official name: Oriental Republic of Uruguay

Capital city: Montevideo

Internet country code: .uy

Flag description: Nine equal horizontal stripes of white (top and bottom) alternating with blue; there is a white square in the upper hoist-side corner with a yellow sun bearing a human face known as the Sun of May with 16 rays that alternate between triangular and wavy

Geographical description: Southern South America, bordering the South Atlantic Ocean, between Argentina and Brazil

Total area: 68,000 sq. mi. (176,000 sq. km.)

Climate: Warm temperate; freezing temperatures almost unknown

Nationality: *noun:* Uruguayan(s); *adjective:* Uruguayan

Population: 3,460,607 (July 2007 CIA est.)

Ethnic groups: European 88%, mestizo 8%, African 4%, Amerindian (practically nonexistent)

Languages spoken: Spanish, Portunol, or Brazilero (Portuguese-Spanish mix on the Brazilian frontier)

Religions: Roman Catholic 66% (less than half of the adult population attends church regularly), Protestant 2%, Jewish 1%, nonprofessing or other 31%

Uzbekistan

Official name: Republic of Uzbekistan

Capital city: Tashkent (Toshkent)

Internet country code: .uz

Flag description: Three equal horizontal bands of blue (top), white, and green separated by red fimbriations with a white crescent moon and 12 white stars in the upper hoist-side quadrant

National anthem: lyrics from poem by A. Aripov, music by M. Burkhanov

Geographical description: Central Asia, north of Afghanistan

Total area: 172,741 sq. mi. (447,400 sq. km.)

Climate: Mostly mid-latitude desert, long, hot summers, mild winters; semiarid grassland in east

Nationality: *noun:* Uzbekistani(s); *adjective:* Uzbekistani

Population: 27,780,059 (July 2007 CIA est.)

Ethnic groups: Uzbek 80%, Russian 5.5%, Tajik 5%, Kazakh 3%, Karakalpak 2.5%, Tatar 1.5%, other 2.5% (1996 est.)

Languages spoken: Uzbek 74.3%, Russian 14.2%, Tajik 4.4%, other 7.1%

Religions: Muslim (mostly Sunnis) 88%, Eastern Orthodox 9%, other 3%

Vanuatu

Official name: Republic of Vanuatu

Capital city: Port-Vila (on Efate)

Internet country code: .vu

Flag description: Two equal horizontal bands of red (top) and green with a black isosceles triangle (based on the hoist side) all separated by a black-edged yellow stripe in the shape of a horizontal Y (the two points of the Y face the hoist side and enclose the triangle); centered in the triangle is a boar's tusk encircling two crossed namele leaves, all in yellow

Geographical description: Oceania, group of islands in the South Pacific Ocean, about three-quarters of the way from Hawaii to Australia

Total area: 4,707 sq. mi. (12,190 sq. km.)

Climate: Tropical; moderated by southeast trade winds from May to October; moderate rainfall from November to April; may be affected by cyclones from December to April

Nationality: *noun:* Ni-Vanuatu(s); *adjective:* Ni-Vanuatu

Population: 211,971 (July 2007 CIA est.)

Ethnic groups: Ni-Vanuatu 94%, European 4%, other Pacific Islanders, Asian 2%

Languages spoken: local languages (more than 100) 72.6%, pidgin (known as Bislama or Bichelama) 23.1%, English 1.9%, French 1.4%, other 0.3%, unspecified 0.7%

Religions: Presbyterian 31.4%, Anglican 13.4%, Roman Catholic 13.1%, Seventh-Day Adventist 10.8%, other Christian 13.8%, indigenous beliefs 5.6% (including Jon Frum cargo cult), other 9.6%, none 1%, unspecified 1.3%

Venezuela

Official name: Bolivarian Republic of Venezuela

Capital city: Caracas

Internet country code: .ve

Flag description: Three equal horizontal bands of yellow (top), blue, and red with the coat of arms on the hoist side of the yellow band and an arc of eight white five-pointed stars centered in the blue band

National anthem: "Gloria al Bravo Pueblo"

National flower: Orchid

National tree: Araguaney

National bird: Turpial

Geographical description: Northern South America, bordering the Caribbean Sea and the North Atlantic Ocean, between Colombia and Guyana

Total area: 352,143 sq. mi. (912,050 sq. km.)

Climate: Tropical; hot, humid; more moderate in highlands

Nationality: *noun:* Venezuelan(s); *adjective:* Venezuelan

Population: 26,023,528 (July 2007 CIA est.)

Ethnic groups: Spanish, Italian, Portuguese, Arab, German, African, indigenous Amerindian

Languages spoken: Spanish (official), numerous indigenous dialects

Religions: nominally Roman Catholic 96%, Protestant 2%, other 2%

Vietnam

Official name: Socialist Republic of Vietnam

Capital city: Hanoi

Internet country code: .vn

Flag description: Red with a large yellow five-pointed star in the center

National anthem: "Tiến quân ca" (The Song of the Marching Troops) by Văn Cao

Geographical description: Southeastern Asia, bordering the Gulf of Thailand, Gulf of Tonkin, and South China Sea, alongside China, Laos, and Cambodia

Total area: 127,243 sq. mi. (331,114 sq. km.)

Climate: Tropical in south; monsoonal in north with hot, rainy season (May to September) and warm, dry season (October to March)

Nationality: *noun*: Vietnamese (singular and plural); *adjective*: Vietnamese

Population: 85,262,356 (July 2007 CIA est.)

Ethnic groups: Kinh (Viet) 86.2%, Tay 1.9%, Thai 1.7%, Muong 1.5%, Khome 1.4%, Hoa 1.1%, Nun 1.1%, Hmong 1%, others 4.1%

Languages spoken: Vietnamese (official), English (increasingly favored as a second language), some French, Chinese, and Khmer; mountain area languages (Mon-Khmer and Malayo-Polynesian)

Religions: Buddhist 9.3%, Roman Catholic 6.7%, Hoa Hao 1.5%, Cao Dai 1.1%, Protestant 0.5%, Muslim 0.1%, none 80.8%

Yemen

Official name: Republic of Yemen

Capital city: Sanaa

Internet country code: .ye

Flag description: Three equal horizontal bands of red (top), white, and black

Geographical description: Middle East, bordering the Arabian Sea, Gulf of Aden, and Red Sea, between Oman and Saudi Arabia

Total area: 203,796 sq. mi. (527,970 sq. km.)

Climate: Mostly desert; hot and humid along west coast; temperate in western mountains affected by seasonal monsoon; extraordinarily hot, dry, harsh desert in east

Nationality: *noun*: Yemeni(s); *adjective*: Yemeni

Population: 22,230,531 (July 2007 CIA est.)

Ethnic groups: Predominantly Arab, but also Afro-Arabs, South Asians, Europeans

Languages spoken: Arabic

Religions: Muslim including Shaf'i (Sunni) and Zaydi (Shi'a), small numbers of Jewish, Christian, and Hindu

Zambia

Official name: Republic of Zambia

Capital city: Lusaka

Internet country code: .zm

Flag description: Green with a panel of three vertical bands of red (hoist side), black, and orange below a soaring orange eagle, on the outer edge of the flag

Geographical description: Southern Africa, east of Angola

Total area: 290,585 sq. mi. (752,614 sq. km.)

Climate: Tropical; modified by altitude; rainy season (October to April)

Nationality: *noun*: Zambian(s); *adjective*: Zambian

Population: 11,477,447 (July 2007 CIA est.)

Ethnic groups: African (more than 70 groups) 98.7%, European 1.1%, other 0.2%

Languages spoken: English (official), major vernaculars include Bemba, Kaonda, Lozi, Lunda, Luvale, Nyanja, Tonga, and about 70 other indigenous languages

Religions: Christian 50%-75%, Muslim and Hindu 24%-49%, indigenous religions 1%

Zimbabwe

Official name: Republic of Zimbabwe

Capital city: Harare

Internet country code: .zw

Flag description: Seven equal horizontal bands of green, yellow, red, black, red, yellow, and green with a white isosceles triangle edged in black with its base on the hoist side; a yellow Zimbabwe bird representing the long history of the country is superimposed on a red five-pointed star in the center of the triangle, which symbolizes peace; green symbolizes agriculture, yellow represents mineral wealth, red symbolizes blood shed to achieve independence, and black stands for the native people

Geographical description: Southern Africa, between South Africa and Zambia

Total area: 150,760 sq. mi. (390,580 sq. km.)

Climate: Tropical; moderated by altitude; rainy season (November to March)

Nationality: *noun*: Zimbabwean(s); *adjective*: Zimbabwean

Population: 12,311,143 (July 2007 CIA est.)

Ethnic groups: African 98% (Shona 82%, Ndebele 14%, other 2%), mixed and Asian 1%, white less than 1%

Languages spoken: English (official), Shona, Sindebele (the language of the Ndebele, sometimes called Ndebele), numerous but minor tribal dialects

Religions: Syncretic Christian and indigenous religions 50%, Christian 25%, indigenous religions 24%, Muslim and other 1%

APPENDIX 11

Legal Holidays by Country

Legal holidays in the following countries are listed in Gregorian calendar order. Jewish holidays and Christian movable holidays are listed according to the range of months in which the day may fall. Muslim holidays appear at the bottom of the list for each country, since their dates are determined by the Muslim lunar calendar.

Afghanistan

Feb 15	Liberation Day
Mar	Nauruz
Apr 28	Victory Day
Aug 19	Independence Day

Muslim holidays:

Muharram	Ashura
Rabi al-Awwa	Mellad Nabi (Mawlid al-Nabi)
1 Ramadan	Ramadan
Shawwal (3 days)	Id al-Fitr
Dhu al-Hijjah (3 days)	Id al-Adha

Albania

Jan 1	New Year's Day
Jan 2	New Year's Holiday
Mar	Nevruz
Mar-Apr	Catholic Easter
Apr-May	Orthodox Easter
May 1	May Day
Oct 19	Mother Teresa Day
Nov 28	Independence Day
Nov 29	National Liberation Day
Dec 25	Christmas

Muslim holidays:

Shawwal	Lesser Bajram (Id al-Fitr)
Dhu al-Hijjah	Greater Bajram (Id al-Adha)

Algeria

Jan 1	New Year's Day
May 1	Labor Day
Jun 19	Anniversary of June 19
Jul 5	Independence Day
Nov 1	Anniversary of the Revolution (1954)

Muslim holidays:

Muharram	Islamic New Year
Muharram	Achoura (Ashura)

Rabi al-Nabi	Mawlid al-Nabi
Shawwal	Id al-Fitr
Dhu al-Hijjah	Id al-Adha

Andorra

Jan 1	New Year's Day
Jan 6	Twelfth Night
Feb-Mar	Carnival
Mar 14	Day of the Constitution
Mar-Apr: Fri before Easter	Good Friday
Mar-Apr: Mon after Easter	Easter Monday
May 1	Labour Day
May-Jun: Mon after Pentecost	Whitsun Monday
Aug 15	Assumption
Sep 8	National Day (Our Lady of Meritxell)
Nov 1	All Saints' Day
Dec 8	Immaculate Conception
Dec 25	Christmas
Dec 26	St. Etienne's Day (Patron of the Capital)

Angola

Jan 1	New Year's Day
Jan 4	Martyrs of Colonial Repression Day
Feb 4	Day Inicio de Luta Armada (Commencement of Armed Struggle Day)
Feb-Mar	Carnival Day
Mar 8	International Women's Day
Mar-Apr: Fri before Easter	Good Friday
Apr 14	Peace and National Reconciliation Day
May 1	International Workers' Day
May 25	Africa Day
Jun 1	International Children's Day
Sep 17	National Hero's Day (Birthday of President Neto)
Nov 2	All Souls' Day
Nov 11	Independence Day
Dec 10	Foundation of the MPLA Workers' Party Day
Dec 25	Family Day (Christmas Day)

Antigua and Barbuda

Jan 1 ....New Year's Day
Mar-Apr: Fri before Easter ....Good Friday
Mar-Apr: Mon after Easter ....Easter Monday
May, first Mon ....Labour Day
May-Jun: Mon after Pentecost ....Whit Monday
Aug, first Mon ....J'ouvert (Carnival)
Aug, first Tues ....Last Lap (Carnival)
Nov 1 ....Independence Day
Dec 9 ....National Heroes Day
Dec 25 ....Christmas Day
Dec 26 ....Boxing Day

Argentina

Jan 1 ....New Year's Day
Mar-Apr: Fri before Easter ....Good Friday
Mar-Apr, first and last days ....Passover
Mar 24 ....National Memorial Day (Truth and Justice Day)
Apr 2 ....Malvinas Veterans and Memorial Day
May 1 ....Labor Day
May 25 ....1810 Revolution Anniversary
Jun 10 ....Islas Malvinas Day
Jun 20 ....Flag Day
Jul 9 ....Independence Day
Aug 17 ....San Martín Day
Sep-Oct ....Yom Kippur
Oct 12 ....Dia de la Raza (Columbus Day)
Dec 8 ....Immaculate Conception
Dec 25 ....Christmas Day

Muslim holidays:

Muharram ....Islamic New Year
Shawwal ....Ending of the Fast (Id al-Fitr)
Dhu al-Hijjah ....Feast of Sacrifice (Id al-Adha)

Armenia

Jan 1-2 ....Amanor (New Year's holiday)
Jan 6 ....Surb Tsnund (Armenian Christmas Day)
Jan 28 ....Army Day
Mar 8 ....International Women's Day
Apr 24 ....Genocide Memorial Day
May 1 ....Labour Day
May 9 ....Victory and Peace Day
May 28 ....First Republic Day
Jul 5 ....Constitution Day
Sep 21 ....Independence Day
Dec 31 ....New Year's Eve

Australia

Jan 1 ....New Year's Day
Jan 26 or following Mon ....Australia Day
Mar, second Mon ....Labour Day
Mar-Apr: Fri before Easter ....Good Friday
Mar-Apr: Fri before Easter ....Holy Saturday
Mar-Apr: Mon after Easter ....Easter Monday
Apr 25 ....Anzac Day
Jun, second Mon ....Queen Elizabeth II Birthday
Nov, first Tues ....Melbourne Cup Day

Dec 25 ....Christmas Day
Dec 26 ....Boxing Day

Austria

Jan 1 ....New Year's Day
Jan 6 ....Epiphany
Mar-Apr: Mon after Easter ....Easter Monday
Apr-Jun ....Ascension Day
May 1 ....Staatsfeiertag (Labour Day)
May-Jun ....Corpus Christi
May-Jun: Mon after Pentecost ....Whit Monday
Aug 15 ....Assumption
Oct 26 ....National Day
Nov 1 ....All Saints' Day
Dec 8 ....Immaculate Conception
Dec 25 ....Christtag (Christmas Day)
Dec 26 ....Stefanitag (St. Stephen's Day)

Azerbaijan

Jan 1 ....New Year's Day
Jan 20 ....Day of the Martyrs
Mar 8 ....International Women's Day
Mar 21 ....Novruz Bayrami
May 9 ....Victory in World War II Day
May 28 ....Republic Day
Jun 15 ....National Salvation Day
Jun 26 ....Army and Navy Day
Oct 18 ....National Independence Day
Nov 12 ....Constitution Day
Nov 17 ....Day of National Revival
Dec 31 ....Day of Solidarity of
Azerbaijanis throughout the World

Bahamas

Jan 1 ....New Year's Day
Mar-Apr: Fri before Easter ....Good Friday
Mar-Apr: Mon after Easter ....Easter Monday
May-Jun: Mon after Pentecost ....Whit Monday
Jun, first Fri ....Labour Day
Jul 10 ....Independence Day
Aug, first Mon ....Emancipation Day
Oct 12 ....Discovery Day
Dec 25 ....Christmas Day
Dec 26 ....Boxing Day

Bahrain

Jan 1 ....New Year's Day
May 1 ....Labor Day
Dec 16 ....National Day

Muslim holidays:

1 Muharram ....Hijra (Islamic New Year)
10 Muharram ....Ashoora
12 Rabi al-Awwal ....Prophet's Birthday (Mawlid al-Nabi)
1-3 Shawwal ....Eid al Fitr (Id al-Fitr)
10-12 Dhu al-Hijjah ....Eid al Adha (Id al-Adha)

Bangladesh

Feb 21 . . . . .Shahid Dibosh (Mother Language Day)
Mar 26 . . . . .Independence Day
Apr-May . . . . .Buddha Purnima
Apr, mid- . . . . .Pahela Baishakh (Bengali New Year)
May 1 . . . . .May Day
Aug 15 . . . . .Bangabandhu National Mourning Day
Aug-Sep . . . . .Janmashtami
Sep-Oct . . . . .Durga Puja
Dec 16 . . . . .Bijoy Dibosh (Victory Day)
Dec 25 . . . . .Christmas

Muslim holidays:

Muharram . . . . .Ashura
Rabi al-Awwal . . . . .Mawlid al-Nabi
15 Shaban . . . . .Shab-e-Barat
Ramadan, last Fri . . . . .Jumat-al-wida
Shawwal . . . . .Id al-Fitr
Dhu al-Hijjah . . . . .Id al-Adha

Barbados

Jan 1 . . . . .New Year's Day
Jan 21 . . . . .Errol Barrow Day
Mar-Apr: Fri before Easter . . . . .Good Friday
Mar-Apr: Mon after Easter . . . . .Easter Monday
Apr 28 . . . . .National Heroes Day
May 1 . . . . .Labour Day
May-Jun: Mon after Pentecost . . . . .Whit Monday
Aug 1 . . . . .Emancipation Day
Aug 5, first Mon .Kadooment Day
Nov 30 . . . . .Independence Day
Dec 25 . . . . .Christmas Day
Dec 26 . . . . .Boxing Day

Belarus

Jan 1-2 .New Year's Day holiday
Jan 7 . . . . .Orthodox Christmas
Mar 8 . . . . .Women's Day
Apr-May, ninth day after
  Orthodox Easter . . . . . . .Radunitsa (Ancestors Veneration)
May 1 . . . . .Labor Day
May 9 . . . . .Victory Day
Jul 3 . . . . .Independence Day
Nov 7 .October Revolution Day
Dec 25 . . . . .Catholic Christmas

Belgium

Jan 1 . . . . .New Year's Day
Mar-Apr: Mon after Easter . . . . .Easter Monday
May 1 . . . . .Labor Day
May-Jun . . . . .Ascension Day
May-Jun . . . . .Whit Monday
Jul 21 . . . . .Independence Day
Aug 15 . . . . .Assumption Day
Nov 1 . . . . .All Saints' Day
Nov 11 . . . . .Armistice Day
Dec 25 . . . . .Christmas Day

Belize

Jan 1 . . . . .New Year's Day
Mar 9 . . . . .Baron Bliss Day
Mar-Apr: Fri before Easter . . . . .Good Friday
Mar-Apr: Sat before Easter . . . . .Holy Saturday
Mar-Apr: Mon after Easter . . . . .Easter Monday
May 1 . . . . .Labour Day
May 24 . . . . .Sovereign's Day/Commonwealth Day
Sep 10 . . . . .National Day
Sep 21 . . . . . . .Independence Day (St. George's Caye Day)
Oct 12 . . . . .Pan American Day
Nov 19 . . . . .Garifuna Settlement Day
Dec 25 . . . . .Christmas Day
Dec 26 . . . . .Boxing Day

Benin

Jan 1 . . . . .New Year's Day
Jan 10 . . . . .National Vodoun Day
                                    (Traditional Religions Day)
Mar-Apr: Mon after Easter . . . . .Easter Monday
May 1 . . . . .Labor Day
May-Jun . . . . .Ascension Day
May-Jun . . . . .Whit Monday
Aug 1 . . . . .Independence Day
Aug 15 . . . . .Assumption
Nov 1 . . . . .All Saints' Day
Dec 25 . . . . .Christmas

Muslim holidays:

Rabi al-Awwal . . . . .Maouloud (Prophet's Birthday)
Shawwal . . . . .Korite (Id al-Fitr)
Dhu al-Hijjah .Tabaski (Id al-Adha)

Bermuda

Jan 1 . . . . .New Year's Day
Mar-Apr: Fri before Easter . . . . .Good Friday
May 24 . . . . .Bermuda Day
Jun, second Mon . . . . .Queen Elizabeth II Birthday
Jul-Aug, Thurs before first
  Mon in Aug . . . . .Emancipation Day (Cup Match)
Jul-Aug, Fri before first
  Mon in Aug . . . . .Somer's Day (Cup Match)
Sep, first Mon . . . . .Labour Day
Oct, second Mon . . . . .Heroes' Day
                                    (Dame Lois Browne-Evans)
Nov 11 . . . . .Rememberance Day
Dec 25 . . . . .Christmas Day
Dec 26 . . . . .Boxing Day

Bhutan

Jan-Mar . . . . .Losar (Tibetan New Year)
Jun 2 . . . . .Coronation Anniversary
Aug 8 . . . . .Independence Day
Nov 11 (3 days) . . . . .Birthday of HM
                          King Jigme Singye Wangchuck
Dec 17 . . . . .National Day

Bolivia

Jan 1 . . . . .New Year's Day
Feb-Mar: Mon and Tues before
  Ash Wednesday . . . . .Carnival
Mar-Apr: Fri before Easter . . . . .Good Friday
May 1 . . . . .Labor Day
May-Jun . . . . .Corpus Christi
Aug 6 .National/Independence Day
Nov 2 . . . . .All Souls' Day
Dec 25 . . . . .Christmas Day

Bosnia and Herzegovina

Jan 1 . . . . .New Year's Day
Mar-Apr, Friday before Easter . . . . .Good Friday
Mar-Apr, Monday after Easter . . . . .Easter Monday
May 1 . . . . .Labor Day
Dec 25 . . . . .Christmas Day

Botswana

Jan 1 . . . . .New Year's Day
Jan 2 . . . . .Public Holiday
Mar-Apr . . . . .Good Friday through Easter Monday
May 1 . . . . .Labor Day
May-Jun . . . . .Ascension Day
Jul 1 . . . . .Sir Seretse Khama Day
Jul 16 . . . . .President's Day
Jul 17 . . . . .Public Holiday
Sep 30 . . . . .Botswana Day
Oct 1 . . . . .Public Holiday
Dec 25 . . . . .Christmas
Dec 26 . . . . .Boxing Day

Brazil

Jan 1 . . . . .New Year's Day
Feb-Mar: Mon and Tues before
  Ash Wednesday . . . . .Carnival
Mar-Apr: Fri before Easter . . . . .Good Friday
Apr 21 . . . . .Tiradentes Day
Apr 23 . . . . .St. George's Day
May 1 . . . . .Labor Day
May-Jun . . . . .Corpus Christi
Sep 7 . . . . .Independence Day
Oct 12 .Our Lady of Aparacida Day
Nov 2 . . . . .All Souls' Day
Nov 15 . . . . .Proclamation of the Republic
Dec 25 . . . . .Christmas Day

Brunei

Jan 1 . . . . .New Year's Day
Jan-Feb . . . . .Chinese New Year
Feb 23 . . . . .National Day
May 31 . . . . .Royal Brunei Armed Forces Day
Jul 15 . . . . .H.M. the Sultan's Birthday
Dec 25 . . . . .Christmas Day

Muslim holidays:

1 Muharram . . . . .First day of Islamic New Year

12 Rabi al-Awwal . . . . .Muhammad's Birthday
                                                  (Mawlid al-Nabi)
27 Rajab . . . . .Isra Mikraj (Laylat al-Miraj)
1 Ramadan . . . . .First day of fasting month
During Ramadan . . . . .Anniversary of the Revelation
                                            of the Quran (Laylat al-Qadr)
1 Shawwal . . . . .Hari Raya (Id al-Fitr)
10-12 Dhu al-Hijjah . . . .(Id al-Adha)

Bulgaria

Jan 1 . . . . .New Year's Day
Mar 3 .National Day/Bulgaria Day
Apr-May: Mon after Easter . . . . .Easter Monday
May 1 . . . . .Labor Day
May 6 . . . . .Day of the Armed Forces
May 24 . . . . .Day of Bulgarian Enlightenment,
                                    Culture and the Slavonic Alphabet
Sep 6 . . . . .National Unification Day
Sep 22 . . . . .Independence Day
Nov 1 . . . . .Enlightenment Leaders Day
Dec 24-26 . . . . .Christmas

Burkina Faso

Jan 1 . . . . .New Year's Day
Jan 3 . . . . .Revolution Day
                                          (Anniversary of the 1966 uprising)
Mar 8 .International Women's Day
Mar-Apr, Monday after Easter . . . . .Easter Monday
Apr-Jun . . . . .Ascension Day
May 1 . . . . .Labor Day
Aug 5 . . . . .Independence Day
Aug 15 . . . . .Assumption
Nov 1 . . . . .All Saints' Day
Dec 11 . . . . . .Proclamation of Independence (National Day)
Dec 25 . . . . .Christmas Day

Muslim holidays:

Rabi al-Awwal . . . . .Mouloud (Mawlid al-Nabi)
Shawwal . . . . .Korite/Aïd El Segheir (Id al-Fitr)
Dhu al-Hijjah . . . . .Tabaski/Aïd El Kebir (Id al-Adha)

Burma. *See* Myanmar

Burundi

Jan 1 . . . . .New Year's Day
Feb 5 . . . . .Unity Day
Apr 6 .President Ntaryamira Day
May 1 . . . . .Labor Day
May-Jun . . . . .Ascension Day
Jul 1 . . . . .Independence Day
Aug 15 . . . . .Assumption
Oct 13 . . . . .Prince Rwagasore Day
Oct 21 . . . . .President Ndadaye Day
Nov 1 . . . . .All Saints' Day
Dec 25 . . . . .Christmas

Muslim holidays:

Shawwal . . . . .Aid-El-Fithr (Id al-Fitr)
Dhu al-Hijjah . . . . .Aid-El-Hadj (Id al-Adha)

Cambodia

Jan 1	New Year's Day
Jan 7	Victory Day (Liberation Day over Genocidal Regime)
Feb	Meak Bochea
Mar 8	International Women's Day
Apr 13-15	Cambodian New Year
Apr-May	Visaka Bochea (Birth, Enlightenment, and Death of Buddha)
May 1	International Labour Day
May 13-15	King's Birthday
May	Royal Ploughing Ceremony
Jun 18	Former Queen Mother's Birthday
Sep 24	Constitution Day
Sep-Oct	Phchum Ben (Ancestors' Day)
Oct 29	King's Coronation Day (Norodom Sihamoni)
Oct 30-Nov 1	Birthday of His Majesty Preah Bat Norodom Sihanouk, King of Cambodia
Oct-Nov	Bonn Om Toak (Water Festival)
Nov 9	Independence Day
Dec 10	International Human Rights Day (U.N.)
Dec 25	Christmas

Cameroon

Jan 1	New Year's Day
Feb 11	Youth Day
Mar-Apr: Fri before Easter	Good Friday
May 1	Labor Day
May 20	National Day
May-Jun	Ascension Day
Aug 15	Assumption
Dec 25	Christmas Day

Muslim holidays:

Shawwal	Djoulde Soumae (Id al-Fitr)
Dhu al-Hijjah	Tabaski (Id al-Adha)

Canada

Jan 1	New Year's Day
Mar-Apr: Fri before Easter	Good Friday
Mar-Apr: Mon after Easter	Easter Monday
May 25, Mon before Victoria Day	(Queen Elizabeth II Birthday observed)
Jul 1	Canada Day
Sep, first Mon	Labour Day
Oct, second Mon	Thanksgiving Day
Nov 11	Remembrance Day
Dec 25	Christmas Day
Dec 26	Boxing Day

Cape Verde

Jan 1	New Year's Day
Jan 13	Democracy and Liberty Day
Jan 20	National Heroes Day
May 1	Labor Day
Jun 1	Youth Day
Jul 5	Independence Day
Aug 15	Assumption

Nov 1	All Saints' Day
Dec 25	Christmas Day

Central African Republic

Jan 1	New Year's Day
Mar 29	Boganda Day
Mar-Apr: Mon after Easter	Easter Monday
May 1	Labor Day
May-Jun	Ascension Day
May-Jun	Whit Monday
Jun 30	Prayer Day
Aug 13	Independence Day
Aug 15	Assumption
Nov 1	All Saints' Day
Dec 1	National Day (Proclamation of the Republic)
Dec 25	Christmas Day

Chad

Jan 1	New Year's Day
Mar-Apr: Mon after Easter	Easter Monday
May 1	Labor Day
Aug 11	Independence Day
Nov 1	All Saints' Day
Nov 28	Proclamation of the Republic
Dec 1	Freedom and Democracy Day
Dec 25	Christmas Day

Muslim holidays:

Rabi al-Awwal	Maouloud Al Nebi (Mawlid al-Nabi)
Shawwal	Korite (Aid al-Fitr)
Dhu al-Hijjah	Tabaski (Id al-Adha)

Chile

Jan 1	New Year's Day
Mar-Apr, Fri before Easter	Good Friday
Mar-Apr, Sat before Easter	Holy Saturday
Mar-Apr, Sat before Easter	Easter
May 1	Labor Day
May 21	Battle of Iquique Day
June 29 (varies)	Sts. Peter and Paul Day
Jul 16	Lady of Carmen Day
Aug 15	Assumption
Sep 18	Independence Day
Sep 19	Army Day
Oct 12 (varies)	Dia de la Raza (Columbus Day)
Nov 1	All Saints' Day
Dec 8	Immaculate Conception
Dec 25	Christmas Day

China

Jan 1	New Year's Day
Jan-Feb (3 days)	Lunar New Year
May 1 (3 days)	Labor Day
Oct 1 (3 days)	National Days

Colombia

Jan 1 ....New Year's Day
Jan 6 ....Epiphany
Mar 19 ....St. Joseph's Day
Mar-Apr: Thurs before Easter ....Holy Thursday
Mar-Apr: Fri before Easter ....Good Friday
Apr-Jun ....Ascension Day
May-Jun ....Corpus Christi
May-Jun: Fri after Corpus Christi ...Sacred Heart of Jesus
May 1 ....Labor Day
Jun 29 (varies) ....Sts. Peter and Paul Day
Jul 20 ....Independence Day
Aug 7 ....Battle of Boyacá Day
Aug 15 ....Assumption
Oct 12 ....Race Day
Nov 1 ....All Saints' Day
Nov 11 ....Cartagena Independence Day
Dec 8 ....Immaculate Conception
Dec 25 ....Christmas Day

Comoros

Jan 1 ....New Year's Day
Mar 18 ....Cheikh Al Maarouf Day
May 1 ....Labor Day
Jul 6 ....Independence Day
Nov 12 ....Journée Nationale Maoré

Muslim holidays:

Muharram ....Islamic New Year
Rabi al-Awwal ....Mouloud (Mawlid al-Nabi)
Rajab ....Laylat al-Miraj
Shawwal ....Ide el Fitr (Id al-Fitr)
Dhu al-Hijjah ....Ide el Kabir (Id al-Adha)

Congo, Democratic Republic of

Jan 1 ....New Year's Day
Jan 4 ....Day of the Martyrs for Independence
Jan 16 ....Heroes' Day (Laurent Kabila)
Jan 17 ....Heroes' Day (Patrice Lumumba)
May 1 ....Labor Day
May 17 ....Liberation Day
Jun 30 ....Independence Day
Aug 1 ....Parents' Day
Dec 25 ....Christmas Day

Congo, Republic of

Jan 1 ....New Year's Day
Mar –Apr ....Easter Monday
Apr-Jun ....Ascension Day
May-Jun, Mon after Pentecost ....Whit Monday
May 1 ....Labor Day
Jun 10 ....Reconciliation Day
Aug 15 ....Independence Day
Nov 1 ....All Saints' Day
Dec 25 ....Christmas

Costa Rica

Jan 1 ....New Year's Day

Mar-Apr ....Holy Week
Apr 11 ....Anniverary of Rivas Battle
(Juan Santamaria Day)
May 1 ....Labor Day
Jul 25 ....Annexation of Guanacaste
Aug 15 ....Assumption (Mother's Day)
Sep 15 ....Independence Day
Oct 12 ....Culture Day/Columbus Day
Dec 25 ....Christmas

Côte d'Ivoire

Jan 1 ....New Year's Day
Mar-Apr: Mon after Easter ....Easter Monday
May 1 ....Labor Day
May-Jun ....Ascension Day
May-Jun ....Whit Monday
Aug 7 ....Independence Day
Nov 1 ....All Saints' Day
Nov 15 ....Peace Day
Dec 25 ....Christmas

Muslim holidays:

Rabi al-Awwal ....Mawlid al-Nabi
Shawwal ....Korite (Id al-Fitr)
Dhu al-Hijjah ....Tabaski (Id al-Adha)

Croatia

Jan 1 ....New Year's Day
Jan 6 ....Epiphany
Mar-Apr: Mon after Easter ....Easter Monday
May 1 ....Labor Day
May-Jun ....Corpus Christi
May 30 ....Statehood Day (National Day)
Jun 22 ....Croatian Uprising Day
Jun 25 ....Croatian Statehood Day
Aug 5 ....Victory and Homeland Gratitude Day
Aug 15 ....Assumption
Oct 8 ....Croatian Independence Day
Nov 1 ....All Saints' Day
Dec 25 ....Christmas
Dec 26 ....St. Stephen's Day

Cuba

Jan 1 ....Liberation Day
Jan 2 ....New Year Public Holiday
May 1 ....Labor Day
Jul 26 and 27 ....National Revolution Day
Oct 10 ....Anniversary of the beginning
of the War of Independence (1868)
Dec 25 ....Christmas
Dec 31 ....End of the Year Public Holiday

Cyprus

Jan 1 ....New Year's Day
Jan 6 ....Epiphany Day
Feb-Mar: 50 days before
Orthodox Easter ....Kathara Deftera (Green Monday)

Mar 25 . . . .(Greek Independence Day
Apr 1 . . . . .EOKA Day (Greek Cypriot National Day)
Apr 23 .Turkish Independence Day
Apr-May: Fri before Orthodox Easter . . . . . . .Good Friday
Apr-May: Mon after Orthodox Easter . . . . .Easter Monday
May 1 . . . . .Labor Day
May 19 . . . . .Ataturk Day
May-Jun . . . . .Kataklysmos Festival (Pentecost)
Aug 15 . . . . .Assumption
Aug 30 . . . . .Turkish Victory Day
Oct 1 . . . . .Cyprus Independence Day
Oct 28 . . . . .Ochi Day
Oct 29 . . . . .Republic of Turkey Day
Dec 24 . . . . .Christmas Eve
Dec 25 . . . . .Christmas Day
Dec 26 . . . . .Boxing Day

Muslim holidays:

12 Rabi al-Awwal . . . .Prophet's Birthday (Mawlid al-Nabi)
1-2 Shawwal . . . . .Ramazan Bayrami (Id al-Fitr)
10-12 Dhu al-Hijjah . . . . . . .Kourban Bayrami (Id al-Adha)

Czech Republic

Jan 1 . . . . .New Year's Day
Mar-Apr: Mon after Easter . . . . .Easter Monday
May 1 . . . . .Labor Day
May 8 . . . . .Liberation Day
Jul 5 . . . . .Sts. Cyril and Methodius Day
Jul 6 . . . . .Jan Hus Day
Sep 28 . . . . .Czech Statehood Day
Oct 28 . . . . .Independence Day
Nov 17 . . . . .Freedom and Democracy Day
Dec 24 . . . . .Christmas Eve
Dec 25 . . . . .Christmas Day
Dec 26 . . . . .St. Stephen's Day

Denmark

Jan 1 . . . . .New Year's Day
Mar-Apr: Thurs before Easter . . . . .Maundy Thursday
Mar-Apr: Fri before Easter . . . . .Good Friday
Mar-Apr: Mon after Easter . . . . .Easter Monday
Apr-May: fourth Fri after Easter . . . . .Store Bededag
(Great Prayer)
Apr-Jun . . . . .Ascension Day
May-Jun: Mon after Pentecost . . . . .Whit Monday
Jun 5 . . . . .Constitution Day
Dec 24 . . . . .Christmas Eve
Dec 25 . . . . .Christmas Day
Dec 26 . . . . .Second Christmas Day

Djibouti

Jan 1 . . . . .New Year's Day
May 1 . . . . .Labor Day
Jun 27 . . . . .Independence Day

Muslim holidays:

1 Muharram . . . . Awal Mouharam (Islamic New Year)
Rabi al-Awwal . . . . .Mawlid al-Nabi
Shawwal (two days) . . . . Id al-Fitr
Dhu al-Hijjah (three days) . . . . .Id al-Adha

Dominica

Jan 1 . . . . .New Year's Day
Feb (two days) . . . . .Carnival
Mar-Apr: Fri before Easter . . . . .Good Friday
Mar-Apr: Mon after Easter . . . . .Easter Monday
May, first Mon . . . . .Labor Day
May-Jun . . . . .Whit Monday
Aug 5 . . . . .Emancipation Day (August Monday)
Nov 3 . . . . .Independence Day
Nov 4 . . . . .Community Day of Service
Dec 25 . . . . .Christmas
Dec 26 . . . . .Boxing Day

Dominican Republic

Jan 1 . . . . .New Year's Day
Jan 6 . . . . .Epiphany
Jan 21 . . . . . . .Day of the Virgin of Altagracia (High Grace)
Jan 26 . . . . .Birthday of Juan Pablo Duarte
Feb 27 . . . . .Independence Day
Mar-Apr: Fri before Easter . . . . .Good Friday
May 1 . . . . .Labor Day
May-Jun . . . . .Corpus Christi
Aug 16 . . . . .Independence Restoration Day
Sep 24 . . . . .Day of the Virgin of Mercedes
Nov 6 . . . . .Constitution Day
Dec 25 . . . . .Christmas Day

East Timor (Timor-Leste)

Jan 1 . . . . .New Year's Day
Mar-Apr: Fri before Easter . . . . .Good Friday
May-Jun . . . . .Corpus Christi
May 1 . . . . .Labor Day
May 20 . . . . .Independence Day
Aug 30 . . . . .Consultation Day (Election Day)
Nov 1 . . . . .All Saints' Day
Nov 2 . . . . .All Souls' Day
Nov 12 . . . . .National Youth Day
Nov 28 . . . . .Independence Proclamation Day
Dec 7 . . . . .National Heroes' Day
Dec 8 . . . . .Immaculate Conception
Dec 25 . . . . .Christmas

Muslim holidays:

1 Shawwal . . . . .Idul Fitri (Id al-Fitr)
Dhu al-Hijjah . . . . .Idul Adha (Id al-Adha)

Ecuador

Jan 1 . . . . .New Year's Day
Feb-Mar . . . . .Carnaval
Mar-Apr: Fri before Easter . . . . .Good Friday
May 1 . . . . .Labor Day
May 24 . . . . .Battle of Pichincha Day
Aug 10 . . . . .National Day
Oct 9 . . . . .Guayaquil Independence Day
Nov 2 . . . . .All Souls' Day
Nov 3 . . . . .Cuenca Independence Day
Dec 25 . . . . .Christmas Day

Egypt

Jan 7	Coptic Christmas
Apr 25	Sinai Liberation Day
Apr-May: Mon after Coptic Easter	Sham El-Nassem
May 1	Labor Day
Jul 23	Revolution Day
Oct 6	Armed Forces Day

Muslim holidays:

1 Muharram	El Hijra (New Year)
12 Rabi al-Awwal	Moulid El Nabi (Muhammad's Birthday)
Shawwal (two days)	Lesser Bairam (Id al-Fitr)
Dhu al-Hijjah (three days)	Great Bairam (Id al-Adha)

El Salvador

Jan 1	New Year's Day
Mar-Apr: Thur, Fri, and Sat before Easter	Maundy Thursday – Holy Saturday
May 1	Labor Day
Aug 3 (four days)	Festival of El Salvador del Mundo (Savior of the World)
Sep 15	Independence Day
Oct 12	Día de la Raza (Columbus Day)
Nov 1 (varies)	Cry of Independence Day
Nov 2	Día de los Difuntos (Day of the Dead or All Souls' Day)
Dec 25	Christmas Day
Dec 31	New Year's Eve

England. *See* United Kingdom

Equatorial Guinea

Jan 1	New Year's Day
Mar-Apr: Sun before Easter	Palm Sunday
Mar-Apr: Fri before Easter	Good Friday
Mar-Apr	Easter Sunday
May-Jun	Corpus Christi
Jun 5	President's Day
Aug 3	Freedom Day
Aug 15	Constitution Day
Oct 12	Independence Day
Dec 8	Immaculate Conception
Dec 25	Christmas Day

Eritrea

Jan 1	New Year's Day
Jan 7	Eritrean Christmas
Jan 19	Timket (Coptic Epiphany)
Feb 10	Fenkil Day
Apr-May: Fri before Easter	Orthodox Good Friday
Apr-May	Tensae (Orthodox Easter)
May 1	May Day
May 24	Liberation Day
Jun 20	Martyrs' Day
Sep 1	Revolution Day
Sep 11	Keddus Johannes (Orthodox New Year)
Sep 27	Meskel

Muslim holidays:

12 Rabi al-Awwal	Muhammad's Birthday (Mawlid al-Nabi)
1 Shawwal	Ed'Al Fetir (Id al-Fitr)
Dhu al-Hijjah	Ed'Al Adha (Id al-Adha)

Estonia

Jan 1	New Year's Day
Feb 24	Independence Day
Mar-Apr: Fri before Easter	Good Friday
Mar-Apr	Easter
May 1	Spring Day
May-Jun	Whit Sunday (Pentecost)
Jun 23	Victory Day
Jun 24	Midsummer's Day/St. John's Day
Aug 20	Restoration of Independence Day
Dec 24	Christmas Eve
Dec 25	Christmas Day
Dec 26	Boxing Day

Ethiopia

Jan 7	Genna (Ethiopian Christmas)
Jan 19	Timket (Ethiopian Epiphany)
Mar 2	Adwa Victory Day
Apr-May: Fri before Easter	Siklet (Good Friday)
Apr-May	Fasika (Easter)
May 1	International Labor Day
May 5	Patriots' Victory Day
May 28	Overthrow of the Derg Regime
Sep 11	Enkutatash (Ethiopian New Year)
Sep 27	Meskel (Finding of the True Cross)

Muslim holidays:

12 Rabi al-Awwal	Muhammad's Birthday (Mawlid al-Nabi)
1 Shawwal	Id Al Fetil (Id al-Fitr)
10-12 Dhu al-Hijjah	Id Al Adaha (Id al-Adha)

Fiji

Jan 1	New Year's Day
Mar	Youth Day
Mar-Apr: Fri before Easter	Good Friday
Mar-Apr: Sat before Easter	Easter Saturday
Mar-Apr: Mon after Easter	Easter Monday
May 28	Ratu Sir Lala Sukuna Day
Jun, third Mon	Queen Elizabeth II Birthday
Oct	Fiji Day
Oct-Nov	Diwali
Dec 25	Christmas Day
Dec 26	Boxing Day

Muslim holiday:

Rabi al-Awwal	Muhammad's Birthday (Mawlid al-Nabi)

Finland

Jan 1	New Year's Day
Jan 6	Epiphany

Mar-Apr, Fri before Easter . . . . .Good Friday
Mar-Apr . . . . .Easter
Mar-Apr, Mon after Easter . . . . .Easter Monday
May 1 . . . . .May Day
May-Jun . . . . .Ascension Day
May-Jun . . . . .Whitsun (Pentecost)
Jun . . . . .Midsummer
Nov, first Sat . . . . .All Saints' Day
Dec 6 . . . . .Independence Day
Dec 24 . . . . .Christmas Eve
Dec 25 . . . . .Christmas Day
Dec 26 . . . . .Boxing Day

France

Jan 1 . . . . .New Year's Day
Mar-Apr: Mon after Easter . . . . .Easter Monday
May 1 . . . . .Labor Day
May 8 . . . . .Victory Day 1945
May-Jun . . . . .Ascension Day
May-Jun: Mon after Pentecost . . . . .Whit Monday
Jul 14 . . . . .Bastille Day
Aug 15 . . . . .Assumption
Nov 1 . . . . .All Saints' Day
Nov 11 . . . . .Armistice Day 1918
Dec 25 . . . . .Christmas Day

Gabon

Jan 1 . . . . .New Year's Day
Mar-Apr: Mon after Easter . . . . .Easter Monday
Apr 17 . . . . .Women's Day
May 1 . . . . .Labor Day
May-Jun . . . . .Whit Monday
Aug 15 . . . . .Assumption
Aug 16-17 . . . . .Independence holiday
Nov 1 . . . . .All Saints' Day
Dec 25 . . . . .Christmas

Muslim holidays:

Shawwal . . . . .Id al-Fitr (Aid el-Fitiry)
Dhu al-Hijjah . . . . .Id al-Adha (Aid El-Kebir)

Gambia

Jan 1 . . . . .New Year's Day
Feb 18 . . . . .Independence Day
Mar-Apr: Fri before Easter . . . . .Good Friday
Mar-Apr: Mon after Easter . . . . .Easter Monday
May 1 . . . . .May Day
Jul 22 . . . . .Revolution Day
Aug 15 . . . . .St. Mary's Day (Assumption)
Dec 25 . . . . .Christmas Day

Muslim holidays:

Rabi al-Awwal . . . . .Mawlid al-Nabi
Shawwal . . . . .Id al-Fitr
Dhu al-Hijjah . . . . .Tabaski (Id al-Adha)

Georgia, Republic of

Jan 1-2 . . . . .New Year's holiday
Jan 7 . . . . .Orthodox Christmas

Jan 19 . . . . .Epiphany
Mar 3 . . . . .Mother's Day
Mar 8 . . . . .Women's Day
Apr 9 . . . . .Independence Restoration Day
Apr-May: Fri before Easter . . . . .Good Friday
Apr-May: Sat before Easter . . . . .Holy Saturday
Apr-May . . . . .Easter
Apr-May: Mon after Easter . . . . .Easter Monday
May 9 . . . . .Victory Day
May 12 . . . . .St. Andrea the First Day
May 26 . . . . .Independence Day
Aug 28 . . . . .Mariamoba (Assumption)
Oct 14 . . . . .Svetitskhovloba
Nov 23 . . . . .Giorgoba (St. George's Day)

Germany

Jan 1 . . . . .New Year's Day
Mar-Apr: Fri before Easter . . . . .Good Friday
Mar-Apr . . . . .Easter
Mar-Apr: Mon after Easter . . . . .Easter Monday
May 1 . . . . .May Day
May-Jun . . . . .Ascension Day
May-Jun . . . . .Pentecost
May-Jun: Mon after Pentecost . . . . .Whit Monday
Oct 3 .Day of German Unity
Dec 25 . . . . .Christmas Day
Dec 26 . . . . .Second Day of Christmas

Ghana

Jan 1 . . . . .New Year's Day
Mar 6 . . . . .Independence Day
Mar-Apr: Fri before Easter . . . . .Good Friday
Mar-Apr: Mon after Easter . . . . .Easter Monday
May 1 . . . . .May Day
Jul 1 . . . . .Republic Day
Dec 5 . . . . .Farmers' Day
Dec 25 . . . . .Christmas Day
Dec 26 . . . . .Boxing Day

Muslim holidays:

1 Shawwal . . . . .Eid El Fitr (Id al-Fitr)
10-12 Dhu al-Hijjah . . . . .Eid Ul Adha (Id al-Adha)

Gibraltar

Jan 1 . . . . .New Year's Day
Mar: second Mon . . . . .Commonwealth Day
Mar-Apr: Fri before Easter . . . . .Good Friday
Mar-Apr: Mon after Easter . . . . .Easter Monday
May: first Mon . . . . .May Day
May: last Mon . . . . .Spring Bank Holiday
Jun: third Mon . . . . .Queen Elizabeth II Birthday
Aug: last Mon . . . . .Late Summer Bank Holiday
Sep 10 .Gibraltar National Day
Dec 25 . . . . .Christmas Day
Dec 26 . . . . .Boxing Day

Greece

Jan 1 . . . . .New Year's Day
Jan 6 . . . . .Epiphany

Mar-Apr: Mon before
Ash Wednesday . . . . . . .Clean Monday (beginning of Lent)
Mar 25 . . . . .Independence Day and
Feast of the Annunciation
Apr-May: Fri before Easter . . . . .Good Friday
Apr-May: Sat before Easter . . . . .Holy Saturday
Apr-May: Mon after Easter . . . . .Easter Monday
May 1 . . . . .Labour Day
May-Jun: Mon after Pentecost . . . . .Whit Monday
Aug 15 . . . . .Assumption Day
Oct 28 . . . . .Ochi Day
Dec 25 . . . . .Christmas Day
Dec 26 . . . . .Second Day of Christmas

Grenada

Jan 1 . . . . .New Year's Day
Feb 7 . . . . .Independence Day
Mar-Apr: Fri before Easter . . . . .Good Friday
Mar-Apr: Mon after Easter . . . . .Easter Monday
May-Jun . . . . .Corpus Christi
May-Jun: Mon after Pentecost . . . . .Whit Monday
May 1 . . . . .Labour Day
Aug (two days) . . . . .Carnival
Aug: first Mon . . . . .Emancipation Day
Oct 25 . . . . .Thanksgiving Day
Dec 25 . . . . .Christmas Day
Dec 26 . . . . .Boxing Day

Guatemala

Jan 1 . . . . .New Year's Day
Apr-May: Wed before Easter . . . . .Holy Wednesday
Apr-May: Thurs before Easter . . . . .Maundy Thursday
Apr-May: Fri before Easter . . . . .Good Friday
Apr-May: Sat before Easter . . . . .Holy Saturday
May 1 . . . . .Labor Day
Jun 30 . . . . .Army Day
Sep 15 . . . . .Independence Day
Oct 20 . . . . .Celebration of the 1944 Revolution
Nov 1 . . . . .All Saints' Day
Dec 24 . . . . .Christmas Eve (afternoon only)
Dec 25 . . . . .Christmas Day
Dec 31 . . . . .New Year's Eve (afternoon only)

Guinea

Jan 1 . . . . .New Year's Day
Mar-Apr: Mon after Easter . . . . .Easter Monday
Apr 3 . . . . .Declaration of the Second Republic
May 1 . . . . .Labor Day
May 25 . . . . .Organization of African Unity Day
Aug 15 . . . . .Assumption Day
Oct 2 . . . . .Independence Day
Nov 1 . . . . .All Saints' Day
Dec 25 . . . . .Christmas Day

Muslim holidays:

Rabi al-Awwal . . . . .Maoloud (Mawlid al-Nabi)
Shawwal . . . . .End of Ramadan (Id al-Fitr)
Dhu al-Hijjah . . . . .Tabaski (Id al-Adha)

Guinea-Bissau

Jan 1 . . . . .New Year's Day
Jan . . . . .National Heroes' Day
Mar 8 . . . . .International Women's Day
May 1 . . . . .Labor Day
Aug 3 . . . . .Martyrs of Colonialism Day
Sep 24 . . . . .Independence Day
Nov 14 . . . . .Readjustment Movement Day
Dec 25 . . . . .Christmas Day

Muslim holidays:

Shawwal . . . . .Id al-Fitr
Dhu al-Hijjah . . . . .Tabaski (Id al-Adha)

Guyana

Jan 1 . . . . .New Year's Day
Feb 23 . . . . .Mashramani (Republic Day)
Mar: full moon day . . . . .Phagwah
Mar-Apr: Fri before Easter . . . . .Good Friday
Mar-Apr: Mon after Easter . . . . .Easter Monday
May 1 . . . . .May Day (Labour Day)
May 26 . . . . .Independence Day
Jul: first Mon . . . . .Caricom Day
Aug . . . . .Freedom Day
Oct-Nov . . . . .Diwali
Dec 25 . . . . .Christmas Day
Dec 26 . . . . .Boxing Day

Muslim holidays:

12 Rabi al-Awwal . . . . . . .Youmon-Nabi (Mawlid al-Nabi)
10-12 Dhu al-Hijjah . . . . .Eid-ul-Azah (Id al-Adha)

Haiti

Jan 1 . . . . .New Year's Day and Independence Day
Jan 2 . . . . .Ancestors' Day
Feb-Mar: Mon through Ash Wednesday . . . . .Carnival
Mar-Apr: Fri before Easter . . . . .Good Friday
Apr 14 . . . . .Pan-American Day
May 1 . . . . .Agriculture and Labor Day
May 18 . . . . .Flag and University Day
May-Jun . . . . .Ascension Day
May-Jun . . . . .Corpus Christi
Aug 15 . . . . .Assumption
Oct 17 . . . . .Anniversary of the death of
Jean-Jacques Dessalines
Oct 24 . . . . .United Nations Day
Nov 1 . . . . .All Saints' Day
Nov 2 . . . . .All Souls' Day
Nov 18 . . . . .Battle of Vertières' Day
Dec 25 . . . . .Christmas Day

Honduras

Jan 1 . . . . .New Year's Day
Apr-May: Thurs before Easter . . . . .Maundy Thursday
Apr-May: Fri before Easter . . . . .Good Friday
Apr-May: Sat before Easter . . . . .Holy Saturday
Mar-Apr . . . . .Easter
Apr 14 . . . . .Day of the Americas (Pan-American Day)

May 1 . . . . .Labor Day
Sep 15 . . . . .Independence Day
Oct 3 . . . . .Day of the Soldier
Oct 12 . . . . .Columbus Day
Oct 21 . . . . .Armed Forces Day
Dec 25 . . . . .Christmas Day

Hong Kong

Jan 1 . . . . .New Year's Day
Jan-Feb . . . . .Lunar New Year (first three days)
Mar-Apr . . . . .Ching Ming (Qing Ming)
Mar-Apr: Fri before Easter . . . . .Good Friday
Mar-Apr: Sat before Easter . . . . .Holy Saturday
Mar-Apr: Mon after Easter . . . . .Easter Monday
Apr-May . . . . .Buddha's Birthday
May 1 . . . . .Labour Day
May-Jun . . . . .Tuen Ng Festival (Dragon Boat Festival)
Jul 1 . . . . .Hong Kong Special Administrative
Region Establishment Day
Oct 1 . . . . .National Day
Sep-Oct . . . . .Day following Mid-Autumn Festival
Sep-Oct . . . . .Chung Yeung Festival
Dec 25 and first following weekday . . . . .Christmas

Hungary

Jan 1 . . . . .New Year's Day
Mar 15 . . . . .Revolution and Independence Day
Mar-Apr: Mon after Easter . . . . .Easter Monday
May 1 . . . . .Labor Day
May-Jun . . . . .Pentecost
May-Jun: Mon after Pentecost . . . . .Whit Monday
Aug 20 . . . . .St. Stephen's Day
Oct 23 . . . . .Republic Day
Nov 1 . . . . .Day of the Dead (All Saints' Day)
Dec 25 . . . . .Christmas Day
Dec 26 .Second Day of Christmas

Iceland

Jan 1 . . . . .New Year's Day
Mar-Apr: Thurs before Easter . . . . .Maundy Thursday
Mar-Apr: Friday before Easter . . . . .Good Friday
Mar-Apr: Mon after Easter . . . . .Easter Monday
Apr 19-25, Thurs between . . . . .Sumardagurinn Fyrsti
(First Day of Summer)
May 1 . . . . .Labour Day
May-Jun . . . . .Ascension Day
May-Jun: Mon after Pentecost . . . . .Whit Monday
Jun 17 . . . . .Independence Day (National Day)
Aug, first Mon . . . . .Commerce Day
Dec 24 . . . . .Christmas Eve (after noon)
Dec 25 . . . . .Christmas Day
Dec 26 . . . . .Boxing Day
Dec 31 . . . . .New Year's Eve (after noon)

India

Jan 26 . . . . .Republic Day
Aug 15 . . . . .Independence Day

Oct 2 . . . . .Gandhi's Birthday
Muslim holidays:
1 Muharram . . . . .Islamic New Year
12 Rabi al-Awwal . . . . . . .Milad-un-Nabi (Mawlid al-Nabi)
1 Shawwal . . . . .Id al-Fitr
10-12 Dhu al-Hijjah . . . .Id ul-Zuha (Bakr-id or Id al-Adha)

Indonesia

Jan 1 . . . . .New Year's Day
Feb . . . . .Chinese New Year
Mar-Apr: Fri before Easter . . . . .Wafat Isa Almasih
(Good Friday)
Apr-May . . . . . . .Waisak Day (Vesak or Buddha's Birthday)
May-Jun . . . . .Ascension Day
Aug 17 . . . . .Independence Day
Dec 25 . . . . .Christmas Day

Muslim holidays:
1 Muharram . . . . Islamic New Year
12 Rabi al-Awwal . . . . . . .Milad-un-Nabi (Mawlid al-Nabi)
27 Rajab . . . . Isra and Miraj of Prophet Muhammad
(Laylat al-Miraj)
1 Shawwal . . . . Id al-Fitr
10-12 Dhu al-Hijjah . . . Id ul-Zuha (Bakr-id or Id al-Adha)

Iran

Feb . . . . .Victory of Islamic Revolution
Mar . . . . .Oil Nationalization Day
Mar 21, around (five days) . . . . .Nowruz (New Year)
Mar-Apr .Islamic Republic Day
Apr 2, around . . . . .Sizdah be-dar (Nature Day)
Mar-Apr .Islamic Republic Day
Jun .Death of Imam Khomeini
Jun . . . . .National Uprising Day (1963)

Muslim holidays:
9 Muharram . . . . .Taasou'a
10 Muharram . . . . .Ashura
20 Safar . . . . .Arba'in-e Hosseini
28 Safar . . . . .Demise of Holy Prophet and
Martyrdom of Imam Hassan
17 Rabi al-Awwal . . . . .Birth of Prophet and
Imam Saadeq (Mawlid al-Nabi)
13 Rajab . . . . .Imam Ali's Birthday
27 Rajab . . . . .Mission of the Holy Prophet (Laylat al-Miraj)
15 Shaban .Birthday of Twelfth Imam
21 Ramadan .Imam Ali's Martyrdom
1 Shawwal . . . . .End of Fasting Month (Id al-Fitr)
25 Shawwal . . . . .Martyrdom of Imam Saadeq
11 Dhu al-Qadah . . . . .Birthday of Imam Reza
10 Dhu al-Hijjah . . . . .Festival of Sacrifices
(Qadir or Id al-Adha)

Iraq

Jan 1 . . . . .New Year's Day
Jan 6 . . . . .Anniversary of Founding of the Iraqi Army
Feb 8 . . . . .Anniversary of 14th Ramadan Revolution
Mar 21 . . . . .Spring Day

Apr 7 ....Anniversary of Founding
the Arab Baath Socialist Party
Apr 9 ....National Day
Apr 17 ....Fao Liberation Day
May 1 ....May Day
Jun 1 ....Oil Nationalization Day
Jul 30 ....Liquidation of Anti-Revolution
Aug 8 ...Day of Victory and Peace over Iranian Aggression
Dec 25 ....Christmas Day

Muslim holidays:
1 Muharram ....Hijra New Year
10 Muharram ....Aashuraa Day (Ashura)
12 Rabi al-Awwal ....Prophet Muhammad's Birthday
(Mawlid al-Nabi)
27 Rajab ....Isra'a and Mi'raj Day (Laylat al-Miraj)
17 Ramadan ....Badder Conquest Day
1-3 Shawwal ....Eid al-Fitr (Id al-Fitr)
10-13 Dhu al-Hijjah ....Eid al-Adha (Id al-Adha)

Ireland

Jan 1 ....New Year's Day
Mar 17 ....St. Patrick's Day
Mar-Apr: Mon after Easter ....Easter Monday
May, first Mon ....May Day Holiday
Jun, first Mon ....June Holiday
Aug, first Mon ....August Holiday
Oct, last Mon ....October Holiday
Dec 25 ....Christmas Day
Dec 26 ....St. Stephen's Day

Israel

Feb-Mar ....Purim
Mar-Apr ....Passover
Apr-May ....Independence Day
May-Jun ....Shavuot
Jul-Aug ....Tisha B'Av
Sep-Oct ....Rosh Hashana
Sep-Oct ....Yom Kippur
Sep-Oct ....Sukkot
Sep-Oct ....Simchat Torah
Oct-Nov ....Ethiopian Sigd Festival
Nov-Dec ....Hanukkah

Italy

Jan 1 ....New Year's Day
Jan 6 ....Epiphany
Mar-Apr ....Easter
Mar-Apr: Mon after Easter ....Easter Monday
Apr 25 ....Liberation Day
May 1 ....Labor Day
Aug 15 ....Assumption Day
Nov 1 ....All Saints' Day
Dec 8 ....Immaculate Conception Day
Dec 25 ....Christmas Day
Dec 26 ....St. Stephen's Day

Ivory Coast. *See* Côte d'Ivoire

Jamaica

Jan 1 ....New Year's Day
Feb-Mar ....Ash Wednesday
Mar-Apr: Fri before Easter ....Good Friday
Mar-Apr: Mon after Easter ....Easter Monday
May 23 ....Labour Day
Aug 1 ....Emancipation Day
Aug 6 ....Independence Day
Oct, third Mon ....National Heroes' Day
Dec 25 ....Christmas Day
Dec 26 ....Boxing Day

Japan

Jan 1 ....New Year's Day
Jan ....Coming-of-Age Day
Feb 11 ....Foundation Day
Mar ....Vernal Equinox Day
Apr 29 ....Showa Day
May 3 ....Constitution Memorial Day
May 4 ....Greenery Day
May 5 ....Children's Day
Jul ....Marine Day
Sep 15 ....Respect-for-the-Aged Day
Sep ....Autumnal Equinox Day
Oct ....Health-Sports Day
Nov 3 ....Culture Day
Nov 23 ....Labor-Thanksgiving Day
Dec 23 ....Emperor's Birthday
Dec 31 ....New Year's Eve

Jordan

Jan 1 ....New Year's Day
May 1 ....Labor Day
May 25 ....Independence Day
Jun 9 ....King Abdullah's Accession to the Throne
Jun 10 ....Great Arab Revolt
Dec 25 ....Christmas Day

Muslim holidays:
1 Muharram ....Hijri New Year
12 Rabi al-Awwal ....Prophet Muhammad's Birthday
(Mawlid al-Nabi)
27 Rajab ....Al-Isra'wal Mi'raj (Laylat al-Miraj)
1 Ramadan ....Ramadan begins
1 Shawwal ....Eid al-Fitr (Id al-Fitr)
10-12 Dhu al-Hijjah ....Eid al-Adha (Id al-Adha)

Kazakhstan

Jan 1-2 ....New Year's holiday
Mar 8 ....International Women's Day
Mar ....Nauryz Meiramy (Spring New Year)
May 1 ....Kazakhstan Peoples Unity Day
May 9 ....Victory Day
Aug 30 ....Constitution Day
Oct 25 ....Republic Day
Dec 16 ....Independence Day

Kenya

Jan 1	New Year's Day
Mar-Apr: Fri before Easter	Good Friday
Mar-Apr: Mon after Easter	Easter Monday
May 1	Labour Day
Jun 1	Madaraka Day
Oct 10	Moi Day
Oct 20	Kenyatta Day
Dec 12	Jamhuri (Independence Day)
Dec 25	Christmas Day
Dec 26	Boxing Day

Muslim holiday:

1 Shawwal	Id ul-Fitr

Kiribati

Jan 1	New Year's Day
Mar 10	Women's Day
Mar-Apr: Fri before Easter	Good Friday
Mar-Apr: Mon after Easter	Easter Monday
Apr 21	Health Day
Jul 7	Uniwaine (Elderly Men) Day
Jul 8	Unaine (Elderly Women) Day
Jul 9	Gospel Day
Jul 12	Independence Day
Aug 11	Youth Day
Oct 6	Teacher's Day
Dec 8	Human Rights Day
Dec 25	Christmas Day
Dec 26	Boxing Day

Korea, North
(Democratic People's Republic of Korea)

Jan 1	New Year's Day
Feb 16	Kim Jong-il's Anniversary
Apr 15	Birthday of Kim Il-sung
Apr 25	Founding of the People's Army
May 1	Labor Day
Jul 27	Victory Day
Aug 15	Liberation Day
Sep 9	National Day
Oct 10	Founding of the Workers' Party
Dec 27	Constitution Day

Korea, South
(Republic of Korea)

Jan 1	New Year's Day
Mar 1	Independence Movement Day (Samil-Jol)
Apr-May	Buddha's Birthday
May 5	Children's Day
Jun 6	Memorial Day
Aug 15	Liberation Day
Oct 3	National Foundation Day
Aug 28	Assumption Day (Orthodox)

Kosovo, Republic of

Jan 1-2	New Year's holiday

Jan 6	Orthodox Christmas
Feb 17	Kosovo Independence Day
Apr 9	Kosovo Constitution Day
Mar-Apr: Mon after Easter	Easter Monday (Catholic)
Mar-Apr: Mon after Easter	Easter Monday (Orthodox)
May 1	Labor Day
May 8	Europe Day
Dec 25	Christmas Day

Muslim holidays:

1 Shawwal	Eid al-Fitr (Id al-Fitr)
10 Dhu al-Hijjah	Eid al-Addha (Id al-Adha)

Kuwait

Jan 1	New Year's Day
Feb 25	National Day
Feb 26	Liberation Day

Muslim holidays:

1 Muharram	Hijri New Year
12 Rabi al-Awwal	Prophet Muhammad's Birthday (Mawlid al-Nabi)
27 Rajab	Ascension of the Prophet (Laylat al-Miraj)
1 Shawwal	Eid al-Fitr (Id al-Fitr)
10-12 Dhu al-Hijjah	Eid al-Adha (Id al-Adha)

Kyrgyzstan

Jan 1	New Year's Day
Jan 7	Orthodox Christmas
Mar 8	International Women's Day
Mar 21	Nooruz (New Year)
Mar 24	National Revolution Day
May 1	International Labor Day
May 5	Constitution Day
May 9	Victory Day
Aug 31	Independence Day
Nov 7	Social Revolution Day

Muslim holidays:

1 Shawwal	Orozo Ait (Id al-Fitr)
Dhu al-Hijjah	Kurban Ait (Id al-Adha)

Laos

Jan 1	New Year's Day
Mar 8	Women's Day
Apr: three days in mid	Lao New Year (Water Festival)
May 1	Labor Day
Jun 1	Children's Day
Oct	Last day of Buddhist Lent
Oct: day after Buddhist Lent ends	Boat Racing Festival
Nov	That Luang Festival
Dec 2	National Day

Latvia

Jan 1	New Year's Day
Mar-Apr: Fri before Easter	Good Friday
Mar-Apr	Easter

Mar-Apr: Mon after Easter ....Easter Monday
May 1 ....Labor Day
May 4 ....Independence Restoration Day
Jun 23 ....Ligo (Midsummer's Eve)
Jun 24 ....Jani (St. John's Day)
Nov 18 ....Independence Day
Dec 25 ....Christmas Day
Dec 26 ....Second Day of Christmas
Dec 31 ....New Year's Eve

Lebanon

Jan 1 ....New Year's Day
Jan 6 ....Epiphany/Armenian Christmas
Feb 9 ....St. Maroun's Day
Mar-Apr: Fri before Catholic Easter ....Good Friday
Mar-Apr ....Catholic Easter
Apr-May: Fri before Orthodox Easter ....Good Friday
Apr-May ....Orthodox Easter
May 1 ....Labor Day
May ....Martyrs' Day
May ....Resistance and Liberation Day
Aug 15 ....Assumption Day
Nov 22 ....Independence Day
Dec 25 ....Christmas Day

Muslim holidays:
1 Muharram ....Hijra New Year
10 Muharram ....Aashuraa Day (Ashura)
12 Rabi al-Awwal ....Prophet Muhammad's Birthday
(Mawlid al-Nabi)
1 Shawwal ....Eid al-Fitr (Id al-Fitr)
10-13 Dhu al-Hijjah ....Eid al-Adha (Id al-Adha)

Lesotho

Jan 1 ....New Year's Day
Mar 11 ....Moshoeshoe's Day
Mar-Apr: Fri before Easter ....Good Friday
Mar-Apr: Mon after Easter ....Easter Monday
May 1 ....Workers' Day
May 25 ....Africa Day/Heroes' Day
May-Jun ....Ascension Day
Jul 17 ....King's Birthday
Oct 4 ....Independence Day
Dec 25 ....Christmas Day

Liberia

Jan 1 ....New Year's Day
Feb 11 ....Armed Forces Day
Mar: second Wed ....Decoration Day
Mar 15 ....J. J. Robert's Birthday
Apr 11 ....Fast and Prayer Day
May 14 ....National Unification Day
Jul 26 ....Independence Day
Aug 24 ....Flag Day
Nov: first Thurs ....Thanksgiving Day
Nov 29 ....President Tubman's Birthday
Dec 25 ....Christmas Day

Libya

Mar 2 ....Declaration of Jamahiriya Day (1977)
Mar 28 ....British Evacuation Day
Jun 11 ....Evacuation of Foreign Bases Day
Sep 1 ....Revolution Day
Oct 7 ....Italian Evacuation Day
Oct 26 ....Day of Mourning
Dec 24 ....Independence Day

Muslim holidays:
Muharram ....Islamic New Year
Rabi al-Awwal ....Mawlid al-Nabi
Shawwal ....Id al-Fitr
Dhu al-Hijjah ....Id al-Adha

Liechtenstein

Jan 1 ....New Year's Day
Jan 6 ....Epiphany
Feb 2 ....Candlemas
Feb-Mar ....Shrove Tuesday
Mar 19 ....Feast of St. Joseph
Mar-Apr: Fri before Easter ....Good Friday
Mar-Apr: Mon after Easter ....Easter Monday
May 1 ....Labor Day
May-Jun ....Ascension Day
May-Jun ....Pentecost
May-Jun ....Whit Monday
May-Jun ....Corpus Christi Day
Aug 15 ....National Day
Sep 8 ....Nativity of Our Lady
Nov 1 ....All Saints' Day
Dec 8 ....Immaculate Conception Day
Dec 24 ....Christmas Eve
Dec 25 ....Christmas Day
Dec 26 ....St. Stephen's Day
Dec 31 ....Silvester (New Year's Eve)

Lithuania

Jan 1 ....New Year's Day
Feb 16 ....Independence Day
Mar 11 ....Restoration of Lithuania's Statehood
Mar-Apr: Mon after Easter ....Easter Monday
Mar-Apr: Tues after Easter ....Easter Tuesday
May 1 ....Labour Day
May: first Sun ....Mothers' Day
Jun 24 ....St. John's Day
Jul 6 ....State Day (Crowning of King Mindaugas)
Aug 15 ....Assumption Day
Nov 1 ....All Saints' Day
Dec 25-26 ....Christmas Day

Luxembourg

Jan 1 ....New Year's Day
Mar-Apr: Mon after Easter ....Easter Monday
May 1 ....May Day
May-Jun ....Ascension Day
May-Jun ....Whit Monday
Jun 23 ....National Day (Grand Duke's Birthday)

Aug 15 . . . . .Assumption
Nov 1 . . . . .All Saints' Day
Dec 25 . . . . .Christmas Day
Dec 26 . . . . .St. Stephen's Day

Macedonia

Jan 1 . . . . .New Year's Day
Jan 6-7 . . . . .Orthodox Christmas
May 1 . . . . May Day
May 24 . . . . .Sts. Cyril and Methodius Day
Aug 2 . . . . .Republic Day
Sep 8 . . . . .Independence Day
Oct 11 . . . . .Uprising Against Facism Day
Oct 23 . . . . .Day of the Macedonian Revolution
Dec 8 . . . . .St. Kliment Ohridski

Madagascar

Jan 1 . . . . .New Year's Day
Mar 8 . . . . .Women's Day (women only)
Mar 29 . . . . .Martyrs' Day
Mar-Apr: Mon after Easter . . . . .Easter Monday
May 1 . . . . .Ascension Day/Labor Day
Jun 26 . . . . .Independence Day
Aug 15 . . . . .Assumption Day
Nov 1 . . . . .All Saints' Day
Dec 25 . . . . .Christmas Day
Dec 30 . . . . .Anniversary of the Republic

Malawi

Jan 1 . . . . .New Year's Day
Jan 15 . . . . .John Chilembwe Day
Mar 3 . . . . .Martyrs' Day
Mar-Apr: Fri before Easter . . . . .Good Friday
Mar-Apr: Mon after Easter . . . . .Easter Monday
May 1 . . . . .Labour Day
May 14 . . . . .Kamuzu Day
Jun 14 . . . . .Freedom Day
Jul 6 . . . . .Republic Day
Oct: second Mon . . . . .Mothers' Day
Dec 25 . . . . .Christmas Day
Dec 26 . . . . .Boxing Day

Malaysia

Jan-Feb . . . . .Chinese New Year
Apr-May . . . . .Wesak Day
May 1 . . . . .Labour Day
Jun .. . . .Birthday Celebration of
SPB Yang di Pertuan Agong
Aug 31 . . . . .National Day
Oct-Nov . . . . .Deepavali
Dec 25 . . . . .Christmas Day

Muslim holidays:

1 Muharram . . . . .Maal Hijrah (Hijra New Year)
12 Rabi al-Awwal . . . . .Maulidur Rasul
(Muhammad's Birthday or Mawlid al-Nabi)
1 Shawwal . . . . .Hari Raya Qurban (Id al-Fitr)
10-12 Dhu al-Hijjah . . . .Hari Raya Aidil Adha (Id al-Adha)

Maldives

Jan 1 . . . . .New Year's Day
Mar . . . . .National Day
Apr 8 .Maldives Embraced Islam
Jul 26-27 . . . . .Independence Day holiday
Nov 3 . . . . .Victory Day
Nov 11 . . . . .Republic Day

Muslim holidays:

1 Muharram . . . . .Islamic New Year
12 Rabi al-Awwal . . . . .Muhammad's Birthday
(Mawlid al-Nabi)
1 Ramadan . . . . .Ramadan begins
1 Shawwal . . . . .Id al-Fitr
10-12 Dhu al-Hijjah . . . . .Id al-Adha

Mali

Jan 1 . . . . .New Year's Day
Jan 20 . . . . .Armed Forces Day
Mar 26 . . . . .Day of the Martyrs
May 1 . . . . .Labor Day
May 25 . . . . .African Unity Day
Sep 22 . . . . .Independence Day
Dec 25 . . . . .Christmas Day

Muslim holidays:

12 Rabi al-Awwal . . . . .Mawlud (Mawlid al-Nabi or
Muhammad's Birthday)
1 Ramadan . . . . .Ramadan begins
1 Shawwal . . . . .Aïd el-Fitr (Id al-Fitr)
10-12 Dhu al-Hijjah . . . .Tabaski (Aïd el-Kébir; Id al-Adha)

Malta

Jan 1 . . . . .New Year's Day
Feb 10 . . . . .Feast of St. Paul's Shipwreck
Mar 19 . . . . .Feast of St. Joseph
Mar 31 . . . . .Freedom Day
Mar-Apr: Fri before Easter . . . . .Good Friday
May 1 . . . . .Workers' Day
Jun 7 . . . . .Commemoration of Uprising of June 7, 1919
Jun 29 . . . . .Feast of Sts. Peter and Paul (Mnarja)
Aug 15 . . . . .Assumption
Sep 8 . . . . .Feast of Our Lady of Victories
Sep 21 . . . . .Independence Day
Dec 8 . . . . .Immaculate Conception
Dec 13 . . . . .Republic Day
Dec 25 . . . . .Christmas Day

Marshall Islands

Jan 1 . . . . .New Year's Day
Mar 1 . . . . .Nuclear Victims' Memorial Day
Mar-Apr: Fri before Easter . . . . .Good Friday
May 1 . . . . .Constitution Day
Jul 4 . . . . .Fishermen's Day
Sep 1 . . . . .Workers' Day
Sep 30 . . . . .Customs Day
Nov 17 . . . . .Presidents' Day
Dec 4 . . . . .Kamolol (Thanksgiving Day)
Dec 25 . . . . .Christmas Day

Mauritania

Jan 1 . . . . .New Year's Day
May 1 . . . . .Labor Day
May 25 . . . . .Journée de l'OUA (Africa Day)
Nov 28 . . . . .Independence Day

Muslim holidays:
1 Muharram . . . . .Islamic New Year
12 Rabi al-Awwal . . . . .Id al Maouloud
(Muhammad's Birthday or Mawlid al-Nabi)
1 Shawwal . . . . .Id al-Fitr
10-12 Dhu al-Hijjah .Id al-Adha

Mauritius

Jan 1-2 . . . . .New Year holiday
Jan-Feb . . . . .Thaipoosam Cavadee
Jan-Feb . . . . .Chinese New Year
Feb-Mar . . . . .Maha Shivaratree
Mar-Apr . . . . .Ougadi (Telegu New Year)
Mar 12 . . . . .National Day
May 1 . . . . .Labour Day
Aug 15 . . . . .Assumption Day
Aug-Sep . . . . .Ganesh Chaturti
Nov 1 . . . . .All Saints' Day
Oct-Nov . . . . .Divali
Dec 25 . . . . .Christmas Day

Muslim holiday:
1 Shawwal . . . . .Id al-Fitr

Mexico

Jan 1 . . . . .New Year's Day
Feb 5 . . . . .Constitution Day
Mar 21 . . . . .Birthday of Benito Juarez
Mar-Apr: Thurs before Easter . . . . .Holy Thursday
Mar-Apr: Fri before Easter . . . . .Good Friday
Apr-May . . . . .Easter
May 1 . . . . .Labor Day
May 5 . . . . .Battle of Puebla (Cinco de Mayo)
Sep 16 . . . . .Independence Day
Oct 12 . . . . .Día de la Raza
Nov 2 . . . . .Día de los Fieles Difuntos
(Day of the Dead; All Souls' Day)
Nov 20 . . . . .Anniversary of the Revolution
Dec 12 . . . . .Our Lady of Guadelupe
Dec 25 . . . . .Christmas Day

Micronesia

Jan 1 . . . . .New Year's Day
May 10 . . . . .FSM Day
Oct 24 .United Nation's Day
Nov 3 . . . . .FSM Independence Day
Nov 11 . . . . .Veterans' Day
Dec 25 . . . . .Christmas Day

Moldova

Jan 1 . . . . .New Year's Day
Jan 7-8 .Orthodox Christmas

Mar 8 .International Women's Day
Apr-May . . . . .Easter
Apr-May: Mon one week after Easter . . . .Memorial Easter
May 1 . . . . .Labor Day
May 9 . . . . .Victory Day
Aug 27 . . . . .Independence Day
Aug 31 . . . . .Limba Noastra National Language Day

Monaco

Jan 1 . . . . .New Year's Day
Jan 27 . . . . .St. Dévôte's Day
Mar-Apr: Mon after Easter . . . . .Easter Monday
May 1 . . . . .Labor Day
May-Jun . . . . .Ascension Day
May-Jun . . . . .Whit Monday
May-Jun . . . . .Fête Dieu (Corpus Christi)
Aug 15 . . . . .Assumption Day
Nov 1 . . . . .All Saints' Day
Nov 19 . . . . .National Day
Dec 8 . . . . .Immaculate Conception
Dec 25 . . . . .Christmas Day

Mongolia

Jan 1 . . . . .New Year's Day
Jan-Feb . . . . .Lunar New Year
Mar 8 . . . . .International Women's Day
Jun 1 . . . . .Mother and Child Day
Jul 11-13 . . . . .National Day (Naadam)
Nov 26 . . . . .Independence Day

Montenegro

Jan 1-2 . . . . .New Year's holiday
Jan 7 . . . . .Orthodox Christmas
Jan 8 . . . . .Second Day of Orthodox Christmas
Mar-Apr: Fri before Easter . . . . . . .Orthodox Good Friday
Mar-Apr: Mon after Easter . . . . .Orthodox Easter Monday
May 1 . . . . .May Day
May 21 . . . . .Independence Day
Jul 13 . . . . .National Day

Morocco

Jan 1 . . . . .New Year's Day
Jan 11 . . . . .Presentation of Independence Proclamation
May 1 . . . . .Labor Day
Jul 30 . . . . .Feast of the Throne
Aug 14 . . . . .Oued Eddahab Allegiance
Aug 20 . . . . .Anniversary of the
Revolution of the King and the People
Aug 21 . . . . .Youth's Day/King's Birthday
Nov 6 . . . . .Green March Day
Nov 18 . . . . .Independence Day

Muslim holidays:
1 Muharram . . . . .Islamic New Year
Rabi al-Awwal . . . . .Muhammad's Birthday
(Mawlid al-Nabi)
Shawwal . . . . .Id al-Fitr
Dhu al-Hijjah . . . . .Id al-Adha

Mozambique

Jan 1	New Year's Day
Feb 3	Heroes' Day
Apr 7	Women's Day
May 1	Workers' Day
Jun 25	Independence Day
Sep 7	Victory Day
Sep 25	Revolution Day
Oct 4	Day of Peace and Reconciliation
Dec 25	Family/Christmas Day

Myanmar

Jan 4	Independence Day
Feb 12	Union Day
Feb-Mar	Full Moon Day of Tabaung
Mar 2	Peasants' Day
Mar 27	Armed Forces Day
Apr, mid	Thingyan (Water Festival)
Apr, mid	Myanmar New Year Day
Apr-May	Full Moon Day of Kason
May 1	May Day (Labor Day)
Jun-Jul	Full Moon Day of Waso (Beginning of Buddhist Lent)
Jul 19	Martyrs' Day
Sep-Oct	End of Buddhist Lent (Thadingyut Festival of Lights)
Oct-Nov	Dewali (Depali Festival Day)
Oct-Nov	Tazaungdaing Festival
Nov (movable)	National Day
Dec 25	Christmas Day

Namibia

Jan 1	New Year's Day
Mar 21	Independence Day
Mar-Apr: Fri before Easter	Good Friday
Mar-Apr: Mon after Easter	Easter Monday
May 1	Workers Day
May 4	Cassinga Day
May 25	Africa Day
May-Jun	Ascension Day
Aug 26	Heroes Day
Dec 10	International Human Rights Day
Dec 25	Christmas Day
Dec 26	Family Day

Nauru

Jan 1	New Year's Day
Jan 31	Independence Day
Mar-Apr: Fri before Easter	Good Friday
Mar-Apr: Mon after Easter	Easter Monday
Mar-Apr: Tues after Easter	Easter Tuesday
May 17	Constitution Day
Sep 25	National Youth Day
Oct 26	Angam Day
Dec 25	Christmas Day
Dec 26	Boxing Day

Nepal

Jan 30	Martyrs' Day
Feb 19	Democracy Day
Feb-Mar	Mahashivrati
Mar 8	International Women's Day
Mar-Apr	Fagu Purnima
Mar-Apr	Ramnawami
Apr	Ghode Jatra
Apr	Nepali New Year
Apr-May	Buddha Day
May 1	May Day
Aug	Janai Purnima
Aug-Sep	Krishnasthami
Sep-Oct	Ghatasthapana
Sep-Oct	Dashain (six days)
Oct-Nov	Tihar (three days)
Dec 25	Christmas

Netherlands

Jan 1	New Year's Day
Mar-Apr: Fri before Easter	Good Friday
Mar-Apr: Mon after Easter	Easter Monday
Apr 29	Queen's Birthday
May 5, every 5 years (2005, 2010, etc)	Liberation Day
May-Jun	Ascension Day
May-Jun	Whit Sunday (Pentecost)
May-Jun	Whit Monday
Dec 25	Christmas Day
Dec 26	Second Day of Christmas

New Zealand

Jan 1-2	New Year's holiday
Feb 6	Waitangi Day
Mar-Apr: Fri before Easter	Good Friday
Mar-Apr: Mon after Easter	Easter Monday
Apr 25	ANZAC Day
Jun, first Mon	Queen Elizabeth II Birthday
Oct, first Mon	Labour Day
Dec 25	Christmas Day
Dec 26	Boxing Day

Nicaragua

Jan 1	New Year's Day
Mar-Apr: Thurs before Easter	Holy Thursday
Mar-Apr: Fri before Easter	Good Friday
May 1	Labor Day
Jul 19	Sandinista Revolution Day
Sep 14	Battle of San Jacinto
Sep 15	Independence Day
Dec 8	Immaculate Conception Day
Dec 25	Christmas Day

Niger

Jan 1	New Year's Day
Mar-Apr: Mon after Easter	Easter Monday
Apr 24	Concord Day

May 1 ....Labor Day
Aug 3 ....Independence Day
Dec 18 ....Republic Day
Dec 25 ....Christmas Day

Muslim holidays:

Rabi al-Awwal ....Mouloud (Muhammad's Birthday
or Mawlid al-Nabi)
27 Ramadan ....Leilat-ul-Kadr (Laylat al-Qadr)
Shawwal ....Id al-Fitr
Dhu al-Hijjah ....Tabaski (Id al-Adha)

Nigeria

Jan 1 ....New Year's Day
Mar-Apr: Fri before Easter ....Good Friday
Mar-Apr: Mon after Easter ....Easter Monday
May 1 ....Labor Day
May 29 ....Democracy Day
Oct 1 ....Independence Day
Dec 25 ....Christmas Day
Dec 26 ....Boxing Day

Muslim holidays:

Rabi al-Awwal .....The Prophet's Birthday (Id el-Maulud)
Shawwal ....Id el-Fitri
Dhu al-Hijjah ....Id el-Kabir (Id al-Adha)

Niue

Jan 1 ....New Year's Day
Feb 6 ....Waitangi Day
Mar-Apr: Fri before Easter ....Good Friday
Mar-Apr: Mon after Easter ....Easter Monday
Apr 25 ....ANZAC Day
Jun: first Mon ....Queen Elizabeth II Birthday
Oct ....Peniamina Gospel Day
Oct ....Constitution Day
Dec 25 ....Christmas Day
Dec 26 ....Boxing Day
Dec-Jan ....Commission Holiday

North Korea. *See* Korea, North

Northern Ireland. See United Kingdom

Norway

Jan 1 ....New Year's Day
Mar-Apr: Sun before Easter ....Palm Sunday
Mar-Apr: Thurs before Easter ....Maundy Thursday
Mar-Apr: Fri before Easter ....Good Friday
Mar-Apr ....Easter Sunday
Mar-Apr: Mon after Easter ....Easter Monday
May 1 ....Labor Day
May 17 ....Constitution Day
May-Jun ....Ascension Day
May-Jun ....Whitsun (Pentecost)
May-Jun ....Whit Monday
Dec 25 ....Christmas Day
Dec 26 ....Second Day of Christmas

Oman

Jan 1 ....New Year's Day
Jul 23 ....Renaissance Day
Nov 18-19 ....National Day holiday

Muslim holidays:

1 Muharram ....Hijri New Year
12 Rabi al-Awwal ....Prophet Muhammad's Birthday
(Mawlid al-Nabi)
27 Rajab ....Isra and Meiraj (Laylat al-Miraj)
Shawwal (four days) ....Id al-Fitr
Dhu al-Hijjah (five days) ....Id al-Adha

Pakistan

Feb 5 ....Kashmir Day
Mar 23 ....Pakistan Day
May 1 ....Labor Day
Aug 14 ....Independence Day
Nov 9 ....Birthday of Muhammad Iqbal
Dec 25 .....Christmas Day and Birthday of Quaid-e-Azam

Muslim holidays:

12 Rabi al-Awwal ....Eid-e-Milad-un-Nabi
(Mawlid al-Nabi)
14 Shaaban ....Shab-e-Barat
1 Shawwal ....Id al-Fitr
10 Dhu al-Hijjah ....Id-ul-Azha (Id al-Adha)

Palau

Jan 1 ....New Year's Day
Mar 15 ....Youth Day
May 5 ....Senior Citizens Day
Jun 1 ....President's Day
Jul 9 ....Constitution Day
Sep: first Mon ....Labor Day
Oct 1 ....Independence Day
Oct 24 ....United Nations Day
Nov: last Thurs ....Thanksgiving Day
Dec 25 ....Christmas Day

Panama

Jan 1 ....New Year's Day
Jan 9 ....National Mourning Day
Feb ....Mardi Gras
Mar-Apr: Fri before Easter ....Good Friday
Mar-Apr: Sat before Easter ....Holy Saturday
Mar-Apr ....Easter
May 1 ....Labor Day
Nov 3 ....Independence from Colombia Day
Nov 4 ....Flag Day
Nov 10 ....Independence Proclamation/
Uprising of Los Santos
Nov 28 ....Independence from Spain Day
Dec 8 ....Mother's Day
Dec 25 ....Christmas Day
Dec 31 ....New Year's Eve

Papua New Guinea

Jan 1 . . . . .New Year's Day
Mar-Apr: Fri before Easter . . . . .Good Friday
Mar-Apr: Sat before Easter . . . . .Holy Saturday
Mar-Apr . . . . .Easter Sunday
Mar-Apr: Mon after Easter . . . . .Easter Monday
Jun: second Mon . . . . .Queen Elizabeth II Birthday
Jul 23 . . . . .Remembrance Day
Sep 16 . . . . .Independence Day
Dec 25 . . . . .Christmas Day
Dec 26 . . . . .Boxing Day

Paraguay

Jan 1 . . . . .New Year's Day
Mar 1 . . . . .Heroes' Day
Mar-Apr: Thurs before Easter . . . . .Holy Thursday
Mar-Apr: Fri before Easter . . . . .Good Friday
May 1 . . . . .Labor Day
May 15 . . . . .Independence Day
Jun 12 . . . . .End of the Chaco War
Aug 15 . . . . .Founding of Asuncion
Sep 29 . . . . .Victory Day
Dec 8 . . . . .Immaculate Conception
Dec 25 . . . . .Christmas Day

Peru

Jan 1 . . . . .New Year's Day
Mar-Apr: Thurs before Easter . . . . .Holy Thursday
Mar-Apr: Fri before Easter . . . . .Good Friday
Mar-Apr . . . . .Easter
May 1 . . . . .Labor Day
Jun 29 . . . . .Sts. Peter and Paul Day
Jul 28-29 . . . . .Independence Day Holiday
Aug 30 . . . . .St. Rose of Lima Day
Oct 8 . . . . .Battle of Angamos
Nov 1 . . . . .All Saints' Day
Dec 8 . . . . .Immaculate Conception
Dec 25 . . . . .Christmas Day

Philippines

Jan 1 . . . . .New Year's Day
Feb 24 . . . . .Edsa Revolution Day
Mar-Apr: Thurs before Easter . . . . .Maundy Thursday
Mar-Apr: Fri before Easter . . . . .Good Friday
Mar-Apr: Sat before Easter . . . . .Black Saturday
Apr 9 . . . . .Araw ng Kagitingan (Bataan Day)
May 1 . . . . .Labor Day
Jun 12 . . . . .Independence Day
Aug: last Sun . . . . .National Heroes Day
Nov 1 . . . . .All Saints' Day
Nov 30 . . . . .Bonifacio Day
Dec 25 . . . . .Christmas Day
Dec 30 . . . . .Rizal Day
Dec 31 . . . . .New Year's Eve

Poland

Jan 1 . . . . .New Year's Day
Mar-Apr . . . . .Easter
Mar-Apr: Mon after Easter . . . . .Easter Monday
May 1 . . . . .Labor Day
May 3 . . . . .Constitution Day
May . . . . .Whit Sunday (Pentecost)
May-Jun . . . . .Corpus Christi
Aug 15 . . . . .Assumption
Nov 1 . . . . .All Saints' Day
Nov 11 . . . . .Independence Day
Dec 25 . . . . .Christmas Day
Dec 26 .Second Day of Christmas

Portugal

Jan 1 . . . . .New Year's Day
Feb-Mar . . . . .Shrove Tuesday
Mar-Apr: Fri before Easter . . . . .Good Friday
Mar-Apr . . . . .Easter
Apr 25 . . . . .Liberty Day
May 1 . . . . .Labor Day
May-Jun . . . . .Corpus Christi
Jun 10 . . . . .National Day
Aug 15 . . . . .Assumption
Oct 5 . . . . .Republic Day
Nov 1 . . . . .All Saints' Day
Dec 1 . . . . .Independence Day
Dec 8 . . . . .Immaculate Conception
Dec 25 . . . . .Christmas Day

Qatar

Dec 18 . . . . .National Day (Independence Day)

Muslim holidays:

Shawwal (four days) . . . . .Id al-Fitr
Dhu al-Hijjah . . . . .Id al-Adha

Romania

Jan 1-2 . . . . .New Year's holiday
Apr-May: Mon after
Orthodox Easter . . . . .Orthodox Easter Monday
May 1 . . . . .Labor Day
Dec 1 . . . . .National Day
Dec 25-26 . . . . .Christmas holiday

Russian Federation

Jan 1-5 . . . . .New Year's holiday
Jan 7 .Russian Orthodox Christmas
Feb 23 .Protector of Motherland Day
Mar 8 . . . . .International Women's Day
May 1 . . . . .Spring and Labor Day
May 9 . . . . . . .Victory Day (Over German Nazism in WWII)
Jun 12 . . . . .Independence Day
Nov 4 . . . . .Unity Day

Rwanda

Jan 1 . . . . .New Year's Day
Feb 1 . . . . .Heroes' Day
Mar-Apr: Fri before Easter . . . . .Good Friday
Mar-Apr: Mon after Easter . . . . .Easter Monday
Apr 7 . . . . .Genocide Memorial Day
May 1 . . . . .Labor Day
Jul 1 . . . . .Independence Day
Jul 4 . . . . .National Liberation Day
Aug 15 . . . . .Assumption
Oct 1 . . . . .Patriotism Day
Dec 25 . . . . .Christmas
Dec 26 . . . . .Second Day of Christmas

St. Kitts and Nevis

Jan 1 . . . . .New Year's Day
Jan 2 . . . . .Carnival Day
Mar-Apr: Fri before Easter . . . . .Good Friday
Mar-Apr: Mon after Easter . . . . .Easter Monday
May: first Mon . . . . .Labour Day
May-Jun . . . . .Whit Monday
Aug 4 . . . . .Emancipation Day
Sep 16 . . . . .National Heroes' Day
Sep 19 . . . . .Independence Day
Dec 25 . . . . .Christmas Day
Dec 26 . . . . .Boxing Day

St. Lucia

Jan 1-2 . . . . .New Year's Holiday
Feb 22 . . . . .Independence Day
May 1 . . . . .Labor Day
Aug 4 . . . . .Emancipation Day
Dec 13 . . . . .National Day
Dec 25 . . . . .Christmas Day
Dec 26 . . . . .Boxing Day

St. Vincent and the Grenadines

Jan 1 . . . . .New Year's Day
Mar 14 . . . . .National Heroes' Day
Mar-Apr: Fri before Easter . . . . .Good Friday
Mar-Apr: Mon after Easter . . . . .Easter Monday
May 5 . . . . .Labor Day
May-Jun . . . . .Whit Monday
Jul: second Mon . . . . .Carnival Monday
Jul: second Tues . . . . .Carnival Tuesday
Aug: first Mon . . . . . .August Monday (Emancipation Day)
Oct 27 . . . . .Independence Day
Dec 25 . . . . .Christmas Day
Dec 26 . . . . .Boxing Day

Samoa

Jan 1-2 . . . . .New Year's Holiday
Mar-Apr: Fri before Easter . . . . .Good Friday
Mar-Apr: Sat before Easter . . . . .Easter Saturday
Mar-Apr: Mon after Easter . . . . .Easter Monday
May: second Mon . . . . .Mothers' Day

Jun 1 . . . . .Independence Day
Aug: second Mon . . . . .Fathers' Day
Oct: Mon after second Sun . . . . .Lotu-a-Tamaiti
Dec 25 . . . . .Christmas
Dec 26 . . . . .Boxing Day

San Marino

Jan 1 . . . . .New Year's Day
Jan 6 . . . . .Epiphany
Feb 5 . . . . .Anniversary of the
  Liberation of the Republic and St. Agatha's Day
Mar 25 .Anniversary of the Arengo
  (National Assembly)
Mar-Apr: Fri before Easter -
  Mon after Easter . . . . .Good Friday - Easter Monday
Apr 1 . . . . .Investiture of the Regent Captains
May 1 . . . . .Labor Day
May-Jun . . . . .Corpus Christi
Jul 28 . . . . .Anniversary of the Fall of Fascism
Aug 15 . . . . .Assumption Day
Sep 3 . . . . .San Marino Foundation Day
Oct 1 . . . . .Investiture of the Regent Captains
Nov 1 . . . . .All Saints' Day
Nov 2 . . . . .All Souls' Day
Dec 8 . . . . .Immaculate Conception
Dec 24 . . . . .Christmas Eve
Dec 25 . . . . .Christmas Day
Dec 26 . . . . .St. Stephen's Day/Boxing Day
Dec 31 . . . . .New Year's Eve

São Tomé and Príncipe

Jan 1 . . . . .New Year's Day
Feb 3 . . . . .Martyrs' Day
May 1 . . . . .Labor Day
Jul 12 . . . . .Independence Day
Sep 6 . . . . .Armed Forces Day
Sep 30 . . . . .Agricultural Reform Day
Dec 21 . . . . .São Tomé Day
Dec 25 . . . . .Christmas Day

Saudi Arabia

Sep 23 . . . . .National Day

Muslim holidays:
1 Shawwal . . . . Id al-Fitr
10 Dhu al-Hijjah . . . . .Id al-Adha

Scotland. *See* United Kingdom

Senegal

Jan 1 . . . . .New Year's Day
Mar-Apr: Mon after Easter . . . . .Easter Monday
Apr 4 . . . . .Independence Day
May 1 . . . . .Labor Day
May-Jun . . . . .Ascension Day
May-Jun . . . . .Pentecost
Aug 15 . . . . .Assumption Day

Nov 1 . . . . .All Saints' Day
Dec 25 . . . . .Christmas Day

Muslim holidays:
1 Muharram . . . . Tamkharit (Islamic New Year)
Rabi al-Awwal . . . . .Maulud (Muhammad's Birthday or Mawlid al-Nabi)
1 Shawwal . . . . .Korite (Id al-Fitr)
10 Dhu al-Hijjah . . . . .Tabaski (Id al-Adha)

Serbia

Jan 1-2 . . . . .New Year's holiday
Jan 7 . . . . .Orthodox Christmas Day
Feb 15 . . . . .National Day
Mar-Apr: Fri before Easter . . . . .Great Friday
Mar-Apr: Mon after Easter . . . . . .Orthodox Easter Monday
Apr 27 . . . . .Constitution Day of the Socialist Republic of Yugoslavia
May 1 . . . . .May Day
Aug 15 . . . . .Assumption
Nov 1 . . . . .All Saints' Day
Dec 25 . . . . .Christmas Day

Seychelles

Jan 1-2 . . . . .New Year Holiday
Mar-Apr: Fri before Easter . . . . .Good Friday
Mar-Apr: Sat before Easter . . . . .Holy Saturday
May 1 . . . . .Labour Day
May-Jun . . . . .Corpus Christi Day
Jun 5 . . . . .Liberation Day
Jun 18 . . . . .National Day
Jun 29 . . . . .Independence Day
Aug 15 . . . . .Assumption Day
Nov 1 . . . . .All Saints' Day
Dec 8 . . . . .Immaculate Conception Day
Dec 25 . . . . .Christmas Day

Sierra Leone

Jan 1 . . . . .New Year's Day
Mar-Apr: Fri before Easter . . . . .Good Friday
Mar-Apr: Mon after Easter . . . . .Easter Monday
Apr 27 . . . . .Independence Day
Dec 25 . . . . .Christmas Day
Dec 26 . . . . .Boxing Day

Muslim holidays:
Rabi al-Awwal . . . . . . .Maoulid-Un-Nabi (Mawlid al-Nabi)
Shawwal . . . . .Id al-Fitr
Dhu al-Hijjah . . . . .Tabaski (Id al-Adha)

Singapore

Jan 1 . . . . .New Year's Day
Jan-Feb . . . . .Chinese New Year
Mar-Apr: Fri before Easter . . . . .Good Friday
Apr-May . . . . .Vesak Day
May 1 . . . . .Labour Day
Aug 9 . . . . .National Day

Oct-Nov . . . . .Deepavali
Dec 25 . . . . .Christmas Day

Muslim holidays:
1 Shawwal . . . . .Hari Raya Pausa (Id al-Fitr)
10 Dhu al-Hijjah . . . . .Hari Raya Hajj (Id al-Adha)

Slovakia

Jan 1 .Republic Day/New Year's Day
Jan 6 . . . . .Epiphany
Mar-Apr: Fri before Easter . . . . .Good Friday
Mar-Apr: Mon after Easter . . . . .Easter Monday
May 1 . . . . .May Day
May 8 . . . . .Victory Day
Jul 5 . . . . .Sts. Cyril and Methodius Day
Aug 29 . . . . .Slovak National Uprising Day
Sep 1 . . . . .Constitution Day
Sep 15 . . . . .Lady Mary of Sorrows, Patron of Slovakia
Nov 1 . . . . .All Saints' Day
Nov 17 . . . . . .Day of the Fight for Freedom and Democracy
Dec 24 . . . . .Christmas Eve
Dec 25 . . . . .Christmas Day
Dec 26 . . . . .Second Day of Christmas

Slovenia

Jan 1-2 . . . . .New Year's holiday
Feb 8 . . . . .Preseren Day
Mar-Apr . . . . .Easter Sunday
Mar-Apr: Mon after Easter . . . . .Easter Monday
Apr 27 . . . . .Day of Uprising against Nazi Occupation
May 1-2 .May Day holiday
May-Jun . . . . .Whit Sunday (Pentecost)
Jun 25 . . . . .National Day
Aug 15 . . . . .Assumption Day
Oct 31 . . . . .Reformation Day
Nov 1 . . . . .All Saints' Day
Dec 25 . . . . .Christmas Day
Dec 26 . . . . .Independence Day

Solomon Islands

Jan 1 . . . . .New Year's Day
Mar-Apr: Fri before Easter -
  Mon after Easter . . . . .Good Friday - Easter Monday
May-Jun . . . . .Whit Monday
Jun: third Fri .Queen's Birthday
Jul 7 . . . . .Independence Day
Dec 25 . . . . .Christmas
Dec 26 . . . . .National Day of Thanksgiving

South Africa

Jan 1 . . . . .New Year's Day
Mar 21 . . . . .Human Rights Day
Mar-Apr: Fri before Easter . . . . .Good Friday
Mar-Apr: Mon after Easter . . . . .Family Day
Apr 27 . . . . .Freedom Day
May 1 . . . . .Workers' Day
Jun 16 . . . . .Youth Day

Aug 9 . . . . National Women's Day
Sep 24 . . . . Heritage Day
Dec 16 . . . . Day of Reconciliation
Dec 25 . . . . Christmas Day
Dec 26 . . . . Day of Goodwill

South Korea. *See* Korea, South

Spain

Jan 1 . . . . New Year's Day
Jan 6 . . . . Epiphany
Mar-Apr: Fri before Easter . . . . Good Friday
Mar-Apr . . . . Easter Sunday
May 1 . . . . Labor Day
Aug 15 . . . . Assumption Day
Oct 12 . . . . National Day
Nov 1 . . . . All Saints' Day
Dec 6 . . . . Constitution Day
Dec 8 . . . . Immaculate Conception Day
Dec 25 . . . . Christmas Day

Sri Lanka

Jan . . . . Tamil Thai Pongal Day
Feb 4 . . . . National Day
Feb-Mar . . . . Maha Sivarathri Day
Mar-Apr: Fri before Easter . . . . Good Friday
Apr 13 . . . . Day prior to Sinhala and Tamil New Year
Apr 14 . . . . Sinhala and Tamil New Year
Apr-May: day following Vesak Full Moon . . . . . Poya Day
May 1 . . . . May Day
Oct-Nov . . . . Deepavali Festival Day
Dec 25 . . . . Christmas Day
Full moon days of each month

Muslim holidays:
Rabi al-Nabi . . . . Milad-Un-Nabi
(Holy Prophet's Birthday or Mawlid al-Nabi)
Shawwal . . . . Id-Ul-Fitr (Ramazan Festival Day
or Id al-Fitr)
Dhu al-Hijjah . . . . Id-Ul-Allah (Hajji Festival Day
or Id al-Adha)

Sudan

Jan 1 . . . . Independence Day
Apr 27 . . . . Coptic Easter
Jun 30 . . . . Revolution Day
Dec 25 . . . . Christmas Day

Muslim holidays:
1 Muharram . . . . Islamic New Year
12 Rabi al-Awwal . . . . Mawlid al-Nabi
1 Shawwal . . . . Id al-Fitr
10 Dhu al-Hijjah . . . . Id al-Adha

Suriname

Jan 1 . . . . New Year's Day
Mar: full moon day . . . . Phagwa

Mar-Apr: Fri before Easter -
Mon after Easter . . . . Good Friday - Easter Monday
May 1 . . . . Labor Day
Jul 1 . . . . Emancipation Day (Keti Koti)
Aug 9 . . . . Indigenous People's Day
Nov 25 . . . . Independence Day
Dec 25 . . . . Christmas Day
Dec 26 . . . . Second Day of Christmas

Muslim holiday:
Shawwal . . . . Id al-Fitr

Swaziland

Jan 1 . . . . New Year's Day
Mar-Apr: Fri before Easter . . . . Good Friday
Mar-Apr: Mon after Easter . . . . Easter Monday
Apr 19 . . . . King's Birthday
Apr 25 . . . . National Flag Day
May 1 . . . . Workers' Day
May-Jun . . . . Ascension Day
Jul 22 . . . . King Father's Birthday
Aug-Sep . . . . Umhlanga Reed Dance
Sep 6 . . . . Somhlolo Day (Independence Day)
Dec 25 . . . . Christmas Day
Dec 26 . . . . Boxing Day
Dec-Jan . . . . Incwala Day

Sweden

Jan 1 . . . . New Year's Day
Jan 6 . . . . Epiphany
Mar-Apr: Fri before Easter . . . . Good Friday
Mar-Apr . . . . Easter Sunday
Mar-Apr: Mon after Easter . . . . Easter Monday
Apr-May . . . . Ascension Day
May 1 . . . . Labor Day
May-Jun . . . . Whit Sunday (Pentecost)
Jun 6 . . . . National Day
Jun . . . . Midsummer's Day
Nov 1 . . . . All Saints' Day
Dec 25 . . . . Christmas Day
Dec 26 . . . . Second Day of Christmas

Switzerland

Jan 1 . . . . New Year's Day
Mar-Apr: Fri before Easter . . . . Good Friday
Mar-Apr . . . . Easter Sunday
Mar-Apr: Mon after Easter . . . . Easter Monday
Apr-May . . . . Ascension Day
May-Jun . . . . Whit Sunday (Pentecost)
May-Jun . . . . Whit Monday
Aug 1 . . . . Swiss National Day
Dec 25 . . . . Christmas Day

Syria

Jan 1 . . . . New Year's Day
Mar 8 . . . . Commemoration of the Revolution
Mar 21 . . . . Mothers' Day

Mar-Apr ....Easter Sunday
Apr 17 ....Commemoration of the Evacuation
May 1 ....May Day (Workers' Holiday)
May 6 ....Martyrs' Day
Dec 25 ....Christmas Day

Taiwan
(Republic of China)

Jan 1 ....New Year's Day/Founding Day
                              of the Republic of China
Jan-Feb ....Chinese New Year
Feb 28 ....Peace Memorial Day
Apr 4 ....Tomb Sweeping Day
May-Jun ....Dragon Boat Festival
Aug-Sep ....Mid-Autumn Festival
Oct 10 ....Double Tenth National Day

Tajikistan

Jan 1 ....New Year's Day
Mar 8 ....International Women's Day
May 1 ....Labor Day
May 9 ....Victory Day
Jun 27 ....Unity Day
Sep 9 ....Independence Day
Nov 6 ....Constitution Day

Tanzania

Jan 1 ....New Year's Day
Jan 12 ....Zanzibar Revolution Day
Mar-Apr: Fri before Easter ....Good Friday
Mar-Apr: Mon after Easter ....Easter Monday
Apr 26 ....Union Day
May 1 ....Labor Day
Jul 7 ....Saba Saba Day
Aug 8 ....Farmers' Day
Oct 14 ....Nyerere Day
Dec 9 ....Independence Day
Dec 25 ....Christmas Day
Dec 26 ....Boxing Day

Muslim holidays:
12 Rabi al-Awwal ....Maulid (Mawlid al-Nabi)
1 Shawwal ....Idd el Fitr
10 Dhu al-Hijjah ....Idd el Haf (Id al-Adha)

Thailand

Jan 1 ....New Year's Day
Feb-Mar ....Makha Bucha Day
Apr 6 ....Chakri Day
Apr ....Songkran Festival
Apr-May ....Wisakha Bucha Day (Buddha's Birthday)
May 5 ....Coronation Day
Aug 12 ....Her Majesty the Queen's Birthday
Oct 23 ....Chulalongkorn Day
Dec 5 ....His Majesty the King's Birthday
Dec 10 ....Constitution Day
Dec 31 ....New Year's Eve

Togo

Jan 1 ....New Year's Day
Jan 24 ....Economic Liberation Day
Mar-Apr: Mon after Easter ....Easter Monday
Apr 27 ....Independence Day
May 1 ....Labor Day
May-Jun ....Ascension Day
May-Jun ....Whit Monday
Jun 21 ....Martyrs' Day
Aug 15 ....Assumption Day
Nov 1 ....All Saints' Day
Dec 25 ....Christmas Day

Muslim holidays:
Shawwal ....Id al-Fitr
Dhu al-Hijjah ....Tabaski (Id al-Adha)

Tonga

Jan 1 ....New Year's Day
Mar-Apr: Fri before Easter ....Good Friday
Mar-Apr: Mon after Easter ....Easter Monday
Apr 25 ....ANZAC Day
Jun 4 ....Emancipation Day
Jul 12 ....Birthday of the Heir to the Crown of Tonga
Aug 1 ......Official Birthday of the Reigning Sovereign of
                              Tonga/Coronation Day
Nov 4 ....National Day
Dec 4 ....King Tupou I Day
Dec 25 ....Christmas Day
Dec 26 ....Boxing Day

Trinidad and Tobago

Jan 1 ....New Year's Day
Mar 30 ....Spiritual Baptist Liberation Shouter Day
Mar-Apr: Fri before Easter ....Good Friday
Mar-Apr: Mon after Easter ....Easter Monday
May 30 ....Indian Arrival Day
May-Jun ....Corpus Christi Day
Jun 19 ....Labour Day
Aug 1 ....Emancipation Day
Aug 31 ....Independence Day
Sep 24 ....Republic Day
Oct-Nov ....Divali
Dec 25 ....Christmas Day
Dec 26 ....Boxing Day

Muslim holiday:
1 Shawwal ....Id-il-Fitr

Tunisia

Jan 1 ....New Year's Day
Mar 20 ....Independence Day
Mar 21 ....Youth Day
Apr 9 ....Martyrs' Day
May 1 ....Labor Day
Jul 25 ....Republic Day
Aug 13 ....Women's Day
Nov 7 ....New Era Day

Muslim holidays:

Muharram . . . . .Ras el am el Hijra (Islamic New Year)
Rabi al-Awwal . . . . .Mouled (Mawlid al-Nabi)
Shawwal . . . . .Aid Esseghir (Id al-Fitr)
Dhu al-Hijjah . . . . .Aid el Kebir (Id al-Adha)

Turkey

Jan 1 . . . . .New Year's Day
Apr 23 . . . . .National Sovereignty and Children's Day
May 19 .Atatürk Commemoration
and Youth & Sports Day
Aug 30 . . . . .Victory Day
Oct 29 . . . . .Republic Day

Muslim holidays:

1 Shawwal (three days) . . . . . . .Seker Bayrami (Eid al-Fitr)
10 Dhu al-Hijjah (four days) . . . . .Kurban Bayrami
(Id al-Adha)

Turkmenistan

Jan 1 . . . . .New Year's Day
Jan 12 . . . . .Memorial Day
Feb 19 . . . . .National Flag Day
Mar 8 .International Women's Day
Mar 21 . . . . .Novruz-Bairam
May 9 . . . . .Victory Day
May 18 .Revival and Unity Day
Oct 6 . . . . .Remembrance Day
Oct 27-28 . . . . .Independence Day holiday
Dec 12 . . . . .Day of Neutrality

Muslim holidays:

Shawwal . . . . .Ramadan-Bairam (Id al-Fitr)
Dhu al-Hijjah . . . . .Kurban-Bairam (Id al-Adha)

Tuvalu

Jan 1 . . . . .New Year's Day
Mar . . . . .Commonwealth Day
Mar-Apr: Fri before Easter -
Mon after Easter . . . . .Good Friday - Easter Monday
May . . . . .Gospel Day (Te Aso o te Tala 'Lei)
Jun: Mon after third Sat . . . . .Queen's Birthday
Aug . . . . .National Children's Day
Oct . . . . .Independence Day
Dec 25 . . . . .Christmas Day
Dec 26 . . . . .Boxing Day

Uganda

Jan 1 . . . . .New Year's Day
Jan 26 . . . . .NRM Anniversary Day
Mar 8 .International Women's Day
Mar-Apr: Fri before Easter . . . . .Good Friday
Mar-Apr: Mon after Easter . . . . .Easter Monday
May 1 . . . . .Labor Day
Jun 3 . . . . .Martyrs' Day
Jun 9 . . . . .National Heroes Day
Oct 9 . . . . .Independence Day

Dec 25 . . . . .Christmas Day
Dec 26 . . . . .Boxing Day

Muslim holidays:

Shawwal . . . . .Id al-Fitr
Dhu al-Hijjah . . . . .Id al-Adha

Ukraine

Jan 1 . . . . .New Year's Day
Jan 7 . . . . .Orthodox Christmas
Mar 8 . . . . .Women's Day
Apr-May . . . . .Easter
Apr-May: Mon after Easter . . . . .Easter Monday
May 1 . . . . .Labor Day
May 9 . . . . .Victory Day
Jun 28 . . . . .Constitution Day
Aug 24 . . . . .Independence Day

United Arab Emirates

Jan 1 . . . . .New Year's Day
Dec 2-3 . . . . .National Day holiday

Muslim holidays:

1 Muharram .Islamic New Year
Rabi al-Awwal . . . . .Muhammad's Birthday
(Mawlid al-Nabi)
Shawwal . . . . .Id al-Fitr
Dhu al-Hijjah . . . . .Id al-Adha

United Kingdom

England and Wales

Jan 1 . . . . .New Year's Day
Mar-Apr: Fri before Easter . . . . .Good Friday
Mar-Apr: Mon after Easter . . . . .Easter Monday
May: first Mon . . . . .Early May Bank Holiday
May: last Mon . . . . .Spring Bank Holiday
Aug: last Mon . . . . .Summer Bank Holiday
Dec 25 . . . . .Christmas Day
Dec 26 . . . . .Boxing Day

Northern Ireland

Jan 1 . . . . .New Year's Day
Mar: third Mon . . . . .St. Patrick's Day
Mar-Apr: Fri before Easter . . . . .Good Friday
Mar-Apr: Mon after Easter . . . . .Easter Monday
May: first Mon . . . . .Early May Bank Holiday
May: last Mon . . . . .Spring Bank Holiday
Jul 12 . . . . .Battle of the Boyne (Orangemen's Day)
Aug: last Mon . . . . .Summer Bank Holiday
Dec 25 . . . . .Christmas Day
Dec 26 . . . . .Boxing Day

Scotland

Jan 1-2 . . . . .New Year's holiday
Mar-Apr . . . . .Good Friday
May: first Mon . . . . .Early May Bank Holiday
May: last Mon . . . . .Spring Bank Holiday
Aug: last Mon . . . . .Summer Bank Holiday

Nov 30 . . . . .St. Andrew's Day
Dec 25 . . . . .Christmas Day
Dec 26 . . . . .Boxing Day

Uruguay

Jan 1 . . . . .New Year's Day
Jan 6 . . . . .Epiphany
Feb . . . . .Carnival (two days)
Mar-Apr: Thurs before Easter . . . . .Maundy Thursday
Mar-Apr: Fri before Easter . . . . .Good Friday
Apr 19 . . . . .Desembarco de los 33 Orientales
May 1 . . . . .Labor Day
May 18 .Batalla de las Piedras
Jun 19 . . . . .Birthday of Artigas
Jul 18 . . . . .Constitution Day
Aug 25 . . . . .Independence Day
Oct 12 .Día de los Américas
Nov 2 . . . . .Día de los Difuntos (All Souls' Day)
Dec 25 . . . . .Christmas Day

Uzbekistan

Jan 1 . . . . .New Year's Day
Mar 8 . . . . .Women's Day
Mar 21 . . . . .Nawruz
May 9 . . . . .Memorial Day
Sep 1 . . . . .Independence Day
Oct 1 . . . . .Teacher's Day
Dec 8 . . . . .Constitution Day

Muslim holidays:
Shawwal . . . . .Id-Al Fitr
Dhu al-Hijjah . . . . .Id-Al Zuha (Id al-Adha)

Vanuatu

Jan 1 . . . . .New Year's Day
Feb 21 . . . . .Fr. Walter Lini Day
Mar 6 . . . . .Custom Chiefs Day
Mar-Apr: Fri before Easter . . . . .Good Friday
Mar-Apr: Mon after Easter . . . . .Easter Monday
May 1 . . . . .Labour Day
May-Jun . . . . .Ascension Day
Jul 24 . . . . .Children's Day
Jul 30 . . . . .Independence Day
Aug 15 . . . . .Assumption Day
Oct 5 . . . . .Constitution Day
Nov 29 . . . . .Unity Day
Dec 25 . . . . .Christmas Day
Dec 26 . . . . .Family Day

Venezuela

Jan 1 . . . . .New Year's Day
Feb-Mar . . . . .Carnival Monday and Tuesday
Mar-Apr: Thurs before Easter . . . . .Maundy Thursday
Mar-Apr: Fri before Easter . . . . .Good Friday
Apr 19 . . . . .Declaration of Independence Day
May 1 . . . . .Labor Day
Jun 24 .Battle of Carabobo Day

Jul 5 . . . . .National Day (Independence Day)
Jul 24 . . . . .Simón Bolívar's Birthday
Oct 12 . . . . .Day of Indigenous Resistance
Dec 25 . . . . .Christmas Day

Vietnam

Jan 1 . . . . .New Year's Day
Jan-Feb (four days) . . . .Lunar New Year (Tet Nguyen Dan)
Apr 15 .Gio to Hung Vuong Day
Apr 30 . . . . .Saigon Liberation Day
May 1 . . . . .International Labor Day
Sep 2 . . . . .National Day

Wales. *See* United Kingdom

Western Samoa. *See* Samoa

Yemen

May 1 . . . . .Labor Day
May 22 . . . . .National Day
Sep 26 . . . . .Revolution Day
Oct 14 . . . . .Liberation Day
Nov 30 . . . . .Independence Day

Muslim holidays:
1 Muharram . . . . .Memory of Prophet's Immigration
(Islamic New Year)
29 Ramadan-3 Shawwal . . . . .Id Al Fitr
9-14 Dhu al-Hijjah . . . . .Id Al Adha

Yugoslavia. *See* Serbia – Montenegro

Zaire. *See* Congo, Democratic Republic of

Zambia

Jan 1 . . . . .New Year's Day
Mar 8 . . . . .International Women's Day
Mar 12 . . . . .Youth Day
Mar-Apr: Fri before Easter . . . . .Good Friday
Mar-Apr: Sat before Easter . . . . .Holy Saturday
Mar-Apr: Mon after Easter . . . . .Easter Monday
May 1 . . . . .Labour Day
May 25 . . . . .African Freedom Day
(Anniversary of OAU's Foundation)
Jul: first Mon . . . . .Heroes' Day
Jul: first Tues . . . . .Unity Day
Aug: first Mon . . . . .Farmers' Day
Oct 24 . . . . .Independence Day
Dec 25 . . . . .Christmas Day

Zimbabwe

Jan 1	New Year's Day
Mar 29	General Elections Day
Mar-Apr: Fri before Easter	Good Friday
Mar-Apr: Sat before Easter	Holy Saturday
Mar-Apr	Easter Sunday
Mar-Apr: Mon after Easter	Easter Monday
Apr 18	Independence Day
May 1	Labour Day
May 25	Africa Day
Aug 11	Heroes' Day
Aug 12	Defense Forces Day
Dec 22	National Unity Day
Dec 25	Christmas Day
Dec 26	Boxing Day

APPENDIX 12

Tourism Information Sources for Countries around the World

The following list includes tourism information sources for countries around the world, except the United States, Canada, and Mexico (*see* Appendix 8) The listings are in alphabetical order by name of the country, with cross references where appropriate to other forms of the countries' names. Within each country listing, listings are in the following order, although each country may not have all offices:

National Tourism Office
Chamber of Commerce
Consulate General
Embassy
Permanent Mission to the United Nations

Afghanistan

Afghanistan Consulate General
360 Lexington Ave
11th Fl
New York, NY 10017
Phone: 212-972-2276; Fax: 212-972-9046

Afghanistan Embassy
2341 Wyoming Ave NW
Washington, DC 20008
Phone: 202-483-6410; Fax: 202-483-6488
www.embassyofafghanistan.org

Afghanistan Permanent Mission to the UN
360 Lexington Ave
11th Fl
New York, NY 10017
Phone: 212-972-1212; Fax: 212-972-1216

Albania

Albania Embassy
2100 'S' St NW
Washington, DC 20008
Phone: 202-223-4942; Fax: 202-628-7342

Albania Permanent Mission to the UN
320 E 79th St
New York, NY 10021
Phone: 212-249-2059; Fax: 212-535-2917

Algeria

Algeria Embassy
2118 Kalorama Rd NW

Washington, DC 20008
Phone: 202-265-2800; Fax: 202-667-2174
www.algeria-us.org

Algeria Embassy - Consular Section
2137 Wyoming Ave NW
Washington, DC 20008
Phone: 202-265-2800; Fax: 202-265-1978
www.algeria-us.org

Algeria Permanent Mission to the UN
326 E 48th St
New York, NY 10017
Phone: 212-750-1960; Fax: 212-759-9538
www.algeria-un.org

Andorra

Andorra Embassy
2 United Nations Plaza
27th Fl
New York, NY 10017
Phone: 212-750-8064; Fax: 212-750-6630
www.andorra.ad

Andorra Permanent Mission to the UN
2 UN Plaza
27th Fl
New York, NY 10017
Phone: 212-750-8064; Fax: 212-750-6630

Angola

US-Angola Chamber of Commerce
1100 Connecticut Ave NW
Suite 1000

Washington, DC 20036
Phone: 202-223-0540; Fax: 202-223-0551
www.us-angola.org

Angola Embassy
2108 16th St NW
Washington, DC 20009
Phone: 202-785-1156; Fax: 202-822-9049
www.angola.org

Angola Permanent Mission to the UN
125 E 73rd St
New York, NY 10021
Phone: 212-861-5656; Fax: 212-861-9295

Anguilla

Anguilla Tourist Marketing Office
246 Central Ave
White Plains, NY 10606
Phone: 914-287-2400; Fax: 914-287-2404
Toll-free: 877-426-4845
www.anguilla-vacation.com

Antigua and Barbuda

Antigua & Barbuda Dept of Tourism & Trade
25 SE 2nd Ave
Suite 300
Miami, FL 33131
Phone: 305-381-6762; Fax: 305-381-7908
Toll-free: 888-268-4227
www.antigua-barbuda.org

Antigua & Barbuda Dept of Tourism & Trade
305 E 47th St
6th Fl
New York, NY 10007
Phone: 212-541-4117; Fax: 212-541-4789
Toll-free: 888-268-4227
www.antigua-barbuda.org

Antigua & Barbuda Consulate General
25 SE 2nd Ave
Suite 300
Miami, FL 33131
Phone: 305-381-6762; Fax: 305-381-7908

Antigua & Barbuda Embassy
3216 New Mexico Ave NW
Washington, DC 20016
Phone: 202-362-5122; Fax: 202-362-5225

Antigua & Barbuda Permanent Mission to the UN
305 E 47th St
6th Fl
New York, NY 10017
Phone: 212-541-4117; Fax: 212-757-1607
www.un.int/antigua

Argentina

Argentina National Tourist Office
1101 Brickell Ave Suite 901

South Tower
Miami, FL 33131
Phone: 305-442-1366; Fax: 305-441-7029
www.sectur.gov.ar

Argentina National Tourist Office
12 W 56th St
New York, NY 10019
Phone: 212-603-0443; Fax: 212-586-1786
www.sectur.gov.ar

Argentine-American Chamber of Commerce Inc
630 5th Ave
25th Fl
New York, NY 10111
Phone: 212-698-2238; Fax: 212-698-2239
www.argentinechamber.org

Argentina Consulate General
245 Peachtree Center Ave
Suite 2101
Atlanta, GA 30303
Phone: 404-880-0805; Fax: 404-880-0806

Argentina Consulate General
205 N Michigan Ave
Suite 4208
Chicago, IL 60601
Phone: 312-819-2620; Fax: 312-819-2612

Argentina Consulate General
3050 Post Oak Blvd
Suite 1625
Houston, TX 77056
Phone: 713-871-8935; Fax: 713-871-0639

Argentina Consulate General
5055 Wilshire Blvd
Suite 210
Los Angeles, CA 90036
Phone: 323-954-9155; Fax: 323-934-9076

Argentina Consulate General
800 Brickell Ave
PH 1
Miami, FL 33131
Phone: 305-373-7794; Fax: 305-373-1598

Argentina Consulate General
12 W 56th St
New York, NY 10019
Phone: 212-603-0400; Fax: 212-541-7746
www.congenargentinany.com

Argentina Embassy
1600 New Hampshire Ave NW
Washington, DC 20009
Phone: 202-238-6400; Fax: 202-332-3171
www.embassyofargentina.us

Argentina Permanent Mission to the UN
1 UN Plaza
25th Fl
New York, NY 10017
Phone: 212-688-6300; Fax: 212-980-8395
www.un.int/argentina

Armenia

Armenia Consulate General
50 N La Cienega Blvd
Suite 210
Beverly Hills, CA 90211
Phone: 310-657-6102; Fax: 310-657-7419

Armenia Embassy
2225 R St NW
Washington, DC 20008
Phone: 202-319-1976; Fax: 202-319-2982
www.armeniaemb.org

Armenia Permanent Mission to the UN
119 E 36th St
New York, NY 10016
Phone: 212-686-9079; Fax: 212-686-3934
www.un.int/armenia

Aruba

Aruba Tourism Authority
1 Financial Plaza
Suite 2508
Fort Lauderdale, FL 33394
Phone: 954-767-6477; Fax: 954-767-0432
Toll-free: 800-862-7822
www.aruba.com

Aruba Tourism Authority
1144 E State St
Suite A-300
Geneva, IL 60134
Phone: 630-262-5580; Fax: 630-262-5581
Toll-free: 800-862-7822
www.aruba.com

Aruba Tourism Authority
1750 Powder Springs Rd
Suite 190
Marietta, GA 30064
Phone: 404-892-7822; Fax: 404-873-2193
www.aruba.com

Aruba Tourism Authority
10655 Six Pines Dr
Suite 145
The Woodlands, TX 77380
Phone: 281-362-1616; Fax: 281-362-1644
Toll-free: 800-862-7822
www.aruba.com

Aruba Tourism Authority
1200 Harbor Blvd
Weehawken, NJ 07086
Phone: 201-330-0800; Fax: 201-330-8757
Toll-free: 800-862-7822
www.aruba.com

Tourism Australia
6100 Center Dr
Suite 1150
Los Angeles, CA 90045
Phone: 310-695-3200; Fax: 310-695-3201
Toll-free: 800-369-6863
www.australia.com

Australia

Australian-American Chamber of Commerce of Hawaii
1000 Bishop St
Honolulu, HI 96813
Phone: 808-526-2242; Fax: 808-534-0475
lava.net/aacc

Australian American Chamber of Commerce of Houston
PO Box 130261
Houston, TX 77219
Phone: 713-527-9688; Fax: 713-527-9688
www.aacc-houston.org

Australian-American Chamber of Commerce of San
  Francisco
PO Box 210508
San Francisco, CA 94121
Phone: 415-485-6718; Fax: 415-485-6832
www.sfaussies.com

Australian New Zealand American Chambers of Commerce
c/o Embassy of Australia
1601 Massachusetts Ave NW
Washington, DC 20036
Phone: 202-797-3028; Fax: 202-797-3457
www.anzaccnational.com

Australia Consulate General
123 N Wacker Dr
Suite 1330
Chicago, IL 60606
Phone: 312-419-1480; Fax: 312-419-1499
www.austemb.org/chicago.html

Australia Consulate General
1000 Bishop St
PH
Honolulu, HI 96813
Phone: 808-524-5050; Fax: 808-531-5142
www.austemb.org/honolulu.html

Australia Consulate General
2049 Century Park E
Century Plaza Towers 19th Fl
Los Angeles, CA 90067
Phone: 310-229-4800; Fax: 310-277-3462
www.austemb.org/losangeles.html

Australia Consulate General
150 E 42nd St
34th Fl
New York, NY 10017
Phone: 212-351-6500; Fax: 212-351-6501
www.australianyc.org

Australia Embassy
1601 Massachusetts Ave NW
Washington, DC 20036
Phone: 202-797-3000; Fax: 202-797-3168
www.austemb.org

Australia Permanent Mission to the UN
150 E 42nd St
33rd Fl
New York, NY 10017
Phone: 212-351-6600; Fax: 212-351-6610
www.australianyc.org

Austria

Austrian Tourist Office
PO Box 1142
New York, NY 10108
Phone: 212-944-6880; Fax: 212-730-4568
www.austria.info/us

US-Austrian Chamber of Commerce
165 W 46th St
New York, NY 10036
Phone: 212-819-0117; Fax: 212-819-0345
www.usatchamber.com

Austria Consulate General
400 N Michigan Ave
Suite 707
Chicago, IL 60611
Phone: 312-222-1515; Fax: 312-222-4113
www.aussenministerium.at

Austria Consulate General
11859 Wilshire Blvd
Suite 501
Los Angeles, CA 90025
Phone: 310-444-9310; Fax: 310-477-9897
www.austria.org/austriaintheus.shtml#5

Austria Consulate General
31 E 69th St
New York, NY 10021
Phone: 212-737-6400; Fax: 212-772-8926
www.austria-ny.org

Austria Embassy
3524 International Ct NW
Washington, DC 20008
Phone: 202-895-6700; Fax: 202-895-6750
www.austria.org

Austria Permanent Mission to the UN
600 3rd Ave
31st Fl
New York, NY 10016
Phone: 917-542-8400; Fax: 212-949-1840
www.un.int/austria

Azerbaijan

Azerbaijan Embassy
2741 34th St NW
Washington, DC 20008
Phone: 202-337-3500; Fax: 202-337-5911
www.azembassy.com

Azerbaijan Permanent Mission to the UN
866 UN Plaza
Suite 560
New York, NY 10017
Phone: 212-371-2559; Fax: 212-371-2784

Bahamas

Bahamas Tourism Office
8600 W Bryn Mawr Ave

Suite 580 N
Chicago, IL 60631
Phone: 773-693-1500; Fax: 773-693-1114
www.bahamas.com

Bahamas Tourism Office
11400 W Olympic Blvd
Suite 204
Los Angeles, CA 90064
Phone: 310-312-9544; Fax: 310-445-8800
Toll-free: 800-439-6993
www.bahamas.com

Bahamas Tourism Office
60 E 42nd St
Suite 1850
New York, NY 10165
Phone: 212-758-2777; Fax: 212-753-6531
Toll-free: 800-823-3136
www.bahamas.com

Bahamas Tourism Office
1200 S Pine Island Rd
Suite 750
Plantation, FL 33324
Phone: 954-236-9292; Fax: 954-236-9282
Toll-free: 800-224-3681
www.bahamas.com

Bahamas Consulate General
25 SE 2nd Ave
Miami, FL 33131
Phone: 305-373-6295; Fax: 305-373-6312

Bahamas Consulate General
231 E 46th St
New York, NY 10017
Phone: 212-421-6420; Fax: 212-688-5926

Bahamas Embassy
2220 Massachusetts Ave NW
Washington, DC 20008
Phone: 202-319-2660; Fax: 202-319-2668

Bahamas Permanent Mission to the UN
231 E 46th St
New York, NY 10017
Phone: 212-421-6925; Fax: 212-759-2135

Bahrain

Bahrain Consulate General
866 2nd Ave
14th Fl
New York, NY 10017
Phone: 212-223-6200; Fax: 212-223-6206
www.un.int/bahrain/consulate.html

Bahrain Embassy
3502 International Dr NW
Washington, DC 20008
Phone: 202-342-1111; Fax: 202-362-2192
www.bahrainembassy.org

Bahrain Permanent Mission to the UN
866 2nd Ave

14th Fl
New York, NY 10017
Phone: 212-223-6200; Fax: 212-319-0687
www.un.int/bahrain

Bangladesh

Bangladesh Consulate General
4201 Wilshire Blvd
Suite 605
Los Angeles, CA 90010
Phone: 323-932-0100; Fax: 323-932-9703
www.bangladeshconsulatela.com

Bangladesh Consulate General
211 E 43rd St
Suite 502
New York, NY 10017
Phone: 212-599-6767; Fax: 212-682-9211

Bangladesh Embassy
3510 International Dr NW
Washington, DC 20008
Phone: 202-244-0183; Fax: 202-244-2771
www.bangladoot.org

Bangladesh Permanent Mission to the UN
227 E 45th St
New York, NY 10017
Phone: 212-867-3434; Fax: 212-972-4038
www.un.int/bangladesh

Barbados

Barbados Tourism Authority
150 Alhambra Cir
Suite 1000
Coral Gables, FL 33134
Phone: 305-442-7471; Fax: 305-774-9497
Toll-free: 800-221-9831
barbados.org/barbados2

Barbados Tourism Authority
3440 Wilshire Blvd
Suite 1207
Los Angeles, CA 90010
Phone: 213-380-2198; Fax: 213-384-2763
barbados.org/barbados2

Barbados Tourism Authority
800 2nd Ave
2nd Fl
New York, NY 10017
Phone: 212-986-6516; Fax: 212-573-9850
Toll-free: 800-221-9831
barbados.org/barbados2

Barbados Consulate General
150 Alhambra Cir
Suite 1000
Coral Gables, FL 33134
Phone: 305-442-1994; Fax: 305-567-2844

Barbados Vice Consulate
3440 Wilshire Blvd

Suite 1207
Los Angeles, CA 90010
Phone: 213-380-2198; Fax: 213-384-2763

Barbados Consulate General
800 2nd Ave
2nd Fl
New York, NY 10017
Phone: 212-867-8435; Fax: 212-986-1030

Barbados Embassy
2144 Wyoming Ave NW
Washington, DC 20008
Phone: 202-939-9200; Fax: 202-332-7467

Barbados Permanent Mission to the UN
800 2nd Ave
2nd Fl
New York, NY 10017
Phone: 212-867-8431; Fax: 212-986-1030
Toll-free: 800-221-9831

Belarus

Belarus Consulate General
708 3rd Ave
21st Fl
New York, NY 10017
Phone: 212-682-5392; Fax: 212-682-5491

Belarus Embassy
1619 New Hampshire Ave NW
Washington, DC 20009
Phone: 202-986-1606; Fax: 202-986-1805
www.belarusembassy.org

Belarus Permanent Mission to the UN
136 E 67th St
4th Fl
New York, NY 10021
Phone: 212-535-3420; Fax: 212-734-4810
www.un.int/belarus

Belgium

Belgian Tourist Office
220 E 42nd St
Suite 3402
New York, NY 10017
Phone: 212-758-8130; Fax: 212-355-7675
www.visitbelgium.com

Belgian-American Chamber of Commerce in the US
101 Hudson St
21st Fl
Jersey City, NJ 07302
Phone: 201-631-8065; Fax: 201-631-8067
www.belcham.org

Belgium Consulate General
230 Peachtree St NW
Suite 2710
Atlanta, GA 30303
Phone: 404-659-2150; Fax: 404-659-8474

Belgium Consulate General
6100 Wilshire Blvd
Suite 1200
Los Angeles, CA 90048
Phone: 323-857-1244; Fax: 323-936-2564

Belgium Consulate General
1065 Avenue of the Americas
22nd Fl
New York, NY 10018
Phone: 212-586-5110; Fax: 212-582-9657
www.diplomatie.be/newyork/

Belgium Consulate General
1065 Ave of the Americas
22nd Fl
New York, NY 10018
Phone: 212-586-5110; Fax: 212-582-9657

Belgium Embassy
3330 Garfield St NW
Washington, DC 20008
Phone: 202-333-6900; Fax: 202-333-3079
www.diplobel.us

Belgium Permanent Mission to the UN
823 UN Plaza
4th Fl
New York, NY 10017
Phone: 212-378-6300; Fax: 212-681-7618
www.un.int/belgium

Belize

Belize Consulate General
4801 Wilshire Blvd Suite 250
Park Mile Plaza
Los Angeles, CA 90018
Phone: 323-634-9900; Fax: 323-634-9903

Belize Embassy
2535 Massachusetts Ave NW
Washington, DC 20008
Phone: 202-332-9636; Fax: 202-332-6888
www.embassyofbelize.org

Belize Permanent Mission to the UN
675 3rd Ave
Suite 1911
New York, NY 10017
Phone: 212-593-0999; Fax: 212-593-0932
www.belizemission.com

Benin

Benin Embassy
2124 Kalorama Rd NW
Washington, DC 20008
Phone: 202-232-6656; Fax: 202-265-1996
www.beninembassy.us

Benin Permanent Mission to the UN
125 E 38th St
New York, NY 10016
Phone: 212-684-1339; Fax: 212-684-2058
www.un.int/benin

Bermuda

Bermuda Dept of Tourism
675 3rd Ave
20th Fl
New York, NY 10017
Phone: 212-818-9800; Fax: 212-983-5289
Toll-free: 800-223-6106
www.bermudatourism.com

Bhutan

Bhutan Permanent Mission to the UN
763 UN Plaza
New York, NY 10017
Phone: 212-682-2268; Fax: 212-661-0551

Bolivia

Bolivia Consulate General
3701 Wilshire Blvd
Suite 1065
Los Angeles, CA 90010
Phone: 213-388-0475; Fax: 213-384-6272

Bolivia Consulate General
211 E 43rd St
Suite 702
New York, NY 10017
Phone: 212-687-0530; Fax: 212-687-0532
www.boliviaweb.com/embassies.htm

Bolivia Embassy
3014 Massachusetts Ave NW
Washington, DC 20008
Phone: 202-483-4410; Fax: 202-328-3712
www.boliviaweb.com/embassies.htm

Bolivia Permanent Mission to the UN
211 E 43rd St
Rm 802
New York, NY 10017
Phone: 212-682-8132; Fax: 212-687-4642

Bonaire

Bonaire Government Tourist Office
10 Rockefeller Plaza
Suite 900
New York, NY 10020
Phone: 212-956-5911; Fax: 212-956-5913
Toll-free: 800-266-2473
www.infobonaire.com

Bosnia and Herzegovina

Bosnia & Herzegovina Consulate General
2109 E St NW
Washington, DC 20037
Phone: 202-337-6478; Fax: 202-337-2909
www.bhembassy.org

Bosnia & Herzegovina Embassy
2109 E St NW

Washington, DC 20037
Phone: 202-337-1500; Fax: 202-337-1502
www.bhembassy.org

Bosnia & Herzegovina Permanent Mission to the UN
866 UN Plaza
Suite 585
New York, NY 10017
Phone: 212-751-9015; Fax: 212-751-9019

Botswana

Botswana Embassy
1531 New Hampshire Ave NW
Washington, DC 20036
Phone: 202-244-4990; Fax: 202-244-4164
www.botswanaembassy.org

Botswana Permanent Mission to the UN
154 E 46th St
New York, NY 10017
Phone: 212-889-2277; Fax: 212-725-5061

Brazil

Brazilian-American Chamber of Commerce of Georgia
PO Box 93411
Atlanta, GA 30377
Phone: 404-880-1551; Fax: 404-880-1555
www.bacc-ga.com

Brazilian-American Chamber of Commerce of Florida
PO Box 310038
Miami, FL 33231
Phone: 305-579-9030; Fax: 305-579-9756
www.brazilchamber.org

Brazilian-American Chamber of Commerce Inc
509 Madison Ave
Suite 304
New York, NY 10022
Phone: 212-751-4691; Fax: 212-751-7692
www.brazilcham.com

Brazil Consulate General
8484 Wilshire Blvd
Suite 711
Beverly Hills, CA 90211
Phone: 323-651-2664; Fax: 323-651-1274
www.brazilian-consulate.org

Brazil Consulate General
20 Park Plaza
Suite 810
Boston, MA 02116
Phone: 617-542-4000; Fax: 617-542-4318
www.consulatebrazil.org

Brazil Consulate General
401 N Michigan Ave
Suite 3050
Chicago, IL 60611
Phone: 312-464-0244; Fax: 312-464-0299

Brazil Consulate General
1233 West Loop S
Suite 1150
Houston, TX 77027
Phone: 713-961-3063; Fax: 713-961-3070
www.brazilhouston.org

Brazil Consulate General
80 SW 8th St
Suite 2600
Miami, FL 33130
Phone: 305-285-6200; Fax: 305-285-6259
www.brazilmiami.org

Brazil Consulate General
1185 6th Ave
New York, NY 10036
Phone: 917-777-7777; Fax: 212-827-0225
www.brazilny.org

Brazil Consulate General
300 Montgomery St
Suite 900
San Francisco, CA 94104
Phone: 415-981-8170; Fax: 415-981-3628
www.brazilsf.org

Brazil Embassy
3006 Massachusetts Ave NW
Washington, DC 20008
Phone: 202-238-2700; Fax: 202-238-2827
Toll-free: 800-727-2945
www.brasilemb.org

Brazil Embassy - Consular Section
3009 Whitehaven St NW
Washington, DC 20008
Phone: 202-238-2828; Fax: 202-238-2818
www.brasilemb.org

Brazil Permanent Mission to the UN
747 3rd Ave
9th Fl
New York, NY 10017
Phone: 212-372-2600; Fax: 212-371-5716
www.un.int/brazil

British Virgin Islands

British Virgin Islands Tourist Board
3450 Wilshire Blvd
Suite 1202
Los Angeles, CA 90010
Phone: 213-736-8931; Fax: 213-736-8935
Toll-free: 800-835-8530
www.bvitourism.com

British Virgin Islands Tourist Board
1270 Broadway
Suite 705
New York, NY 10001
Phone: 212-696-0400; Fax: 212-563-2263
Toll-free: 800-835-8530
www.bvitourism.com

Brunei Darussalam

Brunei Darussalam Embassy
3520 International Ct NW
Washington, DC 20008
Phone: 202-237-1838; Fax: 202-885-0560
www.bruneiembassy.org

Brunei Darussalam Permanent Mission to the UN
771 1st Ave
New York, NY 10017
Phone: 212-697-3465; Fax: 212-697-9889

Bulgaria

Bulgaria Consulate General
121 E 62nd St
New York, NY 10021
Phone: 212-935-4646; Fax: 212-319-5955
www.consulbulgaria-ny.org

Bulgaria Embassy
1621 22nd St NW
Washington, DC 20008
Phone: 202-387-0174; Fax: 202-234-7973
www.bulgaria-embassy.org

Bulgaria Permanent Mission to the UN
11 E 84th St
New York, NY 10028
Phone: 212-737-4790; Fax: 212-472-9865
www.un.int/bulgaria

Burkina Faso

Burkina Faso Embassy
2340 Massachusetts Ave NW
Washington, DC 20008
Phone: 202-332-5577; Fax: 202-667-1882
www.burkinaembassy-usa.org

Burkina Faso Permanent Mission to the UN
866 UN Plaza
Suite 326
New York, NY 10017
Phone: 212-308-4720; Fax: 212-308-4690

Burma. *See* Myanmar

Burundi

Burundi Embassy
2233 Wisconsin Ave NW
Suite 212
Washington, DC 20007
Phone: 202-342-2574; Fax: 202-342-2578
www.burundiembassy-usa.org

Burundi Permanent Mission to the UN
336 E 45th St
12th Fl
New York, NY 10017
Phone: 212-499-0001; Fax: 212-499-0006

Cambodia

Cambodia Embassy
4530 16th St NW
Washington, DC 20011
Phone: 202-726-7742; Fax: 202-726-8381
www.embassyofcambodia.org

Cambodia Permanent Mission to the UN
866 UN Plaza
Suite 420
New York, NY 10017
Phone: 212-223-0676; Fax: 212-223-0425
www.un.int/cambodia

Cameroon

Cameroon Embassy
2349 Massachusetts Ave NW
Washington, DC 20008
Phone: 202-265-8790; Fax: 202-387-3826

Cameroon Permanent Mission to the UN
22 E 73rd St
New York, NY 10021
Phone: 212-794-2296; Fax: 212-249-0533

Cape Verde

Cape Verde Consulate General
607 Boylston St
4th Fl
Boston, MA 02116
Phone: 617-353-0014; Fax: 617-859-9798

Cape Verde Embassy
3415 Massachusetts Ave NW
Washington, DC 20007
Phone: 202-965-6820; Fax: 202-965-1207

Cape Verde Permanent Mission to the UN
27 E 69th St
New York, NY 10021
Phone: 212-472-0333; Fax: 212-794-1398

Cayman Islands

Cayman Islands Dept of Tourism
820 Gessner Rd
Suite 1335
Houston, TX 77024
Phone: 713-461-1317; Fax: 713-461-7409
www.caymanislands.ky

Cayman Islands Dept of Tourism
8300 NW 53rd St
Suite 103
Miami, FL 33166
Phone: 305-599-9033; Fax: 305-599-3766
www.caymanislands.ky

Cayman Islands Dept of Tourism
3 Park Ave
39th Fl
New York, NY 10016

Phone: 212-889-9009; Fax: 212-889-9125
Toll-free: 877-422-9626
www.caymanislands.ky

Cayman Islands Dept of Tourism
18 W 140 Butterfield Rd
Suite 920
Oakbrook Terrace, IL 60181
Phone: 630-705-0650; Fax: 630-705-1383
www.caymanislands.ky

Central African Republic

Central African Republic Embassy
1618 22nd St NW
Washington, DC 20008
Phone: 202-483-7800; Fax: 202-332-9893

Central African Republic Permanent Mission to the UN
51 Clifton Ave
Suite 2008
Newark, NJ 07104
Phone: 973-482-9161; Fax: 973-350-1174

Chad

Chad Embassy
2002 R St NW
Washington, DC 20009
Phone: 202-462-4009; Fax: 202-265-1937
www.chadembassy.org

Chad Permanent Mission to the UN
211 E 43rd St
Suite 1703
New York, NY 10017
Phone: 212-986-0980; Fax: 212-986-0152

Chile

Chile-US Chamber of Commerce
800 Brickell Ave
Suite 900
Miami, FL 33131
Phone: 786-419-2092; Fax: 305-374-4270
www.chileus.org

Chile Consulate General
875 N Michigan Ave
Suite 3352
Chicago, IL 60611
Phone: 312-654-8780; Fax: 312-654-8948

Chile Consulate General
1300 Post Oak Blvd
Suite 1130
Houston, TX 77056
Phone: 713-621-5853; Fax: 713-621-8672

Chile Consulate General
6100 Wilshire Blvd
Suite 1240
Los Angeles, CA 90048
Phone: 323-933-3697; Fax: 323-933-3842

Chile Consulate General
800 Brickell Ave
Suite 1230
Miami, FL 33131
Phone: 305-373-8623; Fax: 305-379-6613

Chile Consulate General
866 UN Plaza
Suite 601
New York, NY 10017
Phone: 212-980-3366; Fax: 212-888-5288
www.chileny.com

Chile Consulate General
6th & Chestnut St
Public Ledger Bldg Suite 1030
Philadelphia, PA 19106
Phone: 215-829-9520; Fax: 215-829-0594

Chile Consulate General
870 Market St
Suite 1058
San Francisco, CA 94102
Phone: 415-982-7662; Fax: 415-982-2384
www.consuladochilesfo.com

Chile Embassy
1732 Massachusetts Ave NW
Washington, DC 20036
Phone: 202-785-1746; Fax: 202-887-5579
www.chile-usa.org

Chile Permanent Mission to the UN
855 2nd Ave
Suite 44
New York, NY 10017
Phone: 212-832-3323; Fax: 212-832-0236
www.un.int/chile

North American-Chilean Chamber of Commerce
30 Vesey St
Suite 506
New York, NY 10007
Phone: 212-233-7776; Fax: 212-233-7779

China

China National Tourist Office
550 N Brand Blvd
Suite 910
Glendale, CA 91203
Phone: 818-545-7507; Fax: 818-545-7506
Toll-free: 800-670-2228
www.cnto.org

China National Tourist Office
350 5th Ave
Suite 6413
New York, NY 10118
Phone: 212-760-8218
www.cnto.org

USA-China Chamber of Commerce
55 W Monroe St
Suite 630
Chicago, IL 60603

Phone: 312-368-9030; Fax: 312-368-9922
www.usccc.org

Chinese Chamber of Commerce of Hawaii
42 N King St
Honolulu, HI 96817
Phone: 808-533-3181; Fax: 808-533-6967
www.ccchi.org

Chinese Chamber of Commerce of Los Angeles
977 N Broadway
Suite E
Los Angeles, CA 90012
Phone: 213-617-0396; Fax: 213-617-2128
www.lachinesechamber.org

Chinese Chamber of Commerce of San Francisco
730 Sacramento St
San Francisco, CA 94108
Phone: 415-982-3000; Fax: 415-982-4720

China People's Republic of Consulate General
1 E Erie St
Chicago, IL 60611
Phone: 312-803-0095; Fax: 312-803-0110
www.chinaconsulatechicago.org

China People's Republic of Consulate General
3417 Montrose Blvd
Houston, TX 77006
Phone: 713-520-1462; Fax: 713-524-7656
www.chinahouston.org

China People's Republic of Consulate General
443 Shatto Pl
Los Angeles, CA 90020
Phone: 213-807-8088; Fax: 213-807-8019
www.chinaconsulatela.org

China People's Republic of Consulate General
520 12th Ave
New York, NY 10036
Phone: 212-244-9392
www.nyconsulate.prchina.org

China People's Republic of Consulate General
1450 Laguna St
San Francisco, CA 94115
Phone: 415-674-2900; Fax: 415-563-0494
www.chinaconsulatesf.org

China People's Republic of Embassy
2300 Connecticut Ave NW
Washington, DC 20008
Phone: 202-328-2500; Fax: 202-588-0032
www.china-embassy.org

China People's Republic of Permanent Mission to the UN
350 E 35th St
New York, NY 10016
Phone: 212-655-6100; Fax: 212-634-7626
www.china-un.org

Colombia

Colombian American Chamber of Commerce
250 Catalonia Ave
Suite 407
Coral Gables, FL 33134
Phone: 305-446-2542; Fax: 305-446-2038
www.colombiachamber.com

Colombia Consulate
5901-C Peachtree Dunwoody Rd
Suite 375
Atlanta, GA 30328
Phone: 770-668-0512; Fax: 770-668-0763

Colombia Consulate General
8383 Wilshire Blvd
Suite 420
Beverly Hills, CA 90211
Phone: 323-653-9863; Fax: 323-653-2964

Colombia Consulate
535 Boylston St
3rd Fl
Boston, MA 02116
Phone: 617-536-6222; Fax: 617-536-9372

Colombia Consulate General
500 N Michigan Ave
Suite 2040
Chicago, IL 60611
Phone: 312-923-1196; Fax: 312-923-1197

Colombia Consulate General
280 Aragon Ave
Coral Gables, FL 33134
Phone: 305-448-5558; Fax: 305-441-9537

Colombia Consulate General
5851 San Felipe
Suite 300
Houston, TX 77057
Phone: 713-527-8919; Fax: 713-529-3395
www.colhouston.org

Colombia Consulate General
10 E 46th St
New York, NY 10017
Phone: 212-370-0004; Fax: 212-972-1725

Colombia Consulate General
595 Market St
Suite 2130
San Francisco, CA 94105
Phone: 415-495-7195; Fax: 415-777-3731

Colombia Embassy
2118 Leroy Pl NW
Washington, DC 20008
Phone: 202-387-8338; Fax: 202-232-8643
www.colombiaemb.org

Colombia Embassy - Consular Section
1101 17th St NW
Suite 1007
Washington, DC 20036
Phone: 202-332-7573; Fax: 202-332-7180
www.colombiaemb.org

Colombia Permanent Mission to the UN
140 E 57th St
5th Fl
New York, NY 10022
Phone: 212-355-7776; Fax: 212-371-2813
www.colombiaun.org

Comoros

Comoros Embassy
866 United Nations Plaza
Suite 418
New York, NY 10017
Phone: 212-750-1637; Fax: 212-750-1657

Comoros Permanent Mission to the UN
866 UN Plaza
Suite 418
New York, NY 10017
Phone: 212-750-1637; Fax: 212-750-1657
www.un.int/comoros

Congo, Democratic Republic of

Congo Democratic Republic of Embassy
1726 M St NW
Washington, DC 20036
Phone: 202-234-7690; Fax: 202-234-2609

Congo Republic of Embassy
4891 Colorado Ave NW
Washington, DC 20011
Phone: 202-726-0825; Fax: 202-726-1860

Congo Democratic Republic of Permanent Mission to the
  UN
866 UN Plaza
Suite 511
New York, NY 10017
Phone: 212-319-8061; Fax: 212-319-8232
www.un.int/drcongo

Congo Republic of Permanent Mission to the UN
866 2nd Ave
2nd Fl
New York, NY 10017
Phone: 212-832-6553; Fax: 212-832-6558
www.un.int/congo

Costa Rica

Costa Rica Consulate General
1870 The Exchange
Suite 100
Atlanta, GA 30339
Phone: 770-951-7025; Fax: 770-951-7073
www.costarica-embassy.org/consular/consulates

Costa Rica Consulate General
203 N Wabash Ave
Suite 702
Chicago, IL 60601
Phone: 312-263-2772; Fax: 312-263-5807
www.costarica-embassy.org/consular/consulates

Costa Rica Consulate
3000 Wilcrest Dr
Suite 112
Houston, TX 77042
Phone: 713-266-0484; Fax: 713-266-1527
www.costarica-embassy.org/consular/consulates

Costa Rica Consulate General
1605 W Olympic Blvd
Suite 400
Los Angeles, CA 90015
Phone: 213-380-7915; Fax: 213-380-5639
www.costarica-embassy.org/consular/consulates

Costa Rica Consulate General
1101 Brickell Ave
Suite 401 North Tower
Miami, FL 33131
Phone: 305-871-7485; Fax: 305-871-0860
www.costarica-embassy.org/consular/consulates

Costa Rica Consulate General
225 W 34th St Suite 1203
Penn Plaza Blvd
New York, NY 10122
Phone: 212-509-3066; Fax: 212-509-3068
www.costarica-embassy.org/consular/consulates

Costa Rica Consulate General
2112 'S' St NW
Washington, DC 20008
Phone: 202-328-6628; Fax: 202-265-4795
www.costarica-embassy.org/consular/consulates

Costa Rica Embassy
2114 'S' St NW
Washington, DC 20008
Phone: 202-234-2945; Fax: 202-265-4795
www.costarica-embassy.org

Costa Rica Permanent Mission to the UN
211 E 43rd St
Rm 903
New York, NY 10017
Phone: 212-986-6373; Fax: 212-986-6842

Cote d'Ivoire (Ivory Coast)

Cote d'Ivoire Embassy
2424 Massachusetts Ave
Washington, DC 20008
Phone: 202-797-0300; Fax: 202-462-9444
www.embaci.com

Cote d'Ivoire Permanent Mission to the UN
46 E 74th St
New York, NY 10021
Phone: 212-717-5555; Fax: 212-717-4492
www.un.int/cotedivoire

Croatia

Croatian National Tourist Office
350 5th Ave
Suite 4003

New York, NY 10118
Phone: 212-279-8672; Fax: 212-279-8683
Toll-free: 800-829-4416
www.croatia.hr

Croatia Consulate General
737 N Michigan Ave
Suite 1030
Chicago, IL 60611
Phone: 312-482-9902; Fax: 312-482-9987
www.croatiaemb.org

Croatia Consulate General
11766 Wilshire Blvd
Suite 1250
Los Angeles, CA 90025
Phone: 310-477-1009; Fax: 310-477-1866
www.croatiaemb.org

Croatia Consulate General
369 Lexington Ave
11th Fl
New York, NY 10017
Phone: 212-599-3066; Fax: 212-599-3106
www.croatiaemb.org

Croatia Embassy
2343 Massachusetts Ave NW
Washington, DC 20008
Phone: 202-588-5899; Fax: 202-588-8936
www.croatiaemb.org

Croatia Permanent Mission to the UN
820 2nd Ave
19th Fl
New York, NY 10017
Phone: 212-986-1585; Fax: 212-986-2011
www.un.int/croatia

Cuba

Cuba Interests Section
Embassy of Switzerland
2630 16th St NW
Washington, DC 20009
Phone: 202-797-8518; Fax: 202-797-8521
www.geocities.com/cubainte

Cuba Permanent Mission to the UN
315 Lexington Ave
New York, NY 10016
Phone: 212-689-7215; Fax: 212-689-9073
www.un.int/cuba

Curacao

Curacao Tourist Board
3361 SW 3rd Ave
Suite 102
Miami, FL 33145
Phone: 305-285-0511; Fax: 305-285-0535
Toll-free: 800-328-7222
www.curacao-tourism.com

Cyprus

Cyprus Tourism Organization
13 E 40th St
New York, NY 10016
Phone: 212-683-5280; Fax: 212-683-5282
www.cyprustourism.org

Cyprus Consulate General
13 E 40th St
New York, NY 10016
Phone: 212-686-6016; Fax: 212-686-3660

Cyprus Embassy
2211 R St NW
Washington, DC 20008
Phone: 202-462-5772; Fax: 202-483-6710
www.cyprusembassy.net

Cyprus Permanent Mission to the UN
13 E 40th St
New York, NY 10016
Phone: 212-481-6023; Fax: 212-685-7316
www.un.int/cyprus

Czech Republic

Czech Center & Tourist Authority
1109 Madison Ave
New York, NY 10028
Phone: 212-288-0830; Fax: 212-288-0971
www.czechcenter.com

Czech Republic Consulate General
10990 Wilshire Blvd
Suite 1100
Los Angeles, CA 90024
Phone: 310-473-0889; Fax: 310-473-9813
www.mzv.cz/losangeles

Czech Republic Consulate General
1109-1111 Madison Ave
New York, NY 10028
Phone: 646-981-4040; Fax: 212-717-5064
www.mfa.cz/newyork

Czech Republic Embassy
3900 Spring of Freedom St NW
Washington, DC 20008
Phone: 202-274-9100; Fax: 202-966-8540
www.mzv.cz/washington

Czech Republic Permanent Mission to the UN
1109 Madison Ave
New York, NY 10028
Phone: 646-981-4000; Fax: 646-981-4099
www.czechembassy.org

Democratic People's Republic of Korea. *See* North Korea

Denmark

Danish Tourist Board
655 3rd Ave

18th Fl
New York, NY 10017
Phone: 212-885-9700; Fax: 212-885-9710
www.visitdenmark.com

Danish-American Chamber of Commerce
885 2nd Ave
18th Fl
New York, NY 10017
Phone: 212-705-4945; Fax: 212-754-1904
www.daccny.com

Denmark Consulate General
211 E Ontario St
Suite 1800
Chicago, IL 60611
Phone: 312-787-8780; Fax: 312-787-8744
www.consulatedk.org

Denmark Consulate General
1 Dag Hammarskjold Plaza 18th Fl
885 2nd Ave
New York, NY 10017
Phone: 212-223-4545; Fax: 212-754-1904
www.denmark.org

Denmark Embassy
3200 Whitehaven St NW
Washington, DC 20008
Phone: 202-234-4300; Fax: 202-328-1470
www.ambwashington.um.dk/en

Denmark Permanent Mission to the UN
885 2nd Ave
18th Fl
New York, NY 10017
Phone: 212-308-7009; Fax: 212-308-3384
www.un.int/denmark

Djibouti

Djibouti Embassy
1156 15th St NW
Suite 515
Washington, DC 20005
Phone: 202-331-0270; Fax: 202-331-0302

Djibouti Permanent Mission to the UN
866 UN Plaza
Suite 4011
New York, NY 10017
Phone: 212-753-3163; Fax: 212-223-1276

Dominica

Dominica Consulate General
800 2nd Ave
Suite 400-H
New York, NY 10017
Phone: 212-599-8478; Fax: 212-808-4975

Dominica Embassy
3216 New Mexico Ave NW
Washington, DC 20016
Phone: 202-364-6781; Fax: 202-364-6791

Dominica Permanent Mission to the UN
800 2nd Ave
Suite 400H
New York, NY 10017
Phone: 212-949-0853; Fax: 212-808-4975

Dominican Republic

Dominican Republic Tourist Board
848 Brickell Ave
Suite 405
Miami, FL 33131
Phone: 305-358-2899; Fax: 305-358-4185
www.dominicanrepublic.com

Dominican Republic Tourist Board
136 E 57th St
Suite 803
New York, NY 10022
Phone: 212-588-1012; Fax: 212-588-1015
Toll-free: 888-374-6361
www.dominicanrepublic.com

Dominican Republic Consulate General
1516 Oak St
Suite 321
Alameda, CA 94501
Phone: 510-864-7777; Fax: 818-504-6617
www.domrep.org

Dominican Republic Consulate General
20 Park Plaza
Statler Bldg Suite 601
Boston, MA 02116
Phone: 617-482-2101; Fax: 617-482-8133
www.domrep.org

Dominican Republic Consulate General
8700 Bryanmawr St Suite 818
Presidents Plaza O'Hare Center
Chicago, IL 60631
Phone: 773-714-4924
www.domrep.org

Dominican Republic Consulate General
1038 Brickell Ave
Miami, FL 33131
Phone: 305-358-3220; Fax: 305-358-2318
consuladodominicanomiami.org

Dominican Republic Consulate General
1501 Broadway
Suite 410
New York, NY 10036
Phone: 212-768-2480; Fax: 212-768-2677
www.domrep.org

Dominican Republic Consulate General
1715 22nd St NW
Washington, DC 20008
Phone: 202-332-6280; Fax: 202-387-2459
www.domrep.org

Dominican Republic Embassy
1715 22nd St NW
Washington, DC 20008

Phone: 202-332-6280; Fax: 202-265-8057
www.domrep.org

Dominican Republic Permanent Mission to the UN
144 E 44th St
4th Fl
New York, NY 10017
Phone: 212-867-0833; Fax: 212-986-4694
www.un.int/dr

Ecuador

Ecuadorian-American Chamber of Commerce of Greater
  Miami
1390 Brickell Ave
Suite 220
Miami, FL 33131
Phone: 305-539-0010; Fax: 305-539-8001
www.ecuachamber.com

Ecuador Consulate General
8484 Wilshire Blvd
Suite 540
Beverly Hills, CA 90211
Phone: 323-658-6020; Fax: 323-658-1198

Ecuador Consulate General
30 S Michigan Ave
Suite 204
Chicago, IL 60603
Phone: 312-338-1002; Fax: 312-338-1004
www.ecuador.org/consulates.htm

Ecuador Consulate General
4200 Westheimer Rd
Suite 218
Houston, TX 77027
Phone: 713-572-8731; Fax: 713-572-8732

Ecuador Consulate General
1101 Brickell Ave
Suite M102
Miami, FL 33131
Phone: 305-539-8214; Fax: 305-539-8313

Ecuador Consulate General
800 2nd Ave
Suite 600
New York, NY 10017
Phone: 212-808-0170; Fax: 212-808-0188
www.consulecuadornewyork.com

Ecuador Consulate General
400 Market St
4th Fl
Newark, NJ 07105
Phone: 973-344-6900; Fax: 973-344-0008
www.consuladoecuadornj.com

Ecuador Consulate General
235 Montgomery St
Suite 944
San Francisco, CA 94104
Phone: 415-982-1819; Fax: 415-982-1833

Ecuador Embassy
2535 15th St NW
Washington, DC 20009
Phone: 202-234-7200; Fax: 202-234-3429
www.ecuador.org

Ecuador Permanent Mission to the UN
866 UN Plaza
Suite 516
New York, NY 10017
Phone: 212-935-1680; Fax: 212-935-1835

Egypt

Egyptian Tourist Authority
630 5th Ave
Suite 2305
New York, NY 10111
Phone: 212-332-2570; Fax: 212-956-6439
Toll-free: 877-773-4978
www.egypttourism.org

American Egyptian Cooperation Foundation
28 E Jackson Blvd
Suite 809
Chicago, IL 60604
Phone: 312-427-9368
www.americanegyptiancoop.org

American Egyptian Cooperation Foundation
1535 West Loop S
Suite 200
Houston, TX 77027
Phone: 713-624-7113
www.americanegyptiancoop.org

American Egyptian Cooperation Foundation
330 E 39th St
Suite 32L
New York, NY 10016
Phone: 212-867-2323; Fax: 212-697-0465
www.americanegyptiancoop.org

American Egyptian Cooperation Foundation
870 Market St
Suite 855
San Francisco, CA 94102
Phone: 415-837-0989; Fax: 415-837-0989
www.americanegyptiancoop.org

Egypt Consulate General
500 N Michigan Ave
Suite 1900
Chicago, IL 60611
Phone: 312-828-9162; Fax: 312-828-9167
www.eg2002.net

Egypt Consulate General
1990 Post Oak Blvd
Suite 2180
Houston, TX 77056
Phone: 713-961-4915; Fax: 713-961-3868

Egypt Consulate General
1110 2nd Ave
Suite 201

New York, NY 10022
Phone: 212-759-7120; Fax: 212-308-7643
www.egyptnyc.net

Egypt Consulate General
3001 Pacific Ave
San Francisco, CA 94115
Phone: 415-346-9700; Fax: 415-346-9480
www.egy2000.com

Egypt Embassy
3521 International Ct NW
Washington, DC 20008
Phone: 202-895-5400; Fax: 202-244-4319
www.egyptembassy.us

Egypt Permanent Mission to the UN
304 E 44th St
New York, NY 10017
Phone: 212-503-0300; Fax: 212-949-5999

El Salvador

El Salvador Consulate General
104 S Michigan Ave
Suite 816
Chicago, IL 60603
Phone: 312-332-1393; Fax: 312-332-4446
www.elsalvador.org/home.nsf/consularinfo

El Salvador Consulate General
2600 Douglas Rd
Suite 104
Coral Gables, FL 33134
Phone: 305-774-0840; Fax: 305-774-0850

El Salvador Consulate General
1555 W Mockingbird Ln
Suite 216
Dallas, TX 75235
Phone: 214-637-0732; Fax: 214-637-1106
www.elsalvador.org/home.nsf/consularinfo

El Salvador Consulate General
1702 Hillendahl Blvd
Houston, TX 77055
Phone: 713-270-6239; Fax: 713-270-9683
www.elsalvador.org/home.nsf/consularinfo

El Salvador Consulate General
3450 Wilshire Blvd
Suite 250
Los Angeles, CA 90010
Phone: 213-383-8580; Fax: 213-383-8599
www.elsalvador.org/home.nsf/consularinfo

El Salvador Consulate General
46 Park Ave
New York, NY 10016
Phone: 212-889-3608; Fax: 212-679-2835
www.elsalvador.org/home.nsf/consularinfo

El Salvador Consulate General
507 Polk St
Suite 280
San Francisco, CA 94102

Phone: 415-771-8524; Fax: 415-771-8522
www.elsalvador.org/home.nsf/consularinfo

El Salvador Embassy
1400 16th St NW
Suite 100
Washington, DC 20036
Phone: 202-595-7500; Fax: 202-232-3763
www.elsalvador.org

El Salvador Permanent Mission to the UN
46 Park Ave
3rd Fl
New York, NY 10016
Phone: 212-679-1616; Fax: 212-725-3467

Equatorial Guinea

Equatorial Guinea Embassy
2020 16th St NW
Washington, DC 20009
Phone: 202-518-5700; Fax: 202-518-5252

Equatorial Guinea Permanent Mission to the UN
242 E 51st St
New York, NY 10022
Phone: 212-223-2324; Fax: 212-223-2366

Eritrea

Eritrea Embassy
1708 New Hampshire Ave NW
Washington, DC 20009
Phone: 202-319-1991; Fax: 202-319-1304

Eritrea Permanent Mission to the UN
800 2nd Ave
18th Fl
New York, NY 10017
Phone: 212-687-3390; Fax: 212-687-3138
www.un.int/eritrea

Estonia

Estonia Consulate General
600 3rd Ave
26th Fl
New York, NY 10016
Phone: 212-883-0636; Fax: 212-883-0648
www.nyc.estemb.org

Estonia Embassy
2131 Massachusetts Ave NW
Washington, DC 20008
Phone: 202-588-0101; Fax: 202-588-0108
www.estemb.org

Estonia Permanent Mission to the UN
600 3rd Ave
26th Fl
New York, NY 10016
Phone: 212-883-0640; Fax: 212-883-0648

Ethiopia

Ethiopia Embassy
3506 International Dr NW
Washington, DC 20008
Phone: 202-364-1200; Fax: 202-587-0195
www.ethiopianembassy.org

Ethiopia Permanent Mission to the UN
866 2nd Ave
3rd Fl
New York, NY 10017
Phone: 212-421-1830; Fax: 212-754-0360
www.un.int/ethiopia

Fiji

Fiji Visitors Bureau
5777 W Century Blvd
Suite 220
Los Angeles, CA 90045
Phone: 310-568-1616; Fax: 310-670-2318
Toll-free: 800-932-3454
www.bulafiji.com

Fiji Embassy
2233 Wisconsin Ave NW
Suite 240
Washington, DC 20007
Phone: 202-337-8320; Fax: 202-337-1996
www.fijiembassy.org

Fiji Permanent Mission to the UN
630 3rd Ave
7th Fl
New York, NY 10017
Phone: 212-687-4130; Fax: 212-687-3963

Finland

Finnish Tourist Board
655 3rd Ave
18th Fl
New York, NY 10017
Phone: 212-885-9700; Fax: 212-885-9710
www.gofinland.org

Finnish American Chamber of Commerce Inc
866 United Nations Plaza
New York, NY 10017
Phone: 212-821-0225; Fax: 212-750-4418
www.finlandtrade.com

Finnish-American Chamber of Commerce on the Pacific
  Coast
PO Box 3058
Tustin, CA 92781
Phone: 714-573-0604; Fax: 714-242-9153
www.faccpacific.com

Finland Consulate General
1801 Century Pk E
Suite 2100
Los Angeles, CA 90067
Phone: 310-203-9903; Fax: 310-203-9186
www.finland.org/en/

Finland Consulate General
866 UN Plaza
Suite 250
New York, NY 10017
Phone: 212-750-4400; Fax: 212-750-4418
www.finland.org/en

Finland Embassy
3301 Massachusetts Ave NW
Washington, DC 20008
Phone: 202-298-5800; Fax: 202-298-6030
www.finland.org

Finland Permanent Mission to the UN
866 UN Plaza
Suite 222
New York, NY 10017
Phone: 212-355-2100; Fax: 212-759-6156
www.un.int/finland

France

French Government Tourist Office
9454 Wilshire Blvd
Suite 210
Beverly Hills, CA 90212
Phone: 310-271-6665; Fax: 310-276-2835
www.franceguide.com

French Government Tourist Office
205 N Michigan Ave
Suite 3770
Chicago, IL 60601
Phone: 312-327-0290
www.franceguide.com

French Government Tourist Office
444 Madison Ave
16th Fl
New York, NY 10022
Phone: 212-838-7800; Fax: 212-838-7855
us.franceguide.com

French-American Chamber of Commerce of Atlanta
321 Pharr Rd
Suite G
Atlanta, GA 30305
Phone: 404-846-2500; Fax: 404-846-2555
www.facc-atlanta.com

French-American Chamber of Commerce of Chicago
35 E Wacker Dr
Suite 670
Chicago, IL 60601
Phone: 312-578-0444; Fax: 312-578-0445
www.facc-chicago.com

French-American Chamber of Commerce of Dallas
2665 Villa Creek Dr
Suite 214
Dallas, TX 75234
Phone: 972-241-0111; Fax: 972-241-0901
www.faccdallas.com

French-American Chamber of Commerce of Houston
5373 W Alabama St

Suite 209
Houston, TX 77056
Phone: 713-960-0575; Fax: 713-960-0495
www.facchouston.com

French-American Chamber of Commerce of Los Angeles
8222 Melrose Ave
Suite 203
Los Angeles, CA 90046
Phone: 323-651-4741; Fax: 323-651-2547
www.frenchchamberla.org

French-American Chamber of Commerce of Florida
14 NE 1st Ave
Suite 1005
Miami, FL 33132
Phone: 305-374-5000; Fax: 305-358-8203
www.faccmiami.com

French-American Chamber of Commerce of Louisiana
2 Canal St
Suite 2426
New Orleans, LA 70130
Phone: 504-561-0070; Fax: 504-592-9999
www.ccife.org/usa/louisiane

French-American Chamber of Commerce of New York
122 E 42nd St
Suite 2015
New York, NY 10168
Phone: 212-867-0123; Fax: 212-867-9050
www.ccife.org/usa/new_york

French-American Chamber of Commerce of Philadelphia
2000 Market St
Suite 2850
Philadelphia, PA 19103
Phone: 215-419-5559; Fax: 215-419-5533
www.faccphila.org

French-American Chamber of Commerce of San Francisco
703 Market St
Suite 450
San Francisco, CA 94103
Phone: 415-442-4717; Fax: 415-442-4621
www.faccsf.com

French-American Chamber of Commerce of the Pacific
  Northwest
2200 Alaskan Way
Suite 490
Seattle, WA 98121
Phone: 206-443-4703; Fax: 206-448-4218
www.ccife.org/usa/seattle

France Consulate General
3475 Piedmont Rd NE
Suite 1840
Atlanta, GA 30305
Phone: 404-495-1660; Fax: 404-495-1661
www.consulfrance-atlanta.org

France Consulate General
31 Saint James Ave
Suite 750
Boston, MA 02116

Phone: 617-832-4400
www.consulfrance-boston.org

France Consulate General
205 N Michigan Ave
Suite 3700
Chicago, IL 60601
Phone: 312-327-5200; Fax: 312-327-5201
www.consulfrance-chicago.org

France Consulate General
777 Post Oak Blvd
Suite 600
Houston, TX 77056
Phone: 713-572-2799; Fax: 713-572-2911
www.consulfrance-houston.org

France Consulate General
10990 Wilshire Blvd
Suite 300
Los Angeles, CA 90024
Phone: 310-235-3200; Fax: 310-312-0704
www.consulfrance-losangeles.org

France Consulate General
1395 Brickell Ave
Suite 1050
Miami, FL 33131
Phone: 305-403-4185; Fax: 305-403-4187
www.consulfrance-miami.org

France Consulate General
1340 Poydras St
Suite 1710
New Orleans, LA 70112
Phone: 504-569-2870; Fax: 504-569-2871
www.consulfrance-nouvelleorleans.org

France Consulate General
934 5th Ave
New York, NY 10021
Phone: 212-606-3680; Fax: 212-606-3614
www.consulfrance-newyork.org

France Consulate General
540 Bush St
San Francisco, CA 94108
Phone: 415-397-4330; Fax: 415-433-8357
www.consulfrance-sanfrancisco.org

France Embassy
4101 Reservoir Rd NW
Washington, DC 20007
Phone: 202-944-6000; Fax: 202-944-6175
www.ambafrance-us.org

France Permanent Mission to the UN
245 E 47th St
44th Fl
New York, NY 10017
Phone: 212-308-5700; Fax: 212-421-6889
www.un.int/france

French West Indies. *See* **Martinique**

Gabon

Gabon Tourist Information Office
347 5th Ave
Suite 805
New York, NY 10016
Phone: 212-447-6700; Fax: 212-447-1532

Gabon Consulate
18 E 41st St
9th Fl
New York, NY 10017
Phone: 212-686-9720; Fax: 212-689-5769

Gabon Embassy
2034 20th St NW
Washington, DC 20009
Phone: 202-797-1000; Fax: 202-332-0668

Gabon Permanent Mission to the UN
18 E 41st St
9th Fl
New York, NY 10017
Phone: 212-686-9720; Fax: 212-689-5769
www.un.int/gabon

Gambia

Gambia Embassy
1156 15th St NW
Suite 905
Washington, DC 20005
Phone: 202-785-1399; Fax: 202-785-1430
www.gambiaembassy.us

Gambia Permanent Mission to the UN
800 2nd Ave
Rm 400F
New York, NY 10017
Phone: 212-949-6640; Fax: 212-856-9820

Georgia

Georgia Embassy
1101 15th St NW
Suite 602
Washington, DC 20005
Phone: 202-387-2390; Fax: 202-393-4537
www.georgiaemb.org

Georgia Permanent Mission to the UN
1 UN Plaza
26th Fl
New York, NY 10017
Phone: 212-759-1949; Fax: 212-759-1823
www.un.int/georgia

Germany

German National Tourist Office
122 E 42nd St
20th Fl
New York, NY 10168
Phone: 212-661-7200; Fax: 212-661-7174
www.visits-to-germany.com

German-American Chamber of Commerce of the Southern
  US Inc
530 Means St NW
Suite 120
Atlanta, GA 30318
Phone: 404-586-6800; Fax: 404-586-6820
www.gaccsouth.com

German-American Chamber of Commerce of the Midwest
  Inc
401 N Michigan Ave
Suite 3330
Chicago, IL 60611
Phone: 312-644-2662; Fax: 312-644-0738
www.gaccom.org

German-American Chamber of Commerce Inc
75 Broad St
21st Fl
New York, NY 10004
Phone: 212-974-8830; Fax: 212-974-8867
www.gaccny.com

German-American Chamber of Commerce Inc - Philadelphia
1600 JFK Blvd Suite 200
4 Penn Center
Philadelphia, PA 19103
Phone: 215-665-1585; Fax: 215-665-0375
www.gaccphiladelphia.com

Representative of German Industry & Trade
1627 'I' St NW
Suite 550
Washington, DC 20006
Phone: 202-659-4777; Fax: 202-659-4779
www.rgit-usa.com

Germany Consulate General
285 Peachtree Center Ave NE
Suite 901
Atlanta, GA 30303
Phone: 404-659-4760; Fax: 404-659-1280

Germany Consulate General
3 Copley Pl
Suite 500
Boston, MA 02116
Phone: 617-536-4414; Fax: 617-536-8573

Germany Consulate General
676 N Michigan Ave
Suite 3200
Chicago, IL 60611
Phone: 312-202-0480; Fax: 312-202-0466
germany.info/chicago

Germany Consulate General
1330 Post Oak Blvd
Suite 1850
Houston, TX 77056
Phone: 713-627-7770; Fax: 713-627-0506
www.germanconsulatehouston.org

Germany Consulate General
6222 Wilshire Blvd
Suite 500
Los Angeles, CA 90048
Phone: 323-930-2703; Fax: 323-930-2805

Germany Consulate General
100 N Biscayne Blvd
Suite 2200
Miami, FL 33132
Phone: 305-358-0290; Fax: 305-358-0307

Germany Consulate General
871 UN Plaza
New York, NY 10017
Phone: 212-610-9700; Fax: 212-610-9702

Germany Consulate General
1960 Jackson St
San Francisco, CA 94109
Phone: 415-775-1061; Fax: 415-775-0187
www.germany.info

Germany Embassy
4645 Reservoir Rd NW
Washington, DC 20007
Phone: 202-298-4000; Fax: 202-298-4249
www.germany-info.org

Germany Permanent Mission to the UN
871 UN Plaza
New York, NY 10017
Phone: 212-940-0400; Fax: 212-940-0402
www.germany-info.org/UN

Ghana

Ghana Consulate General
19 E 47th St
New York, NY 10017
Phone: 212-832-1300; Fax: 212-751-6743

Ghana Embassy
3512 International Dr NW
Washington, DC 20008
Phone: 202-686-4520; Fax: 202-686-4527
www.ghanaembassy.org

Ghana Permanent Mission to the UN
19 E 47th St
New York, NY 10017
Phone: 212-832-1300; Fax: 212-751-6743
www.un.int/ghana

Greece

Greek National Tourist Organization
645 5th Ave
Suite 903
New York, NY 10022
Phone: 212-421-5777; Fax: 212-826-6940
www.gnto.gr

Greece Consulate
3340 Peachtree Rd NE

Tower Place 100 Suite 1670
Atlanta, GA 30326
Phone: 404-261-3313; Fax: 404-262-2798

Greece Consulate General
86 Beacon St
Boston, MA 02108
Phone: 617-523-0100; Fax: 617-523-0511
www.greekembassy.org/consular/boston

Greece Consulate General
650 N Saint Clair St
Chicago, IL 60611
Phone: 312-335-3915; Fax: 312-335-3958
www.greekembassy.org/consular/chicago

Greece Consulate
520 Post Oak Blvd
Suite 450
Houston, TX 77027
Phone: 713-840-7522; Fax: 713-840-0614
www.greekembassy.org/consular/houston

Greece Consulate General
12424 Wilshire Blvd
Suite 800
Los Angeles, CA 90025
Phone: 310-826-5555; Fax: 310-826-8670
www.greekembassy.org/consular/los_angeles

Greece Consulate General
69 E 79th St
New York, NY 10021
Phone: 212-988-5500; Fax: 212-734-8492
www.greekembassy.org/consular/newyork

Greece Consulate General
2441 Gough St
San Francisco, CA 94123
Phone: 415-775-2102; Fax: 415-776-6815
www.greekembassy.org/consular/san_francisco

Greece Embassy
2219 Massachusetts Ave NW
Washington, DC 20008
Phone: 202-939-1300; Fax: 202-939-1324
www.greekembassy.org

Greece Embassy - Consular Section
2217 Massachusetts Ave NW
Washington, DC 20008
Phone: 202-939-1306; Fax: 202-234-2803

Greece Permanent Mission to the UN
866 2nd Ave
13th Fl
New York, NY 10017
Phone: 212-888-6900; Fax: 212-888-4440
www.greeceun.org

Grenada

Grenada Board of Tourism
PO Box 1668
Lake Worth, FL 33460
Phone: 561-588-8176; Fax: 561-588-7267

Toll-free: 800-927-9554
www.grenadagrenadines.com

Grenada Board of Tourism
305 Madison Ave
Suite 2145
New York, NY 10165
Phone: 212-687-9554; Fax: 212-682-4748
www.grenadagrenadines.com

Grenada Consulate General
800 2nd Ave
Suite 400-K
New York, NY 10017
Phone: 212-599-0301; Fax: 212-599-1540
www.grenadaconsulate.org

Grenada Embassy
1701 New Hampshire Ave NW
Washington, DC 20009
Phone: 202-265-2561; Fax: 202-265-2468

Grenada Permanent Mission to the UN
800 2nd Ave
Suite 400-K
New York, NY 10017
Phone: 212-599-0301; Fax: 212-599-1540

Guatemala

Guatemala Consulate General
203 N Wabash Ave
Suite 910
Chicago, IL 60601
Phone: 312-332-1587; Fax: 312-332-4256

Guatemala Consulate General
3013 Fountain View Dr
Suite 210
Houston, TX 77057
Phone: 713-953-9531; Fax: 713-953-9383

Guatemala Consulate General
1625 W Olympic Blvd
Suite 1000
Los Angeles, CA 90015
Phone: 213-365-9251; Fax: 213-365-9245

Guatemala Consulate General
1101 Brickell Ave
Suite 1003-S
Miami, FL 33131
Phone: 305-679-9945; Fax: 305-679-9983

Guatemala Consulate General
57 Park Ave
New York, NY 10016
Phone: 212-686-3837; Fax: 212-447-6947

Guatemala Consulate General
870 Market St
Suite 667
San Francisco, CA 94102
Phone: 415-788-5651; Fax: 415-788-5653

Guatemala Embassy
2220 R St NW
Washington, DC 20008
Phone: 202-745-4952; Fax: 202-745-1908
www.guatemala-embassy.org

Guatemala Permanent Mission to the UN
57 Park Ave
New York, NY 10016
Phone: 212-679-4760; Fax: 212-685-8741
www.un.int/guatemala

Guinea

Guinea Embassy
2112 Leroy Pl NW
Washington, DC 20008
Phone: 202-986-4300; Fax: 202-986-4800

Guinea Permanent Mission to the UN
140 E 39th St
New York, NY 10016
Phone: 212-687-8115; Fax: 212-687-8248
www.un.int/guinea

Guyana

Guyana Consulate General
370 7th Ave
Suite 402
New York, NY 10001
Phone: 212-947-5110; Fax: 212-947-5163
www.guyana.org/govt/govt_offices.html

Guyana Embassy
2490 Tracy Pl NW
Washington, DC 20008
Phone: 202-265-6900; Fax: 202-232-1297
georgetown.usembassy.gov

Guyana Permanent Mission to the UN
801 2nd Ave
5th Fl
New York, NY 10017
Phone: 212-573-5828; Fax: 212-573-6225

Haiti

Haiti Consulate General
545 Boylston St
Rm 201
Boston, MA 02116
Phone: 617-266-3660; Fax: 617-778-6898
www.haiti.org/misyon.htm

Haiti Consulate General
220 S State St
Suite 2110
Chicago, IL 60604
Phone: 312-922-4004; Fax: 312-922-7122
www.haitianconsulate.org

Haiti Consulate General
259 SW 13th St

Miami, FL 33130
Phone: 305-859-2003; Fax: 305-854-7441
www.haiti.org/misyon.htm

Haiti Consulate General
271 Madison Ave
5th Fl
New York, NY 10016
Phone: 212-697-9767; Fax: 212-681-6991
www.haitianconsulate-nyc.org

Haiti Embassy
2311 Massachusetts Ave NW
Washington, DC 20008
Phone: 202-332-4090; Fax: 202-745-7215
www.haiti.org

Haiti Permanent Mission to the UN
801 2nd Ave
Rm 600
New York, NY 10017
Phone: 212-370-4840; Fax: 212-661-8698

Holy See (Vatican City)

Holy See Apostolic Nunciature
3339 Massachusetts Ave NW
Washington, DC 20008
Phone: 202-333-7121; Fax: 202-337-4036
www.vatican.va

Holy See Permanent Observer Mission to the UN
25 E 39th St
New York, NY 10016
Phone: 212-370-7885; Fax: 212-370-9622
www.holyseemission.org

Honduras

Honduras Tourism Institute
299 Alhambra Cir
Suite 226
Coral Gables, FL 33134
Phone: 305-461-0601; Fax: 305-461-0602
Toll-free: 800-410-9608
www.letsgohonduras.com

Honduras Consulate General
4506 W Fullerton Ave
Chicago, IL 60639
Phone: 773-342-8281; Fax: 773-342-8293

Honduras Consulate General
6700 W Loop S
Suite 360
Houston, TX 77401
Phone: 713-667-4693; Fax: 713-667-4284

Honduras Consulate General
3550 Wilshire Blvd
Suite 410
Los Angeles, CA 90010
Phone: 213-383-9244; Fax: 213-383-9309
www.consuladodehonduras.com

Honduras Consulate General
7171 Coral Way
Suite 309
Miami, FL 33155
Phone: 305-269-9399; Fax: 305-269-9445

Honduras Consulate General
World Trade Center 2 Canal St
Suite 2340
New Orleans, LA 70130
Phone: 504-522-3118; Fax: 504-523-0544

Honduras Consulate General
35 W 35th St
6th Fl
New York, NY 10001
Phone: 212-714-9451; Fax: 212-714-9453

Honduras Consulate General
4040 E McDowell Rd
Suite 305
Phoenix, AZ 85008
Phone: 602-273-0173; Fax: 602-273-0547

Honduras Consulate General
600 Houze Way
Suite 3A
Roswell, GA 30076
Phone: 770-645-8881; Fax: 770-645-8808

Honduras Consulate General
870 Market St
Suite 449
San Francisco, CA 94102
Phone: 415-392-0076; Fax: 415-392-6726

Honduras Consulate
1014 M St NW
2nd Fl
Washington, DC 20001
Phone: 202-737-2972; Fax: 202-737-2907
www.hondurasemb.org/visas.htm

Honduras Embassy
3007 Tilden St NW
Suite 4M
Washington, DC 20008
Phone: 202-966-7702; Fax: 202-966-9751
www.hondurasemb.org

Honduras Permanent Mission to the UN
866 UN Plaza
Suite 417
New York, NY 10017
Phone: 212-752-3370; Fax: 212-223-0498
www.un.int/honduras

Hong Kong

Hong Kong Tourism Board
10940 Wilshire Blvd
Suite 2050
Los Angeles, CA 90024
Phone: 310-208-4582; Fax: 310-208-1869
Toll-free: 800-282-4582
www.discoverhongkong.com

Hong Kong Tourism Board
115 E 54th St
2nd Fl
New York, NY 10022
Phone: 212-421-3382; Fax: 212-421-8428
www.discoverhongkong.com

Hungary

Hungarian National Tourist Office
350 5th Ave
Suite 7107
New York, NY 10118
Phone: 212-695-1221; Fax: 212-695-0809
www.gotohungary.com

Hungarian-American Chamber of Commerce of New
  England Inc
111 Huntington Ave
26th Fl
Boston, MA 02199
Phone: 508-347-2742; Fax: 508-347-3831
www.hungarianamericanchamber.com

Hungarian-American Chamber of Commerce in the US Inc
205 De Anza Blvd
PMB 157
San Mateo, CA 94402
Phone: 650-573-7351

Hungary Consulate General
11766 Wilshire Blvd
Suite 410
Los Angeles, CA 90025
Phone: 310-473-9344; Fax: 310-479-5119

Hungary Consulate General
223 E 52nd St
New York, NY 10022
Phone: 212-752-0661; Fax: 212-755-5986

Hungary Embassy
3910 Shoemaker St NW
Washington, DC 20008
Phone: 202-362-6730; Fax: 202-966-8135
www.huembwas.org

Hungary Permanent Mission to the UN
227 E 52nd St
New York, NY 10022
Phone: 212-752-0209; Fax: 212-755-5395
www.un.int/hungary

Iceland

Icelandic Tourist Board
PO Box 4649
Grand Central Station, NY 10163
Phone: 212-885-9700; Fax: 212-885-9710
www.icelandtouristboard.com

Icelandic-American Chamber of Commerce
800 3rd Ave
36th Fl
New York, NY 10022

Phone: 212-593-2700; Fax: 212-593-6269
www.iceland.org/us/nyc/consulate-general/chamber-of-
  commerce

Iceland Consulate General
800 3rd Ave
36th Fl
New York, NY 10022
Phone: 212-593-2700; Fax: 646-282-9369
www.iceland.org/us/nyc/

Iceland Embassy
1156 15th St NW
Suite 1200
Washington, DC 20005
Phone: 202-265-6653; Fax: 202-265-6656
www.iceland.org/us

Iceland Permanent Mission to the UN
800 3rd Ave
36th Fl
New York, NY 10022
Phone: 212-593-2700; Fax: 212-593-6269
www.iceland.org/un/nyc

India

India Tourist Office
3550 Wilshire Blvd
Suite 204
Los Angeles, CA 90010
Phone: 213-380-8855; Fax: 213-380-6111
Toll-free: 800-422-4634
www.tourismofindia.com

India Tourist Office
1270 Ave of the Americas
Suite 1808
New York, NY 10020
Phone: 212-586-4901; Fax: 212-582-3274
Toll-free: 800-953-9399
www.tourismofindia.com

India Consulate General
455 N Cityfront Plaza Dr
Suite 850
Chicago, IL 60611
Phone: 312-595-0405; Fax: 312-595-0417
www.indianconsulate.com

India Consulate General
1990 Post Oak Blvd
Suite 600
Houston, TX 77056
Phone: 713-626-2148; Fax: 713-626-2450
www.cgihouston.org

India Consulate General
3 E 64th St
New York, NY 10021
Phone: 212-774-0600; Fax: 212-861-3788
www.indiacgny.org

India Consulate General
540 Arguello Blvd
San Francisco, CA 94118

Phone: 415-668-0662; Fax: 415-668-9764
www.cgisf.org

India Consulate
2536 Massachusetts Ave NW
Washington, DC 20008
Phone: 202-939-9806
www.indianembassy.org/consular

India Embassy
2107 Massachusetts Ave NW
Washington, DC 20008
Phone: 202-939-7000; Fax: 202-265-4351
www.indianembassy.org

India Permanent Mission to the UN
235 E 43rd St
New York, NY 10017
Phone: 212-490-9660; Fax: 212-490-9656
www.un.int/india

Indonesia

American-Indonesian Chamber of Commerce
317 Madison Ave
Suite 1619
New York, NY 10017
Phone: 212-687-4505; Fax: 212-687-5844
www.aiccusa.org

Indonesia Consulate General
211 W Wacker Dr
8th Fl
Chicago, IL 60606
Phone: 312-920-1880; Fax: 312-920-1881
www.indonesiachicago.org

Indonesia Consulate General
10900 Richmond Ave
Houston, TX 77042
Phone: 713-785-1691; Fax: 713-780-9644

Indonesia Consulate General
3457 Wilshire Blvd
Los Angeles, CA 90010
Phone: 213-383-5126; Fax: 213-487-3971

Indonesia Consulate General
5 E 68th St
New York, NY 10021
Phone: 212-879-0600; Fax: 212-570-6206
www.indony.org

Indonesia Consulate General
1111 Columbus Ave
San Francisco, CA 94133
Phone: 415-474-9571; Fax: 415-441-4320

Indonesia Embassy
2020 Massachusetts Ave NW
Washington, DC 20036
Phone: 202-775-5200; Fax: 202-775-5365
www.embassyofindonesia.org

Indonesia Permanent Mission to the UN
325 E 38th St

New York, NY 10016
Phone: 212-972-8333; Fax: 212-972-9780
www.indonesiamission-ny.org

Iran

Iran Islamic Republic of Interests Section
Embassy of Pakistan
2209 Wisconsin Ave NW
Washington, DC 20007
Phone: 202-965-4990; Fax: 202-965-1073
www.daftar.org

Iran Islamic Republic of Permanent Mission to the UN
622 3rd Ave
34th Fl
New York, NY 10017
Phone: 212-687-2020; Fax: 212-867-7086
www.un.int/iran

Iraq

Iraq Permanent Mission to the UN
14 E 79th St
New York, NY 10021
Phone: 212-737-4433; Fax: 212-772-1794

Ireland

Irish Tourist Board
345 Park Ave
17th Fl
New York, NY 10154
Phone: 212-418-0800; Fax: 212-371-9052
Toll-free: 800-669-9967
www.tourismireland.com

Ireland Chamber of Commerce in the US
556 Central Ave
New Providence, NJ 07974
Phone: 908-286-1300; Fax: 908-286-1200
www.iccusa.org

Ireland-US Council for Commerce & Industry
1156 Ave of the Americas
New York, NY 10036
Phone: 212-921-1414; Fax: 212-730-2232

Ireland Consulate General
535 Boylston St
Boston, MA 02116
Phone: 617-267-9330; Fax: 617-267-6375
www.irelandemb.org/contact.html

Ireland Consulate General
400 N Michigan Ave
Suite 911
Chicago, IL 60611
Phone: 312-337-1868; Fax: 312-337-1954
www.irelandemb.org/chicago.html

Ireland Consulate General
345 Park Ave
17th Fl

New York, NY 10154
Phone: 212-319-2555; Fax: 212-980-9475
www.irelandemb.org/contact.html

Ireland Consulate General
100 Pine St
33rd Fl
San Francisco, CA 94111
Phone: 415-392-4214; Fax: 415-392-0885
www.irelandemb.org/contact.html

Ireland Embassy
2234 Massachusetts Ave NW
Washington, DC 20008
Phone: 202-462-3939; Fax: 202-232-5993
www.irelandemb.org

Ireland Permanent Mission to the UN
885 2nd Ave
19th Fl
New York, NY 10017
Phone: 212-421-6934; Fax: 212-752-4726
www.un.int/ireland

Israel

Israel Government Tourist Office
6380 Wilshire Blvd
Suite 1700
Los Angeles, CA 90048
Phone: 323-658-7463; Fax: 323-658-6543
www.goisrael.com

Israel Government Tourist Office
800 2nd Ave
16th Fl
New York, NY 10017
Phone: 212-499-5660; Fax: 212-499-5645
Toll-free: 888-774-7723
www.goisrael.com

American-Israel Chamber of Commerce Southeast Region
1150 Lake Hearn Dr
Suite 130
Atlanta, GA 30342
Phone: 404-843-9426; Fax: 404-843-1416
www.aiccse.org

America-Israel Chamber of Commerce - Chicago
247 S State St
15th Fl
Chicago, IL 60604
Phone: 312-235-0586; Fax: 312-641-0724
www.americaisrael.org

American-Israel Chamber of Commerce & Industry of
  Minnesota
13100 Wayzata Blvd
Suite 130
Minnetonka, MN 55305
Phone: 952-593-8666; Fax: 952-593-8668
www.aiccmn.org

America-Israel Chamber of Commerce & Industry
3 New York Plaza
10th Fl

New York, NY 10004
Phone: 212-232-8440; Fax: 646-365-3366
www.aicci.net

Israel Consulate General
1100 Spring St NW
Suite 440
Atlanta, GA 30309
Phone: 404-487-6500; Fax: 404-487-6555
www.israelemb.org/atlanta

Israel Consulate General
111 E Wacker Dr
Suite 1308
Chicago, IL 60601
Phone: 312-297-4800; Fax: 312-297-4855
www.embassyofisrael.org/chicago

Israel Consulate General
24 Greenway Plaza
Suite 1500
Houston, TX 77046
Phone: 713-627-3780; Fax: 713-627-0149
www.israelemb.org/tx

Israel Consulate General
6380 Wilshire Blvd
Suite 1700
Los Angeles, CA 90048
Phone: 323-852-5500; Fax: 323-852-5555
www.israelemb.org/la

Israel Consulate General
100 N Biscayne Blvd
Suite 1800
Miami, FL 33132
Phone: 305-925-9400; Fax: 305-925-9451
www.israelemb.org/miami

Israel Consulate General in New York
800 2nd Ave
New York, NY 10017
Phone: 212-499-5300; Fax: 212-499-5455
www.israelfm.org

Israel Consulate
230 S 15th St
Suite 8
Philadelphia, PA 19102
Phone: 215-546-5556; Fax: 215-545-3986

Israel Consulate General
456 Montgomery St
Suite 2100
San Francisco, CA 94104
Phone: 415-844-7500; Fax: 415-844-7555
israelemb.org/sanfran

Israel Embassy
3514 International Dr NW
Washington, DC 20008
Phone: 202-364-5500; Fax: 202-364-5429
www.israelemb.org

Israel Permanent Mission to the UN
800 2nd Ave
New York, NY 10017

Phone: 212-499-5510; Fax: 212-499-5515
www.israel-un.org/

Italy

Italian Government Tourist Board
500 N Michigan Ave
Suite 2240
Chicago, IL 60611
Phone: 312-644-0996; Fax: 312-644-3019
www.italiantourism.com

Italian Government Tourist Board
12400 Wilshire Blvd
Suite 550
Los Angeles, CA 90025
Phone: 310-820-1898; Fax: 310-820-6357
www.italiantourism.com

Italian Government Tourist Board
630 5th Ave
Suite 1565
New York, NY 10111
Phone: 212-245-5618; Fax: 212-586-9249
www.italiantourism.com

Italian American Chamber of Commerce of Chicago
30 S Michigan Ave
Suite 504
Chicago, IL 60603
Phone: 312-553-9137; Fax: 312-553-9142
www.italianchamber.us

Italy-America Chamber of Commerce of Texas Inc
1800 W Loop S
Suite 1120
Houston, TX 77027
Phone: 713-626-9303; Fax: 713-626-9309
www.iacctexas.com

Italy-America Chamber of Commerce West Inc
10350 Santa Monica Blvd
Suite 210
Los Angeles, CA 90025
Phone: 310-557-3017; Fax: 310-557-1217
www.italchambers.net/losangeles

Italy-America Chamber of Commerce Southeast Inc
270 NE 4th St
Suite 2
Miami, FL 33132
Phone: 305-577-9868; Fax: 305-577-3956
www.iacc-miami.com

Italy-America Chamber of Commerce Inc
730 5th Ave
Suite 600
New York, NY 10019
Phone: 212-459-0044; Fax: 212-459-0090
www.italchamber.org

Italy Consulate General
600 Atlantic Ave
17th Fl
Boston, MA 02210
Phone: 617-722-9201; Fax: 617-722-9407

Italy Consulate General
500 N Michigan Ave
Suite 1850
Chicago, IL 60611
Phone: 312-439-8600; Fax: 312-467-1335
www.consnewyork.esteri.it/Consolato_NewYork

Italy Consulate General
4000 Ponce de Leon Blvd
Suite 590
Coral Gables, FL 33146
Phone: 305-374-6322; Fax: 305-374-7945
www.consmiami.esteri.it/Consolato_Miami

Italy Consulate
535 Griswold St
Buhl Bldg Suite 1840
Detroit, MI 48226
Phone: 313-963-8560; Fax: 313-963-8180
www.italconsdetroit.org

Italy Consulate General
1300 Post Oak Blvd
Suite 660
Houston, TX 77056
Phone: 713-850-7520; Fax: 713-850-9113
www.italconshouston.org

Italy Consulate General
12400 Wilshire Blvd
Suite 300
Los Angeles, CA 90025
Phone: 310-820-0622; Fax: 310-820-0727
sedi.esteri.it/losangeles

Italy Consulate General
690 Park Ave
New York, NY 10021
Phone: 212-737-9100; Fax: 212-249-4945
www.italconsulnyc.org

Italy Vice Consulate
1 Gateway Center
Suite 100
Newark, NJ 07102
Phone: 973-643-1448; Fax: 973-643-3043
www.consnewark.esteri.it/Consolato_Newark

Italy Consulate General
150 S Independence Mall West
Public Ledger Bldg Suite 1026
Philadelphia, PA 19106
Phone: 215-592-7329; Fax: 215-592-9808
www.italconphila.org

Italy Consulate General
2590 Webster St
San Francisco, CA 94115
Phone: 415-931-4924; Fax: 415-931-7205
www.italcons-sf.org

Italy Embassy
3000 Whitehaven St NW
Washington, DC 20008
Phone: 202-612-4400; Fax: 202-518-2154
www.italyemb.org

Italy Permanent Mission to the UN
2 UN Plaza
24th Fl
New York, NY 10017
Phone: 212-486-9191; Fax: 212-486-1036
www.italyun.org

Ivory Coast. *See* Cote D'Ivoire

Jamaica

Jamaica Tourist Board
5201 Blue Lagoon Dr
Suite 1101
Miami, FL 33126
Phone: 305-665-0557; Fax: 305-666-7239
Toll-free: 800-233-4582
www.visitjamaica.com

Jamaica Consulate General
25 SE 2nd Ave
Suite 842
Miami, FL 33131
Phone: 305-374-8431; Fax: 305-577-4970

Jamaica Embassy
1520 New Hampshire Ave NW
Washington, DC 20036
Phone: 202-452-0660; Fax: 202-452-0081
www.jamaicaembassy.org

Jamaica Permanent Mission to the UN
767 3rd Ave
9th Fl
New York, NY 10017
Phone: 212-935-7509; Fax: 212-935-7607
www.un.int/jamaica

Japan

Japan National Tourist Organization
515 S Figueroa St
Suite 1470
Los Angeles, CA 90071
Phone: 213-623-1952; Fax: 213-623-6301
www.japantravelinfo.com

Japan National Tourist Organization
1 Rockefeller Plaza
Suite 1250
New York, NY 10020
Phone: 212-757-5640; Fax: 212-307-6754
www.japantravelinfo.com

Japanese Chamber of Commerce & Industry of Chicago
541 N Fairbanks Ct
Suite 2050
Chicago, IL 60611
Phone: 312-245-8344; Fax: 312-245-8355
www.jccc-chi.org/en

Japanese Chamber of Commerce & Industry of Hawaii
400 Hualani St
Suite 20B

Hilo, HI 96720
Phone: 808-934-0177; Fax: 808-934-0178

Japanese Chamber of Commerce & Industry of New York Inc
145 W 57th St
6th Fl
New York, NY 10019
Phone: 212-246-8001; Fax: 212-246-8002
www.jcciny.org

Japanese Chamber of Commerce of Northern California
1875 S Grant St
Suite 760
San Mateo, CA 94402
Phone: 650-522-8500; Fax: 650-522-8300
www.jccnc.org

Japan Consulate General
3601 C St
Suite 1300
Anchorage, AK 99503
Phone: 907-562-8424; Fax: 907-562-8434
www.anchorage.us.emb-japan.go.jp

Japan Consulate General
1 Alliance Ctr 3500 Lenox Rd
Suite 1600
Atlanta, GA 30326
Phone: 404-240-4300; Fax: 404-240-4311
www.japanatlanta.org

Japan Consulate General
600 Atlantic Ave
Federal Reserve Plaza 14th Fl
Boston, MA 02210
Phone: 617-973-9772; Fax: 617-542-1329
www.boston.us.emb-japan.go.jp

Japan Consulate General
737 N Michigan Ave
Suite 1100
Chicago, IL 60611
Phone: 312-280-0400; Fax: 312-280-9568
www.chicago.us.emb-japan.go.jp

Japan Consulate General
1225 17th St
Suite 3000
Denver, CO 80202
Phone: 303-534-1151; Fax: 303-534-3393
www.denver.us.emb-japan.go.jp

Japan Consulate General
400 Renaissance Ctr
Suite 1600
Detroit, MI 48243
Phone: 313-567-0120; Fax: 313-567-0274
www.detroit.us.emb-japan.go.jp

Japan Consulate General
1742 Nuuanu Ave
Honolulu, HI 96817
Phone: 808-543-3111; Fax: 808-543-3170
www.honolulu.us.emb-japan.go.jp

Japan Consulate General
900 Fannin St Suite 3000
2 Houston Center
Houston, TX 77010
Phone: 713-652-2977; Fax: 713-651-7822
www.houston.us.emb-japan.go.jp

Japan Consulate General
350 S Grand Ave
Suite 1700
Los Angeles, CA 90071
Phone: 213-617-6700; Fax: 213-617-6727
www.la.us.emb-japan.go.jp

Japan Consulate General
80 SW 8th St
Brickell Bay View Ctr Suite 3200
Miami, FL 33130
Phone: 305-530-9090; Fax: 305-530-0950
www.miami.us.emb-japan.go.jp

Japan Consulate General
639 Loyola Ave
Suite 2050
New Orleans, LA 70113
Phone: 504-529-2101; Fax: 504-568-9847
www.neworleans.us.emb-japan.go.jp

Japan Consulate General
299 Park Ave
18th Fl
New York, NY 10171
Phone: 212-371-8222; Fax: 212-319-6357
www.cgj.org

Japan Consulate General
Wells Fargo Ctr 1300 SW 5th Ave
Suite 2700
Portland, OR 97201
Phone: 503-221-1811; Fax: 503-224-8936
www.portland.us.emb-japan.go.jp

Japan Consulate General
50 Fremont St
Suite 2300
San Francisco, CA 94105
Phone: 415-777-3533; Fax: 415-974-3660
www.cgjsf.org

Japan Consulate General
601 Union St
Suite 500
Seattle, WA 98101
Phone: 206-682-9107; Fax: 206-624-9097
www.seattle.us.emb-japan.go.jp

Japan Embassy
2520 Massachusetts Ave NW
Washington, DC 20008
Phone: 202-238-6700; Fax: 202-328-2187
www.embjapan.org

Japan Permanent Mission to the UN
866 UN Plaza
2nd Fl
New York, NY 10017

Phone: 212-223-4300; Fax: 212-751-1966
www.un.int/japan

Jordan

Jordan Tourism Board
6867 Elm St
Suite 102
McLean, VA 22101
Phone: 703-243-7404; Fax: 703-243-7406
Toll-free: 877-733-5673
www.seejordan.org

Jordan Embassy
3504 International Dr NW
Washington, DC 20008
Phone: 202-966-2664; Fax: 202-966-3110
www.jordanembassyus.org

Kazakhstan

Kazakhstan Consulate
866 UN Plaza
Suite 586A
New York, NY 10017
Phone: 212-888-3024; Fax: 212-888-3025
www.kazconsulny.org

Kazakhstan Embassy
1401 16th St NW
Washington, DC 20036
Phone: 202-232-5488; Fax: 202-232-5845
www.kazakhembus.com

Kazakhstan Permanent Mission to the UN
866 UN Plaza
Suite 586
New York, NY 10017
Phone: 212-230-1900; Fax: 212-230-1172
www.un.int/kazakhstan

Kenya

Kenya Tourism Board
c/o Carlson Destinationa Marketing Services
PO Box 59159
Minneapolis, MN 55459
Phone: 866-445-3692; Fax: 763-212-2533
Toll-free: 866-445-3692
www.magicalkenya.com

Kenya Embassy
2249 R St NW
Washington, DC 20008
Phone: 202-387-6101; Fax: 202-462-3829
www.kenyaembassy.com

Kenya Permanent Mission to the UN
866 UN Plaza
Rm 486
New York, NY 10017
Phone: 212-421-4740; Fax: 212-486-1985
www.un.int/kenya

Korea, North. *See* **North Korea (Democratic People's Republic of Korea)**

Korea, South. *See* **South Korea (Republic of Korea)**

Kuwait

Kuwait Embassy
2940 Tilden St NW
Washington, DC 20008
Phone: 202-966-0702; Fax: 202-966-0517

Kuwait Permanent Mission to the UN
321 E 44th St
New York, NY 10017
Phone: 212-973-4300; Fax: 212-370-1733
www.kuwaitmission.com

Kyrgyzstan

Kyrgyzstan Embassy
2360 Massachusetts Ave NW
Washington, DC 20008
Phone: 202-449-9822; Fax: 202-386-7550
www.kyrgyzstan.org

Kyrgyzstan Permanent Mission to the UN
866 UN Plaza
Suite 477
New York, NY 10017
Phone: 212-486-4214; Fax: 212-486-5259

Laos

Lao People's Democratic Republic Embassy
2222 'S' St NW
Washington, DC 20008
Phone: 202-332-6416; Fax: 202-332-4923
www.laoembassy.com

Lao People's Democratic Republic Permanent Mission to the
  UN
317 E 51st St
New York, NY 10022
Phone: 212-832-2734; Fax: 212-750-0039
www.un.int/lao

Latvia

Latvia Embassy
2306 Massachusetts Ave NW
Washington, DC 20008
Phone: 202-328-2840; Fax: 202-328-2860
www.latvia-usa.org

Latvia Permanent Mission to the UN
333 E 50th St
New York, NY 10022
Phone: 212-838-8877; Fax: 212-838-8920

Lebanon

Lebanon Consulate General
3031 W Grand Blvd
Suite 560
Detroit, MI 48202
Phone: 313-758-0753; Fax: 313-758-0756

Lebanon Consulate General
660 S Figueroa St
Suite 1050
Los Angeles, CA 90017
Phone: 213-243-0999

Lebanon Consulate General
9 E 76th St
New York, NY 10021
Phone: 212-744-7905; Fax: 212-794-1510
www.lebconsny.org

Lebanon Embassy
2560 28th St NW
Washington, DC 20008
Phone: 202-939-6300; Fax: 202-939-6324
www.lebanonembassyus.org

Lebanon Permanent Mission to the UN
866 UN Plaza
Rm 531-533
New York, NY 10017
Phone: 212-355-5460; Fax: 212-838-2819

Lesotho

Lesotho Embassy
2511 Massachusetts Ave NW
Washington, DC 20008
Phone: 202-797-5533; Fax: 202-234-6815
www.lesothoemb-usa.gov.ls

Lesotho Permanent Mission to the UN
204 E 39th St
New York, NY 10016
Phone: 212-661-1690; Fax: 212-682-4388
www.un.int/lesotho

Liberia

Liberia Consulate General
820 2nd Ave
Suite 1300
New York, NY 10017
Phone: 212-687-1025; Fax: 212-599-3189
www.liberiaconsulate.com

Liberia Embassy
5201 16th St NW
Washington, DC 20011
Phone: 202-723-0437; Fax: 202-723-0436
www.embassyofliberia.org

Liberia Permanent Mission to the UN
820 2nd Ave
Suite 1300
New York, NY 10017
Phone: 212-687-1033; Fax: 212-687-1035

Libya

Libyan Arab Jamahiriya Permanent Mission to the UN
309-315 E 48th St
New York, NY 10017
Phone: 212-752-5775; Fax: 212-593-4787
www.libya-un.org

Liechtenstein

Liechtenstein Embassy
888 17th St NW
Suite 1250
Washington, DC 20006
Phone: 202-331-0590; Fax: 202-331-3221
www.liechtenstein.li

Liechtenstein Permanent Mission to the UN
633 3rd Ave
27th Fl
New York, NY 10017
Phone: 212-599-0220; Fax: 212-599-0064

Lithuania

Lithuania Consulate General
211 E Ontario St
Suite 1500
Chicago, IL 60611
Phone: 312-397-0382; Fax: 312-397-0385
www.ltembassyus.org

Lithuania Consulate General
420 5th Ave
3rd Fl
New York, NY 10018
Phone: 212-354-7840; Fax: 212-354-7911
www.ltembassyus.org

Lithuania Embassy
4590 MacArthur Blvd NW
Suite 200
Washington, DC 20009
Phone: 202-234-5860; Fax: 202-328-0466
www.ltembassyus.org

Lithuania Permanent Mission to the UN
420 5th Ave
3rd Fl
New York, NY 10018
Phone: 212-354-7820; Fax: 212-354-7833
www.un.int/lithuania/lithuania.html

Luxembourg

Luxembourg National Tourist Office
17 Beekman Pl
New York, NY 10022
Phone: 212-935-8888; Fax: 212-935-5896
www.ont.lu

Luxembourg-American Chamber of Commerce
17 Beekman Pl
New York, NY 10022

Phone: 212-888-6701; Fax: 212-935-5896
www.luxembourgbusiness.org

Luxembourg Consulate General
17 Beekman Pl
New York, NY 10022
Phone: 212-888-6664; Fax: 212-888-6116
www.luxembourgnewyork.com

Luxembourg Consulate General
1 Sansome St
Suite 830
San Francisco, CA 94104
Phone: 415-788-0816; Fax: 415-788-0985
www.luxembourgsf.org

Luxembourg Embassy
2200 Massachusetts Ave NW
Washington, DC 20008
Phone: 202-265-4171; Fax: 202-328-8270
www.luxembourg-usa.org

Luxembourg Permanent Mission to the UN
17 Beekman Pl
New York, NY 10022
Phone: 212-935-3589; Fax: 212-935-5896
www.un.int/luxembourg

Macau

Macau Government Tourist Office
1334 Parkview Ave
Suite 300
Manhattan Beach, CA 90266
Phone: 310-545-3430; Fax: 310-545-4221
Toll-free: 866-656-2228
www.macautourism.gov.mo

Macedonia

Macedonia Consulate General
2000 Town Center
Suite 1130
Southfield, MI 48075
Phone: 248-354-5537; Fax: 248-354-5538

Macedonia Embassy
2129 Wyoming Ave
Washington, DC 20008
Phone: 202-667-0501; Fax: 202-667-2131

Macedonia Permanent Mission to the UN
866 UN Plaza
Suite 517
New York, NY 10017
Phone: 212-308-8504; Fax: 212-308-8724
www.un.int/macedonia

Madagascar

Madagascar Embassy
2374 Massachusetts Ave NW
Washington, DC 20008
Phone: 202-265-5525; Fax: 202-265-3034

Madagascar Permanent Mission to the UN
820 2nd Ave
Suite 800
New York, NY 10017
Phone: 212-986-9491; Fax: 212-986-6271

Malawi

Malawi Embassy
1156 15th St NW
Suite 320
Washington, DC 20005
Phone: 202-721-0270; Fax: 202-721-0288

Malawi Permanent Mission to the UN
600 3rd Ave
21st Fl
New York, NY 10016
Phone: 212-317-8738; Fax: 212-317-8729

Malaysia

Tourism Malaysia
818 W 7th St
Suite 970
Los Angeles, CA 90017
Phone: 213-689-9702; Fax: 213-689-1530
Toll-free: 800-336-6842
www.tourism.gov.my

Tourism Malaysia
120 E 56th St
Suite 810
New York, NY 10022
Phone: 212-754-1113; Fax: 212-754-1116
Toll-free: 800-558-6787
www.tourism.gov.my

Malaysia Consulate General
550 S Hope St
Suite 400
Los Angeles, CA 90071
Phone: 213-892-1238; Fax: 213-892-9031

Malaysia Consulate General
313 E 43rd St
New York, NY 10017
Phone: 212-490-2722; Fax: 212-490-2049

Malaysia Embassy
3516 International Ct NW
Washington, DC 20008
Phone: 202-572-9700; Fax: 202-572-9882

Malaysia Permanent Mission to the UN
313 E 43rd St
New York, NY 10017
Phone: 212-986-6310; Fax: 212-490-8576
www.un.int/malaysia

Maldives

Maldives Permanent Mission to the UN
800 2nd Ave

Suite 400-E
New York, NY 10017
Phone: 212-599-6194; Fax: 212-661-6405
www.un.int/maldives

Mali

Mali Embassy
2130 R St NW
Washington, DC 20008
Phone: 202-332-2249; Fax: 202-332-6603
www.maliembassy.us

Mali Permanent Mission to the UN
111 E 69th St
New York, NY 10021
Phone: 212-737-4150; Fax: 212-472-3778
www.un.int/mali

Malta

Malta Consulate
249 E 35th St
New York, NY 10016
Phone: 212-725-2345; Fax: 212-779-7097
www.gov.mt

Malta Embassy
2017 Connecticut Ave NW
Washington, DC 20008
Phone: 202-462-3611; Fax: 202-387-5470

Malta Permanent Mission to the UN
249 E 35th St
New York, NY 10016
Phone: 212-725-2345; Fax: 212-779-7097

Marshall Islands

Marshall Islands Consulate General
1888 Lusitana St
Suite 301
Honolulu, HI 96813
Phone: 808-545-7767; Fax: 808-545-7211
www.rmiembassyus.org

Marshall Islands Embassy
2433 Massachusetts Ave NW
Washington, DC 20008
Phone: 202-234-5414; Fax: 202-232-3236
www.rmiembassyus.org

Marshall Islands Permanent Mission to the UN
800 2nd Ave
18th Fl
New York, NY 10017
Phone: 212-983-3040; Fax: 212-983-3202

Martinique

Martinique Promotion Bureau
444 Madison Ave
16th Fl
New York, NY 10022

Phone: 800-391-4909
www.martinique.org

French West Indies Tourist Board
444 Madison Ave
16th Fl
New York, NY 10022
Phone: 212-838-7800; Fax: 212-838-7855

Mauritania

Mauritania Embassy
2129 Leroy Pl NW
Washington, DC 20008
Phone: 202-232-5700; Fax: 202-319-2623
www.ambarim-dc.org

Mauritania Permanent Mission to the UN
116 E 38th St
New York, NY 10016
Phone: 212-252-0113; Fax: 212-252-0175
Mauritius

Mauritius Embassy
4301 Connecticut Ave NW
Suite 441
Washington, DC 20008
Phone: 202-244-1491; Fax: 202-966-0983
www.maurinet.com/embasydc.html

Mauritius Permanent Mission to the UN
211 E 43rd St
15th Fl
New York, NY 10017
Phone: 212-949-0190; Fax: 212-697-3829

Micronesia

Micronesia Federated States of Consulate
3049 Ualena St
suite 910
Honolulu, HI 96819
Phone: 808-836-4775; Fax: 808-836-6896

Micronesia Federated States of Embassy
1725 'N' St NW
Washington, DC 20036
Phone: 202-223-4383; Fax: 202-223-4391

Micronesia Federated States of Permanent Mission to the
  UN
820 2nd Ave
Suite 17A
New York, NY 10017
Phone: 212-697-8370; Fax: 212-697-8295
www.fsmgov.org/fsmun

Moldova

Moldova Embassy
2101 'S' St NW
Washington, DC 20008
Phone: 202-667-1130; Fax: 202-667-1204
www.embassyrm.org

Moldova Permanent Mission to the UN
35 E 29th St
New York, NY 10016
Phone: 212-447-1867; Fax: 212-447-4067
www.un.int/moldova

Monaco

Monaco Government Tourist Office
565 5th Ave
23rd Fl
New York, NY 10017
Phone: 212-286-3330; Fax: 212-286-9890
Toll-free: 800-753-9696
www.visitmonaco.com

Monaco Permanent Mission to the UN
866 UN Plaza
Suite 520
New York, NY 10017
Phone: 212-832-0721; Fax: 212-832-5358
www.un.int/monaco

Mongolia

Mongolia Embassy
2833 M St NW
Washington, DC 20007
Phone: 202-333-7117; Fax: 202-298-9227
www.mongolianembassy.us

Mongolia Permanent Mission to the UN
6 E 77th St
New York, NY 10021
Phone: 212-861-9460; Fax: 212-861-9464
www.un.int/mongolia

Morocco

Moroccan National Tourist Office
20 E 46th St
Suite 1201
New York, NY 10017
Phone: 212-557-2520; Fax: 212-949-8148
www.tourism-in-morocco.com

Moroccan National Tourist Office
7208 Sand Lake Rd
Suite 204
Orlando, FL 32819
Phone: 407-264-0133; Fax: 407-264-0134
www.tourism-in-morocco.com

Morocco Consulate
10 E 40th St
23rd Fl
New York, NY 10016
Phone: 212-213-9644; Fax: 212-725-4198
www.moroccanconsulate.com

Morocco Consulate General
10 E 40th St
24th Fl
New York, NY 10016

Phone: 212-758-2625; Fax: 212-779-7441
www.moroccanconsulate.com

Morocco Embassy
1601 21st St NW
Washington, DC 20009
Phone: 202-462-7980; Fax: 202-462-7643

Morocco Permanent Mission to the UN
866 2nd Ave
6th & 7th Fl
New York, NY 10017
Phone: 212-421-1580; Fax: 212-980-1512
www.un.int/morocco

Mozambique

Mozambique Embassy
1990 M St NW
Suite 570
Washington, DC 20036
Phone: 202-293-7146; Fax: 202-835-0245
www.embamoc-usa.org

Mozambique Permanent Mission to the UN
420 E 50th St
New York, NY 10022
Phone: 212-644-6800; Fax: 212-644-5972
www.un.int/mozambique

Myanmar (Burma)

Myanmar Embassy
2300 'S' St NW
Washington, DC 20008
Phone: 202-332-3344; Fax: 202-332-4351
www.mewashingtondc.com

Myanmar Permanent Mission to the UN
10 E 77th St
New York, NY 10021
Phone: 212-744-1271; Fax: 212-744-1290

Namibia

Namibia Embassy
1605 New Hampshire Ave NW
Washington, DC 20009
Phone: 202-986-0540; Fax: 202-986-0443

Namibia Permanent Mission to the UN
360 Lexington Ave
Suite 1502
New York, NY 10017
Phone: 212-685-2003; Fax: 212-685-1561
www.un.int/namibia

Nauru

Nauru Permanent Mission to the UN
800 2nd Ave
Suite 400-A
New York, NY 10017
Phone: 212-937-0074; Fax: 212-937-0079

Nepal

Nepal Consulate General
820 2nd Ave
Suite 17B
New York, NY 10017
Phone: 212-370-3988; Fax: 212-953-2038

Nepal Embassy
2131 Leroy Pl NW
Washington, DC 20008
Phone: 202-667-4550; Fax: 202-667-5534
www.nepalembassyusa.org

Nepal Permanent Mission to the UN
820 2nd Ave
Suite 17B
New York, NY 10017
Phone: 212-370-3988; Fax: 212-953-2038
www.un.int/nepal

Netherlands

Netherlands Board of Tourism & Conventions
355 Lexington Ave
19th Fl
New York, NY 10017
Phone: 212-370-7360; Fax: 212-370-9507
Toll-free: 888-464-6552
www.holland.com

Netherlands Chamber of Commerce in the US Inc
267 5th Ave
Suite 301
New York, NY 10016
Phone: 212-265-6460; Fax: 212-265-6402
www.netherlands.org

Netherlands Consulate General
303 E Wacker Dr
Suite 2600
Chicago, IL 60601
Phone: 312-856-0110; Fax: 312-856-9218
Toll-free: 877-388-2443
www.cgchicago.org

Netherlands Consulate General
2200 Post Oak Blvd
Suite 610
Houston, TX 77056
Phone: 713-622-8000; Fax: 713-622-3581
www.nlconsulatehouston.org

Netherlands Consulate General
11766 Wilshire Blvd
Suite 1150
Los Angeles, CA 90025
Phone: 310-268-1598; Fax: 310-312-0989
www.ncla.org

Netherlands Consulate General
701 Brickell Ave
5th Fl
Miami, FL 33131
Phone: 786-866-0480; Fax: 786-866-0497
www.cgmiami.org

Netherlands Consulate General
1 Rockefeller Plaza
11th Fl
New York, NY 10020
Phone: 212-246-1429; Fax: 212-333-3603
www.cgny.org

Netherlands Embassy
4200 Linnean Ave NW
Washington, DC 20008
Phone: 202-244-5300; Fax: 202-362-3430
www.netherlands-embassy.org

Netherlands Permanent Mission to the UN
235 E 45th St
16th Fl
New York, NY 10017
Phone: 212-697-5547; Fax: 212-370-1954
www.pvnewyork.org

New Zealand

New Zealand Tourism Board
501 Santa Monica Blvd
Suite 300
Santa Monica, CA 90401
Phone: 310-395-7480; Fax: 310-395-5453
Toll-free: 866-639-9325
www.newzealand.com/travel

New Zealand Consulate General
222 E 41st St
Suite 2510
New York, NY 10017
Phone: 212-832-4038; Fax: 212-832-7602

New Zealand Consulate General
2425 Olympic Blvd
Suite 600-E
Santa Monica, CA 90404
Phone: 310-566-6555; Fax: 310-566-6556
www.nzcgla.com

New Zealand Embassy
37 Observatory Cir NW
Washington, DC 20008
Phone: 202-328-4800; Fax: 202-667-5227
www.nzembassy.com

New Zealand Permanent Mission to the UN
1 UN Plaza
25th Fl
New York, NY 10017
Phone: 212-826-1960; Fax: 212-758-0827
nzmissionny.org

Nicaragua

Nicaraguan-American Chamber of Commerce
16161 SW 144th Terrace
Miami, FL 33196
Phone: 305-599-2737; Fax: 305-969-4509
www.naccflorida.com

Nicaragua Consulate General
8989 Westheimer St
Suite 103
Houston, TX 77063
Phone: 713-789-2762; Fax: 713-789-3164

Nicaragua Consulate
3550 Wilshire Blvd
Suite 200
Los Angeles, CA 90010
Phone: 213-252-1170; Fax: 213-252-1177

Nicaragua Consulate General
8532 SW 8th St
Suite 270
Miami, FL 33144
Phone: 305-265-1415; Fax: 305-265-1780

Nicaragua Consulate General
820 2nd Ave
Suite 802
New York, NY 10017
Phone: 212-986-6562; Fax: 212-983-2646

Nicaragua Consulate General
870 Market St
Suite 518
San Francisco, CA 94102
Phone: 415-765-6825; Fax: 415-765-6826

Nicaragua Embassy
1627 New Hampshire Ave NW
Washington, DC 20009
Phone: 202-939-6570; Fax: 202-939-6542

Nicaragua Permanent Mission to the UN
820 2nd Ave
Suite 801
New York, NY 10017
Phone: 212-490-7997; Fax: 212-286-0815
www.un.int/nicaragua

Niger

Niger Embassy
2204 R St NW
Washington, DC 20008
Phone: 202-483-4224; Fax: 202-483-3169
www.nigerembassyusa.org

Niger Permanent Mission to the UN
417 E 50th St
New York, NY 10022
Phone: 212-421-3260; Fax: 212-753-6931
www.un.int/niger

Nigeria

Nigeria Consulate General
828 2nd Ave
New York, NY 10017
Phone: 212-850-2200; Fax: 212-687-1476
www.nigeriahouse.com

Nigeria Embassy
3519 International Ct NW
Washington, DC 20008
Phone: 202-986-8400; Fax: 202-362-6981
www.nigeriaembassyusa.org

Nigeria Permanent Mission to the UN
828 2nd Ave
New York, NY 10017
Phone: 212-953-9130; Fax: 212-697-1970

North Korea (Democratic People's Republic of Korea)

Democratic People's Republic of Korea, Permanent Mission
  to the UN
820 2nd Ave
13th Fl
New York, NY 10017
Phone: 212-972-3105; Fax: 212-972-3154

Norway

Norwegian Tourist Board
655 3rd Ave
18th Ave
New York, NY 10017
Phone: 212-885-9700; Fax: 212-885-9710
www.visitnorway.com

Norwegian-American Chamber of Commerce Southwest
  Chapter
2777 Allen Pkwy
Suite 1185
Houston, TX 77019
Phone: 713-526-6222; Fax: 713-521-9473
nacchouston.org

Norwegian-American Chamber of Commerce Upper
  Midwest Chapter
821 Marquette Ave
Suite 800
Minneapolis, MN 55402
Phone: 612-332-3338; Fax: 612-332-1386

Norwegian-American Chamber of Commerce Inc
835 3rd Ave
38th Fl
New York, NY 10022
Phone: 212-421-1655; Fax: 212-838-0374
www.nacc.no

Norwegian-American Chamber of Commerce Northern
  California Chapter
20 California St
6th Fl
San Francisco, CA 94111
Phone: 415-986-0770; Fax: 415-986-7875
www.nacc.no/sanfrancisco

Norwegian-American Chamber of Commerce Southern
  California Chapter
PO Box 3251
Thousand Oaks, CA 91359
Phone: 818-735-0019; Fax: 818-735-0032
www.naccla.org

Norway Consulate General
2777 Allen Pkwy
Suite 1185
Houston, TX 77019
Phone: 713-521-2900; Fax: 713-521-9648
www.norway.org/embassy

Norway Consulate General
821 Marquette Ave
Suite 800
Minneapolis, MN 55402
Phone: 612-332-3338; Fax: 612-332-1386
www.norway.org/embassy

Norway Consulate General
825 3rd Ave
38th Fl
New York, NY 10022
Phone: 212-421-7333; Fax: 212-754-0583
www.norway.org/embassy

Norway Consulate General
20 California St
6th Fl
San Francisco, CA 94111
Phone: 415-986-0766; Fax: 415-986-3318
www.norway.org/embassy

Norway Embassy
2720 34th St NW
Washington, DC 20008
Phone: 202-333-6000; Fax: 202-337-0870
www.norway.org/embassy

Norway Permanent Mission to the UN
825 3rd Ave
39th Fl
New York, NY 10022
Phone: 212-421-0280; Fax: 212-688-0554
www.norway-un.org

Oman

Oman Embassy
2535 Belmont Rd NW
Washington, DC 20008
Phone: 202-387-1980; Fax: 202-745-4933

Oman Permanent Mission to the UN
866 UN Plaza
Suite 540
New York, NY 10017
Phone: 212-355-3505; Fax: 212-644-0070

Pakistan

Pakistan Consulate General
10850 Wilshire Blvd
Suite 1250
Los Angeles, CA 90024
Phone: 310-441-5114; Fax: 310-441-9256

Pakistan Consulate General
12 E 65th St
New York, NY 10021
Phone: 212-879-5800; Fax: 212-517-6987

Pakistan Embassy
3517 International Ct NW
Washington, DC 20008
Phone: 202-243-6500; Fax: 202-686-1534
www.embassyofpakistanusa.org

Pakistan Permanent Mission to the UN
8 E 65th St
New York, NY 10021
Phone: 212-879-8600; Fax: 212-744-7348
www.un.int/pakistan

Palau

Palau Embassy
1700 Pennsylvania Ave NW
Suite 400
Washington, DC 20006
Phone: 202-349-8598; Fax: 202-349-8597
www.palauembassy.com

Panama

Panama Consulate General
24 Greenway Plaza
Suite 1307
Houston, TX 77046
Phone: 713-622-4451; Fax: 713-622-4468
www.conpahouston.com

Panama Consulate General
5775 Blue Lagoon Dr
Suite 200
Mimai, FL 33126
Phone: 305-447-3700; Fax: 305-447-4142

Panama Consulate General
2424 World Trade Ctr
2 Canal St
New Orleans, LA 70130
Phone: 504-525-3458; Fax: 504-524-8960
www.consulateofpanama.com

Panama Consulate General
1212 Ave of the Americas
6th Fl
New York, NY 10036
Phone: 212-840-2450; Fax: 212-840-2469

Panama Consulate General
124 Chestnut St
Philadelphia, PA 19106
Phone: 215-574-2994; Fax: 215-625-4876

Panama Embassy
2862 McGill Terr NW
Washington, DC 20008
Phone: 202-483-1407; Fax: 202-483-8413
www.embassyofpanama.org

Panama Permanent Mission to the UN
866 UN Plaza
Suite 4030
New York, NY 10017
Phone: 212-421-5420; Fax: 212-421-2694

Papua New Guinea

Papua New Guinea Embassy
1779 Massachusetts Ave NW
Suite 805
Washington, DC 20036
Phone: 202-745-3680; Fax: 202-745-3679
www.pngembassy.org

Papua New Guinea Permanent Mission to the UN
201 E 42nd St
Suite 405
New York, NY 10017
Phone: 212-557-5001; Fax: 212-557-5009

Paraguay

Paraguay Consulate General
25 SE 2nd Ave
Suite 705
Miami, FL 33131
Phone: 305-374-9090; Fax: 305-374-5522

Paraguay Consulate General
211 E 43rd St
Suite 1400
New York, NY 10017
Phone: 212-682-9441; Fax: 212-682-9443

Paraguay Embassy
2400 Massachusetts Ave NW
Washington, DC 20008
Phone: 202-483-6960; Fax: 202-234-4508

Paraguay Permanent Mission to the UN
211 E 43rd St
Suite 400
New York, NY 10017
Phone: 212-687-3490; Fax: 212-818-1282
www.un.int/paraguay

Peru

Peru Tourist Office
495 Biltmore Way
Suite 404
Coral Gables, FL 33134
Phone: 305-476-1220
Toll-free: 866-661-7378
www.peru.info/perueng.asp

Peruvian American Chamber of Commerce
9737 NW 41st St
PMB 348
Doral, FL 33178
Phone: 786-221-5890; Fax: 786-221-5834
www.peruvianchamber.org

Peru Consulate General
20 Park Plaza
Suite 511
Boston, MA 02116
Phone: 617-338-2227; Fax: 617-338-2742

Peru Consulate General
180 N Michigan Ave
Suite 1830
Chicago, IL 60601
Phone: 312-782-1599; Fax: 312-704-6969

Peru Consulate General
1001 S Monaco Pkwy
Suite 210
Denver, CO 80224
Phone: 303-355-8555; Fax: 303-355-8555
www.consuladoperu.com

Peru Consulate General
5177 Richmond Ave
Suite 695
Houston, TX 77056
Phone: 713-355-9517; Fax: 713-355-9377
www.consuladoperu.com

Peru Consulate General
3450 Wilshire Blvd
Suite 800
Los Angeles, CA 90010
Phone: 213-252-5910; Fax: 213-252-8130
www.consuladoperu.com/LosAngeles/index10.htm

Peru Consulate General
444 Brickell Ave
Suite M135
Miami, FL 33131
Phone: 305-374-1305; Fax: 305-381-6027
www.consulado-peru.com

Peru Consulate General
241 E 49th St
New York, NY 10017
Phone: 646-735-3828; Fax: 646-735-3866

Peru Consulate General
100 Hamilton Plaza
Suite 1221
Paterson, NJ 07505
Phone: 973-278-3324; Fax: 973-278-0254

Peru Consulate General
870 Market St
Suite 1067
San Francisco, CA 94102
Phone: 415-362-7136; Fax: 415-362-2836

Peru Embassy
1700 Massachusetts Ave NW
Washington, DC 20036
Phone: 202-833-9860; Fax: 202-659-8124
www.embassyofperu.us

Peru Permanent Mission to the UN
820 2nd Ave
Suite 1600
New York, NY 10017
Phone: 212-687-3336; Fax: 212-972-6975

Philippines

Philippine Dept of Tourism

556 5th Ave
1st Fl Mezzanine
New York, NY 10036
Phone: 212-575-7915; Fax: 212-302-6759
www.tourism.gov.ph

US Federation of Philippine American Chambers of
  Commerce Inc
2887 College Ave
Suite 1 Box 106
Berkeley, CA 94705
Phone: 510-548-7952; Fax: 510-845-9901
www.fpacc.com

Philippine American Chamber of Commerce Inc
317 Madison Ave
Suite 520
New York, NY 10017
Phone: 212-972-9326; Fax: 212-687-5844
www.philamchamber.org

Philippines Consulate General
30 N Michigan Ave
Suite 2100
Chicago, IL 60602
Phone: 312-332-6458; Fax: 312-332-3657
www.chicagopcg.com

Philippines Consulate General
2433 Pali Hwy
Honolulu, HI 96817
Phone: 808-595-6316; Fax: 808-595-2581

Philippines Consulate General
3600 Wilshire Blvd
Suite 500
Los Angeles, CA 90010
Phone: 213-639-0980; Fax: 213-639-0990
www.pcgenla.org

Philippines Consulate General
556 5th Ave
New York, NY 10036
Phone: 212-764-1330; Fax: 212-382-1146
www.pcgny.net

Philippines Consulate General
447 Sutter St
6th Fl
San Francisco, CA 94108
Phone: 415-433-6666; Fax: 415-421-2641
www.philippineconsulate-sf.org

Philippines Embassy
1600 Massachusetts Ave NW
Washington, DC 20036
Phone: 202-467-9300; Fax: 202-328-9417
www.philippineembassy-usa.org

Philippines Permanent Mission to the UN
556 5th Ave
5th Fl
New York, NY 10036
Phone: 212-764-1300; Fax: 212-840-8602
www.un.int/philippines

Poland

Polish National Tourist Office
5 Marine View Plaza
Suite 208
Hoboken, NJ 07030
Phone: 201-420-9910; Fax: 201-584-9153
www.polandtour.org

Poland Consulate General
820 N Orleans St
Suite 335
Chicago, IL 60610
Phone: 312-337-8166; Fax: 312-337-7841
www.polishconsulatechicago.org

Poland Consulate General
12400 Wilshire Blvd
Suite 555
Los Angeles, CA 90025
Phone: 310-442-8500; Fax: 310-442-8515
www.polishconsulatela.com

Poland Consulate General
233 Madison Ave
New York, NY 10016
Phone: 212-561-8160; Fax: 646-237-2105
www.polandconsulateny.com

Poland Embassy
2224 Wyoming Ave NW
Washington, DC 20008
Phone: 202-234-3800; Fax: 202-328-2152
www.polandembassy.org

Poland Permanent Mission to the UN
9 E 66th St
New York, NY 10021
Phone: 212-744-2506; Fax: 212-517-6771
www.polandun.org

Portugal

Portuguese Trade & Tourism Office
590 5th Ave
4th Fl
New York, NY 10036
Phone: 646-723-0200; Fax: 212-575-4737
Toll-free: 800-767-8842
www.visitportugal.com

Portuguese Trade & Tourist Office
88 Kearny St
Suite 1770
San Francisco, CA 94108
Phone: 415-391-7080; Fax: 415-391-7147
www.visitportugal.com

Portugal-US Chamber of Commerce
590 5th Ave
4th Fl
New York, NY 10036
Phone: 212-354-4627; Fax: 212-575-4737
portugal-us.com

Portugal Consulate General
699 Boylston St
7th Fl
Boston, MA 02116
Phone: 617-536-8740; Fax: 617-536-2503

Portugal Consulate
628 Pleasant St
Rm 204
New Bedford, MA 02740
Phone: 508-997-6151; Fax: 508-992-1068

Portugal Consulate General
590 5th Ave
3rd FL
New York, NY 10036
Phone: 212-221-3165; Fax: 212-221-3462

Portugal Consulate General
Legal Ctr
1 Riverfront Plaza
Newark, NJ 07102
Phone: 973-643-4200; Fax: 973-643-3900

Portugal Consulate
56 Pine St
6th Fl
Providence, RI 02903
Phone: 401-272-2003; Fax: 401-273-6247

Portugal Consulate General
3298 Washington St
San Francisco, CA 94115
Phone: 415-346-3400; Fax: 415-346-1440

Portugal Consulate
2012 Massachusetts Ave NW
Washington, DC 20036
Phone: 202-332-3007; Fax: 202-387-2768

Portugal Embassy
2012 Massachusetts Ave NW
Washington, DC 20036
Phone: 202-328-8610; Fax: 202-462-3726

Portugal Permanent Mission to the UN
866 2nd Ave
9th Fl
New York, NY 10017
Phone: 212-759-9444; Fax: 212-355-1124
www.un.int/portugal

Puerto Rico

Puerto Rico Convention Bureau
500 Tanca St
Suite 402
San Juan, PR 00901
Phone: 787-725-2110; Fax: 787-725-2133
Toll-free: 800-875-4765
www.meetpuertorico.com

Puerto Rico Tourism Co
901 Ponce de Leon Blvd
Suite 101
Coral Gables, FL 33134

Phone: 305-445-9112; Fax: 305-445-9450
Toll-free: 800-866-7827
www.gotopuertorico.com

Puerto Rico Tourism Co
3575 W Cahuenga Blvd
Suite 620
Los Angeles, CA 90068
Phone: 323-874-5991; Fax: 323-874-7257
Toll-free: 800-874-1230
www.gotopuertorico.com

Puerto Rico Tourism Co
666 5th Ave
15th Fl
New York, NY 10103
Phone: 212-586-6262; Fax: 212-586-1212
Toll-free: 800-223-6530
www.gotopuertorico.com

Puerto Rico Tourism Co
Paseo La Princesa
PO Box 902-3960
Old San Juan, PR 00902
Phone: 787-721-2400; Fax: 787-722-6238
www.gotopuertorico.com

Puerto Rico Chamber of Commerce
PO Box 9024033
San Juan, PR 00902
Phone: 787-721-6060; Fax: 787-721-6060
camarapr.org

Puerto Rican Chamber of Commerce of South Florida
3550 Biscayne Blvd
Suite 306
Miami, FL 33137
Phone: 305-571-8006; Fax: 305-571-8007
www.puertoricanchamber.com

Qatar

Qatar Consulate General
1990 Post Oak Blvd
Suite 810
Houston, TX 77056
Phone: 713-355-8221; Fax: 713-355-8184

Qatar Embassy
2555 M St NW
Washington, DC 20037
Phone: 202-274-1600; Fax: 202-237-0061
www.qatarembassy.net

Qatar Permanent Mission to the UN
809 UN Plaza
4th Fl
New York, NY 10017
Phone: 212-486-9335; Fax: 212-758-4952

Republic of Korea. *See* South Korea

Romania

Romanian National Tourist Office
355 Lexington Ave
19th Fl
New York, NY 10017
Phone: 212-545-8484
www.romaniatourism.com

Romania Consulate General
11766 Wilshire Blvd
Suite 560
Los Angeles, CA 90025
Phone: 310-444-0043; Fax: 310-445-0043
www.consulateromania.org

Romania Consulate General
200 E 38th St
3rd Fl
New York, NY 10016
Phone: 212-682-9120; Fax: 212-972-8463
www.romconsny.org

Romania Embassy
1607 23rd St NW
Washington, DC 20008
Phone: 202-332-4846; Fax: 202-232-4748
www.roembus.org

Romania Permanent Mission to the UN
573-577 3rd Ave
New York, NY 10016
Phone: 212-682-3274; Fax: 212-682-9746
www.un.int/romania

Russia

Russian National Tourist Office
224 W 30th St
Suite 701
New York, NY 10001
Phone: 646-473-2233; Fax: 646-473-2205
Toll-free: 877-221-7120
www.russia-travel.com

Russian-American Chamber of Commerce
1552 Pennsylvania St
Denver, CO 80203
Phone: 303-831-0829; Fax: 303-831-0830
www.russianamericanchamber.org

American-Russian Chamber of Commerce & Industry
1101 Pennsylvania Ave NW
6th Fl
Washington, DC 20004
Phone: 202-756-4943; Fax: 202-362-4634
www.arcci.org

Russian Federation Consulate General
9 E 91st St
New York, NY 10128
Phone: 212-348-0926; Fax: 212-831-9162

Russian Federation Consulate General
2790 Green St
San Francisco, CA 94123
Phone: 415-928-6878; Fax: 415-929-0306
www.consulrussia.org

Russian Federation Consulate General
2001 6th Ave
Westin Bldg Suite 2323
Seattle, WA 98121
Phone: 206-728-1910; Fax: 206-728-1871
www.netconsul.org

Russian Federation Embassy
2650 Wisconsin Ave NW
Washington, DC 20007
Phone: 202-298-5700; Fax: 202-298-5735
www.russianembassy.org

Russian Federation Permanent Mission to the UN
136 E 67th St
New York, NY 10021
Phone: 212-861-4900; Fax: 212-628-0252
www.un.int/russia

Rwanda

Rwanda Embassy
1714 New Hampshire Ave NW
Washington, DC 20009
Phone: 202-232-2882; Fax: 202-232-4544

Rwanda Permanent Mission to the UN
124 E 39th St
New York, NY 10016
Phone: 212-679-9010; Fax: 212-679-9133

Saint Barthelemy

Saint Barthelemy Tourist Office
444 Madison Ave
16th Fl
New York, NY 10022
Phone: 212-838-7800; Fax: 212-838-7855
us.franceguide.com

Saint Kitts and Nevis

Saint Kitts Tourism Authority
414 E 75th St
Suite 5
New York, NY 10021
Phone: 212-535-1234; Fax: 212-734-6511
Toll-free: 800-582-6208
www.stkitts-tourism.com

Saint Kitts & Nevis Embassy
3216 New Mexico Ave NW
Washington, DC 20016
Phone: 202-686-2636; Fax: 202-686-5740
www.stkittsnevis.org

Saint Kitts & Nevis Permanent Mission to the UN
414 E 75th St

Suite 5
New York, NY 10021
Phone: 212-535-1234; Fax: 212-535-6854
www.stkittsnevis.org/unmission.html

Saint Lucia

Saint Lucia Tourist Board
800 2nd Ave
9th Fl
New York, NY 10017
Phone: 212-867-2950; Fax: 212-867-2795
Toll-free: 800-456-3984
www.stlucia.org

Saint Lucia Consulate General
800 2nd Ave
9th Fl
New York, NY 10017
Phone: 212-697-9360; Fax: 212-697-4993
www.un.int/stlucia/consulate.htm

Saint Lucia Embassy
3216 New Mexico Ave NW
Washington, DC 20016
Phone: 202-364-6792; Fax: 202-364-6723

Saint Lucia Permanent Mission to the UN
800 2nd Ave
9th Fl
New York, NY 10017
Phone: 212-697-9360; Fax: 212-697-4993
www.un.int/stlucia

Saint Martin / Saint Maarten

Saint Maarten Tourist Office
675 3rd Ave
Suite 1807
New York, NY 10017
Phone: 212-953-2084; Fax: 212-953-2145
Toll-free: 800-786-2278
www.st-maarten.com

Saint Martin Tourist Office
675 3rd Ave
Suite 1807
New York, NY 10017
Phone: 212-475-8970; Fax: 212-260-8481
Toll-free: 877-956-1234
www.st-martin.org

Saint Vincent and the Grenadines

Saint Vincent & the Grenadines Tourist Information Office
801 2nd Ave
21st Fl
New York, NY 10017
Phone: 212-687-4981; Fax: 212-949-5946
Toll-free: 800-729-1726
www.svgtourism.com

Saint Vincent & the Grenadines Consulate General
801 2nd Ave

21st Fl
New York, NY 10017
Phone: 212-687-4490; Fax: 212-949-5946

Saint Vincent & the Grenadines Embassy
3216 New Mexico Ave NW
Washington, DC 20016
Phone: 202-364-6730; Fax: 202-364-6736
www.embsvg.com

Saint Vincent & the Grenadines Permanent Mission to the
  UN
800 2nd Ave
4th Fl
New York, NY 10017
Phone: 212-599-0950; Fax: 212-599-1020

Samoa

Samoa Embassy
800 2nd Ave
Suite 400-J
New York, NY 10017
Phone: 212-599-6196; Fax: 212-599-0797

Samoa Permanent Mission to the UN
800 2nd Ave
Suite 400J
New York, NY 10017
Phone: 212-599-6196; Fax: 212-599-0797

San Marino

San Marino Permanent Mission to the UN
327 E 50th St
New York, NY 10022
Phone: 212-751-1234; Fax: 212-751-1436

Sao Tome and Principe

Sao Tome & Principe Permanent Mission to the UN
400 Park Ave
7th Fl
New York, NY 10022
Phone: 212-317-0533; Fax: 212-317-0580

Saudi Arabia

Saudi Arabia Consulate General
5718 Westheimer Rd
Suite 1500
Houston, TX 77057
Phone: 713-785-5577; Fax: 713-785-1163

Saudi Arabia Consulate General
2045 Sawtelle Blvd
Los Angeles, CA 90025
Phone: 310-479-6000; Fax: 310-479-2752

Saudi Arabia Consulate General
866 2nd Ave
5th Fl
New York, NY 10017
Phone: 212-752-2740; Fax: 212-688-2719

Saudi Arabia Embassy
601 New Hampshire Ave NW
Washington, DC 20037
Phone: 202-342-3800; Fax: 202-944-5983
www.saudiembassy.net

Senegal

Senegal Tourist Office
350 5th Ave
Suite 3118
New York, NY 10118
Phone: 212-279-1953; Fax: 212-279-1958
www.senegal-tourism.com

Senegal Embassy
2112 Wyoming Ave NW
Washington, DC 20008
Phone: 202-234-0540; Fax: 202-332-6315
www.senegalembassy-us.org

Senegal Permanent Mission to the UN
238 E 68th St
New York, NY 10021
Phone: 212-517-9030; Fax: 212-517-3032
www.un.int/senegal

Serbia and Montenegro

Serbia & Montenegro Consulate General
201 E Ohio St
Suite 200
Chicago, IL 60611
Phone: 312-670-6707; Fax: 312-670-6787
www.scgchicago.org

Serbia & Montenegro Embassy
2134 Kalorama Rd NW
Washington, DC 20008
Phone: 202-332-0333; Fax: 202-332-3933
www.yuembusa.org

Serbia & Montenegro Permanent Mission to the UN
854 5th Ave
New York, NY 10021
Phone: 212-879-8700; Fax: 212-879-8705
www.un.int/serbia-montenegro

Seychelles

Seychelles Embassy
800 2nd Ave
Suite 400C
New York, NY 10017
Phone: 212-972-1785; Fax: 212-972-1786

Seychelles Permanent Mission to the UN
800 2nd Ave
Suite 400C
New York, NY 10017
Phone: 212-972-1785; Fax: 212-972-1786

Sierra Leone

Sierra Leone Embassy
1701 19th St NW
Washington, DC 20009
Phone: 202-939-9261; Fax: 202-483-1793
www.embassyofsierraleone.org

Sierra Leone Permanent Mission to the UN
245 E 49th St
New York, NY 10017
Phone: 212-688-1656; Fax: 212-688-4924

Singapore

Singapore Tourism Board
5670 Wilshire Blvd
Suite 1550
Los Angeles, CA 90036
Phone: 323-677-0808; Fax: 323-677-0801
Toll-free: 800-283-9595
www.visitsingapore.com

Singapore Tourism Board
1156 Ave of Americas
Suite 702
New York, NY 10036
Phone: 212-302-4861; Fax: 212-302-4801
www.visitsingapore.com

Singapore Consulate
231 E 51st St
New York, NY 10022
Phone: 212-223-3331; Fax: 212-826-5028
www.mfa.gov.sg/newyork-consul

Singapore Consulate General
595 Market St
Suite 2450
San Francisco, CA 94105
Phone: 415-543-4775; Fax: 415-543-4788
www.mfa.gov.sg/sanfrancisco

Singapore Embassy
3501 International Pl NW
Washington, DC 20008
Phone: 202-537-3100; Fax: 202-537-0876
www.mfa.gov.sg/washington

Singapore Permanent Mission to the UN
231 E 51st St
New York, NY 10022
Phone: 212-826-0840; Fax: 212-826-2964
www.mfa.gov.sg/newyork

Slovakia

Slovakia Embassy
3523 International Ct NW
Washington, DC 20008
Phone: 202-237-1054; Fax: 202-237-6438
www.slovakembassy-us.org

Slovakia Permanent Mission to the UN
801 2nd Ave

12th Fl
New York, NY 10017
Phone: 212-286-8418; Fax: 212-286-8419
www.un.int/slovakia

Slovenia

Slovenia Consulate
55 Public Sq
Suite 945
Cleveland, OH 44113
Phone: 216-589-9220; Fax: 216-589-9210

Slovenia Consulate General
600 3rd Ave
21st Fl
New York, NY 10016
Phone: 212-370-3006; Fax: 212-370-3581
www.embassy.org/slovenia/offices.htm

Slovenia Embassy
1525 New Hampshire Ave NW
Washington, DC 20036
Phone: 202-667-5363; Fax: 202-667-4563

Slovenia Permanent Mission to the UN
600 3rd Ave
24th Fl
New York, NY 10016
Phone: 212-370-3007; Fax: 212-370-1824
www.un.int/slovenia

Solomon Islands

Solomon Islands Embassy
800 2nd Ave
Suite 400L
New York, NY 10017
Phone: 212-599-6192; Fax: 212-661-8925

Solomon Islands Permanent Mission to the UN
800 2nd Ave
Suite 400L
New York, NY 10017
Phone: 212-599-6192; Fax: 212-661-8925

Somalia

Somalia Permanent Mission to the UN
425 E 61nd St
Suite 702
New York, NY 10021
Phone: 212-688-9410; Fax: 212-759-0651

South Africa

South African Tourism Board
500 5th Ave
20th Fl Suite 2040
New York, NY 10110
Phone: 212-730-2929; Fax: 212-764-1980
Toll-free: 800-593-1318
www.southafrica.net/index.cfm

South Africa Consulate General
200 S Michigan Ave
Suite 600
Chicago, IL 60604
Phone: 312-939-7929; Fax: 312-939-2588

South Africa Consulate General
6300 Wilshire Blvd
Suite 600
Los Angeles, CA 90048
Phone: 323-651-0902; Fax: 323-651-5969
link2southafrica.com

South Africa Consulate General
333 E 38th St
9th Fl
New York, NY 10016
Phone: 212-213-4880; Fax: 212-213-0102
www.southafrica-newyork.net

South Africa Embassy
3051 Massachusetts Ave NW
Washington, DC 20008
Phone: 202-232-4400; Fax: 202-265-1607
www.saembassy.org

South Africa Permanent Mission to the UN
333 E 38th St
9th Fl
New York, NY 10016
Phone: 212-213-5583; Fax: 212-692-2498
www.southafrica-newyork.net

South Korea (Republic of Korea)

Korea National Tourism Organization
737 N Michigan Ave
Suite 910
Chicago, IL 60611
Phone: 312-981-1717; Fax: 312-981-1721
Toll-free: 800-868-7567
english.tour2korea.com

Korea National Tourism Organization
2 Executive Dr
Suite 750
Fort Lee, NJ 07024
Phone: 201-585-0909; Fax: 201-585-9041
Toll-free: 800-868-7567
english.tour2korea.com

Korea National Tourism Organization
5509 Wilshire Blvd Wilshire Blvd
Suite 103
Los Angeles, CA 90036
Phone: 323-634-0280; Fax: 323-634-0281
Toll-free: 800-868-7567
english.tour2korea.com

Korean Chamber of Commerce
3440 Wilshire Blvd
Suite 520
Los Angeles, CA 90010
Phone: 213-480-1115; Fax: 213-480-7521

Korean Chamber of Commerce & Industry in the USA Inc
460 Park Ave
Suite 410
New York, NY 10022
Phone: 212-644-0140; Fax: 212-644-9106
www.kocham.org

Korea Republic of Consulate General
229 Peachtree St
International Tower Suite 500
Atlanta, GA 30303
Phone: 404-522-1611; Fax: 404-521-3169

Korea Republic of Consulate General
455 N City Front Plaza Dr
NBC Tower Suite 2700
Chicago, IL 60611
Phone: 312-822-9485; Fax: 312-822-9849

Korea Republic of Consulate General
2756 Pali Hwy
Honolulu, HI 96817
Phone: 808-595-6109; Fax: 808-595-3046

Korea Republic of Consulate General
1990 Post Oak Blvd
Suite 1250
Houston, TX 77056
Phone: 713-961-0186; Fax: 713-961-3340
www.koreahouston.org/e

Korea Republic of Consulate General
3243 Wilshire Blvd
Los Angeles, CA 90010
Phone: 213-385-9300; Fax: 213-385-1849
www.koreanconsulatela.org

Korea Republic of Consulate General
335 E 45th St
4th Fl
New York, NY 10017
Phone: 646-674-6000; Fax: 646-674-6023
www.koreanconsulate.org

Korea Republic of Consulate General
1 Gateway Ctr
2nd Fl
Newton, MA 02458
Phone: 617-641-2830; Fax: 617-641-2831
www.kcgboston.org

Korea Republic of Consulate General
3500 Clay St
San Francisco, CA 94118
Phone: 415-921-2251; Fax: 415-921-5946
www.koreanconsulatesf.org

Korea Republic of Consulate General
2033 6th Ave
Suite 1125
Seattle, WA 98121
Phone: 206-441-1011; Fax: 206-441-7912
www.mofat.go.kr

Korea Republic of Consulate General
2320 Massachusetts Ave NW
Washington, DC 20008
Phone: 202-939-5661; Fax: 202-342-1597

Korea Republic of Embassy
2450 Massachusetts Ave NW
Washington, DC 20008
Phone: 202-939-5600; Fax: 202-797-0595
www.koreaembassyusa.org

Korea Republic of Permanent Mission to the UN
335 E 45th St
New York, NY 10017
Phone: 212-439-4000; Fax: 212-986-1083
www.un.int/korea

Spain

Tourist Office of Spain
8383 Wilshire Blvd
Suite 960
Beverly Hills, CA 90211
Phone: 323-658-7188; Fax: 323-658-1061
www.okspain.org

Tourist Office of Spain
845 N Michigan Ave
Suite 915-E
Chicago, IL 60611
Phone: 312-642-1992; Fax: 312-642-9817
www.okspain.org

Tourist Office of Spain
1395 Brickell Ave
Suite 1130
Miami, FL 33131
Phone: 305-358-1992; Fax: 305-358-8223
www.okspain.org

Tourist Office of Spain
666 5th Ave
35th Fl
New York, NY 10103
Phone: 212-265-8822; Fax: 212-265-8864
www.okspain.org

Spain-US Chamber of Commerce
350 5th Ave
Suite 2600
New York, NY 10118
Phone: 212-967-2170; Fax: 212-564-1415
www.spainuscc.org

Spain Consulate General
31 St James Ave
Suite 905
Boston, MA 02116
Phone: 617-536-2506; Fax: 617-536-8512
www.spainconsul-ny.org/boston.html

Spain Consulate General
180 N Michigan Ave
Suite 1500
Chicago, IL 60601
Phone: 312-782-4588; Fax: 312-782-1635
www.consulate-spain-chicago.com

Spain Consulate General
1800 Bering Dr
Suite 660

Houston, TX 77057
Phone: 713-783-6200; Fax: 713-783-6166

Spain Consulate General
5055 Wilshire Blvd
Suite 860
Los Angeles, CA 90036
Phone: 323-938-0158; Fax: 323-938-2502

Spain Consulate General
2655 Le Jeune Rd
Suite 203
Miami, FL 33134
Phone: 305-446-5511; Fax: 305-446-0585
www.conspainmiami.org

Spain Consulate General
2102 World Trade Ctr
2 Canal St
New Orleans, LA 70130
Phone: 504-525-4951; Fax: 504-525-4955

Spain Consulate General
150 E 58th St
30th Fl
New York, NY 10155
Phone: 212-355-4080; Fax: 212-644-3751
www.spainconsul-ny.org

Spain Consulate General
1405 Sutter St
San Francisco, CA 94109
Phone: 415-922-2995; Fax: 415-931-9706

Spain Embassy
2375 Pennsylvania Ave NW
Washington, DC 20037
Phone: 202-452-0100; Fax: 202-833-5670
www.spainemb.org

Spain Permanent Mission to the UN
245 E 47th St
36th Fl
New York, NY 10017
Phone: 212-661-1050; Fax: 212-949-7247
www.spainun.org

Sri Lanka

Sri Lanka Consulate General
3250 Wilshire Blvd
Suite 1405
Los Angeles, CA 90010
Phone: 213-387-0210; Fax: 213-387-0216
www.srilankaconsulatela.com

Sri Lanka Consulate
630 3rd Ave
20th Fl
New York, NY 10017
Phone: 212-986-7040; Fax: 212-986-1838
un.cti.depaul.edu/public/Sri_Lanka/0/

Sri Lanka Embassy
2148 Wyoming Ave NW
Washington, DC 20008

Phone: 202-483-4025; Fax: 202-232-7181
www.slembassyusa.org

Sri Lanka Permanent Mission to the UN
630 3rd Ave
20th Fl
New York, NY 10017
Phone: 212-986-7040; Fax: 212-986-1838

Sudan

Sudan Embassy
2210 Massachusetts Ave NW
Washington, DC 20008
Phone: 202-338-8565; Fax: 202-667-2406
www.sudanembassy.org

Sudan Permanent Mission to the UN
305 E 47th St
4th Fl
New York, NY 10017
Phone: 212-573-6033; Fax: 212-573-6160

Suriname

Suriname Consulate General
6303 Blue Lagoon Dr
Suite 325
Miami, FL 33126
Phone: 305-265-4655; Fax: 305-265-4599
www.scgmia.com

Suriname Embassy
4301 Connecticut Ave NW
Suite 460
Washington, DC 20008
Phone: 202-244-7488; Fax: 202-244-5878
www.surinameembassy.org

Suriname Permanent Mission to the UN
866 UN Plaza
Suite 320
New York, NY 10017
Phone: 212-826-0660; Fax: 212-980-7029
www.un.int/suriname

Swaziland

Swaziland Embassy
1712 New Hampshire Ave NW
Washington, DC 20009
Phone: 202-234-5002; Fax: 202-234-8254

Swaziland Permanent Mission to the UN
408 E 50th St
New York, NY 10022
Phone: 212-371-8910; Fax: 212-754-2755

Sweden

Swedish Travel & Tourism Council
655 3rd Ave
18th Fl
New York, NY 10017

Phone: 212-885-9700; Fax: 212-885-9764
www.visitsweden.com

Swedish-American Chambers of Commerce USA Inc
1403 King St
Alexandria, VA 22314
Phone: 703-836-6560; Fax: 703-836-6561
www.sacc-usa.org

Swedish-American Chamber of Commerce Inc Chicago
    Chapter
150 N Michigan Ave
Suite 2800
Chicago, IL 60601
Phone: 312-863-8592; Fax: 312-624-7701
www.sacc-usa.org/chicago

Swedish-American Chamber of Commerce in Colorado
4525 S Decatour St
Englewood, CO 80110
Phone: 720-338-2381; Fax: 720-889-2606
sacc-usa.org/colorado

Swedish-American Chamber of Commerce of Greater Los
    Angeles Inc
10940 Wilshire Blvd
Suite 700
Los Angeles, CA 90024
Phone: 310-478-8613; Fax: 310-444-0424
www.sacc-gla.org

Swedish-American Chamber of Commerce Inc Minnesota
    Chapter
American Swedish Institute
2600 Park Ave
Minneapolis, MN 55407
Phone: 612-991-3001; Fax: 612-333-3914
www.sacc-minnesota.org

Swedish-American Chamber of Commerce Inc New York
    Chapter
570 Lexington Ave
20th Fl
New York, NY 10022
Phone: 212-838-5530; Fax: 212-755-7953
www.saccny.org

Swedish-American Chamber of Commerce Georgia Inc
4775 Peachtree Industrial Blvd
Bldg 300 Suite 300
Norcross, GA 30092
Phone: 770-670-2480; Fax: 770-670-2500
www.sacc-georgia.org

Swedish-American Chamber of Commerce San
    Diego/Tijuana Chapter
1020 Symphony Towers
750 B St
San Diego, CA 92101
Phone: 619-338-4020; Fax: 619-233-9890
www.sacc-sandiego.org

Swedish-American Chamber of Commerce Inc San Francisco
    Chapter
564 Market St
Suite 305

San Francisco, CA 94104
Phone: 415-781-4188; Fax: 415-781-4189
www.sacc-usa.org/sf

Swedish-American Chamber of Commerce Inc Washington
   DC Chapter
1501 M St NW
9th Fl
Washington, DC 20005
Phone: 202-467-2638; Fax: 202-467-2688
sacc-usa.org

Swedish-American Chamber of Commerce Inc New
   England Chapter
49 Walnut St
Bldg 4
Wellesley, MA 02481
Phone: 781-239-3555; Fax: 781-239-3555
www.sacc-ne.org

Sweden Consulate General
10940 Wilshire Blvd
Suite 700
Los Angeles, CA 90024
Phone: 310-445-4008; Fax: 310-473-2229
www.swedenabroad.se/pages/start____7596.asp

Sweden Consulate General
1 Dag Hammarskjold Plaza
885 2nd Ave 45th Fl
New York, NY 10017
Phone: 212-583-2550; Fax: 212-755-2732
www.swedeninfo.com

Sweden Consulate General
120 Montgomery St
Suite 2175
San Francisco, CA 94104
Phone: 415-788-2631; Fax: 415-788-6841
www.swedenabroad.com/pages/start____8372.asp

Sweden Embassy
2900 K St NW
Washington, DC 20007
Phone: 202-467-2600; Fax: 202-467-2699
www.swedenabroad.com/pages/start____6989.asp

Sweden Permanent Mission to the UN
885 2nd Ave
46th Fl
New York, NY 10017
Phone: 212-583-2500; Fax: 212-832-0389
www.un.int/sweden

Switzerland

Switzerland Tourism
608 5th Ave
Suite 202
New York, NY 10020
Phone: 212-757-5944; Fax: 212-262-6116
Toll-free: 800-794-7795
www.myswitzerland.com

Swiss-American Chamber of Commerce
500 5th Ave

Rm 1800
New York, NY 10110
Phone: 212-246-7789; Fax: 212-246-1366
www.amcham.ch

Switzerland Consulate General
1349 W Peachtree St Suite 1000
2 Mid-Town Plaza
Atlanta, GA 30309
Phone: 404-870-2000; Fax: 404-870-2011
www.eda.admin.ch/washington_emb

Switzerland Consulate General
737 N Michigan Ave
Suite 2301
Chicago, IL 60611
Phone: 312-915-0061; Fax: 312-915-0388
www.eda.admin.ch/washington_emb

Switzerland Consulate General
11766 Wilshire Blvd
Suite 1400
Los Angeles, CA 90025
Phone: 310-575-1145; Fax: 310-575-1982
www.eda.admin.ch/washington_emb

Switzerland Consulate General
633 3rd Ave
30th Fl
New York, NY 10017
Phone: 212-599-5700; Fax: 212-599-4266
www.eda.admin.ch/washington_emb

Switzerland Consulate General
456 Montgomery St
Suite 1500
San Francisco, CA 94104
Phone: 415-788-2272; Fax: 415-788-1402
www.eda.admin.ch/washington_emb

Switzerland Embassy
2900 Cathedral Ave NW
Washington, DC 20008
Phone: 202-745-7900; Fax: 202-387-2564
www.swissemb.org

Switzerland Permanent Mission to the UN
633 3rd Ave
29th Fl
New York, NY 10011
Phone: 212-286-1540; Fax: 212-286-1555
www.eda.admin.ch/newyork_miss/e

Syria

Syrian Arab Republic Embassy
2215 Wyoming Ave NW
Washington, DC 20008
Phone: 202-232-6313; Fax: 202-234-9548
www.syrianembassy.us

Syrian Arab Republic Permanent Mission to the UN
820 2nd Ave
15th Fl
New York, NY 10017
Phone: 212-661-1313; Fax: 212-983-4439

Tahiti

Tahiti Tourism
300 Continental Blvd
Suite 160
El Segundo, CA 90245
Phone: 310-414-8484; Fax: 310-414-8490
www.tahiti-tourisme.com

Taiwan

Taiwan Visitors Assn
3731 Wilshire Blvd
Suite 780
Los Angeles, CA 90010
Phone: 213-389-1158; Fax: 213-389-1094
www.taiwan.net.tw

Taiwan Visitors Assn
405 Lexington Ave
37th Fl
New York, NY 10174
Phone: 212-867-1632; Fax: 212-867-1635
www.taiwan.net.tw

Taiwan Visitors Assn
555 Montgomery St
Suite 505
San Francisco, CA 94111
Phone: 415-989-8677; Fax: 415-989-7242
www.taiwan.net.tw

Tajikistan

Tajikistan Embassy
1005 New Hampshire Ave
Washington, DC 20037
Phone: 202-223-6090; Fax: 202-223-6091
www.tjus.org

Tajikistan Permanent Mission to the UN
136 E 67th St
New York, NY 10021
Phone: 212-744-2196; Fax: 212-472-7645

Tanzania

Tanzania United Republic of Embassy
2139 R St NW
Washington, DC 20008
Phone: 202-939-6125; Fax: 202-797-7408
www.tanzaniaembassy-us.org

Tanzania United Republic of Permanent Mission to the UN
201 E 42nd St
Suite 1700
New York, NY 10017
Phone: 212-972-9160; Fax: 212-682-5232

Thailand

Tourism Authority of Thailand
611 N Larchmont Blvd
1st Fl

Los Angeles, CA 90004
Phone: 323-461-9814; Fax: 323-461-9834
Toll-free: 800-842-4526
www.tourismthailand.org

Tourism Authority of Thailand
61 Broadway
Suite 2810
New York, NY 10006
Phone: 212-432-0433; Fax: 212-269-2588
Toll-free: 800-842-4526
www.tourismthailand.org

Thailand Consulate General
700 N Rush St
Chicago, IL 60611
Phone: 312-664-3129; Fax: 312-664-3230
www.thaichicago.net

Thailand Consulate General
611 N Larchmont Blvd
2nd Fl
Los Angeles, CA 90004
Phone: 323-962-9574; Fax: 323-962-2128
www.thai-la.net

Thailand Consulate General
351 E 52nd St
New York, NY 10022
Phone: 212-754-1770; Fax: 212-754-1907
www.thaiconsulnewyork.com

Thailand Embassy
1024 Wisconsin Ave NW
Suite 401
Washington, DC 20007
Phone: 202-944-3600; Fax: 202-944-3611
www.thaiembdc.org

Thailand Permanent Mission to the UN
351 E 52nd St
New York, NY 10022
Phone: 212-754-2230; Fax: 212-688-3029

Timor-Leste

Timor-Leste Embassy
4201 Massachusetts Ave NW
Suite 504
Washington, DC 20008
Phone: 202-966-3202; Fax: 202-966-3205

Timor-Leste Permanent Mission to the UN
866 UN Plaza
Suite 1201
New York, NY 10017
Phone: 212-759-3675; Fax: 212-759-4196
www.un.int/timor-leste

Togo

Togo Embassy
2208 Massachusetts Ave NW
Washington, DC 20008
Phone: 202-234-4212; Fax: 202-232-3190

Togo Permanent Mission to the UN
112 E 40th St
New York, NY 10016
Phone: 212-490-3455; Fax: 212-983-6684

Tonga

Tonga Embassy
250 E 51st St
New York, NY 10022
Phone: 917-369-1025; Fax: 917-369-1024

Tonga Consulate General
360 Post St
Suite 604
San Francisco, CA 94108
Phone: 415-781-0365; Fax: 415-781-3964

Tonga Permanent Mission to the UN
250 E 51st St
New York, NY 10022
Phone: 917-369-1025; Fax: 917-369-1024

Trinidad and Tobago

Trinidad & Tobago Consulate General
1000 Brickell Ave
Suite 800
Miami, FL 33131
Phone: 305-374-2199; Fax: 305-374-3199

Trinidad & Tobago Consulate General
475 5th Ave
4th Fl
New York, NY 10017
Phone: 212-682-7272; Fax: 212-986-2146

Trinidad & Tobago Embassy
1708 Massachusetts Ave NW
Washington, DC 20036
Phone: 202-467-6490; Fax: 202-785-3130

Trinidad & Tobago Permanent Mission to the UN
820 2nd Ave
5th Fl
New York, NY 10017
Phone: 212-697-7620; Fax: 212-682-3580

Tunisia

Tunisia Embassy
1515 Massachusetts Ave NW
Washington, DC 20005
Phone: 202-862-1850; Fax: 202-862-1858

Tunisia Permanent Mission to the UN
31 Beekman Pl
New York, NY 10022
Phone: 212-751-7503; Fax: 212-751-0569

Turkey

Turkish Tourist Office
5055 Wilshire Blvd

Suite 850
Los Angeles, CA 90036
Phone: 323-937-8066; Fax: 323-937-1271
www.tourismturkey.org

Turkish Tourist Office
821 UN Plaza
1st Fl
New York, NY 10017
Phone: 212-687-2194; Fax: 212-599-7568
Toll-free: 877-367-8875
www.tourismturkey.org

Turkey Consulate General
360 N Michigan Ave
Suite 1405
Chicago, IL 60601
Phone: 312-263-0644; Fax: 312-263-1449
www.turkishembassy.org

Turkey Consulate General
1990 Post Oak Blvd
Suite 1300
Houston, TX 77056
Phone: 713-622-5849; Fax: 713-623-6639
Toll-free: 888-566-7656

Turkey Consulate General
6300 Wilshire Blvd
Suite 2010
Los Angeles, CA 90048
Phone: 323-655-8832
www.turkiye.net/lacg

Turkey Consulate General
821 UN Plaza
5th Fl
New York, NY 10017
Phone: 212-949-0160; Fax: 212-983-1293

Turkey Embassy
2525 Massachusetts Ave NW
Washington, DC 20008
Phone: 202-612-6700; Fax: 202-319-1639
www.turkishembassy.org

Turkey Permanent Mission to the UN
821 UN Plaza
10th Fl
New York, NY 10017
Phone: 212-949-0150; Fax: 212-949-0086
www.un.int/turkey

Turkmenistan

Turkmenistan Embassy
2207 Massachusetts Ave NW
Washington, DC 20008
Phone: 202-588-1500; Fax: 202-588-0697
www.turkmenistanembassy.org

Turkmenistan Permanent Mission to the UN
866 UN Plaza
Suite 424
New York, NY 10017
Phone: 212-486-8908; Fax: 212-486-2521

Turks and Caicos Islands

Turks & Caicos Islands Tourism Office
60 E 42nd St
Suite 2817
New York, NY 10165
Phone: 646-375-8830; Fax: 646-375-8835
Toll-free: 800-241-0824
www.turksandcaicostourism.com

Turks & Caicos Islands Tourism Office
60 E 42nd St
Suite 2817
New York, NY 10165
Phone: 646-375-8830; Fax: 646-375-8835
Toll-free: 800-241-0824
www.turksandcaicostourism.com

Tuvalu

Tuvalu Permanent Mission to the UN
800 2nd Ave
Suite 400-D
New York, NY 10017
Phone: 212-490-0534; Fax: 212-808-4975

Uganda

Uganda Embassy
5911 16th St NW
Washington, DC 20011
Phone: 202-726-7100; Fax: 202-726-1727
www.ugandaembassy.com

Uganda Permanent Mission to the UN
336 E 45th St
New York, NY 10017
Phone: 212-949-0110; Fax: 212-687-4517

Ukraine

Ukraine Consulate General
10 E Huron St
Chicago, IL 60611
Phone: 312-642-4388; Fax: 312-642-4385
www.ukrchicago.com

Ukraine Embassy
3350 M St NW
Washington, DC 20007
Phone: 202-333-0606; Fax: 202-333-0817
Toll-free: 800-779-8347
www.ukremb.com

Ukraine Permanent Mission to the UN
220 E 51st St
New York, NY 10022
Phone: 212-759-7003; Fax: 212-355-9455
www.un.int/ukraine

United Arab Emirates

United Arab Emirates Embassy
3522 International Ct NW

Washington, DC 20008
Phone: 202-243-2400; Fax: 202-243-2432
www.uae-embassy.org

United Arab Emirates Permanent Mission to the UN
305 E 47th St
7th Fl
New York, NY 10017
Phone: 212-371-0480; Fax: 212-371-4923

United Kingdom

VisitBritain
551 5th Ave
Suite 701
New York, NY 10176
Phone: 212-986-2266; Fax: 212-986-1188
Toll-free: 800-462-2748
www.visitbritain.com

British-American Chamber of Commerce Great Lakes
  Region
1120 Chester Ave
Suite 470
Cleveland, OH 44114
Phone: 216-621-0222; Fax: 216-696-2582
www.baccgl.org

British-American Business Council of Los Angeles
11766 Wilshire Blvd
Suite 1230
Los Angeles, CA 90025
Phone: 310-312-1962; Fax: 310-312-1914
www.babcla.org

British-American Chamber of Commerce of Miami
200 S Biscayne Blvd
Suite 4143
Miami, FL 33131
Phone: 305-377-0992; Fax: 305-448-7605

British-American Business Council
52 Vanderbilt Ave
20th Fl
New York, NY 10017
Phone: 212-661-4060; Fax: 212-661-4074
www.babc.org

British-American Chamber of Commerce of San Francisco
235 Montogmery St
Suite 907
San Francisco, CA 94104
Phone: 415-296-8645; Fax: 415-296-9649
www.baccsf.org

United Kingdom of Great Britain & Northern Ireland
  Consulate General
Georgia Pacific Ctr 133 Peachtree St NE
Suite 3400
Atlanta, GA 30303
Phone: 404-954-7700; Fax: 404-954-7702
www.britainusa.com/atlanta

United Kingdom of Great Britain & Northern Ireland
  Consulate General
1 Memorial Dr

Suite 1500
Cambridge, MA 02142
Phone: 617-245-4500; Fax: 617-621-0220
www.britainusa.com/boston

United Kingdom of Great Britain & Northern Ireland
 Consulate General
400 N Michigan Ave
Suite 1300
Chicago, IL 60611
Phone: 312-970-3800; Fax: 312-970-3854
www.britainusa.com/chicago

United Kingdom of Great Britain & Northern Ireland
 Consulate
World Trade Ctr 1675 Broadway
Suite 1030
Denver, CO 80202
Phone: 303-592-5200; Fax: 303-592-5209
www.britainusa.com/denver

United Kingdom of Great Britain & Northern Ireland
 Consulate General
1000 Louisiana St
Suite 1900
Houston, TX 77002
Phone: 713-659-6270; Fax: 713-659-7094
www.britainusa.com/houston

United Kingdom of Great Britain & Northern Ireland
 Consulate General
11766 Wilshire Blvd
Suite 1200
Los Angeles, CA 90025
Phone: 310-481-0031; Fax: 310-481-2960
www.britainusa.com/la

United Kingdom of Great Britain & Northern Ireland
 Consulate
1001 Brickell Bay Dr
Suite 2800
Miami, FL 33131
Phone: 305-374-1522; Fax: 305-374-8196
www.britainusa.com/miami

United Kingdom of Great Britain & Northern Ireland
 Consulate General
845 3rd Ave
New York, NY 10022
Phone: 212-745-0200; Fax: 212-754-3062
www.britainusa.com/ny

United Kingdom of Great Britain & Northern Ireland Vice
 Consulate
200 S Orange Ave
Sun Trust Ctr Suite 2110
Orlando, FL 32801
Phone: 407-581-1540; Fax: 407-254-3333
www.britainusa.com/orlando

United Kingdom of Great Britain & Northern Ireland
 Consulate General
1 Sansome St
Suite 850
San Francisco, CA 94104
Phone: 415-617-1300; Fax: 415-434-2018
www.britainusa.com/sf

United Kingdom of Great Britain & Northern Ireland
 Consulate
900 4th Ave
Suite 3001
Seattle, WA 98164
Phone: 206-622-9255; Fax: 206-622-4728
www.britainusa.com/seattle

United Kingdom of Great Britain & Northern Ireland
 Embassy
3100 Massachusetts Ave NW
Washington, DC 20008
Phone: 202-588-6500; Fax: 202-588-7870
www.britainusa.com/embassy

United Kingdom of Great Britain & Northern Ireland
 Permanent Mission to the UN
885 2nd Ave
28th Fl
New York, NY 10017
Phone: 212-745-9200; Fax: 212-745-9316
www.ukun.org

Uruguay

Uruguay Consulate General
1077 Ponce De Leon Blvd
Coral Gables, FL 33134
Phone: 305-443-9764; Fax: 305-443-7802

Uruguay Consulate General
420 Madison Ave
6th Fl
New York, NY 10017
Phone: 212-753-8581; Fax: 212-753-1603
www.conuruyork.org

Uruguay Consulate General
429 Santa Monica Blvd
Suite 400
Santa Monica, CA 90401
Phone: 310-394-5777; Fax: 310-394-5140

Uruguay Embassy
1913 'I' St NW
Washington, DC 20006
Phone: 202-331-1313; Fax: 202-331-8142
www.uruwashi.org

Uruguay Permanent Mission to the UN
866 UN Plaza
Suite 322
New York, NY 10017
Phone: 212-752-8240; Fax: 212-593-0935
www.un.int/uruguay

US Virgin Islands

US Virgin Islands Dept of Tourism
245 Peachtree Center Ave
Suite MB-05
Atlanta, GA 30303
Phone: 404-688-0906; Fax: 404-525-1102
www.usvitourism.vi

US Virgin Islands Dept of Tourism
500 N Michigan Ave
Suite 2030
Chicago, IL 60611
Phone: 888-656-8784; Fax: 312-670-8788
www.usvitourism.vi

US Virgin Islands Dept of Tourism
2655 S LeJeune Rd
Suite 907
Coral Gables, FL 33134
Phone: 305-442-7200; Fax: 305-445-9044
Toll-free: 800-372-8784
www.usvitourism.vi

US Virgin Islands Dept of Tourism
3460 Wilshire Blvd
Suite 412
Los Angeles, CA 90010
Phone: 213-739-0138; Fax: 213-739-2005
www.usvitourism.vi

US Virgin Islands Dept of Tourism
1270 Ave of the Americas
Suite 2108
New York, NY 10020
Phone: 212-332-2222; Fax: 212-332-2223
www.usvitourism.vi

US Virgin Islands Dept of Tourism
PO Box 6400
Saint Thomas, VI 00804
Phone: 340-774-8784; Fax: 340-774-4390
Toll-free: 800-372-8784
www.usvitourism.vi

US Virgin Islands Dept of Tourism
444 N Capitol St NW
Suite 305
Washington, DC 20001
Phone: 202-624-3590; Fax: 202-624-3594
Toll-free: 800-372-8784
www.usvitourism.vi

Uzbekistan

American-Uzbekistan Chamber of Commerce
1717 N St NW
Washington, DC 20036
Phone: 202-828-4111
www.aucconline.com

Uzbekistan Consulate General
801 2nd Ave
20th Fl
New York, NY 10017
Phone: 212-754-7403
www.uzbekconsulny.org

Uzbekistan Embassy
1746 Massachusetts Ave NW
Washington, DC 20036
Phone: 202-887-5300; Fax: 202-293-6804
www.uzbekistan.org

Uzbekistan Permanent Mission to the UN
801 2nd Ave
20th Fl
New York, NY 10017
Phone: 212-486-4242; Fax: 212-486-7998

Vanuatu

Vanuatu Permanent Mission to the UN
800 E 2nd Ave
New York, NY 10004
Phone: 212-920-5700

Vatican City. *See* Holy See

Venezuela

Venezuelan-American Chamber of Commerce of the US
2332 Galiano St
2nd Fl
Coral Gables, FL 33134
Phone: 305-728-7042; Fax: 305-728-7043
venezuelanchamber.org

Venezuela Consulate General
545 Boylston St
3rd Fl
Boston, MA 02116
Phone: 617-266-9368; Fax: 617-266-2350

Venezuela Consulate General
20 N Wacker Dr
Suite 1925
Chicago, IL 60606
Phone: 312-236-9655; Fax: 312-580-1010

Venezuela Consulate General
2925 Briarpark Dr
Suite 900
Houston, TX 77042
Phone: 713-974-0028; Fax: 713-974-1413
www.consulvenhou.org

Venezuela Consulate General
1101 Brickell Ave
Suite 901
Miami, FL 33131
Phone: 305-577-4214; Fax: 305-372-5167

Venezuela Consulate General
World Trade Ctr
2 Canal St Suite 2300
New Orleans, LA 70130
Phone: 504-522-3284; Fax: 504-522-7092
www.neworleans.embavenez-us.org

Venezuela Consulate General
7 E 51st St
New York, NY 10022
Phone: 212-826-1660; Fax: 212-644-7471
consulado-ny.gov.ve

Venezuela Consulate General
311 California St

Suite 620
San Francisco, CA 94104
Phone: 415-955-1982; Fax: 415-955-1970

Venezuela Embassy
1099 30th St NW
Washington, DC 20007
Phone: 202-342-2214; Fax: 202-342-6820
www.embavenez-us.org

Venezuela Permanent Mission to the UN
335 E 46th St
New York, NY 10017
Phone: 212-557-2055; Fax: 212-557-3528
www.un.int/venezuela

Vietnam

Vietnamese-American Chamber of Commerce of Hawaii
PO Box 2011
Honolulu, HI 96805
Phone: 808-545-1889; Fax: 808-734-2315
www.vacch.org

Vietnam Consulate General
1700 California St
Suite 430
San Francisco, CA 94109
Phone: 415-922-1707; Fax: 415-922-1848
www.vietnamconsulate-sf.org

Vietnam Embassy
1233 20th St NW
Suite 400
Washington, DC 20036
Phone: 202-861-0737; Fax: 202-861-0917
www.vietnamembassy.us

Vietnam Permanent Mission to the UN
866 UN Plaza
Suite 435
New York, NY 10017
Phone: 212-644-0594; Fax: 212-644-5732
www.un.int/vietnam

Yemen

Yemen Embassy
2319 Wyoming Ave NW
Washington, DC 20008
Phone: 202-965-4760; Fax: 202-337-2017
www.yemenembassy.org

Yemen Permanent Mission to the UN
413 E 51st St
New York, NY 10022
Phone: 212-355-1730; Fax: 212-750-9613

Zambia

Zambia Embassy
2419 Massachusetts Ave NW
Washington, DC 20008
Phone: 202-265-9717; Fax: 202-332-0826
www.zambiaembassy.org

Zambia Permanent Mission to the UN
237 E 52nd St
New York, NY 10022
Phone: 212-888-5770; Fax: 212-888-5213
www.un.int/zambia

Zimbabwe

Zimbabwe Embassy
1608 New Hampshire Ave NW
Washington, DC 20009
Phone: 202-332-7100; Fax: 202-483-9326
www.zimbabwe-embassy.us

Zimbabwe Permanent Mission to the UN
128 E 56th St
New York, NY 10022
Phone: 212-980-9511; Fax: 212-308-6705

APPENDIX 13

Bibliography

This annotated bibliography contains sources cited or consulted in **HFCWD**, as well as other sources for further reading. Sources marked with the diamond symbol (♦) are cited in the entries in the main text. Sources cited in the bibliography are organized under the following categories:

I. Reference and Other Background Works on Holidays

   A. General Works
   B. Calendars and Time-Reckoning Systems
   C. Festival Organization
   D. Philosophy, Theory, and Analysis of Festivity
   E. Teaching Aids

II. Holidays of Major Religious Traditions

   A. General Works
   B. African
   C. Baha'i
   D. Buddhism
   E. Christianity
   F. Hinduism
   G. Islam
   H. Judaism
   I. Sikhism
   J. Taoism
   K. Zoroastrianism

III. Holidays of Ethnic Groups and Geographic Regions

   A. General Works
   B. Africa
   C. Ancient World (Western)
   D. Asia and the Middle East
      1. General Works
      2. Bangladesh
      3. China and Honk Kong
      4. India and Sri Lanka
      5. Indonesia
      6. Iran
      7. Japan
      8. Korea
      9. Lebanon
      10. Mongolia
      11. Nepal
      12. Philippines
      13. Saudi Arabia
      14. Thailand
      15. Turkey
      16. Vietnam
   E. Caribbean and Latin America
      1. General Works
      2. Cuba
      3. Dominican Republic
      4. El Salvador
      5. Haiti
      6. Jamaica
      7. Mexico
      8. Trinidad
   F. South America
   G. Europe
      1. General Works
      2. Albania
      3. Bulgaria
      4. Czechoslovakia
      5. France
      6. Germany
      7. Greece
      8. Hungary
      9. Italy
      10. Macedonia
      11. Russia
      12. Scandinavia
      13. Soviet Union (former)
      14. Spain
      15. Ukraine
      16. United Kingdom
   H. North America
      1. General Works
      2. Canada
      3. Native North America
      4. United States—General Works and Background on Holidays
      5. United States—Works on the Presidents
      6. United States—Works on the States

IV. Individual Holidays

   A. Christmas
   B. Easter
   C. Fourth of July
   D. Halloween
   E. Mardi Gras
   F. Memorial Day
   G. Mother Day
   H. New Year

♦ Indicates a book cited in the main text

I. REFERENCE AND OTHER BACK-GROUND WORKS ON HOLIDAYS

A. General Works

♦ Augur, Helen. *The Book of Fairs*. Introduction by Hendrik Willem Van Loon. Illustrated by James MacDonald. 1939. Reprint. Detroit: Omnigraphics, Inc., 1992.

> Traces the development of trade, customs, and social life in connection with fairs in history up to the 1939 World's Fair. Includes discussion of fairs and festivals in ancient Tyre, Athens and Rome, the Kinsai Fairs in 13th-century Cathay, festivals in 13th-century France, 15th-century Belgium and Germany, medieval England, Ireland and Scotland, Russia, and the modern expositions. [Cited in the text as *BkFairs-1939*]

♦ Blackburn, Bonnie, and Leofranc Holford-Strevens. *The Oxford Companion to the Year: An Exploration of Calendar Customs and Time-Reckoning*. New York: Oxford University Press, 1999.

> This day-by-day guide presents idiosyncratic inclusion of mostly English holidays. It claims Chambers's *Book of Days* (see below) as its predecessor and includes much the same kind of material. Part I is arranged by month. Each month opens with a brief history of the month's name, concentrating on ancient Rome and ancient Britain, followed with a brief list of some important holidays around the world. Part I also includes essays on the seasons; Oxford, Cambridge, and law terms; the months; the week; days; the Western Church year and its feasts; the Orthodox Church year and its feasts; and other holidays. Part II provides essays on days and times, calendar systems, and dating. [Cited in the text as *OxYear-1999*]

♦ Chambers, Robert, ed. *The Book of Days: A Miscellany of Popular Antiquities in connection with the Calendar, including Anecdote, Biography, & History, Curiosities of Literature, and Oddities of Human Life and Character*. New introduction by Tristram Potter Coffin. 1862-64. Reprint. Detroit: Omnigraphics, Inc., 1990.

> British tome organized chronologically and covering popular Christian festivals and saints' days; seasonal phenomena; folklore of the British Isles, especially that connected with the passing of time and seasons of the year; "Notable Events, Biographies, and Anecdotes connected with the Days of the Year"; "Articles of Popular Archaeology, of an entertaining character, tending to illustrate the progress of Civilization, Manners, Literature, and Ideas in these kingdoms"; and other miscellaneous items. [Cited in the text as *BkDays-1864*]

♦ Cirlot, J. E. *A Dictionary of Symbols*. 2nd ed. Translated by Jack Sage. Foreword by Herbert Read. New York: Philosophical Library, 1971.

> Hundreds of entries on symbols and their significance. Symbols include animals, objects, natural phenomena, places, and mythological and other characters. [Cited in the text as *Dict-Symb-1971*]

♦ Clynes, Tom. *Wild Planet: 1,001 Extraordinary Events for the Inspired Traveler*. Detroit: Gale Research Inc., 1995.

> Light-hearted look at 1,001 festivals around the world, arranged by geographical region. Entries also provide brief notes on transport, accommodations, and other local festivals, as well as contact information. Festival theme index, chronological index, and festival name index. [Cited in the text as *Wild-Planet-1995*]

♦ Corwin, Judith Hoffman. *Harvest Festivals around the World*. Illustrated by the author. Parsippany, NJ: Silver Burdett Press, 1995.

> Introduction to selected harvest festivals in Barbados, Switzerland, England, Nigeria, Ghana, Israel, Japan, China, India, ancient Egypt, Canada, and among Incans and the Hopi Indians for young readers. Includes craft activities and recipes. [Cited in the text as *HarvFestWrld-1995*]

Deems, Edward M., comp. *Holy-Days and Holidays*. 1902. Reprint. Detroit: Gale Research Company, 1968.

> Divided into two major sections—religious and secular holidays—both arranged chronologically. Covers events observed in the United States, Canada, and United Kingdom. For each holiday, the compiler presents an introductory essay, a selection of prose essays, sermons and speeches, an alphabetical list of "suggestive thoughts," and poetry pertaining to the occasion.

♦ Dobler, Lavinia. *Customs and Holidays around the World*. Illustrated and designed by Josephine Little. New York: Fleet Publishing Corporation, 1962.

> Written for children under the supervision of the Rev. Howard V. Harper, this volume describes secular and religious holidays and festivals around the world by season. [Cited in the text as *CustHolWrld-1962*]

♦ Dobler, Lavinia. *National Holidays around the World*. Illustrated and designed by Vivian Browne. New York: Fleet Press Corporation, 1968. 233 pp.

> Covers national and independence days from more than 130 countries. Written for a young audience. Entries are chronologically arranged and provide brief recounting of historical and political circumstances leading up to the observance of the day and a description of the nation's flag. [Cited in the text as *Natl-HolWrld-1968*]

Dossey, Donald E. *Holiday Folklore, Phobias and Fun: Mythical Origins, Scientific Treatments and Superstitious "Cures."* Los Angeles: Outcomes Unlimited Press, Inc., 1992.

> An expert on phobias and anxiety and stress disorders conducts informal survey of origins of various holiday customs—New Year's, St. Valentine's Day, St. Patrick's Day, Friday the 13th, Easter, April Fools' Day, Halloween, Thanksgiving, Christmas—while offering advice on dealing with holiday stress and anxiety. Appendices include some folklore recipes, tips for cognitive refocusing and keying, and list of phobias and symptoms.

♦ Dunkling, Leslie. *Dictionary of Days*. New York: Facts on File, 1988.

> Alphabetical listing of more than 700 named days: local days, fictional days (such as The Day of the Jackal and Lewis Carroll's "unbirthday"), expressions (such as "hey-day" and "turkey day"), generic (e.g., Friday) and technical terms (e.g., sidereal day) as well as names of holidays and other observed events. Much cross-referencing. Emphasis is on providing general-interest etymological information on the name itself in addition to giving basic definition of the day's significance. Often gives Scottish and northern English dialectical forms. Many entries include relevant literary quotations. A special feature is a calendar that chronologically maps the days discussed. [Cited in the text as *DictDays-1988*]

Frazer, James George. *The Golden Bough: A Study in Magic and Religion*. One volume, abridged ed. New York: Collier Books, 1950.

> Numerous festivals are discussed in this classic work on legends, mythology, and religions throughout the world, abridged in one volume.

♦ Indicates a book cited in the main text

♦ Griffin, Robert H., and Ann H. Shurgin, eds. *The Folklore of World Holidays*. 2nd ed. Detroit: Gale Research Inc., 1999.

Chronologically arranged collection of customs, legends, songs, food, superstitions, games, pageants, etc., associated with more than 340 festivals and holidays in over 150 countries. The United States and, for the most part, Canada, are not included. The editor provides a brief explanation of the holiday, followed by excerpts from written material describing actual observances of the event. Bibliographic information for each source follow the excerpts. [Cited in the text as *FolkWrldHol-1999*]

♦ Heinberg, Richard. *Celebrate the Solstice: Honoring the Earth's Seasonal Rhythms Through Festival and Ceremony*. Foreword by Dolores LaChapelle. Wheaton, IL: Quest Books, The Theosophical Publishing House, 1993.

Discusses the celebration of winter and summer solstices and world renewal rites and myths throughout history around the world. Suggests activities for contemporary observance. [Cited in the text as *CelebSols-1993*]

Helfman, Elizabeth S. *Celebrating Nature: Rites and Ceremonies Around the World*. Illustrated by Carolyn Cather. New York: The Seabury Press, 1969.

Describes for young readers celebrations associated with the seasons from ancient times among Egyptians, Hebrews, Babylonians, Greeks, Romans, Ashanti, Yoruba, Ga and Kikuyu peoples in Africa, New Guinea peoples, Thai people, Chinese, Japanese, Hindus, Saora people, Muslims, Incans, Mapuche Indians, Aztecs, and North American Indians, as well as observance of Christian holidays throughout the world. Pronunciation guide. Further reading list. [Cited in the text as *CelebNature-1969*]

♦ Henderson, Helene, ed. *Holiday Symbols and Customs: A Guide to the Legend and Lore behind the Traditions, Rituals, Foods, Games, Animals, and Other Symbols and Activities Associated with Holidays and Holy Days, Feasts and Fasts, and Other Celebrations Covering Calendar, Religious, Historic, Folkloric, National, Promotional, Sporting and Ancient Events, as Observed in the United States and Around the World*. 4th ed. Detroit: Omnigraphics, 2009.

Provides an introduction to the many ways in which people celebrate and find meaning in their holiday traditions. This revised and expanded edition includes over 300 entries that cover such diverse topics as the Academy Awards, Cinco de Mayo, the Hiroshima Peace Ceremony, the Rose Bowl, and Watch Night. Each entry explains the type of holiday, when and where it is observed, and the related symbols and customs. Additional sections include information on tourism organizations for all U.S. states and for nations around the world; contact information for relevant organizations; explanations of secular and religious calendars; and a bibliography and index. [Cited in the text as *HolSymbols-2009*]

Hone, William. *The Every-Day Book; or, Everlasting Calendar of Popular Amusements, Sports, Pastimes, Ceremonies, Manners, Customs, and Events, Incident to Each of the Three Hundred and Sixty-Five Days, in Past and Present Times; Forming a Complete History of the Year, Months, & Seasons, and a Perpetual Key to the Almanack; Including Accounts of the Weather, Rules for Health and Conduct, Remarkable and Important Anecdotes, Facts, and Notices, in Chronology, Antiquities, Topography, Biography, Natural History, Art, Science, and General Literature; Derived from the Most Authentic Sources, and Valuable Original Communications, with Poetical Elucidations, for Daily Use and Diversion*. Introduction by Leslie Shepard. 2 vols. 1827. Reprint. Detroit: Omnigraphics, Inc., 1990.

Each volume presents a different collection of miscellany on holy days, festivals, and anniversaries from January 1 through December 31. Indexes of general subjects, Christian saints, poetry, flowers and plants, and engravings are found in both volumes. Bibliography of works by William Hone.

♦ Humphrey, Grace. *Stories of the World's Holidays*. 1924. Reprint. Detroit: Omnigraphics, Inc., 1990.

Twenty stories for young readers describing the origins of commemorated historical events in the United States, England, France, Italy, China, Japan, Poland, Ireland, Czechoslovakia, and South America, arranged in chronological order. Suggested reading list. [Cited in the text as *StoryWrldHol-1924*]

♦ Ickis, Marguerite. *The Book of Festivals and Holidays the World Over*. Drawings by Richard E. Howard. New York: Dodd, Mead & Co., 1970.

A selection of "holidays and festivals that are current and give promise of continuing indefinitely," 12 chapters in chronological order cover customs and legends associated with New Year's, Epiphany, Lent, Holy Week, Easter, Advent, and Christmas, as well as more than 80 winter, spring, summer, and fall festivals in nearly 50 countries. [Cited in the text as *BkFestHol-Wrld-1970*]

♦ Ingpen, Robert, and Philip Wilkinson. *A Celebration of Customs & Rituals of the World*. New York: Facts on File, 1996.

The first part of the book discusses calendar customs around the world in chronological order by month. Subsequent sections describe life-cycle ceremonies, agricultural customs, social and worship rituals, and art. [Cited in the text as *CelebCust-RitWrld-1996*]

♦ James, E. O. *Seasonal Feasts and Festivals*. 1961. Reprint. Detroit: Omnigraphics, Inc., 1993.

Covers more than 100 season-based rituals, dances, plays, and festivals of the Paleolithic era, vegetation cults, Egypt, Mesopotamia, Palestine, Hebrew, Asia Minor and Greece, Rome, Christianity, and medieval to 18th-century Europe. Examines Egyptian, Babylonian, Greek, Roman, Julian, and Christian calendars. [Cited in the text as *SeasFeast-1961*]

♦ Kindersley, Barnabas, and Annabel Kindersley. *Celebrations! Festivals, Carnivals, and Feast Days from around the World (Children Just Like Me)*. New York: DK Publishing, 1997.

This husband (photographer) and wife (author) traveled around the world collecting photos and stories from children about festivals. Published in association with the United Nations Children's Fund (UNICEF). For young readers. [Cited in the text as *CelebFestCarnFeast-1997*]

♦ Leach, Maria, ed. *Funk & Wagnalls Standard Dictionary of Folklore, Mythology & Legend*. New York: Harper & Row, 1984.

This first one-volume edition contains "a representative sampling," contributions from 34 anthropologists and folklorists of more than 4,500 entries on animals, minerals, vegetables and objects, rituals, festivals and practices, songs, legends and games, and gods, monsters and other entities associated with the folklore and mythology of over 2,000 cultures, peoples, and countries and other geographical regions in the world. More than 50 longer essays surveying the folklore of various cultures and folkloric methodologies, themes and elements conclude with bibliographies. In addition, sources are occasionally inserted throughout in individual entries. [Cited in the text as *Dict-FolkMyth-1984*]

Long, Kim. *The Almanac of Anniversaries*. Santa Barbara: ABC-CLIO, 1992.

♦ Indicates a book cited in the main text

Timeline-like structure provides 25th, 50th, ... 500th anniversaries relating to notable events and people that will take place between 1993 and 2001. Within each year, anniversaries are given chronologically. Calendar Locator chart provides cross-reference of years and milestones.

♦ McFarland, Jeanne. *Festivals*. Morristown, NJ: Silver Burdett Company, 1981.

Brief discussion of some major ancient and modern festivals and holidays throughout the world for younger readers. [Cited in the text as *Festivals-1981*]

♦ Merin, Jennifer, with Elizabeth B. Burdick. *International Directory of Theatre, Dance, and Folklore Festivals*. Westport, CT: Greenwood Press, 1979.

More than 850 festivals involving theater, dance or folklore in over 50 countries are covered. The United States is not included. Entries are organized by country and often contain mailing addresses, phone numbers, contact names, and dates of occurrence. Length of festival description varies from a few lines to a few paragraphs. Festival entries are followed by a country-by-country chronological listing of festivals, bibliography, an appendix listing the number of festivals in each country, and index of festivals by festival name. [Cited in the text as *IntlTh-Folk-1979*]

Nickerson, Betty. *Celebrate the Sun: A Heritage of Festivals Interpreted through the Art of Children from Many Lands*. New York: J. B. Lippincott Company, 1969.

Covers more than 30 holidays worldwide, as well as provides descriptions of such events as spring festivals, weddings, parades, processions, fairs, circuses, and side shows—all accompanied by over 40 paintings by children around the world.

♦ Shemanski, Frances. *A Guide to World Fairs and Festivals*. Westport, CT: Greenwood Press, 1985.

Following the format of *A Guide to Fairs and Festivals in the United States* by the same author, this volume includes entries on more than 280 fairs and festivals held in 75 countries. A country-by-country chronological listing of festivals follows the main text. Appendix lists festivals by type. [Cited in the text as *GdWrldFest-1985*]

♦ Spicer, Dorothy Gladys. *Book of Festivals*. Foreword by John H. Finley. 1937. Reprint. Detroit: Omnigraphics, Inc., 1990.

The main part of the book is broken down into 35 chapters, each covering an ethnic or major religious (Hindu, Jew, and Muslim or Mohammedan) group or nationality. Groups were chosen on the basis of their representation in the United States. Geographic areas covered include Asia, eastern and western Europe, India, the Middle East, and the United States. Within each chapter, holidays and festivals are listed and described in chronological order. Part II of the book is devoted to discussions of the Armenian, Chinese, Gregorian, Hindu, Jewish, Julian, and Mohammedan calendars. Topics include rate of variation between the Julian and Gregorian calendars, dates of Easter computed between 1938 and 1950, and dates of major Jewish holidays computed between 1936 and 1951. The appendix is a glossary of religious and festival terms. The bibliography, with notes, organizes sources by ethnic group or nationality. [Cited in the text as *BkFest-1937*]

Spielgelman, Judith. *UNICEF's Festival Book*. Illustrated by Audrey Preissler. New York: U.S. Committee for UNICEF, 1966.

For young readers. Presents New Year (Enkutatash) in Ethiopia, Divali in India, Now-ruz (Nawruz) in Iran, Hanukkah in Israel, Doll Festival (Hina Matsuri) in Japan, Posadas in Mexico, Sin-terklaas (St. Nicholas's Day) in the Netherlands, end of Ramadan ('Id al-Fitr) in Pakistan, Easter in Poland, Lucia Day (St. Lucy's Day) in Sweden, Songkran in Thailand, and Halloween in Canada and the United States.

♦ Stoll, Dennis Gray. *Music Festivals of the World: A Guide to Leading Festivals of Music, Opera and Ballet*. London: Pergamon Press, Ltd., 1963.

Describes more than 50 music festivals in over 20 countries that run for at least eight days, feature performers known around the world, and show signs of continuing indefinitely. Book is organized into thematic chapters containing essays discussing each event's special features and background and addresses for obtaining tickets. Index of festivals. [Cited in the text as *MusFestWrld-1963*]

♦ Trawicky, Bernard. *Anniversaries and Holidays*. 5th ed. Chicago: American Library Association, 2000.

Organized chronologically, this book offers more than 3,000 short entries on religious and civic holidays and anniversaries marking notable people and events. The first and longest part of the book covers fixed days according to the Gregorian calendar. Months begin with an introductory note covering how the month was named, notable historical events or festivals occurring in the month, and flowers and birthstones associated with it. Entries are grouped together under each date by "Holy Days and Feast Days," "Holidays and Civic Days," and "Anniversaries and Special Events Days." Movable days are listed in the second part of the book and are organized by the Christian, Jewish, Islamic, and Chinese calendars. The annotated bibliography describes more than 400 books and web sites related to primarily U.S. holidays and anniversaries and is broken down by subject. [Cited in the text as *AnnivHol-2000*]

♦ Van Straalen, Alice. *Book of Holidays around the World*. New York: E. P. Dutton, 1986.

Brief datebook-style entries provide at least one observance or anniversary for each day of the year. Photographs and reproductions of literary illustrations and artwork punctuate nearly every page. Appendices offer brief descriptions of Buddhist, Chinese, Christian, Hindu, Islamic, and Jewish calendars, followed by alphabetical listing of movable festivals and holidays. [Cited in the text as *BkHolWrld-1986*]

Walsh, William S. *Curiosities of Popular Customs and of Rites, Ceremonies, Observances, and Miscellaneous Antiquities*. 1914. Reprint. Detroit: Gale Research Company, 1966.

Dictionary-style coverage of Christian, Jewish, Islamic, Buddhist, Japanese, Chinese, Hindu, ancient, and secular holidays and feasts including entries on people, places, customs, and relics associated with them. Also contains entries on birthdays, the months, and various calendars.

Webster, Hutton. *Rest Days; The Christian Sunday, the Jewish Sabbath, and Their Historical and Anthropological Prototypes*. 1916. Reprint. Detroit: Omnigraphics, Inc., 1992.

The standard work on the origin of holy days and their religious and sociological development. Among topics covered are the tabooed days at critical epochs, the holy days, lunar superstitions and festivals, lunar calendars and the week, market days, unlucky days, the Babylonian "evil days," and the Shabattum.

B. Calendars and Time-Reckoning Systems

Achelis, Elisabeth. *The Calendar for Everybody*. 1943. Reprint. Detroit: Omnigraphics, Inc., 1990.

Traces the calendar from its beginning, relating little-known facts about our present calendar and proposes a new calendar

♦ Indicates a book cited in the main text

system and presents advantages to be gained by using it. Discusses the earth's time, the Egyptian, Julian, Gregorian, and world calendars.

Asimov, Isaac. *The Clock We Live On*. Revised ed. Illustrated by John Bradford. New York: Abelard-Schuman, 1965.

The scientist-science fiction writer explains the solar and lunar systems by which humans have learned to tell time. Surveys devices for keeping time, from ancient to modern clocks and calendars. Discussion of solar, lunar, Egyptian, Hebrew, Christian, Julian, Gregorian, and French Revolutionary calendars, and chronological eras.

Aveni, Anthony F. *Empires of Time: Calendars, Clocks, and Cultures*. New York: Kodansha International, 1995.

A far-reaching examination of concepts of time and calendar systems across cultures and throughout history. Discusses historical development and workings of various calendar and time-reckoning schemes, pointing out their contribution to cultural systems as well as illustrating the connection between political power and control over the calendar. Explores the evidence for the earliest known calendar systems, including Neolithic time-reckoning systems, calendar systems of the ancient Greeks, and the Stonehenge controversy. Detailed coverage of the Western (Gregorian), Mayan, Aztec, Incan, and Chinese calendars, as well as discussion of the calendar systems of two tribal groups, the Nuer of East Africa, and the Trobriand Islanders of the Pacific.

Coleman, Lesley. *A Book of Time*. Camden, NJ: Thomas Nelson, Inc., 1971.

Survey of Sumerian, Babylonian, Muslim, Christian, Jewish, Egyptian, Roman, Julian, Gregorian, and French Revolutionary calendars and the proposed World Calendar. Includes discussion of timepieces, clockmakers, navigation, and some theories and literature dealing with time.

Couzens, Reginald C. *The Stories of the Months and Days*. 1923. Reprint. Detroit: Omnigraphics, Inc., 1990.

Explains how the months and days were named, telling stories about the Greek, Roman, Anglo and Saxon gods, goddesses, and emperors with whom they are associated.

Irwin, Keith Gordon. *The 365 Days*. Illustrated by Guy Fleming. New York: Thomas Y. Crowell Company, 1963.

Discusses solar, lunar, and astronomical cycles, ancient calendars of Egypt, Babylon, Chaldea, Rome, and the Mayas. Traces origins and development from the Julian to the Gregorian calendars. Note on various calendars proposed in recent history. Section on dating the observance of Easter and Christmas. Discussion of carbon-dating and tree rings.

Krythe, Maymie R. *All About the Months*. New York: Harper & Row, Publishers, 1966.

Discussion, in chronological order, of how each month was named, anniversaries occurring within each month, lore and literature associated with the month, mention of ancient holidays and festivals, and each month's gem and flower.

O'Neil, W. M. *Time and the Calendars*. Sydney, Australia: Sydney University Press, 1975.

Examines Egyptian, Roman, Babylonian, Indian, Chinese, Meso-American, and Gregorian calendars, and the day, week, month, and year. Appendix gives names of the days in various languages.

Parise, Frank, ed. *The Book of Calendars*. New York: Facts on File, Inc., 1982.

Summarizes the history and organization of the Babylonian, Macedonian, Hebrew, Seleucid, Olympiad, Roman, Armenian, Islamic, Fasli, Zoroastrian, Yezdezred, Jelali, Egyptian, Coptic, Ethiopian, Iranian, Afghanistan, Akbar, Fasli Deccan, Parasuram, Burmese and Arakanse, Chinese, Tibetan, Mayan, Julian, Gregorian, and Christian eras and calendars. Tables throughout convert the various ancient and other calendars to Julian or Gregorian dates or years. Dates of Easter provided from the year 1 through 1999. Calendar of Christian saints. Explanations of the French Revolutionary calendar and the Soviet calendar. Table depicts dates various regions in Europe celebrated New Year's Day.

Richard, E. G. *Mapping Time: The Calendar and Its History*. Oxford, England: Oxford University Press, 1998.

Parts I and II present a history of calendar systems from ancient times, including Babylonian and Near Eastern, Egyptian, Chinese and east Asian, Indian, Mayan and Aztec, Greek, Celtic, Teutonic, Icelandic, Roman and Julian, Jewish, Islamic and Baha'i, Gregorian, and French Republican calendars. Part III provides mathematical formulas for calendar conversions. Part IV contains essays giving brief history of Easter and its dating.

Tannenbaum, Beulah, and Myra Stillman. *Understanding Time: The Science of Clocks and Calendars*. Illustrated by William D. Hayes. New York: Whittlesey House, 1958.

Explanation for young readers of time and clocks, calendars, and other measuring systems used throughout history. Each chapter includes suggested experiments.

C. Festival Organization

Goldblatt, Joe Jeff. *Special Events: The Art and Science of Celebration*. Foreword by Linda Faulkner, Social Secretary to the White House during the Reagan Administration. New York: Van Nostrand Reinhold, 1990.

Guide to the special events industry, including social, retail, corporate and government events, meetings, and conventions. Provides techniques for budgeting, planning, and creating events such as theme parties, awards ceremonies, holidays, fairs, festivals, sporting events, and more. Appendices list related books and organizations and provide the text of the Flag Code.

Wilson, Joe, and Lee Udall. *Folk Festivals: A Handbook for Organization and Management*. Knoxville: The University of Tennessee Press, 1982.

Guide for folklore festival organizers covering such topics as administration, programming concepts, planning, publicity, and production. Part Two describes three folk festivals produced in the United States (Tucson Meet Yourself Festivalssissippi Valley Folk Festival, and Open Fiddlers' Contest), including an interview with a festival performer and samples of media releases and public service announcements.

D. Philosophy, Theory, and Analysis of Festivity

Browne, Ray B., and Michael T. Marsden, eds. The Cultures of Celebrations. Bowling Green, OH: Bowling Green State University Popular Press, 1994.

Collection of 15 case studies from scholars working in areas relating to popular culture studies. Essays analyze various celebrations and forms of entertainment, including Shi'ite rituals, folk festivals in Australia, Lord Mayor's Procession, Columbus celebrations from the 18th to the 20th centuries, and seasonal festivals in Manitoba.

♦ Indicates a book cited in the main text

Cantwell, Robert. *Ethnomimesis: Folklife and the Representation of Culture*. Chapel Hill: The University of North Carolina Press, 1993.

> Describes the Festival of American Folklife, held annually on the Mall in Washington, DC, and discusses it as a cultural artifact that can yield insights on "festivity, identity, and memory."

Cox, Harvey. *The Feast of Fools: A Theological Essay on Festivity and Fantasy*. Cambridge, MA: Harvard University Press, 1969.

> Adapted from the William Belden Noble Lectures given by the author in 1968 at Harvard University. Theological examination of spiritual aspects of festivity and fantasy as practiced in Western cultures. Uses the medieval Feast of Fools and its eventual disappearance as a symbol for thesis that Western civilization needs a rebirth of "the spirit represented by the Feast of Fools."

Falassi, Alessandro, ed. *Time Out of Time: Essays on the Festival*. Albuquerque: University of New Mexico Press, 1987.

> Collection of essays by Goethe, Hemingway and Aldous Huxley, and Victor Turner, Vladimir Propp, and other folklorists describing and analyzing festivals celebrated in Europe, North and South America, Africa, Asia, and Oceania such as the Palio at Siena, the Roman Carnival, bullfighting, Olojo Festival, Carnival at Rio de Janeiro, the Holy Ghost Festival in the Azores, and more.

Handelman, Don. *Models and Mirrors: Towards an Anthropology of Public Events*. Cambridge, England: Cambridge University Press, 1990.

> Analyses of such festivals as the Palio of Siena, Christmas mumming in Newfoundland, observance of Jewish and state holidays in Israel and in Israeli kindergartens, and katchina dancers as well as other forms of public ritual play.

MacAloon, John J., ed. *Rite, Drama, Festival, Spectacle: Rehearsals Toward a Theory of Cultural Performance*. Philadelphia: Institute for the Study of Human Issues, Inc., 1984.

> Papers from 10 scholars in the humanities delivered at the 76th Burg Wartenstein Symposium, sponsored by the Wenner-Gren Foundation for Anthropological Research. Academic essays concerned with various cultural and performative implications of festival and ritual in literature and in actuality: "Liminality and the Performative Genres," Victor Turner; "Charivari, Honor, and the Community in Seventeenth-Century Lyon and Geneva," Natalie Zemon Davis; "'Rough Music' in The Duchess of Malfi: Webster's Dance of Madmen and Charivari Tradition," Frank W. Wadsworth; "Borges's 'Immortal': Metaritual, Metaliturature, Metaperformance," Sophia S. Morgan; "Arrange Me into Disorder: Fragments and Reflections on Ritual Clowning," Barbara A. Babcock; "The Diviner and the Detective," Hilda Kuper; "A Death in Due Time: Construction of Self and Culture in Ritual Drama," Barbara G. Myerhoff; "The Ritual Process and the Problem of Reflexivity in Sinhalese Demon Exorcisms," Bruce Kapferer; "Carnival in Multiple Planes," Roberto Da Matta; and "Olympic Games and the Theory of Spectacle in Modern Societies," John J. MacAloon.

Pieper, Josef. *In Tune with the World: A Theory of Festivity*. Translated by Richard and Clara Winston. New York: Harcourt, Brace & World, Inc., 1965.

> Philosophical essay discusses what festivity means from a predominantly Western and Christian orientation. Includes consideration of festivity in relation to art, labor, and modern commercialization of history.

Thompson, E. P. *Customs in Common: Studies in Traditional Popular Culture*. New York: The New Press, 1993.

> Scholarly study of English working-class culture in the 18th and early 19th centuries. Includes examination of the historical contexts of such events as beating the bounds, the Horn Fair, and others.

Turner, Victor, ed. *Celebration: Studies in Festivity and Ritual*. Washington, DC: Smithsonian Institution Press, 1982.

> This companion volume to the Smithsonian Institution's exhibition of celebratory objects is a collection of essays exploring such topics as objects used in festivals, celebrations as rites of passage, and political, economic and religious festivals. Events included within the discussions are Juneteenth, Penitentes, Trinidad Carnival, Incwala, Juggernaut (Rath Yatra), Dragon Boat Festival in China, Rama festivals in India, German-American Passion Plays in the United States, and more.

E. Teaching Aids

Bauer, Caroline Feller. *Celebrations: Read-Aloud Holiday and Theme Book Programs*. Drawings by Lynn Gates Bredeson. New York: H. W. Wilson Company, 1985.

> Education specialist offers 16 theme book programs dealing with holidays and such invented celebrations as National Nothing Day and Pigmania for teachers and other professionals working with primarily middle-grade children. Each program includes some prose and poetry selections, ideas for bulletin boards, recipes, activities and jokes, and lists of related books marked for various age groups.

Dupuy, Trevor Nevitt, ed. *Holidays; Days of Significance for All Americans*. New York: Franklin Watts, Inc., 1965.

> Intended for elementary-school teachers. Brief essays from contributors to, and members of, the Historical Evaluation and Research Organization cover 27 patriotic holidays and commemorative days observed in the United States. Further reading list.

Green, Victor J. *Festivals and Saints Days: A Calendar of Festivals for School and Home*. Poole, Dorset, England: Blandford Press Ltd., 1978.

> Beginning with New Year's Day and following the calendar, the book covers more than 30 secular, Christian, Jewish, Hindu and Muslim holidays observed in Britain. Also includes Independence Day and Thanksgiving in the United States. Further reading list.

Hopkins, Lee Bennett, and Misha Arenstein. *Do You Know What Day Tomorrow Is? A Teacher's Almanac*. New York: Citation Press, 1975.

> Guide intended to integrate chronologically presented information about people, places, and events with elementary-school curriculum. Provided for each month are a brief explanation of its name, flower and birthstone, representative poem, and descriptive listings in chronological order of events in history, anniversaries associated with notable people, holidays, admission days, and other events that occur on each day of the year. Appendices include a reference bibliography for teachers and list of sources cited.

II. HOLIDAYS OF MAJOR RELIGIOUS TRADITIONS

A. General Works

♦ Bellenir, Karen. *Religious Holidays and Calendars: An Encyclopedic Handbook*. Foreword by Martin E. Marty. 3rd ed. Detroit: Omnigraphics, Inc., 2004.

♦ Indicates a book cited in the main text

This third edition contains more than 100 new entries and is organized into three sections. Part One consists of chapters explaining the history of calendars around the world: Babylonian, Greek, Jewish, Indian, Chinese, Egyptian, Mayan and Aztec, Islamic, Roman, Julian, Gregorian, British, Teutonic, Icelandic, and modern calendar reform movements. Part Two consists of chapters on 17 religious groups. Each chapter provides background of the religion, overview of the religion's calendar, and descriptions of the religion's holidays. Listing of Internet resources. Appendices include: contact information and web sites for sources and organizations offering more information, a bibliography arranged by topic, and a five-year chronological list of holidays. Holiday Index, Calendar Index, and Master Index. [Cited in the text as *RelHolCal-2004*]

♦ Bowker, John, ed. *The Oxford Dictionary of World Religions.* Oxford, England: Oxford University Press, 1997. 1111 pp. Indexes.

More than 80 contributors provide over 8,200 cross-referenced entries on major religions, movements, sects, people, texts, sacred sites, customs, festivals, and ethics. Topic index and index of Chinese headwords. [Cited in the text as *OxDictWrldRel-1997*]

♦ Crim, Keith, ed. *Perennial Dictionary of World Religions* (originally published as *Abingdon Dictionary of Living Religions*). San Francisco: Harper & Row, 1989.

Over 160 scholars contributed more than 1,600 entries on the world's major living systems of faith: deities, saints and other holy figures, religious sites, art and architecture, movements, sects and societies, authors and texts, creeds, prayers, mantras, and spiritual practices. Some bibliography provided throughout in individual entries. Long survey article on each major religion. Good cross-referencing. Guide to abbreviations and pronunciation table. Listing of key entries pertaining to major religions. [Cited in the text as *DictWrldRel-1989*]

♦ Eliadercea, ed. *The Encyclopedia of Religion.* 16 vols. New York: Macmillan, 1987.

A comprehensive collection of articles by leading scholars and religious figures touching on all aspects of religion. Reflects the significant increase in knowledge and changing interpretive frameworks which have marked the study of religion in the last 60 years. Treats religious ideologies and practices, as well as sociological aspects of religions from Paleolithic times to the present. Generates broad view of topics through composite entries joining several articles under a common heading. Articles list works cited and give suggestions for further reading. Ample coverage of non-Western religions. Extensively cross-referenced. [Cited in the text as *EncyRel-1987*]

♦ Gross, Ernie. *This Day in Religion.* New York: Neal-Schuman Publishers, Inc., 1990.

Offers a day-by-day listing of significant events in the world of religion from biblical times to the present. Focuses on Christianity, but some coverage of Judaism and Eastern religions. Includes saints' days, the birth or death of religious leaders or notable figures in the world of religion, appointments, canonizations, feast days, founding dates of organizations and associations, and other important events. [Cited in the text as *DayRel-1990*]

♦ Harper, Howard V. *Days and Customs of All Faiths.* 1957. Reprint. Detroit: Omnigraphics, Inc., 1990.

Part One contains more than 300 entries in chronological order that cover Roman, Jewish, and Christian religious festivals, saints' days and major secular holidays observed, especially in the United States. Part Two consists of chapters covering Jewish customs, major Christian holiday customs, including New

Year's, words and expressions associated with various lore, and wedding customs. [Cited in the text as *DaysCustFaith-1957*]

Hinnells, John R., ed. *The Penguin Dictionary of Religions.* Harmondsworth, Middlesex, England: Penguin Books, 1984.

More than 1,000 entries contributed by 29 scholars cover deities, beliefs, people, places, texts, institutions, practices, rituals, and festivals associated with the world's religions, past and present. List of contents by subject area and contributor. Maps of Europe, ancient Near East and west Asia, Africa, the Indian sub-continent, Southeast Asia, Japan, China, Southwest Pacific and Australasia, North America, Mesoamerica, and Latin America. Substantial bibliography by subject area, cross-referenced with the entries. Synoptic index. General index.

Jones, Lindsay, ed. *Encyclopedia of Religion.* 15 vols. 2nd ed. Detroit: Macmillan Reference USA, 2004.

A broad encyclopedia that addresses religion through a cross-cultural approach, while emphasizing the role of religion in everyday life. Highlights the major religious events celebrated by the world's different religious groups.

Magida, Arthur J., ed. *How to Be a Perfect Stranger: A Guide to Etiquette in Other People's Religious Ceremonies.* Woodstock, VT: Jewish Lights Publishing, 1996.

Provides an overview of the content of and the expected dress and behavior at the services of 20 religious and denominational groups. Covers the Assemblies of God, Baptist, Buddhist, Christian Scientist, Disciples of Christ, Episcopalian, Greek Orthodox, Hindu, Islamic, Jehovah's Witnesses, Jewish, Lutheran, Methodist, Mormon, Presbyterian, Quaker, Catholic, Seventh-day Adventist, and United Church of Christ ceremonies. Lists each group's major religious holidays and their significance. Reviews the calendar systems of the major religions, and furnishes a calendar listing of their holidays for the years 1996 to 1998.

Parrinder, Geoffrey. *A Dictionary of Non-Christian Religions.* Philadelphia: The Westminster Press, 1971.

More than 2,400 entries provide A to Z coverage of people, deities, rites, locations, festivals, texts, philosophies, etc., associated with ancient and living non-Christian religions, including various African religions, Aztec, Baha'i, Buddhism, Confucianism, Hinduism, Islam, Jainism, Judaism, Maori religion, Native American religions, Shinto, Sikhism, Taoism, Theosophy, Yoruba, Zoroastrianism, religions of ancient Rome, Greece, Babylon, and of the Celts, Egyptians, Incans, Mayans, Scandinavians, and others. Cross-referencing. Lists of Egyptian, Chinese, and Islamic dates and dynasties. Further reading list.

♦ Pike, Royston. *Round the Year with the World's Religions.* 1950. Reprint. Detroit: Omnigraphics, Inc., 1993.

Chronologically arranged chapters covering customs, legends, and stories behind religious observances in ancient Rome and Greece, Europe, India, Tibet, China, Japan, and Ceylon (Sri Lanka), and among ancient Romans, Greeks and Egyptians, Jews, Christians, Hindus, Jains, Muslims, Buddhists, Incans, and Aztecs. [Cited in the text as *RoundYr-1950*]

♦ Riggs, Thomas, ed. *Worldmark Encyclopedia of Religious Practices.* 3 vols. Detroit: Gale, 2006.

A three-volume, 1,800-page set that describes current religious practices throughout the world, including festivals and holidays, rituals, rites of passage, dietary practices, modes of dress, and other topics for 13 major religions and 28 religious subgroups. [Cited in the text as *EncycRelPractices-2006*]

♦ Indicates a book cited in the main text

Bibliography

B. African

King, Noel Q. *Religions of Africa: A Pilgrimage into Traditional Religions.* New York: Harper & Row, Publishers, 1970.

> Discusses Ashanti, Yoruba, and others' religious festivals, ceremonies, and customs, such as the Egungun Festival and ceremonies for Yoruba deities, as well as birth, initiation, marriage, and death customs among various African ethnic groups. Notes on pronunciation. Good further reading list, including many works in English.

Lawson, E. Thomas. *Religions of Africa: Traditions in Transformation.* Religious Traditions of the World Series. San Francisco: Harper & Row, 1984.

> Surveys history and religious traditions of the Zulu and Yoruba peoples. Covers customs, legends, and ceremonies associated with birth, puberty, marriage, and death. Festivals described include the Zulu (or Shembe) Festival, New Year's, and the New Yam Festival. Further reading list.

Murphy, Joseph M. *Working the Spirit: Ceremonies of the African Diaspora.* Boston: Beacon Press, 1994.

> Describes history, significance, and performance of religious ceremonies, practices, music, and dances observed through Voodoo in Haiti, Candomblé in Brazil, Santería in Cuba and among Cuban Americans, Revival Zion in Jamaica, and "the Black Church" in the United States, in attempt to show how all are connected to a common spiritual foundation.

C. Baha'i

♦ Smith, Peter. *A Concise Encyclopedia of the Baha'i Faith.* Oxford, England: Oneworld, 2000.

> More than 600 entries introduce people, history, places, sacred texts, beliefs, and tenets of the faith. Cross references. [Cited in the text as *ConEncyBahai-2000*]

Gaver, Jessyca Russell. *The Baha'i Faith: Dawn of a New Day.* New York: Hawthorn Books, Inc., 1967.

> Surveys the development of the Baha'i faith and its major prophets, beliefs, and laws and obligations. Discussion of observance of the Nineteen-Day Feast, New Year (Nawruz), and the Ridvan Festival.

D. Buddhism

♦ Bechert, Heinz, and Richard Gombrich, eds. *The World of Buddhism: Buddhist Monks and Nuns in Society and Culture.* London: Thames and Hudson, 1984.

> Covers the spread of Buddhism and describes tenets and practices. [Cited in the text as *WrldBuddhism-1984*]

Snelling, John. *Buddhist Festivals.* Holidays and Festivals Series. Vero Beach, FL: Rourke Enterprises, Inc., 1987.

> For young readers. Provides historical background on Buddha and discusses Buddhist festivals in Thailand, Sri Lanka, Tibet, and Japan, as well as brief notes on Buddhist observances in Asia, the United States, and Britain. Further reading list.

E. Christianity

Attwater, Donald. *The Penguin Dictionary of Saints.* 2nd ed. revised and updated by Catherine Rachel John. London: Penguin Books, 1983.

> Covers, in alphabetical order, more than 750 saints. Scope is international. Includes obscure and early, as well as more pop-

ular and recent saints. List of emblems associated with saints. Chronological list of feast days.

Bentley, James. *A Calendar of Saints: The Lives of the Principal Saints of the Christian Year.* New York: Facts on File Publications, 1986.

> Brief biographies of more than 300 saints are provided. Inspirational quotes from saints preface each month and also appear throughout. Richly illustrated, over 300 paintings are reproduced.

♦ Brewster, H. Pomeroy. *Saints and Festivals of the Christian Church.* 1904. Reprint. Detroit: Omnigraphics, Inc., 1990.

> Much of the book originally appeared as a series of articles published in the *Union and Advertiser* in Rochester, New York, which the author subsequently revised, adding more material to be published in the form reprinted in 1990. A yearbook of sorts of the Christian calendar, entries are arranged in chronological order, beginning with Advent. At least one saint or church feast is discussed for nearly every day of the year. Chronological list of the bishops and popes of the Christian church since St. Peter. Alphabetical list of canonized saints and others. General Index. [Cited in the text as *SaintFestCh-1904*]

Cowie, L. W., and John Selwyn Gummer. *The Christian Calendar: A Complete Guide to the Seasons of the Christian Year Telling the Story of Christ and the Saints from Advent to Pentecost.* Springfield, MA: G & C Merriam Company, Publishers, 1974.

> Introduction gives historical background on the development of the Christian calendar. Part one discusses each Christian holiday and Sunday of the liturgical year, from Advent to the 24th Sunday after Pentecost, discussing the scripture and/or festival associated with each day covered. Part two provides entries, in chronological order, on saints' days and feasts for every day of the Gregorian year. List of patron saints, in alphabetical order by saint. Glossarial index.

Denis-Boulet, Noële M. *The Christian Calendar.* Vol. 113 of the *Twentieth-Century Encyclopedia of Catholicism.* Translated by P. Hepburne-Scott. New York: Hawthorn Books, 1960.

> Provides historical background on how the Christian calendar evolved from earlier calendars. Discussion of the observance of Sunday, Easter, and other feasts. History of martyrologies. Calendar reforms through history and contemporary reform proposal of a world calendar.

♦ Farmer, David Hugh. *The Oxford Dictionary of Saints.* 2nd ed. Oxford, England: Oxford University Press, 1987.

> Covers, in alphabetical order, more than 1,000 saints venerated in the Christian church—mainly in Great Britain, but this edition also includes some Greek and Russian saints from Eastern Orthodoxy. Bibliographical sources conclude the entries. Appendices include a list of English people who have been candidates for canonization and are associated with a popular cult, a list of patronages of saints, iconographical emblems of saints, places in Great Britain and Ireland associated with saints, and a calendar of feast days for saints. [Cited in the text as *OxDict-Saints-1987*]

Gwynne, Rev. Walker. *The Christian Year: Its Purpose and Its History.* 1917. Reprint. Detroit: Omnigraphics, Inc., 1990.

> Beginning chapters address the purpose and development of the Christian liturgical year. Discussion of Jewish holidays, as well as early Christians' observance of Jewish feasts and transformation of these into Christian feasts. Church calendar is explained, along with technical terms associated with it. History and description of observances of holidays and saints' days. Appendix includes liturgical colors and questions for review or examination.

♦ Indicates a book cited in the main text

Hamilton, Mary. *Greek Saints and Their Festivals*. London: William Blackwood and Sons, 1910.

> Describes the observance of saints' days and other religious, as well as a few secular, holidays as celebrated in Greece, by the Greek Orthodox Church, and in Italy, Sicily, and Sardinia.

Holweck, Frederick George. *A Biographical Dictionary of the Saints, with a General Introduction on Hagiology*. 1924. Reprint. Detroit: Omnigraphics, Inc., 1990.

> Covers thousands of saints—all those venerated in any Christian church, including those not officially canonized but with popular cult following. Brief bibliographical notices.

♦ Metford, J.C.J. *The Christian Year*. London: Thames and Hudson, 1991.

> Explanation of the Christian liturgical year and its feasts, fasts, and other special days. [Cited in the text as *ChristYr-1991*]

Monks, James L. *Great Catholic Festivals*. Great Religious Festivals Series. New York: Henry Schuman, 1951.

> Discusses origins and Catholic observance of Christmas, Epiphany, Easter, Pentecost, Corpus Christi, and Assumption.

New Catholic Encyclopedia. 2nd ed. Washington, DC: Catholic University of America Press, 2003.

> Provides information about persons, institutions, religions, philosophies, scientific developments, and social movements related to the Catholic Church.

Rodgers, Edith Cooperrider. *Discussion of Holidays in the Later Middle Ages*. New York: Columbia University Press, 1940. Reprinted by AMS Press, 1967.

> Examines holy days observed (or not observed), the Church's position on feasts, rules of observance, and nature of actual observance of religious holidays between 1200 and the Reformation.

Secretariat, Bishops' Committee on the Liturgy, National Conference of Catholic Bishops [Gurrieri, John A.]. *Holy Days in the United States*. Washington, DC: United States Catholic Conference, 1984.

> Description of history, meaning, and liturgical and popular observance of the six holy days of obligation, as well as saints' days, with discussion of American saints, and other special days for Roman Catholics in the United States. Questions for discussion and suggested reading list conclude each chapter.

♦ Urlin, Ethel L. *Festivals, Holy Days, and Saints' Days: A Study in Origins and Survivals in Church Ceremonies & Secular Customs*. 1915. Reprint. Detroit: Omnigraphics, Inc., 1992.

> Entries cover, in chronological order, major Christian festivals and saints' days in England and Europe. Some mention of ancient Roman and Greek festivals where they figure in the origins of current Christian feasts. Listing of liturgical colors and the festivals during which they are worn by clergy. English calendar of Christian festivals and saints' days. [Cited in the text as *FestSaintDays-1915*]

Wainwright, Geoffrey, and Karen B. Westerfield Tucker, eds. *The Oxford History of Christian Worship*. Oxford: Oxford University Press, 2006.

> Comprehensive history covers the liturgical traditions of Orthodox, Catholic, Protestant, and Pentecostal traditions throughout the world, and includes material on the cultural contexts of those traditions.

Walshchael, ed. *Butler's Lives of the Saints*. Concise ed. Foreword by Cardinal Basil Hume. San Francisco: Harper & Row, Publishers, 1985.

> Abridgement of the four-volume *Lives of the Saints, or The Lives of the Fathers, Martyrs and other Principal Saints: Compiled from Original Monuments and other authentick records: Illustrated with the Remarks of judicious modern criticks and historians*, by Alban Butler, originally published in London between 1756 and 1759. The original contained nearly 1,500 entries. Later editions expanded to include 2,500. This edition provides biographical sketches and legends associated with one saint for each day of the year, in chronological order. List of patron saints.

Weiser, Francis X. *Handbook of Christian Feasts and Customs: The Year of the Lord in Liturgy and Folklore*. New York: Harcourt, Brace & World, Inc., 1958.

> Part I discusses Christian significance of Sunday and other days of the week, ember days, and rogation days. Part II is organized according to the Christian calendar and presents descriptions of major Christian feasts. Part III deals with the veneration of saints and Mary and provides some background on a few of the most popular saints.

F. Hinduism

Gupte, Rai Bahadur B. A. *Hindu Holidays and Ceremonials with Dissertations on Origin, Folklore and Symbols*. Calcutta and Simla, India: Thacker, Spink & Co., 1919.

> The main text contains dictionary-style entries on Hindu festivals, days and places of worship and ceremony, and mythological and historical persons along with constellations associated with them. Brief glossary precedes main text with entries on animals and plants with folkloric significance.

Mitter, Swasti. *Hindu Festivals*. Holidays and Festivals Series. Vero Beach, FL: Rourke Enterprises, Inc., 1989.

> Background for young readers on Hindu beliefs, history, and festivals inside and outside India. Note on the Hindu calendar and chronological table of Hindu holidays by month.

Sivananda, Sri Swami. *Hindu Fasts and Festivals*. India: The Yoga-Vedanta Forest Academy Press, 1983.

> Explains religious significance and customs and observances of 27 popular Hindu festivals. Also discusses folklore surrounding eclipses and special days. Includes some Hindu prayers. Concludes with an essay on the "Philosophy of Idol Worship."

♦ Stutley, Margaret, and James Stutley. *Harper's Dictionary of Hinduism: Its Mythology, Folklore, Philosophy, Literature, and History*. San Francisco: Harper & Row, 1977.

> Contains 2,500 entries on Hindu history, people, deities, texts, rituals, and other subjects. [Cited in the text as *DictHindu-1977*]

♦ Thomas, Paul. *Hindu Religion, Customs and Manners, Describing the Customs and Manners, Religious, Social and Domestic Life, Arts and Sciences of the Hindus*. 4th rev ed. Bombay, India: D. B. Taraporevala Sons & Co., Ltd., 1960.

> Covers Hindu history and creation theories, the caste system, religious sects, beliefs and practices, philosophy, social and domestic life, superstitions, etiquette, dress and ornamentation, literature and languages, ceremonies, music, dance, the calendar and holidays, architecture, the fine arts, and courtship and love. [Cited in the text as *HinduRelCustManners-1960*]

♦ Underhill, M. M. *The Hindu Religious Year*. London: Oxford University Press, 1921.

♦ Indicates a book cited in the main text

Discussion of festivals celebrated in India, including one chapter devoted to those in the state of Maharashtra. [Cited in the text as *HinduRelYr-1921*]

G. Islam

♦ Ahsan, M. M. *Muslim Festivals. Holidays and Festivals Series.* Vero Beach, FL: Rourke Enterprises, Inc., 1987.

Presents Islamic beliefs, holidays, and rites for young readers. Note on Islamic calendar. Chronological table of Muslim holidays by Islamic month. Further reading list. [Cited in the text as *MusFest-1987*]

Feener, R. Michael. *Islam in World Cultures: Comparative Perspectives.* Santa Barbara.: ABC-CLIO, 2004.

Provides an introduction to the issues relating to Islam in the context of globalization. Analyzes differences in Islamic culture and practice by looking at how Islam interacts with local cultures.

♦ Glassé, Cyril. *The Concise Encyclopedia of Islam.* Introduction by Huston Smith. San Francisco: Harper & Row, 1991.

More than 1,100 entries cover people, places, texts, beliefs, rituals, festivals, and practices associated with the Islamic faith and its branches. Appendices include historical synopsis of the Islamic world, maps of Mecca and description of the Hajj, schematic representation of branches of Islam, genealogical tables, and chronology. [Cited in the text as *ConEncyIslam-1991*]

♦ Gulevich, Tanya. *Understanding Islam and Muslim Traditions: An Introduction to the Religious Practices, Celebrations, Festivals, Observances, Beliefs, Folklore, Customs, and Calendar System of the World's Muslim Communities, Including an Overview of Islamic History and Geography.* Detroit: Omnigraphics, 2004.

Introduces readers to Islam through an examination of its religious observances, customs, holidays, calendar system, and folk beliefs, describing how people around the world express their Muslim identity. The book's 43 chapters are organized into three sections: A Brief Introduction to Islam; Religious Customs and Folklore; and Calendar System, Holidays, and Other Days of Observance. Additional resources, relevant web sites, a glossary of terms, a topical bibliography, and an index are also included. [Cited in the text as *Und-Islam-2004*]

Momen, Moojan. *An Introduction to Shia Islam: The History and Doctrines of Twelver Shiism.* New Haven, CT: Yale University Press, 1985.

A comprehensive treatment of the complex religious movement of Shia Islam.

Musk, Bill A. *Holy War: Why Do Some Muslims Become Fundamentalists?* London: Monarch, 2003.

An informative study of Islamic fundamentalism.

Sanders, Paula. *Ritual, Politics, and the City in Fatimid Cairo.* Albany, NY: State University of New York Press, 1994.

Examines court ritual practices, ceremonial processions, and such festivals as Nawruz, Ramadan, and the Festival of Breaking the Fast ('Id al-Fitr) in fourth- and fifth-century Cairo in terms of social and political culture.

Trimingham, J. Spencer. *Islam in West Africa.* London: Oxford University Press, 1959.

Describes history, beliefs, practices, and observances of Muslim West Africans. Explanation of Islamic calendar, saints, social customs. Glossary-Index of Arabic and African terms. General index.

♦ Von Grunebaum, Gustave E. *Muhammadan Festivals.* Introduction by C. E. Bosworth. New York: Olive Branch Press, 1988.

Provides historical background on Islam, as well as discussion of beliefs, prayers, saints, and worship services. Festivals covered are the pilgrimage to Mecca, Ramadan, Nawruz, Muhammad's birthday (Mawlid al-Nabi), feasts of saints, and the death anniversary of Husain (Ashura). [Cited in the text as *MuhFest-1988*]

H. Judaism

Cashman, Greer Fay. *Jewish Days and Holidays.* Illustrated by Alona Frankel. New York: SBS Publishing, Inc., 1979.

Describes for young readers the history of, and traditions and customs associated with, major Jewish holidays, including the Sabbath. Sidebars depict foods and other items used during celebrations. Concludes with quiz on matching sidebar items with appropriate holiday.

Edidin, Ben M. *Jewish Customs and Ceremonies.* Illustrated by H. Norman Tress. New York: Hebrew Publishing Company, 1941.

A companion to Ben M. Edidin's *Jewish Holidays and Festivals* (see below), intended as an educational supplemental text, describes everyday customs as well as those associated with holidays and other important events, such as birth, bar and bat mitzvah, marriage, burial, and worship.

Edidin, Ben M. *Jewish Holidays and Festivals.* Illustrated by Kyra Markham. 1940. Reprint. Detroit: Omnigraphics, Inc., 1993.

Discusses history, significance, and customs associated with Jewish holidays and anniversaries.

Eisenberg, Azriel. *The Story of the Jewish Calendar.* Wood engravings by Elisabeth Friedlander. New York: Abelard-Schuman, 1958.

A short story of two teenaged boys watching for the new moon prefaces a brief history of the Jewish calendar. Explanation of Jewish holidays and names of months and Sabbaths and their significance. Glossary of Hebrew terms and place-names.

Gaster, Theodor H. *Festivals of the Jewish Year.* New York: William Sloane Associates Publishers, 1953.

Presents origins of Jewish festivals and holy days, draws comparisons to other religious and ethnic holidays, and describes evolving nature of their observance throughout history.

Goldin, Hyman E. *A Treasury of Jewish Holidays: History, Legends, Traditions.* New York: Twayne Publishers, 1952.

Examines Jewish festivals, explaining their meanings, describing customs and traditional beliefs associated with them, and telling the stories of their historical origins. Calendar of Jewish festivals from 1951 to 1971.

Hacohen, Devorah, and Menahem Hacohen. *One People; The Story of the Eastern Jews: Twenty Centuries of Jewish Life in North Africa, Asia and Southeastern Europe.* Introduction by Yigal Allon. Translated by Israel I. Taslitt. New York: Sabra Books, 1969.

Discusses history, folklore, beliefs and customs, ceremonies, and observance of holidays among Jews in Iraq and Kurdistan, Persia, the Caucasus, Bukhara, Morocco, Algeria, Tunisia and Jreba, Libya, Cyrenaica, Egypt, Syria, Yemen, Hadramaut, Aden, Turkey, Salonika, Bulgaria, and India.

♦ Indicates a book cited in the main text

Rockland, Mae Shafter. *The Jewish Party Book: A Contemporary Guide to Customs, Crafts, and Foods*. New York: Schocken Books, 1978.

> Traditional customs, foods, and activities associated with birth, bar and bat mitzvah, marriage, reunions, housewarmings, and holidays. Appendix provides explanation of Jewish calendar and table of holiday dates from 1978 to 2000.

Rosenau, William. *Jewish Ceremonial Institutions*. 3rd rev ed. 1925. Reprint. Detroit: Omnigraphics, Inc., 1992.

> Adapted from a series of lectures given by the author at the Oriental Seminary of the Johns Hopkins University in 1901. Origin and purpose of the synagogue and explanatory commentary on its worship services and customs. Discussion of the Jewish calendar and observance of holidays and festivals at home and at the synagogue. Practices associated with birth, marriage, bar and bat mitzvah, divorce, mourning, and related laws and practices.

Strassfeldchael. *The Jewish Holidays: A Guide and Commentary*. Illustrated by Betsy Platkin Teutsch. New York: Harper & Row, 1985.

> Each of 11 chapters deals with a holiday and its specific practices in depth. Appendices on the Jewish calendar, laws pertaining to holidays, Torah reading list for the holidays, glossary of Hebrew blessings, glossary of Hebrew terms, and dates of holidays to the years 1999-2000.

Trepp, Leo. *The Complete Book of Jewish Observance: A Practical Manuel for the Modern Jew*. New York: Behrman House, Inc./Simon & Schuster, 1980.

> Covers Jewish prayers, practices, customs, and laws in addition to festivals and fasts.

Turck, Mary. *Jewish Holidays*. New York: Crestwood House, 1990.

> Explanations for young readers of reasons for celebrating the holidays, ways in which they are observed, and food, blessings, and prayers associated with them. Brief further reading list.

Turner, Reuben. *Jewish Festivals*. Holidays and Festivals Series. Vero Beach, FL: Rourke Enterprises, Inc., 1987.

> Presents scriptural background for young readers on the Jewish feasts, along with customs and traditions, recipes and food, and activities associated with them. Sections explaining the Jewish calendar, including a calendar of festivals, and the Hebrew alphabet. Further reading list.

Wigoder, Geoffrey, ed. *The Encyclopedia of Judaism*. New York: Macmillan, 1989.

> Several hundred cross-referenced entries cover religious life and development, from the major and minor prophets to dietary laws, from festivals and ceremonies to definitions of concepts and terms.

I. Sikhism

Cole, William Owen, and Piara Singh Sambhi. *The Sikhs: Their Religious Beliefs and Practices*. Boston: Routledge & Kegan Paul, 1978.

> Covers historical background, beliefs, and practices of the Sikh faith, including discussion of founder Guru Nanak and others, scripture, places and style of worship, ethics, ceremonies, birth, marriage and death rites, and calendar of festivals. Appendices cover the Rehat Maryada, or guide to the Sikh way of life; prayers and meditations; population statistics; and explanation of the structure of the Guru Granth Sahib—the scriptural hymns.

♦ Kapoor, Sukhbir Singh. *Sikh Festivals*. Holidays and Festivals Series. Vero Beach, FL: Rourke Enterprises, Inc., 1989.

> Background for young readers on Sikh religious beliefs, history, and ceremonies and festivals. Chronological table of holidays by Hindu month. List of Sikh gurus. Further reading list. [Cited in the text as *SikhFest-1989*]

J. Taoism

Sasochael R. *Taoism and the Rite of Cosmic Renewal*. 2nd ed. Pullman: Washington State University Press, 1990.

> Religious studies professor details his observations of the Chiao Festival at a temple in Taiwan in 1970, and also provides descriptions of other annual events in the Chinese religious calendar.

K. Zoroastrianism

Boyce, Mary. *Zoroastrians: Their Religious Beliefs and Practices*. London: Routledge, 1979.

> Noted Zoroastrian scholar gives history of the religion and describes beliefs and rituals.

III. HOLIDAYS OF ETHNIC GROUPS AND GEOGRAPHIC REGIONS

A. General Works

Countries of the World and Their Leaders Yearbook 2007. Detroit: Gale, 2006.

> Yearbook covering nearly 200 countries based on reports from the U.S. Department of State. Entries typically cover each nation's geography, history, economy, government, political conditions, and state of relations with the United States, as well as detailed travel notes.

♦ Stearns, Peter N., ed. *The Encyclopedia of World History*. Boston: Houghton Mifflin, 2001.

> A broad encyclopedia providing covering of people, nations, and events around the world. [Cited in the text as *EncycWorldHistory-2001*]

Szajkowski, Bogdan. *Political Parties of the World*. 6th ed. London: John Harper Publishing, 2005.

> Extensive material on politics and major political parties for nations around the world.

World and Its Peoples. 11 vols. New York: Marshall Cavendish, 2007.

> Attempts to go beyond superficial and stereotypical information about people around the world by showing how the nations of the modern world became what they are today.

Worldmark Encyclopedia of the Nations. 12th ed. 5 vols. Detroit: Gale, 2006.

> Information on 193 countries and dependencies, with four country volumes arranged by geographic region and one volume focusing on the United Nations.

B. Africa

Baker, Colin. *State of Emergency: Crisis in Central Africa, Nyasaland 1959-1960*. London: Tauris Academic Studies, 1997.

♦ Indicates a book cited in the main text

Covers a critical period in the history of Central Africa and examines the growth of nationalist violence in Malawi (formerly Nyasaland) and the declaration of the state of emergency.

Beier, Ulli. *Yoruba Myths.* Cambridge, England: Cambridge University Press, 1980.

> The author and contributors present 41 myths from Nigeria about Yoruba deities, including Ogun and Oranmiyan.

Brockman, Norbert C. *An African Biographical Dictionary.* 2nd ed. Millerton, NY: Grey House Publishing, 2006.

> Biographical sketch that describes Chilembwe as "the great hero and martyr of Malawi."

♦ Ellis, Royston, and John R. Jones. *Festivals of the World: Madagascar.* (Festivals of the World Series) Milwaukee: Gareth Stevens Publishing, 1999.

> Provides brief introduction to the country, calendar of selected festivals, description of five festivals, craft activities, further reading, and a recipe for young readers. [Cited in the text as *Fest-Wrld: Madag-1999*]

Lentakis, Michael B. *Ethiopia: Land of the Lotus Eaters.* London: Janus Publishing, 2005.

> Offers a definitive explanation of modern history in Ethiopia, covering the last century up until 1994. It attempts to describe the changes that have taken place in Ethiopia over the past century.

Levine, Donald N. *Wax & Gold: Tradition and Innovation in Ethiopian Culture.* Chicago: The University of Chicago Press, 1965.

> Social scientist examines history, traditions, lifestyles, literature, art, and religion of Amhara people in Ethiopia. Festivals discussed include Maskal (Exaltation of the Cross), St. Michael's Day and other saints' days, Christmas (Ganna), and Timqat (Epiphany).

Middleton, John, and Joseph C. Miller, eds. *New Encyclopedia of Africa.* 2nd ed. 5 vols. Detroit: Charles Scribner's Sons, 2007.

> Discusses the culture, history, and politics of African nations, from ancient civilizations to the present day.

Miers, Suzanne, and Igor Kopytoff. *Slavery in Africa: Historical and Anthropological.* Madison: University of Wisconsin Press, 1977.

> Uses case studies and an anthropological viewpoint to examine the social effects of slavery in Africa.

Moran, Mary H. *Liberia: The Violence of Democracy.* Philadelphia: University of Pennsylvania Press, 2006.

> An examination of Liberia's democratic origins and violent history.

♦ Opoku, A. A. *Festivals of Ghana.* Accra, Ghana: Ghana Publishing Corporation, 1970.

> Includes 12 chapters that describe traditional festivals in Ghana. The final section presents photographs of additional festivals celebrated in Ghana. [Cited in the text as *FestGhana-1970*]

O'Toole, Thomas, and Janice E. Baker. *Historical Dictionary of Guinea.* Lanham, MD: Scarecrow Press, 2005.

> A historical dictionary that provides a range of tools: an introductory narrative covering Guinea's political and economic history; a chronology from the earliest known history to the present day; hundreds of cross-referenced dictionary entries

covering people, places, events, institutions, movements, political and social groups, and cultural issues; and an extensive bibliography of current publications.

Townsend, Reginald E., ed. *The Official Papers of William V. S. Tubman, President of Liberia.* London: Longmans, 1968.

> A collection of speeches and written documents by the Liberian president during his years in office, 1944-1971.

Westermarck, Edward. *Ritual and Belief in Morocco.* 2 vols. London: Macmillan and Co., Ltd., 1926.

> Author presents results of on-site research, discussing peoples living in Morocco and their religions, beliefs and practices, saints, charms, and superstitions. Calendar and agricultural rites and festivals are covered in vol. 2. List of tribes and locales.

C. Ancient World (Western)

♦ Adkins, Lesley, and Roy Adkins. *Dictionary of Roman Religion.* Oxford, England: Oxford University Press, 1996.

> More than 1,400 entries discuss Roman mythology, gods, people, temples, and festivals. There is also some coverage of Christianity, Judaismthraism, and ancient Celtic religion. Most entries include bibliographic references. [Cited in the text as *DictRomRel-1996*]

♦ Avery, Catherine B., ed. *The New Century Classical Handbook.* New York: Appleton-Century-Crofts, Inc., 1962.

> This book has more than 6,000 dictionary-style entries, with pronunciations, covering mythological and historical figures, texts, places, festivals, legends, and artifacts in ancient Greece and Rome. Some cross-referencing. [Cited in the text as *NewCentClassHandbk-1962*]

♦ Brumfield, Allaire Chandor. *The Attic Festivals of Demeter and Their Relation to the Agricultural Year.* Salem, NH: Ayer Company, 1981.

> Scholarly investigation of the various Attic (ancient Greek) festivals of Demeter. Covers Proerosia, Thesmophoria, Haloa, Cloaia, the Lesser Mysteries, various harvest festivals, Skira, and the Eleusinian Mysteries. Argues that these festivals attempted to ritually ensure a good harvest and to consolidate community attention on important moments of the agricultural cycle. List of Athenian months. Appendix provides a glossary of Greek agricultural words. General index and index of Greek words. [Cited in the text as *AtticFest-1981*]

♦ Fowler, W. Warde. *The Roman Festivals of the Period of the Republic: An Introduction to the Study of the Religion of the Romans.* London, England: Macmillan and Co., Ltd., 1899. Reprinted in 1925.

> Describes the Roman calendar and Roman festivals of the Republican era in chronological order, from Mensis Martius, or March, to Mensis Februarius, or February. Chronological table of calendar festivals, according to the Republican calendar. Indexes of subjects, Latin words, Latin authors quoted, and Greek authors quoted. [Cited in the text as *RomFest-1925*]

♦ Grantchael. *A Guide to the Ancient World: A Dictionary of Classical Place Names.* New York: H. W. Wilson Company, 1986.

> Covers place names throughout the Mediterranean world and Europe. Gives location, history of settlement, major historical events, incorporation into states or empires, and current remains. Furnishes 15 maps of various European and Mediterranean regions, with ancient place names marked. Provides a bibliography of sources in the following ancient and modern languages: Greek, Latin, Aramaic, Armenian, Coptic, German,

♦ Indicates a book cited in the main text

Hebrew, Syriac, and English. Also lists relevant journals and archeological reports. [Cited in the text as *GdAnctWrld-1986*]

♦ Hammond, N.G.L., and H. H. Scullard. *The Oxford Classical Dictionary*. 2nd ed. Oxford, England: Clarendon Press, 1970.

Covers the ancient Greek and Roman worlds. Treats place names, mythological figures, legends, notable individuals, institutions, customs, natural features, political and administrative units, festivals, cults, and more. Entries are substantial; most list sources. Offers bibliography of books in many languages. Index includes people, places, and things mentioned throughout, but not titles of entries. [Cited in the text as *OxClassDict-1970*]

♦ *Lemprière's Classical Dictionary of Proper Names mentioned in Ancient Authors Writ Large*. 3rd ed. Introduction by R. Willets. London, England: Routledge & Kegan Paul, 1984.

More than 10,000 dictionary-style entries cover historical and mythological figures, places, festivals, and other terms relevant to the classical world from the 12th century B.C. to the 15th century A.D. Chronological table of events, from the Trojan War to the fall of Trebizond in 1461, precedes the text of the Dictionary. Originally published in 1788, this source had particular influence on 19th-century English literature. [Cited in the text as *ClassDict-1984*]

♦ Parke, H. W. *Festivals of the Athenians*. Ithaca, NY: Cornell University Press, 1977.

Describes festivals celebrated in ancient Athens. Part one presents, in chronological order, the festivals associated with a specific calendar date. Part two covers local and movable festivals. Gives background information on Athenian religion and daily life. Includes a calendar of Athenian festivals and a map of Athens showing principal sanctuaries. [Cited in the text as *FestAth-1977*]

♦ Scullard, H. H. *Festivals and Ceremonies of the Roman Republic*. Ithaca, NY: Cornell University Press, 1981.

Describes numerous holidays and ceremonies of the Republic. Part one provides introduction to Roman religion. Part two gives historical background of festivals and identifies (when possible) deity or event celebrated, manner of observance, legends and temple sites associated with the celebration, and references made to the festival in ancient texts. Part three covers other ceremonies, such as those connected with triumphs, ovations, and meetings of the Senate. Provides a map of Rome identifying sites of temples and buildings, a further reading list, a list of Roman calendars and festivals, a complete Roman calendar, and a list of temples and their dates of consecration. [Cited in the text as *FestRom-1981*]

D. Asia and the Middle East

1. General Works

Festivals in Asia. Asian Copublication Programme Series Two. Sponsored by the Asian Cultural Centre for UNESCO. Tokyo: Kodansha International Ltd., 1975.

For young readers. Describes, in chronological order, the New Year in Singapore, Festival of Fire (New Year) in Iran, Dolls' Day and Boys' Day in Japan, Bengali New Year in Bangladesh, the Water Festival in Burma, New Year in Cambodia, New Year in Laos, Sinhala and Tamil New Year in Sri Lanka, and Maytime in the Philippines, often through storytelling.

Jettmar, Karl, ed. *Cultures of the Hindukush: Selected Papers from the Hindu-Kush Cultural Conference Held at MoesgÂrd 1970*. Wiesbaden, Germany: Franz Steiner Verlag, 1974.

These papers and notes by more than a dozen scholars were compiled from the conference in 1970 on cultures of peoples in the valley regions of the Hindukush mountain range in Central Asia, including the Kafirs, Kalasha, and Kom. Topics covered include languages, history, festivals, religion, cosmology, mythology, customs, and political organization.

More Festivals in Asia. Asian Copublication Programme Series Two. Sponsored by the Asian Cultural Centre for UNESCO. Tokyo: Kodansha International Ltd., 1975.

For young readers. Describes, in chronological order, Tano Day in Korea, Eid-ul-Fitr in Pakistan, Lebaran in Indonesia, Hari Raya Puasa in Malaysiad-Autumn Festival in Vietnam, Dasain in Nepal, Diwali Festival of Lights in India, Loy Krathong in Thailand, and the Buzkashi Game in Afghanistan, often through storytelling.

♦ Viesti, Joe, and Diane Hall. *Celebrate! In South Asia*. New York: Lothrop, Lee & Shepard Books, 1996.

Photos and descriptions of nine festivals in Bangladesh, Bhutan, Burma (Myanmar), India, Nepal, Pakistan, and Sri Lanka. [Cited in the text as *CelebSouthAsia-1996*]

2. Bangladesh

Anisujjaman, Samsujjaman Khan, and Syed Manzoorul Islam, eds. *Festivals of Bangladesh*. Dhaka, Bangladesh: Nymphea Publication, 2005.

Covers the celebration of festivals, fasts, and feasts in Bangladesh.

3. China and Hong Kong

Bredon, Juliet, and Igor Mitrophanow. *The Moon Year: A Record of Chinese Customs and Festivals*. Shanghai: Kelly & Walsh, Ltd., 1927.

Chapters on the Chinese calendar, imperial ceremonies, and the many Chinese gods and cults associated with them, including a discussion of the rise of Confucianism, Taoism, and Buddhism. A chapter is then devoted to each month of the Chinese year, describing the observance of festivals within each month.

Burkhardt, V. R. *Chinese Creeds & Customs*. 2 vols. Hong Kong: The South China Morning Post, Ltd., 1953-55.

Author describes customs and observance of more than 20 festivals and ceremonies in China, as well as legends, foods, objects, symbols, and fine arts, and discussion of the calendar. Appendices include list of the 24 segments of the Chinese year, the 10 celestial stems and 12 earthly branches, and a table of Chinese temples that lists each temple's locale, god(s) worshipped, and date founded.

Eberhard, Wolfram. *Chinese Festivals*. Great Religious Festivals Series. New York: Henry Schuman, 1952.

Essays on observance and folklore associated with the New Year, Dragon Boat Festivald-Autumn Festival, Spring Festival, Feast of the Souls, Sending the Winter Dress Festival, and the Weaving Maid and the Cowherd Festival.

Hodous, Lewis. *Folkways in China*. London: Arthur Probsthain, 1929.

Author relates his travels to more than 20 festivals in China, covering history, lore, superstitions, customs, and foods. List of Chinese names.

Latsch, Marie-Luise. *Chinese Traditional Festivals*. Beijing: New World Press, 1984.

♦ Indicates a book cited in the main text

Discusses seven major Chinese festivals and their changing significance through history. Festivals covered are New Year Lantern Festival, Pure Brightness Festival (Qing Ming), Dragon Boat Festivald-Autumn Festival, Honoring the Kitchen God, and the Lunar New Year's Eve.

Qi Xing, comp. *Folk Customs at Traditional Chinese Festivals.* Translated by Ren Jiazhen. Illustrated by Yang Guanghua. Beijing: Foreign Languages Press, 1988.

Describes customary festivities for 13 traditional Chinese festivals, including the Spring Festival, Lantern Festival, Spring Dragon Day, Clear and Bright Festival, Dragon Boat Festival, Heaven's Gift Day, Double Seventh Nightddle of the Year Festivald-Autumn Festival, Double Ninth Day, Eighth Day of the Twelfth Month, Kitchen God's Day, and New Year's Eve. Also gives brief descriptions of 10 minor festivals. Covers major festivals of 15 ethnic minority groups, for example Tibetans and Mongolians, as well as 20 minor ethnic festivals. Appendices explain various elements of the traditional Chinese calendar systems, including the 24 solar terms, the 10 heavenly stems and 12 earthly branches, list modern China's commemorative days, and provide a brief chronology of periods in Chinese history.

Stepanchuk, Carol, and Charles Wong. *Mooncakes and Hungry Ghosts: Festivals of China.* San Francisco: China Books & Periodicals, 1991.

Covers legends, history, foods, superstitions, poems, objects, and customs associated with such major Chinese holidays as New Year, Dragon Boat Festivald-Autumn Festival, Clear Brightness Festival, Feast of the Hungry Ghosts, Festival of the Cowherd and the Weaving Maiden, Tian Hou, Protectress of Seafarers, and Double Yang Day, as well as 12 holidays observed by national minorities in China. Appendices include explanation of the Chinese calendar, listing of major festivals by the calendar, table of related symbols, notes on arranging food, pictorial glossary of symbols, Chinese character glossary, and chronology of dynasties.

Tun Li-Ch'en. *Annual Customs and Festivals in Peking.* Translated by Derk Bodde. 2nd rev ed. Hong Kong: Hong Kong University Press, 1965 (1st ed 1936).

Originally written in 1900, this book describes more than 100 annual events in Peking, arranged chronologically by Chinese month. Appendices discuss the Chinese calendar and list units of measure, English equivalents of Chinese names, dynasties and emperors, and concordance of Chinese and Gregorian calendars from 1957-1984.

Ward, Barbara E., and Joan Law. *Chinese Festivals in Hong Kong.* The Guidebook Company, Ltd., 1993.

Presents 30 Chinese festivals and ceremonies as they are observed in contemporary Hong Kong. Explanation of solar calendar and chart. Map of festival locations. Festival calendar, including table converting solar dates from 1992 to 2004.

4. India and Sri Lanka

Bapat, Tara. *Rituals and Festivals of India.* Bombay: Focus Book, 1991.

Covers Hindu holidays, festivals, and rituals.

♦ Bezbaruah, M. P. *Fairs & Festivals of India.* 5 vols. New Delhi: Gyan Publishing House, 2003.

Provides extensive coverage of various festival and celebrations in India. [Cited in the test as *FairsFestIndia-2003*]

♦ Patil, Vimla. *Celebrations: Festive Days of India.* Bombay, India: India Book House Pvt. Ltd., 1994.

Month-by-month discussion of Hindu, Buddhist, Islamic, Christian, and Jain festivals in India, as well as explanation of Hindu, Islamic, and Zoroastrian calendars. Other chapters deal with women's festivals, life-cycle customs, worship, and symbols of religions practiced in India. [Cited in the text as *CelebFestIndia-1994*]

♦ Sanon, Arun. *Festive India.* Photographs by Gurmeet Thukral. New Delhi: Frank Bros. & Co., 1987.

Text and photos present a portrait of 26 major festivals celebrated in India. The appendix provides a chronological listing of festivals and their locations within the country. [Cited in the text as *FestIndia-1987*]

♦ Welbon, Guy R., and Glenn E. Yocum, eds. *Religious Festivals in South India and Sri Lanka.* New Delhi: Manohar, 1982.

Scholars in anthropology, religious studies, and history of Indian art contribute 12 essays that derive from a workshop at the Conference on Religion in South India. Essays are entitled: "The Hindu Festival Calendar," Karen L. Merrey; "Festivals in Pancaratra Literature," H. Daniel Smith; "The Cycle of Festivals at Parthasarathi Temple," James L. Martin; "The Candala's Song," Guy R. Welbon; "Two Citra Festivals in Madurai," D. Dennis Hudson; "Chronometry, Cosmology, and the Festival Calendar in the Murukan Cult," Fred W. Clothey; "Mahasivaratri: The Saiva Festival of Repentance," J. Bruce Long; "The Festival Interlude: Some Anthropological Observations," Suzanne Hanchett; "The End Is the Beginning: A Festival Chain in Andhra Pradesh," Jane M. Christian; "Kalam Eluttu: Art and Ritual in Kerala," Clifford R. Jones; "The Kataragama and Kandy Asala Peraharas: Juxtaposing Religious Elements in Sri Lanka," Donald K. Swearer; and "An-keliya: A Literary-Historical Approach," Glenn E. Yocum. [Cited in the text as *RelFestSriLank-1982*]

5. Indonesia

♦ Berg, Elizabeth. *Festivals of the World: Indonesia.* (Festivals of the World Series) Milwaukee: Gareth Stevens Publishing, 1997. 32 pp. Illustrated. Glossary. Index.

Provides brief introduction to the country, calendar of selected festivals, description of five festivals, craft activities, further reading, and a recipe for young readers. [Cited in the text as *FestWrld: Indonesia-1997*]

6. Iran

Aghaie, Kamran Scot. *The Martyrs of Karbala: Shi'i Symbols and Rituals in Modern Iran.* Seattle: University of Washington Press, 2004.

Examines Shi'i symbols and rituals to show the effects of modernization on society, politics and religion in Iran.

Daniel, Elton L., and Ali Akbar Mahdi. *Culture and Customs of Iran.* Westport, CT: Greenwood Publishing, 2006.

Presents an overview of contemporary cultural life in Iran, focusing on such topics as geography, religion, social customs, media, and the arts.

Lorentz, John H. *Historical Dictionary of Iran.* Lanham, MD: Scarecrow Press, 2006.

A historical dictionary that provides a range of tools: an introductory narrative covering Iran's political and economic history; a chronology from the earliest known history to the present day; hundreds of cross-referenced dictionary entries covering people, places, events, institutions, movements, political and social groups, and cultural issues; and an extensive bibliography of current publications.

♦ Indicates a book cited in the main text

7. Japan

♦ Ashkenazichael. *Matsuri: Festivals of a Japanese Town.* Honolulu: University of Hawaii Press, 1993.

> Scholarly examination of festivals in the town of Yuzawa in Akita Prefecture. [Cited in the text as *Matsuri-1993*]

♦ Bauer, Helen, and Sherwin Carlquist. *Japanese Festivals.* Garden City, NY: Doubleday & Company, Inc., 1965.

> Essays on 11 major festivals. Chapters on food and flower festivals. Second half of book is a chronological arrangement of Japanese festivals. Back matter includes a pronunciation guide and summary of Japan's history. [Cited in the text as *JapanFest-1965*]

Casal, U. A. *The Five Sacred Festivals of Ancient Japan: Their Symbolism & Historical Development.* Tokyo: Charles E. Tuttle Company, Inc., and Sophia University, 1967.

> Covers historical background, traditions, legends and myths, food, customs, and current observance of the New Year Festival, the Girls' Festival, the Boys' Festival, the Star Festival, and the Chrysanthemum Festival in Japan.

♦ Epstein, Sam, and Beryl Epstein. *A Year of Japanese Festivals.* Illustrated by Gordon Laite. Champaign, IL: Garrard Publishing Company, 1974.

> Descriptions of more than 15 festivals celebrated in Japan. For young readers. [Cited in the text as *YrJapanFest-1974*]

♦ *Illustrated Festivals of Japan.* Japan Travel Bureau, 1993.

> Provides brief information about 271 festivals in Japan and a festival calendar. [Cited in the text as *IllFestJapan-1993*]

♦ Zabilka, Gladys, comp. *Customs and Culture of Okinawa.* Rev ed. Tokyo: Bridgeway Press Books/ Charles E. Tuttle Company, 1959.

> Written for American students whose parents lived on the U.S. military base in Okinawa after World War II, the book contains chapters on the geography, people, schools, arts, industry, religions, festivals, customs, health, fairy tales, and songs (including scores) of Okinawa. [Cited in the text as *CustCultOkinawa-1959*]

8. Korea

♦ Choe Sang-su. *Annual Customs of Korea: Notes on the Rites and Ceremonies of the Year.* Seoul: Seomun-dang Publishing Company, 1983.

> Prominent Korean folklorist describes holiday-related customs, games, foods, and celebrations of the year in chronological order by lunar month. [Cited in the text as *AnnCustKorea-1983*]

Chun Shin-yong, ed. *Customs and Manners in Korea.* Part of the 10-volume Korean Culture Series. Seoul: International Cultural Foundation and Si-sa-yong-o-sa, Inc., 1982.

> Scholars from various academic specialties contribute 10 essays on Korean traditions and values, rituals and rites, mental health, literature and mythology. The essay, "Annual Ceremonies and Rituals," by Choi Gil-sung, discusses the timing, significance, and observance of various festivals throughout Korea. Kim Yol-kyu's "Several Forms of Korean Folk Rituals, Including Shaman Rituals" examines folk dance and festivals.

♦ Ho Siow Yen. *Festivals of the World: South Korea.* (Festivals of the World Series) Milwaukee: Gareth Stevens Publishing, 1998.

> Provides brief introduction to the country, calendar of selected festivals, description of five festivals, craft activities, further reading, and a recipe for young readers. [Cited in the text as *FestWrld: SouthKorea-1998*]

9. Lebanon

AbuKhalil, As'ad. *Historical Dictionary of Lebanon.* Lanham, MD: Scarecrow Press, 1998.

> A historical dictionary that provides a range of tools: an introductory narrative covering Lebanon's political and economic history; a chronology from the earliest known history to the present day; hundreds of cross-referenced dictionary entries covering people, places, events, institutions, movements, political and social groups, and cultural issues; and an extensive bibliography of current publications.

10. Mongolia

♦ Fisher, Frederick. *Festivals of the World: Mongolia.* (Festivals of the World Series) Milwaukee: Gareth Stevens Publishing, 1999.

> Provides brief introduction to the country, calendar of selected festivals, description of five festivals, craft activities, further reading, and a recipe for young readers. [Cited in the text as *FestWrld: Mongolia-1999*]

11. Nepal

Anderson, Mary M. *The Festivals of Nepal.* London: George Allen & Unwin Ltd., 1971.

> Describes, in chronological order of occurrence, more than 30 Hindu, Buddhist, and Nepalese festivals attended in Nepal, as well as legends and customs associated with them.

12. Philippines

♦ Mendoza, Lunita. *Festivals of the World: Philippines.* (Festivals of the World Series) Milwaukee: Gareth Stevens Publishing, 1999.

> Provides brief introduction to the country, calendar of selected festivals, description of five festivals, craft activities, further reading, and a recipe for young readers. [Cited in the text as *FestWrld: Phil-1999*]

13. Saudi Arabia

♦ O'Shea, Maria. *Festivals of the World: Saudi Arabia.* (Festivals of the World Series) Milwaukee: Gareth Stevens Publishing, 1999.

> Provides brief introduction to the country, calendar of selected festivals, description of five festivals, craft activities, further reading, and a recipe for young readers. [Cited in the text as *FestWrld: Saudi-1999*]

14. Thailand

♦ Whyte, Harlinah. *Festivals of the World: Thailand.* (Festivals of the World Series) Milwaukee: Gareth Stevens Publishing, 1998.

> Provides brief introduction to the country, calendar of selected festivals, description of five festivals, craft activities, further reading, and a recipe for young readers. [Cited in the text as *FestWrld: Thailand-1998*]

♦ Indicates a book cited in the main text

15. Turkey

♦ O'Shea, Maria. *Festivals of the World: Turkey*. (Festivals of the World Series) Milwaukee: Gareth Stevens Publishing, 1999.

> Provides brief introduction to the country, calendar of selected festivals, description of five festivals, craft activities, further reading, and a recipe for young readers. [Cited in the text as *Fest-Wrld: Turkey-1999*]

16. Vietnam

Crawford, Ann Caddell. *Customs and Culture of Vietnam*. Foreword by Henry Cabot Lodge. Illustrations by Hau Dinh Cam. Rutland, VT: Charles E. Tuttle Co., Publishers, 1966.

> In addition to providing a calendar and description of festivals and holidays, this book is a survey of mainly South Vietnamese geography, history, culture, religion, education, media, arts, medicine, agriculture, and industry against the backdrop of the Vietnam War. Customs, ceremonies, legends, and points of interest are also included.

♦ McKay, Susan. *Festivals of the World: Vietnam*. (Festivals of the World Series) Milwaukee: Gareth Stevens Publishing, 1997.

> Provides brief introduction to the country, calendar of selected festivals, description of five festivals, craft activities, further reading, and a recipe for young readers. [Cited in the text as *Fest-Wrld: Viet-1997*]

E. Caribbean and Latin America

1. General Works

Houston, Lynn Marie. *Food Culture in the Caribbean*. Westport, CT: Greenwood Publishing, 2005.

> Provides insight into the culture of the Caribbean by focusing on its foods. Looks at the region's foods and eating habits, reviewing distinctive social, cultural, linguistic, geographical, political, and economic characteristics. Includes a historical overview, major foods, cooking, typical meals, eating out, special occasions, recipes, and more.

♦ Milne, Jean. *Fiesta Time in Latin America*. Los Angeles: The Ward Ritchie Press, 1965.

> Organized chronologically, this book discusses more than 80 festivals celebrated in Mexico and Central and South America. Concludes with list of festivals by country. [Cited in the text as *FiestaTime-1965*]

2. Cuba

Bettelheim, Judith, ed. *Cuban Festivals: An Illustrated Anthology*. New York: Garland Publishing, Inc., 1993.

> Scholars from various academic disciplines present essays on Cuban festivals: "The Afro-Cuban Festival 'Day of the Kings'," Fernando Ortiz; "Annotated Glossary for Fernando Ortiz's The Afro-Cuban Festival 'Day of the Kings'," David H. Brown; "Glossary of Popular Festivals," Rafael Brea and José Millet; "Carnival in Santiago de Cuba" and "Appendix: The Tumba Francesa and Tajona of Santiago de Cuba," Judith Bettelheim; and "Flashback on Carnival, a Personal Memoir," Pedro Pérez Sarduy.

3. Dominican Republic

Matibag, Eugenio. *Haitian-Dominican Counterpoint: Nation, State, and Race*. New York: Palgrave, 2003.

> An analysis of the relationship between Haiti and the Dominican Republic, looking at cultural, economic, social, and political ties across the border.

Zakrewski Brown, Isabel. *Culture and Customs of the Dominican Republic*. Westport, CT: Greenwood Press, 1999.

> Presents an overview of contemporary cultural life in the Dominican Republic, focusing on such topics as geography, religion, social customs, media, and the arts.

4. El Salvador

Boyland, Roy. *Culture and Customs of El Salvador*. Westport, CT: Greenwood Publishing, 2001.

> Presents an overview of contemporary cultural life in El Salvador, focusing on such topics as geography, religion, social customs, media, and the arts.

5. Haiti

Dunham, Katherine. *Dance of Haiti*. Foreword by Claude Lévi-Strauss. Photographs by Patricia Cummings. Los Angeles: University of California, 1983.

> In a revised version of her thesis, the dancer-anthropologist surveys religious, social, and festive uses of dance in Haiti, including some commentary on dance and Lent, Mardi Gras, Holy Week, and Easter.

Matibag, Eugenio. *Haitian-Dominican Counterpoint: Nation, State, and Race*. New York: Palgrave, 2003.

> An analysis of the relationship between Haiti and the Dominican Republic, looking at cultural, economic, social, and political ties across the border.

♦ Ngcheong-Lum, Roseline. *Festivals of the World: Haiti*. (Festivals of the World Series) Milwaukee: Gareth Stevens Publishing, 1999.

> Provides brief introduction to the country, calendar of selected festivals, description of five festivals, craft activities, further reading, and a recipe for young readers. [Cited in the text as *Fest-Wrld: Haiti-1999*]

Pamphile, Léon Dénius. *Haitians and African Americans: A Heritage of Tragedy*. Gainesville: University Press of Florida, 2001.

> Studies the relationship between Haitians and African Americans, from the colonial era to the present day.

Perusse, Roland I. *Historical Dictionary of Haiti*. Lanham, MD: Scarecrow Press, 1977.

> A historical dictionary that provides a range of tools: an introductory narrative covering Haiti's political and economic history; a chronology from the earliest known history to the present day; hundreds of cross-referenced dictionary entries covering people, places, events, institutions, movements, political and social groups, and cultural issues; and an extensive bibliography of current publications.

Schiller, Nina Glick, and Georges Eugene Fouron. *Georges Woke Up Laughing: Long-Distance Nationalism*. Durham, NC: Duke University Press, 2001.

> Uses history, autobiography, and ethnography to show the Haitian experience of migration to the United States, with insight into the ongoing effects of globalization.

♦ Indicates a book cited in the main text

6. Jamaica

Mordecai, Martin, and Pamela Mordecai. *Culture and Customs of Jamaica*. Westport, CT: Greenwood Publishing, 2001.

> Presents an overview of contemporary cultural life in Jamaica, focusing on such topics as geography, religion, social customs, media, and the arts.

7. Mexico

Beezley, William H., Cheryl English Martin, and William E. French, eds. *Rituals of Rule, Rituals of Resistance: Public Celebrations and Popular Culture in Mexico*. Wilmington, DE: Scholarly Resources, Inc., 1994.

> Presents 15 papers by scholars at the Eighth Conference of Mexican and North American Historians in San Diego, 1990. Essays analyze popular culture, rituals, customs, and festivals in Mexico in the context of political power and colonial domination.

Burland, C. A. *The Gods of Mexico*. New York: G. P. Putnam's Sons, 1967.

> Alphabetical listing of Aztec gods. Guide to pronunciation. Covers Aztec, Mayan, Toltec, and Olmec cultures, cities, calendar systems, deities, and religions. Aztec ceremonies and festivals described. Appendices discuss Mayan, Aztec, and other Mexican codices and tlachtli, a ball game.

Fergusson, Erna. *Fiesta in Mexico*. Illustrated by Valentín Vidaurreta. New York: Alfred A. Knopf, 1934.

> Account of travel to festivals throughout Mexico, including Pilgrimage to Chalma, Moors and Christians in Tuxpan, La Fiesta de Nuestra Señora de la Soledad in Oaxaca, Passion Play in Tzintzuntzan, Los Voladores in Coxquihui, a Yaqui Indian Pascola, Deer Dance, Coyote Dance, Los Matachines, Holy Week, Good Friday and Holy Saturday in Tlaxcala, Day of the Dead, All Saints' Day and All Souls' Day, Lent, Fiesta of Nuestra Seña de la Santa Vera Cruz, El Viernes de Dolores (fifth Friday in Lent) in Santa Anita, Christmas, and Posadas. Also includes historical discussion of ancient Aztec, Christian, and secular celebrations.

Marcus, Rebecca B., and Judith Marcus. *Fiesta Time in Mexico*. Champaign, IL: Garrard Publishing Company, 1974.

> Intended for young readers, this book describes the following holidays and festivals observed in Mexico: Day of the Dead, Our Lady of Guadalupe, Christmas, New Year's, Day of the Three Kings, St. Anthony the Abbot's Day, Holy Week and Easter, St. John's Day, Mexican Independence Day, Fifth of May, and the Twentieth of November. Pronunciation guide.

♦ Miller, Mary, and Karl Taube. *An Illustrated Dictionary of the Gods and Symbols of Ancient Mexico and the Maya*. New York: Thames and Hudson Ltd., 1993.

> Nearly 300 entries on religion in ancient Mesoamerica include coverage of gods, symbols, sacred sites, practices, and concepts. Two essays precede the entries: one on Mesoamerican cultural history, the other on Mesoamerican religion. [Cited in the text as *GodsSymbAncMex-1993*]

Toor, Frances. *A Treasury of Mexican Folkways: The Customs, Myths, Folklore, Traditions, Beliefs, Fiestas, Dances, and Songs of the Mexican People*. New York: Bonanza Books, 1985.

> Covers agricultural, religious, and folk festivals and ceremonies celebrated by the various peoples in Mexico, including dances, songs, folk arts, legends, riddles, and idiomatic expressions.

8. Trinidad

Hill, Errol. *The Trinidad Carnival: Mandate for a National Theatre*. Austin: University of Texas Press, 1972.

> Historical survey of Trinidad and the Carnival, calypso, and masquerades, including descriptions of observances from the 19th century. Argues that elements of the Carnival and its related traditions should be harnessed toward producing a national theater. Appendices provide an example of calypso drama as well as a list of 50 renowned calypsos.

F. South America

Buechler, Hans C. *The Masked Media: Aymara Fiestas and Social Interaction in the Bolivian Highlands*. The Hague, Netherlands: Mouton Publishers, 1980.

> Anthropologist presents results of fieldwork on festivals, saints' fiestas, and other rituals among the Aymara people in Bolivia. Appendices offer notes on musical instruments employed during different festivals throughout the year; a description of the Fiesta of the Skulls at the main cemetery in La Paz; comparative table of food and drink expenditures for sponsors of rural and urban festivals during the 1960s and 1970s; a fiesta sponsor's list of participants' contributions and involvement with a fiesta held in Lamacachi; and a note on recent use of brass bands in Compi fiestas. Index of authors referenced. Index of subjects.

♦ Jermyn, Leslie. *Festivals of the World: Peru*. (Festivals of the World Series) Milwaukee: Gareth Stevens Publishing, 1998.

> Provides brief introduction to the country, calendar of selected festivals, description of five festivals, craft activities, further reading, and a recipe for young readers. [Cited in the text as *FestWrld: Peru-1998*]

♦ Roraff, Susan. *Festivals of the World: Chile*. (Festivals of the World Series) Milwaukee: Gareth Stevens Publishing, 1998.

> Provides brief introduction to the country, calendar of selected festivals, description of five festivals, craft activities, further reading, and recipes for young readers. [Cited in the text as *FestWrld: Chile-1998*]

G. Europe

1. General Works

♦ Cooper, Gordon. *Festivals of Europe*. 1961. Reprint. Detroit: Omnigraphics, Inc., 1994.

> Tourist-oriented guide provides brief mentions or descriptions of more than 1,000 festivals in 25 Western and Eastern European countries. Arranged alphabetically by country, festivals are discussed by type of event: agricultural, carnival, cultural, national, religious, sporting, trade, wine and food. Chapter offering travel hints. [Cited in the text as *FestEur-1961*]

Cosman, Madeleine Pelner. *Medieval Holidays and Festivals: A Calendar of Celebrations*. New York: Charles Scribner's Sons, 1981.

> Describes customs, activities, food and recipes, music, costume and decoration associated with 12 holidays from the 12th through the 16th centuries, mainly in England, France, Italy, and Germany: Twelfth Night, Valentine's Day, Easter, All Fool's Day, May Daydsummer Eve, St. Swithin's Day, Lammaschaelmas, Halloween, St. Catherine's Day, and Christmas. Further reading list.

Crampton, Richard, and Ben Crampton. *Atlas of Eastern Europe in the Twentieth Century*. London: Routledge, 1997.

♦ Indicates a book cited in the main text

Draws a definitive picture of the changing shape of Eastern Europe from the beginning of the 20th century to the present.

Hanawalt, Barbara A., and Kathryn L. Reyerson, eds. *City and Spectacle in Medieval Europe*. Minneapolis: University of Minnesota Press, 1994.

> Includes 12 papers from a 1991 conference at the University of Minnesota that explore various kinds of ritual and ceremony observed in medieval Europe, including liturgical rites in France, Holy Thursday in Spain, mid-summer in London, accounts of several festivals in medieval Castile, and more.

Johnson, Margaret M. *Festival Europe! Fairs & Celebrations throughout Europe*. Memphis: Mustang Publishing Co., 1992.

> Tourist-oriented guide organized by region. Entries on more than 700 festivals in 21 countries are in chronological order, from May to October. Includes descriptions of types of events held in each country. Addresses of tourist boards are provided.

Madden, Daniel M. *A Religious Guide to Europe*. New York: Macmillan Publishing Co., Inc., 1975.

> Describes making pilgrimages to hundreds of shrines, sanctuaries, and other holy places in more than 15 European countries, from Ireland to Turkey. Travel and accommodation information, as well as descriptions of secular points of interest are provided.

♦ Perl, Lila. *Foods and Festivals of the Danube Lands: Germany, Austria, Czechoslovakia, Hungary, Yugoslavia, Bulgaria, Romania, Russia*. Illustrated by Leo Glueckselig. Cleveland: The World Publishing Company, 1969.

> Discusses foods, festivals, and traditions in countries bordering the Danube River. Provides historical overview on the region and on each country's people and lifestyles, often stretching back to prehistoric times. Heavy coverage of foods prepared and consumed in each country, including recipes. [Cited in the text as *FoodFestDanube-1969*]

♦ Rabin, Carol Price. *Music Festivals in Europe and Britain*. Stockbridge, MA: Berkshire Traveller Press, 1980.

> More than 90 music festivals in 21 European countries are described, arranged by country. Entries provide historical background, type of music offered, notable features and performers from past festivals, contact names, addresses and phone numbers for obtaining tickets and accommodation, and recommended attire. Listing of addresses and phone numbers of government tourist offices. Suggested reading list. [Cited in the text as *MusFestEurBrit-1980*]

♦ Spicer, Dorothy Gladys. *Festivals of Western Europe*. 1958. Reprint. Detroit: Omnigraphics, Inc., 1994.

> Major festivals in 12 western European countries described in more than 250 entries. Some material duplicates or is revised from that found in the author's *Book of Festivals*. Table of dates for Easter and other Christian movable days from 1958 to 1988. Glossary of festival terms. Suggested reading list. Indexes of festivals by country and by names of festivals. [Cited in the text as *FestWestEur-1958*]

2. Albania

Jacques, Edwin E. *The Albanians: An Ethnic History from Prehistoric Times to the Present*. Jefferson, NC: McFarland, 1995.

> A history of Albania that details the struggle of its people to maintain their cultural and linguistic integrity and their ethnic identity despite foreign influence on the country. Includes Albanian, French, Italian and many other documentary sources.

3. Bulgaria

Crampton, R. J. *A Concise History of Bulgaria*. Cambridge: Cambridge University Press, 2005.

> Presents a general introduction to Bulgaria and comments on its historical relationship to Macedonia.

Roudometof, Victor. *Collective Memory, National Identity, and Ethnic Conflict: Greece, Bulgaria, and the Macedonian Question*. Westport, CT: Praeger, 2002.

> In-depth analysis of inter-ethnic relations in the southern Balkans. The author examines the evolution of the Macedonian Question and the production of rival national narratives by Greeks, Bulgarians, and Macedonians

4. Czechoslovakia

Martin, Pat, comp. *Czechoslovak Culture: Recipes, History and Folk Arts*. Iowa City, IA: Penfield Press, 1989.

> Focus is on Czech-American culture, including traditions and stories carried over from Czechoslovakia. Essays on pioneer experiences, observance of holidays, including lengthy treatment of decorating Easter eggs, folk art, foods and recipes. Profiles of famous Czechs and Czech Americans. A partial list of Czech festivals throughout the United States and tips on planning Czech festivals.

5. France

Janvier, Thomas A. *The Christmas Kalends of Provence*. 1902. Reprint. Detroit: Omnigraphics, Inc., 1990. 262 pp. Illustrated.

> Relates tales about rites and celebrations of ancient feasts and festivals practiced in France.

♦ McKay, Susan. *Festivals of the World: France*. (Festivals of the World Series) Milwaukee: Gareth Stevens Publishing, 1998.

> Provides brief introduction to the country, calendar of selected festivals, description of five festivals, craft activities, further reading, and a recipe for young readers. [Cited in the text as *FestWrld: France-1998*]

Ozouf, Mona. *Festivals and the French Revolution*. Translated by Alan Sheridan. Cambridge, MA: Harvard University Press, 1988.

> Historian examines the Revolutionary festivals observed between 1789 and 1799, and their role in the French Revolution. Discussion of Revolutionary calendar. Brief chronology of the Revolution.

6. Germany

Russ, Jennifer M. *German Festivals & Customs*. London: Oswald Wolff, 1982.

> Origins and observance of more than 50 religious, historical, and food festivals, pageants, and social customs and ceremonies. Includes rhymes, food, legends, and songs associated with events. Appendices include list of legal holidays in the Federal Republic of Germany. Subject index. Index of names and places.

7. Greece

Megas, George A. *Greek Calendar Customs*. Athens, Greece: Press and Information Department, 1958.

> Covers customs, beliefs, legends, food, and songs associated with more than 60 saints' days, holidays, festivals, and agricul-

♦ Indicates a book cited in the main text

tural activities in Greece (especially rural traditions), according to the seasons of the year.

Roudometof, Victor. *Collective Memory, National Identity, and Ethnic Conflict: Greece, Bulgaria, and the Macedonian Question.* Westport, CT: Praeger, 2002.

> In-depth analysis of inter-ethnic relations in the southern Balkans. The author examines the evolution of the Macedonian Question and the production of rival national narratives by Greeks, Bulgarians, and Macedonians.

Shea, John. *Macedonia and Greece: The Struggle to Define a New Balkan Nation.* Jefferson, NC: McFarland & Company, 1997.

> Details conflict in the Balkans, specifically focusing on the nations of Macedonia and Greece.

8. Hungary

Dömötör, Tekla. *Hungarian Folk Customs.* Translated by Judith Elliott. Corvina, Budapest, Hungary: Corvina Press, 1972.

> Brief survey of folk customs and beliefs, and their study in Hungary. Discussion of history and observance of seasonal, religious, and secular festivals, as well as birth, marriage, and burial practices.

9. Italy

Ashby, Thomas. *Some Italian Scenes and Festivals.* New York: E. P. Dutton and Company, Inc., c1928.

> Describes several religious and folk festivals observed in Italy, while providing impressions of the landscape and peoples, as well as some historical background.

Toor, Frances. *Festivals and Folkways of Italy.* New York: Crown Publishers, Inc., 1953.

> Describes the author's observations of holidays, festivals, and folk customs in Sicily, southern Italy and Sardinia, and Rome and its outskirts. Appendix includes notes on Italian festas, beliefs, folk arts, and folklore bibliography.

10. Macedonia

Crampton, R. J. *A Concise History of Bulgaria.* Cambridge: Cambridge University Press, 2005.

> Presents a general introduction to Bulgaria and comments on its historical relationship to Macedonia.

Poulton, Hugh. *Who Are the Macedonians?* Bloomington: Indiana University Press, 2000.

> Traces the history of Macedonia from antiquity to the present.

Roudometof, Victor. *Collective Memory, National Identity, and Ethnic Conflict: Greece, Bulgaria, and the Macedonian Question.* Westport, CT: Praeger, 2002.

> In-depth analysis of inter-ethnic relations in the southern Balkans. The author examines the evolution of the Macedonian Question and the production of rival national narratives by Greeks, Bulgarians, and Macedonians.

Shea, John. *Macedonia and Greece: The Struggle to Define a New Balkan Nation.* Jefferson, NC: McFarland & Company, 1997.

> Details conflict in the Balkans, specifically focusing on the nations of Macedonia and Greece.

11. Russia

♦ Whyte, Harlinah. *Festivals of the World: Russia.* (Festivals of the World Series) Milwaukee: Gareth Stevens Publishing, 1997. 32 pp. Illustrated. Glossary. Index.

> Provides brief introduction to the country, calendar of selected festivals, description of five festivals, craft activities, further reading, and a recipe for young readers. [Cited in the text as *FestWrld: Russia-1997*]

12. Scandinavia

Wyndham, Lee. *Holidays in Scandinavia.* Illustrated by Gordon Laite. Champaign, IL: Garrard Publishing Company, 1975.

> Discusses 10 holidays and festivals in Sweden, Norway, and Denmark for young readers. Pronunciation guide.

13. Soviet Union (former)

Petrone, Karen. *Life Has Become More Joyous, Comrades: Celebrations in the Time of Stalin.* Bloomington: Indiana University Press, 2000.

> A social history of such celebrations in the Soviet era as New Year's Day, the anniversary of the 1917 revolution, and other historical and socialist commemorations, and analysis of the role such celebrations played in Soviet life.

Watson, Jane Werner. *A Parade of Soviet Holidays.* Illustrated by Ben Stahl. Champaign, IL: Garrard Publishing Company, 1974.

> Aimed at a young audience, discusses the significance and celebration of more than 20 holidays and festivals observed throughout the former Soviet Union.

14. Spain

♦ Epton, Nina. *Spanish Fiestas (Including Romerías, Excluding Bull-Fights).* New York: A. S. Barnes and Company, 1968.

> Descriptions of Easter, Corpus Christidsummer, Christmas, New Year's, and Carnival celebrations throughout Spain, as well as Moors and Christians fiestas, and more than 30 other festivals, holy days, and romerías (pilgrimages) observed in Spain. [Cited in the text as *SpanFiestas-1968*]

15. Ukraine

♦ Bassis, Vladimir. *Festivals of the World: Ukraine.* (Festivals of the World Series) Milwaukee: Gareth Stevens Publishing, 1998.

> Provides brief introduction to the country, calendar of selected festivals, description of five festivals, craft activities, further reading, and a recipe for young readers. [Cited in the text as *FestWrld: Ukraine-1998*]

16. United Kingdom

Brand, John. *Observations on Popular Antiquities, Chiefly Illustrating the Origin of Our Vulgar Customs, Ceremonies, and Superstitions; with the Additions of Sir Henry Ellis.* London: Chatto and Windus, 1877.

> Chronologically arranged discussion, with historical background, of more than 60 holidays and festivals as observed in western Europe, especially England. Collection of lore on hundreds of items falling under such headings as sports and games, charms and omens, witchcraft and mythology, marriage, childbearing, death, and drinking customs.

♦ Indicates a book cited in the main text

Cameron, David Kerr. *The English Fair*. Thrupp, Stroud, Gloucestershire: Sutton, 1998.

> Beautifully illustrated history of fairs in England from ancient times to the present, based on local sources, interviews, and museum and library archives.

Drake-Carnell, F. J. *Old English Customs and Ceremonies*. New York: Charles Scribner's Sons; London: B. T. Batsford Ltd., 1938.

> Survey of religious, municipal (London), legal, commerciallitary, school, marine, and royal ceremonies, customs and protocol relating to the House of Parliament, and rural festivals and traditions—such as the Furry Dance, Beating the Bounds, and Plough Monday—observed in England.

♦ Hole, Christina. *English Custom & Usage*. 1941-42. Reprint. Detroit: Omnigraphics, Inc., 1990.

> Discusses the celebration of various holidays in England and examines the transformation of pre-Christian observances and rituals into Christian holy days. [Cited in the text as *EngCust-Use-1941*]

♦ Howard, Alexander. *Endless Cavalcade: A Diary of British Festivals and Customs*. London: Arthur Barker Limited, 1964.

> Arranged in chronological order, over 360 entries describe at least one holiday, festival, civic event or custom for every day of the year, as observed in Britain. [Cited in the text as *EndlessCaval-1964*]

Jones, T. Gwynn. *Welsh Folklore and Folk-Custom*. 1930. Reprint. Suffolk, England: D. S. Brewer, 1979.

> Collection of Welsh folklore regarding gods, ghosts, fairies, monsters, caves, lakes, magic, marriage, birth, and death. Recounting of some folk tales. Chapters 9-10 deal with customs concerning such holidays as May Daydsummer, Christmas, New Year's, Easter, Mari Lwyd, and others.

Kightly, Charles. *The Customs and Ceremonies of Britain: An Encyclopaedia of Living Traditions*. London: Thames & Hudson Ltd., 1986.

> Book opens with a Calendar of Customs, listing events and holidays in chronological order. Next, in alphabetical order, more than 200 entries describe the observance and historical background of religious holidays, secular festivals, and other elements of social life. Practices associated with other types of events are discussed under such general headings as "Bells and Bellringing Customs," "Birth," "Civic Customs," "Coronations," "Fairs," and "Harvest Customs." Regional listing of events.

Le Vay, Benedict. *Eccentric Britain: The Bradt Guide to Britain's Follies and Foibles*. Guilford, CT: The Globe Pequot Press, 2000.

> Describes quirky events, practices, customs, people, and places in the United Kingdom. Includes travel and contact information.

♦ Long, George. *The Folklore Calendar*. 1930. Reprint. Detroit: Omnigraphics, Inc., 1990.

> Arranged in chronological order, entries provide historical background for, and cover observance of, more than 40 holidays, festivals, ceremonies, and other events in Great Britain. [Cited in the text as *FolkCal-1930*]

Owen, Trefor M. *A Pocket Guide: The Customs and Traditions of Wales*. Cardiff: University of Wales Press, 1991.

> Discusses agricultural traditions, customs associated with the home and domestic life, Mari Lwyd, St. Thomas's Day, Twelfth Night, Candlemas, St. David's Day, religious and communal observances and events, and eisteddfod from the 19th century to the present day. Historical survey of the study of folk customs in Wales. Selected reading list by chapter.

♦ Palmer, Geoffrey, and Noel Lloyd. *A Year of Festivals: A Guide to British Calendar Customs*. London: Frederick Warne, 1972.

> Discusses the history and current practice of numerous calendar customs in the United Kingdom in chronological order. Also includes chapters on customs in London and fairs and a list of customs according to county. [Cited in the text as *YrFest-1972*]

♦ Spicer, Dorothy Gladys. *Yearbook of English Festivals*. 1954. Reprint. Detroit: Omnigraphics, Inc., 1993.

> Chronologically arranged descriptions of more than 200 English holidays, ceremonies, anniversaries, and local festivals and traditions. Map of England depicting regions and counties. Explanation of Julian and Gregorian calendars and their coexistence in parts of the country. List of movable Christian feasts dependent upon the date of Easter. List of liturgical colors, what they symbolize and when they are used. Table of dates of Easter for 1954 to 1984. Suggested reading list. Indexes by name of event, county, and region. [Cited in the text as *YrbookEngFest-1954*]

Wright, A. R. *British Calendar Customs*. 3 vols. Preface by S. H. Hooke. London: William Glaisher Ltd., 1936.

> Volumes I through III cover popular customs, lore, superstitions, weather omens, and songs associated with holidays and festivals observed in England. Volume I deals with Christian movable holidays from Shrovetide to Corpus Christi, as well as other movable festivals and harvest customs. Volumes II and III survey nearly 100 secular and religious festivals occurring on fixed dates, presented in chronological order.

H. North America

1. General Works

♦ Davis, Alan. *The Fun Also Rises: Travel Guide North America*. San Francisco: Greenline Publications, 1998.

> Travel guide focusing on "the most fun places to be at the right time." For each of 92 events the author provides description of the event, day-by-day plans for attending, travel-related information about accommodations, restaurants, local sights, and nightlife, including contact information. Events and cities are rated for "fun." [Cited in the text as *FunAlsoRises-1998*]

2. Canada

Parry, Caroline. *Let's Celebrate! Canada's Special Days*. Toronto, Ontario, Canada: Kids Can Press Ltd., 1987.

> For young readers. Entries cover more than 250 secular and religious holidays and festivals celebrated in Canada, including Muslim, Hindu, Chinese, Jewish, Baha'i, Sikh, Jaina, Buddhist, and Christian holy days. Entries are organized by season of the year and, in addition to discussion of the holiday's background, include riddles, games, poems, crafts, and other activities. Explanation of the calendar, as well as sidebars providing brief background notes on various religious and ethnic groups.

3. Native North America

♦ Eagle/Walking Turtle. *Indian America: A Traveller's Companion*. Santa Fe: John Muir Publications, 1989.

More than 300 Indian tribes in the United States are listed and arranged by geographical region. Entries provide mailing address and location, phone numbers, public ceremony or powwow dates, visitor information, and historical background. The appendix offers chronological listing of Indian Moons according to tribe; powwow calendar for North America; Indian arts and crafts shows; Navajo rug auctions; museums with major American Indian collections; Indian-owned and -operated museums and cultural centers, stores, rodeos, and community colleges; populations by state as of April 1980; reservations, rancherias and pueblos with population figures; and urban Indian centers in major metropolitan areas. [Cited in the text as *IndianAmer-1989*]

Faris, James C. *The Nightway: A History and a History of Documentation of a Navajo Ceremonial*. Albuquerque: University of New Mexico Press, 1990.

Anthropologist presents a study of recordings of the Navajo Nightway Ceremony and its stories, songs, beliefs, prayers and practices, including sandpainting. Charts and figures detail genealogies of medicine men who have led the Nightway, as well as specific elements of Nightways observed over the last 100 years.

♦ Fergusson, Erna. *Dancing Gods: Indian Ceremonials of New Mexico and Arizona*. Foreword by Tony Hillerman. Albuquerque: University of New Mexico Press, 1931. Sixth paperback printing, 1991.

Describes history, meaning, and performance of religious and social dances and ceremonies observed among the Pueblo, Hopi, Navajo, and Apache peoples, including prayers, customs, and some historical background on each. [Cited in the text as *DancingGods-1931*]

Fewkes, Jesse Walter. *Hopi Snake Ceremonies; An Eyewitness Account*. Selections from Bureau of American Ethnology, Annual Reports Nos. 16 and 19 for the years 1894-95 and 1897-98. Albuquerque: Avanyu Publishing, Inc., 1986.

Reprint of two papers published in annual reports. Author describes ceremonies performed by the Hopi Snake Society during the 1890s.

Fewkes, Jesse Walter. *Tusayan Katcinas and Hopi Altars*. Introduction by Barton Wright. Albuquerque: Avanyu Publishing, Inc., 1990.

Reprint of two texts by Fewkes, one an article, "The Katcina Altars in Hopi Worship," that appeared in the Annual Report of the Board of Regents of The Smithsonian Institution for 1926. Both represent author's late 19th-century endeavor to describe and analyze katchina ceremonials among the Hopis, including the Powamû ceremony.

♦ Hirschfelder, Arlene, and Paulette Molin. *Encyclopedia of Native American Religions*. Updated ed. Foreword by Walter R. Echo-Hawk. New York: Checkmark Books/Facts on File, 2001.

More than 1,200 cross-referenced entries cover religious beliefs, practices, ceremonies, sacred sites, and symbols of more than 80 North American Indian tribes. There are also entries on Native religion-related court cases and legislation. A subject index and a standard index are provided. [Cited in the text as *Ency-NatAmerRel-2001*]

♦ Kavasch, E. Barrie. *Enduring Harvests: Native American Foods and Festivals for Every Season*. Illustrated by Mitzi Rawls. Old Saybrook, CT: The Globe Pequot Press, 1995.

Profiles, in chronological order from September to August, 75 Native festivals in North and South America and provides more than 150 recipes related to the events. Includes a directory of sellers of Native foods. [Cited in the text as *EndurHarv-1995*]

Tiller, Veronica E., ed. *Discover Indian Reservations USA: A Visitors' Welcome Guide*. Foreword by Ben Nighthorse Campbell. Denver: Council Publications, 1992.

Travel-oriented information provided on more than 350 federal and state Indian reservations in 33 states, listed in alphabetical order by state. Entries include a brief profile on the reservation's land, population, and structure, its location and address, cultural institutes, special events (festivals, powwows, rodeos, etc.), businesses and organizations, accommodations, and special restrictions. Appendix I lists tribes alphabetically and gives their location. Appendix II is a powwow directory by state, then month.

4. United States—General Works and Background on Holidays

♦ Anyike, James C. *African American Holidays: A Historical Research and Resource Guide to Cultural Celebrations*. Chicago: Popular Truth, Inc., 1991.

Covers holidays celebrated by slaves between the 17th and 19th centuries as well as Martin Luther King, Jr. birthday observances, Black History Month, African Liberation Day, Juneteenth, Umoja Karamu (Unity Feast), and Kwanzaa. Appendices include timeline of important dates in history and brief historical background on major holidays observed in the United States. List of related sources and organizations. [Cited in the text as *AfrAmerHol-1991*]

Bailey, Carolyn Sherwin. *Stories for Every Holiday*. 1919. Reprint. Detroit: Omnigraphics, Inc., 1990.

Includes 27 stories for young readers about 19 Christian and secular holidays observed in the United States. Arranged in chronological order, beginning with Labor Day.

♦ Coates, Helen R. *The American Festival Guide: A Handbook of More Than 200 Colonial, Homesteading, Western, Spanish, Folk, Rodeo, Sports, Cultural and Other Annual Festivals and Celebrations in the United States and Canada, with a Calendar and a Gazetteer of Festivals for Ready Reference*. 1956. Reprint. Detroit: Omnigraphics, Inc., 1998.

Part One of the book contains detailed descriptions of 10 representative festivals. Part Two covers nearly 200 festivals, arranged by type, in detail. Completing the book are a calendar of festivals, arranged by month, and a gazetteer of festivals, arranged by state. [Cited in the text as *AmerFestGuide-1956*]

Coffin, Tristram P., and Hennig Cohen, eds. *Folklore in America: Tales, Songs, Superstitions, Proverbs, Riddles, Games, Folk Drama, and Folk Festivals with 17 Folk Melodies*. 1966. Reprinted by University Press of America, Inc., 1986.

Presents numerous examples of folk tradition among more than 30 ethnic groups in the United States. Index of ethnic groups and geographic locations. Index of titles and first lines of songs. List of tale types and motifs.

Cohen, Hennig, and Tristram Potter Coffin. *America Celebrates! A Patchwork of Weird & Wonderful Holiday Lore*. Detroit: Visible Ink Press, 1991.

Drawing from oral history and newspaper and journal accounts, this book collects more than 200 traditions, legends, beliefs, superstitions, recipes, food, games, dances, poems, riddles, and music associated with over 60 religious, patriotic, commemorative, agricultural, ethnic, and folk holidays and fes-

♦ Indicates a book cited in the main text

Bibliography

tivals observed among various ethnic, regional, and occupational groups in North America.

♦ Cohen, Hennig, and Tristram Potter Coffin, eds. *The Folklore of American Holidays: A Compilation of More Than 600 Beliefs, Legends, Superstitions, Proverbs, Riddles, Poems, Songs, Dances, Games, Plays, Pageants, Fairs, Foods, and Processions Associated with Over 140 American Calendar Customs and Festivals.* 3rd ed. Detroit: Gale Research Inc., 1999.

Chronologically arranged collection of lore associated with more than 140 holidays and festivals in the United States. Various ethnic, occupational, and religious groups living in the United States are represented. The editors provide brief background information on the event's history, followed by excerpts from written material describing actual observances of the event, as well as accompanying customs, legends, games, recipes, music, etc. Bibliographic information for each source follows the excerpts. Subject Index; Ethnic and Geographic Index; Collectors, Informants, and Translators Index; Song Titles and First Significant Lines Index; and Motif and Tale Types Index. [Cited in the text as *FolkAmerHol-1999*]

♦ Christianson, Stephen G., comp. and ed. *The American Book of Days.* Fourth ed. New York: H. W. Wilson, 2000.

Contains more than 800 entries pertaining to American holidays, festivals, and anniversaries organized by month. Selections reflect events in American history, including entries on each U.S. president and chief justice. There is at least one entry for every day of the year. Entries tend to be lengthy, averaging about 1,300 words. Each month begins with an essay recounting the origin of the month, ancient festivals observed, and the month's birthstone. Nine appendices include essays on "The Calendar," "The Era," "The Days of the Week," "Signs of the Zodiac," a list of "Important Public Holidays and Events," and reprints of the U.S. Constitution, the Declaration of Independence, the Articles of Confederation, and the Mayflower Compact of 1620. [Cited in the text as *AmerBkDays-2000*]

Dillon, Philip Robert. *American Anniversaries; Every Day of the Year; Presenting Seven Hundred and Fifty Events in United States History, from the Discovery of America to the Present Day.* c1918. Reprint. Detroit: Omnigraphics, Inc., 1991.

Opens with a chronology of principal events during World War I and summary of armistice. Book is organized chronologically. At least one anniversary is given for each day of the year. Entries cover anniversaries of historical events and people in politics and legislation, commerce and invention, arts and letters.

♦ Gay, Kathlyn. *African-American Holidays, Festivals, and Celebrations: The History, Customs, and Symbols Associated with Both Traditional and Contemporary Religious and Secular Events Observed by Americans of African Descent.* Detroit: Omnigraphics, 2007.

Presents the history, customs, symbols, and lore of more than 100 diverse African-American holidays and festivals celebrated in the United States. Events covered include contemporary and historical African-American holidays—ranging from slave observances to Kwanzaa. Also covered are holidays and festivals commemorating notable people, historical events, and religious and cultural heritage. Each entry covers the name and date of the holiday or festival; its history and how it was created; when and where it was first celebrated; where and how it is observed today; web sites and contact information for relevant organizations; and suggestions for further reading. [Cited in the text as *AAH-2007*]

♦ Goring, Ruth. *Latino Life: Holidays and Celebrations.* Vero Beach, FL: Rourke Publications, 1995.

Describes family celebrations, religious and patriotic holidays, and folk festivals observed by Hispanic Americans. Includes a calendar of holidays and festivals. For young readers. [Cited in the text as *LatinoLife-1995*]

Greif, Martin. *The Holiday Book: America's Festivals and Celebrations.* New York: The Main Street Press, 1978.

Lengthy entries cover, in chronological order, traditions, customs, and poetry associated with 20 major patriotic, religious, and commemorative holidays observed in the United States. Shorter entries discuss background and observance of 20 more special days.

Gutiérrez, Ramón, and Geneviève Fabre, eds. *Feasts and Celebrations in North American Ethnic Communities.* Albuquerque: University of New Mexico Press, 1995.

Includes 12 essays that analyze celebrations and practices surrounding such events as funerals, holidays such as Halloween and Easter, folk festivals, and harvest rites among African Americans, Hispanics, Filipinos, West Indians, urban and rural Americans, and gays throughout North and South America.

Henderson, Helene, ed. *Patriotic Holidays of the United States: An Introduction to the History, Symbols, and Traditions behind the Major Holidays and Days of Observance.* Detroit: Omnigraphics, Inc., 2006.

Provides a wealth of historical material about national patriotic holidays celebrated in the United States. The book also provides an overview of the United States' form of government, national symbols, political parties, and the development of its national identity, as well as 18 important primary sources relating to the holidays. Other features include a chronology of key historical events, a bibliography, a list of web sites, and an index. [Cited in the text as *PatHols-2006*]

Hobbie, Margaret, comp. *Italian American Material Culture: A Directory of Collections, Sites, and Festivals in the United States and Canada.* Westport, CT: Greenwood Press, 1992.

Lists nearly 100 museum collections related to Italian-American culture, more than 40 sites around the U.S. significant in Italian-American history, and more than 100 religious, folk, agricultural, art, music, food, and commemorative festivals associated with Italian-American material culture. Festival entries provide information on event's location, sponsor address and phone number, dates observed, estimated annual attendance and date first observed, and brief description of festival activities. Sponsor name index. Subject index.

Jaynes, Gerald, ed. *Encyclopedia of African American Society.* 2 vols. Thousand Oaks, CA: Sage Reference, 2005.

A two-volume reference set that describes African-American culture, including music, literature, arts, religion, sports, and social issues.

Levinson, David, and Karen Christensen, eds. *Global Perspectives on the United States: A Nation by Nation Survey.* 2 vols. Great Barrington, MA: Berkshire, 2007.

Explores the image of the United States—its government, people, and culture—from the viewpoints of people around the world.

Litwicki, Ellen M. *America's Public Holidays, 1865-1920.* Washington, DC: Smithsonian Institution Press, 2000.

Examines the influence of the end of the Civil War, the wave of immigration, and the labor movement on the creation and observance of public holidays in the U.S. from 1865 to 1920.

♦ Indicates a book cited in the main text

Murphy, Joseph M. *Santería: African Spirits in America.* Boston: Beacon Press, 1988.

> Traces origins and presents beliefs, rituals, ceremonies, songs, gestures, foods, and herbs associated with the practice of the Santería ("the way of the saints") religion, an Afro-Cuban outgrowth of the Yoruba religion in Nigeria, as observed by African Americans in New York.

Olcott, Frances Jenkins. *Good Stories for Anniversaries.* Illustrated by Hattie Longstreet Price. 1937. Reprint. Detroit: Omnigraphics, Inc., 1990.

> More than 120 stories for children relating to holidays and events in the history of the United States, such as Inauguration Day, Bunker Hill Day, and pioneer days. Arranged chronologically by the school year.

♦ Rabin, Carol Price. *The Complete Guide to Music Festivals in America: Classical, Opera, Jazz, Pops, Country, Folk, Bluegrass, Old-Time Fiddlers, Cajun.* 4th ed. Illustrated by Celia Elke. Great Barrington, MA: Berkshire Traveller Press, 1990.

> Covers more than 150 music festivals in 40 of the United States and territories, as well as Canada, arranged by type of music. Within each section, festivals are listed by the state in which they take place. Entries include a description of the event and addresses and phone numbers to obtain information on purchasing tickets and finding accommodations. Listing of music festivals by location, with maps. Suggested reading list. Index by name of festival. [Cited in the text as *MusFestAmer-1990*]

Sandak, Cass R. *Patriotic Holidays.* New York: Crestwood House, 1990.

> Covers 16 patriotic holidays in the United States, and a handful of others elsewhere, for young readers. Further reading list.

Santino, Jack. *All Around the Year: Holidays and Celebrations in American Life.* Urbana and Chicago: University of Illinois Press, 1994.

> Discusses origins and meanings of holidays observed in the United States, and customs, ephemera, and symbols associated with them.

Schaun, George, and Virginia Schaun. *American Holidays and Special Days.* Illustrations by David Wisniewski. Lanham: Maryland Historical Press, 1986.

> Alphabetical and chronological listings of holidays. List of dates on which states were admitted to the United States. Part I discusses the various calendars, names of the months and days of the week, movable days, and reasons for observance of special days. Part II consists of more than 60 entries on holidays, festivals, and commemorative days observed in the United States in chronological order.

Schibsby, Marian, and Hanny Cohrsen. *Foreign Festival Customs.* Rev ed. New York: American Council for Nationalities Service, 1974.

> Describes Christmas, New Year's, and Easter customs, traditions, and recipes from more than 30 immigrant groups to the United States. Discusses Thanksgiving and harvest traditions from Europe.

♦ Shapiro, Larry. *A Book of Days in American History.* New York: Charles Scribner's Sons, 1987.

> Brief entries are arranged in calendar order and cover at least one event in U.S. history. Focus is on European settlement and history from pre-Revolutionary days through the 1970s. [Cited in the text as *BkDaysAmerHist-1987*]

♦ Shemanski, Frances. *A Guide to Fairs and Festivals in the United States.* Westport, CT: Greenwood Press, 1984.

> Following the format of *A Guide to World Fairs and Festivals* by the same author, this volume covers more than 260 fairs and festivals in the United States, American Samoa, Puerto Rico, and the U.S. Virgin Islands. Entries are arranged alphabetically by state and city, then by territory. Each entry provides a description of the festival's history, purpose, and idiosyncrasies of observance. A state-by-state chronological listing of festivals follows the main text. Appendix lists festivals by type. [Cited in the text as *GdUSFest-1984*]

Spicer, Dorothy Gladys. *Folk Festivals and the Foreign Community.* 1923. Reprint. Detroit: Omnigraphics, Inc., 1990.

> Offers advice on administration and production gleaned from folk festivals organized during the 1920s that were attempts to bond recent immigrants with those born in the United States by fostering understanding and appreciation of cultural diversity.

Thornton, Willis. *Almanac for Americans.* 1941. Reprint. Detroit: Gale Research Company, 1973.

> A "Book of Days of the Republic," arranged chronologically, focuses on patriotic holidays and historical events in the United States.

Tuleja, Tad. *Curious Customs: The Stories Behind 296 Popular American Rituals.* New York: Harmony Books, 1987.

> Provides historical information and occasionally tongue-in-cheek observations on major American holidays as well as customs and superstitions surrounding various social activities including gestures, apparel, etiquette, eating, and courtship.

5. United States—Works on the Presidents

Benbow, Nancy D. Myers, and Christopher H. Benbow. *Cabins, Cottages and Mansions: Homes of the Presidents of the United States.* Gettysburg, PA: Thomas Publications, 1993.

> A foreword by Pres. James A. Garfield's great-grandson leads off detailed entries on each president as well as the featured sites. Black-and-white photos and addresses, telephone numbers and traveling directions are included, as is an entry describing the White House.

Haas, Irvin. *Historic Homes of the American Presidents.* New York: Dover Publications, Inc., 1991.

> Entries on the homes or birthplaces of 35 U.S. presidents include excellent black-and-white photos (some exterior, some interior) and many detailed descriptions of the residences, though length of the entries varies. Addresses, telephone numbers, and traveling directions are included. The White House is also listed.

Kane, Joseph Nathan. *Facts About the Presidents.* New York: H. W. Wilson Company, 1993.

> This is a detailed and exhaustive source for "facts about the presidents." Biographical information on immediate family is included, with selected events of the president's life and administration highlighted. Comparative data (religion, military service and so on) is included along with election information and a section on the vice presidents.

Kern, Ellyn R. *Where the American Presidents Lived, Including a Guide to the Homes that Are Open.* Indianapolis: Cottontail Publications, 1982.

> Presidential lives broken down by years, with black-and-white photos and line drawings, followed by brief descriptions and history of sites with addresses, telephone numbers, and locations on line maps organized geographically.

♦ Indicates a book cited in the main text

Kochmann, Rachel M. *Presidents' Birthplaces, Homes and Burial Sites*. Osage, MN: Osage Publications, 1999.

> Black-and-white photographs accompany the brief text which includes basic facts, dates and a quote from each president. Addresses and traveling directions are listed along with locations on line maps.

Kruh, David, and Louis Kruh. *Presidential Landmarks*. New York: Hippocrene Books, 1992.

> Each entry opens with a two- to three-page overview of each president and his administration, followed by descriptions of sites and addresses, telephone numbers, and traveling directions. An entry on "multi-presidential" sites is also included. Photos are black-and-white.

6. United States—Works on the States

Abate, Frank, ed. *American Places Dictionary: A Guide to 45,000 Populated Places, Natural Features, and Other Places in the United States*. Four volumes. Detroit: Omnigraphics, Inc., 1994.

> Organized first by state, then by county, this reference work provides coverage of the following places throughout the U.S.: states, counties and county equivalents, incorporated places (cities, towns, etc.), unincorporated places (certain townships, villages, Census Designated Places, etc.), American Indian reservations, major military installations, and geographic features. Place entries for each state are preceded by various geographic and demographic data on the state, including symbols and name origin information, a description of the local government, and an essay on the state's history and boundaries. Place entries provide legal place name and status, latitude and longitude, population, land and water areas, notable background information, and name origin. Miscellany on American Places and American Names—Curiosities and Peculiarities. State indexes. Complete index in volume 4.

Kane, Joseph Nathan, Janet Podell, and Steven Anzovin. *Facts about the States*. 2nd ed. New York: H. W. Wilson Company, 1993.

> This reference book presents the following information about each state, organized alphabetically by state: admission date and rank; explanations of state name, nicknames, seal and flag; motto, song, and symbols; geographic and climatic data; national sites; chronology of significant dates in the state's history; demographic data; local government, political history, finances, economy, environment, ethnic groups, educational and cultural facilities; miscellaneous state facts; and bibliography containing fiction and nonfiction works about the state. The District of Columbia and Puerto Rico are also covered. Comparative tables on land areas and shorelines, population, settlement by non-native Americans, geography, finances, transportation, military installations, and educational facilities.

IV. Individual Holidays

A. Christmas

Auld, William Muir. *Christmas Tidings*. 1933. Reprint. Detroit: Omnigraphics, Inc., 1990.

> Describes legends, verse, and such historic liturgies as the Roman Breviary and the Missal.

Auld, William Muir. *Christmas Traditions*. 1931. Reprint. Detroit: Omnigraphics, Inc., 1992.

> This history of Christmas surveys origins, antecedents, changes, and developments of the traditions through the ages.

Covers ancient English carols, the yule log, the tree, bells, and more. Excerpts from literature, legends, and historical accounts.

Ballam, Harry, and Phyllis Digby Morton, eds. *The Christmas Book*. 1947. Reprint. Detroit: Omnigraphics, Inc., 1990.

> Collection of articles and stories by such writers as Charles Dickens, Aldous Huxley, Washington Irving, Bram Stoker, and others on the subject of Christmas. Several holiday quizzes are included, for which the Appendices provide the answers.

Bauer, John E. *Christmas on the American Frontier, 1800-1900*. 1961. Reprint. Detroit: Omnigraphics, Inc., 1993.

> Seventeen chapters cover such topics as "A California Festival of Good Will," "Down a Prairie Chimney," "Giving Christmas to the Indians," and more. Contains eyewitness accounts of frontier holidays.

Buday, George. *The History of the Christmas Card*. 1954. Reprint. Detroit: Omnigraphics, Inc., 1992.

> Traces the rise of the Christmas card and discusses its forerunners, old Christmas card creators, children's cards, religious cards, and wartime Christmas cards. Appendices list artists and designers, old Christmas card sentiment writers, and Christmas card publishers.

Carucci, Laurence Marshall. *Nuclear Nativity: Rituals of Renewal and Empowerment in the Marshall Islands*. Dekalb: Northern Illinois University Press, 1997.

> Anthropologist describes the history, context, and elements of the Kurijmoj festival, the four-month Christmas celebration of the Enewetak people, who, from 1947 to 1980, were forced to live away from their home atoll in the Marshall Islands so the U.S. government could conduct nuclear weapons tests.

Crippen, Thomas G. *Christmas and Christmas Lore*. 1923. Reprint. Detroit: Omnigraphics, Inc., 1990.

> Collection of customs, traditions, and legends relating to Christmas, drawn from chapbooks and pamphlets of the 17th and 18th centuries and from various books dealing with antiquities and legends.

Dawson, W. F. *Christmas: Its Origins and Associations*. 1902. Reprint. Detroit: Omnigraphics, Inc., 1990.

> Arranged chronologically, this book covers the holiday's origin, its historical events, and festive celebrations during the course of 19 centuries. Considers the evolving tradition in Britain and includes information on the celebration of Christmas in various lands.

Duncan, Edmondstoune. *The Story of the Carol*. 1911. Reprint. Detroit: Omnigraphics, Inc., 1992.

> Surveys development of the forms and purposes of carols, as well as the days, feasts, pageants, and religious rites associated with them. Includes words and music to traditional carols. Appendices include brief biographical notes on relevant individuals, glossary, chronological table of development of carols, and list of manuscript carols held in the British Museum.

Foley, Daniel J. *Christmas the World Over: How the Season of Joy and Good Will Is Observed and Enjoyed by Peoples Here and Everywhere*. Illustrated by Charlotte Edwards Bowden. Philadelphia and New York: Chilton Books, 1963.

> Customs and traditions associated with Christmas in more than 30 countries around the world. Heavy coverage of Europe and Latin America.

Foley, Daniel J., ed. *Christmas in the Good Old Days: A Victorian Album of Stories, Poems, and Pictures of the Personalities Who*

♦ Indicates a book cited in the main text

Rediscovered Christmas. 1961. Reprint. Detroit: Omnigraphics, Inc., 1994.

> Anthology of stories and poems written during the Victorian era by such authors as Louisa May Alcott, Washington Irving, Bret Harte, O. Henry, Charles Dickens, Hans Christian Andersen, Herman Melville, and others. Includes brief sketches on the authors.

♦ Gulevich, Tanya. *Encyclopedia of Christmas and New Year's Celebrations: Over 240 Alphabetically Arranged Entries Covering Christmas, New Year's, and Related Days of Observance, Including Folk and Religious Customs, History, Legends, and Symbols from Around the World. Supplemented by a Bibliography and Lists of Christmas Web Sites and Associations, as well as an Index.* Illustrated by Mary Ann Stavros-Lanning. Detroit: Omnigraphics, Inc., 2003.

> Cross-referenced entries discuss Christmas and New Year's folklore, history, customs, foods, and more. Thirty-nine entries deal with Christmas in Europe, Asia, North Africa, the Middle East, and Latin America. Twenty-one entries treat New Year's Day and Eve. Other holidays discussed include Advent, the Assumption, Candlemas, Epiphany, Feast of the Circumcision, Hanukkah, Holy Innocents' Day, Kwanzaa, and numerous saints' days. Appendices include a bibliography, web sites, and information about associations whose missions relate to the holidays. [Cited in the text as *EncyChristmas-2003*]

Hole, Christina. *Christmas and Its Customs: A Brief Study*. Illustrated by T. Every-Clayton. New York: M. Barrows and Company, Inc., 1957.

> Discusses origins of the holiday, as well as garlands, gift giving, carols, food, and legends and superstitions. Also covers Twelfth Night and the New Year.

Hottes, Alfred Carl. *1001 Christmas Facts and Fancies*. 1946. Reprint. Detroit: Omnigraphics, Inc., 1990.

> Facts and fancies, stories and legends gathered from author's personal experiences and obscure literature.

Miles, Clement A. *Christmas in Ritual and Tradition; Christian and Pagan*. 1912. Reprint. Detroit: Omnigraphics, Inc., 1990.

> Part I deals with the Christian observance, examining Latin and European hymns and poetry, liturgy, popular customs, and dramas, pageants, and plays. Part II covers pre-Christian winter festivals and their surviving customs. Includes discussion of the Christmas tree, gifts, cards, and mumming, as well as more than 20 saints' days and other holidays and festivals observed throughout the year in Europe.

Miller, Daniel, ed. *Unwrapping Christmas*. Oxford, England: Clarendon Press, 1993.

> Ten anthropological essays by scholars in various academic fields on contemporary, and international, observance and meaning of Christmas: "A Theory of Christmas" and "Christmas against Materialism in Thailand," Daniel Miller; "Father Christmas Executed," Claude Lévi-Strauss; "The Rituals of Christmas Giving," James Carrier; "Materialism and the Making of the Modern American Christmas," Russell Belk; "Cinderella Christmas: Kitsch, Consumerism, and Youth in Japan," Brian Moeran and Lise Skov; "The English Christmas and the Family: Time out and Alternative Realities," Adam Kuper; "Christmas Cards and the Construction of Social Relations in Britain Today," Mary Searle-Chatterjee; "Christmas Present: Christmas Public," Barbara Bodenhorn; and "The Great Christmas Quarrel and Other Swedish Traditions," Orvar Löfgren.

Schauffler, Robert, ed. *Christmas: Its Origin, Celebration and Significance as Related in Prose and Verse*. New foreword by

Tristram Potter Coffin. 1907. Reprint. Detroit: Omnigraphics, Inc., 1990.

> Collection of prose and poetry, hymns and carols divided into sections on origins, celebration, and the significance and spirit of Christmas.

Sechrist, Elizabeth Hough. *Christmas Everywhere: A Book of Christmas Customs of Many Lands*. Rev ed. Philadelphia: Macrae Smith Company, 1962.

> For young readers. Stories and customs associated with Christmas in 20 locales around the world.

Silverthorne, Elizabeth. *Christmas in Texas*. College Station: Texas A & M University Press, 1990.

> Examines Christmas customs, traditions, including recipes, and folklore of different ethnic groups in Texas, including Hispanic, Chinese, German, French, African American, Scandinavian, Italian, Polish, British, Czech, Wendish, and Orthodox.

Walsh, William S. *The Story of Santa Klaus: Told for Children of All Ages from Six to Sixty*. 1909. Reprint. Detroit: Omnigraphics, Inc., 1991.

> Discusses the origin and development of the Klaus legend, mythological concepts absorbed by Christianity, the Three Kings, Twelfth Night customs, Father Christmas, and Christmas traditions and observances in various countries. Illustrations by artists of all times from Fra Angelico to Henry Hutt.

Weiser, Francis X. *The Christmas Book*. Illustrated by Robert Frankenberg. 1952. Reprint. Detroit: Omnigraphics, Inc., 1990.

> Relates the story of the celebration of Christmas, from the beginning with its gospel and history, through the festivities of the Middle Ages, to the decline and eventual revival of Christmas customs in Europe and the United States. Ancient and familiar hymns are included, as well as a section on holiday breads and pastries.

Wernecke, Herbert H. *Christmas Customs Around the World*. Philadelphia: The Westminster Press, c1959.

> Covers historical background, customs and legends, holiday recipes, and pageants and programs. Describes observance of the holiday in more than 60 countries on all continents.

B. Easter

The Book of Easter. Introduction by William C. Doane. 1910. Reprint. Detroit: Omnigraphics, Inc., 1990.

> Collection of Easter poems, stories, hymns, and essays from various sources including the Bible, and by such writers as Elizabeth Barrett Browning, Walter Pater, Robert Browning, Alfred Tennyson, George Herbert, Thomas Hardy, and others. Reproductions of famous paintings relating to Easter by such artists as Rembrandt, Rubens, and Fra Angelico. Provides historic accounts and descriptions of customs and legends associated with Good Friday, Easter, and the Ascension.

♦ Gulevich, Tanya. *Encyclopedia of Easter, Carnival, and Lent: A Guide to This Season's Joyous Celebration and Solemn Worship, Including Folk Customs, Religious Observances, History, Legends, Folklore, Symbols, and Related Days from Europe, the Americas, and Around the World*. Illustrated by Mary Ann Stavros-Lanning. Detroit: Omnigraphics, Inc., 2002.

> More than 150 cross-referenced entries discuss history, religious celebrations, customs, folklore, foods, and symbols related to Easter, Carnival, and Lent in 20 countries around the world. Also includes entries on Ash Wednesday, Pentecost, May Day,

♦ Indicates a book cited in the main text

Shavuot, Passover, and No Ruz. A bibliography and web sites related to the holiday season are presented in the appendices. [Cited in the text as *EncyEaster-2002*]

Hazeltine, Alice Isabel, and Elva Sophronia Smith, eds. *The Easter Book of Legends and Stories*. Illustrated by Pamela Bianco. 1947. Reprint. Detroit: Omnigraphics, Inc., 1992.

> Compilation of literature relating to Easter including biblical narrative, poems, plays, legends, and stories by such authors as Robert Frost, Emily Dickinson, A. E. Housman, and others. Indexes of authors and titles.

Lord, Priscilla Sawyer, and Daniel J. Foley. *Easter the World Over*. Philadelphia: Chilton Book Company, 1971.

> Discusses origins of, and traditions, practices, rhymes, songs and music, fine arts, and food associated with, Easter, Holy Week, and Carnival or Mardi Gras in the Middle East, United States, Europe, Bermuda, the Caribbean, and South and Central America. Also covers the spring festivals of Ching-ming (Qing Ming) in China and Setsubun in Japan.

C. Fourth of July

Appelbaum, Diana Karter. *The Glorious Fourth: An American Holiday, an American History*. New York: Facts on File, 1989.

> Covers the history and celebration of Independence Day in the United States, from the beginning until the bicentennial festivities in 1976.

Travers, Len. *Celebrating the Fourth: Independence Day and the Rites of Nationalism in the Early Republic*. Amherst.: University of Massachusetts Press, 1997.

> Discusses the early celebrations of the Fourth of July and their role in fostering a new sense of national identity. Describes celebrations in Boston, Philadelphia, and South Carolina from 1777 to 1826.

D. Halloween

Santino, Jack. *The Hallowed Eve: Dimensions of Culture in a Calendar Festival in Northern Ireland*. Lexington: University Press of Kentucky, 1998.

> Clearly written scholarly examination of Halloween as it is celebrated in Northern Ireland, its history, games, and other traditions, based on the author's fieldwork.

Thompson, Sue Ellen, ed. *Halloween Program Sourcebook: The Story of Halloween, Including Excerpts of Stories and Legends, Strange Happenings, Poems, Plays, Activities, and Recipes Focusing on Halloween from the Eighteenth Century to the Present*. Illustrated by Mary Ann Stavros-Lanning. Detroit: Omnigraphics, 2000.

Following an introductory essay on the history of the holiday, the book presents a selection of Halloween-related material to be read, spoken, or performed, as well as craft activities, costume ideas, games, and recipes. Works excerpted or reprinted include those by authors such as Washington Irving, Edgar Allan Poe, Robert Burns, and more. Author and Title Index and Index to First Lines of Poetry.

E. Mardi Gras

Mitchell, Reid. *All on a Mardi Gras Day: Episodes in the History of New Orleans Carnival*. Cambridge, MA: Harvard University Press, 1995.

> Retells the story of a number of incidents occurring on or around Mardi Gras, from the early 1800s to the 1990s. Provides a unique window on the history of Mardi Gras, its meaning to various ethnic and social groups across time, and the history and culture of New Orleans. Gives suggested reading list.

F. Memorial Day

Schauffler, Robert, ed. *Memorial Day; Its Celebration, Spirit, and Significance as Related in Prose and Verse, with a Non-sectional Anthology of the Civil War*. 1940. Reprint. Detroit: Omnigraphics, Inc., 1990.

> Compilation of 140 stories and poems relating the significance of Memorial Day in the United States.

G. Mother's Day

Schauffler, Robert, ed. *Mother's Day; Its History, Origin, Celebration, Spirit, and Significance as Related in Prose and Verse*. 1927. Reprint. Detroit: Omnigraphics, Inc., 1990.

> Collection of poetry and stories about mother-worship in pagan times, mother-love antedating Christianity, and some of the ancient customs and rites honoring mothers throughout the centuries. Suggestions for Mother's Day programs for school exercises also included.

H. New Year

Blackwood, Alan. New Year. *Holidays and Festivals Series*. Vero Beach, FL: Rourke Enterprises, Inc., 1987.

> For young readers. Discusses ancient celebrations of the New Year in Egypt, Babylonia, and Rome, and among Celts. Explanation of the Jewish and Chinese calendars, the Muslim and Hindu New Year, the New Year throughout Asia, the New Year in the United States and Britain, and some mentions of customs in various European countries. Entries on St. Sebastian and St. Basil. Further reading list.

♦ Indicates a book cited in the main text

Indexes

INDEX 1

Chronological Index
Fixed Days and Events

The index below lists entries according to the month or specific date(s) in which they are observed. For each month, those holidays that fall within the month but with no single date are given first; followed by holidays celebrated on specific date(s); followed by those observed at the same time every year, although not on a specific date (e.g., the first Monday, the last week, etc.).

See also the Chronological Index—Movable Days, the Special Subject Index, and the General Index.

Numbers in the index refer to entry numbers, not page numbers

Numbers in the index refer to entry numbers, not page numbers

Numbers in the index refer to entry numbers, not page numbers

Numbers in the index refer to entry numbers, not page numbers

Numbers in the index refer to entry numbers, not page numbers

Numbers in the index refer to entry numbers, not page numbers

Numbers in the index refer to entry numbers, not page numbers

Numbers in the index refer to entry numbers, not page numbers

Numbers in the index refer to entry numbers, not page numbers

Numbers in the index refer to entry numbers, not page numbers

Numbers in the index refer to entry numbers, not page numbers

Numbers in the index refer to entry numbers, not page numbers

Numbers in the index refer to entry numbers, not page numbers

Numbers in the index refer to entry numbers, not page numbers

Numbers in the index refer to entry numbers, not page numbers

Numbers in the index refer to entry numbers, not page numbers

Numbers in the index refer to entry numbers, not page numbers

Numbers in the index refer to entry numbers, not page numbers

Numbers in the index refer to entry numbers, not page numbers

Numbers in the index refer to entry numbers, not page numbers

Numbers in the index refer to entry numbers, not page numbers

Numbers in the index refer to entry numbers, not page numbers

Numbers in the index refer to entry numbers, not page numbers

Numbers in the index refer to entry numbers, not page numbers

Numbers in the index refer to entry numbers, not page numbers

Numbers in the index refer to entry numbers, not page numbers

Numbers in the index refer to entry numbers, not page numbers

Numbers in the index refer to entry numbers, not page numbers

Numbers in the index refer to entry numbers, not page numbers

Numbers in the index refer to entry numbers, not page numbers

Numbers in the index refer to entry numbers, not page numbers

Numbers in the index refer to entry numbers, not page numbers

Numbers in the index refer to entry numbers, not page numbers

Numbers in the index refer to entry numbers, not page numbers

Numbers in the index refer to entry numbers, not page numbers

Numbers in the index refer to entry numbers, not page numbers

Numbers in the index refer to entry numbers, not page numbers

Numbers in the index refer to entry numbers, not page numbers

INDEX 2

Chronological Index
Movable Days

The index below lists entries that are observed according to the dates of non-Gregorian calendars, including the Jewish calendar and Hindu calendar, as well as movable Christian holidays that depend on the date of Easter. Hindu dates are approximate, since some Hindu sects begin reckoning new months at the new moon, while others begin reckoning from the full moon.

The listings for each month are followed by listings of other calendar dates, including those of the lunar Chinese and Buddhist calendars, and dates according to the Islamic and Zoroastrian calendars.

See also the Chronological Index—Fixed Days, the Special Subject Index, and the General Index.

Numbers in the index refer to entry numbers, not page numbers

Numbers in the index refer to entry numbers, not page numbers

Numbers in the index refer to entry numbers, not page numbers

Numbers in the index refer to entry numbers, not page numbers

Numbers in the index refer to entry numbers, not page numbers

Numbers in the index refer to entry numbers, not page numbers

September–October

October–November

Numbers in the index refer to entry numbers, not page numbers

ISLAMIC CALENDAR DATES

Numbers in the index refer to entry numbers, not page numbers

MISCELLANEOUS DATES

INDEX 3

Special Subject Index

This index organizes entries according to six specific subjects. Many of the entries in HFCWD fall into the following subject categories:

Ancient/Pagan
Calendar
Folkloric
Historic
Promotional
Sporting

Some events may be listed in more than one category. For instance, St. Patrick's Day is listed under the Historic Index, because it commemorates a historical person, and the Folkloric Index, for all the folk legends and traditions associated with St. Patrick and his feast day.

See also the Chronological Indexes (Fixed Days and Movable Days) and the General Index.

Ancient / Pagan

Indexed below are holidays rooted in ancient Greece, ancient Rome, or in Europe before the spread of Christianity.

Numbers in the index refer to entry numbers, not page numbers

Calendar

Indexed below are festivals that deal specifically with the calendar or that are held in celebration of the time of the year (solstices and equinoxes), the beginning and end of seasons, etc.

Numbers in the index refer to entry numbers, not page numbers

Folkloric

Indexed below are festivals deeply rooted in folklore and tradition, as well as those celebrating specific folk tales.

Numbers in the index refer to entry numbers, not page numbers

Numbers in the index refer to entry numbers, not page numbers

Numbers in the index refer to entry numbers, not page numbers

Historic

Indexed below are festivals commemorating specific events from history, including battles, the birth dates of famous people, national independence, etc.

Numbers in the index refer to entry numbers, not page numbers

Numbers in the index refer to entry numbers, not page numbers

Numbers in the index refer to entry numbers, not page numbers

Numbers in the index refer to entry numbers, not page numbers

Numbers in the index refer to entry numbers, not page numbers

Numbers in the index refer to entry numbers, not page numbers

Numbers in the index refer to entry numbers, not page numbers

Numbers in the index refer to entry numbers, not page numbers

Numbers in the index refer to entry numbers, not page numbers

Promotional

Indexed below are festivals that promote everything from city, state, and national pride to agricultural products; from activities (quilting, rodeo) to social values (conservation, harmony among peoples).

Numbers in the index refer to entry numbers, not page numbers

Numbers in the index refer to entry numbers, not page numbers

Numbers in the index refer to entry numbers, not page numbers

Special Subject Index

Numbers in the index refer to entry numbers, not page numbers

Numbers in the index refer to entry numbers, not page numbers

Sporting

Indexed below are events that are based on or revolve around sporting events. This index does not include the many fairs and festivals in which games and contests form only a part.

Numbers in the index refer to entry numbers, not page numbers

Numbers in the index refer to entry numbers, not page numbers

INDEX 4

General Index

The General Index lists people, places, institutions, religious and ethnic groups, and names of festivals and holidays by keyword. It also lists other items of significance within the entries. For example, foods, animals, music, customs, and activities closely associated with an event are indexed, as are celebratory elements common to various cultures.

See also the Chronological Indexes (Fixed Days and Movable Days) and the Special Subject Index.

Numbers in the index refer to entry numbers, not page numbers

Numbers in the index refer to entry numbers, not page numbers

Numbers in the index refer to entry numbers, not page numbers

B

Numbers in the index refer to entry numbers, not page numbers

General Index

baptism, Jesus
    See Epiphany
Baptism of the Lord, Feast of the, 0216
Baptists, 2988
Barbados
    Caribbean community commemoration, 0452
    harvest festival, 0664
    independence day, 0217
    jazz festival, 0218
    political holiday, 0223
    settlement festival, 1204
Barbados Independence Day, 0217
Barbados Jazz Festival, 0218
Bar-B-Q Festival, International, 0219
Bard of Armagh Festival of Humorous Verse, 0220
Barnaby Bright
    See St. Barnabas's Day
Barnaby Day
    See St. Barnabas's Day
Barnebirkie, 0077
Barnum Festival, 0221
Barnum, Phineas Taylor (P. T.), 0221
Barók, Bela, 0367
Baron Bliss Day, 0222
baroque music festival, 0162
Barrel Parade
    See Kopenfahrt (Barrel Parade)
Barrow (Errol) Day, 0223
Bartholomew Fair, 0224
Basant Panchami
    See Vasant Panchami (Basant Panchami)
Bascarsija Nights, 0225
baseball, 1547, 2225, 3028
Basket Dance, 0226
basket festival, 1644
basketball, 1580
Basotho people, 1771
Basque Festival
    See St. Ignatius Loyola, Feast of
Basque Festival, National, 0227
Basset Hound Games, 0228
Bastille, 1900
Bastille Day, 0229, 0230, 0446
Bastille Day (Kaplan, Louisiana), 0230
Bastille, Festival de la, 0231
Bat Flight Breakfast, 0232
Bataan Day, 0233
Bath, England, 0168
Bath International Music Festival, 0234
bathing celebrations
    Caribbean, 2543
    India, 0042, 1383, 1455, 1591, 1662, 1671, 2445
    Malaysia, 1620
Baths of Caracalla, 0235
bathtub race, 3010
Batista, Fulgencio, 0670, 0912
Battalion Day
    See Whit-Monday (Whitmonday)

Battle for the Bridge, 1040
Battle of Adwa, 0884
Battle of Ayacucho, 0321
Battle of Bataan, 0233
Battle of Boyacá, 0602
Battle of Britain Day, 0236
Battle of Cannae, 0504
Battle of Carabobo, 2894
Battle of Cuildremne, 2507
Battle of Flodden, 0605
Battle of Flowers (Colombia), 0465
Battle of Flowers (Jersey, Channel Islands), 0237
Battle of Flowers (Vienna, Austria), 0238
Battle of Germantown, Reenactment of, 0239
Battle of Gettysburg, 1025, 1026
Battle of Golden Spurs, 0945
battle of good over evil, 1051
Battle of Iquique, 0542
Battle of Lake Regillus, 0496
Battle of New Orleans Day, 0240
Battle of North Point, 0710
Battle of Olustee Reenactment, 0241
Battle of Pichincha Day, 0811
Battle of Puebla, 0591
Battle of St. George's Caye, 0259
Battle of Tarqui, 0812
Battle of Vönnu, 0881
Battles of Lexington and Concord Day
    See Patriots' Day
Battleship Day
    See Maine Memorial Day
Bavarian culture, 0974
Bawming the Thorn Day, 0242
Bayard, 1032
Bayfest, 0243
Bayou Classic, 0244
Bayou Food Festival, 0013
Bayram
    See Id al-Adha (Feast of Sacrifice; Eid)
Bayreuth Festival, 0245
Bazán family, 0130
Be Kind to Animals Week, 0246
beach festival, 2652
Beaches, Day of the (Día de las Playas), 0247
bean soup, 1690
beans, 0065, 0857, 0860, 0864
Bean-Throwing Festival
    See Setsubun (Bean-Throwing Festival)
bear dance, 2872
Bear Festival
    See Iyomante Matsuri (Bear Festival)
Bear Society Dance, 0248
Beard, Dan C., 0347
Beargrease (John) Sled Dog Marathon, 0249
Beatles, 0002
beauty pageants
    Ireland, 2243
    United States, 1739

Numbers in the index refer to entry numbers, not page numbers

Numbers in the index refer to entry numbers, not page numbers

Numbers in the index refer to entry numbers, not page numbers

Numbers in the index refer to entry numbers, not page numbers

Numbers in the index refer to entry numbers, not page numbers

General Index

Numbers in the index refer to entry numbers, not page numbers

Numbers in the index refer to entry numbers, not page numbers

Día del Oriente
  See Amazon and Galapagos Day
Día del Puno, 0731
Día dos Finados
  See All Souls' Day
Diablos, 0486
Diamond Head Crater Celebration, 0732
Diana (goddess) festival, 1848
dice competition, 0733
Dicing for the Maid's Money Day, 0733
Dick, James, 0911
Dickens, Charles, 0362
Digambaras, 0042, 0697
Diipolia
  See Bouphonia (Buphonia)
Dinagyang, 0734
Dingaan's Day
  See Reconciliation, Day of
Dinkins, David, 0027
Dinosaur Days, 0735
dinosaur festivities, 0735
Dionysia (Bacchanalia), 0736
Dionysus, 0105, 0736
Dioscuri, 0496
Dipolia
  See Bouphonia (Buphonia)
Dipri Festival, 0737
Disabled Persons, International Day of, 0738
Disarmament Week, 0739
Discoverers' Day
  See Columbus Day
Discovery Day, 0740
  See also Columbus Day; Klondike Gold Discovery Day;
    Magellan (Ferdinand) Day
Dismal Days
  See Egyptian Days
Disraeli, Benjamin, 2135
Distaff Day, 0741
Divali
  See Dewali (Divali, Deepavali, Festival of Lights)
divination, 0036
Divine Holy Spirit, Festival of the (Festa do Divino), 0742
djellabahs, 0426
Djibouti Independence Day, 0743
Doan Ngu (Summer Solstice Day), 0744
doctor feast days, 0036
Doctors' Day, 0745
Dodd, Sonora Louise Smart, 0903
Dodge City Days, 0746
Dodge (Geraldine R.) Poetry Festival, 0748
Dodge National Circuit Finals Rodeo, 0747
Dodo Masquerade
  See Boys' Dodo Masquerade
Dog Days, 0749
dog games, 0228
dog sled races
  Alaska, 0089, 0892, 1272, 2777
  Canada, 0451

  Minnesota, 0249
  Northwest Territories, 0451
  Oregon, 1980
dog shows
  Alaska, 0586
  France, 0669
Dog Star, 0749
Doggett, Thomas, 0750
Doggett's Coat and Badge Race, 0750
Dogon people, 0378
dogs, 0228, 0586, 0669,, 0749, 2760
Dogwood Festival, 0751
Dol Purnima, 0752
Doleing Day, 0753
Dol-Jatra
  See Holi
doll festivals
  Japan, 0696, 1189
  Missouri, 1408
  Poland, 1661
Dom Fair, 0754
Domenica delle Palme
  See Palm Sunday (Italy) (Domenica delle Palme)
Dominica
  Caribbean community commemoration, 0452
  creole music festival, 3013
  independence day, 0755
Dominica Independence Day, 0755
Dominican Republic
  Christmas, 0563
  dancing festival, 1707
  independence days, 0756, 0757
  national holiday, 0772
  religious holidays, 0758, 0759
Dominican Republic Independence Day, 0756
Dominican Republic Independence Restoration Day, 0757
Dominican Republic Our Lady of Altagracia (Feast of the
    Virgin of Altagracia, Feast of Our Lady of Altagracia), 0758
Dominican Republic Our Lady of Mercedes Day, 0759
Dominion Day
  See Canada Day
Don Quixote, 0505
donation day, 2028
Dongji (Winter Solstice), 0760
donuts, 2006
Doo Dah Parade, 0761
Dormition of the Most Holy Mother of God
  See Assumption of the Blessed Virgin Mary, Feast of the
Dorsey, Thomas A., 0534
dosmo, 0762
Dosmoche, 0762
Double Fifth
  See Tuan Wu (Double Fifth)
Double Nine Day
  See Chung Yeung
Double Seventh
  See Seven Sisters Festival

Numbers in the index refer to entry numbers, not page numbers

Emancipation Day (Hutchinson, Kansas), 0844
Emancipation Day (Tallahassee, Florida), 0845
Emancipation Day (United States), 0846
Emancipation Day (Washington, D.C.), 0847
Emancipation Proclamation, 0844, 0845, 0846, 0978
Ember Days, 0849
embracing churches, 0596
Emeliyanovs, Galina, 0598
Emeliyanovs, Yuri, 0598
Emerson, Roy, 0170
Emma Naea Rooke, Queen, 0854
Emmerson, Michael, 0255
Empire Day
    See Bonfire Night; Commonwealth Day; Japan National
      Foundation Day
Emume Ibo Uzo
    See Road Building
Encaenia Day, 0850
enchiladas, 2978
end of New Year celebration, 2686
end-of-the-year celebration, 1202
Enescu (George) Festival, 0851
engagements, 0065
England
    See also Great Britain; Scotland; United Kingdom; Wales
    air show, 0236
    archery contest, 1091
    bank holiday, 0214
    begging by the poor, 0753
    bell silence commemoration, 2424
    bell-ringing ceremonies, 2778, 2979
    bird marking, 2672
    birthday commemorations, 1349, 2386, 2400
    boat races, 0316, 1179
    bonfires, 0329
    calendar switch, 0969
    candle auction, 0437
    charity events, 2281, 2759
    cheese-rolling contest, 0518
    Christmas celebration, 1953
    church payment day, 1200
    clothing fair, 0224
    college founding ceremony, 1614
    coronation holiday, 2164
    crossing a home's threshold, 0929
    death commemorations, 2100, 2135
    deer roasting ceremony, 2179
    devil's rock commemoration, 1176
    dice competition, 0733
    ear commemoration, 1904
    elections, 0830, 0831
    embracing churches, 0596
    end-of-the-year celebration, 1202
    farming holiday, 2104
    fig-eating, 0918
    fishing festival, 1006
    flower shows, 0521, 2259
    food celebrations, 0985, 1958, 2027, 2630

    freedom holiday, 1593
    fundraiser for the blind, 1020
    getting rid of meat, 0601
    government budget, 0368
    harvest festival, 1168
    hawthorn tree commemoration, 0242
    hedge-building ceremony, 2101
    historic festival, 1553, 2223
    hobby horse parade, 1733
    honorary degree-awarding, 0850
    hood retrieval game, 1172
    horse racing, 0717, 1070, 1430, 2249
    hospital fundraisers, 0056, 2635
    hunting festivities, 1241, 2044
    lantern night, 2145
    Lenten carnival, 0902
    literary festivals, 0168, 0362
    marriage mock trial, 0779
    military commemorations, 0236, 0662, 0887, 2795
    mining festival, 0781
    mischievous children's night, 1737
    music festivals, 0054, 0234, 0522, 2502, 2755, 3005
    national day of thanksgiving, 0905
    noise-making fair, 2005
    opera festival, 1045
    oyster shell-building, 1106
    political ceremonies, 1557, 1688, 2622
    processions, 0628, 2921
    religious celebrations, 0055, 0104, 0439, 0628, 1059, 1475,
      1773
    rent-payment day, 2052, 2158
    royal birthdays, 0840, 0968
    rushbearing ceremony, 1394
    saint feast days, 2278, 2486, 2494, 2495, 2500, 2502, 2504,
      2513, 2523, 2603
    sporting events, 0341, 0750, 0885, 1077, 1256, 2990
    summer solstice ceremony, 0770
    theater festival, 3052
    tip-collection day, 0346
    trade fairs, 1481, 2526
    unlucky day, 0820
    walking-only day, 2937
    winter solstice festival, 2837
English Opera Group, 0054
Enkutatash, 0852
Enlighteners, Day of the (Den na Buditelite), 0853
Enrile, Juan Ponce, 0915
Entierro de la Sardina
    See Burial of the Sardine
environment celebrations
    Alabama, 0167
    United Nations, 2132, 3019
    United States, 0785, 1095
Eo e Emalani i Alaka i Festival, 0854
Eoff, Dan, 0585
Eostre, 0787
Epidaurus Festival, 0855
epidemics, 0744

Numbers in the index refer to entry numbers, not page numbers

Feast of the Archangel Michael
 See Michaelmas
Feast of the Beheading
 See St. John the Baptist, Martyrdom of
Feast of the Birth
 See Christmas (Spain) (Pascua de Navidad)
Feast of the Circumcision and the Name of Jesus
 See Circumcision, Feast of the
Feast of the Circumcision of Our Lord
 See Circumcision, Feast of the
Feast of the Divine Holy Spirit, 0500
Feast of the Exaltation of the Cross, 0181
Feast of the Harvest
 See Shavuot (Shabuoth)
Feast of the Holy Ghost
 See Divine Holy Spirit, Festival of the (Festa do Divino)
Feast of the Holy Name of Our Lord Jesus Christ
 See Circumcision, Feast of the
Feast of the Lanterns
 See Vesak (Wesak; Buddha's Birthday)
Feast of the Most Holy Body of Christ
 See Corpus Christi
Feast of the Nativity of Our Lady
 See Nativity of the Blessed Virgin Mary, Feast of the
Feast of the Nativity of Our Lord
 See Christmas
Feast of the Nativity of St. John the Baptist
 See St. John's Day
Feast of the North American Martyrs
 See Martyrs of North America, Feast of the
Feast of the Presentation of Christ in the Temple
 See Candlemas
Feast of the Purification of the Blessed Virgin Mary
 See Candlemas
Feast of the Redeemer
 See Redentore, Festa del
Feast of the Sun
 See Inti Raymi Fiesta
Feast of the Virgin of Altagracia
 See Dominican Republic Our Lady of Altagracia (Feast of the Virgin of Altagracia, Feast of Our Lady of Altagracia)
Feast of Torches
 See Imbolc (Imbolg)
Feast of Unleavened Bread
 See Passover
Feast of Waxing Lights
 See Imbolc (Imbolg)
Feast of Weeks
 See Shavuot (Shabuoth)
FeatherFest, 0906
Federation of Bosnia and Herzegovina, 0334
Feira Nacional de Agricultura
 See Agriculture Fair at Santarém, National
fell running, 1077
female
 See women
feminist celebration, 1133

fence-painting competition, 2779
Feralia, 0907
Ferdinand, Archduke, 0334
Ferdinand, King, 0604
Ferdinand, Prince, 0375
Feria de San Marcos
 See St. Mark, Fair of (Feria de San Marcos)
Feriae Latinae
 See Latin Festival (Feriae Latinae)
Ferrara's Buskers' Festival, 0401
fertility celebrations
 ancient Egypt, 1732
 ancient Greece, 0641, 1154, 2747
 ancient Rome, 0949, 1521, 1572, 1975
 Bulgaria, 1474, 1648, 2557
 Netherlands, 2928
 Nigeria, 1985
 Swaziland, 1842
 Ukraine, 1458
 Vanuatu, 1483
Fes Festival of World Sacred Music, 0908
Fesitval of Young Herbs
 See Nanakusa Matsuri (Seven Herbs or Grasses Festival)
Festa Confederada
 See Confederados Reunion
Festa da Luz (Festival of Light), 0909
Festa dei Giglio
 See Lily Festival (Festa dei Giglio)
Festa del Grillo, 0910, 0981
Festa del Perdono
 See Forgiveness, Feast of
Festa di San Nicola
 See St. Nicholas's Day (Italy)
Festa do Bonfim
 See Bonfim Festival (Festa do Bonfim)
Festa do Colete Encarnado
 See Red Waistcoat Festival
Festa do Divino
 See Divine Holy Spirit, Festival of the (Festa do Divino)
Festa dos Tabuleiros
 See Tabuleiros Festival (Festa dos Tabuleiros)
Festival d'Automne
 See Paris Autumn Festival (Festival d'Automme)
Festival d'Avignon
 See Avignon Festival
Festival de Merengue
 See Merengue Festival (Festival de Merengue)
Festival in the City, 0908
Festival International de Jazz de Montréal
 See Montreal Jazz Festival
Festival of Ancient Drama
 See Epidaurus Festival
Festival of Boys
 See Ghanta Karna (Gathyamuga)
Festival of Broken Needles
 See Hari-Kuyo (Festival of Broken Needles)
Festival of Colors
 See Holi

Numbers in the index refer to entry numbers, not page numbers

Numbers in the index refer to entry numbers, not page numbers

Numbers in the index refer to entry numbers, not page numbers

Numbers in the index refer to entry numbers, not page numbers

1244

Numbers in the index refer to entry numbers, not page numbers

Numbers in the index refer to entry numbers, not page numbers

Numbers in the index refer to entry numbers, not page numbers

Netherlands, 0954
Ohio, 0117
Hortobágy Bridge Fair and International Equestrian Festival, 1242
Hosay
See Ashura
Hosay Festival, 1243
Hoshana Rabbah, 1244
hospital fundraisers, 0056, 2635
Hospital Week, National, 1245
Hostos Day, 1246
Hostos, Eugenio Maria de, 1246
Hot Air Balloon Classic, 1247
hot cross bun, 1059
Hot Springs State Park (Thermopolis, Wyoming), 1035
hot summer days, 0749
hound trailing, 1077
House of Parliament, 0905
house-cleaning, 2667
Houses and Gardens, Festival of, 1248
Houston Livestock Show & Rodeo, 1249
Houston, Sam, 0047, 2736
How, John, 0733
Howe, William, 0887
Howl! Festival, 1250
huasos, 0789, 0916
Huguenots, 0224
Human Rights Day, 0281
Human Towers of Valls, 1251
Humor and Satire Festival, International, 1252
humor festival, 1252
Humphrey, Hubert, 0030
Hundred Drums Festival
See Wangala (Hundred Drums Festival)
Hundred Guinea Cup, 0082
Hungary
Carnival, 0469
classical music festival, 0367
food festival, 2682
horse festival, 1242
independence day, 1254
national holiday, 1253
saint feast days, 2564, 2602
Hungary Republic Day, 1253
Hungary Revolution and Independence Day, 1254
Hungry Ghosts Festival
See Ullambana (Hungry Ghosts Festival; All Souls' Feast)
Hunters' Moon, Feast of the, 1255
Huntigowk Day
See April Fools' Day
hunting celebrations
Belgium, 2532
England, 1241, 2044
Hurling the Silver Ball, 1256
Hurricane Speculation Day, 1257
Hurston (Zora Neale) Festival of the Arts and Humanties, 1258

Hus (Jan) Day, 1259
Husayn Ali, 0201
Hussein, 0153
Hussein Day
See Ashura
Hussein Festival
See Hosay Festival
Hussein, Imam al-, 0124, 0125
Hussein, King, 0005
Hussein, Saddam, 0125
Huston, John, 0427
Hutus, 0399
Hyacinthia, 0459

I

"I Am an American" Day
See Citizenship Day
I Madonnari Italian Street Painting Festival, 1260
Ibu Afo Festival, 1261
ice events
Alaska, 1849
China, 1164
Colorado, 1999
Finland, 0924
Ice Worm Festival, 1262
Iceland
arts festival, 2209
Children's Day, 0540
constitution festival, 2752
fishermen's holiday, 2438
food festival, 2753
independence day, 1263
New Year's Eve, 1874
saint feast day, 2609
sea festival, 2349
summer festival, 0928
viking festival, 2914
Iceland Independence Day, 1263
Icelandic Festival, 1264
Icelandic festivals
Canada, 1264
Manitoba, 1264
ice-skating race, 0836
icons, 0513
Id al-Adha (Feast of Sacrifice; Eid), 1265
Id al-Arba'in Shahid
See Forty Martyrs' Day
Id al-Fitr (Eid), 1266
Id al-Fitr (Nigeria), 1267
Id al-Kabir
See Id al-Adha (Feast of Sacrifice; Eid)
Id Mar Jurjus
See St. George's Day (Syria) (Id Mar Jurjus)
Idaho
American Indian ceremony, 1556
boating regatta, 1269

Numbers in the index refer to entry numbers, not page numbers

Numbers in the index refer to entry numbers, not page numbers

Hindu celebrations, 0042, 0152, 0174, 0408, 0409, 0513, 1345
Jain festival, 0697
literary pageant, 2180
marriage celebrations, 1002, 1693
masks, 0532
military commemoration, 1592
monsoon festival, 2718
mythological holiday, 2439
national holiday, 1290
new year, 1331
parade, 0467
Passion play, 2716
pilgrimages, 0075, 2769
prospective matrimonial festival, 2709
purification ceremony, 1001
raft festival, 0266
religious ceremonies, 1376, 1411, 1452, 1455, 1594, 1595, 2408
retreat, 0498
royal festival, 0947
sacred name day, 0084
saint feast days, 2389, 2608
seasonal festival, 1551
Shi'ite religious festival, 0153
Shiva, Lord, festival, 2114
sibling festival, 2177
snake festivals, 1344, 1810
spiritual festival, 2045
spring festivals, 0073, 1205, 1840, 2890
stone-throwing ritual, 0721
sun holiday, 1589
tree worshipping, 0073
water festival, 1203
women's festival, 1002
workers' holiday, 2926
Zoroastrian religion, 0001, 0017
India Republic Day, 1290
Indian Arrival Day, 1291
Indian festivals
    California, 2143
    Trinidad and Tobago, 1291
Indian Market, 1292
Indiana
    automobile racing, 1071, 1293
    autumn festival, 0118
    Dean, James, tribute, 0707
    historic reenactment, 1255
    literary festival, 2214
    turtle festival, 2833
    Wizard of Oz festival, 3000
Indianapolis 500, 1293
indigenous events (Australia), 1007, 1373, 2194
Indigenous Peoples Day
    See Columbus Day
Indonesia
    ballet, 2183
    birthday commemorations, 1384, 2360

Carnival festival, 1460
Children's Day, 0540
dance event, 2183
Hindu festival, 2029
independence day, 1294
new year, 1931
religious celebrations, 0823, 2095
Indonesia Independence Day, 1294
Indra, 0099, 0174
Indra Jatra, 1295
Industrial Day
    See Saba Saba Day
Indy 500
    See Indianapolis 500
information specialists, 0020
initiation ceremony, 2402
Innocents' Day
    See Holy Innocents' Day
Insect-Hearing Festival
    See Freeing the Insects
insects, 0498, 0890, 0981
Insurrection Day
    See Madagascar Martyrs' Day
Interceltique, Festival, 1296
intermarriage, 0917
International Association of Administrative Professionals, 0020
International Bluegrass Music Association, 0314
International Board on Books for Young People (IBBY), 0539
International Centre for Creative Research, 0176
International Cricket Council, 0656
International Festival of Contemporary Music
    See Warsaw Autumn Festival
International Film Festival
    See Cannes Film Festival
International Freedom Festival, 0431
International Istanbul Festival
    See Istanbul Festivals, International
interracial marriage, 0340
Inti Raymi Festival
    See Inti Raymi Fiesta
Inti Raymi Fiesta, 1297
Inti Raymi Pageant
    See Inti Raymi Fiesta
Intruz
    See Carnival (Goa, India)
Inuit Indians, 0008, 1921
    See also American Indians
Inuus, 0904
Invention of the Cross
    See Exaltation of the Cross, Feast of the
Iowa
    American Indian ceremony, 1709
    arts festival, 3004
    balloon festival, 1247
    bicycle racing, 2174
    country music festival, 1960
    covered bridge festival, 1587

General Index

Numbers in the index refer to entry numbers, not page numbers

Numbers in the index refer to entry numbers, not page numbers

K

Numbers in the index refer to entry numbers, not page numbers

Numbers in the index refer to entry numbers, not page numbers

Numbers in the index refer to entry numbers, not page numbers

Meistertrunk Pageant (Master Draught Pageant), 1696
Meitlisonntag, 1697
Melbourne Cup Day, 1698
Melbourne International Comedy Festival, 1699
Melchior, 0858, 0864
Mella, Ramón, 0756, 0772
Memorial Day, 1700
    See also Graveyard Cleaning and Decoration Day
Memorial Day Luminaria at Fredericksburg National
   Cemetery, 1701
memorial days
    Armenia, 0142
    Marshall Islands, 1646
    Myanmar, 1803
    South Korea, 2465
    United States, 1603
    Virginia, 1701
Memory Day
    See Graveyard Cleaning and Decoration Day
Memphis in May International Festival, 1702
Memphis, Tennessee, 0481, 0842
Menelik II, Emperor, 0884
Menuhin Festival, 1703
Menuhin, Yehudi, 0234, 0272
Mercè, Festa de la, 1704
Merchants' Flower Market, 1705
Merdeka Day, 1706
Merengue Festival (Festival de Merengue), 1707
Meritxell, Jungfrau von, 0091
Merrie Monarch Festival, 1708
Mesa, Arizona, 0618
Mescalero Apache Tribe, 0113
Meskwaki Powwow, 1709
    See also American Indians
Messiah Festival, 1710
meteors, 2066
Methodist Church, 0439
Métis, 0008
Mevlana, Festival of, 1711
Mexican folk music festival, 2817
Mexican-American celebration, 1958
Mexico
    agricultural festival, 2534
    American Indian festival, 2324
    animal event, 2258
    autumn feast, 1939
    Aztec commemoration, 1227
    birthday commemoration, 2950
    border festival, 0517
    Carnival, 0472
    Christmas celebration, 0582
    cross commemoration, 0726
    cultural festival, 2323
    dancing, 0472, 0630, 0825, 1115, 2070
    death commemoration, 0065
    drama, 0472
    fire ceremony, 1858
    folk dance festival, 2562

    food festival, 1899
    healing festival, 1903
    horsemen event, 0727
    independence day, 1712
    literary festival, 0505
    Mayan feasts, 0536, 0665
    military commemoration, 0591
    mock church battle, 2568
    Passion play, 2047
    processions, 0630, 1061
    rain festival, 0185
    religious celebrations, 0065, 0630, 0729, 1061, 1218, 1223,
      1283
    religious pilgrimages, 2089
    religious reenactment, 2121
    rodeo, 0727
    saint feast days, 2305, 2491, 2534, 2540, 2599
    spirits, return of the, 0728
    Vernal Equinox, 2899
    Virgin Mary celebrations, 1991, 1994
Mexico Festival of Independence, 1712
Meyboom, 1713
Mezza Quaresima
    See Mid-Lent (Italy)
Miami, Florida, 0458
Miami/Bahamas Goombay Festival, 1714
Mi-Carême, 1715
Michaelmas, 1716
Michaelmas (Norway), 1717
Michigan
    African cultural festival, 0032
    Arab cultural festival, 0121
    arts fair, 0691
    automobile parade, 3007
    automobile show, 1916
    basketball tournament, 1580
    Christmas festivities, 1910
    clothing festival, 2196
    country music festival, 0766
    dairy festival, 0688
    electronic music festival, 0718
    fish festival, 1718
    food festivals, 0322, 0528, 2077
    freedom festival, 0979
    German festival, 0974
    jazz festivals, 0719, 1273
    military commemoration, 1068
    parade, 3007
    Renaissance festival, 1719
    Scottish Highlands festival, 0068
    ship-sinking remembrance, 0817
    sporting event, 1580
    summer festival, 0072
Michigan Brown Trout Festival, 1718
Michigan Renaissance Festival, 1719
Michizane, Sugawara, 2728
Mid-Autumn Festival, 1720
Mid-Autumn Festival (Singapore), 1721

Numbers in the index refer to entry numbers, not page numbers

Numbers in the index refer to entry numbers, not page numbers

Mountain Man Rendezvous, 1783
mountain men, 1097, 1783
Mountain State Forest Festival, 1784
Mouride Brotherhood, 1069
mouriscadas, 0860
movie awards, 0010
Moving Day, 1785
Moxie Festival, 1786
Moyers, Bill, 0748
Mozambique
 combatting illegal trade of wild plants and animals, 1788
 independence day, 1787
 masked dancing, 1723
 peace commemoration, 1789
Mozambique Independence Day, 1787
Mozambique Lusaka Agreement Day, 1788
Mozambique Peace Day, 1789
Mozart Festival
 See Salzburg Festival
Mozart Festival (Mozartfest), 1791
Mozart Week (Mozartwoche), 1792
Mozart, Wolfgang Amadeus, 0088, 0351, 0454, 0616, 0805, 1045, 2282
Mozart (Wolfgang Amadeus), Birthday of, 1790
Mshweshwe
 See Moshoeshoe's Day
Mt. Wakakusa Dead Grass-Burning Event
 See Wakakusayama Yaki (Mount Wakakusa Fire Festival)
Mtskhetoba (Day of Mtskheta)
 See Svetitskhovloba
Muhammad commemorations, 0692, 1675
Mule Days, 1793
Mulid of Shaykh Yusuf Abu el-Haggag (Moulid of Abu el-Haggag), 1794
mullet dogs, 0319
multicultural celebrations
 Finland, 0891
 Florida, 0914
 Texas, 0243
mummers, 0571
Mumping Day
 See Doleing Day
Munich Opera Festival, 1795
Muñoz-Rivera Day, 1796
Muñoz-Rivera, Luis, 1796
Muscat Festival, 1797
Museum Days/Remembering James Dean
 See Dean (James) Festival
Mushroom Festival, 1798
Music and Dance Festival, International, 1799
music awards, 0282
music commemoration
 Austria, 2425
music competition, 0490
music festivals
 See also specific music genres; performing arts events

Acadian, 0011
Alaska, 2437
Antigua and Barbuda, 0108
Arkansas, 2003
Aruba, 0462
Australia, 0018, 0019
Bahamas, 1362
Belgium, 0938
Bulgaria, 1053
Canada, 0011, 0516, 1735, 2160, 2456
Chile, 2915
Connecticut, 2351
Egypt, 0122
England, 0054, 0234, 0522, 2502, 2755, 3005
Finland, 1175, 2336
Florida, 0967
France, 2071, 2277
French Polynesia, 0229
Germany, 1685
Hawaii, 0732
Idaho, 1268, 1961
Ireland, 0939
Israel, 1323
Italy, 0401, 0951
Kansas, 1710
Lebanon, 0044, 0186, 0406
Louisiana, 0984, 2932
Massachusetts, 2702
Michigan, 0718, 0719
New Brunswick, 1735
New Mexico, 2321
New York, 0448
Newfoundland, 2456
Norway, 0268
Portugal, 0392
Prince Edward Island, 0516
Quebec, 2160
Saudi Arabia, 0006
Scotland, 2227
South Africa, 0444
Spain, 1799, 2291, 2328
Switzerland, 1348
Tahiti, 0229
Texas, 0911
United States, 1763
Vermont, 1636
Vietnam, 1537
Wales, 0822
music fundraiser, 0289
Muskogee, State of, 0345
Muskogee-Creek Indians, 0655
Muslim events
 See Islamic events
mustard, 1817
Mut I-ard, 1800

Myanmar
    Buddha's birthday, 1386
    Buddhist festival, 2715
    independence day, 1802
    light festival, 2951
    memorial day, 1803
    military commemoration, 1801
    national holiday, 1805
    new year, 2750
    peasants holiday, 1804
    spirit festival, 2714
    temple celebration, 2419
Myanmar Armed Forces Day, 1801
Myanmar Independence Day, 1802
Myanmar Martyrs' Day, 1803
Myanmar Peasants' Day, 1804
Myanmar Union Day, 1805
Mysteries
    See Eleusinian Mysteries
Mystery Play (Elche), 1806
Mystery Play (Tibet), 1807
mythological celebrations
    ancient Rome, 0457, 0496, 0504, 1187, 1619, 1665
    forest festival, 0904
    Hindu religion, 0275, 1479
    India, 2439

N

Naa Damba, 0692
NAACP Image Awards, 1808
Naadam, 1809
Naag Panchami, 1810
Nabanna, 1811
Nabekamuri Matsuri (Pan-on-Head Festival), 1812
nacimiento, 0563
Nada Festival
    See Kenka Matsuri (Roughhouse Festival)
Nadaam
    See Naadam
Nagoya City Festival, 1813
Naked Festival
    See Hadaka Matsuri (Naked Festival)
naked rope-climbing festival, 1134
naluyuks, 0859
Namahage Festival, 1814
Namahage Sedo Matsuri
    See Namahage Festival
Namibia
    death commemoration, 0495
    military commemoration, 1815
    planting festival, 1930
Namibia Heroes Day, 1815
Nammys
    See Native American Music Awards (Nammys)
Nanakusa Matsuri (Seven Herbs or Grasses Festival), 1816
Napa Valley Mustard Festival, 1817

Napoleon I, 0446
Napoleon III, 0591
Napoleon's Day, 1818
Narak Chaturdashi, 1819
Narcissus Festival, 1820
Nariyal Purnima (Coconut Day), 1821
Narsimha Jayanti, 1822
NASA Day of Remembrance, 1823
NASCAR Winston Cup circuit, 0599, 0703
Nashville, Tennessee, 0642
Nast, Thomas, 0571
Natal Day in Nova Scotia, 1824
Natchez Spring and Fall Pilgrimages, 1825
Natchitoches Christmas Festival, 1826
    See also American Indians
Nation Day
    See Cambodia Victory Day
National Anthem Day
    See Defenders' Day
National Association for the Advancement of Colored
    People (NAACP), 1808
National Association of Black Storytellers, 0303
National Audubon Society, 0166, 0570
National Aviation Day
    See Aviation Day
National Balloon Classic
    See Hot Air Balloon Classic
National Baptist Convention, USA, 0102
National Conference for Community and Justice, 0363
National Constitution Center, 0617
National Council for the Traditional Arts, 0957
National Day
    See Belgium Independence Day; Dutch Liberation Day;
        Ecuador Independence Day; Iceland Independence
        Day; Iran Islamic Republic Day; Malawi Republic
        Day
National Day of Oil
    See Iran Petroleum Nationalization Anniversary
National Enlighteners Day
    See Leaders of the Bulgarian National Revival Day
        (National Enlighteners Day)
national exhibitions, 0433
National Family Week
    See Family Week
national holidays
    See also specific national holiday, e.g., independence
        days
    Andorra, 0091
    Antigua and Barbuda, 0109
    Australia, 0169
    Austria, 0171
    Bahrain, 0203
    Bosnia and Herzegovina, 0334
    Brazil, 0354
    Brunei, 0365
    Bulgaria, 0853
    Burkina Faso, 0389
    Cameroon, 0428

National Reunification Day
    See Ukraine Unification Day (National Reunification Day)
National Velvet, 1070
National Wheat Festival, 2802
National Youth Day
    See Timor Santa Cruz Massacre Day (National Youth Day)
Nations, Festival of (Minnesota), 1827
Nations, Festival of (Montana), 1828
Native American Ceremonies in June at Devils Tower, 1829
Native American Music Awards (Nammys), 1830
Native Americans
    See American Indians;
    See also individual tribes
Native Islander Gullah Celebration, 1831
Nativity of Our Most Holy Lady, the Theotokos
    See Nativity of the Theotokos
Nativity of the Blessed Virgin Mary, Feast of the, 1832
Nativity of the Blessed Virgin Mary, Feast of the (Germany), 1833
Nativity of the Blessed Virgin Mary, Feast of the (Peru), 1834
Nativity of the Theotokos, 1835
nativity scene, 0563
natural resources celebration, 0385
nature appreciation, 2943
Nauru
    independence day, 1836
    population concern, 0092
Nauru Independence Day, 1836
Nauruz
    See Nawruz (Naw roz; No Ruz; New Year)

Nav Roz
　　See Nawruz (Naw roz; No Ruz; New Year)
Nava Varsa
　　See Bisket Jatra
Navabarsha
　　See Bisket Jatra
Navajo Indians, 1837, 1838, 1839, 2406
　　See also American Indians
Navajo Mountain Chant, 1837
Navajo Nation Fair at Window Rock, 1838
Navajo Night Chant, 1839
Navanna
　　See Nabanna
Navaratri
　　See Durga Puja
Navel, Jean-Yves, 0094
Navy (U.S.), 0136
Naw roz
　　See Nawruz (Naw roz; No Ruz; New Year)
Nawruz (Kazakhstan), 1841
Nawruz (Naw roz; No Ruz; New Year), 1840
Nayak, Tirumala, 0947
Nazis
　　Croatia, 0657
　　Czech Republic, 2641
　　Germany, 1451
　　Israel, 1209
　　Netherlands, 0782
　　Poland, 2110
　　Russia, 2907
Ncwala, 1842
N'cwala, 1843
Nebraska
　　agricultural holiday, 0126
　　American Indian dance festival, 2972
　　bird event, 0651
　　chicken festival, 2959
　　Czech festival, 0679
　　frontier days, 0987
　　horse racing, 0987
　　livestock exposition, 0041
　　rodeo, 0041
　　western heritage festival, 1844
NEBRASKAland DAYS, 1844
Nebuchadnezzar, King, 0147, 1011
Nebuta Matsuri, 1845
Nedele velikonocnní, 0791
needle festival, 1166
Nefertiti, 0009
Negro History Week
　　See Black History Month
Neighbor Day, 1846
Nelson Day
　　See Trafalgar Day
Nemean Games, 1847
Nemoralia, 1848
Nenana Ice Classic, 1849

Neopagan events
　　bonfires, 0925
　　Celtic festivals, 0667
　　harvest festivals, 1575
　　Imbolc, 1279
　　Sabbat, 2267
　　summer solstice, 0770
　　vernal equinox, 1274
Nepal
　　animal festival, 2760
　　animal sacrifice, 0780
　　Buddha holiday, 1655
　　chariot procession, 2189
　　death commemorations, 0993, 1030, 1295
　　donation day, 2028
　　fathers commemoration, 1048
　　flower festival, 0780
　　good over evil festival, 0780
　　monsoon festival, 2718
　　national holiday, 1850
　　pole ceremony, 0288
　　religious holiday, 2408
　　royal birthday, 1427
　　sibling festival, 2177
　　snake festival, 1810
　　sun holiday, 1589
Nepal Democracy Day, 1850
Neri-Kuyo, 1851
Netherlands
　　arts festival, 0886
　　bonfire, 0796
　　children's festival, 1569
　　cultural festival, 1206
　　fertility ceremony, 2928
　　fishermen's holiday, 1377
　　flower festivals, 0954, 1407, 1705
　　flower-gathering, 0722
　　golf, 0361
　　harvest procession, 1047
　　heroism commemoration, 1512
　　horticultural exhibition, 0954
　　ice-skating race, 0836
　　military event, 1852
　　national holiday, 0782
　　new year, 1868
　　political ceremony, 2137
　　religious holidays, 0796, 0808, 1649, 2022, 2415
　　royal birthday, 1360
　　winter festival, 0313
Netherlands Antilles, 2426
Netherlands Military Tattoo, 1852
Neto, Antonio Agostinho, 0096
Nettle Day
　　See Shick-Shack Day (Shik-Shak Day, Shicsack Day, Shig-Shag Day)
Neujahr
　　See New Year's Day (Germany)

General Index

Denmark, 1874
Ecuador, 1876
Germany, 1877
Iceland, 1874
Japan, 1968
Nigeria, 1261
Romania, 1874
Scotland, 1874
Spain, 1878
United States, 1874, 2952, 2953
New Year's Eve (Brazil), 1875
New Year's Eve (Ecuador), 1876
New Year's Eve (Germany) (Silvesterabend), 1877
New Year's Eve (Japan)
    See Omisoka
New Year's Eve (Spain), 1878
New Year's Eve Watch Night
    Georgia (state), 2952
    Pennsylvania, 2953
New Year's Parade of Firemen (Dezome-shiki), 1879
New York
    abolition movement, 2816
    African-American festivals, 1167, 2097
    American Indian festival, 2637
    balloon festival, 2473
    birthday commemorations, 0764, 2236
    canoe regatta, 1013
    chamber music festival, 1674
    classical music festival, 2334
    dance festivals, 0693, 2334
    death commemoration, 1654
    discovery day, 2900
    film festival, 2800
    flower festival, 1535
    French festival, 0446
    gay rights commemoration, 2632
    horse racing, 0261
    jazz festival, 2040
    lights festival, 1533
    literary celebrations, 0300, 1250
    military commemorations, 0386, 0941
    music concert, 0448
    onion festival, 0767
    parade, 0027
    peace festival, 3023
    procession, 1036
    religious festival, 1188
    running races, 1880, 2938
    saint feast day, 2294
    slavery commemoration, 1574
    women's rights celebration, 2619
New York City Fire Department, 0941
New York City Marathon, 1880
New York City Police Department, 0941
New Zealand
    agricultural show, 1882
    arts festival, 1881
    military commemoration, 0111

national holiday, 2935
    shearing competition, 1054
    yacht race, 0082
New Zealand Day
    See Waitangi Day
New Zealand Festival, 1881
New Zealand National Agricultural Fieldays, 1882
Newfoundland
    arts festivals, 2456
    birthday commemoration, 0397
    Christmas Eve, 0571
    music festivals, 2456
    poetry celebration, 0397
    provincial holiday, 1883
Newfoundland Discovery Day, 1883
Newman, Robert, 0101
Newport Harbor Christmas Boat Parade, 1884
Newport Jazz Festival
    See JVC Jazz Festival
Newport Music Festival, 1885
Newport to Bermuda Race, 1886
Nez Perce Indians, 0537, 1556
    See also American Indians
Ngan Duan Sib (Tenth Lunar Month Festival), 1887
Nganja, Feast of, 1888
Ngmayem Festival, 1889
Ngoc Son Temple Festival, 1890
Ngondo Festival, 1891
Ngoni tribe, 1843
Ngouabi, Marien, 0615
Nguillatun, 1892
Niagara Falls, 1533
Nicaragua
    independence day, 1894
    military commemoration, 1893
Nicaragua Battle of San Jacinto Day, 1893
Nicaragua Independence Day, 1894
Nice Carnaval, 1895
Nicklaus, Jack, 0361
Nicodemus Emancipation and Homecoming Celebration, 1896
Nicolaus Esterházy, Prince, 0367
Niemeyer, Oscar, 0464
Nieuwjaarsdag
    See New Year's Day (Netherlands) (Nieuwjaarsdag)
Niger
    male beauty contest, 1012
    national holiday, 1897
    rain celebration, 0674
    seasonal celebration, 0276
Niger Republic Day, 1897
Nigeria
    ancestor commemoration, 1950
    Children's Day, 0540
    cleaning festival, 2846
    cultural festival, 2316
    dead, honoring the, 0178
    dead, visits from the, 1943

Northwest Folklife Festival, 1922
Northwest Territories
    American Indian sporting event, 1921
    dog sled race, 0451
    winter sports festival, 0451
Norway
    branch-striking holiday, 2417
    cattle herding, 1717
    Christmas celebrations, 0562, 2556
    cuckoo superstition, 1679
    Easter festival, 2284
    food festival, 2124
    moving day, 1785
    music festival, 0268
    national holiday, 2285
    religious celebrations, 0797, 2529
    saint feast day, 2581
    skiing, 0077, 1208
    sporting event, 1208
    spring festival, 1923
    sun festival, 2653
    winter fair, 1089
    winter sports, 0797
Norway Constitution Day (Syttende Mai), 1923
Norway's Liberation Day
    See Norway Constitution Day (Syttende Mai)
Norway's National Day
    See Norway Constitution Day (Syttende Mai)
Norwegian festivals
    Iowa, 1913
    Minnesota, 2681
Norwegian spruce tree, 0562
Nosa Senhora dos Navegantes
    See Assumption of the Blessed Virgin Mary, Feast of the
Nossa Senhora da Agonia
    See Our Lady of Sorrows Festival
Nossa Señora da Penha
    See Our Lady of the Rock, Festival of
Notre Dame de la Prospérité
    See Annunciation of the Blessed Virgin Mary, Feast of the (Belgium)
Notre Dame la Consolatrice des Affligés
    See Octave of Our Lady, Consoler of the Afflicted
Nova Scotia
    Acadian celebration, 0011
    birthday commemoration, 1824
    Christmas Eve, 0571
    food festival, 0100
    Scottish cultural festival, 0992
Novena, 0578
Novrus Bairam
    See Nawruz (Naw roz; No Ruz; New Year)
Nubaigai
    See Obzinky
nuclear fallout, 1646
Nuestra Señora de Guadalupe
    See Our Lady of Guadalupe, Fiesta of
Nuestra Señora de Itatí, 1924

Nuestra Señora de los Angeles
    See Our Lady of the Angels, Feast of
Nuestra Señora de Mercedes, 0759
Nuestra Senora de Peñafrancia, Feast of, 1925
Nuits de Fourvière, 1926
Numa Pompilius, 0033
Nunavut Day, 1927
Nusardil, 1928
Nutcrack Night
    See Halloween; Halloween (Ireland)
nuts, 0267
Nuuk Snow Festival, 1929
Nyambinyambi, 1930
Nyepi, 1931
Nytaarsdag
    See New Year's Day (Denmark) (Nytaarsdag)

O

Oak Apple Day
    See Shick-Shack Day (Shik-Shak Day, Shicsack Day, Shig-Shag Day)
Oak Ball Day
    See Shick-Shack Day (Shik-Shak Day, Shicsack Day, Shig-Shag Day)
Oakley (Annie) Festival, 1932
Oath Monday, 1933
Ober, Randy, 0415
Oberammergau Passion Play, 1934
Obon Festival, 1935
Oburata Kofi, 0043
Obzinky, 1936
Ocevi, 0541
Ochi Day, 1937
Ochichi, 0541
Octave of Our Lady, Consoler of the Afflicted, 1938
Octave of the Birth of Our Lord
    See Circumcision, Feast of the
October Feasts, 1939
October Horse Sacrifice, 1940
October Revolution of 1917, 0323
October War of 1973, 0135
October War of Liberation Anniversary, 1941
Odalan (Temple's Birthday), 1942
Odo Festival, 1943
Odunde Festival, 1944
Odwira, 1945
office managers, 0020
ofrendas, 0728
Oglala Lakota Sioux Indians, 0653
    See also American Indians;
    See also Sioux Indians
Oglethorpe Day
    See Georgia Day
Oglethorpe, James Edward, 1015
Ohgiwe
    See Dead, Feast for the

Numbers in the index refer to entry numbers, not page numbers

Numbers in the index refer to entry numbers, not page numbers

Paczki Day, 2006
Padua Purim
>   *See* Purims, Special
Paepcke, Walter, 0155
Pafos Aphrodite Festival Cyprus, 2007
pagan events
>   Great Britain, 1480
>   Italy, 2079
>   North Carolina, 0439
>   Scotland, 1480
Pageant of Peace
>   *See* Lighting of the National Christmas Tree
Pageant of the Golden Tree, 2008
Pageant of the Lamas
>   *See* Mystery Play (Tibet)
Paha Sapa, 1049
Paine (Thomas) Day, 2009
painting festival, 1260
Paitishahem (Patishahya; Feast of Bringing in the Harvest), 2010
Pak Tai, 0530
Pakistan
>   birthday commemoration, 1299
>   cultural festival, 2383
>   death commemorations, 2381, 2866
>   national holidays, 2011, 2012, 2013
>   Passion play, 2716
>   pilgrimage, 0698
>   saint feast day, 2608
>   winter festival, 0514
Pakistan Day, 2011
Pakistan Independence Day, 2012
Pakistan Kashmir Solidarity Day, 2013
Palau Independence Day, 2014
Palestine, 2450
Palio, Festival of the, 2015
Palio of the Contrade
>   *See* Palio, Festival of the
Palio of the Goose and River Festival, 2016
Palm Sunday, 0918, 2017
Palm Sunday (Austria), 2018
Palm Sunday (Finland), 2019
Palm Sunday (Germany) (Palmsonntag), 2020
Palm Sunday (Italy) (Domenica delle Palme), 2021
Palm Sunday (Netherlands) (PalmZondag), 2022
Palm Sunday (United States), 2023
Palmsonntag
>   *See* Palm Sunday (Germany) (Palmsonntag)
PalmZondag
>   *See* Palm Sunday (Netherlands) (PalmZondag)
palo sebo, 0447
Pan American Day, 2024
Panama
>   Carnival, 0473
>   independence day, 2025
>   log-throwing contest, 0208
>   parade, 0473
>   religious celebrations, 0290, 1224

Panama Independence Days, 2025
Panathenaea, 2026
Pancake Day, 2027
Panchadaan, 2028
Panguni Uthiram
>   *See* Panguni Uttiram (Panguni Uthiram)
Panguni Uttiram (Panguni Uthiram), 2029
Panic of 1873, 0294
Pan-on-Head Festival
>   *See* Nabekamuri Matsuri (Pan-on-Head Festival)
pantomimes, 0566
Panza, Sancho, 0505
Papa Festival, 2030
Papa Noel, 0581
papal festival, 2589
papier-mâché dolls, 0696
papier-mâché festival, 1845
Papua New Guinea
>   animal festival, 2080
>   independence day, 2031
>   nature appreciation, 2943
>   tribal culture festival, 1781
Papua New Guinea Independence Day, 2031
papyrus, 0406
parachutists, 0358
Parada del Sol, 2032
Parade of Nations, 0959
parades
>   *See also* processions
>   African American, 0027
>   Arizona, 2888
>   Austria, 0238
>   baby, 0191
>   Bahamas, 0199
>   Bolivia, 0486
>   California, 0143, 0292, 0761, 1315, 2793
>   Channel Islands, 0237
>   Finland, 0923
>   Georgia (state), 2585
>   Germany, 1019
>   Illinois, 0283
>   India, 0467
>   Japan, 0508, 0687, 1879
>   Marinique and Guadeloupe, 0471
>   Michigan, 3007
>   New Jersey, 0191
>   Panama, 0473
>   pirate, 0345
>   Spain, 0442
>   Switzerland, 0477
>   United Arab Emirates (UAE), 0014
>   Virgin Islands (U.S.), 0478
>   Wisconsin, 1084
Paraguay
>   independence day, 2033
>   saint feast days, 2289, 2302
Paraguay Independence Day, 2033
paralysis, 0694

Numbers in the index refer to entry numbers, not page numbers

Pfingstrosen
See Pentecost
Phagwa, 2072
phallic symbols, 0075
Phansa
See Waso (Buddhist Rains Retreat)
Phat Dan Day
See Vesak (Wesak; Buddha's Birthday)
Phchum Ben, 2073
Philadelphia, Pennsylvania, 0835
Philip II of Spain, 0482
Philippines
dancing, 0734
death commemoration, 2219
farming festival, 0447
harvest festival, 1736
independence day, 2074
lantern festival, 1031
military commemoration, 0233
religious celebrations, 0165, 0299, 0889, 0953, 1225, 1925
revolution commemoration, 0915
saint feast day, 2596
spirit ceremony, 1038
theater festivals, 1766, 1769
Philippines Independence Day, 2074
Phillip, Arthur, 0169
phone-throwing contest, 1744
photography festivals, 0094
Phra Buddha Bat Fair, 2075
physically disabled, 2526
Pickett (Bill) Invitational Rodeo, 2076
Pickett's Charge, 1026
Pickle Festival, 2077
Pickle Market
See Bettara-Ichi
pickled radishes, 0273
picnics, 3056
Pied Piper of Hamelin, 0974
Pied Piper Open Air Theater, 2078
Piedigrotta, Festival of, 2079
Piedmont blues, 0377
pierced ears, 0443
Pierrot, 0479
Pig Festivals, 2080
Pig's Face Feast, 2081
pig's head, 0665
pig-slaughtering festival, 1417
Pike Festival, National, 2082
Pilgrim celebrations
Forefather's Day, 0962
Pilgrim Progress Pageant, 2084
Thanksgiving, 2085, 2743
Pilgrim Festivals, 2083
Pilgrim Progress Pageant, 2084
Pilgrim Thanksgiving Day (Plymouth, Massachusetts), 2085
Pilgrimage of Our Lady of Valme, 2086
Pilgrimage of Saut d'Eau, 2087
Pilgrimage of the Dew, 2088

Pilgrimage to Chalma, 2089
Pilgrimage to Mecca (Hajj), 2090
Pilgrimage to Moulay Idriss, 2091
Pilgrimage to Qoyllur Riti, 2092
Pilgrimage to Shrine of Father Laval, 2093
Pilgrimage to Souvenance, 2094
Pilgrimage to the Tomb of Sunan Bayat, 2095
pilgrimages
Alaska, 2530
Haiti, 2087, 2094
India, 0075, 2769
Indonesia, 2095
Mauritius, 2093
Mexico, 2089
Morocco, 2091
Pakistan, 0698
Peru, 2092
Saudi Arabia, 2090
Senegal, 1069
Shi'ite Muslims, 0124, 0125
Spain, 2086, 2088
Sri Lanka, 0016
Pilula, 0598
Pine Battle of Vinuesa, 2096
Pineda, Alonzo Alvarez, 0366
Pinkster Day, 2097
Pinochet, Augusto, 0543
pinole, 0665
pioneer celebrations
Arizona, 1760
Australia, 2000
British Columbia, 0360
Canada, 0360
Utah, 0081
Pioneer Day
See Mormon Pioneer Day
piradzini, 0573
pirate festivals
Florida, 0345, 1008
Texas, 0366
Virginia, 0304
Pirates Week, 2098
pisanki, 1062
Pitcher Fair
See Kumbh Mela (Pitcher Fair)
Pitkäperjantai
See Good Friday
Pitra Visarjana Amavasya, 2099
Pius XI, Pope, 0556
Pius XII, Pope, 0158
Plague Sunday, 2100
planned town festival, 1856
planting festivals
Mali, 0378
Namibia, 1930
Planting the Penny Hedge, 2101
Plataea, 0684
Plebeian Games (Ludi Plebeii), 2102

Numbers in the index refer to entry numbers, not page numbers

Pleureuses, Ceremony of, 2103
plotkeles, 0573
Plough Monday, 0608, 2104
Pluto, 0834
Plymouth, Massachusetts, 0962
pochoveras, 0825
poetry celebrations
    Colombia, 2105
    Japan, 2871
    Macedonia, 2638
    Nevada, 0646
    New Jersey, 0748
    North Dakota, 0689
    Northern Ireland, 0220
    Oregon, 0934
    Scotland, 0397
    United States, 2106
Poetry Festival of Medellín, International, 2105
Poetry Month, National, 2106
poison, 2539
Pol Pot, 0423
Poland
    Christmas celebrations, 0558, 2983
    classical music festival, 2946
    college festival, 1368
    constitution holiday, 2108
    doll festival, 1661
    folk festival, 1478
    food festival, 2006
    independence day, 2109
    Jewish cultural festival, 1343
    national holidays, 2110, 2111
    peasant holiday, 2832
    religious holidays, 0798, 1062
    religious pilgrimage, 0297
    saint feast day, 2488
    spring ritual, 1661
    wheat harvest festival, 0767
    wreath festival, 2980
Polar Bear Swim Day, 2107
poles, 0288, 0327, 0350, 0447, 0762, 2608
Polish Constitution Day, 2108
Polish Independence Day, 2109
Polish Liberation Day, 2110
Polish Solidarity Day, 2111
political commemorations
    Barbados, 0223
    Bermuda, 2064
    England, 1557, 2622
    Germany, 1933
    Hong Kong, 1234
    Isle of Man, 2839
    Netherlands, 2137
    North Korea, 3008
    Pennsylvania, 0866
    San Marino, 2307
    Sweden, 1679
    Tunisia, 2823

    United States, 1287
    Vermont, 2794
Polk County Ramp Festival, 0633
Polka Festival, National, 2112
Pollera Day, 0473
Pollux, 0496
Pongal, 2113
poor people, 0857, 0865, 0869, 2506
Poor Richard's Almanac, 0976
Pooram, 2114
poppies, 0149
Poppy Day
    See Veterans Day
Pops, Boston, 0338
population awareness, 0092, 3024
Porciúncula, 0963
Pori International Jazz Festival, 2115
porridge, 0575
Portland Rose Festival, 2116
Portobelo, Panama, 0290
Portugal
    agricultural fair, 0034
    animal festival, 2197
    Carnival, 0475
    charity for poor, 2685
    dancing, 0475, 0860
    death commemorations, 0065, 2118
    full moon celebration, 2686
    harvest festival, 2685
    independence day, 2120
    Islamic festival, 1307
    military commemoration, 2117
    music festival, 0392
    national holiday, 2119
    new year, 1870
    religious celebrations, 0065, 0149, 0627, 0860, 1108, 1226, 1989, 2034
    saint feast days, 1216, 2446, 2542, 2569, 2615
    Virgin Mary celebrations, 1989, 1993, 1995
Portugal Day
    See Portugal National Day
Portugal Liberation Day, 2117
Portugal National Day, 2118
Portugal Republic Day, 2119
Portugal Restoration of Independence Day, 2120
Portuguese celebrations
    California, 0407
    Massachusetts, 0307
Posadas, 0582, 2121
Poseidon, 0663
Poson, 2122
Posviceni
    See Obzinky
Potato Blossom Festival, 2123
Potato Days, 2124
potatoes, 1270
pots and pans, 0158
poverty, 0857, 0865, 0869, 2506

Numbers in the index refer to entry numbers, not page numbers

Delaware, 2144
New Hampshire, 1395
Punchinello, 0479
Punjabi American Festival, 2143
Punkin Chunkin World Championship, 2144
Punky (Punkie) Night, 2145
Punxsutawney Phil, 1107
puppet festivals
Canada, 1623
Czech Republic, 2146
Japan, 1194
Quebec, 1623
Vietnam, 2746
Puppeteers, Festival of, 2146
puppets, 0193
puppy-dog pie, 0596
Pura Besakih, 0823
Purcell, Henry, 0616
purification ceremonies
China, 0533
Ghana, 1945
India, 1001
Japan, 2728
Pakistan, 0514
Purim, 2147
Purims, Special, 2148
purnima, 0408
Purple Heart Day, 2149
Pushkar Mela, 2150
pussy willows, 0791
Putrada Ekadashi, 2151
putz, 0579
pysanky, 0802
Pythian Games, 2152

Q

Qatar Independence Day, 2153
Qiantang River Tidal Bore Watching Festival, International, 2154
Qing Dynasty, 0763
Qing Ming Festival (Ching Ming Festival), 2155
Qoyllur Riti, Peru, 2092
Quadragesima Sunday, 2156
Quadrilles of San Martin, 2157
Quakers, 0972
Quarter Days, 2158
Quartier d'été, 2159
Quasimodo Sunday
See Low Sunday
Quebec
Acadian festival, 0011
comedy festival, 1364
music festivals, 1757, 2160
puppet festival, 1623
saint feast day, 2489
winter carnival, 2161

Quebec City Festival of Sacred Music, 2160
Quebec Winter Carnival, 2161
Quecholli, 2162
Quechua Indians, 0181, 0435
Queen Elizabeth's Day
See Queen's Day (England)
Queen's Birthday (Thailand), 2163
Queen's Day (England), 2164
Queenship of Mary, 2165
Queima das Fitas
See Burning of the Ribbons (Queima das Fitas)
Quema de Judas, La
See Burning of Judas
Quema del Diablo, La
See Burning the Devil
Quiché Indians, 0291, 0625
Quinta Feira da Espiga
See Ascension Day (Portugal)
Quintaine, La, 2166
Quirinalia, 2167
Quirinalia festival, 0964
Quirinus, 0964
Quist, Adrian, 0170
Qur'an, 1501, 2181

R

rabbit
See Easter Bunny
Räben-Chilbi, 2168
Race of the Ceri, 2169
Race of the Cow, 0643
Race Relations Sunday, 2170
Race Unity Day, 2171
racial discrimination elimination day, 0838
Radha Ashtami, 2172
radishes, 0273, 1899
Radunitsa, 2173
raft festival, 0266
RAGBRAI, 2174
Raghunathji, 0780
Raid on Redding Ridge, 2175
Rain Dance
See Nyambinyambi
rain events
England, 2603
Japan, 2696
Mexico, 0185
Namibia, 1930
Niger, 0674
Rain-Calling Ceremony
See Nyambinyambi
Rainforest World Music Festival, 2176
Rains Retreat, 0146
rake festival, 2787
Raksha Bandhan, 2177

Rally Day, 2178
Ram Roasting Fair, 2179
Rama Leela Festival, 2180
Rama, Lord, 0513, 0723, 0780
Rama V, King, 0587
Ramadan, 2181
Ramanavami (Ram Navami), 2182
Ramayana, 0532, 0780
Ramayana Ballet, 2183
Rameaux
    See Palm Sunday
Ramírez, Juan Sánchez, 0756, 0772
Ramos, Fidel, 0915
Ramos, Thomas Vincent, 1005
ramp (plant), 0633
rams, 0153
Ramses, 0009
Rand Easter Show
    See Rand Show
Rand Show, 2184
Ransom, Stanley A., 0300
Rara (Ra-Ra), 2185
Ras al-Am
    See Nawruz (Naw roz; No Ruz; New Year)
Rasa Leela Festival, 2186
Rashtriya Prajatantra Divas
    See Nepal Democracy Day
Rath Yatra, 2187
Ratification Day, 2188
Rato (Red) Machhendranath, 2189
Rat's Wedding Day, 2190
Rattlesnake Roundup
    See Morris Rattlesnake Roundup
rattlesnake round-ups
    Pennsylvania, 1770
    Texas, 2677
Ravana, 0723, 0780
Ravello Music Festival, 2191
Ravinia Festival, 2192
Reagan, Ronald, 0617
Reconciliation, Day of, 2193
Reconciliation Week, National, 2194
Recovery
    See Exaltation of the Cross, Feast of the
red bean stew, 0760
Red Earth Native American Cultural Festival, 2195
Red Festival Day
    See Red Flannel Festival
Red Flannel Festival, 2196
Red Rum, 1070
Red Waistcoat Festival, 2197
Redentore, Festa del, 2198
Reed Dance, 2199
Reek Sunday, 2200
Rees, Thomas, 0454
Reform Judaism commemoration, 2268
Reformation Day, 2201

Reformation Sunday
    See Reformation Day
Refreshment Sunday
    See Mothering Sunday
Regatta of the Great Maritime Republics, 2202
Regency era, 0168
reggae music celebrations (Jamaica), 1637, 2203
Reggae Sumfest, 2203
Register's Annual Great Bicycle Ride Across Iowa
    See RAGBRAI
Re-Horakhty, 0009
reinado, 0600
reindeer, 0558, 2204
Reindeer Driving Competition, 2204
religious celebrations
    See also individual religions
    ancient Greece, 0834
    ancient Israelites, 2083
    ancient Rome, 0988, 2037
    Argentina, 1281, 1924
    Arizona, 0803
    Armenia, 0309
    Austria, 0864, 2018
    Baha'i religion, 0196
    Bali, 0995
    Bangladesh, 0287, 1376
    Belgium, 0103, 0160, 0488, 0787, 1057, 1210, 1214, 1649, 2058
    Bermuda, 1058
    Bhutan, 2749
    Bolivia, 0435
    Brazil, 0500, 0742, 3046
    Bulgaria, 0788
    California, 0794, 2370
    Cameroon, 0888
    Canada, 0859
    Chile, 0789, 1072, 2768
    Colombia, 2138, 2269
    Cyprus, 0790, 1388
    Czech Republic, 0791, 1221
    Delaware, 0031
    Dominican Republic, 0758, 0759
    Egypt, 0792, 0946
    El Salvador, 0826, 0952
    England, 0055, 0439, 0628, 1059, 1475, 1773
    Ethiopia, 0787, 1003, 2358, 2575, 2765
    Finland, 1476, 2019
    Florida, 0856
    France, 0061, 0156, 0627, 0857, 0865, 0986, 1649, 2035
    Germany, 0629, 0793, 0858, 0986, 1381, 1651, 2020
    Great Britain, 0456
    Greece, 0856, 0965, 1442, 1835, 2026, 2754
    Guatemala, 0063, 0159, 0291, 2362
    Guinea, 0153
    Guyana, 0153
    Haiti, 1222
    Hawaii, 0948
    Hindus, 0042, 0274

Numbers in the index refer to entry numbers, not page numbers

Numbers in the index refer to entry numbers, not page numbers

Numbers in the index refer to entry numbers, not page numbers

Numbers in the index refer to entry numbers, not page numbers

Numbers in the index refer to entry numbers, not page numbers

General Index

Numbers in the index refer to entry numbers, not page numbers

Numbers in the index refer to entry numbers, not page numbers

Numbers in the index refer to entry numbers, not page numbers

T

Numbers in the index refer to entry numbers, not page numbers

General Index

Numbers in the index refer to entry numbers, not page numbers

Numbers in the index refer to entry numbers, not page numbers

General Index

Numbers in the index refer to entry numbers, not page numbers

Victory over Japan Day
    See V-J Day (Victory over Japan Day)
Vidalia Onion Festival, 2908
Vielle de la Saint Jean, La
    See St. John's Eve (France) (La Vielle de la Saint Jean)
Vienna Festival, 2909
Viernes Santo
    See Good Friday (Mexico) (Viernes Santo)
Vietnam
    autumn harvest festival, 0590
    birthday commemoration, 1196
    death commemorations, 2742, 2910
    firecrackers, 0927
    lunar new year, 1571
    military action, 2733
    moon goddess holiday, 1720
    music festival, 1537
    national holidays, 2275, 2911
    new year, 2733
    puppet festival, 2746
    royal holiday, 1473
    saint festival, 1890
    souls festival, 2851
    summer solstice, 0744
    Veterans Memorial anniversary, 2912
Vietnam Ancestors Death Anniversary, 2910
Vietnam National Day, 2911
Vietnam Veterans Memorial Anniversary, 2912
Vietnam War, 2733
Vietnamese commemoration of the Virgin Mary, 1631
Vieux Carré, 0984
Vighnesa/Vighneswara, 1000
Vigil of Easter
    See Holy Saturday
Vigil of Epiphany
    See Epiphany Eve (Austria)
Vignerons, Fête des (Winegrowers' Festival), 2913
Viking celebrations
    British Isles, 1353
    Iceland, 2914
    United States, 1513
Viking chieftain, 0989
Viking Festival, 2914
Viligia, La
    See Christmas Eve (Italy) (La Vigilia)
Viña del Mar International Song Festival, 2915
Vinalia, 2916
Vinalia Priora
    See Vinalia
Vinalia Rustica
    See Vinalia
Vincy Carnival, 2917
Vinegar Festival, International, 2918
Vinegrower's Day, 2919
Vintage Computer Festivals, 2920
Vintners' Procession, 2921
vipukelka, 0924
Virgen de Candelaria, 0435

Virgen de la Soledad
    See Our Lady of Solitude, Fiesta of
Virgen de Los Angeles Day, 2922
Virgen del Rosario, 1072
Virgen del Socavón, 0486
Virgin Islands (U.S.)
    Carnival, 0478
    national holiday, 2796
    weather safety day, 1257
Virgin Mary celebrations
    Belgium, 0103, 0160
    Bolivia, 0435
    Brazil, 1987, 1998
    Costa Rica, 1996
    Dominican Republic, 0758, 0759
    El Salvador, 0952
    England, 1475
    France, 1992
    Guatemala, 0159
    Italy, 0161, 1988
    Luxembourg, 1938
    Mexico, 1991, 1994
    Missouri, 1631
    Peru, 0436, 1834
    Poland, 0297
    Portugal, 1989, 1993, 1995
    Spain, 1806, 2086, 2923
    United States (southwestern), 1990
    worldwide, 0158, 1835
Virgin of the Pillar, Feast of the, 2923
Virgin of the Rosary, 1072
Virginia
    African folk life celebration, 0765
    birthday commemorations, 1340, 2949
    bluegrass festival, 1954
    food festival, 2397
    historic commemorations, 1328, 3053
    horse-corralling festival, 0548
    jousting festival, 1357
    memorial day, 1701
    military commemorations, 0119, 0940
    pirate festival, 0304
    Scottish festival, 2924
    summer festival, 3001
Virginia Scottish Games, 2924
Vishnu, 0042, 0073, 0086, 0699, 0720, 1030, 1821
Vishu
    See Vaisakh
"Visit from St. Nicholas, A" (Moore), 0571
Visitation, Feast of the, 2925
Víspera de San Juan, La
    See St. John's Eve (Spain)
visual arts festivals
    See arts festivals
Visvakarma Puja, 2926
Vivaldi, Antonio, 0616
Vixakha Bouxa
    See Vesak (Wesak; Buddha's Birthday)

Numbers in the index refer to entry numbers, not page numbers

General Index

Numbers in the index refer to entry numbers, not page numbers

Numbers in the index refer to entry numbers, not page numbers

Title Codes for Sources Used in the Dictionary

AAH-2007
Gay, Kathlyn. *African-American Holidays, Festivals, and Celebrations.* Omnigraphics, 2007.

AfrAmerHol-1991
Anyike, James C. *African American Holidays.* Popular Truth, 1991.

AmerBkDays-2000
Christianson, Stephen G., comp. and ed. *The American Book of Days.* 4th ed. H.W. Wilson, 2000.

AmerFestGuide-1956
Coates, Helen R. *The American Festival Guide.* 1956. Reprint. Omnigraphics, 1998.

AnnCustKorea-1983
Choe Sang-su. *Annual Customs of Korea.* Seo-mun-dang Pub. Co., 1983.

AnnivHol-2000
Trawicky, Bernard. *Anniversaries and Holidays.* 5th ed. American Library Association, 2000.

AtticFest-1981
Brumfield, Allaire Chandor. *The Attic Festivals of Demeter and Their Relation to the Agricultural Year.* Ayer Co., 1981.

BkDays-1864
Chambers, Robert, ed. *The Book of Days.* 1862-64. Reprint. Omnigraphics, 1990.

BkDaysAmerHist-1987
Shapiro, Larry. *A Book of Days in American History.* Charles Scribner's Sons, 1987.

BkFairs-1939
Augur, Helen. *The Book of Fairs.* 1939. Reprint. Omnigraphics, 1992.

BkFest-1937
Spicer, Dorothy Gladys. *Book of Festivals.* 1937. Reprint. Omnigraphics, 1990.

BkFestHolWrld-1970
Ickis, Marguerite. *The Book of Festivals and Holidays the World Over.* Dodd, Mead, 1970.

BkHolWrld-1986
Van Straalen, Alice. *Book of Holidays around the World.* W.P. Dutton, 1986.

CelebCustRitWrld-1996
Ingpen, Robert, and Philip Wilkinson. *A Celebration of Customs & Rituals of the World.* Facts on File, 1996.

CelebFestCarnFeast-1997
Kindersley, Barnabas, and Annabel Kindersley. *Celebrations! Festivals, Carnivals, and Feast Days from around the World.* DK Pub., 1997.

CelebFestIndia-1994
Patil, Vimla. *Celebrations: Festive Days of India.* India Book House, 1994.

CelebNature-1969
Helfman, Elizabeth S. *Celebrating Nature.* The Seabury Press, 1969.

CelebSols-1993
Heinberg, Richard. *Celebrate the Solstice.* Quest Books, The Theosophical Pub. House, 1993.

CelebSouthAsia-1996
Viesti, Joe and Diane Hall. *Celebrate! In South Asia.* Lothrop, Lee & Shepard Books, 1996.

ChristYr-1991
Metford, J.C.J. *The Christian Year.* Thames and Hudson, 1991.

ClassDict-1984
Lempriere's Classical Dictionary of Proper Names Mentioned in Ancient Authors Writ Large. 3rd ed. Routledge & Kegan Paul, 1984.

ConEncyBahai-2000
Smith, Peter. *A Concise Encyclopedia of the Baha'i Faith.* Oneworld, 2000.

ConEncyIslam-1991
Glassé, Cyril. *The Concise Encyclopedia of Islam.* Harper & Row, 1991.

CustCultOkinawa-1959
Zabilka, Gladys, comp. *Customs and Culture of Okinawa.* Rev. ed. Bridgeway Press Books/Charles E. Tuttle Co., 1959.

CustHolWrld-1962
Dobler, Lavinia. *Customs and Holidays around the World.* Fleet Pub. Corp., 1962.

DancingGods-1931
Fergusson, Erna. *Dancing Gods.* University of New Mexico Press, 1931.

DayRel-1990
Gross, Ernie. *This Day in Religion.* Neal Schuman Pub., 1990.

DaysCustFaith-1957
Harper, Howrd V. *Days and Customs of All Faiths.* 1957. Reprint. Omnigraphics, 1990.

DictDays-1988
Dunkling, Leslie. *Dictionary of Days.* Facts on File, 1988.

DictFolkMyth-1984
Leach, Maria, ed. *Funk & Wagnalls Standard Dictionary of Folklore, Mythology & Legend.* Harper & Row, 1984.

DictHindu-1977
Stutley, Margaret, and James Stutley. *Harper's Dictionary of Hinduism.* Harper & Row, 1977.

DictRomRel-1996
Adkins, Lesley, and Roy Adkins. *Dictionary of Roman Religion.* Oxford University Press, 1996.

DictSymb-1971
Cirlot, J.E. *A Dictionary of Symbols.* 2nd ed. Philosophical Library. 1971.

DictWrldRel-1989
Crim, Keith, ed. *Perennial Dictionary of World Religions.* Harper & Row, 1989.

EncyChristmas-2003
Gulevich, Tanya. *Encyclopedia of Christmas and New Year's Celebrations.* 2nd ed. Omnigraphics, 2003.

EncyEaster-2002
Gulevich, Tanya. *Encyclopedia of Easter, Carnival and Lent.* Omnigraphics, 2002.

EncyNatAmerRel-2001
Hirschfelder, Arlene, and Paulette Molin. *Encyclopedia of Native American Religions.* Checkmark Books/Facts on File, 2001.

EncyRel-1987
Eliade, Mircea, ed. *The Encyclopedia of Religion.* Macmillan, 1987.

EndlessCaval-1964
Howard, Alexander. *Endless Cavalcade.* Arthur Barker Ltd., 1964.

EndurHarv-1995
Kavasch, E. Barrie. *Enduring Harvests.* Glove Pequot Press, 1995.

EngCustUse-1941
Hole, Christina. *English Custom & Usage.* 1941-42. Reprint. Omnigraphics, 1990.

FestAth-1977
Parke, H.W. *Festivals of the Athenians.* Cornell University Press, 1977.

FestEur-1961
Cooper, Gordon. *Festivals of Europe.* 1961. Reprint. Omnigraphics, 1994.

FestGhana-1970
Opoku, A. A. *Festivals of Ghana.* Ghana Pub. Corp., 1970.

FestIndia-1987
Sanon, Arun. *Festive India.* Frank Bros. & Co., 1987.

Festivals-1981
McFarland, Jeanne. *Festivals.* Silver Burdett Co., 1981.

FestRom-1981
Scullard, H.H. *Festivals and Ceremonies of the Roman Republic.* Cornell University Press, 1981.

FestSaintDays-1915
Urlin, Ethel L. *Festivals, Holy Days, and Saints' Days.* 1915. Reprint. Omnigraphics, 1992.

FestWestEur-1958
Spicer, Dorothy Gladys. *Festivals of Western Europe.* 1958. Reprint Omnigraphics, 1994.

FestWrld: Chile-1998
Roraff, Susan. *Festivals of the World: Chile.* Gareth Stevens Pub., 1998.

FestWrld: France-1998
McKay, Susan. *Festivals of the World: France.* Gareth Stevens Pub., 1998.

FestWrld: Haiti-1999
Ngcheong-Lum, Roseline. *Festivals of the World: Haiti.* Gareth Stevens Pub., 1999.

FestWrld: Indonesia-1997
Berg, Elizabeth. *Festivals of the World: Indonesia.* Gareth Stevens Pub., 1997.

FestWrld: Madag-1999
Ellis, Royston, and John R. Jones. *Festivals of the World: Madagascar.* Gareth Stevens Pub., 1999.

FestWrld: Mongolia-1999
Fisher, Frederick. *Festivals of the World: Mongolia.* Gareth Stevens Pub., 1999.